The Lincoln Writing Dictionary for Children

The Lincoln Writing Dictionary for Children

Harcourt Brace Jovanovich, Publishers

SAN DIEGO   NEW YORK   LONDON

Credits and Acknowledgments

Editor-in-Chief: Christopher Morris

Associate Editor: Margaret Syverson

Staff Editors: Amy Rosen, Daniel Hammer, Tracy Annis

Art & Design Consultant: Rubin Pfeffer

Contributing Editors: Cheryl Jeffrey, Judy Cannon, Andrew Robinson, Rosalinda Johnson, William Butler, Janet Rak, Gregory Moore, Kris Groh, Michael Kilpatrick, Elaine Smyth

Editorial Research: Gloria Tierney

Manuscript Preparation: Janice Mullen, Annalee Bradbury, Elizabeth Sears, Joyce Rice

Text Illustrations: B.J. Hoopes-Ambler, Michael Adams, Sharron O'Neill, Al Fiorentino, Howard Friedman, Walter Stuart, Helen Davie, Len Ebert

Cover Design: Vaughn Andrews

Cover Photo: Bard Martin/The Image Bank West

Photo Research: Nancy Tobin, Lois Briggs, Dawn Kilgore

Photo Credits: *See pages 900-901.*

ISBN 0-15-152394-0

To the Reader

In Abraham Lincoln's time, people would look up words in dictionaries, naturally, but they also *read* dictionaries. The dictionary that Lincoln himself used when he was President still exists and is owned by the editor-in-chief of *this* dictionary. In its margins, you can see pencil notes that Lincoln made from time to time as he browsed through the book.

Why did reading the dictionary—not just finding single words quickly—go out of fashion? Mainly because certain features of earlier dictionaries disappeared over the years. Earlier dictionaries took their clues from literature—to show the use of a word, they presented a quotation from a noted author. Second, these earlier books contained essays on the origin and uses of language. Third, they offered the reader guidance on correct usage—on what words and phrases best conveyed meaning, on choosing one form over another.

All those lost features have been restored in this new *Lincoln Dictionary*. When looking up a word, you will find quotations from the works of over 500 different writers—including almost every famous author in American and British literature. Sprinkled through the pages of this dictionary are 600 short essays on the art and craft of writing. And, since we recognize that readers turn to a dictionary for guidance and advice, these essays express the *opinions* of the *Lincoln Dictionary* editors. Some uses of language are disputed by various experts. We take a stand whenever there is doubt about new words or sound usage.

The *Lincoln Dictionary* is a modern book. Its editors had an advantage: computer techniques. The selection of words for this book is based on a computerized survey of over 10,000,000 (ten million) words of running text, that is, sentences and paragraphs. This is the first large-scale survey of general reading materials carried out in America since the 1930's. The *Lincoln Dictionary* is the sole dictionary to apply computer tabulation to selections from widely-read novels and short stories, from children's books and textbooks and encyclopedias, from magazines and newspapers and government publications—about 2,000 different documents in all. Each word in the survey is scored according to the number of different documents it appears in (called "Range") and the total number of times it occurs (called "Frequency"). The survey covers *modern* English as it is used by people who write well.

This dictionary also includes over 750 illustrations, and is the first to offer a combination of styles—not only color drawings, but also color and black-and-white photos, and fine art. Please read the captions under the illustrations; some of these are also meant to be read as "tips" on writing. Essays on writing appear in alphabetical order, just as entries do, and each one is placed on the same page as the corresponding entry word. (For example, see page 605. There you'll find both a definition of the word *revise* and an essay on *revising* a paper.)

This is a completely new dictionary—not an updated version of an earlier work. It contains 35,000 entry words, including the newest accepted terms from science, history, politics, and so on. As you look up these words, we hope you'll also read the nearest essay on writing or turn to another nearby entry. There are almost one million total words of information in this book.

English is the world's international language in commerce, technology, science, and diplomacy. It has a fascinating past and a glorious future. English is a major part of *your* future. Writing well is a significant accomplishment, and to learn good writing you need guidance from teachers, writers, and, yes, dictionary makers. We think it is fitting to use Abraham Lincoln's name because he was among the American Presidents who are praised for superb writing—Jefferson, Madison, Grant, Theodore Roosevelt, and Woodrow Wilson are others. Like them, all of us would like to be able to write in a clear and interesting way about what we know, what we believe, and what we seek.

Guide to the Dictionary

The Entry: A dictionary is a long list of words in alphabetical order. Each word in this list has information that goes with it, telling how to write the word, how to say it, and how to use it in a sentence. All this information is called an *entry*. *Shown in blue.*

Word Order: Entry words are in alphabetical order. Words beginning with **a** come first, then **b** words, and so on. All the **a** words are also alphabetical—**ab-** words come before **ac-** words, and so on.
Note: It doesn't matter if an entry is two words instead of one. It is still placed according to all its letters, not by the first word only. (This kind of entry is called a *compound word* or *compound entry*.) *Shown in green.*

Guide Words: To find the proper page for a certain entry, check the *guide words* at the top of the page. They tell the first and last entry word on a page. For example, ''haze'' would be on this page, because it is between the guide words ''haven'' and ''he.'' *Shown in yellow.*

Spelling: An entry begins with the *entry word*. This entry word is printed in very heavy black type, **like this.** It shows the word's correct spelling. *Shown in orange.*

Repeated Spellings: Sometimes the same spelling of a word is repeated twice. This means that there are two different words spelled the same way. (These pairs of words are called *homographs*.) *Shown in red.*

Syllable Division: Larger words are divided into parts called *syllables*. The break between one syllable and the next is shown by a black dot, like this: **syl•la•ble.** *Shown in purple.*
Note: When a word does not show any dots, this means it has only one syllable.
Note: To find the syllable breaks for a compound entry, look up the two individual words in the entry. *Shown in purple.*

Pronunciation: Appearing next after the entry word is the *pronunciation*. This shows the proper way to say the word. The pronunciation is printed in ordinary type inside a pair of brackets, like this: [   ]. *Shown in blue.*
Note: Syllables in the pronunciation are divided by a space, not by dots.

fad [fad] *noun, plural* **fads.** something that is very popular for a short time but then goes out of fashion: At one time there was a *fad* at colleges to see how many people could squeeze into a telephone booth. The 'Twist' was a dance *fad* of the early 1960's.

coast [kōst] *noun, plural* **coasts. 1.** the edge of land touching the ocean. **2.** an area of land near the ocean. —*verb,* **coasted, coasting.** to move without effort or power; slide: They *coasted* down the snowy hill on their sleds.

coast•al [kōst′ əl] *adjective.* of or near a coast: *coastal* waters, a *coastal* town.

Coast Guard a part of the United States armed forces that guards the coast and rescues boats and ships in trouble.

haze [hāz] *noun, plural* **hazes.** a thin layer of smoke, mist, or dust in the air: A *haze* of cigarette smoke hung over the room.

brass [bras] *noun.* a yellow metal made of copper and zinc melted together. Brass can be made into various shapes and is used to make ornaments, bowls, and musical instruments.

meal¹ [mēl] *noun, plural* **meals.** the food served or eaten at one time: a *meal* of soup and a salad.

meal² *noun, plural* **meals.** corn or other grain that has been ground up into a coarse powder.

short•ly [shôrt′ lē] *adverb.* in a short time; soon: Mom went to the store; she left a note saying she'll be back *shortly.*

short•stop [shôrt′ stäp′] *noun, plural* **short-stops.** in baseball, the position between second and third base, or a player who plays there.

short story a work of fiction that is shorter than a novel. [LOOK UP **story** FOR SYLLABLE DIVISION.]

add [ad] *verb,* **added, adding. 1.** to put numbers together to find out how much they come out to be: to *add* 2 and 2. **2.** to put a thing with something else: to *add* salt to food, to *add* a room to a house. **3.** to say something more: '''The people hardly know us,' she *added.*'' (Frank O'Connor)

Accent Marks: If a word has more than one syllable, one part of the word is spoken more loudly, or with more force, than the rest of the word. This louder part of the word has what is called the *accent* or *stress*. The accent is shown by a long black mark, like this [′]. *Shown in green*.
Note: For some words, there are two kinds of accents. The other kind is for a syllable spoken with some force, but not as much as a regular accent. This kind of syllable gets a secondary accent mark, like this [′]. *Shown in yellow.*
Here are the two marks again, to show the difference [′ ′].

Different Pronunciations: Some words can be spoken correctly in more than one way. Then there are two different pronunciations given for the word. The one listed first is not necessarily better or more correct than the second; it's the one that our research shows to be used more often. *Shown in orange.*
Note: See the page "Pronunciation Symbols" opposite page 1 for more information.

Part of Speech: The pronunciation is followed by the *part of speech*. It is printed in italic letters, *like this*. Shown in red. The part of speech is a way to put a word into a certain group, according to how it is used. The parts of speech are: *noun, pronoun, verb, adjective, adverb, preposition, conjunction, interjection.*
Note: The dictionary has more information about these part-of-speech terms under their own entries in the book, and also under the writing article PARTS OF SPEECH (page 554).

Other Forms of the Word: If the entry word has other forms, these come after the part of speech. These other forms of the word are also in black type, like the main entry word itself, though the type is not quite as dark, **like this.** *Shown in purple.* These are the forms a word may have:

Type of Word	Other Forms	Example
noun	plural	sock**s**, apple**s**
verb	past tense	work**ed**
	past participle	work**ed**
	present participle	work**ing**
adjective	comparative	high**er**
	superlative	high**est**

a•quar•i•um [ə kwar′ ē əm] *noun, plural* **aquariums** or **aquaria. 1.** a glass bowl or tank containing living fish, other water animals, and water plants. **2.** a building that has a collection of fish and other water animals.

aq•uat•ic [ə kwät′ ik] *adjective.* **1.** living in water: Whales are *aquatic* animals. **2.** taking place in or on water: Swimming and water polo are *aquatic* sports.

aq•ue•duct [ak′ wə dukt′] *noun, plural* **aqueducts.** a large pipe or man-made channel that carries water to places that are far away. Aqueducts make it possible to build cities and grow crops in areas that once were deserts.

da•ta [dat′ ə *or* dā′ tə] *noun.* **1.** things that are known; facts or figures; information: The U.S. Census provides a large amount of *data* about the American people. **2.** any information that is contained in a computer: "*Data* (is) anything that goes into a computer, everything stored in a computer's memory, and anything that comes out." (Peter McWilliams)

pru•dent [proo′ dənt] *adjective, more/most.* looking ahead to possible risks or problems; showing care and good judgment. ◆ The fact of being prudent is **prudence.**

prune[1] [proon] *noun, plural* **prunes.** a plum that is dried and used as food.

prune[2] *verb,* **pruned, pruning.** to cut off certain parts from a plant to help it grow or make it look better: Fruit trees are often *pruned* so that they will produce better fruit.

sad [sad] *adjective,* **sadder, saddest. 1.** not happy; feeling sorrow: The boy was *sad* to be all alone away from his home and family. **2.** causing or showing this feeling: *sad* news, a *sad* voice. —**sadly,** *adverb* —**sadness,** *noun.*

sad•den [sad′ ən] *verb,* **saddened, saddening.** to make or become sad: "She was surprised and *saddened* to see that there were tears in his eyes." (Charles Dickens)

sad•dle [sad′ əl] *noun, plural* **saddles.** a seat for a rider on the back of a horse. —*verb,* **saddled, saddling. 1.** to put a saddle on: to *saddle* a horse. **2.** to put a load on; burden: "She wants an exciting father, and what's she got? She's *saddled* with me." (Graham Greene)

Note: Not all nouns in the dictionary show a plural form. A plural means "more than one," and some nouns don't apply to things that can be counted. *Shown in blue.*

Note: Sometimes an adjective is too long to add **-er/-est.** Then the forms given are *more/most.* *Shown in green.* Also, some adjectives don't show either **-er/-est** or *more/most.* It's not always possible to say that there is "more" of something. *Shown in yellow.*

Definitions: The heart of the entry is the definition. This is the part of the entry that tells what the word means. It appears in ordinary type. *Shown in orange.*

Numbered Definitions: When a word has more than one meaning, the definitions are numbered—**1, 2,** and so on. *Shown in red.* The meaning that comes first is the one that is most common and most basic to the word. This "core meaning" is followed by the other meanings. They are listed according to how closely they relate to the core meaning.

Note: A definition listed as #5 is not used as often as one listed #1, but this does not indicate that #1 is the "true meaning" or "most correct meaning." All meanings in this dictionary are valid uses of the word. *Shown in purple.*

Different Parts of Speech: Many words are used with more than one part of speech. For such words, the first part of speech given is the one that is most common and most basic. *Shown in blue.* All the meanings for this part of speech appear together—all the noun meanings, for example. Then come all the verb meanings, or all the adverb meanings, or whatever. *Shown in green.*

Examples: After the definition comes the example sentence (or example phrase). This example shows how the word is used. A colon signals the beginning of an example, like this **:** The key word in the example is printed in italic type, *like this.* *Shown in yellow.*

Note: The definition and the example support each other and should be read together. Often the example is needed to explain the meaning of the word more fully. *Shown in orange.*

Note: Some definitions are followed by two (or more) examples, to show that a particular meaning can apply in slightly different ways. *Shown in red.*

pot•ter•y [pät′ ər ē] *noun.* **1.** pots, dishes, vases, and other such things shaped from clay and hardened by heat. **2.** the art or business of making such things.

pow•er•ful [pou′ ər fəl] *adjective, more/most.* having great power; strong: Jet planes have *powerful* engines. **—powerfully,** *adverb.*

pow•er•less [pou′ ər lis] *adjective.* without power; not able to do or help something.

lamp [lamp] *noun, plural* **lamps.** a device that gives off light. Modern lamps use electric bulbs to give light. Kerosene or oil lamps were used before homes had electricity.

lan•guage [lang′ gwij] *noun, plural* **languages.** **1.** spoken or written words; human speech. Language is the means by which people tell their thoughts, ideas, and feelings to others. **2.** the particular system of words used in a certain country or by a certain large group of people: the English *language.* **3.** the words used in a certain field or activity: the *language* of science. **4.** the way in which words are used; wording: She asked her lawyer to study the *language* of the contract. **5.** a way of expressing thoughts and feelings without using words: sign *language,* body *language.*

ba•by [bā′ bē] *noun, plural* **babies. 1.** a young child; an infant. **2.** the youngest one in a family or group. **3.** a person who acts in a very childish way. **—verb, babied, babying.** to treat like a baby; give a lot of attention to: Her parents *baby* her by buying her every toy she wants. **—adjective. 1.** for or like a baby: *baby* clothes, a *baby* carriage. **2.** very young: a *baby* animal.

deep [dēp] *adjective,* **deeper, deepest. 1.** going far down from the top or surface: The Atlantic Ocean is 28,000 feet *deep* just north of Puerto Rico. **2.** going far from the front to the back: Their yard is 75 feet wide and 150 feet *deep.* **3.** having a low pitch: The actor James Earl Jones has a very *deep* voice. **4.** in an extreme state or condition, as if deep under water: The baby fell into a *deep* sleep. Sue didn't hear me because she was *deep* in thought. **—adverb.** in a way that is deep; far in, down, or back: "The dark eyes looked *deep* into Winston's own." (George Orwell) **—deeply,** *adverb:* "There was something wrong with him, no doubt, *deeply* wrong." (John Galsworthy)

Quotations: Some of the example sentences were written for this dictionary. Other examples were taken from the writings of famous authors. (See pages 894-899 for a list of these authors.) When the example is from a famous author, the sentence is in quotation marks and the author's name follows. *Shown in purple.*

References: Sometimes the definition will have a word written in small capital letters, LIKE THIS. This identifies a word that is difficult, but that cannot be left out of the definition, because it is too important. The entry for the word in capitals will give more information to help understand this definition. *Shown in blue.* At other times, the definitions will have a word in black type, **like this**. *Shown in green.* This means that the entry word is a form of another word. Refer to that word for the full definition.

"Diamond" Notes: The definition of a word will often contain a diamond sign, like this: ♦ This shows that extra information will follow. The diamond signals that this information is not part of the regular definition. *Shown in yellow.*
Note: You will sometimes see the terms *Informal* or *Slang* used to describe a certain meaning that is not suited to serious, formal writing. Each of these usage terms is explained in its own writing article.

Sub-Entries: A main entry often includes other entries that are related to the entry word. These related words are called **sub-entries**. They are printed in black type, **like this**. A sub-entry has the same meaning as the entry word, but differs from it in some way. The difference may be in spelling, in the use of a capital letter, or in the adding of an ending, such as **-ly** or **-ness**. It may also be that the sub-entry is a phrase which uses the entry word in a special way. *Shown in orange.*

Writing Articles: The writing articles are printed inside colored boxes. A writing article is separate from the entry for a word, but it appears on the same page as its entry word. The article begins with its title in black letters, followed by an explanation or discussion of how the word relates to writing. *Shown in red.*
Note: When the entry word is in Column 'B' (the right-hand column on the page), then the beginning of the article is indented. In this example, **journals** is indented because the entry for the word **journal** is in Column B.

e·merge [i murj´] *verb*, **emerged, emerging. 1.** to come out or up; appear: "My train *emerged* from the tunnel into sunlight . . ." (F. Scott Fitzgerald) **2.** to become known; develop: "The district was beginning to take shape, the people to *emerge* as separate personalities." (James Herriot)

gas [gas] *noun, plural* **gases. 1.** one of the three basic forms of matter, along with a LIQUID and a SOLID. A gas does not have a certain shape and does not occupy a fixed space. Air itself is a gas, and it is made up of other gases such as hydrogen and oxygen. **2.** a gas or mixture of gases burned for cooking or heating. **3.** a short word for GASOLINE. ♦ Something in the form of a gas is **gaseous.**

led [led] the past form of **lead.**

bal·lot [bal´ ət] *noun, plural* **ballots. 1.** a paper or other item used for voting. **2.** the number of votes cast in an election.—*verb*, **balloted, balloting.** to vote by using a ballot: The *balloting* was very heavy in this year's election for senator. ♦ *Ballot* comes from an Italian word meaning "a little ball." Many years ago, people voted by putting a little colored ball into a box.

odd [äd] *adjective*, **odder, oddest. 1.** not as it should be or is expected to be; not normal; strange; unusual: Painting by modern artists often show *odd* shapes and designs. The characters in *Alice in Wonderland* act in *odd* ways. Something that is very strange or unusual is an **oddity. 2.** of numbers, not able to be divided exactly by 2. **3.** happening from time to time; occasional: Gail does *odd* jobs in her spare time. **4.** not part of a matched pair or set: an *odd* sock. —**oddly,** *adverb.* —**oddness,** *noun.*

journals Many writing teachers keep a journal in which they write something day's entry may be as long as a page, or as line. A diary and a journal are similar; the is that a journal describes outside events, while a more on the writer's private thoughts. Some journal in which they record important Defoe did in his famous *Journal of the* however, a journal does not have to deal with stories. In his journal, the British author George record of the things he bought, the work he the house, the weather, and the animals and One good time to keep a journal is when

Pronunciation Symbols

[a] This is the "short a" or "flat a" sound, as in *apple* or *hat*.

[ā] This is the "long a" sound, as in *age* or *cake*. It's actually two sounds put together. Say [e] and [ē] together very quickly and you'll hear [ā].

[âr] This is the "air" sound, as in *care* or *bear*. This is a "short a" with an [r] sound after it. This [r] makes the [a] sound longer.

[ä] This is the "broad a" or "ah" sound, as in *calm* and father. This sound is also used for the letter "o" in words like *hot* and *odd*.

[e] This is the "short e" sound, as in *end* or *pet*.

[ē] This is the "long e" sound, as in *eat* or *we*.

[i] This is the "short i" sound, as in *inch* or *sit*.

[ī] This is the "long i" sound, as in *ice* or *time*. It's actually two sounds put together. Say [ä] and [ē] together very quickly and you'll hear [ī].

[o] This is the "short o" sound. Speakers of American English don't use this sound. People from Great Britain use it in words such as *hot* or *odd*.

[ô] This is the "aw" or "broad o" sound, as in *law* or *awful*. It's often followed by an [r] sound, as in *orange* or *court*. [r] makes the vowel sound longer.

[oo] This is the "flat u" sound, as in *book* or *put*. Be careful not to confuse [oo] with the [o͞o] sound.

[o͞o] This is the "ooh" sound, as in *pool, ooze,* or *who*. This is a longer sound than the [oo] sound.

[oi] This is the "oy" sound, as in *oil* or *toy*. It's actually two sounds. Say [ô] and [ē] together very quickly and you'll hear [oi].

[ou] This is the "ow" sound, as in *owl* or *out*. It's actually two sounds. Say [ä] and [o͞o] together very quickly and you'll hear [ou].

[u] This is the "short u" or "uh" sound, as in *cut* or *done*. This sound is very much the same as [ə]. [u] appears instead of [ə] in a word that has only one syllable, or in a syllable that has an accent.

[ə] This is the "schwa" sound. It often occurs in English for a vowel that it is not stressed (does not have an accent). The schwa sound can be spelled with *a* (as in *above*), *e* (as in *listen*), *i* (as in *pencil*), *o* (as in *melon*), or *u* (as in *circus*).

[yo͞o] This is actually two sounds together, [y] and [o͞o]. This [yo͞o] sound is sometimes called the "long u" sound, as in *use* or *fuel*.

[th] There is only one special symbol for consonants in this dictionary. [th] is the ordinary "th" sound, as in *think* or *moth*. This is the other "th" sound, which is called the "voiced th." Examples of the [th] sound are the words *these* or *bother*.

Other consonants follow the spelling of the word: [b] as in *bug*, [d] as in *dog*, [h] as in *hot*, [p] as in *pet*, [r] as in *run*, and so on.

[′] This is an *accent mark*. It shows the part of a word that is spoken with the most stress, or force—in other words, the part that sounds the loudest.

[′] This is a *secondary accent mark*. It shows a part of a larger word that has some force, but not as much as the primary accent mark [′].

In the dictionary itself, you will find a Pronunciation Key at the bottom of each right-hand page. The Key has six different sections that follow each other to explain different pronunciation symbols.

a, A [ā] *noun, plural* **a's, A's. 1.** the first letter of the English alphabet. **2.** the highest grade or level.

a [ə *or* ā] a word used before a noun or adjective that begins with a CONSONANT sound: *a* house, *a* car, *a* nice yard, two hundred dollars *a* month. The word **a** is an *indefinite article.*

ab•a•cus [ab′ ə kəs] *noun, plural* **abacuses.** a frame with rows of beads that slide back and forth, used to do arithmetic problems. The abacus has been used for thousands of years and is considered to be the earliest form of computer.

a•ban•don [ə ban′ dən] *verb,* **abandoned, abandoning.** to give up or leave completely; desert: The crew *abandoned* the burning ship. ♦ Often used as an adjective: An old *abandoned* car lay rusting on the side of the road. "The room felt cold, exposed, and *abandoned.*" (V.S. Naipaul)

ab•bey [ab′ ē] *noun, plural* **abbeys.** a building where people live who belong to a religious community.

ab•bre•vi•ate [ə brē′ vē āt′] *verb,* **abbreviated, abbreviating.** to make a word shorter by leaving out some of the letters: People often *abbreviate* "United States of America" as "U.S.A."

ab•bre•vi•a•tion [ə brē′ vē ā′ shən] *noun, plural* **abbreviations.** a shorter form of a word, written with some of the letters left out. The *abbreviation* for "Doctor" is "Dr."

ab•do•men [ab′ də mən] *noun, plural* **abdomens. 1.** the part of the body between the chest and the hips. It contains the stomach and other important DIGESTIVE organs. ♦ An **abdominal** [ab däm′ ə nəl] pain or illness is one that affects this part of the body. **2.** the rear part of an insect or spider whose body has three parts.

abbey English kings and queens are crowned at the ancient Westminster Abbey in London.

a•bide [ə bīd′] *verb,* **abided, abiding. 1. abide by.** to obey or follow: Members of the club must *abide by* the rules. **2.** to put up with: I can't *abide* her constant complaining.

> **abbreviations** The word *abbreviate* first meant "to cut something short." An abbreviation is a shortened form of a name or word. "Mass." is easier to write than "Massachusetts." But you would not write "Mass." in a regular sentence where the word is not part of a list or an address: "The first battle of the Revolutionary War took place in Massachusetts."

ab•di•cate [ab′ də kāt′] *verb,* **abdicated, abdicating.** to give up a power or responsibility: In 1936 Edward VIII *abdicated* as King of England. His brother then became king. ♦ The act of abdicating is **abdication.**

a•bil•i•ty [ə bil′ ə tē] *noun, plural* **abilities.** the power or skill to do something: A new baby does not have the *ability* to walk. "Louis was greatly admired for his *ability* as a swimmer." (E.B. White)

A

a•ble [ā′ bəl] *adjective,* **abler, ablest.** having the power or skill to do something: Penguins are not *able* to fly. She's been sick for quite a while, but she should be *able* to go back to school next Monday. (Anne Frank)

-able a *suffix* meaning that some task can be done, such as "climbable" or "touchable." A wash<u>able</u> sweater is one that can be washed.

ab•nor•mal [ab nôr′ məl] *adjective, more/most.* not normal: 102° is an *abnormal* body temperature (98.6° is normal).

a•board [ə bôrd′] *adverb* or *preposition.* on board; in or on a ship, train, or plane.

a•bol•ish [ə bäl′ ish] *verb,* **abolished, abolishing.** to put an end to; get rid of: Some people think that laws allowing parking meters should be *abolished.*
♦ The act of abolishing something is **abolition:** The *abolition* of slavery in the U.S. officially took place in 1863.

a•bo•li•tion•ist [a′ bə lish′ ə nist] *noun, plural* **abolitionists.** a person who wanted to end slavery in the United States in the years before the Civil War.

ab•o•rig•i•ne [ab′ ə rij′ ə nē] *noun, plural* **aborigines. 1.** one of a group of people who lived in Australia for thousands of years before the first European settlers came. **2.** one of any group of people who lived in an area from the earliest known time.

a•bound [ə bound′] *verb,* **abounded, abounding.** to be plentiful: Fish *abound* in that lake. "The whole neighborhood *abounds* with local tales, haunted spots, and twilight superstitions." (Washington Irving)

a•bout [ə bout′] *preposition.* **1.** having to do with: We saw a movie *about* wolves. **2. about to.** at the point of; ready to: The game is *about to* start. —*adverb.* nearly; almost: The meal cost *about* twenty dollars. We're just *about* finished.

a•bove [ə buv′] *preposition.* **1.** higher than; over: The bird flew just *above* the waves. Her work is *above* average. "*Above* the world is stretched the sky." (Edna St. Vincent Millay) **2.** too good or honorable for: He's *above* cheating simply to get a good mark. —*adverb.* in a higher place: The stars were shining *above.* —*adjective.* in an earlier part: The *above* entry on this page is "about."

a•bridge [ə brij′] *verb,* **abridged, abridging.** to make a book or essay shorter by eliminating words, sentences, or paragraphs.

a•broad [ə brôd′] *adverb.* away from one's own country: She is going to study *abroad* next year, either in France or Italy.

a•brupt [ə brupt′] *adjective, more/most.* sudden and unexpected: The picnic came to an *abrupt* end when it started to rain. —**abruptly,** *adverb:* "He had stopped the cab so *abruptly* that the cab behind bumped smack into him." (Sylvia Plath)

ab•scess [ab′ ses] *noun, plural* **abscesses.** a condition where a thick, yellowish liquid called PUS collects in a part of the body because of an infection. It causes soreness and swelling.

ab•sence [ab′ səns] *noun, plural* **absences.** the fact of being absent: What's the reason for his *absence* from school? Plants cannot grow in the *absence* of light.

aborigine The word *aborigine* comes from two Latin words meaning "from the beginning." It was first used to name early dwellers in Italy. Now, the word is used mainly for the original natives of Australia, such as this man.

ab•sent [ab′ sənt] *adjective.* **1.** not present; away or missing: Three students didn't go on the trip because they were *absent* that day. ♦ A person who is absent is called an **absentee** [ab′ sən tē′]. **2.** not paying attention; absent-minded. —**absently,** *adverb:* "He looked *absently* around the room." (J.D. Salinger)

ab•sent•mind•ed [ab′ sənt mīn′ dəd] *adjective, more/most.* not paying attention to what is going on; forgetful: He was so *absentminded* that he bumped into a tree while he was walking along reading a book. —**absentmindedly,** *adverb.*

ab•so•lute [ab′ sə loot′] *adjective.* complete; total: There was *absolute* silence in the room. King Henry VIII of England had *absolute* power over his country. —**absolutely,** *adverb.* completely: "The house was *absolutely* quiet. No one was about." (Oscar Wilde)

absolute zero the lowest possible temperature, at which there is absolutely no heat and no motion of any kind. (about −460° Fahrenheit). This is the lowest temperature in theory; nothing has ever actually been this cold.

ab•sorb [əb sôrb′ *or* əb zôrb′] *verb,* **absorbed, absorbing. 1.** to take in or soak up: Paper towels *absorb* water. "He leaned back and *absorbed* the sun." (Marjorie Kinnan Rawlings) **2.** to hold a person's interest or attention: "Rainsford leaned across the table, *absorbed* in what his host was saying." (Richard Connell)

ab•stain [ab stān′] *verb,* **abstained, abstaining.** to keep back from doing something: 50 senators voted 'yes,' 45 voted 'no,' and 5 *abstained.* "I will *abstain* from all intentional wrongdoing and harm . . ." (*The Physician's Oath*)

ab•stract [ab′ strakt *or* ab strakt′] *adjective,* *more/most.* having to do with an idea or thought, rather than a certain object or person: "Truth" and "beauty" are *abstract* words.

a•cad•e•my [ə kad′ ə mē] *noun, plural* **academies. 1.** a college or school, sometimes one for a particular field of study: the U.S. Naval *Academy,* the Royal *Academy* of Music. **2.** a group of writers, scientists, or scholars: The French *Academy* rules on matters concerning the French language.

ac•cel•er•ate [ak sel′ ə rāt′] *verb,* **accelerated, accelerating.** to speed up; move faster: The car *accelerated* as it pulled out to pass the truck. "He *accelerated* his pace and was soon far ahead." (John McPhee)

—acceleration, *noun:* The *acceleration* of an object that is dropped through the air is about 32 feet per second for each second that it continues to fall.

---

abstract words To keep your writing lively and colorful, try not to use too many abstract words. Such words are sometimes vague or too broad in meaning. You could write: "A new season had arrived and brought with it visible changes." Now compare that to Laura Ingalls Wilder's way of writing about fall in *Little House on the Prairie:* "The tree-tops along the creek were colored now. Oaks were reds and yellows and browns and greens. Cottonwoods and sycamores and walnuts were sunshiny yellow. The sky was not so brightly blue, and the wind was rough." Do you see things more clearly this way? Of course, abstract words shouldn't always be avoided, as in this use of *motion:* "The genius of Americans was found in motion: They either went to new places or remade what was at hand." (William Jovanovich)

---

ab•surd [ab surd′ *or* ab zurd′] *adjective,* *more/most.* not true or sensible; silly; foolish: People who go on that TV game show have to wear *absurd*-looking costumes. ♦ The state of being absurd is **absurdity. —absurdly,** *adverb.*

a•bun•dant [ə bun′ dənt] *adjective,* *more/most.* more than enough; plentiful: *abundant* rainfall. **—abundance,** *noun:* "An *abundance* of trees grew up from the bottom of the ravine, blocking his view." (Virginia Hamilton)

a•buse [ə byo͞oz′] *verb,* **abused, abusing. 1.** to treat in a bad or cruel way: The dog had been beaten, left without food, and otherwise *abused.* **2.** to use in the wrong way: The judge *abused* his position by taking bribes from criminals. **—**[ə byo͞os′] *noun, plural* **abuses. 1.** harsh or cruel treatment: This football helmet is made to take a lot of *abuse.* **2.** a wrong use.

a•byss [ə bis′] *noun, plural* **abysses** [ə bis′ əz]. a large, very deep hole in the earth.

ac•a•dem•ic [ak′ ə dem′ ik] *adjective.* having to do with colleges and universities: Professor Jones is leaving the *academic* world to take a job in business. An *academic* course in high school is one that prepares a student for college.

ac•cel•er•a•tor [ak sel′ ə rā′ tər] *noun, plural* **accelerators.** a pedal on the floor of a car that controls the flow of gas to the engine. The car speeds up when it is pressed down.

ac•cent [ak′ sent] *noun, plural* **accents. 1.** a certain way of talking shared by the people from one country or place: a Russian *accent,* a Midwestern *accent.* **2.** a stronger tone of voice used in saying a part of a word: In the word "accept," the *accent* is on the second syllable; in "access," it is on the first. **3.** an ACCENT MARK. **—***verb,* **accented, accenting.** to say a part of a word in a stronger way: The word "fortify" is *accented* on the first syllable.

accent mark either of two marks [′] or [′] used to show where the accent falls in a word. The part of a word spoken with the most force has

---

Pronunciation Key: A–F			
a	and; hat	ch	chew; such
ā	ate; stay	d	dog; lid
â	care; air	e	end; yet
ä	father; hot	ē	she; each
b	boy; cab	f	fun; off

(Turn the page for more information.)

A

[´], a **primary accent** mark, as in *áccess* [ak´ses] or *accept* [ak sept´]. Some longer words also have [´], a **secondary accent** mark showing an accent for another syllable, as in *accelerate* [ak sel´ ə rāt´].

ac•cept [ak sept´] *verb,* **accepted, accepting. 1.** to take something that is offered or given: The teacher *accepted* a gift from her students. He won't *accept* less than $1,000 for that car. **2.** to agree to or believe: At first people would not *accept* the idea that the earth moves around the sun. —**acceptance,** *noun:* The author gave a party to celebrate the *acceptance* of his new novel by a publisher.

ac•cept•a•ble [ak sep´ tə bəl] *adjective.* good enough to be accepted: His report was *acceptable* because he included enough information. —**acceptably,** *adverb:* All of the actors performed *acceptably,* but no one was really outstanding.

ac•cess [ak´ ses] *noun, plural* **accesses.** a way or means to get in or to have something: The only *access* to the beach is that stairway down the cliff. This computer system provides *access* to a lot of information. —*verb,* **accessed, accessing.** to gain access to: You can *access* the information by hooking up the computer to a telephone line. ◆ Something that can be accessed is **accessible:** The cabin is on top of a high mountain and is not *accessible* by car.

ac•ces•sor•y [ak ses´ ə rē] *noun, plural* **accessories. 1.** something that is not necessary, but that goes along with a more important thing to make it more useful or attractive: That car comes with a number of *accessories,* such as air conditioning and a stereo radio. **2.** someone who helps another person to commit a crime, or who hides the person after the crime: He was sentenced by the judge as an *accessory* in the robbery of the store.

ac•ci•dent [ak´ sə dənt] *noun, plural* **accidents. 1.** something bad or unlucky that happens without being planned or expected. Two cars crashing, a dish breaking, and a person falling and getting hurt are accidents. **2.** anything else that happens without being planned or expected: The ball hit his bat by *accident* while he was trying to get out of the way.

ac•ci•dent•al [ak´ sə dent´ əl] *adjective.* happening by accident: The moving company will pay for any *accidental* damage to the furniture while it's being moved. —**accidentally,** *adverb:* "America was discovered *accidentally* by a great seaman (Columbus) who was looking for something else." (Samuel Eliot Morison)

ac•claim [ə klām´] *verb,* **acclaimed, acclaiming.** to give praise or applause to: "She would be the one student honored, her painting . . . *acclaimed* as the best of the year." (Langston Hughes) —*noun.* praise or applause.

ac•cli•mate [ak´ lə māt´] *verb,* **acclimated, acclimating.** to get used to a new place: It is often hard for a student to *acclimate* himself to a new high school.

ac•com•mo•date [ə käm´ ə dāt´] *verb,* **accommodated, accommodating. 1.** to have room for: "Another boat was being made ready to *accommodate* the crowds." (E.B. White) **2.** to do a favor for; help out: "Why don't you tell Howard you've simply got to work in New York? You're too *accommodating,* dear." (Arthur Miller)

ac•com•mo•da•tion [ə käm´ ə dā´ shən] *noun, plural* **accommodations. 1.** something that accommodates; a help or favor. **2.** *also,* **accommodations.** a place to stay for the night. ◆ This word is frequently misspelled because of its double consonants. Think of Mi<u>ss</u>i<u>ss</u>ippi when you spell *accommodation.*

ac•com•pa•ni•ment [ə kum´ pə nē mənt] *noun, plural* **accompaniments. 1.** anything that accompanies something else: In England, Yorkshire pudding is a common *accompaniment* to roast beef. **2.** music that is played or sung as a background for the main part.

accompany The great singer Billie Holdiay being accompanied by another famous jazz artist, the piano player Art Tatum.

ac•com•pa•ny [ə kum´ pə nē] *verb,* **accompanied, accompanying. 1.** to go along with something or someone else: Today's forecast is for snow *accompanied* by high winds. "Mrs. Townsend *accompanied* me outside the house." (Marjorie Kinnan Rawlings) **2.** to play or sing a musical accompaniment. ◆ A person who does this is an **accompanist.**

A

ac•com•plice [ə käm′ plis] *noun, plural* **accomplices.** a person who helps another to commit a crime or do something wrong: The robbers' *accomplice* blocked the road so that the police couldn't follow them.

ac•com•plish [ə käm′ plish] *verb,* **accomplished, accomplishing.** to carry out or finish something: The workers *accomplished* the task of repairing the roadway. **—accomplishment,** *noun:* "Her main *accomplishment* was . . . playing the piano." (T. H. White)

ac•com•plished [ə käm′ plisht] *adjective, more/ most.* good at something; skilled; expert: an *accomplished* musician.

ac•cord [ə kôrd′] *noun.* **1.** agreement; accordance: Everyone on the committee is in *accord* as to how the money should be spent. **2. of one's own accord.** by a person's own choice: "We shall disappear *of our own accord* and not wait until they come to fetch us." (Anne Frank) **—accordingly** [ə kôr′ ding lē] *adverb:* in the right or necessary way: It's going to be a very fancy party, so dress *accordingly.*

ac•cord•ance [ə kôrd′ əns] *noun.* agreement: He was told to act in *accordance* with the instructions in the letter.

ac•cord•ing to [ə kôr′ ding] **1.** in agreement with: She filled out the form *according to* the directions at the top of the page. **2.** as stated by; on the authority of: *According to* the map, there was once an Indian village on this spot.

ac•cor•di•on [ə kôr′ dē ən] *noun, plural* **accordions.** a musical instrument that is held in the hands and played with a keyboard and buttons. The sound is made by moving the center folds in and out. ♦ *Accordion* doors are usually made of wood, plastic, or cloth; when opened they fold up like an accordion.

ac•count [ə kount′] *noun, plural* **accounts. 1.** a statement or record of how something happened: The book *We* is an *account* of how Charles Lindbergh flew alone across the Atlantic Ocean. **2.** a record kept by a business of how much money goes out and how much comes in. **3.** a sum of money that is kept in a bank: a checking *account*, a savings *account.* **4. on**

account of. because of: The baseball game was called *on account of* rain. ". . . an old general who had been put there *on account of* his rank." (Somerset Maugham) *—verb,* **accounted, accounting. to account for.** to explain or give a reason for: How do you *account for* the fact that you didn't hand in your report on time?

ac•count•ant [ə kount′ ənt] *noun, plural* **accountants.** a person whose work is keeping track of the money spent and taken in by a business or a person. ♦ The work done by an accountant is **accounting.**

ac•cu•mu•late [ə kyōō′ myə lāt′] *verb,* **accumulated, accumulating.** to gather up; collect: ". . . the almost unbelievable amount of snow that can *accumulate* in that part of the state." (John McPhee) **—accumulation,** *noun:* His room has quite an *accumulation* of old magazines because he hates to throw anything away.

ac•cu•ra•cy [ak′ yə rə sē] *noun.* freedom from mistakes or errors; being accurate: There are many stories about Robin Hood's *accuracy* with a bow and arrow.

accuracy Accuracy, when lacking, can ruin even the best-written paper. Be sure of your facts when you write. If you aren't sure, check them. Don't write, "All Canadians speak French and English" just because you have a friend from there who said it is so. Check this dictionary, or check an encyclopedia. Accuracy also applies to the precise meaning of words. If a woman runs in fear or anger out of a room, it is more accurate to say, "She fled" than "She left."

ac•cu•rate [ak′ yə rət] *adjective, more/most.* without errors or mistakes; correct; exact: an *accurate* answer, an *accurate* clock, an *accurate* typist. **—accurately,** *adverb:* "Most of the countries in the world take censuses now, but they don't all do it very *accurately.*" (Isaac Asimov)

ac•cuse [ə kyōōz′] *verb,* **accuse, accusing.** to say that a person has done something wrong or committed a crime: "Are you *accusing* me of stealing?" she asked angrily. The store manager had *accused* her of taking some video tapes. **—accusingly,** *adverb:* When he realized his wallet was gone, he looked *accusingly* at the man standing next to him. ♦ The act of accusing a person of something is an **accusation**

Pronunciation Key: G–N			
g	give; big	k	kind; cat; back
h	hold	l	let; ball
i	it; this	m	make; time
ī	ice; my	n	not; own
j	jet; gem; edge	ng	having
(Turn the page for more information.)			

5

A

[ak′ yə zā′ shən]: "There is possibly some truth in the *accusation* that we are making laws simply because they look nice on the books." (Thomas Merton)

ac•cus•tomed [ə kus′ təmd] *adjective, more/most.* **1.** usual; regular: He sat in his *accustomed* seat at the front of the bus. **2. accustomed to.** used to: She's always lived in Florida, so she's not *accustomed to* cold weather.

ac•knowl•edge [ak näl′ ij] *verb,* **acknowledged, acknowledging. 1.** to admit that something is true: The bank *acknowledged* that it had made a mistake in its records. "It was on this day that the Olinka *acknowledged* . . . defeat." (Alice Walker) **2.** to show that something has been received: They never *acknowledged* my letter, so it may have been lost in the mail. **—acknowledgment** or **acknowledgement,** *noun.*

---

acknowledgment This is one of the few words in English that has two correct spellings. It may be either *acknowledgment* or *acknowledgement.* The first one is used much more often in American English, but the other—with the extra e—is often found in British writing. Sometimes a writer goes against normal spelling either out of error or as a whim. Hemingway called one of his books *A Moveable Feast,* yet *movable* is the spelling in most dictionaries.

---

ace [ās] *noun, plural* **aces. 1.** a playing card with a single spot, the highest card in most games. **2.** a person who is very good at something: Sue's an *ace* at computer games. ♦ Often used as an adjective: the team's *ace* quarterback.

ache [āk] *noun, plural* **aches.** a pain, especially a dull pain that goes on and on. **—verb,** **ached, aching. 1.** to have an ache: "His legs began to *ache* with cold." (Doris Lessing) **2.** to want very much: She's *aching* to go to that party.

a•chieve [ə chēv′] *verb,* **achieved, achieving.** to do or carry out; accomplish: Elvis Presley *achieved* his dream of becoming a famous singer. "They were trying to make it easier for Nancy Lee to *achieve* learning." (Langston Hughes) ♦ An **achiever** is a person who achieves something: A high *achiever* in school is a very good student.

a•chieve•ment [ə chēv′ mənt] *noun, plural* **achievements.** something that is achieved: Michelangelo's greatest *achievement* as a painter was the ceiling of the Sistine Chapel in Rome. "But there must be something satisfying in having done it, a sort of feeling of *achievement.*" (Barbara Pym) ♦ An **achievement test** is a test of how much a student has learned about a certain subject over a period of time.

ac•id [as′ əd] *noun, plural* **acids.** one of a large group of chemicals that have a sour taste, that will turn LITMUS PAPER red, and that react with certain metals to produce HYDROGEN gas. Strong acids are poisonous and can burn through things. **—adjective, more/most. 1.** sour or bitter in taste. **2.** sharp or bitter in manner: That critic is famous for his *acid* remarks about movies he doesn't like. ♦ The quality of being acid is **acidity** [ə sid′ ə tē].

ac•ne [ak′ nē] *noun.* a skin disease in which a person has small, raised sores called PIMPLES on the face and upper body. Acne is most often found among teenagers and usually disappears as they grow older.

acorn An oak tree with its acorn. There is a saying, "From small acorns do large oaks grow." This saying is an *axiom* [ak′ sē əm].

a•corn [ā′ kôrn] *noun, plural* **acorns.** the nut of an oak tree.

a•cous•tics [ə kōōs′ tiks] *plural noun.* **1.** the science that studies how sound is made and how it carries. **2.** the qualities of a place that make it easy or hard to hear sounds in it. **—acoustic,** *adjective.* having to do with sound: *Acoustic* tile is meant to absorb sound.

ac•quaint [ə kwānt′] *verb,* **acquainted, acquainting.** to make familiar with; get to know about: The new girl soon got *acquainted* with the other students in her class.

ac•quaint•ance [ə kwānt′ əns] *noun, plural* **acquaintances. 1.** a person whom one knows, but who is not a close friend. **2.** the state of being acquainted: I have some *acquaintance* with opera, but I've never actually been to a performance.

ac•quire [ə kwīr′] *verb,* **acquired, acquiring.** to come to have; get: The museum has just *acquired* a famous painting by Pablo Picasso. "If you stay long enough in a room the view . . . *acquires* a great value." (Ernest Hemingway) ◆ Something that is acquired is an **acquisition** [ak′ wə zish′ ən]: The XYZ Company's latest *acquisition* is a small computer business.

act [akt] *noun, plural* **acts. 1.** something that is done: a thoughtful *act,* an *act* of kindness. **2.** the doing of something: The basketball player was fouled in the *act* of shooting the ball. **3.** a law: The 55 mile-per-hour speed limit was set by an *act* of Congress. **4.** one part of a play or show: a clown *act,* a ballet with three *acts.* —*verb,* **acted, acting. 1.** to do something: The firemen *acted* quickly to put out the flames. **2.** to behave in a certain way: He's been *acting* very strangely the last few days. "You're both good boys, just *act* that way." (Arthur Miller) **3.** to play a part in a show or movie: Elizabeth Taylor has been *acting* in films since she was a child.

acquit *Acquit* first meant "to put something to rest." If you wrote, "he was acquitted," you'd be referring to someone's being freed of charges (legal complaints) against him. What's wrong with this sentence: "She was acquitted from her position?" It is not only a doubtful use of the word, it is also fancy. Short, strong words tend to improve writing. Hence, "She was fired from her job."

ac•quit [ə kwit′] *verb,* **acquitted, acquitting.** to declare in a court of law that a person is not guilty of a crime: Once someone has been *acquitted,* the person cannot be charged with that same crime again. ◆ When a person is acquitted, it is an **acquittal** [ə kwit′ əl].

a•cre [ā′ kər] *noun, plural* **acres. 1.** a way of measuring the area of land. An acre is equal to 43,560 square feet, which is slightly smaller than a football field (about 48,000 square feet). **2. acres.** lands: We drove past *acres* and *acres* of wheat. ◆ The number of acres in a piece of land is its **acreage** [ā′ krij *or* ā′ kər ij].

ac•ro•bat [ak′ rə bat′] *noun, plural* **acrobats.** a person who is good at physical stunts such as jumping, tumbling, balancing in the air, and swinging from things. —**acrobatic,** *adjective:* The ballet dancer made an *acrobatic* leap through the air.

ac•ro•nym [ak′ rə nim′] *noun, plural* **acronyms.** a word made from the first letters of the name of something. Some acronyms are written as ordinary words: *radar* = *r*adio *d*etection *a*nd *r*anging. Some are sets of initials: CARE = *C*ooperative for *A*merican *R*elief *E*verywhere.

a•cross [ə crôs′] *preposition.* **1.** from one side to the other of: There is an old story that George Washington threw a silver dollar *across* the Rappahannock River. **2.** on the opposite side of: She lives *across* the street from us. —*adverb.* from one side to the other: The Mississippi River was 80 miles *across* during the floods of 1927.

ac•tion [ak′ shən] *noun, plural* **actions. 1.** the doing of something: He likes western movies because they have lots of *action.* **2.** something that is done; an act: a kind *action.* **3.** the way that something works: the *action* of the heart, the *action* of a medicine, the *action* of waves against the shore. **4.** fighting in war: He won a medal for bravery in *action.* **5. in action.** moving or at work; active.

acrobat Circus acrobats often perform tumbling acts from a springboard.

Pronunciation Key: O–S

ō	over; go	ou	out; town
ô	all; law	p	put; hop
oo	look; full	r	run; car
o͞o	pool; who	s	set; miss
oi	oil; boy	sh	show

(Turn the page for more information.)

A

action verb a verb that tells about something that is happening. *Walk, eat,* and *hunt* are action verbs, and so are *help, think,* and *enjoy,* but *is* and *were* are not.

ac•ti•vate [ak′ tə vāt′] *verb,* **activated, activating.** to make active: If anyone opens this door, it will *activate* the burglar alarm.

ac•tive [ak′ tiv] *adjective, more/most.* **1.** in action; moving or working: Many animals are *active* at night rather than in the daytime. Texas has many *active* oil wells. **2.** full of action; lively: an *active* baby. She has a very *active* mind and enjoys learning new things. **3.** in grammar, using a verb to show the subject of the sentence doing or causing the action. In the sentence "He planted some flowers," *planted* is an *active* verb. In the sentence "That tree *was planted* last summer," *was planted* is a PASSIVE verb. ◆ A sentence with an active verb is said to be in the **active voice.**
—**actively,** *adverb:* He is still *actively* involved with the business, though his son is now in charge.

ac•u•punc•ture [ak′ yōō pungk′ chər] *noun.* a form of medical treatment first used in China. It eases pain and disease through the use of very thin needles that are inserted and rotated at certain places in the body.

a•cute [ə kyōōt′] *adjective, more/most.* **1.** sharp and strong: an *acute* pain. "My table manners had become a source of *acute* embarrassment to all of them." (Willie Morris) **2.** quick in noticing things; sharp: "Her hearing became more *acute.* She took fright at the least sound." (Liam O'Flaherty) **3.** very important; serious; urgent: That country has an *acute* shortage of doctors.

ad [ad] *noun, plural* **ads.** a short word for ADVERTISEMENT.

A.D. an abbreviation used in giving dates. "476 A.D." means 476 years after the birth of Christ. ◆ A.D. is short for *Anno Domini,* a Latin phrase meaning "in the year of our Lord."

Ad•ams [ad′ əmz] **1. John,** 1735–1826, the second president of the United States, from 1797 to 1801.

active verbs Many experts on writing, George Orwell, E.B. White, and others have said that it is better to use active verbs than passive ones. That is, write, "Jim painted the house," instead of "The house was painted by Jim." In this situation, the active voice is more direct. The passive has its uses, of course. You can write, "This house was built in 1970" if you don't know who designed or paid for the building. But if you know John Jones built it, use the active voice: "John built it in 1970."

ac•tiv•ist [ak′tə vist] *noun, plural* **activists.** a person who takes strong action in support of some cause: Martin Luther King was an *activist* for civil rights for black people.

ac•tiv•i•ty [ak tiv′ ə tē] *noun, plural* **activities. 1.** something that is done or to be done: She's involved in a lot of after-school *activities* such as soccer, ballet lessons, and Girl Scouts. **2.** the state of being active; action: There's a lot of *activity* at the house across the street; someone must be moving in.

ac•tor [ak′ tər] *noun, plural* **actors.** a person who acts in a play, movie, or TV show.

ac•tress [ak′ tris] *noun, plural* **actresses.** a woman or girl who acts in a play, movie, or TV show.

ac•tu•al [ak′ chōō əl] *adjective, more/most.* in fact; real: This drawing shows the *actual* size of the animal. What is the *actual* cost of that car, including the cost of the extra features?
—**actually,** *adverb:* "The dress rehearsal, which was timed to begin at seven-thirty, *actually* began at ten forty-five." (Noel Coward)

2. John Quincy, 1767–1848, the sixth president of the United States, from 1825 to 1829. He was the son of John Adams.

Adam's apple [ad′ əmz] a lump in the front of the throat that is seen to move when a person talks or swallows. ◆ The name comes from the Bible story of Adam eating the apple; the lump is more prominent in men than in women.

a•dapt [ə dapt′] *verb* **adapted, adapting.** to change in order to fit a new situation: The writer is going to *adapt* his book so it can be made into a movie. "All these plants and animals have *adapted* themselves wonderfully to their desert environment." (Richard Erdoes) ◆ An **adapter** is something that adapts one thing to another: He used an *adapter* to connect the computer to his TV set.

add [ad] *verb,* **added, adding. 1.** to put numbers together to find out how much they come out to be: to *add* 2 and 2. **2.** to put a thing with something else: to *add* salt to food, to *add* a room to a house. **3.** to say something more: "The people hardly know us,' she *added.*" (Frank O'Connor)

ad•dict [ad′ ikt] *noun, plural* **addicts.** a person who cannot control his need for something that is harmful, especially a harmful drug.

ad•dict•ed [ə dikt′ id] *adjective.* not able to do without something harmful: to be *addicted* to cocaine. "There were some waiters and cooks *addicted* to petty stealing." (Claude McKay) ◆ The state of being addicted to something is **addiction** [ə dik′ shən]

ad•di•tion [ə dish′ ən] *noun, plural* **additions.** **1.** the adding of numbers together in arithmetic. **2.** the act of adding one thing to another: The *addition* of those two new players has really helped the team. **3.** a thing that is added: ". . . enough yard between the house and the river to allow for *additions.*" (Ken Kesey) **4. in addition (to).** also; besides: *In addition to* winning the spelling bee, she was also second in the science fair.

ad•di•tion•al [ə dish′ ə nəl] *adjective.* that is added; extra: She brought an *additional* can of gas when she drove across the desert. —**additionally,** *adverb: Additionally,* the winners of this contest will have a chance at another prize.

ad•di•tive [ad′ ə tiv] *noun, plural* **additives.** something that is added to another thing to improve it: Certain foods contain *additives* to give them color or flavor, or to keep them fresh.

a•dept [ə dept′] *adjective, more/most.* very good at something; skillful: He is *adept* at making things with his hands. "She was also surprisingly *adept* at speaking without moving her lips." (George Orwell)

ad•e•quate [ad′ ə kwit] *adjective, more/most.* as much as is needed; enough: Very few trees grow in the desert because there isn't *adequate* rainfall. "Usually he was answered in short but *adequate* sentences by either the cowboy or the Easterner." (Stephen Crane) —**adequately,** *adverb:* These instructions don't *adequately* explain how to use the computer.

ad•he•sive [ad hē′ siv] *adjective, more/most.* able to stick to something; sticky: *Adhesive* tape is used to hold bandages in place. —*noun, plural* **adhesives.** something that is adhesive, such as tape, glue, or paste.

ad•ja•cent [ə jā′ sənt] *adjective.* next to; near: There is a parking lot *adjacent* to the restaurant. "She turned away and crossed the grass to an *adjacent* path." (Ernest K. Gann)

ad•jec•tive [ad′ jə tiv] *noun, plural* **adjectives.** a word that tells something about a noun or pronoun, such as: a *new* car; *three* pencils; *brown* shoes; a *big* mistake. *Funny* is an adjective in "He told a *funny* story," "The movie was very *funny*," "Say something *funny*," and "It seems *funny* that no one saw her leave."

adjectives We use adjectives when we want to tell something specific about a noun. "The *black* car was hard to see in the twilight." Or: "The *old, stooped* woman could not see the car coming." What's the risk in using adjectives? If they help so much, then why not use them often or even always? Here's the risk: If you let a whole description or impression rest mainly on an adjective you are a lazy—and boring—writer. When you write about some person or thing, let the entire content of your paper do the describing, rather than just leaving it up to a few adjectives in the beginning. "The boy was funny" is a good sentence if you go on to show instances of his being humorous. "The girl was pretty" really doesn't say much. Was she "vain" also? Did she wear nice clothes? Did she smile?

ad•dress [ə dres′ *or* ad′ res] *noun, plural* **addresses.** **1.** the place where someone lives or something is located: Cathy's *address* is 37 North Avenue. **2.** the writing on a piece of mail that tells where it is to be sent. **3.** a speech: The President gave an *address* at the UN. **4.** a certain number in the memory of a computer that helps it to locate a piece of information. —[ə dres′] *verb,* **addressed, addressing. 1.** to write the address on a piece of mail. **2.** to speak to a certain person or group: "'You're mighty pretty,' Mrs. May said, *addressing* herself to the smallest girl." (Flannery O'Connor)

ad•join [ə join′] *verb,* **adjoined, adjoining.** to be next to or near: "His narrow bedroom faced east with a view of the blank brick side of the *adjoining* house." (E.L. Doctorow)

Pronunciation Key: T–Z			
t	ten; date	v	very; live
th	think	w	win; away
<u>th</u>	these	y	you
u	cut; butter	z	zoo; cause
ur	turn; bird	zh	measure

(Turn the page for more information.)

A

ad•journ [ə jurn′] *verb,* **adjourned, adjourning.** to stop until a later time: We'll *adjourn* the meeting for now and start again in the morning. **—adjournment,** *noun.*

ad•just [ə just′] *verb,* **adjusted, adjusting. 1.** to change or move something to make it work better: She *adjusted* the TV set because the picture was too dark. "He took out his glasses and *adjusted* them on the end of his nose." (Morley Callaghan) **2.** to become used to something; adapt: He's had trouble *adjusting* to his new schedule at work. ♦ Something that can be adjusted is **adjustable:** The seats in this car are *adjustable* to several different positions.

ad•just•ment [ə just′ mənt] *noun, plural* **adjustments.** the act of adjusting, or something that is adjusted: Making the *adjustment* from high school to college is hard for some students.

ad-lib [ad′ lib′] *verb,* **ad-libbed, ad-libbing.** to say or do something that is made up on the spot rather than planned beforehand: In the middle of Barbara's speech, a light bulb broke, and smiling, she *ad-libbed* that it was a great way to keep an audience awake. *—noun, plural* **ad-libs.** something that is said or done in this way: Johnny Carson is famous for his *ad-libs.*

ad•min•is•ter [ad min′ əs tər] *verb,* **administered, administering. 1.** to be in charge of; manage: A school is *administered* by the principal. **2.** to give out; apply: The police *administered* first aid to the injured man. **3.** to give in an official way: The Chief Justice *administered* the oath of office to the President.

ad•mi•ra•ble [ad′ mər ə bəl *or* ad′ mrə bəl] *adjective, more/most.* that should be admired; very good: He's made an *admirable* effort to improve his school work in this past term. **—admirably,** *adverb.*

admiral Admiral Chester Nimitz led the U.S. Navy in the Pacific in World War II. Here he is shown at the surrender of Japan in 1945, with General Douglas MacArthur and Admiral William F. Halsey.

ad•mi•ral [ad′ mə rəl *or* ad′ mrəl] *noun, plural* **admirals.** the highest ranking officer in the Navy. From lowest to highest, the four grades of admiral are **rear admiral, vice admiral, admiral,** and **admiral of the fleet.** ♦ The first navy commanders to be called admirals were in the Arab fleets that traveled to Europe in about 900 A.D.

> **administer** *Administer* is a fine word with a precise meaning. It is derived from a Latin word meaning "to serve." Unfortunately, some writers want more Latin word endings than they need. *Administer* is a good case in point. An *administrator* is someone who administers in an organization, who sets policy and approves procedures. Nowadays, Americans are beginning to say "administrate." That is pointless. Why give up a good word for another of the same sort that is merely long and fancy?

ad•min•is•tra•tion [əd min′ əs trā′ shən] *noun, plural* **administrations. 1.** the act of administering something: the *administration* of justice, the *administration* of a medicine. **2.** the people in control of a business or group: the *administration* of a college. **3. the Administration.** the President of the U.S., together with his advisers and the heads of the various departments of government. **4.** the period of time when a President is in office. 1961 was the first year of the Kennedy *Administration.*

—administrative [ad min′is trā′ tiv], *adjective:* The mayor of a big city has to have *administrative* ability.

ad•mi•ra•tion [ad′ mə rā′ shən] *noun.* the act of admiring; a strong feeling of respect or pleasure: Ronald Reagan spoke of his *admiration* for President Franklin D. Roosevelt.

ad•mire [ad mīr′] *verb,* **admired, admiring. 1.** to feel great respect for; think highly of: "Everybody *admired* her as a remarkably fine and brave little woman." (Tennessee Williams) **2.** to think of with great pleasure: I was just *admiring* your new dress.**—admirer,** *noun.*

ad•mis•sion [ad mish′ ən] *noun, plural* **admissions. 1.** the act of admitting something: This letter is actually an *admission* by the criminal that he is guilty. **2.** the act of allowing someone to enter a place: *admission* to a college. **3.** the price to enter a place: *Admission* to the movie is five dollars.

ad•mit [ad mit′] *verb*, **admitted, admitting. 1.** to say against one's will that something is true: He finally *admitted* that he had stolen the money. **2.** to agree with something in a slow or reluctant way: "You must *admit* she was right." (Somerset Maugham) **3.** to allow to go in: Children under three will be *admitted* to the park for free. Peggy was *admitted* to law school last week. —**admittance** [ad mit′ əns], *noun:* There is no *admittance* to the beach after dark.

a•do•be [ə dō′ bē] *noun, plural* **adobes. 1.** a building block made of clay that has been mixed with straw and dried in the sun. **2.** a building made of such bricks.

ad•o•les•cent [ad′ ə les′ ənt] *noun, plural* **adolescents.** a person who is no longer a child but not yet an adult; a young teenager. —*adjective, more/most.* having to do with adolescents: Judy Blume is a popular writer of *adolescent* fiction. ♦ The time of life when a person is an adolescent is called **adolescence.**

a•dopt [ə däpt′] *verb*, **adopted, adopting. 1.** to receive into one's family a child of other parents and raise it as one's own: The right to *adopt* a child must be given by law. **2.** to take and use as one's own: French cooking has been *adopted* in many other countries. **3.** to accept something in a formal way: The school *adopted* a new textbook after a vote by the teachers. ♦ A person who adopts a child is an **adoptive** parent.

adobe An adobe house built by Pueblo Indians in Taos, New Mexico. *Adobe* was originally Arabic meaning "brick." When the Arabs ruled Spain they built such buildings, and after the Spanish came to America they called Indian dwellings "adobes."

a•dorn [ə dôrn′] *verb*, **adorned, adorning.** to add something pretty to; decorate: The table was *adorned* with fresh flowers. —**adornment,** *noun.*

A•dri•at•ic Sea [ā′ drē at′ ik] a part of the Mediterranean Sea between Italy and Yugoslavia.

a•drift [ə drift′] *adverb* or *adjective.* drifting; not guided: The storm set many boats *adrift* in the harbor. "I was *adrift* all of a sudden, and I had to . . . find out who I was and where I was and what I was doing." (John D. MacDonald)

a•dult [ə dult′ *or* ad′ ult] *noun, plural* **adults. 1.** a person who is fully grown; a grown-up. Someone who is over twenty-one is considered to be an adult. **2.** an animal or plant that is fully

---

adopt/adapt The words *adopt* and *adapt* look and sound somewhat the same. You can use the "inside" of the word to help you tell them apart. *Opt* means "to choose." To adopt something means to choose that thing: "Miller School has *adopted* the nickname "Mustangs." *Apt* means "right." Think of how to adapt something means to make it suitable or right: "Some animals *adapt* to cold weather by growing a heavier coat of fur."

---

a•dop•tion [ə däp′ shən] *noun, plural* **adoptions.** the act of adopting: the *adoption* of a child. The mayor favors the *adoption* of a new law to limit growth in our town.

a•dore [ə dôr′] *verb*, **adored, adoring.** to love and admire greatly: "She is such a good mother. She *adores* her children." (D.H. Lawrence) "I thought he was the most wonderful boy I'd ever seen. I *adored* him from a distance for five years." (Sylvia Plath) —**adorable,** *adjective:* That is an *adorable* dress. —**adoration** [ad′ ə rā′ shən[, *noun:* The Italian painter Botticelli painted a famous painting showing the *adoration* of Jesus by the Three Wise Men.

grown. —*adjective.* **1.** that is an adult; fully grown: an *adult* bird, an *adult* tree. "It was probably the first time in his *adult* life that he had ever cried." (John Cheever) **2.** meant for adults: an *adult* education course, an *adult* novel.

Pronunciation Key: [ə] Symbol

The [ə] or *schwa* sound occurs in syllables without an accent. It can be spelled with any vowel, such as **a** in above, **e** in listen, **i** in pencil, **o** in melon, **u** in circus. It can also be a combination of vowels, such as **io** in action, **ai** in mountain, **iou** in precious.

(Turn the page for more information.)

ad•vance [ad vans′] *verb,* **advanced, advancing.**
1. to move forward: The fullback *advanced* the ball twelve yards. "He *advanced* to Rainsford and held out his hand." (Richard Connell) **2.** to help the progress of: This discovery will *advance* the cause of science. **3.** to pay money before it is due: ". . . asking if the whole five thousand could not be *advanced* at once, as she was in debt." (D.H. Lawrence) —*noun, plural* **advances. 1.** a forward movement: The army made an *advance* of ten miles. **2.** progress or improvement: There have been many *advances* recently in the field of computers. **3.** money paid before it is due. **4. advances.** a first step to being friendly: She didn't respond to his *advances.* —*adjective.* ahead of time: *advance* notice, an *advance* payment.

ad•vanced [ad vanst′] *adjective, more/most.*
1. ahead of others of the same kind: The Aztec Indians had an *advanced* civilization. **2.** beyond the first level: an *advanced* course in mathematics. **3.** very old: a person of *advanced* age.

ad•vance•ment [ad vans′ mənt] *noun, plural* **advancements.** the act of advancing: *advancements* in medicine. She'll have a good chance for *advancement* with that company.

ad•van•tage [ad van′ tij] *noun, plural* **advantages. 1.** anything that is helpful or useful: "Mammals also have an *advantage* in having a larger brain than any other kind of animal has." (Isaac Asimov) **2. take advantage of. a.** to make good use of; benefit from: "As soon as they were released from the army, they *took advantage of* all the benefits." (Flannery O'Connor) **b.** to treat someone in an unfair way: "I thought so well of Biff, even though he's always *taken advantage of* me." (Arthur Miller)

ad•van•ta•geous [ad′ vən tā′ jəs] *adjective, more/most.* giving an advantage; helpful: She's in the *advantageous* position of being accepted by all four of the colleges she applied to.

—**advantageously,** *adverb:* The new hotel is *advantageously* located next to the airport.

ad•ven•ture [ad ven′ chər] *noun, plural* **adventures. 1.** something that involves danger and excitement; a difficult or risky experience: There have been many movies about the *adventures* of early settlers in the Old West. **2.** any unusual or exciting experience: We had quite an *adventure* getting here through all that snow. ♦ A person who looks for and enjoys adventure is an **adventurer.**

ad•ven•tur•ous [ad ven′ chə rəs] *adjective, more/most.* **1.** enjoying adventures; ready to take risks. **2.** full of danger; risky: They made an *adventurous* journey down the Amazon River. ♦ Another word with the same meaning is **adventuresome** [ad ven′ chər səm].

ad•verb [ad′ vurb′] *noun, plural* **adverbs.** a word that tells something about a verb, an adjective, or another adverb. An adverb can show "how much" (It's *very* late); "in what way" (The train moved *slowly*); "when" (They left *early*); or "where" (Put the chair *here*). ♦ An **adverbial phrase** is one that is used as an averb, such as "The tree swayed *back and forth* in the wind."

adverbs Adverbs are one of several parts of speech that make other parts more precise or more colorful. Adjectives modify (change or add to) nouns. "Jane's hair was a *light* brown." Adverbs modify verbs. "Jane spoke *sharply* to her husband." Both adverbs and adjectives are very useful to a clever writer. But if used too often, an adverb can weaken rather than strengthen a verb: You don't need to write: "The baby crawled *slowly* toward the open door. He cried *sadly* when I closed it." Crawling is slow. Someone who cries is sad. Similarly, don't pile on too many adverbs: "My mother was *gaily, happily, joyously* willing to help." Go back to the examples of *slowly* and *sadly.* You can say: "The boat moved *slowly* away from the dock. She smiled *sadly* as she watched it go." "Smile," written alone, would make the reader think that the person was happy, not sad.

ad•ver•sar•y [ad′ vər ser′ ē] *noun, plural* **adversaries.** a person or group that is against another; an enemy or opponent: France and Germany have been *adversaries* in many wars.

ad•verse [ad vurs′ *or* ad′ vərs] *adjective, more/most.* not good or helpful; unfavorable: The patient had an *adverse* reaction to the medicine, so the doctor stopped using it.

ad•ver•si•ty [ad vur′ sə tē] *noun, plural* **adversities.** something that is bad or unfavorable; a trouble or difficulty: Wagon trains traveling west had to endure Indian attacks, sudden storms, desert heat, and many other *adversities.*

ad•ver•tise [ad′ vər tīz′] *verb,* **advertised, advertising.** to tell about something in an advertisement: Dr. Pepper and other soft drink companies often *advertise* on television. "Evan's Circus was *advertised* to come to town." (Ring Lardner) —**advertiser,** *noun:* That supermarket is a regular *advertiser* in the local paper.

particles of a solid or liquid held in a gas. Aerosols can be manufactured and sealed inside containers, to be released as a spray or foam. Paints, hair spray, shaving cream, and many other products are sold in this form.

advertising writing Advertising writers have to get people's attention in order to sell their products. First, they use simple, direct language: "If you want to feel ready to lick the world in the morning, eat Buzzle Breakfast Flakes." Then, too, their writing is personal, to draw the reader in: "How many times have you said, I ought to go to Markey's because of the cheap prices? Well, you don't have to wish or hope—go to Markey's today!" Sometimes advertising writers go too far. In fact, they show us what not to do as writers, as when they say things with no real meaning: "The Pirate is the toughest car on the road." Or, an ad will say just for effect: "Life is not worth living without a Zinger Chocolate Bar." Of course, they also make mistakes on purpose, so their message will be remembered: "Lyon Paints Ain't Lyin' About Low Prices."

ad•ver•tise•ment [ad′ vər tīz′ mənt *or* ad vurt′- əz mənt] *noun, plural* **advertisements.** any public statement that tells what is good or special about a product or service. Advertisements can be printed in newspapers and magazines, broadcast on TV and radio, or sent through the mail. They are used to sell things or to tell about jobs and services. ◆ The business of making advertisements is **advertising.**

ad•vice [ad vīs′] *noun.* something that is said to a person about what he or she should do: The members of the Cabinet give *advice* to the President. "I regard you as a very brilliant man, Bernard. I value your *advice.*" (Arthur Miller)

ad•vise [ad vīz′] *verb,* **advised, advising. 1.** to give advice: A lawyer *advises* people about matters relating to the law. **2.** to tell about something; inform: The pilot *advised* the passengers that the flight had been delayed. ◆ A person who advises is an **adviser** or **advisor.**

ad•vo•cate [ad′ və kāt′] *verb,* **advocated, advocating.** to say that something is a good idea; be in favor of: Senator Smith *advocates* lower taxes and less government spending. —[ad′ və kit] *noun, plural* **advocates.** a person who advocates something: Susan B. Anthony was an *advocate* of equal rights for women.

aer•i•al [âr′ ē əl] *noun, plural* **aerials.** a radio or television antenna. —*adjective.* in or from the air: an *aerial* photograph, an *aerial* attack.

aer•o•naut•ics [âr′ ə nô′ tiks] *plural noun.* the science or art of designing, making, and flying aircraft. ◆ An **aeronautical** engineer is one who works in this field.

aer•o•sol [âr′ ə sôl *or* âr′ ə säl] *noun, plural* **aerosols.** a substance made up of very tiny

aer•o•space [âr′ ō spās′] *noun.* all the area above the earth; the earth's atmosphere and the space beyond it.

aes•thet•ic [es thet′ ik] *adjective.* having to do with beauty in art or nature: "Music gives him his greatest *aesthetic* pleasure." (Janet Flanner)

a•far [ə fär′] *adverb.* **from afar.** from far away: We heard a faint voice coming *from afar.*

af•fair [ə fâr′] *noun, plural* **affairs. 1.** anything that has to be done or dealt with; a job or piece of business: That really isn't any of his *affair.* ◆ This meaning is often plural: a magazine that reports on current *affairs.* ". . . each man and woman going about the *affairs* of the moment."

aerial In the late 1940's, the skyline of American cities changed as TV aerials appeared on the rooftops.

Pronunciation Key: Accent Marks

[′] is the normal accent mark. It shows where the main stress falls on a word.
[′] is a secondary accent mark. It shows a lighter stress than the primary accent. For example:
tel • e • vis • ion [tel′ə vizh′ən]
(Turn the page for more information.)

A

(Katherine Anne Porter) **2.** any thing or happening: The party was a delightful *affair*. The "Dreyfus *Affair*" was a famous case of a man sent to prison for a crime he didn't commit.

af•fect[1] [ə fekt/] *verb,* **affected, affecting. 1.** to do something to; have an effect on: A shortage of oil would *affect* everyone in this country. **2.** to make a person feel very strongly about something: They were very *affected* by the movie about a missing child.

affect[2] *verb,* **affected, affecting.** to pretend to have or feel: That actor *affects* a British accent, but he's actually from Texas. ◆ This word is often used as an adjective: "In an *affected* high-pitched voice she cried, 'Oh, little girl, have you a penny to spare?'" (Eudora Welty) ◆ Something that is done in this way is an **affectation** [af/ ek tā/ shən].

dress was *affixed* to the package. —[af/ iks/] *noun, plural* **affixes.** a letter or letters attached to a word to change the meaning; a PREFIX or SUFFIX. In the word *unfriendly, un-* and *-ly* are affixes.

af•flict [ə flikt/] *verb,* **afflicted, afflicting.** to cause pain or suffering to: Arthritis is a disease that often *afflicts* older people. ◆ Something that afflicts is an **affliction:** Helen Keller overcame the *afflictions* of blindness and deafness to become a famous writer.

af•flu•ent [af/ lo͞o ənt *or* ə flo͞o/ ənt] *adjective,* **more/most.** having a lot of money or property; wealthy; rich: Beverly Hills is an *affluent* community where movie stars live.

af•ford [ə fôrd/] *verb,* **afforded, affording. 1.** to have enough money for: She can *afford* to buy a new car, but she can't *afford* an expensive one

affected writing If a writer is trying too hard to be proper and correct, instead of writing in a natural way, he might say: "We are given no option and will have to endure the party tonight." This sentence is fancy and unnatural—it's affected, that is, it is seeking to create a fancy impression. It's better to write: "We have to go to the party, so let's get it over with." Which do you prefer: "She has a prickly personality." or, "She has a way of seeming offended or oddly hurt or acting as if she was ignored."

af•fec•tion [ə fek/ shən] *noun, plural* **affections.** a feeling of love or friendship: to have *affection* for your family. She has great *affection* for her dog.

af•fec•tion•ate [ə fek/ shə nit] *adjective, more/most.* having or showing affection: an *affection-ate* smile, an *affectionate* letter from an old friend.—**affectionately,** *adverb.*

af•fi•da•vit [af/ ə dā/ vit] *noun, plural* **affidavits.** a written statement swearing that something is true: All the players on the team had to sign an *affidavit* saying that they did not use illegal drugs.

af•fil•i•ate [ə fil/ ē āt/] *verb,* **affiliated, affiliating.** to join or connect with: He's been *affiliated* with that company for over 30 years. —[ə fil/ ē-it] *noun, plural* **affiliates.** a person or thing that is affiliated: The three major television networks have *affiliates* in many cities around the country. —**affiliation,** *noun.*

af•firm•a•tive [ə fur/ mə tiv] *adjective.* saying that something is true; meaning "yes:" "I certainly do" is an *affirmative* answer to the question "Do you like pizza?" —*noun, plural* **affirmatives:** He answered her question in the *affirmative.*

af•fix [ə fiks/] *verb,* **affixed, affixing.** to fasten or attach something: A label with a mailing ad-

with a lot of extras. "We could not *afford* a cabin, but slept down below decks." (Thomas Merton) **2.** to be able to do something without causing harm: Our star quarterback is the one player we can't *afford* to lose.

Af•ghan•i•stan [af gan/ ə stan/] a country in southwestern Asia. *Capital:* Kabul. *Area:* 250,000 square miles. *Population:* 16,681,000.

a•fire [ə fīr/] *adverb* or *adjective.* on fire: Lightning set the roof of the old barn *afire.* "All the houses had been crushed and many were *afire.*" (John Hersey) ◆ Other words that are formed in the same way are **afoot** (He lost his horse and had to return to camp *afoot*); **afloat** (That aircraft carrier is one of the largest ships *afloat*); and **afield** (His search for the ancient city took him far *afield*).

a•fraid [ə frād/] *adjective, more/most.* **1.** feeling scared; full of fear; frightened: He's *afraid* to go in the water because he can't swim. **2.** feeling sorry or concerned about something: I'm *afraid* I'll have to ask you to come back tomorrow instead. "Aren't you *afraid* you'll make her very unhappy?" (Somerset Maugham)

Af•ri•ca [af/ ri kə] the second-largest continent, located south of Europe between the Atlantic Ocean and the Indian Ocean.

Af•ri•can [af′ ri kən] *noun, plural* **Africans.** a person from Africa. especially a black person who is a native of Africa. —*adjective.* having to do with Africa: *African* art, an *African* language.

Africa Snow-covered Mt. Kenya towers high above the African landscape at the equator.

Af•ro-A•mer•i•can [af′ rō ə mer′ i cən] *noun, plural* **Afro-Americans.** a black American whose ancestors came from Africa. —*adjective.* having to do with black Americans.

remembered that: "But *after all* I had to work, and there was no other work to be got." (Sherwood Anderson)

af•ter•math [af′ tər math′] *noun, plural* **aftermaths.** a thing that comes after as a result of something else: There was flooding along the coast in the *aftermath* of the storm.

af•ter•noon [af′ tər nōōn′] *noun, plural* **afternoons.** the time between noon and evening, ending at sunset.

af•ter•ward [af′ tər wərd] *adverb.* at a later time: They went for a swim, and *afterward* they sat in the sun.

♦ Another form of this word with the same meaning is **afterwards** [af′ tər wərdz]: "Charlotte was not at dinner, but she came down *afterwards.*" (Henry James)

a•gain [ə gen′] *adverb.* once more; another time: They took half an hour for lunch, and then went back to work *again.* "Oh, it sounds so funny, say it *again.*" (Jean Fritz)

a•gainst [ə genst′ *or* ə ginst′] *preposition.* **1.** in a way that is opposite to: Smoking is *against* the rules in this school. The North fought *against* the South in the Civil War. **2.** so as to hit or touch: "His face was *against* the stone." (John Hersey)

Afro-American This is one of several words used to describe black people. It is not a new word—it came into English before the Civil War—but only in recent years has it become common. Other nationalities who came to this country are sometimes called Italian-Americans, Irish-Americans, Mexican-Americans, and so on. *Afro-American* indicates persons who originally came to this country from Africa. Generally, it takes two or three generations before this kind of word usage begins to occur frequently. You would probably not, in the 1980's or 1990's, speak of "Thailand-Americans" or "Vietnamese-Americans." It's odd that you have to stay and work in America a while before you earn a double name. Why do you think this is?

aft [aft] *adverb.* toward the back of a ship or aircraft: to walk *aft.*

af•ter [af′ tər] *preposition.* **1.** later in time than: It's ten minutes *after* three. She takes piano lessons *after* school. **2.** behind or following: "*i* before *e* except *after c.*" She ran *after* the ball. —*adverb.* following in time or place: The store opened at 9:00, and we got there shortly *after.* —*conjunction.* following the time that: They opened the windows *after* the rain stopped.
♦**After** is also used as an adjective to form words with certain nouns, such as **aftereffect, afterlife, aftertaste,** and **afterthought.**

after all 1. in spite of; nevertheless: I didn't think she was going to the party, but she decided to come *after all.* **2.** it should be

age [āj] *noun, plural* **ages. 1.** the amount of time that a person, animal, or plant has been alive: He started college at the *age* of eighteen. **2.** the amount of time that a thing has existed: What's the *age* of that painting? **3.** a certain period of time: old *age,* the computer *age,* the Middle *Ages.* **4. ages.** a long time: "How is old Jem? I haven't seen him for *ages.*" (Doris Lessing)

Pronunciation Key: A–F

a	and; hat	ch	chew; such
ā	ate; stay	d	dog; lid
â	care; air	e	end; yet
ä	father; hot	ē	she; each
b	boy; cab	f	fun; off

(Turn the page for more information.)

A

—*verb*, **aged, aging.** to make or grow old: Certain kinds of cheese are *aged* to make them taste better. "Mr. and Mrs. Greenleaf had *aged* hardly at all. They had no worries, no responsibilities." (Flannery O'Connor)

a•ged [ā′ jid] *adjective.* **1.** old: an *aged* grandparent, medical care for the *aged.* **2.** [ājd] having a certain age: a child *aged* six.

a•gen•cy [ā′ jən sē] *noun, plural* **agencies. 1.** a company or person that does business for others: an advertising *agency.* A travel *agency* makes arrangements for people to go on trips. **2.** a department of the government: the Central Intelligence *Agency.*

a•gen•da [ə jen′ də] *noun.* **1.** a list of things to be talked about at a meeting. **2.** *Informal.* any plan of things to be done: What have you got on the *agenda* for this weekend?

a•gent [ā′ jənt] *noun, plural* **agents. 1.** a person who does business for others: an insurance *agent.* She is an *agent* for several famous movie stars. **2.** a person who works for a government agency. ♦ A **secret agent** is a spy. **3.** something that produces a certain effect: This shampoo contains several different cleansing *agents.*

ag•gra•vate [ag′ rə vāt] *verb,* **aggravated, aggravating. 1.** to make someone angry by bothering them; irritate or annoy: You know it *aggravates* me when you have the TV on so loud. "Don't repeat my words, please. It's a most *aggravating* habit." (George Bernard Shaw) **2.** to make worse: Joe *aggravated* an old knee injury when he slipped on the stairs. —**aggravation,** *noun.*

policy as leader of Nazi Germany. **2.** willing to fight or compete against others; strong and forceful: an *aggressive* car salesman. —**aggressively,** *adverb:* That basketball player plays defense very *aggressively.* —**aggressiveness,** *noun.*

ag•ile [aj′ əl] *adjective, more/most.* able to move in a quick and graceful way: an *agile* ballet dancer, an *agile* basketball player. ♦ Someone who is agile has **agility** [ə jil′ ə tē]: "She moved with great *agility* for such an old woman." (Madeleine L'Engle)

ag•i•tate [aj′ ə tāt′] *verb,* **agitated, agitating. 1.** to move back and forth: A washing machine *agitates* clothes. **2.** to stir up the feelings of; disturb or excite: "It was absurd nowadays to be *agitated* at the thought of traveling by air. Everybody did it." (Noel Coward) **3.** to try and stir up public opinion in support of some cause. ♦ A person who does this is an **agitator.**

a•glow [ə glō′] *adjective* or *adverb.* glowing. ♦ Other words that are formed in the same way are **agleam** and **aglitter.**

ag•nos•tic [ag näs′ tik] *noun, plural* **agnostics.** A person who believes that no one can know or prove that God exists, but who does not say definitely that there is no God. ♦ See also ATHEIST on page 49.

a•go [ə gō′] *adverb.* in the past; before now: They went home about five minutes *ago.*

ag•o•nize [ag′ ə nīz′] *verb,* **agonized, agonizing. 1.** to suffer great pain. ♦ This meaning is often used as an adjective: "With every step the *agonizing* pain mounted until he thought his head would burst." (Walter Farley) **2.** to make

---

aggravate When it was first used in English in the early 1500's, *aggravate* meant "to make heavy." The meanings that are used today are "to make worse" and "to bother or annoy." *Annoy* came into use around the year 1600. Nowadays, writers tend to use *aggravate* for *annoy.* It's not a serious crime! Yet, the fact is that by not being precise in the use of two words you can lose one of them. *Aggravate* has two different senses but *annoy* doesn't: "His bad mood was *aggravated* by her shouting at him." You cannot use *annoy* for *aggravate* in that sentence. So, if people keep mixing them up, as in "He was *aggravated* by the telephone's ringing," *aggravate* could lose its special sense and become only a fancier substitute for *annoy.*

---

ag•gres•sion [ə gresh′ ən] *noun, plural* **aggressions. 1.** an attack made without good reason: The country committed an act of *aggression* when its troops suddenly attacked a neighboring country. **2.** behavior or actions that are strong and forceful.

ag•gres•sive [ə gres′ iv] *adjective, more/most.* **1.** attacking without good reason; warlike: Adolf Hitler followed an *aggressive* foreign

a great effort; struggle: He *agonized* over whether to tell the police what he had seen.

ag•o•ny [ag′ ə nē] *noun, plural* **agonies.** very great pain: to be in *agony* from a broken leg.

a•gree [ə grē′] *verb,* **agreed, agreeing. 1.** to have the same idea about something: I *agree* with you that we should take a side road instead of the main highway. **2.** to be willing to do: The bank *agreed* to lend her money for a new car.

3. in grammar, to go with another word in the proper way: The verb "is" *agrees* with the pronouns "he" and "she"; it does not *agree* with the pronoun "they." **4. agree with.** to be good or healthful for: Hot, spicy foods don't *agree with* him.

a•gree•a•ble [ə grē′ ə bəl] *adjective, more/most.* **1.** ready to agree; willing: Is she *agreeable* to your suggestion? **2.** nice; pleasant: "I've spent *agreeable* years on a mountain lake and came to enjoy the clear Caribbean . . ." (John Barth) **—agreeably,** *adverb.*

> **agreement** The agreement between a verb and noun is very important. If you write, "The six men is in trouble," you have made a bad sentence. "Six" is plural; therefore "are" rather than "is" is required. How would you choose between the following words: "A woman (speak/speaks) on that subject tonight." "Martin Luther King's mourners (was/were) united."

a•gree•ment [ə grē′ mənt] *noun, plural* **agreements. 1.** an understanding or arrangement between two people or groups: Countries can have peace *agreements* or trade *agreements* with each other. The Johnsons signed a letter of *agreement* stating that they were willing to sell the house for $100,000. **2.** the state of agreeing; having the same idea: "Whenever you accept our views we shall be in full *agreement* with you." (Moshe Dayan) **3.** in grammar, the matching of two words in the proper way: A verb must be in *agreement* with its subject.

ag•ri•cul•ture [ag′ rə kul′ chər] *noun.* the science or business of farming. **—agricultural** [ag′ rə kul′ chər əl], *adjective.* having to do with farming: an *agricultural* college. The Cherokee Indians were an *agricultural* people.

a•head [ə hed′] *adverb.* **1.** in or to the front: Mary was ten yards *ahead* of the second-place runner. There was only one car on the road *ahead.* **2.** in a better or more advanced position:

The Lions were six points *ahead* at the half. Todd is way *ahead* of the rest of the class in math. **3.** to or for the future; forward: Set the clock *ahead* one hour tonight for the start of Daylight Saving Time.

aid [ād] *noun, plural* **aids. 1.** help or support: The lifeguard quickly came to his *aid* when he

got knocked down by a wave. **2.** something that is helpful: A hearing *aid* is a device that makes sounds louder. **—verb, aided, aiding.** to help: It is against the law to *aid* a criminal in committing a crime.

aide [ād] *noun, plural* **aides.** someone who aids; a helper or assistant: The President was accompanied on the trip by several of his *aides.*

AIDS [ādz] a disease in which the body completely loses the power to fight off other diseases. ◆ The name is an ACRONYM for Acquired Immune Deficiency Syndrome.

ail [āl] *verb,* **ailed, ailing. 1.** to cause illness or trouble for: Grandpa loves to walk along the beach; he says it's good for whatever *ails* you. **2.** to be sick: "You mustn't pay attention to old Addie. She's *ailing* today." (Eudora Welty)

ail•ment [āl′ mənt] *noun, plural* **ailments.** something that ails a person; an illness, especially a minor illness.

aim [ām] *verb,* **aimed, aiming. 1.** to point a gun or other weapon at a target: to *aim* an arrow, to *aim* a bomb at a building. **2.** to point or direct at someone or something: Be sure you *aim* the camera carefully. **3.** to have a certain goal or purpose: Ted doesn't know much about working with computers yet, but he *aims* to learn in a hurry.

—noun, plural **aims. 1.** the fact of aiming: The hockey player's *aim* was off, and his shot missed the net. **2.** a goal or purpose: "His only *aim* in life had been to get as much fun out of it as possible." (Somerset Maugham)

> **ain't** There is an old saying, "*Ain't* ain't in the dictionary." This was intended to remind people that *ain't* is not "proper English." As you can see, this dictionary does not include the word. If we did, it would have been entered right here. People do use *ain't* in speaking, and you will hear it in popular songs, and in stories to show how certain characters talk. But in your own writing, *ain't* is a sign of carelessness. It does not take more time to write, "is not" or "are not."

	Pronunciation Key: G–N		
g	give; big	k	kind; cat; back
h	hold	l	let; ball
i	it; this	m	make; time
ī	ice; my	n	not; own
j	jet; gem; edge	ng	having

(Turn the page for more information.)

A

air [âr] *noun, plural* **airs. 1.** what we breathe to stay alive. Air is all around the earth and is a mixture of gases, mainly NITROGEN and OXYGEN. **2.** fresh air: Open the windows and get some *air* in here. **3.** the air above the earth; the sky: The sailors threw their hats in the *air* and cheered. **4.** the general feeling or appearance of something: There's an *air* of mystery about that old house. "He had the *air* of a man who has found his place in life." (Katherine Mansfield) **5. airs.** an unnatural way of acting to impress others: Even after she became famous she never put on *airs* with her old friends.
—*verb,* **aired, airing. 1.** to place in the air or let air through: to *air* out a room. **2.** to bring out into the open; make known: The school held a meeting so that the parents could *air* their opinions. **3. on (off) the air.** that is (or is not) being broadcast: That TV show has been *on the air* for twelve years. **4. up in the air.** not decided; uncertain: Her plans for the summer are still *up in the air.*

air•borne [âr′bôrn′] *adjective.* carried by the air: Plants often spread from place to place by means of *airborne* seeds. *Airborne* troops attacked the enemy fort.

airborne Modern armies use airborne troops to strike quickly behind enemy lines. These American paratroopers are landing during a training exercise.

air-con•di•tion [âr′kən dish′ən] *verb,* **air-conditioned, air-conditioning.** to provide a place with air conditioning.
♦ Often used as an adjective: an *air-conditioned* building.

air conditioning a system of treating the air in a room, building, car, or other closed place. Air conditioning makes the air cooler and also drier and cleaner.
♦ An **air-conditioner** is a machine used for air conditioning.

air•craft [âr′kraft′] *noun, plural* **aircraft.** anything that is made to travel through the air, such as an airplane, a helicopter, or a glider.

aircraft carrier a large warship that carries planes. It has a flat deck that the planes can use to land and take off and a lower deck (called a hangar) where they are stored.

aircraft carrier *U.S.S. Dwight D. Eisenhower,* a modern aircraft carrier using nuclear power.

air•line [âr′līn′] *noun, plural* **airlines.** a company whose business is moving people and goods from place to place by aircraft. ♦ A plane used by an airline is an **airliner.**

air•mail [âr′māl′] *noun.* a system of sending mail by means of aircraft. —*verb,* **airmailed, airmailing.** to send something by airmail.
♦ Also used as an adjective and adverb: an *airmail* letter, to send a package *airmail.*

air•man [âr′mən] *noun, plural* **airmen.** a rank in the U.S. Air Force that is below the rank of a sergeant.

air•plane [âr′plān′] *noun, plural* **airplanes.** a vehicle that flies in the air. An airplane flies in spite of being heavier than the air itself. Airplanes have fixed or two-position wings and are powered by jet engines or propellers.

air•port [âr′pôrt′] *noun, plural* **airports.** an area with places for airplanes to land and take off. An airport also has a building or buildings to take care of passengers and cargo, and other buildings to store and service airplanes.

air•space [âr′spās′] *noun.* the air or sky above a country, legally agreed among nations to be part of that country's territory.

air•tight [âr′tīt′] *adjective, most/most.* **1.** so tight that air cannot get in or out: an *airtight* container. **2.** not having any weak points that can be attacked: He had an *airtight* alibi for the day of the crime.

aisle The aisle of St. Bartholomew the Great Church in London, England. This center aisle is also called a *nave* [nāv].

aisle [īl] *noun, plural* **aisles.** a long, narrow space to walk through, such as the passage between rows of seats in a church or theater or the area between counters in a store.

rolling toward him. —*verb,* **alarmed, alarming.** to make afraid: "'Don't be *alarmed,*' said Rainsford. 'I'm no robber.'" (Richard Connell) ◆ Often used as an adjective: an *alarming* report about an approaching hurricane.

A•las•ka [ə las′ kə] a U.S. state in the northwest corner of North America bordered by Canada. *Capital:* Juneau. *Nickname:* "Last Frontier." *Area:* 590,000 square miles. *Population:* 400,000.

Al•ber•ta [al bur′ tə] a province in western Canada. *Capital:* Edmonton. *Area:* 255,000 square miles. *Population:* 2,200,000.

al•bi•no [al bī′ nō] *noun, plural* **albinos.** a person or animal that lacks normal coloring in the skin, hair, and eyes, and that is thought of as being white-colored and having reddish eyes.

al•bum [al′ bəm] *noun, plural* **albums. 1.** a long-playing record or tape. An album usually has a number of selections performed by the same person or group or in the same style. **2.** a

aisle *Aisle* is a "hard" word in spelling tests. Only about 3% of fifth-graders seem to get it right, and only about 13% in grade seven. The reason *aisle* is difficult to spell is that the letters *ai* have the sound [ī]. It sounds exactly like another word, *isle,* meaning "island." If you are listening to a speech and you hear *aisle* or *isle*—both sounding the same—then you need to find out from the *context,* that is, words preceding and succeeding the word. For example, if the speaker says, "He was stranded on an *isle,*" you know it's an island. If instead he says, "He went up the *aisle* on leaving the theater," you know it is a walkway.

a•jar [ə jär′] *adjective* or *adverb.* partly open: "Seeing that Dick's door was slightly *ajar,* we looked in to see if he was there." (Thomas Wolfe)

Al•a•bam•a [al′ ə bam′ ə] a state in the southeastern U.S. *Capital:* Montgomery. *Nickname:* "Heart of Dixie." *Area:* 51,600 square miles. *Population:* 3,890,000.

a la carte [ä′ lə kärt′] a French expression meaning "from the card." In a restaurant, if you order *a la carte* you pick certain foods that are separately priced. With a **fixed-price** menu, you order a whole meal at one price.

Al•a•mo [al′ ə mō] a fort in San Antonio, Texas where a small force of Texans was killed after holding off a much larger group of Mexican soldiers during the Texas Revolution.

a•larm [ə lärm′] *noun, plural* **alarms. 1.** something that makes a noise to warn people or to wake them up: a fire *alarm,* a burglar *alarm.* I slept late because the *alarm* didn't go off. **2.** a sudden feeling of being afraid: He was filled with *alarm* when the parked car suddenly began

book with blank pages to hold stamps, photographs, autographs, or the like.

Al•bu•quer•que [al′ bə kur′ kē] the largest city in New Mexico. *Population:* 332,000.

al•che•my [al′ kə mē] *noun.* an early form of chemistry practiced in the Middle Ages. Alchemy was the study of ways to turn ordinary metals into gold through the use of magic and secret formulas. ◆ A person who practiced alchemy was known as an **alchemist.**

al•co•hol [al′ kə hôl] *noun, plural* **alcohols. 1.** a type of liquid that has no color or smell and can catch fire easily. Alcohol is the substance in beer, wine, whisky, and so on that can make a

Pronunciation Key: O–S			
ō	over; go	ou	out; town
ô	all; law	p	put; hop
oo	look; full	r	run; car
o͞o	pool; who	s	set; miss
oi	oil; boy	sh	show

(Turn the page for more information.)

A

person drunk. Different kinds of alcohol are used in medicines, as a fuel, and for many other products. **2.** any drink that has alcohol in it: Some religions have rules against the use of *alcohol.*

alfalfa An alfalfa plant and its leaf. Alfalfa is made into a sweet-smelling hay that is a rich food for farm animals.

al•co•hol•ic [al′ kə hô′ lik]   *adjective,   more/ most.* containing alcohol: an *alcoholic* drink, *alcoholic* fuels. —*noun, plural* **alcoholics.** a person who suffers from alcoholism.

al•co•hol•ism [al′ kə hô liz′ əm] *noun.* a disease in which a person has a habit of drinking too much alcohol and suffers physical and mental damage because of this.

al•cove [al′ kōv′] *noun, plural* **alcoves.** a small part of a room that is partly closed off from the rest of the room.

ale [āl] *noun, plural* **ales.** an alcoholic drink that is like beer but has a darker color and a more bitter taste.

a•lert [ə lurt′] *adjective, more/most.* **1.** watching very carefully; ready for something to happen: An *alert* guard noticed that the door had been broken open. "They turned and watched him with narrowed, *alert* dark eyes." (Doris Lessing) **2.** quick to learn or understand: a person with an *alert* mind. —*noun, plural* **alerts.** a signal that warns of danger: There was an air raid *alert* as the enemy bombers approached. —*verb,* **alerted, alerting.** to make alert; warn: Paul Revere *alerted* the Americans of the coming of British troops. —**alertly,** *adverb:* The dog stood *alertly* near the door. —**alertness,** *noun.*

Al•ex•an•der the Great [al′ ig zan′ dər] 356– 323 B.C., king of Macedonia (a former country in southern Europe) and ruler of a large empire reaching from Egypt to India.

al•fal•fa [al fal′ fə] *noun.* a plant with purple flowers that is related to clover. It is grown as food for cattle and horses.

al•gae [al′ jē] *plural noun.* a large group of plants that live in water. Algae do not have leaves, roots, and stems, but they do have CHLOROPHYLL. Seaweed is a type of algae.

♦ The singular form of this word is **alga** [al′ gə]. As with many other words in science, *algae* is taken directly from Latin. Changing **-a** to **-ae** is a standard way to form the plural of nouns in Latin.

algae This green seaweed is *kelp,* which is a common form of algae.

al•ge•bra [al′ jə brə] *noun.* a form of mathematics that uses letters to stand for numbers that are not known.

♦ The statement "$3x + 10 = 9y - 5$" is an **algebraic** expression [al′ jə brā′ ik].

algebra Algebra comes from an expression in Arabic meaning "putting things together," because in algebra numerals and letters are placed together to form an equation. In the early Middle Ages, the Arabs were more advanced in mathematics than Western Europe. They introduced the science of algebra to the West. The first use of the word *algebra* was in the title of a book written in the 800's by an Arab mathematician, Muhammad ibn Musa. Why do so many Arab words begin with al-, such as *alcohol, alkali,* and *algebra?* What do you think the *al-* prefix means in Arabic? It means "the."

Al•ge•ri•a [al jēr′ ē ə] a country in northwestern Africa. *Capital:* Algiers. *Area:* 919,000 square miles. *Population:* 21,000,000.

al•go•rithm [al′ gə rith′ əm] *noun, plural* **algorithms.** a way of finding the answer to a problem by going through a series of rules or procedures step by step. Many computer operations are performed by means of algorithms.

a•li•as [ā′ lē əs] *noun, plural* **aliases.** a name that a person uses other than his real name, especially a false name that a criminal uses to hide his true identity.

al•i•bi [al′ ə bī] *noun, plural* **alibis. 1.** a claim that a person was somewhere else when a crime took place and therefore could not have been involved in it. **2.** any excuse for a mistake or failure: "*Alibi* Ike" is a famous story about a baseball player who blamed someone else whenever he missed the ball. —*verb,* **alibied, alibiing.** to give an alibi or excuse.

a•li•en [ā′ lē ən *or* āl′ yən] *noun, plural* **aliens. 1.** a person who is not a citizen of the country in which he is living. **2.** a being in a science fiction story that comes from another planet. —*adjective, more/most.* **1.** having to do with another country; foreign: Some countries have passed laws to keep out *alien* workers. **2.** very different or strange: a movie about *alien* creatures from Mars. **3.** not natural: "To do something like this was still *alien* to my nature. I held back." (William Melvin Kelley)

a•li•e•nate [ā′ lē ə nāt′ *or* āl′ yə nāt′] *verb,* **alienated, alienating. 1.** to cause to become unfriendly: He's *alienated* many of his old friends by bragging about his new job. **2.** to remove or separate from a group: The soldier felt *alienated* from society when he came back from the war. —**alienation,** *noun.*

a•light[1] [ə līt′] *verb,* **alighted** or **alit, alighting.** to get or come down from a higher place: She *alighted* from the horse. "Many different kinds of flies used to *alight* on the railing." (I.B. Singer)

alight[2] *adjective.* lighted up: "His eyes were *alight* with friendship." (James Herriot)

a•lign [ə līn′] *verb,* **aligned, aligning. 1.** to bring into line: The mechanic *aligned* the wheels of the car. **2.** to join or cooperate with: Great Britain is usually *aligned* with the U.S. on foreign policy. —**alignment,** *noun:* The wheels of the car were out of *alignment.*

a•like [ə līk′] *adjective, more/most.* like one another; similar: Dad says that all rock songs sound *alike* to him. —*adverb.* in the same way: That teacher treats everyone in her class *alike.*

al•i•men•ta•ry canal [al′ ə men′ trē] a long tube in the body through which food passes to be digested, absorbed, and then removed as waste matter. It begins at the mouth and includes the ESOPHAGUS, stomach, and intestines.

al•i•mo•ny [al′ ə mō′ nē] *noun.* a certain sum of money approved by a judge for living expenses, paid regularly by a person to a former wife or husband after they have been legally divorced.

a•live [ə līv′] *adjective, more/most.* **1.** having life; not dead; living. **2.** in existence; active: The custom of celebrating Thanksgiving has been kept *alive* for over 350 years. "The river was *alive* with many kinds of ducks chasing each other round." (L.M. Boston)

al•ka•li [al′ kə lī′] *noun, plural* **alkalis** or **alkalies.** one of a large group of chemicals that have a bitter taste and combine with an acid to form a salt. —**alkaline** [al′ kə līn′], *adjective:* The soil in desert regions is usually very *alkaline.*

all [ôl] *adjective.* **1.** with nothing missing or left out; the whole of: They stayed awake *all* night. **2.** every one of: "*All* men are created equal." (Thomas Jefferson) —*adverb.* **1.** completely; entirely: His answers were *all* correct. **2.** for each side: The score was tied, six *all.* —*noun.* everything one has: She gave her *all* to win the race. —*pronoun.* everyone or everything: *All* was quiet on the lake at dawn.

at all 1. under any conditions: Billy finished his dinner, but he didn't drink any milk *at all.* **2.** in any way: She wasn't *at all* upset.

Al•lah [ä′ lə] *noun.* the name of the Supreme Being in the Muslim religion.

al•lege [ə lej′] *verb,* **alleged, alleging.** to state positively that a person has committed a certain crime, but without presenting proof: It's been *alleged* that he stole the money, but he has not yet gone on trial. ◆ Often used as an adjective: an *alleged* bank robber, the *alleged* driver of the getaway car. —**allegedly,** *adverb: Allegedly,* he stole secret military plans.

al•le•giance [ə lē′ jəns] *noun.* a being true or faithful to something; loyalty: to feel *allegiance* to one's country. ◆ The **Pledge of Allegiance** is a statement of loyalty to the United States.

Pronunciation Key: T–Z			
t	ten; date	v	very; live
th	think	w	win; away
th	these	y	you
u	cut; butter	z	zoo; cause
ur	turn; bird	zh	measure

(Turn the page for more information.)

al•ler•gic [ə lur′ jik] *adjective, more/most.* **1.** having an allergy: to be *allergic* to chocolate or to cat hair. **2.** *Informal.* having a strong dislike for: Why won't you help me move this stuff—are you *allergic* to hard work?

al•ler•gy [al′ ər jē] *noun, plural* **allergies.** a reaction of the body against something that is not harmful in itself and that does not bother other people. Things that often cause allergies are dust, animal hair, pollen, and certain kinds of food and medicine.

al•ley [al′ ē] *noun, plural* **alleys. 1.** a long narrow space between buildings, especially one at the side or rear of a row of buildings. **2.** see **bowling alley.**

al•li•ance [ə lī′ əns] *noun, plural* **alliances.** an agreement to work together or combine for some purpose; an allying: an *alliance* between two nations. The General Motors Corporation formed an *alliance* with a Japanese auto company to make a new kind of car.

al•lied [al′ īd *or* ə līd′] *adjective.* being an ally; joined or connected in some way: Biology and chemistry are *allied* subjects.

al•li•ga•tor [al′ ə gā′ tər] *noun, plural* **alligators.** a large water animal with thick, tough skin. An alligator is a reptile very much like the crocodile but with a shorter, flatter head. Alligators live in swamps in the Southeastern United States and in China.

al•lot [ə lät′] *verb,* **allotted, allotting.** to give as a share; give out: You should *allot* ten minutes for each part of the test. "The car *allotted* to me was a tiny Austin." (James Herriot) —**allotment,** *noun:* The dealer gets an *allotment* of twenty new cars a month from the factory. ♦ Note the difference between the noun phrase "a lot." as in "*a lot* of mistakes," and the verb *allot.*

fact that these jeans are going to shrink when they're washed.

al•low•ance [ə lou′ əns] *noun, plural* **allowances. 1.** a sum of money set aside for a certain purpose: Suzie gets a weekly *allowance* for helping her parents with the housework. The store is offering an *allowance* of $100 on any old TV set traded in to buy a new one. **2. make allowance(s) for.** to allow for.

alligator The American alligator. The word *alligator* comes from Spanish *el lagarto,* "the lizard," The English word was first used in print in 1568 by the explorer Job Hortrop.

al•loy [al′ oi] *noun, plural* **alloys.** a metal made by melting and mixing together other metals. Some alloys are an improvement over the metals that combine to make them, as by being harder, stronger, or lighter. Others combine a valuable metal such as gold or silver with a cheaper one. Steel and bronze are alloys. —*verb,* **alloyed, alloying.** to make an alloy: Copper is *alloyed* with zinc to make brass.

all right *All right* and *alright* are two different forms that mean the same thing and sound the same. How does one choose between them? There's no good reason to choose *all right*—except that good writers and educated readers tend to use it. "'Do you want me to read to you?' 'All right. If you want to.'" (Ernest Hemingway) A similar instance is *all ready* and *already,* although you don't have to choose. *All ready* means that things are in order. "The Girl Scouts are *all ready* for their camping trip." But *already* is an adverb that signifies time. "He was *already* home when it happened."

al•low [ə lou′] *verb,* **allowed, allowing. 1.** to let something happen; permit: There's no parking *allowed* on this street. **2.** to let have; give or provide: They *allowed* extra time to get to the airport. **3. allow for.** to take into account; make an adjustment for: You have to *allow for* the

all right 1. not hurt or sick: The car went off the road, but the driver was *all right.* **2.** good enough; satisfactory: The food in that restaurant is *all right,* but it's not worth the prices they charge. **3.** a way of saying "yes": *All right,* you can stay up to watch the end of the movie.

al•ly [al′ī *or* ə lī′] *noun, plural* **allies.** a person, group, or country that joins with another for some purpose: The President worked with his *allies* in Congress to get the law passed. —*verb,* **allied, allying.** to join with another as an ally: Cuba is *allied* with the Soviet Union.

a•lone [ə lōn′] *adjective.* **1.** not with others: Dad is *alone* tonight because the rest of the family went to the movies. **2.** only: Water *alone* won't make those flowers grow; you have to give them plant food. —*adverb.* by oneself or itself: An old cabin stood *alone* in the valley.

---

ally When the word *ally* was first used in English, it referred to the joining together of two people through marriage. Because two powerful families could be allied through the marriage of their children (such as princes and princesses of different countries), the word then came to mean the joining together of countries or groups. If you write, "He was my *ally*," you are not saying the same thing as "I tried to *ally* myself with him." Here, the spelling is the same, the meaning similar, but one is used as a noun and the other is a verb and each has a separate, if *allied,* meaning.

---

al•ma•nac [ôl′ mə nak′] *noun, plural* **almanacs.** a book that contains facts about many different subjects. The first almanacs had calendars and gave information about the weather, the rising and setting of the sun and the moon, and so on. Almanacs now also include facts about countries, states, and cities and lists of famous people or of important dates in history.

al•might•y [ôl mī′ tē] *adjective.* having complete power; all-powerful: *almighty* God. ♦ **The Almighty** is a name for a Supreme Being or God.

al•mond [ä′ mənd] *noun, plural* **almonds.** a small nut that is eaten alone or used as a flavoring for candy and other foods. The almond tree is related to the peach.

alpaca The alpaca lives high in the Andes Mountains of South America.

al•most [ôl′ mōst] *adverb.* very close to, but not actually; nearly: It's *almost* six o'clock. "Ella May and Beatrice came *almost* every day to visit me." (Marjorie Kinnan Rawlings)

let alone not to mention: "Clasby never had the patience to sit through one whole morning, *let alone* four." (Jessamyn West)

a•long [ə lông′] *preposition.* by the length of; beside the long part of: The car raced *along* the highway. —*adverb.* **1.** forward: She walked *along* quickly. **2.** near or with someone: You can bring a friend *along* if you want.

a•long•side [ə lông′ sīd′] *preposition or adverb.* along or by the side: There were several boats *alongside* the dock. The policeman waved the car off the road and stopped his patrol car *alongside.*

a•loof [ə lo͞of′] *adjective, more/most.* not very friendly; removed or distant: Dr. Stern has an *aloof* manner toward his patients, but away from his office he's very friendly. —*adverb.* at a distance: "The newcomer was pleasant in his manner . . . but for some reason he kept *aloof* from the other boys." (F. Scott Fitzgerald)

a•loud [ə loud′] *adverb.* out loud. "Gertrude could not bear having anyone read *aloud* to her." (Janet Flanner)

al•pac•a [al pak′ ə] *noun, plural* **alpacas.** an animal that is related to the camel and lives in the mountains of South America. It has fine, long wool that is used to make clothing.

al•pha•bet [al′ fə bet′] *noun, plural* **alphabets.** the letters used to write a language, arranged in their set order from beginning to end. In English this order is A, B, C, and so on.

Pronunciation Key: [ə] Symbol

The [ə] or *schwa* sound occurs in syllables without an accent. It can be spelled with any vowel, such as a in above, e in listen, i in pencil, o in melon, u in circus. It can also be a combination of vowels, such as io in action, ai in mountain, iou in precious.

(Turn the page for more information.)

A

al•pha•bet•i•cal [al′ fə bet′ i kəl] *adjective.* arranged according to the alphabet: In a telephone book people's names appear in *alphabetical* order. —**alphabetically,** *adverb:* The words in this dictionary are listed *alphabetically.*

al•pha•bet•ize [al′ fə bə tīz′] *verb,* **alphabetized, alphabetizing.** to arrange something in alphabetical order: A computer can *alphabetize* a group of words automatically.

Alps [alps] a mountain system of south-central Europe that extends from southern France through Italy, Switzerland and Austria into Yugoslavia.

Alps The Alps are famous for their beautiful scenery, with high mountains towering over historic farms and villages.

al•read•y [ôl red′ ē] *adverb.* **1.** before now or before a certain time: I've *already* seen that movie. "Arthur had *already* thought the question over and found the answer." (Henry James) **2.** so soon: Are you leaving *already?* You just got here.

al•so [ôl′ sō] *adverb.* as well; besides; too: He washed the car, and he *also* cleaned the inside.

al•tar [ôl′ tər] *noun, plural* **altars.** a table or raised place used as a center for religious services. ◆ An **altar boy** is a boy who helps the priest during a Catholic religious service.

al•ter [ôl′ tər] *verb,* **altered, altering.** to make or become different in a certain way; change somewhat: The store *altered* the coat to make it shorter. —**alteration,** *noun:* Does the store charge extra for *alterations?*

al•ter•nate [ôl′ tər nāt] *verb,* **alternated, alternating. 1.** to take turns; go one after another: In a game of checkers, the two players *alternate* in moving their pieces. **2.** to move back and forth from one to another: The weather has *alternated* between clear days and cloudy ones all this

month. —[ôl′ tər nit] *adjective.* **1.** by turns; one and then another: Mom and Mrs. Jackson drive us to school on *alternate* days. **2.** in place of another; as a substitute: The main highway was blocked off, so they had to take an *alternate* route. —[ôl′ tər nit] *noun, plural* **alternates.** a person or thing that takes the place of another; a substitute. —**alternately,** *adverb:* "The grizzlies . . . *alternately* play the clown and sleep." (Jean Stafford)

alternating current (AC) an electric current that alternates by first flowing in one direction and then in the other, back and forth at regular intervals. The electricity in homes and other buildings uses alternating current. ◆ See also DIRECT CURRENT.

al•ter•na•tive [ôl tur′ nə tiv] *noun, plural* **alternatives. 1.** a choice between two or more things: For her art project, she has the *alternative* of doing either a painting or a clay sculpture. ". . . all the *alternatives* which were likely to face me on the high seas." (Joseph Conrad) **2.** one single choice of this kind: If he keeps missing class, the teacher will have no *alternative* but to give him an 'F' for the course. —*adjective.* giving a choice: They discussed several *alternative* ways of solving the problem.

al•though [ôl thō′] *conjunction.* in spite of; though: *Although* Vincent van Gogh sold only one painting in his own lifetime, today he is one of the world's most famous artists.

al•ti•tude [al′ tə tōōd′] *noun, plural* **altitudes.** the height that something is above the ground or above sea level: Denver is called "The Mile High City" because it has an *altitude* of about one mile.

al•to [al′ tō] *noun, plural* **altos. 1.** the lowest singing voice for a woman, or the highest for a man. An alto is higher than a TENOR and lower than a SOPRANO. **2.** a musical instrument with the same range: an *alto* saxophone.

al•to•geth•er [ôl′ tə geth′ ər] *adverb.* **1.** completely; entirely: "Only a few months ago the mine had closed down *altogether.*" (Eric Knight) **2.** with all included; counting all: There are eight of us going *altogether,* so we'll have to take two cars.

a•lu•mi•num [ə lōō′ mə nəm] *noun.* a lightweight, silver-white metal that is a chemical element. Aluminum is the most common metal in the earth's surface. It is easily shaped, it conducts heat and electricity well, and it does not rust or tarnish easily. Aluminum is used for many purposes, such as in making wire, pots and pans, aircraft and automobile parts, and machinery. ♦ **Aluminum foil** is a very thin sheet of metal used in cooking and storing food.

a•lum•nus [ə lum′ nəs] *noun, plural* **alumni** [ə lum′ nī]. a person who has attended a certain college or school: Harvard University has many famous *alumni,* including President Franklin D. Roosevelt and the great poet T.S. Eliot. ♦ A form of this word that is used to refer to a girl or woman is **alumna** [ə lum′ nə], *plural* **alumnae** [ə lum′ nē].

al•ways [ôl wāz] *adverb.* at all times; all the time: "On the table there was *always* just one object: an old Bible." (Thomas Wolfe)

am [am *or* əm] *verb.* a form of the verb BE that is used with "I" to tell about the present: I *am* taking piano lessons this year.

A.M. or **a.m.** a way to show that a certain time is in the morning. A.M. means between midnight and noon; P.M. means between noon and midnight.

AM one of the two main kinds of signals used by home and car radios. In AM radio the signal is sent out the same number of times per second, but the strength of the signal changes. In FM radio the strength stays the same, but the timing changes.

a•mass [ə mas′] *verb,* **amassed, amassing.** to gather or collect: "Soon (he) had *amassed* the largest personal fortune in the world." (J.D. Salinger)

Am•a•zon [am′ ə zän′] the longest river in South America. It flows from the Andes Mountains in Peru across northern Brazil to empty into the Atlantic Ocean.

Amazon In ancient Greek stories, the Amazons were a tribe of fierce woman warriors. The river got its name because one of the first explorers of the area claimed that he had been attacked by a tribe of Indian women.

am•bas•sa•dor [am bas′ ə dər] *noun, plural* **ambassadors.** a person who lives in a foreign country and serves as the chief representative of his or her government in that country: the United States *Ambassador* to Great Britain.

---

amateur The word *amateur* comes from the Latin word for "love." The idea is that amateurs do something because they love to do it, not because they get paid for it. That's the original meaning of the word. Later, *amateur* began to be used to describe someone who is not expert or talented: "Her performance in the play was *amateurish.*"

---

am•a•teur [am′ ə chər *or* am′ ə tər] *noun, plural* **amateurs. 1.** a person who does something because he enjoys it, not because he is paid to do it: A professional tennis player gets prize money for winning a match, but an *amateur* does not. **2.** a person who does not have skill or experience: This table is obviously the work of an *amateur*—all the legs are crooked. —*adjective.* of or by an amateur: There is an *amateur* golf tournament at the club this week.

a•maze [ə māz′] *verb,* **amazed, amazing.** to surprise greatly: The guards were *amazed* to find that the prisoner had disappeared from his locked cell. ♦ Often used as an adjective: "He gained strength with *amazing* speed." (Liam O'Flaherty) —**amazingly,** *adverb.* in an amazing way: "They were all *amazingly* beautiful." (Robert Heinlein) —**amazement,** *noun.*

am•ber [am′ bər] *noun.* a hard, clear, yellow or brown substance that is used to make beads and jewelry. Amber is a FOSSIL from the RESIN of pine trees that grew millions of years ago.

am•bi•dex•trous [am′ bə deks′ trəs] *adjective.* able to use both hands equally well. Most people are either right- or left-handed rather than truly ambidextrous. —**ambidextrously,** *adverb.*

Pronunciation Key: Accent Marks

[′] is the normal accent mark. It shows where the main stress falls on a word.
[′] is a secondary accent mark. It shows a lighter stress than the primary accent. For example:
tel • e • vis • ion [tel′ ə vizh′ ən]
(Turn the page for more information.)

am·big·u·ous [am big′ yōō əs] *adjective, more/ most.* having more than one possible meaning; not clear: The sentence "Melissa gave her baby sister Laura a sweater that was too small for her" is *ambiguous.* It doesn't tell clearly whether the sweater is too small for Melissa (it could be an old one that she's handing down to her sister) or too small for Laura (it could be a gift that's the wrong size).

am·bi·tion [am bish′ ən] *noun, plural* **ambitions.** a strong desire to become a success or get something: Mike's *ambition* is to become an astronaut some day.

am·bi·tious [am bish′ əs] *adjective, more/most.* having a strong desire to succeed or to become something: Al has *ambitious* plans to build a house all by himself. "Mother was *ambitious* for me. She wanted me to rise in the world." (Sherwood Anderson) **—ambitiously,** *adverb.*

official document: The Constitution was *amended* in 1920 to give women the right to vote. **2.** to change something for the better: Let me *amend* that remark; I didn't mean to suggest that the accident was your fault.

a·mend·ment [ə mend′ mənt] *noun, plural* **amendments.** a change in a law or official document: The first ten *amendments* to the Constitution are called "The Bill of Rights."

A·mer·i·ca [ə mer′ i kə] **1.** all the lands of the Western Hemisphere, including North, Central, and South America. **2.** the United States.

A·mer·i·can [ə mer′ i kən] *noun, plural* **Americans. 1.** a person born or living in the United States. **2.** any person born or living in North or South America. *—adjective.* **1.** having to do with the United States. **2.** having to do with North America and South America: The racoon and the skunk are *American* animals.

> **American** Writers usually mean the United States when they write of "American" events or persons. Even though Canada and Mexico are also in North America, they are not usually included in the expression *American:* "*American* literature produced many interesting writers, Twain, Longfellow, Frost, among others." You would not include here Carlos Fuentes (Mexican) or Malcolm Lowry (Canadian). This is not an unusual practice. Although Britain is part of Europe geographically, you wouldn't write that Shakespeare or Milton was a European writer.

am·bu·lance [am′ byə ləns] *noun, plural* **ambulances.** a car or truck that is specially equipped to carry sick and injured people to the hospital. ◆ The word *ambulance* was the first used in the French army in the early 1800's. It comes from a word meaning "walk." An ambulance was a "walking hospital" that moved with the army.

am·bush [am′ boosh] *noun, plural* **ambushes.** a surprise attack by someone who is hidden: The captain suspected an enemy *ambush,* so he waited until dark to move his troops. *—verb,* **ambushed, ambushing.** to make a surprise attack from a hidden place.

a·me·ba [ə mē′ bə] (*also spelled* **amoeba**) *noun, plural* **amebas.** a tiny, simple form of animal life that can only be seen by using a microscope. An ameba constantly changes its body shape as it moves and takes in food. Amebas live in water and in soil and as PARASITES in larger animals.

a·men [ā′ men′ *or* ä′ men′] *interjection.* a word that means "so be it." "Amen" is spoken at the end of a prayer. It is also used to show that you strongly agree with something another person has just said.

a·mend [ə mend′] *verb,* **amended, amending. 1.** to make a change in the wording of a law or

American Indian a member of the tribes of people who lived in North and South America before the first European explorers came.

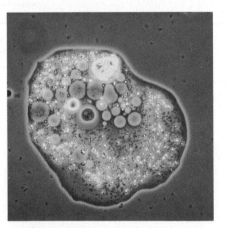

ameba A microscopic photo of an ameba living in water.

American Revolution see **Revolutionary War.**

a·mi·able [ā′ mē ə bəl] *adjective, more/most.* friendly and easy-going; good-natured: The *amiable* store clerk always had a kind word for her customers.

a•mid [ə mid′] *preposition*. in the middle of; surrounded by: One tall tree stood *amid* the smaller bushes along the river bank.

ment gave *amnesty* to soldiers who fought for the Confederate Army.

a•moe•ba [ə mē′ bə] see **ameba**.

among/between At one time students were taught that *between* should only be used when two things or two persons are involved: "It was a secret *between* John and Jane." *Among* was said to be used properly when more than two objects or persons are mentioned: "Let's keep this information *among* ourselves," he said to John, Jane, and Henry. But the distinction is weakening in today's speech. Some fine writers ignore it. "We had only two thin blankets *between* the four of us." (George Orwell) *Between* may seem more natural when the things are thought of separately, rather than as a group. "There was nothing so fine *between* all the four great rivers." (Howard Pyle)

a•miss [ə mis′] *adjective*. not as it should be; wrong or out of order: He knew something was *amiss* when he came home and saw that his front window had been forced open.

am•mo•nia [ə mōn′ yə] *noun, plural* **ammonias**. a strong-smelling, colorless gas that is a mixture of NITROGEN and HYDROGEN. Ammonia mixed with water is often used for household cleaning.

am•mu•ni•tion [am′ yə nish′ ən] *noun*. **1.** bullets, shells, bombs, missiles, and other such weapons that can be fired or launched against an enemy. **2.** facts or arguments that can be used to support some statement or point of veiw. He had a lot of *ammunition* when he came to the meeting to prove that the committee was spending too much money.

am•ne•sia [am nē′ zhə] *noun*. a temporary or permanent loss of memory. Amnesia is usually caused by an injury to the head or by a great emotional shock.

am•nes•ty [am′ nis tē] *noun, plural* **amnesties**. a general pardon given to a group of people who have committed an offense against the government: After the Civil War, the U.S. Govern-

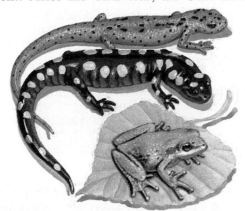

amphibian Three of the most common amphibians—a *newt* (top), a *salamander* (center), and a *frog* (bottom).

a•mong [ə mung′] *preposition*. **1.** in the middle of; surrounded by: "Bees were at work *among* the flowers." (James Herriott) **2.** one of: *Gone with the Wind* is *among* my favorite movies. **3.** in shares to each of: He divided the candy equally *among* the eight children at the party. **4.** throughout the group of: The partners in that business often argue *among* themselves. ♦ Another form of this word is **amongst**: "It would be hard to choose *amongst* them." (Ring Lardner)

a•mount [ə mount′] *noun, plural* **amounts**. **1.** the total number or quantity; the sum: Do you know the *amount* of money in your bank account? **2.** any quantity: He puts only a small *amount* of salt on his food. —*verb*, **amounted, amounting**. **1.** to add up to; total: "The filled sacks and bushels *amount* to many hundred pounds." (Marjorie Kinnan Rawlings) **2.** to develop into; become: "I'm going to try to *amount* to something in life." (Sherwood Anderson)

am•pere [am′ pēr] *noun, plural* **amperes**. in electricity, the standard unit for measuring the strength of a current; called **amp** for short. ♦ This word comes from the name of Andre Marie *Ampere*, a French scientist.

am•phib•i•an [am fib′ ē ən] *noun, plural* **amphibians**. one of a group of cold-blooded animals with backbones. Amphibians have moist skin without scales or fur. They can live either in or out of water. Frogs and salamanders are amphibians.

Pronunciation Key: A–F			
a	and; hat	ch	chew; such
ā	ate; stay	d	dog; lid
â	care; air	e	end; yet
ä	father; hot	ē	she; each
b	boy; cab	f	fun; off

(Turn the page for more information.)

A

am•phib•i•ous [am fib′ ē əs] *adjective.* **1.** having to do with or belonging to the amphibians: Toads are *amphibious* animals. **2.** able to operate either on land or in water: an *amphibious* vehicle.

amphitheater An ancient amphitheater in Greece. The famous Greek tragedies of ancient times were performed in theaters like this.

am•phi•the•a•ter [am′ fə thē′ ə tər] *noun, plural* **amphitheaters.** an oval or round building used as a theater or sports arena. It has a stage or playing surface in the center and rows of seats that rise up one behind the other.

am•ple [am′ pəl] *adjective,* **ampler, amplest.** enough or more than enough; plenty: They have an *ample* supply of firewood for the winter. ". . . the Badger's plain but *ample* supper." (Kenneth Grahame)

am•pli•fi•er [am′ plə fī′ ər] *noun, plural* **amplifiers.** a device for increasing the strength of an electronic signal. An amplifier is used as part of a stereo system to make the sound louder.

am•pli•fy [am′ plə fī′] *verb,* **amplified, amplifying. 1.** to make a signal stronger: In the days before sound was *amplified* by microphones, public speakers had to have loud and powerful voices. **2.** to make larger or more complete: The President issued a written statement to *amplify* his brief remarks at the airport.

am•pu•tate [am′ pyoo tāt′] *verb,* **amputated, amputating.** to cut off a limb of the body in a surgical operation. **—amputation,** *noun.*

Am•ster•dam [am′ stər dam′] the official capital and largest city of the Netherlands. Population: 800,000.

a•muse [ə myooz′] *verb* **amused, amusing. 1.** to cause to laugh or smile: Everyone in the audience was *amused* by the three clowns. **2.** to give pleasure to; entertain: It was too rainy to play outside, so she *amused* herself with a book.

a•muse•ment [ə myooz′ mənt] *noun, plural* **amusements. 1.** the condition of being amused: Jack always tells jokes at lunch for the *amusement* of the other students. **2.** something that amuses: "His *amusements* were golf in summer and going to concerts in winter." (Edmund Wilson)

a•mus•ing [ə myoo′ zing] *adjective, more/most.* bringing amusement to someone: He told us several *amusing* stories about his days in the navy. "Thank you for a most *amusing* evening." (Richard Connell) **—amusingly,** *adverb.*

an [an *or* ən] the form of the word **a** used before a word that begins with a VOWEL sound: *an* egg, *an* orange, *an* anchor, ten dollars *an* hour. The word **an** is an *indefinite article.*

an•a•con•da [an′ ə kän′ də] *noun, plural* **anacondas.** a very large, powerful snake found in South America. The anaconda is not poisonous, but it can coil around an animal and crush it to death.

anaconda The South American anaconda is related to the boa constrictor. It can grow to be 25 feet long and 3 feet around.

a•nal•o•gy [ə nal′ ə jē] *noun, plural* **analogies.** a likeness between two things that are not alike in other ways: an *analogy* between the arms of a human and the tentacles of an octopus.

a•nal•y•sis [ə nal′ ə sis] *noun, plural* **analyses** [ə nal′ə sēz′]. **1.** the separating of something into its basic parts to find out what it is made of. **2.** a careful and detailed study of something: The museum's *analysis* of the painting showed that it was a genuine work by Rembrandt.

an•a•lyze [an′ ə līz′] *verb,* **analyzed, analyzing. 1.** to separate something into its basic parts to find out what it is made of: "The traces of the poison found inside those holes are being *analyzed.*" (John D. MacDonald) **2.** to study something carefully and in detail: The football coach *analyzed* films of the other team's games to learn about their style of play.

A

an•ar•chy [an′ ər kē′] *noun.* a condition in which people are not controlled in any way by government, laws, or rules. ◆ A person who favors this kind of situation in politics is an **anarchist** [an′ ər kist′].

a•nat•o•my [ə nat′ ə mē] *noun, plural* **anatomies. 1.** the body or parts of an animal or plant: The *anatomy* of a frog is like that of a toad. **2.** a branch of science that studies the body structure of animals and plants. ◆ This word first meant "cutting up." Early studies in anatomy were made by cutting up dead animals.

anchoring. 1. to keep a boat or ship in place with an anchor. **2.** to stay in one place, as if held by an anchor: The outfielder remained *anchored* to the spot as the ball sailed past.

an•cient [ān′ shənt] *adjective, more/most.* **1.** having to do with times long past: ". . . some *ancient* conqueror, such as Caesar, or Alexander the Great, or Hannibal." (Tennessee Williams) **2.** very old: "Cinderella" is an *ancient* story. **—the ancients,** *plural noun.* the people who lived in ancient times, such as the early Egyptians, Greeks, and Romans.

and It was once considered incorrect to begin a sentence with "and." The reasoning was: If you've got another statement to make on the same subject, then tie it to the first statement by use of punctuation: "She had reasons for acting *and,* clearly, she was afraid of losing her job." But famous writers often ignore the rule: "*And* as I walked on I was lonely no longer." (F. Scott Fitzgerald) "*And* I haven't got any money at all." (Ernest Hemingway) The risk is that you can write this way too regularly—and end up with choppy sentences: "I opened the door. *And* the dog ran out. *And* my mother complained."

Andes The Andes form a barrier along the western coast of South America. These are the Patagonian Andes, which are in the southernmost part of this mountain range.

an•ces•tor [an′ ses′ tər] *noun, plural* **ancestors.** a person in one's family line who lived a long time ago; an ancient relative: The *ancestors* of the Apache Indians came to the Southwest about 1000 years ago. ◆ All a person's ancestors as a group is his or her **ancestry** [an′ ses′ trē]: "There are Haitians able to trace their *ancestry* back to African kings." (James Baldwin)

an•chor [ang′ kər] *noun, plural* **anchors. 1.** a very heavy iron weight that is lowered into the water from a boat or ship to hold it in place. **2.** something that is like an anchor in giving strength or support: "Sons are the *anchor* of a mother's life." (Sophocles) **—verb,** **anchored,**

and [and *or* ənd *or* ən] *conjunction.* a word used to connect two words, phrases, or sentences: apples *and* oranges. She likes to play soccer, read books, *and* watch TV. He asked me to come along, *and* I quickly said yes.

An•des [an′ dēz] a large mountain system of western South America that extends from one end of the continent to the other. It is the largest mountain range in the world.

an•ec•dote [an′ ik dōt′] *noun, plural* **anecdotes.** a short story that tells something funny or interesting: The history teacher told several *anecdotes* about Lincoln while the class was studying the Civil War.

a•ne•mi•a [ə nē′ mē ə] *noun.* an unhealthy condition in which the body does not have enough red blood cells. A person with anemia looks pale and feels tired and weak. ◆ Someone who suffers from this is **anemic.**

an•es•thet•ic [an′ is thet′ ik] *noun, plural* **anesthetics.** a drug or other substance that causes a loss of feeling in the body. Anesthetics are given by doctors to their patients so that they will not feel pain during an operation.

Pronunciation Key: G–N			
g	give; big	k	kind; cat; back
h	hold	l	let; ball
i	it; this	m	make; time
ī	ice; my	n	not; own
j	jet; gem; edge	ng	having

(Turn the page for more information.)

A

an•gel [ān′ jəl] *noun, plural,* **angels. 1.** in certain religions, a heavenly spirit or being who serves as a messenger of God and watches over people. **2.** a person who is thought of as especially good and kind like an angel: She was such an *angel* to take care of the children while their mother was sick.

An•glo-Sax•on [ang′ glō sak′ sən] *noun, plural* **Anglo-Saxons. 1.** a member of one of the tribes that came from what is now Germany and Scandinavia to invade England about 1500 years ago. **2.** the language of the Anglo-Saxon people. This was the earliest form of what is now the English language.

Anglo-Saxon words Anglo-Saxon words came into English before other kinds of words. Mainly, English consists of Anglo-Saxon words, and Latinate ("Latin-like") words that entered the language from French. Anglo-Saxon words are household, personal, or basic terms: *dog, hand, kill, joke, fun, water.* Latinate words are usually longer, and less precise: *formation, administration, substantial.* As a writer, when in doubt, use Anglo-Saxon words. "She said no" is better than "She replied in the negative." Sometimes, however, a Latinate word wins out because English speakers think it's high-class. For example, the plain word "visit" has been replaced by "visitation." Not only is the meaning not improved, but also the original meaning of *visitation* is lost. Look it up in a large dictionary.

an•ger [ang′ gər] *noun.* the strong feeling that a person has toward someone or something that hurts, opposes, or annoys him: "With sudden *anger* he balled up a dishcloth he was holding and threw it down hard on the floor." (Carson McCullers) —*verb,* **angered, angering.** to make angry: Several players *angered* the coach by fooling around during practice.

an•gry [ang′ grē] *adjective,* **angrier, angriest. 1.** showing or feeling anger: an *angry* remark. The sales clerk was *angry* after the two customers tried on clothes for an hour but didn't buy anything. **2.** sore and painful: Suzie had an *angry* red mark on her leg where the stick hit her. **—angrily,** *adverb.* in an angry way: "He said *angrily,* 'We've got to finish. Don't move!'" (Graham Greene)

an•guish [ang′ gwish] *noun.* very great pain or suffering; agony. **—anguished,** *adjective:* ". . . *anguished* voices spoke up from within the wreckage: 'Please help! Get us out!'" (John Hersey)

an•i•mal [an′ ə məl] *noun, plural* **animals. 1.** a living thing that is not a plant. Animals can move about freely and feed on plants or other animals; plants cannot move about, and they manufacture their own food. Animals typically have a nervous system and sense organs, such as those for sight and hearing. **2.** any animal other than a human being. ♦ *Animal* is one of the most common words in English, but it is not an old term as English words go. It was almost never used before the 1600's, and it does not appear at all in the King James Bible (1611).

an•i•mate [an′ ə māt′] *verb,* **animated, animating.** to give life to; make lively: "Farnon's manner became more and more *animated.* His eyes glittered and he talked rapidly." (James Herriot) —[an′ ə mit] *adjective.* having life; living: A stone is not an *animate* object. ♦ Another form of this word is **animated** [an′ ə mā′ tid]: An **animated cartoon** is one in which the figures move as if they were alive.

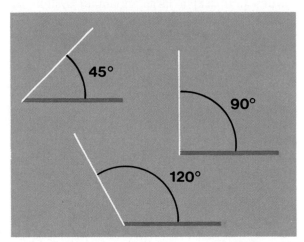

angles The three types of angles—**acute** (less than 90 degrees), **right** (exactly 90 degrees), and **obtuse** (more than 90 degrees).

an•gle [ang′ gəl] *noun, plural* **angles. 1.** the shape formed by an area between two straight lines or flat surfaces that join each other at a given point. Two walls that meet in a corner of a room form an angle. **2.** a point of view: The news reporter asked her editor to give her an *angle* on the story she had to write. —*verb,* **angled, angling.** to move at an angle.

an•kle [ang′ kəl] *noun, plural* **ankles.** the joint where the foot connects to the leg.

an•nex [ə neks′] *verb,* **annexed, annexing.** to add to something larger: The U.S. government *annexed* Hawaii and Alaska as states. "We lived in a kitchen to which four other rooms were *annexed.*" (Alfred Kazin) —[an′ eks] *noun, plural* **annexes.** a building used as an addition to another building: The school built an *annex* to provide more classrooms.

an•ni•hi•late [ə nī′ ə lāt′] *verb,* **annihilated, annihilating.** to destroy completely; wipe out of existence: General Custer and all his troops were *annihilated* at the Battle of Little Bighorn.

an•ni•ver•sa•ry [an′ ə vur′ sə rē] *noun, plural,* **anniversaries.** the return each year of a special date: They celebrate their wedding *anniversary* on February 15.

an•nounce [ə nouns′] *verb,* **announced, announcing.** **1.** to give public notice of; make known: "One night toward Christmas she *announced* that she was leaving." (Thomas Wolfe) **2.** to state the arrival of: A servant at the door *announced* the guests as they walked in. **3.** to introduce or tell about something on radio or TV: President Reagan used to *announce* college football games.

an•nounce•ment [ə nouns′ mənt] *noun, plural* **announcements.** a public notice that makes something known: "'This is D-Day,' came the *announcement* over the English radio." (Anne Frank)

She has an *annual* salary of $30,000. **3.** living and growing for only one year or season: Corn and wheat are *annual* plants. —*noun, plural* **annuals.** a plant or other thing that is annual.

an•nul [ə nul′] *verb,* **annulled, annulling.** to do away with; declare to be invalid: The court *annulled* the teenage couple's marriage because they were too young to be legally married.

a•non•y•mous [ə nän′ ə məs] *adjective.* **1.** from or by a person who does not want to give his name: The college received a large sum of money from an *anonymous* giver. **2.** of unknown name; not known: The tales of "The Arabian Nights" were written by an *anonymous* author. **—anonymously,** *adverb.* He called the police *anonymously* to tell them where the bank robbers were hiding.

an•o•rex•i•a [an′ ə rek′ sē ə] *noun.* a serious disease that causes a person to lose all desire to eat, because of his or her great concern about being overweight. ♦ A person who has anorexia is **anorexic** [an′ ə rek′ sik].

an•oth•er [ə nuth′ ər] *adjective.* **1.** one more; an additional: C̄an I have *another* soda, please? **2.** different: I want to try on *another* jacket, because this one's too small. **3.** of the same kind as; The team's new quarterback could be *another* Joe Namath. —*pronoun.* **1.** an additional one; one more; He ate his ice cream cone and then ordered *another.* **2.** a different one: "Nobody knows why one person is lucky and *another* unlucky." (D. H. Lawrence)

---

answers Answers in newspaper reporting are interesting. It's said that a reader wants to know—about a fire, a dance, an election, a track meet—the five W's, *who, what, where, when, why.* Most reporters are reminded from time to time that the five W's ought to be answered in the first or second paragraph of an article.

---

an•nounc•er [ə noun′ sər] *noun, plural* **announcers.** **1.** a person on radio or television who introduces programs and performers, identifies the station, or reads the news. **2.** any person who announces something: The *announcer* at the basketball game asked the crowd to stand for the national anthem.

an•noy [ə noi′] *verb,* **annoyed, annoying.** to bother or disturb; make somewhat angry; irritate: The noise in the street outside *annoyed* her while she was trying to study. ♦ Often used as an adjective: He has an *annoying* habit of interrupting other people.

an•nu•al [an′ yo͞o əl] *adjective.* **1.** happening or done once a year; yearly: He went to the doctor for his *annual* checkup. **2.** in or for one year:

an•swer [an′ sər] *noun, plural* **answers.** **1.** something spoken or written in return to a question; a reply: The *answer* to "What is 6 × 9?" is 54. **2.** something done in response: I rang the doorbell three times, but there was no *answer.* **3.** a way of dealing with a problem or difficulty: Finding a better-paying job would be the *answer* to his worries about money. —*verb,*

Pronunciation Key: O–S			
ō	over; go	ou	out; town
ô	all; law	p	put; hop
oo	look; full	r	run; car
o͞o	pool; who	s	set; miss
oi	oil; boy	sh	show

(Turn the page for more information.)

A

answered, answering. **1.** to speak or write in reply: "She said she loved getting letters but hated *answering* them." (Katherine Anne Porter) **2.** to act in response to something: Will you please *answer* the phone? **3.** to agree with; conform to: He *answers* to the description of the car thief.

ant [ant] *noun, plural* **ants.** a small insect that lives in large groups called colonies. Ants live in tunnels that they make in the ground or in wood. They are related to bees and wasps.

an•tag•o•nism [an tag′ə niz′ əm] *noun, plural* **antagonisms.** a being against something or somebody; a bad or angry feeling: "We used to be so united, and now I feel there's a great wall of *antagonism* between us." (Somerset Maugham)

an•tag•o•nize [an tag′ə nīz′] *verb,* **antagonized, antagonizing.** to arouse anger or bad feelings in someone: The comedian *antagonized* the audience by making fun of the way they were dressed. "Go easy, Jane, don't *antagonize* them . . ." (Mary Elizabeth Vroman)

Antarctica Paradise Bay in Antarctica. The North Pole is in the Arctic; the South Pole is in Antarctica. Using Latin, *anti-* means "opposite," or "on the other side."

Ant•arc•ti•ca [ant ärk′ ti kə] the fifth-largest continent, located within the **Antarctic Circle** on the South Pole.

ant•eat•er [ant′ ē′ tər] *noun, plural* **anteaters.** an animal with a very long, narrow head and a long, sticky tongue that it uses to eat ants and other insects. Anteaters have long claws that they use to dig into ant hills.

an•te•lope [an′ tə lōp′] *noun, plural* **antelope** or **antelopes.** a slender animal that has long horns and runs very fast. Antelope look like deer, but they are actually related to goats and cows. They are found in Africa and southern Asia. ◆ The PRONGHORN of North America is sometimes also called an antelope.

an•ten•na [an ten′ ə] *noun, plural* **antennas** (for #1) or **antennae** [an ten′ ī] (for # 2). **1.** a metal rod or wire used to receive or send out radio or television signals; an aerial. **2.** one of the pair of long, thin feelers on the head of an insect or of a water animal such as a crab or lobster.

an•them [an′ thəm] *noun, plural,* **anthems.** a song that gives praise to one's country: The "Star-Spangled Banner" is the national *anthem* of the United States.

An•tho•ny [an′ thə nē] **Susan B.,** 1820–1906, American leader of the movement to gain women the right to vote.

an•thro•pol•o•gy [an′ thrə päl′ ə jē] *noun.* the study of how the human race developed and of the way of life of different groups of people around the world. ◆ A person who is an expert in anthropology is an **anthropologist** [an′ thrə-päl′ ə jist]. Anthropologists study how the people of a certain place and time act and what they believe in. —**anthropological,** *adjective.*

an•ti- a *prefix* meaning: **1.** opposed to; against: President Lincoln was antislavery. **2.** acting against: Antifreeze keeps water from freezing.

an•ti•bi•ot•ic [an′ ti bī ät′ ik] *noun, plural* **antibiotics.** a substance that can kill or slow the growth of germs which cause disease. In medicine, antibiotics are produced artificially from BACTERIA or MOLDS. PENICILLIN is an antibiotic.

an•ti•bod•y [an′ ti bäd′ ē] *noun, plural* **antibodies.** a substance that is produced in the blood and that can act against the effect of disease germs or infection. Antibodies can make the body able to resist certain illnesses.

antelope The *oryx* [ôr′ iks], an antelope found in the Arabian and African deserts.

A

an•tic•i•pate [an tis′ ə pāt′] *verb*, **anticipated, anticipating. 1.** to look forward to; expect: They *anticipate* a large crowd at the game tonight. **2.** to deal with in advance: The Secret Service *anticipated* trouble and provided the President with extra security.
♦ The act of anticipating is **anticipation**: ". . . a terrific photographer, with an exceptional talent for *anticipation*, his lens always pointing in the right direction at the right moment." (Dick Francis)

antonyms There are many kinds of dictionaries that writers use: geographical (places), biographical (famous persons), rhyming (aid to writing verse), foreign words and phrases, and antonym-synonym. Look up SYNONYM in this book. Now use a synonym here: "She was happy, no more than that, she was _____." Now use an antonym here: "She wasn't cautious; no, worse than that, she was _____."

an•ti•dote [an′ ti dōt′] *noun, plural* **antidotes. 1.** something that works against the harmful effects of a poison: The *antidote* for that poison is to drink milk or warm water. **2.** a thing that works against something bad or harmful: Getting to know new people can be a good *antidote* for loneliness.

an•ti•freeze [an′ tē frēz′ *or* an′ ti frēz′] *noun.* something added to a liquid to keep it from freezing. The antifreeze used in car radiators has a lower freezing point than water.

an•ti•his•ta•mine [an′ ti his′ tə min] *noun.* a drug that is used to treat colds and such allergies as HAY FEVER and ASTHMA.

an•tique [an tēk′] *adjective, more/most.* of times long ago; made or done long ago: She bought an *antique* clock at an old farmhouse in Vermont.
—*noun, plural* **antiques.** something valuable that was made long ago.

ant•ler [ant′ lər] *noun, plural* **antlers.** one of the bony growths on the head of a deer, moose, or elk. Antlers usually grow in pairs. They are shed each year and then grow back again the next.

an•to•nym [an′ tə nim] *noun, plural* **antonyms.** a word that has a meaning that is opposed to the meaning of another word. "Hostile," "rude," and "cold" all can be antonyms for "friendly." "Hurry" and "rush" can be antonyms for "delay."

an•vil [an′vəl] *noun, plural* **anvils.** a heavy iron or steel block on which metal is hammered into shape by hand. In earlier times, blacksmiths used anvils in their work.

anx•i•e•ty [ang zī′ ə tē] *noun, plural* **anxieties. 1.** an uneasy feeling of worry or nervousness about what might happen: "They always felt an *anxiety* in the house. There was never enough money." (D. H. Lawrence) **2.** a great desire for something; eagerness: Her *anxiety* to win the contest led her to send in fifty different entries.

anx•ious [ang′ shəs] *adjective, more/most.* **1.** worried or uneasy about what might happen; nervous; fearful: "He spoke so seriously that I grew very *anxious*." (Anne Frank) **2.** wanting something very much; eager: "I sure am *anxious* to get out there and fish." (William Saroyan) **—anxiously,** *adverb:* in an anxious way: "The last day! Forty-two faces waiting *anxiously* for report cards." (Mary Elizabeth Vroman)

anxious It is sometimes said that the word *anxious* has only one correct meaning, that of being worried: "They were *anxious*, but did their best to make a joke of it." (Somerset Maugham) The meaning of "eager" is thought of as a new meaning, and therefore somehow incorrect. Actually, *anxious* has been used to mean "eager" since the 1700's, by many different writers. It's nice to think that you can use both words. "I am *anxious* about passing the test." "She's a student who is *eager* to learn."

an•ti•sep•tic [an′ ti sep′ tik] *noun, plural* **antiseptic.** a substance that kills or stops the growth of germs that cause infections. IODINE and ALCOHOL are commonly-used antiseptics.

an•ti•tox•in [an′ ti täk′ sin] *noun, plural* **antitoxins.** a kind of ANTIBODY that protects the body against a particular disease.

Pronunciation Key: T–Z			
t	ten; date	v	very; live
th	think	w	win; away
th	these	y	you
u	cut; butter	z	zoo; cause
ur	turn; bird	zh	measure

(Turn the page for more information.)

an•y [en′ē] *adjective.* **1.** one out of many: Take *any* seat you want. **2.** some: Have you seen *any* good movies lately? **3.** every: *Any* politician has to be able to give speeches in public. —*pronoun.* anybody or anything: She wanted to buy some raspberries, but they didn't have *any.* —*adverb.* at all: It can't get *any* hotter than it is right now.

an•y•bod•y [en′ē bud′ē *or* en′ē bäd′ē] *pronoun.* any person; anyone: "'We're not afraid of *anybody*,' Les said, scowling and trying to scare her." (Erskine Caldwell) —*noun. Informal.* an important person: Everybody who is *anybody* in this town is going to be at the mayor's party.

an•y•how [en′ē hou′] *adverb.* in any case; anyway: I don't care if I'm not invited to the party, because I don't want to go *anyhow.*

any more or **an•y•more** [en′ē môr′] *adverb.* now; nowadays: I guess that store is still open, but we never go there *any more.*

an•y•one [en′ē wun′] *pronoun.* any person; anybody: Did anyone call for me while I was out?

an•y•place [en′ē plās′] *adverb.* to, in, or at any place; anywhere: Just set the box down *anyplace* until I decide what to do with it.

an•y•thing [en′ē thing′] *pronoun.* any thing: I have to go to the store, I don't have *anything* in the house for dinner.

an•y•time [en′ē tīm′] *adverb.* at any time: You can water the lawn *anytime* you want, as long as you do it today.

an•y•way [en′ē wā′] *adverb.* in any case; at any rate: It didn't matter that I couldn't play, because the game was rained out *anyway.*

an•y•where [en′ē wâr′] *adverb.* in, at, or to any place: There are no assigned seats in this class; students can sit *anywhere* they want. The paper's due tomorrow, but she's not *anywhere* near being finished.

a•or•ta [ā ôr′tə] *noun, plural* **aortas.** the main artery of the body that carries the blood from the left side of the heart to all parts of the body except the lungs.

A•pa•che [ə pach′ē] *noun, plural* **Apaches.** a member of an American Indian tribe living in the Southwest.

anyone The word *anyone* is singular, obviously, because it has "one" in it. Therefore, textbooks on writing teach that the correct pronoun to use with *anyone* is "his" or "her." We might say, "Anyone who wants to go on the class trip should have *his* money in by Friday." Some people say that this usage is unfair to females. The sentence should read ". . . his or her money . . ." This is awkward. It's easier to say "If you want to go on the class trip, you should have your money . . ."

ape Three common members of the ape family—a *gorilla* (left), an *orangutan* (top right), and a *chimpanzee* (lower right).

a•part [ə pärt′] *adverb.* **1.** away from each other in space or time: In football the two goal lines are 100 yards *apart.* **2.** in or to pieces: We took our radio *apart* to see what it was made of. **3.** to one side; aside: The new boy stood *apart* from the rest of the children on the playground.

a•part•heid [ə pär′tīd *or* ə pär′tīt] *noun.* in the Republic of South Africa, a policy of dealing unfairly with nonwhite groups, mainly blacks, in housing, jobs, voting, and other civil rights.

a•part•ment [ə pärt′mənt] *noun, plural* **apartments.** a room or set of rooms to live in.

ap•a•thy [ap′ə thē] *noun.* a feeling of not caring; a lack of interest; indifference: "Here was a patient too far gone to care. His lack of expression seemed to show the *apathy* of the desperately ill." (Robert Heinlein) ◆ A person who has this feeling is **apathetic** [ap ə thet′ik].

ape [āp] *noun, plural* **apes.** a large animal related to the monkey. It has no tail and can stand and walk on two feet. Chimpanzees, gorillas, and orangutans are kinds of apes. —*verb,* **aped, aping.** to copy the actions of someone else, as an ape is thought to do; imitate; mimic: The comedian *aped* John Wayne's way of walking and talking.

a•phid [ā′ fəd] *noun, plural* **aphids.** a very small insect that feeds by sucking juices from plants.

a•piece [ə pēs′] *adverb.* for each one; each: Jenny and her sister earned $5 *apiece* for raking up the leaves in their neighbor's yard.

a•pol•o•gize [ə päl′ ə jīz′] *verb,* **apologized, apologizing.** to say one is sorry; make an apology: "John, I want you to *apologize* to Miss Monk for disturbing the class." (James Gould Cozzens)

♦ When someone apologizes, he or she is **apologetic** [ə päl′ ə jet′ ik]: He was *apologetic* after spilling his soda in my lap.

a•pol•o•gy [ə päl′ ə jē] *noun, plural* **apologies.** words that say one is sorry for doing something wrong or for bothering or hurting someone.

A•pos•tle [ə päs′ əl] *noun, plural* **Apostles. 1.** one of the twelve early followers of Jesus Christ. **2. apostle.** someone who closely follows another person or a cause or idea.

a•pos•tro•phe [ə päs′ trə fē] *noun, plural* **apostrophes.** a punctuation mark ['] that is used: **1.** to show that one or more letters have been left out of a word: *He's* means "he is." *Weren't* means "were not." **2.** to show who owns or has something: "*Sharon's* coat means "the coat that belongs to Sharon." **3.** to show the plural of a letter or number: Dennis won the poker hand with a pair of 9's.

ap•par•ent [ə par′ ənt] *adjective, more/most.* **1.** able to be seen easily; plain to see: It's *apparent* that he's been sick, because he looks so pale and tired. **2.** clear to the mind; obvious: "With each remark the force of her dislike became more and more *apparent.*" (F. Scott Fitzgerald) **3.** seeming to be real or true: I gave him a book on sharks because of his *apparent* interest in the subject, but he hasn't even opened it.

ap•par•ent•ly [ə par′ ənt lē] *adverb.* as far as anyone can tell; seemingly: "*Apparently* none of them went to school." (Marjorie Kinnan Rawlings)

ap•peal [ə pēl′] *verb,* **appealed, appealing. 1.** to ask for help or sympathy: The Red Cross *appealed* for volunteer workers to help the earthquake victims. **2.** to be attractive or interesting: The idea of working long hours on weekends does not *appeal* to her at all. ♦ Often used as an adjective: an *appealing* smile, a car with an *appealing* design. **3.** in law, to ask that a case be tried again in a higher court: The defense lawyer decided to *appeal* after his client was convicted. —*noun, plural* **appeals. 1.** a request for sympathy: The minister made an *appeal* for funds to build a new church. **2.** the power to attract or interest: Rock music has a great *appeal* for many young people. **3.** the act of appealing to a higher court.

ap•pear [ə pēr′] *verb,* **appeared, appearing. 1.** to come into view; be seen: "At the same moment, Dick Prosser *appeared* in the doorway of the shack." (Thomas Wolfe) **2.** to seem to

---

apostrophe Possibly one of the hardest punctuation rules to remember has to do with an apostrophe that tells you someone owns a thing. "Janet is a girl. Janet's dog is a beagle." Now, that's easy. What do you write when "Janet's" family is mentioned? Let's say her family name is Jones. Do you write (1) "The Jone's dog" or (2) "The Jones' dog" or (3) "The Jones's dog"? In this dictionary we know No. 1 is wrong. We prefer No. 2 over No. 3, although both are correct.

Ap•pa•la•chi•an Mountains [ap′ ə lā′ chən] a mountain system of eastern North America that extends from southeast Canada to Alabama.

ap•pa•rat•us [ap′ ə rat′ əs] *noun, plural* **apparatus** or **apparatuses.** the tools or equipment used for a certain purpose or to do a certain job: The movie crew set up their cameras, lights, microphones, and other *apparatus.*

ap•par•el [ə par′ əl] *noun.* things to wear; clothing: In this store, children's *apparel* is on the third floor.

be: We didn't know until later that Mark was upset, because he had *appeared* to be in a good mood. **3.** to come before the public: Sir Laurence Olivier has often *appeared* in plays by

---

Pronunciation Key: [ə] Symbol

The [ə] or *schwa* sound occurs in syllables without an accent. It can be spelled with any vowel, such as **a** in above, **e** in listen, **i** in pencil, **o** in melon, **u** in circus. It can also be a combination of vowels, such as **io** in action, **ai** in mountain, **iou** in precious.

(Turn the page for more information.)

A

Shakespeare. **4.** to come formally into a court of law: She has to *appear* next week to answer a speeding ticket.

ap•pear•ance [ə pēr′ əns] *noun, plural* **appearances. 1.** the act of appearing or coming into view: In old Western movies people were often saved by the sudden *appearance* of the U.S. Cavalry. **2.** the way a person or thing looks: "This gave her face a curious, clean, tanned *appearance*." (James Gould Cozzens) **3.** the act of coming before the public: Barbra Streisand made her first *appearance* in movies in 1968.

ap•pen•di•ci•tis [ə pen′ di sī′ tis] *noun.* a condition in which the appendix becomes sore and swollen. In serious cases of appendicitis, the appendix has to be removed by surgery.

ap•pen•dix [ə pen′ diks] *noun, plural* **appendixes** or **appendices** [ə pen′ də sēz′]. **1.** a thin, closed tube in the abdomen, attached to the large intestine. It has no useful function in the body. **2.** a section of writing at the end of a report or book that gives additional information.

ap•pe•tite [ap′ i tīt′] *noun, plural* **appetites. 1.** a desire to eat food: Julie always has a big *appetite* when she's on a camping trip. **2.** any strong desire for something: Kelly has a great *appetite* for learning, so she's always reading books.

ap•pe•tiz•er [ap′ i tī′ zər] *noun, plural* **appetizers.** a small amount of food or drink served at the beginning of a meal to make one hungry for the main course. Foods such as shrimp, clams, or cheese and crackers are often used as appetizers.

ap•plause [ə plôz′] *noun.* approval or enjoyment shown by clapping the hands: The crowd burst into *applause* when the band finished the song.

ap•ple [ap′ əl] *noun, plural* **apples.** a firm round fruit that has a thin red, yellow, or green skin. Apples have white flesh that surrounds a core of small seeds. Apple trees grow in cool climates.

apple

ap•pli•ance [ə plī′ əns] *noun, plural* **appliances.** any small machine or device that is used to do a particular job around the house. Dishwashers, toasters, clothes dryers, refrigerators, and vacuum cleaners are appliances.

ap•pli•cant [ap′ lə kənt] *noun, plural* **applicants.** a person who applies for something, especially for a job.

---

appetizers In a restaurant, an appetizer is the beginning part, or course, of the meal. In writing you can also create an appetizer, something interesting leading to the main part, something that makes you hungry for more information. The first sentence of E.B. White's book *Charlotte's Web* is: "'Where's Papa going with that ax?' said Fern to her mother as they were setting the table for breakfast." Leaving the house with an ax at breakfast time? What's going on? George Orwell starts his famous novel *1984* with: "It was a bright cold day in April and the clocks were striking thirteen." Clocks that say thirteen? What's going on? In writing it's sometimes useful not to start right out with the main course of the story. Let your reader have a taste, get his attention.

---

ap•plaud [ə plôd′] *verb,* **applauded, applauding. 1.** to show approval or enjoyment by clapping the hands: The audience *applauded* the actors when the play was over. **2.** to praise or approve something: The newspapers *applauded* the mayor's efforts to bring new business to the city.

ap•pli•ca•tion [ap′ li kā′ shən] *noun, plural* **applications. 1.** a form or paper that you fill out to get or do something: an *application* for a job, an *application* for a driver's license, an *application* to get into college. **2.** the act of applying: It took several *applications* of glue to hold the picture frame together.

ap•ply [ə plī′] *verb,* **applied, applying. 1.** to put on: She *applied* suntan oil to her arms so that they wouldn't get sunburned. **2.** to make use of: In tomorrow's game we'll try to *apply* what we've learned in practice this week. **3.** to have to do with; relate to: The "No Parking" rule for this street doesn't *apply* on Sundays. **4.** to make a request to get or do something: She is *applying* to the same college her mother went to.

ap•point [ə point′] *verb,* **appointed, appointing. 1.** to name a person to some job or position; choose; select: The President *appointed* Professor Chase to a special council on computer education. **2.** to set a time or place to do something: "She met him at the *appointed* time in the Plaza lobby." (F. Scott Fitzgerald)

ap•point•ment [ə point′ mənt] *noun, plural* **appointments. 1.** an agreement to meet someone at a certain time and place: I have an *appointment* at the doctor at 3:00. **2.** the selection of a person to fill a job or position.

ap•praise [ə prāz′] *verb,* **appraised, appraising.** to set or decide the value of something: The jeweler *appraised* the diamond ring at two thousand dollars. **—appraiser,** *noun.*

ap•pre•ci•ate [ə prē′ shē āt′] *verb,* **appreciated, appreciating. 1.** to realize the worth or value of something: "Father was a well-read man and could *appreciate* an intelligent talker." (Frank O'Connor) **2.** to be grateful for: "The horse appeared to *appreciate* having his sore foot

ap•pre•hen•sion [ap′ ri hen′ shən] *noun, plural* **apprehensions. 1.** a feeling of fear about what might happen; being worried or afraid: "This cheered him, cleared away all his *apprehensions . . .*" (John Cheever) **2.** the act of apprehending; an arrest or capture.

apprentice Benjamin Franklin became a famous printer after working as an apprentice in the printing shop of his brother James.

ap•pren•tice [ə pren′ tis] *noun, plural* **apprentices. 1.** in earlier times, a young person who worked for a skilled worker in order to learn his skill or trade. In return for his training, an apprentice had to work for a certain period of time for little or no pay.

> **apprenticeship** Of all the arts only writing has never, in history, been regarded as a profession or skill or trade in which an apprentice (beginner) worked for a master artist for a number of years to learn his craft and so become licensed to write on his own. In the old days there were guilds (clubs that licensed artisans) for architects, silversmiths, sculptors, musicians, and others. Yet, writing is also a process in which persons have to begin, to learn, to become known by professional writers. To become a good writer—and not just on the hope of becoming a writer by trade—WRITE. Write in a diary; write letters; work for school newspapers.

lifted off the ground." (James Herriot) **3.** to increase in value: That land will *appreciate* greatly when the new highway is built.

ap•pre•ci•a•tion [ə prē′ shē ā′ shən] *noun.* **1.** the act of valuing something; a favorable opinion: Helen has a real *appreciation* of art and loves to spend time in museums. **2.** a feeling of thanks for something; being grateful: The Girl Scout troop gave their leader a present in *appreciation* for all her work during the year.

ap•pre•hend [ap′ ri hend′] *verb,* **apprehended, apprehending.** to hold or catch a person; capture: The police *apprehended* the robbers.

♦ This was was called an **apprenticeship** [ə pren′ tis ship]. **2.** any person who is learning a skill or trade through practical experience. **—***verb,* **apprenticed, apprenticing.** to hire or place someone as an apprentice.

Pronunciation Key: Accent Marks

[′] is the normal accent mark. It shows where the main stress falls on a word.
[′] is a secondary accent mark. It shows a lighter stress than the primary accent. For example:
tel • e • vis • ion [tel′ə vizh′ən]
(Turn the page for more information.)

A

ap•proach [ə prōch′] *verb,* **approached, approaching. 1.** to come near or nearer to: They *approached* the growling dog cautiously. "When Stuart saw the great wave *approaching,* he jumped for the rigging." (E.B. White) **2.** to present an idea or request: He *approached* the boss with a plan for opening a new office in another city.
—*noun, plural* **approaches. 1.** the act of approaching; coming near: Dark clouds warned of the *approach* of a storm. **2.** the way used to get nearer a place: A fallen tree blocked the *approach* to the cabin. **3.** the way in which an idea or request is presented: The best *approach* in dealing with her is to come right to the point.

ap•pro•pri•ate [ə prō′ prē it] *adjective, more/most.* right for a situation; proper or correct: It is *appropriate* to say "I'm sorry" when you have hurt someone's feelings. "Father had just got a new rod the day before, which made the idea of fishing all the more *appropriate.*" (Stephen Leacock)
—[ə prō′ prē āt′] *verb,* **appropriated, appropriating. 1.** to use for a special purpose: The state *appropriated* money to build a new dam. **2.** to take something for oneself, especially in an improper way: The dishonest bank teller *appropriated* funds and hid them in his own account. —**appropriately,** *adverb.*

ap•prov•al [ə prōō′ vəl] *noun.* **1.** a good opinion; praise: The boss showed his *approval* of Fred's work by giving him a raise. **2.** permission or consent: She has to have her parents' *approval* before she can take an after-school job.

ap•prove [ə prōōv′] *verb,* **approved, approving. 1.** to think well of; have a good opinion: Years ago people didn't *approve* of men and women attending the same college. **2.** to give permission or consent to something: The mayor and the city council *approved* the plans for the new shopping center.—**approvingly,** *adverb:* "He nodded approvingly and said, 'That's right. You've got it.'" (Thomas Wolfe)

ap•prox•i•mate [ə präk′ sə mit] *adjective, more/most.* about the same as; close to: The *approximate* driving time from here to Chicago is eight hours. ♦ **Approximately** means nearly or close to: The population of our town is *approximately* five thousand people. —[ə präk′ sə māt′] *verb,* **approximated, approximating.** to come close to; estimate: Can they *approximate* how long it's going to take to fix the car?
♦ An **approximation** is an estimate or guess: I think this house is 100 years old, but that's only an *approximation.*

ap•ri•cot [ap′ ri kät *or* ā′ prə kät] *noun, plural* **apricots.** a round, yellowish-orange fruit that looks like a small peach. Apricot trees grow in warm climates.

apricot This is actually one of the many al- words that came into English from the Arabs (see p. 20). It comes from two Arabic words meaning "the apricot."

A•pril [ā′ prəl] *noun.* the fourth month of the year. April has 30 days.

a•pron [ā′ prən] *noun, plural* **aprons.** a piece of cloth or other material tied loosely around the body to protect clothing.

apt [apt] *adjective, more/most.* **1.** inclined to do or be; likely: From the way those clouds look, it's *apt* to rain soon. **2.** right for the occasion; fitting: an *apt* remark. **3.** quick to learn: an *apt* student.

ap•ti•tude [ap′ ti tōōd′] *noun, plural* **aptitudes.** a natural ability to do something; talent: She has shown real *aptitude* for working with computers.
♦ An **aptitude test** is one that shows which subjects people could learn best or what kind of work they could do well.

a•quar•i•um [ə kwar′ ē əm] *noun, plural* **aquariums** or **aquaria. 1.** a glass bowl or tank containing living fish, other water animals, and water plants. **2.** a building that has a collection of fish and other water animals.

aq•uat•ic [ə kwät′ ik] *adjective.* **1.** living in water: Whales are *aquatic* animals. **2.** taking place in or on water: Swimming and water polo are *aquatic* sports. ♦ *Aquatics* are sports that take place in the water.

A

aq•ue•duct [ak′wə dukt′] *noun, plural* **aque-ducts.** a large pipe or man-made channel that carries water to places that are far away. Aqueducts make it possible to build cities and grow crops in areas that once were deserts.

aqueduct This aqueduct carries water to the city of Los Angeles.

Ar•ab [âr′əb] *noun, plural* **Arabs.** a member of a group of people who speak a language called **Arabic** [âr′ə bik]. These people once lived only in ARABIA, but now live in other regions of the Middle East, Asia, and Africa. —*adjective.* having to do with the Arabs. ◆ **Arabian** [ə rā′bē-ən] is another word that means the same as *Arab.*

A•ra•bi•a [ə rā′bē ə] a large desert area in southwestern Asia. It is a peninsula between the Red Sea and the Persian Gulf.

Arabic numerals the signs commonly used to write numbers; the figures 0, 1, 2, 3, 4, 5, 6, 7, 8, 9. ◆ These are called Arabic numerals because the Europeans first learned them from the Arabs.

ar•bi•trar•y [är′bə trer′ē] *adjective.* not according to any rule or reasons; based on one's feelings or wishes: The teacher asked Jeff to pick a number from one to ten, and he made an *arbitrary* choice of seven. —**arbitrarily,** *adverb.*

ar•bi•trate [är′bə trāt′] *verb,* **arbitrated, arbitrating.** to settle a dispute: A state official was called in to *arbitrate* when the company and its striking employees could not agree on their pay. ◆ The process of helping two sides come to an agreement is called **arbitration.** A person who does this is an **arbiter** or **arbitrator.**

ar•bor [är′bər] *noun, plural* **arbors.** an area that is shaded by trees, shrubs, or vines. ◆ **Arbor Day** is a spring day set aside by some states for planting trees.

arc [ärk] *noun, plural* **arcs.** a part of a curved line, especially part of a circle: The letter "C" is made by drawing an *arc.*

ar•cade [är kād′] *noun, plural* **arcades. 1.** a covered passageway, usually with shops along the sides. **2.** a place where people pay money to play different types of games, especially electronic games run by computer. This is also called a **video arcade.**

arch [ärch] *noun, plural* **arches. 1.** a curved piece of metal or wood that supports the weight of something built over an open space. **2.** a monument or other building that forms an arch or arches. **3.** the raised part of the bottom of the foot. —*verb,* **arched, arching. 1.** to form into an arch; bend or curve: "Fiske opened his eyes and *arched* his eyebrows." (Thomas Wolfe) **2.** to curve over an open space: The rainbow *arched* across the river.

arch The Memorial Arch at Valley Forge, Pennsylvania, honors George Washington and his troops, who suffered through a very harsh winter here in 1777-78.

ar•chae•ol•o•gy [är′kē äl′ə jē] (*also spelled* **archeology**) *noun.* the scientific study of the life and customs of people of ancient times. Archaeology is especially important in studying peoples who did not leave written records.

Pronunciation Key: A–F			
a	and; hat	ch	chew; such
ā	ate; stay	d	dog; lid
â	care; air	e	end; yet
ä	father; hot	ē	she; each
b	boy; cab	f	fun; off

(Turn the page for more information.)

A

♦ A person who is an expert in archaeology is an **archaeologist** [är′ kē äl′ ə jist]. Archaeologists dig into the earth to find the remains of ancient cities and buildings. **—archaeological,** *adjective.* having to do with archaeology or archaeologists.

---

archaic words Archaic words are those that people rarely use any more, but that are still part of our language. How can that be? The answer is these words survive because they are found in certain books of long ago that continue to be read. The King James Bible was published in 1611, and William Shakespeare wrote his famous plays and sonnets between 1590 and 1612. Today, hundreds of millions of people still read these works. People know archaic words because of famous lines such as "Ye (You) are the salt of the earth" (*Matthew 5:13*) or "When that the poor have cried, Caesar *hath* (has) wept" (*Julius Caesar*).

---

ar•cha•ic [är kā′ ik] *adjective.* belonging to an earlier time; out of date: After cars were invented, horse-drawn carriages became *archaic.* The use of "ye" to mean "you" is *archaic.*

arch•bish•op [ärch′ bish′ əp] *noun, plural* **archbishops.** a bishop having the higest rank. An archbishop is leader of all the churches in his district. ♦ This district is called an **archdiocese** [ärch dī′ ə sis *or* ärch dī′ ə sēz′].

ar•che•ol•o•gy [är′ kē äl′ ə jē] see **archaeology.**

arch•er [är′ chər] *noun, plural* **archers.** a person who uses a bow and arrow to hunt or to shoot at a target. ♦ The sport or skill of shooting a bow and arrow is called **archery.**

ar•chi•pel•a•go [är′ kə pel′ ə gō] *noun, plural* **archipelagos.** a group of many islands: The country of Indonesia is an *archipelago.*

ar•chi•tect [är′ kə tekt] *noun, plural* **architects.** **1.** a person who designs buildings, bridges, and other structures and then makes sure that they are built correctly. **2.** anyone who designs or develops something: Ray Kroc of McDonald's was one of the leading *architects* of the modern fast-food business.

ar•chi•tec•ture [är′ kə tek′ chər] *noun.* **1.** the art or science of designing and planning buildings. **2.** a particular style of building: Modern *architecture* often features unusual shapes and designs. **—architectural,** *adjective:* Frank Lloyd Wright is a well-known *architectural* leader.

Arc•tic [ärk′ tik] **1. Arctic Ocean.** the ocean surrounding the North Pole. **2. Arctic Circle.** an imaginary circle around the northern part of the earth. North of this point no trees grow and there is no daylight during the winter.

are [är] *verb.* a form of the verb BE that is used with "you," "we," or "they" to tell about the present: You *are* late. They *are* already gone.

ar•e•a [âr′ ē ə] *noun, plural* **areas. 1.** a measured space or surface: The *area* of the kitchen is about 100 square feet. **2.** any particular place or region: the New York City *area.* **3.** a particular field of interest or work: Computer science is a rapidly-growing *area.*

a•re•na [ə rē′ nə] *noun, plural* **arenas. 1.** in ancient Rome, an open space where fights or contests were held as sport. **2.** a similar modern building for sports events, circuses, and shows. **3.** any place of conflict or competition: the *arena* of politics.

arena The Silverdome, a large modern arena in Michigan, is enclosed to keep out the weather.

aren't [ärnt] a *contraction* meaning "are not."

Ar•gen•ti•na [är′ jən tē′ nə] a country in the southeastern part of South America. *Capital:* Buenos Aires. *Area:* 1,072,000 square miles. *Population:* 27,862,000.

ar•gue [är′ gyoo] *verb,* **argued, arguing. 1.** to have a disagreement; quarrel: The children *argued* about who would clean up the living room. My dad and Uncle Michael spend hours *arguing* about politics. **2.** to give reasons for a point of view: This book *argues* that William Shakespeare actually did not write his famous plays.

A

ar•gu•ment [är′ gyə mənt] *noun, plural* **argu-ments. 1.** a disagreement or quarrel: There was a loud *argument* over whether the base runner was safe or out. **2.** a point of view or reason: His *argument* for not eating red meat is that it's bad for your health.

ar•id [âr′ id] *adjective, more/most.* having little or no rain: "The Pueblos were all good farmers who could grow corn in the sand of *arid* de-serts." (Richard Erdoes)

a•rise [ə rīz′] *verb,* **arose, arisen, arising. 1.** to stand up; get up: He *arose* from his chair to answer the doorbell. **2.** to move upward; rise up: "In these lakes you will enjoy warm waters *arising* from hidden springs." (E.B. White) **3.** to come into being; appear: Many problems *arose* with the new computer because the com-pany hadn't tested it carefully enough.

ar•is•toc•ra•cy [ar′ i stäk′ rə sē] *noun, plural* **aristocracies. 1.** a class of people having a very high standing in society. Kings, queens, and dukes are part of the aristocracy. **2.** any group of people thought of as having a great deal of power, intelligence, or ability. ♦ A person who belongs to the aristocracy is an **aristocrat.**

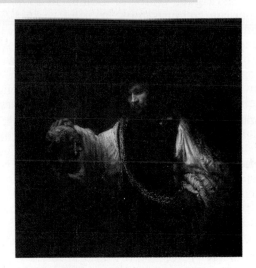

Aristotle A great thinker, Aristotle, as painted by a great artist, Rembrandt. This is *Aristotle Contemplating the Bust of Homer* (Homer was a great poet.)

Ar•is•tot•le [âr i stät′ əl] 384–322 B.C., Greek philosopher. He was the teacher of Alexander the Great.

a•rith•me•tic [ə rith′ mə tik] *noun.* the branch of mathematics that includes adding, subtract-ing, multiplying, and dividing.

Ar•i•zo•na [âr ə zō′ nə] a state in the southwest-ern U.S. *Capital:* Phoenix. *Nickname:* "Grand Canyon State." *Area:* 113,900 square miles. *Population:* 2,860,000.

ark [ärk] *noun, plural* **arks. 1.** in the Bible, a boat built by Noah to save his family and a pair of each kind of animal during a large flood. **2.** any similar boat or ship.

Arizona Monument Valley in Arizona, where wind and water over millions of years have left monumental rocks standing.

Pronunciation Key: G–N

g	give; big	k	kind; cat; back
h	hold	l	let; ball
i	it; this	m	make; time
ī	ice; my	n	not; own
j	jet; gem; edge	ng	having

(Turn the page for more information.)

A

Ar•kan•sas [är′kən sô′] a state in the south-central U.S. *Capital:* Little Rock. *Nickname:* "Land of Opportunity." *Area:* 53,100 square miles. *Population:* 2,291,000.

arm¹ [ärm] *noun, plural* **arms. 1.** either of the two upper parts of the human body between the shoulder and the hands. **2.** something that works or is shaped like an arm: the *arm* of a chair, the *arm* of a record player.

arm² *noun, plural* **arms.** any kind of weapon, such as a gun, knife, or bomb: In 1775 the American colonists took up *arms* against England. —*verb,* **armed, arming. 1.** to supply with weapons: The angry mob *armed* themselves with rocks, sticks, and broken bottles. **2.** to supply with anything that gives strength or power: The senator was *armed* with enough facts to answer all the questions of his critics.

ar•ma•da [är mä′də] *noun, plural* **armadas.** a large group of warships. ♦ The **Spanish Armada** was the fleet of warships from Spain that was defeated by the English in 1588.

armadillo The nine-banded armadillo is the only one found in the U.S. *Armadillo* comes from a Spanish word meaning "little armored thing."

ar•ma•dil•lo [är mə dil′ō] *noun, plural* **armadillos.** a small insect-eating animal found in South America and southern North America. It is covered with a shell of hard, jointed plates.

ar•ma•ment [är′mə mənt] *noun, plural* **armaments. 1.** all of the country's war forces and supplies, including its army, navy, and air force. **2.** the act of arming for war: In the 1930's Adolf Hitler ordered the *armament* of Nazi Germany. ♦ This meaning is often used with a prefix, as in **rearmament** or **disarmament.**

ar•mi•stice [är′mə stis] *noun, plural* **armistices.** an agreement by two sides to stop fighting; a truce. ♦ November 11 is **Armistice Day** (Veteran's Day) in the United States because it is the anniversary of the end of World War I.

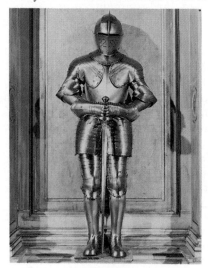

armor This suit of armor for a knight was made in Italy over 500 years ago.

ar•mor [är′mər] *noun.* **1.** in earlier times, a strong covering worn to protect the body during battle. Metal armor was used by knights in the Middle Ages. **2.** any kind of hard cover that serves as protection, such as a turtle's shell or the metal plates on a tank, plane, or warship. —**armored** [är′mərd] *adjective.* covered with or protected by armor: an *armored* car.

ar•mor•y [är′mə rē] *noun, plural* **armories.** a place where weapons are stored.

---

armada/armadillo The words *armada* and *armadillo* both come from Spanish. They came into English in the 1500's. This was a time when many Spanish words entered the English language. Spain was then at the height of its power, and the English navy fought the Spanish Armada for control of the seas. After Christopher Columbus reached the New World in 1492, many Spanish explorers traveled there. They found a number of animals and plants that were not known in Europe, and they made up words to name them—such as *armadillo*. In this dictionary you will several times note that words enter American English because a dominant or leading country used the word. In this case, it's Spain. In other instances, Great Britain or France. Words are left behind, so to speak, by conquering nations. In North America the English, the French, and the Spanish were explorers or invaders, and they held power over large parts of the continent.

arm•pit [ärm′pit′] *noun, plural* **armpits.** the hollow place under the arm at the shoulder.

arms [ärmz] *plural noun.* **1.** weapons. **2.** see **coat of arms.**

Arm•strong [ärm′strông′] **1. Louis ("Satchmo"),** 1900–1971, American jazz musician. **2. Neil,** born 1930, American astronaut, the first person to walk on the moon.

Armstrong Louis Armstrong was a trumpet player who started his career with New Orleans jazz.

ar•my [är′mē] *noun, plural* **armies. 1.** a large group of soldiers who are armed and trained to fight wars on land. **2.** a group of people who are organized for a common goal: The Salvation *Army* works to help poor or needy people. **3.** any large group of people or animals; a crowd: "An ever-growing *army* of people jostled at my heels." (George Orwell)

Arn•old [är′nəld] **Benedict,** 1741–1801, American general in the Revolutionary War who became a traitor.

a•ro•ma [ə rō′mə] *noun, plural* **aromas.** a pleasing smell or fragrance: The campers awoke to the *aroma* of coffee brewing on an open fire.

a•rose [ə rōz′] *verb.* the past tense of **arise.**

a•round [ə round′] *preposition.* **1.** in a circle about: to sail *around* the world. "The girl's fingers were gripped like a baby's *around* her thumb." (Flannery O'Connor) **2.** on all sides of: "I asked him to watch what went on *around* him." (Doris Lessing) **3.** along or to the side of: Put the trash can *around* on the side of the house. **4.** here and there in: They wandered *around* the city for several hours. **5.** somewhat near: They left *around* eight o'clock. —*adverb.* **1.** in a circle: The top spun *around* and *around.*

2. in distance about: Giant redwood trees measure 100 feet *around.* **3.** on all sides: The team gathered *around* the coach.

a•rouse [ə rouz′] *verb,* **aroused, arousing. 1.** to stir up; excite: The newspaper's headline *aroused* his interest, so he bought a copy. **2.** to wake up; awaken: The sound of the smoke alarm quickly *aroused* the family.

ar•range [ə rānj′] *verb,* **arranged, arranging. 1.** to put into order: These books are *arranged* according to their subjects. **2.** to plan for something; prepare: "I *arranged* for the school bus to stop at the entrance." (Marjorie Kinnan Rawlings) **3.** to change a piece of music from the way it was first written. This is done so that it can be performed by different instruments or voices than it was written for, or to change the style of the music.

ar•range•ment [ə rānj′mənt] *noun, plural* **arrangements. 1.** the act of arranging something, or the thing that is arranged: "It seemed a comfortable *arrangement* for the brother and sister to live together." (Barbara Pym) **2.** the act of arranging a piece of music. **3.** plans or preparations: All week long we've been making *arrangements* for Betsy's birthday party.

ar•rest [ə rest′] *verb,* **arrested, arresting. 1.** to stop and hold someone by power of the law: The police promised they would try to find the thief and *arrest* him. **2.** to stop something from going on; check: This medicine will *arrest* the infection in his leg. —*noun, plural* **arrests.** the act of arresting: A TV news show filmed the *arrest* of the robbers.

ar•ri•val [ə rī′vəl] *noun, plural* **arrivals. 1.** someone or something that has arrived: All the seats on the train are taken, so any late *arrivals* will have to stand. **2.** the act of arriving: "The *arrival* of spring meant different things to different people." (Beverly Cleary)

ar•rive [ə rīv′] *verb,* **arrived, arriving. 1.** to come to or reach a place: We *arrived* at the hotel at about eight o'clock. "A few minutes later, two policemen *arrived* from town." (Thomas Wolfe) **2.** to come to or reach a goal or object: The judge has not yet *arrived* at a decision in the case.

Pronunciation Key: O–S			
ō	over; go	ou	out; town
ô	all; law	p	put; hop
oo	look; full	r	run; car
o͞o	pool; who	s	set; miss
oi	oil; boy	sh	show

(Turn the page for more information.)

A

ar·ro·gant [âr′ ə gənt] *adjective, more/most.* having a feeling that you are better than other people; too proud; conceited: an *arrogant* remark, an *arrogant* attitude. —**arrogance** [âr′ ə gəns], *noun.* too much pride; conceit: After winning the beauty contest, Pam lost many friends because of her *arrogance.*

ar·row [âr′ ō] *noun, plural* **arrows. 1.** a long, narrow stick with a sharp point at the front end and feathers on the back. Arrows are shot from a bow. **2.** something shaped like an arrow. The road sign had an *arrow* pointing the way to the state highway. ◆ The pointed end of an arrow is called an **arrowhead.**

ar·se·nal [ärs′ nəl *or* är′ sə nəl] *noun, plural* **arsenals.** a place where military equipment is made or kept.

ar·se·nic [ärs′ nik *or* är′ sə nik] *noun.* a grayish-white powder that is a strong poison. Arsenic is used to get rid of rats or harmful insects and as a weed killer.

ar·son [är′ sən] *noun.* the crime of purposely setting fire to a building or other property. ◆ A person who commits this crime is an **arsonist** [är′ sə nist].

art [ärt] *noun, plural* **arts. 1.** the act of doing something that has beauty or special meaning. Art is meant to bring pleasure to people and to last over the years. Poetry, ballet dancing, and classical music are forms of art. **2.** the area of art that involves creating objects to be looked at; painting, drawing, or sculpture: The Museum of Modern *Art* in New York has famous works by Van Gogh and Picasso. **3.** any activity that requires special skill or talent to do well: the *art* of cooking, the *art* of making friends, the *art* of selling, the *art* of conversation.

ar·ter·y [är′ tə rē] *noun, plural* **arteries. 1.** any of the tubes that carry blood away from the heart to all parts of the body. Arteries differ from VEINS, which carry the blood back to the heart. **2.** a main road or channel that carries things from place to place: The Golden State Freeway is a major traffic *artery* moving through Los Angeles.

ar·thri·tis [är thrī′ tis] *noun.* a disease that makes a person's joints swollen and painful.

ar·thro·pod [är′ thrə päd] *noun, plural* **arthropods.** any of a large group of animals having jointed legs and bodies that are divided into parts. Arthropods include spiders, crabs, and insects.

Ar·thur [är′ thər] **Chester A.,** 1829–1886, the twenty-first president of the United States, from 1881 to 1885.

ar·ti·choke [är′ tə chōk′] *noun, plural* **artichokes.** a tall plant having a large flower head with thick leaves. The leaves are cooked and eaten as a vegetable.

artichoke An artichoke plant with a close-up of the vegetable. The name *artichoke* comes from Arabic.

ar·ti·cle [är′ ti kəl] *noun, plural* **articles. 1.** any particular object or item: Billy had left various *articles* of dirty clothing scattered around his room. "She gave him the money so he could pay for the *articles* himself." (Mary Elizabeth Vroman) **2.** a complete piece of writing on a factual subject in a newspaper, magazine, or book. **3.** a separate section of a document or legal paper: The powers of Congress are described in *Article* I of the U.S. Constitution. **4.** in grammar, one of the words used regularly before nouns. The words *a* and *an* are **indefinite articles,** and the word *the* is the **definite article.**

ar·tic·u·late [är tik′ yə lit] *adjective, more/most.* expressing oneself well; speaking clearly: Richard Burton was known as a very *articulate* actor. —[är tik′ yə lāt′] *verb,* **articulated, articulating.** to speak clearly.

ar·ti·fi·cial [är′ tə fish′ əl] *adjective, more/most.* **1.** made by people, not by nature; not natural: Plastic is an *artificial* substance. Many football stadiums now use an *artificial* playing surface instead of grass. **2.** not sincere or real; pretended: Jim tried to hide his disappointment over not winning the contest with an *artificial* smile. —**artificially,** *adverb.*

artificial intelligence the functions that a computer can perform that are somewhat like human thinking, such as learning how to respond to various problems, how to find answers, and how to reach decisions.

A

artificial respiration the forcing of air into and out of the lungs of a living person whose breathing has stopped. Artificial respiration is used to save the lives of people who have nearly drowned or who have stopped breathing from an accident or illness.

ar•til•ler•y [är til′ ə rē] *noun.* **1.** large and heavy guns used in warfare, such as cannons or rockets. **2.** the branch of an army that uses artillery.

ar•tist [är′ tist] *noun, plural* **artists. 1.** a person who is skilled in one of the arts, such as painting, music, literature, or dancing. **2.** a person who can do something with special skill or talent: Lisa is a real *artist* at getting along with different kinds of people.

ar•tis•tic [är tis′ tik] *adjective, more/most.* **1.** having to do with art or artists: That museum has a display of *artistic* treasures from ancient Egypt. **2.** showing special skill or talent: The banquet table had an *artistic* arrangement of flowers.
—**artistically,** *adverb.* in an artistic way: Her books of poetry don't sell a lot of copies, but they're very well thought of *artistically*.

as [az] *adverb.* **1.** to the same amount; equally: Her hands felt *as* cold *as* ice. **2.** for example: We've seen such animals *as* coyotes and bobcats near our house. —*conjunction.* **1.** in the same way that: Please do just *as* the instructions say. **2.** at the same time that; while: He caught the ball just *as* he was tackled. **3.** because; since: *As* there are no seats left, we'll have to stand. —*preposition.* **1.** like: He went to the party dressed *as* a pirate. **2.** doing the work of: She just got a job *as* an editor.

ascended to the rank of general when he was only 38 years old.

as•cent [ə sent′] *noun, plural* **ascents. 1.** the act of rising or climbing up: "The first recorded *ascent* of Mont Blanc, the highest mountain in Europe, was not until 1706." (Daniel Boorstin) **2.** the act of rising to a higher rank or level.

ash[1] [ash] *noun, plural* **ashes.** the soft, grayish-white powder that is left after something has completely burned.

ash[2] *noun, plural* **ashes.** a kind of shade tree that has a strong, springy wood which is used for making furniture, tool handles, and baseball bats.

a•shamed [ə shāmd′] *adjective, more/most.* **1.** feeling shame or disgrace: "I am not *ashamed* of my grandparents for having been slaves." (Ralph Ellison) **2.** not willing to do something because of shame: He was *ashamed* to admit that he didn't remember her.

a•shore [ə shôr′] *adverb.* on or to the shore: to go *ashore* from a ship.

A•sia [ā′ zhə] the largest continent in the world, east of Europe and north of the equator.

Asia Minor a peninsula in western Asia that is now the Asian part of Turkey. It was the site of many ancient civilizations.

A•sian [ā′ zhən] *noun, plural* **Asians.** a person born or living in Asia. —*adjective.* having to do with Asia: Buddhism is an important *Asian* religion.

a•side [ə sīd′] *adverb.* **1.** on or to one side: "The girls stood *aside*, talking among themselves, looking over their shoulders at the

---

as/like In speaking, people often use *like* as a conjunction: "I'm so tired it feels *like* my feet are about to fall off." In writing, however, this usage is not accepted as correct. Writers use *as, as if,* or *as though* rather than *like*: "I felt myself drawn *as* a fish is drawn on a line." (Stephen Vincent Benét) "He was bumping his feet together *as if* he had trouble walking." (Flannery O'Connor) "Her voice was cracking *as though* she was doing a dramatic performance." (Nancy Willard)

---

as•bes•tos [as bes′ təs] *noun.* a grayish mineral that will not burn. It can be separated into long fibers to make fireproof materials, such as clothing for firefighters. It is now known to be dangerous to health if used in building construction, and people who work with asbestos must use special precautions.

as•cend [ə send′] *verb,* **ascended, ascending. 1.** to go up; rise or climb: "We *ascended* the eighty steps." (Ray Bradbury) **2.** to move upward in rank or level: Douglas MacArthur

boys." (Shirley Jackson) **2.** away or apart: She tries to set *aside* a few minutes every morning to do her exercises.

Pronunciation Key: T–Z

t	ten; date	v	very; live
th	think	w	win; away
th	these	y	you
u	cut; butter	z	zoo; cause
ur	turn; bird	zh	measure

(Turn the page for more information.)

ask [ask] *verb,* **asked, asking. 1.** to raise a question in order to get information: The teacher *asked* what the largest river in the world was. **2.** to put a question to someone: Jason *asked* his sister where she had left the hair dryer. **3.** to make a request or demand: Mike *asked* for help with his homework. Whoever takes this job will be *asked* to work on weekends. **4.** to try to get as a price: The Bakers are *asking* $80,000 for their house. **5.** to invite: We've *asked* them to dinner on Saturday night. He's *asking* for trouble by being so rude to the boss.

a•sleep [ə slēp′] *adjective.* **1.** sleeping: "I thought if I pretended to be *asleep* the knocking might go away." (Sylvia Plath) **2.** having no feeling; numb: My foot was *asleep* because I sat too long on the hard floor. —*adverb.* to sleep: "He had just fallen *asleep,* it seemed, when someone was shaking him." (V.S. Naipaul)

as•par•a•gus [ə spar′ ə gəs] *noun.* a plant that is grown for food. The tender, young asparagus stalks are eaten as a vegetable.

asparagus Asparagus is a member of the lily family and is related to the *asparagus fern,* a popular house plant.

as•pect [as′ pekt] *noun, plural* **aspects. 1.** appearance; look: The old house had a frightening *aspect,* because it was so dark and gloomy. **2.** a particular way that something can be looked at or thought of: The jury carefully studied every *aspect* of the case before reaching its verdict.

as•phalt [as′ fôlt] *noun.* **1.** a thick, sticky, blackish-brown substance that comes from under the ground. Asphalt can also be made from petroleum. **2.** a hard, smooth material that is used to pave roads, made from asphalt and other materials such as sand and gravel.

as•pire [ə spīr′] *verb,* **aspired, aspiring.** to want very much to reach a certain goal: She *aspires* to become a doctor. —**aspiration,** [as′ pə rā′ shən] *noun, plural* **aspirations:** He has *aspirations* of becoming a famous mystery writer.

as•pi•rin [as′ prin *or* as′ pər in] *noun, plural* **aspirins.** a drug that is used in the form of pills to reduce pain and fever.

ass [as] *noun, plural* **asses. 1.** a donkey. **2.** *Slang.* a silly or stupid person; a fool.

as•sas•si•nate [ə sas′ ə nāt′] *verb,* **assassinated, assassinating.** to murder an important or famous person, especially a political leader. ◆ A person who does this is an **assassin** [ə sas′ in]. ◆ The act of assassinating someone is an **assassination** [ə sas′ i nā′ shən]: The *assassination* of Czar Nicholas of Russia occurred on July 16, 1918. ◆ Until very recently, it was thought incorrect to use *assassinate* to describe the murder of anyone other than a head of state, a king or president, or the head of a church. Nowadays, many writers use *assassinate* when describing the murder of a prominent public figure, as in the case of singer John Lennon.

as•sault [ə sôlt′] *noun, plural* **assaults. 1.** in law, a threat or attempt to hurt another person. **2.** any sudden and violent attack: Mexican troops made many *assaults* on the Alamo before the Texans were finally defeated. —*verb,* **assaulted, assaulting.** to attack violently: "He walked nervously toward the men, as if he expected to be *assaulted.*" (Stephen Crane)

as•sem•ble [ə sem′ bəl] *verb,* **assembled, assembling. 1.** to gather or collect in one place: Chris had *assembled* his rock collection for a science project. "Patients, doctors, and nurses *assembled* to see them off." (Somerset Maugham) **2.** to fit or put together: The child's riding toy had to be *assembled* before it could be used.

aspects Some words, like *aspect* and *area,* are useful because they apply to a lot of different situations. Almost any subject or problem in the world can have "aspects" to it, or have certain "areas" within it. Because of this, these words are sometimes used in a vague way: "I first met him in the *area* of 1966." (John Mitchell) Be careful with these words, because they are so general. Instead of saying, "The soccer coach looks at several *aspects* in judging a player," why not be specific? "In judging a player, the coach looks at four things: first, speed; second, ball skills; third, endurance; fourth, intelligence."

as•sem•bly [ə sem′ blē] *noun, plural* **assemblies.** **1.** the gathering together of a group of people: The U.S. Constitution states that there can be no laws against peaceful *assembly.* **2. Assembly.** a body of lawmakers, as in some states or foreign countries. **3.** the act of collecting or putting together: In modern auto factories, much of the *assembly* of a car is done by robots.

assembly A meeting of the General Assembly of the United Nations in New York City.

as•sess [ə ses′] *verb,* **assessed, assessing. 1.** to decide the worth or value of: Mrs. Pratt's house is *assessed* at $70,000. The government flew over the flooded area to *assess* the amount of damage that had been done. **2.** to charge a fee or tax to: Club members are *assessed* $20 each month for the use of the swimming pool. **—assessment,** *noun.*

as•set [as′ et] *noun, plural* **assets. 1.** something useful or valuable; an advantage: Oil deposits

problems for our math homework. **2.** to make definite; set: The judge *assigned* a date for the trial. **3.** to choose or appoint to some task or duty: Those soldiers have been *assigned* to a military base in Germany. "Ella May was *assigned* to sit beside me." (Marjorie Kinnan Rawlings)

as•sign•ment [ə sīn′ mənt] *noun, plural* **assignments. 1.** the act of assigning: The teacher made seating *assignments* for the class on the first day of school. **2.** something that is assigned: The reporter's *assignment* was to write about the two candidates for governor.

as•sist [ə sist′] *verb,* **assisted, assisting.** to give aid or support; help: An usher in a theater *assists* people in finding their seats. In doing his research, the professor was *assisted* by several of his students. **—***noun, plural* **assists.** a play that helps another player to score in sports such as hockey, basketball, and soccer.

as•sist•ance [ə sis′ təns] *noun, plural* **assistances.** the act or fact of assisting; help: Older people sometimes use a cane for *assistance* in walking.

as•sis•tant [ə sis′ tənt] *noun, plural* **assistants.** any person who gives aid or support; a helper: She is an *assistant* to the president of that company. **—***adjective.* acting to help; assisting: The *assistant* store manager is in charge when the manager is out.

as•so•ci•ate [ə sō′ shē āt′] *verb,* **associated, associating. 1.** to bring together or connect in one's mind: Most people *associate* Thanksgiving with a large turkey dinner. **2.** to join together with as a friend, fellow worker, or the like: Do you know which hospital Dr. Ward is *associated* with? **—**[ə sō′ shē it] *noun, plural* **associates.** a person who is joined with others; a friend, fellow worker, or the like.

asset *Asset* comes from a saying used long ago in English courts of law, "to have enough." A person who died with assets was a person who left enough valuable things to pay any debts he owed. Nowadays, *asset* has three meanings that are related: "She was an *asset* to the company, a good executive." "She sold all her *assets* in order to take a long trip." "The company is broke. It owes more than the value of its *assets.*"

are a great *asset* to many Middle Eastern countries. "Perhaps his greatest *asset* was his voice, which was rich in tone . . ." (Noel Coward) **2. assets.** all the things a person or business owns that are worth money: Our family's *assets* include our house, car, and bank accounts.

as•sign [ə sīn′] *verb,* **assigned, assigning. 1.** to give out work: The teacher *assigned* twenty

Pronunciation Key: [ə] Symbol

The [ə] or *schwa* sound occurs in syllables without an accent. It can be spelled with any vowel, such as **a** in above, **e** in listen, **i** in pencil, **o** in melon, **u** in circus. It can also be a combination of vowels, such as **io** in action, **ai** in mountain, **iou** in precious.

(Turn the page for more information.)

A

—[ə sō′shē it] *adjective.* **1.** joined with others: Sandra Day O'Connor became an *associate* justice of the Supreme Court in 1981. **2.** having less than full rights or privileges: The *associate* members of that law firm do not share in the profits of the firm the way the partners do.

as•so•ci•a•tion [ə sō′shē ā′shən] *noun, plural* **associations. 1.** an organization of people joined together for a common purpose: He belongs to an *association* to help fight cruelty to animals. **2.** the fact of joining or being connected: The author Saul Bellow has had a long *association* with the University of Chicago.

as•sort•ed [ə sôr′tid] *adjective.* of different kinds or varieties: The dessert shelf held *assorted* cakes, pies, and cookies.

as•sort•ment [ə sôrt′mənt] *noun, plural* **assortments.** a group of assorted things: "Inside the hall there was piled a large *assortment* of packages and parcels." (J.R.R. Tolkien)

as•sume [ə sōōm′] *verb,* **assumed, assuming. 1.** to believe something is true; suppose: I *assume* you've studied for the test. She *assumed* the plane would take off on time because the weather was clear. ♦ Often used as a conjunction: We'll get there about noon, *assuming* traffic isn't too heavy. **2.** to take on for oneself; undertake: As publisher of the newspaper, Mr. Miller *assumed* responsibility for what was printed in it. **3.** to take control of; take over: The sergeant *assumed* command after all the officers were wounded.

as•sump•tion [ə sump′shən] *noun, plural* **assumptions.** the act of assuming, or something that is assumed: The scientist Copernicus questioned earlier *assumptions* that the sun and planets moved around the earth.

as•sur•ance [ə shoor′əns] *noun, plural* **assurances. 1.** a statement to make a person sure or certain: She gave the boss her *assurance* that she could finish the job on time. "At the bottom of the label was the *assurance,* 'Never Fails to Give Relief.'" (James Herriot) **2.** belief in one's ability; self-confidence. ♦ This is also called **self-assurance.**

as•sure [ə shoor′] *verb,* **assured, assuring. 1.** to make certain or sure: She checked the stove to *assure* herself that it had been turned off. ♦ Often used as an adjective: "He dealt with things with a light, easy, and *assured* touch." (Somerset Maugham) **2.** to tell in a definite way: "'I'll stick to it all right,' Charlie *assured* him." (F. Scott Fitzgerald)

as•ter [as′tər] *noun, plural* **asters.** A star-shaped garden flower that is usually white, pink, blue, or purple.

aster The ancient Greeks thought of the aster as having blossoms in the shape of a star. The name comes from their word for "star."

as•ter•isk [as′tə risk′] *noun, plural,* **asterisks.** a star-shaped mark or symbol [*]. It is used in printing or writing to tell the reader to look elsewhere on the page for more information.

asterisk Probably the most famous use of the word *asterisk* occurred in the baseball record books. When Roger Maris hit 61 home runs in 1961, he beat Babe Ruth's record of 60 home runs in a single season. (Both played for the New York Yankees.) Because some people disliked having to admit that Ruth (who was not only a great hitter but also, originally, a great pitcher) was no longer the home run leader, an asterisk was placed in record books next to Maris's total. At the bottom of the page it was pointed out that Maris hit his 61 homers in a season of 162 games, whereas Ruth had hit 60 in a shorter season of 154 games.

as•ter•oid [as′tə roid′] *noun, plural* **asteroids.** one of several thousand small, rocky bodies that orbit around the sun. Most asteroids rotate between the planets Mars and Jupiter.

asth•ma [az′mə] *noun.* a disease that causes a person to have trouble breathing and to have fits of wheezing and coughing. A person can get asthma from many things, such as from being allergic to dust, animal hair, or certain plants. —**asthmatic,** *adjective* or *noun.*

as•ton•ish [ə stän′ ish] *verb,* **astonished, astonishing.** to surprise greatly; shock or amaze: "The driver was *astonished* to see bricks bouncing in the road ahead of him." (Graham Greene) —**astonishment,** *noun.* great surprise; amazement: They watched in *astonishment* as the magician seemed to disappear.

as•tound [ə stound′] *verb,* **astounded, astounding.** to surprise or shock greatly; amaze; astonish: Mrs. Kline was *astounded* at the news that she had won a new car.

a•stray [ə strā′] *adverb.* straying; away from the right path or direction: "I was somehow very small and very lost and lonely like a child *astray* in the snow." (Frank O'Connor)

as•trol•o•gy [ə sträl′ ə jē] *noun.* the study of the position of the stars and planets to determine the effect that they have on events and on people's lives. Some people believe astrology can be used to predict the future. ◆ A person who practices astrology is called an **astrologer.**

as•tro•naut [as′ trə nôt′] *noun, plural* **astronauts.** a person who is trained to travel in a spacecraft to outer space. ◆ The word astronaut is only about 50 years old, but it goes back to two ancient Greek words meaning "star sailor" or "star traveler."

as•tro•nom•i•cal [as′ trə näm′ i kəl] *adjective, more/most.* **1.** having to do with astronomy. **2.** very large, like the numbers in astronomy: The citizens complained that the cost of the proposed new town hall was *astronomical.*

as•tron•o•my [ə strän′ ə mē] *noun.* the scientific study of the sun, moon, stars, and other heavenly bodies. It includes information on where they are located, what they are made up of, and how they work. ◆ A person who is an expert in astronomy is an **astronomer.**

a•sy•lum [ə sī′ ləm] *noun, plural* **asylums. 1.** a place that gives care and shelter to orphans, the blind, those who are very poor, and so on. ◆ In former times, a hospital for mentally ill people was called an **insane asylum. 2.** protection given to a person who flees his own country and enters another country.

at [at *or* ət] *preposition.* **1.** in, on, by, or near: *at* home, *at* school, *at* the front door. **2.** in the direction of; toward: to shoot an arrow *at* a target. **3.** on or near the time of: to leave *at* 6:00, to retire from a job *at* age 65. **4.** in the condition of: *at* war, *at* rest. **5.** in the amount of: *at* 60 miles per hour, *at* a high price.

ate [āt] *verb.* the past tense of **eat.**

a•the•ist [ā′ thē ist] *noun, plural* **atheists.** a person who states that there is no Supreme Being or God. —**atheism,** *noun.*

Ath•ens [ath′ ənz] the capital of Greece, in the southeastern part of the country. *Population:* 885,000. —**Athenian,** *adjective; noun.*

ath•lete [ath′ lēt] *noun, plural* **athletes.** a person who takes part in sports or games that require strength, speed, and skill, such as baseball or football. ◆ The word *athlete* comes from a Greek expression meaning "I try for a prize." In ancient Greece, athletes competed for prizes in games, such as the Olympics.

ath•let•ic [ath let′ ik] *adjective, more/most.* **1.** having to do with an athlete or athletics: an *athletic* club, a store that sells *athletic* equipment. **2.** strong and vigorous: Sally is very *athletic* in spite of her small size. —**athletics,** *plural noun.* sports and games that require strength, speed, and skill.

At•lan•tic [at lan′ tik] the second-largest ocean in the world, separating North and South America from Europe and Africa.

Atlas An Italian statue of the god Atlas.

at•las [at′ ləs] *noun, plural* **atlases. 1.** a book that is a collection of maps. **2. Atlas.** a god of the ancient Greeks who was thought to support the world on his shoulders. The earliest books of maps often had a picture of Atlas holding up the world.

Pronunciation Key: Accent Marks

[′] is the normal accent mark. It shows where the main stress falls on a word.
[′] is a secondary accent mark. It shows a lighter stress than the primary accent. For example:

tel • e • vis • ion [tel′ə vizh′ən]

(Turn the page for more information.)

A

> **atmosphere** The atmosphere of a place is the certain feeling it creates in people who come there. Writers can describe an imaginary place so well that we can later see real places that remind us of it. Raymond Chandler's descriptions of Los Angeles are of this sort, full of atmosphere. "I got down to Montemar Vista as the light began to fade, but there was a fine sparkle on the water and the sun was breaking far out in long smooth curves. Montemar Vista was a few dozen houses of various sizes and shapes hanging by their teeth and eyebrows to a spur of mountain and looking as if a good sneeze would drop them down on the box lunches on the beach."

at•mos•phere [at′ məs fēr′] *noun, plural* **atmospheres. 1.** the air surrounding the earth: No one had ever traveled beyond the earth's *atmosphere* before the first manned space flights. **2.** the mass of air and gases that surround any star, planet, or other heavenly body: Mars has a thin *atmosphere* made up mainly of carbon dioxide. **3.** the general mood or feeling of a place: ". . . the special *atmosphere* of the theater." (Doris Lessing)

at•mos•pher•ic [at′ məs fēr′ ik] *adjective.* of or in the atmosphere. ◆ **Atmospheric pressure** is the pressure produced by the weight of the earth's atmosphere. It is about 14.7 pounds per square inch at sea level and becomes less as the altitude becomes higher.

a•tom [at′ əm] *noun, plural* **atoms.** an extremely tiny unit of matter that cannot be seen with the naked eye. An atom was once thought to be the smallest unit of matter in the universe. It is now known to contain even smaller parts called PROTONS and NEUTRONS, which appear in a core or NUCLEUS in the center of the atom, and ELECTRONS, which surround the nucleus. An atom is the smallest particle of a chemical element that can either unite with other elements or exist by itself.

a•tom•ic [ə täm′ ik] *adjective.* **1.** of or having to do with atoms: *atomic* research. **2.** using atomic energy: an *atomic* submarine.

atomic bomb a very powerful bomb whose great explosion results from splitting the NUCLEI of atoms of a very heavy chemical element, such as URANIUM or PLUTONIUM.

atomic energy the energy that exists within atoms. Certain atoms can be made to release some of their energy very slowly, as in a NUCLEAR REACTOR, or very quickly, as in an atomic bomb, either by splitting or combining the nuclei of atoms.

a•tone [ə tōn′] *verb,* **atoned, atoning.** to make up for or correct a wrong: The judge felt that giving the man a prison term of only six months would not be enough to *atone* for such a serious crime. **—atonement,** *noun.*

a•tro•cious [ə trō′ shəs] *adjective, more/most.* **1.** very cruel or horrible: Both the North and the South suffered *atrocious* losses in the Battle of Gettysburg. **2.** very bad; of poor quality: His behavior at the party was absolutely *atrocious.* ◆ Something that is atrocious is an **atrocity** [ə träs′ ə tē].

at•tach [ə tach′] *verb,* **attached, attaching. 1.** to fasten to or on; connect: She *attached* a rope to the sailboat. "A whistle was *attached* to an elastic cord around my wrist." (James Gould Cozzens) **2.** to add on at the end: He *attached* his signature to the contract. **3.** to hold by feelings of love or affection: Stan is very *attached* to his dog.

at•tach•ment [ə tach′ mənt] *noun, plural* **attachments. 1.** a connection through feelings of love or affection: "I asked if he was engaged or had any special girl friend, but he said he made a point of keeping free of such *attachments.*" (Sylvia Plath) **2.** a fastening together; connecting. **3.** an extra part or device that can be added to something: This camera has a flash *attachment* for taking indoor photos.

atomic bomb The first nuclear weapon was the atomic bomb, shown here during a test at Bikini Atoll, a deserted island in the Pacific. Later, a more powerful bomb was created, the *hydrogen* bomb. Now, the general term is used: *nuclear* energy, *nuclear* science, *nuclear* bombs.

at•tack [ə tak′] *verb,* **attacked, attacking. 1.** to set upon with force; try to injure: The robber was *attacked* by the guard dogs when he broke into the building. Japan *attacked* Pearl Harbor on December 7, 1941. **2.** to speak or write against: The city council *attacked* the mayor's plan to close the town swimming pool. **3.** to act against in a harmful way: An outbreak of disease *attacked* the city. **4.** to begin to work on or deal with: The entire class *attacked* the science project with great energy. —*noun, plural* **attacks. 1.** the act of attacking. **2.** the sudden coming on of a disease or illness: an *attack* of flu. —**attacker,** *noun.*

at my aunt's wedding. **2.** the number of people attending an event: The *attendance* at the basketball game was 12,000. **3.** a written record of who is present or not present: The teacher took *attendance* each morning at 8:30.

at•ten•tion [ə ten′ shən] *noun, plural* **attentions. 1.** the act or power of watching, listening, or fixing one's mind on something: The President's speech held the audience's complete *attention.* **2.** a military position in which a soldier stands very straight with his arms at his sides, feet together, and eyes straight ahead. —*interjection.* a command to a soldier to stand at attention.

> **attacking a paper** "Attacking a paper" means getting started on writing it. The blank page is hard to deal with—that's why we say that it has to be "attacked." John O'Hara wrote hundreds of short stories in his lifetime. The critic Frank McShane described O'Hara's method of getting started: "Often he would sit at his typewriter and start by thinking of two people whose faces he had seen. He would put the people together in a restaurant or an airplane, and they would begin to talk." As the two characters talked in O'Hara's mind, he would write down what he "overheard" them saying and soon they became real people in his mind. Carlos Fuentes, the great Mexican writer, advises writers to begin their day by reading something they have already written, just to remind themselves they can—and did—write well.

at•tain [ə tān′] *verb,* **attained, attaining. 1.** to gain something through hard work or talent; achieve: Frances Perkins was the first woman to *attain* a position as a member of the President's Cabinet. **2.** to arrive at, reach: "The *Abraham Lincoln* could *attain* a speed of 10.3 knots." (Jules Verne)

at•tempt [ə tempt′] *verb,* **attempted, attempting.** to make an effort to do something; try: I *attempted* to explain what had actually happened, but he wouldn't listen. —*noun, plural* **attempts. 1.** an effort or try: "But in my *attempt* to climb, I found that I was unable to do so." (Frank R. Stockton) **2.** an attack: an *attempt* on a person's life.

at•tend [ə tend′] *verb,* **attended, attending. 1.** to be present at a place or an event: In our state children have to *attend* school for 100 days a year. **2.** to give care or thought to; pay attention to: The firemen *attended* to the accident victims. The boss asked him to *attend* to the problem at once. **3.** to go with as a servant or companion: The queen was *attended* by her ladies in waiting. ◆ A person who attends someone or something is an **attendant.**

at•ten•dance [ə ten′ dəns] *noun.* **1.** the act of attending: The entire family was in *attendance*

at•ten•tive [ə ten′ tiv] *adjective, more/most.* **1.** paying close attention: an *attentive* listener. **2.** courteous and polite: an *attentive* host. —**attentively,** *adverb:* "His father listened *attentively* with his head cocked on one side." (Morley Callaghan)

at•tic [at′ ik] *noun, plural* **attics.** a space or room directly below the roof of a house or other building, above the other rooms.

at•ti•tude [at′ ə tood′] *noun, plural* **attitudes. 1.** a way of thinking, acting, or feeling: Jeff's good *attitude* toward school has helped improve his grades. **2.** a position of the body that suggests a certain action or feeling: ". . . his hands held palm to palm in an *attitude* of prayer." (Carson McCullers)

at•tor•ney [ə tur′ nē] *noun, plural* **attorneys. 1.** a person licensed to practice law; a lawyer. ◆ Also known as an **attorney-at-law. 2.** any

Pronunciation Key: A–F			
u	and, hat	sh	show; such
ā	ate; stay	d	dog; lid
â	care; air	e	end; yet
ä	father; hot	ē	she; each
b	boy; cab	f	fun; off

(Turn the page for more information.)

A

person who is given the right to act in another person's place, especially in legal or business matters. ◆ This is called a **power of attorney.**

at·tract [ə trakt´] *verb,* **attracted, attracting. 1.** to draw the interest of: "Momma and Poppa's voices kept *attracting* his attention." (Katherine Anne Porter) **2.** to draw toward itself: A magnet *attracts* both iron and steel.

at·trac·tion [ə trak´ shən] *noun, plural* **attractions. 1.** the act or power of attracting. **2.** a thing that attracts: "The village's only real *attraction* is the hot spring water." (James Baldwin)

at·trac·tive [ə trak´ tiv] *adjective, more/most.* having the power of attracting someone or something: She's an *attractive* woman. They made the owner of the house an *attractive* offer for the property. **—attractively,** *adverb.* **—attractiveness,** *noun.*

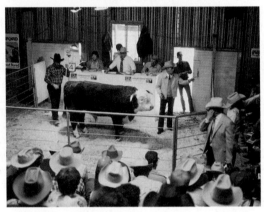

auction A cattle auction, with the *auctioneer* [ôk´ shə nēr´] shown to the right of the animal.

auc·tion [ôk´ shən] *noun, plural* **auctions.** a public sale at which something is sold to the person who offers the highest price for it. **—verb, auctioned, auctioning.** to sell something at an auction.

au·di·ence [ô´ dē əns] *noun, plural* **audiences. 1.** a group of people who listen to or watch a certain event, such as a TV or radio program, a play, concert, or show, or a game or other sports event. **2.** all the people who appreciate and support something: Mark Twain's books

have always had a large *audience* in this country. **3.** a formal meeting with a person of importance or high position: It is Kathy's dream to have an *audience* with the Pope.

au·di·o [ô´ dē ō´] *adjective.* **1.** having to do with sound. **2.** having to do with sending or receiving sound by means of a TV, radio, or the like: Stereos and tape recorders are *audio* equipment. **—noun, plural** **audios.** any electronic equipment that sends or receives sound.

au·di·tion [ô dish´ ən] *noun, plural* **auditions.** a short performance to show or test the ability of a singer, actor, dancer, or other performer: an *audition* for a new Broadway play. **—verb, auditioned, auditioning.** to take part in an audition: Several actors *auditioned* for the starring role in the play.

au·di·to·ri·um [ô´ də tôr´ ē əm] *noun, plural* **auditoriums.** a large room in a school, theater, or other building where people can gather for a show or meeting.

Au·gust [ô´ gəst] *noun.* the eighth month of the year. August has 31 days.

auk [ôk] *noun, plural* **auks.** a black and white sea bird found in cold northern waters. Auks have a heavy body, webbed feet, a short tail, and short wings that they use as paddles.

aunt [ant *or* änt] *noun, plural* **aunts. 1.** the sister of one's father or mother. **2.** the wife of one's uncle.

Aus·tin [ôs´ tən] the capital of the state of Texas. *Population:* 345,000.

Aus·tral·ia [ô strāl´ yə] **1.** the smallest continent in the world, located southeast of Asia. This island continent is occupied by one nation, the **Commonwealth of Australia. 2.** a country that includes this continent and **Tasmania.** *Capital:* Canberra. *Area:* 2,967,900 square miles. *Population:* 14,927,000. **—Australian,** *adjective; noun.*

Aus·tri·a [ô´ strē ə] a country in central Europe. *Capital:* Vienna. *Area:* 32,400 square miles. *Population:* 7,555,000. **—Austrian,** *adjective; noun.*

au·then·tic [ô then´ tik] *adjective, more/most.* **1.** being correct, reliable, or true: That book is an *authentic* account of the first women's rights

audience One of the most important things for a writer to have is a sense of audience. Your audience is the person or many persons you are writing for. It can be your teacher. It can be a classmate or a family member. Perhaps you're writing in hope that you will be published. Perhaps you're writing for yourself, in a diary or journal. Always ask yourself about your audience: (1) Who will read this? (2) What style of writing is proper for that reader? (3) What must I do to hold the attention of my reader or readers?

A

convention in 1840. **2.** not false; real; genuine: an *authentic* signature of George Washington. ♦ The state of being authentic is **authenticity** [ô′ then tis′ ə tē].

> **author** It is merely not a good use of English to write, "Who *authored* this book?" Instead, write, "Who *wrote* this book?" Writing is written. Writers are authors. It is not necessary to muddy the waters by making a good noun, *author*, into a not-so-good verb when a fine verb, *writing*, is already available.

au•thor [ô′ thər] *noun, plural* **authors. 1.** a person who writes a book, article, poem, or other such work. **2.** any person who begins or creates something: He is the *author* of the city's new plan for saving water.

au•thor•i•ty [ə thôr′ ə tē] *noun, plural* **authorities. 1.** the power or right to act, command, or make decisions: The captain of the ship had complete *authority* over the crew. **2.** a person or group that has command or certain powers: Mrs. Fischer was appointed to the city's housing *authority*. **3. authorities.** people who enforce the law: We'll have to report the missing money to the *authorities*. **4.** a respected source of information or advice: That teacher is an *authority* on the Civil War. ♦ Many English words that have to do with government and politics came from Latin, by means of the Norman French who invaded the British Isles in 1066. As rulers they brought French (therefore Latin) words to governing. *Authority* comes from a word meaning "master" or "leader."

au•thor•ize [ô′ thə rīz′] *verb,* **authorized, authorizing. 1.** to give authority or power to someone: The board of directors of the company *authorized* him to buy some land for a new office building. **2.** to approve something officially or legally: "Papers *authorizing* your travel . . . will be at your office in the morning." (James Michener)

au•to [ô′ tō] *noun, plural* **autos.** a short word for **automobile.**

au•to•bi•og•ra•phy [ô′ tə bī äg′ rə fē] *noun, plural* **autobiographies.** the story of a person's life written by that person. **—autobiographical,** *adjective.*

au•to•graph [ô′ tə graf′] *noun, plural* **autographs.** the signature of a person, especially a famous person, in his or her own handwriting. **—verb,** **autographed, autographing.** to write an autograph in or on: The writer *autographed* a copy of her latest book.

au•to•mat•ic [ô′ tə mat′ ik] *adjective.* **1.** acting or working by itself: an *automatic* elevator, an *automatic* garage door opener. **2.** done without thinking: Breathing and blinking the eyes are usually *automatic*. **3.** of a gun, able to fire again and again by itself if the trigger is held down. **—noun, plural** **automatics.** any machine or device that is automatic, especially an automatic gun. **—automatically,** *adverb.* **1.** in an automatic way: That door closes *automatically*. **2.** without thinking: "She soaped the blue shirts without seeing them, rubbing them up and down *automatically*." (Marjorie Kinnan Rawlings)

au•to•ma•tion [ô′ tə mā′ shən] *noun.* a system of working where machines are operated by themselves or by other machines, rather than by people.

au•to•mo•bile [ô′ tə mə bēl′] *noun, plural* **automobiles.** a vehicle that has four wheels and is driven by an engine powered by gasoline or diesel fuel. An automobile is smaller than a truck or bus and is intended mainly to carry passengers rather than goods. ♦ *Automobile* was originally a French word; it came into use in about 1890. It is a combination of two words meaning "self-moving"—an automobile moves by itself instead of being pulled by horses.

au•top•sy [ô′ täp sē] *noun, plural* **autopsies.** a medical examination of a dead body to find out the cause of death.

au•tumn [ô′ təm] *noun.* the season of the year between summer and winter; the fall.

aux•il•ia•ry [ôg zil′ yər ē] *adjective.* giving extra aid or support; helping: The hospital has *auxiliary* power in case the electricity goes off. The police chief added *auxiliary* officers to his staff during the riot. **—noun, plural** **auxiliaries. 1.** a person or thing that is added to give aid or support. **2.** a group within a larger group: The town's Elk Club has a women's *auxiliary*.

auxiliary verb a verb used with other verbs, such as *can, have, do,* or *will.*

Pronunciation Key: G–N			
g	give; big	k	kind; cat; back
h	hold	l	let; ball
i	it; this	m	make; time
ī	ice; my	n	not; own
j	jet; gem; edge	ng	having

(Turn the page for more information.)

A

a·vail·a·ble [ə vāl′ ə bəl] *adjective, more/most.* **1.** that can be had or obtained: These running shoes are *available* in four different colors. **2.** that can be used: The school's computers are *available* to all classes. ◆ The state of being available is **availability** [ə vāl′ə bil′ ə tē].

av·a·lanche [av′ ə lanch′] *noun, plural* **avalanches. 1.** a large, sudden fall of snow and ice down a mountain or over a cliff. **2.** something that is like an avalanche: "He carried in so much wood and built such a high structure with it that his mother walked in fear of an *avalanche* of oak." (John Steinbeck)

av·e·nue [av′ ə nōō′] *noun, plural* **avenues. 1.** road or street, especially a wide main road. **2.** a way to reach or accomplish something: an *avenue* to success.

av·er·age [av′ rij] *noun, plural* **averages. 1.** the number that is found by dividing the sum of two or more quantities by the number of quantities: The *average* of 9, 12, 15, and 20 is 14. **2.** the usual or ordinary amount or kind: Last month's rainfall was much higher than the *average* for April. —*adjective.* **1.** found by figuring the average: the *average* price of a new car, the *average* speed of an airplane over the course of a trip. **2.** usual or ordinary: Penny is about *average* in height and weight for her age. —*verb,* **averaged, averaging. 1.** to find the average of: to *average* a set of numbers. **2.** to have as an average: Kim *averaged* 20 points a game in basketball this year.

a·vi·a·tion [ā′ vē ā′ shən] *noun.* the art, science, or business of building and flying airplanes or other aircraft. ◆ A person who flies an aircraft is an **aviator.** The words *aviation* and *aviator* come from the Latin term *avis,* which means "bird."

av·o·ca·do [av′ ə kä′ dō *or* äv′ ə kä′ dō] *noun, plural* **avocados.** a pear-shaped tropical fruit with yellowish, buttery flesh and a single large seed. Avocados are eaten in salads and Mexican dishes.

a·void [ə void′] *verb,* **avoided, avoiding.** to keep away from: "They were all terrified of him, and some of the kids would go a mile to *avoid* him." (Frank O'Connor)

a·wait [ə wāt′] *verb,* **awaited, awaiting.** to wait for: "The townspeople stood on the station siding . . . *awaiting* the coming of the night train." (Willa Cather)

a·wake [ə wāk′] *verb,* **awoke** or **awaked, awaking. 1.** to wake up: "He *awoke* chilled and sick. There was no sun." (Jack London) **2.** to make active; stir up: His high school English teacher *awoke* in him a great love of poetry. —*adjective.* **1.** not asleep: "He had been lying *awake* ever since the first slight noise." (Edgar Allan Poe) **2.** alert to something; aware: In the early 1900's few people were *awake* to the danger of air pollution.

a·wak·en [ə wā′ kən] *verb,* **awakened, awakening.** to wake up: "A little after one o'clock I was *awakened* by the ringing of a bell." (Thomas Wolfe)

a·ward [ə wôrd′] *verb,* **awarded, awarding. 1.** to give as a prize or reward: The Olympic champions were *awarded* gold medals. **2.** to grant by the decision of a court: The jury *awarded* $10,000 to each injured person. —*noun, plural* **awards.** something that is awarded: The author Robert Penn Warren has received many *awards* for his books.

a·ware [ə wâr′] *adjective, more/most.* knowing or realizing something; conscious: "He was *aware* that the captain was calling his name." (Stephen Crane) —**awareness,** *noun.*

avocado An avocado cut away to show the seed. The word *avocado* comes from the American Indians. The Spanish explorers who first saw this fruit had no name for it because it didn't grow in Europe.

a·way [ə wā′] *adverb.* **1.** from this or that place: Dave can't decide whether to go *away* to college or go to the college right in town. **2.** in another place; absent: She's *away* from her office right now. **3.** in another direction; aside: "He headed *away* from the swamp." (Richard Connell) **4.** from or out of one's possession or use: "When you're through with a book, you just throw it *away*." (Isaac Asimov) **5.** at or to an end; out of existence: "Old soldiers never die, they just fade *away*." (Douglas MacArthur)

A

—*adjective*. **1.** at a distance: He lives two miles *away* from school. **2.** not present; absent; gone: She's been *away* on business for a week.

a•while [ə wīl′] *adverb*. for a short time; briefly: "We stopped so the boy could look at the river *awhile*." (S.E. Hinton)

awhile The adverb *awhile* is always written as one word: "He and Pa talked *awhile*, and then they went off into the woods together." (Laura Ingalls Wilder) The two-word expression "a while" is a noun, meaning "a time." It is usually used with another word in between—"a long while," "a little while." The question of usage reminds us why we need dictionaries. If you are not quite sure how *awhile* is used—and you have read it both ways many times—guessing won't do. Go to a dictionary.

awe [ô] *noun*. great wonder, mixed with fear or respect: "What we brought to the University . . . was a great *awe* before the splendid quotations on its buildings and the walls of its libraries." (Willie Morris)

awe•some [ô′ səm] *adjective, more/most*. causing a feeling of awe: The Statue of Liberty is an *awesome* sight.

aw•ful [ô′ fəl] *adjective, more/most*. **1.** causing fear or terror; terrible: The icy road caused an *awful* accident. **2.** very bad or unpleasant: She thinks fried eggs taste *awful*. **3.** very large; great: I have an *awful* lot of work to do. —*adverb*. very; "It's a long time to wait. You'll get *awful* tired waiting." (John Steinbeck)

awk•ward [ôk′ wərd] *adjective, more/most*. **1.** without ease or grace; clumsy: He *limped* on his sore leg in an *awkward* way. **2.** difficult or embarrassing: "'Will your husband be coming back soon?' I asked to break the rather *awkward* silence." (Barbara Pym)

awl [ôl] *noun, plural* **awls.** a pointed tool used for making holes in leather or wood.

aw•ning [ô′ ning] *noun, plural* **awnings.** a piece of canvas, metal, plastic, or other material, used above a window or door to shelter the inside of the building from sun or rain.

ax or **axe** [aks] *noun, plural* **axes.** a tool with a sharp metal blade attached to a handle. It is used for cutting wood.

awful A hundred years ago *awful*, meaning more or less what *awesome* now means, was quite often used by writers. Here, it shows the flexibility of English that *awful*, having other meanings, more or less gave up the particular meaning of *awesome*. Why is this a good variation whereas *administrate* for *administer* (see p.10) is not?

aw•ful•ly [ô′ flē] *adverb*. **1.** in a terrible or unpleasant way: He behaved *awfully* at the party. **2.** very much so; extremely: "I'm getting *awfully* tired, Ben." (Arthur Miller)

ax•is [ak′ sis] *noun, plural* **axes** [ak′ sēz]. a straight line, usually unseen, around which a body turns or seems to turn. The earth rotates on an imaginary axis.

ax•le [ak′ səl] *noun, plural* **axles.** a rod or bar on which a wheel or pair of wheels turns.

aye or **ay** [ī] *noun, plural* **ayes.** a vote of "yes."

a•za•lea [ə zāl′ yə] *noun, plural* **azaleas.** a small bush with clusters of bright flowers.

a•zure [azh′ ər] *noun* or *adjective*. a bright, clear blue color.

azalea

Pronunciation Key: O–S			
ō	over; go	ou	out; town
ô	all; law	p	put; hop
oo	look; full	r	run; car
o͞o	pool; who	s	set; miss
oi	oil; boy	sh	show

(Turn the page for more information.)

Bb

b,B [bē] *noun, plural* **b's, B's. 1.** the second letter of the alphabet. **2.** the second highest grade or level.

Bab•bage [bab′ ij] **Charles,** 1792–1871, English inventor whose research began the development of the modern computer.

ba•boon [ba bōōn′] *noun, plural* **baboons.** a large, hairy monkey with a face like a dog. Baboons live together in large groups in open areas of Africa and Asia.

baboon The hamadras baboon, which lives on the grassy plains of northern Africa.

ba•by [bā′ bē] *noun, plural* **babies. 1.** a young child; an infant. **2.** the youngest one in a family or group. **3.** a person who acts in a very childish way. —*verb,* **babied, babying.** to treat like a baby; give a lot of attention to: Her parents *baby* her by buying her every toy she wants. —*adjective.* **1.** for or like a baby: *baby* clothes, a *baby* carriage. **2.** very young: a *baby* animal.

ba•by-sit [bā′ bē sit′] *verb,* **baby-sat, baby-sitting.** to take care of a child or children while the parents are away from home for a short time. ♦ A **babysitter** is someone who babysits for a child.

Bach [bäk] **Johann** [yō′ hän] **Sebastian,** 1685–1750, German composer and organist.

bach•e•lor [bach′ lər] *noun, plural* **bachelors.** a man who is not married, especially one who has never been married.

back [bak] *noun, plural* **backs. 1.** the part of the human body opposite the front, from the neck to the end of the spine. **2.** the upper part of an animal's body. **3.** the part of anything that is away from or opposite the front: the *back* of a chair, the *back* of a room, the *back* of a book. **4.** in football, a player whose position is in the backfield. —*verb,* **backed, backing. 1.** to move backward: "She slowly *backed* out of the room and then began to move downstairs." (Paul Zindel) **2.** to support or help: I'm *backing* Stacy for school president. —*adjective.* **1.** away from or opposite the front: a *back* door, the *back* yard. **2.** not current; past: a *back* issue of a newspaper. —*adverb.* **1.** toward the rear: She sat *back* in her chair. Put the milk *back* in the refrigerator. **2.** to the former place or time: "He began to think *back* over the day." (Marjorie Kinnan Rawlings)

back•board [bak′ bôrd′] *noun, plural* **backboards.** in basketball, a flat board that is behind the basket.

back•bone [bak′ bōn′] *noun, plural* **backbones. 1.** the line of jointed bones down the middle of the back; the spine or spinal column. Humans are part of a large group of animals with backbones, that also includes other mammals, birds, reptiles, and fish. **2.** the most important or strongest part of something: Our star pitcher is the *backbone* of the team. **3.** strength of mind; courage: Sir Francis Chichester of England showed a lot of *backbone* when he sailed a small boat around the world by himself.

back•field [bak′ fēld′] *noun, plural* **backfields.** in football, the players who stand behind the line at the beginning of a play.

back•fire [bak′ fīr′] *noun, plural* **backfires. 1.** a loud, quick noise caused by an explosion of gasoline in an engine. **2.** a fire that is purposely

B

set in front of a forest fire or grass fire to stop it from spreading. —*verb,* **backfired, backfiring. 1.** to make a backfire. **2.** to come out in the opposite way than was hoped for: His plan to lose weight by running *backfired* because it made him so hungry that he ended up eating twice as much.

---

background What is the best background for a writer? Some writers have had exciting jobs. Herman Melville was a sailor on a whaling ship. Mark Twain was a Mississippi riverboat pilot. Jack London was a gold prospector in the Yukon. On the other hand, many outstanding writers have led quiet lives. Henry David Thoreau said, "I have traveled a good deal in Concord." He meant that he'd found a lot of things to write about without leaving his little home town. The American poet Emily Dickinson never left Amherst, Massachusetts. It's not clear, TV still being fairly new, how much future writers can imagine the world outside—so much is brought into our houses!

---

back•ground [bak′ground′] *noun, plural* **backgrounds. 1.** the ground or scene behind a main object: In the painting "Mona Lisa," there are hills and water in the *background.* **2.** a position that does not get attention: The coach prefers to stay in the *background* and let his players take the credit for winning. **3.** the events or experiences that lead up to something: For this job you need a good *background* in math and science. ♦ Also used as an adjective: This report gives some *background* information on tomorrow's meeting.

back•ward [bak′wərd] *adverb.* (*also,* **backwards**) **1.** toward the back: He looked *backward* over his shoulder. **2.** with the back forward: She put her sweater on *backward.* **3.** opposite to the usual way: to count *backward* from ten to one. —*adjective, more/most.* **1.** toward the back: a *backward* glance, a *backward* movement. **2.** behind in learning or development: a *backward* area of the world.

ba•con [bā′kən] *noun.* a food made from the side or back of a pig. Bacon is salted or smoked and usually fried in thin slices.

bac•te•ri•a [bak tēr′ē ə] *plural noun.* cells that are so tiny they can be seen only under a microscope. Bacteria are found in soil, air, and water, and on or in plants and animals. Some kinds cause diseases, such as PNEUMONIA, and other kinds are helpful, as in making cheese and vinegar. ♦ The singular form of this word is **bacterium** [bak tēr′ē əm]. A **bacterial** infection is one that is caused by bacteria.

♦ *Bacteria* comes from a Greek word meaning "little rods." When scientists first saw bacteria under a microscope, they thought that they looked like little rods.

bad [bad] *adjective,* **worse, worst. 1.** not good: a *bad* movie, a *bad* smell, food that is *bad* for your health. He's always in a *bad* mood when he first wakes up in the morning. **2.** rotten or spoiled: a *bad* apple, *bad* meat. **3.** sorry: "Billy Buck felt *bad* about his mistake." (John Steinbeck) —**badness,** *noun.*

bade [bād] a past tense of **bid:** "He stopped and *bade* us good-day." (James Joyce)

badge [baj] *noun, plural* **badges.** a mark or sign that shows a person belongs to a certain group or has done a special thing. Police officers wear or carry badges to identify themselves.

badger The North American badger can dig a hole very rapidly, using its long, powerful claws to scoop out the dirt.

badg•er [baj′ər] *noun, plural* **badgers.** an animal with short legs, long, sharp claws, and heavy gray fur. Badgers live under the ground and feed at night.

Pronunciation Key: A–F			
a	and; hat	ch	chew; such
ā	ate; stay	d	dog; lid
â	care; air	e	end; yet
ä	father; hot	ē	she; each
b	boy; cab	f	fun; off

(Turn the page for more information.)

B

—*verb,* **badgered, badgering.** to annoy or nag: The movie star seldom went out in public because fans were always *badgering* her for autographs. ◆ This verb meaning came about because in olden times people used to use dogs to attack and annoy a badger as a kind of sport.

bad•ly [bad′lē] *adverb.* **1.** in a bad way: Our team lost the game, but we really didn't play that *badly.* **2.** very much: "Anything in the world was possible, according to my mother, if you wanted it *badly* enough." (Nancy Willard)

bad•min•ton [bad′mit ən] *noun.* a game for two or four people, played by hitting a small feathered object called a **shuttlecock** [shut′əl käk′] over a high net with a racket. ◆ This game was first played at *Badminton,* a country estate in England.

baf•fle [baf′əl] *verb,* **baffled, baffling.** to confuse or puzzle; bewilder: The police were *baffled;* all the windows and doors were still locked, yet the diamonds had been stolen.

bag [bag] *noun, plural* **bags. 1.** a soft container that is made of paper, cloth, or plastic and that is usually open at the top. It is used to carry food, clothes, or other items. **2.** something that can be used like a bag, such as a woman's purse or a suitcase. —*verb,* **bagged, bagging. 1.** to put into a bag: to *bag* groceries. **2.** to catch or capture, as if in a bag: The hunter *bagged* three ducks.

bag•gage [bag′ij] *noun.* suitcases, bags, or packages that people carry on a trip; luggage.

bag•gy [bag′ē] *adjective,* **baggier, baggiest.** hanging loosely: a *baggy* pair of pants.

Bagh•dad or **Bag•dad** [bag′dad′] the capital of Iraq. *Population:* 3,500,000.

bagpipes Long ago, bagpipes were used to lead Scottish soldiers into battle. Today they are often played in parades and ceremonies.

bag•pipe [bag′pīp′] *noun, plural* **bagpipes.** a musical instrument played by blowing air

through a tube into a leather bag and forcing it out through several pipes. The bagpipe is played in Scotland.

bail[1] [bāl] *verb,* **bailed, bailing. 1.** to scoop water out of a boat: When the canoe began to sink, we started *bailing* with cups and buckets. **2. bail out.** to jump out of an airplane with a parachute.

bail[2] *noun.* money given in return for a prisoner's being let out of jail until the time of his trial. The money is a promise that the person will return to court for the trial.

bait [bāt] *noun, plural* **baits. 1.** something used to attract fish or animals so that they can be caught. Worms, bits of food, and artificial flies are types of bait used to catch fish. **2.** anything that attracts a person to do something: The magazine offered a chance to win a free car as *bait* to get new subscribers. —*verb,* **baited, baiting. 1.** to put bait on: to *bait* a fish hook. **2.** to tease or torment: The crowd *baited* the speaker by shouting insults at him.

bake [bāk] *verb,* **baked, baking. 1.** to cook something by heating it in an oven: to *bake* bread, to *bake* potatoes. **2.** to dry out or make hard by heating: These clay pots were *baked* in the sun.

bak•er [bā′kər] *noun, plural* **bakers.** a person who bakes and sells bread, rolls, cakes, and other foods. ◆ A **bakery** is a place where baked foods are made or sold.

baking soda a white powder used in baking to make cakes, breads, and other foods rise. It can also be used to help relieve an upset stomach. ◆ Another name for this powder is SODIUM BICARBONATE.

bal•ance [bal′əns] *noun, plural* **balances. 1.** a steady, even position of the body: The tightrope walker held out her arms to keep her *balance.* "When one wing is shorter than the other, the *balance* of the bird is upset." (E.B. White) **2.** a condition that is steady or equal: "I'm trying to get man back into *balance* with the environment." (John McPhee) **3.** a scale or object for weighing things by putting them in balance with a known amount of weight. **4.** an amount left over or remaining: She's going to pay part of the cost of the sofa now, and then pay the *balance* when it's delivered to her house. **5.** the amount of money in a certain business account: My bank book shows a *balance* of $200. His auto loan has an unpaid *balance* of $1,800.

—*verb,* **balanced, balancing. 1.** to put or keep in a steady position: "He carried the cup of hot milk carefully, *balancing* it in his hands." (Marjorie Kinnan Rawlings) **2.** to figure the amount of money in an account: to *balance* a checkbook. ◆ Also used as an adjective: This book shows how you can eat a *balanced* diet for better health.

ball² *noun, plural* **balls.** a large, formal dance.

bal·lad [bal′ əd] *noun, plural* **ballads.** a song or poem that tells a story.

bal·last [bal′ əst] *noun, plural* **ballasts.** a heavy material used to keep something steady. Rocks or iron can be used to give a ship ballast.

balanced writing Jack Kerouac wrote several novels, the best-known being *On the Road.* For that book he fed a huge roll of paper into a typewriter and then typed hour after hour, sometimes without stopping. He took this roll of paper to a publisher—it was his manuscript! Some people are the opposite of Kerouac, writing and rewriting sentences a hundred times. Why not try to keep a balance between these two extremes?

Bal·boa [bal bō′ ə] **Vasco de,** 1475–1519, Spanish explorer who discovered the Pacific Ocean.

bal·co·ny [bal′ kə nē] *noun, plural* **balconies. 1.** a raised section that extends out from an apartment house or other building. **2.** an upper floor with seats that extend out over the main floor, as in a theater or church.

bald [bôld] *adjective,* **balder, baldest. 1.** having little or no hair on the head. **2.** without a natural covering: *bald* spots in a lawn from lack of water. **3.** simple or plain: "I don't want to set down a series of *bald* facts in a diary like most people do." (Anne Frank)

bald eagle a large North American eagle with a white neck and head. The bald eagle is the national symbol of the United States.

bale [bāl] *noun, plural* **bales.** a large bundle of things wrapped together to be stored or sent somewhere: a *bale* of cotton. —*verb,* **baled, baling.** to make into a bale: to *bale* hay.

balk [bôk] *verb,* **balked, balking. 1.** to stop short and refuse to move or act: "The horse *balked* and shied away from her." (Lloyd Alexander) **2.** in baseball, a play in which the pitcher starts to pitch and then stops. —*noun, plural* **balks.** the act of balking. If a pitcher commits a balk, the runners move up one base.

ball¹ [bôl] *noun, plural* **balls. 1.** a round object used in many sports and games, such as baseball, football, soccer, golf, tennis, and so on. **2.** anything having a roundish shape like this: a snow*ball*, a *ball* of string, a cannon*ball*. **3.** baseball or a similar game played with a ball: The umpire says "Play *ball*" to start a baseball game. **4.** in baseball, a pitch that is not a strike. A pitch is a ball if the batter doesn't swing at it and it doesn't pass over the plate between his shoulders and his knees. —*verb,* **balled, balling.** to form the shape of a ball: He *balled* up the letter and threw it in the wastebasket.

ball bearing a small metal ball that sits in a groove. Ball bearings are used in machinery to help parts move more easily.

bal·le·ri·na [bal′ ə rē′ nə] *noun, plural* **ballerinas.** a girl or woman ballet dancer.

bal·let [ba lā′ *or* bal′ ā] *noun, plural* **ballets. 1.** an artistic form of dancing that uses special jumps, spins, and movements. A ballet usually tells a story through dance and music. **2.** a group of dancers who perform a ballet. ◆ Of the two pronunciations given above, the second one [bal′ ā] is more common in British English.

ballet The world-famous ballet dancers Mikhail Baryshnikov and Gelsey Kirkland perform in a scene from *The Nutcracker.*

Pronunciation Key: G–N

g	give; big	k	kind; cat; back
h	hold	l	let; ball
i	it; this	m	make; time
ī	ice; my	n	not; own
j	jet; gem; edge	ng	having

(Turn the page for more information.)

bal·loon [bə lōōn/] *noun, plural* **balloons.** a bag filled with air or gas. Small rubber balloons are used as children's toys or for decoration. Much larger balloons filled with a special gas such as HELIUM can be attached to a basket or cabin to carry people above the earth. —*verb,* **ballooned, ballooning.** to puff out or grow larger, as a balloon does when it is filled with air: "All the windows were open and the lace curtains *ballooned* gently toward the street." (James Joyce)

balloon A hot air balloon rises when the air inside it is heated. As the air cools, the balloon will come back to earth.

bal·lot [bal/ ət] *noun, plural* **ballots. 1.** a paper or other item used for voting. **2.** the number of votes cast in an election. —*verb,* **balloted, balloting.** to vote by using a ballot: The *balloting* was very heavy in this year's election for senator. ◆ *Ballot* comes from an Italian word meaning "a little ball." Many years ago, people voted by putting a little colored ball into a box.

ball·point pen [bôl/ point/] a pen having a small ball on its point that transfers ink onto paper.

ball·room [bôl/ room/] *noun, plural* **ballrooms.** a large room used for dancing or for holding parties or meetings.

balm·y [bä/ mē] *adjective,* **balmier, balmiest.** mild and pleasant: Hawaii generally has *balmy* weather.

bal·sa [bôl/ sə] *noun, plural* **balsas.** a tropical tree that has strong but light wood. **Balsa wood** is used to make boats and model airplanes.

bal·sam [bôl/ səm] *noun.* **1.** a pleasant-smelling oil that is used in making perfumes and varnish-

es. **2.** any plant that produces balsam, such as the **balsam fir** tree.

Bal·tic Sea [bôl/ tik] an inland sea of northern Europe that is connected to the Atlantic.

Bal·ti·more [bôl/ tə môr/] a city and seaport of Maryland. *Population:* 787,000.

bamboo A bamboo plant can grow to be 100 feet tall. *Bamboo* comes from Malayan, a language spoken in the area where these trees first grew.

bam·boo [bam bōō/] *noun, plural* **bamboos.** a tall grass that grows like a tree. It has hollow, jointed stems that are used to make such items as fishing poles, furniture, and window blinds.

ban [ban] *verb,* **banned, banning.** to forbid by law or in an official way; prohibit: The city has *banned* smoking in all public buildings. —*noun, plural* **bans.** an official order that bans something: There is a *ban* on motorboats at this lake.

ba·nan·a [bə nan/ ə] *noun, plural* **bananas.** a curved, finger-shaped fruit that grows in bunches and has a yellow skin when ripe. The banana plant grows in tropical areas and has very large leaves.

band¹ [band] *noun, plural* **bands. 1.** a narrow strip of material: a rubber *band.* She wore a gold *band* on her finger. **2.** a stripe or ring of color: Coral snakes are marked by *bands* of black, red and yellow. —*verb,* **banded, banding.** to put a band on: Scientists *band* wild birds to keep track of where they go.

band² *noun, plural* **bands. 1.** a group of people playing musical instruments together. **2.** any group of people, animals, or objects: Robin Hood and his *band* of outlaws.

—*verb*, **banded, banding.** to form a band; unite: The neighbors *banded* together to protest heavy traffic on their streets.

band•age [ban′ dij] *noun, plural* **bandages.** a piece of cloth or tape used to cover or protect a cut or injury. —*verb*, **bandaged, bandaging.** to put a bandage on: The doctor *bandaged* her hand.

ban•dan•a [ban dan′ ə] *noun, plural* **bandanas.** (also spelled **bandanna**) a large handkerchief or scarf with a bright color or pattern.

ban•dit [ban′ dit] *noun, plural* **bandits.** a robber or outlaw, especially one who is part of a gang.

bang [bang] *noun, plural* **bangs.** a loud, sharp noise. —*verb*, **banged, banging.** to make a loud, sharp noise: "Asher raced up the stairs and *banged* on our door." (I.B. Singer)

Ban•gla•desh [bang′ glə desh′] a country in southeast Asia, bordered by India. *Capital:* Dacca. *Area:* 55,100 square miles. *Population:* 93,000,000.

bangs [bangz] *plural noun.* hair cut short in a straight line across the forehead.

ban•ish [ban′ ish] *verb*, **banished, banishing. 1.** to force to leave a country: King Richard I *banished* his brother Prince John for trying to take over as king. **2.** to send or drive away: "She *banished* such thinking and concentrated on the blue of the sky overhead." (Ernest K. Gann) —**banishment**, *noun.*

ban•is•ter [ban′ is tər] *noun, plural* **banisters.** a railing along a staircase, supported by upright pieces of wood or metal.

ban•jo [ban′ jō] *noun, plural* **banjos** or **banjoes.** a musical instrument something like a guitar, with a long neck and a round body. It is played by picking the strings with the fingers.

have dealings with a bank: We *bank* at First National. **2.** to put in a bank: Sue always *banks* part of her salary each month.

bank² *noun, plural* **banks. 1.** the land along the edge of a river or stream. **2.** a heap or mound: a *bank* of earth, a cloud *bank.* —*verb*, **banked, banking. 1.** to form into a bank: The plow *banked* the snow at the edge of the road. **2.** to slant a road so that the outer edge is higher than the inner: to *bank* the curves of a race track.

bank³ *noun, plural* **banks.** a group of similar things together in a row: Their office has a large *bank* of computers.

bank•er [bangk′ ər] *noun, plural* **bankers.** a person whose business is banking, especially someone who manages a bank.

bank•rupt [bangk′ rupt] *adjective.* not able to pay one's bills. A court of law can declare a person or business to be bankrupt if they owe more in debt than they have money to pay. —*verb*, **bankrupted, bankrupting.** to make bankrupt. ♦ The state of being bankrupt is **bankruptcy** [bangk′ rəpt sē]. ♦ *Bankrupt* once meant "broken table." A *bank* was a table where people carried on business dealings. If a person had no money and couldn't pay his bills, the table he used would be broken to show that he wasn't allowed to do business there.

ban•ner [ban′ ər] *noun, plural* **banners. 1.** a strip of cloth with letters or pictures on it representing something: The school soccer team has a *banner* with the names of all the players. **2.** a flag: 'The Star-Spangled *Banner.*' —*adjective.* unusually good; outstanding: It was a *banner* year for the farmers in our state.

ban•quet [bang′ kwit] *noun, plural* **banquets.** a large formal dinner given to honor someone or as part of a celebration.

---

bank Teachers who work with student writers sometimes use a system called a Word Bank to help their students write. The Word Bank is a list of key words or phrases having to do with a certain topic. Suppose you want to write a story about a trip to the beach. Your Word Bank might include the words *water, sand,* or *sunbathers,* or the phrases "glint on the waters," "reddened sands," or "white-painted sunbathers." You could "withdraw" these words from the bank as you go about writing your story.

---

bank¹ [bangk] *noun, plural* **banks. 1.** a place whose business is to keep money safe and to carry on other dealings with money, such as making loans, exchanges, and check payments. ♦ This business is called **banking. 2.** a place where a large supply of something is kept, as a bank keeps a supply of money: the blood *bank* of a hospital. —*verb*, **banked, banking 1.** to

Pronunciation Key: O–S			
ō	over; go	ou	out; town
ô	all; law	p	put; hop
oo	look; full	r	run; car
o͞o	pool; who	s	set; miss
oi	oil; boy	sh	show

(Turn the page for more information.)

B

B

bap•tism [bap/ tiz əm] *noun, plural* **baptisms.** a religious ceremony in which a person is sprinkled with water or dipped under water. Baptism is a symbol of the washing away of the person's sins. It is performed when someone is first admitted to a Christian church.

bap•tize [bap/ tīz/] *verb,* **baptized, baptizing.** to carry out a ceremony of baptism: The minister *baptized* my baby sister.

bar [bär] *noun, plural* **bars. 1.** a straight piece of wood, metal, or other material that is longer than it is wide: a *bar* of soap, a candy *bar,* the *bars* on the windows of a jail. **2.** something that blocks the way; a barrier. **3.** a straight band or stripe of color. **4.** a room with a long counter where alcoholic drinks are served. **5.** in music, one of the straight lines drawn from top to bottom across a STAFF to divide it into units of time called MEASURES. **6.** one of these units of musical time; a measure. **7.** the work or profession of a lawyer: A *bar* examination is a test that a person must pass to be allowed to practice law. —*verb,* **barred, barring. 1.** to close or fasten with a bar: He *barred* the door of the cabin. **2.** to block or keep out: For many years women were *barred* from voting in this country.

barb [bärb] *noun, plural* **barbs.** a sharp point that sticks out backwards from the object it is attached to. Fish hooks, arrows, and spears have barbs.

bar•bar•i•an [bär bar/ ē ən] *noun, plural* **barbarians. 1.** a person who is not civilized; a savage. **2.** a person who is very crude or bad-mannered: "I see so few people to talk to nowadays that I have turned into a sort of *barbarian.*" (Katherine Mansfield) ♦ Someone who is a barbarian is **barbarous.**

stop animals from leaving or entering the property.

bar•ber [bär/ bər] *noun, plural* **barbers.** a person whose work is cutting people's hair.

bare [bâr] *adjective,* **barer, barest. 1.** having no covering or clothing; naked: In winter the trees are *bare* of leaves. **2.** empty: The store's shelves were *bare* after the big sale. —*verb,* **bared, baring.** to make bare; reveal or uncover: The dog *bared* its teeth when the man tried to come into the yard. She *bared* her feelings to her best friend. ♦ Remember the difference between *bare* and *bear,* as in "He couldn't *bear* (not *bare*) the thought of hurting her."

bare•ly [bâr/ lē] *adverb.* only just; scarcely: "When I speak my voice is *barely* a whisper." (Judy Blume)

bar•gain [bär/ gən] *noun, plural* **bargains. 1.** something for sale that is a good value at its price; a good buy: This sweater is a real *bargain* at $20, because it's a famous brand and made of 100% wool. **2.** an agreement between two people or two groups; a deal: Tim made a *bargain* with his mother that he could watch TV late on Friday night if he went to bed early all week. —*verb,* **bargained, bargaining. 1.** to try to reach a bargain: Jill tried *bargaining* with the car owner, but he still wouldn't lower his price. **2. bargain for.** to be ready for; expect: Taking care of the baby was a lot more work than he had *bargained for.*

barge [bärj] *noun, plural* **barges.** a large boat with a flat bottom. Barges are often used to carry freight on rivers and lakes. —*verb,* **barged, barging.** to push or shove rudely: "People would *barge* into his sanctuary, asking questions, making demands . . ." (Robert Heinlein)

barbarian *Barbarian* was first used by the Greeks and Romans to describe tribes of the ancient world who were not as civilized as they. Later, writers in English who disliked uses of words that were either mistaken or worn-out, called such words "barbarisms." Here's a case: "Uninterested" means you're not interested. "Disinterested" means you are neutral, neither for or against something. Yet, people do say "disinterested" to mean "uninterested"—and thus lose a good word. Of this, the writer Berton Roueche said, "Please, let's not give in to this *barbarity!*"

bar•be•cue [bär/ bə kyōō/] *noun, plural* **barbecues. 1.** a grill, stove, or pit for cooking food outdoors over hot coals or an open fire. **2.** a meal with food cooked in this way. —*verb,* **barbecued, barbecuing.** to cook food in this way: to *barbecue* a steak.

barbed wire a kind of wire that has barbs on it, often used for fences on farms and ranches to

bar•i•tone [bar/ i tōn/] *noun, plural* **baritones.** a male singer with a range lower than a TENOR and higher than a BASS.

bark¹ [bärk] *noun, plural* **barks.** the outer covering on a tree trunk or branches. —*verb,* **barked, barking.** to scrape the skin from: She *barked* her knee when she fell off her bike.

bark² *noun, plural* **barks.** the short, sharp sound

made by a dog or similar animal. —*verb*, **barked, barking. 1.** to make this sound. **2.** to speak in a sharp, angry way: The sergeant *barked* out an order to the new recruits.

bar•ley [bär′lē] *noun.* a plant whose grain is used for food and to make beer and whiskey.

bar mitz•vah [mits′ və] a religious ceremony for a Jewish boy at the age of thirteen. It serves to recognize that he has become an adult and can take a full role in the Jewish religion. ◆ A similar ceremony for a girl is a **bas mitzvah.**

curved wood pieces held together with metal hoops. **2.** something shaped like a barrel: A bullet travels through the *barrel* of a gun. —*verb*, **barreled, barreling.** to travel very fast: The racing car *barreled* around the turn.

bar•ren [bar′ ən] *adjective, more/most.* **1.** not able to produce new offspring: a *barren* cow. **2.** not able to produce much: Only cactus will grow in this *barren* desert. That book was just published, but it is absolutely *barren* of new ideas.

B

barren writing *Barren* is a word with strong meanings. A young woman who cannot bear children is called *barren.* A desert is said to be *barren* (though the amount of animal life there is surprising). Can writing be barren? Yes. Sparse writing—Hemingway's short, direct sentences—is not that. Neither is tragic drama with its sad scenes—Shakespeare's *King Lear,* for example. But if your writing lacks force or conveys no pictures in the reader's mind, it is barren. Test your writing. What do you see clearly, or feel strongly, as you read?

barn [bärn] *noun, plural* **barns.** a farm building used to store grain, hay, and farming equipment and as a shelter for cows, horses, and other animals.

bar•na•cle [bär′ nə kəl] *noun, plural* **barnacles.** a small shellfish that attaches itself to underwater objects, such as rocks or the bottom of ships.

ba•rom•e•ter [bə räm′ ə tər] *noun, plural* **barometers. 1.** an instrument used to determine changes in the weather by measuring the amount of pressure in the air. **2.** something that gives notice of a change: Politicians often use public opinion polls as a *barometer* of the mood of the voters.

bar•on [bar′ ən] *noun, plural* **barons. 1.** a nobleman of the lowest rank in Great Britain and other European countries. **2.** a person who has great wealth and power in a certain area: an oil *baron,* a cattle *baron.*

bar•racks [bar′ iks] *noun, plural* **barracks.** a large building or group of buildings where soldiers live, as on a military base.

bar•ra•cu•da [bar′ ə koo′ də] *noun, plural* **barracuda** or **barracudas.** a fish with a long narrow body and many sharp teeth.

bar•rage [bə razh′] *noun, plural* **barrages. 1.** a rapid firing of guns, cannon, or the like; a *barrage* of machine-gun fire. **2.** any continuous series of many things of the same kind: a *barrage* of questions, a *barrage* of criticism.

bar•rel [bar′ əl] *noun, plural* **barrels. 1.** a large, round container with curving sides and a flat top and bottom. A barrel is usually made of

bar•ri•cade [bar′ ə kād′] *noun, plural* **barricades.** a barrier that is set up for protection or to block the way: The soldiers set up *barricades* in the streets to stop the enemy from advancing. —*verb*, **barricaded, barricading.** to set up or build a barricade.

barracuda Barracuda are found in warm ocean areas close to the shore. Their strong bodies and very sharp teeth make them fierce enemies to other fish.

Pronunciation Key: T–Z			
t	ten; date	v	very; live
th	think	w	win; away
<u>th</u>	these	y	you
u	cut; butter	z	zoo; cause
ur	turn; bird	zh	measure

(Turn the page for more information.)

B

bar•ri•er [bar′ē ər] *noun, plural* **barriers.** something that is in the way: The police put a wooden *barrier* across the road to stop traffic. When people have a language *barrier*, they cannot understand each other because they speak different languages.

---

baseball There is a story that baseball was invented in 1839 by Abner Doubleday in Cooperstown, New York. That's why the Baseball Hall of Fame was placed in that city. Sports, like words, have many origins, some of them doubtful. The English long ago played a game like baseball, called "rounders." And the famous novelist Jane Austen wrote about a girl whose parents were upset that she enjoyed sports so much: "Catherine (preferred) cricket, *baseball*, riding on horseback, and running about the country to books." Austen wrote this in 1794, 25 years before Abner Doubleday was born.

---

bar•ter [bär′tər] *verb,* **bartered, bartering.** to trade one thing for another without using money: "Captain John Smith was able to *barter* over two hundred pounds of corn for a few pounds of glass beads." (Jean Fritz) —*noun.* the act of bartering: "If you made *barter* deals, the IRS will be looking for income to be reported." (Sylvia Porter) ◆ *Barter* is thought to be related to a word meaning "cheat" or "trick" with the idea that someone would try to barter by giving something worthless for something valuable.

Bar•ton [bär′tən] **Clara,** 1821–1912, the founder of the American Red Cross.

base¹ [bās] *noun, plural* **bases. 1.** the lowest part of something; bottom: The *base* of the Statue of Liberty is nearly 150 feet high. **2.** the main part of something: Paint with a water *base* is easier to clean up than paint with an oil *base*. **3.** a goal in certain children's games: "Anyone around my *base* is it!" **4.** any of the four corners of a baseball infield that a player must touch to score a run. **5.** a place where many ships, planes, or other military forces are kept. **6.** a number that is used as a standard for counting: Our ordinary numbering system has a *base* of ten; computers often use a *base* of two. **7.** a chemical that can join with an ACID to form a SALT. A base will make LITMUS paper turn blue. —*verb,* **based basing. 1.** to put something on a base: Many U.S. soldiers are *based* in Germany. **2.** to serve as a base or support for something: *The Miracle Worker* is a play *based* on the life of Helen Keller.

base² *adjective, more/most.* **1.** low in value: Lead is a *base* metal, not a precious one. **2.** not honorable; low or mean: "She was a lady, and he was so dreadfully below her . . . he was only a *base* servant." (Henry James)

base•ball [bās′bôl′] *noun, plural* **baseballs. 1.** a game played with a bat and ball by two teams of nine players. It is played on a field with four bases that form the shape of a diamond. The object of the game is to score a run by touching the bases in order. **2.** the ball used in this game.

base•ment [bās′mənt] *noun, plural* **basements.** the lowest floor of a building, usually partly or completely underground.

bash•ful [bash′fəl] *adjective, more/most.* afraid to meet new people; timid; shy: "Down they went, feeling a little *bashful*, for they seldom went to parties." (Louisa May Alcott)

Barton A photo of Clara Barton during the Civil War, taken by the famous American photographer Matthew Brady.

ba•sic [bā′sik] *adjective, more/most.* forming the base or most important part; fundamental: *Basic* training is the training that a soldier gets in his first few weeks of service. "Karl Marx was certain he would discover the *basic* laws of life and society." (Milovan Djilas) —**basics,** *plural noun.* the simplest but most important parts of something: "The educational tools to be used were the so-called *basics*—reading, writing, arithmetic." (Paul Brandwein)

BA•SIC [bā′sik] *noun.* (also spelled **Basic**) a simple language used to program a computer.

BASIC uses common English words to give instructions to the computer. ◆ The name BASIC stands for Beginner's All-purpose Symbolic Instruction Code.

ba·si·cal·ly [bā′ sik lē] *adverb.* for the most part; chiefly; mainly: Although he was in a bad mood this morning, he's *basically* very easy to get along with.

---

basically *Basically* is overused in writing—out of laziness, basically. It is an easy way to fill out a sentence. Recently, Booth Gardner, Governor of the state of Washington, announced a plan to fine himself 25 cents every time he used the word. "It's *basically* a bad habit," he said after it was pointed out that he had said the word 18 different times in one news conference. Suppose you wrote, "The Arctic is known *basically* for its cold weather" or "I'm not the type *basically* who plays cards." What does the word add to either sentence? You should use the word where it stands for something in itself; for example, "It is fear, *basically*, that causes prejudice."

---

ba·sil [baz′ əl *or* bā′ zəl] *noun.* a sweet-smelling plant with small white flowers that belongs to the mint family. Its leaves are used for seasoning food.

bass The name *bass* comes from a word meaning "sharp" or "rough," which probably referred to the sharp fins a bass has on its back.

ba·sin [bā′ sən] *noun, plural* **basins. 1.** a round, hollow bowl used for holding water or other liquid. **2.** a hollow place containing water: The Mortons keep their boat at the town yacht *basin.* **3.** an area of land from which water runs down into a river: "No other river has so vast a *basin* as the Mississippi—it draws its water supply from twenty-eight states." (Mark Twain)

ba·sis [bā′ səs] *noun, plural* **bases** [bā′ sēz]. the most important part of something; foundation:

The Bible is the *basis* of the Christian religion. "The *basis* of our political system is the rights of the people." (George Washington)

bas·ket [bas′ kət] *noun, plural* **baskets. 1.** a container used to hold and carry food, clothes, or other things. A basket is made by putting together strips of wood, plastic, wire, or some other light material. **2.** a large metal ring that is used as the goal in basketball. **3.** a score of two points made by putting the ball through this ring: Nancy scored six *baskets* in the game.

bas·ket·ball [bas′ kət bôl′] *noun, plural* **basket-balls. 1.** a game played with a large round ball by two teams of five players each. The object of the game is to put the ball through the other team's goal, or basket. **2.** the ball used in this game.

bass¹ [bās] *noun, plural* **basses. 1.** a man who has the lowest singing voice. **2.** a musical instrument that has this range: a *bass* guitar. ◆ This and many other English words having to do with music come from Italian—in this case, the word *basso,* meaning low.

bass² [bas] *noun, plural* **bass** or **basses.** a large family of fish found all over the world. Bass live either in salt or fresh water and are often caught for food or sport. Common types are the **striped bass** and the **black bass.**

bass drum [bās] the largest kind of drum. It makes a very deep sound.

bas·set hound [bas′ ət] a small dog with short, thick legs, a long, heavy body, and long, drooping ears.

bas·soon [bə sōōn′] *noun, plural* **bassoons.** a long musical instrument that makes a low sound. It is made of a long, bent wooden tube

---

Pronunciation Key: [ə] Symbol

The [ə] or *schwa* sound occurs in syllables without an accent. It can be spelled with any vowel, such as a in above, e in listen, i in pencil, o in melon, u in circus. It can also be a combination of vowels, such as io in action, ai in mountain, iou in precious.

(Turn the page for more information.)

B

B

with metal keys. It is played by blowing into a curved mouthpiece.

bass vi•ol [bās vī′ əl] a musical instrument that looks like a large violin and makes deep, low tones. It is the largest and lowest-sounding stringed instrument.

baste¹ [bāst] *verb,* **basted, basting.** to pour butter, juice, melted fat, or another liquid over meat while it is cooking to give it flavor: This recipe says the turkey should be *basted* with butter.

baste² *verb,* **basted, basting.** in sewing, to make large, loose stitches so that the material is held in place until it can be stitched permanently.

bat¹ [bat] *noun, plural* **bats. 1.** a long wooden stick used to hit the ball in baseball and similar games. **2. at bat.** having a turn to hit in baseball or a similar game. —*verb,* **batted, batting.** to hit a ball with a bat.

bat² *noun, plural* **bats.** a small, furry flying animal with a body like a mouse and wings of thin skin. Bats hunt for food at night and locate objects by sending out a sound and following the echo. ◆ *Bat²* is a separate word from *bat¹* and once had a different spelling, with a *k* rather than a *t.*

batch [bach] *noun, plural* **batches.** a quantity made or used at one time: He baked a *batch* of cookies.

bath [bath] *noun, plural* **baths. 1.** the washing of the body in water. **2.** the water used for this. **3.** a bathroom or bathtub.

bathe [bāth] *verb,* **bathed, bathing. 1.** to take a bath. **2.** to give a bath to; wash: The nurse *bathed* his cut hand. **3.** to spread over or surround, as if in a bath: After running a mile, he was *bathed* in sweat. The TV news studio was *bathed* in bright lights.

bathing suit a piece of clothing worn for swimming.

bath•room [bath′ room′] *noun, plural* **bathrooms.** a room having a toilet, sink, and often a bathtub or shower.

bath•tub [bath′ tub′] *noun, plural* **bathtubs.** a large tub to bathe in.

ba•ton [bə tän′] *noun, plural* **batons.** a long, thin stick used for a special purpose, as by a drum majorette, the conductor of an orchestra, or a runner in a relay race.

bat•tal•i•on [bə tal′ yən] *noun, plural* **battalions.** a large group of soldiers in an army, usually made up of two or more companies. ◆ *Battalion* once meant "a small battle." The

meaning then was shifted to the group of soldiers who fought such a battle.

bat•ter¹ [bat′ ər] *noun, plural* **batters.** a person who takes a turn to hit the ball in baseball.

batter² *noun, plural* **batters.** a mixture of flour and eggs with milk, water, or another liquid. Batter is used to make such foods as pancakes, cakes, and biscuits and to coat other foods for cooking, such as fish or chicken.

batter³ *verb,* **battered, battering.** to hit again and again; strike hard: "With hoofs *battering* on the ground, the stallion appeared and charged down the hill." (John Steinbeck) —**battered,** *adjective.* beaten or worn by hard use: "She produced her *battered* handkerchief and began to twist it into shreds." (T.H. White)

bat•ter•y [bat′ ər ē] *noun, plural* **batteries. 1.** an electric cell or group of cells that supply current and energy: We couldn't start the car because the *battery* was dead. **2.** in law, the act of illegally hitting or harming somebody. **3.** a group of cannons or other large guns that are fired together. **4.** any group of people or things that are connected or work together: The President spoke into a *battery* of microphones from all the different TV channels.

bat•tle [bat′ əl] *noun, plural* **battles. 1.** a long, hard fight between enemies in war. ◆ The place where a battle is fought is a **battlefield. 2.** any hard struggle or contest: Tonight's championship game will be quite a *battle.* Mom always has a *battle* trying to get Jamie to go to bed on time. —*verb,* **battled, battling.** to carry on a battle against; fight: Doctors are still *battling* cancer. "Flowers . . . *battling* with a jungle of weeds." (James Herriot)

baton A baton being used by the famous orchestra conductor, Leonard Bernstein. The word *baton* first meant a club or weapon. The way a conductor waves his baton was thought to be like waving a weapon in the air.

bat•tle•ship [bat′ əl ship′] *noun, plural* **battle-ships.** a very large warship with heavy armor and powerful guns. Battleships were the largest and most important warships from the late 1800's until World War II.

bawl [bôl] *verb,* **bawled, bawling. 1.** to cry loudly. **2.** to make a loud noise: "The cows were *bawling* in distress and the calves were crying back at them." (Katherine Anne Porter) **3. bawl out.** *Informal.* to scold or criticize loudly: The sergeant *bawled out* the two privates for not having their shoes shined.

bay¹ [bā] *noun, plural* **bays.** a large part of a sea or lake that is partly enclosed by land: San Francisco *Bay,* Cape Cod *Bay.*

bay² *noun, plural* **bays. 1.** the long, deep barking of a dog. **2. at bay.** the position of an animal or person that is kept away or kept from moving: The police kept the angry mob *at bay.* —*verb,* **bayed, baying.** to bark with a long, deep sound: The dog *bayed* at the moon.

bay³ *noun, plural* **bays. 1.** a reddish-brown color. **2.** a horse that has this color. —*adjective.* reddish-brown.

bay⁴ *noun, plural* **bays.** any of several trees, such as the laurel, whose leaf (a **bay leaf**) is used to give flavor in cooking.

bay•o•net [bā′ ə net′] *noun, plural* **bayonets.** a long knife that is attached to the front end of a rifle, used for hand-to-hand fighting.
♦ *Bayonet* comes from Bayonne, a city in France where these weapons were first made.

battleship The battleship *U.S.S. New Jersey* fires her huge guns. American battleships take the names of states of the Union.

be [bē] a special kind of verb that does not show action. **Be** means: **1.** to have reality; exist or live: "To *be* or not to *be* . . ." (Shakespeare: *Hamlet*) **2.** to have a certain character or quality: Can it *be* true? Please *be* a friend and help me out. **3.** to occupy a certain position or condition: I will *be* at home at six. You'll *be* in trouble if you don't finish your report on time. **4.** to take place; happen: Their wedding will *be* sometime in March.
♦ **Be** is used to join the subject of a sentence to another word: **1.** to an adjective that tells about the subject: This soup *is* delicious. **2.** to a noun that refers to the same thing: Emily Dickinson *was* a great poet. Peas and beans *are* vegetables.

---

bayou This word comes into English from French. It also is a Choctaw word. The Choctaws are an American Indian tribe. What connection do they have with the French language? The fact is that the bayou country of Louisiana, where the Choctaws lived, was once a royal colony of France. The French colonists took this word from the Choctaw language and made it part of their language. When the area became part of the United States, the word *bayou* passed over into American English.

---

bay•ou [bī′ yo͞o] *noun, plural* **bayous.** a slow-moving stream that flows through swampy land into or out of a river, lake, or gulf. Bayous are found in the southern U.S., especially in Louisiana.

ba•zaar [bə zär′] *noun, plural* **bazaars. 1.** a sale of things for a special purpose: The church held a *bazaar* to raise money for a new building. **2.** a marketplace or street lined with shops and booths, as in Oriental countries. ♦ *Bazaar* comes from a Persian word meaning "market."

B.C. an abbreviation for "*Before Christ.*" It is used for giving dates. 500 B.C. means 500 years before the birth of Christ.

♦ **Be** is also used with other verbs: **1.** with the present participle: She *is writing* a novel. **2.** with the past participle to form the PASSIVE: The planet Pluto *was discovered* in 1930. **3.** with the INFINITIVE to show the future: This land *is to become* the new soccer field.

Pronunciation Key: Accent Marks

[′] is the normal accent mark. It shows where the main stress falls on a word.
[′] is a secondary accent mark. It shows a lighter stress than the primary accent. For example:

tel • e • vis • ion [tel′ə vizh′ən]
(Turn the page for more information.)

B

beach [bēch] *noun, plural* **beaches.** a flat area along the edge of an ocean, lake, or other body of water, usually covered with sand or small rocks. —*verb,* **beached, beaching.** to move or go onto a beach: to *beach* a boat. "The big Air Force planes seemed *beached* in the fog, like stranded whales." (James Houston)

bea•con [bē′kən] *noun, plural* **beacons.** a light or fire used as a signal, such as a lighthouse that warns or guides ships.

bead [bēd] *noun, plural* **beads. 1.** a small, round piece of glass, wood, metal, or plastic. It has a hole through it so that it can be put on a string or wire with other pieces like it. **2.** any small, round object like this: The runner's forehead was covered with *beads* of sweat. —*verb,* **beaded, beading.** to decorate something with beads.

bea•gle [bē′gəl] *noun, plural* **beagles.** a small hunting dog with short legs, drooping ears, and a smooth coat.

beak [bēk] *noun, plural* **beaks. 1.** the hard, horny mouth parts of a bird; bill. **2.** anything that sticks forward in the shape of a bird's beak: the *beak* of a pitcher.

beak•er [bē′kər] *noun, plural* **beakers. 1.** a thin glass or metal container with a small lip for pouring. Beakers are used in laboratories to hold chemicals. **2.** a large drinking glass or cup that has a wide mouth.

beam [bēm] *noun, plural* **beams. 1.** a long, strong piece of wood or steel, used in buildings to support a floor or ceiling. **2.** a ray of light: *beams* of sunlight, the *beam* of a flashlight. —*verb,* **beamed, beaming. 1.** to send out rays of light; shine: The sun was *beaming* in through the window. **2.** to smile brightly or happily: "The storekeeper was *beaming.* He was a happy man." (E.B. White)

bean [bēn] *noun, plural* **beans. 1.** a smooth, flat seed of certain plants that is eaten as a vegetable, such as a **lima bean** or **kidney bean. 2.** the long pod in which bean seeds grow. Some kinds of bean pods are eaten as vegetables, such as STRING BEANS. **3.** any other seed that looks like a bean: coffee *beans.*

bear¹ [bâr] *noun, plural* **bears.** a large animal with a thick, furry coat, a very short tail, and very sharp claws.

bear² *verb,* **bore, borne** or **born, bearing. 1.** to carry or support; hold up: We didn't go skating on the pond because the ice wasn't thick enough to *bear* our weight. **2.** to put up with; endure: "Please leave Helen out of it. I can't *bear* to hear you talk about her like that." (F. Scott Fitzgerald) **3.** to bring forth or give birth

to: This apple tree *bears* delicious fruit. **4.** to hold in the mind: Jack still *bears* a grudge against me for what I said about him.

beard [bērd] *noun, plural* **beards. 1.** the hair that grows on a man's face. **2.** something like a beard, such as the hair on a goat's chin.

bear•ing [bâr′ing] *noun, plural* **bearing. 1.** the way a person stands, walks, and acts: She moves with the graceful *bearing* of a ballet dancer. **2.** a connection in thought or meaning: "I mention this because it has some *bearing* on what is to follow." (Joseph Conrad) **3. bearings.** a sense of where one is or is going: "He got his *bearings* from a weather vane which showed the four directions of the world." (William Steig) **4.** a part of a machine that holds a moving part and allows it to move more easily.

beast [bēst] *noun, plural* **beasts. 1.** any animal other than man, especially a large four-footed animal. **2.** *Informal.* a person who is very rude, cruel, or brutal. —**beastly,** *adjective.*

beat [bēt] *verb,* **beat, beaten** or **beat, beating. 1.** to hit again and again; pound: Rain was *beating* against the windows. The dog ran away because it was *beaten* by its owner. **2.** to get the better of; defeat: The American hockey team *beat* the Soviets in the 1980 Olympics. **3.** to move back and forth in a regular way: "The bird stretched its neck and *beat* its wings." (Lloyd Alexander) **4.** to stir rapidly; mix with force: He *beat* the eggs with milk for the French toast. **5.** *Informal.* to confuse; bewilder: It *beats* me how we could have lost that book. —*noun, plural* **beats. 1.** a blow or stroke made over and over: They

Alaskan brown bear   grizzly bear

polar bear   black bear

could hear the distant *beat* of the drums. **2.** a single throb or pulse: the *beat* of the heart. **3.** a unit of time or accent in music. **4.** a regular route or round that is followed by someone in a job: a police officer's *beat.* —*adjective. Informal.* very tired; exhausted.

beau·ti·ful [byōō′ tə fəl] *adjective, more/most.* pleasing to see or hear; giving pleasure to the senses or the mind: a *beautiful* woman, *beautiful* music, a *beautiful* painting, a *beautiful* day.

> **beautiful** "Our team played a beautiful game today." "That's a great idea—absolutely beautiful." The word *beautiful* can be used not only to describe persons, but also events and ideas. It can be overused for this reason. Try on occasion "lovely" as the poet Wordsworth does: "Thy mind shall be a mansion for all lovely forms." Or as the novelist George Meredith did: "'You're lovely, Bella.' She drank in his homage."

beau·ty [byōō′ tē] *noun, plural* **beauties. 1.** the quality of being beautiful; a quality that is pleasing to look at, hear, or think about: Many people enjoy going to the mountains to appreciate the *beauty* of nature. **2.** a person or thing that is beautiful: The Swedish actress Greta Garbo was a famous *beauty* during the early days of movies.

bea·ver [bē′ vər] *noun, plural* **beavers.** a furry animal with a broad, flat tail and webbed hind feet for swimming. Beavers use their strong front teeth for gnawing down trees to build dams and nests in streams. Beaver fur was once considered very valuable and was often used for coats and hats.

beaver The beaver is one of the few animals to actually construct its own dwelling. Beaver lodges (homes) and dams are made of sticks, logs, and rocks held together by mud.

be·came [bi kām′] *verb.* the past tense of **become:** Donna *became* a doctor after graduating from medical school.

be·cause [bi kuz′] *conjunction.* for the reason that; since: We were late *because* there was a traffic jam. I can't go *because* I have work to do. **because of** on account of; by reason of: He can't pitch today *because of* a sore arm.

beck·on [bek′ ən] *verb,* **beckoned, beckoning.** to signal to someone with a movement of the hand or head: "A lean , silent man at a shadowy table in a corner . . . *beckoned* to the newcomer." (James Thurber)

be·come [bi kum′] *verb,* **became, become, becoming. 1.** to grow to be; come to be: He *became* very excited when he heard the good news. "She is changing, *becoming* quiet and thoughtful." (Alice Walker) **2.** to look good on; suit: That blue dress *becomes* you because it matches your eyes. **3. become of.** to happen to: "But what has *become of* your beautiful piano?" (Katherine Mansfield)

be·com·ing [bi kum′ ing] *adjective, more/most.* having the right effect; fitting; suitable: That's a very *becoming* blouse you have on.

bed [bed] *noun, plural* **beds. 1.** a piece of furniture made for sleeping or resting on. **2.** any place to sleep or rest: The puppies slept on a *bed* of old newspapers in the kitchen. **3.** a small area to grow things: a flower *bed.* **4.** a layer at the bottom of something: a river *bed,* a *bed* of gravel. —*verb,* **bedded, bedding.** to put in a bed or go to bed: The campers decided to *bed* down at the foot of the mountain.

bed·ding [bed′ ing] *noun.* sheets, blankets, and other materials for a bed.

bed·room [bed′ room′] *noun, plural* **bedrooms.** a room used for sleeping.

bed·spread [bed′ spred′] *noun, plural* **bedspreads.** a cover for a bed that goes over the sheets and blankets.

Pronunciation Key: A–F			
ă	and; hat	ch	chew; such
ā	ate; stay	d	dog; lid
â	care; air	e	end; yet
ä	father; hat	ē	she; each
b	boy; cab	f	fun; off

(Turn the page for more information.)

B

bee [bē] *noun, plural* **bees. 1.** an insect with four wings, a hairy body, and usually a stinger. Bees gather POLLEN and NECTAR from flowers. Some bees live together in large groups in beehives and make honey and **beeswax. 2.** a gathering of people to do something together: Our school district is holding a spelling *bee.*

---

bee We often use animals to form figures of speech. You are as "busy as a bee," as "hardworking as a beaver," as "industrious as an ant," because these are thought of as active animals. You can "have a beef" with someone (an argument or complaint). In the stock market, people who are keen on buying stocks are called "bulls" and those who are doubtful (sellers) are said to be "bears." Even on Wall Street, no one likes being called a "sheep" (someone who just goes along with the crowd).

Beethoven A painting of Ludwig van Beethoven, one of the greatest composers in the history of music.

beech [bēch] *noun, plural* **beeches.** a tree having smooth light-gray bark and dark-green leaves. It produces a sweet-tasting nut.

beef [bēf] *noun.* the meat of a steer, cow, or bull. **Beefsteak** is a slice of beef for broiling or frying. ◆ *Beef* has a plural form, **(beeves)** that is occasionally used, especially in older writing. Thomas Jefferson wrote of "collecting *beeves* in our Southern countries."

bee•hive [bē/ hīv/] *noun, plural* **beehives. 1.** a hive or house for bees. **2.** a busy place: The shopping center was a *beehive* of activity the weekend before Christmas.

been [bin] *verb.* the past participle of **be:** There has *been* a lot of snow this month.

beer [bēr] *noun, plural* **beers. 1.** an alcoholic drink made from a mixture of water and a specially-treated grain called MALT, and then flavored with a fruit called HOPS. **2.** a soft drink made from the roots or leaves of various plants: root *beer*, ginger *beer.*

beet [bēt] *noun, plural* **beets.** the thick, fleshy root of a certain kind of leafy plant. The **red beet** is eaten as a vegetable. Sugar is made from the **white beet.**

Bee•tho•ven [bā/ tō vən] **Ludwig van,** 1770–1827, German composer.

bee•tle [bēt/ əl] *noun, plural* **beetles.** an insect that has biting mouth parts, two hard front wings, and two hind wings. When it is not flying, the front wings form a case to cover the hind wings. Some kinds of beetles cause damage to plants.

beetle Three common types of beetles, the ladybug (left), sweet potato weevil (center), and the cucumber beetle (right).

be•fall [bi fôl/] *verb,* **befell, befallen, befalling.** to happen or happen to: Many difficulties *befell* the Christian pilgrims of the Middle Ages as they journeyed to the Holy Land.

be•fore [bi fôr/] *preposition.* **1.** earlier than: We got there at ten minutes *before* six. **2.** in front of; ahead of: The prisoner stood *before* the judge. —*adverb.* **1.** earlier: This class ends at two o'clock and not a minute *before.* **2.** at any time in the past; until now: Have you ever seen this movie *before?* —*conjunction.* **1.** earlier than the time when: We managed to play three innings *before* it started to rain. **2.** rather than; instead of: I'd wait in line all night outside the theater *before* I'd miss this concert.

be•fore•hand [bi fôr′hand′] *adverb.* ahead of time: The store opens at 9:00 A.M., but the workers get there an hour *beforehand.*

beg [beg] *verb,* **begged, begging. 1.** to ask for something as a gift because one is poor or needy: The homeless man in the park *begged* people for money. **2.** to ask as a favor in a serious or polite way. to *beg* someone's pardon. "She kept *begging* me, with a sorrowful face, to tell her what she had done wrong." (Sylvia Plath)

be•gan [bi gan′] *verb.* the past tense of **begin:** "Her mother leaned back and *began* to cry." (James Baldwin)

beg•gar [beg′ər] *noun, plural* **beggars. 1.** a person who begs, especially one who lives by begging. **2.** a very poor person.

do what is right: "Don't be difficult. *Behave* yourself and they might go easy on you." (Robert Heinlein)

be•hav•ior [bi hāv′yər] *noun, plural* **behaviors.** a way of acting; behaving: The scientists studied the *behavior* of gorillas in the wild. Kate's *behavior* in class has been very good lately.

be•hind [bi hīnd′] *preposition.* **1.** at or toward the back of: In baseball the catcher stands *behind* the batter. "She pushes her hair *behind* her ears." (Ann Beattie) **2.** later than; after: The train is *behind* schedule today. **3.** less advanced than: He's *behind* the other students in math because he's been sick so much lately. **4.** in support of: Congress is *behind* the President's plan. —*adverb.* **1.** at the back; in the rear: He hit the other car from *behind.* **2.** in a place or condition that is left: Tim stayed *behind* at the lake after his friends went home. **3.** not on time; slow; late: Gerald is *behind* in the payments on his new car.

---

beginning a sentence For good reason, sentences usually begin with a noun (subject), as in "*Trains* don't run through this town anymore." or "*Jack* kicked a field goal." But some writers add variety by using a conjunction or an adverb: "*But* she says her favorite gift is the kite I built her. *And* it is very beautiful . . ." (Truman Capote) "*Then* suddenly it burst through the tree line and raced down the hill toward her." (Flannery O'Connor) You can also put a phrase in front of the subject instead of after it: "Standing before the wheel he felt alone . . ." (Ralph Ellison)

---

be•gin [bi gin′] *verb,* **began, begun, beginning. 1.** to do the first part: The class will *begin* a new history lesson today. **2.** to come into being; start to exist: The play *begins* at eight o'clock.

be•gin•ner [bi gin′ər] *noun, plural* **beginners.** a person who is starting to do something for the first time: Cathy is a good ice skater for a *beginner.*

be•gin•ning [bi gin′ing] *noun, plural* **beginnings.** the first part of something; the time or place that something begins: The *beginning* of the book was boring, but it got exciting later on.

be•gun [bi gun′] *verb.* the past participle of **begin:** The movie has already *begun,* so we'd better get to our seats.

be•half [bi haf′] *noun.* **1.** one's interest or side: The family's lawyer will speak on their *behalf.* **2. on behalf of** or **in behalf of.** in the interest of; for: On *behalf of* all the members, I'd like to welcome you to our club.

be•have [bi hāv′] *verb.* **behaved, behaving. 1.** to act or do in a certain way: "We *behaved* like two children let loose in the thick of an adventure." (Katherine Mansfield) **2.** to act properly;

be•hold [bi hōld′] *verb,* **beheld, beholding.** to look upon; see: "My heart leaps up when I *behold* a rainbow in the sky." (William Wordsworth)

beige [bāzh] *noun; adjective.* a pale-brown or grayish-tan color

be•ing [bē′ing] *verb.* the present participle of **be:** She's *being* more careful about her work lately. —*noun, plural* **beings. 1.** life or existence: The modern computer came into *being* about forty years ago. **2.** a person or animal; a living creature: Science-fiction writers often describe *beings* from other planets.

Bei•rut [bā rōōt′] the capital and main port of Lebanon, located on the Mediterranean Sea. *Population:* 702,000.

Pronunciation Key: G–N

g	give; big	k	kind, cat, back
h	hold	l	let; ball
i	it; this	m	make; time
ī	ice; my	n	not; own
j	jet; gem; edge	ng	having

(Turn the page for more information.)

B

Bel·fast [bel´fast] the capital of Northern Ireland. *Population:* 363,000.

bel·fry [bel´frē] *noun, plural* **belfries.** a tower or other place where bells are hung.

Bel·gium [bel´jəm] a country in northern Europe. *Capital:* Brussels. *Area:* 11,800 square miles. *Population:* 9,900,000. **—Belgian,** *adjective; noun.*

Bel·grade [bel´gräd] the capital and largest city of Yugoslavia. *Population:* 975,000.

be·lief [bi lēf´] *noun, plural* **beliefs. 1.** something that is thought to be true or real: It was once a common *belief* that the sun moved around the earth. **2.** the acceptance of something as true or real: He has a strong *belief* in God. **3.** confidence; trust: "And the mother, who had a great *belief* in herself . . ." (D.H. Lawrence)

be·lieve [bi lēv´] *verb,* **believed, believing. 1.** to think of as true or real: Many people *believe* that there is life on other planets. **2.** to have confidence or trust in: "I don't know the meaning of half those long words, and . . . I don't *believe* you do either." (Lewis Carroll) **3.** to think; suppose: I *believe* that she's gone away for the weekend. **4. make believe.** to pretend: The children put a blanket between two chairs and *made believe* it was a tent in the woods.

bell [bel] *noun, plural* **bells. 1.** a hollow object that makes a ringing sound. It is shaped like a cup and is usually made of metal. **2.** anything that makes a ringing sound: Did you hear the door*bell* ring? **3.** anything shaped like a bell: the *bell* of a trumpet.

bell The Liberty Bell in Philadelphia is a famous symbol of freedom for the United States.

Bell [bel] **Alexander Graham,** 1847–1922. American inventor of the telephone. He was born in Scotland.

bel·low [bel´ō] *verb,* **bellowed, bellowing.** to make a loud, deep noise, like the sound made by a bull: " 'Quiet!' *bellowed* the tent leader. 'I want quiet in this tent!' " (E.B. White) *—noun, plural* **bellows.** a loud, deep noise; a roar: "He shouted to her, a *deep bellow* like a hound makes . . ." (Nathanael West)

bel·lows [bel´ōz] *plural noun.* a device that sucks in air when its sides are spread out and blows the air out when they are pushed together. One kind of bellows is used to blow air on a fire to make it burn faster. Other kinds are used in musical instruments, such as the accordion.

bellows *Bellows* is Old English for "blowing bag." But *bellow* meaning a roar, or snort, cannot be traced to its origin. It may come from another Old English word meaning "to be very angry."

bel·ly [bel´ē] *noun, plural* **bellies. 1.** the part of the body that contains the stomach; the abdomen. **2.** a lower part of something that is thought to be like this part of the body: the *belly* of a ship. The airplane had to land on its *belly* after the wheels failed to come down. *—verb,* **bellied, bellying.** to swell out; bulge: The ship's sails *bellied* in the wind.

be·long [bi lông´] *verb,* **belonged, belonging. 1.** to have a proper place: These tools *belong* in the garage. **2. belong to. a.** to be the property of; be owned by: "They worked in the fields all day long together, the fields which *belonged to* Eric's father." (James Baldwin) **b.** to be a member of: She *belongs to* a hiking club.

be·long·ings [bi lông´ingz] *plural noun.* the things a person owns; possessions: ". . . the horse-drawn wagon that carried our furniture and ragged *belongings.*" (I.B. Singer)

be·lov·ed [bi luv´id] *adjective, more/most.* dearly loved: "These pleasures and pastimes, these games and frolics, these *beloved* sights and sounds . . ." (E.B. White) —*noun.* a person who is dearly loved: "Let my *beloved* come into his garden . . ." *(The Bible: The Song of Solomon)*

be•low [bi lō′] *adverb.* **1.** in or at a lower place: Most of the ship's cargo is stored *below.* "He could see the two other boys down *below.*" (Richard Wilbur) **2.** less than zero on a temperature scale: It's 15 degrees *below* today. —*preposition.* lower than; beneath: On this page the word "Berlin" is *below* the picture.

belt [belt] *noun, plural* **belts. 1.** a strip of leather, cloth, or other material that is worn around the waist to hold up clothing or as a decoration. **2.** a place or area that is thought of as being like a belt: Iowa and Illinois are in the farm *belt* of the U.S. **3.** a long circular band that turns two or more wheels or moves things from one place to another: A fan *belt* turns a fan to cool a car's engine. —*verb,* **belted, belting. 1.** to put a belt on or around: to *belt* a dress. **2.** to hit hard: The batter *belted* the pitch out of the park.

bench [bench] *noun, plural* **benches. 1.** a long seat for several people: a park *bench.* **2.** a strong table for working on: a carpenter's *bench.* **3.** the place where a judge sits in a courtroom: The lawyer approached the *bench* for a short discussion with the judge. **4.** the official position of a judge or judges: The governor appointed her to the *bench.* —*verb,* **benched, benching.** to keep a player out of a game: The coach *benched* Walt because he missed two practices this week.

bend [bend] *verb,* **bent, bending. 1.** to make or become curved or crooked: "I should *bend* a hairpin in the shape of a fishhook." (E.B. White) **2.** to move part of the body lower; stoop down; bow: "Opening his eyes, he saw *bending* over him a man in a black coat." (O. Henry) —*noun, plural* **bends.** a curve or turn; angle: When you come to the *bend* in the road, go to the right.

be•neath [bi nēth′] *preposition.* **1.** in a lower place; under; below: "The seal must have heard the sound *beneath* the water." (James Houston) **2.** not worthy of: You're a good student; copying someone else's work is *beneath* you. —*adverb.* under; below: Put the red blanket on top and the blue one *beneath.*

ben•e•fit [ben′ ə fit] *noun, plural* **benefits. 1.** something that is good or helpful; an advantage: Running each day has been a *benefit* to his health. **2.** a public event or entertainment for some person or special cause: The singing

group gave a *benefit* concert for poor children in Africa. **3. benefits.** money paid to a person by the government or an insurance agency: He received unemployment *benefits* after he was laid off from his job at the factory. **4.** something of value that a worker receives from his employer in addition to regular pay, such as vacations and holidays, health insurance, or a pension. ◆ These are also called **fringe benefits.** —*verb,* **benefited, benefiting. 1.** to be helpful to; be good for: Since he's so tired and run-down, a long rest will certainly *benefit* him. **2.** to receive help; profit: The oil companies have *benefited* from better methods of oil drilling.

bent [bent] *verb.* the past form of **bend:** She *bent* over and picked up the paper she'd dropped. —*adjective.* **1.** not straight; curved or crooked **2.** set in one's mind; determined: She is *bent* on becoming a famous actress.

be•ret [bə rā′] *noun, plural* **berets.** a soft, round, flat cap, usually made of wool or felt.

Ber•ing Sea [ber′ ing] a northern arm of the Pacific Ocean, between Alaska and Siberia.

Berlin The Brandenburg Gate, built in 1791, is a famous landmark in Berlin. It stands at the border of this divided city, just in front of the Berlin Wall.

Ber•lin [bər lin′] a city in east-central Germany. It is now divided into **East Berlin,** the capital of East Germany, and **West Berlin,** a part of West Germany. *Population: 3,039,000.*

Pronunciation Key: O–S			
ō	over; go	ou	out; town
ô	all; law	p	put; hop
oo	look; full	r	run; car
o͞o	pool; who	s	set; miss
oi	oil; boy	sh	show

(Turn the page for more information.)

B

Ber•mu•da [bər myoo′ də] a group of British islands in the western Atlantic Ocean.

ber•ry [ber′ ē] *noun, plural* **berries.** a small, juicy fruit that can be eaten, such as a strawberry or raspberry.

ber•serk [bə zurk′ *or* bə surk′] *adjective.* crazy with anger; in a wild rage: The wounded elephant went *berserk* and charged at the hunter.

berth [burth] *noun, plural* **berths. 1.** a place for sleeping on a ship, train, or airplane. **2.** a place to dock a ship.

be•side [bi sīd′] *preposition.* **1.** at the side of; near: "Nick stopped and picked up a Wagner apple from *beside* the road." (Ernest Hemingway) **2.** away or apart from the main point or issue: Whether or not he wants to go is *beside* the point, because we don't have any more tickets anyway. **3. beside oneself.** very upset or excited: "The Swan Boat passengers were *beside themselves* with joy and excitement." (E.B. White)

be•sides [bi sīdz′] *adverb.* in addition; also: He owns three cars and a motorcycle *besides.*

—*adverb.* the *superlative* of **well. 1.** in the most excellent way: I think this is the dress that fits you *best.* **2.** to the highest degree; most: Which of those books did you like *best?*

—*noun.* **1.** a person or thing that is the most excellent: That store sells the *best* in leather goods. **2.** one's finest effort or condition: Let's do our *best* to finish the project today. **3.** good wishes; greetings. Give Amy my *best* when you see her.

bet [bet] *noun, plural* **bets. 1.** an agreement between two people that the one who is wrong about a thing will pay money or something of value to the one who is right. People make bets on who will win a game, race, election, or other contest. **2.** the amount risked in a bet: Dennis made a $2 *bet* on the Super Bowl that the Giants would win.

—*verb,* **bet** or **betted, betting. 1.** to agree to a bet: "I *bet* twenty-five cents we beat you to my house." (James Houston) **2.** to be confident about; believe strongly: I'll *bet* it's going to rain this weekend.

> **beside/besides** The word *beside* cannot be used in place of *besides.* *Besides* means "also" or "in addition to." "That plane will hold 15 people, *beside* the two pilots." That would be a very crowded cockpit, if they were all sitting next to the pilots! The correct form should be ". . . *besides* the two pilots."

—*preposition.* in addition to: There were ten people at Cathy's birthday party *besides* Cathy.

be•siege [bi sēj′] *verb,* **besieged, besieging. 1.** to surround and try to capture: The Germans *besieged* the Russian city of Leningrad for three years during World War II. **2.** to crowd around from all directions: Dozens of teenagers *besieged* the rock star as he got out of his limousine. The winner of the lottery was *besieged* with letters from people asking for money.

be•tray [bi trā′] *verb,* **betrayed, betraying. 1.** to help the enemy; be a traitor: Benedict Arnold plotted with John André to *betray* the American post at West Point. **2.** to be unfaithful to; be false to: I know my friend won't *betray* me by telling my secrets to others. **3.** to show or reveal something that one would like to hide: His shaking hands *betrayed* his nervousness as he read his report. ◆ The act of betraying someone or something is a **betrayal.**

> **better/best** The word *better* is used for comparing two things, and *best* is used for comparing three or more. The writers of this dictionary were taught that. (They also were taught that "better" likens two things as well as compares them. Nowadays that's not crucial, but it helps to remember that we *compare* similar things, but *contrast* differing things.) You can't say, "Steven Spielberg directed *E.T.* and *Jaws. E.T.* is the best movie of the two." You could say it, but you'd be ruining a good vocabulary. *E.T.* may be the best movie you've ever seen—but if you write this you're clearly saying you've seen three or more.

best [best] *adjective.* the *superlative* of **good. 1.** of the highest quality; most excellent: Cherie is the *best* player on our soccer team. **2.** most favorite: He is my *best* friend.

bet•ter [bet′ ər] *adjective.* the *comparative* of **good. 1.** of higher quality; more excellent: This is a *better* air conditioner than our old one, which hardly ever worked. **2.** improved in

B

health or condition: She is much *better* after resting in bed all weekend. **3.** larger: We'll be away the *better* part of a week. —*adverb.* the *comparative* of **well. 1.** in a more excellent way: The car runs much *better* since we had it tuned up. **2.** more: They've been living here *better* than fifteen years.
—*noun, plural* **betters. 1.** the more excellent of two: Which is the *better* of these two cameras? **2. betters.** people who are thought of as better or higher in some way, such as people who have a high position in society. —*verb,* **bettered, bettering. 1.** to make better; improve: He tried to *better* himself by studying hard in school. **2.** to do better than; outdo: Roy *bettered* the school record in the mile run.

be•tween [bi twēn′] *preposition.* **1.** in the place or time that separates two things: Put the lamp *between* the two chairs. The library is open *between* ten and six. She earns *between* fifteen and twenty dollars a week from babysitting. **2.** having to do with; involving: There will be a meeting next week *between* the mayor and the governor. ♦ See AMONG for more information. **3.** in relation to or along with another: How can you tell the difference *between* a crocodile and an alligator?
♦ The correct phrase is "between you and *me,*" not "between you and I." Since it is being used here as a preposition, *between* takes an object, *me.*
—*adverb.* in the place or time separating: He owns those two farms and the pond *between.*

bev•er•age [bev′ rij] *noun, plural* **beverages.** a liquid for drinking; any drink. Milk, orange juice, soda, and coffee are beverages.

be•ware [bi war′] *verb.* be on guard against; watch out for: They had a sign on their fence that said 'Beware of the Dog.' "*Beware* of those trees. Better mark them on the map." (Antoine de St. Exupèry)

be•wil•der [bi wil′ dər] *verb,* **bewildered, bewildering.** to confuse completely; puzzle: We couldn't get that computer program to run because we were completely *bewildered* by the instructions. ♦ The state of being bewildered is **bewilderment:** "He shook his head, full of some *bewilderment* he couldn't communicate." (John Fowles)

be•witch [bi wich′] *verb,* **bewitched, bewitching. 1.** to cast a magic spell over: In old folk tales, people were often *bewitched* by the music of fairies dancing in the forest. **2.** to charm or fascinate very much, as if by a magic spell: The actress's charm and beauty completely *bewitched* the audience.

be•yond [bi yänd′] *preposition.* **1.** on or to the far side of: "*Beyond* the railroad tracks was the river." (James Baldwin) **2.** farther on than: His winning jump was two feet *beyond* the second place jump. **3.** later than; past: Billy stayed awake *beyond* his usual bedtime. **4.** outside a person's knowledge or understanding: This math lesson is completely *beyond* me. —*adverb.* farther away: The balloon sailed over the fence and into the trees *beyond.*

bi•as [bī′ əs] *noun, plural* **biases. 1.** a strong feeling about something without good reason; prejudice: The teacher tried never to show any *bias* for or against a particular student. **2.** a slanting line across the weave of a fabric: Some sewing patterns must be cut on the *bias* of the cloth. —*verb,* **biased, biasing.** to cause to have a bias: The mayor claims that both local newspapers are *biased* and never print anything good about him.

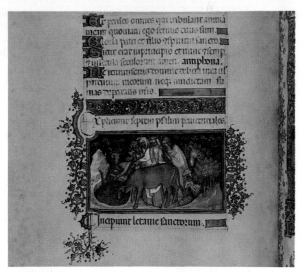

Bible A page from a very early Bible, the Codice Landau Finaly. The Latin writing tells the story of Moses striking a rod against a rock to bring forth water.

Bi•ble [bī′ bəl] *noun.* **1.** the sacred book of writings of the Christian religion, consisting of the OLD TESTAMENT and the NEW TESTAMENT. The Old Testament is also sacred to the Jewish religion. **2. bible.** any book that is accepted as

Pronunciation Key: T–Z			
t	ten; date	v	very; live
th	think	w	win; away
<u>th</u>	these	y	you
u	cut; butter	z	zoo; cause
ur	turn; bird	zh	measure

(Turn the page for more information.)

the highest authority in its field: Dr. Benjamin Spock's *Baby and Child Care* is often considered to be the *bible* of child-raising, because it has been used by millions of parents for over 40 years. ◆ The word *Bible* comes from the same Greek word that gives is *bibliography*. The ancient Greeks got their paper for writing from the city of Byblos, and their word for "book" came from this.

Bib·li·cal [bib′ lə kəl] *adjective* (also spelled **biblical**) having to do with the Bible; found in the Bible: Adam and Eve are the first man and woman in the *Biblical* account of the beginning of life.

---

bibliography There are four points of information in a bibliography: Who wrote the book or article? What is its title? Who published it and when? To make a bibliography, arrange all your sources in alphabetical order. Do this according to the last name of the author—Adams, Henry; Bell, Daniel; Tuchman, Barbara; and so on. Then list the name of the book, underlining it—North and South— and give the publisher's name and the copyright date—Harcourt Brace Jovanovich, 1984. Sometimes, bibliographies give the publisher's city—New York or Chicago or San Diego. A magazine article is usually put in quotes rather than underlined—"Happy Dreams," Time, Dec. 6, 1992. That way, the magazine is identified by the underlining.

---

bib·li·og·ra·phy [bib′ lē äg′ rə fē] *noun, plural* **bibliographies.** a list of books or articles about a particular subject, or by a particular author. A bibliography often appears in a book of information or a factual report to show which sources the writer consulted for information.

bi·cy·cle [bī′ sik əl] *noun, plural* **bicycles.** a light vehicle with two large wheels, one behind the other. It has a seat, handlebars for steering, and two foot pedals to turn the back wheel. —*verb,* **bicycled, bicycling.** to ride a bicycle.

bighorn The hoofs of the bighorn sheep are specially formed to give it the ability to climb steep rocks.

bid [bid] *verb,* **bade** or **bid, bidden** or **bid, bidding. 1.** to say as a greeting; tell: to *bid* someone good morning. **2.** to say as an order; command: "He must be taught, and trained, and *bid* go forth." (Shakespeare, *Julius Caesar*) **3.** to offer a certain price for something: She *bid* two hundred dollars for the antique chair at the auction. —*noun, plural* **bids. 1.** an offer to pay or accept a certain price: The contract to build the new school was awarded to the company that gave the lowest *bid.* **2.** an attempt to obtain or become: The mayor is making a serious *bid* to become a U.S. Senator. —**bidder,** *noun:* That land will be sold to the highest *bidder.*

bid·ding [bid′ ing] *noun, plural* **biddings. 1.** an order; command: The sailors moved quickly at the captain's *bidding.* **2.** the making of a bid: In 1987 the *bidding* on a famous painting by Van Gogh reached nearly $40 million.

bide [bīd] *verb,* **bided, biding.** to wait: They are going to *bide* their time on buying a new car until they find one they really want.

big [big] *adjective,* **bigger, biggest. 1.** great in amount or size; large: They live in a *big* house that has six bedrooms. **2.** grown up or older: He got that baseball glove from his *big* brother. **3.** important: The World Series is a *big* event for baseball fans.

big·horn [big′ hôrn′] *noun, plural* **bighorn** or **bighorns.** a large, wild sheep of the Rocky Mountains. Bighorn sheep are known for their large, curling horns.

big·ot [big′ ət] *noun, plural* **bigots.** a person who will not accept any opinion or belief that is different from his own; a person who is prejudiced. —**bigoted,** *adjective.*

bike [bīk] *noun, plural* **bikes.** a short word for **bicycle.**

bill¹ [bil] *noun, plural* **bills. 1.** a statement of money owed for things bought or used, or for work done: a grocery *bill,* a doctor *bill.* The repairman gave her a *bill* for the work on the TV set. **2.** a piece of paper money: a twenty-dollar *bill*. **3.** a proposed law: The President spoke in favor of the new tax *bill* that was before the Senate. **4.** a printed advertisement or public notice: In restaurants, "*bill* of fare" is a name for a menu. —*verb*, **billed, billing. 1.** to send a statement of money owed: The dentist *billed* me for cleaning my teeth. **2.** to an*nounce* or advertise by bills or posters: That singer is *billed* as the main attraction in next week's show. ◆ The word *bill* at first meant a written statement in a court of law. The court could order a person to pay money he owed.

bill² *noun*, *plural* **bills. 1.** the hard, projecting mouth parts of a bird; a beak. **2.** anything that looks like a bird's bill, such as the mouth of a turtle.

bill•board [bil′ bôrd′] *noun*, *plural* **billboards.** a large board used to display advertisements or announcements to the public. Billboards are often placed along highways.

bill•fold [bil′ fōld′] *noun*, *plural* **billfolds.** a small folding case, usually made of leather or cloth, that is used for carrying paper money, credit cards, and identification papers.

bil•liards [bil′ yərdz] *noun*. **1.** a game in which a long, thin stick called a CUE is used to hit small, hard balls against each other on a cloth-covered table with raised edges. **2.** another name for the game of **pool.**

bin [bin] *noun*, *plural* **bins.** an enclosed box or space for storing loose items, such as grain or coal.

bin•a•ry [bī′ nə rē] *adjective*. **1.** made up of two things or parts: Scientists have discovered *binary* stars that move together through space. ◆ A **binary number** system uses only "1" and "0" to express all numbers. It has a base of 2, rather than 10 as the decimal system does. **2.** having only two choices or possibilities, such as a light switch that says "ON/OFF." Computers use a binary system in which information is processed as a series of choices between one of two conditions.

bind [bind] *verb*, **bound, binding. 1.** to tie or fasten together: The bundle of papers was *bound* with string. **2.** to unite or keep something together, as by love, law, or duty: The witness was *bound* to tell the truth. **3.** to fasten in a cover: Today publishers *bind* books with special machinery, but years ago they were *bound* by hand. ◆ A **binder** is a person or thing that binds, such as a business that binds books or a cover used to hold loose papers together.

bi•noc•u•lars [bə näk′ yə lərz] *plural noun.* a device used to make distant objects appear closer and larger. It is made up of two small telescopes fastened together for use with both eyes.

biography We can all learn something about this kind of writing from what is considered the greatest biography written in English, James Boswell's *The Life of Samuel Johnson.* Try to know the person well. Boswell knew Johnson at first hand, as a friend, but few biographers know great figures in history. Most often, you need to read books and articles about your subject. Don't just list dates and facts in a person's life—tell their importance. Avoid general statements that could apply just as easily to any other writer, general, president—whoever is the subject of your article. Remember that personal details are interesting. For example, General Thomas Jonathan Jackson got his nickname 'Stonewall' in the Civil War because he held his ground during fierce fighting at the Battle of Bull Run. Another general saw him and said, "There stands Jackson like a stone wall."

bil•lion [bil′ yən] *noun*, *plural* **billions.** one thousand million, written as 1,000,000,000. Someone with a billion dollars is a **billionaire.**

Bill of Rights a name given to the first ten amendments to the U.S. Constitution, because they deal with the protection of human rights.

bil•low [bil′ ō] *noun*, *plural* **billows.** a great wave or rising of something, such as a large mass of water, smoke, or steam. —*verb*, **billowed, billowing.** to swell or rise in a great mass: "Smoke *billowed* out of a window on a high floor." (I.B. Singer)

bi•og•ra•phy [bī äg′ rə fē] *noun*, *plural* **biographies.** the written history of a person's life. —**biographical,** *adjective*: Carl Sandburg's life of Lincoln is a famous *biographical* work.

Pronunciation Key: [ə] Symbol

The [ə] or *schwa* sound occurs in syllables without an accent. It can be spelled with any vowel, such as **a** in above, **e** in listen, **i** in pencil, **o** in melon, **u** in circus. It can also be a combination of vowels, such as **io** in action, **ai** in mountain, **iou** in precious.

(Turn the page for more information.)

B

bi•ol•o•gy [bī äl′ ə jē] *noun.* the scientific study of plants and animals. Biology is the study of the physical makeup of living things and the way that they grow, produce new offspring, and relate to their environment. Biology also deals with the origin and history of life on earth and the way living things are distributed over the earth. ♦ An expert in biology is a **biologist.** **—biological,** *adjective:* Zoology is a *biological* science.

bi•on•ic [bī än′ ik] *adjective.* **1.** having to do with bionics. **2.** using electronic and mechanical devices to replace a human body part: A popular TV series dealt with the great strength of a *bionic* man.

bi•on•ics [bī än′ iks] *noun.* the science of studying how the body is formed and how it does something, in order to design a machine or other artificial device to do the same thing. Examples of this are studying birds in order to design aircraft, or studying the human brain and nervous system to design computers.

birch [burch] *noun, plural* **birches.** a tree with hard wood and smooth white bark that is easily peeled off in thin layers. Some North American Indian tribes used long strips of birch bark to make canoes.

bird [burd] *noun, plural* **birds.** any one of a large group of animals that have wings and a body covered with feathers. Birds have a backbone and are warm-blooded. They lay eggs and most kinds can fly.

birth [burth] *noun, plural* **births. 1.** the act of being born from a mother's body; the beginning of life: the *birth* of a baby. **2.** the start or beginning of something: the *birth* of the Space Age. ". . . this nation, under God, shall have a new *birth* of freedom;" (Abraham Lincoln)

birth•day [burth′ dā′] *noun, plural* **birthdays. 1.** the day on which a person was born. **2.** the date on which this day falls in later years: Cathy celebrated her twelfth *birthday* last Saturday.

birth•place [burth′ plās′] *noun.* **1.** the place where someone was born. **2.** the place where something began: Ancient Greece is considered to be the *birthplace* of democracy.

bis•cuit [bis′ kit] *noun, plural* **biscuits.** a small roll, bread, or cake baked from a dough made with flour and baking powder, baking soda, or yeast. ♦ *Biscuit* has the same *bi-* root as words like *binoculars* and *binary*. It first meant "twice cooked."

bish•op [bish′ əp] *noun, plural* **bishops. 1.** in the Christian church, a high-ranking clergyman or minister, especially one who is in charge of a church district or DIOCESE. **2.** in chess, a piece that can move diagonally on the board.

bi•son [bī′ sən] *noun, plural* **bison.** a large wild animal related to the ox. A bison has short horns, a humped back, and a shaggy mane.

bison This famous American animal is called a *buffalo* but is actually a *bison*. Pioneers on the western prairie thought it was a buffalo—an animal they already knew of from Asia and Africa—and they began to use this name.

bit[1] [bit] *noun, plural* **bits. 1.** a small piece or amount: There's just a *bit* of cake left. **2.** a short period of time: We'll have to wait a *bit* for the next bus.

bit[2] *noun, plural* **bits. 1.** the metal part of a bridle that fits into a horse's mouth to control its movements. **2.** a tool that is used for cutting or drilling.

bit[3] *verb.* the past tense of **bite.**

bit[4] *noun, plural* **bits.** the smallest unit of information that can be stored and used by a computer.

bite [bīt] *verb,* **bit, bitten, biting. 1.** to cut, tear, or hold with the teeth: to *bite* into an apple. **2.** to wound with fangs, a stinger, or teeth: Does that dog *bite?* Several people have been *bitten* by rattlesnakes near here. **3.** to cause a sharp pain to; sting: "The air *bit* her cheeks . . . with cold." (Laura Ingalls Wilder) **4.** to take or swallow bait: The fish were really *biting* on the lake this morning. **—noun, plural** **bites. 1.** the act of biting. **2.** a wound or injury that comes from biting: an insect *bite*. **3.** a small bit of food taken at one time; a mouthful: He took a *bite* out of the sandwich. **4.** a light meal; snack: Do we have time to stop for a *bite* of lunch?

bit•ten [bit′ ən] *verb.* the past participle of **bite.**

bit•ter [bit′ ər] *adjective, more/most* or **bitterer, bitterest. 1.** having a sharp, unpleasant taste: The medicine left a *bitter* taste in his mouth. **2.** very harsh or sharp; stinging: ". . . the *bitter* wind cutting my shoulders through my thin coat." (Katherine Anne Porter) **3.** hard to bear; painful: Losing the game in the last inning was a *bitter* disappointment for the team. **4.** having angry or unhappy feelings: He's very *bitter* about the fact that he was fired from his job. **—bitterly:** *adverb:* "Mr. Parnell began *bitterly* protesting at being abandoned." (Lloyd Alexander) **—bitterness,** *noun:* "She accepted the situation without *bitterness*." (Somerset Maugham)

are the remains of giant stars that have collapsed from the weight of their own gravity.

black•mail [blak⁄ māl⁄] *verb,* **blackmailed, blackmailing.** to get money or a favor from someone by threatening to tell something bad about the person: The mayor was being *blackmailed* by someone who knew that as a young man he had served five years in prison under a different name. **—noun.** the crime of blackmailing someone, or the money or favor given for this: to pay *blackmail.*

B

---

black The term *black* is now the word generally accepted by Americans of African ancestry. "Negro" is still used occasionally, but "colored" is not. The change to "black" was noted in the speeches and writing of Martin Luther King, Jr. In his famous 1963 speech "I Have a Dream," he used "Negro" sixteen times. However, Malcolm X and other leaders of that time argued in favor of the term "black," saying that "Negro" was inaccurate and insulting. By the time of his "I've Been to the Mountaintop" speech in 1968, King himself used the term "black" instead of "Negro."

---

black [blak] *noun, plural* **blacks. 1.** the darkest color; the color of tar, coal, or the print in this book; the opposite of white. **2.** *also,* **Black.** a name used to describe the members of a certain race of people who generally have dark skin. **—adjective,** **blacker, blackest. 1.** having the color black. **2.** *also,* **Black.** of or having to do with black people: *black* history. **3.** without light: The night was *black* with no moon out.

black•ber•ry [blak⁄ ber⁄ ē] *noun, plural* **blackberries.** a small black berry that grows on a prickly bush and is sweet-tasting and juicy. Blackberries are used for making jam and pies.

black•bird [blak⁄ burd⁄] *noun, plural* **blackbirds.** any of several birds that are so called because the male is mostly black. The male **redwing blackbird** has a bright red marking on each wing.

black•board [blak⁄ bôrd⁄] *noun, plural* **blackboards.** a smooth, hard surface that is used for writing or drawing with chalk, as in a school classroom. Blackboards are made of slate or other hard materials. ◆ Because such a board is now often light green or another color rather than black, it is also called a **chalkboard.**

black•en [blak⁄ ən] *verb,* **blackened, blackening. 1.** to make or become black in color: "A ring of fire had *blackened* palms and oaks for a hundred feet around." (Marjorie Kinnan Rawlings) **2.** to do harm to; speak evil of: to *blacken* a person's reputation.

black hole an object in outer space with a pull of gravity so strong that not even light can escape. Astronomers believe that black holes

blackout The skyline of New York City during a total blackout in the summer of 1977.

black•out [blak⁄ out⁄] *noun, plural* **blackouts. 1.** the shutting down of electrical power in a certain area. This can happen by accident, such as during a storm, or it can be done in wartime as a protection against an attack at night. **2.** a loss of consciousness for a short time: He has been suffering from *blackouts* ever since his car accident. ◆ Also used as a verb: The pilot almost *blacked out* when his plane went into a steep dive. **3.** a temporary ban or shutdown:

Pronunciation Key: Accent Marks

[⁄] is the normal accent mark. It shows where the main stress falls on a word.
[⁄] is a secondary accent mark. It shows a lighter stress than the primary accent. For example:

tel • e • vis • ion [tel⁄ə vizh⁄ən]

(Turn the page for more information.)

B

There was a news *blackout* during the U.S. invasion of Grenada.

black·smith [blak′smith′] *noun, plural* **blacksmiths.** a person who works with iron by heating it and shaping it with a hammer. A blacksmith can make horseshoes and iron tools.

black widow a poisonous black spider. The female has red markings on its belly and is known to eat the male after mating.

blad·der [blad′ər] *noun, plural* **bladders. 1.** a small, bag-like body part that holds waste liquid called URINE before it is expelled from the body. **2.** a flexible bag, usually made of rubber, that fits inside a ball or other container and holds air or fluid.

blade [blād] *noun, plural* **blades. 1.** the sharp, flat cutting edge of a knife, sword, or tool. **2.** a thin, flat part that is like the blade of a knife: the *blade* of an oar, the *blade* of a propeller, a *blade* of grass.

blame [blām] *verb,* **blamed, blaming. 1.** to hold responsible for something wrong or bad: The book *Unsafe at Any Speed* by Ralph Nader *blamed* American auto companies for making cars that weren't safe. **2.** to find fault with: I don't *blame* you for being upset about that, but you have to try to forget about it. —*noun.* responsibility for something wrong or bad: Ted put the *blame* on his sister for breaking the window, but it was really his fault.

bland [bland] *adjective,* **blander, blandest.** not irritating; mild; soothing: a *bland* diet. "It was so *bland* they had to keep adding garlic to create any taste at all." (Tom Wolfe)

blan·ket [blang′kit] *noun, plural* **blankets. 1.** a large, heavy cloth to keep a person warm, used mainly as a covering on a bed. **2.** anything that can cover things as a blanket does: a *blanket* of fog. —*verb,* **blanketed, blanketing.** to cover with or as if with a blanket: The snow *blanketed* everything in the city. "A heavy silence *blanketed* the room." (James Herriot)

blanket This Indian woman from Bolivia is weaving a blanket made from the wool of the llama.

blare [blâr] *verb,* **blared, blaring.** to sound loudly and harshly: "A radio was *blaring* dance music . . ." (Arthur C. Clarke) —*noun, plural* **blares.** a loud, harsh sound: We heard the *blare* of sirens as the fire trucks raced by.

blank page Ernest Hemingway once said that a writer cannot escape from facing a blank page each day he writes. Georges Simenon, a Belgian-born French author of mystery stories, has dealt with the blank page well enough to write over 300 books in his lifetime. He told his publisher, William Jovanovich, that it's best to start a story by thinking of a person, how he looks, speaks, moves. That might also be good advice for someone writing a factual report on history or politics or art. In much writing, individual persons are the center of interest.

blank [blangk] *adjective,* **blanker, blankest. 1.** without printing or writing: a *blank* page. **2.** vacant or empty: "Their smiles were pleasant and *blank* as air." (Vera Cleaver) —*noun, plural* **blanks. 1.** a space to be filled in on a form or document: Write your name in the *blank* space at the top of the page. **2.** a form or document having such spaces: Do you have any entry *blanks* for the contest? **3.** a cartridge having gunpowder, but no bullet. A blank makes a noise like a bullet being shot.

blast [blast] *noun, plural* **blasts. 1.** a strong rush or gust of air: ". . . terrible *blasts* of hot air and showers of cinders." (John Hersey) **2.** an explosion: The dynamite *blast* could be heard for miles. **3.** a loud noise: a trumpet *blast.* —*verb,* **blasted, blasting. 1.** to blow apart with an explosion: "His shotgun went off by mistake, *blasting* a hole in the ceiling." (E.B. White) **2. blast off.** to launch a rocket or spacecraft.

blaze¹ [blāz] *noun, plural* **blazes. 1.** a bright, glowing fire or flame: We stepped back from the *blaze* of the campfire. **2.** a bright, glowing light. **3.** a bright display: During the spring, the fields were a *blaze* of colorful wildflowers. —*verb,* **blazed, blazing. 1.** to burn brightly: "The room was warm and the logs in the fireplace were *blazing.*" (Walter Farley) **2.** to shine or glow strongly: "The sun *blazed* down upon them." (George Orwell)

blaze[2] *verb,* **blazed, blazing.** to mark a trail, as by cutting a mark in a tree. —*noun, plural* **blazes.** a mark to show where a trail is.

blaz·er [blā′ zər] *noun, plural* **blazers.** a sports jacket in navy blue or another solid color.

bleach [blēch] *verb,* **bleached, bleaching.** to make something white or light-colored by using chemicals or by exposing it to the sun: to *bleach* clothing, to *bleach* one's hair. —*noun, plural* **bleaches.** a soap or chemical used for this.

bleak [blēk] *adjective,* **bleaker, bleakest. 1.** exposed to the wind and weather; bare: "Somewhere beyond those *bleak* hills lay the Great Bear Lake." (John McPhee) **2.** cold and unpleasant; a *bleak* winter day. **3.** depressing or gloomy: "Our school was in a *bleak* building that had once been a warehouse." (Yong Ik Kim) —**bleakly,** *adverb.*

bled [bled] *verb.* the past form of **bleed.**

bleed [blēd] *verb,* **bled, bleeding. 1.** to lose blood from a wound or injury: The cut on his leg was *bleeding* badly. **2.** to lose sap or other fluids: Sap *bled* from the maple tree into the bucket. **3.** to feel sorrow or grief: Her heart *bled* for the parents of the lost child.

blem·ish [blem′ ish] *noun, plural* **blemishes.** a flaw or mark that spoils the appearance or quality of something: a *blemish* on the skin.

---

blends Writers often create *blends* by putting parts of two words together, especially in political writing. "Reaganomics" means President Reagan's policies on economics. "Workfare" means that people must work if they are given money by the government (a blend of *welfare,* in which money is given to needy people without putting them in jobs, and, of course, *work*). How do you think "motel" came about? Or "smog?" Or "brunch?" Blends that are cleverly formed, such as these, often stay in the language. Those that are too artificial, though, can take away from the quality of writing. There are over 600,000 English words already available for your use, without any new blends being created. Use your dictionary!

bleachers Chicago Cub fans fill the bleachers at Wrigley Field to cheer for their team. The name *bleachers* comes from the idea of people "bleaching" in the hot sun while sitting there.

bleach·ers [blēch′ ərs] *noun.* a section of open seats for people to watch a game, contest, parade, or other outdoor event.

—*verb,* **blemished, blemishing.** to spoil the appearance or quality of something: The mayor's reputation has been *blemished* by the rumor that he received illegal payments.

blend [blend] *verb,* **blended, blending. 1.** to mix or put together so that the parts cannot be separated: He *blended* the juices for the fruit punch. **2.** to shade together a little at a time: "I am distracted by a lizard. How perfectly he *blends* into his surroundings." (Judy Blume) **3.** to mix in with; go together: The detective tried to *blend* in with the crowd so that the suspect wouldn't know he was being followed. —*noun, plural* **blends. 1.** something that has been blended; a mixture: That coffee is a special *blend* of several different kinds of beans. **2.** a word that is made by joining parts of two or more words

Pronunciation Key: A–F			
a	and; hat	ch	chew; such
ā	ate; stay	d	dog; lid
â	care; air	e	end; yet
ä	father; hat	ē	she; each
b	boy; cab	f	fun; off

(Turn the page for more information.)

together: The word "brunch" is a *blend* of "*br*eakfast" and "*lunch*."

blen•der [blen′dər] *noun, plural* **blenders.** an electrical appliance for mixing foods or liquids together.

bless [bles] *verb,* **blessed, blessing. 1.** to ask God's help or favor for: *Bless* you for all that you've done for us. **2.** to make holy or sacred: The priest *blessed* the altar of the new church. **3.** to praise or honor as holy: to *bless* the Lord. **4.** to bring happiness or favor to: All their children have been *blessed* with good health. Hawaii is *blessed* with a warm, mild climate.

bless•ed [bles′id *or* blest] *adjective, more/ most.* **1.** that has been blessed; holy: "*Blessed* be the name of the Lord." (The Bible: *Job*) **2.** bringing happiness or favor: The birth of a baby is often called a *blessed* event. "What sky! What light! . . . It is a *blessed* thing to be alive in such weather . . ." (Samuel Beckett)

bless•ing [bles′ing] *noun, plural* **blessings. 1.** a prayer or request for God's help or favor. **2.** approval or honor: The queen gave her *blessing* to her son's plans to be married. **3.** something that brings happiness or satisfaction: This rain is a *blessing* after all that dry weather.

blew [bloo] *verb.* the past tense of **blow:** "The fruit had been picked and the fall wind *blew* through the trees." (Ernest Hemingway)

blight [blīt] *noun, plural* **blights. 1.** any one of several diseases that cause plants to dry up and die. **2.** something that ruins or destroys: Those burned-out old buildings are a *blight* on the landscape.

blimp [blimp] *noun, plural* **blimps.** a very large balloon that is filled with a gas that is lighter than air and that can be steered through the air.

blind [blīnd] *adjective,* **blinder, blindest. 1.** not able to see; without sight: Baby raccoons are *blind* when they are born. **2.** hard to see; hidden or concealed: There was a *blind* curve in the road. **3.** not able to see or notice: She was *blind* to her son's faults. **4.** done only with electronic and mechanical instruments: ". . . *blind* flying through a sea of clouds in the mountains." (Antoine de St. Exupèry) —*verb,* **blinded, blinding.** to make blind: "The bright September sun hit their faces and *blinded* them." (Louise Fitzhugh) "There was a *blinding* flash of light and the guests all blinked." (J.R.R. Tolkien) —**blindly,** *adverb:* "She felt herself go *blindly* spinning through sudden blackness." (Lloyd Alexander) ♦ The condition of being blind is **blindness.**

blind•fold [blind′fōld′] *noun, plural* **blind-**

folds. a piece of cloth or other material used to cover the eyes so that a person cannot see. —*verb,* **blindfolded, blindfolding.** to cover a person's eyes with a blindfold.

blink [blingk] *verb,* **blinked, blinking. 1.** to open and shut the eyes quickly: The smoke made her *blink* constantly. "Suddenly I found myself *blinking* back tears." (Jean Fritz) **2.** to flash on and off: a *blinking* traffic signal. —*noun, plural* **blinks. 1.** a quick flash of light. **2. on the blink.** *Informal.* not working: Our TV set is *on the blink* today.

bliss [blis] *noun.* a feeling of perfect happiness and joy. —**blissful,** *adjective.* full of bliss: a *blissful* smile. —**blissfully,** *adverb:* "He tells her the motel owner is *blissfully* happy." (Ann Beattie)

blis•ter [blis′tər] *noun, plural* **blisters. 1.** a painful bump on the surface of the skin filled with a watery liquid. It is usually caused by a burn or by constant rubbing. **2.** any small bubble or swelling on a surface: The hot sun caused *blisters* to appear on the painted wall. —*verb,* **blistered, blistering.** to form or have blisters on: A sunburn may *blister* the skin. "All I see coming out of your scheme is a sprained back and *blistered* fingers." (Lloyd Alexander)

blizzard Traffic moves slowly through a blizzard in Washington, D.C. *Blizzard* is an American word that first came into popular use during a very hard winter in 1880-81.

bliz•zard [bliz′ard] *noun, plural* **blizzards.** a very heavy snowstorm with strong winds and cold temperatures.

bloat [blōt] *verb,* **bloated, bloating.** to swell or puff up: The horse's stomach was *bloated* from drinking too much water.

blob [bläb] *noun, plural* **blobs.** a small drop or lump of a soft, wet, or sticky substance: a *blob* of paint. Penny dropped a *blob* of ice cream on her dress.

block [bläk] *noun, plural* **blocks. 1.** a solid piece of wood, stone, ice, or another hard material, usually having one or more flat sides. **2.** a square area enclosed by four streets: The neighbors on our *block* are very friendly. **3.** the length of one side of a block: Their house is three *blocks* from the school. **4.** a group or set of things: The school drama club bought a *block* of tickets to a Broadway play. **5.** something that is in the way; an obstacle: The police put up a road*block* to stop the robbers from escaping. **6.** a wooden or metal frame holding one or more pulleys, used with a rope for lifting heavy items. A set of these pulleys is called a **block and tackle.**
—*verb,* **blocked, blocking. 1.** to get in the way of; keep from moving: "Kayak pushed out the piece of ice that he used to *block* the entrance." (James Houston) ◆ Often used with **up** or **out:** "The traffic that had been *blocked up* was moving again." (S.E. Hinton) "Edna *blocked out* all their voices." (Paul Zindel) **2.** in football and other sports, to get in the way of an opposing player so that he cannot move past.

block·ade [blä kād'] *noun, plural* **blockades.** the blocking of a place by an army or navy to stop things from going in or out: In 1948 the Soviet Union set up a land and water *blockade* of West Berlin, and supplies could only be brought into the city by air. —*verb,* **blockaded, blockading.** to close off with a blockade: During the Civil War the Union navy *blockaded* the Southern coast.

blond or **blonde** [bländ] *adjective,* **blonder, blondest. 1.** having a light-yellowish color: *blond* hair. **2.** having light-colored hair. —*noun, plural* **blonds** or **blondes.** a person with light-colored hair. ◆ For girls and women the word is usually spelled **blonde,** and for boys and men it is usually spelled **blond.**

blood [blud] *noun.* **1.** the red liquid in the body that is pumped by the heart through the VEINS and ARTERIES. Through the **bloodstream,** blood carries oxygen and digested food to all parts of the body and carries away waste products. **2.** family relationship; ancestry: Queen Elizabeth is related by *blood* to Queen Victoria. **3. in cold blood.** without feeling; in a cruel and deliberate way: to kill a person *in cold blood.* "A blow *in cold blood* neither can nor should be forgiven." (George Bernard Shaw)

blood·hound [blud'hound'] *noun, plural* **bloodhounds.** a large reddish-brown dog with droopy ears and loose skin around its face. Bloodhounds have a very sharp sense of smell and are used to track people who are lost or who are wanted by the police.

blood pressure the amount of force that the blood has as it presses against the walls of the arteries while being pumped by the heart. Blood pressure that is too high or too low can be dangerous to a person's health.

blood vessel any of the tubes that blood passes through in the body, such as the veins, arteries, and CAPILLARIES.

blood·y [blud'ē] *adjective,* **bloodier, bloodiest. 1.** covered or stained with blood: a *bloody* wound, a *bloody* bandage. **2.** having much loss of life: a *bloody* battle.

B

block style In writing, typing, and word processing, the *block style* or *block form* means that new paragraphs are not indented—that is, the first line of a paragraph is not moved in from the left margin. Business letters usually are written in block style, in which case extra space is left between paragraphs to show that a break occurs. The difference between block style and indenting in a business letter is a matter of custom. Judge for yourself which style you prefer; there is no hard and fast rule. In a school report or a personal letter, though, you should indent the paragraphs.

bloom [bloom] *noun, plural* **blooms. 1.** a blossom or flower. **2.** the time of being in flower: The apple trees are all in *bloom.* **3.** a time of freshness and health: the *bloom* of youth. —*verb,* **bloomed, blooming. 1.** to bear flowers; blossom: "Wild roses *bloomed* everywhere." (Vera Cleaver) **2.** to show freshness and health: "Joan's cheeks *bloomed* like good apples." (Sylvia Plath)

blos·som [bläs'əm] *noun, plural* **blossoms. 1.** a flower or group of flowers, especially of a tree or plant that bears fruit: peach *blossoms.* **2.** the time of being in flower: The cherry trees are in

	Pronunciation Key: G–N		
g	give; big	k	kind; cat; back
h	hold	l	let; ball
i	it; this	m	make; time
ī	ice; my	n	not; own
j	jet; gem; edge	ng	having

(Turn the page for more information.)

B

blossom. —*verb,* **blossomed, blossoming. 1.** to bear flowers; bloom: The tulips *blossomed* early this year. **2.** to grow or develop: Cathy has really *blossomed* into a good soccer player this season.

blot [blät] *noun, plural* **blots. 1.** a stain or spot: The ink left a *blot* on the paper. **2.** something that spoils or disgraces: Those two speeding tickets are a *blot* on his driving record. —*verb,* **blotted, blotting. 1.** to spot or stain. **2.** to soak up; dry: She *blotted* the spilled milk with a paper towel.

blot out 1. to hide or cover completely: "Suddenly a dark cloud swept across the sun, *blotting* it *out* and leaving the earth in shadow." (E.B. White) **2.** to do away with completely: He tried to *blot out* the memory of the car accident.

blot•ter [blät′ər] *noun, plural* **blotters. 1.** a piece of soft, thick paper used in writing to soak up wet ink. **2.** a book for keeping records. A **police blotter** is a record of arrests kept in a police station.

blouse [blous *or* blouz] *noun, plural* **blouses.** a piece of woman's clothing for the upper body, similar to a shirt for men.

blow[1] [blō] *verb,* **blew, blown, blowing. 1.** to move with speed and force by wind or air: "Next morning a cold wind was *blowing,* and storm clouds were rolling up . . ." (Laura Ingalls Wilder) **2.** to send out air, as with the breath: He *blew* on the soup to cool it off. **3.** to move by a current of air: The fan *blew* the papers off the desk. The roof *blew* off the barn during a tornado. **4.** to make a sound by a current of air: to *blow* a bugle. The referee *blew* his whistle to stop the game. **5.** to shape or form with air: to *blow* bubbles, to *blow* glass.

blow out 1. to put out or go out by blowing: She *blew out* the candles on her birthday cake. The lights *blew out* during the storm last night. **2.** to burst suddenly: A tire *blew out* when we drove over the broken glass. ◆ Also used as a noun: Our car had a *blowout* on the freeway.

blow up 1. to fill with air or gas: to *blow up* a balloon. **2.** to damage or destroy by an explosion: The terrorists planted a bomb to *blow up* the building. **3.** to make something larger: to *blow up* a photograph. This issue has been *blown up* way beyond its real importance. **4.** *Informal.* to become very angry.

blow[2] *noun, plural* **blows. 1.** a sudden hard hit with the fist or with a weapon: The boxer took a hard *blow* to the chin. "The *blows* of the axe echoed back and forth." (Marjorie Kinnan Rawlings) **2.** a sudden happening that causes

sorrow or misfortune: Losing the race to his little sister was a real *blow* to his pride.

blow•er [blō′ər] *noun, plural* **blowers. 1.** any person or thing that blows: He works as a glass *blower.* **2.** a fan or other machine that forces air to blow: They used a snow *blower* to clear the snow off the driveway.

blown [blōn] *verb.* the past participle of **blow:** The storm has *blown* snow all over the road. —*adjective.* **1.** no longer working: The lights went out because of a *blown* fuse. **2.** formed by blowing air: *blown* glass.

blow•torch [blō′tôrch′] *noun, plural* **blowtorches.** a small torch that burns gas to send out a very hot flame, used for working on metal.

blub•ber [blub′ər] *noun.* the fat of whales, seals, and other sea animals, used as a source of oil. —*verb,* **blubbered, blubbering.** to cry in a noisy way.

blue [blo͞o] *noun, plural* **blues. 1.** the color of the daytime sky on a clear day. **2.** see **blues.** —*adjective,* **bluer, bluest. 1.** having the color blue. **2.** *Informal.* sad; unhappy: She's really *blue* about failing that math test.

blue•ber•ry [blo͞o′ber′ē] *noun, plural* **blueberries.** a small, sweet-tasting blue berry that grows on either a low or a tall shrub.

bluebird Bluebirds often nest in holes in trees and in bird houses provided by humans.

blue•bird [blo͞o′burd′] *noun, plural* **bluebirds.** a small North American songbird with bluish-colored feathers on its back.

blue•col•lar [blo͞o′käl′ər] *adjective.* having to do with work that is done with the hands by workers wearing special uniforms or work clothes, as opposed to work done in an office by people wearing dress clothes: Factory work is a *blue-collar* job.

◆ The name comes from the fact that such

workers often wear *blue* work shirts, while office (WHITE-COLLAR) workers often wear white ones.

blue•jay [bloo′ jā′] *noun, plural* **bluejays.** a bird of eastern North America with a crest on its head and a bright blue back and wings. It is known for its noisy cry.

blue jeans pants made from a heavy blue denim cloth.

blue•print [bloo′ print′] *noun, plural* **blueprints. 1.** a copy of a building plan, map, or drawing showing lines against a background of another color. For many years blueprints always had white lines on a blue background, but now the lines are often blue or black on white. **2.** any detailed plan or outline: This book claims to give its readers a *blueprint* for success in business.

blues [blooz] *plural noun.* **1.** low spirits; sadness: He's had the *blues* since he broke up with his girlfriend. **2.** a type of music that is typically slow and sad-sounding. The blues began among black people in the southern United States.

bluff[1] [bluf] *verb,* **bluffed, bluffing. 1.** in a card game, to pretend that you have a much better hand than you really do in order to fool the other players. **2.** to try to fool other people by acting braver, stronger, or more sure of oneself than one actually is: He says he'll quit the team if he doesn't get to be the starting quarterback, but he's only *bluffing.* —*noun, plural* **bluffs.** the act of bluffing: Joe always acts tough, but it's really just a *bluff.*

bluff The Mohegan Bluffs of Block Island, part of the state of Rhode Island.

bluff[2] *noun, plural* **bluffs.** a high, steep cliff or river bank. —*adjective.* rough or rude, but in a well-meaning way: He has a *bluff* manner that makes people think he's unfriendly.

blun•der [blun′ dər] *verb,* **blundered, blunder-**ing. **1.** to make a stupid or careless mistake: He *blundered* when he locked his car keys inside the car. **2.** to move in a clumsy way: The boys *blundered* through the weeds looking for the lost ball. —*noun, plural* **blunders.** a stupid or careless mistake: The newspaper made a real *blunder* when they ran a story on the mayor next to one about a bank robber and mixed up the pictures of the two men.

blunt [blunt] *adjective,* **blunter, bluntest. 1.** having a dull edge or point; not sharp: a *blunt* knife. "The nails were flat and *blunt* and shiny." (John Steinbeck) **2.** speaking without worrying about the feelings of others; very plain and direct: "He has a *blunt,* rough way of talking that irritates a lot of people." (S.E. Hinton) —*verb,* **blunted, blunting.** to make something dull or blunt. —**bluntly,** *adverb:* To put it *bluntly,* your team really doesn't have any chance of winning the championship. —**bluntness,** *noun.*

blur [blur] *verb,* **blurred, blurring.** to make less clear or make hard to see: Hold the camera still or you'll *blur* the photo. He spilled some water on his paper and *blurred* the last few words on the page. —*noun, plural* **blurs.** something that is not clear or is hard to see: The race car passed so quickly that it was just a *blur.*

blush [blush] *verb,* **blushed, blushing.** to become red in the face, as from embarrassment, shame, or excitement: The boy *blushed* when he realized he had given the wrong answer. —*noun, plural* **blushes.** a reddening of the face: "There was always a lovely *blush* of color in her cheeks." (Ernest K. Gann)

blus•ter [blus′ tər] *verb,* **blustered, blustering. 1.** to blow in a violent and stormy way: The storm continued to *bluster* all day. **2.** to talk or act in a noisy and threatening manner: That politician is always *blustering* about how the U.S. should declare war on Cuba.

bo•a con•stric•tor [bō′ ə kən strik′ tər] a large, non-poisonous snake that is found in southern Mexico and in Central and South America. It kills small animals by coiling around them and squeezing them to death. It can reach a length of 10 to 15 feet.

Pronunciation Key: O–S

ō	over; go	ou	out; town
ô	all; law	p	put; hop
oo	look; full	r	run; car
oo	pool; who	s	set; miss
oi	oil; boy	sh	show

(Turn the page for more information.)

B

boar [bôr] *noun, plural* **boars. 1.** a wild hog with a hairy coat and a long snout, found in Europe, Africa, and Asia. **2.** a male pig.

boar The wild boar has a good sense of smell that helps it find and dig up roots and other food on the ground.

board [bôrd] *noun, plural* **boards. 1.** a flat, thin piece of sawed wood, generally longer than it is wide. **2.** a flat piece of hard material that is used for a special purpose: an ironing *board,* a chess *board.* **3.** meals furnished for pay. ♦ Used especially in the phrase **room and board. 4.** a group of people who direct or control an organization: a school *board.* The **board of directors** of a company runs the company on behalf of those who own stock in it. —*verb,* **boarded, boarding. 1.** to cover with boards or other such material: They *boarded* up the windows of the beach house for the winter. **2.** to get or give meals for pay: She *boarded* with a friend while her parents were overseas. **3.** to enter or get on a ship, plane, train, or the like: Passengers for Dallas can now *board* at Gate 12.

boarding house a house or building where a room and meals are provided for pay.

boast [bōst] *verb,* **boasted, boasting. 1.** to talk in a very proud way about oneself; brag: All week she's been *boasting* that she's going to win the race on Saturday. **2.** to take pride in having: Our town *boasts* three new shopping centers. —*noun, plural* **boasts.** something that one brags about: Muhammad Ali was famous for his *boasts* about what a great boxer he was. —**boastful,** *adjective.*

boat [bōt] *noun, plural* **boats. 1.** a small, open vessel that is moved through the water by oars, sails, or engines. **2.** a ship or vessel of any size: Today most travelers to Europe go by plane rather than by *boat.* —*verb,* **boated, boating.** to use a boat: to go *boating* on a lake.

bob [bäb] *verb,* **bobbed, bobbing. 1.** to move up and down or side to side with short, jerky motions: The empty soda can *bobbed* on the surface of the water. **2.** to cut the hair short: In the 1920's many women *bobbed* their hair. —*noun, plural* **bobs. 1.** a short, jerky movement. **2.** a small weight or float at the end of a line, especially a fishing line or PLUMB LINE. **3.** a short haircut.

bob•cat [bäb′kat′] *noun, plural* **bobcats.** a small wildcat of North America that has a yellowish-brown coat with dark spots and a short tail.

bob•o•link [bäb′ə lingk′] *noun, plural* **bobolinks.** a songbird found in North and South America. It is related to the blackbird and is named for the sound of its call.

bob•sled [bäb′sled′] *noun, plural* **bobsleds.** a long sled having two sets of runners, a steering wheel, and brakes. It moves on a steep, curving course made of icy snow.

bobsled The word *bobsled* comes from the idea that it moves rapidly up and down in a "bobbing" motion as it goes downhill.

bob•white [bäb′wīt′] *noun, plural* **bobwhites.** a North American quail whose grayish body is marked with brown and white spots. Its name comes from the sound of its call.

bod•i•ly [bäd′ə lē] *adjective* or *adverb.* having to do with the body: This insurance policy pays for damage to the car as well as any *bodily* injury to the passengers. The fireman lifted up the two boys and carried them *bodily* out of the building.

bod•y [bäd′ē] *noun, plural* **bodies. 1.** all of a person or an animal; the entire form that makes up a living thing: The normal temperature of the human *body* is 98.6°. **2.** a dead person or animal; a corpse. **3.** the main part of a person or animal, other than the head and the limbs: A dachshund has short legs and a long *body*. **4.** the main part of something: the *body* of an automobile, the *body* of a letter. **5.** a mass or group: Lake Michigan is a large *body* of water. The entire student *body* cheered for the football team at the big pep rally. The stars and planets are known as heavenly *bodies*. **6.** the quality of being full or thick: This shampoo is supposed to give more *body* to your hair.

is 212° Fahrenheit or 100° Celsius. **2.** *Informal.* the point at which somebody becomes hot with anger: Be careful not to tease her —she's got a low *boiling point.*

bois·ter·ous [boi′stər əs *or* boi′strəs] *adjective, more/most.* rough and noisy: On New Year's Eve a *boisterous* crowd waits in New York's Times Square for the clock to signal the start of the new year. **—boisterously,** *adverb:* "The rooster crowed *boisterously* under the window." (Marjorie Kinnan Rawlings)

B

---

body of a letter In a letter, the *body* is the main part, where the message is contained. The body is everything that comes after the salutation line "Dear so and so" and after any personal comment that isn't part of the message. For example, "Dear John: I hope you are well and back at work. Do let me know." Then comes the body: "On that bid you made to build the garage, we need more drawings and . . . ." Note this: Never try to be familiar or friendly when writing to a company or government agency, if you are asking for a job. Go right to the body of the letter. Most executives throw away letters of the sort that start, "Good morning, Mr. Jones. I think I can make your morning even better if you'll spend a minute to read what I have to say about myself."

---

bod·y·guard [bäd′ē gärd′] *noun, plural* **bodyguards.** someone whose job is to protect and guard another person. Government leaders, movie stars, and other famous persons often have bodyguards.

bog [bäg] *noun, plural* **bogs.** a wet, soft area near water; a swamp or marsh.
—*verb,* **bogged, bogging. to bog down.** to sink or slow down, in or as if in a bog: The plan for the new town hall is *bogged down* because no one can agree on where to build it.

Bo·go·tá [bō′ gə tä′] the capital of Colombia. *Population:* 4,500,000.

boil¹ [boil] *verb,* **boiled, boiling. 1.** to heat a liquid so that bubbles are formed and steam rises. **2.** to cook in boiling water: to *boil* potatoes. ♦ Often used as an adjective: *boiled* beef. **3.** to become very angry or upset: When Tim found out his bicycle had been stolen, he was really *boiling.* —*noun.* the condition of boiling: Put the vegetables in the pot when the water comes to a *boil.*

boil² *noun, plural* **boils.** a painful red swelling under the skin, caused by an infection. A boil has a hard core and is often filled with PUS.

boil·er [boi′lər] *noun, plural* **boilers. 1.** a large tank for holding hot water or steam, used to heat a building or to produce power for an engine. **2.** a pan or pot in which water or another liquid is boiled, as for cooking.

boiling point 1. the temperature at which a liquid begins to boil. The boiling point of water

bold [bōld] *adjective,* **bolder, boldest. 1.** daring and brave; taking risks: The *bold* pilot flew his helicopter right over the enemy fort to rescue the hostages. **2.** not polite; rude: The *bold* boy helped himself to four pieces of cake without asking if anyone else at the table wanted any. **—boldly,** *adverb.* in a bold way: "She looked Burdick *boldly* in the eyes." (Lloyd Alexander) **—boldness,** *noun.*

bold·face [bōld′fās′] *noun.* a kind of printing type in which the letters stand out because they are heavy and black, **like this** or like this.

Bol·í·var [bō lē′ vär] **Simón** [sē′ mōn], 1783–1830, Venezuelan general who freed much of South America from Spanish rule.

Bo·liv·i·a [bə liv′ē ə] an inland country in the western part of South America. *Capitals:* Sucre; La Paz. *Area:* 424,100 square miles. *Population:* 5,900,000. **—Bolivian,** *adjective; noun.*

boll [bōl] *noun, plural* **bolls.** the seed pod of a plant such as cotton or FLAX. ♦ The **boll weevil** is a grayish beetle with a long, thin snout that lays its eggs in cotton plants. It can cause great damage to cotton crops.

	Pronunciation Key: T–Z		
t	ten; date	v	very; live
th	think	w	win; away
<u>th</u>	these	y	you
u	cut; butter	z	zoo; cause
ur	turn; bird	zh	measure

(Turn the page for more information.)

bo•lo•gna [bə lō′ nē] *noun*. a type of sausage or sandwich meat, made with seasoned beef or pork or now sometimes with turkey or chicken.

bologna The word *bologna* has a very unusual spelling, with the ending *gna*. This is because the word comes from the name of a place, Bologna (a large city in Italy). *Bologna* was at first called a "Bologna sausage," because it was a special kind of sausage made in that city. People sometimes spell it as "baloney" or "boloney" to be closer to its sound, but the original spelling *bologna* is the correct one. Can you think of other food names we get from places? *Frankfurter* and *hamburger* are examples.

bol•ster [bōl′ stər] *verb*, **bolstered, bolstering.** to support or give strength to: David has *bolstered* his chances of winning the spelling bee by studying the word list every night. —*noun, plural* **bolsters. 1.** a long, narrow pillow or cushion. **2.** a thing that supports.

bolt [bōlt] *noun, plural* **bolts. 1.** a single flash of lightning. **2.** a sliding bar used to fasten a door. **3.** a pin or rod with a head on one end and a screw thread on the other. A bolt is used with a nut to hold things in place. **4.** a sudden, quick movement: The dog made a *bolt* for the door. **5.** a large roll of cloth, wallpaper, or the like. —*verb*, **bolted, bolting. 1.** to make a sudden, quick movement; dash: The deer *bolted* away when it heard the hunters coming. **2.** to fasten a door with a bolt: "He's got the house *bolted* front and back." (Walter Farley) **3.** to eat food too quickly without chewing: Sam *bolted* down his breakfast and ran out the door.

bomb [bäm] *noun, plural* **bombs.** a container filled with material that will explode or burn, used as a weapon. A bomb goes off when it hits something or when it is set off by a fuse or timer. —*verb*, **bombed, bombing.** to drop or set off a bomb; attack with bombs: to *bomb* a city, to *bomb* a building.

bom•bard [bäm bärd′] *verb*, **bombarded, bombarding. 1.** to attack with bombs or heavy gunfire: The enemy planes *bombarded* the fort until the soldiers surrendered. ♦ The act of doing this is **bombardment. 2.** to attack or overwhelm, as if by bombing: The lawyer *bombarded* the witness with questions about what he had done on the night of the crime.

Bom•bay [bäm bā′] the largest city in India, located on the Arabian Sea. *Population:* 6,000,000.

bomb•er [bäm′ ər] *noun, plural* **bombers. 1.** an airplane that is specially made for dropping bombs. **2.** a person who bombs: The building was destroyed by a terrorist *bomber*.

bo•nan•za [bə nan′ zə] *noun, plural* **bonanzas.** something that brings a person great wealth or good luck, such as an oil well or a gold mine.

bond [bänd] *noun, plural* **bonds. 1.** something that holds or fastens things together, such as glue, rope, chains, and so on: The prisoner broke loose from his *bonds* and escaped. **2.** something that unites people: "Each felt drawn to the other by a mysterious *bond* of affection." (E.B. White) **3.** a note from a government or public agency promising to pay back a loan, usually with interest. When a town wants to raise money for a new courthouse or library, it may issue bonds for sale to the public. —*verb*, **bonded, bonding.** to stick or connect to; join with a bond: Hold the two pieces together until the glue has time to dry and *bond* them.

bond•age [bän′ dij] *noun*. the condition of being a slave or captive: "She has held all the Munchkins in *bondage* for years, making them slave for her day and night." (L. Frank Baum)

bone [bōn] *noun, plural* **bones.** a hard piece that is part of the skeleton of a human or another animal having a backbone. —*verb*, **boned, boning.** to take the bones out of: to *bone* a fish before eating it.

bon•fire [bän′ fīr] *noun, plural* **bonfires.** a large, bright fire built outdoors.

bon•go drums [bäng′ gō] (also, **bongos**) two small drums joined together and played with the hands.

bomber B-25 bombers were land-based planes, but they are shown here on the deck of the aircraft carrier U.S.S. Hornet. They are about to take off for General James Doolittle's famous bombing raid on Japan.

B

bon•net [bän′it] *noun, plural* **bonnets. 1.** a type of hat tied under the chin and having a large, wide brim, formerly worn by women and girls. **2.** a similar hat worn by babies. **3.** an Indian headdress made of feathers: a Cheyenne war *bonnet*.

bo•nus [bō′nəs] *noun, plural* **bonuses.** something extra given to a person as a reward;

er for writing on: a note*book*, an address *book*. **3.** one part of a very large book: *Genesis* is the first *book* of the Bible.
—*verb*, **booked, booking. 1.** to arrange ahead of time: Jim *booked* an airplane flight home for the holidays. **2.** to record charges against someone: The police *booked* him on suspicion of robbing a jewelry store.

B

---

book reports Book reports that quickly get down to business are the best kind. First, give a summary of what the book is about. Next, give your opinion about the plot, style, or importance of the book. Then finish with one or two sentences that will leave the reader with a strong impression of your views. The problem in many reports is that the opening summary is too long and the following opinion is too short. Don't go on and on with details of the book's content—your report isn't supposed to be a substitute for reading the book itself.

---

something more than is owed or expected: At Thanksgiving, each of the factory workers got a free turkey as a *bonus* from the company.

bon•y [bō′nē] *adjective,* **bonier, boniest. 1.** of or like bone: The nose is formed of a *bony* material called cartilage. **2.** having many bones: a *bony* fish. **3.** having bones that stick out or that are large and noticeable: a tall, *bony* basketball player.

boo [boo] *interjection.* a sound made to scare or surprise someone, or to show dislike or disapproval. —*verb*, **booed, booing:** The crowd *booed* when the tennis player threw his racket on the ground after he lost the match.

book [book] *noun, plural* **books. 1.** printed sheets of paper fastened together and having a cover. **2.** blank sheets of paper fastened togeth-

book•keep•er [book′kē′pər] *noun, plural* **bookkeepers.** a person who keeps track of the accounts and records of a business. ♦ The work of a bookkeeper is called **bookkeeping.**

book•let [book′lit] *noun, plural* **booklets.** a small book, usually with a thin paper cover.

boom¹ [boom] *noun, plural* **booms. 1.** a loud, hollow, deep sound: the *boom* of thunder, the *boom* of an explosion. **2.** a time of rapid growth or activity: There was a *boom* in Alaska after gold was discovered there. —*verb*, **boomed, booming. 1.** to make a loud noise: " 'You'll punch nobody!' *boomed* the cop. 'Come along.' " (Louise Fitzhugh) **2.** to grow or increase rapidly: "Long lines of people were waiting to get aboard for the next ride. Business was *booming*." (E.B. White)

boom² *noun, plural* **booms.** a long pole or beam. One kind is used in a boat to keep the bottom of a sail stretched. Another kind holds a microphone for making TV shows and movies.

boom•er•ang [boo′mə rang] *noun, plural* **boomerangs.** a flat, curved piece of wood that can be thrown so that it circles and returns to the thrower. Boomerangs come from Australia and were used as weapons by the ABORIGINES.

Boone [boon] **Daniel,** 1734?–1820, American pioneer and frontiersman.

Boone *Daniel Boone Escorting Settlers Through the Cumberland Gap,* by the American painter George Caleb Bingham. The term "gap" refers to a place in a mountain range where it is easier to pass through.

Pronunciation Key: [ə] Symbol

The [ə] or *schwa* sound occurs in syllables without an accent. It can be spelled with any vowel, such as **a** in above, **e** in listen, **i** in pencil, **o** in melon, **u** in circus. It can also be a combination of vowels, such as **io** in action, **ai** in mountain, **iou** in precious.

(Turn the page for more information.)

B

boost [boost] *verb,* **boosted, boosting. 1.** to lift up or raise; push up: "He led the sheep to the stairs, and then step by step he lugged and *boosted* her upward." (Laura Ingalls Wilder) **2.** to make bigger or grander; increase: Winning the art contest has really *boosted* Jerry's self-confidence. —*noun, plural* **boosts. 1.** a push or shove upward. **2.** an increase or improvement: a *boost* in sales during the Christmas season.

boot [boot] *noun, plural* **boots.** a kind of shoe covering the foot, ankle, and lower part of the leg. Boots are made of leather or rubber and are usually heavier and stronger than ordinary shoes. —*verb,* **booted, booting. 1.** to kick: The soccer player *booted* the ball. **2.** *Informal.* to start the operating system in a computer.

booth [booth] *noun, plural* **booths. 1.** a stand or place where things are displayed or sold: a ticket *booth* at a theater. The publishing company had several *booths* at the book fair. **2.** a small, closed space or compartment: a telephone *booth,* a voting *booth.*

bor•der [bôr′dər] *noun, plural* **borders. 1.** a dividing line or boundary, as between two states or countries: The Rio Grande forms part of the *border* between the U.S. and Mexico. **2.** the edge or rim of something: The wedding dress was made of satin with a *border* of lace. —*verb,* **bordered, bordering. 1.** to be at the border of: New Jersey *borders* New York and Pennsylvania. **2.** to put a border on: The vegetable garden was *bordered* with a row of colorful flowers. **3. border on.** to be near or close to: That plan is so silly it *borders on* insanity.

bore¹ [bôr] *verb,* **bored, boring.** to make tired or restless by being dull or uninteresting: The movie *bored* the man so much that he fell asleep. "He *bored* them with long stories about his experiences . . . at camp." (Walker Percy)

—*noun, plural* **bores.** a person or thing that is dull or uninteresting: I'm not going to invite him to the party—he's such a *bore.* ◆ The condition of being bored is **boredom** [bôr′dəm].

bore² *verb,* **bored, boring.** to make a hole or tunnel; dig or drill: The mole *bored* his way through the lawn. The carpenter *bored* a hole in the board.

bore³ *verb.* the past tense of **bear²:** "The wind *bore* coldness with it, and the men began to shiver." (Stephen Crane)

bor•ing [bôr′ing] *adjective, more/most.* causing boredom; dull or uninteresting: "The grown-ups made friends and talked their usual *boring* grown-up talk." (Jean Fritz)

boring writing If you can mentally see or hear what you want to write, discuss it with details, with "pictures." Professional writers try to start out in a dramatic way, as Stephen Crane does in "The Open Boat:" "None of them knew the color of the sky. Their eyes glanced level, and were fastened upon the waves that swept toward them. These waves were of the hue of slate, save for the tops, which were of foaming white, and all of the men knew the colors of the sea. The horizon narrowed and widened, and dipped and rose, and at all times its edge was jagged with waves that seemed thrust up in points like rocks." What would a boring writer do in this situation? Imagine shortening Crane's story as follows: "The men in the boat were tired. They just sat around waiting for something to happen, hoping to see shore or another boat." Not every writer can be clever or witty or inventive or widely traveled, of course. But any writer can ask himself, "Is this something I myself would stop to read?" If you answer "No," then start again.

born [bôrn] *verb.* a past participle of **bear²:** Andrew was *born* on January 8, 1980. —*adjective.* by birth or natural ability: Although Terry has never taken a lesson, it's clear she's a *born* musician.

born-a•gain [bôrn′ ə gen′] *adjective.* having a new, very strong faith in Jesus Christ. ◆ This word comes from the saying of Jesus in the Bible, "Except a man be *born again,* he cannot see the Kingdom of God."

borne [bôrn] *verb.* a past participle of **bear².**

bor•ough [bur′ō] *noun, plural* **boroughs. 1.** in some states, a town or village that governs itself. **2.** one of the five main sections of New York City.

bor•row [bär′ō] *verb,* **borrowed, borrowing. 1.** to take or get something with the understanding that it will later be returned to its owner: Janice *borrowed* two dollars from her friend because she forgot her lunch money. **2.** to take and use as one's own, adopt; English has *borrowed* many words from other languages.

bottlenecks A *bottleneck* is a term for a situation where a writer gets part of the way through a paper and then gets stuck. One way to avoid a bottleneck is to work in the form of complete drafts. Do your entire first draft before you try to produce anything in final form. The usual reason for a bottleneck is that the writer tries to develop a perfect finished version right away, and then becomes upset when this doesn't work. Read what famous writers have to say about writing—they know that the first draft can never be perfect.

bos•om [booz′ əm] *noun.* the chest or breast. —*adjective.* very close and dear: Those two boys are *bosom* buddies.

boss [bôs] *noun, plural* **bosses.** a person who tells others what to do; someone who is in charge: Who is her *boss* at work? —*verb,* **bossed, bossing.** to tell someone what to do; give orders: He started his own business because he didn't want to be *bossed* around by other people. ◆ A **bossy** person is someone who likes to tell others how to act.

Bos•ton [bôs′ tən] the capital of the state of Massachusetts. *Population:* 563,000.

bot•a•ny [bät′ ə nē] *noun.* the scientific study of plants. Botany includes the study of what kind of plants there are, what they are made of, how and where they grow, and how they can help or harm humans. ◆ A **botanist** is an expert in the field of botany. —**botanical,** *adjective:* A *botanical* garden is a large area where plants are displayed and studied.

both [bōth] *adjective.* the two; one as well as the other: *Both* girls are good ice skaters. —*pronoun.* the two together: Only one of the twins went to the party, although *both* were invited. —*conjunction; adverb.* together; equally: *Both* Japan and Germany sell a lot of cars in the United States. Aluminum is *both* light and strong.

both•er [bäth′ ər] *verb,* **bothered, bothering. 1.** to trouble or annoy: Don't *bother* Mom with so many questions while she's reading. **2.** to take the trouble to do something: I'm not going to *bother* to wash the car because it's supposed to rain this afternoon. "Let it alone, son! Don't you *bother* about it." (D.H. Lawrence) —*noun, plural* **bothers.** something that annoys or troubles: Would it be too much of a *bother* for you to give me a ride to school?

bot•tle [bät′ əl] *noun, plural* **bottles.** a glass or plastic container used to hold liquids. A bottle usually has a narrow neck through which the liquid can be poured and a cap or spout to seal it. —*verb,* **bottled, bottling,** to put in a bottle: to *bottle* soda or fruit juice. ◆ A company that bottles drinks is a **bottler.**

bot•tle•neck [bät′ əl nek′] *noun, plural* **bottle-necks. 1.** a narrow space in a road that cars must move through slowly, as if going through the neck of a bottle: "Traffic was pouring across and pedestrians were building up at the corner in a *bottleneck.*" (Stephen King) **2.** anything that slows progress or movement: They've been trying to finish that project for months, but they keep running into *bottlenecks.*

Boston The Boston Pops Orchestra is famous for its outdoor concerts on the banks of the Charles River.

bot•tom [bät′ əm] *noun, plural* **bottoms. 1.** the lowest part of something: the *bottom* of a box, the *bottom* of a bottle. **2.** land under water: The lake *bottom* was muddy and covered with weeds. **3.** the most basic part: "She wished . . . from the *bottom* of her heart that she had never left home." (James Baldwin) —*adjective.* lowest or last: The milk is on the *bottom* shelf of the refrigerator.

Pronunciation Key: Accent Marks

[′] is the normal accent mark. It shows where the main stress falls on a word.

[′] is a secondary accent mark. It shows a lighter stress than the primary accent. For example:

tel • e • vis • ion [tel′ə vizh′ən]

(Turn the page for more information.)

B

♦ Something that is **bottomless** has no bottom, or seems to have no bottom: a *bottomless* pit in the earth.

bottom line 1. the last line of a business report, showing how much money the company made or lost. **2.** *Informal.* the final result or most important part of something: The *bottom line* of the President's speech is that he is opposed to any plan to raise taxes.

bough [bou] *noun, plural* **boughs.** a large branch of a tree.

bought [bôt] *verb.* the past form of **buy.**

boul·der [bōl′dər] *noun, plural* **boulders.** a very large, rounded rock resting above or partly above the ground.

boul·e·vard [bool′ə värd′] *noun, plural* **boulevards.** a wide city street or avenue, often lined with trees.

boulevard The *Boulevard de Montmartre* in Paris, France, as painted by the famous French artist Camille Pissarro in 1897.

bounce [bouns] *verb,* **bounced, bouncing. 1.** to hit something and spring up or back: The ball *bounced* before the outfielder could catch it. **2.** *Informal.* to have a check returned by the bank without being paid: Since she had no money in her account, her check *bounced.* —*noun, plural* **bounces.** the act of bouncing; a jump or spring.

bound¹ [bound] *verb.* the past form of **bind:** This book has been *bound* with leather. —*adjective.* **1.** fastened by bonds or as if by bonds: The prisoner was *bound* to a chair. She's been house*bound* ever since she got the flu last week. **2.** certain; sure: We're *bound* to be late if we don't go faster. **3.** obliged or determined: "Run if you're *bound* to! You'll be glad enough to come back . . ." (Laura Ingalls Wilder)

bound² *verb,* **bounded, bounding. 1.** to leap or jump: "They saw a deer *bounding* away through the underbrush." (Vera Cleaver) **2.** to bounce back after striking something: The ball *bounded* off the backboard. —*noun, plural* **bounds.** a leap or jump.

bound³ *noun, plural* **bounds.** a limit or line marking the edge; boundary: The pass went over his head and out of *bounds.* That crude remark was beyond the *bounds* of good taste. —*verb,* **bounded, bounding.** to form the boundary of: "The river that *bounded* the meadow drew her like a charm." (Philippa Pearce)

bound⁴ *adjective.* intending to go; going: The train on Track 16 is *bound* for Philadelphia.

bound·a·ry [boun′drē] *noun, plural* **boundaries.** the limit or edge of something; a dividing line: the *boundary* between the U.S. and Canada, the *boundary* between science and religion.

boun·ty [boun′tē] *noun, plural* **bounties.** a reward for killing certain dangerous animals or capturing or killing an escaped criminal: That state has a *bounty* on coyotes.

bou·quet [bōō kā′ *or* bō kā′] *noun, plural* **bouquets. 1.** a bunch of flowers, especially when tied together and given as a gift. **2.** a delicate smell or aroma: the *bouquet* of a fine wine.

bout [bout] *noun, plural* **bouts. 1.** a match or contest: a boxing *bout.* **2.** a certain period of time, especially a period of illness: I had a *bout* of the flu last week.

bow The modern bow is a very exact scientific instrument.

bow¹ [bō] *noun, plural* **bows. 1.** a weapon that

shoots arrows, made of a thin piece of curved wood or other material, with a string called a **bowstring** tied from one end to the other. **2.** a knot with loops, as on a shoelace or on a ribbon for a gift or package. **3.** a stick of wood with a string stretched along its length, used to play a violin or other stringed instrument.

bow² [bou] *verb,* **bowed, bowing. 1.** to bend forward at the waist to show respect or politeness: Men are supposed to *bow* when they meet the Queen of England. **2.** to bend the head forward: She *bowed* her head in sorrow. **3.** to give in; submit: The school *bowed* to the parents' wishes and agreed to begin a new math program.

bow³ [bou] *noun, plural* **bows.** the front part of a boat or ship.

bow•els [bou′əls] *plural noun.* **1.** the INTESTINES. **2.** the deepest part of something: The miners worked in the *bowels* of the earth.

bowl² *verb,* **bowled, bowling. 1.** to play the game of bowling. ♦ A person who plays this game is a **bowler. 2.** to get a certain score in bowling: to *bowl* 300. **3. bowl over.** to knock down or surprise, as if with a rolling ball: The dog almost *bowled* me *over* when he ran by.

bow•leg•ged [bō leg′id] *adjective, more/most.* having legs that curve outward at the knees, as if in the shape of a bow.

bowl•ing [bō′ling] *noun.* a game played by rolling a heavy ball down a wooden lane known as a **bowling alley.** The object is to knock down ten wooden pins at the end of the alley.

box¹ [bäks] *noun, plural* **boxes. 1.** a container used to hold things. A box is shaped like a square or rectangle and has four sides, a bottom, and a top or opening. Boxes can be made of wood, cardboard, or other material. **2.** the amount a box contains: He ate a *box* of crackers. **3.** a special closed-in area like a box: the

---

bowl *Bowl* comes from the Latin word *bulla,* meaning "bubble." The idea is that a bubble looks like a small ball. The word *boil* comes from *bulla,* too, because water forms bubbles as it boils. If you look at *bulla,* you can see that it's also very close to another common English word, *bullet.* But a modern bullet isn't round like a ball. Do you think the word is connected to *bulla* anyway? Why not read something about what early bullets were like and see what you think then?

---

bowl¹ [bōl] *noun, plural* **bowls. 1.** a rounded, hollow dish or container: a soup *bowl,* a salad *bowl,* a mixing *bowl.* **2.** any bowl-shaped part or place: the *bowl* of a spoon. **3.** a large, rounded stadium for football and other sports events: The Miami Dolphins play their home games in the Orange *Bowl.* **4.** a football game played after the regular season between two specially-invited teams. The first games of this kind were played in the Rose Bowl stadium in Pasadena, California, near Los Angeles.

bowl The Rose Bowl is the site of the oldest and most famous bowl game in college football.

batter's *box* in baseball, a *box* in a theater. —*verb,* **boxed, boxing.** to put in a box: The movers *boxed* the dishes and glasses carefully.

box² *verb,* **boxed, boxing. 1.** to take part in the sport of boxing. **2.** to hit with the open hand or fist: to *box* someone on the ear.

box•car [bäks′kär] *noun, plural* **boxcars.** a box-shaped railroad car, used for carrying freight.

box•er [bäks′ər] *noun, plural* **boxers. 1.** a person who takes part in the sport of boxing. **2.** a medium-sized dog with a short, smooth tan or brownish coat, a sturdy build, and a short, square face.

box•ing [bäks′ing] *noun.* the sport of fighting with the fists according to certain rules.

boy [boi] *noun, plural* **boys.** a male child who is not yet a man or adult.

Pronunciation Key: A–F			
a	and; hat	ch	chew; such
ā	ate; stay	d	dog; lid
â	care; air	e	end; yet
ä	father; hat	ē	she; each
b	boy; cab	f	fun; off

(Turn the page for more information.)

B

> **boycott** *Boycott* comes from a person's name. Captain Charles Boycott was an Englishman who lived in Ireland in 1880. At that time, Englishmen owned much of the Irish farmland and many Irish farmers paid rent to the English. Most often, these English landlords did not even live in Ireland and therefore used agents to collect the rent. Captain Boycott was one such agent. As a form of protest against him, the Irish together refused to pay him the rents, would not sell food or goods to his household, and would not speak to him or his family. Nowadays, if one boycotts a company, or even a whole nation, one is protesting against it and hoping to change it. For other "people words," look up *braille, pasteurize,* and *volt.*

boy•cott [boi′kät′] *noun, plural* **boycotts.** a plan by many people to refuse to do business or have dealings with someone. People carry on a boycott as a way of protesting something or of forcing a change in policy. —*verb,* **boycotted, boycotting.** to take part in a boycott: In 1955–56 the black people of Montgomery, Alabama *boycotted* the city bus lines because they were not allowed to sit in the front of the bus.

boy•hood [boi′hood′] *noun, plural* **boyhoods.** the time of life when one is a boy.

boy•ish [boi′ish] *adjective, more/most.* of or like a boy; fit for boys: a *boyish* grin, *boyish* energy. —**boyishly,** *adverb.*

brace•let [brās′lit] *noun, plural* **bracelets.** a small band or chain worn as an ornament around the wrist, arm, or ankle.

brack•et [brak′it] *noun, plural* **brackets. 1.** a piece of wood or metal that is fastened to a wall to hold something up. **2.** one of a pair of symbols [ ] that are used to enclose numbers, letters, or words. **3.** a group or category into which something can be placed: the 12 to 16 age *bracket,* the 50% income tax *bracket.* —*verb,* **bracketed, bracketing. 1.** to put numbers or words in brackets. **2.** to place together in the same group: Students are often *bracketed* for spelling lessons by how they do in reading.

> **brackets** Brackets look like this: [ ] Parentheses look like this: ( ) There is a simple rule on the difference between them. Parentheses are part of a sentence—sometimes a whole sentence is put in parentheses. They are meant to be read like the other text. For example: "Cathy took his remarks (and his note) to mean he was satisfied." But brackets are working tools, so to speak. An editor correcting an article will use brackets to make comments, as will a writer giving instructions to a typist. "[Don't underline any of the words.]"

boy scout a member of the **Boy Scouts,** an organization that teaches boys outdoor skills, physical fitness, and good citizenship.

brace [brās] *noun, plural* **braces. 1.** something used as a support or to hold things together: She put a wooden *brace* under the shelf so that it would hold the heavy books. He wore a *brace* on his leg to help him in walking. **2. braces.** a set of wires and bands used to straighten the teeth. **3.** a handle used to hold a drill or bit. **4.** a pair, especially a pair of animals: The hunter shot a *brace* of pheasants. —*verb,* **braced, bracing. 1.** to hold or make steady; give strength or support: "One hand was on his hip and the other *braced* his knee, as though he had a pain in his side." (Virginia Hamilton) **2.** to prepare for something difficult or for a shock: *Brace* yourself, I have to tell you some bad news. **3.** to fill with energy; refresh: She likes to take a cold, *bracing* shower when she gets up in the morning.

brag [brag] *verb,* **bragged, bragging.** to speak highly about yourself or what you have done;

brace A brace can be used to aid in walking for a person who has a physical disorder.

praise yourself too much; boast. ◆ A person who brags a lot is a **braggart** [brag′ərt].

Brahms [brämz] **Johannes** [yō hä′nəs], 1833–1897, German composer and pianist.

braid [brād] *noun, plural* **braids.** a strip made by weaving or twisting together three or more long pieces of cloth, hair, or other material. —*verb,* **braided, braiding.** to make a braid: The swimmer *braided* her hair to keep it out of her eyes.

braille Louis Braille, who invented the Braille alphabet, was himself blind from the age of three.

braille [brāl] *noun.* a system of printing and writing for blind people. Braille consists of six raised dots used in many combinations to represent letters, words, and so on. Blind people read by touching the dots with their fingertips.

brain [brān] *noun, plural* **brains. 1.** a large, soft mass of grayish nerves and tissue inside the skull. The brain is the center of the NERVOUS SYSTEM in humans and animals. It controls our thoughts and actions. **2. brains.** the mind; intelligence. **3.** *Informal.* a very intelligent person: Todd is a real *brain* at math. —*verb,* **brained, braining.** to hit someone hard on the head.

brain•wash [brān′wäsh′ *or* brān′wôsh′] *verb,* **brainwashed, brainwashing. 1.** to force someone to change his beliefs by putting great mental pressure on him: While the soldier was in a prison camp, he was *brainwashed* into becoming a spy for the enemy. **2.** to persuade someone in an unfair or deceptive way: This book claims that TV commercials *brainwash* people into buying things they don't need.

brake¹ [brāk] *noun, plural* **brakes.** a part that stops or slows a turning wheel or a moving vehicle, such as a bicycle, car, or train. —*verb,* **braked, braking.** to slow down or stop something by using a brake or brakes: "His car almost went over the side of a hill . . . but he *braked* just in time." (Paul Zindel)

brake² *noun, plural* **brakes.** an area covered by bushes and shrubs.

bram•ble [bram′bəl] *noun, plural* **brambles.** a bush or rough shrub with thorns or prickly stems, such as a blackberry bush.

bran [bran] *noun.* the ground-up outer shells or husks of grain. Bran from wheat, rye, or corn is used in cereal, flour, and bread.

branch [branch] *noun, plural* **branches. 1.** a part of a tree that grows out from the trunk. **2.** anything that is thought of as coming out from the main part, as a branch does from a tree: a *branch* of a railroad. Our town has a main library downtown and several *branches* in other neighborhoods. **3.** any part or division: Botany is a *branch* of biology. **4.** a place in a computer program where there is a choice of one or more steps. —*verb,* **branched, branching. 1.** to divide or separate from the main part: This road *branches* off from the main highway just outside the city. **2. branch out.** to extend or add to something: Because her restaurant was so popular, she decided to *branch out* and open two more.

brand [brand] *noun, plural* **brands. 1.** a type or kind of something: a *brand* of soap. That's my favorite *brand* of potato chips. ◆ The name of a particular product made by a certain company is a **brand name:** "Ivory" is the *brand name* for a well-known kind of soap. **2.** a mark or sign made with a hot iron on the skin of cattle or other animals to show who owns them. In former times, a similar mark was burned on the skin of a criminal as a sign of disgrace. —*verb,* **branded, branding. 1.** to put a brand on: to *brand* cattle. **2.** to be marked or identified in a bad way: The soldier was *branded* a coward after he ran away before a battle.

brand-new [brand′ noo *or* bran′ noo′] *adjective.* completely new: a *brand-new* car, a *brand-new* building.

Pronunciation Key: G–N			
g	give; big	k	kind; cat; back
h	hold	l	let; ball
i	it; this	m	make; time
ī	ice; my	n	not; own
j	jet; gem; edge	ng	having

(Turn the page for more information.)

B

breaking sentences into parts
Simple sentences have, usually, a noun and verb without any additions: "I went home." Compound sentences usually are two statements connected by an "and" or "but" and tend to have either a comma or semi-colon. Complex sentences are more complicated than compound ones and involve phrases and clauses. Here's a use of "but": "It was slow work for one man at a time, *but* they were unwilling to leave Kaph by himself." (Ursula K. LeGuin) Here's a use of a semi-colon: "The eastbound train was plowing through a January snowstorm; the dull dawn was beginning to show gray . . ." (Willa Cather) Here's a use of a dash: "He had had the one chance that all men have—he had had the chance of life." (Henry James) What punctuation would you use here? "Harry was alert but not fearful and he could think clearly even as the sound came nearer." [ANSWER: Comma after "fearful."]

brass [bras] *noun.* a yellow metal made of copper and zinc melted together. Brass can be made into various shapes and is used to make ornaments, bowls, musical instruments, and other things.

brave [brāv] *adjective,* **braver, bravest.** having the will to do something dangerous; showing courage; bold: The *brave* girl rescued her little brother from the burning house. "Few there were *brave* enough to visit a house at the edge of a graveyard." (Meindert DeJong) —*verb,* **braved, braving.** to face danger in a brave way; take risks: He *braved* the snowstorm to find the lost campers. —*noun, plural* **braves.** an American Indian warrior.

brav•er•y [brāv′rē] *noun.* the quality of being brave; courage.

brawl [brôl] *noun, plural* **brawls.** a wild, noisy argument or fight: There was a *brawl* at the end of the hockey game. —*verb,* **brawled, brawling.** to fight or argue loudly.

Bra•zil [brə zil′] the largest country in South America. *Capital:* Brasilia. *Area:* 3,286,400 square miles. *Population:* 128,900,000. **—Brazilian,** *adjective; noun.*

breach [brēch] *noun, plural* **breaches. 1.** a gap or opening made by a break in something: The soldiers charged through a *breach* in the enemy lines. **2.** a breaking of a law or promise. In law, **breach of contract** means the failure to obey the terms of a contract. —*verb,* **breached, breaching.** to make an opening in; break through.

bread [bred] *noun, plural* **breads. 1.** a food made by mixing flour or meal with water or milk and then baking it in an oven. **2.** the food needed to live: our daily *bread.* —*verb,* **breaded, breading.** to coat food with bread crumbs for cooking: to *bread* fish.

breadth [bredth] *noun.* the distance from side to side; width.

break [brāk] *verb,* **broke, broken, breaking. 1.** to make something come apart in pieces; smash, split, or crack: to *break* a glass, to *break* the shell of an egg, to *break* a bone in one's leg. **2.** to come apart; go into pieces: That cup will *break* if she drops it. **3.** to make or become useless or damaged: Stop fooling around with the radio or you'll *break* it. **4.** to fail to keep or obey: to *break* a promise, to *break* the law. **5.** to do better than: to *break* the school record in a race. **6.** to change or become weaker: Her voice *broke* as she read the sad letter. He's trying to *break* the habit of biting his nails.

—*noun, plural* **breaks. 1.** a broken place: a *break* in a bone, a *break* in a wall. "People lived as they had always done; there was no *break* between past and present." (V.S. Naipaul) **2.** the act of breaking: a jail *break,* a *break* in the weather, the *break* of day. They stopped work and took a *break* for lunch. **3.** a chance or opportunity: a lucky *break.* "I might have been given a bad *break,* but I've got an awful lot to live for." (Lou Gehrig)

break down 1. to fail to work; stop working: The car *broke down* on the highway. **2.** to become very upset: The witness *broke down* and cried when he tried to describe how the crash happened.

break in 1. to go in by force: Someone *broke in* last night and stole our TV set. **2.** to get ready for use or work: to *break in* a new baseball glove. **3.** to interrupt: Several reporters *broke in* with questions as the mayor read his statement.

break into to go in by force: to *break into* a bank vault.

break out 1. to have a rash or other disorder on the skin. **2.** to begin suddenly: The fire *broke out* in the storeroom. "Suddenly he *broke out* into loud sobs." (Somerset Maugham) **3.** to escape: to *break out* of jail.

break up 1. to separate or scatter into parts: The fog should *break up* by noon. **2.** to bring or come to an end: to *break up* a fight. The marriage *broke up*. **3.** to laugh or cause to laugh: That TV show always *breaks* me *up*.

break•down [brāk′ doun′] *noun, plural* **breakdowns. 1.** the failure to work, move, or act properly: The car had a *breakdown* on the road. **2.** a failing in health, especially a mental collapse; also known as a **nervous breakdown.**

breaker Powerful breakers crash against the rocks at Point Lobos, Monterey, California.

break•er [brā′ kər] *noun, plural* **breakers. 1.** a wave that breaks on shore or on a rock. **2.** any person or thing that breaks: A circuit *breaker* stops the flow of electricity through a circuit.

breath [breth] *noun, plural* **breaths. 1.** the air that is taken into the lungs and forced out when breathing. **2.** the ability to breathe easily: She lost her *breath* as she climbed the steep hill. **3.** a slight breeze: "There was no sound but the *breath* of the south wind." (Marjorie Kinnan Rawlings)

breathe [brēth] *verb,* **breathed, breathing. 1.** to take air into the lungs and force it out: He was *breathing* heavily after running so hard. **2.** to say quietly; whisper: Don't *breathe* a word of this to anybody or I'll get into a lot of trouble.

bred [bred] *verb.* the past form of **breed:** "This is the place I was born, *bred,* and raised." (Sam Shepard)

breech•es [brich′ əz] *plural noun.* an old-fashioned style of trousers that end or are fastened at the knees.

breed [brēd] *verb,* **bred, breeding. 1.** to produce young: Many wild animals will not *breed* when they are kept in zoos. **2.** to raise animals or plants of a particular type: to *breed* hunting dogs, to *breed* roses. **3.** to bring up; train: She's been *bred* to be well-mannered and polite. **4.** to bring about; cause: Some people believe that slum areas *breed* crime. —*noun, plural* **breeds.** a particular type of animal or plant: Collies are a *breed* of dog.

breed•ing [brē′ ding] *noun.* **1.** the act of producing young. **2.** the way someone is taught to behave: a person of good *breeding*.

breakfast *Breakfast* literally means "to break the fast." A "fast" is a time when a person avoids eating, usually for religious reasons. *Breakfast* came about because sleeping hours are like fasting hours—you don't eat during such a time. Hence, people called the first meal of the day "a breaking of the fast," although nothing religious was involved. "Break" lends itself to many meanings beyond the mere tearing, crushing, or snapping of things. "Breakdown" is used when a political meeting doesn't reach a conclusion. It can also refer to a person's suffering a "mental" disorder. "Breakup" can refer to the abrupt ending of a partnership, business, or friendship.

break•fast [brek′ fəst] *noun, plural* **breakfasts.** the first meal of the day; the morning meal.

break•through [brāk′ thrōō] *noun, plural* **breakthroughs.** a sudden finding or advance: Dr. Jonas Salk's experiments led to a *breakthrough* in preventing polio.

breast [brest] *noun, plural* **breasts. 1.** the front part of the body from the neck to stomach; the chest. **2.** a gland in women and female animals that gives milk.

breast•bone [brest′ bōn′] *noun, plural* **breastbones.** the long narrow bone at the front of the chest to which the ribs are attached.

breeze [brēz] *noun, plural* **breezes. 1.** a light, gentle wind: A warm *breeze* blew in from the ocean. **2.** *Informal.* something easy to do: Passing the test was a *breeze* for him because he studied so hard. —**breezy,** *adjective.*

Pronunciation Key: O–S			
ō	over; go	ou	out; town
ô	all; law	p	put; hop
oo	look; full	r	run; car
ōō	pool; who	s	set; miss
oi	oil; boy	sh	show

(Turn the page for more information.)

brew [brōō] *verb,* **brewed, brewing. 1.** to make beer, ale, or a similar drink by soaking, boiling, and FERMENTING malt or hops. **2.** to prepare other drinks such as tea or coffee by soaking or boiling. **3.** to begin to take form; start to happen: A strike is *brewing* at the factory because the workers are very unhappy. —*noun, plural* **brews.** beer or another drink made by brewing.

bri•ar [brī′ ər] *noun, plural* **briars.** (also spelled **brier**) a bush or plant with many thorns, such as a wild rose or blackberry.

bribe [brīb] *noun, plural* **bribes.** an offer of money or something valuable in return for doing something wrong: The dishonest salesman offered the mayor a *bribe* to get the city to buy products from his company. —*verb,* **bribed, bribing.** to give or offer a bribe: He tried to *bribe* the policeman to tear up the traffic ticket he got for speeding.

brick [brik] *noun, plural* **bricks. 1.** a block of clay that has been baked to make it hard. Bricks are used in making walls, fireplaces, sidewalks, and so on. **2.** a set or group of bricks: a red *brick* schoolhouse. **3.** any object shaped like a brick: a *brick* of cheese. —*verb,* **bricked, bricking.** to cover or close up with bricks: They *bricked* up the opening in the wall.

brick A bricklayer uses mortar to hold bricks together. The bricks are laid in rows called *courses,* according to a pattern called a *bond.* (This is American bond.)

bride [brīd] *noun, plural* **brides.** a woman who is about to be married or who was just married. —**bridal,** *adjective:* a white *bridal* gown.

bride•groom [brīd′ grōōm′] *noun, plural* **bridegrooms.** a man who is about to be married or who was just married.

bridge [brij] *noun, plural* **bridges. 1.** a structure that crosses a river, valley, road, or other obstacle so that people can go from one side to the other. **2.** the bony upper part of the nose. **3.**

a platform above the main deck of a ship. **4.** a card game played by two pairs of partners. —*verb,* **bridged, bridging. 1.** to make a bridge over: to *bridge* a river. **2.** to go across or over: The company is coming out with a new computer to *bridge* the gap between their high-priced office model and their cheaper home computer.

bridge The Golden Gate Bridge stretches 4200 feet across San Francisco Bay to join San Francisco to Marin County.

bri•dle [brīd′ əl] *noun, plural* **bridles.** the part of a horse's harness that fits around its head and is used to guide and control it. A bridle is made up of a BIT, straps to hold the bit in the horse's mouth, and REINS. —*verb,* **bridled, bridling. 1.** to put a bridle on: to *bridle* a horse. **2.** to hold back; keep in control; restrain: She had to *bridle* her anger when the boys made fun of her.

brief [brēf] *adjective,* **briefer, briefest.** short in time or length: The minister made a few *brief* announcements at the end of the service. "The woman pushed back in her chair for a *brief* second" (William Armstrong) —*verb,* **briefed, briefing.** to give information or instructions: The commander *briefed* his pilots just before their mission. —*noun, plural* **briefs.** in law, a summary of facts or arguments to be used by a lawyer in preparing a court case. —**briefly,** *adverb.*

brief•case [brēf′ kās′] *noun, plural* **briefcases.** a flat case with a handle, used for carrying business or school papers, books, and other such items.

bri•er [brī′ ər] *noun, plural* **briers.** see **briar.**

brig [brig] *noun, plural* **brigs. 1.** a sailing ship having two masts and square sails. **2.** a navy prison, especially one on a ship.

B

bri•gade [bri gād′] *noun, plural* **brigades. 1.** a large unit of troops in the army. **2.** a group of people organized for a certain purpose: Steve's dad serves in a volunteer fire *brigade.*

bright [brīt] *adjective,* **brighter, brightest. 1.** giving off or showing much light; shining: "The *bright* sunlight of an April morning woke her." (Langston Hughes) "Marian saw the old woman's eyes grow *bright* and turn toward her." (Eudora Welty) ◆ This meaning is also used as an adverb: The stars were shining *bright.* **2.** strong in color: Mr. Wilson's new car is *bright* red. **3.** smart; clever: The students in that class are very *bright.* —**brightly,** *adverb:* Margaret smiled *brightly* as she opened her birthday presents. —**brightness,** *noun:* the *brightness* of the sun on a clear day.

bril•liant [bril′ yənt] *adjective,* more/most. **1.** shining brightly; sparkling: a *brilliant* light, a *brilliant* diamond. **2.** excellent; outstanding: The actress who played Lady Macbeth gave a *brilliant* performance. **3.** very intelligent: a *brilliant* idea. Albert Einstein was a *brilliant* scientist.

brim [brim] *noun, plural* **brims. 1.** the upper edge of a glass, cup, bowl, or similar container: The pitcher of lemonade was filled to the *brim.* **2.** the outer edge of something: Cowboy hats have a wide *brim.* —*verb,* **brimmed, brimming.** to fill to the brim; overflow: "My eyes were so *brimming* with sunlight I couldn't see anything." (Nancy Willard)

brine [brīn] *noun.* **1.** water that is very salty. Brine is used to preserve and store pickles and other foods. **2.** the ocean; sea water.

bring about to make happen; cause: Computers will *bring about* many changes in the way businesses are run.

bring out to present to the public: That studio is *bringing out* five new movies this month.

bring up 1. to care for or raise a child: She's been *brought up* to be very polite to adults. **2.** to mention; suggest: I'll *bring up* the subject at the next meeting.

brink [bringk] *noun, plural* **brinks. 1.** the upper edge or top of a steep place: The mountain climber stood at the *brink* of the cliff. **2.** the point or moment just before something is likely to happen: two countries at the *brink* of war.

brisk [brisk] *adjective,* **brisker, briskest. 1.** quick and active; lively: The men were walking at a *brisk* pace. **2.** cool and refreshing: "*Brisk* winds were blowing every which way." (John Hersey) —**briskly,** *adverb:* "He began to walk *briskly* up Fifth Avenue." (F. Scott Fitzgerald)

bris•tle [bris′ əl] *noun, plural* **bristles.** a short, stiff hair, as on a hog or other animal. Bristles are used to make brushes. —*verb,* **bristled, bristling. 1.** to have the hairs on the back rise stiffly when excited or angry: "The strange dog stood *bristling* and showing his teeth." (Laura Ingalls Wilder) **2.** to stand up straight like bristles: The young soldier's hair was cut so short it *bristled.*

Brit•ish [brit′ ish] *adjective.* having to do with Great Britain. —*noun.* **the British.** the people of Great Britain.

British Co•lum•bi•a [kə lum′ bē ə] a province of western Canada. *Capital:* Victoria. *Area:* 366,300 square miles. *Population:* 2,750,000.

---

bring/take There is a small difference between the words *bring* and *take.* The idea is one of direction. You bring something to a place as in "Bring in the mail." You take something away from a place as in "Take out the garbage." This is a good distinction, but, as often happens in language, there are idioms or sayings that differ from the ordinary use of words. We speak of "take-home pay," "taking in money," or of a store "taking on new workers." One way to test a choice of words is to say them aloud. Does it sound right to say "Please take that can of peanuts to me"?

---

bring [bring] *verb,* **brought, bringing. 1.** to take along or carry with one: Don't forget to *bring* enough money with you on the trip. Katie *brings* her lunch to school every day. **2.** to cause to come about or happen: Winter *brings* colder weather. **3.** to cause to reach a certain state or condition: to *bring* a car to a stop, to *bring* water to a boil. He couldn't *bring* himself to tell her what had really happened. **4.** to sell for: That house will *bring* a high price if it's ever put on the market.

brit•tle [brit′ əl] *adjective,* more/most. hard and easily broken; breaking with a snap: "In the

Pronunciation Key: T–Z			
t	ten; date	v	very; live
th	think	w	win; away
th	these	y	you
u	cut; butter	z	zoo; cause
ur	turn; bird	zh	measure

(Turn the page for more information.)

winter the wash would become as *brittle* as glass and almost break when touched." (I.B. Singer)

broad [brôd] *adjective,* **broader, broadest. 1.** large from side to side: The school playground covers a *broad* area. "A *broad* stretch of coast lay before the eyes of the men." (Stephen Crane) **2.** large in range; not limited: The senator's speech took a *broad* view of the problem of world hunger. **3.** bright and clear. ◆ This meaning is used in the phrase **broad daylight:** His bike was stolen from in front of his house in *broad daylight.*

broad•cast [brôd′kast′] *verb,* **broadcasted, broadcasting. 1.** to send out programs or information by radio or television. **2.** to make something known over a wide area: The rumor that the company was moving to a new city was quickly *broadcast* all over the building. —*noun, plural* **broadcasts.** a program sent out to the public by radio or television: a news *broadcast.*

broc•co•li [bräk′ə lē] *noun, plural* **broccoli.** a plant whose thick green stems are eaten as a vegetable.

broil [broil] *verb,* **broiled, broiling. 1.** to cook very close to a fire or other source of heat: He *broiled* the fish on an outdoor grill. **2.** to be very hot: Desert animals come out at night to avoid the *broiling* heat of the daytime.

broil•er [broi′lər] *noun, plural* **broilers. 1.** the part of a stove that is used for broiling. **2.** a young chicken for broiling.

broke [brōk] *verb.* the past tense of **break:** He got a ticket when he *broke* the speed limit on the highway. —*adjective. Informal.* having little or no money: I'd like to go to the movies with you, but I can't—I'm *broke.*

bron•chi•al tubes [bräng′kē əl] *noun.* the tubes that connect the windpipe and lungs. Air flows to and from the lungs through the bronchial tubes.

bron•chi•tis [bräng kī′təs] *noun.* a soreness and swelling in the bronchial tubes causing a cough and chest pains.

brontosaurus The brontosaurus was up to 67 feet long and weighed about 30 tons. It spent much of its time standing in water to help support its weight.

bron•to•sau•rus [brän′tə sôr′əs] *noun, plural* **brontosauruses.** a huge, plant-eating dinosaur with a very small head and a long neck and tail.

bronze [bränz] *noun.* **1.** a hard metal made of copper and tin, used for statues, medals, jewelry, and machine parts. **2.** a reddish-brown color like that of bronze. —*adjective.* reddish-brown. —*verb,* **bronzed, bronzing.** to make the color of bronze: His skin was *bronzed* from months of working outdoors.

---

broke How can you write good English at one moment and poor English at another with the same word? We are back to idioms, which are sayings commonly used. "If it's not broke, don't fix it." This idiom means, "Don't change something just for the sake of change" (you'll probably end up making things worse). "I didn't wake up on time this morning because my alarm clock was broke," is not at all the same sort of use. Your reader will think you haven't been studying English. "Broken" is needed here, not "broke." Here are other "broke" idioms: "He went broke." "She was broke, penniless."

---

bro•ken [brō′kən] *verb.* the past participle of **break:** Three state records were *broken* in last week's track meet. —*adjective.* **1.** that has or shows a break: *broken* glass. There was a *broken* yellow line down the center of the road. **2.** damaged or ruined as if by a break: a *broken* promise, a *broken* heart. He was a *broken* man after his business failed.

brooch [brōch] *noun, plural* **brooches.** a large piece of jewelry fastened to the clothing with a clasp or pin.

brood [brood] *noun, plural* **broods. 1.** all the young birds that are hatched from eggs laid at the same time by one mother: The hen watched over her *brood* of chicks. **2.** *Informal.* all the children in one family.

B

—*verb,* **brooded, brooding. 1.** to sit on eggs so that they will hatch. **2.** to worry or think about something for a long time: "I stared up at the star-studded sky and *brooded* about what there was before the creation of the world." (I.B. Singer)

brook [brook] *noun, plural* **brooks.** a small stream of fresh water.

brook A small brook cuts a crooked path through this meadow in the Rocky Mountains of Canada.

broom [broom] *noun, plural* **brooms. 1.** a brush with a long handle, used for sweeping. **2.** a bush with yellow flowers, small leaves, and thin branches. In early times brooms were made from these branches.

broth [brôth] *noun, plural* **broths.** a thin soup made from the water used to cook meat, fish, or vegetables.

broth•er [bruth′ ər] *noun, plural* **brothers. 1.** a boy or man who has the same parents as another person. **2.** a male member of the same group or club. **3.** a male member of a religious order who is not a priest.

broth•er•hood [bruth′ ər hood′] *noun, plural* **brotherhoods. 1.** the state of being a brother or brothers. **2.** a group of people who are part of the same club or group.

broth•er-in-law [bruth′ ər ən lô′] *noun, plural* **brothers-in-law. 1.** the brother of one's husband or wife. **2.** the husband of one's sister.

brought [brôt] *verb.* the past form of **bring.** "Miss Dietrich was the kind of teacher who *brought* out the best in her students." (Langston Hughes)

brow [brou] *noun, plural* **brows. 1.** the part of the face between the eyes and the hair; the forehead. **2.** the eyebrow. **3.** the upper edge of a steep place: "An old horse appeared over the *brow* of a hill." (John Steinbeck)

brown [broun] *noun, plural* **browns.** a dark color like that of coffee, chocolate, or mud. —*verb,* **browned, browning.** to make or become brown: She *browned* the meat before putting it in the stew.

Brown [broun] **John,** 1800–1859, American leader of an anti-slavery movement.

brown•ie [brou′ nē] *noun, plural* **brownies. 1.** a small flat chocolate cake that usually has nuts in it. **2.** a kind elf in fairy tales who does good things for people. **3. Brownie.** a girl who belongs to the junior division of the Girl Scouts.

browse [brouz] *verb,* **browsed, browsing. 1.** to look through or at something in a casual way: "I *browse* around, picking a book off the shelf, skimming it, then putting it back." (Judy Blume) **2.** to feed on grass, leaves, or twigs: We could see the deer *browsing* in the meadow.

bruise [brooz] *noun, plural* **bruises. 1.** an injury to the body that does not break the skin but leaves a black and blue mark. **2.** a similar injury to the outside of a fruit, vegetable, or plant. —*verb,* **bruised, bruising.** to cause a bruise on: The grocer accidentally *bruised* the apples by dropping them. "The children were filthy and *bruised,* but none of them had a single cut or scratch." (John Hersey)

bru•nette [broo net′] *adjective.* brown or dark-brown in color: *brunette* hair. —*noun, plural* **brunettes.** a person with dark-brown hair.

brush¹ [brush] *noun, plural* **brushes.** a tool used to sweep, clean, smooth, or paint something. Brushes are made of bristles, wire, or hair attached to a handle. —*verb,* **brushed, brushing. 1.** to sweep, clean, smooth, or paint with a brush: to *brush* one's hair, to *brush* one's teeth. **2.** to touch lightly in passing: "I held open the door and she *brushed* past me without a word." (James Herriott)

brush² *noun, plural* **brushes. 1.** an area where small trees, shrubs, and bushes grow together: We saw a rabbit hiding in the *brush.* **2.** branches or twigs that are broken off from trees.

Pronunciation Key: [ə] Symbol

The [ə] or *schwa* sound occurs in syllables without an accent. It can be spelled with any vowel, such as a in above, e in listen, i in pencil, o in melon, u in circus. It can also be a combination of vowels, such as io in action, ai in mountain, iou in precious.

(Turn the page for more information.)

B

bru·tal [brōōt′ əl] *adjective, more/most.* like a brute; cruel or savage: The soldiers made a *brutal* attack on the village. ◆ The state of being brutal is **brutality:** The man claimed that after he was arrested he was a victim of police *brutality.*

brute [brōōt] *noun, plural* **brutes. 1.** an animal, as opposed to a human; a beast. **2.** a savage or cruel person. —*adjective.* of or like a brute; without mind or feeling: They were helpless against the *brute* force of the tornado.

bub·ble [bub′ əl] *noun, plural* **bubbles. 1.** a round, thin film of liquid shaped like a ball and filled with air or gas. Bubbles often form from soapy water and can float in the air. **2.** a round space filled with air or gas inside a liquid or solid: There are *bubbles* in these ice cubes. —*verb,* **bubbled, bubbling.** to form bubbles: "She lifted the lid of the *bubbling* kettle." (Laura Ingalls Wilder)

Bu·chan·an [byōō kan′ ən] **James,** 1791–1868, the fifteenth president of the United States, from 1857 to 1861.

buck [buk] *noun, plural* **bucks. 1.** the male of deer and certain other animals, such as an antelope, rabbit, or goat. **2.** *Slang.* a dollar: I asked Jimmy to lend me a *buck* for a hot dog. —*verb,* **bucked, bucking. 1.** to jump suddenly with the back arched and the head down: The horse *bucked* and threw its rider to the ground. **2.** to move in a sudden, jerky way: "The car *bucked* a few times and then roared down the street." (Louise Fitzhugh)

buck·et [buk′ it] *noun, plural* **buckets.** a deep, round container with a handle, used for carrying water, dirt, sand, and other things.

buck·le [buk′ əl] *noun, plural* **buckles.** a fastening that holds together the two ends of something, such as a belt or strap. —*verb,* **buckled, buckling. 1.** to fasten with a buckle: We *buckled* our seat belts before the plane took off. **2.** to bend or bulge: His knees *buckled* when he tried to lift the heavy box. The road *buckled* in the desert heat. **3. buckle down.** to work very hard: They *buckled down* and got the job finished.

buck·skin [buk′ skin′] *noun, plural* **buckskins.** a soft leather with a yellowish-tan color, made from the skin of a deer or sheep.

buck·wheat [buk′ wēt′] *noun, plural* **buckwheats.** a plant with small seeds that are ground into flour or that are used as feed for animals.

bud [bud] *noun, plural* **buds.** a small growth or swelling on a plant that will later develop into a flower, leaf, or branch. —*verb,* **budded, budding.** to form or put forth buds: "The trees were freshly *budded* out with pale blooms." (Katherine Anne Porter) —**budding,** *adjective.* beginning to grow or develop: Michael is a *budding* star in basketball.

Bu·da·pest [bōōd′ ə pest′] the capital of Hungary. *Population:* 2,075,000.

Bud·dha [bōōd′ ə] 563?–483 B.C., the founder of the Buddhist religion.

Buddha The Golden Buddha, a statue in a Buddhist temple in Thailand.

Bud·dhism [bōō′ diz əm] *noun.* the religion founded by BUDDHA and based on his teachings. Buddhism is an important religion in many countries of Asia. ◆ A follower of Buddhism is known as a **Buddhist** [bōō′ dist].

bud·dy [bud′ ē] *noun, plural* **buddies.** *Informal.* a very close friend; pal.

budge [buj] *verb,* **budged, budging.** to cause something to move a little: We couldn't *budge* the heavy rock. We asked him to change his mind, but he just won't *budge.*

budg·et [buj′ it] *noun, plural* **budgets.** a plan for spending money. A budget shows how much money is expected to be spent for certain things within a certain time. —*verb,* **budgeted, budgeting.** to plan in or as if in a budget: The publishing company *budgeted* $100,000 to pay for advertising that new book. Jennifer has to *budget* her time better so she won't have to stay up so late doing her homework. ◆ Budget once meant a bag used to carry money. When a government spent money, it was said to "open the budget."

Bue·nos Ai·res [bwā′ nəs âr′ ēz] the capital of Argentina. *Population:* 2,950,000.

buff [buf] *noun, plural* **buffs. 1.** a soft, strong leather made from the skin of a buffalo or ox. **2.** a yellowish-brown color like that of this leather. **3.** a person who is very interested in some activity or subject: a computer *buff*, a science fiction *buff*. —*adjective.* yellowish-brown. —*verb,* **buffed, buffing.** to polish or shine something with or as if with this kind of leather: He *buffed* his shoes with a rag.

buf•fa•lo [buf′ ə lō] *noun, plural* **buffalo** or **buffaloes. 1.** a large. wild ox of North America, having a humped back and a large, shaggy head with short horns. ◆ This animal is more correctly known as a BISON. **2.** any of several kinds of large wild oxen with long, curving horns, found in Asia and Africa.

buffalo This African Cape buffalo lives near water. It has horns that meet like a helmet on top of its head.

Buf•fa•lo [buf′ ə lō] a city in western New York State, on Lake Erie. *Population:* 358,000.
Buf•fa•lo Bill [buf′ ə lō bil′] 1846–1917, American army scout and showman. His real name was **William F. Cody.**
buff•er [buf′ ər] *noun, plural* **buffers. 1.** something that comes between two things to soften a blow or shock: The teacher listened to each boy's complaints about the other and tried to act as a *buffer* between them. **2.** a small country that serves as a barrier between two larger countries that are in conflict; also known as a **buffer state** or **zone. 3.** a storage area in a computer that holds information that is to be printed or transferred elsewhere, so that the main memory can continue to operate.
buf•fet[1] [boo′ fā *or* bə fā′] *noun, plural* **buffets. 1.** a piece of furniture with a flat top that is used for serving food or storing dishes and silverware. **2.** a meal laid out on a buffet or table so that people can serve themselves.

buf•fet[2] [buf′ it] *verb,* **buffeted, buffeting.** to pound or strike again and again: The little sailboat was *buffeted* by strong winds and high waves.

bug [bug] *noun, plural* **bugs. 1.** any of a large group of insects that have thickened front wings and mouth parts that are used for biting and sucking. **2.** any insect or animal like a true bug, such as an ant, spider, beetle, and so on. **3.** *Informal.* a germ that causes disease: a flu *bug.* **4.** *Informal.* something wrong in the operation of a machine, especially a mistake in a computer program that keeps it from working in the right way. **5.** *Informal.* a small microphone that is hidden in a place to pick up private conversations. —*verb,* **bugged, bugging. 1.** *Informal.* to hide a microphone in: to *bug* a room. **2.** *Slang.* to bother or annoy: Mom's always *bugging* me about keeping my room clean.

bug•gy [bug′ ē] *noun, plural* **buggies. 1.** a light carriage with four wheels, pulled by a single horse. **2.** a baby carriage.

bugle A bugle is played during a military ceremony at the Tomb of the Unknown Soldier in Washington. The word *bugle* comes from a Latin word for "ox." The first bugles were made from ox horns.

bu•gle [byōo′ gəl] *noun, plural* **bugles.** a brass musical instrument that is shaped like a trumpet. Bugles were once used by the army to give signals in battle and are now used in funerals and other military ceremonies. ◆ A person who plays a bugle is called a **bugler.**

Pronunciation Key: Accent Marks
[′] is the normal accent mark. It shows where the main stress falls on a word.
[′] is a secondary accent mark. It shows a lighter stress than the primary accent. For example:
tel • e • vis • ion [tel′ə vizh′ən]
(Turn the page for more information.)

B

build [bild] *verb,* **built, building. 1.** to make something by putting parts or materials together: to *build* a house, a road, a bridge, or a ship. **2.** to form little by little; develop: to *build* a business. "I had so much *love* building up in me." (Paul Zindel) —*noun, plural* **builds.** the way something or someone is formed: He got his powerful *build* by lifting weights.

build•er [bil/dər] *noun, plural* **builders.** a person who builds something, especially a person whose work is putting up buildings.

build•ing [bil/ding] *noun, plural* **buildings. 1.** something that is built for use by people or to store things; a structure with walls and a roof, such as a house, store, school, or hotel. **2.** the act or business of putting up buildings.

bull [bool] *noun, plural* **bulls. 1.** the full-grown male of cattle. **2.** the full-grown male of certain other large animals, such as an elephant, moose, whale, or seal. ♦ For those animals whose male is called a bull, the female is called a cow.

bull•dog [bool/dôg/] *noun, plural* **bulldogs.** a heavy, powerful dog with short legs, a large head, and very strong jaws.

bull•doz•er [bool/dō/zər] *noun, plural* **bulldozers.** a large tractor with a heavy metal blade in front. Bulldozers have powerful motors and are used for moving rocks, earth, and trees.

bul•let [bool/it] *noun, plural* **bullets.** a small piece of rounded or pointed metal that is shot from a gun or rifle.

bulletins In its earlier uses *bulletin* was a "short account" and in French a "passport," so that today when we hear on TV that a news bulletin follows, we expect something short, current, and serious. "A Globe Airways jetliner carrying 128 people has just made a forced landing in a cornfield, six miles short of Wheeler Airport. The pilot reports no serious injuries on board. Now to correspondent Susan Bloom at the airport." This bulletin uses two sentences to tell *who, what, when, where,* and *how.* Think of the "bulletin technique" in three easy steps: Keep it short; lead with the most important item; give details afterward.

built [bilt] *verb.* the past form of **build:** "Children are playing in the yards. Someone has already *built* a snowman." (Ann Beattie)

bulb [bulb] *noun, plural* **bulbs. 1.** a round part of certain plants, such as the onion, lily, or tulip. A bulb grows underground and produces a new growth of the plant. **2.** anything that is shaped like a bulb, such as an electric light bulb.

Bul•gar•i•a [bool gar/ē ə] a country in southeastern Europe, on the Black Sea. *Capital:* Sofia. *Area:* 42,900 square miles. *Population:* 8,900,000. —**Bulgarian,** *adjective; noun.*

bulge [bulj] *noun, plural* **bulges.** a part that swells out: The apple made a *bulge* in his pocket. —*verb,* **bulged, bulging.** to swell out: "His pockets *bulged* with loose silver and balled-up notes." (James Herriot) "Aqueduct Racetrack's great stands *bulged* and overflowed." (Walter Farley)

bulk [bulk] *noun.* **1.** great size or volume: In spite of its *bulk,* a tiger is very fast and graceful. **2.** the largest part: The *bulk* of the population of California lives in cities along the coast. ♦ Something that has great bulk is **bulky:** The little boy was dressed for the cold weather in a *bulky* sweater and jacket.

bul•le•tin [bool/ə tən] *noun, plural* **bulletins. 1.** a short announcement giving the latest news about something: The TV station interrupted its regular program to give a *bulletin* about a fire in a paint factory. **2.** a small magazine or newspaper published regularly by a group or organization: The church *bulletin* has an announcement of a picnic this coming Saturday.

bulletin board 1. a board on which notices and other items are posted, as at a school, store, or other public place. **2.** a message center that operates by computer, so that someone can leave messages which other people can read on their own computer screens.

bull•fight [bool/fīt/] *noun, plural* **bullfights.** a sport in which a person known as a **bullfighter** or **matador** [mat/ə dôr/] tries to kill a bull with a sword in a certain way. Bullfights are held in Spain, Mexico, and South America.

bull•frog [bool/frôg/] *noun, plural* **bullfrogs.** a large frog that has a loud, deep croak.

bull's-eye [boolz/ ī/] *noun, plural* **bull's-eyes. 1.** the center circle of a target. **2.** a shot that lands in this circle.

bul•ly [bool/ē] *noun, plural* **bullies.** a person who fights or picks on people who are smaller and weaker: That *bully* always knocks down the smallest boy on the other team. —*verb,* **bullied, bullying.** to act like a bully; frighten someone into doing something: He *bullied* the girls into sharing their lunch money with him.

bum [bum] *noun, plural* **bums.** *Slang.* **1.** a person who does not work and tries to live by begging from others. **2.** a person who is thought of as bad or worthless.

bum•ble•bee [bum′bəl bē′] *noun, plural* **bumblebees.** a large bee that has a thick, hairy body and makes a loud, humming sound.

bumblebee Bumblebees are important to the growing of plants. They travel from one plant to another to gather pollen. This serves to *pollinate* the plants so that they can produce new offspring.

bump [bump] *verb,* **bumped, bumping. 1.** to move or hit against suddenly and heavily: The two cars *bumped* into each other. Brian accidentally *bumped* the lamp and knocked it over. **2.** to move in an uneven, jerky, way: The car *bumped* along the old dirt road. —*noun, plural* **bumps. 1.** a heavy knock or blow: We felt a *bump* as the plane's wheels touched the ground. **2.** a swelling or lump: He has a *bump* on his head where the baseball hit him. —**bumpy,** *adjective:* a *bumpy* plane flight.

bump•er [bum′pər] *noun, plural* **bumpers.** a heavy metal bar that is attached to the front and back of a car, truck, or bus. The bumper protects the body of the car from damage when it is hit. —*adjective.* very large: There was a *bumper* crop of corn in our state this year.

bun [bun] *noun, plural* **buns. 1.** a small bread roll, often sweetened or having raisins or spices. **2.** a roll of hair worn on the top or back of the head.

bunch [bunch] *noun, plural* **bunches.** any group of things growing or placed together: a *bunch* of

carrots or bananas. She left a *bunch* of papers on the desk. —*verb,* **bunched, bunching.** to gather in a bunch: The cattle were *bunched* together along the fence. "He took off his rough cap and *bunched* it in his thick hand." (Katherine Anne Porter)

bun•dle [bun′dəl] *noun, plural* **bundles.** a number of things tied or wrapped together: a *bundle* of old newspapers. ". . . great *bundles* of fireworks of all sorts and shapes." (J.R.R. Tolkien)

verb, **bundled, bundling. 1.** to tie or wrap: He *bundled* the pile of dead branches and took them to the dump. **2. bundle up.** to dress warmly: She made sure the baby was *bundled up* for the cold day.

bun•ga•low [bung′gə lō′] *noun, plural* **bungalows.** a small one-story house or cottage.

bunk [bungk] *noun, plural* **bunks.** a narrow bed that is built in or set against a wall like a shelf. **Bunk beds** are often arranged in pairs, one above the other.

bunk•er [bung′kər] *noun, plural* **bunkers.** a chamber built below the ground with walls of steel and concrete. Bunkers are used for protection in wartime.

bun•ny [bun′ē] *noun, plural* **bunnies.** a rabbit: the Easter *bunny.*

Bun•sen burner [bun′sən] a small instrument that burns a mixture of gas and air to produce a very hot blue flame. Bunsen burners are often used in laboratories for scientific testing.

bunt [bunt] *verb,* **bunted, bunting.** in baseball, to hit a pitch lightly on purpose, so that it goes only a short distance. —*noun, plural* **bunts.** a baseball that has been bunted.

bu•oy [bōō′ē *or* boi] *noun, plural* **buoys. 1.** a floating object that is anchored in the water. Buoys are used to show ships where they may safely go in a harbor or channel or to warn them of dangerous rocks and shallow places at sea. **2.** a ring made of some kind of floating material, used to keep a person afloat in the water ♦ Also known as a **life buoy.** —*verb,* **buoyed, buoying. 1.** to keep a person from sinking; keep afloat. **2.** *also,* **buoy up.** to lift up the spirits or

	Pronunciation Key: A–F		
a	and; hat	ch	chew; such
ā	ate; stay	d	dog; lid
â	care; air	e	end; yet
ä	father; hat	ē	she; each
b	boy; cab	f	fun; off

(Turn the page for more information.)

B

mood of: The passengers on the stalled train were *buoyed up* by the news that help was on the way.

buoy•ant [boi′ənt *or* boo′yənt] *adjective, more/most.* **1.** able to float in water: Cork is a very *buoyant* wood. **2.** cheerful: Mark's *buoyant* personality always puts me in a good mood. ◆ The state of being buoyant is **buoyancy.**

bur [bur] *noun, plural* **burs.** see **burr.**

bur•den [bur′dən] *noun, plural* **burdens. 1.** something that is carried; a load: "He put his *burden* down and straightened up." (Katherine Anne Porter) **2.** something that is hard to bear: "The move from the small farm to the big city was a *burden* and a problem for the family." (I.B. Singer)
—*verb,* **burdened, burdening.** to put a burden on: "They were heavily *burdened* with blanket packs which were strapped to their shoulders." (Jack London) "This snowstorm that was gathering, and that was to *burden* my first flight . . ." (Antoine de St. Exupéry)

bu•reau [byoor′ō] *noun, plural* **bureaus. 1.** a chest of drawers for clothing. **2.** a department of the government: the Federal *Bureau* of Investigation. **3.** an office or agency: the news *bureau* of a TV station.

bu•reauc•ra•cy [byoo räk′rə sē] *noun, plural* **bureaucracies. 1.** a system of running a government or business in which there are many different departments and everyone does a certain job according to very strict rules. **2.** any system in which there is a lot of delay and unnecessary work because rules are followed too strictly. ◆ A person who works in a bureaucracy is called a **bureaucrat** [byoor′ə krat′].

(J.R.R. Tolkien) —*adjective.* that has been buried: *buried* treasure.

bur•lap [bur′lap] *noun.* a coarse cloth woven from the thick fibers of certain plants. It is used mainly to make bags.

bur•ly [bur′lē] *adjective,* **burlier, burliest.** strong and sturdy; husky: "O'Brien was a large, *burly* man with a thick neck . . ." (George Orwell)

Burma Most of the Burmese people live in small farm villages such as this. The country has only one large city, Rangoon.

Bur•ma [bur′mə] a country in southeast Asia, near India and China. *Capital:* Rangoon. *Area:* 261,000 square miles. *Population:* 37,200,000. —**Burmese,** *adjective; noun.*

burn [burn] *verb,* **burned** or **burnt, burning. 1.** to be on fire or set fire to: A candle was *burning* in the window. Chris *burned* some of his old school papers in the fireplace. **2.** to damage or

---

bureaucratic writing Notice the difference between fancy, lengthy, unnecessarily complicated uses of words and simple uses:

Bureaucratic Writing	Simple Writing
"in that time frame"	"at that time"
"she was not supportive of the hospital"	"she didn't help the hospital"
"delayed appropriations caused the personnel not to be compensated"	"because the money ran out the workers weren't paid"

---

bur•glar [bur′glər] *noun, plural* **burglars.** a person who breaks into a house or building to steal something. ◆ This crime is known as **burglary** [bur′glər ē].

bur•i•al [ber′ē əl] *noun, plural* **burials.** the act of placing a dead body in a grave or tomb.

bur•ied [ber′ēd] *verb.* the past form of **bury:** "There must be great secrets *buried* there."

destroy by fire or heat: She *burned* the cookies when she left them in the oven too long. **3.** to make by fire or heat: He accidentally *burned* a hole in his sweater. **4.** to feel hot; give a feeling of heat to: The baby's forehead *burned* with fever. **5.** to use for light or heat: Our camping stove *burns* kerosene oil. —*noun, plural* **burns.** damage or an injury caused by fire or heat: There were several cigarette *burns* on the rug.

burn•er [bur′nər] *noun, plural* **burners.** the part of a stove or furnace from which the flame or heat comes.

burnt [burnt] *verb.* the past form of **burn.**

burr [bur] *noun, plural* **burrs.** (also spelled **bur**) **1.** any seed or plant part with a rough, prickly covering that causes it to stick to things. **2.** a plant that has burrs.

bur•ro [bur′ō] *noun, plural* **burros.** a small donkey.

bur•row [bur′ō] *noun, plural* **burrows. 1.** a hole or tunnel dug in the ground by an animal to live or hide in. **2.** something that is like a burrow: ". . . an elaborate network of tunnels and *burrows* that linked all the various buildings of the hospital." (Sylvia Plath) —*verb,* **burrowed, burrowing. 1.** to dig a hole in the ground: The gopher *burrowed* holes in the lawn. **2.** to search by digging under or through: Shirley *burrowed* through her dresser drawers looking for her necklace. **3.** to go into something, as if in a burrow: "He *burrowed* down into his sleeping bag." (James Houston)

burst [burst] *verb,* **burst, bursting. 1.** to break open suddenly: The dam *burst* under the weight of too much water. "The beautiful bubble grew and . . . *burst* into thin air." (Katherine Anne Porter) **2.** to be full to the point of almost breaking open: The suitcase was *bursting* with clothes. "She wanted to have time to calm down. . . . She didn't want to be *bursting* with excitement." (Langston Hughes) **3.** to come or go suddenly: "Farnon *burst* into the room." (James Herriot) "At the loss of that tooth . . . I *burst* into tears." (Nancy Willard) —*noun, plural* **bursts.** a sudden outbreak: "They shot away from the porch in a *burst* of wild, furious speed." (Vera Cleaver) "There was a *burst* of applause from the onlookers." (Somerset Maugham)

bur•y [ber′ē] *verb,* **buried, burying. 1.** to place a dead body in a grave or tomb. **2.** to cover up with or as if dirt: Our dog likes to *bury* bones in the with dirt. "'Why did I ever take this up?' he cried, *burying* his face in his hands." (Michael

Bond) "She had *buried* all worry about her own welfare." (Robert Heinlein)

bus [bus] *noun, plural* **buses** or **busses. 1.** a large motor vehicle with rows of seats for carrying many passengers. **2.** an electrical pathway that sends information from one part of a computer to another: Data is transferred from the computer's memory to the printer by means of a *bus.* —*verb,* **bused, busing,** or **bussed, bussing.** to send or go by bus: to *bus* students to school. ♦ This meaning is also used as a noun.

bush [boosh] *noun, plural* **bushes.** a low woody plant; a shrub. A bush is smaller than a tree and has branches closer to the ground. The same plant may be called a bush or tree, depending on its size.

bush•el [boosh′əl] *noun, plural* **bushels.** a unit of measure for dry items such as grain, fruit, and vegetables. A bushel is the same as 4 pecks or 32 dry quarts.

bush•y [boosh′ē] *adjective,* **bushier, bushiest.** thick and spreading like a bush: Squirrels have *bushy* tails.

business letters (1) Business letters are short and usually fit on one page, or at the most, two pages. (2) Business letters are serious. You don't tell jokes or ramble on about yourself in a business letter. (3) Business letters are carefully checked for spelling and punctuation before mailing. (4) Business letters are neat. A badly-typed letter gives the impression of a lazy, inefficient person. (5) Business letters go right to the point—which is why they are called 'business.' They state their purpose in the first paragraph.

busi•ness [biz′nis] *noun, plural* **businesses. 1.** the work a person does to earn money; one's job or occupation: He doesn't drive that car on weekends because he only uses it for *business.* **2.** the making, buying, and selling of goods, or the exchange of services for money: *Business* has been good at the new shopping center this year. **3.** a store, company, or factory that does business: The Simpsons sold their clothing *business.* **4.** an event or affair; matter: Cleaning out the attic was a messy *business.* What's this *business* about the city planning to close that school? **5.** one's interest or concern: If he doesn't want to go with us, that's his *business.*

Pronunciation Key: G–N			
g	give; big	k	kind; cat; back
h	hold	l	let; ball
i	it; this	m	make; time
ī	ice; my	n	not; own
j	jet; gem; edge	ng	having

(Turn the page for more information.)

B

busi•ness•man [biz′ nis man′] *noun, plural* **businessmen.** a man who owns a business or works in a business.

busi•ness•wom•an [biz′ nis woom′ ən] *noun, plural* **businesswomen.** a woman who owns a business or works in a business.

bus•ing or **bus•sing** [bus′ ing] *noun.* the act or policy of sending children to school by bus, especially to a school other than the one in their own area in order to have a balance of white and minority students in the schools.

bus•y [biz′ ē] *adjective,* **busier, busiest. 1.** doing something; occupied; active: Mom is *busy* washing the dishes. **2.** having a lot of activity: The road to the beach is very *busy* on summer weekends. **3.** in use: His phone has been *busy* all afternoon. —*verb,* **busied, busying.** to keep busy: "Sport tried to *busy* himself by looking in the icebox." (Louise Fitzhugh)

but [but] *conjunction.* on the other hand: I'd love to go, *but* I have to study. —*preposition.* except: She works every day *but* Sunday.

but "He pulled the brake. *But* it did not hold. . . ." (Eudora Welty) Beginning a new sentence with *but* is a good way to break up what would have been a very long sentence: "Her shoulder wasn't as comfortable as it should have been. *But* she closed her eyes, trying to force sleep." (Joyce Carol Oates) It can also give force to a short statement: "Now she is free, and she thinks, I must run while there is time. *But* she does not go." (Katherine Anne Porter) You should not use "but" if what you create is a choppy, incomplete sentence: "Everyone in the class was there. *But* Amy."

bust [bust] *noun, plural* **busts. 1.** a statue of a person's head, shoulders, and the upper part of the chest. **2.** a woman's bosom. **3.** *Informal.* something that is unsuccessful; a complete failure: "A trumpeter swan that couldn't trumpet was a *bust* as far as she was concerned." (E.B. White)

bus•tle [bus′ əl] *verb,* **bustled, bustling.** to move about in a busy, excited way: "He slammed down the lid and *bustled* over to the door." (James Herriot) —*noun.* noisy, excited activity: the *bustle* of department store shoppers at Christmas time.

—*adverb.* only: He left here *but* a minute ago.

butch•er [booch′ ər] *noun, plural* **butchers. 1.** a person whose work is cutting and selling meat. **2.** a person who kills in a cruel or brutal way. —*verb,* **butchered, butchering.** to kill or cut up for meat: to *butcher* a steer.

but•ler [but′ lər] *noun, plural* **butlers.** a man who is the head servant in a household.

butt¹ [but] *noun, plural* **butts. 1.** the thicker or larger end of something, such as a tool or weapon: the *butt* of a rifle. **2.** the end of something that is left over, such as a cigarette.

butt² *verb,* **butted, butting.** to push or strike a blow with the head or horns: Male mountain goats often *butt* heads with each other. —*noun, plural* **butts.** a blow with the head or horns.

butt³ *noun, plural* **butts.** a person who is the target of teasing or a joke.

but•ter [but′ ər] *noun, plural* **butters. 1.** a solid, yellowish fat that is separated from milk or cream by churning, often used as a spread on bread and for cooking. **2.** another food that spreads like butter, such as peanut butter. —*verb,* **buttered, buttering.** to spread with butter: to *butter* toast.

but•ter•cup [but′ ər kup′] *noun, plural* **buttercups.** any of a large number of plants with yellow flowers shaped like cups.

but•ter•fly [but′ ər flī′] *noun, plural* **butterflies.** an insect with a thin body and four large brightly-colored wings. There are many different kinds of butterflies.

butterfly The name *butterfly* is said to come from the word *butter.* Many common butterflies have the golden-yellow color of butter.

but•ter•milk [but′ər milk′] *noun.* a drink that is made from the liquid left when milk is made into butter.

but•ter•scotch [but′ər skäch′] *noun.* a candy or flavoring made from brown sugar and butter.

buzz word *Informal.* a new and important-sounding word that is used with a special meaning in a certain business or activity: John likes to use a lot of computer *buzz words* to impress his friends.

buzz words When people start using certain new terms repeatedly, these are called *buzz words,* meaning they are all around, buzzing like flies. Computers, a new device, created the buzz words "feedback," "input," "interface," "on-line," and "user-friendly." Sometimes, such words are effective. But when they become overfancy, it's best to choose plain English. "If you have any downtime this week, I hope you and Dave can interface and give me some input on this idea." Can you rewrite this sentence in plain English?

but•ton [but′ən] *noun, plural* **buttons.** **1.** a round, flat piece of plastic, metal, brass, or other material that is used to fasten clothing or to decorate it. **2.** a knob that is pushed or turned to make something work, such as a machine, electric light, elevator, doorbell, and so on. —*verb,* **buttoned, buttoning.** to fasten with a button or buttons.

but•tress [but′tris] *noun, plural* **buttresses.** something strong and heavy built against a wall to hold it up and strengthen it. —*verb,* **buttressed, buttressing.** to make something stronger with or as if with a buttress: to *buttress* a wall. She *buttressed* her argument by presenting a long list of facts and statistics.

buy [bī] *verb,* **bought, buying.** to pay money to get something: to *buy* a book, to *buy* a car. —*noun, plural* **buys.** a bargain: They got a good *buy* on that house.

buy•er [bī′ər] *noun, plural* **buyers.** **1.** any person who buys something. **2.** a person whose work is to buy things for a company: Mr. Sanchez is a shirt *buyer* for Hall's Department Store.

buzz [buz] *verb,* **buzzed, buzzing.** **1.** to make a low humming sound, as bees do. **2.** to be full of activity and talk: The crowd was *buzzing* with excitement as they waited for the big race to begin. **3.** to fly an airplane low over something. —*noun, plural* **buzzes.** a low humming sound, like that of a bee.

buz•zard [buz′ərd] *noun, plural* **buzzards.** a very large bird of prey with a sharp beak, sharp claws, and dark feathers. A buzzard is a kind of hawk.
♦ Some kinds of VULTURES are also called buzzards, such as the turkey vulture.

buzz•er [buz′ər] *noun, plural* **buzzers.** an electrical device that makes a buzzing sound as a signal.

by [bī] *preposition.* **1.** near; beside: Leave the paper *by* the door. **2.** through the work of: a play *by* Shakespeare. **3.** through the use of: He left town *by* train. **4.** according to: to play *by* the rules. **5.** no later than: I hope to finish *by* noon. **6.** as a result of: He made his money *by* working hard. **7.** in the measure or amount of: to win *by* a mile, to buy soda *by* the case. —*adverb.* **1.** past: Is that Jim's car going *by?* **2.** to or at someone's place: Stop *by* for a visit.

by•gone [bī′gôn′] *adjective.* in the past; gone by; former: The old farmer loved to talk about the *bygone* days of his youth. —*noun, plural* **bygones.** something past: Let's forget about our disagreement and let *bygones* be *bygones.*

by•pass [bī′pas′] *noun, plural* **bypasses.** **1.** a road that passes around a city or a downtown area. **2.** an operation to allow blood to pass around a damaged blood vessel. —*verb,* **bypassed, bypassing.** to go around: The new highway *bypasses* the downtown business section.

by•prod•uct [bī′präd′əkt] *noun, plural* **byproducts.** something that is the result of making something else: Buttermilk is a *byproduct* of butter.

by•stand•er [bī′stan dər] *noun, plural* **bystanders.** a person who is standing nearby when something happens: Several *bystanders* saw the robber run out of the bank.

byte [bīt] *noun, plural* **bytes.** a group of digits, usually eight, that a computer stores as one unit in its memory.

Pronunciation Key: O–S			
ō	over; go	ou	out; town
ô	all; law	p	put; hop
oo	look; full	r	run; car
o͞o	pool; who	s	set; miss
oi	oil; boy	sh	show

(Turn the page for more information.)

Cc

c, C [sē] *noun, plural* **c's, C's. 1.** the third letter of the alphabet. **2.** the third-highest grade or level.

cab [kab] *noun, plural* **cabs. 1.** a car with a driver who is paid to take someone where they want to go; a taxi. **2.** the enclosed part of a truck, crane, or other large vehicle where the driver or operator sits.

cab•bage [kab′ij] *noun, plural* **cabbages.** a plant having a rounded head of firm, closely-

cab•i•net [kab′nit] *noun, plural* **cabinets. 1.** a piece of furniture that has shelves and drawers for holding things: a kitchen *cabinet* for dishes and glasses. Business offices use filing *cabinets* to hold letters and papers. **2.** *also,* **Cabinet.** a group of people chosen by the head of a government to give advice on policy. The U.S. Cabinet includes the Secretaries of State, Defense, and the Treasury, and the heads of other important government departments.

cabinet *Cabinet* at one time meant a small room. Now, it means a piece of furniture. However, the older meaning is still used in politics. The first "cabinet" was a small room where the King of England's advisers held meetings. Through metaphor, the word then came to be used for the whole group of advisers. How's this for a combination of metaphors: "The *chair* (actually, a person who runs a meeting) suggested that the *motion* (a proposal to do something) be *tabled* (put down on a table, put aside)."

folded leaves of green or red. Cabbage is eaten as a vegetable.

cab•in [kab′in] *noun, plural* **cabins. 1.** a small, simple house made of logs or rough boards. **2.** a private room on a passenger ship where people stay during a trip. **3.** the main section of an airplane where the passengers sit.

caboose The caboose always comes at the end of the train. It is typically the bright-red color shown here.

ca•ble [kā′bəl] *noun, plural* **cables. 1.** a strong, thick rope made of twisted wire or fibers. Cables are used for holding up bridges or pulling heavy machines. **2.** a bundle of wires protected by a covering or insulation, used to carry electricity. Telephone and telegraph systems use cables to carry messages from one place to another. **3.** a message sent by electric cable. ♦ Also known as a **cablegram.** —*verb,* **cabled, cabling.** to send a message by cable.

cable car a vehicle carried through the air on an overhead cable or pulled along the ground on an underground cable.

cable television or **cable TV** a system in which television shows are sent through a cable instead of over the air waves. People pay a fee for cable TV service in order to get better reception or to receive programs that are not offered on the regular channels.

ca•boose [kə bōōs′] *noun, plural* **cabooses.** the last railroad car on a freight train, used by the train workers.

ca•ca•o [kə kā′ ō] *noun, plural* **cacaos.** an ever-green tree whose seeds are used to make cocoa and chocolate. This tree grows in warm tropical climates. ♦ *Cacao* comes from an American Indian word; the Indians were the first to grow this plant.

cactus The Saguaro cactus is a spectacular sight in the American Southwest. It can grow as much as fifty feet high.

cac•tus [kak′ təs] *noun, plural* **cactuses** or **cacti.** a plant that has a thick green trunk and branch-es covered with sharp needlelike spines instead of leaves. Cactus grows in hot dry places.

cad•die or **cad•dy** [kad′ ē] *noun, plural* **cad-dies.** someone who carries golf clubs for a golfer. —*verb,* **caddied, caddying.** to act as a caddie.

ca•det [kə det′] *noun, plural* **cadets.** a person training to be an officer in the armed forces, especially a student in a military school.

caf•feine [ka fēn′] *noun.* a bitter white sub-stance that is found in coffee, tea, chocolate, and cola drinks. Caffeine makes the body more active and can keep a person from feeling sleepy. Too much caffeine can cause a person to be very nervous.

cage [kāj] *noun, plural* **cages. 1.** an enclosed place with wire or bars for keeping animals or birds, as in a zoo or circus. **2.** anything shaped or used like a cage: Deep-sea divers sometimes use *cages* for protection while they are studying sharks. —*verb,* **caged, caging.** to put something into a cage.

Cai•ro [kī′ rō] the capital of Egypt, on the Nile River. *Population:* 6,200,000.

cake [kāk] *noun, plural* **cakes. 1.** a soft, sweet food made by baking flour, sugar, flavorings, and eggs. Cakes are sometimes covered with icing. **2.** a thin batter that is fried or baked, such as a pancake. **3.** any hard mass that is like a cake: a *cake* of soap.
—*verb,* **caked, caking.** to form or harden into a solid mass: "Her fingers dug out the *caked* snow." (Laura Ingalls Wilder)

ca•lam•i•ty [kə lam′ ə tē] *noun, plural* **calami-ties.** something that causes great suffering or misery: "It seemed a small loss to others, but to Jo it was a dreadful *calamity*." (Louisa May Alcott)

cal•ci•um [kal′ sē əm] *noun.* a soft, silver-white chemical element that is found in marble, chalk, shells, and in such foods as milk and cheese. Calcium is important in the diet be-cause it is needed for strong teeth and bones.

cal•cu•late [kal′ kyə lāt′] *verb,* **calculated, cal-culating. 1.** to get the answer to a problem by using arithmetic: Mom *calculated* how many miles per gallon we got on our car trip. **2.** to

cadet Word history often tells us about world history. In old times in several countries it was the custom that land and other possessions go only to the oldest son. His brothers and sisters got nothing. This custom is called *primogeniture* [prī′mō jen′i tər]. This meant "first birth," as can be seen from other words like *primary* and *generation*. Now here's one result of language and history running together. The word *cadet* first meant "a younger son or brother." As a younger son did not inherit anything, he tended to join the army and he was called a "cadet" when he joined.

Cae•sar [sē′ zər] **Julius,** 100?–44 B.C., Roman general, statesman, and author.

ca•fé [ka fa′] *noun, plural* **cafes.** a small restau-rant or bar.

caf•e•te•ri•a [kaf′ ə tēr′ ē ə] *noun, plural* **cafe-terias.** a type of restaurant where customers order food that is on display at a counter and then carry it to tables to eat.

Pronunciation Key: A–F

a	and; hat	ch	chew; such
ā	ate; stay	d	dog; lid
â	care; air	e	end; yet
ä	father; hat	ē	she; each
b	boy; cab	f	fun; off

(Turn the page for more information.)

C

think out with common sense or reason; estimate: Sioux Indians used to *calculate* time by figuring how long it took the sun to pass over a tent pole. **3.** to plan or design: The commercials on that TV show are *calculated* to appeal to young children. ♦ Often used as an adjective: A **calculated risk** is one that a person thinks about beforehand and is willing to take.

cal•i•ber [kal′ ə bər] *noun.* **1.** the size of a bullet: A 38-*caliber* bullet is fired from a gun whose barrel is 38/100 of an inch across. **2.** ability or quality: a college of the highest *caliber.*

Cal•i•for•nia [kal′ ə fôrn′ yə] a state in the western U.S., on the Pacific Ocean. *Capital:* Sacramento. *Nickname:* "Golden State." *Area:* 158,700 square miles. *Population:* 24,724,000.

calculate Some words in mathematics are Arabic, including *algebra*, but *calculator* is Roman in origin. To count, Romans would often place small stones in clusters of two or three or four—whatever—on the ground. The word *calculus* meant "a small stone, a pebble." Nowadays, we have calculators that run on electricity or on batteries. But what does it mean to say, "She is a *calculating* woman"? It means she's careful (she can count the stones!), but worse, she's *not* careful about other people, always figuring what suits her best. When we say that someone is a calculating person, we don't mean this as a compliment, even though it seems to suggest a careful thinker. Such people are thought to analyze a situation in terms of what will benefit them, as if they were adding up the pluses and minuses.

cal•cu•la•tion [kal′ kyə lā′ shən] *noun, plural* **calculations.** the act or result of calculating.

cal•cu•la•tor [kal′ kyə lā′ tər] *noun, plural* **calculators.** a small machine that can solve number problems automatically. Calculators have keyboards with buttons for numbers and for adding, subtracting, or doing other mathematical operations.

cal•cu•lus [kal′ kyə ləs] *noun.* an advanced form of mathematics used to figure out problems in which the quantities are constantly changing, such as finding the speed of a falling object at one given moment in its fall.

Cal•cut•ta [kal kut′ ə] a major city and port in eastern India. *Population:* 3,291,000.

cal•en•dar [kal′ ən dər] *noun, plural* **calendars.** **1.** a chart showing the days, weeks, and months of the year in order. **2.** a schedule or list of coming events: A court *calendar* tells the cases that are coming before a judge on certain days. ♦ Protestants and Catholics use the **Gregorian Calendar**, named for Pope Gregory. Orthodox Christians, including Serbs, Russians and Greeks, use the older **Julian Calendar**, named for Julius Caesar.

calf¹ [kaf] *noun, plural* **calves.** **1.** the young of cattle. **2.** leather made from the skin of a calf, also known as **calfskin.** **3.** the young of certain other large animals, such as seals and elephants.

calf² *noun, plural* **calves.** the muscular back part of the lower leg, between the knee and ankle.

Cal•ga•ry [kal′ gə rē] a city in southwestern Alberta, Canada. *Population:* 595,000.

call [kôl] *verb,* **called, calling. 1.** to speak or say in a loud voice; shout or cry: The coach *called* to his players from the sidelines. **2.** to ask or command to come: to *call* a dog, to *call* a taxi. **3.** to refer to by a name; give a name to: The teacher doesn't want us to *call* her by her first name. **4.** to describe or identify as: The umpire *called* him safe. **5.** to get in touch by telephone: We'll *call* you tomorrow when we get to town. **6.** to make a short visit. **7.** to stop or put off: The game was *called* when it got too dark to play. —*noun, plural* **calls. 1.** a loud cry or shout: a *call* for help. **2.** the sound made by a bird or animal. **3.** the act of getting in touch with someone by telephone. **4.** a short visit: He paid a *call* on his grandmother on his way to the city. **5.** a need or demand: The Medal of Honor is given for courage "above and beyond the *call* of duty."

call•er [kôl′ ər] *noun, plural* **callers.** a person or thing that calls, such as someone who calls on the phone or makes a short visit.

cal•lus [kal′ əs] *noun, plural* **calluses.** a spot on the skin that has become thick and hard because of constant rubbing.

calm [käm *or* kälm] *adjective,* **calmer, calmest. 1.** quiet and still; not moving: I feel safer swimming in the ocean when it's *calm.* **2.** not nervous or excited: "Above all, you must be *calm* . . . and think things through." (Robert Heinlein) —*noun.* a time or feeling of quiet and stillness: The "*calm* before the storm" is an expression for a time of quiet just before something suddenly happens. —*verb,* **calmed, calming.** to make or to become calm: The boy *calmed* down when he realized he really hadn't been hurt. **—calmly,** *adverb:* "The man's voice spoke *calmly,* as if he had never been sad or angry in his life." (Beverly Cleary)

can go for several days without drinking water. The kind with two humps is called a **Bactrian camel** and is found in central Asia. The kind with one hump is also known as a DROMEDARY.

camera The English author Christopher Isherwood wrote a book, *I Am a Camera,* using the notion that his characters took pictures of where they were and whom they knew. Other writers are said to use "cinematic" style—vivid, short scenes of description and movement. A critic praised Laura Ingalls Wilder as "a very cinematic writer." Here is one of her passages: "They watched striped snakes rippling between the grass stems or lying so still that only their tiny flickering tongues and glittering eyes showed they were alive . . . And sometimes there'd be a great gray rabbit, so still in the lights and shadows of a grass clump that you were near enough to touch him before you saw him."

cal•o•rie [kal′ ə rē] *noun, plural* **calories. 1.** a unit for measuring the amount of heat in something. A **small calorie** is equal to the amount of heat needed to raise the temperature of one gram of water one degree Celsius. A **large calorie** is equal to 1000 small calories. **2.** the large calorie, used as a way to measure the amount of heat or energy that is supplied by eating a certain food: People who are on a diet often have to count how many *calories* they eat each day.

Cam•bo•di•a [kam bō′ dē ə] a country in southeast Asia. *Capital:* Phnom Penh. *Area:* 69,900 square miles. *Population:* 6,100,000. ♦ Also known as **Kampuchea** [kam′ pōō chē′ ə] **—Cambodian,** *adjective; noun.*

came [kām] *verb.* the past tense of **come:** That letter you wanted just *came* in the mail.

camel The camel is called "the ship of the desert." It can travel over the hot sands of the Sahara or Arabian Desert for days with almost no food or water.

cam•el [kam′ əl] *noun, plural* **camels.** a large, hoofed animal with a humped back and a long neck. Camels are used in the deserts of Africa and Asia for riding and carrying loads, and they

cam•er•a [kam′ rə] *noun, plural* **cameras. 1.** a device for taking photographs or motion pictures in which light passes through a small opening called a LENS. The light then forms an image which is recorded on film or some other light-sensitive material. **2.** a similar device used in television to form a picture and send it out as an electronic signal for broadcasting. ♦ A **cameraman** is a person whose work is operating a motion picture or TV camera.

camouflage The lizard's body color provides camouflage from larger animals as it rests on a rock. *Camouflage* first meant "to cover or hide the head."

cam•ou•flage [kam′ ə fläj′ *or* kam′ ə fläzh′] *noun, plural* **camouflages. 1.** the act of changing or disguising the appearance of troops, weapons, planes, and other military equipment so that it will be hard for the enemy to see them. **2.** any disguise or false appearance that serves

Pronunciation Key: G–N

g	give; big	k	kind; cat; back
h	hold	l	let; ball
i	it; this	m	make; time
ī	ice; my	n	not; own
j	jet; gem; edge	ng	having

(Turn the page for more information.)

C

to hide something: A polar bear has a natural *camouflage* because it is the same white color as the snow and ice around it. —*verb*, **camouflaged, camouflaging.** to try to hide something by changing its color or appearance: Soldiers' uniforms are often *camouflaged* by giving them the brown and green color of trees and plants.

camp [kamp] *noun, plural* **camps.** an outdoor area where people live in tents or cabins for a time. —*verb*, **camped, camping.** to set up or live in a camp: The boy scouts *camped* in the woods. ♦ The sport of doing this is **camping.**

campaign The ancient Romans used the word *campus* to mean "field." From this Latin word we get several common English words, one being a college campus itself. We also get *camp*: an open field where an army pitches its tents. Another such word is *campaign*, which comes from the practice in ancient times when armies fought only in summer months and usually in open fields. Nowadays, *campaign* is also used in many public affairs: There are campaigns against harmful drugs, alcohol, etc. Politicians, like ancient armies, launch campaigns in the open—on radio and television—every two or four or six years.

cam•paign [kam pān/] *noun, plural* **campaigns. 1.** in a war, a series of actions planned and carried out to win a certain objective: the North African *campaign* of World War II. **2.** the activities that a political candidate carries on to try to win office. **3.** any series of actions to gain a certain goal: The company planned an advertising *campaign* to introduce their new brand of soap. —*verb*, **campaigned, campaigning.** to take part in a campaign: to *campaign* for President, to *campaign* for greater safety on the highways. —**campaigner,** *noun:* Franklin D. Roosevelt and Ronald Reagan are thought of as highly skilled *campaigners.*

camp•er [kam/ pər] *noun, plural* **campers. 1.** a person who camps. **2.** a car or trailer that is built for use on camping trips.

cam•pus [kam/ pəs] *noun, plural* **campuses.** the land or grounds of a school or college.

can¹ [kan *or* kən] *verb*, past tense **could.** *Can* is a special verb that is often used with other verbs in these meanings: **1.** to be able to or know how to: The baby *can* walk already. *Can* you speak French? Yes, I *can*. **2.** to have the right to: In the U.S., people *can* vote when they're eighteen. **3.** to be allowed: Mom says I *can* go to the game tonight if I finish my homework first.

can² [kan] *noun, plural* **cans. 1.** a metal container that is filled with food or liquid and then sealed to keep out air: a *can* of beans, a *can* of tomato juice. **2.** the amount that is in a can: Add four *cans* of water to make the lemonade.

3. any similar container with a lid: a garbage *can*, a gasoline *can*, a *can* of motion picture film. —*verb*, **canned, canning.** to preserve food by putting it into a can: to *can* peaches.

Can•a•da [kan/ ə də] a country in the northern part of North America. It is the second-largest country in the world. *Capital:* Ottawa. *Area:* 3,851,000 square miles. *Population:* 24,554,000.

Ca•na•di•an [kə nā/ dē ən] *noun, plural* **Canadians.** a person who lives in or comes from Canada. —*adjective.* having to do with Canada.

ca•nal [kə nal/] *noun, plural* **canals.** a waterway that is dug across land. Canals are used to make a body of water deeper so that boats can pass through, to connect two bodies of water that are separated by land, or to carry water to dry lands for farming.

canal The Dutch city of Amsterdam is famous for its system of canals throughout the city.

ca•nar•y [kə nâr/ ē] *noun, plural* **canaries.** a small yellow singing bird that is often kept as a pet. ♦ The canary gets its name from the *Canary* Islands, where it first became known. The ancient Romans called these the "Islands of Dogs" because they found many wild dogs there. In Latin, *canis* is the word for dog.

can•cel [kan/ səl] *verb*, **canceled, canceling** or **cancelled, cancelling. 1.** to take back or do away with; end or stop: Dale had to *cancel* his trip to

Denver because he was sick. **2.** to mark out a check or postage stamp with lines so that it cannot be used again.

can•cer [kan′sər] *noun, plural* **cancers. 1.** a very harmful disease in which certain body cells grow and develop much faster than is normal and destroy healthy tissues. Many forms of cancer can cause death. **2.** something very bad that spreads in a harmful way: One of President Nixon's staff called the Watergate scandal a *cancer* on the Presidency.

can•did [kan′dəd] *adjective, more/most.* **1.** open and direct in telling the truth; frank: "To tell you my private and *candid* opinion, I think . . . he's a spy of Colgan's." (James Joyce) **2.** not posed: a *candid* photograph.

can•di•date [kan′də dāt′] *noun, plural* **candidates.** a person who seeks or is being considered for some office or honor: Jimmy Carter was a *candidate* for President in 1976 and 1980. The company is interviewing several *candidates* for that job. ♦ The word *candidate* once meant "dressed in white." Candidates in ancient Rome wore pure white robes as a symbol of honesty.

can•dle [kan′dəl] *noun, plural* **candles.** a stick of wax, TALLOW, or another solid fat, molded around a string or wick that is burned to give light. A **candlestick** is used to hold a candle.

can•dy [kan′dē] *noun, plural* **candies.** a sweet food made of sugar or syrup, often mixed with chocolate, nuts, or fruits. —*verb,* **candied, candying.** to coat with sugar: *candied* apples.

cane [kān] *noun, plural* **canes. 1.** a long, thin stick to lean on for help in walking. **2.** the long, slender stem of certain tall grass plants, used to make furniture. **3.** a plant having such stems, such as bamboo or sugarcane.

can•ni•bal [kan′ə bəl] *noun, plural* **cannibals.** a person who eats human flesh. ♦ The fact of being a cannibal is **cannibalism.**

can•non [kan′ən] *noun, plural* **cannons** or **cannon.** a very large and heavy gun that is set on a base or mounted on wheels. Cannons were used in warfare in earlier times. A **cannonball** is the solid metal ball fired from a cannon.

can•not [kan′ät *or* kə nät′] *verb.* the opposite of **can;** can not.

canoe The word *canoe* comes from the American Indians. It's said this was one of the first Indian words that Columbus heard when he came to the New World.

ca•noe [kə nōō′] *noun, plural* **canoes.** a light, narrow boat that is pointed at both ends and is moved by paddles. —*verb,* **canoed, canoeing.** to ride in or paddle a canoe.

can't [kant] *verb.* the contraction for **cannot.**

can't/cannot These words mean the same thing. *Can't* is more common—the HBJ Word Survey shows it is used about four times as often as *cannot.* Is there any reason, then, to choose *cannot*? Yes. It is a serious and more formal word than *can't.* It gives more force to the sentence: "Man *cannot* live by bread alone." "A house divided against itself *cannot* stand." (Abraham Lincoln) "We *cannot* walk alone . . . We *cannot* turn back." (Martin Luther King)

can•ta•loupe [kan′tə lōp′] *noun, plural* **cantaloupes.** a kind of melon with a thick, rough skin and sweet, juicy orange flesh.

can•teen [kan tēn′] *noun, plural* **canteens. 1.** a small, flat container for carrying water or other liquids to drink. **2.** a store at a school, factory, or military post that sells food and drinks.

Can•ton [kan′tän′] a river port city in southern China. *Population:* 1,800,000. ♦ Also known as **Guangzhou** [gwang′jō′].

can•vas [kan′vəs] *noun, plural* **canvases.** a strong, coarse cloth made of cotton, FLAX, or

Pronunciation Key: O–S

ō	over; go	ou	out; town
ô	all; law	p	put; hop
oo	look; full	r	run; car
ōō	pool; who	s	set; miss
oi	oil; boy	sh	show

(Turn the page for more information.)

HEMP. Canvas is used for sails, tents, and bags, and as a covering. Artists' oil paintings are often painted on a piece of canvas.

canyon Canyon de Chelly in Arizona, the home of an ancient Indian civilization. *Canyon* is from Spanish *cañon*; the Spanish explorers were the first Europeans to see the canyons of the American Southwest.

can•yon [kan′ yən] *noun, plural* **canyons.** a deep valley with high, steep sides. A canyon often has a river flowing through it.

a *capacity* of ten gallons. **2.** mental or physical power; ability: "Some people could do it, but Mrs. Oliver was bitterly aware of not having the proper *capacity*." (Agatha Christie) **3.** a position or function: Bernard Baruch served several U.S. Presidents in the *capacity* of personal adviser.

cape¹ [kāp] *noun, plural* **capes.** a piece of outer clothing worn over the shoulders like a coat, but having no sleeves.

cape² *noun, plural* **capes.** a large piece of land that sticks out into an ocean or lake.

cap•i•tal [kap′ ə təl] *noun, plural* **capitals. 1.** the larger form of a letter of the alphabet, as is used at the beginning of a person's name. **2.** the city where the government of a state or country is located. **3.** money or anything that can be used to earn more money; wealth. All the money, property, or other valuable things that a business or person owns is capital. —*adjective.* **1.** most important; main: a *capital* city. **2.** having to do with CAPITAL PUNISHMENT: Murder is a *capital* offense. **3.** having to do with capital or wealth: Money gained or lost from selling property is known as a **capital gain** or **capital loss.**

capital letters In general, there are four occasions to use capital letters: (1) To begin a sentence: "**T**he only thing we have to fear is fear itself." (2) To name a particular person or place: **F**ranklin **D. R**oosevelt; **H**yde **P**ark, **N**ew **Y**ork. (3) To give the title of a person, group, or event: **P**resident **R**oosevelt and **K**ing **G**eorge; the **S**upreme **C**ourt; the **N**ew **D**eal. (4) To identify important words in the title of a book, movie, song, etc.: **S**unrise at **C**ampobello; "**H**appy **D**ays **A**re **H**ere **A**gain." (Of course, we also capitalize the word **I** at all times.)

cap [kap] *noun, plural* **caps. 1.** a hat that fits closely over the head, usually without a brim but often with a VISOR. **2.** something that is shaped or works like a cap: a bottle *cap.* The dentist put a *cap* on her broken tooth. **3.** a small explosive wrapped in paper, used in toy guns to make a noise like a bullet firing. —*verb,* **capped, capping. 1.** to put a cap on; cover: He *capped* the jelly jar. Snow *capped* the mountains. **2.** to follow with something as good or better: She played well the whole game, and then to *cap* it off she scored the winning basket.

ca•pa•ble [kā′ pə bəl] *adjective, more/most.* **1.** able to do something: He's *capable* of doing better in school. "Roseberg was *capable* of very hard work and of long hours of concentration." (Winston Churchill) **2.** able to do something well; efficient: She's a very *capable* worker.

ca•pac•i•ty [kə pas′ ə tē] *noun, plural* **capacities. 1.** the amount that can be held by a container or a space: My car's gas tank has

cap•i•tal•ism [kap′ ə təl iz′ əm] *noun.* a system in which individual people and companies rather than the government hold and control the money, or CAPITAL. Under capitalism, the things needed to do business, such as land, factories, and goods, are privately owned and are operated to make money for the owners.

cap•i•tal•ist [kap′ ə təl ist] *noun, plural* **capitalists.** a person who believes in or supports the policy of capitalism.

cap•i•tal•ize [kap′ ə təl īz′] *verb,* **capitalized, capitalizing. 1.** to write or print a capital letter; begin a word with a capital letter: Always *capitalize* the first word of a sentence. **2.** to provide a business with capital: That company is *capitalized* by many wealthy investors. **3.** to use to advantage; gain or profit from: The Raiders *capitalized* on their opponents' fumble at the ten-yard line and scored a touchdown.

capital punishment the act or policy of putting someone to death as the penalty for a crime.

capitol/capital The words *capitol* and *capital* sound exactly alike, and they both refer to important places in government. But they are two different words, because while a capital is the city which is the center of government, the actual building where lawmakers and government workers carry out their duties is a capitol: "Washington, D.C., is the *capital* of the United States. The Senate works in the *Capitol* Building." Think of land and you might see the "a" in *capital*. Think of offices and you might see the "o" in *capitol*.

cap•i•tol [kap′ ə təl] *noun, plural* **capitols. 1. Capitol.** the building in Washington, D.C. where the United States Congress meets. **2.** the building in a state capital where the state lawmakers meet.

Capitol The United States Congress meets in the Capitol Building in Washington, D.C.

cap•size [kap′ sīz] *verb,* **capsized, capsizing.** to turn upside down; turn over. ♦ Usually used of a boat: "If the boat had *capsized* he would have tumbled . . . out upon the ocean." (Stephen Crane)

cap•sule [kap′ səl] *noun, plural* **capsules. 1.** a very small container of medicine that can be swallowed whole. **2.** the part of a plant that holds and protects its seeds. **3.** a part of a space vehicle that separates from the rest of the vehicle in flight. Astronauts ride in the capsule of a spacecraft. —*adjective.* in a brief form; condensed: The newspaper's movie listings give a *capsule* description of each movie playing in town.

cap•tain [kap′ tən] *noun, plural* **captains. 1.** the rank of an officer in the armed forces. In the army, a captain ranks above a lieutenant and below a major. **2.** the person who is in command of a ship. **3.** any person who is in command of a group; a leader: the *captain* of a soccer team. —*verb,* **captained, captaining.** to act as captain; lead; command: to *captain* a ship.

cap•tion [kap′ shən] *noun, plural* **captions.** the words used with a picture in a book, magazine, or newspaper to tell something about what is in the picture. The picture of the Capitol on this page has a caption under it.

cap•tive [kap′ tiv] *noun, plural* **captives.** someone who is locked up; a prisoner. —*adjective.* **1.** held as a prisoner; not free: A zoo has *captive* animals. **2.** held within bounds, as if one were a prisoner: The passengers in the cab were a *captive* audience for the driver's jokes. ♦ The state of being a captive is **captivity:** "It's against the law to hold one of these wild birds in *captivity*." (E.B. White)

cap•ture [kap′ chər] *verb,* **captured, capturing. 1.** to catch and hold a person or thing; take control of: We *captured* the butterfly with a net. The British *captured* Washington, D.C. in the War of 1812. **2.** to catch and hold, as if capturing a person: The paintings of Frederic Remington *captured* the color and excitement of the Old West. —*noun, plural* **captures.** the act of capturing: There was a $10,000 reward for the *capture* of the bank robbers.

car [kär] *noun, plural* **cars. 1.** a motor vehicle with four wheels and a motor; an automobile. **2.** any similar vehicle used to carry people or things: a railroad *car*, a street*car.*

Ca•ra•cas [kə rä′ kəs] the capital of Venezuela. *Population:* 1,280,000.

car•a•mel [kar′ ə məl] *noun, plural* **caramels. 1.** a smooth, chewy brown candy, usually cut into small cubes. **2.** sugar that has melted and turned brown from being cooked slowly, used in flavoring cookies and other foods.

car•at [kar′ ət] *noun, plural* **carats. 1.** a unit of weight used to measure precious stones, such as

C

Pronunciation Key: T–Z			
t	ten; date	v	very; live
th	think	w	win; away
th	these	y	you
u	cut; butter	z	zoo; cause
ur	turn; bird	zh	measure

(Turn the page for more information.)

117

diamonds. A carat equals 1/5 of a gram. **2.** a measure of pure gold or gold mixed with other metals. ♦ This meaning is usually spelled **karat.**

car•a•van [kar′ ə van′] *noun, plural* **caravans.** a traveling group of people or vehicles: a *caravan* of army tanks and trucks.

car•bo•hy•drate [kär′ bō hī′ drāt] *noun, plural* **carbohydrates.** a food substance of sugar or starch made by green plants from carbon dioxide, water, and the energy supplied by the sun. Foods such as bread, noodles, and potatoes have high amounts of carbohydrates in them. Carbohydrates supply energy to the body.

car•bon [kär′ bən] *noun.* a chemical element found in some amount in all living things. Coal, petroleum, and diamonds are almost pure carbon.

carbon di•ox•ide [dī äk′ sīd] a heavy gas with no odor, formed from carbon and oxygen. Carbon dioxide is a part of the air that humans and other living things breathe out. Plants need carbon dioxide to produce food through a process called PHOTOSYNTHESIS. Carbon dioxide is also formed when fuels such as gas, oil, or coal are burned for energy.

carbon mon•ox•ide [mə näk′ sīd] a very poisonous gas that has no color or smell. It is formed when carbon burns but does not completely burn up, as in a gasoline engine.

car•bu•re•tor [kär′ bə rā′ tər] *noun, plural* **carburetors.** a part of a gasoline engine that mixes air and gasoline into a fine mist that will burn to run the engine.

car•cass [kär′ kəs] *noun, plural* **carcasses.** the dead body of an animal, especially when it is ready to be cut up for meat.

card [kärd] *noun, plural* **cards. 1.** a small, flat piece of stiff paper, cardboard, or plastic with printing on it. A card usually has a rectangular shape. There are many different kinds of cards, such as greeting cards, library cards, school report cards, and so on. **2.** one of a set of 52 cards divided into four suits and marked with special symbols and numbers, used in playing various games. **3. cards.** any game played with playing cards.

card•board [kärd′ bôrd′] *noun.* a stiff piece of thick paper, used for making boxes and some types of cards.

car•di•nal [kärd′ nəl] *noun, plural* **cardinals. 1.** an official in the Catholic Church having the second highest rank, just under the Pope. **2.** a bright-red color. This is the color of the robes and hats worn by Roman Catholic cardinals. **3.**

a bright-red songbird of North America with a crest of feathers on its head. —*adjective.* **1.** of first importance; primary: The *cardinal* rule of good pitching is to be able to throw strikes. **2.** having a bright-red color.

cardinal The cardinal got its name because its bright red feathers reminded people of the red robes worn by cardinals in the Catholic Church.

cardinal number a number that indicates how many of something there are, such as *three* days or *four* houses.

care [kâr] *noun, plural* **cares. 1.** a feeling of being worried or troubled; concern: She's always in such a good mood that you'd think she didn't have a *care* in the world. **2.** close attention: The box of glasses was marked "Handle with *Care.*" **3.** a looking after; custody or keeping: to be in the *care* of a nurse. I'm going to take *care* of my neighbor's dog while she's away. —*verb,* **cared, caring. 1.** to be interested in or concerned with: She *cares* a great deal about her schoolwork. I don't *care* where we eat as long as it's cheap. **2.** to wish or want: Would you *care* to have some more tea?

ca•reer [kə rēr′] *noun, plural* **careers. 1.** the work that a person does for a living: Anne is planning a *career* as a lawyer. **2.** the general course of a person's life: Bill Bradley had an outstanding *career* as a basketball player before he became a U.S. Senator.

care•free [kâr′ frē′] *adjective, more/most.* free of troubles or worry; without care: The children seemed completely *carefree* as they ran and played in the park.

care•ful [kâr′ fəl] *adjective, more/most.* paying close attention; using care: Please be *careful* with that hot soup. —**carefully,** *adverb:* She drove very *carefully* during the snowstorm.

care•less [kâr′ lis] *adjective, more/most.* **1.** not giving enough attention; not caring: He was *careless* in painting the wall and left a lot of bare spots. **2.** done without being careful; showing lack of care: It was a *careless* mistake for John to leave the stove on when he went out. **—carelessly,** *adverb:* She wrote the report very *carelessly,* and it was filled with spelling mistakes. **—carelessness,** *noun:* That forest fire was caused by a camper's *carelessness* .

ca•ress [kə res′] *verb,* **caressed, caressing.** to touch or stroke in a loving way: She *caressed* the baby's head while it lay sleeping. **—noun,** *plural* **caresses.** a tender, loving touch.

care•tak•er [kâr′ tā′ kər] *noun, plural* **caretakers.** a person whose job is to look after another's property, such as a house or land.

car•go [kär′ gō] *noun, plural* **cargoes** or **cargos.** the load of goods that is carried by a ship, plane, or other vehicle; freight.

Caribbean The Caribbean island of Antigua. The name *Caribbean* comes from the Carib Indians, a tribe that lived in this area at the time of Columbus.

Car•ib•be•an Sea [kar′ ə bē′ ən *or* kə rib′ ē ən] a part of the Atlantic Ocean between the West Indies and Central and South America.

car•i•bou [kar′ ə boo′] *noun, plural* **caribou** or **caribous.** a type of large deer that lives in colder northern regions. It is the only type of deer in which both the male and female have antlers. ♦ This animal is considered to be the same as the one known in Europe as a REINDEER.

car•na•tion [kär nā′ shən] *noun, plural* **carnations.** a flower with a sweet, spicy smell and many colorful petals.

Car•ne•gie [kär′ nə gē] **Andrew,** 1835–1919, American businessman who later gave much of his money to charity. He was born in Scotland.

car•ni•val [kär′ nə vəl] *noun, plural* **carnivals.** a show or festival that has rides, games, and other amusements. ♦ The word *carnival* comes from the Latin *carne,* meaning "meat" (as does *carnivorous*). In the Middle Ages, people could not eat meat during Lent, a period of 40 days before Easter. A carnival was a celebration just before Lent began.

car•niv•o•rous [kär niv′ ə rəs] *adjective,* feeding on the flesh of other animals; meat-eating: Lions are *carnivorous* animals.

car•ol [kar′ əl] *noun, plural* **carols.** a song of joy and celebration, especially a Christmas song. **—verb,** **caroled, caroling.** to sing songs of joy and celebration: A group of our neighbors go *caroling* every Christmas Eve. **—caroler,** *noun.*

car•ou•sel [kar′ ə sel′] *noun, plural* **carousels.** (also spelled **carrousel**) a MERRY-GO-ROUND.

carp [kärp] *noun, plural* **carp** or **carps.** a large freshwater fish found in ponds and streams, often used for food.

car•pen•ter [kär′ pən tər] *noun, plural* **carpenters.** a person whose work is building and fixing things made of wood, such as houses.

car•pet [kär′ pit] *noun, plural* **carpets. 1.** a soft, heavy floor covering made from wool or other fibers. **2.** anything that covers like a carpet: "They relaxed on a *carpet* of moss." (William Steig) **—verb,** **carpeted, carpeting.** to cover with a carpet: They *carpeted* the bedroom and the hallway.

car pool an arrangement by a group of car owners in which the members of the group take turns driving each other to work or driving their children to school.

car•riage [kar′ ij] *noun, plural* **carriages. 1.** a four-wheeled vehicle that carries passengers and is usually pulled by a horse or horses. **2.** a small vehicle that is pushed by hand and used to carry a baby or doll. **3.** a movable part of a machine that supports or carries other moving parts: a typewriter *carriage.*

car•ri•er [kar′ ē ər] *noun, plural* **carriers. 1.** any

C

Pronunciation Key: [ə] Symbol

The [ə] or *schwa* sound occurs in syllables without an accent. It can be spelled with any vowel, such as **a** in above, **e** in listen, **i** in pencil, **o** in melon, **u** in circus. It can also be a combination of vowels, such as **io** in action, **ai** in mountain, **iou** in precious.

(Turn the page for more information.)

C

person or thing that carries something: a mail *carrier*. **2.** see **aircraft carrier**. **3.** a person or animal that does not suffer from a disease but carries the germs and can pass them on.

Car•roll [kar′əl] **Lewis,** 1832–1898, English novelist, the author of *Alice in Wonderland*. His real name was **Charles L. Dodson.**

car•rot [kar′ət] *noun, plural* **carrots.** the long orange root of a common garden plant, often eaten as a vegetable.

car•ry [kar′ē] *verb,* **carried, carrying. 1.** to hold or support something while moving it from one place to another: Please *carry* these towels upstairs. The Amazon *carries* more water than any other river in the world. **2.** to have with oneself or itself: She always *carries* some extra money in case she needs it. **3.** to move from one place to another: The singer's voice *carried* to the last row of the theater. **4.** to have for sale: Does that store *carry* cameras? **5.** to win or capture: In the 1984 election Ronald Reagan *carried* every state but Minnesota.

carry on 1. to take part in; conduct: to *carry on* a conversation, to *carry on* business. **2.** to behave or talk in a foolish or very excited way.
carry out to put into action; accomplish: to *carry out* a plan.

Car•son [kär′sən] **Kit (Christopher),** 1809–1868, American frontiersman and scout.

cart [kärt] *noun, plural* **carts. 1.** a strong two-wheeled vehicle used for carrying loads. Carts are usually pulled by oxen, mules, or horses. **2.** a lightweight vehicle that is pushed or pulled by hand: Mary loaded her groceries into the shopping *cart.* —*verb,* **carted, carting.** to carry something in or as if in a cart: It took all morning to *cart* the trash to the dump.

Car•ter [kär′tər] **Jimmy (James Earl),** born 1924, the thirty-ninth president of the United States, from 1977 to 1981.

car•ti•lage [kär′tə lij] *noun.* a strong, flexible body tissue that is not as hard as bone but is able to support softer tissues in the same way that bone does. The nose and the outer part of the ear are made of cartilage.

car•ton [kärt′ən] *noun, plural* **cartons.** a container of cardboard, paper, or plastic that comes in different shapes and sizes and can hold a variety of things: a milk *carton.*

car•toon [kär tōōn′] *noun, plural* **cartoons. 1.** a drawing or sketch that shows something funny or tells a story. Cartoons usually appear in magazines and newspapers. A **political cartoon** gives an opinion on politics in a humorous or exaggerated drawing. ♦ A person who draws cartoons is a **cartoonist. 2.** a group of cartoons arranged in a short series in a newspaper; a comic strip. **3.** a movie made up of a continuous series of drawings.

car•tridge [kär′trij] *noun, plural* **cartridges. 1.** a small metal, plastic, or paper case filled with gunpowder and a bullet, used for firing from a gun. **2.** a small case that holds something for use in a machine or device, such as film for a camera, ink for a pen, the needle in a record player, or tape for a tape recorder.

carve [kärv] *verb,* **carved, carving. 1.** to cut or slice cooked meat into pieces: to *carve* a turkey, to *carve* roast beef. **2.** to cut or shape something out of a solid block: to *carve* a statue. **3.** to decorate or make by cutting: Many students had *carved* their names in the old desk. ♦ Something that is carved is a **carving.**

Car•ver [kär′vər] **George Washington** 1864–1943, American plant scientist.

Carver A painting of George Washington Carver by the American artist Betsy Graves.

cas•cade [kas kād′] *noun, plural* **cascades. 1.** a waterfall or series of waterfalls. **2.** something that seems to move like a waterfall: "Sister Irene recognized nothing in his *cascade* of words. " (Joyce Carol Oates) —*verb,* **cascaded, cascading.** to fall in or like a cascade: When the pipe broke, water *cascaded* down the steps.

case¹ [kās] *noun, plural* **cases. 1.** an example of something: This is an obvious *case* of cheating, because every one of his answers is exactly the same as hers. **2.** the actual facts or state of affairs: They expected the building to be finished this month, but that's not the *case*. **3.** an illness or injury, or a person who is ill or injured: a *case* of measles. **4.** a matter that is being handled by the police or other officials, or being tried in a court of law: a murder *case*.

in case or **in case of** if it should happen that; if: Buy some more milk just *in case* we run out.

people to be in a play, movie, or television program: Judy Garland was *cast* as Dorothy in *The Wizard of Oz*. **6.** to record a vote: She *cast* her ballot for Sue to be the team captain.

case English has words that are like tools. If you use them correctly, you make a good sentence. Take the term *case*. In English, case is the difference in pronouns: *him, her, me; he, she, I.* "Mom drives Dave and *I* to school." "Dave and *me* like to sit in the front seat." What's wrong in those two sentences? "I," like "he" and "she," is nominative—that is, it's like a noun. "Me," like "him" and "her," is objective, that is, the object of the noun. "I hit the ball." "The ball hit me."

case² *noun, plural* **cases.** a box, bag, or other container used to hold and carry things: a camera *case,* a *case* of soda, a *case* of motor oil.

cash [kash] *noun.* **1.** money on hand in the form of bills and coins; ready money. **2.** money or a check paid at the time of buying something: Is she going to pay *cash,* or charge it to her credit card? —*verb,* **cashed, cashing.** to give or get cash for: to *cash* a check.

cash•ew [kash′o͞o] *noun, plural* **cashews.** a small, curved nut that can be eaten. It grows on an evergreen tree that is found in hot, wet climates.

cash•ier [ka shĕr′] *noun, plural* **cashiers.** a person in a store, restaurant, or bank who takes in or pays out money to customers.

cash•mere [kazh′mĕr *or* kash′mĕr] *noun, plural* **cashmeres.** a very soft, fine wool that comes from the hair of a certain kind of goat living in the high mountains of Asia.

cas•ket [kas′kit] *noun, plural* **caskets.** a box to hold the body of a dead person; a coffin.

Cas•pi•an Sea [kas′pē ən] the largest saltwater lake in the world. It lies between southeastern Europe and southwestern Asia.

cas•se•role [kas′ə rōl′] *noun, plural* **casseroles.** **1.** a heavy cooking dish in which food can be baked and served. **2.** food cooked in such a dish.

cas•sette [kə set′] *noun, plural* **cassettes.** a small plastic box that holds magnetic tape to be loaded into a tape player or tape recorder.

cast [kast] *verb,* **casted, casting. 1.** to throw through the air: The fisherman *cast* his line into the water. **2.** to cause to fall on or over: "The dim light from the cabin window *cast* long shadows." (William Armstrong) **3.** to direct or turn: "Sara *cast* one of her quick looks about her." (Frances Hodgson Burnett) **4.** to make or form something by pouring a liquid or soft material into a mold and letting it harden: The artist *cast* a statue in bronze. **5.** to choose

—*noun, plural* **casts. 1.** a stiff bandage made of plaster and cloth, used for holding a broken bone or injured part of the body in place while it heals. **2.** the actors in a play, movie, or television program. **3.** the act of casting; a throw. **4.** something that is cast in a mold.

cast iron a form of iron that has been melted and poured into molds. It is strong and heavy and is used to make frying pans, stoves, radiators, and machine parts.

castle The Alcazar, a famous castle in Spain built in the 11th century. We use the term *castle in Spain* to mean "a daydream or imaginary scheme."

cas•tle [kas′əl] *noun, plural* **castles. 1.** a very large building or group of buildings with thick walls, towers, and many rooms. Castles were built in the Middle Ages to give protection against attack. Kings, princes, and other pow-

Pronunciation Key: Accent Marks

[′] is the normal accent mark. It shows where the main stress falls on a word.

[′] is a secondary accent mark. It shows a lighter stress than the primary accent. For example:

tel • e • vis • ion [tel′ə vizh′ən]
(Turn the page for more information.)

C

erful rulers lived in castles. **2.** one of the pieces in the game of chess, also known as ROOK.

Cas•tro [kas′ trō] **Fidel,** born 1926, Cuban revolutionary leader, the ruler of Cuba since 1959.

cas•u•al [kazh′ wəl *or* kazh′ ȯo̅ əl] *adjective, more/most.* **1.** happening by chance; not expected: a *casual* meeting on the street between two old friends. **2.** without strong feeling or concern: Mary has a *casual* friendship with the women in her office. **3.** not formal; relaxed: He was dressed in *casual* clothes for the picnic. —**casually,** *adverb.*

cas•u•al•ty [kazh′ əl tē] *noun, plural* **casualties. 1.** a person who is seriously injured or killed in an accident, or a soldier who is killed, wounded, or missing in battle. **2.** a person or thing that is hurt or destroyed by some event: Several older stores downtown were *casualties* of the loss of business to a new shopping center.

cat [kat] *noun, plural* **cats. 1.** a small, furry animal with a long tail and sharp claws, often kept as a pet. **2.** any of the larger animals that belong to the same family as the pet cat, such as a lion, tiger, leopard, bobcat, or mountain lion.

catch [kach *or* kech] *verb,* **caught, catching. 1.** to take hold of something that is moving with the hands: to *catch* a ball. **2.** to capture or trap: to *catch* a fish, to *catch* a butterfly in a net. **3.** to become fastened or stuck: She *caught* her sweater on a nail. **4.** to discover by surprise: Mom *caught* Chris eating candy just before dinner. **5.** to be in time for: to *catch* a bus or a train. **6.** to suddenly have or get: The log *caught* fire. Don't go out without your jacket—you might *catch* cold. **7.** *Informal.* to see or hear: I'm sorry; I didn't *catch* your name. —*noun, plural* **catches. 1.** the act of catching something. **2.** something that holds or fastens: the *catch* on a bracelet. **3.** something that is caught: a *catch* of fish. **4.** a game of throwing and catching a ball. **5.** a hidden trick or difficulty: That offer of free land can't be true; there has to be a *catch* somewhere.

catch•er [kach′ ər *or* kech′ ər] *noun, plural* **catchers. 1.** a player in baseball whose position is behind home plate and who catches pitches that are not hit. **2.** any person or thing that catches: A dog*catcher* catches stray dogs that are running loose.

---

catch 22 The expression "catch 22" means a 'no-win' situation—either way you go, it's wrong. This is a new expression, from Joseph Heller's novel *Catch-22.* There are also older variations on "catch 22." "Six of one, half a dozen of the other." "Heads I win, tails you lose." The ancient Greeks used "between Scylla and Charybdis." The Strait of Messina, in the Mediterranean Sea, had on one side a rocky place called Scylla, on the other a whirlpool called Charybdis. A ship passing through was in great danger whichever way it went. A current expression, "between a rock and a hard place," sounds like the ancient Greek.

---

cat•a•log [kat′ ə lôg′] *noun, plural* **catalogs. 1.** a list of things in a certain order. A library has a **card catalog** giving an alphabetical list of all its books by author, title, and subject. **2.** a book or file containing such a list: Stores mail out *catalogs* listing the things they have for sale. A college *catalog* tells about the courses that students can take. —*verb,* **cataloged, cataloging.** to list in a catalog: to *catalog* the paintings owned by a museum.

cat•a•logue [kat′ ə lôg′] *noun, plural* **catalogues.** *verb,* **catalogued, cataloguing.** another spelling of **catalog.**

cat•a•ract [kat′ ə rakt′] *noun, plural* **cataracts. 1.** a very large waterfall. **2.** a condition of the eye in which the lens becomes cloudy and light is blocked from entering.

ca•tas•tro•phe [kə tas′ trə fē] *noun, plural* **catastrophes.** a sudden and terrible disaster, such as an earthquake, flood or plane crash.

catch 22 *Informal.* a problem that cannot be solved because two different rules or conditions automatically cancel each other out: Tony can't get a job after school because he doesn't have any experience; the *catch 22* is that the only way to get experience is to have a job.

cat•e•go•ry [kat′ ə gôr′ ē] *noun, plural* **categories.** a group of things that are thought of as being alike in some way; a class: Milk, cheese, and butter are part of the *category* of dairy foods. ◆ Something that has to do with a category is **categorical** [kat′ i gôr′ ə kəl] —**categorically,** *adverb.*

ca•ter [kā′ tər] *verb,* **catered, catering. 1.** to supply food, drink, and other services for a party or special event: to *cater* a wedding. ◆ A person or business that does this is a **caterer. 2.** to please someone by providing what the person needs or wants: That hotel *caters* to business travelers. **3.** to give a special or unfair

C

cattle *Cattle* means steers or cows. In medieval French, *cattle* was a variation of the word *chattel*. *Chattel* is today a legal term referring to movable possessions that are not real estate: that is, furniture and equipment. Cattle were, therefore, chattel. The most valuable movable possessions in olden times were livestock—chickens, ducks, etc.—and the most valuable livestock was cattle. It follows, doesn't it? Even though cattle are very useful to man, it is a negative comment when a group of people are said to be like cattle. This means that they move or act as one large, unthinking mass, rather than doing things individually. The idea is that they form a "herd," like a herd of cattle.

advantage. The newspaper editorial said that the President's new tax plan *caters* to big business.

cat•er•pil•lar [kat′ ər pil′ ər] *noun, plural* **caterpillars.** a small, worm-like stage in the growth of moths and butterflies. A caterpillar is the LARVA, or first stage, in the growth of these insects.

caterpillar Four common types of caterpillars. The two on the left will become moths and the two on the right will be butterflies. *Caterpillar* comes from a Latin word meaning "a little hairy cat."

cat•fish [kat′ fish′] *noun, plural* **catfish** or **catfishes.** a type of fresh-water fish that has long feelers on the side of the head that look somewhat like a cat's whiskers.

ca•the•dral [kə thē′ drəl] *noun, plural* **cathedrals.** the official church of a BISHOP. Many large, impressive cathedrals were built in Europe during the Middle Ages.

Cath•er•ine the Great [kath′ rən] 1729–1796, the ruler of Russia from 1763 to 1796.

Cath•o•lic [kath′ lik] *adjective.* having to do with the branch of the Christian church that is headed by the Pope. —*noun, plural* **Catholics.** a person who is a member of the Catholic church. ♦ Another name for this is the **Roman Catholic Church.** —*adjective.* **catholic.** having to do with a broad area; general; widespread: a person with *catholic* tastes in reading.

cat•tle [kat′ əl] *plural noun.* the large animals with hoofs and short horns that are commonly raised for meat, milk, and hides; cows, bulls, and steers as a group.

caught [kôt] *verb.* the past form of **catch:** "She *caught* me by surprise." (Louise Fitzhugh)

cau•li•flow•er [kô′ li flou′ ər] *noun.* a plant with a large round head made up of tightly-packed white flowers, often eaten as a vegetable.

caulk [kôk] *verb,* **caulked, caulking.** to fill in holes and cracks in a building or a boat to keep out air or water: to *caulk* the edges of a bathtub or shower. —*noun.* a soft or sticky material that is used to caulk.

cathedral Notre Dame de Paris (Our Lady of Paris) is located on an island in the Seine River. It is probably the world's best-known cathedral. Built between the years 1163 and 1250, it is an example of the *Gothic* style of architecture.

Pronunciation Key: A–F

a	and; hat	ch	chew; such
ā	ate; stay	d	dog; lid
â	care; air	e	end; yet
ä	father; hat	ē	she; each
b	boy; cab	f	fun; off

(Turn the page for more information.)

123

C

cause [kôz] *noun, plural* **causes. 1.** a thing or person that makes something happen: What was the *cause* of all that noise? Our history class is studying the *causes* of the Civil War. **2.** a reason for acting in a certain way: There's no *cause* to be upset about what happened. **3.** a goal or purpose that a person believes in: That group is working for the *cause* of peace. —*verb,* **caused, causing.** to make something happen; be the cause of: The forest fire was *caused* by lightning.

cave [kāv] *noun, plural* **caves.** a natural hollow place in the side of a mountain or under the ground, usually with an opening to the surface. —*verb,* **caved, caving. to cave in.** to fall in or down: After the blast, the walls of the building *caved in* quickly.

cave man a human being who lived in a cave thousands of years ago.

cav•ern [kav′ ərn] *noun, plural* **caverns.** a large cave, usually caused by an underground stream.

cause and effect In a cause-and-effect paragraph, you begin by describing some situation or event. "I fell down that day and, later, because I had to wear a plaster cast, I met someone I'd never have seen otherwise." Now, that's a cause leading to an effect. "The nurse who cut off the cast, once my leg had healed, told me of a job at the hospital." Now, that's an effect. The point is: at the beginning let your reader know where you will end.

cau•tion [kô′ shən] *noun, plural* **cautions. 1.** the act of being careful or watchful to avoid trouble or danger: Motorists were warned to use *caution* in driving because of the icy roads. **2.** a warning: The workmen who were fixing the highway put up a *caution* sign. —*verb,* **cautioned, cautioning.** to tell to be careful; warn: Dad *cautioned* us not to swim in the deep water alone.

cau•tious [kô′ shəs] *adjective, more/most.* being careful; using caution: The mountain climbers were very *cautious* on the narrow ledge. —**cautiously,** *adverb:* "He approached the bear cub *cautiously.*" (Marjorie Kinnan Rawlings)

cav•al•ry [kav′ əl rē] *noun, plural* **cavalries. 1.** in earlier times, a group of soldiers who fought on horseback. **2.** a modern fighting unit that uses tanks and helicopters.

cav•i•ty [kav′ ə tē] *noun, plural* **cavities. 1.** a hollow place or hole, as in the ground. **2.** a hollow place in a tooth caused by DECAY.

CB short for **citizens' band,** a range of radio frequencies that can be used by private citizens, as opposed to frequencies that are used by broadcasting stations, police departments, aircraft, and so on.

cease [sēs] *verb,* **ceased, ceasing.** to stop: "IBM said that it will *cease* production next month of its PC Jr. home computer." (Andrew Pollack)

cedar The true cedar tree is not found in the Americas. It is an ancient plant that is mentioned in the Bible.

cavalry "Cavalryman's Breakfast on the Plains," a painting done in about 1890 by the famous Western artist Frederic Remington.

ce•dar [sē′ dər] *noun, plural* **cedars.** an evergreen tree with thick, rough bark, soft needles, and reddish wood with a pleasant smell.

ceil·ing [sē′ ling] *noun, plural* **ceilings. 1.** the inside top part of a room, opposite the floor. **2.** the upper limit; top: The government put a *ceiling* on the price of gasoline. **3.** the highest that an aircraft can fly: That plane has a *ceiling* of 50,000 feet.

cel·e·brate [sel′ ə brāt′] *verb,* **celebrated, celebrating. 1.** to observe a certain day or time with special activities: to *celebrate* Christmas. Next month they will *celebrate* their 25th wedding anniversary. **2.** to have a party or enjoy oneself to honor a special occasion: The whole city *celebrated* when the home team won the World Series. **3.** to perform a religious ceremony: to *celebrate* Mass. **4.** to honor or praise someone or something. ♦ Usually used as an adjective: "He had been a *celebrated* pilot of naval airships." (John McPhee)

cel·e·bra·tion [sel′ ə brā′ shən] *noun, plural* **celebrations.** the act of celebrating: The author had a big *celebration* when his book reached number one on the best-seller list.

ce·leb·ri·ty [sə leb′ rə tē] *noun, plural* **celebrities.** a person who is famous and who is often seen on television or written about in newspapers and magazines.

cel·er·y [sel′ rē] *noun.* a garden plant with long, light-green stalks, eaten as a vegetable.

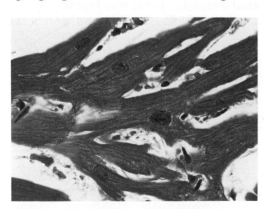

cell A greatly enlarged view of several muscle cells in the human heart. This meaning comes from the sense of a prison cell—a cell looks like a small, enclosed room.

cell [sel] *noun, plural* **cells. 1.** a very small, plain room, especially one in a prison where prisoners live. **2.** the basic unit of the body of a living thing. A cell has a center part called the NUCLEUS, which is surrounded by a fluid called PROTOPLASM and enclosed in a thin wall or membrane. **3.** a container holding substances that can produce electricity by means of chemical action.

cel·lar [sel′ ər] *noun, plural* **cellars.** a room or rooms under a house or under the ground; a basement.

cello The most famous cello player of the 20th century, Pablo Casals of Spain.

cel·lo [chel′ ō] *noun, plural* **cellos.** a musical instrument shaped like a violin, but larger and having a lower tone. It is held upright between the knees and is played with a bow.

cel·lo·phane [sel′ ə fān′] *noun.* a clear, thin material made from cellulose and used for wrapping items such as food and packages.

cel·lu·lose [sel′ yə lōs′] *noun.* a substance that forms the cell wall of a plant. When it is processed, cellulose can be used to make paper, plastics, cloth, and other materials.

Cel·si·us [sel′ shəs *or* sel′ sē əs] *adjective.* having to do with or measured by the **Celsius scale,** which is a way of showing temperature. A Celsius scale shows 0 degrees as the temperature at which water freezes and 100 degrees as the temperature at which water boils. ♦ This is also known as a CENTIGRADE SCALE. ♦ The name *Celsius* comes from Anders Celsius, a Swedish scientist who developed this system.

ce·ment [sə ment′] *noun, plural* **cements. 1.** a powdery gray mixture that is made by heating LIMESTONE and clay to a high temperature. When cement is mixed with water, the mixture

C

Pronunciation Key: G–N

g	give; big	k	kind; cat; back
h	hold	l	let; ball
i	it; this	m	make; time
ī	ice; my	n	not; own
j	jet; gem; edge	ng	having

(Turn the page for more information.)

C

dries to become very hard like stone. Cement is used in making buildings, roads, and sidewalks. **2.** any soft, sticky substance that hardens to hold things together: Rubber *cement* is used as a glue for household items. —*verb*, **cemented, cementing.** to join together or cover with or as if with cement.

cem•e•ter•y [sem′ ə ter′ ē] *noun, plural* **cemeteries.** a place where dead people are buried; a graveyard.

cen•sor [sen′ sər] *noun, plural* **censors.** a person whose job is to examine books, movies, or the like to remove parts that are thought to be harmful or improper: U.S. television networks have *censors* who review a program before it goes on the air.—*verb*, **censored, censoring.** to act as a censor: In World War II soldiers' letters were *censored* to take out information that might help the enemy. ◆ The act or fact of censoring something is **censorship:** Communist countries use *censorship* to make sure that nothing is published or broadcast that criticizes the government.

cen•sus [sen′ səs] *noun, plural* **censuses.** an official count of all the people who live in a certain country, state, or city. The national census of the U.S. is taken every ten years.

cent [sent] *noun, plural* **cents.** a coin of the U.S. and Canada, the smallest coin in value. One hundred cents is equal to one dollar.

cen•ti•pede [sen′ tə pēd′] *noun, plural* **centipedes.** a small animal like a worm, with a long flat body, many pairs of legs, and two poisonous front fangs.

centipede The form *cent-* means "one hundred," but a centipede may actually have as many as 170 legs. The first pair of legs are poisonous fangs.

cen•tral [sen′ tral] *adjective.* **1.** in or near the middle; in between: *Central* America is between North America and South America. The railroad station is in the *central* part of the city. **2.** most important; main: Scrooge is the *central* character of the story "A Christmas Carol."

Central America the southernmost part of the continent of North America, southeast of Mexi-

center "Man's concept of his place in the universe was centered *around* himself and the place where he lived." (Simpson & Beck) "People like to deny how much of our culture is centered *around* television." (Stephen Gottlieb) This is acceptable English, but not really elegant, precise English. In mathematics, a center is a single point, a reference for other locations. Other things can be around a center, but the center can't go around anything else! Try this: "The President centered his talk *on* jobs."

cen•ter [sen′ tər] *noun, plural* **centers. 1.** the exact middle point of a circle, equally distant from every point on the edge. **2.** the middle point or part of anything: Put the table in the *center* of the room. **3.** the main point of activity or attention: San Francisco is the banking *center* of northern California. **4.** a player whose position is in the middle of the playing area in such sports as basketball, football, and hockey. —*verb*, **centered, centering.** to put in the middle or center: *Center* the picture on the wall.

cen•ti•grade [sen′ tə grād′] *adjective.* another name for **Celsius.**

cen•ti•me•ter [sen′ tə mē′ tər] *noun, plural* **centimeters.** a basic measure of length in the METRIC SYSTEM, equal to 1/100 of a meter.

co. Central America includes the countries of **Belize** [bə lēz′], **Costa Rica** [kôs′ tə rē′ kə], El Salvador, Guatemala, Honduras, Nicaragua, and Panama.

cen•tu•ry [sen′ chə rē] *noun, plural* **centuries. 1.** any period of 100 years' time: From 1848 to 1948 was a *century*. **2.** any of the 100-year periods before or since the birth of Jesus Christ: We now live in the 20th *century*. 1776 was in the 18th *century*.

ce•ram•ic [sə ram′ ik] *noun, plural* **ceramics. 1. ceramics.** the art of making things such as bricks, bowls, and pots by shaping and baking clay. **2.** something made from clay in this way. ◆ Also used as an adjective: That room has a *ceramic* tile floor.

ce•re•al [sēr′ē əl] *noun, plural* **cereals. 1.** seeds or grains that come from certain grass plants such as wheat, rice, oats, corn, and rye. **2.** a breakfast food made of these seeds or grains. Cornflakes and oatmeal are cereals.

cer•e•mo•ny [ser′ə mō′ nē] *noun, plural* **ceremonies. 1.** an act or series of acts carried out in a special way or by special rules: Wedding *ceremonies* are performed today much as they were hundreds of years ago. **2.** very polite behavior based on formal rules. ◆ Something is done according to ceremony is **ceremonial** or **ceremonious:** The crowning of a king or queen of England is a very *ceremonial* occasion.

cer•tain [sur′ tən] *adjective, more/most.* **1.** known to be true or right; positive; sure: Are you absolutely *certain* that you locked the door? **2.** sure to be or happen: A wrong turn on that mountain road means a *certain* accident. **3.** settled or agreed on: To become an airline pilot you must have a *certain* number of hours of flying time. **4.** not named or stated, but known: *Certain* wild animals are active only at night. Coffee comes from a *certain* plant that grows in hot climates. ◆ The state or feeling of being certain is **certainty:** "I had an absolute *certainty* that I should see again what I had already seen." (Henry James)

cer•tain•ly [sur′ tən lē] *adverb.* surely or definitely; without a doubt: She *certainly* studied hard for that math test. "He *certainly* hated to be left alone in a place like Chicago." (Bernard Malamud)

cer•tif•i•cate [sər tif′ ə kit] *noun, plural* **certificates.** an official form or document giving information about something: A birth *certificate* tells the date and place of a person's birth.

Cer•van•tes [sər vän′ tās] **Miguel De,** 1547–1616, Spanish writer, author of *Don Quixote.*

chain [chān] *noun, plural* **chains. 1.** a row of links or rings joined to each other. Chains are usually made of metal and are used to fasten or pull things. **2.** silver or gold links made into a necklace or bracelet. **3.** a series of things or happenings connected to each other: The Boston Tea Party was part of the *chain* of events that led up to the American Revolution. A **chain store** is one of a group of stores of the same kind owned by the same company. —*verb,* **chained, chaining.** to fasten or hold with a chain: He *chained* his bike to the post so that no one could take it.

chair [châr] *noun, plural* **chairs.** a piece of furniture for one person to sit on. A chair usually has four legs and a back, and sometimes has arm rests on each side. —*verb,* **chaired, chairing.** to serve as chairman: Phyllis will *chair* the committee meeting.

C

chairman *Chairman* is of course male, A *man* is male. In today's world, we tend to say *chairperson,* so that it refers to either a man or a woman. Sometimes, *chairwoman* is used. But *chair* by itself has been used for many years. In 1939, John Steinbeck wrote in his famous novel *The Grapes of Wrath:* " 'Give our names, Jessie. Mention our names to Mix' Joad, Jessie's the Chair,' she explained." In a legislature, the person conducting a meeting is called "the chair," as in, "The *chair* now calls for a vote," Which word should you use in your writing? It depends on which an organization prefers to use, and on what the person prefers to be called.

chair•man [châr′ mən] *noun, plural* **chairmen. 1.** the person who is in charge of a meeting. **2.** a person who is in charge of a company or group: He is *chairman* of the English department at the state university. ◆ The **chairman of the board** of a company is the head of the company.

chair•wom•an [châr′ woom′ ən] *noun, plural* **chairwomen.** a woman who is in charge of a meeting or group.

chalk [chôk] *noun, plural* **chalks. 1.** a soft, white rock made up mostly of tiny seashells. Chalk is used to make cement, lime, and fertilizer. **2.** a piece of this substance used for writing or drawing. —*verb,* **chalked, chalking. 1.** to write, draw, or mark with chalk: She *chalked* a line on the sidewalk. **2. chalk up.** to score or earn: to *chalk up* ten points in a game.

chalk•board [chôk′ bôrd′] *noun, plural* **chalkboards.** large green or black board used for writing on with chalk.

chal•lenge [chal′ ənj] *verb,* **challenged, chal-**

Pronunciation Key: O–S			
ō	over; go	ou	out; town
ô	all; law	p	put; hop
oo	look; full	r	run; car
ōō	pool; who	s	set; miss
oi	oil; boy	sh	show

(Turn the page for more information.)

lenging. 1. to call to a fight or contest: Our sixth-grade team *challenged* the other school to a touch football game. **2.** to ask for proof that something is true or correct: The police *challenged* his story of what had happened to the missing money. **3.** to demand effort or work: That teacher believes in trying to *challenge* her students. ◆ Often used as an adjective: "Now he confronted the most *challenging*, the deepest part of the stream." (William Steig) —*noun, plural* **challenges. 1.** a call to take part in a contest or fight. **2.** a call or demand to find out who someone is: The soldier halted at the sentry's *challenge*. **3.** a job or task that calls for a lot of effort: That advanced math class should really be a *challenge* for him.

cham•ber [chām′ bər] *noun, plural* **chambers. 1.** a private room in a house, especially a bedroom. **2.** a large room where lawmakers meet together, or the group itself: The Senate is the upper *chamber* of Congress. ◆ In many cities, a **chamber of commerce** works to help business in the town. **3.** *also,* **chambers.** a judge's private meeting room in a courthouse. **4.** any enclosed place like a chamber: The *chamber* of a gun is where the bullet goes.

chameleon The chameleon can change its color in reaction to outside conditions. Because of this, the word is sometimes used to describe people who change their beliefs or habits to suit the situation.

cha•me•leon [kə mēl′ yən *or* kə mē′ lē ən] *noun, plural* **chameleons.** a small lizard that can change the color of its skin. It is often thought that it does this to match the color of its surroundings, but actually the change is a reaction to light and heat or to possible danger.

cham•pi•on [cham′ pē ən] *noun, plural* **champions. 1.** the winner of first place in a contest or game: Joe Louis was heavyweight boxing

champion for twelve years, longer than any other man. **2.** a person who fights for or defends other people or a cause: Robin Hood was thought of as the *champion* of the poor in old England. ◆ A **championship** is the position of being a champion: The *championship* of professional football is known as the Super Bowl.

chance [chans] *noun, plural* **chances. 1.** an opportunity or occasion to do something: "Please write to me, soon as you have a *chance*." (Alice Walker) **2.** something that is likely to happen; a possibility: There's a *chance* that it will rain this afternoon. **3.** fate or luck: "It was a matter of *chance* that I should have rented a house in one of the strangest communities in North America." (F. Scott Fitzgerald) **4.** a risk or gamble: Don't take *chances* by swimming alone in such rough water. —*verb,* **chanced, chancing. 1.** to happen accidentally: Julie *chanced* to meet a friend from home while traveling in Europe. **2.** to risk: Let's leave now; I don't want to *chance* being late.

chan•de•lier [shan′ də lēr′] *noun, plural* **chandeliers.** a light fixture that hangs down from the ceiling and has several branches to hold lights.

change [chānj] *verb,* **changed, changing. 1.** to become or make different: I was glad when the weather *changed* and it was hot enough to go swimming. She *changed* her mind about dinner and decided to have fish instead of steak. **2.** to put on other clothes or coverings: He *changed* into his sneakers for gym class. **3.** to exchange money, such as dollars for coins. —*noun, plural* **changes. 1.** the act or result of changing: They had a *change* of plans and decided to drive instead of taking the bus. **2.** something that takes the place of something else; something new or different: **3.** money returned when one gives a larger amount for something than what it costs. **4.** coins, as opposed to paper money: a *change* purse.

chan•nel [chan′ əl] *noun, plural* **channels. 1.** a means of carrying an electronic signal to a radio or television set through a certain range of frequencies. **2.** the path followed by a river, or the deepest part of a river or other waterway. **3.** a body of water joining two larger bodies: The English *Channel* connects the North Sea to the Atlantic Ocean. **4. channels.** the official or proper way of proceeding in a business or other organization: In the army you have to go through *channels* to get something done. —*verb,* **channeled, channeling** or **channelled, channelling. 1.** to form a channel. **2.** to send as if through a channel; direct: Mary has *channeled* all her energy into her studies.

chant [chant] *noun, plural* **chants.** a singing or shouting of the same words or tunes over and over again. Chants are often used during religious services or at sports events. —*verb,* **chanted, chanting.** to sing or shout a chant.

Cha•nu•kah [ha′ nə kə] another spelling of **Hanukkah.**

cha•os [kā′ äs] *noun.* a state of great confusion; a complete lack of order: There was complete *chaos* in the city after an ice storm knocked out all electrical power.

chap[1] [chap] *verb,* **chapped, chapping.** to make or become dry, rough or cracked. ♦ Usually used as an adjective: *chapped* lips.

chap[2] *noun, plural* **chaps.** *Informal.* a boy or man; fellow: "That's the *chap* who looks after things up here." (Michael Bond)

chap•el [chap′ əl] *noun, plural* **chapels. 1.** a small church. **2.** a small area within a larger church, used for special religious services or private prayer.

chap•lain [chap′ lən] *noun, plural* **chaplains.** a religious leader who holds services for members of the armed forces or for people in a prison, school, or hospital.

chaps [chaps] *plural noun.* heavy leather pants worn by cowboys over their regular pants to protect their legs. Chaps are fastened around the waist but have no seat.

chap•ter [chap′ tər] *noun, plural* **chapters. 1.** one section of a book: *Chapter* nine of my science book is about electricity. **2.** a period of life or time that is thought of as like a chapter in a book: The settling of the Old West was an exciting *chapter* in American history. **3.** a branch of a club or other organization: The Red Cross has *chapters* in many different cities.

char [chär] *verb,* **charred, charring.** to partly burn something: a *charred* piece of wood.

and so on. **3.** good personal qualities: "Peter hasn't enough *character* yet, not enough willpower, too little courage and strength." (Anne Frank) **4.** a person in a movie, play, book, or story: Walt Disney's most famous *characters* are Mickey Mouse and Donald Duck. **5.** *Informal.* a person who is thought of as odd or unusual. **6.** a letter, number, or other mark used in printing. **7.** the minimum amount of information handled by a computer.

char•ac•ter•is•tic [kar′ ik tə ris′ tik] *noun, plural* **characteristics.** a special quality or feature that makes a person or thing what it is. —*adjective, more/most.* being a special quality or feature of someone or something; typical: The use of very strong, bright colors is *characteristic* of the paintings of Vincent van Gogh. —**characteristically,** *adverb.*

char•ac•ter•ize [kar′ ik tə rīz′] *verb,* **characterized, characterizing. 1.** to be a characteristic of: A camel is *characterized* by its humped back. **2.** to tell about the character of: In the book *Charlotte's Web,* Wilbur the pig is *characterized* as being kind and friendly.

char•coal [chär′ kōl′] *noun.* a black substance that is made by heating wood in a container with very little air. Charcoal is used for drawing pictures, as a filter to make air or water pure, or for fuel, as in outdoor cooking.

charge [chärj] *verb,* **charged, charging. 1.** to ask as a price or payment: That store *charges* $3.00 to rent a video tape. **2.** to pay later for something that is bought now: She's going to *charge* that dress and pay for it at the end of the month. **3.** to accuse or blame in an official way: The police have *charged* the driver with speeding. **4.** to attack by rushing at something: "Like a black thunderbolt the bull *charged,* the rush of his great body shaking the earth." (Walter Farley) **5.** to load with electricity: The gas

C

character In a story a person is called a character. If he's the main character, and if the story is fiction, he is also called the hero—that's a literary form meaning "chief character" and has nothing to do with bravery. You will someday run into the words "protaganist" and "antagonist." These terms describe the character who acts or speaks for some cause— "pro"—and the character who opposes it—"ant(e)."

char•ac•ter [kar′ ik tər] *noun, plural* **characters. 1.** all the qualities and features of a thing or place that make it different from others: The city of Paris has a special *character* that draws visitors from all over the world. **2.** what a person really is like as shown by the way he or she thinks, talks, or acts. A person's character may be strong or weak, honest or dishonest,

Pronunciation Key: T–Z			
t	ten; date	v	very; live
th	think	w	win; away
<u>th</u>	these	y	you
u	cut; butter	z	zoo; cause
ur	turn; bird	zh	measure

(Turn the page for more information.)

C

charisma *Charisma* goes back to a Greek word that meant "a special gift or favor from God." It has been in English since the 1600's, usually in connection with persons who were thought to be possessed by special powers—beyond those ordinary persons had. Today, people associate it with politics, especially when it is used to describe President Kennedy's personality and political style or President Reagan's. *Charisma* was originally a much stronger word than *charm*, given its religious origin, and it suggested a special kind of leader—someone who could move a nation with the force of his personality, such as Mahatma Gandhi. As often happens with language, the word became weaker through overuse. Many politicians and business leaders are now said to be *charismatic*, and the word now often means simply "having the personality to attract or influence others."

station attendant *charged* our car battery. —*noun, plural* **charges. 1.** the cost of something; price: There is a $2.00 *charge* to get in to the museum. **2.** responsibility, care, or control. ◆ Often used in the phrase **in charge:** The sales manager is *in charge* of the sales force. **3.** the amount of electricity in a substance: The batteries had a weak *charge*, so the flashlight was dim. **4.** a formal or legal accusing or blame for something wrong: The men were arrested on a *charge* of robbery. **5.** a rushing attack: "The *Charge* of the Light Brigade" is a poem about a famous battle.

charge account a service based on an agreement between a store or bank and its customer that the customer may buy things, charge them to his account, and pay for them later.

chariot In his four-horse chariot, the Emperor Marcus Aurelius makes his entry into Rome. This is a *relief* sculpture, done in about the year 160 A.D.

char•i•ot [char′ē ət] *noun, plural* **chariots.** a cart on two wheels that is pulled by horses. In ancient times, chariots were used in races, wars, and parades.

cha•ris•ma [kə riz′ mə] *noun.* a special power or ability that a person has to make others admire him and want to follow him; great charm or personal appeal.

char•i•ta•ble [char′ ə tə bəl] *adjective, more/ most.* **1.** having to do with charity: The Red Cross is a *charitable* organization. The amount of a *charitable* contribution can be taken off a person's income tax. **2.** giving money or help to the poor or needy; generous. **3.** kind and understanding: She thought his painting looked awful, but she made a *charitable* comment that he must have worked hard on it. —**charitably,** *adverb:* After Bobby struck out the coach said *charitably*, "You almost hit that last one."

char•i•ty [char′ ə tē] *noun, plural* **charities. 1.** kindness and forgiveness in dealing with other people. **2.** a gift of money or other help to the poor or needy. **3.** an organization or fund for helping people who are poor or needy, such as the Red Cross or the Salvation Army.

Char•le•magne [shär′ lə mān′] 742–814, king of what is now France and ruler of the Holy Roman Empire.

Char•lotte [shär′ lət] the largest city in North Carolina. *Population:* 314,000.

charm [chärm] *noun, plural* **charms. 1.** the power to attract or please people: She's very well-liked by her classmates because she has great *charm*. "Its *charm* was that everything was light and airy, happy like spring, with a lot of blue sky, paper-white clouds . . ." (James Baldwin) **2.** a magic object, saying, or action that is supposed to bring good luck or keep away evil: People sometimes carry a rabbit's foot as a lucky *charm*. **3.** a small ornament that hangs from a bracelet or other piece of jewelry. —*verb,* **charmed, charming.** to attract or please greatly: They were *charmed* by the Valentine card their daughter made for them. ◆ Often used as an adjective: a *charming* dress.

chart [chärt] *noun, plural* **charts. 1.** information that is given in a neat or orderly way, in the form of a GRAPH, diagram, or list of facts and figures. Charts are used to show such information as weather, population, sales, and so on. **2.** a map, especially a map for sailors that shows how deep water is and where things are located. —*verb,* **charted, charting. 1.** to make a map of: The explorer Amerigo Vespucci *charted* the coastline of South America. **2.** to show or record on a chart: That TV show *charts* the most popular records each week.

char•ter [chär′tər] *noun, plural* **charters. 1.** an official written document or paper that gives special rights and responsibilities to people. Certain companies, such as airlines or television stations, must have a government charter to do business. **2.** an agreement to rent or lease a bus, airplane, or car for a special purpose. —*verb,* **chartered, chartering.** to rent or lease by charter: to *charter* a bus.

chauf•feur [shō′fər *or* shō fur′] *noun, plural* **chauffeurs.** someone whose work is driving other people around in a car.

cheap [chēp] *adjective,* **cheaper, cheapest. 1.** having a low price; not expensive: Table salt is *cheap* to buy. **2.** charging low prices: a *cheap* restaurant. **3.** not made or done well; of poor quality: That *cheap* toy broke the first time they played with it. **4.** not willing to give or spend money; stingy. —**cheaply,** *adverb.*

cheat [chēt] *verb,* **cheated, cheating. 1.** to act in a way that is not fair; be dishonest. to *cheat* on a test by copying someone's answers, to *cheat* at cards by looking at the other players' hands. **2.** to take in a dishonest way: to *cheat* a person out of his money. —*noun, plural* **cheats.** a person who cheats. ◆ Also called a **cheater.**

check [chek] *noun, plural* **checks. 1.** a test or careful look at something to see if it is right or as it should be: Before starting the car, she made a quick *check* to make sure the children

---

checklists In courses on writing, the use of checklists has become a popular idea. A checklist is a list of elements that need to be gone over before handing in a paper. Here are three main elements: (1) Does the title fit the text? Don't be over-fancy here. A paper on weather stations shouldn't be titled, "Eyes Above." (2) Is the punctuation correct? Don't turn your paper in without testing. For example: "She said, go home!" What's wrong? (3) Does the end add to the beginning? If you start out, "This is the story of a girl's fight against an early death," don't merely repeat these words at the end. By then you have told the reader a great deal and can summarize it. A hard thing to learn, yet the simplest, is that a story, true-to-life or fiction, ought to have a beginning and a middle and an end.

---

chase [chās] *verb,* **chased, chasing. 1.** to go after something quickly; try to catch: The little boy *chased* his ball as it rolled down the hill. **2.** to cause to run away; drive away: She *chased* the rabbit out of the garden. —*noun, plural* **chases.** the act of chasing or running after: The escaped bank robbers led the police on a wild *chase.*

chat [chat] *verb,* **chatted, chatting.** to talk in a light, friendly way. —*noun, plural* **chats:** The two men had a *chat* about the weather.

chat•ter [chat′ər] *verb,* **chattered, chattering. 1.** to make a quick, rattling sound: " 'Stay still,' Kayak hissed through his teeth, now *chattering* from cold and fear." (James Houston) **2.** to talk quickly about unimportant things: "All during the dance Jody had joked and laughed and *chattered* . . ." (Sylvia Plath). —*noun.* the act or sound of chattering.

Chau•cer [chô′sər] **Geoffrey** [jef′rē], 1340–1400, English poet, the author of *The Canterbury Tales.*

had their seat belts on. **2.** a mark [✔] to show that something has been looked at or tested: Put a *check* next to each correct answer. **3.** a written order to a bank to pay a certain amount of money to the person or business named on the paper. **4.** a piece of paper showing how much a person owes for buying food in a restaurant. **5.** a ticket, tag, or slip of paper to show that a thing has been left to be picked up later. **6.** something that stops or holds back: A *check* in hockey is a play to keep another player from moving forward. **7.** a pattern of squares: a jacket with black and white *checks.*

Pronunciation Key: [ə] Symbol

The [ə] or *schwa* sound occurs in syllables without an accent. It can be spelled with any vowel, such as a in above, e in listen, i in pencil, o in melon, u in circus. It can also be a combination of vowels, such as io in action, ai in mountain, iou in precious.

(Turn the page for more information.)

—*verb*, **checked, checking. 1.** to test or examine something to see if it is right or as it should be: to *check* the oil in a car engine. **2.** to put a check mark next to something. **3.** to get information for something: He *checked* his dictionary to find out what the word meant. **4.** to leave something to be picked up later: He *checked* his hat and coat at the door when he went into the restaurant. **5.** to stop or hold back: to *check* the spread of a disease. **6.** to mark with a pattern of squares. ♦ Usually used as an adjective: a *checked* dress. **7. check in.** to register as a guest: to *check in* at a hotel. **check out.** to pay one's bill for being a guest and leave.

check•ers [chek′ ərz] *plural noun.* a game for two people in which each player has twelve flat, round pieces to move. It is played on a **checkerboard**, which has 64 squares of two different colors, usually red and black.

check•up [chek′ up′] *noun, plural* **checkups. 1.** a medical examination given by a doctor or dentist. **2.** any careful examination of something to find out what condition it is in: Mom's bringing her car in for a 5000-mile *checkup.*

cheek [chēk] *noun, plural* **cheeks. 1.** the wide, fleshy part of the face between the nose and the ear. **2.** a bold, rude way of acting: She had the *cheek* to push into line ahead of the others.

cheer [chēr] *noun, plural* **cheers. 1.** good feelings or good spirits; happiness. **2.** a shout of happiness, encouragement, or praise: The children gave a *cheer* when they saw Santa Claus step from the helicopter. ♦ A **cheerleader** is someone who leads people in cheering at a football game or other sports event. —*verb*, **cheered, cheering. 1.** to make or become happy: The flowers we sent to Lou in the hospital really *cheered* him up. **2.** to give a cheer: The crowd *cheered* for the winning runner.

cheer•ful [chēr′ fəl] *adjective, more/most.* **1.** full of happiness or good feelings: "His greatest charm was this *cheerful* . . . way of making friends with people." (Frances Hodgson Burnett) **2.** bringing cheer: a *cheerful* smile, a *cheerful* bouquet of flowers.

cheese [chēz] *noun, plural* **cheeses.** a food made from milk. Cheese is made by separating a solid material called CURDS from milk and pressing it into a solid block or cake.

chee•tah [chē′ tə] *noun, plural* **cheetahs.** a large, wild cat with spots like a leopard, found in Africa and Asia. Cheetahs can run faster than any other animal.

cheetah All members of the cat family are hunters, but only the cheetah is fast enough to catch such swift prey as antelope or gazelles. It can reach a speed of 70 miles per hour. The name *cheetah* is from Hindi (a language of India) meaning "spotted" or "colorful."

chef [shef] *noun, plural* **chefs.** the chief cook of a restaurant.

chem•i•cal [kem′ i kəl] *noun, plural* **chemicals.** any substance that can cause other substances to change or that is the result of other substances reacting to each other. Chemicals can be either ELEMENTS, which are basic substances, or COMPOUNDS, which are made up of two or more elements. —*adjective.* **1.** having to do with chemistry: *chemical* engineering. **2.** made by or using chemicals: a *chemical* reaction. **Chemical warfare** uses poisonous or harmful substances such as poison gas.

chem•ist [kem′ ist] *noun, plural* **chemists.** a scientist who is trained in chemistry.

chemist *Chemist* and *chemistry* come from the word *alchemist.* In the Middle Ages, an alchemist was a person who tried to turn ordinary metals into gold. Alchemists also tried to find a magic substance called an *elixir* [i lik′sər], which would cure all diseases and, even better, allow people to live forever. Obviously, the alchemists never succeeded. But from experiments in their vain search for the magical elixir, they did in fact learn many facts about the nature of chemical elements. From the pseudo (fake) science of alchemy, the true science of chemistry was born.

chem•is•try [kem′is trē] *noun.* **1.** the science that studies different substances to determine what they are made of, what qualities they have, and how they change when they combine or react with other substances. **2.** the way that a group of people or things mix or go together: The coach of the basketball team tried to put together a lineup that would have just the right *chemistry.*

cher•ish [cher′ish] *verb,* **cherished, cherishing.** to love and treat with great care; hold dear: Lisa *cherishes* her new pet puppy.

cher•ry [cher′ē] *noun, plural* **cherries. 1.** a small, round red fruit with smooth skin and a pit in the center, often eaten raw or in pies and other desserts. Cherries grow in clumps on trees in cool climates. **2.** a bright-red color like that of a cherry.

cherry A cherry tree in full bloom, with a closeup of the fruit. The word originally meant "stone fruit," referring to the hard pit at the center.

chess [ches] *noun.* a game for two people in which each player has 16 pieces that move in different ways according to certain rules. The object of chess is to trap the other player's main piece (the king) so that it cannot move.

chest [chest] *noun, plural* **chests. 1.** the upper front part of the body. The heart and lungs are inside the chest, enclosed by the ribs. **2.** a large, strong box used to keep things in: a tool *chest,* a toy *chest.* **3.** a large wooden piece of furniture having several drawers, used for holding or storing clothing and other things.

chest•nut [ches′nut′] *noun, plural* **chestnuts. 1.** a sweet, reddish-brown nut that can be eaten. It grows inside a prickly case until it is ripe. Almost all American chestnut trees have

been killed by a fungus disease. **2.** a reddish-brown color like a chestnut, or something that has this color.

chew [cho͞o] *verb,* **chewed, chewing.** to grind and crush food or other things with the teeth. —*noun, plural* **chews.** something that is chewed: a *chew* of tobacco. ◆ **Chewing gum** is made from the gum of certain tropical trees.

Chiang Kai-Shek [chang′ kī shek′] 1887–1975, Chinese general and political leader.

Chicago In 1914 poet Carl Sandburg called Chicago "City of the Big Shoulders" and "a tall bold slugger." A modern view of the lakefront skyline shows that these descriptions still fit the city today.

Chi•ca•go [shi kä′ gō] a city in Illinois, on Lake Michigan. It is the third-largest city in the U.S. *Population:* 3,000,000.

chick [chik] *noun, plural* **chicks.** a young chicken or other young bird.

chick•a•dee [chik′ ə dē] *noun, plural* **chickadees.** a small gray North American bird with black and white markings and a black head. It was named for the sound of its call.

chick•en [chik′ ən] *noun, plural* **chickens.** a type of bird that is often raised for its eggs and meat; a hen or rooster.

chicken pox [päks] a mild disease that easily spreads from one person to another, found most often in children. Chicken pox causes a fever and small red sores on the body.

Pronunciation Key: Accent Marks

[′] is the normal accent mark. It shows where the main stress falls on a word.
[′] is a secondary accent mark. It shows a lighter stress than the primary accent. For example:

tel • e • vis • ion [tel′ə vizh′ən]

(Turn the page for more information.)

C

chief [chēf] *noun, plural* **chiefs.** the person who is the head of a group; a leader: A fire *chief* is in charge of a fire department. An Indian *chief* is the leader of a tribe. ♦ A **chieftain** is the leader of a tribe or clan. —*adjective.* **1.** being the highest in rank; most powerful: The **Chief Justice** of the Supreme Court is the head of the Court. **2.** most important; main: The *chief* crops grown in the U.S. are wheat and corn. "Mr. Bilbo Baggins became once again the *chief* topic of conversation." (J.R.R. Tolkien) —**chiefly,** *adverb.* for the most part; largely, mainly: Lemonade is *chiefly* water with some lemon juice and sugar.

child [chīld] *noun, plural* **children. 1.** a young boy or girl. **2.** a person's son or daughter of any age: Mr. and Mrs. Jones have one *child* and three grandchildren. ♦ **Childhood** is the time in a person's life when he or she is a child.

child One of the odd things about English is that the plural of *child* is not "childs," but *children.* There are no other common English words that form the plural in this way. However, at one time the plurals for the words *brother* and *sister* were "brethren" and "sistern." *Brethren* occurs in the Bible. "The war has actually begun! Our *brethren* are already in the field," Patrick Henry declared in 1775. As the English language developed, the *-ren* ending was added to *child* to make it like these other two words. For many years *child* also had another common plural, *childer,* but this went out of use in the 1600's. Surprisingly, the regular form "childs" was almost never used even in early times.

child•ish [chīld′ish] *adjective, more/most.* **1.** for or like a child: *childish* games such as tag or hide-and-go-seek. **2.** not suitable for an adult; not mature: He lost his temper in a *childish* way when he found out the store was out of what he wanted.

chil•dren [chil′drən] *noun.* the plural of **child.**

Chil•e [chil′ē] a country on the southwest coast of South America. *Capital:* Santiago. *Area:* 292,300 square miles. *Population:* 11,500,000.

chil•i [chil′ē] *noun, plural* **chilies. 1.** the dried seed pod of a kind of red pepper, used to make a hot seasoning for food. **2.** a dish flavored with chili peppers, made with meat and usually beans.

chill [chil] *noun, plural* **chills. 1.** a mild but uncomfortable coldness: "It was true autumn with a touch of *chill* in the air." (Lionel Trilling) **2.** a feeling of being cold, often with shivering: I got a *chill* from waiting for the bus in the rain. —*verb,* **chilled, chilling.** to make or become cold: "The rain that afternoon had *chilled* the air." (Carson McCullers) ♦ Also used as an adjective: "He awoke *chilled* and sick. There

was no sun." (Jack London) —*adjective.* being unpleasantly cold; chilly: a *chill* wind.

chill•y [chil′ē] *adjective, more/most.* **1.** too cold to feel pleasant; giving a chill: a *chilly* November wind. **2.** not warm or friendly: The senator got a *chilly* reaction when he spoke in favor of raising taxes.

chime [chīm] *noun, plural* **chimes. 1.** a bell or pipe tuned to a note of a musical scale. Chimes are played by being hit with small, padded hammers. **2.** the ringing or piping sounds made when these bells or pipes are played. —*verb,* **chimed, chiming.** to make a musical sound by striking or ringing bells: "The clock on the wall *chimed* midnight." (Vera Cleaver).

chim•ney [chim′nē] *noun, plural* **chimneys.** a hollow, upright structure, usually of brick or stone, that carries smoke from a fireplace or furnace to the outside of the building.

chim•pan•zee [chim′pan zē′] *noun, plural* **chimpanzees.** a small, brownish-black ape that lives in trees in Africa. Chimpanzees are among the most intelligent animals.

chimpanzee The chimpanzee is one of the few creatures besides humans to make use of tools. The animal's name comes from a native African word.

chin [chin] *noun, plural* **chins.** the bony part of the face below the mouth and above the neck. The chin is the front part of the lower jaw. —*verb,* **chinned, chinning.** to pull oneself up to an overhead bar until the chin is higher than the bar.

chi•na [chī′ nə] *noun.* **1.** a fine, glasslike pottery that is made of clay or porcelain and baked twice. This pottery was first made in the country of China. **2.** dishes, vases, and other things made of china.

Chi•na [chī′ nə] **1.** the country with the largest population in the world, located in east Asia. *Capital:* Peking (Beijing). *Area:* 3,691,500 square miles. *Population:* 1,031,880,000. ◆ Also known as the **People's Republic of China. 2. Nationalist China.** another name for TAIWAN.

China Sea a part of the western Pacific Ocean along the west coast of Asia.

Chi•nese [chī nēz′] *noun, plural* **Chinese. 1.** a person born in China or whose family or ancestors are from China. **2.** the language spoken in China. —*adjective.* of or having to do with China or its people.

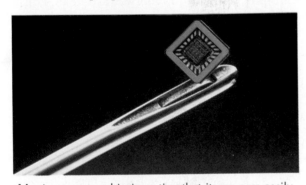

chip A computer chip is so tiny that it can pass easily through the eye of a needle, as shown in this greatly-enlarged view.

chip [chip] *noun, plural* **chips. 1.** a small piece that has been broken or cut off: He picked up the *chips* of wood after he finished chopping the log. **2.** a thin slice of food, especially a potato chip. **3.** a small disk used as a counter in certain games, such as poker. **4.** a very tiny flake of material, usually SILICON, that has been specially treated to carry the circuits that are needed to operate a computer. —*verb,* **chipped, chipping. 1.** to break or cut off a small piece of something: They *chipped* the old paint off the wall before putting on the new coat. **2. chip in.** to give one's share of money or help; contribute: Everyone *chipped in* to buy a gift for the teacher.

chipmunk The chipmunk can climb trees, but spends most of its time on the ground collecting seeds and nuts. The name comes from an Indian word.

chip•munk [chip′ mungk′] *noun, plural* **chipmunks.** a small North American animal with brown fur and a striped back. Chipmunks are related to squirrels.

chis•el [chiz′ əl] *noun, plural* **chisels.** a tool with a sharp edge at the end of a metal blade. A chisel is used to shape or cut wood, stone, or metal. —*verb,* **chiseled, chiseling.** to shape or cut something with a chisel.

chiv•al•ry [shiv′ əl rē] *noun.* **1.** the good qualities that the knights of the Middle Ages were supposed to have. Chivalry includes honor, bravery, politeness, and the protection of the weak. **2.** very polite or kind behavior, especially by a man toward a woman. ◆ A person or an action that shows chivalry is **chivalrous.**

chlo•rine [klôr′ ēn] *noun.* a greenish-yellow poisonous gas with a strong, unpleasant odor. Chlorine is a chemical element used to kill germs and clean things. Compounds of chlorine are used to treat water in swimming pools.

chlo•ro•phyll [klôr′ ə fil] *noun.* the substance in plants that gives them their green color. Chlorophyll uses sunlight to make food for the plant from the elements in air and water by means of a process known as PHOTOSYNTHESIS.

choc•o•late [chäk′ lət *or* chôk′ lət] *noun, plural* **chocolates. 1.** a food made from CACAO beans that have been ground up and roasted and then mixed with sugar and other things. It is used

Pronunciation Key: A–F			
a	and; hat	ch	chew; such
ā	ate; stay	d	dog; lid
â	care; air	e	end; yet
ä	father; hat	ē	she; each
b	boy; cab	f	fun; off

(Turn the page for more information.)

C

to flavor ice cream, cakes, and other desserts. **2.** candy made of chocolate or flavored with chocolate. **3.** a sweet drink made of chocolate mixed with milk or water, usually served hot. **4.** a dark-brown color like that of chocolate. —*adjective.* **1.** made of or flavored with chocolate. **2.** having a dark-brown color.

C

choose [chooz] *verb,* **chose, chosen, choosing. 1.** to pick or select from a group: Please *choose* a book from this list for your book report. We can *choose* either soup or salad to start the meal. **2.** to decide or prefer to do something: "I do not *choose* to run for President in 1928." (Calvin Coolidge)

choosing a topic Writing should fit, somewhat as clothing does. Don't force a size 10 subject into a size 6 paper. Pick a subject that's too big ("Rocks," "Europe," "Deserts") and you'll never get your paper down to the proper size. Pick one that's too small ("The Ocotillo Plant") and you won't find enough information to fill out your paper. Use the library as a guide. If your topic has 30 or 40 different references, it's too broad. One or two, and obviously it's too narrow. This is not easy. You want detail but not too much. You want to generalize but not vaguely. A good rule is this: See the forest, but look for the trees.

choice [chois] *noun, plural* **choices. 1.** the act of choosing; selecting one from a group: She had to make a *choice* of which dress to wear to the party. **2.** the chance or right to choose: Mom gave us a *choice* of hamburgers or hot dogs for lunch. **3.** a person or thing that is chosen. —*adjective,* **choicer, choicest.** of high quality; excellent: We had *choice* seats in the middle of the front row.

choir [kwīr] *noun, plural* **choirs.** a group of singers who sing together in a church or school.

choke [chōk] *verb,* **choked, choking. 1.** to stop or block the breathing of a person or animal: The thick smoke *choked* the firemen. **2.** to be unable to breathe or swallow normally: He was

chop [chäp] *verb,* **chopped, chopping. 1.** to cut by hitting with something sharp: to *chop* wood. She *chopped* down the tree with an ax. **2.** to cut into small pieces: He *chopped* up some onions for the stew. —*noun, plural* **chops. 1.** a quick, sharp blow. **2.** a small piece of meat with a rib in it: lamb *chops*, pork *chops*.

Cho•pin [shō′ pan] Frederic, 1810–1849, Polish composer and pianist.

chop•sticks [chäp′ stiks′] *plural noun.* a pair of long, thin sticks for eating solid food, used mainly in Asian countries.

chord [kôrd] *noun, plural* **chords.** a combination of three or more musical notes that are sounded at the same time.

chore Chore is an American word that came into use in the early 1800's. It first meant "the return of a certain time." If an event occurs day after day, like milking cows or delivering newspapers, it became known as a chore. Gradually it lost the previous meaning and began to gain a negative tone, as in, "Buying a birthday present for Jerry is always a real chore." A tiring and unpleasant job, one repeated from time to time, is now called a chore.

choking on a piece of meat caught in his throat. **3.** to hold back or stop: "I don't know why the words remained *choked* up within me." (Moss Hart) **4.** *Informal.* to do badly in a tense situation because of nervousness. —*noun, plural* **chokes. 1.** the act of choking. **2.** a part of a gasoline engine that cuts down the flow of air into the engine.

cho•les•ter•ol [kə les′ tə rôl′] *noun, plural* **cholesterols.** a white, fatty substance found in food that comes from animals. If too much cholesterol builds up in the blood vessels, it can cause problems to health.

chore [chôr] *noun, plural* **chores. 1.** a small job around a house or farm that has to be done regularly: One of my *chores* is taking out the garbage. **2.** any unpleasant or difficult task: Doing those math problems was a real *chore.*

cho•rus [kôr′ əs] *noun, plural* **choruses. 1.** a group of singers or dancers who perform together: My parents are going to hear me sing in the school *chorus.* **2.** a part of a song that is sung after each verse. **3.** something said by many people at the same time: It was hard to hear the politician speak over the *chorus* of "boo's" from the audience. —*verb,* **chorused,**

chorusing. to sing or speak at the same time: The class *chorused* "yes" when asked if they were looking forward to summer vacation.

chose [chōz] *verb.* the past tense of **choose.**

cho·sen [chō′zən] the past participle of **choose:** Melissa was *chosen* by her classmates to be student body president.

chow·der [chou′dər] *noun, plural* **chowders.** a thick soup made of fish or vegetables, usually with milk and potatoes.

Christ [krīst] *noun.* JESUS, the founder of the Christian religion.

chris·ten [kris′ən] *verb,* **christened, christening.** **1.** to receive someone into a Christian church by a special ceremony known as BAPTISM; baptize. **2.** to give a certain name to a person at baptism. **3.** to give a name to: The new submarine was *christened* "U.S.S. Dolphin." ◆ The ceremony of naming or receiving someone as a Christian is a **christening.**

Chris·tian [kris′chən] *noun, plural* **Christians.** a person who believes in Jesus Christ and follows his teachings; a follower of any religion based on Jesus' teachings. —*adjective.* **1.** having to do with Jesus Christ or his teachings: Easter Sunday is a *Christian* holiday. **2.** believing in Jesus Christ and following his teachings: a *Christian* elementary school. **3.** following the example of Christ; showing a gentle, helpful, loving nature: Mother Teresa shows a *Christian* spirit in her work to help the poor.

Chris·ti·an·i·ty [kris′chē an′ə tē] *noun.* **1.** the religion based on the teachings of Jesus Christ; the Christian religion. **2.** all Christians as a group.

Christ·mas [kris′məs] *noun, plural* **Christmases.** a holiday to celebrate the birth of Jesus Christ. It falls on December 25.

Christmas tree a pine or other evergreen tree, real or artificial, that is decorated with lights and ornaments at Christmas time.

chro·mi·um [krō′mē əm] *noun.* a hard, gray metal that is a chemical element. Chromium does not rust and can be polished to a bright, silvery shine. It is often used to cover other metals or as part of a mixture of metals. ◆ Also called **chrome.**

chron·ic [krän′ik] *adjective.* lasting a long time; coming back again and again: Common *chronic* illnesses are asthma, arthritis, and rheumatism. He's a *chronic* complainer who never seems to enjoy anything. —**chronically,** *adverb:* to be *chronically* ill.

chron·i·cle [krän′ə kəl] *noun, plural* **chroni-** cles. a record of events in the order in which they happened; a history: Shakespeare took the plots of many of his plays from "The *Chronicles* of England, Scotland, and Ireland" by Raphael Holinshed. —*verb,* **chronicled, chronicling.** to make a chronicle of: The voyages of Christopher Columbus are *chronicled* in the book *Admiral of the Ocean Sea.*

chrys·an·the·mum [kri san′thə məm] *noun, plural* **chrysanthemums.** a round flower with many petals. Chrysanthemums blossom in the fall and grow in many colors.

chrysanthemum Chrysanthemums ("mums" for short) flower during days of short sunlight, and thus are a popular autumn decoration.

chuck·le [chuk′əl] *verb,* **chuckled, chuckling.** to laugh softly and quietly: "Jody heard his father and Billy Buck *chuckling* and he knew it was a joke of some kind." (John Steinbeck) —*noun, plural* **chuckles.** a soft, quiet laugh.

chunk [chunk] *noun, plural* **chunks.** **1.** a thick piece or lump: a *chunk* of ice. The stew had *chunks* of meat in it. **2.** *Informal.* a large amount: Homework takes a big *chunk* of time out of my day.

church [church] *noun, plural* **churches.** **1.** a building for Christian religious services. **2.** any building for the public worship of God. **3.** *also,*

C

Pronunciation Key: G–N

g	give; big	k	kind; oat; back
h	hold	l	let; ball
i	it; this	m	make; time
ī	ice; my	n	not; own
j	jet; gem; edge	ng	having

(Turn the page for more information.)

Church. a particular branch of the Christian religion: The Pope is the head of the Catholic *Church.* **4.** religion in general: "Separation of *church* and state" means separating religious activities from the actions of government.

Chur•chill [church′ hil′] **Winston,** 1874–1965, British statesman, writer, and orator, prime minister of Great Britain during World War II.

churn [churn] *noun, plural* **churns.** a container in which cream or milk can be shaken and beaten to make butter, often used in former times. —*verb,* **churned, churning. 1.** to use a churn. **2.** to move or stir with a rough motion, like that of a churn: "His feet *churned* the waves as though he were running on top of the water." (E.B. White)

chute [shoōt] *noun, plural* **chutes.** a steep slide or tube down which things can be moved or dropped to an opening at the other end: a mail *chute,* a laundry *chute,* a coal *chute.*

ci•der [sī′ dər] *noun, plural* **ciders.** the juice that is pressed from apples, used as a drink and to make vinegar.

ci•gar [si gär′] *noun, plural* **cigars.** a small, tight roll of tobacco leaves prepared for smoking.

cig•a•rette [sig′ ə ret′] *noun, plural* **cigarettes.** a small roll of finely-cut tobacco leaves that is wrapped tightly in a thin white paper to be smoked.

Cin•cin•na•ti [sin′ sə nat′ ē] a city in the southwestern part of Ohio. *Population:* 385,000.

cin•der [sin′ dər] *noun, plural* **cinders.** a piece of wood or coal that is partly burned and no longer flaming.

cin•e•ma [sin′ ə mə] *noun, plural* **cinemas.** another name for a motion picture or a motion picture theater.

cin•na•mon [sin′ ə mən] *noun.* a reddish-brown spice made from the dried inner bark of a certain tropical tree, used to flavor cookies, pies, and other foods.

Churchill A protrait of Sir Winston Churchill by the famous photographer Yousuf Karsh of Ottawa, taken in 1941.

cir•cle [sur′ kəl] *noun, plural* **circles. 1.** a line that curves around to meet itself without a break. Every part of the line is the same distance from a point inside at the center. **2.** anything that is shaped like a circle: The square dancers all joined hands in a *circle.* **3.** a group of people who have the same interests: a *circle* of friends. "My father was well known in the best *circles* in this kingdom . . ." (William Makepeace Thackeray)—*verb,* **circled, circling. 1.** to draw or form a circle around: Please *circle* the correct answer. **2.** to move around in a circle: The plane *circled* the airfield, waiting for permission to land.

cir•cuit [sur′ kət] *noun, plural* **circuits. 1.** a path that ends where it began; a going around: The earth makes a *circuit* around the sun. **2.** a route over which a person or group makes regular trips: A *circuit* judge is one who holds court in different towns within a district. **3.** a path through which an electric current flows: Our air conditioner is on its own *circuit* because it needs more power than the other appliances.

cinquains Language-arts courses often have students write a *cinquain* [sing′kān]. The term comes from the French word for "five." It can refer to any poem, or section of a poem, that is five lines long. In student writing, though, a cinquain usually has a certain pattern:

Line 1: A noun (the title)	Hawk	Sailboat
Line 2: Two adjectives	Graceful, free	Sleek, elegant
Line 3: Three verbs	Sailing, soaring, swooping	Slicing, leaning, gliding
Line 4: A verb phrase	Watching from the sky	Dancing to wind music
Line 5: Another noun	Warrior	Freedom

cir•cu•lar [sur′kyə lər] *adjective.* **1.** having a round shape; in the form of a circle: The full moon looks *circular.* "Next he began a *circular* wall, laying flat stones one on top of another." (Farley Mowat) **2.** moving in a circle: The model plane flew in a *circular* path over the field. —*noun, plural* **circulars.** a printed letter, announcement, or advertisement that is sent out to a large number of people.

cir•cu•late [sur′kyə lāt′] *verb,* **circulated, circulating. 1.** to move around and back to a starting point; go in a circuit: Blood *circulates* from the heart through the body and back to the heart. **2.** to move about; spread: There's a rumor *circulating* around the office that the company is planning to move to another city.

cir•cu•la•tion [sur′kyə lā′shən] *noun, plural* **circulations. 1.** a going around; movement in a circuit: They put in an attic fan to help the *circulation* of air through the house. **2.** the movement of blood through the blood vessels. ◆ The path of blood circulation in the body is the **circulatory system** [sur′kyə lə tôr′ē]. **3.** the number of copies of a newspaper or magazine that are sold for each issue.

cir•cum•fer•ence [sər kum′frəns] *noun, plural* **circumferences. 1.** a line that forms the outside of a circle. **2.** the distance around the edge of something round: The *circumference* of the earth is about 25,000 miles.

cir•cum•stance [sur′kəm stans′] *noun, plural* **circumstances. 1.** a condition, fact, or event that happens with something else and has an effect on it: What were the *circumstances* that led up to the crime? **2.** luck or chance: She was the victim of *circumstance* because her car was parked right under the tree when it fell. **3. circumstances.** the state or condition of something: a person in poor financial *circumstances.* Under the *circumstances,* he has no choice but to pay the fine.

cir•cus [sur′kəs] *noun, plural* **circuses.** a large show with clowns, acrobats, trained animals, and other performers. Circuses usually travel from town to town and give their shows under a big tent.

cite [sīt] *verb,* **cited, citing. 1.** to repeat someone else's words; quote: In Martin Luther King's speeches, he often *cited* the Bible. **2.** to use as an example; refer to: President Reagan *cited* Sandra Day O'Connor's record as a judge when he nominated her for the Supreme Court. ◆ Something that is cited is a **citation:** This dictionary has many *citations* from famous writers.

cit•i•zen [sit′ə zən] *noun, plural* **citizens. 1.** someone who is an official member of a country, either by being born there or by choosing to live there and become a member. Citizens have certain rights, such as voting, and certain responsibilities, such as obeying the laws and paying taxes. **2.** anyone who lives in a town or city; a resident: She's a *citizen* of Los Angeles.

cit•i•zen•ship [sit′ə zən ship′] *noun.* the fact of being a citizen, and the rights and responsibilities that go with this fact.

citrus Four citrus fruits: an orange and grapefruit (rear), and a lime and lemon (front).

cit•rus [sit′rəs] *noun, plural* **citruses** or **citrus.** any one of a certain family of fruit trees that grow in warm areas, such as oranges, grapefruits, lemons, or limes.

cit•y [sit′ē] *noun, plural* **cities. 1.** a large area where many people live and work. Cities are larger than towns or villages and have their own local government, usually headed by a mayor. **2.** the people of a city: The *city* has decided to make both 5th and 6th Avenue one-way streets.

civ•ic [siv′ik] *adjective.* **1.** having to do with a city. **2.** having to do with a citizen or citizenship: They attend the town council meetings because of their interest in *civic* affairs. —**civics,** *noun.* the study of the rights and responsibilities of citizens as a subject in school.

C

C

civ·il [siv′ əl] *adjective.* **1.** having to do with a citizen or citizenship. **Civil liberties** are the freedoms that citizens have to think, speak, and act as they wish, as long as other people are not harmed. **2.** not connected with military or church affairs: *The sailor's case was tried in a civil court rather than by the Navy. The couple was married in a civil ceremony at City Hall.* **3.** within a country or state. **Civil defense** is the defense of a country against an air attack on its territory. **4.** polite; courteous: *The least you could do is give me a civil answer.*

ci·vil·ian [sə vil′ yən] *noun, plural* **civilians.** a person who is not a member of the armed forces or a police force. —*adjective.* having to do with civilians: *Police detectives usually wear civilian clothes rather than regular uniforms.*

civ·i·li·za·tion [siv′ ə lə zā′ shən] *noun, plural* **civilizations. 1.** a condition of human society in which people have progressed in their knowledge of art, science, government, farming, trade, and so on: *Civilization has taken thousands of years to develop.* **2.** the way of life of a particular people or nation: *the ancient civilizations of Greece and Rome.*

civ·i·lize [siv′ ə līz′] *verb,* **civilized, civilizing.** to change from a primitive condition of life to a more developed one: *The ancient Romans tried to civilize the European tribes they conquered with their knowledge of government, building, and agriculture.* ◆ Also used as an adjective: *a civilized nation, civilized customs.*

civil rights the rights and privileges of a citizen. Civil rights in the United States are guaranteed by the Constitution, which gives each citizen freedom of speech and religion, the right to vote, and equal protection under the law.

civil service an area of government service that is not connected with the armed forces, the lawmaking branch, or the courts. **Civil servants,** such as post office employees, are appointed on the basis of scores on public examinations, rather than being chosen by politicians.

war was fought in Spain from 1936 to 1939. **2. Civil War.** the war in the United States between the North and the South, from 1861 to 1865.

claim [klām] *verb,* **claimed, claiming. 1.** to ask for or take as one's own: *The winner of the contest claimed his prize.* In 1889, settlers in Oklahoma were allowed to *claim* land that had once belonged to the Indians. **2.** to say that something is true; declare as a fact: *"He claimed I didn't know anything about fishing or hunting."* (William Saroyan) —*noun, plural* **claims. 1.** a demand for something as one's own: *After the accident, we filed a claim with the insurance company for the damage to the car.* **2.** a statement that something is true: *They all laughed at Jimmy's claim of having seen a flying saucer.* **3.** a thing that is claimed, especially land: *The miner found gold on his claim.*

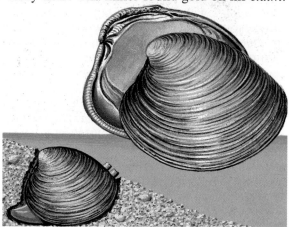

clam The *quahog* [kō′ häg] is a clam often used for food along the Atlantic Coast. Its unusual name comes from an Indian word. Cherrystones and littlenecks are two smaller sizes of this clam.

clam [klam] *noun, plural* **clams.** an animal that has a soft body and a double shell that is joined by a hinge. Clams are found in either salt or fresh water. Many kinds are good to eat. —*verb,* **clammed, clamming:** to dig for clams in the sand or mud.

Civil War For many years the term "Civil War" was considered to be a form of prejudice on the part of Northerners against Southerners, who in 1861 maintained they had seceded from the Union to form a new republic. To them a civil war meant that the Southerners were outlaws, rebels against the legal government. For that reason textbooks and other references used "War Between the States." Nowadays, almost all Americans, North, South, West, East, use the term "Civil War."

civil war 1. a war between two opposing groups of citizens within the same country: *A civil*

clamp [klamp] *noun, plural* **clamps.** a device used for gripping or holding things together

tightly. It is usually made up of two parts that can be tightened with a screw or spring.
—*verb*, **clamped, clamping. 1.** to hold together with a clamp: Tom *clamped* the two blocks of wood until the glue was dry. **2. clamp down.** to be strict: The judge *clamped down* on speeders by giving heavy fines.

clan [klan] *noun, plural* **clans. 1.** a group of families who are all related to the same ancestor: In ancient Scotland the members of one *clan* often fought against another. **2.** a group of relatives: The whole Doyle *clan* is coming to our house for dinner.

clap [klap] *verb*, **clapped, clapping. 1.** to hit together loudly: The teacher *clapped* her hands to get the students' attention. **2.** to applaud by hitting the hands together: The audience *clapped* after the singer finished. **3.** to slap with an open hand: "She *clapped* her spare hand to her hurt ankle . . ." (T.H. White) —*noun, plural* **claps. 1.** a sharp, sudden noise: a *clap* of thunder. "Margot closes her book with a *clap*." (Anne Frank) **2.** a friendly slap.

clar•i•fy [klar′ ə fī′] *verb*, **clarified, clarifying. 1.** to make clear or pure: Butter is *clarified* by heating it. **2.** to make something easier to understand; explain: The instruction book helped to *clarify* the way the computer works.

clar•i•net [klar′ ə net′] *noun, plural* **clarinets.** a musical instrument with a mouthpiece and a long body shaped like a tube. It is played by blowing into the mouthpiece and pressing the keys or covering the holes with the fingers.

clar•i•ty [klar′ ə tē] *noun.* the state of being clear; clearness: I like that singer because of the *clarity* of her voice.

clash [klash] *verb*, **clashed, clashing. 1.** to hit or come together with a loud, harsh sound. **2.** to come into conflict; disagree strongly: The politician *clashed* with his opponent over whether to cut the defense budget. **3.** to not match well: The red pants *clash* with that green shirt—why don't you wear the white shirt instead? —*noun, plural* **clashes. 1.** a loud, harsh sound. **2.** a strong disagreement; conflict.

clasp [klasp] *noun, plural* **clasps. 1.** something that holds two objects or parts together, such as a buckle or hook: Linda asked me to fasten the *clasp* on her necklace. **2.** a strong grip or hold. —*verb*, **clasped, clasping. 1.** to fasten with a clasp: He *clasped* the bracelet on his wrist. **2.** to hold or grip strongly: "The two men *clasped* hands in a friendly way." (F. Scott Fitzgerald)

class [klas] *noun, plural* **classes. 1.** any group of people or things that are alike in some way: All birds belong to a *class* of animals called "Aves." **2.** a group of students who meet or are taught together. ◆ A person in the same class as another is a **classmate. 3.** a meeting of such a group: I have to see the teacher after *class* today. ◆ School classes are held in a **classroom. 4.** a group of students who have graduated or will graduate in the same year: the *class* of 1990. **5.** a division or rank based on quality: A first-*class* ticket on an airplane costs more than a regular seat. **6.** *Informal.* high quality or elegance; excellence: People think of Cary Grant and Grace Kelly as movie stars with a lot of *class*.
—*verb*, **classed, classing.** to put in a class; classify: Pablo Picasso is usually *classed* as a Spanish painter, even though he lived most of his life in France.

classics At first, classic or classical literature meant the writings of the ancient Greeks and Romans, the epic poetry of Homer and the prose of Caesar and Cicero. By the nineteenth century a classic also meant a work—from any country—that has been recognized as a masterpiece over a long period of time. Mark Twain joked that "A classic is a book which people praise and don't read." But his own book, *Huckleberry Finn*, is now an American classic, both highly praised and widely read. Some modern works can be thought of as classics, such as Sinclair Lewis's novel *Main Street* (1920), T. S. Eliot's poem *The Waste Land* (1922), and Arthur Miller's play *Death of a Salesman* (1949).

clas•sic [klas′ ik] *noun, plural* **classics. 1.** a great book or work of art that has been thought of highly for a long time: William Shakespeare's plays are *classics* of literature. **2.** anything that is thought of as highly outstanding in its field: The 1957 Ford Thunderbird is a *classic* of American car making. **3. the classics.** the literature of ancient Greece and Rome: For many

Pronunciation Key: T–Z

t	ten; date	v	very; live
th	think	w	win; away
<u>th</u>	these	y	you
u	cut; butter	z	zoo; cause
ur	turn; bird	zh	measure

(Turn the page for more information.)

C

years, *the classics* were the main course of study in American private schools. —*adjective, more/most.* **1.** of the highest quality in literature or art: *Moby Dick* and *Huckleberry Finn* are *classic* American novels. **2.** being of very high quality in its field: a *classic* car, a *classic* building. **3.** very typical and obvious: The accident was a *classic* example of careless driving.

clas•si•cal [klas′i kəl] *adjective.* **1.** *also,* **Classical.** having to do with ancient Greece and Rome, or with their literature, art, and culture: The White House and the U.S. Capitol Building are designed in a *classical* style. **2.** having to do with CLASSICAL MUSIC: The violin is a *classical* instrument.

classical music a serious form of music that follows certain formal rules and standards that were set down in Europe in the 1700's and early 1800's. Symphonies and operas are types of classical music.

clas•si•fi•ca•tion [klas′ ə fə kā′ shən] *noun, plural* **classifications.** the act or result of classifying: the *classification* of plants according to where they grow.

clas•si•fy [klas′ ə fī] *verb,* **classified, classifying. 1.** to place in a class or group: to *classify* mail according to Zip Code. "He *classified* shirts and suits just as carefully as he did birds and mammals." (Jules Verne) **2.** to keep secret: to *classify* information about a military weapon. ♦ Often used as an adjective: **Classified advertising** in a newspaper divides the ads into groups according to what they are for.

clat•ter [klat′ ər] *verb,* **clattered, clattering.** to make a loud, rattling noise: "Sheridan's troops *clattered* up the avenue." (W.A. Swanberg) —*noun, plural* **clatters.** a clattering noise: "She made a light *clatter* in the kitchen." (Marjorie Kinnan Rawlings)

claus•tro•pho•bi•a [klôs′ trə fō′ bē ə] *noun.* a very strong and unusual fear of being in a small, crowded, or enclosed place, such as an elevator or closet.

claw [klô] *noun, plural* **claws. 1.** a sharp, curved nail on the foot of an animal or bird. **2.** one of the grasping parts on the limb of a lobster or crab. **3.** anything shaped like a claw, such as the part of a hammer used to pull out nails. —*verb,* **clawed, clawing.** to scratch, tear, or dig with claws or hands: The searchers *clawed* through the dirt to get to the buried treasure.

clay [klā] *noun, plural* **clays.** a kind of soft, fine earth that can be shaped when it is wet but that hardens when it is dried or baked. Clay is used to make bricks and pottery.

Clay [klā] Henry, 1777–1852, American political leader and orator.

clean [klēn] *adjective,* **cleaner, cleanest. 1.** free from dirt or stain; not dirty: The players changed into *clean* clothes after the game. **2.** free from wrong; honorable or fair: The mayor was proud of her *clean* record in politics. **3.** complete; total: The prisoners made a *clean* escape. **4.** neat or even: an automobile with *clean* lines, a person with *clean*-cut features. —*verb,* **cleaned, cleaning.** to make clean: to *clean* a floor, to *clean* a suit of clothes. ♦ Often used with **up** or **out:** Please *clean up* your room before you go out. All the students *cleaned out* their desks at the end of the year.

clean•er [klēn′ ər] *noun, plural* **cleaners. 1.** a person or business whose work is cleaning things: He took his suit to the *cleaners.* **2.** a machine or substance that is used for cleaning: a rug *cleaner,* an oven *cleaner.*

clean•li•ness [klen′ lē nis] *noun.* the condition of being clean.

clause The term clause refers to a part within a sentence. How, then, does it differ from a phrase? Neither one is a complete sentence. The difference is that a clause has its own subject and verb, but a phrase does not. "Watching TV" is a phrase; "While I was watching TV" is a clause. "While I was watching TV, the power suddenly went off," is two clauses making up a sentence. The first is a *dependent clause,* and the second is an *independent clause.* Why is it important to know this difference? Because independent clauses can be written as separate sentences, but dependent clauses cannot. The words "While I was watching TV" would not be a sentence, but a sentence fragment. As for phrases, they are never sentences.

clause [klôz] *noun, plural* **clauses. 1.** a part of a sentence that has a subject and a verb. **2.** a single part of a law, treaty, or any other written agreement: There is a *clause* in her lease for the apartment stating that pets are not allowed.

clean•ly [klēn′ lē] *adverb.* in a clean way: The sharp saw cut *cleanly* through the board. —[klen′ lē] *adjective,* **cleanlier, cleanliest.** always neat and clean: Cats are very *cleanly* animals.

cleanse [klenz] *verb,* **cleansed, cleansing.** to make clean: The nurse *cleansed* the soldier's wound. ♦ A substance that is used for cleaning is called a **cleanser.**

clench [klench] *verb,* **clenched, clenching.** to hold or press together tightly: to *clench* one's fists. "He *clenched* his jaw, trying to look like Agent 007." (Louise Fitzhugh)

clear writing A college professor once told his students in a writing class, "Orwell is your textbook." George Orwell's essays and fiction are models of fine modern English. Orwell himself said that when he wrote, he tried to create "Prose like a windowpane" so that readers would picture the scene he was describing. In a famous essay, "Politics and the English Language," Orwell warned against the use of vague phrases such as "with respect to," "by the fact that," or "have the effect of." He said that such writing was merely "gumming together long strips of words." What writing should consist of, he said, was "picking out words for the sake of their meaning and inventing images in order to make the meaning clearer."

clear [klēr] *adjective,* **clearer, clearest. 1.** easy to see through: The lake water was so *clear* that she could see all the way to the bottom as she stood on the dock. **2.** free from anything that darkens; bright: a sunny day with *clear* skies. **3.** easy to see, hear, or understand: a *clear* voice, *clear* handwriting. —*verb,* **cleared, clearing. 1.** to make or become clear: "After helping his mother *clear* the table and wash the dishes, he got ready." (Donald Sobol) **2.** to move away so as to make clear: "As the dust *cleared,* he made out that it was not so serious." (Walker Percy) **3.** to free from something that blocks: "My voice cracks. I cough, *clear* my throat, and say it again." (Judy Blume) **4.** to go over or by without touching: The horse *cleared* the fence. **5.** to free from blame or guilt: The lawyer was sure that the new evidence would *clear* the defendant.
—**clearly,** *adverb:* "Tom could always hear what went on next door as *clearly* as if he were there himself." (Philippa Pearce)

clear•ance [klēr′əns] *noun, plural* **clearances. 1.** the act or fact of clearing: People who work on secret military projects have to get *clearance* from the government. **2.** a sale to clear out merchandise from a store. **3.** the amount of clear space between two things: The *clearance* between the highway and the bridge overhead is 14 feet.

clear•ing [klēr′ing] *noun, plural* **clearings.** an area of land in a forest where there are no trees and bushes.

cleav•er [klē′vər] *noun, plural* **cleavers.** a knife with a broad, heavy blade and a short handle, used by butchers to cut up meat.

clef [klef] *noun, plural* **clefs.** in music, a printed mark that shows the pitch of the notes. There are three clefs: **G (treble), F (bass),** and **C (tenor or alto).**

Cle•o•pa•tra [klē′ə pat′rə] 69–30 B.C., the queen of Egypt from 51 to 30 B.C.

Cleopatra An ancient Roman coin showing an image of Cleopatra.

cler•gy [klur′jē] *noun, plural* **clergies.** ministers, priests, and rabbis, as a group; the people whose job is religious work. ♦ A man who is a member of the clergy is a **clergyman.**

clerk [klurk] *noun, plural* **clerks. 1.** a person who sells goods at a store. **2.** a person whose work is to keep records and other papers in order in an office. —*verb,* **clerked, clerking.** to work as a clerk: After law school she *clerked* for one of the Supreme Court Justices.

Cleve•land [klēv′lənd] a city in the northeastern part of Ohio, on Lake Erie. *Population:* 574,000.

Pronunciation Key: [ə] Symbol

The [ə] or *schwa* sound occurs in syllables without an accent. It can be spelled with any vowel, such as **a** in above, **e** in listen, **i** in pencil, **o** in melon, **u** in circus. It can also be a combination of vowels, such as **io** in action, **ai** in mountain, **iou** in precious.

(Turn the page for more information.)

Cleve•land [klēv′lənd] **(Stephen) Grover,** 1837–1908, the twenty-second and twenty-fourth president of the United States, from 1885 to 1889 and from 1893 to 1897.

climax A climax is the high point of a story. Think of the plot of a story as a line:

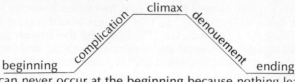

The climax can never occur at the beginning because nothing leads up to the high point. (It *could* end a story. "Denouement" [dā′ noō mänt′] is a literary term meaning "winding down." (In French it means untying a knot.) In most stories the climax comes shortly before the end. Doris Lessing's story "Through the Tunnel," tells of a boy's struggle to swim underwater through a long tunnel. At the end of the story, Jerry, the boy, is sitting at lunch with his mother. The climax has already taken place one page earlier, when Jerry finally succeeds in his effort to get through the tunnel.

clev•er [klev′ ər] *adjective,* **cleverer, cleverest. 1.** having a quick mind; smart; bright: The *clever* detective figured out right away who had stolen the jewels. "The people of Olinka . . . are *clever* people about most things, and understand new things very quickly." (Alice Walker) **2.** showing skill or quick thinking: a *clever* idea. **—cleverly,** *adverb.* **—cleverness,** *noun.*

cliché "One man's meat is another man's poison." That saying can be called a *cliché.* A cliché [klē′ shā] is an overused expression that becomes stale and so weakens writing. It's fun to make up lists of clichés: "last but not least," "in this day and age," "hook, line, and sinker," "few and far between," "flat as a pancake," "selling like hotcakes," "good as gold," "nothing ventured, nothing gained," and "crash" (meaning lie down or sleep). Make your own list. It will help you avoid the use of clichés.

click [klik] *noun, plural* **clicks.** a short, sharp sound. **—***verb,* **clicked, clicking. 1.** to make this sound. **2.** *Informal.* to fit or work together smoothly: Suddenly everything *clicked* in his mind and he understood how to solve the math problem.

cli•ent [klī′ ənt] *noun, plural* **clients. 1.** someone who uses the services or advice of a professional person. A lawyer, accountant, real estate agent, or social worker all have clients. **2.** any customer of a store or business. ♦ A group of clients is a **clientele** [klī′ ən tel′].

cliff [klif] *noun, plural* **cliffs.** a high, steep surface of rock or earth that rises sharply above the land or water below.

cli•mate [klī′ mət] *noun, plural* **climates. 1.** the usual weather that a place has. Climate includes the temperature, rain or snow, winds, and the amount of sunshine in a region. **2.** a section of the country having a certain type of weather: Arizona has a dry *climate.* **3.** the main attitude or feeling that a certain group or place has: the *climate* of public opinion.

cli•max [klī′ maks′] *noun, plural* **climaxes.** the most exciting or important part of something; the point of highest interest: The *climax* of a movie usually comes just before the end.

climb [klīm] *verb,* **climbed, climbing. 1.** to go up something, especially by using the hands and feet: to *climb* a mountain, to *climb* over a fence. ♦ This meaning is also used to tell about moving down or to the side: to *climb* down from a horse, to *climb* out of bed. **2.** to move upward, as if by climbing; rise: The plane *climbed* to 30,000 feet. That book has *climbed* to number one on the bestseller list. ♦ A **climbing plant** is one that grows by climbing a wall or other support. Ivy is a type of climbing plant.**—***noun, plural* **climbs. 1.** the act of climbing: Their *climb* to the top of the hill took two hours. **2.** a place to be climbed: This mountain is a dangerous *climb* for beginners.

clinch [klinch] *verb,* **clinched, clinching. 1.** to hold on to another person tightly, as in boxing or wrestling. **2.** to nail or fasten something firmly. **3.** to come to a final agreement or conclusion; settle: Our basketball team has already *clinched* the league championship even though there are three games left to play. **—***noun, plural* **clinches.** the act of clinching.

cling [kling] *verb,* **clung, clinging. 1.** to stick or hold tightly to something: When she took the clothes out of the dryer, the socks were *clinging* to each other. **2.** to refuse to give up; stay attached to: She still *clings* to the idea that she's a famous singer, even though she hasn't made a record in years.

clin•ic [klin′ik] *noun, plural* **clinics. 1.** a place where people can get medical help without having to stay in a hospital. **2.** any place where people can get help or learn certain skills: a reading *clinic.*

clip¹ [klip] *verb,* **clipped, clipping. 1.** to cut with a pair of scissors or shears; trim: to *clip* a hedge, to *clip* an article out of the newspaper. **2.** to cut something short, as if by clipping: "He spoke each word so clearly, in a *clipped* kind of way." (Mary Norton) —*noun, plural* **clips.** a quick rate of moving: The old man moved at quite a surprising *clip* on his morning walk.

clip² *noun, plural* **clips.** an object that holds things together: a paper *clip,* a tie *clip.* A **clipboard** is used to hold sheets of paper in place for writing. —*verb,* **clipped, clipping.** to hold things together with a clip: She *clipped* the check to her letter.

clipper ship A Currier & Ives print of the *Three Brothers,* a famous American clipper ship. At this time (1875) it was the largest sailing ship in the world.

clip•per [klip′ ər] *noun, plural* **clippers. 1.** a tool used to cut or clip things: fingernail *clip-*

pers. **2.** a large sailing ship of the 1880's that was built to travel at a fast speed; also called a **clipper ship.**

clip•ping [klip′ ing] *noun, plural* **clippings. 1.** a story, picture, or advertisement cut out of a newspaper or magazine. **2.** anything that is cut off or clipped from something else.

> **clique** *Clique* comes from an Old English word meaning "make noise." It's hard to connect that with its present-day meaning. A clique is a small group of people who think themselves special and might act together against another—quietly, usually. How would you define several choices of words: "group," "set," "crowd," "gang," "club"? Here are hints: you wouldn't say a "stylish gang" or a "violent set" or an "elite crowd."

clique [klēk *or* klik] *noun, plural* **cliques.** a small group of people who keep to themselves and do not mix with others.

cloak [klōk] *noun, plural* **cloaks. 1.** a loose outer garment that covers the body. **2.** something that covers up or hides, as a cloak covers the body: The prisoners escaped under the *cloak* of darkness. —*verb,* **cloaked, cloaking.** to cover up or hide: The Navy's plans for a new jet fighter have been *cloaked* in secrecy.

clock [kläk] *noun, plural* **clocks.** an object that shows the time of day. A clock is meant to be left in one place rather than carried around or worn as a watch is.

◆ A **digital clock** shows the time directly in numbers. An **analog clock** has a dial with hands pointing to the time.

—*verb,* **clocked, clocking.** to measure time with a clock: The police *clocked* the speeding car at 80 miles per hour.

clock•wise [kläk′ wīz′] *adjective* or *adverb.* moving in the same direction as the hands of a clock.

clog [kläg] *verb,* **clogged, clogging.** to stop up; block: Dead leaves *clogged* the storm drain. The road was *clogged* with traffic. —*noun, plural* **clogs. 1.** a shoe with a thick wooden or cork bottom. **2.** something that causes clogging.

clone [klōn] *noun, plural* **clones. 1.** a living plant or animal that is produced from only one

---

Pronunciation Key: Accent Marks

[′] is the normal accent mark. It shows where the main stress falls on a word.
[′] is a secondary accent mark. It shows a lighter stress than the primary accent. For example:
tel • e • vis • ion [tel′ə vizh′ən]
(Turn the page for more information.)

C

C

parent. The clone has GENES that are identical to the parent plant or animal it was taken from. **2.** something that is an exact copy or close imitation: That TV show is so popular that several *clones* of it are already on the air. —*verb,* **cloned, cloning.** to grow as a clone: Scientists can *clone* bacteria for use in research.

close¹ [klōz] *verb,* **closed, closing. 1.** to cover up a space or passage; make not open; shut: to *close* a door, to *close* your mouth. **2.** to bring together the parts of: "Miss Friel *closed* her book with a snap." (Brian Moore) **3.** to bring or come to an end: to *close* a letter with "Yours truly," to *close* a bank account by taking out all the money. **4.** to stop operating or working: The office *closed* for the holiday. ◆ Often used with **up** or **down:** Mr. Ross *closed up* the store and went home. The factory may *close down* because business is so slow. ◆ This word is also used as an adjective: The President made a few *closing* remarks before ending the press conference.—*noun, plural* **closes.** the closing of something; the end or finish: the *close* of school. "The day was drawing to a *close.*" (Dylan Thomas)

close-up [klōs′up′] *noun, plural* **close-ups.** a picture in which something appears at a close or short range: Movies and television shows use *close-ups* to show the expression on people's faces.

clot [klät] *noun, plural* **clots.** a soft lump formed from a liquid that becomes thick: a blood *clot.* —*verb,* **clotted, clotting.** to form a clot: When blood is exposed to air, it starts *clotting.*

cloth [klôth] *noun, plural* **cloths. 1.** a material made by weaving or knitting cotton, silk, wool, or other fibers. It is used to make clothes, blankets, curtains, and many other things. **2.** a piece of this material used for a special purpose: a table*cloth,* a wash*cloth,* a dish*cloth.*

clothe [klōth] *verb,* **clothed** or **clad, clothing. 1.** to put clothes on; dress: The character of Darth Vader is always *clothed* in black. **2.** to provide with clothes: to feed and *clothe* a family. **3.** to cover: After the snowstorm, every tree on the street was *clothed* in white.

clothes [klōz] *plural noun.* things worn to cover the body, such as shirts, pants, dresses, jackets, coats, and so on.

---

close of a paper This is a general term for the end of any piece of writing. It includes the ending of a story or the conclusion of an essay. What is a good close? Try these suggestions: (1) Make it neat. It should be a clean break, and shouldn't leave the reader hanging. (2) Keep it short. If you need more than a paragraph to wrap things up, this isn't really a close. (3) Keep it straight. Don't reach for a joke, a tricky phrase, or a puzzling question. (4) Make it specific. Don't search for a sweeping statement that will summarize the whole paper; just stop.

---

close² [klōs] *adjective,* **closer, closest. 1.** not far apart in space, time, or feeling; near: She can walk to school because she lives so *close.* It's getting *close* to Christmas. Karen has a very *close* friend who's in her Girl Scout troop. **2.** without enough air or space: This room is very *close* with the windows shut tight. ◆ **Close quarters** is a very tight or crowded place. **3.** giving careful thought or attention: to take a *close* look at something. **4.** nearly even: a *close* election for class president. —*adverb.* in a close way; near: "I'll walk ahead and you stay *close* behind me." (James Houston) —**closely,** *adverb:* They watched *closely* as she explained how to work the computer. —**closeness,** *noun.*

close call a narrow escape from danger or difficulty.

clos•et [kläz′ət] *noun, plural* **closets.** a small room or cabinet for hanging clothes and storing things.

cloth•ing [klō′thing] *noun.* things worn to cover the body; clothes.

cloud The majestic thunderhead, or *cumulonimbus* [kyoom′yə lō nim′bəs] cloud hanging over the woods is a sign that a storm is coming.

cloud [kloud] *noun, plural* **clouds. 1.** a white, gray, or dark mass floating high in the sky.

Clouds are made of tiny drops of water or ice hanging in the air. ◆ A **cloudburst** is a sudden, heavy rainfall. **2.** any mass or grouping of things like a cloud: a *cloud* of dust. A *cloud* of insects swarmed around the streetlight. —*verb,* **clouded, clouding. 1.** to cover or become covered with clouds: The morning sky was clear, but by noon it *clouded* over. **2.** to make or become darker or less clear: His face *clouded* when he heard the bad news.

cloud•y [kloud′ē] *adjective,* **cloudier, cloudiest. 1.** covered with clouds: a *cloudy* sky, *cloudy* weather. **2.** not clear: *cloudy* water in a muddy pond. Her memory is a bit *cloudy* as to exactly what happened that day.

clove [klōv] *noun, plural* **cloves.** the dried flower bud of a certain tropical tree. Cloves have a sharp smell and taste and are used as a spice to give flavor in cooking.

clo•ver [klō′vər] *noun, plural* **clover.** a plant with leaves formed in three small, round parts and white, red, or purple flower heads. Clover is used as food for cows and to make soil richer.

clown [kloun] *noun, plural* **clowns. 1.** a person whose work is to make others laugh by doing tricks, acting silly, and wearing funny clothes. Clowns often entertain at circuses or parades.

thing: a swimming *club,* a chess *club,* a garden *club.* **4.** a black clover leaf design like this [♣], found on a playing card. **5. clubs.** the suit of cards that has this design. —*verb,* **clubbed, clubbing.** to hit or beat with a club or stick.

clue [kloo] *noun, plural* **clues.** something that helps a person solve a problem or mystery: After the robbery the police looked for *clues,* such as the robber's fingerprints. She hasn't a *clue* as to who sent her that Valentine card.

clump [klump] *noun, plural* **clumps. 1.** a thick group or cluster: a *clump* of dirt. ". . . a creek and a *clump* of yellow willow trees." (Katherine Mansfield) **2.** a heavy, clumsy sound. —*verb,* **clumped, clumping. 1.** to form in a clump. **2.** to walk with a heavy, clumsy sound: The little boy *clumped* around the house wearing his father's shoes.

clum•sy [klum′zē] *adjective,* **clumsier, clumsiest. 1.** not moving smoothly; awkward: The *clumsy* puppies fell over each other as they tried to get out of the box. **2.** not well made, said, or done: He gave a *clumsy* excuse for not having his homework finished. —**clumsily,** *adverb.* —**clumsiness,** *noun.*

clung [klung] *verb.* the past form of **cling:** The child *clung* to his mother's hand.

C

clustering Many teachers of writing now recommend a technique called "clustering." It's used during the first stage of writing, after you've chosen your topic but before you begin to write. You take the topic and write it on a sheet of paper. Then, you "cluster" around it the important facts or qualities that can be connected to it. You use this as a starting point for your paper.

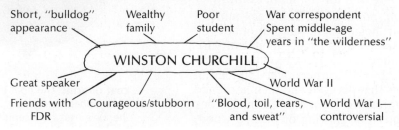

2. anyone who tells jokes or acts in a foolish way to make others laugh: Matt is the class *clown* at school. —*verb,* **clowned, clowning.** to behave like a clown; act silly: She was *clowning* around on her bicycle and ran into a fence.

club [klub] *noun, plural* **clubs. 1.** a heavy stick that is used to hit something. People fought with clubs before more modern weapons were invented. **2.** one of the long sticks used to hit the ball in the game of golf. **3.** a group of people who have joined together to do some special

clus•ter [klus′tər] *noun, plural* **clusters.** a group of similar things growing or gathered

Pronunciation Key: A–F			
a	and; hat	ch	chew; such
ā	ate; stay	d	dog; lid
â	care; air	e	end; yet
ä	father; hot	ē	she; each
b	boy; cab	f	fun; off

(Turn the page for more information.)

C

together: a *cluster* of flowers. —*verb,* **clustered, clustering.** to be in a cluster: "The sailors were *clustered* out of the rain in the doorways of the station." (John Updike)

clutch [kluch] *verb,* **clutched, clutching. 1.** to hold or grasp tightly: "From behind she suddenly *clutched* the child with her sharp little fingers." (Eudora Welty) **2.** to reach for; try to grab: The mountain climber *clutched* at a rock as he started to slip off the ledge. —*noun, plural* **clutches. 1.** a part in an automobile or other machine that connects or disconnects the motor from the other working parts. **2.** a tense or critical situation in a game or contest.

clut•ter [klut′ ər] *noun.* a group of things scattered about in a disorganized way; a mess: One corner of the office was filled with old magazines, empty boxes, and other *clutter.* —*verb,* **cluttered, cluttering.** to scatter or toss about; mess up: The artist's studio was *cluttered* with half-finished pictures, paint cans, brushes, and rags.

co- a *prefix* meaning "with another, together:" Robert Redford was Paul Newman's *co*star in the movie *The Sting.*

coach [kōch] *noun, plural* **coaches. 1.** a person who is in charge of a team in football, basketball, and other sports. **2.** any person who teaches or trains a performer or athlete: a singing *coach,* a tennis *coach.* **3.** a large, closed carriage on wheels that is pulled by horses. **4.** a section of seats on a bus, train, or airplane that is less expensive than other sections. —*verb,* **coached, coaching.** to act as a coach: His older sister is *coaching* him for the math exam.

coal [kōl] *noun, plural* **coals. 1.** a black mineral that gives off heat when burned, made up mostly of CARBON with a small amount of various other minerals. Coal is found in layers underground. It was formed over millions of years by plants that decayed and then hardened under great pressure from the earth or rock above. **2.** a piece of glowing or burned wood, coal, or charcoal.

coarse [kôrs] *adjective,* **coarser, coarsest. 1.** not smooth or fine; rough: In winter, horses have a *coarse* coat. **2.** made up of large parts or pieces: *coarse* soil, *coarse* salt. **3.** not having good manners; acting in a rough or crude way; rude. —**coarsely,** *adverb.* —**coarseness,** *noun.*

coast [kōst] *noun, plural* **coasts. 1.** the edge of land touching the ocean. **2.** an area of land near the ocean. —*verb,* **coasted, coasting.** to move without effort or power; slide: They *coasted* down the snowy hill on their sleds.

coast•al [kōs′ təl] *adjective.* of or near a coast: *coastal* waters, a *coastal* town.

Coast Guard a part of the United States armed forces that guards the coast and rescues boats and ships in trouble.

coat [kōt] *noun, plural* **coats. 1.** a piece of clothing with sleeves, usually worn outdoors over other clothing. **2.** the hair or fur of an animal: a lamb's wooly *coat.* **3.** a thin layer of something that covers a surface: a *coat* of paint. —*verb,* **coated, coating.** to cover with a thin layer of something: The fruit was *coated* with sugar to make candy. "We *coat* the surface of the earth with beer cans and chemicals, asphalt and old television sets." (John McPhee)

coat•ing [kō′ ting] *noun, plural* **coatings.** a thin layer of something that covers a surface; a coat.

coat of arms a design that shows the sign or symbol of a family, club, school, or other group. Long ago a soldier wore a coat of arms on his shield to show the family or kingdom he belonged to.

coat of arms The coat of arms of Christopher Columbus. The section on the lower left represents the lands that he discovered.

coax [kōks] *verb,* **coaxed, coaxing.** to try to get something in a nice or gentle way; persuade: They tried to *coax* the dog into the car by offering it some food.

cob [käb] *noun, plural* **cobs.** a short word for **corncob.**

co•balt [kō′ bôlt′] *noun.* a shiny silver-white metal that is similar to iron and nickel. Cobalt is a chemical element. It is often mixed with other metals in ALLOYS and used to make magnets, steel, and paint, or as a coloring material.

cobra The king cobra of southeast Asia is the largest poisonous snake in the world. It can grow to be 18 feet long.

co•bra [kō′ brə] *noun, plural* **cobras.** a large, very poisonous snake found in Africa and Asia. When excited, the cobra puffs out the skin around its neck into a flat hood.

cob•web [käb′ web′] *noun, plural* **cobwebs.** another word for **spiderweb.**

co•caine [kō kān′] *noun.* a habit-forming drug made from the leaves of a South American plant called **coca** [kō kə]. The use of cocaine is against the law and can be extremely dangerous to one's health.

cock•pit [käk′ pit′] *noun, plural* **cockpits.** the part of an aircraft where the pilot and other crew members sit.

cock•roach [käk′ rōch′] *noun, plural* **cock-roaches.** a brown or black insect with a flat, oval body and long feelers. Cockroaches are household pests that come out at night to feed.

cock•tail [käk′ tāl′] *noun, plural* **cocktails. 1.** a mixed alcoholic drink, especially one served before a meal. **2.** seafood, fruit, or fruit juices served at the start of a meal: a shrimp *cocktail.*

cock•y [käk′ ē] *adjective,* **cockier, cockiest.** too sure of oneself; too self-confident; conceited.

co•coa [kō′ kō] *noun.* **1.** a dark brown powder made by crushing the dried seeds of the CACAO tree. This powder gives a chocolate taste to foods. **2.** a hot drink made by mixing cocoa with sugar and milk or water.

co•co•nut [kō′ kə nut′] *noun, plural* **coconuts.** a large, round fruit that comes from the **coconut palm** tree. It has a thick, hard shell with sweet white meat and a milky liquid inside.

co•coon [kə kōōn′] *noun, plural* **cocoons.** a silky covering that is spun by an insect to protect it while it is in an inactive stage of life called a PUPA. A caterpillar lives in a cocoon while it is developing into a moth or butterfly.

cod [käd] *noun, plural* **cod** or **cods.** a fish found in northern areas of the Atlantic Ocean. Cod are caught in large numbers for food.

code *Code* is taken from an old word referring to a collection of laws. But the word has other deep roots. In Latin, *codex* was a block of wood split into leaves or tablets. When Harcourt Brace Jovanovich published Leonardo da Vinci's *Codex Atlanticus,* it was twelve huge volumes of drawings and text, yet *codex* could also apply to a single volume. The famous Code of Hammurabi was a set of laws laid down by a Middle Eastern ruler 4000 years ago. The modern meaning of *code* involves secret symbols, a system of secret communication. In World War II the Americans "broke" the Japanese radio code and for a time knew what orders were sent out from Tokyo to admirals and generals in battle.

Co•chise [kō chēs′] 1812?–1874, Apache Indian chief.

cock [käk] *noun, plural* **cocks. 1.** a male chicken; a rooster. **2.** the male of certain other birds that are used for food. —*verb,* **cocked, cocking. 1.** to tilt or tip; turn up: "He sat there with his head *cocked* to one side, very coolly." (Tom Wolfe) **2.** to pull back the hammer of a gun: The hunter *cocked* his rifle.

cocker spaniel a small dog with long ears and silky hair.

code [kōd] *noun, plural* **codes. 1.** a set of words, signs, or symbols used to send messages. Codes are often used to keep messages short or secret.

Pronunciation Key: G–N

g	give; big	k	kind; cat; back
h	hold	l	let; ball
i	it; this	m	make; time
ī	ice; my	n	not; own
j	jet; gem; edge	ng	having

(Turn the page for more information.)

2. in a computer, a method of presenting information and instructions in a form that can be understood by the computer. **3.** a system of laws arranged in an orderly way: The building *code* says that the swimming pool must have a high fence around it. **4.** any set of rules or principles for doing things: a *code* of honor. —*verb,* **coded, coding.** to put into code: to *code* a message.

cof•fee [kôf′ ē] *noun, plural* **coffee** or **coffees. 1.** a dark brown, hot drink made of the crushed and roasted seeds of a plant that grows in warm, moist climates. **2.** the seeds or beans of this plant.

coffee A coffee bush is shown with its berries (above), each containing two coffee beans (below). The word *coffee* comes from Arabic. The Arabs were the first people to raise coffee plants.

cof•fin [kôf′ in] *noun, plural* **coffins.** a box or case in which the body of a dead person is placed to be buried.

coil [koil] *noun, plural* **coils.** anything made by winding something around in a circle many times; a connected series of circles: a *coil* of rope, a *coil* of wire. —*verb,* **coiled, coiling.** to wind in a coil: Andrew *coiled* up the hose.

coin U.S. coins from the first half of the 20th century. The Indian cent and Liberty quarter (left); Buffalo nickel and Walking Liberty half dollar (center); Mercury dime and Peace dollar (right).

coin [koin] *noun, plural* **coins.** a flat, round piece of metal used as money. —*verb,* **coined, coining. 1.** to make coins from metal: The U.S. government *coins* money at several mints around the country. **2.** to make up; invent: President Harry Truman *coined* the phrase, "The buck stops here."

co•in•cide [kō′ ən sīd′] *verb,* **coincided, coinciding. 1.** to happen at the same time. **2.** to be alike or identical: The police aren't sure how the accident happened because the witnesses' stories don't *coincide* at all.

co•in•ci•dence [kō in′ sə dəns] *noun, plural* **coincidences.** two things happening at the same time or place that seem to have been planned or arranged, but actually happen together by accident: It was a *coincidence* that the baby was born on her mother's birthday.

coincidence/chance Coincidence and chance are both elements in telling a story. By *chance,* two travelers might happen to stop at the same place. However, if the two were actually brothers, who met without planning to do so, that would be a *coincidence.* This is what happens in Thomas Hardy's story, "Three Strangers" in which three men accidentally meet at a lonely cottage. If you use coincidence too often, you are a lazy storyteller: instead of constructing events so that chance brings people together, you might have unbelievable coincidences—say, two brothers meet after thirty years and find they've married two sisters. Literary critic Laurence Perrine suggests three rules: (1) The coincidence should not appear at the end. In "The Three Strangers," it takes place early in the story. (2) The coincidence should be important, but not the crucial event. Hardy uses coincidence to get things moving; the real action comes after the meeting. (3) The coincidence should be believable. It *is* unusual that the three men meet. But they are all traveling to or from the same place, and the cottage is the only resting place along the way.

co•la [kō′lə] *noun, plural* **colas.** (also spelled **kola**) **1.** a tree that grows in warm tropical regions. **Cola nuts** contain CAFFEINE and are used to flavor soft drinks. **2.** any of various dark-colored soft drinks flavored with cola nuts or a similar-tasting substance.

cold [kōld] *adjective,* **colder, coldest. 1.** having a low temperature; not hot: a *cold* winter day. The water was too *cold* for us to go swimming. **2.** not feeling warm; chilly: She was *cold,* so she put on a sweater. **3.** not friendly or kind: He gave me a *cold* look when I accidentally stepped on his foot. —*noun, plural* **colds. 1.** a lack of heat: Some house plants will die if left out in the *cold.* **2.** a common illness that causes sneezing, a running nose, and coughing. —**coldly,** *adverb:* "They looked at her *coldly,* as if they were finding fault with her." (D.H. Lawrence) —**coldness,** *noun.*

cold-blooded [kōld′ blud′ əd] *adjective, more/ most.* **1.** having a body temperature that changes as the nearby air or water becomes colder or warmer. Fish, frogs, turtles, and snakes are cold-blooded animals. **2.** having no feelings or emotions; cruel, a *cold-blooded* murderer.

col•lab•o•rate [kə lab′ ə rāt′] *verb,* **collaborated, collaborating. 1.** to work together; work with others: The two authors *collaborated* on a book about Thomas Jefferson. **2.** to help an enemy against one's own country. ♦ The act of collaborating is **collaboration.**

col•lar [käl′ ər] *noun, plural* **collars. 1.** the band or strip around the neck of a coat, shirt, or dress. **2.** a band or chain worn around the neck of an animal, such as a dog or cat. **3.** anything that is like a collar, such as a ring that holds a rod or pipe in place. —*verb,* **collared, collaring. 1.** to put a collar on. **2.** to catch as if by the collar: The storekeeper *collared* the thief as he was sneaking out the door with a radio.

col•lar•bone [käl′ ər bōn′] *noun, plural* **collarbones.** the bone that connects the shoulder bone to the breastbone. ♦ In medicine this bone is known as the **clavicle** [klav′ ə kəl].

col•league [käl′ ēg] *noun, plural* **colleagues.** someone who is in the same business or with the same company as another; a fellow worker: While the doctor was away on vacation, one of his *colleagues* treated his patients for him.

col•lect [kə lekt′] *verb,* **collected, collecting. 1.** to bring together in a group; gather together; assemble: The campers *collected* some wood for a fire. "A crowd which had followed him down the lane *collected* outside the door." (James Joyce) **2.** to gather for a hobby, study, or display: Rosa *collects* stamps from all over the world. **3.** to get as payment: Nick *collected* money from the people on his paper route. ♦ To be **collected** means to be calm and relaxed.

col•lec•tion [kə lek′ shən] *noun, plural* **collections. 1.** the act of gathering together or collect-

C

---

collaboration In writing, collaboration refers to two (or more) people writing together. For example, school textbooks are normally prepared by a number of writers rather than a single one. The earliest dictionaries were compiled by a single person, such as Samuel Johnson in England and Noah Webster in the United States. Now reference books are less personal and are usually written by a group of editors. On the other hand, novels and short stories are almost never written in collaboration. One special form of collaboration is called GHOST WRITING. (See page 329.)

---

col•lage [kə lazh′] *noun, plural* **collages.** a picture that is made by gluing pieces of materials such as paper, cloth, and yarn to a surface.

col•lapse [kə laps′] *verb,* **collapsed, collapsing. 1.** to fall down or fall in: The shed *collapsed* when a huge tree fell on it. **2.** to lose strength; break down: "Out of breath, . . . he *collapsed* in a heap." (Lloyd Alexander) **3.** to fail completely or suddenly: "His whole life would be ruined, all his plans for the future would *collapse.*" (E.B. White) ♦ Something that can be folded together is **collapsible:** a *collapsible* beach chair, —*noun, plural* **collapses.** the act or fact of collapsing: the *collapse* of an old building, the *collapse* of a business.

ing: Garbage *collection* is once a week in our town. **2.** something collected: a *collection* of dust on an old set of books. **3.** a group of things gathered for a hobby, study, or display: "The photograph is one of a *collection* by a famous photographer." (S.E. Hinton)

Pronunciation Key: O–S

ō	over; go	ou	out; town
ô	all; law	p	put; hop
oo	look; full	r	run; car
o͞o	pool; who	s	set; miss
oi	oil; boy	sh	show

(Turn the page for more information.)

C

col·lec·tor [kə lek′ tər] *noun, plural* **collectors.** someone or something that collects: a coin *collector,* a tax *collector.*

Co·lom·bi·a [kə lum′ bē ə] a country in north-eastern South America. *Capital:* Bogotá. *Area:* 439,800 square miles. *Population:* 28,800,000.

colons A colon, like a period, shows a full stop in writing. It differs in that it is used within the sentence. It signals, in effect, "what follows." It has three common uses: (1) Before a list of items: "It was full of all sorts of things that you find in barns: ladders, grindstones, pitchforks, monkey wrenches . . . "(E.B. White) (2) To introduce a quotation: "She heard someone running behind her, a breathless exclamation: 'Sister Irene!'" (Joyce Carol Oates) (3) To separate two parts of a sentence, when the second explains the first: "It was night: the stars were glittering, the trees standing black and still." (Doris Lessing)

col·lege [käl′ ij] *noun, plural* **colleges.** a school of higher learning beyond a high school. A college offers a course of study, usually for four years, and students who complete this course receive a special certificate called a DE-GREE or diploma. **2.** a special school within an entire UNIVERSITY for instruction in one particular area: a teacher's *college,* a medical *college.* ◆ Something that has to do with college is **collegiate** [kə lē′ jit].

col·lide [kə līd′] *verb,* **collided, colliding.** to strike or bump together in a rough or violent way; crash: Two cars *collided* at the highway exit. "He bounced out the door, *colliding* with his father who was rushing to the table." (Louise Fitzhugh)

col·lie [käl′ ē] *noun, plural* **collies.** a large dog with a long, thin face and long, thick hair.

collie The collie is a popular breed that has often been featured in movies and TV shows. It was first used by Scottish farmers to guard sheep.

col·li·sion [kə lizh′ ən] *noun, plural* **collisions.** the act of colliding; hitting together; a crash: "He had to swim with his head above water to avoid *collisions.*" (John Cheever)

co·lon¹ [kō′ lən] *noun, plural* **colons.** a mark of punctuation [:] that is used to call attention to a certain group of words that follow, as in "For example:"

colon² *noun, plural* **colons.** the lower part of the large intestine.

colo·nel [kur′ nəl] *noun, plural* **colonels.** an officer's rank in the army, below a general and above a major. ◆ A **lieutenant colonel** ranks below a full colonel.

colonial Colonial houses are often found in New England. This was the style built during colonial times, in the 1600's and 1700's.

co·lo·ni·al [kə lō′ nē əl] *adjective.* **1.** having to do with a colony or colonies: Calcutta was the central city of Britain's *colonial* government in India. ◆ The policy of ruling other areas as colonies is called **colonialism:** Many European countries practiced *colonialism* in Africa and Asia in the 1800's. **2.** having to do with the thirteen original colonies in America: *colonial* history. ◆ The word **Colonial** refers to a style of furniture or buildings that imitates the style of this original colonial period.

col·o·nize [käl′ ə nīz′] *verb,* **colonized, colonizing.** to set up or live in a colony: The Romans *colonized* England in the year 43 A.D.

col•o•ny [kälʹ ə nē] *noun, plural* **colonies. 1.** a group of people who leave their own country to settle in another area that is under the control of that country: A *colony* of English settlers landed at Jamestown, Virginia, in 1607. **2.** an area of land that is ruled by a distant country: Mexico was once a *colony* of Spain. **3. the Colonies.** the thirteen former British colonies that became the first states of the United States. ♦ A person living in the Colonies was a **colonist. 4.** a group of people who live near each other and are alike in some way: The "Left Bank" section of Paris was a well-known artists' *colony* in the 1920's. **5.** a group of animals or plants of the same kind living together: Sea lions and seals gather in *colonies*.

col•or [kulʹ ər] *noun, plural* **colors. 1.** the quality of a thing that comes from the way light strikes it and then is sensed by the eyes. Color can make the thing look different from another thing having the same size and shape. **2.** any one of the different ways in which this quality is sensed by the eyes. There are three **primary colors**—red, blue, and yellow. Other colors, such as green, purple, or orange, are combinations of these primary colors. **3.** the color of a person's skin: "The right of citizens of the United States to vote shall not be denied . . . on account of . . . *color*." (U.S. Constitution) **4.** a lively or interesting quality: The books of Charles Dickens captured the *color* of life in 19th-century London. **5. the colors.** the flag of a certain country or military unit: "Have your troops hoist *the colors* to its peak." (Douglas MacArthur) —*verb,* **colored, coloring.** to give color; add color: The little child *colored* the walls with a crayon. "Her face *colored* scarlet as the words came out." (Brian Moore)

Col•o•rad•o [kälʹ ə räʹ dō] **1.** a state in the west-central U.S. *Capital:* Denver. *Nickname:* "Centennial State." *Area:* 104,200 square miles. *Population:* 3,050,000. **2.** a river of the southwestern U.S. that flows from the Rocky Mountains of Colorado to the Gulf of Mexico.

col•or-blind [kulʹ ər blīndʹ] *adjective.* not able to see the difference between certain colors. ♦ The fact of being color-blind is **color-blindness.**

col•ored [kulʹ ərd] *adjective.* **1.** having color: He kept the white and *colored* clothes separate when he did his wash. **2.** having to do with the black race, or any race that is not white.

col•or•ful [kulʹ ər fəl] *adjective, more/most.* **1.** full of color: Henri Matisse was known for his *colorful* paintings. **2.** interesting or exciting:

She wrote a *colorful* description of her trip.

col•or•ing [kulʹ ər ing] *noun, plural* **colorings. 1.** the way something or someone is colored: The *coloring* of maple trees changes in fall. **2.** a thing that gives color or changes the color of something: hair *coloring*, food *coloring*.

colt [kōlt] *noun, plural* **colts.** a young horse, especially a male.

Co•lum•bus [kə lumʹ bas] the capital of the state of Ohio. *Population:* 565,000.

Columbus This medal of Christopher Columbus was created for the Columbian Exposition in Chicago in 1892. This was a celebration of the 400th anniversary of Columbus's voyage.

Co•lum•bus [kə lumʹ bəs] **Christopher,** 1451–1506, Italian explorer who discovered America for Spain in 1492.

col•umn [kälʹ əm] *noun, plural* **columns. 1.** a tall, slender post or pillar, usually made of wood or stone, that stands upright to support a roof or other part of a building. In modern buildings, columns are often used for decoration rather than as an actual support. **2.** anything long and slender like a column: a *column* of smoke. A *column* of ants trailed along the ground. **3.** a narrow vertical section of words or figures: You are now reading the right-hand *column* of this page **4.** a regular article or feature in a newspaper or magazine, usually written by the same person. ♦ A person who writes a column is called a **columnist.**

C

Pronunciation Key: T–Z			
t	ten; date	v	very; live
th	think	w	win; away
th	these	y	you
u	cut; butter	z	zoo; cause
ur	turn; bird	zh	measure

(Turn the page for more information.)

co·ma [kō′ mə] *noun, plural* **comas.** a state of long, deep unconsciousness from which a person cannot be awakened, caused by an injury or illness.

comb [kōm] *noun, plural* **combs. 1.** a plastic or metal object with teeth, used to arrange or style the hair. **2.** a thick, fleshy, red piece of skin on top of the head of a rooster or similar bird. —*verb,* **combed, combing. 1.** to arrange or style the hair with a comb. **2.** to search for something very carefully: The police *combed* the area looking for the escaped prisoners.

com·bat [käm′ bət] *noun, plural* **combats. 1.** a battle or war between two military forces: The Purple Heart is a medal given to any U.S. soldier wounded in *combat.* —[kəm bat′] *verb,* **combated, combating.** to fight or struggle against: Dr. Jonas Salk found a medicine to *combat* the spread of the disease polio.

com·bi·na·tion [käm′ bə nā′ shən] *noun, plural* **combinations. 1.** something that is formed by combining things: A mule is a *combination* of a horse and a donkey. "My mother's eyes lit up with a *combination* of excitement and curiosity." (Paul Zindel) **2.** the act of combining: The *combination* of red and blue makes purple. **3.** a series of numbers or letters used to open a lock.

com·bine [kəm bīn′] *verb,* **combined, combining.** to put together; join or unite; mix: She *combined* flour, butter, and water to make a pie crust. ◆ Often used as an adjective: "Under the *combined* attack of wind and sea . . ." (Armstrong Sperry) —[kam′ bīn′] *noun, plural* **combines.** a machine used to harvest wheat.

boil. She hopes her wish will *come* true. **4.** to be from a certain place: Janet *comes* from a small town in North Dakota. **5.** to be available; exist: This shirt *comes* in four different colors.

co·me·di·an [kə mē′ dē ən] *noun, plural* **comedians. 1.** a person whose work is entertaining others by telling jokes or doing funny things, as in a movie or on TV. **2.** a funny person.

com·e·dy [käm′ ə dē] *noun, plural* **comedies.** a play, movie, or television program that is funny and that has a happy ending. ◆ A **situation comedy** is a TV comedy show that uses the same characters in a series of programs.

comet Halley's Comet moving across the sky in 1986. *Comet* comes from a Greek term meaning "long hair." The idea is that the tail of a comet looks like this.

com·et [käm′ it] *noun, plural* **comets.** a heavenly body that travels in a long path around the sun and has a bright head and a long streaming tail. It is thought to be a mass of ice, frozen gases, and dust.

combining sentences Good writers combine short sentences to help the flow of their writing and keep it lively. Here are some short sentences that well-known writers have combined for a better effect. See if you can feel the difference, and then practice with your own writing. Two sentences together: "The captain saw a floating stick, and they rowed to it." (Stephen Crane) "It was now midnight, and my task was drawing to a close." (Edgar Allan Poe) Now three sentences: "The sun set; the dusk fell on the stream, and lights began to appear along the shore." (Joseph Conrad) "The east-bound train was plowing through a January snowstorm; the dull dawn was beginning to show grey when the engine whistled a mile out of Newark." (Willa Cather)

com·bus·tion [kəm bus′ chən] *noun.* the process of burning: The power of a car engine comes from the *combustion* of fuel.

come [kum] *verb,* **came, come, coming. 1.** to go or move toward a place: Our dog always *comes* when he's called. **2.** to reach a certain place; arrive: *Come* home before dark. Winter *comes* early in Alaska. **3.** to reach a certain point or condition: Heat the soup until it *comes* to a

com·fort [kum′ fərt] *noun, plural* **comforts. 1.** a feeling of being free from worry, pain, or sorrow, and of having one's needs satisfied: to live in *comfort.* "There was a certain *comfort* in having her near me, for I did not want to be alone." (Isak Dinesen) **2.** a person or thing that gives this feeling: The motel's ad said "We offer all the *comforts* of home." —*verb,* **comforted, comforting.** to give comfort to someone who is upset or in pain or difficulty: The mother *comforted* her little boy after he had a bad dream.

com•fort•a•ble [kumf′tər bəl *or* kum′fər tə-bəl] *adjective, more/most.* **1.** giving comfort: *comfortable* clothes, a *comfortable* bed. "He was no millionaire . . . but he had a *comfortable* income." (I.B. Singer) **2.** feeling comfort; at ease: "You feel mighty free and easy and *comfortable* on a raft." (Mark Twain) —**comfortably,** *adverb:* This car can seat five people *comfortably*.

com•ic [käm′ ik] *noun, plural* **comics. 1.** a person who tells funny stories or jokes that make people laugh; a comedian. **2.** a COMIC STRIP or COMIC BOOK. —*adjective, more/most.* funny or amusing: Amelia Bedelia is a *comic* character who always gets mixed up about language. ♦ Another form of this word is **comical.**

comic strip a group of simple cartoon drawings telling a joke or story. A **comic book** is a series of comic strips put together in the form of a booklet or magazine.

com•ma [käm′ ə] *noun, plural* **commas.** a mark of punctuation [,] that is used: **1.** to separate parts of a sentence: Wood floats, but iron doesn't. **2.** to set off items in a series: Tea is grown in India, China, and Japan. It was a cold, dark, dreary day. **3.** to separate parts of a name, date, or address: John D. Rockefeller, Jr. June 6, 1944. El Paso, Texas.

com•mand [kə mand′] *verb,* **commanded, commanding. 1.** to give orders to; order; direct: "She slammed supper on the table and *commanded* everybody to eat and be quick about it." (Vera Cleaver) **2.** to have power or authority over: Robert E. Lee *commanded* the Army of Northern Virginia in the Civil War. **3.** to receive or demand as one's due: That singer *commands* a high fee for a personal appearance. —*noun, plural* **commands. 1.** an order or direction: The dog sat up at his owner's *command*. **2.** the power to give orders: to be in *command* of a ship. **3.** the power or ability to make use of something: Winston Churchill had a great *command* of the English language. **4.** an instruction to a computer to perform a certain operation.

com•mand•er [kə man′ dər] *noun, plural* **commanders. 1.** a person in command; a leader. **2.** an officer's rank in the navy, below a captain. A **lieutenant commander** ranks next below a commander.

com•mand•ment [kə mand′ mənt] *noun, plural* **commandments. 1.** a command or law. **2. Commandment.** one of the **Ten Commandments,** the ten supreme laws of human actions given by God to Moses, as told in the Bible.

com•mem•o•rate [kə mem′ ə rāt′] *verb,* **commemorated, commemorating.** to honor the memory of some person or event: In 1976 the U.S. *commemorated* its 200th anniversary as a nation. —**commemoration,** *noun.*

com•mence [kə mens′] *verb,* **commenced, commencing.** to begin; start: The awards ceremony will *commence* at eight o'clock.

commas As we speak, we can delay between words for a moment to show a break in thought. The comma does for writing what this pause does in speech. From the Pulitzer Prize-winning author Alice Walker, here are examples of four uses of the comma: (1) To set off individual words: "Mr. Sweet was a tall, thinnish man . . ." (2) To set off a phrase within the sentence: "I ran to the phone, called the airport, and within four hours I was speeding along the dusty road to Mr. Sweet's." (3) To set off a clause: "When he was leaving, my mother said to us that we'd better sleep light that night." (4) To divide the parts of a compound sentence: "Mr. Sweet used to call me his princess, and I believed it."

com•mence•ment [kə mens′ mənt] *noun, plural* **commencements. 1.** the beginning or start of something. **2.** the ceremony of graduating from a school or college.

com•ment [käm′ ent] *noun, plural* **comments.** a remark, statement, or opinion about someone or something: The teacher wrote some *comments* on Ron's science report. —*verb,* **commented, commenting.** to make a comment: The TV reporter asked the senator to *comment* on the story in that morning's paper.

Pronunciation Key: [ə] Symbol

The [ə] or *schwa* sound occurs in syllables without an accent. It can be spelled with any vowel, such as a in above, e in listen, i in pencil, o in melon, u in circus. It can also be a combination of vowels, such as io in action, ai in mountain, iou in precious.

(Turn the page for more information.)

C

com•merce [käm′ ərs] *noun.* the buying and selling of goods, especially on a large scale between different places or countries: "Interstate *commerce*" means business that goes on between people in different states.

com•mer•cial [kə mur′ shəl] *noun, plural* **commercials.** an advertisement on TV or radio. —*adjective, more/most.* having to do with business or trade: A *commercial* airliner is one that flies passengers and goods to make money, as compared to a private plane or a military aircraft. —**commercially,** *adverb.*

com•mis•sion [kə mish′ ən] *noun, plural* **commissions.** 1. a group of people given the power or authority to do a certain job: The mayor set up a *commission* on education to study problems in the city's schools. 2. a position of power or authority, especially a rank in the armed forces. 3. a payment of money to a person for carrying out or arranging the sale of something: That real estate agent gets a *commission* of 6% on the price of each house she sells. 4. the act of doing something; a committing: the *commission* of a crime. 5. **out of (in) commission.** out of (in) active use or service: The U.S. took most of its battleships *out of commission* after World War II. —*verb,* **commissioned, commissioning.** 1. to give power or authority to: The artist was *commissioned* to do a painting for a new postage stamp. ♦ A **commissioned officer** is one who has received a written commission for his rank. 2. to put into active service: The aircraft carrier *Nimitz* was *commissioned* in 1975.

com•mis•sion•er [kə mish′ ən ər] *noun, plural* **commissioners.** 1. a person who is in charge of a department of the government: a fire *commissioner*, a traffic *commissioner*. 2. an official who is in charge of a sports league: the *commissioner* of major-league baseball.

com•mit [kə mit′] *verb,* **committed, committing.** 1. to do or perform something wrong or bad: to *commit* murder, to *commit* an error in baseball. "In his heart was the pain of having *committed* a crime." (E.B. White) 2. to be put in the care or charge of: The court *committed* him to a mental hospital for treatment. 3. to promise or assign to something: She's *committed* to working there all summer. "You are the kind of man who, once *committed*, would give his life for what he believes in." (John D. MacDonald)

com•mit•ment [kə mit′ mənt] *noun, plural* **commitments.** the fact of being committed to something: Peg couldn't go on the trip; she had too many other *commitments*.

com•mit•tee [kə mit′ ē] *noun, plural* **committees.** a group of people who work together for a common purpose: Jeff is on the refreshment *committee* for the school dance. In Congress, the Armed Services *Committee* deals with matters relating to the Army, Navy, and Air Force.

com•mod•i•ty [kə mäd′ ə tē] *noun, plural* **commodities.** anything that can be bought or sold, especially raw materials produced by farming or mining: Corn, lumber, and silver are commodities.

com•mon [käm′ ən] *adjective,* **commoner, commonest** or *more/most.* 1. appearing or happening often; usual or familiar: Dogs are a *common* household pet. 2. widespread; general: "It was *common* knowledge that Marcia had recently had a serious operation." (Barbara Pym) 3. having to do with people in general; public: "The Congress shall have power . . . to provide for the *common* defense of the United States." (U.S. Constitution) 4. shared by two or more people or groups: "We and the Africans will be working for a *common* goal: the uplift of black people everywhere." (Alice Walker) 5. of no special rank or quality; average; ordinary: the *common* man, *common* table salt. 6. of low quality; cheap or vulgar. —*noun, plural* **commons.** 1. an area of public land used by the people of a town or community: Boston *Common* is the oldest public park in the U.S. 2. **in common.** equally with another or others: "The only thing . . . they had *in common* was that they both loved watching horror movies." (Paul Zindel) —**commonly,** *adverb:* It was once *commonly* believed the earth was flat.

common sense good judgment that comes from everyday experience rather than from special knowledge; ordinary intelligence: Mom has read a lot of books on how to raise children, but she still feels it's mainly a matter of *common sense.*

com•mon•wealth [käm′ ən welth′] *noun, plural* **commonwealths.** 1. all the people who live in a nation or state. 2. a nation or state that is governed by the people. ♦ Certain states of the U.S. have the official name **Commonwealth,** such as Massachusetts and Virginia. 3. *also,* **Commonwealth of Nations.** an organization made up of Great Britain and countries that were once ruled by Britain, such as Canada, India, and Australia.

com•mo•tion [kə mō′ shən] *noun, plural* **commotions.** a loud, noisy disturbance: "There was a tremendous *commotion*—wings beating, feet racing, water churned to a froth." (E.B. White)

com•mu•ni•cate [kə myōō′ nə kāt′] *verb,* **communicated, communicating.** to share or exchange information, feelings, or thoughts; speak or write to someone: People don't *communicate* by letter today as much as they did before the telephone was invented.

com•mu•ni•ca•tion [kə myōō′ nə kā′ shən] *noun, plural* **communications. 1.** the act of communicating; A coach should have good *communication* with the players on his team. **2.** what is communicated; the information or ideas given. **3. communications.** a system that is used to communicate, such as TV, radio, or telephone.

com•mun•ion [kə myōōn′ yən] *noun, plural* **communions. 1.** a close sharing of thoughts or feelings. **2. Communion.** a religious ceremony observed by Christian churches, in which bread and wine are blessed in memory of the last meal eaten by Jesus.

com•mun•ism [käm′ yə niz′ əm] *noun.* **1.** an economic system in which all property, goods, and services belong to the government rather than to individual people or private companies. Under communism all people are supposed to share equally in what is produced. **2.** *also,* **Communism.** a policy of government based on this system.

com•mun•ist [käm′ yə nist] *adjective.* (àlso spelled **Communist**). having to do with communism: The Soviet Union is a *communist* country. ♦ A **Communist Party** is a political party that favors communism. —*noun, plural* **communists.** a person who favors communism or belongs to a Communist Party.

com•mu•ni•ty [kə myōō′ nə tē] *noun, plural* **communities. 1.** a group of people who live in the same area, such as a neighborhood or town. A **community center** is a building that serves the general public in such an area. **2.** the area or town itself: San Antonio, Texas is a rapidly-growing *community.* **3.** any group of people

joined together by common interest: A nun is a member of a religious *community.*

com•mute [kə myōōt′] *verb,* **commuted, commuting.** to travel regularly to and from one's place of work, especially over a long distance. ♦ A person who does this is a **commuter.**

com•pact[1] [käm′ pakt′ *or* kəm pakt′] *adjective, more/most.* **1.** packed together tightly: The newspapers were bundled in a *compact* pile. **2.** taking up a small amount of space or room: a *compact* stereo system. —[kəm pakt′] *verb,* **compacted, compacting.** to pack together tightly. ♦ A **compactor** is a machine that compacts trash or garbage into a tight bundle.

—[käm′ pakt′] *noun, plural* **compacts. 1.** a small case used to hold a woman's face powder. **2.** a car that is smaller than a regular-sized model. The smallest car models are called **subcompacts.**

com•pact[2] [käm′ pakt] *noun, plural* **compacts.** an agreement between different countries or groups. ♦ The **Mayflower Compact** was the first official set of rules for government in America.

com•pan•ion [kəm pan′ yən] *noun, plural* **companions. 1.** a person who spends time with another; a friend: "My cousin Sandy had up to that time been my only really close *companion.*" (Edmund Wilson) ♦ The friendship between companions is known as **companionship. 2.** any person who goes along with another: First prize in this contest is a free trip to London for the winner and a *companion.*

C

communication People using language communicate orally (by speech) or by writing. What are some advantages of writing over speech? (1) Writing is usually more precise—you can go back to edit a paragraph, if need be, but you don't "re-speak." Lawyers, doctors, and business people write down important communication, because it avoids the problem of "That's not exactly what I said." (2) Writing has a greater capacity. Early peoples had to memorize a long poem or story to keep it in existence, but now we can write it down. We can also write down huge amounts of factual information (as in this dictionary), far beyond what anyone could memorize. (3) Writing endures. William Shakespeare lived in England 400 years ago. Today, no one can state for certain anything that he said during his life, but his written words are known the world over.

Pronunciation Key: Accent Marks

[′] is the normal accent mark. It shows where the main stress falls on a word.
[′] is a secondary accent mark. It shows a lighter stress than the primary accent. For example:

tel • e • vis • ion [tel′ ə vizh′ ən]

(Turn the page for more information.)

C

com•pa•ny [kum′ pə nē] *noun, plural* **companies. 1.** a group of people who join together to do business; a firm or business: IBM is the largest computer *company* in the U.S. **2.** any group of people joined together for some purpose: the New York City Ballet *Company*. **3.** someone who visits; a guest or guests: They're having *company* over for dinner tonight. **4.** a group of friends; companions. **5.** companionship: She's a friendly person who enjoys the *company* of others. **6.** a unit of soldiers in the army, under the command of a captain.

com•pa•ra•ble [käm′ prə bəl] *adjective.* able to be compared; similar: New York City is *comparable* in size to London and Tokyo.

com•par•a•tive [kəm par′ ə tiv] *adjective.* **1.** making a comparison: Bob made a *comparative* study of the two cars before deciding which one to buy. **2.** according to a comparison; compared to others: San Diego is a *comparative* newcomer to the list of America's largest cities. —*noun, plural* **comparatives.** in grammar, a form of an adjective or adverb that gives the idea of comparison: "Higher" and "better" are *comparatives.* —**comparatively,** *adverb.* by comparison; John Kennedy was *comparatively* young when he became President.

com•pare [kəm pâr′] *verb,* **compared, comparing. 1.** to find out or show how a thing is different from or like something else: *Compare* your answers with the answer key in the back of the book. **2.** to say that a thing is like something else: A famous poem about President Lincoln *compared* him to the captain of a ship. "I have been studying how I may *compare* this prison where I live unto the world." (Shakespeare; *King Richard II*) **3.** to be similar in quality to: I like frozen corn, but it really can't *compare* with fresh corn that's just been picked.

Japanese methods of doing business. **2.** a likeness; similarity: California and Montana are about the same size, but there's no *comparison* in the number of people they have. **3.** in grammar, a change in the form of an adjective or adverb to show a difference in amount or quality.

com•part•ment [kəm pärt′ mənt] *noun, plural* **compartments.** a separate division or part; a section: The refrigerator has different *compartments* for butter, cheese, meat, and vegetables. ◆ A car has a **glove compartment** to hold small items such as gloves, maps, and so on.

compass A hand compass of the type used by campers and hikers to find direction in the wilderness.

com•pass [kum′ pəs *or* käm′ pəs] *noun, plural* **compasses. 1.** an instrument that shows direction by means of a magnetic needle that always points north towards the magnetic North Pole. **2.** an instrument with two legs joined at the top, used to draw circles or measure distance.

com•pas•sion [kum pash′ ən] *noun.* the quality of feeling deeply sorry for others who are

---

comparisons James Jones' novel *From Here to Eternity* describes how the U.S. Army enlisted man, Private Prewitt plays "Taps" on the bugle. The first note was long: "Held long like thirty years." The second note was short: "Short like a ten-minute break is short." ("Thirty years" was the full time of service for a career soldier; "ten-minute break" refers to a short rest period during a march.) Because they fit the setting of his story, Jones choose these particular comparisons to show the idea of "short" and "long." They relate directly to army life—the life of Private Prewitt. F. Scott Fitzgerald describes Tom Buchanan's house in *The Great Gatsby:* "The lawn started at the beach and ran toward the front door for a quarter of a mile, jumping over sun-dials and brick walks and burning gardens . . ." Having read this, which do you think Tom is, a piano player or a football player?

---

com•par•i•son [kəm par′ ə sən] *noun, plural* **comparisons. 1.** the act of comparing: This book gives a *comparison* of the American and

suffering or in distress, and wanting to help them. ◆ A person who has this feeling is **compassionate.**

com•pat•i•ble [kəm pat′ ə bəl] *adjective, more/ most.* **1.** able to get along or go well together: The business broke up because the two owners just weren't *compatible* with each other. **2.** of a computer system, able to work with a different type of system: This software program will not run on that computer because they are not *compatible.*

com•pel [kəm pel′] *verb,* **compelled, compelling.** to make someone do something under force: "He had said he might soon be *compelled* to leave her awhile." (Theodore Dreiser)

com•pen•sate [käm′ pən sāt′] *verb,* **compensated, compensating. 1.** to make up for something that is lacking: Peter had to study extra hard to *compensate* for missing a week of classes. **2.** to pay: The lawyer expects to be fully *compensated* for all the time she's spent on that case. **—compensation,** *noun:* Glasses are a *compensation* for weak eyesight.

satisfied: Last year's champions were too *complacent* this season and lost their first five games. **—complacently,** *adverb.*

com•plain [kəm plān′] *verb,* **complained, complaining. 1.** to say that something is wrong or unfair; be unhappy or annoyed: Many of the people in back *complained* that it was too hard to see what was going on. **2.** to make a formal report or statement that something is wrong: to *complain* to the police.

com•plaint [kəm plānt′] *noun, plural* **complaints. 1.** the act of complaining; an expression of unhappiness; finding fault: "Their voices . . . sounded cross and loud and full of *complaint.*" (Sylvia Plath) **2.** the cause of complaining: The teacher's only *complaint* about Mark is that sometimes he talks too much in class. **3.** a formal statement or report of complaining; a charge: They filed a *complaint* with the police against the boys who broke their window.

complement/compliment It's easy to confuse *compliment*—to praise—with *complement*, because they are pronounced alike. Nowadays, you hear of "complimentary tickets," a fancy way of saying "free tickets." You can also "pay someone a compliment." Odd, isn't it, that these two common uses of *compliment* call for opposite actions: giving free and paying? To make things worse, *complement* comes from a word meaning a ceremony or tribute, and *compliment*—with the *i* instead of the *e*—also has the sense of ceremony and tribute. Look up the definitions of each in the dictionary—that will make things better!

com•pete [kəm pēt′] *verb,* **competed, competing.** to take part in some kind of contest or game; try to win: Beverly wants to *compete* in the school science fair.

com•pe•tent [käm′ pə tənt] *adjective, more/ most.* able to do what is needed; capable; efficient: She is a *competent* worker. ♦ The state of being competent is **competence.**

com•pe•ti•tion [käm′ pə tish′ ən] *noun, plural* **competitions. 1.** the act of competing; trying to win a contest or game: Katie plays a lot of different sports because she loves *competition.* **2.** a contest or game: a swimming *competition.*

com•pet•i•tive [kəm pet′ ə tiv] *adjective, more/ most.* **1.** liking to win or compete: a person with a *competitive* personality. **2.** having to do with or using competition: The airline industry is a highly *competitive* business.

com•pet•i•tor [kəm pet′ ə tər] *noun, plural* **competitors.** someone who competes; a rival: CBS, NBC, and ABC are the chief *competitors* in the television industry.

com•pla•cent [kəm plā′ sənt] *adjective, more/ most.* comfortable with one's position; self-

com•ple•ment [käm′ plə mənt] *noun, plural* **complements.** something that makes a thing whole or complete: The sauce was a good *complement* for the meat. **—**[käm′ plə ment′] *verb,* **complemented, complementing.** to make whole or complete: Her new shoes *complement* her dress perfectly. ♦ Something that complements is **complementary.**

com•plete [kəm plēt′] *adjective, more/most.* **1.** not missing anything; having all parts; whole; entire: He has a *complete* set of Mark Twain's books. ". . . a large picnic *complete* with watermelon, fresh fruit, and barbecue." (Alice Walker) **2.** ended; finished: When will the new highway be *complete?* **3.** total; full: "There were a few moments of *complete* silence . . ."

Pronunciation Key: A–F

a	and; hat	ch	chew; such
ā	ate; stay	d	dog; lid
â	care; air	e	end; yet
ä	father; hat	ē	she; each
b	boy; cab	f	fun; off

(Turn the page for more information.)

(Mary Norton) —*verb*, **completed, completing.**
1. to add what is missing; make whole: Jean *completed* the puzzle by putting in the last piece. **2.** to bring to an end; finish: You have to *complete* the test within one hour. "He had just *completed* his training at the Eastern Medical University." (John Hersey)

com•plete•ly [kəm plēt′ lē] *adverb*. in every way; totally; entirely: Parts of San Francisco were *completely* destroyed during the earthquake of 1906.

com•ple•tion [kəm plē′ shən] *noun, plural* **completions. 1.** the act of completing something: The *completion* of the new bridge is scheduled for next year. **2.** a completed condition: An architect designs a building and also sees the project through to *completion.*

com•plex [kəm pleks′ *or* käm′ pleks′] *adjective, more/most.* **1.** hard to explain or understand: "The search for rules, the only way to understand such a vast and *complex* universe . . ." (Carl Sagan) **2.** made up of many parts: Los Angeles has a *complex* system of highways. ♦ The state of being complex is **complexity:** the *complexity* of Einstein's scientific theories. —[käm′ pleks] *noun, plural* **complexes. 1.** something made up of many parts: Over 5,000 people live in that housing *complex.* **2.** a continuing feeling of worry or concern about some fault or problem: I don't know why she has such a *complex* about her looks; she's really very pretty.

com•pli•cat•ed [käm′ plə kā′ tid] *adjective, more/most.* hard to do or understand: "A huge, *complicated* machine . . . with many tubes and wires . . ." (James Thurber)

com•pli•ca•tion [käm′ plə kā′ shən] *noun, plural* **complications.** something that complicates; a difficult condition or situation.

com•pli•ment [käm′ plə mənt *or* käm′ plə ment′] *verb*, **complimented, complimenting.** to say something good to or about someone; give praise to a person: He *complimented* Betty's new hair style. The teacher *complimented* Laura on the poem she wrote. —*noun, plural* **compliments. 1.** something nice said to or about a person: They've received many *compliments* about their beautiful flower garden. **2. compliments.** greetings; good wishes.

com•pli•men•ta•ry [käm′ plə men′ tər ē] *adjective, more/most.* **1.** being or showing a compliment: The critics made *complimentary* remarks about her performance. **2.** given away free: Anyone who works here gets a *complimentary* parking space in the basement.

com•ply [kəm plī′] *verb*, **complied, complying.** (usually used with **with**) to act in agreement with something, such as a rule or request: If you drive a car, you must *comply with* the traffic laws. ♦ The act of complying is **compliance** [kəm plī′ əns].

com•po•nent [kəm pō′ nənt] *noun, plural* **components.** one of the separate units that make up a system or machine: A stereo system has

---

complex sentences A complex sentence is like a compound sentence—it has more than a single subject and verb. The difference is that in a complex sentence only one part is worded so that it could stand alone. To give variety to your writing, you can combine two sentences into one complex sentence. Here is Charles Dickens' in *Great Expectations*, with two complex sentences: "When I reached home, my sister was very curious to know all about Miss Havisham's . . ." "My sister was not in a very bad temper when we presented ourselves in the kitchen . . ." And here is Dickens with a compound-complex sentence: "When I ran home from the churchyard, the forge was shut up, and Joe was sitting alone in the kitchen."

---

com•plex•ion [kəm plek′ shən] *noun, plural* **complexions. 1.** the natural color and appearance of the skin, especially the face. **2.** the general appearance or nature of something: The *complexion* of the neighborhood changed after those old buildings were torn down.

com•pli•cate [käm′ plə kāt′] *verb*, **complicated, complicating. 1.** to make harder to do or understand: Don't *complicate* your report by adding those long tables of statistics. **2.** to make worse or more severe: His illness was *complicated* by high blood pressure.

several different *components*, such as loudspeakers, a tape player, and a tuner.

com•pose [kəm pōz′] *verb*, **composed, composing. 1.** to make up something; put together: Air is *composed* of oxygen and other gases. **2.** to write or create: to *compose* poetry. "One day, he *composed* a love song for Serena." (E.B. White) **3. compose oneself.** to make oneself calm or relaxed: She was nervous before her speech, but she *composed herself* and got through it easily.

com•pos•er [kəm pō′ zər] *noun, plural* **compos-**

ers. a person who composes something, especially one who creates a piece of music: Wolfgang Amadeus Mozart was the *composer* of "The Magic Flute."

compound sentence a sentence having two or more parts that could each be separate sentences on their own. "Bees have six legs, but spiders have eight legs" is a compound sentence.

compound sentences A compound sentence consists of two or more parts. Each part forms a complete sentence with its own subject and verb. Why not just have two sentences, then? Often, the clauses in a compound sentence are very short, and they'd sound choppy as separate sentences: "The dogs slept; one of them was having a dream." (Eudora Welty) "He wasn't hungry, it was lovely weather, and he had the whole country before him." (Mark Helprin) Sometimes, a compound sentence has a better flow or rhythm: "It was only the tip of his shoe that caught the stranger, but he went flying out of the door with his collecting box under his arm." (Stephen Vincent Benét)

com•pos•ite [kəm päz′ it] *adjective.* made up of a number of different parts: This book gives a *composite* account of the battle through interviews with many of the men who were there.

com•po•si•tion [käm′ pə zish′ ən] *noun, plural* **compositions. 1.** the act of composing: the *composition* of a poem or a piece of music. **2.** something that is composed: Chopin created many beautiful *compositions* for the piano. **3.** the parts of something that make up the whole: The scientist wanted to know the *composition* of the rock. **4.** a piece of writing done as a school assignment.

com•po•sure [käm pō′ zhər] *noun.* the state of being calm and relaxed; being composed: The basketball player kept his *composure* even though the fans were yelling at him.

compound word a word made up of two or more parts that are words in themselves, such as *high school, high-class,* or *highway.*

com•pre•hend [käm′ pri hend′] *verb,* **comprehended, comprehending.** to grasp with the mind; understand mentally: "I said the words I saw on the page without *comprehending* their meaning." (John D. MacDonald)

com•pre•hen•sion [käm′ pri hen′ shən] *noun.* the act or power of understanding something: Reading *comprehension* is the ability to understand and remember what you have read.

com•press [kəm pres′] *verb,* **compressed, compressing.** to force into a smaller space; press or squeeze together: She *compressed* the pile of clothes so that they would all fit into the suitcase. ♦ Often used as an adjective: Cer-

compounds English constantly creates new words by putting existing words together. Compounds are formed by such combinations as: noun-noun (*basketball, typewriter*), adjective-noun (*greenhouse, highchair*), verb-adverb (*shutdown, breakout*), and noun-adjective (*childlike, effortless*). How should compounds be written? There are three possibilities—as one word (*airmail*), with a hyphen (*air-mail*), or as two separate words (*air mail*). If you are not sure, look it up in a dictionary as you are writing.

com•pound [käm′ pound′] *adjective.* made up of two or more parts: Oak trees have a *compound* leaf. ♦ The **compound eye** of an insect is made up of many different small parts, each of which can see part of an object. —*noun, plural* **compounds. 1.** in chemistry, a substance formed by combining two or more ELEMENTS: Water is a *compound* of hydrogen and oxygen. **2.** anything that is a combination of parts. **3.** a COMPOUND WORD. —[käm′ pound′ *or* kəm-pound′] *verb,* **compounded, compounding. 1.** to mix together; combine: to *compound* a medicine. **2.** to make worse: Don't *compound* the problem by complaining about it so much.

tain machines are run by the power of *compressed* air. ♦ A machine like this is a **compressor.** —[käm′ pres′] *noun, plural* **compresses.** a soft cloth or pad applied to a part of the body to treat a wound or injury.

Pronunciation Key: G N

g	give; big	k	kind; cat; back
h	hold	l	let; ball
i	it; this	m	make; time
ī	ice; my	n	not; own
j	jet; gem; edge	ng	having

(Turn the page for more information.)

C

com•pres•sion [kəm presh′ ən] *noun.* the act of compressing something, especially the fuel mixture in a car engine.

com•prise [kəm prīz′] *verb,* **comprised, comprising.** to be made up of; consist of; include: The tiny village was *comprised* of two stores, a gas station, and a post office.

com•pro•mise [käm′ prə mīz′] *noun, plural* **compromises.** the settling of a disagreement by each side giving up something: Mom wanted to eat out and Dad wanted her to fix dinner at home; their *compromise* was to have a pizza delivered to the house. —*verb,* **compromised, compromising.** to reach a compromise.

com•pul•so•ry [kəm pul′ sər ē] *adjective.* required by law or force: Going to school is *compulsory* for children in the U.S.

com•pute [kəm pyoot′] *verb,* **computed, computing.** to find out by using mathematics; calculate: They *computed* the cost of putting a swimming pool in their back yard. ◆ The act of computing is **computation** [käm′ pyə tā′ shən].

computer The first electronic computer, the ENIAC, shown in 1946 with one of its designers, J.P. Eckert. It took up an entire room, and required a huge amount of electric power to operate it.

com•put•er [kəm pyoo′ tər] *noun, plural* **computers.** a machine that is able to handle complicated problems or tasks by breaking them down into simple steps that it can do very fast. A computer can keep a large amount of information stored in a small place by changing it into a code. In order to work, a computer needs HARDWARE (the machine itself) and SOFTWARE (programs that tell the machine what to do).

com•rade [käm′ rad] *noun, plural* **comrades.** a close companion or friend.

con•cave [kän kāv′ *or* kän′ kāv′] *adjective,*

more/most. having a shape that curves inward; the opposite of CONVEX. The inside of a bowl or cup is concave.

con•ceal [kən sēl′] *verb,* **concealed, concealing.** to keep secret or out of sight; hide secretly: "Hyde listened to their plans, *concealed* behind a tree." (James Thurber) ◆ Also used as an adjective: The police arrested him for carrying a *concealed* weapon.

con•cede [kən sēd′] *verb,* **conceded, conceding.** **1.** to admit that something is true, usually against one's will: Dad *concedes* that we haven't used our boat as much as we expected to, but he still thinks it was worth buying. **2.** to accept a loss; give up: The losing candidate *conceded* soon after the polls closed.

con•ceit•ed [kən sē′ təd] *adjective, more/most.* having too high an opinion of oneself; too proud: She's very *conceited* and is always talking about how pretty she is. ◆ The feeling of being conceited is **conceit.**

computer Students with the Apple II, a popular modern computer. This small machine can do much more than the room-sized ENIAC could.

con•ceive [kən sēv′] *verb,* **conceived, conceiving.** to form in the mind; think of; imagine: It's hard to *conceive* of the size of the universe. ◆ Something that can be conceived is **conceivable:** No woman has ever been elected President, but it's *conceivable* that one could be.

con•cen•trate [kän′ sən trāt′] *verb,* **concentrated, concentrating. 1.** to focus the mind on something; pay close attention: On the last day before Christmas vacation the children had a hard time *concentrating* on their schoolwork. **2.** to gather or collect in one place: The U.S. auto industry is *concentrated* in Detroit. **3.** to make a mixture stronger or thicker, especially by reducing the amount of water. ◆ Usually used as an adjective: *concentrated* orange juice.

—*noun, plural* **concentrates.** a mixture that is concentrated.

con•cen•tra•tion [kän′ sən trā′ shən] *noun, plural* **concentrations. 1.** close attention: "He ate with great *concentration,* as though he were doing a math problem with his teeth." (Louise Fitzhugh) **2.** the act or fact of concentrating, or something concentrated: The U.S. has large *concentrations* of troops in West Germany.

concentration camp a prison camp where people are held who are considered to be enemies of the government, especially one of the German prison camps where many Jews and others opposed by the Nazis died during World War II.

con•cept [kän′ sept′] *noun, plural* **concepts.** a general idea or thought: The teacher explained the *concept* of inflation by comparing the prices of common foods in 1955 and 1985. ♦ Something that has to do with a concept or concepts is **conceptual:** That history book arranges events in a *conceptual* way, rather than by when they happened.

con•cep•tion [kən sep′ shən] *noun, plural* **conceptions. 1.** the act of conceiving: the *conception* of a plan. **2.** an idea or concept: I have no *conception* of how this computer actually works.

con•cern [kən surn′] *verb,* **concerned, concerning. 1.** to be about; have to do with: There's a story in today's paper *concerning* the new shopping center. **2.** to be of interest or importance to; affect: This is a private matter and really doesn't *concern* you. **3.** to make troubled or anxious; worry: Her poor schoolwork *concerned* her parents. "You're obviously upset and that *concerns* me." (David Mamet) —*noun, plural* **concerns. 1.** something that is of importance or interest: My main *concern* is that we finish the job on time. **2.** something that causes trouble; a worry: "He became full of *concern,* and shook his head and sighed." (J.R.R. Tolkien) **3.** a company or business: "I'm in business in Prague, representing a couple of *concerns* there." (F. Scott Fitzgerald)

con•cerned [kən surnd′] *adjective, more/most.* **1.** troubled or anxious; worried: "'Are you okay?' said Kate, looking him over, her face serious, *concerned.*" (Louise Fitzhugh) **2. as far as one is concerned.** in one's opinion. "*As far as he was concerned,* the conversation was over." (S.E. Hinton)

con•cern•ing [kən sur′ ning] *preposition.* having to do with; about: The detective wants to question him *concerning* the missing jewels.

con•cert [kän′ sərt] *noun, plural* **concerts.** a public performance of music, especially one with a number of musicians or singers.

con•cer•to [kən cher′ tō] *noun, plural* **concertos.** a musical composition for one or more solo instruments, such as a piano or violin, accompanied by an orchestra.

con•ces•sion [kən sesh′ ən] *noun, plural* **concessions. 1.** the act of conceding, or what is conceded: As a *concession* to their age, the younger runners were given a head start. **2.** a right to do something granted by the government or another authority: a *concession* to sell refreshments at a football stadium.

conch The conch can move about rapidly on the ocean bottom by pressing against the sand with its long, claw-like arm, called an *operculum.*

conch [kängk *or* känch] *noun, plural* **conches.** a tropical sea animal having a large, one-piece shell with a spiral shape. The shell is often brightly colored.

con•cise [kən sīs′] *adjective, more/most.* expressing a lot of thought or meaning in a few words: a *concise* short story. Lincoln's "Gettysburg Address" is a *concise* speech.

con•clude [kən klood′] *verb,* **concluded, concluding. 1.** to end something: The World Series *concludes* the baseball season. **2.** to form an opinion; come to believe: After studying the two crimes, the police have *concluded* that they were committed by the same person.

Pronunciation Key: O–S			
ō	over; go	ou	out; town
ô	all; law	p	put; hop
oo	look; full	r	run; car
oo	pool; who	s	set; miss
oi	oil; boy	sh	show

(Turn the page for more information.)

con•clu•sion [kən kloo′ zhən] *noun, plural* **con-clusions. 1.** the end or final part of something: The *conclusion* of the movie will be shown after the next commercial. **2.** something decided by thinking; a judgment or decision: He came to the *conclusion* that he won't have time to take a vacation this summer. ◆ To **jump to conclusions** means to make a judgment or decision too quickly, without enough information.

con•dense [kən dens′] *verb,* **condensed, con-densing. 1.** to change from a gas or vapor to a liquid: "The warm, steamy air began to *condense* on the windows . . ." (Jeffery Paul Chan) **2.** to make thick or more compressed. **3.** to make shorter by taking out some parts. ◆ This word is often used as an adjective: *condensed* milk, a *condensed* version of Dickens' novel *David Copperfield.*

C

conclusion The conclusion of a paper is the opinion you present at the end. Most reports, essays, biographies, etc., have a beginning, middle, and conclusion (end). What are some problems to avoid in writing a conclusion? (1) The incomplete conclusion: "So in spite of its bad points, this was an interesting book." (What bad points? The writer forgot to mention any.) Any statement you make in the conclusion has to be supported by earlier facts or argument. (2) The 'lame' conclusion: "And that's all I could find out about Amelia Earhart." Be positive in your conclusion; don't just let it trail off. (3) The obvious conclusion: "So that's why I think we need a longer lunch hour." In this case, it would be better to end before the conclusion!

con•crete [kän′ krēt *or* kän krēt′] *noun.* a mix-ture of cement, sand, gravel, and water that becomes very hard when dry. Concrete is used for sidewalks and as a building or road materi-al. —*adjective.* **1.** made of concrete: a *concrete* walk. **2.** having to do with things that can be seen or felt, as opposed to something sensed with the mind: A book, a pencil, or a desk are *concrete* objects.

◆ The act of condensing is **condensation** [kän′ dən sā′ shən]: Dew is a *condensation* of water vapor from the air.

con•di•tion [kən dish′ ən] *noun, plural* **condi-tions. 1.** the way something or someone is: Dan always keeps his car in good *condition.* **2.** a state of health or physical fitness: "Stuart touched his toes ten times every morning to keep himself in good *condition.*" (E.B. White)

concrete words *The King's English* (by Fowler & Fowler) says "Prefer the concrete word to the abstract." *The Elements of Style* (by Strunk & White) says the same thing. How does this apply to the student writer? "In our social studies course, we use a textbook and some support materials." "Support materials?" What does that mean? Use specific, concrete terms: ". . . a workbook, a test, an atlas, a dictionary, and a compact disc. You don't have to completely avoid abstract terms—"anger," "beauty," and "intelligence" are good words. Just remember two things: (1) Avoid vague abstract terms like "areas under consideration" and "the dynamics of the situation." (2) Be specific. When you mention "beauty," show what are the features of a person or object that lend it beauty.

con•cus•sion [kən kush′ ən] *noun, plural* **con-cussions. 1.** an injury to the brain caused by a hard blow or fall. **2.** a hard blow or violent shaking, as from an explosion.

con•demn [kən dem′] *verb,* **condemned, con-demning. 1.** to strongly disapprove of someone or something: That parents' group *condemns* the amount of violence shown on TV. **2.** to state the punishment of a guilty person: The judge *condemned* the convicted man to five years in prison. **3.** to say officially that some-thing is not safe or fit for use: That building has been *condemned* because of fire damage.

3. a requirement necessary for something else to happen: "He agreed at once to continue on in the store under the *conditions* Morris offered." (Bernard Malamud) **4. conditions.** a state of affairs; circumstances: The coal miners went on strike in hope of improving their working *conditions.* —*verb,* **conditioned, conditioning.** make or become used to some-thing: She's doing a lot of running to *condition* herself for the marathon race. ◆ Something that depends on a certain condition is **condi-tional:** Our agreement to buy the house is *conditional* on our selling our old house.

con•do•min•i•um [kän′ dəm in′ ē əm] *noun,*
plural **condominiums. 1.** an apartment building
in which each of the apartments is individually
owned, rather than the entire property having
one owner. **2.** an apartment in such a building.

con•dor [kän′ dôr] *noun, plural* **condors.** a very
large bird with a bare head and neck. A condor
is a kind of vulture. Condors are found in the
mountains of California and South America.

con•duct [kän′ dəkt] *noun, plural* **conducts.** the
way someone acts or behaves: According to
Billy's teacher, his *conduct* in class has been
very good. —[kən dukt′] *verb,* **conducted, con-**
ducting. 1. to act in a certain way; behave. **2.** to
carry on or carry out: to *conduct* business. The
police are *conducting* an investigation of how
the fire started. **3.** to be in charge of; lead: to
conduct an orchestra. **4.** to be a path for; carry:
Aluminum *conducts* heat very well.

con•duc•tor [kən duk′ tər] *noun, plural* **con-**
ductors. 1. a person who directs an orchestra or
other musical group. **2.** a person in charge of
passengers on a train, bus, or streetcar. The
conductor often has the job of collecting fares.
3. something that conducts: Rubber is not a
good *conductor* of electricity.

cone [kōn] *noun, plural* **cones. 1.** a figure that
has a round, flat base and is pointed at the other
end. **2.** anything shaped like a cone. Ice cream
is often served in cones. **3.** the fruit of a pine or
other evergreen tree, made up of hard, overlapping scales. It bears the seeds of the tree.

con•fed•er•a•cy [kən fed′ ər ə sē *or* kən fed′ rə-
sē′] *noun, plural* **confederacies. 1.** a group of
countries, states, or people joined together:
The "Five Nations" was a group of Indian
tribes that united to form the Iroquois *confeder-*
acy. **2. the Confederacy.** the eleven southern
states that left the United States in 1860 and
1861. ◆ These states formed the **Confederate**
States of America.

con•fed•er•ate [kən fed′ ər it *or* kən fed′ rit]
noun, plural **confederates. 1.** a person, group,
or country who joins with another for a common purpose: The leader of the gang and his
confederates were caught by the police. **2. Con-**
federate. a person who fought for or supported
the Confederacy. —*adjective.* **1.** belonging to a
confederacy. **2. Confederate.** having to do with
the Confederacy.

con•fed•er•a•tion [kən fed′ ə rā′ shən] *noun,*
plural **confederations.** the act of forming a
confederacy, or the confederacy itself: In
1781 the American states formed a *confederation.*
◆ The constitution of these states was known

as the **Articles of Confederation.** It was replaced
by the U.S. Constitution in 1787.

con•fer [kən fur′] *verb,* **conferred, conferring.**
1. to meet and talk things over; have a discussion: The baseball player *conferred* with his
lawyer and business agent before signing the
new contract. **2.** to give an honor or award:
". . . this honor you have *conferred* upon my
painting." (Langston Hughes)

con•fer•ence [kän′ frəns] *noun, plural* **confer-**
ences. 1. a meeting to discuss something: Mrs.
Tate had a *conference* with her son's teacher to
go over his schoolwork. ◆ A meeting at which
news reporters can ask someone questions is a
press conference. 2. a group of teams or organizations: the American Football *Conference.*

con•fess [kən fes′] *verb,* **confessed, confessing.**
1. to say that one has done something that is
wrong or against the law: He *confessed* that he
had stolen the money. "I can usually tell when
he's hiding something and I keep after him till
he *confesses.*" (Ring Lardner) **2.** to make
known: What did you say? I must *confess* I
wasn't listening. **3.** to tell one's sins to a priest.

Confederate A painting of the famous
Confederate general Thomas Jonathan
'Stonewall' Jackson at the Battle of Bull
Run, July 21, 1861.

Pronunciation Key: T–Z

t	ten; date	v	very; live
th	think	w	win; away
th	these	y	you
u	cut; butter	z	zoo; cause
ur	turn; bird	zh	measure

(Turn the page for more information.)

con·fes·sion [kən fesh′ ən] *noun, plural* **confessions.** the confessing of something: "This is a *confession* that concerns only you. I lied to you, you see." (Anthony Burgess)

confetti Crowds often throw confetti as a way of celebrating at a parade or other such event as at this political *motorcade* in Mexico.

con·fet·ti [kən fet′ ē] *noun.* tiny pieces of colored paper thrown in the air to celebrate something, as at a wedding or parade.

con·fide [kən fīd′] *verb,* **confided, confiding.** **1.** to tell as a secret: "Would she have *confided* something like that to anyone other than you?" (John D. MacDonald) **2.** to show or put trust in someone: "I hope I shall be able to *confide* in you completely . . ." (Anne Frank)

con·fi·dence [kän′ fə dəns] *noun, plural* **confidences. 1.** a firm faith in oneself and belief in one's abilities: Winning the first four games has given our team a lot of *confidence.* **2.** faith or trust in someone or something else: I have a lot of *confidence* that what she says is true. **3.** trust that a secret will be kept by someone: I'm telling you this in strict *confidence.*

always knew how to decide and what to do in any situation." (Edmund Wilson) "I know this term is going to bring you luck. I can almost taste it, that's how *confident* I am." (Nancy Willard) —**confidently,** *adverb:* "I looked *confidently* at Pop, waiting for the explanation." (S.E. Hinton)

con·fi·den·tial [kän fə den′ shəl] *adjective.* told or written as a secret: ". . . a *confidential* tone quite unusual in him, as if he were taking her into an important secret." (Katherine Anne Porter) —**confidentially,** *adverb:* "Alix lowered his voice *confidentially.* 'He's in Paris, but he doesn't come here anymore. Paul doesn't allow it.'" (F. Scott Fitzgerald)

con·fine [kən fīn′] *verb,* **confined, confining.** to hold or keep within limits: to be *confined* to prison. Each speaker was asked to *confine* his remarks to five minutes. —[kän′ fīn′] *noun, plural* **confines.** a limit; boundary. ◆ Usually used in the plural: "It detains the water bird and prevents him from leaving the *confines* of this public park." (E.B. White) ◆ The state of being confined is **confinement:** A prisoner who is kept apart from other prisoners is said to be in solitary *confinement.*

con·firm [kən furm′] *verb,* **confirmed, confirming. 1.** to show something to be true or correct: The movie star *confirmed* the rumors that he was about to be married. **2.** to agree to or approve officially: The Senate *confirmed* the arms agreement. **3.** to make sure of an appointment or arrangement: "I waited to the end of the week for Brandon to *confirm* our date for Saturday." (Paul Zindel) **4.** to admit a person to a church or synagogue as a full member. —**confirmed,** *adjective.* not likely to change: I doubt that he'll ever get married; he's really a *confirmed* bachelor.

confidence "I am an enormously talented man, after all. It's no use pretending that I am not, and I was bound to succeed." This quotation comes from George Bernard Shaw, a famous Irish-born dramatist. Sounds as if he had smooth sailing as a writer, doesn't it? Actually, in the first nine years of his professional writing career, his average income as an author was one cent per day—one cent. In nine years he sold a total of one article, one poem, and one advertisement. The critic Archibald Henderson called this "one of the most devastating initial failures in literary history." Yet Shaw kept on writing, and finally became known the world over. His plays are probably quoted more often than any other English author, except for Shakespeare. As Henderson said, it was "only confidence in his own powers" that enabled him to rise above his early failures.

con·fi·dent [kän′ fə dənt] *adjective, more/most.* having confidence; believing strongly: "One felt that he was completely *confident*—that he

con·fir·ma·tion [kän′ fər mā′ shən] *noun, plural* **confirmations. 1.** the act of confirming something: She phoned the restaurant for *confirma-*

tion of her reservation for dinner. **2.** something that confirms; proof: At the present time there is no *confirmation* for that rumor. **3.** the ceremony of admitting someone to full membership in a church or synagogue.

con•fis•cate [kän′ fəs kāt′] *verb,* **confiscated, confiscating.** to take property away by authority: The police *confiscated* the stolen radios. —**confiscation,** *noun.*

con•flict [kän′ flikt] *noun, plural* **conflicts. 1.** a long fight or struggle; a war: armed *conflict* between two countries. **2.** a clash of opinions or ideas; a strong disagreement: There is a *conflict* in Congress over the new tax law. **3.** a situation with opposing needs or conditions: She can't come to the meeting because there's a *conflict* in her schedule. ◆ A **conflict of interest** is when a person has two opposing interests in the same matter. —[kən flikt′] *verb,* **conflicted, conflicting.** to be in conflict; disagree: He can get an after-school job as long as it doesn't *conflict* with his studies.

The *confused* passenger boarded a plane for Auckland, New Zealand instead of Oakland, California. **2.** to mistake one person or thing for another: People often *confuse* the words "affect" and "effect" or "minor" and "miner."

con•fu•sion [kən fyoo′ zhən] *noun, plural* **confusions. 1.** a confused condition or situation: There was a lot of *confusion* in the streets when the traffic lights went out. **2.** the mistaking of one person or thing for another: The fact that Tim and his twin brother look so much alike leads to a lot of *confusion.*

Con•go [käng′ gō] **1.** a river of central Africa that flows from Zaire to the Atlantic; also known as the **Zaire River. 2.** a country in west-central Africa. *Capital:* Brazzaville. *Area:* 132,000 square miles. Population: 1,625,000.

con•grat•u•late [kən grach′ ə lāt′] *verb,* **congratulated, congratulating.** to give praise or good wishes to someone for their success or good fortune: We *congratulated* Maria for winning first prize in the poster contest.

C

conflict *Conflict* refers to the contest or struggle that is the heart of a story, that makes it move to a conclusion. It may be a conflict with nature, as in "To Build a Fire" (Jack London) in which a man is lost in a vast area of snow, or between one person and another, as in "The Most Dangerous Game" (Richard Connell) in which a cruel man who loves hunting decides that another man is the best kind of prey, or between one person and a general group, as in "All Summer in a Day" (Ray Bradbury). It may also be a conflict within nature, as in "The Wild Goat's Kid" (Liam O'Flaherty), or within one person, as in "A Sunrise on the Veld" (Doris Lessing). The term "conflict" does not literally mean a fight or argument.

con•form [kən fôrm′] *verb,* **conformed, conforming.** to act according to certain customs or rules: The movie director expected all the actors to *conform* to his way of working. ◆ Someone who tries to make sure his own behavior conforms to others is a **conformist.**

con•front [kən frunt′] *verb,* **confronted, confronting. 1.** to meet face to face, especially in a bold or challenging way: "He stopped where she was standing and *confronted* her directly." (Flannery O'Connor) **2.** to bring face to face with: The man confessed to the burglary when he was *confronted* with the stolen goods. ◆ The act of confronting is **confrontation.**

Con•fu•cius [kən fyoo′ shəs] 551?–479 B.C., Chinese philosopher.

con•fuse [kən fyooz′] *verb,* **confused, confusing. 1.** to make uncertain or disordered; mix up: "He knew no English, and the sound of the strange language all about him *confused* him." (Willa Cather) ◆ Often used as an adjective:

con•grat•u•la•tion [kən grach′ ə lā′ shən] *noun, plural* **congratulations.** the act of congratulating. **2. congratulations.** praise or good wishes: The other people in the office offered him *congratulations* on the birth of his new grandchild.

con•gre•gate [käng′ grə gāt′] *verb,* **congregated, congregating.** to gather together in a crowd; assemble: Hundreds of people *congregated* at the park to hear the free concert.

con•gre•ga•tion [käng′ grə gā′ shən] *noun, plural* **congregations. 1.** the act of congregating;

Pronunciation Key: [ə] Symbol

The [ə] or *schwa* sound occurs in syllables without an accent. It can be spelled with any vowel, such as **a** in above, **e** in listen, **i** in pencil, **o** in melon, **u** in circus. It can also be a combination of vowels, such as **io** in action, **ai** in mountain, **iou** in precious.

(Turn the page for more information.)

a gathering of people or things. **2.** a group of people who gather for a religious service.

con•gress [kän′ grəs] *noun, plural* **congresses. 1.** a group of people who meet officially to make laws. ♦ The **Continental Congress** was the law-making body of the 13 colonies during the American Revolution. **2. Congress.** the law-making branch of the United States government. Congress is made up of the SENATE and the HOUSE OF REPRESENTATIVES. **3.** a formal meeting of representatives to set policy: The *Congress* of Vienna was a famous meeting of the nations of Europe in 1814–15.

Congress President Franklin D. Roosevelt speaks to Congress on December 8th, 1941, the day after Japan attacked the U.S. forces at Pearl Harbor. Roosevelt is asking Congress to declare war.

con•gress•man [käng′ grəs mən] *noun, plural* **congressmen.** a member of Congress, especially of the House of Representatives.

con•gress•wom•an [käng′ grəs woom′ ən] *noun, plural* **congresswomen.** a female member of Congress, especially of the House of Representatives.

combination: The state police worked in *conjunction* with the FBI to help solve the crime.

con•nect [kə nekt′] *verb,* **connected, connecting. 1.** to join or fasten together: We *connected* the trailer to the car bumper. **2.** to think of one thing with another; associate: I *connect* summer with hot days and trips to the beach. **3.** to join with another or others; have a relation to: The police believe he is *connected* with organized crime. ♦ Often used as an adjective: To fly from here to New York, you have to get a *connecting* flight in Dallas.

Con•nect•i•cut [kə net′ i kət] a state in the northeastern U.S. *Capital:* Hartford. *Nickname:* "Constitution State." *Area:* 5,000 square miles. *Population:* 3,155,000.

con•nec•tion [kə nek′ shən] *noun, plural* **connections. 1.** the act of connecting; the joining of things: The proper *connection* of the wires for this stereo system is explained in the instruction book. **2.** the fact of being connected: I couldn't tell who was on the phone because the *connection* was so bad. **3.** a connecting of two planes, trains, or other means of transportation.

con•quer [käng′ kər] *verb,* **conquered, conquering. 1.** to get the better of in war or conflict; defeat by force: Cortés sailed from Spain to Mexico to *conquer* the Aztec Empire. **2.** to overcome or gain control of: to *conquer* a disease. She's *conquered* her fear of flying and now enjoys traveling by plane.

con•quer•or [käng′ kər ər] *noun, plural* **conquerors.** a person who conquers: Caesar and Alexander were great *conquerors* of the ancient world. "This England never did nor never shall, lie at the proud foot of a *conqueror*." (Shakespeare, *King John*)

con•quest [kän′ kwest′] *noun, plural* **conquests. 1.** the act of conquering: the *conquest* of an enemy in war, the *conquest* of outer space.

conjunctions Conjunctions serve to join words, phrases, or clauses within a sentence. You can use them to link sentences together, so that you avoid a long series of short, simple sentences: "He picked up the two heavy bags. He carried them around the station to the other tracks. He looked up the tracks. He did not see the train." That sounds like "Hemingway style." It is in fact from a story by Ernest Hemingway, "Hills Like White Elephants." However, in the story the actual passage reads: "He picked up the two heavy bags and he carried them around the station to the other side of the tracks. He looked up the tracks but could not see the train."

con•junc•tion [kən jungk′ shən] *noun, plural* **conjunctions. 1.** a word used to join words, phrases, and sentences. *And, but,* and *if* are common *conjunctions.* **2.** a joining together;

2. something that is conquered: France's Grand Army of the Republic made many *conquests* in Europe in the early 1800's under the command of Napoleon.

con•science [kän′ shəns] *noun, plural* **con-sciences.** a sense of what is right and wrong that makes one feel sorry or guilty for having done something bad: No one saw him copying the answers on the test, but later his *conscience* bothered him and he told the teacher what he had done.

con•sci•en•tious [kän′ shē en′ shəs] *adjective, more/most.* **1.** trying to do what is right; following one's conscience. ◆ A **conscientious objector** is someone who refuses to fight in the armed forces because he believes war is wrong. **2.** having or showing great care or effort: She's a very *conscientious* student.

con•scious [kän′ shəs] *adjective, more/most.* **1.** able to see and feel; awake. **2.** able to realize some fact or feeling; aware: "Basil was *conscious* that he was the most unpopular boy at school." (F. Scott Fitzgerald) **3.** done on purpose; intentional: "He swallowed and made a *conscious* effort to speak quietly." (Irwin Shaw) **—consciously,** *adverb.* in a conscious way; on purpose: He's *consciously* trying to be more polite to his parents.

con•scious•ness [kän′ shəs nəs] *noun.* **1.** the condition of being conscious or awake: The diver lost *consciousness* when his head hit the diving board. **2.** a person's conscious thoughts and feelings; awareness: "Our whole past experience is continually in our *consciousness* . . ." (Charles Peirce)

con•sent [kən sent′] *verb,* **consented, consenting.** to give permission; agree to: The city *consented* to close off Main Street for the Thanksgiving Day parade. **—noun, plural consents.** permission; agreement: "On my word of honor as a gentleman, I will never marry without my mother's *consent.*" (William Makepeace Thackeray)

con•se•quence [kän′ sə kwens′] *noun, plural* **consequences. 1.** the result or outcome of some action or happening: "As a *consequence* of a chance event the rest of his life was to be changed." (Walker Percy) **2.** importance: Which candidate wins the election is of no *consequence* to me. **3. take the consequences.** to accept what happens because of one's actions: "You were free to do as you chose and *take the consequences.*" (Lloyd Alexander)

con•se•quent•ly [kän′ sə kwent′ lē] *adverb.* as a result; therefore: "He had to paddle with the bamboo, and *consequently* each trip took a very long time." (John Hersey)

con•ser•va•tion [kän′ sər vā′ shən] *noun.* **1.** the act of conserving: Driving at a steady speed is helpful in the *conservation* of fuel. **2.** the protection and careful use of natural resources such as forests, lakes and rivers, minerals, and wild animals. ◆ A person who supports this type of conservation is a **conservationist.**

conservation Conservationists from the U.S. Forest Service replant an area with pine trees. The previous growth in the area was destroyed by a fire.

con•serv•a•tive [kən sur′ və tiv′] *adjective, more/most.* **1.** wanting to keep things as they have been; against change. In politics, people who are conservative generally believe that the government should hold to the values of the past and take a limited role in human affairs. **2.** not taking chances; cautious or careful: That football coach favors a *conservative* game and never tries long passes or tricky plays. **3.** following a modest style; not showy: The bank president dressed in a very *conservative* way and always wore a gray or navy blue suit. **—noun, plural conservatives.** a person who is conservative. **—conservatively,** *adverb.*

con•sid•er [kən sid′ ər] *verb,* **considered, considering. 1.** to think about carefully: The judge told the jury to *consider* all the evidence before reaching a decision. ◆ Also used as an adjective: The doctor's *considered* opinion is that there is no need for the patient to have an operation. **2.** to think of as; believe to be: "I was never allowed to go to the moving pictures, for my mother *considered* the films silly and cheap." (James Gould Cozzens) **3.** to take into

C

Pronunciation Key: Accent Marks

[′] is the normal accent mark. It shows where the main stress falls on a word.

[′] is a secondary accent mark. It shows a lighter stress than the primary accent. For example:

tel • e • vis • ion [tel′ ə vizh′ən]

(Turn the page for more information.)

account; allow for: She plays the piano very well, if you *consider* that she's only had a few lessons. **4.** to be thoughtful of; respect: to *consider* the feelings of other people.

con·sid·er·a·ble [kən sid′ ər ə bəl] *adjective.* worth noticing or considering; rather large: A *considerable* number of people wrote letters to the network about that TV show. **—considerably,** *adverb:* The patient has improved *considerably* since last night.

con·sid·er·ate [kən sid′ ə rət] *adjective, more/most.* thoughtful of the feelings of other people: It was *considerate* of Billy to send a card to his sick friend. **—considerately,** *adverb.*

con·sid·er·a·tion [kən sid′ ə rā′ shən] *noun, plural* **considerations. 1.** thoughtfulness for the feelings of other people: He kept the radio turned down low out of *consideration* for his neighbors. **2.** careful thought: After much *consideration,* they finally decided to sell their house and buy a larger one. **3.** something to be thought of or taken into account: Good gas mileage is the most important *consideration* for her in choosing a new car.

con·sid·er·ing [kən sid′ ər ing] *preposition.* taking into account; allowing for: I thought that actress was very good, *considering* this was her first movie.

con·sist [kən sist′] *verb,* **consisted, consisting. consist of:** to be made up of: James Joyce's book *Ulysses* is 800 pages long, but it *consists of* the events of one single day.

con·sis·ten·cy [kən sis′ tən sē] *noun, plural* **consistencies. 1.** a certain degree of thickness or stiffness: The soup was so thin that it had almost the *consistency* of water. **2.** the fact of keeping to the same way of acting or thinking: He has no *consistency* as a bowler; one game he rolls 200 and the next 140.

con·sis·tent [kən sis′ tənt] *adjective, more/most.* **1.** staying to one way of acting or thinking: That shortstop is a *consistent* fielder who rarely makes an error. **2.** in agreement: The accused man claimed he was at his job the day of the crime, but that wasn't *consistent* with his company's work records. **—consistently,** *adverb:* Julia *consistently* scores over 90 on her math tests.

con·sole¹ [kən sōl′] *verb,* **consoled, consoling.** to comfort someone who is disappointed or sad: We *consoled* my little brother after his team lost the championship game. ◆ Something that consoles is a **consolation** [kän′ sə lā′ shən]: The winner gets a new car, and the others each get $50 as a *consolation* prize.

con·sole² [kän′ sōl] *noun, plural* **consoles. 1.** the cabinet of a television, radio, or stereo that is designed to rest on the floor. **2.** the DISPLAY screen of a computer.

con·so·nant [kän′ sə nənt] *noun, plural* **consonants. 1.** a sound in speech that is made when the flow of air through the mouth is blocked by the lips, teeth, or tongue. **2.** a letter of the alphabet that stands for such a sound; any letter that is not a vowel.

con·spic·u·ous [kən spik′ yōō əs] *adjective, more/most.* easily seen or noticed; attracting attention: Lew was *conspicuous* in the class picture because he was so much taller than the other students.

con·spir·a·cy [kən spēr′ ə sē] *noun, plural* **conspiracies.** secret planning with others to do something wrong or against the law: a *conspiracy* to overthrow the government of a country. ◆ A person who takes part in a conspiracy is a **conspirator.**

con·stant [kän′ stənt] *adjective.* **1.** not changing; staying the same: The airliner flew at a *constant* speed of 550 miles per hour. **2.** going on all the time; not stopping: the *constant* roar of a waterfall. Three days of *constant* rain turned the field to mud. **3.** happening over and over; continuous: Our TV set gets *constant* use. She's getting tired of his *constant* complaining about his job. **—constantly,** *adverb:* Food in this freezer is kept *constantly* at zero degrees.

constellation The Pleiades and other stars make up the constellation of Taurus the Bull. The ancient Greeks named the star cluster Pleiades after a story about seven sisters.

con·stel·la·tion [kän′ stə lā′ shən] *noun, plural* **constellations.** a group of stars that form a pattern in the sky. Constellations were named long ago for things they were thought to look like, such as the Big Dipper or Great Bear.

con•sti•tute [kän′ stə toot′] *verb*, **constituted, constituting.** to make up; form: Twelve people *constitute* a jury in most trials. "Many persons have a wrong idea of what *constitutes* true happiness." (Helen Keller)

con•sti•tu•tion [kän′ stə too′ shən] *noun, plural* **constitutions. 1.** the basic laws and principles used to govern a nation or state: The governor called for some changes in the state *constitution*. **2. the Constitution.** the written set of laws used to govern the United States. **3.** the general condition of a person's body: "He wanted his sons to . . . have strong *constitutions*." (F. Scott Fitzgerald)

Constitution An original copy of the Constitution, showing the famous "We the People" opening written large above the rest of the document.

con•sti•tu•tion•al [kän′ stə too′ shən əl] *adjective.* **1.** allowed by the Constitution: Laws against freedom of speech are not *constitutional.* **2.** having to do with a constitution: a *consti-*

con•struc•tion [kən struk′ shən] *noun, plural* **constructions. 1.** the act of constructing something; building: the *construction* of a new highway. **2.** the business or work of building houses, apartments, offices, and so on.

con•struc•tive [kən struk′ tiv] *adjective, more/most.* helping to make better; having a useful purpose: The teacher's *constructive* criticism helped me to see what I was doing wrong.

con•sult [kən sult′] *verb*, **consulted, consulting.** to go to for advice or information: to *consult* a doctor. "Mr. Lenehan took out a silver watch, *consulted* it, snapped the case shut." (Brian Moore. ♦ The act of consulting is a **consultation** [kän′ səl tā′ shən].

con•sult•ant [kən sul′ tənt] *noun, plural* **consultants.** a person who gives expert or professional advice: The auto company hired a *consultant* to study how to produce cars more cheaply.

con•sume [kən soom′] *verb*, **consumed, consuming. 1.** to use up: A car engine *consumes* fuel. **2.** to destroy: The fire *consumed* the building before the fire trucks arrived. **3.** to eat or drink, especially a large amount: At half time the team *consumed* several gallons of water. **4.** to take up all the attention or energy of: He's been *consumed* by his work lately.

con•sum•er [kən soo′ mər] *noun, plural* **consumers.** anyone who buys and uses things. A person who buys groceries is a consumer.

con•sump•tion [kən sump′ shən] *noun.* the using up of something, or the amount that is used up: The *consumption* of fuel in an automobile is greater at 75 miles per hour than 55.

contact The word *contact* has been around for several hundred years, but only in this century has it been used in the sense of "get in touch with:" "If the skin rash lasts for more than three or four days, *contact* your doctor." At one time, books on the rules of good writing scorned such use. Why ruin a good word like *contact* when you have other words at hand: *call, telephone, ask, write, speak, summon,* etc.? *Contact* means literally "to touch a person." Actually, what bothered rule-makers was that *contact* is a noun turned into a verb. But the same holds true of *telephone,* doesn't it?

tutional amendment, a country with a *constitutional* government.

con•strict [kən strikt′] *verb*, **constricted, constricting.** to make or become smaller or narrower: "My throat *constricted* with fear." (I.B. Singer)

con•struct [kən strukt′] *verb*, **constructed, constructing.** to make by putting parts together or combining things; build: Several new office buildings are being *constructed* downtown.

con•tact [kän′ takt] *noun, plural* **contacts. 1.** the act of touching; touching together: We

Pronunciation Key: A–F

a	and; hat	ch	chew; such
ā	ate; stay	d	dog; lid
â	care; air	e	end; yet
ä	father; hat	ē	she; each
b	boy; cab	f	fun; off

(Turn the page for more information.)

heard the noise of the airplane wheels coming in *contact* with the runway. **2.** a relation or connection: Mom keeps in *contact* with her old friends from high school. **3.** a person one knows who can be of help or influence: That reporter has a lot of good *contacts* in the city government. —*verb,* **contacted, contacting.** to get in touch with; make connection with: "I had *contacted* the doctor, asking him to stop by . . ." (Ann Beattie) ♦ See article on p. 171.

contact lens a small, thin plastic lens worn over the eyeball instead of eyeglasses to correct poor vision.

con•ta•gious [kən tā′ jəs] *adjective, more/most.* **1.** easily spread from person to person by some kind of contact: Chicken pox is a *contagious* disease. **2.** causing the same feeling or action in others: "His mouth curled up at the bottom into a *contagious* smile." (Paul Zindel)

con•tain [kən tān′] *verb,* **contained, containing. 1.** to be able to hold; have inside: This can *contains* a pound of coffee. **2.** to have as a part; include: Ice cream *contains* sugar. "Tom's letters to his parents *contained* nothing but brief, dry reports of a dull life . . ." (Philippa Pearce) **3.** to keep to oneself; hold back; control: "The woman was eating roasted peanuts that smelled so good he could hardly *contain* his hunger." (Ralph Ellison)

con•tem•po•rar•y [kən tem′ pə rer′ ē] *adjective, more/most.* **1.** belonging to the same time: Shakespeare and Galileo are *contemporary* figures in history; both were born in 1564. **2.** current; modern: Saul Bellow is the only *contemporary* American author to win the Nobel Prize, in 1976. —*noun, plural* **contemporaries.** a person living at the same time as another.

con•tempt [kən tempt′] *noun.* **1.** a feeling that someone or something is mean, cruel, or worthless. ♦ A person feeling contempt is **contemptuous** [kən temp′ chŏŏ əs]: "Suddenly, I realized I had done something wrong, and I felt *contemptuous* of myself." (I.B. Singer) **2.** *also,* **contempt of court.** in a court of law, the crime of failing to obey or show respect for a judge or for proper courtroom procedure.

con•tend [kən tend′] *verb,* **contended, contending. 1.** to fight or struggle: Early farmers in New England had to *contend* with harsh weather and rocky soil. **2.** to take part in a contest; compete: Thirty-two teams are *contending* for the state basketball championship. **3.** to argue in favor of; claim: Many experts *contend* that running is good for your health. ♦ A person who contends is a **contender:** Terry could have been a *contender* for the heavyweight boxing championship.

content and form A famous Canadian critic of modern writing, Marshall McLuhan wrote, "The medium is the message." He meant by this that you cannot really separate content—what you intend to be understood, your thoughts or feeling, from the form (or way) you say it. He argued that television or the movies or a daily newspaper changes the content of a story even if the writer is unaware of it. How can you test this theory? Try this: before you write a book report or any other kind of theme, put the main points in newspaper headline form, as if it were front-page news. Then take your main points and turn them into a set of questions and answers—as if you were being interviewed on TV. What changes occur in the content?

con•tain•er [kən tā′ nər] *noun, plural* **containers.** anything used to hold or contain something, such as a box, can, bottle, or jar.

con•tam•i•nate [kən tam′ ə nāt′] *verb,* **contaminated, contaminating.** to make dirty or impure: The town's water supply was *contaminated* by chemical wastes. —**contamination,** *noun.*

con•tem•plate [kän′ təm plāt′] *verb,* **contemplated, contemplating. 1.** to look at in a thoughtful way: "Burden *contemplated* the painting of Jefferson." (Gore Vidal) **2.** to think about carefully: "It was the only future she had ever *contemplated* really, a home, children, the love of some man . . ." (Theodore Dreiser) —**contemplation,** *noun.*

con•tent[1] [kän′ tent] *noun, plural* **contents. 1.** what something holds; what is contained: Airlines examine the *contents* of passengers' bags to make sure they are not carrying weapons. ". . . a nation where they will not be judged by the color of their skin but by the *content* of their character." (Martin Luther King) **2.** something that is written or said: the *contents* of a letter. ♦ The **table of contents** of a book is a list of what the book contains.

con•tent[2] [kən tent′] *adjective,* *more/most.* happy with what one has; satisfied: "Come on now, all you young men, all over the world . . . Don't be *content* with things as they are." (Winston Churchill)

—verb, **contented, contenting.** to make content; satisfy: She was all alone in the house, so she *contented* herself with reading a book. —noun. a feeling of being content. ◆ This is also called **contentment:** "From sheer happiness, (he) spread his chest with a sigh of full *contentment*." (Kenneth Grahame)

con•tent•ed [kən ten′ tid] *adjective, more/most.* satisfied; content: "They both looked *contented* and well fed." (Dick Francis)

con•test [kän′ test] *noun, plural* **contests.** a game, race, or other event to be won; a struggle or competition: a dance *contest*, a cooking *contest*. She won a new car by entering a *contest* through the mail. —[kən test′] *verb,* **contested, contesting. 1.** to fight or struggle over; compete for: France and Germany *contested* the border area of Alsace in several wars. **2.** to question or challenge: The losing candidate *contested* the results of the election.

con•test•ant [kən tes′ tənt] *noun, plural* **contestants.** a person who takes part in a contest; a competitor: Jill would like to be a *contestant* on a TV game show.

con•tin•u•al [kən tin′ yōō əl] *adjective.* **1.** happening again and again; frequent: It was hard for her to study with the *continual* phone calls she got from her friends. **2.** going on without stopping; continuous: a *continual* noise. —**continually,** *adverb:* "The animal blinked *continually* in the sunshine." (Jack London)

con•tin•ue [kən tin′ yōō] *verb,* **continued, continuing. 1.** to go on without stopping; keep happening: The rain *continued* for two days. "The phone rang, and Edna let it *continue* ringing." (Paul Zindel) **2.** to start again after stopping: This story will be *continued* in next month's issue. **3.** to stay in the same place or situation; remain: Mrs. Barlow plans to *continue* in her present job until she's 65 years old. ◆ The continuing of something is a **continuation.**

con•tin•u•ous [kən tin′ yōō əs] *adjective.* going on without a stop: the *continuous* movement of the waves in the ocean, the *continuous* flow of traffic on a busy highway. —**continuously,** *adverb:* Santa Fe, New Mexico has served *continuously* as a capital city since the early 1600's.

context "Will you *stand* here?" the major asked the general. "No. We will withdraw one hundred yards to the edge of the wood," the general replied. What do you make of this question and answer? Is the general on a stool or a ladder? No. Look at the context. If these sentences occur in a story of warfare, you know immediately that "stand" means to "take a position in order to attack or fight the enemy." *Context* comes from Latin, meaning "to weave together." The context of a statement is like the cloth, and the statement is like a thread in that cloth.

con•text [kän′ text] *noun, plural* **contexts.** the other words or sentences that surround a particular word or sentence and are important to how it is understood: The senator complained that his remarks were taken out of *context* when they were quoted in the newspaper and did not show his true feelings.

con•ti•nent [kän′ tə nənt] *noun, plural* **continents. 1.** one of the seven large land areas of the earth. The continents are Africa, Asia, North America, South America, Europe, Australia, and Antarctica. Europe and Asia are actually part of the same land area (EURASIA), but are thought of as separate continents because they have had a different history and culture. **2. the Continent.** the continent of Europe, apart from Great Britain.

con•ti•nen•tal [kän′ tə nen′ təl] *adjective.* **1.** having to do with a continent: Hawaii is not part of the *continental* U.S. **2. Continental.** having to do with the continent of Europe: *Continental* food.

con•tour [kän′ toor] *noun, plural* **contours.** the outline or shape of something: We saw the *contour* of the coastline from the plane.

con•tract [kän′ trakt] *noun, plural* **contracts.** an agreement that has the force of law and is usually written down. It states that two or more people or groups agree to do or not do certain things. —[kən trakt′] *verb,* **contracted, contracting. 1.** to make or become shorter or smaller; draw together: The pupils of the eyes *contract* when the light becomes brighter. **2.** to make an agreement by contract: That company has *contracted* to build a new shopping center.

C

Pronunciation Key: G–N

g	give; big	k	kind; cat; back
h	hold	l	let; ball
i	it; this	m	make; time
ī	ice; my	n	not; own
j	jet; gem; edge	ng	having

(Turn the page for more information.)

3. to get something that is bad or not wanted, such as an illness: "He *contracted* dreadful hay fever . . ." (Walker Percy)

con•trac•tion [kən trak′shən] *noun, plural* **contractions. 1.** a word formed by putting together two words with a certain letter or letters left out: "She's not" and "she isn't" are *contractions* for "she is not." **2.** the act of contracting: The *contraction* of the heart pushes the blood to the arteries.

con•trac•tor [kän′ trak tər] *noun, plural* **contractors.** a person or company that agrees to do work for a certain price, especially building work.

con•tra•dict [kän′ trə dikt′] *verb,* **contradicted, contradicting.** to say the opposite of; say to be wrong or untrue: Fred said he heard a wolf near the camp, but John *contradicted* him and said it was just a dog. ♦ Something that contradicts is a **contradiction:** There were a number of *contradictions* between what the politician promised before the election and what he actually did when he took office. ♦ Something that involves a contradiction is **contradictory:** "He who hesitates is lost" and "Look before you leap" are two old sayings that are *contradictory.*

con•tral•to [kən tral′ tō] *noun, plural* **contraltos. 1.** the lowest female singing voice. **2.** a singer who has such a voice.

con•trar•y [kän′ trer ē] *adjective, more/most.* **1.** completely different; opposite or opposed: My sister and I have *contrary* tastes in music; she likes classical music and I like rock. **2.** [*also,* kən trer′ ē] liking to argue or oppose; stubborn: Steven is the most *contrary* person I know; he always does the opposite of what he's told. —*noun, plural* **contraries. 1.** something that is opposite. **2. on (to) the contrary** exactly the opposite; the opposite is true.

with the blinding glare of the noon sun." (Eugene O'Neill) —[kän′ trast′] *noun, plural* **contrasts. 1.** the comparing of things to show a difference: Business at that store has been very good this month, in *contrast* with last month. **2.** a person or thing that shows such a difference: There is a great *contrast* between the lives of the rich and the poor in that country.

con•trib•ute [kən trib′ yo͞ot] *verb,* **contributed, contributing. 1.** to give money or help: The rich man *contributed* a valuable painting to the city art museum. **2.** to supply writing to a newspaper or magazine. **3. contribute to.** to help to bring about: Many different players have *contributed to* the team's success this season. ♦ A person who contributes is a **contributor:** James Thurber was a leading *contributor* to the *New Yorker* magazine for many years.

con•tri•bu•tion [kän′ trə byo͞o′ shən] *noun, plural* **contributions.** the act of contributing, or something that is contributed: a *contribution* to the Red Cross. "'You should ring for the ambulance,' said Marcia, making her first *contribution* to the discussion." (Barbara Pym)

con•trive [kən trīv′] *verb,* **contrived, contriving. 1.** to make or form something, especially in a clever way: "It was one of those pictures which are so *contrived* that the eyes follow you about when you move." (George Orwell) **2.** to plan or scheme to do something: Tom Sawyer *contrived* to have his friends paint his fence for him. ♦ Something that is **contrived** is false or artificial: The plot of that movie was very *contrived*—every time the hero was in trouble someone would suddenly appear to save him.

con•trol [kən trōl′] *verb,* **controlled, controlling. 1.** to have power over; rule; command: Great Britain *controlled* India for many years. **2.** to direct the course of; regulate: This dial

---

contrast Effective writers use contrast. They mix short sentences with long ones, and ordinary, concrete words with abstract ones. Shortly after Sir Winston Churchill became British Prime Minister in World War II, he gave his first speech to the House of Commons. The nation listened for what Churchill would offer as the new leader. He began with long sentences— one had 74 words—and with abstract words such as "administration," "complexity," "undertaking," and "preliminary." Then he said: "I have nothing to offer but blood, toil, tears, and sweat."

---

con•trast [kən trast′] *verb,* **contrasted, contrasting. 1.** to compare two things in order to show a difference between them: "The Odd Couple" *contrasts* Felix Unger, who is very neat and fussy, with his messy roommate Oscar Madison. **2.** to show differences when compared: "Beneath them is deep cool shade, *contrasting*

controls the heat in the building. **3.** to hold back; keep down: She was angry, but she managed to *control* her temper. —*noun, plural* **controls. 1.** the act or fact of controlling: The government used price *controls* to try to hold down the cost of food. **2.** a holding back; check: "He sounded calm, completely in *control* of himself." (S.E. Hinton) **3. controls.** the instruments used to run a machine: the *controls* of an airplane. ◆ A **controller** is a person who controls something, especially a person who has charge of money matters for a business or a branch of government.

control tower a tower on an airfield from which workers direct the taking off and landing of airplanes. A person who does this work is an **air traffic controller.**

control tower The control tower at Orlando, Florida's International Airport, one of the world's busiest airports.

con•tro•ver•sial [kän′ trə vur′ shəl] *adjective, more/most.* causing a lot of argument or disagreement: The Vietnam War was a very *controversial* event in American history.

con•tro•ver•sy [kän′ trə vur′ sē] *noun, plural* **controversies.** an argument or dispute; a strong disagreement: Gerald Ford's decision to pardon former President Nixon was a source of *controversy.*

con•ven•ience [kən vēn′ yəns] *noun, plural* **conveniences. 1.** the quality of being convenient; ease and comfort: The motel provides free transportation to the airport for the *convenience* of its guests. **2.** something that is convenient; a thing that saves time or effort: "We were unfamiliar with such *conveniences* as hot running water or a bathroom." (I.B. Singer)

con•ven•ient [kən vēn′ yənt] *adjective, more/most.* **1.** suited to one's needs or purposes; right for the situation: We can meet at whatever time and place is *convenient* for you. **2.** easy to reach or get to; handy: Their house is *convenient* to the town park. **—conveniently,** *adverb.*

con•vent [kän′ vent] *noun, plural* **convents.** a building in which a group of nuns live together under certain religious rules.

con•ven•tion [kən ven′ shən] *noun, plural* **conventions. 1.** a formal meeting for a special purpose: The Republicans and Democrats each hold a *convention* every four years to choose their candidates for President and Vice President. **2.** an accepted or approved way of acting; a custom.

con•ven•tion•al [kən ven′ shən əl] *adjective, more/most.* **1.** following the accepted practice; customary: Shaking hands when meeting someone is a *conventional* thing to do in this country. **2.** of the usual or ordinary type; commonplace: He has very *conventional* taste in food and doesn't like to try new foreign dishes. **—conventionally,** *adverb:* "She always said the right thing, took the *conventionally* right attitude. . . ." (Tennessee Williams)

con•ver•sa•tion [kän′ vər sā′ shən] *noun, plural* **conversations.** a talk between two or more people; talking.

conversation Laurence Sterne in his best-known book, *Tristram Shandy,* made this remark, "Writing, when properly managed (as you may be sure I think mine is), is but a different name for conversation." Now, he does not mean that the language used in speaking is the best choice of words for writing—often it is not so. He did mean that a writer and his reader have a relationship, much as do friends talking over lunch. Sterne said that a good writer respects the reader's being able to understand and does not "talk down" to the reader. "The truest respect which you can pay the reader's understanding is to . . . leave him something to imagine, in his turn, as well as yourself." When you tell a story, don't list every single detail. Certain things can be merely suggested, rather than stated directly. Let the readers use their imagination, too.

Pronunciation Key: O–S

ō	over; go	ou	out; town
ô	all; law	p	put; hop
oo	look; full	r	run; car
o͞o	pool; who	s	set; miss
oi	oil; boy	sh	show

(Turn the page for more information.)

C

con•verse [kən vurs′] *verb,* **conversed, conversing.** to have a conversation: She *conversed* with her neighbor over the fence.

con•ver•sion [kən vur′ zhən] *noun, plural* **conversions.** the act of converting: The *conversion* of iron into steel requires a high level of heat.

con•vert [kən vurt′] *verb,* **converted, converting. 1.** to change from one thing to another: "How is it possible for the body to *convert* yesterday's lunch into today's muscles?" (Carl Sagan) **2.** to change one's religion or beliefs: "Mr. Kernan . . . had been *converted* to the Catholic faith at the time of his marriage." (James Joyce) —[kän′ vurt′] *noun, plural* **converts.** a person who has been persuaded to accept a new religion or belief.

con•vert•i•ble [kən vur′ tə bəl] *adjective.* able to change into something else: She bought a *convertible* sofa that can also be used as a bed.' —*noun, plural* **convertibles.** a car with a soft top that folds down toward the back.

con•vex [kän veks′ *or* kän′ veks] *adjective, more/most.* curved or rounded outward: Contact lenses are curved to fit the *convex* shape of the eyeball.

con•vey [kən vā′] *verb,* **conveyed, conveying. 1.** to move or carry something to another place: Today TV signals are often *conveyed* by cable rather than through the air. ◆ A **conveyance** is something that moves people or things from place to place, such as a bus, truck, or airplane. **2.** to communicate some thought or feeling; make known: "Most of the time a nod or a grunt would carry all the meaning that she wanted to *convey* to him." (Ralph Ellison)

con•vict [kən vikt′] *verb,* **convicted, convicting.** to find by a court of law that someone is guilty of a crime: He was *convicted* of stealing a gold watch from the jewelry store. —[kän′ vikt] *noun, plural* **convicts.** someone who has been convicted of a crime and is in prison serving a sentence.

con•vic•tion [kən vik′ shən] *noun, plural* **convictions. 1.** the act of proving that a person is guilty of a crime: John's *conviction* for speeding will stay on his driving record for another three years. **2.** a strong belief about something: Because of his religious *convictions,* he won't work on Sunday.

con•vince [kən vins′] *verb,* **convinced, convincing.** to make someone believe something; persuade: "Laura . . . finally *convinced* him that he must vote for Norman Thomas." (Tennessee Williams) "I'm *convinced* that you can do the work and keep up with your grade . . ."

(Madeleine L'Engle) ◆ Also used as an adjective: The witness told a *convincing* story of what he had seen.

con•voy [kän′ voi′] *noun, plural* **convoys.** a number of ships, trucks, or other vehicles traveling together in a group. In wartime, naval vessels often go in a convoy as a protection against attack.

convoy A convoy of U.S. Navy ships in the Indian Ocean. The aircraft carrier *U.S.S. Midway,* center, is being escorted by smaller ships.

cook [kook] *verb,* **cooked, cooking.** to make food ready to eat by heating it: Has the meat *cooked* long enough? —*noun, plural* **cooks.** a person who cooks. ◆ The verb is also used to form other nouns such as **cooking, cookbook,** and **cookout.**

cook•ie [kook′ ē] (also spelled **cooky**) *noun, plural* **cookies.** a small, sweet cake that is usually flat and round.

cool [kool] *adjective,* **cooler, coolest. 1.** lacking warmth; a little cold: a *cool* day in early fall. Put the butter in a *cool* place so it doesn't melt. ◆ Something that keeps food or drink cool is a **cooler. 2.** not excited; calm: Some of the passengers were nervous during the storm, but the flight crew remained *cool.* **3.** not friendly or interested: He smiled as she passed, but she gave only a *cool* nod in reply. **4.** *Informal.* outstanding in some way, as in style or appearance. —*noun.* **1.** something that lacks warmth; a cool place or thing: The *cool* of the early morning. **2.** *Slang.* one's temper: to lose or keep your *cool.* —*verb,* **cooled, cooling.** to make something cool: The fan *cooled* the hot room. "Mr. Rocque was so mad that it took him a minute to *cool* down." (Louise Fitzhugh) —**coolly,** *adverb.* —**coolness,** *noun.*

Coo•lidge [koo′ lij] **Calvin,** 1872–1933, the thirtieth president of the United States, from 1923 to 1929.

coop [ko͞op] *noun, plural* **coops.** a cage for keeping chickens or small animals. —*verb,* **cooped, cooping.** (usually used with **up**) to keep in a small space, as if in a coop: "Be good for him to be out in the sun. No animal likes to be *cooped up* too long." (John Steinbeck)

co-op [kō′äp′] *noun, plural* **co-ops.** a short word for **cooperative.**

Coo·per [ko͞o′pər] **James Fenimore,** 1789–1851, American novelist.

co·op·er·ate [kō äp′ə rāt′] *verb,* **cooperated, cooperating.** to act with another or others to do something; work together: "People had to *cooperate,* and work together to build irrigation ditches along the banks of the river." (Isaac Asimov)

co·op·er·a·tion [kō äp′ə rā′shən] *noun.* the act or process of cooperating; working together: Making a Hollywood movie requires the *cooperation* of a great number of people.

co·op·er·a·tive [kō äp′ rə tiv] *adjective, more/most.* willing to work with or help others: That author is always *cooperative* when younger writers ask her for advice.
—*noun, plural* **cooperatives.** something owned and operated by the people who use it: If an apartment building is a *cooperative,* it means the people who live there form a group to own and run the building.

co·or·di·nate [kō ôr′də nāt′] *verb,* **coordinated, coordinating.** to cause different things to work together well: The brain *coordinates* the movements of the body.

♦ Often used as an adjective: A ballet dancer must be very well-*coordinated.* —**coordination,** *noun.* When a baby first learns to walk, it does not have good *coordination.*

cop [käp] *noun, plural* **cops.** *Informal.* a police officer.

cope [kōp] *verb,* **coped, coping.** to handle a difficult situation with success: "We are having enough trouble today without having to *cope* with your foolishness." (E.B. White)

Co·per·ni·cus [kə pur′nə kəs] **Nicolaus,** 1473–1543, Polish astronomer who was the founder of modern astronomy.

co·pi·lot [kō′pī′lət] *noun, plural* **copilots.** the assistant pilot of an aircraft.

cop·per [käp′ər] *noun.* **1.** a reddish-brown metal that is used to make pennies and other coins, electrical wire, and other products. Copper is a chemical element. It is a good conductor of heat and electricity. **2.** a reddish-brown color like that of copper.

copper A new finish and reinforcement is given to the copper torch of the Statue of Liberty for its 100th anniversary celebration in 1986.

cop·per·head [käp′ər hed′] *noun, plural* **copperheads.** a poisonous snake with a reddish-colored head. Copperheads are found in the eastern and southern United States.

copying *Copying* we all know to mean: writing the words of another person or, by using electronic copiers, running off pages of a text to make one or ten or a hundred copies. Now, consider the word *copyright.* Whose right is being mentioned in this legal term? It is the right of the author not to have his or her writing copied to such an extent that the writer loses ownership of a novel or play or essay. Look in the front of this dictionary. © means that Harcourt Brace Jovanovich, the publisher, owns the right to publish (make copies for sale) of this dictionary, but that no one else can do so without obtaining the publisher's permission.

cop·y [käp′ē] *noun, plural* **copies. 1.** something that is made to look or be just like something

Pronunciation Key: T–Z

t	ten; date	v	very; live
th	think	w	win; away
<u>th</u>	these	y	you
u	cut; butter	z	zoo; cause
ur	turn; bird	zh	measure

(Turn the page for more information.)

C

else; an imitation: This dress is a *copy* of one by a famous Paris designer. **2.** one of a number of newspapers, magazines, books, tapes, and so on printed or made at the same time. —*verb,* **copied, copying. 1.** to make a copy of something; duplicate: to *copy* a poem out of a book. **2.** to be like; imitate: Young people sometimes *copy* the way a popular singer or movie star looks and dresses. ♦ A **copier** is a machine that makes copies of letters and other papers, as in an office.

cop•y•right [kăp′ ē rīt′] *noun, plural* **copyrights.** the right by law to be the only one to publish, produce, or sell a certain artistic work, such as a book, movie, or piece of music.

cor•al [kôr′ əl] *noun.* **1.** a rock-like material made up of the skeletons of tiny sea animals that live in warm waters. **2.** the animal that produces this material. A **coral reef** is a large formation of coral like a wall in shallow water. **3.** a pinkish-red color like that of coral.

coral snake The poisonous North American coral snake bites but does not strike at its victim as most snakes do.

coral snake a small poisonous snake with red, yellow, and black bands. It is found in the southern United States.

cord [kôrd] *noun, plural* **cords. 1.** a kind of heavy string that is thicker and stronger than ordinary string. **2.** a covered wire used to connect an electric lamp or appliance to a power outlet. **3.** a part of the body that is thought of as like a cord: the spinal *cord,* the vocal *cords.* **4.** a unit of measure for a pile of cut firewood. A cord is eight feet wide by four feet high by four feet deep.

cor•dial [kôr′ jəl] *adjective, more/most.* warm and friendly: Our doctor always gives a *cordial* greeting to each patient who comes to see her. **—cordially,** *adverb.* She gave us a wave and smiled *cordially.*

cor•du•roy [kôr′ də roi] *noun.* a woven cloth with small ridges running lengthwise that look like cords. Corduroy is usually made from cotton and is a soft but long-wearing fabric.

core [kôr] *noun, plural* **cores. 1.** the hard central part of an apple, pear, or similar fruit. The core contains the seeds of the fruit. **2.** the central or most important part of something: the *core* of the earth. This article really gets to the *core* of the problem. —*verb,* **cored, coring.** to take or cut out the core of something: to *core* an apple.

cork [kôrk] *noun, plural* **corks. 1.** the thick outer bark of a certain type of oak tree. Cork is very light and floats easily. It is used to make floor coverings, bulletin boards, and other things. **2.** something made from cork, especially a bottle stopper. —*verb,* **corked, corking.** to put a cork in a bottle opening.

cork•screw [kôrk′ skroo′] *noun, plural* **corkscrews.** a hand tool used to pull corks out of bottles. The corkscrew has a strong spiral wire that is screwed into the cork and a handle used to pull the wire and cork out of the bottle.

corn[1] [kôrn] *noun.* a tall green plant that has large ears covered with rows of yellow or white KERNELS. Corn is eaten as a vegetable and is used as feed for farm animals. It is also used to make many other food products, such as **corn oil, cornmeal, cornstarch, corn bread, cornflakes,** and so on.

corn[2] *noun, plural* **corns.** a painful area where the skin has become hard and thick, especially on the toe.

corn•cob [kôrn′ kăb′] *noun, plural* **corncobs.** the tough, woody core of an ear of corn. Corn kernels grow in rows on the corncob.

cor•ne•a [kôr′ nē ə] *noun, plural* **corneas.** the clear outer layer on the surface of the eyeball. It covers the IRIS and the PUPIL.

cor•ner [kôr′ nər] *noun, plural* **corners. 1.** the point where two lines, walls, or other surfaces come together: the *corner* of a room, the *corner* of a piece of paper. **2.** the place where two streets come together. **3.** a secret, private, or faraway place: The zoo displayed animals from all *corners* of the earth. **4.** a difficult or embarrassing position: He got himself into a tight *corner* when he used his credit card to charge a lot of things he couldn't afford. —*verb,* **cornered, cornering.** to force someone into a corner: The wolves *cornered* the deer. She *cornered* the doctor at the party and told him a long story about all her various aches and pains.

corn•y [kôr′ nē] *adjective,* **cornier, corniest.** *Informal.* very old-fashioned, simple, or sentimental: a *corny* joke. The movie had a *corny* plot about a grouchy old man who finally became friendly because of a cute little puppy he found.

Co•ro•na•do [kôr′ ə nä′ dō] **Francisco Vasquez de,** 1510–1554, Spanish explorer of the southwestern United States.

cor•o•nar•y [kôr′ ə ner′ ē] *adjective.* having to do with the heart or with the two arteries that supply blood directly to the heart.

cor•o•na•tion [kôr′ ə nā′ shən] *noun, plural* **coronations.** the crowning of a new king or queen: The *coronation* of Queen Elizabeth II took place in 1952.

cor•por•al [kôr′ prəl] *noun, plural* **corporals.** a rank in the army, below a sergeant and above a private.

cor•po•ra•tion [kôr′ pə rā′ shən] *noun, plural* **corporations.** a business or other group that is allowed by law to act as if it were one single person. The legal rights and obligations of a corporation are separate from those of the people who own or work for it. —**corporate** [kôr′ pə rit] *adjective.* having to do with corporations: the *corporate* income tax rate.

corps [kôr] *noun, plural* **corps** [kôrz]. **1.** a military group that is trained for a special purpose: the Marine *Corps,* a medical *corps.* **2.** any group of people working together: The President made a few remarks to the press *corps.*

corpse [kôrps] *noun, plural* **corpses.** the body of a dead person.

cor•pus•cle [kôr′ pus′ əl] *noun, plural* **corpuscles.** any of the small red or white cells that make up the blood.

cor•ral [kə ral′] *noun, plural* **corrals.** a fenced area or pen for keeping horses, cattle, or other animals.

cor•rect [kə rekt′] *adjective, more/most.* **1.** having no mistakes; right: the *correct* spelling of a word. The *correct* answer to "What is the largest state?" is "Alaska." **2.** following certain rules or standards; proper: Wearing shorts and a T-shirt is not a *correct* way to dress for a church wedding. —*verb,* **corrected, correcting. 1.** to mark or point out the mistakes in something: to *correct* a test paper. **2.** to change to make right or proper: to *correct* a child for acting rude. ◆ Something that corrects is **corrective:** People with poor eyesight have to wear *corrective* lenses when they drive a car. —**correctly,** *adverb:* She answered all the questions on the test *correctly.* —**correctness,** *noun.*

corrections Someone once wrote a publisher to ask if a story could be submitted for publication by Harcourt Brace Jovanovich without the author's worrying over "minor errors like spelling and grammar." The publisher replied as follows: "If you don't care how you dress when in public, or if you don't mind being confused by the words in street signs that give directions, then I suppose you also do not care whether your writing is worth anyone's attention. Good punctuation, accurate spelling, and careful grammar are so important that there is no argument against them. If you are not serious about what you mean to say, why should any reader take you seriously?"

cor•rec•tion [kə rek′ shən] *noun, plural* **corrections.** the act of correcting, or something that corrects: Our teacher always makes her *corrections* on our papers with red ink.

cor•re•spond [kôr′ ə spänd′] *verb,* **corresponded, corresponding. 1.** to agree with something; match: The number of places at the table should *correspond* with the number of guests at the party. **2.** to be similar to; be like: The Hawaiian word "aloha" *corresponds* to either "hello" or "good-bye." **3.** to write or exchange letters. ◆ The act of corresponding is **correspondence:** Newspapers publish *correspondence* from their readers.

cor•re•spon•dent [kôr′ ə spänd′ ənt] *noun, plural* **correspondents. 1.** a person who corresponds with another by letter. **2.** a person who sends in a news report to a newspaper, TV station, and so on, especially from a distant place.

cor•ri•dor [kôr′ ə dər] *noun, plural* **corridors.** a long, narrow hallway or passage in a building, usually with doors opening from it.

C

Pronunciation Key: [ə] Symbol

The [ə] or *schwa* sound occurs in syllables without an accent. It can be spelled with any vowel, such as a in above, e in listen, i in pencil, o in melon, u in circus. It can also be a combination of vowels, such as io in action, ai in mountain, iou in precious.

(Turn the page for more information.)

C

cor•rode [kə rōd/] *verb,* **corroded, corroding.** to wear away little by little over a period of time: Metal can be *corroded* by rust or acids. ♦ The process or result of corroding is **corrosion.** A thing that can cause corrosion, such as acid, is **corrosive.**

cor•rupt [kə rupt/] *adjective, more/most.* having poor morals; dishonest; crooked: The *corrupt* politician accepted a secret payment to change his vote. —*verb,* **corrupted, corrupting.** to cause someone to be dishonest; make corrupt. ♦ The state of being corrupt is **corruption:** The new mayor promised to eliminate *corruption* in the city government.

> **corruption of language** "The Corruption of English" is a recent essay by the critic John Simon. He, like others who use the term "corruption," mean it to be a stronger word than "mistake" or "error." They are saying that certain ways of using language can be dishonest and harmful, rather than just incorrect. George Orwell wrote, "If thought corrupts language, language can also corrupt thought." He argued that if people do not use a particular word correctly, the word will lose its force and have only a vague, general meaning. An example of this can be seen in the word "republic." This originally meant a free government. Now, almost every country in the world calls itself a "republic" or "democratic republic," even if the government is run by a dictator who allows no freedom to speak or vote. If someone says, "We just intend to rid our town of undesirables," ask who they are, "the undesirables," and who decides they are that, and on what authority they can be removed.

cor•sage [kôr sazh/] *noun, plural* **corsages.** a flower or arrangement of flowers worn by a woman on the shoulder or wrist.

Cor•tés [kôr tez/] **Hernando,** 1485–1547, Spanish explorer and conqueror of Mexico.

cos•met•ic [käz met/ ik] *noun, plural* **cosmetics.** a powder, cream, or other material used to make the face, hair, or skin look more attractive. ♦ Usually used in the plural: Lipstick, eyeshadow, and rouge are *cosmetics.*

cos•mic [käz/ mik] *adjective.* relating to the whole universe, especially to the stars and galaxies. **Cosmic rays** are high-speed particles that reach the earth from outer space.

cost [kôst] *noun, plural* **costs. 1.** the price of something; the amount paid: What was the *cost* of that coat? **2.** the loss of something; a sacrifice: The Panama Canal was built at the *cost* of a great many workers' lives. —*verb,* **cost, costing. 1.** to have as a price: That book *costs* $19.95. **2.** to cause the loss of something: The outfielder's error *cost* his team the game.

cost•ly [kôst/ lē] *adjective,* **costlier, costliest. 1.** costing a lot; expensive: Hospital care in the U.S. is *costly.* **2.** causing a great loss: It was a *costly* victory because many lives were lost.

cos•tume [käs/ tōōm] *noun, plural* **costumes. 1.** clothes worn to dress up as someone or something else: He wore a Frankenstein *costume* for Halloween. **2.** the style of clothing worn by the people of a certain place or time: When the tourists arrived in Hawaii, they were greeted by a band wearing colorful native *costumes.* ♦ **Costume jewelry** is made from inexpensive materials rather than precious stones.

cot [kät] *noun, plural* **cots.** a lightweight, narrow bed, usually having a folding frame.

cot•tage [kät/ ij] *noun, plural* **cottages.** a small house, especially one for vacation use at the beach or in the mountains.

cot•ton [kät/ ən] *noun.* a plant that produces seeds covered with fluffy white fibers that are processed to make cloth and thread. The fibers and the cloth are also called cotton. ♦ Often used as an adjective: a *cotton* dress.

cotton Shown here are the blossoms of the cotton plant, a seed case, and the puffy cotton ball. The word *cotton* comes from the Arabs, who introduced this plant to Europe in the Middle Ages.

cot•ton•mouth [kät′ ən mouth′] *noun, plural* **cottonmouths.** a poisonous snake of North America, usually known as a WATER MOCCASIN.

cottonmouth The poisonous cottonmouth gets its name from the white color of its mouth. It is also known as a *water moccasin.*

cot•ton•tail [kät′ ən tāl′] *noun, plural* **cottontails.** a North American rabbit with brown or gray fur and a short, fluffy white tail.

cot•ton•wood [kät′ ən wood′] *noun, plural* **cottonwoods.** a type of POPLAR trcc that grows near streams and rivers in North America. Cottonwood seeds have white hairs that look like cotton fibers.

couch [kouch] *noun, plural* **couches.** a large piece of furniture that two or more people can sit on; a sofa.

cou•gar [kōō′ gər] *noun, plural* **cougars.** a large, wild cat of North America, more often known as a MOUNTAIN LION.

cough [kôf] *verb,* **coughed, coughing.** to force air from the lungs with a sudden effort and loud noise. —*noun, plural* **coughs. 1.** the sudden, loud sound made when a person is coughing. **2.** an illness that causes a person to cough often.

could [kood] *verb.* the past form of **can:** "It was very hard to get a ball past Louis—he *could* return almost any shot." (E.B. White) ◆ **Could** is also used in place of CAN or MAY to make a statement less strong: *Could* you please put this away for me? I'm not sure whose jacket that is—it *could* be Jim's.

could•n't [kood′ ənt] *verb.* the contraction for **could not.**

coun•cil [koun′ səl] *noun, plural* **councils. 1.** a group of people who meet to discuss a problem or make a decision: a *council* of church leaders, a student *council* at a school. **2.** an elected group of people who make laws: a city *council.*

coun•sel [koun′ səl] *noun.* **1.** ideas or opinions about what to do; advice; guidance: The President often consults the cabinet for *counsel* on problems of government. **2.** a person who gives legal advice; a lawyer: In the U.S., any person accused of a crime has the right to *counsel.* —*verb,* **counseled, counseling.** to give advice or guidance to: Mr. Arnold *counseled* his son not to drop out of school.

coun•se•lor [koun′ slər] *noun, plural* **counselors. 1.** a person who advises or guides: Meg's college *counselor* helped her decide which courses to take. **2.** a lawyer: the *counselor* for the defense. **3.** a person who is in charge of activities at a children's camp.

count[1] [kount] *verb,* **counted, counting. 1.** to find the amount or number of something; add up: The highway department is going to *count* how many cars use the bridge each day. **2.** to name or write numbers in order: to *count* to fifty. **3.** to include when adding up or thinking about something: There were 30 people in the class picture, *counting* the teacher. **4.** to be taken into account: You have to take off from behind this line, or else your jump won't *count.* —*noun, plural* **counts. 1.** the act of counting. **2.** a number obtained by counting; a total; sum: At the *count* of three I'll say "go" to start the race. **3.** a charge against a person in a court of law: He is accused of three *counts* of burglary.

count on. to expect or depend on: "I was *counting on* selling her and her husband a whole . . . load of goods." (Eugene O'Neill)

count[2] *noun, plural* **counts.** a nobleman of high rank in some European countries.

count•down [kount′ doun′] *noun, plural* **countdowns.** a way of marking the time left before the start of an event by counting backwards to zero. A countdown is used to time the launching of a spacecraft.

count•er[1] [koun′ tər] *noun, plural* **counters. 1.** a long, flat surface where customers in restaurants, banks, or stores are served, or where things are displayed. Kitchens and bathrooms also have counters that are used to work on or to hold things. **2.** an object used for counting or keeping score, as in a game.

C

Pronunciation Key: Accent Marks

[′] is the normal accent mark. It shows where the main stress falls on a word.
[′] is a secondary accent mark. It shows a lighter stress than the primary accent. For example:

tel • e • vis • ion [tel′ ə vizh′ ən]
(Turn the page for more information.)

C

counter² *adverb* or *adjective.* opposed to something; in the opposite way: The man acted *counter* to his lawyer's advice and agreed to give the police a full statement of what had happened. They wanted to sell the house for $100,000; she offered $90,000, and they made a *counter* offer of $95,000. ◆ This meaning is often used in compounds to give the idea of opposing or going against something, as in **counterattack, counteroffensive,** and **counterspy.** —*verb,* **countered, countering.** to oppose something; go or act in the opposite way: The boxer *countered* the other fighter's punch.

country music a type of music that began in rural areas of the southern United States. Country music songs often tell about the lives and problems of ordinary people. ◆ This music is also called **country and western** to include the style of music that developed from the cowboy songs of the Old West.

coun•try•side [kun′ trē sīd′] *noun, plural* **countrysides.** an area outside the city; a rural area.

coun•ty [koun′ tē] *noun, plural* **counties.** one of the sections into which a state or country is divided. A county has its own local government.

---

counter- The word *counter* is used as a prefix meaning "in the opposite direction" or "against." Knowing this, you can probably figure out the meaning of words such as *counterattack, counterclockwise, counteract,* and *counteroffer. Counter-* is close in meaning to "anti-," as in "anti-terrorist laws." But it is broader in meaning. Notice you could not make an "anti-offer" when bargaining to buy a car. "Anti-" means one is strongly opposed, as in "anti-communism."

---

coun•ter•clock•wise [koun′ tər kläk′ wīz′] *adverb, adjective.* in a direction opposite to the way the hands of a clock move: You turn a lid *counterclockwise* to take it off a jar.

coun•ter•feit [koun′ tər fit] *verb,* **counterfeited, counterfeiting.** to copy something in order to fool or cheat people by using the copy in place of the real thing: He *counterfeited* tickets for the rock concert and sold them to people outside the stadium. —*adjective.* not the real thing; meant to cheat people: a *counterfeit* $20 bill. —*noun, plural* **counterfeits.** something that is counterfeit.

coun•ter•part [koun′ tər part′] *noun, plural* **counterparts.** a person or thing that is like another or acts in the same way: The prime minister of Canada is the *counterpart* of the president of the United States.

coun•tess [koun′ təs] *noun, plural* **countesses.** a woman who is married to a count, or who holds the same rank as a count.

coun•try [kun′ trē] *noun, plural* **countries. 1.** an area of land that is under the same government; a nation. A country has certain set borders, and the people who live there are not under any government higher than that of the country itself. **2.** any area of land of a certain type: The American Midwest is good farming *country.* **3.** an area of land away from cities and towns; a rural area: She works in New York City, but spends her weekends in the *country.* —*adjective.* having to do with areas away from the city; rural, an old *country* inn.

cou•ple [kup′ əl] *noun, plural* **couples. 1.** two things that are the same or that go together; a pair: I have a *couple* of tickets for the ballgame tomorrow. **2.** two people who are thought of together because they are married, engaged, partners in a dance or game, and so on: Mom and Dad went out to dinner with two other *couples.* —*verb,* **coupled, coupling.** to put together; join: The railroad cars were *coupled* to the engine at the freight yard.

cou•pon [kōō′ pän *or* kyōō′ pän] *noun, plural* **coupons.** a printed piece of paper that can be traded for money or merchandise or used to get a cheaper price on a product: Mom uses her *coupons* at the supermarket to save money.

cour•age [kur′ ij] *noun.* a quality of being able to face danger or pain without giving in to being afraid; bravery: "Did you know that an Arabian horse is the only breed with the *courage* to face a lion?" (Walter Farley)

cou•ra•geous [kə rā′ jəs] *adjective, more/most.* showing or having courage; brave: a *courageous* act, a *courageous* person.

course [kôrs] *noun, plural* **courses. 1.** a moving from one point to another; movement through space or time: The passengers can watch a movie during the *course* of the flight. **2.** a certain direction in which something moves or goes: The ship's *course* was due west. **3.** a way of acting or of doing something: "I know not what *course* others may take . . ." (Patrick Henry) **4.** an open area used for games or races: a golf *course.* **5.** a series of classes in a particular subject: an English *course,* a driver education *course.* **6.** one part of a meal: They had soup before the main *course.*

of course without a doubt; certainly: Any list of the world's great cities must *of course* include Paris. ♦ Often used as an answer in conversation: "Is it OK if I borrow your newspaper?" "*Of course.*"

court [kôrt] *noun, plural* **courts. 1.** an official meeting at which a judge holds trials and settles legal matters: a traffic *court.* **2.** the place where such a meeting is held; a courtroom or courthouse. **3.** a judge or judges. **4.** a space set up for a certain game or sport: a tennis *court,* a basketball *court.* **5.** see **courtyard. 6.** the home of a king, queen, or other royal ruler: Hampton *Court* was the palace of King Henry VIII of England. **7.** respect or honor: to pay *court* to someone. —*verb,* **courted, courting. 1.** to pay attention to in order to get a favor from: The politician *courted* several wealthy businessmen with the hope that they'd give money to his campaign. **2.** to spend time with or pay attention to a person one hopes to marry: Grandpa showed us an old picture taken when he and Grandma were *courting.* **3.** to act so as to get or bring on something, especially something bad: They're *courting* disaster by building that house so close to the edge of the cliff.

cour•te•ous [kur′tē əs] *adjective, more/most.* polite and considerate toward other people: The children were always *courteous* to their friends' parents. —**courteously,** *adverb:* I was surprised at the way the taxi driver *courteously* opened the door and helped us in. —**courteousness,** *noun.*

cour•te•sy [kur′tə sē] *noun, plural* **courtesies.** polite and considerate behavior or manners; being courteous.

court•house [kôrt′hous′] *noun, plural* **courthouses.** a building used for trials and other legal matters. A room used for this purpose is a **courtroom.**

court-mar•tial [kôrt′mär′shəl] *noun, plural* **courts-martial.** a military court that tries members of the armed forces for offenses against military law. —*verb,* **court-martialed, court-martialing:** to bring someone to trial in such a court: Private Smith was *court-martialed* for hitting an officer.

court•yard [kôrt′yärd′] *noun, plural* **courtyards.** a small open space or yard that is enclosed by buildings or walls.

cous•in [kuz′ən] *noun, plural* **cousins. 1.** the son or daughter of one's aunt or uncle. **2.** any relative that has the same great-grandparents or other ancestor.

cove [kōv] *noun, plural* **coves.** a small bay or inlet that is sheltered by land.

cove This large cove is located in the U.S. Virgin Islands in the Caribbean.

cov•er [kuv′ər] *verb,* **covered, covering. 1.** to place or put something over or on: She *covered* the sleeping baby with a blanket. **2.** to spread over the surface of; lie over or on: "Every rock seemed to be *covered* with crabs." (Jeffery Paul Chan) **3.** to travel or go over: "He had not *covered* more than ten miles that day." (Jack London) **4.** to deal with; include: This social studies course *covers* American history up to 1865. **5.** to watch over or guard: The police are *covering* all the roads out of town. **6.** to have as one's work or interest: Several reporters are at court today to *cover* a murder trial.

—*noun, plural* **covers. 1.** something that covers: to put a *cover* on a chair or sofa. **2.** the outside of a book, magazine, record album, or the like. **3.** *also,* **covers.** a blanket or bedspread used to cover a bed. **4.** something that protects or hides: The soldiers took *cover* behind a tree.

cover up to hide or conceal: They *covered up* the trap with leaves so that the animals wouldn't see it. The teller tried to *cover up* the fact that he was stealing money. ♦ Also used as a noun: The 'Watergate' scandal began with a *cover-up* of a burglary.

C

Pronunciation Key: A–F			
a	and; hat	ch	chew; such
ā	ate; stay	d	dog; lid
â	care; air	e	end; yet
ä	father; hat	ē	she; each
b	boy; cab	f	fun; off

(Turn the page for more information.)

coverage A publisher once asked one of his authors to write a short article on the topic of American Literature. The author said, "Now, that's hard. It would be easier for me if you wanted a *long* article instead of a short one." In general, it's harder to write a short paper on a very broad topic than it is to write a long paper on a small subject. Entire novels have been written about the events of one single day (such as *Appointment in Samarra* by John O'Hara or *Mrs. Dalloway* by Virginia Woolf). Could you write two pages that cover the entire Civil War? If you are interested in this topic, and your assignment is a two-page paper, why not write about a single battle or a single person?

C

cov•er•age [kuv′ rij] *noun.* **1.** the amount of space or time that a newspaper or TV program gives to report a news event. **2.** the amount and extent of something covered by insurance: She has $10,000 *coverage* for damage to her car in an accident.

cov•er•ing [kuv′ ring] *noun, plural* **coverings.** anything that covers, protects, or hides: A rug is a floor *covering.*

cov•et [kuv′ it] *verb,* **coveted, coveting.** to want very much to own or have something, especially a thing belonging to another person: "No one in Olinka owns a bicycle, but one of the road-builders has one, and all the Olinka men *covet* it and talk of some day purchasing their own." (Alice Walker)

cow [kou] *noun, plural* **cows. 1.** the full-grown female of CATTLE. **2.** the full-grown female of certain other large animals, such as the moose, whale, or elephant. ♦ For those animals whose female is called a cow, the male is called a BULL and the young a CALF.

cow•ard [kou′ ərd] *noun, plural* **cowards.** a person who is not brave or courageous; someone who shows fear in a shameful way or who is easily frightened: "I hung my head, just the way *cowards* do in books." (Jean Fritz)

cow•ard•ly [kou′ ərd lē] *adjective, more/most.* not brave or courageous; showing fear in a shameful way: In *The Wizard of Oz,* the Cowardly Lion was even afraid of the little dog Toto and cried whenever he was scared. ♦ The state of being cowardly is **cowardice.**

cow•boy [kou′ boi′] *noun, plural* **cowboys.** a man who takes care of cattle on a ranch, usually on horseback.

cow•er [kou′ ər] *verb,* **cowered, cowering.** to move away in fear of something: "A wild glare from me was enough to make the dogs *cower* back in their chairs." (James Herriot)

coy•o•te [kī ō′ tē *or* kī′ ōt′] *noun, plural* **coy-otes** or **coyote.** a North American animal that is related to the wolf. Coyotes are native to the West but are now also found elsewhere.

co•zy [kō′ zē] *adjective,* **cozier, coziest.** warm and comfortable: a soft, *cozy* chair. "The kitchen felt warm and *cozy* with the rain outside." (Louise Fitzhugh)

crab [krab] *noun, plural* **crabs. 1.** a water animal that has a wide, flat body covered by a hard shell. Crabs have four pairs of legs and a pair of front claws. Many kinds of crabs are used as food. **2.** *Informal.* someone who is cross and bad-tempered; a grouch.

crab apple a small, sour apple that is used to make jelly.

crab grass a weed grass that has thick, heavy leaves and spreads very quickly. Crab grass is a pest in lawns and gardens because it grows in place of other plants.

crack [krak] *verb,* **cracked, cracking. 1.** to break without coming completely apart; split: The glass *cracked* when I dropped it into the sink. **2.** to make a sudden, sharp noise: "The tree groaned, ripping and *cracking* in a shower of bark and splinters." (Lloyd Alexander) **3.** to

coyote Unlike the wolf, which moves in a pack, most coyotes live and hunt alone. They are often found living near people and may even raid garbage cans.

hit with a sharp, hard blow: "And my head! *Cracked* it on the ceiling . . . feel as though it's coming in half." (Mary Norton) **4.** to cause to fail or come apart: His voice *cracked* as he read the sad letter. The secret agent *cracked* the enemy's code. —*noun, plural* **cracks. 1.** a narrow break or split in something that is still in one piece: This teacup has a *crack* in it. **2.** a narrow space or opening: "He ran . . . to a door that showed a *crack* of light." (O. Henry) **3.** a sudden, sharp noise: the *crack* of a whip. **4.** a sharp, hard blow.

crack down to become more strict with rules or laws: The police are *cracking down* on speeders by giving out more tickets. ◆ Also used as a noun: a *crackdown* on the sale of illegal drugs.

crack up to crash: Marty *cracked up* his car during the ice storm. ◆ Also used as a noun: There was a bad *crackup* on the highway.

crack•er [krak/ər] *noun, plural* **crackers.** a thin, crisp piece of food made in the same way as bread.

crack•le [krak/əl] *verb,* **crackled, crackling.** to make a quick, sharp, snapping sound: "A fire was *crackling* in the fireplace." (Raymond Chandler) —*noun, plural* **crackles:** We heard the *crackle* of wood burning.

cra•dle [krā/dəl] *noun, plural* **cradles. 1.** a small bed for a newborn baby, usually on rockers. **2.** the place where something starts, in the way that a person's life is thought of as starting in a cradle: "And then Boston—Boston is the *cradle* of the Revolution." (Arthur Miller) —*verb,* **cradled, cradling.** to hold as if in a cradle: "He continued across the room, *cradling* something close to his narrow chest." (J.D. Salinger)

craft [kraft] *noun, plural* **crafts. 1.** a special skill in doing or making something with the hands. Sewing, woodworking, and making pottery and baskets are crafts. ◆ A man who does this kind of work is a **craftsman:** "He had a few skilled *craftsmen*—carpenters, plumbers, electricians, and so on." (Ronald Reagan) **2.** (*plural,* **craft**) a boat, ship, or aircraft: A warning was sent to all small *craft* on the ocean because of the coming storm. **3.** skill in fooling or tricking others; cunning.

craft•y [kraf/tē] *adjective,* **craftier, craftiest.** smart and clever in a sly, tricky way; cunning: The *crafty* fox easily escaped from the dogs that were chasing him. —**craftily,** *adverb.* —**craftiness,** *noun.*

crag [krag] *noun, plural* **crags.** a rough, steep rock or cliff.

cram [kram] *verb,* **crammed, cramming. 1.** to force something into a tight place: "The road was still *crammed* with great, glittering decorated buses, with motor bike taxis, and with cars. " (Doris Lessing) "His cottage was *crammed* with books." (T.H. White) **2.** to study hard for a test at the last minute: Suzie's in her room *cramming* for tomorrow's exam.

cramp [kramp] *noun, plural* **cramps. 1.** a sudden, sharp pain that comes from the tightening of a muscle: Bill got a *cramp* in his leg from swimming in the cold lake. **2. cramps.** sharp pains in the stomach or abdomen. —*verb,* **cramped, cramping. 1.** to have or cause to have a cramp. **2.** to crowd into a tight space: "She feels *cramped* when anyone besides them is in the apartment." (Ann Beattie)

cranberry The word *cranberry* is thought to be related to *crane,* because these birds live in the same swampy areas where the plant grows.

cran•ber•ry [kran/ber/ē] *noun, plural* **cranberries.** a sour, shiny red berry that grows in wet places. Cranberries are used to make sauce, juice, and jelly.

crane [krān] *noun, plural* **cranes. 1.** a tall water bird with a long neck and very long, thin legs. **2.** a large machine with a long, movable arm. It is used to move heavy weights, as in the building of a road or tall building. —*verb,* **craned, craning.** to stretch out the neck as a crane does: The people in the back of the crowd *craned* their necks to see the famous movie star.

Pronunciation Key: G–N			
g	give; big	k	kind; cat; back
h	hold	l	let; ball
i	it; this	m	make; time
ī	ice; my	n	not; own
j	jet; gem; edge	ng	having

(Turn the page for more information.)

Crane [krān] **Stephen**, 1871–1900, American novelist and short-story writer.

crank [krangk] *noun, plural* **cranks. 1.** a handle or rod that is turned to make a machine work. **2.** a person who is very odd or who has very strange ideas. **3.** a person who is often angry or irritated. —*verb,* **cranked, cranking.** to use or turn a crank: Long ago cars had to be *cranked* to start the engine.

crank•y [krangk′ē] *adjective,* **crankier, crankiest.** often angry or irritated; grouchy: Chris is always *cranky* when his mother makes him clean his room.

crash [krash] *verb,* **crashed, crashing. 1.** to go against something suddenly in a hard, noisy way: "The cupboard came *crashing* to the floor with everything that was in it." (Meindert DeJong) **2.** to fail or collapse suddenly: When the stock market *crashed* in 1929, thousands of people lost their money. **3.** of a computer, to completely stop working, as from a loss of electrical power. —*noun, plural* **crashes. 1.** the act of crashing: an airplane *crash,* a car *crash.* **2.** the noise made by this: The bowl fell with a *crash* on the kitchen floor. **3.** a sudden failure or collapse, as of a business. —*adjective.* showing a very great effort over a short time: a *crash* diet. Mary is taking a *crash* course in Spanish because her company just transferred her to Mexico.

crate [krāt] *noun, plural* **crates.** a large box made of strips of wood. Fruits and vegetables are often packed in crates. —*verb,* **crated, crating.** to pack things in a crate.

crater A deep crater formed on the surface of the moon.

cra•ter [krā′tər] *noun, plural* **craters.** a large hole in the ground, shaped like a bowl: There are many *craters* on the surface of the moon that were caused by meteors hitting it.

crawl [krôl] *verb,* **crawled, crawling. 1.** to move slowly on the hands and knees, as a baby does before it learns how to walk. **2.** to move in a way that is like the crawling of a baby: ". . . plants that creep and *crawl* in the green grass forests." (Margaret Wise Brown) **3.** to be completely covered or filled with something: "Welcome to the Philadelphia Zoo, which *crawls* with rare mammals, birds, reptiles, amphibians, and fish . . ." (E.B. White) —*noun, plural* **crawls. 1.** the act of crawling; a slow way of moving: Traffic slowed to a *crawl* during the heavy rainstorm. **2.** a type of swimming stroke in which the swimmer lies face down in the water and moves the arms overhead.

cray•fish [krā′fish′] *noun, plural* **crayfish** or **crayfishes.** a small fresh-water animal that looks like a lobster and can be eaten. It is also called a **crawfish** [krô′fish].

crayfish Crayfish like to hide under rocks or burrow in the mud during daylight hours.

cray•on [krā′än] *noun, plural* **crayons.** a short stick of colored wax or chalk, used for drawing.

cra•zy [krā′zē] *adjective,* **crazier, craziest. 1.** not having a healthy mind; insane. **2.** not sensible; foolish; silly: Running outside in the snow in a bathing suit was a *crazy* thing for him to do. **3.** *Informal.* very excited or enthusiastic: "I'm *crazy* about horses. I've always been that way." (Sherwood Anderson) ◆ Something that is very popular for a short time is a **craze.**

Crazy Horse [krā′zē hôrs′] 1844?–1877, Sioux Indian chief.

creak [krēk] *verb,* **creaked, creaking.** to make a sharp, squeaking sound: "The wind . . . made the trees *creak* as branches scratched against each other." (Walter Farley) —*noun, plural* **creaks:** The old gate swung open with a *creak.*

C

cream [krēm] *noun, plural* **creams. 1.** the thick, yellowish part of milk that has fat in it. It rises to the top when whole milk is left standing. Cream can be separated from the milk for making butter or for use in other foods. **2.** something that is smooth and thick like cream: shaving *cream*, skin *cream*. ♦ A thing that is like cream or that has a lot of cream in it is **creamy. 3.** the color of cream; a pale-yellow shade of white. **4.** the best part of something, as cream is thought to be the best part of milk: The *cream* of pro basketball players will be playing in next week's All-Star Game.

crease [krēs] *noun, plural* **creases.** a line or mark made by folding or pressing something: a *crease* in a pair of pants. —*verb,* **creased, creasing.** to put a crease in something: " 'I was only joking,' he said, *creasing* his face into a smile." (Michael Bond)

cre·ate [krē āt′] *verb,* **created, creating.** to cause something new to come into being: The new shopping center is going to *create* a lot of business for our town.

cre·a·tion [krē ā′ shən] *noun, plural* **creations. 1.** the creating of something: "That was the wonderful thing about true *creation*. You made something nobody else on earth could make but you . . ." (Langston Hughes) **2.** something that has been created: The Vietnam Veterans' Memorial in Washington was the *creation* of a young artist named Maya Lin. **3. (the) Creation.** the creating of the universe by God.

cre·a·tion·ism [krē ā′ shə niz′ əm] *noun.* the belief that the universe and all living things on earth were created by God from nothing, as described in the Bible. ♦ A person who believes in or supports creationism is a **creationist.**

cre·a·tor [krē ā′ tər] *noun, plural* **creators. 1.** a person who creates something: Charles Schulz is the *creator* of the "Peanuts" characters. **2. (the) Creator.** a name for God.

cre·a·ture [krē′ chər] *noun, plural* **creatures. 1.** an animal of any kind: rattlesnakes, lizards, and other *creatures* of the desert. "The Native American was a brother to all *creatures*." (Stewart Udall) **2.** any human being: "What marvelous *creatures* we are!" (Winston Churchill) **3.** a strange or frightening being: We saw a movie about *creatures* from outer space.

cre·den·tials [krə den′ shəlz] *plural noun.* papers or letters that identify a person or give him the authority to do something: No one is admitted to the secret military base without showing the proper *credentials*.

cred·it [kred′ it] *noun, plural* **credits. 1.** a way of buying something and paying for it at a later date: The Wilsons bought a new TV set on *credit*. **2.** an amount of money in a person's favor in a business account: Claire returned the sweater to the store, and they gave her a $20 *credit*. **3.** praise or honor for doing something: The scientist shared the *credit* for her discovery with her two assistants. **4.** belief or faith in something; trust: "He knew more about her than anybody would give him *credit* for." (Bernard Malamud) **5.** a unit of work in college or school: Betty is taking sixteen *credits* this term. —*verb,* **credited, crediting.** to get or give credit for something: DeSoto is *credited* with discovering the Mississippi River.

credit card a small plastic card that allows the person named on it to have credit when paying for things, as at a store, restaurant, hotel, or gas station.

creative writing At one time, the term "creative writing" was a term used to refer to works that call on the imagination—novels, short stories, plays, and poems. People did not use the term to mean factual works such as essays, reports, or news articles. Today, teachers of writing usually don't make this distinction. Good writing, whatever its form, takes some amount of skill and imagination. Actually, all writing is creative writing. The English writer Sir J. F. Stephen said, "Orignality does not consist in saying what no one has ever said before, but in saying exactly what you think yourself."

cre·a·tive [krē ā′ tiv] *adjective,* *more/most.* **1.** able to create things; good at making new things or having new ideas: Shakespeare's plays show that he was a very *creative* person. ♦ The quality of being creative is **creativity** [krē′ ā tiv′ tē]. **2.** having or showing creativity: Heather did a very *creative* science project in which she put together a homemade radio.

Pronunciation Key: O–S

ō	over; go	ou	out; town
ô	all; law	p	put; hop
oo	look; full	r	run; car
ōō	pool; who	s	set; miss
oi	oil; boy	sh	show

(Turn the page for more information.)

C

cred•i•tor [kred′ ə tər] *noun, plural* **creditors.** a person or business to whom money is owed by someone else.

creek [krēk] *noun, plural* **creeks.** a small body of water that flows into a larger river.

creek A creek winds through the woodlands of Quebec, Canada. The pronunciation "crick," which is still heard in some places, comes from the fact that the word used to be spelled as *crick* or *crike.*

creep [krēp] *verb,* **crept, creeping. 1.** to move slowly and quietly; crawl: "He *creeps* across the narrow beams, as steady as a cat." (Mabel Watts) **2.** to move or spread slowly: ". . . the lofty sky, with gray clouds *creeping* quietly over it." (Leo Tolstoy) **3.** to feel as if things are crawling over one's skin: The monster movie was so scary it made my flesh *creep.* —*noun, plural* **creeps. 1. the creeps.** *Informal.* a feeling of being frightened or very uncomfortable: "'He's crazy,' he repeated, 'He gives me *the creeps.*'" (Carson McCullers) **2.** *Slang.* a person who is thought of as very odd, annoying, or disgusting.

crepe [krāp] *noun, plural* **crepes. 1.** a soft thin cloth with fine lines and folds in it. **Crepe paper** has a wrinkled surface that looks like this cloth. **2.** a small, thin pancake.

crept [krept] the past form of **creep:** "While Major was speaking four rats had *crept* out of their holes." (George Orwell)

cres•cent [kres′ ənt] *noun, plural* **crescents. 1.** the shape of the moon when only a thin, curved part of it can be seen. **2.** something that has this shape.

crest [krest] *noun, plural* **crests. 1.** a group of feathers that sticks up on top of a bird's head. **2.** the highest part of something, such as a hill or wave: "The sea was quite choppy, with great waves topped by white *crests.*" (Idries Shah)

crev•ice [krev′ əs] *noun, plural* **crevices.** a narrow opening or crack: "The *crevices* in the rock seemed to get smaller as he climbed higher." (Mark Helprin)

crew [krōō] *noun, plural* **crews. 1.** all the people who work on board a ship or aircraft: That jet airliner has a *crew* of fourteen. **2.** a group of people working together on a certain job: a road *crew,* the camera *crew* for a TV program.

crib [krib] *noun, plural* **cribs. 1.** a small bed for a baby. A crib has high sides with bars to keep the baby from falling out. **2.** a small farm building that holds grain or corn. **3.** a box or trough that horses or cattle eat from.

crick•et[1] [krik′ ət] *noun, plural* **crickets.** a black or brown insect with long legs that looks like a small grasshopper. The male makes a chirping sound by rubbing its front wings together.

cricket[2] *noun.* an outdoor game something like baseball, played with a ball by two teams of eleven players each. It is played in Great Britain and countries of the British Commonwealth.

cricket The game of cricket being played by a team from the British West Indies. The name comes not from the insect, but from a word for the bat used to play the game.

cried [krīd] *verb.* the past form of **cry.**

crime [krīm] *noun, plural* **crimes. 1.** something that is against the law, especially something serious for which a person can be punished: Murder and robbery are *crimes.* **2.** something thought of as cruel or very bad: It's a *crime* to throw away all that perfectly good food when so many people could use it.

crim•i•nal [krim′ ə nəl] *noun, plural* **criminals.** a person who has committed a crime. —*adjective, more/most.* **1.** having to do with crime: A *criminal* lawyer defends people who are accused of crimes. **2.** being a crime: Stealing a car or breaking into someone's house are *criminal* acts. **3.** like a crime; very bad or cruel.

crim•son [krim′zən] *noun.* a deep red color. —*adjective.* having this color.

crip•ple [krip′əl] *noun, plural* **cripples.** a person who is not able to move some part of the body in the normal way because of an injury or disease. —*verb,* **crippled, crippling. 1.** to make a person into a cripple: Franklin D. Roosevelt was *crippled* by polio. **2.** to make helpless or useless; cause great damage to: The rainstorm *crippled* the city, knocking down telephone poles, electrical wires, and trees.

cri•sis [krī′səs] *noun, plural* **crises** [krī′sēz]. an important point at which great change will take place; a time of danger or great difficulty: The Civil War was a *crisis* in American history.

crisp [krisp] *adjective,* **crisper, crispest. 1.** hard and dry, but easily broken into pieces: *crisp* toast. **2.** fresh and firm; not wilted: *crisp* vegetables such as raw carrots and celery. **3.** cool and refreshing; brisk: a *crisp,* clear October day. **4.** short and exact; showing no doubt: "The words and sentences were all *crisp* and clear." (F. Scott Fitzgerald) —*verb,* **crisped, crisping.** to make or become crisp. —**crisply,** *adverb:* The captain *crisply* shouted out orders to the crew. —**crispness,** *noun.*

criss•cross [kris′crôs′] *verb,* **crisscrossed, crisscrossing.** to mark with or have a pattern of lines that cross one another. ◆ This word is also used as a noun, adjective, or adverb with the same meaning.

crit•ic [krit′ik] *noun, plural* **critics. 1.** a person whose work is to judge what is good or bad about a book, play, painting, or other artistic work. **2.** a person who finds fault with someone or something: Senator Jones has been a very strong *critic* of the President's new tax plan.

crit•i•cal [krit′ə kəl] *adjective,* more/most. **1.** looking for faults; likely to disapprove: Her older brother is a *critical* person who points out every little mistake she makes. **2.** having to do with a critic or critics: If a book is a *critical* success, it means that most critics thought it was good. **3.** having to do with a crisis; very serious or dangerous: The lost campers had a *critical* shortage of food and water.

◆ Hospitals use the term *critical* for a patient whose condition is so serious that he or she is in danger of dying. —**critically,** *adverb.* in a critical way: The boss looked *critically* at Judy as she walked in two hours late.

crit•i•cism [krit′i siz′əm] *noun, plural* **criticism. 1.** the act of finding fault; disapproval. His teacher has to be very careful in dealing with him because he gets so upset at *criticism.* **2.** the act of saying what is good or bad about a book, movie, or the like.

criticism Does criticism have to be negative? Here is a case where a word has both an ordinary and a literary meaning. "He *criticized* the President's budget" means that he is opposed to, or unfavorable to it. But the literary word *criticism* has to do with examining and judging, either favorably or unfavorably. In the original Greek meaning, *criticism* meant judgment, neither especially good nor bad. James Joyce and T.S. Eliot, two of the greatest modern writers, benefited from the criticism of a fellow writer, Ezra Pound.

crit•i•cize [krit′i sīz] *verb,* **criticized, criticizing. 1.** to find fault with something; disapprove: She was upset because her boyfriend *criticized* her new hair style. **2.** to judge what is good or bad about something; act as a critic.

croak [krōk] *noun, plural* **croaks.** a deep, harsh sound, such as that made by a frog. —*verb,* **croaked, croaking.** to make this sound.

cro•chet [krō shā′] *verb,* **crocheted, crocheting.** to make clothing by connecting loops of thread or yarn with a hooked needle.

Crock•ett [kräk′it] **David (Davy),** 1786–1836, American frontiersman and politician.

croc•o•dile [kräk′ə dīl′] *noun, plural* **crocodiles.** a large animal with short legs, a long tail, thick scaly skin, and a long, narrow head. It is a reptile living in rivers and swamps in warm areas of the U.S., Africa, and Asia.

Crom•well [kräm′wel] **Oliver,** 1599–1658, English general and statesman, the ruler of England from 1653 to 1658.

crook [krook] *noun, plural* **crooks. 1.** a person who is not honest; a criminal. **2.** a bent or curved part: Sara held the cat in the *crook* of her arm. —*verb,* **crooked, crooking.** to curve or hook.

C

Pronunciation Key: T–Z

t	ten; date	v	very; live
th	think	w	win; away
th	these	y	you
u	cut; butter	z	zoo; cause
ur	turn; bird	zh	measure

(Turn the page for more information.)

crook•ed [krook/id] *adjective, more/most.* **1.** not straight; bent or twisted: They followed a *crooked* path through the bushes. The Mississippi River has a *crooked* course. **2.** not honest: The man had a *crooked* scheme to sell people land he really didn't own.

crop [kräp] *noun, plural* **crops. 1.** *also,* **crops.** a plant grown to be used as food or to make something: Corn and wheat are important *crops* in the U.S. **2.** the amount of a certain plant grown and harvested at one time. **3.** a group of people or things that appear at the same time, as a crop does: The Dodgers have a whole *crop* of new players this spring. **4.** a pouch in the neck of a bird, near the bottom of its throat. Food is partly digested in the crop. **5.** a short whip with a loop at the end, used in horseback riding. —*verb,* **cropped, cropping.** to cut off the top or outside of; trim: to *crop* a photograph.

cro•quet [krō/kā] *noun.* an outdoor game played by hitting wooden balls through a series of wire hoops known as WICKETS. The player hits the ball with a wooden stick known as a MALLET.

cross [krôs] *noun, plural* **crosses. 1.** an object or mark formed by a stick or bar with another bar across it in the shape of a "T" or an "X." In ancient times people were put to death by hanging them on a large wooden cross. **2. the cross.** the symbol of the Christian religion, representing the cross on which Jesus died. **3.** a small emblem or medal in the shape of a cross: The Navy *Cross* is awarded for bravery. **4.** a mixing of different kinds of animals or plants: A mule is a *cross* between a horse and a donkey. —*verb,* **crossed, crossing. 1.** to go from one side of something to the other: "Let us *cross* over the river, and rest under the trees." (Stonewall Jackson) **2.** to draw a line through: Melissa *crossed* out the word that was spelled wrong. **3.** to put or place one thing across another: "She *crossed* her legs so that I would not fail to notice her white cowboy boots." (Nancy Willard) **4.** to disagree with or oppose: They didn't like the boss's idea, but no one was about to *cross* him. —*adjective,* **crosser, crossest. 1.** placed or going across: A *cross*road is one that crosses another road. **2.** angry or grouchy: The baby is really *cross* this morning because he didn't get enough sleep.

cross•bow [krôs/bō/] *noun, plural* **crossbows.** a weapon with a small bow set across a wooden bar or stock. Crossbows were used in the Middle Ages.

cross•ing [krôs/ing] *noun, plural* **crossings.** a place where something crosses or is crossed: A street sign saying "school *crossing*" means children cross there on their way to school.

cross section 1. a slice or cutting made straight across an object. **2.** a view or drawing showing the inside of something, as if it were cut open in this way. **3.** a sampling of a typical group of people as a way to show something about a much larger group.

cross•word puzzle [krôs/wurd/] a puzzle with sets of squares to be filled in with letters forming words. Clues are given to help fill in the words. It is so called because the words *cross* each other and can be read either across or down.

crotch [kräch] *noun, plural* **crotches.** the place where the body divides into two legs.

crouch [krouch] *verb,* **crouched, crouching.** to stoop down or bend low; squat: "He had already moved back, *crouching* to leap." (James Baldwin) —*noun, plural* **crouches.** a position of crouching: A catcher in baseball gets into a *crouch* as he waits for the pitch.

crow[1] [krō] *noun, plural* **crows.** a large, shiny black bird that makes a harsh noise that sounds like "caw."

crow Crows have long been considered pests by farmers, but studies show that they eat thousands of harmful insects each year.

crow[2] *verb,* **crowed, crowing. 1.** to make a loud cry, as a rooster does: The rooster *crowed* as soon as the sun started to rise. **2.** to speak in a happy or proud way: "'I'm good,' she *crowed.* 'I'm better than you.'" (Nancy Willard)

crow•bar [krō/bär/] *noun, plural* **crowbars.** a heavy steel or iron bar bent slightly at one end, used to lift or pry heavy things.

crucial You will see this word used frequently in literature. It is derived from *crux*, which in Latin means a cross. Now, how does it explain what is crucial? It is not a religious term. It is taken from the metaphor of a cross: where two directions meet. Good writers like to keep the meaning of the word so that it signifies that an important occasion has arisen and an important decision must be made. "It is crucial. Either keep the job and hope for a raise. Or quit the job and look for a better one." Of course, *crucial* can mean "important," "serious," even "final." But none of those is quite the same. The closest word to *crucial* is *momentous.* Look up that word.

C

crowd [kroud] *noun, plural* **crowds. 1.** a large number of people gathered together in one place: There was a *crowd* of over 50,000 people at today's football game. **2.** a certain group of people: He got into trouble by hanging around with a bad *crowd.* —*verb,* **crowded, crowding.** to put or force too many people or things into too small a space. ". . . many thousands of people so *crowded* together you can see almost nothing else." (Isaac Asimov)

crown This historic Italian crown dates back to the 800's. According to legend, it contains a nail taken from the cross of Jesus.

crown [kroun] *noun, plural* **crowns. 1.** a special covering or ornament for the head, worn by a king, queen, or other ruler as a sign of power. Crowns often are made of gold and have jewels set in them. **2.** the rank or power of a king or queen. **3.** a wreath of flowers worn on the head as a sign of winning some honor. **4.** an honor or championship: the heavyweight boxing *crown.* **5.** the highest point of something: The top of the head is called the *crown.* —*verb,* **crowned, crowning. 1.** to give royal power to a ruler by placing a crown on the head. King George VI was *crowned* in 1936. **2.** to cover the top of: a mountain peak *crowned* with snow.

CRT short for **cathode-ray tube,** a tube where slender beams shine on a screen to make a glowing light. Most computers have a display like a TV screen that is called a CRT.

cru•cial [kroo′shəl] *adjective, more/most.* being a very important test or issue; of deciding importance: In 1954 the Supreme Court made its *crucial* decision that black and white school children could not be kept separate by law.

cru•ci•fix•ion [kroo′sə fiks′shən] *noun, plural* **crucifixions. 1.** the act of crucifying a person. Long ago people who committed certain crimes were punished by *crucifixion.* **2. the Crucifixion.** the putting to death of Jesus Christ on the cross. ♦ A cross with a figure of Jesus on it is called a **crucifix.**

cru•ci•fy [kroo′si fī′] *verb,* **crucified, crucifying.** to kill someone by nailing or tying their hands and feet to a cross: The ancient Romans sometimes *crucified* criminals and slaves.

crude [krood] *adjective,* **cruder, crudest. 1.** in a raw or natural state: *Crude* oil has to be treated with special chemicals before it can be used in automobiles. **2.** not done or made with skill; rough: The *crude* map showed a row of X's for mountains. **3.** without taste or good manners; not polite.

cru•el [kroo′əl] *adjective,* **crueler, cruelest. 1.** willing or eager to give pain and suffering to others; not kind; brutal: Hitler was a *cruel* dictator. **2.** causing pain and suffering: The Constitution states that "*cruel* and unusual punishment" cannot be given as a penalty for a crime. "A *cruel* blast of wind swept out of the north, driving chilling swirls of icy fog around them." (James Houston) —**cruelly,** *adverb.*

cru•el•ty [krool′tē] *noun, plural* **cruelties.** the quality of being cruel; a cruel action: The man was arrested for *cruelty* to animals because he let his pet dog starve to death.

Pronunciation Key: [ə] Symbol

The [ə] or *schwa* sound occurs in syllables without an accent. It can be spelled with any vowel, such as a in above, e in listen, i in pencil, o in melon, u in circus. It can also be a combination of vowels, such as io in action, ai in mountain, iou in precious.

(Turn the page for more information.)

cruise [krōōz] *verb,* **cruised, cruising. 1.** to go by ship from place to place, especially for enjoyment. **2.** to move or ride in an easy way: "The Chief turned the loaded bus east at 110th Street and *cruised . . .* down Fifth Avenue." (J.D. Salinger) ♦ The **cruising speed** of a plane, ship, or car is the speed at which it makes the best use of fuel. —*noun, plural* **cruises.** a trip by ship taken for enjoyment.

cruis•er [krōōz/ ər] *noun, plural* **cruisers. 1.** a large warship that is faster than a battleship but has fewer guns. **2.** a motorboat with a cabin for living on board.

crumb [krumb] *noun, plural* **crumbs. 1.** a tiny piece of dry food, especially a baked food such as bread, cake, or a cracker or cookie. **2.** a very small bit or amount: Starting with just a few *crumbs* of evidence, the detective finally figured out who the killer was.

crum•ble [krum/ bəl] *verb,* **crumbled, crumbling. 1.** to break into small bits: He *crumbled* the dry bread and fed it to the birds. **2.** to fall into pieces: ♦ Often used as an adjective: Nothing is left of that ancient city but the *crumbling* ruins of a few buildings.

crunch [krunch] *verb,* **crunched, crunching.** to move with or make a noisy, crackling sound. —*noun, plural* **crunches.** the act or sound of crunching.

cru•sade [krōō sād/] *noun, plural* **crusades. 1. Crusade.** one of a series of wars fought between 1095 and 1291 by the Christians of Europe to try to capture the Holy Land where Jesus lived from the Muslims. **2.** a strong movement or fight for something good or against something bad: a *crusade* for human rights, a *crusade* against traffic accidents. —*verb,* **crusaded, crusading:** to take part in a crusade: Martin Luther King *crusaded* for civil rights for black people.

cru•sad•er [krōō sād/ ər] *noun, plural* **crusaders. 1. Crusader.** a person who took part in one of the Crusades. **2.** any person who takes part in a crusade: Ralph Nader has been a strong *crusader* for safer automobiles.

crush [krush] *verb,* **crushed, crushing. 1.** to press or squeeze something hard enough to break or harm it: "He could *crush* a beer can with one hand . . ." (Nancy Willard) **2.** to crowd or press tightly: "They were all *crushed* in the doorway as the whole school seemed to arrive at once." (Louise Fitzhugh) —*noun, plural* **crushes. 1.** the act of crushing, or the state of being crushed: There was a *crush* of people around the exit from the subway station. **2.** a strong and often foolish liking for a person, usually lasting a short time: My brother Bill has a *crush* on a beautiful movie star.

crust [krust] *noun, plural* **crusts. 1.** the hard, crisp outer part of bread, rolls, or pies. **2.** any hard outer covering or layer: a *crust* of snow. The earth's *crust* is about 5 to 25 miles deep. —*verb,* **crusted, crusting.** to cover or become covered with a crust.

crus•ta•cean [krus tā/ shən] *noun, plural* **crustaceans.** any of a large group of animals that have a hard shell and a jointed body and live mostly in water. Crustaceans include lobsters, crabs, shrimp, crayfish, and barnacles.

crustacean Many crustaceans are eaten as food, such as the blue crab that is shown here. It is found along the Atlantic coast of North America.

crutch [kruch] *noun, plural* **crutches. 1.** a support used to help a lame person walk. **2.** anything that gives help or support to some-

crusade This is another word that derives from "cross." The knights who fought in the Crusades in the period 1150 to 1400 often wore a cross painted on their armor or shields. The Crusaders were Christians who wanted to free Jerusalem from the Muslims who controlled the ancient Holy Land. Nowadays, *crusade* is used to describe a moral campaign or struggle that someone takes very seriously. The civil rights movement of the 1960's was called a *crusade.* People speak of "a *crusade* against drug use." *Crusade* can be over-used. To say, "We are *crusading* for better road repairs on Highway I-4," is to make the word trivial.

thing that is weak: For math students, a calculator can be a *crutch* that keeps them from working out problems on their own.

cry [krī] *verb,* **cried, crying. 1.** to shed tears; weep. **2.** to make a loud call; shout: "Watch out for that rock!" she *cried.* —*noun, plural* **cries. 1.** a loud call or shout. **2.** the special sound that an animal makes: "Nights were filled with the lonely *cry* of the loon." (Holling C. Holling)

crys•tal [kris′təl] *noun, plural* **crystals. 1.** a solid object with flat surfaces that form a regular pattern; *crystals* of salt or sugar. Snowflakes are *crystals.* **2.** a clear mineral that has no color and can be seen through. Crystal looks like pure ice, and is a form of QUARTZ. **3.** a very fine, clear glass used to make vases, plates, bowls, and other things.

crystal Fine crystal from the famous manufacturer Steuben Glass.

cub [kub] *noun, plural* **cubs. 1.** the young of certain animals, such as the wolf, lion, or tiger. **2.** a person who is young and inexperienced: After he got out of high school, Ernest Hemingway was a *cub* reporter for the Kansas City Star.

Cu•ba [kyoo′bə] an island country in the Caribbean Sea, south of Florida. *Capital:* Havana. *Area:* 44,218 square miles. *Population:* 10,500,000. —**Cuban,** *adjective; noun.*

cube [kyoob] *noun, plural* **cubes. 1.** a solid figure with six flat, square sides that are equal in size. **2.** something shaped like a cube: Peg fed the horse some *cubes* of sugar. **3.** the result of multiplying a number by itself twice: The *cube* of 3 is 27 because 3×3×3=27.

cu•bic [kyoo′bik] *adjective.* **1.** having the shape of a cube: Children's toy blocks are *cubic* in shape. **2.** having length, width, and thickness. ◆ A **cubic foot** is a unit of measure equal

to the volume of a cube one foot high, one foot wide, and one foot deep.

cub scout a member of the **Cub Scouts,** the junior division of the Boy Scouts.

cuck•oo [koo′koo] *noun, plural* **cuckoos.** a brown bird with a long tail whose call sounds like its name. The European cuckoo lays its eggs in the nests of other birds instead of hatching them itself.

cucumbers

cu•cum•ber [kyoo′kəm bər] *noun, plural* **cucumbers.** a long, tough-skinned green vegetable that is often used for salads or made into pickles.

cud [kud] *noun, plural* **cuds.** the partly-chewed food that cows, sheep, and certain other animals bring back into the mouth from the stomach to be chewed again for easier digestion.

cue[1] [kyoo] *noun, plural* **cues. 1.** in a play or movie, a certain speech, movement, or other signal used to tell an actor to begin to do something: When she opens the letter, that's your *cue* to walk on stage. **2.** any hint or suggestion as to what to do: For a lot of people who watch TV, when a commercial comes on it's a *cue* to change the channel. —*verb,* **cued, cuing.** to give a person a cue: When I want you to start your speech I'll *cue* you with a hand signal.

Pronunciation Key: Accent Marks

[′] is the normal accent mark. It shows where the main stress falls on a word.
[′] is a secondary accent mark. It shows a lighter stress than the primary accent. For example:

tel • e • vis • ion [tel′ ə vizh′ən]

(Turn the page for more information.)

C

C

cue² *noun, plural* **cues.** a long, thin stick used to hit a ball in the game of pool or billiards.

cuff¹ [kuf] *noun, plural* **cuffs.** a band or fold of cloth at the bottom of a shirt sleeve or pants leg. **2. off the cuff.** without preparation: That candidate often makes mistakes when he speaks *off the cuff.*

cuff² *verb,* **cuffed, cuffing.** to strike with the open hand; slap. —*noun, plural* **cuffs.** a blow with the open hand.

cui•sine [kwi zēn′] *noun, plural* **cuisines.** a style or type of cooking: French *cuisine.* "Imagine a *cuisine* offering a hundred styles of soup and 18 kinds of cheese." (Erik Eckholm)

cul•prit [kul′ prit] *noun, plural* **culprits.** someone who is guilty of a crime or of doing something wrong.

cul•ti•vate [kul′ tə vāt′] *verb,* **cultivated, cultivating. 1.** to prepare the ground for growing crops; plant and care for crops: The farmer *cultivated* the garden plot by turning over the soil and putting down fertilizer. ◆ The act of cultivating land is **cultivation. 2.** to improve or develop something through effort, as if raising a crop of plants: Alice tried to *cultivate* a friendship with her wealthy neighbor.

cul•ture [kul′ chər] *noun, plural* **cultures. 1.** all the beliefs and ways of acting that are common to a certain group of people at a certain time in history. Culture is made up of such things as the way people live, the work they do and the things they use for work, and the god or gods they believe in. **2.** the qualities found in a human society that is highly developed, such as art, science, and education: The Renaissance was a time when *culture* was at a high point in western Europe. **3.** good taste, good manners, and an appreciation for learning and the arts: a person of great *culture.* **5.** the growing of bacteria or viruses for scientific study.

cun•ning [kun′ ing] *adjective, more/most.* clever at fooling others; tricky; sly: The burglars had a *cunning* plan for robbing the store. —*noun.* cleverness at fooling others. —**cunningly,** *adverb.*

cup [kup] *noun, plural* **cups. 1.** a small open container, usually with a handle, used mainly to hold coffee, tea, soup, and other hot drinks. **2.** a unit of measure in cooking. One cup equals eight ounces of liquid or sixteen tablespoons. —*verb,* **cupped, cupping.** to make into the shape of a cup: Tom *cupped* his hands together to get a drink of water from the stream.

cup•board [kub′ ərd] *noun, plural* **cupboards.** a cabinet or closet with shelves, used for storing dishes, food, and other items.

cup•cake [kup′ kāk′] *noun, plural* **cupcakes.** a small cake baked in a cup-shaped pan.

curb [kurb] *noun, plural* **curbs. 1.** the raised concrete edge along the side of a street: He parked his car close to the *curb.* **2.** something that holds back or restrains: That senator wants to put a *curb* on government spending for military weapons. —*verb,* **curbed, curbing.** to hold back or control something: Many people believe drinking grapefruit juice *curbs* your appetite and helps you lose weight.

curd•le [kurd′ əl] *verb,* **curdled, curdling. 1.** of milk, to form into a thick substance called **curds.** Curds separate from the thin, watery part of milk (the WHEY) when it turns sour. **2.** to make or become very thick: The sauce *curdled* when the pan got too hot.

cure [kyōōr] *verb,* **cured, curing. 1.** to bring or come back to health, especially by the use of medical treatment: The doctor *cured* her rash with a new kind of skin cream. **2.** to get rid of something that is thought to be like a sickness: I've finally *cured* myself of the habit of biting my nails. **3.** to preserve or treat something by drying, smoking or salting: Meat or fish can be *cured* by drying them in the sun. —*noun, plural* **cures.** something that cures: At this time there is no *cure* for the common cold.

cur•few [kur′ fyōō] *noun, plural* **curfews. 1.** a rule or law saying that people have to be off the streets by a fixed time of night. **2.** any rule that something must end by a certain time of night: The players on the football team have a 10:00 *curfew* the night before a game.

curfew *Curfew* comes from a French expression meaning "cover the fire." In the Middle Ages, a bell would ring at a certain hour every night. The bell was a signal to the people of the town to cover (with metal grates), or put out, their fires for the evening. This was done so that fires would not, once started, spread in the middle of the night while people slept. Now people say things like, "The airport has a midnight *curfew:* no planes can land or take off after twelve." This is an extended meaning of the word. It's far from the idea of "covering a fire," but it still keeps to the basic sense of an evening deadline. Look up *deadline.*

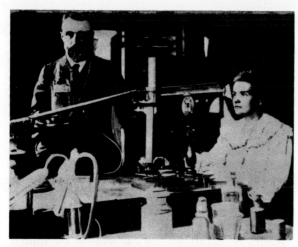

Curies Marie Curie and her husband Pierre at work in their laboratory in France. Marie Curie is the only person to win two separate Nobel Prizes in science.

Cu•rie [kyŏŏr′ ē] **Marie,** 1867–1934, French chemist, born in Poland.

cu•ri•os•i•ty [kyŏŏr′ ē äs′ ə tē] *noun, plural* **curiosities. 1.** a strong interest in finding out about different things and people: "He had the *curiosity* to open the door and listen, and look after them." (Charles Dickens) **2.** something that is very strange, rare, or unusual: The "Spruce Goose" was the largest plane ever built, but it flew only once and is now just a *curiosity.*

cu•ri•ous [kyŏŏr′ ē əs] *adjective, more/most.* **1.** very interested in finding out about things and people: " 'How was it down there?' asked Mr. Little, who was always *curious* to know about places he had never been to." (E.B. White) **2.** wanting to know about things that are not one's proper concern; nosy. **3.** very strange, rare, or unusual: "Many *curious* metal objects caught the faint light and winked and glared from the walls like shining teeth." (James Houston) —**curiously,** *adverb.* in a curious way: *Curiously* enough, Thomas Jefferson and John Adams both died on July 4, 1826, fifty years to the day after the U.S. was founded.

curl [kurl] *verb,* **curled, curling. 1.** to form into coils or rings: to *curl* one's hair. **2.** *also,* **curl up.** to move or be in a curved shape: "He looked as if he might *curl up* and go to sleep any minute." (Walter R. Brooks) —*noun, plural* **curls.** anything that forms a curl. —**curly,** *adjective: curly* hair. ♦ A **curler** is a device used to make the hair curly.

cur•rant [kur′ ənt] *noun, plural* **currants.** a small red or black sour-tasting berry that grows in bunches on a prickly bush. Currants are usually dried and are used in cooking and in making jelly.

cur•ren•cy [kur′ ən sē] *noun, plural* **currencies.** the form of money that a country uses: U.S. *currency* is based on the dollar.

cur•rent [kur′ ənt] *adjective, more/most.* belonging to the present time: *Current* events are the things that are going on now. I can't send her a Christmas card because I don't have her *current* address. —*noun, plural* **currents. 1.** a flow of moving gas or liquid; a stream: a *current* of air. The twigs floated with the *current* of the river. **2.** a flow of electricity through a wire or other object: The thicker a wire, the more *current* it can carry. **3.** a general trend: The *current* of public opinion seems to support the President's decision. —**currently,** *adverb.* at this time; now: There are *currently* about 50,000 people living in our town.

current usage Dictionaries say that their comments about language are based on "current usage." What does this mean? "Current usage" is the language that people use at the present time, but the situation is tricky. Just because a form is common doesn't make it part of current usage—this dictionary doesn't include "lite" or "thru," even though they are used all the time. Current usage is based on this rule or definition: It is the language that educated people accept as correct at the present time. How can we know what words are accepted currently? By use of a computer, we created the HBJ Word Survey—a study of millions of words from current books, magazines, and newspapers.

cur•ric•u•lum [kə rik′ yə ləm] *noun, plural* **curriculums.** all the subjects that are offered in a school as a course of study: An elementary school *curriculum* includes reading, English, spelling, math, science, and social studies.

Pronunciation Key: A–F

a	and; hat	ch	chew; such
ā	ate; stay	d	dog; lid
â	care; air	e	end; yet
ä	father; hat	ē	she; each
b	boy; cab	f	fun; off

(Turn the page for more information.)

C

curse [kurs] *noun, plural* **curses. 1.** a wish that evil or harm will happen to someone, often made by calling on God or a spirit: In old fairy tales, a wicked witch would sometimes put a *curse* on people to make them sleep for a long time or to turn them into animals. **2.** trouble or evil that happens to someone, as if from a curse: War is a *curse* of mankind. **3.** a word or words used in swearing; language that is considered very rude to use. —*verb,* **cursed, cursing. 1.** to call for a curse on someone or something: That famous diamond is said to be *cursed* because so many people who have owned it have had terrible bad luck. **2.** to use bad language; swear. **3.** to cause or be caused harm by a curse: She is *cursed* with a bad back that aches all the time.

cur•sor [kur′sər] *noun, plural* **cursors.** a marker on a computer screen that shows the place on the screen where the person is working. A cursor may be a small line, a spot of light, or an arrow or other shape.

cur•tain [kur′tən] *noun, plural* **curtains. 1.** a large piece of fabric hung across a room or over a window. **2.** a large hanging cloth or screen that separates the stage of a theater from the audience. **3.** anything that covers or hides something as a curtain does: A thick *curtain* of fog hung over the valley. —*verb,* **curtained, curtaining.** to provide with a curtain: In a hospital room each patient's bed usually can be *curtained* off from the rest of the room.

curtsy A little girl gives a curtsy as she presents a gift to Queen Elizabeth of Great Britain.

curt•sy [kurt′sē] *noun, plural* **curtsies.** for a woman or girl, a way of bending the body to show respect, as to a king or queen.

—*verb,* **curtsied, curtsying.** to make a curtsy. Men and boys bow instead of doing this.

curve [kurv] *noun, plural* **curves. 1.** a line that bends smoothly in one direction: the *curve* of a rainbow, the *curve* of the earth. **2.** anything that is shaped like a curve; a round or bending part: He slowed the car when he came to a *curve* in the road. **3.** *also,* **curveball.** a pitch in baseball that moves to the side, from right to left if the pitcher is righthanded. —*verb,* **curved, curving.** to move in or have the shape of a curve: A long driveway *curves* around in front of the house.

cush•ion [kush′ən] *noun, plural* **cushions. 1.** a pillow filled with a soft material and used for sitting, lying, or resting. **2.** something that is like a cushion: A Hovercraft is a vehicle that travels over water on a *cushion* of air. —*verb,* **cushioned, cushioning. 1.** to supply with a cushion. **2.** to soften or reduce a shock, as a cushion would: The soft snow *cushioned* the skier's fall. The company gave him six months' extra pay to *cushion* the blow of being fired.

cus•tard [kus′tərd] *noun, plural* **custards.** a sweet dessert made of milk, eggs, and sugar.

Cus•ter [kus′tər] **George Armstrong,** 1839–1876, American general, killed along with all his troops by Indians at the Battle of Little Bighorn.

cus•to•di•an [kəs tō′dē ən] *noun, plural* **custodians. 1.** a person who takes care of someone or something: She is the *custodian* of the sculpture collection at the art museum. **2.** a person who takes care of a public building; a janitor.

cus•to•dy [kus′tə dē] *noun, plural* **custodies.** the condition of being under the care of something or someone in authority: The police held the suspected bank robbers in *custody.*

cus•tom [kus′təm] *noun, plural* **customs. 1.** the way things are normally done by people in general; a usual way of acting that goes on over the years: It is a *custom* in the U.S. to eat turkey on Thanksgiving Day. **2.** one person's usual way of acting; a habit: "It was his *custom* after dinner to take a walk." (James Thurber) **3. customs.** a tax paid on goods brought into a country from somewhere else, or the office that inspects these goods and collects the tax. —*adjective.* made in a special way for one person: a *custom* home, *custom* clothes.

cus•tom•ar•y [kus′tə mer′ē] *adjective, more/ most.* what is commonly or usually done; based on custom: It is *customary* to give presents on someone's birthday. —**customarily,** *adverb:* That door is *customarily* kept locked.

cus·tom·er [kus′ tə mər] *noun, plural* **customers.** someone who buys something or uses some service, especially a person who buys something at a store.

cut [kut] *verb,* **cut, cutting. 1.** to make an opening in something with a sharp tool or edge: to *cut* wood, to *cut* a cake, to *cut* a hole in a wall. **2.** to have or get an injury from something sharp: She *cut* her finger on the broken glass. **3.** to move or go as if by cutting: The cold wind *cut* through her thin jacket. He *cut* across the field on his way home from school. **4.** to make something shorter or smaller, by or as if by cutting: to *cut* one's hair or fingernails. Several scenes were *cut* from that movie when it was shown on TV. —*noun, plural* **cuts. 1.** something that is cut or that comes from cutting: He got a *cut* on his foot when he stepped on the broken glass. Prime rib is an expensive *cut* of beef. **2.** the act of taking away or making smaller: a *cut* in taxes or in pay.

cut off 1. to separate by cutting, or as if by cutting: to *cut off* a branch from a tree. The mountain town was *cut off* by a snowstorm. **2.** to disconnect: I was just talking to Ed on the phone, but we were *cut off.*

cute [kyo͞ot] *adjective,* **cuter, cutest.** pretty and charming; pleasing to the eye or mind: a *cute* baby. The little girl wore a *cute* new dress. ♦ **Cute** is usually used for something that is attractive in a light or delicate way, as opposed to something large, important, or serious.

cut·ter [kut′ ər] *noun, plural* **cutters. 1.** a person who cuts, especially someone whose job is cutting things: a diamond *cutter.* **2.** a tool that cuts out shapes: a cookie *cutter.* **3.** a small, fast boat, especially an armed boat used by the Coast Guard.

cut·ting [kut′ ing] *noun, plural* **cuttings. 1.** a piece cut off something. the art project. **2.** a stem or twig cut from a plant and able to grow roots and develop into a new plant. —*adjective.* **1.** sharp and able to cut: the *cutting* edge of a knife. **2.** hurting another's feelings; insulting: a *cutting* remark.

cy·cle [sī′ kəl] *noun, plural* **cycles. 1.** something that happens regularly in the same order over and over again: The four seasons of the year are a *cycle.* **2.** a series of acts making one complete operation: A washing machine *cycle* includes soaking, washing, rinsing, and spinning. **3.** a short word for BICYCLE, MOTORCYCLE, TRICYCLE, and so on. —*verb,* **cycled, cycling.** to ride a bicycle, motorcycle, and so on.

cy·clone [sī′ klōn′] *noun, plural* **cyclones. 1.** a violent windstorm; a tornado. **2.** a storm in which winds move rapidly in a circle around a center of low air pressure, which also moves.

cyl·in·der [sil′ ən dər] *noun, plural* **cylinders. 1.** a hollow shape like that of a pipe or tube. **2.** something having this shape. —**cylindrical,** *adjective:* Tennis balls come in *cylindrical cans.*

cym·bal [sim′ bəl] *noun, plural* **cymbals.** a musical instrument that is a round metal plate, played by being struck together with another cymbal or hit with a drumstick.

cyn·i·cal [sin′ i kəl] *adjective, more/most.* believing that people always act in a selfish way and that there is little good in the world: When a woman gave a million dollars to build a new hospital, Dick made the *cynical* remark that she only did it to get her name on the building. ♦ A person who has this attitude is a **cynic.**

cypress The famous Monterey Cypress tree on the coast of California is a favorite subject for both photographers and painters, because of its unusual twisted shape.

cy·press [sī′ prəs] *noun, plural* **cypresses.** an evergreen tree that has dark, scale-like leaves, hard reddish wood, and small cones.

czar [zär] *noun, plural* **czars.** the title of the emperors who ruled Russia until the Soviet revolution of 1917.

Czech·o·slo·va·ki·a [chek′ ə slə väk′ ē ə] a country in east-central Europe. *Capital:* Prague. *Area:* 49,373 square miles. *Population:* 15,600,000. —**Czechoslovakian,** *adjective; noun.*

C

Pronunciation Key: G–N

g	give; big	k	kind; cat; back
h	hold	l	let; ball
i	it; this	m	make; time
ī	ice; my	n	not; own
j	jet; gem; edge	ng	having

(Turn the page for more information.)

Dd

d,D [dē] *noun, plural* **d's, D's. 1.** the fourth letter of the alphabet. **2.** the fourth highest grade or level.

dab [dab] *verb,* **dabbed, dabbing.** to touch in a light or gentle way: "She *dabbed* at her eyes with a tiny handkerchief." (Theodore Dreiser) —*noun, plural* **dabs.** a light or gentle touch.

dab·ble [dab′əl] *verb,* **dabbled, dabbling. 1.** to splash in or out of water: The boys *dabbled* their feet in the water. **2.** to do or work at something a little, but not in a serious way: Jim likes to *dabble* at writing poetry, but he's never tried to get anything published.

dachs·hund [däks′hoond′] *noun, plural* **dachshunds.** a small dog with a long body, very short legs, and drooping ears.

dad [dad] *noun, plural* **dads.** father. Children often call their father Dad or Daddy.

daffodil A famous poem by William Wordsworth says, "I saw a crowd, a host, of golden daffodils."

daf·fo·dil [daf′ə dil′] *noun, plural* **daffodils.** a plant that has long, thin leaves and yellow or white flowers. Daffodils grow from bulbs and bloom in the spring.

dag·ger [dag′ər] *noun, plural* **daggers.** a small knife with a short pointed blade, used in former times as a weapon.

dai·ly [dā′lē] *adjective.* done, happening, or appearing every day: a *daily* flight from New York to Chicago. Grandpa likes to take a *daily* morning walk around the park. —*adverb.* day after day; every day: Please water the grass *daily* while we're away. —*noun, plural* **dailies.** a newspaper that is printed every day.

dain·ty [dān′tē] *adjective,* **daintier, daintiest.** pretty or graceful in a light, delicate way: The ballet dancer took small, *dainty* steps. "She was a *dainty* little figure, with a white neck . . . and a slender waist." (Nathaniel Hawthorne) —**daintily,** *adverb:* "She was peeling a fig *daintily* with a knife." (Pearl Buck)

dair·y [dâr′ē] *noun, plural* **dairies. 1.** a place where milk and cream are made into butter and cheese, or where milk products are sold. **2.** a farm where cows are kept for milk and milk products.

dai·sy [dā′zē] *noun, plural* **daisies.** a plant that has a flower of white, pink, or yellow petals around a yellow center.

Dal·las [dal′əs] the second-largest city in Texas, in the northeastern part of the state. *Population:* 905,000.

dam [dam] *noun, plural* **dams.** a wall built across a river or creek to hold back the flow of water. —*verb,* **dammed, damming.** (usually used with **up**) to build a dam across; hold back by a dam: Beavers often *dam up* a stream to form a pond.

dam·age [dam′ij] *noun, plural* **damages.** harm or injury that makes something less valuable or useful: The *damage* to crops from the heavy rainstorm cost the local farmers a lot of money. —*verb,* **damaged, damaging.** to harm or injure; hurt: The accident *damaged* the front of the car. He *damaged* his reputation as an actor by quitting the play just before opening night.

Da•mas•cus [də mas′ kəs] the capital of Syria. It is one of the oldest cities in the world. *Population:* 1,200,000.

damp [damp] *adjective,* **damper, dampest.** a little wet; moist: "It was a gray day, without sun, and there was a *damp* feeling of coming rain in the air." (Andre Norton) —*noun.* a slight wetness; moisture: the *damp* of a spring evening at the seashore. —**dampness,** *noun.*

dan•ger•ous [dān′ jər əs] *adjective, more/most.* full of or causing danger: That is a *dangerous* road because there are so many sharp curves. "'I've always thought,' said Rainsford, 'that the Cape Buffalo is the most *dangerous* of all big game.'" (Richard Connell)

dan•gle [dang′ gəl] *verb,* **dangled, dangling.** to hang or swing loosely: The night watchman carried a bunch of keys *dangling* from a chain.

dangling phrases Think for a moment of this. you are about to enter an automobile and someone says, "Since it is Tuesday, you might want to telephone first." What does Tuesday have to do with the car or with telephoning? Here's another instance. "Leaving the city, the lights were spread out below us like a blanket." Who was leaving the city? It sounds as if "the lights" were. In both sentences there are dangling phrases, that is, parts of a statement that seem wrongly attached to the main message. To improve the first sentence, "Since it is Tuesday you might telephone the library to make sure it's open before you leave." In the second, try this: "Leaving the city, we saw the lights spread out below us . . ." Or you could even change the sentence: "As we left the city, the lights were spread out below us. . . ." Do you see why "dangling" is a good word here? Most dangling phrases are participles, verbs with "ing" endings.

damp•en [dam′ pən] *verb,* **dampened, dampening. 1.** to make or become damp: She *damp-ened* the cloth and wiped off the table. **2.** to make less happy or pleasant: "He's never out to *dampen* your spirits or to hurt you." (Alice Walker)

dance [dans] *verb,* **danced, dancing. 1.** to move the body in a certain pattern of steps or movements in time to music. ♦ A person who dances is called a **dancer. 2.** to move in a quick or lively way: ". . . masses of wild flowers, all *dancing* in the spring breeze." (Walter Farley) —*noun, plural* **dances. 1.** a particular set of steps or movements in time to music: The waltz is a famous *dance* that began in Europe in the 1700's. **2.** a party where people dance: I'm going to the school *dance* this Friday.

dan•de•li•on [dan′ də lī′ ən] *noun, plural* **dan-delions.** a plant with a bright yellow flower and long leaves with ragged edges. Dandelion leaves are sometimes eaten in salads.

dan•druff [dan′ drəf] *noun.* small pieces of dry skin that form on the scalp and flake off.

dan•ger [dān′ jər] *noun, plural* **dangers. 1.** a chance that something bad or harmful will happen: The highway was closed because of the *danger* from the brush fire nearby. "In a bullfight . . . there is always *danger,* and there is always death." (Ernest Hemingway) **2.** something that can cause danger: The school nurse showed a film on the *dangers* of smoking.

Dan•te [dän′ tā] 1265–1321, Italian poet, the author of *The Divine Comedy.*

dandelion The word *dandelion* comes from French, *dent de lion* (tooth of the lion). The leaves were thought to look like teeth.

Pronunciation Key: A–F			
a	and; hat	ch	chew; such
ā	ate; stay	d	dog; lid
â	care; air	e	end; yet
ä	father; hat	ē	she; each
b	boy; cab	f	fun; off

(Turn the page for more information.)

D

Dan•ube [dan′yo̅o̅b] the second-longest river in Europe. It flows from West Germany to the Black Sea.

dare [dâr] *verb,* **dared, daring. 1.** to challenge a person to do something difficult or dangerous: Jason *dared* his sister Stacey to climb to the top of the tree. **2.** to be brave enough to do something. ♦ Often used with another verb: "She could not stay there, but *dared* she try to go on?" (Andre Norton) **3.** to be bold or rude enough to do something: "How *dare* you ask the little Kelveys into the courtyard? You know . . . you're not allowed to talk to them." (Katherine Mansfield) —*noun, plural* **dares.** a challenge.

dar•ing [dâr′ing] *adjective, more/most.* willing to take chances; having courage: Charles Lindbergh was a *daring* pilot. —*noun.* courage; bravery: The defenders of the Alamo are remembered for their *daring.*

dark [därk] *adjective,* **darker, darkest. 1.** having little or no light: a *dark* night, a *dark* room. **2.** not light in color; almost black: *dark* hair, a *dark* suit of clothes. **3.** sad or gloomy: "He has a *dark* future—he hates everything." (F. Scott Fitzgerald) —*noun.* **1.** a lack of light; darkness: Little children are sometimes afraid of sleeping in the *dark.* **2.** night; nighttime: Billy's mother told him to be home before *dark.* **3. in the dark.** without knowing; not aware: The press was kept *in the dark* about whether the mayor was planning to run again. —**darkness,** *noun.*

dark•en [där′kən] *verb,* **darkened, darkening.** to make or become dark: The sky *darkened* and it began to rain.

dar•ling [där′ling] *noun, plural* **darlings.** a person who is loved very much. —*adjective, more/most.* **1.** very much loved: The birthday card said "To my *darling* wife." **2.** cute or charming: What a *darling* hat that is!

darn [därn] *verb,* **darned, darning.** to sew up a hole in a piece of clothing: He *darned* an old sock that was worn out at the heel.

dart [därt] *noun, plural* **darts.** a thin, pointed weapon that looks like a small arrow. **Darts** is an indoor game in which darts are thrown at a target on the wall. —*verb,* **darted, darting.** to make a quick, sudden movement: "From the cliff I could see canoes *darting* here and there." (Scott O'Dell)

Dar•win [där′win] **Charles,** 1809–1882, English scientist who developed the theory of EVOLUTION.

> **dashes** A dash is used to show a sudden break in the middle of a sentence, as if one thought interrupts another: "Hicksey showed me—in fact, he showed us all." (James Gould Cozzens) A dash is also used to show where a speaker suddenly stops or is interrupted: "'Mr. Weinstein'—'Call me Allen!' he said sharply." (Joyce Carol Oates) Writers may use a pair of dashes to set off a part in the middle of a sentence: "Old Misery —whose real name was Thomas—had once been a builder and decorator." (Graham Greene) "She kind of liked snakes—except cottonmouths and rattlers—because she found them funny." (Jean Stafford) Remember, though, that a dash is a strong form of punctuation. Use it only when you want to show a major break in the sentence.

dash [dash] *verb,* **dashed, dashing. 1.** to move quickly; rush: The people at the park *dashed* for their cars when the thunderstorm started. **2.** to move or throw with great force; smash: "The breaking waves *dashed* high on the rock-bound coast." (Felicia Hemans) **3. dash off.** to do or finish something very quickly: "He *dashed off* the list of calls each morning with such speed . . ." (James Herriot) —*noun, plural* **dashes. 1.** a short, fast race: a forty-yard *dash.* **2.** any sudden, quick movement: "The door was open. He could make a *dash* for it down the hall." (Langston Hughes) **3.** a small amount: John put a *dash* of pepper sauce into the soup. **4.** a punctuation mark like this [—]. A dash is used to show that part of a word has been left out (May 5th, 19—) or to show a break in a sentence: "Undoubtedly it was colder than fifty below—how much colder he did not know." (Jack London)

dash•board [dash′bôrd′] *noun, plural* **dashboards.** a panel in an automobile directly in front of the driver. The dashboard has certain controls for the car and dials that give the driver information such as how fast the car is going and how much gas, oil, and water it has.

dash•ing [dash′ing] *adjective, more/most.* having a lot of energy and style: The actor played a *dashing* young navy officer.

da•ta [dat′ə *or* dā′tə] *noun.* **1.** things that are known; facts or figures; information: The U.S. Census provides a large amount of *data* about the American people. **2.** any information that is contained in a computer: "*Data* (is) anything that goes into a computer, everything stored in a computer's memory, and anything that comes out." (Peter McWilliams)

data base a large collection of information stored in a computer; also called a **data bank.**

date•line [dāt′līn] *noun, plural* **datelines. 1.** a line at the beginning of a newspaper article that tells where the article was written. **2.** *also,* **date line.** an imaginary line running north and south through the Pacific Ocean. East of the line, it is one day earlier than it is west of the line.

---

data The word *data* comes from Latin, where it is a plural word—the singular form in Latin is *datum.* Because of this, writers before the 1950's tended to use it as a plural in English also: "These *data* refer only to operating units . . ." (Robert & Helen Lynd) The singular form is more common today: "There are blank spaces where the actual *data* is to be input." (Personal Computing Magazine) "The *data* is, literally, what is given." (Cleanth Brooks) Whether you use *data* as plural or singular, don't overuse it. "Information" or "facts" "descriptions" or "statements" might be the word you want instead of *data.*

---

date[1] [dāt] *noun, plural* **dates. 1.** the certain time when something happens or will happen, shown by the day, month, or year: Please be sure to write the *date* on your letter. The *date* of Abraham Lincoln's birth was February 12, 1809. **2.** an appointment to meet someone or be somewhere: They made a *date* to go to the movies on Saturday night. **3.** someone of the opposite sex with whom one has a date. —*verb,* **dated, dating. 1.** to mark with a date: This old coin is *dated* 1873. He signed the check, but he forgot to *date* it. **2.** to assign a date to; show the age of: The celebration of Mother's Day *dates* from the early 1900's. **3.** to have a date with someone.

date[2] *noun, plural* **dates.** the sweet, brownish fruit of the **date palm** tree. Dates have been an important food in the Middle East for thousands of years.

daugh•ter [dôt′ər] *noun, plural* **daughters. 1.** a person's female child. **2.** a female thought of as being related to something: The "*Daughters* of the American Revolution" are women whose ancestors fought in the Revolutionary War.

daugh•ter-in-law [dôt′ər ən lô′] *noun, plural* **daughters-in-law.** the wife of a person's son.

Dav•is [dā′vis] **Jefferson,** 1808–1889, the president of the Confederate States of America during the Civil War.

dawn Dawn breaks over a misty valley in the farming area of central California.

dawn [dôn] *noun, plural* **dawns. 1.** the time when the day begins; the first light of day. **2.** the

date palm The date palm tree with a close-up of the fruit. The pit is seen in the cut-away view of the dried fruit.

Pronunciation Key: G–N

g	give; big	k	kind; cat; back
h	hold	l	let; ball
i	it; this	m	make; time
ī	ice; my	n	not; own
j	jet; gem; edge	ng	having

(Turn the page for more information.)

beginning of something: The launching of Sputnik in 1957 was the *dawn* of the Space Age. —*verb*, **dawned, dawning. 1.** to begin to be day; grow light: "A lovely Sunday morning *dawned* without a cloud." (Louisa May Alcott) **2.** to begin to be clear to the mind: It suddenly *dawned* on the general that there was an enemy spy among his men.

◆ Often used as an adjective: "A light flashed on . . . a *dazzling* circle, shining straight in their eyes." (Mary Norton) **2.** to amaze or surprise: "The horses . . . were all of a *dazzling* and powerful beauty." (Walter Farley)

D.C. 1. an abbreviation for DISTRICT OF COLUMBIA. **2.** *also,* **DC.** an abbreviation for DIRECT CURRENT.

---

dead Death is primarily a biological term: an animal or human being dies, ceases to function forever. But death is used as a metaphor very often. "After the third quarter of the football game, our passing attack *died.*" "The deal is *dead.* The buyer won't make another offer." "Why argue about a *dead* issue?" "It's like beating a *dead* horse." The adverb is also used for other than biological purposes. "His humor was *deadly.* Everyone got speared by his sharp, witty remarks." Of course you could also use the word literally: "The canned food was *deadly* for the six people who ate it."

---

day [dā] *noun, plural* **days. 1.** the time when the sun is out; the opposite of night: The shortest *day* of the year is in December. **2.** one period of 24 hours; the time from one midnight to the next: April has 30 *days.* **3.** a special day: Thanksgiving *Day,* St. Patrick's *Day.* **4.** the part of the day spent working: She works a seven-hour *day* and a five-*day* week. **5.** a time in history; age: In Shakespeare's *day* many people believed in ghosts and witches.

day•break [dā′brāk′] *noun, plural* **daybreaks.** the beginning of the day; dawn.

day-care center [dā′ kâr′] a place that takes care of young children during the daytime.

day•dream [dā′drēm′] *noun, plural* **daydreams.** pleasant thinking or wishing about things one would like to do or have happen. —*verb,* **daydreamed, daydreaming.** to have a daydream: Stan didn't hear what his boss said; he was *daydreaming* about going fishing.

day•light [dā′līt′] *noun.* **1.** the light of day; light from the sun. **2.** the dawn; daybreak.

daylight-saving time the time when clocks are set one hour ahead of STANDARD TIME to give extra daylight in the evening. It begins in late spring and lasts until early fall.

day•time [dā′tīm′] *noun.* the time when it is day and not night.

daze [dāz] *verb,* **dazed, dazing.** to make unable to think clearly, as from a blow on the head; confuse or stun: "He sat down again, *dazed,* trying to remember just what it was she had said." (Pearl Buck) —*noun, plural* **dazes.** a confused or stunned condition.

daz•zle [daz′ əl] *verb,* **dazzled, dazzling. 1.** to make blind or almost blind with too much light.

dead [ded] *adjective,* **deader, deadest. 1.** not alive; no longer having life: The flowers are *dead* because I forgot to water them. **2.** never having had life: Rocks are *dead* objects. Most scientists believe that Mars is a *dead* planet. **3.** without feeling, activity, or energy: We couldn't call home because the phone was *dead.* Latin is a *dead* language. **4.** complete or absolute, like death: There was *dead* silence in the room. The arrow hit the target *dead* center. —*noun.* **1.** people who are no longer living: ". . . these *dead* shall not have died in vain." (Abraham Lincoln) **2.** the darkest, coldest, or most quiet part: the *dead* of night, the *dead* of winter. —*adverb.* **1.** completely: to stop *dead,* to be *dead* wrong about something. **2.** directly: The sailors saw an island *dead* ahead of them.

dead•en [ded′ən] *verb,* **deadened, deadening.** to make dull or weak: "The cold *deadened* all sound." (John Cheever)

dead end 1. a street or passageway that has no way out at the other end. **2.** a situation or course of action that does not lead on to something further. ◆ Also used as an adjective: She'll never get anywhere in her career if she doesn't get out of that *dead-end* job.

dead•line [ded′līn′] *noun, plural* **deadlines.** a set time by which something must be done or finished: Friday is the *deadline* for turning in our book reports.

dead•ly [ded′lē] *adjective,* **deadlier, deadliest. 1.** causing or able to cause death; fatal: A gun is a *deadly* weapon. **2.** intending to kill or destroy: *deadly* enemies, a *deadly* fight.

Dead Sea a salt lake on the border between Israel and Jordan. It is the lowest point on earth.

Death Valley Death Valley was once the site of a large lake; now it receives less than two inches of rain per year. The hottest temperature in the history of North America was recorded here, 134°F.

deaf [def] *adjective,* **deafer, deafest. 1.** not able to hear or to hear well. ♦ The condition of being deaf is **deafness. 2.** not willing to listen or pay attention: The king was *deaf* to the people's protests.

deaf•en [def′ ən] *verb,* **deafened, deafening:** to make someone deaf: The loud blast *deafened* him for a short time. ♦ Often used as an adjective: a *deafening* roar.

deal [dēl] *verb,* **dealt, dealing. 1.** to have to do with; be about: That book *deals* with John F. Kennedy's time as President. **2.** to act or behave toward others in a certain way: Mrs. Jones *deals* fairly with all of the students in her class. **3.** to buy and sell things; do business: My uncle's store *deals* in antique furniture. **4.** to give out or distribute: It's Harry's turn to *deal* the cards. —*noun, plural* **deals. 1.** a bargain or agreement: Sam made a *deal* to buy the used car. **2. a good deal** or **a great deal.** a large amount; a lot: "He also learned *a great deal* by using his own eyes and ears." (C.S. Lewis)

deal•er [dē′ lər] *noun, plural* **dealers. 1.** a person who buys and sells things to make a living: an automobile *dealer.* **2.** a person who deals the cards in a card game.

dealt [delt] the past form of **deal.**

dear [dēr] *adjective,* **dearer, dearest. 1.** much loved; beloved: My sister is very *dear* to me. **2.** highly regarded: "*Dear* Sir" is a polite way to begin a letter. —*noun, plural* **dears.** a person who is loved. —*interjection.* an expression of surprise or trouble: Oh *dear!* I must have left my wallet in the store! —**dearly,** *adverb:* "Dorothy played with Toto, and loved him *dearly.*" (L. Frank Baum)

death [deth] *noun, plural* **deaths. 1.** the end of life in people, animals, or plants. **2.** something thought of as like death; the destroying of something: Competition from television brought about the *death* of radio soap operas.

Death Valley a desert valley in eastern California. It contains the lowest point in the Western Hemisphere (282 feet below sea level).

de•bate [di bāt′] *noun, plural* **debates. 1.** a discussion or argument about the reasons for and against something: The school board had a *debate* about whether or not to close Oak Hill School. **2.** a contest in which two sides formally argue for and against a question. —*verb,* **debated, debating. 1.** to argue or discuss some issue: The Senate *debated* about changing the income tax system. **2.** to think about; consider: Suzie is *debating* about going to camp this summer. —**debater,** *noun.*

debate The first Presidential debate in 1960 between John Kennedy (left) and Richard Nixon (right). Many people felt that Kennedy won the election largely because of his performance in this debate.

de•bris [də brē′] *noun.* scattered pieces or remains from something that has been broken or destroyed; ruins or rubble.

debt [det] *noun, plural* **debts. 1.** money that is owed by one person or business to another. **2.** anything that is due to one person from another: We owe the fire department a *debt* of thanks for saving our house from burning. **3.**

Pronunciation Key: O–S			
ō	over; go	ou	out; town
ô	all; law	p	put; hop
oo	look; full	r	run; car
o͞o	pool; who	s	set; miss
oi	oil; boy	sh	show

(Turn the page for more information.)

D

the state of owing money. ♦ Usually used in the phrases **in debt** and **out of debt.** Someone who owes a debt is a **debtor.**

de•but [də byōō′ or dā′ byōō′] *noun, plural* **debuts. 1.** the first public appearance of an actor or singer, or the first performance of a show or movie: Jane Fonda's movie *debut* was in *Tall Story* in 1960. **2.** any first appearance or attempt: Japanese cars made their *debut* in the U.S. in the early 1950's. **3.** a formal party given to introduce a young lady into society.

dec•ade [dek′ād′] *noun, plural* **decades.** a period of ten years.

de•cal [dē′ kal *or* di kal′] *noun, plural* **decals.** a design or picture transferred from specially-prepared paper to glass, wood, and other surfaces. Decals are put on car windows, model planes, children's riding toys, and so on.

de•cay [di kā′] *noun.* **1.** the slow rotting of animal or plant matter: I brush after each meal to avoid tooth *decay.* **2.** a gradual decline into a poor or weak condition: Turkey's Ottoman Empire went through a long period of *decay* before it finally was dissolved after World War One. —*verb,* **decayed, decaying.** to suffer from decay; rot or cause to have rot.

de•ceased [di sēst′] *adjective.* dead; no longer living: The relatives of the *deceased* woman gathered at her funeral. —**the deceased,** *noun.*

de•ceit [di sēt′] *noun, plural* **deceits.** something that deceives; a dishonest action: The government sometimes checks TV commercials to make sure they are free of *deceit.* ♦ A person who uses deceit is **deceitful:** The *deceitful* salesman told them the car was in good condition even though he knew it needed lots of repairs.

de•cen•cy [dē′ sən sē] *noun.* the quality of being decent.

de•cent [dē′ sənt] *adjective, more/most.* **1.** accepted by people as meeting the standards of good taste; proper and respectable: *decent* behavior. It's not *decent* to make fun of someone who is handicapped. **2.** fairly good; satisfying: She always tries to eat a *decent* meal for breakfast. He's been looking for weeks, but he still can't find a *decent* after-school job. —**decently,** *adverb.*

de•cep•tion [di sep′ shən] *noun, plural* **deceptions.** the act of deceiving, or something that deceives.

de•cep•tive [di sep′ tiv] *adjective, more/most.* **1.** likely to deceive; not honest: The *deceptive* advertisement said the motel was right on the ocean when it was actually two miles inland. **2.** giving a false idea or impression; misleading: That house is *deceptive;* it looks small from the outside, but it's actually got plenty of room. —**deceptively,** *adverb.* —**deceptiveness,** *noun.*

dec•i•bel [des′ ə bəl] *noun, plural* **decibels.** a unit for measuring how loud a certain sound is. Ordinary conversation in a room is usually about 50 decibels.

de•cide [di sīd′] *verb,* **decided, deciding. 1.** to make up one's mind: He *decided* to wear his blue suit rather than the gray one. **2.** to judge or settle a question or argument: The jury *decided* in favor of the accused man and he was set free.

de•cid•ed [di sī′ did] *adjective, more/most.* definite or certain; sure: Many people believe that children who go to preschool have a *decided* advantage when they get to first grade. —**decidedly,** *adverb.*

---

deceive Two sets of words have grown up from the root word *deceive.* The two groups are *deceit, deceitful, deceitfully* and *deception, deceptive, deceptively.* Since a root word usually doesn't develop two separate forms in this way, is there a difference between the two? Yes. *Deceit* and *deceitful* are always negative and always indicate dishonesty. (J. Edgar Hoover, the former FBI director, wrote a book on spies in America called *Masters of Deceit.*) However, *deception* and *deceptive* could be dishonest, but they can also suggest fooling people in a way that is not harmful. We can speak of a pitcher with a *deceptive* throwing motion, or the way certain animals have *deceptive* body markings to hide them from larger animals.

---

de•ceive [di sēv′] *verb,* **deceived, deceiving.** to make someone believe something that is not true; fool or mislead: Desert mirages *deceive* people into thinking they are seeing water that actually isn't there.

De•cem•ber [di sem′ bər] *noun, plural* **Decembers.** the twelfth and last month of the year. December has 31 days.

de•cid•u•ous [di sij′ ōō əs] *adjective.* shedding its leaves every year: The maple is a *deciduous* tree.

dec•i•mal [des′ məl *or* des′ ə məl] *adjective.* based on the number ten. —*noun, plural* **decimals.** a fraction with a denominator of 10 or a multiple of 10 such as 100 or 1000. This is also called a decimal fraction. The decimal fraction

.5 is another way of writing 5/10, and .75 is another way of writing 75/100. ◆ The period before a decimal fraction, such as .5 or .75, is called a **decimal point.**

de•ci•sion [di sizh′ ən] *noun, plural* **decisions.** **1.** the act or result of having one's mind made up; a definite conclusion: Julie has made a *decision* to go to law school after college. **2.** a firm or determined way of thinking.

de•ci•sive [di sī′ siv] *adjective, more/most.* **1.** deciding something completely; giving a clear result: In the first Super Bowl, Green Bay scored a *decisive* victory by beating Kansas City 35-10. **2.** showing decision; firm or determined: a *decisive* person, a *decisive* answer. —**decisively,** *adverb.* —**decisiveness,** *noun.*

deck [dek] *noun, plural* **decks. 1.** one of the floors on a ship or boat that divides it into different levels. **2.** a platform that is like the deck of a ship or boat: That house has a *deck* that overlooks the lake. **3.** a set of playing cards. —*verb,* **decked, decking.** to decorate or dress: He was all *decked* out in a brand-new suit.

dec•la•ra•tion [dek′ lə rā′ shən] *noun, plural* **declarations.** the announcing or making known of something; a formal statement: When the tourists returned to the U.S., they had to give a written *declaration* of all the things they had bought overseas.

Declaration of Independence The easiest thing to notice on the Declaration is the signature of John Hancock, president of the Continental Congress.

Declaration of Independence a statement presented on July 4, 1776, that declared the thirteen American colonies to be a free country independent of England.

de•clare [di klâr′] *verb,* **declared, declaring.** **1.** to announce or make something known in a formal way: The mayor *declared* a holiday in honor of the astronauts. The U.S. *declared* war on Japan in World War II. **2.** to state in a definite way; say strongly: "The rents, *declared* Babbitt, were too low . . ." (Sinclair Lewis)

de•cline [di klīn′] *verb,* **declined, declining.** **1.** to refuse in a polite way to do or accept something: George Washington *declined* to run for a third term as President. **2.** to become less or grow weaker; decrease: At one time many people traveled to Europe by ship, but business *declined* after the jet airliner was developed. **3.** to move or slope downward: "The sun was *declining* and I wished to be on the road by nightfall." (E.M. Forster) —*noun, plural* **declines.** a slow weakening or lessening: Spanish power in Europe began its *decline* during the reign of King Philip II in the late 1500's.

de•code [dē kōd′] *verb,* **decoded, decoding.** to change secret writing into ordinary words: The spy *decoded* the secret message.

de•com•pose [dē′ kəm pōz′] *verb,* **decomposed, decomposing.** to decay or rot: The old oranges we left outside *decomposed* after several weeks. ◆ The process of decomposing is **decomposition.**

dec•o•rate [dek′ ə rāt′] *verb,* **decorated, decorating. 1.** to make more beautiful: We *decorated* the Christmas tree with lights and ornaments. **2.** to give a medal or badge to: The navy *decorated* the sailor for his bravery. **3.** to add paint, wallpaper, or new furnishings to a room. ◆ Someone whose work is decorating rooms is a **decorator.**

dec•o•ra•tion [dek′ ə rā′ shən] *noun, plural* **decorations. 1.** the act of decorating something. **2.** something that decorates; an ornament. **3.** a medal or badge.

dec•o•ra•tive [dek′ rə tiv *or* dek′ ə rə tiv] *adjective, more/most.* serving to decorate; ornamental: a *decorative* bowl of flowers.

de•coy [dē′ koi] *noun, plural* **decoys. 1.** a model of a bird that is used by hunters to attract real birds within shooting distance or into a trap.

Pronunciation Key: T–Z			
t	ten; date	v	very; live
th	think	w	win; away
<u>th</u>	these	y	you
u	cut; butter	z	zoo; cause
ur	turn; bird	zh	measure

(Turn the page for more information.)

2. someone who leads another person into danger or into a trap: The policewoman dressed as an old lady to act as a *decoy* and catch the muggers. —[di koi′] *verb,* **decoyed, decoying.** to act as or use a decoy; lure.

de•crease [di krēs′] *verb,* **decreased, decreasing.** to make or become less: That senator wants to *decrease* government spending for military weapons. —[dē′ krēs *or* di krēs′] *noun, plural* **decreases. 1.** a lessening or decline of something: After the team dropped into last place, there was a *decrease* in attendance at their games. **2.** the amount by which something becomes less.

de•cree [di krē′] *noun, plural* **decrees.** an official order or decision: In 1534 King Henry VIII issued a *decree* declaring himself to be the head of the new Church of England. —*verb,* **decreed, decreeing.** to order or decide something by a decree.

ded•i•cate [ded′ə kāt′] *verb,* **dedicated, dedicating. 1.** to set apart for or direct to a special purpose or use: Mother Teresa of India has *dedicated* her life to working with the poor. ♦ Often used as an adjective: He is a very *dedicated* scientist who puts all his energy into his work. **2.** to address a book or other work to a person as a sign of respect or affection: Herman Melville *dedicated* his novel *Moby Dick* to the famous author Nathaniel Hawthorne.

ded•i•ca•tion [ded′ə kā′ shən] *noun, plural* **dedications. 1.** the act or fact of dedicating: a *dedication* at the front of a book, the *dedication* of a new church. **2.** the state or attitude of being dedicated: She'd get better grades if she had more *dedication* to her studies.

de•duct [di dukt′] *verb,* **deducted, deducting.** to take away one amount from another; subtract: A person can *deduct* the cost of certain things from the income tax he owes.

de•duc•tion [di duk′ shən] *noun, plural* **deductions. 1.** the act of deducting: That store offers a *deduction* of 5 percent for prompt payment in cash. **2.** a thing that is deducted. A **tax deduction** is something a taxpayer is allowed to subtract from the tax owed. ♦ If a thing can be deducted from taxes, it is **deductible.**

deed [dēd] *noun, plural* **deeds. 1.** something done; an act or action: He did a good *deed* by helping us fix our flat tire. **2.** a written, legal agreement stating who owns a house or piece of property.

deep [dēp] *adjective,* **deeper, deepest. 1.** going far down from the top or surface: The Atlantic Ocean is 28,000 feet *deep* just north of Puerto

Rico. **2.** going far from the front to the back: Their yard is 75 feet wide and 150 feet *deep.* **3.** having a low pitch: The actor James Earl Jones has a very *deep* voice. **4.** in an extreme state or condition, as if deep under water: The baby fell into a *deep* sleep. Sue didn't hear me because she was *deep* in thought. —*adverb.* in a way that is deep; far in, down, or back: "The dark eyes looked *deep* into Winston's own." (George Orwell) —**deeply,** *adverb:* "There was something wrong with him, no doubt, *deeply* wrong." (John Galsworthy).

deer Three well-known types of deer. Two are from North America, the mule deer (rear) and the white-tailed deer (left). The red deer (right) is found in Europe.

deer [dēr] *noun, plural* **deer** or **deers.** a fast-running wild animal that has hoofs and chews its CUD. A male deer has antlers that it sheds every year and grows back the next year. There are many different kinds of deer found in various parts of the world.

de•face [di fās′] *verb,* **defaced, defacing.** to damage the appearance of; mar: Someone *defaced* the painting by slashing it with a knife.

de•feat [di fēt′] *verb,* **defeated, defeating.** to win a victory over; beat in a battle or contest: The army *defeated* the rebels who tried to take over the city. We *defeated* the other team by two touchdowns. —*noun, plural* **defeats.** a loss in a contest or battle: Lee was very disappointed about his *defeat* in the school election.

de•fect [di fekt′ *or* dē′ fekt] *noun, plural* **defects.** something that takes away from the quality of a thing; a fault or weakness: The Tylers are very upset with their new car because it has so many minor *defects.* —[di fekt′] *verb,* **defected, defecting.** to leave one's country or group in order to join another: *The famous Russian ballet dancer Mikhail Baryshnikov defected and moved to the U.S.* ♦ A person who defects is a **defector.**

de•fec•tive [di fek′ tiv] *adjective, more/most.* having a defect or defects: *The plane lost power because of a defective engine.*

de•fend [di fend′] *verb,* **defended, defending. 1.** to guard against attack or danger; protect: *A force of 180 Texans defended the Alamo against the Mexican army.* **2.** to act, speak, or write in favor of someone or something under attack: *The president of the company defended his decision to close down two factories.* **3.** to serve as a lawyer for a person who is accused of a crime. ♦ A person who defends someone or something is a **defender.**

de•fense [di fens′] *noun, plural* **defenses. 1.** the act of defending: *The senator spoke in defense of his plan to raise taxes.* **2.** a person or thing that defends: *The U.S. has a strong defense in the Army, Navy, and Air Force.* **3.** a lawyer or lawyers who defend an accused person. **4.** [*also,* dē′ fens] in sports such as football and basketball, a player or players who try to stop the other team from scoring. ♦ Someone or something that has no defense is **defenseless.**

the judgment or opinion of another person: *They deferred to Susan on which trail to take up the mountain, because no one else had climbed it before.* **—deference** [def′rəns], *noun.*

de•fi•ance [di fī′ əns] *noun, plural* **defiances.** the act or attitude of defying; a refusal to obey or show respect.

de•fi•ant [di fī′ ənt] *adjective, more/most.* showing defiance: *John Paul Jones is famous for giving the defiant answer "I have not yet begun to fight" when asked to surrender.* **—defiantly,** *adverb.*

de•fi•cien•cy [di fish′ ən sē] *noun, plural* **deficiencies. 1.** a lack of something that is needed or important: *a vitamin deficiency.* **2.** the amount by which something is lacking; shortage: *When the bank teller checked her cash drawer, she found a deficiency of $1000.*

de•fi•cient [di fish′ ənt] *adjective, more/most.* lacking something that is needed or important: *Many years ago sailors often became ill at sea because their diet was deficient in fruits and vegetables.*

def•i•cit [def′ ə sit] *noun, plural* **deficits.** a situation in which there is less than is needed: *There is a deficit in the federal budget because the government spends more than it takes in.*

D

---

defining terms Let's suppose that you are writing a "how-to" paper. Your topic is "How to Use a VCR." In the middle of the paper, you say, "If you have to leave the room for a minute while you're watching something, hit Freeze Frame. If a loud commercial comes on, just use the Mute button." Wait a minute. Maybe your readers don't know as much about VCR's as you do. Define your terms, please. You have just used two terms that may be unfamiliar—*freeze frame* and *mute.* You should go back and edit your paper this way: ". . . hit Freeze Frame. That's a control that will stop (freeze) the picture at the frame it's on." And this way: ". . . use the Mute button. That will turn off (mute) the sound completely."

---

de•fen•sive [di fens′ siv] *adjective, more/most.* **1.** protecting or guarding against attack: *In the Civil War, both sides dug deep trenches as a defensive measure.* **2.** having to do with defense in sports: *A linebacker is a defensive player in football.* **3.** expecting to be attacked or criticized: *He is very defensive at work and feels he has to explain everything he does to his boss.* **—defensively,** *adverb:* *"She stands and listens defensively, as if the music held some meaning that threatened her."* (Eugene O'Neill)

de•fer¹ [di fur′] *verb,* **deferred, deferring.** to put off until a later time; delay; postpone: *"He wrote we would have to defer the project for a year."* (George Plimpton) ♦ Something that defers is a **deferment.**

defer² *verb,* **deferred, deferring.** to give in to

de•fine [di fīn′] *verb,* **defined, defining. 1.** to give the meaning of a word or group of words: *This dictionary defines the word "deity" as "a god or goddess."* **2.** to describe or tell exactly; make clear: *The company prepared job descriptions to define what each worker was supposed to do.* **3.** to set the limits or boundary of: *The fence defines where our property ends.*

Pronunciation Key: [ə] Symbol

The [ə] or *schwa* sound occurs in syllables without an accent. It can be spelled with any vowel, such as **a** in above, **e** in listen, **i** in pencil, **o** in melon, **u** in circus. It can also be a combination of vowels, such as **io** in action, **ai** in mountain, **iou** in precious.

(Turn the page for more information.)

D

def·i·nite [def′ ə nit] *adjective.* beyond doubt; certain; clear: Is it *definite* that Mr. Edwards won't be teaching here next year? "Yes" and "no" are *definite* answers, but "maybe" is not. —**definitely,** *adverb:* "Miss Beach is supposed to have written quite *definitely* that she was not interested." (Janet Flanner)

def·i·ni·tion [def′ ə nish′ ən] *noun, plural* **definitions.** an explanation of the meaning of a word or group of words: On this page the word "degree" has five *definitions* and a writing article.

de·form [di fôrm′] *verb,* **deformed, deforming.** to spoil the shape or appearance of; make ugly: The constant heavy winds had *deformed* the tree by bending its branches in an odd way.

de·frost [di frôst′] *verb,* **defrosted, defrosting.** to make free of ice or frost; thaw out. ♦ A **defroster** is a device that melts or removes ice, as on a car windshield.

deft [deft] *adjective, more/most.* quick and skillful; clever: The magician's *deft* movements made it easy for him to hide the coin in his hand. —**deftly,** *adverb.*

de·fy [di fī′] *verb,* **defied, defying.** to challenge boldly; resist: The defenders of the fort were able to *defy* a much larger force.

de Gaulle [di gôl′] **Charles,** 1890–1970, French general and statesman.

de·gree [di grē′] *noun, plural* **degrees. 1.** a step or stage in a process or series: I learned how to operate the computer by *degrees* over a period of several weeks. **2.** the amount or extent of something: Burns on the skin are measured by *degree.* First *degree* murder is more serious than third *degree.* **3.** a unit for measuring temperature: Water freezes at 32 *degrees* Fahrenheit. **4.** a unit for measuring an angle or an arc of a circle: A square has four angles of 90 *degrees.* **5.** an official title given for completing a certain course of study: a *degree* in English.

de·i·ty [dē′ ə tē] *noun, plural* **deities.** a god or goddess: All of the planets but Earth are named for *deities* of the ancient world.

de·ject·ed [di jek′ tid] *adjective, more/most.* sad or depressed; discouraged: "George felt so utterly lonely and *dejected* that he wanted to weep." (Sherwood Anderson)

Del·a·ware [del′ ə wâr′] **1.** a state on the east coast of the U.S. *Capital:* Dover. *Nickname:* "First State." *Area:* 2,100 square miles. *Population:* 600,000. **2.** a river that flows through New York, Pennsylvania, New Jersey, and Delaware to the Atlantic.

de·lay [di lā′] *verb,* **delayed, delaying. 1.** to put off until a later time; postpone: The opening of the new shopping center has been *delayed* until summer. **2.** to cause to be late: Our bus was *delayed* by the snowstorm. —*noun, plural* **delays.** a delaying or being delayed: There will be a *delay* of 30 minutes before takeoff.

del·e·gate [del′ ə git *or* del′ ə gāt′] *noun, plural* **delegates.** a person chosen to act or speak for others: Jeanne Kirkpatrick served as the U.S. *delegate* to the United Nations from 1981 to 1985. —[del′ ə gāt′] *verb,* **delegated, delegating. 1.** to appoint someone as a delegate. **2.** to give authority or duties to another: The head of a large business has to *delegate* certain responsibilities to the people who work for him.

de·lete [di lēt′] *verb,* **deleted, deleting.** to cross out or remove something written or printed: She *deleted* several paragraphs from her story because they slowed down the plot. ♦ Something that is deleted is a **deletion.**

de·lib·er·ate [di lib′ ər it] *adjective, more/most.* **1.** done or said on purpose: Murder is the *deliberate* killing of another person. I'm sorry I forgot to send you a birthday card; it wasn't *deliberate.* **2.** slow and careful; not hurried: Marsha is very *deliberate* when she's taking a test. —[di lib′ ə rāt′] *verb,* **deliberated, deliber-**

---

degree *Degree* is a term of measurement. "It is ninety *degrees* outside." "The ship was off course by ten *degrees.*" Degree also is used in grammar to measure words.

Least	Next	Most
high	higher	highest
silly	sillier	silliest

These degrees are called positive (least) as in *good,* comparative (next) as in *better,* and superlative (most) as in *best.* If you listen to sportscasters on radio or television, you'll often hear mistaken uses of degree. "He's one of the *better* players in the league." "He has a *very unique* batting stance." In the first sentence, *best* is the right word. As for the second, *unique* means one of a kind—you can't be more or less unique. What is wrong with this? "Harriet said the villain in the movie was the frighteningest she'd ever seen." Here's a clue: some words need *more* or *most* to show degree.

ating. to think carefully; consider: They *deliberated* for days before they decided to buy the new house. —**deliberately,** *adverb.* in a deliberate way: "He read the letter slowly and *deliberately . . .* his mouth silently forming the words." (John O'Hara)

de·lib·er·a·tion [di lib′ə rā′ shən] *noun, plural* **deliberations. 1.** the act or fact of deliberating: After much *deliberation,* she made up her mind to accept the new job. **2.** *also,* **deliberations.** a discussion of the arguments for or against something.

del·i·ca·cy [del′ ə kə sē] *noun, plural* **delicacies. 1.** a being delicate; fineness: the *delicacy* of a spider web. **2.** a rare or choice food: Caviar is thought of as a *delicacy* by many people.

del·i·cate [del′ ə kit] *adjective,* more/most. **1.** very finely made or shaped: a *delicate* piece of lace. **2.** light and pleasing: the *delicate* scent of an expensive perfume. **3.** easily hurt or damaged; "Carrie had always been *delicate,* she could not stand such cold much longer." (Laura Ingalls Wilder) **4.** very sensitive: "Choosing a jury is always a *delicate* task." (Clarence Darrow) —**delicately,** *adverb:* "Treading *delicately* like a cat, Aslan stepped from stone to stone across the stream." (C.S. Lewis)

del·i·ca·tes·sen [del′ ə kə tes′ ən] *noun, plural* **delicatessens.** a store that sells foods that are ready to eat, such as cheese, cold meats, salads, and sandwiches.

de·li·cious [di lish′ əs] *adjective,* more/most. very pleasing to the taste or smell: a *delicious* cake, the *delicious* smell of bread being baked. —**deliciously,** *adverb.* —**deliciousness,** *noun.*

de·light [di līt′] *noun, plural* **delights.** great pleasure or happiness; joy: The little boy smiled with *delight* when his birthday cake was brought into the room. "Frodo welcomed his old friend with surprise and great *delight.*" (J.R.R. Tolkien) —*verb,* **delighted, delighting. 1.** to give great pleasure or joy: The babysitter *delighted* the children with funny stories and jokes. "The King who *delighted* in music, had frequent concerts at Court." (Jonathan Swift) **2.** to have or take great pleasure: He *delights* in teasing his younger sister.

de·light·ful [di līt′ fəl] *adjective,* more/most. very pleasing; giving joy: "All sorts of *delightful* things happened, and good times really seemed to have come." (Louisa May Alcott) —**delightfully,** *adverb:* The weather's been *delightfully* warm and clear this week.

de·lir·i·ous [di lēr′ ē əs] *adjective.* **1.** out of one's mind for a time from illness or an injury:

The patient was *delirious* from a very high fever and kept calling to people who weren't actually there. **2.** wildly excited: The girls were *delirious* with joy when they got to meet the famous rock star. —**deliriously,** *adverb.*

de·liv·er [di liv′ ər] *verb,* **delivered, delivering. 1.** to carry and give out; hand over; distribute: The mail carrier *delivered* a post card to my house. That pizza shop *delivers* pizza in our neighborhood. **2.** to speak or utter; say: Abraham Lincoln *delivered* the Gettysburg Address on November 19, 1863. **3.** to send to a target: to *deliver* a blow in boxing. **4.** to give birth to a baby, or help a woman to give birth. **5.** to set free or rescue from something: The Lord's Prayer asks God to "*deliver* us from evil."

de·liv·er·y [di liv′ rē] *noun, plural* **deliveries. 1.** the act of carrying or handing over something to a place or person: The milk truck made a *delivery* to the school lunch room. **2.** a way of speaking or singing: The actor's *delivery* was so clear that people could hear him easily even in the back row. **3.** the act of giving birth.

delta A view of the Nile River delta, taken from far above the earth by a communications satellite.

del·ta [del′ tə] *noun, plural* **deltas.** a mass of sand, mud, and earth at the mouth of a river. A delta is shaped like a fan or triangle. The Mississippi and Nile rivers have large deltas.

de·mand [di mand′] *verb,* **demanded, demanding. 1.** to ask for very strongly or forcefully;

Pronunciation Key: Accent Marks

[′] is the normal accent mark. It shows where the main stress falls on a word.
[′] is a secondary accent mark. It shows a lighter stress than the primary accent. For example:

tel • e • vis • ion [tel′ə vizh′ən]
(Turn the page for more information.)

insist: The angry workers *demanded* a raise in pay and more time off. "They *demanded* the truth from her and she gave it quite simply." (Pearl Buck) **2.** to call for; require: Opera singing *demands* a good, strong voice. —*noun, plural* **demands. 1.** the act of demanding: The President declared that he would not give in to the *demands* of the terrorists. **2.** something that is demanded: A mother of young children has a lot of *demands* on her time. ◆ Also used as an adjective: Being police chief of a large city is a very *demanding* job.

de•mon [dē′mən] *noun, plural* **demons. 1.** a bad or evil spirit; a devil. **2.** a person who is very cruel or wicked. **3.** a person who has a lot of energy or determination: Grandpa has his hands full trying to take care of Jennie—she's a real little *demon*.

dem•on•strate [dem′ ən strāt′] *verb,* **demonstrated, demonstrating. 1.** to show clearly or explain: In 1876 Alexander Graham Bell *demonstrated* the first telephone. **2.** to take part in a public display to protest or to make demands

---

democracy *Democracy* and *republic* are close in meaning but are not the same. By strict definition, *republic* refers to a government where the people are ruled by representatives whom they elect. In a *democracy*, the people may rule directly. In ancient Greece, citizens gathered to vote on government policies, and today in parts of New England, they still do this. Obviously, you could not ask all the citizens of Los Angeles or the State of Alabama to vote directly on main issues. They vote for representatives to act for them. But there is nothing wrong in the saying that the United States is both a republic and a democracy, because democracy now describes a people who can act and live freely without loss of their civil rights.

---

de•moc•ra•cy [di mäk′ rə sē] *noun, plural* **democracies. 1.** a government that is run by the people who live under it. In a **direct democracy** the voters themselves make the laws, as was done in ancient Greece. More common today is an **indirect democracy,** where the voters elect representatives who make the laws, as is the case with the U.S. Congress. **2.** a country in which the government is a democracy, such as the United States.

dem•o•crat [dem′ ə krat′] *noun, plural* **democrats. 1.** a person who favors democracy. **2. Democrat.** a person who belongs to or supports the Democratic Party.

dem•o•crat•ic [dem′ ə krat′ ik] *adjective, more/most.* **1.** having to do with or favoring democracy: Great Britain, Canada, and Japan have a *democratic* system of government. **2.** favoring equal rights or treatment for all people: The owner of that company is a very *democratic* person who treats all his workers fairly. **3. Democratic.** having to do with the Democratic Party.

Democratic Party one of the two major political parties in the United States, along with the REPUBLICAN PARTY.

de•mol•ish [di mäl′ ish] *verb,* **demolished, demolishing.** to destroy completely; tear down; wreck: "Their church was on a hill; it has since been *demolished* by a hurricane." (John Updike) ◆ The act of demolishing something is **demolition** [dem′ ə lish′ ən].

for something: Many people *demonstrated* outside the jail, urging that prisoners be given better treatment. ◆ A person who demonstrates is a **demonstrator.**

dem•on•stra•tion [dem′ ən strā′ shən] *noun, plural* **demonstrations. 1.** the act of demonstrating; something that shows clearly or explains: The salesman gave us a *demonstration* of how the computer worked. **2.** a public show or

Democratic Party The symbol of the Democrats, the donkey, was first used by President Andrew Jackson. In this famous political cartoon of the 1880's by Thomas Nast, the donkey stands for "Copperheads" (northern Democrats who were sympathetic to the South).

parade to protest or to demand something: A *demonstration* was held in front of the power company to oppose their plan to raise the cost of electricity.

de•mote [di mōt′] *verb*, **demoted, demoting.** to put back to a lower grade or rank: The sergeant was *demoted* to private after he disobeyed an officer's orders. ♦ The fact of being demoted is a **demotion.**

den [den] *noun, plural* **dens. 1.** a wild animal's home or resting place, especially a large animal such as a lion, bear, or wolf. **2.** something thought of as like a den, such as a hiding place for criminals. **3.** a small room in a house where a person can read, study, or watch television. **4.** a group of Cub Scouts.

de•ni•al [di nī′ əl] *noun, plural* **denials.** the act of denying; saying that something is not true.

den•im [den′ əm] *noun, plural* **denim** or **denims. 1.** a sturdy cotton cloth, often used for work or sports clothes. **2. denims.** pants or overalls made of denim.

Den•mark [den′ märk′] a country in northern Europe. *Capital:* Copenhagen. *Area:* 16,600 square miles. *Population:* 5,180,000. **—Danish,** *adjective; noun.*

de•nom•i•na•tion [di näm′ ə nā′ shən] *noun, plural* **denominations. 1.** a religious group: Presbyterians, Methodists, and Lutherans are different *denominations* of the Protestant Church. **2.** one unit of things in a system: A dime is a *denomination* of money.

de•nom•i•na•tor [di näm′ ə nā′ tər] *noun, plural* **denominators.** the number below the line in a fraction, showing the number of equal parts the whole is divided into: In the fraction 3/4, 4 is the *denominator* and 3 is the NUMERATOR.

disapproval of; condemn: The new candidate for governor *denounced* the way her opponent had been running the state. ♦ The act of denouncing is **denunciation.**

dense [dens] *adjective,* **denser, densest.** closely packed together; thick: The fog was so *dense* that we could only see a few feet in front of us. "Already a *dense* mass of people was blocking the south side of the square." (George Orwell) **—densely,** *adverb:* ". . . a long island *densely* covered with tall palm forest." (Thor Heyerdahl)

den•si•ty [den′ sə tē] *noun, plural* **densities. 1.** the state of being dense. **2.** the amount of something within a certain unit or area: Japan has a higher population *density* than the United States.

dent [dent] *noun, plural* **dents.** a place where the surface of something has been pushed in by a hard blow: There was a *dent* in the roof of the car from where a branch fell on it. —*verb,* **dented, denting.** to make a dent in: to *dent* the fender of a car.

den•tal [den′ təl] *adjective.* **1.** having to do with the teeth: Eating fresh fruit rather than sweets promotes *dental* health. **2.** having to do with a dentist: *Dental* school usually lasts three years.

den•tist [den′ tist] *noun, plural* **dentists.** a person who is professionally trained to take care of people's teeth. ♦ The profession of a dentist is **dentistry** [den′ tis trē].

den•tures [den′ chərz] *plural noun.* a set of false teeth.

Den•ver [den′ vər] the capital of the state of Colorado. *Population:* 494,000.

de•ny [di nī′] *verb,* **denied, denying. 1.** to say something is not true: Even though the police

---

denotation *Denotation* means that a word signifies this or that particular meaning. "The *denotation* was clear: she spoke of wood rotting under the pier, and not of the pilings below the pier." *Connotation* means that a word suggests or hints at this or that meaning. "We realized that she was unfair to the actor by her *connotations*; she kept saying he was 'young' when she really mean 'inexperienced,' and she said he spoke with an accent when in fact she meant that he was a poor speaker."

---

de•note [di nōt′] *verb,* **denoted, denoting. 1.** to be a sign of; show: "A red and yellow sky . . . *denoted* the approach of darkness." (Charles Dickens) **2.** to be a name for; mean: The word "lion" *denotes* a certain wild animal of the cat family. **—denotation,** *noun.*

de•nounce [di nouns′] *verb,* **denounced, denouncing.** to speak openly against; show strong

a	and; hat	ch	chew; such
ā	ate; stay	d	dog; lid
â	care; air	e	end; yet
ä	father; hat	ē	she; each
b	boy; cab	f	fun; off

(Turn the page for more information.)

found the TV set in his house, he *denied* that he stole it from the store. **2.** to refuse to give or allow: The Constitution says that the right to vote shall not be *denied* on account of a person's race or sex.

de•o•dor•ant [dē ō′ dər ənt] *noun, plural* **deodorants.** a substance that hides bad smells. Deodorants are used to remove the smell of PERSPIRATION or to cover up odors in a room.

dependent clause Something that is *dependent* depends or relies on another thing. This word is used in the term "dependent clause," which is an important idea in writing. A clause is a part of a sentence. To say that a clause is "dependent" means that it depends on another part of the sentence. Why is this important? Because a dependent clause cannot stand alone as a separate sentence. It must be joined to the words it depends on. "Take notes on your topic. Before you start your paper." What's wrong here? "Before you start your paper" doesn't make sense alone, even though it has a subject and a verb. It cannot be a sentence by itself, but has to be joined to the first sentence: "Take notes on your topic before you start your paper."

de•part [di pärt′] *verb,* **departed, departing. 1.** to go away; leave: The bus will *depart* from in front of school at three o'clock. **2.** to change from the usual way: They *departed* from their usual custom of having turkey for Thanksgiving and had roast beef instead.

de•part•ment [di pärt′ mənt] *noun, plural* **departments.** a special part or division of something: the women's clothing *department* of a store, the English *department* of a high school. The fire *department* and police *department* are two parts of city government.

department store a large store that sells many different things and is divided into separate departments for each type of item sold.

de•par•ture [di pär′ chər] *noun, plural* **departures. 1.** the going away of someone or something: "The arrival or *departure* of any ship was the biggest event in the little harbor town." (Armstrong Sperry) **2.** a change from the usual way: Going camping was a real *departure* for Mom because she usually hates the outdoors.

de•pend [di pend′] *verb,* **depended, depending.** (usually used with **on**) **1.** to rely on for help or support: Larry *depends on* his mother to wake him up in the morning because he always oversleeps. **2.** to be controlled or determined by: Whether Danny can watch that show or not *depends on* how much homework he has. **—dependence,** *noun.*

de•pend•a•ble [di pen′ də bəl] *adjective, more/most.* able to be depended on; reliable or trustworthy: Dad doesn't want a fancy car —just a *dependable* one that'll get him to work.

de•pend•ent [di pen′ dənt] *adjective, more/most.* **1.** relying on the help of someone or something: The Red Cross is *dependent* on contributions for the money it needs. **2.** controlled or determined by: Whether or not we hold the party outdoors is *dependent* on the weather. **—noun, plural** **dependents.** any person who relies on another for help or support: Children are *dependents* of their parents.

de•pict [di pikt′] *verb,* **depicted, depicting.** to show in a picture or by words: Vincent Van Gogh's paintings often *depict* flowers and fields. The books of Laura Ingalls Wilder *depict* pioneer life.

de•plore [di plôr′] *verb,* **deplored, deploring.** to be very sorry about and consider to be wrong: The mayor *deplored* the lack of parks and playgrounds in the city.

de•port [di pôrt′] *verb,* **deported, deporting.** to order a person to leave a country of which he is not a citizen: The U.S. *deported* the criminal 'Lucky' Luciano to his native country, Italy.

de•pos•it [di päz′ it] *verb,* **deposited, depositing. 1.** to put money or valuable things in a bank or safe place. **2.** to put or set down: He *deposited* the package on the front steps. **3.** to pay money as a promise to do something or to pay more later: "When she found the apartment, she *deposited* the first month's rent at once." (Langston Hughes) **—noun, plural** **deposits. 1.** something put in a bank or safe place: a *deposit* of $100 in a savings account. ♦ A person who makes a deposit is a **depositor. 2.** money paid as a promise to do something or to pay more later. **3.** a mass of material that has built up through the action of nature: a *deposit* of dirt at the mouth of a river. There are large gold *deposits* in South Africa.

de•pot [dē′ pō] *noun, plural* **depots. 1.** a railroad or bus station. **2.** a place for storing things, especially military supplies.

de•pre•ci•ate [di prē′ shē āt′] *verb,* **depreciated, depreciating.** to fall or cause to fall in price or value: Most new cars *depreciate* a lot in their first year. ♦ The process of depreciating is **depreciation**.

de•press [di pres′] *verb*, **depressed, depressing. 1.** to make sad or gloomy: It *depressed* her to stay home alone while all her friends were at the dance. ♦ Often used as an adjective: "Even the scenery was *depressing*. There was nothing to see but the snow blowing over the road." (Tom Wolfe) **2.** to press down: To open the emergency door of an airplane, you *depress* a lever. **3.** to cause to sink to a lower level: Car sales have been *depressed* this month.

de•pres•sion [di presh′ ən] *noun, plural* **depressions. 1.** sadness or low spirits; a gloomy feeling: He sank into a deep *depression* after he lost his job. **2.** a low or sunken place in the surface of something: "At last they found the track again—a faint *depression* in the grass." (Walter Farley) **3.** a time when business is very bad and a great many people are out of work. ♦ The time in the 1930's when there was such a condition is known as the **Depression** or the **Great Depression**.

de•prive [di prīv′] *verb*, **deprived, depriving.** (usually used with **of**) to keep from having or doing; take away: Tina's mother sometimes punishes her by *depriving* her *of* watching her favorite TV show.

depth [depth] *noun, plural* **depths. 1.** how deep something is; the distance from top to bottom or from front to back: The *depth* of the Pacific Ocean in one part is almost seven miles. **2.** *also,* **depths.** the deepest or most central part of something: the *depths* of a mine. **3.** *also,* **depths.** the part that is thought of as most extreme or severe: the *depths* of winter, to be in the *depths* of despair. **4.** deep learning, thinking, or feeling: Benjamin Franklin was a man of great *depth*. **5. in depth.** in a thorough way; in detail: to study a problem *in depth*.

dep•u•ty [dep′ yə tē] *noun, plural* **deputies.** a person appointed to work for or take the place of another: a sheriff's *deputy*. The mayor is assisted by several *deputy* mayors.

de•riv•a•tive [di riv′ ə tiv] *noun, plural* **derivatives. 1.** something that is derived: Wine and vinegar are *derivatives* of grapes. **2.** a word that is derived from another word, such as "kindly" and "kindness" from "kind." —*adjective.* that is derived: The Rolling Stones' Mick Jagger has a *derivative* singing style that was copied from black singers of the southern U.S.

de•rive [di rīv′] *verb*, **derived, deriving.** (usually with **from**) **1.** to get from a certain source:

Cocoa is *derived from* cacao seeds. The word "derrick" *derives from* a man's name. **2.** to get or receive: She *derived* a lot of satisfaction *from* helping her little brother with his art project. ♦ The deriving of something is **derivation**.

de•rog•a•to•ry [di räg′ ə tôr′ ē] *adjective*. showing no respect; insulting: The candidate made *derogatory* remarks about his opponent.

derrick The tall framework of an oil derrick rises from the ocean in a southern California oil field.

der•rick [der′ ik] *noun, plural* **derricks. 1.** a large machine for lifting and moving heavy things. Derricks are used on ships to load crates and containers or lift heavy nets filled with fish. **2.** a tower or frame over an oil well that supports machinery for drilling.

de•scend [di send′] *verb*, **descended, descending. 1.** to move from a higher to a lower place: "Caspian found himself *descending* a dark stairway into the earth." (C.S. Lewis) "The grey warm evening of August had *descended* upon the city." (James Joyce) **2.** to come down from an earlier source: The writer F. Scott Fitzgerald was *descended* from Francis Scott Key, the author of the "Star-Spangled Banner." **3.** to move in a sudden attack: A swarm of locusts *descended* on the crops.

Pronunciation Key: G–N			
g	give; big	k	kind; cat; back
h	hold	l	let; ball
i	it; this	m	make; time
ī	ice; my	n	not; own
j	jet; gem; edge	ng	having

(Turn the page for more information.)

D

de•scen•dant [di sen′dənt] *noun, plural* **descendants.** a person or animal that comes from certain ancestors: Modern racehorses are *descendants* of Arabian horses that were brought to England about 300 years ago.

de•scent [di sent′] *noun, plural* **descents. 1.** a moving from a higher to a lower place: The airplane pilot began his *descent* into Los Angeles Airport. **2.** family origin; ancestry: President Kennedy was of Irish *descent.* **3.** a downward slope: The ski trail makes a sharp *descent* just past this turn. **4.** a sudden attack.

des•cribe [di skrīb′] *verb,* **described, describing.** to give a picture of something in words; tell or write about something: "They told him how to find the field hospital. They *described* its exact location." (Stephen Crane)

adjective: "I liked to walk through the town after midnight, when the streets were *deserted.*" (Dylan Thomas) **2.** to go away from a place where one should stay: The soldier who was supposed to be on guard duty *deserted* his post. ◆ The fact or crime of leaving in this way is **desertion,** and a person who does this is a **deserter. 3.** to leave when needed or called for: "His strength suddenly *deserted* him and he had to sit down." (J.M. Coetzee)

de•serve [di zurv′] *verb,* **deserved, deserving.** to be entitled to have or get; have the right to: After working so hard all year, she *deserves* a vacation. He *deserves* to be punished for acting so fresh to his grandmother. ◆ Someone who deserves something is **deserving:** The scholarship will be awarded to a *deserving* student.

description "Her voice was sweet, and reminded him of elms, of lawns, of those glass arrangements that used to be hung from porch ceilings to tinkle in the summer wind." (John Cheever) "Her voice is full of money . . . the jingle of it, the cymbals' song of it . . ." (F. Scott Fitzgerald) "Veda was at a piano, playing. Then suddenly the miracle voice was everywhere, going through glass and masonry as though they were air." (James M. Cain) These sentences can be thought of as another way of saying, "She had a musical voice." But that's a vague sentence, and it doesn't give us much information. Notice that the writers use short, exact words in their description—"lawns," "money," "glass," "air." These are *analogies:* they try to give you a sense of something that can't be recorded on the printed page—the sound of a woman's voice.

de•scrip•tion [di skrip′shən] *noun, plural* **descriptions. 1.** the telling of how a person or thing looked, felt, or acted, or how an event took place; an account of something. **2.** kind; variety: The pond was a home for wildlife of every *description*—birds, fish, frogs, snakes, and even racoons and skunks.

de•scrip•tive [di skrip′tiv] *adjective.* serving to describe: "Beautiful" is a *descriptive* word.

de•seg•re•gate [dē seg′rə gāt′] *verb,* **desegregated, desegregating.** to stop the practice of separating or SEGREGATING people of different races: After World War II the armed forces were *desegregated* by order of President Truman. **—desegregation,** *noun.*

des•ert[1] [dez′ərt] *noun, plural* **deserts.** a very dry area of land. A desert is usually sandy and has little plant life. **—adjective. 1.** having to do with a desert: Cactus is a *desert* plant. **2.** having no people: *Robinson Crusoe* is about a man who was shipwrecked on a *desert* island.

de•sert[2] [di zurt′] *verb,* **deserted, deserting. 1.** to go away or leave: The wild animals *deserted* that area as soon as people started putting up houses there. ◆ Usually used as an

de•sign [di zīn′] *noun, plural* **designs. 1.** a plan or drawing that shows how something will look or will be made. A design can show a building, a car or other machine, a piece of clothing or furniture, or a page of a book. **2.** a certain pattern or arrangement of lines, colors, or shapes: American Indian rugs and blankets have very colorful *designs.* **3.** an idea or purpose in the mind: Do the police think the fire

desert This barren desert in the mountains of Chile, South America, is appropriately named 'Moon Valley.'

started by accident or by *design?* **4. designs.** sly or evil plans to get or take something: The king was worried that his younger brother had *designs* on the throne. —*verb,* **designed, designing. 1.** to make a plan or drawing to show how something will be made; to *design* a house, to *design* the package for a new brand of cereal. **2.** to plan or make for a certain purpose; intend: This dictionary is *designed* for use by students. —**designer,** *noun.*

des•ig•nate [dez′ ig nāt′] *verb,* **designated, designating. 1.** to mark or point out; show: That sign with the arrow *designates* the trail back to camp. **2.** to call by a special name or title: The person who graduates with the highest marks will be *designated* "valedictorian." **3.** to choose; name: "Voas was a Navy lieutenant who was *designated* as the astronauts' training officer." (Tom Wolfe)

designated hitter a baseball player who does not play in the field but bats in place of a weaker hitter, usually the pitcher.

de•sir•a•ble [di zīr′ ə bəl] *adjective, more/most.* worth wanting or having; good or helpful: You don't have to know how to type for that job, but it's certainly *desirable.* —**desirably,** *adverb.*

de•sire [di zīr′] *verb,* **desired, desiring.** to wish or long for; want to have: The hotel promised to provide its guests with anything they might *desire.* —*noun, plural* **desires.** a strong wish or longing to have something: "While he had no *desire* to eat, he knew that he must eat to live." (Jack London)

de•spair [di spâr′] *noun.* **1.** a feeling of having completely lost hope: "Anton tramped the streets for several days sleeping in doorways until he was in utter *despair.*" (Willa Cather) **2.** something that causes this feeling: That girl is the *despair* of her teacher because she never pays attention in class. —*verb,* **despaired, despairing.** to lose hope: "I have often *despaired,* but something always happens to start me hoping again." (C.S. Lewis)

des•per•ate [des′ prit *or* des′ pər it] *adjective, more/most.* **1.** being reckless or wild because all hope is gone; feeling despair: The *desperate* criminal swore that the police would never capture him alive. **2.** causing despair; very bad or dangerous: The skin diver was in a *desperate* situation when he suddenly came face to face with a shark. —**desperately,** *adverb:* "She was no longer herself. *Desperately* she fought for control." (Andre Norton) ◆ The feeling of being desperate is **desperation:** The pilot looked in *desperation* for a safe place to land.

de•spise [di spīz′] *verb,* **despised, despising.** to feel great dislike for; hate or scorn: "She had *despised* him for the evil he had done." (Bernard Malamud) ◆ Something that is despised is **despicable** [də spik′ ə bəl].

de•spite [di spīt′] *preposition.* in spite of: Janet went to school today *despite* the fact that she has a bad cold.

des•sert [di zurt′] *noun, plural* **desserts.** a sweet or tasty food served at the end of a meal, such as fruit, ice cream, pie, or cake.

D

---

dessert/desert This is one of the "troublesome pairs" in English. The verb form of *desert* even has the same pronunciation as dessert—[di zurt′]. People often leave the second s off *dessert,* or do the opposite and spell the verb *desert* with two s's. Remember this pattern:

    1) the dry land area: *desert* [dez′ ərt]
    2) the end of a meal: *dessert* [di zurt′]
    3) a verb, "to leave:" *desert* [di zurt′]

---

desk [desk] *noun, plural* **desks.** a piece of furniture with a flat top, used for writing or reading. Most desks have drawers or compartments for papers and other things.

des•o•late [des′ ə lit] *adjective, more/most.* **1.** without people; deserted: "There are three trees but otherwise the land looks waste and *desolate.*" (Paul Scott) **2.** very unhappy: "Now that I am without you, all is *desolate.*" (Conrad Aiken) —**desolation,** *noun.*

de So•to [di sō′ tō] **Hernando,** 1496?–1542, Spanish explorer.

des•ti•na•tion [des′ tə nā′ shən] *noun, plural* **destinations.** a place where someone or something is going or is sent: The sign on the bus said its *destination* was Market Street.

Pronunciation Key: O–S

ō	over; go	ou	out; town
ô	all; law	p	put; hop
oo	look; full	r	run; car
o͞o	pool; who	s	set; miss
oi	oil; boy	sh	show

(Turn the page for more information.)

D

des•tine [des′tin] *verb,* **destined, destining.** to be decided ahead of time, as if by fate: The *Titanic* set out on its first voyage with great excitement, but the ship was *destined* never to arrive in New York.

des•ti•ny [des′tə nē] *noun, plural* **destinies. 1.** what happens to a person or thing; one's fortune or fate in life: It was Winston Churchill's *destiny* to lead his country in its time of greatest danger. **2.** the power that is thought to control what happens; fate.

de•stroy [di stroi′] *verb,* **destroyed, destroying. 1.** to ruin or wreck completely; put an end to: In A.D. 79 the Roman city of Pompeii was *destroyed* by a volcano. **2.** to put to death a badly injured or sick animal: The great race horse Ruffian had to be *destroyed* after breaking her leg in a race.

de•stroy•er [di stroi′ ər] *noun, plural* **destroyers. 1.** a small, fast warship that is armed with large guns and various other weapons. **2.** a person or thing that destroys: In the Hindu religion, the god Shiva is the *destroyer* of life.

de•struc•tion [di struk′ shən] *noun.* a destroying or being destroyed; ruin: The tornado left *destruction* in its path—cars were smashed, houses were knocked down, and trees were blown across the road.

de•struc•tive [di struk′ tiv] *adjective, more/most.* **1.** causing great damage or ruin: a *destructive* fire, a *destructive* hurricane. **2.** wanting or tending to destroy or tear down: The *destructive* boy broke all the windows of the bus.

de•tach [di tach′] *verb,* **detached, detaching.** to unfasten and separate; disconnect: Gary *detached* the wheels from the toy car. She *detached* the sales tags from her new dress.

de•tached [di tacht′] *adjective, more/most.* **1.** not connected or joined to something else: Our garage is *detached* from the house. **2.** not

taking sides; free from strong feelings. ◆ The state of being detached is **detachment:** "This gave him a certain *detachment,* the easy manner of an onlooker and an observer." (Willa Cather)

detail Detail, detail, detail. It's always needed in writing. You can have too much detail, of course, but nine out of ten times you will need more than you put in the first draft of a story or report or letter. "The Senator was impressive." That's a good sentence, but not as good as: "The Senator spoke with a booming voice, yet he also listened; and when he led a discussion he was careful not to ride roughshod over others." If you write a report on *Moby Dick,* Herman Melville's great novel, don't just say, "Captain Ahab had a wooden leg." Use detail: first, make the verb better than "had." "He hobbled" or "he strode" on his false leg. Melville tells us Ahab's leg is not actually of wood, but ivory—it is made from the jawbone of a whale. That needs to be said. This detail expresses Ahab's mad desire to find and kill the huge white whale Moby Dick, which had, on an earlier voyage, overturned a whaling boat and torn off Ahab's leg.

de•tail [di tāl′ *or* dē′ tāl] *noun, plural* **details. 1.** a small or less important point or fact: My brother gave us all the *details* of the baseball game, from the first pitch to the last. **2.** *also,* **details.** the act or fact of dealing with things one at a time: Making a dress involves a lot of *details.* **3.** a small group of people who have a special duty: The sergeant ordered a *detail* of six soldiers to clear the trees off the road. —[di tāl′] *verb,* **detailed, detailing. 1.** to describe or tell fully. **2.** to appoint or choose for a special task: Mrs. Edwards has been *detailed* to collect the money for the picnic.

destroyer A modern U.S. Navy destroyer.

de•tain [di tān′] *verb,* **detained, detaining.** to stop from going; hold back. The man was *detained* by the police for questioning. "A young woman . . . laid her hand on his arm to *detain* him." (James Joyce)

de•tect [di tekt′] *verb,* **detected, detecting.** to find out about; discover; notice: A smoke alarm *detects* the presence of smoke in the air. ◆ The act of detecting is **detection:** "Nobody ever escaped *detection,* and nobody ever failed to confess." (George Orwell) ◆ Something that detects is a **detector:** Airlines use a metal *detector* to try to prevent people from bringing a gun on to a plane.

de•tec•tive [di tek′ tiv] *noun, plural* **detectives. 1.** a police officer whose work is to find out information that can be used to solve a crime and capture the criminal. **2.** *also,* **private detective.** a private citizen whose work is to solve crimes or to find out information about people. —*adjective.* having to do with detectives.

de•ter [di tur′] *verb,* **deterred, deterring.** to stop from doing because of fear or doubt; prevent or discourage: The growling dog *deterred* the little boy from walking across the lawn. ◆ Something that deters is a **deterrent:** The mayor feels that putting more police on the streets will be a *deterrent* to crime.

de•ter•gent [di tur′ jənt] *noun, plural* **detergents.** a cleaning powder or liquid used like soap. Detergents are used to wash dishes, clothing, walls and floors, and so on.

de•te•ri•o•rate [di tēr′ ē ə rāt′] *verb,* **deteriorated, deteriorating.** to make or become worse: That house has really *deteriorated* because nobody has kept up with the painting or repairs. ◆ The state of being deteriorated is **deterioration:** They hadn't seen him in several years, so they were surprised at the *deterioration* in his health.

de•ter•mi•na•tion [di tur′ mə nā′ shən] *noun, plural* **determinations. 1.** great firmness in carrying something out; a strong purpose: Helen Keller's great *determination* led her to become a famous writer and speaker even though she was both blind and deaf. **2.** a deciding or settling of something.

de•ter•mine [di tur′ min] *verb,* **determined, determining. 1.** to decide or settle definitely: If a vote in the Senate is tied, the Vice President votes to *determine* the outcome. **2.** to be the reason for a certain result; have a direct effect on: The ratings for a TV show *determine* whether or not it is kept on the air.

de•ter•mined [di tur′ mind] *adjective, more/most.* having one's mind made up firmly; showing a strong will: The *determined* look on her face showed how much she wanted to win. "I hauled at Mason's arm, *determined* to keep him inside." (S.E. Hinton)

de•test [di test′] *verb,* **detested, detesting.** to dislike very much; hate: Mom *detests* movies that show a lot of killing and violence.

de•tour [dē′ toor] *noun, plural* **detours.** a route that is different from or less direct than the regular way: Because the main highway was flooded, we had to make a *detour* on an old two-lane road. —*verb,* **detoured, detouring.** make or use a detour: "'I'm going to fly straight,' I tell him. 'I don't plan on *detouring* at all.'" (Charles Lindbergh)

de•tract [di trakt′] *verb,* **detracted, detracting.** (usually used with **from**) to take away from the looks or value of something: People who are trying to sell their house are careful to clean up any dirt that might *detract* from its appearance.

De•troit [di troit′] the largest city in the state of Michigan, and the center of the U.S. auto industry. *Population:* 1,210,000.

dev•as•tate [dev′ ə stāt′] *verb,* **devastated, devastating.** to destroy completely; ruin: The farmer's crops were *devastated* by the unexpected snowstorm. —**devastation,** *noun.*

de•vel•op [di vel′ əp] *verb,* **developed, developing. 1.** to grow or cause to grow; bring or come into being: Oak trees *develop* from acorns. Thomas Edison *developed* the first successful electric lamp. **2.** in photography, to use chemicals on exposed film or plates in order to bring out a picture. ◆ Someone or something that develops is a **developer,** such as a person or company that builds real estate developments.

de•vel•op•ment [di vel′ əp mənt] *noun, plural* **developments. 1.** the act or process of developing: the *development* of the United States from thirteen small colonies into a large nation. **2.** an event or happening: The TV station gave a bulletin about the latest *developments* in the case of the missing child. **3.** a group of houses or other buildings built by the same builder and following the same model or models.

de•vi•ate [dē′ vē āt′] *verb,* **deviated, deviating.** to change from the usual way. In Little League baseball they *deviate* from the major league rule and play only six innings instead of nine. —**deviation,** *noun.*

D

Pronunciation Key: T–Z

t	ten; date	v	very; live
th	think	w	win; away
th	these	y	you
u	cut; butter	z	zoo; cause
ur	turn; bird	zh	measure

(Turn the page for more information.)

device *Device* is a useful word with a wide range of meanings. A device can be almost anything that is produced by human thought or effort—a tool, a machine, a plan, a method of doing something, even a scheme or trick. This idea of a scheme or trick carries over into writing. A "plot device" is an action or situation that the writer uses to make things happen in the story. Rather crude plot devices are found in daytime TV serial stories. (Do you know why such television shows are called "soap operas"? It's because they so often depend on ads from laundry soap and detergents.) All the principal characters in a show work together, or live next to each other, or eat their meals together. This ordinarily wouldn't happen in real life, but it gives the writer an excuse to have the characters constantly meeting each other so that the plot can move along.

D

de•vice [di vīs′] *noun, plural* **devices. 1.** anything that is built or made by people to be used for a certain purpose. Any tool or machine is a device. **2.** a plan or scheme; trick: A mother bird will fly quickly out of its nest as a *device* to draw attention from the baby birds in the nest.

dev•il [dev′ əl] *noun, plural* **devils. 1. the Devil.** the chief spirit of evil; also called SATAN. The Devil is thought of as the ruler of Hell and is shown in pictures as a man with a pointed beard, horns, a pointed tail, and hoofs. **2.** a person thought of as very evil and cruel, like the Devil. **3.** a person who is full of energy or mischief: Jimmy scribbled all over my new book, that little *devil!*

dev•il•ish [dev′ ə lish *or* dev′ lish] *adjective, more/most.* like the devil, as in being evil, full of mischief, and so on: "I don't have any idea who ate the cookies," Joey said with a *devilish* grin.

de•vi•ous [dē′ vē əs] *adjective, more/most.* **1.** not direct or straight: That cab driver took the most *devious* route possible to get here; we paid $20 for a trip that should have cost $8. **2.** not honest or straightforward: He had a *devious* reason for staying home from school today; there was a test that he hadn't studied for. —**deviously**, *adverb.* —**deviousness**, *noun.*

de•vise [di vīz′] *verb,* **devised, devising.** to think up; plan or invent: "The sign language and simple words my mother *devised* to communicate with the Americans . . ." (Ernesto Galarza)

de•vote [di vōt′] *verb,* **devoted, devoting.** to give attention, time, or help to: This floor of the museum is *devoted* to modern American art. "I want to *devote* my life to Christian service." (Flannery O'Connor) ♦ Often used as an adjective: The dog has been a *devoted* companion to the old man for many years.

de•vo•tion [di vō′ shən] *noun, plural* **devotions. 1.** the fact of being devoted. **2. devotions.** prayers or other religious acts.

de•vour [di vour′] *verb,* **devoured, devouring. 1.** to eat in a very hungry or greedy way: "I felt hungry and snatched a thick double-slice of bread and butter . . . This I *devoured.*" (Jack London) **2.** to take up something eagerly, as if eating food: Peter loves to read and just *devours* books. "The black horse *devoured* the track with his long strides . . ." (Walter Farley)

dew [doo] *noun.* small drops of water that form from the night air and collect on the ground or another surface.

di•a•be•tes [dī′ ə bē′ tis *or* dī′ ə bē′ tēz] *noun.* a serious disease in which there is too much sugar in the blood. This happens when the blood does not have enough of a substance known as INSULIN. ♦ A person who has diabetes is a **diabetic** [dī′ ə bet′ ik].

di•a•crit•i•cal mark [dī′ ə krit′ ə kəl] a mark or sign put over or under a letter to show how it sounds.

di•ag•no•sis [dī′ əg nō′ sis] *noun, plural* **diagnoses** [dī′ əg nō′ sēz]. **1.** a finding based on a careful study of a person by a doctor to determine if the person has a certain disease or unhealthy condition. **2.** any careful study to find out why a certain problem exists: The mechanic's *diagnosis* is that the car needs a new fuel pump.

di•ag•o•nal [dī ag′ ə nəl] *adjective.* having a slanting direction: The letter 'X' is made with two *diagonal* lines. —**diagonally**, *adverb:* "He walked *diagonally* across the street." (Raymond Chandler)

di•a•gram [dī′ ə gram′] *noun, plural* **diagrams.** a drawing, plan, or figure that shows or explains how something works, how it is made, or how it is arranged: The model plane came with step-by-step *diagrams* for putting it together. —*verb,* **diagramed, diagraming.** to make a diagram or show by a diagram: English textbooks *diagram* sentences to show how they are formed.

di•al [dī′ əl] *noun, plural* **dials.** the front or face

if dying: "At noon on Tuesday the blizzard ended. Then the wind *died* down." (Laura Ingalls Wilder) "He was too tired to shovel the fire into life, and saw the last flame *die*." (Dylan Thomas) **3.** to want very much; wish: I'm *dying* to find out who will win the Academy Award for best actress.

die² *noun, plural* **dies. 1.** a metal device used to stamp, mark, or shape things. Dies cut the threads on nuts and bolts and stamps the design on coins. **2.** one of a pair of DICE.

die•sel [dē′zəl] *noun, plural* **diesels.** an engine that burns a heavy form of oil as a fuel instead of gasoline. Ships, heavy trucks, locomotives, and some automobiles have diesel engines.

the same as each other; separate: "Cougar," "mountain lion," and "puma" are three *different* names for the same animal. **3.** not like most others; Lois has very *different* taste in clothes and never dresses like her classmates. —**differently**, *adverb:* The twins always wear their hair *differently* so that people can tell them apart.

dif•fi•cult [dif′ə kəlt *or* dif′ə kult′] *adjective, more/most.* **1.** hard to do, make, or understand; not easy: It's often *difficult* for Japanese people to say the letter "L" because their language doesn't have this sound. **2.** hard to get along with or please: He's a *difficult* child who never does what his parents want.

D

diet What different meanings this word has! It means "one's usual food" and, in reverse, it can mean a special intake of food (to lose weight, for example, or regain health). Also, a *diet* is an assembly or lawmaking group—as in Japan, where the Diet is like the U.S. Congress. Both senses relate to "day." The food meaning of the words comes from ancient Greek for "how one proceeds daily." The assembly meaning is from Latin meaning a "day," as in a day's journey or a day's work. As you probably know, a lot of ancient Rome's vocabulary derived from the Greeks.

di•et [dī′ət] *noun, plural* **diets. 1.** the food and drink that is eaten by a person or animal: In many countries rice is the main part of the daily *diet.* The *diet* of a skunk is made up mostly of insects and smaller animals. **2.** a special selection of food and drink that a person chooses because of health reasons or to gain or lose weight: Craig is on a low-salt *diet* because he has high-blood pressure. —*verb,* **dieted, dieting.** to eat according to a certain diet: Shelley *dieted* for several weeks and lost 15 pounds.

dif•fer [dif′ər] *verb,* **differed, differing. 1.** to be different: A wolf and a fox are similar animals, but they *differ* in size and color. **2.** to have another opinion; disagree.

dif•fer•ence [dif′rəns] *noun, plural* **differences. 1.** the fact of being unlike someone or something else; being different: There's a big *difference* between watching a ballgame on TV and actually being at the park. **2.** the way or amount of being different: The *difference* between diet soda and regular soda is that diet sodas don't have sugar. **3.** the amount left after one quantity is subtracted from another: The *difference* between 30 and 20 is 10. **4.** a disagreement: The company and its employees held a meeting to settle their *differences* over the new work rules.

dif•fer•ent [dif′rənt] *adjective, more/most.* **1.** not like someone or something else; not alike: Grandpa's old home town is very *different* today than it was when he was a boy. **2.** not

dif•fi•cul•ty [dif′ə kul′tē] *noun, plural* **difficulties. 1.** the fact of being difficult: "Eustace walked with *difficulty*, almost with pain . . ." (E.M. Forster) **2.** something that is difficult: They've been having some financial *difficulties* since they bought that big new house.

dig [dig] *verb,* **dug, digging. 1.** to break up, turn over, or remove the earth. **2.** to make or get by digging: to *dig* a hole, to *dig* a well, to *dig* for clams or for gold. **3.** to push or poke, as if digging a hole: to *dig* your elbow into someone's ribs. **4.** to get or search for something with difficulty, as if one were digging in the earth: Kelly went to the library and *dug* up some interesting facts for her history report.

di•gest [dī jest′ *or* di jest′] *verb,* **digested, digesting. 1.** to break down or change food in the mouth, stomach, and intestines to simpler forms that can be taken in and used by the body. **2.** to think over something for a time to gain a better understanding: "Please, turn back and read this letter over. It is too packed with . . . thought to *digest* the first time." (F.

Scott Fitzgerald) —[dī**/** jest] *noun, plural* **digests.** a shortened version of a long book or article.

di•ges•tion [dī jes**/** chən *or* di jes**/** chən] *noun, plural* **digestions.** the process or method of digesting.

di•ges•tive [dī jes**/** tiv *or* di jes**/** tiv] *adjective.* relating to or helping in digestion. The **digestive system** is the group of organs that digest food and eliminate wastes from the body.

dig•it [dij**/** it] *noun, plural* **digits. 1.** a finger or toe. **2.** a numeral, especially one of the numerals from 0 to 9.

dig•i•tal [dij**/** ə təl] *adjective.* having to do with or showing information directly in number form: a *digital* clock or watch.

dig•ni•fied [dig**/** nə fīd**/**] *adjective, more/most.* having or showing dignity: ". . . a handsome, *dignified* old house with well-kept lawns reaching down to the water's edge." (Kenneth Grahame)

dig•ni•ty [dig**/** nə tē] *noun, plural* **dignities. 1.** a quality of being worthy and honorable that commands the respect of other people: "We can never be satisfied as long as our children are . . . robbed of their *dignity* by signs stating 'For Whites Only.'" (Martin Luther King) **2.** pride in one's character or position: The boss always has other people answer the phone for him because he thinks it's beneath his *dignity* to do it himself. **3.** a calm, serious and formal manner: She managed to keep her *dignity* even after the waiter spilled soup all over her.

dike The famous Zuyder Zee dike of Holland.

dike [dīk] *noun, plural* **dikes.** (also spelled **dyke**) a wall, dam, or other structure built to hold back water. Dikes are built to prevent flooding from a sea, river, or other body of water.

di•lap•i•dat•ed [də lap**/** ə dā**/** tid] *adjective, more/most.* partly fallen down or broken from lack of care: a *dilapidated* old house.

di•lem•ma [də lem**/** ə] *noun, plural* **dilemmas.** a situation in which either of two choices is just as bad as the other; a problem with no easy solution: The congressman has a real *dilemma* about that bill—he knows the voters back home are against it, but all the leaders of his own party insist that he vote for it.

dil•i•gent [dil**/** ə jənt] *adjective, more/most.* careful and hard-working; not lazy: Melissa is very *diligent* about getting her homework done on time. —**diligently,** *adverb.*

di•lute [di lo͞ot**/** *or* dī lo͞ot**/**] *verb,* **diluted, diluting. 1.** to make thinner or weaker by adding a liquid: The directions said to *dilute* the soup mix with one can of water. **2.** to weaken by adding or mixing in something: Her speech made some good points, but the effect was *diluted* by the boring statistics she included.

dim [dim] *adjective,* **dimmer, dimmest. 1.** having or giving little light; not bright: Through the fog we could see one *dim* light at the end of the dock. **2.** not clear or distinct; vague: "There was no moon, and the cedar boughs were but *dim* shadows against a gray sky." (Mary Norton) **3.** not seeing, hearing, or understanding well: Old Shep's eyesight had grown *dim* over the years. —*verb,* **dimmed, dimming.** to make or grow dim: "The air smelled of morning and the stars were *dimming*." (Doris Lessing)

dime [dīm] *noun, plural* **dimes.** a coin of the U.S. and Canada, worth 10 cents.

di•men•sion [di men**/** shən] *noun, plural* **dimensions.** the measurement of the length, width, or height of something. —**dimensional,** *adjective:* A cube is a three-*dimensional* figure.

di•min•ish [di min**/** ish] *verb,* **diminished, diminishing.** to make or become smaller in size or importance: "You would be surprised how the sale of hairpins has *diminished;* we are seldom asked for them." (Beatrix Potter) "They disappear as a single *diminishing* shape, gray fading to darkness." (Barry Lopez)

di•min•u•tive [di min**/** yə tiv] *adjective, more/most.* very small; tiny: The playground was empty except for the *diminutive* figure of one young child playing alone.

dim•ple [dim**/** pəl] *noun, plural* **dimples.** a small hollow place in something, especially the cheeks or the chin.

din [din] *noun, plural* **dins.** a loud, annoying noise that goes on for some time: "The bright warm sunlight was streaming through the window, and he could hear the *din* of traffic." (James Joyce)

dine [dīn] *verb,* **dined, dining.** to eat dinner: They like to *dine* out at least once a week.

diner A popular diner in Wilkinsburg, Pennsylvania. Diners got their name because they were shaped like the dining car of a railroad train.

din•er [dī′ nər] *noun, plural* **diners. 1.** a person who is eating a meal, especially dinner. **2.** *also,* **dining car.** a railroad car where meals are served. **3.** a small restaurant shaped like a dining car.

SUPPER. **2.** a special dinner in honor of some person or event.

di•no•saur [dī′ nə sôr′] *noun, plural* **dinosaurs.** one of a group of reptiles that lived on earth millions of years ago, but have now completely died out. The largest were bigger than any other land animal that has ever lived.

dinosaur The dinosaurs in the front, triceratops (left), and stegosaurus (right) used protective horns, spikes, and plates as a defense against giant meat-eaters such as allosaurus (rear).

dinosaur The poet William Shakespeare refers to an elephant or a whale, rather than a dinosaur, when he wants to give an image of huge size. *Dinosaur* comes from two Greek words meaning "terrible lizard," but the ancient Greek writers don't mention the animal. Nor does it appear in the writings of ancient Rome or the Middle Ages. In fact, before the 1800's no one knew that these creatures had once existed. In 1822, a young Englishwoman named Mary Ann Mantell found some huge teeth that were later identified as coming from a plant-eating dinosaur. The word *dinosaur* was made up in 1841 by a British scientist, Richard Owen. Today, we use the expression "dinosaur" for something large, clumsy, out-of-date, etc: "That 1965 car is a real gas-guzzling *dinosaur.*"

din•ghy [ding′ ē] *noun, plural* **dinghies.** a small rowboat, especially one used to go ashore from a larger boat.

din•gy [din′ jē] *adjective,* **dingier, dingiest.** dark and dirty in appearance; not bright; dull: The white kitchen curtains had turned a *dingy* gray from dirt and smoke.

dining room a room where dinner and other meals are served.

din•ner [din′ ər] *noun, plural* **dinners. 1.** the main meal of the day, served in the evening. When the main meal is eaten in the middle of the day it is sometimes called dinner rather than lunch, and the evening meal is then called

dip [dip] *verb,* **dipped, dipping. 1.** to put into or under water or another liquid for a short time: Julie *dipped* her hand into the lake to find out how cold the water was. **2.** to reach inside a thing to take something out: He *dipped* into the bag and took out a handful of popcorn. **3.** to

Pronunciation Key: A–F				
a	and; hat		ch	chew; such
ā	ate; stay		d	dog; lid
â	care; air		e	end; yet
ä	father; hat		ē	she; each
b	boy; cab		f	fun; off

(Turn the page for more information.)

lower and then quickly raise again: "The American flag should not be *dipped* to any person or thing." (U.S. Flag Code) **4.** to drop or go down: "The sun had *dipped* out of sight behind a bank of clouds." (John P. Marquand) —*noun, plural* **dips. 1.** the act of dipping one's body in the water; a quick swim. **2.** a liquid into which something is dipped: Sheep *dip* is used to kill insects and disease on the animals' skin. **3.** a soft food mixture into which other foods can be dipped: onion *dip*. **4.** a sinking or drop: Be careful of that *dip* in the road up ahead.

diph·the·ri·a [dif thēr′ē ə *or* dip thēr′ē ə] *noun.* a serious disease of the throat that makes breathing difficult.

di·plo·ma [di plō′ mə] *noun, plural* **diplomas.** a printed piece of paper given by a school or college to show that a student has graduated and has completed a certain course of study.

diploma A diploma is nicknamed a "sheepskin." For many years diplomas were written on a fine grade of paper called *parchment*, which was made from a sheep's skin.

dip·lo·mat [dip′ lə mat′] *noun, plural* **diplomats. 1.** a person whose job is to represent his or her country in dealings with other countries around the world. **2.** any person who is good at dealing with other people. ♦ The art or work of being a diplomat is **diplomacy:** Count Metternich of Austria was considered a master of *diplomacy* for his shrewd dealings with other countries.

dip·lo·mat·ic [dip′ lə mat′ ik] *adjective, more/ most.* **1.** having to do with diplomats or their work: The U.S. and China resumed normal *diplomatic* relations in 1979. **2.** showing skill in dealing with another person's feelings: When he said, "Don't you think my little son is really cute?" she gave the *diplomatic* answer, "He looks just like you." —**diplomatically,** *adverb.*

dip·per [dip′ ər] *noun, plural* **dippers. 1.** a cup with a long handle that is used to lift water or other liquids. **2.** either of two groups of stars in the northern sky shaped somewhat like a dipper. The larger group is the **Big Dipper** and the smaller is the **Little Dipper.**

di·rect [di rekt′] *verb,* **directed, directing. 1.** to be in charge of the activity or dealings of; manage or control: Mrs. Hall *directs* the daily operations of the bank. **2.** to order or command: "The captain *directed* the cook to take one oar at the stern." (Stephen Crane) **3.** to tell or show someone the way: Could you *direct* me to the nearest telephone? **4.** to send to a particular place; point or aim: "He sat with . . . his eyes *directed* to a corner of the floor." (Robert Louis Stevenson) —*adjective, more/most.* **1.** going from one point to another in line or by the shortest route: He took a *direct* flight from Boston to Dallas. **2.** following the truth; honest: A witness in court has to give *direct* answers. **3.** in an exact way; exact: The general gave his men a *direct* order.

direct current (D.C.) an electric current that flows in only one direction at a constant rate. Today ordinary household electricity uses ALTERNATING CURRENT (A.C.) instead.

di·rec·tion [di rek′ shən] *noun, plural* **directions. 1.** the act or fact of directing; management or control: The Boston Pops Orchestra was under the *direction* of Arthur Fiedler for almost 50 years. **2.** something that is directed; an order or command: He pulled his car to the side of the road at the police officer's *direction.* **3. directions.** information or instructions on how to get to a place or do a certain thing: The man gave us *directions* to the bus station. Read the *directions* on the box carefully before you use that pancake mix. **4.** the line along which something moves or the way it faces: "We sailed in, following the *direction* of the waves." (Thor Heyerdahl)

di·rect·ly [di rekt′ lē] *adverb.* **1.** in a direct line or way; straight: A famous instruction in the game of 'Monopoly' is "Go *directly* to Jail. Do not pass Go." **2.** at once; immediately: She should be here *directly.* **3.** exactly or absolutely: His opinions about politics are *directly* opposite to mine.

direct object in grammar, the person or thing that receives the action that is expressed by a verb. In the sentence "I bought a shirt," "a shirt" is the direct object because it tells what was bought.

di·rec·tor [di rek′ tər] *noun, plural* **directors. 1.** any person who directs something: the *direc-*

dis- *Dis-* is a common prefix in English that carries the meaning of "not" or "the opposite of." It is most often attached to verbs, such as *dislike, disappear, disobey,* or *disagree.* It is also used with nouns (*disrespect, disadvantage*), and with adjectives (*dishonest, disloyal*). *Disaster* originally meant a "bad star." When something very bad happened to a person, he was said to have "a bad star." (In the Middle Ages people believed that the stars and planets could control what happened to them.) By the way, look at the article on page 230 on "dispatch." That does not have the negative meaning. No one said language follows iron-clad rules!

tor of a summer camp. **2.** a person who is in charge of the performance of a play, movie, or television show: John Ford was the *director* of many famous Western movies. **3.** a person who controls the affairs of a business as a member of the BOARD OF DIRECTORS.

di•rec•to•ry [di rek′trē] *noun, plural* **directories.** a book or sign containing a list of names, addresses, and other facts. A telephone book is a directory.

dirigible The most famous dirigible was the German Zeppelin. It is shown here at Lakehurst, New Jersey in 1937. Shortly after this it tragically exploded and burned at this very spot.

dir•i•gi•ble [dir′ ə jə bəl] *noun, plural* **dirigibles.** a large balloon shaped like a long tube. It is driven by a motor and can be steered.

dirt [durt] *noun.* **1.** dust, mud, grease, or other such material that makes things unclean. **2.** loose earth or soil, as in a garden. **3.** something thought of as nasty, worthless, or very unpleasant: That gossip magazine prints all the latest *dirt* about movie stars.

dirt•y [dur′tē] *adjective,* **dirtier, dirtiest. 1.** not clean; soiled by dust, mud, grease, or the like: The little boy washed his *dirty* hands before eating. **2.** nasty or mean; not nice: Why did you give me such a *dirty* look when I said that? The fans always boo him because he's such a *dirty* player.

dis•a•bil•i•ty [dis′ ə bil′ ə tē] *noun, plural* **disabilities.** the fact of being disabled, or something that disables: Blindness is a severe *disability*.

dis•a•ble [dis ā′ bəl] *verb,* **disabled, disabling.** to take away the normal ability to do something; cripple: The disease arthritis *disables* many people. ◆ Often used as an adjective: The movie *Coming Home* deals with a *disabled* veteran of the Vietnam War.

dis•ad•van•tage [dis′ əd van′ tij] *noun, plural* **disadvantages. 1.** something that makes it harder to do a thing or to succeed: Being Catholic was thought to be a *disadvantage* in running for President until John Kennedy won in 1960. **2.** an unfavorable condition or situation.

dis•a•gree [dis′ ə grē′] *verb,* **disagreed, disagreeing. 1.** to fail to agree; differ in opinion: The town wants to close Parker School, but many of the parents *disagree.* **2.** to be unlike each other; be different: The answer I got for that problem *disagrees* with the one in the book. **3.** to have a bad or unpleasant effect on; be harmful: Mom never eats mushrooms because they *disagree* with her.

dis•a•gree•a•ble [dis′ ə grē′ ə bəl] *adjective, more/most.* **1.** likely to disagree; hard to get along with: "He was the proudest, most *disagreeable* man in the world, and everybody hoped he would never come there again." (Jane Austen) **2.** bad or unpleasant: cold, *disagreeable* weather. Cleaning out the cellar was a dirty, *disagreeable* job. —**disagreeably,** *adverb.*

dis•a•gree•ment [dis′ ə grē′ mənt] *noun, plural* **disagreements.** the act of disagreeing: They had a serious *disagreement* and aren't speaking to each other.

Pronunciation Key: G–N

g	give; big	k	kind; cat; back
h	hold	l	let; ball
i	it; this	m	make; time
ī	ice; my	n	not; own
j	jet; gem; edge	ng	having

(Turn the page for more information.)

D

> **disc or disk** For most words in English, there is only one correct way to spell the word. *Disk* is one of the few that has a variant spelling—a second form of the word that is equally correct. This variant (*disc*) does not occur as often as the preferred spelling *disk*, but the c form can be seen in words like *discus, disc jockey,* and *discotheque.* The main reason that *disk* is more common today is that this is the spelling preferred by the computer industry, where it is frequently used in terms such as "hard disk," "disk drive" and "disk operating system."

dis•ap•pear [dis′ ə pēr′] *verb,* **disappeared, disappearing. 1.** to go out of sight: The moon *disappeared* behind the clouds. **2.** to pass away or go out of existence; end completely: Dinosaurs *disappeared* millions of years ago. "His anger *disappeared* like bubbles from water turned off at the boil." (Brian Moore)

dis•ap•pear•ance [dis′ ə pēr′ əns] *noun, plural* **disappearances.** the act or fact of disappearing: The Missing Persons Bureau deals with the *disappearance* of people from their homes.

dis•ap•point [dis′ ə point′] *verb,* **disappointed, disappointing.** to fail to live up to one's hopes, wishes, or desires: Maria will *disappoint* her parents if she doesn't make the honor roll. ♦ Often used as an adjective: That game was a very *disappointing* loss for our team.

dis•ap•point•ment [dis′ ə point′ mənt] *noun, plural* **disappointments. 1.** the act or feeling of being disappointed. **2.** something or someone that disappoints: I usually like that actor's movies, but his latest was a real *disappointment.*

dis•ap•prove [dis′ ə proov′] *verb,* **disapproved, disapproving.** to have a feeling or belief against; not approve: My parents *disapprove* of skateboarding because they think it's too dangerous. Mr. Jensen wanted a new computer for his office, but the boss *disapproved* his request. —**disapproval,** *noun.*

dis•arm [dis ärm′] *verb,* **disarmed, disarming. 1.** to take away weapons from: The police *disarmed* the prisoners. **2.** to make harmless: to *disarm* a bomb. **3.** to reduce, limit, or do away with the armed forces or military weapons of a country. ♦ The act of disarming a country is **disarmament:** the *disarmament* of Germany after World War II.

dis•as•ter [di zas′ tər] *noun, plural* **disasters.** any event that causes great suffering or loss such as a flood, fire, earthquake, train wreck, or plane crash. ♦ Something that causes a disaster is **disastrous:** a *disastrous* hurricane. —**disastrously,** *adverb.*

dis•be•lief [dis′ bi lēf′] *noun, plural* **disbeliefs.** lack of belief: Doug's face showed *disbelief* when his picture won first prize.

disc [disk] *noun, plural* **discs.** another spelling of **disk.**

dis•card [dis kärd′] *verb,* **discarded, discarding. 1.** in card games, to put down a card that one does not want or need in one's hand. **2.** to throw away or give up something: She went through her desk and *discarded* some old school papers. —[dis′ kärd] *noun, plural* **discards.** the act of discarding, or something that is discarded.

dis•cern [di surn′] *verb,* **discerned, discerning.** to notice or recognize with the senses or the mind: "Suddenly some of the steam begins to advance, and, peering through it, you *discern* Aunt Elizabeth." (Upton Sinclair).

dis•charge [dis chärj′] *verb,* **discharged, discharging. 1.** to release or let go; dismiss: The prisoner was *discharged* from jail after serving a three-year sentence. She was *discharged* from her job because she missed so many days of work for no reason. **2.** to unload or remove cargo or passengers. **3.** to fire or shoot: to *discharge* a rifle. **4.** to give off or let out water or other liquid; flow: The Potomac River *discharges* into Chesapeake Bay. —[dis′ chärj] *noun, plural* **discharges. 1.** a release from work or service; a dismissal: Jim received an honorable *discharge* from the army. **2.** the act of discharging: the *discharge* of fluid from an infected cut.

dis•ci•ple [di sī′ pəl] *noun, plural* **disciples. 1.** someone who believes in and closely follows the teachings of another person: Martin Luther King has been called a *disciple* of Mahatma Gandhi. **2.** *also,* **Disciple.** one of the twelve early followers of Jesus.

dis•ci•pline [dis′ ə plin] *noun, plural* **disciplines. 1.** strict training given to improve the body, mind, or character: Becoming an Olympic athlete takes years of *discipline.* **2.** an attitude of obedience and self-control that results from such training: "*Discipline* is the soul of an army." (George Washington) **3.** punishment given to train or correct. **4.** an area of knowledge or education: Mathematics and science are related *disciplines.*

—*verb*, **disciplined, disciplining. 1.** to give discipline to; train: Indians hunting for game *disciplined* themselves to stand for hours without moving. **2.** to punish in order to train or correct: He's hard to control in school because his parents never *discipline* him at home.

disc jockey a person whose job is playing recorded music, as on the radio.

disc jockey The name *disc jockey* came from the idea that this person handles or manages records ("discs") as a rider ("jockey") handles a horse.

dis•close [dis klōz′] *verb*, **disclosed, disclosing. 1.** to bring into view; uncover: The ruins of the ancient city of Pompeii were accidentally *disclosed* many years later by some people digging a well. **2.** to reveal something that had been secret or hidden: The bank *disclosed* that one of their officers had been secretly transferring money into his own account. ♦ Something that is disclosed is a **disclosure**: President Nixon had to resign after the *disclosure* of serious wrongdoing in his administration.

disconnected the phone so that no one could call while she was taking a bath.

dis•con•tent•ed [dis′ kən ten′ tid] *adjective, more/most.* not content; unhappy or dissatisfied: Jerry was *discontented* with his job because the pay was so low.

dis•con•tin•ue [dis′ kən tin′ yōō] *verb*, **discontinued, discontinuing.** to stop using or doing; end: "He left a note for the milkman to *discontinue* service." (Peter DeVries)

dis•co•theque [dis′ kə tek′] *noun, plural* **discotheques.** a nightclub or other place where people go to dance to recorded music.

dis•count [dis′ kount] *noun, plural* **discounts.** an amount that is less than the regular or full price: At the end of the summer this store sells bathing suits at a 50% *discount.* —[dis kount′ or dis′ kount] *verb*, **discounted, discounting.** to sell at a discount: to *discount* clothing.

dis•cour•age [dis kur′ ij] *verb*, **discouraged, discouraging. 1.** to cause to lose courage or hope: Failing her first driving test did not *discourage* Sara from trying again to get her license. ♦ Often used as an adjective: "It's just that you can't really help them and it's so *discouraging*—it's all for nothing." (F. Scott Fitzgerald) **2.** to try to prevent from doing something: His parents *discouraged* him from trying out for football because they were afraid he'd get hurt.

dis•cour•te•ous [dis kur′ tē əs] *adjective, more/most.* not showing courtesy; rude; impolite: a *discourteous* remark.

dis•cov•er [dis kuv′ ər] *verb*, **discovered, discovering. 1.** to find out something that people

D

discover Did Columbus discover America? The word *discover* means to find something that was not known before. When Columbus reached America, several million people were already living there—the various Indian tribes. So it can hardly be said that America was an unknown place. But America was unknown to the people of the Old World (Europe, Asia, and Africa). Those people learned about America from the news of Columbus's voyage. Therefore it is correct to say, "Columbus *discovered* America." Recently, on television a young child asked, "Who invented electricity?" This is incorrect because *invent* means to bring something new into existence. Electricity as a force in nature has always been present—it needed to be discovered, not invented.

dis•co [dis′ kō] *noun, plural* **discos. 1.** a short word for **discotheque. 2.** a style of popular music with a strong, steady beat.

dis•col•or [dis kul′ ər] *verb*, **discolored, discoloring.** to change to a weaker or less attractive color: Cigarette smoking can *discolor* the teeth.

dis•con•nect [dis′ kə nekt′] *verb*, **disconnected, disconnecting.** to break a connection: Mom

Pronunciation Key: O–S			
ō	over; go	ou	out; town
ô	all; law	p	put; hop
oo	look; full	r	run; car
o͞o	pool; who	s	set; miss
oi	oil; boy	sh	show

(Turn the page for more information.)

did not know about before: Mary Ann Mantell, a young Englishwoman, is credited with *discovering* the first dinosaur bones in 1837. **2.** to find out; learn: I was halfway to school when I *discovered* I'd left my lunch at home.

dis•cov•er•y [dis kuv′ rē] *noun, plural* **discoveries. 1.** the act of discovering; finding something that people did not know about: the *discovery* of America by Columbus in 1492, the *discovery* of gold in California in 1848. "Childhood used to end with the *discovery* that there is no Santa Claus." (James Thurber) **2.** something that is discovered: The idea that germs cause disease was an important scientific *discovery*.

dis•creet [dis krēt′] *adjective, more/most.* very careful about what one says or does; showing good judgment: Nancy was *discreet* in not revealing her friend's secret. "I followed at a *discreet* distance, so I was not noticed." (Wole Soyinka) ◆ The fact of being discreet is **discretion** [dis kresh′ ən].—**discreetly,** *adverb.*

dis•crim•i•nate [dis krim′ ə nāt] *verb,* **discriminated, discriminating. 1.** to treat certain people unfairly or differently from others: It is against the law in the U.S. to *discriminate* against women in hiring workers. **2.** to notice a difference between; distinguish: He is color-blind and can't *discriminate* between red and green.

dis•crim•i•na•tion [dis krim′ ə nā′ shən] *noun, plural* **discriminations. 1.** the act or policy of treating people unfairly because of their race, religion, nationality, sex, or age. **2.** the ability to make or see differences; good judgment: Her parents think she should show more *discrimination* in her choice of friends.

discus From the shape of the discus we can see how this relates to our modern word *dish.*

dis•cus [dis′ kəs] *noun, plural* **discuses.** a flat, heavy disk that is thrown for distance as a sports event.

dis•cuss [dis kus′] *verb,* **discussed, discussing.** to talk over or write about a subject: The class *discussed* their plans for the school fair. This magazine article *discusses* housing problems in our city.

dis•cus•sion [dis kush′ ən] *noun, plural* **discussions.** the act of discussing; talk or writing about a certain subject: Mom and Dad had a lively *discussion* about next week's election for mayor.

dis•dain [dis dān′] *noun.* a feeling that someone or something is not worthy or is beneath oneself: The senator treated the reporter's silly question with *disdain*.

dis•ease [di zēz′] *noun, plural* **diseases.** a condition that prevents the body or a body part from working in its normal way; a sickness or illness. People, animals, and plants can all suffer from diseases. A disease is a condition caused by an infection, growth, or the like, rather than by an accident or a wound. ◆ Something that has a disease is **diseased:** They cut away a *diseased* limb from the old elm tree.

dis•grace [dis grās′] *noun, plural* **disgraces. 1.** a loss of honor or respect; shame: The mayor had to resign in *disgrace* when it was learned he had used city money to build a house for himself. **2.** something that causes such a lack of honor or respect: Mom says it's a real *disgrace* that a city as big as ours doesn't have even one art museum. —*verb,* **disgraced, disgracing.** to bring disgrace to: He *disgraced* his family when he was sent to prison for murder.

dis•grace•ful [dis grās′ fəl] *adjective, more/most.* causing or deserving disgrace. —**disgracefully,** *adverb.*

dis•guise [dis gīz′] *verb,* **disguised, disguising. 1.** to change or hide the way one looks: The spy *disguised* himself as an enemy soldier so that he could take photos of the secret army base. **2.** to hide or conceal: She tried to *disguise* her fear of the dog by acting friendly. —*noun, plural* **disguises.** something that changes or hides the way one really looks: Sherlock Holmes often wore *disguises* so that criminals wouldn't know who he was.

dis•gust [dis gust′] *noun.* a strong feeling of dislike caused by something very bad or unpleasant: The smell of the rotten meat filled her with *disgust*. —*verb,* **disgusted, disgusting.** to cause a feeling of disgust. ◆ Often used as an adjective: She gave him a *disgusted* look when he said he'd eaten snails and frog's legs on his trip to France. "They were *disgusting*-looking and very dirty . . ." (F. Scott Fitzgerald)

dish [dish] *noun, plural* **dishes. 1.** a plate or shallow bowl used to hold or serve food. **2.** a certain type of food: Pizza is her favorite *dish*. **3.** a television antenna in the shape of a large dish, used to receive signals from a satellite. —*verb,* **dished, dishing.** to put or serve in a dish: "When he arrived home at four o'clock his dinner was ready to be *dished* up." (D.H. Lawrence)

dis•hon•est [dis än′ist] *adjective, more/most.* not honest: It is *dishonest* to lie, cheat, or steal. ♦ Being dishonest is **dishonesty.**

dis•hon•or [dis än′ər] *noun.* loss of honor or respect; disgrace; shame: The general brought *dishonor* to himself by giving secrets to the enemy. —*verb,* **dishonored, dishonoring.** to cause dishonor: Doctors have to promise not to *dishonor* the medical profession.

dis•hon•or•a•ble [dis än′ər ə bəl] *adjective, more/most.* causing or deserving dishonor; not honorable. —**dishonorably,** *adverb.*

dish•wash•er [dish′ wäsh′ ər *or* dish′ wôsh′ ər] *noun, plural* **dishwashers. 1.** a machine that automatically washes dishes and other kitchen items. **2.** a person whose job is washing dishes.

dis•in•fect•ant [dis′ in fekt′ ənt] *noun, plural* **disinfectants.** any substance used to destroy disease-causing germs, harmful bacteria, or viruses: The nurse put a *disinfectant* on his cut.

dis•in•te•grate [dis in′ tə grāt′] *verb,* **disintegrated, disintegrating.** to break up or separate into many small pieces: The soft rock *disintegrated* when I hit it with the hammer. ♦ The fact of disintegrating is **disintegration.**

dish A satellite dish to pick up TV signals has become a common sight in the U.S. in recent years. The name comes from its dish-like shape and appearance.

phonograph record. **2.** a metal or plastic plate with a magnetic surface, used in a computer to store information.

disk drive a computer device that reads and records information on a disk. A disk drive spins the disk very fast to locate the information needed.

dis•like [dis līk′] *verb,* **disliked, disliking.** to not like; disapprove of or object to: "She didn't *dislike* housework, but she *disliked* so much of it." (Willa Cather) —*noun, plural* **dislikes.** a feeling of not liking someone or something.

dis•lo•cate [dis′ lō kāt′] *verb,* **dislocated, dislocating. 1.** to force a bone out of its joint: He *dislocated* his shoulder when he fell. ♦ The fact of being dislocated is **dislocation. 2.** to put out of order; disrupt.

> **disinterested** Older persons are often sad about the changing of English, because good meanings of a word are lost. A case in point is *disinterested.* Here is a recent quotation from a newspaper: "After the game, a reporter suggested to Abdul-Jabbar that the Lakers had seemed a bit *disinterested.*" This sentence should read " . . . a bit *uninterested.*" *Uninterested* means you are not curious about or involved with an event or a person. Now another example: " . . . committees with names suggesting that they are *disinterested* groups in favor of justice. They actually get much of their money from such conservative sources as business and large farm owners." (Anthony Lewis) The second sentence uses *disinterested* correctly to mean "neither for nor against; not biased; neutral." Unfortunately, some writers nowadays ignore this distinction. Doing so, they lose a perfectly fine word.

dis•in•ter•est•ed [dis in′ tris tid] *adjective, more/most* **1.** not having a selfish or personal interest; not prejudiced; fair: A judge should take a *disinterested* view of the cases that come before the court. **2.** *Informal.* not having any interest at all; uninterested. (See note above.)

disk [disk] *noun, plural* **disks.** (also spelled **disc**) **1.** a thin, round, flat object, such as a coin or

Pronunciation Key: T Z			
t	ten; date	v	very; live
th	think	w	win; away
<u>th</u>	these	y	you
u	cut; butter	z	zoo; cause
ur	turn; bird	zh	measure

(Turn the page for more information.)

D

dis•loy•al [dis loi′ əl] *adjective, more/most.* not loyal; unfaithful: It was *disloyal* of her friend to criticize her behind her back. ◆ The act or fact of being disloyal is **disloyalty.**

dis•o•bey [dis′ ə bā′] *verb,* **disobeyed, disobeying.** to refuse or fail to obey: Many drivers *disobeyed* the 55-mile-per-hour speed limit when it was first put into effect.

> **dismal** The word *dismal* carries the idea of something bad, but it does not have the same *dis-* root as words like *disaster* and *disease* (see p. 225). *Dismal's* sense of bad comes from the "mal" part of the word. We can see this same root, Latin *malus,* in words such as *malice.* The original form of *dismal* was *dies mali,* meaning "evil days." In the Middle Ages, people believed that bad things were more likely to happen on certain unlucky days. These days were marked on the calendar as "dies mali." (There is one remaining example of these "dismal days"—Friday the 13th.) *Dismal* is often used in writing. It suggests not only something bad, but a feeling of darkness, gloom, and great sorrow: ". . . the weather was cold and threatening, the way dreary, the footing bad, darkness coming on . . . Now that we were out upon the *dismal* wilderness . . ." (Charles Dickens)

dis•mal [diz′ məl] *adjective, more/most.* causing gloom or sadness; depressing: "The farther they went the more *dismal* and lonely the country became." (L. Frank Baum) **—dismally,** *adverb:* "The long night hours dragged *dismally* and endlessly on." (Jim Kjelgaard)

dis•may [dis mā′] *noun.* a strong, sudden feeling of alarm or great disappointment: She was filled with *dismay* when she realized she had left her purse with all her money on the train. **—verb, dismayed, dismaying.** to feel dismay: They were *dismayed* to see the brush fire racing toward their house.

dis•miss [dis mis′] *verb,* **dismissed, dismissing. 1.** to tell or allow to go: The teacher *dismissed* the class at 3:00. **2.** to remove a person from a job or position; fire: The company *dismissed*

dis•or•der [dis ôr′ dər] *noun, plural* **disorders. 1.** lack of order; confusion: "There was no trace of *disorder* or confusion in the neat cabin." (Bret Harte) **2.** an unhealthy or harmful condition: a mild stomach *disorder* **—verb, disordered, disordering.** to throw into confusion. ◆ Usually used as an adjective: "Her face was shiny with tears, and her hair was *disordered.*" (John Cheever)

dis•or•der•ly [dis ôr′ dər lē] *adjective, more/most.* **1.** not neat or tidy; confused: a *disorderly* room. **2.** causing a disturbance; rowdy or wild in behavior: The *disorderly* crowd of soccer fans threw papers and bottles onto the field.

dis•or•gan•ized [dis ôr′ gə nīzd] *adjective, more/most.* not organized; without order or arrangement; confused.

> **dispatch** The word is both a verb ('send quickly') and a noun (an official message that is sent quickly). The statesman and writer Lord Chesterfield, who lived in the 1700's, is best known for his letters to his son. In a letter of February 5, 1750, he told him, "*Dispatch* is the soul of business." He said, "At your age, you have no right nor claim to laziness . . . . Never put off until tomorrow what you can do today." It's odd that Lord Chesterfield became famous for these letters, yet almost nothing is known about the son who was so publicly scolded.

three employees for stealing supplies from the warehouse. ◆ The fact of dismissing or being dismissed is a **dismissal.**

dis•mount [dis mount′] *verb,* **dismounted, dismounting.** to get off or down from something one is mounted on, especially a horse.

Dis•ney [diz′ nē] **Walter (Walt),** 1901–1966, American cartoonist, movie producer, and popular entertainer.

dis•o•be•di•ent [dis′ ə bē′ dē ənt] *adjective, more/most.* refusing to obey; not following orders. ◆ Being disobedient is **disobedience.**

dis•patch [dis pach′] *verb,* **dispatched, dispatching.** to send off to a person or place: "She'd written over three hundred descriptions of Manny Fox and *dispatched* them to sheriffs throughout the South . . ." (Truman Capote) **—noun, plural** **dispatches.** a written message or report: The reporter sent a *dispatch* to his newspaper from the scene of the battle.

dis•pel [dis pel′] *verb,* **dispelled, dispelling.** to make disappear; drive away: "Morning light did little to *dispel* the effects of the nightmare." (Frank Herbert)

dis•pense [dis pens′] *verb,* **dispensed, dispensing. 1.** to give out; distribute: This machine *dispenses* soft drinks. **2. dispense with.** to do without or get rid of: When a movie is shown on TV they usually *dispense with* the list of names at the end of the film.

dis•perse [dis purs′] *verb,* **dispersed, dispersing.** to move or scatter in different directions; break up: The police *dispersed* the angry mob by spraying them with water.

dis•place [dis plās′] *verb,* **displaced, displacing. 1.** to take the place of; replace: Push-button telephones have largely *displaced* the older dial phones. **2.** to remove from its normal place. ♦ A **displaced person** is someone who has been forced to leave his country, as by a war.

dis•play [dis plā′] *verb,* **displayed, displaying.** to show for others to see: Buster Keaton was called 'The Great Stone Face' because he never *displayed* any feelings in his movies. —*noun, plural* **displays. 1.** the act or fact of displaying: a *display* of anger. **2.** the part of a computer that shows the operator the information that is being worked on. For most computers, the display looks like a TV screen.

that is **disposable** is meant to be thrown away after use instead of being used over and over.

dis•po•si•tion [dis′ pə zish′ ən] *noun, plural* **dispositions. 1.** a person's usual way of acting, thinking, or feeling: "She had a lively, playful *disposition* which delighted in anything ridiculous." (Jane Austen) **2.** the arrangement or settling of something.

dis•prove [dis proov′] *verb,* **disproved, disproving.** to prove something to be false or incorrect: Jim said he had stayed in the house studying all weekend, but his fresh sunburn *disproved* it.

dis•pute [dis pyoot′] *verb,* **disputed, disputing. 1.** to argue or fight about something; struggle against: The two countries *disputed* for years over a small strip of land on their border. **2.** to question the truth of something; deny: The government *disputed* the millionaire's claim that he owed no income tax. —*noun, plural* **disputes.** an argument or struggle.

dis•qual•i•fy [dis kwal′ ə fī′] *verb,* **disqualified, disqualifying.** to make or declare not qualified or unfit for something: Mary was *disqualified* from the race for bumping another runner off the track. —**disqualification,** *noun.*

D

Disraeli Benjamin Disraeli was a great prime minister of the British Empire (in 1868 and again in 1874–1880) who was also a good writer, a novelist—he published seven novels between 1836 and 1847 and two more after 1870. Quite a few politicians have been literary figures: Julius Caesar, the Emperor Napoleon, Abraham Lincoln, Winston Churchill, Ulysses S. Grant, among others. For the most part, politicians in our time use "ghostwriters" whose names are not put on the speeches or essays the politician gives out. This is an acceptable practice nowadays, except when it's not clear what the politician said and what was borrowed. For example, this happened when Senator Robert Kennedy became known for the lines, "You see things; and you say, 'Why?' But I dream things that never were; and I say, 'Why not?'" This stirring quote was actually the words of the great British playwright, George Bernard Shaw.

dis•please [dis plēz′] *verb,* **displeased, displeasing.** to not please; annoy or offend: Sally *displeased* her brother by following him around when he had friends over to visit.

dis•pos•al [dis pō′ zəl] *noun.* **1.** the act of getting rid of something. **2.** the power to use or control something: Each salesman for that company has a car at his *disposal.* **3.** a device under a kitchen sink that grinds up soft kitchen garbage so that it can be washed down the drain, also called a **garbage disposal.**

dis•pose [dis pōz′] *verb,* **disposed, disposing. 1.** to get rid of; throw away: He *disposed* of the trash by taking it to the dump. **2.** to deal with or settle: Let's *dispose* of this problem before we start discussing anything else. ♦ Something

Dis•rae•li [diz rā lē] **Benjamin** (1804-1881), British political leader and author.

dis•re•gard [dis′ ri gärd′] *verb,* **disregarded, disregarding.** to pay little or no attention to; ignore: She *disregarded* the teacher's instructions and ended up doing the problem the wrong way. —*noun.* lack of attention or respect; neglect: *disregard* for the law.

Pronunciation Key: [ə] Symbol

The [ə] or *schwa* sound occurs in syllables without an accent. It can be spelled with any vowel, such as a in above, e in listen, i in pencil, o in melon, u in circus. It can also be a combination of vowels, such as io in action, ai in mountain, iou in precious.

(Turn the page for more information.)

D

dis•re•pair [dis′ ri pâr′] *noun.* the state of needing major repairs: "The town was in great *disrepair* —no building was without a broken window, no street without a wrecked car … (Paul Theroux)

dis•re•spect [dis′ ri spekt′] *noun.* a lack of respect; rudeness: Talking out of turn in class shows *disrespect* for the other students. ◆ A person who acts this way is **disrespectful.**

dis•rupt [dis rupt′] *verb,* **disrupted, disrupting.** to put out of order; break up or upset: The woman *disrupted* the trial by shouting out loudly that the witness was telling a lie. —**disruption,** *noun.*

dis•sat•is•fied [dis sat′ is fīd′] *adjective, more/most.* not satisfied or pleased; discontented: We were very *dissatisfied* with the new computer we bought because it was so hard to learn to use. ◆ The feeling of being dissatisfied is **dissatisfaction.**

dis•sect [di sekt′ *or* dī sekt′] *verb,* **dissected, dissecting.** to cut something apart in order to examine or study it: The science class *dissected* a frog to study its digestive system.

dis•sent [di sent′] *verb,* **dissented, dissenting.** to think or feel differently; disagree: The movie *Twelve Angry Men* tells of how one man on a jury *dissented* when the eleven others thought the accused person was guilty. ◆ Also used as an adjective: When the U.S. Congress declared war on Japan in 1941, there was only one *dissenting* vote. —*noun, plural* **dissents.** the act of dissenting.

dis•solve [di zälv′] *verb,* **dissolved, dissolving.** 1. to mix or become mixed into a liquid: The sugar *dissolved* when I stirred it in my tea. 2. to break up; end: to *dissolve* a marriage.

dis•tance [dis′ təns] *noun, plural* **distances.** 1. the amount of space between two things, places, or points: The *distance* between New York and Los Angeles is about 3,000 miles. 2. a place or point far away: "In the *distance,* fireworks began going off." (E.B. White) 3. a feeling or attitude of being unfriendly.

dis•tant [dis′ tənt] *adjective, more/most.* 1. far away in space or time; not near: As he lay in bed he heard the *distant* sound of a train whistle. 2. separated by a certain amount: "The airstrip is a few long fields *distant* from my house." (Annie Dillard) 3. not friendly: No matter how hard he tried to please her, she remained cool and *distant.*

dis•till [dis til′] *verb,* **distilled, distilling.** to heat a liquid until it becomes a gas or VAPOR and then cool it until it becomes a liquid again. Liquids are distilled to make them pure or to remove substances that are not wanted. ◆ The process of distilling something is called **distillation** [dis′ tə lā′ shən]: the *distillation* of gasoline from crude oil.

dis•tinct [dis tingkt′] *adjective, more/most.* 1. different from others; not the same; separate: Frogs and toads are similar but *distinct* animals. 2. easy to sense or understand; clear; definite. —**distinctly,** *adverb:* "I was very careful to pronounce my 'sirs' *distinctly,* in order that he might know that I was polite." (Richard Wright)

dis•tinc•tion [dis tingk′ shən] *noun, plural* **distinctions.** 1. the act or fact of making or noticing a difference. 2. a feature or characteristic that makes one thing different from another: The shape of the jaw is one *distinction* between an alligator and a crocodile. 3. honor or excellence: The Nobel Prize is given for great *distinction* in literature, science, and other fields.

dis•tinc•tive [dis tingk′ tiv] *adjective, more/most.* showing a difference from others; special; characteristic: Many old-time movie stars had very *distinctive* voices, such as Cary Grant, Katherine Hepburn, and James Stewart.

dis•tin•guish [dis ting′ gwish] *verb,* **distinguished, distinguishing.** 1. to know the difference between; tell apart: The players' uniforms were so covered with mud we could hardly *distinguish* one team from the other. 2. to cause a difference; make distinct: "Our minds are our *distinguishing* characteristic . . . We are not stronger or swifter than many other animals. . . . We are only smarter." (Carl Sagan) 3. to bring honor or recognition to oneself. ◆ Often used as an adjective: The convention will be attended by a number of *distinguished* scientists from around the world.

dis•tort [dis tôrt′] *verb,* **distorted, distorting.** 1. to twist or bend something out of its normal or true form: Amusement parks have trick mirrors that *distort* the way people look. 2. to change from its true meaning: The news article *distorted* the mayor's remarks. ◆ Something that is distorted is a **distortion:** We have to get our TV fixed because there's a lot of *distortion* in the picture.

dis•tract [dis trakt′] *verb,* **distracted, distracting.** to take someone's attention away from what they are thinking or doing: Tom didn't hear what his friend said because the pretty girl walking by *distracted* him. ◆ Also used as an adjective: Catherine gave me a *distracted* smile and kept her eyes glued to the TV set.

♦ Something that distracts is a **distraction:** It's hard for him to study on the school bus with all its *distractions*.

> **distractions** When teachers of writing speak of "distractions," they don't refer to a student's writing while listening to loud music on the radio. "Distractions" are insertions of fact or opinion into the body of a paper that serve to distract the reader. (They're also called "detours," "sidetracks," or "digressions.") Suppose you were writing a book report on C. S. Lewis's *The Lion, the Witch, and the Wardrobe*. "Until I read this, I never knew that a science fiction book is like fantasy. I mean that a story can be 'unreal' while being scientific also." Now, where are you going? You've introduced a subject broader than your topic, and you will find it hard to get back to saying what Lewis's book is about and what you think of it. You have, in fact, distracted yourself as well as the reader.

dis•tress [dis tres′] *noun, plural* **distresses. 1.** a feeling of great pain or sorrow; misery; grief: Losing his job caused him quite a lot of *distress*. **2.** danger, trouble, or great need: The Coast Guard rescued the ship that was in *distress*. —*verb,* **distressed, distressing.** to cause distress to a person.

dis•trib•ute [dis trib′ yo͞ot] *verb,* **distributed, distributing. 1.** to give something out in shares; deal out: The bakery *distributes* bread to stores all over town. **2.** to spread out; scatter: She *distributed* the grass seed evenly over the lawn.

dis•tri•bu•tion [dis′ trə byo͞o′ shən] *noun, plural* **distributions.** the act or fact of distributing: The supply sergeant had charge of the *distribution* of uniforms to the soldiers.

dis•trib•u•tor [dis trib′ yə tər] *noun, plural* **distributors. 1.** a person or thing that distributes, especially someone whose business is distributing goods for sale. **2.** a device in a gasoline engine that distributes an electric current to the spark plugs.

dis•trict [dis′ trikt] *noun, plural* **districts. 1.** an area of a country, state, or city that is officially marked for a special purpose: a school *district*. The U.S. House of Representatives has 435 election *districts*. **2.** any general area with a special use or character: The financial *district* of New York is known as Wall Street.

district attorney a lawyer who acts for the government in a certain district, such as a city or county. The district attorney represents the government against someone accused of a crime.

District of Columbia a federal district of the U.S. between Maryland and Virginia. It consists of the city of Washington, the capital of the U.S. *Population:* 675,000.

dis•trust [dis trust′] *verb,* **distrusted, distrusting.** to not trust; be suspicious of; doubt.

—*noun.* lack of trust: The customer looked at the long, complicated sales contract with *distrust*.

dis•turb [dis turb′] *verb,* **disturbed, disturbing. 1.** to make uneasy, upset, or nervous: ". . . the quarrel had deeply *disturbed* Schwartz and he slept badly." (Bernard Malamud) **2.** to break in on; interrupt; bother: "She sat reading through the morning hours . . . and no one *disturbed* her." (Pearl Buck)

dis•turb•ance [dis tur′ bəns] *noun, plural* **disturbances.** the act or fact of disturbing: The loud motorcycles were quite a *disturbance* as they roared through the neighborhood.

ditch [dich] *noun, plural* **ditches.** a long, narrow hole dug along the ground. Ditches are used to drain off or carry water.

dive [dīv] *verb,* **dived** or **dove, diving. 1.** to jump or go head first into water: You can't *dive* at this end of the pool because it isn't deep enough. **2.** to move downward through the air quickly and at a steep angle: The fighter plane *dived* toward the enemy ship. **3.** to go, move, or drop suddenly: "The rabbit *dived* into a hole beneath a pile of rocks." (Jim Kjelgaard) —*noun, plural* **dives. 1.** a head-first jump into water: Peggy made a beautiful *dive* from the high board. **2.** a quick, steep movement downward.

div•er [dī′ vər] *noun, plural* **divers. 1.** any person who dives into water. **2.** a person who works or explores under the water. **3.** a bird that dives into water for its food.

di•verse [di vurs′ *or* dī′ vərs] *adjective, more/ most.* not the same; different: The people of the U.S. come from *diverse* backgrounds.

Pronunciation Key: Accent Marks

[′] is the normal accent mark. It shows where the main stress falls on a word.
[′] is a secondary accent mark. It shows a lighter stress than the primary accent. For example:
tel • e • vis • ion [tel′ə vizh′ən]
(Turn the page for more information.)

D

D

di•ver•sion [di vur′zhən] *noun, plural* **diversions. 1.** a change or turning aside from a planned direction. **2.** something that draws away attention: A smoke bomb in the street created a *diversion* while the two men robbed the store. **3.** something that relaxes or amuses: Watching TV is my favorite *diversion.*

di•ver•si•ty [di vur′sə tē] *noun, plural* **diversities.** the state of being unlike; difference; variety: Newspapers in the Soviet Union are not allowed to express any *diversity* of opinion.

di•vert [di vurt′] *verb,* **diverted, diverting. 1.** to change the direction in which something moves: The sign *diverted* us to another road. **2.** to draw attention to another direction: A song on the radio *diverted* Greg's attention from his homework. **3.** to entertain; amuse: He made funny faces to *divert* the crying baby.

di•vide [di vīd′] *verb,* **divided, dividing. 1.** to separate into parts, pieces, or groups; split: The state of Nebraska was settled according to a law that *divided* the land into sections of 640 acres each. **2.** to separate into parts and give some to each; share: The three winners *divided* the prize money. **3.** to show how many times one number is contained in another: 300 *divided* by 10 is 30. **4.** to separate into opposing sides: The senators were *divided* on the question of raising taxes. —*noun, plural* **divides.** a high area of land that separates two river systems flowing in different directions.

di•vis•i•ble [di viz′ə bəl] *adjective.* capable of being evenly divided: The number 10 is *divisible* by the numbers 10, 5, 2, and 1.

di•vi•sion [di vizh′ən] *noun, plural* **divisions. 1.** the act of dividing: the *division* of a large farm into smaller plots for houses. **2.** one of the parts into which something is divided: the Western *Division* of the National Baseball League. **3.** something that divides or separates. **4.** in arithmetic, the process of dividing one number by another. **5.** a large unit of an army.

di•vi•sor [di vī′zər] *noun, plural* **divisors.** a number by which another is to be divided. When you divide 8 by 4, the *divisor* is 4.

di•vorce [di vôrs′] *noun, plural* **divorces.** the official ending of a marriage by a court of law. —*verb,* **divorced, divorcing. 1.** to end a marriage by law. **2.** to separate from: The company president tried to *divorce* himself from the day-to-day details of the business.

diz•zy [diz′ē] *adjective,* **dizzier, dizziest.** having or causing a light-headed feeling of spinning around and being about to fall: Riding on the "Jet-Go-Round" ride always makes me feel *dizzy.* ◆ The feeling of being dizzy is **dizziness.**

DNA a chemical substance found in the cells of all living things. DNA is an acid that carries the characteristics of an animal or plant from the parent to its offspring. DNA determines the way in which a child resembles its parents.

dividing words One of the editors of this dictionary says that he finds it hard to divide a word at the end of a line unless he thinks of its syllables. For example, "Joyce ran toward the door and suddenly threw her com-pact against it." Only years after he left college did he realize that there is really no rule that a word at the end of a line has to be divided strictly by syllables. It would make just as much sense if you divided "compact" into "comp-act." Are there no general rules, then? Not so. Use these: (1) Don't leave a single letter by itself on a line, as by dividing "a-wake" or "stere-o." (2) Divide compound words between their parts, as in "break-fast" or "home-work." (3) Separate a prefix or suffix, as in "pre-school" or "kind-ness." (4) When a word has a double consonant in the middle, divide between these two letters, as in "ham-mer" or "pep-per."

div•i•dend [div′ə dend] *noun, plural* **dividends. 1.** a number that is to be divided by another number: When you divide 8 by 4, the *dividend* is 8. **2.** money that is earned by a company as a profit and then divided among the people who own shares of the company.

di•vine [di vīn′] *adjective.* **1.** having to do with or like God or a god; religious; sacred: the Cathedral of St. John the *Divine.* **2.** given by God: In the Middle Ages there was a belief that kings had a **divine right** to rule, meaning that their power came directly from God.

do [do̅o̅] *verb,* **did, done, doing. 1.** to cause a certain action to happen; carry out; perform: to *do* a job, to *do* business. **2.** to finish a certain task; complete: She has to *do* her homework before she can watch TV. ◆ Usually used in the past participle: I'll be *done* in about five minutes. **3.** to act in a certain way: to *do* your best. This car can *do* 100 miles an hour. **4.** to bring about a certain result: A few days off will *do* him good. **5.** to deal with a certain thing: to *do* one's hair; to *do* the dishes. **6.** to be satisfactory: That box will *do* for a picnic table.

Do is also used with other verbs as a HELPING VERB: **1.** to ask a question: *Do* you know the Johnsons? Where *do* they live? **2.** with the word "not" Wolves *do not* like to live near people. **3.** to stand for another verb that was just used: No one else in my family likes fish, but I *do*. (*like* fish) **4.** to make something that is said stronger: I *do* hope you'll be able to go with us.

> **do** The HBJ Word Survey shows that the verb *do* ranks among the 50 most common words in English, counting all its forms such as *done* and *did*. In spite of this, people sometimes make mistakes with the word, by confusing the different forms. "I know who *done* it." "She *do* so know what happened." You could tell right away that these sentences were incorrect, couldn't you? *Done* can only be used with another verb, in expressions such as "have done" or "was done." When the verb appears alone, *did* is correct: "I know who *did* it." *Do* is used with *I, you, we,* or *they,* but with *he/she/it* (called the third person), *does* is correct: "She *does* so know what happened."

dock[1] [däk] *noun, plural* **docks.** a place for boats or ships to tie up. Docks have platforms for loading and unloading cargo and passengers. —*verb,* **docked, docking. 1.** to bring a boat or ship into a dock. **2.** to join two spacecraft together in space.

dock[2] *verb,* **docked, docking. 1.** to take some away; make less: The boss *docked* Joe's pay last week because he missed three days of work. **2.** to cut off the end of an animal's tail or ears.

doc•tor [däk′tər] *noun, plural* **doctors. 1.** a person who has been specially trained and is licensed by law to treat sickness or injury and preserve health. A surgeon and a dentist are two types of doctors. **2.** a person who has the highest degree that a university gives: a *Doctor*

of Law. A **Doctor of Philosophy (Ph.D.)** degree is given in such subjects as biology, history, or English.

doc•trine [däk′trin] *noun, plural* **doctrines. 1.** something that is believed by a group of people, especially the official beliefs of a certain religion. **2.** an official statement of government policy: The **Monroe Doctrine** stated that the U.S. was opposed to European countries interfering in the Americas.

doc•u•ment [däk′yə mənt] *noun, plural* **documents. 1.** a written or printed statement that gives official proof or information about something. A birth certificate and a driver's license are documents. **2.** a printed copy of information from a computer. —*verb,* **documented, documenting.** to prove something by a document or documents: The man *documented* his claim that the old house actually belonged to him.

doc•u•men•ta•ry [däk′yə men′trē] *noun, plural* **documentaries.** a movie or television program that gives factual information about a real-life subject.

dodge [däj] *verb,* **dodged, dodging. 1.** to keep away from something by moving quickly: The batter *dodged* the baseball that was thrown at him. **2.** to get away from something in a tricky way; cleverly avoid: The witness *dodged* the lawyer's questions by claiming he had suddenly lost his memory. —*noun, plural* **dodges. 1.** a quick move to avoid something; an act of dodging. **2.** a trick used to fool or cheat someone: The man tried to use a tax *dodge* so that he wouldn't have to pay income taxes.

do•do [dō′ dō] *noun, plural* **dodos** or **dodoes.** a large bird that once lived on islands in the

dodo The dodo became extinct very quickly when sailors came to the islands where it lived. They hunted it for food and rats from the ships ate its eggs.

	Pronunciation Key: A–F		
a	and; hat	ch	chew; such
ā	ate; stay	d	dog; lid
â	care; air	e	end; yet
ä	father; hat	ē	she; each
b	boy; cab	f	fun; off

(Turn the page for more information.)

Indian Ocean. The dodo had small wings and was not able to fly. People killed the dodo for food, and today none of those birds exist.

doe [dō] *noun, plural* **does** or **doe. 1.** a female deer. **2.** the female of several other animals for which the male is known as a BUCK, such as the antelope or rabbit.

does [duz] *verb.* a present form of the verb **do.**

does•n't [duz′ ənt] a contraction of **does not.**

dog [dôg] *noun, plural* **dogs.** a four-legged animal that barks and is closely related to the wolf. There are many separate breeds of dogs that differ from each other in size and appearance. —*verb,* **dogged, dogging.** to follow closely, as a dog follows a trail: to *dog* a person's footsteps.

dogwood The beautiful white and pink blossoms of the dogwood tree bring color to the southern U.S. in the spring.

dog•wood [dôg′ wood′] *noun, plural* **dogwoods.** a tree that has flowers with a greenish-yellow center and pink or white leaves that look like petals. Dogwoods blossom in the spring.

doll [däl] *noun, plural* **dolls.** a child's toy that looks like a baby, a child, or a grown person.

dol•lar [däl′ ər] *noun, plural* **dollars.** the basic unit of money in the United States and Canada. One dollar is equal to 100 cents.

dol•phin [däl′ fin] *noun, plural* **dolphins.** a water animal that is related to the whale, but is smaller. It has a long snout like a bird's beak and two flippers. Dolphins are mammals rather than fish. Dolphins are very intelligent and can be trained to do things.

do•main [dō mān′] *noun, plural* **domains.** all the land under the control of one ruler or government: Julius Caesar's *domain* as emperor included what is now Spain and France.

dome [dōm] *noun, plural* **domes. 1.** a large, round roof that looks like an upside-down bowl. Domes are built on a round base or one with many sides. The U.S. Capitol Building in Washington has a dome. **2.** anything shaped like a dome: ". . . the pale *domes* of soft-boiled eggs in blue egg cups." (Sylvia Plath)

do•mes•tic [də mes′ tik] *adjective, more/most.* **1.** having to do with a home, household, or family: Cooking, washing, and cleaning are *domestic* chores. **2.** not wild; tame: Common *domestic* animals include dogs, cats, cows, and horses. **3.** of one's own country; not foreign: They served a *domestic* wine from California.

dom•i•nant [däm′ ə nənt] *adjective, more/most.* having the greatest power or influence; most important; controlling: In British government the House of Commons is *dominant.* Blue is the *dominant* color in that room.

dom•i•nate [däm′ ə nāt′] *verb,* **dominated, dominating.** to rule or control by power, size, or importance: The Boston Celtics *dominated* pro basketball for many years. ♦ The dominating of something is called **domination:** For many years Egypt was under the *domination* of other countries.

Do•min•i•can Republic [də min′ i kən] a country in the West Indies, on the eastern part of the island of **Hispaniola** [his′ pan yō′ lə] *Capital:* Santo Domingo. *Area:* 18,000 square miles. *Population:* 5,675,000.

do•min•ion [də min′ yən] *noun, plural* **dominions. 1.** rule or control: The Bible says that "man has *dominion* over every living thing on the earth." **2.** land under the control of a ruler or government.

dolphin The dolphin is known for its ability to leap high out of the water. Exactness in language rests in good part with checking a dictionary—a dolphin is not a fish. It is a sea mammal, warm-blooded with lungs and therefore dependent on breathing air.

dom•i•no [dăm′ ə nō′] *noun, plural* **dominoes.** one of a set of small black tiles or pieces of wood marked with dots, used for playing the game of **dominoes.**

do•nate [dō′ nāt′] *verb,* **donated, donating.** to give as a gift; present; contribute: to *donate* money to the Red Cross, to *donate* a valuable painting to a museum.

do•na•tion [dō nā′ shən] *noun, plural* **donations.** the act of donating, or something that is donated; a gift or contribution.

done [dun] *verb.* the past form of **do:** She's *done* very well in math this year. —*adjective.* **1.** completed; finished: I'd like to read that magazine if you're *done* with it. **2.** cooked enough: Check the oven to see if the meat is *done* yet.

don•key [dăng′ kē] *noun, plural* **donkeys.** an animal related to the horse, but smaller and having longer ears. Donkeys are often used to pull or carry loads.

do•nor [dō′ nər] *noun, plural* **donors.** any person who donates or provides something: a blood *donor,* the *donor* of a painting.

don't [dōnt] *verb.* the contraction for "do not."

donkey The sturdy and reliable donkey is an important pack animal in many countries, as shown here in Iran. It is known for being very stubborn if mistreated.

dope [dōp] *noun, plural* **dopes. 1.** *Slang.* an illegal drug, such as opium or heroin. **2.** *Slang.* a very stupid person. **3.** a thick varnish or similar liquid used to treat a surface or hold parts together.

dor•mant [dôr′ mənt] *adjective.* not active for a period of time: The volcano Mt. St. Helens had been *dormant* for years before it suddenly

don't The difference between *don't* and *doesn't* is a serious matter of speaking and writing well. A careful person who has several years of schooling does not say: "It *don't* matter to me." Your ear tells you what is good or bad usage: "We *don't* like you" is correct, as is "They *don't* have to reply." It's not always true, though, that *doesn't* is the singular and *don't* the plural. For example, the correct form is "I *don't,*" not "I *doesn't.*" Yet *he/she/it* (a singular) always calls for *doesn't.* Dylan Thomas begins a famous poem with the line, "*Do not* go gentle into that good night." However, *don't* is more natural for ordinary conversation and friendly letters.

doom [do͞om] *noun, plural* **dooms.** a terrible fate; ruin or death: The warden led the condemned prisoner to his *doom.* —*verb,* **doomed, dooming. 1.** to subject to a terrible fate: The spy was *doomed* to spend the rest of his life in prison. **2.** to make bad luck, failure, or destruction certain: That business was *doomed* from the start because they never had enough money to operate.

door [dôr] *noun, plural* **doors. 1.** a movable part that is used to open or close the entrance to something, such as a room, building, or car or other vehicle. **2.** a doorway.

door•step [dôr′ stěp′] *noun, plural* **doorsteps.** a step or flight of steps leading up to the outside door of a building.

door•way [dôr′ wā′] *noun, plural* **doorways. 1.** an opening in a wall that leads in and out of a room or building and is closed by a door. **2.** a way of getting to some place or goal.

erupted in 1980. The Dark Ages is the name for a time when learning and art were *dormant* in Europe.

dor•mi•to•ry [dôr′ mə tôr′ ē] *noun, plural* **dormitories.** a building with many bedrooms. Colleges have dormitories for students.

dose [dōs] *noun, plural* **doses.** a certain amount of a medicine taken at one time.

dot [dät] *noun, plural* **dots.** a small, round spot or mark like this: [. . .] —*verb,* **dotted, dotting. 1.** to mark with a dot or dots: The teacher

Pronunciation Key: G N		
g	give; big	k kind; cat; back
h	hold	l let; ball
i	it; this	m make; time
ī	ice; my	n not; own
j	jet; gem; edge	ng having

(Turn the page for more information.)

D

reminded Jim to *dot* his "i's." **2.** to be scattered here and there: ". . . a beautiful country, with green meadows *dotted* with bright flowers . . ." (L. Frank Baum)

the funniest picture I've seen this year. **2.** a state of being uncertain or undecided: With only half the votes counted, the results of the election are still in *doubt*.

> **double negatives** A "double negative" is a statement that uses two negative words to express one negative idea, such as "I *don't* know *nothing* about it" or "I *didn't* have *no* breakfast this morning." Double negatives are not necessary—just one negative word will carry the same meaning. In fact, "I don't know nothing about it" could be strictly taken to mean "I do know *something* about it," which is a positive statement. Writers of fiction may purposely use double negatives in the speech of a character, to show that the person is not educated or polished. For example, in John Steinbeck's novel about poor Oklahoma farmers, *The Grapes of Wrath*, the character Muley says, "I *don't* go *no* place and I *don't* leave *no* place." Sometimes writers even use a triple negative: "*Nor nobody* else heard them *neither*." (Flannery O'Connor)

D

dou•ble [dub/ əl] *adjective.* **1.** twice as many or twice as much: He got *double* pay for working all day Sunday. **2.** made for two people or made up of two similar parts: *double* doors, a *double* bed, a *double*-barreled shotgun. **3.** having two different sides or qualities: The word "politician" has a *double* meaning. —*adverb.* **1.** two together; in pairs: He saw *double* after he got hit in the head. **2.** twice as much: If he doesn't pay that parking ticket now he'll be charged *double*. —*noun, plural* **doubles. 1.** a number or amount that is twice as much. **2.** a person or thing like another: The star's *double* appeared in the scene that showed him riding a horse. **3.** in baseball, a hit that allows the batter to get to second base. —*verb,* **doubled, doubling. 1.** to make or become twice as many or twice as much: The boss *doubled* Joan's salary. **2.** to fold or bend as if to make double: "He was almost *doubled* over from trying to catch his breath." (S. E. Hinton)

dou•ble-cross [dub/ əl krôs/] *verb,* **double-crossed, double-crossing.** to cheat or betray someone by promising to do one thing and then doing another: One bank robber *double-crossed* the rest of the gang by disappearing with all the stolen money himself. —*noun.* the act of double-crossing someone.

dou•ble•head•er [dub/ əl hed/ ər] *noun, plural* **doubleheaders.** two games played one after the other on the same day.

double play a play in baseball in which two runners are put out.

doubt [dout] *verb,* **doubted, doubting.** to not believe or trust; feel uncertain; question: I only met him once years ago, so I *doubt* that he'll remember me. —*noun, plural* **doubts. 1.** a feeling of not believing or trusting: I had my *doubts* about that movie, but it turned out to be

doubt•ful [dout/ fəl] *adjective, more/most.* in doubt; uncertain: "Their eyes were *doubtful*. For the first time he felt them wondering if it was going to be easy to get home." (Pearl Buck) —**doubtfully,** *adverb.*

dough [dō] *noun, plural* **doughs.** a soft, thick mixture of flour, liquid, and other ingredients, used to make such foods as bread, cookies, pies, and so on.

dough•nut [dō/ nut/] *noun, plural* **doughnuts.** a small cake of sweetened dough cooked in fat. Doughnuts are usually shaped like rings with holes in the middle.

Doug•lass [dug/ ləs] **Frederick,** 1817–1895, American author and leader in the anti-slavery movement.

dove A dove played an important part in the Bible story of Noah's Ark. Also in the Bible is the famous line: "And the voice of the turtle (turtledove) is heard in our land." (from the *Song of Solomon*)

dove[1] [duv] *noun, plural* **doves.** a small bird that looks like a pigeon. Doves have a thick body and make a cooing sound.

dove² [dōv] *verb.* a past tense of **dive:** She *dove* into the water.

down¹ [doun] *adverb.* **1.** from a higher place to a lower one; toward the ground: The ball rolled *down* the hill. The whole family sat *down* for dinner. **2.** to a place that is further away: Go *down* to the store and get some milk. **3.** to or in a lower position or condition: The price of calculators has gone *down* since they first came out. **4.** to a condition that is weaker, quieter, less active, or the like: The car slowed *down*. Please turn *down* the radio. **5.** from an earlier to a later time: a story that comes *down* from the Middle Ages. —*adjective.* **1.** going downward; directed down: a *down* escalator. **2.** in a lowered position or state: The price of milk is *down* this week. **3.** feeling ill or sad: Bobby is *down* with the flu again. **4.** not working; out of order: All the bank's computers are *down* today. —*preposition.* moving down along, through, or into: Katie slid *down* the slide. —*verb*, **downed, downing.** to go or bring down; make go down: He *downed* three glasses of lemonade. —*noun, plural* **downs.** in football, any of the four chances that the team with the ball has to move forward at least ten yards.

down² *noun.* the fine, soft feathers baby birds have before they grow adult feathers. ◆ Something soft and fluffy like down is **downy.**

down•heart•ed [doun′ här′ tid] *adjective.* sad; depressed.

down payment a payment of part of the price of something at the time of buying it, with the rest of the amount to be paid later.

down•pour [doun′ pôr′] *noun, plural* **down-pours.** a very heavy rainstorm.

down•town [doun′ toun′] *adverb, adjective.* in the main part or business center of a town or city.

down•ward [doun′ wərd] (*also,* **downwards**) *adverb, adjective.* from a higher to a lower place or position; down.

doze [dōz] *verb*, **dozed, dozing.** to sleep lightly; nap: "He was just *dozing* off to sleep when he heard his name." (Irwin Shaw)

doz•en [duz′ ən] *noun, plural* **dozens** or **dozen.** a group or set of twelve things.

drab [drab] *adjective*, **drabber, drabbest.** not bright or interesting; dreary; dull: The city's waterfront is a *drab* landscape of old warehouses and rotting piers.

draft [draft] *noun, plural* **drafts. 1.** a current of air indoors: "The floor and the walls were so solid that not the smallest cold *draft* came in." (Laura Ingalls Wilder) **2.** something that controls the flow of air, as in a furnace. **3.** a sketch, plan, or rough copy of something to be made or written: The lawyer prepared several *drafts* of the letter before she was sure it was correct. **4.** the process of selecting someone to serve for a special purpose: During World War II, many men were called to war by the *draft*. **5.** a drink such as beer that is drawn from a barrel or other large container, rather than stored in a bottle or can. —*verb*, **drafted, drafting. 1.** to make a draft: The architect *drafted* the plans for the new office building. **2.** to select someone for a special purpose: Each year pro football teams *draft* the top college players. —*adjective.* **1.** used for pulling heavy loads: Horses and oxen are *draft* animals. **2.** ready to be drawn from a container: *draft* beer.

---

drafts The drafts of a term paper in school, or of the manuscript for a book, are the different stages needed to produce a finished copy. How many drafts should you write? As many as it takes to make your writing concise and clear. Here's a rough draft: "The park was closed, not all day however, because the police said children played." Here's a revised draft: "The police closed the park every evening, after it was shown that it was dangerous for children to play there in the dark." Here's a different example: "The men were tired and looked for trees." This first draft isn't clear. Why were they looking? A revised version, another draft, would go like this: "Being tired and thirsty from working in the hot summer sun, the men looked for some trees to rest under."

---

down•right [doun′ rīt′] *adjective.* complete; certain; a *downright* lie. —*adverb.* completely: to be *downright* mad.

down•stairs [doun′ starz′] *adverb, adjective.* down the stairs; on or to a lower floor.

down•stream [doun′ strēm′] *adverb, adjective.* in the same direction that the water flows in a stream or river.

Pronunciation Key. O–S			
ō	over; go	ou	out; town
ô	all; law	p	put; hop
oo	look; full	r	run; car
o͞o	pool; who	s	set; miss
oi	oil; boy	sh	show

(Turn the page for more information.)

drafts•man [drafts′ mən] *noun, plural* **draftsmen. 1.** a person who draws designs or plans for buildings, machinery, or other structures. **2.** an artist who can draw very well: "Ingres ranks among the finest *draftsmen* in the history of painting." (Willard Misfeldt)

draft•y [draf′ tē] *adjective,* **draftier, draftiest.** exposed to or letting in currents of air: a *drafty* old barn.

drag [drag] *verb,* **dragged, dragging. 1.** to pull slowly and with great effort along the ground or floor; haul: "They *dragged* the mattress into the kitchen and made their bed on the floor." (Nathanael West) **2.** to go very slowly: The meeting *dragged* on until almost midnight. **3.** to trail along the ground: ". . . slowly she came to meet him, *dragging* the heavy cape." (Katherine Mansfield) **4.** to search the bottom of a body of water with a net or hook: The police *dragged* the lake for the missing gun.

drag•on [drag′ ən] *noun, plural* **dragons.** in old stories and legends, a beast that breathes out fire and smoke. It is usually shown as a huge winged lizard with large claws.

drag•on•fly [drag′ ən flī′] *noun, plural* **dragonflies.** a large insect with a long, thin body and four narrow wings. Dragonflies live near fresh water and eat other insects.

drain [drān] *verb,* **drained, draining. 1.** to draw off or flow off slowly: "All the blood had been *drained* out of my face till my tan looked like a layer of brown paint over white." (S.E. Hinton) **2.** to make empty or dry by letting water flow off: "The pot had been *drained* of water and dumped on its side." (Bernard Malamud) **3.** to use up; exhaust: "He was tired, *drained* of his energy." (C. S. Forester) "Slowly, the heat *drained* the spirit from them. . . ." (John Knowles) —*noun, plural* **drains. 1.** a pipe or other opening that draws off liquids: the *drain* in a sink. **2.** a thing that uses up or exhausts something: Leaving a car's headlights on causes a *drain* on the battery.

dragon The old tale of St. George slaying the dragon, as shown in a painting done by the great Italian artist Raphael in about 1505.

drain•age [drā′ nij] *noun.* the process of draining off water or other liquids: The holes in the flower pot are for *drainage.*

drake [drāk] *noun, plural* **drakes.** a male duck.

dra•ma [drä′ mə] *noun, plural* **dramas. 1.** a story written to be acted out by actors on a stage; a play. **2.** the art of writing or presenting plays: Shakespeare is the leading figure of English *drama.* **3.** an event in real life that is like a drama: The TV reporter described the *drama* of the spacecraft blasting off for Mars.

dra•mat•ic [drə mat′ ik] *adjective, more/most.* **1.** having to do with drama. **2.** like a drama; full of excitement or feeling: a *dramatic* rescue of a child from a burning building. She's very *dramatic* about her problems and makes them seem more serious than they really are. —**dramatically,** *adverb:* Professional wrestlers react very *dramatically* when they are supposedly hurt in the ring.

---

dramatization In novels or short stories, the term *dramatization* refers to the way a character is presented ("dramatized") to the reader. In Charles Dickens' *Great Expections:* "(Joe) was a mild, good-natured, sweet-tempered, easygoing, foolish, dear fellow." That is one form of dramatization—a direct description by the author. Another way is indirect—using the character's own speech and actions. For example, Joe speaks to a prisoner who has stolen a pie from him: "God knows you're welcome to it, so far as it was ever mine . . . We don't know what you have done, but we wouldn't have you starved to death for it, poor miserable fellow creature." Which of these methods is better? Is it better to describe a character, or to let him or her speak? The answer is: do both.

dram•a•tist [dräm′ə tist] *noun, plural* **dramatists.** a person who writes plays; a playwright.

dram•a•tize [dräm′ə tīz′] *verb,* **dramatized, dramatizing. 1.** to write or present something as a drama: William Gibson *dramatized* the life of Helen Keller in the play *The Miracle Worker.* **2.** to present something in a dramatic way: That teacher *dramatizes* the events of history to make them more interesting.

drank [drangk] *verb.* the past tense of **drink.**

drape [drāp] *verb,* **draped, draping.** to hang a cover loosely over something: He *draped* his jacket over the back of the chair. "The fields and lower woods lay in ghostly silence before him, *draped* in a lightly veiled mist." (Walter Farley) **—drapes,** *plural noun.* cloth that hangs in long, loose folds in front of a window.

dra•per•y [drā′ prē] *noun, plural* **draperies.** (usually used in the plural) see **drapes.**

dras•tic [dras′ tik] *adjective, more/most.* very strong or serious: The mayor took *drastic* steps to deal with the water shortage.

draw [drô] *verb,* **drew, drawn, drawing. 1.** to make a picture with a pen, pencil, or other writing tool: Mickey likes to *draw* pictures of jet planes. **2.** to pull, drag, or haul: Six horses *drew* the wagon. "You can *draw* the curtains and sit by the fire." (Dylan Thomas) **3.** to bring or come close: The musician *drew* a crowd on the street. "Their headlights seemed to *draw* the raindrops, like moths." (Amado Muro) **4.** to pull out or up; remove: to *draw* a gun, to *draw* a cork from a bottle, to *draw* a number in a contest. **5.** to get; receive: I *drew* ten dollars from the bank. "As I tell everybody, I *draw* my own conclusions." (Eudora Welty) **6.** to pull air: to *draw* a deep breath. **—noun, plural draws. 1.** the act of taking a pistol and aiming it. **2.** a game or contest that ends in a tie.

draw•back [drô′ bak′] *noun, plural* **drawbacks.** something bad or unpleasant about a situation; a problem or disadvantage: The main *drawback* to living there is the long, cold winters.

draw•bridge [drô′ brij′] *noun, plural* **drawbridges.** a bridge made to be moved up or down to allow or prevent crossing.

draw•er [drôr] *noun, plural* **drawers.** a box-shaped container that fits into a piece of furniture, such as a desk, cabinet, or chest. It is open at the top so that things can be placed inside.

draw•ing [drô′ ing] *noun, plural* **drawings. 1.** a picture or design made by putting lines on a surface with a pencil, pen, or the like. **2.** the selection of a winning ticket or chance in a RAFFLE or LOTTERY.

drawl [drôl] *verb,* **drawled, drawling.** to talk slowly, drawing out one's words. **—noun.** the speech of a person who drawls: People from Texas are thought of as speaking with a *drawl.*

drawn [drôn] *verb.* the past participle of **draw.**

dread [dred] *verb,* **dreaded, dreading.** to have a great fear of what is to come; be very afraid: "His eyes were not those of mortal man, so that Sig *dreaded* them and was glad they were not turned in his direction." (Andre Norton) **—noun.** a feeling of great fear about something in the future: "Romney, half sick with *dread* for what lay ahead . . ." (Vera & Bill Cleaver) **—adjective.** (also, **dreaded**) causing great fear: a *dread* disease, a *dreaded* criminal.

dread•ful [dred′ fəl] *adjective, more/most.* **1.** causing fear; terrible: ". . . at the dead hour of night, amid the *dreadful* silence of that old house. . . ." (Edgar Allan Poe) **2.** of poor quality; bad; awful: That new TV show is absolutely *dreadful.* **—dreadfully** *adverb:* "I was *dreadfully* frightened." (Daniel Defoe)

dream [drēm] *noun, plural* **dreams. 1.** pictures, thoughts, and feelings that come to the mind during sleep: Judy had a *dream* that she was flying over the treetops. **2.** something imagined while awake; a daydream. **3.** something that one hopes for and imagines coming true: Brian's *dream* is to become a famous rock star. **—verb,** **dreamt** or **dreamed, dreaming. 1.** to have a dream or daydream: "How should an old man spend his days if not in *dreaming* of his well-spent past?" (John Galsworthy) **2.** to think of as possible; imagine: "I work harder here than I ever *dreamed* I could work." (Alice Walker) **—dreamer,** *noun.*

dreamt [dremt] *verb.* the past tense of **dream.**

dream•y [drē′ mē] *adjective,* **dreamier, dreamiest.** like a dream: They spent a *dreamy* summer afternoon drifting down the river. She gave me a *dreamy* look as though she hadn't heard a word I said.

drear•y [drēr′ ē] *adjective,* **drearier, dreariest.** very sad; depressing: a cold, wet, *dreary* day. "He had taken a *dreary* road, darkened by all the gloomiest trees of the forest." (Nathaniel Hawthorne)

Pronunciation Key· T–7

t	ten; date	v	very; live
th	think	w	win; away
th	these	y	you
u	cut; butter	z	zoo; cause
ur	turn; bird	zh	measure

(Turn the page for more information.)

D

dredge [drej] *noun, plural* **dredges.** a large floating machine that scoops up mud from the bottom of a river, stream, or channel in order to make it deeper. —*verb,* **dredged, dredging. 1.** to scoop out with or as if with a dredge: "Even the children *dredged* up their pennies." (Alice Walker)

drench [drench] *verb,* **drenched, drenching.** to make completely wet; soak: "I had no idea it had begun to rain so hard. Why, you're *drenched,* sir!" (Rod Serling)

dress [dres] *noun, plural* **dresses. 1.** a type of clothing worn by women or girls that is a top and a skirt in one piece. **2.** a particular style of clothing: Evening *dress* is a style worn to a formal party. —*verb,* **dressed, dressing. 1.** to put clothes on; to wear clothes. **2.** to prepare or take care of something in a special way, as if putting on clothing: to *dress* a turkey for the oven. The nurse *dressed* his infected foot. **3. dress up.** to wear formal or fancy clothes.

dress•er[1] [dres′ ər] *noun, plural* **dressers.** a large piece of furniture, having drawers and used for storing clothes.

dresser[2] *noun, plural* **dressers.** a person that dresses, especially someone who dresses in a certain way: a fancy *dresser.*

dress•ing [dres′ ing] *noun, plural* **dressings. 1.** the act of getting dressed; putting on clothes. **2.** a bandage put on a cut or other wound. **3.** a type of sauce used on salads and other foods. **4.** a mixture of bread crumbs and seasoning; also called STUFFING.

drew [droo] *verb.* the past tense of **draw.**

drib•ble [drib′ əl] *verb,* **dribbled, dribbling. 1.** to flow and trickle in drops: "Water *dribbled* across her face and into her half-open mouth." (Andre Norton) **2.** in basketball or soccer, to move the ball along by short bounces or kicks. —*noun, plural* **dribbles. 1.** a small amount of liquid; a series of drops. **2.** the act of dribbling the ball in basketball or soccer. ♦ A person who dribbles a ball is a **dribbler.**

dried [drīd] *verb.* the past form of **dry:** "Nick wanted to catch grasshoppers for bait before the sun *dried* the grass." (Ernest Hemingway)

dri•er [drī′ ər] *adjective.* the COMPARATIVE form of **dry.**

dri•est [drī′ ist] *adjective.* the SUPERLATIVE form of **dry.**

drift [drift] *verb,* **drifted, drifting. 1.** to be moved or carried along by wind or water currents: The balloon *drifted* slowly up over the trees. **2.** to pile up or gather in heaps because of the wind or water: "They took long steps, because the wind had *drifted* the snow almost up to their knees." (Mark Helprin) **3.** to move without any purpose or goal: "They had spent a year in France for no particular reason, and then *drifted* here and there wherever people played polo and were rich together." (F. Scott Fitzgerald) —*noun, plural* **drifts. 1.** loose material that is piled by wind or moving water: The snow*drift* was so high he couldn't see over it. **2.** the direction of movement of water or wind. **3.** the general idea or meaning of something: Could you go over that again—I didn't get your *drift.*

drift•wood [drift′ wood′] *noun, plural* **driftwoods.** old pieces of wood floating on water or washed up on shore.

driftwood A twisted piece of driftwood is washed ashore on a beach in Massachusetts.

drill [dril] *noun, plural* **drills. 1.** a tool used to cut round holes in wood and other hard materials. **2.** teaching or training by doing something over and over: Our class has a spelling *drill* three times a week. Fire *drills* show people how to leave a burning building safely. —*verb,* **drilled drilling. 1.** to cut a hole with a drill: The dentist *drilled* her tooth. **2.** to teach or train by repeating over and over: "There wasn't much I could help her with except to *drill* her on pronunciation—the 'L' and 'R' sounds." (Wakako Yamauchi)

drink [dringk] *verb,* **drank, drunk, drinking. 1.** to swallow water or any other liquid: He *drank* two glasses of orange juice. **2.** to drink alcohol. **3.** to soak in or soak up; absorb: The dry grass *drank* up the water from the sprinkler. **4. drink in.** to take in through the senses or the mind: "His eyes *drank in* all the things that a born dog man will see in a dog." (Jim Kjelgaard) —*noun, plural* **drinks. 1.** any liquid that one can drink. **2.** an alcoholic drink.

drip [drip] *verb,* **dripped, dripping.** to fall in

drops: "The sweat popped out on his forehead and *dripped* down on his shirt." (Langston Hughes) —*noun, plural* **drips. 1.** liquid drops that fall or drip from something. **2.** the sound made by something dripping: The steady *drip* of the faucet kept me awake half the night.

drive [drīv] *verb,* **drove, driven, driving. 1.** to control or direct the movement of a car or other vehicle. **2.** to go or carry in a car or other vehicle: Mom has to *drive* Melissa to soccer practice. **3.** to move or cause to move: to *drive* a nail into a board, to *drive* a herd of cattle. **4.** to force to act in a certain way: Stop making that terrible noise! You're *driving* me crazy! —*noun, plural* **drives. 1.** a ride in a car or another vehicle: It's a long *drive* from our house to the beach. **2.** a street or driveway: Lake Shore *Drive.* **3.** a strong, organized effort to do something: We're starting a paper *drive* to raise money for the club. **4.** a long hit in golf, baseball, or other games.

drive-in This term came into use after World War II. It was first applied to eating places and to movies, as seen here. Then banks put tellers at drive-in windows. These are all U.S. devices. Other countries don't seem to be in as big a hurry as Americans!

drive-in [drīv′ in′] *noun, plural* **drive-ins.** a movie theater, bank, restaurant, or the like where customers are served in their cars.

driv•er [drī′ vər] *noun, plural* **drivers. 1.** a person who drives a car or other vehicle. **2.** a golf club with a wooden head, used to hit long shots.

drive•way [drīv′ wā′] *noun, plural* **driveways.** a private road that is between a house or building and the street.

driven [driv′ ən] *verb.* the past participle of **drive.**

driz•zle [driz′ əl] *verb,* **drizzled, drizzling.** to rain lightly in small drops. —*noun.* a fine rain or mist.

dromedary The one-humped dromedary can travel as far as one hundred miles a day in the desert on very little food and water.

drom•e•dar•y [dräm′ ə der′ ē] *noun, plural* **dromedaries.** a type of camel that has one hump, found in Arabia and North Africa.

drone [drōn] *verb,* **droned, droning. 1.** to make a low, humming sound that goes on and on. **2.** to speak in a tone of voice that is boring or monotonous: The speaker *droned* on for hours about his idea for changing the name of the state capital. —*noun, plural* **drones. 1.** a low, continuous humming noise. **2.** a male bee that has no sting and does not gather honey. **3.** a person who lives off the work of others.

drool [drool] *verb,* **drooled, drooling.** to let the liquid in the mouth drip down one's face.

droop [droop] *verb,* **drooped, drooping.** to sink or hang down: "Her eyes *drooped* and she fell off to sleep." (Edward S. Fox)

drop [dräp] *verb,* **dropped, dropping. 1.** to fall or let fall; lower: She accidentally *dropped* her wallet on the sidewalk. The temperature *dropped* ten degrees in an hour before the storm. **2.** to deliver to a certain place or person: I'll *drop* you a letter when I have time. **3.** to make a short, casual visit: Let's *drop* over to Stacey's house and see what she's doing. **4.** to stop or be stopped from continuing an activity: Karen *dropped* ballet lessons because she was

---

Pronunciation Key: [ə] Symbol

The [ə] or *schwa* sound occurs in syllables without an accent. It can be spelled with any vowel, such as **a** in above, **e** in listen, **i** in pencil, **o** in melon, **u** in circus. It can also be a combination of vowels, such as **io** in action, **ai** in mountain, **iou** in precious.

(Turn the page for more information.)

getting behind in her studies. **5.** to leave out; omit: For verbs that end in "e," such as "like," you *drop* the "e" before adding "ing."
—*noun, plural* **drops. 1.** a tiny amount of a liquid with a rounded shape like a ball: *Drops* of rain rolled off the roof. **2.** candy or medicine with a rounded shape like this: cough *drops*, lemon *drops*. **3.** the act of dropping or falling, or the fall itself. **4.** the distance between two levels, one higher and one lower: There's a sixty-foot *drop* between the top of the cliff and the river below. **5.** a place where something may be left or dropped for someone else.

drop off 1. to deliver to a place: *Drop off* this package at the Post Office. **2.** to become less; weaken: Sales of that computer have really *dropped off* lately. **3.** to fall asleep: "After he *dropped off* to sleep, she sat holding his hand." (Willa Cather)

drop out to stop attending or taking part in something: to *drop out* of school, to *drop out* of the Girl Scouts. ♦ Often used as a noun: The city is setting up a special program for high school *dropouts*.

drop•per [dräp′ ər] *noun, plural* **droppers.** a small tool for measuring out a medicine or other liquid one drop at a time.

drought An area in northern Africa that was once green farmland, now showing the effects of a severe drought.

drought [drout] *noun, plural* **droughts.** a long period of time when there is no rain: All the crops died because of the summer *drought*.

drove[1] [drōv] *verb.* the past tense of **drive.**

drove[2] *noun, plural* **droves. 1.** a bunch of animals moving together, especially cattle or other farm animals. **2.** a crowd of people: "Somehow I had not expected to see any white people in Africa, but they are here in *droves*." (Alice Walker)

drown [droun] *verb,* **drowned, drowning. 1.** to die because water or another liquid fills the lungs so that there is no air to breathe. **2.** to cover up one sound with a louder sound: "They tried to *drown* him out with an angry roar." (Thomas Wolfe) "The noise of the wind and sea *drowned* more distant sounds." (Ken Follett)

drowse [drouz] *verb,* **droused, drousing.** to sleep lightly; be partly awake: "She lay and *drowsed*, hoping in her sleep that the children would keep out and let her rest a minute." (Katherine Anne Porter)

drow•sy [drou′ zē] *adjective,* **drowsier, drowsiest.** not fully awake; sleeping lightly: Sitting by the quiet pond in the warm sunshine made him very *drowsy.* —**drowsily,** *adverb:* "'Good children,' the old man said *drowsily.* He seemed half asleep." (Pearl Buck)

drug [drug] *noun, plural* **drugs. 1.** a medical substance used to treat or cure disease or pain in the body; a medicine: Aspirin and penicillin are commonly-used modern *drugs.* **2.** a substance that has a strong effect on the mind or body and that can become habit-forming: Heroin, cocaine, and marijuana are illegal *drugs.* —*verb,* **drugged, drugging.** to give a drug to a person: In spy movies people are often *drugged* to get them to tell secrets.

drug•gist [drug′ ist] *noun, plural* **druggists.** a person who has a license to make and sell drugs; a pharmacist.

drug•store [drug′ stôr′] *noun, plural* **drugstores.** a store that sells drugs and medicines along with other items.

drum [drum] *noun, plural* **drums. 1.** a musical instrument made up of a hollow frame shaped like a bowl or circle with a tight cover. The cover is struck with the hands or with sticks to make a sound. **2.** any container shaped like a drum: Gasoline is sometimes stored in 500-gallon *drums.* —*verb,* **drummed, drumming. 1.** to beat on or play a drum. **2.** to make repeated sounds like drum beats: "The Governor *drummed* on the table with his fingers." (Somerset Maugham) **3.** to force with steady or repeated efforts: We finally *drummed* it into our dog's head not to chase cars down the street.

drum major a person who is the leader of a marching band.

drum ma•jor•ette [mā′ jə ret′] a girl or woman who twirls a baton at the front of a marching band.

drum•mer [drum′ ər] *noun, plural* **drummers.** a person who plays a drum or drums.

drum·stick [drum/stik/] *noun, plural* **drum-sticks. 1.** the wooden stick used to beat a drum. **2.** the lower part of the leg from a cooked bird, such as chicken or turkey.

drunk [drungk] *verb.* the past participle of **drink:** The other guests had *drunk* all the lemonade by the time we got there. —*adjective,* **drunker, drunkest.** not in proper control of one's thoughts or actions because of drinking too much alcohol. —*noun, plural* **drunks.** a person who is drunk.

dry [drī] *adjective,* **drier, driest. 1.** having very little or no water; not damp or wet: Let me get you a *dry* towel. Arizona has a *dry* climate. **2.** needing a drink; thirsty. **3.** boring; dull: Ann thought her American history textbook was very *dry.* —*verb,* **dried, drying.** to make or become dry.

dry-clean [drī/ klēn] *verb,* **dry-cleaned, dry-cleaning.** to clean clothes by using chemicals instead of water. A business that does this is called a **dry-cleaner.**

dry·er [drī/ ər] (also spelled **drier**) *noun, plural* **dryers.** an appliance for drying wet things: a hair *dryer,* a clothes *dryer.*

dry goods cloth, ribbons, thread, and other such items.

du·al [dōō/ əl] *adjective.* made up of or having two matching or similar parts; double: Passenger airplanes have *dual* controls for the pilot and co-pilot.

du·bi·ous [dōō/ bē əs] *adjective,* **more/most.** causing or feeling doubt; uncertain: The Senator was *dubious* about whether the new bill would ever become a law.

Dub·lin [dub/ lin] the capital of the Republic of Ireland. *Population:* 545,000.

duch·ess [duch/ is] *noun, plural* **duchesses.** the wife or widow of a DUKE.

duck¹ *verb,* **ducked, ducking. 1.** to lower the head quickly; bend down: Tim *ducked* to miss the tree branch that was sticking out. **2.** to push under water for a short time: The boys were

splashing and *ducking* each other in the pool. **3.** to avoid or dodge: The movie star *ducked* the reporters who wanted to interview her.

duck² [duk] *noun, plural* **ducks. 1.** a water bird that has waterproof feathers, webbed feet, and a broad bill. **2.** the female of this bird. The male bird is called a DRAKE.

duck Four types of North American ducks. The wood duck (left), hooded merganser (right), mallard (center), and pintail (rear).

duck·ling [duk/ ling] *noun, plural* **ducklings.** a young or baby duck.

duct [dukt] *noun, plural* **ducts.** a tube or pipe that holds moving air or liquid: They installed heating *ducts* in the new office.

due to It's generally agreed that "due to" can be used to mean the same thing as "because of." However, some books on writing—such as Wilson Follett's *Modern American Usage*—do not accept the following use of "due to:" "His car skidded *due to* the icy road." Here, they say, "because of" is more accurate. But it's doubtful that people will stop using "due to" this way. Why? Well, language changes. Fifty years ago, many people in the U.S. used, instead of "due to," "owing to." Only in other English-speaking countries has that term survived. A British language expert could probably still tell you the precise use of "because of," "owing to," and "due to," although English newspapers usually don't make such distinctions any longer.

due [dōō] *adjective.* **1.** owed to someone as a debt or right: Don't worry, you'll get every cent that is *due* you. **2.** proper or suitable: "In *due* time I quieted down . . ." (Anne Frank)

Pronunciation Key: Accent Marks

[/] is the normal accent mark. It shows where the main stress falls on a word.
[/] is a secondary accent mark. It shows a lighter stress than the primary accent. For example:

tel • e • vis • ion [tel/ə vizh/ən]
(Turn the page for more information.)

D

3. expected, required, or promised: The book reports are *due* Friday. —*noun, plural* **dues. 1.** something that is deserved; something due: to give a person his *due*. **2. dues.** money that is paid by members to belong to a club or organization. —*adverb.* straight; directly: The island of Cuba is *due* south of Florida. **due to.** because of: The game had to be put off *due to* rain.

du·el [dōō′ əl] *noun, plural* **duels. 1.** a fight between two people to settle a quarrel or point of honor. Duels were once fought with swords or pistols by men of the upper class. **2.** any fight or struggle between two opposing sides: the *duel* in baseball between the batter and the pitcher. —*verb,* **dueled, dueling.** to fight or take part in a duel.

du·et [dōō et′] *noun, plural* **duets.** a piece of music that is written for two instruments or two voices.

dug [dug] *verb.* the past tense of **dig.**

dugout The Brooklyn Dodgers' dugout on opening day of the 1954 season. The team is lined up on the top step of the dugout in the order they batted that day. From left: Junior Gilliam, Pee Wee Reese, Duke Snider, Jackie Robinson, Roy Campanella, Gil Hodges, Carl Furillo, Billy Cox, Carl Erskine.

dug·out [dug′ out′] *noun, plural* **dugouts. 1.** a small shelter next to a baseball field where the players sit when they are not batting or playing in the field. **2.** a canoe made from a hollowed-out log.

duke [dōōk] *noun, plural* **dukes.** a noble title or rank that is just below a prince.

dull [dul] *adjective,* **duller, dullest. 1.** not sharp or pointed; blunt: I can't cut the cardboard with these *dull* scissors. **2.** not clear or sharp to the senses: a *dull* color. Grandpa sometimes gets a *dull* pain in his back on damp days. **3.** slow to learn or understand; not alert. **4.** not exciting; boring: "I'm sure you must find Belfast *dull* after New York, after all that excitement." (Brian Moore) —*verb,* **dulled, dulling.** to make or become dull.

dumb [dum] *adjective,* **dumber, dumbest. 1.** not able to speak: a deaf and *dumb* person. **2.** *Informal.* stupid; foolish.

dumb·bell [dum′ bel′] *noun, plural* **dumbbells.** a short bar with a heavy knob at each end, used for exercising.

dumb·found·ed [dum′ found′ id] *adjective, more/most.* (also spelled **dumfounded**) astonished; amazed: "We didn't say a thing. We just stood there *dumbfounded*—not knowing which way we'd been fooled." (Langston Hughes)

dum·my [dum′ ē] *noun, plural* **dummies. 1.** a copy of a human figure, used as a substitute for a person: The dressmaker used a *dummy* of the movie actress to make her costumes for a film. **2.** anything made to look like something else and be used in its place: When a book is being made, the publisher uses a *dummy* of the pages to show what they will look like.

dump [dump] *verb,* **dumped, dumping.** to get rid of; unload in a pile: "Someone just *dumped* a whole garbage can of orange peels out the window." (J.D. Salinger) —*noun, plural* **dumps. 1.** a place to throw out trash and garbage. **2.** *Slang.* a very messy place.

dune [dōōn] *noun, plural* **dunes.** a ridge of sand that is piled and shaped by the wind.

dunes Although much of the American desert is covered by low-growing plants, the image it calls up in many people's minds is of vast empty sand dunes, as seen here.

dun·ga·rees [dung′ gə rēz′] *plural noun.* pants or overalls made from heavy cloth; also called JEANS.

dun·geon [dun′ jən] *noun, plural* **dungeons.** a dark underground prison or cell.

du·pli·cate [dōō′ plə kit] *noun, plural* **duplicates.** something that is an exact copy or just like something else: "Both of these rooms were exactly alike in every detail. Even the pictures were *duplicates*." (Nathanael West) —*adjective.* exactly like something else: a *duplicate* set of car keys. —[doō′plə kāt′] *verb,* **duplicated, duplicating. 1.** to make an exact copy: Xerox machines are used to *duplicate* letters. **2.** to do or make again; repeat: Can last season's Super Bowl winners *duplicate* their victory this year?

dur•ing [door′ ing] *preposition.* throughout or at some point in the course of: "The ice, which had softened *during* the night, began to melt." (E.B. White)

dusk [dusk] *noun.* the time of evening just before dark; twilight: "When the short days of winter came, *dusk* fell before we had well eaten our dinner." (James Joyce)

dust bowl A dust storm in Cimarron County, Oklahoma in 1936, in the area known as the Dust Bowl. Arthur Rothstein's famous photograph shows a farmer and his sons running to their storm cellar to escape the winds.

dust [dust] *noun.* fine, dry particles of dirt: A cloud of *dust* surrounded the car as it raced down the dirt road. —*verb,* **dusted, dusting. 1.** to wipe or brush dust off some surface: She *dusts* the furniture every week. **2.** to sprinkle or powder something: The sweet rolls were *dusted* with powdered sugar. ◆ Something covered with dust, or appearing this way, is **dusty:** The noon sun beat down on the deserted and *dusty* street.

Dutch [duch] a name for the people who live in the Netherlands.

du•ty [doō′ tē] *noun, plural* **duties. 1.** something one ought to do because it is right, proper, or the law: It is a citizen's *duty* to vote in elections. **2.** a certain task or type of work that is called for by a particular job: "My primary *duties* would be helping with the children and teaching a kindergarten class or two." (Alice Walker) **3.** a tax paid to the government for goods brought into a country.

dwarf [dwôrf] *noun, plural* **dwarfs** or **dwarves. 1.** a full grown person, animal, or plant that is smaller than normal. **2.** in fairy tales, a very small man who has magic powers. —*verb,* **dwarfed, dwarfing.** to cause to appear small: We felt *dwarfed* by the tall trees in the redwood forest.

dwell [dwel] *verb,* **dwelt** or **dwelled, dwelling. 1.** to live in or make one's home: The moose *dwells* in northern forests. ◆ A **dweller** is a person who lives somewhere: The Cliff *Dwellers* were American Indians who lived along the walls of high canyons in the Southwest. **2. dwell on.** to think, write, or speak about at length: The professor was known to *dwell on* his favorite subject for hours at a time.

dwell•ing [dwel′ ing] *noun, plural* **dwellings.** the place where someone lives, one's home: "The houses of the Munchkins were odd-looking *dwellings,* for each was round with a big dome for a roof." (L. Frank Baum)

dwin•dle [dwin′ dəl] *verb,* **dwindled, dwindling.** to slowly become less or smaller: ". . . a long corridor of doors, *dwindling* in the distance . . ." (Anne Morrow Lindbergh)

dye [dī] *noun, plural* **dyes.** a substance used to change the color of things such as food, hair, and cloth. —*verb,* **dyed, dyeing.** to add color to or change the color of something: Cindy *dyed* her old sweater bright red.

dy•ing [dī′ ing] *verb.* a present form of **die.**

dy•nam•ic [dī nam′ ik] *adjective, more/most.* having great energy and enthusiasm: Mary Lou Retton's *dynamic* performance in the 1984 Olympics made her famous in the U.S.

dy•na•mite [dī′ nə mīt′] *noun.* a very powerful explosive, often used in blasting rocks. Dynamite is usually packed in sticks and exploded by lighting a fuse. It is made from NITROGLYCERINE. —*verb,* **dynamited, dynamiting.** to blow up with dynamite: The highway department *dynamited* the hillside to build a new road.

dy•nas•ty [dī′ nəs tē] *noun, plural* **dynasties.** a series of leaders or rulers who are from the same family: China was ruled by the Ching *dynasty* from 1644 to 1912.

Pronunciation Key: A–F			
a	and; hat	ch	chew; such
ā	ate; stay	d	dog; lid
â	care; air	e	end; yet
ä	father; hot	ē	she; each
b	boy; cab	f	fun; off

(Turn the page for more information.)

Ee

e, E [ē] *noun, plural* **e's, E's.** the fifth letter of the alphabet.

each [ēch] *adjective.* one of two or more people or things: *Each* state in the U.S. is represented by two senators. —*pronoun.* every one: *Each* of the soldiers had to take a turn standing guard. —*adverb.* for or to every one: Those sodas cost fifty cents *each*.

ea·ger [ē′gər] *adjective, more/most.* wanting to do or have something very much: "The children stepped closer. They were *eager* to hear about how he could make them . . . rich." (Donald Sobol) —**eagerly,** *adverb:* "Edmund and Lucy *eagerly* bent forward to see what was in Peter's hand." (C.S. Lewis)

ea·gle [ē′gəl] *noun, plural* **eagles.** a large bird with a long hooked beak, strong claws, and broad wings. Eagles have very keen eyesight and feed on small animals. The **bald eagle** is the national bird and symbol of the United States.

ear¹ [ēr] *noun, plural* **ears. 1.** the part of the body that people and animals use to hear, located on either side of the head. The human ear is divided into three parts: the **outer ear, middle ear,** and **inner ear. 2.** the ability to use the sense of hearing: a person with a good *ear* for music or for language.

ear² *noun, plural* **ears.** the part of corn, wheat, and other grain plants on which the seeds grow.

eagle Large, powerful, and graceful, the eagle is seen as the ruler of the skies. It has been used as a national symbol throughout history—ancient Rome, the Austrian empire, and Nazi Germany are other examples besides the United States.

ear·drum [ēr′drum′] *noun, plural* **eardrums.** a thin layer of tissue that separates the middle ear from the inner ear. The eardrum moves back and forth when sound waves strike it and carries the sound to the inner part of the ear.

Ear·hart [âr′härt′] **Amelia,** 1897–1937, American aviator, the first woman to fly alone across the Atlantic Ocean.

ear "Muriel said, 'Usually we have a goose. My daddy brings a goose from the Eastern Shore. Or don't you care for goose. Would you rather just a turkey? A duck? What are you used to eating, Macon?'" (Anne Tyler) One critic said that Tyler has "a perfect ear," because of the way Muriel and her other characters talk. A writer with a "good ear" can create characters who speak in a natural way, as people do ordinarily. Another writer with a keen ear is John O'Hara: "They said I wasn't supposed to take a job that I had to stand up all the time. I'll have to look for work that I can be sitting down. I thought of a telephone operator. They train you, and you don't have to have a high school diploma." This is not "correct English" in every respect, but it is the way O'Hara's character would talk in real life. By the way, curse words are used by a lot of people, but they become unreal and boring when used repeatedly in writing. Readers suspect the writer of lacking an "ear" when all they read is foul language.

earl [url] *noun, plural* **earls.** a title of noble rank in Great Britain.

ear•ly [ur′lē] *adjective,* **earlier, earliest. 1.** happening near the beginning: He takes an *early* bus to the city so that he can be at the office by 8:00. These flowers are at their best in *early* summer. **2.** before the usual time: Chris ate an *early* dinner tonight because he had a baseball game at 5:30. **3.** of a time long ago; ancient: The Leakey family has found much evidence of *early* man in East Africa. —*adverb:* **1.** near the beginning: Dairy farmers have to get up *early* in the morning. **2.** before the usual time: Mom always gets to the station *early* so she won't miss her train.

earn [urn] *verb,* **earned, earning. 1.** to get paid for working: Brian *earns* $25 a week from his paper route. **2.** to get something one deserves because of hard work or effort: Ice skater Katerina Witt trained for years before *earning* a gold medal in the 1988 Olympics.

ear•nest [ur′nist] *adjective, more/most.* strong in one's purpose; serious and sincere: He's making an *earnest* attempt to control his bad temper. —**earnestly,** *adverb:* "Jimmy did not study very *earnestly* . . ." (James Joyce)

earn•ings [ur′ningz] *plural noun.* **1.** money that has been earned by work: "He invested his *earnings* in his brother's education." (Harper Lee) **2.** the amount of money that a company makes after all its expenses are paid; profit.

ear•phone [ēr′fōn′] *noun, plural* **earphones.** a device worn on the ear for listening to a radio, tape player, telephone, or the like.

ear•ring [ēr′ring′] *noun, plural* **earrings.** a piece of jewelry worn on the ear.

earth [urth] *noun, plural* **earths. 1.** *also,* **Earth.** the planet we live on. Earth is the fifth-largest planet in the solar system and is the third in distance from the sun. **2.** the land surface of the earth, as opposed to the oceans or the sky; soil or dirt: Helen raked the loose *earth* from around the plants in her garden.

earth•ly [urth′lē] *adjective.* **1.** of the earth or the world: "I will talk of things heavenly or things *earthly.*" (John Bunyan) **2.** practical; possible: I wish you'd throw out that broken-down old chair; it's of no *earthly* use to anybody.

earth•quake [urth′kwāk′] *noun, plural* **earthquakes.** a strong shaking or trembling of the ground. Earthquakes happen when rock or other material moves suddenly under the ground. A major earthquake can break the surface of the earth and cause great damage.

earth•worm [urth′wurm′] *noun, plural* **earthworms.** a common worm that lives in the soil. Earthworms have long tube-like bodies that they stretch out or bunch up in order to move in the ground.

ease [ēz] *noun.* **1.** freedom from worry, trouble, or pain: Mr. Dixon looks forward to a life of *ease* when he retires from his job next year. **2.** freedom from difficulty or great effort: "He ran with such *ease* that his strides seemed to be a single flowing movement." (Walter Farley) **3. at ease. a.** a military command to stand in a relaxed position with the feet apart. **b.** a feeling of being relaxed or without worry: "For some reason they were not altogether *at ease* with each other." (Tennessee Williams) —*verb,* **eased, easing. 1.** to make free from worry, trouble, or pain; make easier: Sally took some medicine to *ease* the soreness in her throat. **2.** to move slowly and carefully: "Gray took a deep breath and *eased* himself back away from me against the wall." (William Styron)

ea•sel [ē′zəl] *noun, plural* **easels.** a stand or rack for holding signs or pictures. Artists often use an easel to hold a painting while it is being painted.

earth Planets usually have Greek or Roman names; Mars, Venus, Jupiter, Mercury, and Saturn were all Roman gods. *Earth,* however, is Old English. The early Saxon tribes who named the earth didn't know of the other planets.

E

	Pronunciation Key: A–F		
a	and; hat	ch	chew; such
ā	ate; stay	d	dog; lid
â	care; air	e	end; yet
ä	father; hot	ē	she; each
b	boy; cab	f	fun; off

(Turn the page for more information.)

eat It is possible, even today, to find educated persons in Britain saying "et" for "eat." In a similar fashion, Englishmen used "ain't" as perfectly proper usage about two hundred years ago. An American writing "et" or "ain't" today would be criticized by his readers. Words become "proper" or "improper" over the years. One group of language experts in the 1940's even said that some words ought to be dated!

eas•i•ly [e′ zə lē] *adverb, more/most.* **1.** without trying hard; with no difficulty: Our dog can *easily* jump that fence into the yard next door. **2.** without doubt or question: That movie was *easily* the best one I've seen all summer.

east [ēst] *noun.* **1.** the direction that the sun comes from when it rises in the morning. **2.** *usually,* **East.** any place or region in that direction. **3. the East. a.** the eastern part of the United States, especially the states along the Atlantic Ocean north of Maryland. **b.** the land to the east of Europe; the Orient. —*adjective.* **1.** toward the east: the *east* side of a street. **2.** coming from the east: an *east* wind. —*adverb.* toward the east: The plane flew *east.*

East•er [ēs′ tər] *noun, plural* **Easters.** a Christian holiday to celebrate Christ's rising from the dead. It comes on the Sunday after the first full moon of spring, between March 22nd and April 25th.

east•ern [ēs′ tərn] *adjective.* **1.** coming from the east: In California, *eastern* winds from the desert are hot and dry. **2.** toward the east: He lives at the *eastern* end of the valley. **3. Eastern. a.** having to do with the eastern part of the U.S.: The *Eastern* states are those of New England, and New York, New Jersey, and Pennsylvania. An **Easterner** is a person born or living in the East. **b.** having to do with Asia or the nearby islands; Oriental.

Eastern Hemisphere the half of the earth that lies east of the Atlantic Ocean and consists of the continents of Europe, Africa, Asia and Australia.

East Germany the northeastern part of Germany, now a separate country called the **German Democratic Republic.** *Capital:* East Berlin. *Area:* 41,800 square miles. *Population:* 16,750,000.

east•ward [ēst′ wərd] *adverb, adjective.* toward the east.

eas•y [ē′ zē] *adjective,* **easier, easiest. 1.** needing only a little work or effort; not hard to do: an *easy* job, an *easy* subject in school. **2.** not hard to please: She's an *easy* teacher who always gives a lot of A's. **3.** free from pain, worry, or trouble: to lead an *easy* life.

eat [ēt] *verb,* **ate, eaten, eating. 1.** to chew and swallow food: to *eat* an apple. Lions *eat* meat. **2.** to have a meal: to *eat* lunch. Do you want to *eat* before or after the game? **3.** to wear away or destroy as if by eating: Rust is *eating* away at the paint on my car.

eaves [ēvz] *plural noun.* the lower part of a roof that hangs out over the side of the building.

eaves•drop [ēvz′ dräp′] *verb,* **eavesdropped, eavesdropping.** to listen to other people talking without their knowing about it: By *eavesdropping* at the door, Mary Ann found out that her parents had bought her a bicycle for Christmas. —**eavesdropper,** *noun.*

ebb [eb] *noun, plural* **ebbs.** the flowing of the ocean tide away from the shore; also called **ebb tide.** —*verb,* **ebbed, ebbing. 1.** of the tide, to flow out. **2.** to grow less; weaken or decline: In a marathon race a runner's strength often begins to *ebb* after about 20 miles.

ebb tide This is the ancient abbey of Mont Saint Michel on the English Channel. During the ebb tide (shown here) the land around it is exposed. At high tide the entire area becomes an island surrounded by the sea once more.

eb•on•y [eb′ ə nē] *noun.* a hard, heavy wood that comes from trees grown in Africa and Asia. Ebony is used to make the black keys of a piano, and for other woodwork.

ec•cen•tric [ik sen′ trik] *adjective, more/most.* not in the normal or usual way; odd; peculiar: Her neighbors thought Hilda was very *eccentric* because she kept more than fifty cats in her house.

echo [ek′ō] *noun, plural* **echoes.** a sound that is heard again because it bounces off a surface and comes back: He likes to sing in the shower —he thinks the *echo* makes his voice sound better. —*verb,* **echoed, echoing. 1.** to send back the sound of something; make an echo: "One of the girls screamed. Her long . . . cry *echoed* back instantly from the cliffs." (Gilbert Highet) **2.** to repeat what has already been said: When I visited the Gettysburg battlefield, Lincoln's famous speech *echoed* in my mind.

e•clipse [i klips′] *noun, plural* **eclipses.** a darkening or hiding of the sun, the moon, or a planet. This is usually caused by the passing of another heavenly body. A **solar eclipse** occurs when the moon passes between the sun and the earth, partly or completely hiding the sun. A **lunar eclipse** occurs when the earth passes between the sun and the moon, causing the earth's shadow to partly or completely darken the moon. —*verb,* **eclipsed, eclipsing. 1.** to cause or form an eclipse. **2.** to make something else seem less important; overshadow: Ronald Reagan's early fame as a movie star has been *eclipsed* by his later success in politics.

eclipse A solar eclipse was an event that was greatly feared in ancient times. People would think that the gods had taken away the sun for good as a punishment.

e•col•o•gy [i käl′ ə jē *or* ē käl′ ə jē] *noun.* **1.** the scientific study of how plants and animals relate to each other and to their environment. **2.** a situation in which there is a balanced relationship between living things and their environment: "If dead trees are not left to rot, the *ecology* of the wilderness is disturbed." (John McPhee) —**ecological,** *adjective.*

ec•o•nom•ic [ek′ ə näm′ ik *or* ē′ kə näm′ ik] *adjective.* having to do with money, or with the making, selling, or using of goods and services: The President proposed a new *economic* program that would lower taxes.

ec•o•nom•i•cal [ek′ ə näm′ ə i kəl *or* ē′ kə näm′ ə kəl] *adjective, more/most.* using or operating with little waste; saving money: Mom says it's more *economical* to shop at a big supermarket than at small local stores. —**economically,** *adverb:* He wants a car that runs *economically* because he has to drive a long distance to work.

ec•o•nom•ics [ek′ ə näm′ iks *or* ē′ kə näm′iks] *noun.* the study of the making, selling, and using of goods and services. Economics includes the study of such matters as money, income, business, and taxes. ♦ An **economist** [i kän′ ə mist] is an expert in economics.

e•con•o•mize [i kän′ ə mīz′] *verb,* **economized, economizing.** to limit the spending of money or the use of something; not be wasteful: If we start to *economize* now, we'll be able to save enough to take a vacation next summer.

e•con•o•my [i kän′ ə mē] *noun, plural* **economies. 1.** the way that the money and goods of a country are developed and used by its people: The *economy* of the U.S. was at a low point during the Great Depression. **2.** the careful use of money, goods, or other resources.

ec•sta•sy [ek′ stə sē] *noun, plural* **ecstasies.** very great happiness or delight: "Slowly, wonderingly, a grin of *ecstasy* began to stretch itself across Paul's face." (Mary Norton) —**ecstatic** [ek stat′ ik], *adjective:* "Hidden birds sprang forth, filling the air with glad, *ecstatic* music." (Mary Mapes Dodge)

Ec•ua•dor [ek′ wə dôr′] a country in northwest South America, on the Pacific Ocean. *Capital:* Quito. *Area:* 106,000 square miles. *Population:* 8,500,000.

ed•dy [ed′ ē] *noun, plural* **eddies.** a current of water, wind, smoke, or the like moving in a circle. —*verb,* **eddied, eddying.** to move in this way.

Ed•dy [ed′ ē] **Mary Baker,** 1821–1910, American religious leader, the founder of the Christian Science Church.

edge [ej] *noun, plural* **edges. 1.** the line or place where something ends: The glass fell off the *edge* of the table. The cabin was on the *edge* of

---

Pronunciation Key: G–N

g	give; big	k	kind; cat; back
h	hold	l	let; ball
i	it; this	m	make; time
ī	ice; my	n	not; own
j	jet; gem; edge	ng	having

(Turn the page for more information.)

a forest. **2.** the cutting side of a blade or tool. —*verb,* **edged, edging. 1.** to give an edge to; border: The dress was *edged* with lace. **2.** to move carefully or little by little: "They *edged* the table through the doorway." (Laura Ingalls Wilder)

ed•i•ble [ed′ ə bəl] *adjective.* safe or fit to eat: Some wild mushrooms are *edible* and some are poisonous.

Ed•in•burgh [ed′ ən bur′ ō] the capital of Scotland. *Population:* 470,000.

ed•i•tor [ed′ i tər] *noun, plural* **editors. 1.** any person who edits written material. **2.** a person who is in charge of a newspaper, magazine, reference book, or other large publication, or of one of its departments. **3.** a person employed by a book publisher to correct and otherwise improve written material and to carry out other tasks necessary for the publishing of the material as a book. **4.** a person who edits a film or tape recording. ◆ The work that is done by an editor is **editing.**

> **editing** The process of editing on a newspaper, or in magazine and book publishing companies, has two different parts: copy editing and content editing. Content editing includes major changes such as adding a new paragraph or writing a different ending, or moving a paragraph from one section to another. Copy editing is the last and most technical stage. A copy editor checks on accurate spelling, on mistakes in grammar, on making sure that the words used are exactly the ones intended. This editor also checks the names of places and people. When you write a school paper, you have to be an author, editor, and copy editor—all three. You can't afford to hire others, so you must revise, check, revise and check, again and again!

E

Ed•i•son [ed′ i sən] **Thomas Alva,** 1847–1931, American inventor.

ed•it [ed′ it] *verb,* **edited, editing. 1.** to check, correct, and otherwise prepare the writing of another person to be published: Maxwell Perkins *edited* the novels of Thomas Wolfe. **2.** to check, correct, and otherwise improve one's own writing: Sharon *edited* her history report before she handed it in to the teacher. **3.** to prepare a film, tape recording, or the like by arranging and cutting the available materials.

ed•i•to•ri•al [ed′ i tôr′ ē əl] *noun, plural* **editorials. 1.** a newspaper or magazine article that gives the editor's or publisher's opinion on some issue, rather than simply reporting facts. **2.** a similar statement of opinion given by the management of a TV or radio station. —*adjective.* **1.** having to do with an editorial: In a newspaper, political cartoons appear on the *editorial* page. **2.** having to do with an editor or with editing: to make *editorial* changes in a paper.

> **editorials** If you have an assignment to write an editorial, here are some steps to follow: 1) State your opinion right away, and state it clearly: "The city should put a traffic light at the intersection of Valley Road and Conway Drive." 2) Provide some background information. An editorial is not like a news story—there the writer gives a lot of facts to describe what has happened, but doesn't state his own views about it. However, an editorial has to have facts to support the opinions: "There is no light on the corner now, just a stop sign. Conway Drive used to be a quiet side street. But in the past year or so . . ." 3) Give the reasons for your position: "There should be a light because so many children pass that way on their way to school. In the last month, there have been three bad accidents . . ." 4) Re-state your position at the end, using different wording: "For all these reasons, we need a light there as soon as possible."

e•di•tion [i dish′ ən] *noun, plural* **editions. 1.** the form in which a book is printed: Many novels are available in both hardcover and paperback *editions.* **2.** one of many copies of a book, newspaper, or magazine published at one time: The first *edition* of a famous book is often worth a lot of money. That history book is out of date and the publisher is working on a new *edition.*

Ed•mon•ton [ed′ mən tən] the capital of Alberta, Canada. *Population:* 535,000.

ed•u•cate [ej′ ə kāt′] *verb,* **educated, educating.** to develop or train a person's mind or character in a certain way; teach: Both her parents were *educated* at the University of Iowa.

◆ A person whose work is educating people is an **educator.**

ed•u•ca•tion [ej′ ə kā′ shən] *noun, plural* **educations. 1.** the development of the mind and character through study and training; the gaining of knowledge about the world in general or about some particular subject. **2.** a certain type of knowledge and training: To get that job, you have to have at least a high-school *education.* **3.** the study of teaching and the methods and problems of teaching.

ed•u•ca•tion•al [ej′ ə kā′ shən əl] *adjective, more/most.* **1.** having to do with education: The book *Why Johnny Can't Read* deals with *educational* issues in the U.S. **2.** giving information or knowledge: an *educational* television series. Working with handicapped children was really an *educational* experience for her.

Ed•ward VIII [ed′ wərd] 1894–1972, the king of England in 1936. He gave up the throne and became **Duke of Windsor.**

eel [ēl] *noun, plural* **eels.** a long, thin fish that looks like a snake and has smooth, slimy skin.

ee•rie [ēr′ ē] *adjective,* **eerier, eeriest.** strange and scary; frightening: People claim to have seen an *eerie* shape drifting through that old graveyard at night. ". . . with *eerie* shadows cast by the lantern light suddenly looming on all sides." (Erskine Caldwell) **—eerily,** *adverb:* Although it was the middle of the day, the streets were *eerily* quiet and deserted.

ef•fect [i fekt′] *noun, plural* **effects. 1.** something that happens because of something else: One *effect* of closing the highway for repairs has been heavy traffic on local streets. The *effects* of that medicine last for about five hours. **2.** the power to change or influence something: The 55 mile-per-hour speed limit went into *effect* in 1975. **3. effects.** belongings; property: The school provides lockers where students can keep personal *effects.* **4. in effect. a.** in force or operation. **b.** in actual fact; really: When President Woodrow Wilson became very ill in his second term, his wife was *in effect* the leader of the country. **—verb, effected, effecting.** to make happen; cause: The new owner has *effected* many changes in the way the business is run.

ef•fec•tive [i fek′ tiv] *adjective, more/most.* **1.** able to change or influence something: Martin Luther King was a very *effective* speaker. **2.** in force; in effect: A new law against smoking in public buildings becomes *effective* next month. **—effectively,** *adverb:* That weed killer worked very *effectively* in our garden.

ef•fi•cien•cy [i fish′ ən sē] *noun.* the state of being efficient: New cars have a sticker telling the fuel *efficiency* of the engine.

ef•fi•cient [i fish′ ənt] *adjective, more/most.* getting results without wasting time or effort: Our new air conditioner is much more *efficient* in keeping the house cool than the old fan was. The new school principal seems to be very *efficient* at her job. **—efficiently,** *adverb:* He can keep track of his business more *efficiently* since he got a home computer.

ef•fort [ef′ ərt] *noun, plural* **efforts. 1.** the use of energy or force to do something; hard work: For all their *effort,* they couldn't move the huge log that blocked the road. **2.** a try or attempt: Paul has been making a real *effort* to get along better with his sister. **—effortless,** *adjective.* with little or no effort. **—effortlessly,** *adverb.*

egg The eggs of various birds—at rear, an ostrich; front, left to right, a turkey, a tinamou (whose egg is noted for its shiny surface), an owl, and a robin.

egg¹ [eg] *noun, plural* **eggs. 1.** a round or oval object produced from the body of a female bird, fish, insect, or reptile, from which the young hatches out. **2.** a special cell that is produced in the body of a woman or a female animal. It can join with a male cell to develop into a new baby or animal.

egg² *verb,* **egged, egging.** to encourage to do something, especially something one should not do or does not want to do: While the two boys argued, several others *egged* them on to fight.

egg•plant [eg′ plant′] *noun, plural* **eggplants.** a vegetable that is shaped like a large egg, having a shiny purple skin.

E

Pronunciation Key. O–S			
ō	over; go	ou	out; town
ô	all; law	p	put; hop
oo	look; full	r	run; car
o͞o	pool; who	s	set; miss
oi	oil; boy	sh	show

(Turn the page for more information.)

E

e•go [ē′ gō] *noun, plural* **egos. 1.** a feeling in the mind that makes a person aware that he or she is different from others; the self. **2.** a feeling of being better than others; a very high opinion of oneself: He's the star pitcher of the team, but the other players don't like him because of his big *ego*.

e•gret [ē′ grit] *noun, plural* **egrets.** a tall bird with a long neck, a pointed bill, and long white feathers. The egret is a type of HERON.

Egypt Two ancient symbols of Egypt, the camel and the pyramid. These are the Giza pyramids, built over 4500 years ago on the Nile River near Cairo.

E•gypt [ē′ jipt] a country in northeast Africa, on the Mediterranean and Red Seas. In ancient times Egypt was an important center of civilization. *Capital:* Cairo. *Area:* 386,200 square miles. *Population:* 43,500,000. —**Egyptian,** *adjective; noun.*

eight [āt] *noun, plural* **eights;** *adjective.* one more than seven; 8. —**eighth,** *adjective; noun.*

Ein•stein [īn′ stīn′] **Albert,** 1879–1955, German scientist who later lived in the United States. He made some of the most important discoveries in the field of modern physics.

Ei•sen•how•er [ī′ zən hou′ ər] **Dwight David,** 1890–1969, American general in World War II and the thirty-fourth president of the United States, from 1953 to 1961.

or the other of two things: There are two new movies in town, but I haven't seen *either* of them. —*conjunction.* (used with **or**) We can have *either* potatoes *or* rice with the chicken. —*adverb.* also; besides: Greg didn't go to the party, and his sister didn't *either*.

e•ject [i jekt′] *verb,* **ejected, ejecting.** to throw or push out: The manager was *ejected* from the game for arguing with the umpire. Tom *ejected* the tape from the VCR before turning it off.

e•lab•o•rate [i lab′ ər it] *adjective, more/most.* worked out or developed in careful detail: *Elaborate* plans were made for the President's visit to New York. —[i lab′ ə rāt′] *verb,* **elaborated, elaborating.** to work out with great care; add details: Mr. Jones sent out a report to *elaborate* on what he had said at the meeting. —**elaborately,** *adverb.*

Einstein He became so famous for his brilliant theories that today we use "Einstein" as a symbol for intelligence, as in "He's a real *Einstein*" or "It doesn't take any *Einstein* to figure that one out."

e•lapse [i laps′] *verb,* **elapsed, elapsing.** to pass or go by: He lost his driver's license for speeding, and one year has to *elapse* before he can get a new one.

either or "Either Steve or John will pitch in today's game." This sentence shows that *either* and *or* are words which give you a choice of one out of two. Therefore, a singular verb is used. "Either Steve or John *are* going to pitch" is incorrect. "Either Steve or John *is* going . . ." is the correct usage. Some writers argue that the "Either Steve or John are" form is used so often that there's no point in correcting people. We don't agree. Even though it's probable that people nowadays will say: "The program will feature David *and/or* Jane," a language purist would use: "The program will feature David or Jane, or both."

ei•ther [ē′ thər *or* ī′ thər] *adjective.* one or the other: We can take *either* road, but Highway 5 usually has less traffic than 15. —*pronoun.* one

e•las•tic [i las′ tik] *adjective, more/most.* able to be stretched or squeezed and then return to its original shape: Rubber is an *elastic* material.

—*noun, plural* **elastics.** something that is elastic, such as a rubber band.

el•bow [el′ bō] *noun, plural* **elbows. 1.** the joint that connects the upper and lower arm. **2.** something with the shape of a bent elbow, such as a piece of pipe. —*verb,* **elbowed, elbowing.** to push or shove using the elbows: "Boys *elbowed* each other and stared at girls . . ." (Andrea Lee)

eld•er [el′ dər] *adjective.* being older than another person, especially a brother or sister: Peggy is named after her father's *elder* sister. —*noun, plural* **elders. 1.** a person who is older: "That's no way to speak to a woman nearly eighty years old . . . I'd have you respect your *elders,* young man." (Katherine Anne Porter) **2. the elder.** the older of two people with the same name: The famous painting *The Harvesters* is by Pieter Brueghel the *Elder.*

eld•er•ly [el′ dər lē] *adjective.* at or near old age; quite old: Arthritis is a more common disease among *elderly* people than young ones. —*noun.* **the elderly.** older people as a group.

eld•est [el′ dist] *adjective.* being the oldest in a family: Queen Elizabeth's *eldest* son Charles will follow her to the throne.

e•lect [i lekt′] *verb,* **elected, electing. 1.** to make a choice by voting: Franklin D. Roosevelt was *elected* President four times. **2.** to choose or decide on a certain course of action: In certain court cases a person can *elect* either to be tried by a jury or by a judge. ". . . a van which Welch had *elected* to pass on a sharp bend between two stone walls." (Kingsley Amis)

e•lec•tion [i lek′ shən] *noun, plural* **elections.** the act or fact of choosing someone by voting: *Elections* for the House of Representatives are held every two years.

e•lec•tive [i lek′ tiv] *adjective.* **1.** having to do with an election: Dwight Eisenhower was elected President even though he had never run for *elective* office before. **2.** done by choice: An *elective* subject in school is one that a student chooses to take besides required courses. —*noun, plural* **electives.** something that is done by choice.

e•lec•tric [i lek′ trik] *adjective.* **1.** having to do with electricity; producing or worked by electricity: an *electric* motor, *electric* lights, an *electric* guitar. **2.** caused by or containing electricity: an *electric* shock. **3.** very exciting: an *electric* acting performance by Meryl Streep.

e•lec•tri•cal [i lek′ tri kəl] *adjective.* having to do with electricity: Modern homes have many types of *electrical* appliances.

electric eel an eel-like fish that can produce a strong electric shock. Electric eels are found in fresh water in South America.

e•lec•tri•cian [i lek′ trish′ ən] *noun, plural* **electricians.** a person whose work is installing, fixing, or operating electrical wiring and equipment.

e•lec•tric•i•ty [i lek′ tris′ ə tē] *noun.* **1.** a basic form of energy that is produced by a current of ELECTRONS flowing rapidly through a wire or other object. Electricity is used for many purposes, such as to give light, make heat, provide power to motors, and run TV sets and radios. **2.** electric current: They shut off the *electricity* when they closed up their beach house for the winter.

e•lec•tro•cute [i lek′ trə kyōōt′] *verb,* **electrocuted, electrocuting.** to kill by using a very strong electric current.
♦ A machine used to electrocute criminals is an **electric chair.**

e•lec•trode [i lek′ trōd′] *noun, plural* **electrodes.** the place where electricity leaves or enters an electrical device or battery.

e•lec•tro•mag•net [i lek′ trō mag′ nit] *noun, plural* **electromagnets.** a piece of iron or steel that becomes a magnet when wrapped with a wire that has an electric current running through it.

e•lec•tron [i lek′ trän′] *noun, plural* **electrons.** a very tiny bit of matter, too small to be seen. Electrons make up the part of an ATOM that surrounds the central NUCLEUS. An electron has a NEGATIVE charge of energy; the nucleus contains other particles with a POSITIVE charge, called PROTONS.

e•lec•tron•ic [i lek trän′ ik] *adjective.* having to do with electrons or electronics: *Electronic* music uses sounds that are produced or changed by means of electricity. —**electronically,** *adverb.*

electronic mail a way of sending messages electronically, by means of a computer. One person enters a message in his computer which another person can then read on the screen of his own computer.

E

Pronunciation Key: T–Z			
t	ten; date	v	very; live
th	think	w	win; away
th	these	y	you
u	cut; butter	z	zoo; cause
ur	turn; bird	zh	measure

(Turn the page for more information.)

E

e•lec•tron•ics [i lek′ trän′ iks] *noun.* **1.** the scientific study of how electrons act and move. The field of electronics includes telephones, radios, TV sets, record and tape players, computers, and so on. **2.** the area of business and industry that deals with electronic products such as computers and TV sets.

el•e•gant [el′ ə gənt] *adjective, more/most.* of a very rich and fine quality; having beauty and style: Princess Diana's *elegant* dress was admired by everyone at the party. ◆ The state of being elegant is **elegance.**

elegant writing "Rebecca did not make for the carriage; but as soon as she perceived her old acquaintance Amelia seated in it, acknowledged her presence by a gracious nod and smile and by kissing and shaking her fingers playfully in the direction of the vehicle." (William Makepeace Thackeray) "Macomber's wife had not looked at him nor he at her and he had sat by her in the back seat with Wilson sitting in the front seat." (Ernest Hemingway) These sentences describe similar situations, but they were written about 100 years apart. Did you guess that Thackeray's is the older of the two? In the 1800's, he and other writers used a style that draws on long phrases and clauses and on long words. Hemingway became famous for using the plain style. Which is the right style? Neither and both are. In literature there are fads. In time, the fads disappear and a reader doesn't criticize. Jane Austen's style as old-fashioned or a novelist today as being "too modern." Great writing is not progressive—the art doesn't grow by stages and depend on discoveries to become better—not like science, for example. Ancient Greek playwrights were great 3000 years ago and are great today.

el•e•ment [el′ ə mənt] *noun, plural* **elements.**
1. any one of the more than a hundred basic substances or materials from which all other things are made. An element has atoms of only one kind and cannot be broken down into any simpler substance by ordinary chemical means. Carbon, oxygen, and hydrogen are common elements in nature. **2.** one of the basic parts of something: Interesting characters and exciting action are *elements* of a good story. **3.** the most natural place or setting: Fish can only live in their own *element,* which is water. **4. the elements.** the forces of nature, such as wind, rain and snow.

el•e•men•ta•ry [el′ ə men′ trē] *adjective, more/most.* dealing with basic rules and principles: *elementary* science, an *elementary* course in arithmetic.

elementary school a school for children that includes the first six grades and usually kindergarten. Certain elementary schools may include up to grade eight, and some others end at grade five.

el•e•phant [el′ ə fənt] *noun, plural* **elephants.** the largest of all land animals. Elephants have a gray body, a long trunk, big, floppy ears, and two tusks of ivory.

el•e•vate [el′ ə vāt′] *verb,* **elevated, elevating.** to raise or lift to a higher level: He's supposed to keep his sprained ankle *elevated* so that the swelling will go down. ◆ An **elevated railway** has tracks above the ground.

el•e•va•tion [el′ ə vā′ shən] *noun, plural* **elevations. 1.** the height above sea level of a certain place: La Paz, Bolivia has the greatest *elevation* of any capital city in the world, over 12,000 feet. **2.** a raised place: "Muroc was up in the high *elevations* of the Mojave Desert." (Tom Wolfe) **3.** a lifting or raising up of something.

el•e•va•tor [el′ ə vā′ tər] *noun, plural* **elevators.** an enclosed car or cage that carries people and things up and down inside a building. Elevators operate by using cables and a motor to make them go from one floor to another.

elf [elf] *noun, plural* **elves.** in stories, a tiny being with magical powers. Elves are usually full of mischief and play tricks on people.

elephant The two types of elephants. The Asian elephant (left) has small ears and two humps on the forehead. The African elephant (right) has large ears touching the shoulder and a curved forehead.

el·i·gi·ble [el′ ə jə bəl] *adjective.* having what is required to be or do something; officially qualified: A person under the age of 35 is not *eligible* to run for President. "In order for him to be *eligible* to play he must keep up his studies." (James Thurber) ◆ The state of being eligible is **eligibility** [el′ ə jə bil′ ə tē].

e·lim·i·nate [i lim′ ə nāt′] *verb,* **eliminated, eliminating.** to leave out or get rid of: She was *eliminated* from the spelling bee when she missed the word "psyche." ◆ The act of eliminating is **elimination:** The doctors' group took out an ad calling for the *elimination* of smoking on all passenger airplanes

El·i·ot [el′ ē ət] **1. Thomas Stearns (T. S.),** 1888–1965, English poet and critic, born in the United States. **2. George,** 1819–1880, English novelist. Her real name was **Mary Ann Evans.**

Elizabeth Queen Elizabeth I (left) and Elizabeth II. Why does British royalty use Roman numerals (I, II) and not Arabic ones (1, 2)? Arabic numerals did not come into use in Europe until the late Middle Ages; by then a Roman numbering system for rulers had been long established.

E·liz·a·beth I [i liz′ ə bəth] 1533–1603, the queen of England from 1558 to 1603.

Elizabeth II, born 1926, the queen of England since 1952.

elk [elk] *noun, plural* **elks** or **elk.** a large deer of North America, the male of which has very large antlers. This animal is also known as a **wapiti** [wäp′ i tē].

elm [elm] *noun, plural* **elms.** a tall shade tree with broad leaves and arching branches. Its strong, hard wood is used for building crates and boxes. Since the 1930's most North American elm trees have died from a fungus called **Dutch elm disease.**

e·lope [i lōp′] *verb,* **eloped, eloping.** to go away secretly to get married, usually without the permission of one's parents.

el·o·quent [el′ ə kwənt] *adjective, more/most.* having the ability to speak and use words well: Winston Churchill's *eloquent* speeches inspired the British people to fight on against the Germans in World War II. ◆ The state of being eloquent is **eloquence.**

El Pas·o [el pas′ ō] a city in western Texas. *Population:* 425,000.

El Sal·va·dor [sal′ və dôr′] the smallest country in Central America. *Capital:* San Salvador. *Area:* 8,130 square miles. *Population:* 4,375,000.

else [els] *adjective.* other or different: Who *else* besides Kelly got an 'A' on the test? —*adverb.* **1.** in a different manner, time, or place: Manero's is closed today—is there anyplace *else* good to eat in town? **2.** otherwise: We'd better leave now or *else* we'll be late.

else·where [els′ wâr′] *adverb.* somewhere else; in another place: The field is flooded, so our game will have to be played *elsewhere.*

e·lude [i lood′] *verb,* **eluded, eluding.** to avoid being caught or found: The bank robbers *eluded* the police and got away. They've been trying to solve that problem for days, but so far the solution has *eluded* them.

elves [elvz] *noun.* the plural of **elf.**

e·man·ci·pate [i man′ sə pāt′] *verb,* **emancipated, emancipating.** to set someone or something free from slavery or from being unfairly controlled.
◆ The act of being freed in this way is **emancipation.** The **Emancipation Proclamation** issued by Abraham Lincoln on January 1, 1863, freed all slaves in the Confederate states.

em·bank·ment [im bangk′ mənt] *noun, plural* **embankments.** a raised bank or wall of earth, stones, or blocks, used to hold back water or to hold up a road.

em·bar·go [im bär′ gō] *noun, plural* **embargoes.** a government order forbidding certain ships to enter or leave its ports.

em·bark [im bärk′] *verb,* **embarked, embarking. 1.** to go on a ship to take a trip. **2.** to start out; set out: After college she *embarked* on a career in banking.

E

Pronunciation Key: [ə] Symbol

The [ə] or *schwa* sound occurs in syllables without an accent. It can be spelled with any vowel, such as a in above, e in listen, i in pencil, o in melon, u in circus. It can also be a combination of vowels, such as **io** in action, **ai** in mountain, **iou** in precious.

(Turn the page for more information.)

em·bar·rass [im bar′ əs] *verb,* **embarrassed, embarrassing.** to make someone feel uneasy, nervous, or ashamed: Mike gets *embarrassed* when his grandmother tells stories about the silly things he did when he was a baby. ◆ Often used as an adjective: It was an *embarrassing* moment for Laura when she spelled her boss's name wrong in a letter.

em·bar·rass·ment [im bar′ əs mənt] *noun, plural* **embarrassments.** the feeling of being embarrassed: Todd was filled with *embarrassment* when the teacher caught him sleeping during class.

em·bas·sy [em′ bə sē] *noun, plural* **embassies.** the official home and place of work of an AMBASSADOR and his or her assistants in another country: the U.S. *Embassy* in London.

em·bed [im bed′] *verb,* **embedded, embedding.** to place or fix something firmly: The king's crown was *embedded* with jewels.

em·ber [em′ bər] *noun, plural* **embers.** a glowing coal or piece of wood from a fire, especially one that is no longer burning in flames.

em·bez·zle [im bez′ əl] *verb,* **embezzled, embezzling.** to steal money or goods that one is supposed to take care of. ◆ A person who does this is an **embezzler.**

em·blem [em′ bləm] *noun, plural* **emblems.** an object or sign that stands for something; a symbol: The bald eagle is an *emblem* of the United States. The *emblem* of the Girl Scouts is a three-leaf clover.

em·brace [im brās′] *verb,* **embraced, embracing.** to hold or take in one's arms as a sign of love or affection; hug. —*noun, plural* **embraces.** the act of embracing someone: ". . . a confused whirl of *embraces,* kisses, backslaps, handshakes, and loud greetings of all sorts." (Eugene O'Neill)

em·broi·der [im broi′ dər] *verb,* **embroidered, embroidering. 1.** to stitch designs with thread onto a piece of cloth: The pillowcases were *embroidered* with red and gold leaves. ◆ These designs are called **embroidery** [im broi′ dər ē]. **2.** to add extra details to the facts; exaggerate: My Uncle Leo *embroiders* his stories about his boyhood.

em·bry·o [em′ brē ō] *noun, plural* **embryos.** an early form of a plant or animal that is developing from an egg or a seed. A plant inside a seed, a bird inside an egg, and a baby inside a human mother or an animal are all embryos.

em·er·ald [em′ rəld] *noun, plural* **emeralds. 1.** a valuable bright-green stone or gem. Emeralds are used in fine jewelry. **2.** the green color of this stone. —*adjective.* having this color: Ireland is called "The *Emerald* Isle" because of its many green fields.

e·merge [i murj′] *verb,* **emerged, emerging. 1.** to come out or up; appear: "My train *emerged* from the tunnel into sunlight . . ." (F. Scott Fitzgerald) **2.** to become known; develop: "The district was beginning to take shape, the people to *emerge* as separate personalities." (James Herriot)

e·mer·gen·cy [i mur′ jən sē] *noun, plural* **emergencies.** a serious, sudden, and unexpected happening that needs quick action: Police officers and firefighters must be able to handle different types of *emergencies.* —*adjective.* having to do with or used for an emergency: an *emergency* exit, fire trucks and other *emergency* vehicles.

Em·er·son [em′ ər sən] **Ralph Waldo,** 1803–1882, American poet and essayist.

em·i·grant [em′ ə grənt] *noun, plural* **emigrants.** a person who leaves his own country to live in another one: The famous scientist Albert Einstein was an *emigrant* from Germany to the United States.

em·i·grate [em′ ə grāt] *verb,* **emigrated, emigrating.** to leave one's own country to settle in another: "He had *emigrated* to America from Ireland when he was a very young man." (A. Conan Doyle) —**emigration,** *noun.*

em·i·nent [em′ ə nənt] *adjective, more/most.* above others in power or position; famous and respected: Marie Curie was an *eminent* scientist. ◆ The state of being eminent is **eminence.**

e·mit [i mit′] *verb,* **emitted, emitting.** to give out or send forth: The burning building *emitted* a terrible heat. "The scream she *emitted* was heard at the dockyards a mile away." (Paul Gallico)

emerald The huge Gachala emerald from a mine in Colombia, South America. It weighs 858 carats, or almost one pound.

emotion in writing In Ray Bradbury's famous science-fiction story, "All Summer in a Day," a group of children are on the planet Venus, where it has rained without stopping for seven years. Then the sun comes out briefly and they are happy: "And the jungle burned with sunlight as the children, released from their spell, rushed out, yelling, into the springtime." They turn sad when the rain begins again: "They turned and started to walk back toward the underground house, their hands at their sides, their smiles vanishing away." And they feel guilty for harming Margot: "They could not meet each other's glances. Their faces were solemn and pale. They looked at their hands and feet, their faces down." Note that emotion, feelings, are shown by description that involves sounds, movements, gestures. In writing, it's never good enough to generalize emotions: "He was sad." "She was hopeful." You need to flesh out feelings, use detail. You need to show, rather than just tell.

e•mo•tion [i mō′ shən] *noun, plural* **emotions.** a strong feeling of any kind: "Wally was one of those people who didn't mind showing their *emotions*, happiness, rage, frustration, whatever." (Tom Wolfe)

e•mo•tion•al [i mō′ shən əl] *adjective, more/most.* **1.** having to do with a person's feelings: The wedding was an *emotional* time for the bride's mother, who cried at one time and laughed at another. **2.** easily excited or moved by feelings: Young children are very *emotional* and show their feelings easily. **3.** showing or causing strong feeling: Patrick Henry is remembered for his *emotional* speeches on liberty and patriotism. **—emotionally,** *adverb.*

em•per•or [em′ pər ər] *noun, plural* **emperors.** a person who rules an EMPIRE. The title of "emperor" was used mainly in former times.

em•pha•tic [em fat′ ik] *adjective, more/most.* giving emphasis; very definite: "I thanked her and thanked her again, nodding to be *emphatic*." (Kate Simon) **—emphatically,** *adverb.*

em•pire [em′ pīr] *noun, plural* **empires. 1.** a group of countries under one ruler or government: the Roman *Empire*, the British *Empire.* **2.** any large area or activity that is ruled over by one person: John D. Rockefeller once controlled a vast oil *empire.*

em•ploy [im ploi′] *verb,* **employed, employing. 1.** to pay someone to work; hire: The store plans to *employ* more people for the holiday season. **2.** to make use of; use: Some early automobiles *employed* steam or electricity for power instead of gasoline. **—noun.** the fact of being employed: The man was secretly a spy in the *employ* of a foreign government.

emphasis How can you give a word emphasis in writing? CAPITALS, SMALL CAPITALS, *italics*, **boldface,** or underlining show emphasis. For writing done by hand or with a typewriter, though, emphasis can only be shown in three ways: by capitals, by underlining, or by use of quotation marks. Underlining is usually a better way to do it: "The Mississippi is not just a river. It's the river." Save capitals to show that someone who is talking has said one word very loudly: "Jimmy did WHAT? Mom asked." In general, you should use emphasis carefully, and not overdo it. Like anything else, too much is usually less rather than more. A person who shouts all the time can't get attention when he really needs it. In writing, also, use a calm voice until you need a stronger one.

em•pha•sis [em′ fə sis] *noun, plural* **emphases** [em′ fə sēz′] **1.** special importance or attention given to something: In judging high school students for admission to college, great *emphasis* is placed on their grades and test scores. **2.** extra force or meaning given to a certain word or part of a word.

em•pha•size [em′ fə sīz′] *verb,* **emphasized, emphasizing.** to give emphasis to; stress: At one time colleges *emphasized* Latin over all other subjects, but now only a few students even take the subject at all.

em•ploy•ee [im ploi′ ē] *noun, plural* **employees.** a person who is paid to work for someone else: That company has over 2000 *employees.*

Pronunciation Key: Accent Marks

[′] is the normal accent mark. It shows where the main stress falls on a word.
[′] is a secondary accent mark. It shows a lighter stress than the primary accent. For example:

tel • e • vis • ion [tel′ə vizh′ən]
(Turn the page for more information.)

em•ploy•er [im ploi′ ər] *noun, plural* **employers.** a person or company that pays others to do work: He's worked for several different *employers* in the past few years.

em•ploy•ment [im ploi′ mənt] *noun, plural* **employments. 1.** the fact of employing or being employed. **2.** the work that someone does; a job: Marian is looking for some kind of *employment* in the publishing business.

em•press [em′ pris] *noun, plural* **empresses.** a woman who rules an EMPIRE.

emp•ty [emp′ tē] *adjective.* **1.** having nothing inside: She put a carton of milk and two *empty* glasses on the table. The house has been *empty* ever since the owner moved out last month. **2.** having no force or value: Professional wrestlers often make *empty* threats against their opponents before a match. —*verb,* **emptied, emptying. 1.** to make or become empty: Fred *emptied* the waste basket into a garbage can outside. The train *emptied* as soon as we pulled into the station. **2.** to flow out; pour out: Many other rivers *empty* into the Mississippi. ♦ The fact of being empty is **emptiness.**

e•mu [ē′ myoo] *noun, plural* **emus.** a large bird of Australia that looks like an ostrich. An emu can run very fast, but it cannot fly.

en•a•ble [in ā′ bəl] *verb,* **enabled, enabling.** to make able to do something; give the ability to: "I afterwards sold them to *enable* me to buy Burton's *Historical Collections.*" (Benjamin Franklin)

en•act [in akt′] *verb,* **enacted, enacting. 1.** to make into law: The state *enacted* a law against child abuse. **2.** to act out or perform a role in a play: to *enact* the part of the Queen in *Hamlet.*

e•nam•el [i nam′ əl] *noun, plural* **enamels. 1.** a smooth, hard, glossy coating used to protect or decorate metal or clay objects, such as pots and pans. **2.** a glossy paint that dries to a hard finish. —*verb,* **enameled, enameling.** to cover or coat with enamel.

en•chant [in chant′] *verb,* **enchanted, enchanting. 1.** to put a magic spell on: In old tales, people are often *enchanted* by witches or fairies. **2.** to charm greatly, as if by magic: Luciano Pavarotti's beautiful voice has *enchanted* listeners all over the world. ♦ Often used as an adjective: a story about an *enchanted* forest, a beautiful movie star with an *enchanting* smile. —**enchantment,** *noun.*

en•cir•cle [in sur′ kəl] *verb,* **encircled, encircling.** to form or move in a circle: "This pasture was smaller than the last (and) *encircled* almost entirely by woods." (Flannery O'Connor)

en•close [in klōz′] *verb,* **enclosed, enclosing. 1.** to surround and shut in: Their back yard is *enclosed* by a chain fence. **2.** to include with something else in an envelope or package: Jill *enclosed* a picture of herself inside the letter.

en•core [än′ kôr′] *noun, plural* **encores. 1.** a call made by the audience for a singer or other performer to continue after the end of the regular show. **2.** a performance done after the audience has called for an encore: For his *encore,* the singer sang "Ave Maria."

en•count•er [in koun′ tər] *verb,* **encountered, encountering.** to come up against; meet: "One morning, as he was coming up to the hotel, he *encountered* Mrs. Travis." (John Galsworthy) —*noun, plural* **encounters.** a meeting, especially one that is unexpected or difficult: Kevin has had several *encounters* with dogs while delivering newspapers, but he's never been bitten.

en•cour•age [in kur′ ij] *verb,* **encouraged, encouraging. 1.** to give courage or hope to someone: Laura's teacher *encouraged* her to enter her project in the state science fair. ♦ Often used as an adjective: The patient shows *encouraging* signs of making a full recovery. **2.** to help bring about or make happen: The city is trying to *encourage* the building of new office buildings downtown. —**encouragingly,** *adverb:* The coach spoke *encouragingly* to Terry before she went up to bat.

en•cour•age•ment [in kur′ ij mənt] *noun, plural* **encouragements. 1.** something that encourages someone: The audience's applause was an *encouragement* to the nervous speaker. **2.** the act or fact of encouraging: The publishers didn't accept her book, but they gave her a lot of *encouragement* to go on with her writing.

en•cy•clo•pe•di•a [in sī′ klə pē′ dē ə] *noun, plural* **encyclopedias.** a book or set of books giving information about many things. An encyclopedia has articles explaining facts about a great number of subjects or about many different areas of one large subject.

end [end] *noun, plural* **ends. 1.** the last part: The movie was so boring that we left long before the *end.* **2.** the part where something begins or stops: Their house is at the *end* of Cole Street. **3.** the point in time where something no longer goes on or exists: the *end* of the day, the *end* of the nineteenth century. **4.** a final purpose or goal: "Those who won our independence believed that the final *end* of the state was to make men free. ." (Louis Brandeis) —*verb,* **ended, ending.** to bring to an end; stop: to *end* a letter. The movie *ends* at 9:45.

en·dan·ger [in dān′ jər] *verb*, **endangered, endangering.** to cause someone or something to be in danger: She *endangered* her own life to save the baby from the burning house.

endangered species Some of the American animals that are endangered species—the condor (above), eagle, wolf, and bighorn sheep.

endangered species a kind of animal or plant that exists in such small numbers that it is likely to die out completely unless it is protected. Giant pandas and tigers are among the endangered species of Asia.

end·ing [end′ ing] *noun, plural* **endings.** the end of something, especially the last part of a

en·dorse [in dôrs′] *verb*, **endorsed, endorsing. 1.** to talk or act in favor of someone or something; support publicly: Congressman Smith *endorsed* the President's bid for re-election. **2.** to write one's name on the back of a check: You have to *endorse* this check before the bank will cash it. **—endorsement**, *noun.*

en·dow [in dou′] *verb*, **endowed, endowing. 1.** to give money or property to a person or an organization: "Mr. Yerkes had established the Yerkes Observatory and *endowed* it with millions." (Saul Bellow) **2.** to give a special talent or ability: She was *endowed* with a beautiful singing voice. **—endowment**, *noun.*

en·dur·ance [in door′ əns] *noun.* the power or ability to endure: Jack built up his *endurance* for soccer by running five miles a day. Teaching first grade calls for patience and *endurance.*

en·dure [in door′] *verb*, **endured, enduring. 1.** to put up with; hold out under: She *endured* the pain of her broken leg until the doctors were able to help her. **2.** to continue or last: The plays of Shakespeare have *endured* for almost 400 years. ♦ Also used as an adjective: Thanksgiving is an *enduring* custom in the U.S.

en·e·my [en′ ə mē] *noun, plural* **enemies. 1.** a person who tries to hurt or wishes harm to another; someone who is strongly against another person. **2.** a country at war with another country. **3.** anything that is dangerous or harmful: An elephant has no *enemies* in nature, except man.

---

endings There are many ways to end a story. In some modern stories, the writer just stops. "Then it comes to me:" is the ending of the novel *Frieze*, by Cecile Pineda. In the past, however, writers were expected to provide a clear ending that brought the plot to a close. Here are two endings written in the same year (1894) by famous British writers of the Victorian Age. First, *By England's Aid*, by G.A. Henty: "Dolores had, two or three years after her arrival in England, embraced the faith of her husband; and although she complained a little at times of the English climate, she never once regretted the step she had taken in leaving her native Spain." Now, Rudyard Kipling's "Rikki-tikki-tavi:" "Rikki-tikki had a right to be proud of himself. But he did not grow too proud, and he kept that garden as a mongoose should keep it, with tooth and jump and spring and bite, till never a cobra dared show its head inside the walls." Is the traditional "neat ending" a better choice for student writers in their stories? The editors of this book think so.

---

book, movie, or play: Shirley Jackson's story "Charles" is famous for its surprise *ending.*

end·less [end′ lis] *adjective.* **1.** seeming to have no end or stopping point; going on and on: "Those animals that are called camels live in a place of *endless* sand." (Alex Haley) **2.** without end: A circle is an *endless* figure. **—endlessly**, *adverb.*

Pronunciation Key: A–F			
a	and; hat	ch	chew; such
ā	ate; stay	d	dog; lid
â	care; air	e	end; yet
ä	father; hat	ē	she; each
b	boy; cab	f	fun; off

(Turn the page for more information.)

E

en•er•get•ic [en′ ər jet′ ik] *adjective, more/most.* full of energy: Ted was tired from a busy day, but after a good night's sleep he felt *energetic* again. "Great-grandfather's wife was a delicate, yet strong and *energetic* lady." (Shawn Hsu Wong) —**energetically,** *adverb.*

en•er•gy [en′ ər jē] *noun, plural* **energies.** **1.** any kind of power that can cause things to move or do other kinds of work. Sun, wind, and moving water are all sources of energy; so are coal, gasoline, and electricity. **2.** the strength or will to do something: Yesterday I had enough *energy* to work all day, but today I'm really tired. **3.** *usually,* **energies.** the power to work; effort: She's devoting all her *energies* to finishing her social studies report.

en•force [in fôrs′] *verb,* **enforced, enforcing.** to make sure that a law or rule is obeyed: "A one-hour parking limit is *enforced* during business hours." (John Updike) —**enforcement,** *noun:* The head law-*enforcement* officer of a city is the police chief.

en•gage [in gāj′] *verb,* **engaged, engaging. 1.** to promise or agree to marry a person. ♦ Often used as an adjective: The *engaged* couple planned for a June wedding. **2.** to hire someone for a job; employ: "The American *engaged* him at last at three dollars . . ." (Joseph Conrad) **3.** to take part in something; participate: "Now we are *engaged* in a great civil war . . ." (Abraham Lincoln)

en•gage•ment [in gāj′ mənt] *noun, plural* **engagements. 1.** a promise or agreement to be married: Bob and Mary held a party to announce their *engagement.* **2.** a meeting or appointment: Mrs. Bishop's secretary reminded her she had a dinner *engagement* that evening. **3.** the fact of being hired for work: That singer has a two-week *engagement* in Las Vegas. **4.** a battle in a war.

en•gine [en′ jin] *noun, plural* **engines. 1.** a machine that uses energy to make something move or run; a motor. An engine may get its power from gasoline, oil, electricity, steam, or other sources of energy. **2.** a railroad car with a motor to pull other cars; a locomotive.

en•gi•neer [en′ jə nēr′] *noun, plural* **engineers. 1.** a person who is trained in engineering; someone who plans and builds such things as engines and other machines, automobiles and airplanes, and bridges, roads, or buildings. **2.** a person whose work is running a railroad engine. **3.** a person who runs or takes care of machinery or technical equipment. —*verb,* **engineered, engineering. 1.** to plan, build, or manage as an engineer: The roads of the ancient Romans were very well *engineered,* and some are still used today. **2.** to manage or carry out: Mr. Willis *engineered* a big deal for his company to buy out another firm.

en•gi•neer•ing [en jə nēr′ ing] *noun.* a field of work that takes the laws and principles of science and applies them to plan, build, and operate things that are useful to humans. The different branches of engineering include such activities as building a dam or a canal, drilling for oil, making paints or plastic, developing a computer, and designing a spacecraft.

Eng•land [ing′ glənd] a country that is the main part of Great Britain. It is separated from Europe by the **English Channel.** *Capital:* London. *Area:* 50,400 square miles. *Population:* 46,550,000.

Eng•lish [ing′ glish] *noun.* **1.** the language that was first spoken in England and that is now also spoken in the United States and in other countries that were once ruled by Great Britain, such as Canada and Australia. **2. the English.** the people of England. —*adjective.* having to do with England or the English language.

en•grave [in grāv′] *verb,* **engraved, engraving. 1.** to carve letters, pictures, or designs into a surface: The doctor's name was *engraved* on a brass plate on his office door. **2.** to cut designs into a hard surface to be used for printing, or to print something using such a surface: We received an *engraved* invitation to my cousin's wedding. **3.** to be deeply impressed on the mind, as if by engraving: The scene of the battlefield was *engraved* in his memory forever.

engine A historic locomotive engine on the Erie Railway. The large grating on the front is called a "cowcatcher." It was used to push animals and other things off the track so that they wouldn't delay or derail the train.

♦ Something that is engraved is an **engraving**.

engraving Detail from an engraving done in 1498 by the great German artist Albrecht Durer.

en•gulf [in gulf′] *verb*, **engulfed, engulfing.** to completely surround and swallow up: The flood waters *engulfed* the house. "... a moment of terror had *engulfed* him." (Frank Herbert)

en•large [in lärj′] *verb*, **enlarged, enlarging.** to make or become bigger: They're going to *enlarge* their house by building a room over the garage. Microscopes *enlarge* things that are too small to be seen by the eye alone. —**enlargement**, *noun*: He made an *enlargement* of the photo.

en•light•en [in līt′ ən] *verb*, **enlightened, enlightening.** to cause to understand, give knowledge to: Reading Laura Ingalls Wilder's books has really *enlightened* me about pioneer life on the prairie. ♦ The fact of being enlightened is **enlightenment. The Enlightenment** was a time in the 1700's when great advancements were made in science, learning, and political thought.

en•list [in list′] *verb*, **enlisted, enlisting.** to choose to join the army, navy, or another branch of the armed forces. —**enlistment**, *noun*: Joe signed up for a four-year *enlistment* in the Marines. ♦ An **enlisted man** is someone in the armed forces who is not an officer.

e•nor•mous [i nôr′ məs] *adjective*, *more/most.* much bigger than is usual; huge: "An *enormous* castle, lighted as by the light of many moons, stood upon a hill a mile away." (James Thurber) ". . . he had an *enormous* respect for what he called serious writers." (Graham Greene) —**enormously**, *adverb*.

enormous Some people, when they find that an established author makes an error, say: "Homer nods." This means that even the first great storyteller in history, Homer, occasionally slipped into error. John Updike is one of the best American novelists alive. But Updike may have nodded when he wrote: "We in America have from the beginning been . . . reforming the *enormity* of nature we were given, which we took to be hostile." *Enormity* strictly refers to something very wrong or bad, as in "the enormity of a crime." *Enormousness* is a word that means "large size." Do you agree that this distinction is needed? The television reporter Leslie Stahl wrote: "Given the *enormity* of this landslide vote for President Reagan . . . " What do you think that means?

en•hance [in hans′] *verb*, **enhanced, enhancing.** to make better; add to: Salt and pepper are often used to *enhance* the flavor of food. —**enhancement**, *noun*.

en•joy [in joi′] *verb*, **enjoyed, enjoying. 1.** to get joy or pleasure from; like to do: On weekends Dad *enjoys* watching football on TV. **2.** to have the use or benefit of: to *enjoy* good health. **3. enjoy oneself.** to have a good time: I hope you *enjoyed yourself* at the party.

en•joy•ment [in joi′ mənt] *noun*. the act or fact of enjoying something; pleasure: Many airline flights now show movies for the *enjoyment* of the passengers. ♦ Something that gives enjoyment is **enjoyable**: We spent a very *enjoyable* day at the beach yesterday.

e•nough [i nuf′] *adjective*. not too much and not too little; just the right amount: The meeting room didn't have *enough* chairs for everyone, so some people had to stand. —*noun:* We're low on gas, but we've got *enough* to get home. —*adverb:* She ran the race just fast *enough* to win.

Pronunciation Key: G–N			
g	give; big	k	kind; cat; back
h	hold	l	let; ball
i	it; this	m	make; time
ī	ice; my	n	not; own
j	jet; gem; edge	ng	having

(Turn the page for more information.)

E

en•rage [in rāj′] *verb,* **enraged, enraging.** to make very angry; fill with rage: "The colonel . . . became so *enraged* with Clevinger that he beat his fist down upon the table . . ." (Joseph Heller)

en•rich [in rich′] *verb,* **enriched, enriching.** **1.** to make rich or richer: The nation of Saudi Arabia has been *enriched* by the deposits of oil on its land. **2.** to make better by adding something; improve: ". . . light winds began to sift the loose ashes over the fields, *enriching* the soil." (Alex Haley) —**enrichment,** *noun.*

en•roll [in rôl′] *verb,* **enrolled, enrolling.** to take in a new member, or become a new member: "I was six and ready to be *enrolled* in the first grade." (Kate Simon)

en•roll•ment [in rôl′ mənt] *noun, plural* **enrollments. 1.** the act or process of enrolling. **2.** the number of people enrolled: Brian's high school has an *enrollment* of about 800 students.

en•sign [en′ sən] *noun, plural* **ensigns. 1.** a flag or banner that is flown on a ship to represent a country or organization. **2.** the lowest-ranking officer of the Navy or Coast Guard.

en•sure [in shoor′] *verb,* **ensured, ensuring.** (also spelled **insure**) to make sure or certain; guarantee: He bought a special double lock for the door to *ensure* that no one could break in. The Constitution *ensures* certain rights for all American citizens.

en•tan•gle [in tang′ gəl] *verb,* **entangled, entangling. 1.** to get caught in, or as if in, a tangle or net: The fishing line got *entangled* in some seaweed. That oil company has been *entangled* in a long court battle over drilling on public land. —**entanglement,** *noun.*

en•ter [en′ tər] *verb,* **entered, entering. 1.** to come or go into: to *enter* a room or a building. **2.** to begin; start: Next month that store will *enter* its tenth year of business. **3.** to sign up or register; enroll: Matt *entered* his rabbit in the pet show. Marsha will be *entering* high school this fall. **4.** to put down an item or figure in a book: The bank teller *entered* my deposit in my bankbook. **5.** to cause something to be recorded or included: The things said in Congress are *entered* in the Congressional Record. —*noun.* a command that is given to a computer to record a certain item of information.

en•ter•prise [en′ tər prīz′] *noun, plural* **enterprises. 1.** something that is done, especially something complicated or difficult: "The *enterprise* the Army had undertaken . . . was the development of supersonic jet and rocket planes." (Tom Wolfe) **2.** the carrying on of business activity: In most countries the airlines are government-owned, but in the U.S. they are part of private *enterprise.*

en•ter•tain [en′ tər tān′] *verb,* **entertained, entertaining. 1.** to keep interested and amused; please: The puppies kept the children *entertained* for hours. "Once in the boat we were *entertained* by the songs of our boatman." (Alice Walker) ♦ Also used as an adjective: We saw a very *entertaining* dance show at the county fair. **2.** to have a guest or guests: Her parents often *entertain* on weekends. **3.** to have in mind; consider: He's *entertaining* the idea of going to Europe next summer.

en•ter•tain•er [en′ tər tān′ ər] *noun, plural* **entertainers.** a person who entertains others, especially someone who works as a singer, actor, or comedian.

en•ter•tain•ment [en′ tər tān′ mənt] *noun, plural* **entertainments. 1.** the act of entertaining; keeping people amused or interested. **2.** something that is amusing or entertaining: A clown show provided the *entertainment* at Esther's birthday party.

en•thu•si•asm [in thoo′ zē az′ əm] *noun.* a strong feeling of excitement and interest; a great liking: Pete Rose is famous among baseball fans for his *enthusiasm* for the game.

en•thu•si•as•tic [in thoo′ zē as′ tik] *adjective, more/most.* full of enthusiasm; showing or having excitement and interest: Mom wasn't too *enthusiastic* about going camping at first, but she really enjoyed it. —**enthusiastically,** *adverb:* Billy always eats his green vegetables, but he doesn't do it very *enthusiastically.*

en•tire [in tīr′] *adjective.* with nothing left out; complete; whole: We were really tired after spending the *entire* day shopping. "Yesterday, I was going to run the *entire* New York City Marathon course . . ." (Jimmy Breslin) —**entirety** [in tīr′ tē], the complete amount.

en•tire•ly [in tīr′ lē] *adverb.* completely; fully: "She looks *entirely* different off the stage. I thought she was much better-looking." (Dorothy Parker)

en•ti•tle [in tīt′ əl] *verb,* **entitled, entitling. 1.** to give a right or privilege to: Buying a ticket for the bus *entitles* you to ride, but not to have a seat. **2.** to give a title to; call: The famous detective Sherlock Holmes first appeared in a story *entitled A Study in Scarlet.*

en•trance¹ [en′ trəns] *noun, plural* **entrances. 1.** a door or passageway through which someone enters a place: The *entrance* to the garden is between two rose bushes. **2.** the act of entering: ". . . the sound of someone's *entrance* through the corridor-door stopped him." (Dashiell Hammett) **3.** the permission or right to go in; admission: Barry wasn't allowed *entrance* to the restaurant because he wasn't wearing a shirt or shoes.

surround or go with a certain person or thing: Students become better readers in school if reading is important in their home *environment.*—**environmental,** *adjective: Environmental* studies have shown that certain insect poisons cause damage to plants.

environment Los Angeles, California has been the home ground of many writers. Nathanael West and Raymond Chandler wrote there. Joan Didion was born and educated in northern California and lives now in Los Angeles. This huge city, like other cities, can produce writers who reflect their *environment,* that is, the persons, places, things around them. Nathanael West saw Hollywood as a deadly environment, because there illusion and reality often made the same impressions. Raymond Chandler, who wrote great crime novels, found the L.A. environment not crowded, yet complicated. His detective, "Marlowe," was always looking for connections between people. Joan Didion seems to find eccentric people, odd happenings in all parts of L.A., yet, even if she is not surprised by this, it seems to make her weary. Now, what are these remarks? They are *criticism*—see page 189.

en•trance² [in trans´] *verb,* **entranced, entrancing.** to fill with wonder and delight: We were *entranced* by the graceful performance of the great ballet dancer.

en•trust [in trust´] *verb,* **entrusted, entrusting.** to trust someone to take charge of or deal with something: "Your grandfather *entrusted* you to my care." (Eugene O'Neill)

en•try [en´ trē] *noun, plural* **entries. 1.** a place where you can enter; an entrance: The *entry* to the fort was guarded by soldiers. **2.** the act of entering: The actress made a dramatic *entry* onto the stage. **3.** something that is entered: an *entry* in a race or contest. **4.** a written item in a record or book. **5.** a word that is recorded in a dictionary. In this book "entitle" is a **main entry** that also includes the other entries "entitled" and "entitling."

en•vel•op [en vel´ əp] *verb,* **enveloped, enveloping.** to cover completely; wrap up: Weeds had grown up around the old shed and almost *enveloped* the walls.

en•ve•lope [en´ və lōp´ *or* än´ və lōp´] *noun, plural* **envelopes.** a thin, flat paper covering used to hold a letter or other piece of writing, used especially for mailing.

en•vi•ous [en´ vē əs] *adjective, more/most.* feeling or showing envy; jealous: Some of the other students were *envious* of Kelly's good grades, so they made fun of her for studying so much.

en•vi•ron•ment [in vī´ ro mont *or* in vī´ rən-mənt] *noun, plural* **environments. 1.** the natural conditions that make up the area in which a plant, animal, or person lives, such as air, water, and land: Lizards are often found in a desert *environment.* **2.** all the conditions that

en•vy [en´ vē] *noun.* **1.** a feeling of wanting what someone else has; jealousy: When he saw his friend's new car, he was filled with *envy.* **2.** a person or thing causing this feeling. —*verb,* **envied, envying.** to feel envy about something; be jealous: He *envies* his sister because she's so much better at sports than he is.

en•zyme [en´ zīm] *noun, plural* **enzymes.** a substance produced by living cells to help body activity take place. Enzymes can affect or speed up chemical actions in body cells, such as digestion.

ep•ic [ep´ ik] *noun, plural* **epics. 1.** a long poem telling about real or imaginary heroes and their adventures. **2.** any long story with lots of action, characters, and details: The movie *Gone With the Wind* is an *epic* of the Civil War. —*adjective.* having to do with or like an epic: Homer's *Odyssey* is an *epic* poem. Alone in a tiny plane, Amelia Earhart made an *epic* flight across the Atlantic.

ep•i•dem•ic [ep´ ə dem´ ik] *noun, plural* **epidemics.** the rapid spread of a disease to many people at the same time: More than 20 million people died in a flu *epidemic* in 1918. **2.** the rapid spread or outbreak of something bad that is thought of as like a disease: There's been an *epidemic* of robberies in town lately.

E

Pronunciation Key: O–S			
ō	over; go	ou	out; town
ô	all; law	p	put; hop
oo	look; full	r	run; car
o͞o	pool; who	s	set; miss
oi	oil; boy	sh	show

(Turn the page for more information.)

E

ep·i·sode [ep′ ə sōd′] *noun, plural* **episodes.** one part of a series of events in a story or in real life: The most-watched TV show ever was the last *episode* of MASH. "She saw this *episode* of her life closed." (D.H. Lawrence)

e·qual [ē′ kwəl] *adjective.* **1.** having the same amount, size, or volume as something else: Three teaspoons are *equal* to one tablespoon. **2.** affecting everyone in the same way: In business, **equal opportunity** means that all people have the same chance to do something, whatever their race, sex, religion, and so on. **3.** having enough ability or strength to do something: After training for a year, he finally felt he was *equal* to running in a marathon. —*verb,* **equaled, equaling.** to be equal to something else: Five plus five *equals* ten. No one has yet *equaled* Joe DiMaggio's record of hitting in 56 straight games. —*noun, plural* **equals.** someone or something that is the equal of another. —**equally,** *adverb:* New York is almost *equally* distant from Boston and Washington.

e·qual·i·ty [i kwal′ ə tē] *noun.* the condition of being equal, especially in economic or political rights.

e·qua·tion [i kwā′ zhən] *noun, plural* **equations.** a mathematical statement showing that two things are equal, such as $3x - 6 = 9$.

e·qua·tor [i kwā′ tər] *noun, plural* **equators.** the imaginary line around the center of the earth at a point halfway between the North and South Poles. —**equatorial,** *adjective.* having to do with or near the equator: Ecuador and Kenya are *equatorial* countries. ♦ *Equator* is related to the word *equal.* The idea is that this line divides the earth into two equal parts.

e·qui·nox [ē′ kwə näks′] *noun, plural* **equinoxes.** one of the two times during the year when the sun is directly over the equator, causing day and night to be equal in length. The **spring equinox** falls about March 21 and the **fall equinox** about September 23.

e·quip [i kwip′] *verb,* **equipped, equipping.** to provide what is needed: This car is *equipped* with power steering and power brakes.

e·quip·ment [i kwip′ mənt] *noun.* **1.** the things that are provided for a particular purpose or job: Camping *equipment* includes tents and sleeping bags. **2.** the act of providing such things: the *equipment* of an army with uniforms and weapons.

e·quiv·a·lent [i kwiv′ ə lənt] *adjective.* being the same or about the same; equal: 32 degrees Fahrenheit is *equivalent* to 0 degrees Celsius. The word "weep" is *equivalent* in meaning to "cry." —*noun.* something that is the same or equal: The winner of the contest gets $10,000, or the *equivalent* in foreign money.

e·ra [ir′ ə] *noun, plural* **eras.** a certain period of history or time that is thought of as one part: The time when Queen Elizabeth I ruled England was called the Elizabethan *era.*

e·rase [i rās′] *verb,* **erased, erasing. 1.** to remove by rubbing out or wiping off: Dave *erased* the wrong answer on his paper. The waves *erased* all traces of our footprints from the shore. **2.** to remove completely, as if by rubbing out: Rosemary accidentally *erased* two songs from her brother's tape recording.

e·ras·er [i rā′ sər] *noun, plural* **erasers.** something that is used to remove or rub out unwanted marks, especially writing on a page.

e·rect [i rekt′] *adjective, more/most.* straight up; not bent: When a soldier is at attention he has to stand *erect.* —*verb,* **erected, erecting. 1.** to build or put up: "Great dikes have been *erected* . . . to keep the ocean where it belongs." (Mary Mapes Dodge) **2.** to put into an upright position: to *erect* a tent.

Er·ie [ēr′ ē] **1. Lake Erie.** the fourth largest of the Great Lakes. It separates the U.S. and Canada at New York State. **2. Erie Canal.** a historic waterway in New York State, between Albany and Buffalo.

ermine The coat of the ermine turns white in winter to give it camouflage against a background of snow. During the rest of the year, its fur is brown.

er·mine [ur′ min] *noun, plural* **ermines** or **ermine.** a small wild animal that looks like a weasel and is raised for its valuable fur.

e·rode [i rōd′] *verb,* **eroded, eroding.** to wear or wash away slowly: The Colorado River *eroded* the area known as the Grand Canyon. ♦ Also used as an adjective: "The air was full of light dust blown by the breeze from the *eroding* mountains." (John Steinbeck) —**erosion** [i rō′ zhən] *noun.* the process of eroding.

er•rand [erʹ ənd] *noun, plural* **errands. 1.** a short trip for the purpose of doing something, such as going to a store or to the bank, picking up or delivering something, and so on. **2. to run an errand.** to make such a trip.

Es•ki•mo [esʹ kə mō] *noun, plural* **Eskimos. 1.** a member of a group of people who live in Alaska, Canada, and other Arctic areas. **2.** the language spoken by Eskimos. —*adjective.* having to do with Eskimos or their language.

> **errors in print** "I lost a jackit that belonged to my brother. This was the the first time I wore it. I shouldn't have wornit without asking him." Each of these sentences shows a careless error. Did you spot them? ("Jacket" mispelled as "jackit," "the" written twice, "worn" and "it" joined as one word) Errors in print do creep through, no matter how carefully editors go over something before it is published. The error of the "double the" is especially hard to catch. Have you found errors in this book? If you have, please write and let us know what they are.

er•ror [erʹ ər] *noun, plural* **errors. 1.** something that is incorrect; a mistake: Bonnie made three *errors* while typing the page. **2.** in baseball, a wrong play made by a fielder that allows a runner or batter to be safe when he should have been out.

e•rupt [i ruptʹ] *verb,* **erupted, erupting. 1.** to break or burst out violently: The volcano Mt. St. Helens *erupted* in May of 1980. **2.** to develop or appear suddenly: "A burst of laughter *erupted* from Leto." (Frank Herbert) —**eruption,** *noun:* the *eruption* of lava from a volcano.

es•ca•la•tor [esʹ kə lāʹ tər] *noun, plural* **escalators.** a moving stairway that carries people from one floor to another, as in a store, airport, or other public building.

es•cape [es kāpʹ] *verb,* **escaped, escaping. 1.** to get away or get free; break loose: The prisoners *escaped* by hiding in a laundry truck. After the accident, dangerous gases *escaped* from the tank cars. **2.** to avoid something harmful or dangerous: The tornado destroyed the house, but luckily the family *escaped* injury. **3.** to slip out of one's mind or memory, as if escaping: Jim, this is Mr. . . . I'm sorry, your name *escapes* me. —*noun, plural* **escapes. 1.** the act or fact of escaping: The outlaw John Dillinger was famous for his daring *escapes* from prison. **2.** something that takes one's mind away from worries, problems, or cares.

es•cort [esʹ kôrtʹ] *noun, plural* **escorts. 1.** someone or something that goes along with another for protection or as an honor: a police *escort.* A destroyer serves as an *escort* to larger ships such as aircraft carriers. **2.** a man who goes along with a woman to a dance or party. —[es kôrtʹ] *verb,* **escorted, escorting.** to act as an escort: In World War II fighter planes *escorted* bombers to their target.

eruption A recent eruption of Kilauea Iki Volcano in Hawaii, as liquid lava flows down.

e•soph•a•gus [i säfʹ ə gəs] *noun.* the tube through which food passes from the mouth to the stomach.

ESP *noun.* the ability to know about things through some means other than the ordinary use of the five senses (sight, hearing, and so on). People with ESP supposedly can predict the future, tell what other people are thinking, or know about an event that is happening somewhere else. ◆ ESP is short for e̲xtra̲se̲nso-ry perception.

es•pe•cial•ly [es peshʹ əl ē] *adverb.* **1.** more than usual; in a special way: The weather's

Pronunciation Key. T–Z

t	ten; date	v	very; live
th	think	w	win; away
th	these	y	you
u	cut; butter	z	zoo; cause
ur	turn; bird	zh	measure

(Turn the page for more information.)

been *especially* cold this month. **2.** in a way more than others; particularly: My little brother likes the characters on "Sesame Street," *especially* Big Bird and Cookie Monster.

es•pi•o•nage [es′ pē ə nazh′] *noun.* the act or practice of spying, especially to get secret information about the military or political activities of a foreign government.

es•teem [ə stēm′] *verb,* **esteemed, esteeming.** to think highly of; respect: "Jack Bamborough's books were not only *esteemed;* they also brought in money." (Aldous Huxley) —*noun.* great respect: admiration.

es•ti•mate [es′ tə mit] *noun, plural* **estimates.** a judgment of the amount or quality of something; a general but careful guess: The garage

> **essay** "Essay" is a word that has an important history. The French writer Montaigne wrote short pieces of prose on various subjects. He called them *Essais,* in French, "tries" or "attempts." He sought to explain his views, to reveal his convictions. In the course of this, he invented the essay. An essay is usually short. Essays often appear in newspapers or magazines. William Safire, a writer for the *New York Times,* even calls his newspaper column "Essay." Much of the writing you do as a student takes the form of an essay, such as book reports or editorials. American writers whose essays are quoted in this dictionary include Henry David Thoreau, Mark Twain, E.B. White, James Baldwin, Joan Didion, and John McPhee.

E

es•say [es′ ā] *noun, plural* **essays.** a short piece of writing about a true subject, especially one that tells the writer's point of view.

es•sence [es′ əns] *noun, plural* **essences. 1.** the basic quality of something that makes it what it is: The *essence* of "Mr. Rogers'" appeal to young children is his relaxed and friendly manner on the air. **2.** a concentrated substance made from a plant or drug: The *essences* of certain flowers are used for making perfume.

es•sen•tial [ə sen′ shəl] *adjective, more/most.* of the greatest importance; necessary; basic: Studying is *essential* to getting good grades. —*noun, plural* **essentials.** something that is necessary or basic. —**essentially,** *adverb:* There are a few final touches left to do, but the house is *essentially* finished.

es•tab•lish [ə stab′ lish] *verb,* **established, establishing. 1.** to create or begin; set up: Harvard University was *established* in 1636, making it the oldest U.S. college. **2.** to prove to be true or correct: It was *established* that he was at home at the time of the crime.

es•tab•lish•ment [ə stab′ lish mənt] *noun, plural* **establishments. 1.** something that is established, especially a place of business: That bank is the oldest *establishment* in town. **2.** the act or fact of establishing.

es•tate [ə stāt′] *noun, plural* **estates. 1.** a large piece of land, usually with a large, impressive home on it. **2.** everything that a person owns, especially the money and property that is left to others at the time of death: After Howard Hughes died his *estate* was valued at almost $500 million.

gave us an *estimate* of the cost of repairing the car. —[es′ tə māt′] *verb,* **estimated, estimating.** to form a general opinion; make an estimate. —**estimation** [es′ tə má′ shən], *noun.*

etc. an abbreviation of the Latin phrase **et cetera,** meaning "and so forth:" Japan is known for making TV sets, radios, stereos, *etc.*

etching Detail from an etching by Rembrandt done in 1648, a self-portrait of the artist.

etch [ech] *verb,* **etched, etching. 1.** to engrave a picture or image by using acid to burn the design into a metal plate. An **etching** is then made by putting ink on the plate and pressing it against paper. **2.** to create a clear picture or image, as if by etching: "Never would he forget that moment when they had seen the first pearly outlines of the snow-covered mountains *etched* against the sky." (Pearl Buck)

e•ter•nal [i tur′ nəl] *adjective.* **1.** continuing or lasting forever: the *eternal* movement of the ocean tides. Rome is known as the "*Eternal City*" because of its long history. **2.** seeming to continue or last forever: An *eternal* complaint of teenagers is that their parents don't understand them. —**eternally,** *adverb.*

e•ter•ni•ty [i tur′ nə tē] *noun, plural* **eternities.** **1.** time that goes on forever; time without end. **2.** a period of time that seems to go on forever: We waited an *eternity* before our train finally arrived.

eth•ics [eth′ iks] *plural noun.* **1.** the study of what is good and bad, and of right and wrong ways of acting. **2.** a set of rules or standards for a certain person or group: According to medical *ethics,* doctors should not tell people about the problems of patients they are treating.

eth•i•cal [eth′ ə kəl] *adjective, more/most.* following correct standards of ethics; proper or right: For many years it was not considered *ethical* for a lawyer to advertise for new clients.

E•thi•o•pi•a [ē′ thē ō′ pē ə] a country in eastern Africa, on the Red Sea. *Capital:* Addis Ababa. *Area:* 470,000 square miles. *Population:* 32,150,000. —**Ethiopian,** *adjective; noun.*

eth•nic [eth′ nik] *adjective.* having to do with people who share the same language, culture, homeland, and so on: Irish, Italians, and Mexicans are among the *ethnic* groups in the U.S.

et•i•quette [et′ ə kət] *noun.* the rules of correct social behavior: Interrupting someone who is speaking and talking with food in your mouth are not proper *etiquette.*

et•y•mol•o•gy [et′ ə mäl′ ə jē] *noun, plural* **etymologies.** the history of a word, telling where it came from and what it first meant.

Eu•rope [yoor′ əp] the sixth largest continent, east of the Atlantic Ocean and west of the Ural Mountains and Black Sea.

Eu•ro•pe•an [yoor′ ə pē′ ən] *noun, plural* **Europeans.** a person born or living in Europe. —*adjective.* having to do with Europe or its culture.

e•vac•u•ate [i vak′ yoo āt′] *verb,* **evacuated, evacuating.** to leave or go away from: People were *evacuated* by helicopter after the river overflowed and flooded the town. —**evacuation,** *noun.*

e•vade [i vād′] *verb,* **evaded, evading.** to escape or avoid through clever planning: The thief managed to *evade* the police. The witness tried to *evade* the lawyer's question by talking about something else. ◆ The act of evading something is **evasion.**

e•val•u•ate [i val′ yoo āt′] *verb,* **evaluated, evaluating.** to judge or figure the value or condition of something: to *evaluate* a painting or a piece of furniture. The boss *evaluated* each of the workers to decide which ones should get a raise in pay. —**evaluation,** *noun.*

e•vap•o•rate [i vap′ ə rāt′] *verb,* **evaporated, evaporating. 1.** to change from a liquid into a gas or VAPOR: The water I spilled on the driveway *evaporated* in the hot sun. **2.** to fade away; disappear: Hope of finding the lost plane began to *evaporate* after several days with no news. —**evaporation,** *noun.*

eve [ēv] *noun, plural* **eves.** the evening or day before a certain day or holiday: Christmas *Eve,* New Year's Eve. Lynn still hadn't finished packing on the *eve* of her trip to Australia.

e•ven [ē′ vən] *adjective, more/most.* **1.** completely flat and smooth; level: They planted the

etymology Often in this dictionary the reader is given the etymology of a word, that is, the origin and history of the word. For most readers etymology is not important. But if you are trying hard to augment your vocabulary—where does "augment" come from?—then knowing the original and various meanings of a word going all the way back to Greek or Latin or Old French or Anglo-Saxon is useful. Words have a nationality, you might say, like people. Can you say effectively, "She was the *architect* of my hopes?" Look up ARCHITECT and see what you think.

eu•ca•lyp•tus [yoo′ kə lip′ təs] *noun, plural* **eucalyptuses** or **eucalyptus.** a tall tree that comes from Australia and now grows in the western U.S. and other warm, dry climates.

Eur•a•sia [yoo rā′ zhə] Europe and Asia, thought of as a single continent because they are part of the same land area. —**Eurasian,** *adjective; noun.*

Pronunciation Key: [ə] Symbol

The [ə] or *schwa* sound occurs in syllables without an accent. It can be spelled with any vowel, such as **a** in above, **e** in listen, **i** in pencil, **o** in melon, **u** in circus. It can also be a combination of vowels, such as **io** in action, **ai** in mountain, **iou** in precious.

(Turn the page for more information.)

E

E

garden on an *even* piece of ground. **2.** not changing; steady: to drive at an *even* speed. Our teacher has an *even* temper and rarely gets upset. **3.** at the same height: The corn was *even* with the top of the fence. **4.** being the same or equal: The score was *even* at 3 to 3. **5.** exact: An **even number** is one that can be divided exactly by 2, with nothing left over, such as 4, 10, 36, and so on. —*adverb.* **1.** still; yet: It's *even* colder today than it was yesterday. **2.** surprising as it may seem: We all enjoyed the rock concert, *even* Grandpa. —*verb,* **evened, evening.** to make or become even: to *even* the score in a game. —**evenly,** *adverb:* "She tried to breathe *evenly* and slowly." (Andre Norton)

eve•ning [ēv′ning] *noun, plural* **evenings.** the time between late afternoon and night; the late part of the day. —*adjective.* having to do with evening: Supper is an *evening* meal.

e•vent [i vent′] *noun, plural* **events. 1.** something that happens, especially an important happening: The marriage of Prince Charles and Lady Diana was a great social *event* in Britain. **2.** a contest in a sports program or series: Carl Lewis won three *events* in the 1984 Olympics. **3. in the event of.** if something happens; in case of: *In the event of* a tie, the prize money will be divided between the two winners. **4. in any event.** in any case; no matter what.

e•ven•tu•al [i ven′ choo̅ əl] *adjective.* happening at some later time or at the end; final: The *eventual* result of the French and Indian War was that France lost all its power in the New World. —**eventually,** *adverb.* at the end; finally: I don't know where the cat went, but *eventually* she'll get hungry and come back home.

ev•er [ev′ ər] *adverb.* **1.** at any time: Have you *ever* been to Disney World? **2.** always: People in fairy tales are said to live happily *ever* after. **3.** in any way: How did you *ever* find that?

Everglades The Everglades is filled with cypress and mangrove trees. It is one of the largest swamps in the world, though its area has been reduced in recent years.

Ev•er•glades [ev′ ər glādz] a large swampy region in southern Florida.

ev•er•green [ev′ ər grēn′] *adjective.* having leaves or needles that stay green all year long. —*noun, plural* **evergreens.** a tree, shrub, or plant whose leaves or needles stay green year-round. Pines and firs are evergreens.

eve•ry [ev′ rē] *adjective.* **1.** all of the ones in a group; each: That supermarket is open *every* day, even holidays. **2.** all that is possible: He was given *every* chance to make up the work, but he never did it. **3. every other.** skipping one each time: *Every other* year, there is a new election in the House of Representatives.

eve•ry•bod•y [ev′ rē bud′ ē *or* ev′ rē bäd′ ē] *pronoun.* every person; everyone: "*Everybody* in the family thought he had been awfully good about the whole thing." (E.B. White)

eve•ry•day [ev′ rē dā′] *adjective.* that happens every day; usual; ordinary: Jeff didn't even act excited—you'd think meeting a movie star was an *everyday* event for him.

---

everyone Because "body" and "one" refer to a single thing, words such as *everyone* and *everybody* are considered to be singular. This is fairly easy to remember when no pronoun is involved: "The decks were deserted, no one was near them, *everyone was* dressing for dinner." (Conrad Aiken) It gets tricky when a pronoun follows. A strict rule says use the singular: "*Everyone* needs to respect and take pride in *his* native way of speaking." (Monroe Spears) (In today's custom that could also be "his or her.") Many writers feel that a pronoun later in a sentence calls for the plural: "Experience is the name *everyone* gives to *their* mistakes." (Oscar Wilde) This is especially true when it's not clear from the situation who the "one" or "body" actually is: "You act as a decoy. If you see *anybody* we know, lure *them* away." (Nancy Willard)

Ev•er•est, Mount [ev′ rəst] the highest mountain in the world, in the Himalayas on the border between Tibet and Nepal.

eve•ry•one [ev′ rē wun′] *pronoun.* every person: Julie invited *everyone* in her class to her birthday party.

eve•ry•thing [ev′rē thing′] *pronoun.* **1.** all things: ". . . snow, sleet, rain, hail, *everything* that can come down from heaven but tadpoles and spiders." (Jessamyn West) **2.** all that matters or is important: "Winning isn't *everything*, but wanting to win is." (Vince Lombardi)

eve•ry•where [ev′rē wâr′] *adverb.* in all places: Jimmy's dog follows him *everywhere*.

e•vict [ē vikt′] *verb,* **evicted, evicting.** to force a person by law to move out of a place: He was *evicted* from his apartment for not paying his rent. —**eviction,** *noun.*

ev•i•dence [ev′ə dəns] *noun.* anything that shows or makes clear; proof: The murderer's fingerprints were the only *evidence* the police could find.

ev•i•dent [ev′ə dənt] *adjective, more/most.* easy to see or understand; obvious: "From her breathing it was *evident* that she was going off to sleep again." (George Orwell) —**evidently,** *adverb.* as it seems: "They are all chattering and laughing loudly. They *evidently* have some secret joke in common." (Eugene O'Neill)

e•vil [ē′vəl] *adjective, more/most.* **1.** against what is good or right; very bad; wicked: an *evil* person, an *evil* crime. **2.** causing harm: an *evil* drug, an *evil* habit. —*noun, plural* **evils.** **1.** being evil; wickedness: The Lord's Prayer asks God to "deliver us from *evil.*" **2.** something that is evil: "The *evil* that men do lives after them." (Shakespeare, *Julius Caesar*)

ev•o•lu•tion [ev′ə lōō′shən] *noun, plural* **evolutions. 1.** the scientific theory that all living plants and animals came from fewer and simpler forms of life, and that these forms changed over millions of years into the many different forms that exist on the earth today. **2.** any slow, gradual change or development: The Magna Carta was an important event in the *evolution* of British democracy.

e•volve [i välv′] *verb,* **evolved, evolving.** to slowly grow, develop, or change: Charles Darwin set forth the theory that man *evolved* from the apes. The current space shuttle *evolved* from a simple rocket designed many years ago.

ewe [yōō] *noun, plural* **ewes.** a female sheep.

ex- a *prefix* meaning: **1.** in the past but not now; former: An *ex*-actor is a former actor. **2.** out of: An *exit* is a way out.

ex•act [ig zakt′] *adjective, more/most.* without anything wrong; having no mistakes; correct; precise: The *exact* time now is 8:52 A.M., and 30 seconds. Supermarkets have scales that show the *exact* weight of food. —**exactly,** *adverb:* "Zabeth knew *exactly* what the people of her village wanted, and how much they would be willing or able to pay for it." (V.S. Naipaul)

ex•ag•ger•ate [ig zaj′ə rāt′] *verb,* **exaggerated, exaggerating.** to make something seem more than it really is: I know Stan loves ice cream, but he's *exaggerating* when he says he eats a half gallon every day. ♦ Something that is exaggerated is an **exaggeration.**

exaggeration Exaggeration is often used in writing to create a certain effect, such as humor. Writers can use exaggeration to criticize: "Then, the next morning, in chapel, he made a speech that lasted about ten hours. He started off with about fifty corny jokes." (J.D. Salinger, *The Catcher in the Rye*) Exaggeration is used in serious situations, too. Albert Camus' novel *The Stranger* begins with the line: "Mother died today, or maybe it was yesterday." Camus wants to show that the character Meursault is totally cold and without feeling, so he exaggerates his lack of interest in this tragic event. In Franz Kafka's *The Trial,* a character spends many years in courts without ever learning what crime he's charged with. This is using exaggeration within what seems a normal context—lawyers, witnesses, courts. Kafka was depicting life under the "thought control" of a dictatorship. "I had a *Kafkaesque* experience" means that an event occurred which seemed normal or routine at first but became so exaggerated as to frustrate or puzzle the observer.

ex•am [ig zam′] *noun, plural* **exams.** a short word for **examination:** I have to study for tomorrow's science *exam.*

ex•am•i•na•tion [ig zam′ə nā′shən] *noun, plural* **examinations. 1.** the act of examining; a careful study: She's going to the doctor for a complete physical *examination.* "He made an anxious *examination* of the paper, turning it in

---

Pronunciation Key: Accent Marks

[′] is the normal accent mark. It shows where the main stress falls on a word.
[′] is a secondary accent mark. It shows a lighter stress than the primary accent. For example:

tel • e • vis • ion [tel′ə vizh′ən]

(Turn the page for more information.)

E

all directions." (Edgar Allan Poe) **2.** a test in school or college.

ex•am•ine [ig zam′ in] *verb,* **examined, examining. 1.** to look at closely and carefully; inspect; check: The detective *examined* the note that the thief had left behind. "He looked me over as though he were *examining* a prize poodle." (Richard Wright) **2.** to question closely: Lawyers in court *examine* witnesses.

> **examples** The author Norman Mailer once presented two different ways of describing something. First: "A strong man came into the room." The other way: "A man entered. He was holding a walking stick, and for some reason, he now broke it in two like a twig." Which version did he say was better? He chose the second one, because it gets the point across by example. As Mailer points out, if he only says the man is "strong," we (the readers) have to take his word for it. We have no evidence. But when the man snaps the walking stick in two, we have direct proof.

ex•am•ple [ig zam′ pəl] *noun, plural* **examples. 1.** something that shows what other things of the same kind are like; a usual or typical member of a group: Cactus and sagebrush are *examples* of plants that can grow in the desert. **2.** a person or thing that is imitated; a model: "You bear your loss with such courage, and *set the example* for us all." (Lloyd Alexander) **3.** a problem: The teacher wrote the math *example* on the blackboard so that she could explain it.

ex•as•per•ate [ig zas′ pə rāt′] *verb,* **exasperated, exasperating.** to annoy or irritate greatly; make angry: I get really *exasperated* when I can't get my computer to work the way it's supposed to. —**exasperation,** *noun:* "'Why can't you let me help you?' she demanded in *exasperation*." (F. Scott Fitzgerald)

ex•ca•vate [eks′ kə vāt′] *verb,* **excavated, excavating. 1.** to take out or make by digging; dig out: The workers *excavated* dirt from the yard for a swimming pool. **2.** to uncover by digging: The scientists *excavated* an ancient Indian village from the canyon walls.

ex•ceed [ik sēd′] *verb,* **exceeded, exceeding.** to be more than; go beyond: In summer the temperature here often *exceeds* 100 degrees. The movie *Heaven's Gate* was supposed to cost $11 million to make, but it *exceeded* its budget by $25 million. —**exceedingly,** *adverb:* very; unusually: "You have come at an *exceedingly* inconvenient time. I am very busy." (Evelyn Waugh)

ex•cel [ik sel′] *verb,* **excelled, excelling.** to do better or be better than others: My friend Larry *excels* as a math student.

ex•cel•lence [ek′ sə ləns] *noun.* the state of having very high quality; being excellent: Brazil is known for the *excellence* of its soccer teams and has won three world championships.

ex•cel•lent [ek′ sə lənt] *adjective, more/most.* of very high quality; very, very good; outstanding: They had an *excellent* dinner at the finest restaurant in town. Swimming is considered an *excellent* form of exercise. —**excellently,** *adverb.*

ex•cept [ik sept′] *preposition.* not including; other than; leaving out: All the months have 30 or 31 days, *except* February. —*conjunction.* only; but: I'd love to go with you, *except* that I have homework to do.

ex•cep•tion [ik sep′ shən] *noun, plural* **exceptions. 1.** the fact of being left out: All of Ian Fleming's books are about James Bond, with the *exception* of one children's book. **2.** a person or thing that is left out or different: Very few countries still have kings or queens, but Britain is an *exception.*

ex•cep•tion•al [ik sep′ shən əl] *adjective, more/most.* out of the ordinary; very unusual, especially in a good way: All the students in that class are bright, and one or two are *exceptional.* —**exceptionally,** *adverb:* We've had *exceptionally* nice weather lately.

ex•cess [ik ses′ *or* ek′ ses] *noun, plural* **excesses. 1.** an amount that is too much or that is more than usual: Diabetes is a disease in which there is an *excess* of sugar in the blood. **2.** the amount by which one thing is more than another. **3. in excess of.** more than: The Kodiak bear can weigh *in excess of* 1600 pounds. —[ek′ ses] *adjective.* more than is needed or is usual; extra: Before cooking the meat, Mom trimmed off all the *excess* fat.

ex•ces•sive [ik ses′ iv] *adjective, more/most.* more than is needed or wanted; too much: Doctors warn against putting an *excessive* amount of salt on food. —**excessively,** *adverb:* She's *excessively* concerned about her appearance and is always looking in the mirror.

ex•change [iks chānj′] *verb,* **exchanged, exchanging.** to take or give one thing for another;

E

trade: The sweater didn't fit her, so the store *exchanged* it for a smaller size. —*noun, plural* **exchanges. 1.** the giving or taking of one thing for another: There was an *exchange* of gifts at the office Christmas party. Dan cleaned out the Moores' yard in *exchange* for getting to use their swimming pool. **2.** a place where things are exchanged or traded: the New York Stock *Exchange.*

ex•cite [iks sīt′] *verb,* **excited, exciting.** to cause to have strong and lively feelings; stir up; arouse. Mom doesn't let us play with the baby at bedtime because we'll *excite* him and he won't sleep.

ex•cit•ed [ik sīt′ əd] *adjective, more/most.* having strong and lively feelings: The crowd gave an *excited* cheer as the rock star appeared on stage. —**excitedly,** *adverb:* The children ran *excitedly* to open their presents.

ex•cite•ment [ik sīt′ mənt] *noun, plural* **excitements. 1.** the condition of being excited: "'A home run!' everybody yelled in *excitement.*" (Eleanor Estes) **2.** something that excites.

ex•cit•ing [ik sīt′ ing] *adjective, more/most.* causing excitement; an *exciting* movie, an *exciting* basketball game. —**excitingly,** *adverb.*

ex•claim [iks klām′] *verb,* **exclaimed, exclaiming.** to speak or cry out suddenly in surprise or with strong feeling: "Watch out for that snake!" she *exclaimed.*

ex•cla•ma•tion [eks′ klə mā′ shən] *noun, plural* **exclamations.** something that is exclaimed: "A long silence was broken by a sudden *exclamation* from Holmes . . ." (A. Conan Doyle) ♦ A sentence with an exclamation is an **exclamatory sentence.**

can hold 60 people, *excluding* the driver. ♦ The act or fact of excluding is **exclusion** [iks kloo′ zhən].

ex•clu•sive [iks kloo′ siv] *adjective, more/most.* **1.** belonging to only one person or group; not shared with others: The President gave an *exclusive* interview to a reporter from *Time* magazine. **2.** letting in only a few people and keeping out others: an *exclusive* country club.

ex•cur•sion [ik skur′ zhən] *noun, plural* **excursions.** a trip taken for enjoyment: an *excursion* to the seashore.

ex•cuse [ik skyooz′] *verb,* **excused, excusing. 1.** to forgive for a wrong that is not really bad or serious: Please *excuse* me for stepping on your foot. **2.** to let off from doing something or being in a place: Danny asked his mother if he could be *excused* from the dinner table. —[ik skyoos′] *noun, plural* **excuses.** something that excuses; a reason that explains something: Ryan's *excuse* for missing soccer practice was that he had a dentist's appointment.

ex•e•cute [ek′ sə kyoot′] *verb,* **executed, executing. 1.** to carry out; do: An Olympic diver has to be able to *execute* certain standard dives. **2.** to put into effect; enforce: Congress makes laws and the President *executes* them. **3.** to put someone to death, especially according to law for a crime that the person has committed.

ex•e•cu•tion [ek′ sə kyoo′ shən] *noun, plural* **executions. 1.** the act of executing; carrying out or putting into effect: the *execution* of a captain's orders by the ship's crew. **2.** the executing of a person, especially by a legal order. ♦ A person who carries out the execution of a criminal is an **executioner.**

E

---

exclamation points The famous writer F. Scott Fitzgerald once made this comment: "Using a lot of exclamation points is like laughing at your own jokes." He meant that you don't have to be your own audience. Let the reader react. An exclamation point in a story says, "This is exciting," or "This is surprising," the way laughing at your own joke says, "This is funny." If you write the story well, your readers will know that something is exciting or surprising, and you won't need a lot of exclamation points to remind them. How would you edit the following? "Finally she got all the ribbons and wrapping paper off and opened the box. It was completely empty! She couldn't believe it! What a mean trick! It had to be Ted's idea!"

---

exclamation point a punctuation mark [!] used after an exclamation or at the end of an exclamatory sentence, also called an **exclamation mark.**

ex•clude [iks klood′] *verb,* **excluded, excluding. 1.** to keep from entering; shut out: An 'R' movie rating *excludes* people under 17 unless they're with an adult. **2.** to not include: This bus

E

ex•ec•u•tive [ig zek′ yə tiv] *noun, plural* **executives. 1.** any person who manages or helps to manage a business or other organization. **2.** the part of a government that manages its affairs and puts laws into effect. In the U.S., the **Executive Branch** is headed by the President. —*adjective.* **1.** having to do with managing a business or other organization: The Chief *Executive* Officer of a company is the person who is the head of the company. **2.** having to do with the executive branch of government.

ex•empt [ig zempt′] *verb,* **exempted, exempting.** to free from a duty or obligation; excuse; release: Certain property is *exempted* from property taxes, such as churches and hospitals. ♦ The fact of exempting is an **exemption:** to get an *exemption* from jury duty.

ex•er•cise [ek′ sər sīz′] *noun, plural* **exercises. 1.** activity of the body that is meant to promote good health or to develop some ability or good quality: Running, swimming, and playing tennis are popular forms of *exercise.* **2.** a question or problem that gives practice: There are *exercises* at the end of each chapter of that textbook. **3.** the use of a certain power or ability: *The Prince* by Machiavelli is a famous book on the *exercise* of political power. **4. exercises.** a ceremony or program: high-school graduation *exercises.* —*verb,* **exercised, exercising. 1.** to do a form of exercise. **2.** to make use of; put into practice: to *exercise* the right to vote. "She had to *exercise* all her self-control not to cry." (Somerset Maugham)

ex•ert [ig zurt′] *verb,* **exerted, exerting. 1.** to make use of; apply: The President is *exerting* all his influence to get that bill passed by the Senate. **2. exert oneself.** to make an effort: try hard: Eric hates to *exert himself* in school; he studies just enough to get by. —**exertion,** *noun.*

ex•hale [eks hāl′] *verb,* **exhaled, exhaling.** to breathe out: to *exhale* air from the lungs.

ex•haust [ig zôst′] *verb,* **exhausted, exhausting. 1.** to use up completely: "It was almost silent up here, since he had *exhausted* his rocket fuel." (Tom Wolfe) **2.** to make very tired. ♦ Usually used as an adjective: "He crawled out of bed like an *exhausted* swimmer leaving the surf." (Nathanael West) —*noun, plural* **exhausts. 1.** the waste gases or smoke that escape from an engine. **2.** the pipe in an automobile that carries these gases away; also called an **exhaust pipe.**

ex•haus•tion [ig zôs′ chən] *noun.* the state of being exhausted: When they reached the mountaintop, the climbers sank to the ground in *exhaustion.*

ex•hib•it [ig zib′ it] *verb,* **exhibited, exhibiting. 1.** to show a sign of; reveal: to *exhibit* fear or nervousness. **2.** to put on display; show in public: Pablo Picasso first *exhibited* his paintings in Paris when he was only 20. —*noun, plural* **exhibits.** something that is exhibited.

ex•hi•bi•tion [ek′ sə bish′ ən] *noun, plural* **exhibitions. 1.** the act of exhibiting: Many tennis fans dislike that player because of his *exhibitions* of bad temper. **2.** a public display; a show: an *exhibition* of furniture from colonial times. In sports, an **exhibition game** is one that does not count as part of the regular season.

ex•hil•a•rate [ig zil′ ə rāt′] *verb,* **exhilarated, exhilarating.** to cause to feel fresh, happy, and lively: He opened the window and breathed in the *exhilarating* mountain air.

ex•ile [eg′ zīl *or* ek′ sīl] *noun, plural* **exiles. 1.** the state of being forced to leave one's country: Juan Perón lived in *exile* in Spain after he was overthrown as ruler of Argentina. **2.** a person who has been forced to leave his country: Many Cuban *exiles* now live in the U.S. —*verb,* **exiled, exiling.** to send a person into exile: After Germany lost World War I, the German emperor was *exiled.*

ex•ist [ig zist′] *verb,* **existed, existing. 1.** to be real: There are many stories about Robin Hood, but it's not known if he actually *existed.* **2.** to take place; be present: ". . . a warm friendship *existed* between these two men." (Armstrong Sperry) **3.** to continue to live; have life: "His life would be lonely until he too, died, ceased to *exist* . . ." (James Joyce)

ex•ist•ence [ig zis′ təns] *noun.* the fact of existing; being real: In the Middle Ages many people believed in the *existence* of ghosts. Part of Tennessee was once the separate state of Franklin, which is no longer in *existence.*

exhaust The exhaust of jet engines trails across the sky as the Navy's Blue Angels flying team performs.

ex•it [eg′ zit *or* ek′ sit] *noun, plural* **exits. 1.** a way out: We left the theater by the side *exit*. To get to their house, take the highway to *exit* 51. **2.** the act of leaving: Linda made a quick *exit* from the party when she saw her old boyfriend. —*verb*, **exited, exiting.** to make an exit; go out; leave: The passengers *exited* from the plane.

ex•ot•ic [ig zät′ ik] *adjective, more/most.* from another part of the world; foreign; strange: *exotic* birds such as the peacock or ostrich. Paul Gauguin is known for his *exotic* paintings of the South Seas.

studio has every *expectation* that their new movie will be a big success.

ex•pe•di•ent [ik spēd′ ē ənt] *adjective, more/most.* that is useful or helpful to a person, but is not necessarily fair or right: After Nazi Germany defeated France in World War II, some French leaders found it *expedient* to take sides with the Germans.

ex•pe•di•tion [ek′ spə dish′ ən] *noun, plural* **expeditions.** a long trip or journey made for a special reason: The Lewis and Clark *Expedition* explored western America to the Pacific Ocean.

expanding a paper Two editors of this dictionary do not agree on some fine points. One says, "It only takes a half hour or so to get a haircut. It takes weeks or months for your hair to grow back. In the same way, it's easier to make a piece of writing shorter than to make it longer." But another says the hardest effort in writing is to be brief. He once asked a professor at Princeton University to write a history of English literature in 5000 words. The professor replied, "It would be easier if you gave me 50,000 words instead of 5000." The first editor has also said, "Suppose you have an assignment to write a report of at least five pages. You should "overwrite" it by 10% or 20%". The second disagrees. "It's hard enough to write clearly," he argues, "without deliberately writing more than you truly expect to use in a final draft." Which editor do you agree with? What has been your experience in writing papers for history or literature classes?

E

ex•pand [ik spand′] *verb,* **expanded, expanding.** to make or become larger: A balloon *expands* when you blow air into it. In 1968 the National Hockey League *expanded* from six teams to twelve.

ex•panse [ik spans′] *noun, plural* **expanses.** a wide and open space; a broad area: We drove through a large *expanse* of desert.

ex•pan•sion [ik span′ shən] *noun, plural* **expansions. 1.** the expanding of something: Heat causes the *expansion* of metal. That company is interested in *expansion* and plans open a new office. **2.** something formed by expanding.

ex•pect [ik spekt′] *verb,* **expected, expecting. 1.** to look forward to; think something will probably come or happen: Jimmy's been watching for the mailman all morning; he's *expecting* a package from Grandma. **2.** to think of as right or proper; require: "After a snowstorm they are *expected* to sweep the feathery covering away . . ." (Mary Mapes Dodge)

ex•pect•ant [ek spek′ tənt] *adjective.* looking forward to or waiting for something to happen: An *expectant* mother is a woman who is *expecting*—who is going to have a baby. ♦ A person's **life expectancy** is how long the person is expected to live.

ex•pec•ta•tion [ek′ spek tā′ shən] *noun, plural* **expectations.** the act or fact of expecting: The

ex•pel [ik spel′] *verb,* **expelled, expelling. 1.** to force someone to leave a group or place for some wrongdoing: The college *expelled* several students for cheating on exams. **2.** to force out from the body: Whales *expel* air through a hole in the top of the head.

ex•pend•i•ture [ik spen′ di chər] *noun, plural* **expenditures.** something that is used up or spent, especially money.

ex•pense [ik spens′] *noun, plural* **expenses. 1.** the amount of money something costs; the price or charge for something: Travel *expenses* for a business trip can include plane fare, a hotel room, and meals. **2.** a cause or reason for spending money: Adding a new bedroom to the house was a big *expense*. **3.** a loss or sacrifice: She works very long hours, but not at the *expense* of her health.

ex•pen•sive [ik spen′ siv] having a high price; costing a lot of money: Milk is more *expensive* now than it was 20 years ago. "He's given me

Pronunciation Key: G–N			
g	give; big	k	kind; cat; back
h	hold	l	let; ball
i	it; this	m	make; time
ī	ice; my	n	not; own
j	jet; gem; edge	ng	having

(Turn the page for more information.)

an *expensive* Swiss watch." (John Fowles) —**expensively,** *adverb.* She dresses very *expensively* in the latest Paris fashions.

son or reasons for: How do you *explain* the fact that you're two hours late? ◆ Something that explains is **explanatory** [ik splan′ ə tôr′ ē].

> **explanation** A common writing assignment for students is one that calls for explaining how something happened or who someone was. A large part of explanation is what is abbreviated as "how to." Writing of this kind might explain how to cook pancakes, how to make a jack-o-lantern, or how to ride a skateboard. George Orwell's "A Nice Cup of Tea" is a case of "how to" in the hands of a master stylist. Orwell shows how, in eleven steps, you can be orderly and logical, but not boring. His directions are clear and reveal his own voice, with his own tone and wit visible. One reason to learn how to write "how to" is that it requires that you always use two simple tools: detail and order. In business, in law, medicine, engineering, these two are the tools of success.

ex•per•i•ence [ik spēr′ ē əns] *noun, plural* **experiences. 1.** some thing that happens to a person; an event in one's life: I'll never forget the *experience* of visiting New York and seeing the Statue of Liberty. **2.** knowledge or skill that is gained by doing something: He has 12 years' *experience* as a teacher. —*verb,* **experienced, experiencing.** to go through; have happen to: to *experience* pain. Our train *experienced* several delays because of the snowstorm.

ex•per•i•ment [ik sper′ ə mənt] *noun, plural* **experiments. 1.** a careful study under controlled conditions to discover or prove some fact or law of science: We did an *experiment* in class to show what happens to plants if they don't get any sunlight. **2.** any test or trial to find something out: That school is going to have year-round classes as an *experiment* to see if the children learn better. —*verb,* **experimented, experimenting.** to find out by testing; make an experiment: The coach *experimented* with several different lineups before finding the best one.

ex•per•i•men•tal [ik sper′ ə men′ təl] *adjective.* used for or having to do with an experiment: an *experimental* drug. That car is an *experimental* model that hasn't gone into production yet. —**experimentally,** *adverb.*

ex•pert [ek′ spərt] *noun, plural* **experts.** a person who knows a lot about something or is very good at it: a computer *expert.* —*adjective, more/most.* knowing a lot or having a lot of skill; being an expert: an *expert* photographer.

ex•pire [ik spīr′] *verb,* **expired, expiring.** to come to an end; go out of use or out of existence: Marty needs to get a new driver's license because his old one just *expired.*

ex•plain [ik splān′] *verb,* **explained, explaining. 1.** to make something clear or easy to understand: Our teacher *explained* the meaning of the word "photosynthesis." **2.** to give the rea-

ex•plan•a•tion [ek′ splə nā′ shən] *noun, plural* **explanations. 1.** the explaining of something; clearing up a difficulty or mistake: the *explanation* of an arithmetic problem. **2.** something that explains; a reason: The police have no *explanation* for how the money disappeared.

ex•plic•it [ik splis′ it] *adjective, more/most.* clearly stated or shown: That company has very *explicit* rules on how people are supposed to dress in the office. —**explicitly,** *adverb:* The sign *explicitly* says that dogs aren't allowed here.

ex•plode [ik splōd] *verb,* **exploded, exploding. 1.** to burst suddenly with a loud noise; blow up: The firecracker *exploded* just after we lit the fuse. **2.** to burst forth suddenly and noisily: The audience *exploded* with laughter.

ex•ploit [eks′ ploit] *noun, plural* **exploits.** a brave or daring action: T.H. White's books tell of the *exploits* of King Arthur and his knights. —[ik sploit′] *verb,* **exploited, exploiting. 1.** to make use of something so as to help oneself: Great Britain *exploited* the large deposits of oil in the North Sea. **2.** to use unfairly; help oneself in a selfish way: "A few greedy people . . . are *exploiting* her for the sake of publicity." (Walter Farley) —**exploitation,** *noun.*

ex•plor•a•tion [eks′ plə rā′ shən] *noun, plural* **explorations.** the act of exploring: the *exploration* of the American Southwest by Francisco de Coronado.

ex•plore [ik splôr′] *verb,* **explored, exploring. 1.** to travel to an unknown or little-known place to learn more about it: At different times in history people have *explored* the American West, central Africa, the bottom of the ocean, and the surface of the moon. **2.** to go through a place that is not familiar: Heather likes to go *exploring* in the woods behind her house. **3.** to look into closely; examine: The government is *exploring* ways to improve the tax system.

ex•plor•er [ik splôr′ ər] *noun, plural* **explorers.** a person who explores something.

ex•plo•sion [ik splō′ zhən] *noun, plural* **explosions. 1.** the blowing up of something suddenly and noisily; the act of exploding: the *explosion* of a bomb. **2.** a sudden and sharp increase: The state of California has had a population *explosion* since World War II.

explosion The destruction of an old building to make way for new construction. This picture is just seconds after the planned explosion of dynamite charges.

ex•plo•sive [ik splō′ siv] *adjective, more/most.* likely to explode or cause an explosion: The sign on the truck warned that it was carrying *explosive* gas. —*noun, plural* **explosives.** something that can explode or cause an explosion. Dynamite is an explosive.

ex•port [ik spôrt′ *or* eks′ pôrt] *verb,* **exported, exporting.** to send goods to other countries for trade or sale: Colombia *exports* coffee to the United States. —[eks′ pôrt] *noun, plural* **exports. 1.** something that is sold or traded to another country: Wheat is a major *export* of the United States. **2.** the process of exporting.

ex•pose [ik spōz′] *verb,* **exposed, exposing. 1.** to leave without protection; uncover: On his first day at the beach he tried not to *expose* himself to the sun for too long. **2.** to make something known; reveal: The newspaper *exposed* the mayor's connection with organized crime. **3.** to become subject to; allow to have an effect: Jimmy just came down with chicken pox, so I guess everyone else in his class has been *exposed.* **4.** to allow light to reach a photographic film or plate.

ex•po•sure [ik spō′ zhər] *noun, plural* **exposures. 1.** the act of exposing, or the fact of being exposed: *Exposure* to the sun can cause a sunburn. The reporter won a Pulitzer Prize for

his *exposure* of a scandal in city government. **2.** a condition in which a person is exposed to severe weather: The campers who were lost in a snowstorm almost died of *exposure.* **3.** the time taken to get an image on a photographic film: A camera used for action photographs should have a short *exposure.*

ex•press [ik spres′] *verb,* **expressed, expressing. 1.** to tell in words; state: The film critic wrote a review *expressing* her opinion of the movie. **2.** to show a thought or feeling in some way other than by words: Clapping hands is a way to *express* praise for someone. —*adjective.* **1.** clear and definite; certain: Mrs. Charlton gave money to the city with the *express* wish that it be used for a park. **2.** going or sent quickly: An *express* train or bus makes only a few stops instead of stopping at every regular stop. ♦ Also used as an *adverb:* to send a package *express.* —*noun, plural* **expresses.** an express train, bus, mail service, or the like. —**expressly,** *adverb.* clearly; definitely: Dr. Marsh offered to help her, but she said he'd come *expressly* to see Dr. Cole.

ex•pres•sion [ik spresh′ ən] *noun, plural* **expressions. 1.** the putting of thoughts or feelings into words or actions: He sent us a gift as an *expression* of thanks for our help. **2.** a look on the face that shows a certain thought or feeling: "She had been married to him for eight years and knew every *expression* of his face and every thought in his mind." (Somerset Maugham) **3.** a common word, phrase, or saying: "Cold as ice," "cool as a cucumber," and "warm as toast" are well-known *expressions.* ♦ Something that is full of expression is **expressive:** "He had fine hazel eyes, large and *expressive* . . ." (Pearl Buck)

ex•press•way [ik spres′ wā] *noun, plural* **expressways.** a wide highway with many lanes built for fast and direct traveling without traffic lights or side streets.

ex•quis•ite [ik skwiz′ it] *adjective, more/most.* having a special delicate beauty or charm; very finely made or done: "We have a man who does the most *exquisite* woodworking." (Andrea Lee) —**exquisitely,** *adverb:* "Every movement

E

Pronunciation Key: O–S			
ō	over; go	ou	out; town
ô	all; law	p	put; hop
oo	look; full	r	run; car
ōō	pool; who	s	set; miss
oi	oil; boy	sh	show

(Turn the page for more information.)

she made was *exquisitely* graceful and *exquisitely* right." (Noel Coward)

ex•tend [ik stend′] *verb,* **extended, extending. 1.** to make longer; lengthen: The state plans to *extend* the old highway to join Route 40. ♦ Also used as an adjective: Mrs. Slater made an *extended* visit to her daughter's family. **2.** to reach or stretch out: "From one shore, a point of land *extended* out into the pond." (E.B. White) **3.** to give or offer: to *extend* help, to *extend* a welcome to someone.

ex•tinct [ik stingkt′] *adjective.* **1.** of a certain animal or group of people, no longer existing; having died out: Dinosaurs are *extinct* animals. The Yahi Indians of northern California became *extinct* when the last member of the tribe died in 1916. **2.** no longer active or in use: "Two campfires, almost *extinct,* glowed red . . ." (Evelyn Waugh) ♦ The state of being extinct is **extinction:** The American buffalo was once threatened with *extinction* because so many were killed during the late 1800's.

> **extended meanings** Stephen Crane wrote of men lost at sea in "The Open Boat." "As darkness settled finally, the shine of the light, lifting from the sea in the south, changed to full gold. On the northern horizon a new light appeared, a small bluish gleam on the edge of the waters. These two lights were the furniture of the world. Otherwise there was nothing but waves." "Furniture?" How can lights be furniture? For sailors lost at sea in a rowboat, the open sea is the whole world to them. It is empty and frightening, like a deserted house at night. Calling two faint lights "furniture" makes the reader sense the desolation, the bare hopes of the sailors. Crane's clever use of "furniture" makes the scene come to life.

ex•ten•sion [ik sten′shən] *noun, plural* **extensions. 1.** a stretching out; addition: We built an *extension* onto our garage so that we'd have room to park our trailer. Income tax is due April 15th, but it is possible to get an *extension* until August 15th. **2.** an extra telephone connected with the main one.

ex•ten•sive [ik sten′siv] *adjective, more/most.* covering a large area or having a large size; great: Australia has an *extensive* desert in the center of the continent. The new boss made *extensive* changes when he took over the company. **—extensively,** *adverb.*

ex•tent [ik stent′] *noun, plural* **extents.** the length or amount to which something extends; the size of a thing: The mayor flew over the fire area to judge the *extent* of the damage.

ex•te•ri•or [ik stēr′ē ər] *adjective.* outer or outside: *Exterior* paint is used on the outside walls of a house. **—***noun, plural* **exteriors. 1.** an outer part or surface: That car model has a choice of six colors for the *exterior.* **2.** an outward appearance or manner: Underneath his rough *exterior* he's actually very kind.

ex•ter•mi•nate [ik stur′mə nāt′] *verb,* **exterminated, exterminating.** to get rid of by killing off completely; wipe out: to *exterminate* rats, insects, or other household pests. ♦ A person who does this is an **exterminator.**

ex•ter•nal [ik stur′nəl] *adjective.* on or of the outside; outer: A medicine for *external* use is meant to be put on the skin but not swallowed. The State Department deals with the *external* affairs of the U.S. **—externally,** *adverb.*

ex•tin•guish [ik sting′gwish] *verb,* **extinguished, extinguishing.** to put out: We *extinguished* the campfire by throwing water on it.

ex•tin•guish•er [ik sting′gwish ər] *noun, plural* **extinguishers.** see **fire extinguisher.**

ex•tor•tion [ik stôr′shən] *noun.* the crime of getting money, favors, or something of value from a person by force or threat.

ex•tra [eks′trə] *adjective.* more than what is usual or needed; additional: She usually leaves at 5:00, but today she got *extra* pay for working until 7:00**—***noun, plural* **extras. 1.** something added to what is usual or needed: Our new car has a lot of *extras,* such as a tape deck and air conditioning. **2.** a special edition of a newspaper that reports something very important. **—***adverb.* more than usual: "I know it's an *extra* cold night." (Mary Mapes Dodge)

ex•tract [ik strakt′] *verb,* **extracted, extracting. 1.** to take or pull out, usually with some effort: The dentist *extracted* Jim's wisdom tooth. **2.** to get out by pressing, heating, or some other process: ". . . a machine which could *extract* the juice of two hundred oranges in half an hour . . ." (F. Scott Fitzgerald) **—**[eks′trakt] *noun, plural* **extracts.** a substance that has been made by extracting: vanilla *extract.*

ex•tra•cur•ric•u•lar [eks′trə kə rik′yə lər] *adjective.* connected with a school, but not part of the regular course of study: *Extracurricular* activities include working on the school paper, playing on the football team, or being in the band.

ex•tra•or•di•nar•y [ik strôr′də nar′ē] *adjective,*

more/most. very unusual; remarkable; exceptional: "*Extraordinary* silence this evening, I strain my ears and do not hear a sound." (Samuel Beckett)

ex•trav•a•gant [ik strav′ ə gənt] *adjective, more/ most.* **1.** spending money in a careless or wasteful way: The federal government is often accused of paying *extravagant* amounts for ordinary items such as screwdrivers and ashtrays. **2.** going beyond what is reasonable; too extreme: That movie star always has *extravagant* demands when he makes a picture, such as having special food flown in from Paris. ♦ The state of being extravagant is **extravagance.**

ex•treme [ik strēm′] *adjective, more/most.* **1.** far beyond what is usual; very great or severe: Antarctica is a region of *extreme* cold. The zoo workers approached the tiger with *extreme* care. **2.** very far; farthest: "They slept at the *extreme* back of the house . . . (A. Conan Doyle) **3.** very far from what is ordinary or typical: The Nazis were an *extreme* political party. ♦ A person who has extreme views in politics is an **extremist.** —*noun, plural* **extremes. 1.** something that is extreme: California has great *extremes* of altitude—from the lowest point in the U.S. to 14,000-foot mountains. **2.** the greatest or highest degree: to do something in the *extreme.* **3. go to extremes.** to do something in an extreme way; do more than is sensible or right. —**extremely,** *adverb:* to be *extremely* happy, to do something that is *extremely* dangerous.

ex•trem•i•ty [ik strem′ ə tē] *noun, plural* **extremities. 1.** the state of being extreme; the farthest point or highest degree. **2. extremities.** the hands and feet.

eye [i] *noun, plural* **eyes. 1.** the part of the body with which people and animals see. **2.** the colored part of the eye; the IRIS: Jill has blue *eyes.* **3.** a look or gaze: His *eye* fell upon a letter that had been left on the table. **4.** something thought of as like an eye in some way, such as the hole in a needle that the thread goes

through, the dark spots on a potato from which new plants can grow, or the center of a storm. **5.** the power to use the eyes well; an ability to see, recognize, or appreciate things: a batter with a good *eye* in baseball, a movie director with an *eye* for spotting talented young actors. —*verb,* **eyed, eying,** or **eyeing.** to watch carefully or closely: ". . . a vast face which *eyed* him from the opposite wall." (George Orwell)

catch one's eye to attract one's attention: The pretty girl *caught his eye* as she walked by.

keep an eye on to watch carefully; look after: The police are *keeping an eye on* the bank because they think it might be robbed.

eye•ball [i′ bôl′] *noun, plural* **eyeballs.** the round part of the eye that the eyelids close over.

eye•brow [i′ brou′] *noun, plural* **eyebrows.** the hair that grows along the bony part of the face above each eye.

eye•glass•es [i′ glas′ iz] *plural noun.* a pair of lenses in a frame worn in front of the eyes to help make the sight better; more often called GLASSES.

eye•lash [i′ lash′] *noun, plural* **eyelashes.** one of the small hairs growing in a row along the edge of the eyelid.

eye•lid [i′ lid′] *noun, plural* **eyelids.** the fold of skin that can open and close over the eye.

eye•sight [i′ sīt′] *noun.* the ability to see; vision: They tested her *eyesight* before she was given a driver's license.

E

extreme statements "Return of the Lost Riders is the greatest movie I've ever seen. (I used to think it was the first Lost Riders, but this is even better.) Cal Trenton has to be the best actor in Hollywood. The chase scenes are the most exciting of any movie ever made." Extreme words, especially superlatives such as "greatest," "best," or "most"—can be powerful tools for a writer, but if they are used too often, they lose effect. It's like the old story of "The Boy Who Cried Wolf," who was always making extreme claims and demands for help, so much so that when he really was attacked no one came in answer to his cries. If a writer says a lot of artists are "the greats," how will he describe Michelangelo or Shakespeare? He will have worn out his superlatives!

eye•tooth [i′ tōōth′] *noun, plural* **eyeteeth.** either of the two pointed teeth in the upper front part of the mouth.

Pronunciation Key: T–Z

t	ten; date	v	very; live
th	think	w	win; away
th	these	y	you
u	cut; butter	z	zoo; cause
ur	turn; bird	zh	measure

(Turn the page for more information.)

f, F [ef] *noun, plural* **f's, F's. 1.** the sixth letter of the alphabet. **2.** a grade or mark showing a student has failed a certain subject.

fable An early edition of Aesop's Fables showing the famous tale ''The Fox and the Grapes.''

fa•ble [fā′bəl] *noun, plural* **fables.** a story made up to teach a lesson. Fables usually are about animals that act and talk like people.

fab•u•lous [fab′yə ləs] *adjective, more/most.* **1.** like a fable or story; beyond belief; amazing: They must have paid a *fabulous* amount of money for such a beautiful house. **2.** *Informal.* very good; outstanding; excellent: Have you seen that movie yet? It's really *fabulous!*

face [fās] *noun, plural* **faces. 1.** the front part of the head, where the eyes, nose and mouth are. **2.** a look or expression, especially one that shows anger or dislike. She made a *face* when she tasted the sour pickle. **3.** the front or upper part of something: the *face* of a mountain, the *face* of a playing card. **4.** personal pride; self-respect. ◆ Usually used in the expressions **save face** or **lose face.** —*verb,* **faced, facing. 1.** to turn the face toward: ''Sally was standing with her back to her mother, *facing* the long bathroom mirror.'' (Anne Morrow Lindbergh) **2.** to have the front toward: ''The end wall *facing* us has two windows in its upper story . . .'' (Eugene O'Neill) **3.** to meet with directly; deal with: ''Miss Briggs was used to *facing* the world alone . . .'' (Langston Hughes)

fables A *fable* is sometimes thought of as being the same thing as a folk tale, but it's actually just one kind of tale. (See FOLK TALES) In fables, animal characters act human, usually with the purpose of warning listeners against bad habits. They are *moral* lessons told as stories. The best known *fabulist* (fable writer) is Aesop, who lived about 600 B.C. Here are the lessons in two Aesop tales: ''The Ant and the Grasshopper'' tells about the value of hard work and preparing for the future. ''The Tortoise and the Hare'' tells that the race is not always to the swiftest; continuous effort can overcome speed. The best modern fable is George Orwell's *Animal Farm* (1946). It contains the famous line: ''All animals are equal, but some are more equal than others.'' Orwell was writing about dictatorships, especially Communist ones, where there is the pretense that all citizens are free and equal, although this is not the truth.

fab•ric [fab′rik] *noun, plural* **fabrics.** any material made by weaving or knitting threads. Fabric is made from natural fibers such as cotton, wool, or silk, and from man-made fibers such as POLYESTER.

fa•cial [fā′shəl] *adjective.* having to do with the face: In silent movies, actors showed their thoughts through their *facial* expressions. —*noun, plural* **facials.** a treatment to improve the appearance of the face.

fa•cil•i•ty [fə sil′ ə tē] *noun, plural* **facilities.**
1. ease or skill in doing something: The magician had amazing *facility* with a deck of cards and was able to do many tricks. **2.** *also,* **facilities.** something that makes things easier or that serves a certain purpose: The school has a language *facility* with tape recordings, foreign books, magazines, and videotapes.

fact [fakt] *noun, plural* **facts. 1.** something that is known to be true or real; something that exists or that has happened: It's a *fact* that the earth moves around the sun. **2.** any information presented as true or real: The principal's leaving school—is that a *fact?*

fac•tor [fak′ tər] *noun, plural* **factors.** something that helps to bring about or cause something else; one part of a situation: The main *factor* in our choosing that car was its many safety features. "The brisk wind . . . had died out and would be no *factor* in the race." (Walter Farley)

fac•to•ry [fak′ trē *or* fak′ tə rē] *noun, plural* **factories.** a building or group of buildings where goods are made to be sold, especially one where large quantities of a product are made by machines.

fac•tu•al [fak′ chōō əl] *adjective.* having to do with or based on facts: "George Washington was the first president of the United States" is a *factual* statement **—factually** *adverb:* a news article that is *factually* correct.

fad [fad] *noun, plural* **fads.** something that is very popular for a short time but then goes out of fashion: At one time there was a *fad* at colleges to see how many people could squeeze into a telephone booth. The 'Twist' was a dance *fad* of the early 1960's.

fade [fād] *verb,* **faded, fading. 1.** to lose color or brightness: "The sun was down, and a cool pale evening was quietly *fading* into night." (J.R.R. Tolkien) **2.** to disappear slowly; grow dim or faint: They stood watching the train until it *faded* into the distance. "The heavy scowl *faded* from Conly's face as McCann marched briskly toward them." (James Joyce)

Fahr•en•heit [fâr′ ən hīt′] *noun.* a scale of temperature in which 32 degrees is the point when water freezes and 212 degrees is the point when it boils. **—adjective.** according to this scale: The hottest temperature recorded in the U.S. was 134 degrees *Fahrenheit.*

fail [fāl] *verb,* **failed, failing. 1.** to get less than a satisfactory score or mark; not pass: to *fail* a test, to *fail* a math course, to *fail* seventh grade. **2.** to not do what is intended; not succeed: The high jumper tried three times to clear the bar but *failed* each time. **3.** to not act or work as is expected: The pilot had to land suddenly after one of the plane's engines *failed.* The accused man *failed* to appear in court for his trial. **4.** to lose strength; become weak. ♦ Usually used as an adjective: Our old dog has *failing* eyesight.

---

factual reports A popular TV hero of the 1950's was Joe Friday, a Los Angeles police detective played by Jack Webb. He always said, when interviewing a witness of some crime, "Just the facts, Ma'am." Sergeant Friday kept running into people who told him of remote things—describing a dog, for instance, instead of describing a car that stood idling near a store that was robbed. Let's suppose you're writing a factual report for social studies—on Benedict Arnold, let's say. Keep Joe Friday's "facts" motto in mind in these ways: (1) Don't try to enter a person's mind. "It was at this moment Arnold decided to become a traitor." How do you know what he was thinking? Did he say it in a letter? Did he tell someone? (2) Don't confuse fact and opinion. "The person who was really to blame was Arnold's wife. Without her, he never would have acted as he did." How can you prove this? (3) Don't assume something if there are no facts to support it. "Obviously, there were others included in the plot; Arnold and André couldn't have done it all alone." Again, are there facts that you can present to support this idea?

---

fac•ul•ty [fak′ əl tē] *noun, plural* **faculties. 1.** all of the teachers at a school or college. Parents can meet with the *faculty* at Back-to-School Night. **2.** a special skill or talent for doing something: Judy takes a lot of interest in other people and has a real *faculty* for making friends. **3.** a natural power of the mind or senses: the *faculty* of sight.

Pronunciation Key: A–F

a	and; hat	ch	chew; such
ā	ate; stay	d	dog; lid
â	care; air	e	end; yet
ä	father; hat	ē	she; each
b	boy; cab	f	fun; off

(Turn the page for more information.)

—*noun.* **without fail.** without failure; surely; certainly.

fail•ure [fāl′yər] *noun, plural* **failures. 1.** the act or fact of failing: Gerald Ford retired from politics after his *failure* to be elected President in 1976. **2.** a condition of not working or acting properly: heart *failure,* an electrical power *failure* caused by a thunderstorm. **3.** a person or thing that fails: The Broadway play *Kelly* was a complete *failure* and closed after giving only one performance.

faint [fānt] *adjective,* **fainter, faintest. 1.** not clearly seen, heard, or smelled; weak or dim: "The sky was very blue and soft, the stars rather *faint* because the moon was full." (Willa Cather) "From somewhere far away there floated the *faint* shouts of children." (George Orwell) **2.** feeling weak and dizzy. —*noun, plural* **faints.** a condition in which a person appears to suddenly fall asleep for a short time and does not know what is happening. Great pain, a loss of blood, or a shock to the mind can cause someone to fall into a *faint.* —*verb,* **fainted, fainting.** to fall into a faint. —**faintly,** *adverb.*

fair[1] [fâr] *adjective,* **fairer, fairest. 1.** not choosing or favoring one side over another; honest: The teacher tried to be *fair* in deciding who had written the best story. **2.** following the rules in a proper way: *fair* play in a game. **3.** in baseball, not FOUL. **4.** not too good and not too bad; average: Beth did a *fair* job of washing the car—she missed a few dirty spots. **5.** of the skin, light in coloring. **6.** of weather, clear and sunny. **7.** pleasing to look at; beautiful: The mayor greeted the visitors by saying, "Welcome to our *fair* city." —*adverb.* in a fair way; fairly: "The other two cheated, but Joe played *fair.*" (Arthur C. Clarke) —**fairness,** *noun.*

fair[2] *noun, plural* **fairs. 1.** a large public event where farm products and farm animals are shown and offered for sale: Doug's rabbit won a blue ribbon at the State *Fair* last summer. **2.** a large showing of goods, products, or objects: Each year thousands of people in the publishing business attend the Frankfurt Book *Fair.* At a **World's Fair** there are displays and exhibits from many different nations and companies. **3.** any display or show of items of a certain kind: Ellen's working on a big project for the school science *fair.*

fair•ly [fâr′lē] *adverb.* **1.** in an honest or fair way: She quit her job because she felt she wasn't being treated *fairly* by her boss. **2.** for the most part; somewhat; rather: "Mrs. Hall thinks he should be back *fairly* soon." (James Herriott)

fair•y [fâr′ē] *noun, plural* **fairies.** a small, make-believe person who has magical powers.

faith [fāth] *noun, plural* **faiths. 1.** a strong belief in something; confidence; trust: Mom's going to take the new car on the trip—she doesn't have much *faith* in the old station wagon. **2.** a thought or belief that is not based on facts or proof: I have *faith* that whoever finds my wallet will return it to me. **3.** a belief and trust in God. **4.** a particular way or system of believing in God; a religion: the Muslim *faith.*

faith•ful [fāth′fəl] *adjective, more/most.* **1.** having faith or trust; loyal; devoted: "He took along his *faithful* mule Queenie to carry supplies." (Donald Sobol) **2.** keeping to the facts; true; accurate: Several people saw the thief, but only one witness could give a *faithful* description of him. —**faithfully,** *adverb:* "Sally worked *faithfully* in the house throughout the hottest months." (Langston Hughes) —**faithfulness,** *noun.*

fake [fāk] *noun, plural* **fakes.** a person or thing that is not what it should be or seems to be: That was supposed to be a valuable old painting, but it's actually a cheap *fake.* —*verb,* **faked, faking. 1.** to act so to fool or deceive; pretend: The quarterback *faked* a pass and then ran around end. Joey *faked* an upset stomach so that he wouldn't have to eat his vegetables. **2.** to make something seem real in order to fool: The man who posed as a doctor *faked* a letter of recommendation from a famous hospital. ♦ Often used as an adjective: *fake* money, a *fake* fur coat.

falcon One of the fastest birds, the falcon can dive out of the sky at speeds up to 180 miles per hour.

fal•con [fäl′kən *or* fôl′kən] *noun, plural* **falcons.** a bird that is related to the hawk, having long wings, a hooked bill and strong claws. Falcons fly very fast and can be trained to hunt and kill other birds and small animals.

familiar words When you write, you don't have to avoid using a familiar word over and over. A famous linguist (Sir Arthur Quiller-Couch) once advised writers not to turn fancy. He said that if you are writing about Lord Byron it is ridiculous to avoid writing "Byron" over and over by calling him "the lame poet" or "the exiled poet" or "the titled poet." But there's a difference between getting fancy and using familiar words in new ways. Our Word Survey showed that well-known writers prefer to use simple words in different contexts when there's a chance. For example: "It was snowing and Kenny watched the large flakes melt against the window. They ran down the glass in long *sad* drips." (Maurice Sendak) "There were bitter winters when the snow *cried* under his heel . . ." (A. B. Guthrie) ". . . there were now only the desolate sandboxes knee-deep in crusted ice. When he crossed the hills the wind blew cold as *misery* . . ." (F. Scott Fitzgerald) "By seven o'clock the air was *blind* with sweeping snow, the earth was carpeted, the streets were *numb*." (Thomas Wolfe).

fall [fôl] *verb,* **fell, fallen, falling. 1.** to move or go down from a higher place: A cold rain was *falling.* A tear *fell* from his eye. **2.** to go down suddenly from a standing or sitting position: to *fall* on an icy sidewalk. **3.** to become lower in amount or position: The temperature began *falling* when the sun went down. **4.** to take place on a certain date: My birthday will *fall* on a Sunday this year. **5.** to pass into a certain state or condition: to *fall* asleep, to *fall* in love. How could you *fall* for that old trick? —*noun, plural* **falls. 1.** the season of the year between summer and winter; also called AUTUMN. **2.** the act or fact of falling: a *fall* from a tree, a heavy snow*fall,* or rain*fall,* the *fall* of the Roman Empire.

fall•out [fôl′out] *noun.* the RADIOACTIVE dust that falls to the ground after a nuclear bomb explodes.

falls [fôlz] *plural noun.* a place where a river makes a sudden drop; a waterfall.

false [fôls] *adjective,* **falser, falsest. 1.** not true, right, or correct; wrong: "Water flows uphill" is a *false* statement. **2.** not real; artificial: *false* teeth, *false* eyelashes. **3.** meant to fool or deceive; not honest or actual: The criminal used a *false* name. That drawer has a *false* bottom for hiding things. ◆ A **falsehood** is a lie. —**falsely,** *adverb:* The movie *The Wrong Man* was a true story of someone who was *falsely* accused of murder.

fal•ter [fôl′tər] *verb,* **faltered, faltering.** to become unsteady; not go straight on; hesitate. ◆ Often used as an adjective: The nervous young actress read her opening lines in a *faltering* voice.

fame [fām] *noun.* the fact of being famous; being well known: Elizabeth Taylor first gained *fame* as a movie star when she was only twelve years old.

fa•mil•iar [fə mil′yər] *adjective, more/most.* **1.** often seen or heard; well-known; common: Surfers are a *familiar* sight at California beaches. "You have seen yourself a thousand times in the mirror . . . no sight is more *familiar.*" (Walker Percy) **2.** knowing something well: Marsha is *familiar* with that kind of computer and can use it easily. ◆ The state of being familiar is **familiarity** [fə mil yer′ə tē].

fam•i•ly [fam′lē] *noun, plural* **families. 1.** a mother, father, and their children: Tickets to the fair are $2 each, or $7 for a whole *family.* **2.** the children of a mother and father: They've been married two years and are planning to start a *family* soon. **3.** a group of people related to each other; relatives: At Thanksgiving our whole *family* has a big dinner at my grandmother's house. **4.** a large group of related things: Lions and tigers are members of the cat *family.* English, French, and Russian all belong to the Indo-European *family* of languages. —*adjective.* suited to an entire family, both children and adults: a *family* restaurant, a movie that is good *family* entertainment.

fam•ine [fam′in] *noun, plural* **famines.** a very serious lack of food in a certain place. Famines can happen if the main food people rely on is destroyed or does not grow. Many people may starve to death during a famine.

fa•mous [fā′məs] *adjective, more/most.* known to many people; very well-known: William

Pronunciation Key: G N			
g	give; big	k	kind; cat; back
h	hold	l	let; ball
i	it; this	m	make; time
ī	ice; my	n	not; own
j	jet; gem; edge	ng	having

(Turn the page for more information.)

F

Shakespeare is England's most *famous* writer. The state of Colorado is *famous* for its mountain scenery.

fan[1] [fan] *noun, plural* **fans. 1.** a machine that uses an electric motor to turn several blades very quickly to make air move, as for cooling a room or a car engine. **2.** a piece of stiff, flat paper or other material in the shape of a half-circle, held in the hand and moved to make a cool breeze. —*verb,* **fanned, fanning. 1.** to move air with or as if with a fan: The people on the hot bus *fanned* themselves with their newspapers. **2.** to spread out like an open fan: The searchers *fanned* out through the woods to look for the lost child.

fan[2] *noun, plural* **fans.** somebody who follows or admires a certain activity, group, or person: a country music *fan,* a New York Yankee *fan,* a *fan* of Clint Eastwood movies.

fa•nat•ic [fə nat′ ik] *noun, plural* **fanatics.** a person who is much too serious or enthusiastic about something; someone who goes too far: Mahatma Gandhi was killed by a Hindu *fanatic* who believed Gandhi was too friendly to other religions. —*adjective.* being a fanatic; much too serious or enthusiastic: They are such *fanatic* followers of Nebraska football that everything in their house has the team's red and white colors.

fan•cy [fan′ sē] *adjective,* **fancier, fanciest.** not plain or simple; very decorated or elegant: a *fancy* dress, a *fancy* car, a basketball player known for his *fancy* moves. —*verb,* **fancied, fancying. 1.** to picture in the mind; imagine: "*Fancy* you hitting a ball farther than anyone else." (Michael Bond) **2.** to like very much; be fond of: He *fancies* brightly-colored shirts and neckties. —*noun, plural* **fancies. 1.** the power to picture something in the mind; imagination. **2.** an odd or unusual idea or wish: He had a sudden *fancy* for a sandwich made of peanut

butter and pickles. **3.** a liking for someone or something; fondness.

fang [fang] *noun, plural* **fangs.** a long, pointed tooth, as of a dog, wolf, or snake, especially a poisonous snake.

fan•tas•tic [fan tas′ tik] *adjective, more/most.* **1.** seeming to come from fantasy rather than reality; very strange; odd: The firelight cast *fantastic* shapes on the walls of the darkened room. **2.** hard to accept as real; amazing: Those diamonds must be worth a *fantastic* amount of money. **3.** very good; outstanding: "The chocolate and candies have become more . . . *fantastic* and delicious all the time." (Roald Dahl) —**fantastically,** *adverb.*

fantasy The word *fantasy,* tracing it back to Latin, means "a picture in the mind." In short, it's something that is imagined but not actually seen. In a fantasy, a writer creates a place or situation not part of the real world. How does the writer transport the reader to this imaginary world? Usually, by a change in time—the story either goes far back in time, before history, or forward to a future time. For example, *The Time Machine,* by H. G. Wells, was written in the year 1895 but is set in the year 802701. In the late 1890's Jules Verne wrote about the future; many of the fantastic things he described actually came true in later years, including aircraft, submarines, and television. There's still another kind of fantasy in which no particular time, past or future, is described. The best example is *The Wizard of Oz,* by L. Frank Baum, in which the character Dorothy finds that no time at all has passed on earth during her long visit to the land of Oz.

fan•ta•sy [fan′ tə sē] *noun, plural* **fantasies. 1.** something that is made up or pictured in the mind; something imaginary: "She felt as though she had slipped from the real world into *fantasy.*" (Andre Norton). **2.** a story, movie, or the like that deals with an imaginary world: *The Invisible Man* and *The War of the Worlds* are well-known *fantasies* by the British author H. G. Wells.

far [fär] *adverb,* **farther** or **further, farthest** or **furthest. 1.** at or to a great distance; not near in space or time: to live *far* from town, to look *far* out to sea, to study *far* into the night. **2.** at or to a certain point in space or time. ♦ Usually used in the phrase **as (so) far as:** I'll ride along with you *as far as* the corner. **3.** very much: She's by *far* the fastest runner in the class. —*adjective,* **farther, farthest** or **further, furthest. 1.** at a distance; not near: a *far* country. **2.** more distant; farther away: The golfer's shot landed on the *far* side of the hole.

far•a•way [fär′ ə wä′] *adjective.* **1.** far away; distant: "He listened to the *faraway* bells that echoed softly against the . . . mountain walls." (Maurice Sendak) **2.** not paying close attention, as if looking at something in the distance:

"There was a *faraway* expression on her face and her eyes were dreamy." (Mary Norton)

fare [fâr] *noun, plural* **fares. 1.** the money a person pays to travel by public transportation, as on a bus, train, airplane, or ship. **2.** a person who pays for a ticket to ride; a passenger: The cab driver was complaining because he'd only had one *fare* all morning. **3.** food; a meal: When she's camping out she gets along on plain and simple *fare*.
—*verb,* **fared, faring.** to get along; do: "I wondered how Granger had *fared* fifty yards up the road." (Graham Greene)

Far East the countries of eastern Asia; the Orient.

fare•well [fâr′wel′] *noun, plural* **farewells;** *interjection.* good-bye and best wishes.
—*adjective.* at the end or the time of leaving; final: Dwight D. Eisenhower gave a famous *farewell* address at the end of his term as President.

farm [färm] *noun, plural* **farms.** an area of land where animals or crops are raised for food, especially a place where this is done as a business. —*verb,* **farmed, farming.** to own or work on a farm.

farm•er [fär′mər] *noun, plural* **farmers.** any person who lives or works on a farm, especially someone whose job is farming.

far•sight•ed [fär′sī′tid] *adjective, more/most.* **1.** able to see things far away more clearly than things that are close up. **2.** able to judge what will happen in the future.

coming." (L.M. Boston) —**fascination,** *noun:* She has a *fascination* with old furniture and spends hours searching through antique shops.

fas•cism [fash′iz əm] *noun.* a modern form of government in which a dictator and the dictator's political party have complete power over the country. ♦ A person who believes or supports fascism is called a **fascist.** Fascist governments are very strongly opposed to SOCIALISM or COMMUNISM.

fash•ion [fash′ən] *noun, plural* **fashions. 1.** a style of clothing, especially a new or current style of women's clothing. **2.** the newest style or custom in the way someone dresses, talks, or acts: "There is a *fashion* in Harlem now for boys to wear something called knickers . . ." (Alice Walker) **3.** the particular way something is done: "There were many men in the common room, most of them eating in a hurried *fashion*." (Andre Norton) —*verb,* **fashioned, fashioning.** to give shape or form to; make: ". . . most of the days I spent *fashioning* a spear to catch the giant devilfish." (Scott O'Dell) ♦ Something that is in fashion is **fashionable.**

fast¹ [fast] *adjective,* **faster, fastest. 1.** moving or acting with speed; going quickly; rapid; swift: a *fast* runner, a *fast* worker, a *fast* trip. **2.** of a watch or clock, ahead of the correct time. **3.** loyal; faithful: Ellen and Diane are *fast* friends. —*adverb.* **1.** in a fast way; quickly; rapidly: to swim *fast,* to learn something *fast.* **2.** tightly or firmly: "He stopped and held *fast* to the tree." (Walter Farley)

---

farther/further If you were in school during the 1950's, your English textbook would have told you to make a distinction between *farther* and *further.* This distinction is that *farther* should be used only for actual distances from one place to another, and *further* for things that are not physically measured: "He took ten steps *farther.*" "She simply couldn't deal with him any *further.*" Our Word Survey found that writers don't observe this distinction. Even some excellent writers in the past didn't make the choice. For example, for a distance that can be measured: "She was born in the village, and had never been *further* away from it than Colebrook or perhaps Darnford." (Joseph Conrad) For something non-physical: "I advise you to go no *farther* with your vocabulary." (F. Scott Fitzgerald) In the last decades of the twentieth century, it's safe to say you can use either word and have it stand for both meanings.

---

far•ther [fär′th ə r] *adverb* or *adjective.* a COMPARATIVE form of **far.**

far•thest [fär′thist] *adverb* or *adjective.* a SUPERLATIVE form of **far.**

fas•ci•nate [fas′ə nāt′] *verb,* **fascinated, fascinating.** to attract and interest very much; charm: "Roger was *fascinated* to watch him working, to see the chips flying and the shape

Pronunciation Key: O–S			
ō	over; go	ou	out; town
ô	all; law	p	put; hop
oo	look; full	r	run; car
o͞o	pool; who	s	set; miss
oi	oil; boy	sh	show

(Turn the page for more information.)

fast² *verb,* **fasted, fasting.** to choose to eat little or no food for reasons of health or because of one's religious or political beliefs: During the month of Ramadan all Muslims must *fast* during daylight hours. —*noun, plural* **fasts.** a day or time of eating little or no food. People sometimes go on a fast as a way to call attention to a cause or to bring about a change in some policy.

fas•ten [fas′ ən] *verb,* **fastened, fastening.** to close up, attach, or connect; make fast: "She wrapped herself in a blanket-sized towel and *fastened* it near her shoulder . . ." (Mark Helprin) **2.** to fix firmly; direct: "The people *fasten* their eyes upon the coming boat . . ." (Mark Twain) "He tried to *fasten* his attention on the letter." (Kingsley Amis)

fast-food [fast′ food′] *adjective.* offering foods that can be quickly prepared and served, such as hamburgers and French fries. Fast-food restaurants are usually part of a large operation that serves a standard menu at each location. ♦ People in this business often prefer to use the term **fast-service.**

fast food The McDonald's fast-food empire grew from this single location in Des Plaines, Illinois, a suburb of Chicago.

fat [fat] *noun, plural* **fats.** a soft white or yellow substance found in the body of a person or animal, and in the seeds, nuts, and fruits of plants. Fat is an important source of energy for the human body. However, too much fat in the body is harmful to health. —*adjective,* **fatter, fattest. 1.** having a lot of fat or too much fat. **2.** having much in it; full: a *fat* wallet. That basketball star just signed a *fat* new contract.

fa•tal [fāt′ əl] *adjective,* **more/most. 1.** causing death: a *fatal* fire, a *fatal* plane crash. ♦ A **fatality** [fā′ tal′ ə tē] is a death that occurs violently or by a sudden accident. **2.** very bad; causing harm or ruin: a *fatal* mistake, a *fatal* flaw in a machine. ". . . the long lake which ended at the *fatal* rapids under the Stone House." (Farley Mowat) —**fatally,** *adverb:* to be *fatally* wounded in battle.

fate [fāt] *noun, plural* **fates. 1.** a power beyond human control that is thought to decide the way things happen in the world: "*Fate* now proceeded to deal me several harsh blows . . ." (John O'Hara) ". . . it was as if some *fate* in me forced me to see it." (Eugene O'Neill) **2.** something that happens to a person as if by fate; one's fortune or destiny: "However, this is your *fate* and so it must be." (Andre Norton) **3.** the end or final result of something; outcome: The Supreme Court will determine the *fate* of that case.

fa•ther [fä′ thər] *noun, plural* **fathers. 1.** the male parent of a child. **2.** a man or thing thought of as like a father, because of beginning something or causing it to develop: George Washington is known as "The *Father* of His Country." The Indians called the Mississippi River "The *Father* of the Waters." **3.** the **Father** or **Our Father.** a name for God. **4. Father.** a title for a Catholic priest. —*verb,* **fathered, fathering.** to be or act as a father to: to *father* a child.

fa•ther-in-law [fä′ thər in lô′] *noun, plural* **fathers-in-law.** the father of one's husband or wife.

Father's Day a holiday in honor of fathers, celebrated on the third Sunday of June.

fath•om [fath′ əm] *noun, plural* **fathoms.** a unit of length equal to six feet. Fathoms are used to measure the depth of water. —*verb,* **fathomed, fathoming. 1.** to find the depth of water. **2.** to come to understand; get to the true meaning of: "I used to study him . . . trying to *fathom* the secret of his appeal." (James Herriott)

fa•tigue [fə tēg′] *noun.* a feeling of being very tired from a long period of work or mental strain. —*verb,* **fatigued, fatiguing.** to cause a person to be very tired.

fat•ten [fat′ ən] *verb,* **fattened, fattening.** to make or become fat: The farmer *fattened* the pigs by feeding them extra corn. ♦ Food that is likely to make a person fat is said to be **fattening.**

fau•cet [fô′ sit] *noun, plural* **faucets.** a device that turns the flow of water from a pipe on or off.

Faulk•ner [fôlk′ nər] **William,** 1897–1962, American novelist.

F

fault The huge San Andreas Fault that runs down through the center of the state of California has been responsible for several large, destructive earthquakes and many minor ones.

fault [fôlt] *noun, plural* **faults. 1.** something in a person's character or way of acting that is not as it should be; a personal weakness: ". . . just now I was staring at you, but that's only an awful *fault* of mine." (Katherine Mansfield) **2.** a mistake or weak point in the way something works or is made; a flaw: a *fault* in an electrical wiring system. **3.** the responsibility for something that is wrong: "It's not the Dutch people's *fault* that we're having such a miserable time." (Anne Frank) **4.** a crack or break in the earth that causes the mass of rock on one side to move against the mass on the other side. Earthquakes are likely to take place along a fault. **5. at fault.** in the wrong; deserving blame: Which of the two drivers was *at fault* in the accident? —*verb,* **faulted, faulting.** to find fault with someone; blame: She was just trying to help—you can't *fault* her for that. —**faulty,** *adverb:* a car with *faulty* brakes.

fa•vor [fā′vər] *noun, plural* **favors. 1.** an act that helps someone; a kind act: Could you do me a *favor* and put this box in the garage? **2.** a condition of being liked, accepted, or approved: The movie actress was out of *favor* with the public because of her unpopular statements about politics. ♦ Often used in the expression **in (one's) favor:** The score was 3-2 *in favor* of the home team. **3.** a small gift given to each guest at a party. —*verb,* **favored, favoring. 1.** to do a favor for: I hope you will *favor* me with a prompt answer to this letter. **2.** to think of with favor; support or approve: Chuck is always complaining that his mother *favors* his younger sister over him. **3.** to treat in a special or careful way: He says his leg is all right now, but he's still *favoring* it when he runs.

fa•vor•a•ble [fāv′rə bəl] *adjective, more/most.* **1.** showing favor; approving or liking: That new play has gotten very *favorable* reviews. **2.** in one's favor; promising; encouraging: Old sailing ships had to wait for *favorable* winds and tides to leave the harbor. —**favorably,** *adverb:* The senator spoke *favorably* about the President's new plan.

fa•vor•ite [fāv′rit] *adjective.* thought of with the most favor; best-liked: Math is his *favorite* subject in school. Her *favorite* writer is Laura Ingalls Wilder. —*noun, plural* **favorites. 1.** someone or something that is liked best or favored over others. ♦ The practice of showing favor to a person in an unfair way is **favoritism. 2.** someone who is expected to win a game or contest: The Royals are the *favorites* in the American League West this year.

fawn [fôn] *noun, plural* **fawns.** a young deer less than one year old.

fawn This word is used specifically to refer to a young deer. The term *fawn* goes back to the Latin word for "child."

fear [fēr] *noun, plural* **fears.** a bad feeling that danger, pain, or something unknown is near: Ever since she was bitten when she was very young, my sister has had a *fear* of dogs. —*verb,* **feared, fearing. 1.** to have fear; be afraid of something: to *fear* snakes, to *fear* flying in an airplane. **2.** to be worried or anxious about what will happen: The king *feared* that his enemies would rise up against him. —**fearful,** *adjective.*

Pronunciation Key: T–Z			
t	ten; date	v	very; live
th	think	w	win; away
th	these	y	you
u	cut; butter	z	zoo; cause
ur	turn; bird	zh	measure

(Turn the page for more information.)

fear•less [fēr′lis] *adjective, more/most.* having or showing no fear; very brave. —**fearlessly,** *adverb.* —**fearlessness,** *noun.*

feast [fēst] *noun, plural* **feasts. 1.** a large or special meal with a lot of food. **2.** a religious holiday or celebration; a festival. —*verb,* **feasted, feasting.** to have a feast; eat very well.

feat [fēt] *noun, plural* **feats.** an act or deed that shows great skill, strength, or daring: One of Houdini's magic *feats* was escaping from a locked trunk underwater while tied in ropes and chains.

feath•er [feth′ər] *noun, plural* **feathers.** a light growth that covers and protects a bird's skin. Feathers keep birds warm and help them to fly.

fea•ture [fē′chər] *noun, plural* **features. 1.** an important or special thing that stands out; something that gets attention or is especially noticed: The main *feature* of that house is the large back yard with a swimming pool. **2.** a single part of the face or body: Her best *feature* is her pretty blue eyes. **3.** the main film of a motion picture program; a full-length movie. **4.** a special story in a newspaper or magazine. —*verb,* **featured, featuring.** to have as a feature; give importance to: That restaurant *features* fresh seafood.

F

income taxes. Spying, kidnaping, and bank robbery are *federal* crimes.

fed•er•a•tion [fed′ə rā′shən] *noun, plural* **federations.** an organization of nations, states, or other groups into one unit: The American *Federation* of Labor is a large group of labor unions.

fee [fē] *noun, plural* **fees.** money asked or paid for a service or right; a charge: There is a $2 *fee* to enter the museum. The doctor's *fee* for an office visit is $25.

fee•ble [fē′bəl] *adjective,* **feebler, feeblest.** not strong; weak: The cabin was dark except for the *feeble* light of an old lantern. "She made a *feeble* attempt to go back, but Agba held her firmly . . ." (Marguerite Henry) —**feebly,** *adverb.*

feed [fēd] *verb,* **fed, feeding. 1.** to give food to: She *feeds* the baby every four hours. He *fed* an apple to a horse. **2.** to take food into the body; eat: ". . . the small animals were *feeding* close to camp." (Ernest Hemingway) **3.** to provide or supply with some important material: to *feed* information into a computer. "Captain Wilder sat *feeding* little sticks into the fire." (Ray Bradbury) —*noun, plural* **feeds.** food for animals, especially farm animals: chicken *feed.*

feedback When a word is altered from its usual meaning and applied to something else, this is called a *metaphor.* Words in science are often used as metaphors. In Webster's *Collegiate Dictionary* there occurs this example, "Using *metaphor,* we say that computers have senses and a memory." (William Jovanovich). The process also works in reverse—we take words from science and use them in ordinary language. *Input* is information put into a computer, or a statement made by someone—at a conference, say. *Feedback* is both a technical and biological term meaning that new information is returned to its source—your nerves furnish *feedback* to your brain. The ordinary word *hardware* was taken to apply to computer machinery, then a new word *software* was created to match this, as a way to describe the coded programs that make the computer machines work. Most books on writing say that terms such as *feedback* and *input* are overused in ordinary writing, yet it can be also said that a good metaphor is one that works.

Feb•ru•ar•y [feb′yoo er′ē *or* feb′roo er′ē] *noun.* the second month of the year. February has 28 days, except for every fourth year (LEAP YEAR), when it has 29.

fed [fed] the past form of **feed.**

fed•er•al [fed′rəl] *adjective.* **1.** having to do with a nation that is formed by the coming together or agreement of many states: The United States has a *federal* government. **2.** having to do with the national government, as opposed to state or local government: *federal*

feed•back [fēd′bak′] *noun, plural* **feedback. 1.** a process by which a machine gets back information about how it is working and then adjusts itself according to this information. **2.** information about how some process or plan is working: The principal wants the parents to give her some *feedback* on her idea.

feed•er [fēd′ər] *noun, plural* **feeders. 1.** a device used to give feed to animals: a bird *feeder.* **2.** a device that feeds in some material: A Xerox machine has a paper *feeder.*

feel bad(ly) "She plays the piano *well*" (adverb). "She is a *good* piano player (adjective). It is not good English to use the adjective in place of the adverb, as in "She plays the piano *good*." There is one small group of verbs that does not follow this pattern. These are the verbs that describe the senses: *feel, look, sound,* and *seem.* With these words, the verb actually describes the subject rather than expressing action. Thus, they are followed by an adjective—we say "She looks *tired*" rather than "She looks *tiredly.*" The one verb in this group where the issue is not clear is *feel.* Should you say "I *feel bad* about what happened" or "I *feel badly*"? The usage expert Roy Copperud made a survey of many current dictionaries and usage books. He found that both these forms were considered to be acceptable. The editors of this dictionary don't agree with this. We recommend that you use only "feel bad," not "feel badly."

feel [fēl] *verb,* **felt, feeling. 1.** to find out about by touching: *Feel* this melon and tell me if you think it's ripe yet. "Ralph edged forward, *feeling* his way over the uneven surface as though he were blind." (William Golding) **2.** to be aware of by touch: to *feel* a pain in your leg. "He *felt* the dry, uncomfortable gravel under his evening shoes . . ." (Ian Fleming) **3.** to have a sense of in the mind; be aware of: to *feel* sick, to *feel* glad, to *feel* regret. **4.** to think or believe: I'm going to vote for Mrs. Barlow because I *feel* she's the best person for the job. —*noun.* the way something seems to the touch: The wool sweater had a rough *feel.*

feel•er [fē′lər] *noun, plural* **feelers. 1.** a part of an insect's body that is used for feeling; an antenna. **2.** a suggestion or hint to find out what people think or might do: When the mayor wanted to run for re-election, he sent out *feelers* to the labor unions to see if they would be willing to support him.

feel•ing [fē′ling] *noun, plural* **feelings. 1.** the ability to feel by touching; the sense of touch. **2.** a certain sense that the body or mind feels: a *feeling* of pain, a *feeling* of happiness. **3. feelings.** the sensitive part of a person's nature; one's pride: When she said my new haircut looked funny, she hurt my *feelings.* **4.** a way of thinking; an opinion or belief: I think that's a good idea; what's your *feeling* about it?

feet [fēt] *noun.* the *plural* of **foot.**

feign [fān] *verb,* **feigned, feigning.** to put on a false show of something; pretend: "I walked on *feigning* not to have noticed her . . ." (Iris Murdoch)

feint [fānt] *noun, plural* **feints.** a pretended movement or attack made to fool someone. —*verb,* **feinted, feinting.** to make such a false move.

fell¹ [fel] the past tense of **fall:** He tripped and *fell* over a crack in the sidewalk.

fell² *verb,* **felled, felling. 1.** to hit and knock down: The knight *felled* his enemy. **2.** to cut down: to *fell* a tree.

fel•low [fel′ō] *noun, plural* **fellows. 1.** any man or boy: Eddie went bowling with some of the *fellows* from his office. **2.** a person who is like another; a companion or equal. ◆ Also used as an adjective: Meryl Streep is highly respected by her *fellow* actresses.

fel•low•ship [fel′ō ship′] *noun, plural* **fellowships. 1.** friendship among the members of a group; companionship. **2.** a position or sum of money given to a student for advanced study: "I was . . . awarded the Guggenheim *Fellowship,* which would enable me to live and work abroad for a year." (Thomas Wolfe)

fel•o•ny [fel′ə nē] *noun, plural* **felonies.** a very serious crime that can be punished by a long prison term or sometimes even by death. Stealing a car is a felony; parking a car near a fire hydrant is a MISDEMEANOR.

felt¹ [felt] the past form of **feel.**

felt² *noun.* a heavy cloth made by rolling and pressing wool, fur, or other material together. Slippers and hats are often made of felt.

fe•male [fē′māl] *noun, plural* **females. 1.** a woman or girl. **2.** an animal that can give birth to young or lay eggs. —*adjective.* **1.** having to do with women or girls: Sandra Day O'Connor was the first *female* justice of the Supreme Court. **2.** of or relating to an animal that is a female: A *female* pig is called a sow.

F

Pronunciation Key: [ə] Symbol

The [ə] or *schwa* sound occurs in syllables without an accent. It can be spelled with any vowel, such as **a** in above, **e** in listen, **i** in pencil, **o** in melon, **u** in circus. It can also be a combination of vowels, such as **io** in action, **ai** in mountain, **iou** in precious.

(Turn the page for more information.)

feminine words Some languages divide nouns according to *gender,* or sex. That is, a word is considered to be either masculine, feminine, or neuter (neither masculine or feminine). This can be confusing to an English speaker studying a foreign language. For example, in Latin the word for "apple" is *malum,* which is masculine, but "apple tree" is feminine, *malus.* Also, the Latin word for "finger" is masculine, but "hand" is feminine, and "arm" is neuter. The only way that gender is shown in English is by the ending of certain words that describe a person's work or activity: *businessman-businesswoman, actor-actress.* In most cases, English either uses a word that does not signal gender— *painter, carpenter, nurse*—or uses "man" for the general form— *fisherman, foreman, gunman.* In the past, there were more male-female pairs of words, such as *aviator-aviatrix, poet-poetess.* But these fell out of use because they were thought to suggest that the female version of the word was less than the male—that a woman poet was so unusual that a separate name was needed for her.

fem•i•nine [fem/ ə nin] *adjective, more/ most.* **1.** of or having to do with women or girls: "Actress" is the feminine form of the word "actor." **2.** typical of or suitable for women.

fem•i•nism [fem/ ə niz/ əm] *noun.* **1.** the idea or belief that women should have the same basic rights and chances as men. **2.** a movement to gain equal rights and treatment for women in society, business, and politics. ♦ A **feminist** is a person who believes in or supports feminism.

fence [fens] *noun, plural* **fences.** a structure built in the form of a railing or wall to mark off or protect a certain piece of land. A fence is put up to keep people and animals in or out. —*verb,* **fenced, fencing. 1.** to put a fence around a certain area of land. ♦ Usually used with **in** or **off:** "She had *fenced in* a hundred acres once, digging the post holes herself . . ." (Katherine Anne Porter) **2.** to fight with swords; take part in the sport of FENCING.

fenc•ing [fen/ sing] *noun.* the sport or art of fighting with swords.

fend [fend] *verb,* **fended, fending. 1.** (used with **off**) to defend oneself; fight against: "Drew *fended off* the low branches . . ." (James Dickey) **2. fend for oneself.** to try to get along without help; look after oneself.

fend•er [fen/ dər] *noun, plural* **fenders.** a metal guard or frame that sticks out over the wheels of a car or bicycle. Fenders protect the wheels and tires and keep off mud or water.

fer•ment [fər ment/] *verb,* **fermented, fermenting. 1.** to cause a chemical change that forms bubbles of gas, as when sugar changes to alcohol: When grapes *ferment,* wine is formed. ♦ This process of change is called **fermentation** [fur/ men tā/ shən]. **2.** to cause unrest or trouble. ♦ Also used as a noun: a time of political *ferment.*

Fer•mi [fer/mē] **Enrico,** 1901–1954, American scientist, born in Italy.

fern [furn] *noun, plural* **ferns.** a plant that has many large, green feathery leaves. Ferns do not have flowers or true seeds, but produce new plants by means of tiny SPORES. Several thousand types of ferns grow throughout the world, usually in wet places.

fe•ro•cious [fə rō/ shəs] *adjective, more/most.* very strong and violent; fierce: A tiger is a *ferocious* animal. "Rose has that *ferocious* Vermont Yankee pride . . ." (Alice Adams) —**ferociously,** *adverb:* "She was chewing so *ferociously* upon a piece of gum . . ." (Roald Dahl) ♦ The state of being ferocious is **ferocity** [fə räs/ ə tē]: "From beneath their broad-brimmed hats of palm leaf gleamed eyes which . . . had a kind of animal *ferocity.*" (Nathaniel Hawthorne)

Fer•rar•o [fə rär/ ō] **Geraldine,** born 1935, the first woman to be a major-party candidate for vice-president.

fencing A fencing match in Montreal, Canada. The tips of the foils are blunted, but can still injure an eye, so the fencers use face masks for protection.

ferret The black-footed ferret of the North American plains is endangered because its main food source, the prairie dog, has become scarce.

fer•ret [fer′ it] *noun, plural* **ferrets.** a small animal that looks like and is related to the weasel. In Europe ferrets have been trained to hunt mice, rats, and rabbits by driving them out of their holes.

Fer•ris wheel [fer′ is] a large wheel that spins around in the air and has seats for passengers, found at fairs and amusement parks.

fer•ry [fer′ ē] *noun, plural* **ferries.** a boat that goes back and forth to carry people, cars, and goods across a river or other narrow body of water. —*verb,* **ferried, ferrying.** to go in a ferry or other such boat: ". . . he put Page aboard his yacht and had him *ferried* to Nassau, a hundred miles away." (George Plimpton).

ferry The Staten Island ferry brings commuters from the island across New York Bay to work in Manhattan.

fer•tile [fur′ təl] *adjective,* **more/most.** 1. good for plants to grow in; able to produce crops and plants easily: *fertile* soil, a *fertile* area. 2. of an animal or plant, able to produce eggs, seeds, pollen, or young. 3. able to produce many thoughts or ideas: a *fertile* imagination. ◆ The state of being fertile is **fertility** [fər til′ ə tē].

fer•ti•lize [fur′ təl īz] *verb,* **fertilized, fertilizing.** 1. to place POLLEN or SPERM into a plant or female animal to develop a seed: Bees *fertilize* flowers by carrying pollen from one plant to the next. 2. to use fertilizer on: to *fertilize* a lawn or a garden. ◆ The process of fertilizing something is **fertilization.**

fer•ti•liz•er [fur′ tə lī′ zər] *noun, plural* **fertilizers.** a substance used to make the soil richer and to help plants grow. Fertilizers include natural materials such as waste matter or crushed bones from animals, as well as certain chemicals.

fes•ti•val [fes′ tə vəl] *noun, plural* **festivals.** 1. a day or time of celebrating: a harvest *festival,* a religious *festival.* 2. a series of entertainments or cultural events of the same kind over several days: the Cannes Film *Festival.*

fetch [fech] *verb,* **fetched, fetching.** to go after and bring back: "Peter went up to the loft to *fetch* some old newspapers." (Anne Frank) "I'm hungry . . . could you *fetch* me a little bit to eat." (William Styron)

feud [fyo͞od] *noun, plural* **feuds.** a long, bitter fight or quarrel: In the 1800's there was a famous *feud* in the hills of Kentucky between the Hatfield and McCoy families—it lasted more than 30 years and at least 20 people were killed. —*verb,* **feuded, feuding.** to take part in a feud: He's *feuding* with his neighbors because their dog is always digging up his lawn.

fe•ver [fē′ vər] *noun, plural* **fevers.** 1. a body temperature that is higher than the usual or normal level, which is 98.6°F. for most people. A fever is not a sickness in itself, but is one of the most common signs that a person is sick. 2. a disease that causes a high fever, such as **yellow fever** or **scarlet fever.** 3. a state of being very excited or upset: "While I huddled on a chair in a *fever* of terror . . ." (Russell Baker)

few [fyo͞o] *adjective,* **fewer, fewest.** not many: There are only a *few* stores in that small town. —*noun; pronoun.* a small number; not many: A lot of people entered the 50-mile bike race, but only a *few* finished the entire course.

fi•an•cée [fē′ än sā′ or fē än′ sā] *noun, plural* **fiancées.** a woman to whom a man is engaged to

F

Pronunciation Key: Accent Marks

[′] is the normal accent mark. It shows where the main stress falls on a word.
[′] is a secondary accent mark. It shows a lighter stress than the primary accent. For example:

tel • e • vis • ion [tel′ə vizh ′ən]

(Turn the page for more information.)

be married. ♦ A man to whom a woman is engaged to be married is a **fiancé** [fē′ än sä′ or fē än′ sä].

fi•ber [fī′ bər] *noun, plural* **fibers.** a long, thin, thread-like piece of material: Cotton, wool, or silk *fibers* are used to make clothing.

fi•ber•glass [fī′ bər glas′] *noun.* a strong, long-lasting material made of fine threads of glass. Fiberglass is used to make fabrics, parts for cars, planes, and boats, building materials, and many other common products.

the *field* of medicine. —*verb,* **fielded, fielding.** in baseball, to catch a batted ball.

field•er [fēl′ dər] *noun, plural* **fielders.** a baseball player who plays out in the field and tries to catch the ball.

field goal 1. a score of three points in football, made by kicking the ball between the goal posts. **2.** a score of two points in basketball.

field hockey a form of hockey played on a field between two teams of eleven players each, using a hard rubber ball.

> **fiction** "For truth is always strange, stranger than *fiction,*" (Lord Byron) Here, Byron says that "real life" has more bizarre or unusual events than a storyteller can make up. Such a made-up story is fiction, whether it is called a novel or a short story or a narrative poem or a play. The verb form of this word is *fictionalize,* as in: "Robert Penn Warren's novel *All the King's Men* is a *fictionalized* biography of Huey Long, a famous Southern politician." The idea that fiction is invented by the writer suggests that poetry and drama fall under the label of *fiction.* Usually they do not. *Fiction* refers mainly to writing that is in prose form. The best-known award in American literature is the Pulitzer Prize; one of the awards given each year is "for *fiction* in book form by an American author." But there are also separate Pulitzer Prizes for poetry and for drama. The category Fiction includes only short stories and novels—such as the novel *All the King's Men,* which won the Pulitzer Prize for Fiction in 1947.

F

fic•tion [fik′ shən] *noun.* **1.** a form of writing in which the writer makes up the characters and the things that happen, instead of writing about real people and events. Novels and short stories are kinds of fiction. **2.** anything that is made up or imagined: Do you really believe what he says about his uncle being a rock star? I think it's pure *fiction.* —**fictional,** *adjective:* Paul Bunyan is a *fictional* character.

fic•ti•tious [fik tish′ əs] *adjective.* **1.** having to do with writing that is fiction; fictional. **2.** not true or real: The criminal gave the police a *fictitious* name when he was arrested.

fid•dle [fid′ əl] *noun, plural* **fiddles.** a popular name for the VIOLIN, especially when it is used to play country or folk music. ♦ A person who plays the fiddle is a **fiddler.** —*verb,* **fiddled, fiddling.** to play a fiddle.

fidg•et [fij′ it] *verb,* **fidgeted, fidgeting.** to move in a restless or nervous way: "I stood there *fidgeting* on the sidewalk, zipping the zipper of my jacket up and down." (S.E. Hinton)

field [fēld] *noun, plural* **fields. 1.** any piece of land that has few or no trees; open land. **2.** a piece of land that is used for growing crops: a cotton *field,* a corn *field.* **3.** any area of land used for a certain purpose: a football field, an oil *field,* a battle*field.* **4.** an area of activity or interest: Rosalyn Yalow won a Nobel Prize in

fiend [fēnd] *noun, plural* **fiends. 1.** *also,* **Fiend.** an evil spirit; a devil. **2.** a very cruel or wicked person. **3.** *Informal.* someone who is very devoted to something: Grandma is a real fresh-air *fiend* and keeps the windows wide open even in winter. —**fiendish,** *adjective.* being or like a fiend; cruel; wicked.

fierce [fērs] *adjective,* **fiercer, fiercest. 1.** likely to attack or cause harm; savage: A grizzly bear is a *fierce* animal. **2.** very strong or dangerous; violent: "The wind blew in *fierce* gusts as we left the village, stinging our faces with sand." (Scott O'Dell) —**fiercely,** *adverb:* "My kid brother and I would battle *fiercely* over who would get . . . the Sunday color comics." (Jean Shepherd)

fi•es•ta [fē es′ tə] *noun, plural* **fiestas.** a celebration or festival, especially in a Spanish-speaking country.

fife [fīf] *noun, plural* **fifes.** a small instrument like a flute, making a high sound. The fife was often played in marching bands during the American Revolution.

fifth [fifth] *noun, plural* **fifths;** *adjective.* the number five in a series.

fig [fig] *noun, plural* **figs.** the sweet, pear-shaped fruit of a bush or tree that grows in warm climates. Figs are usually eaten as a dried fruit, but can also be eaten fresh off the tree.

fight [fīt] *noun, plural* **fights. 1.** an occasion when people try to hurt each other with weapons or fists; a battle or struggle. **2.** an occasion when people attack each other with words; a quarrel or argument: Betty and her sister had a big *fight* about who was supposed to clean up the kitchen. **3.** any contest or struggle against some opposing force: Susan B. Anthony was a leader in the *fight* to gain women the right to vote. **4.** a boxing match. —*verb,* **fought, fighting. 1.** to use fists or weapons against: The Americans *fought* the British in the War of 1812. **2.** to argue or quarrel: Kevin often *fights* with his brother about which TV show to watch. **3.** to take part in a contest or struggle: "The wind is so strong that they have to *fight* their way through it." (Katherine Mansfield)

fight•er [fīt′ ər] *noun, plural* **fighters. 1.** any person who fights: Andrew Jackson was famous as an Indian *fighter* before he became President. **2.** a person who fights in the sport of boxing; a boxer. **3.** a fast war plane with a crew of one or two, used to attack enemy planes and ground troops.

fig•ur•a•tive [fig′ yər ə tiv] *adjective.* using words in a way that goes beyond or away from their ordinary meaning. For example, Arthur Miller wrote that, "A salesman is way out there in the blue, riding on a smile and a shoeshine." He was using "blue" and "riding" in a *figurative* way, to mean roughly "the world" and "getting along." —**figuratively,** *adverb.*

—*verb,* **figured, figuring. 1.** to use numbers to find an answer. **2.** to be important or stand out: The fact that the book was easy to use *figured* in the teacher's decision to choose it for her class. **3.** to think or believe: I *figured* you must have had car problems when you didn't show up on time. **4. figure out.** to find an answer or explanation: Mom helped Dad *figure* out how to put the new lawnmower together.

fig•ure•head [fig′yer hed′] *noun, plural* **figureheads.** someone who holds a high position but does not have real power; The president of the Soviet Union is a *figurehead*; the head of the Communist Party is the real leader.

figure of speech an expression that uses words in a different way from their ordinary meaning. Carl Sandburg's "The fog comes in on little cat feet" and T.S. Eliot's "The yellow fog that rubs its back upon the windowpanes" are figures of speech.

figure skating a form of ice skating in which the skaters have to form certain figures on the ice or carry out certain movements.

file[1] [fīl] *noun, plural* **files. 1.** a folder, cabinet, or other container to hold papers, letters, cards, and so on. **2.** a set of papers arranged in some order: The doctor kept a *file* of all her patient's records. **3.** a line of people, animals, or things behind one another: Indians used to move through a forest in single *file*. **4.** in a computer, a collection of records or facts that have to do with the same subject.

> **figurative words** "After that day a new life began for Johnny, and he flourished like a poor little plant that has struggled out of some dark corner into the sunshine." (Louisa May Alcott) "The muffled tongue of Big Ben tolled nine by the clock as the cortege [funeral procession] left the palace, but on history's clock it was sunset, and the sun of the old world was setting in a dying blaze of splendor never to be seen again." (Barbara Tuchman) These two quotations are examples of *figurative* language. The writer is using familiar, realistic things—in one case, a plant; in the other a clock, and the sun. But these things are being used in a figurative way—they refer to an idea rather than to the object itself. Why not pick up a favorite book of your own, and look for figurative language there?

fig•ure [fig′ yər] *noun, plural* **figures. 1.** a symbol that stands for a number: 1, 2, 7, 14, 57, and so on are *figures*. **2.** an amount shown in numbers: The company published their sales *figures* for last year. **3.** the shape or outline of something; form: The skaters traced circular *figures* on the ice. **4.** the shape or form of a person's body: Susan watches what she eats so she'll keep her slim *figure*. **5.** a person, especially a well-known or important person: "Your father was a *figure* of glamour and excitement in their rather dull lives." (Pearl Buck)

—*verb,* **filed, filing. 1.** to put away or store in a file; to *file* a letter. **2.** to send in to or put on an official record: They *filed* a claim with their

Pronunciation Key: A–F			
a	and; hat	ch	chew; such
ā	ate; stay	d	dog; lid
â	care; air	e	end; yet
ä	father; hat	ē	she; each
b	boy; cab	f	fun; off

(Turn the page for more information.)

insurance company for the damage to the car. **3.** to move in a line or file: "Quietly we *filed* out of the village along the trail . . ." (Scott O'Dell)

file² *noun, plural* **files.** a steel tool used to grind, smooth, and polish hard objects. A file has small, rough ridges in its surface that evenly cut away small amounts of material. —*verb,* **filed, filing.** to use or cut with a file: Tom *filed* down the sharp edge on the door.

fill [fil] *verb,* **filled, filling. 1.** to put as much into something as it will hold: to *fill* a glass with water, to *fill* up the gas tank of a car. **2.** to take up all the space of an area: The crowd had *filled* the stadium by the start of the game. "A heavy Georgia spring *filled* the morning air with sunshine." (Langston Hughes) **3.** to close or stop up by putting something in: The dentist *filled* the cavity in her tooth. **4.** to supply what is needed or asked for: The butcher *filled* Mrs. Bishop's meat order. **5.** to write information on a paper or form: *Fill* in each blank with the correct answer. Joanna *filled* out an application for a new library card. —*noun.* **1.** an amount that fills or satisfies: to eat or drink your *fill.* **2.** something used to fill an area of ground, such as dirt or gravel.

fil•let [fi lā′] *noun, plural* **fillets.** (also spelled **filet**) a slice of meat with no bones and very little fat.

fill•ing [fil′ ing] *noun, plural* **fillings. 1.** a material used to fill a cavity in a tooth. **2.** anything used to fill something: a *pie filling.*

film [film] *noun, plural* **films. 1.** a narrow strip of plastic or other material that is used with a camera to take photographs. The film is covered with a chemical substance that changes when it is exposed to light. **2.** a movie: *Robin Hood* is Andrew's favorite *film.* **3.** a thin layer or coating over something: There was a *film* of dust on top of the dresser. —*verb,* **filmed, filming.** to take photographs on film; make a movie: Mr. Johnston *filmed* his daughter's soccer game.

fil•ter [fil′ tər] *noun, plural* **filters. 1.** a device through which a liquid or gas is passed in order to clean out substances that are harmful or unwanted. Gasoline engines use different types of filters to remove dirt from air, oil, and fuel. **2.** any material used for this purpose, such as paper, cloth, charcoal, or sand. —*verb,* **filtered, filtering. 1.** to pass a liquid or gas through a filter: to *filter* drinking water. Air conditioners *filter* dust out of the air. **2.** to pass or move slowly, as if through a filter: "The light from the stars *filtered* through the beeches and elms and pines . . ." (Walter Farley)

filth [filth] *noun.* sickening, disgusting, or terrible dirt.

filth•y [fil′ thē] *adjective,* **filthier, filthiest.** covered with filth; very, very dirty: "The kitchen sink was full nearly to the brim with *filthy,* greenish water . . ." (George Orwell)

fin [fin] *noun, plural* **fins. 1.** one of the thin, flat parts that fish move to swim and keep their balance in the water. Fins are also found on water animals such as dolphins and whales. **2.** a flat rubber shoe shaped like a fin, used by swimmers for greater speed in the water. **3.** any object that looks like a fin, as on the body of a car.

finalize "Then, around midnight, the decisions are *finalized*." (Peter Jones) "The title insurance is *finalized* when the loan is closed." (Robert Kratovil) "Yankees *finalize* Whitson's contract." *(New York Times)* How do you feel about the word *finalize*? As these quotes show, it's obviously part of our language, yet several books on writing criticize this as a weak word, a word that doesn't add anything to the good old-fashioned word "finish." Those who favor the word *finalize* argue that it does add something to the language. As you can see from the quotes above, *finalize* usually refers to the ending of a long process in business or law, a process that involves a number of people. What do you think? Would you vote to admit *finalize* to the "club" of acceptable words?

Fill•more [fil′ môr] **Millard,** 1800–1874, the thirteenth president of the United States, from 1850 to 1853.

fil•ly [fil′ ē] *noun, plural* **fillies.** a young female horse.

fi•nal [fin′ əl] *adjective.* **1.** coming at the end of something; being the end; last: the *final* chapter of a book. The Super Bowl is the *final* game of the pro football season. **2.** having or allowing no further discussion or change: In this contest, the decision of the judges will be *final.* —*noun, plural* **finals. 1.** also, **finals.** the last test or examination of a course in school or college. **2.** usually, **finals.** the last or deciding game in a match or series.

fi•nal•ly [fī′ nə lē *or* fīn′ lē] *adverb.* at the end; at last: We *finally* found the car keys after looking for half an hour.

fi•nance [fī nans′ *or* fī′ nans] *noun, plural* **finances. 1.** the control or management of money for a government, business, or person; matters dealing with money. **2. finances.** the amount of money owned by a person or group: That company's *finances* are at a very low level right now. —*verb,* **financed, financing.** to provide money for someone or something: Public schools are *financed* by taxes.

fi•nan•cial [fī nan′ shəl] *adjective.* having to do with finance; dealing with money: Newspaper reports on the stock market and on the price of gold appear in the *financial* section. —**financially,** *adverb:* a person who is doing well *financially.*

finch [finch] *noun, plural* **finches.** songbirds with a short, strong beak. Canaries, and sparrows are kinds of finches.

find [fīnd] *verb,* **found, finding. 1.** to happen or come upon by accident: to *find* a dollar bill on the sidewalk. **2.** to look for and locate; get something that is hidden or lost: We finally *found* Mom's wedding ring behind her dresser. **3.** to get or obtain by effort: to *find* a job. How does she *find* the time to do housework when she's so busy all day? **4.** to learn or discover something that was not known: to *find* the answer to a math problem. **5.** to meet with a certain thing or condition: Kangaroos are *found* in Australia. "I went in, and *found* myself in an empty room . . ." (V.S. Naipaul) —*noun, plural* **finds.** something that is found, especially something valuable: That old painting is a real *find.*

fine[1] [fīn] *adjective,* **finer, finest. 1.** of high quality; very good or excellent: a *fine* meal, *fine* weather for a picnic. **2.** very small or thin: Some dictionaries are written in *fine* print. "The sand was as smooth and *fine* and white as icing sugar." (Mary Norton) —*adverb.* **1.** also, **finely.** so as to be very thin or small: Chop the vegetables *fine* for the stew. **2.** in an exact way: to *fine*-tune a piano. **3.** *Informal.* very well: Suzie's doing *fine* in school.

fine[2] *noun, plural* **fines.** an amount of money that is paid as a penalty for breaking a law or rule: The library charges a *fine* when books are not returned on time. —*verb,* **fined, fining.** to punish by charging a fine: The judge *fined* the man $100 for speeding.

fin•ger [fing′ gər] *noun, plural* **fingers.** one of the five parts that form the end of the hand,

also referred to as four fingers and a thumb. —*verb,* **fingered, fingering.** to touch something with the fingers.

fin•ger•nail [fing′ gər nāl′] *noun, plural* **fingernails.** the thin, hard covering on the end of the finger.

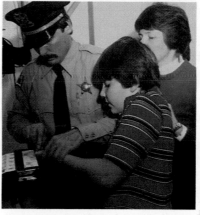

fingerprint This boy is taking part in a nationwide fingerprinting program to help identify lost children. At right is a close-up of a print.

fin•ger•print [fing′ gər print′] *noun, plural* **fingerprints.** a pattern made by pressing the inside tip of the finger against a surface. Each person's fingerprints have a different pattern from all other people, so they can be used to identify the person. —*verb,* **fingerprinted, fingerprinting.** to record the fingerprints of someone.

fin•ish [fin′ ish] *verb,* **finished, finishing. 1.** to bring or come to the end; complete: Mom *finished* painting Cathy's room this morning. "When I *finished* grammar school I had to go to work." (Richard Wright) **2.** to use until gone; use up: Mary *finished* a quart of milk by herself at breakfast. **3.** to put a final coat or surface on something: The cabinets were *finished* with a dark-colored stain. —*noun, plural* **finishes. 1.** the end of something: the *finish* of a race. **2.** the final coat or surface of something.

Fin•land [fin′ lənd] a country in northern Europe, on the Baltic Sea. *Capital:* Helsinki. *Area:* 130,100 square miles. *Population:* 4,810,000. —**Finnish,** *adjective; noun.*

\	Pronunciation Key: G–N		
g	give; big	k	kind, cat, back
h	hold	l	let; ball
i	it; this	m	make; time
ī	ice; my	n	not; own
j	jet; gem; edge	ng	having

(Turn the page for more information.)

295

F

fi•ord [fē′ôrd *or* fyôrd] (also spelled **fjord**) *noun, plural* **fiords.** a narrow inlet of the sea between tall, steep cliffs.

fir [fur] *noun, plural* **firs.** a tall evergreen tree that bears upright cones and that is related to the pine tree. Fir trees usually grow in northern areas and are an important source of lumber.

fire [fīr] *noun, plural* **fires. 1.** the flame, heat, and light caused by something burning. **2.** burning that causes damage or harm: a forest *fire.* **3.** a very strong feeling, like being on fire: "Sometimes I wish I had the *fire* of Jackie Robinson to speak out and tell the black man's story." (Joe Louis) **4.** the shooting of a gun: rifle *fire,* cannon *fire.* —*verb,* **fired, firing. 1.** to dismiss from a job: The company *fired* him because he was always late for work. **2.** to shoot a gun. **3.** to cause something to burn: to *fire* up a furnace. **4.** to arouse strong feelings: to *fire* a person's imagination.

fire•arm [fīr′ärm′] *noun, plural* **firearms.** a weapon that is carried and fired by one person, such as a shotgun, rifle, or pistol.

fire•crack•er [fīr′krak′ər] *noun, plural* **firecrackers.** a paper tube that contains a small amount of explosive and a fuse.

fire drill the practicing of what to do and where to go in order to leave a school or office building in case of fire.

fire escape a metal stairway or ladder on the outside of a building, to be used to leave the building in case of fire.

fire extinguisher a small metal container having chemicals that can be sprayed on a fire to put it out.

fire•fight•er [fīr′fī′tər] *noun, plural* **firefighters.** a person whose job is to put out dangerous fires; a fireman.

fire•fly [fīr′flī′] *noun, plural* **fireflies.** a small kind of beetle that gives off short flashes of light from the rear part of its body when it flies in the dark; also called a **lightning bug.**

fire•man [fīr′mən] *noun, plural* **firemen. 1.** a person whose job is to put out dangerous fires. **2.** a person whose work is looking after a fire, as in a furnace or locomotive engine.

fire•place [fīr′plās′] *noun, plural* **fireplaces.** a structure built to contain a fire for heating or cooking. Fireplaces are made of a fireproof material, such as brick, and have a chimney to carry away the smoke.

fire•proof [fīr′proōf′] *adjective, more/most.* made of materials that will not burn, or will not burn easily.

fire•works [fīr′wurks′] *plural noun.* firecrackers, skyrockets, and other such explosives that make loud noises and fill the sky with brightly-colored lights.

fireworks A display of fireworks at the Statue of Liberty during a Fourth of July celebration.

firm¹ [furm] *adjective,* **firmer, firmest. 1.** not giving way to pressure; hard; solid: *firm* ground, a *firm* mattress. **2.** not easily moved; strong or steady: "She braced herself and took a *firm* hold . . ." (Lloyd Alexander) **3.** not likely to change; staying the same: We made a *firm* offer to buy the house. —*adverb.* not moving or changing: "The doctor held *firm* for once and said let them go." (Ken Kesey) —**firmly,** *adverb.* Pack the dirt down *firmly* around the edges of the plant. —**firmness,** *noun.*

firm² *noun, plural* **firms.** a business company, especially one formed by two or more partners: a *firm* of lawyers.

first [furst] *adjective.* being number one; before all others: January is the *first* month of the year. —*adverb.* **1.** before anyone or anything else: Heather finished *first* in the race. If you want to watch TV you'll have to clean your room *first.* **2.** for the first time: Radio programs were *first* broadcast in the U.S. in 1920. —*noun, plural* **firsts. 1.** someone or something that is first. **2.** the beginning: At *first* they didn't get along, but now they're good friends.

first aid immediate help or treatment given to someone who is injured or sick, before regular medical help is available.

first class 1. a class of mail that includes letters, more expensive than other classes but also delivered faster. 2. the best and most expensive class of seating and service on a plane, train, or ship. —**first-class,** *adjective.*

first•hand [furst′ hand′] (also spelled **first-hand**) *adjective; adverb.* from the original source or place; direct: A *firsthand* description of an event is one given by someone who was there when it happened.

you because it will *fit* under the seat. 2. to be suitable or right for: That actor really *fits* the part of Sir Lancelot because he's young and handsome. —*adjective,* **fitter, fittest.** 1. having what is needed for a purpose; suitable; right: *The New York Times* says that it publishes "All the News That's *Fit* to Print." 2. in good physical condition; healthy: She exercises to keep *fit.* —*noun, plural* **fits.** the way something fits: That blouse is a perfect *fit* for you.

first person A first-person novel is one in which the writer speaks as "I," which means that the writer is also a character in the story. If the story is told without the writer appearing in it as "I," then it's a *third-person* story (See PERSON for more information.) Sometimes, however, the "I" is used but doesn't refer to the writer directly or obviously. This is first person fiction with a special twist. George Orwell, who was very tall and thin, and who went to a famous school, wrote a first-person novel about how the world seemed to a short, fat man with ordinary schooling, George Bowling. Emily Brontë stepped even farther out of character when she wrote *Wuthering Heights*—her first-person character was a man, Mr. Lockwood. Perhaps the writer who made the greatest departure though, was Anna Sewell, author of the children's classic *Black Beauty*. This novel is told in the first person—by a horse.

F

fish [fish] *noun, plural* **fish** or **fishes.** any of a large group of animals that live in water. Fish have a long backbone and breathe by means of GILLS. Almost all fish have fins to aid in swimming and balancing, and small plates on their skin called scales. —*verb,* **fished, fishing.** 1. to catch fish or try to catch fish for food or as a sport. ♦ This work or sport is known as **fishing.** 2. to draw or pull out as if by fishing: Joe *fished* a quarter out of his pocket. 3. to try to get something in an indirect or roundabout way: "For all my *fishing,* I could never find out what she thought of me." (Mary McCarthy)

fish•er•man [fish′ ər mən] *noun, plural* **fishermen.** a person who fishes, either for a living or for sport.

fishing rod a long pole made of wood or other materials and having a hook and line attached for catching fish. Most fishing rods have a reel that holds extra line.

fis•sion [fish′ ən] *noun.* 1. the process of splitting apart the center or NUCLEUS of an atom to release large amounts of energy. 2. the dividing of a cell or simple living thing into parts as a means of producing new individuals.

fist [fist] *noun, plural* **fists.** a hand that is closed with the fingers tightly folded into the palm.

fit¹ [fit] *verb,* **fit** or **fitted, fitting.** 1. to be or cause to be the right size and shape: This sweater doesn't *fit*—I'd better try on a larger size. You can take this bag on the plane with

fit² *noun, plural* **fits.** a sudden attack or show of strong feeling: a coughing *fit.* Tony's going to have a *fit* when he sees that big scratch on his car door.

Fitz•ger•ald [fits jer′ əld] **F. Scott,** 1896–1940, American novelist and short-story writer.

five [fīv] *noun, plural* **fives;** *adjective.* one more than four; 5.

fix [fiks] *verb,* **fixed, fixing.** 1. to cause something that is not working properly to act in the proper way; repair: to *fix* a broken chair. 2. to prepare or arrange in a certain way: to *fix* your hair. Mom always *fixes* a big turkey dinner on special holidays. 3. to make firm or secure: They have just *fixed* the date for their wedding. 4. to direct or hold steadily: "Her eyes were *fixed* on the colored lights strung over our table . . ." (Joan Didion) 5. to secretly arrange the outcome of a game or contest ahead of time: In 1919 the World Series was *fixed,* and gamblers paid the White Sox to lose on purpose. —*noun, plural* **fixes.** 1. a difficult or

Pronunciation Key: O–S			
ō	over; go	ou	out; town
ô	all; law	p	put; hop
oo	look; full	r	run; car
oo̅	pool; who	s	set; miss
oi	oil; boy	sh	show

(Turn the page for more information.)

F

unpleasant situation: We'll be in quite a *fix* if we get a flat tire, because there's no spare. **2.** the act of fixing a game or contest.

fix•ture [fiks′ chər] *noun, plural* **fixtures. 1.** something in a building that is fastened in place to stay: Sinks, bathtubs, and ceiling lights are common household *fixtures.* **2.** a person or thing thought of as being fixed in place: Mr. Lewis is a *fixture* at the train station—he's been selling papers at the same stand for twenty years.

flag [flag] *noun, plural* **flags. 1.** a piece of cloth having designs, symbols, and colors on it, used to represent a country, state, or other organization. **2.** a small piece of colored cloth, used for giving signals: In auto racing, a yellow *flag* tells drivers to slow down. —*verb,* **flagged, flagging.** to stop or signal something with or as if with a flag. ♦ Usually used with **down:** Travis tried to *flag down* a taxi, but the driver didn't see him and drove right by.

Flag Day June 14th, a day when people fly the American flag in honor of the fact that on that day in 1777 Congress chose the official U.S. flag.

flair [flâr] *noun, plural* **flairs.** a natural talent: a *flair* for writing. She has a real *flair* for designing clothes.

flake [flāk] *noun, plural* **flakes.** a small, thin, flat piece of something, such as snow, dried paint, soap, breakfast cereal, and so on. —*verb,* **flaked, flaking.** to come off in flakes; peel: Paint was *flaking* off the garage wall.

flank [flangk] *noun, plural* **flanks. 1.** either side of the body of an animal or person, between the ribs and the hip. **2.** an area to the side: The general sent his cavalry forces to attack the enemy's left *flank.* —*verb,* **flanked, flanking.** to be by or at the side of someone or something: "Two rows of royal guards *flanked* the entrance." (Marguerite Henry)

flan•nel [flan′ əl] *noun.* a soft, woven cotton cloth that is used to make shirts and other clothing, blankets, sheets, and so on.

flap [flap] *verb,* **flapped, flapping. 1.** of a bird, to move the wings up and down. **2.** to wave loosely and noisily, like the beating of a bird's wings: "The wind *flapped* her shirt round her like a flag." (C.S. Forester) —*noun, plural* **flaps.** something that is attached at only one edge so that it can move freely: a tent *flap,* a *flap* on an envelope.

flare [flâr] *verb,* **flared, flaring. 1.** to burn suddenly and with a bright glow: The charcoal *flared* when Dad lit the lighter fluid. "The sun was *flaring* over the ridge . . ." (Walter Farley) "The square was lit almost as bright as day by *flaring* torches and moonlight . . ." (Sherley Anne Williams) **2.** to spread out or open up: This skirt is designed to *flare* from the hips. **3. flare up.** to show sudden anger or strong feeling. —*noun, plural* **flares. 1.** an emergency device that gives off a bright light, used for signals at sea, by motorists whose cars have broken down, and so on. **2.** a bright light lasting for a short time.

---

flair/flare Let's distinguish between these two similar words. *Flare* refers to a kind of light or flash: "The policemen lighted *flares,* which gave the scene a theatrical, tragic air." (Anais Nin) *Flair* refers to a natural gift or talent: "Yet even then she had a an air of grace, a marvelous *flair,* such as comes from nature alone." (Walter Farley)

---

flame [flām] *noun, plural* **flames. 1.** the glowing gas that rises up from a fire, usually seen as an orange or yellow band of light. **2.** *also,* **flames.** a state of blazing fire: The house was in *flames* when the firefighters arrived. —*verb,* **flamed, flaming. 1.** to burn or blaze with flames. **2.** to show red or glow, as if burning: "She was *flaming* with anger." (Saul Bellow)

fla•min•go [flə ming′ gō] *noun, plural* **flamingos** or **flamingoes.** a water bird that lives in warm areas. Flamingos have pink or red feathers, a very long neck, and long thin legs.

Flan•ders [flan′ dərz] a former country in northern Europe, now mostly in Belgium, with parts in the Netherlands and France. —**Flemish,** *adjective; noun.*

flamingo Both flamingo parents take turns sitting on the egg, and also feeding the young chick once it has hatched from the egg.

flash [flash] *noun, plural* **flashes. 1.** a sudden bursting out of light or flame: a *flash* of lightning. **2.** a very short time: Quick as a *flash* she grabbed the baby before he could fall. **3.** a sudden feeling or thought: "Ah—they had it, he knew with a *flash* of recognition." (Anne Morrow Lindbergh) **4.** a short word for FLASHLIGHT or FLASHBULB. —*verb,* **flashed, flashing. 1.** to give off or show a sudden, brief light. **2.** to move quickly or suddenly: The skier *flashed* by us on her way down the hill. **3.** to show for a moment: A message *flashed* across the TV screen. —*adjective.* happening suddenly: a *flash* flood, a *flash* fire.

flash•bulb [flash′bulb′] *noun, plural* **flashbulbs.** an electric lamp that burns very brightly for a moment, used for taking photographs indoors or in dim light.

flash•light [flash′līt′] *noun, plural* **flashlights.** a small battery-powered electric light that is usually held in the hand.

flash•y [flash′ē] *adjective,* **flashier, flashiest.** very showy; fancy; gaudy: a *flashy* dresser, a *flashy* sports car.

flask [flask] *noun, plural* **flasks.** a small glass bottle with a narrow neck or opening, especially one used in medicine to hold liquids.

flats The Bonneville Salt Flats in the Utah desert are often used for automobile speed racing because of their empty, perfectly flat surface.

flat¹ [flat] *adjective,* **flatter, flattest. 1.** having a surface that goes straight across; smooth and even; level: The top of a table is *flat.* **2.** lying stretched or spread out: She was *flat* on her back on the sofa. **3.** not changing; fixed: The garage charges a *flat* rate of $15 for an oil change, no matter how long it takes. **4.** in music: **a.** half a step lower than the natural pitch: Brahms' Piano Concerto in B *Flat.* **b.** lower than the true or proper pitch: Her

voice sounded *flat* on that last song. **5.** of a tire, not having enough air. —*noun, plural* **flats. 1.** a flat surface or part: "He rushed over to the desk, and began to pound it with the *flat* of his hand." (James Herriot) **2.** a musical symbol [♭] for playing a note one-half step below the natural pitch. —*adverb.* **1.** in a flat manner or position: to lie *flat* on the floor. **2.** exactly: Bob Hayes won the Olympic 100-meter race in ten seconds *flat.* —**flatly,** *adverb.* —**flatness,** *noun.*

flat² *noun, plural* **flats.** a group of rooms on one floor; an apartment.

flat•fish [flat′fish′] *noun, plural* **flatfish** or **flatfishes.** a fish that has a thin, flat body and lives along the bottom in shallow ocean water. Flatfish have both eyes on the upper side of the body, which is dark-colored while the lower side is white.

flat•ten [flat′ən] *verb,* **flattened, flattening.** to make or become flat: "Again Holmes *flattened* out the paper upon his plate." (A. Conan Doyle)

flat•ter [flat′ər] *verb,* **flattered, flattering. 1.** to try to please a person by giving praise that is false or exaggerated: Eddie always *flatters* his older sister about how smart she is so that she'll help him do his homework. **2.** to please or make happy: "I was *flattered* that she wanted to speak to me, because of all the older girls I admired her most." (F. Scott Fitzgerald) **3.** to make something seem more attractive than it really is: Grandpa says that photograph *flatters* him because it makes him look much younger.

flat•ter•y [flat′ər ē] *noun.* kind words or praise that are not true or are not deserved: In the fable of "The Fox and the Crow," the fox uses *flattery* to get some cheese away from the crow.

fla•vor [flā′vər] *noun, plural* **flavors. 1.** a certain quality that a food has which is sensed by the tongue and mouth; a particular taste: My favorite *flavor* of ice cream is chocolate. **2.** a special quality that a thing has which makes it different from others: The room was decorated with ship's models, paintings of the ocean, and other objects that gave it the *flavor* of the sea. —*verb,* **flavored, flavoring.** to add something to give taste or flavor.

Pronunciation Key: T–Z			
t	ten; date	v	very; live
th	think	w	win; away
<u>th</u>	these	y	you
u	cut; butter	z	zoo; cause
ur	turn; bird	zh	measure
(Turn the page for more information.)			

F

flavor As you read these writing articles, you will often find us speaking of "metaphors," "images," or "figures of speech" —the twisting or turning of words to create fresh pictures in the mind. Note this use of the word *flavor:* "Maloney was fond of saying that every good lie must be *flavored* with a little truth, as whiskey with water." (John McGahern) "Whiskey" represents a lie and "water" the truth. How about this choice of words? "Another mountain rose, desolate with *dead rocks* and starving little black bushes." (John Steinbeck) He chose to call the rocks "dead" and the bushes "starving." While a bush can't really starve, it can wither and die. One more: "It was too far to see any details; it seemed to me then simply a low-lying patch of *dim* blue in the *uncertain* blue-gray sea." (H. G. Wells) Do you see how the whole sentence leads up to the words "dim" and "uncertain"?

fla•vor•ing [flā vər ing] *noun, plural* **flavorings.** something that is added to give flavor to food or drinks.

flaw [flô] *noun, plural* **flaws. 1.** a crack, scratch, or other mark that takes away from the value of something: The jeweler found only one small *flaw* in the diamond. **2.** a small fault or problem: The movie had a good plot except for one *flaw*—they never explained how the detective got out of the locked room. —*verb,* **flawed, flawing:** to cause to have a flaw: The skater's beautiful performance was *flawed* only by one slight fall she took at the end.

flax [flaks] *noun.* a plant with blue flowers and long, slender stems. Fibers from this plant are spun into thread that is then used to weave cloth. Flax seed is used to make oil and animal feed.

flea [flē] *noun, plural* **fleas.** a small, wingless insect that lives by sucking blood from animals and people. Fleas can carry diseases which they pass on by biting through the skin.

flee [flē] *verb,* **fled, fleeing.** to run or get away: "The bird took fright and *fled* with a clatter of wings." (George Orwell)

fleece [flēs] *noun.* the wool coat of a sheep. —*verb,* **fleeced, fleecing.** to cut the fleece off a sheep.

fleet[1] [flēt] *noun, plural* **fleets. 1.** a group of naval warships under one command. **2.** any group of ships or vehicles: a *fleet* of buses.

fleet[2] *adjective,* **fleeter, fleetest.** moving very fast; swift: The jaguar is a *fleet* animal. —**fleetly,** *adverb.*

flesh [flesh] *noun.* **1.** the part of the body that covers the bones; muscles and other tissues. **2.** the meat of an animal used as food. **3.** the part of fruits and vegetables that can be eaten.

flew [floo] *verb.* the past tense of **fly.**

flex [fleks] *verb,* **flexed, flexing.** to bend and move a muscle or a certain part of the body:

"He *flexed* and un*flexed* his arm muscles." (James T. Farrell)

flex•i•ble [flek′ sə bəl] *adjective,* *more/most.* **1.** able to bend easily without breaking: The baby's toy was made of *flexible* plastic. **2.** able to change to meet different needs or conditions: The hours for that job are *flexible,* as long as you work 40 hours a week.

flick [flik] *noun, plural* **flicks.** a quick, snapping movement: a *flick* of the wrist. —*verb,* **flicked, flicking.** to make such a movement: He *flicked* on the porch light.

flick•er[1] [flik′ ər] *verb,* **flickered, flickering. 1.** to shine or glow with an uneven light: "There was no light but the endless *flickering* of stars." (Marjorie Kinnan Rawlings) **2.** to move back and forth in a quick, uneven way: "He had difficulty controlling the thoughts that *flickered* through his mind." (Walter Farley) —*noun, plural* **flickers.** a flickering light or action: "Her eyes were closed against the *flicker* of the television screen." (Joan Didion)

flicker[2] *noun, plural* **flickers.** a North American woodpecker with a spotted breast and yellow or red markings on the head and tail.

fleet A famous world-wide cruise of the American Great White Fleet in 1908. Here the ships are entering the harbor of Rio de Janiero, Brazil.

fli•er [flī′ ər] *noun, plural* **fliers.** (also spelled **flyer**) **1.** anything that flies, such as a bird or insect. **2.** a person who flies in an airplane. **3.** a single piece of paper with an advertisement or announcement printed on it.

flight[1] [flīt] *noun, plural* **flights. 1.** the use of wings to move through the air: the *flight* of an eagle. **2.** a movement through the air by some type of aircraft: the *flight* of a balloon or rocket. **3.** a scheduled trip by airplane: *Flight* 155 goes from New York to San Diego. **4.** something that goes above or beyond the usual limits: a *flight* of fancy, *flights* of the imagination. **5.** the steps leading from one floor of a building to another.

flight[2] *noun, plural* **flights.** the act of running or breaking away to be free; an escape.

flight attendant a person who is a member of the crew of a passenger airplane, and whose job is to give information and instructions, serve meals and drinks, and perform other services to aid the passengers. ♦ Also called a STEWARD or STEWARDESS.

flim•sy [flim′ zē] *adjective,* **flimsier, flimsiest.** light and weak; likely to break or give way: The toy was so *flimsy* that it fell apart the first time he played with it.

flinch [flinch] *verb,* **flinched, flinching.** to suddenly back away in fear or pain: The boy *flinched* when the dog jumped toward him.

fling [fling] *verb,* **flung, flinging.** to throw or move something with great force: "She spun the car around so sharply Stephen was almost *flung* out of the seat." (Katherine Anne Porter) —*noun, plural* **flings. 1.** the act of flinging; a sudden throw. **2.** a short time for doing something that one enjoys: "She was only having her *fling.* When the time came she'd settle down and make a good wife." (Pearl Buck)

flint [flint] *noun, plural* **flints.** a hard rock that will make a spark of fire when it is scratched against a piece of iron or steel. Flint was used to start fires before matches were invented, and is still used today in cigarette lighters. Flint is a type of QUARTZ.

flip [flip] *verb,* **flipped, flipping. 1.** to turn over in the air: to *flip* a pancake in a pan. **2.** to toss or move with a quick motion of the hand: to *flip* an electric light switch, to *flip* through the pages of a book. "He *flipped* the reins against the horse's shoulders and rode away." (John Steinbeck) —*noun, plural* **flips. 1.** a sudden move or toss in the air: A *flip* of a coin will decide which team kicks off. **2.** a somersault made from a standing position.

flip•per [flip′ ər] *noun, plural* **flippers. 1.** in some water animals, a wide, flat body part used in swimming. Whales and seals have flippers. **2.** a rubber shoe shaped somewhat like an animal's flipper, used by swimmers and skin divers; also called a FIN.

flirt [flurt] *verb,* **flirted, flirting. 1.** to act friendly to a member of the opposite sex in a light, playful way. **2.** to deal with something serious in a light or playful way: He *flirted* with danger by walking too close to the edge of the cliff. —*noun, plural* **flirts.** a person who likes to flirt with members of the opposite sex.

flit [flit] *verb,* **flitted, flitting.** to move about rapidly and lightly: "Mrs. Parsons' eyes *flitted* nervously from Winston to the children and back again." (George Orwell) "A picture of three boys walking along the bright beach *flitted* through his mind." (William Golding)

float Two types of floats—a diving float kept above water by empty barrels and an inflatable plastic float.

float [flōt] *verb,* **floated, floating. 1.** to be held up by the surface of a liquid or by the air: She *floated* on her back in the lake. "White clouds *floated* over a pink sky." (Katherine Mansfield) **2.** to move on a current of air or water: The boat *floated* away from the dock. —*noun, plural* **floats. 1.** something that floats on the water, such as a cork on a fishing line. **2.** a platform on a lake for diving or sunbathing. **3.** a stage or platform on wheels that carries an exhibit in a parade.

flock [fläk] *noun, plural* **flocks. 1.** a number of animals of the same kind that live or move

F

Pronunciation Key: [ə] Symbol

The [ə] or *schwa* sound occurs in syllables without an accent. It can be spelled with any vowel, such as **a** in above, **e** in listen, **i** in pencil, **o** in melon, **u** in circus. It can also be a combination of vowels, such as **io** in action, **ai** in mountain, **iou** in precious.

(Turn the page for more information.)

F

together: a *flock* of sheep, a *flock* of geese. **2.** a large group of people: A *flock* of teenagers waited in line to buy tickets for the rock concert. **3.** a group of people who follow a certain minister or other religious leader. —*verb,* **flocked, flocking.** to move together in a group or crowd: The voters *flocked* to the polls to cast their ballots on Election Day.

floe [flō] *noun, plural* **floes.** a large, flat piece of floating ice.

flood [flud] *noun, plural* **floods. 1.** a large flow of water over dry land, especially one that causes loss or damage. **2.** any large outpouring like a flood: The writer received a *flood* of angry letters after he wrote an article attacking President John Kennedy. —*verb,* **flooded, flooding. 1.** to cover over with water: The river overflowed its banks and *flooded* the countryside. **2.** to fill or pour into in large amounts or numbers: "The full moon *flooded* the fields with light . . ." (Walter De la Mare) **3.** to supply too much fuel to an engine, so that it does not work properly.

flood The first meaning of *flood* was "the flowing in of the tide," as in Shakespeare's famous line, "There is a tide in the affairs of men, which taken at the flood leads on to victory."

floor [flôr] *noun, plural* **floors. 1.** the bottom surface of a room that a person walks or stands on. **2.** the bottom surface of anything: the ocean *floor.* It's a 1500-foot drop to the *floor* of the canyon. **3.** one level or story of a building: Miss Wright's office is on the tenth *floor.* —*verb,* **floored, flooring. 1.** to build a floor in a house or building. **2.** to knock down to the floor: The boxer *floored* his opponent with a hard punch. **3.** *Informal.* to confuse or surprise: Most of the test was easy, but that last question really *floored* me.

flop [fläp] *verb,* **flopped, flopping. 1.** to move or jump about in an awkward way: The fish began to *flop* wildly as the fisherman lifted it out of the water. **2.** to fall or drop in a loose, relaxed way: After her long trip she *flopped* into bed and fell asleep right away. —*noun, plural* **flops. 1.** a flopping movement or noise. **2.** *Informal.* a complete failure: The new television program was a real *flop* and was taken off the air after only three weeks.

floppy disk [fläp′ ē] a thin, flexible piece of plastic that has computer information stored on it. It can be fitted into a computer to display the data or perform a function.

flo•ral [flôr′ əl] *adjective.* having to do with or like flowers: a *floral* arrangement, wallpaper with *floral* designs.

Florence The Duomo, a famous church in Florence.

Flor•ence [flôr′ əns] a city in central Italy. *Population:* 460,000. —**Florentine** [flôr′ən tīn′], *adjective; noun.*

Flor•i•da [flôr′ i də] a state in the southeastern U.S. It is a long peninsula between the Atlantic Ocean and the Gulf of Mexico. *Capital:* Tallahassee. *Nickname:* "Sunshine State." *Area:* 58,500 square miles. *Population:* 10,440,000.

flo•rist [flôr′ ist] *noun, plural* **florists.** a person who is in the business of growing or selling flowers and small plants.

floun•der[1] [floun′ dər] *verb,* **floundered, floundering.** to move or act in a clumsy way; struggle or stumble: The horse *floundered* in the water as it tried to climb up the river bank. The actor *foundered* when he couldn't remember his line.

flounder[2] *noun, plural* **flounder** or **flounders.** a small saltwater flatfish that is often eaten as food.

flour [flour] *noun, plural* **flours.** a powder or meal made by grinding and sifting cereal grains, especially wheat. Flour is used to make bread, cake, cookies, spaghetti, and other foods.

flour•ish [flur′ ish] *verb,* **flourished, flourishing.**

1. to grow or develop well: "He was prepared to make gardens *flourish* where deserts had been." (Doris Lessing) **2.** to be at its most active or successful point: The Aztec civilization *flourished* in Mexico in the 1400's and early 1500's. **3.** to wave about in a bold or showy way: "This photo proves my client is innocent!" the lawyer shouted, *flourishing* it in front of the jury. —*noun, plural* **flourishes. 1.** a bold or showy display of something: He held the door open for her with an exaggerated *flourish*. **2.** a fancy addition or decoration, especially in a person's handwriting.

ENZA. Influenza is a virus disease that spreads easily and resembles a bad cold. Its symptoms include a fever, a cough, and muscle aches.

flue [flo̅o̅] *noun, plural* **flues.** an enclosed passageway that provides an escape for smoke or hot air. A fireplace or furnace has a flue.

fluff [fluf] *noun, plural* **fluffs.** light, soft material, like a cotton ball or the fur of a kitten. —*verb,* **fluffed, fluffing.** to make into a light, soft mass: She *fluffed* up the pillows when she made the bed. —**fluffy,** *adjective:* "Almanzo loved light, *fluffy* buckwheat pancakes . . ." (Laura Ingalls Wilder)

flout/flaunt Any book on correct English is sure to have an article on the difference between *flout* and *flaunt*. These words are not common. Our Word Survey shows that neither word is used often enough to qualify for entry in this dictionary. In case you should ever encounter them in reading, you can tell them apart this way. *Flout* means to defy something. *Flaunt* means to show off. They are often used incorrectly. "55-mph law here to stay, but drivers *flaunt* it every day." (Headline in the *San Diego Union*) That should have been *flout*. "I know you're happy you found that money, but don't *flout* it by running around waving it in the air." That should be *flaunt*.

flow [flō] *verb,* **flowed, flowing. 1.** to move along in a stream: The Mississippi River *flows* south. Blood *flows* through the body. **2.** to move in a steady, smooth way: "A crowd *flowed* over London Bridge . . ." (T.S. Eliot) **3.** to move or hang in a loose, graceful way. ♦ Often used as an adjective: *flowing* hair, *flowing* handwriting. —*noun, plural* **flows.** the act of flowing: the *flow* of air from a fan, the *flow* of electricity through a wire, the *flow* of traffic along a highway.

flow•er [flou′ər] *noun, plural* **flowers. 1.** the part of a plant that blooms and produces seeds or fruit; a blossom. Many flowers are beautifully colored and are used as decoration. **2.** a plant with flowers, especially a small plant grown for the beauty of its flowers. **3.** the finest part or best time of something: During the 1400's, Renaissance art was in full *flower* in the city of Florence. —*verb,* **flowered, flowering. 1.** to produce or have flowers; blossom: Most plants *flower* in the spring. **2.** to come to full growth; flourish.

flow•er•y [flou′ər ē] *adjective.* **1.** having many flowers: The hillside was a *flowery* mass of color. **2.** using fancy or showy language: In the 1800's politicians often had *flowery* nicknames, such as "The Plumed Knight" (James G. Blaine) or "The Silver-Tongued Orator" (William Jennings Bryan).

flown [flōn] *verb.* the past participle of **fly.**

flu [flo̅o̅] *noun.* a short form of the word INFLU-

flu•id [flo̅o̅′ id] *noun, plural* **fluids.** a substance that is able to flow or move freely; a liquid or gas. A fluid takes on the shape of the container that holds it. —*adjective, more/most.* **1.** capable of flowing; not solid or rigid: Cheese becomes *fluid* when it is heated. **2.** having a relaxed, flowing appearance or style: the *fluid* movements of a great ballet dancer.

flung [flung] *verb.* the past form of **fling.**

fluo•res•cent [flə res′ ənt] *adjective.* able to give out light when acted on by certain forms of energy, especially ULTRAVIOLET RAYS. A **fluorescent lamp** is a narrow tube that sends out a white light when electricity passes through fluorescent materials in the tube.

fluo•ride [flôr′ īd] *noun, plural* **fluorides.** a chemical that is added to drinking water and toothpaste for the purpose of reducing tooth decay. Fluorides are compounds of the chemical element **fluorine** [flôr′ ēn] with other elements. ♦ The process of adding fluoride to drinking water is called **fluoridation** [flôr′ ə dā′ shən].

F

Pronunciation Key: Accent Marks

[′] is the normal accent mark. It shows where the main stress falls on a word.
[′] is a secondary accent mark. It shows a lighter stress than the primary accent. For example:

tel • e • vis • ion [tel′ə vizh′ən]
(Turn the page for more information.)

F

flur•ry [flur′ē] *noun, plural* **flurries. 1.** a short, light burst of wind, snow, or rain. **2.** a sudden outburst of feeling or activity; a stir: There was a *flurry* of activity in the office when the new boss suddenly walked in.

flush¹ [flush] *verb,* **flushed, flushing. 1.** to turn red in the face because of a sudden rush of blood to the skin; blush: "The prince's face *flushed* with anger . . ." (Mark Twain) **2.** to wash or rinse something with a flow of water. **3.** to scare out of hiding: The dog *flushed* the rabbit from the underbrush.

flush² *adjective; adverb.* being level or even: We pushed the sofa *flush* against the wall.

flus•ter [flus′tər] *verb,* **flustered, flustering.** to make nervous or confused: The yelling of the crowd *flustered* the goalie and he completely missed an easy shot.

flute [floot] *noun, plural* **flutes.** a musical instrument made up of a long, metal pipe with several holes that are covered by the fingers or by metal parts called keys.

flut•ter [flut′ər] *verb,* **fluttered, fluttering. 1.** to flap the wings so as to move in a rapid and uneven way. The butterfly *fluttered* from flower to flower. **2.** to move with a quick, uneven motion: "Flags of both countries . . . *fluttered* against the sky." (Marguerite Henry) **3.** to go about in a restless or nervous way: Ann *fluttered* around the apartment, trying to straighten things up before her guests arrived. —*noun, plural* **flutters. 1.** a quick, uneven movement. **2.** a state of nervous excitement.

fly¹ [flī] *verb,* **flew, flown, flying. 1.** to move through the air by means of wings, or by the force of wind. **2.** to move or travel through the air in an aircraft: to *fly* to Los Angeles, to *fly* food and medicine to the victims of a flood. **3.** to move or float in the air: The kite *flew* higher as she let out the string. **4.** to move or pass quickly: The dog *flew* out the door and ran after the neighbor's cat. Is it Friday already? This week has really *flown* by. **5.** in baseball, to hit a ball high into the air. ◆ The past form of this meaning is usually **flied**: The batter *flied* out to left field to end the inning. —*noun, plural* **flies. 1.** a cloth flap that covers a zipper or row of buttons on a pair of pants or other clothing. **2.** a baseball hit in the air; also called a **fly ball.**

fly² *noun, plural* **flies. 1.** a type of flying insect having a single pair of wings. The most common fly is the housefly, but mosquitoes and gnats are also flies. **2.** any of various other flying insects, such as the butter*fly* or dragon*fly*. **3.** a fishhook decorated with small feathers and

other ornaments to look like a fly or other insect.

fly•er [flī′ər] *noun, plural* **flyers.** another spelling of **flier.**

flying fish an ocean fish with side fins that look like wings. It uses these fins to jump up and glide above the water.

flying fish

flying saucer a saucer-shaped object that is said to fly across the sky, supposedly flown by beings from outer space. People claim to have seen flying saucers at various places in the world.

flying squirrel a type of North American squirrel having winglike folds of skin on each side of the body that allow it to make long, sailing leaps through the air.

FM one of the two main types of radio broadcasting signal, along with AM. In FM radio, the frequency of the radio wave is made higher or lower to match the sound being broadcast.

foam [fōm] *noun, plural* **foams.** a mass of tiny bubbles. Foam can be found on the top of a soft drink or inside the mouth of an animal that is sick or very hot. Some fire extinguishers contain a special foam for putting out fires. —*verb,* **foamed, foaming.** to form into foam: "The boiling beans roared, *foaming* up, but did not quite run over." (Laura Ingalls Wilder).

foam rubber a soft kind of rubber full of tiny bubbles of air, used for making cushions, pillows, and mattresses.

fo•cus [fō′kəs] *noun, plural* **focuses. 1.** the point in the distance at which several rays of light meet after going through a glass lens or being reflected in a mirror. **2.** a position in which something must be placed in order to be seen or understood clearly: The TV is out of *focus* and the picture looks really fuzzy. **3.** a center of activity or interest: Tomorrow's football game was the *focus* of attention at school today. —*verb,* **focused, focusing. 1.** to adjust a lens or the eyes to get a sharper image or picture: to *focus* a pair of binoculars. **2.** to direct or fix attention on: "He breathed the sweet night air and *focused* his senses and his wits." (Ian Fleming)

fod•der [fäd′ ər] *noun, plural* **fodders.** dry, rough food, such as corn stalks and hay, given to cattle and other farm animals.

foe [fō] *noun, plural* **foes.** an enemy or opponent: "Heyward had given one of his pistols to Hawkeye, and together they rushed . . . toward their *foes.*" (James Fenimore Cooper)

fog A layer of fog settles over farmland in Ketcham, Idaho, near the Sawtooth National Forest.

fog [fôg *or* fäg] *noun, plural* **fogs. 1.** a misty cloud of small water drops that collects close to the ground or over a body of water. Fog can appear when winds blow warm, most air over a cooler surface. **2.** a confused state of mind: I'm sorry I didn't hear what you said—I've been in such a *fog* all morning. —*verb,* **fogged, fogging.** to cover with a fog; produce a fog: She slowed the car because the windshield had *fogged* up.

fog•gy [fôg′ ē *or* fäg′ ē] *adjective,* **foggier, foggiest. 1.** full of fog; misty: a *foggy* morning. **2.** not clear; confused: a *foggy* idea.

foil¹ [foil] *verb,* **foiled, foiling.** to prevent a person from carrying out a plan; stop from succeeding: The guards *foiled* the prisoners' attempt to escape.

foil² *noun, plural* **foils.** metal that has been flattened into a very thin, paper-like sheet: Aluminum *foil* is used to wrap food.

fold [fōld] *verb,* **folded, folding. 1.** to bend something over itself one or more times: to *fold* a letter before putting it into an envelope, to *fold* clean clothes after taking them out of the dryer. ◆ Often used as an adjective: a *folding* chair or table. **2.** to draw close to the body: The

bird *folded* its wings. **3.** to fail or close: That business will have to *fold* if sales don't pick up soon. —*noun, plural* **folds.** a part that is folded, or a mark made by folding.

fold•er [fōl′ dər] *noun, plural* **folders. 1.** a folded piece of stiff paper or plastic, used to keep loose sheets of paper together. **2.** a booklet made of pieces of folded paper: The travel agent gave us several *folders* on vacations in Europe.

fo•li•age [fō′ lē ij *or* fō′ lij] *noun.* all the leaves on a certain tree or plant: The Swamp Maple tree has bright red *foliage* in the fall.

folk [fōk] *noun, plural* **folk** or **folks. 1.** people of a certain type or group: city *folk,* young *folk,* poor *folks.* **2.** a person's parents or other relatives: Cindy brought her boyfriend home to meet her *folks.* **3.** people in general: Most *folks* around this town are friendly and down-to-earth. —*adjective.* having to do with the ordinary people of an area, especially farm people, and with the way of life that they have passed down from one generation to another: "Feed a cold and starve a fever" is a saying in *folk* medicine. ◆ **Folk music** and **folk songs** are played and sung by such people.

F

folk art The Pennsylvania Dutch region of eastern Pennsylvania is known for its colorful folk art.

folk art a type of art that is created by ordinary or unknown people rather than by trained artists, and that includes common objects and tools as well as paintings and sculptures.

Pronunciation Key: A–F			
a	and; hat	ch	chew; such
ā	ate; stay	d	dog; lid
â	care; air	e	end; yet
ä	father; hat	ē	she; each
b	boy; cab	f	fun; off

(Turn the page for more information.)

folk dance a traditional dance developed and passed down by the people of a certain country or region. Many folk dances began hundreds of years ago as ceremonies or celebrations.

folk•lore [fōk′ lôr′] *noun.* the stories and beliefs handed down by a people over the years.

folk tale a story that was told hundreds of years ago and that has been passed down over time by word of mouth: "Cinderella" and "Jack and the Beanstalk" are well-known *folk tales.*

fond [fänd] *adjective,* **fonder, fondest. 1.** (used with **of**) having a warm or loving feeling toward: "They were both *fond of* music and went to the opera together." (Willa Cather) **2.** showing this feeling: She has *fond* memories of the summers she spent at Cape Cod. **—fondly,** *adverb.* **—fondness,** *noun.*

fon•dle [fän′ dəl] *verb,* **fondled, fondling.** to stroke or handle in a loving way; caress: Laurie *fondled* the little kitten.

> **folk tales** The oldest form of literature is the folk tale. These stories originally were *oral* literature—that is, passed along by one person telling aloud the story to others, who repeat the story from memory. Folk tales began so far back in human history that it's not possible to date them. Idries Shah, a noted collector of tales, has published an Egyptian story that was first written down over 3000 years ago. Research by Shah and others has shown that the same basic stories are found all over the world, at all times in history. For example, the Indians of eastern North America told of a poor young girl, Oochigeaskw, who is treated very badly by her two cruel sisters. Both sisters hope to marry a handsome young man, but he ends up marrying Oochigeaskw instead. Does this sound familiar? It should—it's an Indian version of "Cinderella." In fact, there are more than 300 different versions of "Cinderella." How was the same story told in so many places? No one knows. But there is this possibility: in storytelling, there are not hundreds upon hundreds of possible plots or story lines. Aristotle, the Greek philosopher, said that there are only four main causes of events and that all others are variations of these four.

fol•low [fäl′ ō] *verb,* **followed, following. 1.** to come or go after: Jackie's dog *followed* him to the playground. March *follows* February. **2.** to move or continue along a certain course: *Follow* this road until you come to the main highway. **3.** to act according to; obey: to *follow* a person's advice. **4.** to watch or observe closely: You've never heard of Yogi Berra? You must not *follow* baseball. **5.** to understand clearly: Can you explain that? I don't *follow* you.

fol•low•er [fäl′ ō ər] *noun, plural* **followers. 1.** someone who follows or supports a person, cause, or idea: a *follower* of Ronald Reagan, a *follower* of the Muslim religion. **2.** any person or thing that follows: Timmy does whatever his friends do, because he's such a *follower.*

fol•low•ing [fäl′ ō ing] *noun, plural* **followings. 1.** a group of people who follow or support some person, cause, or idea: Many American authors have a large *following* in the Soviet Union, such as Jack London. **2. the following.** the things listed next. —*adjective:* coming right after; next: The plane leaves at 10:00 P.M. and gets to New York the *following* morning.

fol•ly [fäl′ ē] *noun, plural* **follies.** a complete lack of good judgment; being foolish: It was sheer *folly* for him to buy that worthless desert land in hopes of finding gold on it.

food [fōōd] *noun, plural* **foods. 1.** something that people eat, especially something solid, as opposed to a liquid. **2.** any substance that living things take in to keep them alive, give them strength and energy, and help them grow.

fool [fōōl] *noun, plural* **fools. 1.** a person who does not have good judgment or good sense; a silly or stupid person. **2.** in former times, a person at the court of a king who was supposed to amuse people by doing silly things; a jester. —*verb,* **fooled, fooling. 1.** to act dishonestly toward; trick; deceive: "I know you're thinking already how you can *fool* me and break the promise you've just made." (Eugene O'Neill) **2.** to speak in a joking way; pretend: We're not really moving away . . . I was only *fooling* when I said it. **3.** to act in a playful or silly way: John got in trouble for *fooling* around in class. Don't *fool* with the fire alarm—it might go off.

fool•ish [fōō′ lish] *adjective,* more/most. **1.** showing a lack of good judgment or good sense; acting like a fool: It would be *foolish* of him to try to go up the mountain alone, since he has no experience as a climber. **2.** like a fool: She felt *foolish* when she realized she'd poured orange juice instead of milk on her cereal.

foot [foot] *noun, plural* **feet. 1.** the body part attached to the end of the leg, used for standing or moving. **2.** something thought of as like a foot, because it is located at the end or lower part: "He lay curled up at the *foot* of the stairs." (James Joyce) **3.** a unit of length equal to 12 inches.

foot•ball [foot′bôl′] *noun, plural* **footballs. 1.** a game played on a large field by two teams of eleven players each. The team that has the ball tries to carry or kick it over the other team's goal line. **2.** the ball used in this game. **3.** in countries other than the U.S. and Canada, the game of soccer.

foot•hill [foot′hil′] *noun, plural* **foothills.** a low hill at the base of a large mountain or mountain range.

foot•ing [foot′ing] *noun, plural* **footings. 1.** a safe placing of the feet, or a safe surface for standing: "The waves grew so high that the people under the bridge could no longer keep their *footing*." (John Hersey) **2.** a position or relationship: The new business is on a sound *footing*.

foot•note [foot′nōt′] *noun, plural* **footnotes.** a note at the bottom of a page that refers to something written on that page.

leave *for* school in the morning. **3.** in order to serve the purpose stated: to eat fish *for* dinner, to use an old box *for* a table. **4.** to benefit the person or thing stated: to vote *for* Laura as class president. **5.** because of the reason stated: to get an 'A' *for* excellent work, to jump *for* joy. **6.** considering the thing stated: Today's very cold *for* May. She's quite a good swimmer *for* a six-year old. **7.** in place of the thing stated: What's the French word *for* "bread?" —*conjunction:* "My heart broke again, *for* it was plain that I had got to learn this troublesome river both ways."(Mark Twain)

for•age [fôr′ij] *noun.* food for cattle, horses, and other farm animals, such as grass or small plants. —*verb,* **foraged, foraging.** to move about in search of food or other supplies: "When the snow continued day after day, it became necessary for him and Sandy to go *foraging*." (Beatrix Potter)

for•bid [fər bid′] *verb,* **forbade, forbidden, forbidding.** to order not to do; rule against; prohibit: The city zoning law *forbids* the use of that land for stores or other businesses. ◆ Often used as an adjective: A part of Peking, China is

F

> **footnotes** Printers call the top of a page "head," and the bottom is the "foot." Thus the name *footnote,* which is a note at the bottom of a page of text. Why put anything at the bottom? Usually, a writer wants to show where he got his information, or he wants to include an interesting bit of information without letting it interfere with the flow of the main text. To use a footnote, put a small number "1" after the end of a sentence and then repeat the number at the bottom the page and make the note. Here's an example: "A recent book explains how the Indians kept track of time by watching the way a shadow from the sun slowly changed position."[1] (If you have more than one footnote on the same page, use the numbers 2, 3, and so on.)
>
> ---
>
> [1]Evan S. Connell, Son of the Morning Star, p. 303.

foot•print [foot′print′] *noun, plural* **footprints.** an outline or impression made by a person's foot: to make *footprints* in the sand, to track *footprints* across a kitchen floor.

foot•step [foot′step′] *noun, plural* **footsteps. 1.** a forward movement made by placing one foot ahead of the other. **2.** the sound made by taking a step: "Suddenly she heard Alban's *footstep*." (Somerset Maugham) **3. follow in someone's footsteps.** to follow or imitate the example of another person.

for [fôr] *preposition.* **1.** to the distance, time, or amount stated: to walk *for* three miles, a magazine that sells *for* two dollars. **2.** directed to the person or thing stated: a movie *for* children, to

known as the *Forbidden* City because at one time Westerners were not allowed to go there.

for•bid•ding [fər bid′ing] *adjective, more/most.* looking dangerous or unfriendly; causing fear: "The landscape is absolutely *forbidding*, with mountains towering on all four sides." (James Baldwin)

	Pronunciation Key; G–N		
g	give; big	k	kind; cat; back
h	hold	l	let; ball
i	it; this	m	make; time
ī	ice; my	n	not; own
j	jet; gem; edge	ng	having
	(Turn the page for more information.)		

F

force [fôrs] *noun, plural* **forces. 1.** the ability to cause something to move or to happen; power; energy: The *force* of the wind blew down several trees. **2.** in science, anything that changes the size or shape of an object, or makes it move or stop moving: The *force* of gravity causes things to fall to the ground. **3.** the use of physical power on a person or thing: The policemen had to use *force* to get the prisoner into the police car. **4.** a power that influences the mind or thoughts: Do you really like that cereal, or do you just eat it by *force* of habit? **5.** a group of people organized for some purpose: The IBM Company has a large sales *force*. **6. forces.** an army or other military unit: U.S. naval *forces* were on patrol in the Indian Ocean. —*verb,* **forced, forcing. 1.** to use force against some object: "The wind is blowing so hard that they have to *force* the door shut behind them." (Ann Beattie) **2.** to make a person do something: The robbers *forced* him to open the safe. The movie was so boring that she had to *force* herself to stay awake.

front part of the arm between the elbow and the wrists.

fore•cast [fôr′kast′] *verb,* **forecast** or **forecasted, forecasting.** to tell what is likely to happen; predict: The TV weatherman *forecast* light rain for tomorrow. —*noun, plural* **forecasts.** the act of forecasting; a prediction.

fore•fa•ther [fôr′fä′thər] *noun, plural* **forefathers.** a relative in the distant past; an ancestor: "I am a Shawnee. My *forefathers* were warriors." (Tecumseh)

fore•fin•ger [fôr′fing′gər] *noun, plural* **forefingers.** the finger closest to the thumb, also known as the index finger.

fore•ground [fôr′ground′] *noun, plural* **foregrounds. 1.** the part of a photograph or a painting that seems to be nearest to the person looking at it. **2.** *also,* **forefront.** a position of attention or importance.

fore•head [fôr′əd or fôr′hed′] *noun, plural* **foreheads.** the upper part of the face, between the eyes and the hair.

foreign words "I heard my grandmother's voice: 'What are you making a *tsimmes?*' It was what she would ask my mother when, say, I had cut myself while doing something I shouldn't have done, and her daughter was busy bawling me out." (Philip Roth) The word *tsimmes* is probably new to you—it's from Yiddish, a German-based language spoken by some Jews. Here it means "a fuss" or "a big deal." Writers may use foreign words to show how a certain character speaks, as Roth does here. Or they may use the foreign version of a familiar expression. Edgar Allan Poe's story "The Cask of Amontillado" ends with "*In pace requiescat!*" a Latin phrase meaning "Rest in peace!" There's a danger in using too many foreign expressions. You can confuse your readers, for one thing. For another, there's the risk of a writer simply showing off her or his thinking in another language. Nobody wants to read something like this: "You are a junak," his mother told him proudly, "Fala Boju," but he was embarrassed and asked her to stop, saying "Dosta." (The language here is Serbo-Croatian.)

force•ful [fôrs′fəl] *adjective, more/most.* having the power or force to influence people: a *forceful* argument. Martin Luther King was a *forceful* speaker. —**forcefully,** *adverb.* —**forcefulness,** *noun.*

ford [fôrd] *noun, plural* **fords.** an area of a river or stream that is shallow enough to walk or ride across. —*verb,* **forded, fording.** to cross at a shallow place: to *ford* a stream.

Ford [fôrd] **1. Gerald R.,** born 1913, the thirty-eighth president of the United States, from 1974 to 1977. **2. Henry,** 1863–1947, American automobile manufacturer.

fore [fôr] *adjective; adverb.* in or toward the front; forward: the *fore* part of an aircraft. —*noun.* the front part, especially of a ship.

fore•arm [fôr′ärm′] *noun, plural* **forearms.** the

for•eign [fôr′ən] *adjective.* **1.** away from one's own country: A passport gives a person permission for *foreign* travel. **2.** relating to another country: Students at that school have to take a *foreign* language, such as French or German. **3.** not belonging naturally: a cinder or other *foreign* substance in the eye.

for•eign•er [fôr′ə nər] *noun, plural* **foreigners.** a person who is in a country other than his or her own.

fore•man [fôr′mən] *noun, plural* **foremen. 1.** a person whose job is to be in charge of a group of workers at a factory, warehouse, farm, or the like. **2.** the member of a jury who acts as its chairman and spokesman.

fore•most [fôr′mōst′] *adjective.* most important; leading: Leontyne Price is one of the *foremost* opera singers of modern times. That book has some funny parts, but it's first and *foremost* a mystery story.

fore•run•ner [fôr′run′ər] *noun, plural* **forerunners.** something that comes before or prepares the way for something else: Silent movies were the *forerunners* of today's sound films.

fore•see [fôr′sē′] *verb,* **foresaw, foreseen, foreseeing.** to expect something to happen before it does; see or know ahead of time: The city hadn't *foreseen* that the new school would be so crowded, and now they have to add extra classrooms.

fore•sight [fôr′sīt′] *noun.* the ability to foresee things; being able to look ahead and prepare for the future: Mom had the *foresight* to bring along extra gas in case we ran out.

forest Before the coming of the Europeans, much of the eastern half of North America was covered by deciduous forests such as this one in Michigan.

for•est [fôr′ist] *noun, plural* **forests.** a large area of land having many trees and other plants; woods.

fore•tell [fôr tel′] *verb,* **foretold, foretelling.** to tell something that will happen in the future: Some people believe it's possible to *foretell* events from the position of the stars.

for•ev•er [fôr ev′ər] *adverb.* **1.** without ever ending; for all time: In 1933 the famous scientist Albert Einstein left Germany *forever* and lived the rest of his life in the U.S. **2.** again and again; many times or all the time: I wish Jason would bring his own pen to school—he's *forever* borrowing mine.

fore•word [fôr′wərd] *noun, plural* **forewords.** a section at the front of a book that tells something about it.

for•feit [fôr′fit] *verb,* **forfeited, forfeiting.** to give up or lose something because of a fault or mistake: The Lions had to *forfeit* the baseball game because only six of their players showed up. —*noun, plural* **forfeits.** the thing that is given up or lost.

forge¹ [fôrj] *noun, plural* **forges.** a furnace used to heat metal so that it becomes soft and can be hammered into various shapes. —*verb,* **forged, forging. 1.** to shape metal by heating and hammering it. **2.** to create something with a lot of effort: to *forge* an alliance between two countries that were enemies. **3.** to make something false and pretend it is real: to *forge* another person's signature on a check.

forge² *verb,* **forged, forging.** to push on with slow but steady progress: The hikers *forged* ahead through the snowstorm.

for•ger•y [fôr′jər ē] *noun, plural* **forgeries.** the crime of making or copying something in a false way and presenting it as the real thing: That painting is supposed to be by Van Gogh, but it's actually a *forgery.* ♦ A person who commits this crime is a **forger.**

for•get [fər get′] *verb,* **forgot, forgotten, forgetting. 1.** to not be able to call to mind something that was once known; not remember: His first name's Jim, but I *forget* his last name. **2.** to fail to remember to do, bring, or get something: Carol *forgot* to write her name on her paper. Dad *forgot* his raincoat on the train.

for•get•ful [fər get′fəl] *adjective, more/most.* likely to forget; having a poor memory. —**forgetfulness,** *noun.*

for•give [fər giv′] *verb,* **forgave, forgiven, forgiving. 1.** to stop feeling angry toward and no longer want to blame or punish: The Bible often speaks of *forgiving* people for what they've done wrong. I hope you'll *forgive* me for getting here so late. **2.** to take away the obligation to pay back a debt: to *forgive* a loan. The act of forgiving or being willing to forgive someone is **forgiveness.**

for•go [fôr gō′] *verb,* **forwent, forgone, forgoing.** (also spelled **forego**) to give up; do without: They chose to *forgo* lunch and keep on working. "The adults decided to *forgo* the pool, but Uncle Karl insisted they change into swimsuits . . ." (John Barth)

F

Pronunciation Key: O–S			
ō	over; go	ou	out; town
ô	all; law	p	put; hop
oo	look; full	r	run; car
o͞o	pool; who	s	set; miss
oi	oil; boy	sh	show

(Turn the page for more information.)

fork [fôrk] *noun, plural* **forks. 1.** a small kitchen tool having two or more points attached to a handle, used to pick up and hold food. **2.** a large farm tool with a similar shape; a pitchfork. **3.** a point where something divides into two or more parts: a *fork* in the road. Birds often build nests in the *fork* of a tree. —*verb,* **forked, forking. 1.** to use a fork. **2.** to divide into branches: The road *forks* at the bottom of the hill.

for•lorn [fôr′lôrn′] *adjective, more/most.* sad and lonely: A *forlorn*-looking stray puppy followed him home from school.

form [fôrm] *noun, plural* **forms. 1.** the outward appearance that something has; the shape or outline of a thing: Certain road signs are in the *form* of a triangle. **2.** an example of something; a kind or type: Wind is a *form* of energy. Democracy is the *form* of government used in the U.S. **3.** a manner or style of doing something: The diver put in a lot of practice to improve his *form.* **4.** a piece of paper having blanks to be filled in with information. **5.** a certain way that a word is used: "Forged" and "forging" are *forms* of the verb "forge." —*verb,* **formed, forming. 1.** to be or cause to be in a certain form: She cut the paper to *form* a star. **2.** to take on a form; come to be: Ice had *formed* on the windows. A line *formed* outside the ticket office. **3.** to bring into being; cause to be: to *form* a club, to *form* a plan for doing something. **4.** to be the form or nature of; be: Desert *forms* most of the state of Nevada. **5.** to change the form of a word in a certain way: Most nouns in English *form* the plural by adding "s" or "es."

for•mal [fôr′məl] *adjective, more/most.* **1.** following strict customs or rules: Laura received a *formal* invitation to her cousin's wedding. The lawyers drew up a *formal* agreement for the sale of the house. **2.** suitable for wearing to an important ceremony or event: a *formal* dress. ♦ Also used as a noun: Lynn bought a new *formal* for the Emerald Ball. **3.** very proper and polite; not relaxed: The boss is really *formal* around the office and never calls people by their first names, even if he's known them for years. —**formally,** *adverb;* —**formality,** *noun.*

for•mat [fôr′mat′] *noun, plural* **formats. 1.** the size, shape, and style of a book or magazine: This dictionary has an alphabetical *format.* **2.** any system or arrangement for doing something; a plan.

for•ma•tion [fôr mā′shən] *noun, plural* **formations. 1.** the act of forming something: the *formation* of rust on iron, the *formation* of a person's character. **2.** something that is formed, especially in nature: a cloud *formation,* a rock *formation.* **3.** the particular way that something is formed: a group of aircraft flying in *formation,* a football team that uses the 'I' *formation.*

for•mer [fôr′mər] *adjective.* **1.** during the past; at an earlier time: *Former* Presidents of the U.S. are still protected by the Secret Service after they leave office. **2.** the first of two things that were just named or mentioned: "When Jane and Elizabeth were alone, the *former* . . . expressed to her sister how very much she admired him." (Jane Austen) —**formerly,** *adverb:* The Republic of Ireland was *formerly* part of Great Britain.

for•mu•la [fôr′myə lə] *noun, plural* **formulas. 1.** a set of symbols and figures used in chemistry or mathematics to express some rule: NaCl is the *formula* for salt. The *formula* for the area of a rectangle is: area = length × width. **2.** a list of the things that make up a medicine, fuel, or other substance: In 1985 many people became

---

formal language Formal writing uses longer sentences, longer words, and more abstract words than *informal* writing. Compare language with clothing. Formal clothing is for special, important occasions—a wedding, a funeral, a church service. Informal clothing is for casual use—relaxing or playing a sport. In a similar way, formal writing is used for serious topics, such as a political speech or a business report. Informal writing is for everyday situations—a letter to a friend, or a note left for a family member. Yet, if you have to choose formal or informal, the editors of this dictionary urge you to lean toward the informal. James Fenimore Cooper's famous novel *The Last of the Mohicans* has this passage: "By heaven! There is a human form, and it approaches. Stand to your arms, my friends, for we know not whom we encounter." This is a formal way of saying, "Get ready, men, there's a stranger coming." Now for some informal language, Harry Truman's first remarks when he became President after the death of Franklin D. Roosevelt: "Boys, did you ever have a load of hay fall on you?" When they told me yesterday what had happened, I felt like the moon, the stars and all the planets had fallen on me."

upset when the *formula* for Coca-Cola was changed. **3.** a certain set of methods that will lead to some result: a *formula* for success. **4.** a special milk-like liquid for a baby to drink.

for•sake [fôr sāk′] *verb,* **forsook, forsaken, forsaking.** to leave behind and give up completely: In Charles Dickens' book *Great Expectations,* the character Pip becomes a rich man in London and *forsakes* his old country friend Joe Gargery.

for•syth•i•a [fôr sith′ē ə] *noun, plural* **forsythias.** a shrub with yellow, bell-shaped flowers that grow in clusters and bloom in early spring.

fort An 1855 painting of Fort Pierre, a U.S. Army fort in the Dakota Territory. The city of Pierre later grew up here and became the capital of South Dakota.

fort [fôrt] *noun, plural* **forts. 1.** a strong building for defense against an enemy attack. **2.** an area where a large number of soldiers and weapons are regularly located.

forth [fôrth] *adverb.* **1.** forward in direction or time: ". . . men walking back and *forth* in the hallway inside the building . . ." (Jimmy Breslin) **2.** out into sight or view: "Young Goodman Brown came *forth* into the street . . ." (Nathaniel Hawthorne)

for•ti•fy [fôr′tə fī] *verb,* **fortified, fortifying. 1.** to make strong against possible attack: In early times cities were *fortified* by the building of high walls. **2.** to make stronger; give support to: He *fortified* himself with several cups of hot coffee before heading out into the cold. **3.** to add a substance to food to make it more healthful: Breakfast cereals are often *fortified* with vitamins and minerals.

for•tress [fôr′tris] *noun, plural* **fortresses.** a fort, especially a large fort.

for•tu•nate [fôr′chə nit] *adjective, more/most.* having or bringing a good result; lucky: I was

fortunate enough to get there just before they sold the last tickets. "You don't know how *fortunate* you are that your life is so pleasantly arranged for you." (Pearl Buck) **—fortunately,** *adverb:* She left her history notes on the bus, but *fortunately* the driver found them and gave them back to her.

for•tune [fôr′chən] *noun, plural* **fortunes. 1.** a large amount of money or property; great wealth: That movie star's house must be worth a *fortune.* **2.** something that will happen in the time to come; fate: Chinese restaurants often give people a *fortune* cookie that has a saying about the future, such as "You will take a long journey." **3.** chance or luck: to have good *fortune.*

for•tune-tell•er [fôr′chən tel′ər] *noun, plural* **fortune-tellers.** someone who claims to be able to tell what will happen in the future. Common methods of **fortune-telling** include looking in a crystal ball, studying a person's palm, picking out playing cards, and examining tea leaves.

Fort Worth a city in northeastern Texas. Population: 385,000.

fo•rum [fôr′əm] *noun, plural* **forums. 1.** *also,* **Forum.** in ancient Rome, a large public square that was the center of the city. Government meetings, business dealings, and other important activities took place in the Forum. **2.** a meeting where issues are discussed in public.

for•ward [fôr′wərd] *adverb.* (also spelled **forwards**) to or toward the front: The players lined up and each one stepped *forward* as his name was called. The police are hoping someone will come *forward* with information about the crime. **—adjective, more/most. 1.** at or near the front: The pilot sits in the *forward* part of the plane. **2.** acting in too bold a way; rude: It was a bit *forward* of him to ask her for a date five minutes after they first met. **—verb, forwarded, forwarding. 1.** to send mail ahead to a new address: When we moved, our mail was *forwarded* to our new apartment. **2.** to help or advance: to *forward* the cause of world peace. **—noun, plural** **forwards.** a player whose position is at the front in certain games, such as basketball, soccer, and hockey.

F

Pronunciation Key: T–Z			
t	ten; date	v	very; live
th	think	w	win; away
th	these	y	you
u	cut; butter	z	zoo; cause
ur	turn; bird	zh	measure

(Turn the page for more information.)

fos•sil [fäs′ əl] *noun, plural* **fossils.** the hardened remains of an animal or plant that lived thousands of years ago. Fossils are preserved in rock, earth, ice, or other substances.

fossil A fossil of the Priscarara fish, found in Wyoming in 1984. It is about 50 to 60 million years old.

fos•ter [fôs′ tər] *adjective.* having to do with the care of children by people who are not their parents by birth or by adoption: *foster* care, a *foster* child or parent.

Fos•ter [fôs′ tər] **Stephen,** 1826–1864, American songwriter.

fought [fôt] *verb.* the past form of **fight.**

foul [foul] *adjective, more/most.* **1.** having a very unpleasant smell or taste; disgusting; rotten: *foul* air in a room that hasn't been opened for months, the *foul* odor of burning rubber. **2.** of weather, rainy and stormy: a *foul* day. **3.** very bad; wicked; evil: *foul* crimes. **4.** not polite or decent: *foul* language. —*noun, plural* **fouls. 1.** in sports and games, a move or play that is against the rules: The soccer player committed a *foul* by tripping an opposing player. **2.** in baseball, a ball hit outside the foul lines; also called a **foul ball.** —*verb,* **fouled, fouling. 1.** to make something foul: ". . . the water and the shore beneath were *fouled* with greenwhite slime." (James Joyce) **2.** to make or become tangled: The boy *fouled* his kite in the branches of the tree. **3.** to break a rule in a game or sport; commit a foul.

foul line either of the two lines in baseball that run from home plate through first or third base to the end of the outfield. A ball must be hit inside the lines to allow the batter to reach base.

found[1] [found] *verb.* the past form of **find.**

found[2] *verb,* **founded, founding.** to bring into being; start; establish: The city of Detroit was *founded* in 1701 by Antoine de la Cadillac.

foun•da•tion [foun dā′ shən] *noun, plural* **foundations. 1.** the lowest part of a house or other building, which supports the rest of the building. **2.** the base or support on which something rests or depends; basis: The Constitution is the *foundation* of our system of government. **3.** the act of founding or establishing something. **4.** an organization that is set up to provide money for certain worthy causes, such as education, science research, and the arts.

found•er [foun′ dər] *noun, plural* **founders.** a person who founds or establishes something.

found•ry [foun′ drē] *noun, plural* **foundries.** a place where metal is melted and shaped to make various products.

foun•tain [fount′ ən] *noun, plural* **fountains. 1.** a device that creates a small stream of water for drinking. **2.** a stream of water that is made to shoot up in the air or to flow among specially-designed statues and pools. **3.** a natural stream of water rising up from the earth.

fountain The famous Trevi fountain in Rome. It was the scene of the popular movie *Three Coins in the Fountain.*

four [fôr] *noun, plural* **fours;** *adjective.* one more than three; 4. —**fourth,** *adjective; noun.*

Fourth of July a national holiday in the U.S., in honor of the adoption of the Declaration of Independence on July 4, 1776; also called **Independence Day.**

fowl [foul] *noun, plural* **fowl** or **fowls. 1.** any of various large birds that are raised for food, such as chickens, geese, turkeys, or ducks. **2.** any bird, especially a wild bird hunted for food.

fox [fäks] *noun, plural* **foxes.** a wild animal that has a pointed nose and ears, a bushy tail, and thick fur. It is related to the wolf. The **red fox** is found in wooded areas in most parts of North America.

frac•tion [frak′ shən] *noun, plural* **fractions.**

1. a number that is one or more of the equal parts of a whole or a group. A fraction is shown as two numbers with a line between them; the first number is divided by the second. **2.** a very small part of a whole: a *fraction* of a second.

frac•ture [frak′chər] *verb,* **fractured, fracturing.** to crack or break a bone: Linda *fractured* her ankle when she fell down the stairs. —*noun, plural* **fractures.** a crack in a bone.

frag•ile [fraj′əl] *adjective, more/most.* easy to break or destroy; delicate; frail: a *fragile* wine glass with a very thin stem.

"The Colonel stood *framed* in the doorway . . . clearly lighted by a torch he carried." (Andre Norton) **3.** to make an innocent person seem guilty by means of tricks or false proof: ". . . a deliberate plot to *frame* an innocent man." (Barbara Tuchman)

frame•work [frām′wurk′] *noun, plural* **frameworks.** the basic structure around which a thing is built.

France [frans] a country in western Europe. *Capital:* Paris. *Area:* 211,000 square miles. *Population:* 54,000,000.

---

fragments In grammar, a *sentence fragment* is a group of words that's not complete by itself, because it lacks a noun or a verb, or both. For example: "But a sudden piece of glass on a sidewalk. Or a nickel tune in a music box. A shadow on a wall at night. And I would remember." (Carson McCullers) Langston Hughes, the splendid black American author, wrote: "He walked up the steps of the church. He knocked at the door. No answer. He tried the handle. Locked." There are fragments underlined in both quotations. Writers may purposely use fragments to show that a character's thought or action is interrupted. Sometimes, they use fragments to imitate patterns of speech. Generally, for a student writer it's best to avoid fragments, especially in factual reports. Here's the kind of sentence you might watch out for. This is from a recent newspaper ad: "We offer you the best buyer-protection plan. Of any American-made car." That fragment has no purpose. It's just bad writing.

---

frag•ment [frag′mənt] *noun, plural* **fragments.** **1.** a small piece broken off from an object: "Piggy leaned forward and put a *fragment* of wood on the fire." (William Golding) **2.** a small or incomplete part: ". . . he had heard in his early years such *fragments* of tales and half-remembered stories . . ." (J.R.R. Tolkien)

fra•grance [frā′grəns] *noun, plural* **fragrances.** a pleasant smell, as of flowers or perfume: "The rains had ended, and . . . the air was heavy with the *fragrance* of lush wild blooms and fruits." (Alex Haley) —**fragrant,** *adjective.*

frail [frāl] *adjective,* **frailer, frailest.** thin and weak in body or form; not strong: "They were *frail* men and it was all they could do to keep the sheet level." (James Herriot)

frame [frām] *noun, plural* **frames. 1.** a group of connecting parts that gives support or shape to something: Some Indian tribes made boats by stretching animals skins over a wooden *frame.* **2.** a hard border or case into which something is placed: a picture *frame,* the *frame* of a window or door. **3.** the form of a person's body: a woman with a small *frame.* **4. frame of mind.** the state of a person's thoughts or feelings; mood. —*verb,* **framed, framing. 1.** to put a frame around; to *frame* a painting or a photograph. **2.** to set within a background or border:

fran•chise [fran′chīz] *noun, plural* **franchises. 1.** the right to vote in an election. **2.** a right to operate or do business, given by a government body or by a company: the Atlanta *franchise* in major-league baseball. They have a *franchise* to operate a McDonald's restaurant.

Fran•co [frang′kō] **Francisco,** 1892–1975, Spanish general, the ruler of Spain from 1936 to 1975.

frank [frangk] *adjective,* **franker, frankest.** honest and open in expressing what one thinks and feels; sincere: "To be perfectly *frank* with you, I worry about money a great deal." (John Cheever) —**frankly,** *adverb.* —**frankness,** *noun.*

frank•furt•er [frangk′fər tər] *noun, plural* **frankfurters.** a piece of cooked meat that is formed into a long, thin, reddish tube, usually made of beef or beef and pork. Frankfurters are a type of SAUSAGE and are often served in a

---

F

Pronunciation Key: [ə] Symbol

The [ə] or *schwa* sound occurs in syllables without an accent. It can be spelled with any vowel, such as a in above, e in listen, i in pencil, o in melon, u in circus. It can also be a combination of vowels, such as io in action, ai in mountain, iou in precious.

(Turn the page for more information.)

F

roll with mustard and other seasonings. ◆ Also called a HOT DOG or a **frank.**

Frank•lin [frangk′lin] **Benjamin,** 1706–1790, American patriot, statesman, scientist, and author.

Franklin This portrait was done in 1767 by a London artist, David Martin, after Franklin went there to speak before the British House of Commons.

fran•tic [fran′tik] *adjective, more/most.* not in control of one's feelings; very excited with fear, worry, anger, or pain: "The journey uphill was made in dashes and rests, a *frantic* rush up a few yards and then a rest." (John Steinbeck) **—frantically,** *adverb:* ". . . everybody searching *frantically* for the precious remaining tickets." (Roald Dahl)

fra•ter•ni•ty [frə tur′nə tē] *noun, plural* **fraternities.** a male social club, especially at a college or university. Most fraternities use letters of the Greek alphabet to form their names.

fraud [frôd] *noun, plural* **frauds. 1.** a dishonest act or trick, especially one that cheats someone: The store owner was arrested for *fraud* because he sold cheap machine-made blankets as "hand-made Navaho Indian blankets." **2.** a person or thing that is not what is claimed; a fake. ◆ Someone or something that is a fraud is **fraudulent** [frô′jə lənt].

fray [frā] *verb,* **frayed, fraying.** to wear away and separate into loose threads; become ragged or worn: "His clothing was of rich stuff, but old and slightly *frayed* in places." (Mark Twain)

freak [frēk] *noun, plural* **freaks. 1.** a person, animal, or plant that has developed in a way that is very unusual or unnatural. **2.** a highly unusual thing or event: By a *freak* of nature, the town of Holt, Missouri once had 12 inches

of rainfall in just 42 minutes. ◆ Also used as an adjective: Famous pitcher 'Goose' Gossage once was put out of action by a *freak* accident—he hurt himself while sneezing.

freck•le [frek′əl] *noun, plural* **freckles.** a very small brown spot on the skin, usually caused by being exposed to sunlight.

free [frē] *adjective,* **freer, freest. 1.** not costing anything; with no cost: The telephone company gives a *free* phone book to each of its customers. **2.** not under the control or power of another: a *free* country. **3.** not held or kept in; not confined: The prisoner went *free* when the charges against him were dropped. **4.** not troubled or bothered; clear: Make sure the motor is *free* of dust. **5.** not busy or in use: I have two *free* afternoons a week now that my piano lessons are over. **—adverb.** at no cost: Children under six years old can ride the bus *free.* **—verb, freed, freeing.** to make or set free: to *free* an animal from a trap. **—freely,** *adverb:* to speak *freely* about a problem.

free•dom [frē′dəm] *noun, plural* **freedoms. 1.** the state of being free: When the jury found him innocent, the accused man was given his *freedom.* **2.** the right to be free; being able to act, think, speak, and write as one wishes: The Bill of Rights of the U.S. Constitution gives certain *freedoms* to all Americans, such as *freedom* of speech, *freedom* of the press, and *freedom* of religion. **3.** the condition of being free of a burden, worry, or the like.

free enterprise a system or policy of doing business with little or no control by the government; also called a **free market.**

free•hand [frē′hand′] *adjective; adverb.* drawn or written by hand, without the use of special measurements: a *freehand* sketch.

free•way [frē′wā′] *noun, plural* **freeways.** an express highway that does not charge a toll.

freeze [frēz] *verb,* **froze, frozen, freezing. 1.** to change from a liquid to a solid by cold. **2.** to become covered or filled with ice: "The fire had gone out and the pipes had *frozen.*" (Eleanor Estes) **3.** to make or become very cold: Why don't you put a coat on—you'll *freeze* with just that thin sweater. **4.** to stop moving suddenly, as if turning to ice: Deer often *freeze* in their tracks when they hear some other animal. **5.** to set or fix at a certain amount: The mayor wants to *freeze* rents in the city at the present level. **—noun, plural** **freezes. 1.** a period of very cold weather: A January *freeze* destroyed the orange crop. **2.** the act of freezing: The company ordered a *freeze* on pay raises.

freez·er [frē′zər] *noun, plural* **freezers. 1.** a separate part of a refrigerator that has a temperature below freezing, used to make ice, freeze food, and store frozen foods. **2.** a special refrigerator used for this same purpose.

freight [frāt] *noun.* **1.** the act or business of moving goods by land, air, or water: We sent the package by air *freight*. **2.** the goods carried in this way, as in a plane, ship, or truck: Railroad trains are often used to move *freight*. ♦ A **freighter** is a ship used for carrying freight.

Fre·mont [frē′mänt′] **John C.,** 1813–1890, American general and western explorer.

French [french] *noun.* **1. the French.** the people of France. **2.** the language of France. —*adjective.* having to do with France, its people, or their language.

French fries potatoes cut in thin strips and fried in deep fat until they are brown and crisp.

French horn a brass musical instrument that is made up of a long, coiled tube, widening into the shape of a bell. It is played by blowing into a curved mouthpiece while pressing a series of valves.

letter in English that has the highest *frequency* is *e*. **3.** the number of times per second that a radio wave is broadcast.

fre·quent [frē′kwent] *adjective, more/most.* happening again and again; taking place often: People living along the Gulf of Mexico have to expect *frequent* rainstorms. —*verb,* **frequented, frequenting.** to often be in a certain place: to *frequent* a restaurant, to *frequent* or a museum. —**frequently,** *adverb.*

fresh [fresh] *adjective,* **fresher, freshest. 1.** in its good and natural condition, because it was just gathered, caught, or produced: *fresh* fruit and vegetables, *fresh* fish, *fresh* milk. **2.** just made or done: *fresh* bread, *fresh* animal tracks in the snow. He had a *fresh* cut on his leg. **3.** another and different: The family decided to move to Australia to get a *fresh* start in life. **4.** not stale; cool or refreshing: *fresh* air, a *fresh* breeze. **5.** of water, not part of the ocean; not salty. **6.** not polite; rude: The boy gave a *fresh* answer when the teacher asked him to be quiet. —**freshly,** *adverb:* "The spring breezes blew *freshly* from green fields far away." (Louisa May Alcott) —**freshness,** *noun.*

French words In 1066, a French-speaking army from Normandy defeated the English at the Battle of Hastings and took control of England. For about 200 years, French, not Anglo-Saxon, was the language used by people in government, law, the church, and the arts. As time went by, the Normans began to think of themselves as English rather than French, and a mix of Latin (from the French) and Germanic languages (from the Anglo-Saxons mainly) became English. The strength of English is found in that mixture. Here's a sentence that uses mostly Latinate words: "She communicated an expression that terminated the exchange." Here's the same thought in words of Germanic origin: "She scowled. It ended the talk." Now, a contrast, with one English word and one French, both meaning *quiet*. Can you tell which of the key words is French and which is Anglo-Saxon? "Outside, the wind was higher than ever, and the old man started nervously at the sound of a door banging upstairs. A *silence* unusual and depressing settled upon al three . . ." (W. W. Jacobs) "Midafternoon's a quiet time in any season. In winter with snow on the ground, no leaves to rustle and bare limbs rigid as rock, against a cloudless sky, the *hush* is deepest of all." (Jessamyn West)

fren·zy [fren′zē] *noun, plural* **frenzies.** a state of wild, excited feelings or activity: The mob was in a *frenzy* as they shouted for the police to release the prisoner. "Christmas Eve she spent in *frenzies* of baking—cakes, pies, gingerbread cookies . . ." (Russell Baker)

fre·quen·cy [frē′kwən sē] *noun, plural* **frequencies. 1.** the fact of being frequent; happening again and again: The other actors were annoyed by the *frequency* with which the star showed up late for filming. **2.** the number of times that something happens or appears: The

fresh·en [fresh′ən] *verb,* **freshened, freshening.** to make fresh. ♦ Usually used with **up:** to *freshen up* a room with a new coat of paint.

F

fresh•man [fresh′ mən] *noun, plural* **freshmen.** a student in the first year of high school or college.

fresh•wa•ter [fresh′ wô′ tər] *adjective.* living in water that is not salty: Trout are *freshwater* fish.

fret [fret] *verb,* **fretted, fretting.** to make or become worried, angry, or upset, especially over something small or unimportant: He always *frets* if his bus to work arrives a few minutes late.

Freud [froid] **Sigmund,** 1856–1939, Austrian medical scientist who founded the system of psychoanalysis to deal with people's mental problems.

fric•tion [frik′ shən] *noun.* **1.** the rubbing of one object against another: He got a blister from the *friction* of his sneaker rubbing against his toe. **2.** a force that slows down or stops the movement of two objects that touch each other: A stone will slide on ice more easily than dirt because the ice has less *friction.* **3.** the effect of opposing forces or ideas; conflict; disagreement: There's a lot of *friction* between the two candidates for mayor.

Fri•day [frī′ dā] *noun, plural* **Fridays.** the sixth day of the week.

fried [frīd] *verb.* the past form of **fry.** ♦ Often used as an adjective: *fried* chicken, *fried* potatoes.

Frie•dan [frē dan′] **Betty,** born 1921, American author and women's rights leader.

friend [frend] *noun, plural* **friends. 1.** a person whom one knows well and likes, but who is not a family member; someone that a person likes to spend time with. **2.** a person who helps or supports someone or something: He is a *friend* of the opera and gave a lot of money for the new concert hall.

friend•ly [frend′ lē] *adjective,* **friendlier, friendliest. 1.** like a friend; warm or kind: a *friendly* smile, a *friendly* neighbor. Karen gave me some *friendly* advice about how to get along with the coach. **2.** without anger or fighting; on good terms: The U.S. has troops on the soil of certain *friendly* nations. Dad and Uncle Bob had a *friendly* argument about politics.

friend•ship [frend′ ship] *noun, plural* **friendships.** the feeling between friends; the relationship of being friends.

fright [frīt] *noun, plural* **frights. 1.** a feeling that something very bad is just about to happen; a sudden feeling of deep fear or alarm. **2.** something that looks shocking, ugly, or ridiculous: The outfit she wore on Halloween made her look a *fright.*

fright•en [frīt′ ən] *verb,* **frightened, frightening. 1.** to make or become suddenly afraid or alarmed; fill with fright: "Those creatures *frightened* me so badly that my heart is beating yet." (L. Frank Baum) ♦ Often used as an adjective: "The natives looked *frightened,* jumped back into the canoe, and disappeared." (Thor Heyerdahl) **2.** to drive away by scaring: The dog *frightened* away the birds by barking at them. **—frightful,** *adjective.*

frig•id [frij′ id] *adjective, more/most.* **1.** very, very cold: People who live in Alaska have to get used to *frigid* weather. **2.** cold and unfriendly in manner: His girlfriend gave him a *frigid* look when she saw him paying attention to another girl.

fringe [frinj] *noun, plural* **fringes. 1.** an edge of hanging threads or cord used as a decoration on curtains, bedspreads, clothing, and so on. **2.** the part away from the middle; the edge: He stayed on the *fringe* of the group, never quite joining the conversation. **—verb,** **fringed, fringing.** to make a fringe for: ". . . dark blue eyes, *fringed* with long, black lashes." (Laura Ingalls Wilder)

Fris•bee [friz′ bē] *noun, plural* **Frisbees.** a trademark for a dish-shaped plastic object that people throw to each other as a game.

---

friendly letters "Friendly letter" is a term used to describe a letter to a friend or family member, as opposed to a BUSINESS LETTER. What's the key to writing a good friendly letter? Make it natural, so that the voice you use in friendly conversations comes through in your friendly letters. Also, make the content fit the interests of your reader. Books on writing often say that you should begin by writing your address at the top of the page, but in fact most people don't do this (though many do use writing paper with their address printed on it). Most people just begin with the date and "Dear ____." At the end, you can write a friendly close, such as "Your friend" or "Best wishes." You should suit your closing to your reader, just as you suit the content of the letter. Are you aware that people today don't write friendly letters nearly as often as in the past? Why do you think this is so?

friv•o•lous [friv′ ə ləs] *adjective, more/most.* not serious or important; silly: Supermarket newspapers often have *frivolous* articles about men from outer space, miracle diets and cures for disease, and famous people coming back from the dead.

frog [frôg] *noun, plural* **frogs.** a small animal with webbed feet, smooth skin, no tail, and strong back legs that it uses for jumping. Frogs are good swimmers and usually live in or near water.

frog

frol•ic [fräl′ ik] *verb,* **frolicked, frolicking.** to play happily: The children *frolicked* in the swimming pool for hours. —*noun, plural* **frolics.** a happy time or party.

from [frəm *or* främ] *preposition.* **1.** used to show a starting place or time: George Washington was *from* Virginia. Big-league baseball is played *from* April to October. **2.** used to show a starting point or position: She got a letter *from* home. He took a dollar *from* his pocket. **3.** used to show the source or cause: Bread is made *from* flour. She felt really tired *from* working so late. **4.** used to show a difference: Some people have trouble telling red *from* green.

front [frunt] *noun, plural* **fronts. 1.** a part that is forward or near the beginning; the opposite side from the back: She wrote her name on the *front* of her notebook. **2.** the land at the edge of a street or body of water: They have a home on the ocean *front.* **3.** in a war, a place where the fighting is going on. **4.** an outward appearance that is different from what is real: He was very nervous, but he tried to keep up a bold *front.* **5.** in weather, the division between two masses of air that have different temperatures: a cold *front.*
—*adjective.* facing or near the front; in front: the *front* door of a house. Newspapers print important news on the *front* page.

—*verb,* **fronted, fronting.** to look out on; face: "In warm weather she would walk around the little lake *fronting* her apartment." (Langston Hughes)

fron•tier [frän′ tēr′] *noun, plural* **frontiers. 1.** the last edge of a settled area before the part that is not built up or developed begins: the Western *frontier* of the U.S. in the 1800's. **2.** the border area between two countries. **3.** any place or area of knowledge that has not yet been fully explored or developed: the *frontiers* of space, the *frontiers* of medical science.

frost [frôst] *noun, plural* **frosts. 1.** a covering of thin ice that forms when cold temperatures freeze the water vapor in the air. **2.** weather cold enough to cause freezing. —*verb,* **frosted, frosting.** to cover with frost: The windshield *frosted* up as they sat in the car talking. **—frosty,** *adjective:* We could see our breath in the *frosty* air.

frost Tiny crystals of frost cover these red berries. Frost can be damaging to many fruit crops, especially at unexpected times of the year.

Frost [frôst] **Robert,** 1874–1963, American poet.

frost•bite [frôst′ bīt′] *noun.* damage to a part of the body caused by freezing. Frostbite usually affects the hands, feet, and face. —*verb,* **frostbit, frostbitten, frostbiting.** to injure by exposure to extreme cold. ◆ Usually used as an adjective: *frostbitten* toes.

F

Pronunciation Key: A–F			
a	and; hat	ch	chew; such
ā	ate; stay	d	dog; lid
â	care; air	e	end; yet
ä	father; hat	ē	she; each
b	boy; cab	f	fun; off

(Turn the page for more information.)

frost•ing [frôs′ ting] *noun, plural* **frostings.** a sweet mixture of sugar, butter, and flavoring, used to decorate a cake or cookies; also called ICING.

frown [froun] *verb,* **frowned, frowning. 1.** to draw the eyebrows together so that lines appear in the forehead. People frown when they are upset or angry, when they are thinking hard, when the light is very bright, and so on. **2. frown on.** to be against; disapprove: "He never allowed me to talk to him in the office and *frowned on* meeting anywhere near it . . ." (Iris Murdoch) —*noun, plural* **frowns.** the act of frowning.

froze [frōz] *verb.* the past tense of **freeze.**

fro•zen [frō′ zən] *verb.* the past participle of **freeze:** "Softly, *frozen* . . . with fear, she turned the door handle." (D. H. Lawrence)

fruit [froot] *noun, plural* **fruit** or **fruits. 1.** a sweet, juicy plant part that is good to eat, often served as a snack or for dessert. Apples, oranges, strawberries, bananas, grapes, and peaches are popular fruits. **2.** the part of any flowering plant that contains the seeds.

frus•trate [frus′ trāt] *verb,* **frustrated, frustrating. 1.** to prevent or block from reaching a goal: The firemen fought the brush fire all day, but the hot, dry winds *frustrated* their efforts to put it out. **2.** to have a feeling of being discouraged, irritated, or helpless: Dad really got *frustrated* trying to fix the air conditioner. ◆ Also used as an adjective: "Fitzgerald, a *frustrated* athlete, admired Hemingway's reputation as an athlete and war hero." (Noel Fitch)

frus•tra•tion [frus trā′ shən] *noun, plural* **frustrations. 1.** the feeling of being frustrated: Pam threw her tennis racket in *frustration* after she lost the match. **2.** something that causes this.

fry [frī] *verb,* **fried, frying.** to cook food in a pan, usually with hot oil or fat: He *fried* some bacon for breakfast. —*noun, plural* **fries.** a meal of fried food: a fish *fry.*

fudge [fuj] *noun.* a soft candy, usually made of chocolate, sugar, milk, and butter, and sometimes nuts.

fu•el [fyool] *noun, plural* **fuels.** anything that is burned to provide heat or power, such as wood coal or oil.

fu•gi•tive [fyoo′ jə tiv] *noun, plural* **fugitives.** a person who is running away or has run away, especially someone who is trying to escape from the law.

ful•fill [fəl fil′] *verb,* **fulfilled, fulfilling. 1.** to cause to happen; carry out: to *fulfill* a promise. It was many years before her dream of going to Paris was finally *fulfilled.* **2.** to satisfy; meet: to *fulfill* the requirements for a job. —**fulfillment,** *noun.*

full [fool] *adjective,* **fuller, fullest. 1.** holding as much or as many as possible: a *full* bucket of water. The hotel is *full,* so we'll have to stay somewhere else. **2.** with nothing missing; complete: a *full* deck of cards, a *full* day's work. **3.** having a large amount: It was summer and the town was *full* of tourists. **4.** to the greatest amount or degree: to go at *full* speed, to use a cleaning liquid at *full* strength. **5.** of the body, having a rounded shape: a *full* face. **6.** of clothes, wide or loose-fitting: a *full* skirt. —*adverb.* **1.** completely; entirely: He filled the bag *full* of apples. **2.** straight on, directly: to look a person *full* in the face. —**fullness,** *noun.*

full•back [fool′ bak′] *noun, plural* **fullbacks.** a football or soccer player who stands farthest back behind the front line.

Ful•ton [ful′ tən] **Robert,** 1765–1815, American inventor and engineer who developed the first successful steamboat.

ful•ly [fool′ ē] *adverb.* **1.** totally; completely: "He repeated, but more *fully,* what he had said in the first place to Anne." (Somerset Maugham) **2.** at least; no less than: "She blinked. Her mouth opened for *fully* five seconds." (Dick Francis)

-ful English suffixes and prefixes give writers a great range in the choice of words. The suffix *-ful,* meaning "full of" or "having the qualities of," is used to turn nouns into adjectives, as in *hope/hopeful* and *beauty/beautiful.* What are the advantages of adding a suffix to a noun, rather than using a completely different adjective? First, the force of the noun comes through in the adjective; second, a much greater variety of words becomes available. Note the *ful* adjectives in the following: "Now it came, wind and rain, shrieking down from the west in unbelievable contrast to the *delightful* weather of only half an hour before." (C.S. Forester) "Yes, they all knew as soon as they saw me that I would be a *wonderful* addition to the group." (John D. MacDonald) English makes it easy to avoid lengthy constructions. In some other languages, if you want to say "delightful," you must use several words.

fum·ble [fum′ bəl] *verb,* **fumbled, fumbling. 1.** to feel around in a clumsy way: "He *fumbled* at his belt for a thong on which were strung several large keys." (Andre Norton) **2.** to handle something awkwardly: The announcer *fumbled* the introductions and called the guest of honor by the wrong name. **3.** to lose hold of; drop: The quarterback *fumbled* the ball and the other team recovered it. —*noun, plural* **fumbles.** the act of fumbling a ball.

fume [fyo̅o̅m] *noun, plural* **fumes.** (usually used in the plural) a smoke or gas that has a bad smell or is harmful: We could smell the *fumes* from the old bus. —*verb,* **fumed, fuming. 1.** to give off fumes. **2.** to be very angry or irritated: Uncle Eddie was really *fuming* after another driver cut in front of us on the road.

fun [fun] *noun.* **1.** a time of playing, enjoying oneself, or being amused; a good time: Andrew always has *fun* at the beach. **2.** someone or something that causes enjoyment or amusement: Disneyland is great *fun* for children. Tom was no *fun* at the party because all he did was complain about how bored he was. **3. make fun of.** to laugh at in a cruel or unkind way; tease.

func·tion [fungk′ shən] *noun, plural* **functions. 1.** the proper activity or use of a person or thing; role; purpose: The *function* of the chairman is to be in charge of the meeting. **2.** a formal social event or ceremony: The Al Smith Dinner is an important political *function* in New York City. —*verb,* **functioned, functioning.** to serve a function; work or act: An old-time cowboy's hat also *functioned* as a pillow or a water bucket.

fund [fund] *noun, plural* **funds. 1.** money set aside or raised for a special purpose: The United Negro College *Fund* provides money for the education of black students. **2. funds.** money that is available for use: The new bridge will be paid for by both state and federal *funds.* **3.** a supply of something that is ready for use: A dictionary is a *fund* of information about words. —*verb,* **funded, funding.** to provide funds for: Public TV programs are often *funded* by large corporations.

fun·da·men·tal [fun′ də ment′ əl] *adjective, more/most.* forming a necessary or very important part; basic; essential: The law of gravity is a *fundamental* principle of science. —*noun, plural* **fundamentals.** a basic principle or part: Blocking and tackling are the *fundamentals* of football. —**fundamentally,** *adverb.*

fu·ner·al [fyo̅o̅n′ rəl *or* fyo̅o̅′ nər əl] *noun, plural* **funerals.** a religious service or other special ceremony held for a dead person, especially at the time the person is buried.

fun·gus [fung′ gəs] *noun, plural* **fungi** [fun′ gī *or* fun′ jī], **funguses.** one of a very large group of plants that have no flowers or leaves and lack green coloring matter. Mushrooms and mold are fungi.

fungus This type of fungus, known as *bracket fungus,* often grows on tree limbs.

fun·nel [fun′ əl] *noun, plural* **funnels. 1.** a utensil with a wide cone or cup at one end that narrows to a thin tube at the other. A funnel is used to avoid spilling while pouring a liquid into a container with a small opening. **2.** the smokestack of a steamship or steam engine.

fun·ny [fun′ ē] *adjective,* **funnier, funniest. 1.** causing laughter; amusing: a *funny* joke, a *funny* story, a *funny* movie. **2.** unusual in a strange way; odd; peculiar: That's *funny*—I left my book here five minutes ago and now it's gone. "The car kept rocking and made us both feel *funny.*" (F. Scott Fitzgerald)

fur [fur] *noun, plural* **furs. 1.** the thick, soft hair that covers the skin of many types of animals. Tigers, bears, and rabbits have fur. **2.** a coat made from animal fur. —**furry,** *adjective.*

fu·ri·ous [fyo̅o̅r′ ē əs] *adjective, more/most.* **1.** filled with or showing great anger; in a rage: Mr. Francis was *furious* when we broke his

	Pronunciation Key: G–N		
g	give; big	k	kind; cat; back
h	hold	l	let; ball
i	it; this	m	make; time
ī	ice; my	n	not; own
j	jet; gem; edge	ng	having

(Turn the page for more information.)

F

lent or extreme; very strong or fierce: The racing cars roared around the track at a *furious* pace. **—furiously,** *adverb:* "She sits Betty up and *furiously* shakes her." (Arthur Miller)

fur•nace [fur′ nis] *noun, plural* **furnaces.** an enclosed chamber where fuel is burned to produce heat. Furnaces are used to heat houses and other buildings.

furnace In this *blast furnace* used for steelmaking, temperatures can reach as high as 3000° F.

F

fur•nish [fur′ nish] *verb,* **furnished, furnishings. 1.** to supply or decorate with furniture: She *furnished* her den with antique furniture ♦ Often used as an adjective: A *furnished* apartment is rented with furniture in it. **2.** to supply what is needed; provide: The Colorado River *furnishes* water to five different states.

fur•ni•ture [fur′ ni chər] *noun.* movable items, such as tables, chairs, sofas, and beds, that are used in a home or office to sit or lie down on, work at, keep things in, and so on.

fur•ther [fur′ thər] a COMPARATIVE form of **far.** *adjective.* additional; more: I'd like to take that empty box, if you don't have any *further* use for it. —*adverb.* **1.** to a greater degree or amount; more: The police are going to look *further* into the matter. **2.** at a more distant point; farther. See FARTHER for more information. —*verb,* **furthered, furthering.** to help the progress of; support or advance: to *further* the cause of highway safety.

fur•ther•more [fur′ thər môr′] *adverb.* in addition to; besides; also: That road is much too narrow, and *furthermore* it's not well lighted.

fur•thest [fur′ thist] *adjective; adverb.* a SUPERLATIVE form of **far.**

fu•ry [fyoor′ ē] *noun, plural* **furies.** the state of being furious: the *fury* of a tornado. The manager was in a *fury* when the umpire made a bad call against his team.

fuse [fyooz] *noun, plural* **fuses. 1.** a piece of cord or other easily-burned material that is used to set off a bomb or other explosive. **2.** a strip of metal in an electric circuit that melts and breaks the circuit when the current becomes too strong. Newer buildings use a **circuit breaker** for this purpose rather than a fuse. —*verb,* **fused, fusing. 1.** to melt or soften by heating: The heat of the fire had *fused* the plastic toy into a shapeless lump. **2.** to unite by or as if by melting: Layers of glass are *fused* to make car windshields that won't shatter.

fu•se•lage [fyoo′ sə läzh′ *or* fyoo′ sə lij] *noun, plural* **fuselages.** the main body of an airplane, holding the crew, passengers, and cargo. The wings and tail are attached to the fuselage.

fu•sion [fyoo′ zhən] *noun.* **1.** the act of fusing; melting together. **2.** in science, the combining of two atomic NUCLEI to form a heavier NUCLEUS. Fusion creates huge amounts of nuclear energy, as in the hydrogen bomb.

fuss [fus] *noun, plural* **fusses. 1.** great attention to small or unimportant things: "When the airport officials saw the big white birds out on the airstrip, they raised a terrible *fuss*." (E.B. White) **2.** a great show of interest or affection: "Yankel had made a *fuss* about how big and pretty I'd become . . ." (Kate Simon) —*verb,* **fussed, fussing.** to make a fuss. ♦ A person who fusses or is hard to please is **fussy:** ". . . *fussy* customers who behaved as if the goods in her store belonged to them." (I.B. Singer)

fu•tile [fyoot′ əl] *adjective.* having no effect; not successful: ". . . six weeks of seemingly endless, *futile* day-after-day searching . . ." (Alex Haley) —*futilely,* *adverb:* "I went on *futilely* trying to unscrew nuts which wouldn't unscrew . . ." (Dick Francis)

fu•ture [fyoo′ chər] *noun, plural* **futures. 1.** the time that is yet to come: The new shopping center will be opening in the near *future.* **2.** a chance of success: "He knew he had a big *future* in front of him." (F. Scott Fitzgerald) **3.** in grammar, a verb that shows action in the time to come. —*adjective.* happening in the future: If it gets too dark, we'll stop the game and finish it at some *future* date.

fuzz [fuz] *noun.* fine, loose fibers or hair, as on a peach.

fuzz•y [fuz′ ē] *adjective,* **fuzzier, fuzziest. 1.** like or covered with fuzz: a *fuzzy* caterpillar. **2.** not clear; blurred; hazy: Sometimes we can get that channel on our TV set, but it's always very *fuzzy.*

g, G [jē] *noun, plural* **g's, G's.** the seventh letter of the alphabet.

gadg•et [gaj′ it] *noun, plural* **gadgets.** a name for any small tool or machine: Dad is always buying the latest kitchen *gadgets,* such as electric knife sharpeners, ice cream mixers, juice makers, and so on. ". . . the fellow I saw in one of the picture magazines who made himself a *gadget* to warm his shoes." (Ralph Ellison)

galaxy This term comes from a Greek word for "milk." The ancient Greeks used this word to describe the only galaxy they knew, the Milky Way. They thought of it as "milky" because they saw a broad streak of speckled white arched across the night sky—almost like a stream of spilled milk. (The stars appeared much brighter to the ancients than they do to us today. Nowadays, the sky is filled with artificial light.) In writing, the word *galaxy* is used to suggest "many" and "important" and "celebrated." "*Philadelphia Story* features Cary Grant, Katherine Hepburn, and James Stewart, three of the brightest stars in the Hollywood *galaxy.*" Or, "San Francisco, like New Orleans, offers tourists a *galaxy* of fine restaurants."

gag [gag] *noun, plural* **gags. 1.** something put in or across the mouth to stop a person from talking or crying out, such as a scarf or handkerchief. **2.** a joke: The comedian told a *gag* about a three-legged horse that ran in triangles. —*verb,* **gagged, gagging. 1.** to stop someone from talking or crying out by using a gag. **2.** to not be able to swallow; choke: to *gag* on a large piece of meat.

Ga•ga•rin [gə gär′ ən] **Yuri,** 1934–1968, Russian astronaut, the first person to fly in space.

gai•ly [gā′lē] *adverb.* in a gay or happy way; joyfully: "From the Yacht Club's veranda someone waved at them *gaily.*" (James Jones)

gain [gān] *verb,* **gained, gaining. 1.** to come to have; get or win, especially by some effort: In football, a team must *gain* ten yards in four plays or the other team gets the ball. "She *gained* control of herself and stood there staring at me." (Robert Penn Warren) **2.** to get as an increase or addition: The baby has *gained* a lot of weight in the past year. **3. gain on.** to catch up to; get closer: The red car was *gaining on* the others in the race. —*noun, plural* **gains. 1.** something that is gained. **2.** *also,* **gains.** an increase in value; profit: If someone sells a house for more than it cost to buy it, there is a *gain* on the sale.

gait [gāt] *noun, plural* **gaits.** a way of stepping, walking, or running: A horse's fastest *gait* is called a gallop.

gal•ax•y [gal′ ək sē] *noun, plural* **galaxies.** a group of many millions of stars. There are millions of different galaxies in the universe. The Earth, sun, and other planets in our solar system are part of the Milky Way galaxy.

gale [gāl] *noun, plural* **gales. 1.** in weather reports, a wind that blows with a speed of 32 to 63 miles per hour. **2.** any very strong wind: "He was in the stern, hearing the roar of the *gale* and the smashing waves against the boat." (Walter Farley) **3.** a sudden noise that is like a strong wind: *gales* of laughter.

Ga•li•leo [gal′ ə lā′ ō] 1564–1642, Italian astronomer and physicist.

G

gal·lant [gal′ ənt] *adjective, more/most.* **1.** showing a brave or noble spirit; heroic: By a *gallant* effort, the firefighters were able to rescue the man from the burning building. **2.** very polite or respectful. **—gallantly,** *adverb.*

gall bladder [gôl] a small organ in the body near the liver. It holds a liquid known as **gall** or BILE that helps to digest food.

gal·ler·y [gal′ rē *or* gal′ ə rē] *noun, plural* **galleries. 1.** a room or building where works of art are shown or sold. **2.** the highest balcony of a theater, church, or other such building.

gal·ley [gal′ ē] *noun, plural* **galleys. 1.** a long, low ship with sails and oars, used in early times, especially in the Greek and Roman navies. Slaves or prisoners were often forced to do the rowing. **2.** the kitchen of an airplane or ship.

game [gām] *noun, plural* **games. 1.** something that is done to have fun or as a way of playing: a *game* of tag, a *game* of catch. **2.** a way of playing in which there are certain rules and one side tries to win; a sport or contest: a baseball *game*, a card *game*, a *game* of Monopoly. **3.** wild animals, birds, or fish hunted or caught for sport or food—*adjective,* **gamer, gamest. 1.** full of spirit and courage; brave: a *game* boxer. **2.** ready; willing: Who's *game* for a swim?

gan·der [gan′ dər] *noun, plural* **ganders.** a full-grown male goose.

Gan·dhi [gän′ dē] **1. Mohandas,** 1869–1948, Indian political and religious leader. He was also known as **Mahatma Gandhi. 2. Indira,** 1917–1984, the prime minister of India from 1966 to 1977 and from 1980 to 1984.

---

galley Workers in the publishing business speak of *galley proofs* or *galleys,* which are long columns of type before illustrations (if any) or page numbers are added to arrange the type into *pages.* Editors read the galleys to make additions to the text or make cuts. Also they correct grammar and usage, and check on the accuracy of names, places, and events that are discussed there. There was, in the good old days, *linotype,* a whole line of text set or cast in one block of type, and *monotype,* with each letter cast separately into ruled lines. Today, instead of metal type, a computer can generate paper or film with type that can be used in printing. However, the term *galley* is still used for a printer's proof. Technology has changed, but the idiom hasn't. (Look up IDIOM if you are not sure what's meant here.)

---

gal·lon [gal′ ən] *noun, plural* **gallons.** a unit of measure for liquids. A gallon is equal to four quarts, or 3.785 liters.

gal·lop [gal′ əp] *noun, plural* **gallops.** the fastest way of running for a horse or other four-footed animal. During a gallop, all four feet come off the ground at once. —*verb,* **galloped, galloping.** to move or ride at a gallop.

gal·lows [gal′ ōz] *noun, plural* **gallows** or **gallowses.** a wooden frame on which criminals are put to death by hanging.

ga·losh·es [gə läsh′ iz] *plural noun.* boots or overshoes made of rubber or plastic, worn to protect the feet from rain or snow.

gam·ble [gam′ bəl] *verb,* **gambled, gambling. 1.** to try to win money on the outcome of some game or other event whose result cannot be known ahead of time. This is known as **gambling.** Common forms of gambling include betting on card games or on horse races and other sports events. ♦ A person who gambles is a **gambler. 2.** to take a chance on any future event that is uncertain: Ben didn't study the lesson, and *gambled* that the teacher wouldn't call on him. —*noun, plural* **gambles.** something that is uncertain or dangerous; a risk.

gang [gang] *noun, plural* **gangs. 1.** a number of people who act together to do something that is against the law; a group of criminals: Jesse James led a famous *gang* of train robbers in the 1880's. **2.** a group of young people from one area who form a group under a certain name. Gang members often commit minor crimes and fight with other gangs. **3.** any group of people who work or act together: A road *gang* repaired the holes in the highway.
—*verb,* **ganged, ganging. gang up.** to act against as a group: Tim and Jeff often *gang up* on their little sister.

gang·plank [gang′ plangk′] *noun, plural* **gangplanks.** a movable board used as a bridge to get on or off a ship.

gang·ster [gang′ stər] *noun, plural* **gangsters.** a member of a gang of criminals: Al Capone was a famous *gangster.*

gap [gap] *noun, plural* **gaps. 1.** an open space; an opening or break: a *gap* in a fence, a *gap* between a person's front teeth. **2.** an opening or pass between mountains: Daniel Boone took settlers west through the Cumberland *Gap* in the Appalachians. **3.** a blank or empty space: *gaps* in a person's memory.

gape [gāp] *verb,* **gaped, gaping. 1.** to stare at something with the mouth wide open, as in great surprise: ". . . holding Papa's hand and *gaping* at the wonder of it." (Russell Baker) **2.** to be or become wide open: "When the white lid *gaped* open, she dropped the can inside." (Kay Boyle) ♦ Often used as an adjective: There was a *gaping* hole in the fence where the car had crashed through.

ga•rage [gə räzh′] *noun, plural* **garages. 1.** building or part of a building used for parking a car. **2.** a place or business for repairing cars.

garage sale a sale of personal belongings such as old furniture, toys, or clothes, held in or in front of the seller's garage.

gar•bage [gär′ bij] *noun.* waste food and other unwanted things that are thrown away from a kitchen.

gar•den [gärd′ ən] *noun, plural* **gardens.** a small area of land where vegetables or flowers are grown. —*verb,* **gardened, gardening.** to work in a garden. ♦ A person who takes care of a lawn or garden is a **gardener.**

gar•de•nia [gär dēn′ yə] *noun, plural* **gardenias.** a yellow or white flower with smooth, waxy petals and a very strong, sweet smell. Gardenias grow on an evergreen bush.

gardenia The heavy fragrance of the gardenia makes it an attractive shrub. It has thick blossoms and shiny leaves.

Gar•field [gär′ fēld′] **James,** 1831–1881, the twentieth president of the United States, in 1881.

gar•gle [gär′ gəl] *verb,* **gargled, gargling.** to rinse the inside of the mouth and throat with liquid: The doctor said I should *gargle* with warm salt water to help my sore throat.

gargoyle A gargoyle seems to be gazing out over Paris from the Cathedral of Notre Dame. Gargoyles were used to keep rainwater off the walls of a cathedral; the water ran from the roof to a spout in the gargoyle's mouth.

gar•goyle [gär′ goil] *noun, plural* **gargoyles.** a very ugly or frightening stone figure, part human and part animal. Churches and other buildings of the Middle Ages often had gargoyles on the edge of the roof.

gar•lic [gär′ lik] *noun.* a plant that looks like a small onion. The bulb of the garlic plant has a very strong smell and taste and is used for flavor in cooking.

gar•ment [gär′ mənt] *noun, plural* **garments.** any piece of clothing.

gar•net [gär′ nit] *noun, plural* **garnets.** a deep-red gem used in jewelry.

gar•nish [gär′ nish] *noun, plural* **garnishes.** something put on or around food to make it look more attractive. Radishes, parsley, and lemon slices are often used as garnishes. —*verb,* **garnished, garnishing.** to decorate food with a garnish.

gar•ri•son [gar′ ə sən] *noun, plural* **garrisons. 1.** a fort or place where soldiers are stationed. **2.** the soldiers at such a fort.

gar•ter [gär′ tər] *noun, plural* **garters.** an elastic strap or band that holds up a stocking.

garter snake a brown or green North American snake with yellow stripes. Garter snakes are harmless to humans.

G

Pronunciation Key: G–N			
g	give; big	k	kind; cat; back
h	hold	l	let; ball
i	it; this	m	make; time
ī	ice; my	n	not; own
j	jet; gem; edge	ng	having

(Turn the page for more information.)

gas [gas] *noun, plural* **gases. 1.** one of the three basic forms of matter, along with a LIQUID and a SOLID. A gas does not have a certain shape and does not occupy a fixed space. Air itself is a gas, and it is made up of other gases such as hydrogen and oxygen. **2.** a gas or mixture of gases burned for cooking or heating. **3.** a short word for GASOLINE. ◆ Something in the form of a gas is **gaseous.**

gash [gash] *noun, plural* **gashes.** a long, deep cut or wound: "The trees had had broad *gashes* chipped off on one side." (Lois Lenski) —*verb,* **gashed, gashing.** to make a gash in something.

gas mask a mask worn over the nose and mouth, having a filter to keep out harmful chemicals, smoke, or gases in the air.

gas•o•line [gas′ə lēn′] *noun.* a liquid fuel that burns very easily, made from PETROLEUM. Gasoline is used to run cars and trucks, airplanes, boats, lawn mowers, and many other vehicles.

gasp [gasp] *verb,* **gasped, gasping.** to breathe in air suddenly or with difficulty: "They sucked and *gasped* at the thin, thin air . . ." (Ray Bradbury) —*noun, plural* **gasps.** the act of gasping.

gas station a place that sells gasoline. Some gas stations also repair and service cars and trucks.

gate [gāt] *noun, plural* **gates.** a part in a fence or wall that opens and closes like a door.

gate•way [gāt′ wā′] *noun, plural* **gateways. 1.** an opening in a fence that can be closed with a gate. **2.** a way to get someplace or do something: "The Latin School was the *gateway* to Harvard University . . ." (Theodore H. White)

gath•er [gath′ ər] *verb,* **gathered, gathering. 1.** to come or bring together: "The crowd began to *gather* in the Capitol Plaza long before noon." (Arthur Schlesinger) **2.** to pick up or collect: to *gather* flowers. "He *gathered* his energies together and took the hill at a jog." (Jeffery Paul Chan) **3.** to put together in the mind: "You *gather* I'm sure, that I like English food. I do" (James Beard) **4.** to bring together in folds: The dress was *gathered* at the waist.

gath•er•ing [gath′ ə ring] *noun, plural* **gatherings.** the act or fact of coming together; a meeting: "This was a *gathering* of all the tribes . . ." (Tom Wolfe)

gaud•y [gô′ dē] *adjective,* **gaudier, gaudiest.** bright and colorful in a showy way; having too much decoration: The piano player Liberace was known for his *gaudy* style of dressing.

gauge [gāj] *noun, plural* **gauges. 1.** an instrument for measuring the amount or size of something. Different types of gauges measure temperature, air or water pressure, and the level of water or other liquid. **2.** a standard measure for certain manufactured objects. There are gauges for the thickness of a wire and the distance between two railroad tracks. —*verb,* **gauged, gauging. 1.** to measure something by means of a gauge. **2.** to judge or estimate something, as if by using a gauge: to *gauge* a person's character.

gaunt [gônt] *adjective,* **gaunter, gauntest.** very thin and bony in an unhealthy way, as if sick or starving: ". . . the horses were *gaunt* from the terrible journey . . ." (Marguerite Henry)

gauze [gôz] *noun.* a very thin, loosely-woven cloth that can be easily seen through, often used to make bandages.

gave [gāv] the past tense of **give.**

gav•el [gav′ əl] *noun, plural* **gavels.** a small wooden hammer that is tapped to call for order or attention, as by a judge in a courtroom.

gay [gā] *adjective,* **gayer, gayest. 1.** happy and full of fun; cheerful: "He was very *gay* and lighthearted and quite forty years younger, as he walked out the door." (Arthur C. Clarke) **2.** brightly-colored: ". . . there were hooked oval rugs with *gay* flower patterns." (Mary O'Hara)

gaze [gāz] *verb,* **gazed, gazing.** to look at something steadily for a long time, without looking away; stare: "They *gazed* curiously at the strange new visitor." (P. L. Travers)

gazelle Gazelles live on dry, open plains in Africa and Asia.

ga•zelle [gə zel′] *noun, plural* **gazelles.** a graceful animal that looks like a small deer and has curved horns and slender legs. Gazelles are good jumpers and can run very fast.

gear [gēr] *noun, plural* **gears. 1.** a wheel having teeth that fit into the teeth of another wheel. Gears are used to allow motion to be passed from one part of a machine to another, so as to control speed, power, or direction. **2.** an arrangement of such wheels in an automobile. **3.** a group of connected parts in a machine that have a certain purpose: the landing *gear* of an airplane. **4.** the equipment needed for a certain activity: mountain-climbing *gear.* —*verb,* **geared, gearing.** to fit to a certain purpose; make suitable: That computer program is *geared* to businesses rather than home use.

geese [gēs] *noun.* the plural of **goose.**

Gei·ger counter [gī′ gər] a device used to find and measure RADIOACTIVITY.

armed forces. In former times, a general was someone who was in command of an army. In the U.S. armed forces today, a general ranks above a colonel. ◆ There are five ranks of general, having from five stars down to one: **General of the Army (Air Force), general, lieutenant general, major general,** and **brigadier** [brig′ ə dēr′] **general.**
—*adjective.* **1.** having to do with everyone or with the whole; not limited: That beach is not open to the *general* public, only to people who live in this town."Over the past five years there's been a *general* breakdown of law and order . . ." (Sam Shepard) **2.** not giving details; not specific or exact: I'm not a mechanic, but I've got a *general* idea how a car engine works. **3. in general.** as a rule; usually; generally: *In general,* mammals live on land.

′generalize To *generalize* is to make a general or broad statement that covers a lot of particular things. "Americans waste time watching television, because it's no better than staring at street traffic." This is called a *sweeping generalization*—presenting a general opinion as fact. Generalizations can be useful in a factual report, when you generalize to state finally the basic points made in your paper as in, "A lot of television is devoted to movies and old series." Even so, you have to be careful. How much is "a lot of television"? Two hours a day? Ten hours? This is a *vague generalization*. A good place to use generalizations is to introduce a topic, or to conclude it. Start with a generalization: "New York is a city of commercial cathedrals, huge structures of business." Then, be specific: "The 'twin towers' of the World Trade Center reach 110 stories." "Wall Street is a tiny canyon between buildings." "Skyscrapers make space vertical, using air as land."

gel·a·tin [jel′ ə tən] *noun.* a clear substance like jelly, used as a food and in making drugs, photographic film, and glue. It is made from the bones, skin, and other parts of animals.

gem [jem] *noun, plural* **gems. 1.** a valuable stone that has been cut and polished; a jewel. Diamonds, emeralds, and other precious stones are gems. **2.** a person or thing that is very special or valuable, like a gem: The boss said his new assistant is a real *gem.*

gene [jēn] *noun, plural* **genes.** one of the very tiny parts of matter found in all animal and plant cells, serving to determine which characteristics a parent passes on to its offspring. There are thousands of genes in the nucleus of a cell, arranged in long chain-like structures called **chromosomes** [krō′ mə sōmz′]. Genes determine what color a person's eyes and hair will be and influence other qualities such as height and weight.

gen·er·al [jen′ rəl *or* jen′ ər əl] *noun, plural* **generals.** an officer of the highest rank in the

gen·er·al·ize [jen′ rə līz *or* jen′ ə rə līz] *verb,* **generalized, generalizing. 1.** to form a general rule or conclusion: Ratings of TV shows note which programs a few thousand people watch and then *generalize* about what the entire country watches. **2.** to state an idea that is too broad or too general: Just because you've had trouble with your car, don't *generalize* and say that all American cars are badly made. ◆ The act of generalizing is a **generalization.**

gen·er·al·ly [jen′ rə lē] *adverb.* **1.** as a rule; in most cases; usually: "When I'm out somewhere, I *generally* just eat a Swiss cheese sand-

Pronunciation Key: O S			
ō	over; go	ou	out; town
ô	all; law	p	put; hop
oo	look; full	r	run; car
o͞o	pool; who	s	set; miss
oi	oil; boy	sh	show

(Turn the page for more information.)

wich and a malted milk." (J. D. Salinger) **2.** among most people; widely; commonly: It's not *generally* known that the U.S. once sent troops into Russia to oppose the Communists.

gen•er•ate [jen′ ə rāt′] *verb,* **generated, generating.** to cause to be; bring about; produce: A bolt of lightning can *generate* a spark that touches off a forest fire. That article in the school paper *generated* a lot of discussion.

gen•er•a•tion [jen′ ə rā′ shən] *noun, plural* **generations. 1.** one step in the line of descent in a family. **2.** a group of people born in the same period of time: ". . . the torch has been passed to a new *generation* of Americans, born in this century . . ." (John F. Kennedy) **3.** a period of about 30 years, or roughly the time from the birth of one generation of a family to the next. **4.** a stage in the development of a certain product or device: Remington Rand's UNIVAC was a first-*generation* computer developed in 1951. **5.** the act of generating: The force of a waterfall can be used for the *generation* of electric power.

gen•er•a•tor [jen′ ə rā′ tər] *noun, plural* **generators.** a machine that produces electricity from other forms of energy, as by burning fuel.

ge•ner•ic [jə ner′ ik] *adjective.* **1.** having to do with a general group; not special: Pasta is a *generic* name for spaghetti, noodles, macaroni, and so on. **2.** not sold under a brand name or trademark: *Generic* products usually have a lower price than brand-name items. **3.** *Slang.* of poor quality: Don't buy anything there—their clothes are really *generic.*

gen•er•os•i•ty [jen′ ə räs′ ə tē] *noun, plural* **generosities.** the quality of being generous, or a generous action.

gen•er•ous [jen′ rəs *or* jen′ ər əs] *adjective, more/most.* **1.** willing and happy to give to others; not selfish: "He is a nice man and *generous,* is always sending Henry presents . . ." (Sherwood Anderson) **2.** large in amount: Lou took a *generous* helping of the birthday cake. **—generously,** *adverb.*

ge•net•ics [jə net′ iks] *noun.* the area of biology that includes the study of how certain characteristics are passed on from parent to child through the GENES. **—genetic,** *adjective.* having to do with genetics: The **genetic code** is the arrangement of genes that transfers *genetic* information from parent to child.

Ge•ne•va [jə nē′ və] a city in southwestern Switzerland. *Population:* 154,000.

Gen•ghis Khan [gen′ gis kän′] 1162?–1227, Mongolian general who conquered much of Asia and eastern Europe.

generic products Generic foods are easily identified on the shelf by their plain, simple, black-and-white labels.

gen•ial [jēn′ yəl] *adjective, more/most.* cheerful and friendly; pleasant: "Mr. Shepherd was a *genial* man who . . . gave the children nickels and took the boys fishing." (Shirley Jackson)

ge•nie [jē′ nē] *noun, plural* **genies.** in Arabian folk tales, a spirit with great magical powers. In the story of Aladdin, a genie appears when a magic lamp is rubbed and gives Aladdin three wishes.

gen•ius [jēn′ yəs] *noun, plural* **geniuses. 1.** a person who has a very outstanding mind; someone who is able to produce great thoughts or lasting works of art or science. **2.** the mental ability that such a person has: Shakespeare's plays and Einstein's scientific theories are

genius *Genius* is a powerful word which in its strict sense applies to no more than a few thousand persons in the history of the world—Leonardo, Einstein, Shakespeare, Mozart, for example. Because the word is so powerful, it's an impressive way to describe a person—even if you know, literally, the person is no Shakespeare. The term can mean only "someone who is very good at something." A genius may be an advertising copywriter, a businessman who has created a chain of stores, a writer of many best-selling novels. In general, such usage weakens the basic meaning of the word. It's better to say, "He's a genius at ad copy or at creating jobs or at writing popular suspense stories."

works of *genius*. **3.** any person who is thought of as very intelligent or as highly skilled at some mental activity: a *genius* at planning a political campaign, a *genius* at writing advertising copy.

gen•tle [jent′əl] *adjective,* **gentler, gentlest. 1.** not hard, rough, or wild: a *gentle* horse that is easy to ride, to give a person a *gentle* tap on the arm. **2.** not having great force; soft, low, or mild: a *gentle* rain, a *gentle* breeze.

---

gentle We know what a man is. What is a *gentleman*? The form *gen-* has to do with a person's birth or family. Jews call Christians "gentiles," which means "a person who is not of Jewish birth." The origin of the term *gentle* has nothing to do with being soft and kind by nature. In the Middle Ages, a gentle person was someone born into a high-ranking family. The poet Geoffrey Chaucer says of one of his characters in *The Canterbury Tales*: "He was a very perfect, gentle knight." "A gentle knight" meant "a noble knight." As time went on, the term *gentle* described the way a person of high birth was trained to act. Such people were thought of as being kind and polite; a *gentle man* did not treat people in a rough or harsh way.

---

gen•tle•man [jent′əl mən] *noun, plural* **gentle-men. 1.** in former times, a man born into a good family and having a high social position: ". . . a man with such good manners, such fine clothes, so like a *gentleman*." (Henry James) **2.** a man who is honorable and treats others well. **3.** a polite way to refer to any man: "Ladies and *gentlemen,* may I have your attention, please."

gen•tly [jent′lē] *adverb.* in a gentle way: "Spring air entered *gently* in warm breezes that smelled of flowers and trees." (Mark Helprin)

gen•u•ine [jen′ yōō in] *adjective, more/most.* **1.** actually what it seems to be; not false; real: a *genuine* diamond, a *genuine* painting by Rembrandt. **2.** not pretended; honest; sincere: to make a *genuine* effort to help a person. —**genuinely,** *adverb:* "Several smiling faces seemed *genuinely* pleased to see me." (Dick Francis)

ge•og•ra•phy [jē äg′rə fē] *noun.* the study of the natural features of the earth, such as mountains, deserts, and bodies of water, and of natural events such as plant and animal life and climate. Geography also studies human features of the earth, such as the cities and countries people live in and the resources and products they use. —**geographical,** *adjective.*

ge•ol•o•gy [jē äl′ ə jē] *noun.* the scientific study of the rocks, soil, and other minerals that make up the earth's crust. Geology also includes the study of how these materials were formed, how they are arranged in layers, and how they have changed throughout the history of the earth. ◆ An expert in geology is a **geologist.** —**geological,** *adjective.*

ge•om•e•try [jē äm′ ə trē] *noun.* the branch of mathematics that is concerned with the study of points, lines, angles, shapes, and solid figures. Geometry is used to determine the shape and size of an object or the distance between two points. —**geometric** or **geometrical,** *adjective.*

George III [jôrj] 1738–1820, the king of England during the American Revolution.

Geor•gia [jôr′ jə] a state in the southeastern U.S. *Capital:* Atlanta. *Nickname:* "Peach State." *Area:* 58,900 square miles. *Population:* 5,650,000.

geranium A very popular house and garden plant, the geranium is grown for its bright, showy flowers.

ge•ra•ni•um [jə rā′ nē əm] *noun, plural* **gerani-ums.** a plant with clusters of red, pink, or white flowers and thick, round leaves.

Pronunciation Key: T–Z			
t	ten; date	v	very; live
th	think	w	win; away
<u>th</u>	these	y	you
u	cut; butter	z	zoo; cause
ur	turn; bird	zh	measure

(Turn the page for more information.)

G

ger•bil [jur′bəl] *noun, plural* **gerbils.** a small, furry animal like a mouse, with a long tail and long hind legs. Gerbils are often kept as pets.

germ [jurm] *noun, plural* **germs. 1.** any one of many types of tiny plants or animals that can be seen only through a microscope and that can cause disease. **2.** the earliest form of a living thing, especially the part of a seed, nut, or bud that can sprout into a new plant: wheat *germ*. **3.** the earliest form or beginning of something: the *germ* of an idea.

Ger•man [jur′mən] *noun, plural* **Germans. 1.** a person born or living in Germany. **2.** the language spoken in Germany. —*adjective.* having to do with Germany or the German language.

German shepherd a large, strong dog with thick black or brown fur, first bred in Germany to herd sheep. They are often trained to work with police and to guide blind people.

Ger•ma•ny [jur′mə nē] a country in western Europe. After World War II, it was divided into EAST GERMANY and WEST GERMANY.

ger•mi•nate [jur′mə nāt′] *verb,* **germinated, germinating.** to start growing or developing; sprout: This grass seed will *germinate* about a week after it's planted.

Ge•ron•i•mo [jə rän′ə mō′] 1829–1909, Apache Indian chief.

ges•ture [jes′chər] *noun, plural* **gestures. 1.** a movement of the hands, head, or other part of the body to show what a person thinks or feels: The teacher made a *gesture* for silence in the noisy class by putting his finger over his lips. **2.** some action that is done to show a certain feeling: a *gesture* of friendship. —*verb,* **gestured, gesturing.** to make a gesture.

get [get] *verb,* **got, got** or **gotten, getting. 1.** to come to have for oneself: to *get* a job, to *get* a birthday present, to *get* an 'A' on a test. **2.** to cause to be or to happen: to *get* a haircut, to *get* lunch, to *get* ready for bed. **3.** to be or become: to *get* sick, to *get* lost, to *get* married, to *get* mad about something. **4.** to move or go to a place: to *get* home late. Can you *get* this sweater into your suitcase? **5.** to understand: to *get* a joke, to *get* the point of a story. **6.** to have to or need to: "I've *got* to finish this report today."

Get•tys•burg [get′ēz burg′] a town in southern Pennsylvania where an important Civil War battle was fought.

geyser The Riverside Geyser is on the bank of the Firehole River, in Yellowstone National Park, Wyoming.

gey•ser [gī′zər] *noun, plural* **geysers. 1.** a spring that shoots hot water and steam into the air from time to time. Some geysers can shoot hundreds of feet high. **2.** anything that rises into the air like a geyser: ". . . a little *geyser* of dirt spouted out on either side." (Jim Kjelgaard)

Gha•na [gä′nə] a country in western Africa. *Capital:* Accra. *Area:* 91,900 square miles. *Population:* 12,400,000.

ghast•ly [gast′lē] *adjective,* **ghastlier, ghastliest.** causing great fear; horrible: The movie *Psycho* is about a series of *ghastly* murders.

ghet•to [get′ō] *noun, plural* **ghettos** or **ghettoes. 1.** in former times, a section of a European city where Jewish people were forced to live by law. **2.** in modern times, a part of a city where many members of a minority group live because they are poor or are not accepted by other groups. Ghettos often are very crowded and have old, run-down buildings.

getaway What is the difference between "departing" or "leaving" and a "getaway"? If a criminal "made his getaway," it means he escaped. If you are tired after a year's schoolwork, you could say, "I need to make a quick *getaway* the day after school closes." If the President left for a weekend rest at Camp David, you would not say, "The President made his *getaway* from the White House."

ghost [gōst] *noun, plural* **ghosts. 1.** the spirit of a dead person as it supposedly appears to living people, usually thought of as a pale or shadowy form like a human figure. **2.** something very dim or faint, like a ghost: The *ghost* of a smile crossed her face. We don't have a *ghost* of a chance of beating that team. **3.** short for GHOST-WRITER. —**ghostly,** *adjective.* like a ghost: A *ghostly* shape seemed to float past the window of the old deserted house.

ghost•writ•er [gōst′ri′tər] *noun, plural* **ghost-writers.** a person who writes a book for some-one else who then takes the credit as the book's author.

GI *noun, plural* **GI's.** a nickname for a soldier in the U.S. Army, especially during World War II.

gi•ant [jī′ənt] *noun, plural* **giants. 1.** a creature that is much larger than an ordinary person. Giants often appear in Greek myths and in folk tales like "Jack and the Beanstalk." **2.** a person who is much taller and heavier than usual: Wilt Chamberlain was a *giant* among pro basketball players at 7′2″ and nearly 300 pounds. **3.** any person or thing having great power or influ-ence: IBM is a *giant* in the computer industry. —*adjective:* being a giant; very large: Macy's in New York is a *giant* department store covering an entire city block.

gid•dy [gid′ē] *adjective,* **giddier, giddiest. 1.** feeling as if one's head is spinning; dizzy. **2.** not at all serious; silly; playful: to be in a *giddy* mood.

gift [gift] *noun, plural* **gifts. 1.** something that is given; a present: a birthday *gift.* **2.** a special talent that a person has: "He had a *gift* for languages, and spoke all the local dialects." (Somerset Maugham) —**gifted,** *adjective.* hav-ing a special talent: She is a *gifted* pianist. A *gifted* child is one who is very intelligent.

gi•gan•tic [jī gan′ tik] *adjective, more/most.* like a giant; very large; huge: "No room seemed big enough for his *gigantic* frame." (Edna Ferber) "One entire wall was covered by a *gigantic* chart of the English Channel." (Cornelius Ryan)

gig•gle [gig′ əl] *verb,* **giggled, giggling.** to laugh in an excited or silly way, especially in a high voice. —*noun, plural* **giggles.** such a laugh.

Gi•la monster [hē′ lə] a large, poisonous lizard found in the southwestern U.S. It has bead-like scales with black and orange or pink markings.

gill [gil] *noun, plural* **gills.** the body part that fish and many other water animals use for breathing. The gills take in oxygen from the water.

gim•mick [gim′ik] *noun, plural* **gimmicks.** *In-formal.* a clever way to attract attention: The company is looking for some *gimmick* to help sell their new product.

gin¹ [jin] *noun, plural* **gins.** a strong, colorless alcoholic drink that is made from grain and flavored with juniper berries.

gin² *noun, plural* **gins.** a machine that separates seeds from cotton; also called a **cotton gin.**

gin•ger [jin′ jər] *noun, plural* **gingers.** a spice with a strong, sharp taste, used in food and medicine. Ginger comes from the root of a tropical plant.

ginger ale a carbonated soft drink flavored with ginger.

gin•ger•bread [jin′ jər bred′] *noun, plural* **gin-gerbreads.** a dark, sweet cake or cookie fla-vored with ginger and molasses.

gi•raffe [jə raf′] *noun, plural* **giraffes.** a large African mammal with long legs, a very long neck, and a light-colored coat with brown patches. Giraffes are the tallest living animals.

giraffe The giraffe can feed on the upper leaves of a tree, reaching food that is too high for other plant-eating animals.

G

Pronunciation Key: [ə] Symbol

The [ə] or *schwa* sound occurs in syllables without an accent. It can be spelled with any vowel, such as **a** in above, **e** in listen, **i** in pencil, **o** in melon, **u** in circus. It can also be a combination of vowels, such as **io** in action, **ai** in mountain, **iou** in precious.

(Turn the page for more information.)

gir·der [gur′dər] *noun, plural* **girders.** a large, long beam, usually made of steel. Girders are used to support a floor or to serve as a frame for a building, bridge, or other structure.

girl [gurl] *noun, plural* **girls.** a female child who is not yet a woman or adult.

---

girl In earlier days, *girl* was a word with a wider range. It meant "child" or "young person," and believe it or not, it could mean either a male or a female. By Shakespeare's time (about the year 1600), this meaning had faded away, and people used the word *girl* only to refer to females. For hundreds of years no one thought it wrong to call a female who was, say, thirty years of age, "girl." But women who work in business now object to being referred to as "girls," because they think this suggests that they and their work are not as serious or important as men and their work. They criticize uses such as "I'll have my *girl* (my secretary) type that up for you" or "Give this to the *girl* (the receptionist) at the front desk." Newspapers used to carry want ads for the job of "Girl Friday" or "Gal Friday" meaning an office worker who is a "go-fer," fetching meals, answering telephones, running errands, putting off unwelcome callers. Because of the objection, this description is almost never used today. (The term "Girl Friday" came from a character in a book—Robinson Crusoe's Man Friday. Do you know what the connection is?)

---

girl·hood [gurl′hood′] *noun, plural* **girlhoods.** the time of life when one is a girl.

girl·ish [gur′lish] *adjective.* of or like a girl; fit for girls.

girl scout a member of the **Girl Scouts,** an organization that teaches girls outdoor skills, physical fitness, and good citizenship.

give [giv] *verb,* **gave, given, giving. 1.** to take something that one has and pass it to another person as a present: I'm going to *give* Lois a book for her birthday. **2.** to hand over or let have: *Give* me the salt please. I'll *give* you two dollars for that picture. **3.** to provide or supply: a cow that *gives* a lot of milk. a teacher who *gives* attention to all her students, **4.** to cause to have or to happen: The car's been *giving* us trouble lately. **5.** to perform or put on: to *give* a speech, to *give* a party. **6.** to move or bend under pressure: The door *gave* slightly as he leaned against it.

giv·en [giv′ən] *verb.* the past participle of **give.** —*adjective.* that has been stated or decided: You must finish the test within a *given* time.

gla·cier [glā′shər] *noun, plural* **glaciers.** a huge mass of ice that moves very slowly down a mountain or over land. A glacier is formed over a long period of time from snow that has not melted. At one time glaciers covered much of North America and Europe. —**glacial,** *adverb.* of or like a glacier: *Glacial* deposits of clay and sand can form hills or ridges in the earth.

glad [glad] *adjective,* **gladder, gladdest.** feeling good about something; happy or pleased: Jen-

nifer was *glad* she got an "A" on her test. —**gladly,** *adverb:* I'm sure she'll *gladly* help you out. —**gladness,** *noun.*

glad·i·a·tor [glad′ē ā′tər] *noun, plural* **gladiators.** in ancient Rome, a man who fought another man or an animal as a public entertainment. Gladiators sometimes were paid fighters, but usually were slaves, prisoners, or criminals who were forced to fight.

glad·i·o·lus [glad′ē ō′ləs] *noun, plural* **gladioli** [glad′ē ō′lē] or **gladioluses.** a plant having stiff, sword-shaped leaves and large flowers that grow in bright clusters along a long stem.

glam·our [glam′ər] *noun.* (also spelled **glamor**) a power of charm and beauty that can attract people: The Eiffel Tower, sidewalk cafes, and beautiful women dressed in the latest fashions all add to the *glamour* of Paris. —**glamorous,** *adjective:* having glamour: Old Hollywood movies often featured *glamorous* stars such as Marlene Dietrich.

glacier The broad Muir glacier coming down into Glacier Bay in Alaska. Glaciers are millions of years old and move slowly over time cutting paths through mountains.

G

glance [glans] *verb,* **glanced, glancing. 1.** to look at something quickly for a short time: "Alec *glanced* at his wristwatch as he hurried away . . ." (Walter Farley) **2.** to hit something at a slant and fly off to one side: He threw a rock that *glanced* off the side of the house. —*noun, plural* **glances.** a quick look.

gland [gland] *noun, plural* **glands.** one of the organs that makes a special substance which is used or released by the body. Glands produce such things as tears or sweat, juices to digest food, and cells to fight disease germs. The liver, kidneys, and stomach are important glands.

glare [glâr] *noun, plural* **glares. 1.** a strong, harsh light: "The *glare* from the sun and snow blinded him." (Arthur Schlesinger) **2.** an angry look or stare: "I put down my glass and fixed Mrs. Pumphrey with a severe *glare*." (James Herriot) —*verb,* **glared, glaring. 1.** to shine with a strong, harsh light: "Yancey strolled out into the *glaring* sunshine . . ." (Edna Ferber) **2.** to give an angry look or stare: "He sat *glaring* at his companion in a snarling silence." (Booth Tarkington)

glass [glas] *noun, plural* **glasses. 1.** a hard material that can be seen through and that will break easily. Glass is used to make windows, bottles, light bulbs, and many other products. It is made by melting together a mixture of sand and certain other materials, such as SODA and LIME, and then rapidly cooling the mixture. **2.** a container of glass or plastic that is used for drinking: Sue drank two *glasses* of orange juice with her breakfast. **3.** something made of glass, such as a mirror or telescope. **4. glasses.** a pair of lenses made of glass or plastic, used to help people see better; also called **eyeglasses.**

glass•y [glas′ē] *adjective,* **glassier, glassiest. 1.** looking like glass: There was no wind and the sea was bright and *glassy.* **2.** of the eyes, having a dull, fixed expression; not lively or alert.

glaze [glāz] *noun, plural* **glazes.** a thin, shiny coating over something: The sidewalk was covered with a *glaze* of ice. —*verb,* **glazed, glazing. 1.** to put a thin coating on: to *glaze* doughnuts. **2.** to put glass in or on: That house has double-*glazed* windows to keep in heat. **3.** of the eyes, to become glassy. ♦ A person who cuts and installs glass is a **glazier** [glā′zhər].

gleam [glēm] *noun, plural* **gleams.** a bright flash or beam of light: "The sky had been a dark gray all day, with not a *gleam* of sun." (Willa Cather) —*verb,* **gleamed, gleaming.** to shine brightly: "Some distant lamp or lighted window *gleamed* below me." (James Joyce) ♦ Often used as an adjective: "Snowball opened his mouth and showed two rows of *gleaming* white teeth, sharp as needles." (E. B. White)

glee [glē] *noun.* great happiness or joy; delight: The children laughed with *glee* at the clown. —**gleeful,** *adjective.* —**gleefully,** *adverb.*

glen [glen] *noun, plural* **glens.** a small, narrow valley.

Glenn [glen] **John,** born 1921, American astronaut and politician, the first American to orbit the earth.

glide [glīd] *verb,* **glided, gliding. 1.** to move smoothly and easily with little effort: "She wished that she could go dancing at Mouquin's and *glide* about the floor . . . flowing with the music." (Mark Helprin) **2.** of an aircraft, to travel through the air without using a motor or other form of power. —*noun.* the act or fact of gliding.

glider This World War II glider was used for landings behind enemy lines.

glid•er [glī′dər] *noun, plural* **gliders. 1.** an aircraft without a motor that glides on air currents. **2.** a swinging outdoor seat hung from a frame or ceiling.

glim•mer [glim′ər] *noun, plural* **glimmers. 1.** a faint, unsteady light: He saw the *glimmer* of a campfire in the distance. **2.** a weak sign; trace: Even though it had rained all day, they still had a *glimmer* of hope that the game could be played. —*verb,* **glimmered, glimmering.** to shine with a faint, unsteady light.

Pronunciation Key: Accent Marks

[′] is the normal accent mark. It shows where the main stress falls on a word.
[′] is a secondary accent mark. It shows a lighter stress than the primary accent. For example:

tel • e • vis • ion [tel′ə vizh′ən]
(Turn the page for more information.)

G

glimpse [glimps] *noun, plural* **glimpses.** a short, quick look at something: "He could now and then as the sea flattened catch a *glimpse* of clear sand below . . ." (James Jones) —*verb,* **glimpsed, glimpsing.** to get a quick view; see for a moment: He *glimpsed* someone waving from the back seat as the car raced by.

glis·ten [glis′ ən] *verb,* **glistened, glistening.** to shine with a soft, reflected light; sparkle: ". . . Alec watched the sun's rays *glisten* on the white snow." (Walter Farley)

glit·ter [glit′ ər] *verb,* **glittered, glittering.** to shine with bright flashes; sparkle brightly: ". . . a big gate, all studded with emeralds that *glittered* so in the sun." (L. Frank Baum) —*noun.* **1.** something that glitters or seems to glitter: "There was a *glitter* of tears for a moment." (Dick Francis) **2.** an attractive or showy quality; glamour: the *glitter* of Hollywood.

gloat [glōt] *verb,* **gloated, gloating.** to think about something with selfish delight or satisfaction: Dennis *gloated* over beating his older sister in the checker game.

globe [glōb] *noun, plural* **globes. 1.** any object or shape that is round like a ball: an electric light *globe.* "Looking up, we saw great *globes* of white flame floating in the sky." (Jill Paton Walsh) **2.** the earth: an ocean liner that circles the *globe.* **3.** a round object showing a model of the earth or the sky. —**global,** *adjective:* global war. Hunger is a *global* problem.

glo·ri·fy [glôr′ ə fī′] *verb,* **glorified, glorifying. 1.** to praise or give glory to. **2.** to cause something to seem better or more important than it actually is: Many current movies and television shows are criticized for *glorifying* violence.

glo·ri·ous [glôr′ ē əs] *adjective, more/most.* **1.** having or deserving great praise or glory: The patriot Samuel Adams said of the first battle of the Revolution, "What a *glorious* morning for America!" **2.** very beautiful or splendid; magnificent; grand: "Balloons in brilliant primary colors . . . rising from the green-grass in *glorious* jumbled rainbows." (Dick Francis) —**gloriously,** *adverb.*

glo·ry [glôr′ ē] *noun, plural* **glories. 1.** great honor or praise that comes to a person for some success; great fame: Abner Doubleday got all the *glory* for inventing baseball, though it turned out later he had nothing to do with it. **2.** great beauty or splendor: "The warm *glory* of afternoon sunlight made him start and blink his eyes." (Aldous Huxley) **3.** a person or thing that brings great honor or pride: The American flag is often called "Old *Glory.*"

glos·sa·ry [gläs′ ər ē] *noun, plural* **glossaries.** a list of difficult or special words with their meanings. A glossary appears at the end of a book or article to explain words used in the text.

glove [gluv] *noun, plural* **gloves.** a covering for the hand, especially one with a separate part for each finger.

glossary A *glossary* is "a collection of glosses." But what then is a gloss? A *gloss* is a short comment or explanation, telling the meaning of a rarely-used or specialized word. You have seen glosses in your textbooks. A word is given an asterisk* as it appears in the text, and then the gloss appears at the bottom of the page (or at the end of the chapter.) In this way, it's like a FOOTNOTE (see p. 307). A *glossary* collects all the glosses in alphabetical order at the back of the book. Should you gloss words in your own writing? Probably not. When you use an unfamiliar word, explain it right away with a following phrase or sentence: "Pioneer children usually wore clothes made of linsey-woolsey, a rough, homemade cloth that was a mixture of wool with linen and cotton." "Their supper was usually johnnycake or hoecake made from ground corn."

gloom [glōōm] *noun.* **1.** dim light; darkness: "To chase away the *gloom* the family threw pine-branches on their fire . . ." (Nathaniel Hawthorne) **2.** low spirits; sadness; sorrow.

gloom·y [glōō′ mē] *adjective,* **gloomier, gloomiest. 1.** partly or completely dark; dim: "It was winter: November, with late *gloomy* dawns and a cold wind . . ." (Iris Murdoch) **2.** causing or full of sorrow or low spirits; sad: "The housekeeper departed, and he and I sat in *gloomy* silence." (Bertrand Russell)

glow [glō] *noun, plural* **glows. 1.** a soft, steady light or shine: the *glow* of candles, the *glow* of hot coals in a fireplace. **2.** a warm, bright color of the skin. **3.** a warm or happy feeling: "A wonderful *glow* of life and freedom came upon her . . ." (John Galsworthy) —*verb,* **glowed, glowing. 1.** to give off a soft, steady light: "A yellow lantern *glowed* on the front porch." (Richard Wright) **2.** to have a shining, healthy color: Her cheeks *glowed* pink. **3.** to have or show a warm feeling: to *glow* with pride.

glue [glōō] *noun, plural* **glues.** any sticky substance used to hold or join things together, especially a thick liquid made by boiling animal skin and parts. —*verb,* **glued, gluing. 1.** to stick things together with glue: He *glued* the broken chair leg back together. **2.** to fasten or hold tight, as if with glue: Eric's eyes were *glued* to the TV set as he watched his favorite show.

glum [glum] *adjective,* **glummer, glummest.** in low spirits; sad; gloomy: She feels really *glum* after being sick in the house with chicken pox all week. —**glumly,** *adverb.*

gnarled [närld] *adjective, more/most.* having a rough, twisted look: The old tree was *gnarled* and its branches were like twisted arms.

gnat [nat] *noun, plural* **gnats.** a tiny biting insect having two wings. There are many kinds of gnats found in all parts of the world.

gnaw [nô] *verb,* **gnawed, gnawing. 1.** to bite at and chew so as to wear away: The puppy was *gnawing* on a bone. **2.** to cause pain or worry, as if by chewing: "Fear was *gnawing* at her . . ." (Edna Ferber) "Oh, Celie, this thing has been *gnawing* away at her all these years!" (Alice Walker)

gnome [nōm] *noun, plural* **gnomes.** in old stories, a dwarf or other tiny creature who lives under the ground and guards treasures, such as gold or silver. ♦ *Gnome* comes from an old word meaning "wise," with the idea that gnomes had special knowledge of the earth.

gnu [nōō *or* nyōō] *noun, plural* **gnus** or **gnu.** a large African antelope with curved horns, a tail like a horse, and a head and humped shoulders like a buffalo.

are things *going* with you lately? **7.** to be suited; fit: That purple shirt doesn't *go* with the orange skirt.

goad [gōd] *noun, plural* **goads. 1.** a pointed stick used to make cattle or other farm animals move. **2.** something that forces a person to move or act. —*verb,* **goaded, goading.** to force to move or act; drive or annoy as if with a goad: "She seldom managed nowadays to *goad* me into a reply to her insults." (Dick Francis)

goal [gōl] *noun, plural* **goals. 1.** something that a person wants and tries for; an aim or purpose: Ruth studied very hard to reach her *goal* of getting straight A's. "I believe this nation should commit itself to achieving the *goal* . . . of landing a man on the moon . . ." (John F. Kennedy) **2.** in certain games such as football,

gnu A herd of gnu on the plains of Kenya, in east-central Africa. This animal is also known as a *wildebeest* [wil′də bēst′].

go/say *Go* is one of the most widely-used words in English. In the 13-volume *Oxford English Dictionary,* the definitions for this two-letter word take up 37 columns of type. One definition that is not included in the *OED,* though, is the use of "go" to mean "say," as in "I asked Heather why she was mad at me. So she *goes,* 'Who said I was mad?' And then I *go,* 'You did!'" This is a very recent meaning of the word. It probably comes from the use of *go* to mean "have a certain wording," as in: "How does that song *go?*" or "'All's well that ends well,' as the old saying *goes.*" Because this is such a new and informal meaning, we recommend you avoid it in your writing. The word *say* does a perfectly good job and doesn't need to be replaced.

go [gō] *verb,* **went, gone, going. 1.** to move from one place to another; move along: to *go* home, to *go* to New York City. **2.** to take part in or do: to *go* shopping, to *go* to college. **3.** to reach or extend: Does this road *go* to town? **4.** to be in a state of; become: to *go* to sleep, to *go* hungry. **5.** to have a place; belong: Those books *go* on the second shelf. **6.** to turn out; happen: How

Pronunciation Key: A–F			
a	and; hat	ch	chew; such
ā	ate; stay	d	dog; lid
â	care; air	e	end; yet
ä	father; hot	ē	she; each
b	boy; cab	f	fun; off
(Turn the page for more information.)			

soccer, basketball, or hockey, a space which players must reach or get the ball or puck into in order to score. **3.** a point won by reaching the goal in such a game.

goal·ie [gō′ lē] *noun, plural* **goalies.** the player in a game who is in charge of protecting the goal and keeping the other team from scoring.
♦ Also called a **goalkeeper** or **goaltender.**

goat [gōt] *noun, plural* **goats.** an animal with short horns, rough hair, and a tuft of hair like a beard under its chin. Goats are related to sheep and are raised for their milk, meat, and hair. Wild goats usually live in mountain areas.

goat·ee [gō tē′] *noun, plural* **goatees.** a short, pointed beard, thought of as like the hair on a goat's chin.

gob·ble¹ [gäb′ əl] *verb,* **gobbled, gobbling.** to eat in a very fast, noisy way; eat quickly and greedily: ". . . they started to *gobble* the food . . . as if it was the best thing they'd eaten in their lives." (Andrea Lee)

gobble² *noun, plural* **gobbles.** a harsh sound like that made by a male turkey. —*verb,* **gobbled, gobbling.** to make this sound.

gob·lin [gäb′ lin] *noun, plural* **goblins.** in old stories, an ugly elf or spirit that plays evil tricks on people.

God [gäd] *noun.* the name for the being who is believed to be the maker and ruler of the world, worshiped as being all-powerful, present everywhere, and continuing forever.

god [gäd] *noun, plural* **gods.** a being who is believed to live forever and have powers far beyond those of ordinary people. In ancient Greece and Rome, people worshipped many different gods and told stories about them.

god·child [gäd′ chīld′] *noun, plural* **godchildren.** in the Christian religion, a child for whom two adults act as sponsors at the ceremony of baptism. These two **godparents** (the **godfather** and **godmother**) promise to help, if necessary, with the child's religious training.

god·dess [gäd′ is] *noun, plural* **goddesses.** a female god: The ancient Romans worshipped Venus as the *goddess* of love.

go·ing [gō′ ing] *verb.* the present participle of **go.** —*noun, plural* **goings. 1.** the act of going; leaving: That house has strange comings and *goings* at all hours of the night. **2.** the conditions for some form of travel or journey: The rain turned to snow, and the *going* got very slippery. —*adjective.* in existence or operation: the *going* price for something. I think the Mercedes is the best car *going*.

gold A fortune in gold bars on display in a London bank. Gold in a raw form or in bars like this is called *bullion* [bul′ yən].

gold [gōld] *noun.* **1.** a soft, heavy, very valuable yellow metal used to make jewelry and coins. Gold is a chemical element. **2.** something thought of as very valuable or special, like gold: a person with a heart of *gold.* **3.** a bright-yellow color like gold.

gold·en [gōld′ ən] *adjective.* **1.** made of or containing gold. **2.** having the color or shine of gold; deep, bright yellow. **3.** very good or excellent; very valuable: a *golden* opportunity. **4.** having to do with the fiftieth year in a series: His grandparents have just celebrated their *golden* wedding anniversary.

gold·en·rod [gōld′ ən räd′] *noun, plural* **goldenrods.** a tall plant with long stalks of small yellow flowers. Goldenrod blooms in late summer or early fall.

gold·fish [gōld′ fish′] *noun, plural* **goldfish** or **goldfishes.** a small freshwater fish that usually has an orange-gold color, often kept in home aquariums or ponds.

gold mine A gold mine in South Africa, which is now the world's chief source of gold. We also use the expression "a gold mine" to mean "a source of money or riches."

G

golf [gälf] *noun.* an outdoor game in which a player hits a small, hard ball with special clubs having iron or wooden heads. The object of the game is to use as few strokes as possible to hit the ball into a series of holes called a **golf course.** —*verb,* **golfed, golfing.** to play the game of golf. —**golfer,** *noun.*

gone [gôn] the past participle of **go.**

gong [gông] *noun, plural* **gongs.** a round metal plate that makes a deep ringing sound when it is struck with a hammer.

—*interjection.* a word used to show surprise: "Oh, my *goodness!*" she said when she found the money in the street.

goods [goodz] *plural noun.* **1.** anything made to be bought or sold; merchandise: That store sells all its *goods* at discount prices. "In the great tent the country people had spread out their *goods*—butter, cheese, eggs, honey, and the like." (Howard Pyle) **2.** the things that belong to someone; belongings: household *goods.* **3.** cloth; fabric: dress *goods.*

---

good/well Do you know how to choose between these words? *Good* is an adjective and therefore modifies (adds to) a noun: "She's a *good* tennis player." *Well* is an adverb and therefore modifies (adds to) a verb: "She plays tennis *well*." A mistake that some people make is to use *good* as an adverb. "She plays tennis *good*." *Well* should be used there. You can say, "John felt *good*," and mean he was cheerful and energetic. If you say "John felt *well*," you suggest that earlier he was ill or not at ease. You shouldn't write "I don't sing *good*." You should write "These clothes look *good*." What's the distinction here? Some verbs link with adjectives, not adverbs. These are "sense" verbs such as *look, feel,* or *sound.* We say "That idea *sounds good* to me" (not "sounds well") and "The cool rain really *felt good* on my skin" (not "felt well").

---

good [good] *adjective,* **better, best. 1.** having the right qualities; above average; not poor or bad: a *good* student, *good* weather, to have a *good* time at a party. **2.** honest and kind; not evil: a *good* deed, a person with a *good* character. **3.** as it should be; all right: *good* health, a *good* appetite. **4.** useful or helpful for a certain purpose: *good* advice, a *good* exercise for losing weight. **5.** proper or correct: *good* manners, to use *good* English. **6.** in use or effect: This train ticket is *good* for one month. **7.** at least the amount stated: We waited a *good* half hour for him to arrive. —*noun, plural.* something that is good: A long vacation would really do her a lot of *good.*

good•bye or **good-by** [good′ bī′] *interjection; noun.* what someone says to another person when one or the other is leaving.

Good Friday the Friday before Easter. It is set aside in Christian churches as the anniversary of the day Jesus died on the cross.

good-na•tured [good′ nā′ chərd] *adjective, more/most.* having a kind and friendly nature; pleasant; cheerful. ♦ The word **good** is used to form other compound words that have the same meaning, such as **good-hearted, good-humored,** and **good-tempered.**

good•ness [good′ nis] *noun.* **1.** the quality of being good. **2.** the quality of having a good character; caring for others; kindness.

goose The Canada goose is known for its honking call and for flying in long, V-shaped formations as it migrates.

goose [goos] *noun, plural* **geese.** a web-footed water bird that looks like a duck but is larger and has a longer neck. Some kinds of geese are wild, such as the **Canada goose,** and others are

G

Pronunciation Key: G–N

g	give; big	k	kind; cat; back
h	hold	l	let; ball
i	it; this	m	make; time
ī	ice; my	n	not; own
j	jet; gem; edge	ng	having

(Turn the page for more information.)

tame, such as the large white variety that is raised for meat.

go·pher [gō′fər] *noun, plural* **gophers.** a small, furry North American animal that lives in long tunnels that it burrows under the ground. Gophers have very long teeth and large claws that are used for digging, and large cheek pouches used to carry food.

gorge [gôrj] *noun, plural* **gorges.** a deep, narrow valley that has steep and rocky walls on either side, usually formed by a river that runs through it. —*verb,* **gorged, gorging.** to eat a very large amount of food; stuff oneself with food: He *gorged* himself at the picnic, eating three helpings of everything.

gor·geous [gôr′jəs] *adjective, more/most.* very beautiful to look at: a *gorgeous* sunset, *gorgeous* flowers, a *gorgeous* movie star.

gorilla Although it has a reputation for being very fierce, the gorilla is really fairly shy and gentle.

go·ril·la [gə ril′ə] *noun, plural* **gorillas.** a very large, strong ape. Gorillas have a broad, heavy chest and shoulders, long arms, and short legs. They live in the rain forests of central Africa and feed on fruits and vegetables.

gos·pel [gäs′pəl] *noun, plural* **gospels. 1. Gospel.** in the Bible, any of the first four books of the New Testament, which tell of the life of Christ and are thought to have been written by his Apostles, Matthew, Mark, Luke, and John. **2.** the teachings of Jesus and his Apostles. **3.** anything believed or accepted as absolutely true: That's the *gospel* truth—she told me so herself.

gos·sip [gäs′ ip] *noun, plural* **gossips. 1.** talk or news about the personal lives of other people that is not kind and often is not true: Supermarket newspapers print *gossip* about TV stars and other famous people. **2.** a person who likes to spread gossip. —*verb,* **gossiped, gossiping.** to repeat stories and rumors about other people; spread gossip.

got [gät] **1.** the past tense of **get:** I *got* two letters in the mail today. **2.** a past participle of **get:** "That's not the kind of log house I've *got* in mind." (Bobbie Ann Mason)

got·ten [gät′ ən] a past participle of **get:** "I had about *gotten* over the fear that I'd stop breathing during the night." (Garrison Keillor)

gouge [gouj] *noun, plural* **gouges. 1.** a tool with a curved, hollow blade, used to make holes or grooves in wood. **2.** a deep hole, groove, or cut: The lawn mower accidentally bumped against the fence and left a big *gouge* in the fence post. —*verb,* **gouged, gouging.** to make a gouge.

gourd [gôrd] *noun, plural* **gourds.** a rounded fruit with a hard, outer shell. Gourds grow on vines and are related to pumpkins and squash. The shells are used as decorations or as cups, bowls, and dippers.

gourd Several colorful varieties of gourds.

gour·met [goor mā′] *noun, plural* **gourmets.** a person who has a great appreciation for fine food and drink and knows a lot about them. —*adjective.* having to do with or suited for a gourmet: *gourmet* meals, a *gourmet* cook.

gov·ern [guv′ ərn] *verb,* **governed, governing. 1.** to be in charge of a country, state, city, or other body; rule: The United States is *governed* by the President and the Congress. **2.** to be in charge of something; control or manage: "She *governed* her house cunningly and firmly." (James Joyce) **3.** to decide or influence the

G

govern To *govern* is to steer or lead a community as provided by its politics and laws. It also means that someone exercises authority. In England, a *governess* is a woman hired to look after children — she is a substitute for the parents who are often away or socially busy. The verb has no special quality. Hitler *governed* Germany ruthlessly, as a dictator. American Presidents *govern* under a system of "checks and balances," i.e., the Congress and Supreme Court share authority with the President. In the U.S., the heads of state governments are also "governing." In parts of the British Commonwealth (as in Canada), there is a Governor-General who has an authority but who is appointed by the British Queen as her representative. Can you name three synonyms for *govern?* (Try *rule* for one.)

nature of something; determine: The movements of the moon *govern* the flow of ocean tides.

gov•ern•ment [guv′ər mənt *or* guv′ ərn mənt] *noun, plural* **governments. 1.** a system of controlling a country, state, city, or other body and managing its affairs: The U.S. and Canada have a democratic form of *government*. **2.** the act of ruling; governing. **3.** the group of people who manage or govern a certain place.

gov•er•nor [guv′ə nər *or* guv′ ər nər] *noun, plural* **governors. 1.** a person who is the head of a state government in the United States. **2.** a person who manages a colony or territory on behalf of the ruling country: William Bradford was a famous *governor* of the Plymouth Colony in Massachusetts. **3.** an official who is in charge of an organization: Movie Oscars are awarded by the Motion Picture Academy's board of *governors*. **4.** a device that controls the speed of a machine, especially one that keeps an engine from going too fast.

gown [goun] *noun, plural* **gowns. 1.** a woman's dress, especially a long, formal dress worn for special occasions: a wedding *gown*. **2.** a long, loose robe worn for an important event, as by a judge in a courtroom or a minister in church. **3.** a long, loose robe or similar garment: a dressing *gown*, a night*gown*.

grab [grab] *verb,* **grabbed, grabbing. 1.** to take hold of suddenly by the hand: He *grabbed* his coat and ran out the back door. **2.** to take something in a sudden or hasty way: to *grab* a bite to eat before going out, to *grab* a taxi to the airport. —*noun, plural* **grabs.** the act of grabbing: "Greatly alarmed, he made a *grab* at the side of the boat . . ." (Kenneth Grahame)

grace [grās] *noun, plural* **graces. 1.** a way of moving that is smooth and easy and beautiful to see: Champion figure skater Peggy Fleming was known for her *grace* on the ice. **2.** a highly pleasing or agreeable quality; charm: Their home is decorated with *grace* and style. **3.** a

feeling of kindness or politeness: He pushed right past us and didn't even have the *grace* to say "Excuse me." **4.** a period of extra time that is allowed for something: The hotel's checkout time is noon, but they allow a three-hour *grace* period before they charge for an extra day. **5.** a short prayer of thanks given before a meal. —*verb,* **graced, gracing.** to add grace to: Freshly-cut flowers *graced* the dining table.

grace•ful [grās′ fəl] *adjective, more/most.* **1.** showing or having grace; moving in a smooth and beautiful way: a *graceful* ballet dancer. **2.** having charm; very pleasant and agreeable: Ronald Reagan is thought of as a *graceful* politician who is good at avoiding difficult situations. —**gracefully,** *adverb.*

gra•cious [grā′ shəs] *adjective, more/most.* showing kindness and courtesy; well-mannered. —**graciously,** *adverb.*

grack•le [grak′ əl] *noun, plural* **grackles.** a large American blackbird with a long tail, shiny black feathers, and a very harsh cry.

grade [grād] *noun, plural* **grades. 1.** one year or level of school: Students in the twelfth *grade* are called seniors. **2.** a letter or number showing how well a student has done; a mark: Sheila got a *grade* of 'B' on her book report. **3.** one level on a scale of value: "Choice" and "Prime" are *grades* of beef. **4.** the amount of slope on a road, hill or railroad track: a hill with a steep *grade.* —*verb,* **graded, grading. 1.** to give a grade or mark to: The teacher *graded* the test papers. **2.** to place according to level or quality: to *grade* eggs by their size. **3.** to change the amount of slope in an area of ground: The

G

Pronunciation Key: O–S			
ō	over; go	ou	out; town
ô	all; law	p	put; hop
oo	look; full	r	run; car
o͞o	pool; who	s	set; miss
oi	oil; boy	sh	show
(Turn the page for more information.)			

bulldozer *graded* the hillside so that a house could be built there.

grade school a school that includes grades one to six and usually kindergarten; more often called ELEMENTARY SCHOOL.

grad•u•al [graj′ōō əl] *adjective, more/most.* happening little by little; changing or moving slowly: There was a *gradual* drop in the temperature, and we started to feel chilly. —**gradually,** *adverb.*

grad•u•ate [graj′ōō āt′] *verb,* **graduated, graduating. 1.** to complete a full course of study at a school or college and be given a certificate or paper showing this: My cousin just *graduated* from law school. **2.** to mark off something in equal amounts for measuring: a *graduated* measuring cup. **3.** to advance to some higher level or status: "The three-year-old had *graduated* from a cot to a bed . . ." (Ken Follett) —[graj′ōō it] *noun, plural* **graduates.** a person who has graduated from a school or college: To get that job, you have to be a high-school *graduate.*

grad•u•a•tion [graj′ōō ā′shən] *noun, plural* **graduations. 1.** a ceremony to honor people who have graduated: The seniors wore caps and gowns during their *graduation.* **2.** the act or fact that has been grafted on to another place. **2.** money or other favors gained in a dishonest way because of one's position, especially by a politician or public official.

grain [grān] *noun, plural* **grains. 1.** the seed of wheat, corn, rice, and other such food plants. **2.** a tiny, hard piece of something: a *grain* of salt, a *grain* of sand. **3.** the lines or marks that run through wood, stone, meat, and other substances: It's easier to saw this wood if you cut along the *grain.* **4.** the smallest possible amount; a tiny bit: I don't think there's a *grain* of truth in his story.

gram [gram] *noun, plural* **grams.** a way of measuring weight. The gram is the basic unit of weight in the metric system. There are about 28 grams in an ounce.

gram•mar [gram′ ər] *noun.* **1.** the way in which words are used in a language. When a person has a certain thought to express, grammar determines how the person should form this thought into a sentence that will sound natural and correct to other people. **2.** the use of words according to these rules: It's not correct *grammar* to say "they was here."

grammar school another name for an ELEMENTARY SCHOOL.

---

grammar Language experts say that speech is natural, that you are born with an innate (natural or basic) ability to speak sentences. But reading is not natural in this way. It has to be taught. Writing is also not natural. Teaching good writing is the hardest teaching (and learning) job of all. Grammar is the structure of language. When we begin speaking as infants we use grammar without knowing what it is. Later, in school we are taught English grammar. It has two parts: *syntax* and *usage.* Syntax deals with language as an orderly system, with nouns and verbs, with ways to state meaning. Usage has to do with common terms in a language. Should you use *infer* or *imply*? (See p. 397.) On a job, should you use *shall* or *will*? (See p. 692.)

---

of graduating: Jed needs to pass only two more courses for *graduation.*

graf•fi•ti [grə fē′ tē] *plural noun.* words or drawings scribbled or painted in a public place without permission, as on a wall, sidewalk, rock, and so on.

graft [graft] *verb,* **grafted, grafting. 1.** to put a bud or twig from one plant into a cut or slit on another plant, so that the two will grow together: Fruit trees are often *grafted* to make them grow faster or produce better fruit. **2.** to move a piece of skin or bone from one part of the body to another, or from one person to another: Doctors *graft* healthy skin onto an area of a person's body that has been badly burned or injured. —*noun, plural* **grafts. 1.** something

graffiti Graffiti on the western side of the Berlin Wall.

gram•mat•i•cal [grə mat′ i kəl] *adjective.* **1.** having to do with grammar: The teacher marked several *grammatical* errors on my paper. **2.** according to grammar; following the rules of grammar: It's not *grammatical* to say "He don't know nothing."—**grammatically,** *adverb.*

grand [grand] *adjective,* **grander, grandest. 1.** very large and impressive; magnificent; splendid: The MGM *Grand* is one of the biggest and most expensive hotels in Las Vegas. **2.** greatest in size or importance; main: the *Grand* Canal in Venice, Italy. ♦ This meaning is often used to form compound nouns: **grand opera,** a **grand piano,** a **grand duke** or **grand duchess. 3.** taking in everything; complete: She won $3,000 on the quiz show today and $5,000 yesterday, for a *grand* total of $8,000. **4.** very good; excellent: "To him, a horse was the *grandest* animal in the world." (Walter Farley)

Grand Canyon A winter view of the canyon from Yaki Point.

Grand Canyon a very large and deep canyon formed by the Colorado River in northwestern Arizona.

grand•child [grand′ chīld′] *noun, plural* **grandchildren.** the child of one's son or daughter; a granddaughter or grandson.

grand•daugh•ter [grand′ dôt′ ər] *noun, plural* **granddaughters.** the daughter of one's son or daughter.

grand•fa•ther [grand′ fä′ thər] *noun, plural* **grandfathers.** the father of one's mother or father.

grandfather clock a clock in a tall, narrow cabinet that stands on the floor.

grand jury a special kind of jury that studies the facts of a case and then decides whether or not someone should be accused of a crime and put on trial.

grand•moth•er [grand′ muth′ ər] *noun, plural* **grandmothers.** the mother of one's mother or father.

grand•par•ent [grand′ per′ ənt] *noun, plural* **grandparents.** the parent of one's mother or father; a grandmother or grandfather.

grand•son [grand′ sun′] *noun, plural* **grandsons.** the son of one's son or daughter.

grand•stand [grand′ stand′] *noun, plural* **grandstands.** the main seating area for people at a parade, fair, or sports event. Grandstands are made of sloping rows of seats and are sometimes covered by a roof.

gran•ite [gran′ it] *noun.* a hard, heavy type of rock that is often used in buildings and monuments.

gra•no•la [grə nō′ lə] *noun.* a dry breakfast or snack food made of rolled oats, wheat germ, brown sugar or honey, and sometimes dried fruit and nuts.

grant [grant] *verb,* **granted, granting. 1.** to give or allow what one asks: In old stories, a person is often *granted* three wishes by a fairy or genie. **2.** to admit to be true; agree: "*Granted* he was a nice tricky runner, but he was so small that when somebody hit him he flew 10 feet." (Jack Kerouac) **3. take for granted.** to be aware of without questioning or thinking about: "She didn't really mind housekeeping so much. She *took* it *for granted,* and did it just because it was there to be done." (Aldous Huxley) —*noun, plural* **grants. 1.** something that is granted. ♦ A **land grant** is property given by the government to a person, as for farming. **2.** money that is provided for education or the arts: Professor Chase received a $30,000 *grant* to begin work on a biography of the author Eudora Welty.

Grant [grant] **Ulysses S.,** 1822–1885, American general in the Civil War and the eighteenth president of the United States, from 1869 to 1877.

grape [grāp] *noun, plural* **grapes.** a small, juicy, round fruit that grows in bunches on vines. Grapes are usually green or purple and have a smooth, thin skin. They are eaten raw and are also used to make juice, wine, raisins, and jam.

Pronunciation Key: T–Z			
t	ten; date	v	very; live
th	think	w	win; away
th	these	y	you
u	cut; butter	z	zoo; cause
ur	turn; bird	zh	measure

(Turn the page for more information.)

grape•fruit [grāp′frōōt′] *noun, plural* **grape-fruit** or **grapefruits.** a round fruit with a pale-yellow skin and white, yellow, or pink pulp. Grapefruit are like oranges, but are larger and more sour in taste.

grape•vine [grāp′vīn′] *noun, plural* **grape-vines. 1.** a vine that grapes grow on. **2.** a secret or informal way of passing news or rumors from person to person: I heard through the *grapevine* at school that Steve and his girlfriend had a big fight last night.

grass [gras] *noun, plural* **grasses. 1.** one of a large family of green plants that have long, thin leaves and grow throughout the world. Members of this family include sugarcane, bamboo, reeds, and cereal grasses such as wheat, rice, and corn. **2.** any of the various types of grass plants that are used to cover lawns, playgrounds, and sports fields, or grown in fields and pastures as feed for farm animals. Common grasses include rye, **bluegrass,** and **Bermuda grass. —grassy,** *adjective.*

grapevine I heard through the *grapevine* that the club secretary was leaving town." The "grapevine" is a route or series of places through which rumor and gossip are carried from one person to another. It's an unofficial way of passing information in, say, a business office or a school. What is the connection between the grapevine that is a plant, and "rumors" or "inside information"? During the Civil War, messages were sent by means of a "grapevine telegraph," so called because its wires were thought to extend in a complicated, twisting pattern, like the shape of a spreading grapevine. That's what some dictionaries say. But this dictionary isn't so sure of that origin for *grapevine.* Maybe it's like the idiom, "The real McCoy." There are at least fifteen different explanations for that expression and all of them, therefore, are suspect! Dictionaries are not without error, after all.

G

graph [graf] *noun, plural* **graphs.** a drawing that shows how certain numbers or facts relate to each other. Graphs use a set of lines, bars, or pictures to show many different types of information.

graph•ic [graf′ik] *adjective, more/most.* **1.** having to do with or shown by a graph: a *graphic* record of the average monthly temperature for a place. **2.** having to do with drawing, printing, photography, and other ways of representing images or words on a surface: The **graphic arts** include the design and printing of books, magazines, and advertisements. **3.** very realistic or true to life, as if shown in a picture: This book gives a *graphic* picture of the lives of poor farm workers. —*noun, plural* **graphics.** a graphic image, especially one that appears on a television or computer screen: That new video game really has great *graphics.*

graph•ite [graf′īt] *noun.* a soft, black mineral that is a form of carbon. Graphite is used for lead in pencils.

grasp [grasp] *verb,* **grasped, grasping. 1.** to take hold of firmly with the hands: **2.** to take hold of with the mind; understand: "I think I *grasped* quite soon what was going on and where I was and all that." (Kingsley Amis) —*noun, plural* **grasps. 1.** a firm hold or grip. **2.** the fact of grasping with the mind; understanding: He just started the course and doesn't have a good *grasp* of the subject yet.

grass•hop•per [gras′häp′ər] *noun, plural* **grasshoppers.** an insect that has wings and long powerful legs that it uses for jumping.

grate[1] [grāt] *noun, plural* **grates. 1.** a frame of iron bars placed over a window or other opening; also called a **grating. 2.** a frame of iron bars to hold burning fuel in a furnace or fireplace.

grate[2] *verb,* **grated, grating. 1.** to grind or shred into small pieces by rubbing against a rough surface: He *grated* the carrots and added them to the salad. **2.** to make a harsh, grinding noise by rubbing or scraping: "The bottom of the boat *grated* on the sand." (John P. Marquand) **3.** to be unpleasant or irritating: The way she chews gum so loudly really *grates* on my nerves.

grate•ful [grāt′fəl] *adjective, more/most.* feeling or showing thanks for some favor or for something good that has happened: to be *grateful* to a friend for her kind words, to be *grateful* for a clear, sunny day after a week of rain. **—gratefully,** *adverb:* He smiled *gratefully* as the police car pulled over to help him.

grat•i•fy [grat′ə fī′] *verb,* **gratified, gratifying.** to give pleasure or satisfaction to; please: She was *gratified* by the good report the boss wrote about her. **—gratification,** *noun.*

grat•i•tude [grat′ə tōōd′] *noun.* a feeling of being grateful; feeling thanks for a favor or for something good: "I accept this award with *gratitude* and pride . . ." (Langston Hughes)

grave¹ [grāv] *noun, plural* **graves. 1.** a hole dug in the ground to bury a dead body. **2.** any place of death or burial: It is sometimes said that a ship which sinks has gone to a watery *grave.*

grave² *adjective,* **graver, gravest. 1.** of great importance; very serious: Being president of the U.S. is a *grave* responsibility. **2.** very dangerous or threatening; causing great concern: The patient is in *grave* condition. **3.** very serious in manner; solemn: "He kept the *grave* look on his face for a moment. And then he smiled." (Tom Wolfe) —**gravely,** *adverb.*

grav•el [grav′əl] *noun.* a loose mixture of pebbles and small pieces of rock, often used for making driveways and roads.

gravestone The grave of Colonel George Armstrong Custer at the site of the Battle of Little Bighorn.

grave•yard [grāv′yard′] *noun, plural* **graveyards.** a place where dead people are buried; a cemetery.

grav•i•tate [grav′ə tāt′] *verb,* **gravitated, gravitating. 1.** to move or tend to move by the force of gravity. **2.** to move or be attracted by a strong influence: At first everyone at the party was scattered around the room, but as time went on they all *gravitated* toward the refreshment table.

grav•i•ta•tion [grav′ə tā′shən] *noun.* the force that causes any two bodies in the universe to tend to move toward one another; the force of gravity. Gravitation keeps the planets in their orbits and holds the gases of the sun together.

grav•i•ty [grav′ə tē] *noun.* **1.** the force that pulls things toward the center of the earth. Gravity causes things to have weight and to fall to earth when they are dropped. **2.** the state of being grave; seriousness; importance: "Not until darkness closed in did he realize what he had done. Then the *gravity* of it struck him." (Marguerite Henry)

gra•vy [grā′vē] *noun, plural* **gravies.** the juices that drip from meat while it is cooking, or a sauce made from these juices.

gray [grā] *noun, plural* **grays.** (also spelled **grey**) **1.** a color that is a mixture of black and white. **2.** not cheerful or bright: a *gray* winter day. —*adjective.* having the color gray. ♦ The spelling *grey* is more often used in Great Britain.

graze¹ [grāz] *verb,* **grazed, grazing.** of a cow, sheep, or other such animal, to feed on growing grass: "At length the buffalo began to appear, *grazing* in herds on the great prairies which then bordered the river." (Mark Twain)

graze² *verb,* **grazed, grazing.** to touch or scrape lightly: "Butterflies *grazed* Shaun's nose, leaving the powder from their wings." (Marguerite Henry)

grease [grēs] *noun.* **1.** soft, melted animal fat: We poured the bacon *grease* into a can. **2.** any thick, oily substance: He put some *grease* on the bicycle wheel to make it turn more easily. —*verb,* **greased, greasing.** to rub or put grease on: I *greased* the frying pan so that the meat wouldn't stick to it.

greas•y [grē′sē] *adjective,* **greasier, greasiest. 1.** covered or soiled with grease. **2.** containing grease or fat; oily: *greasy* food.

great [grāt] *adjective,* **greater, greatest. 1.** much better than is usual; of very high quality; excellent: The Mona Lisa is a *great* painting. Washington and Lincoln are thought of as *great* presidents. **2.** very large or important: the *Great* Wall of China. **3.** much more than usual: *great* happiness, a *great* deal of money. It came as a *great* surprise to me. **4.** very good; first-rate: a *great* vacation, a restaurant that serves *great* hamburgers. **5.** of a relative, belonging to the next earlier generation: They have four grandchildren and two *great*-grandchildren.

Great Bri•tain [brit′ən] a country located on a large island off the coast of western Europe. It is made up of England, Scotland, Wales, and Northern Ireland. *Capital:* London. *Area:* 94,200 square miles. *Population:* 56,200,000.

Great Dane [dān] a very tall, powerful dog with a short, smooth coat.

G

Pronunciation Key: [ə] Symbol

The [ə] or *schwa* sound occurs in syllables without an accent. It can be spelled with any vowel, such as **a** in above, **e** in listen, **i** in pencil, **o** in melon, **u** in circus. It can also be a combination of vowels, such as **io** in action, **ai** in mountain, **iou** in precious.

(Turn the page for more information.)

Great Lakes a chain of five large lakes in east-central North America. They are Lake Superior, Michigan, Huron, Erie, and Ontario.

Great Plains a large area of flat land east of the Rocky Mountains, extending from northern Texas up to Canada.

Great Salt Lake a large salt lake in northwestern Utah.

much *greed* that he wanted everything he owned turned into gold.

greed•y [grēd′ē] *adjective,* **greedier, greediest. 1.** showing greed; wanting very much to have more than one needs or more than one's share. **2.** wanting to eat or drink a very large amount of food. **—greedily,** *adverb:* "Lena eats *greedily,* bending over her plate . . ." (Andrea Lee)

Greek In the 200's B.C., there were occasional meetings, and sometimes wars, between the ancient Greeks and ancient Romans. The Greeks were more advanced and sophisticated as a culture and society. One result was that the Romans borrowed many ideas and customs from them. When Rome became the dominant empire in the West, its Latin language developed into several local forms—French, Spanish, Italian, Portuguese, Romanian, and so on. After the year 1066, when the French-speaking Normans ruled England, many words that had begun in Greek, then moved to Latin, and then to French, finally entered English. Thus, Greek words are often found in English in government *(democracy, politics),* science *(arithmetic, geography, machine, physics),* and learning and art *(school, drama, poetry, architecture, music).* Even in modern times Greek words have come into English. Examples are *astronaut,* which comes from the ancient Greek words for "star" and "sailor," and *telephone,* which is from the words meaning "far off" and "sound."

great•ly [grāt′lē] *adverb.* very much; highly: The passengers were *greatly* relieved when the pilot said they'd flown clear of the storm.

Greece [grēs] a country in southeastern Europe that includes many islands in the Aegean Sea. In ancient times Greece was an important center of learning and civilization. *Capital:* Athens. *Area:* 50,900 square miles. *Population:* 9,700,000.

Greece The Parthenon, a very famous temple in Athens, Greece.

greed [grēd] *noun, plural* **greeds.** a selfish desire to get more than one's fair share of something; a very great wish for money, power, and so on: An old folk tale tells of a king who had so

Greek [grēk] *noun, plural* **Greeks. 1.** a person born or living in Greece. **2.** the language of Greece. **—***adjective.* having to do with Greece, its people, or their language.

green [grēn] *noun, plural* **greens. 1.** the color of growing grass and leaves. **2.** an area of ground that is covered with grass: New England towns often have a village *green* in the center. **3.** on a golf course, the area of smooth, short grass around the hole. **4. greens.** green leaves and stems of plants that are used for food. **—***adjective.* **greener, greenest. 1.** having the color green. **2.** covered with growing plants, grass, or leaves: "In England's *green* and pleasant land . . ." (William Blake) **3.** not full-grown; not ripe: *green* tomatoes. **4.** without training; not experienced: He's a good young player, but he's too *green* to be in the major leagues.

green•house [grēn′ hous′] *noun, plural* **greenhouses.** a building made of glass or plastic, used for growing plants all year round in a controlled temperature.

Green•land [grēn′ lənd] an island in the North Atlantic, off northeastern Canada, belonging to Denmark. It is the largest island in the world. *Area:* 840,000 square miles. *Population:* 54,000.

greet [grēt′] *verb,* **greeted, greeting. 1.** to welcome or speak to a person in a friendly or polite way: She *greeted* her grandmother with a big hug. **2.** to respond to; meet or receive: They *greeted* the good news with a loud cheer.

greet•ing [grēt′ing] *noun, plural* **greetings.**
1. the act or words of a person who greets someone; a welcome: She got a friendly *greeting* from her neighbor as he walked by.
2. greetings. a friendly message that someone sends: Christmas *greetings.*

gre•nade [grə nād′] *noun, plural* **grenades.** a small bomb that can be thrown by hand or fired by a rifle.

grew [grōō] *verb.* the past tense of **grow.**

grey [grā] *noun, plural* **greys.** another spelling of **gray.**

grey•hound [grā′hound′] *noun, plural* **greyhounds.** a slender dog with long legs, a smooth coat, and a long nose.

greyhound Greyhounds are the fastest runners of any breed of dog, and are often used for racing.

grid•dle [grid′əl] *noun, plural* **griddles.** a flat, heavy metal plate used to cook pancakes, bacon, and other foods.

grief [grēf] *noun, plural* **griefs.** great sadness or suffering, as at the death of a loved one; great sorrow.

griev•ance [grē′vəns] *noun, plural* **grievances.** something that is thought of as a reason for being angry or upset; a complaint: The workers presented a list of their *grievances* to the head of the company.

grieve [grēv] *verb,* **grieved, grieving.** to feel grief; be very sad: The entire country *grieved* over the death of President John F. Kennedy in 1963.

griev•ous [grē′vəs] *adjective, more/most.* very serious or severe; causing grief or suffering: ". . . Caesar was ambitious: If it were so, it is a *grievous* fault," (Shakespeare, *Julius Caesar*) —**grievously,** *adverb.*

grill [gril] *noun, plural* **grills.** a framework of metal bars to hold food for cooking over an open fire: We broiled the hamburgers on the *grill.* —*verb,* **grilled, grilling. 1.** to broil food on a grill. **2.** to question severely for a long time: The police *grilled* the suspect for hours before he finally admitted he'd been lying.

grim [grim] *adjective,* **grimmer, grimmest.**
1. causing fear; horrible or frightening: Jack London's "To Build a Fire" is a *grim* tale of a man freezing to death. **2.** very stern or harsh; forbidding: "So we stood there in *grim* silence, unwilling to ask more questions." (Donald Sobol) —**grimly,** *adverb:* "Ahab was now found *grimly* clinging to his boat's broken half . . ." (Herman Melville)

grim•ace [grim′əs] *noun, plural* **grimaces.** a tight, twisted expression on the face, as from pain or annoyance: "Her face wrinkled up in a *grimace* of disgust." (Aldous Huxley) —*verb,* **grimaced, grimacing.** to make a grimace.

grime [grīm] *noun.* a heavy layer of dirt that covers or is rubbed deep into a surface: The mechanic's hands were covered with *grime* after he finished working on the car engine. —**grimy,** *adjective.*

grin [grin] *verb,* **grinned, grinning.** to smile in a very happy way; have a wide smile. —*noun, plural* **grins.** a wide, very happy smile.

grind [grīnd] *verb,* **ground, grinding. 1.** to crush or chop into small pieces or a fine powder: to *grind* coffee beans, to *grind* beef for hamburgers. **2.** to make something smooth or sharp by rubbing it against something rough: to *grind* a knife to sharpen it. **3.** to rub together harshly and noisily: People who are nervous sometimes *grind* their teeth when they're asleep. **4. grind out.** to produce something in a steady, mechanical way, as if grinding things with a machine: The critics never like his books, but he *grinds out* a new one every year anyway. ◆ Something that grinds is a **grinder.**

grind•stone [grīnd′stōn′] *noun, plural* **grindstones. 1.** a flat, circular stone that is turned to sharpen knives, tools, and so on. **2. keep one's nose to the grindstone.** to keep working hard at some task or problem.

G

Pronunciation Key: Accent Marks

[′] is the normal accent mark. It shows where the main stress falls on a word.
[′] is a secondary accent mark. It shows a lighter stress than the primary accent. For example:

tel • e • vis • ion [tel′ə vizh′ən]
(Turn the page for more information.)

G

grip [grip] *noun, plural* **grips. 1.** a tight, strong hold; a firm grasp: "He dug his toes and his fingers into the ice, getting a *grip* to pull himself backwards." (Eleanor Estes) **2.** a full hold; control: "Now, now, Jim, get a *grip* on yourself. Take it easy, old boy." (James Herriot) **3.** a part to take hold of; a handle: the *grip* on a golf club. —*verb,* **gripped, gripping.** to hold something in a tight, strong way: "He *gripped* the boy's shoulder with fingers as strong as the claw of an eagle." (Marguerite Henry)

grit [grit] *noun, plural* **grits. 1.** very small bits of sand, stone, dirt, or the like: *Grit* blew into her face and hair as she walked along the beach. **2.** *Informal.* bravery; courage.

grits [grits] *noun.* coarsely ground corn, oats, or wheat used as a breakfast cereal.

grizzly bear The name *grizzly* comes from a word meaning "gray." Don't mix this up with *grisly,* which has the same sound but means "horrible."

griz•zly bear [griz′lē] a very large, fierce bear of western North America. Grizzly bears have long claws and brown or black fur tipped with gray.

gro•cer•y [grōs′rē *or* grōs′ə rē] *noun, plural* **groceries. 1.** a store that sells food and household supplies. A grocery is smaller than a supermarket and is usually not part of a larger chain of stores. ♦ A person who owns or runs a grocery is a **grocer. 2. groceries.** food and household supplies.

groom [grōōm] *noun, plural* **grooms. 1.** a person whose work is taking care of horses. **2.** short for **bridegroom.** —*verb,* **groomed, grooming. 1.** to take care of a horse, as by washing, brushing, and feeding it. **2.** to make neat and clean in appearance. ♦ Usually used as an adjective: a person who is very well-*groomed.* **3.** to prepare someone for a certain job or responsibility: The coach is *grooming* him to be next year's quarterback.

groove [grōōv] *noun, plural* **grooves.** a long, narrow cut or track: the *grooves* in a phonograph record. There were *grooves* in the dirt road where the heavy truck had passed. —*verb,* **grooved, grooving.** to make a groove in.

grope [grōp] *verb,* **groped, groping. 1.** to feel about with the hands in an uncertain way because one cannot see clearly: "Often there was no hallway light, which meant *groping* around in the darkness . . ." (Russell Baker) **2.** to search in one's mind, as if feeling for something: He was daydreaming when the teacher called on him, and he had to *grope* for the right answer.

gross [grōs] *adjective,* **grosser, grossest. 1.** with nothing taken out; total: A person's *gross* income is the total amount that is earned before any taxes are paid. **2.** obviously wrong or bad: a *gross* error. **3.** not polite or proper; disgusting; vulgar: a *gross* remark, a *gross* habit. —*noun, plural* **grosses** or **gross. 1.** the total amount. **2.** a group of twelve dozen or 144, used as a way of measuring goods in business.

> **gross** *Gross* has three common adjective meanings. There's the sense of "a person's *gross* (total) income," that of "a *gross* (obviously bad) mistake," and that of "a *gross* (vulgar or disgusting) habit of using the back of your hand to wipe your mouth while eating." The third sense of *gross* isn't a new meaning; Shakespeare used it 400 years ago. Yet, it is now almost too common in the speech and writing of young people: "Oh, how *gross!*" "Stop it, that's *gross!*" The problem is that *gross* in this sense is used so often that the other two meanings can be lost. Remember how we've often said that a good word can get worn out from overuse? (Other such "well-worn words" are *basically* and *beautiful.*)

groan [grōn] *noun, plural* **groans.** a deep, sad sound that people make when they are in pain, unhappy, or upset. —*verb,* **groaned, groaning.** to give a deep, sad sound; make a groan.

gro•tesque [grō tesk′] *adjective, more/most.* having a strange, unnatural appearance; ugly in a frightening way: Maurice Sendak's books often show *grotesque* monsters.

grouch [grouch] *noun, plural* **grouches.** a person who is bad-tempered and complains a lot; someone who is often in a bad mood. —**grouchy,** *adjective.*

ground[1] [ground] *noun, plural* **grounds. 1.** the solid part of the earth's surface; the earth; land: A pass in football must be caught before it touches the *ground.* **2. grounds.** the land around a house or school. **3.** *also,* **grounds.** an area of land that is used for a certain purpose: picnic *grounds,* a camp *ground,* a fair *ground.* **4.** *also,* **grounds.** a cause for thinking or doing something; a reason: The police believe they have *grounds* for charging him with the crime. **5. grounds.** small pieces of coffee that settle at the bottom of a cup or pot. —*verb,* **grounded, grounding. 1.** to force to stay on the ground or come down to the ground: Our plane was *grounded* for several hours by the ice storm. **2.** to cause to hit the bottom of a river or other body of water. **3.** to connect an electric wire with the ground so that its circuit will be safely completed. **4.** in baseball, to hit a ball so that it bounces or rolls along the ground.

ground[2] *verb.* the past form of **grind**: Grains of wheat are *ground* to make flour.

ground·hog [ground′ hôg′] *noun, plural* **groundhogs.** a small animal with a plump body and a bushy tail; usually called a WOODCHUCK.

grove [grōv] *noun, plural* **grove.** a group of trees standing together: an orange *grove.*

grow [grō] *verb,* **grew, grown, growing. 1.** of a living thing, to become bigger in size: My brother *grew* three inches last year. **2.** to live and be able to develop: Lemon trees *grow* in warm areas. **3.** to cause or allow to grow: to *grow* tomatoes, to *grow* a beard. **4.** to become larger; increase: The city of Los Angeles *grew* rapidly after World War II. **5.** to become: to *grow* old, to *grow* tired of something. **6. to grow up.** to become an adult.

growl [groul] *verb,* **growled, growling. 1.** to make a deep, low, rumbling sound in the throat, as a dog does when it is angry or as a sign of warning. **2.** to speak in a tone of voice like this. —*noun, plural* **growls.** a growling sound.

grown [grōn] *verb.* the past participle of **grow.**

grown-up [grōn′ up′] *noun, plural* **grown-ups.** a person who is fully grown; an adult.

growth [grōth] *noun, plural* **growths. 1.** the process of growing: the *growth* of a child, the *growth* of a plant. **2.** something that has grown: A wart is a *growth* on the skin. There was a thick *growth* of woods along the fence.

grub [grub] *noun, plural* **grubs.** a beetle or other insect after it has been hatched from an

G

group editing In recent years, a technique called group editing has become popular in courses on writing. In group editing, a student's first draft is read by a few other students. They get together with the writer and suggest ways that the paper can be improved. Their suggestions are general ones, such as "Change the wording of your title." or "Add more information to your first paragraph." Group editing does not deal with specific issues, such as "Put a comma in that sentence" or "Check the spelling of that name." It's also important that the people in the group express their comments in a positive way. For example, not "Who is this guy Uncle Jimmy anyway? Who needs him?" but rather "The character of Uncle Jimmy seems interesting, but you need to connect him more closely to the rest of the story."

group [groop] *noun, plural* **groups. 1.** a number of persons or things together: A *group* of people were waiting outside for the store to open. **2.** a number of persons or things that belong together or are thought of together: All the children in Karen's reading *group* are using the same book. The state of Hawaii is a *group* of islands in the Pacific Ocean. —*verb,* **grouped, grouping.** to form into or belong to a group: Oranges, lemons, limes, and grapefruit are *grouped* together as citrus fruits.

grouse [grous] *noun, plural* **grouse** or **grouses.** a bird that has a plump body and brown, black, or gray feathers. Grouse look somewhat like chickens and are hunted as a game bird.

egg and before it is a fully-grown insect. A grub looks like a worm.

grudge [gruj] *noun, plural* **grudges.** a feeling of anger or dislike against a person that has been felt for a long time: The two neighbors didn't speak for years because of an old *grudge* about one man's tree falling against the other's house.

Pronunciation Key: A–F			
a	and; hat	ch	chew; such
ā	ate; stay	d	dog; lid
â	care; air	e	end; yet
ä	father; hot	ē	she; each
b	boy; cab	f	fun; off

(Turn the page for more information.)

—*verb*, **grudged, grudging.** to refuse to give or allow: "Daddy doesn't *grudge* us these times together . . ."(Anne Frank)

gru•el•ing [grōō′ ling] *adjective, more/most.* very difficult or tiring: The 400-meter hurdles is a *grueling* race.

grue•some [grōō′ səm] *adjective, more/most.* causing fear or disgust; horrible: "You looked as if you'd been watching some frightful *gruesome* operation." (Kingsley Amis)

gruff [gruf] *adjective,* **gruffer, gruffest. 1.** deep and harsh; rough-sounding: The policeman told them in a *gruff* voice to stop blocking the sidewalk. **2.** not friendly or polite; rough: My uncle has a *gruff* way of dealing with people, but underneath it he's really nice.

grum•ble [grum′ bəl] *verb,* **grumbled, grumbling.** to show unhappiness or discontent; complain in a low, angry voice.

grunt [grunt] *noun, plural* **grunts.** a short, deep, harsh sound. —*verb,* **grunted, grunting.** to make a short, deep, harsh sound: "He could hear the wild boar *grunting* and coughing in his hole." (Marguerite Henry)

guar•an•tee [gar′ ən tē′] *noun, plural* **guarantees. 1.** a promise to fix or replace something or to give back the money paid for it, if something goes wrong with it during a certain period of time: We have a three-year *guarantee* on our new microwave oven. **2.** a way of being certain that something will happen or will be done: "The Bill of Rights . . . is every American's *guarantee* of freedom." (Harry Truman) —*verb,* **guaranteed, guaranteeing. 1.** to give a guarantee for: This car is *guaranteed* for the first 5000 miles of driving. **2.** to make sure or certain: "No one can *guarantee* success in war . . ." (Winston Churchill)

G

guerrilla These guerrilla fighters from Afghanistan took part in the conflict between their country and the U.S.S.R.

guard The "changing of the guard" takes place outside London's Buckingham Palace, as one guard relieves another at his post.

guard [gärd] *verb,* **guarded, guarding. 1.** to watch over; protect from harm; keep safe: Soldiers *guarded* the entrance to the fort. **2.** to watch over to keep from escaping or keep under control: Several policemen *guarded* the prisoner on his way to court. **3.** in sports, to stay close to a player on the other team to try to keep him from scoring. —*noun, plural* **guards. 1.** a policeman, soldier, or other person who watches over or protects someone or something. **2.** anything that protects or provides safety: Soccer players wear shin *guards* in case another player kicks them. **3.** in football, one of the two offensive players who line up at either side of the center, or a defensive player who lines up across from the center. **4.** in basketball, either of the two players whose position is farther away from the basket when their team has the ball.

guard•i•an [gär′ dē ən] *noun, plural* **guardians. 1.** a person chosen by law to take care of someone who is young or who is not able to take care of himself: The boy's aunt and uncle were appointed by the court to be his *guardians* after his parents died in an accident. **2.** something that guards or protects: The U.S. Constitution is called a *guardian* of freedom.

Gua•te•ma•la [gwä′ tə mä′ lə] a country in Central America, south of Mexico. *Capital:* Guatemala City. *Area:* 42,000 square miles. *Population:* 7,450,000.

guer•ril•la [gə ril′ ə] *noun, plural* **guerrillas.** a member of a small group of soldiers who make quick surprise attacks in enemy territory.

guess [ges] *verb,* **guessed, guessing. 1.** to have an idea about something without being sure that it is right; decide when one does not know exactly: "I watched him very closely, for I wanted to try to *guess* what was in his mind." (John Hersey) **2.** to judge by guessing: to *guess* a person's age, to *guess* at the correct answer on a test. **3.** to believe or suppose: I'm not sure what time it is—I *guess* about 3:30. —*noun, plural* **guesses.** an opinion formed without having enough information to be sure; the act of guessing.

guest [gest] *noun, plural* **guests. 1.** someone who is at another person's home for a meal or a visit: We have four *guests* coming over for dinner tonight. **2.** someone who stays at a hotel or motel.

guided missile a missile that is guided along a certain course throughout its flight by an automatic control inside it or by radio signals that it receives from the ground.

guild [gild] *noun, plural* **guilds. 1.** in the Middle Ages, a group of businessmen or skilled workers who were involved with the same kind of work, such as merchants, bakers, or tailors. Guilds served to protect the interests of members and set rules for doing business. **2.** a modern organization that is similar to a guild. ♦ Some modern labor unions are called guilds: Hollywood movie actors belong to the Screen Actor's *Guild.*

guest "Who was the *host* of this party?" You are asking who it is who gave the party, whose house it was held in, who paid for the food, etc. A *guest* is someone who's invited to such a meal or get-together. Television talk shows have a host, a person who invites others to come on as guests, to talk or sing, or both. When he or she is on vacation, it's common to say that the person taking the chair is a "guest host." *Guest host* is an example of an oxymoron [ăk′ si môr′ ən]. That is a combination of two words that seem to mean the opposite thing: "His feeble attempt at a joke was greeted with a *deafening silence.*" Oxymorons are used in literature. Ring Lardner said of a fellow author, Ernest Hemingway, "Few men can stand the *strain* of *relaxing* with him." This was a humorous way of saying that Hemingway's idea of relaxing was to take on some kind of heavy physical activity, tiring and even dangerous, such as boxing, deep-sea fishing, or big-game hunting.

guid•ance [gīd′ əns] *noun.* **1.** the act or fact of guiding: Thomas Wolfe often received *guidance* in his writing career from his editor Maxwell Perkins. **2.** advice or direction given to students as to which courses to take, what career to follow, how to deal with personal problems, and so on. **3.** something that guides, such as an automatic system for guiding a plane, ship, or spacecraft.

guide [gīd] *noun, plural* **guides. 1.** a person who leads a group of explorers, soldiers, campers, or other such people through an area that they are not familiar with. **2.** a person whose work is leading visitors through a museum, famous building, amusement park, or the like; also called a **tour guide. 3.** anything that shows the way or shows how something should be done: "Let your conscience be your *guide*" is a well-known old saying. **4.** a book that shows how to do something or gives facts about something: A school textbook comes with a teacher's *guide* that explains how to use the lessons. —*verb,* **guided, guiding. 1.** to serve as a guide: Kit Carson often *guided* Army troops through Indian country. **2.** to lead in a certain way: "She took him arm and *guided* him across the room." (John Cheever)

guilt [gilt] *noun, plural* **guilts. 1.** the fact of having done wrong or broken the law: The evidence in the case convinced the jury of the man's *guilt.* **2.** a feeling of having done something wrong; shame: He felt a lot of *guilt* after he hurt his little sister.

guilt•y [gil′ tē] *adjective,* **guiltier, guiltiest. 1.** having been convicted of a crime in a court of law: to be *guilty* of murder. **2.** having done something wrong; deserving blame or punishment: It turned out that the thief got in because a night watchman was *guilty* of forgetting to lock the door. **3.** feeling or showing guilt: Todd gave his mother a *guilty* look when she asked him what had happened to the rest of the cookies.

Guin•ea [gin′ē] a country in west Africa. *Capital:* Conakry. *Area:* 95,000 square miles. *Population:* 8,300,000.

Pronunciation Key: G–N			
g	give; big	k	kind; cat; back
h	hold	l	let; ball
i	it; this	m	make; time
ī	ice; my	n	not; own
j	jet; gem; edge	ng	having

(Turn the page for more information.)

guin•ea pig [gin′ ē] a small, furry animal with short ears, short legs, and no tail. Guinea pigs are often kept as pets or used in scientific experiments.

guinea pig The guinea pig is not a pig and is not from the African country of Guinea. It is a rodent from South America. Its name is one of those "wrong turns" of language that sometimes occur.

gui•tar [gi tär′] *noun, plural* **guitars.** a musical instrument with a long neck and six or more strings. Guitars are played by plucking or strumming the strings. Electric guitars are used to give louder and different sounds.

gulf [gulf] *noun, plural* **gulfs. 1.** an area of an ocean or sea that is partly enclosed by land. A gulf is usually larger and deeper than a bay. **2.** a great separation or difference: The strike is likely to go on because there's a wide *gulf* between the two sides.

Gulf Stream a warm ocean current flowing from the Gulf of Mexico across the Atlantic to western Europe.

gull [gul] *noun, plural* **gulls.** a bird with gray and white feathers, webbed feet, and long wings. Gulls live on or near bodies of water.

gul•li•ble [gul′ ə bəl] *adjective, more/most.* easily tricked or fooled; believing almost anything: She was so *gullible* that she believed him when he told her that he spent his summer vacation making a movie in Hollywood.

gul•ly [gul′ ē] *noun, plural* **gullies.** a narrow ditch or trench cut in the earth by heavy rains or running water.

gulp [gulp] *verb,* **gulped, gulping. 1.** to swallow in a quick or greedy way: The man *gulped* down his cup of coffee when he saw his train pulling into the station. **2.** to swallow air out of fear or nervousness; gasp. —*noun, plural* **gulps.** a large, quick swallow.

gum[1] [gum] *noun, plural* **gums. 1.** a thick, sticky juice that comes from different trees and plants. Gum is used to coat the back of a stamp or the flap of an envelope. It is also used to make candies and chemicals. **2.** gum that is sweetened for chewing; also called **chewing gum.**

gum[2] *noun, plural* **gums.** the firm pink flesh around the teeth.

gun [gun] *noun, plural* **guns. 1.** a weapon that shoots bullets or shells through a metal tube. Rifles, pistols, and cannons are types of guns. **2.** any device that looks like a gun and shoots something out: We painted the house with a spray *gun.* —*verb,* **gunned, gunning. 1.** to shoot or hunt with a gun: to go *gunning* for rabbits. **2.** to speed up a motor or engine suddenly: "Lewis *gunned* past the Olds and up the ramp onto the freeway." (James Dickey)

gun•pow•der [gun′ pou′ dər] *noun, plural* **gunpowders.** a powder that explodes when set on fire. Gunpowder was once widely used in guns. It is now mainly used in fireworks and in blasting.

gup•py [gup′ ē] *noun, plural* **guppies.** a small, brightly-colored tropical fish. Guppies are often kept in home aquariums.

gur•gle [gur′ gəl] *verb,* **gurgled, gurgling.** to make a low, uneven, bubbling sound: "Thirst made her aware of the sound of *gurgling* waters." (Jean Auel)

gull Three types of gulls—Bonaparte's gull (top left); Western (right); Black-backed (right).

gush [gush] *verb,* **gushed, gushing.** to pour out suddenly and in a large amount: The water *gushed* out of the broken hydrant. "The crowd began to *gush* forth from the doors of the church." (Nathaniel Hawthorne) —*noun, plural* **gushes.** a sudden, heavy flow: a *gush* of blood from a bad cut.

gust [gust] *noun, plural* **gusts. 1.** a sudden, strong rush of wind: "A fresh *gust* of wind took

G

the house and shook it . . ." (Madeleine L'Engle) **2.** a sudden outburst of feeling: *A gust of laughter broke out from the audience when the clown fell down.* —*verb,* **gusted, gusting.** to move in a gust: *The winds were gusting at up to 50 miles per hour.*

gut [gut] *noun, plural* **guts. 1.** the digestive system, especially the intestines. **2.** a strong thread made from the intestines of an animal. Tennis racket strings and fishing lines are sometimes made of gut. **3. guts.** *Slang.* courage; bravery: *"I'm glad to know we still have men in the Senate who have the guts to do what they believe to be right."* (Alan Drury) —*verb,* **gutted, gutting.** to completely remove or destroy the inside of: *to gut a fish to prepare it for cooking. Fire gutted the old house.*

Gu•ten•berg [gōōt′ ən burg′] **Johannes,** 1390?–1468, German printer who was the inventor of printing with movable type.

gut•ter [gut′ ər] *noun, plural* **gutters. 1.** a ditch along the side of a street for carrying off water. **2.** a pipe or trough along the lower edge of a roof that carries off rain water. **3.** the groove along either side of a bowling alley.

guy[1] [gī] *noun, plural* **guys.** a rope, chain, or wire used to steady or fasten something: *Guy wires are used to hold up a large tent.*

gymnastics A gymnast performs on the equipment known as a *side horse* or *pommel horse.*

with the use of bars, mats, and other equipment in a gymnasium. ♦ A person who takes part in this sport is a **gymnast.** —**gymnastic,** *adjective.*

Gyp•sy [jip′ sē] *noun, plural* **Gypsies.** a person belonging to a wandering group of people who are thought to have come from India hundreds of years ago.

gypsy moth a small moth whose caterpillar stage causes great damage to trees by eating their leaves.

gy•ro•scope [jī′ rə skōp′] *noun, plural* **gyroscopes.** a wheel that is mounted so that it can

G

---

guy *Guy* is one of the few English words to come from a person's name. Guy Fawkes led the Gunpowder Plot of 1605. This was a secret plan to blow up the building in which the English Parliament sat and to kill King James I. The explosion was designed to take place on November 5th, but officials of the government found out and broke the rebellion. As time passed, November 5th became a holiday in England. People set off fireworks and paraded through the streets with a figure of Guy Fawkes dressed in strange, ragged clothes. The word *guy* then came to mean anyone with an odd or frightening appearance. Finally, people in America began to use *guy* to mean "any man," or any ordinary man. (The wonderful musical comedy *Guys and Dolls* used New York street talk for "men and women.") When you use *guy,* remember that it is a word for conversation with friends but not for serious writing.

---

guy[2] *noun, plural* **guys.** *Informal.* any man or boy: *"'Who?' he asked . . . 'Anybody. First guy in the alphabet. I don't care.'"* (Philip Roth)

gym [jim] *noun, plural* **gyms. 1.** short for GYM-NASIUM. **2.** a course in physical education that is taught in a school or college.

gym•na•si•um [jim nā′ zē əm] *noun, plural* **gymnasiums.** a room or building with equipment for physical exercise or training and for indoor sports.

gym•nas•tics [jim nas′ tiks] *noun.* a sport in which certain jumps and movements are done

move around an axis in any direction. While the wheel is spinning, it resists tilting by shifting the axis in the opposite way that the base is tilted. Large gyroscopes are used to keep ships and airplanes steady.

Pronunciation Key: O–S			
ō	over; go	ou	out; town
ô	all; law	p	put; hop
ōō	look; full	r	run; car
ōō	pool; who	s	set; miss
oi	oil; boy	sh	show

(Turn the page for more information.)

h, H [āch] *noun, plural* **h's, H's.** the eighth letter of the alphabet.

hab•it [hab′ it] *noun, plural* **habits. 1.** something a person does so often or for so long that it is done without thinking. A habit is usually hard to stop or control: He has a *habit* of biting his fingernails. "She had a *habit* of blinking whenever she began to speak, as if she couldn't get out the first word . . ." (Paul Scott) **2.** a usual way of acting or behaving; custom: "I . . . lay wondering why the milkman had appeared some two hours before his *habit.*" (MacKinlay Kantor) **3.** a special kind of clothing: Until recent years, all nuns wore *habits.* A **riding habit** is an outfit worn for horseback riding.

had [had] *verb.* the past form of **have:** Sally *had* to leave school early today.

had•dock [had′ ək] *noun, plural* **haddock** or **haddocks.** an ocean fish found in the northern Atlantic, often used for food.

had•n't [had′ ənt] the contraction for "had not."

hag•gard [hag′ ərd] *adjective, more/most.* having deep lines in one's face; looking as if one is sick, in pain, or very tired.

hai•ku [hī′ kōō′] *noun, plural* **haiku** or **haikus.** a form of poetry that originated in Japan. A haiku is made up of three lines that do not rhyme, with five syllables in the first line, seven in the second, and five in the third.

haiku Students like to write haiku poems because this form of poetry is short and simple, and does not have to rhyme. Haiku poetry began in Japan as comic verse, but soon was used for serious thoughts. Nature is usually mentioned in the first line of a haiku. If there are strong feelings, the poem hints at them rather than stating them directly. A haiku is meant to seem simple on the surface, but to leave the reader with a lot of food for thought. Here are examples from two famous haiku poets. (The 5-7-5 syllable count often changes when a Japanese poem is translated into English.) "The old pond/A frog jumps in/The sound of the water." (Matsuo Basho) "The falling flower/I saw drift back to the branch/Was a butterfly." (Moritake)

ha•bit•u•al [hə bich′ ōō əl] *adjective.* **1.** done over and over again, like a habit: "Martha went on smiling her *habitual* smile . . ." (Aldous Huxley) **2.** done or acting by habit: a *habitual* liar, a *habitual* criminal. **3.** usual or regular; customary: He sat in his *habitual* seat at the front of the bus. **—habitually,** *adverb.*

hack [hak] *verb,* **hacked, hacking. 1.** to cut or chop roughly with heavy blows: Jed *hacked* up the old box to use for firewood. **2.** to cough with harsh, dry sounds.

hack•er [hak′ ər] *noun, plural* **hackers.** a person who likes to experiment with computers; someone who is interested in computers as a hobby.

hail¹ [hāl] *noun, plural* **hails. 1.** small lumps of ice that fall from the sky during a storm. A **hailstorm** usually occurs during a thunderstorm. A single lump of hail is a **hailstone. 2.** a heavy shower of something, thought of as like hail falling from the sky: a *hail* of bullets during a battle. **—verb, hailed, hailing.** to pour down as hail: It *hails* more often in spring than in other seasons.

hail² *verb,* **hailed, hailing. 1.** to get someone's attention by shouting or waving: The man *hailed* a cab by waving his newspaper in the air. **2.** to give honor or approval to; praise: "There were few who did not *hail* him as a true military genius . . ." (Joseph Heller) **3. hail from.** to come from a certain place. —*interjection.* a cheer or welcome called out to someone: The official song for greeting the President is "*Hail to the Chief.*"

hair [hâr] *noun, plural* **hairs. 1.** a very thin, fine growth like a thread on the skin of people and animals. Much of the hair on a human body grows on the top of the head. **2.** a mass or covering of such growths. ♦ A **hairdo** or **hair-style** is the way a person wears the hair.

hair•cut [hâr′kut′] *noun, plural* **haircuts.** the act of cutting the hair, or the style in which it is cut.

hair•y [hâr′ē] *adjective,* **hairier, hairiest.** covered with hair; having a lot of hair.

Hai•ti [hā′tē] a country in the West Indies, on the western part of the island of Hispaniola. *Capital:* Port-au-Prince. *Area:* 10,700 square miles. *Population:* 5,100,000. —**Haitian,** [hā′shən], *adjective; noun.*

half [haf] *noun, plural* **halves. 1.** one of two equal parts of something: She ate *half* of the orange and gave the other *half* to her friend. **2.** in certain sports, one of the two equal time periods that make up a game. —*adjective.* **1.** amounting to half; being a half: a *half*-gallon of milk. **2.** related through one parent only: a *half* brother or sister. —*adverb.* **1.** to the amount of one half: The gas tank is *half* full. **2.** partly or nearly: Colleen was so tired that she was *half* asleep during dinner.

the window open *halfway.* **2.** not full or complete; part way: to do a *halfway* decent job.

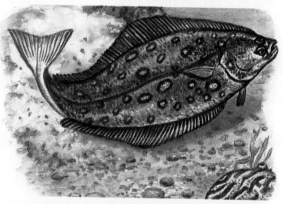

halibut

hal•i•but [hal′ə bət] *noun, plural* **halibut** or **halibuts.** a very large fish with a flat body, often used for food. Halibut are found in northern waters of the Pacific and Atlantic.

hall [hôl] *noun, plural* **halls. 1.** a long, narrow area in a building, on to which other rooms open; a way of passing through a house or building. ♦ Also called a **hallway. 2.** a space or room just inside the entry to a house or building: We left our wet boots in the front *hall* to dry. **3.** a large room or building for meetings or other public gatherings: a dining *hall,* a concert *hall.* **4.** a building containing offices of local government: The mayor's office is at City *Hall.*

H

> **half** There are strict meanings to some words as well as less strict ones. In mathematics, *half* means 50%. "A *half-hearted* attempt to do something" means a person did not really try hard. *Half* here does not mean literally "50%," but rather "not all the way." To "try to solve a problem by *half measures*" means the steps taken aren't enough to deal with the matter. A "*half-baked* idea" is one that wasn't given enough thought. It's interesting that all these "half" words tend to have a negative meaning. The saying goes that a cheerful person will look at a glass of water and say it's half full, while a gloomy person says it is half empty. But with "half" words, the negative view has won out.

half•back [haf′bak′] *noun, plural* **halfbacks. 1.** in football, an offensive player who runs with the ball or catches passes; now more often called a **running back. 2.** in soccer, a player whose position is between the forwards and the defenders; also called a **midfielder.**

half•mast [haf′ mast′] *noun.* (also called **half-staff**) the position of a flag when it is partly or halfway down from the top of a pole. Flags are flown at half-mast to honor a person who has just died.

half•way [haf′wā *or* haf′wā′] *adjective; adverb.* **1.** half the way between two things: Leave

Hal•low•een [hal′ə wēn′] *noun, plural* **Hallow-eens.** the evening of October 31st. Children celebrate Halloween by dressing up in costumes, playing tricks and games, and collecting candy and other treats.

Pronunciation Key: A–F

a	and; hat	ch	chew; such
ā	ate; stay	d	dog; lid
â	care; air	e	end; yet
ä	father; hot	ē	she; each
b	boy; cab	f	fun; off

(Turn the page for more information.)

ha•lo [hā′lō] *noun, plural* **halos** or **haloes. 1.** in art, a shining circle of light shown around the head of Jesus, an angel, or another holy person. **2.** a ring of light that appears to surround the moon or sun in cold, misty weather.

halo A halo of ice crystals around the sun.

halt [hôlt] *verb,* **halted, halting.** to stop for a time: "(He) *halted* his horse on the steep hillside as he studied the scene below." (Rod Serling) —*noun, plural* **halts.** a stopping of something: "The train came to a sudden, jolting *halt.*" (Paul Theroux)

hal•ter [hôl′tər] *noun, plural* **halters.** a rope or strap used to lead or tie a horse or other animal. A halter usually fits over the animal's nose and behind its ears.

halve [hav] *verb,* **halved, halving. 1.** to divide into two equal parts; divide in half: to *halve* a grapefruit. **2.** to reduce by half: He *halved* the recipe to make a meal for two people rather than four.

halves [havz] *noun.* the plural of **half.**

ham [ham] *noun, plural* **hams. 1.** the meat from the back leg of a hog. Ham is often salted or smoked before being eaten. **2.** a person who sends and receives radio messages as a hobby on home equipment (a **ham radio**). **3.** *Informal.* an actor who uses a very showy, exaggerated style to get the audience's attention.

ham•burg•er [ham′bur′gər] *noun, plural* **hamburgers. 1.** ground beef. **2.** a sandwich consisting of a round, flat piece of cooked ground beef inside a bun. ◆ The word *hamburger* comes from an earlier name, Hamburg Steak, from the city of Hamburg, Germany.

Ham•il•ton [ham′əl tən] **Alexander,** 1757–1804, American patriot and statesman.

ham•mer [ham′ər] *noun, plural* **hammers. 1.** a tool with a heavy metal head attached to a long handle, used to drive nails and shape metal.

2. something that looks like or is used like a hammer: The *hammer* of a gun hits the firing pin to make the gun go off. —*verb,* **hammered, hammering. 1.** to hit with a hammer: to *hammer* a nail into a board. **2.** to hit with a hard blow: He *hammered* the table with his fist.

ham•mock [ham′ək] *noun, plural* **hammocks.** a swinging cot or bed made of netting or sturdy cloth that is hung between two supports.

ham•per¹ [ham′pər] *verb,* **hampered, hampering.** to get in the way of; block: The detectives' efforts to find the thief were *hampered* by the fact that no one in the neighborhood would give them any information.

hamper² *noun, plural* **hampers.** a large basket or container with a cover: a picnic *hamper,* a clothes *hamper* for dirty laundry.

ham•ster [ham′stər] *noun, plural* **hamsters.** a small, furry animal with a plump body, a short tail, and cheek pouches. Hamsters are part of the rodent family. They are often kept as pets.

hamster

Han•cock [han′käk′] **John,** 1737–1793, American patriot who was the first person to sign the Declaration of Independence.

hand [hand] *noun, plural* **hands. 1.** the end of the arm from the wrist down, made up of the palm, four fingers, and the thumb. **2.** something thought of as like a hand: the *hands* of a clock. **3.** a round of applause; clapping: They gave the singer a big *hand.* **4.** handwriting: He signed the letter in a shaky *hand.* **5.** **hands.** control or possession: The secret formula is now in the *hands* of the enemy. **6.** a part in doing something; share; role: Everyone on the team had a *hand* in our winning the game. **7.** a worker: The farmer had a hired *hand* who helped him with the work. **8.** the cards a player holds in a card game, or one round in a game. —*verb,* **handed, handing.** to give or pass with the hand: John *handed* a dollar to the sales clerk to pay for the magazine.

H

hand Obviously, the hand is central in language because until recent times most work was done with human hands, not machines. Think of clothing being made *by hand*, a person who keeps extra food *on hand*, a custom *handed down* from early times, someone who *lends a hand* to a friend in need, or *having the upper hand* in a struggle. As old as some "hand" expressions are, others are very new. Within the past ten years, for example, the phrase "hands-on" has become popular. "Hands-on experience" means learning by actually operating a machine or traveling as a salesman, as opposed to taking a course in how to do it. A "hands-on" manager in business is said to be one who gets directly involved with employees in their daily office or factory routine.

hand•bag [hand′bag′] *noun, plural* **handbags.** a bag or case used to carry small personal items such as keys, money, a comb, and so on; a purse.

hand•ball [hand′bôl′] *noun, plural* **handballs.** a game for two or four players who take turns hitting a ball against a wall with their hands. The object of the game is to hit the ball in such a way that the next player cannot hit it back.

hand•book [hand′book′] *noun, plural* **handbooks.** a small book that has basic information about a certain subject: the Boy Scout *Handbook*, a *handbook* of English grammar.

hand•cuff [hand′kuf′] *noun, plural* **handcuffs.** one of two metal rings that lock around a person's wrist. Handcuffs are joined together by a chain and are used to stop a prisoner from using his hands. —*verb,* **handcuffed, handcuffing.** to put handcuffs on a person.

hand•ful [hand′fool′] *noun, plural* **handfuls.** 1. the amount a hand can hold at one time: She took a big *handful* of popcorn from the box. 2. a small number or amount: At the Alamo a *handful* of Texans fought to hold off a huge Mexican army.

hand•i•cap [han′dē kap′] *noun, plural* **handicaps.** 1. a mental or physical problem that makes it very hard for a person to do things that other people can do without difficulty. Some physical handicaps include being blind or deaf, having lost an arm or leg, or being unable to walk or move the body normally. 2. anything that makes it harder for a person to do something; a disadvantage: Not having the proper education can be a *handicap* in trying to get a job. 3. an advantage or disadvantage given in a race or contest to try to make the chances of winning equal for all: In a horse race, faster horses carry more weight as a *handicap*. —*verb,* **handicapped, handicapping.** to have a handicap: "I began to realize how much his injury had *handicapped* him . . ." (John O'Hara)

hand•i•capped [han′dē kapt′] *adjective.* having a physical or mental handicap; disabled:

Parking lots have to provide special parking spaces for *handicapped* people.

hand•i•craft [han′dē kraft′] *noun, plural* **handicrafts.** an art or occupation that calls for care and skill in the use of the hands. Making pots and weaving baskets are handicrafts.

hand•ker•chief [hang′kər chif] *noun, plural* **handkerchiefs.** a soft, square piece of cloth used to wipe the nose, eyes, or face.

han•dle [hand′əl] *noun, plural* **handles.** the part of an object that is held by the hand. A car door, a pair of scissors, and a frying pan all have handles. —*verb,* **handled, handling.** 1. to hold or touch with the hands: She *handled* the Christmas bulbs very carefully as she unpacked them. 2. to deal with or manage something, as if holding it in the hands: Mrs. Simmons' job at the department store is to *handle* complaints from customers. 3. to act or move in a certain way: This car *handles* very well on icy roads. 4. in business, to sell or deal in a certain item: "Bookshops and even ordinary shops refused to *handle* the book." (V.S. Naipaul)

han•dle•bars [hand′əl bärz′] *plural noun.* the curved bar above the front wheel of a bicycle or motorcycle. The rider holds the handlebars for steering.

hand•shake [hand′shāk′] *noun, plural* **handshakes.** the holding and shaking of another person's right hand as a greeting or to show friendship or agreement.

hand•some [han′səm] *adjective,* **handsomer, handsomest.** 1. of a man or boy, good-looking; having a pleasing appearance. 2. good-looking in a way that is thought of as strong or dignified: ". . . a red cardinal bird, *handsome* and spar-

Pronunciation Key: G–N			
g	give; big	k	kind; cat; back
h	hold	l	let; ball
i	it; this	m	make; time
ī	ice; my	n	not; own
j	jet; gem; edge	ng	having
(Turn the page for more information.)			

kling in the winter sun.'' (Marguerite Henry) **3.** fairly large or impressive; generous in size or amount: "The company made a *handsome* profit that year . . ." (John K. Galbraith) **—handsomely,** *adverb:* "Probably no general in British history had been so *handsomely* rewarded . . ." (William L. Shirer)

hand•spring [hand′ spring′] *noun, plural* **handsprings.** a leap in which a person springs onto his hands with his feet in the air, then flips over onto his feet again.

hand•writ•ing [hand′ rī′ ting] *noun, plural* **handwritings. 1.** writing done by hand, rather than typed or printed by a machine. **2.** the style or look of a person's writing: His *handwriting* is hard to read because the letters are so small.

hand•y [han′ dē] *adjective,* **handier, handiest. 1.** within easy reach; at hand; nearby: Mom keeps a flashlight and candles *handy* in case the power goes off. **2.** good at working with one's hands; skillful: If you're *handy* with a needle and thread, would you sew this button back on for me? **3.** helpful or easy to use; convenient: This little vacuum cleaner is quite a *handy* thing to have for cleaning out odd places.

hang [hang] *verb,* **hung, hanging. 1.** to fix or fasten something from above, leaving the lower part free: to *hang* wet clothes on a line, to *hang* a picture on a wall. **2.** to bend over or bend down: to *hang* your head in shame or in sorrow. **3.** (**hanged, hanging.**) to put a person to death by hanging him from a rope tied around his neck. ◆ A person who hangs criminals is a **hangman. 4.** to float above; be in the air over: "The new moon *hung* over Agha's shoulder . . ." (Marguerite Henry) —*noun.* **1.** the way something hangs: the *hang* of a jacket. **2.** *Informal.* the skill or ability to do something easily: I just can't seem to get the *hang* of this new computer.

are hung. **2.** anything used to hang something, such as a hook for hanging a picture.

hang glider A hang glider can hold a person aloft by means of rising currents.

hang glider a large, kite-like object that sails through the air carrying one person who hangs from a frame attached to the glider.

hang•nail [hang′ nāl′] *noun, plural* **hangnails.** a piece of skin hanging loose near a fingernail.

hang•out [hang′ out′] *noun, plural* **hangouts.** *Informal.* a place where someone spends free time: In our town Nick's Pizza Parlor is a big *hangout* for teenagers.

hang•up [hang′ up′] *noun, plural* **hangups.** *Informal.* a worry or problem that prevents a person from acting in a normal way: The boss has such a *hangup* about being short that he won't hire anyone taller than he is.

Han•ni•bal [han′ ə bəl] 247–183 B.C., general of Carthage (a former country in North Africa) who won famous victories over the Romans.

Ha•noi [ha noi′] the capital of Vietnam, in the northern part of the country. *Population:* 2,570,000.

hang "Depend upon it, sir, when a man knows he is to be *hanged* in a fortnight [two weeks' time], it concentrates his mind wonderfully." (Samuel Johnson) Dr. Johnson, the most famous dictionary editor of all time, was obviously very careful in his choice of words. You'll note that he said *hanged* rather than *hung.* You do say, "She *hung* a sign above her store." Strictly speaking, though, when the word is used to refer to hanging as a form of execution, the correct past form is *hanged,* not *hung.* Is it worth struggling to preserve this small distinction in modern English? The editors will stand by Dr. Johnson. We can't argue that it's terrible to use *hung,* but Dr. Johnson also said, in the Preface to his Dictionary, "Let us make some struggles for our language."

hang•ar [hang′ ər] *noun, plural* **hangars.** a shed or building where airplanes are kept.

hang•er [hang′ ər] *noun, plural* **hangers. 1.** a wire, wood, or plastic frame on which clothes

Ha•nuk•kah [hä′ nə kə] (also spelled **Chanukah**). a Jewish holiday that usually falls in early December. It is celebrated by lighting candles over a period of eight nights.

hap•pen [hap′ ən] *verb*, **happened, happening.**
1. to take place; occur: The fire *happened* at about 10 o'clock last night. **2.** to take place without plan or reason; occur by chance: Her birthday *happens* to be the same day as mine. **3.** to come upon by chance or accident: While reading the book, I *happened* on a dollar bill stuck between the pages. **4.** to cause a change, especially a bad change: What *happened* to the radio? It was working fine yesterday.

hap•pen•ing [hap′ ə ning] *noun, plural* **happenings.** something that happens; an incident or event.

hap•pi•ness [hap′ ē nis] *noun.* the state of being happy.

hap•py [hap′ ē] *adjective,* **happier, happiest.**
1. having or showing a good feeling; pleased with what is happening: "I feel *happy*—deep down. All is well." (Katherine Mansfield) **2.** having or showing good luck; fortunate: By a *happy* accident two passengers didn't show up and we got their seats. **3.** pleased or willing: The doctor won't be in on Monday, but he'll be *happy* to see you on Tuesday. —**happily,** *adverb.*

hard [härd] *adjective,* **harder, hardest. 1.** solid and firm to the touch; not easy to bend or push in: The ice was as *hard* as a rock. **2.** not easy to do or understand; difficult: a *hard* job, a *hard* math problem, a *hard* person to get along with. **3.** full of sorrow, pain, or trouble: a *hard* life, to have *hard* luck. **4.** not gentle or kind: a person with a *hard* heart, a judge who is *hard* on criminals. **5.** having great force or strength: a *hard* punch, a *hard* rain. —*adverb.* in a hard way: to hit a ball *hard,* to study *hard* for a test.

hard copy a printed copy of information from a computer.

hard disk a hard plate made from metal or clay and coated with magnetic material, used in a computer to store a very large amount of information.

hard•en [härd′ ən] *verb,* **hardened, hardening.** to make or become hard: The melted candle wax *hardened* as it cooled. The workers have *hardened* their position and the strike will probably go on a long time.

Hard•ing [här′ ding] **Warren G.,** 1865–1923, the twenty-ninth president of the United States, from 1921 to 1923.

---

happily Normally, the form *-ly* means "in a _____ way." This is an adverb suffix added at the end of an adjective. Thus, *carefully* means "in a careful way," *quickly* means "in a quick way," and so on. With some adjectives, however, this rule is not strictly followed: "*Happily* Red Smith did exist." (Shana Alexander) This does not mean that Red Smith (a famous sportswriter) lived "in a happy way." It means, "It is a happy thing that for us that Red Smith was around." Other words used in a similar way are *sadly, luckily, fortunately, apparently,* and *clearly.* Language critics don't object to the use of any of these words. But they are not consistent. [See HOPEFULLY on p. 375] The editors of this dictionary think that *hopefully* is no worse than *happily,* as in: "*Happily,* the building will be sold."

---

har•ass [hə ras′ *or* har′ əs] *verb,* **harassed, harassing.** to bother or annoy someone again and again: He bought a lot of things that he couldn't pay for, and now he's constantly being *harassed* by bill collectors. ♦ The fact of being harassed is **harassment.**

har•bor [här′ bər] *noun, plural* **harbors. 1.** an area of water that is protected from the rougher waters of an ocean, river, or lake. A harbor provides a safe place for ships or boats to stay. **2.** a place thought of as safe or protected like a harbor; a shelter: "It was a cool spot, . . . a very *harbor* from the raging streets." (Charles Dickens) —*verb,* **harbored, harboring. 1.** to give shelter or protection, especially to someone or something bad: to *harbor* an escaped criminal. **2.** to hold or keep within the mind: to *harbor* a grudge against someone.

hard•ly [härd′ lē] *adverb.* **1.** only just; almost not: "Tears blinded her eyes until she could *hardly* see where she was going." (Lois Lenski) **2.** surely or probably not: You could *hardly* expect the plane to wait just for you.

hard•ship [härd′ ship′] *noun, plural* **hardships.** something that causes sorrow, pain, or trouble: Early pioneers on the American frontier had to put up with a lot of *hardships.*

Pronunciation Key: O–S

ō	over; go	ou	out; town
ô	all; law	p	put; hop
oo	look; full	r	run; car
ōō	pool; who	s	set; miss
oi	oil; boy	sh	show

(Turn the page for more information.)

H

hard•ware [härd′wâr′] *noun.* **1.** metal parts used to make and fix other items. Tools, nails, screws, and locks are kinds of hardware. **2.** the machine parts and devices that make up a computer, such as a display screen, a keyboard, disks, wires, and a printer. Hardware is the "hard" or physical parts of the computer, as opposed to the information or programs stored inside, which are SOFTWARE. **3.** weapons or machinery used in war: military *hardware.*

hard•wood [härd′wood′] *noun, plural* **hardwoods.** the heavy, strong wood of certain trees, used for floors, furniture, and so on. Oak, maple, and mahogany are hardwoods.

har•dy [här′dē] *adjective,* **hardier, hardiest.** strong and healthy; able to stand hardships: A geranium is a *hardy* plant because it can stand both the hot sun and the cold.

hare The long hind legs of the hare make it better at leaping and running than its close relative the rabbit.

hare [hâr] *noun, plural* **hares.** a furry animal that is very much like a rabbit, but with longer ears and longer hind legs.

harm [härm] *noun.* **1.** something that causes pain, damage, or loss; an injury or hurt: The severe hailstorm caused great *harm* to the orange crop. **2.** something that is wrong or evil: I don't see any *harm* in using a calculator to do my math homework. —*verb,* **harmed, harming.** to cause or feel harm: Driving a car for a long time without changing the oil may *harm* the engine.

harm•ful [härm′fəl] *adjective,* *more/most.* causing or able to cause harm; damaging: Eating too many sweets can be *harmful* to your teeth. —**harmfully,** *adverb.*

harm•less [härm′lis] *adjective,* *more/most.* causing no harm: Some snakes are poisonous, but most are *harmless* to man. —**harmlessly,** *adverb.*

har•mon•i•ca [här män′i kə] *noun, plural* **harmonicas.** a small rectangular musical instrument with one or more rows of metal reeds. It is held in the hand and played by blowing air through the reeds.

har•mo•ni•ous [här mō′nē əs] *adjective,* *more/most.* showing or having harmony: a *harmonious* meeting between the leaders of two friendly nations. —**harmoniously,** *adverb.*

har•mo•nize [här′mə nīz′] *verb,* **harmonized, harmonizing. 1.** in music, to add another set of notes to the main melody when writing, playing, or singing the music. **2.** to add notes to a musical melody to form CHORDS. **3.** to go together with others in a smooth or pleasing way. The flowers in the painting *harmonize* with the flower pattern in the wallpaper.

har•mo•ny [här′mə nē] *noun, plural* **harmonies. 1.** a combination of musical notes sounded at the same time in a pleasant-sounding way. **2.** musical notes played or sung to go along with a melody. **3.** a state of being in agreement or at peace: There has been *harmony* between the U.S. and Canada for over 200 years.

har•ness [här′nis] *noun, plural* **harnesses. 1.** a set of leather straps and bands used to attach a horse or other work animal to a wagon, plow, or other vehicle to be pulled. **2.** any set of straps used to fasten or control something: a parachute *harness.* —*verb,* **harnessed, harnessing. 1.** to put a harness on a work animal. **2.** to control and put to work: Electricity can be generated by *harnessing* the power of a waterfall.

harp A harp being played by a member of the Florida Symphony Orchestra.

harp [härp] *noun, plural* **harps.** a stringed musical instrument shaped like a very large triangle

H

with a curved top. A harp is played by plucking the strings with the fingers. ♦ A person who plays the harp is a **harpist.**

harpoon An Eskimo using a harpoon to spear a seal in Robert Flaherty's classic movie, *Nanook of the North* (1922).

har•poon [här′ po͞on′] *noun, plural* **harpoons.** a spear with a rope attached to it. Harpoons are thrown by hand or shot from guns. They are used to kill or capture whales and other large sea animals. —*verb,* **harpooned, harpooning.** to kill or catch with a harpoon.

harp•si•chord [härp′ sə kôrd′] *noun, plural* **harpsichords.** a stringed musical instrument with a keyboard. It looks like a small piano and is an earlier form of this instrument.

an adjective: The soldier had had some *harrowing* experiences during the war.

harsh [härsh] *adjective,* **harsher, harshest.** **1.** painful or unpleasant to the senses; rough: The *harsh* wind blew through her thin coat. ". . . in the rays of a very clear and *harsh* electric light." (Mark Helprin) **2.** not kind; cruel or severe: The Roman emperor Nero was a *harsh* ruler. —**harshly,** *adverb:* "It has been said that life has treated me *harshly . . .*" (Helen Keller) —**harshness,** *noun.*

har•vest [här′ vist] *noun, plural* **harvests. 1.** the gathering or picking of a crop when it is ripe: The corn will be ready for *harvest* in another few weeks. **2.** a crop that is gathered: The potato *harvest* was small this year because of the bad weather. —*verb,* **harvested, harvesting.** to gather in a crop: to *harvest* wheat. ♦ A machine that harvests crops is a **harvester.**

has [haz] *verb.* the third person, present singular tense of **have.**

hash [hash] *noun.* a mixture of chopped meat and potatoes, onions, or other vegetables cooked as a meal. —*verb,* **hashed, hashing.** *Informal.* **hash over** or **hash out.** to talk about; discuss: The two opposing groups met to *hash out* their problems.

has•n't [haz′ ənt] a contraction for **has not.**

has•sle [has′ əl] *Informal. noun, plural* **hassles. 1.** something that bothers; a problem or difficulty. **2.** an argument or fight.

H

> **hassle** This is a new word that has only been widely used for about ten years. You'll note we label it "Informal" in this dictionary. You would not write in a history paper, "The American colonists complained that this Act would allow British soldiers to *hassle* them whenever they wished." As time goes by, *hassle* may be accepted in serious writing. Benjamin Franklin once objected to the word *opposed,* as well as to using *notice* as a verb. Today, no one objects to either of these. However, *dope* (meaning a stupid person) has been in English for 150 years, but it still isn't accepted as a serious word, and probably never will be. *Hassle* may make it, and it may not.

Har•ri•son [hâr′ ə sən] **1. William Henry,** 1773–1841, the ninth president of the United States, in 1841. **2. Benjamin,** 1833–1901, the twenty-third president, from 1889 to 1893. He was the grandson of William Henry Harrison.

har•row [har′ ō] *noun, plural* **harrows.** a heavy frame with rows of metal teeth or disks. A harrow is used to break up ground into smaller pieces after it has been plowed. —*verb,* **harrowed, harrowing. 1.** to prepare land with a harrow: "He had plowed and *harrowed* the ground and sowed the grain." (Laura Ingalls Wilder) **2.** to cause pain or worry. ♦ Used as

—*verb,* **hassled, hassling.** to bother or annoy a person: My friend Jerry says that his mom is always *hassling* him about the way he wears his hair.

Pronunciation Key: T–Z

t	ten; date	v	very; live
th	think	w	win; away
<u>th</u>	these	y	you
u	cut; butter	z	zoo; cause
ur	turn; bird	zh	measure

(Turn the page for more information.)

haste [hāst] *noun.* **1.** speed in getting something done; quickness: "She took an apple quickly, as if the basket might disappear if she didn't make *haste*." (Flannery O'Connor) **2.** too much of a hurry; careless speed: In her *haste* to catch the bus, she forgot her school books.

has•ten [hā′sən] *verb,* **hastened, hastening.** to move or act quickly; hurry: "Skinker and Arthur *hastened* to move Mrs. Witcher's desk and push it against the wall." (Iris Murdoch)

hast•y [hās′tē] *adjective,* **hastier, hastiest. 1.** done with speed; quick; speedy: When Dad brought some friends home for dinner, Mom made a *hasty* trip to the store for more chicken. **2.** done too quickly: He made a *hasty* judgment without finding out all the facts of the matter. —**hastily,** *adverb:* "He picked up his clothes *hastily* and ran to unlock the front door." (Beryl Bainbridge) —**hastiness,** *noun.*

hat [hat] *noun, plural* **hats.** a covering worn on the head. A hat usually has a CROWN that fits over the top of the head and a BRIM that goes around below this.

hatch¹ [hach] *verb,* **hatched, hatching. 1.** of a baby bird, fish, reptile, and so on, to come out of an egg. **2.** to plan or bring forth: ". . . he began *hatching* a scheme to ship Uncle Charlie south." (Russell Baker)

hatch² *noun, plural* **hatches. 1.** an opening or small door in the deck of a ship, leading to a lower level. **2.** any trap door or small opening like this.

hatch•et [hach′it] *noun, plural* **hatchets.** a small ax with a short handle, used with one hand.

hate [hāt] *verb,* **hated, hating. 1.** to dislike very, very much; have strong, deep feelings against: Members of the Nazi Party in Germany were taught to *hate* people of other races and religions. **2.** to want to avoid; dislike: Mike *hates* eating green vegetables. I *hate* to tell you this, but I lost that book you lent me. —*noun, plural* **hates.** a deep, strong dislike.

ha•tred [hā′trid] *noun.* a deep, strong feeling against a person or thing; hate.

haugh•ty [hô′tē] *adjective,* **haughtier, haughtiest.** having or showing too much pride; feeling better than other people: The *haughty* movie star wouldn't have anything to do with her old friends after she became famous.

haul [hôl] *verb,* **hauled, hauling. 1.** to pull or drag with effort: "For days and days, he had been *hauling* logs from the creek bottoms . . ." (Laura Ingalls Wilder) **2.** to move or carry: The boat *hauled* a load of coal down the river. —*noun, plural* **hauls. 1.** a strong pulling or dragging; the act of hauling. **2.** a distance that something moves or goes: We'd better stop for gas now—it's a long *haul* from here to the next town. **3.** an amount collected: For Halloween we got a big *haul* of candy from our neighbors.

haunch [hônch] *noun, plural* **haunches.** the part of the body around the hips and hind legs: The dog sat back on its *haunches,* begging for food.

haunt [hônt] *verb,* **haunted, haunting. 1.** to visit or return to a place as a ghost, spirit, or other strange form: "The people in the village began to believe that the woods were *haunted* . . . by the ghosts of all the dead men." (John O'Hara) **2.** to visit a place often: "He *haunted* the market place, the Horse Fair, the stables of the inns." (Marguerite Henry) **3.** to stay in the mind or come to mind often: "An old wish returned to *haunt* the shoemaker: that he had had a son instead of a daughter . . ." (Bernard Malamud) —*noun, plural* **haunts.** a place that is often visited: "Orchestra Hall, the Arts Institute, the Civic Opera House were among his favorite *haunts*." (Andrew Greeley)

have [hav] *verb,* **had, having. 1.** to be in possession of; own or hold: Do you *have* a pencil I could borrow? I *have* an idea for earning some money. **2.** to own or hold as a quality or feature: A tiger *has* stripes on its body. September *has* thirty days. **3.** to go through; experience: to *have* breakfast, to *have* a cold, to *have*

---

have/of Can you choose the correct sentence here? "I *should of* known that would happen." "I *should have* known that would happen." When you see the two forms together, it's probably obvious to you that *have* is correct; *of* is not a verb form. Nevertheless, student writers do make this mistake. The reason is that *have,* when it's spoken as part of a verb phrase, is not stressed. So it sounds the same as *of,* about like this: [uv]. This kind of spelling mistake is called a *sound error*—replacing one word with another that has the same sound.

---

hate•ful [hāt′fəl] *adjective,* **more/most. 1.** causing or deserving hate: a *hateful* crime. **2.** feeling or showing hate. —**hatefully,** *adverb.*

a good time at a party. **4.** to cause to happen or be done; bring about: to *have* your hair cut. I'll *have* Dad pick you up at 3:00. **5.** to carry on; be part of: to *have* a talk with someone. We're going to *have* a dance at school on Friday. **6.** to give birth to: to *have* a baby. ◆ **Have** is also used with other verbs: **1.** to form the PERFECT tense: We *have lived* here for six years. **2.** with **to,** to show need or obligation: I *have to leave* now.

ha•ven [hā′vən] *noun, plural* **havens.** a place of safety or rest; shelter: ". . . all of us saw the cabin as a *haven* from what obviously would have been very cold ground." (John McPhee)

have•n't [hav′ənt] the contraction for **have not.**

Ha•wai•i [hə wɪ′ e] **1.** a state made up of a group of islands in the central Pacific Ocean. *Capital:* Honolulu. *Nickname:* "The Aloha State." *Area:* 6,500 square miles. *Population:* 995,000. **2.** the largest island of this group. —**Hawaiian,** *adjective; noun.*

hawk[1] [hôk] *noun, plural* **hawks.** a large bird of prey having a sharp, hooked bill and powerful feet with sharp, curved claws. Hawks catch and eat many different kinds of small animals.

hawk The hawk's eyesight, eight times sharper than a human's, allows it to spot mice and other prey from high in the air.

hawk[2] *verb,* **hawked, hawking.** to offer goods for sale in a public place by calling out or shouting; peddle: He has a job *hawking* peanuts and popcorn at the baseball stadium.

Haw•thorne [hô′thôrn′] **Nathaniel,** 1804–1864, American novelist and short-story writer.

hay [hā] *noun.* grass, clover, or other plants that have been cut and dried for use as food for horses, cattle, and other farm animals.

Hayes [hāz] **Rutherford D.,** 1822–1893, the nineteenth president of the United States, from 1877 to 1881.

hay fever an allergy that causes sneezing, a stuffy nose, and itchy eyes. Hay fever is caused by breathing the pollen of certain plants.

hay•stack [hā′ stak′] *noun, plural* **haystacks.** a large pile of hay stacked outdoors.

haz•ard [haz′ ərd] *noun, plural* **hazards.** something that can cause harm or injury; a risk or danger: That pile of old newspapers and boxes is a real fire *hazard.* ◆ Something that is a hazard is **hazardous:** People in the army can get extra pay for *hazardous* duty. —*verb,* **hazarded, hazarding.** to take a risk.

Hawaii Beaches such as this one on the island of Kauai attract thousands of tourists to Hawaii.

haze [hāz] *noun, plural* **hazes.** a thin layer of smoke, mist, or dust in the air: A *haze* of cigarette smoke hung over the room.

ha•zel [hā′ zəl] *noun, plural* **hazels. 1.** a tree with light brown nuts that can be eaten. **2.** a light-brown or greenish-brown color.

ha•zy [hā′ zē] *adjective,* **hazier, haziest. 1.** covered by or blurred with haze: a *hazy* summer afternoon. **2.** not clear; dim; blurred: "It is possible that my memory of these events will have grown *hazy* with time." (Kazuo Ishiguro)

H-bomb [āch′ bäm′] *noun.* short for **hydrogen bomb.**

he [hē] *pronoun.* **1.** the boy, man, or male animal that has been mentioned; that male one: I called Jim on the phone, but *he* wasn't home. **2.** a person whose sex is not mentioned; any one person: There is an old saying, "*He* who hesitates is lost." —*noun, plural* **he's.** a male: Is your cat a *he* or a she?

Pronunciation Key: [ə] Symbol

The [ə] or *schwa* sound occurs in syllables without an accent. It can be spelled with any vowel, such as **a** in above, **e** in listen, **i** in pencil, **o** in melon, **u** in circus. It can also be a combination of vowels, such as **io** in action, **ai** in mountain, **iou** in precious.

(Turn the page for more information.)

he or she Until recently, writers used *he* (and therefore *his* and *him*) in sentences where the sex of the person being written about was not needed or wasn't clear. "The article says it's a good idea for a principal to live in the same town where *he* works. It helps *him* to understand problems in *his* school." Many people now feel that this usage is unfair. (A principal can just as easily be a woman.) One solution to the problem is to use the phrases "he or she," and so on. However, a series of these expressions can make for awkward wording: ". . . live in the town where *he or she* works, help *him or her* solve problems of *his or her* school." Why not change the sentence? ". . . a good idea for principals to live in the same town where *they* work . . ." or ". . . for a principal to live and work in the same town . . ."

head [hed] *noun, plural* **heads. 1.** the top part of the body, containing the eyes, ears, mouth, nose, and brain. **2.** the power of the brain; the mind: She has a good *head* for figures. I didn't understand that book; it was way over my *head*. **3.** anything thought of as like a head in shape or position: a *head* of lettuce, the *head* of a pin. A tape player has a magnetic *head* to record or play sound. **4.** something that is at the top or front: to stand at the *head* of the stairs, to march at the *head* of a parade. **5.** a person who is at the top; a leader: In Canada the prime minister is the *head* of the government. **6.** (*plural,* **head**) one of a group of cattle or other such animals: That ranch has about 800 *head* of cattle. **7.** an important or crucial point: to bring matters to a *head*, to have a problem come to a *head*. **8. heads.** the side of a coin having a face on it. —*verb,* **headed, heading. 1.** to move in a certain direction; go toward: to *head* south. **2.** to be or go at the head of; lead: He *heads* a large insurance company. **3.** in soccer, to strike the ball with the head. ♦ A play of this kind is called a **header.** —*adjective.* being the head: the *head* chef in a restaurant.

head•ache [hed′āk′] *noun, plural* **headaches.** a pain in the head.

head•band [hed′band′] *noun, plural* **headbands.** a strip of cloth or other material worn around the head, as to keep the hair out of the eyes or for decoration.

head•dress [hed′dres′] *noun, plural* **headdresses.** a covering or decoration for the head. The chiefs of certain American Indian tribes used to wear large and fancy headdresses.

head•ing [hed′ing] *noun, plural* **headings.** something written at the top of a page, such as the first part of a letter, the title of a page, chapter, or book, and so on.

head•light [hed′līt′] *noun, plural* **headlights.** a bright light attached to the front of a car, bicycle, or other such vehicle.

head•line [hed′līn′] *noun, plural* **headlines. 1.** several words printed in larger and darker type at the beginning of a newspaper article, telling what the story is about. **2.** a similar title above a magazine article or an advertisement.

head•long [hed′lông′] *adverb; adjective.* **1.** *also,* **headfirst.** with the head first. **2.** without thinking things through; in a hasty way.

head-on [hed′än′] *adverb; adjective.* with the head or front first: The two cars hit *head-on.*

head•phone [hed′fōn′] *noun, plural* **headphones.** a radio or telephone receiver held against the ear by a band worn across the head.

head•quar•ters [hed′kwôr′tərz] *noun.* **1.** a main location or office for the operations of an army, police force, or other such group: The soldiers were waiting for an order from *headquarters.* **2.** the main office of a business or other organization.

headlines A good newspaper headline makes a person pick up the paper and read the story. After President Gerald Ford refused certain grants of Federal aid to New York City at a time of financial crisis for the city, the *New York Daily News* carried this headline: "FORD TO CITY: DROP DEAD!" As this example shows, the key to a good headline is to use short, powerful words. Headline space is limited, and long, fancy words don't get the job done. For example, a recent *New York Times* news story could be summed up as "Attorney General Edwin Meese provides a positive description of the routine of the Reagan Presidency." Note how much shorter the headline words are: "MEESE PAINTS WHITE HOUSE IN KIND HUES." Also, soft, even poetic words are used here. "MEESE PAINTS WHITE HOUSE IN KIND COLORS" is flat, not suggestive.

head·strong [hed′strông′] *adjective, more/most.* determined to have one's own way; not giving in; stubborn.

head·way [hed′wā′] *noun.* forward motion or progress: We couldn't make much *headway* driving through the heavy snowstorm.

heal [hēl] *verb,* **healed, healing. 1.** to make or become well; return to health: Doctors *heal* the sick. **2.** to repair or make right: The passing of time *healed* the bad feelings between them.

health [helth] *noun.* **1.** a condition in which the body and mind are as they should be; being free from sickness and feeling well: Eating the proper foods is important to *health*. **2.** the condition of the body and mind, whether good or bad: He wants to retire from his job because he's been in poor *health* for several years.

health food any food that is believed to be much better for the health than other types of food, such as raw fruits and vegetables, or breads or cereals made from natural grains.

health·ful [helth′fəl] *adjective, more/most.* good for the health: Eating a balanced diet is a *healthful* practice.

health·y [hel′thē] *adjective,* **healthier, healthiest. 1.** having or showing good health: a baby with a *healthy* glow on its cheeks. **2.** helping the health: Swimming is considered to be a *healthy* exercise. **3.** large in amount: The old sailor had a *healthy* respect for the power of the sea.

heap [hēp] *noun, plural* **heaps. 1.** a group of things thrown together; a pile: Jane tossed the *heap* of dirty clothes into the laundry basket. **2.** *Informal.* a large number or amount: to be in a *heap* of trouble. —*verb,* **heaped, heaping. 1.** to pile in a heap: "Kunta had begun digging into the *heaping* plateful of food she had set before him." (Alex Haley) **2.** to give or provide in large amounts: "And so when praise was *heaped* upon her . . ." (Pearl Buck)

hear [hēr] *verb,* **heard, hearing. 1.** to take in sound through the ear: to *hear* a noise outside, to *hear* the phone ringing. **2.** to pay attention to; listen to: The judge wants to *hear* all the evidence before he makes his decision. **3.** to get a message or information about; learn or find out: Did you *hear* what happened to Ellen this morning? **4. hear of.** to know of; be aware of: I've never *heard of* that actor before.

hear·ing [hēr′ing] *noun, plural* **hearings 1.** the sense by which sounds are received by the ear. **2.** the act of getting information: *Hearing* that John was moving away was a big surprise to us. **3.** an official meeting or trial allowing someone the chance to be heard: a *hearing* in court.

hearing aid a small electronic device worn on the ear to make sounds louder, used by people who have problems with hearing.

heart [härt] *noun, plural* **hearts. 1.** a large hollow muscle that pumps blood to all parts of the body. **2.** the heart thought of as the center of a person's feelings: Marc congratulated the runner who had beaten him, but his *heart* really wasn't in it. **3.** energy and courage: a football player with a lot of *heart*. **4.** the center or main part of something: Police headquarters is located in the *heart* of the city. **5.** a heart-shaped design like this [♥], as on a playing card or a Valentine. **6. hearts.** the suit of cards having this shape. **7. by heart.** by memory: She learned a poem *by heart* for the school play.

heart·ache [härt′āk′] *noun, plural* **heartaches.** a deep feeling of sorrow or grief.

heart attack a sudden failure of the heart to work normally, often resulting in death or in serious damage to the body.

heart·beat [härt′bēt′] *noun, plural* **heartbeats.** a single pumping movement of the heart.

heart·bro·ken [härt′brō′kən] *adjective, more/most.* suffering great sorrow or grief.

hearth In colonial times, a family would do all its cooking at a hearth like this.

hearth [härth] *noun, plural* **hearths.** the floor of a fireplace and the area around it. A hearth is usually made of brick or stone.

Pronunciation Key: Accent Marks

[′] is the normal accent mark. It shows where the main stress falls on a word.

[′] is a secondary accent mark. It shows a lighter stress than the primary accent. For example:

tel • e • vis • ion [tel′ə vizh′ən]

(Turn the page for more information.)

H

heart•y [härt′ē] *adjective*, **heartier, heartiest.**
1. showing warmth and feeling; friendly: Hank had a *hearty* laugh that made you want to laugh along with him. **2.** strong and healthy: a *hearty* meal, a person with a *hearty* appetite.
—**heartily**, *adverb*. —**heartiness**, *noun*.

heat [hēt] *noun*. **1.** a form of energy that causes the temperature of something to become higher. Heat is produced by the sun, by fire, by FRICTION, and by certain chemical reactions. **2.** a high temperature; being hot: *Heat* is used to soften steel for shaping it. She didn't like living in Arizona because of the *heat*. **3.** warm air supplied to a room or building: to turn up the *heat* on a cold day. **4.** a point of strong feelings or excitement: In the *heat* of the game he forgot all about his sore leg. —*verb*, **heated, heating.** to make warm or hot; give heat to: to *heat* a house, to *heat* soup before serving it. ◆ Also used as an adjective: a *heated* garage. A *heated* argument has strong, angry feelings.

heat•er [hēt′ər] *noun, plural* **heaters.** a device that provides heat, as to a building or car. Stoves, radiators, furnaces, and fireplaces are types of heaters.

heath [hēth] *noun*. **1.** a low, evergreen shrub related to heather. **2.** an area of open land where heath and other low plants grow.

heath•er [heth′ər] *noun, plural* **heathers.** a low, evergreen shrub that has purplish flowers. It is native to Scotland and England.

heave [hēv] *verb*, **heaved, heaving. 1.** to lift, raise, or throw with great effort: They *heaved* the heavy logs into the back of the truck. **2.** to breathe with great effort: We all *heaved* a sigh of relief when the lost boy was found.

heav•en [hev′ən] *noun, plural* **heavens. 1.** *also,* **Heaven.** in religious teaching, the place where God lives and where good people go after they die, usually thought of as a place of complete happiness above the sky and the universe. **2.** *also,* **the heavens.** the area above the earth; the sky: The *heavens* seemed to open up and rain began to pour down. **3.** a state of great happiness like heaven: She was in *heaven* when she got to meet her favorite movie star.

heav•en•ly [hev′ən lē] *adjective, more/most.*
1. having to do with heaven: *heavenly* angels.
2. of or in the sky: The stars and planets are *heavenly* bodies. **3.** like heaven; bringing great happiness: They spent a *heavenly* vacation cruising through the Hawaiian Islands.

heav•i•ly [hev′ə lē] *adverb*. in a heavy way: "With a groan the burro fell *heavily* on his side." (Marguerite Henry)

heav•y [hev′ē] *adjective*, **heavier, heaviest.**
1. having a lot of weight; hard to pick up or move: a *heavy* rock, a *heavy* suitcase. **2.** having more than the usual weight for its kind: a *heavy* sweater, *heavy* cardboard. **3.** greater than usual in size or amount: a *heavy* rain, *heavy* traffic, a *heavy* meal, a person who is a *heavy* smoker, *heavy* voting in an election. **4.** seeming to be under a great weight: moist, *heavy* air, a sad and *heavy* heart. —**heaviness**, *noun*.

He•brew [hē′brōō] *noun, plural* **Hebrews. 1.** a member of one of the Jewish tribes of ancient times. **2.** the language spoken by these people. Hebrew is one of the official languages of Israel and is also used in the religious ceremonies of Judaism.

hec•tic [hek′tik] *adjective, more/most.* filled with activity; busy in a hurried or confusing way: It was really *hectic* trying to get to school on time after we all slept too late.

he'd [hēd] the contraction for "he had" or "he would."

hedge In the gardens of the famous Louvre Museum of Paris, the hedges are grown and trimmed into beautiful designs.

hedge [hej] *noun, plural* **hedges.** a row of closely-planted shrubs or low trees. Hedges form a boundary or fence in a yard or garden. —*verb*, **hedged, hedging. 1.** to close in or separate something with a hedge: The back yard was *hedged* with shrubs. **2.** to avoid giving a direct answer: The candidate for mayor *hedged* when the reporters questioned him about what he planned to do about the high crime rate in the city.

hedge•hog [hej′hôg′] *noun, plural* **hedgehogs.** an insect-eating animal related to the porcupine. It has a pointed snout and is covered with sharp, stiff spines. When it is frightened, it rolls into a ball with its spines pointed out for protection.

H

heed [hēd] *verb,* **heeded, heeding.** to pay attention to: to *heed* a person's advice. He failed to *heed* the stop sign and kept driving right along. —*noun.* one's attention; notice: "It began to drizzle but . . . she paid it no *heed.*" (Brian Moore)

heel [hēl] *noun, plural* **heels. 1.** the rounded back part of the foot below the ankle. **2.** the part of a shoe or sock at the heel. **3.** anything that has the shape or position of a heel: The *heel* of the hand is the lower part of the palm.
verb, **heeled, heeling.** to follow on the heels of; follow closely: The dog trainer taught the puppy to *heel* at his side.

heft•y [hef′tē] *adjective,* **heftier, heftiest.** heavy or large: a *hefty* weight-lifter.

heif•er [hef′ər] *noun, plural* **heifers.** a young cow that has not had a calf.

height [hīt] *noun, plural* **heights. 1.** the distance from the top to the bottom of something: Ellen's *height* is five feet, four inches. **2.** the state of having great height; being high: I had already guessed that he was a basketball player, because of his *height.* **3.** *also,* **heights.** a high place: He didn't want to go up on the roof because he's afraid of *heights.* Washington *Heights* is the highest section of New York City. **4.** the highest point; peak: August is the *height* of the tourist season in Europe.

height•en [hīt′ən] *verb,* **heightened, heightening.** to make higher or greater; increase: The sound of footsteps outside the door *heightened* his fear of being alone in the house.

heir [âr] *noun, plural* **heirs.** a person who has the right to own or hold money, property, or a title after the owner dies; a person who inherits something: Queen Elizabeth's oldest son Prince Charles is the *heir* to the British throne.

helicopter This rescue helicopter is used at Yosemite National Park in California.

hel•i•cop•ter [hel′i käp′tər] *noun, plural* **helicopters.** an aircraft without wings that is lifted up by two large blades that are driven by a motor. The blades, called **rotors** [rō′tərz], turn horizontally above the helicopter to hold it in the air.

he•li•um [hē′lē əm] *noun.* a very light gas that has no color or smell and does not burn. Helium is a chemical element that is found in very small amounts in the earth's atmosphere, but in large amounts in the sun and stars. It is used to fill balloons because it is lighter than air.

hell [hel] *noun, plural* **hells. 1.** *also,* **Hell.** in religious teaching, the place where evil people are punished after death, often thought of as being a fiery region beneath the earth that is ruled over by the Devil. **2.** something that causes great suffering; a very bad place or condition: "War is *hell.*" (William Tecumseh Sherman)

he'll [hēl] the contraction for "he will."

---

heir Like many other terms having to do with law or money matters, *heir* came into English from Old French. It goes back to a time (the 1200's) when the French-speaking Normans had control of the English court system. Today, it is sometimes thought that the word *heir* is used after the person with money or property has died and his children or relatives, his *heirs,* are given an inheritance. This is the legal sense of the term. In general use, "He is an *heir* to the Smithers oil fortune" can mean either that he has already received an inheritance, or that he'll probably receive one in the future.

◆ A woman who is an heir is also called an **heiress.**

heir•loom [âr′lo͞om′] *noun, plural* **heirlooms.** a valuable piece of property that is handed down from one person to another: That old painting is an *heirloom* that once belonged to my great-grandmother.

held [held] *verb.* the past form of **hold.**

H

Pronunciation Key: A–F

a	and; hat	ch	chew; such
ā	ate; stay	d	dog; lid
â	care; air	e	end; yet
ä	father; hot	ē	she; each
b	boy; cab	f	fun; off

(Turn the page for more information.)

hel•lo [he lō/ *or* hə lō/] *interjection; noun, plural* **hellos.** a word of greeting used when meeting someone or talking on the telephone.

helm [helm] *noun, plural* **helms. 1.** the wheel used for steering a ship. **2.** a position of control like the helm of a ship: With a new governor at the *helm*, things should get better in our state.

hel•met [hel/ mit] *noun, plural* **helmets.** a hard covering worn to protect the head in certain sports, in warfare, in doing dangerous work, and so on.

help [help] *verb*, **helped, helping. 1.** to do part of the work; do what is needed or wanted: Mom *helped* Peter with his homework. People wear glasses to *help* them see better. **2.** to keep from; avoid or prevent: She couldn't *help* crying during the sad part of the movie. **3. help oneself.** to serve oneself: *Help yourself* to some of the cookies. —*noun, plural* **helps. 1.** the act of helping; aid; assistance: We never could have done it without her *help*. **2.** a person or thing that helps. **3.** a hired worker or workers, especially someone paid to do housework.

space for us to stand, *hemmed in* by the furniture." (Iris Murdoch)

Hemingway The author in 1939, working on his novel *For Whom the Bell Tolls*.

Hem•ing•way [hem/ ing wā/] **Ernest,** 1899–1961, American novelist and short-story writer.

Hemingway Jim Bishop, the author of many best-selling books, one being *The Day Lincoln Was Shot*, said that when he sat down to write each day, he always began by reading something from the works of Ernest Hemingway. "I hoped that his style would rub off on me." What was the famous "Hemingway style?" Contests are often held in which people compete to write in this style. A typical entry might read, "The rain stopped. We felt the wind blow. The wind was warm. It was good." These writers assume that Hemingway used very short sentences and simple words. This is half right; he did use simple words. But go back to the real Hemingway, the opening of a story from his first collection: "The rain stopped as Nick turned into the road that went up through the orchard. The fruit had been picked and the fall wind blew through the bare trees. Nick stopped and picked up a Wagner apple from beside the road, shiny in the brown grass from the rain." Hemingway did use sentences of natural length. Contrary to what many people seem to think, he didn't often use repetition, nor did he avoid adjectives.

H

help•ful [help/ fəl] *adjective, more/most.* giving help: *helpful* advice. Ian finds it *helpful* to use a dictionary. —**helpfully,** *adverb.*

help•ing [help/ ing] *noun, plural* **helpings.** one serving of food; a portion: Chris really liked Dad's beef stew and had a second *helping.*

help•less [help/ lis] *adjective, more/most.* not being able to take care of oneself or to act without help: A newborn baby is *helpless.* —**helplessly,** *adverb.* —**helplessness,** *noun.*

hem [hem] *noun, plural* **hems.** the smooth edge on the bottom of a piece of clothing. A hem is made by turning the rough edge under and sewing it in place. —*verb*, **hemmed, hemming. 1.** to put a hem on: to *hem* a skirt. **2. hem in.** to close in; surround: "There was just enough

hem•i•sphere [hem/ is fēr/] *noun, plural* **hemispheres.** one-half of the earth. The **Northern Hemisphere** and the **Southern Hemisphere** are divided by the EQUATOR. The **Western Hemisphere** and the **Eastern Hemisphere** are not divided by an exact line in this way, but the Western Hemisphere is thought of as North and South America.

hem•lock [hem/ läk/] *noun, plural* **hemlocks. 1.** a large evergreen tree similar to a pine, having reddish bark, flat needles, and drooping branches. **2.** a poisonous plant that has hollow stems and clusters of white flowers.

hemp [hemp] *noun, plural* **hemps.** a tough fiber made from the stems of a tall green plant, used to make rope and cloth.

hen [hen] *noun, plural* **hens. 1.** an adult female chicken. **2.** the adult female of certain other birds, such as a turkey or pheasant.

hence [hens] *adverb.* **1.** as a result; for this reason: The state of Georgia began as a colony under King George II, *hence* the name Georgia. **2.** from this time: ". . . a place where they could meet after work, four evenings *hence*." (George Orwell)

Hen•ry [hen′ rē] **Patrick,** 1736–1799, American patriot and orator.

Henry VIII 1491–1547, the king of England from 1509 to 1547.

her [hur] *pronoun.* **1.** the pronoun SHE when used as an object: Give me Eve's address so I can send *her* a letter. **2.** the pronoun SHE when used as a possessive: I don't know Eve's address, but I do have *her* phone number.

her•ald [her′ əld] *noun, plural* **heralds.** in former times, a person who carried messages for a king and gave important news. —*verb,* **heralded, heralding.** to give a message or sign of: "The morning seemed to *herald* a glorious day." (Ford Madox Ford)

herb [urb *or* hurb] *noun, plural* **herbs.** any plant whose stems, leaves, roots, or seeds are used for flavoring food or as a medicine. Common herbs include parsley, basil, mint, and sage.

herd [hurd] *noun, plural* **herds. 1.** a group of farm animals or other large animals that feed or stay together: a *herd* of cattle, a *herd* of wild elephants. **2.** a person who herds animals: a goat*herd.* —*verb,* **herded, herding. 1.** to gather a group of animals into a herd. **2.** to form or gather into a large group: "The two women *herded* the children inside." (Lois Lenski)

here [hēr] *adverb.* **1.** in, at, or to this place: Jason, you stand *here,* next to Brian. *Here* comes our bus now. **2.** at the time being spoken about; now: *Here* it is Thursday, and we still haven't heard from her. I don't agree with that, and *here's* why. —*noun.* this place: Do you know how to get to Route 22 from *here?* —*interjection.* a word used to get someone's attention: Look *here,* you can't park right in front of our driveway.

here•by [hēr bī′ *or* hēr′ bī] *adverb.* by the means of this; by this action: The mayor said, "I *hereby* declare today a city holiday in honor of our world champion baseball team!"

he•red•i•tar•y [hə red′ i ter′ ē] *adjective.* **1.** able to be passed on from a parent to its offspring: Color blindness is *hereditary.* **2.** passing from a parent to a child by inheritance: Kings and queens are *hereditary* rulers.

he•red•i•ty [hə red′ i tē] *noun, plural* **heredities.** the process by which living things pass on their characteristics from parent to child. All humans, animals, and plants do this through tiny substances called GENES within the cells of the body. When a person is born, heredity determines such things as whether the person is male or female, and the color of the skin, hair, and eyes. It also influences the height and general body shape the person will grow to have.

her•i•tage [her′ i tij] *noun, plural* **heritages.** what has been handed down from the past; the beliefs and customs that people take from earlier generations: The *heritage* of America includes such things as the Thanksgiving and Fourth of July holidays, the spirit of the pioneers who settled the West, and the rights granted by the Constitution.

her•mit [hur′ mit] *noun, plural* **hermits.** a person who chooses to live alone, away from other people. In former times people often became hermits for religious reasons.

he•ro [hēr′ ō] *noun, plural* **heroes. 1.** a person who is admired by others for his great achievements or outstanding qualities: President John Kennedy has been the *hero* of many young people in politics. Martin Luther King and Jackie Robinson are among the leading *heroes* of black people. **2.** a person who shows great courage: Audie Murphy was the best-known American *hero* of World War II, earning more medals than any other soldier. **3.** the leading male character in a book, play, or movie.

he•ro•ic [hi rō′ ik] *adjective, more/most.* **1.** having to do with a hero: Sir Thomas Malory wrote *heroic* tales of King Arthur and his knights. **2.** showing the qualities of a hero; very brave or outstanding: The lifeguard made a *heroic* rescue of the drowning man.

her•o•in [her′ ō in] *noun.* a powerful drug that is made from MORPHINE. Heroin was once used to kill pain and cause sleep, but it is now illegal because it is very dangerous and habit-forming.

her•o•ine [her′ ō in] *noun, plural* **heroines. 1.** a woman who is admired by others for her great achievements or outstanding qualities: Joan of Arc is the national *heroine* of France. **2.** a

Pronunciation Key: G–N			
g	give; big	k	kind; cat; back
h	hold	l	let; ball
i	it; this	m	make; time
ī	ice; my	n	not; own
j	jet; gem; edge	ng	having

(Turn the page for more information.)

woman who shows great courage: Jan was a real *heroine* for pulling those children out of the burning car. **3.** the leading female character in a book, play, or movie: Scarlett O'Hara is the *heroine* of *Gone With the Wind*.

her•o•ism [her′ō iz′ əm] *noun.* the quality of being a hero: The Silver Star is a U.S. Army medal for *heroism* in battle.

her•on [her′ ən] *noun, plural* **herons.** a wading bird that has very long legs, a long, slender neck, and a narrow head with a sharply-pointed bill.

hero sandwich a sandwich made from a small loaf of bread filled with meats, cheeses, and lettuce, tomatoes, and so on.

her•ring [her′ ing] *noun, plural* **herring** or **her-rings.** a small saltwater fish that lives mainly in colder waters of the North Atlantic. It is very important as food and is either eaten fresh, or smoked or salted.

hers [hurz] *pronoun.* a possessive form of SHE: This book is mine and that one is *hers*.

heron The Great Blue Heron is the largest heron in the Americas. Herons nest together in groups called *heronries*.

hex•a•gon [hek′ sə gän′] *noun, plural* **hexa-gons.** in mathematics, a closed figure having six sides and six angles.

hey [hā] *interjection.* a word used to attract someone's attention or to show a certain feeling: *Hey!* That was my soda you just drank!

---

herself/himself This pair of words has several different uses. First, they refer to an earlier noun or pronoun: "You know that picture in Laura's bedroom? She painted it *herself*." Second, they are used to stress that a certain person is doing something: "The principal *herself* taught our class today after our teacher had to leave." A third use of the word is slightly informal, that of "a person's true self:" "Mom says she's not really *herself* in the morning until she has breakfast." Also, there's a special use of the word in Irish or Scottish English. "Himself" is an important man, a boss. It is often used in a teasing way to refer to the "head man" of a household: "Watch that the little ones don't make so much noise, would you? *Himself* is trying to sleep."

H

her•self [hur′ self′] *pronoun.* **1.** her own self: My little sister just learned to tie her shoes by *herself*. **2.** a stronger form of SHE or HER, used to call attention to the person that was just mentioned. **3.** her usual or normal self: Katie was up very late last night and she's not really *herself* today.

he's [hēz] the contraction for "he is" or "he has."

hes•i•tant [hez′ ə tənt] *adjective, more/most.* stopping or waiting because one is not sure; not wanting to act: He's *hesitant* about trying out for the basketball team, because he's not sure if he's good enough. **—hesitantly,** *adverb.*

hes•i•tate [hez′ ə tāt′] *verb,* **hesitated, hesitat-ing.** to stop or wait for a time; be slow in acting: Billy *hesitated* at the edge of the diving board before jumping off. "Sitting, pen in hand, she *hesitated* over what to say next." (Shirley Jack-son) **—hesitation,** *noun:* When they offered her the new job, she accepted without *hesitation*.

hi [hī] *interjection.* a word used to greet people, like "hello."

hi•ber•nate [hī′ bər nāt′] *verb,* **hibernated, hi-bernating.** of an animal, to spend a long period of time in a very quiet and inactive state like sleep. Bears and some other animals hibernate during the winter and live off fat that is stored in their bodies. ◆ This period of rest is called **hibernation.**

hic•cup [hik′ up′] *noun, plural* **hiccups. 1.** a sudden gasp of breath that one cannot control, producing a short, clicking sound. A hiccup is caused by a sudden tightening of the breathing muscles. **2. the hiccups.** the condition of having hiccups one after the other. **—verb,** **hiccupped, hiccupping.** to have hiccups.

hick•o•ry [hik′ ər ē] *noun, plural* **hickories.** a tall North American hardwood tree with gray bark. Hickory nuts can be eaten.

hid [hid] *verb.* the past tense of **hide:** Andrew *hid* in the closet to surprise his sister.

hid•den [hid′ ən] *verb.* the past participle of **hide**: Dad had *hidden* the Easter eggs so well that it took us a long time to find them.

hide¹ [hīd] *verb,* **hid, hidden** or **hid, hiding. 1.** to put or keep out of sight: Mom always *hides* the cookies so that we won't eat them between meals. **2.** to keep secret; conceal: Phil tried to *hide* his disappointment when Heather's poem won the prize instead of his.

hide² *noun, plural* **hides.** the skin of an animal. Hides are used to make leather for shoes, clothing, and other products.

hide-and-seek [hīd′ ən sēk′] *noun.* a children's game in which some players hide and another or others seek (try to find) them.

hid•e•ous [hid′ ē əs] *adjective, more/most.* very ugly or frightening; horrible: a movie about *hideous* monsters that come back from the dead. "They made such *hideous* howlings and yellings, that I had never indeed heard the like." (Daniel DeFoe) **—hideously,** *adverb.*

hide•out [hīd′ out′] *noun, plural* **hideouts.** a safe place to hide, especially one used by a criminal to hide from the law. "A lonely island, miles off the coast—it was an ideal *hideout.*" (Ken Follett)

hi•er•o•glyph•ics [hī′ rō glif′ iks] *plural noun.* a form of writing in which pictures and symbols, rather than words, are used to represent ideas. The Egyptians and other ancient peoples used hieroglyphics before they developed the alphabet. A **hieroglyphic** of two wavy lines means "water" in many American Indian languages.

high [hī] *adjective,* **higher, highest. 1.** going far up above the ground; tall: a *high* building. California's tallest mountains are called the *High* Sierras. **2.** at a point far above the ground: a balloon that is *high* in the air. **3.** at the stated distance above the ground: That fence is about five feet *high.* **4.** greater than is normal or usual: *high* winds, *high* prices, *high* blood pressure, to have a *high* opinion of someone. **5.** above others in rank or importance: a *high* court, a *high* government official. **6.** of music or other sound, nearer to the top of the range of sound that the human ear can hear. —*noun, plural* **highs. 1.** something that is high; a high place or point: Today's temperature of 105° was a new *high* for this date. **2.** a weather condition in which there is a central area of air with higher pressure than the areas around it. —*adverb.* to a high place or point: to hit a ball *high* in the air.

high•jack [hī′ jak′] *verb,* **highjacked, highjacking.** another spelling of **hijack.**

high jump a sports event where a person jumps over a bar set between two poles. The winner is the one who clears the bar at the highest level.

highlands A cottage in the Highlands of Scotland.

high•light [hī′ līt′] *noun, plural* **highlights. 1.** a point or area showing bright light, as in a painting or photograph. **2.** the most interesting or important part of something: The *highlights* of the baseball game were shown on the six o'clock news. —*verb,* **highlighted, highlighting.** to show or serve as a highlight: The mayor complained that the newspapers always *highlighted* bad news about the city and ignored the good things.

high•ly [hī′ lē] *adverb.* **1.** to a great degree; very much; very: This restaurant was *highly* recommended by one of our neighbors. **2.** in a good or favorable way: Cathy's teachers think very *highly* of her writing ability.

High•ness [hī′ nis] *noun, plural* **Highnesses.** a title of respect used when addressing royalty: Her Royal *Highness* Queen Elizabeth II.

high-rise [hī′ rīz′] *noun, plural* **high-rises.** a tall building that has many stories or floors.

high school the school attended after elementary school and junior high school, usually including grades nine to twelve.

high seas the open waters of the ocean that are not under the control of any country.

high•way [hī′ wā′] *noun, plural* **highways.** a public road that is a main route.

Pronunciation Key: O–S			
ō	over; go	ou	out; town
ô	all; law	p	put; hop
oo	look; full	r	run; car
o͞o	pool; who	s	set; miss
oi	oil; boy	sh	show

(Turn the page for more information.)

high•way•man [hī′wā′mən] *noun, plural* **high-waymen.** in former times, someone who robbed travelers on a public road.

hi•jack [hī′jak′] *verb,* **hijacked, hijacking. 1.** to take over a truck or other vehicle while it is on the road in order to steal its cargo. **2.** to take control of an airplane by force in order to make certain demands, such as the payment of ransom money, the release of political prisoners, and so on. —**hijacker,** *noun.*

hike [hīk] *verb,* **hiked, hiking.** to go on a long walk, especially one that is taken for exercise or enjoyment: The Girl Scouts *hiked* to a lake on the other side of the hill. —*noun, plural* **hikes.** a long walk.

hi•lar•i•ous [hi ler′ē əs] *adjective, more/most.* very funny; full of or causing loud laughter: Mom thinks Peter Sellers' Pink Panther movies are absolutely *hilarious.*

hill [hil] *noun, plural* **hills. 1.** a raised piece of ground that is higher than the surrounding land, but smaller than a mountain. **2.** a small heap or pile: There are a lot of ant *hills* in our back yard.

hill•y [hil′ē] *adjective,* **hillier, hilliest.** having many hills: San Francisco is a *hilly* city.

hilt [hilt] *noun, plural* **hilts.** the handle of a sword or dagger.

him [him] *pronoun.* the pronoun HE when used as an object: If that's Doug on the phone, ask *him* to call back later.

Himalayas A village in the Himalayas, just below Mount Everest, the world's tallest mountain.

Hi•ma•la•yas [him′ə lā′yəz] a range of mountains between Tibet and India that contains the highest mountains in the world. —**Himalayan,** *adjective.*

him•self [him self′] *pronoun.* **1.** his own self: Bob cut *himself* while he was shaving. **2.** his

usual or normal self: Don't be upset with Jeff for acting so rude; he's just not *himself* today. **3.** a stronger form of HE or HIM, used to call attention to the person mentioned: This copy of the book was signed by the author himself.

hind [hīnd] *adjective.* at the back; rear. ♦ Used to refer to animals: Bears can stand on all four legs or on just their *hind* legs.

hin•der [hin′dər] *verb,* **hindered, hindering.** to get in the way of; hold back or delay; interfere with: The strong winds *hindered* the campers' efforts to put up their tent and get a fire started. ♦ Something that hinders is a **hindrance.**

Hin•du [hin′dōō′] *noun, plural* **Hindus.** a member of the religion (**Hinduism**) to which most people of India belong.

hinge [hinj] *noun, plural* **hinges.** a jointed piece that allows a door, gate, lid, or other swinging part to open or move.

hint [hint] *noun, plural* **hints. 1.** a piece of information that is meant to help someone answer a question or to do something more easily: You still can't guess? All right, I'll give you a *hint*—his last name begins with 'S.' **2.** a slight amount of something that can barely be noticed: It was only February, but there was a *hint* of spring in the air. —*verb,* **hinted, hinting.** to suggest something without saying it directly; show by a hint: "I bet you have to get up really early tomorrow," she *hinted* when she wanted her guests to go home.

hip [hip] *noun, plural* **hips.** the bony part on either side of the human body where the legs join the body.

hip•po•pot•a•mus [hip′ə pät′ə məs] *noun, plural* **hippopotamuses.** a very large, heavy animal that lives in or near lakes, rivers, or ponds in central and southern Africa. It has a broad body, short legs, and thick gray or brown skin without hair.

hire [hīr] *verb,* **hired, hiring. 1.** to get someone to do work for pay; employ: ". . . a grower who was *hiring* pickers for his apple and peach crops." (Lois Lenski) **2.** to get the use of something for a time in return for payment; rent: to *hire* a cab, to *hire* a hall for a dance. —*noun.* the act or fact of hiring: Several places at the lake have fishing boats for *hire.*

Hi•ro•shi•ma [hir′ō shē′mə] a city in Japan that was destroyed by an atomic bomb during World War II.

his [hiz] *pronoun.* the pronoun HE when used as a possessive: Mike left *his* jacket at the park yesterday. Phil and I sit next to each other—this desk is mine and that one's *his.*

Hispanic The usual rule for referring to members of a certain ethnic group is to use the term that they themselves prefer. Thus *black* is now the proper term for that group of people, though at one time it was considered usual and proper to say *Negro*. The situation is not as clear with people from Latin America who are in the United States. The Federal government uses the term *Hispanic*. However, many people of this group dislike that word and prefer the term *Latin* or *Latino*. They feel that *Hispanic* suggests too close a connection with the European culture of Spain, while *Latino* better describes the culture of Latin America. Also, some people who came to the U.S. from Mexico refer to themselves as *Chicanos* while others dislike this word and use the term *Mexican-American*. Because it has such a broad meaning, "Hispanic" is probably the word that will win out.

His•pan•ic [his pan′ ik] *adjective.* having to do with the countries of South and Central America that speak the Spanish language; Latin American. —*noun.* **1.** a person who lives in Latin America. **2.** a person in the United States whose ancestors came from Latin America.

hiss [his] *verb,* **hissed, hissing. 1.** to make a sharp, long 's' sound: Air *hissed* out of the hole in the bicycle tire. **2.** to show anger or dislike by making this sound: At plays in earlier times, the audience used to *hiss* when the villain appeared on stage. —*noun, plural* **hisses.** a hissing sound.

his•to•ri•an [his tôr′ ē ən] *noun, plural* **historians.** a person who studies or writes about history.

his•tor•ic [his tôr′ ik] *adjective, more/most.* important or famous in history: the *historic* day when man first set foot on the moon. *Historic* places in the U.S. include Plymouth Rock, the Alamo, and Pearl Harbor.

days of World War I. **3.** the study of past events, especially as a subject in school.

hit [hit] *verb,* **hit, hitting. 1.** to go hard against; give a blow to: to *hit* a person with your hand in a fight. The car went off the road and *hit* a tree. **2.** to affect in a bad way, as if with a blow: The news that she'd failed the test *hit* her hard. **3.** to come to; reach: Stay on this road and you'll *hit* the main highway in about a mile. —*noun, plural* **hits. 1.** the act or fact of hitting. **2.** something that is very popular: The movie *Star Wars* was a big *hit* when it first came out. ♦ Often used as an adjective: a *hit* song. **3.** in baseball, a ball that is hit by the batter so that he can reach base safely.

hit-and-run [hit′ ən run′] *adjective.* having to do with a road accident in which the driver who caused the accident immediately drives away from the scene, instead of remaining there as is required by law.

historic, historical There's a small but significant difference between these similar words. Something *historic* is important in history: "Before his *historic* voyages, Christopher Columbus had some 30 years of practical experience in seamanship." (Arthur Schlesinger) *Historical* means simply "having to do with history." Samuel Eliot Morison (a great historian himself) said that a historian's job was "to throw light on *historical* darkness." Please note also that the correct form is "a historic occasion" or "a historical study." Some people mistakenly believe that these words take *an,* but the rule in English is both very simple and very consistent: words with a vowel sound take *an*; words with a consonant sound (such as *h*) take *a.* Arthur Schlesinger said of a friend, "Frank Bourgin, *a historical* pioneer."

his•tor•i•cal [his tôr′ i kəl] *adjective.* **1.** having to do with history: a *historical* museum. *North and South* is a *historical* novel about the Civil War. **2.** *Informal.* historic: a *historical* site.

his•to•ry [his′ trē *or* his′ tə rē] *noun, plural* **histories. 1.** all the things that have happened in the time before now; all past events: George Washington is one of the most important figures in American *history.* **2.** a story or record of certain past events: Barbara Tuchman's book *The Guns of August* is a *history* of the early

hitch [hich] *verb,* **hitched, hitching. 1.** to fasten or tie something with a rope, strap, or the like: to *hitch* a horse to a wagon. **2.** to move or raise

Pronunciation Key: T–Z

t	ten; date	v	very; live
th	think	w	win; away
<u>th</u>	these	y	you
u	cut; butter	z	zoo; cause
ur	turn; bird	zh	measure

(Turn the page for more information.)

with a jerking motion: "Watching himself in the mirror, Studs *hitched* up his football pants." (James T. Farrell) **3.** to HITCHHIKE: to *hitch* a ride on a truck.
—*noun, plural* **hitches. 1.** something that hitches; a fastening: A trailer *hitch* is used to connect a trailer to a car. **2.** an unexpected problem or delay: The robbery would have gone off without a *hitch* if the burglars hadn't set off the alarm at the end. **3.** a jerking motion: He's having trouble hitting the ball because he has such a *hitch* in his swing. **4.** any of several types of knots used to fasten things.

hitch•hike [hich′hīk′] *verb,* **hitchhiked, hitchhiking.** to travel by walking or standing at the side of a road and trying to get free rides from passing cars or trucks. ◆ A person who does this is a **hitchhiker.**

Hit•ler [hit′lər] **Adolf,** 1889–1945, the dictator of Nazi Germany from 1933 to 1945.

hive [hīv] *noun, plural* **hives.** (also called a **beehive**) **1.** a place, either man-made or natural, where bees live. **2.** a very busy, active place; a place crowded with people.

hives [hīvz] *noun.* a painful skin condition in which red, itchy patches or bumps form on the skin, usually caused by an allergy.

hoard [hôrd] *verb,* **hoarded, hoarding.** to gather and store away a secret supply of something: People sometimes *hoard* food if they think there's going to be a shortage. Jamie said his Halloween candy is all gone, but I know he's still *hoarding* some. —*noun, plural* **hoards.** a supply that is gathered and kept hidden: ". . . he had found a way to increase his little *hoard* of cash money." (Sterling North)

hoarse [hôrs] *adjective,* **hoarser, hoarsest.** having a harsh or rough sound: The game was so exciting and I yelled so much I had a *hoarse* voice afterwards.

been *hobbling* around on crutches since he hurt his leg skateboarding. **2.** to tie an animal's legs together so that it cannot run away: Cowboys on the range sometimes used to *hobble* their horses at night. **3.** to keep from moving or acting freely; hinder: The team has been *hobbled* because their two best players are out with injuries. —*noun, plural* **hobbles.** something that is used to hobble an animal.

hob•by [häb′ē] *noun, plural* **hobbies.** something that a person does regularly for enjoyment in his or her free time. Popular hobbies include gardening, photography, stamp collecting, and building models. —**hobbyist,** *noun.*

Ho Chi Minh [hō′ chē′ min′] 1890–1969, Vietnamese revolutionary leader.

hock•ey [häk′ē] *noun.* **1.** a game played on ice by two teams of six players each. The players wear skates and use long, curved sticks to try to hit a small, hard rubber disk called a PUCK into the other team's goal. **2.** a similar game played on a field; more often called **field hockey.**

hoe [hō] *noun, plural* **hoes.** a tool with a thin, flat blade at the end of a long handle, used mainly to dig up weeds and loosen the soil around plants. —*verb,* **hoed, hoeing.** to use a hoe: to *hoe* a garden.

hog [häg or hôg] *noun, plural* **hogs. 1.** a pig raised for its meat. **2.** any animal of the pig family. Wild hogs called "razorbacks" live in part of the southern U.S. **3.** *Informal.* a dirty, greedy, or selfish person: A "road *hog*" is a driver who stays in the middle of the road and won't let anyone by. —*verb,* **hogged, hogging.** *Informal.* to take more than one's share: Jim *hogged* all the cookies and didn't give us any.

ho•gan [hō′gən] *noun, plural* **hogans.** an earth house used by the Navaho Indians, made by covering logs, poles, or stones with mud, which then dries to form a hard surface.

hoaxes Hoaxes in literature have been very common over the years. The nature of writing is such that there's no way to tell who really wrote a story or poem, or when it was written. One of the most famous literary hoaxes involved the Rowley Poems. These were supposedly the work of a British monk of the 1400's. A poet named Thomas Chatterton "discovered" them in the late 1700's. It turned out later that he had written them himself, using an old-fashioned style.

hoax [hōks] *noun, plural* **hoaxes.** a story or trick meant to fool people: The 'Cardiff Giant' was a famous *hoax*—it was supposed to be the body of a man 10 feet tall and thousands of years old, but it was really a fake made of stone.

hob•ble [häb′əl] *verb,* **hobbled, hobbling. 1.** to walk in an awkward way or with a limp: Todd's

hoist [hoist] *verb,* **hoisted, hoisting.** to lift or raise up: to *hoist* the sails on a ship. "He *hoisted* himself up on one of the windowsills and sat there." (Eleanor Estes) —*noun, plural* **hoists. 1.** a machine or device used to lift or raise something heavy: Dock workers use a *hoist* to lift cargo out of a ship. **2.** the act of lifting.

hold¹ [hōld] *verb,* **held, holding. 1.** to take and keep in one's hands: *Hold* my books while I open the door. **2.** to keep in a certain place or position: Mom told Billy to *hold* still while she cut his hair in the back. The news reporter was being *held* prisoner by terrorists. **3.** to be able to keep, contain, or support: Our car's gas tank *holds* twelve gallons. **4.** to control or possess: The President of the U.S. *holds* office for four years. **5.** to carry on; conduct: to *hold* a meeting, to *hold* a garage sale. —*noun, plural* **holds. 1.** the act or fact of holding something with the hands; a grasp or grip. **2.** a controlling power or influence: The Soviet dictator Joseph Stalin kept a tight *hold* on his country. **3.** a way of interrupting a telephone call so that a person is not on the line but is not completely disconnected: She put the caller on *hold* so that she could answer another call.

hold² *noun, plural* **holds.** the area of a ship or airplane where cargo is stored.

hold•er [hōl′dər] *noun, plural* **holders.** a person or thing that holds: For many years Jesse Owens was the *holder* of the world record in the long jump. ♦ Often used to form other words: a pot*holder,* a knife*holder.*

hold•ing [hōl′ding] *noun, plural* **holdings.** something that is held or owned: an oil company with large *holdings* in Alaska.

hold•up [hōld′up′] *noun, plural* **holdups. 1.** a robbery by someone who has or pretends to have a weapon. **2.** a delay: A strike at the factory caused a *holdup* of shipments. ♦ Also used as a verb: An armed gang *held up* Gilman's Jewelry Store this morning. Sorry we're late—we were *held up* by a traffic jam.

hole [hōl] *noun, plural* **holes. 1.** an open place in something solid: a *hole* in a sock, a *hole* in a tooth. Moles and gophers live in *holes* in the ground. **2.** a place where something is missing; a gap: He claims he had nothing to do with the crime, but there are several *holes* in his story. **3.** in golf, a shallow opening in the ground into which the player must hit the ball.

hol•i•day [häl′ə dā′] *noun, plural* **holidays.** a day when most people do not work and business offices are closed, usually because of the celebration of some special day or event: Major *holidays* in the U.S. include the Fourth of July, Thanksgiving, Christmas, and New Year's Day.

Hol•land [häl′ənd] another name for THE NETHERLANDS.

hol•low [häl′ō] *adjective,* **hollower, hollowest. 1.** having a hole or empty space inside: Basketball and soccer are played with a *hollow* ball.

Owls often make their nests in *hollow* trees. **2.** suggesting a sound made in an empty place; deep and dull: ". . . a *hollow* whistling sound, as if she were blowing across the mouth of a bottle." (Beverly Cleary) —*noun, plural* **hollows. 1.** an empty space; a hole: The old dirt road was filled with ruts and *hollows.* **2.** a low area of land with hills around it; a small valley: The country singer Loretta Lynn often sings about her home in Butcher *Hollow,* Kentucky. —*verb,* **hollowed, hollowing.** to make an empty space: Before you carve a pumpkin into a jack-o-lantern, you have to *hollow* it out. —**hollowly,** *adverb.*

hol•ly [häl′ē] *noun, plural* **hollies.** an evergreen plant that has bright red berries and shiny green leaves with sharp, pointed edges. Holly is often used as a decoration at Christmas.

Hollywood A view of the famous hillside "Hollywood" sign.

Hol•ly•wood [häl′ē wood′] an area in Los Angeles, California, that is the center of the U.S. movie and television industries.

ho•lo•caust [häl′ə kôst′] *noun, plural* **holocausts. 1.** great destruction or loss of life, especially because of fire. **2.** *usually,* **the Holocaust.** the mass killing of European Jews by Nazi Germany during World War II.

hol•ster [hōl′stər] *noun, plural* **holsters.** a leather case for carrying a pistol, usually worn attached to a belt or on a strap across the shoulder.

Pronunciation Key: [ə] Symbol

The [ə] or *schwa* sound occurs in syllables without an accent. It can be spelled with any vowel, such as **a** in above, **e** in listen, **i** in pencil, **o** in melon, **u** in circus. It can also be a combination of vowels, such as **io** in action, **ai** in mountain, **iou** in precious.

(Turn the page for more information.)

H

ho•ly [hō′lē] *adjective,* **holier, holiest. 1.** having to do with God; deserving worship; sacred: the *Holy* Bible. Jerusalem is a *holy* city of the Christian, Jewish, and Muslim religions. In Christianity, the **Holy Spirit** or **Holy Ghost** is the spirit of God. **2.** very religious; like a saint: a *holy* man of the Hindu religion.

home [hōm] *noun, plural* **homes. 1.** the place where a person lives: She worked late and didn't get *home* until 7:00. **2.** the place where an animal lives: Beavers make their *homes* in ponds and streams. **3.** the place where something comes from or is typically found: Hollywood is the *home* of the American movie business. **4.** a place that cares for ill or handicapped people, or people with special needs: a nursing *home.* **5.** the goal or point to be reached in certain games, such as hide-and-seek. **6.** in baseball, the base at which the batter stands to hit and which a runner must reach to score a run; also called **home plate. 7. at home. a.** at or in one's home. **b.** relaxed and comfortable; at ease: She's just started driving and doesn't feel *at home* behind the wheel yet. —*adjective.* **1.** having to do with or used in the home: *home* cooking, a *home* computer. **2.** having to do with or being in a base or home area: the *home* office of a company. The *home* team in baseball bats last. —*adverb.* to or at one's home: to stay *home* for the weekend.

home•mak•er [hōm′mā′kər] *noun, plural* **homemakers.** a person who manages a home and takes care of household work.

Hom•er [hō′mər] Greek poet of the 8th or 9th century B.C. who wrote the *Iliad* and the *Odyssey.*

home•room [hōm′room′] *noun, plural* **homerooms.** a school classroom where a group of pupils report in the morning for an attendance check, to receive announcements, and so on.

home run a hit in baseball that allows the batter to run around all the bases and score a run; also called a **homer.**

home•sick [hōm′sik] *adjective, more/most.* sad and lonely because of being away from one's home and family. —**homesickness,** *noun.*

home•spun [hōm′spun′] *adjective.* **1.** of cloth or clothing, made at home: a *homespun* shirt. **2.** simple and ordinary; not fancy: Abraham Lincoln was known for his *homespun* jokes and stories.

home•stead [hōm′sted] *noun, plural* **homesteads. 1.** a house and the land around it, especially a small farm with its land and buildings. **2.** a piece of land given by the government to a person who lives on it and farms it: The **Homestead Act** of 1862 granted 160 acres of land to anyone who would live there as a farmer for five years.

---

home The many "home" words in English come from the idea of home as the main or central place, the place where something begins. *Home plate* in baseball is one obvious example of this. In Great Britain, the government department that deals with matters within the country is called the *Home* Office, and the counties just outside the city of London are known as the *Home* Counties. *Home* is one of the oldest words in English; it's been used for over 1000 years. In all that time, probably the best definition of the word was the one provided by the poet Robert Frost, in "The Death of the Hired Man" (1914). He wrote, "Home is the place where, when you have to go there, They have to take you in."

---

home economics the study of how to manage a household, including cooking, family relations, and consumer education.

home•land [hōm′land′] *noun, plural* **homelands.** the country where a person was born or has his or her home.

home•ly [hōm′lē] *adjective,* **homelier, homeliest. 1.** unattractive in appearance; not handsome or pretty; plain. **2.** typical of life at home; simple: They ate a *homely* supper of soup and bread.

home•made [hōm′mād′] *adjective.* made at home; not made in a factory or by a professional: Cookie companies often try to copy the taste of *homemade* cookies.

home•town [hōm′toun′] (also spelled **home town**) *noun, plural* **hometowns.** the town or city where a person was born or grew up, or where a person lives.

home•ward [hōm′wərd] *adverb; adjective.* (*also,* **homewards**) toward home: to sail *homeward,* a *homeward* journey.

home•work [hōm′wərk] *noun.* **1.** school lessons or studying done outside of the regular class period. **2.** reading or study done to prepare for something: The mayor had an answer ready for all the reporters' questions; she must have really done her *homework.*

hom•i•cide [häm′ə sīd′] *noun, plural* **homicides.** the act of killing another person. The killing may be against the law, such as a MURDER. It may also be an accidental killing, or a **justifiable homicide** [jus′ tə fī′ ə bəl], as when a person kills someone who has attacked him.

hom•i•ny [häm′ ə nē] *noun.* a food made from kernels of dried white corn with the hulls removed. Hominy is usually ground up and boiled before eating.

ho•mog•e•nized milk [hə mäj′ ə nīzd′] milk in which the cream has been mixed evenly throughout the milk so that it will not rise to the top. ♦ This process is called **homogenization** [hə mäj′ ə ni zā′ shən].

ho•mo•graph [häm′ ə graf′] *noun, plural* **homographs.** a word that is spelled the same way as another word, but has a different meaning. A baseball *bat* and the *bat* that flies through the air are homographs.

sided cells, built by honeybees in their nest to hold honey and young bees. —*verb,* **honeycombed, honeycombing.** to fill with spaces, tunnels, or patterns similar to a bee's honeycomb: The island was *honeycombed* with caves and tunnels dug by the defending troops.

hon•ey•dew melon [hun′ ē dōō′] a smooth, white or pale-green melon with sweet green flesh.

hon•ey•moon [hun′ ē mōōn′] *noun, plural* **honeymoons. 1.** a trip or vacation taken by a couple who have just been married. **2.** a pleasant or peaceful period at the start of something: The news reporters didn't criticize the governor much when he first took office, but now the *honeymoon* is over. —*verb,* **honeymooned, honeymooning.** to be on or have a honeymoon: They *honeymooned* in Hawaii.

---

homographs The Greek form *homo* means "same." In Greek, *graph* is "writing" (as in *autograph*); *phone* is "sound" (as in *telephone*), and *nym* is "word" or "name" (as in *synonym*). A *homograph* has the same writing (spelling) as another word. It may have the same sound, as in "electric *light*," "a *light* rain." Or it may have a different sound, as in "rain and *winds*" "a road that *winds*." But homographs always have a different meaning. *Homophones* have the same sound but a different meaning: *so, sew, sow. Homonym* has a less exact meaning; any homograph or homophone can be called a homonym.

---

ho•mo•nym [häm′ ə nim′] *noun, plural* **homonyms.** a word that has the same sound as another but a different meaning.

ho•mo•phone [häm′ ə fōn′] *noun, plural* **homophones.** a word that has the same sound as another, but a different meaning and spelling. The words *to, two,* and *too* are homophones.

hon•est [än′ ist] *adjective, more/most.* **1.** not lying, cheating, or stealing; able to be trusted; fair and truthful: The teacher had left her answer book open on the desk, but Mary was too *honest* to copy from it. **2.** showing these qualities; without lying, cheating, or stealing: an *honest* answer. —**honestly,** *adverb.*

hon•es•ty [än′ is tē] *noun.* the quality of being honest: There are many old stories about the *honesty* of George Washington, such as his saying, "I cannot tell a lie" when his father asked him if he had done something wrong.

hon•ey [hun′ ē] *noun, plural* **honeys. 1.** a sweet, thick liquid that is made by certain bees called **honeybees.** Honey comes from NECTAR, a thin liquid that bees gather from flowers. People eat honey or use it to sweeten things. **2.** a name for a person who is loved; darling; dear.

hon•ey•comb [hun′ ē kōm′] *noun, plural* **honeycombs.** a wax structure formed of six-

honeysuckle

hon•ey•suck•le [hun′ ē suk′ əl] *noun, plural* **honeysuckles.** a climbing vine or bush that has

H

Pronunciation Key: Accent Marks

[′] is the normal accent mark. It shows where the main stress falls on a word.
[′] is a secondary accent mark. It shows a lighter stress than the primary accent. For example:

tel • e • vis • ion [tel′ ə vizh′ən]
(Turn the page for more information.)

many brightly-colored, sweet-smelling flowers with the shape of a tube.

Hong Kong Hong Kong Harbor as seen from Victoria Peak, 1800 feet above the city.

Hong Kong [häng′ käng′] a British colony on the southeastern coast of China. *Capital:* Victoria. *Area:* 400 square miles. *Population:* 5,150,000.

honk [hängk] *noun, plural* **honks.** a loud, harsh sound, such as that made by a goose or by a car horn. —*verb,* **honked, honking.** to make or cause to make this sound: Jim *honked* his horn and waved as he drove by his friend's house.

Hon•o•lu•lu [hän′ ə lo͞o′ lo͞o] the capital city of Hawaii, on the island of Oahu. *Population:* 395,000.

hon•or [än′ ər] *noun, plural* **honors. 1.** a sense of what is right to do; being fair and honest: He's a man of *honor* who would never go back on a promise. **2.** good name; reputation: She gave the teacher her word of *honor* that she had done the whole project by herself. **3.** a sign of great respect; a special recognition or award: Winning the Nobel Prize in literature is a great *honor* for an author. **4. Honor.** a title of respect for a judge, mayor, or other high official. ♦ Used in the phrase **Your (His, Her) Honor. 5. honors.** a special mention or recognition given to a student for outstanding work: to graduate with *honors.* —*verb,* **honored, honoring.** to show great respect for; give honor to.

hon•or•a•ble [än′ ər ə bəl *or* än′ rə bəl] *adjective, more/most.* **1.** having or showing a sense of honor; doing what is right, fair, and honest: Turning in the $100 bill you found on the bus was an *honorable* thing to do. **2.** deserving or bringing honor or great respect. ♦ An **honorable mention** is a recognition or award given to someone who has done very well, but not well enough to win top honors. —**honorably,** *adverb.*

hon•or•ar•y [än′ ə rer′ ē] *adjective, more/most.* **1.** given or done as an honor: Colleges often award *honorary* degrees to famous people. **2.** as an honor only; without actual duties or rights: Dad got a certificate making him an *honorary* deputy sheriff of Deadwood County.

hood [hood] *noun, plural* **hoods. 1.** a protective covering for the head and neck, usually attached to the collar of a coat or jacket. **2.** a hinged metal cover over the engine of an automobile. **3.** something that looks or acts like a hood: Our new stove has a *hood* over it to draw out smoke.

hood•lum [hood′ ləm] *noun, plural* **hoodlums.** a rough, nasty person who disobeys the law and causes trouble or damage: My grandmother was knocked down by three young *hoodlums* who stole her purse.

hoof [hoof *or* hoof] *noun, plural* **hoofs** or **hooves.** a hard, tough covering that protects the foot of a horse, cow, deer, pig, or similar animal. —**hoofed,** *adjective.*

hook [hook] *noun, plural* **hooks. 1.** a bent or curved piece of metal, wood, plastic, or another strong material: He hung his jacket on the *hook* in the hall. **2.** a curved piece of metal with a sharp point at one end, used for catching fish. —*verb,* **hooked, hooking. 1.** to fasten, hold, or catch with a hook: to *hook* a trailer to a car. "That was a trout. He had been solidly *hooked.*" (Ernest Hemingway) **2.** to form a hook or a hook shape: Mary *hooked* her arm through her mother's as they crossed the street. **3. hook up.** to set up a piece of electrical equipment so that it is ready to work. ♦ Also used as a noun: a telephone *hookup.*

hoop Plastic *hula hoops* were a very popular toy for a short time in the 1950's.

hoop [hoop] *noun, plural* **hoops. 1.** a band or flat ring in the form of a circle: Metal *hoops* are

H

hopefully "I have fought this for some years, and will fight it till I die." (Hal Borland) "This is one that makes me physically ill." (Harold Taylor) "I have sworn eternal war on this." (A. B. Guthrie, Jr.) "I deplore it, I curse it and I'm losing the war." (Red Smith) What is the enemy that these well-known writers oppose with such anger? Is it a cruel dictator? A terrible disease? Actually, it's a word, a simple, fairly common word—*hopefully*. These people, and many other writers, object to the modern use of the word to mean "I hope that" or "It's to be hoped that." "*Hopefully*, people won't believe everything that they read about us." (Diana, Princess of Wales) These critics argue that the only correct meaning of *hopefully* is "in a hopeful way:" "*Hopefully*, I look for signs of bobcat or coyote but find none." (Edward Abbey) The editors of this dictionary are in sympathy with those who want to limit *hopefully* to this meaning, but we say that it's too late. *Hopefully* has dug itself into ordinary speech, and in any event, it isn't much worse than *happily*. (See p. 355)

used to hold wooden barrels together. Women used to wear *hoops* under their dresses to hold their skirts out. **2.** a circular ring used as a child's toy. Many years ago, children used to roll hoops as a street game. Plastic **hula hoops** were a popular toy in the 1950's. **3.** another name for the basket in basketball.

hoot [ho͞ot] *noun, plural* **hoots. 1.** the sound an owl makes. **2.** a sound like this, used to show anger or disappointment. —*verb,* **hooted, hooting.** to make this sound.

Hoo•ver [ho͞o′vər] **Herbert,** 1874–1964, the thirty-first president of the United States, from 1929 to 1933.

hop¹ [häp] *verb,* **hopped, hopping.** to move with short, quick jumps: "Duke grabbed his foot and went *hopping* about the stable like a one-legged bird." (Marguerite Henry) —*noun, plural* **hops.** a short jump or movement: The shortstop caught the ball on the first *hop*.

hop² *noun, plural* **hops. 1.** a climbing vine with clusters of greenish flowers that look like small pine cones. **2. hops.** the dried ripe flower clusters of this plant, used to give flavor to beer.

hope [hōp] *verb,* **hoped, hoping.** to want something and believe that it is possible; wish and expect that something will happen: "I *hope* your train won't be too crowded, that you'll get a seat." (Barbara Pym) —*noun, plural* **hopes. 1.** a strong wish for something and a belief that it will happen: Keith has *hopes* of getting an 'A' in English this term. **2.** a person or thing that gives hope.

hope•ful [hōp′fəl] *adjective, more/most* **1.** having or showing hope: Brad is very *hopeful* that his sore leg will get better in time for Saturday's race. **2.** giving cause for hope; promising: The downtown area still needs a lot of cleaning up, but there are a few *hopeful* signs that things are getting better.

hope•ful•ly [hōp′fə lē] *adverb.* **1.** in a hopeful way: "A dozen times he started up to peer *hopefully* about for dawn. But the night was a thousand hours long." (Jim Kjelgaard) **2.** *Informal.* it is hoped; let us hope that.

hope•less [hōp′lis] *adjective, more/most.* not having or giving any chance of success; without hope: The plane leaves in 20 minutes and we're still 15 miles from the airport—I'd have to say things look *hopeless.* —**hopelessly,** *adverb.* —**hopelessness,** *noun.*

Hopi The Hopi indians of the American Southwest are famous for their beautiful *kachina* dolls, which are used in religious ceremonies.

Pronunciation Key: A–F			
a	and; hat	ch	chew; such
ā	ate; stay	d	dog; lid
â	care; air	e	end; yet
ä	father; hot	ē	she; each
b	boy; cab	f	fun; off

(Turn the page for more information.)

hop•per [häp′ ər] *noun, plural* **hoppers. 1.** an insect or animal that hops. ♦ Used in compound words: a grass*hopper*. **2.** a place for storing grain, coal, and other such items. It is usually wide open at the top with a smaller opening at the bottom to let the contents out.

hop•scotch [häp′ skäch′] *noun.* a child's game in which a stone or other object is thrown onto a pattern of numbered squares on the ground. A player has to hop through the squares in a certain way to pick up the object.

horde [hôrd] *noun, plural* **hordes.** a large group; a crowd or swarm: I left the sugar out and a *horde* of ants invaded the kitchen table.

hor•i•zon [hə rī′ zən] *noun, plural* **horizons. 1.** the distant line where the land or sea appears to touch the sky: "An evening star appeared above the *horizon*." (Sterling North) **2.** the limit or range of a person's experience or knowledge: Four years of college study has really broadened her *horizons*.

hor•i•zon•tal [hôr′ ə zänt′ əl] *adjective.* in line with the ground or horizon; straight across; level: The walls of a room are VERTICAL and the floor and ceiling are *horizontal*. Gymnasts do exercises on long **horizontal bars** placed above the floor. —**horizontally,** *adverb.*

adjective. having horns or something like horns: a *horned* owl.

horned toad [hôrnd] a small, brown or grayish lizard that has sharp spikes like horns on its head and body. Horned toads live mainly in dry areas of the southwestern United States and Mexico. ♦ This animal is more correctly called a **horned lizard.**

hor•net [hôr′ nit] *noun, plural* **hornets.** a large type of wasp that has a painful sting.

hornet

hor•ri•ble [hôr′ ə bəl] *adjective, more/most.* **1.** causing horror; very frightening or shocking; terrible: Seeing the skyscraper on fire was a

horrible This word is an example of how English vocabulary exists on three different levels. At the first level is the original, strong meaning of the word: "a *horrible* plane crash." The second level is the extended meaning: "a *horrible*-tasting medicine." As you can see, this gives a much stronger effect than *bad* or *unpleasant*. A writer has to be careful about the third, weakened sense of the word. "What a *horrible* movie! We walked out halfway through!" Here, *horrible* can mean only "I don't like that." Now, the word has lost almost all the force it had in its first sense.

hor•mone [hôr′ mōn] *noun, plural* **hormones.** a chemical substance made in certain glands of the body and carried by the bloodstream to various body parts. Hormones control body growth and development and regulate activities such as breathing, digestion, and perspiration.

horn [hôrn] *noun, plural* **horns. 1.** a hard, permanent growth on the head of certain animals, such as cattle, sheep, goats, or rhinoceroses. Horns usually are curved and pointed and grow in pairs. **2.** any one of a group of musical instruments played by blowing into a narrow opening at one end of a large curved tube. The earliest of these instruments were made from animal horns; modern instruments are usually made of brass. Trumpets, trombones, and tubas are horns. **3.** a device in a car, truck, or other vehicle that can make a loud noise as a warning to someone in the way. —**horned,**

horrible sight. **2.** very bad or unpleasant; awful: Rotten eggs have a *horrible* smell.—**horribly,** *adverb.*

hor•rid [hôr′ id] *adjective, more/most.* **1.** causing great fear or shock; horrible: ". . . *horrid* shapes, and shrieks, and sights unholy." (John Milton) **2.** very bad or unpleasant.

hor•ri•fy [hôr′ ə fī′] *verb,* **horrified, horrifying. 1.** to cause a feeling of horror; fill with great fear or shock: Mrs. Ellis was *horrified* to find that someone had stolen her brand-new car. **2.** to surprise in an annoying or unpleasant way: His parents were *horrified* by his progress report—he's failing every subject.

hor•ror [hôr′ ər] *noun, plural* **horrors. 1.** a feeling of great fear or shock; terror: ". . . her hands clutched to her face in *horror*, the tiger at her feet." (James M. Cain) **2.** something that causes this feeling: the *horrors* of war.

H

horse [hôrs] *noun, plural* **horses. 1.** a large, grass-eating animal having four legs with hoofs and a flowing mane and tail. Horses are strong and fast and are used for riding. **2.** a frame with legs that is used to hold something up, as a horse supports a rider. A carpenter uses a **sawhorse** to support a board while he cuts it. **3.** in gymnastics, a padded block with legs that is used for vaulting exercises.

horse•back [hôrs′ bak′] *adverb; noun.* on the back of a horse: In early America the mail was delivered by riders on *horseback.*

horse chestnut a tall shade tree that has large, shiny brown nuts and clusters of large white flowers.

horse•fly [hôrs′ flī′] *noun, plural* **horseflies.** a large fly that bites horses and other animals and sucks their blood.

horse•pow•er [hôrs′ pou′ ər] *noun.* a unit used for measuring the power of an engine. One horsepower is equal to the amount of power needed to lift 550 pounds one foot in one second: He bought a lawnmower with a three-*horsepower* motor.

horse•rad•ish [hôrs′ rad′ ish] *noun, plural* **horseradishes.** a tall, whitish herb with a large, sharp-tasting root. The root is mashed with vinegar to make a strong, spicy seasoning for food.

horse•shoe [hôrs′ shoo′] *noun, plural* **horseshoes. 1.** a U-shaped piece of metal that is nailed to the bottom of a horse's hoof to protect it. **2. horseshoes.** a game in which players throw a horseshoe or an object shaped like this, so that it will land on or near a post in the ground.

horseshoe crab a sea animal having a large shell shaped like a horseshoe and a spiny tail. It is actually more closely related to spiders than to crabs. Horseshoe crabs have existed in the same form for millions of years.

hor•ti•cul•ture [hôr′ tə kul′ chər] *noun.* the study and practice of growing fruits, vegetables, flowers, and decorative plants.

hose [hōz] *noun, plural* **hoses. 1.** a tube made of rubber, plastic, or other material that can be easily bent, used to move water or another liquid, as for watering a garden, spraying water on a fire, or moving gasoline from a pump into a car's gas tank. **2.** socks; stockings; also called **hosiery** [hō′ zhər ē].
—*verb,* **hosed, hosing.** to spray with a hose: Mr. Weiss *hoses* down the sidewalk outside his store every morning.

hos•pi•ta•ble [hä spit′ ə bəl] *adjective, more/most.* friendly to guests or visitors; giving a warm welcome: ". . . their *hospitable* traditions that made them ask me in for a 'bit o' dinner.'" (James Herriot) —**hospitably,** *adverb.*

hos•pi•tal [häs′ pit əl] *noun, plural* **hospitals.** a place where doctors and nurses work and where there are special rooms and equipment to take care of people who are sick or hurt or otherwise in need of medical care.

hos•pi•tal•i•ty [häs′ pə tal′ ə tē] *noun.* generous and friendly treatment of guests or visitors; a warm welcome: "They made a point . . . of offering *hospitality* to frightened or stranded foreigners." (V. S. Naipaul)

hos•pi•tal•ize [häs′ pit əl īz′] *verb,* **hospitalized, hospitalizing.** to put a person in the hospital for medical treatment. —**hospitalization,** *noun.*

host¹ [hōst] *noun, plural* **hosts. 1.** a person who invites and entertains guests: The *host* of the party announced that dinner was ready. **2.** a person who is the main performer on a television variety show or talk show: Johnny Carson has been the *host* of the "Tonight Show" for many years. —*verb,* **hosted, hosting.** to act as a host: to *host* a dinner.

host² *noun, plural* **hosts.** a very large number; a multitude: A *host* of shoppers poured through the doors as the special sale began.

hos•tage [häs′ tij] *noun, plural* **hostages.** a person who is held as a prisoner until certain demands have been met: The terrorists held the plane crew and passengers as *hostages* and demanded the release of other terrorists being held in prison.

host•ess [hōs′ tis] *noun, plural* **hostesses.** a woman who invites and entertains guests; a female host.

hos•tile [häs′ təl] *adjective, more/most.* **1.** showing anger or dislike; unfriendly: When I asked him to move out of the way, his only answer was a *hostile* stare. **2.** of or belonging to an enemy: The town was attacked by *hostile* troops.

hos•til•i•ty [hä stil′ ə tē] *noun, plural* **hostilities. 1.** a feeling of being unfriendly; anger or dislike: **2. hostilities.** acts of war.

Pronunciation Key: G–N

g	give; big	k	kind; cat; back
h	hold	l	let; ball
i	it; this	m	make; time
ī	ice; my	n	not; own
j	jet; gem; edge	ng	having

(Turn the page for more information.)

H

hot [hät] *adjective,* **hotter, hottest. 1.** having a high temperature; very warm: a *hot* day, *hot* water, a *hot* oven. **2.** having a sharp, burning taste: This pepper sauce is really *hot.* **3.** easily excited; violent: Watch how you deal with him because he's got a *hot* temper. **4.** very active or successful: She's the *hottest* young actress around and is being offered many starring roles. **5.** close to something being followed or looked for: The police are *hot* on the trail of the escaped criminal. **6.** *Informal.* recently stolen or obtained in an illegal way: The police stopped him because he was driving a *hot* car.

hot dog 1. a long, thin sausage served in a roll; also called a FRANKFURTER. **2.** *Slang.* a person who shows off or who likes a lot of attention.

ho•tel [hō tel´] *noun, plural* **hotels.** a place that rents rooms for sleeping, and usually offers meals as well.

hound [hound] *noun, plural* **hounds.** a type of dog with droopy ears, a very good sense of smell, and a deep bark. Hounds were originally trained to hunt animals. Beagles, foxhounds, and dachshunds are hounds. —*verb,* **hounded, hounding.** to follow someone in an annoying way; pester: The reporter *hounded* the movie star for days until she finally agreed to give him an interview.

hour [our] *noun, plural* **hours. 1.** a period of sixty minutes: From 6:52 to 7:52 is one *hour.* **2.** one of the points of time indicating such a period: That radio station gives news on the *hour* and the half-hour. **3.** the amount of distance that can be traveled in one hour: It's about two *hours* from here to Los Angeles. **4.** a certain point in time: Mom doesn't like to get calls at dinner *hour.* **5. hours.** a fixed time for doing something: a doctor's *hours.* The store's *hours* are from nine to six.

hour•ly [our´ lē] *adjective; adverb.* **1.** occurring every hour: There are *hourly* flights from here to Chicago. **2.** figured by the hour: You can rent the boat for an *hourly* or daily rate.

house [hous] *noun, plural* **houses. 1.** a building for one family or a few people to live in, separate from other buildings. **2.** the people living in a house; a household: Lee had a bad nightmare and his yelling woke up the whole *house.* **3.** any building used for a certain purpose: a dog*house,* an apartment *house.* We saw a movie at the Rye Play*house.* **4.** a royal family or other important family: The *House* of Rothschild was once the leading banking group in Europe. **5.** a group of people who make laws: The Senate is the upper *house* of Congress.

6. an audience in a theater: There was a full *house* at the school play. —[houz] *verb,* **housed, housing.** to provide a place for someone or something to live, stay, or be kept: Colleges *house* their students in buildings called dormitories.

house•boat [hous´ bōt´] *noun, plural* **houseboats.** a large, flat-bottomed boat equipped so that people can live on it.

house•fly [hous´ flī´] *noun, plural* **houseflies.** a common type of fly that lives in or around people's homes and eats food and household garbage. It sometimes spreads diseases.

house•hold [hous´ hōld´] *noun, plural* **households.** all the people living together in one house. —*adjective.* **1.** having to do with a house: *household* jobs such as cooking, cleaning, and washing dishes. **2.** very well-known; common; familiar: "Xerox" became a *household* word after the company's copying machine became famous.

house•keep•er [hous´ kē´ pər] *noun, plural* **housekeepers.** a person whose work is taking care of a house and doing housework.

House of Representatives The chamber where the U.S. House of Representatives meets.

House of Representatives one of the two branches of the U.S. Congress. There are 435 members of the House, who are elected to two-year terms. The number of representatives per state is determined by the number of people living there.

house•wife [hous´ wīf´] *noun, plural* **housewives.** a married woman who takes care of household work and the needs of a family. A housewife is usually someone who does not work at a job outside the home.

house•work [hous´ wurk´] *noun.* the work done in a home, such as cleaning, cooking, washing, ironing, and so on.

hous•ing [hou′zing] *noun, plural* **housings.**
1. houses as a group; places to live. The city is building new public *housing* downtown. **2.** a covering that protects the moving parts of a machine: the *housing* on an electric drill.

Hous•ton [hyōō′stən] the largest city in Texas, in the southeastern part of the state. *Population:* 1,600,000.

hov•er [huv′ər] *verb,* **hovered, hovering. 1.** to stay in the air over one spot: "The helicopter . . . *hovered* over the flooded houses." (Lois Lenski) "A silver curve of the moon *hovered* already in the western sky." (F. Scott Fitzgerald) **2.** to stay close to; remain near: "When he awoke, Jake Irons was up and *hovering* over a fire . . ." (Marguerite Henry)

—*noun, plural* **howls.** a loud, wailing cry: "The big wolf's . . . mouth opened and a long *howl* rose toward the sky." (Laura Ingalls Wilder)

hub [hub] *noun, plural* **hubs. 1.** the center part of a wheel. ♦ A **hubcap** is a metal cap that fits over the hub of an automobile's wheels. **2.** a center of activity: The city of Boston was once called "the *Hub*" because it was so important in the life of early New England.

huck•le•ber•ry [huk′əl ber′ē] *noun, plural* **huckleberries.** a small, shiny berry that looks like a blueberry but is darker and smaller. Huckleberries grow on small, low bushes.

hud•dle [hud′əl] *verb,* **huddled, huddling.** to crowd together in a tight group; bunch up: "The grass roof leaked in a dozen places, and

---

how-to papers A "how-to" paper is a common assignment for students in a writing course. The idea is to give a step-by-step explanation of how to do some task or operation. A real challenge is to take something that seems completely obvious, because we do it so often, and explain that. Examples of this are topics such as "how to boil water," "how to wash a car," or "how to catch a baseball." Here are some "how-to" steps for a how-to paper: (1) Proceed step by step, from the beginning. (2) Use simple terms, not technical ones. (3) Give exact details of the procedure. (4) Don't leave any step out, even if it seems obvious.

---

how [hou] *adverb.* **1.** in what way or by what means: *How* do you work this computer? *How* do you say "friend" in Spanish? **2.** in what condition or state: *How* is Jean since her operation? **3.** to what degree or amount: *How* did you like the movie? *How* much does that camera cost? —*conjunction.* the fact that; the way that: "Remember *how* he waved to me?" (Arthur Miller)

the men *huddled* together for warmth." (John Toland) —*noun, plural* **huddles.** a group crowded or bunched together: In football, the team with the ball forms a *huddle* to call the next play.

Hud•son River [hud′sən] a river in eastern New York that flows south to the Atlantic Ocean at New York City.

hue [hyōō] *noun, plural* **hues.** a color, or a

H

---

however Our Word Survey shows that the conjunction *however* is one of the most common words in English. *However,* it is not nearly as common in novels and stories as it is in nonfiction writing (such as this article). One reason is that a story tends to move along in a line headed for a climax, and then wind down. *However* is a word that argues with something just said. It tends to slow action. In a factual article, the writer can move back and forth, presenting one point, then a contrast. This kind of movement often calls for *however.* When you use this conjunction, set it off with a comma. This applies whether it begins the sentence ("Teddy Roosevelt was a small and sickly child. *However,* he worked hard to build himself up.") or comes within the sentence ("TR had supported Taft; *however,* he soon came to disagree with him.")

---

how•ev•er [hou ev′ər] *conjunction.* in spite of that; but still; yet: I thought that joke was really funny—*however,* no one else laughed or even cracked a smile. —*adverb.* in whatever way: Just put the boxes in the closet *however* they fit.

howl [howl] *verb,* **howled, howling.** to make a long, loud crying sound: "She could hear wind *howling* in the chimneys." (Madeleine L'Engle)

Pronunciation Key: O–S			
ō	over; go	ou	out; town
ô	all; law	p	put; hop
oo	look; full	r	run; car
ōō	pool; who	s	set; miss
oi	oil; boy	sh	show

(Turn the page for more information.)

shade of a color: The winter sky had a grayish *hue.*

hug [hug] *verb,* **hugged, hugging. 1.** to put the arms around someone or something and hold it close: "Karen was still *hugging* her big rag doll." (Lois Lenski) **2.** to stay close to: The small rowboat *hugged* the shore to avoid the rough waves in open water. —*noun, plural* **hugs.** a close, tight hold.

huge [hyoōj] *adjective.* having a great size; very large; enormous: Elephants are *huge* animals. Our Christmas party was a *huge* success.

hull [hul] *noun, plural* **hulls. 1.** the sides and bottom of a ship: a sailboat with a wooden *hull.* **2.** the outer covering of a seed. A pea pod and a nutshell are hulls.

hum [hum] *verb,* **hummed, humming. 1.** to make a soft, musical sound while keeping the lips together: If you *hum* that tune for me, maybe I can remember the words. **2.** to make a low, even, buzzing sound. —*noun, plural* **hums.** a soft sound like that made by a bee: the *hum* of a fan as it cools a room.

hu•man [hyoō′mən] *adjective.* having to do with a person or people: The *human* body has twelve pairs of rib bones. Great writers such as Shakespeare and Dickens give a true picture of *human* nature. —*noun, plural* **humans.** a person. ◆ Also called a **human being.**

hu•mane [hyoō mān′] *adjective, more/most.* acting as a person should toward human beings or animals; showing human kindness: The *Humane* Society acts to protect children and animals from being treated in a cruel way.

hu•man•i•ty [hyoō man′ə tē] *noun.* **1.** the human race; all people as a group. **2.** the state of being humane; kindness.

hum•ble [hum′bəl] *adjective,* **humbler, humblest. 1.** not proud; modest: Although she was born wealthy and became the wife of a President, Eleanor Roosevelt was a *humble* person

who did not place herself above others. ◆ The quality of being humble is **humility** [hyoō mil′ə tē]. **2.** not large or important: Abraham Lincoln rose from *humble* beginnings to become a great President. —*verb,* **humbled, humbling.** to make humble: The boys thought they had quite a good soccer team, so it really *humbled* them when the girls' team beat them. —**humbly,** *adverb:* "Clematis kept himself *humbly* a little in the rear." (Booth Tarkington)

hu•mid [hyoō′mid] *adjective, more/most.* of the air, damp or moist: a hot, *humid* July day.

hu•mid•i•ty [hyoō mid′ə tē] *noun.* the amount of water vapor in the air: The *humidity* is higher near the ocean than it is in the desert.

hu•mil•i•ate [hyoō mil′ē āt′] *verb,* **humiliated, humiliating.** to make someone feel foolish or worthless; make ashamed: It *humiliated* him to finish last in the race after he had told everyone he was going to win. "It's *humiliating* to let the whole world know that you're broke and need money." (William Inge) —**humiliation,** *noun.*

hum•ming•bird [hum′ing burd′] *noun, plural* **hummingbirds.** a small, brightly-colored American bird with a long, narrow beak. Hummingbirds move their wings with great speed to fly forward, backward, or sideways, or to hover in one place. One kind of hummingbird is the smallest bird in the world.

hu•mor [hyoō′mər] *noun, plural* **humors. 1.** something that is funny; something that makes people laugh: The *humor* of the Peanuts character Snoopy comes from the way he thinks and acts like a person rather than a dog. **2. sense of humor.** the ability to make people laugh or to appreciate something funny. **3.** the way a person feels; one's mood: to be in a good or bad *humor.* —*verb,* **humored, humoring.** to give in to what someone wants; go along with a person's mood or wishes: Mom knew that Eddie's leg really wasn't badly hurt, but just to *humor* him she put a bandage on it anyway.

humor There's no way to analyze exactly what is funny or humorous. What we can do, though, is to describe some of the techniques that authors have used to achieve this effect in writing. *The Unexpected:* Humor can come from something surprising that happens in the story. At the end of Shirley Jackson's "Charles" we suddenly learn that the boy who keeps telling his mother about a bad boy (Charles) at school is really the bad boy himself. *The Unaware Storyteller:* In Stephen Leacock's "How We Kept Mother's Day," the narrator seems to think a fishing trip is just the perfect way to spend Mother's Day. *Actions That Don't Suit the Situation:* This can be either treating a serious matter as if it were a joke, as the barber does in Ring Lardner's "Haircut," or being serious about a comical matter, as in Kingsley Amis' *Lucky Jim,* where Jim gets caught in ridiculous situations but always handles them as if they were everyday events.

H

hu•mor•ist [hyōō′ mər ist] *noun, plural* **humorists.** a person who speaks or writes in a funny way, especially someone who writes humorous books or stories.

hu•mor•ous [hyōō′ mər əs] *adjective, more/most.* full of humor; funny: *James Thurber is known for* humorous *stories like "The Night the Bed Fell."* —**humorously,** *adverb.*

hump [hump] *noun, plural* **humps.** a rounded part that sticks up: *Camels and buffalo have* humps *on their backs.*

hu•mus [hyōō′ məs] *noun.* the dark brown part of the soil that is formed by material from dead plants. Humus is rich in substances that help plants grow.

hunch [hunch] *verb,* **hunched, hunching.** to bend over; to form a hump: *". . . a fire burning by the side porch and a few tired souls* hunched *over in black leather jackets."* (Allen Ginsberg) —*noun, plural* **hunches.** a guess made because of a strong feeling: *I had a* hunch *it would rain, so I brought along my umbrella.*

hun•dred [hun′ drid] *noun, plural* **hundreds;** *adjective.* ten times ten; 100. —**hundredth,** *noun; adjective.*

hung [hung] *verb.* the past form of **hang:** *"She blew upon a silver whistle that* hung *around her neck."* (L. Frank Baum)

Hun•ga•ry [hung′ gə rē] a country in central Europe. *Capital:* Budapest. *Area:* 35,900 square miles. *Population:* 10,725,000. —**Hungarian,** *adjective; noun.*

Hungary The Danube River flows through the center of Budapest, Hungary's capital city.

hun•ger [hung′ gər] *noun, plural* **hungers. 1.** a feeling of wanting or needing food: *Eating those few crackers wasn't enough to take away her* hunger. **2.** a strong wish or need for anything. —*verb,* **hungered, hungering.** to have a strong need or wish for something: *The teacher*

saw that the child was hungering *for praise, and she always made kind remarks about his work.*

hun•gry [hung′ grē] *adjective,* **hungrier, hungriest. 1.** needing or wanting food. **2.** having a strong need or wish for something: *Prince John of England was* hungry *for power and plotted to remove his brother from the throne.* —**hungrily,** *adverb.*

hunk [hungk] *noun, plural* **hunks.** a big piece or lump; a chunk: *The keeper tossed several* hunks *of meat into the lion's cage.*

hunt [hunt] *verb,* **hunted, hunting. 1.** to chase wild animals in order to catch or kill them: *The Plains Indians used to* hunt *buffalo.* **2.** to chase after a person in the same way: *The police are* hunting *for the men who robbed the Sunrise Bank.* **3.** to search hard for something: *to* hunt *for a lost pair of socks.* —*noun, plural* **hunts. 1.** a chase made to catch or kill: *a deer* hunt. *State and local police are carrying on a man*hunt *for the escaped killer.* **2.** a search to find something: *an Easter egg* hunt.

hunt•er [hunt′ ər] *noun, plural* **hunters.** a person or animal that hunts, especially one that hunts wild animals.

hurdle Runners in the women's 400-meter low hurdles in the 1984 Olympics.

hur•dle [hurd′ əl] *noun, plural* **hurdles. 1.** a fence or small frame that is to be jumped over during a race. **2. hurdles.** a race in which runners jump over a series of such barriers. **3.** a problem or obstacle that has to be overcome:

Pronunciation Key: T–Z			
t	ten; date	v	very; live
th	think	w	win; away
<u>th</u>	these	y	you
u	cut; butter	z	zoo; cause
ur	turn; bird	zh	measure

(Turn the page for more information.)

"He had language difficulties, and I helped him over some *hurdles.*" (Herman Wouk) —*verb,* **hurdled, hurdling.** to leap over something. ◆ An athlete who runs in a hurdle race is a **hurdler.**

hurl [hurl] *verb,* **hurled, hurling.** to throw something hard and fast: "'A ball!' cried Gamesh, *hurling* his glove in the air." (Philip Roth)

Hu•ron, Lake [hyŏŏr′ än] the second largest of the Great Lakes, between the state of Michigan and Ontario, Canada.

hur•rah [hə rä′] or **hur•ray** [hə rā′] *noun; interjection.* a shout used to show excitement or great happiness.

hurricane A yacht club in New England is struck by the force of "Hurricane Carol" in 1954.

hur•ri•cane [hur′ ə kān′] *noun, plural* **hurricanes.** a large, powerful storm with strong, swirling winds and heavy rains. To be officially called a hurricane, a storm must have winds blowing at 75 miles per hour or more.

hur•ried [hur′ ēd] *adjective.* moving or done more quickly than usual: rushed; hasty: She got up too late, so she only had a *hurried* breakfast of half a muffin and a glass of juice. —**hurriedly,** *adverb.*

hur•ry [hur′ ē] *verb,* **hurried, hurrying.** to move more quickly than usual; rush: He had to *hurry* through the airport because he was late for his plane. —*noun, plural* **hurries.** the act of moving fast; or the wish or need to move fast: "I'm sorry we're in such a *hurry,* but we've got a taxi waiting." (William Inge)

hurt [hurt] *verb,* **hurt, hurting. 1.** to cause pain to; injure: Gary *hurt* his arm when he fell off his bike. **2.** to feel pain: Grandpa says his knees *hurt* whenever the weather is cold and damp. **3.** to cause pain to a person's feelings; make sad or upset: It *hurt* her when she wasn't invited to the party. **4.** to have a bad effect on; harm:

Failing that test will really *hurt* his chances of getting a good mark for the course. —*noun, plural* **hurts.** something that hurts; an injury.

hur•tle [hurt′ əl] *verb,* **hurtled, hurtling.** to move with great speed; rush with force: "The shaggy little creature kicked, bucked, . . . and even *hurtled* straight up the walls." (James Herriott)

hus•band [huz′ bənd] *noun, plural* **husbands.** a man to whom a woman is married.

hush [hush] *verb.* **hushed, hushing. 1.** to make quiet: to *hush* a crying baby. "The announcer spoke in *hushed* tones as if he were describing a tennis match . . ." (Tom Wolfe) **2. hush up.** to keep secret: The mayor wanted to *hush up* the story that he was once in jail as a young man. —*noun.* a time of complete quiet; silence. —*interjection:* "*Hush!*" she said to the noisy children.

husk [husk] *noun, plural* **husks.** the dry outside covering of corn or certain other fruits and vegetables. —*verb,* **husked, husking.** to remove the husk from: to *husk* corn.

husk•y[1] [hus′ kē] *adjective,* **huskier, huskiest. 1.** big and strong: a *husky* weightlifter. **2.** deep and rough-sounding: a *husky* voice.

husky[2] *noun, plural* **huskies.** a large, strong dog with a thick, bushy coat. Huskies are used in the far north to pull dogsleds.

hus•tle [hus′ əl] *verb,* **hustled, hustling. 1.** to move or work quickly and with lots of energy: Randy really has to *hustle* to deliver all the newspapers on his route each morning. The police *hustled* the protesters out of the mayor's office. **2.** *Informal.* to try to make money in a clever and energetic way, especially by doing something that is not completely honest. —*noun, plural* **hustles.** the act or fact of hustling: Baseball player Pete Rose became famous for his *hustle* on the field. ◆ A person who hustles is a **hustler.**

hut [hut] *noun, plural* **huts.** a small, roughly-built house or other shelter.

hy•a•cinth [hī′ ə sinth′] *noun, plural* **hyacinths.** a plant with a cluster of bell-shaped flowers. Hyacinths grow from bulbs and have long leaves that grow from the base of the stem.

hy•brid [hī′ brid] *noun, plural* **hybrids.** a plant or animal that comes from parents of two different kinds. A mule is a hybrid that comes from crossing a female horse and a male donkey. Hybrids are important in developing better varieties of plants and farm animals. ◆ Also used as an adjective: *hybrid* roses, *hybrid* cattle that produce more milk.

H

hy•drant [hī′ drənt] *noun, plural* **hydrants.** a wide, thick water pipe that stands above ground near a street. Hydrants are connected to main water pipes under the ground. They provide water for fighting fires or washing the streets.

hydrofoil A hydrofoil [hī′ drə foil′] has fins that lift it out of the water to increase its speed.

hy•dro•gen [hī′ drə jən] *noun.* a gas that cannot be seen, tasted, or smelled, but that burns easily. Hydrogen is the lightest of all chemical elements. It mixes with oxygen to make water, and is more common than any other element.

hydrogen bomb a very powerful bomb that gets its energy from the FUSION of hydrogen atoms to form helium atoms. It is the most powerful explosive weapon ever produced.

hy•e•na [hī ēn′ ə] *noun, plural* **hyenas.** a wild animal of Africa and Asia that looks something like a dog. Hyenas have a large head with strong jaws, and make a cry that sounds like a person laughing.

hy•giene [hī′ jēn′] *noun.* the things that people do to keep their bodies clean and healthy. Washing the body and hair and brushing the teeth are important parts of hygiene.

hymn [him] *noun, plural* **hymns.** a song of praise to God. People sing hymns as part of a religious service.

hy•phen [hī′ fən] *noun, plural* **hyphens.** a short line [-] used to join two words, as in "merry-go-round" or "a two-day trip." In a book, a hyphen is also used to separate the parts of a word at the end of a line.

hy•phen•ate [hī′ fə nāt′] *verb,* **hyphenated, hyphenating.** to put a hyphen in: to *hyphenate* the word *self-respect.*

hyp•no•sis [hip nō′ sis] *noun.* the state of mind of a person who has been hypnotized. Hypnosis is used in medicine to prevent people from feeling pain or to treat forms of mental illness. **—hypnotic,** *adjective.*

hyp•no•tism [hip′ nə tiz′ əm] *noun.* the act or practice of hypnotizing a person. ♦ A **hypnotist** is someone who is able to do this.

hyp•no•tize [hip′ nə tīz′] *verb,* **hypnotized, hypnotizing.** to put a person in a special state of mind in which he is very relaxed, as if asleep, but is still able to move and to sense things around him.

hyp•o•crite [hip′ ə krit′] *noun, plural* **hypocrites.** a person who pretends to have good qualities he does not actually have; someone who speaks of being honest, kind, and so on, but doesn't really act that way. ♦ The fact of being a hypocrite is **hypocrisy** [hi päk′ rə sē]. **—hypocritical** [hip′ ə krit′ ə kəl], *adjective.*

hys•ter•i•cal [his ter′ i kəl] *adjective, more/most.* **1.** losing control of oneself because of fear, sorrow, or other strong feelings: "Alan went quite *hysterical.* He cried for days without stopping . . ." (Peter Shaffer) **2.** *Informal.* very funny.

Pronunciation Key: [ə] Symbol

The [ə] or *schwa* sound occurs in syllables without an accent. It can be spelled with any vowel, such as **a** in above, **e** in listen, **i** in pencil, **o** in melon, **u** in circus. It can also be a combination of vowels, such as **io** in action, **ai** in mountain, **iou** in precious

(Turn the page for more information.)

H

Ii

i, I [ī] *noun, plural* **i's, I's.** the ninth letter of the alphabet.

I *pronoun.* the person who is speaking or writing: My sister takes piano lessons but *I* don't.

> **I/me** Can you see the mistake in this sentence? "Laura and me went to the library today." It should be "Laura and I . . ." It's also incorrect to say, "The librarian told Laura and I about some new books that just came in." However, this correct English may be losing out. Many people in law, medicine, and business, college-trained people, say, "He told George and I the story." In this dictionary, and in textbooks, fiction, and nonfiction published by HBJ, we still hold fast to the proper uses of "I" and "me." But we realize it may be a losing battle. Still, if you want to be considered a careful speaker and writer, why should *you* give in to this mistake?

ice [īs] *noun, plural* **ices. 1.** water that has been made solid by cold; frozen water. Ice forms when the temperature of water falls to 32°F (0°C). **2.** a frozen dessert made with sweetened fruit juice. —*verb,* **iced, icing. 1.** to make cold or keep cold with ice: ♦ Usually used as an adjective: *iced* tea or coffee. **2.** to become covered with ice; freeze: The lake often *ices* over at this time of year.

Ice Age a period of time when glaciers covered large parts of the surface of the earth. The most recent Ice Age began about 1.75 million years ago and ended about 10,000 years ago.

ice•berg [īs′burg′] *noun, plural* **icebergs.** a very large piece of ice that has broken off a glacier and is floating in the ocean. Icebergs can be dangerous to ships.

ice•boat [īs′bōt′] *noun, plural* **iceboats. 1.** a vehicle used for traveling over ice, consisting of a light framework with runners like ice skates and a large sail. **2.** an ICE-BREAKER.

ice•box [īs′bäks′] *noun, plural* **iceboxes. 1.** a heavy box or chest in which food is cooled with ice. Iceboxes were used before the development of the electric refrigerator. **2.** another name for a REFRIGERATOR.

ice•break•er [īs′brāk′ər] *noun, plural* **icebreakers.** a large, heavy ship used to break a path through ice so that other ships can pass.

ice•cap [īs′kap′] *noun, plural* **icecaps.** a permanent layer of ice and snow that covers an area of land and slopes downward from a high center. Antarctica is covered by an icecap.

ice cream a smooth, frozen food that is served as a dessert, made of milk or cream with various sweeteners and flavorings.

ice hockey see **hockey.**

Ice•land [īs′lənd] an island country in the North Atlantic, east of Greenland. *Capital:* Reykjavik. *Area:* 39,770 square miles. *Population:* 236,000. —**Icelandic,** *adjective; noun.*

ice skate a shoe with a metal blade attached to the bottom, used for skating on ice.

ice-skate [īs′ skāt′] *verb,* **ice-skated, ice-skating.** to skate on ice. —**ice-skater,** *noun.*

iceberg This iceberg is even larger than it seems. About 90% of an iceberg is below the water.

icicle Water running off the roof of this house has formed icicles during freezing temperatures.

i•ci•cle [ī′ si kəl] *noun, plural* **icicles.** a pointed, hanging piece of ice formed by water that freezes as it drips.

ic•ing [ī′ sing] *noun, plural* **icings.** a sweet, smooth mixture of sugar, eggs, butter, and flavoring that is used to cover and decorate cakes, cookies, and other baked goods; also called **frosting.**

i•cy [ī′ sē] *adjective,* **icier, iciest. 1.** covered with ice: Be careful walking to school because the sidewalks are very *icy.* **2.** very cold; like ice: an *icy* wind. **3.** cold and unfriendly: Peggy gave her brother an *icy* stare when he made fun of her.

I'd [īd] the contraction for "I had" or "I would."

I•da•ho [ī′ də hō′] a state in the northwestern U.S. *Capital:* Boise. *Nickname:* "Gem State." *Area:* 83,600 square miles. *Population:* 944,000.

i•de•a [ī dē′ ə] *noun, plural* **ideas. 1.** a thought, plan, or picture that has been formed in the mind; something that exists in the mind: Sharon has a good *idea* for her science project. Whose *idea* was it to put those huge statues on Mt. Rushmore? **2.** a certain belief or opinion: I had no *idea* that you and Jeff were cousins. **3.** the purpose or point of something: The *idea* of baseball is to score more runs than the other team.

i•de•al [ī dē əl *or* ī dēl′] *noun, plural* **ideals. 1.** a person or thing that is thought of as being perfect; a perfect example. Getting an A in the course—that's the *ideal*—but I'd settle for a B. **2. ideals.** standards for thinking or acting: Eleanor Roosevelt was a person of high *ideals.*

—*adjective, more/most.* being exactly what is wanted or hoped for; the best possible: Sitting in the sun on a quiet beach in Hawaii—to me that's the *ideal* vacation. —**ideally,** *adverb:* "*Ideally* they should build their own dwellings to their own needs." (Beryl Bainbridge)

i•de•al•ist [ī dē′ ə list] *noun, plural* **idealists.** a person who has high ideals; someone who believes in acting according to strict standards of what is good or right. ◆ The beliefs of an idealist are called **idealism:** The movie *Mr. Smith Goes to Washington* is about a young senator whose *idealism* makes it hard for him to accept the real world of politics. —**idealistic,** *adjective: Idealistic* young people often join the Peace Corps to work in a poor country.

i•den•ti•cal [ī den′ ti kəl] *adjective.* **1.** being exactly alike: That airline's planes all have *identical* blue-and-white markings on the tail. **2.** being the very same: The two golfers hit long shots that landed in almost the *identical* spot on the green. —**identically,** *adverb.*

i•den•ti•fi•ca•tion [ī den′ tə fi kā′ shən] *noun, plural* **identifications. 1.** the act of identifying; recognizing someone or something: The robbery victim made an *identification* of the thief from a police lineup. **2.** something that is used to prove who a person is: The bank asked him for some *identification* before they would cash his check, so he showed his driver's license.

i•den•ti•fy [ī den′ tə fī′] *verb,* **identified, identifying. 1.** to know or show that some person or thing is who or what you say it to be; recognize: She *identified* the suitcase as the one she'd lost by the yellow tape on the handle. **2. identify with. a.** to think one thing is the same as another; consider the same: People sometimes *identify* happiness *with* having a lot of money. **b.** to feel something in common with: I could really *identify with* the main character in that book, because I live in a small farming town just like he did.

i•den•ti•ty [ī den′ tə tē] *noun, plural* **identities. 1.** who a person is, or what a thing is: The movie star wore a big hat and dark glasses to hide her *identity* from the crowd of fans. **2.** the fact of being identical.

I

Pronunciation Key: A–F

a	and; hat	ch	chew; such
ā	ate; stay	d	dog; lid
â	care; air	e	end; yet
ä	father; hat	ē	she; each
b	boy; cab	f	fun; off

(Turn the page for more information.)

idioms "He let the cat out of the bag." "She was in the doghouse." "Outside, it was raining cats and dogs." All these are idioms. The individual words do not carry their usual meaning, but go together to create an expression with a special meaning. A sprinkling of idioms can make a piece of writing sound lively, but if you overload the piece with idioms, the lively tone becomes forced, and the reader soon tires of it. James Thurber made fun of this style in his story, "The Catbird Seat." In it, a character constantly uses idioms such as "sitting in the catbird seat" (in a good spot, doing fine) and "tearing up the pea patch" (going wild). He has a New York City office worker using these idioms, which in fact are Southern farm expressions.

id·i·om [id′ē əm] *noun, plural* **idioms. 1.** a group of words whose meaning cannot be understood by putting together the regular meaning of each separate word in the group, such as "keep an eye on," "play it by ear," or "put your nose to the grindstone." **2.** the way of speaking that is typical of a certain group of people: ". . . the homely *idiom* of our old north country speech." (Beatrix Potter) —**idiomatic,** *adjective:* "Keep your chin up" is an *idiomatic* expression.

id·i·ot [id′ē ət] *noun, plural* **idiots. 1.** a word formerly used in medical science to describe a person with very low intelligence, who cannot take care of himself. **2.** a very foolish or stupid person: "Only an *idiot* would build a boat in the middle of the woods." (Lloyd Alexander) ♦ Something **idiotic** is very foolish or stupid.

i·dle [īd′ əl] *adjective,* **idler, idlest. 1.** not working or busy; doing nothing: All the teams in the league have games today except the Lions, who are *idle* until next Saturday. **2.** not willing to work; lazy: "I do . . . spend less money, and less time lost in *idle* company." (Samuel Pepys) **3.** not producing anything useful; worthless: *idle* gossip. Paula says my big plans for the future are nothing more than *idle* talk. —*verb,* **idled, idling. 1.** to spend time doing nothing: "He had to do something with himself; he couldn't just *idle* away more hours around the barn." (Alex Haley) **2.** to run a motor or machine slowly and out of gear: "He left the pickup truck *idling* by the side of the diner as he always did." (John Gardner)

—**idly,** *adverb:* "I cannot sit *idly* by in Atlanta and not be concerned about what happens in Birmingham." (Martin Luther King)

i·dol [īd′ əl] *noun, plural* **idols. 1.** an object or other image that is worshipped as a god. An idol is usually a statue or similar figure. **2.** a person who is greatly admired or loved: Babe Ruth was the *idol* of many baseball fans in the 1920's. ♦ To **idolize** someone means to admire the person very much: Teenagers often *idolize* popular movie stars or rock singers.

if [if] *conjunction.* **1.** in the event that; should it happen that: *If* it rains today, the game will be played on Friday. *If* you don't want potatoes, you can have rice instead. **2.** whether: Do you know *if* we have school next Monday? **3.** that: Is it all right *if* I borrow your pen for a minute?

igloo An igloo in the Canadian Arctic region. In the Eskimo language "igloo" means "house," but in English it's used only for the well-known "ice house."

ig·loo [ig′ lōō] *noun, plural* **igloos.** a dome-shaped house made from blocks of ice or snow, often used by the Eskimos in former times. Igloos were built as a temporary shelter while hunting or traveling in the winter months, but usually not as a permanent home.

ig·ne·ous [ig′ nē əs] *adjective.* of rocks, produced by the cooling and hardening of very hot materials. When lava from a volcano hardens, it forms a type of **igneous rock.**

ig·nite [ig nīt′] *verb,* **ignited, igniting. 1.** to set fire to something; cause to burn. **2.** to begin to burn; catch on fire: "In thirty seconds the rocket would *ignite* right underneath his back." (Tom Wolfe)

ig·ni·tion [ig nish′ ən] *noun, plural* **ignitions. 1.** the act of setting on fire or catching fire: the *ignition* of gasoline in a car engine. **2.** an electrical system that starts the engine of a car, boat, or other vehicle.

I

ig•no•rance [igʹ nər əns] *noun.* the fact or state of being ignorant; not knowing: In his *ignorance*, he tried to make the flashlight work without putting in any batteries. The saying, "*Ignorance* of the law is no excuse" means that you can't claim the reason you broke a certain law is that you didn't know about it.

ig•no•rant [igʹ nər ənt] *adjective, more/most.* **1.** not knowing much; having little or no knowledge and education: "It's a great thing, an Oxford University education! Me, I'm only a poor *ignorant* Dublin man." (Brendan Behan) **2.** not aware of a certain thing; not knowing: "Dickens' only reference to the game (cricket) shows that he was *ignorant* of its rules." (George Orwell) **3.** showing a lack of information or knowledge: He made the *ignorant* remark that America is the only country which builds jet airliners. **—ignorantly,** *adverb.*

ig•nore [ig nôrʹ] *verb,* **ignored, ignoring.** to pay no attention to; not take notice of: Linda *ignored* me by walking right past without saying hello.

i•gua•na [i gwäʹ nə] *noun, plural* **iguanas.** a large lizard with a row of spines along its back. It is found in very warm parts of the Americas.

iguana This North American desert iguana is unusual among desert animals; it actually prefers to be out in the hot temperatures of midday and hunts during that time.

ill [il] *adjective.* **1.** having a disease; not healthy; sick: He's been *ill* with the flu for several days now. **2.** bad or harmful: The farmer's business is suffering from the *ill* effects of bad weather. **3. ill at ease.** not comfortable; uneasy: The boss is very *ill at ease* about giving speeches and usually has one of his assistants do it. **—adverb.** in a bad or harmful way: There is an old saying, "Do not speak *ill* of the dead." ♦ Often used in combination with another words, such as **ill-tempered, ill-mannered,** and so on. **—noun,**

plural **ills. 1.** a sickness; disease. **2.** something that is bad or harmful.

I'll [īl] the contraction for **I will.**

il•le•gal [i lēʹ gəl] *adjective.* not legal; against the law. **—illegally,** *adverb:* He got a ticket because his car was *illegally* parked.

Il•li•nois [il ə noiʹ] a state in the north-central U.S., bordered by Lake Michigan. *Capital:* Springfield. *Nickname:* "The Inland Empire." *Area:* 56,400 square miles. *Population:* 11,448,000.

il•lit•er•ate [i litʹ ər it] *adjective.* **1.** not able to read or write at all; having no education: In the Middle Ages most poor farmers were *illiterate.* **2.** not able to read and write well enough to get along in the world; having a poor education: Some experts consider that a person in the U.S. who cannot read a newspaper or write out a check is *illiterate.* **—noun, plural** **illiterates.** a person who is illiterate. ♦ The fact of being illiterate is **illiteracy.**

ill•ness [ilʹ nis] *noun, plural* **illnesses. 1.** the fact or state of being ill; disease: Our teacher is out today because of *illness.* **2.** a certain disease: Polio was a very dangerous *illness* until doctors learned how to prevent it in the 1950's.

il•lu•mi•nate [i lo͞oʹ mə nāt/] *verb,* **illuminated, illuminating.** to light up; shine light on: "A bright light *illuminated* the entire scene." (Richard Vasquez) **—illumination,** *noun.*

il•lu•sion [i lo͞oʹ zhən] *noun, plural* **illusions. 1.** something that fools the eyes, ears, or other senses: The circus clown wore stilts to create the *illusion* that he was ten feet tall. "The thin red second hand swung smoothly round the dial, giving the *illusion* of time rapidly passing." (Kingsley Amis) **2.** a false idea or belief: In early times people had the *illusion* that the earth was flat.

il•lus•trate [ilʹ əs trāt/] *verb,* **illustrated, illustrating. 1.** to add a picture to a book or other written work in order to explain it, give it decoration, or make it more interesting: The artist N.C. Wyeth *illustrated* such well-known books as *Treasure Island* and *The Last of the Mohicans.*

I

Pronunciation Key: G–N

g	give; big	k	kind; cat; back
h	hold	l	let; ball
i	it; this	m	make; time
ī	ice; my	n	not; own
j	jet; gem; edge	ng	having

(Turn the page for more information.)

◆ A person who does this is called an **illustrator. 2.** to explain something by giving an example or by comparing it to something else: This dictionary *illustrates* the meaning of words by showing how they are used by famous writers.

il·lus·tra·tion [il′ əs trā′ shən] *noun, plural* **illustrations. 1.** a picture that is used to explain or decorate something written. **2.** something used to explain; an example: Falling leaves are a good *illustration* of the law of gravity.

il·lus·tri·ous [i lus′ trē əs] *adjective, more/most.* famous because of outstanding works or actions; great: Dame Margot Fonteyn had an *illustrious* career as a ballet dancer.

im·age [im′ ij] *noun, plural* **images. 1.** a copy or likeness of something: Ted is the *image* of his father. **2.** a picture formed when light shines in a mirror or through a camera lens: "As the great ship's *image* had expanded on the television screen in the secret control room . . ." (Arthur C. Clarke) **3.** a picture formed in the mind: "The center of her mind was filled with the *image* of the great, white clock at the railway station." (James Baldwin) **4.** public opinion about a person or thing; the way something is thought of by people: Movie actor John Wayne had the *image* of a strong, fearless hero. The oil company hired a new advertising agency to try to improve their *image*. **5.** in writing, a word or words used to suggest a certain picture to the mind: "Every word in the poem contains some *image*, some appeal to the senses: The

gray sea, the long black land, the yellow half-moon . . ." (Laurence Perrine) ◆ The use of words in this way by a writer is called **imagery** [im′ ij rē].

i·mag·i·nar·y [i maj′ ə ner′ ē] *adjective.* existing only as a picture in the mind; not real: My little sister has an *imaginary* friend that she pretends to play with when she's alone. The countries of North and South Korea are divided by an *imaginary* line called the 38th Parallel.

> **imagination** All good writers depend on their faculties of imagination. Whether a writer invents a story in a time or at a place he could not know personally, or whether he uses his own examples, he still needs the tools of imagination. Probably the most noted description of the Civil War's fighting is *The Red Badge of Courage,* by Stephen Crane. Crane wasn't even born when the Civil War was fought, yet he imagined what it was like. You can help your imagination of course. Crane listened to the stories of many veterans who had actually fought in the Civil War. You can also read books or do other research about it. Crane studied the photos of Civil War battlefields taken by Matthew Brady.

i·mag·i·na·tion [i maj′ ə nā′ shən] *noun, plural* **imaginations. 1.** the ability of the mind to create something new or different, or to create a new or different use for something that already exists: Mickey Mouse, Donald Duck, Disneyland, and many popular movies for children were all the product of Walt Disney's *imagination.* **2.** something imagined: Tommy thought he heard someone sneaking around outside the house, but it was just his *imagination.*

i·mag·i·na·tive [i maj′ ə nə tiv] *adjective, more/most.* showing or having a good imagination: *The Wizard of Oz* is an *imaginative* story about a girl who gets lost in a strange land.

i·mag·ine [i maj′ in] *verb,* **imagined, imagining. 1.** to form an idea or image in the mind; have a mental picture of something: "One way to do this is to *imagine* all the people in the world spread out evenly." (Isaac Asimov) **2.** to believe to be true; suppose; guess: I *imagine* you'll be at Gail's party tomorrow, won't you? **3.** to have an idea about something, especially a

> **images** "On this 10th day of June, 1940, the hand that held the dagger has struck it into the back of its neighbor." President Franklin D. Roosevelt said that when the dictator Benito Mussolini sent his Italian troops into France. It was an important event of World War II. He might have been content just to say, "Today, Italy has declared war on France." Why, then, did he choose the image of the dagger? Roosevelt wanted to show that he felt Mussolini was a coward, declaring war on France after Germany had already weakened France and France was about to fall. President Roosevelt also said after the attack on Pearl Harbor, "Yesterday, December 7th, 1941—a date which will live in *infamy* . . ." (You can look up the word *infamy* on p. 396.)

wrong or untrue idea: He *imagines* that people are making fun of him because he wears braces, so he tries not to smile. ◆ Something that can be imagined is **imaginable:** "Fields of yellow and brown coral and . . . smaller patches of almost every color and color combination *imaginable.*" (James Jones)

im•i•tate [im′ ə tāt′] *verb,* **imitated, imitating.** **1.** to try to act or be like someone or something else; follow an example; copy: A mockingbird can *imitate* the call of almost any other bird. **2.** to look like; resemble: Artificial playing fields are colored green to *imitate* real grass.

im•i•ta•tion [im′ ə tā′ shən] *noun, plural* **imitations. 1.** the act of imitating; copying: My uncle can do a really good *imitation* of Jimmy Stewart and sound just like him. **2.** a copy of something else: an *imitation* of a famous painting. —*adjective.* made to look like something else; not real: She decided to buy an *imitation* fur coat because real furs are so expensive.

im•ma•ture [im′ ə choor′ *or* im′ ə toor′] *adjective, more/most.* **1.** not fully grown or developed; not ripe: *Immature* tomatoes are hard and green. **2.** not acting according to one's age; behaving in a childish way.

im•me•di•ate [i mē′ dē it] *adjective.* **1.** happening at once; without delay: The townspeople are completely cut off by flood waters and need *immediate* help. **2.** close; near: Only the *immediate* family came to her wedding—her cousins weren't invited. —**immediately,** *adverb:* "I needed money—not *immediately* but in the future." (William Saroyan)

im•mense [i mens′] *adjective, more/most.* of very great size; huge: "The hotels were *immense*—five times as big as the Grand Central . . . in Dublin." (Brian Moore) "The country to her had been an *immense* surprise and delight." (Isak Dinesen) —**immensely,** *adverb:* "I am *immensely* fond of you all . . ." (J.R.R. Tolkien) —**immensity,** *noun.*

im•mi•grant [im′ ə grənt] *noun, plural* **immigrants.** a person who comes into a foreign country to live after leaving the country where he or she was born.

im•mi•grate [im′ ə grāt′] *verb,* **immigrated, immigrating.** to go to live in a country in which one was not born: Thousands of people *immigrate* to the United States from other countries every year. ◆ The process of immigrating is called **immigration.**

im•mi•nent [im′ ə nənt] *adjective.* about to happen; likely to occur soon: The darkening sky warned us that a storm was *imminent.*

im•mor•al [i môr′ əl] *adjective, more/most.* not moral; wicked; evil. ◆ The fact of being immoral is **immorality** [im′ ôr al′ ə tē].

im•mor•tal [i môrt′ əl] *adjective.* **1.** living forever; never dying: Religion teaches that God is *immortal.* **2.** lasting forever: William Shakespeare's *immortal* plays. ◆ The state of being immortal is **immortality** [im′ ôr tal′ətē].

im•mune [i myoon′] *adjective.* **1.** protected from a disease: People are generally *immune* to chicken pox after they have had it once. **2.** not affected by; free from: That author claims he's *immune* to criticism and never pays attention to the reviews of his books. ◆ The fact of being immune is **immunity.**

im•pact [im′ pakt] *noun, plural* **impacts. 1.** the striking of one object against another; a collision: "The screen became suddenly blank as the missile destroyed itself on *impact.*" (Arthur C. Clarke) **2.** the force or effect of something: ". . . the tide of democracy, socialism, and communism had had dramatic *impact* on the people of Japan, and they too set up a cry for change." (John Toland)

im•pair [im pâr′] *verb,* **impaired, impairing.** to take away from the strength or quality of; make less; weaken: Poor eating habits may *impair* a person's health.

immigrant An immigrant family from Italy arrives at Ellis Island, New York City, in this photograph taken by Lewis Hine in around 1910.

Pronunciation Key: O–S

ō	over; go	ou	out; town
ô	all; law	p	put; hop
oo	look; full	r	run; car
ōō	pool; who	s	set; miss
oi	oil; boy	sh	show

(Turn the page for more information.)

impala The swift impala is able to leap 30 feet in the air and run at about 50 miles per hour.

im·pal·a [im pal′ ə] *noun, plural* **impalas.** a small reddish or brown African antelope with curved horns. An impala can run very fast and make long, high leaps through the air.

im·par·tial [im pär′ shəl] *adjective, more/most.* not favoring one person or side more than another; not partial; fair: The judge and jury should be *impartial* as they hear the facts of a criminal case. —**impartially,** *adverb.*

im·pa·tient [im pā′ shənt] *adjective, more/most.* not willing to put up with delay or problems; not patient:". . . to those who were *impatient* to leave, each minute had seemed endless." (Helen MacInnes) —**impatiently,** *adverb.* —**impatience,** *noun:* "The line always moved too slowly for him, and you could pick him out by his *impatience* and restlessness." (Upton Sinclair)

im·peach [im pēch′] *verb,* **impeached, impeaching.** to make a formal charge that a government official is guilty of a crime or serious wrong: The House of Representatives can vote to *impeach* the President, who is then put on trial by the Senate. ◆ The fact of impeaching a public official is **impeachment.**

im·pede [im pēd′] *verb,* **impeded, impeding.** to get in the way of; hinder; obstruct: "He broke his leg and worked with the cast *impeding* him for months." (Isaac Asimov) ◆ Something that impedes is an **impediment** [im ped′ ə mənt].

im·per·a·tive [im per′ ə tiv] *adjective, more/most.* **1.** not to be avoided or put off; absolutely necessary; urgent: The pilot realized it was *imperative* that they land at once because they were so low on fuel. **2.** in grammar, expressing a command: "Slow down!" is an *imperative* sentence. —*noun, plural* **imperatives.** a verb or sentence that expresses a command.

im·per·fect [im pur′ fikt] *adjective.* not perfect; having faults: ". . . his youth, his *imperfect* English, and odd appearance kept important clients at a distance." (W.A. Swanberg) —**imperfection** [im′ pər fek′ shən], *noun:* an *imperfection* in a diamond.

im·per·i·al [im pēr′ ē əl] *adjective.* having to do with an empire, or an emperor or empress: The emperor of Japan lives in the *Imperial* Palace.

im·per·i·al·ism [im pēr′ ē ə liz′ əm] *noun.* the policy of controlling the government or territory of another country. During the 1800's, Britain, France, and other nations of Europe practiced imperialism in Africa and ruled much of the land there. ◆ A person who follows or supports this policy is an **imperialist.**

im·per·son·ate [im pur′ sə nāt] *verb,* **impersonated, impersonating.** to pretend to be someone else; copy the looks and actions of another person: The man was arrested for *impersonating* a police officer. —**impersonation,** *noun.* Comedian Rich Little is famous for his *impersonations* of movie stars and politicians.

im·ple·ment [im′ plə mənt] *noun, plural* **implements.** a tool or piece of equipment that is used to do a particular job: A shovel and a rake are common gardening *implements.* —[im′ plə ment′] *verb,* **implemented, implementing.** to put into action: to *implement* a plan.

im·ply [im plī′] *verb,* **implied, implying.** to express something without saying it directly; suggest; hint: "His expression *implied* that there

imply/infer These are not common words, but "watchdogs" of the English language become aroused when people use them incorrectly. *Imply* means "to suggest; hint at; say in an indirect way:" "You stand there boldly denying that you did it, and to cover up your own guilt you are willing to *imply* that your king might be the thief." (William Steig) "The village of Loma is built, as its name *implies,* on a low round hill . . ." (John Steinbeck) *Infer* means "to learn in an indirect way; guess at without being told:" "My images about Africa had been largely *inferred* from Tarzan movies . . ." (Alex Haley) "She can consider the context of the word and *infer* its meaning." (Carolyn Paine)

I

was something wrong with a mother who wanted to leave her child." (Mark Helprin) ◆ Something that is implied is an **implication** [im′ plə kā′ shən].

im•po•lite [im′ pə līt′] *adjective, more/most.* not polite; having bad manners; rude. —**impolitely,** *adverb.* —**impoliteness,** *noun.*

im•port [im pôrt′] *verb,* **imported, importing.** to bring in something from a foreign country for sale or use: The United States *imports* coffee from Colombia and Brazil. "Charles Boyer has gone to Hollywood to become the latest *imported* American movie star." (Janet Flanner) —[im′ pôrt′] *noun, plural* **imports. 1.** something that is imported. **2.** importance: a matter of great *import.*

away soon because it's making you *impossible!*" (Judy Blume) —**impossibly,** *adverb.* —**impossibility** [im′ päs ə bil′ ə tē], *noun.*

im•pos•tor [im päs′ tər] *noun, plural* **impostors.** a person who pretends to be someone else in order to gain or get something: At the 1985 Emmy Awards, an *impostor* tried to accept an award that wasn't really his.

im•press [im pres′] *verb,* **impressed, impressing. 1.** to have a strong effect on the mind or feelings, especially in a good way: The mayor *impressed* me as a very intelligent woman. "He had been so *impressed* by me that he was going to make me a representative of the Curtis Publishing Company." (Russell Baker) **2.** to make a mark or pattern by pressing.

impressions Eudora Welty once described the origin of a story, "The Worn Path." "One day I saw a solitary old woman like Phoenix. She was walking; I saw her, at middle distance, in a winter country landscape, and watched her slowly make her way across my line of vision. The sight of her made me write the story." Welty then invented the rest of the story to fit her fleeting impression of the woman. She proceeded to create a life that fit the woman's appearance. A first impression does not make a story in itself, but it is a good starting point. A person's face, a song or conversation overheard, a flash of memory of some place—all can be impressions that lead a writer into a complete story.

im•por•tance [im pôrt′ əns] *noun.* the state or quality of being important. This book deals with the *importance* of eating proper foods.

im•por•tant [im pôrt′ ənt] *adjective, more/most.* worth caring about or being concerned with; having some value or meaning: Getting good grades in school is *important* to her. The front page of a newspaper gives the most *important* news stories of the day.

im•pose [im pōz′] *verb,* **imposed, imposing. 1.** to take unfair advantage; force oneself on someone: Oh, I'd love to stay for dinner—are you sure I wouldn't be *imposing?* ◆ Something that is imposed is an **imposition** [im′ pə zi′ shən]. **2.** to set up or apply by force: to *impose* a new tax on cigarettes, to *impose* military rule on a country. ◆ Something that is **imposing** is large and impressive: Niagara Falls is an *imposing* sight.

im•pos•si•ble [im päs′ ə bəl] *adjective, more/most.* **1.** not able to be or to happen; not possible: It's *impossible* to drop a stone and have it go upward instead of falling to the ground. **2.** not able to be done: "For a moment John March found it *impossible* to speak." (John P. Marquand) **3.** hard to put up with or get along with; very unpleasant or difficult: "Whatever's wrong with you I hope it goes

im•pres•sion [im presh′ ən] *noun, plural* **impressions. 1.** a strong effect produced in the mind; an idea or feeling about what something is like: It's very hard to sell a house if people get a bad *impression* of it as they first walk up to the door. "I've tried to get in touch with you several times . . . In fact, I have the *impression* you are avoiding me." (Evelyn Waugh) **2.** a mark or pattern made on a surface by pressing: Many famous movie stars have left an *impression* of their hands and feet in wet cement at the Chinese Theater in Hollywood. **3.** an imitation of the way someone speaks, acts, or looks; an impersonation.

im•pres•sive [im pres′ iv] *adjective, more/most.* having a powerful effect on the mind or feelings; making a strong or lasting impression: Notre Dame Cathedral in Paris is an *impressive* sight. —**impressively,** *adverb.* —**impressiveness,** *noun.*

I

Pronunciation Key: T–Z

t	ten; date	v	very; live
th	think	w	win; away
th	these	y	you
u	cut; butter	z	zoo; cause
ur	turn; bird	zh	measure

(Turn the page for more information.)

im•print [im´ print´] *noun, plural* **imprints. 1.** a mark made by pressing: We followed the *imprint* of the truck's tires in the mud. **2.** an influence or effect that is thought of as being like this: The life of Napoleon made a great *imprint* on the French nation. —[im print´] *verb,* **imprinted, imprinting.** to make an imprint: The company's name was *imprinted* on its envelopes.

im•pris•on [im priz´ ən] *verb,* **imprisoned, imprisoning.** to put in prison; lock up. —**imprisonment,** *noun.*

im•prob•a•ble [im präb´ ə bəl] *adjective.* not likely to occur or be true; not probable; unlikely: Dick told an *improbable* story about how his dog ate his homework paper.

im•prop•er [im präp´ ər] *adjective, more/most.* not correct; wrong: He got a ticket for making an *improper* left turn from the center lane. —**improperly,** *adverb.*

improper fraction a fraction that is greater than or equal to 1, such as 6/5 and 4/4.

im•prove [im prōōv´] *verb,* **improved, improving.** to make or become better: My piano playing is *improving* because I've been practicing every day. Thomas Edison didn't make the very first electric light bulb, but he greatly *improved* on what had been done before.

im•prove•ment [im prōōv´ mənt] *noun, plural* **improvements. 1.** the act or fact of improving; making or becoming better: Tim's grades show a lot of *improvement* since he started studying more. **2.** a person or thing that is better; something that adds value: When they bought the house they put aside extra money to pay for a new roof and other *improvements.*

im•pro•vise [im´ prə vīz] *verb,* **improvised, improvising. 1.** to make up and perform something without preparing beforehand: The speech she had written was too short and she had to *improvise* for the last few minutes. **2.** to make or build from whatever materials are available: Musicians in the West Indies often *improvise* musical instruments out of old steel cans. ◆ Something that is improvised is an **improvisation** [im präv´ ə zā´shən].

im•pu•dent [im´ pyə dənt] *adjective, more/most.* showing no respect; too bold and forward; rude. —**impudence,** *noun.*

im•pulse [im´ puls´] *noun, plural* **impulses. 1.** a sudden wish to act; something decided without real thought: *Impulse* buying means buying something you don't really need, just because you like it. "Airplanes were scarce in Persia. When Miller saw one, he felt an *impulse* to run to the mountains and . . . reach up and touch it." (John McPhee) **2.** a sudden wave or force: *Impulses* of the nervous system carry messages to the brain. ◆ A person who acts according to impulse is **impulsive.**

in- English has two similar forms that mean "not," *in-* and *un-*. "Along with these bananas, . . . we also gathered some pineapples of *unbelievable* size." (Jules Verne) "The sky was scattered once more with the *incredible* lamps of stars." (William Golding) (*Believable* and *credible* both mean "able to be believed.") *In-* has three other forms. Before *r,* the prefix changes to *ir-:* "A peculiar noise was going on, a scuffling, *irregular* noise . . ." (C. S. Lewis) Before *l* it is *il-:* "We were in the middle lane. A quick left turn would be *illegal.*" (Hunter Thompson) Before *'m,' 'b,'* or *'p,'* it is *im-:* "He refused to compromise any longer with an *immoral* position." (James Michener)

in [in] *preposition.* **1.** inside: Put your shoes *in* the closet. **2.** into: Get *in* the car **3.** at a certain place: She was born *in* Florida. **4.** at a certain time: I'll be finished *in* an hour. **5.** to or at a certain condition: to be *in* pain, to get *in* trouble, to leave *in* a hurry. **6.** by a certain way or method: to sign a letter *in* ink, to pay for something *in* cash. —*adverb.* inside or within: It might rain, so bring the wash *in.*

inauguration The inauguration of Calvin Coolidge as President in 1925. He had already served two years in office following the death of Warren G. Harding.

in•au•gu•rate [in ô´ gyə rāt´] *verb,* **inaugurated, inaugurating. 1.** to put a person into a high

I

office with a formal ceremony: The President of the United States is *inaugurated* on January 20th of the year following the election. ♦ This is called an **inauguration. 2.** to officially begin something important: The Wright brothers' first flight *inaugurated* the age of air travel.

In•ca [ingk′ə] *noun, plural* **Inca** or **Incas.** a member of an Indian tribe that had a highly-advanced civilization in the mountains of South America in the years 1200-1500.

Inca The Inca were known for beautiful craftwork such as this carved jaguar's head. South American Indians regarded this animal as a symbol of courage.

in•cense¹ [in′ sens′] *noun, plural* **incenses.** a substance that has a sweet smell when it is burned. Incense is used in certain religious ceremonies.

incense² [in sens′] *verb,* **incensed, incensing.** to make very angry: It *incenses* him to have to pay so much money in income taxes.

in•cen•tive [in sen′ tiv] *noun, plural* **incentives.** something that makes a person want to try harder or do more work: Bill's father offered to buy him a new bike as an *incentive* to make him get better grades.

inch [inch] *noun, plural* **inches.** a unit of measure for length. Twelve inches equal one foot. An inch is equal to 2.54 centimeters. —*verb,* **inched, inching.** to move very slowly, a little bit at a time: "He watched the bumper-to-bumper traffic *inching* its way north." (E.L. Doctorow)

in•ci•dent [in′ sə dənt] *noun, plural* **incidents. 1.** something that happens; an event: James Thurber's stories often describe amusing *incidents* from his boyhood in Ohio. **2.** a minor conflict; an occurrence of violence: There are hard feelings between those two countries because of the many *incidents* along their border.

in•ci•den•tal [in sə dən′ təl] *adjective.* along with something else; in addition: *Incidental* expenses on a business trip are small items other than the cost of travel, a room, and meals.

in•ci•den•tal•ly [in sə dent′ lē] *adverb.* by the way; along with something else: Yes, I really like the Matt Christopher books—*incidentally,* don't you still have one of them that you borrowed from me?

in•cin•er•a•tor [in sin′ ə rā′ tər] *noun, plural* **incinerators.** a furnace that is used to burn trash or garbage.

in•cli•na•tion [in′ klə nā′ shən] *noun, plural* **inclinations. 1.** a liking for something or a favoring of some point of view; a preference: She really likes where she's living now and doesn't have the least *inclination* to move. **2.** a surface that is at an angle; a slope or slant.

in•cline [in klīn′] *verb,* **inclined, inclining. 1.** to be or move at an angle; slant; slope: "I *inclined* my head slightly in a sort of nod or bow." (Iris Murdoch) **2.** to lean toward in the mind; favor: I'm *inclined* to agree with you about that. **3.** to be likely to; tend: "Becky . . . had never really mastered multiplication tables and was *inclined* to confuse sevens and nines . . ." (Robert Heinlein) —[in′ klīn′ *or* in klīn′] *noun, plural* **inclines.** a slanted or sloped surface.

inclined plane a flat, or plane, surface that slopes downward at an angle to meet the ground. Something can be moved up an inclined plane more easily than it can be lifted.

in•clude [in klood′] *verb,* **included, including. 1.** to be made up of; have as a part; contain: This recipe *includes* sugar, flour, and milk. **2.** to put into a group; take in or put in: Any list of popular American movies would have to *include Gone With the Wind.* "I say 'we' because they always try to *include* me in everything they do . . ." (Alice Walker)

in•come [in′ kum′] *noun, plural* **incomes.** all the money that comes in to a person or business for work that is done, things that are sold, or property that is owned.

I

Pronunciation Key: [ə] Symbol

The [ə] or *schwa* sound occurs in syllables without an accent. It can be spelled with any vowel, such as **a** in above, **e** in listen, **i** in pencil, **o** in melon, **u** in circus. It can also be a combination of vowels, such as **io** in action, **ai** in mountain, **iou** in precious.

(Turn the page for more information.)

income tax a tax that the government collects on the income earned by a person or a business. Income taxes in the U.S. are collected by the federal government, most states, and some cities.

in•cor•rect [in′ kə rekt′] *adjective.* not correct or proper; wrong: an *incorrect* answer. —**incorrectly,** *adverb.*

in•deed [in dēd′] *adverb.* in truth or fact; really: "Are we going to give up without a fight?" the speaker shouted. "No *indeed!*"

in•def•i•nite [in def′ ə nit] *adjective, more/most.* not clear or exact; not definite: The project will begin at some *indefinite* date in the future. —**indefinitely:** Let's get this settled soon; we don't want it to drag on —*indefinitely.*

indenting Indenting is used in two ways. First, you indent the first line of a new paragraph—the indenting in fact is what signals that there's a new paragraph. Second, you indent a list, series of facts, or other such separate information, to make it stand out. In business letters, the start of a new paragraph is often signaled by skipping a line rather than by indenting. But in books and in newspapers and magazines, the normal style is to indent. This is also the style you should use in your own writing. How much should you indent? An indent of five letter spaces is about right.

in•crease [in krēs′] *verb,* **increased, increasing.** to make or become larger in size or amount: She *increased* the speed of her car so she could pass the truck in front of her. —[in′ krēs′] *noun, plural* **increases. 1.** the amount by which something is made larger: The workers are asking for a 15% *increase* in pay. **2.** the act of increasing; growth: ". . . a population *increase* of almost one million a year." (John Toland)

in•creas•ing•ly [in krēs′ ing lē] *adverb.* more and more: It's becoming *increasingly* difficult to find a home at a cheap price in our town.

in•cred•i•ble [in kred′ ə bəl] *adjective, more/most.* hard to believe or imagine; amazing: ". . . the slashing stride that covered the turf at an almost *incredible* speed." (Dick Francis) "Two or three of these boxes were a load. Six of them were an *incredible* amount." (Jerome Weidman) —**incredibly,** *adverb.*

in•dent [in dent′] *verb,* **indented, indenting.** to start a line of a written work farther to the right than other lines: to *indent* the first line of a paragraph.

in•de•pen•dence [in′ di pen′ dəns] *noun.* the fact of being independent; freedom.

Independence Day another name for the holiday more often known as the FOURTH OF JULY.

in•de•pen•dent [in di pen′ dənt] *adjective, more/most.* **1.** not under the control of another country; not ruled by others; free: The U.S. and Canada are *independent* nations. **2.** thinking or acting for oneself; not depending on others: My great-grandmother is very *independent* and insists on doing all her own shopping and housework even though she's almost 90. **3.** not connected with others; separate: He's decided to leave his job with the TV network to set up an *independent* film company.

independent clauses A clause is a group of words within a sentence, with its own noun and verb. It can be either an *independent* or a *dependent* clause. "While the words yet seemed to hang in the air, Shane was moving toward the front of the room." (Jack Schaefer) The underlined clause is *dependent;* it's not a complete sentence. The other clause is *independent;* it could stand alone as a sentence. Why is it useful to join two independent clauses as one sentence? "It was empty and the doors there were closed." (Schaefer) He could have written, "It was empty. The doors there were closed." Why didn't he? Because the statements are so short. They read more smoothly when joined together.

in•cu•ba•tor [in′ kyə bā′ tər] *noun, plural* **incubators. 1.** a heated container used in hospitals for newborn babies who are born too early or who have serious health problems. **2.** a heated container used for hatching eggs artificially.

in•debt•ed [in det′ id] *adjective, more/most.* in the debt of; owing something: Jack feels *indebted* to you for all the help you gave him.

in•dex [in′ deks] *noun, plural* **indexes. 1.** an alphabetical list at the end of a book that shows the page or pages where information on a particular subject can be found. **2.** something that shows a certain value or quality: The Dow-Jones Average is an *index* of the price of 30 important stocks. —*verb,* **indexed, indexing.** to put a topic or name in an index.

I

index finger the finger next to the thumb; also called the FOREFINGER.

In•di•a [in′dē ə] a country in southern Asia. *Capital:* New Delhi. *Area:* 1,269,400 square miles. *Population:* 726,155,000.

India One of the world's most famous and most beautiful buildings, the Taj Mahal in Agra, India. It was built in 1630-1648.

Rudy jerk his head, *indicating* he wanted to talk to Mariana alone." (Richard Vasquez) **2.** to point out; show: "There is a . . . secret map, with marks and crosses, *indicating* where the jewels lie hidden." (James Thurber) —**indicator,** *noun.*

in•di•ca•tion [in′ də kā′ shən] *noun, plural* **indications.** something that indicates; a sign: "There was not much *indication* that the hurricane had passed that way: only a few trees and signs down . . ." (Thomas Pynchon) ". . . two well-dressed ladies, neither of whom gave the slightest *indication* that they knew I was there." (Larry McMurtry)

in•dict [in dīt′] *verb,* **indicted, indicting.** to charge someone with a crime or offense: For certain serious crimes, a person must be *indicted* by a grand jury before he or she can be put on trial. —**indictment,** *noun.*

in•dif•fer•ent [in dif′ rənt] *adjective, more/most.* not caring one way or the other how something happens or turns out: Dad and Jeff got really excited watching the World Series, but Mom was *indifferent.* —**indifference,** *noun.*

India Some writers like to gather facts to use them at a later occasion. Take India and Argentina, for example. India is the second-largest country in population in the world, with 800,000,000 people. It occupies 1,269,000 square miles. Argentina is not much smaller in geography. It's about 1,073,400 square miles, or about 85% the size of India. But its population is about 32,000,000, which is only about 4% the size of India's population. Is this just "trivia?" No. You can draw a lot of inferences, from learning this, about history, religion, culture, exploration, settlement of territory.

In•di•an [in′ dē ən] *noun, plural* **Indians. 1.** a member of one of the groups of people who lived in North or South America before the European explorers came; also called an AMERICAN INDIAN or a NATIVE AMERICAN. **2.** a person born or living in India. —*adjective.* **1.** having to do with the American Indian people. **2.** having to do with the people of India.

In•di•an•a [in′ dē an′ ə] a state in the north-central U.S. *Capital:* Indianapolis. *Nickname:* "Hoosier State." *Area:* 36,300 square miles. *Population:* 5,500,000.

In•di•an•ap•o•lis [in′ dē ə nap′ ə lis] the capital of the state of Indiana. *Population:* 705,000.

Indian Ocean an ocean east of Africa, west of Australia, and south of Asia.

Indian summer a short period of mild, warmer weather in late autumn.

in•di•cate [in′ də kāt′] *verb,* **indicated, indicating. 1.** to be a sign of; reveal or suggest: "The questions of the five military judges *indicated* their doubts . . ." (Barbara Tuchman) "He saw

in•di•ges•tion [in′ də jes′ chən] *noun.* a pain or uncomfortable feeling that comes after eating, as from eating too much or too quickly.

in•dig•nant [in dig′ nənt] *adjective, more/most.* surprised and angry about something that is thought to be unfair: She was *indignant* that someone would suggest she had to cheat to pass the test. —**indignantly,** *adverb:* ". . . there was Charles Wallace standing *indignantly* in front of her, his hand on his hips." (Madeleine L'Engle) —**indignation** [in′ dig nā′ shən], *noun.*

in•di•rect [in′ də rekt′] *adjective, more/most.* **1.** not in a straight path or line; not direct. **2.** not directly mentioned or connected: When he

I

Pronunciation Key: Accent Marks

[′] is the normal accent mark. It shows where the main stress falls on a word.
[′] is a secondary accent mark. It shows a lighter stress than the primary accent. For example:

tel • e • vis • ion [tel′ ə vizh′ ən]

(Turn the page for more information.)

said, "I'll think it over," it was really an *indirect* way of saying "no." Jill took up tennis for the exercise, but an *indirect* benefit is that she's met several new friends. **—indirectly,** *adverb.*

indirect object in grammar, a noun or pronoun that is affected by the action of the verb, but doesn't receive the action directly as a direct object does. In the sentences "Lou sent me a postcard from Florida" or "Give me a call tomorrow," "me" is an indirect object.

in•di•vid•u•al [in də vij′ o͞o əl]   *adjective.* **1.** being a certain one; single and separate from others; particular: "I saw not a crowd but the set faces of *individual* men and women." (Ralph Ellison) **2.** by or meant for one: The cereal package had twelve small boxes, each with an *individual* serving. **—noun,** *plural* **individuals. 1.** a single person or thing, as opposed to a group. **2.** a person thought of in a particular way: "Dan Maloney is just the kind of rugged *individual* the Toronto hockey team needs." (Ken McKenzie) **—individually,** *adverb:* The teacher met with each student *individually* to talk about their science projects.

in•di•vid•u•al•it•y [in də vij′ o͞o al′ ə tē]   *noun, plural* **individualities.** a quality that makes someone or something different from others.

in•di•vis•i•ble [in′ də viz′ ə bəl] *adjective.* **1.** in mathematics, not able to be divided evenly; leaving a remainder: 17 is *indivisible* by all smaller numbers except 1. **2.** not able to be divided or separated: The Pledge of Allegiance says the United States is an *indivisible* nation.

In•do•ne•sia [in′ də nē′ zhə]   a country of southeast Asia that includes over 3000 islands. *Capital:* Jakarta. *Area:* 789,000 square miles. *Population:* 156,900,000. **—Indonesian,** *adjective; noun.*

in•door [in′ dôr′] *adjective.* of or taking place inside a house or other building: an *indoor* swimming pool. Bowling is an *indoor* sport.

in•doors [in′ dôrz′] *adverb.* inside a house or other building: to stay *indoors* on a rainy day.

in•duce [in do͞os′] *verb,* **induced, inducing.** to cause or lead someone to act in a certain way: "What on earth *induced* her to behave as she did, I never could understand." (Oscar Wilde) ♦ Something that induces is an **inducement.**

in•dus•tri•al [in dus′ trē əl] *adjective.* **1.** having to do with or made by industry: Cars and trucks are *industrial* products. **2.** having highly-developed industry: Japan and West Germany are *industrial* countries.

industrial arts a school subject that teaches the skills needed for work in industry.

in•dus•tri•al•ize [in dus′ trē əl īz′] *verb,* **industrialized, industrializing.** to develop a system of industries in a country or area: Belgium was the second country in Europe to *industrialize,* after Great Britain. **—industrialization,** *noun.*

Industrial Revolution the period of time in history when machines were developed to produce goods, and forms of energy such as steam, coal, oil, and electricity began to be used. The Industrial Revolution began in late 1700's.

in•dus•tri•ous [in dus′ trē əs] *adjective, more/most.* working hard: "You are very properly proud of having been *industrious* enough to make money . . ." (George Bernard Shaw) **industriously,** *adverb.*

in•dus•try [in′ dəs trē] *noun, plural* **industries. 1.** the producing and selling of machine-made goods; the work of factories and manufacturing plants. Industry takes natural materials and uses machines to convert them into things that are sold. **2.** manufacturing and business activity in general: The mayor has a plan to bring new *industry* to our town. **3.** a particular type of manufacturing or business: the steel *industry,* the television *industry.* **4.** hard work; steady effort: "I had told him he had not enough *industry* and self-discipline to make himself anything." (Iris Murdoch)

in•ert [in urt′] *adjective.* **1.** slow to move or act; not moving. "He lay at first *inert,* like a man either dead or dreaming." (John Hersey) **2.** of a chemical substance, not able or not likely to react or combine with other chemicals: Helium is an *inert* gas that does not burn.

in•er•tia [in ur′ shə] *noun.* in science, a property of all matter that keeps a thing from being moved when it is still or from being stopped when it is moving, unless it is acted on by an outside force.

in•ev•i•ta•ble [in ev′ ə tə bəl] *adjective.* **1.** that cannot be avoided; sure to happen: "As long as there are . . . nations possessing great power, war is *inevitable.*" (Albert Einstein) **2.** happening very often; expected: Be ready for the *inevitable* delay where Routes 5 and 20 come together. **—inevitably,** *adverb.*

in•fa•mous [in′ fə məs] *adjective, more/most.* having a bad or evil reputation: an *infamous* criminal. ♦ The state of being infamous is **infamy** [in′ fə mē].

in•fant [in′ fənt] *noun, plural* **infants.** a very young child or baby. ♦ **Infancy** [in′ fən sē] is the time of being an infant.

in•fan•tile paralysis [in′ fən tīl′] a virus disease, more often called POLIO.

infantry U. S. infantrymen in a "chow line" during the World War II Battle of the Bulge (Christmas, 1944).

in•fan•try [in′ fən trē] *noun, plural* **infantries.** the part of an army made up of soldiers trained and equipped to fight on foot.

in•fect [in fekt′] *verb,* **infected, infecting. 1.** to cause disease by allowing germs to enter the body: His cut got dirt in it and became *infected.* **2.** to spread easily from one person to another: "Mr. Fleagle loved *Macbeth* . . . but he lacked the gift of *infecting* others with his own passion." (Russell Baker) ◆ Something that can infect is **infectious:** The common cold is an *infectious* disease. "Jane and Michael couldn't help laughing too, because Mr. Wigg's (laugh) was so *infectious.*" (P.L. Travers)

in•fec•tion [in fek′ shən] *noun, plural* **infections. 1.** the fact of being infected: Hospital operating rooms are specially cleaned to prevent *infection.* **2.** a disease caused by germs infecting the body, especially a painful swelling where germs have entered an open cut or sore.

in•fer [in fur′] *verb,* **inferred, inferring.** to know or learn something by judging the facts or by noticing something, rather than by being told directly: He seemed curious to know more

about her, or so she *inferred* from the way his eyes kept following her. ◆ Something that is inferred is an **inference** [in′ fər əns].

in•fer•i•or [in fēr′ ē ər] *adjective, more/most.* lower in quality, value, or rank; not as good or as high: Kelly is so good in math that she makes the rest of the class feel *inferior.* ◆ The state of being inferior is **inferiority** [in fēr′ ē ôr′ ə tē]. An **inferiority complex** is a strong and disturbing feeling that one is not as important or as good at things as other people are.

in•field [in′ fēld′] *noun, plural* **infields.** in baseball: **1.** the area of the field marked off by the bases and their baselines. **2.** the players whose positions are in the infield; the first, second, and third baseman and the shortstop. **—infielder,** *noun.*

in•fi•nite [in′ fə nit] *adjective.* **1.** having no limits or boundaries; going on without end: "I sat on the bed and stared out into *infinite* space." (Woody Allen) **2.** very great; as much as is possible: It takes *infinite* patience to be a good kindergarten teacher. ◆ The fact of being infinite is **infinity** [in fin′ ə tē]. **—infinitely,** *adverb:* "They thought that America was a glowing land reaching *infinitely* high from the middle of a gentle sea." (Mark Helprin)

in•fin•i•tive [in fin′ ə tiv] *noun, plural* **infinitives.** in grammar, a verb form made up of the word "to" and the basic form of a verb, such as "She likes *to swim*" or "I have *to leave.*"

infinitives An infinitive is any verb phrase with the word "to" in it. "To" is followed by another verb, usually an action verb: "They rode this time because it was too far *to walk* . . ." (William Faulkner) Sometimes, the verb is a form of BE ". . . knowing all the time that sooner or later she would have *to be* brave . . ." (Faulkner) In some cases, a writer may leave off the verb and have only "to," if it is clear from the rest of the sentence what is meant: "But he didn't answer, and his father didn't wait for him *to.*" (to answer) (Faulkner) The one tricky use of the infinitive is when it appears as a noun. Although it's a verb form, it can be used as the subject of a sentence: "*To delay* will mean certain failure." This special use is usually found in poetry. For example: "*To be* or not *to be:* That is the question." (William Shakespeare) or "*To err* [make a mistake] is human, *to forgive* divine." (Alexander Pope)

in•flame [in flām′] *verb,* **inflamed, inflaming. 1.** to have or cause to have an INFLAMMATION: His

I

Pronunciation Key: A–F

a	and; hat	ch	chew; such
ā	ate; stay	d	dog; lid
â	care; air	e	end; yet
ä	father; hat	ē	she; each
b	boy; cab	f	fun; off

(Turn the page for more information.)

throat was *inflamed* because of an infection. **2.** to make angry or greatly excited: The speaker *inflamed* the crowd with a speech calling for riot and revolution.

in•flam•ma•ble [in flam′ ə bəl] *adjective.* easily set on fire; able to burn easily: Gasoline is *inflammable.*

in•flam•ma•tion [in flə mā′ shən] *noun, plural* **inflammations.** a condition where part of the body becomes swollen, hot, and painful.

in•flate [in flāt′] *verb,* **inflated, inflating. 1.** to expand or swell by filling with air or another gas: You *inflate* a toy balloon by blowing into it. ♦ Something that can be inflated is **inflatable. 2.** to increase or enlarge beyond what it should be. ♦ Usually used as an adjective: a movie star with an *inflated* idea of his own importance.

in•fla•tion [in flā′ shən] *noun, plural* **inflations. 1.** a situation in which the prices of important goods and services go up rapidly and a given amount of money will purchase less than it did before. **2.** the act of inflating.

in•flec•tion [in flek′ shən] *noun, plural* **inflections.** in language: **1.** a change in the form of a word because of the way it is used. "Inflated" and "inflating" are **inflected forms** of the verb "inflate." **2.** a change in the level or pitch of the voice to show meaning.

in•flu•ence [in′ floo əns] *noun, plural* **influences. 1.** the power to cause a change or to have some effect: The pull of the moon's gravity has an *influence* on the tides. **2.** the power to affect a person's mind or actions without using force: The mayor tried to use his *influence* with the judge to get the case dropped. **3.** a person or thing that has this power: Ernest Hemingway was an *influence* on many American writers. —*verb,* **influenced, influencing.** to have an influence on: The fact that this town has such good schools *influenced* our family to move here.

in•flu•en•tial [in′ floo en′ shəl] *adjective, more/ most.* having or using influence: Pablo Picasso was a very *influential* figure in modern art.

in•flu•en•za [in′ floo en′ zə] *noun.* a disease like a very bad cold; more often called **flu.**

in•form [in fôrm′] *verb,* **informed, informing. 1.** to give information to a person; let know; tell: The letter *informed* her that she had to appear for jury duty. **2.** to tell something that is secret or that will harm a person: The police solved the case when one of the jewel thieves *informed* on the rest of the gang. ♦ A person who informs against another is an **informer.**

in•for•mal [in fôr′ məl] *adjective, more/most.* **1.** not formal; casual; relaxed: Dad plays basketball in an *informal* league where there are no uniforms and they don't really keep score. **2.** of language, used in everyday conversation and friendly writing, but not appropriate for more serious situations. —**informally,** *adverb.*

informal After a defeat for his party in elections for Congress, President Lincoln was asked how he felt. "Well," he said, "I feel like the boy back in Kentucky who stubbed his toe while running to see his sweetheart. I'm too big to cry, and it hurts too much to laugh." That's an example of informal language. Lincoln also used formal language, as in the Gettysburg Address when he began: "Fourscore and seven years ago, our forefathers brought forth on this continent a new nation . . ." There's a place for both styles; it depends on which is more appropriate in a given situation. For example, business executives now receive letters from strangers that begin, "Good morning, Mr. Smith." Such a greeting is too informal for this situation, and such letters are usually tossed aside. Similarly, some letters of this kind are too formal. They use such stilted language, they are so long-winded, so awkward in wording, that the reader cannot find out what is really being said. Those letters, too, are tossed aside.

in•for•ma•tion [in′ fər mā′ shən] *noun.* **1.** a group of facts that are known about something; things that help you to learn about a thing or know what it is like: A dictionary is a book of *information* about words. **2.** a service provided to answer customers' questions and give other facts: When Janet moved, I got her new phone number by calling *information.* ♦ Something that gives information is **informative.**

in•gen•ious [in jēn′ yəs] *adjective, more/most.* showing or having a lot of imagination; very clever: In 1831 inventor Cyrus McCormick developed an *ingenious* machine for harvesting wheat. ♦ The quality of being ingenious is **ingenuity** [in′ jə noo′ ə tē].

in•gre•di•ent [in grē′ dē ənt] *noun, plural* **ingredients.** any one of the parts in a mixture: Flour is the main *ingredient* of bread. Interesting characters are an important *ingredient* of a good novel.

I

in·hab·it [in hab′ it] *verb*, **inhabited, inhabiting.** to live in or on: Animals that *inhabit* the desert have become used to living without much water. "This country . . . belongs to the people who *inhabit* it." (Abraham Lincoln)

in·hab·i·tant [in hab′ ə tənt] *noun, plural* **inhabitants.** a person or animal that lives in a place for a length of time: The Indians were the first human *inhabitants* of North America.

in·hale [in hāl′] *verb*, **inhaled, inhaling.** to breathe into the lungs: Firemen wear gas masks so that they won't *inhale* dangerous smoke.

in·her·it [in her′ it] *verb*, **inherited, inheriting. 1.** to get money, property, or personal possessions from someone who has died: Carrie *inherited* her grandmother's wedding ring along with some antique furniture. **2.** to get a quality or characteristic from one's parent or ancestors: Alex *inherited* his father's blue eyes and red hair. "She *inherits* her mother's sense of humor and energy." (Clifford Odets)

in·her·i·tance [in her′ ə təns] *noun, plural* **inheritances.** something that is inherited: His grandfather left him an *inheritance* of ten thousand dollars.

in·hu·man [in hyōō′ mən] *adjective, more/ most.* without human kindness; cruel; brutal. ◆ The quality of being inhuman is **inhumanity.**

i·ni·tial [i nish′ əl] *noun, plural* **initials.** the first letter of a word or name. —*adjective.* coming or belonging at the beginning; first; earliest: The *initial* sound of the word "capital" is [kap]. —*verb*, **initialed, initialing.** to mark or sign one's initials: The banker *initialed* the paper to show he had approved the loan. —**initially,** *adverb.*

i·ni·ti·ate [i nish′ ē āt′] *verb*, **initiated, initiating. 1.** to be the first one to do something; set up; start: The music teacher *initiated* a new program to have concerts at the school. **2.** to make a person a member of a group or club by some special ceremony: "I recall being *initiated* into the Mañana Club one night at the Governor's Mansion, in a ceremony which involved being blindfolded . . ." (Joan Didion) —**initiation,** *noun.*

i·ni·ti·a·tive [i nish′ ə tiv] *noun, plural* **initiatives. 1.** the ability to begin or carry out an action; energy in doing things for oneself: Senator Charles Percy had so much *initiative* that he had his own business while still in high school and became head of a large company at the age of 29. **2.** the first step in doing something; the lead: "He had sent a message to Kotali. He had done so on his own *initiative.*" (Paul Scott)

in·ject [in jekt′] *verb*, **injected, injecting. 1.** to force a fluid through the skin with a special needle: The dentist *injected* some medicine into her gums to make her mouth numb. **2.** to put in a comment or suggestion: Instead of just reading the announcement as it was written, Cliff tried to *inject* some humor into it.

in·jec·tion [in jek′ shən] *noun, plural* **injections. 1.** the forcing of a liquid medicine or other fluid into the body with a special hollow needle: Doctors give people *injections* against diseases such as measles or smallpox. **2.** something that is injected: "'I wish I knew you better,' the President confessed with a sudden *injection* of charm in his voice." (Allen Drury)

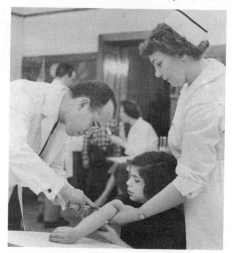

injection Dr. Jonas Salk gives an injection to 8-year-old Susan Blomstein, one of the first children to receive the new vaccine against polio, in 1954.

in·jure [in′ jər] *verb*, **injured, injuring.** to cause pain or harm to; damage; hurt: The football player *injured* his knee when he was tackled.

in·ju·ry [in′ jər ē] *noun, plural* **injuries.** the act or fact of injuring; something that brings pain or harm: The train went off the track and there were several *injuries* among the passengers.

in·jus·tice [in jus′ tis] *noun, plural* **injustices.** a lack of justice; something that is not fair or right: In early America women faced the *injustice* of not being allowed to vote.

I

Pronunciation Key: G–N

g	give; big	k	kind; cat; back
h	hold	l	let; ball
i	it; this	m	make; time
ī	ice; my	n	not; own
j	jet; gem; edge	ng	having

(Turn the page for more information.)

ink [ingk] *noun, plural* **inks.** a colored liquid that is used for writing, drawing, or printing. ◆ An **inkwell** is a container used to hold ink. —*verb*, **inked, inking.** to put ink on: The policeman *inked* the suspect's fingers in order to take his fingerprints. —**inky,** *adjective:* Certain sea animals such as the octopus can release an *inky* liquid to hide themselves from an enemy.

ink•ling [ing′kling] *noun.* a slight suggestion or hint: "Thinking they were absolutely alone, they had no *inkling* his eyes were upon them." (Virginia Hamilton)

in•laid [in′lād′] *adjective.* set into the surface as a decoration: The music box had a design of *inlaid* gold. ◆ A decoration made in this way is an **inlay.**

in•land [in′lənd] *adjective.* away from the coast or border: Kansas is an *inland* state. —*adverb.* in or toward the inner part: The hurricane along the coast is expected to move *inland.*

in-law [in′lô′] *noun, plural* **in-laws.** a relative by marriage instead of by birth. A person's in-laws include the husband's or wife's parents, brothers, and sisters.

in•let [in′let′] *noun, plural* **inlets.** a narrow strip of water leading from a larger body of water into the land.

inlet Annisquam Inlet in Gloucester, Mass.

in•mate [in′māt′] *noun, plural* **inmates.** a person who is confined in a prison, mental hospital, or the like.

inn [in] *noun, plural* **inns. 1.** in former times, a small hotel by the roadside providing rooms and meals for travelers. **2.** a modern hotel or restaurant in the style of a historic inn.

in•ner [in′ər] *adjective.* **1.** located farther in; inside: The doctor sees her patients in an *inner* office. **2.** more private; more secret: People often keep a diary to record their *inner* feelings.

in•ning [in′ing] *noun, plural* **innings.** in baseball, one of the playing periods into which a game is divided. In an inning, each team has a chance to bat until they have made three outs.

in•no•cence [in′ə səns] *noun.* the state or quality of being innocent: The jury believed in the woman's *innocence* and found her "not guilty."

in•no•cent [in′ə sənt] *adjective, more/most.* **1.** free from doing wrong or committing a crime; without guilt: The lawyer said that his client was *innocent* because he was out of the country when the robbery took place. **2.** causing or meaning no harm: Don't be upset by what she said—it was just an *innocent* remark. **3.** not aware of evil or sin; simple and trusting. —**innocently,** *adverb.*

in•no•va•tion [in′ə vā′shən] *noun, plural* **innovations.** a new idea or method of doing something: "For the villagers, television was the biggest *innovation* since the airplane." (Joe McGinniss) ◆ Someone who is good at thinking up or starting new things is **innovative.**

in•oc•u•late [in äk′yə lāt] *verb,* **inoculated, inoculating.** to protect a person or animal from a disease by giving him a special substance containing dead or weakened germs of that disease. This makes the body build up a protection against the disease. —**inoculation,** *noun.*

in•put [in′poot′] *noun.* **1.** any form of data or program instructions entered into a computer from an outside source. **2.** any comments or advice thought of as being like this: Mrs. Selman has some good ideas for the Christmas party, but she needs to get the principal's *input.*

in•quire [in kwīr′] *verb,* **inquired, inquiring.** to get more information about something by asking questions: He *inquired* at the post office to see if they'd found the missing letter.

in•quir•y [in kwīr′ē *or* in′kwə rē] *noun, plural* **inquiries.** the act or fact of inquiring: The mayor's office conducted an *inquiry* to find out if any city employees were involved in the real estate scandal.

in•quis•i•tive [in kwiz′ə tiv] *adjective, more/most.* eager to learn; curious: "He was *inquisitive* and he didn't understand and he wanted to know." (Graham Greene)

in•sane [in sān′] *adjective, more/most.* **1.** having a serious mental illness: For many years the courts have ruled that a grown person who cannot tell the difference between right and wrong is legally *insane.* **2.** without sense; very foolish; wild: He's got some *insane* scheme to attach a sail to the back of the car as a way of saving gasoline. —**insanely,** *adverb.*

I

in•san•i•ty [in san′ ə tē] *noun.* the condition of being insane; mental illness.

in•scribe [in skrīb′] *verb,* **inscribed, inscribing.** to write, carve, or mark letters on something: "Emma Lazarus, who wrote those lines *inscribed* on the Statue of Liberty . . ." (Alfred Kazin)

in•scrip•tion [in skrip′ shən] *noun, plural* **inscriptions.** something that is inscribed: When he retired from his job, Grandpa got a gold watch with the *inscription* "For forty years of loyal service."

in•sect [in′ sekt] *noun, plural* **insects.** a small animal with six legs, no backbone, and a body divided into three main parts. Most insects have wings. Beetles, moths, ants, bees, flies, mosquitoes, cockroaches, and grasshoppers are among the hundreds of thousands of kinds of insects in the world.

in•sec•ti•cide [in sek′ tə sīd′] *noun, plural* **secticides.** a chemical poison or other substance used to kill insects and other pests.

in•se•cure [in′ sə kyoor′] *adjective, more/most.* **1.** likely to fail or give way; not firm or steady: The climber had only an *insecure* hold on the rock and was afraid he would fall. **2.** not confident and relaxed; uncertain; fearful: Jeff has a lot of talent as an artist, but he's so *insecure* about his ability that he'll never show his work to anyone. ♦ The state of being insecure is **insecurity.**

in•sen•si•tive [in sen′ sə tiv] *adjective, more/most.* not aware of or not caring about the feelings of others; not sensitive: She made an *insensitive* remark about Dave's new braces that really hurt him.

in•sert [in surt′] *verb,* **inserted, inserting.** to put, set, or place in: "Gruber *inserted* the key into the lock and twisted." (Bernard Malamud) —[in′ surt] *noun, plural* **inserts.** something put in or set in: This Sunday's newspaper has a lot of *inserts* from stores advertising big sales. —**insertion,** *noun.*

in•side [in′ sīd′ *or* in sīd′] *noun, plural* **insides.** the part that is in; the inner part: the *inside* of a house, the *inside* of a box. —*adjective.* **1.** being in, on, or toward the inside: an *inside* wall, an *inside* pocket of a jacket. **2.** from the inside of some group: The police think the robbery was an *inside* job, because whoever did it knew where the jewels were hidden. —*adverb; preposition.* in, on, or toward the inside.

in•sig•ni•a [in sig′ nē ə] *noun, plural* **insignia** or **insignias.** a badge, medal, or special mark showing that a person holds some position or honor. People in the armed forces wear various insignia to show which part of the service they are in, their rank, and their special branch of service (infantry, submarines, and so on).

in•sig•ni•fi•cant [in′ sig nif′ ə kənt] *adjective, more/most.* not significant; small in number, size, or value; unimportant: Their train trip went smoothly, with one *insignificant* delay of ten minutes. —**insignificance,** *noun.*

in•sist [in sist′] *verb,* **insisted, insisting.** to stand up strongly for one's idea or position; say in a firm way: Our teacher *insists* that we do our science projects ourselves instead of having our parents work on them.

in•som•ni•a [in säm′ nē ə] *noun.* the condition of being unable to fall asleep or to get a normal amount of sleep.

in•spect [in spekt′] *verb,* **inspected, inspecting.** to look at closely and carefully; examine: Jet airliners have to be *inspected* regularly to make sure they do not have mechanical problems.

in•spec•tion [in spek′ shən] *noun, plural* **inspections.** the act of inspecting: "A careful *inspection* showed them that . . . the cart would travel no longer." (Kenneth Grahame)

in•spec•tor [in spek′ tər] *noun, plural* **inspectors.** **1.** a person whose work is to inspect something: A fire *inspector* inspects buildings to determine if they have the proper protection against fires. **2.** a high-ranking police officer.

insignia A Marine gunnery sergeant in his dress uniform with Marine Corps insignia.

Pronunciation Key: O–S

ō	over; go	ou	out; town
ô	all; law	p	put; hop
oo	look; full	r	run; car
o͞o	pool; who	s	set; miss
oi	oil; boy	sh	show

(Turn the page for more information.)

inspiration In comic strips and cartoons, characters often are hit with a sudden inspiration. This is usually shown by a light bulb glowing over the character's head. When you are trying to come up with an idea for a story, you might wish there was such a "writer's light bulb" to get you going. But inspiration in writing is rare. The Italian novelist Alberto Moravia said, "I trust in inspiration, but I don't sit back and wait for it every day." The fact is that inspiration is no more than a writer's having the desire to write and a subject to write about. Without one, the other is useless. How can you start if you find yourself staring at a blank piece of paper? The Mexican writer Carlos Fuentes advises, "Read something you wrote before—just to prove to yourself that you can write."

in•spir•a•tion [in ́spə rā ́shən] *noun, plural* **inspirations. 1.** a force that stirs the mind or feelings: The speeches of Patrick Henry gave *inspiration* to the American colonists. **2.** a person or thing that has this power: The sight of snow-covered Mount Fuji has been an *inspiration* for many Japanese artists.

in•spire [in spīr ́] *verb,* **inspired, inspiring. 1.** to cause strong feelings or a strong wish to do something important: The Scottish chieftain Robert Bruce was *inspired* to keep fighting by watching the struggles of a spider trying to spin a web. **2.** to cause a certain action, feeling, or thought: The movie *Citizen Kane* was *inspired* by the life of William Randolph Hearst.

in•stall [in stôl ́] *verb,* **installed, installing 1.** to put a mechanical device in place and set it up for use: to *install* a telephone, to *install* an air conditioner. **2.** to place a person in a position or office by means of some ceremony: "Alan Shepard was . . . *installed* as a national hero on the order of Lindbergh." (Tom Wolfe) **—installation,** *noun:* If you buy that dishwasher, there's an extra charge for *installation.*

in•stall•ment [in stôl ́mənt] *noun, plural* **installments. 1.** one of a series of payments: She paid for the TV set in 24 monthly *installments* of $25 each. **2.** one of several parts of a magazine or newspaper story, TV series, or the like.

in•stance [in ́stəns] *noun, plural* **instances. 1.** a single situation in which some general point is true; an example or case: Coyotes usually don't live near people, but in some *instances* they are found in major cities. **2. for instance.** as an example; such as: Mississippi has produced some outstanding writers—*for instance,* William Faulkner, Richard Wright, Eudora Welty.

in•stant [in ́stənt] *noun, plural* **instants. 1.** a very short time; a moment: "He awoke at dawn this Christmas morning. For a brief *instant* he could not remember where he was." (Pearl Buck) **2.** a certain moment or point in time: "I saw him almost the same *instant,* sir, that Captain Ahab did . . ." (Herman Melville)

—adjective. 1. without delay; immediate: When I asked if I could borrow his radio his answer was an *instant* 'no.' **2.** of foods, needing very little time or effort to prepare: *instant* coffee, *instant* cake mix. **—instantly,** *adverb.*

in•stead [in sted ́] *adverb.* **1.** in place of another: He usually drives to work, but today he took the bus *instead.* **2. instead of.** rather than; in place of: Do you want juice *instead of* milk?

in•step [in ́step ́] *noun, plural* **insteps.** the top part of the foot between the toes and ankle, or the part of a shoe covering this.

in•stinct [in ́stingkt] *noun, plural* **instincts. 1.** an inner force that causes an animal to act in a certain way. Instinct is something the animal is born with, rather than something it learns or decides to do: Spiders spin webs and birds build nests by *instinct.* **2.** *also,* **instincts.** a natural feeling or ability: "The only advice, indeed that one person can give another about reading is to . . . follow your *instincts.*" (Virginia Woolf)

in•stinc•tive [in stingk ́tiv] *adjective.* **1.** coming from instinct: Bees have an *instinctive* habit of storing honey in their hives. **2.** as if by instinct; automatic: When a plane flies low overhead, people's *instinctive* reaction is to duck their heads. **—instinctively,** *adverb.*

in•sti•tute [in ́stə tōōt ́] *noun, plural* **institutes.** a school, organization, or society set up for a special purpose: The Massachusetts *Institute* of Technology is a leading university for math and science education. **—verb, instituted, instituting.** to set up or establish; start: "If we *institute* an entrance exam to keep out those who can't read or write . . ." (Kingsley Amis)

in•sti•tu•tion [in ́stə tōō ́shən] *noun, plural* **institutions. 1.** an organization set up for some public purpose, such as a hospital, school, or library. **2.** an established custom or practice: Marriage is an *institution* in many societies. **3.** a person who has long been connected with some place or activity: Katherine Hepburn is a Hollywood *institution* who has won three Best Actress awards over a span of fifty years.

in•struct [in strukt⁄] *verb,* **instructed, instructing. 1.** to give skill or knowledge to; teach: The salesman *instructed* us in the correct way to operate the computer. **2.** to give an order or direction: The police *instructed* all motorists to drive with care because of the icy roads.

in•struc•tion [in struk⁄shən] *noun, plural* **instructions. 1.** the act or fact of teaching. **2. instructions.** the steps or rules involved in doing something; directions: Don't start the test until you've read all the *instructions.* ♦ Something that gives instruction is **instructive.**

in•struc•tor [in struk⁄tər] *noun, plural* **instructors. 1.** a person who instructs; a teacher: Peggy's working as a diving *instructor* at the town pool this summer. **2.** a college teacher who ranks below a professor.

in•stru•ment [in⁄ strə mənt] *noun, plural* **instruments. 1.** an object that makes musical sounds, such as a piano, violin, trumpet, or drum. **2.** a device used to do a certain kind of work; a tool: A scalpel is an *instrument* used by a doctor for an operation. **3.** a device that records information: A car's dashboard has *instruments* telling the car's speed, how many miles it has gone, and so on.

in•stru•men•tal [in⁄ strə men⁄ təl] *adjective, more/most.* **1.** serving to get something done; useful; helpful: A reward is being offered for any evidence that is *instrumental* in the capturing of the criminal. **2.** for or by musical instruments: The orchestra recorded an *instrumental* version of the Beatles' song "Yesterday."

in•su•late [in⁄ sə lāt⁄] *verb,* **insulated, insulating. 1.** to cover, fill, or surround something with a special material in order to slow or stop the flow of heat, sound, or electricity: to *insulate* an attic to keep heat from escaping during the winter. **2.** to separate from others: "Great wealth was a frightful handicap; it *insulated* you from living." (Mary McCarthy)

in•su•la•tion [in⁄ sə lā⁄ shən] *noun.* **1.** any material that insulates something. **2.** the act or fact of insulating.

in•sult [in sult⁄] *verb,* **insulted, insulting.** to say something bad about a person, or treat the person in a rude way; show a lack of respect: "The fact that he never bothered to remember our names was *insulting.*" (Maya Angelou) —[in⁄ sult] *noun, plural* **insults.** something said or done to hurt a person's feelings.

in•sur•ance [in shoor⁄ əns] *noun.* **1.** a way of protecting against the loss of a large amount of money because of something bad happening, such as a person dying or becoming very ill, or property being damaged or stolen. To get insurance, a person makes an agreement to pay a regular amount of money at certain times. In return, the insurance company promises that it will pay a much larger amount if loss or damage should take place. **2.** anything that is thought of as a protection against loss or damage: We were winning 1-0 late in the game, but we wanted to get another goal as *insurance.*

in•sure [in shoor⁄] *verb,* **insured, insuring. 1.** to get or have insurance for something: People *insure* their life or health, their home or car, or valuable property such as jewelry and diamonds. **2.** to make certain; ensure: "They'll take twice as long and make a hundred extra . . . models to *insure* themselves against another failure." (Ray Bradbury)

in•te•grate [in⁄ tə grāt⁄] *verb,* **integrated, integrating.** to bring parts together into a whole: *The Long Hot Summer* was a movie that *integrated* several of William Faulkner's stories into a single movie. **2.** to make open or available to people of all races: to *integrate* a public school system. ♦ Often used as an adjective: an *integrated* neighborhood.

insulation This man is blowing fiberglass insulation into the ceiling space of this new house. The thick pink pads on the walls and ceiling are also a form of insulation.

Pronunciation Key: T–Z

t	ten; date	v	very; live
th	think	w	win; away
th	these	y	you
u	cut; butter	z	zoo; cause
ur	turn; bird	zh	measure

(Turn the page for more information.)

integration The first real test of integration in the South was at Little Rock, Arkansas in 1957. U.S. troops had to escort black students to school.

in•te•gra•tion [in′ tə grā′ shən] *noun.* the act or policy of allowing people of all races to have equal access to schools, parks, restaurants, hotels, and other public areas.

in•tel•lec•tu•al [in′ tə lek′ choo əl] *adjective.* having to do with the mind or intellect; mental: She's well over 80, but her *intellectual* powers are as strong as ever. —*noun, plural* **intellectuals.** a person who is intelligent and well-educated, and who has an interest in the arts and other activities of the mind. —**intellectually,** *adverb.*

in•tel•li•gence [in tel′ ə jəns] *noun.* **1.** the ability to use the mind to do such things as learning new things, understanding ideas, remembering facts, and solving problems. **2.** information about the activities and plans of another country: The United States uses the Central *Intelligence* Agency to obtain information about other nations.

in•tel•li•gent [in tel′ ə jənt] *adjective, more/ most.* having or showing intelligence; able to use the mind well; smart; bright: an *intelligent* student who gets high marks. Dan asked an *intelligent* question that showed he'd listened carefully. —**intelligently,** *adverb.*

in•tend [in tend′] *verb,* **intended, intending. 1.** to have in mind as a plan or purpose; mean to: "I *intend* to prevent it, even if I have to break down these bars!" (Rod Serling) **2.** to mean for a certain person or use: The present was *intended* for both boys, not just Jimmy.

in•tense [in tens′] *adjective, more/most.* **1.** very great or strong; extreme: *Intense* heat is used to melt iron for making steel. **2.** full of strong feelings; very emotional. —**intensely,** *adverb:* "He disliked Mrs. Johnson *intensely*." (Nathanael West) —**intensity,** *noun.*

in•ten•si•fy [in tens′ ə fī] *verb,* **intensified, intensifying.** to make or become more intense: "Their objections only *intensified* Martha's stubborn determination to have her own way." (Aldous Huxley)

in•tent [in tent′] *adjective, more/most.* **1.** directed toward a certain plan or purpose: "These people ignored the children entirely, seeming to be completely *intent* on their own business." (Madeleine L'Engle) **2.** having or showing deep feeling; intense: "She asked me where I was from, her face *intent* with strong interest." (Amado Muro) —**intently,** *adverb.*

in•ten•tion [in ten′ shən] *noun, plural* **intentions. 1.** something that a person plans or intends to do; a purpose or aim: "And I had the high *intention* of reading many other books besides." (F. Scott Fitzgerald) **2. intentions.** plans or goals: "The books on the refrigerator remind her of her better *intentions*, but she decides that first she'll see what's on TV." (Robert Coover)

in•ten•tion•al [in ten′ shən əl] *adjective.* done on purpose; not accidental; deliberate; intended: an *intentional* insult. I'm sorry our dog got into your yard; it certainly wasn't *intentional* on our part. —**intentionally,** *adverb.*

interceptor A modern interceptor fighter plane, the U.S. Navy's F-14 "Tomcat."

in•ter•cept [in′ tər sept′] *verb,* **intercepted, intercepting.** to stop or catch something on its way from one person or place to another; interrupt; block: The fighter planes were sent out to *intercept* the enemy bombers before they could reach the city. ♦ The act of intercepting something is an **interception,** such as a play in football where the defensive team catches a pass that was meant for an offensive player. —**interceptor,** *noun.*

in•ter•est [in′ trist *or* in′ tər ist] *noun, plural* **interests. 1.** a feeling of wanting to put one's attention on something and know more about it: "She pays careful attention to everything he does, watches with *interest* . . ." (Ann Beattie) **2.** something that causes this feeling: He's working as a waiter right now, but his real *interest* is acting. **3.** *also,* **interests.** something that helps a person; an advantage or benefit. **4.** a sum of money paid for the use of someone else's money. A bank pays interest to a person who leaves money in the bank for saving, and charges interest to a person who borrows money. —*verb,* **interested, interesting.** to catch or hold the attention; cause to have an interest: We're always getting calls from people who try to *interest* us in buying things for the house.

in•ter•est•ed [in′ tris tid *or* in′ tə res′ tid] *adjective, more/most.* **1.** having or showing an interest; paying attention. **2.** having a personal concern: The mayor is going to have a meeting of all *interested* parties regarding the new park.

in•te•ri•or [in tēr′ ē ər] *noun, plural* **interiors. 1.** the inside or inner part: Our car is white on the outside, with a blue *interior.* **2.** a region away from the coast or border; an inland area: Brazil has several large cities near the ocean, but not many people live in the *interior.* —*adjective.* of or having to do with the inner part: an *interior* wall. ♦ An **interior decorator** designs and decorates the interior of a room or building.

in•ter•jec•tion [in′ tər jek′ shən] *noun, plural* **interjections.** a word or phrase that shows a sudden strong feeling. "Ouch!" "Help!" and "Hey!" are interjections.

in•ter•me•di•ate [in′ tər mē′ dē it] *adjective.* in the middle; in between: The *intermediate* ice-skating class is for people who already know how to skate, but aren't ready to start advanced figure skating yet. An **intermediate school** comes between the lower and upper grades.

interesting writing Are there any specific methods you can use to make your writing more interesting? Yes. Try to use details, not generalities. Try to use words that relate to the senses: how does a thing feel, smell, sound, look? In the opening chapter of Charles Dickens' *Great Expectations,* this is how the main character Pip describes his childhood home: "Ours was the marsh country, down by the river, within twenty miles of the sea. My first vivid impression of things seems to me to have been gained on a memorable raw afternoon toward evening. At such a time I found out for certain that this bleak place was the churchyard; and that Philip Pirrip, late of this parish, and Georgiana, wife of the above, were dead and buried. I knew that the dark flat wilderness beyond was the marshes; and that the low leaden line beyond was the river; and that this distant savage lair from which the wind was rushing was the sea; and that the small bundle of shivers growing afraid of it all and beginning to cry was Pip."

in•ter•est•ing [in′ tris ting *or* in′ tə res′ ting] *adjective, more/most.* causing or creating interest: I just read an *interesting* article about how the ocean liner *Titanic* was found at the bottom of the sea. —**interestingly,** *adverb.*

in•ter•fere [in′ tər fēr′] *verb,* **interfered, interfering. 1.** to get in the way; interrupt or block: "She liked to be busy, so why *interfere* with her pleasure?" (Graham Greene) **2.** to get involved with the affairs of others without being asked; meddle: When Jimmy and his friends argue, you shouldn't *interfere.*

in•ter•fer•ence [in′ tər fēr′ əns] *noun.* **1.** the act or fact of interfering: The U.S. has often accused the Soviet Union of *interference* in the affairs of other countries. **2.** something that interrupts or disturbs a radio or television signal, such as the noise of a nearby station. **3.** in sports, blocking or getting in the way of a player on the other team.

in•ter•mis•sion [in′ tər mish′ ən] *noun, plural* **intermissions.** a break between the parts of a play or other performance.

in•ter•nal [in tur′ nəl] *adjective.* **1.** in or having to do with the inside of the body: Doctor Olsen practices *internal* medicine. After the accident, the man had two cracked ribs and was suffering from *internal* bleeding. **2.** having to do with matters within a country or organization: The **Internal Revenue Service** collects tax on money that is earned within the U.S. or by U.S. citizens. —**internally,** *adverb.*

Pronunciation Key: [ə] Symbol

The [ə] or *schwa* sound occurs in syllables without an accent. It can be spelled with any vowel, such as **a** in above, **e** in listen, **i** in pencil, **o** in melon, **u** in circus. It can also be a combination of vowels, such as **io** in action, **ai** in mountain, **iou** in precious.

(Turn the page for more information.)

in•ter•na•tion•al [in′tər nash′ ən əl] *adjective.* having to do with two or more nations; between nations: *international* trade, *international* waters, the *International* Court of Justice. —**internationally,** *adverb.*

in•ter•pret [in tur′ prit] *verb,* **interpreted, interpreting. 1.** to take something that has just been said in one language and repeat it in another. ♦ A person who does this is an **interpreter.** **2.** to understand or explain something in a certain way: He *interpreted* her silence to be a sign that she was angry at him. **3.** to perform or depict in a certain way: to *interpret* a piece of music. —**interpretation,** *noun:* Richard Burton was well-known for his *interpretation* of Shakespeare's *Hamlet.*

in•ter•val [in′ tər vəl] *noun, plural* **intervals.** a period of time or space between: "There was always about two seconds' delay, and taking that *interval* into account . . ." (Dick Francis) "Much rain also in these days, though with some *intervals* of fair weather." (Daniel Defoe)

in•ter•vene [in′ tər vēn′] *verb,* **intervened, intervening. 1.** to come or be between: "Half-way across the hall he heard the sound of Bertrand's laugh, but well muffled by an *intervening* door." (Kingsley Amis) **2.** to come in to settle a dispute or to stop something from happening: Mr. Evans was going to fire Dan from his job at the store, but Mrs. Evans *intervened* and convinced him to give the boy another chance. —**intervention** [in′ tər ven′ shən], *noun.*

interviews Conducting an interview is a common assignment for student writers. Here are a few suggestions: (1) Let the person talk. TV's Johnny Carson is known for drawing out his guests, rather than interrupting with his own remarks. (2) Keep the comments in the form of natural speech. Chicago author Studs Terkel edits his "oral history" interviews to sound like people talking, rather than to be formal and correct like written language. (3) Use the person's own voice. Novelist Ernest Hemingway served as a war correspondent in World War II. His interviews made lively reading, but as one critic pointed out, "Wherever he goes on the battlefront he somehow manages to find soldiers who talk exactly like characters from Hemingway."

in•ter•ro•gate [in ter′ ə gāt′] *verb,* **interrogated, interrogating.** to question someone in an official or formal way, especially about a crime. —**interrogation,** *noun.*

in•ter•rog•a•tive [in′ tə räg′ ə tiv] *adjective.* having the form of a question: "Who was that on the phone?" is an *interrogative* sentence.

in•ter•rupt [in′ tə rupt′] *verb,* **interrupted, interrupting. 1.** to break in while someone else is talking: "If I *interrupted* the conversation with a question, four or five adults (would) . . . say 'Children should be seen, and not heard.'" (Russell Baker) **2.** to stop or break in on something: The television program was suddenly *interrupted* for a news bulletin.

in•ter•rup•tion [in tə rup′ shən] *noun, plural* **interruptions.** the act or fact of interrupting: The modern Olympic Games have been held every four years, with *interruptions* during World War I and World War II. "Felicity listened without *interruption* . . . never seeming to take her grave, sweet eyes from his face." (Paul Gallico)

in•ter•sect [in′ tər sekt′] *verb,* **intersected, intersecting.** to meet and cross each other: The letter X is formed by two lines that *intersect.* ♦ A place where two things intersect is an **intersection:** The New York Library is at the *intersection* of Fifth Avenue and 42nd Street.

in•ter•view [in′ tər vyoo′] *noun, plural* **interviews. 1.** a meeting or conversation in which one person asks another person questions in order to get information: The mayor gave an *interview* to a reporter from Channel 39 News. **2.** a meeting at which a person is asked questions to determine if he or she is qualified for some job or position: The new department store will open next year and is holding *interviews* for sales people. —*verb,* **interviewed, interviewing.** to have an interview with: The movie star was *interviewed* by a number of newspaper reporters. —**interviewer,** *noun.*

in•tes•tine [in tes′ tin] *noun, plural* **intestines.** a long, twisting tube in the body that runs downward from the stomach and that is important in digesting food. The intestine is made up of the **small intestine** and **large intestine.**

in•ti•mate [in′ tə mit] *adjective, more/most.* known very well; close and well-acquainted: *intimate* friends. —**intimacy,** *noun:* "During their long separation their letters were creating an *intimacy* between them . . ." (Russell Baker)

in•tim•i•date [in tim′ ə dāt′] *verb,* **intimidated, intimidating.** to threaten or frighten; make afraid: Before World War II, Nazi Germany held huge military rallies to *intimidate* smaller

I

introductions "They threw me off the hay truck at noon." That is the first line of a famous novel, *The Postman Always Rings Twice,* by James M. Cain. In a novel or short story, there are no preliminaries. "Hit the ground running" is a good rule. Now, let's turn to factual articles, and to nonfiction books (history, biography, current affairs, etc.) At Harcourt Brace Jovanovich, it is more and more the advice of editors to authors of such books, "Don't delay the reader by prefaces and introductions. Begin. Don't tell the readers what they're about to read. Let them begin." Not all authors are willing to follow this advice. HBJ has on occasion yielded, saying to an author, "Fine, use your introduction, only call it Chapter One."

neighboring countries. The hitters on our team were *intimidated* by the fast pitcher on the other team. **—intimidation,** *noun.*

in•to [in′ tōō] *preposition.* **1.** to the inside of: Put the carrots *into* the stew. **2.** so as to hit against: He backed the car right *into* a tree. **3.** so as to be in a certain place or condition: At 32°F water turns *into* ice. After college Mona plans to go *into* teaching. **4.** *Informal.* very interested in or involved with: Joey is really *into* country music now.

in•tox•i•cate [in täk′ sə kāt′] *verb,* **intoxicated, intoxicating. 1.** to make drunk from too much alcohol. **2.** to fill with great excitement: ". . . *intoxicated* with the sparkle, the ripple, the scents and the sounds and the sunlight." (Kenneth Grahame) **—intoxication,** *noun.*

in•tra•mu•ral [in′ trə myoo′ rəl] *adjective.* between or among members of the same school: an *intramural* basketball game.

in•tri•cate [in′ tri kit] *adjective, more/most.* very hard to understand, follow, or do; complicated; involved: A spider's web has an *intricate* pattern. The mystery stories of Agatha Christie often have an *intricate* plot, with many different characters who could be the killer. **—intricacy,** *noun.* **—intricately,** *adverb.*

in•trigue [in trēg′] *verb,* **intrigued, intriguing. 1.** to make curious or interested: England's Stonehenge monument has long *intrigued* people, because no one knows who built it, or how and why they did it. **2.** to plot or scheme in a sly, secret way: The spies *intrigued* against the government. **—**[in′ trēg *or* in trēg′] *noun, plural* **intrigues.** a secret plan or scheme.

in•tro•duce [in′ trə doos′] *verb,* **introduced, introducing. 1.** to make known or acquainted for the first time: The teacher *introduced* the new student to the rest of the class. **2.** to bring into use or notice, especially for the first time: In 1964, Ford *introduced* the popular Mustang automobile. **3.** to begin; start: Newspaper columnist Liz Smith *introduces* each of her columns with a short quotation.

in•tro•duc•tion [in′ trə duk′ shən] *noun, plural* **introductions. 1.** the act of introducing: Spanish explorers were responsible for the *introduction* of horses into the Americas. **2.** the act of introducing people to each other. **3.** something that serves to introduce: That course is an *introduction* to computer programing. **4.** a part at the beginning of a book, play, or the like that tells something about it.

in•trude [in trood′] *verb,* **intruded, intruding.** to come in without being invited or wanted. ◆ Someone who intrudes is an **intruder:** She called the police to report an *intruder* on her neighbor's property. **—intrusion,** *noun.*

in•vade [in vād′] *verb,* **invaded, invading. 1.** to enter with force as an enemy; attack: World War II began in 1939 when Nazi Germany *invaded* Poland. **2.** to enter in great numbers: Thousands of college football fans *invade* Dallas each year for the Texas-Oklahoma game. **3.** to enter where one is not wanted; intrude.

in•va•lid [in′ və lid] *noun, plural* **invalids.** a sick, weak, or disabled person who is not able to care for himself. **—**[in val′ id] *adjective.* not valid; without force or effect: A check is *invalid* if you don't sign it.

in•val•u•a•ble [in val′ yə bəl] *adjective.* having a value that is beyond measure; priceless: Leonardo's *Mona Lisa* is an *invaluable* painting.

in•va•sion [in vā′ zhən] *noun, plural* **invasions.** the act or fact of invading: The World War II *invasion* of France by Allied soldiers was called 'D-Day.' Novelist J.D. Salinger sued to stop a book from being written about him, saying it was an *invasion* of his privacy.

I

Pronunciation Key: Accent Marks

[′] is the normal accent mark. It shows where the main stress falls on a word.
[′] is a secondary accent mark. It shows a lighter stress than the primary accent. For example:

tel • e • vis • ion [tel′ ə vizh′ ən]

(Turn the page for more information.)

inventing characters Inventing a character does not mean making up someone who is totally different from people in the real world. Famous writers usually base their characters on people they know, or know of. For example, Mark Twain drew some of the characters in his most popular books, *Tom Sawyer* and *Huckleberry Finn,* from people in his home town of Hannibal, Missouri. Twain knew a carefree, independent boy named Tom Blankenship who probably was the model for Huckleberry Finn. Twain didn't write about people exactly as they were; the real-life person was the starting point for the story character.

in•vent [in vent′] *verb,* **invented, inventing. 1.** to make or think of for the first time; create something new: Thomas Edison *invented* the movie camera and phonograph. **2.** to make up; think up: Every time Jerry's late, he *invents* some wild excuse to try to explain it.

in•ven•tion [in ven′ chən] *noun, plural* **inventions. 1.** the act or fact of inventing: The *invention* of the printing press made it possible to make many copies of a book at one time. **2.** something invented: The computer has become one of the most important *inventions* of modern times. **3.** the power to invent things. ◆ A person with this ability is **inventive:** Charles Dickens was an *inventive* author who created many well-known characters.

in•ven•tor [in ven′ tər] *noun, plural* **inventors.** a person who invents something.

in•ven•to•ry [in′ vən tôr′ ē] *noun, plural* **inventories. 1.** a detailed list of items on hand, especially the items that a business has available for sale: The publishing company's *inventory* showed how many books were in the warehouse and what they were worth. **2.** all of the articles listed: The store holds a sale every August to reduce its *inventory* of bathing suits.

in•ver•te•brate [in vur′ tə brāt] *adjective.* of an animal, having no backbone. —*noun, plural* **invertebrates:** Insects, worms, jellyfish, and lobsters are *invertebrates.*

in•vest [in vest′] *verb,* **invested, investing. 1.** to put money in use in order to make more money in the future: People *invest* in real estate because they expect the price of land to go up. ◆ A person who invests is an **investor. 2.** to spend time or energy in order to get some benefit: She's *invested* years in ballet lessons, hoping to get on the stage some day. **3.** to give a certain quality to: "Once *invested* with meaning, words became magic . . ." (Gore Vidal)

in•ves•ti•gate [in ves′ tə gāt] *verb,* **investigated, investigating.** to look into carefully in search of information; try to learn the facts about: The policeman *investigated* the murder case by questioning everyone who might have seen the killer. —**investigator,** *noun.*

in•ves•ti•ga•tion [in ves′ tə gā′ shən] *noun, plural* **investigations.** the act of investigating; a careful search or examination.

in•vest•ment [in vest′ mənt] *noun, plural* **investments. 1.** the fact of investing; using money to earn a future profit: Bank savings accounts are a common form of *investment.* **2.** something in which money is invested.

in•vis•i•ble [in viz′ ə bəl] *adjective.* not able to be seen; not visible: Air and sound are *invisible.* ". . . by her magic acts (the witch) made the iron *invisible* to human eyes." (L. Frank Baum)

in•vi•ta•tion [in′ və tā′ shən] *noun, plural* **invitations.** the act or fact of inviting: For his birthday party Andrew sent *invitations* to all the boys in his class.

in•vite [in vīt′] *verb,* **invited, inviting. 1.** to ask someone to come somewhere or do something: "They didn't *invite* me to sit down at their table . . . but I sat down anyway." (J.D. Salinger) **2.** to be likely to cause; bring on: The mayor is just *inviting* criticism by being seen in public with a suspected crime leader. —**inviting,** *adjective:* "Nothing at that moment could be more *inviting* to Dunsey than the bright fire on the brick hearth." (George Eliot)

in•vol•un•tar•y [in väl′ ən ter′ ē] *adjective.* **1.** not done by choice; not voluntary: An *involuntary* crime is one that a person did not purposely try to commit. **2.** happening without thought or control; automatic: Breathing is mainly an *involuntary* action. —**involuntarily,** *adverb.*

in•volve [in välv′] *verb,* **involved, involving. 1.** to have as a necessary part; include: Her job *involves* a lot of typing. **2.** to bring into a difficult or damaging situation: President Nixon had to resign from office because he was *involved* in the Watergate scandal. **3.** to take up all one's attention; absorb: He's very *involved* in his work and doesn't see much of his family.

in•volved [in välvd′] *adjective, more/most.* hard to follow or understand; complicated: He gave us a long and *involved* explanation of what was wrong with the car's engine.

I

in•volve•ment [in välv′ mənt] *noun, plural* **involvements.** the fact of being involved: George Washington's farewell address warned against America's *involvement* in foreign wars.

in•ward [in′ wərd] *adverb.* (*also,* **inwards**). toward the inside or center: The door to the kitchen opens *inward.* —*adjective.* toward or on the inside. —**inwardly,** *adverb.*

i•o•dine [ī′ ə dīn] *noun.* **1.** a chemical element that is used in medicine and in photography. **2.** a liquid medicine that contains iodine, used to treat cuts and prevent infections.

I•o•wa [ī′ ə wə] a state in the midwestern U.S., bordered by the Mississippi River to the east. *Capital:* Des Moines. *Nickname:* "Hawkeye State." *Area:* 56,300 square miles. *Population:* 2,915,000.

IQ [ī′ kyoo′] *noun.* short for *Intelligence Quotient,* a way of indicating a person's intelligence by comparing his or her score on a standard test with the scores of others. An IQ of 100 represents the average score.

I•ran [i ran′ *or* i rän′] a country in southwest Asia, on the Persian Gulf and Caspian Sea. *Capital:* Teheran. *Area:* 637,000 square miles. *Population:* 41,000,000. ◆ Formerly known as **Persia** [pur′ zhə] —**Iranian,** *adjective; noun.*

I•raq [i rak′ *or* i räk′] a country in southwest Asia, bordered by the Persian Gulf, Iran, and Saudi Arabia. *Capital:* Baghdad. *Area:* 168,000 square miles. *Population:* 14,600,000. —**Iraqi,** *adjective; noun.*

Ireland This view of Killary Harbor shows why Ireland is known as the Emerald Isle.

Ire•land [īr′ lənd] **1.** a large island in the North Atlantic off western Europe. It contains the **Republic of Ireland** and NORTHERN IRELAND. **2.** the republic that occupies much of this island. *Capital:* Dublin. *Area:* 26,600 square miles. *Population:* 3,600,000.

iris Grown from a bulb, the iris divides quickly into many plants in the garden.

i•ris [ī′ ris] *noun, plural* **irises. 1.** the colored part of the eye around the pupil. It controls the amount of light that enters the eye. **2.** a plant that has long leaves and large flowers of different colors.

I•rish [ī′ rish] *noun.* **the Irish.** the people of Ireland, or people whose ancestors are from Ireland. —*adjective.* having to do with Ireland or its people.

Irish setter [set′ ər] a tall, slender hunting dog with a silky, reddish coat.

i•ron [ī′ ərn] *noun, plural* **irons. 1.** a hard, grayish metal that is a chemical element. Iron is needed in the body by all plants, animals, and people to live and grow. **Iron ore** is used to make steel for tools and machines. **2.** something that is made from iron, such as a golf club with a metal head or a device used for branding cattle. **3.** a household appliance made up of a handle attached to a flat metal surface that can be heated. It is used to press wrinkles out of clothes. —*adjective.* **1.** made of iron. **2.** strong and hard, as if made of iron: He has an *iron* will and never gives up once he's decided to do something. —*verb,* **ironed, ironing. 1.** to press or smooth with a heated iron: to *iron* a shirt. **2. iron out.** to smooth out or solve problems.

I

Pronunciation Key: A–F

a	and; hat	ch	chew; such
ā	ate; stay	d	dog; lid
â	care; air	e	end; yet
ä	father; hat	ē	she; each
b	boy; cab	f	fun; off

(Turn the page for more information.)

i·ron·ic [ī rän′ ik] *adjective, more/most.* showing or full of irony: In the story "The Most Dangerous Game," it is *ironic* that Rainsford, the world-famous hunter, is hunted down like an animal himself. ◆ Another form of this word is **ironical. —ironically,** *adverb.*

i·ro·ny [ī′ rə nē] *noun, plural* **ironies.** something that is the opposite of what is naturally expected or what would usually happen.

ir·reg·u·lar [i reg′ yə lər] *adjective, more/most.* **1.** not usual or normal: an *irregular* heartbeat. ◆ Something irregular is an **irregularity** [i reg′ yə lar′ ə tē]. **2.** in grammar, not following the normal pattern: The verb "make" is *irregular,* because the past form is "made" rather than "maked." **—irregularly,** *adverb.*

ir·re·sist·i·ble [ir′ i zis′ tə bəl] *adjective, more/most.* too strong to be resisted: the *irresistible* force of a hurricane. Those cookies were so *irresistible* that I ate the whole box.

ir·re·spon·si·ble [ir′ i spän′ sə bəl] *adjective, more/most.* without a sense of responsibility; not reliable or trustworthy: I can't ask Doug to watch the baby, because he's very *irresponsible* and might just let her wander off by herself.

ir·ri·gate [ir′ ə gāt] *verb,* **irrigated, irrigating.** to supply land or crops with water from another place, through a system of canals or pipes.

ir·ri·ga·tion [ir′ i gā′ shən] *noun.* the process of irrigating, or a system for doing this.

ir·ri·ta·ble [ir′ ə tə bəl] *adjective, more/most.* easily made angry or upset; quick to become irritated. **—irritably,** *adverb.*

ir·ri·tate [ir′ ə tāt′] *verb,* **irritated, irritating.** **1.** to make angry or impatient; annoy; bother: Dad gets really *irritated* when he's caught in heavy traffic on the way to work. **2.** to make sore or sensitive: Cutting raw onions often *irritates* a person's eyes.

ir·ri·ta·tion [ir′ ə tā′ shən] *noun, plural* **irritations.** the fact of being irritated, or something that does this: That's a very strong soap that can cause a skin *irritation.*

is [iz] *verb.* a form of the verb BE used with "he," "she," or "it" to tell about the present: Los Angeles *is* the biggest city in California.

Is·lam [iz′ läm] *noun.* a name for the religion that was founded by the prophet Muhammad; the MUSLIM religion. **—Islamic,** *adjective.*

> **irony** If by coincidence a person who hates or dislikes his neighbor moves to another part of town, only to find that his neighbor has by chance also moved, again right next door—that's *irony.* Irony is the unexpected turn of events that almost make you believe some giant hand is monitoring people to get the right effect. In O. Henry's "The Ransom of Red Chief," two men kidnap a boy and demand a ransom from his family, but the boy is such a nuisance that in the end the kidnappers have to pay his parents to take him back. In his story "The Gift of the Magi," a poor young married couple face a bleak Christmas. The wife cuts her beautiful long hair and sells it so she can buy her husband a chain for his watch, while at the same time her husband sells the watch to buy her a set of expensive, fashionable combs.

is·land [ī′ lənd] *noun, plural* **islands. 1.** a body of land that is completely surrounded by water. ◆ All land on earth is actually surrounded by water, but *island* usually refers to a land area smaller than a continent. **2.** something thought of as like an island: A traffic *island* is a place in the middle of a wide street where people can stand while crossing the street.

isle [īl] *noun, plural* **isles.** another word for an island, especially a small island. ◆ Usually used in poetry and other writing.

is·n't [iz′ ənt] the contraction for **"is not."**

i·so·late [ī′ sə lāt′] *verb,* **isolated, isolating.** to set or keep apart from others; separate: Prisons sometimes *isolate* the most dangerous criminals in a different area from the other prisoners. ◆ Often used as an adjective: "These mountains seemed as *isolated* as the surface of Mars." (Joe McGinniss) ◆ The state of being isolated is **isolation.**

irrigation Irrigation ditches allow the Central Valley of California to be the nation's largest vegetable-growing area even though it receives very little rainfall.

I

Is•ra•el [iz′ rē əl] a country in southwest Asia, on the Mediterranean Sea. *Capital:* Jerusalem. *Area:* 8,000 square miles. *Population:* 4,200,000. —**Israeli,** *adjective; noun.*

made a list of the *items* I needed to pack for my trip. **2.** a piece of news: I read an *item* in today's paper saying that Janet's older sister got married.

> **it's/its** When *he* owns a watch, it is *his.* When *she* owns a watch, it is *hers.* When a church group takes money for a new building, it is *theirs.* But what happens if *it* owns something? Suppose the city of Boston owned the building? Then you would say "*its* building." So far, so good. But then what do you make of *it's?* It looks like a possessive (*his, her, their, its*); it sounds like a possessive, but *it's* not. Now, *you* decide the difference between "it" and "it's" by reading over these examples.

is•sue [ish′ o͞o] *noun, plural* **issues. 1.** a single copy of a newspaper or magazine: The first *issue* of *Time* Magazine came out in 1923. **2.** a subject that is being talked about or considered; a matter to be dealt with: In the 1968 election for President, the Vietnam War was a major *issue.* **3.** something that is sent or given out: There was a special *issue* of postage stamps for the 1984 Olympic Games. —*verb,* **issued, issuing.** to send or give out: to *issue* uniforms to new soldiers. The mayor *issued* a statement to announce plans for a new city park.

Is•tan•bul [is′ tan bool′] a city in northwestern Turkey. *Population:* 2,700,000.

it [it] *pronoun.* **1.** the thing or animal that has been mentioned; that one: You can have this book—I'm finished reading *it.* **2.** a condition that is mentioned: *It* looks like rain. **3.** a subject that is mentioned: How far is *it* to the beach? How did you like *it* in New York?

I•tal•ian [i tal′ yən] *noun, plural* **Italians. 1.** a person who was born in Italy or whose family comes from Italy. **2.** the language of Italy. —*adjective.* having to do with Italy, its people, or their language.

i•tal•ic [i tal′ ik] *adjective.* of printing, having the letters slanting to the right, rather than straight up and down (Roman type). *These words are printed in italic type.* —**italics,** *noun.*

It•a•ly [it′ ə lē] a country in southern Europe. *Capital:* Rome. *Area:* 117,000 square miles. *Population:* 57,900,000.

itch [ich] *noun, plural* **itches. 1.** an irritating or slightly painful feeling in the skin, that makes one want to scratch or rub the place where it is to make the feeling go away. **2.** a restless, uneasy feeling or desire. —*verb,* **itched, itching. 1.** to feel or cause to feel an itch. **2.** to have a strong, restless desire to do something: "I had been *itching* to get away all afternoon . . ." (Russell Baker) —**itchy,** *adverb.*

i•tem [ī′ təm] *noun, plural* **items. 1.** a single thing; one of something: an *item* of clothing. I

it'll [it′ əl] the contraction for **it will.**

its [itz] *adjective.* the pronoun IT when used as a possessive; belonging to it: New Jersey got *its* name from an island near England.

it's [itz] a contraction for **"it is"** or **"it has."**

it•self [it self′] its own self: This oven can turn *itself* off and on automatically with a timer.

I've [īv] the contraction for **"I have."**

i•vo•ry [īv′ rē] *noun, plural* **ivories. 1.** a hard, white substance that forms a very long, pointed tooth called a TUSK in elephants and certain other animals. **2.** a creamy-white color like that of ivory.

ivory This ivory whale tusk shows the carving style known as *scrimshaw,* which was practiced as a handicraft by American sailors of the 1800's.

i•vy [ī′ vē] *noun, plural* **ivies. 1.** a vine that has shiny leaves and grows by climbing up walls or along the ground. **2.** a plant that is like ivy, such as POISON IVY.

	Pronunciation Key: G–N		
g	give; big	k	kind; cat; back
h	hold	l	let; ball
i	it; this	m	make; time
ī	ice; my	n	not; own
j	jet; gem; edge	ng	having

(Turn the page for more information.)

I

j, J [jā] *noun, plural* **j's, J's.** the tenth letter of the alphabet.

jab [jab] *verb,* **jabbed, jabbing.** to hit someone or something with a short, quick blow: Patrick *jabbed* the other player with his elbow as they were fighting for the ball under the basket. —*noun, plural* **jabs.** a short, quick blow, as with something sharp.

jack [jak] *noun, plural* **jacks. 1.** a tool or machine used for lifting heavy objects a short distance off the ground. A jack is used to lift the end of a car high enough to work underneath it or change a flat tire. **2.** a playing card with a picture of a young man on it. A jack ranks between a ten and a queen. **3. jacks.** a game using small, star-shaped metal pieces which players quickly pick up while bouncing a small ball. —*verb,* **jacked, jacking.** to lift something with a jack: He *jacked* up the car so that he could change the flat tire.

jack•al [jak′əl] *noun, plural* **jackals.** a wild animal that is related to the dog. Jackals live on the plains of Africa and Asia. They often eat the remains of small animals that have been killed by other animals.

jack•et [jak′it] *noun, plural* **jackets. 1.** a short coat for the upper body, ending at the waist or hips. **2.** an outer covering that is thought of like a jacket, such as the skin of a potato or a paper wrapping that protects the cover of a book.

jack-in-the-box [jak′ in thə bäks′] *noun, plural* **jack-in-the-boxes.** a toy made up of a box with a doll inside that pops out when the lid is opened.

jack•knife [jak′nīf′] *noun, plural* **jackknives. 1.** a large, strong pocketknife with blades that fold into the knife handle. **2.** a dive in which the diver bends forward while in the air to touch the toes and then straightens out. —*verb,* **jackknifed, jackknifing.** to bend or fold like a jackknife: Traffic on the expressway was stalled after a large trailer truck *jackknifed* and turned over.

jack-o'-lan•tern [jak′ ə lan′tərn] *noun, plural* **jack-o'-lanterns.** a pumpkin that has been hollowed out and carved with holes to look like a face, used for decoration at Halloween. A candle or light is often placed inside the jack-o'-lantern to show the carved face.

jack-o'-lantern This word came from the expression "Jack with the lantern," a nickname for a night watchman carrying a lantern.

jack•pot [jak′ pät′] *noun, plural* **jackpots.** the largest prize in a contest or game: Murray won a *jackpot* of $10,000 on the TV game show.

jack rabbit a large hare that lives on the plains of western North America, having a thin body, very long ears, and large, strong back legs. They are very fast runners.

Jack•son [jak′sən] **1. Andrew,** 1767–1845, American general and the seventh president of the United States, from 1829 to 1837. **2. Thomas Jonathan ("Stonewall"),** 1824–1863, American Confederate general in the Civil War.

Jack•son•ville [jak′ sən vil′] the largest city in Florida, in the northeastern part of the state. *Population:* 545,000.

jade [jād] *noun.* a hard, green stone used in jewelry and carvings.

jag•ged [jag′id] *adjective.* cut or shaped in a rough, uneven way, often with sharp points: the *jagged* glass of a broken window. "It was twi-

412

light and the mountains looked *jagged* against the sky as though they had been cut out of black paper." (Noel Coward)

jaguar The jaguar is the most powerful wild cat of the Western Hemisphere. It ranged up into the southwestern United States until the early 1900's.

jag•uar [jag′ wär] *noun, plural* **jaguars.** a large, wild cat having yellowish-brown fur with black spots. Jaguars are found in Mexico and in Central and South America.

jail [jāl] *noun, plural* **jails. 1.** a building for keeping people who have been arrested and are waiting for trial, or who have been found guilty of a minor crime. **2.** any place where prisoners are kept; a prison. —*verb,* **jailed, jailing.** to put someone into jail.

jam¹ [jam] *verb,* **jammed, jamming. 1.** to push or squeeze into a tight space: "The passengers *jammed* the deck and crowded the railing for a breath of air." (E.L. Doctorow) **2.** to hurt by squeezing or crushing: Diane *jammed* her hand when she slammed the drawer shut. **3.** of a moving part, to get stuck and stop working: These door handles sometimes *jam* in really cold weather. **4.** in radio, to send out signals that interfere with a broadcast: The Soviet Union often *jams* programs coming into the country from the West. —*noun, plural* **jams. 1.** a group of people or things that are crowded tightly together; a traffic *jam.* **2.** a bad situation: We'll be in a real *jam* if the car breaks down; it's 30 miles to the next town.

jam² *noun, plural* **jams.** a sweet, thick, sticky food made from cooked fruit and sugar. Jam is eaten on bread and with other foods.

Ja•mai•ca [jə mā′ kə] an island country in the West Indies, south of Cuba. *Capital:* Kingston. *Area:* 4,400 square miles. *Population:* 2,300,000. —**Jamaican,** *adjective; noun.*

jan•gle [jang′ gəl] *verb,* **jangled, jangling.** to make a sharp ringing or rattling sound: "Meg awoke to the *jangling* of her alarm clock . . ." (Madeleine L'Engle)

jan•i•tor [jan′ i tər] *noun, plural* **janitors.** a person whose job is to clean a building and take care of it.

Jan•u•ar•y [jan′ yoo er′ ē] *noun.* the first month of the year. January has thirty-one days.

Ja•pan [jə pan′] a country of eastern Asia that is made up of four main islands and many smaller islands. *Capital:* Tokyo. *Area:* 145,000 square miles. *Population:* 120,000,000.

Jap•a•nese [jap′ ə nēz′] *noun, plural* **Japanese. 1.** a person born or living in Japan. **2.** the language of Japan. —*adjective.* having to do with Japan, its people, or their language.

Japanese beetle a large insect having a green body and reddish wings, that came into the United States from Japan. Japanese beetles are major pests that feed on plants and destroy crops.

jail/prison There's a difference between these two words. *Jail* refers to a local building used to hold people for a short time, while they are waiting for trial or serving a short sentence. *Prison* is the place where a convicted criminal serves out a sentence. Our Word Survey shows that *prison* is used about twice as often as *jail.* One reason for this is that *jail* is not used as a metaphor, but *prison* is. Writers use *prison* to stand for a condition in which a person is trapped, confined, and so on. For example: "We think of the key, each in his *prison*" (T. S. Eliot) "But the civilized man has the habits of the house. His house is a *prison.*" (Henry David Thoreau)

jar¹ [jär] *noun, plural* **jars.** a glass or clay container used to hold food. Such foods as peanut butter, jelly, and pickles come in jars.

jar² *verb,* **jarred, jarring. 1.** to move by shaking; cause to shake violently: The earthquake *jarred* the house. "He drove his fist on the table so that the plates *jarred* . . ." (John Cheever) **2.** to

Pronunciation Key: A–F			
a	and; hat	ch	chew; such
ā	ate; stay	d	dog; lid
â	care; air	e	end; yet
ä	father; hat	ē	she; each
b	boy; cab	f	fun; off
(Turn the page for more information.)			

J

have an upsetting effect on; disturb or shock: ". . . when I opened the sitting room door the noise *jarred* in my head." (James Herriot) —*noun, plural* **jars.** the act or fact of jarring; a shaking or shock.

jar•gon [jär′ gən] *noun, plural* **jargons. 1.** the special words used in a certain activity or profession: That doctor explains things to her patients simply instead of using medical *jargon.* **2.** writing that is hard to understand because it is full of long or unfamiliar words.

> **jargon** Suppose a lawyer writes: "In the event of time constraints, it is advised that you waive the final section." He is using *jargon*—fussy and stiff language which he may think a lawyer needs to use. "If you're short of time, skip the last part" would be good English and would mean the same thing. In a specialized occupation, there are many words and phrases that are not used in general writing, but that are important in that field. But there also can be *jargon*—the overuse of long, complicated words that are not really needed, especially when dealing with people outside the field. Police jargon uses words like *perpetrator* for "criminal." Business people use phrases like "time frame," "targeted goals," and "implementing policy."

jave•lin [jav′ə lin] *noun, plural* **javelins.** a long, thin, light-weight spear that is thrown for distance in track and field contests. In ancient times javelins were used for hunting or as weapons in war.

javelin A javelin throw by the former world record holder, Tom Petranoff of the United States.

jaw [jô] *noun, plural* **jaws. 1.** the upper and lower bony parts of the mouth. The jaws hold the gums and teeth. **2.** the part of a tool that holds or grips something: the *jaws* of a trap.

jay [jā] *noun, plural* **jays.** any of a group of brightly-colored, noisy birds. The best-known type in North America is the blue jay.

jay•walk [jā′ wôk′] *verb,* **jaywalked, jaywalking.** to break a traffic law while walking across the street, as by crossing against a red light or in the middle of a block. **—jaywalker,** *noun.*

jazz [jaz] *noun.* a type of popular music that was developed by black musicians and singers in the southern U.S. Jazz usually has a strong beat and lively rhythm. Jazz musicians often make up their own notes and change rhythms as they play, rather than following a certain written composition.

jeal•ous [jel′ əs] *adjective, more/most.* disliking another person because of something he or she has or can do: Stacy is *jealous* of her friend Kim because Kim has such beautiful clothes.

jeal•ous•y [jel′ ə sē] *noun, plural* **jealousies.** the feeling of being jealous: Dave doesn't really think your skateboard looks silly; he just said that out of *jealousy* because he doesn't have one.

jeans [jēns] *noun.* pants or overalls made of a heavy and strong cotton cloth. Because for many years these pants were always dark blue, they are also called **bluejeans.**

jeep [jēp] *noun, plural* **jeeps.** a small powerful automobile made for traveling over rough roads and doing various kinds of work. It was first used in World War II for driving in places where there were no good roads.

Jeff•er•son [jef′ ər sən] **Thomas,** 1743–1826, American statesman and writer, the third president of the United States, from 1801 to 1809.

jell [jel] *verb,* **jelled, jelling.** to take on a firm and definite shape: After several weeks of meetings, the plans for the company's new line of business have finally started to *jell.*

jel•ly [jel′ ē] *noun, plural* **jellies.** a clear, firm food usually made by cooking fruit juice with sugar. Jelly is served with other foods, such as bread or meat, or used as a filling for pastries.

jel•ly•fish [jel′ ē fish′] *noun, plural* **jellyfish** or **jellyfishes.** a sea animal that is shaped like an umbrella and has a soft body that looks like jelly. A jellyfish has many long, trailing parts, called TENTACLES, that can cause a painful sting.

jeop•ar•dy [jep′ ər dē] *noun.* the danger of death, loss, or great harm: The Coast Guard

J

warned everyone on the island that they were in *jeopardy* from the approaching hurricane.

jerk [jurk] *noun, plural* **jerks.** a quick, sharp pull or twist: When she saw her little brother making faces at her through the window, she lowered the shade with a *jerk.* —*verb,* **jerked, jerking.** to move with a quick, sudden motion: "He *jerks* the cloth off the table, sending the dishes rattling to the floor." (William Inge)

jerk•y [jurk′ē] *adjective.* having a jerking motion; moving by sudden stops and starts: a *jerky* subway ride. The movie character "Annie Hall" speaks in a nervous, *jerky* way, interrupting herself in the middle of every sentence. —**jerkily,** *adverb:* "Her body moved *jerkily* about, her head bobbed from side to side." (Kingsley Amis)

jer•sey [jur′zē] *noun, plural* **jerseys. 1.** a type of soft cloth knitted from cotton, wool, or other materials. **2.** a pullover shirt or sweater made from this material, often used as part of a sports uniform.

Jerusalem This is a holy city for the three great religions of the West. Seen here are the Wailing Wall (Jewish) and the Dome of the Rock (Muslim). Nearby is the spot where Jesus was crucified (Christian).

Je•ru•sa•lem [jə roo′ sə ləm] an ancient Middle Eastern city that is now the capital of Israel. It is a holy city of the Jewish, Christian, and Muslim religions. *Population:* 400,000.

jest [jest] *noun, plural* **jests.** something said or done for fun; a joke: He claims he just said that in *jest,* but I think he really meant to hurt her feelings. ♦ In the Middle Ages, a **jester** was a man whose job was to entertain a king, queen, or other ruler by doing foolish tricks and telling jokes.

—*verb,* **jested, jesting.** to speak or act in fun: "The test is going to be today instead of next week? Surely you *jest!*"

Je•sus or **Jesus Christ** [jē′ zəs krīst] about 4 B.C.–about 29 A.D., the founder of the Christian religion, believed by Christians to be the son of God.

jet [jet] *noun, plural* **jets. 1.** a powerful stream of gas, liquid, or vapor that is forced through a small opening by great pressure: The fireboat sent *jets* of water high into the air. **2.** an aircraft powered by a jet engine. —*verb,* **jetted, jetting.** to shoot out in a stream; spurt: Water from a broken lawn sprinkler *jetted* high in the air.

jet engine an engine used in airplanes, rockets, and other such vehicles. It draws in air, mixes it with fuel, and burns this mixture to produce a blast of hot gases. This stream, or *jet,* of hot gas is forced out the rear to move the aircraft forward.

jet lag a feeling of being tired and slightly ill, coming after a long airplane flight through several time zones. It comes about because a person's body must adjust to the change in time from one place to the other.

jet•ty [jet′ē] *noun, plural* **jetties.** a wall of rocks, concrete, or other material built out into the ocean or another body of water. A jetty is used to break the force of waves or to control the flow of water.

Jew [joo] *noun, plural* **Jews. 1.** a person who follows the Jewish religion, called JUDAISM. **2.** a member of the group of people who followed Moses, as told in the Old Testament; a Hebrew.

jew•el [joo′ əl *or* jool] *noun, plural* **jewels. 1.** a diamond, ruby, emerald, or other such precious stone; a gem: the crown *jewels* of the British Royal family. **2.** a person or thing thought of as very valuable or outstanding, like a jewel: The city of Cairo, Egypt is sometimes called "the *Jewel* of the Nile."

jew•el•er [jool′ ər] *noun, plural* **jewelers.** a person who makes, sells, or repairs jewelry and watches.

jew•el•ry [joo′ əl rē *or* jool′ rē] *noun.* rings, necklaces, earrings, pins, and other such orna-

J

Pronunciation Key: G–N			
g	give; big	k	kind; cat; back
h	hold	l	let; ball
i	it; this	m	make; time
ī	ice; my	n	not; own
j	jet; gem; edge	ng	having

(Turn the page for more information.)

ments that people wear. Jewelry is usually made of a precious metal such as gold or silver, often with gems set it. ♦ **Costume jewelry** is inexpensive ornaments meant to look like precious stones.

Jew·ish [jōō′ ish] *adjective.* having to do with Jews or their religion or culture: Yom Kippur is a *Jewish* holiday.

jig [jig] *noun, plural* **jigs.** a lively dance, or the music for this dance.

jig·gle [jig′ əl] *verb,* **jiggled, jiggling.** to move back and forth with a small, quick motion; wiggle; shake: Please don't *jiggle* the table while I'm writing.

jig·saw [jig′ sô] *noun, plural* **jigsaws.** a special saw for cutting wavy or curving lines.

jigsaw puzzle a puzzle in which small cardboard or wooden pieces that have been cut in irregular shapes are fitted together to complete a picture.

jin·gle [jing′ gəl] *verb,* **jingled, jingling.** to make a gentle ringing sound: "She got up, patting a pocket in which keys *jingled*." (Dashiell Hammett) —*noun, plural* **jingles. 1.** a jingling sound, as of small metal objects hitting against each other. **2.** a short verse or tune that is easy to remember: McDonald's "You deserve a break today" and Coca-Cola's "I'd like to teach the world to sing" are popular modern *jingles.*

Joan of Arc A modern medal showing Joan of Arc with her sword and battle armor.

Joan of Arc [jōn′ əv ärk′] 1412?–1431, French saint and military leader, the national heroine of France.

job [jäb] *noun, plural* **jobs. 1.** any form of work for which a person is paid: Diane has an after-school *job* at the supermarket. **2.** anything that is worked at or done: Laura did a really nice *job* on her social studies project. "It's my *job* to ask the questions, yours to answer them." (Peter Shaffer)

jock·ey [jäk′ ē] *noun, plural* **jockeys.** a person who is paid to ride a horse in a horse race.

jog [jäg] *verb,* **jogged, jogging.** to run at a slow, even pace, as for training or exercise: My mom *jogs* two miles every morning. ♦ A person who does this is a **jogger.** —*noun, plural* **jogs.** a slow, steady pace like that used for jogging.

John XXIII [jän] 1881–1963, the pope of the Roman Catholic Church from 1958 to 1963.

John Paul II born 1920, the pope of the Roman Catholic Church since 1978.

John·son [jän′ sən] **1. Andrew,** 1808–1875, the seventeenth president of the United States, from 1865 to 1869. **2. Lyndon B.,** 1908–1973, the thirty-sixth president of the United States, from 1963 to 1969. **3. Samuel,** 1709–1784, English author and dictionary editor.

join [join] *verb,* **joined, joining. 1.** to put or bring together to become one: For this dance, all the dancers *join* hands in a circle. The jeweler made a bracelet by *joining* tiny gold links. **2.** to come together with; connect: ". . . the border country where Massachusetts *joins* Vermont and New Hampshire." (Stephen Vincent Benét) **3.** to meet with or keep company with: Can you *join* us for lunch tomorrow? **4.** to become a member of; become part of: to *join* a club, to *join* the army.

joint [joint] *noun, plural* **joints. 1.** a place in the body where two or more bones are joined, usually in such a way that they can move. The wrist, elbow, knee, and ankle bones have joints. **2.** the place where two or more things join together: The plumber tightened the *joint* between the pipes so that the water wouldn't leak out. —*adjective.* shared by two or more people: My parents have a *joint* bank account. Mrs. Lee and her sister June are the *joint* owners of the clothing store. —**jointly,** *adverb.*

joke [jōk] *noun, plural* **jokes. 1.** a very short story that is told to make people laugh. **2.** something that is done to be funny: Peter filled the sugar bowl with salt as a *joke*, but Dad didn't laugh when he put some in his coffee. **3.** something that is ridiculous or that cannot be taken seriously: The 55-mile-an-hour speed limit on that highway is really a *joke;* people go 70 or more all the time. —*verb,* **joked, joking.** to tell or make jokes.

jok·er [jō′ kər] *noun, plural* **jokers. 1.** a person who tells jokes or likes to play jokes. **2.** an extra playing card that has a picture of a joker on it, used as a wild card in certain games.

J

journals Many writing teachers recommend that students keep a journal in which they write something each day. The day's entry may be as long as a page, or as short as one line. A diary and a journal are similar; the difference is that a journal describes outside events, while a diary focuses more on the writer's private thoughts. Some writers keep a journal in which they record important events, as Daniel Defoe did in his famous *Journal of the Plague Year.* However, a journal does not have to deal with major news stories. In his journal, the British author George Orwell kept a record of the things he bought, the work he did around the house, the weather, and the animals and plants he saw. One good time to keep a journal is when you go on a trip. Many famous journals have dealt with travel, such as those of Samuel Johnson (Scotland), Graham Greene (Africa, Mexico), and John Steinbeck (the U.S.).

jol•ly [jäl′ē] *adjective,* **jollier, jolliest.** full of fun; very cheerful; merry.

jolt [jōlt] *verb,* **jolted, jolting.** to move or shake roughly: "You got into a little open car and *jolted* along through the darkness for fifteen minutes." (Isaac Asimov) —*noun, plural* **jolts. 1.** a sudden rough movement; a bump or jerk: "They climbed into the plane. A little *jolt,* and they were off." (Aldous Huxley) **2.** a sudden shock or surprise: Hearing about the accident gave me a terrible *jolt.*

information from the Almanac . . ." (Carson McCullers)

jour•nal [jur′nəl] *noun, plural* **journals. 1.** a record of daily events that someone writes about his or her life or work. **2.** a newspaper or magazine: The *Ladies' Home Journal* is a popular woman's magazine.

jour•nal•ism [jur′nə liz′əm] *noun.* the work or profession of gathering and presenting the news, as by a newspaper or magazine, or by a radio or TV station.

journalism It might seem that journalism is not good training for a writer of fiction. A novelist or short-story writer makes up his story and shapes it as he wishes, while the key to good reporting is presenting the facts and leaving out your opinion. However, several noted American authors came to fiction from journalism, such as Mark Twain, Stephen Crane, Ernest Hemingway, and Damon Runyon. Certain principles of journalism apply equally well to other forms of writing: (1) Use a strong lead that will get people's attention. (2) Don't write to impress your readers, but to inform them. (3) Keep your audience in mind. Think of how much they know about your subject, and what approach you have to take to hold their interest. (4) Give details, and be accurate about them. Describe individual people, rather than groups, trends, or movements.

Jones [jōnz] **John Paul,** 1747–1792, American naval officer in the Revolutionary War, born in Scotland.

Jor•dan [jôr′dən] a country in southwest Asia, between Israel and Saudi Arabia. *Capital:* Amman. *Area:* 37,500. *Population:* 3,500,000. —**Jordanian** [jôr′dā′nē ən], *adjective; noun.*

Jo•seph [jō′səf] **1.** in the Bible, the husband of Mary, the mother of Jesus. **2. Chief Joseph,** 1840?–1904, Nez Perce Indian Chief.

jos•tle [jäs′əl] *verb,* **jostled, jostling.** to push or bump roughly: "I jumped around behind the counter and *jostled* him out of the way." (Raymond Chandler)

jot [jät] *verb,* **jotted, jotting. jot down.** to write a short, quick note: The witness *jotted down* the bank robbers' license number as their car sped away. "Sometimes she paused to *jot down* some

jour•nal•ist [jur′nəl ist] *noun, plural* **journalists.** a person whose work is journalism, especially someone who reports news stories for a newspaper.

jour•ney [jur′nē] *noun, plural* **journeys. 1.** a trip from one place to another, especially a long trip: "By land or by water it was a difficult *journey,* and took two days." (V.S. Naipaul) **2.** the distance or time needed for a journey. **3.** any movement through time or space that is

Pronunciation Key: O–S			
ō	over; go	ou	out; town
ô	all; law	p	put; hop
oo	look; full	r	run; car
ōo	pool; who	s	set; miss
oi	oil; boy	sh	show

(Turn the page for more information.)

thought of as long or difficult like a journey: "Death and sorrow will be the companions of our *journey . . .*" (Winston Churchill) —*verb,* **journeyed, journeying.** to take a long trip; make a journey: In the 1840's, many pioneers *journeyed* to the West over the Oregon Trail.

jo·vi·al [jō′ vē əl] *adjective, more/most.* full of good humor; merry or jolly: ". . . a man with twinkling greenish eyes set in a round *jovial* face." (Dashiell Hammett)

jowls [joulz] *plural noun.* loose, hanging folds of flesh around the lower jaw and throat.

joy [joi] *noun, plural* **joys. 1.** a feeling of being very happy or pleased; gladness; delight: She shouted with *joy* when her name was announced as the prize winner. **2.** a thing that brings happiness: "A thing of beauty is a *joy* forever" (John Keats)

Joyce [jois] **James,** 1882–1941, Irish author.

joy·ful [joi′ fəl] *adjective, more/most.* feeling, showing, or causing joy; full of joy: The fans

of something: a person who is a good *judge* of character. —*verb,* **judged, judging. 1.** to act as a judge in a court of law or a contest. **2.** to make a decision about the value or quality of something: That coach always picks good players for his team because he's very good at *judging* talent. **3.** to form an opinion or estimate of: "He *judged* her to be a year or so younger than himself." (James Joyce)

judg·ment [juj′ mənt] *noun, plural* **judgments** (also spelled **judgement**). **1.** an official decision given by a judge or a jury in a court of law: The *judgment* of the court was that the man should be sentenced to six months in prison. **2.** the ability to decide something: She shows good *judgment* in choosing her friends. **3.** an opinion reached after thinking carefully about something.

ju·di·cial [joo dish′ əl] *adjective.* having to do with judges or courts of law: The Supreme Court is the highest level of the U.S. *judicial* system.

> **judgment (judgement)** This is one of the rare English words that has two equally correct spellings. Either *judgment* or *judgement* is acceptable; they are *variant spellings* of the same word. Our Word Survey shows that the form *judgment,* without the e, is much more common. In American English, this is the spelling that is almost always used. The general trend in modern American English is to use the shorter and simpler spellings. Thus *traveling* is preferred to *travelling,* *busing* to *bussing, airplane* to *aeroplane* and *programing* to *programming.*

gave a *joyful* shout as the winning home run sailed over the fence. —**joyfully,** *adverb:* "Vlemk smiled and threw up his hands as *joyfully* as an old man when he sees his son." (John Gardner)

joy·ous [joi′ əs] *adjective, more/most.* filled with joy; very happy: It was a *joyous* day when my brother came home safe from the war. —**joyously,** *adverb.* —**joyousness,** *noun.*

Jua·rez [wär′ ez] **Benito,** 1806–1872, Mexican political leader.

Ju·da·ism [joo′ dē iz′ əm] *noun.* the religion of the Jewish people as set forth in the Old Testament of the Bible. Judaism was one of the earliest religions to believe in only one God.

judge [juj] *noun, plural* **judges. 1.** a public official who is in charge of a court of law and who decides questions of law at a trial. The judge sets the punishment of a guilty person. In some court cases, the judge decides if the person on trial is guilty or innocent. **2.** someone who decides the winner of a contest: The winner in such sports as figure skating, diving, and gymnastics is chosen by *judges.* **3.** a person who gives an opinion about the value or quality

ju·do [joo′ dō] *noun.* a form of wrestling or fighting developed in Japan as a way of defending oneself without weapons. In judo a person uses the opponent's own weight and force as a way to throw or pin him.

Benito Juarez

jug [jug] *noun, plural* **jugs.** a round container with a small handle and a narrow neck, used for holding liquids.

jug·gle [jug′ əl] *verb,* **juggled, juggling. 1.** to toss up balls or other objects and keep them moving continuously through the hands and

J

into the air: The clown *juggled* three oranges at once. ◆ A person who can do this is a **juggler**. **2.** to deal with several problems, situations, or tasks all at the same time: She's trying to *juggle* two part-time jobs, her housework, and caring for her children.

juggler The connection between jugglers and clowns is shown by the fact that *juggle* goes back to a Latin word meaning "to joke."

juice [jo͞os] *noun, plural* **juices. 1.** the liquid from fruit, vegetables, or meat: orange *juice,* tomato *juice,* roast beef cooking in its own *juices.* **2.** a natural fluid in the body: Digestive *juices* act to digest food.

juic•y [jo͞os′ē] *adjective,* **juicier, juiciest.** having a lot of juice: fresh, *juicy* peaches.

juke•box [jo͞ok′bäks′] *noun, plural* **jukeboxes.** a record player that plays music when money is put into a slot and a certain song is selected.

Ju•ly [joo lī′] *noun.* the seventh month of the year. July has thirty-one days.

jum•ble [jum′bəl] *verb,* **jumbled, jumbling.** to mix or throw about in a confused way: Torn wrappings from presents were *jumbled* all around the Christmas tree. —*noun, plural* **jumbles.** "She walked down the street with its *jumble* of cheap shops . . ." (Brian Moore)

jum•bo [jum′bō] *adjective.* very large: a *jumbo*-size jar of peanut butter. A Boeing 747 is a *jumbo* jet.

jump [jump] *verb,* **jumped, jumping. 1.** to use the legs to move up into the air: The football player *jumped* up to catch the pass that was over his head. **2.** to go over something by jumping: The horse *jumped* the fence. **3.** to make a sudden or quick movement: "The steamer gave a sudden hoot of its siren which made me *jump*." (Noel Coward) **4.** to go up

quickly in value or amount; rise: The price of lettuce at the supermarket just *jumped* from 29¢ to 79¢ a head. —*noun, plural* **jumps. 1.** the act of jumping; a leap or spring. **2.** something to be jumped over: In that race the runners have to go over a water *jump*. **3.** a sudden movement: Gary gave a *jump* when the phone rang loudly.

jump•er[1] [jum′pər] *noun, plural* **jumpers.** a person or thing that jumps.

jumper[2] *noun, plural* **jumpers.** a dress with no sleeves or collar. Jumpers are usually worn over sweaters or blouses.

jump•y [jum′pē] *adjective,* **jumpier, jumpiest.** easily frightened; nervous: I felt *jumpy* being alone in the house all night.

junc•tion [jungk′shən] *noun, plural* **junctions. 1.** a place where things join or cross: a railroad *junction*. The city of St. Louis is at the *junction* of the Mississippi and Missouri Rivers. **2.** the act of joining.

June [jo͞on] *noun.* the sixth month of the year. June has thirty days.

jun•gle [jung′gəl] *noun, plural* **jungles. 1.** an area of tropical land that is covered with thick masses of trees, vines, and bushes. **2.** a place or situation that is thought of as like a jungle, as by being dangerous or hard to deal with: the *jungle* of big business.

jun•ior [jo͞on′yər] *adjective.* **1.** the younger of two. A son who is given the same name as his father is called "junior." **2.** having a lower rank or position: a *junior* vice president of a company. In the army, a second lieutenant is a *junior* officer. **3.** of or in the next to last year of high school or college. —*noun, plural* **juniors. 1.** a person who is in the junior year of high school or college. **2.** a person who is younger than another: They're in the same grade, but she's ten months his *junior*.

junior high school a school between elementary school and high school. A junior high school includes the seventh and eighth grades, and sometimes sixth or ninth grade as well.

ju•ni•per [jo͞o′nə pər] *noun, plural* **junipers.** an evergreen tree or bush. Junipers have bluish-purple fruits that look like berries.

Pronunciation Key: T–Z			
t	ten; date	v	very; live
th	think	w	win; away
<u>th</u>	these	y	you
u	cut; butter	z	zoo; cause
ur	turn; bird	zh	measure

(Turn the page for more information.)

junk The word *junk* was first used by sailors. When ropes or cables were put in position on a sailing ship, any short, extra pieces that were left over were called *junk*. "Pieces of junk" were used for odd jobs, to fix or fasten equipment, or were simply thrown away. The word *junk* came to refer to anything that was not valuable. Here are four uses of "junk." You might hear today: "Mom gave me $3.00 for helping her clean out all the old *junk* in the basement." "The Cambodian refugees set to sea aboard a *junk*." "He's as mean as a *junk*yard dog." "He works on Wall Street selling *junk* bonds." If you can't figure out each of these uses from this dictionary, go to a larger one.

junk¹ [jungk] *noun.* old, worn-out things that have no use or value; things to be thrown away; trash: We've got to clear out all that *junk* that's lying around the garage. —*verb,* **junked, junking.** to get rid of as useless or worthless; throw out: to *junk* a broken-down old car.

junk² *noun, plural* **junks.** a flat-bottomed Chinese boat with square sails.

junk Chinese families often live aboard junks such as this one on the Kiang River south of Kweilin, China.

junk food *Informal.* popular foods that are believed to have little or no food value. Candy, cookies, soft drinks, potato chips, and other snacks are thought of as junk food.

Ju•pi•ter [jōō′pə tər] *noun.* **1.** the largest planet in the solar system. Jupiter is the fifth-closest planet to the sun. **2.** The chief god in the religion of the ancient Romans.

jur•or [joor′ər] *noun, plural* **jurors.** a person who serves on a jury. There are usually twelve jurors on a jury.

jur•y [joor′ē] *noun, plural* **juries.** in a court of law, a group of people officially chosen to listen to the evidence at a trial and to decide on a verdict.

just [just] *adverb.* **1.** only or merely: The ball didn't break the window; it *just* bounced off it. **2.** in the exact way; exactly: The baby looks *just* like her mother. **3.** not by much; barely: He got

there *just* in time to catch his train. **4.** a very short while ago; very recently: You want Amy? I'm sorry, she *just* left. **5.** very; completely: That picture would look *just* perfect over our fireplace. —*adjective, more/most.* **1.** as it should be; honest and right; fair: The Bill of Rights provides for *just* treatment of all citizens. **2.** as is one's due; earned or deserved: I don't blame you for being angry—you certainly have *just* cause for it.

jus•tice [jus′tis] *noun, plural* **justices. 1.** the quality of being just; honest and fair treatment according to honor or law. **2.** a judge of the United States Supreme Court. The Supreme Court has eight **Associate Justices** and one **Chief Justice. 3.** the carrying out of the law: The U.S. Department of *Justice* enforces federal laws. **4.** the state of being proper or correct: How could we lose when we played so much better than they did—there's no *justice* to it!

jus•ti•fy [jus′tə fī′] *verb,* **justified, justifying. 1.** to show that something is fair and reasonable: A taxpayer must be prepared to *justify* any claims he makes that lower his taxes. **2.** to provide a good reason for something that would otherwise be thought of as bad: The man claimed he was *justified* in pulling his gun because the three teenagers had threatened to attack him. —**justification** [jus′tə fə kā′shən], *noun:* ". . . the boy has *justification* for the kick—she hit him first." (John Cheever)

jut [jut] *verb,* **jutted, jutting.** to stick up or out: ". . . his little legs bent back so that his knees *jutted* outwards." (Carson McCullers)

jute [jōōt] *noun.* a plant fiber that is used to make rope and BURLAP. Jute grows mostly in tropical areas of Asia.

ju•ve•nile [jōō′və nəl *or* jōō′və nīl′] *adjective, more/most.* **1.** for or about children or young people: *Alice in Wonderland* is one of the world's best-known *juvenile* books. **2.** suitable only for a young child; childish; immature: You won't play unless you get to pitch the whole game—don't you think that's a *juvenile* attitude? —*noun, plural* **juveniles.** a young person.

J

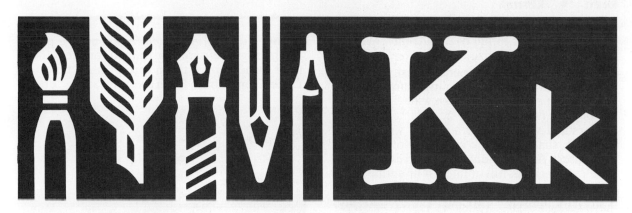

k, K [kā] *noun, plural* **k's, K's.** the eleventh letter of the alphabet.

Kaf•ka [käf′ kə] **Franz,** 1883–1924, German author, living in Czechoslovakia.

ka•lei•do•scope [kə lī′ də skōp′] *noun, plural* **kaleidoscopes.** a tube that contains pieces of colored glass at one end and a small hole at the other. When a person looks through the hole and turns the tube, two mirrors inside reflect the changing patterns of the moving glass.

kangaroo A mother kangaroo with its baby, known as a "joey."

kan•ga•roo [kang′ gə roo′] *noun, plural* **kanga-roos.** an animal that lives in Australia. It has small front legs and very strong back legs that it uses for jumping along the ground. The female kangaroo carries her young in a pouch on the front of her body.

Kan•sas [kan′ zəs] a state in the midwestern U.S. *Capital:* Topeka. *Nickname:* "Sunflower State." *Area:* 82,300 square miles. *Population:* 2,408,000.

Kansas City a city in western Missouri. *Population:* 450,000.

kar•at [kar′ ət] *noun, plural* **karats.** *(also spelled* **carat***)* a unit of measure to show the amount of gold in a certain metal mixture. Pure gold is 24 karats, but most gold jewelry is either 18 or 14 karats.

ka•ra•te [kə rä′ tē] *noun.* a Japanese style of fighting in which the hands, elbows, feet, and knees are used instead of weapons.

ka•ty•did [kā′ tē did′] *noun, plural* **katydids.** a large green insect that looks somewhat like a grasshopper. The male makes a shrill noise that sounds like its name by rubbing its two front wings together.

kay•ak [kī′ ak] *noun, plural* **kayaks. 1.** a light-weight Eskimo canoe that is propelled by one long oar with a paddle at each end. **2.** a lightweight modern canoe that looks like this.

kayak Eskimos have used kayaks for thousands of years. The traditional kayak has a light frame of wood or bone covered with animal skin, and an opening for the paddler.

keel [kēl] *noun, plural* **keels. 1.** a wooden or steel piece that runs down the whole length of the bottom of a ship or boat. The keel is the main support of a ship's structure. **2.** a fin-shaped piece that is attached to the bottom of a sailboat and hangs down into the water to keep the boat upright. **3. on an even keel.** steady; balanced: "How could she get things back *on a more even keel?*" (Mary Norton) —*verb,* **keeled, keeling.** (used with **over**) **1.** to turn upside-down; capsize: Our boat *keeled over in* the big waves. **2.** to fall over suddenly: When I heard I'd won the prize, I nearly *keeled over.*

keen [kēn] *adjective,* **keener, keenest. 1.** having a sharp cutting edge or point; sharp: a knife with a *keen* edge. ". . . a *keen* wind had started to blow." (Andrea Lee) **2.** able to think or understand well; bright: a person with a *keen* mind. **3.** sharp or quick in the use of the mind or senses: A bloodhound has a *keen* sense of smell. **4. keen on.** full of interest or enthusiasm; eager: "He wasn't too *keen on* visiting Mr. Curry by himself." (Michael Bond) —**keenly,** *adverb:* "He worked slowly and carefully, *keenly* aware of his danger." (Jack London)

keep [kēp] *verb,* **kept, keeping. 1.** to have or hold for a time; have and not give up: I don't want that pen you borrowed; you can *keep* it. **2.** to continue in a certain position or condition: *Keep* going on this road until you come to Route 20. This is a light jacket, but it really *keeps* me warm. **3.** to put or hold in a certain place: to *keep* a car in a garage, to *keep* money in a bank. **4.** to hold back; prevent: The noise next door *kept* her from sleeping. **5.** to take care of; manage: to *keep* house, to *keep* the books for a company. **6.** to carry out or continue in the proper way: to *keep* a promise, to *keep* a secret. **7.** to make a regular record of or in: to *keep* a diary. "I'm *keeping* an account of everything. I'll pay every penny back." (Arthur Miller)

keep•er [kēp′ər] *noun, plural* **keepers.** a person who takes care of or is in charge of something: The zoo animals were given food by their *keeper.* ◆ Often combined with other words, as in shop*keeper,* gate*keeper,* or goal*keeper.*

keep•sake [kēp′sāk′] *noun, plural* **keepsakes.** something that is kept or given in memory of a person: When my friend moved out of town, she gave me one of her bracelets as a *keepsake.*

keg [keg] *noun, plural* **kegs.** a small barrel: a *keg* of beer, a *keg* of nails.

Kel•ler [kel′ər] **Helen,** 1880–1968, American lecturer and author who was both blind and deaf.

kelp [kelp] *noun.* a large brown seaweed. Some kinds of kelp are used to make products such as fertilizer and iodine.

Kennedy [ken′i dē] **1. John F.,** 1917–1963, the thirty-fifth president of the United States, from 1961 to 1963. **2.** his father, **Joseph P.,** 1888–1969, American businessman and government official. **3.** his brothers, **Robert F.,** 1925–1968, and **Edward M. (Ted),** born 1932, American political leaders.

ken•nel [ken′əl] *noun, plural* **kennels.** a place where dogs are raised or trained, or are left by their owners to be taken care of for a time. ◆ *Kennel* comes from Latin *canis,* meaning "dog."

Kentucky The world's most famous horse race is the Kentucky Derby, held each May at Churchill Downs race track in Louisville, Kentucky.

Ken•tuck•y [kən tuk′ē] a state in the east-central U.S. *Capital:* Frankfort. *Nickname:* "Bluegrass State." *Area:* 40,400 square miles. *Population:* 3,700,000.

Ken•ya [ken′yə] a country in east-central Africa. *Capital:* Nairobi. *Area:* 224,900 square miles. *Population:* 18,200,000. —**Kenyan,** *adjective; noun.*

kept [kept] *verb.* the past form of **keep.**

ker•chief [kur′chif] *noun, plural* **kerchiefs. 1.** a piece of cloth worn over the head or around the neck. **2.** a handkerchief.

ker•nel [kurn′əl] *noun, plural* **kernels. 1.** a grain or seed of wheat or corn. **2.** the soft part inside the shell of a nut, fruit, or seed. **3.** the

Helen Keller

K

central or most important part of something: A famous study of English explained the language in terms of a few *kernel* sentences.

ker•o•sene [ker′ ə sēn′] *noun.* a thick, light-colored oil that is made from petroleum. Kerosene is used as fuel for such things as lamps, stoves, and jet engines.

ketch•up [kech′ əp] *noun (also spelled* **catsup)** a thick red sauce that is made of tomatoes, onions, salt, sugar, and spices. Ketchup is used to add flavor to hamburgers and other foods. ♦ The word *ketchup* comes from Chinese.

ket•tle [ket′ əl] *noun, plural* **kettles. 1.** a metal pot, usually having a lid, used for boiling liquids or cooking foods. **2.** a closed metal container with a small opening, used for heating water; also called a **teakettle.**

ket•tle•drum [ket′ əl drum′] *noun, plural* **kettledrums.** a large, deep-sounding drum with a bowl-shaped copper or brass body.

key¹ [kē] *noun, plural* **keys. 1.** a small piece of metal with a special shape, that fits into a lock to open or close it. **2.** anything shaped or used like a key: a *key* to open a coffee can. Some old clocks are wound with a *key.* **3.** a thing that solves or explains something: The note that the

key² *noun, plural* **keys.** a low island or reef, as off the coast of southern Florida.

Key [kē] **Francis Scott,** 1779–1843, the author of the "Star-Spangled Banner," the national anthem of the United States.

key•board [kē′ bôrd′] *noun, plural* **keyboards.** a set of keys in rows on a piano, typewriter, computer, or the like. —*verb,* **keyboarded, keyboarding.** to use a computer keyboard. —**keyboarder,** *noun.*

key•pad [kē′ pad′] *noun, plural* **keypads.** a small set of keys with numbers and symbols, as on an electronic calculator or a computer.

key•stone [kē′ stōn′] *noun, plural* **keystones. 1.** the middle stone at the top of an arch. The keystone holds the other stones of the arch in place. **2.** the part or element on which other parts depend: Pennsylvania is called the *Keystone* State because it was in a central position among the original 13 states.

khak•i [kak′ ē] *noun.* **1.** a light, yellowish-brown or tan color. **2.** a heavy cotton cloth having this color, often used for military uniforms.

Khru•shchev [krōōsh′ chef] **Nikita,** 1894–1971, the ruler of the Soviet Union from 1958 to 1964.

key words   Courses that teach the writing process often use the technique of CLUSTERING (see p. 147). The group of words that form the cluster branch off from a *key word* placed at the center. Let's say you want to write a story of mystery and suspense. You start with a key word that sums up the effect you want for your story—*fear, scary, horror,* or whatever. Then you note things that are suggested by this key word, such as "dark night," "strange noises," "deserted old house," "monsters," "going back in time," "ghosts," "people who aren't what they seem," and "surprise ending." Remember that your key word is what's important. You might look at the list above and say, "I'm going to write a horror story that's different, one that takes place at high noon, on a sunny day, in a big park, with nothing but ordinary people around." Then those are the ideas that you develop around your key word.

victim left was the *key* to finding out who killed him. This math book has an answer *key* in the back. **4.** the most important element or part: "That money was the *key* to everybody's future happiness." (Russell Baker) **5.** one of a set of buttons or parts that is pressed down to play a musical instrument or use a machine: typewriter *keys,* the black *keys* on a piano. **6.** in music, a scale or set of notes in which the notes are all related to each other and are based on one note (the **keynote**): a song written in the *key* of G. —*adjective.* **1.** very important; major: The computer company is having problems because several of their *key* employees left to form their own company. **2. keyed up.** excited or nervous; tense.

kick [kik] *verb,* **kicked, kicking. 1.** to hit or strike with the foot: He *kicked* a rock down the street ahead of him. **2.** to strike out with the foot or feet: The swimmer *kicked* harder as she neared the finish line. **3.** to make or do by kicking: to *kick* up dust, to *kick* a field goal in football. **4.** of a gun, to spring back when fired.

Pronunciation Key: A–F			
a	and; hat	ch	chew; such
ā	ate; stay	d	dog; lid
â	care; air	e	end; yet
ä	father; hat	ē	she; each
b	boy; cab	f	fun; off

(Turn the page for more information.)

K

5. kick out. *Informal.* to dismiss or remove someone, especially suddenly or in a forceful way: He was *kicked out* of college for cheating on an exam. —*noun, plural* **kicks. 1.** a hit or blow with the foot. **2.** the springing back of a gun when it is fired. **3.** *Informal.* a feeling of excitement or pleasure: Grandpa got a big *kick* out of the present Billy gave him. **4.** *Informal.* a strong new interest or concern: Dad is on a money-saving *kick* lately.

kick•off [kik′ ôf′] *noun, plural* **kickoffs.** in football or soccer, a kick that puts the ball into play at the beginning of each half or after a score has been made. ♦ Also used as a verb: The Sharks won the coin toss and decided to *kick off.*

kid [kid] *noun, plural* **kids. 1.** a young goat. **2.** soft leather made from the skin of this animal: *kid* gloves. **3.** a child or young person. —*adjective. Informal.* younger: I had to bring my *kid* brother along to the movies with me. —*verb,* **kidded, kidding.** to make fun of or joke with someone: Mom likes to *kid* Billy about how much time he spends combing his hair.

kill•er [kil′ ər] *noun, plural* **killers.** a person or thing that kills, especially someone who kills another person.

killer whale The killer whale, a mammal, is also called the *orca,* from its Latin name.

killer whale a large black-and-white whale that feeds on large fish and on water animals such as seals and walruses.

---

kid The word *kid,* when used to mean "a child," is informal English. Most informal words are fairly new, but to use *kid* in speaking of human beings, not animals, has been found in print as far back as 1599. It became popular in the 1800's. For example, in 1841 Lord Shaftesbury, a famous British government leader, wrote: "I passed a few days happily with my wife and *kids.*" Using *kid* or *kids* when speaking of children is easier than using *siblings,* a more formal word meaning "brothers and sisters." Most people do not use *sibling,* yet nowadays it does appears in writing because it is a way to express the idea of "either a brother or a sister:" "Student writers will often have characters in their stories who are based on their *siblings.*"

---

kid•nap [kid′ nap′] *verb,* **kidnapped** or **kidnaped, kidnapping** or **kidnaping.** to take away and hold someone by force. ♦ A person who does this is a **kidnapper.** A kidnapper usually demands money or something else in return for letting the kidnapped person go free.

kid•ney [kid′ nē] *noun, plural* **kidneys.** one of a pair of body organs in the abdomen that separate waste matter (called URINE) from the bloodstream to be passed out of the body through the BLADDER.

kill [kil] *verb,* **killed, killing. 1.** to end the life of; cause to die: Wolves live by *killing* other animals. **2.** to put an end to; destroy; ruin: A low mark on that test *killed* my chances of getting an 'A' for the course. **3.** to use up free time: Our train doesn't leave until six, so we'll have to *kill* an hour walking around the city. **4.** *Informal.* to cause great pain; hurt badly: This toothache is really *killing* me. —*noun, plural* **kills.** the act of killing, or an animal that is killed.

kiln [kiln] *noun, plural* **kilns.** a furnace or oven for burning, baking, or drying things at a very high temperature. Kilns are used to make bricks, pottery, and charcoal.

ki•lo [kē′ lō] *noun, plural* **kilos.** short for KILOGRAM or KILOMETER.

kil•o•gram [kil′ ə gram′] *noun, plural* **kilograms.** the basic unit of weight in the metric system. A kilogram is equal to 1000 grams, or about 2.2 pounds.

ki•lom•e•ter [ki läm′ ə tər *or* kil′ ə mē′ tər] *noun, plural* **kilometers.** a unit of length in the metric system. A kilometer is equal to 1000 meters, or about .62 miles.

kil•o•watt [kil′ ə wät′] *noun, plural* **kilowatts.** a unit of measure for electrical power. A kilowatt is equal to 1000 watts.

kilt [kilt] *noun, plural* **kilts.** a pleated, plaid skirt that reaches to the knees. Kilts are a traditional form of clothing among men in Scotland.

kimono Japanese women wearing colorful silk kimonos.

ki•mo•no [ki mō′ nə *or* ki mō′ nō] *noun, plural* **kimonos.** a long loose robe or gown that has wide sleeves and is tied with a wide sash called an **obi.** In Japan, kimonos are a traditional form of clothing for both men and women.

kin [kin] *noun.* a person's family; relatives: If she dies, the property will be passed on to her next of *kin.* **—kinship,** *noun.*

kin•dle [kind′ əl] *verb,* **kindled, kindling. 1.** to set on fire; start something burning: "The children huddled around the stove . . . while she *kindled* the fire." (Erskine Caldwell) **2.** to stir up or excite; arouse: "A museum is now supposed to *kindle* the imagination . . ." (Joan Didion)

kin•dling [kind′ ling] *noun.* small pieces of material used to start a fire, such as twigs, brush, leaves, paper, or thin branches.

kind•ly [kīnd′ lē] *adjective,* **kindlier, kindliest.** warm and friendly; kind: "He couldn't help having a *kindly* feeling for somebody who had been so good to him." (P.L. Travers) *—adverb.* **1.** in a kind way: to act *kindly* toward someone. **2.** as a favor; please: Will you *kindly* move your package so that I can sit down? **—kindliness,** *noun.*

kind•ness [kīnd′ nis] *noun, plural* **kindnesses.** the quality of being kind, or a kind act: I know you had to tell him 'no,' but I appreciate your *kindness* in doing it so nicely.

king [king] *noun, plural* **kings. 1.** a man who is the ruler of a country, and whose power has been passed down from his father or another relative: Prince Charles will become *king* of

---

kind "A lemon is a *kind* of fruit." That is a correct use of "kind of." Now, note this: "What *kind of a* car does he drive?" There is no reason to add "a" here. That's not a serious mistake in writing, but mixing the singular with the plural is serious. Here's a case in point. "You can only find *these kind* of books in a public library." Either make both words singular ("find *this kind* of book") or make both plural ("*these kinds* of books"). Finally, there's the phrase *kind of,* meaning "somewhat" or "rather:" "He said 'OK,' but he seemed *kind of* unhappy about it." It's suitable to use this phrase in a letter to a friend, but not in more formal writing, as in "By this time, relations between the two countries had become *kind of* strained." You could say "somewhat strained" or, better yet, just "strained."

---

kind¹ [kīnd] *adjective,* **kinder, kindest. 1.** wanting to help others and make them happy; friendly; caring: He was very *kind* to stop and help us fix our flat tire. **2.** showing or coming from a feeling of caring; warm and generous: a *kind* heart. Her *kind* words made him feel less upset about what happened.

kind² *noun, plural* **kinds. 1.** a group of things that are alike in some way; a type: A whale is not a fish, but a *kind* of mammal. There are many *kinds* of food at a supermarket. **2. kind of.** more or less; rather; somewhat: "It was getting *kind* of chilly, so I pulled the sweatshirt hood up over my head." (Lawrence Yep)

kin•der•gar•ten [kin′ dər gärt′ ən] *noun, plural* **kindergartens.** a class in school that comes before the first grade.

Great Britain when Queen Elizabeth dies or leaves the throne. **2.** a person or thing that is thought of like a king, as by being very important or powerful: The lion is sometimes called the *king* of beasts. Elvis Presley was known as the *King* of Rock and Roll. **3.** a playing card with a picture of a king on it. A king ranks between a queen and an ace. **4.** the most important piece in the game of chess or checkers.

Pronunciation Key: G–N

g	give; big	k	kind; cat; back
h	hold	l	let; ball
i	it; this	m	make; time
ī	ice; my	n	not; own
j	jet; gem; edge	ng	having

(Turn the page for more information.)

K

King Martin Luther King delivering the 'I Have a Dream' speech at the March on Washington, August 28, 1963.

King [king] **Martin Luther,** 1929–1968, American civil-rights leader and orator.

king•dom [king′ dəm] *noun, plural* **kingdoms.**
1. a country that is ruled by a king or queen.
2. one of the three main groups into which the natural world is divided. They are the **animal kingdom,** the **plant kingdom,** and the **mineral kingdom.**

king•fish•er [king′ fish ər] *noun, plural* **kingfishers.** a bright colored bird with a crested head and pointed bill. Kingfishers feed on fish and insects.

king-size [king′ sīz′] *adjective.* extra large: a *king-size* bed.

king snake a large, nonpoisonous snake found in southern and western North America.

kink [kingk] *noun, plural* **kinks. 1.** a short, tight curl or twist in hair, wire, rope, or the like: There was a *kink* in the garden hose and the water didn't flow smoothly. **2.** a pain or stiffness in a muscle; a cramp. **3.** a small problem or difficulty in the working of something: It's basically a good plan, but there are a few *kinks* that have to be worked out. —*verb,* **kinked, kinking.** to curl or twist sharply; form a kink.

Kip•ling [kip′ ling] **Rudyard,** 1865–1936, English author.

kiss [kis] *verb,* **kissed, kissing.** to touch with the lips as a sign of love, affection, or greeting: I *kissed* my mom good-bye when I left for school. —*noun, plural* **kisses.** a touch with the lips as a sign of love, affection, or greeting.

kit [kit] *noun, plural* **kits. 1.** a set of parts that are to be put together by the buyer: Model airplanes and cars often come in a *kit.* **2.** a small set of tools or equipment for a certain purpose: a first-aid *kit,* a sewing *kit.*

kitch•en [kich′ ən] *noun, plural* **kitchens.** a room where food is cooked.

kite [kīt] *noun, plural* **kites. 1.** a light object that is flown in the air at the end of a long string, made up of a frame that is covered with paper, plastic, or cloth. **2.** a hawk with long, pointed wings, a forked tail, and a hooked bill.

kit•ten [kit′ ən] *noun, plural* **kittens.** a young cat.

knack [nak] *noun.* a special talent or skill; the ability to do something easily: "She was a lucky woman who had . . . a *knack* of writing what quite a lot of people wanted to read." (Agatha Christie)

knap•sack [nap′ sak′] *noun, plural* **knapsacks.** a canvas or leather bag used to carry clothes, camping equipment, and so on. It is strapped over the shoulders and carried on the back.

knead [nēd] *verb,* **kneaded, kneading. 1.** to mix a soft mass such as dough or clay by pressing or working it with the hands: to *knead* bread dough before baking it. **2.** to press and rub with the hands; massage: "He *kneaded* the muscle with his right hand . . ." (Philip Roth)

knee [nē] *noun, plural* **knees.** the joint of the leg between the thigh and the lower leg, or the area around this joint.

knee•cap [nē′ kap′] *noun, plural* **kneecaps.** the flat, movable bone in front of the knee. Its medical name is the **patella** [pə tel′ ə].

king snake

kneel [nēl] *verb,* **knelt** or **kneeled, kneeling.** to go down or rest on a bent knee or knees: "The grass was wet and cold as he *knelt* on the bank . . ." (Ernest Hemingway) "She *kneeled* on the ground . . . and dug up the sandy soil." (John Steinbeck)

knew [noo] *verb.* the past tense of **know.**

knick•ers [nik′ ərz] *plural noun.* short trousers with legs fitting tightly just below the knee, formerly worn by boys and young men.

knife [nīf] *noun, plural* **knives.** a tool made of a sharp blade attached to a handle, used for cutting or as a weapon. —*verb,* **knifed, knifing.** **1.** to cut or stab with a knife. **2.** to move quickly through, as if by cutting: The speedboat *knifed* through the water.

knit [nit] *verb,* **knitted** or **knit, knitting. 1.** to make cloth or clothing by looping yarn or thread together with long needles or with a machine: Aunt Jean *knitted* Andrew a sweater. **2.** of a broken bone, to grow together: His broken wrist *knitted* well as it healed.

knight English has several common words that use the spelling *kn-* but the [n] sound. Silent-'k' words include *knife, knight, knee, knob, knock,* and *know.* At one time the [k] was actually heard in such word—something like [kuh-nife], [kuh-nite], [kuh-nee], and so on. The [k] sound dropped off over time because people found the ''k-n'' combination hard to pronounce. However, the letter *k* was retained anyway, which makes for an odd spelling. All these *kn-* words came into English from Germanic languages, of which Anglo-Saxon was one. The Angles and the Saxons invaded England at various times from the year 400 A.D. to 1000 A.D. Their languages did have a *kn-* or *cn-* pattern. Even though no later English words followed this pattern, *know, knife, knee,* etc., are such old words, and so common, that they have kept their odd form.

knight [nīt] *noun, plural* **knights. 1.** in the Middle Ages, an armed warrior who fought on horseback and gave his loyalty to a king or other ruler. Knights pledged to defend the Christian church and to act according to a code of honor. **2.** in modern Great Britain, a man who holds an honorary rank of knight because of great achievements or service to his country. A knight uses the title 'Sir' before his name. **3.** a piece in the game of chess that is usually shaped like a horse's head. —*verb,* **knighted, knighting.** to raise to the rank of knight: In former times a man was *knighted* by being tapped on the shoulder with a sword.

knight An early 16th-century Italian painting of knights in battle.

knight•hood [nīt′hood′] *noun.* **1.** the rank of a knight: In the Middle Ages a king could grant *knighthood* to any man who showed great bravery in battle. **2.** knights as a group, or the beliefs and customs of knights: *Knighthood* in Europe developed about the year 1100, and faded away in the 1400's.

knives [nīvz] the plural of **knife.**

knob [näb] *noun, plural* **knobs. 1.** a rounded handle for opening a door or drawer: The doors in that old house have brass door *knobs.* **2.** a round handle for operating a radio, television set, or other such device. **3.** any rounded part like this, such as a lump on the trunk of a tree. —**knobby,** *adjective.*

knock [näk] *verb,* **knocked, knocking. 1.** to strike with a hard blow or blows; hit: to *knock* on a door. **2.** to hit with a noise; bang: The old car's engine was *knocking* badly. **3.** to hit and cause to fall: ''. . . the force of the thunderstorm had *knocked* one of the rain gutters loose.'' (John Cheever) —*noun, plural* **knocks. 1.** a sharp, hard blow: ''Suddenly a double *knock* deep below made the whole house rattle.'' (George Orwell) **2.** a pounding or clanking noise in a car engine: This new gasoline formula is supposed to have an anti-*knock* compound.

knock out 1. to hit so hard as to make unconscious: The boxer *knocked out* his opponent in the first round.
♦ Also used as a noun: to win a fight by a *knockout.* **2.** *Informal.* to make a very great effort: ''He was just as tired as I was, but he was *knocking* himself *out* not to show it.'' (S.E. Hinton)

Pronunciation Key: O–S

ō	over; go	ou	out; town
ô	all; law	p	put; hop
oo	look; full	r	run; car
o͞o	pool; who	s	set; miss
oi	oil; boy	sh	show

(Turn the page for more information.)

knoll [nōl] *noun, plural* **knolls.** a small, rounded hill.

knot [nät] *noun, plural* **knots. 1.** a fastening made by tying together pieces of string, rope, or thread: a *knot* in a shoelace or a necktie. **2.** a tight tangle of hair. **3.** a small group; a cluster: A *knot* of people were standing near the accident to see if anyone was hurt. **4.** a hard, dark, roundish spot in wood or in a board. A knot is a place where a branch grew out from the trunk of a tree. **5.** a hard mass or lump: Mike has a *knot* on his head where he bumped it. **6.** a measure of speed for ships, boats, and aircraft. A knot is equal to one NAUTICAL MILE, or 6,076 feet, per hour. A ship moving at a speed of 20 knots is going about 23 miles per hour. —*verb,* **knotted, knotting.** to tie in or with a knot.

knot·ty [nät′ē] *adjective,* **knottier, knottiest. 1.** having many knots: a room with walls made of *knotty* pine paneling. **2.** hard to explain, understand, or deal with: a *knotty* problem.

know [nō] *verb,* **knew, known, knowing. 1.** to have information in the mind; be certain of the truth or facts about: I *know* she lives on Grand Avenue, but I don't *know* which house it is. **2.** to be familiar with; have experience with: I've *known* him since we were in seventh grade together. **3.** to have learned; be skilled in: My little sister already *knows* how to ride a two-wheeler. You have to *know* Spanish to get that job. **4.** to tell apart from others; identify or recognize: You'll *know* him by the big cowboy hat he always wears.

know·ledge [näl′ij] *noun.* **1.** what a person knows; facts and ideas; information: "His *knowledge* of history and science seems complete . . ." (Arthur C. Clarke) **2.** what is generally known; learning: scientific *knowledge,* medical *knowledge.* **3.** the fact of knowing; understanding or awareness: I'm sorry to hear he's in the hospital; I had no *knowledge* he'd been ill.

♦ A person who has a great deal of knowledge is **knowledgeable** [näl′ij ə bəl].

known [nōn] *verb.* the past participle of **know.**

—*adjective.* generally recognized or accepted: a *known* fact, a man who is a *known* criminal.

knuck·le [nuk′əl] *noun, plural* **knuckles.** a joint of a finger, especially one of the joints between the finger and the rest of the hand.

ko·a·la [kō ä′lə] *noun, plural* **koalas.** a furry, chubby animal of Australia that looks like a small bear but is actually related to the kangaroo. Koalas live in trees and feed on one certain type of eucalyptus tree.

koala A koala holding onto a eucalyptus branch.

Ko·ran [kô rän′] *noun.* the sacred book of the Muslim religion, believed to have been revealed to Muhammad by the angel Gabriel.

Ko·re·a [kə rē′ə] a former country in eastern Asia, on the **Korean Peninsula.** It is now divided into NORTH KOREA and SOUTH KOREA. — **Korean,** *adjective; noun.*

ko·sher [kō′shər] *adjective.* of food, prepared according to the traditional rules of the Jewish religion.

Ku·wait [kōō wāt′] **1.** a country in southwest Asia, on the Persian Gulf. *Area:* 6,500 square miles. *Population:* 1,600,000. **2.** the capital and chief port of Kuwait. *Population:* 80,000. —**Kuwaiti,** *adjective; noun.*

K

knowledge of a subject "Write about what you know." It's the advice of all teachers of writing. Here, we want to go over it again because some student writers think it means, "Write about what you've *experienced*—(personally seen or heard or done)." But you know about things in other ways than by direct experience. Suppose you have an assignment to write about what your town was like 50 years ago. You could (1) Look up old magazine and newspaper issues and books in the library. (2) Use your imagination. Is there a shopping center that used to be farmland? Are there historical markers on buildings or street signs? How was the city first named?

l, L [el] *noun, plural* **l's, L's.** the twelfth letter of the alphabet.

lab [lab] *noun, plural* **labs.** short for **laboratory:** Our class did an interesting experiment in science *lab* today.

la•bel [lā′ bəl] *noun, plural* **labels. 1.** a piece of cloth or paper attached to something to tell what it is or give other information about it; a mailing *label* on a package, the *label* on the inside of a jacket. **2.** a word or phrase used to describe or name something: In this dictionary, words are given part-of-speech *labels.* —*verb,* **labeled, labeling. 1.** to put a label on: The movers *labeled* each box before they loaded it in the truck. **2.** to describe or name something with a label; name or call: "He could not *label* the smells as yet, but he was sorting them out in his mind." (Marguerite Henry)

la•bor [lā′ bər] *noun, plural* **labors. 1.** hard work, especially physical work: The story of the *Labors* of Hercules tells of twelve difficult things that this Greek hero had to do. **2.** working people as a group, especially people who work with their hands. ♦ An organization of such people is a **labor union.** —*verb,* **labored, laboring. 1.** to work hard; toil: "Often they *labored* far into the night . . . and the late passer-by would see the little light burning in the printing shop." (Edna Ferber) **2.** to move slowly and with difficulty: "For fifteen minutes, twenty, half an hour, he *labored* slowly toward where he thought the porthole should be." (Isaac Asimov) —**laborious** [lə bôr′ ē əs] *adjective.* needing much labor.

lab•o•ra•to•ry [lab′ rə tôr′ ē] *noun, plural* **laboratories.** a room or building with special equipment for scientific research or experiments.

Labor Day a holiday in the United States to honor working people. It is celebrated on the first Monday in September.

la•bor•er [lā′ bər ər] *noun, plural* **laborers.** a person who does work, especially physical work.

lace [lās] *noun, plural* **laces. 1.** a cord or string used to pull or hold things together: a shoe*lace.* **2.** a fabric that is woven of fine threads in a loose, open pattern: a *lace* tablecloth, *lace* on a wedding dress. —*verb,* **laced, lacing. 1.** to fasten with a lace or laces: to *lace* up a pair of ice skates. **2.** to make a loose, woven pattern like lace: ". . . brown washed pieces of wood *laced* with hundreds of tiny hairline cracks." (Donald Barthelme) —**lacy,** *adjective.*

lace A French woman practices the ancient art of lacemaking. Lace was once considered so valuable that the term "lace-curtain" was used to mean "fashionable" or "wealthy."

lack [lak] *verb,* **lacked, lacking.** to be without; be in need of: "You can't spin a web, Wilbur . . . You *lack* two things needed to spin a web." (E.B. White) "And with me beside you, you

Pronunciation Key: A–F			
a	and; hat	ch	chew; such
ā	ate; stay	d	dog; lid
â	care; air	e	end; yet
ä	father; hot	ē	she; each
b	boy; cab	f	fun; off

(Turn the page for more information.)

shall not *lack* a friend." (T.S. Eliot) —*noun.* the state of being without something; need: "I've got dark rings under my eyes from *lack* of sleep." (Anne Frank) "We manufacture almost nothing because of our *lack* of wood." (Irving Stone)

lac•quer [lak′ ər] *noun, plural* **lacquers.** a substance used to give something a protective, shiny coat, as on the surface of wood. —*verb,* **lacquered, lacquering.** to coat with lacquer.

la•crosse [lə krôs′] *noun.* a game played on a large field between two teams of ten players, who use a special racket with a long handle and a net on the end to catch and throw a small, hard ball. Points are scored by throwing the ball into a goal.

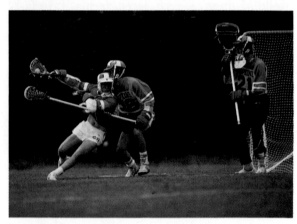

lacrosse This word is French, meaning 'the crosier.' A *crosier* is a hooked stick. Once used by shepherds, it's now carried by bishops in religious ceremonies.

lad [lad] *noun, plural* **lads.** a word for a boy or young man.

lad•der [lad′ ər] *noun, plural* **ladders. 1.** a device used for climbing up or down. It has two long side rails with rungs between them to step on. **2.** a way of moving up or making progress: She hopes that getting in to such a good college will be the first step on the *ladder* to success.

lad•en [lād′ ən] *adjective, more/most.* filled or loaded down with: "*Laden* with trade goods— striped cloth, scarlet hoods, hats, strings of coral . . ." (Daniel Boorstin)

la•dle [lād′ əl] *noun, plural* **ladles.** a bowl-shaped spoon with a long handle, used to scoop out liquids. —*verb,* **ladled, ladling.** to spoon out or dip: "She *ladled* food into pans big enough to wash in." (Marjorie Kinnan Rawlings)

la•dy [lā′ dē] *noun, plural* **ladies. 1.** a woman who has a high social position. **2. Lady.** in England, a title given to a woman of noble

rank: The Princess of Wales held the title *Lady* Diana before she married Prince Charles. **3.** a woman or girl with very polite manners and habits: Mom told Cathy to act like a *lady* and stop shouting at her little brother. **4.** any woman: There was a letter in our mailbox that was actually for the *lady* across the street.

ladybug The ladybug is often released by the hundreds into gardens to eat insects that infest flowers and crops.

la•dy•bug [lā′ dē bug′] *noun, plural* **ladybugs.** (also called a **ladybird**) a small, round insect that is red or orange and has black spots on its back. Ladybugs eat several kinds of insects that are harmful to plants.

lag [lag] *verb,* **lagged, lagging.** to fall behind: "She passed me, and complained that I *lagged* behind." (Samuel Johnson) —*noun, plural* **lags.** a delay or following after.

la•goon [lə gōōn′] *noun, plural* **lagoons.** a shallow area of water that is partly cut off from a larger body of water by a narrow strip of land or by a coral reef.

laid [lād] the past form of **lay:** "He *laid* down his little parcel wrapped in newspaper and took off his hat." (Robert Penn Warren)

lain [lān] the past participle of **lie:** ". . . he lifted from the ground a black cloak that had *lain* there hidden by the darkness." (J.R.R. Tolkien)

lair [lâr] *noun, plural* **lairs.** the den or place where a wild animal lives, especially a bear, wolf, or other large animal.

lake [lāk] *noun, plural* **lakes.** a body of fresh or salt water that is completely surrounded by land.

lamb [lam] *noun, plural* **lambs. 1.** a young sheep. **2.** the meat of a young sheep.

lame [lām] *adjective,* **lamer, lamest. 1.** not able to walk well because of being hurt or disabled; limping. **2.** sore, stiff, or painful: a *lame* back, a *lame* shoulder. **3.** not effective; weak: a *lame* excuse for not doing something. "When the old man in baggy pants came on to make *lame* jokes that no one laughed at . . ." (Kate Simon) —*verb,* **lamed, laming.** to make lame.

la•ment [lə ment′] *verb,* **lamented, lamenting.** to express deep sorrow or regret: "The same sweet sad music comes from the tree again, as if its spirit were playing . . . a last *lamenting* farewell." (Eugene O'Neill)

lamp [lamp] *noun, plural* **lamps.** a device that gives off light. Modern lamps use electric bulbs to give light. Kerosene or oil lamps were used before homes had electricity.

lance [lans] *noun, plural* **lances.** a long spear made of wood and having a sharp metal tip. Lances were once used as a weapon in battle, as by knights in the Middle Ages. —*verb,* **lanced, lancing.** to cut open with a sharp knife or instrument: The doctor *lanced* the infected sore on her skin so that it could drain.

land [land] *noun, plural* **lands. 1.** the part of the earth's surface that is not covered by water. **2.** land thought of as property; real estate: Mr. Raymond is buying up a lot of *land* near the new highway. **3.** land thought of as being of a certain type: farm *land,* the High*lands* of Scotland. **4.** a country or its people: The Star-Spangled Banner calls America "the *land* of the free." —*verb,* **landed, landing. 1.** to arrive or bring to shore: Columbus *landed* in the New World on October 12, 1492. **2.** to bring or come down to the ground from the air: to *land* an aircraft. **3.** to bring a fish out of the water. **4.** to get or obtain something, as if landing a fish: That advertising agency has just *landed* a big new account.

land•ing [land′ing] *noun, plural* **landings. 1.** the act of coming to land from the water or the air: an airplane *landing,* the *landing* of a spacecraft. **2.** a place where passengers land, or cargo is unloaded. **3.** a wide, flat area in a stairway between flights of stairs.

land•lord [land′lôrd′] *noun, plural* **landlords.** a person who owns apartments, houses, or rooms that he rents to other people. ♦ A woman who does this is a **landlady.**

land•mark [land′märk′] *noun, plural* **landmarks. 1.** a familiar or easily-seen object that is used as a guide: Maps for sailors include *landmarks* such as tall buildings, water towers, high smokestacks, and so on. **2.** an event or discov-ery that is important in history: ". . . the ancient *landmarks* set up in the Bill of Rights." (Luther Youngdahl) ♦ Often used as an adjective: the Supreme Court's *landmark* decision to outlaw school segregation.

land•scape [land′skāp′] *noun, plural* **landscapes. 1.** a view of a certain large area of land: The entire *landscape* was covered with an icy layer of snow. **2.** a painting or photograph showing a view of such an area, especially one of farms, woods, and so on. —*verb,* **landscaped, landscaping.** to plant trees, shrubs, flowers, lawns, and other plants according to a certain plan, especially in order to make an area more beautiful.

landscape A landscape painting, *The Valley of the Yosemite,* by Albert Bierstadt (American, 1830-1902).

land•slide [land′slīd′] *noun, plural* **landslides. 1.** a sliding or falling down of rock and soil from a mountain, hill, or slope. **2.** the fact of winning an election by a large number of votes: The 1972 election for President was a *landslide* for Richard Nixon; he won 49 states out of 50.

lane [lān] *noun, plural* **lanes. 1.** a narrow, often winding path or road: ". . . a picture of rolling country, leafy *lanes,* cheerful cottages, and well-kept big houses." (Michael Robbins) **2.** a division of a road for a single line of traffic going in one direction. **3.** any narrow line or way: In a 100-yard dash, each runner must stay in his own *lane.* **4.** in bowling, the long strip of floor down which the ball is rolled.

Pronunciation Key: G–N			
g	give; big	k	kind; cat; back
h	hold	l	let; ball
i	it; this	m	make; time
ī	ice; my	n	not; own
j	jet; gem; edge	ng	having

(Turn the page for more information.)

L

language change The English language changes over time, but the changes are slight and hard to notice. If you were to compare a list of the common words used in 1920 and the common words used today, you'd see that about 98% of them are the same. The main difference is the introduction of new words to describe modern inventions—*radio, TV, jet, computer, astronaut,* and others. (See *laser* on the next page.) Even if you were to go back to the 1700's, you'd find that almost all of today's common words were already in use. The core of English has not changed much since William Shakespeare wrote, four centuries ago. Some critics argue that it's all right to use a new word that clearly "fills a hole" in the language, such as *computer.* But you should avoid slang terms that really don't add anything new, such as "bad" meaning "good" and "gross" meaning "offensive."

lan•guage [lang′gwij] *noun, plural* **languages. 1.** spoken or written words; human speech. Language is the means by which people tell their thoughts, ideas, and feelings to others. **2.** the particular system of words used in a certain country or by a certain large group of people: the English *language.* **3.** the words used in a certain field or activity: the *language* of science. **4.** the way in which words are used; wording: She asked her lawyer to study the *language* of the contract. **5.** a way of expressing thoughts and feelings without using words: sign *language,* body *language.*

language arts a school subject that studies the English language, including grammar, writing, and usually speaking and listening skills.

lan•tern [lan′tərn] *noun, plural* **lanterns.** a covering or container for holding a light, usually having a handle so that it can be carried. Most lanterns have glass sides or openings through which the light can shine.

La•os [lous *or* lä′ōs] a country in southeast Asia, bordered by China and Vietnam. *Area:* 91,500 square miles. *Population:* 3,800,000. **—Laotian,** [lā ō′shən] *adjective; noun.*

lap¹ [lap] *noun, plural* **laps.** the front part of the body of a person who is sitting down, from the waist to the knees.

lap² *verb,* **lapped, lapping.** to place something so it lies partly over something else; overlap: "The sofa in the parlor was too short for her, her feet *lapped* over the edges . . ." (Carson McCullers) *—noun, plural* **laps.** the entire length of something, or the entire distance around: The football coach told all the players to run two *laps* around the track.

lap³ *verb,* **lapped, lapping. 1.** to drink by licking up with the tongue: "The kitten was *lapping* milk out of a saucer." (Madeleine L'Engle) **2.** to splash or move against gently: ". . . to walk along the ocean, in the wet sand, with the ocean *lapping* at my feet." (Judy Blume)

la•pel [lə pel′] *noun, plural* **lapels.** the flap of fabric folded back on either side of the front of a jacket or coat.

lapse [laps] *noun, plural* **lapses. 1.** a small error or slip: After he hurt his head in a car accident, he was bothered by *lapses* of memory. **2.** a passage of time; an interval: She just started taking piano lessons again after a two-year *lapse.* *—verb,* **lapsed, lapsing.** to gradually slip or pass away: The two passengers talked to each other as the plane took off but then *lapsed* into silence as the flight went on.

lar•ce•ny [lär′sə nē] *noun, plural* **larcenies.** in law, the crime of stealing money or property.

lard [lärd] *noun.* a white, greasy substance that is made from the melted fat of hogs. Lard is used in cooking.

large [lärj] *adjective,* **larger, largest. 1.** more than the usual size, amount, or number; big: Los Angeles is a *large* city. ". . . more than one hundred thousand, the *largest* crowd ever to watch a horse race in New York City." (Walter Farley) **2. at large. a.** on the loose; escaped; free: Three prisoners broke out of jail and are *at large* somewhere in the city. **b.** as a whole: This magazine is just sent to doctors and is not sold to the public *at large.*

large•ly [lärj′lē] *adverb.* to a great amount or extent; mostly; mainly: The central part of Australia is *largely* desert.

lar•i•at [lar′ē ət] *noun, plural* **lariats.** a long rope with a sliding loop at one end, used to rope cattle and horses on a ranch.

lark¹ [lärk] *noun, plural* **larks.** a small gray-brown bird that sings while it is in flight. The **skylark** is common in Europe; the **horned lark** is found in North America.

lark² *noun, plural* **larks.** something done for fun or amusement: "This was his first trip . . . and he seemed to regard it as a bit of a *lark.*" (Tom Wolfe)

larkspur The plant gets its name from the distinctive "spur" that extends upward from the flower. In former times it was called the *lark-heel*.

lark·spur [lärk′ spur′] *noun, plural* **larkspurs.** a plant with tall spikes of blue, pink, or white flowers; also called **delphinium** [del fin′ ē əm].

lar·va [lär′ və] *noun, plural* **larvae** [lär′ vē] **1.** an early stage of an insect's life cycle, when it looks like a worm. A caterpillar is the larva of a butterfly or moth. **2.** an early stage of development of a fish or water animal that looks different from its adult form.

lar·ynx [lar′ ingks] *noun, plural* **larynxes.** the upper part of the throat between the tongue and the WINDPIPE. The sound of the voice is produced in the larynx by means of the VOCAL CORDS. ◆ **Laryngitis** [lar′ ən jī′ tis] is a painful swelling of the larynx, often causing a hoarse, faint voice.

la·ser [lā′ zər] *noun, plural* **lasers.** a device that produces a very narrow and very powerful beam of light traveling in a single direction. Laser beams are used for many purposes, as for melting or cutting metal, for sending long-distance telephone, radio, and TV signals, for performing surgical operations, and for printing information from a computer.

lash¹ [lash] *noun, plural* **lashes. 1.** a stroke or blow given with a whip: On old sailing ships a sailor might be given ten *lashes* as a punishment for doing something wrong. **2.** a hair growing from the edge of the eyelid; an eyelash. —*verb,* **lashed, lashing. 1.** to strike with or as if with a whip: "The leather reins *lashed* his face." (Walter Farley) **2.** to move or strike suddenly: "Suddenly the rain began to *lash* against the window." (Madeleine L'Engle)

lash² *verb,* **lashed, lashing.** to tie with a cord or rope: "The inside of the plane was loaded with freight *lashed* into place with strong ropes." (James Houston)

lass [las] *noun, plural* **lasses.** a word for a girl or young woman.

las·so [las′ ō *or* la sōō′] *noun, plural* **lassos** or **lassoes.** a long rope with a sliding loop at one end; a lariat. —*verb,* **lassoed, lassoing.** to rope with a lasso: to *lasso* a steer.

last¹ [last] *adjective.* **1.** coming after all others; at the end: We missed the *last* bus home and had to walk all the way. **2.** most recent: I saw a great movie on TV *last* night. **3.** not likely or expected: Bart was the *last* person I expected to meet at the art museum. —*adverb.* **1.** at the end: The letter 'z' comes *last* in the alphabet. **2.** most recently: The police asked her where she had *last* seen the missing jewelry. —*noun.* **1.** a person or thing that is last. **2. at last.** at the end; finally.

last² *verb,* **lasted, lasting. 1.** to go on until a certain time or point; not end; continue: Tonight's meeting will *last* about an hour. **2.** to remain in use or in good condition: This car has *lasted* nearly five years with no major repairs.

last³ a block or form shaped like a person's foot, used in making or repairing shoes.

latch [lach] *noun, plural* **latches.** a device used to hold a door or gate closed. It usually has a bar of metal or wood that fits into a notch. —*verb,* **latched, latching.** to fasten a door or gate in this way.

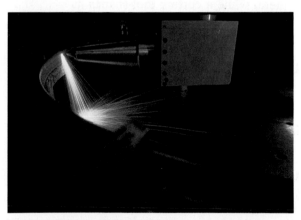

laser Using an industrial laser beam to cut holes in a jet engine part.

Pronunciation Key: O–S			
ō	over; go	ou	out; town
ô	all; law	p	put; hop
oo	look; full	r	run; car
o͞o	pool; who	s	set; miss
oi	oil; boy	sh	show

(Turn the page for more information.)

late [lāt] *adjective,* **later, latest. 1.** coming after the expected or proper time: He missed the bus and was *late* for school. **2.** occurring near the end of some period of time: Automobiles were first used in the *late* 1800's. **3.** not long past; recent: Donna always wears the *latest* style in clothing. **4.** having died: On her bedroom table she keeps a picture of her *late* husband. —*adverb.* **1.** after the proper or expected time. **2.** toward the end of a certain time: The maple tree in our yard loses its leaves *late* in the fall.

late•ly [lāt′lē] *adverb.* not long ago; recently: Have you seen any good movies *lately?*

Latin America the countries in the Western Hemisphere south of the U.S. People of these countries speak Spanish or Portuguese, languages that come from Latin.

lat•i•tude [lat′ə tōōd′] *noun, plural* **latitudes. 1.** a way of measuring distance on the earth according to position north or south of the equator, using imaginary lines that run east and west. Latitude is measured in degrees; each degree represents about 69 miles (111 kilometers). **2.** freedom of action or expression: Our teacher gives us a lot of *latitude* in choosing a topic for a report.

latter/former "Before Washington D.C. was built, two other cities were the capital of the U. S., New York and Philadelphia. The *former* was the capital from 1785 to 1790, and the *latter* from 1790 to 1800." *Former* means "the first of two things just mentioned" and *latter* means "the second of two." Here's another instance. "Two villages on the site, Hamburg and Georgetown, were absorbed into Washington, D.C. Only the *latter* still exists as a section of Washington." You don't have to use *former/latter* in your writing, of course. The first example could have read, "New York was the capital from 1785 to 1790, and Philadelphia from . . ."

lat•er•al [lat′ər əl] *adjective.* coming from or having to do with the side: A *lateral* pass in football goes to the side rather than forward. —**laterally,** *adverb.*

lathe [lāth] *noun, plural* **lathes.** a machine used for holding and spinning a piece of wood or metal while a cutting tool shapes it.

lath•er [lath′ər] *noun, plural* **lathers. 1.** a thick white foam made by rapidly mixing soap and water. **2.** a foam caused by heavy sweating, especially on a horse. —*verb,* **lathered, lathering.** to make a lather.

Lat•in [lat′ən] *noun, plural* **Latins. 1.** the language that was spoken in ancient Rome and the Roman Empire. **2.** a person who speaks one of the languages that come from Latin, such as Italian, French, Spanish, or Portuguese. **3.** a person born in or coming from LATIN AMERICA. —*adjective.* **1.** having to do with the Latin language. **2.** having to do with Latin America.

lat•ter [lat′ər] *adjective.* **1.** the second of two things that were just named or mentioned. **2.** nearer the end; later: Utah became a state in the *latter* part of the 19th century.

lat•tice [lat′is] *noun, plural* **lattices.** a structure made of thin wooden or metal strips placed across each other with open spaces between them, often used as a fence or as a frame for growing plants.

laugh [laf] *verb,* **laughed, laughing.** to make the special sounds and movements of the face that show one is happy or finds something funny: to *laugh* at a joke, to *laugh* at a funny movie or TV show. —*noun, plural* **laughs.** the act or sound of laughing.

laugh•ter [laf′tər] *noun.* the act or sound of laughing.

launch[1] [lônch] *verb,* **launched, launching. 1.** to put a boat or ship into the water: "We all went to the cove and watched him *launch* the big

Latin More than half of our English words come from Latin. They came in by an indirect route. One might think that because the Romans controlled the British Isles during the period of 43 A.D. to 476 A.D., they left behind their Latin language. It didn't happen that way. The Anglo-Saxon tribes who began the English language picked up only a handful of Latin words, such as *school, candle,* and *fever.* But Latin, the basis of French, Italian, and Spanish, came to Britain when the French-speaking Normans conquered England in 1066. Soon afterward, thousands of Latin words entered English through the route of the Normans. Native English words tend to be simpler than their Latinate equivalents—*dog/canine; house/residence; get/acquire; have/possess.*

canoe." (Scott O'Dell) **2.** to send an aircraft, spacecraft, or other vehicle into the air: *The first space shuttle was launched in 1981.* **3.** to start out on something, as if setting out in a ship: ". . . when Uncle Hal *launched* on his suppertime stories." (Russell Baker) —*noun, plural* **launches.** the act of launching: "The four flight decks were crammed with aircraft, none quite set for *launch*." (Herman Wouk)

launch² *noun, plural* **launches.** an open motorboat, especially one used for short trips on a harbor or the like.

launching pad a special platform or structure from which rockets and missiles are launched into the air; also called a **launch pad.**

laun•der [lôn′ dər] *verb,* **laundered, laundering.** to wash or wash and iron clothes.

laun•dry [lôn′ drē] *noun, plural* **laundries. 1.** a place or business where clothes and other fabrics are washed. **2.** clothes that have just been washed or that need to be washed.

lau•rel [lôr′ əl] *noun, plural* **laurels. 1.** an evergreen shrub that has stiff, fragrant leaves. In ancient times, laurel wreaths were given to people as a sign of victory in a battle or contest. **2. laurels.** honor or fame. **3. rest on one's laurels.** to be satisfied with what one has already done.

lava A spectacular lava flow during the eruption of Kilauea volcano in Hawaii.

la•va [lä′ və *or* lav′ ə] *noun.* **1.** the red-hot, melted rock that flows out of a volcano when it erupts. **2.** the hardened rock that forms from the cooling of this substance.

lav•a•to•ry [lav′ ə tôr′ ē] *noun, plural* **lavatories. 1.** a small sink or basin in a bathroom. **2.** a bathroom, especially a public one.

lav•en•der [lav′ ən dər] *noun, plural* **lavenders. 1.** a small plant related to mint. It has light-purple flowers and a strong, sweet smell. **2.** a light purple color.

lav•ish [lav′ ish] *adjective, more/most.* given in great amounts; very generous: "It made a *lavish* display set out on the table—knives, forks, salad forks, more forks for the pie . . ." (Shirley Jackson) —*verb,* **lavished, lavishing.** to give or spend very freely: "Nazar had *lavished* much love and attention on the young horse." (Walter Farley) —**lavishly,** *adverb.*

law [lô] *noun, plural* **laws. 1.** a rule made and enforced by the government of a country, state, or city, to be followed by the people who live there: *There is a law in our state that people have to be 16 years old to get a driver's license.* **2.** a system or set of these rules: *Robbery and murder are against the law.* **3.** the profession of a lawyer or a judge. **4.** any rule that must be obeyed: *English soccer leagues follow the laws of the Football Association.* **5.** a statement in science or mathematics about something that always takes place in a certain way when certain conditions are present: *Sir Isaac Newton's three laws of motion.* **6.** any similar statement about what is expected to happen in a certain situation: '*Murphy's Law*' says that "anything that can go wrong, will."

law•ful [lô′ fəl] *adjective.* allowed or recognized by law; legal: *the lawful arrest of a suspected criminal.* —**lawfully,** *adverb.*

law•less [lô′ lis] *adjective, more/most.* not ruled or controlled by laws: *the lawless frontier towns of the Old West.*

lawn [lôn] *noun, plural* **lawns.** an area around a house or building that is planted with grass.

lawn•mow•er [lôn′ mō′ ər] *noun, plural* **lawnmowers.** a machine with revolving blades, used to cut grass.

law•suit [lô′ sōōt′] *noun, plural* **lawsuits.** a court case that does not come from a criminal charge against someone. A lawsuit asks the court to decide a claim or question between two sides: *The lawsuit claimed that the author had copied parts of his best-selling novel out of someone else's book.*

law•yer [lô′ yər] *noun, plural* **lawyers.** a person who is trained and licensed to give people advice about the law and to represent them in court.

Pronunciation Key: T–Z			
t	ten; date	v	very; live
th	think	w	win; away
<u>th</u>	these	y	you
u	cut; butter	z	zoo; cause
ur	turn; bird	zh	measure

(Turn the page for more information.)

lay/lie Remember that *lay* means you put something down. A hen *lays* eggs, a mother *lays* a blanket over a sleeping child. *Lie* shows position and does not mean that someone is acting upon another person or thing. She's going to *lie* down to rest, an island *lies* several miles offshore. The confusing thing is that the past tense of *lie* is *lay*. "After lunch he *lay* down on the sofa to rest." *Laid* is the past form of *lay*: "She *laid* the packages on the table." This is standard English, but it could be losing out. In a hospital, you may hear nurses and doctors say, "*Lay* down now." Also, some doctors say *nauseous* when they mean *nauseated*. (*Nauseous* means "causing an upset stomach," as in "*nauseous* fumes from an old bus;" *nauseated* means "having an upset stomach.") In hospitals there are various kinds of verbal surgery.

lay¹ [lā] *verb,* **laid, laying. 1.** to place or set: Just *lay* the package on that table. **2.** to put down and attach in place: to *lay* a carpet, to *lay* tiles for a kitchen floor. **3.** of a bird, to produce an egg or eggs. **4. lay off.** to dismiss from a job: The company had to *lay off* 60 workers at the Smithtown factory because business was slow.

lay² *verb.* the past tense of **lie.**

lay•er [lā′ər] *noun, plural* **layers. 1.** a single thickness or level of something: Roman roads were built with four *layers* of material. "A double *layer* of clothes never hurts anyone in the winter . . ." (E.L. Konigsburg) **2.** a person or thing that lays: a brick*layer.*

lay•off [lā′ ôf′] *noun, plural* **layoffs. 1.** the act of laying off a worker or workers. **2.** any period of not being active.

la•zy [lā′ zē] *adjective,* **lazier, laziest. 1.** not liking to work or be active; not willing to do things: His room is always a mess because he's too *lazy* to clean it up. **2.** suggesting or causing a lazy feeling: a *lazy,* slow-moving stream, a *lazy* summer day. **—lazily,** *adverb:* "A bird circled *lazily* above them . . ." (Walter Farley) **—laziness,** *noun.*

LCD an abbreviation for *Liquid Crystal Display.* Liquid crystal reacts to electric impulses by changing its color. Watches, calculators, and portable computers often use an LCD display to show letters and numbers.

lead¹ [lēd] *verb,* **led, leading. 1.** to show the way; go along before or with: "Jack *led* the way down the rock and across the bridge." (William Golding) **2.** to go first or be ahead of others: At the half our team was *leading,* 6–0. **3.** to go or reach in a certain direction; be a way to: ". . . marble steps were seen, *leading* downwards into darkness." (Lewis Carroll) **4.** to be in charge of; direct or control: to *lead* an orchestra, to *lead* troops in battle. **5.** to live life in a certain way: Mr. Sims has *led* a quiet life since he retired. **—***noun, plural* **leads. 1.** the fact of being ahead, or the amount that one is ahead: The Wolves have a three-game *lead* with

only six games left to play. **2.** the position of guiding or giving direction: If you're not sure how to do it, just follow her *lead.* **3.** the main or most important part in a play, film, or other performance. **4.** an answer or discovery; a clue: The police got a good *lead* in the robbery case from an unknown telephone caller.

lead² [led] *noun, plural* **leads. 1.** a soft, heavy gray metal that is easily bent or shaped. Lead is a chemical element and one of the oldest known metals. It is used in batteries for cars and planes, in some kinds of paint and gasoline, and in making pipes, protective shields, and storage tanks. **2.** the substance in a pencil that makes writing marks, made of a mineral (GRAPHITE) that looks something like lead.

lead•er [lē′ dər] *noun, plural* **leaders.** someone who leads: a band *leader,* a cheer*leader.* In the Soviet Union the head of the Communist Party is the *leader* of the country. ♦ The fact or quality of being a leader is **leadership.**

leaf [lēf] *noun, plural* **leaves. 1.** one of the thin, flat green parts growing from a stem or branch on trees, bushes, flowers, grass, and other plants. Leaves make food for the plant. **2.** a sheet of paper from a book or magazine; a page: A loose-*leaf* notebook has pages that can be removed. **3.** a very thin sheet of metal, especially gold. **4.** an extra piece that is inserted in or folded out from a table to make it larger. **—***verb,* **leafed, leafing. 1.** of a plant, to produce or grow leaves. **2.** to quickly glance at and turn pages: to *leaf* through a magazine.

leaf•let [lēf′ lit] *noun, plural* **leaflets.** a small booklet or sheet of paper: At the museum entrance we got a *leaflet* telling where the different exhibits were.

leaf•y [lēf′ ē] *adjective,* **leafier, leafiest.** covered with or having many leaves: *leafy* vegetables such as spinach and lettuce.

league¹ [lēg] *noun, plural* **leagues. 1.** a group of sports teams that play against each other: the National Football *League,* a bowling *league.* **2.** a group of people or organizations joined for

L

a common purpose: the *League* of Women Voters. The *League* of Nations was an earlier form of the United Nations.

league² *noun, plural* **leagues.** a old measure of distance equal to about three miles, once used in European countries.

leak [lēk] *noun, plural* **leaks. 1.** a crack or hole that allows something to pass through by accident: a *leak* in a roof that lets in rain, a *leak* in a tire caused by a nail. **2.** information that was supposed to be secret, but that somehow becomes known: The President didn't want to announce the new Cabinet members yet, but there was a *leak* somewhere and all the newspapers got the story. —*verb,* **leaked, leaking.** to cause or have a leak. —**leaky,** *adjective.*

Leaning Tower The Leaning Tower of Pisa, a famous bell tower in Italy, looks like it is about to fall over, but it has stood this way for over 600 years.

lean¹ [lēn] *verb,* **leaned, leaning. 1.** to go at an angle; not be straight up and down: "Paul was *leaning* over Miss Price's shoulder examining her book." (Mary Norton) **2.** to rest against someone or something: "The boy crossed his knees and *leaned* back in his chair." (John Gardner) **3.** to count on for support; rely or depend: to *lean* on a friend during a difficult time. **4.** to have a tendency toward; favor: The jury hasn't decided yet, but everyone thinks they're *leaning* toward a guilty verdict.

lean² *adjective,* **leaner, leanest. 1.** having very little fat: a tall, *lean* basketball player. Round steak is a *lean* cut of meat. **2.** not producing or having enough; scarce: a *lean* harvest. This was a *lean* year for the movie business.

leap [lēp] *verb,* **leaped** or **leapt, leaping. 1.** to make a jump or spring, especially a high, sudden jump: "Porpoises *leaped* gracefully around us, some not twenty feet away." (Ernie Pyle) **2.** to make a sudden or eager move like this: "The electricity suddenly came on and the kitchen *leapt* into bright light." (Iris Murdoch) —*noun, plural* **leaps.** the act of leaping.

leap year a year with 366 days instead of 365. The extra day, February 29, is added every four years so that the calendar year will be the same as the time it takes the earth to circle the sun.

learn [lurn] *verb,* **learned, learning. 1.** to come to know something one did not know before, or be able to do something one could not do: to *learn* to read, to *learn* a foreign language. "'Fern,' he said gently, 'you will have to *learn* to control yourself.'" (E.B. White) **2.** to fix in the mind; memorize: The actor has to *learn* his lines for the play. **3.** to come to know or realize; find out: When we got there we *learned* that the tickets don't actually go on sale until tomorrow.

learn•ed [lur´nid] *adjective, more/most.* having or showing much education or knowledge: "He's been curing himself, you know. He's a very *learned* doctor." (Lewis Carroll)

learn•ing [lur´ning] *noun.* the act or process of learning, or the knowledge and skill that comes from this: Colleges and universities are referred to as institutions of higher *learning.*

learning disability a term used to describe various problems that cause a child to have difficulty learning things in school.

lease [lēs] *noun, plural* **leases.** a written agreement between the owner of property and someone who rents this property, stating the length of time the property will be rented and the amount to be paid. —*verb,* **leased, leasing.** to rent by means of a lease: Today many people *lease* new automobiles rather than buying them.

leash [lēsh] *noun, plural* **leashes.** a strap or chain fastened to a collar to lead or hold a dog or other animal. —*verb,* **leashed, leashing.** to hold or lead an animal with a leash.

least [lēst] *adjective.* the smallest: A penny is worth the *least* amount of any American coin.

Pronunciation Key: [ə] Symbol

The [ə] or *schwa* sound occurs in syllables without an accent. It can be spelled with any vowel, such as a in above, e in listen, i in pencil, o in melon, u in circus. It can also be a combination of vowels, such as io in action, ai in mountain, iou in precious.

(Turn the page for more information.)

—adverb. to the smallest amount: Franklin Pierce is one of the *least*-known American Presidents. *—noun.* **1.** the smallest in size or importance: The *least* you could do is say you're sorry. **2. at least. a.** not less than: She tries to get *at least* eight hours sleep a night. **b.** in any case; at any rate: They did beat us, but *at least* it was a close game.

leath•er [leth′ ər] *noun, plural* **leathers.** a material made by cleaning and tanning the skin of an animal. Leather is used to make shoes, belts, gloves, purses, jackets, and many other items. Most leather comes from cattle, though other animals are also used.

leave[1] [lēv] *verb,* **left, leaving. 1.** to go away from a place: Our train *leaves* in ten minutes. **2.** to withdraw from; quit: to *leave* school and get a job. **3.** to cause to be or stay in a certain place: to *leave* food on your plate, to *leave* footprints on the kitchen floor. **4.** to cause to be or stay in a certain condition: They *left* the window shades down while they were away. **5.** to give to someone else to do or use: "He *left* it to me to ask the questions." (V.S. Naipaul) **6.** to give to another when one dies, as in a will.

leave[2] *noun, plural* **leaves. 1.** official permission to be absent from work, school, or military duty: My cousin is home on *leave* from the Air Force. **2.** permission to do something.

ledge [lej] *noun, plural* **ledges. 1.** a narrow shelf that sticks out from a wall: a window *ledge.* **2.** a flat, narrow place like this on the side of a cliff or mountain.

Lee [lē] **Robert E.,** 1807–1870, American general, the leading commander of the Confederate Army during the Civil War.

Lee Robert E. Lee painted by the famous American artist N. C. Wyeth. General Lee rode this horse, Traveller, throughout the Civil War.

leave alone/let alone "I was to stick with the first grade and he would stick with the fifth. In short, I was to *leave* him *alone.*" (Harper Lee) "Can I have a little peace if I go down in the cellar? Will you *let* me *alone* then?" (James Thurber) One expert on usage, Bergen Evans, says that *leave alone* and *let alone* are equally correct. But another expert, Roy Copperud, argues that something is lost when *let alone* is not used. His reasoning is that *leave* has a stronger meaning, the sense of "go away." Thus an exact use of *leave alone* would be: "The rest of the class went inside and *left* him *alone* on the playground." Our recommendation is: Use either *let* or *leave alone,* whichever sounds more natural. But avoid "*leave* him be," "*leave* her do it by herself," and other such phrases for which *let* is clearly more correct.

leaves [lēvz] *noun.* the plural of **leaf.**

Leb•a•non [leb′ ə nən] a country in southwest Asia, on the Mediterranean Sea. *Capital:* Beirut. *Area:* 4,000 square miles. *Population:* 3,400,000. **—Lebanese,** *adjective; noun.*

lec•ture [lek′ chər] *noun, plural* **lectures. 1.** a prepared speech or talk given to an audience, especially as part of a course of study in a college. **2.** a serious talk that warns or scolds someone: Andy got a *lecture* from Mom about not leaving his toys all over the floor. *—verb,* **lectured, lecturing.** to give a lecture. **—lecturer,** *noun.*

led [led] *verb.* the past form of **lead.**

leech [lēch] *noun, plural* **leeches. 1.** a worm that lives in water and damp soil. It sucks the blood of other animals for food. **2.** *Slang.* a person who tries to gain money or favors from others without doing anything in return.

leek [lēk] *noun, plural* **leeks.** a vegetable related to the onion. A leek has long, thick green leaves and a narrow white bulb.

left[1] [left] *noun, plural* **lefts.** the opposite of the right; the side that the heart is on in the body, and that you start to read from on a line of words. *—adjective.* on or being the left: a *left* shoe. *—adverb.* to the left: to turn *left.*

left[2] *verb.* the past form of **leave.**

L

left-hand [left′ hand′] *adjective.* on or toward the left: Put that in the *left-hand* drawer.

left-hand·ed [left′ hand′ id] *adjective.* **1.** using the left hand more often or more easily than the right. **2.** done with or using the left hand: a *left-handed* shot in basketball. **3.** not as it usually is or as it should be: A "*left-handed* compliment" is one that actually turns out to be something of an insult.

left·o·ver [left′ ō′ vər] *noun, plural* **leftovers.** something that remains or is left, such as food after a meal. ♦ Also used as an adjective: Danny used some *leftover* wood to build a fort for his toy soldiers.

leg [leg] *noun, plural* **legs. 1.** one of the parts of the body that support a person or animal while standing or walking. **2.** the part of a piece of clothing that covers the leg. **3.** something that is shaped or used like a leg: the *leg* of a table. **4.** one part or stage of a trip or effort: Bob ran the first *leg* of the relay race.

le·gal [le′ gəl] *adjective.* **1.** having to do with the law: Mrs. Stacy went to a lawyer for *legal* advice when she decided to start her own business. **2.** according to law; allowed by law: a *legal* parking space.

2. like a legend; very famous: the *legendary* home run feats of Babe Ruth.

leg·i·ble [lej′ ə bəl] *adjective, more/most.* of writing or printing, able to be read; easy to read: *legible* handwriting. —**legibly,** *adverb:* Please type your answers or print them *legibly.*

legend The Robin Hood legend has come down from 12th-century England.

legends A *legend* is a story about a seemingly real person, usually one who performs amazing or heroic feats. There are famous legends of Robin Hood and his band of outlaws, and of King Arthur and his Knights of the Round Table. Arthur is thought to be modeled after several early British kings, and Robin Hood may be based on the life of an English nobleman. Legends can also tell of real people, as a way of showing their outstanding qualities. Often, the legend is good fun, good for its color and imagination. For example, it's known that George Washington was a strong man who could throw a heavy weight a great distance. It's also accepted as fact that he was very honest. However, it's certainly a legend that he once threw a silver dollar across a half-mile wide river, or that as a boy he said "I cannot tell a lie" when asked by his father who chopped down a cherry tree. From the point of view of the storyteller, a legend can be defined as "an improvement on the facts."

leg·end [lej′ ənd] *noun, plural* **legends. 1.** a story passed down by people over many years. A legend is usually not known to be true for certain but is based in some way on facts. Legends often tell about make-believe heroes such as Robin Hood, or tell make-believe stories about real heroes such as George Washington. **2.** a person who is very famous in a certain way, especially while still alive: Charles Lindbergh became a *legend* in his own time by making the first flight alone across the Atlantic.

leg·end·ar·y [lej′ ən der′ ē] *adjective, more/most.* **1.** having to do with legends: the *legendary* knights of King Arthur's Round Table.

le·gion [lē′ jən] *noun, plural* **legions. 1.** a large military unit of the ancient Roman army, made up of several thousand soldiers. **2.** any large military force. **3.** a very large number: The singer's London concerts are always sold out because she has *legions* of fans there.

Pronunciation Key: Accent Marks

[′] is the normal accent mark. It shows where the main stress falls on a word.
[′] is a secondary accent mark. It shows a lighter stress than the primary accent. For example:

tel • e • vis • ion [tel′ ə vizh′ ən]

(Turn the page for more information.)

L

leg•is•late [lej′ is lāt′] *verb*, **legislated, legislating.** to make or pass a law or laws. ♦ The act or fact of doing this is **legislation**: The city council is considering new *legislation* to ban smoking in public places.

leg•is•la•tive [lej′ is lā′ tiv] *adjective*. **1.** having the power to create and pass laws: In the United States, Congress is the *legislative* branch of the federal government. **2.** having to do with the making of laws.

leg•is•la•tor [lej′ is lā′ tər] *noun*, *plural* **legislators.** a person who makes laws; someone who belongs to a law-making body.

leg•is•la•ture [lej′ is lā′ chər] *noun*, *plural* **legislatures.** a group of people elected to create and pass laws: a state *legislature*.

le•git•i•mate [lə jit′ ə mit] *adjective*, *more/most*. **1.** according to the law; legal: The court ruled that she had a *legitimate* claim to the property. **2.** according to what is right or proper: She had a *legitimate* reason for missing school today. **—legitimately**, *adverb*.

lei Visitors to Hawaii are often greeted by island girls who present them with flower leis.

lei [lā *or* lā′ē] *noun*, *plural* **leis.** a wreath of fresh flowers worn around the neck, especially one worn as a custom in Hawaii.

lei•sure [lē′ zhər *or* lezh′ ər] *noun*. a condition or time of not having to work; free time to do as one wishes: Golf and fishing are popular *leisure*-time activities in the U.S. **—leisurely**, *adjective*: "Learn to live at a *leisurely* pace. You live longer." (Lanford Wilson)

lem•on [lem′ ən] *noun*, *plural* **lemons. 1.** a juicy yellow fruit that has a sour taste. Lemons grow on trees in warm climates and are related to grapefruits, oranges, and limes. **2.** a bright yellow color like that of a lemon. **3.** *Informal*. a car or other machine that is badly made or has many things wrong with it.

lem•on•ade [lem′ ən ād′] *noun*, *plural* **lemonades.** a drink made of lemon juice, sugar, and water.

lend [lend] *verb*, **lent, lending. 1.** to let someone have or use something for a while: Uncle Dave *lent* us his car while ours was being fixed. **2.** to give someone money that is to be paid back by a stated time, usually at a certain rate of INTEREST: The bank is going to *lend* them the money to build an extra bedroom on their house. **3.** to give or add; provide: The fireworks show should *lend* a lot of excitement to the evening. "A mop of straw-colored hair *lent* his face a boyish look." (Ian Fleming)

length [length] *noun*, *plural* **lengths. 1.** the distance of a thing from one end to the other end: The *length* of the boat is sixteen feet. **2.** the amount of time from beginning to end; the time something lasts: The movie was about two hours in *length*. **3.** a piece of something that is long: a *length* of rope. **4.** the fact or condition of being long: I was able to get through the book quickly, in spite of its *length*. **5.** the extent to which something is taken or carried out: That movie star has gone to great *lengths* to keep unwanted visitors away from her home.

length•en [length′ ən] *verb*, **lengthened, lengthening.** to make or become longer: "Jake *lengthened* his stride and crossed the road . . ." (Kingsley Amis) "The shadows *lengthened* and the wind grew *chilly*." (J.M. Coetzee)

length•wise [length′ wīz] *adverb; adjective:* in the direction of the length: The hallway measures 32 feet *lengthwise*.

leng•thy [leng′ thē] *adjective*, *more/most*. very long; too long: Cuban leader Fidel Castro is known for giving *lengthy* speeches, and once spoke at the UN for almost five hours.

len•ient [lēn yənt *or* le′nē ənt] *adjective*, *more/most*. not strict or harsh in dealing with someone under one's authority: a *lenient* parent. "Most of his professors were *lenient* and helped him along." (James Thurber)

Le•nin [len′ in] **Vladimir Ilyich (Nikolai),** 1870–1924, Russian communist leader, the first ruler of the Soviet Union.

Len•in•grad [len′ ən grad] a city in the northwest Soviet Union, by the Gulf of Finland. *Population:* 4,100,000.

lens [lenz] *noun*, *plural* **lenses. 1.** a piece of glass or other material that is curved to make light rays move apart or come together. A lens can make objects look larger or closer. Lenses are used in cameras, eyeglasses, telescopes, and so on. **2.** the clear, colorless part of the eye that focuses light rays onto the RETINA.

lent [lent] *verb.* the past form of **lend.**

Lent [lent] *noun.* in the Christian religion, a period of forty days before Easter. In some Christian churches Lent is a season of fasting and of denying oneself certain pleasures.

butter on her food lately. —*adverb.* to a smaller amount: He decided to take the *less*-traveled side road instead of the main highway. —*preposition.* minus; without: The new car will cost about $10,000, *less* $2,000 for trading in our old car. —*noun.* a smaller amount or part; something that is less.

less•en [les′ ən] *verb,* **lessened, lessening.** to make or become less.

less/fewer *Less* applies to things that can't be counted as single units: "She's trying to use *less* salt on her food." You can't say "fewer salt." *Fewer* applies to individual things that can be counted: "Unfortunately *fewer* than seven paying customers showed up." (John J. O'Connor, *New York Times* critic). We studied many examples of these two words for this dictionary. We find that in all kinds of writing, people now tend to use *less*, whatever the situation: "But *less* than 100 miles to the north . . ." (Robert Lindsay, news reporter) "*Less* than 200 Texans occupied the fort." (Joseph Conlin, historian) There are several common phrases that use *less*, even though strictly it should be *fewer*: No one ever writes "25 words or *fewer*," or "ten miles, more or *fewer*." We suggest you "follow your ear" rather than trying to figure out whether a certain quantity can be counted. Use *fewer* only when it sounds natural.

Leonardo A self-portrait by Leonardo da Vinci.

Le•o•nar•do da Vin•ci [lē′ ə när′ dō də vin′- chē] 1452–1519, Italian painter, sculptor, architect, engineer, and scientist.

leop•ard [lep′ ərd] *noun, plural* **leopards.** a large wild cat that lives in Africa and Asia. Most leopards have a yellowish coat with black spots, but a few are all black.

le•o•tard [lē′ ə tärd′] *noun, plural* **leotards.** a thin, one-piece garment that stretches to fit tightly over the body from the shoulders to the hips, worn for dancing, exercising, and so on.

less [les] *adjective.* not as great in amount; not as much: She's been trying to use *less* salt and

less•er [les′ ər] *adjective, adverb.* being smaller; of less size or amount: to choose the *lesser* of two evils in a situation. She enjoys visiting *lesser*-known vacation spots.

les•son [les′ ən] *noun, plural* **lessons. 1.** something to be learned in school; an exercise, reading, or other activity that is assigned and taught: a math *lesson.* **2.** any form of study or instruction to learn something or to gain some skill: swimming *lessons,* driving *lessons,* piano *lessons.* **3.** an experience or event in life that gives knowledge or understanding: After his accident, Jeff learned his *lesson* and drove more carefully.

let [let] *verb,* **let, letting. 1.** to cause to happen or be willing to have happen; allow or permit: Mom *let* us stay up late to watch the end of the movie. **2.** to allow to move or go in a certain way: to *let* a dog into the house, to *let* air out of a tire. **3.** to rent: a room to *let.*

le•thal [lē′ thəl] *adjective, more/most.* able to cause death; deadly: A knife is a *lethal* weapon.

let's [lets] the contraction for "let us:" *Let's* stop for lunch in the next town.

Pronunciation Key: A–F			
a	and; hat	ch	chew; such
ā	ate; stay	d	dog; lid
â	care; air	e	end; yet
ä	father; hot	ē	she; each
b	boy; cab	f	fun; off

(Turn the page for more information.)

L

let·ter [let′ ər] *noun, plural* **letters. 1.** a mark or sign that stands for a speech sound and is used to spell words. The word "lettuce" has seven letters. **2.** a written message: I received a *letter* in the mail from my cousin yesterday. —*verb,* **lettered, lettering.** to mark with letters: On the door was a sign with 'KEEP OUT' *lettered* in red.

let·tuce [let′ əs] *noun, plural* **lettuces.** a plant with large green leaves. Several different kinds of lettuce are eaten in salads and in sandwiches.

leu·ke·mi·a [loo kē′ mē ə] *noun.* a very serious blood disease in which the body makes too many white blood cells.

lev·ee [lev′ ē] *noun, plural* **levees.** a wall built up along a river bank to keep the water from overflowing during a flood.

lev·el [lev′ əl] *adjective.* **1.** having a flat surface: to build a house on *level* ground. **2.** at the same height or position: She cut the top of the rose bush so that it was *level* with the fence. **3.** steady; even: to speak in a *level* tone of voice. —*noun, plural* **levels. 1.** something that is level, especially one floor or story of a building. **2.** the height of something: Mountains are measured according to distance above sea *level.* **3.** the position of something in a rank or scale: All the students in that class can read at their proper grade *level.* **4.** a device used to show whether or not something is level. —*verb,* **leveled, leveling. 1.** to make level: They *leveled* the ground to make a soccer field. **2.** to knock down to the ground; tear down: The wrecking crew *leveled* the old building to make way for a new shopping center. **3.** to deal with in a straight, direct way; be honest: "Well, you see Brooke, I might as well *level* with you. There are three other girls . . . who gave good readings too." (Bonnie Zindel)

lev·er [lev′ ər *or* lēv′ ər] *noun, plural* **levers. 1.** a rod or bar used to lift things or to pry things open. When a lever is used to lift something, it is supported between the two ends by a fixed object called a **fulcrum** [ful′ krəm], and is pushed down on one end to raise the weight at the other end. **2.** a rod or bar that is moved to control or operate a machine: a gearshift or parking brake *lever* in a car.

lev·y [lev′ ē] *verb,* **levied, levying.** to order to be paid: to *levy* a tax; to *levy* a fine.

Lew·is [loo′ is] **Meriwether,** 1774–1809, American explorer who with **William Clark,** 1770–1838, explored the western U.S.

Lewis & Clark A painting of Lewis and Clark with their guide, the Indian woman Sacajewa.

Lex·ing·ton [lek′ sing tən] a town in eastern Massachusetts, near Boston, where the first battle of the American Revolution was fought.

li·a·bil·i·ty [lī ə bil′ ə tē] *noun, plural* **liabilities. 1.** the fact of being liable for some wrong or crime: *Liability* insurance pays money to the victim of an accident. **2.** the fact of being likely. **3. liabilities.** all the money that a person or business owes; debts. **4.** something that hinders or holds back; a disadvantage: The car's lack of power is a real *liability* on these hilly roads.

li·a·ble [lī′ bəl] *adjective, more/most.* **1.** responsible by law; legally bound to pay: If a child destroys someone's property the parents are *liable* for the damage done. **2.** likely: Don't put those glasses so close to the edge; they're *liable* to fall off. "A sheep-herder gets company so seldom that when he does get a chance to talk he's *liable* to say almost anything." (Ernie Pyle)

li•ar [lī′ ər] *noun, plural* **liars.** a person who tells lies.

li•brar•y [lī′ brer′ ē *or* lī′ brâr′ ē] *noun, plural* **libraries. 1.** a room or building where a large collection of books is kept for public or general use. Modern libraries also have magazines, newspapers, records, films, videotapes, and so on. **2.** a collection of books in a person's home. **3.** any large collection of films, photos, records, or the like.

library When you write a report, the encyclopedias and other reference books in a library are important to you, as are biographies and histories and books on current affairs. But you shouldn't rely only on factual books. Suppose you're writing a paper on the Great Depression of the 1930's. Your public library may also have a file of magazines and newspapers that were published in the 1930's. Look into them; that way you can examine direct evidence about the period. You may also want to read a novel or play written in the period—your librarian can help you find one. Your library might have special local materials about the 1930's, such as a history of your city, or a collection of "oral history" tapes.

lib•er•al [lib′ rəl *or* lib′ ər əl] *adjective, more/most.* **1.** wanting to make changes in something with the goal of improving it; in favor of change. In politics, people who are liberal generally believe that the government should take an active role in human affairs and create new laws and programs that will solve social problems. **2.** willing to give freely; generous: Mr. Adams has been a *liberal* supporter of the local art museum. **3.** not exact or strict: A *liberal* translation of the French phrase "c'est la vie" is "that's the way it goes." —*noun, plural* **liberals.** a person who is liberal, especially in politics. —**liberally,** *adverb.*

lib•er•ate [lib′ ə rāt] *verb,* **liberated, liberating.** to set free: The Germans took over the city of Paris during World War II, but it was *liberated* by the Allies in August 1944. —**liberator,** *noun:* Simon Bolivar is known as 'The *Liberator*' because of his role in freeing South America from Spanish rule.

Li•be•ri•a [lī bēr′ ē ə] a country in western Africa. *Capital:* Monrovia. *Area:* 43,000. *Population:* 2,100,000. —**Liberian,** *adjective; noun.*

lib•er•ty [lib′ ər tē] *noun, plural* **liberties. 1.** the state of being free from the control or rule of others; being able to act, speak, and think as one wishes. **2.** a certain type of freedom; a right or power to do something. **Civil liberties** in the U.S. are the rights granted to citizens by the Constitution. **3.** the fact of being free of control or restrictions. "School was recently over for the summer, and the feeling of *liberty* sat uneasily on most of them." (Shirley Jackson)

li•brar•i•an [lī brer′ ē ən *or* lī brâr′ ē ən] *noun, plural* **librarians.** someone who is in charge of a library, or someone who works at a library.

Lib•ya [lib′ ē ə] a country in northern Africa, on the Mediterranean. *Capital:* Tripoli. *Area:* 679,400. *Population:* 3,300,000. —**Libyan,** *adjective; noun.*

lice [līs] *noun.* the plural of **louse.**

li•cense [lī′ sens] *noun, plural* **licenses. 1.** legal permission to do or own something, given by a government body: People need a *license* to do such things as drive a car, own a dog, get married, operate a business, and so on. **2.** the card, paper, or other document that gives proof of this permission. **3.** freedom that is taken too far; too much freedom. —*verb,* **licensed, licensing.** to give a license to a person: A doctor must be *licensed* to practice medicine.

li•chen [lī′ kən] *noun, plural* **lichens.** a small plant without flowers that grows on rocks, trees, or along the ground.

lick [lik] *verb,* **licked, licking. 1.** to pass the tongue over: to *lick* an ice cream cone, a cat *licking* its paws. **2.** *Informal.* to defeat: "That means he has won first prize. I guess you're *licked,* Wilbur." (E.B. White) —*noun, plural* **licks. 1.** a movement of the tongue over something. **2.** *also,* **salt lick.** a natural salt deposit that animals can lick. **3.** *Informal.* a small amount: Get Joe to help you move those boxes —he hasn't done a *lick* of work all day.

Pronunciation Key: G–N			
g	give; big	k	kind; cat; back
h	hold	l	let; ball
i	it; this	m	make; time
ī	ice; my	n	not; own
j	jet; gem; edge	ng	having

(Turn the page for more information.)

L

lic•o•rice [lik′ə rish *or* lik′ rish] *noun.* **1.** a black, sweet-tasting flavoring that is made from the roots of a certain plant. **2.** candy that is flavored with licorice.

lid [lid] *noun, plural* **lids. 1.** a movable cover for a container; a top: the *lid* of a garbage can. **2.** an eyelid.

lie¹ [lī] *verb,* **lay, lain, lying. 1.** to put one's body in a flat position on a surface: to *lie* in bed. **2.** to be or rest on a surface: "Soon her eye fell on a little glass box that was *lying* under the table." (Lewis Carroll) **3.** to be in a certain place or condition: "Lambert Field *lies* in farming country . . ." (Charles Lindbergh) **4.** to be found; be; exist: "Only a hundred years *lies* between the age of electricity and the age of steam." (Arthur C. Clarke)

lie² *noun, plural* **lies.** something that a person says, knowing that it is not true. —*verb,* **lied, lying.** to tell a lie.

lieu•ten•ant [lōō ten′ ənt] *noun, plural* **lieutenants. 1.** a military or police officer ranking next below a captain. In the army, the two ranks of lieutenant are **first lieutenant** and **second lieutenant.** In the navy, the two ranks are **lieutenant** and **lieutenant junior grade. 2.** someone who acts on behalf of a higher authority; a deputy: The president of the company sent two of his *lieutenants* to check on the problems.

life [līf] *noun, plural* **lives. 1.** the quality that makes people, plants, and animals different from rocks, machines, and other such things. Something that has life can develop young like itself and can grow in size until it reaches adult form. It can move its body about or have movement within the body, and react to its surroundings. **2.** the time between birth and death; one's lifetime. **3.** a living person: More than 1500 *lives* were lost when the *Titanic* sank. **4.** living things as a group: This book deals with animal *life* in Australia. **5.** the period during which something is in use or in effect: the *life* of a car, the *life* of a contract or a loan. **6.** energy; spirit: Marty is always the *life* of the party. **7.** a particular way of living: a quiet *life, life* in colonial New England. **8.** human existence in general: "When a man is tired of London, he is tired of *life* . . ." (Samuel Johnson)

life•boat [līf′ bōt′] *noun, plural* **lifeboats.** an open boat used for saving lives at sea. Lifeboats are carried on large boats or ships.

life•guard [līf′ gärd′] *noun, plural* **lifeguards.** a person who works at a beach or swimming pool to rescue swimmers or protect them from danger.

life•less [līf′ lis] *adjective.* without life; having no life or spirit: "And he had not thought his fingers could go *lifeless* in so short a time." (Jack London) "His voice had turned dull and *lifeless,* and Laurie knew the disappointment that was in him." (Edward S. Fox)

life•like [līf′ līk′] *adjective, more/most.* looking as if alive; copying real life: a *lifelike* painting.

life•long [līf′ lông′] *adjective.* for all one's life; lasting through life: a *lifelong* friend.

life preserver an article worn around the body to keep a person floating in water, such as a **life jacket** or **life belt.**

life-size [līf′ sīz′] *adjective.* of the same size as the person or thing being shown: a *life-size* statue.

life•time [līf′ tīm′] *noun, plural* **lifetimes.** the period of time a person lives or a thing lasts; the time of being alive.

lift [lift] *verb,* **lifted, lifting. 1.** to raise into the air; take to a higher position; pick up: She *lifted* the suitcase and put it in the trunk of the car. "A car sped past, *lifting* a great cloud of yellow-brown dust." (Richard Wright) **2.** to rise and go; go away: "The morning fog had *lifted,* giving way to a clear day." (Marguerite Henry) **3.** to go up; be raised to a higher level: Their spirits were *lifted* by the news that help was on the way. —*noun, plural* **lifts. 1.** the act of lifting. **2.** a ride in a car or other vehicle: Can you give me a *lift* to the post office? **3.** a happy feeling; a rise in spirits: Grandma likes to have a cup of tea because she says it gives her a *lift.* **4.** a machine or device for lifting. **5.** a moving cable with seats attached: The ski *lift* takes skiers to the top of the mountain.

lift-off [lift′ ôf′] *noun, plural* **lift-offs.** the firing or takeoff of a rocket or spacecraft.

lifeboat This cruise ship is equipped with enough lifeboats (seen hanging on the side) to hold all of the passengers and crew in case of an emergency.

lig·a·ment [lig′ ə mənt] *noun, plural* **ligaments.** a band of strong tissues that connects bones or holds organs of the body in place.

light[1] [līt] *noun, plural* **lights. 1.** the form of energy that makes it possible for us to see, given off by the sun, an electric bulb, and so on. **2.** anything that gives off light, especially an electric lamp: Turn off the *lights* downstairs when you go to bed. **3.** something used to set fire to something else: She asked him to give her a *light* for her cigarette. **4.** a way of seeing or regarding something: to shed new *light* on a problem, to look at something in a different *light.*
—*verb,* **lit** or **lighted, lighting. 1.** to burn or cause to burn: "He *lit* a fire in the stove." (Leslie Silko) "Royal *lighted* a candle . . ." (Laura Ingalls Wilder) **2.** to make bright; give brightness to: One 100-watt bulb will *light* the whole room well enough. **3.** to make or become lively or bright: A smile *lit* up Carol's face when she recognized her old friend. —*adjective,* **lighter, lightest. 1.** not dark; bright: It gets *light* about 6:30 AM at this time of year. **2.** pale in color: Her hair is *light* brown—almost blonde.

light[2] *adjective,* **lighter, lightest. 1.** having little weight; not heavy: a *light* cotton shirt. Feathers and sponges are *light.* **2.** having less than the usual weight for its kind: a *light* truck. Aluminum is a *light* metal. **3.** small in amount or degree: a *light* meal, a *light* snowfall, a person who is a *light* sleeper. **4.** moving easily; graceful: The gymnast was *light* on her feet. **5.** not serious; meant to entertain: Dad likes *light* reading such as spy stories and Westerns. **6.** low in fat or calories: *light* beer, canned fruit in *light* syrup. —*adverb.* in a light way: Mark always travels *light* when he goes camping and carries everything in one small pack. —**lightly,** *adverb:* "She laughed *lightly* and clapped her hands . . ." (Walter Farley) —**lightness,** *noun.*

light[3] *verb,* **lighted** or **lit, lighting.** to come down from flight: "Two ravens came flying and *lit* in the tree above him." (Howard Pyle)

light·en[1] [līt′ ən] *verb,* **lightened, lightening.** to make or become lighter or less dark; brighten.

light·en[2] *verb,* **lightened, lightening. 1.** to make less heavy; make lighter: The boss *lightened* her work load because she had too much to do. **2.** to make or become more cheerful.

light·er [lī′ tər] *noun, plural* **lighters. 1.** a device that produces a small flame to light a cigarette or cigar. **2.** a person or thing that lights. In the old days of gas lamps, a lamp*light-er* went around and lit the street lamps.

light-heart·ed [līt′ här′ tid] *adjective, more/most.* cheerful and carefree; without worry: "They laughed until they were weak. It was good to be *light-hearted* . . ." (Marjorie Kinnan Rawlings) —**lightheartedness,** *noun.*

lighthouse The North Head Lighthouse at the entrance to the Columbia River in Washington.

light·house [līt′ hous′] *noun, plural* **lighthouses.** a tower with a very bright, powerful light at the top. Lighthouses are built along the coast near dangerous places in the water, so that their light can warn and guide ships.

light·ning [līt′ ning] *noun.* a sudden flash of light in the sky. Lightning is formed by a powerful charge of electricity between clouds, or between clouds and the ground. This electric charge also produces the sound of thunder.

lightning Summer lightning over a Pennsylvania farm.

Pronunciation Key: O–S			
ō	over; go	ou	out; town
ô	all; law	p	put; hop
oo	look; full	r	run; car
ōō	pool; who	s	set; miss
oi	oil; boy	sh	show

(Turn the page for more information.)

L

lightning rod a metal rod that is attached to the top of a building to protect it against damage from lightning, by conducting the electric charge harmlessly into the ground.

light pen a pen-shaped device that is connected to a computer by a wire that sends a tiny beam of light. A light pen is used to give information directly to the computer.

light year the distance that light travels in one year. A light year is almost six trillion miles. Light years are used in measuring very great distances in space, such as the distance between stars or planets.

lik•a•ble [līk′ ə bəl] (also spelled **likeable**) *adjective, more/most.* easy to like; pleasant.

like•ly [līk′ lē] *adjective,* **likelier, likeliest.** **1.** more or less certain to happen; to be expected; probable: Dark clouds in the sky mean it's *likely* to rain. **2.** seeming to be true; reliable: His story just doesn't sound *likely*. **3.** right for the time or purpose; fitting: a *likely* spot for a picnic. —*adverb.* probably.

like•ness [līk′ nis] *noun, plural* **likenesses.** **1.** the fact of being alike. **2.** a copy or picture: "I knew she would hate to have her *likeness* taken. For nearly forty years she had refused to be photographed." (Mary McCarthy)

like•wise [līk′ wiz] *adverb.* in the same way; also: The coach stood with his arms spread wide and told the players to do *likewise*.

---

like/as In the 1960's, a TV commercial featured the line, "Winstons taste good, *like* a cigarette should." Then, a new version appeared. A young man said the same line, but an older man, an "English professor" type, wagged his finger in a scolding way and said, "You mean, *as* a cigarette should." This misuse of *like* became so famous a mistake that language purists now say, making fun of an awkward usage, "That sounds *like* a Winston ad." What then is the mistake? *Like* is a preposition: "The wind through the fir trees made a sound *like* a human voice." (Ernie Pyle) (Here, it joins the noun phrase "a human voice" to the rest of the sentence.) *Like* as a conjunction should be avoided. Here's a usage that can be improved: "Because, *like* they say, it's better to give. And receive." (Ad for Apple Computers) This would be better if it read, "as they say." Now a correct example: "She glanced around the glowing room *as if* someone might be watching her." (E.M. Forster)

---

like¹ [līk] *verb,* **liked, liking. 1.** to feel good toward something or someone; be fond of; enjoy: to *like* ice cream, to *like* to read. **2.** to feel about; judge; regard: How did you *like* that movie? **3.** to want; wish: Would you *like* some more cake? The principal would *like* to see you in her office. —**likes,** *plural noun.* the things a person enjoys or favors.

like² *preposition.* **1.** being the same as something else in some way; similar; alike: Carrie looks a lot *like* her older sister. **2.** what one expects of; typical of: It's just *like* Larry to forget his homework. **3.** much the same as; in the same way as: "I was *like* a child again, learning everything for the first time." (Jamake Highwater) **4.** for example; such as: Collectors pay huge prices for paintings by famous artists *like* Van Gogh and Picasso. **5.** in the manner or condition stated: Do you feel *like* eating out tonight? It looks *like* rain. —*adjective, more/most.* exactly or nearly the same. —*noun.* **1.** a person or thing like another; an equal. **2. and the like.** and others of the same kind; and so on: peas, beans, corn, *and the like*.

like•li•hood [līk′ lē hood′] *noun, plural* **likelihoods.** the fact of being likely; probability.

li•lac [lī′ läk] *noun, plural* **lilacs. 1.** a bush with clusters of tiny, sweet-smelling purple, pink, or white flowers. **2.** a pale pinkish-purple color.

lily The white Washington lily (left), wood lily (right), and tiger lily (below).

lil•y [lil′ ē] *noun, plural* **lilies. 1.** a plant with large, brightly-colored flowers shaped somewhat like a bell. The lily grows from a bulb and has narrow leaves. Common types include the white **Easter lily** and the orange **tiger lily. 2.** any other plant like a lily, such as the WATER LILY.

lily of the valley a plant that has small, bell-shaped white flowers growing down one side of its stem.

Li•ma [lē′mə] the capital and largest city of Peru. *Population:* 2,900,000.

li•ma bean [lī′mə] a flat, pale green bean that is cooked and eaten as a vegetable.

limb [lim] *noun, plural* **limbs. 1.** one of the larger branches growing out from the trunk of a tree. **2.** a leg, arm, or other such body part.

lim•ber [lim′bər] *adjective, more/most.* able to move or bend easily; flexible: "His shoulders and arms were still strong and *limber* . . ." (Laurence Yep) —*verb,* **limbered, limbering.** (used with **up**) to make or become limber.

lime[1] [līm] *noun, plural* **limes.** the light-green, juicy fruit of a certain tree that grows in warm climates. Limes are related to lemons and oranges and have a sour taste.

lime[2] *noun.* a white powder made up of calcium and oxygen. Lime is made by burning limestone. It is used for such purposes as making cement, glass, fertilizer, and insect poison.

lim•er•ick [lim′rik] *noun, plural* **limericks.** a humorous poem that has five lines. The first and second lines both rhyme with the last line. The third and fourth lines are shorter in length and rhyme with each other.

lime•stone [līm′stōn′] *noun, plural* **limestones.** a type of rock that is used for building and for making lime. Limestone is formed mainly from the shells and bones of sea animals.

lim•it [lim′it] *noun, plural* **limits. 1.** the farthest edge or point that one can go to; the point where something stops: I thought we should run another lap around the track, but Dad said four was his *limit.* **2.** *also,* **limits.** the edge or boundary of a certain area: the Detroit city *limits.* **3.** the greatest amount or number that is officially allowed: The speed *limit* on this highway is 55 miles per hour. —*verb,* **limited, limiting.** to set a limit: "What are your questions? Please remember that our time is *limited.*" (Isaac Asimov) ♦ Something that limits is a **limitation.**

lim•ou•sine [lim′ə zēn′] *noun, plural* **limousines.** a very large and expensive automobile that usually has a glass panel between the front and back seats. Limousines are driven by a paid driver while the passengers sit in back.

limp[1] [limp] *verb,* **limped, limping.** to walk in an uneven way, with less weight on one leg, usually because of pain or injury. —*noun, plural* **limps.** a limping walk or movement.

limp[2] *adjective,* **limper, limpest.** not stiff or firm; drooping: "Then his breath explodes out of him, and he falls back *limp* against the wall." (Ken Kesey) —**limply,** *adverb:* "He held out his hand and David shook hands *limply.*" (Shirley Jackson)

Lin•coln [ling′kən] **Abraham,** 1809–1865, the sixteenth president of the United States, from 1861 to 1865.

Lind•bergh [lind′burg′] **1. Charles,** 1902–1974, American aviator who was the first to fly across the Atlantic alone. **2.** his wife, **Anne Morrow Lindbergh,** born 1906, American author.

Lindbergh Charles A. Lindbergh and his wife, Anne Morrow Lindbergh.

line[1] [līn] *noun, plural* **lines. 1.** a long, thin mark: a white *line* down the middle of a highway. Notebook paper has *lines* to write on. **2.** a long, thin piece of string, rope, or the like: a fishing *line,* a clothes*line,* a telephone *line.* **3.** a border or edge marked by or as if by a line: Eric was the first runner to cross the finish *line.* **4.** a wrinkle or mark on the skin. **5.** a group of people or things side by side or one behind the other: They stood in *line* all day to get tick-

Pronunciation Key: T–Z			
t	ten; date	v	very; live
th	think	w	win; away
th	these	y	you
u	cut; butter	z	zoo; cause
ur	turn; bird	zh	measure

(Turn the page for more information.)

ets for the rock concert. **6.** a row of words on a page: *A sonnet is a poem with 14* lines. **7. lines.** the words spoken by an actor or actress. **8.** a system of transportation: *a bus* line, *a rail* line, *an air*line. **9.** a type of goods for sale: *a* line *of clothes.* **10.** a person's job or business: *What* line *of work is he in?* **11.** in football, the group of players who stand alongside the ball at the start of a play. —*verb,* **lined, lining. 1.** to mark with lines: *to* line *a baseball field.* **2.** to form into a line; place or arrange in line: "*Every street is* lined *and double-*lined *with trees.*" (Doris Lessing) ♦ Often used with **up.**

line² *verb,* **lined, lining. 1.** to cover the inside of: *to* line *gloves with fur. We put away the Christmas ornaments in a box* lined *with newspaper.* **2.** to be used as a lining or covering for: "*The walls were* lined *with TV screens.*" (Donald Sobol)

lin•e•ar [lin′ ē ər] *adjective.* **1.** made of lines; using a line or lines. **2.** having to do with length: *Feet and miles are* linear *measurements.*

lin•en [lin′ ən] *noun, plural* **linens. 1.** a strong cloth made from the stalks of a plant called FLAX. Linen is used to make dresses, suits, and tablecloths. **2.** *also,* **linens.** household articles such as tablecloths, sheets, towels, and napkins, made of linen or a similar fabric.

lin•er¹ [lī′ nər] *noun, plural* **liners.** a ship or airplane that carries passengers on a regular route: *The* Queen Mary *is a famous ocean* liner.

liner² *noun, plural* **liners.** something used as a lining: *a trash can* liner.

line•up [līn′ up′] *noun, plural* **lineups. 1.** a line of people arranged by the police so that a victim or witness can identify a suspect in a crime. **2.** a list of the players who are taking part in a game.

lin•ger [ling′ ər] *verb,* **lingered, lingering.** to stay on longer than usual; move or go away slowly: "*He* lingered *on the corner awhile, not pressed for time.*" (Booth Tarkington) "*The last note echoed from the halls of the Ritz and* lingered *over the Public Garden.*" (E.B. White)

lin•ing [lī′ ning] *noun, plural* **linings.** a layer of material that covers the inside surface of something: *the* lining *of a coat.*

link [link] *noun, plural* **links. 1.** a ring or loop that is part of a chain. **2.** something that is like a link in a chain; a connection: links *of sausage.* Some men's shirts are fastened with cuff links rather than buttons. **3.** anything that joins things as if by a chain: *This old photo album is a* link *to the past.* —*verb,* **linked, linking.** to join or connect: *The Golden Gate Bridge* links *San Francisco to Marin County.*

li•no•le•um [lin ōl′ ē əm] *noun, plural* **linoleums.** a smooth floor covering that is made of a mixture of linseed oil and ground wood put on a cloth backing.

lin•seed oil [lin′ sēd] *noun.* a yellowish oil that comes from the seed of the FLAX plant, used to make paints, linoleum, varnishes, and ink.

lint [lint] *noun.* tiny bits of thread or fluffy material from yarn or cloth. Lint often collects on clothes in a washing machine or a dryer.

lion Lions live together in a large group called a *pride.* The female lion, or *lioness* (below), does most of the hunting, while the male (above) guards the territory of the pride.

li•on [lī′ ən] *noun, plural* **lions.** a large, powerful animal of the cat family that lives in Africa. A few lions are also found in India. Lions have a smooth brown coat and a long tail. A male lion has a shaggy mane around the neck, head, and shoulders.

lip [lip] *noun, plural* **lips. 1.** one of the two movable folds of flesh that form the opening to the mouth. **2.** the edge or rim of a container or opening: *the* lip *of a coffee mug.*

lip•stick [lip′ stik] *noun, plural* **lipsticks.** a stick of wax and coloring used to color the lips.

liq•uid [lik′ wid] *noun, plural* **liquids.** one of the three basic forms of matter; something that is not a GAS or a SOLID. A liquid differs from a solid in that it flows freely and will fit the shape of its container. It differs from a gas in that it has a definite volume and will not expand to fill the container. A liquid will become a gas if heated to a certain point, or a solid if cooled to a certain point. —*adjective.* in the form of a

L

liquid: *liquid* crystal, *liquid* oxygen. This medicine comes either as pills or in *liquid* form.

liq•uor [lik′ ər] *noun, plural* **liquors.** a strong alcoholic drink such as gin, vodka, or scotch.

lit•er [lēt′ ər] *noun, plural* **liters.** (also spelled **litre**) a basic unit of measure for liquid in the metric system. A liter is equal to about 1.06 quarts of liquid.

> **literal meaning** The *literal* meaning of a word is its basic and obvious and familiar one, the one you'll find in the dictionary. For example: "When ice melts, it turns into a *liquid*, water." That is a literal use of the word *liquid*. But words can also move away from their literal sense: "On hot summer nights, we'd sit on the porch and listen to the Dodger game from the radio inside. Red Barber's *liquid* voice would flow gently across the night air." This is a figurative use of the word *liquid* (see FIGURATIVE). It takes the literal idea of *liquid* meaning "water," but applies it to something that cannot actually flow like water.

Lis•bon [liz′ bən] the capital of Portugal. *Population:* 800,000.

lisp [lisp] *noun, plural* **lisps.** a way of saying the sounds of "s" and "z" improperly, to sound like "th" in "them" or "thing." —*verb,* **lisped, lisping.** to speak with a lisp.

list¹ [list] *noun, plural* **lists.** a series of names, numbers, or other things written one after the other as a record of information: Mom makes a shopping *list* when she goes to the supermarket. They sent the letter to everyone whose name was on the mailing *list.* —*verb,* **listed, listing.** to make a list of; enter in a list.

list² *noun, plural* **lists.** a tilt or slant to one side. —*verb,* **listed, listing:** The ship was *listing* badly after it got stuck on a sand bar.

lit•er•al [lit′ ər əl] *adjective, more/most.* following the exact wording or meaning; word for word: A personal attack on someone is said to be "ad hominem;" this is a Latin expression whose *literal* meaning is "to the man."

lit•er•al•ly [lit′ ər ə lē] *adverb.* **1.** using words according to their exact or strict meaning: If you said, "He told a few jokes to break the ice," you would not be using the word "ice" *literally.* **2.** really; actually: "It was not hard for Alec to believe that the horse the natives called 'Firetail' could *literally* walk the sky." (Walter Farley)

lit•er•ar•y [lit′ ər rer′ ē] *adjective, more/most.* having to do with literature: Edmund Wilson is a famous American *literary* critic.

> **literary style** Compare how two British writers describe visits to foreign places: "My gentleness and good behavior had gained so far on the emperor and his court, and indeed upon the army and people in general, that I began to conceive hopes of getting my liberty in a short time. I took all possible methods to cultivate this favorable disposition." "You couldn't keep any secrets for five hours in this border town. Lucia had only been twenty-four hours in the place, but she knew all about Mr. Joseph Calloway. The only reason I didn't know about him (and I'd been in the place two weeks) was because I couldn't talk the language any more than Mr. Calloway could." The first example shows the literary style of the 18th-century author Jonathan Swift, the second the plain style of the modern author Graham Greene. "Literary style" means graceful, polished, carefully-phrased writing.

lis•ten [lis′ ən] *verb,* **listened, listening.** to try to hear; to pay attention in order to hear: to *listen* to music, to *listen* to what someone is saying. —**listener,** *noun:* That radio program has more *listeners* than any other show in this city.

list•less [list′ lis] *adjective, more/most.* without power or energy; tired or uninterested: "He lay there in bed, *listless* and worn out . . ." (Walter Farley) —**listlessly,** *adverb.*

lit [lit] *verb.* a past form of **light:** She *lit* the candles on the birthday cake.

lit•er•ate [lit′ ə rit] *adjective, more/most.* **1.** able to read and write; not ILLITERATE. **2.** knowing a lot about literature and culture; well-read.

Pronunciation Key: [ə] Symbol

The [ə] or *schwa* sound occurs in syllables without an accent. It can be spelled with any vowel, such as **a** in above, **e** in listen, **i** in pencil, **o** in melon, **u** in circus. It can also be a combination of vowels, such as **io** in action, **ai** in mountain, **iou** in precious.

(Turn the page for more information.)

449

lit•er•a•ture [lit′ ər ə chər] *noun.* **1.** writing that has outstanding quality; written works that show imagination, powerful ideas, beauty, or great style in a way that has lasting value. **2.** novels, poems, and other works of imagination in general, as opposed to factual writing. **3.** a leaflet, booklet, or other printed material to advertise or promote something: Dan asked the company to send him some *literature* on their new computer.

lit•mus paper [lit′ məs] a type of paper used in chemical tests. It is soaked in a special chemical dye (**litmus**). Litmus paper will turn red if dipped into an acid solution and blue if dipped into one that is alkaline (a base).

lit•ter [lit′ ər] *noun, plural* **litters. 1.** bits of paper and other waste material lying around; rubbish. **2.** a number of young animals born at one time to the same mother: Lions usually have two or three cubs in a *litter.* **3.** a stretcher for carrying sick or wounded people.

2. to keep up life; feed or support oneself: A hawk *lives* on rabbits, mice, and other small animals. **3.** to make one's home: Giraffes *live* in Africa. My friend Karen *lives* across the street from us. **4.** to spend one's life or time in a certain way: to *live* dangerously, to *live* like a king.

live² [līv] *adjective.* **1.** having life; not dead: He keeps a *live* rattlesnake as a pet. **2.** burning or glowing: The campers poured water over the *live* coals to put them out. **3.** carrying electricity: The storm knocked down a light pole, and a *live* wire was dangling over the street. **4.** of a TV program, shown while actually taking place, rather than being taped or filmed for later showing. ◆ Also used as an adverb: The President's speech was shown *live.*

live•li•hood [līv′ lē hood′] *noun, plural* **livelihoods.** the way a person earns a living.

live•ly [līv′ lē] *adjective,* **livelier, liveliest.** full of life or energy: *lively* music, a person with a

lively writing Lively writing has "punch;" you feel what the author describes. How can you achieve a lively style? Use details. "The sky was dark" isn't as lively as "The sky was blank, black, not showing holes where the stars shine through." Here's how Doris Lessing describes a boy walking barefoot: "Now he felt the chilled dust push up between his toes, and he let the muscles of his feet spread and settle into the shapes of the earth, and he thought: I could walk a hundred miles on feet like these!" Use verbs that show action, movement, tension. Here's how Nadine Gordimer describes a train coming into a station: "The train called out, along the sky; but there was no answer; and the cry hung on: I'm coming . . . I'm coming. The engine flared out now, big, whisking a dwindling body behind it; the track flared out to let it in. Creaking, jerking, jostling, gasping, the train filled the station." Use surprise to add liveliness. Saki, the British short-story writer, wrote, "You might keep my luggage until I wire my address. There are only a couple of trunks and some golf clubs and a leopard cub."

—*verb,* **littered, littering.** to scatter trash or other things in a careless way: "He looked down quickly at the floor and saw it *littered* with empty cigarette boxes and discarded paper bags." (V.S. Naipaul)

lit•tle [lit′ əl] *adjective,* **littler, littlest. 1.** small in size or amount; not big: Add a *little* water when you cook the vegetables. **2.** not fully grown; young: Mike gave his old toy trucks to his *little* brother. **3.** small in importance: He has to clear up a few *little* problems at the office. —*adverb.* not much; slightly: to feel a *little* tired or a *little* sick. —*noun.* a small amount: Let me have a *little* of that bread.

Little Big•horn [big′ hôrn′] a river in Montana near where George Custer and his troops were wiped out by Sioux and Cheyenne Indians.

live¹ [liv] *verb,* **lived, living. 1.** to be alive; have life: George Washington *lived* in the 1700's.

lively imagination. —*adverb.* in a lively way: to step *lively.*

liv•er [liv′ ər] *noun, plural* **livers. 1.** a very important organ of the body. It performs more different functions than any other organ, including digesting fats, storing vitamins, and cleaning the blood. The liver is the largest gland in the human body. **2.** the liver of an animal used as food, such as a calf or chicken.

lives [līvz] *noun.* the plural of **life.**

live•stock [līv′ stäk′] *noun.* animals raised on a farm or ranch. Cows, horses, pigs, and sheep are livestock.

liv•ing [liv′ ing] *verb.* the participle of **live.** —*adjective.* **1.** having life; not dead; alive: The elephant is the largest *living* land animal. **2.** having to do with life or a certain way of life: George Orwell wrote a famous book about the poor *living* conditions of English coal miners. **3.** still in use; active: English is a *living* language. —*noun, plural* **livings. 1.** the fact or condition of being alive. **2.** a way of supporting oneself or earning the means to live: She earns her *living* by giving ballet lessons. **3.** a certain way of life: suburban *living*.

living room a main room in a house for general use, as for entertaining guests, reading, watching television, and so on.

liz•ard [liz′ərd] *noun, plural* **lizards.** any of a large group of animals that usually have a scaly body, four legs, and a long tail. Lizards are reptiles and are usually found in warm climates.

lizard Three North American lizards. The collared lizard (left), the alligator lizard (above right), and the five-lined skink (below).

lla•ma [lä′mə] *noun, plural* **llamas** or **llama.** a South American animal that is related to the camel but is smaller and has no hump. Llamas are raised for their thick, soft wool.

load [lōd] *noun, plural* **loads. 1.** something that is lifted or carried: I opened the door for Mrs. Lewis because she was carrying a *load* of books. **2.** the amount of weight that can be supported by something at one time: That moving van will carry a *load* of 40,000 pounds. **3.** something that weighs on the mind; a burden or worry: I found my missing ring—that really takes a *load* off my mind. **4.** *Informal.* any large amount of something: I can't go to the game— I've still got *loads* of homework to do. —*verb,* **loaded, loading. 1.** to put a load in or on something. **2.** to put a charge of gunpowder or ammunition into a gun: to *load* a rifle. **3.** to put something needed into a machine; to *load* a dishwasher, to *load* a camera with film.

loaf[1] [lōf] *noun, plural* **loaves. 1.** a mass of bread baked in one large piece. **2.** anything shaped like a loaf of bread: a meat *loaf*.

loaf[2] *verb,* **loafed, loafing.** to spend time doing little or nothing; rest or relax in a lazy way: "They stood *loafing* at the corner, telling jokes and laughing." (Betty Smith)

loaf•er [lō′fər] *noun, plural* **loafers. 1.** a person who loafs; a lazy person. **2.** a type of slip-on shoe.

loan [lōn] *noun, plural* **loans. 1.** money that is given for a time and paid back later, usually with INTEREST: a bank *loan* for a new car. **2.** anything that is borrowed: That painting by Picasso is on *loan* from a museum in Spain. —*verb,* **loaned, loaning.** to give something as a loan; lend: I *loaned* him money to get into the movie after he left his wallet home.

lob•by [läb′ē] *noun, plural* **lobbies. 1.** a waiting room or hall at the entrance to a hotel, theater, apartment, or other public building. **2.** a person or organized group that works to try to get lawmakers to vote in a certain way: The gun *lobby* opposed a law to control the sale of firearms. ♦ A person who does this is a **lobbyist.** —*verb,* **lobbied, lobbying.** to try to get lawmakers to vote in a certain way. The farmers *lobbied* in favor of a law giving special low rates to farms for the use of water.

lob•ster [läb′stər] *noun, plural* **lobsters.** a sea animal with a hard outer shell and no backbone, often eaten as food. Lobsters have five pairs of legs with large claws on the front pair.

lobster A lobster's natural coloring is brown or green. Its shell becomes red only after it is cooked.

Pronunciation Key: Accent Marks

[′] is the normal accent mark. It shows where the main stress falls on a word.

[′] is a secondary accent mark. It shows a lighter stress than the primary accent. For example:

tel • e • vis • ion [tel′ə vizh′ən]
(Turn the page for more information.)

L

lo•cal [lō′ kəl] *adjective.* **1.** having to do with a certain place, especially the town or neighborhood one lives in: *Local* news stories are about things that happen in the newspaper's own area. People can get income tax forms at their *local* post office or library. **2.** of a bus, train, or subway, making all or most of the stops on a certain route. —*noun, plural* **locals.** a local bus, subway or train. —**locally,** *adverb.*

lo•cal•i•ty [lō kal′ i tē] *noun, plural* **localities.** a local area, such as a neighborhood or town.

lo•cate [lō′ kāt′] *verb,* **located, locating. 1.** to be or exist in a certain place: The city of Chicago is *located* on Lake Michigan. **2.** to put in a certain place: They've decided to *locate* their new store on Route 110. **3.** to find the position of; search out: Hawks have sharp eyesight and can *locate* their prey from far off.

lo•ca•tion [lō kā′ shən] *noun, plural* **locations. 1.** a place where something is located: The new football stadium has an excellent *location* near two main highways. **2.** the act or fact of locating. **3.** a place used in filming a movie or TV show that is not in a studio: That movie was shot on *location* in the Arizona desert.

> **location** Anthony Burgess, a British critic and novelist, said that one test of a great writer is the ability to describe a location so well in a story that it influences our view of the real world. For example, real-estate ads often carry the phrase "Gatsby mansion." This means a home in the style of the waterfront mansion that is an important location in F. Scott Fitzgerald's *The Great Gatsby.* A recent magazine article said that an office building in Los Angeles showed "the Chandler style." (Raymond Chandler's detective hero Philip Marlowe worked out of a small, dusty office at the back of a low-rent building.) Chandler said that when he wanted to describe a place, he would go to an actual location like it and study the place carefully, for as long as half a day.

lock¹ [läk] *noun, plural* **locks. 1.** a small device used to keep a door, window, drawer, or other object fastened until it is opened by a key or by some other special means. **2.** a part of a canal or waterway closed off with gates. The water level can be raised or lowered within it to allow a ship to go from one body of water to another. **3.** in old firearms, the part where the charge or cartridge is exploded. —*verb,* **locked, locking. 1.** to fasten with a lock: to *lock* up a beach house for the winter. **2.** to shut or hold in place: In our car the steering wheel *locks* when the engine is not running. **3.** to join or hold firmly in place, as if with a lock: The police officers *locked* their arms together to hold back the crowd.

lock² *noun, plural* **locks. 1.** a piece of hair from the head. **2. locks.** the hair of the head: a young child with curly *locks.*

lock•er [läk′ ər] *noun, plural* **lockers.** a small closet or cabinet that can be locked, used for storing personal belongings in a public place.

lock•et [läk′ it] *noun, plural* **lockets.** a small metal case for a picture, a lock of hair, or another such memento. A locket is usually worn on a chain around the neck.

lock•smith [läk′ smith′] *noun, plural* **locksmiths.** a person whose work is making, installing, or fixing locks.

lo•co•mo•tive [lō′ kə mō′ tiv] *noun, plural* **locomotives.** a railroad car with an engine, used for pulling or pushing other cars.

lo•cust [lō′ kəst] *noun, plural* **locusts. 1.** a type of grasshopper that travels in swarms of millions of insects. Locusts can eat all the plants in their path and cause great damage to farm crops. **2.** a tree with small, feathery leaves and sweet-smelling white flowers.

lode [lōd] *noun, plural* **lodes.** a deposit of metal ore in the earth: The Comstock *Lode* was the richest silver deposit ever found in the U.S.

lodge [läj] *noun, plural* **lodges. 1.** a house or cottage, especially one used for a special purpose: a hunting *lodge,* a ski *lodge.* **2.** a branch of a larger organization or club: My uncle belongs to a local *lodge* of the Elks Club. —*verb,* **lodged, lodging. 1.** to live in a place for a time: "He rather enjoyed the voyage, for he was well fed and well *lodged* . . ." (Jules Verne) **2.** to be stuck or caught in something: The football was *lodged* in the tree between two branches. **3.** to place a formal charge or complaint: ". . . to plead innocent to the charges the Lieutenant had *lodged* against him." (Joseph Heller)

lodg•ing [läj′ ing] *noun, plural* **lodgings. 1.** a place to sleep or live in for a while: Several families had to seek *lodging* in the church basement after a flood ruined their homes. **2. lodgings.** a rented room or rooms in someone else's home. ♦ A person who lives in another person's home and pays rent is a **lodger.**

L

loft [lôft] *noun, plural* **lofts. 1.** an open space or room under the roof of a building; an attic. **2.** any large, open space in a building used as work or storage area. **3.** an open area under the roof of a barn, used for storing hay.

loft•y [lôf′tē] *adjective,* **loftier, loftiest. 1.** very high: "High above them towered *lofty* peaks, some snow-covered." (Walter Farley) **2.** high and noble; grand: John Kennedy's first speech as President expressed *lofty* goals for America. **3.** very proud; arrogant: "The policeman seemed drawn away from them in spirit, wrapped in *lofty* silence." (Mary Norton) —**loftily,** *adverb.*

Well-known logos of U.S. companies include golden arches for McDonald's, and a snow-covered mountain for Paramount Pictures.

loin [loin] *noun, plural* **loins. 1.** the part of the body on each side of the backbone, between the ribs and hips. **2.** a cut of meat from this part of a cow, pig, or other animal.

loi•ter [loi′tər] *verb,* **loitered, loitering. 1.** to stand or stay around an area doing nothing: Some boys were *loitering* on the street corner, watching the cars go by. **2.** to move or do something slowly; linger: "The twins were *loitering* over their cereal, and Mrs. Walpole, with one eye on the clock . . ." (Shirley Jackson)

logbooks In early times, ships did not have accurate instruments to judge their speed. Sailors threw overboard a wooden log attached to a line. Speed was calculated by the rate at which this log-line trailed out behind the ship. The captain kept a "log-book" in which he recorded the log's movement. As time went on, the logbook became a daily record of events that affected the ship and its cargo and crew. "Thanks be to God, the air is as soft as in April in Seville [a port city in southern Spain], and it's a pleasure to be in it, so fragrant it is." That entry was made by a captain in his log on October 8, 1492. You know that captain. The value of a logbook for student writers is daily writing practice. It could be something as obvious as the weather—that's what Christopher Columbus noted in his log, four days before he discovered America.

log [lôg] *noun, plural* **logs. 1.** a large, rough piece of wood cut from a tree, with the bark still on it. **2.** a daily record of the events of a ship's voyage; also called a **logbook. 3.** any similar record of events: The truckdriver's *log* showed how long his trip took, and when and where he stopped. —*verb,* **logged, logging. 1.** to chop down trees and cut them into pieces. ♦ A person who does this work is a **logger. 2.** to make a record of something in a log: All visitors to the office have to *log* in at the front desk.

log•ic [läj′ik] *noun.* **1.** an exact form of thinking that follows certain methods to reach a proper conclusion. A basic principle of logic is that if something belongs to a group, and all members of the group have a certain quality, then the thing must have this quality: A dolphin is a whale. All whales live in the water. Therefore, all dolphins live in the water. **2.** correct thinking of any kind: *Logic* indicates there were at least two robbers, because no one could move that heavy box alone.

log•i•cal [läj′i kəl] *adjective, more/most.* **1.** according to the rules of logic. **2.** showing correct thinking; reasonable; sensible: This will be Danny's first plane trip, so it's only *logical* that he's nervous. —**logically,** *adverb.*

lo•go [lō′gō] *noun, plural* **logos.** a sign or mark that identifies a business or other organization.

lol•li•pop or **lol•ly•pop** [läl′ē päp′] *noun, plural* **lollipops** or **lollypops.** a piece of hard candy on the end of a stick.

London The Thames River flows through London.

Lon•don [lun′dən] the capital of Great Britain, in southern England. *Population:* 6,700,000.

Pronunciation Key: A–F			
a	and; hat	ch	chew; such
ā	ate; stay	d	dog; lid
â	care; air	e	end; yet
ä	father; hat	ē	she; each
b	boy; cab	f	fun; off

(Turn the page for more information.)

Lon·don [lun′ dən], **Jack,** 1876–1916, American author.

lone [lōn] *adjective.* **1.** not with another; alone: There was a *lone* pine tree in the middle of the field. **2.** being just one; only; single: "A *lone* adult in a house of children . . ." (Julia O'Faolain).

lone·ly [lōn′ lē] *adjective,* **lonelier, loneliest. 1.** unhappy about being alone; wanting to be with friends or to be in touch with other people: "He would have felt *lonely* and homesick, had Charlotte not been with him." (E.B. White) **2.** causing a person to have this feeling: "I must go down to the seas again, to the *lonely* sea and the sky," (John Masefield) **3.** not visited by people; deserted: "Our street was always quiet and often *lonely* with little to watch from our front porch." (Ernesto Galarza) **—loneliness,** *noun.* the fact of being lonely: "The thought of being alone on the island . . . filled my heart with *loneliness.*" (Scott O'Dell)

lone·some [lōn′ səm] *adjective, more/most.* **1.** unhappy about being alone; lonely: "Oh, it's a *lonesome* thing, being an umpire. There are men who won't talk to you the rest of your life." (Philip Roth) **2.** making one feel lonely: "She played the piano for him and filled his *lonesome* hours." (Irving Stone)

long¹ [lông] *adjective,* **longer, longest. 1.** being a great distance from one end to the other; not short: a *long* tunnel under a river. A giraffe has a *long* neck. **2.** lasting a great time or extent: a *long* speech, a *long* wait in a doctor's office. **3.** having a certain length or time: a race one mile *long.* The movie was two hours *long.* **4.** of vowel sounds, spoken like the name of the letter itself; having a sound that is more drawn out: The **i** in "life" is a *long* **i**. **—adverb. 1.** for a great amount of time: You can wait here for her; she won't be gone *long.* **2.** for or during a certain time; throughout: It snowed all night *long.*

long² *verb,* **longed, longing.** to want very much; have a great desire for: "You'd have thought he'd be *longing* to get out in the air after being caged up all week." (Peter Shaffer)

Long Beach a port city in southern California. *Population:* 365,000.

long·hand [lông′ hand′] *noun.* normal handwriting in its full form, as opposed to SHORTHAND, typing, or machine printing.

longhorn Longhorn cattle on a Texas ranch. The University of Texas sports teams use "Longhorns" as their nickname.

long·horn [lông′ hôrn′] *noun, plural* **longhorns.** a breed of cattle that has very long, spreading horns. Large numbers of longhorns were raised for beef in the southwestern U.S. in the 1800's.

long·ing [lông′ ing] *noun, plural* **longings.** a feeling of wanting something very much; a strong desire: "I couldn't help feeling a *longing* to have lots of fun myself for once." (Anne Frank) **—adjective.** feeling or showing longing: "A man across from us ordered blueberry pie, and Mom cast a *longing* glance at it." (Nancy Willard) **—longingly,** *adverb:* "Almanzo . . . looked *longingly* at the bright-eyed colts." (Laura Ingalls Wilder)

long and short sentences A good way to make your writing flow is to mix long and short sentences. "He just kept showing his teeth and snarling, and when she tried to get past him he kept in front of her and snapped at her. That scared her." (Laura Ingalls Wilder) That's a sentence of 26 words, followed by one of three words. A series of sentences of the same length can form a boring pattern. In our study of famous modern writers, we found that they often begin a passage with long sentences of description, then follow with a short sentence to sum up the scene. In George Orwell's *The Road to Wigan Pier,* he begins one paragraph in this way: "I remember a winter afternoon . . ." Then he presents two sentences of description—the first is 36 words long, the second is 51. These provide details such as "factory chimneys sending out plumes of smoke" and "The canal path was a mixture of cinders and frozen mud." Then comes a short sentence: "It was horribly cold."

L

lon•gi•tude [iän′jə tōōd′] *noun, plural* **longi-tudes.** a way of measuring distance on the earth according to an imaginary line drawn between the North and South Pole. Longitude is measured in degrees east or west of this line, according to lines running north and south.

look [look] *verb,* **looked, looking. 1.** to use the eyes to see: to *look* out the window, to *look* at a picture. **2.** to appear to be; seem: You *look* tired today. "He was thirty-four years old, and *looked* sixty." (Mark Twain) **3.** to face in a certain direction: "The upstairs windows *looked* out over the tree-lined street." (Erskine Caldwell) —*noun, plural* **looks. 1.** the act of looking: Take a *look* at this picture in today's paper. **2.** a certain way of looking; an appearance or expression: She had a worried *look* on her face as she read the letter. Shakespeare's character Cassius is described as having "a lean and hungry *look*." **3. looks.** personal appearance; what one looks like: a movie star who is famous for his good *looks*.

look•out [look′out′] *noun, plural* **lookouts. 1.** a person whose job it is to watch carefully for something: The ship's *lookout* spotted another ship in the distance. **2.** a careful watching for something: The police were told to be on the *lookout* for a white pickup truck with the license plate KF-79.

loom¹ [lōōm] *noun, plural* **looms.** a machine or frame for weaving thread into cloth.

loom² *verb,* **loomed, looming. 1.** to rise up into view as a large shape: "On this gray morning the castle *loomed* up over everything . . ." (Cornelius Ryan) **2.** to come into the mind as large or threatening: ". . . thirty million dollars? The figure *loomed* in Sport's mind." (Louise Fitzhugh)

loon [lōōn] *noun, plural* **loons.** a water bird with short legs, webbed feet, and a black head. Loons are good swimmers and divers and use their long, sharp beaks to catch fish. They are known for their loud cry, which sounds like a wild, crazy laugh.

loop [lōōp] *noun, plural* **loops. 1.** the rounded part of a string or rope that crosses itself.

2. anything that has or makes a loop: The fighter plane made a *loop* in the sky. —*verb,* **looped, looping.** to make or form a loop: He *looped* the rope around the pony's neck.

loop•hole [lōōp′hōl′] *noun, plural* **loopholes.** a way of avoiding a rule or law without actually breaking it: That company didn't owe any income tax last year because they took advantage of several *loopholes* in the tax code. "I was confident, as usual, that I had discovered the *loophole* in their argument." (Wole Soyinka)

loose [lōōs] *adjective,* **looser, loosest. 1.** not fastened or attached tightly: "He has a *loose* tooth and he wiggles it with his fingers." (Judy Blume) **2.** not tied or fastened at all; free: One of our cows got *loose* and Dad had to go after it. **3.** not fitting tightly: a *loose* sweater. **4.** not strict or exact: I made a *loose* count of the fans at the game and guessed there were about 200 people there. —*adverb.* in a loose way: A set of keys hung *loose* at his belt. —**loosely,** *adverb.* —**looseness,** *noun.*

loose/lose The correct use of these words may seem obvious because they sound different and carry very different meanings. It's surprising, though, how often *loose* is misused for *lose*. "I wish to apologize to you for *loosing* my temper yesterday." Unless the person became so angry that he began to throw things around, *losing* is the correct word here. The verb *loose* means only "to let free; to let go." "She *loosed* the boat from its moorings." (George Eliot) "Belton had gone into the stable and had himself *loosed* the animal." (Anthony Trollope)

loos•en [lōō′sən] *verb,* **loosened, loosening.** to make or become loose: "He took off his jacket, *loosened* his tie and switched on the desk fan." (John Gregory Dunne)

loot [lōōt] *noun.* things of value that have been stolen: One of the jewel thieves was caught, but the other escaped with the *loot*. —*verb,* **looted, looting.** to steal or rob, especially to steal property from a store or home during a riot, war, or other disturbance. ◆ A person who does this is a **looter.**

lop•sid•ed [läp′sī′did] *adjective, more/most.* leaning too far to one side; larger or heavier on one side than the other: "He carried a *lopsided* old suitcase which was tied with a rope." (Carson McCullers)

Pronunciation Key: G–N

g	give; big	k	kind; cat; back
h	hold	l	let; ball
i	it; this	m	make; time
ī	ice; my	n	not; own
j	jet; gem; edge	ng	having

(Turn the page for more information.)

lord [lôrd] *noun, plural* **lords. 1.** in the Middle Ages, a man who held a high rank in a kingdom. A lord lived in a castle or large house and ruled over the other people living around it. **2.** a person who holds great power or rules over others. **3. Lord.** in Great Britain, a title for a man of noble rank: *Lord* Mountbatten was a famous commander in the British armed forces. —*verb,* **lorded, lording.** (used with **over**) to act in a proud or bossy way toward others.

Lord or **the Lord** a title for God or for Jesus.

Los Angeles [lôs an′jə ləs] a city in southern California, on the Pacific Ocean. It is the second-largest city in the U.S. *Population:* 3,080,000.

Los Angeles A complicated system of freeways connects this huge city.

los•er [lōō′zər] *noun, plural* **losers. 1.** any person or thing that loses: the *loser* of a football game. **2.** someone who often loses or is very unsuccessful.

loss [lôs] *noun, plural* **losses. 1.** the fact of losing something: This year our soccer team had a record of eight wins and six *losses.* **2.** something that is lost: No one was hurt in the accident, but the car was a total *loss.* **3.** in business, the amount by which money paid out during a certain time is greater than money taken in.

lost [lôst] the past form of **lose:** The skater *lost* her balance and fell to the ice. —*adjective.* that is missing or that cannot be found: a *lost* dog.

lot [lät] *noun, plural* **lots. 1.** a large number or amount: *Lots* of people have been calling to ask about the car Dad has for sale. **2.** a piece of land: a parking *lot,* a used-car *lot.* **3.** a number of persons or things of one group: I know this Christmas tree is a bit small, but it's the best of the *lot.* **4.** a piece of paper, straw, wood, or the like, used to decide something by chance: People sometimes draw *lots* to see who will get or do something. **5.** the deciding of something by chance. **6.** one's fate or fortune: He feels it's his *lot* in life to become a rich man some day. —*adverb:* very much: Our new house is a *lot* bigger than our other one.

lo•tion [lō′shən] *noun, plural* **lotions.** a smooth liquid mixture used on the skin as to soften, protect, or heal it: hand *lotion,* suntan *lotion.*

lots, a lot Both these expressions have good standing in English. However, they are better suited to everyday conversation than serious writing. "Can't I get those sneakers, Mom? *Lots of/Many* kids at school have that color." Which is more natural as a spoken sentence? "Roosevelt and the nation faced *many/a lot of* problems when he took the oath of office." And here? Also, remember that it's better to use an exact phrase, if one is possible, than the vague expressions *lots of* or *many.* "After we had cleared the sunny and the shady areas, both, we put down about ten handfuls of [not "a lot of" or "many"] seeds, throwing them thicker in the shady area because we knew some would not grow."

lose [lōōz] *verb,* **lost, losing. 1.** to come to be without something; forget or not know where something is: to *lose* a pen, to *lose* a set of car keys. **2.** to fail to keep or have: to *lose* your temper, to *lose* interest in something. **3.** to fail to win; not win: to *lose* a war, to *lose* an election, to *lose* an argument. **4.** to have taken away: to *lose* a job. The old man had *lost* his hearing. **5.** to have less of: to *lose* weight on a special diet. The company *lost* money on their personal-computer business. **6.** to be completely taken up with: "He was *lost* in his thoughts when the telephone rang." (Ian Fleming)

lot•ter•y [lät′ər ē] *noun, plural* **lotteries.** a contest where the winners are selected by lot or chance. Many states of the U.S. now sell lottery tickets to raise money for the government, with large cash prizes being offered to the winners.

lo•tus [lō′təs] *noun, plural* **lotuses.** a large colorful flower that has broad leaves and that floats in the water.

loud [loud] *adjective,* **louder, loudest. 1.** having a great or strong sound; noisy: The TV was on so *loud* that I didn't hear the phone ring. **2.** having colors too bright to be pleasing; not in good taste: a *loud* shirt with green, purple, and orange designs. —*adverb:* in a loud way: "I raised it (the whistle) to my lips and blew good and *loud.*" (Nancy Willard) —**loudly,** *adverb.* —**loudness,** *noun.*

loud•speak•er [loud′ spē′ kər] *noun, plural* **loudspeakers. 1.** a device for making sounds louder. Loudspeakers are used for making announcements in public places. **2.** the part of a TV, radio, or stereo that sends out sound.

Lou•i•si•an•a [lŏō ē′ zē an′ ə] a state in the south-central U.S., on the Gulf of Mexico. *Capital:* Baton Rouge. *Nickname:* "Pelican State." *Area:* 48,500 square miles. *Population:* 4,300,000.

Lou•is•ville [lŏō′ ē vil′] the largest city in Kentucky, on the Ohio River. *Population:* 300,000.

lounge [lounj] *verb,* **lounged, lounging. 1.** to stand or sit in a comfortable, relaxed way: "(They) *lounged* in whatever shade could be found in the hot, dry, dusty street." (Edna Ferber) **2.** to move or act in a relaxed way: He *lounged* around the house on Sunday afternoon, reading the paper and watching TV. —*noun, plural* **lounges.** a room in a public building where a person can relax.

louse [lous] *noun, plural* **lice.** a tiny insect with no wings. Lice live on people and animals by sucking their blood.

lous•y [lou′ zē] *adjective,* **lousier, lousiest.** *Slang.* very bad or unpleasant.

We all had a *lovely* time at Cathy's birthday party. —**loveliness,** *noun.*

lov•er [luv′ ər] *noun, plural* **lovers. 1.** someone who loves another person: Romeo and Juliet are a famous pair of young *lovers.* **2.** a person who loves a certain thing: a dog *lover,* a *lover* of the theater.

low [lō] *adjective,* **lower, lowest. 1.** close to the ground or surface; not high or tall: Strawberries grow on a *low* bush. **2.** below the usual or general level: to speak in a soft, *low* voice. It hasn't rained at all lately and the lake is getting *low.* **3.** below the normal amount: 'Madman Marty's' TV store is known for its *low* prices. **4.** of little value or quality; bad; poor: Kenny was upset that he got such a *low* mark on the test. **5.** deep in pitch: a singer with a *low* voice. **6.** sad or unhappy: Denise has been feeling *low* since she broke up with her boyfriend. —*adverb,* **lower, lowest.** at or to a low place or level: The plane flew *low* over the treetops. —*noun, plural* **lows.** something that is low: The temperature was an all-time *low* for this date. —**lowly,** *adjective.* having a low rank or position.

low•er [lō′ ər] *adjective.* the COMPARATIVE form of **low:** a *lower* floor of a building, students in the *lower* grades. —*verb,* **lowered, lowering. 1.** to bring or move down: "He *lowered* his voice to a whisper." (John Toland) **2. lower oneself.** to act in a wrong or unworthy way.

---

love/like A word can often be made more intense by another word that carries a stronger meaning, or, to put it another way, "turns up the heat." For example, *love* means "like very much," *furious* means "very angry," *exhausted* means "very tired," *ancient* means "very old." You can write that someone is *tired* after working for two hours, but is *exhausted* after working all day without stopping. You can refer to the *old* U.S. Route 66 and an *ancient* Roman highway. The only thing to be careful about is to make sure that the stronger word fits the situation and is not an exaggeration.

---

love [luv] *noun, plural* **loves. 1.** a very deep, strong feeling of caring for another person, as between members of the same family, two people of the opposite sex, or very close friends. **2.** a great liking for something: a *love* of music, *love* for your country. She has a great *love* of traveling and has been around the world twice. **3.** a person for whom one feels love. —*verb,* **loved, loving. 1.** to have a very deep, strong feeling of caring for someone: to *love* your parents. **2.** to like very much: Jerry *loves* chocolate ice cream.

love•ly [luv′ lē] *adjective,* **lovelier, loveliest. 1.** very pleasing to look at; beautiful: a *lovely* girl, a *lovely* view of spring flowers blooming on a hillside. **2.** very nice or pleasant; delightful:

low•er•case [loī′ ər kaīs′] *adjective; noun.* of a word or letter, written in small letters; not in capital letters.

loy•al [loi′ əl] *adjective,* **more/most.** true to a person, country, or idea; faithful: "I wanted her to stay always, wanted to know she would be my *loyal* partner." (Bonnie Zindel) —**loyally,** *adverb.*

Pronunciation Key: O–S

ō	over; go	ou	out; town
ô	all; law	p	put; hop
oo	look; full	r	run; car
ōō	pool; who	s	set; miss
oi	oil; boy	sh	show

(Turn the page for more information.)

loy•al•ty [loi′ əl tē] *noun, plural* **loyalties.** the fact or condition of being loyal: "You see my kind of *loyalty* was *loyalty* to one's country." (Mark Twain)

lu•bri•cant [lōō′ bri kənt] *noun, plural* **lubricants.** a substance such as oil or grease that is very slippery, used on the moving parts of machinery to help them move smoothly.

lu•bri•cate [lōō′ brə kāt′] *verb,* **lubricated, lubricating.** to put oil or grease on the moving parts of a machine so that they will move easily and smoothly.—**lubrication,** *noun.*

luck [luk] *noun.* **1.** the way some things happen in life by accident, without being controlled or planned; fate: The winner of a lottery or a dice game is decided by *luck.* **2.** success or good fortune as a result of this; good luck: People sometimes carry a rabbit's foot or other object that they think will bring them *luck.*

luck•i•ly [luk′ ə lē] *adverb.* in a lucky way; by good luck; fortunately: The car slid off the road, but *luckily* no one was hurt.

luck•y [luk′ ē] *adjective,* **luckier, luckiest. 1.** having or showing good luck: "Maybe if we're *lucky* . . . we'll get there before the storm closes in on us." (James Houston) **2.** thought of as bringing good luck: College basketball coach Lou Carnesecca had a *lucky* sweater that he wore to every game one season.

lug [lug] *verb,* **lugged, lugging.** to pull or carry with great effort; drag: "He *lugged* his suitcase to the end of the block, and stood waiting for a streetcar." (Richard Wright)

lug•gage [lug′ ij] *noun.* the suitcases and bags that a traveler takes along on a trip; baggage.

luke•warm [lōōk′ wôrm′] *adjective.* **1.** slightly warm; neither hot nor cold: She soaked her sore foot in *lukewarm* water. **2.** showing little interest or enthusiasm; not eager: The critic gave the movie a *lukewarm* rating of two stars out of a possible five.

lull [lul] *verb,* **lulled, lulling.** to make or become calm; quiet down: "After a while the *motion* of the train lulled him into a shallow sleep." (Ken Follett) —*noun, plural* **lulls.** a brief period of calm: a *lull* in the fighting during a battle.

lul•la•by [lul′ ə bī] *noun, plural* **lullabies.** a soft song to lull a baby to sleep. "Rock-a-Bye-Baby" is a well-known lullaby.

lum•ber[1] [lum′ bər] *noun.* boards and planks cut from logs.

lumber[2] *verb,* **lumbered, lumbering.** to move in a noisy, clumsy way: The heavily-loaded garbage truck *lumbered* down the street.

lumberjack These early lumberjacks have just made an 'undercut'. The tree will then be sawed on the other side so that it will fall in this direction.

lum•ber•jack [lum′ bər jak′] *noun, plural* **lumberjacks.** a person whose work is cutting down trees to be turned into lumber.

lu•mi•nous [lōō′ mə nəs] *adjective, more/most.* giving off light; glowing; shining: "She woke and looked at the *luminous* hands of the clock on the bed table." (John Gregory Dunne)

lump [lump] *noun, plural* **lumps. 1.** a small, solid piece of something having no special shape: a *lump* of coal, a *lump* of clay. **2.** a swelling or bump: Roy had a *lump* on his head where the baseball hit him. —*verb,* **lumped, lumping. 1.** to form into a lump or lumps. **2.** to put together in one group: "You could not *lump* men together and measure them by any rule." (Laura Ingalls Wilder) —**lumpy,** *adjective.*

lu•nar [lōō′ nər] *adjective.* having to do with the moon: In a *lunar* eclipse, the moon passes through the earth's shadow.

lu•na•tic [lōō′ nə tik] *noun, plural* **lunatics.** someone who is mentally ill or who acts in a very wild and foolish way.

lunch [lunch] *noun, plural* **lunches.** a meal eaten in the middle of the day, between breakfast and dinner. —*verb,* **lunched, lunching.** to eat lunch.

lunch•eon [lun′ chən] *noun, plural* **luncheons.** lunch, especially a special or formal lunch.

lung [lung] *noun, plural* **lungs.** one of a pair of large organs in the chest that are used for breathing. The lungs take in oxygen from the air and transfer it into the blood, then remove a waste product, carbon dioxide, from the blood to be breathed out.

L

-ly The ending *-ly* is used to make adjectives (which modify nouns) into adverbs (which modify verbs). "He spoke in a quiet [adjective] voice [noun]. He spoke [verb] quietly [adverb]." Errors are easy to spot: "We can get this done *easy*." "Turn the key *slow* to the right." These should correctly read: "Get this done *easily*." "Turn the key *slowly*." Many words use the same form for both the adjective and the adverb (a *fast* driver; to drive *fast*). Further, sometimes the "ly" rule doesn't apply. It's natural and correct to say "Go slow," "Take it easy," "Hold on tight," or "Cut the meat thin."

lunge [lunj] *noun, plural* **lunges.** a sudden movement or rush forward: The outfielder made a *lunge* for the ball as it dropped in front of him. —*verb,* **lunged, lunging.** to make a sudden movement forward: "He *lunged* over the counter suddenly, snatching at her hand . . ." (John Gardner)

lure [lŏŏr] *noun, plural* **lures. 1.** something that strongly attracts or tempts a person: She tried to keep her mind on her homework, but the *lure* of the beautiful spring day outside made it difficult. **2.** an artificial bait used to catch fish. —*verb,* **lured, luring.** to attract strongly; tempt: "You act as a decoy. If you see anybody we know, *lure* them away." (Nancy Willard)

lurk [lurk] *verb,* **lurked, lurking.** to wait out of sight; hide or move in a sneaky way: "There was no one hiding behind the front seats. No one *lurking* round the edges of the car park." (Dick Francis)

lush [lush] *adjective,* **lusher, lushest.** thick, rich, and healthy: "The grass here, watered by underground springs, was even more *lush* than outside the wall." (Walter Farley)

Lu•ther [lŏŏ′ thər] **Martin,** 1483–1546, German religious leader who was one of the founders of the Protestant religion.

Lux•em•bourg or **Lux•em•burg** [luk′ səmburg′] **1.** a country in western Europe. *Area:* 998 square miles. *Population:* 400,000. **2.** the capital and largest city of Luxembourg. *Population:* 77,000.

lux•u•ri•ous [luk zhoor′ ē əs *or* lug zhoor′ē əs] *adjective, more/most.* very rich, splendid, or expensive: They stayed at a *luxurious* hotel on the beach in Hawaii. —**luxuriously,** *adverb.*

lux•u•ry [luk′ shər ē *or* lug′ shər ē] *noun, plural* **luxuries. 1.** something that gives pleasure but is not considered necessary, especially something that is expensive: *luxuries* such as imported foods and wines or custom-made clothing. **2.** a very rich, splendid, or costly way of living.

lye [lī] *noun.* a strong, dangerous substance used in making soap and cleaning fluids. Lye is made by soaking wood ashes in water.

ly•ing[1] [lī′ ing] the present participle of **lie**[1]: She was *lying* on the couch, resting.

lying[2] the present participle of **lie**[2]: The police think he's *lying* about where he was that night.

lymph [limf] *noun.* a clear liquid in the tissues of the body. Lymph brings food and oxygen to the cells of the body and carries away waste products. This process is carried out by a system of **lymphatic** [lim fat′ ik] vessels and **lymph glands** or **lymph nodes** [nōdz].

lynx

lynx [lingks] *noun, plural* **lynx** or **lynxes.** a wild animal of the cat family, with long legs, a short tail, and fur in bunches around its ears. One type of lynx is found in the northern U.S. and Canada.

ly•ric [lir′ ik] *noun, plural* **lyrics. 1. lyrics.** the words to a song, as opposed to the melody. **2.** a short poem that tells a poet's personal feelings. —*adjective.* (*also,* **lyrical**) expressing strong, deep feelings: a *lyric* poem.

Pronunciation Key: T–Z			
t	ten; date	v	very; live
th	think	w	win; away
<u>th</u>	these	y	you
u	cut; butter	z	zoo; cause
ur	turn; bird	zh	measure

(Turn the page for more information.)

m, M [em] *noun, plural* **m's, M's.** the thirteenth letter of the alphabet.

ma'am [mam] *noun, plural* **ma'ams.** the contraction of **madam.**

mac·a·ron·i [mak′ ə rō′ nē] *noun.* a type of noodle that is shaped like a small, short tube. Macaroni is cooked in boiling water before being eaten.

Mac·Ar·thur [mək är′ thər] **Douglas,** 1880–1964, American general in World War II.

machete The word *machete* [mə shet′ ē] is from Spanish. It is a heavy knife used in Latin America to cut crops and brush.

Ma·chi·a·vel·li [mäk′ ē ə vel′ ē] **Niccolo,** 1469–1527, Italian philosopher who wrote *The Prince,* a famous work on political strategy.

ma·chine [mə shēn′] *noun, plural* **machines.** **1.** any device that uses energy and motion to do work. Most machines combine moving and fixed parts. Automobiles, dishwashers, printing presses, and computers are all types of machines. **2.** *also,* **simple machine.** a basic device that makes it easier to do physical work, such as lifting or moving something. The six simple machines are the lever, pulley, wedge, screw, wheel and axle, and inclined plane. **3.** a group of people who seem to act in an automatic way, like a machine: Years ago, many large U.S. cities were run by political *machines* who picked all candidates and controlled elections.

machine gun an automatic rifle that fires bullets rapidly as long as the trigger is pressed.

ma·chin·er·y [mə shēn′ ə rē] *noun.* **1.** machines as a group: The John Deere Company makes tractors and other farm *machinery.* **2.** the working parts of a machine or machines: The elevator isn't working because something got caught in the *machinery.* ♦ A person who works with machinery is a **machinist.**

mack·er·el [mak′ ər əl] *noun, plural* **mackerel** or **mackerels.** a large ocean fish that is often caught for food. Its body is blue-green above and silvery-white below.

mad [mad] *adjective,* **madder, maddest. 1.** feeling or showing anger; angry: "I couldn't say anything because I was too *mad.* I walked out and slammed the door behind me." (S.E. Hinton) **2.** not in one's right mind; insane. **3.** not sensible; very foolish: He has a *mad* scheme for raising penguins in his back yard. **4.** wild and confused: The children made a *mad* scramble across the lawn as the Easter egg hunt began. **5.** of a dog, having a very dangerous disease called RABIES that causes the dog to run about wildly and attack people. **—madly,** *adverb.* **—madness,** *noun.*

ma·dam [mad′ əm] *noun.* a polite way of speaking to a woman: "*Madam,* your table is ready now," the waiter told her.

made [mād] the past form of **make.**

made-up [mād′ up′] *adjective.* not real or true; imaginary: He told a *made-up* story about his dog eating his homework.

Mad·i·son [mad′ i sən] **James,** 1751–1836, the fourth president of the United States, from 1809 to 1817, and chief writer of the U.S. Constitution.

Ma•drid [mə drid′] the capital and largest city of Spain, in the central part of the country. *Population:* 3,200,000.

mag•a•zine [mag′ ə zēn′ or mag′ ə zēn′] *noun, plural* **magazines. 1.** a printed collection of writing, often with pictures, that is published at regular times, usually every week or every month. **2.** the part of a gun or rifle that contains the bullets. **3.** a room for storing explosives or ammunition: In old warships, gunpowder was kept in a *magazine* below decks.

mag•ne•si•um [mag nē′ zē əm *or* mag nē′ zhəm] *noun.* a lightweight, silvery-white metal that burns with a brilliant white light. Magnesium is a chemical element. It is used to make metal alloys.

mag•net [mag′ nit] *noun, plural* **magnets. 1.** a piece of metal, rock, or other material that has the power to attract iron and steel toward it. **2.** anything that strongly attracts people to it: A *magnet* school is one that offers special programs to attract students from a wide area.

> **magazine articles** A newspaper article is usually written in an upside-down "triangle" or "pyramid" style (see TRIANGLE), with the important information packed up front in the article. This is not a "rule" for writing newspaper articles; rather, it's a tradition. Writers are not sure how much of their copy will be cut before it's set in type. For magazines, the problem of cutting usually does not exist. The writer is asked to submit a certain number of lines or words. Thus, the important information can be spread more evenly throughout the article. If you want to try your hand at magazine writing, try *Highlights* or *Cobblestone*, which publish writing by students. There's even one magazine at least, *Stone Soup*, that is made up completely of writing sent in by readers.

Ma•gel•lan [mə jel′ ən] **Ferdinand,** 1480?–1521, Portuguese navigator who led the first expedition to sail around the world.

mag•got [mag′ ət] *noun, plural* **maggots.** a young fly that has just hatched from its egg. A maggot is the LARVA state of a fly and has a thick, soft body like a worm, with no legs and no separate head.

ma•gic [maj′ ik] *noun.* **1.** a special power that is supposed to make a person able to control what happens or to do things that would otherwise be impossible. The practice of magic makes use of certain sayings, objects, and actions that are thought to have this power. **2.** the performing of certain tricks that seem impossible as a show, such as pulling a rabbit out of a hat. **3.** a powerful effect that seems to work by magic; Basketball star Earvin Johnson is called 'Magic' because of his ability to fool the other team with quick, unexpected passes. —*adjective.* having to do with the power of magic: "He's got a *magic* peach in his hand, grown in heaven for the gods . . . a person eats that peach and that person lives forever." (Laurence Yep)

mag•i•cal [maj′ i kəl] *adjective.* of or done by magic: Cinderella's fairy godmother used her *magical* powers to turn a pumpkin into a beautiful carriage. —**magically,** *adverb.*

ma•gi•cian [mə jish′ ən] *noun, plural* **magicians. 1.** a person who performs magic tricks to entertain people: The *magician* Harry Houdini was famous for his amazing escapes. **2.** a person who supposedly has true magical powers.

mag•net•ic [mag net′ ik] *adjective, more/most.* **1.** having the properties of a magnet: Compass needles are *magnetic* and show direction by pointing to the north. **2.** having a great power to attract, as if by a magnet: Ballet teacher George Balanchine had a very *magnetic* personality and many of the world's great dancers came to study with him.

magnetic pole 1. either of the two points of a magnet where the magnetic force is strongest. **2.** either of two points on the earth's surface where the magnetic force is strongest. The North Pole and the South Pole are close to, but not exactly at, the magnetic poles.

mag•net•ism [mag′ nə tīz′ əm] *noun.* **1.** the power that a magnet has to attract iron, steel, and other metals. Electric currents, certain metals, and the earth itself have magnetism. **2.** a great power to attract or charm others.

mag•net•ize [mag′ nə tīz′] *verb,* **magnetized, magnetizing.** to cause something to become magnetic.

mag•ni•fi•cent [mag nif′ ə sənt] *adjective, more/most.* very grand, beautiful, or outstanding: As

	Pronunciation Key: A–F		
a	and; hat	ch	chew; such
ā	ate; stay	d	dog; lid
â	care; air	e	end; yet
ä	father; hot	ē	she; each
b	boy; cab	f	fun; off

(Turn the page for more information.)

M

our plane landed in Washington we had a *magnificent* view of the city, with the Capitol Building and the Washington Monument lighting up the sky. **—magnificence,** *noun.*

mag•ni•fy [mag′ nə fī′] *verb,* **magnified, magnifying. 1.** to make something look larger than it actually is: *Magnifying* objects with a microscope allows people to study things that normally could not be seen by the human eye. **2.** to make something seem greater or more important than it really is; exaggerate: Rod sometimes *magnifies* a small personal problem to the point where he can think of nothing else.

magnifying glass a lens that causes things to appear larger than they really are.

mag•ni•tude [mag′ nə tood′] *noun.* size or importance: The *magnitude* of a star indicates how bright it appears in the sky.

magnolia A magnolia tree with a close-up of its blossoms.

mag•no•lia [mag nō′ lē ə *or* mag nōl′ yə] *noun, plural* **magnolias.** a North American tree or shrub that has large white, pink, yellow, or purple flowers.

mag•pie [mag′ pī] *noun, plural* **magpies.** a noisy black-and-white bird that has a long tail and a thick bill. Magpies are related to crows.

ma•hog•a•ny [mə häg′ ə nē] *noun, plural* **mahoganies. 1.** an evergreen tree that grows in tropical climates. Its strong, reddish-brown wood is of very high quality and is often used to make furniture and musical instruments. **2.** a dark reddish-brown color like this wood.

maid [mād] *noun, plural* **maids. 1.** a woman servant, especially one who does household work such as washing and cleaning. **2.** an unmarried girl or young woman; a maiden.

maid•en [mād′ ən] *noun, plural* **maidens.** an old word for a girl or young woman who is not married. **—adjective.** first; earliest: The ocean liner *Titanic* sunk on its *maiden* voyage.

maiden name the family name of a woman before she is married.

maid of honor an unmarried woman who is the bride's main attendant at a wedding.

mail[1] [māl] *noun, plural* **mails. 1.** letters, packages, postcards, and the like sent from one place to another by the post office. **2.** the public system by which mail is sent and delivered: She sent out the invitations to her birthday party by *mail.* **—verb,** **mailed, mailing.** to send by mail.

mail[2] in the Middle Ages, a type of armor made of small metal plates or rings linked together, used to protect the body during battle.

mail•man [māl′ mən] *noun, plural* **mailmen.** a person who picks up and delivers the mail; also called a **mail carrier.**

main [mān] *adjective.* the first in size or importance: The Colorado is the *main* river of the southwestern U.S. The *main* reason I liked the book was that the story was very exciting. **—noun, plural** **mains.** a large pipe that carries water, gas, electricity, or the like to or from a central location.

main idea Paragraphs are best constructed by beginning with a main idea, then adding details to support or expand that idea. When you shift to another main idea, you can start a new paragraph. In "The Way to Rainy Mountain," N. Scott Momaday begins one paragraph with this main idea: "Once there was a lot of sound in my grandmother's house, a lot of coming and going, feasting and talk." Then, the rest of the paragraph gives supporting details: "The summers there were full of excitement and reunion . . . They made loud and elaborate talk among themselves . . . they prepared meals that were banquets." Then a contrasting idea introduces a new paragraph: "Now there is a funeral silence in the rooms, the endless wake of some final word. The walls have closed in upon my grandmother's house." The main idea often is presented in one simple, direct sentence. Momaday begins other paragraphs with "I returned to Rainy Mountain in July." "I like to think of her as a child." and "A dark mist lay over the Black Hills, and the land was like iron."

Maine [mān] a state at the northeast tip of the U.S. *Capital:* Augusta. *Nickname:* "Pine Tree State." *Area:* 33,200 square miles. *Population:* 1,200,000.

mainframe This mainframe computer is being used to handle millions of ticket requests for the Summer Olympic Games.

main•frame [mān′frām′] *noun, plural* **mainframes.** a very powerful computer that is able to process huge amounts of information. One mainframe can handle information for many different terminals that are connected to it.

main•land [mān′land′ *or* mān′lənd] *noun, plural* **mainlands.** the main land mass of an area or continent, apart from outlying islands.

main•ly [mān′lē] *adverb.* for the most part; chiefly: ". . . a bookcase full of paperback books, *mainly* classics which she had never read." (John LeCarré)

main•tain [mān tān′] *verb,* **maintained, maintaining. 1.** to continue or carry on in the same way: The jetliner *maintained* an even speed of 550 miles per hour. **2.** to keep in good condition; take care of: to *maintain* a car by having regular service work done. **3.** to say strongly; declare; insist: He was arrested for the robbery, but he *maintained* he'd been at home asleep when it happened.

main•te•nance [mān′tə nəns] *noun.* the act or fact of maintaining something: People who own apartments in that building pay a monthly fee for *maintenance* of the grounds around it.

maize [māz] *noun.* another name for the corn plant, used especially in British English.

ma•jes•tic [mə jes′tik] *adjective, more/most.* having or showing majesty; very grand or dignified. —**majestically,** *adverb.*

maj•es•ty [maj′is tē] *noun, plural* **majesties. 1. Majesty.** the title used when speaking to a king or queen. **2.** a very grand and impressive quality: the *majesty* of Niagara Falls.

ma•jor [mā′jər] *adjective.* **1.** great in size or importance: Corn is a *major* crop of American farmers. **2.** greater than another or others; main: There are 26 teams in the *major* leagues in baseball. —*noun, plural* **majors. 1.** a rank in the Army, Air Force, or Marines, above a captain and below a lieutenant colonel. **2.** a student's main area of study in college: Eileen is a history *major.*

ma•jor•i•ty [mə jôr′ə tē] *noun, plural* **majorities. 1.** the greater of two numbers; more than half: The *majority* of Americans live in or near large cities. **2.** the difference between a larger and a smaller number: The 99th Congress had 54 Republican senators and 46 Democrats, so the Republicans had a *majority* of 8.

make [māk] *verb,* **made, making. 1.** to bring something into being, especially by putting parts or materials together: My aunt sews really well and *makes* all her own clothes. Dad's going to *make* beef stew for dinner tonight. **2.** to cause something to happen; bring about: to *make* a noise, to *make* a telephone call, to *make* plans to do something. **3.** to cause someone or something to be in a certain condition: I don't eat mushrooms because they *make* me sick. Mrs. Davis was just *made* a vice-president of her company. **4.** to force someone to act in a certain way: The school put speed bumps in the parking lot to *make* people slow down. **5.** to go on or get on: to *make* a 6:30 train, to *make* the honor roll at school. **6.** to gain or earn: to *make* $2.50 an hour as a babysitter. —*noun, plural* **makes.** the way in which something is made; a brand or style: That's a really nice TV set—what *make* is it?

make-be•lieve [māk′ bi lēv′] *noun.* something that is not real; something made up. The story of *Alice in Wonderland* takes place in a world of *make-believe.* ♦ Also used as an adjective.

mak•er [mā′kər] *noun, plural* **makers.** a person or thing that makes something: That store has low prices on clothing by famous *makers.* ♦ Often used in combination with other words: a dress*maker,* a watch*maker.*

make•up [māk′up′] *noun, plural* **makeups. 1.** certain substances that are put on the face.

M

Women wear lipstick and powder as makeup to look more attractive. Actors often wear special makeup to appear much older, to look frightening or silly, and so on. **2.** the particular way that something is formed or arranged: The chart gave the *makeup* of the Executive Branch of the government.

ma·lar·i·a [mə lâr′ē ə] *noun.* a disease that causes a high fever, sweating, and severe chills. Malaria is carried from one person to another by the female of certain types of mosquitoes, which transmit the disease when they bite someone. Many people die from malaria in tropical areas of the world.

Ma·lay·sia [mə lā′zhə] a country in southeast Asia that consists of the southern **Malay Peninsula** and the northern part of the island of **Borneo** [bôr′nē ō]. *Capital:* Kuala Lumpur. *Area:* 127,400 square miles. *Population:* 15,000,000. —**Malaysian,** *adjective; noun.*

male [māl] *adjective.* **1.** having to do with the sex that can be the father of young: A *male* elephant is called a bull. **2.** having to do with men or boys: Until recently such colleges as Yale and Dartmouth had only *male* students. —*noun, plural* **males.** a male person or animal.

mal·ice [mal′is] *noun.* a wish to hurt someone on purpose: He was upset by the low mark the teacher gave his paper, but he realized she didn't do it out of *malice.* ◆ Something that is done with malice is **malicious.**

ma·lig·nant [mə lig′nənt] *adjective, more/ most.* tending to cause harm; harmful; dangerous: Cancer is a *malignant* growth in the body caused by cells growing out of control.

mall [môl] *noun, plural* **malls. 1.** a public walkway that is closed to auto traffic. **2.** a shopping center, especially one that is enclosed and has a central walkway with shops on either side.

mall The Grand Avenue Mall in Milwaukee, Wisconsin.

mal·lard [mal′ərd] *noun, plural* **mallards.** a very common wild duck found in many parts of the world. The female has a brownish body with blue bands on the wings, and the male has a green head, a white band around the neck, a reddish-brown chest, and a gray back.

mal·let [mal′it] *noun, plural* **mallets. 1.** a hammer that has a short handle and a wooden head. **2.** a hammer with a long handle, used to strike the ball in games such as polo and croquet.

mal·nu·tri·tion [mal′ nōō trish′ ən] *noun.* a weak and unhealthy condition of the body caused by eating too little food or eating the wrong foods.

malt [môlt] *noun.* **1.** a cereal grain, usually barley, that is soaked in warm water until it sprouts and then is dried. Malt is used in making beer and other alcoholic beverages. **2.** a drink made with milk, ice cream, powdered malt, and flavorings; also called a **malted milk.**

ma·ma [ma′mə] *noun, plural* **mamas.** a word for "mother."

mam·mal [mam′əl] *noun, plural* **mammals.** a type of animal that is warm-blooded, has a backbone, and usually has fur or hair on its body. Female mammals can produce milk for their young. Except for one special group, the young of mammals are born alive, rather than hatched from eggs. Mammals include humans, dogs, cattle, mice, and whales.

mammoth The bones of the mammoth are often found in North America. Entire bodies have been discovered frozen in the glaciers of Siberia.

mam·moth [mam′əth] *noun, plural* **mammoths.** a type of elephant that lived in ancient times. The last ones died out about ten thousand years ago. —*adjective.* very large; huge: Brazil's national soccer team plays in a *mammoth* stadium that holds 200,000 people.

M

man Here's a quote from an old encyclopedia article on MAN: "When *man* learned to build and heat shelters, to sew warm clothing . . . *he* began to move . . ." Let's compare this to a newer encyclopedia. Under MAN we find no article at all. Instead, there's a note that says "See HUMAN BEING." There, we find, "As *people* improved their hunting skills, *they* obtained large amounts of meat." What caused this change? Many women have objected to the use of *man* to refer to people in general. (We see this usage in familiar phrases such as "All *men* are created equal"in the Declaration of Independence and "*Man* does not live by bread alone" in the Bible.) If you asked a politician to choose between the two usages, he'd probably say that the Declaration and the Bible are right and so, too, are modern feminists. What do *you* think?

man [man] *noun, plural* **men. 1.** a full-grown male person; a male who is no longer a boy. **2.** any human being, male or female: "Hardly a *man* is now alive, Who remembers that famous day and year . . ." (Henry Wadsworth Longfellow) **3.** the human race; mankind: ". . . a struggle against the common enemies of *man* . . ." (John F. Kennedy) —*verb,* **manned, manning.** to supply with people for work: "Under his command more than half a million men *manned* defenses along a tremendous length of coastline." (Cornelius Ryan)

man•age [man′ij] *verb,* **managed, managing. 1.** to be in charge of something; control; direct: to *manage* a store, to *manage* a business. **2.** to be able to deal with a situation, especially a difficult one; get along: "He found two minnows in a large pool . . . and *managed* to catch them in his tin bucket." (Jack London)

man•age•ment [man′ij mənt] *noun, plural* **managements. 1.** the act of managing something: That newspaper column gives advice on money *management*. **2.** the act of managing a business, especially the skill of directing the work of other people. **3.** the people who manage a particular company.

man•ag•er [man′i jər] *noun, plural* **managers.** a person who manages something: an office *manager*, the sales *manager* of a large clothing store, the *manager* of a movie theater.

man•do•lin [man′də lin *or* man′də lin′] *noun, plural* **mandolins.** a small musical instrument somewhat like a guitar. A mandolin has a pear-shaped body and four pairs of strings.

mane [mān] *noun, plural* **manes.** a growth of long, thick hair on the neck and shoulders of some animals, such as horses and male lions.

ma•neu•ver [mə noo′ vər] *noun, plural* **maneuvers. 1.** a planned movement of military troops or ships: Washington's crossing the Delaware River to win the Battle of Trenton has been called the most brilliant *maneuver* of the Revolutionary War. **2. maneuvers.** such movements carried out as a training exercise: The Seventh Fleet is on *maneuvers* in the Indian Ocean this month. **3.** a clever plan or action, usually one meant to fool or trick someone: "He feels that . . . the steps taken by the government are mere political *maneuvers* leading nowhere." (Thomas Merton) —*verb,* **maneuvered, maneuvering. 1.** to move or guide something: "There was the usual delay as passengers *maneuvered* their luggage through the door." (P.D. James) **2.** to plan cleverly; scheme: Joe *maneuvered* to get himself seated next to his boss at dinner.

man•ga•nese [mang′ gə nēz] *noun.* a brittle, silver-gray metal that is used in producing steel. Manganese is a chemical element.

man•ger [mān′ jər] *noun, plural* **mangers.** an open box or bin where hay or other food is put for farm animals to eat.

man•go [mang′ gō] *noun, plural* **mangoes** or **mangos.** a juicy, yellowish-red fruit that has a roundish shape and a sweet taste. Mangos grow on an evergreen tree found in tropical climates.

man•hole [man′ hōl′] *noun, plural* **manholes.** an opening in the street for a worker to pass through to work on something under the ground, such as a telephone cable.

man•hood [man′ hood′] *noun.* the fact or time of being a man.

man•i•a [mā′ nē ə *or* mān′ yə] *noun, plural* **manias. 1.** a mental illness that can cause a person to become violent or very excited. **2.** a very strong liking for something: "Peter has a *mania* for crossword puzzles at the moment and hardly does anything else." (Anne Frank)

Pronunciation Key: O–S			
ō	over; go	ou	out; town
ô	all; law	p	put; hop
oo	look; full	r	run; car
oo	pool; who	s	set; miss
oi	oil; boy	sh	show

(Turn the page for more information.)

ma•ni•ac [mā′ nē ak′] *noun, plural* **maniacs.** a person who is violently insane.

man•i•cure [man′ ə kyoor′] *noun, plural* **mani-cures.** the care and treatment of the fingernails, including cleaning, shaping, and often polishing. —*verb,* **manicured, manicuring.** to give a manicure. ♦ Usually used as an adjective: "His hands were white, small, and beautifully *manicured.* (Christopher Isherwood)

Ma•nil•a [mə nil′ ə] the capital and largest city of the Philippines, on Manila Bay. *Population:* 1,600,000.

ma•nip•u•late [mə nip′ yə lāt′] *verb,* **manipu-lated, manipulating. 1.** to use the hands to operate or work something, especially with skill: He quickly *manipulated* the keys of the computer and a colorful design appeared on the screen. **2.** to use skill to control or influence others, especially in an unfair or dishonest way: "She used to lie awake nights, thinking of what she could do to *manipulate* people into waiting on her." (Paul Zindel) ♦ The act or fact of manipulating is **manipulation.**

Man•i•to•ba [man′ i tō′ bə] a province in central Canada. *Capital:* Winnipeg. *Area:* 251,000 square miles. *Population:* 1,100,000.

man•kind [man′ kīnd′ *or* man′ kīnd′] *noun.* human beings as a group; the human race.

man•ner•ism [man′ ər iz′ əm] *noun, plural* **mannerisms.** a way of acting that is unusual or easy to notice, and that is done as a habit: "His movements are exact and wooden and he has a *mannerism* of standing and sitting in stiff, posed attitudes . . ." (Eugene O'Neill)

man•or [man′ ər] *noun, plural* **manors. 1.** a large house and area of land owned by a lord in the Middle Ages. On a manor, peasants were allowed to farm some of the land in exchange for food or goods. **2.** a very large house or mansion.

man•sion [man′ shən] *noun, plural* **mansions.** a very large, expensive home with many rooms and usually a large area of land around it.

man•slaugh•ter [man′ slô′ tər] *noun, plural* **manslaughters.** in law, the killing of a human being in a way that is wrong, but that is not done on purpose as is the case with murder. Examples of manslaughter might be killing a person during a fight or by driving a car in a dangerous way.

man•tel [man′ təl] *noun, plural* **mantels.** a shelf located above a fireplace. ♦ Also called a **mantelpiece.**

man•tis [man′ tis] *noun, plural* **mantises.** another name for the PRAYING MANTIS. ♦ Also called a **mantid** [man′ tid].

manuals Many professional writers have two books close at hand as they write, first, a dictionary, and second, a manual of style. A style manual deals with the use of periods, commas, and other marks of punctuation. It shows when to use capital letters and how to deal with abbreviations, numbers, and other "non-word" forms. A manual also tells you the proper form for footnotes, bibliographies, and indexes. Three leading style manuals are *The Chicago Manual of Style* (University of Chicago), *Words Into Type* (Prentice-Hall), and *Webster's Standard American Style Manual* (Merriam-Webster). The most popular (in sales) of all English handbooks over the past fifty years is the *Harbrace College Handbook* (Harcourt Brace Jovanovich), which is used as a style guide by college students. For style notes written for a younger student, you don't have to look any further than the writing articles in this dictionary.

man-made [man′ mād′] *adjective.* created by people rather than by nature; artificial: Plastic is a *man-made* material.

man•ner [man′ ər] *noun, plural* **manners. 1.** the way in which something happens or is done: She packed the glasses in the box in a very careful *manner.* **2.** a certain way of acting or behaving: "Her *manner* was quiet and friendly." (Kingsley Amis) **3. manners.** a way of behaving that is considered polite or proper: "He learned good *manners:* he trained himself to rise and give his chair to a lady." (Carson McCullers) **4.** a kind or type: The harbor was filled with all *manner* of small boats.

man•u•al [man′ yōō əl] *adjective.* **1.** having to do with the hands; involving the use of the hands: Cutting down trees, laying bricks, and painting a house are forms of *manual* labor. **2.** not operating automatically: A *manual* type-writer does not run on electricity. —*noun, plural* **manuals.** a book of instructions on how to do something; a handbook or guidebook: A person buying a new car gets an owner's *manu-al* showing how it works.

man•u•fac•ture [man′ yə fak′ chər] *verb,* **man-ufactured, manufacturing. 1.** to make a product in large amounts by means of machines: to *manufacture* trucks, to *manufacture* clothing.

M

2. to make something in a regular or organized way, as if by manufacturing: Green plants can *manufacture* their own food. "Unless they *manufactured* their own air, they were forced to return to the surface from time to time . . ." (Jules Verne) —*noun, plural* **manufactures.** the act of manufacturing, or something that is manufactured. —**manufacturer,** *noun:* West Germany is a leading auto *manufacturer.*

ma•nure [mə noŏr′] *noun.* waste products of animals, such as cattle or chickens, used as a fertilizer to enrich the soil.

the world. Maple wood is strong and hard and is used to make furniture. The best-known North American maple tree is the **sugar maple,** whose sap is used to make **maple syrup.**

mar [mär] *verb,* **marred, marring. 1.** to damage or spoil the appearance of: The top of the antique table was *marred* by several deep scratches. "Above them the blue sky hung like an endless dome *marred* by not one single cloud." (James Houston) **2.** to spoil the quality of; damage: The team's easy victory was *marred* by a serious injury to their quarterback.

---

manuscript The original meaning of *manuscript* was "a written work done by hand." (*Manus* is Latin for "hand.") In the Middle Ages, manuscripts of the Bible and other religious books were produced by monks. These manuscripts were beautifully decorated with illustrations, designs, special letters, and so on. Decorated manuscripts of this kind—called *illuminated manuscripts*—are regarded as art treasures today, such as the Book of Kells in Ireland. (The publisher of this dictionary holds the notion that the custom of using paragraphs began in the Middle Ages, to give these monk-artists a chance to illuminate the first letter of the first word of a paragraph. He points out that the ancient Greek authority Aristotle does not even mention the paragraph in his commentary on the art of writing.) The modern meaning of *manuscript* is the "working copy" of a book or article, before it is typeset and printed. Authors and publishers often abbreviate the term *manuscript* as *ms.* or *MS.*

---

man•u•script [man′ yə skript′] *noun, plural* **manuscripts. 1.** in early times, a book or paper written by hand. **2.** in modern times, a typewritten or handwritten copy of a book, article, or other piece of writing, prepared by a writer for typesetting and printing by a publisher.

man•y [men′ ē] *adjective.* **1.** being a large number; great in number: *Many* Americans watch the Super Bowl on TV each year. **2.** being a certain number: How *many* times have you seen that movie? —*noun; pronoun.* a large number: A lot of people enter that contest, but not *many* win anything.

Mao Tse-Tung [mou′ dzə doōng′] 1893–1976, Chinese communist leader, ruler of the People's Republic of China from 1949 to 1976. ♦ Also spelled **Mao Zedong.**

map [map] *noun, plural* **maps.** a drawing, chart, or other picture that shows a certain place and its important features, such as oceans, rivers, mountains, countries, cities, roads, and so on. —*verb,* **mapped, mapping. 1.** to make a map of; show on a map: Amerigo Vespucci was the first to *map* the coastline of South America. **2. map out.** to plan something in careful detail, as if making a map: The auto company has *mapped out* a big advertising campaign.

ma•ple [mā′ pəl] *noun, plural* **maples.** a tall tree that grows widely in the northern half of

maple The close-up view shows the winged seed pod, the green leaf of summer, and the gold leaf of fall.

Pronunciation Key: T–Z

t	ten; date	v	very; live
th	think	w	win; away
<u>th</u>	these	y	you
u̅	cut; butter	z	zoo; cause
ur	turn; bird	zh	measure

(Turn the page for more information.)

mar•a•thon [mar′ ə thän′] *noun, plural* **marathons. 1.** a foot race of 26 miles and 385 yards, run over roads and open ground rather than around a track. **2.** any very long race or competition: *In the 1930's people took part in dance* marathons *where they tried to dance for several days at a time.* ◆ The marathon race gets its name from the Battle of Marathon in 490 B.C., in which the Greeks defeated the Persians. A runner carried news of the battle to the city of Athens—a distance of about 26 miles. Legend has it that the runner fell dead just after giving the news.

marathon Joan Benoit winning the first Olympic marathon for women at the 1984 Games at Los Angeles.

mar•ble [mär′ bəl] *noun, plural* **marbles. 1.** a very hard, smooth stone that is used in buildings, floors, and statues. Marble is formed from heated limestone and is usually white or streaked with different colors. **2. marbles.** a children's game played with small balls that were once made of marble, but now are glass. Players take turns shooting their marbles to knock other players' marbles out of a ring. **3.** a ball of marble or glass used in this game.

march [märch] *verb,* **marched, marching. 1.** to walk with regular, even steps, as is done by soldiers, members of a band, people in a parade, and so on. **2.** to walk or move in a steady, determined way: *"Without looking at Bryan and Fay, he* marched *up the aisle in the direction of one of the exit doors."* (Noel Coward) —*noun, plural* **marches. 1.** the act of marching, or the distance marched: *The soldiers made a forced* march *of 40 miles in one day.* **2.** a piece of music with a strong steady beat, used for marching: *"Pomp and Circumstance" is a well-known* march *that is often played at school graduation ceremonies.*

March *noun.* the third month of the year. March has thirty-one days.

mare [mâr] *noun, plural* **mares.** the female of a horse or related animal, such as a donkey or zebra.

mar•ga•rine [mär′ jə rən] *noun, plural* **margarines.** a soft, smooth food that is used in place of butter. Margarine is made from vegetable oil and coloring or flavoring. ◆ This is also called **oleo** [ō′ lē ō] or **oleomargarine.**

mar•gin [mär′ jin] *noun, plural* **margins. 1.** the blank space between the edges of a page and the printed or written part. **2.** an extra part or amount in addition to what is needed: *President Nixon won the 1972 election by a wide* margin. *Planes landing at that small airfield have to be careful, because there's very little* margin *for error.* —**marginal,** *adjective: The teacher made some* marginal *comments on Michael's paper.* —**marginally,** *adverb.*

Ma•rie An•toi•nette [mə rē′ an′ twə net′] 1755–1793, the queen of France at the time of the French Revolution.

mar•i•gold [mar′ ə gōld′] *noun, plural* **marigolds.** a garden plant that has orange, yellow, or red flowers.

mar•i•jua•na [mar′ ə wä′ nə] *noun.* the dried leaves and flowers of a certain plant called HEMP. Marijuana is a drug that is sometimes smoked for its effect on the mind and feelings. It is against the law to sell, have, or use marijuana in the U.S.

ma•rine [mə rēn′] *adjective.* **1.** having to do with the ocean: *marine* mammals such as whales and dolphins. **2.** having to do with ships and boats: *He bought some paint for his sailboat at the* marine *supply store.* —**Marine,** *noun, plural* **Marines.** a member of the U.S. Marine Corps.

Marine Corps a branch of the U.S. Armed Forces under the Department of the Navy. Marines are trained and equipped to take part in landing operations during battle.

mar•i•o•nette [mar′ ē ə net′] *noun, plural* **marionettes.** a puppet or doll that is moved from above by pulling strings or wires attached to its feet, hands, head, and so on.

mark [märk] *noun, plural* **marks. 1.** anything on a surface that shows where something else has touched the surface, such as a spot, a line, a chip, and so on: *The baby left finger* marks *on the wall.* **2.** a line, sign, or symbol written or printed to show something: *The teacher put a check* mark *next to each right answer.* **3.** a letter or number used in school to show the level a student has earned; a grade: *Dave got the highest* mark *on the math test.* **4.** something

marks for editing In publishing, the marks used for editing a piece of writing are standard throughout the industry. The system has to be uniform, so that authors, editors, and typesetters can clearly understand each other. If you look in an English textbook, you may see a chart of these editing marks. There is also a chart of editing marks at the back of this dictionary.

used to show a certain position or place: a book *mark*. The runners were on their *mark* and the race was about to start. **5.** a thing that serves as a sign or symbol of something else: In business, when a person has a large corner office, it is usually a *mark* of importance within the company. **6.** a goal or target that is aimed at: Robin Hood was known for always hitting the *mark* with his arrows. The company's sales fell far short of the *mark* this month. —*verb,* **marked, marking. 1.** to make a mark: "Mason was standing against the kitchen doorway, trying to *mark* off how tall he was." (S.E. Hinton) **2.** to give a school mark to; grade: to *mark* a test paper. **3.** to be a mark or feature of; show or indicate: "The wind *marked* the swift approach of dawn . . ." (Walter Farley)

mark•er [mär′kər] *noun, plural* **markers. 1.** something that marks a spot: Sit where you see the place *marker* with your name on it. **2.** a pen or other tool used for marking or writing.

mar•ket [mär′kit] *noun, plural* **markets. 1.** a store or other place where certain goods are sold: We bought some steaks at the meat *market*. **2.** the public buying and selling of goods or services: The Watsons decided to put their house on the *market* and move into an apartment. **3.** buyers of a certain type: That science fiction movie was intended for the teenage *market*. **4.** a demand for something that is for sale: There is a large *market* for TV sets and VCR's in the U.S. —*verb,* **marketed, marketing. 1.** to sell or put up for sale: Italian shoe companies often *market* their products in other countries. ◆ **Marketing** is the process by which companies try to find buyers for their products and influence them to buy. Advertising and selling are major parts of marketing. **2.** to go shopping for food and supplies.

mar•lin [mär′lən] *noun, plural* **marlin** or **marlins.** a fish living in deep ocean waters. ◆ The **blue marlin** is a popular game fish.

mar•ma•lade [mär′mə lād] *noun, plural* **marmalades.** a jam made by boiling oranges or other fruit with sugar.

ma•roon¹ [mə rōōn′] *verb,* **marooned, marooning. 1.** to put a person on shore in a deserted or isolated place and leave him there: In olden times, a ship's captain would sometimes ma-

roon sailors on a deserted island as a punishment for wrongdoing. **2.** to leave someone alone or helpless in such a way; strand: Rickey complained that he was be *marooned* at the cabin all weekend with no car to get away.

maroon² *noun, plural* **maroons;** *adjective.* a dark brownish-red color.

mar•riage [mar′ij] *noun, plural* **marriages. 1.** the fact of being married: My grandparents have had a long and happy *marriage*. **2.** the act or ceremony of marrying; a wedding.

mar•row [mar′ō] *noun.* the soft substance that fills the hollow central part of a bone.

mar•ry [mar′ē] *verb,* **married, marrying. 1.** to legally join a man and a woman as husband and wife: In almost all states a man and woman have to be 18 to get *married* without their parents' permission. **2.** to take someone for one's husband or wife: She *married* her high-school sweetheart.

marlin The marlin has a spear-like upper jaw that measures about two feet long. It may weigh as much as 400 pounds.

Pronunciation Key: [ə] Symbol

The [ə] or *schwa* sound occurs in syllables without an accent. It can be spelled with any vowel, such as a in above, e in listen, i in pencil, o in melon, u in circus. It can also be a combination of vowels, such as io in action, ai in mountain, iou in precious.

(Turn the page for more information.)

Mars [märz] *noun.* **1.** the seventh-largest planet in the solar system. Mars has two moons and is the fourth planet in distance from the sun. **2.** the god of war in the religion of the ancient Romans.

marsh [märsh] *noun, plural* **marshes.** an area of soft, low land that is partly or completely covered by water.

mar•shal [mär′shəl] *noun, plural* **marshals. 1.** a kind of police officer who works for the federal court and has duties like those of a sheriff. **2.** the chief of the police or fire departments of some cities. **3.** a person in charge of a parade or ceremony. —*verb,* **marshaled, marshaling.** to arrange in proper order; organize: The lieutenant *marshaled* his troops on the parade ground. "He rose and paced around the small bleak room, as if he were *marshaling* his thoughts . . ." (Helen MacInnes)

Mar•shall [mär′shəl] **1. John,** 1755–1835, the chief justice of the U.S. Supreme Court from 1801 to 1835. **2. George C.,** 1880–1959, American general and statesman. **3. Thurgood,** born 1908, the first black justice of the Supreme Court.

marsh•mal•low [märsh′mel′ō] *noun, plural* **marshmallows.** a soft white candy covered with powdered sugar.

mar•su•pi•al [mär soo′pē əl] *noun, plural* **marsupials.** a group of animals that are found mostly in Australia. A female marsupial has a pouch on the outside of her body in which she can carry and nurse her young. Marsupials include the kangaroo, koala, and wombat, and also the opossum, which lives in the Americas.

mar•tial [mär′shəl] *adjective.* having to do with war; suitable for war.

martial arts certain methods of self-defense or fighting developed in Oriental countries such as Japan and China, involving hand-to-hand fighting without weapons. The martial arts include karate and judo.

martial law temporary rule by an army over an area of its own country. Martial law may be declared if there is an emergency where the civil government cannot control the country, as during wartime, rioting, or a natural disaster.

mar•tin [mär′tən] *noun, plural* **martins.** a bird that belongs to the swallow family, having dark feathers and a forked tail.

mar•tyr [mär′tər] *noun, plural* **martyrs. 1.** a person who is killed or is made to suffer greatly because of his religion or beliefs: Some early Christians were *martyrs* who were killed by the

Romans because they chose to worship Jesus. **2.** a person who dies or suffers greatly in serving some cause: "Ku Klux Klansmen shot and killed civil rights volunteer Viola Liuzzo; and the movement had another *martyr.*" (Stephen B. Oates)

mar•vel [mär′vəl] *noun, plural* **marvels.** someone or something that is very surprising, outstanding, or unusual: The development of the artificial heart is one of the *marvels* of modern medicine. —*verb,* **marveled, marveling** or **marvelled, marvelling.** to be filled with wonder or amazement; astonish: "Airplanes he *marveled* at, but they did not come close enough to frighten him." (Mary Norton)

mar•vel•ous [mär′vəl əs] *adjective, more/most.* **1.** causing wonder or great surprise; astonishing; amazing: It was a *marvelous* sight as our plane flew low over the Grand Canyon. **2.** very good; excellent; splendid: We had a *marvelous* time on our vacation in New York City. —**marvelously,** *adverb.*

Marx [märks] **Karl,** 1818–1883, German political philosopher and writer whose theories (known as **Marxism**) form the basis for modern socialism and communism.

Mary [mâr′ē] **1.** in the Bible, the mother of Jesus, known as the **Virgin Mary. 2. Mary Queen of Scots,** 1542–1587, the queen of Scotland from 1542 to 1587.

Mar•y•land [mar′ə lənd] a state on the east coast of the U.S. *Capital:* Annapolis. *Nickname:* "Old Line State." *Area:* 10,600 square miles. *Population:* 4,270,000.

Maryland At the U.S. Naval Academy in Annapolis, Maryland, students (called *midshipmen* in navy terms) line up for inspection.

mas•cot [mas′kät] *noun, plural* **mascots.** an animal, person, or thing that is supposed to bring good luck: My brother's high school football team has a bulldog for a *mascot.*

mas•cu•line [mas′kyə lin] *adjective, more/ most.* of or belonging to men or boys: "King," "prince," and "duke" are *masculine* titles.

mash [mash] *verb,* **mashed, mashing.** to beat or crush something into a soft mass: *mashed* potatoes. ". . . her sheets and her nightgown, which lay all *mashed* together in a pile on the floor." (Nancy Willard) —*noun, plural* **mashes.** a soft mixture of grain and warm water that is used for feeding horses and other animals.

mask [mask] *noun, plural* **masks. 1.** a covering worn to protect or hide the face: Firefighters often wear *masks* when they enter a smoke-filled building. **2.** anything that hides or covers something like a mask: His smile was a *mask* that hid his true feeling of disappointment. —*verb,* **masked, masking. 1.** to cover with a mask: The Lone Ranger was a famous *masked* cowboy hero of early radio and TV. **2.** to hide or cover up: "Their front windows were *masked* by hedges and shrubs." (Raymond Chandler) ". . . he *masked* his sorrow in silence." (Marguerite Henry)

ma•son•ry [mā′sən rē] *noun.* **1.** the trade or work of building things with stone or brick. ♦ A person who does such work is a **mason. 2.** something built of stone or brick, such as a wall or a fireplace.

mas•quer•ade [mas′kə rād′] *noun, plural* **masquerades.** a party or dance where people wear masks and costumes. —*verb,* **masqueraded, masquerading.** to look like or pretend to be someone else; pose.

mass [mas] *noun, plural* **masses. 1.** a body of matter that has no particular shape; an indefinite amount of something: The heavy rains left a *mass* of dirt at the bottom of the driveway. **2.** a large quantity or amount: The hillside was covered with a *mass* of wildflowers. **3. masses** or **the masses.** ordinary or average people as a group; the common people. **4.** the amount of matter that a given body contains. Mass causes a thing to have a certain weight from the pull of gravity, and it is not affected if the thing changes in form. —*verb,* **massed, massing.** to gather or form into a mass. —*adjective:* **1.** of or including many people: Farmers from the Midwest held a *mass* protest in Washington this week. **2.** on a large scale: Radio and TV are forms of *mass* communication. ♦ **Mass produc tion** is the use of machinery and standard methods to make many items of the same product, such as a car.

Mass *noun, plural* **Masses.** the main religious service in the Catholic Church and in some other Christian churches.

Massachusetts The historic Minuteman Statue in Lexington, Mass., site of the first battle of the American Revolution.

Mas•sa•chu•setts [mas′ə chōō′sits] a state in the northeastern U.S., on the Atlantic Ocean. *Capital:* Boston. *Nickname:* "Bay State." *Area:* 8,300 square miles. *Population:* 5,800,000.

mas•sa•cre [mas′ə kər] *noun, plural* **massacres.** a cruel and bloody killing of many people or animals: In the "St. Valentine's Day *Massacre*" on February 14, 1929, Chicago gangsters dressed as police shot down seven members of another gang. —*verb,* **massacred, massacring.** to kill in this way.

mas•sage [mə säzh′] *noun, plural* **massages.** a treatment of the body by rubbing, stroking, and striking certain parts, as to relax the muscles, reduce pain, improve blood circulation, and so on. —*verb,* **massaged, massaging.** to give someone a massage.

mas•sive [mas′iv] *adjective, more/most.* having great size or mass; strong and heavy; huge.

mast [mast] *noun, plural* **masts.** a long pole that rises straight up from the deck of a ship, used to hold up the sails.

mas•ter [mas′tər] *noun, plural* **masters. 1.** a person who has power or control over others: The dog ran over as soon as its *master* called. **2.** a person who has great skill or is a great expert at something: The **Old Masters** is a name given to the great European painters of the 1400–1600's, such as Leonardo da Vinci and Rembrandt. **3. Master.** a word used instead of

---

Pronunciation Key: Accent Marks

[′] is the normal accent mark. It shows where the main stress falls on a word.
[′] is a secondary accent mark. It shows a lighter stress than the primary accent. For example:

tel • e • vis • ion [tel′ə vizh ′ən]

(Turn the page for more information.)

"Mister," to address a small boy. —*adjective.* **1.** very skilled at working or doing things with the hands: a *master* carpenter, a *master* mechanic. **2.** most important; main: a *master* bedroom. A *master* copy of something is the original form that is used to make other copies. **3.** being in control of a system or operation: a *master* switch, a *master* plan. —*verb,* **mastered, mastering. 1.** to become the master of; bring under control: She *mastered* her fear of speaking in public and gave a speech to the entire school. **2.** to become an expert in; become skillful at: Danny hasn't been able to *master* a two-wheel bike yet. ♦ The fact of mastering something is **mastery.**

thick or tangled mass: a *mat* of hair, a *mat* of weeds. —*verb,* **matted, matting.** to become tangled in a thick mass.

match[1] [mach] *noun, plural* **matches.** a thin piece of wood or cardboard coated on one end with a chemical that will catch on fire when it is rubbed against a rough surface.

match[2] *noun, plural* **matches. 1.** a person or thing that is equal to or very much like another: Nancy is a great tennis player and is a *match* for any of the boys in her class. **2.** someone or something that goes well with another: That blue sweater would be a good *match* for your gray pants. **3.** a game or contest: a chess *match.*

---

masterpiece There were three ranks of workers in the Middle Ages. An *apprentice* was a boy or young man who trained, usually for seven years, to learn a craft; he received room and board, but no pay. An apprentice was then promoted to become a *journeyman*, a man with enough skill to perform the work, but one who did not own his own shop. He was paid by a *master,* the owner of a business. To become a master, a worker had to produce a piece of work good enough to be accepted by other masters. This was his *masterpiece*. The word then came to be applied to other forms of great achievement: "In 1805 Herman Melville completed his *masterpiece, Moby-Dick* or *The Whale*." (William Rose Benét). Our only warning about this word is the same as with other "high-powered" words—apply it only when it truly fits the situation.

---

mas•ter•piece [mas′tər pēs′] *noun, plural* **masterpieces.** an outstanding work or accomplishment, especially in the arts.

mas•to•don [mas′tə dän′] *noun, plural* **mastodons.** a large animal that once lived in many parts of the world but is now extinct. It was related to the modern elephant.

mat [mat] *noun, plural* **mats. 1.** a small piece of material used as a floor covering: People often have a welcome *mat* outside their front door so that visitors can wipe their feet. **2.** a small piece of material put under a dish, lamp, or other such object to protect a surface or act as a decoration: She set the table with place *mats* and matching napkins. **3.** a thick pad used on the floor of a gymnasium or other sports area to protect someone in falling or jumping. **4.** a

—*verb,* **matched, matching. 1.** to be similar or go well together: "Jackrabbits began to show the change from brown to white, to *match* the coming snow." (A.B. Guthrie) **2.** to be the same as: In the game of 'Go Fish,' you put together cards that *match.* **3.** to compete with as an equal: "He kept to that long stride and she had to hop-skip to *match* it." (Andre Norton)

mate [māt] *noun, plural* **mates. 1.** one of a pair: I'm looking for the *mate* to this sock. **2.** a husband or wife. **3.** the male or female of a pair of animals or birds: A female lion does much more hunting than its *mate.* **4.** an officer on a ship: On a merchant ship, the first *mate* ranks just below the captain. —*verb,* **mated, mating.** of animals, to join together for breeding.

ma•ter•i•al [mə tir′ē əl] *noun, plural* **materials.**

---

material for a story How do you get material for a story? Here are a few possibilities. (1) <u>Your experiences</u>. Many writers develop stories from things that happened to them personally. Usually, it's better if the experience is the starting point for a story, rather than the story being an exact description of what happened. (2) <u>Experiences of others</u>. You can listen to people talk about their interesting experiences, and draw on that. (3) <u>Current events</u>. Writers often skim through the daily papers looking for odd or interesting events. (4) <u>Events in history</u>. A writer can create a story by placing characters against a background of historical events. (5) <u>Classic stories</u>. It's said there are no new stories, only the same ones told over and over.

1. what something is made of or used for: Wood is a common building *material*. **2.** cotton or other such fabric for clothing. —*adjective, more/most.* **1.** of or in the form of matter; physical. **2.** having to do with the body or the physical world: *material* needs such as food and clothing. —**materially,** *adverb.*

ma•ter•i•al•is•tic [mə tir′ ē ə lis′ tik] *adjective, more/most.* much too concerned with material things; caring too much about what one owns or has: She's a very *materialistic* girl who always has to have the latest in clothes.

ma•ter•i•al•ize [mə tir′ ē ə līz] *verb,* **materialized, materializing. 1.** to take on a physical form; become a material being: Old stories about Count Dracula claimed he could *materialize* as a wolf or a bat. ". . . two riders *materialized* out of the mist." (Iris Murdoch) **2.** to become real: He promised to help us, but so far nothing has *materialized.*

ma•ter•nal [mə tur′ nəl] *adjective, more/most.* **1.** of or like a mother: *maternal* pride. **2.** related through the mother's side of the family: Your mother's father is your *maternal* grandfather.

math [math] *noun.* short for **mathematics.**

math•e•mat•i•cal [math′ ə mat′ i kəl *or* math′-mat′ i kəl] *adjective.* having to do with mathematics: Many people now use pocket calculators for *mathematical* operations.

math•e•mat•ics [math′ ə mat′ iks *or* math′-mat′ iks] *noun.* the study of numbers, quantities, and shapes, and of the way these things are measured and related to one another. Arithmetic, algebra, and geometry are branches of mathematics. ♦ A person who is an expert in mathematics is called a **mathematician.**

things are made up of matter. Matter can be a solid, liquid, or gas. **2.** anything that is to be dealt with or thought about; a subject that is given attention: The *Wall Street Journal* reports on business and financial *matters.* **3.** an unpleasant or difficult situation; a problem. ♦ Used in the phrase **the matter:** What's *the matter* with Judy? She hasn't said a word all morning. —*verb,* **mattered, mattering.** to be important; make a difference: Buy some paper towels at the store—it doesn't *matter* which brand.

mat•tress [mat′ rəs] *noun, plural* **mattresses.** a thick pad that is used for sleeping on. A mattress usually fits within the frame of a bed.

ma•ture [mə choor′ *or* mə toor′] *adjective, more/most.* **1.** fully grown or developed: *Mature* oak trees can be 100 feet high. **2.** having to do with or suitable for an adult: When a movie is rated "For *Mature* Audiences Only," younger people can't see it without an adult. —*verb,* **matured, maturing.** to become full-grown; become an adult. —**maturity,** *noun.*

max•i•mum [maks′ sə məm] *noun, plural* **maximums.** the greatest or highest number or point: The gas tank of our car holds a *maximum* of 15 gallons. —*adjective.* greatest or highest possible: The U.S. government has set a *maximum* highway speed limit of 55 miles per hour.

may [mā] *verb,* past tense **might. May** is a special verb that is used with other verbs in these meanings: **1.** it is more or less likely: I can't find my jacket—I *may* have left it at school. **2.** it is allowed: Swimmers *may* use any part of the beach south of 28th Street. **3.** it is to be hoped that: "*May* the gods heap misfortune on your head!" (Jean Fritz)

may/can Have you ever had a conversation like this? You ask: "Can I read your newspaper?" The answer: "Yes, you can. But you *may* not." The person was pointing out the difference between *can,* meaning "be able to " and *may,* meaning "be allowed to." But this distinction is weakening. Even the very strict *Harper's Dictionary of Contemporary Usage* admits, "It is only fair to say that the distinction is often ignored." The advantage of *can* is that it carries both ideas in the same words. Also, *may* has a more common meaning, "It's possible; it's somewhat likely." Thus "I *may* have the day off" is unclear. We do recommend you use "*May* I" when asking for permission to do something; it sounds more polite.

mat•i•nee [mat′ ə nā′] *noun, plural* **matinees.** a play or other performance in the afternoon.

ma•tron [mā′ trən] *noun, plural* **matrons. 1.** a married woman: the *matron* of honor at a wedding. **2.** a woman who is in charge of others, as at a hospital or prison.

mat•ter [mat′ ər] *noun, plural* **matters. 1.** anything that has weight and takes up space. All

Pronunciation Key: A–F

a	and; hat	ch	chew; such
ā	ate; stay	d	dog; lid
â	care; air	e	end; yet
ä	father; hot	ē	she; each
b	boy; cab	f	fun; off

(Turn the page for more information.)

May *noun.* the fifth month of the year. May has 31 days.

may•be [mā′bē] it may be; it's possible; perhaps: Dad is half an hour late—*maybe* he got caught in traffic.

may•on•naise [mā′ə nāz′ *or* mā′ə nāz′] *noun.* a thick dressing for salads, sandwiches, and other foods. Mayonnaise is made of egg yolks, oil, vinegar or lemon juice, and seasonings, beaten together until thick.

may•or [mā′ər] *noun, plural* **mayors.** a person who is elected as the head of a city or town government.

maze A maze formed from hedges at the historic Chateau of Villandry in France.

maze [māz] *noun, plural* **mazes. 1.** a complicated series of paths through which it is hard to find one's way: "The building is such a *maze* of stairs and doors and wide white corridors that you can easily lose your way." (Ernie Pyle) **2.** any complicated situation like a maze: He finds the income tax system very confusing and says it's a *maze* of rules and forms.

Mc•Kin•ley [mə kin lē] **1. William.** 1843–1901, the twenty-fifth president of the United States, from 1897 to 1901. **2. Mount McKinley.** the highest mountain in North America, in south-central Alaska (20,320 feet high).

me [mē] *pronoun.* the pronoun **I** when used as an object: Call *me* tomorrow morning. Please pass *me* the milk. Darryl lent this tape to *me.*

Mead [mēd] **Margaret,** 1901–1978, American anthropologist.

mead•ow [med′ō] *noun, plural* **meadows.** a large area of grassy land, especially one where farm animals feed or where hay is grown.

mead•ow•lark [med′ō lärk′] *noun, plural* **meadowlarks.** a common songbird of North America that has a brownish back and wings and a yellow breast with a black bar across it.

mea•ger [mē′gər] *adjective, more/most.* very little; small in quantity; poor: The soldiers in the prison camp were allowed only a *meager* diet of rice and a few bits of fish.

meal¹ [mēl] *noun, plural* **meals.** the food served or eaten at one time: a *meal* of soup and a salad.

meal² *noun, plural* **meals.** corn or other grain that has been ground up into a coarse powder.

mean¹ [mēn] *verb,* **meant, meaning. 1.** to have the sense of; carry the thought of: The words "create" and "manufacture" *mean* "make." **2.** to want to do or say; have in mind or as a purpose: She lives on Elm Street; no, I *mean* Oak Street. **3.** to be a sign of: A solid yellow line in the road *means* cars aren't supposed to cross it. **4.** to have a certain effect: "Having such an important pig was going to *mean* plenty of extra work." (E.B. White)

mean² *adjective,* **meaner, meanest. 1.** wanting to hurt others; not kind or good; nasty; cruel. **2.** hard to handle or deal with; tough: That pitcher throws a *mean* fastball. "The lock . . . was brass and big as a dinner plate and had a *mean* look." (Nancy Willard) **3.** low in rank or quality; poor. ◆ This last meaning is used mostly in older writing.

Mt. McKinley The Indian name for this mountain is *Denali,* which means "The Great One."

mean³ *noun, plural* **means. 1.** something that is halfway between two extremes; a middle point, condition, or action. **2.** in mathematics, the sum of a series of items divided by the number of items; the average: The *mean* of the numbers from 1 to 11 is 6. **3. means.** the way that something is done or can be done: "He looked about for some *means* of making himself comfortable . . ." (Alice Walker) **4. means.** money or property; wealth: "In fact our *means* are dreadfully small." (Henry James) —*ad-*

M

jective. being in a mean or middle position; average: The *mean* temperature here in January is about 30 degrees.

me•an•der [mē an′ dər] *verb,* **meandered, meandering.** to follow a slow, wandering course: "*Meandering* mountain streams watered the lush green grass and the air was warm without being hot." (Walter Farley)

mean•ing [mē′ ning] *noun, plural* **meanings.** the way a thing is meant; what is intended: The Spanish word "adios" has the same *meaning* as English "good-bye." "The full *meaning* of the night's events hit me, and I began crying." (Harper Lee) —**meaningful,** *adjective.* having a serious meaning; important. —**meaningless,** *adjective.* having no meaning.

---

meaning of a story At one time, writers would directly state the meaning or *moral* of a story. They would would pause in the middle of the action to address the reader: "Perhaps, reader, I have another illustration, which will set my intention in still a clearer light before you." (Henry Fielding, *Amelia;* 1752). The idea behind this was that a story should contain a message or lesson. It was up to the author to make sure the reader understood this message. You may have read old fables or folk tales that end with a moral like: "One good turn deserves another." Nowadays, this isn't done. The attitude in modern writing is that meaning should not be stated directly, because the same story can mean different things to different readers.

---

meant [ment] *verb.* the past form of **mean:** "I learned more and more to know what he *meant* and what he wanted me to do." (Anna Sewell)

mean•time [mēn′ tīm′] *noun.* **in the meantime.** in the time between: "'And his clothes must go to the cleaners.' 'But what will he wear *in the meantime?*'" (Mary Norton)

mean•while [mēn′ wīl′] *adverb.* **1.** in the time between; in the meantime: It was a full minute since she had entered the room. *Meanwhile,* nobody else had moved or said a word. **2.** at the same time: I'll get down the Christmas lights; *meanwhile,* you start putting the ornaments on the tree.

mea•sles [mē′ zəlz] *noun.* **1.** a disease that is caused by a virus and that can spread easily from one person to another. It causes people to break out in red spots on the skin, have a fever, and have a cough and other symptoms of a bad cold. **2.** any similar virus disease, such as **German measles.**

meas•ure [mezh′ ər] *verb,* **measured, measuring. 1.** to find out how big something is, what it weighs, how much of it there is, and so on: Common instruments for *measuring* include a ruler, a scale, and a thermometer. **2.** to measure a certain size or amount: Paper for typewriters *measures* 8-1/2 by 11 inches. **3.** to mark off by measuring: "(He) watched her *measure* out the black tea leaves into the pot." (John Fowles)

—*noun, plural* **measures. 1.** a way of measuring something: Pounds, inches, and degrees are common units of *measure* in the U.S. **2.** something used to measure, such as a **tape measure** or a **measuring cup. 3.** a way of judging something; a standard: Grades in school are not necessarily a true *measure* of intelligence. **4.** an amount that can be measured: She is a college teacher, and she's also had some *measure* of success as a writer. **5.** an action done to make something happen: Speed bumps were put in the school parking lot as a safety *measure.* **6.** a bar of music.

meas•ure•ment [mezh′ ər mənt] *noun, plural* **measurements. 1.** the act of measuring; a way of finding the size or amount of a thing. **2.** the size or amount found by measuring: Items used to build a house come in standard *measurements.*

meat [mēt] *noun, plural* **meats. 1.** the flesh of an animal that is eaten for food. Beef and pork are kinds of meat. The flesh of birds or fish is not usually called meat. **2.** the part of anything that can be eaten: coconut *meat,* the *meat* of a walnut. **3.** the main part of something: Newspaper reporters learn to get the *meat* of their story into the first few sentences.

Mec•ca [mek′ ə] a city in Saudi Arabia. It is the birthplace of Muhammad and the holiest city of the Muslim religion. *Population:* 400,000.

me•chan•ic [mə kan′ ik] *noun, plural* **mechanics.** a person who is skilled at fixing or working with machines: an auto *mechanic.*

Pronunciation Key: G–N			
g	give; big	k	kind; cat; back
h	hold	l	let; ball
i	it; this	m	make; time
ī	ice; my	n	not; own
j	jet; gem; edge	ng	having

(Turn the page for more information.)

M

> **mechanics** In writing, the term *mechanics* refers to the "working parts" of language—the basic rules that govern the way words appear in print. Mechanics includes *punctuation* (such as where to use a comma in a sentence), *capitalization* (such as which words to capitalize in a title), and *form* (such as how to set up a paper; how to arrange a table of contents and a bibliography; how to present quotations and footnotes). Mechanics is important. For example, there's no doubt that a mystery story is more interesting if the writer knows how to use quotation marks properly to indicate speech by the characters.

me•chan•i•cal [mə kan′ i kəl] *adjective.* **1.** using or having to do with machines or tools: *mechanical* drawing, *mechanical* engineering. **2.** made or worked by a machine: a *mechanical* teddy bear that can walk and talk. **3.** acting like a machine; without any feeling or expression. —**mechanically,** *adverb:* "Without taking her eyes off his face, she *mechanically* pulled on her long gloves." (Isak Dinesen)

interfere in other people's business in a rude or unwanted way: Whenever my uncle comes to visit he starts *meddling* in the kitchen and telling Mom she doesn't cook things the right way. —**meddler,** *noun.*

me•di•a [mē′ dē ə] *noun.* **1.** the plural of **medium. 2.** *also,* **the media.** the means of public communication, such as newspapers, television, and radio.

> **media** When we add words from other languages, we usually change them to fit the patterns of English. For example, we get *auditorium* from Latin. In Latin, a word like this would form its plural by changing the "um" to "a"—*auditoria*. But in English we say "Madison High School has one of the largest *auditoriums* of any school in the state." (It's not a good idea to use fancy Latin endings like "stadia" for "stadiums.") A few words retain their Latin form even when used in English. "Television, radio, newspapers, and news magazines are the important news *media* in the U.S." Here, the word *media* is a plural of *medium.* The plural is formed in the Latin way, by changing "um" to "a." "The mayor claims that the *media* is trying to force him out of office." Strictly speaking, this sentence should read "the *media* <u>are</u> trying," because *media* is a plural word.

me•chan•ics [mə kan′ iks] *noun.* **1.** the branch of science that deals with motion, and with the effect of force on bodies in motion or at rest: *Mechanics* is used in designing an aircraft or building a bridge. **2.** the way in which some action is carried out: The famous pitcher Tom Seaver wrote a book on the *mechanics* of pitching.

mech•a•nism [mek′ ə niz′ əm] *noun, plural* **mechanisms. 1.** the working parts of a machine: the *mechanism* of a watch or a clock. **2.** the arrangement the parts of a large or complicated system: the *mechanism* of the Federal government.

med•al [med′ əl] *noun, plural* **medals.** a round, flat piece of metal something like a coin, having a design or writing on it. Medals are often given as awards for bravery in war or for some outstanding achievement: The winner of an event in the Olympic Games gets a gold *medal.* ◆ A **medallion** is a large, round medal, or an ornament shaped like this.

med•dle [med′ əl] *verb,* **meddled, meddling.** to

med•i•cal [med′ i kəl] *adjective.* having to do with the study and use of medicine: a *medical* school, a problem needing *medical* attention.

Med•i•care [med′ i kâr] *noun.* government health insurance in the United States that pays medical bills for people who are 65 years of age and older. ◆ **Medicaid** is a similar program for people of all ages who cannot afford to pay for medical care.

med•i•ca•tion [med′ ə kā′ shən] *noun.* **1.** something used to treat disease or relieve pain; a medicine: The doctor gave her some *medication* for her skin rash. **2.** the act of treating someone with medicine.

med•i•cine [med′ ə sən] *noun, plural* **medicines. 1.** a drug or other substance that is used to treat, prevent, or cure disease or to relieve pain or injuries. ◆ Something used this way is said to be **medicinal** [mə dis′ ə nəl]. **2.** the science of treating and understanding disease. Medicine deals with methods or efforts to keep people alive, keep them in good health, and help them not to suffer.

M

medicine man among the early American Indians and certain other groups, a person believed to have special powers to cure sickness and deal with evil spirits.

me•di•e•val [med′ē′vəl *or* mid′ē′vəl] *adjective.* having to do with the Middle Ages: *medieval* art. *Medieval* warfare involved knights fighting in armor.

me•di•o•cre [mē′dē ō′kər] *adjective.* not unusual or outstanding; average or below-average; not very good: He didn't study much this year and got only *mediocre* grades.

med•i•tate [med′ə tāt′] *verb,* **meditated, meditating.** to think for a period of time about something; focus the mind in a serious way. People often meditate for religious reasons, to relax, to clear their mind of problems, and so on. —**meditation,** *noun.*

Mediterranean The Italian village of Portovenere, in northern Italy, on the Mediterranean Sea. The word *Mediterranean* means "middle of the earth." To the ancient Greeks and Romans, this sea was the center of the world.

Med•i•ter•ra•ne•an Sea [med′i tə rā′nē ən] a large inland sea between Europe, Asia, and Africa.

me•di•um [mē′dē əm] *noun, plural* **mediums** or **media. 1.** something that is in the middle: She's trying to find a happy *medium* between being too strict with her children and letting them do whatever they want. **2.** the certain conditions in which something lives or acts: According to this book, sandy soil is the proper *medium* for growing strawberry plants. **3.** a form of communication or expression: "If I could have learned to sew . . . we might have found a *medium* in which to communicate." (Mary McCarthy) **4.** a person who supposedly can receive messages that are sent by dead people to their living relatives or friends.

—*adjective.* having a middle position; in the middle: a *medium*-sized shirt, a steak cooked *medium* rather than rare or well-done.

med•ley [med′lē] *noun, plural* **medleys. 1.** a mixture of songs or tunes performed together: She sang a *medley* from the musicals of Rodgers and Hammerstein. **2.** a mixture of things that do not ordinarily go together.

meek [mēk] *adjective,* **meeker, meekest.** having a shy or gentle nature; not confident or aggressive; mild. —**meekly,** *adverb:* "The little fellow blushed and *meekly* followed Salters forward." (Rudyard Kipling)

meet [mēt] *verb,* **met, meeting. 1.** to come face to face with; come upon: I happened to *meet* my friend at the supermarket this afternoon. **2.** to be introduced to: Dad, I'd like you to *meet* my teacher, Mr. Simpson. **3.** to keep an appointment with: I told Jeff I'd *meet* him in front of the theater at 7:15. **4.** to come together with; join: The yard has a row of bushes that *meets* the back fence. **5. meet with.** to experience: to *meet with* bad weather. —*noun, plural* **meets.** a gathering for competition: a track *meet.*

meet•ing [mē′ting] *noun, plural* **meetings. 1.** a gathering of a group of people, especially one that is arranged for a certain purpose: The publishing company held a *meeting* of all its salesmen to introduce the year's new books. **2.** the act of coming together.

Me•ir [mī ēr′] **Golda,** 1898–1978, the prime minister of Israel from 1969 to 1974.

mel•an•chol•y [mel′ən käl′ē] *adjective, more/ most.* **1.** feeling sad or depressed; low in spirits; gloomy: "'Only it is so very lonely here,' Alice said in a *melancholy* voice; and . . . two large tears came rolling down her cheeks." (Lewis Carroll) **2.** causing this feeling: ". . . the boat floating on the darkening river with *melancholy* trees on either side." (Katherine Mansfield) —*noun.* low spirits; sadness.

Mel•bourne [mel′bərn] a seaport city in southeastern Australia. *Population:* 3,000,000.

mel•low [mel′ō] *adjective,* **mellower, mellowest. 1.** soft, full, and rich: a singer with a *mellow* voice. **2.** made wise and gentle by age and

Pronunciation Key: O–S			
ō	over; go	ou	out; town
ô	all; law	p	put; hop
oo	look; full	r	run; car
o͞o	pool; who	s	set; miss
oi	oil; boy	sh	show

(Turn the page for more information.)

M

experience: That actress used to be very nervous and quick-tempered, but she's become *mellow* over the years. —*verb*, **mellowed, mellowing.** to make or become mellow.

mel•o•dra•ma [mel′ ə drä′ mə] *noun, plural* **melodramas.** a play, movie, or book in which the characters act in a very exaggerated way. ♦ Something that is like melodrama is **melodramatic:** I know Linda was happy to win the prize, but it was a bit *melodramatic* of her to fall to the floor when she heard the news.

mel•o•dy [mel′ ə dē] *noun, plural* **melodies. 1.** a series of musical notes that make up a tune: The "Star-Spangled Banner" was written to the *melody* of an old British song. **2.** the main part of a piece of music.

mem•brane [mem′ brān′] *noun, plural* **membranes.** a thin layer of skin or tissue that lines parts of the body.

me•men•to [mə men′ tō] *noun, plural* **mementos** or **mementoes.** something that serves as a reminder of an event or time in the past; a souvenir: Karen keeps those theater tickets as a *memento* of her vacation in New York.

mem•o [mem′ ō] *noun, plural* **memos. 1.** in business, a note or short letter written to someone within the same company: The boss sent out a *memo* saying that the office would be closed for Washington's Birthday. **2.** any brief note or letter written to remind a person of something. ♦ The full form of this word is **memorandum** [mem′ ə ran′ dəm].

memos In business, memo writing has certain rules that are important to both the memo writer (who is hoping to be promoted as he proceeds through his career) and the reader (who wants clear and recent information). (1) Be brief. A long memo makes a demand on the reader. (2) Lead with the main point. If the message is that employees should have parking stickers on their cars, say it up front. (3) Use simple, direct language. Phrases such as "It has been determined that" or "An extensive study has revealed that" fill up the page but don't contribute anything to meaning. Recently, the head of a large American company sent a memo to the staff to announce that a court fight of great importance for the company had finally ended. The first sentence read, "It's over!"

♦ Something that is musical or full of melody is **melodious** [mə lō′ dē əs]: "She spoke in a low, soft, warmly *melodious* voice that soothed those who listened." (Betty Smith)

mel•on [mel′ ən] *noun, plural* **melons.** a large fruit that grows on a vine. Melons have a sweet, juicy pulp that can be eaten. Cantaloupes and watermelons are well-known types of melons.

melt [melt] *verb*, **melted, melting. 1.** to change from a solid into a liquid by heating: The ice cubes *melted* into water in the hot sun. He poured *melted* butter over the popcorn. **2.** to turn to liquid; dissolve: The sugar *melted* in the cup of tea. **3.** to disappear gradually; fade: ". . . Alec wished that he could *melt* into the night." (Walter Farley) **4.** to make or become gentler or milder; soften: "He can sing Al Jolson's greatest hits in a way that *melts* your heart." (Nancy Willard)

Mel•ville [mel′ vil′] **Herman,** 1819–1891, American novelist, author of *Moby Dick.*

mem•ber [mem′ bər] *noun, plural* **members.** a person, animal, or thing that belongs to a certain group: Our neighbor is a *member* of the city fire department. Lions and tigers are *members* of the cat family. ♦ The fact of being a member is **membership.**

mem•o•ra•ble [mem′ rə bəl *or* mem′ə rə bəl] *adjective.* that is worth remembering; important: "Other people, so I have read, treasure *memorable* moments in their lives." (Walker Percy)

memorial The Lincoln Memorial in Washington D.C.

me•mo•ri•al [mə môr′ ē əl] *noun, plural* **memorials.** something that serves to honor the memory of an important person or event: In

1982 the Vietnam *Memorial* was dedicated in Washington, D.C., to honor those killed in the Vietnam War.

Memorial Day a holiday to remember and honor American servicemen who died fighting for the United States. Memorial Day was originally on May 30th and is now on the last Monday in May.

mem•o•rize [mem′ ə rīz′] *verb,* **memorized, memorizing.** to learn by heart; commit to memory: Actors in a stage play have to *memorize* their lines. "Rab made Johnny *memorize* the twenty-two names." (Esther Forbes)

mem•or•y [mem′ rē *or* mem′ ə rē] *noun, plural* **memories. 1.** the ability to remember things: Mayor Smith has a great *memory* and never forgets people's names once he's met them. **2.** someone or something that is remembered: I have pleasant *memories* from my childhood of the summers I spent on a lake in Connecticut. **3.** all that can be remembered: He forgot his sheet music and had to sing the song from *memory.* **4.** the place in a computer that stores all the information put into it, and that gives instructions to other parts of the machine to handle the information.

Mem•phis [mem′ fis] a city in southwestern Tennessee, on the Mississippi River. *Population:* 650,000.

men [men] *noun.* the plural of **man.**

men•ace [men′ is] *noun, plural* **menaces.** something that can cause harm; a threat; danger: The newspaper editorial referred to subway crime as a *menace* to the entire city. "When he spoke she was frightened by the *menace* in his voice." (John Le Carré) —*verb,* **menaced, menacing.** to put in danger; threaten. ♦ Usually used as an adjective: "It shook its head, making a *menacing* motion with its horns." (Marjorie Kinnan Rawlings) —**menacingly,** *adverb:* "The bear edged away to one side, growling *menacingly.*" (Jack London)

mend [mend] *verb,* **mended, mending. 1.** to put back in good condition; repair; fix: "I *mended* that little vase you broke." (Iris Murdoch) **2.** to get better; heal or improve: Her sprained ankle has *mended* and now she's running again. "I always promised to *mend* my bad ways." (Claude Brown) —*noun, plural* **mends.** a place that has been mended.

men•tal [men′ təl] *adjective.* **1.** having to do with the mind: a *mental* test, *mental* health. **2.** having to do with people suffering from a disease of the mind: *mental* illness, a *mental* hospital, a *mental* patient. —**mentally,** *adverb.*

men•tion [men′ shən] *verb,* **mentioned, mentioning.** to speak or write about; refer to: "Well, do you remember that photograph I *mentioned* to you?" (Peter Shaffer) "He looked up as his name was *mentioned.*" (Isaac Asimov) —*noun, plural* **mentions.** the fact of mentioning; a statement or reference: There was no *mention* of the accident in today's paper.

men•u [men′ yoo] *noun, plural* **menus. 1.** a list of the food and drinks that are available in a restaurant or other eating place, along with their prices. **2.** in a computer, a list on the screen showing the different things that the person using the program may choose to do.

mer•chan•dise [mur′ chən dīs *or* mur′ chən dīz] *noun.* things that are bought and sold; goods: That store sells books, magazines, newspapers, and other such *merchandise.*

mer•chant [mur′ chənt] *noun, plural* **merchants. 1.** a person in the business of buying and selling goods for a profit: a coffee *merchant.* **2.** a person who owns or is in charge of a store; a storekeeper. —*adjective.* having to do with business or trade: a *merchant* ship.

merchant marine the ships of a nation that are used to carry goods bought from or sold to other countries.

Mercury The planet Mercury, in a photo by the Mariner 10 spacecraft.

Mer•cu•ry [mur′ kyə rē] *noun.* **1.** the smallest planet in the solar system. Mercury is the

---

Pronunciation Key: T–Z

t	ten; date	v	very; live
th	think	w	win; away
<u>th</u>	these	y	you
u	cut; butter	z	zoo; cause
ur	turn; bird	zh	measure

(Turn the page for more information.)

479

closest planet to the sun. **2.** the ancient Roman god who served as a messenger for other gods and was the god of roads and travel.

mer•cu•ry [mur′ kyə rē] *noun.* a heavy silver-white metal that is a chemical element. Mercury is a liquid at normal temperatures. It is used in thermometers to indicate the temperature, and in lamps, switches, and batteries.

mer•cy [mur′ sē] *noun, plural* **mercies. 1.** kind or gentle treatment given to someone who is under one's control or power, especially by not giving punishment that is deserved or expected: Friends of the convicted man asked the judge to have *mercy* on him and give him a light sentence. **2.** something one is thankful for; a blessing: It's a *mercy* that someone saw the smoke and called the fire department. —**merciful,** *adjective.* —**merciless,** *adjective.*

mere [mēr] *adjective,* **merer, merest.** nothing more or less than; only: There was a *mere* scratch on his leg, but he shouted and cried as if it had been broken.

mere•ly [mēr′ lē] *adverb.* not more than; only: I'm not trying to interfere; I *merely* want to help you.

merge [murj] *verb,* **merged, merging. 1.** to come together as one; join: Cars entering a highway have to *merge* with the passing traffic. **2.** in business, to join together two or more companies as a single company: In 1985 the General Electric Company *merged* with RCA to form a huge electronics company.

merg•er [mur′ jər] *noun, plural* **mergers.** the act or fact of merging, especially the merging of two businesses to form a single company.

me•rid•i•an [mə rid′ ē ən] *noun, plural* **meridians.** one of a group of imaginary lines on the earth from the North Pole to the South Pole. Meridians are used to indicate LONGITUDE, which shows position on the earth's surface. ◆ A line passing through Greenwich, England is the **prime meridian.** Distances east and west are measured according to this line.

mer•it [mer′ it] *noun, plural* **merits. 1.** the fact of having value or worth; having a good quality: Boy Scouts can earn *merit* badges for doing certain worthwhile things. "His writing in history, criticism, and politics had considerable *merit.*" (James Boswell) **2. merits.** the actual facts or qualities of something, whether good or bad. —*verb,* **merited, meriting.** to be worthy of something; have a right to; deserve.

mer•maid [mur′ mād′] *noun, plural* **mermaids.** an imaginary creature of the sea that has the head and upper body of a woman, and the

lower body and tail of a fish. In olden times sailors told stories of seeing beautiful mermaids who tried to lure them off their ships.

mer•ry [mer′ ē] *adjective,* **merrier, merriest.** full of fun and good cheer; very happy; jolly: At Christmastime people often wish each other '*Merry* Christmas.' —**merrily,** *adverb.*

mer•ry-go-round [mer′ ē gō round′] *noun, plural* **merry-go-rounds.** an amusement ride that consists of a round platform that turns, with seats in the shape of horses and other animals; also called a CAROUSEL.

mesa A mesa in Monument Valley, Utah. *Mesa* comes from the Spanish word for "table."

me•sa [mā′ sə] *noun, plural* **mesas.** a hill or mountain with steep sides and a very flat top. Mesas are common in the southwestern United States and in northern Mexico.

mesh [mesh] *noun, plural* **meshes.** a net made of fine, tightly connected threads or wires. Mesh is used for window screens and kitchen strainers. —*verb,* **meshed, meshing.** to fit together; fit into place: The gears of a car *mesh* when the driver shifts to a different gear.

Mes•o•po•ta•mi•a [mes′ ə pə tā′ mē ə] an ancient region in southwest Asia, now part of Iraq. It was one of the earliest centers of modern civilization. —**Mesopotamian,** *adjective; noun.*

mes•quite [mes kēt′] *noun.* a low, thorny shrub that grows in the American Southwest and other hot, dry climates.

mess [mes] *noun, plural* **messes. 1.** a place that is dirty and unpleasant, with useless or unwanted things lying around: "Jane wasn't kidding about her room. It's a *mess,* with clothes scattered all over the place." (Judy Blume) **2.** a situation that is unpleasant, confusing, or hard to deal with: He got himself into a real *mess* when he borrowed Dad's car without asking. **3.** in the armed forces, a place for a large group

M

of people to eat. —*verb*, **messed, messing, mess up.** to make a mess: The baby *messed up* my puzzle, and now I can't find half the pieces.

mes•sage [mes′ij] *noun, plural* **messages.**
1. information passed on from one person to another or others, especially by sending it through a third party: Dave wasn't home when I called, so I left a *message* with his sister to have him call me back. **2.** an official statement or speech: The "State of the Union" address is the President's yearly *message* to Congress. **3.** a lesson, moral, or other point contained in a story: The *message* of the movie was that a criminal is always punished in the end.

mes•sen•ger [mes′ən jər] *noun, plural* **messengers.** a person who carries messages, packages, and so on from one place to another.

mes•sy [mes′ē] *adjective,* **messier, messiest.** in a mess; dirty; untidy: a *messy* room with newspapers all over the floor. **—messiness,** *noun.*

met [met] *verb.* the past form of **meet.**

me•tab•o•lism [mə tab′ə liz′ əm] *noun, plural* **metabolisms.** all the processes that a living plant or animal carries on within itself in order to stay alive. These processes include changing food and water into new tissues or into energy, and breaking down and removing waste products. **—metabolic** [met′ ə bäl′ ik], *adjective.*

metamorphosis Follow the arrows: the first stage is the egg; next is the caterpillar, then the *pupa,* inside a cocoon. The final stage is an adult Alfalfa Butterfly.

met•a•mor•pho•sis [met′ ə môr′ fə sis] *noun, plural* **metamorphoses. 1.** in lower animals, a series of complete changes in body form that take place from birth to the adult stage. **2.** any complete or very obvious change: Over the years that her TV show was on the air, the actress made a complete *metamorphosis* from an awkward teenager to a beautiful young woman.

metaphor Metaphor is one of the most important tools a writer can use. "On the other side the hill rose up sharply and at the top the *jagged rotten teeth* of the mountain showed against the sky." (John Steinbeck) (An expression using *like, as,* or another such word to make a comparison is a SIMILE.) Robert Frost speaks of "the *dust* of snow" falling from a tree, Charles Dickens of "the smooth white *sheet* of snow upon the roofs." Bret Harte describes snow as "a *sea* of white," and Dylan Thomas says that snow "*swam* and drifted out of the trees." The purpose of a metaphor is to give a new look at something. George Orwell said, "Never use a metaphor or simile that you are used to seeing in print." That could apply to "a blanket of snow" or "white as snow." Instead, try to create a new metaphor. Willa Cather describes snow-covered fields as *"wrapped* in a white *silence."* Thomas Wolfe writes that as snow fell "the air was *blind,* the earth was *carpeted,* the streets were *numb."*

met•al [met′ əl] *noun, plural* **metals.** any of a large group of substances, such as iron, gold, lead, aluminum, and copper. Metals are chemical elements, or are alloys made by combining one element with another. In general, metals are heavy, have a shiny grayish or whitish color, and can conduct heat and electricity well. Most metals can be melted, hammered into a thin sheet, or drawn out into a wire.

me•tal•lic [mə tal′ ik] *adjective.* made of, containing, or like metal: *metallic* paints, a gray, *metallic* color.

met•a•phor [met′ ə fôr′] *noun, plural* **metaphors.** a way of describing something by suggesting that it is like another thing. Writers

Pronunciation Key: [ə] Symbol

The [ə] or *schwa* sound occurs in syllables without an accent. It can be spelled with any vowel, such as **a** in above, **e** in listen, **i** in pencil, **o** in melon, **u** in circus. It can also be a combination of vowels, such as **io** in action, **ai** in mountain, **iou** in precious.

(Turn the page for more information.)

often use metaphor to tell about a person or a place. For example: "I stared back at the lights of Bay City . . . scattered points of light drew together and became a jeweled bracelet in the show window of the night." (Raymond Chandler) —**metaphorical,** *adjective:* American cities often have *metaphorical* nicknames, such as "The Gateway to the West" (St. Louis) and "The City with the Big Shoulders" (Chicago).

me•te•or [mē′tē ər] *noun, plural* **meteors.** a piece of metallic or rocky matter from space that falls at a high speed to the earth. As the meteor moves through the air in the earth's atmosphere, it becomes extremely hot and glows white, creating a brief flash of light across the sky.

me•te•or•ic [mē′tē ôr′ik] *adjective.* **1.** having to do with a meteor. **2.** happening very quickly or in a brief time, like a meteor moving through the sky: The Apple Computer Company had a *meteoric* rise to become one of America's largest companies.

me•te•or•ite [mē′tē ə rīt′] *noun, plural* **meteorites.** a meteor that has fallen to earth without being totally burned up. Some meteorites have left craters in the earth more than a mile wide.

me•te•or•ol•o•gy [mē′tē ə räl′ə jē] *noun.* a science that studies weather and the events in the earth's atmosphere that produce weather conditions. ◆ An expert in meteorology is a **meteorologist.**

me•ter[1] [mē′tər] *noun, plural* **meters.** a way of measuring how long something is, or how far it is between two places. The meter is the basic unit of measure in the METRIC SYSTEM. It is equal to 39.37 inches, or just over 3-1/4 feet.

meter[2] *noun, plural* **meters.** any device or machine used to measure or record the amount of something: Photographers sometimes use a light *meter* to tell how much light is in a room. An electric *meter* on a house shows how much electricity is being used. ◆ Also used in compounds such as thermo*meter,* speedo*meter.*

meter[3] *noun, plural* **meters. 1.** in poetry, a regular arrangement of words in a line, according to which words are accented (spoken strongly) and which are not. The meter of a poem is determined by which syllable in a group of two or three gets the accent, such as to*day,* *dai*ly, or *yes*terday. **2.** in music, a similar pattern of rhythm, based on the number of strong and weak beats in a measure.

meter Most poems are written with a regular and repeated pattern of sound. John McCrae's famous poem "In Flanders Fields" begins with the line "In Flanders fields the poppies blow." ("In Flanders fields the poppies blow." ("da-DUM da-DUM da-DUM da-DUM.") Then comes "Between the crosses, row on row." ("da-DUM da-DUM da-DUM da-DUM" again.) As you can see (and hear) both lines follow the same rising-and-falling pattern of syllables. There are four sets of sounds, each having a weak (that is, softer) syllable, followed by a strong one (that is, louder).

me•te•or•oid [mē′tē ə roid′] *noun, plural* **meteoroids.** the name for a meteor in space, outside the earth's atmosphere. ◆ A **meteor shower** takes place when the earth passes through a large group of meteoroids as it moves through space.

meth•od [meth′əd] *noun, plural* **methods.** a way of doing something: This book claims to present a new *method* of losing weight. The police think one man committed all three robberies, because the same *method* of entering the house was used each time.

methods of writing In writing a story, do you start with a beginning event and then make up the rest as you go along? Or do you work out the whole plot in your mind before you begin to write? William Faulkner said that he began by creating a character, and then, "Once he stands up on his feet and begins to move, all I do is trot along behind him with a paper and pencil . . ." Anthony Burgess said that he writes and rewrites page one until he has it right, then does page two, and so on. Some writers actually begin the story with the end: "I always know the ending; that's where I start." (Toni Morrison). A very famous remark relating to this was made by Edward Gibbon, whose *Decline and Fall of the Roman Empire* is one of the greatest histories ever written. He said, "Once I got the first sentence right, the rest followed."

M

me·thod·i·cal [mə thäd′ i kəl] *adjective, more/most.* acting according to a method; exact; orderly: "It was impossible to tell whether the new servant would turn out as absolutely *methodical* as his master required . . ." (Jules Verne) —**methodically,** *adverb.*

met·ric [met′ rik] *adjective.* **1.** having to do with the metric system: a *metric* ruler. The 100-meter dash is the *metric* equivalent of the 100-yard dash. **2.** *also,* **metrical.** having to do with meter in poetry or music.

metric system a system of measurement that is based on units of ten. In the metric system, the *meter* is the basic way to measure length, and the *kilogram* (1000 grams) is the basic measurement for weight, or mass. The *liter* is usually used to measure capacity (how much something holds). Most countries use the metric system, but the United States generally uses what is called the **English system** or **traditional system** (feet, miles, pounds, gallons, and so on).

me·trop·o·lis [mə träp′ ə lis] *noun, plural* **metropolises.** a very large and important city, such as Tokyo, Mexico City, Paris, and so on. ◆ The word *metropolis* goes back to an ancient Greek term meaning "mother city."

met·ro·pol·i·tan [met′ rə päl′ ə tən] *adjective.* having to do with a large city: the New York *Metropolitan* Museum of Art. ◆ A **metropolitan area** is made up of a central city and its nearby smaller towns and suburbs.

Mex·i·can [mek′ sə kən] *noun, plural* **Mexicans.** a person born or living in Mexico. —*adjective.* having to do with Mexico, its people, or their culture.

Mex·i·co [mek′ si ko] **1.** a country in southern North America, south of the U.S. *Capital:* Mexico City. *Area:* 761,700 square miles. *Population:* 71,000,000. **2. Gulf of Mexico.** a part of the Atlantic Ocean east of Mexico and South of the U.S.

Mexico City the capital of Mexico, in the south-central part of the country. *Population:* 15,000,000.

Mi·am·i [mī am′ ē] a city in southeastern Florida. *Population:* 348,000.

mice [mīs] *noun.* the plural of **mouse.**

Mi·chel·an·ge·lo [mī′ kəl an′ jə lō] 1475–1564, Italian painter and sculptor.

Mich·i·gan [mish′ ə gən] **1.** a state in the north-central U.S., bordered by Lakes Michigan, Huron, Erie, and Superior. *Capital:* Lansing. *Nickname:* "Wolverine State." *Area:* 58,200 square miles. *Population:* 9,300,000. **2.** the third largest of the Great Lakes.

mi·crobe [mī′ krōb′] *noun, plural* **microbes.** a living thing so small that it cannot be seen without a microscope; also called a MICROORGANISM. ◆ This word is usually used for those microorganisms that cause disease.

mi·cro·com·put·er [mī′ krō kəm pyoo′ tər] *noun, plural* **microcomputers.** (also called a **micro**) a small computer that has all its functions stored on a MICROPROCESSOR.

mi·cro·film [mī′ krə film′] *noun, plural* **microfilms.** film on which images have been reduced to a very small size. Microfilm is viewed with a projector that enlarges the image.

mi·cro·or·gan·ism [mī′ krō ôr′ gən iz əm] *noun, plural* **microorganisms.** a very tiny living thing that can only be seen with a microscope. Bacteria and viruses are microorganisms. ◆ The study of such organisms is called **microbiology.**

mi·cro·phone [mī′ krə fōn′] *noun, plural* **microphones.** an instrument that changes sound waves into electrical signals. Microphones are used to make sound louder, to broadcast radio and TV shows, and to record sound for movies, phonograph records, and tape recordings.

mi·cro·pro·cess·or [mī′ krō prä′ ses ər] *noun, plural* **microprocessors. 1.** a single CHIP that contains all of the things that a computer uses to process information. **2.** another name for a MICROCOMPUTER.

Mexico City The *Paseo* is the main street of the "City of Mexico." It has a series of landscaped circles with a monument in each circle.

Pronunciation Key: Accent Marks

[′] is the normal accent mark. It shows where the main stress falls on a word.

[′] is a secondary accent mark. It shows a lighter stress than the primary accent. For example:

tel • e • vis • ion [tel′ə vizh′ən]

(Turn the page for more information.)

mi·cro·scope [mī′ krə skōp′] *noun, plural* **microscopes.** a device that is used to look at something that is too small to be seen with the eye alone. A microscope uses a combination of lenses to make the object look much larger. Microscopes are often used in science to study bacteria, body cells, and so on.

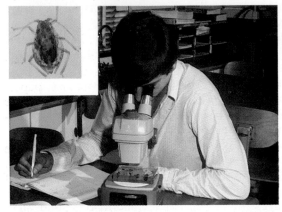

microscope A student uses a microscope to view the tiny aphid, seen in the inset at upper left magnified at 20X (twenty times life size).

mi·cro·scop·ic [mī′ krə skäp′ ik] *adjective.* **1.** not able to be seen without a microscope: An ameba is a *microscopic* form of life. **2.** with or as if with a microscope: The photo showed a *microscopic* view of pond algae. The sergeant made a *microscopic* examination of the soldier's locker.

mi·cro·wave [mī′ krō wāv′] *noun, plural* **microwaves.** an electric wave that has a very short length, used in radar and to send long-distance television signals.

microwave oven an oven that uses microwaves to cook foods much more quickly than a gas or electric oven.

mid [mid] *adjective.* at or in the middle. ♦ Usually used in compounds: a man in his *mid*-thirties. The canoe struck a rock in *mid*stream.

mid·dle [mid′ əl] *adjective.* at or near the center; away from the sides, the front and back, or the beginning and end: I sat in the *middle* seat on our plane trip, between Mom and Dad. —*noun, plural* **middles.** something that is in this place or position: a road with a white line down the *middle*. The phone always seems to ring when we're right in the *middle* of eating dinner.

middle age the time of life when a person is not young and not old; the age from about forty to about sixty. ♦ Also used as an adjective: a *middle-aged* man.

Middle Ages the period in European history between ancient times and the beginning of modern times. The Middle Ages is usually considered to have started in the year 476, when the Western Roman Empire fell, and ended in about 1500, when life in Europe began to change greatly.

middle class the group of people who rank in the middle in a society. They have more money than those in the poor, lower class, but less money than the rich, upper class. ♦ Also used as an adjective: a house in a *middle-class* neighborhood.

Middle East a region of northeastern Africa and southwestern Asia, the site of many ancient civilizations. It includes such modern nations as Libya, Egypt, Lebanon, Syria, Israel, Jordan, Iran, Iraq, and Saudi Arabia.

Middle West a region of the U.S. that includes the states of Ohio, Indiana, Michigan, Illinois, Wisconsin, Minnesota, Iowa, and Missouri. ♦ Also known as the **Midwest.**

mid·get [mij′ it] *noun, plural* **midgets. 1.** a very small person. A midget is much smaller than an ordinary adult but has a normal body shape and normal intelligence. **2.** a very small thing compared to others of its kind: a *midget* racing car.

mid·night [mid′ nīt′] *noun.* twelve o'clock at night; the middle of the night.

midst [midst] *noun.* the middle: "We are in the *midst* of the longest heat wave Atlantic City has seen in twenty-five years." (Judy Blume)

mid·way [mid′ wā] *adjective; adverb:* in the middle; halfway. —*noun, plural* **midways.** an amusement park at a fair, circus, or carnival, usually including rides and games.

might¹ [mīt] *verb.* the past form of **may.**

---

micro-/macro- These two prefixes came into English from Greek, through the route of Latin. They are a contrasting pair. *Micro-* means "very small; tiny; minute." *Macro-* means the opposite, "very large; very great.".Both words are used to form scientific and cultural terms (although *micro-* is far more common). *Macroeconomics* studies broad, general trends of economics. A *microclimate* is the particular climate of one small area. The two words are sometimes used in contrast with each other. For example, a *microcosm* [mī′ krō käz′ əm] is a very specific, limited view of a subject, while a *macrocosm* [ma′ kro käz′ əm] is a wide, general view.

M

might[2] *noun.* great strength or power: "He pulled with all his *might* and the window came open." (Maurice Sendak)

might•y [mī′ tē] *adjective,* **mightier, mightiest.** showing great strength or power; very strong: Songs and poems often refer to the *mighty* ocean. A famous old saying about writing is "The pen is *mightier* than the sword." —*adverb. Informal.* very: He'll be *mighty* upset if he doesn't get to go with us. —**mightily,** *adverb.*

mi•grant [mī′ grənt] *noun, plural* **migrants.** **1.** an animal that regularly moves its home each year because of changes in the weather, the food supply, or other conditions: Canada geese are *migrants* that fly south for winter months. **2.** a person who travels from one place to another to work. **Migrant workers** are often hired to pick fruit, vegetables, or other crops during the season when they are ripe.

mi•grate [mī′ grāt′] *verb,* **migrated, migrating.** **1.** of animals, to move from one place to another at a certain time each year: Whales in the northern Pacific *migrate* thousands of miles south every winter to bear their young. **2.** of people, to move from one place to live in another because of certain problems or conditions: "We had *migrated*, in 1901, from Indiana to Montana, where my father was to be the first principal of the Teton County High School." (A.B. Guthrie).

migration A group of barren-ground caribou migrating across the tundra of northern Canada.

mi•gra•tion [mī′ grā′ shən] *noun, plural* **migrations.** the act or fact of migrating: Caribou form herds of up to 100,000 animals during their *migration.*

mike [mīk] *noun, plural* **mikes.** a short word for MICROPHONE.

mild [mīld] *adjective,* **milder, mildest. 1.** not having great force; not rough or harsh: a *mild* winter with warm temperatures. She had a *mild* headache, but she went to work anyway. **2.** calm and gentle: In movies Woody Allen usually plays a *mild*-mannered character. **3.** not strong in taste or smell; not sharp, sour, or bitter: a *mild* wine, a *mild* Cheddar cheese.

mil•dew [mil′ dōō′] *noun.* a fungus disease that attacks plants and some products made from plant or animal matter, such as leather, paper, or cloth. Mildew grows in closed areas where dampness is trapped. —*verb,* **mildewed, mildewing.** to become coated with mildew.

mild•ly [mīld′ lē] *adverb.* **1.** in a mild way: The nurse spoke *mildly* to the nervous little boy. **2.** slightly: "The farmers were *mildly* hopeful of a good rain before long." (John Steinbeck)

mile [mīl] *noun, plural* **miles. 1.** a way of measuring distance. It is equal to 5280 feet, or about 1.6 kilometers. **2. nautical mile.** a way of measuring distance for sea or air travel, equal to about 6080 feet.

mile•age [mī′ lij] *noun.* **1.** the number of miles that have been traveled or that are to be traveled: What's the *mileage* from Trenton to Dover? **2.** the number of miles that a vehicle can travel on one gallon of fuel: Diesel engines usually get better *mileage* than ordinary gas engines. **3.** *Informal.* an amount or period of use: Uncle Carl has really gotten a lot of *mileage* out of that old winter coat of his.

mile•stone [mīl′ stōn′] *noun, plural* **milestones. 1.** a marker placed alongside a road to show the distance in miles to a certain place. **2.** something that is a sign of progress or of some important event: Winning the Oscar for Best Actress was a *milestone* in her career.

mil•i•tant [mil′ ə tənt] *adjective, more/most.* ready to fight or struggle; aggressive: a *militant* political party that wants to overthrow the present government. —*noun, plural* **militants.** a person who is militant: In 1979, Iranian *militants* attacked and took over the U.S. embassy in Teheran.

Pronunciation Key: A–F			
a	and; hat	ch	chew; such
ā	ate; stay	d	dog; lid
â	care; air	e	end; yet
ä	father; hot	ē	she; each
b	boy; cab	f	fun; off

(Turn the page for more information.)

M

mil•i•tar•y [mil′ ə ter′ ē] *adjective.* having to do with soldiers, the armed forces, or war: People train to become army officers at the U.S. *Military* Academy. —*noun.* **the military.** the armed forces of a country.

mi•li•tia [mə lish′ ə] *noun, plural* **militias.** a group of citizens who are given military training so that they can help the armed forces during a war or other emergency. The Minutemen were a militia during the American Revolution.

milk [milk] *noun, plural* **milks. 1.** a white liquid food made in the bodies of female mammals to feed their babies. Cow's milk is often used as food by people. **2.** the white juice of certain fruits or plants: coconut *milk.* —*verb,* **milked, milking. 1.** to draw milk from an animal: to *milk* a cow. —**milky,** *adjective:* "Her face had turned a *milky* yellow color." (George Orwell)

milk•shake [milk′ shāk′] *noun, plural* **milkshakes.** a chilled drink made of flavored milk and ice cream, whipped or shaken together.

milk•weed [milk′ wēd′] *noun.* a plant that is filled with a milky juice and has large, silky seed pods.

Milky Way 1. a white path of stars that can be seen across the night sky. The Milky Way is made up of billions of stars. **2. Milky Way Galaxy.** a galaxy that includes the stars seen as the Milky Way. Earth and the other planets orbiting the sun are part of this galaxy.

mill The Currier and Ives print *The Old Grist Mill,* (1863). The word *grist* means grain that is ground in a mill.

mill [mil] *noun, plural* **mills. 1.** a large machine that grinds wheat or other grain into flour or meal. **2.** any similar machine to crush or grind food: pepper *mill.* **3.** a building containing machines to grind grain. ◆ A person who owns or operates a mill is a **miller. 4.** a building where large machines make a certain product: a paper *mill,* a steel *mill.* —*verb,* **milled, milling.**

1. to grind or make something with a mill. **2.** to move around in a circle or moving mass with no special direction: "There we were, thousands and thousands of us, *milling* around the border like cattle . . ." (Edna Ferber)

mil•li•me•ter [mil′ ə mē′ tər] *noun, plural* **millimeters.** a unit of measure equal to one-thousandth of a meter, or about .03937 inch.

mil•lion [mil′ yən] *noun, plural* **millions.** one thousand times one thousand; 1,000,000. —**millionth,** *adjective; noun.*

mil•lion•aire [mil′ yən âr′] *noun, plural* **millionaires.** a person who has a million dollars or more in money or property.

Mil•ton [milt′ ən] **John,** 1608–1674, English poet, author of *Paradise Lost.*

Mil•wau•kee [mil wô′ kē] a city in southeastern Wisconsin, on Lake Michigan. *Population:* 640,000.

mim•e•o•graph [mim′ ē ə graf′] *noun, plural* **mimeographs.** a machine that is used to make copies of written pages, or a copy made from such a machine. —*verb,* **mimeographed, mimeographing.** to make copies with this machine.

mim•ic [mim′ ik] *verb,* **mimicked, mimicking. 1.** to copy someone or something; imitate: Children sometimes *mimic* other children to make fun of them. **2.** to resemble closely in appearance: The viceroy butterfly *mimics* the monarch butterfly because birds are less likely to eat the monarch. —*noun, plural* **mimics.** a person or animal that mimics. ◆ The fact of mimicking something else is **mimicry.**

mince [mins] *verb,* **minced, mincing. 1.** to cut or chop meat or other food into very small pieces. **2.** to choose words very carefully; keep from saying something directly: "I do not *mince* matters in front of the family . . ." (T.S. Eliot)

mince•meat [mins′ mēt′] *noun.* a sweet filling for pie. Mincemeat is made of spices, raisins, finely cut fruits, and sometimes meat.

mind [mīnd] *noun, plural* **minds. 1.** the part of a person that can think; the part that learns, knows, remembers, and decides things. **2.** the ability of the mind to think and feel; intelligence. **3.** a normal state of the mind: We speak of a person losing his *mind,* being out of his *mind,* and so on. **4.** the use of the mind; one's thoughts or attention: He almost had an accident because he didn't keep his *mind* on the road. **5.** one's opinion or point of view: to change your *mind,* to make up your *mind.* —*verb,* **minded, minding. 1.** to take care of; watch over: to *mind* a baby. **2.** to not like something; be against; object to: Do you *mind* if I borrow this book? **3.** to pay attention to; be concerned about. ♦ This meaning is used in special phrases such as **mind your manners, mind your own business** or **never mind:** Just pick up the big pieces of wood; *never mind* about those little sticks.

mine[1] [mīn] *pronoun.* the one that belongs to me: On the way back I rode Cathy's bike and she rode *mine.*

mine[2] *noun, plural* **mines. 1.** a place where people dig into the earth to take out useful or valuable substances, such as coal, iron, copper, silver, gold, uranium, and so on. **2.** a thing that is thought of as being like a mine, because it is a source of something useful or valuable: She's been guiding visitors around the park for years and is a *mine* of information about the place. **3.** a bomb or other explosive charge that is hidden under the ground or the water. A mine is set to explode when someone moves or touches it. —*verb,* **mined, mining. 1.** to take out something useful or valuable from the ground: Today most of the world's diamonds are *mined* in South Africa. ♦ This work is called **mining. 2.** to hide bombs underground or underwater: The harbor had been *mined* to keep enemy ships from entering.

min•er [mīn′ ər] *noun, plural* **miners.** a person who works in a mine.

min•er•al [min′ ər əl] *noun, plural* **minerals. 1.** a solid substance that is found in nature, but which is not alive and is not formed from plant or animal matter. Rocks are made up of different minerals. Lead, iron, gold, and quartz are minerals. **2.** any natural substance that is taken from the earth because it is useful or valuable, such as coal, oil, natural gas, salt, or sand.

min•gle [ming′ gəl] *verb,* **mingled, mingling. 1.** to mix with another thing; combine: "The little sandy-haired woman gave a squeak of *mingled* fear and disgust." (George Orwell) **2.** to mix with other people; be part of a group: ". . . her party is going badly, when her guests sit in corners and refuse to *mingle.*" (Dorotl Parker)

min•i•a•ture [min′ ē ə chər *or* min′ ə chər] *noun, plural* **miniatures. 1.** something that is a smaller copy of something else: "Beside her stood a small girl, a *miniature* of her mother." (James Houston) **2.** a very small painting. At one time many European artists painted miniatures of people to be worn inside a locket or other piece of jewelry. —*adjective.* very small; tiny: a *miniature* poodle. ♦ **Miniature golf** is played in an area much smaller than a regular course.

min•i•mum [min′ ə məm] *noun, plural* **minimums.** the smallest amount; the least possible: You have to get a *minimum* of 30 questions right to pass the test. —*adjective.* being the lowest or smallest amount: The police and fire departments usually require that a person be a certain *minimum* height to join the force.

minimum wage the lowest rate of pay for workers that is allowed by law. A company may not pay less than the minimum wage.

min•is•ter [min′ i stər] *noun, plural* **ministers. 1.** in the Protestant church, a person who has charge of religious services; the head of a church. **2.** in countries other than the U.S., the head of a large department of the government: The British Foreign *Minister* is a position similar to the U.S. Secretary of State. **3.** a person who is sent to a foreign country to represent his or her government. A minister ranks below an AMBASSADOR. —*verb,* **ministered, ministering.** to take care of; give help to: "Aunt Alexandra *ministered* to Francis, wiping his tears away with her handkerchief." (Harper Lee)

min•is•try [min′ ə strē] *noun, plural* **ministries. 1.** the office or work of a minister. **2.** a department of government headed by a minister: In Israel the armed forces are under the control of the *Ministry* of Defense.

mink Minks hunt near water and on land. Their diet includes frogs, rabbits, and snakes.

mink [mingk] *noun, plural* **minks** or **mink.** a small animal related to the weasel. It is valued for its thick, beautiful brown fur. In the wild, minks live in wooded areas near water.

Pronunciation Key: G–N

g	give; big	k	kind; cat; back
h	hold	l	let; ball
i	it; this	m	make; time
ī	ice; my	n	not; own
j	jet; gem; edge	ng	having

(Turn the page for more information.)

M

Min•ne•ap•o•lis [min′ē ap′ə lis] a city in eastern Minnesota, on the Mississippi River. *Population:* 375,000.

Min•ne•so•ta [min′ə sō′tə] a state in the north-central U.S., bordered by Canada. *Capital:* St. Paul. *Nickname:* "Gopher State." *Area:* 84,100 square miles. *Population:* 4,200,000.

min•now [min′ō] *noun, plural* **minnows.** any one of a group of small freshwater fish. Many different types of minnows are found in North America and in most other parts of the world.

min•u•end [min′yōō end′] *noun, plural* **minuends.** in mathematics, the number from which another number is subtracted: In the problem 5−2=3, the *minuend* is 5.

mi•nus [mī′nəs] *preposition.* **1.** made less by; less: Eight *minus* two is six. **2.** *Informal.* without: Jerry finished the race *minus* his left shoe. —*adjective.* **1.** less than or lower than: In that course, a grade of 80 to 82 is a B *minus.* **2.** less than zero: The coldest temperature ever in Florida was *minus* two degrees.

> **minor/miner** These two words are often confused. People write, "It's only a *miner* problem" because they think of the *-er* ending of words like *smaller* and *lesser.* Or they write, "This disease is found among coal *minors,*" thinking of *sailor, actor, inventor,* and so on. Let's get these words straight. The person who works in a mine—just remember the e in that word—is a *miner.* Think of the word for something that a miner takes from the earth, *mineral.* The word meaning "smaller, lesser" is *minor.* In law, a young child is called a *minor.* Think of the word that comes from this, *minority.*

mi•nor [mī′nər] *adjective.* **1.** not of great size or importance; unimportant: We've never had any trouble with the car except for a few *minor* repairs. **2.** not as important as another or others; smaller; lesser: The Utica Blue Sox are a *minor*-league team in baseball. —*noun, plural* **minors.** a person who is under the age set by law for certain things, such as voting, serving in the military, signing a contract, and so on. In most states of the U.S., a minor is someone under 18.

mi•nor•i•ty [mə nôr′ə tē] *noun, plural* **minorities. 1.** the smaller of two unequal numbers; less than half: The poll showed that only a *minority* of those asked were for the idea—it was 34% for, 66% against. **2.** *also,* **minority group.** a group of people who are of a different race, nationality, or religion than a larger group living in the same area: The U.S. government recognizes by law several *minorities,* including Blacks, American Indians, Hispanics, and Asian-Americans. ◆ Often used as an adjective: That company has a plan to hire more *minority* workers.

mint¹ [mint] *noun, plural* **mints. 1.** a plant used for flavoring such foods as jelly, ice cream, gum, and tea. **2.** a candy flavored with mint.

mint² *noun, plural* **mints. 1.** a place where the national government of a country makes the coins and paper money used in the country. **2.** *Informal.* a large amount of money: That's a beautiful watch—it must have cost you a *mint.* —*verb,* **minted, minting.** to make money in a mint: to *mint* quarters. —*adjective.* in perfect condition; like new. ◆ Usually used in the phrase **in mint condition.**

—*noun, plural* **minuses.** *also,* **minus sign.** a sign [−] showing that something is to be subtracted.

min•ute¹ [min′it] *noun, plural* **minutes. 1.** a way of measuring time. One minute is equal to sixty seconds, and sixty minutes make one hour. **2.** a very small amount of time; a moment: I knew she was your sister the *minute* I saw her. **3. minutes.** a written record of what was said or done at a meeting. **4.** one sixtieth part of an area that is measured in degrees, such as an arc or angle: The exact center of North America is in the state of North Dakota at a longitude of 100 degrees, 10 *minutes.*

mi•nute² [mī nōōt′] *adjective,* **minuter, minutest. 1.** very, very small; tiny: They found some *minute* specks of gold dust in the shallow river water. **2.** made up of many fine points; very careful or exact: The drawings of Leonardo da Vinci are famous for their *minute* detail.

mint Coins must be perfect to pass inspection by this employee at the Royal Canadian Mint.

M

mis- "These included misconstruction of documents, miscitation and misidentification of publications, misleading translations, misquotations, misattribution . . ." (Henry A. Turner, American historian) That is a barrage of "mis" words! The form *mis-* is what is called a "negative prefix." That is, it means "not." A negative prefix has the effect of changing a word so that it means the opposite; it generally carries the sense of "bad," "badly," "wrong," or "lacking." "It was rare in her experience to so *miscalculate* . . ." [calculate wrongly] (Mary Gordon) "Looking back upon a dreadful *misspent* life . . ." [spent badly] (Daniel Defoe) Turner's statement above may seem hard to read. But remember that the prefix can be separated. If you take *identification* and add the idea of "badly" or wrongly" to it, you can see what the word means.

min·ute·man [min′ it man′] *noun, plural* **min·utemen.** a volunteer soldier of the American Revolution. Minutemen were not part of the regular Army, but they were ready to fight "at a minute's notice."

mir·a·cle [mir′ ə kəl] *noun, plural* **miracles.** **1.** an amazing event that goes beyond the laws of nature. Many religions tell of miracles performed by a holy leader, such as curing people who are sick or dying. In the Bible, the miracles of Jesus include turning water into wine, walking on water, and bringing a dead man back to life. **2.** any event that is very amazing, lucky, or surprising: "A young spider knows how to spin a web without any instructions from anybody. Don't you regard that as a *miracle?*" (E.B. White)

mi·rac·u·lous [mə rak′ yə ləs] *adjective, more/ most.* **1.** highly amazing; wonderful; marvelous: to make a *miraculous* recovery from a disease. **2.** having to do with a religious miracle: a *miraculous* medal showing the appearance of the Virgin Mary. —**miraculously,** *adverb.*

mi·rage [mi räzh′] *noun, plural* **mirages. 1.** a sight that seems to appear but is not actually there. People driving in the desert on a hot day often see what looks like a lake far off in the distance. This mirage is caused by currents of hot air that change the way light rays from the sky reach the eyes. **2.** something that is not what it seems or that cannot come true; an illusion.

mir·ror [mir′ ər] *noun, plural* **mirrors. 1.** a smooth, shiny surface that reflects the image of whatever is in front of it. Most mirrors are made of glass with a thin coating of silver, aluminum, or other metal on the back. **2.** anything thought of like a mirror in showing or reflecting something in an exact way: The stock market is a *mirror* of what business conditions are in general. —*verb,* **mirrored, mirroring.** to reflect with or as if with a mirror: "A crackling fire was *mirrored* in the gleaming brass of the hearth." (James Herriot)

mis·cel·la·ne·ous [mis′ ə lā′ nē əs] *adjective.* being a number of things that are different from each other; not fitting into a single group: Mom has a big kitchen drawer where she keeps pencils, bottle openers, scissors, string, glue, and other *miscellaneous* items.

mis·chief [mis′ chif] *noun.* **1.** an act that causes some trouble or damage, but is not seriously bad: At Halloween children sometimes do *mischief,* such as putting soap on people's windows. **2.** a feeling of wanting to tease or cause harm: Billy's thoughts were full of *mischief* as he took down the can of spray paint.

mis·chie·vous [mis′ chi vəs] *adjective, more/ most.* **1.** full of or caused by mischief: "There was something *mischievous* about her sometimes, you could see she was looking for trouble, in a nice way." (John Fowles) **2.** suggesting mischief: " . . . eyes that could be one moment *mischievous* or laughing and in the next moment sad." (William L. Shirer)

mis·de·mean·or [mis′ di mē′ nər] *noun, plural* **misdemeanors.** in law, a crime that is less serious than a FELONY. A misdemeanor is punished by a fine, a work program, or a short jail sentence, rather than a long prison term.

mi·ser [mī′ zər] *noun, plural* **misers.** a person who loves money for its own sake. A miser lives like a poor person even though he is rich, in order to avoid spending money. —**miserly,** *adjective.*

mis·er·a·ble [miz′ ər ə bəl] *adjective, more/ most.* **1.** feeling or causing misery; very unhappy: ". . . the boy who had spent *miserable* holidays alone in an empty school." (L.M.

Pronunciation Key. O–S			
ō	over; go	ou	out; town
ô	all; law	p	put; hop
oo	look; full	r	run; car
o͞o	pool; who	s	set; miss
oi	oil; boy	sh	show

(Turn the page for more information.)

M

Boston) **2.** of very poor quality; very bad: "When their crude shelter was finished, it looked like nothing but another *miserable* pile of ice." (James Houston) —**miserably,** *adverb.*

mis•er•y [miz′ ər ē] *noun, plural* **miseries.** a feeling of great pain or suffering; great unhappiness: a poor, homeless person who lives in *misery.*

mis•fit [mis′ fit] *noun, plural* **misfits.** a person who does not seem to fit in to a place or group: Mike felt like a *misfit* when he moved to a new high school and didn't know anyone there.

mis•for•tune [mis fôr′ chən] *noun, plural* **misfortunes. 1.** a lack of good fortune; bad luck: ". . . we've had the *misfortune* to lose our money." (Henry James) **2.** an unlucky or unfortunate event; something bad that happens.

mis•giv•ing [mis giv′ ing] *noun, plural* **misgivings.** an idea that things might turn out wrong; feelings of doubt or worry: Danny had never been away from home before, so his mother watched him go with some *misgivings.*

mis•guid•ed [mis gī′ dəd] *adjective, more/most.* led in the wrong way; led into wrong actions or ideas: He made a *misguided* attempt to give her advice, and ended up hurting her feelings.

mis•hap [mis′ hap] *noun, plural* **mishaps.** an unlucky accident, especially one that is not serious: The old car's dented fenders and scratched doors showed clearly the various *mishaps* it had gone through over the years.

to a wrong action or idea: "Don't ever be *misled* by his backwoodsy ways; he's a very sharp operator, level-headed as they come." (Ken Kesey) ♦ Often used as an adjective: Distances in the desert are very *misleading,* and things often look closer than they really are.

mis•place [mis plās′] *verb,* **misplaced, misplacing. 1.** to put something in a place and forget where it is: I *misplaced* my flashlight and had to use some matches instead. **2.** to put in the wrong place: That big beautiful house really looks *misplaced* in the middle of a block of old, rundown cottages.

miss¹ [mis] *verb,* **missed, missing. 1.** to fail to connect in some way; not hit, catch, or get something: to swing at and *miss* a pitch in baseball, to arrive late at the station and *miss* the train. **2.** to not do what is expected or intended; fail to do, see, or know: to *miss* a hard question on a test, to *miss* three days of school because of being sick. **3.** to not connect with something bad; get away from; avoid: Dad likes to leave the office late so that he'll *miss* all the rush-hour traffic. **4.** to notice that something is lost or absent: I left my jacket at Linda's house, but I was halfway home before I *missed* it. **5.** to feel sad because someone is not there: "He had *missed* her that month she had been out in Milton." (Esther Forbes) —*noun, plural* **misses.** the fact of missing, or something that misses: He hit the target four times and had only one *miss.*

Miss/Mrs./Ms. The word *Ms.* was put into dictionaries almost as soon as it came into popular use. *Ms.* filled a hole in the language. "*Miss* Mary Smith" means a woman who is not married; "*Mrs.* Smith" means one who is or has been married. "*Ms.* Smith" can refer to any woman, whether married or not, just as "*Mr.* Smith" tells us nothing about whether a man is married. Some unmarried women prefer *Miss,* others prefer *Ms.* There are also married women who prefer *Ms.* to *Mrs.* When you write to a woman you know, you'll probably know which title she uses for herself. What about a woman you don't know? Then, *Ms.* is the safest choice.

mis•judge [mis juj′] *verb,* **misjudged, misjudging.** to judge in a way that is wrong or incorrect: I think you're *misjudging* Holly—she isn't unfriendly, she's just very shy. —**misjudgment,** *noun.*

mis•lay [mis lā′] *verb,* **mislaid, mislaying.** to put something in a place and forget where it is; misplace: Dad *mislaid* his car keys and had to borrow Mom's.

mis•lead [mis lēd′] *verb,* **misled, misleading. 1.** to lead or guide in the wrong direction: Don't let that old map *mislead* you; Highway 40 goes around the city now, not through it. **2.** to lead

miss² *noun, plural* **misses. 1. Miss.** a title used for a woman or girl who is not married. **2.** any young woman or girl: Excuse me, *Miss,* do you know if Dr. Orta's office is in this building?

mis•sile [mis′ əl] *noun, plural* **missiles.** any object that is thrown or shot through the air, especially a weapon such as an arrow, bullet, rocket, or GUIDED MISSILE.

mis•sing [mis′ ing] *adjective.* **1.** not present or found; lost: Magazines and posters often show pictures of *missing* children. **2.** lacking or absent: Mom bought some glue to put the *missing* leg back on the chair.

M

mis•sion [mish′ ən] *noun, plural* **missions.**
1. the sending forth of a person or group to perform a special job: The search pilot's *mission* was to locate the enemy aircraft carriers. **2.** a church or other place where missionaries do their work: In the 1700's the Spanish priest Junipero Serra established many Catholic *missions* among the Indians of southern California. **3.** a purpose or task in life that one feels chosen for or required to do: "The poet Virgil has said that the *mission* of the Roman is to rule." (Robert Graves).

mis•sion•ar•y [mish′ ən er′ ē] *noun, plural* **missionaries.** a person who is sent forth by a church to teach and help spread the religion of that church, especially in a foreign country.

Mis•sis•sip•pi [mis′ i sip′ ē] **1.** a state in the south-central U.S., bordered on the west by the Mississippi River. *Capital:* Jackson. *Nickname:* "Magnolia State." *Area:* 47,700 square miles. *Population:* 2,551,000. **2.** the chief river of the U.S., flowing from northern Minnesota to the Gulf of Mexico.

Mis•sou•ri [mi zoor′ ē] **1.** a state in the central U.S., bordered on the east by the Mississippi River. *Capital:* Jefferson City. *Nickname:* "'Show Me' State." *Area:* 69,700 square miles. *Population:* 4,951,000. **2.** the longest river in the U.S., flowing from the Rocky Mountains to join the Mississippi in eastern Missouri.

mission The mission of San Antonio de Padua, near Monterey, California.

and time again, the kids went home by *mistake* to different houses." (Ken Kesey) —*verb,* **mistook** or **mistaken, mistaking.** to make a mistake; understand something in the wrong way.

mis•tak•en [mis tā′ kən] *adjective.* being a mistake; not correct; wrong: People are sometimes frightened of king snakes because of a *mistaken* belief that they are poisonous. —**mistakenly,** *adverb.*

---

misspellings A well-known teacher of writing, Donald Graves, said, "Good spelling is the final face shown to an audience . . . poor spelling may say 'I don't particularly care about my content, nor you, the reader.'" Can you learn correct spelling? Of course. Are some people "born" spellers? Yes, even though it can't be scientifically proved. Some good writers have been notoriously bad spellers. Yet, if you want a good career you will sooner or later have to write reports, memos, and letters. Good spelling makes you look better, the way it makes good prose look better.

---

mis•spell [mis spel′] *verb,* **misspelled** or **misspelt, misspelling.** to spell a word incorrectly.

mist [mist] *noun, plural* **mists. 1.** a cloud of very fine drops of water in the air; a light fog. **2.** anything that makes things dim or cloudy like a mist: "Her eyes were instantly clouded over with a *mist* of tears." (Flannery O'Connor) —*verb,* **misted, misting. 1.** to become covered with a mist: The car windows were *misted* over from the damp spring night. **2.** to rain in fine drops; come down as mist.

mis•take [mis′ tāk′] *noun, plural* **mistakes.** something that is not correct; something done, said, or thought in the wrong way: The teacher marked the spelling *mistakes* on my paper. "The houses looked so much alike that, time

mis•ter [mis′ tər] *noun, plural* **misters. 1. Mister.** a title used before a man's name. In writing, it is usually abbreviated as **Mr. 2.** a way of speaking to a man whose name is not known: Hey, *Mister,* you left your car headlights on!

mis•tle•toe [mis′ əl tō′] *noun, plural* **mistletoes.** a plant with small light-green leaves and white

---

Pronunciation Key: T–Z

t	ten; date	v	very; live
th	think	w	win; away
<u>th</u>	these	y	you
u	cut; butter	z	zoo; cause
ur	turn; bird	zh	measure

(Turn the page for more information.)

M

berries. Mistletoe grows as a PARASITE on the branches of trees. It is often used as a Christmas decoration.

mis•tress [mis′tris] *noun, plural* **mistresses.** a girl or woman who has power or control over others: The horse ran over to the fence when it saw its *mistress* standing there.

mist•y [mis′tē] *adjective,* **mistier, mistiest. 1.** clouded or covered with mist: a *misty* morning, a *misty* mountaintop. **2.** not clear; vague: These poems are written in a strange, *misty* style that is very difficult to understand.

mis•un•der•stand [mis′un dər stand′] *verb,* **misunderstood, misunderstanding.** to understand incorrectly; not understand: We *misunderstood* her directions and got off at Miller Road instead of Fort Miller Road.

mis•un•der•stand•ing [mis′un dər stand′ing] *noun, plural* **misunderstandings. 1.** a failure to understand; lack of understanding. **2.** a minor argument or quarrel; a disagreement.

mis•use [mis yōoz′] *verb,* **misused, misusing.** to use in the wrong way: People sometimes *misuse* "don't" in sentences such as "He don't live there any more." —[mis yōos′] *noun, plural* **misuses.** an incorrect or wrong use.

mite [mīt] *noun, plural* **mites.** a tiny animal that is related to the spider. Mites live off stored foods, on plants, or on larger animals such as cattle and horses. Some kinds burrow into the skin of humans.

mitt [mit] *noun, plural* **mitts. 1.** a baseball glove that is worn on one hand to catch the ball: a first baseman's *mitt.* **2.** a mitten.

mit•ten [mit′ən] *noun, plural* **mittens.** a covering used to keep the hands warm. A mitten is like a glove but covers the four fingers together, with only the thumb having a separate part.

mix [miks] *verb,* **mixed, mixing. 1.** to put different things together as one or in one group: to *mix* ice cream, milk, and chocolate syrup for a milkshake. **2.** to join with other people at a party or other social gathering; make friends: She is very shy and finds it hard to *mix* with the other girls. **3. mix up.** to put together in a confusing way: I dialed Carl's number wrong because I *mixed up* the last two numbers. ♦ Also used as a noun: We almost got on the wrong plane because there was a *mix-up* at the gate. —*noun, plural* **mixes. 1.** a food that is sold partly prepared, with some ingredients already mixed: cake *mix.* **2.** any group of different things: an unusual *mix* of guests at a dinner.

mixed [miskt] *adjective.* **1.** made up of more than one kind: a can of *mixed* nuts. **2.** made up

of both males and females: a *mixed* bowling league.

mixed number a number that is made up of a whole number and a fraction such as 66⅔.

mix•er [mik′sər] *noun, plural* **mixers. 1.** a machine for mixing different things together: a concrete *mixer,* a paint *mixer.* **2.** any person or thing that mixes: He's very popular at parties because he's such a good *mixer.* **3.** a dance or party given so that people can meet each other.

mix•ture [miks′chər] *noun, plural* **mixtures.** something that is made up of different things or ingredients; something that is mixed: Her expression was a *mixture* of surprise and anger.

moan [mōn] *noun, plural* **moans.** a long, low sound, especially one that comes from pain or suffering: "He heard a *moan* and a few feet below him he saw Kayak clinging to the icy rockface." (James Houston) —*verb,* **moaned, moaning. 1.** to give a moan or a sound like this. **2.** to speak with moans; complain: Cathy's been *moaning* about how much homework she has to do tonight.

moat [mōt] *noun, plural* **moats.** a deep, wide ditch that is usually filled with water. In the Middle Ages, moats were dug around castles or towns for protection against enemies. Moats are sometimes used today to keep animals confined to a certain place in a zoo.

moat A large moat surrounds this castle, Bishop's Palace, in Wells, England.

mob [mäb] *noun, plural* **mobs. 1.** a large, excited group of people who are likely to cause harm or break the law: An angry *mob* surrounded the jail, throwing rocks at the police. **2.** a gang of criminals: the Capone *Mob.* ♦ Also used as an adjective: *Mob* violence broke out as two rival gangs fought each other. —*verb,* **mobbed, mobbing.** to form a large, excited crowd: Thousands of screaming fans *mobbed* the airport to greet the winning Super Bowl team.

M

mo•bile [mō′ bəl] *adjective, more/most.* **1.** able to move or be moved easily: Linemen in pro football have to be not only big but also *mobile.* **2.** able to move or change in position: In the Middle Ages society was not *mobile* —a person born into a poor family had almost no chance of advancing in the world. —[mō′ bēl′] *noun, plural* **mobiles.** a modern type of sculpture in which parts hang from wires or strings, so that they can move in the air.

mobile home a type of home that is not attached permanently to its foundation. People usually live in the home in one place, but it is possible to move it to another place.

moc•ca•sin [mäk′ ə sin] *noun, plural* **moccasins. 1.** a soft leather shoe with a soft sole and no heel, first made and worn by North American Indians. **2.** see WATER MOCCASIN.

mock [mäk] *verb,* **mocked, mocking.** to laugh at or make fun of someone, especially by copying the person's speech or actions: "Their eyes met hers; their grins *mocked* the old confident smile she had lost." (Ken Kesey) —*adjective.* being an imitation; make-believe; fake: "The boy's mother pushed his shoulder in *mock* annoyance." (John Barth) —**mockery,** *noun.*

mock•ing•bird [mäk′ ing burd] *noun, plural* **mockingbirds.** a gray-and-white American songbird that mocks, or imitates, the sounds of many other kinds of birds.

mode [mōd] *noun, plural* **modes.** a way of doing something; manner; means: "The handwriting is very difficult to read, even by those who are best acquainted with Johnson's *mode* of penmanship." (James Boswell)

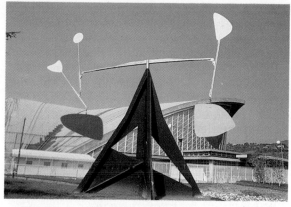

mobile The mobile "Three Up, Three Down," by the famous American sculptor Alexander Calder, who invented this art form in the early 1930's.

of what something should be like: "I believe the British government forms the best *model* the world ever produced . . ." (Alexander Hamilton) **4.** a person whose job is to wear new clothes, jewelry, cosmetics, and so on to show them for sale, as in an advertisement or a fashion show. **5.** a person who poses for pictures by an artist or photographer. —*verb,* **modeled, modeling. 1.** to make or design a model: Andy *modeled* a dinosaur out of clay. **2.** to work as a model: to *model* clothes. **3.** to use something as an example: The U.S. Capitol Building is *modeled* after the buildings of ancient Greece and Rome. —*adjective.* **1.** being a model or copy: A builder of houses often has a *model* home for buyers to visit. **2.** serving as a good example; being a model for others: a *model* citizen.

---

models for writing A "model for writing" is an example. It gives you a picture of how to write certain things—letters, memos, applications for work, stories, and the like. One kind of model is the *literary model* -which is to say a model taken from the work of a professional author. Let's say your assignment is to write an on-the-spot report about a baseball game. You might read Heywood Broun's "The Ruth Is Mighty and Shall Prevail" or John Updike's "Kid Bids Hub Fans Adieu" (about Ted Williams' last game). Another kind is the *instructor's model.* Here, you would read a baseball story written by the editors of the grammar or language textbook you are using. A third kind is the *student model.* Here, you would read a paper of this kind written by another student writer like yourself.

---

mod•el [mäd′ əl] *noun, plural* **models. 1.** something made as a copy or example of something else, especially in a smaller form than the original: Chris collects *models* of ships and planes from World War II. **2.** a certain style or type of some product that is manufactured: The 1964 Ford Mustang was a very popular *model* of car. **3.** a person or thing that is a good example

Pronunciation Key: [ə] Symbol

The [ə] or *schwa* sound occurs in syllables without an accent. It can be spelled with any vowel, such as **a** in above, **e** in listen, **i** in pencil, **o** in melon, **u** in circus. It can also be a combination of vowels, such as **io** in action, **ai** in mountain, **iou** in precious.

(Turn the page for more information.)

mo•dem [mō′ dəm] *noun, plural* **modems.** in a computer, a device that allows it to communicate with other computers, usually over telephone lines. A modem allows information and instructions to be passed between computers.

mod•er•ate [mäd′ ər it] *adjective.* **1.** neither too great nor too little; not extreme: The city of San Diego is famous for its *moderate* climate; temperatures in January and July are only about 15 degrees apart. ◆ The fact of being moderate is **moderation.** —*noun, plural* **moderates.** a person who has moderate ideas or opinions, especially in politics: President Dwight Eisenhower was known as a *moderate* whose policies were neither very conservative nor very liberal. —[mäd′ ə rāt] *verb,* **moderated, moderating.** to make or become less extreme. —**moderately,** *adverb: moderately*-priced clothing.

modest for her to walk around the house after her bath wearing just a towel. —**modestly,** *adverb:* "Although he spoke *modestly,* it soon became clear that he was an expert." (Christopher Isherwood)

mod•est•y [mäd′ ə stē] *noun.* the fact of being modest: Baseball star Steve Garvey is known for his *modesty* and says that his success came from good fortune, hard work, the help of his teammates, and so on.

mod•i•fi•ca•tion [mäd′ ə fə kā′ shən] *noun, plural* **modifications.** the act or fact of modifying something; a change: This car is much the same as last year's model, with a few slight *modifications.*

mod•i•fi•er [mäd′ ə fī′ ər] *noun, plural* **modifiers.** in grammar, a word that goes with another word and affects its meaning.

modifiers The word *modify* means "to change." "These police cars are standard models that have been *modified* with more powerful engines." A word that affects the meaning of another word in a sentence is a *modifier.* You can write, "A man came in and walked over to our table. Mr. Jones looked up at him." Or, you can write: "A *big* man came in and walked *slowly* over to our table. Mr. Jones *nervously* looked up at him." You've now told a lot more about this scene just by adding a few modifiers, the adjective *big* and the adverbs *slowly* and *nervously.* Grammar books say a modifier "limits the meaning" of a word. This may be true in one sense, in that "a nervous look" has a more narrow meaning than simply "a look," which could be "casual," "bored," "aimless," any or all of these. A better statement would be that modifiers *expand* or *add* to the meaning of words.

mod•ern [mäd′ ərn] *adjective,* *more/most.* **1.** having to do with the present time or with the recent past: VCR's, personal computers, and microwave ovens are *modern* inventions. **2.** not old-fashioned; up-to-date: *modern* furniture, a *modern* hairstyle. —*noun, plural* **moderns.** a person who is modern or who has modern ideas. ◆ To make something more modern is to **modernize** it: The house was built in 1920, but the kitchen was *modernized* just last year.

modern art a style of art that first became popular in the early 1900's, in which artists show unusual shapes, colors, and designs rather than presenting things as they appear in nature.

mod•est [mäd′ ist] *adjective, more/most.* **1.** not thinking too highly of yourself; not talking about what you are good at or calling attention to things you have done. **2.** not grand, impressive, or fancy; plain and simple: "Live Oak Camp is *modest* by most standards, having no swimming pool, public showers, view of the sea, or cable TV . . ." (Wright Morris) **3.** decent and proper in a quiet way, as in one's dress or actions: Mom tells my little sister that it isn't

mod•i•fy [mäd′ ə fī] *verb,* **modified, modifying.** **1.** to make different in some way; change somewhat: The plans for the meeting have been *modified* to allow the principal to make a few special remarks at the end. **2.** in grammar, to limit the meaning of another word or describe what it means: In Rudyard Kipling's line, "The great gray-green, greasy Limpopo River," all of the other words *modify* "Limpopo River."

mod•ule [mäj′ ool *or* mäd′ yool] *noun, plural* **modules.** **1.** a separate unit of a spacecraft that has a special use and can be separated from the rest of the craft. **2.** in a computer, any device that is a separate unit and that can be added to the computer system. A printer, a disk drive, and a mouse are types of modules.

moist [moist] *adjective,* **moister, moistest.** slightly wet; damp: *moist* air, to wipe off something with a *moist* rag. ◆ To **moisten** something means to make it moist: "He *moistened* his upper lip by running his tongue over it." (James Joyce)

mois•ture [mois′ chər] *noun.* a small amount of water or other liquid that forms on something.

M

mo•lar [mō′ lər] *noun, plural* **molars.** one of the large teeth at the back of the mouth that have a broad surface for grinding food. There are twelve molars in an adult's mouth.

mo•las•ses [mə las′ iz] *noun.* a thick, sweet brown syrup that is produced when sugarcane is made into sugar. Molasses is used in making gingerbread, cookies, candy, and other foods.

mold[1] [mōld] *noun, plural* **molds.** a hollow container that is used to give something a certain shape. A liquid or a soft material such as wax is poured into the mold and allowed to harden. The mold is then removed to leave the object with the mold's shape. Machine parts, coins, plastic toys, and many other things are made in molds. —*verb,* **molded, molding. 1.** to form something into shape with or as if with a mold: to *mold* bread dough into the shape of a loaf. **2.** to give something a certain form or character, as if with a mold: The coach *molded* a group of young players into a great team.

mold[2] *noun, plural* **molds.** a tiny, simple plant that cannot produce its own food. It is a type of FUNGUS. Mold can be seen as a soft, fuzzy growth, often bluish or greenish in color, that is found on such foods as bread, cheese, and fruit. —*verb,* **molded, molding.** to develop or become covered with mold.

mold•ing [mōl′ ding] *noun, plural* **moldings. 1.** the process of molding or an object that is molded. **2.** a strip of wood, plaster, or other material used as a decoration on the edge of a wall, window, or doorway.

mold•y [mōl′ dē] *adjective,* **moldier, moldiest. 1.** covered with mold: a *moldy* orange, *moldy* bread. **2.** having a stale, damp smell: a *moldy* old cabinet in the corner of a basement.

mole[1] [mōl] *noun, plural* **moles.** a small raised spot on the skin, usually brownish or black.

mole Although moles create a problem by digging up lawns, their digging helps keep soil rich.

mole[2] *noun, plural* **moles. 1.** a small animal that lives in burrows underground. Moles have tiny eyes that are covered by fur, powerful front feet for digging, and soft grayish fur. **2.** a spy who works secretly within the government of an opposing country.

mol•e•cule [mäl′ ə kyool′] *noun, plural* **molecules.** the smallest particle into which a substance can be divided and still keep the same qualities as the original substance. A molecule is made up of two or more ATOMS. A molecule of water has two atoms of hydrogen and one of oxygen. —**molecular** [mə lek′ yə lər] *adjective.*

mol•lusk [mäl′ əsk] *noun, plural* **mollusks.** one of a large group of animals having a soft body and no backbone. Most mollusks live in the ocean, such as clams, oysters, and octopuses. Other kinds live on land, such as snails and slugs, or in fresh water.

molt [mōlt] *verb,* **molted, molting.** of an animal, to shed the feathers, skin, shell, or hair at a certain time to allow for new growth. Birds, snakes, insects, lobsters, and some mammals are among the animals that molt.

mol•ten [mōl′ tən] *adjective.* in liquid form because of having been melted by great heat: Volcanoes often spill *molten* rock called lava.

mom [mäm] *noun, plural* **moms.** mother. Children often call their mother "Mom" or "Mommy."

mo•ment [mō′ mənt] *noun, plural* **moments. 1.** a very short period of time; an instant: "I can't stay more than a *moment.* I'm late as it is." (Peter Shaffer) **2.** a certain point in time: "The *moment* the doors closed he ran back . . . and picked up the telephone." (E.L. Doctorow)

mo•men•tar•y [mō′ mən ter′ ē] *adjective.* lasting only a short time; for a moment: "When he drank, the tea was so cold it brought a *momentary* pain to his forehead." (John Gardner) —**momentarily,** *adverb.* for or in a moment: "It's bright outside. They both stop, *momentarily* blinded by the glare." (Ann Beattie)

mo•men•tous [mō men′ təs] *adjective, more/ most.* very important; significant: It was a *momentous* event when Richard Nixon became the first American president to visit the People's Republic of China.

Pronunciation Key: Accent Marks

[′] is the normal accent mark. It shows where the main stress falls on a word.
[′] is a secondary accent mark. It shows a lighter stress than the primary accent. For example:

tel • e • vis • ion [tel′ ə vizh ′ən]
(Turn the page for more information.)

mo•men•tum [mō men′ təm] *noun, plural* **momentums. 1.** the amount of force that a moving object has as a result of its combined weight and speed: A ball will gain *momentum* as it rolls down a hill. **2.** any force that grows or advances: She was far behind the other candidates early in the race, but her campaign is gaining *momentum* as the election gets closer.

mon•arch [män′ ərk] *noun, plural* **monarchs. 1.** a ruler who is not elected to power, but takes over at the death of a parent or other relative and then rules for life. Kings, queens, and emperors are monarchs. **2.** a North American butterfly with orange and black wings.

mon•ar•chy [män′ ər kē] *noun, plural* **monarchies. 1.** a form of government having a monarch. **2.** a country ruled by a monarch, such as Saudi Arabia. Countries such as Spain, Denmark, and Great Britain are called **limited** or **constitutional monarchies** because a person has the title of king or queen but little actual power.

mon•as•ter•y [män′ əs ter′ ē] *noun, plural* **monasteries.** a building or buildings where a group of monks live according to certain religious rules.

Mon•day [mun′ dā] *noun, plural* **Mondays.** the second day of the week.

Mo•net [mō nā′] **Claude,** 1840–1926, French painter.

Monet The Impressionist painters got their name from this painting, Claude Monet's *Impression: Sunrise.*

mon•ey [mun′ ē] *noun, plural* **moneys. 1.** objects that are in the form of coins or paper bills and that have a certain accepted value, for use in buying and selling things or in paying for work done. **2.** any system of using certain objects in this way. At different times in history gold, stones, shells, beads, and many other things have been used as money. **3.** a large amount of money; wealth.

Mon•go•li•a [mäng gō′ lē ə] **1.** a historic region in east-central Asia, now divided into the **Mongolian People's Republic** and northern China. **2.** this republic. *Capital:* Ulan Bator. *Area:* 604,300 square miles. *Population:* 1,800,000. —**Mongolian,** *adjective; noun.*

mon•goose [mäng′ gōōs′] *noun, plural* **mongooses.** a small, fierce animal that can move very quickly and that is known for its ability to kill rats and poisonous snakes, such as the cobra. It is found in Africa and in India and other parts of southern Asia.

mon•grel [mäng′ rəl] *noun, plural* **mongrels.** a dog or other animal that is a mixture of different breeds. ◆ Such a dog is often called a **mutt.**

monitor This weather station uses television monitors to display information about weather conditions.

mon•i•tor [män′ ə tər] *noun, plural* **monitors. 1.** a student who is given a special duty in school, such as helping teachers take attendance, keeping order in the hall or lunchroom, and so on. **2.** someone or something used to keep watch or look for signs of trouble: Hospitals often connect a patient to a heart *monitor* to alert the hospital staff in case of a problem. **3.** a television set used in a broadcasting studio to display what is being broadcast. **4.** the screen that displays information in a computer, or a television set that can be connected to a computer, VCR, or the like to provide a picture for it. —*verb,* **monitored, monitoring.** to watch over or check on something: The new class schedule seems to be working well, but the principal is going to *monitor* the situation carefully.

monk [mungk] *noun, plural* **monks.** a man who has become a member of a certain religious order and lives a life of prayer under special rules set by that order, such as not being married or owning property.

monkey Two South American monkeys (left), the red howler monkey and the spider monkey (center). The patas monkey (right) is African.

mon·key [mung′kē] *noun, plural* **monkeys.** one of a family of animals having long arms and legs, hands with thumbs, and a long tail. Monkeys usually live in trees, are very good climbers and are among the most intelligent animals. —*verb,* **monkeyed, monkeying.** *Informal.* to play around with something in a foolish way.

monkey wrench a tool with a handle attached to a movable clamp that can be adjusted to fit different sizes of nuts and bolts.

mon·o·gram [män′ ə gram] *noun, plural* **monograms.** a person's initials written together in a fancy way. Monograms are used on towels, stationery, clothing, and other such items. —*verb,* **monogrammed, monogramming.** to mark with a monogram.

without allowing others to speak: "If one person does all the talking, that's a *monologue*." (S.E. Hinton)

mo·nop·o·lize [mə näp′ ə līz] *verb,* **monopolized, monopolizing. 1.** to have or get complete control of some type of business; have a monopoly. **2.** to have complete control of something: Older children sometimes feel that a new baby *monopolizes* their mother's time.

mo·nop·o·ly [mə näp′ ə lē] *noun, plural* **monopolies. 1.** in business, a situation where one company has complete control of a certain product or service, and there are no other companies selling the same thing. If a company has a monopoly on something, someone who wants to buy it has no choice but to buy from that company. **2.** a company or other organization that has this complete control: At one time, John D. Rockefeller's Standard Oil Company was a *monopoly* in the U.S. oil industry. **3.** complete control over any situation, as if by a monopoly: Sara doesn't want anyone else to talk at the meetings; she thinks she has a *monopoly* on all the good ideas.

mon·o·rail [män′ ə rāl′] *noun, plural* **monorails.** a railway system with cars that ride on a single rail or track elevated above the ground.

mo·not·o·nous [mə nät′ ə nəs] *adjective, more/most.* **1.** continuing without change at the same level: "The sound of *monotonous* axe blows rang through the forest . . ." (Stephen Crane) **2.** tiring or boring because of a lack of change; dull: Dad thinks that riding to work on the train is really *monotonous*, and he's always looking for ways to pass the time. ♦ This feeling or quality is called **monotony.**

monologue In a monologue, one character talks on and on, making a full statement of some sort, even if no other characters are present. For student writers, the monologue is a good writing device. You can write a monologue just as if you were telling a story out loud to friends. The risk with a monologue is that it can limit the writer. The readers know only what the main character tells them, and the effect of a single long conversation can be boring. Writers avoid this by using the storyteller to reveal important information. If you were writing a story in monologue form, let's say you have your character start speaking normally, as if he'd just sat down next to a stranger on an airplane or in a hotel lobby. As we read on, though, we realize that he is sitting in a prison cell. The listener is his new cell mate.

mon·o·logue [män′ ə lôg′] *noun, plural* **monologues. 1.** a play or part of a play during which one actor speaks alone: "To be or not to be" is the beginning of a famous *monologue* in Shakespeare's play *Hamlet.* **2.** a series of jokes or stories told by one person: Johnny Carson always has a *monologue* to begin his "Tonight Show." **3.** any long speech given by one person,

Pronunciation Key: A–F			
a	and; hat	ch	chew; such
ā	ate; stay	d	dog; lid
â	care; air	e	end; yet
ä	father; hot	ē	she; each
b	boy; cab	f	fun; off

(Turn the page for more information.)

Mon•roe [mən rō′] **James,** 1758–1831, the fifth president of the United States, from 1817 to 1825. He issued the Monroe Doctrine in 1823.

mon•soon [män soon′] *noun, plural* **monsoons.** **1.** a strong, steady wind that blows in southern Asia and the Indian Ocean. Summer monsoons blow from the ocean and cause heavy rains. In the winter they blow from the land and bring dry weather. **2.** this season of summer rain, or a heavy rainstorm during this season.

mon•ster [män′ stər] *noun, plural* **monsters.** **1.** a huge, imaginary creature that has a strange and frightening appearance. Old folk tales often tell of dragons, sea serpents, and other such monsters. **2.** a person who is very cruel or evil. **3.** any person or thing that is very large: The Chicago Bears football team is nicknamed "The *Monsters* of the Midway."

mon•strous [män′ strəs] *adjective, more/most.* **1.** not natural or normal, especially in an ugly or frightening way. **2.** very wrong or evil: Prisoners in the Nazi concentration camps were treated with *monstrous* cruelty. **3.** very large; huge: ". . . a muffled roar of energy, as though some *monstrous* gigantic machine were spinning its wheels at breakneck speed." (Roald Dahl) **—monstrously,** *adverb.*

Mon•tan•a [män tan′ ə] a state in the northwestern U.S., bordered by Canada. *Capital:* Helena. *Nickname:* "Treasure State." *Area:* 147,100 square miles. *Population:* 801,000.

Mon•te•vi•de•o [män′ tə vi dā′ ō] the capital of Uruguay, on the Rio de la Plata. *Population:* 1,230,000.

month [munth] *noun, plural* **months.** one of the twelve parts into which the year is divided.

month•ly [munth′ lē] *adjective.* **1.** done or happening once a month: *National Geographic* is a *monthly* magazine. **2.** of or for a month: *Monthly* sales of new cars for December were way up this year. *—adverb.* once a month; every month. *—noun, plural* **monthlies.** a magazine published once a month.

Mont•re•al [män′ trē ôl′] the largest city in Canada, in southern Quebec on the St. Lawrence River. *Population:* 1,085,000.

monument This monument in Washington, D.C. is part of the Vietnam War Memorial.

mon•u•ment [män′ yə mənt] *noun, plural* **monuments.** **1.** a statue, building, or other object that is built to honor and preserve the memory of some important person or event. **2.** an outstanding work or achievement that brings honor to a person's memory: After Sir Christopher Wren designed the famous St. Paul's church in London, he wrote on a small stone in the very center, "If you seek his *monument,* look around you." ◆ Something that is very large or important is **monumental.**

mood [mood] *noun, plural* **moods.** a certain feeling that a person has; a person's state of mind: to be in a good *mood.* "Sometimes when he was not in a *mood* to read he would stand at the window and watch the snow." (John Gardner) ◆ A person who changes moods quickly, or who is often in a bad mood, is **moody.**

mood Let's look at how two writers set the mood of a story in the opening lines. "During the whole of a dull, dark, and soundless day in the autumn of the year, when the clouds hung oppressively low in the heavens, I had been passing alone, on horseback, through a singularly dreary tract of country, and at length found myself, as the shades of the evening drew on, within view of the melancholy House of Usher." (Edgar Allan Poe) "On a peg by the front door hung a starling in a wooden cage and at the back door stood a spring house, the cold spring water running between crocks of yellow-skinned milk. At the front gate a moss-rose said welcome and on a trellis over the parlor window a Prairie Queen nodded at the roses in the parlor carpet." (Jessamyn West) Both describe the same kind of place, a house in the country. Which opening sets a cheerful mood? Which sets a gloomy mood? How does each writer get this effect?

M

moon [mōōn] *noun, plural* **moons. 1.** a heaven-ly body that revolves around the earth about once every 29½ days. The light that appears to shine from the moon is actually light reflected from the sun. The moon has a rocky surface of craters and mountains with no water or atmos-phere. **2.** a similar body that revolves around another planet: Titan is one of the 23 *moons* of Saturn. —*verb,* **mooned, mooning.** to spend time in a lazy or wasteful way: "Claudius has been wasting his time *mooning* about the Apol-lo Library." (Robert Graves)

moon•light [mōōn′lĭt′] *noun.* the light that comes from the moon. ♦ Often used as an adjective: We took a *moonlight* cruise around the lake. —*verb,* **moonlighted, moonlighting.** to work at another job besides one's full-time job, especially at night: He works for the Parks Department and *moonlights* as a cab driver.

moor[1] [mōōr] *verb,* **moored, mooring.** to fasten or tie a boat in place: Several large navy ships were *moored* in the harbor. ♦ The place where a ship does this is called a **mooring.**

moor[2] *noun, plural* **moors.** a large area of open, empty land with few trees on it. There are moors in parts of England and Scotland.

moose

moose [mōōs] *noun, plural* **moose.** a large ani-mal that belongs to the deer family. A moose has a heavy body with large humped shoulders, long legs, and a large head. The male has wide, flat antlers. Moose are found in North America and in northern parts of Europe and Asia.

mop [măp] *noun, plural* **mops.** a household tool used for cleaning floors, having a long handle that ends in a sponge or a bundle of thick soft string. —*verb,* **mopped, mopping. 1.** to use a mop. **2.** to use a cloth or other material to soak up moisture, as a mop would: He *mopped* his brow with a handkerchief.

mope [mōp] *verb,* **moped, moping.** to move slowly, in a dull, sad way: "Billy Bob *moped* around for days, picking things up, dropping them again . . ." (Truman Capote)

mo•ped [mō′ped] *noun, plural* **mopeds.** a small, light bicycle that can be pedaled and that also has a low-powered engine.

mor•al [môr′əl] *adjective.* **1.** having to do with what is right and wrong: Justin found five dollars on the playground and had to make a *moral* decision about whether to turn it in. **2.** what is right by these standards; honest or good: The store owner was a *moral* man who would never cheat a customer. **3.** having to do with the mind or spirit rather than with action: "Neeley stood by and said nothing. His func-tion was to come along for *moral* support." (Betty Smith)—*noun, plural* **morals. 1. morals.** a person's beliefs or actions in matters of right and wrong. **2.** a lesson about right and wrong: The *moral* of *The Wizard of Oz* is "There's no place like home." —**morally,** *adverb.*

mor•ale [mə ral′] *noun.* the state of mind of a person or a group; how people feel about their situation in life or about what will happen to them in the future: *Morale* in the office has really improved since the boss started asking people personally about their complaints.

mo•ral•i•ty [mə ral′ə tē] *noun, plural* **moralit-ies. 1.** the right or wrong of something. **2.** right conduct; acting in the proper way. **3.** a set of moral standards: middle-class *morality.*

mor•bid [môr′bid] *adjective,* **more/most.** hav-ing to do with death, disease, or other such matters, especially in a way that is unpleasant or unnatural: "It was a dream with a lot of *morbid* visions about death . . ." (Paul Zindel) —**morbidly,** *adverb:* "She was *morbidly* afraid that we would be poisoned." (Wole Soyinka)

more [môr] *adjective.* **1.** greater in number or amount: *More* people live in California than in Nevada. **2.** additional; extra: You'd better bring some *more* money in case we decide to eat out. —*noun.* a larger or extra amount. —*adverb.* **1.** to a greater number or amount: Color TV's cost *more* than black-and-white ones. **2.** in addi-tion; again: I'll try to call her once *more.*

Pronunciation Key: G–N			
g	give; big	k	kind; cat; back
h	hold	l	let; ball
i	it; this	m	make; time
ī	ice; my	n	not; own
j	jet; gem; edge	ng	having

(Turn the page for more information.)

M

more•o•ver [môr′ō′vər] *adverb.* not only that; besides; also.

morn [môrn] *noun, plural* **morns.** a short word for morning, used especially in poems.

morn•ing [môr′ning] *noun, plural* **mornings.** **1.** the early part of the day, from the time the sun rises or a person gets up until noon. **2.** any time between midnight and noon.

morning glory a climbing vine with white, purple, or blue flowers that are shaped something like a bell. The flowers open in the early morning and then close for the rest of the day.

Mo•roc•co [mə räk′ō] a country in northwest Africa, on the Atlantic and the Mediterranean. *Capital:* Rabat. *Area:* 172,400 square miles. *Population:* 21,100,000. —**Moroccan,** *adjective; noun.*

Morse [môrs] **Samuel F. B.,** 1791–1872, American inventor and artist who made the first practical telegraph.

Morse Code [môrs] a system of short and long signals, or dots and dashes, that represent letters of the alphabet. The Morse Code was once the most common method of sending long-distance messages. It was named after Samuel F. B. Morse.

mor•sel [môr′səl] *noun, plural* **morsels.** a small bit or piece of something: "He had eaten nothing all day . . . he had refused to touch a *morsel* of food." (Albert Payson Terhune)

mor•tal [môr′təl] *adjective.* **1.** sure to die at some time: All living things are *mortal.* ♦ The fact of being mortal is **mortality. 2.** causing death, or able to cause death: *mortal* combat. **3.** very serious or intense: a *mortal* sin. —**mortally,** *adverb:* to be *mortally* wounded.

mor•tar [môr′tər] *noun, plural* **mortars. 1.** a material made of a mixture of sand, water, and lime or cement. It is used in building to hold bricks or stones together. **2.** a small, light cannon with a short barrel, used to fire shells in a high arc over a short distance. **3.** a thick, heavy bowl in which substances are crushed into a fine powder with a tool called a **pestle.** The use of a mortar and pestle was once very common in preparing drugs and medicines.

mort•gage [môr′gij] *noun, plural* **mortgages.** an agreement by which someone borrows money to buy a house or other property, or borrows against the value of real estate that is already owned. If the borrower does not pay back the loan, the lender can take ownership of the property. —*verb,* **mortgaged, mortgaging.** to place a mortgage on property.

mo•sa•ic [mō zā′ik] *noun, plural* **mosaics.** a picture or design made of many small pieces of colored glass or tile that are fastened together. Mosaic art was very important in the Roman Empire and in the early Middle Ages.

Mo•ses [mō′zis] in the Bible, the Hebrew leader who received the Ten Commandments.

Mos•cow [mäs′kou] the capital of the Soviet Union, in the western part of the country. *Population:* 7,850,000.

Moscow Red Square, Moscow. Though red stands for the Communist Party, the square got its name long before the Communist era. The name comes from a Russian word that means both "the color red" and "beautiful."

Mos•lem [mäz′ləm] *noun, plural* **Moslems.** another spelling of **Muslim.**

mosque [mäsk] *noun, plural* **mosques.** a Muslim temple or place of worship. The **Great Mosque** in Mecca is considered to be the center of the Muslim religion.

mos•qui•to [məs kē′tō] *noun, plural* **mosquitos** or **mosquitoes.** a small, flying insect that is found in all parts of the world, especially in hot, damp places. Female mosquitoes can sting humans and animals and suck their blood. Some kinds pass on dangerous diseases when they bite, such as malaria and yellow fever.

moss [môs] *noun, plural* **mosses.** a type of small green plant that has no flowers and that grows together in clumps to form a soft, dense mat. Moss is found growing in shady, damp places on the surface of rocks, at the base of trees, or along the ground. —**mossy,** *adjective.*

most [mōst] *adjective.* **1.** the greatest in number or amount: California has the *most* people of any U.S. state. **2.** to a great extent or amount; nearly all: *Most* Americans own a television set. —*adverb.* to the greatest amount: William Shakespeare is the world's *most* famous writer. —*noun.* the greatest number or amount: We'll be gone about two hours, or three at the *most.*

M

most•ly [mōst′ lē] *adverb.* for the most part; largely; mainly: The weather report said today will be *mostly* sunny.

mo•tel [mō tel′] *noun, plural* **motels.** a place for people who are traveling by car to spend the night, usually located near a highway or other main road.

moth [môth] *noun, plural* **moths.** any of a very large group of insects that are found throughout the world. Moths are very much like butterflies, but are less brightly-colored, have smaller wings and larger bodies, and are active mainly at night. Some kinds of moths are harmful because of the damage they cause to trees, food plants, or clothing.

moth•er [muth′ ər] *noun, plural* **mothers. 1.** the female parent of a child. **2.** a woman or thing thought of as like a mother: People speak of England as the *mother* country of the United States. ♦ **Mother nature** is the world of animals, plants, and so on, apart from man. —*verb,* **mothered, mothering.** to be or act as a mother to.

moth•er-in-law [muth′ ər in lô′] *noun, plural* **mothers-in-law.** the mother of one's husband or wife.

Mother's Day a holiday in honor of mothers, celebrated on the second Sunday of May.

mo•tion [mō′ shən] *noun, plural* **motions. 1.** the fact of moving; not staying still; movement: "The otter likes to lie on its back, floating up and down to the *motion* of the waves . . ." (Scott O'Dell) **2.** one single or particular way of moving: To show that a pitch is a strike, an umpire makes a *motion* with his right hand. **3.** in a meeting, a plan or suggestion that is stated in a certain way and put forward for a vote or decision: Sara made a *motion* that the meeting be ended. —*verb,* **motioned, motioning.** to make a motion; move the hand or body as a signal to do something. —**motionless,** *adjective:* "They made out the dim form of a crocodile lying *motionless* on the sandy bottom." (Armstrong Sperry)

motion picture 1. a series of pictures which appear on a screen very quickly one after the other, so that it seems there is one continuing picture in which people and objects move. **2.** a particular story presented in this form; more often called a MOVIE or FILM.

mo•ti•vate [mō′ tə vāt′] *verb,* **motivated, motivating.** to give someone a motive or reason to do something. —**motivation,** *noun.* the fact of motivating; something that causes a person to act: The famous acting teacher Stanislavsky

said that actors should understand the *motivation* of the character they were playing.

mo•tive [mō′ tiv] *noun, plural* **motives. 1.** the reason that a person does something; a cause to act: The desire for religious freedom was the main *motive* for the Pilgrims coming to America. **2.** the reason that a person commits a crime: After a bomb was found in the company offices, the police questioned all former employees that they thought might have a *motive.*

mo•tor [mō′ tər] *noun, plural* **motors.** a machine that changes power into motion. Motors are used to make other machines work, as in a washing machine, vacuum cleaner, electric fan, and so on. —*adjective.* **1.** run by a motor: a *motor* scooter. **2.** having to do with cars or other motor vehicles: *Motor* Trend magazine reports on the auto industry. **3.** having to do with motion, especially the motion of the body: Very young children usually don't have enough *motor* control to catch a baseball or ride a bicycle.

mo•tor•boat [mō′ tər bōt′] *noun, plural* **motorboats.** a boat, especially a small boat, that is powered by a motor.

mo•tor•cy•cle [mō′ tər sī′ kəl] *noun, plural* **motorcycles.** a two-wheeled vehicle that is powered by a gasoline motor, somewhat like a bicycle but larger and heavier.

mo•tor•ist [mō′ tər ist] *noun, plural* **motorists.** a person who drives a car.

mot•to [mät′ ō] *noun, plural* **mottoes** or **mottos.** a short phrase or sentence that sums up what a person or group believes in or stands for; a guiding idea or principle: The *motto* of the U.S. Marine Corps is "Always Faithful."

mound [mound] *noun, plural* **mounds. 1.** a hill or heap of dirt, stones, or other such material: When gophers dig a hole, they leave a *mound* of earth around the entrance. **2.** in baseball, the raised ground in the center of the infield from which the pitcher throws the ball to the batter. **3.** a large pile or mass of something: "I still have a *mound* of documents—government papers, secret instructions, and unpublished notes and interviews . . ." (Theodore H. White)

Pronunciation Key: O–S

ō	over; go	ou	out; town
ô	all; law	p	put; hop
oo	look; full	r	run; car
ōō	pool; who	s	set; miss
oi	oil; boy	sh	show

(Turn the page for more information.)

501

mount[1] [mount] *verb,* **mounted, mounting. 1.** to go or climb up something: "Two soldiers were *mounting* the steps of the staircase . . ." (E.L. Doctorow) **2.** to get up on: to *mount* a horse. **3.** to set firmly in place; fix: For her science report she *mounted* several photographs on a large sheet of cardboard. **4.** to go up in amount or level; rise; increase: The number of delays on that railroad has been *mounting* in recent months. —*noun, plural* **mounts. 1.** a horse or other animal for riding. **2.** a frame or support for mounting something, such as a painting.

mount[2] *noun, plural* **mounts.** a short word for **mountain,** often used in names: *Mount* Whitney, *Mount* McKinley, *Mount* Everest.

moun•tain [moun′tən] *noun, plural* **mountains. 1.** a large mass of land that rises high above the land around it. The difference between a mountain and a high hill is not exact, but a mountain is usually thought of as being 2,000 feet or more above its surroundings. ◆ A group or series of mountains is called a **mountain range. 2.** a large pile or amount of something; a heap: "Both men ate *mountains* of potatoes." (Ken Follett)

mountain lion This is one of the rarest and most solitary of the big cats. It's known by many other names, such as *puma, cougar, panther,* and *catamount.*

mountain lion a large wild cat that is found in the mountains of North and South America.

moun•tain•ous [moun′tən əs] *adjective, more/most.* **1.** having many mountains: Switzerland is a *mountainous* country. **2.** like a mountain; very high or large: Sunset Beach in Hawaii is famous for its *mountainous* waves.

mourn [môrn] *verb,* **mourned, mourning.** to be very sad over the loss of someone or something; feel great sorrow: "We come together today to *mourn* the deaths of seven brave Americans (the Challenger astronauts), to share the grief that we all feel . . ." (Ronald Reagan) ◆ A **mourner** is a person who mourns for someone.

mourn•ful [môrn′fəl] *adjective, more/most.* feeling great sorrow; very sad: "I felt a *mournful* sinking at the heart, and muttered: 'I shall never see my friends again—never, never again.' " (Mark Twain) —**mournfully,** *adverb.*

mourn•ing [môr′ning] *noun.* **1.** the act of showing great sadness over a death or loss. **2.** black clothing worn to show sorrow over someone's death.

mouse [mous] *noun, plural* **mice. 1.** a small, furry animal with a pointed nose, large, sharp front teeth, and a long tail. There are many kinds of mice found in different parts of the world. **2.** *Informal.* a person who is very shy or easily frightened. **3.** a small device used to give instructions to a computer without the use of the keyboard, thought to be shaped somewhat like a mouse.

mous•tache another spelling of **mustache.**

mouth [mouth] *noun, plural* **mouths. 1.** the opening in the face of a person or animal through which food and drink is taken into the body, and by which sounds are made. **2.** an opening that is thought of as being like a mouth: New York City is at the *mouth* of the Hudson River. —*verb,* **mouthed, mouthing.** to move the mouth in a certain way: "Mulai Ismael *mouthed* each word slowly, as if it gave off a pleasant taste." (Marguerite Henry)

mouth•piece [mouth′pēs′] *noun, plural* **mouthpieces.** the part of an object that is put near or between the lips. Telephones and some musical instruments have mouthpieces.

mouth•wash [mouth′wäsh′ *or* mouth′wôsh′] *noun, plural* **mouthwashes.** a liquid, usually flavored, that is used for rinsing out the mouth and freshening the breath.

move [mo͞ov] *verb,* **moved, moving. 1.** to change the place where something is; go or cause to go from one place to another: Mom *moved* the blue chair from the living room to the den. The train *moved* slowly away from the station. **2.** to change the place where one lives: When Cathy was six, her family *moved* from New York to California. **3.** to begin to take action; act: After the owner's son took over the business, he *moved* quickly to hire a number of new people. **4.** to make a formal suggestion at a meeting; make a MOTION. **5.** to cause a person to act or feel in a certain way: "She was *moved* almost to tears . . ." (John Hersey)

—*noun, plural* **moves. 1.** the act of moving: The phone rang, but no one made a *move* to answer it. The mayor announced his latest *move* to try to settle the teachers' strike. **2.** the act of moving a piece in a game, or a turn to do this: In chess, the player with the white pieces has the first *move.* ♦ Something that can be moved is **movable** or **moveable.**

much [much] *adjective,* **more, most. 1.** being a large amount; great in amount: He's looking for a used car that doesn't cost *much* money. **2.** being a certain amount: How *much* does it cost to get in to the zoo? —*adverb:* I don't like seafood very *much.* —*noun; pronoun:* "For of those to whom *much* is given, *much* is required . . ." (John F. Kennedy)

movement Good writers often use the technique of *movement* to describe a scene, showing one spot, then another, and still another, the way a movie camera moves around a scene to show different views. Here's how Eudora Welty uses movement in "The Corner Store." First, she's across the street from the store: "Our Little Store rose right up from the sidewalk; standing in a street of family houses . . ." After a description of the outside of the store comes this: "Running in and out of the sun, you met what seemed total obscurity [darkness] inside." This begins a description of the inside of the store. She moves up to describe things on the shelves high overhead, then down to show things at the eye level of a small child. Finally, she moves in close for a "tight shot"—a detailed description of one thing. This is an ice barrel filled with cold drinks, where she spends a nickel to buy her favorite kind of soda. She then leaves and ends with, "That was good-bye."

move•ment [mo͞ov′ mənt] *noun, plural* **move- ments. 1.** the act of moving: Beaches are formed by the *movement* of the waves against the shore. **2.** the moving parts of a machine: the *movement* of a watch. **3.** the efforts or actions of a group of people: In the late 1960's, the peace *movement* opposed American involvement in the Vietnam War. **4.** one part of a larger piece of music, such as a symphony.

mov•er [mo͞o′ vər] *noun, plural* **movers. 1.** a person or business whose work is moving furniture and other belongings from one place to another. **2.** any person or thing that moves.

mov•ie [mo͞o′ vē] *noun, plural* **movies. 1.** a story or other work of entertainment or education, presented in the form of a motion picture; also called a FILM. **2. movies.** the showing of a movie, or a theater where movies are shown.

mov•ing [mo͞ov′ ing] *adjective,* **more/most. 1.** that moves or is able to move: to oil the *moving* parts of a machine, to shoot at a *moving* target. **2.** having a strong effect on the feelings: Walt Whitman wrote a *moving* poem on the death of President Lincoln.

mow [mō] *verb,* **mowed** or **mown, mowing.** to cut grass or other such growing plants in a lawn or field. —**mower,** *noun.*

Mo•zart [mōt′ särt] **Wolfgang Amadeus,** 1756– 1791, Austrian composer.

Mr. [mis′ tər] a title used before a man's name.

Mrs. [mis′ iz] a title used before a married woman's name.

Ms. [miz] a title used before a woman's name.

mu•cus [myo͞o′ kəs] *noun.* a thick slippery liquid that coats and protects the inside of the mouth, throat, and other parts of the body. When a person has a cold, the nose and throat produce too much mucus.

mud [mud] *noun.* dirt that is soft, wet, and sticky. —**muddy,** *adjective.*

mud•dle [mud′ əl] *verb,* **muddled, muddling.** to mix up; confuse: "I'm not sure that I haven't got it a little *muddled* in my mind." (Mary Norton)

muff [muf] *noun, plural* **muffs. 1.** a soft, thick roll of fur open at each end for warming the hands. At one time women carried a muff in cold weather. **2.** a clumsy or awkward mistake. ♦ This meaning is also used as a verb.

muf•fin [muf′ in] *noun, plural* **muffins.** a small piece of bread like a little cake, baked in a small container and usually eaten hot.

muf•fle [muf′ əl] *verb,* **muffled, muffling.** to make a sound softer or weaker: "They worked together, quickly, quietly, their voices *muffled* by the fog." (James Houston)

muf•fler [muf′ lər] *noun, plural* **mufflers. 1.** a device used to soften the noise made by the

Pronunciation Key: T–Z			
t	ten; date	v	very; live
th	think	w	win; away
th	these	y	you
u	cut; butter	z	zoo; cause
ur	turn; bird	zh	measure

(Turn the page for more information.)

M

> **multiple meanings** A good dictionary lists *multiple meanings* (two or more meanings for the same word). It's sometimes thought that a word has only one proper meaning, and that its other meanings are weaker or less correct. Actually, all meanings given in this dictionary are equally correct. The one listed as #1 is the most common or most basic. The others follow according to how common they are, or how closely they relate to the core meaning. For example, the main meaning of *rest* is "to lie down and *rest*." But it has other meanings: "A small wool hat *rested* on the top of his nose." (Washington Irving) "Her body was half-turned toward him and he could feel her eyes *resting* on his face." (Roald Dahl) ". . . gray granite rocks, *resting* above the lake, facing west." (Leslie Silko)

engine of a car, truck, bus, or the like. **2.** a scarf that is wrapped around the neck for warmth.

mug [mug] *noun, plural* **mugs.** a large, heavy drinking cup that has a flat bottom, straight sides, and usually a handle. —*verb,* **mugged, mugging.** to suddenly attack someone in order to rob the person, especially on the street. ♦ Someone who robs in this way is a **mugger.**

mug•gy [mug′ē] *adjective,* **muggier, muggiest.** warm and damp; humid: "The night was as hot and *muggy* as the day had been; not a breath of air, not so much as a cricket stirring." (John Gardner)

Mu•ham•mad [moo häm′id] 570?–632, the founder of the Muslim religion and its chief prophet.

mul•ber•ry [mul′ber′ē] *noun, plural* **mulberries.** a tree having dark, reddish-purple berries that can be eaten.

mulch [mulch] *noun, plural* **mulches.** loose material such as leaves, grass, wood chips, and so on, spread around plants to protect them against cold, heat, or dryness. —*verb,* **mulched, mulching.** to cover with mulch.

mule A farmer uses a team of eight mules to pull a cultivator and make the soil ready for planting.

mule [myool] *noun, plural* **mules.** an animal that is produced by mating a female horse and a male donkey. A mule looks somewhat like a horse, but has the long ears and tail of a donkey. Mules are used as work animals.

mul•ti•ple [mul′tə pəl] *adjective.* being more than one; many: *Multiple* copies of a letter can be made quickly on a Xerox machine. —*noun, plural* **multiples.** a number that is the result of multiplying one number by another.

mul•ti•pli•ca•tion [mul′tə plə kā′shən] *noun.* in mathematics, a short way of adding a number to itself a certain number of times. The multiplication of 16×4 is the same as $16 + 16 + 16 + 16$ (64).

mul•ti•pli•er [mul′tə plī′ər] *noun, plural* **multipliers.** the number used to multiply another number. If you multiply 10 by 3, 3 is the *multiplier* and 10 is the **multiplicand.**

mul•ti•ply [mul′tə plī] *verb,* **multiplied, multiplying. 1.** in mathematics, to perform the operation of multiplication. **2.** to become greater in number, especially very quickly or by a large amount: When there are no larger animals to hunt them, rabbits *multiply* rapidly. "Books read to her, and others which she read herself, *multiplied* her vocabulary." (Helen Keller)

mul•ti•tude [mul′tə tood′] *noun, plural* **multitudes.** a very large number of people or things: The Indian leader Mahatma Gandhi attracted vast *multitudes* when he gave a speech.

mum•ble [mum′bəl] *verb,* **mumbled, mumbling.** to speak in a soft way with the mouth partly closed, so that one cannot be understood: A stage actor is trained to speak his words very clearly instead of *mumbling.*

mum•my [mum′ē] *noun, plural* **mummies.** a dead body that has been preserved and kept from decaying. This was done especially by the ancient Egyptians, who believed that dead people needed their bodies to live on in the next world. Egyptian mummies were treated with chemicals, wrapped in cloth, and kept sealed in a special tomb.

mumps [mumps] *noun.* a disease that causes a painful swelling in the lower cheeks and around the jaw, making it difficult to chew or swallow.

munch [munch] *verb,* **munched, munching.** to chew or eat something in a noisy way.

mu·ni·ci·pal [myo͞o nis′ ə pəl] *adjective.* having to do with a city or its government: a *municipal* court, *municipal* parks.

mural The mural *Construction*, by the Missouri artist Thomas Hart Benton.

mu·ral [myo͞or əl] *noun, plural* **murals.** a large painting or design on a wall.

mur·der [mur′ dər] *noun, plural* **murders.** the killing of one person by another on purpose, in a way that is against the law. —*verb,* **murdered, murdering.** to commit the crime of murder. ◆ A person who does this is a **murderer.** —**murderous,** *adjective.*

murk·y [mur′ kē] *adjective,* **murkier, murkiest.** very dark or cloudy: the *murky* water of a muddy pond, a *murky* night as fog rolls in.

mur·mur [mur′ mər] *noun, plural* **murmurs.** a soft, low sound that goes on and on: From our hotel room near the beach, you could hear the *murmur* of the ocean far below. —*verb,* **murmured, murmuring.** to make this sound: "Pa Forrester leaned close to Penny and *murmured* in a low voice." (Marjorie Kinnan Rawlings)

mus·cle [mus′ əl] *noun, plural* **muscles. 1.** a type of body tissue made up of strong fibers that can be tightened or relaxed, causing body parts to move. Muscles are used to do work, such as walking, running, or lifting things. They also help the body to automatically perform such activities as breathing, chewing and digesting food, and circulating the blood. **2.** a particular body part made up of this tissue: The biceps and triceps are arm *muscles.* **3.** strength of the muscles; physical strength.

mus·cu·lar [mus′ kyə lər] *adjective, more/most.* **1.** having well-developed muscles; strong: "Geoff Hurst was superbly built, tall, with immensely *muscular* thighs, a fine jumper . . ." (Brian Glanville) **2.** having to do with the muscles: *muscular* aches and pains.

mu·se·um [myo͞o zē′ əm] *noun, plural* **museums.** a building used to keep and display works of art, or things of value and interest from other fields, such as history, science, technology, or animal and plant life.

mush·room [mush′ ro͞om′] *noun, plural* **mushrooms.** a type of plant that has a stalk with a cap on top shaped like a cup or umbrella. A mushroom is a kind of fungus. Many kinds of mushrooms can be eaten; some others are poisonous and are called TOADSTOOLS. —*verb,* **mushroomed, mushrooming.** to suddenly appear or grow, in the way that mushrooms spring from the ground: What at first seemed to be a minor crime has *mushroomed* into a huge scandal.

mu·sic [myo͞o′ zik] *noun.* **1.** the art of making sounds that are beautiful or pleasing to the ear, and of putting these sounds together in a pattern that expresses a certain feeling. **2.** a particular way of arranging these sounds; a musical composition: For the song "Oklahoma," Oscar Hammerstein wrote the words and Richard Rodgers wrote the *music.* **3.** the notes of a musical composition set down on paper: Many early jazz musicians could not read *music* and created their own version of a song. **4.** a sweet or pleasing sound like music: ". . . the *music* of dancing winds and of brave winds whistling in the rigging." (Samuel Eliot Morison)

mu·si·cal [myo͞o′ zə kəl] *adjective, more/most.* **1.** having to do with music: A piano is a *musical* instrument. **2.** having a pleasing sound like music: "The packed snow creaked underfoot and everywhere I could hear a *musical* trickle and drip as the noon sun thawed icicles." (Sylvia Plath) —*noun, plural* **musicals.** a stage show or movie that includes songs and dancing as well as ordinary spoken words. Well-known American musicals include *The Sound of Music* and *My Fair Lady.* —**musically,** *adverb.*

mu·si·cian [myo͞o zish′ ən] *noun, plural* **musicians.** a person who plays or sings music, especially someone who does this in a show.

mus·ket [mus′ kit] *noun, plural* **muskets.** a gun with a very long barrel that was used in warfare before the rifle was invented, as in the American Revolution.

Pronunciation Key: [ə] Symbol

The [ə] or *schwa* sound occurs in syllables without an accent. It can be spelled with any vowel, such as a in above, e in listen, i in pencil, o in melon, u in circus. It can also be a combination of vowels, such as io in action, ai in mountain, iou in precious.

(Turn the page for more information.)

505

musk•mel•on [musk′ mel′ ən] *noun, plural* **muskmelons.** a large, sweet fruit that has a hard rind, small seeds, and juicy flesh. Cantaloupes are a type of muskmelon.

musk ox [musk] a large animal that is somewhat like a buffalo, having long, curving horns and a coat of thick, shaggy hair. It is found in far northern areas of North America.

musk•rat [musk′ rat′] *noun, plural* **muskrats.** a small rodent with dark brown fur that lives in wet, swampy areas of North America. Muskrats have a long, flat tail and webbed rear feet for swimming.

muskrat Although it has an unpleasant "musky" odor, the muskrat actually gets its name from the Indian word for this animal.

Mus•lim [muz′ ləm *or* mo͞oz′ ləm] *noun, plural* **Muslims.** (also spelled **Moslem**) a member of the religion that worships Allah as the one true God and Muhammad as his prophet. Muhammad founded the Muslim religion in the early 600's. This religion is called ISLAM. —*adjective.* of or having to do with this religion.

mus•lin [muz′ lən] *noun.* a type of cotton cloth that may be either light or heavy in weight, used to make such items as blouses, sheets, and table cloths.

mus•sel [mus′ əl] *noun, plural* **mussels.** a type of water animal that can be eaten. Mussels have a two-part shell with a bluish-black color. They are related to clams.

Mus•so•li•ni [mo͞o′ sə lē′ nē] **Benito,** 1883–1945, the dictator of Fascist Italy from 1922 to 1943.

must [must] *verb.* **Must** is a special verb used with other verbs to show: **1.** that something is absolutely certain: A person *must* have food and water to live. **2.** that something is likely: Who's that at the door? It *must* be Brian. **3.** that something is needed or required: Yes, I'm afraid we *must* be leaving now. ◆ This meaning

is also used as a noun: You've got to hand in your paper by Friday; it's an absolute *must.*

mus•tache [mus′ tash′ *or* məs tash′] (also spelled **moustache**) *noun, plural* **mustaches.** hair that is grown on a man's upper lip.

mus•tang [mus′ tang] *noun, plural* **mustangs.** a small wild horse of the American Southwest.

mus•tard [mus′ tərd] *noun, plural* **mustards.** **1.** a yellow or brownish-yellow paste or powder with a sharp taste, used to give flavor to meats and other foods. **2.** the plant from which this seasoning is made.

mus•ter [mus′ tər] *verb,* **mustered, mustering. 1.** to call or bring people together; assemble: The troops were *mustered* on the parade ground for inspection by the visiting general. **2.** to gather from inside oneself; summon up: She finally *mustered* up enough nerve to sing a number in the school talent show.

mute [myo͞ot] *adjective.* **1.** not having the normal power to speak. **2.** not willing to speak; silent: They asked the prisoner question after question, but he simply sat *mute* in his chair. —*noun, plural* **mutes. 1.** a person who cannot speak. **2.** a device that is attached to a musical instrument, such as a trumpet or trombone, to soften the tone of the notes played. —*verb,* **muted, muting.** to make softer: The streets were oddly quiet as the deep snow *muted* the sounds of passing traffic. —**mutely,** *adverb.*

mu•ti•late [myo͞o′ tə lāt′] *verb,* **mutilated, mutilating. 1.** to cause serious injury to a person. **2.** to cause great damage to something: An insane man *mutilated* the valuable painting by slashing it with a knife. —**mutilation,** *noun.*

mu•ti•ny [myo͞o′ tə nē] *noun, plural* **mutinies. 1.** an attempt by the crew of a naval ship to take command of the ship away from the captain. **2.** any rebellion by a group against its leaders: In the Sepoy *Mutiny* of 1857, Indian soldiers in the British army fought against their British commanders. —*verb,* **mutinied, mutinying.** to take part in a mutiny. —**mutinous,** *adjective.*

mut•ter [mut′ ər] *verb,* **muttered, muttering.** to speak in a low tone that cannot be clearly understood: "Mr. Morgan did not look up from his maps, but he *muttered* a greeting." (James Houston)

mut•ton [mut′ ən] *noun.* the meat from a full-grown sheep.

mu•tu•al [myo͞o′ cho͞o əl] *adjective.* shared or felt by two or more people or groups: "He didn't like Sandmeyer, and he was sure the feeling was *mutual.*" (Arthur C. Clarke) ◆ In a **mutual fund,** the money invested by many

M

people is combined into one account for buying stocks and bonds.

muz•zle [muz′əl] *noun, plural* **muzzles. 1.** the nose, mouth, and jaws of an animal. **2.** a set of straps or other covering device that fits over an animal's mouth to keep it from biting. **3.** the opening in the end of a gun barrel where the bullet comes out. —*verb,* **muzzled, muzzling.** to put a muzzle on a dog or other animal.

mys•ter•y [mis′tər ē] *noun, plural* **mysteries. 1.** something that cannot be explained or understood by normal means; something that is hidden or unknown: In 1975, the famous labor leader Jimmy Hoffa disappeared and was never seen again; what happened to him is a *mystery.* **2.** a book, movie, TV show or other story in which there is a crime or other unexplained problem that has to be solved.

myths A myth is a story told by early people to explain the features of the natural world. For example, a myth might say that thunder is caused by gods fighting in the sky, or that a group of lakes was created when a giant dipped his fingers into the earth. Because a myth gives a scientifically false explanation, it also means "a false story or belief." For example, the book *The Myth of the Farm Family* argues that American farming is actually not done by single hard-working families but by large, "faceless" corporations. Scholars study the myths of the ancient Greeks, the Celts of Ireland, the Teutonic people of Scandinavia and Germany, and the American Indians, among others. Finally, myths make great stories. Modern writers who have drawn on Greek myths include poets W.B. Yeats and T.S. Eliot, novelist James Joyce, and dramatist Eugene O'Neill.

my [mī] *pronoun.* of or belonging to me: I think that's *my* book, not yours. I like to wear *my* hair short in summer.

myr•tle [mur′təl] *noun, plural* **myrtles. 1.** a sweet-smelling evergreen shrub or tree that has pink or white flowers and shiny leaves. **2.** a vine that grows along the ground and has shiny leaves and blue flowers.

myth [mith] *noun, plural* **myths. 1.** a story from very early times that tries to explain why things happen as they do, such as the weather, the change of seasons, or the creation of the world, animals, and human beings. **2.** a story or idea that is not true: It's a *myth* that the koala is a kind of bear; it's actually related to the kangaroo.

myself "My friend and me are working on a science project together." This should be "My friend and I." As the subject of the sentence, it needs *I,* a subject pronoun, rather than *me,* an object pronoun. What about this? "The teacher chose Jessica, Daniel, and I to be readers for the school play." Here, *me* is correct, because it's the object of the verb *chose.* So what do people do when they've been wrong with *me,* and also wrong with *I?* They try to avoid the problem completely: "My friend and *myself* are working . . ." "She chose Jessica, Daniel and *myself*" *Myself* might seem to be a good "middle ground" between *I* and *me,* but it isn't used that way—check the definition.

my•self [mī self′] *pronoun.* my own self: I painted this picture *myself.* You don't have to help me; I'll do it *myself.* ♦ Note that *myself* has to follow "I" or "me" in a sentence. It is not used alone.

mys•te•ri•ous [mis′tir′ē əs] *adjective, more/ most.* full of mystery; hard to explain or understand: "The full moon glowed like a *mysterious* spaceship sailing through the clouds." (James Houston) "Those things are controlled by certain *mysterious* laws that people on earth don't know or understand." (Tennessee Williams) —**mysteriously,** *adverb:* "They arrive from nowhere . . . camp for a few days and nights and then disappear as *mysteriously* as they came." (George Orwell)

myth•i•cal [mith′ə kəl] *adjective.* (also spelled **mythic**) having to do with myths or legends: It's not certain if there was a real King Arthur in England, or if he was just a *mythical* character.

my•thol•o•gy [mi thäl′ə jē] *noun, plural* **mythologies.** myths as a group; a collection of myths and legends.

Pronunciation Key: Accent Marks
[′] is the normal accent mark. It shows where the main stress falls on a word.
[′] is a secondary accent mark. It shows a lighter stress than the primary accent. For example:
tel • e • vis • ion [tel′ə vizh′ən]
(Turn the page for more information.)

M

n, N [en] *noun, plural* **n's, N's.** the fourteenth letter of the alphabet.

nag [nag] *verb,* **nagged, nagging. 1.** to complain to a person over and over about some problem or fault: "My aunt was furious and *nagged* him about giving it to me, because I was too young." (Jill Paton Walsh) **2.** to bother or annoy again and again: "Sam's question *nags* at her." (Ann Beattie) ♦ Often used as an adjective: a *nagging* backache. —*noun, plural* **nags.** a person who nags: Whenever Mom tells Chris to clean his room, he says she's just being a *nag.*

nail [nāl] *noun, plural* **nails. 1.** a long, thin piece of metal with a pointed end and a flat, circular top. Nails are hammered into pieces of wood or other material to hold them together or fasten them to something. **2.** the flat, hard layer protecting the top end of a person's finger or toe. —*verb,* **nailed, nailing.** to fasten something together with nails.

na•ive [nī ēv′] *adjective, more/most.* not having experience or knowledge; believing or accepting things without question: It was a bit *naive* of him to expect that the computer would be as easy to use as the advertisements claimed.

na•ked [nā′ kid] *adjective.* **1.** having no clothing or other covering; bare. **2.** without the usual or natural covering: "We stood under a willow tree, and I noticed that the long *naked* branches were yellow and thick with buds." (Andrea Lee) **3.** with nothing to hide or disguise it; plain: the *naked* truth.

name [nām] *noun, plural* **names. 1.** the word or words by which someone or something is known. **2.** an insulting word or words: She got angry when the other girls called her *names.* **3.** the fact of having one's name well-known; fame: Barbra Streisand had already made a *name* for herself as a singer before she became a movie actress.

   —*verb,* **named, naming. 1.** to give a name to someone or something. **2.** to mention by name; identify: Can you *name* all the Presidents of the U.S.? **3.** to choose for some position or honor: The school has just *named* a new principal. **4.** to settle on; decide: I'd like to buy that painting—just *name* your price.

name•ly [nām′ lē] *adverb.* that is to say: In 1959 the U.S. added two more states—*namely,* Alaska and Hawaii.

nap¹ [nap] *noun, plural* **naps.** a short sleep, especially during the day. —*verb,* **napped, napping.** to sleep for a short time; take a nap.

nap² *noun, plural* **naps.** a soft, fuzzy surface on some types of cloth or leather.

nap•kin [nap′ kin] *noun, plural* **napkins.** a square piece of cloth or paper used at meals to keep food and drink off the clothes and to wipe the hands and mouth.

Napoleon A portrait of the young Napoleon, by Antoine Gros.

Na•po•leon I [nə pō′ lē ən] or **Napoleon Bonaparte** [bō′ nə pärt], 1769–1821, French general and political leader.

nar•cis•sus [när sis′ əs] *noun, plural* **narcissuses** or **narcissus.** a type of spring plant that grows from a bulb, having white or yellow flowers with a cup-shaped part in the center.

nar•cot•ic [när kät′ ik] *noun, plural* **narcotics.** a powerful type of drug that when taken in small amounts as a medicine can relieve or take away pain, cause sleep, and generally dull the senses. If taken in large amounts, narcotics can cause great damage to a person's system. Heroin, morphine, and opium are types of narcotics.

(Richard Wright) They still haven't decided which car to buy, but they've *narrowed* it *down* to two choices. —*noun, plural* **narrows.** a thin or narrow part in a body of water. —**narrowly,** *adverb:* "A great chunk of the kitchen ceiling fell one winter, *narrowly* missing our mother." (James Baldwin)

---

narrowing a topic Topics for reports come in three sizes: too broad, too narrow, and just right. When student writers have a problem getting started with a paper, it's usually because their topic is too broad. Let's say you want to do a social-studies report on California. Instead of trying to do the entire history of California, you can choose a single year, a year that was typical of a whole era or was especially notable because of some event. 1849, the year of the California gold rush, is such a year. When choosing a topic, check your library. Look at an encyclopedia. Then look in the card catalog for books on the topic. Are there 60 books available as sources? Does the topic get a 30-page article in the encyclopedia? If so, then it's too big. Narrow it.

---

nar•rate [nar′ āt′] *verb,* **narrated, narrating.** **1.** to serve as the NARRATOR of a movie, play, and so on. **2.** to tell a story, especially in a book. ♦ A **narrative** is a story or tale.

na•sal [nā′ zəl] *adjective.* having to do with the nose: the *nasal* passages.

Nash•ville [nash′ vil′] the capital of the state of Tennessee. *Population:* 456,000.

---

narration In *first-person narration,* the author tells the story by using "I." In Ernest Hemingway's *The Sun Also Rises,* a typical chapter begins, "When *I* woke in the morning *I* went to the window and looked out." In *third-person narration,* the author is not a character, but an observer. The characters are described by third-person pronouns—*he, she, they.* Hemingway's *The Old Man and the Sea* begins, "*He* was an old man who fished alone in a skiff in the Gulf Stream and *he* had gone eighty-four days without taking a fish." *Second-person narration* uses *you* to make the reader part of the story. Hemingway's "In Another Country" is a first-person narrative. But at one point he shifts to second-person: "Always, though, *you* crossed the bridge across the canal to enter the hospital. It was warm, standing in front of her charcoal fire, and the chestnuts were warm afterward in *your* pocket."

---

nar•ra•tor [nar′ āt ər *or* nar′ ə tər] *noun, plural* **narrators. 1.** a person who speaks along with the action of a film, play, TV show, or the like, to tell the audience what is going on or to give background information. **2.** anyone who tells or writes a story. ♦ The words spoken or written by a narrator are **narration.**

nar•row [nar′ ō] *adjective,* **narrower, narrowest. 1.** having a slender width; not broad or wide: The wagon train crossed the river at its *narrowest* point. **2.** small in amount or extent; limited: The mayor takes advice only from a *narrow* group of old friends. ♦ Someone who is **narrow-minded** has very strict opinions and does not like to change his ways of thinking. **3.** almost not enough; close to failing: "Charlotte felt greatly relieved to see him go. It had been a *narrow* escape." (E.B. White) —*verb,* **narrowed, narrowing.** to make or become narrow: "Taylor's eyes *narrowed* and when he spoke there was a note of anger in his voice."

na•stur•ti•um [nə stur′ shəm] *noun, plural* **nasturtiums.** a plant with bright orange, yellow, or red flowers and round leaves.

nas•ty [nas′ tē] *adjective,* **nastier, nastiest. 1.** acting in a rude or angry way; mean; cruel: a *nasty* remark, a person with a *nasty* temper. **2.** very serious or harmful: a *nasty* cut, a *nasty* cold. "They say a *nasty* storm system is moving in over us." (James Houston) —**nastily,** *adverb.* —**nastiness,** *noun.*

na•tion [nā′ shən] *noun, plural* **nations. 1.** a place that has certain borders and its own form

---

Pronunciation Key: A–F			
a	and; hat	ch	chew; such
ā	ate; stay	d	dog; lid
â	care; air	e	end; yet
ä	father; hot	ē	she; each
b	boy; cab	f	fun; off

(Turn the page for more information.)

of government, and is not part of any larger area of government; a country: "A *nation* may be said to consist of its territory, its people, and its laws." (Abraham Lincoln) **2.** the people of a nation. **3.** a large and organized tribe: the Zulu *nation* of southern Africa.

na•tion•al [nash′nəl *or* nash′ ə nəl] *adjective.* having to do with or belonging to a nation: The President of the U.S. is chosen in a *national* election. —*noun, plural* **nationals.** a citizen of a certain nation: After the 1979 revolution in Iran, American *nationals* were ordered to leave the country. —**nationally,** *adverb.*

na•tion•al•ism [nash′ nə liz′ əm] *noun.* **1.** a feeling of belonging to a certain nation and of wanting that nation to rule itself independently: After World War II *nationalism* led many African countries to demand self-government. ♦ A person who supports nationalism is a **nationalist. 2.** a deep feeling of loyalty to one's own country, especially the idea that it is superior to other countries and that its interests are more important. ♦ A person who has this attitude is **nationalistic.**

na•tion•al•i•ty [nash′ nal′ ə tē *or* nash′ ə nal′ ə tē] *noun, plural* **nationalities. 1.** the fact of being a citizen of a certain country. **2.** a group of people having the same homeland, language, and culture.

na•tive [nā′ tiv] *noun, plural* **natives. 1.** a person who was born or grew up in a certain place: Ronald Reagan lived for many years in California, but was a *native* of Illinois. **2.** an animal, plant, or group of people that has lived in a place from the earliest times. —*adjective.* **1.** having to do with the place where a person was born or grew up: Both of Andy's parents are *native* New Yorkers. **2.** living or growing somewhere from the earliest times. Potatoes now are found all over Europe, but they are *native* to America. **3.** having to do with a person's birth: Joseph Conrad became one of the greatest

English novelists even though his *native* language was Polish.

Native American a member of the group of people native to North and South America, also called an INDIAN or AMERICAN INDIAN. ♦ Many people of this group now prefer *Native American* to *Indian*, but this is not yet completely established as the correct term.

na•tiv•i•ty [nə tiv′ ə tē] *noun.* **the Nativity.** the birth of Jesus Christ.

nat•u•ral [nach′ ə rəl] *adjective, more/most.* **1.** made by or found in nature; not caused or produced by people; not artificial: The Grand Canyon, Niagara Falls, and Death Valley are famous *natural* wonders of the U.S. **2.** having to do with nature, as opposed to people: Gravity is a *natural* law. **3.** happening normally in nature or in life; usual; ordinary: The man seemed to have died of *natural* causes, but one detective suspected he'd been murdered. "I knew the *natural* sounds of the city at this hour . . ." (Russell Baker) **4.** present from birth; not needing to be taught: Elvis Presley is thought of as a singer with great *natural* talent. **5.** not pretended or artificial: The actress gave a very *natural* performance. —*noun, plural* **naturals.** a person who has a natural talent or ability: The great baseball player 'Shoeless Joe' Jackson was a *natural* as a hitter.

natural language "Make your writing talk," says Sheridan Baker in *The Complete Stylist.* "Write in a way that comes naturally," say Strunk & White in *The Elements of Style.* Try to write the way you speak. It's better to begin with a "natural voice" than with a pretense to fancy style. Yet, that's just one part of the advice. If you read a printed record of an actual conversation, you'll be surprised at how rambling, disorganized, and error-filled it seems. "And then, uh . . . you know we don't have to do it this way, so I said to him, Jimmy, I said, Jimmy, um . . . like I don't think this is really going to work." So "write as you speak" doesn't mean that good writing is speech written down. What "natural voice" does for you is to get you started. Just imagine you must tell someone of a condition or situation that is urgent. Also, you can rehearse your words by saying them aloud to yourself. Then, begin to write.

nat•u•ral•ist [nach′ rəl ist] *noun, plural* **naturalists.** a person who studies nature, especially someone who studies plants and animals living in nature. ♦ This study is called **natural history.**

nat•u•ral•ize [nach′ rə līz] *verb,* **naturalized, naturalizing.** to become part of another country or place. ♦ Usually used as an adjective: Albert Einstein was a *naturalized* citizen of the U.S.; he was born in Germany.

nat•u•ral•ly [nach′ rə lē] *adverb.* **1.** by nature; without anything artificial: "Her hair was *naturally* black, black as a raven's wing." (Mary McCarthy) **2.** in a normal, natural way: For her photographs she tries to get people to sit or stand *naturally*. **3.** as would be expected; of course: The restaurant's Thanksgiving menu features turkey, *naturally*.

natural resources things supplied by nature that are important for human life. Water, minerals, and plants are natural resources.

na•ture [nā′chər] *noun, plural* **natures. 1.** *also,* **Nature.** the world and everything in it that is not made by people, such as animals, plants, mountains, oceans, the weather, the planets, and so on. **2.** the world of wildlife and the outdoors. **3.** the basic qualities or characteristics that make something what it is: Of course that song is loud; rock music is loud by *nature*. **4.** type; kind: She enjoys bike riding, jogging, hiking, and things of that *nature*.

naught [nôt] *noun.* nothing; zero.

naugh•ty [nô′tē] *adjective,* **naughtier, naughtiest.** behaving in the wrong way; not obedient; bad: The *naughty* puppy chewed up the newspaper and scattered the pieces all over.

nau•se•a [nô′zē ə *or* nô′zh ə] *noun.* a feeling of being sick to one's stomach or about to vomit. ♦ Often used as an adjective: "The night before the examination Douglas (MacArthur) could not sleep, and after breakfast he was *nauseated*." (William Manchester) ♦ Something that causes this feeling is **nauseous** or **nauseating**. Note that *nauseous* means "making sick," not "being sick."

nau•ti•cal [nô ti kəl] *adjective.* having to do with sailors, the ocean, or ships: "Port" and "starboard" are the *nautical* terms for left and right.

Navajo A Navajo child wearing traditional tribal clothing.

Nav•a•jo [năv′ə hō′] *noun, plural* **Navajo** or **Navajos.** (also spelled **Navaho**) an American Indian tribe living in the southwestern U.S.

na•val [nā′vəl] *adjective.* having to do with the navy or with warships: Navy officers are trained at the U.S. *Naval* Academy.

na•vel [nā′vəl] *noun, plural* **navels.** a small round mark on the abdomen of people and other mammals that is made when the cord connecting a newborn baby to its mother is cut.

nav•i•gate [nav′ə gāt] *verb,* **navigated, navigating. 1.** to control or steer a ship or aircraft: In 1966 Sir Francis Chichester *navigated* a small sailboat around the world alone. **2.** to travel on or over a certain body of water: The Frenchman Louis Joliet was the first European to *navigate* the upper Mississippi River.

nav•i•ga•tion [nav′ə gā′shən] *noun.* **1.** the science or method of determining where a ship or aircraft is, how far it has traveled, and what direction it is going in: In earlier times, *navigation* was done by studying the position of the sun, moon, and stars and the direction of the wind. **2.** the act of navigating: The U.S. began the *navigation* of space satellites in 1960.

nav•i•ga•tor [nav′ə gā′tər] *noun, plural* **navigators. 1.** a person who plans and directs the course of a ship or airplane; someone who navigates. **2.** in earlier times, a person who led a voyage by ship to explore unknown lands, such as Christopher Columbus.

na•vy [nā′vē] *noun, plural* **navies. 1.** *also,* **Navy.** the part of a country's armed forces that has to do with war on the seas, including all its warships and the officers and sailors who serve on them, along with aircraft and other weapons and supplies. **2.** a very dark blue color like that of some naval uniforms; also called **navy blue.**

nay [nā] *adverb.* an older word for "no." —*noun, plural* **nays.** a vote of "no."

Naz•a•reth [naz′ə rith] an ancient town in what is now Israel, where Jesus spent his early life.

Na•zi [nä′tsē] *noun, plural* **Nazis.** a member of the political party that ruled Germany under Adolf Hitler from 1933 to 1945.

near [nēr] *adverb,* **nearer, nearest.** at a short distance or time away; not far; close: As the baby tried to walk her mother stood *near*. —*adjective.* **1.** close by; not far away: The new

Pronunciation Key: G–N			
g	give; big	k	kind; cat; back
h	hold	l	let; ball
i	it; this	m	make; time
ī	ice; my	n	not; own
j	jet; gem; edge	ng	having

(Turn the page for more information.)

shopping center will open in the *near* future. **2.** done or missed by a small amount: a *near* accident, a shot that was a *near* miss. **3.** close in feeling or relationship: "My teacher is so *near* to me that I scarcely think of myself apart from her." (Helen Keller) —*preposition.* close to; by: to live *near* the ocean. —*verb,* **neared, nearing.** to come close or closer to; approach: The ship was *nearing* land. —**nearness,** *noun.*

near•by [nēr bī′] *adjective; adverb.* not far away; close: He pulled off some leaves from a *nearby* tree. Most of the people who work in that office live *nearby.*

near•ly [nēr′ lē] *adverb.* almost but not quite; close to; practically: The auditorium was *nearly* full for the school play.

near•sight•ed [nēr′ sī′ tid] *adjective, more/most.* unable to see things that are far away as clearly as a person with normal eyesight can.

neat [nēt] *adjective,* **neater, neatest. 1.** being clean and in good order; arranged as it should be; tidy: He stacked all his note cards in *neat* piles on his desk. **2.** done in a skillful or clever way: How did you get that light to turn on by itself? That's a *neat* trick. **3.** *Informal.* very good; fine: "She was really cute, with gold hair and light-green eyes and the *neatest* gold freckles all over her face." (S.E. Hinton) —**neatly,** *adverb.* —**neatness,** *noun.*

Ne•bras•ka [nə bras′ kə] a state in the midwestern U.S. *Capital:* Lincoln. *Nickname:* "Cornhusker State." *Area:* 77,200 square miles. *Population:* 1,586,000.

nec•es•sar•i•ly [nes′ ə ser′ ə lē] *adverb.* in a way that must be or that cannot be avoided: Just because the house is old doesn't *necessarily* mean it needs a lot of repairs.

nec•es•sar•y [nes′ ə ser′ ē] *adjective, more/most.* **1.** that must be done or had; needed; required: Before you begin to make the stew, get together all the *necessary* ingredients. **2.** that cannot be avoided; that must be; certain. ♦ A **necessary evil** is something bad a person must put up with to get something good.

ne•ces•si•ty [nə ses′ ə tē] *noun, plural* **necessities. 1.** something needed or required: The old saying, "*Necessity* is the mother of invention" means that people invent things because they need them. **2.** the fact of being necessary.

neck [nek] *noun, plural* **necks. 1.** the part of the body that connects the head to the shoulders. **2.** the part of clothing that fits around the neck: He wears shirts with a size 16 *neck.* **3.** something thought to be like a neck, as by being long and narrow: the *neck* of a soda bottle.

neck•er•chief [nek′ ər chif] *noun, plural* **neckerchiefs.** a square of cloth that is folded and worn around the neck like a scarf, especially by western cowboys.

neck•lace [nek′ lis] *noun, plural* **necklaces.** jewelry that is worn around the neck as an ornament, such as a chain of gold or silver, a string of beads or pearls, and so on.

neck•tie [nek′ tī′] *noun, plural* **neckties.** a long, narrow strip of cloth worn around the neck and under the collar and tied in front in a knot or a bow. Men usually wear a necktie when they are dressed in a suit.

nec•tar [nek′ tər] *noun, plural* **nectars.** a sweet liquid found in the center of some flowers, collected and used by bees to make honey.

need [nēd] *noun, plural* **needs. 1.** the lack of something that is useful, important, or wanted: Her paper had a lot of careless mistakes and showed a *need* for more time and effort. **2.** *usually,* **needs.** something that is useful, important, or wanted: the *needs* of a newborn baby. **3.** something that must be done; an obligation: "A young fellow like Bernie has lots of time, no *need* to rush through life." (Brian Moore) **4.** condition of being without something important; being poor or in difficulty. —*verb,* **needed, needing. 1.** to want and be without; have a need for: After rolling around in the mud the dog *needed* a good bath. **2.** to be obligated; have to: You don't *need* to pick me up; I'll walk home.

needlepoint A farm woman of Virginia's Blue Ridge Mountains working on her needlepoint.

nee•dle [nēd′ əl] *noun, plural* **needles. 1.** a small, thin tool that is usually made of metal, used in sewing to move thread through cloth. One end has a hole to which thread is fastened and the other end has a sharp point. **2.** a long, slender rod used in knitting to hold and form the stitches. **3.** a thin, pointed needle-shaped leaf found on certain trees, such as the pine, spruce, or fir. **4.** a hollow tube with a sharp, thin point that is used to inject medicine or another liquid into the body. **5.** any of various other things that are long, thin, and pointed like a needle: the *needle* of a compass, a diamond *needle* for a record player. —*verb,* **needled, needling.** to bother or annoy a person; tease.

need•less [nēd′lis] *adjective.* not necessary or needed: Steve went to a lot of *needless* trouble washing the dishes by hand when he could have just used the dishwasher. —**needlessly,** *adverb.*

need•y [nē′dē] *adjective,* **needier, neediest.** not having what is needed to live on; poor.

neg•a•tive [neg′ə tiv] *adjective, more/most.* **1.** saying or meaning "no;" showing that something is not true, not to be done, and so on: Shaking the head from side to side is a *negative* answer. **2.** not helpful or friendly; not positive: Bernie has a very *negative* attitude toward New York City ever since he was almost robbed on a visit there. **3.** of a number, being less than zero. **4.** having one of the two opposite electrical charges: In a battery, the *negative* pole is marked with a minus sign (−) and the positive with a plus (+). **5.** showing that a certain disease or harmful condition is not present: Chris was afraid he'd broken his finger, but luckily the X-rays were *negative.* —*noun, plural* **negatives. 1.** a word or phrase that says or means "no". **2.** in photography, an image on a piece of film that is developed into a print.

to do; leave undone: "It was a sad thing that Father had *neglected* to tell me about the Finch family . . ." (Harper Lee) —*noun.* the fact or condition of being neglected. The house hasn't been painted for years and years—it's a sad case of *neglect.*

neg•li•gent [neg′lə jənt] *adjective, more/most.* caused by or showing neglect; not doing what one should; careless: The storekeeper was *negligent* when he didn't fix the broken stairs in his shop and someone fell down them. ♦ The fact of being negligent is **negligence.**

ne•go•ti•ate [ni gō′shē āt′] *verb,* **negotiated, negotiating. 1.** to talk over a problem or issue in order to reach an agreement or to make arrangements: The two countries were *negotiat-*

negative This negative will produce a black-and-white photo of President Lincoln when it is processed.

---

negatives English has a rule that only one negative word is needed to express a negative idea. That is, if you use *no, never, none, nothing, nobody,* or another such word, don't follow it up with another negative in the same statement. "'I *don't* want *nothing,*' Nancy said." (William Faulkner) This is a *double negative*—two words used to express the same negative idea. The correct form is "I don't want *anything.*" Some writers know the rule but deliberately avoid it—for effect. They do this to give a realistic sound to the speech of a certain character, as Faulkner did in writing about uneducated people in the rural South. Misuse of the negative is one of the most serious errors a writer can make. If you read, "Deserts are places that don't have no rain," you would assume the writer is careless or perhaps badly trained.

---

neg•lect [ni glekt′] *verb,* **neglected, neglecting. 1.** to not give the proper attention or care to: "In the days that followed, Mr. Zuckerman was so busy entertaining visitors that he *neglected* his farm work." (E.B. White) ♦ Often used as an adjective: "He could think of nothing to do alone and as the afternoon wore on he felt lonely and *neglected.*" (L.M. Boston) **2.** to fail

N

ing a peace treaty to end the war between them. **2.** to go safely on or over: "He cautiously *negotiated* a flight of stairs . . . and came to a landing." (Mark Helprin)

ne•go•ti•a•tion [ni gō′ shē ā′ shən] *noun, plural* **negotiations.** the act or fact of negotiating, or something that is negotiated: Mr. Snyder has just begun *negotiations* to sell his business to a large out-of-town company.

Ne•gro [nē′ grō] *noun, plural* **Negroes.** a member of a race of people who generally have dark skin, now usually referred to as BLACKS. —*adjective.* of or having to do with black or Negro people. ◆ See BLACK on p. 77 for more information.

Neh•ru [nā′ rōō] **Jawaharlal** [jə wä′ har läl′], 1889–1964, the first prime minister of India, from 1947 to 1964.

neigh•bor [nā′ bər] *noun, plural* **neighbors. 1.** a person who lives next door or nearby. **2.** a person or thing located next to another: There weren't enough books for the whole class, so Suzy had to share hers with her *neighbor.* —**neighboring,** *adjective.* close by; near: The war in Vietnam spread to the *neighboring* countries of Laos and Cambodia. —**neighborly,** *adjective.* like a good neighbor; friendly.

neigh•bor•hood [nā′ bər hood′] *noun, plural* **neighborhoods. 1.** one particular area that is within a larger city or town and that has certain characteristics of its own: We have to go downtown to see a movie because there's no theater in our *neighborhood.* ◆ Also used as an adjective: to play basketball at the *neighborhood* park. **2.** all the people who live in a certain area: Stop making so much noise! You'll wake up the whole *neighborhood!*

is used in tubes to light up signs and lamps because it glows when electricity is applied to it. Neon is a chemical element.

neon The dazzling neon lights of the Ginza district in Tokyo, Japan.

Ne•pal [nə pôl′ *or* nā pôl′] a country between India and Tibet, in the Himalayas. *Capital:* Katmandu. *Area:* 54,400 square miles. *Population:* 15,100,000.

neph•ew [nef′ yōō] *noun, plural* **nephews. 1.** the son of a person's brother or sister. **2.** the son of a person's brother-in-law or sister-in-law.

Nep•tune [nep′ tōōn] *noun.* **1.** the fourth-largest planet in the solar system, and the eighth in distance from the sun. **2.** the ancient Roman god of the sea.

nerve [nurv] *noun, plural* **nerves. 1.** a fiber or bundle of fibers connecting the brain and spinal cord to other parts of the body, such as the eyes, ears, muscles, and organs. Nerves carry

neither This word should be followed by *nor,* not *or.* "He can neither speak *nor* hear but he reads my lips easily." (Walter Farley) "That night there was neither thunder *nor* snow." (L.M. Boston) Please note also that *neither* is singular, and takes a singular verb. On the front of the main New York City Post Office, there is a sign in huge letters. It is a quotation from the ancient Greek writer Herodotus, which has become a motto of the postal service: "*Neither* snow, *nor* rain, *nor* heat, *nor* gloom of night, *stays* [not 'stay'] these carriers from their appointed rounds."

nei•ther [nē′ thər *or* nī′ thər] *adjective.* not one or the other: "He was a rather skinny boy, *neither* large nor small for fourteen." (Esther Forbes) —*pronoun:* Do you want to have pie or cake? *Neither,* I'm going to skip dessert. —*conjunction:* Mom isn't home right now, and *neither* is Dad.

ne•on [nē′ än] *noun.* a gas that has no color or smell and is found in small amounts in the air. It

the messages to and from the brain that make the body work. **2.** strength of the mind or will; courage; bravery: After the near-crash the pilot lost his *nerve* and refused to fly again. **3.** the fact of being rude or impolite: ". . . You have the *nerve* to tell me you were only courting me because you thought I might put money in your restaurant." (Brian Moore) **4. nerves.** a feeling of being upset or nervous; nervousness.

ner•vous [nur′vəs] *adjective, more/most.*
1. quick to become upset or excited; not relaxed; tense: "Billy got more and more *nervous,* afraid the girl might not show up, afraid
she might." (Ken Kesey) **2.** showing this feeling: "Barney had long, *nervous* hands that were
usually drumming out a tune or scratching his
arm or doing something . . ." (Laurence Yep)
3. having to do with the nerves or the mind: a
nervous breakdown. Polio and epilepsy are
nervous disorders. —**nervously,** *adverb:* "He
was *nervously* shifting the phone from ear to
ear while he talked." (Hunter Thompson)
—**nervousness,** *noun.*

nervous system the network in the body made
up of the brain, spinal cord, and nerves.

nest [nest] *noun, plural* **nests. 1.** a place built by
a bird from grass, mud, twigs, or other materials, and used for laying its eggs and raising its
young. **2.** a similar place used by other animals,
such as fish, turtles, or snakes. **3.** any shelter or
comfortable home. —*verb,* **nested, nesting.** to
make or live in a nest.

nes•tle [nes′əl] *verb,* **nestled, nestling.** to settle
down or lie in a comfortable place: "The boy
nestled himself upon my shoulder and pretended to go to sleep." (Mark Twain)

net¹ [net] *noun, plural* **nets. 1.** a fabric made of
thread, cord, or rope woven or knotted togeth-
er, leaving evenly-spaced openings. Nets are
used to catch, stop, or hold things: a fishing *net,*
a hair *net,* a butterfly *net.* **2.** a net used as a goal
or dividing line in such games as tennis, volleyball, hockey, or soccer. **3.** anything that catches
and holds things like a net: to be caught in the
net of fate. —*verb,* **netted, netting.** to catch in a
net: Gary *netted* a beautiful rainbow trout on
his last fishing trip.

net² *adjective.* **1.** left after all charges, costs, and
allowances have been made: The *net* weight of
a truckload of furniture is the weight of the
furniture itself, not counting the weight of the
truck. **2.** after everything has been taken into
account; final: The new magazine was tested in
six different cities, but the *net* result was that
people weren't very interested in it. —*verb,*
netted, netting. to receive as a profit: They
netted $20,000 on the sale of their house.

Neth•er•lands, the [neth′ ər ləndz] a country in
northwestern Europe, on the North Sea. *Capital:* Amsterdam. *Area:* 15,800 square miles.
Population: 14,500,000.

net•tle [net′əl] *noun, plural* **nettles.** a tall,
prickly plant that has hairs on its leaves and
stem that sting the skin when touched.

net•work [net′wurk′] *noun, plural* **networks.**
1. a system or pattern of crossing lines, wires,
routes, or the like: A *network* of blood vessels
can be seen through the skin on your hand.
"They connected with other vines and other
branches, forming a *network* that shut out hard
sunlight." (Virginia Hamilton) **2.** a group of
radio or TV stations in different places that are
joined together so that they can use the same
broadcasts. **3.** a system of computers connected
to each other so that they can share and exchange information. **4.** any connected group or
system: the Hilton Hotel *network.* —*verb,* **net-
worked, networking.** to cooperate with a group
of others to do or get something, especially to
advance in business.

neu•tral [noo′trəl] *adjective, more/most.* **1.** not
taking sides in a war, argument, or contest:
Sweden was *neutral* in World War II and did not
fight with either the Allies or the Axis countries. ♦ The fact of being neutral is **neutrality**
[noo tral′ ə tē]. **2.** having little or no color, or a
color that blends easily with others: Gray, tan,
and cream are *neutral* colors. **3.** in chemistry,
neither an acid nor a base: a *neutral* solution.
—*noun.* a position of gears in an automobile in
which no power is sent from the engine to the
wheels. ♦ To make something neutral is to
neutralize it.

Netherlands This windmill is typical of many
found in the Netherlands. The term *Netherland*
literally means "Lower Land."

Pronunciation Key: T–Z

t	ten, date	v	very, live
th	think	w	win; away
th	these	y	you
u	cut; butter	z	zoo; cause
ur	turn; bird	zh	measure

(Turn the page for more information.)

neu·tron [nōō′ trän′] *noun, plural* **neutrons.** in an atom, a tiny particle that has neither a positive nor a negative charge of electricity. Neutrons and PROTONS together make up almost all the mass of the nucleus of the atom. Neutrons are found in all atoms except hydrogen.

Ne·vad·a [nə väd′ ə *or* nə vad′ ə] a state in the western U.S. *Capital:* Carson City. *Nickname:* "Silver State." *Area:* 110,500 square miles. *Population:* 881,000.

nev·er [nev′ ər] *adverb.* not at any time; not ever: "That was such a happy summer Laura wanted it *never* to end." (Laura Ingalls Wilder)

nev·er·the·less [nev′ ər thə les′] *adverb; conjunction:* in any case; in spite of that; anyway: I'm afraid I won't be able to go, but *nevertheless,* thanks for asking me.

new [nōō] *adjective,* **newer, newest. 1.** made or done just now or a short time ago; not in being for long; not old: At the end of the winter, trees grow *new* leaves. **2.** just seen, found, or learned about; not known before: In 1930 scientists discovered a *new* planet and named it Pluto. **3.** being in a place or condition for only a short time: Suzanne has just started her *new* job. **4.** taking the place of what was there before: a *new* edition of a book. **5.** beginning again: a *new* moon, the beginning of a *new* day.

New·ark [nōō′ ərk] a city in northeastern New Jersey. *Population:* 329,000.

New Bruns·wick [brunz′ wik] a province in southeastern Canada, northeast of Maine. *Capital:* Fredericton. *Area:* 28,300 square miles. *Population:* 696,000.

New England the northeastern part of the U.S. that includes Maine, New Hampshire, Vermont, Massachusetts, Rhode Island, and Connecticut. ◆ These states were first settled by Puritans from England.

New England A view of a Vermont town in autumn, showing a classic New England feature, the three-story steepled church.

New·found·land [nōō′ fənd lənd] **1.** a large island off the southeastern coast of Canada. **2.** a province of southeastern Canada that includes this island and Labrador on the mainland. *Capital:* St. John's. *Area:* 158,200 square miles. *Population:* 597,000.

New Hampshire [hamp′ shər] a state in the northeastern U.S., bordered by Canada. *Capital:* Concord. *Nickname:* "Granite State." *Area:* 9,300 square miles. *Population:* 951,000.

New Jer·sey [jur′ zē] a state on the middle Atlantic coast of the U.S. *Capital:* Trenton. *Nickname:* "Garden State." *Area:* 7,800 square miles. *Population:* 7,450,000.

new·ly [nōō′ lē] *adverb.* not long ago; recently; lately. ◆ Used in combination with an adjective: a *newly*-completed highway, a *newly*-married couple.

◆ A **newlywed** is a person who has been recently married.

New Mexico The red cliffs of Jemez Canyon near Los Alamos, New Mexico.

New Mexico a state in the southwestern U.S., bordered by Mexico to the south. *Capital:* Santa Fe. *Nickname:* "Land of Enchantment." *Population:* 1,360,000.

New Or·leans [ôr′ lənz *or* ôr lēnz′] a port city in southeastern Louisiana, on the Mississippi River. *Population:* 560,000.

news [nōōz] *noun.* **1.** a newspaper, television, or radio report about something important that has recently happened or become known. **2.** any report about something that has recently happened: Every week Grandma sends us a letter with all the latest *news* about the family.

news·cast [nōōz′ kast′] *noun, plural* **newscasts.** a radio or television program on which news events are reported.

◆ A person who presents the news on such a show is a **newscaster.**

N

newspapers "Camembert cheese, Bordeaux wine, and Parisian newspapers fill the shelves of Guinea's first supermarket." This is the lead for a recent news story in the *New York Times*. You've probably heard that a news story should lead with Who/What/Where/When/Why. However, it doesn't really work that way. *Where* and *when* appear in the dateline: "Seattle, Oct. 6. This summer the rain country's rains failed." Many stories don't have a *who*, such as this "rain" story. *What* is too general; the entire story is the answer to that. Finally, very few stories say *why*. The *Times* had a story in that issue about a food critic who gave false information in a book; the reporter did not attempt to say *why* this happened. So why is the "Five W's" a popular guideline for student writers? Because it reminds you to do these things: Concentrate on the facts; lead with the most important thing; be specific. Note that the writer did not say, "Products from France fill the shelves . . ."

news•pa•per [nōōz′ pā′ pər] *noun, plural* **newspapers.** a paper printed and sold each day or each week to report the news to the public. Newspapers also contain other writing besides news stories, such as editorials and columns, as well as advertisements.

newt [nōōt] *noun, plural* **newts.** a small, brightly-colored animal with smooth skin, short legs, and a long tail. It lives part of the time in water and part on land.

New Testament the second part of the Bible. It is a record of the life and teachings of Jesus Christ and his followers.

New•ton [nōōt′ ən] **Sir Isaac,** 1642–1727, English mathematician and philosopher who discovered the laws of gravity.

New World North and South America; the Western Hemisphere.

New Year or **New Year's Day** the first day of a calendar year.

New York [yôrk] **1.** a state on the east coast of the U.S. *Capital:* Albany. *Nickname:* "Empire State." *Area:* 49,600 square miles. *Population:* 17,700,000. **2.** *also,* **New York City.** a city in southeastern New York State, at the mouth of the Hudson River. It is the largest city in the U.S. *Population:* 7,080,000.

New Zea•land [zē′ lənd] a country on two main islands in the southwestern Pacific, near Australia. *Capital:* Wellington. *Area:* 102,900 square miles. *Population:* 3,200,000.

next [nekst] *adjective.* just after this one or after the one before: The new store will open *next* month. ♦ Also used as an adverb or a preposition: First you turn on the key; *next* you step on the gas. Their house is *next* to the park.

next door in or at the nearest house, building, or room. ♦ Also used as an adjective: a *next-door* neighbor.

Ni•ag•a•ra Falls [nī ag′ rə] a large waterfall on the U.S.-Canadian border between New York State and Ontario.

nib•ble [nib′ əl] *verb,* **nibbled, nibbling.** to take quick, small bites: "Minnows nosed up the current, flashing in the sun, *nibbling* at Jeremiah's bare toes." (Sterling North)

Nic•a•ra•gua [nik′ ə rä′ gwə] a country in Central America south of Honduras, with coastlines on the Pacific and the Caribbean. *Capital:* Managua. *Area:* 50,200 square miles. *Population:* 3,000,000. —**Nicaraguan,** *adjective; noun.*

nice [nīs] *adjective,* **nicer, nicest.** pleasing or good in some way, as by being kind, friendly, well done, well made, and so on: She's a *nice* person who always helps out her friends. It was a *nice* day for a picnic, with clear, sunny skies. —**nicely,** *adverb.*

niche [nich] *noun, plural* **niches. 1.** a hollowed-out or sunken place in a wall, used to hold something for decoration, such as a small statue or a vase. **2.** a place or activity for which a person is well-suited: Cathy has finally found her *niche* with the new company after holding several different jobs.

nick [nik] *noun, plural* **nicks. 1.** a small cut or chip on the edge or surface of something. **2. in the nick of time.** at the final moment; just in time. —*verb,* **nicked, nicking.** to make a nick.

nick•el [nik′ əl] *noun, plural* **nickels. 1.** a strong, hard, silver-colored metal that is often combined with other metals. Nickel is a chemical element. **2.** a U.S. coin worth five cents, made from a mixture of nickel and copper.

nick•name [nik′ nām′] *noun, plural* **nicknames.** a name used in place of a person's real

---

Pronunciation Key: [ə] Symbol

The [ə] or *schwa* sound occurs in syllables without an accent. It can be spelled with any vowel, such as **a** in above, **e** in listen, **i** in pencil, **o** in melon, **u** in circus. It can also be a combination of vowels, such as **io** in action, **ai** in mountain, **iou** in precious.

(Turn the page for more information.)

N

name. A nickname can be simply a short form of the person's name, such as Joe (Joseph) Namath. It can also be a description of the person, such as 'Bear' Bryant. —*verb*, **nicknamed, nicknaming.** to give a nickname to a person.

nic•o•tine [nik′ ə tēn′] *noun.* a poison that is found in small amounts in the leaves, roots, and seeds of tobacco plants. Nicotine is one of the harmful substances in cigarettes. It is used as an insect poison and in some medicines.

niece [nēs] *noun, plural* **nieces. 1.** the daughter of a person's brother or sister. **2.** the daughter of a brother-in-law or sister-in-law.

Ni•ge•ri•a [nī jēr′ ē ə] a country in western Africa, on the Gulf of Guinea. *Capital:* Lagos. *Area:* 357,000 square miles. *Population:* 84,800,000. —**Nigerian,** *adjective; noun.*

night [nīt] *noun, plural* **nights.** the time when it is dark; the time between sunset and sunrise.

night•gown [nīt′ goun′] *noun, plural* **nightgowns.** a loose, dress-like garment worn to bed by women and girls.

night•in•gale [nīt′ ən gāl′] *noun, plural* **nightingales.** a small, reddish-brown bird with a gray or white underside. The males are known for their beautiful songs, often sung at night.

Night•in•gale [nīt′ ən gāl′] **Florence,** 1820–1910, English nurse, the founder of modern nursing.

night•ly [nīt′ lē] *adjective; adverb.* happening or done every night: a *nightly* news broadcast.

nim•ble [nim′ bəl] *adjective,* **nimbler, nimblest.** moving in a light, graceful way; agile. —**nimbly,** *adverb:* ". . . a bullfighter, waving his red cape in front of the bull and stepping *nimbly* aside . . ." (Beverly Cleary)

nine [nīn] *noun, plural* **nines;** *adjective.* one more than eight; 9. —**ninth,** *adjective; noun.*

nine•ty [nīn′ tē] *noun, plural* **nineties;** *adjective.* nine times ten; 90. —**ninetieth,** *adjective; noun.*

nip [nip] *verb,* **nipped, nipping. 1.** to give a quick, sharp bite: The dog *nipped* the boy's leg. **2.** to cut off by pinching: to *nip* dead leaves off a plant. **3.** to sting with cold; chill. —*noun, plural* **nips. 1.** a small, quick bite. **2.** a biting chill: a *nip* in the air on a fall morning.

nip•ple [nip′ əl] *noun, plural* **nipples. 1.** a round tip at the center of the breast, through which a baby drinks milk from its mother. **2.** a soft rubber mouthpiece on a baby's bottle that the baby sucks to get milk or another liquid.

ni•tro•gen [nī′ trə jən] *noun.* a gas that has no color, smell, or taste. It makes up about 70% of the air and is found in all living things. Nitrogen is a chemical element.

Nix•on [nik′ sən] **Richard M.,** born 1913, the thirty-seventh president of the United States, from 1969 to 1974.

no [nō] *adverb.* **1.** the opposite of "yes;" a word used to mean that something can't be, won't be, shouldn't be, and so on. **2.** not any; not at all: Entries to the contest must be mailed *no* later than Friday.

no/any "He didn't have *no* idea what the matter was, of course." (Mark Twain). "It didn't take *no* private detective to figure out who had played me this little joke." (Ring Lardner). By remembering the rule about NEGATIVES (see p. 513), you were able to spot the errors in these sentences, weren't you? Because the negative idea has already been signaled by *didn't* ("did not"), the correct form is *any,* not *no.* Of course, Twain and Lardner knew the *no/any* rule; they were breaking it on purpose to present a certain kind of character. When the barber in Lardner's story "Haircut" says, "Jim won't need no shavin' mug no more . . ." he tells us something about character. In factual writing, *any* is always used when there is another negative in the statement.

night•mare [nīt′ mâr′] *noun, plural* **nightmares. 1.** a dream that is frightening or disturbing; a bad dream: Last night I had a *nightmare* that I was falling out of my apartment window. **2.** a frightening or horrible experience that is thought of as being like a bad dream: We ran out of gas halfway across the bridge at rush hour—what a *nightmare!*

Nile [nīl] the longest river in the world, flowing north from Lake Victoria in central Africa to the Mediterranean in Egypt.

—*adjective:* Let me help you —it's *no* trouble. —*noun, plural* **nos.** a vote or answer of "no."

No•bel [nō bel′] **Alfred,** 1833–1896, Swedish chemist who invented dynamite. He established a fund for the Nobel Prizes.

Nobel Prize an international award given each year for very important work in certain fields. Prizes have been awarded since 1901 for physics, chemistry, medicine, literature, and advancing the cause of peace. A prize in economic science was added in 1969.

no·bil·i·ty [nō bil′ ə tē] *noun, plural* **nobilities.**
1. people who are born into or who are given a high rank or title in society. Kings, queens, princes, princesses, counts, barons, and so on make up the nobility. **2.** the quality or fact of being noble.

no·ble [nō′ bəl] *adjective,* **nobler, noblest.**
1. having a high rank or title in society. **2.** having great value or character; distinguished; outstanding: In Shakespeare's *Julius Caesar,* Mark Antony praises Brutus by calling him "the *noblest* Roman of them all." **3.** very grand or impressive in appearance; splendid: "These clipper ships of the early 1850's were . . . the *noblest* of all sailing vessels, and the most beautiful creations of man in America." (Samuel Eliot Morison) —*noun, plural* **nobles.** a person of high rank or title. ◆ Such a person is also called a **nobleman** or **noblewoman.** —**nobly,** *adverb.*

no·bod·y [nō′ bud′ ē *or* nō′ bäd′ ē] *pronoun.* no person; not anybody; no one: "*Nobody* likes the man who brings bad news." (Sophocles) —*noun, plural* **nobodies.** a person of no importance: "I didn't want you to think I was just some *nobody.*" (F. Scott Fitzgerald)

noc·tur·nal [näk tur′ nəl] *adjective.* having to do with or happening at night: *Nocturnal* animals such as the owl or raccoon sleep during the day and are active at night.

nois·y [noi′ zē] *adjective,* **noisier, noisiest.** full of noise; making a lot of noise: "I hate that *noisy* place—buzzing with trucks and airplanes." (James Houston) —**noisily,** *adverb:* "Mr. Dedalus threw his knife and fork *noisily* on his plate." (James Joyce)

no·mad [nō′ mad] *noun, plural* **nomads. 1.** a member of a tribe or group that often moves from place to place, rather than staying in one permanent home: Certain American Indian tribes were *nomads* who followed the buffalo across the Great Plains. ◆ A group that does this is **nomadic. 2.** any person who wanders about from place to place.

nom·i·nate [näm′ ə nāt] *verb,* **nominated, nominating. 1.** to choose someone to run for office. **2.** to name to a high office or position: The President has the power to *nominate* new justices for the Supreme Court. "By the time I'm twenty I'll have helped so many people that they'll *nominate* me for the Guiness Book of World Records." (Nancy Willard).

nom·i·na·tion [näm′ ə nā′ shən] *noun, plural* **nominations.** the act or fact of nominating. ◆ A person who is nominated is a **nominee.**

non·cha·lant [nän′ shə länt′] *adjective, more/ most.* not showing much interest or effort; cool; casual: Dave's only had his license for a week, but he tries to act very *nonchalant,* as if he'd been driving for years. —**nonchalantly,** *adverb.*

none Language experts argue over the use of *none.* Some take it to mean "no one," and say it's a singular word. Others say that a word should fall naturally in line with other words in the sentence, and that if *none* is used to refer to a plural noun, it should take a plural verb. In our own survey of teachers and writers, we found that usage was divided. Some writers use the singular: "Notes could be tightly soaked and folded . . . to make sure *none was* intercepted along the way." (Joyce Maynard) Others use the plural: "But this morning Leo did not look into his face and *none* of the men *were* talking." (Carson McCullers) "We recommend the second choice, using *none* as a plural. "None of the men *was* talking" is awkward, because there's a strong plural word near the verb, *men.* But we are not necessarily right. "It's an open case," as lawyers and detectives say.

nod [näd] *verb,* **nodded, nodding. 1.** to move the head up and down. **2.** to do this as a sign to show that one agrees, is saying 'yes,' and so on. —*noun, plural* **nods:** "So, with a *nod* of thanks to his friends, he went on his walk . . ." (A.A. Milne)

noise [noiz] *noun, plural* **noises. 1.** a sound that is loud, unpleasant, or unwanted: Mom asked the boys not to make so much *noise* while she was talking on the phone. **2.** any sound: He heard a *noise* outside, and looked out the window to see what it was.

none [nun] *pronoun.* not one; not any: She tried several keys in the lock, but *none* fit. —*adverb.* not at all: That store is *none* too cheap.

Pronunciation Key: Accent Marks

[′] is the normal accent mark. It shows where the main stress falls on a word.
[′] is a secondary accent mark. It shows a lighter stress than the primary accent. For example:
tel • e • vis • ion [tel′ ə vizh′ ən]
(Turn the page for more information.)

non•sense [nän′sens′] *noun.* talk or actions that do not make sense; things that have a foolish meaning or no meaning at all.

noo•dle [nōōd′ əl] *noun, plural* **noodles.** a mixture of flour, water, and egg dried into flat strips. Noodles come in different sizes and shapes and are used in soups, stews, and other meals. ♦ *Noodle* comes from the German word for this food.

noon [nōōn] *noun.* twelve o'clock in the daytime; the middle part of the day.

no one not one person; nobody: I rang the doorbell, but *no one* answered.

noose [nōōs] *noun, plural* **nooses.** a loop of rope or cord with a knot that tightens at the end when it is pulled.

nor [nôr] *conjunction.* and not: Something that is lukewarm is neither hot *nor* cold.

nor•mal [nôr′ məl] *adjective.* **1.** as it should be; healthy and natural: The *normal* temperature of the body is 98.6 degrees. **2.** as it usually is; like most others; typical: We've had a lot more than the *normal* amount of rain this month. —**normally,** *adverb:* I really enjoyed *The Sound of Music,* even though *normally* I don't like musicals.

north [nôrth] *noun.* **1.** the direction to your right when you face the sun as it goes down at night; the opposite of south. **2.** *usually,* **North.** any place or region in that direction. **3. the North. a.** the states that fought against the Confederate states (the SOUTH) in the Civil War; the Union states. **b.** the region roughly north of Washington, D.C. and east of Ohio; more often called the **East** or **Northeast.** —*adjective.* **1.** toward the north: the *north* side of Chicago. **2.** coming from the north: a *north* wind. —*adverb.* toward the north: to travel *north.*

North America the northern continent of the Western Hemisphere that includes Canada, the U.S., Mexico, and Central America.

North Car•o•li•na [kar′ ə lī′ nə] a southern state of the U.S., on the Atlantic coast. *Capital:* Raleigh. *Nickname:* "Tarheel State." *Area:* 52,600 square miles. *Population:* 6,020,000.

North Da•ko•ta [də kō′ tə] a state in the north-central U.S., bordered by Canada. *Capital:* Bismarck. *Nickname:* "Sioux State." *Area:* 70,700 square miles. *Population:* 670,000.

north•ern [nôr′ thərn] *adjective, more/most.* **1.** in or toward the north. **2.** coming from the north: a cold *northern* air mass. **3. Northern.** of or in the North. ♦ A **Northerner** is a person born or living in the north.

Northern Ireland a part of Great Britain in the northeastern corner of the island of Ireland. *Capital:* Belfast. *Area:* 5,500 square miles. *Population:* 1,500,000.

northern lights A view of the northern lights near Fairbanks, Alaska.

northern lights bands of bright light and color seen in the northern sky at night, especially in the Arctic regions; also called the **aurora bore-alis** [ə rôr′ ə bor′ ē al′ əs].

North Korea a country that occupies the northern part of the Korean Peninsula. *Capital:* Pyongyang. *Area:* 46,500 square miles. *Population:* 19,300,000.

North Pole the northernmost point of the earth, near the middle of the Arctic Ocean.

North Sea a part of the Atlantic Ocean between Great Britain and northern Europe.

North Star a bright star in the northern sky, almost directly above the North Pole; also called **Polaris.**

Nor•way [nôr′ wā] a country in northern Europe, west of Sweden. *Capital:* Oslo. *Area:* 128,200 square miles. *Population:* 4,200,000. —**Norwegian,** *adjective; noun.*

Norway A ship passes between mountains in one of the many picturesque *fiords* [fē′ordz] in Norway.

nose [nōz] *noun, plural* **noses. 1.** the part of the face or head that is used for breathing and smelling. **2.** the sense of smell: a dog with a good *nose*. **3.** an ability to sense or search out things: a reporter with a good *nose* for news. **4.** something that sticks out in front, like a nose: the *nose* of an airplane. —*verb*, **nosed, nosing. 1.** to use the nose: "The fawn *nosed* about the room, smelling of one man after the other . . ." (Marjorie Kinnan Rawlings) **2.** to search for something in a prying or annoying way; snoop.

words or sentences that a person writes down to help remember some larger thought or idea. **3.** a short comment or item of information in a book to explain something or to refer to another place in the book. **4.** notice or attention: Take *note* of what she says. **5.** a little bit; a hint or suggestion: There was a *note* of sadness in her voice. **6.** one musical sound, or the sign representing this sound. A written note shows how long a certain sound is to be held and how high or low it is.

notes "Why do I have to write notes before I do a research paper? Why can't I write a first draft right from the source books?" There are good answers here. First of all, writing from the source is not possible if you do research in the library and then write at home. Many sources can't be taken out of the library—encyclopedias, magazine collections, and so on. Also, most libraries limit you to a certain number of books on any given topic. Second, if you have three or four primary sources and three or four secondary ones, you can't write a report with eight books spread open in front of you. Third, you can't get a one-gallon paper from one gallon of facts. You need to boil down the information by writing crisply, and of course boiling water lessens it. Also, going from book to note card to paper helps you avoid direct use of the wording of the source. This is known as *plagiarism*.

nos•tril [näs′tril] *noun, plural* **nostrils.** one of the two outer openings of the nose. The nostrils are the passageways through which air is pulled into the body by the lungs.

nos•y [nōz′ē] *adjective,* **nosier, nosiest.** concerned with things that are not one's business: It's *nosy* to open other people's mail or listen in on their phone calls.

not [nät] *adverb.* in no way: A whale is *not* a fish; it's a mammal.

no•ta•ble [nō′tə bəl] *adjective,* *more/most.* worth being noticed; important; outstanding. —*noun, plural* **notables.** a person who is notable: The opening of the new bridge will be attended by the governor, the mayor, and various other *notables.* —**notably,** *adverb.*

no•ta•tion [nō tā′shən] *noun, plural* **notations. 1.** a short note: to make a *notation* in the margin of a paper. **2.** a system of symbols used to represent something: The + sign is a mathematical *notation.*

notch [näch] *noun, plural* **notches.** a small, V-shaped cut made on the edge or surface of something: Pioneers often would make a *notch* in a tree with an ax to show others coming through the woods where the trail was. —*verb,* **notched, notching.** to cut a notch in something.

note [nōt] *noun, plural* **notes. 1.** a short letter or message: Ryan left his mother a *note* to say he'd gone up the street to his friend's house. **2.** a few

—*verb,* **noted, noting. 1.** to write down: Mr. Ames *noted* the license plate of the car that had caused the accident. **2.** to pay careful attention to; notice.

note•book [nōt′bŏŏk′] *noun, plural* **notebooks.** a book with blank pages for taking notes or for writing or drawing.

noted [nō′tid] *adjective, more/most.* famous; well-known: a *noted* singer, a *noted* author.

noth•ing [nuth′ing] *noun.* **1.** no thing or things; not anything. **2.** zero: The Blues won by a score of one to *nothing.* **3.** something that is not at all important: Don't worry about this cut, it's *nothing* but a tiny scratch. —*adverb.* not in any way; not at all.

no•tice [nō′tis] *noun, plural* **notices. 1.** a short printed or written message that announces something: There was a *notice* on the bulletin board saying that somebody had lost a wallet. **2.** a warning or action that shows something is about to happen: "His hand rested on the door handle, prepared to slam it shut at a moment's

Pronunciation Key: A–F			
a	and; hat	ch	chew; such
ā	ate; stay	d	dog; lid
â	care; air	e	end; yet
ä	father; hot	ē	she; each
b	boy; cab	f	fun; off

(Turn the page for more information.)

N

notice.'' (Christopher Isherwood) **3.** a formal statement ahead of time that someone will be moving, leaving a job, or the like. **4.** the fact of knowing about or being aware of something; attention: ''There was an air raid going on, but we weren't taking much *notice*.'' (Jill Paton Walsh) —*verb*, **noticed, noticing.** to pay attention to; see or sense: Did you *notice* that Jan has changed her hair style? ◆ Something that can be noticed is **noticeable.**

no•ti•fy [nō′tə fī] *verb*, **notified, notifying.** to make some information known to a person; announce something: The bank's letter *notified* her that her car loan had been approved. —**notification** [nō′ti fə kā′shən], *noun.*

no•tion [nō′shən] *noun, plural* **notions. 1.** a vague or general idea about something: ''It happened so suddenly, Thomas had the *notion* that time had stopped.'' (Virginia Hamilton) **2.** a sudden or odd desire to do something: ''Eventually I put the map away, but the *notion* of (going to) Alaska lingered on.'' (Joe McGinniss) **3. notions.** small items that are used in sewing, such as needles, thread, pins, and ribbons.

> **notorious** *Notorious* means not just ''famous,'' but ''famous for something bad.'' ''Al Capone was a *notorious* criminal.'' ''That restaurant is *notorious* for its high prices and rude waiters.'' Some writers nowadays use *notorious* in a positive way: ''We [Texas A & M] get some good students from this program, and we also get some *notoriety*.'' (Laurence Cress). We think you should avoid this, and use *notorious* only in the narrower sense. If it comes to mean simply *famous*, and if *notoriety* equals *fame*, then English has lost something. Here's an example of how *fame* and *notoriety* are different. ''For *fame* awaited him in England, not the false kind he had already brought on himself, not cheap *notoriety*, but real *fame*.'' (Malcolm Lowry)

no•to•ri•ous [nō tôr′ē əs] *adjective, more/most.* well-known for something bad; famous in a bad way: ''Dutch Schultz was Newark's most *notorious* gangster.'' (Russell Baker) ◆ The fact of being notorious is **notoriety** [nō′tə rī′ə tē]. —**notoriously,** *adverb.*

noun [noun] *noun, plural* **nouns.** a word that names a person, place, or thing. A noun can act as the subject of a verb (The *dog* just got out), the object of a verb (I forgot to close the *door*), or the object of a preposition (He ran across the *street*). Many nouns tell about things that can be counted, and they can be changed from singular to plural by adding **-s** or **-es.**

nour•ish [nur′ish] *verb,* **nourished, nourishing.** to provide food and other things to plants and animals so that they can live and grow. ◆ Usually used as an adjective: Cake and cookies are not thought to be as *nourishing* as fruits and vegetables.

nour•ish•ment [nur′ish mənt] *noun.* **1.** what is needed to keep plants and animals alive and growing: The patient is having stomach problems and is only allowed to have liquid *nourishment.* **2.** the act or fact of nourishing.

no•va [nō′və] *noun, plural* **novas** or **novae.** a star that explodes and sends huge masses of matter into space. It becomes tremendously bright for a time and then fades to its former lower level of brightness.

No•va Sco•tia [nō′və skō′shə] a province on the east coast of Canada. *Capital:* Halifax. *Area:* 21,400 square miles. *Population:* 850,000.

nov•el [näv′əl] *noun, plural* **novels.** a written story that is long enough to fill a book. A novel tells about people and events made up by the author, rather than presenting actual facts or history. —*adjective, more/most.* not known before; new and unusual: The mayor has just presented a *novel* idea for what to do with the old riverfront area—build a series of floating department stores.

nov•el•ist [näv′ əl ist] *noun, plural* **novelists.** a person who writes novels.

nov•el•ty [näv′ əl tē] *noun, plural* **novelties. 1.** something that is novel; a new and unusual thing: ''Indians were no *novelty* to the townspeople of Wichita. Sabra had seen them all her life.'' (Edna Ferber) **2.** the fact of being novel; being new: At first he used his home computer all the time, but the *novelty* soon wore off and he lost interest. **3. novelties.** small, inexpensive objects bought for amusement, such as toys, games, cheap jewelry, and so on.

No•vem•ber [nō vem′bər] *noun.* the eleventh month of the year. November has thirty days.

nov•ice [näv′ is] *noun, plural* **novices. 1.** a person who is new to a job or activity; a beginner: Many sports have *novice* events for people who are just starting to compete. **2.** a person who is taken into a religious order for a trial period.

now [nou] *adverb.* **1.** at this time; at the present: She was born in Ohio but *now* lives in New York. **2.** at once; right away: We'd better leave *now* or we'll miss the bus. —*conjunction.* considering that; since: *Now* that it's stopped raining, we can finish the game. —*noun.* the present time: He should have been here by *now*.

now•a•days [nou′ ə dāz′] *adverb.* these days; now: *Nowadays* most people own a TV set.

no•where [nō′ wâr′] *adverb.* at, to, or in no place: "One moment he was walking just behind them, and the next he was *nowhere* to be seen." (Mary Norton)

noz•zle [näz′ əl] *noun, plural* **nozzles.** a small opening or spout at the end of a hose or pipe: the *nozzle* of a firefighter's hose.

nui•sance [nōō′ səns] *noun, plural* **nuisances.** something or someone that annoys or causes trouble; a bother: "There is a bird known as the 'camp robber.' He is a huge *nuisance* because he gets into the cabin and eats up your food." (Ernie Pyle)

numb [num] *adjective.* **1.** having lost feeling or movement: ". . . the water was icy cold—so cold that their ankles ached and their feet went *numb*." (Jack London) —*verb,* **numbed, numbing.** to make numb: "The cold nipped Almanzo's eyelids and *numbed* his nose." (Laura Ingalls Wilder) —**numbly,** *adverb.*

numbers How should numbers be treated in writing? Should they be words (eight, forty-nine), or numerals (80, 49)? It's obvious that these uses look strange: "A car pulled up to the house and 2 men got out." "Two" is better here. "Lou Gehrig played in two thousand one hundred thirty big-league baseball games in a row." "2130" is better here. A small number looks odd as a numeral, and a large one looks odd in word form. But where's the dividing line between large and small? The usual style in print is to write out one to ten as words and use numerals after that. Larger round numbers are also written out, such as fifty, six hundred, or four million. Be consistent with whichever style you use. Don't write "14" in one place and "fourteen" just after. Also, always use the word form to begin a sentence.

nu•cle•ar [nōō′ klē ər] *adjective.* **1.** having to do with a nucleus: *nuclear* particles. **2.** using power from the nucleus of an atom: A hydrogen bomb is a *nuclear* weapon. **3.** having to do with nuclear weapons: *nuclear* war.

nuclear energy power or energy that can be released from the nucleus of an atom.

nuclear reactor a device that produces a very large amount of energy from a small amount of fuel by means of the force of atomic energy. Nuclear reactors are sometimes used instead of coal or oil to produce electric power.

nu•cle•us [nōō′ klē əs] *noun, plural* **nuclei** or **nucleuses.** **1.** the tiny roundish center of an animal or plant cell that controls the cell's growth and other important activities. **2.** the central part of an atom that contains PROTONS and NEUTRONS. The nucleus has a positive charge of electricity. **3.** the central or most important part of something.

nudge [nuj] *verb,* **nudged, nudging.** to push or move something slightly, in a gentle way: "He . . . *nudged* him with an elbow and he and the little boy laughed." (Shirley Jackson) *noun, plural* **nudges:** to give someone a *nudge*.

nug•get [nug′ it] *noun, plural* **nuggets. 1.** a rough lump of gold or other precious metal as it is found in nature. **2.** a small thing that is very valuable: a *nugget* of information.

num•ber [num′ bər] *noun, plural* **numbers. 1.** how many there are of something; the amount of things in a group: Fresh corn is sold by the *number* of ears, not by the weight. **2.** a sign or word that tells how many, such as 6, six,

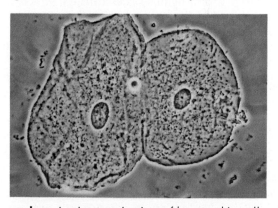

nucleus A microscopic view of human skin cells from inside the mouth. The nucleus is seen as a darker ring near the center of each cell.

Pronunciation Key: G N

g	give; big	k	kind; cat; back
h	hold	l	let; ball
i	it; this	m	make; time
ī	ice; my	n	not; own
j	jet; gem; edge	ng	having

(Turn the page for more information.)

N

sixteenth, 60th, and so on. **3.** a certain number that is given or assigned to someone: Do you know Jill's telephone *number*? **4.** a large but not exact amount: A *number* of people have told her how nice her new car looks. —*verb,* **numbered, numbering. 1.** to give a number or numbers to: The houses on our block are *numbered* from 2100 to 2200. **2.** to amount to; include: "In winter the population of Tarbox *numbers* something less than seven thousand." (John Updike) **3.** to limit the number of: It's starting to get dark much earlier now, and the days are *numbered* before winter will be here.

nu•mer•al [nōōm′ rəl *or* nōō′ mər əl] *noun, plural* **numerals.** a sign or symbol that represents a certain number or quantity.

nu•mer•a•tor [nōō′ mə rā′ tər] *noun, plural* **numerators.** in a fraction, the number above the line rather than below. In the fraction 1/4, 1 is the numerator and 4 is the DENOMINATOR.

nu•mer•i•cal [nōō mer′ i kəl] *adjective.* having to do with a number or numbers; expressed by numbers: 6 + 2 = 8 is a *numerical* equation. —**numerically,** *adverb*

nu•mer•ous [nōō′ mə rəs] *adjective, more/ most.* being or made up of a large number; very many: ". . . newspapers, magazines, writing paper, stamps, and other items too *numerous* to mention." (Michael Bond)

nun [nun] *noun, plural* **nuns.** a woman who belongs to a religious order through which she dedicates her life to serving God. Nuns do not marry and usually live together as part of a group. They do such work as teaching, caring for the sick, and helping the poor.

nurse [nurs] *noun, plural* **nurses. 1.** a person who is specially trained to take care of sick people and carry on other medical duties. Nurses work in hospitals or in private homes, and also in **nursing homes** where elderly or ill people are cared for. **2.** a person hired to take care of children in the family's home; also called a **nursemaid.** —*verb,* **nursed, nursing. 1.** to act as a nurse; care for the sick: to *nurse* a person back to health. **2.** to treat something in a careful and gentle way: "Roane jerked away, *nursing* her bitten hand." (Andre Norton) "(He) *nursed* his second cup of coffee." (Isaac Asimov) **3.** to feed a baby its mother's milk.

nurs•er•y [nurs′ rē *or* nur′ sər ē] *noun, plural* **nurseries. 1.** a room or place for babies or young children. **2.** a place where plants are grown and sold.

nursery rhyme a short song or poem for children, such as "Jack and Jill Went Up the Hill."

nursery school a school for young children who are not old enough to go to kindergarten; now usually called a PRESCHOOL.

nut Four types of nuts. The walnut and the acorn (top), the pecan and the hazelnut (bottom).

nut [nut] *noun, plural* **nuts. 1.** the dry fruit of certain plants, made up of a hard outer shell with a seed inside. Walnuts, almonds, and cashews are nuts. **2.** a small piece of metal with a hole in the center, through which a bolt is turned or screwed. **3.** *Slang.* a person who is thought of as odd, foolish, or crazy.

nut•crack•er [nut′ krak′ ər] *noun, plural* **nutcrackers. 1.** a tool used to crack open the hard outer shell of a nut. **2.** a bird related to the crow, that lives on pine nuts.

nut•meg [nut′ meg] *noun, plural* **nutmegs.** a sweet-smelling spice made from grinding the seeds of a certain evergreen tree.

nu•tri•ent [nōō′ trē ənt] *noun, plural* **nutrients.** the special elements found in food that people, animals, and plants need to live and grow, such as proteins and vitamins.

nu•tri•tion [nōō trish′ ən] *noun.* **1.** the fact of taking in food; nourishment: Good *nutrition* is very important to health. **2.** the process by which food is taken in and used by living things.

nu•tri•tious [nōō trish′ əs] *adjective, more/ most.* of food, having or giving nourishment; healthful: She began to feel better when she started eating a more *nutritious* diet.

ny•lon [nī′ län] *noun.* a strong artificial material that is used for many purposes, such as to make clothing, rope, or brushes, and for machine parts.

nymph [nimf] *noun, plural* **nymphs.** in stories of the ancient Greeks and Romans, one of a group of beautiful goddesses who lived in woods, trees, water, and so on.

o, O [ō] *noun, plural* **o's, O's.** the fifteenth letter of the alphabet.

oak [ōk] *noun, plural* **oaks.** one of a large group of trees having large, notched leaves and nuts that are called acorns. An oak tree has strong, hard wood which is used in building and in making furniture.

Oak•land [ōk/lənd] a city in California, on San Francisco Bay. *Population:* 340,000.

oar [ôr] *noun, plural* **oars.** a long pole with a flat blade at one end, used for rowing a boat.

o•a•sis [ō ā/ sis] *noun, plural* **oases. 1.** an area in the middle of a desert where trees and other plants can grow because there is a water supply. **2.** any place or thing that is thought of as giving comfort or relief, as an oasis does in the desert.

oath [ōth] *noun, plural* **oaths. 1.** a strict promise by a person to tell the truth, obey the law, act in the proper way, or the like: The President and other government officials take an *oath* of office when they begin to serve. **2.** a word or phrase used to express anger or other strong feelings in a rude and improper way; a curse.

oats [ōtz] *plural noun.* **1.** a grain that is related to wheat, used in breakfast cereals and as food for horses and other animals. **2. oat.** the tall grass plant that produces this grain. ♦ **Oatmeal** is a cereal made from oats.

o•be•di•ent [ō bē/ dē ənt] *adjective, more/most.* willing to obey; doing what one is told or is supposed to do: an *obedient* dog, a child who is *obedient* to his parents. ♦ The fact of being obedient is **obedience:** *Obedience* to a commanding officer is an important part of a soldier's training. **—obediently,** *adverb:* "The pupils filed *obediently* down the aisles and dropped into their seats." (E.B. White)

o•bey [ō bā/] *verb,* **obeyed, obeying. 1.** to do what one is told or asked to do: "She *obeyed* him; she always did as she was told." (Maxine Hong Kingston) **2.** to follow a rule, or law: to *obey* the speed limit on the highway.

objects In some languages, a noun changes according to whether it is the subject or the object in a sentence. This doesn't occur in English. "He saw a *wolf*" is the same form as "The *wolf* was standing near the lake." (The first "wolf" is a direct object; the second is a subject.) The only time there's a subject-object change in English is for pronouns: *I/me, we/us, he/him, she/her* (*you* and *it* don't change). "Jeff and me aren't friends any more" is incorrect because the object pronoun *me* has been used as a subject. ("Jeff and I" is correct.) Another thing to remember: subject-verb-object is the basic pattern of English sentences. It follows the natural way that we tell how something happened. "My uncle (S) bought (V) a new car (O). He (S) traded in (V) his old one (O)."

ob•ject [äb/ jikt *or* äb/ jekt/] *noun, plural* **objects. 1.** a real thing that can be seen and touched: Radio waves can go through walls and other solid *objects.* **2.** a person or thing that draws the attention or that causes certain feelings: The large gift-wrapped box was the *object* of great curiosity among the children. **3.** something aimed at or worked toward; a purpose or goal: The *object* of chess is to capture the other player's pieces. **4.** in grammar: **a.** a word that receives the action of a verb; a DIRECT OBJECT. **b.** a word that is affected by the action

O

of a verb; an INDIRECT OBJECT. **c.** a word that relates to a preposition. In the sentence, "Bill sent a card to his grandmother on her birthday," "card" is the direct object, "grandmother" is the indirect object, and "birthday" is the object of the preposition "on."
—[äb jekt′] *verb*, **objected, objecting. 1.** to be against; oppose: "Does your Uncle Joseph *object* to smoking?" (Robert Louis Stevenson) **2.** to give a reason against: "I suggested that they should dig at some other place. But to this they *objected* . . ." (Frank R. Stockton)

ob•jec•tion [äb jek′ shən] *noun, plural* **objections.** the fact of objecting, or a reason for this: "Mr. Secretary, we have no *objection* to publicity. In fact, we insist on it." (Robert Heinlein) **—objectionable,** *adjective.*

ob•jec•tive [äb jek′ tiv] *adjective, more/most.* dealing with facts and real things, rather than with opinions or personal feelings: The reporter was *objective* in his articles about the two candidates for mayor and didn't favor either one. —*noun, plural* **objectives.** the goal or purpose of something: When the army landed on the enemy beach, their *objective* was to capture a nearby airfield. **—objectively,** *adverb.*

given: "I am *obliged* to Mr. Astle for his ready permission to copy the following letters . . ." (James Boswell) **3.** to do someone a favor: ". . . he was fond of the Mole, and would do most anything to *oblige* him." (Kenneth Grahame) ◆ A person who is glad to do favors for others is **obliging.**

o•blique [ō blēk′] *adjective.* **1.** not straight; slanting. An **oblique angle** is either more or less than 90°. **2.** not direct or clear: an author with an *oblique* style of writing.

o•blit•e•rate [ə blit′ ə rāt′] *verb,* **obliterated, obliterating.** to completely destroy; wipe out or erase: "In his absence she had somehow *obliterated* the evidence . . ." (Ken Follett)

o•bliv•i•on [ə bliv′ ē ən] *noun.* the state of being completely forgotten: Robert Southey was a famous writer of the 1800's, but he has passed into *oblivion.* ◆ A person who is **oblivious** to something does not notice it: "The British soldiers went about their business as though *oblivious* of the many hostile, curious eyes watching them" (Esther Forbes)

ob•long [äb′ lông′] *adjective.* having a shape that is longer than it is wide. —*noun, plural* **oblongs.** a rectangle that is not a square.

---

objective approach Here are two writers describing a fire: "It made me weep to see it. The churches, houses, and all on fire and flaming at once; and a horrid noise the flames made, and the crackling of houses at their ruin. So home with a sad heart . . ." (Samuel Pepys) "But high above and all around, the fire was burning, more vivid than the sun, throwing spirals of smoke in the air like the smoke from a volcano. Thirty-three cabins burned, and twelve thousand acres of forest still burning endangered countless homes below the fire." (Anaïs Nin) Pepys tells us directly how he feels. ("It made me weep to see it," and so on.) Nin doesn't include her own feelings. Her method is the *objective* approach, while his is *subjective,* or personal. Does this mean an objective writer doesn't care about how he feels? No. Suppose you were writing about a forest fire near your home. "We stopped eating and went out to look. An orange line ran along the top of the ridge and then slanted down the mountainside. It was shaped like a giant number 7." You don't need to add, "I was worried about our house." Let the readers use *their* imagination.

---

ob•li•gate [äb′ lə gāt′] *verb,* **obligated, obligating.** to make someone do something because it is right or is required by law: Eddie was *obligated* to pay the parking ticket.

ob•li•ga•tion [äb′ lə gā′ shən] *noun, plural* **obligations. 1.** the fact of being obligated, or something that obligates; a duty. **2.** money or something else that is owed; a debt.

o•blige [ə blīj′] *verb,* **obliged, obliging. 1.** to make someone feel that something should be done; force to happen: "He has been *obliged* to pay off all his debts." (George Orwell) **2.** to make a person thankful for something done or

ob•nox•ious [äb näk′ shəs] *adjective, more/most.* very rude or unpleasant; nasty: Betty's *obnoxious* behavior spoiled the party for everyone. **—obnoxiously,** *adverb.*

o•boe [ō′ bō] *noun, plural* **oboes.** a woodwind musical instrument made up of a long tube that has a double reed for the mouthpiece.

ob•scene [äb sēn′ *or* əb sēn′] *adjective, more/most.* going against accepted standards of what is decent or moral: TV shows don't allow performers to make *obscene* remarks on the air.
◆ **Obscenity** [äb sen′ ə tē] is the fact of being obscene, or an example of this.

O

ob•scure [əb skyo͞or′] *adjective, more/most.*
1. not easy to understand; not clear: The author Gertrude Stein is known for *obscure* statements like "A rose is a rose is a rose" and "There is no there there." **2.** not likely to be noticed; not well-known: "New York is full of people who are quite content to live *obscure* lives in some out-of-the-way corner of the city." (Walker Percy) —*verb*, **obscured, obscuring.** to make obscure; hide from view: "Out of a brown field rose the mountain, partially *obscured* by mist." (Beryl Bainbridge) ♦ **Obscurity** [əb skyo͞or′ ə tē] is the fact of being obscure.

ob•serve [əb zurv′] *verb,* **observed, observing.**
1. to see and notice; pay attention to: A neighbor *observed* two men running from the building just before the fire broke out. "She wore, Edward *observed,* a dark blue velvet suit . . ." (Anaïs Nin) **2.** to watch carefully for a special purpose: "Never before had I been able to *observe* these creatures alive and free in their environment." (Jules Verne) **3.** to follow or obey a certain custom or rule: Memorial Day is now *observed* on the last Monday in May. **4.** to make a comment or remark: "My uncle *observed* that it was now getting late." (William

observation In writing, *observation* means being able to look at a scene and notice its special details and features. What is the test of how well you observe and then write what you see? Usually, the test is found in your use of verbs, which describe action. The temptation to use *do* or *have* should be resisted. Use verbs that are specific. Here's an observation of an underwater scene: "I *kicked* hard so that I'd *clear* the coral that *challenged* my hand with sharp edges. I *slithered* past the coral to *grasp* the sea grass. My lungs were *pumping,* my legs *tingling* . . ." Now, here's another test of observation, this one from the British suspense writer Ian Fleming: "Everywhere the jeweled reef fish *twinkled* and *glowed* and the giant anemones of the Indian Ocean *burned* like flames in the shadows." Note the strong, vivid verbs—Fleming says that the brightly-colored anemones (a flower-like sea creature) "burned like flames."

ob•ser•va•tion [äb′ zər vā′ shən] *noun, plural* **observations. 1.** the fact of observing or being observed: Railroad trains sometimes have an *observation* car for people to look out at the passing scenery. **2.** the act of observing something in a scientific way and noting what is seen. **3.** a comment or remark: The speaker started by making a few *observations* about how crowded the meeting hall was.

ob•serv•a•to•ry [əb zur′ və tôr ē] *noun, plural* **observatories.** a building with telescopes and other scientific equipment for observing and studying the planets, stars, and other objects in the heavens.

Makepeace Thackeray) ♦ Someone who is **observant** is quick or careful to observe.

ob•serv•er [əb zur′ vər] *noun, plural* **observers.** a person who observes: "The Arctic Ocean can seem utterly silent . . . to an *observer* standing far above." (Barry Lopez)

ob•sess [əb ses′] *verb,* **obsessed, obsessing.** to fill the mind completely with one idea in a way that is not normal or healthy. —**obsession,** *noun:* In the book *Moby Dick,* Captain Ahab's *obsession* with the white whale causes him to follow it all across the world.

ob•so•lete [äb sə lēt′] *adjective, more/most.* not used any more; out of date: Many devices once used in American homes are now *obsolete,* such as iceboxes, washboards, and carpet sweepers.

ob•sta•cle [äb′ stə kəl] *noun, plural* **obstacles.** something that blocks or stands in the way: "The main *obstacle* to the success of the Utah landing was a body of water known as the Douve River." (Cornelius Ryan)

observatory The Mauna Kea Observatory in Hawaii is located almost 14,000 feet above sea level.

Pronunciation Key: G–N

g	give; big	k	kind; cat; back
h	hold	l	let; ball
i	it; this	m	make; time
ī	ice; my	n	not; own
j	jet; gem; edge	ng	having

(Turn the page for more information.)

O

ob•sti•nate [äb′ sti nit] *adjective.* not wanting to change or cooperate; stubborn: "He wouldn't admit there was anything wrong. How very *obstinate* some people are." (Christopher Isherwood) **—obstinacy,** *noun.* **—obstinately,** *adverb.*

ob•struct [əb strukt′] *verb,* **obstructed, obstructing. 1.** to make passage or movement difficult; block up: "Torres Strait is about a hundred miles wide, but it is *obstructed* by all kinds of islands, reefs, and rocks which make it nearly impossible to sail through." (Jules Verne) **2.** to be in the way or view of: The trees on our neighbor's property *obstruct* our view of the lake. **—obstruction,** *noun:* the fact of obstructing, or something that obstructs.

ob•tain [əb tān′] *verb,* **obtained, obtaining.** to get or gain, especially through some effort; acquire: "Most of the food the Cook family ate was *obtained* by hunting or fishing." (Joe McGinniss) ◆ Something that can be obtained is **obtainable.**

ob•tuse [äb toos′] *adjective.* **1.** slow to learn or understand: "Her mother was deliberately *obtuse* about what had happened . . ." (Alice Walker) **2.** of an angle, greater than 90°.

ob•vi•ous [äb′ vē əs] *adjective, more/most.* very easy to see or understand; plain; clear: It's *obvious* that those two boys are brothers because they look so much alike. **—obviously,** *adverb:* "Sylvia was *obviously* musical—when she was two and a half she had already begun to sing." (Aldous Huxley)

oc•ca•sion [ə kā′ zhən] *noun, plural* **occasions. 1.** the time when a certain event takes place; a certain point in time: "I did say on one *occasion* that I'd never allow her to appear in a theater of mine again." (Noel Coward) **2.** a time that is favorable or proper for something to happen; an opportunity. **3.** a special event or point in time: "But a birthday, I always feel, is a great *occasion,* taken too much for granted these days." (Harold Pinter)

oc•ca•sion•al [ə kā′ zhən əl] *adjective, more/most.* happening only once in a while; not regular or frequent: "There wasn't much business at this time of the year, only *occasional* tourists and some hunters or fishermen." (Bernard Malamud) **—occasionally,** *adverb.*

oc•cu•pant [äk′ yə pənt] *noun, plural* **occupants.** a person who occupies a place: "The coffee-room had no other *occupant* . . . than the gentleman in brown." (Charles Dickens) ◆ The fact of occupying is **occupancy.**

oc•cu•pa•tion [äk′ yə pā′ shən] *noun, plural* **occupations. 1.** the kind of work a person regularly does to earn money. **2.** the fact of occupying: the *occupation* of Japan by the U. S. after World War II.

occupations for writers There are three basic kinds of work for professional writers. *Independent authors* may write novels, nonfiction books, magazine articles, even film or TV scripts over a long career. An author who has established a reputation can depend on receiving not only fees, but also royalties for writing. (A *royalty* is a percentage of the sale price of a book—a 10% royalty on a $20.00 book is $2.00 per copy.) *Staff writers* work for a company as employees and are paid a salary. They are given writing assignments by the company. *Freelance writers* work for themselves. They set their own hours and usually choose their own projects. Often, they are known for specialized writing—science or politics or encyclopedias, or textbooks of various kinds. They usually work in their homes. They are paid a one-time fee for a piece of work.

oc•cu•py [äk′ yə pī′] *verb,* **occupied, occupying. 1.** to take up the space of; fill: "That part of the earth's surface *occupied* by water is . . . over 94 billion acres." (Jules Verne) **2.** to take up one's time or attention: "While she made the tea I *occupied* myself by looking at her books . . ." (Barbara Pym) **3.** to take and keep possession of a place: During World War II the German army *occupied* Paris.

oc•cur [ə kər′] *verb,* **occurred, occurring. 1.** to take place; happen: The accident *occurred* at about 5:00 yesterday afternoon. **2.** to be found; appear; exist: 'E' is the letter that *occurs* most often in English words. **3.** to suggest itself; come to mind: "Did it ever *occur* to you that maybe you've got just as many problems as he does?" (Paul Zindel)

oc•cur•rence [ə kur′ əns] *noun, plural* **occurrences. 1.** something that occurs; an event: An eclipse of the moon is an unusual *occurrence.* **2.** the act of occurring.

o•cean [ō′ shən] *noun, plural* **oceans. 1.** the large body of salt water that covers about three-fourths of the surface of the earth. **2.** any one of the four main parts into which this water is divided; the Atlantic, Pacific, Indian, or Arctic Ocean.

o·cean·og·ra·phy [ō′ shən äg′ rə fē] *noun.* the science or study of the ocean and its animals and plants. ◆ A person who studies oceanography is an **oceanographer.**

oc·e·lot [äs′ ə lät *or* ō′ sə lət] *noun, plural* **ocelots.** a medium-sized wild cat that has a yellowish coat with a pattern of black spots and stripes. Ocelots are found in the southwestern U.S., Mexico, and parts of South America.

o'clock [ə kläk′] *adverb.* of or by the clock, used in stating an exact hour of the day: The movie starts at eight *o'clock.*

O'Connor U.S. Supreme Court Justice Sandra Day O'Connor.

O'Con·nor [ō kän′ ər] **Sandra Day,** born 1930, the first woman justice of the United States Supreme Court.

oc·ta·gon [äk′ tə gän] *noun, plural* **octagons.** a flat plane figure that has eight angles and eight sides. —**octagonal** [äk tag′ ə nəl], *adjective.*

oc·tave [äk′ tiv *or* äk′ tāv] *noun, plural* **octaves.** in music: **1.** the range between the lowest and highest note of one musical scale. There are seven whole tones and five half tones between the lowest and the highest tone. **2.** a series of eight notes or tones of a musical scale. The lowest tone is an octave below the highest.

Oc·to·ber [äk tō′ bər] *noun.* the tenth month of the year. October has thirty-one days.

oc·to·pus [äk′ tə pəs] *noun, plural* **octopuses.** a salt-water animal having a soft body with no backbone and eight long arms called TENTA-CLES. The tentacles have rows of small suction pads underneath to help the octopus grip on to rocks and food.

odd [äd] *adjective,* **odder, oddest. 1.** not as it should be or is expected to be; not normal; strange; unusual: Painting by modern artists often show *odd* shapes and designs. The characters in *Alice in Wonderland* act in *odd* ways. ◆ Something that is very strange or unusual is an **oddity. 2.** of numbers, not able to be divided exactly by 2. **3.** happening from time to time; occasional: Gail does *odd* jobs in her spare time. **4.** not part of a matched pair or set: an *odd* sock. —**oddly,** *adverb.* —**oddness,** *noun.*

odds [ädz] *plural noun.* **1.** a number used to show the chance that a certain thing is true or will happen: If you flip a coin, the *odds* are 50–50 that it will turn up heads. **2.** the general chance that something is true or will happen: She loves Virginia Hamilton's books, so the *odds* are that she's already read this one.

o·dor [ō′ dər] *noun, plural* **odors.** a scent or smell, especially one that is unpleasant: They put a fan over the stove to carry off smoke and kitchen *odors.*

of [uv, äv, *or* əv] *preposition.* **1.** belonging to: the back *of* your leg, the price *of* a car. **2.** having or containing: a glass *of* water, a deck *of* cards. **3.** named as; that is: the City *of* New York, the age *of* 21. **4.** having to do with: the Chief *of* Police, to be afraid *of* dogs. **5.** in relation to: ten minutes *of* four.

O

octopus The octopus usually measures between one and three feet in length, but some kinds may reach ten feet.

Pronunciation Key: O S

ō	over; go	ou	out; town
ô	all; law	p	put; hop
oo	look; full	r	run; car
ōō	pool; who	s	set; miss
oi	oil; boy	sh	show

(Turn the page for more information.)

O

off [ôf *or* äf] *adverb.* **1.** away from or free from: The bird flew *off.* Take your coat *off.* ◆ Also used as a preposition: Sue gets *off* work at 4:30. **2.** not active or working: Turn the radio *off.* ◆ Also used as an adjective: The game is *off* because of the rain. **3.** less than usual: Everything in the store is selling for 20% *off.*

of•fend [ə fend′] *verb,* **offended, offending.** to cause someone to feel upset or angry; hurt a person's feelings; insult: "You left me in the dark as to matters which you should have explained to me years ago. I am extremely hurt and *offended.*" (George Bernard Shaw)

of•fend•er [ə fen′ dər] *noun, plural* **offenders.** a person who does something wrong, especially someone who breaks a rule or law.

of•fense [ə fəns′] *noun, plural* **offenses. 1.** the breaking of a rule or law; a crime: The judge gave him only a small fine because it was his first *offense.* **2.** the fact of offending someone, or something that causes this. **3.** [ô′ fens] the attacking of an enemy or opponent, as in a battle. **4.** [ô′ fens] in sports such as football or basketball, the team or players who have the ball and are trying to score.

of•fen•sive [ə fen′ siv] *adjective, more/most.* **1.** causing someone to be offended: That teacher is able to tell students what's wrong with their papers without being *offensive.* **2.** [ô′ fen siv] having to do with offense in warfare or in sports: An *offensive* fighter plane is used to attack enemy forces. Quarterback is an *offensive* position in football. —*noun, plural* **offensives.** the act or fact of making an attack: The Tet *Offensive* was an important event in the Vietnam War.

of•fer [ô′ fər] *verb,* **offered, offering. 1.** to present something that may or may not be taken: She *offered* her guest a glass of lemonade. **2.** to be willing to do something: "Jody *offered* to help in the kitchen, but Grandma sent him away." (Marjorie Kinnan Rawlings) **3.** to put forward as a suggestion or an attempt: The dealer *offered* us $2000 for our old car. "I'm curious to hear what he has to *offer.* Then we'll take it or leave it." (Samuel Beckett) —*noun, plural* **offers.** the act of offering, or something that is offered.

of•fer•ing [ô′ fər ing] *noun, plural* **offerings.** something given; a contribution: They gave an *offering* of ten dollars to the church.

off•hand [ôf′ hand′] *adjective, adverb.* without thought or planning: a careless, *offhand* remark. I'm not sure how far it is to school from here—*offhand,* I'd say about two miles.

of•fice [ôf′ is] *noun, plural* **offices. 1.** a building or other place where the work of a business is carried on: a doctor's *office.* He went to the post *office* to buy stamps. **2.** an important position, especially in government: the *office* of President of the United States.

of•fi•cer [ôf′ ə sər] *noun, plural* **officers. 1.** a person who has a certain high rank in the armed forces, such as a general or captain. **2.** a policeman or policewoman. **3.** a person who holds an important position: In that business, contracts can only be signed by someone who is an *officer* of the company.

of•fi•cial [ə fish′ əl] *noun, plural* **officials. 1.** a person who holds an office or position of authority: City *officials* have approved the plans to build a new park near us. **2.** in sports, a person who decides when a rule has been broken and what the penalty should be, such as a referee in football. —*adjective, more/most.* **1.** having to do with a position of authority: a mayor's *official* duties. **2.** having been decided or determined by officials: Our *official* school colors are blue and white. —**officially,** *adverb:* A newly-elected President *officially* takes office on January 20th.

off•set [ôf′ set′] *verb,* **offset, offsetting.** to make up for; balance: The company got a lot of sales from its new store in the shopping mall to *offset* the loss of business downtown.

off•shoot [ôf′ shoot′] *noun, plural* **offshoots.** a thing that grows or branches out from something else: Many spy movies of the 1960's were *offshoots* of the James Bond movies.

off•shore [ôf′ shôr′] *adjective; adverb.* away from the shore: an *offshore* breeze, *offshore* drilling for oil.

off•spring [ôf′ spring′] *noun, plural* **offsprings** or **offspring.** the young of a person, animal, or plant.

of•ten [ôf′ ən] *adverb, more/most* or **oftener, oftenest.** happening again and again: "The night was fair and crisp, as nights *often* are just before Christmas." (E.B. White) The restaurant is right near her office and she eats there *often.*

oh [ō] *interjection.* a word used to show a certain feeling, such as surprise, happiness, or fear.

O•hi•o [ō hī′ ō] **1.** a state in the east-central U.S., on Lake Erie. *Capital:* Columbus. *Nickname:* "Buckeye State." *Area:* 41,200 square miles. *Population:* 10,791,000. **2.** a river flowing southwest from southwestern Pennsylvania to the Mississippi.

O

oil wells A 1919 photograph of a famous oil field near Wichita Falls, Texas that produced a record amount of oil from its wells.

oil [oil] *noun, plural* **oils. 1.** a thick, dark liquid that is found in the earth and that is used to make gasoline and other fuels; also called PE-TROLEUM. **2.** any of various other thick, greasy substances that are usually in a liquid form, will float on water, and will burn easily. Oils may be mineral, vegetable, or animal, and are used for cooking, for fuel, or to make machines run more smoothly. **3.** a paint made by mixing coloring material with an oil, or a painting using such paints. —*verb,* **oiled, oiling.** to put oil on something: to *oil* a new baseball glove so that it will be softer and more flexible.

oil•y [oil′ē] *adjective,* **oilier, oiliest.** of, like, or containing oil.

oint•ment [oint′ mənt] *noun, plural* **ointments.** an oily cream put on the skin to soften it or to cure a skin disorder: The doctor gave me an *ointment* for my poison ivy rash.

Oklahoma City, the capital of Oklahoma, in the central part of the state. *Population:* 403,000.

old [ōld] *adjective,* **older, oldest. 1.** having lived for a long time; not young: *Old* age is usually said to begin at 65 or 70. **2.** having existed or been in use for a long time: an *old* car, an *old* joke about a talking dog. **3.** having a certain age: The Kentucky Derby is a race for three-year-*old* horses. **4.** former; earlier: I get more homework now than at my *old* school.

old•en [ōl′ dən] *adjective.* long ago; in earlier times: Witches and fairies often appear in the stories of *olden* days.

old-fash•ioned [ōld′ fash′ ənd] *adjective, more/most.* **1.** having to do with past times; out-of-date: *Old-fashioned* radios were made of wood and were very large. **2.** favoring old ways and ideas: People of the Amish religion lead an *old-fashioned* life and avoid the use of modern clothing and inventions.

Old Testament a collection of writings that tell about the religion, history, and culture of the ancient Hebrews. The Old Testament forms the complete Jewish Bible and the first part of the Christian Bible.

o•le•o•mar•ga•rine [ō′ lē ō mär′ jə rin] *noun.* (*also,* **oleo.**) a smooth, soft substance used in place of butter, more often called MARGARINE.

ol•ive [äl′ iv] *noun, plural* **olives. 1.** a small oval fruit that is yellow-green or black in color and has a hard pit in the center. Olives come from a small evergreen tree that is grown in hot, dry areas. **2.** a dull greenish-brown color.

olive oil a green or yellow oil pressed from olives. It is used in salad dressings and in cooking.

OK How is this word spelled? Is it *OK,* or does it have periods, *O.K.?* Or is it *okay?* You'll find each of these spellings appearing in print. Our survey shows that OK (capitals, no periods) is now the most common form. This is the one we recommend for your use. Remember that when OK is a verb, it needs an apostrophe: "They can't go ahead until the boss OK's it." Is OK a proper word to use in writing? If you're writing a story, it's acceptable to use it in the speech of your characters. But avoid it in a factual report, a business letter, or other such formal writing. It obviously is wrong to write, "General Crook promised the Indians they would be OK if they moved to the reservation." Use "would not be harmed" or "would be safe."

OK [ō′ kā′] *adverb; adjective; interjection.* (*also* spelled **O.K., Okay,** or **okay**) all right; fine: If you want to use my book, it's *OK* with me. —*verb,* **OK'd, OK'ing.** to approve; say ‘yes to.

O•kla•ho•ma [ō′ klə hō′ mə] a state in the southwestern U.S. *Nickname:* "Sooner State." *Area:* 69,900 square miles. *Population:* 3,177,000.

Pronunciation Key: T–Z			
t	ten; date	v	very; live
th	think	w	win; away
th	these	y	you
u	cut; butter	z	zoo; cause
ur	turn; bird	zh	measure

(Turn the page for more information.)

O

O•lym•pic Games [ə lim′ pik] *noun.* (also, **Olympics.**) **1.** an international sports competition held once every four years, each time in a different country. Athletes from all over the world take part in these events, which are divided into the **Summer Olympics** and the **Winter Olympics. 2.** a contest in sports, poetry, and music that was held every four years at Olympia in ancient Greece and that was the model for the modern Olympics.

O•ma•ha [ō′ mə hô′] a city in eastern Nebraska, on the Missouri River. *Population:* 314,000.

om•e•let [äm′ lit] *noun, plural* **omelets.** a food made from a mixture of eggs beaten with milk or water, and then cooked and folded over. Often a filling such as cheese or meat is added.

o•men [ō′ mən] *noun, plural* **omens.** a happening that is thought of as a sign of good or bad luck in the future: A black cat crossing your path is said to be a bad *omen*, but finding a four-leaf clover is believed to be a good *omen*.

om•i•nous [äm′ ə nəs] *adjective,* more/most. being a bad omen; seeming to tell of something bad to come; threatening: ". . . they caught glimpses of ancient walls of stone, and the ruins of towers: they had an *ominous* look." (J.R.R. Tolkien) **—ominously,** *adverb.*

o•mit [ō mit′] *verb,* **omitted, omitting.** to leave out; not include or do: "Tell her everything you can about the place where you spent your childhood. *Omit* no detail, no matter how small." (Frank Herbert) ◆ Something that is omitted is an **omission** [ō mi′ shən].

on [än] *preposition.* **1.** held up by something and touching it: to put dishes *on* the table, to hang a picture *on* a wall, to wear a ring *on* your finger, to ride *on* a horse. **2.** located at or near: a house *on* the beach, a city *on* the Mexican border. **3.** having to do with the thing or condition stated: a book *on* Africa, to go *on* a trip, to leave *on* Friday, to talk *on* the phone, a dress that is *on* sale. —*adverb.* **1.** so as to be touching or covering: Heather put her raincoat

on. **2.** so as to be in use or operation: to turn the TV *on.* ◆ Also used as an adjective: All the lights were *on* when we got home.

once [wuns] *adverb.* **1.** one time: That magazine comes out *once* a month. **2.** at a certain time in the past, but no longer: New York was *once* the capital of the United States. —*conjunction.* as soon as; when: That will be a beautiful building *once* it is finished.

on•com•ing [än′ kum′ ing] *adjective.* getting closer; nearing: "He heard the roar of an *oncoming* truck." (William F. Buckley)

one [wun] *noun, plural* **ones. 1.** the number that is larger than zero and less than two, also written 1. **2.** a single person or thing. —*adjective.* being a single person or thing: She only missed *one* problem on the test. —*pronoun.* **1.** a single person or thing: *One* of the glasses is cracked. **2.** any person; anyone: That wasn't much of a meal, but *one* can hardly expect great food at those prices.

one Either *one* or *you* can be used to mean "anyone; a person; people in general." American writers tend to use *you*: "The lake had never been what *you* would call a wild lake." (E.B. White) "*You* can't pick up a book these days without getting involved . . ." (Jean Kerr) British writers tend to use *one*: "*One* should not, however, begin a paragraph with an 'and' or 'but.' If *one* did . . ." (Robert Graves) Some even use it when the subject could be *I* or *we*: "They aren't our sort, and *one* must face the fact." (E. M. Forster) Americans might say that *you* is direct and friendly, and that *one* sounds stuffy. The British might reply that *you* is forward and impolite. It's simply a difference in style—the difference being that American English is generally, although not always, less formal than British English.

one•self [wun′ self′] *pronoun.* one's own self.

one-sid•ed [wun′ sī′ did] *adjective,* more/most. **1.** having one side much stronger than the other: It was a *one-sided* game, with our team winning 42 to 0. **2.** favoring one side over another; unfair: That book on the Kennedy family seemed very *one-sided*, listing many of their problems but almost no good points.

one-way [wun′ wā′] *adjective.* moving or allowing movement in only one direction: a *one-way* street, a *one-way* train ticket.

on•ion [un′ yən] *noun, plural* **onions.** a vegetable that is often used in cooking, having a sharp taste and a strong smell. Onions grow as bulbs below the surface of the ground, just above the roots of the plant.

on-line [än′ līn′] *adjective.* of computer equipment, being connected directly with a central computer and ready to operate.

on•look•er [än′ look′ ər] *noun, plural* **onlookers.** a person who looks on; a spectator.

on•ly [ōn′lē] *adjective.* without any others of the same kind or type; alone: An *only* child has no brothers and sisters. The bat is the *only* mammal that can fly. —*adverb.* **1.** and nothing else; and that is all: The medicine label said, "Use *only* as directed." **2.** merely; just: Mozart began to write music when he was *only* five.

Ontario In Ottawa, Ontario (Canada's capital), the Royal Canadian Mounted Police (a symbol of Canada) line up for inspection.

On•tar•i•o [än târ′ē ō] **1.** a province in central Canada. *Capital:* Toronto. *Area:* 412,600 square miles. *Population:* 8,625,000. **2.** the smallest of the Great Lakes, between the U.S. and Canada.

on•to [än′tōō] *preposition.* to a position on or upon: The skater stepped *onto* the ice.

o•pal [ō′pəl] *noun, plural* **opals.** a gem that shows slight changes in color when seen under different light conditions.

o•paque [ō pāk′] *adjective, more/most.* not allowing light to pass through; not transparent.

o•pen [ō′pən] *adjective, more/most.* **1.** allowing things to pass through; not shut: A bird flew in through the *open* window. **2.** not covered, sealed, fastened, and so on: an *open* can of soda, to cook food on an *open* fire. **3.** having a clear space: the *open* country of the American Southwest. **4.** ready for business; doing business: The office is *open* from nine to five. —*verb,* **opened, opening. 1.** to make or become open: to *open* a book and begin to read. **2.** to begin; start: That movie *opens* with a view of mountain scenery. —*noun.* **the open.** Deer usually live in woods but can also be seen in *the open.* —**openly,** *adverb.* so as to be seen or noticed: "The students in the first row or two were staring *openly* at him now." (Anita Desai)

o•pen•er [ō′pə nər] *noun, plural* **openers. 1.** a tool used to open bottles, cans, or other sealed containers. **2.** any device that opens something: an automatic garage-door *opener.* **3.** the first of a series of events or contests: the *opener* of the baseball season.

o•pen•ing [ō′pən ing] *noun, plural* **openings. 1.** an open space; a hole: A big moth got in through an *opening* in the screen door. **2.** a job or position that is available or not yet filled: There are several *openings* for sales people at the new department store. **3.** the beginning of something: the *opening* of a new play.

opening lines You need to "grab" the reader with your very first sentence. Good writers know that. "On the third day after they moved to the country he came walking back from the village carrying a basket of groceries and a twenty-four yard coil of rope." (Katherine Anne Porter) Porter's line makes us ask, "Twenty-four yards of rope? Just after he moved there? What's that for?" When you start a story, instead of writing, "To begin with . . ." or "Susan Slade was ten years old and lived with her mother" or "Bolton is a small town in the suburbs," why not make the reader curious? Here's an example: "A man stood upon a railroad bridge in northern Alabama, looking down into the swift water twenty feet below." (Ambrose Bierce) Now, a plain opening, one to make you wonder: "One dollar and eighty-seven cents. That was all. And sixty cents of it was in pennies." (O. Henry, "The Gift of the Magi")

on•ward [än′wərd] *adverb, adjective. (also,* **onwards)** in or to a forward direction or position.

ooze [ōōz] *verb,* **oozed, oozing. 1.** to move or leak out slowly; seep: "If your foot touched the bottom, black mud *oozed* between your toes." (John Mortimer) **2.** to seem to act in this way: "Justin fairly *oozed* politeness and good humor." (John Jakes)

Pronunciation Key: Accent Marks

[′] is the normal accent mark. It shows where the main stress falls on a word.
[′] is a secondary accent mark. It shows a lighter stress than the primary accent. For example:

tel • e • vis • ion [tel′ə vizh′ən]
(Turn the page for more information.)

O

opera One of America's most famous opera stars, Beverly Sills, performs as 'Rosina' in the *Barber of Seville.*

op•er•a [äp′ rə *or* äp′ ə rə] *noun, plural* **operas.** a musical play in which all or most of the characters' lines are sung rather than spoken.
♦ Something that has to do with opera is **operatic** [äp′ ə rat′ ik].

op•er•ate [äp′ ə rāt′] *verb,* **operated, operating.**
1. to run or work in a certain way: The city bus line doesn't *operate* after midnight. **2.** to control the way something runs or functions: to *operate* a sewing machine. That airline *operates* a large fleet of wide-body jets. **3.** to cut into a person's body as a medical procedure; perform surgery: Dr. Nichols *operated* on Jim's knee after he hurt it playing football.

op•er•a•tion [äp′ ə rā′ shən] *noun, plural* **operations. 1.** the act or fact of working or running something: This booklet explains the *operation* of the computer. **2.** the act of cutting into a person's body by a doctor to take out a diseased part or correct some harmful condition. **3.** a military movement of troops, supplies, or equipment: The World War II plan to land

Allied Forces in North Africa was called "*Operation* Torch." **4.** an organized activity for a certain purpose: a rescue *operation.*

op•er•a•tor [äp′ ə rā′ tər] *noun, plural* **operators. 1.** a person who works for a telephone company giving information and assistance to customers. **2.** any person who runs or operates something. a computer *operator.*

op•er•et•ta [äp′ ə ret′ ə] *noun, plural* **operettas.** a short, often funny opera with many of the words spoken rather than sung to music.

o•pin•ion [ə pin′ yən] *noun, plural* **opinions. 1.** information that is based on what a person believes, rather than on what can be shown to be true or real: It's a fact that New York has more people than any other U.S. city; it's an *opinion* that New York has more good restaurants than Chicago. **2.** a particular idea or judgment formed in this way; what a person thinks about something: He has a high *opinion* of his own intelligence and is always telling people what to do. **3.** the judgment of an expert, formed after careful thought: Dr. Evans told her she needs an operation, but she's going to get a second *opinion* from another doctor.

opinion Most textbooks on writing have a lesson on opinions and make a distinction between opinion and fact. (Look up both words.) What do the editors of this dictionary think? (1) <u>Fact and opinion go together.</u> If you state an opinion, give factual details along with it. If you speak of Hawaii's beauty, then give facts about the beaches and the mountains to support this opinion. (2) <u>Fact and opinion depend on each other.</u> *Word Book Encyclopedia* says "Hawaii's mild climate [opinion] and beautiful scenery [opinion] make the state one of the favorite year-round playgrounds of the world [fact]." The article then goes on to give facts about Hawaii's tourist industry, having already established that Hawaii is beautiful and pleasant. (3) <u>There are different degrees of opinion.</u> It's not necessary to say that "Hawaii is the prettiest state." "One of the prettiest states" is just as effective, and it avoids an extreme statement.

o•pi•um [ō′ pē əm] *noun.* a powerful and dangerous drug made from a certain type of poppy plant. It is sometimes used in medicine to relieve pain or cause sleep, but it can easily become habit-forming. Heroin and morphine are made from opium.

o•pos•sum [ə päs′ əm] *noun, plural* **opossums.** a small, four-legged animal that lives in trees and carries its young in a special pouch. When it becomes very frightened, it sometimes lies completely still and appears to be dead. ♦ This animal is also called a **possum.**

op•po•nent [ə pō′ nənt] *noun, plural* **opponents.** a person or group on the opposite side in a contest or struggle; someone who is against another: The mayor is running for election again against three *opponents.*

op•por•tu•ni•ty [äp⁄ ər too⁄ nə tē] *noun, plural* **opportunities.** a favorable time or situation; a chance: She wants to tell the boss about her idea, but the right *opportunity* hasn't come up.

op•pose [ə pōz⁄] *verb,* **opposed, opposing.** to be against; act or go against: In the Hundred Years' War England *opposed* France.

op•po•site [äp⁄ ə zit] *noun, plural* **opposites.** something that is completely different from another thing: Hot and cold or night and day are *opposites.* —*adjective.* **1.** completely different: "Old" and "new" have *opposite* meanings. **2.** across from; facing: The cities of Minneapolis and St. Paul are on *opposite* sides of the Mississippi River.

op•po•si•tion [äp⁄ ə zish⁄ ən] *noun.* **1.** the act or fact of opposing; being against: The senator announced his *opposition* to the President's new tax plan. **2.** an opposing group: That team is changing its schedule next year because they want to have stronger *opposition.*

op•press [ə pres⁄] *verb,* **oppressed, oppressing. 1.** to rule by unfair and cruel methods: The American colonists felt they were *oppressed* by British rule and fought to become free. **2.** to cause a heavy, dull feeling of being sad or tired.

remained *optimistic* and kept talking about what he would do when he got better. ◆ This kind of hopeful, cheerful attitude is **optimism,** and a person who has it is an **optimist.**

op•tion [äp⁄ shən] *noun, plural* **options. 1.** the right to make a choice, or the thing that is chosen: Air conditioning and a stereo radio are popular *options* in a car. **2.** the right to buy or sell something at a future date: She's renting the house with an *option* to buy later.

op•tion•al [äp⁄ shən əl] *adjective.* left to one's choice, not required: The teacher gave an *optional* homework assignment that students could do for extra credit.

op•tom•e•trist [äp täm⁄ ə trist] *noun, plural* **optometrists.** a person trained and licensed to examine people's eyes and prescribe eyeglasses or contact lenses to correct their eyesight.

or [ôr] *conjunction.* The word **or** is used to show a choice, in these ways: **1.** one of a group of things: Do you want milk *or* juice? Those pens come with black, blue, *or* red ink. **2.** the second of only two things: Close the door *or* the dog will get out. **3.** one of two ways of saying the same thing: This plant is called a Saguaro *or* Giant Cactus.

O

oral history This is a fairly recent term. It means interviewing people who have been important in politics or business or art, or who have had an unusual experience. Let's say you decide to interview older people about what your town was like 40 years ago. (1) Use a tape recorder. It's more accurate than written notes, and people will speak more naturally than if you write down everything they say. (2) Edit the remarks to remove the usual pauses and delays in speech—"ah," "uh," "and so," etc. (3) Guide the person toward the subject. Instead of "I guess you've seen a lot of changes in this town over 40 years," ask instead, "What buildings on Main Street are the same as when you were a boy?" "Was there a track field when you went to the old Central High?" (4) Don't break in on the person's train of thought. "That's interesting about Bloch's Drug Store. But you said it was on Elm Place; Mr. Lowe told me it was on *Oak.*" You're there to ask and listen—not to have a conversation. You can check for yourself later where it was.

◆ Something that oppresses is **oppressive:** "The heat was terribly *oppressive,* and the huge sunlight flamed . . ." (Oscar Wilde)

op•pres•sion [ə presh⁄ ən] *noun.* the fact of being oppressed, or something that oppresses.

op•ti•cal [äp⁄ ti kəl] *adjective.* (*also,* **optic**) having to do with the eye or the sense of sight: the *optic* nerve. ◆ An **optical illusion** is when a person seems to see something that is not actually there.

op•ti•mis•tic [äp⁄ tə mis⁄ tik] *adjective, more/ most.* expecting things to turn out well; looking at the good side of a situation rather than the bad side: Even while he was very sick, he

o•ral [ôr⁄ əl *or* ō⁄ rəl] *adjective.* **1.** spoken rather than written: Early folk tales were an *oral* form of storytelling. **2.** having to do with the mouth: A dentist who operates on someone's teeth or jaw is an *oral* surgeon. —**orally,** *adverb.*

Pronunciation Key: Accent Marks

[⁄] is the normal accent mark. It shows where the main stress falls on a word.
[ˏ] is a secondary accent mark. It shows a lighter stress than the primary accent. For example:

tel • e • vis • ion [tel⁄ə vizh⁄ən]
(Turn the page for more information.)

O

or•ange [ôr**/** inj] *noun, plural* **oranges. 1.** a round fruit with a thick reddish-yellow skin and sweet, juicy pulp. Oranges are CITRUS fruits related to lemons, limes, and grapefruits. **2.** the color that is like this fruit.

orangutan The peaceful orangutan is an endangered animal. Its name means 'man of the woods' in Malaysian.

o•rang•u•tan [ô rang**/** ə tan] *noun, plural* **orang-utans.** a large ape that lives in trees on certain islands of southern Asia. Orangutans have long arms, short legs, and shaggy reddish-brown hair.

o•ra•tor [ôr**/** ə tər] *noun, plural* **orators.** a person who makes a speech in public: American political leaders who are considered great *orators* include Franklin D. Roosevelt and Martin Luther King. ◆ An **oration** is a speech, especially a long and formal speech. ◆ The art of public speaking is called **oratory.**

or•bit [ôr**/** bit] *noun, plural* **orbits. 1.** the path of a heavenly body as it moves in a circle around another heavenly body: The *orbit* of the earth around the sun takes 365 days. **2.** the path of a man-made satellite or spacecraft around the earth. **3.** any movement or area thought of as being like an orbit: "When he moved from the *orbit* of his house to an office, restaurant, airport, a new city . . ." (Brian Moore) —*verb,* **orbited, orbiting.** to move in an orbit around the earth or another heavenly body.

or•chard [ôr**/** chərd] *noun, plural* **orchards.** an area of land where fruit trees are grown.

or•ches•tra [ôr**/** kəs trə] *noun, plural* **orches-tras. 1.** a group of musicians who play various instruments under the direction of a leader called a conductor. A modern **symphony or-chestra** consists of about 100 musicians divided among string, woodwind, brass, and percussion instruments. **2.** the musical instruments that are played by such a group. **3.** the place just in front of the stage where the musicians sit to play in a theater, or the seats near this area.

or•chid [ôr**/** kid] *noun, plural* **orchids.** one of a large family of flowering plants that grow all over the world. The flowers are valued for their unusual shape and showy colors.

orchid Several kinds of beautiful and exotic orchids.

or•dain [ôr dān**/**] *verb,* **ordained, ordaining. 1.** to decide or order by law or authority: "We, the people of the United States . . . do *ordain* and establish this Constitution . . ." (Preamble to the U.S. Constitution) **2.** to appoint someone to be a minister, priest, or rabbi by a formal ceremony.

or•deal [ôr dēl**/** *or* ôr**/** dēl**/**] *noun, plural* **or-deals.** a very difficult or painful test or experi-ence: The soldier survived the *ordeal* of being in an enemy prison camp for several years.

or•der [ôr**/** dər] *noun, plural* **orders. 1.** a com-mand or direction given to a person to do something or act in a certain way: People in the armed forces must follow an officer's *orders*. **2.** a certain way in which things are placed in relation to each other: Words in a dictionary are listed in alphabetical *order*. **3.** a situation in which things are arranged or done in the proper way: I couldn't call home because the phone is out of *order*. **4.** a serving of food in a restau-rant. **5.** a request to buy, sell, or supply goods in business: That computer company just got a large *order* from the government. **6.** a group of related people or things: Cats and dogs both belong to the meat-eating *order* of animals. **7. in order to.** so as to; for the purpose of: They planted some trees *in order to* have shade for the back yard.

—*verb,* **ordered, ordering. 1.** to tell someone to do something; give a command: The judge *ordered* that the prisoner be set free. **2.** to ask for; request: Mom called the restaurant and *ordered* a pizza.

or•der•ly [ôr′dər lē] *adjective, more/most.* **1.** placed in a neat way; in order: She kept all her clothes arranged in very *orderly* rows in her closet. **2.** not causing trouble or making noise: A friendly and *orderly* crowd stood outside the airport fence waiting for the President's plane. —*noun, plural* **orderlies.** a worker whose job is to keep things in order, as in a hospital.

or•di•nal number [ôr′də nəl] a number that shows position in a series. Fourth, fifth, and sixth are ordinal numbers; three, four, and five are CARDINAL NUMBERS.

or•di•nar•i•ly [ôr′də ner′ə lē] *adverb.* in most cases; normally; usually: He left work early tonight, but *ordinarily* he stays late.

or•di•nar•y [ôr′də ner′ē] *adjective, more/most.* being as it usually is or is expected to be; normal; common: The *ordinary* U.S. high school goes from grade nine to twelve.

ore [ôr] *noun, plural* **ores.** any rock or mineral that contains a certain amount of a valuable metal, such as iron.

Or•e•gon [ôr′ə gän *or* ôr′ə gən] a state in the northwestern U.S., on the Pacific Ocean. *Capital:* Salem. *Nickname:* "Beaver State." *Area:* 97,000 square miles. *Population:* 2,650,000.

or•gan [ôr′gən] *noun, plural* **organs. 1.** a musical instrument that has pipes of different sizes through which air is blown to produce many different tones. An organ is played with a set or sets of keyboards. ♦ A person who plays this instrument is called an **organist. 2.** a part of an animal or plant that does a particular job. The heart, eyes, lungs, and stomach are the organs in the human body. **3.** a means of communication: Newsletters that give news about events within a company are called "house *organs.*"

or•gan•ic [ôr gan′ik] *adjective.* **1.** having to do with organs of the body. **2.** having to do with living things, as opposed to artificial products: Cover the plant's roots with *organic* materials such as wood chips, dead leaves, or grass. **3.** of food, grown without artificial fertilizers or pest controls: *organic* vegetables.

or•gan•ism [ôr′gə niz′əm] *noun, plural* **organisms.** any living animal or plant.

or•gan•i•za•tion [ôr′gə nə zā′shən] *noun, plural* **organizations. 1.** a group of people who are joined together for some purpose: a parent-teacher *organization* at a school, the World Health *Organization.* **2.** the act or fact of organizing; putting things together according to a system.

or•gan•ize [ôr′gən īz′] *verb,* **organized, organizing. 1.** to put things together according to some plan or system; arrange in an orderly way: Factual books in a library are *organized* by subject. "Everything was *organized* to get the planes off without delay." (James Houston) **2.** to bring people together into a group: In the 1880's Samuel Gompers *organized* what became the largest American labor union.

o•ri•ent [ôr′ē ent] *verb,* **oriented, orienting. 1.** to place or locate in a certain position: "The salesman watched Lucas pause, squinting at the trees to *orient* himself . . ." (William Faulkner) **2.** to make or become familiar with a new situation. —**orientation,** *noun:* New high school students go through *orientation* at the beginning of the year.

O•ri•ent [ôr′ē ent] *noun.* the countries of eastern Asia, such as Japan, China, and Korea.

O•ri•en•tal [ôr′ē en′tal] *noun, plural* **Orientals.** a person who is from the Orient or whose family came from the Orient. —*adjective.* having to do with the Orient.

or•i•gin [ôr′ə jin] *noun, plural* **origins.** the point from which something comes; the cause, beginning, or source: The *origin* of the Mississippi River is a lake in northern Minnesota.

organ The huge pipe organ at the Reverend Robert Schuller's Crystal Cathedral in California.

O

originality Are you *original* only when you write poems and stories and create a wholly new work? No. There's another kind of originality. It applies to factual writing, where the challenge is to take the facts available to everyone, yet present them in an original way. If you are writing about a county in Ireland where your grandfather was born, you might begin by mentioning famous Irish songs, 'The Irish Soldier Boy,' or 'The Irish Rebel,'or 'The Wild Colonial Boy.' All of these are about young men. All are a way to point out how the Irish have so often been involved in fighting in wars and in rebelling against English rule. Or you could begin by writing, "The potato is a seed in Irish life and history. Because of the Potato Famine of 1845–47, when Ireland's potato crop failed, many Irish left for America."

o•rig•i•nal [ə rij′ ə nəl] *adjective, more/most.*
1. not in being before; not copied; completely new: When a movie is an "*original* screenplay," this means the story was not taken from a book, a play, or an earlier movie. **2.** having to do with the origin or beginning; earliest; first: The U.S. flag has thirteen stripes to stand for the *original* thirteen states. ◆ The fact of being original is **originality** [ə rij′ ə nal′ ə tē]: The teacher said that Beth's science project showed a lot of *originality.* —*noun, plural* **originals.** something that is original, rather than a copy or imitation.

o•rig•i•nal•ly [ə rij′ ə nəl ē] *adverb.* at first; from the start: The city of Detroit was *originally* a fort used by French fur traders.

o•rig•i•nate [ə rij′ ə nāt] *verb,* **originated, originating. 1.** to bring into being; cause to be; invent: The Thanksgiving holiday was *originated* by the early Pilgrim settlers. **2.** to come to be; start; begin: She got on the plane at Dallas, but the flight *originated* in New York.

o•ri•ole [ôr′ ē ōl′] *noun, plural* **orioles.** a songbird that has orange and black or yellow and black feathers.

or•na•ment [ôr′ nə mənt] *noun, plural* **ornaments.** something that is added to give beauty; something pretty; a decoration: to put *ornaments* on a Christmas tree. —*verb,* **ornamented, ornamenting.** to decorate with ornaments; add beauty to: "She sat there with her extremely pretty hands, *ornamented* with very brilliant rings . . ." (Henry James) —**ornamental,** *adjective: ornamental* flowers.

or•nate [ôr nāt′] *adjective, more/most.* having much decoration; fancy; showy: The palace of French kings at Versailles has very *ornate* furnishings.

or•phan [ôr′ fən] *noun, plural* **orphans.** a child whose parents are dead. ◆ An **orphanage** is a home that takes care of orphans.

or•tho•don•tist [ôr′ thə dän′ tist] *noun, plural* **orthodontists.** a dentist who specializes in straightening teeth.

or•tho•dox [ôr′ thə däks] *adjective, more/most.* **1.** following the usual or accepted way; typical; customary: The *orthodox* method of setting a table is to put the forks on the left and knives and spoons on the right. **2.** having or following generally-accepted beliefs: This book gives the *orthodox* view of George Washington—that he was a great leader and hero. **3. Orthodox. a.** having to do with a group of Christian churches that separated from the Roman Catholic Church in early times. ◆ This church is called the **Eastern Orthodox Church. b.** having to do with a branch of the Jewish religion that follows very strict customs and traditions.

Orwell George Orwell is recognized as one of the three or four great prose writers of the 20th century, and is called "the conscience of modern writers." Here are some of his thoughts on writing: "Good prose is like a window pane." "So long as I remain alive and well I shall continue to feel strongly about prose style, to love the surface of the earth, and to take pleasure in solid objects and scraps of useless information." "A scrupulous [very careful] writer, in every sentence that he writes, will ask himself at least four questions, thus: What am I trying to say? What words will express it? What image or idiom will make it clearer? Is this image fresh enough to have an effect?"

Or•well [ôr′ wel] **George,** 1903–1940, English author. His real name was **Eric Blair.**

Os•lo [äz′ lō] the capital and largest city of Norway. *Population:* 452,000.

os•mo•sis [äz mō′ sis *or* äs mō′ sis] *noun.* the movement of fluid through a MEMBRANE until it becomes mixed with fluid on the other side of that membrane. Osmosis allows fluid to move through cell walls in the human body.

ostrich The ostrich is the largest living bird, weighing up to 300 pounds and standing about 8 feet tall.

os•trich [äs′trich] *noun, plural* **ostriches.** a very large African bird that has long legs and a long neck. An ostrich cannot fly, but it can run very fast. Ostriches are the largest of all living birds.

oth•er [uth′ər] *noun, plural* **others. 1.** being the one of two that is left; remaining: You carry this box and I'll take the *other* one. **2.** not the same as was just mentioned; not this one or ones: Andy is taller than the *other* boys in his class. **3.** in the recent past: I ran into Greg at the supermarket the *other* day. **4. every other.** every second one: That writer's column appears in the paper *every other* morning. —*pronoun:* Jill got there at five, but the *others* didn't arrive until six.

other•wise [uth′ər wīz] *adverb.* other than that; in a different way or a different condition: "They came to visit her, bringing news she *otherwise* would not have heard." (Alice Walker) —*conjunction.* or else: "We've got to have some rules, *otherwise* it will be too confusing . . ." (E.B. White)

Ot•ta•wa [ät′ə wə] the capital of Canada, in southeastern Ontario. *Population:* 304,000.

ot•ter [ät′ər] *noun, plural* **otters** or **otter.** a small animal that is related to the weasel, with a long, slender body, webbed feet, and thick brown fur. Otters live in or near the water.

ouch [ouch] *interjection.* a word used to express sudden pain.

ought [ôt] **ought** is used with other verbs to show: **1.** that something is right or should be done: Anyone riding in a car *ought* to wear a seat belt. **2.** that something can be expected to happen: They *ought* to be here any minute now.

ounce [ouns] *noun, plural* **ounces. 1.** a unit of weight equal to 1/16 of a pound, or about 28

grams in the metric system. **2.** a unit of measure for liquids. 16 **fluid ounces** equal one pint. **3.** a little bit: I didn't have an *ounce* of strength left after the soccer game was over.

our [our] *adjective.* of us; belonging to us: My brother and I took *our* dog to the park.

ours [ourz] *pronoun.* the one or ones that belong to us or have to do with us: Both cars are the same make, but *ours* is newer.

our•selves [our selvz′] *pronoun.* our own selves: We made lunch *ourselves* while Mom was at the store.

out [out] *adverb.* **1.** away from the inside: He took a shirt *out* of the closet. **2.** away from the usual place: The doctor has stepped *out* for a minute. **3.** so as to be at an end: to put *out* a fire, to fill *out* a form, to check *out* of a motel. **4.** so as to be seen or known: The sun came *out* from behind a cloud. **5.** so as to be available for use: to give *out* free tickets, to check *out* a book from the library. —*adjective.* **1.** not a choice; not possible: Going to the beach this weekend is *out* unless I can get all my homework done. **2.** not in style; not in fashion: Very long hair for men was popular in the late 1960's but is now *out.* **3.** in baseball, no longer at bat and not safely on base.

otter A sea otter diving for a clam. The otter will open the tightly-closed shell by smashing it against a rock. This is an unusual use of "hands" and "tools" by an animal.

Pronunciation Key: G–N

g	give; big	k	kind; cat; back
h	hold	l	let; ball
i	it; this	m	make; time
ī	ice; my	n	not; own
j	jet; gem; edge	ng	having

(Turn the page for more information.)

O

out·board motor [out′bôrd′] a small motor attached to the outside back part of a boat.

out·break [out′brāk′] *noun, plural* **outbreaks.** the act of breaking out: There was an *outbreak* of measles at our school last month.

out·burst [out′burst′] *noun, plural* **outbursts.** a bursting out of some strong feeling or action: "There was a sudden *outburst* of voices from the entrance hall." (Christopher Isherwood)

out·cast [out′kast′] *noun, plural* **outcasts.** a person who is cast out or rejected by a group.

out·come [out′kum′] *noun, plural* **outcomes.** the way that something comes out; the end or result: The sports section listed the *outcome* of Sunday's pro football games.

out·cry [out′krī′] *noun, plural* **outcries. 1.** a loud cry; a scream. **2.** a strong public protest: The mayor hired more policemen as a result of the public *outcry* against crime in the streets.

out·dat·ed [out dā′tid] *adjective, more/most.* out of date; old-fashioned: "Aeroplane" and "flying machine" are *outdated* words for "airplane."

out·do [out dōō′] *verb,* **outdid, outdone, outdoing.** to do better than; surpass: Each TV store tried to *outdo* all the others with bigger and bigger sales and discounts.

out·door [out′dôr′] *adjective.* done or used in the open, rather than in a house or building: Fishing and hiking are *outdoor* sports. **—outdoors,** *adverb.*

out·er [ou′tər] *adjective.* on the outside; farther out: Coats and jackets are *outer* clothing.

Nancy wore a pretty green *outfit* to the party. **3.** a group of people who work together: My dad and Mr. Lewis were in the same *outfit* in the army. **—verb, outfitted, outfitting.** to provide the necessary clothing or equipment for something: to *outfit* people for a canoe trip.

out·go·ing [out′gō′ing] *adjective, more/most.* **1.** going out; departing; leaving: The west runway is being used for *outgoing* flights. **2.** mixing easily with other people; friendly and talkative: He enjoys being a salesman because he's such an *outgoing* person.

out·grow [out′grō′] *verb,* **outgrew, outgrown, outgrowing. 1.** to grow too big for: Dave has already *outgrown* the shirt I gave him last Christmas. **2.** to leave behind as one grows older; grow away from: My little sister has *outgrown* the habit of sleeping with her dolls.

out·ing [ou′ting] *noun, plural* **outings.** a short trip or walk outdoors for pleasure: Our family went on an *outing* to the beach today.

out·law [out′lô′] *noun, plural* **outlaws.** a person who often breaks the law; a criminal: Jesse James and Billy the Kid were famous *outlaws* of the Old West. **—verb, outlawed, outlawing.** to declare to be against the law: The 13th Amendment to the Constitution *outlawed* slavery.

out·let [out′let] *noun, plural* **outlets. 1.** a place for something to get out; an opening or exit: the *outlet* of a lake, the *outlet* of a drainpipe. **2.** a way of expressing or releasing something: Mom bought Jimmy a punching bag to use as an *outlet* for his energies. **3.** a place in a wall where an electric device can be plugged in.

outlines For a full-length report in social studies, science, or literature, teachers usually require a formal outline along with the paper itself. Often this outline has to be handed in while the paper is still in progress. Students sometimes question this. Their idea is that the outline should be done after the paper is finished, because it's too hard to tell before then what the outline should include. Actually, doing an outline is not just a formal exercise. The key to putting together a factual paper is order—the sequence in which the information is presented. Whenever people carry out some task—building a house, planting a garden, whatever—they act in a certain 1, 2, 3 order. This is what an outline does—it gives the 1, 2, 3 order in which you will present information in your paper. That's why teachers want it done while the paper is in progress.

out·field [out′fēld′] *noun, plural* **outfields.** in baseball: **1.** the part of the field beyond the infield. **2.** the three players who play in the outfield. The **outfielders** are the left fielder, right fielder, and center fielder.

out·fit [out′fit′] *noun, plural* **outfits. 1.** a set of the articles or equipment needed for doing something: a camping *outfit.* **2.** a set of clothes:

out·line [out′līn′] *noun, plural* **outlines. 1.** a line that marks the outer edge or boundary of something and shows its shape: The *outline* of Lake Superior looks something like the head of a wolf. **2.** a drawing that shows only the outer edge of something. **3.** a short list or plan that gives the main points of a longer report, speech, article, or the like.

—*verb*, **outlined, outlining. 1.** to make or give an outline: At the meeting the boss will *outline* his plan to open a new office. **2.** to show something in outline.

out•look [out′look′] *noun, plural* **outlooks. 1.** what can be seen from a place; a view. **2.** a way of thinking or feeling about things: She's basically a happy person and has a very positive *outlook* on life. **3.** a view of the future; the way things are expected to happen.

out•ly•ing [out′lī′ing] *adjective*. located far from the center or main part; distant: There are about 5,000 people living in this area, including all the *outlying* farms.

out•num•ber [out′num′bər] *verb*, **outnumbered, outnumbering.** to be larger in number than; be more than.

out-of-date [out′ əv dāt′] *adjective, more/most*. no longer in style or use; outdated.

out•post [out′pōst′] *noun, plural* **outposts. 1.** a small group of soldiers placed away from a main army camp as a guard against surprise attacks. **2.** any group or settlement far away from the main location.

out•put [out′poot′] *noun*. **1.** the amount of something produced: That auto factory has an *output* of 1,000 cars a day. **2.** the act of putting forth something: the *output* of electrical energy from a generator. **3.** in computers, any information that comes out of the computer and can be understood by the user.

out•rage [out′rāj′] *noun, plural* **outrages. 1.** an action that is very cruel or wrong, and that causes great harm: "When man destroys the life and beauty of nature, there is the *outrage*." (G.M. Trevelyan) **2.** angry feelings caused by an injury or insult: The President made a speech on national television to express his *outrage* over the airplane hijacking. —*verb*, **outraged, outraging.** to make very angry; offend greatly; insult.

out•ra•geous [out rā′ jəs] *adjective, more/most*. **1.** very cruel or wrong: an *outrageous* crime. **2.** very bad or insulting; shocking: The cab driver wants $50 just to go from here to the airport? That's *outrageous!* —**outrageously,** *adverb*.

out•rig•ger [out′rig′ər] *noun, plural* **outriggers.** a float attached to a canoe by a frame to help keep the canoe from turning over, used especially in the islands of the South Pacific.

out•right [out′rīt′] *adjective*. complete; total: an *outright* lie. —*adverb*. **1.** completely; entirely: They finally paid off the loan on their house and now own it *outright*. **2.** directly; honestly: She told him *outright* what she thought of him.

out•set [out′set′] *noun*. the beginning; the start: We've been having trouble with our new car right from the *outset*.

out•side [out′sīd′] *noun, plural* **outsides.** the opposite of inside; the outer side, surface, or part: Megan put a big "Keep Out!" sign on the *outside* of her door. —*adverb*. on or to the outside; outdoors: Let's go *outside* and have a game of catch. —*preposition*. to the outer side of: She lives fifteen miles *outside* Chicago. —*adjective*. **1.** on, to, or from the outside: the *outside* walls of a house. **2.** very small; not likely; slight: We've only got an *outside* chance of winning the game. ♦ A person who does not belong to a certain group is an **outsider.**

out•skirts [out′skurts′] *plural noun*. the edge or outer area of a town or other place: This bus line runs all the way to the *outskirts* of the city.

out•smart [out′smärt′] *verb*, **outsmarted, outsmarting.** to use one's mind to get the better of another; be more clever than: The "Uncle Remus" folk tales tell of how a rabbit *outsmarts* a fox and a bear.

out•spo•ken [out′spō′kən] *adjective, more/most*. saying what one thinks or feels without holding back; speaking one's mind freely: My cousin is very *outspoken* and is always giving her opinion about things.

out•stand•ing [out′stan′ding] *adjective, more/most*. **1.** better than others; standing out from

outrigger Outrigger canoes have been used for centuries in the Hawaiian Islands. The outrigger helps keep the craft afloat in rough seas.

O

Pronunciation Key: O S

ō	over; go	ou	out; town
ô	all; law	p	put; hop
oo	look; full	r	run; car
oo	pool; who	s	set; miss
oi	oil; boy	sh	show

(Turn the page for more information.)

O

the rest: Larry won an award as the *outstanding* student in his class. **2.** not paid or settled: There is still $2,000 *outstanding* on the loan she took out to buy that car. —**outstandingly,** *adverb.*

out·ward [out′wərd′] *adverb.* (*also,* **outwards**) toward the outside: Fire exit doors in a public place always open *outward.* —*adjective.* that is seen; outer: He gave an *outward* appearance of being calm, even though he was nervous inside. —**outwardly,** *adverb.*

out·weigh [out′wā′] *verb,* **outweighed, outweighing. 1.** to weigh more than. **2.** to be greater in value or importance than: There are a few things Ted doesn't like about his new school, but the good points *outweigh* the bad.

out·wit [out′wit′] *verb,* **outwitted, outwitting.** to get the better of; outsmart.

o·val [ō′vəl] *adjective.* shaped like an egg: The Indianapolis 500 auto race takes place on an *oval* track. —*noun, plural* **ovals.** something that has an oval shape.

o·va·ry [ō′və rē] *noun, plural* **ovaries. 1.** the part of a female animal in which eggs are produced. **2.** the part of a plant in which seeds are formed.

ov·en [uv′ən] *noun, plural* **ovens. 1.** a kitchen appliance with an enclosed space that can be heated for cooking food inside it. **2.** any similar device used to heat or dry things: a pottery *oven.*

o·ver [ō′vər] *preposition.* **1.** higher than and not touching; above: We flew *over* the Grand Canyon on our way to California. **2.** from one side to the other of: The Bear Mountain Bridge goes *over* the Hudson River. **3.** on or across the surface of; covering: She had on a jacket *over* her sweater. **4.** higher in amount or position; more than: Don't spend *over* ten dollars on the birthday present. **5.** during the time of: She's visiting her family *over* the Christmas holidays. **6.** about; concerning: Don't get upset *over* such a little thing. —*adverb:* **1.** down from an upright position: The dog knocked the lamp *over.* **2.** to another place or person: Jerry came *over* to see me today. **3.** another time; again: I spilled juice on my homework paper and had to do it *over.* —*adjective.* at an end; finished: We left as soon as the movie was *over.*

o·ver·all [ō′vər ôl′] *adjective; adverb.* including everything; as a whole: The *overall* cost of the meal was $33, with the tax and the tip.

o·ver·alls [ō′vər ôls′] *plural noun.* sturdy, loose-fitting work trousers with a top piece that covers the chest, held up by straps that go over the shoulders.

o·ver·board [ō′vər bôrd′] *adverb.* **1.** over the side of a ship or boat into the water: A passenger fell *overboard,* but the crew rescued him. **2. go overboard.** to go too far; become too intense or excited about something.

o·ver·cast [ō′vər kast′] *adjective, more/most.* of the sky, covered over with clouds; somewhat dark.

o·ver·coat [ō′vər kōt′] *noun, plural* **overcoats.** a long, heavy coat worn over other clothes for warmth.

o·ver·come [ō′vər kum′] *verb,* **overcame, overcome, overcoming. 1.** to get the better of; defeat: "He learned to write on a blackboard and *overcame* his dislike of the sound of scraping chalk." (V.S. Naipaul) **2.** to make helpless or weak: The fireman was *overcome* by smoke from the fire.

o·ver·crowd [ō′vər kroud′] *verb,* **overcrowded, overcrowding.** to put too many people or things in; crowd too much. ◆ Usually used as an adjective: an *overcrowded* subway car.

o·ver·do [ō′vər doo′] *verb,* **overdid, overdone, overdoing. 1.** to do or use too much: People who are just starting to exercise shouldn't *overdo* it the first day. **2.** to cook too long or too much. ◆ Usually used as an adjective: The roast beef was dry and *overdone.*

o·ver·dose [ō′vər dōs′] *noun, plural* **overdoses.** too large a dose: He accidentally took an *overdose* of the medicine because he didn't read the label correctly. —*verb,* **overdosed, overdosing.** to give or take too large a dose.

o·ver·due [ō′vər doo′] *adjective.* past the usual or proper time; not done or paid at the time due: The fine for *overdue* library books is 10¢ a day. After 45 years in movies, Henry Fonda finally won a long-*overdue* Oscar for Best Actor.

o·ver·flow [ō′vər flō′] *verb,* **overflowed, overflowing. 1.** to flow over the top or beyond the usual limits: Before the Aswan Dam was built the Nile River *overflowed* its banks almost every year. **2.** to spill or spread over; be very full or too full: "There were bookshelves above the cot, and more bookshelves, *overflowing* with books . . ." (Joe McGinniss) —*noun, plural* **overflows.** something that flows over.

o·ver·grow [ō′vər grō′] *verb,* **overgrew, overgrown, overgrowing. 1.** to grow over; cover with growth: Weeds had *overgrown* the old shed. **2.** to grow too much; grow too fast. ◆ Usually used as an adjective: The once-beautiful valley is now *overgrown* with shopping centers and housing developments.

o•ver•hand [ō/vər hand/] *adjective, adverb.* with the hand moving above the shoulder: Pitchers in softball are not allowed to throw the ball *overhand.*

o•ver•haul [ō/vər hôl/] *verb,* **overhauled, overhauling. 1.** to make complete repairs or improvements, as by taking apart: The mechanic *overhauled* the car engine. **2.** to catch up to; overtake: The speedboat quickly *overhauled* the slow fishing boat. —*noun, plural* **overhauls.** the act of overhauling something.

o•ver•head [ō/vər hcd/] *adverb, adjective.* above the head: He ducked as a bird flew just *overhead.* Until recent years phone and electric companies used *overhead* wires. —*noun, plural* **overhead.** the general costs of running a business, aside from the cost of making and selling the company's products. Rent, taxes, repairs, heat, and electricity are part of overhead.

o•ver•hear [ō/vər hēr/] *verb,* **overheard, overhearing.** to hear something that one is not meant to hear: I was in the other room and *overheard* my parents planning a surprise birthday party for me.

o•ver•lap [ō/vər lap/] *verb,* **overlapped, overlapping. 1.** to rest on something and partly cover it: The roof was made of flat *overlapping* stones. **2.** to connect with or partly touch: Their years at the college *overlapped;* she was a freshman when he was a senior.

very polite. **3.** to have a view of from a higher place: "The windows of the office *overlooked* the athletic field." (Paul Zindel)

o•ver•night [ō/vər nīt/] *adverb; adjective.* **1.** during or through the night: Cathy is staying *overnight* at her friend Katie's house. **2.** very quickly; suddenly: "We struck oil. *Overnight,* then, my ten was worth two hundred . . ." (V.S. Naipaul)

o•ver•pass [ō/vər pas/] *noun, plural* **overpasses.** a bridge or road that crosses over a road, canal, or railroad.

o•ver•pow•er [ō/vər pou/ər] *verb,* **overpowered, overpowering.** to defeat by greater power; get the better of: He's so much bigger and stronger than the players he goes up against that he just *overpowers* them.

o•ver•rule [ō/vər rool/] *verb,* **overruled, overruling.** to rule against; decide against: The Supreme Court can *overrule* decisions made by lower courts.

o•ver•seas [ō/vər sēz/] *adverb; adjective:* across the sea; abroad: He's going to join the army and hopes to serve somewhere *overseas.*

o•ver•sight [ō/vər sīt/] *noun, plural* **oversights.** a careless mistake that is not made on purpose.

o•ver•sleep [ō/vər slēp/] *verb,* **overslept, oversleeping.** to sleep too long; sleep past the time one wanted to wake up.

overstatement Here's a recent letter to the editor in a local newspaper: "The colonists fought for their freedom in 1776. Now let's all fight for *our* freedom, the right to wear T-shirts at Orange Glen High School." Searching for a strong image to make his point, the writer has actually weakened the point, making his wish more trivial by comparing it to a great historic event. Suppose you wrote: "I had a sleepover party and we stayed up all night. The next morning my bedroom looked like a tornado went through it. Sleepy, but awake, I felt like giant hammers were pounding my brain. Mom was mad enough to kill all of us." At this point, your readers would say, do you need all that? Tornadoes, giant hammers, murder? You may think you need to "shout" to get the reader's attention. Actually, if you do this, your message is harder to hear, not easier.

o•ver•load [ō/vər lōd/] *verb,* **overloaded, overloading.** to put too much of a load on: to *overload* a moving truck with furniture. —*noun, plural* **overloads:** Too many electrical appliances working at once can put an *overload* on a power system.

o•ver•look [ō/vər look/] *verb,* **overlooked, overlooking. 1.** to fail to see or notice; miss: The detective Sherlock Holmes was known for finding important clues that the police had *overlooked.* **2.** to choose not to see or pay attention to; ignore: The teacher *overlooked* Mike's rude remark because he was usually

o•ver•take [ō/vər tāk/] *verb,* **overtook, overtaken, overtaking.** to catch up with: "The riders were too swift to *overtake,* and too many to oppose." (J.R.R. Tolkien)

Pronunciation Key: T Z

t	ten; date	v	very; live
th	think	w	win; away
th	these	y	you
u	cut; butter	z	zoo; cause
ur	turn; bird	zh	measure

(Turn the page for more information.)

O

o•ver•throw [ō′vər thrō′] *verb*, **overthrown, overthrowing.** to remove from power; defeat or destroy: The Shah of Iran ruled his country for 38 years but was finally *overthrown* by a Muslim revolution. ◆ Also used as a noun: Fidel Castro took power in Cuba after the *overthrow* of the Batista government.

o•ver•time [ō′vər tīm′] *noun, plural* **overtimes. 1.** extra time worked beyond regular working hours, or the pay for this time. ◆ Also used as an adjective or adverb: *overtime* pay, to work three hours *overtime.* **2.** in sports, an extra amount of time to decide the winner of a game that has ended in a tie.

o•ver•ture [ō′vər chər] *noun, plural* **overtures. 1.** a musical composition played by an orchestra to introduce a longer musical work such as a ballet or opera. **2.** an offer or proposal to begin something: Anwar Sadat of Egypt made *overtures* toward Israel that finally led to a peace agreement between the two countries.

o•ver•weight [ō′vər wāt′] *adjective, more/ most.* having too much weight.

o•ver•whelm [ō′vər welm′] *verb,* **overwhelmed, overwhelming.** to overcome completely; overpower; crush: "Dulcie was so *overwhelmed* that she could scarcely think what to say." (Barbara Pym)

owe [ō] *verb,* **owed, owing. 1.** to have to pay; be required to pay: I *owe* Nancy five dollars that I borrowed from her. **2.** to have to give: He *owes* me an apology for wrecking my bike. **3. owing to.** because of: "Daniel nearly missed his flight, *owing to* a traffic snarl-up." (John Fowles)

owl [oul] *noun, plural* **owls.** a bird with a large round head, large eyes, and a short, hooked bill. Owls hunt at night for mice, frogs, snakes, and insects.

owl Two common North American owls, the great horned owl (left) and the snowy owl.

own [ōn] *adjective.* of or belonging to oneself or itself: Tim fixed his *own* breakfast because his parents were still asleep. —*verb,* **owned, owning. 1.** to have as belonging to one; possess: to *own* a car, to *own* a house. **2.** to admit; confess: "His age was forty-eight, and he *owned* to forty-four." (George Orwell)

own•er [ō′nər] *noun, plural* **owners.** a person who owns something. ◆ The fact of owning something is **ownership.**

ox [äks] *noun, plural* **oxen.** the full-grown male of cattle. Oxen are used as work animals or for beef.

ox•en [äks′ən] the *plural* of **ox.**

ox•ide [äk′sīd] *noun, plural* **oxides.** a compound of oxygen and another element.

ox•i•dize [äk′sə dīz] *verb,* **oxidized, oxidizing.** to combine a chemical substance with oxygen. ◆ The process of oxidizing is **oxidation.** The rusting of metal is an example of oxidization.

ox•y•gen [äk′sə jin] *noun.* a gas that has no color or smell. Oxygen is the most common chemical element in the world. Water is mostly oxygen, and the air is about one-fifth oxygen. Plants, animals, and people all need oxygen to live. **Liquid oxygen** is used as a rocket fuel.

oyster The giant Pacific oyster may grow to be 12 inches across. It can be found attached to rocks or pilings.

oys•ter [ois′tər] *noun, plural* **oysters.** a sea animal that has a soft body inside a rough shell with two parts. Oysters are found in warm shallow water along coasts. Many kinds of oysters are eaten as food. Some oysters produce pearls inside their shells.

o•zone [ō′zōn′] *noun.* a form of oxygen that has a sharp, fresh odor and is produced by an electric charge in the air. The **ozone layer** of the earth's atmosphere keeps harmful rays from the sun from reaching the surface of the earth.

p, P [pē] *noun, plural* **p's, P's.** the sixteenth letter of the alphabet.

pace [pās] *noun, plural* **paces. 1.** one step taken in walking or running, or the length of such a step. **2.** the speed with which some activity is done: "At a brisk *pace* I could do the walk from Queen's Gate Terrace in about twenty minutes." (Iris Murdoch) **3.** a fast movement of a horse in which both the legs on one side of the animal move forward at the same time. ♦ A race horse that runs in this way is a **pacer.** —*verb,* **paced, pacing. 1.** to walk back and forth again and again: "He seemed as restless as a Bengal tiger *pacing* back and forth inside its cage." (James Herriot) **2.** to measure the length of something with paces: The referee *paced* off a five-yard penalty.

Pa•cif•ic Ocean [pə sif′ ik] the largest ocean in the world. It extends from the Arctic to the Antarctic between the Americas and Asia.

pac•i•fist [pas′ ə fist] *noun, plural* **pacifists.** a person who believes that differences between people and nations should be settled by peaceful methods rather than by war. ♦ This belief is called **pacifism.**

large amount of something bad: a *pack* of thieves, a *pack* of lies. —*verb,* **packed, packing. 1.** to put something in a box, suitcase, or other container: to *pack* clothes for a trip. **2.** to fill something up: "Each day the courtroom was *packed* as tightly as the space would permit." (James Weldon Johnson)

pack•age [pak′ ij] *noun, plural* **packages. 1.** something wrapped, tied, or sealed inside a box, bag, or other such container: In a supermarket meat is sold in *packages.* **2.** a number of things grouped together and thought of as one: The airline is offering a vacation *package* that includes air fare, hotels, and all meals. ♦ Often used as an adjective: The movie star and her husband signed a *package* deal to make a movie together. —*verb,* **packaged, packaging.** to wrap or make into a package: When we bought the camera, film was already *packaged* with it.

pact [pakt] *noun, plural* **pacts.** an agreement between people or countries to deal with each other in a certain way or do certain things: The Munich *Pact* was an agreement signed in 1938 by Great Britain, France, Germany, and Italy, turning certain lands over to Germany.

---

padding "'What an unlucky day this is,' thought Suzie Stern. She had never known such bad luck, not a single day as unlucky as this one. Bad, bad luck." This is "padding," adding unnecessary words to make a story or article longer. Padding is boring; it repeats something the reader already knows. If your subject is too small, enlarge it. For example, an article on seals can be expanded by including other marine mammals: walruses, sea lions, and dolphins. Another way to prevent padding is to ask yourself: Have I covered too short a period of time, or too narrow a location?

---

pack [pak] *noun, plural* **packs, 1.** a number of things that are wrapped or tied together to be carried by a person or animal on the back: Campers often carry food and equipment in *packs.* **2.** a group of things of the same type that go together: a *pack* of playing cards, a six-*pack* of soda. Wolves hunt for game in *packs.* **3.** a

pad [pad] *noun, plural* **pads. 1.** a number of sheets of paper glued or stuck together along one end, used for writing. **2.** a small ink-soaked cushion in a box, used to put ink on a rubber stamp for marking something. **3.** a thick, soft piece of material used to make furniture or clothing more comfortable; also called **pad-**

P

page format There are certain generally-used customs as to how the *format* (the design) of a handwritten or typed paper should be presented. First, your side margins should be at least one-half inch for a handwritten paper. For a typed paper, the usual side margin is one inch, or slightly more. Don't make the margins too wide because this creates a "ladder" appearance. Allow proper margins at the top and bottom of the page also—for typing, at least one inch, but not over one and a half. Always number all the pages of your paper at the *top—including* the first page. If you put your name or the title of your paper on every page, put the page number at the right, not in the center.

ding. **4.** a similar material used to protect something: Football and hockey players wear shoulder *pads*. **5.** the under part of an animal's paw that is thick and soft like a cushion. —*verb*, **padded, padding. 1.** to cover or line something with a pad or cushion: The workmen *padded* the walls of the elevator while they were loading the furniture onto it. **2.** to make something longer by adding more words than are necessary. ◆ See writing article on p. 545. **3.** to walk with soft, quiet steps: "He slipped out of bed and *padded* silently across to the window." (Stephen King)

pad•dle [pad′əl] *noun, plural* **paddles. 1.** a long-handled pole that is wider at the bottom, used in the water to move and steer a canoe or other small boat. **2.** a small, flat board with a handle, used to hit the ball in table tennis and other such games. —*verb,* **paddled, paddling. 1.** to move a canoe or boat with a paddle. **2.** to move the hands and feet with short strokes when swimming: The dog *paddled* across the pond. **3.** to hit someone with a paddle or the hand as a punishment.

pad•dock [pad′ək] *noun, plural* **paddocks. 1.** a small, fenced area of grass for horses to graze or exercise. **2.** an enclosed area at a racetrack where the horses are put on display.

pad•dy [pad′ē] *noun, plural* **paddies.** a field used for growing rice.

pad•lock [pad′läk′] *noun, plural* **padlocks.** a lock that can be put on or taken off something. It has a curved bar that twists open when unlocked. The bar can be put through a ring and then snapped and locked into its own base. —*verb,* **padlocked, padlocking.** to lock something with a padlock.

pa•gan [pā′gən] *noun, plural* **pagans.** a person who either worships many gods or believes there is no god at all. In earlier times, the word meant someone who was not a Christian, Jew, or Muslim. Most people in ancient Greece and Rome were pagans. ◆ Also used as an adjective: *pagan* customs, a *pagan* ceremony.

page[1] [pāj] *noun, plural* **pages.** one side of a sheet of paper in a book, newspaper, or magazine.

page[2] *noun, plural* **pages. 1.** in the Middle Ages, a boy who was in training to become a knight and who acted as a knight's servant. **2.** a young person who carries messages or does other errands for people: *Pages* work for members of Congress in the U.S. Capitol Building. —*verb,* **paged, paging.** to try to find someone in a public place by having his name called out: We had my uncle *paged* at the airport to tell him where to meet us.

pag•eant [paj′ənt] *noun, plural* **pageants. 1.** a play or show about some event in the past. People in a pageant dress in the costumes of the time they are showing. **2.** a large and colorful parade or ceremony for an important event: the Rose Bowl *pageant.*

pagoda A pagoda in Kyoto, Japan. The term *pagoda* comes from India, where Buddhism began.

pa•go•da [pə gō′də] *noun, plural* **pagodas.** a building having several stories, each with a roof around it that curves upward. Pagodas have been built as houses of worship for the Buddhist religion in China, Japan, and other countries of Asia.

paid [pād] *verb.* the past form of **pay**: She *paid* for the sweater with a check.

pail [pāl] *noun, plural* **pails.** a round, open container with a flat bottom and a curved handle for carrying it; a bucket: Little children playing at the beach often carry sand in *pails.*

pain [pān] *noun, plural* **pains. 1.** a bad feeling that is sensed in or on the body, that a person does not like having, and that shows something is wrong. A headache, a cut on the arm, or an upset stomach can cause pain. **2.** a feeling like this in the mind; sadness: the *pain* of having a family member die. **3. pains.** great care or effort: She took *pains* to make sure that every word of her report was correct. **4.** *Informal.* a person or thing that is very unpleasant or annoying; a nuisance: Tommy's being a real *pain* today and keeps trying to ruin our game.— *verb,* **pained, paining.** to cause or feel pain.

Paine [pān] **Thomas,** 1737–1809, American patriot and author.

pain•ful [pān′fəl] *adjective.* **1.** causing pain: A sprained ankle can be a very *painful* injury. **2.** causing worry or concern: Both girls wanted very badly to play the leading part, and it was a *painful* decision for the teacher to choose just one of them. —**painfully,** *adverb.*

paint [pānt] *noun, plural* **paints.** a coloring matter that is mixed with water, oil, or some other liquid. Paint is put on walls and other surfaces to color, decorate, or protect them. —*verb,* **painted, painting. 1.** to cover something with paint: to *paint* a wall. **2.** to make a picture or a design with paint: Eddie *painted* a picture of a log cabin in art class. **3.** to tell about something so as to create a picture in the mind: Joe had *painted* such a glowing picture of his new job that we were all surprised when he quit after two weeks.

paint•er [pān′tər] *noun, plural* **painters. 1.** a person whose work is painting things, such as walls, buildings, signs, bridges, and so on. **2.** a person who paints pictures; an artist.

paint•ing [pān′ting] *noun, plural* **paintings. 1.** a picture made with paints. **2.** the art of painting pictures: She's studying the history of American *painting* at college this year. **3.** the act of putting on paint.

pair [pâr] *noun, plural* **pairs. 1.** a set of two things that are together or are supposed to be together: a *pair* of socks, a *pair* of shoes. **2.** one thing made up of two similar parts: a *pair* of eyeglasses, a *pair* of scissors, a *pair* of pants. **3.** two people or animals that go or work together: Farmers used to use a *pair* of mules or oxen to pull a plow. —*verb,* **paired, pairing.** to make or form a pair.

pa•ja•mas [pə ja′məz] *noun.* a set of clothes that are worn for sleeping, usually made up of a shirt and trousers or shorts.

Pak•i•stan [pak′i stan′ *or* päk′i stän′] a country in southern Asia, west of India. *Capital:* Islamabad. *Area:* 310,400 square miles. *Population:* 89,200,000. —**Pakistani,** *adjective; noun.*

pal [pal] *noun, plural* **pals.** *Informal.* a good friend.

palace Buckingham Palace in London, the official home of British kings and queens since 1837.

pal•ace [pal′is] *noun, plural* **palaces. 1.** a very large and grand building that is an official home of a king, queen, or other ruler. **2.** any very large and impressive house or building: Many stage shows in New York City were held at the *Palace* Theater.

pal•ate [pal′it] *noun, plural* **palates. 1.** the inside upper part of the mouth. The bony front part is the **hard palate.** The fleshy back part is the **soft palate. 2.** the sense of taste: a food critic who is known for his good *palate.*

pale [pāl] *adjective,* **paler, palest. 1.** without the usual amount of color in the face: You look a little *pale* today; are you feeling sick? **2.** of a light shade; not bright: The *pale* moonlight cast soft shadows from the trees and buildings. —*verb,* **paled, paling.** to turn pale: She *paled* when the plane suddenly started to bump.

Pal•es•tine [pal′is tīn′] a historic region in southwestern Asia, now divided between Israel and Jordan. —**Palestinian,** *adjective; noun.*

Pronunciation Key: A–F			
a	and; hat	ch	chew; such
ā	ate; stay	d	dog; lid
â	care; air	e	end; yet
ä	father; hot	ē	she; each
b	boy; cab	f	fun; off

(Turn the page for more information.)

P

P

pal•ette [pal´it] *noun, plural* **palettes.** a thin board used by artists to mix paints. A palette usually has an oval shape with a hole for the thumb.

pal•i•sades [pal´ə sādz] *plural, noun.* a line of steep cliffs rising beside a river.

pal•lid [pal´id] *adjective, more/most.* lacking the usual or normal color; pale: "The lad was actually *pallid* with rage." (Oscar Wilde) —**pallor,** *noun.*

palm[1] [päm] *noun, plural* **palms.** the inside of the hand between the wrist and the fingers. —*verb,* **palmed, palming.** to hold or hide something in the hand: "His hands were so big. Big enough to *palm* a basketball." (Judy Blume)

palm[2] *noun, plural* **palms.** a tree that has a long trunk with no branches and a cluster of broad leaves at the top. The leaves are shaped like huge feathers or fans. Palm trees grow in warm climates, especially in the tropics.

pal•met•to [pal met´ō] *noun, plural* **palmettoes.** a type of palm tree that grows in the southeastern United States.

Palm Sunday the Sunday before Easter. According to the Bible, when Jesus returned to Jerusalem on this day, the people there greeted him by laying palm branches before his path.

pal•o•mi•no [pal´ə mē´nō] *noun, plural* **palominos.** a horse having a golden coat and a cream-colored or white mane and tail.

pam•pas [pam´pəs] *noun.* a name used in South America for an area of wide, grassy plains with no trees.

pan [pan] *noun, plural* **pans. 1.** a shallow, open container, usually made of metal and having a handle, used for cooking foods: a frying *pan,* a sauce *pan.* **2.** any shallow metal container like this, such as one used to sift gold ore from earth or gravel. —*verb,* **panned, panning. 1.** to separate gold from earth or gravel by washing it in a pan. **2.** to criticize strongly: I thought the new play was good, but the newspaper and TV critics really *panned* it.

Pan•a•ma [pan´ə mä´] **1.** the southernmost country of Central America. *Capital:* Panama City. *Area:* 29,200 square miles. *Population:* 2,013,000. **2. Panama Canal.** a ship canal that connects the Atlantic and Pacific Oceans. —**Panamanian** [pan´ə mä´nē ən], *adjective; noun.*

Panama Canal An aerial view of ships passing through the Panama Canal.

Panama Canal As it happens, the Atlantic entrance to the Panama Canal is not east of the Pacific entrance, as you might expect. Is this unusual fact truly important to a writer? No. Is it important that Windsor, Ontario (Canada) is in part *south,* not north of Detroit, Michigan? Again, no. But—some geographical features, especially borders, *are* important as subjects for writing. The 38th parallel in Korea is one. The Rio Grande, between the U.S. and Mexico, is another. The Rhine River and the Danube River in Europe are still others. Any one of these could be a good subject for a paper.

pam•per [pam´pər] *verb,* **pampered, pampering.** to treat someone in too kind a way; give too much attention to; spoil: She *pampers* her dog so much that she cooks a special meal for it every night. ◆ Also used as an adjective: ". . . a *pampered* child who has always had her own way for the asking." (Margaret Mitchell)

pam•phlet [pam´flit] *noun, plural* **pamphlets.** a small, short book with a paper cover; a booklet: The power company sent us a *pamphlet* on ways to use less electricity.

pan•cake [pan´kāk´] *noun, plural* **pancakes.** a thin, flat cake made in a pan or on a griddle by frying a mixture called BATTER, usually made of milk, eggs, and flour.

pan•cre•as [pan´krē əs] *noun.* a large gland behind the stomach that helps digest foods.

pan•da [pan´də] *noun, plural* **pandas. 1.** a large animal that looks something like a bear; also called a **giant panda.** Pandas have shaggy coats with black-and-white markings and live in the bamboo forests of southern China. **2.** a small, reddish-brown animal that looks something like a raccoon; also called a **lesser panda**. It lives in the mountains of southern Asia.

pane [pān] *noun, plural* **panes.** a sheet of glass that is set into a door or window frame.

pan•el [pan′ əl] *noun, plural* **panels. 1.** a section of a wall or door that is different from the rest of the surface, as by being of a different material, design, or color: a wooden door with glass *panels.* ◆ A group of panels joined together is called **paneling. 2.** a board with dials and controls for operating something: an instrument *panel* in an airplane. **3.** a group of people who meet to talk about or judge something: On that radio show, people can get business advice from a *panel* of experts. —*verb,* **paneled, paneling.** to decorate or fit with panels: The walls of their family room are *paneled* with pine.

pang [pang] *noun, plural* **pangs.** a sudden, sharp pain or feeling inside: I ate a quick snack to get rid of my hunger *pangs.*

pan•ic [pan′ ik] *noun, plural* **panics.** a sudden feeling of great fear that makes a person or an animal want to get away quickly: When the theater caught fire, the crowd went into a *panic* and charged for the exits. —*verb,* **panicked, panicking.** to feel or cause panic: "If you are ever in real trouble, don't *panic.* Sit down and think about it." (Louise Fitzhugh) —**panicky,** *adjective.*

pan•o•ram•a [pan′ ə ram′ ə] *noun, plural* **panoramas.** a wide and complete view of an area: "In the distance is the *panorama* of a typical small Midwestern town, including a grain elevator, a railway station . . ." (William Inge) —**panoramic,** *adjective:* From the tower, we had a *panoramic* view of the Grand Canyon.

pan•sy [pan′ zē] *noun, plural* **pansies.** a small garden flower with five round petals that overlap each other.

pant [pant] *verb,* **panted, panting.** to breathe very hard and fast in short breaths: The runners were *panting* heavily after the race.

pan•ther [pan′ thər] *noun, plural* **panthers** or **panther.** a large, wild cat or leopard, especially one with a black coat.

pan•to•mime [pan′ tə mīm] *noun, plural* **pantomimes. 1.** the act or art of telling about something by moving the body, hands, and face without talking; silent acting. ◆ A person who does this is called a **mime. 2.** a show that is acted out with no talking. —*verb,* **pantomimed, pantomiming.** to show or act something out in pantomime: Early movies had no sound and the actors had to *pantomime* the story.

pan•try [pan′ trē] *noun, plural* **pantries.** a small room or closet for storing food, dishes, or other kitchen items.

pants [pants] *plural noun.* clothing for the lower half of the body from the waist to the ankles, divided to cover each leg separately; also called trousers or slacks.

pa•pa•ya [pə pī′ yə *or* pə pä′ yə] *noun, plural* **papayas.** a sweet yellowish fruit that looks and tastes like a melon. The papaya tree grows in tropical climates and looks like a palm tree.

pa•per [pā′ pər] *noun, plural* **papers. 1.** a material used for writing on and for printing books, magazines, and newspapers. Paper is usually made from wood, or from rags or grasses. It is also used in place of cloth for towels, napkins, tissues, and so on, and it has many other uses, as for making bags, packages, and cartons. **2.** a single piece or sheet of this material: She wrote her name on her test *paper.* **3.** a piece of paper with information on it: Dad bought the car, and the dealer is drawing up the *papers* now. **4.** a written report or other such assignment in school. **5.** short for NEWSPAPER. **6.** short for WALLPAPER. —*verb,* **papered, papering.** to cover with wallpaper: to *paper* a room.

pa•per•back [pā′ pər bak′] *noun, plural* **paperbacks.** a book that has a soft paper cover instead of a hard one. (The other kind is called a **hardcover** or **hardback.**)

panther Black panthers are actually jaguars or leopards in a dark color stage. This color helps conceal them from their prey.

Pronunciation Key: G–N

g	give; big	k	kind; cat; back
h	hold	l	let; ball
i	it; this	m	make; time
ī	ice; my	n	not; own
j	jet; gem; edge	ng	having

(Turn the page for more information.)

papier mâché [pā′ pər mə shā′] a mixture of shredded papers and glue that is used to make dolls, puppets, models, and other such things. Papier mâché is hard when it dries.

pap•ri•ka [pa prē′ kə] *noun, plural* **paprikas.** a reddish spice made from sweet red peppers, used in cooking to flavor and decorate foods.

pa•py•rus [pə pī′ rəs] *noun.* **1.** a tall water plant or reed that grows in swamps or near rivers in Europe and Africa. **2.** a very early form of paper that was made from this plant, used by the ancient Egyptians, Greeks, and Romans.

been called a tropical *paradise* because of its beautiful scenery and lovely weather.

par•a•dox [par′ ə däks′] *noun, plural* **paradoxes.** a statement or situation that contains two opposing ideas but in fact has some truth to it: A famous *paradox* of modern architecture is "less is more"—that is, a building with less decoration actually appears more artistic. —**paradoxical,** *adjective.*

par•af•fin [par′ ə fin] *noun.* a white substance like wax, made from petroleum. Paraffin is used in making candles and wax paper.

---

paragraphs There is nothing in the fundamental nature of English that requires the use of paragraphs. A book of 1000 pages could possibly be printed as a single paragraph. But paragraphs do help the reader to pick out key points, and they make the page easier on the eye by breaking up the text. To decide where to begin a new paragraph, an old-fashioned method is the best. Start with a TOPIC SENTENCE that gives the MAIN IDEA of the paragraph, then provide a series of sentences to explain more about this main idea. Then, break for a new paragraph as you introduce a new idea. Also, don't make paragraphs too long or too short. A paragraph that takes up 25 lines on a 30-line page does not create enough of a break on the page. A paragraph of only one or two lines does give you a break, and is fine, but if you have a series of these short paragraphs, your page may look ragged. Save the one-sentence or two-sentence paragraph for a significant or dramatic statement.

---

par [pär] *noun.* **1.** a fixed or stated amount: the *par* value of a share of stock. **2.** in golf, a fixed score that a player should be able to get on a hole if he hits each shot properly. **3.** a normal or usual condition: She hasn't been feeling up to *par* lately.

par•a•chute [par′ ə shoot′] *noun, plural* **parachutes.** a large piece of fabric shaped like an umbrella, which unfolds in midair to slow the fall of something dropping from a great height. A parachute allows people or packages dropped from an airplane to reach the ground safely. —*verb,* **parachuted, parachuting.** to drop down by parachute: The test pilot *parachuted* to safety just before his plane crashed.

pa•rade [pə rād′] *noun, plural* **parades. 1.** a public march or movement in honor of a person or a special event. In a parade, people, marching bands, vehicles, floats, and so on pass before a crowd along a certain route. **2.** any procession of a large group of people: There has been a *parade* of people in and out of the boss's office all day. —*verb,* **paraded, parading. 1.** to march in a parade. **2.** to display in a proud way; show off: She always *parades* her wealth by wearing very expensive clothes and jewelry.

par•a•dise [par′ ə dīs′] *noun.* **1.** another name for HEAVEN. **2.** a place or condition of perfect beauty or happiness: The island of Tahiti has

par•a•graph [par′ ə graf′] *noun, plural* **paragraphs.** one part of a piece of writing starting on a new line and usually set in, or INDENTED, from the other lines.

Par•a•guay [par′ ə gwā′] an inland country in central South America. *Capital:* Asunción. *Area:* 157,000 square miles. *Population:* 3,360,000. —**Paraguayan,** *adjective; noun.*

par•a•keet [par′ ə kēt′] *noun, plural* **parakeets.** a small bird that is a type of parrot, often kept as a pet. Parakeets have brightly-colored feathers and very long tails. They can be trained to repeat words and sounds that they hear.

par•al•lel [par′ ə lel] *adjective, adverb.* of two lines or paths, going in the same direction but always staying the same distance apart, without meeting or crossing: Railroad tracks have two *parallel* rails. "Then the grizzly moved off at a distance and walked *parallel* to him all the way." (John McPhee) —*noun, plural* **parallels. 1.** a parallel line or surface. **2.** a situation in which two things are closely connected: This article draws a *parallel* between the 55-mile-per-hour speed limit and the drop in highway accidents. **3.** imaginary lines parallel to the equator around the earth's surface, used to show degrees of LATITUDE: The countries of North and South Korea are divided by the 38th *Parallel.* —*verb,* **paralleled, paralleling. 1.** to lie

P

parallel structure In writing; the term *parallel structure* means that the different elements of a sentence match each other. "We had bad weather all week—rain, wind, and cloudy." This sentence is not parallel because there is a shift in part of speech. Did you spot it? The correct form could be, "We had rain, wind, and clouds" (all nouns) or it could be "It was rainy, windy, and cloudy" (all adjectives). The words in a list like this should have the same form. Parallel structure can also be a matter of style, as well as grammatical correctness. "We assure you: the work will be finished on time; you're going to be pleased with it; our price is surprisingly low." This would be smoother and stronger if the statements were parallel: ". . . we'll be finished on time; you'll be pleased with our work; you'll be surprised at our low price."

in a parallel direction. **2.** to have a close connection: The baseball careers of Willie Mays and Mickey Mantle *paralleled* each other—they came to the big leagues the same year, 1951.

par•al•lel•o•gram [par′ ə lel′ ə gram′] *noun, plural* **parallelograms.** a figure or shape that has four sides, with the two opposite sides running parallel to each other.

pa•ral•y•sis [pə′ ral′ ə sis] *noun,* the loss of feeling or movement in a part of the body, especially when this loss is complete and permanent. This is usually caused by damage to the nerves affecting that part of the body. ◆ A person whose lower body suffers from paralysis is a **paraplegic** [par′ ə plē′ jik].

par•a•lyze [par′ ə līz′] *verb,* paralyzed, paralyzing. **1.** to take away the power to feel or move a part of the body: Pro football player Darryl Stingley's arms and legs were *paralyzed* after he broke his neck in a game. **2.** to make unable to act or function; make helpless: A complete power failure *paralyzed* the city for several hours.

par•a•me•ci•um [par′ ə mē′ sē əm] *noun, plural* **parameciums** or **paramecia.** a very tiny water animal that can only be seen through a microscope. A paramecium is made up of only one cell with fine hairs called **cilia** [sil′ ē ə] that help it to swim and gather food.

par•a•med•ic [par′ ə med′ ik] *noun, plural* **paramedics.** a person who is trained to assist doctors or to give emergency medical treatment to people who have had an accident or suddenly become ill.

par•a•noid [par′ ə noid′] *noun, plural* **paranoids.** a person who has a strong, abnormal feeling that other people unfairly dislike him and want to cause him harm. ◆ Also used as an adjective.

par•a•pro•fes•sion•al [par′ ə prə fesh′ nəl] *noun, plural* **paraprofessionals.** a person who works with and helps professional workers, such as a teacher's assistant or a lawyer's aide.

par•a•site [par′ ə sīt′] *noun, plural* **parasites. 1.** a plant or animal that lives on or in a larger plant or animal, which is called the HOST. A parasite takes its food from the host and may cause disease or damage to it. Fleas, ticks, and tapeworms are parasites. **2.** a person who lives completely off another or others, without doing anything useful on his own.

par•a•sol [par′ ə sôl′] *noun, plural* **parasols.** a small, light umbrella used to protect against the sun.

par•a•troop•er [par′ ə trōō′ pər] *noun, plural* **paratroopers.** a soldier who is specially trained and equipped to parachute from an airplane into a battle area. ◆ Such soldiers are members of the **paratroops.**

par•cel [pär′ səl] *noun, plural* **parcels. 1.** something that is wrapped up; a package. ◆ The sending of such packages through the mail is called **parcel post. 2.** a piece of real estate: Mr. Bowers owns several *parcels* of land near the

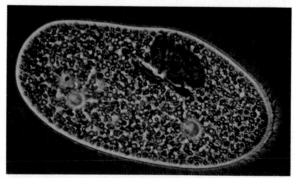

paramecium A microscopic view of a paramecium showing the hairlike *cilia* that help it move in water.

Pronunciation Key: O–S

ō	over; go	ou	out; town
ô	all; law	p	put; hop
oo	look; full	r	run; car
ōō	pool; who	s	set; miss
oi	oil; boy	sh	show

(Turn the page for more information.)

downtown area. —*verb*, **parceled**, **parceling**. (used with **out**) to divide or give out in parts: "Jem *parceled out* our roles: I was Mrs. Radley . . . Dill was old Mr. Radley." (Harper Lee)

parch [pärch] *verb*, **parched**, **parching**. to make or become very hot and dry: Her throat felt *parched* after her long drive in the desert sun.

P

![parchment page from a Hebrew Bible]

parchment A parchment page from a Hebrew Bible.

parch·ment [pärch′mənt] *noun*, *plural* **parchments**. **1.** sheep or goat skins that are specially prepared for writing on. College diplomas are often written on parchment. In earlier times, important documents such as the Magna Carta were written on parchment. **2.** a high-quality paper that is made to look like parchment.

par·don [pär′dən] *verb*, **pardoned**, **pardoning**. **1.** to free someone without punishment for a crime or offense: The Governor *pardoned* the prisoner because of new evidence that showed he wasn't guilty. **2. pardon me** or **I beg your pardon**. please excuse me: *Pardon me*, I didn't hear what you said. —*noun*, *plural* **pardons**. the act of pardoning: In 1974 President Ford granted Richard Nixon a *pardon* for any crimes he might have committed as President.

pare [pâr] *verb*, **pared**, **paring**. **1.** to cut or peel off the skin of a fruit or vegetable: to *pare* an apple. **2.** to cut down; reduce: The company has to *pare* down its travel expenses.

par·ent [pâr′ənt] *noun*, *plural* **parents**. **1.** a mother or father. ♦ **Parenthood** is the fact of being a parent. **2.** an animal or plant that produces another of its own kind. **3.** anything thought of as being like a father or mother: When a company owns several smaller companies it is called the *parent* company.

pa·ren·the·sis [pə ren′thə sis] *noun*, *plural* **parentheses** [pə ren′thə sēz]. one of a pair of curved lines ( ) used in writing. Parentheses are used to set apart a word or phrase within a sentence. For example: "The length of the race is 10,000 meters (about 6.2 miles)."

Par·is [par′is] the capital of France, on the Seine River. *Population:* 2,300,000.—**Parisian**, *adjective; noun.*

par·ish [par′ish] *noun*, *plural* **parishes**. an area served by one church and its priest or minister.

park [pärk] *noun*, *plural* **parks**. **1.** a special piece of public land set aside for people to use for rest and enjoyment. **2.** a large area of land that is left in its natural form for public use: Yellowstone National *Park* is famous for its beautiful scenery. —*verb*, **parked**, **parking**. to stop or leave a car or other vehicle for a time. —**parking**, *noun*. the act of parking a car, or the place for parking. ♦ Often used as an adjective: a *parking* lot, a *parking* meter.

par·ka [pär′kə] *noun*, *plural* **parkas**. a heavy fur or cloth jacket with a hood.

parka Famous polar explorer Robert Peary, wearing an Eskimo fur parka.

park·way [pärk′wā′] *noun*, *plural* **parkways**. a wide highway or street along which trees, bushes, and grass have been planted.

par·lia·ment [pär′lə mənt] *noun*, *plural* **parliaments**. **1.** a group of people who have been given the power to make the laws of a country. ♦ Something that has to do with a parliament is **parliamentary**. Meetings of a city council or a student government are conducted according to the rules of **parliamentary procedure. 2. Parliament**. the body of law makers that governs Great Britain. Parliament is made up of the House of Lords and the House of Commons.

par·lor [pär′lər] *noun*, *plural* **parlors**. **1.** a special room in a home where guests are entertained. Houses built in recent times do not have a separate room called a parlor. **2.** a room or building used for a certain type of business: a beauty *parlor*, an ice cream *parlor*.

pa•ro•chi•al [pə rō′ kē əl] *adjective.* having to do with a parish of the Catholic Church: a *parochial* school.

pa•role [pə rōl′] *noun, plural* **paroles.** the release of a person in prison before the full length of his sentence has been served. A person on parole must follow certain rules or be sent back to prison. —*verb,* **paroled, paroling.** to release a prisoner on parole.

par•rot [par′ ət] *noun, plural* **parrots.** a large bird with brightly-colored feathers, a short, hooked beak, and a long tail. Parrots can be taught to copy human speech and other sounds. —*verb,* **parroted, parroting.** to copy another person's words or actions exactly.

pars•ley [pärs′ lē] *noun.* a small green plant with many tiny, curly leaves. Parsley is often used to flavor foods such as soups or stews and to decorate other foods.

par•tial [pär′ shəl] *adjective.* **1.** not all; only a part; not complete: The photo was only big enough to show a *partial* view of the building. **2.** favoring one side over another; prejudiced: The umpire seemed to be *partial* to the home team and called all the close pitches in their favor. **3.** especially fond of or attracted to: to be *partial* to ice cream. —**partially,** *adverb:* The kick was *partially* blocked and landed in front of the goal posts.

par•tic•i•pate [pär tis′ ə pāt′] *verb,* **participated, participating.** to join with others in doing something; take part: Our teacher tries to get everybody to *participate* in class discussions. ♦ The fact of participating is **participation.**

par•ti•ci•ple [pär′ tə sip′ əl] *noun, plural* **participles.** in grammar, either of two verb forms used with other verbs to form certain tenses. The **present participle** of the verb is usually formed with the ending *-ing*. The **past participle** is usually formed with the ending *-ed*.

P

participles A common mistake in writing involves the *dangling participle*. It "dangles," or hangs, from the sentence, without referring clearly to anything. "Being the youngest of six children, Pam loved to play volleyball." What does the participle ("Being the youngest ") have to do with the rest of the sentence, with volleyball? Usually, when writers let a participle "dangle," it's because they have a connection in mind for it, but haven't made the connection clear on the page. Perhaps this writer knows that Pam's older brothers and sisters all played volleyball, and that they always included her in their games to make up a team. But the *reader* doesn't know that. (See also DANGLING PHRASES.)

pars•nip [pärs′ nip] *noun, plural* **parsnips.** a plant whose thick, white or yellow root is cooked and eaten as a vegetable.

par•son [pär′ sən] *noun, plural* **parsons.** a minister or other clergyman.

part [pärt] *noun, plural* **parts. 1.** something that belongs to a thing, but is not all of the thing: *Part* Two of the movie will be shown tomorrow night. **2.** one of the pieces that are put together to make up a whole thing: Headlights and spark plugs are *parts* of a car. **3.** a character acted by an actor in a play or movie. **4.** a line that is made in the hair, with some hair being combed to one side and the rest on the other. **5. take part.** to do something along with others: Sara *takes part* in soccer at her high school. —*verb,* **parted, parting. 1.** to come between; break up; separate: The speedboat *parted* the waters. **2.** to leave one another; go different ways; separate: "The two men *parted* at the door, shaking hands." (William F. Buckley) —*adjective.* not full or complete; partial. —*adverb.* in part; partly: A mule is *part* horse and *part* donkey.

par•ti•cle [pär′ ti kəl] *noun, plural* **particles.** a tiny piece or bit: *particles* of dust.

par•tic•u•lar [pər tik′ yə lər] *adjective, more/ most.* **1.** apart from others; being a certain one: You can buy a TV with stereo sound, but this *particular* set doesn't have it. "There were no special schools in Lawton Beach for his *particular* talents . . ." (E.L. Konigsburg) **2.** special; unusual: This book should be of *particular* interest to nature lovers. **3.** paying close attention to details: My uncle is very *particular* about food. —*noun, plural* **particulars.** a single or separate fact or detail. —**particularly,** *adverb.* especially: You'll enjoy that movie, *particularly* if you like action.

Pronunciation Key: T–Z			
t	ten; date	v	very; live
th	think	w	win; away
th	these	y	you
u	cut; butter	z	zoo; cause
ur	turn; bird	zh	measure

(Turn the page for more information.)

part•ing [pär′ting] *noun.* the act or fact of going away. ◆ Often used as an adjective: The President made a few *parting* remarks to the crowd before he got on the plane.

par•ti•san [part′i zən] *noun, plural* **partisans.** a person who strongly favors some cause or idea. ◆ Often used as an adjective: a *partisan* speech, *partisan* politics.

par•ti•tion [pär tish′ən] *noun, plural* **partitions.** a wall, panel, or screen that divides a space into smaller parts: The company set up *partitions* to divide a large open area into individual offices. —*verb,* **partitioned, partitioning. 1.** to separate by a wall, panel, or screen. **2.** to divide into parts or sections: The Louisiana Territory was purchased from France and later *partitioned* into states.

part•ly [pärt′lē] *adverb.* in part; not completely: *partly* cloudy weather.

part•ner [pärt′nər] *noun, plural* **partners. 1.** in business, someone who joins with another person or persons in running a company and who shares in the profits or losses of that company. **2.** a person who dances with another person. **3.** one of two people who play together on the same side in a game: Doubles is a form of tennis in which each player has a *partner.*

part•ner•ship [pärt′nər ship′] *noun, plural* **partnerships.** the fact of being a partner, or a business that is run by partners.

par•ty [pär′tē] *noun, plural* **parties. 1.** a gathering of a group of people to have a good time or to mark some special occasion: a birthday *party.* **2.** a group of people who act or work together in politics to try to win elections: the Republican or Democratic *Party.* **3.** any group of people who act together: A search *party* found the boy who was lost in the woods. **4.** any one person: With this phone, you can put your *party* on hold and talk to someone else.

pass [pas] *verb,* **passed, passing. 1.** to move beyond; go past: Cars on a highway are supposed to *pass* other cars on the left. **2.** to go from one place or condition to another; move: "The first ten minutes of breakfast *passed* in complete silence." (George Orwell) **3.** to complete some test or problem in an acceptable way: To get a driver's license, she had to *pass* a written exam and a road test. **4.** to vote in favor of; approve: The bill became a law after it was *passed* by the Senate. **5.** to hand or throw from one person to another: *Pass* me the butter. The soccer player *passed* the ball to her teammate. **6.** to use up or spend time: He got there early and *passed* the time reading a book.—*noun, plural* **passes. 1.** in sports, the act of throwing the ball from one player to another. **2.** a piece of paper that allows a person to do something or go past a certain point. **3.** an opening or gap to go through: Wagon trains used to cross the Rocky Mountains through the South *Pass.*

parts of speech This is a holdover from Latin, which has clearly-defined parts of speech. Latin is an *inflected* language—its words change meaning or serve as different parts of a sentence when their endings change. English is not an inflected language. In Latin, a noun can be placed after a verb in a simple sentence; the word endings make the thought clear. In English, words must be placed in a certain order; confusion occurs if they are out of order. To know the parts of speech in English is helpful because we can then correct or improve our language. You need to know that *nouns* or *pronouns* are used either as the subject of a sentence or the object of a *verb.* You need to know that *adjectives* modify nouns or pronouns, that *adverbs* modify verbs. You need to know that *conjunctions* join parts of a sentence, that *articles* go before nouns, and that *prepositions* show position.

part of speech one of the basic classes into which words are grouped according to how they are used. The parts of speech in English are noun, pronoun, verb, adjective, adverb, preposition, conjunction, and interjection.

par•tridge [pär′trij] *noun, plural* **partridges** or **partridge.** a bird that has a plump body and gray, white, and brown feathers.

part-time [pärt′ tīm′] *adjective; adverb.* for only part of the usual working day or week: Steve goes to college and has a *part-time* job in the evenings working as a waiter.

pas•sage [pas′ij] *noun, plural* **passages. 1.** a way of passing from one point to another; a way through: The water route above North America is called the Northwest *Passage.* **2.** the act of going forward; a movement or journey: "It (the ice) was really too thin for safe *passage.*" (John Jakes) **3.** the fact of passing: the *passage* of time. **4.** a small part of a written work or piece of music, presented by itself: In her speech she quoted *passages* from the Bible.

pas•sage•way [pas′ij wā′] *noun, plural* **passageways.** a way along which a person or thing can pass; a passage: The old castle had many secret *passageways* from one room to another.

pas•sen•ger [pas′ ən jər] *noun, plural* **passengers.** a person who gets a ride in a bus, train, airplane, or other such vehicle.

pass•ing [pas′ ing] *noun, plural* **passings. 1.** the act of going by or going past. **2. in passing.** while dealing with something else; incidentally: During his speech the mayor mentioned *in passing* that his son had just gotten married. —*adjective.* **1.** moving by; going by: Someone waved to me from the window of the *passing* train. **2.** for only a short time; brief: Dave had a *passing* interest in golf last year.

pas•sion [pash′ ən] *noun, plural* **passions. 1.** a very strong feeling: Love, hate, and anger are *passions.* **2.** a very strong liking: She has a *passion* for art and goes to the museum almost every weekend. —**passionate,** *adjective.*

words. a secret word or phrase that a person has to know in order to pass a guard, get into a special place, and so on.

past [past] *noun.* **1.** the time that has come before now; what has already happened: In the *past,* people did all their work by hand rather than with machines. **2.** the PAST TENSE. —*adjective.* **1.** in the time gone by; before now; earlier: We haven't had any rain for the *past* two months. **2.** of an earlier time; former: The U.S. Secret Service still protects *past* Presidents after they leave office. —*preposition.* beyond in place or amount: The dog ran *past* me and out the door. The bus usually gets here about five minutes *past* eight. —*adverb.* going by; beyond: Jed honked his horn at us as he drove *past.*

past•a [päs′ tə] *noun.* a food made by mixing flour and water into paste or dough. Spaghetti, macaroni, and noodles are types of pasta.

passive It's often said that when the active voice is used it tends to make the verb strong, and when the passive is used it tends to make the verb sound weak or wordy. Is that always the case? No. For example, here's a use of the passive. See if you think it's weak: "There was a terrible accident at the corner." "What happened?" "A man was killed." A weak passive is "The ball was hit by John." The active "John hit the ball" is stronger, clearer, and more direct. We use the passive when the thing receiving the action is the important part of the sentence: "I've been robbed!" Lincoln's Gettysburg Address says "Now we are engaged in a great civil war," not, "A great civil war engages us." We also use the passive when the thing that causes the action is not mentioned, or not known: "All men are created equal." Writers and readers of English can disagree on fine points. The publisher of this dictionary says, "Whenever possible, use present tense, active voice." The chief editor of this dictionary thinks that's good advice but overstated.

pas•sive [pas′ iv] *noun. (also,* **passive voice***)* in grammar, a verb form showing that something happens to the subject, rather than the subject causing it to happen. In the sentence, "Judy *was stung* by a bee," the verb is in the passive. —*adjective.* not acting or responding, especially at a time when one should act or is expected to act: "She is much too soft and *passive* for my liking and . . . gives in about everything." (Anne Frank) —**passively,** *adverb.*

Pass•o•ver [pas′ ō vər] *noun.* a Jewish holiday that celebrates the escape of Jews from slavery in Egypt in ancient times. Passover comes in the spring and lasts for eight days.

pass•port [pas′ port′] *noun, plural* **passports.** an official paper given to a person by the government of his or her country. It identifies the person as a citizen of the country and gives permission to travel to other countries.

pass•word [pas′ wurd′] *noun, plural* **pass-**

paste [pāst] *noun, plural* **pastes. 1.** a soft mixture that is used to stick paper and other things together, often made of flour and water. **2.** anything that is soft and sticky like this: tooth*paste,* a sauce made with tomato *paste, paste* wax for a car. —*verb,* **pasted, pasting.** to stick or fasten with paste: The children *pasted* down pictures for their art project.

pas•tel [pas tel′] *noun, plural* **pastels. 1.** a soft chalk used like a crayon for drawing pictures, or a picture drawn with these chalks. **2.** a soft, pale color such as pink or tan.

Pronunciation Key: [ə] Symbol

The [ə] or *schwa* sound occurs in syllables without an accent. It can be spelled with any vowel, such as **a** in above, **e** in listen, **i** in pencil, **o** in melon, **u** in circus. It can also be a combination of vowels, such as **io** in action, **ai** in mountain, **iou** in precious.

(Turn the page for more information.)

Louis Pasteur

Pas•teur [pas tŏŏr′] **Louis** [lŏŏ′ē], 1822–1895, French chemist who developed the process of pasteurization for milk.

pas•teur•ize [pas′ chə rīz′] *verb,* **pasteurized, pasteurizing.** to heat milk or another food hot enough to kill harmful germs that are present in it. Pasteurizing milk makes it safer to drink. ♦ This is called **pasteurization.**

pas•time [pas′ tīm′] *noun, plural* **pastimes.** a pleasant way of passing the time, such as a game, sport, or hobby: Baseball is often called America's national *pastime.*

pas•tor [pas′ tər] *noun, plural* **pastors.** a person who is in charge of a Christian church.

pas•try [pā′ strē] *noun, plural* **pastries. 1.** sweet, baked foods such as pies. **2.** the dough that is used to make the crusts of such foods.

past tense in grammar, a form of a verb showing something that happened in the past, or that existed in the past.

pas•ture [pas′ chər] *noun, plural* **pastures. 1.** a field or piece of land covered with plants that are eaten by farm animals such as cows, horses, and sheep. **2.** the grass and other growing plants that these animals feed on.

pat [pat] *verb,* **patted, patting. 1.** to touch or strike softly with an open hand; tap: She *patted* the dog's head. **2.** to shape or flatten by tapping lightly: "The ladies sat down. They shook their clothes and they *patted* their hair." (Eleanor Estes) —*noun, plural* **pats. 1.** a gentle stroke or tap. **2.** a small, flat piece of butter.

patch [pach] *noun, plural* **patches. 1.** a small piece of material used to cover a hole or rip in clothing: Suzie wore an old pair of blue jeans with *patches* on the knees. **2.** a piece of cloth or bandage put over a wound or injury for protection: an eye *patch.* **3.** a small area that is different from what is around it: There were still some *patches* of snow on the ground. —*verb,* **patched, patching. 1.** to put a patch on; mend. **2. patch up.** to make right; settle: to *patch up* a quarrel between two old friends.

patch•work [pach′ wurk′] *noun.* pieces of cloth of different sizes and colors that are sewn together, often in a pattern. Patchwork is often used on QUILTS.

pat•ent [pat′ ənt] *noun, plural* **patents.** an official paper given by a government to a person or company. The **patentholder** has the right to be the only one to make, use, or sell an invention for a certain number of years. —*verb,* **patented, patenting.** to get a patent for something: People can *patent* new machines, products, and ways of doing things.

patent leather a type of leather that has a very smooth, shiny surface. Patent leather is used to make shoes, belts, and purses.

pa•ter•nal [pə tur′ nəl] *adjective.* **1.** of or like a father: The boss takes a *paternal* attitude toward his young employees. **2.** related through the father's side of the family: Your father's mother is your *paternal* grandmother.

path [path] *noun, plural* **paths. 1.** a way or trail on which people or animals walk: He shoveled a *path* through the snow to the mailbox. **2.** a line along which something or someone moves; a route: He wasn't paying attention and almost stepped into the *path* of an oncoming car.

past tense This is the *simple past:* "She *washed* her hair last night." The *past progressive* tells about a past action that was interrupted: "She *was washing* her hair when suddenly the lights went off." The *past perfect* tells about one action that ended before another began: "She *had* always *used* Glitzo Shampoo, but then she switched to Sun Brite." In a story, you can choose whether you want to set it in the past or the present. The present tense can make the readers feel that the action is going on right in front of them: "The door is slightly open. She pushes it wide and walks slowly over to the desk. At the desk a small, middle-aged man sits, dressed in a dark blue suit. He's leaning back in the chair taking a nap. When she walks closer, she sees that his eyes are open wide, staring, unmoving."

pathetic The word *pathetic* originally had a strong meaning. Something *pathetic* caused a person to feel very sad, or to feel sorry for someone: "The firing stopped and the battlefield fell silent, except for the *pathetic* cries of the wounded." As is often the case with strong words that refer to horror, suffering, and so on, *pathetic* then came to take on a weaker meaning, that of "very bad, worthless": "He made one last *pathetic* attempt to fold the map correctly and then simply crumpled it up in a ball." Because there are many simpler ways to say "bad," we recommend you save *pathetic* for its stronger meaning. Use it to refer to things that cause great sorrow.

pa•thet•ic [pə thet′ ik] *adjective, more/most.* **1.** causing a very sad feeling; full of sorrow; pitiful: Watching the poor man look through the trash can for food was a *pathetic* sight. **2.** *Informal.* very bad or unsuccessful; worthless. —**pathetically,** *adverb:* "'No one ever listens to me,' he said *pathetically.*" (Anita Desai)

pa•tience [pā′ shəns] *noun.* the fact of being patient; the ability to deal calmly with trouble or delay: Sometimes when we get stuck in traffic, my dad loses his *patience* and starts yelling at the other drivers.

pa•tient [pā′ shənt] *adjective, more/most.* able to deal with delays and problems without immediately getting upset; willing to wait for something: That teacher is very *patient* with her students and doesn't mind going over the same thing several times. —*noun, plural* **patients.** a person who is staying in a hospital or is being treated by a doctor. —**patiently,** *adverb.*

pat•i•o [pat′ ē ō] *noun, plural* **patios. 1.** an outdoor space near a house that is usually paved with stone or tile and is used for cooking, eating, or relaxing. **2.** an inner yard or court that is open to the sky. Houses in Spain and Mexico are often built around patios.

pa•tri•ot [pā′ trē ət] *noun, plural* **patriots.** a person who loves his or her country and gives it loyal support. ◆ The feeling of someone who is a patriot is **patriotism.**

pa•tri•ot•ic [pā′ trē ät′ ik] *adjective, more/most.* showing or feeling love and support for one's country: The songwriter George M. Cohan became famous for *patriotic* tunes such as "It's a Grand Old Flag."

pa•trol [pə trōl′] *verb,* **patrolled, patrolling.** to go through or around an area to guard it and make sure there is no trouble: "Day and night they (cats) *patrolled* the barn keeping mice and rats from feed-bins." (Laura Ingalls Wilder) —*noun, plural* **patrols. 1.** the act of patrolling an area. A police car that does this is a **patrol car. 2.** a small group of soldiers, ships, or airplanes sent out to locate or find out about enemy forces. **3.** a small group of Boy Scouts.

pa•tron [pā′ trən] *noun, plural* **patrons. 1.** a person who regularly buys at a certain store or restaurant. **2.** someone who helps or supports a person, group, or cause: The wealthy Italian nobleman Lorenzo de Medici was a *patron* of the artists Michelangelo and Botticelli. **3. patron saint.** a saint who is believed to give special protection to a certain person or place: St. Andrew is the *patron saint* of Scotland. ◆ The fact of being a patron is **patronage.**

pat•tern [pat′ ərn] *noun, plural* **patterns. 1.** the way in which colors, shapes, or lines are arranged; a design: The board in checkers has a *pattern* of red and black squares. **2.** a guide or model that is to be followed in making something: a dress *pattern.* **3.** a set of actions or conditions that continue or are repeated: The police think the same person is behind all the robberies because they follow a certain *pattern.* —*verb,* **patterned, patterning.** to make according to a pattern; follow a model: "The examinations were *patterned* after regular classroom sessions." (John Jakes)

Paul [pôl] **Saint,** died in about 67 A.D., one of the disciples of Jesus and an early Christian missionary.

pause [pôz] *verb,* **paused, pausing.** to stop for a short time and then continue; stop in the middle of something: "He *paused* to collect his thoughts . . ." (William L. Shirer) —*noun, plural* **pauses.** a short stop or rest.

pave [pāv] *verb,* **paved, paving. 1.** to cover a street, walk, or other such place with a hard, level surface: The sidewalk was *paved* with concrete. **2. pave the way.** to go before something and prepare the way; make it easier for something to happen.

P

Pronunciation Key: Accent Marks

[′] is the normal accent mark. It shows where the main stress falls on a word.
[′] is a secondary accent mark. It shows a lighter stress than the primary accent. For example:

tel • e • vis • ion [tel′ə vizh ′ən]
(Turn the page for more information.)

P

pave•ment [pāv′mənt] *noun, plural* **pavements.** **1.** a paved surface, such as a street, sidewalk, or parking lot. **2.** the concrete, stone, or other such material used for this.

pa•vil•ion [pə vil′yən] *noun, plural* **pavilions.** **1.** a large, fancy tent used for shows or parties. **2.** an open building with a roof and a raised wooden floor, used in a park or at a fair.

paw [pô] *noun, plural* **paws.** the foot of a four-footed animal that has claws or nails, such as a cat or dog. —*verb,* **pawed, pawing.** **1.** to strike or touch with a paw or foot. **2.** to handle something in a rough or awkward way.

pawn[1] [pôn] *verb,* **pawned, pawning.** to leave something valuable with a person in order to get a loan: to *pawn* a watch. ♦ A person whose business is loaning money in this way is a **pawnbroker.**

pawn[2] *noun, plural* **pawns.** **1.** in the game of chess, the least valuable piece. **2.** a person used unfairly by someone else to gain an advantage.

pay [pā] *verb,* **paid, paying.** **1.** to give money to someone in return for something or for work done: to *pay* ten dollars for a shirt, to *pay* for a plane ticket. **2.** to give money to settle or take care of: to *pay* a phone bill. **3.** to be worth doing or having: Once he's made up his mind, it doesn't *pay* to argue with him. **4.** to have to put up with or suffer: ". . . until they stand before the bar of justice and *pay* the extreme penalty." (Lloyd Alexander) **5.** to do, say, or make some stated action: to *pay* attention in class, to *pay* a visit to a friend, to *pay* someone a compliment. —*noun.* money that is given for work or goods.

pay•ment [pā′mənt] *noun, plural* **payments.** **1.** the act of paying. **2.** the amount that is paid: The *payments* on his car loan are $165 a month.

pay•roll [pā′rōl′] *noun, plural* **payrolls.** a list of workers to be paid, and the amount of money to be paid.

pea [pē] *noun, plural* **peas.** a small, round, green seed that is eaten as a vegetable. Peas grow inside long green pods on a low-growing garden plant.

peace [pēs] *noun.* **1.** a time in which fighting is not going on; the state of being free from war. **2.** a time when things are quiet and calm; freedom from trouble or disorder: "One early summer Sunday, the sun over the churchyard sent its *peace* and warmth into the little house." (Meindert De Jong)

Peace Corps an agency of the United States government that sends volunteer workers to help poor people in foreign countries improve their living conditions.

peace•ful [pēs′fəl] *adjective, more/most.* **1.** in a state of peace; free from fighting or trouble; calm: Mark loves to hike alone through the woods because it's so quiet and *peaceful* there. **2.** not wanting to fight; not warlike: The Cherokee Indians were a *peaceful* tribe of farmers and traders. —**peacefully,** *adverb.*

peach [pēch] *noun, plural* **peaches.** **1.** a sweet, round, juicy fruit that has a smooth, fuzzy skin and a hard pit inside. Peach trees are found in most areas of the world with a mild climate. **2.** a yellowish-pink color like the skin of a peach.

pea•cock [pē′käk′] *noun, plural* **peacocks** or **peacock.** the male of a large bird (the **peafowl**) that has brilliant green, blue, and gold tail feathers that spread out like a fan. The female of this bird is called a **peahen.**

peak [pēk] *noun, plural* **peaks.** **1.** the pointed top of a mountain or hill. **2.** a mountain, especially one that stands alone: Pike's *Peak* is a famous mountain in Colorado. **3.** any pointed top or end: The part of a baseball cap that sticks out in front is called a *peak.* **4.** the highest point: "The excitement . . . reached its *peak* the following Saturday." (Eleanor Estes)

peal [pēl] *noun, plural* **peals.** **1.** the loud ringing of a set of bells. **2.** any long, loud sound like this: "Their clever remarks sent her into merry *peals* of laughter." (Margaret Mitchell) —*verb,* **pealed, pealing.** to sound out in a peal; ring out.

peanut The peanut is not a nut; it is actually a member of the pea family.

pea•nut [pē′nut′] *noun, plural* **peanuts.** a plant seed that grows in pods that ripen underground. Peanuts look and taste like nuts and have many uses. They are eaten whole or ground to make peanut butter, and peanut oil is used in cooking.

peanut butter a soft creamy food that is used to make sandwiches and as a spread on crackers.

pear [pâr] *noun, plural* **pears.** a sweet, juicy fruit with a smooth yellowish skin. Pear trees are found in mild climates throughout the world.

pearl A pearl inside the shell of the oyster in which it was formed.

pearl [purl] *noun, plural* **pearls. 1.** a small, round gem that is formed inside the shell of a certain kind of oyster. Most pearls have a soft white or cream-colored shine. **2.** something that looks like or has the color of a pearl: She was wearing a *pearl*-gray silk blouse. **3.** something thought of as very special or valuable like a pearl: The great basketball player Earl Monroe was called "The *Pearl*" because of his fancy moves and passes. **—pearly,** *adjective.*

Pearl Harbor a naval base near Honolulu, Hawaii, where Japanese planes attacked U.S. forces on December 7th, 1941, to bring about America's entry into World War II.

peas•ant [pez′ ənt] *noun, plural* **peasants. 1.** in earlier times, one of a group of people in Europe who lived and worked on small farms. **2.** in modern countries, a farmer or farm worker who is poor and uneducated.

peat [pēt] *noun.* a kind of rich soil that is found in swampy areas. Peat is made up of decayed plants. It is used as fertilizer and as a fuel.

peb•ble [peb′ əl] *noun, plural* **pebbles.** a small stone that is smooth and round, especially one found in or near water.

pe•can [pi kän′ *or* pi kan′] *noun, plural* **pecans.** a small oval nut that grows on a tree. Pecans have a sweet taste and are used in cooking.

peck[1] [pek] *verb,* **pecked, pecking.** to strike or poke at something as a bird does with its beak: The chickens were *pecking* at some seeds on the ground. **—noun, plural** **pecks. 1.** a short stroke made by pecking. **2.** a light, quick kiss: a *peck* on the cheek.

peck[2] *noun, plural* **pecks. 1.** a unit of measure for grain, fruit, vegetables, and other dry things. A peck is equal to eight quarts, or one-fourth of a bushel. **2.** *Informal.* a great deal; a large amount: a *peck* of trouble.

pe•cu•liar [pi kyool′ yər] *adjective, more/most.* **1.** not as it should be or usually is; odd or strange: "Jamie laughed a *peculiar*, high clicking laugh which Eric had not heard before, which he did not like . . ." (James Baldwin) **2.** belonging only to one certain person or thing: Bengal tigers are *peculiar* to India.

pe•cu•li•ar•i•ty [pi kyool′ yar′ ə tē] *noun, plural* **peculiarities.** the fact of being odd or peculiar; something that is not normal: It is a *peculiarity* of the Manx cat that it has no tail.

ped•al [ped′ əl] *noun, plural* **pedals.** a lever that is worked or operated by the foot to control machinery. A bicycle is moved by pushing down on the pedals. Pedals are used to control the brakes or gas in a car. **—verb,** **pedaled, pedaling.** to work or use the pedals of something: to *pedal* a bicycle.

ped•dle [ped′ əl] *verb,* **peddled, peddling.** to carry small goods from place to place for sale: People often *peddle* fruit and other food in the streets of big cities. ♦ A person who sells things in this way is a **peddler.**

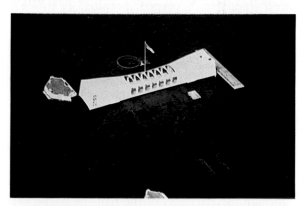

Pearl Harbor A monument to the American sailors who died at Pearl Harbor—below it can be seen the sunken wreckage of the battleship *Arizona.*

P

Pronunciation Key: A–F			
a	and; hat	ch	chew; such
ā	ate; stay	d	dog; lid
â	care; air	e	end; yet
ä	father; hot	ē	she; each
b	boy; cab	f	fun; off

(Turn the page for more information.)

ped•es•tal [ped′ is təl] *noun, plural* **pedestals.** **1.** the base on which a statue or column stands. **2.** any base on which something stands or is supported.

ped•es•tri•an [pə des′ trē ən] *noun, plural* **pedestrians.** a person who travels on foot; someone who walks on the street, as opposed to someone who is in a car, truck, bus, and so on.

pe•di•a•tri•cian [pē′ dē ə trish′ ən] *noun, plural* **pediatricians.** a doctor whose specialty is taking care of babies and children and dealing with illnesses of childhood. ♦ This branch of medicine is called **pediatrics** [pē′ dē at′ riks].

ped•i•gree [ped′ ə grē′] *noun, plural* **pedigrees.** a line of ancestors of a person or animal; a family tree: That horse's *pedigree* includes a winner of the Kentucky Derby.

peek [pēk] *verb,* **peeked, peeking.** to look quickly or secretly: Billy *peeked* into the box to see if his birthday present was inside. —*noun, plural* **peeks.** a quick or secret look.

peel [pēl] *noun, plural* **peels.** the skin or outer covering of certain fruits or vegetables: a lemon *peel,* a banana *peel.* —*verb,* **peeled, peeling. 1.** to remove the skin or outer covering from: to *peel* potatoes. **2.** to remove something in this way; strip off: Sharon *peeled* the address label from the magazine. **3.** to come off in pieces or thin strips: Skin was *peeling* off her shoulders where she had gotten sunburned.

peep¹ [pēp] *verb,* **peeped, peeping. 1.** to look quickly or secretly; peek: "Taylor went to the window and pulled back the curtain slightly and *peeped* out." (Richard Wright) **2.** to come partly into view; begin to be seen: "He saw the bright rim of the moon just *peeping* over the horizon." (James Thurber) —*noun, plural* **peeps.** a quick or secret look; a peek.

peep² *noun, plural* **peeps.** any little, high sound like those made by a young bird or chicken. —*verb,* **peeped, peeping.** to make such a sound.

peer¹ [pēr] *verb,* **peered, peering.** to look closely at something to see it clearly: "*Peering* through the darkness of the hall, he found the door he was looking for." (Woody Allen)

peer² *noun, plural* **peers. 1.** a person who has the same rank or quality as another; an equal: Babe Ruth had no *peers* among the baseball players of his time. **2.** a person who has a noble title, such as a duke. —**peerless,** *adjective.* having no peer or equal; very outstanding.

peg [peg] *noun, plural* **pegs.** a piece of wood or metal that fits into a surface. Pegs are used to fasten things together, hang things on, plug holes, and so on. —*verb,* **pegged, pegging.** to fasten or hold with pegs: The campers *pegged* the tent to hold it in place.

Pe•king [pē′ king′] the capital of the People's Republic of China. *Population:* 8,860,000. ♦ Also known as **Beijing** or **Peiping.**

Peking The Forbidden City in Peking, where at one time no Westerner was allowed to set foot.

pel•i•can [pel′ i kən] *noun, plural* **pelicans.** a large water bird with a long bill and webbed feet. The pelican has a large pouch under its lower bill that it uses for holding the fish it catches.

pel•let [pel′ it] *noun, plural* **pellets. 1.** a small ball made of some hard substance: Hail falls from the sky in *pellets* called hailstones. **2.** a bullet or piece of shot for a gun.

pelt¹ [pelt] *verb,* **pelted, pelting. 1.** to attack by throwing things at: The angry mob *pelted* the police with rocks and bottles. **2.** to hit or move against something heavily: The rain *pelted* down on the roof.

pelt² *noun, plural* **pelts.** the skin of an animal with the fur or hair still on it.

pen¹ [pen] *noun, plural* **pens.** a tool used for writing or drawing with ink.

pen² *noun, plural* **pens. 1.** a small, enclosed yard for cows, chickens, pigs, or other farm animals. **2.** any small enclosed area: a baby's play*pen.* —*verb,* **penned, penning.** to shut up animals in a pen.

pe•nal•ize [pen′ əl īz *or* pē′ nəl īz] *verb,* **penalized, penalizing.** to give a penalty to: In hockey, a player who trips someone is *penalized* by being kept off the ice for two minutes.

pen•al•ty [pen′ əl tē] *noun, plural* **penalties. 1.** a punishment for breaking a rule or law: Many states now allow the death *penalty* for the crime of murder. **2.** in sports, a disadvantage that is placed on a team or player for breaking the rules: a five-yard *penalty* in football.

P

pen·cil [pen′ səl] *noun, plural* **pencils.** a thin, pointed tool that is used for writing and drawing. Pencils are usually made of a stick of black or colored material inside a wood covering. —*verb,* **penciled, penciling.** to write, draw, or mark with a pencil: Mom *penciled* in the time of my piano lesson on the calendar.

pen·du·lum [pen′ jə ləm *or* pen′ də ləm] *noun, plural* **pendulums.** a weight that is hung from a fixed point so that it can swing back and forth. Some clocks have pendulums to control the movement of the parts.

pen·e·trate [pen′ ə trāt′] *verb,* **penetrated, penetrating. 1.** to go into or pass through: "Suddenly a dim light *penetrated* the darkness." (Walter Farley) "The roar of traffic *penetrated* the room." (John R. Tunis) **2.** to explore and learn about; understand: "For a whole hour I remained lost in these thoughts, trying to *penetrate* this mystery . . ." (Jules Verne)

penguin The male of the emperor penguin hatches the egg. He keeps the egg warm on top of his feet, covering it with his belly.

pen·guin [peng′ gwin] *noun, plural* **penguins.** a black-and-white sea bird with narrow wings like flippers. Penguins cannot fly but use their wings for swimming. They live in large colonies of thousands of birds, in Antarctica or other waters south of the equator.

pen·i·cil·lin [pen′ ə sil′ in] *noun.* a powerful medicine used to kill bacteria that cause diseases and infections. Penicillin is an ANTIBIOTIC made from a certain plant mold.

pen·in·su·la [pə nin′ sə lə] *noun, plural* **peninsulas.** a piece of land that is almost surrounded by water and is connected to a larger body of land. The state of Florida is a peninsula.

pen·i·ten·tia·ry [pen′ ə ten′ shər ē] *noun, plur-*

al **penitentiaries.** a federal or state prison for people who are found guilty of serious crimes.

pen·man·ship [pen′ mən ship′] *noun.* the act or art of writing by hand; handwriting.

pen name a name that an author uses in place of his or her real name. "Mark Twain" was the pen name of Samuel Langhorne Clemens.

pen·nant [pen′ ənt] *noun, plural* **pennants. 1.** a long, narrow flag that is shaped like a triangle. Pennants are used by ships for signaling and by sports teams as emblems or banners. **2.** in baseball and other sports, a banner given as an award for winning a championship.

Penn·syl·va·nia [pen′ səl vān′ yə] a state in the east-central U.S. *Capital:* Harrisburg. *Nickname:* "Keystone State." *Area:* 45,300 square miles. *Population:* 11,865,000.

pen·ny [pen′ ē] *noun, plural* **pennies. 1.** a coin of the United States or Canada that is worth one cent, or 1/100 of a dollar. **2.** a British coin worth 1/100 of a pound.

pen·sion [pen′ shən] *noun, plural* **pensions.** a sum of money that is paid regularly by a company to someone who used to work for the company but is now retired.

pen·ta·gon [pen′ tə gän′] *noun, plural* **pentagons. 1.** a figure that has five sides and five angles. **2. the Pentagon. a.** a five-sided building in Arlington, Virginia that is the headquarters of the U.S. Department of Defense. **b.** the Department of Defense itself, or U.S. military leaders in general: The *Pentagon* has asked for a larger budget this year.

pent·house [pent′ hous′] *noun, plural* **penthouses.** an apartment built on the top floor or roof of a building, usually more expensive to live in than other apartments in the building.

pe·o·ny [pē′ ə nē] *noun, plural* **peonies.** a garden plant with large pink, red, or white flowers.

peo·ple [pē′ pəl] *noun, plural* **people** or **peoples. 1.** men, women, and children; persons as a group: The Rose Bowl football stadium holds 100,000 *people.* **2.** all of the persons who form a certain nation, state, or other such place: "We the *People* of the United States . . ." **3.** the members of a certain group; persons who have

P

	Pronunciation Key: G–N		
g	give; big	k	kind; cat; back
h	hold	l	let; ball
i	it; this	m	make; time
ī	ice; my	n	not; own
j	jet; gem; edge	ng	having

(Turn the page for more information.)

something in common: rich *people*, young *people*. **4. the people.** persons in general, the average person: Abraham Lincoln was famous for saying, "You can't fool all of *the people* all the time." —*verb*, **peopled, peopling.** to fill with people; populate.

pep [pep] *noun.* the fact of being lively and having a lot of energy: The puppy was full of *pep* as it ran around the yard. —*verb*, **pepped, pepping.** to fill with energy: A quick run on a cold morning always *peps* me up.

pep•per [pep′ ər] *noun, plural* **peppers. 1.** a seasoning with a sharp, spicy taste that is widely used to flavor meat, vegetables, and other kinds of food. Pepper plants have small berries called **peppercorns** that are dried and then ground up into a powder. **2.** any of several garden plants with large, hollow fruits that are green, red, or yellow. Peppers are eaten as a vegetable or are used to flavor other foods. —*verb*, **peppered, peppering. 1.** to season food with pepper. **2.** to hit or shower with small things, as if putting pepper on food: "About this time her conversation became *peppered* with references to 'next term.'" (George Orwell)

pep•per•mint [pep′ ər mint′] *noun, plural* **peppermints. 1.** a small plant that belongs to the mint family. The oil from peppermint is used to flavor candy, chewing gum, and toothpaste. **2.** a candy that is flavored with peppermint oil.

per•cent [pər sent′] *noun.* (also spelled **per cent**) a certain number of parts out of 100 parts: Ten *percent* of one hundred is ten. The symbol for percent is **%**. A **percentile** [pər sen′ tīl] is a point on a scale of 100 that shows how many within a group are at or below that point.

per•cen•tage [pər sen′ tij] *noun, plural* **percentages. 1.** a part of the whole stated in hundreds; percent: The *percentage* of American homes with a TV set is about 98%. **2.** a part of some larger whole: Mr. Evans says that if I help him sell the Christmas trees, there'll be a *percentage* in it for me.

perch[1] [purch] *noun.* **1.** a bar or branch on which a bird can rest. **2.** any high place for sitting or standing: The climbers looked down toward the valley from their *perch* on the side of the mountain. —*verb*, **perched, perching. 1.** of a bird, to sit or rest on a perch. **2.** to place or sit high up: "Mrs. Murray was sitting *perched* on her high stool, writing away . . ." (Madeleine L'Engle)

perch[2] *noun, plural* **perches.** one of a large family of freshwater fish found in North America and Europe. The **yellow perch** is a small fish popular for fishing and for food. Other fish in this family include the pike and pickerel.

per•cus•sion [pər kush′ ən] a musical instrument that is played by striking or shaking it, such as a drum, cymbal, or xylophone.

perfect This is what is called an *absolute* word. When a pitcher pitches a *perfect* game, it doesn't just mean it was a very good game. It means that not one single player on the other team got on base in the entire game. Some statements don't mean literally perfect. "Clear Lake is the *perfect* vacation spot" or "The Dazzler is the *perfect* car for a big family." No one would pounce on those statements as bad English, but they are weak uses of *perfect*. Here's the question this dictionary raises again and again: If you misuse a word you might *lose* it!

per [pur] *preposition.* **1.** for each: The cost of renting the movie is $2.00 *per* day. The school is going to supply one computer *per* classroom. **2.** *Informal.* according to: He prepared the report *per* the boss's instructions.

per•ceive [pər sēv′] *verb,* **perceived, perceiving. 1.** to become aware of through the senses; see, hear, taste, smell, or feel: "While he was talking, he *perceived* a person standing at the window." (James Boswell) ◆ The act of perceiving something is **perception. 2.** to sense with the mind; understand; realize: "Her mind struggled with the problem, while *perceiving* that there was no solution." (George Orwell) ◆ A person who is **perceptive** is quick to sense and understand things.

per•fect [pur′ fikt] *adjective, more/most.* **1.** that cannot be made better; having no faults or mistakes; exactly as it should be: A grade of 100% on a test is a *perfect* score. **2.** just as a person wishes or needs it to be; ideal; excellent: It was a *perfect* day for the beach—warm, clear, and sunny. **3.** *Informal.* total; complete: On plane trips he always likes to talk to the person next to him, even if it's a *perfect* stranger. **4.** having to do with the PERFECT TENSE. —[pər fekt′] *verb,* **perfected, perfecting.** to make perfect; remove errors or faults from.

per•fec•tion [pər fek′ shən] *noun.* **1.** the state of being perfect. **2.** the act or process of making something perfect: Polio became a much less dangerous disease after the *perfection* of a medicine to combat it. ◆ A person who seeks or expects perfection is a **perfectionist.**

per•fect•ly [pur′ fikt lē] *adverb.* **1.** in a perfect way: In gymnastics, someone who performs *perfectly* in an event gets a score of 10. **2.** very much; totally; completely: "Except for a little hair round the base of the skull, he was *perfectly* bald." (Christopher Isherwood)

perfect tense in grammar, a verb tense formed with "have" or "had" and another verb. It is used to show an action that began in the past, such as "Jack *had* already *left* when we got there," or "We *have lived* here for six years."

per•fo•rate [pur′ fə rāt′] *verb,* **perforated, perforating.** to make a hole or holes through. ◆ Usually used as an adjective: Paper that is *perforated* has many tiny holes along a line so that it can be easily torn off there.

per•form [pər fôrm′] *verb,* **performed, performing. 1.** to carry out a certain work or action; do: "Jubal . . . watched Mike attempt to *perform* a dive exactly as Dorcas had just *performed* it." (Robert Heinlein) **2.** to do something before the public, such as singing, acting, or dancing; put on a show of some kind. **3.** to work or operate in the proper way: a car that *performs* well on rough roads.

per•for•mance [pər fôr′ məns] *noun, plural* **performances. 1.** a play, musical program, or other such entertainment that is presented before an audience. **2.** the act of performing or doing something: His *performance* at work has improved since he was switched to a different department. **3.** the way that a machine performs or operates: Expensive sports cars have high-*performance* engines.

per•form•er [pər fôr′ mər] *noun, plural* **performers.** a person who performs or entertains in public, such as a singer, dancer, or actor.

per•fume [pur′ fyo͞om] *noun, plural* **perfumes. 1.** a specially-prepared liquid that has a sweet, pleasant smell, worn by women on the body or clothing. **2.** a sweet, pleasant smell; fragrance: "The familiar *perfumes* of wildflowers filled

Kunta's nostrils as he ran." (Alex Haley) —[pər fyo͞om′] *verb,* **perfumed, perfuming.** to fill with a sweet, fragrant odor: a *perfumed* handkerchief.

per•haps [pər haps′] *adverb.* it is possible; maybe: This story is by P.L. Travers—*perhaps* you've heard of her book *Mary Poppins.*

per•il [per′ əl] *noun, plural* **perils.** a serious chance of harm or loss; danger: "The *Perils* of Pauline" was an old movie series about a woman who was always escaping from danger. —**perilous,** *adjective:* ". . . for a *perilous* few minutes it was like being in a rowboat on a stormy sea." (Bernard Malamud) —**perilously,** *adverb.*

pe•rim•e•ter [pə rim′ ə tər] *noun, plural* **perimeters. 1.** the length of the boundary around a figure or area: the *perimeter* of a rectangle. **2.** the outer boundary of an area.

pe•ri•od [pir′ ē əd] *noun, plural* **periods. 1.** a mark [.] used in writing to show the end of a sentence. It is also used after numbers in a list or at the end of an ABBREVIATION. **2.** a certain part of a school day: lunch *period.* **3.** a certain time in history: the Civil War *period.* **4.** any amount or portion of time: Ice hockey is played in three *periods* of twenty minutes each.

---

periods The obvious use of a period is to end a sentence. Periods also have certain special uses, as in numbers ("It cost $2.50" "He hit .320 last year") and in abbreviations (Dr. Wilson, Mrs. Hayes, Kurt Vonnegut, Jr.). There's really no trick to ending a sentence with a period—as long as you don't get careless and forget to do it. A sentence that is a statement always ends with a period. "*Moon Patrol* is playing at the Star Cinema. It starts at 3:00." Sentences that are demands or appeals or questions end with other punctuation marks: "Stop!" "Help!" "Why?" A *direct question* takes a question mark, "Do you want to go see it?" But an *indirect question* takes a period: "Ask Kate if she wants to go."

---

pe•ri•od•ic [pir′ ē äd′ ik] *adjective.* happening over and over again, especially at regular times: This car is supposed to have *periodic* oil changes every 5,000 miles. —**periodically,** *adverb.*

pe•ri•od•i•cal [pir′ ē äd′ i kəl] *noun, plural* **periodicals.** a magazine or other publication that comes out at a regular time, usually once or twice a month. —*adjective.* **1.** having to do with a periodical. **2.** another word for PERIODIC.

Pronunciation Key: O–S			
ō	over; go	ou	out; town
ô	all; law	p	put; hop
o͝o	look; full	r	run; car
o͞o	pool; who	s	set; miss
oi	oil; boy	sh	show

(Turn the page for more information.)

P

periscope A U. S. Navy officer mans the periscope aboard a modern nuclear submarine.

per·i·scope [per′ ə skōp′] *noun, plural* **periscopes. 1.** a special device used in a submarine to see things above the surface of the water. Periscopes use mirrors to reflect an image down a tube to the eye of the viewer. **2.** any similar device used to see things that otherwise would be blocked from view.

per·ish [per′ ish] *verb,* **perished, perishing.** to lose one's life; die, especially in a violent or tragic way: "Our fathers (the Pilgrims) were Englishmen which came over this great ocean, and were ready to *perish* in this wilderness." (William Bradford)

per·ish·a·ble [per′ ish ə bəl] *adjective, more/ most.* of food, likely to spoil or decay rapidly: Meat, fish, milk, and bread are *perishable.* **—perishables,** *noun.*

per·ju·ry [pur′ jə rē] *noun, plural* **perjuries.** in law, the crime of telling a lie in court after swearing to tell the truth.

perk [purk] *verb,* **perked, perking.** (usually used with **up**) **1.** to pick up or lift quickly: The dog's ears *perked up* when he heard the family car turn into the driveway. **2.** to become more lively or cheerful: "Once we started eating, people would *perk up* and be jolly." (Jean Fritz) **—perky,** *adjective*: She's a happy, friendly person with a *perky* personality.

per·ma·nent [pur′ mə nənt] *adjective, more/ most.* lasting or meant to last for a long time without change; not temporary: Mailboxes along the street have to be attached to something *permanent* in the ground, such as a metal or wooden post. The U.N. Security Council has ten members who serve two-year terms and five *permanent* members. ◆ The fact of being permanent is **permanence. —***noun, plural* **permanents.** a treatment for the hair to produce a long-lasting curl. **—permanently,** *adverb.*

per·mis·sion [pər mish′ ən] *noun.* the fact of permitting; allowing a person to do something: People under a certain age cannot get married without their parents' *permission.*

per·mit [pər mit′] *verb,* **permitted, permitting. 1.** to agree that a person may do something; let; allow: Our town does not *permit* people to let their dogs run loose in the street. **2.** to make possible; allow to happen: The picnic will be held Saturday, weather *permitting.* **—**[pur′ mit] *noun, plural* **permits.** a written statement from some authority allowing something: a fishing *permit.* Dale got a learner's *permit* to drive as soon as he was sixteen.

per·pen·dic·u·lar [pur′ pən dik′ yə lər] *adjective.* **1.** straight up and down: the *perpendicular* walls of a canyon. **2.** at a right angle to a line or surface: Trees usually grow *perpendicular* to the ground.

per·pet·u·al [pur pech′ ᴏᴏ əl] *adjective.* **1.** going on forever; never stopping; eternal: A *perpetual* motion machine would be one that could work forever without stopping or wearing out. **2.** happening over and over; going on for a very long time: ". . . a race whose people have waged *perpetual* war for thousands of years." (Walter Farley) **—perpetually,** *adverb:* "She was *perpetually* telling him to do this and to do that." (Henry James)

per·plex [pər pleks′] *verb,* **perplexed, perplexing.** to make very confused or puzzled; bewilder: "The boy hearing his name, yet not sure where the sound of his father's voice came from, stood *perplexed* . . ." (John Toland)

per·se·cute [pur′ sə kyᴏᴏt′] *verb,* **persecuted, persecuting.** to treat a person or group in a way that is cruel or very unfair, especially over a long time: Members of the Mormon religion finally settled in Utah after they were *persecuted* in several other places. **—persecution,** *noun:* the *persecution* of the Jews by the Nazis.

Per·shing [pur′ shing] **John J.,** 1860–1948, American general, commander of the U.S. forces in World War I.

Persian Gulf [pur′ zhən] an inlet of the Arabian Sea between Iran and Arabia.

per·sim·mon [pər sim′ ən] *noun, plural* **persimmons.** a reddish-orange fruit that grows on a certain North American tree. Persimmons are very sour when green, but are sweet and soft when ripe.

per·sist [pər sist′] *verb,* **persisted, persisting. 1.** to continue doing something in spite of problems or difficulty: "He had *persisted* in his efforts to continue his education despite his father's opposition.'' (Sherley Anne Williams) **2.** to go on and on; continue: "Danny . . . tried to brush from his mind a thought that *persisted* in staying there. He had always dreamed of having a dog like this." (Jim Kjelgaard)

per·sis·tent [pər sis′tənt] *adjective, more/most.* **1.** continuing in a stubborn way; not giving up: "She knew that the kitten would try again, it being in the nature of cats to be unendingly *persistent.*" (Meindert DeJong) ♦ The fact of being persistent is **persistence. 2.** going on and on; lasting; enduring: a *persistent* backache. **—persistently,** *adverb.*

per·son [pur′sən] *noun, plural* **persons. 1.** a human being; a man, woman, or child. **2.** in language, a word showing either who is speaking (the **first person**), who is spoken to (the **second person**) or being spoken about (the **third person**). **3. in person.** physically there; present: He had to appear *in person* to pay the traffic fine, rather than sending the money by mail.

ality. **2.** personal qualities that are pleasing to others: In choosing people to be cheerleaders, she looks for someone who has a lot of *personality.* **3.** a person who is well-known: Barbara Walters is a famous TV news *personality.*

per·son·al·ly [pur′sən əl ē] *adverb.* **1.** by oneself rather than through someone else; in person; directly: "I will *personally* hand my letter to him when I see him again." (Judy Blume) **2.** as far as oneself is concerned; speaking for oneself: A lot of my friends watch that TV show, but *personally,* I think it's silly. **3.** in a personal way: "Hope you don't take her remarks too *personally.*" (John Jakes)

per·son·nel [pur′sə nel′] *noun.* **1.** all the people who work in a company or organization: With the Christmas season coming, the store will have to hire more sales *personnel.* **2.** the department of a company that handles matters having to do with personnel, such as hiring new workers or dealing with problems on the job.

person The *first person* is *I, me, we, us,* the one who is speaking. The *second person* is *you,* the one who is being spoken to. The *third person* is anyone being spoken about—*he, she, it, they, him, her, them.* All nouns and proper names use the third person. Of course, a writer may use either the first, second, or third person. In general, factual writing is best cast in the third person. School reports especially read better if you leave yourself out of the text. In fiction, writers use either the first or the third person. For student writers, we recommend the third person. The story will be more effective if you stand back from its locale and action. Even if the main character is based on yourself, use the third person: "*He* did such and such" or "*She* said so and so." But we have to admit that it's sometimes harder to write in the third person than in the first person.

per·son·al [pur′sən əl] *adjective, more/most.* **1.** having to do with only one person rather than with people in general; private: The company doesn't like it when people make a lot of *personal* phone calls during business hours. "I just can't tell some stranger all about my *personal* life." (Beth Henley) **2.** directed toward a certain person, especially in a way that is rude or prying: Instead of sticking to political issues, the candidate made a lot of *personal* remarks about his opponent's family. **3.** done in person: a *personal* appearance by a famous rock singer. **4.** having to do with the body: Things like soap, toothpaste, and deodorant are called *personal*-care products.

per·son·al computer a small computer meant to be used on its own by one person.

per·son·al·i·ty [pur′sən al′ə tē] *noun, plural* **personalities. 1.** the way a person acts; all the habits, feelings, and other such qualities that show what someone is like: He's well-liked by his classmates because he has a friendly *person-*

per·spec·tive [pər spek′tiv] *noun, plural* **perspectives. 1.** in art, a way of painting or drawing a picture so that things in the background seem to be farther away and harder to see, as they would be in a real-life view of the same scene. **2.** a certain way of thinking about or judging something; a point of view: To put the size of the state of Alaska in its proper *perspective,* it is larger than the next three biggest states put together.

per·spi·ra·tion [pur′spə rā′shən] *noun.* **1.** the moisture that is given off through the pores of the skin; sweat. **2.** the process of giving off this moisture.

Pronunciation Key: T–Z			
t	ten; date	v	very; live
th	think	w	win; away
th	these	y	you
u	cut; butter	z	zoo; cause
ur	turn; bird	zh	measure

(Turn the page for more information.)

P

per•spire [pər spīr/] *verb,* **perspired, perspiring.** to give off perspiration; sweat.

per•suade [pər swād/] *verb,* **persuaded, persuading.** to make a person do or believe something; win over; convince: "He tried to *persuade* his father to have nothing to do with the offer." (Upton Sinclair) ♦ The act or fact of persuading is **persuasion** [pər swā/ zhən].

per•tain [pər tān/] *verb,* **pertained, pertaining.** to be related to; have to do with: "Tillet was his own bookkeeper and examined every bill *pertaining* to the operation of Mont Royal." (John Jakes) ♦ Something that has to do with the matter at hand is **pertinent:** "She had the knack of sensing what was *pertinent* information and what was junk." (John D. MacDonald)

Peru The ancient ruins of Machu Picchu, Peru, once a walled Inca city.

Pe•ru [pə roō/] a country in western South America, on the Pacific between Ecuador and Bolivia. *Capital:* Lima. *Area:* 482,300 square miles. *Population:* 17,995,000. —**Peruvian,** *adjective; noun.*

per•vade [pər vād/] *verb,* **pervaded, pervading.** to go or spread throughout: "Like all seaside towns it was *pervaded* by the smell of fish." (Virginia Woolf) —**pervasive,** *adjective:* "At night the juke box music from the pavilion *pervaded* the cabin." (James Jones)

pe•so [pā/ sō] *noun, plural* **pesos.** a coin that is used in Mexico and other Spanish-speaking countries.

pes•si•mis•tic [pes/ ə mis/ tik] *adjective, more/ most.* expecting things to turn out badly; looking at the bad side of a situation rather than the good side. ♦ This kind of negative attitude is called **pessimism,** and a person who has it is a **pessimist:** Dad is a real *pessimist* about our car;

every time he hears it make a strange noise he thinks it's about to break down completely.

pest [pest] *noun, plural* **pests. 1.** an animal, insect, or plant that destroys crops or causes other damage: Mice and ants are common household *pests.* ♦ A chemical used to kill pests is a **pesticide. 2.** a person who is very annoying; a nuisance.

pes•ter [pes/ tər] *verb,* **pestered, pestering.** to bother or annoy: "I'd let him drive in, and *pester* him to let me drive back." (S.E. Hinton)

pet [pet] *noun, plural* **pets. 1.** a dog, cat, bird, fish or other tame animal that is kept by people as a companion or for amusement. **2.** a person who is treated with special kindness; a favorite: A student who seems to be very popular with the teacher may be called "teacher's *pet.*" —*adjective.* **1.** treated or kept as a pet: a *pet* monkey. **2.** best liked; favorite: The company put a lot of money into that building because it's the boss's *pet* project. —*verb,* **petted, petting.** to pat or touch in a kind and gentle way: She *petted* the puppy on the head.

pet•al [pet/ əl] *noun, plural* **petals.** one of the parts of a flower. The petals give the flower its special shape and bright color.

Pe•ter [pē/ tər] **Saint,** died in about 64 A.D., one of the disciples of Jesus, considered to be the first pope.

pe•ti•tion [pə tish/ ən] *noun, plural* **petitions.** a formal paper directed to the government or another authority, requesting that some action take place: All the people in our neighborhood signed a *petition* to the city council asking that a traffic light be put on the corner. —*verb,* **petitioned, petitioning.** to submit such a request.

Petrified Forest Petrified logs lie scattered on the ground in the Petrified Forest in Arizona.

pet•ri•fy [pet/ rə fī] *verb,* **petrified, petrifying. 1.** to become hard like stone over a very long period of time. ◆ Usually used as an adjective: *petrified* wood, the *Petrified* Forest in Arizona. **2.** to make or become unable to move, as if turned to stone: "Charlie climbed on to the bed and tried to calm the three old people who were still *petrified* with fear." (Roald Dahl)

pe·tro·le·um [pə trō′lē əm] *noun.* a thick, oily liquid that can burn easily, usually found underground. Petroleum is believed to have formed from plant or animal remains that were buried under rock for millions of years. It is used for making fuels such as gasoline, natural gas, kerosene, heating oil, and for many other industrial products.

pet·ti·coat [pet′ē kōt′] *noun, plural* **petticoats.** a type of skirt that is worn under another skirt or dress; a slip.

pet·ty [pet′ē] *adjective,* **pettier, pettiest. 1.** of little value; not important: I hate to eat lunch with her because she always has some *petty* complaint about the food. **2.** too concerned with details that are not important; narrow-minded. **3.** lower in rank: A *petty* officer in the Navy ranks below a regular officer.

pe·tu·nia [pə tōō′ nyə] *noun, plural* **petunias.** a garden plant that produces many brightly-colored flowers.

petunia A close-up of a brilliant purple blossom.

pew [pyōō] *noun, plural* **pews.** a long bench for people to sit on in church.

pew·ter [pyōō′ tər] *noun.* a gray metal that is a mixture of tin and other metals, usually lead and copper. Pewter was often used in early America for dishes, bowls, candlesticks, and other such articles.

phan·tom [fan′ təm] *noun, plural* **phantoms.** an image that appears to be real, but does not

actually exist: "The *phantom* deer arise/and all lost, wild America/Is burning in their eyes." (Stephen Vincent Benét)

phar·aoh [fâr′ ō *or* fā′ rō] *noun, plural* **pharoahs.** (also spelled **Pharoah**). the title given to the rulers of ancient Egypt.

phar·ma·cist [fär′ mə sist] *noun, plural* **pharmacists.** a person who is trained and licensed to prepare and sell medicines; a druggist.

phar·ma·cy [fär′ mə sē] *noun, plural* **pharmacies. 1.** a store where drugs and medicines are prepared and sold. **2.** the act or work of preparing drugs and medicines.

phase [fāz] *noun, plural* **phases. 1.** one stage of development for a person or thing: A caterpillar is a *phase* in the life of a butterfly. My brother is going through a *phase* where he sits in his room all day listening to rock music. **2.** any of the stages of the moon's cycle as viewed from earth, such as the full moon.

pheas·ant [fez′ ənt] *noun, plural* **pheasants.** a long-tailed bird with brightly-colored feathers. Pheasants are hunted for food or sport.

phe·nom·e·non [fə näm′ ə nän′] *noun, plural* **phenomenons** or **phenomena. 1.** any fact or event in nature that can be observed or studied, especially one that is unusual or interesting: "UFO's are back in the news, and it is high time we took a serious look at this *phenomenon*." (Woody Allen) **2.** someone or something that is very unusual or remarkable: "She became something of a local *phenomenon* in plantation society because it was believed she could not smile." (Alice Walker) —**phenomenal,** *adjective.* very unusual; amazing.

Phil·ip·pines [fil′ ə pēnz′] an Asian country made up of over 7,000 islands in the western Pacific north of Indonesia. *Capital:* Manila. *Area:* 115,000 square miles. *Population:* 51,995,000. —**Filipino,** *adjective; noun.*

phil·o·den·dron [fil′ ə den′ drən] *noun, plural* **philodendrons.** a climbing plant with shiny, heart-shaped leaves.

phi·los·o·pher [fi läs′ ə fər] *noun, plural* **philosophers. 1.** a person who has a great knowledge of philosophy or has studied questions of phi-

P

Pronunciation Key: [ə] Symbol

The [ə] or *schwa* sound occurs in syllables without an accent. It can be spelled with any vowel, such as **a** in above, **e** in listen, **i** in pencil, **o** in melon, **u** in circus. It can also be a combination of vowels, such as **io** in action, **ai** in mountain, **iou** in precious.

(Turn the page for more information.)

losophy. **2.** any person who thinks deeply or makes judgments about the nature of life: Will Rogers was called the "Cowboy *Philosopher*" because of his wise and funny comments.

phil·o·soph·i·cal [fil ə säf′ ə kəl] *adjective, more/most.* (*also,* **philosophic**) **1.** having to do with philosophy: St. Augustine's *City of God* is a famous *philosophical* work of the Middle Ages. **2.** dealing with problems in a calm, accepting way: a person who has a *philosophical* attitude toward life.

phil·o·so·phy [fi läs′ ə fē] *noun, plural* **philosophies. 1.** the study of the nature and meaning of life. Philosophy deals with such questions as how to think and learn, what is true or real, what is right and wrong, and how to judge art and beauty. **2.** such a system of thought followed by a particular person or group: The ideas in the Declaration of Independence were influenced by the *philosophy* of John Locke. **3.** any set of beliefs that determines how a person acts; a guide to living: Work hard and play hard—that's his *philosophy*.

Phoe·nix [fē′ niks] the capital of the state of Arizona. *Population:* 789,000.

phone [fōn] *noun, plural* **phones.** short for TELEPHONE. —*verb,* **phoned, phoning.** to call someone on the telephone.

pho·net·ics [fə net′ iks] *noun.* the study of the sounds people make when they speak and how these sounds are produced.

pho·ny [fō′ nē] *adjective,* **phonier, phoniest.** *Informal.* not real; false; fake: "Ben . . . sent a *phony* message to keep anyone from realizing that he had disappeared." (Robert Heinlein) —*noun, plural* **phonies.** a person or thing that is not genuine; a fake.

phos·pho·rus [fäs′ fər əs] *noun.* a chemical element that is found in several different forms. The basic form is a yellowish, waxy substitute that is very poisonous and glows in the dark. It will start to burn if left out in the air at ordinary temperatures. Another form of phosphorus is needed by plants and animals in order to grow.

pho·to [fō′ tō] *noun, plural* **photos.** a short word for PHOTOGRAPH.

pho·to·cop·y [fō′ tō käp′ ē] *noun, plural* **photocopies.** an exact copy of something written or printed on a page, made by a special photographic process. —*verb,* **photocopied, photocopying.** to make a photocopy of something. —**photocopier,** *noun.*

pho·to·graph [fō′ tə graf′] *noun, plural* **photographs.** a picture made with a camera. A photograph is produced when light rays enter the camera through a small opening and strike a piece of film that is sensitive to light. An image called a NEGATIVE appears on the film, and this is then treated with special chemicals to develop the photograph. —*verb,* **photographed, photographing.** to make a photograph of something. —**photographic,** *adjective.*

---

phonetic spelling Boxing manager Joe Jacobs was known for his colorful language. Once, when his fighter lost a very close decision, Jacobs shouted into the ring microphone, "We wuz robbed!" Another time, he left a sick bed to go to the World Series, only to have his team lose. His comment was, "I should of stood in bed." Actually, all of us say "was" to sound like "wuz," and "should have" to sound like "should of." *Wuz* and *of* are *phonetic spellings*, meaning they match the sound of the word. Jacobs' remarks were written this way to fit in with his misuse of grammar—"We was robbed" for "We were robbed" and "I should have stood [stayed] in bed." Professional writers use phonetic spellings to show that a certain character is not well schooled.

—**phonetic,** *adjective:* having to do with the sounds of speech: The *phonetic* symbol [ē] is used to show the "long e" sound of *me* or *eat*.

pho·nics [fän′ iks] *noun.* a way of teaching people to read by showing how the letters used in writing stand for certain speech sounds.

pho·no·graph [fō′ nə graf′] *noun, plural* **phonographs.** a device for playing records; also called a **record player.** A phonograph has a needle that picks up sound from the grooves of a record as it turns, and plays the sound through a loudspeaker or speakers.

pho·to·graph·er [fə täg′ rə fər] *noun, plural* **photographers.** a person who takes photographs, especially someone who does this as a job.

pho·to·graph·y [fə täg′ rə fē] *noun.* the art or work of taking photographs.

pho·to·syn·the·sis [fō′ tō sin′ thə sis] *noun.* the process by which green plants make food from the water and carbon dioxide they take in. These plants have a substance called CHLOROPHYLL that allows them to change the energy of sunlight into food.

phrases A phrase is less than a sentence, but more than a word. It's a group of words that go together, but that are not complete in meaning and therefore cannot act as a sentence. A common mistake in writing is to present a phrase as if it were a sentence: "After that, she didn't say a single word to me. For the rest of the year." This second "sentence" is really a phrase; it doesn't have a subject and verb. (It should be joined somehow to the previous sentence.) If someone asked you, "How much longer are you taking that music class?" and you answer, "For the rest of the year," it's not incorrect. The subject and verb are understood: "*I'm taking* it for the rest of the year." In general, though, each sentence must have its own subject and verb, unless it is a direct response to the sentence before.

P

phrase [frāz] *noun, plural* **phrases. 1.** a group of two or more words that go together to express an idea, but do not form a complete sentence. **2.** a short expression or saying that carries a certain meaning and is easily remembered; a slogan or motto: Presidents are often known by special *phrases* that describe their policies, such as Roosevelt's "New Deal" and Kennedy's "New Frontier." —*verb,* **phrased, phrasing.** to say or write something in a particular way: "Not a half-bad idea. I'd have to think how to *phrase* it though." (Louise Fitzhugh)

phys•i•cal [fiz′ i kəl] *adjective, more/most.* **1.** having to do with the body: Anybody who wants to play on the football team has to have a *physical* examination from the team doctor. **2.** having to do with solid, material things that can be seen, as opposed to thoughts or feelings: Carson McCullers wrote a famous story, "A Tree, A Rock, A Cloud"—all these things are *physical* objects. ♦ The **physical sciences** are those that deal with earth, matter, and the universe, such as physics, chemistry, and geology. —**physically,** *adverb:* "*Physically* he was quite different from the local people. He was taller, more muscular." (V.S. Naipaul)

physical education a school subject that has to do with sports, exercise, and other such physical activities.

phy•si•cian [fi zish′ ən] *noun, plural* **physicians.** a person who is trained and licensed to practice medicine; a doctor.

phys•ics [fiz′ iks′] *noun.* the science that studies matter and the forces in the universe that act on matter, such as motion, heat, light, sound, electricity, and magnetism. Physics includes the study of atoms, atomic particles, and nuclear energy. ♦ A person who is an expert in physics is a **physicist** [fiz′ ə sist].

pi [pī] *noun.* a number equal to about 3.14, which is obtained by dividing the distance around any circle by the distance across the circle. Pi is represented in mathematics by the Greek letter π.

pi•an•o [pē an′ ō] *noun, plural* **pianos.** a large musical instrument with a keyboard. A musical sound is made by pressing a key, which causes a felt-covered hammer to strike a certain metal string. ♦ A person who plays the piano is a **pianist** [pē′ ə nist].

Pi•cas•so [pi kä′ sō] **Pablo,** 1881–1973, Spanish painter.

Picasso Pablo Picasso in his studio.

pic•co•lo [pik′ ə lō] *noun, plural* **piccolos.** a small flute that produces sounds an octave higher than the regular flute.

pick[1] [pik] *verb,* **picked, picking. 1.** to take just one from a group; choose; select: *Pick* a card from the deck and I'll tell you what it is. **2.** to take up with the hands; gather: to *pick* flowers, to *pick* corn. **3.** to act on in a wrong or dishonest way: Someone *picked* his pocket in the subway and stole his money. "'I'm good at

P

picking locks, Kate,' he said. 'I used to be a burglar.'" (Nancy Willard) **4.** to play a guitar or other such instrument with the fingers. **5. pick a fight.** to start a fight or argument. **6. pick on.** to bother or make fun of; tease. —*noun, plural* **picks. 1.** something that is chosen from a group; a choice: Take your *pick* of any kind of candy you want. **2.** a small piece of plastic or other hard material used to play a guitar, banjo, or other such instrument.

pick² *noun, plural* **picks. 1.** a tool consisting of a curved bar sharpened at each end and attached to a long wooden handle; also called a **pickax.** A pick is used to break up hard ground, rocks, paved surfaces, and so on. **2.** any tool with a sharp point used to break up or poke at something: an ice *pick,* a tooth*pick.*

pick•pock•et [pik′ päk′ it] *noun, plural* **pickpockets.** a person who steals things by taking them out of someone's pocket.

pick•up [pik′ up′] *noun, plural* **pickups. 1.** the act of picking up something: There is no trash *pickup* today because of the holiday. **2.** a quick increase in speed: A diesel engine doesn't have as much *pickup* as a regular gas engine. **3.** a small truck with an open back for carrying light loads; also called a **pickup truck.**

pic•nic [pik′ nik] *noun, plural* **picnics. 1.** a meal in which food is taken along to a park or other outdoor place and eaten there. **2.** *Informal.* a very pleasant or easy task: "Trying to recover fifteen or twenty Sunday papers in a pitch-black hallway was no *picnic.*" (Russell Baker) —*verb,* **picknicked, picnicking.** to go on a picnic.

picturing a scene The British writer Raymond Chandler lived most of his life in Southern California. He wrote famous mystery stories such as *Farewell, My Lovely, Lady in the Lake,* and *The Big Sleep.* Two critics who admired Chandler's writing published a book of photographs called *Raymond Chandler's Los Angeles.* Since Chandler's books were fiction, how is it possible to publish photographs of the scenes in them? Because he describes places so well that readers can actually *picture* them. What are some "Chandler methods" *you* can use? (1) Give *exact* detail: "There were two hundred and eighty steps up to Cabrillo Street." (2) Use metaphor: ". . . at the edge a few unbeatable wild flowers hung on like naughty children that won't go to bed." (3) Describe shabby, little-known places in the same picturesque way as famous or beautiful ones: "1644 West 54th Place was a dried-out brown house with a dried-out brown lawn in front of it. There was a large bare patch around a tough looking palm tree."

pick•er•el [pik′ ər əl] *noun, plural* **pickerels** or **pickerel.** a freshwater fish that is often caught for food or sport. It has a long, thin body and a narrow, pointed head with many sharp teeth. The pickerel belongs to the pike family.

pick•et [pik′ it] *noun, plural* **pickets. 1.** a pointed stake or post driven into the ground. A group of these can be used to make up a **picket fence. 2.** a soldier or soldiers assigned to stand guard outside a camp or fort. **3.** a person who stands or marches back and forth outside a building to protest something. Pickets may be seen carrying signs outside a business where there is a strike going on, or in front of public buildings as a political protest. —*verb,* **picketed, picketing.** to stand or march as a picket: People often *picket* outside the White House to try to get the President to change some policy.

pick•le [pik′ əl] *noun, plural* **pickles.** any food, especially a cucumber, that has been preserved and flavored by keeping it in a mixture of salt water or vinegar for a time. —*verb,* **pickled, pickling.** to preserve food in this way. ♦ Usually used as an adjective: *pickled* beets.

pic•ture [pik′ chər] *noun, plural* **pictures. 1.** something that shows what a person or thing looks like; a drawing, painting, photograph or the like: A one-dollar bill has a *picture* of George Washington on it. **2.** what is seen on a television or movie screen: The *picture* is always fuzzy when I get Channel 13 on this set. **3.** a movie: In 1939 *Gone With the Wind* won the Academy Award for Best *Picture.* **4.** an image in the mind: The author Jack London gave a very realistic *picture* of the great San Francisco earthquake. —*verb,* **pictured, picturing. 1.** to make a picture of: Paintings of Jesus usually *picture* him as a tall, thin man with long hair. **2.** to form an image in the mind; imagine: "I had frequently *pictured* to myself what Margot would look like." (Christopher Isherwood) **3.** to give a picture of in words; describe.

pic•tur•esque [pik′ chə resk′] *adjective, more/ most.* like a picture, especially by being very beautiful, interesting, or artistic: "The beams were painted red or blue or black, according to the owner's taste, and this gave the houses a very *picturesque* look." (Mark Twain)

pie [pī] *noun, plural* **pies.** a food made up of a pastry crust and a filling of fruit, vegetables, or meat, usually baked in a shallow round pan.

piece [pēs] *noun, plural* **pieces. 1.** something that has been cut, broken, or otherwise taken off a larger thing: a *piece* of string, a *piece* of cake, a *piece* of glass. **2.** a single thing that is part of some larger group or is an example of the group: a *piece* of land, a *piece* of paper. **3.** one part of a set: He plays the drums in a six-*piece* band. This jigsaw puzzle has over 500 *pieces*. **4.** a single work in painting, music, writing, and so on. **5.** an example of something: Elaine's term paper was a fine *piece* of work. **6.** a coin: A quarter is a twenty-five cent *piece.* —*verb,* **pieced, piecing.** to join pieces together: Jack tried to *piece* together the broken coffee cup with glue.

pier A Pacific Ocean pier at Cayucos, on the California coast near Monterey.

pier [pēr] *noun, plural* **piers. 1.** a structure built out from the shore over the water and used as a boat dock or as a walkway. **2.** a large post or pillar used to hold up a bridge or a building.

pierce [pērs] *verb,* **pierced, piercing.** to go through or make a hole through something: "Just then a shaft of sunlight *pierced* the window of the stable." (Marguerite Henry) ♦ Often used as an adjective: "He had one of those very *piercing* whistles that are practically never in tune . . ." (J.D. Salinger)

Pierce [pērs] **Franklin,** 1804–1869, the four-teenth president of the United States, from 1853 to 1857.

pig [pig] *noun, plural* **pigs. 1.** a four-legged animal with a fat body, short legs, a broad nose, and a short curly tail; also called a hog or swine. Pigs are raised on farms to provide meats such as pork, sausage, and bacon, and for many other products such as lard and leath-er. **2.** *Slang.* a person who is thought to have

bad qualities that are connected with pigs, such as being dirty, eating too much, or being greedy and selfish.

pi•geon [pij′ ən] *noun, plural* **pigeons.** a common bird with short legs and a plump body. Various kinds of pigeons are found throughout the world. Pigeons and doves are actually the same type of bird, and the pigeon that is often seen in large cities is also called a **rock dove.**

pig•gy•back [pig′ ē bak] *adjective; adverb.* carried on a person's shoulders or back: The father carried his little boy *piggyback.*

piggy bank a small bank for children, often shaped like a pig, into which coins are put through a slot in the top.

pig•ment [pig′ mənt] *noun, plural* **pigments. 1.** a colored substance that is mixed with liquid to make dyes, inks, and paints. **2.** a natural coloring material in plants and animals: Chlorophyll is a *pigment* in plant cells that gives them a green color.

pig•tail [pig′ tāl′] *noun, plural* **pigtails.** hair that has been made into a braid or braids at the side or the back of the head.

pike [pīk] *noun, plural* **pike** or **pikes.** one of a family of long, thin freshwater fish with a large mouth and many sharp teeth. Pike are popular for game fishing and for food.

pike Pike hide behind logs and underwater plants to hunt other fish.

Pronunciation Key: A–F			
a	and; hat	ch	chew; such
ā	ate; stay	d	dog; lid
â	care; air	e	end; yet
ä	father; hot	ē	she; each
b	boy; cab	f	fun; off

(Turn the page for more information.)

P

pile¹ [pīl] *noun, plural* **piles. 1.** several or many things of the same kind lying on top of each other: a wood *pile*, a *pile* of old newspapers. **2.** an amount of some loose material arranged in a hill or mound: a sand *pile*. **3.** *Informal.* a large amount: He claims to have *piles* of money invested in the stock market. —*verb*, **piled, piling. 1.** to stack or heap so as to form a pile: "Both sides of the pavement were *piled* high with great banks of hard snow." (Eleanor Estes) **2.** to crowd together as if in a pile: "All three of us would *pile* on Lem's white mare and go for miles across the countryside." (S.E. Hinton)

pile² *noun, plural* **piles.** a heavy post of concrete, wood, or steel used to help hold up a bridge, pier, or building; also called a **piling.**

pile³ *noun, plural* **piles.** the soft thick fibers on the surface of a carpet or on materials such as VELVET.

Pilgrims "The First Thanksgiving at Plymouth, Massachusetts," a historic painting by Jenny A. Brownscombe. The Pilgrims were the first to celebrate the Thanksgiving holiday, in the Plymouth Colony in 1621.

pil•grim [pil′grim] *noun, plural* **pilgrims. 1.** a person who travels to a holy place for religious reasons: In the Middle Ages, many Christian *pilgrims* visited the Holy Land where Jesus lived. ♦ A journey of this kind is called a **pilgrimage:** All Muslims are supposed to make a *pilgrimage* to Mecca at least once in their lives. **2. Pilgrim.** one of the group of English settlers who traveled to Plymouth, Massachusetts, in 1620 to seek religious freedom.

pill [pil] *noun, plural* **pills.** medicine in the form of a small ball or tablet that is swallowed whole. Aspirin often comes in the form of pills.

pil•lar [pil′ər] *noun, plural* **pillars. 1.** an upright column that either holds up a building or stands by itself as a monument. **2.** a person who

is thought of as an important source of strength or support: "He and my father were the *pillars* of the family, highly successful in their respective professions." (Edmund Wilson)

pil•low [pil′ō] *noun, plural* **pillows.** a cushion made of feathers or other soft material, used as a support for the head while lying down. ♦ A **pillowcase** is a cloth cover for a pillow.

pi•lot [pī′lət] *noun, plural* **pilots. 1.** a person who flies an aircraft or spacecraft. **2.** a person who is specially trained to steer ships into and out of a harbor or in dangerous waters. —*verb*, **piloted, piloting.** to act as a pilot; steer or guide: Only someone with special training can *pilot* a jet aircraft. "She (the teacher) *piloted* the older ones through long division to fractions." (George Orwell)

pim•ple [pim′pəl] *noun, plural* **pimples.** a small reddened bump on the skin, often sore and having PUS inside.

pin [pin] *noun, plural* **pins. 1.** a very small, short length of metal with a point at one end and a flat head at the other. A pin is used to fasten pieces of cloth or paper together. **2.** any similar thing used to hold or fasten: a hair*pin*, a clothes*pin*. **3.** an ornament with a clasp for attaching it to clothing. **4.** in the game of bowling, one of the ten bottle-shaped wooden pieces to be knocked down by the ball. —*verb*, **pinned, pinning. 1.** to fasten or join together with a pin: She wore a flower *pinned* to her dress. **2.** to hold in one place: The wrestler won the match by *pinning* his opponent. "He was *pinned* to the spot now, by a steely look from his mother." (Penelope Lively)

pin•a•fore [pin′ə fôr′] *noun, plural* **pinafores.** a piece of clothing that is like an apron, worn by a girl or woman over a dress or alone as a sleeveless dress.

pinch [pinch] *verb*, **pinched, pinching. 1.** to press very tightly between the thumb and finger, or between hard surfaces: He *pinched* his little sister's arm, and now she has a black-and-blue mark there. **2.** to make tight or wrinkled: "His face was *pinched* with bitterness or illness." (John Cheever) —*noun, plural* **pinches. 1.** the act of squeezing hard on a person's skin. **2.** a very small amount of something, such as can be held between the thumb and finger: He added a *pinch* of salt to the soup. **3.** a time of sudden difficulty or trouble; an emergency: Don't throw away that old lantern—we can always use it in a *pinch* if the lights go out.

pinch hitter in baseball, a player who bats in place of another.

pine The ponderosa or Western yellow pine, with a close-up view of the needles and cone.

pine[1] [pīn] *noun, plural* **pines. 1.** any one of a large group of evergreen trees that bear CONES and have long, very thin leaves called needles. **2.** the wood of a pine tree.

pine[2] *verb,* **pined, pining.** to become weak or sick from sadness or from wanting something too much: Mom says that Sharon's just *pining* away since her boyfriend went off to college.

pine•ap•ple [pīn′ ap′ əl] *noun, plural* **pineapples.** the sweet, juicy fruit of a certain plant that grows in tropical climates. Pineapples have a tough brownish skin and stiff, pointed leaves on top. Many pineapples are grown in Hawaii.

pink [pingk] *noun, plural* **pinks. 1.** a pale red color. **2.** a garden plant bearing pink or white flowers with a sweet smell.

pin•point [pin′ point′] *verb,* **pinpointed, pinpointing.** to place or determine exactly: "The bear *pinpoints* in her mind the spot where the seal now rests." (Barry Lopez)

pint [pīnt] *noun, plural* **pints.** a unit of measure. A pint is equal to 16 ounces, or one-half quart. It equals 0.47 liters in the metric system.

pin•to [pin′ tō] *noun, plural* **pintos.** a horse with patches of white and other colors on its body.

pin•wheel [pin′ wēl] *noun, plural* **pinwheels.** a toy with paper or plastic blades fastened with a pin through the center. It spins when a person blows against it or the wind blows it.

pi•o•neer [pī′ ə nir′] *noun, plural* **pioneers. 1.** one of the first people to live in a new land, preparing the way for others: Daniel Boone was a famous *pioneer* who founded settlements on the Kentucky frontier in the late 1700's. **2.** a person who does something first and leads the way for others: Thomas Edison was a *pioneer* in the use of electricity. —*verb,* **pioneered, pioneering.** to act as a pioneer: The Apple Company *pioneered* in the sale of small and inexpensive computers.

pipe [pīp] *noun, plural* **pipes. 1.** a long, hollow tube used to carry water, steam, oil, and other liquids or gases from one place to another. Pipes carry water into and out of a house. **2.** a tube with a small bowl at one end, used to hold tobacco for smoking. **3.** the long, tube-shaped part of certain musical instruments, such as the organ. —*verb,* **piped, piping. 1.** to carry by a pipe or pipes: Oil is *piped* from Alaska to the lower forty-eight states. **2.** to play music or give a signal on a pipe: to *pipe* a tune on a bagpipe. **3.** to speak up or be heard: " 'Dusty Miller—let me hear your voice.' 'Here it is,' *piped* Dusty." (Esther Forbes)

pipeline The Alaska Pipeline snakes down a hill.

pipe•line [pīp′ līn′] *noun, plural* **pipelines. 1.** a series of connected pipes used to carry oil, water, gas, or the like over long distances. **2.** a direct way to get news or information: "Sylvia maintained an exclusive . . . *pipeline* to sources that no correspondent had succeeded in reaching." (Erskine Caldwell)

pi•ra•nha [pə rän′ ə] *noun, plural* **piranhas** or **piranha.** a fierce fish of the Amazon River that has very sharp teeth. Piranhas are small but swim in huge groups to attack their prey.

P

Pronunciation Key: G–N			
g	give; big	k	kind; cat; back
h	hold	l	let; ball
i	it; this	m	make; time
ī	ice; my	n	not; own
j	jet; gem; edge	ng	having
(Turn the page for more information.)			

pirate N.C. Wyeth's cover painting for Robert Louis Stevenson's classic pirate book, *Treasure Island*.

pi•rate [pī′ rit] *noun, plural* **pirates. 1.** a person who attacks and robs a ship at sea. ♦ The crime of being a pirate is **piracy** [pī′ rə sē′]. **2.** any person who takes and uses the work or property of others in a way that is against the law: People sometimes rent a videotape of a movie and then make a *pirate* copy for their own use. —*verb,* **pirated, pirating.** to make copies of a movie, record album, computer program, or the like, and sell or use them illegally.

pis•til [pis′ təl] *noun, plural* **pistils.** the part of a flower where the seeds are produced.

pis•tol [pis′ təl] *noun, plural* **pistols.** a small gun that is held and fired in one hand; also called a **handgun.**

pis•ton [pis′ tən] *noun, plural* **pistons.** in a machine, a solid part that fits inside a hollow cylinder and moves back and forth by pressure, as from steam or from a liquid such as oil, or from a controlled explosion, as in a gasoline engine. The pistons in a car engine provide movement that is then transferred to the wheels to make them turn.

pit¹ [pit] *noun, plural* **pits. 1.** a hole in the ground, especially one made by digging something out: a sand *pit.* In open-*pit* mining, minerals are taken out from a large, open hole in the ground. **2.** a small hole or hollow in the surface of anything: The gravel on the road made *pits* in the paint of our car. —*verb,* **pitted, pitting. 1.** to make pits in something. **2.** to match one person or group against another: The boxer was *pitted* against the former champion.

pit² *noun, plural* **pits.** the hard seed in the middle of certain fruits, such as a peach or cherry.

pitch¹ [pich] *verb,* **pitched, pitching. 1.** in baseball, to throw the ball to the batter. **2.** to throw or toss anything in this way: *Pitching* horseshoes was once a very popular sport in the U.S. **3.** to fall roughly forward, or go roughly up and down: "The boat *pitched* so wildly that in one breath you could see the ship and in the next it had gone." (Scott O'Dell) **4.** to set up a camp or tent. **5.** to set at a certain level of sound: "The voice . . . was so low *pitched* that the crowd held its breath in order to hear." (Edna Ferber) **6. pitch in.** to start to work: "All the girls agreed to *pitch in* and help out." (Paul Zindel) —*noun, plural* **pitches. 1.** a throw by the pitcher in baseball. **2.** the level of a certain sound, in terms of how high or low it is: A singer who can sing each note exactly at the right level is said to have perfect *pitch.*

pitch² *noun, plural* **pitches.** a black, gummy substance made from tar, used to pave streets or to make things waterproof. —*adjective.* very dark or black, like pitch.

pitch•er¹ [pich′ ər] *noun, plural* **pitchers.** a container with a handle on the side and a lip for pouring liquids.

pitcher² *noun, plural* **pitchers.** in baseball, the player who throws the ball to the batter.

pitch•fork [pich′ fôrk′] *noun, plural* **pitch-forks.** a fork with a long handle that is used on farms to lift and throw hay or straw.

pit•fall [pit′ fôl′] *noun, plural* **pitfalls.** a hidden problem or danger: The test seems easy enough, but there are several *pitfalls* if you don't read the instructions carefully enough.

pit•i•ful [pit′ i fəl] *adjective, more/most.* **1.** causing a feeling of pity: "His voice cracked as he spoke, and I guessed he was thinking about sights too *pitiful* to put in words." (Jean Fritz) **2.** *Informal.* badly done; poor: The Dodgers lost today 14–0? That's really *pitiful.*

Pitts•burgh [pits′ burg′] a city in southwestern Pennsylvania. *Population:* 424,000.

pit•y [pit′ ē] *noun, plural* **pities. 1.** a feeling of being sorry about the unhappiness or suffering of another person: "This little lady, she took *pity* on me when I was practically starving." (William Inge) **2.** a cause for sorrow or regret: "Isn't it a *pity* I had to sell my lovely guitar?" (Eleanor Estes) —*verb,* **pitied, pitying.** to feel pity for someone.

piv•ot [piv′ ət] *noun, plural* **pivots.** a shaft or pin on which something turns: The needle of a compass rests on a *pivot* that allows it to move freely in order to point north. —*verb*, **pivoted, pivoting.** to turn around on or as if on a pivot: "Charles *pivoted* on the heel of his boot and ran." (John Jakes)

plac·id [plas′id] *adjective*, *more/most.* calm and quiet; peaceful: the *placid* surface of an empty lake at nightfall, a person with an easy-going, *placid* nature.

plagiarism If you copy a writer's work it's a crime called *plagiarism*. The law is clear. You cannot copyright a title. You cannot copyright an idea. You *can* copyright the text of a novel, even if another would have the same title. It's the *expression* of an idea that can be copyrighted, not the idea itself. Does that mean you cannot "quote" from a book? No. You can quote sentences, even paragraphs, as long as you identify the author. You can *paraphrase* a writer's essay, for example—using your words In place of his own here and there—as long as you do so briefly, and name the author whose work you are using.

piz·za [pēt′sə] *noun*, *plural* **pizzas.** a food made up of a thin baked crust covered with tomato sauce, cheese, and seasonings, often topped with other things, such as sausages, mushrooms, onions, and so on. Pizza was first made in Italy and is now a very popular food in the U.S. and other countries.

pla·gia·rize [plā′jə rīz] *verb*, **plagiarized, plagiarizing.** to copy and pass off as one's own the writing or words of another. ◆ The fact of doing this is called **plagiarism.**

plague [plāg] *noun*, *plural* **plagues. 1.** a very serious disease with a high fever and chills, spreading rapidly from one person to another.

placement If a certain phrase or clause is not correctly placed in the sentence, usually the problem is one of *distance:* it needs to be placed closer to the word or subject it relates to. "There's a meeting about playing a soccer game with Juniper School in the principal's office." The phrase *in the principal's office* is misplaced. "There's a meeting in the principal's office . . ." Now try this: "Juniper has new uniforms for their soccer players that are blue and gold." The clause "that are blue and gold" could refer to *soccer players*, but it actually refers to *uniforms*. You could edit this sentence in several ways. "Juniper has new blue-and gold uniforms for their soccer players." "Juniper's new soccer uniforms are blue and gold." "The Juniper soccer players have new blue-and-gold uniforms."

place [plās] *noun*, *plural* **places. 1.** a certain part of space; any point in space thought of by itself: The land is mostly woods, except for a few *places* where the trees were cleared away. **2.** a house, city, or other such location on the earth: People often say, "New York City is a great *place* to visit, but I wouldn't want to live there." **3.** a room, building, or other area used for a certain purpose: a fire*place,* a show*place.* **4.** a position for a certain person: Set another *place* at the table; Jim's staying for dinner. **5.** any position in time, space, rank, and so on: People use a bookmark to mark the *place* where they stopped reading. **6.** a name for a short street: My friend Jason lives at 37 Goodwin *Place.*
—*verb*, **placed, placing. 1.** to put something in a certain place or position. **2.** to identify something by connecting it with the proper facts, location, and so on: She looks familiar to me, but I just can't *place* her at the moment. ◆ The act or fact of placing is **placement:** Schools sometimes use *placement* tests to determine what class a student should be put in.

It is caused by a certain type of bacteria carried by fleas. In the Middle Ages this disease swept through Europe and Asia and killed millions of people. It is also known as **bubonic plague** [byōō′bän′ik] or the **Black Plague** or **Black Death. 2.** any quickly-spreading and dangerous disease; an epidemic: The Bible tells of Egypt being set upon by a *plague* of locusts. —*verb*, **plagued, plaguing.** to trouble or distress; cause to suffer: "I've been *plagued* with sore throats." (Tennessee Williams)

plaid [plad] *noun*, *plural* **plaids. 1.** a pattern of evenly-spaced squares formed by stripes of different colors that cross each other. **2.** any fabric having this pattern.

Pronunciation Key: O–S			
ō	over; go	ou	out; town
ô	all; law	p	put; hop
oo	look; full	r	run; car
o͞o	pool; who	s	set; miss
oi	oil; boy	sh	show

(Turn the page for more information.)

P

plain [plān] *adjective,* **plainer, plainest. 1.** easy to see, hear, or understand: I found the pen right away—it was out in *plain* sight, on the table. **2.** not fancy or elegant; without decoration: The Pilgrims of Massachusetts wore *plain,* dark clothing. **3.** not very good-looking; unattractive; homely. **4.** very direct in expressing thoughts and feelings; frank: A famous book of interviews with President Harry Truman was called *Plain Speaking.* **5.** with nothing else added; by itself: I'll have a *plain* hamburger, with no catsup or mustard. **—plainly,** *adverb:* "Now, take your time, and tell me *plainly* what you want." (Robert Louis Stevenson) **—***noun,* *plural* **plains.** a large area of land that is flat or nearly flat.

plain•tiff [plān′tif] *noun, plural* **plaintiffs.** in law, a person who brings a complaint to court in a lawsuit. If someone sues a company, that person is the plaintiff and the company is the DEFENDANT.

plan [plan] *noun, plural* **plans. 1.** a way or idea worked out ahead of time for what to do or how to do it: If you don't have any *plans* for tonight, why don't we go to a movie? **2.** a drawing or diagram showing how to make something or how something is arranged: the *plans* for a new house. ♦ A person who makes plans is a **planner. —***verb,* **planned, planning.** to think about or work out how to do something; make a plan: I got home at four, just as I *planned.*

plane¹ [plān] *noun, plural* **planes. 1.** any smooth, flat surface: *Plane* geometry deals only with flat surfaces, rather than solid objects. **2.** a level or grade of development: to keep a conversation on a high *plane* by talking only about serious subjects. **3.** a short word for AIRPLANE.

plane² *noun, plural* **planes.** a hand tool with a wide, sharp blade that is used to smooth away the rough parts of a wooden surface. **—***verb,* **planed, planing.** to use a plane on something: to *plane* a table top.

plan•et [plan′it] *noun, plural* **planets. 1.** one of the large round bodies that move in an orbit around the sun. The nine planets are Mercury, Venus, Earth, Mars, Jupiter, Saturn, Uranus, Neptune, and Pluto. **2.** any similar body in another solar system.

plan•e•tar•i•um [plan′ə tar′ē əm] *noun, plural* **planetariums.** a building with a domed ceiling on which the movements of the sun, planets, moon, stars, and other heavenly bodies are displayed, using special equipment.

plank [plangk] *noun, plural* **planks.** a long, heavy, flat piece of wood that has been sawed:

The workmen laid down *planks* for people to walk on while they were repairing the sidewalk.

plank•ton [plangk′tən] *noun.* the mass of very tiny plants and animals that float with the current on an ocean or lake. Many sea animals live by eating plankton.

plant [plant] *noun, plural* **plants. 1.** a living thing that is not an animal. Most plants can make their own food, which animals cannot. They normally stay in one place, while animals can move from place to place. **2.** a vegetable, flower, or other small form of plant life, as opposed to a larger tree or shrub. **3.** a building where something is made or manufactured; a factory: Books are produced in a printing *plant.* **—***verb,* **planted, planting. 1.** to set a plant or seed into the ground so that it can grow. **2.** to set very firmly in place: "Henry *planted* his elbows on the counter and shook his head." (John Gardner)

A COTTON PLANTATION ON THE MISSISSIPPI.

plantation *Cotton Plantation on the Mississippi,* a Currier and Ives print.

plan•ta•tion [plan tā′shən] *noun, plural* **plantations.** a large farm or estate where one crop is grown and the work is done by workers who live there. There were many plantations in the South before the Civil War.

plant•er [plan′tər] *noun, plural* **planters. 1.** a person or thing that plants. **2.** a person who owns or runs a plantation: George Washington was a *planter* in Virginia. **3.** a container in which decorative plants are grown.

plaque [plak] *noun, plural* **plaques. 1.** a flat board or piece of metal that has writing or designs on it. Plaques are often placed at a historic spot to give information, or given as an award for something. **2.** a thin film left by food on the surface of teeth. Plaque contains bacteria that can cause cavities.

plas•ma [plaz′mə] *noun.* the clear, almost colorless liquid part of the blood, in which red and white blood cells are suspended. Plasma is what makes the blood able to flow through the body.

plas•ter [plas′tər] *noun.* a mixture of lime, sand, and water that becomes hard as it dries. Plaster is used as a coating to protect or decorate walls and ceilings. —*verb*, **plastered, plastering. 1.** to cover a wall or ceiling with plaster. **2.** to cover closely, as if with plaster: "It was raining . . . his hair was *plastered* round his head like a cap." (Truman Capote)

plas•tic [plas′tik] *noun, plural* **plastics.** an artificial material that is soft and can be shaped when it is hot. When it cools, it becomes very hard. Many common items are made partly or completely of plastic. —*adjective*. **1.** made of plastic: a *plastic* toy, a *plastic* drinking cup. **2.** able to be molded or shaped: Sculpture is often called a *plastic* art, because it involves shaping things from stone, clay, or wood. **3.** *Informal.* not natural or real; fake.

plate [plāt] *noun, plural* **plates. 1.** a round, nearly flat dish from which food is eaten. **2.** one serving at a meal: The cost of the fund-raising dinner is $50 a *plate*. **3.** a thin, flat, smooth piece of metal or other such material: Battleships and tanks are protected by steel *plates*. **4.** a thin piece of metal that is stamped, printed, or engraved: a car license *plate*. Each person's office had a name *plate* on the door. **5.** one of the large sections into which the earth's crust is divided. **6.** knives, forks, serving dishes, or the like, coated with a thin layer of silver or gold. —*verb*, **plated, plating.** to cover with a thin layer of metal, such as gold or silver.

platform giving their positions on the issues.

plat•i•num [plat′ə nəm] *noun.* a valuable metal that looks like silver. Platinum is very heavy and is easily shaped. It is used to make jewelry, and in tools and machinery. Platinum is a chemical element.

Pla•to [plā′tō] 428?–348? B.C., Greek philosopher.

pla•toon [plə toon′] *noun, plural* **platoons.** a small group of soldiers under the command of a lieutenant. A platoon is part of a company and is made up of two or more squads.

plat•ter [plat′ər] *noun, plural* **platters.** a large plate for serving food, usually having an oval shape: a turkey *platter*.

plat•y•pus [plat′ə pəs] *noun, plural* **platypuses.** an animal that has a bill like a duck, webbed feet, a broad flat tail, and dark brown fur. They are unusual among mammals in that they lay eggs, rather than having their young born alive. They live along rivers in Australia.

play [plā] *verb*, **played, playing. 1.** to do something for fun; pass the time in an enjoyable way: The children *played* in the sand near the water. **2.** to take part in a certain sport or game: to *play* baseball, to *play* checkers. **3.** to act out a part on the stage, in a movie, and so on. **4.** to make music or sound: to *play* a tune on the piano. **5.** to handle or deal with something in a careless or wrong way: Children are often warned not to *play* with matches. **6.** to act in a certain way: to *play* a trick on someone. Let's *play* it safe and get there ahead of time.

plays Playwriting, like all other forms of writing, has special features and customs. In a play all the writing is in the form of speech—the characters talk, and in so doing bring out their attitudes, their desires, their hopes and fears. The audience learns about the past of the characters from what they themselves say. Sometimes this leads to forced dialogue, where a character states something the other person already knows, just to get this information to the audience: "CARL: 'You've been my trusted business partner for many years, Fred. We've been friends since college. Now, tell me . . .'" A good playwright avoids this sort of unnatural speech by having another character ask Carl, "How long have you known Fred, anyway?" This allows for a natural "background" on Fred.

pla•teau [pla tō′] *noun, plural* **plateaus.** a large, flat area of land that is higher than the land around it: The Columbia *Plateau* covers 100,000 square miles in the northwestern U.S.

plat•form [plat′fôrm] *noun, plural* **platforms. 1.** a floor or flat surface that is raised off the ground: The mayor stood on a *platform* as he spoke to the crowd. **2.** a statement of beliefs and policies: Before an election for President, the Democrats and Republicans each issue a

—*noun, plural* **plays. 1.** a way of having fun or enjoying oneself. **2.** a story that is acted out on

Pronunciation Key: T–Z

t	ten; date	v	very; live
th	think	w	win; away
th	these	y	you
u	cut; butter	z	zoo; cause
ur	turn; bird	zh	measure

(Turn the page for more information.)

stage, a drama. **3.** an action or movement in a game: The shortstop made a great *play* on the ground ball. **4.** a certain way of acting: a person who has a sense of fair *play*.

play•er [plā′ ər] *noun, plural* **players. 1.** a person who takes part in a game or sport: There are five *players* on a basketball team. **2.** a person who plays a musical instrument: a piano *player*. **3.** a machine that reproduces something that was recorded before: a tape *player*. **4.** an actor or actress: The *Player's* Club was a famous club for actors in the 1800's.

play•ful [plā′ fəl] *adjective, more/most.* **1.** wanting to play; full of fun: a *playful* puppy or kitten. **2.** not serious; joking: He gave his friend a *playful* punch on the arm, but he wasn't really mad at him. **—playfully,** *adverb.*

play•ground [plā′ ground′] *noun, plural* **playgrounds.** an outdoor area where children can play, usually having swings, slides, and other such equipment.

play•mate [plā′ māt′] *noun, plural* **playmates.** a child that another plays with; a friend.

play•pen [plā′ pen′] *noun, plural* **playpens.** a small folding pen with bars or netting on the sides, used to keep babies and very young children in one place while they are playing.

play•wright [plā′ rīt′] *noun, plural* **playwrights.** a person who writes plays.

plaza The Piazza San Marco, a plaza that is the historic center of Venice, Italy.

pla•za [plä′ zə *or* plaz′ ə] *noun, plural* **plazas.** a square or other open public area in a city.

plea [plē] *noun, plural* **pleas. 1.** a serious request for something; an appeal: The mayor made a *plea* to all citizens to save water during the long dry spell. **2.** in law, the answer that an accused person gives in court to the charges made against him: a *plea* of not guilty.

plead [plēd] *verb,* **pleaded** or **pled, pleading. 1.** to make a serious request; ask for something with deep feeling: " 'Please don't drive so fast,' Edna *pleaded*." (Paul Zindel) **2.** to respond to a charge in court: to *plead* guilty.

pleas•ant [plez′ ənt] *adjective, more/most.* **1.** that pleases the mind or senses; giving pleasure; enjoyable: We spent a *pleasant* day relaxing at the beach. **2.** having nice manners or behavior; friendly: Tommy's kindergarten teacher has a warm, *pleasant* manner. **—pleasantly,** *adverb.*

please [plēz] *verb,* **pleased, pleasing. 1.** to cause someone to feel good; give pleasure to: "I tried to *please* my father by bringing home good marks." (Anita Desai) **2.** to like or wish to do; prefer; choose: "You work hard, but you work as you *please*, and no man can tell you to go or come." (Laura Ingalls Wilder) ◆ Also used to ask a person politely to do something: "*Please* listen to what I have to say." (Jules Verne)

pleas•ing [plē′ zing] *adjective, more/most.* giving pleasure; pleasant: a person with a *pleasing* smile, wallpaper that has a *pleasing* combination of colors.

plea•sure [plezh′ ər] *noun, plural* **pleasures. 1.** a feeling of being happy or enjoying oneself; the feeling of liking something: "I have taken much *pleasure* in our walks and talks together." (Anthony Burgess) "It was a *pleasure* to me to be able to do something for you . . ." (Tennessee Williams) **2.** fun or enjoyment, as opposed to work: Was his trip to New York for business or for *pleasure*? ◆ Often used as an adjective: The harbor was filled with sailboats, speedboats, and other *pleasure* craft.

pleat [plēt] *noun, plural* **pleats.** a flat fold made in cloth by folding it over on itself and sewing or pressing it in place. **—pleated,** *adjective.* having pleats: a *pleated* skirt.

pled [pled] *verb.* a past form of **plead.**

pledge [plej] *noun, plural* **pledges. 1.** a serious promise or agreement that is meant to be kept: The *Pledge* of Allegiance to the American flag is a promise to be loyal to the United States. **2.** something valuable given to guarantee that a loan will be paid back. **—verb,** **pledged, pledging.** to make a pledge; promise: "President Carter has *pledged* himself to cutting down on government." (Art Buchwald)

plen•ti•ful [plen′ ti fəl] *adjective, more/most.* present in a full or large amount; more than enough; abundant: "The strawberries were so *plentiful,* you could stand in one spot and pick them by the handful." (Jean Fritz)

plen•ty [plen′tē] *noun.* as much or more than is needed; a full supply: "He believed in eating *plenty* of what we in Harlem called 'soul food.'" (Malcolm X)

pli•ers [plī′ərz] *plural noun.* a tool that looks somewhat like a pair of scissors, with two handles and two short grips that close tightly together. Pliers are used for holding, bending, or cutting things.

plod [pläd] *verb,* **plodded, plodding. 1.** to walk slowly and heavily: "The horses *plodded* across the prairie, mile on mile, mile on mile." (Edna Ferber) **2.** to do something slowly and with a lot of effort: He's not a quick learner—he just *plods* along with a lesson until he finally gets it. —**plodder,** *noun.*

plop [pläp] *verb,* **plopped, plopping.** to move or go with a flat, heavy sound: "Marsh *plopped* his books down on a chair." (Paul Zindel)

plot [plät] *noun, plural* **plots. 1.** a secret plan to do something, especially something bad or wrong: The Gunpowder *Plot* of 1605 was a plan by a group of English rebels to blow up the House of Parliament and kill the king. **2.** a small area or piece of ground: Grandpa grows tomatoes on a little *plot* behind the garage. **3.** the main story or action in a book, play, movie, or the like. —*verb,* **plotted, plotting. 1.** to make a secret plan or plot. **2.** to make a map, diagram, or chart of: The weather service *plotted* the path of the coming storm.

plow to work the soil or to move snow. **2.** to move along with a strong effort: ". . . the long column of ships *plowing* steadily across the English Channel behind him." (Cornelius Ryan) ◆ This word is also spelled **plough.**

plow American farms traditionally used a walking plow attached to a horse to prepare a field for planting; this work is now done by machinery

pluck [pluk] *verb,* **plucked, plucking. 1.** to pull or pick something off or out: "Birds' eggs freshly *plucked* from their nests . . ." (Jerzy Kosinski) **2.** to pull the feathers off a chicken or other such bird to prepare it for cooking. **3.** to grasp at; pull at: "She hurried through brambles that *plucked* at her skirt." (Lloyd Alexander) —*noun, plural* **plucks. 1.** the act of plucking at something; a pull or tug. **2.** courage; bravery.

---

plot The plot of a story is the series of events in the story, the line of action. It's been said that all stories about the Old West, in movies and books and on TV, show one of only four basic plots, each involving a struggle with a powerful outside force: outlaws (as in *High Noon, Hombre*); Indians *(Fort Apache, Stagecoach);* greedy landowners *(Shane);* lust for gold and other wealth *(Treasure of the Sierra Madre).* There may be more, but the point is that writers do not need to be wholly original in thinking up a plot. Take realistic characters and put them in a believable situation where they must deal with a problem. Then you have a story. It doesn't matter if the same basic plot has been used somewhere else—what counts is *telling* the story and *creating* characters. Use natural language; choose exact details; surprise the reader. All that will give an old plot new life!

---

plo•ver [pluv′ər *or* plō′vər] *noun, plural* **plovers.** a medium-sized bird that has a short, pointed bill, a short tail, and long, pointed wings. Plovers are usually brown or black above and white below. They live on beaches and other open areas near water.

plow [plou] *noun, plural* **plows. 1.** a large, heavy farm tool used for breaking up and turning the soil to prepare it for planting. **2.** something that works like a plow, especially a snowplow. —*verb,* **plowed, plowing. 1.** to use a

◆ A **plucky** person is one who shows a lot of courage: Emma Edmonds was a *plucky* young girl who became a spy during the Civil War.

Pronunciation Key: [ə] Symbol

The [ə] or *schwa* sound occurs in syllables without an accent. It can be spelled with any vowel, such as **a** in above, **e** in listen, **i** in pencil, **o** in melon, **u** in circus. It can also be a combination of vowels, such as **io** in action, **ai** in mountain, **iou** in precious.

(Turn the page for more information.)

P

plug [plug] *noun, plural* **plugs. 1.** a piece of wood, metal, or other material used to fill or cover a hole: A *plug* is used in a bathtub to keep the water from running out. **2.** a device attached to the end of an electric wire or cord, used to make an electrical connection. It has points sticking out that fit into similar holes in a SOCKET. **3.** the socket itself. —*verb,* **plugged, plugging. 1.** to fill or stop up: "They even *plugged* the keyhole and the cracks around the door with cotton and newspapers." (Eleanor Estes) **2.** to put the plug of an electrical device into an outlet. **3.** to work slowly but steadily: to *plug* away at a school assignment.

plum A plum tree with a detail of the fruit.

plum [plum] *noun, plural* **plums. 1.** a small, round, juicy fruit that grows on a small tree. Plums usually have a smooth purple or red skin. **2.** a dark reddish-purple color.

plum•age [ploo′mij] *noun.* a bird's feathers: The peacock has beautiful *plumage.*

plumb [plum] *noun, plural* **plumbs.** a small weight hung from the end of a string or rope, used to measure how deep something is or to see if something is straight up and down: The builder used a *plumb* to make sure the wall was straight. ♦ This is also called a **plumb bob,** and

the line is called a **plumb line.** —*verb,* **plumbed, plumbing.** to test or measure with a plumb.

plumb•er [plum′ər] *noun, plural* **plumbers.** a person whose work is putting in and repairing water pipes and fixtures.

plumb•ing [plum′ing] *noun.* the system of pipes and fixtures that brings water to a building and carries waste water away.

plume [ploom] *noun, plural* **plumes. 1.** a large, showy feather: A cockatoo has a bright yellow *plume* on top of its head. **2.** a feather or cluster of feathers worn for decoration: The Confederate general Jeb Stuart often wore a *plume* on his hat. **3.** something that looks like a feather: A *plume* of smoke drifted up from the fire.

plum•met [plum′it] *verb,* **plummeted, plummeting.** to drop or fall suddenly: "Suddenly the magpie *plummeted* from its perch . . ." (Meindert DeJong)

plump [plump] *adjective,* **plumper, plumpest.** having a full or round figure; fat in a pleasing or healthy way: a baby with *plump* arms and legs.

plun•der [plun′dər] *verb,* **plundered, plundering.** to steal goods or valuable things from a place; rob: Thieves *plundered* the tomb of King Tut of ancient Egypt and stole much of what was stored there. —*noun.* goods or valuables taken in this way; loot.

plunge [plunj] *verb,* **plunged, plunging. 1.** to go or move quickly and with force: "She *plunged* her arms and face, her whole head, into the icy water." (Ursula K. LeGuin) **2.** to make a sudden and complete change: "The room was *plunged* into darkness, total darkness." (Jules Verne) **3.** to begin something in a hurried or hasty way: "Uncle Jack *plunged* into another long tale about an old Prime Minister . . ." (Harper Lee) —*noun, plural* **plunges.** the act of plunging; a quick jump or movement.

plu•ral [ploor′əl] *noun, plural* **plurals.** the form of a word used to show more than one. The plural of "door" is "doors." —*adjective.* showing more than one.

plurals The normal way to form the plural in English is to add *s* to the end of the word. Words ending with the sounds [ch], [s], [sh], [x], or [z] add *es*: dish es, match es, box es. What is interesting is that some words don't follow the regular patterns. If a noun ends in a consonant plus *y* , it changes *y* to *i* and adds *es*: ten penn ies. Some nouns that end with *f* form the plural by changing *f* to *v* and adding *es:* autumn lea ves. Some words for animals use the same form for singular and plural: one deer, two deer. A few common words change the vowel sound in the middle: one foot, two feet/that man; those men. Finally, some nouns don't have any plural at all, because they describe ideas rather than things and can't be counted—*homework, courage, music, news, happiness, peace.*

plus [plus] *preposition.* **1.** added to; and: Four *plus* four is eight. **2.** *Informal.* along with; and also: I invited six boys from my class, *plus* my younger brother. —*adjective.* **1.** more than or higher than: A grade of 85 would be a B, and 89 is a B *plus.* **2.** greater than zero. —*noun, plural* **pluses.** a sign (+) showing that something is to be added; also called a **plus sign.**

plush [plush] *adjective,* **plusher, plushest.** very rich and impressive; luxurious: a lawn with a thick, *plush* growth of grass, a *plush* apartment building in the most expensive part of town.

Plu•to [ploo′tō] *noun.* **1.** the planet that is farthest from the sun. **2.** the ancient Greek god of the dead and of the underworld, a region below the earth.

plu•to•ni•um [ploo tō′nē əm] *noun.* a metal that is a chemical element. Plutonium is produced artificially for use in nuclear reactors and atomic weapons. It gives off large amounts of radiation and is very easily exploded.

ply•wood [plī′wood] *noun.* a strong board that is often used in building, made of several thin sheets of wood glued together.

P.M. or **p.m.** a way to show that a certain time is in the afternoon or evening. ♦ P.M. means from noon until midnight; A.M. means between midnight and noon.

pneu•mo•nia [nə mōn′yə *or* noo mōn′yə] *noun.* a serious disease of the lungs, usually caused by infection from bacteria or viruses. People with pneumonia may get a sore throat, a high fever, chest pains, and a dry cough.

pock•et [päk′it] *noun, plural* **pockets. 1.** a small bag sewn inside clothing, used to hold items such as money, keys, pens or pencils, and so on. **2.** any small compartment that is like this: Passenger airplanes have a *pocket* on the back of each seat to hold magazines and newspapers. **3.** a small area that is different from what is around it: The divers found an air *pocket* inside the sunken ship. —*adjective.*

small enough to fit inside a pocket, or meant for carrying in a pocket: a *pocket* watch, a *pocket* camera. —*verb,* **pocketed, pocketing.** to put something in a pocket: "He *pockets* the twenty dollars that is in the letter." (Ann Beattie)

pock•et•book [päk′it book′] *noun, plural* **pocketbooks.** a woman's bag used to carry small items such as a wallet, keys, a checkbook, a comb, and so on; a purse.

pock•et•knife [päk′it nīf′] *noun, plural* **pocketknives.** a small knife with one or more blades that fold up into the handle, so that it can be safely carried in a pocket.

pod [päd] *noun, plural* **pods.** a plant part that is a shell or case in which seeds grow. When it is ripe, a pod splits open and releases its seeds. Peas and beans grow inside pods.

Poe [pō] **Edgar Allan,** 1809–1849, American poet and short-story writer.

po•em [pō′əm] *noun, plural* **poems.** a form of writing that expresses ideas or feelings through the sound and rhythm of words, as well as through their meaning. A poem has shorter lines than ordinary writing, and each line ends at a certain place that is decided by the writer. In many poems, different lines have the same sound at the end and the same pattern of sounds within the line.

poems One of the hardest terms to define is *poem.* What do poems have in common? Many have different lines that end with the same sound. But others, such as Shakespeare's dramas, use *blank verse,* where the lines do not rhyme. They often have a regular pattern of sound, called METER, but many modern poems are written as *free verse,* with neither rhyme nor meter. Poems are usually short, compared to novels or stories. But Thomas Hardy's *The Dynasts* is hundreds of pages long. Almost all poems feature METAPHOR—the use of words in a way other than their ordinary meaning. Yet prose also uses metaphor. A definition of poetry is that it can be a song, a story, a play, almost anything at all—but it always is characterized by *intensity of word use.* Words are made to carry more subtle meanings and are made to create distinctive sounds. In a poem, words are concentrated and intricately arranged.

po•et [pō′it] *noun, plural* **poets.** a person who writes poems.

po•et•ic [pō et′ik] *adjective, more/most.* having to do with or like a poem: The haiku is a *poetic* form that is popular in Japan.

Pronunciation Key: Accent Marks

[′] is the normal accent mark. It shows where the main stress falls on a word.
[′] is a secondary accent mark. It shows a lighter stress than the primary accent. For example:

tel • e • vis • ion [tel′ə vizh′ən]
(Turn the page for more information.)

P

po•et•ry [pō′ ə trē] *noun.* **1.** the art or process of writing poems. **2.** poems as a part of literature: Great figures of English *poetry* include Chaucer, Shakespeare, and Milton. **3.** something thought of as very beautiful, like a poem: The ballet dancing of Mikhail Baryshnikov has been called pure *poetry*.

point•less [point′ ləs] *adjective, more/most.* without purpose or meaning; having no point: It's *pointless* to send in an entry for the contest now—the deadline was last Monday.

point of view the way a person looks at or judges things; a viewpoint.

point of view A writer's *point of view* is the way he or she chooses to look at a story, to observe what the characters are doing. A writer who uses the *personal point of view* acts as a character in the story and directly tells the readers what he sees, hears, and thinks. In Daniel Keyes' "Flowers for Algernon," we learn of the changes in Charlie's mind through Charlie's own comments. With the *single point of view*, the writer is not part of the story, but he still can see into the mind of one character. Writers use this when the key to the story is understanding the thoughts of one character, as in James Thurber's "The Secret Life of Walter Mitty." With the *general point of view*, the writer can see into the mind of more than one character. In Saki's "The Story-Teller," a man and a woman travel in a railway coach together; the story hinges on what they are thinking about each other. A writer who uses the *observer's point of view* doesn't look into anyone's mind. The reader must judge the characters' thoughts by the way they act and what they say. In O.Henry's "A Retrieved Reformation," the surprise ending of the story would be completely lost if the characters' thoughts were revealed.

poin•set•ti•a [poin set′ ə *or* poin set′ ē ə] *noun, plural* **poinsettias.** a plant with very bright-red leaves that look like flowers, surrounding tiny yellow buds that are the actual flowers. Poinsettias are popular Christmas decorations.

point [point] *noun, plural* **points. 1.** a sharp, thin end: the *point* of a pencil or a knife. **2.** a narrow piece of land that sticks out into the water: Montauk *Point* is at the end of Long Island. **3.** any particular area or spot of land: The South Pole is the *point* on earth that is farthest south. **4.** a dot, period, or other such mark used in writing. **5.** a certain time, position, or condition: The boiling *point* of water is 212° F. **6.** the main thought that explains the idea or purpose of something: The *point* of her article was that we need more parking spaces around the school. **7.** a single idea, fact, or characteristic: Spelling is one of his weak *points*. **8.** one unit of scoring in a game: A touchdown counts six *points*. —*verb,* **pointed, pointing. 1.** to show the way or indicate something: "The clock over the ticket office *pointed* to one forty-seven." (Kingsley Amis) **2.** to aim or turn in a certain direction: to *point* a gun.

point•er [poin′ tər] *noun, plural* **pointers. 1.** something used to point to things: Teachers sometimes use a *pointer* to show something on the blackboard. **2.** a hunting dog that is trained to show the position of game by standing very still and pointing the head toward it. **3.** a helpful piece of advice.

poise [poiz] *verb,* **poised, poising.** to balance or hold steady in one place: "His notebook was out and his pencil *poised*." (John Gregory Dunne) "The combined armies were *poised* for the final assault." (John Toland) —*noun.* **1.** a feeling of being calm and in control of oneself. **2.** the act of holding steady; balance.

poi•son [poi′ zən] *noun, plural* **poisons.** a substance that can kill or seriously harm a person, animal, or plant. Common chemical poisons include arsenic, lye, and lead. Poison is contained in the bite of many snakes and insects, and also in certain plants. —*verb,* **poisoned, poisoning. 1.** to cause injury or death with a poison. **2.** to add poison to: South American Indian tribes used to *poison* the tips of their arrows. **3.** to have a very bad influence: The play *Othello* tells of how Iago *poisons* Othello's mind by causing him to mistrust his wife.

poison ivy a North American plant that has shiny leaves made up of three leaflets. The oil of this plant can cause a severe, itchy skin rash when it is touched. ♦ Another form of the plant is called **poison oak.**

poi•son•ous [poi′ zən əs] *adjective, more/most.* containing poison; causing death or harm by poison: The copperhead is a *poisonous* snake.

poke [pōk] *verb,* **poked, poking. 1.** to push against with a pointed object; give a sharp blow: He *poked* holes in the paper with the point of a knife. **2.** to thrust or stick out: The turtle *poked* its head out of its shell. **3.** to move or act very slowly: The old truck was *poking* along in the right lane. **4. poke fun at.** to make jokes about; tease. —*noun, plural* **pokes.** a sharp, quick blow.

pok·er[1] [pō′kər] *noun, plural* **pokers.** a pointed metal rod used to stir up or tend a fire.

poker[2] *noun.* a card game in which players make bets that their cards have, or will have, a higher value than the other players' hands. The player with the best hand wins the money.

Po·land [pō′lənd] a country in north-central Europe, on the Baltic Sea. *Capital:* Warsaw. *Area:* 120,500 square miles. *Population:* 36,150,000. —**Polish,** *adjective; noun.*

po·lar [pō′lər] *adjective.* having to do with the North or South Pole: a *polar* expedition.

polar bear a large bear with heavy white fur. Polar bears live near the North Pole and in nearby northern regions.

polar bear

pole[1] [pōl] *noun, plural* **poles.** a long, slender rod or post of wood, metal, or another material: a fishing *pole,* a telephone *pole,* a flag*pole.*

pole[2] *noun, plural* **poles. 1.** the north or south end of the earth's AXIS. **2.** either of the two ends of a magnet where the opposite magnetic forces are the strongest.

pole vault a track-and-field sport in which a person jumps over a high bar by setting a long pole into the ground and using it to lift himself up over the bar.

po·lice [pə lēs′] *plural noun.* a group of people who work for the government to keep order, enforce the law, prevent crime, and arrest or charge people who are thought to have committed crimes. A member of a police force is called a **police officer, policeman,** or **policewoman.** —*verb,* **policed, policing.** to control or keep order with police: The downtown streets were heavily *policed* during the President's visit.

pol·i·cy[1] [päl′ə sē] *noun, plural* **policies.** a plan that guides the way something is done; a set of rules or ideas for action: The "New Deal" was Franklin D. Roosevelt's *policy* to end the Great Depression. That restaurant has a *policy* that no credit cards are accepted.

policy[2] *noun, plural* **policies.** a written agreement or contract between an insurance company and a person whose life or property is insured.

po·li·o [pō′lē ō] *noun.* a very serious disease of the nervous system that is easily spread from one person to another. It can cause damage to the muscles, PARALYSIS (being unable to move), and even death. It is most likely to occur in children, but a vaccine has been developed that has made polio quite rare today. ♦ Other names for the disease are **poliomyelitis** [pō′lē ō mī′ ə lī′ tis] and **infantile paralysis.**

po·lish [päl′ish] *verb,* **polished, polishing. 1.** to make something shiny and smooth, as by rubbing with a cloth or other such material: to *polish* a floor, to *polish* a pair of shoes. **2.** to make smooth or neat; work on to take out problems and rough spots: The Senator spent several hours *polishing* the speech he's giving tomorrow night. **3. polish off.** to finish completely: "He had swallowed the doughnut and also *polished off* the drink." (Alice Walker) —*noun, plural* **polishes. 1.** a hard, smooth, shiny surface. **2.** something used to produce such a surface: nail *polish,* furniture *polish.*

po·lite [pə līt′] *adjective,* **politer, politest.** having or showing good manners; acting toward other people in a nice and proper way: "Excuse me," "please," and "thank you" are *polite* ways of speaking. —**politely,** *adverb.* —**politeness,** *noun.*

po·li·ti·cal [pə lit′ ə kəl] *adjective, more/most.* **1.** having to do with politics; concerning the activities of government: The Republicans and Democrats are the two major *political* groups in the U.S. **2.** concerned with gaining power or advantage by influencing others: He only made the team because of *political* reasons—his father is a good friend of the coach. —**politically,** *adverb.*

P

Pronunciation Key: A–F

a	and; hat	ch	chew; such
ā	ate; stay	d	dog; lid
â	care; air	e	end; yet
ä	father; hot	ē	she; each
b	boy; cab	f	fun; off

(Turn the page for more information.)

politician The tone that a word carries can be positive (good), negative (bad), or neutral (neither good nor bad). The literal meaning of *politician* is neutral, "a person who takes part in politics." However, *politician* now can be an insult. If you said of someone in the business world, "Mr. X is a real *politician*," in theory it could mean he's good at sensing what people want and responding to it. But what it really means is that he has no strong beliefs of his own, that he wants to be on the popular side of issues, and that he tries to win favor with people in power. Because of the negative tone of *politician*, people in politics prefer *political leader*, which is neutral, or *statesman*, which is very positive. (Though it's been said that the definition of a *statesman* is any *politician* who's been out of office for twenty years.)

pol•i•ti•cian [päl′ ə tish′ ən] *noun, plural* **politicians. 1.** a person who is elected to public office or is running for office, such as a mayor, governor, or senator. **2.** any person who works for a political party or is involved in politics. **3.** a person who is skillful in dealing with other people in order to gain some advantage.

pol•i•tics [päl′ ə tiks] *noun.* **1.** the science or practice of holding public office or taking part in government. **2.** a person's attitudes or beliefs about government: My dad's *politics* are very conservative. **3.** competition for influence or power over other people: Mrs. Bailey opened her own business after she got tired of the office *politics* in her old job.

Polk [pōlk] **James K.,** 1795–1849, the eleventh president of the United States, from 1845 to 1849.

pol•ka [pōl′ kə *or* pō′ kə] *noun, plural* **polkas.** a lively folk dance that began in central Europe.

polka dot one of a pattern of dots that are evenly spaced and repeated.

poll [pōl] *noun, plural* **polls. 1.** the process of casting and counting votes in an election. **2.** *also,* **polls.** the place where votes are cast and counted: The *polls* were open from 8 A.M. to 8 P.M. on Election Day. **3.** a way of getting information about what a group of people think by asking certain questions. —*verb,* **polled, polling. 1.** to get information by using a poll: Auto makers often *poll* car buyers to find out what kind of car they prefer. **2.** to receive a certain number of votes in an election.

pol•len [päl′ ən] *noun.* in flowers, the fine yellow powder that contains the male part of the plant. These male cells join with the female cells of the same plant or a related one to produce seeds. ◆ This process is called **pollination** [päl′ ə nā′ shən]

pol•lute [pə lo͞ot′] *verb,* **polluted, polluting.** to put something into the air, a body of water, or an area of land that makes it dirty or harmful to living things: The air in cities can be *polluted* by car exhaust or by smoke from factories. ◆ Also used as an adjective: *polluted* air.

pol•lu•tion [pə lo͞o′ shən] *noun.* the act or fact of polluting: The famous "London fog" of the 1890's was actually not fog, but *pollution* in the city's air caused by smoke from coal fires. ◆ Something that pollutes is a **pollutant.**

po•lo [pō′ lō] *noun.* a game played on a large grassy field by two teams of riders on horseback. The players use long-handled mallets to try to knock a wooden ball into a goal.

Po•lo [pō′ lō] **Marco,** 1254–1324?, Italian traveler who wrote about his visits to China.

pol•y•es•ter [päl′ ē es′ tər] *noun.* an artificial fiber made from chemicals, often used for making clothes and fabric.

pol•y•gon [päl′ i gän′] *noun, plural* **polygons.** in mathematics, any figure that has three or more straight sides.

pol•yp [päl′ ip] *noun, plural* **polyps. 1.** a simple water animal that has a body shaped like a tube or cup with the open end forming a mouth. **2.** a growth in or on the body that is not normal.

pom•e•gra•nate [päm′ ə gran′ it] *noun, plural* **pomegranates.** a reddish fruit shaped like an apple, with many small seeds that are covered with a juicy pulp.

pom•pous [päm′ pəs] *adjective,* more/most. acting very proud and important; too serious and formal: The headwaiter in that fancy restaurant is known for the *pompous* way he deals with customers. —**pompously,** *adverb.*

pon•cho [pän′ chō] *noun, plural* **ponchos.** a loose type of clothing made of a large piece of material with a hole in the middle for the head to go through. Ponchos are worn over other clothes to keep a person warm or dry.

pond [pänd] *noun, plural* **ponds.** a small, shallow body of fresh water that is completely surrounded by land. Ponds may be formed by nature or dug by people, as on a farm.

pon•der [pän′dər] *verb,* **pondered, pondering.** to think about something very seriously: "There was a more serious problem. He lay in his bunk *pondering* upon it." (Stephen Crane)

po•ny [pō′ nē] *noun, plural* **ponies.** a type of horse that is small when fully grown. Ponies are usually under five feet tall at the shoulder.

pony express a system for delivering mail that was used between Missouri and California in 1860–61. The mail was carried by a series of riders who changed horses along the route.

po•ny•tail [pō′ nē tāl′] *noun, plural* **ponytails.** a hairstyle in which the hair is drawn back and fastened at the back of the head so that it hangs down like a horse's tail.

poodle

poo•dle [pōōd′ əl] *noun, plural* **poodles.** a dog with thick, curly hair, used as a hunting dog in Europe in earlier times.

pool¹ [pōōl] *noun, plural* **pools. 1.** *also,* **swimming pool.** a large tank of water for swimming and diving, either set into the ground or above it, also called a **swimming pool. 2.** a body of still water: Their garden has a small *pool* with goldfish and water lilies. **3.** a small amount of any liquid; a puddle: There was a *pool* of water on the floor below the refrigerator.

pool² *noun, plural* **pools. 1.** a game played with hard balls on a large table that has six holes called pockets. A player uses a long stick called a cue to hit one white ball (the cue ball) against the fifteen colored balls so that they drop into the pockets. **2.** an arrangement by which a group of people share work or effort: People in a car *pool* take turns driving. —*verb,* **pooled, pooling.** to put things together for common use; share: When we *pooled* our money, we had just enough to buy a large pizza.

poor [poor] *adjective,* **poorer, poorest. 1.** not having enough money to pay for things that are needed, such as decent food, clothing, or shelter. **2.** not as good or as much as is expected or needed; bad: D minus is a *poor* grade in school. **3.** worth feeling sorry for; needing pity or care: I hope they can rescue those *poor* miners who are trapped in the coal mine. —**poorly,** *adverb.*

pop¹ [päp] *verb,* **popped, popping. 1.** to make or cause to make a sudden, short sound: He *popped* the balloon with a pin. **2.** to go quickly up or out; move in a sudden way: "What he saw as he walked up to the display counter made his eyes *pop.*" (Peter DeVries) ". . . words that had *popped* into his head a second before he opened his mouth." (Sherley Anne Williams) —*noun, plural* **pops. 1.** a short, sharp sound: the *pop* of a cork being pulled from a bottle. **2.** short for SODA POP.

pop² *Informal.* short for POPULAR: *pop* music.

pop grammar A number of writers have campaigned to keep English "pure," such as Edwin Newman, Theodore Bernstein, John Simon, and William Safire. They complain about modern uses of words or phrases, and they argue that the language has seriously declined from a time, about 30 or 40 years ago, when people did use it carefully and precisely. They could be called *purists,* but their opponents call them *pop grammarians.* It's said that pop (popular) grammar is not a serious, accurate view of the language. Critics of pop grammar argue that these writers have not studied language history and thus are unaware that language change is natural, even useful. Though many dictionary makers oppose these purists, we support their efforts. We don't agree with those who say English is "falling apart," but concern over corrections makes people aware of misuse of the language. These writers *care* about the language. That alone is useful!

P

Pronunciation Key: G–N			
g	give; big	k	kind; cat; back
h	hold	l	let; ball
i	it; this	m	make; time
ī	ice; my	n	not; own
j	jet; gem; edge	ng	having
(Turn the page for more information.)			

pop•corn [päp′kôrn′] *noun.* a type of corn with kernels that pop open and become white and puffy when they are heated.

pope [pōp] *noun, plural* **popes.** (*also,* **Pope**) the head of the Catholic Church.

pop•lar [päp′lər] *noun, plural* **poplars.** a tall, thin tree that grows quickly and has pointed leaves. Poplar trees have light, soft wood.

poppy The colorful poppy is a favorite subject for artists.

pop•py [päp′ē] *noun, plural* **poppies.** a plant with large, round flowers that are usually red, yellow, or white. An illegal drug called OPIUM is made from one kind of poppy.

pop•u•lar [päp′yə lər] *adjective, more/most.* **1.** liked or enjoyed by many people: "The beach there is *popular* because it is public and because it is beautiful." (E.L. Konigsburg) **2.** having many friends; well-liked: "If she wants to remain *popular* she has to start thinking of other people's feelings." (John O'Hara) **3.** having to do with people in general; of or by the people: State governors in the U.S. are elected by a *popular* vote. **4.** accepted by many people; widespread; common: There is a *popular* belief that boys are better at math than girls.

pop•u•lar•i•ty [päp′yə lar′ə tē] *noun.* the fact or condition of being popular: At the height of his *popularity* in the 1950's, Elvis Presley had four different records in the top ten at once.

popular music music such as rock, country and western, jazz, or folk music, as opposed to CLASSICAL MUSIC that is written for ballets, operas, or symphony orchestras.

pop•u•late [päp′yə lāt] *verb,* **populated, populating. 1.** to live in a certain place; inhabit: The state of Minnesota is *populated* by many people whose families come from Norway or Sweden. **2.** to provide people for an area: Mormon pioneers *populated* the Salt Lake Valley.

pop•u•la•tion [päp′yə lā′shən] *noun, plural* **populations. 1.** the total number of people who live in a place, or all these people as a group: The *population* of New York City is about seven million. **2.** a particular group of people or animals: the bird *population* of an area.

pop•u•lous [päp′yə ləs] *adjective, more/most.* having many people; full of people.

por•ce•lain [pôr′slin *or* pôr′sə lin] *noun.* a very fine kind of china that is so thin that light can be seen through it. It is made by baking a special clay at high temperatures. Cups, dishes, and vases are made with porcelain.

porch [pôrch] *noun, plural* **porches.** a section that is attached to a house or other building, usually covered by a roof but having open sides.

por•cu•pine [pôr′kyə pīn′] *noun, plural* **porcupines.** an animal that is covered with long, sharp quills, which it uses to protect itself against attack.

porcupine When it is frightened, the porcupine raises its quills and lashes its tail but contrary to folk belief it cannot "shoot" its quills.

pore[1] [pôr] *noun, plural* **pores.** a very small opening that allows liquid or air to go through: There are *pores* in the skin through which sweat can pass. Water escapes from a plant leaf through *pores* in the surface of the leaf.

pore[2] *verb,* **pored, poring.** (used with **over**) to look at and study very carefully; examine: "Her father sat at a tiny brown table *poring* over a map." (Alice Walker)

pork [pôrk] *noun.* the meat of a pig or hog.

por•poise [pôr′pəs] *noun, plural* **porpoises** or **porpoise.** a warm-blooded sea animal that looks like a small whale, with a round head and a blunt snout. Porpoises are very intelligent, and are trained to do tricks and perform in shows.

P

586

por•ridge [pôr′ ij] *noun.* a soft breakfast food made by boiling oatmeal or other cereal in water or milk until it thickens, often eaten in earlier times.

port [pôrt] *noun, plural* **ports. 1.** a place where boats and ships can dock or anchor; a harbor: The ship had to put into *port* because of the warnings of a storm. **2.** a city that has a harbor where ships can load and unload their cargo and passengers: New Orleans is an important *port* on the Gulf of Mexico. **3.** the left side of a ship or aircraft as you are facing the front.

port•a•ble [pôr′ tə bəl] *adjective,   more/most.* easy to move from one place to another; able to be carried: Ted brought his *portable* radio to the beach with him.

por•ter [pôr′ tər] *noun, plural* **porters. 1.** a person who is hired to carry luggage or packages, as in a hotel or at a railroad station. **2.** a person who assists passengers on a train.

port•fo•li•o [pôrt fō′ lē ō′] *noun, plural* **portfolios.** a folder or case for holding loose papers and other materials.

port•hole [pôrt′ hōl′] *noun, plural* **portholes.** a small, round window in the side of a ship or boat to let in air and light.

por•tion [pôr′ shən] *noun, plural* **portions. 1.** a part of some larger thing or amount; a share: Everyone who goes on the trip will pay a *portion* of the cost. **2.** a serving of food: That restaurant is known for its large *portions.* —*verb,* **portioned, portioning.** to divide or give out something in portions.

por•trait [pôr′ trit *or* pôr′ trāt] *noun, plural* **portraits. 1.** a painting or photograph of a person. A portrait usually shows only the face, but sometimes the whole body is shown. **2.** a realistic description of something in words: James Joyce's famous book on his childhood is called *A Portrait of the Artist as a Young Man.*

por•tray [pôr′ trā′] *verb,* **portrayed, portraying. 1.** to show in a picture: The artist Norman Rockwell often *portrayed* ordinary scenes from small-town American life. **2.** to create a picture of something in words; describe: In the book *Mommie Dearest,* movie star Joan Crawford was *portrayed* by her daughter as a cruel and selfish woman. **3.** to act out a certain part in a play, film, or the like. ◆ The act or fact of portraying something is a **portrayal.**

Por•tu•gal [pôr′ chə gəl] a country in southwestern Europe, on the Atlantic Ocean. *Capital:* Lisbon. *Area:* 34,350 square miles. *Population:* 10,286,000. —**Portuguese,** *adjective; noun.*

pose [pōz] *noun, plural* **poses.** a way of standing or sitting; a position of the body: Ballet dancers have to be able to hold certain *poses.* —*verb,* **posed, posing. 1.** to hold or place in position for a picture: The family *posed* in front of the fireplace for a photo for their Christmas cards. **2. pose as.** to pretend to be: In the James Bond spy novels, Bond *poses as* a businessman from the "Universal Export Company." **3.** to put forward; present: to *pose* a question.

po•si•tion [pə zish′ ən] *noun, plural* **positions. 1.** the place where a person or thing is: Old-time sailors guided their ships by the *position* of the sun, moon, and stars. **2.** the place where a person or thing is supposed to be; the proper or assigned place: Katie's *position* on the soccer team is right wing. **3.** the way someone or something is placed: The nurse put the patient in a comfortable *position* in bed. **4.** a particular situation or condition: "Nothing makes him happier than to be in a *position* to say 'I told you so.'" (Christopher Isherwood) **5.** a way of thinking; point of view: The reporters questioned the congressman about his *position* on defense spending.

portrait The most famous portrait ever painted, the *Mona Lisa* by Leonardo da Vinci.

Pronunciation Key: O–S			
ō	over; go	ou	out; town
ô	all; law	p	put; hop
oo	look; full	r	run; car
o͞o	pool; who	s	set; miss
oi	oil; boy	sh	show

(Turn the page for more information.)

P

pos•i•tive [päz′ ə tiv] *adjective, more/most.* **1.** with no doubt; absolutely sure; certain: Don't put down your answer until you're *positive* that it's right. **2.** that agrees with or approves of something: "Yes" is a *positive* answer to a question. **3.** meant to make things better; helpful or useful: The teacher always tries to put *positive* comments on her students' papers so they won't get discouraged about writing. **4.** of a number, being larger than zero. **5.** having one of the two possible electrical charges. A flashlight battery has a NEGATIVE charge at one end and a positive charge at the other end. **6.** of a medical test, showing that a certain disease or harmful condition is present. **7.** of an adjective, showing the simple form, when there is no comparison: The *positive* form of "slower" is "slow." —*noun, plural* **positives.** an image on film that shows the light and dark areas as they actually appear, rather than reversed as in a negative.

pos•i•tive•ly [päz′ ə tiv′ lē] *adverb.* **1.** in a positive way: The car was *positively* identified as the one that was stolen last month. **2.** *Informal.* actually; indeed: "It is boiling hot, we are *positively* melting." (Anne Frank)

pos•sess [pə zes′] *verb,* **possessed, possessing. 1.** to have or keep for oneself; own: "There were more planes here than he thought were *possessed* by the entire Royal Air Force." (Ken Follett) **2.** to feel or have a very strong influence that takes over one's mind or will: "He was *possessed* with a wild notion of rushing out into the streets and taking a train to Detroit." (F. Scott Fitzgerald) **3.** to be under the control of a spirit, especially an evil one.

pos•ses•sion [pə zesh′ ən] *noun, plural* **possessions. 1.** the fact of possessing something: In football a team must gain ten yards in four plays, or else they lose *possession* of the ball. **2.** something owned; a belonging: The family lost all of their *possessions* in the flood. "My one other physical *possession* was a portable typewriter . . ." (A. B. Guthrie) **3.** a territory under the rule of an outside government: The island of Bermuda is a British *possession.*

pos•ses•sive [pə zes′ iv] *adjective, more/most.* **1.** in grammar, showing that something belongs to a certain person or thing: In the sentence "Sue wore a flower in her hair," "her" is a *possessive* pronoun. **2.** wanting very much to own or completely control something: She's

pos•se [päs′ ē] *noun, plural* **posses.** a group of men gathered by a sheriff to help as law officers for a time, as to capture a criminal or to keep order in an emergency. Posses were used in earlier times, as in the American West.

very *possessive* about her boyfriend and gets very angry if he even talks to another girl. —*noun, plural* **possessives.** a word that shows possession. In the sentence "We're going to Peggy's house," "Peggy's" is a possessive.

pos•si•bil•i•ty [päs′ ə bil′ ə tē] *noun, plural* **possibilities. 1.** the fact of being possible: Scientists say there is no *possibility* of building a machine that can run constantly on its own power. **2.** something that is possible: We need to pick a place to have the pizza party—what are the *possibilities?*

pos•si•ble [päs′ ə bəl] *adjective, more/most.* **1.** that can be, happen, or be done: It's *possible* for a woman to be elected President of the U.S., but it has not happened so far. **2.** that could be used, considered, or done: Each question on the test had four *possible* answers.

pos•si•bly [päs′ ə blē] *adverb.* **1.** according to what is possible: We can't *possibly* finish all this work today. **2.** it is possible that; perhaps: I'm not sure how many people were there—500, *possibly* 600.

pos•sum [päs′ əm] *noun, plural* **possums.** another word for an OPOSSUM.

post¹ [pōst] *noun, plural* **posts.** a piece of wood, metal, or other such material that is placed upright in the ground to support something: a fence *post.* —*verb,* **posted, posting.** to put up a notice: The names of the students who won awards were *posted* on the bulletin board.

post² *noun, plural* **posts. 1.** the place where a soldier, guard, or police officer is supposed to be when he is on duty. **2.** a place where soldiers are stationed; a fort. **3.** a job or position, especially an appointed position in the government: Henry Kissinger held the *post* of Secretary of State in President Nixon's cabinet. **4.** short for TRADING POST. —*verb,* **posted, posting.** to station or place at a particular spot: Several Secret Service men were *posted* at the entrance to the White House.

post³ *noun, plural* **posts. 1.** a system to carry letters, packages, and so on; the mail. **2.** one delivery of mail. —*verb,* **posted, posting. 1.** to mail a letter or package. **2. keep (someone) posted.** to let someone know the latest news: While my brother was away I *kept him posted* on how the local teams were doing.

post•age [pōst′ ij] *noun.* the amount of money charged by the post office for sending something by mail.

postage stamp see **stamp.**

post•al [pōs′ təl] *adjective.* having to do with mail or post offices: the U.S. *Postal* Service.

post•card [pōst′ kärd′] *noun, plural* **postcards.** a small card used for sending short notes through the mail. Post cards usually have a picture on one side and space for the address and message on the other side.

poster An 1899 circus poster.

post•er [pōs′ tər] *noun, plural* **posters.** a large printed sign, often with an illustration or photograph, used for advertising or as decoration: Outside the theater there was a *poster* giving information about the show.

post•man [pōst′ mən] *noun, plural* **postmen.** another name for a MAILMAN.

post•mark [pōst′ märk′] *noun, plural* **postmarks.** an official mark placed on mail to cancel the stamp and show the date and place of mailing. —*verb,* **postmarked, postmarking.** to stamp mail with a postmark.

post•mas•ter [pōst′ mas′ tər] *noun, plural* **postmasters.** the person in charge of a post office.

post office an official government office that accepts, sorts, and delivers mail and sells postage stamps.

post•pone [pōst pōn′] *verb,* **postponed, postponing.** to put off until some later time: The soccer game was *postponed* until the next day because the field was too wet. ◆ The act of postponing something is a **postponement.**

pos•ture [päs′ chər] *noun, plural* **postures.** the way a person holds or carries the body when standing, sitting, or walking.

P

P

pot [pät] *noun, plural* **pots. 1.** a deep, usually round container used for holding food and liquids in cooking: a tea*pot*, a *pot* of soup. **2.** a container for a growing plant. —*verb,* **potted, potting.** to put something in a pot. ♦ Usually used as an adjective: a *potted* plant.

po·tas·si·um [pə tas′ ē əm] *noun.* a soft, light, silver-white metal that is often found in the earth. It is used to make soap, fertilizer, explosives, and many other things, and it is also needed for growth by plants and animals. Potassium is a chemical element.

po·ta·to [pə tā′ tō] *noun, plural* **potatoes.** a round or oval-shaped vegetable that grows under the ground as part of a leafy plant. Potatoes are white inside with a brown or reddish skin, and are cooked before they are eaten.

po·tent [pōt′ ənt] *adjective, more/most.* having great strength or force; very powerful: a *potent* drug. Her letter presents a *potent* argument in favor of the new law.

poul·try [pōl′ trē] *noun.* chickens, turkeys, ducks, geese, and other such birds that are raised for their meat or eggs.

pounce [pouns] *verb,* **pounced, pouncing.** to jump down on something suddenly to grab or stop it: The hawk *pounced* on the jackrabbit. —*noun, plural* **pounces.** a sudden leap or swoop to attack.

pound¹ [pound] *noun, plural* **pounds. 1.** the standard unit for measuring weight in the United States. A pound is made up of sixteen ounces, and is equal to about .45 kilograms in the metric system. **2.** the basic unit of money in Great Britain and some other countries. ♦ An amount in pounds is written with the symbol (£): Ten pounds is £ 10.

pound² *verb,* **pounded, pounding. 1.** to hit hard over and over; hit heavily: "Then I heard somebody *pounding* on the front door." (Nancy Willard) **2.** to beat or crush something down into a powder or mass, as by hitting it

---

potential "The plane pulled up at the last second and just missed the other plane, avoiding a *potential* disaster." The plane didn't *avoid* a potential disaster; there *was* a potential disaster. "The Blues have a lot of *potential* this season. Last year's team won the league, and almost all of those players are back this season." Strictly speaking, the Blues don't have a lot of *potential*; they have power, strength, talent, or whatever. There are two elements in the word *potential*. One is that a certain power, or force, or ability is present. The other is the sense that it's possible, or likely, this power will go into effect. It's unused power, waiting to be tapped.

---

po·ten·tial [pə ten′ chəl] *adjective.* that is able to be or happen; possible but not yet true or real: "Anyone who wants to sell a car in Los Alamos parks it here and *potential* buyers come to see what's available." (Judy Blume) —*noun, plural* **potentials.** a quality that is able to develop: He isn't much of a basketball player yet, but he has a lot of *potential* because he's so tall.

po·tion [pō′ shən] *noun, plural* **potions.** in folk tales and beliefs, a drink that is supposed to have magical powers to act as a medicine, a poison, a way of making someone go to sleep or fall in love, and so on.

pot·ter [pät′ ər] *noun, plural* **potters.** a person who makes pottery by hand.

pot·ter·y [pät′ ər ē] *noun.* **1.** pots, dishes, vases, and other such things shaped from clay and hardened by heat. **2.** the art or business of making such things.

pouch [pouch] *noun, plural* **pouches. 1.** a soft container that is open at the top; a bag or sack: Mail carriers carry letters in a *pouch*. **2.** a part of an animal that is like a bag: Chipmunks have cheek *pouches* to hold food.

with a heavy object: "There was no grass on this square, just hard dirt, *pounded* down by children playing games here." (Eleanor Estes) **3.** to have the feeling or sound of something beating hard: "My heart was *pounding* so loud I thought sure he'd hear it." (S.E. Hinton)

pound³ *noun, plural* **pounds.** an official place for keeping stray dogs and other animals until

pottery An Irish potter "throws," or shapes, a handcrafted piece of pottery on a potter's wheel.

their owners claim them or new owners can be found. Usually the owner must pay a charge or fine before the animal can be released.

pour [pôr] *verb,* **poured, pouring. 1.** to cause a liquid to move or flow in a steady stream: to *pour* milk into a glass. **2.** to move in a steady way, like liquid flowing out of a container: "So many people *pour* out of the building that she might not see him anyway." (Ann Beattie) **3.** to rain hard: "Rain *poured* from the black sky upon the empty dockyard." (Ray Bradbury) **4.** **pour out,** to tell about something freely; talk openly: "He was a good listener. People *poured out* their souls to him and he didn't make them feel uncomfortable." (V.S. Naipaul)

pout [pout] *verb,* **pouted, pouting.** to push out the lips with a frown to show that one is angry or upset: The little girl *pouted* when her father told her she couldn't watch her favorite TV show. —*noun, plural* **pouts.** a pouting look.

pov•er•ty [päv′ ər tē] *noun.* the fact of being poor; being without money for things that are basic and necessary to life.

pow•der [pou′ dər] *noun, plural* **powders. 1.** fine bits or dust made by grinding or crushing something solid: He smashed the soft rock with a hammer and it turned to *powder.* **2.** fine bits of material used for a certain purpose: baking *powder,* face *powder.* **3.** short for GUNPOWDER. —*verb,* **powdered, powdering. 1.** to cover or sprinkle something with powder: The actress *powdered* her face before she went in front of the cameras. **2.** to make or turn something into a powder: *powdered* sugar, *powdered* milk.

producers had a lot of *power* and could force an actor to appear in a certain picture. **5.** someone or something having this quality: The U.S. and the Soviet Union are the major *powers* in the world today. **6.** in mathematics, the number of times that a number is multiplied by itself to get a certain result: 7 to the second *power* is 49 (7 × 7). —*verb,* **powered, powering.** to provide with power: Early railroad trains were *powered* by steam. —*adjective.* powered by a motor: a *power* lawn mower.

pow•er•ful [pou′ ər fəl] *adjective, more/most.* having great power; strong: Jet planes have *powerful* engines. —**powerfully,** *adverb.*

pow•er•less [pou′ ər lis] *adjective.* without power; not able to do or help something.

prac•ti•cal [prak′ ti kəl] *adjective, more/most.* **1.** having to do with what is real and actual, rather than with theories or ideas: This book gives a lot of *practical* advice on how to grow flowers. **2.** suited for actual use; useful: Grandma likes to give *practical* gifts like a shirt or a sweater, rather than toys. **3.** showing good sense; reasonable: " 'What are you going to use for money?' asked his *practical* wife." (E.B. White)

practical joke a trick that is played to tease someone or to make a person seem foolish.

prac•ti•cal•ly [prak′ tik lē] *adverb.* **1.** very close to, but not quite; nearly: The game is *practically* over—there's only a minute left. **2.** in a practical or useful way.

prac•tice [prak′ tis] *verb,* **practiced, practicing. 1.** to do something again and again to become

practice In sports, in music, in dancing, in writing, too, practice helps. A piano player can practice by playing the scales, a basketball player can practice free throws, and so on. But how can you practice writing? First of all, any time you write you are improving your ability to state matters clearly and forcefully. Second, you always have the opportunity to edit your own writing as you go along. Third, you can directly practice writing by keeping a journal, in which you write down brief passages several times a week. This can be only a few lines, or as much as a paragraph or two. Here are some entries from a notebook kept by F. Scott Fitzgerald: "The wind searched the walls for old dust." "A sound of clinking waiters." "The silvery 'Hey!' of a telephone." "The pavements grew sloppier and the snow in the gutters melted into dirty sherbet."

pow•er [pou′ ər] *noun, plural* **powers. 1.** the fact of being able to do something; an action that one can do: Only humans have the *power* to speak. **2.** a force that can move things or do work; energy: electric *power,* a nuclear *power* plant. **3.** electricity: Our *power* went off during last night's storm. **4.** the ability to control or influence others: Old-time Hollywood movie

Pronunciation Key: [ə] Symbol

The [ə] or *schwa* sound occurs in syllables without an accent. It can be spelled with any vowel, such as **a** in above, **e** in listen, **i** in pencil, **o** in melon, **u** in circus. It can also be a combination of vowels, such as **io** in action, **ai** in mountain, **iou** in precious.

(Turn the page for more information.)

P

better at it: Workbooks are used in school to *practice* what is taught in a lesson. **2.** to do or carry on a certain action: A person on a diet has to *practice* a lot of self-control. **3.** to follow or carry on some activity in a regular way: A person must have a special license to *practice* law. ◆ Also used as a noun: She has a successful medical *practice*. —*noun, plural* **practices. 1.** the act or fact of practicing: I'm afraid I've gotten a bit out of *practice* at the piano. **2.** actual use or action: It seemed like a good plan in theory, but in *practice* it turned out to be too expensive. **3.** the usual way something is done; a custom or habit: The boss made it a *practice* to take new workers on a tour of the building.

prai·rie [prar′ē] *noun, plural* **prairies.** a large open area of flat or rolling land that is covered with grass and has very few trees or none at all.

prairie dog The prairie dog gets its name from the barking sound it makes as a warning.

prairie dog a small, furry animal that lives on the prairies of western North America. Prairie dogs live in underground burrows in colonies that may include thousands of animals.

praise [prāz] *noun.* words that show that someone likes or thinks highly of a person or thing; words showing something is good. —*verb,* **praised, praising. 1.** to give praise to someone; speak favorably about. **2.** to worship or give honor to God.

prance [prans] *verb,* **pranced, prancing. 1.** of a horse, to step or spring forward with high, lively steps. **2.** to move or walk in a proud, happy way like this: The winner of the TV game show *pranced* around the stage when her prizes were announced.

prank [prangk] *noun, plural* **pranks.** a joke or trick: They played a *prank* on Richard by putting a frog in his desk at school.

pray [prā] *verb,* **prayed, praying.** to give a prayer; address words or thoughts to God: The minister asked everyone in church to *pray* for the sick man who was in the hospital.

pray·er [prā′ ər] *noun, plural* **prayers. 1.** thoughts or words directed to God: The *Lord's Prayer.* **2.** the fact of praying: The family had a moment of silent *prayer* before they began to eat. **3.** *Informal.* a hope or chance: If this traffic doesn't let up, we don't have a *prayer* of getting to the airport on time.

praying mantis

praying mantis a large green or brown insect related to the grasshopper; also called a MANTIS or MANTID. It feeds on many other kinds of insects. ◆ The name comes from the way it stands with its front legs raised and held together, like a person holding his hands up to pray.

preach [prēch] *verb,* **preached, preaching.** to speak in public about God or religion.

preach·er [prē′ chər] *noun, plural* **preachers.** a person who preaches, especially in a church.

pre·car·i·ous [pri kar′ē əs] *adjective, more/ most.* not safe or secure; dangerous: "With one hand he clung to the side rods of his *precarious* roost . . ." (Edna Ferber) —**precariously,** *adverb:* ". . . an electric fan perched *precariously* on a swaying pile of books and papers." (Laurence Yep)

pre·cau·tion [pri kô′ shən] *noun, plural* **precautions.** something done ahead of time to avoid danger or harm: Before the trip she had the car checked and serviced as a *precaution* against a breakdown on the road.

pre·cede [pri sēd′] *verb,* **preceded, preceding.** to come before; go ahead of: "The dunes loomed black in the long silence that *precedes* a storm." (Meindert DeJong) ◆ Often used as an adjective: Don't answer the questions until you've read the *preceding* lesson.

pre•ce•dent [pres′ ə dent] *noun, plural* **precedents.** something used as an example or guide for the future: In law, a judge's decision in a case is often used as a *precedent* in later cases.

pre•cinct [prē′ singkt′] *noun, plural* **precincts.** a part of a city that is considered to be a separate area, as for voting or for police and fire protection.

pre•cious [presh′ əs] *adjective, more/most.* **1.** having great worth, because of being very rare or expensive; very valuable: "Water, in this burning land, was a *precious* thing to be measured out like wine." (Edna Ferber) "The holidays are so short that every minute is *precious*." (Tennessee Williams) ◆ Gold and silver are called **precious metals,** and diamonds, emeralds, and rubies are **precious stones.** **2.** greatly loved; dear: "Her parents always told her she was this *precious* little thing." (Paul Zindel) —**preciousness,** *noun.*

prec•i•pice [pres′ i pis] *noun, plural* **precipices.** a very steep, high wall of rock or earth; a cliff.

pre•cip•i•tate [pri sip′ ə tāt′] *verb,* **precipitated, precipitating.** to cause something bad to hap-

pre•cis•ion [pri sizh′ ən] *noun.* the quality of being precise or exact: "With a sort of military *precision* that astonished him, she outlined the route that he was to follow." (George Orwell)

pre•co•cious [pri kō′ shəs] *adjective, more/most.* of a child, learning and doing things at a much earlier age than other children: TV situation comedies often feature *precocious* youngsters who talk and act like adults.

pre•da•tor [pred′ ə tər] *noun, plural* **predators.** an animal that lives by hunting other animals for food. Hawks, wolves, and sharks are predators. —**predatory** [pred′ ə tôr′ ē] *adjective.*

pred•e•ces•sor [pred′ ə ses′ ər] *noun, plural* **predecessors.** someone or something that comes before; a person or thing that precedes: The new mayor blamed the city's problems on his *predecessors* in the office of mayor.

pre•dic•a•ment [pri dik′ ə mənt] *noun, plural* **predicaments.** a difficult or embarrassing problem that a person is not sure how to deal with: Heather's in a bit of a *predicament* this weekend —she's supposed to go on a Girl Scout trip, but she hasn't finished her science report yet.

predicate "A sentence must have a subject and a predicate." This is basic to all languages. A noun followed by a verb is a basic form of expression that allows human beings to complete and state their thoughts. The noun serves as the *subject* of the sentence, and the verb serves as the *predicate.* "*Ted* wanted to see a movie: *He* checked the paper. *Crash Landing* was playing at Cinema Nine. *The first show* was at 2:00." Here, the subject is in *italics,* the predicate is underlined. The subject identifies who or what carries out an action. It has a noun or pronoun, or a participle acting as a noun. The predicate identifies the action that is taken by the subject. (Above, the verbs are *wanted, to see, checked, was playing,* and *was.*) The predicate always contains a verb.

pen suddenly: "If any of them chose that moment to *precipitate* a war, France would have to fight without an ally." (Barbara Tuchman)

pre•cip•i•ta•tion [pri sip′ ə tā′ shən] *noun.* any form of water that falls from the sky. Precipitation may be either rain, snow, hail, or sleet.

pre•cise [pri sīs′] *adjective, more/most.* **1.** having the proper order or details; strictly as it should be; exact: Jet aircraft have very *precise* instruments to measure speed and distance. **2.** acting or speaking in an exact, careful way: "When a man lives in a house by himself he gets very *precise* habits . . ." (Ernest Hemingway)

pre•cise•ly [pri sīs′ le] *adverb.* **1.** in a precise or accurate way; exactly: "As on this summer night at *precisely* 9:26, at *precisely* 5,050 feet . . ." (Ernest K. Gann) **2.** especially; particularly: "Yet what now interests me is *precisely* this . . ." (Doris Lessing)

pred•i•cate [pred′ i kit] *noun, plural* **predicates.** in grammar, one of the two basic parts that make up a sentence. The SUBJECT tells what the sentence is about. The predicate usually comes after it; it tells what the subject is or does.

pre•dict [pri dikt′] *verb,* **predicted, predicting.** to tell about something that will happen: Weather reports *predict* what the next day's weather will be like. "The day after the Boston Tea Party John Adams had *predicted* that it would arouse the country." (William L. Shirer)

Pronunciation Key: Accent Marks

[′] is the normal accent mark. It shows where the main stress falls on a word.

[′] is a secondary accent mark. It shows a lighter stress than the primary accent. For example:

tel • e • vis • ion [tel′ ə vizh′ ən]

(Turn the page for more information.)

pre·dic·tion [pri dik′shən] *noun, plural* **predictions.** the act of predicting, or something that is predicted: Sports reporters often make *predictions* as to who will win an upcoming game.

P

pre·face [pref′is] *noun, plural* **prefaces.** a short, separate part at the beginning of a book or speech that tells something about the main part: In the *Preface* to his famous dictionary, Dr. Samuel Johnson explained his ideas for how dictionaries should be made.

pre·fer [pri fur′] *verb,* **preferred, preferring.** to like one person or thing better than another; choose one over another: "I'd have *preferred* chocolate chip mint, but I ate my vanilla." (Judy Blume)

pref·er·a·ble [pref′rə bəl] *adjective.* that is to be preferred: The report can be handwritten, but typing is *preferable.* —**preferably,** *adverb:* He wants to sit in the non-smoking section of the plane, *preferably* by a window.

pref·er·ence [pref′rəns *or* pref′ər əns] *noun, plural* **preferences.** the fact of preferring one thing to another: We can take either Route 15 or Route 5—what's your *preference*?

pre·fix [prē′fiks′] *noun, plural* **prefixes.** a group of letters put before a word to change the meaning. *Un-* and *non-* are prefixes meaning "not," as in "*un*known" or "*non*fiction."

history began, which was about 6,000 years ago: Scientists believe that farming began in the Middle East in *prehistoric* times. ◆ This period of time is known as **prehistory.**

> **preface** An opening section in a book may be called a *preface, introduction,* or *foreword.* You may be interested to hear from a well-known publisher on this subject: "Most of these pieces of writing that appear before the body of the text are quite useless. Why should an author tell you what he is just about to tell you? If you call most long introductions Chapter One the same result is attained. Moreover, most prefaces contain an author's thanks to all the people who aided her—librarians, other scholars, her husband, her editor or professor. Such expressions of gratitude can just as effectively become "postfaces," at the end of a book."

prej·u·dice [prej′ə dis] *noun, plural* **prejudices. 1.** a strong feeling against another person because of the race, religion, or group he or she belongs to, rather than because of something this particular person has done. **2.** any general opinion that is used to judge a situation in place of the facts of this situation: My little brother has a real *prejudice* against new foods—he says "I don't like that" before he's even tasted it. —*verb,* **prejudiced, prejudicing.** to cause a person to have a prejudice. ◆ Usually used as an adjective: He has a *prejudiced* attitude toward foreign-made cars and would never buy one.

pre·lim·i·nar·y [pri lim′ə ner′ē] *adjective.* done or happening before the main or most important part; coming before: Before the boss agrees to start the project, he wants a *preliminary* report on how much it will cost.

pre·ma·ture [prē′mə choor′ *or* prē′mə toor′] *adjective, more/most.* before the usual or normal time; too early: A *premature* baby is one that is born before its body has had the proper development. —**prematurely,** *adverb:* a young man with *prematurely* gray hair.

> **prefixes** There are two ways in which prefixes are used in English. First, many words that already exist have been formed by adding a prefix to a root word. Taking *pre-* ("before") itself, we have words such as *preview,* "to see before", *prehistory,* "a time before written history", and *prejudice* "judging beforehand". Second, we can create new words with a prefix, as in *pre-pay* a bill by paying beforehand, take a *pre-test* in school before the course starts, or *pre-register* by mail before the official registration date. You can even invent a word: "A tadpole is a *pre-frog.*" Did you notice that the newer *pre-* words have a hyphen after the prefix? When a new word is formed this way, it uses a hyphen because people aren't used to this particular combination. As time goes on, it's accepted as a single word.

preg·nant [preg′nənt] *adjective.* of a female human or animal, having young growing inside the body before birth. ◆ The fact of being pregnant is **pregnancy** [preg′nən sē′].

pre·his·tor·ic [prē′his tôr′ik] *adjective.* having to do with the period of time before written

pre·mier [pri mir′] *noun, plural* **premiers.** in some countries, the person who is the chief officer of the government. The office of Premier is like that of Prime Minister in Great Britain. —*adjective:* highest or most important; first: John Milton was the *premier* poet of his day.

♦ A **premiere** is the first performance of a new play, movie, or other such work.

prem•ise [prem′is] *noun, plural* **premises. 1.** a basic statement or fact that is accepted as true and used as the starting point for a certain way of thinking: The *premise* of the Declaration of Independence is that all people are born with certain rights which no ruler or government can take away. **2. premises.** a piece of land and the buildings on it: This apartment house does not allow any pets to be kept on the *premises*.

pre•mi•um [prē′mē əm] *noun, plural* **premiums. 1.** something extra offered to persuade a person to do or buy something: Banks sometimes offer a *premium* to anyone who opens a new account. **2.** the amount paid at one time for an insurance policy. **3. put (place) a premium on.** to value something highly. —*adjective.* having higher value or quality: *premium* gasoline.

prep•a•ra•tion [prep′ə rā′shən] *noun, plural* **preparations. 1.** the fact of preparing, or something done to prepare: "In the morning he made *preparations* to depart for the coast." (John Jakes) **2.** something prepared for a certain purpose, such as food or medicine. ♦ Something done for preparation is **preparatory** [prep′ər ə tôr′ē]: A **preparatory school** (**prep school**) prepares students for college.

pre•pare [pri pâr′] *verb,* **prepared, preparing. 1.** to get ready for something that is going to happen; make or become ready: "Mrs. Wong comes out of the house, *prepared* for rain." (Ann Beattie) **2.** to make something by putting things together: to *prepare* dinner.

pre•pos•ter•ous [pri päs′ trəs] *adjective, more/most.* not making sense; very silly or foolish; ridiculous: The man told a *preposterous* story about being kidnapped by creatures from outer space. —**preposterously,** *adverb.*

pre•school [prē′ skool′] *noun, plural* **preschools.** a school that is for children who are too young to enter kindergarten and that is not part of the public school system. —*adjective.* having to do with children who are below school age.

pre•scribe [pri skrīb′] *verb,* **prescribed, prescribing. 1.** of a doctor, to order a certain treatment or medicine for a patient: When doctors write "t.i.d." it means they are *prescribing* that a medicine be taken three times a day. **2.** to set as a rule to be followed; order: H.W. Fowler's *Modern English Usage* is famous for *prescribing* how to use the language.

pre•scrip•tion [pri skrip′shən] *noun, plural* **prescriptions.** a written order from a doctor to use a certain medicine or follow a certain treatment: The doctor gave Tony a *prescription* for his sore throat.

pres•ence [prez′əns] *noun.* **1.** the condition of being in a certain place; being present: "Colonel, sir, your *presence* is requested immediately at the laboratory." (Sam Shepard) **2.** the way that a certain person appears or acts: "B.B. King is a great, warm *presence* when he performs . . ." (Andrea Lee)

pres•ent[1] [prez′ənt] *adjective.* **1.** being in a certain place at a certain time: A student who is in school is marked '*present.*' **2.** going on now; at this time; current: He wants to leave his

prepositions In the 1700's, people thought of Latin as the model for other languages, and they made rules for English to match those of Latin. A Latin sentence normally ends with the verb, and therefore a preposition cannot come at the end. (*Preposition* literally means "placed before.") Thus, the rule that an English sentence should not end with a preposition was for a long time held to be strictly correct. Some writers still follow this rule: "As a writer I feel I have fewer tools with which to work." (Peter S. Prescott) [not "to work with."] But unlike Latin, English has many verb phrases in which a preposition follows the verb. Breaking up such a phrase creates awkward wording. "In Chicago I had a computer to work with" is good English, in the view of many teachers. The most famous comment on this rule was made by Sir Winston Churchill, who's supposed to have said: "This is the sort of nonsense up with which I will not put."

prep•o•si•tion [prep′ə zish′ən] *noun, plural* **prepositions.** in grammar, a word relating a noun or pronoun to another word. In "The ball rolled down the hill," "down" is a preposition. It shows the relationship of the noun "hill" to the rest of the sentence. —**prepositional** [prep′ə zish′ə nəl], *adjective:* In the sentence above, "down the hill" is a **prepositional phrase.**

Pronunciation Key: A–F

a	and; hat	ch	chew; such
ā	ate; stay	d	dog; lid
â	care; air	e	end; yet
ä	father; hot	ē	she; each
b	boy; cab	f	fun; off

(Turn the page for more information.)

present job and get one that pays more. —*noun*. **1.** the present time. **2. for the present** or **at present.** now: "Mr. Kurtz was *at present* in charge of the trading post." (Joseph Conrad) **3.** short for PRESENT TENSE.

pres•ent² [prez′ ənt] *noun, plural* **presents.** something that is passed on from one person to another to keep, as a sign of love, good feelings, being grateful, and so on: People get *presents* on their birthdays or at Christmas. —[pri zent′] *verb*, **presented, presenting. 1.** to give something as a present. **2.** to put something before the public or a group; show or display: The high school drama club is *presenting Our Town* this year. **3.** to introduce a person, especially in a formal way: After the show the members of the cast were *presented* to the Queen. ◆ Something that is fit to be seen or presented is **presentable. 4.** to bring forward; cause to be: The lock on this door is broken—that *presents* a problem.

pres•en•ta•tion [prez′ ən tā′ shən] *noun, plural* **presentations.** the act of presenting, or something that is presented.

pres•ent•ly [prez′ ənt lē] *adverb*. **1.** at the present time; now: "If she was *presently* convinced that the year was 1921 . . ." (Julia O'Faolain) **2.** in or after a little while; soon: "*Presently* a door opened and several children appeared in it." (Flannery O'Connor)

present tense in grammar, a verb form showing something that happens or exists at the present time.

pre•serve [pri zurv′] *verb*, **preserved, preserving. 1.** to keep from harm; keep safe; protect: An old saying when people were in danger was, "May the saints *preserve* us." **2.** to keep in the same state; keep up; maintain: "The sheltered life had *preserved* her youthful appearance." (Somerset Maugham) **3.** to prepare food so that it will not rot or spoil: People often *preserve* fruit by boiling it and storing it in airtight jars. —*noun, plural* **preserves. 1.** an area of forest or other wild land where wild animals are protected. **2. preserves.** fruit that has been cooked with sugar and made into jam or jelly.

pre•side [pri zīd′] *verb*, **presided, presiding.** to be in charge; control or direct: "Their day began with a meeting at 9:15. Wilson *presided* and scheduled what was to be done during the day." (George Plimpton)

pres•i•den•cy [prez′ ə den′ sē] *noun, plural* **presidencies. 1.** the office of president: John Kennedy was the youngest person ever elected to the *presidency* of the U.S. **2.** the term during which a president holds office.

pres•i•dent [prez′ ə dənt] *noun, plural* **presidents. 1. President.** the head of the government in the United States. **2.** the highest-ranking officer in other countries, such as France or the Soviet Union. In such countries, the president is often the official head of the government, but not the actual leader. **3.** the officer in charge of a club, college, or other such organization. **4.** a high-ranking officer of a business. In some companies, the president is the highest officer,

---

present tense The present tense tells about action happening *now*, at this time. Actually, English has *two* present tenses. The *simple present tense*, in spite of its name, does not tell about action that is going on at the present time. For this, we use the *present progressive tense* (think of how *progress* means "going on, going forward"). It uses BE plus an action verb: "Who <u>is</u> <u>making</u> all that noise?" If someone called you on the phone and asked, "What are you doing?" you wouldn't say, "I <u>watch</u> TV." That would be the simple present. You'd use the present progressive: "I'm <u>watching</u> TV." These are the main uses of the simple present tense: (1) To show a habit or an ongoing action: "He <u>goes</u> to Rose School." "I <u>love</u> mysteries." (2) To show a general truth or condition: "Water <u>flows</u> downhill." "He who <u>laughs</u> last <u>laughs</u> best." (3) To describe a situation in a story: "A man <u>comes</u> up to me and <u>says</u> . . ."

---

pres•er•va•tion [prez′ ər vā′ shən] *noun*. the act of preserving: The Sierra Club is very concerned with the *preservation* of wildlife in this country. "I speak today for the *preservation* of the Union." (Daniel Webster)

pre•serv•a•tive [pri zur′ və tiv] *noun, plural* **preservatives.** anything that is used to preserve something: In earlier times, salt was often used as a *preservative* to keep meat from spoiling.

but in most large U.S. companies there is a chairman of the board above the president. ◆ Something that has to do with a president is **presidential:** a *presidential* election.

press [pres] *verb*, **pressed, pressing. 1.** to push against something in a firm, steady way: "Then he *pressed* his face close to the window." (Rudyard Kipling) "Brady *pressed* his lips together." (Jean Fritz) **2.** to make clothing smooth, as with an iron. **3.** to move or go with force: "The sun stood directly overhead, *pressing* its heat down upon the town." (Esther Forbes) **4.** to ask for something in a strong way: "When I rose a second time he again *pressed* me to stay." (James Boswell) ◆ Often used as an adjective: "While there I received a *pressing* invitation to come immediately down to Trenton." (Henry James)

—*noun, plural* **presses. 1.** a machine used to press things: A wine *press* crushes grapes to make wine. **2.** a machine that prints newspapers, magazines, or books; also called a PRINTING PRESS. **3.** newspapers, magazines, radio, and TV, or the people who report for them: The U.S. Constitution guarantees freedom of the *press.* **4.** the fact of pressing: "The main *press* of people stood opposite a booth or stage . . ." (Virginia Woolf)

press A *pressman* checks the flow of ink on a color printing press.

on; force or influence strongly: His parents *pressure* him to do well in school and sports.

pres•tige [pres tēzh′ *or* pres tēj′] *noun.* respect or high position that comes from some outstanding accomplishment. ◆ Something that has prestige is **prestigious** [prə stij′ əs].

pre•sume [pri zōōm′] *verb,* **presumed, presuming. 1.** to accept something as true without full proof; suppose; assume: Dave wants to borrow Dad's power drill—I *presume* he knows how to work it. **2.** to do something without having the right or permission. ◆ Someone who presumes in this way is **presumptuous** [pri zum′ chōō əs]: "It is highly *presumptuous* to sit in judgment . . . over other people's work and talent." (John Simon) —**presumably,** *adverb:* "The facts at hand *presumably* speak for themselves . . ." (J.D. Salinger)

pre•tend [pri tend′] *verb,* **pretended, pretending. 1.** to act as if something is true or real when it is not; put on a false show: "I *pretended* to read through the magazine, flipping the pages over even though I wasn't looking at the pictures or the words." (Laurence Yep) **2.** of a child, to imagine something is true as a game; make believe: "When he sat in front he *pretended* he was driving a racing car." (Louise Fitzhugh) ◆ Something that is pretended is a **pretense:** "The American walked away, making a great *pretense* of not being in a hurry." (V.S. Naipaul)

pret•ty [prit′ ē] *adjective,* **prettier, prettiest. 1.** pleasing to the eyes; nice to look at; attractive: a *pretty* girl, a *pretty* flower. **2.** pleasing to

pretty The word *pretty* once was a general word used in praise or approval of a person or thing, somewhat like the modern word *nice.* A "pretty man" was one who had a proper appearance or displayed pleasing qualities: "He observed they were *pretty men,* meaning, not handsome, but stout warlike fellows." (Sir Walter Scott) It also had the sense of "a great deal, a considerable amount:" "(This) brought a *pretty* sum into his pocket." (William Makepeace Thackeray) *Pretty* has kept one general meaning, the sense of "somewhat, rather:" "It gets *pretty* cold here in the fall." This use of the word has been in the language since the 1500's. But you should be careful about overusing it. If you met a person aged ninety, you'd say, "He's very (or remarkably) old," not "He's pretty old."

pres•sure [presh′ ər] *noun, plural* **pressures. 1.** the force that is caused by one thing pushing against another: The air *pressure* in these tires is supposed to be 28 pounds per square inch. **2.** a strong force or influence to do something: A high-*pressure* salesman is one who pushes very hard to make customers buy.

—*verb,* **pressured, pressuring.** to put pressure

Pronunciation Key: O–S			
ō	over; go	ou	out; town
ô	all; law	p	put; hop
oo	look; full	r	run; car
ōō	pool; who	s	set; miss
oi	oil; boy	sh	show

(Turn the page for more information.)

P

prewriting "Prewriting" is anything that a writer does before actually starting to write. The term *prewriting* is fairly new. The earliest use of it we've found was in 1968. Obviously, then, writers were able to get along for many centuries without prewriting. This has led some critics to charge that this is not a new method at all, but just a name that lumps together various techniques which writers have always used to get started (interviewing, research, note-taking, outlining, etc.). However, prewriting does call for the use of several new techniques, such as CLUSTERING (see p. 147). The idea of "prewriting" developed because teachers noticed that the most difficult thing for student writers was getting started. Prewriting is intended to ease the student into the paper through a series of steps leading up to the first draft.

the senses in any way: a *pretty* song. —*adverb.* somewhat; rather: "The store's *pretty* empty, it being Thursday afternoon." (John Updike) —**prettily,** *adverb.* **prettiness,** *noun.*

pret•zel [pret′ səl] *noun, plural* **pretzels.** a thin roll of dough that is shaped like a knot or stick and baked until it is crisp. Pretzels are usually salted on the outside.

pre•vail [pri vāl′] *verb,* **prevailed, prevailing. 1.** to be in general use; be common. ◆ Usually used as an adjective: Along the Pacific Coast, the *prevailing* winds blow to the east. **2.** to be the strongest; win out: "Love and truth . . . in the long run no force can *prevail* against them." (Mahatma Gandhi) ◆ Something that prevails is **prevalent** [prev′ ə lənt]: "The belief, *prevalent* in all their homes . . ." (Alice Walker)

pre•vent [pri vent′] *verb,* **prevented, preventing. 1.** to keep something from happening, especially something that is bad or not wanted: "The door had a metal pole built into it to *prevent* its being opened from the outside." (James Baldwin) **2.** to keep a person from doing something; hold back or stop: "A bad attack of flu has *prevented* me from writing to you until today." (Anne Frank) ◆ Something that serves or intends to prevent is **preventive:** a *preventive* medicine.

pre•ven•tion [pri ven′ shən] *noun.* the act or fact of preventing something: fire *prevention,* accident *prevention.*

pre•view [prē′ vyoo′] *noun, plural* **previews. 1.** an advance showing of a movie, play, or the like before its regular opening. **2.** any advance showing or example: The designer gave a *preview* of the new fashions he'll be selling in the stores this fall.

pre•vi•ous [prē′ vē əs] *adjective.* coming or made before something else; earlier: She piled up all the newspapers that had come during the *previous* week. —**previously,** *adverb:* The store put in a computer to keep track of their bills— *previously* everything was done by hand.

prey [prā] *noun.* **1.** an animal that is hunted and killed by another animal for food. **2.** a person who is hurt or taken advantage of by another; a victim. —*verb,* **preyed, preying.** (used with **on**) **1.** to hunt animals for food: Eagles *prey on* small animals, fish, and snakes. **2.** to harm or take advantage of: The police are looking for a robber who's been *preying on* elderly people.

price [prīs] *noun, plural* **prices. 1.** the amount of money paid or asked for something to be sold. **2.** what a person has to give up to get something that is wanted: The Union Army won the Battle of Gettysburg, but they paid a terrible *price* in the lives that were lost. —*verb,* **priced, pricing. 1.** to set a certain price for something: All the gifts at the school Christmas fair were *priced* at $3.00 or less. **2.** to find out the price of something: Before we bought our new TV, we *priced* TV sets at other stores.

prick [prik] *verb,* **pricked, pricking.** to make a tiny hole with a sharp, pointed object: The nurse *pricked* Damon's finger to get a blood sample. ◆ Also used as a *noun:* a pin *prick.*

prickly pear

prick•ly [prik′ lē] *adjective,* **pricklier, prickliest.** having small sharp points or thorns. ◆ A **prickly pear** is a type of cactus plant that has wide, flat stems and bright yellow flowers. It bears red or purple pear-shaped fruit.

pride [prīd] *noun.* **1.** a proper sense of one's worth and ability; self-respect: My grandmother takes a lot of *pride* in her beautiful flower garden. **2.** a person or thing that is highly thought of: Their baby is their *pride* and joy. **3.** too high an opinion of oneself; a feeling that one is better than other people. —*verb,* **prided, priding, pride oneself on,** to take pride in; think highly of: "Mrs. Creery *prided herself on* knowing human nature." (George Orwell)

pried [prīd] *verb.* the past tense of **pry.**

priest [prēst] *noun, plural* **priests. 1.** in the Catholic Church and other Christian churches, a man who has been specially trained and given the power to lead religious ceremonies. ♦ A man who is a priest is a member of the **priesthood. 2.** a leader of various other religions: a high *priest* of the ancient Aztec Indians.

pri•ma•ry [prī′mer ē] *adjective.* **1.** first in importance: She wants to go to that college for several reasons, but the *primary* one is that they have such a good science department. **2.** first in order or time: the *primary* grades in school. —*noun, plural,* **primaries.** an election in which members of the same party run against each other to see who will be the party's candidate in the general election. —**primarily,** *adverb.*

primary color one of the three basic colors—red, yellow, and blue—that can combine with each other to make all the other colors.

pri•mate [prī′māt] *noun, plural* **primates.** one of the group of mammals made up of human beings and the animals that resemble them most closely, the apes and monkeys.

prime [prīm] *adjective.* **1.** first in importance or value; primary: "The *prime* pilot for the X-1 was a man whom Bell regarded as the best of the breed." (Tom Wolfe) ♦ **Prime time** for television is the hours in the evening when the most people are watching. The **prime rate** of interest is the rate which a bank charges its best customers for loans. **2.** of meat or other food, of the best quality: *prime* ribs of beef. —*noun.* the best time or condition: A pro baseball player is in his *prime* at the age of about 28 to 32. —*verb,* **primed, priming.** to get someone or something ready; prepare: To *prime* a pump means to put water into it so that it will work.

prime minister the head of the government in Great Britain, and in Canada and other countries whose government system is modeled after Britain's. He or she is usually the leader of the party that has a majority in the legislature.

prime number a number that cannot be divided evenly except by itself and by 1, such as 17.

prim•er [prim′ər] *noun, plural* **primers. 1.** a reading book that is used by beginning readers. **2.** any textbook or instruction book for those beginning a subject. **3.** [prī′mər] paint or other such material used to prepare a surface for painting.

prim•i•tive [prim′ə tiv] *adjective, more/most.* **1.** having to do with the earliest times or stages of something, especially the development of living things on earth: *Primitive* humans used tools of wood, rock, and bone because they did not know how to work with metal. **2.** not advanced; simple and crude: Artists in the Middle Ages used a *primitive* form of the camera to trace pictures on a screen. **3.** having to do with a very simple, flat style of painting that appears to have been done by a child, or a person with no artistic training. —*noun, plural* **primitives.** a person who is primitive or who creates art in a primitive style.

prim•rose [prim′rōz′] *noun, plural* **primroses.** a garden plant with trumpet-shaped flowers of various colors that grow in clusters.

prince [prins] *noun, plural* **princes. 1.** the son of a king or queen. **2.** the husband of a ruling queen. **3.** a male ruler or very high-ranking noble, especially the ruler of a small country or territory: Areas of India were ruled by *princes* when it was part of the British Empire.

Prince Edward Island an island province in southeastern Canada, in the Gulf of St. Lawrence. *Capital:* Charlottetown. *Area:* 2,180 square miles. *Population:* 118,000.

prin•cess [prin′sis] *noun, plural* **princesses. 1.** the daughter of a king or queen. **2.** the wife of a prince.

prin•ci•pal [prin′sə pəl] *noun, plural* **principals. 1.** the person who is in charge of a school. **2.** an original amount of money that is borrowed or invested, not counting interest paid or income earned on the money. **3.** a person who has a leading or important position: The *principals* in a business deal are the people who own or control the companies involved. —*adjective.* first in importance; main: The *principal* problem with the new shopping center is that it doesn't have enough parking.

Pronunciation Key: G–N

g	give; big	k	kind; cat; back
h	hold	l	let; ball
i	it; this	m	make; time
ī	ice; my	n	not; own
j	jet; gem; edge	ng	having

(Turn the page for more information.)

P

principle "In traditional life stories, even the *principle* character is male." (Letty Cottin Pogrebin) The correct word here is *principal*, not *principle* as it now appears. (The "*principal* character" would be the main or major character.) *Principle* means a basic idea, belief, or rule: "If there is one *principle* deeply rooted in the mind of every American, it is that we shall have nothing to do with conquest." (Thomas Jefferson). *Principle* is always a noun. *Principal* is mainly an adjective but can also be a noun, as in "the *principal* of an elementary school." Think of major or main as relating to principal; belief, idea, or rule as relating to principle. There's also an old method used for many years by school teachers: "The principal is your pal."

prin•ci•ple [prin′ sə pəl] *noun, plural* **princi-ples. 1.** any important belief or truth that serves as the starting point for other ideas, or as a guide to action: The *principle* of democracy is that people should choose their own leaders. **2.** a law of nature or science that is stated in a certain way: Archimedes' *Principle* says that an object floating in water is held up by a force equal to its own weight.

print [print] *verb,* **printed, printing. 1.** to write words with straight, separate letters. **2.** to put words on paper by machine, as for a newspa-per, book, magazine, or the like. **3.** to include certain writing in a newspaper or magazine; publish: The newspaper *printed* Mom's letter to the editor. —*noun, plural* **prints. 1.** letters made by printing: Books for early readers usu-ally have large *print*. **2. in (out of) print.** printed in a book and available (or not available) for sale. **3.** a mark made by pressing on or into something. ♦ Usually used in compounds: a foot*print*, a finger*print*. **4.** a copy of a photo-graph made from film. **5.** a painting or other picture reproduced by printing. **6.** fabric or clothing with a design pressed or marked on it: a summer dress with a flower *print*.

print•er [prin′ tər] *noun, plural* **printers. 1.** a person or business that prints books, maga-zines, or other such material. **2.** a device that is connected to a computer to print information from the computer.

printing press a machine that rapidly prints letters, words, or pictures on paper.

print•out [print′ out′] *noun, plural* **printouts.** the printed material that comes out of a com-puter printer.

pri•or [prī′ ər] *adjective.* coming before; earli-er: Students taking this test are not supposed to have any *prior* knowledge of what the questions are. ♦ Also used in the phrase **prior to:** The witness said he had never seen the man *prior to* the day of the crime.

pri•or•i•ty [prī ôr′ ə tē] *noun, plural* **priorities. 1.** the right to be first because of need or importance: In a hospital emergency room, a patient whose life is in danger takes *priority* over someone with a less serious problem. **2.** something that is first in importance: When the pioneers settled in the West, their top *priority* was to be near a water supply.

prism [priz′ əm] *noun, plural* **prisms.** a solid glass object that can break rays of light into the individual colors of the rainbow.

pris•on [priz′ ən] *noun, plural* **prisons.** a place where people found guilty of a crime are forced to stay for a certain time as a punishment.

pris•on•er [priz′ nər] *noun, plural* **prisoners. 1.** a person who is forced to stay in a prison. **2.** any person who is held by force; a captive. ♦ A **prisoner of war** is a soldier who is captured and held by the enemy during a war.

pri•va•cy [prī′ və sē] *noun, plural* **privacies.** the fact of being private; being away from the notice or attention of others: "We never opened anyone else's mail. We respected each other's *privacy*." (Paul Zindel)

pri•vate [prī′ vit] *adjective, more/most.* **1.** not having to do with or belonging to people in general; not public: You can't park there be-cause it's a *private* road. **2.** not working for the government or holding government office: a *private* detective. The general decided to leave the army and take a job in *private* industry. **3.** not meant to be shared with or known by others; personal: ". . . each of them needing to be alone with his *private* thoughts and feel-ings." (William Steig) —*noun, plural* **privates.** a soldier having the lowest rank. A **private first class** ranks below a corporal.

priv•i•lege [priv′ lij] *noun, plural* **privileges.** a special right given to a person or group of people: Only students who have passed all their subjects have the *privilege* of going on the boat trip. "I had the *privilege* of being one of the few outsiders to cross the finished bridge before it was opened." (Ernie Pyle) ♦ Someone who is **privileged** has special advantages in life, such as having more money or a higher place in society.

prize [prīz] *noun, plural* **prizes.** something won in a game or contest: First *prize* in a race in the Olympics is a gold medal. —*verb,* **prized, prizing.** to think very highly of something.

pro [prō] *noun, plural* **pros.** a short form of PROFESSIONAL: a golf *pro.* —*adjective:* Pro football is played on Sundays.

prob•lem [prob′ləm] *noun, plural* **problems. 1.** something that is hard to deal with, and that can cause trouble: Dad brought the car back to the dealer because he's having *problems* with the steering. **2.** a question for which an answer is needed, as in a school lesson: For math homework, we did the *problems* on page 140.

problem in a story When you write a story, there has to be a crisis of some sort, a problem that needs solving, a person in a situation that must change, a conflict between groups that will cause change. There is a *setting*, of course. Where does the story occur? In a house, in a factory, on a street? There are *characters*, of course, the persons who are in the setting and who are affected by the problem, or *crux*, of the story. "Every Thanksgiving, our family gets together at one relative's house for dinner." "Uncle Don was the host for this year's dinner." "Suddenly Thanksgiving morning Uncle Don decided that we should all go to a restaurant instead of eating at home—all 23 of us." *Now* you have a story, because you've created a setting (house and restaurant), a character (Don), and a problem (23 people going to dinner on the spur of the moment).

prob•a•bil•i•ty [präb′ ə bil′ ə tē] *noun, plural* **probabilities. 1.** in mathematics, a number or statement showing how likely it is that something will happen: If you pick a playing card out of a deck, the *probability* that it will be red is 1 out of 2. **2.** the fact of being probable; the chance that something will happen or is true.

prob•a•ble [präb′ ə bəl] *adjective, more/most.* fairly certain to happen or be true: Jones is the *probable* starting pitcher for the Blues today. The fire department said that the *probable* cause of the fire was a leaky gas line.

prob•a•bly [präb′ ə blē] *adverb.* almost certain or definite; bound to be; likely: I'm not sure how I cut my foot—*probably* on a piece of glass.

pro•ba•tion [prō bā′ shən] *noun, plural* **probations. 1.** a period of time when a person who was found guilty of a crime is under the control of a court and must act in a proper way. A person who is very young or who commits a minor crime may be put on probation instead of being sent to prison. **2.** a set period of time for testing a person: In that company, new workers have a three-month *probation* period to make sure they can do the work.

probe [prōb] *noun, plural* **probes. 1.** a careful study of something to investigate a certain problem: The Senate questioned many suspected gang leaders as part of its *probe* into organized crime. **2.** a device or tool used to explore or test something. —*verb,* **probed, probing.** to carry out a careful search or investigation. "He carefully *probed* the ice before him." (James Houston)

pro•ce•dure [prə sē′ jər] *noun, plural* **procedures.** the proper or correct way to do something, especially a set of steps to be done in order: The bank gave her a booklet explaining the *procedure* for applying for a home loan.

pro•ceed [prə sēd′] *verb,* **proceeded, proceeding. 1.** to go on or move forward; continue: The car stopped at the stop sign and then *proceeded* through the intersection. **2.** to carry on an activity: "He *proceeded* with his task and never turned his head toward me." (Emily Brontë)

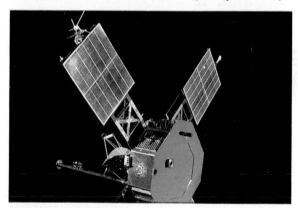

probe A model of a space probe sent to explore the planet Venus.

Pronunciation Key: T–Z			
t	ten; date	v	very; live
th	think	w	win; away
<u>th</u>	these	y	you
u	cut; butter	z	zoo; cause
ur	turn; bird	zh	measure
(Turn the page for more information.)			

P

pro•ceed•ings [prə sē′ dingz] *noun.* **1.** things that happen or are done; events. **2.** a record of things done at a meeting or in court.

pro•ceeds [prō′ sēdz′] *noun, plural* **proceeds.** the amount of money gained from a sale or other business activity: The *proceeds* from the Little League candy sale will be used to buy new uniforms for the players.

pro•cess [präs′ es] *noun, plural* **processes. 1.** a series of actions done in a certain way to make or do something: The house is a mess because they're in the *process* of painting all the bedrooms. **2.** a series of events in nature that happen in a certain way: The *process* by which green plants make food is called "photosynthesis." —*verb,* **processed, processing.** to prepare or do something using a series of steps: A computer *processes* information.

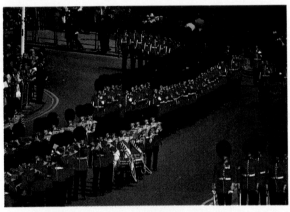

procession The procession known as the "Trooping of the Colors" is held on the birthday of Queen Elizabeth II.

pro•ces•sion [prə sesh′ ən] *noun, plural* **processions. 1.** the act of moving forward in an even, orderly way: "Clouds drifted across the sky in an endless *procession*." (E.B. White) **2.** a group of people moving in this way: "Soon I was heading a *procession* of five or six boys to the schoolroom." (Wole Soyinka)

pro•ces•sor [prä′ ses′ ər] *noun, plural* **processors.** a person or thing that processes something: A computer that is used for writing is called a word *processor*. A food *processor* is an appliance used in cutting and preparing foods.

pro•claim [prō klām′ *or* prə klām′] *verb,* **proclaimed, proclaiming.** to make known or announce to the public: "There was a notice in the window which *proclaimed* that all the rooms were taken." (John Le Carré)

pro•cla•ma•tion [präk′ lə mā′ shən] *noun, plural* **proclamations.** an official public announcement.

pro•cras•ti•nate [prō kras′ tə nāt′] *verb,* **procrastinated, procrastinating.** to put off something that should be done; delay without good reason: Bill *procrastinated* on his history report and had to do all the work the night before it was due. —**procrastination,** *noun.*

pro•cure [prō kyoor′] *verb,* **procured, procuring.** to get or have something, usually by special care or effort: "A college friend had *procured* a ticket to the White House." (William L. Shirer)

prod [präd] *verb,* **prodded, prodding. 1.** to push or jab with something pointed: to *prod* a mule with a stick to get it to move. **2.** to urge or press a person to do something. —*noun, plural* **prods.** the act of prodding, or a thing used for this: Ranchers sometimes use a cattle *prod* to move cattle.

prod•i•gy [präd′ ə jē] *noun, plural* **prodigies. 1.** a child or young person who is very brilliant or who has some amazing talent: Bobby Fischer was a chess *prodigy* who was the best player in America at the age of 14. **2.** something wonderful or amazing: "These algae are a real *prodigy* of creation, one of the marvels of universal plant life." (Jules Verne)

pro•duce [prə doos′] *verb,* **produced, producing. 1.** to make or build something from certain materials; manufacture: The United States *produces* most of the world's jet airliners. **2.** to bring forth from something grown or from animals: Maple trees *produce* a sap that is used for maple syrup. **3.** to bring into being; cause to exist: "The Nautilus could *produce* its own light in the ocean depths." (Jules Verne) **4.** to bring forth into view; show: "He *produced* a large key ring from the pocket of his jacket." (Stephen King) **5.** to bring a play, movie, TV show, or the like before the public. —[prō′ doos] *noun.* fresh vegetables or fruit grown for sale.

produce The produce section of the famous Pike Place Market in Seattle, Washington.

pro•duc•er [prə dōō′ sər] *noun, plural* **produc-ers. 1.** a person or thing that produces some-thing: Saudi Arabia is one of the world's largest *producers* of oil. **2.** a person in charge of the producing of a play, movie, and so on.

pro•duct [präd′ əkt] *noun, plural* **products. 1.** a thing that is made or manufactured; something produced: Milk, cheese, and butter are known as dairy *products*. **2.** in mathematics, the num-ber you get when you multiply two other num-bers: The *product* of 6 times 2 is 12. **3.** anything that comes from thought or action; a result: This book is obviously the *product* of a lively and creative mind.

pro•duc•tion [prə duk′ shən] *noun, plural* **pro-ductions. 1.** the act or fact of producing some-thing: Typesetting, printing, and binding are part of the process of book *production*. **2.** something that is produced: a *production* of the play *Romeo and Juliet*.

pro•duc•tive [prə duk′ tiv] *adjective, more/most.* **1.** able to produce things, especially in large amounts: John O'Hara was a *productive* author who wrote hundreds of short stories and many novels. ◆ The ability to produce things is **productivity** [prō′ dək tiv′ ə tē]. **2.** able to pro-duce a useful result: The homeowners' meeting wasn't very *productive* because several people took up all the time with minor complaints.

pro•fess [prə fes′] *verb,* **professed, professing. 1.** to openly declare or claim something. **2.** to claim something in a false way: "When ques-tioned about his age, (he) *professed* to know absolutely nothing." (Carson McCullers)

pro•fes•sion [prə fesh′ ən] *noun, plural* **profes-sions. 1.** a type of work that calls for special education and training and that usually requires some license or official permission to do the work. **2.** any work thought of as a profession: "He was a barber by *profession*." (William Saroyan) **3.** the public stating of a belief or feeling: The knight made a *profession* of his loyalty to the king.

pro•fes•sion•al [prə fesh′ ən əl] *noun, plural* **professionals. 1.** in sports, an athlete who is paid to play, as opposed to one who plays for enjoyment. **2.** a person who works in a profes-sion, such as a doctor, dentist, lawyer, and so on. —*adjective, more/most.* **1.** in sports, being a professional; being paid to play: The Super Bowl is the championship of *professional* foot-ball. **2.** doing something for pay that others do without pay: a *professional* writer, a *profession-al* dancer. **3.** having to do with a profession: A bill from a lawyer may say on it, "For *profes-sional* services." **4.** done in a skillful way, as if

by a professional: The workmen did a very *professional* job of building that wall.
—**professionally,** *adverb:* "*Professionally* speaking this was the highest moment of his career." (C.S. Forester)

pro•fes•sor [prə fes′ ər] *noun, plural* **profes-sors. 1.** a title for the highest rank of teacher at a college or university. **2.** any teacher at a college or university.

pro•file [prō′ fīl′] *noun, plural* **profiles. 1.** the view or outline of something as seen from the side, especially the human face: U.S. coins show *profiles* of such presidents as Lincoln, Washington, and Jefferson. **2.** a short descrip-tion of a person or thing: The school newspaper published a *profile* of the new principal.

pro•fit [präf′ it] *noun, plural* **profits.** any money that a business has left over after all its costs have been paid. The profit is the difference between the amount taken in from sales and the amount paid to get those sales. —*verb,* **profit-ed, profiting. 1.** to make a profit; gain money. **2.** to gain or benefit from something: to *profit* from experience. "I shall *profit* by your knowl-edge." (Dashiell Hammett)

prof•it•a•ble [präf′ it ə bəl] *adjective, more/most.* **1.** making or giving a profit. **2.** giving a gain or benefit: It was a *profitable* visit to the library for Ellen, because she found all the books she needed. —**profitably,** *adverb.*

pro•found [prə found′] *adjective, more/most.* **1.** having or showing a deep knowledge or understanding: the *profound* wisdom of ancient philosophers such as Plato and Socrates. **2.** very strongly felt; very great: "There was such lone-someness up there, such a *profound* cold still-ness." (Ernie Pyle) —**profoundly,** *adverb.*

pro•gram [prō′ gram′] *noun, plural* **programs. 1.** a show on television or radio: a news *pro-gram*. **2.** a list or announcement giving informa-tion about a show, meeting, or other such activity: a *program* for a Broadway play, a *program* for a big-league baseball game. **3.** the performance or meeting itself: Kevin's class is going to sing "Jingle Bells" in the school's Christmas *program*. **4.** a plan or set of activities to be done: an exercise *program*, the U.S. space

---

Pronunciation Key: [ə] Symbol

The [ə] or *schwa* sound occurs in syllables without an accent. It can be spelled with any vowel, such as **a** in above, **e** in listen, **i** in pencil, **o** in melon, **u** in circus. It can also be a combination of vowels, such as **io** in action, **ai** in mountain, **iou** in precious.

(Turn the page for more information.)

P

program. **5.** in computers, a set of instructions allowing the computer to carry out a certain job. —*verb,* **programmed, programming** or **programed, programing. 1.** to enter instructions into a computer so that it can perform a certain function. **2.** to cause a person to act in an automatic way, as if controlled by a computer: "He would like to try to control his dreams; *program* his mind for what would happen while he was asleep." (Paul Zindel)

pro•gram•mer [prō′gram′ər] *noun, plural* **programmers.** (also spelled **programer**) a person who develops programs for use in a computer. ♦ The act of doing this is called **programming.**

pro•gress [präg′res] *noun.* **1.** the act of moving forward toward some goal: Cathy is supposed to clean out her old magazines, but she isn't making much *progress* because she keeps stopping to read them. **2.** a gradual change or improvement: The Dark Ages is a name for a period when mankind made very little *progress.* **3. in progress.** happening at the time; going on. —[prə gres′] *verb,* **progressed, progressing.** to move forward or toward some goal; advance: "The waves increased in size as he *progressed* into deeper waters." (Ken Follett) ♦ The act of progressing is **progression.**

pro•gres•sive [prə gres′iv] *adjective, more/ most.* **1.** moving forward or upward step by step: A *progressive* tax system means that people who earn more money pay a higher rate of tax. **2.** wanting progress or change in politics and social issues: The *Progressive* Movement of the early 1900's was an effort to improve conditions in the U.S. **3.** in grammar, showing that an action is in progress: "The baby *is taking* a nap" is in the present *progressive* tense. —*noun, plural* **progressives.** a person who favors change or reform.

pro•hib•it [prō hib′it] *verb,* **prohibited, prohibiting.** to officially forbid by law or other authority: Smoking is now *prohibited* in many public places.

pro•hi•bi•tion [prō′ə bi′shən] *noun, plural* **prohibitions. 1.** the act of prohibiting something: "There were repeated *prohibitions* against all private and commercial air traffic in the area." (E.L. Doctorow) **2. Prohibition.** the period of time in the U.S. between 1920 and 1933, when it was against the law to buy, sell, or make alcoholic drinks.

pro•ject [präj′ekt] *noun, plural* **projects. 1.** a large-scale effort or plan to carry out some important task: America's effort to develop the first atomic bomb was called the Manhattan

Project. **2.** a special assignment done by students as part of their studies: Andrew's science *project* is a study of how ants get their food. **3.** *also,* **housing project.** a group of apartment buildings, especially one that is part of a government program to provide housing for poor people, the elderly, and so on. —[prə jekt′] *verb,* **projected, projecting. 1.** to reach forward; stick out: "The houses were of wood, with the second story *projecting* over the first." (Mark Twain) **2.** to cause something to be seen or heard over a distance: Stage actors have to learn to *project* their voices. **3.** to think forward as to how something will turn out; make a prediction: TV news shows analyze the early voting in an election and *project* the winner.

pro•jec•tile [prə jek′təl] *noun, plural* **projectiles.** any object that is thrown or hurled through the air, such as a stone, a bullet, or a guided missile.

pro•jec•tion [prə jek′shən] *noun, plural* **projections. 1.** a part that projects: There were *projections* of rocky cliffs along the seashore. **2.** the act or fact or projecting: Most TV sets use rear *projection,* which means that the picture comes from behind the screen.

Prohibition Federal agents pouring whiskey down a sewer during the era of Prohibition.

pro•jec•tor [prə jek′tər] *noun, plural* **projectors.** a machine that shows a picture on a screen by means of a beam of light and special lenses. Different types of projectors are used in movie theaters, large-screen TV sets, and so on.

pro•long [prə lông′] *verb,* **prolonged, prolonging.** to make something longer, especially longer than is usual or necessary; extend: Doctors search for new methods to *prolong* human life. "There was a *prolonged* and not particularly cheerful silence." (John Mortimer)

prom [präm] *noun, plural* **proms.** a formal dance given by a high school or college class, especially at the end of the school year.

prom·i·nent [präm′ ə nənt] *adjective, more/ most.* **1.** important and well-known; having a high position: The meeting was attended by the mayor and other *prominent* people in our town. **2.** easy to notice or see; obvious: Supermarkets put items on sale in a *prominent* position at the front of the store. **3.** standing or sticking out: "He had small quick eyes set above his *prominent* cheekbones . . ." (James Houston) ◆ The fact of being prominent is **prominence.**

pro·mise [präm′ is] *noun, plural* **promises. 1.** a statement by a person that he or she surely will do something, or that something surely will happen. **2.** a sign of something that might happen in the future: "It was full daylight, with every *promise* of a fine day." (C.S. Forester) *—verb,* **promised, promising. 1.** to give a promise. Mom was mad that Ted borrowed the car without asking, and he *promised* her he wouldn't do it again. **2.** to give a reason to expect something to happen.

promontory The promontory known as "Devil's Elbow," on the coast of Oregon.

pro·mon·to·ry [präm′ ən tôr′ ē] *noun, plural* **promontories.** a high point of land or rock that extends outward: "Where the river joins the sea, there is a *promontory* or cliff rising straight up hundreds of feet to form the last outpost of land." (William Styron)

pro·mote [prə mōt′] *verb,* **promoted, promoting. 1.** to move a person up in rank or grade: The police officer was *promoted* to the rank of sergeant. **2.** to help the growth or development of something: The European Common Market was formed to *promote* trade among the member countries. **3.** to try to sell or advance some product: The movie star has gone on several TV talk shows to *promote* her new book.

pro·mo·tion [prə mō′ shən] *noun, plural* **promotions. 1.** the act or fact of promoting: His company just gave him a *promotion* to sales manager. **2.** a certain activity designed to help the sales or progress of something: the *promotion* of a new brand of soap.

prompt [prämpt] *adjective,* **prompter, promptest. 1.** at the correct or expected time; not late: It's not like her to keep us waiting for so long; she's usually very *prompt.* **2.** done without delay; quick: Whenever the company gets a letter of complaint from a customer, they give it a *prompt* reply. *—verb,* **prompted, prompting. 1.** to cause someone to act without delay: Seeing Linda all by herself at lunch *prompted* me to ask her to sit with us. **2.** to remind a speaker of something he or she is supposed to say: to *prompt* an actor who can't remember his next line. **—promptly,** *adverb.* **—promptness,** *noun.*

prone [prōn] *adjective, more/most.* **1.** likely to act or be a certain way: A person who is accident-*prone* is likely to have a lot of accidents. **2.** lying flat with the front or face downward: Soldiers are trained to fire a rifle while lying in a *prone* position.

prong [prông] *noun, plural* **prongs. 1.** one of the sharp points of a fork or other such tool. **2.** any sharp pointed end like this.

prong·horn [prông′ hôrn′] *noun, plural* **pronghorns.** a large, fast-running animal that has a light brown coat and curved horns with prongs. It lives in flat, open areas of western North America. It is often called an antelope but is actually a separate type of animal.

pronghorn

Pronunciation Key: Accent Marks

[′] is the normal accent mark. It shows where the main stress falls on a word.

[′] is a secondary accent mark. It shows a lighter stress than the primary accent. For example:

tel • e • vis • ion [tel′ə vizh′ən]

(Turn the page for more information.)

P

pronouns When using a pronoun: ask, "What is its form?" Ask also, "What does it refer to?" The first question is important because form can change according to the way the pronoun is used in the sentence. We say "He hit the ball" when the pronoun is the subject, "The ball hit him" when the pronoun is an object, and "That is his ball" when the pronoun shows possession. "Dave and me played tennis yesterday" or "Mom left some cake as a snack for Dave and I," are incorrect uses of the pronoun. Sometimes, a pronoun's reference is not clear, and if that happens, then the sentence won't be clear. "Uncle Mike told Dad to take the side roads. He hates driving on the main highway." Does "he" mean "Dad" or "Uncle Mike?" Make the reference clear: "Uncle Mike knows that Dad hates driving on the main highway, so he told Dad to . . ."

pro•noun [prō′ noun′] *noun, plural* **pronouns.** in grammar, a word used in place of a noun to refer to a person, place, or thing. In the sentence "I lent him my jacket," "I" is a **subject pronoun,** "him" is an **object pronoun,** and "my" is a **possessive pronoun.**

pro•nounce [prə nouns′] *verb,* **pronounced, pronouncing. 1.** to speak the sound of a word or letter: In English the letter **c** may be *pro-*

♦ Used in combination with a noun: water-*proof* seat covers, a bullet*proof* vest for a policeman, a sound*proof* recording studio.

proof•read [proōf′ rēd′] *verb,* **proofread** [proōf′ red′], **proofreading.** to read over a piece of writing before it is finished, in order to find and correct any mistakes that it may have.
♦ A person who does this work is called a **proofreader.**

proofreading This step takes place after you're finished writing. There's no point in checking a paragraph for punctuation if you're not sure that you will keep it in the final paper. Professional proofreaders use different methods to look for errors. Some read the paper aloud and say the punctuation marks and capital letters: "We (capital 'W') stopped at Ben's (capital 'B,' apostrophe 's') house. (period)" This makes you more conscious of missing items. Others read through several times, looking for a certain kind of mistake each time. Some read the paper out of order (p. 2, then 5, 1, 4, etc.). This is because when you read along naturally, you concentrate more on the story line and you aren't as likely to spot proofreading errors.

nounced with the sound of [s] or [k]. **2.** to state something in an official or serious way: "The verdict was *pronounced* by the foreman in a strong, clear voice which filled the courtroom, 'Not Guilty.'" (James Weldon Johnson)

pro•nounced [prə nounst′] *adjective.* easy to notice; obvious: "He has a *pronounced* limp when he walks." (Claude Brown)

pro•nun•ci•a•tion [prə nun′ sē ā′ shən] *noun, plural* **pronunciations.** the act of pronouncing a word or letter, or the way that it is pronounced.

proof [proōf] *noun, plural* **proofs. 1.** papers, facts, or any other sure way to show that something is true: People use their birth certificate as *proof* of how old they are. **2.** in science or mathematics, the process of determining if a certain statement is true. **3.** a trial copy of a photograph or a piece of writing, to be checked over for mistakes and problems before the printing of the final copies. **4.** a measure of the amount of alcohol in an alcoholic drink. —*adjective.* able to protect against something that is harmful or unwanted.

prop [präp] *verb,* **propped, propping. 1.** to keep something in place by placing a support under or against it: The window wouldn't stay up, so we had to *prop* it open with a stick. **2.** to place or be in a leaning or resting position: "He *propped* the book against his knees and began reading." (George Orwell) —*noun, plural* **props. 1.** something used to keep a thing in place or keep it from falling. **2.** an object used as part of a scene in a play or movie, not including the actors' costumes or the background scenery. **3.** a short word for PROPELLER.

prop•a•gan•da [präp′ ə gan′ də] *noun.* **1.** a method of trying to make people think or believe something. Propaganda usually gives only one side of an issue, and often slants the truth or even tells lies. **2.** information in this form: During World War II, German *propaganda* broadcasts by "Lord Haw Haw" tried to convince the British to give up.

pro•pel [prə pel′] *verb,* **propelled, propelling.** to make something move in a certain direction or keep it moving: "I wanted to stay and explore, but Calpurnia *propelled* me up the aisle ahead of her." (Harper Lee)

pro•pel•ler [prə pel′ər] *noun, plural* **propellers.** a device that has blades sticking out from a shaft that turns very rapidly. The blades produce a force that is used to move an aircraft through the air or a boat through the water.

propeller The propeller of a modern private aircraft, the Piper Cheyenne.

pro•per [präp′ər] *adjective, more/most.* **1.** suited to a certain use or purpose; fitting; correct: "The men had neither *proper* clothing nor food enough to see them through the winter." (Barry Lopez) "I like to make a *proper* job of anything I take on. See it through to the end." (Penelope Lively) **2.** in the most correct sense of the word; strictly speaking: The Dallas Cowboys actually play in the suburb of Irving, not in the city *proper.* —**properly,** *adverb.*

proper noun or **proper name** a noun that names one particular person, place, or thing and is spelled with a capital letter.

prop•er•ty [präp′ər tē] *noun, plural* **properties.** **1.** anything that is owned by a person: Stealing is taking something that is not your *property.* **2.** a certain area of land: Oceanfront *property* in southern California is very expensive. **3.** a particular quality or fact about something: It is a *property* of iron to be attracted by a magnet.

proph•e•cy [präf′ə sē] *noun, plural* **prophecies.** **1.** the act of telling or warning about something that is supposed to happen in the future. Prophecy is usually thought of as coming from God or from some special power, rather than from facts or reason. **2.** something that is said in this way: The *prophecies* of Nostradamus, a French writer of the 1500's, supposedly describe many events that took place in later years.

proph•e•sy [präf′ə sī] *verb,* **prophesied, prophesying.** to tell or give a prophecy.

proph•et [präf′it] *noun, plural* **prophets. 1.** a person who tells or delivers a message that comes from God: The Bible tells about Hebrew *prophets* such as Isaiah, Abraham, and Jeremiah. **2.** a person who claims to be able to tell what will happen: He is a financial *prophet* who writes a newspaper column predicting what the stock market will do. ◆ Something that is **prophetic** [prə fet′ik] tells about the future.

pro•por•tion [prə pôr′shən] *noun, plural* **proportions. 1.** the amount or size of something when compared to something else: When mixing the salad dressing, use the *proportion* of three parts oil to one part vinegar. **2.** *also,* **proportions.** the size or extent of something: What started out as a minor dispute between the two countries is now taking on the *proportions* of a major war. **3.** a proper or balanced relationship between the parts of a thing: The artist drew the picture so that the horse's head was in *proportion* with its body.

pro•pos•al [prə pō′zəl] *noun, plural* **proposals. 1.** the act or fact of proposing: the *proposal* of a motion at a committee meeting. **2.** something that is proposed; a plan or suggestion: The city council is studying the Smith Company's *proposal* to build a new hotel on the lakefront. **3.** an offer of marriage.

pro•pose [prə pōz′] *verb,* **proposed, proposing. 1.** to put something forward to be considered; suggest: "When we left the dining room, she *proposed* to show me over the rest of the house." (Charlotte Brontë) **2.** to plan to do something: "First, how do you *propose* to get this tree to the river?" (Lloyd Alexander) **3.** to make an offer of marriage.

pro•po•si•tion [präp′ə zish′ən] *noun, plural* **propositions. 1.** something that is proposed; a proposal: *Proposition* 13 was a famous measure in California to cut the cost of government spending. **2.** a statement put forward for argument or discussion: The Gettysburg Address says that this country is "dedicated to the *proposition* that all men are created equal."

pro•pri•e•tor [prə prī′ə tər] *noun, plural* **proprietors.** a person who owns something, especially the owner of a small business or store.

pro•pul•sion [prə pul′shən] *noun.* the act or

	Pronunciation Key: A–F		
a	and; hat	ch	chew; such
ā	ate; stay	d	dog; lid
â	care; air	e	end; yet
ä	father; hot	ē	she; each
b	boy; cab	f	fun; off

(Turn the page for more information.)

process of propelling something: Modern fighter aircraft are powered by jet *propulsion.*

prose [prōz] the usual form of written language; writing that is not poetry.

> **prose** Any form of writing that is not poetry is *prose.* Prose is what we speak, and what we write generally, whether in the form of newspaper articles, novels, short stories, encyclopedia entries, and so on. Prose is the form that you use for most of your school writing, too. How do you judge how well prose is written? In newspaper articles, facts are the key element of prose. In a narrative, dialogue (the speech of the characters) might be what a critic notices. In an essay, elegance and grace can be achieved. Prose can be highly distinctive and personal, as in Tom Wolfe's *The Right Stuff.* Or, a writer's prose can be so subtly controlled that it is almost "invisible"—the reader is not aware of the author's hand. George Orwell, E. B. White, Joseph Mitchell, Lillian Ross, John McPhee, and Joan Didion write that way.

pros•e•cute [präs′ ə kyōōt′] *verb,* **prosecuted, prosecuting.** to bring someone to trial in a court of law for a crime or offense: He was *prosecuted* for stealing a car. ♦ A lawyer who prosecutes a case on behalf of the government is a **prosecutor.** This side of the case is the **prosecution.**

pros•pect [präs′ pekt] *noun, plural* **prospects.** **1.** something that can be expected or looked forward to; a strong hope or possibility: "Is there any *prospect* of this money coming after all?" (Christopher Isherwood) **2.** a person who is a possible candidate or customer: She made three sales this morning, and also lined up several good *prospects.* **3.** a view looking out over an area: When asked what the most beautiful view in Scotland was, Samuel Johnson said, "The noblest *prospect* which a Scotchman ever sees is the road that leads to England." —*verb,* **prospected, prospecting.** to search for something valuable: In 1849 many people came to California to *prospect* for gold.

pros•pec•tive [prə spek′ tiv] *adjective.* likely to be; very possible: They want to sell their house and have shown it to two *prospective* buyers.

pros•pec•tor [präs′ pek′ tər] *noun, plural* **prospectors.** a person who searches an area for gold, oil, uranium, or other such valuable materials.

pros•per [präs′ pər] *verb,* **prospered, prospering.** to do very well; be successful: His restaurant business has really *prospered.*

pros•per•i•ty [präs per′ ə tē] *noun.* the condition of doing very well or being successful: When the U.S. was struggling to get out of the Depression, the Democratic Party had the saying "*Prosperity* is just around the corner."

pros•per•ous [präs′ pər əs] *adjective, more/ most.* having wealth or good fortune; successful: *prosperous* farm land, a *prosperous* businessman who owns the largest store in town.

pro•tect [prə tekt′] *verb,* **protected, protecting.** to keep or guard from harm: Secret Service men *protect* the President when he travels. The car has a special coating to *protect* the paint.

pro•tec•tion [prə tek′ shən] *noun, plural* **protections. 1.** the fact of keeping someone or something from harm: "When Shawn was afraid, he came running to Agba for *protection.*" (Marguerite Henry) **2.** something that prevents damage or harm: Many toothpastes contain a chemical called fluoride as a *protection* against tooth decay.

pro•tec•tive [prə tek′ tiv] *adjective, more/most.* serving to protect: Jerry says his mother is too *protective* and watches him too closely.

pro•tein [prō′ tēn′] *noun, plural* **proteins.** a substance found in all living animals and plant cells. Proteins are necessary for human life to exist. Foods such as eggs, milk, meat, beans, and cheese are good sources of *protein.*

pro•test [prō′ test′] *noun, plural* **protests.** something said or done to show that a person disagrees with some policy, action, or decision: In the 1960's there were *protests* against the U.S. involvement in the Vietnam War. ♦ A person who acts in this way is a **protester.** —[*also,* prə test′] *verb,* **protested, protesting.** to make a protest; object: In baseball a team can *protest* a game if they feel that the umpire has not followed the rules properly.

Pro•tes•tant [prät′ is tənt] *noun, plural* **Protestants.** a person of the Christian religion who does not belong to a Catholic or an Orthodox church. Protestant churches include the Lutherans, Presbyterians, Methodists, and Baptists.

pro•ton [prō′ tän] *noun, plural* **protons.** a basic particle of an atom found in the NUCLEUS of the atom. A proton has a positive electrical charge.

pro•to•plasm [prō′ tə plaz′ əm] *noun.* a basic substance that is the living matter of every plant or animal cell. Protoplasm is like a clear jelly with no color, and it is enclosed by a membrane that forms the wall of the cell.

pro•to•zo•an [prō′ tə zō′ ən] *noun, plural* **pro-tozoans** *or* **protozoa.** one of a group of tiny animals that have only one cell.

pro•trude [prō trood′] *verb,* **protruded, pro-truding.** to stick out: "He was holding the hoe with the end of the handle *protruding* about six inches from his right fist." (John Le Carré)

proud [proud] *adjective,* **prouder, proudest.**
1. being pleased with something you have made or done, or something that relates to you: Andy was very *proud* of the picture he painted in his kindergarten art class and showed it to everyone in the family. **2.** causing or able to cause this feeling: It was a *proud* moment for Jan's parents when she graduated from college. **3.** thinking too highly of oneself; conceited: "Do not be too *proud* to accept help from anyone who can give it, Miss Richards." (Mary Elizabeth Vroman) —**proudly,** *adverb.*

prove [proov] *verb,* **proved** or **proven, proving.**
1. to show that something is true or as it is said it to be: The French scientist Louis Pasteur was the first to *prove* that bacteria cause disease. **2.** to turn out to be: "He *proved* to be a nice, friendly cop, however, and gave them directions instead of a ticket." (Wright Morris)

pro•verb [präv′ ərb] *noun, plural* **proverbs.** a short, well-known saying that contains a certain truth or makes a certain point: "A stitch in time saves nine" and "He who laughs last laughs best" are well-known *proverbs.*

pro•vid•ing [prə vī′ ding] *conjunction.* on the condition that; provided: "He can buy mine any time he wants to, *providing* he offers me a decent price." (John O'Hara)

pro•vince [präv′ ins] *noun, plural* **provinces.** a large division or part of a country, similar to a U.S. state: Alberta is a *province* of Canada.

pro•vin•cial [prə vin′ shəl] *adjective.* **1.** of or related to a province: Vancouver is the seat of *provincial* government in British Columbia. **2.** having to do with small towns or farm areas, especially in a way that is thought of as old-fashioned or narrow-minded: A person with a *provincial* attitude will not accept new or different ideas.

pro•vi•sion [prə vizh′ ən] *noun, plural* **provisions.** **1.** the act or fact of providing: A company pension plan is a *provision* for a worker's retirement. **2. provisions.** food supplies; food: "*Provisions* to last a whole winter have to be brought up in autumn." (Doris Lessing) —**provisional,** *adjective.* for the time being: Alexander Kerensky led the *provisional* government that followed the Russian Revolution, but he was overthrown after a short time.

pro•voke [prə vōk′] *verb,* **provoked, provoking.** **1.** to cause to happen; bring about: ". . . do nothing that might *provoke* any public outbreak." (T.S. Eliot) **2.** to excite or stir up: The British tax on tea *provoked* the American colonists to hold the protest known as the

proved/proven "Here, an accused person is innocent until *proved* guilty." Or would you write, ". . . until *proven* guilty?" Some language critics take a tough stand on this issue. Sheridan Baker states that *proven* isn't a verb at all. Another critic, Theodore Bernstein, allows that it is a verb, but says it's Scottish English, not American English. What does our Word Survey show? We found that *proven* is generally used as a verb. In the past, *proved* was far more common. However, in the past 25 years or so *proven* has become just as common: "He [an American general] believed, and in this he was *proven* correct, that air power could destroy Japan." (Theodore H. White) Our recommendation is: use either *proved* or *proven,* whichever one sounds more natural to you.

pro•vide [prə vīd′] *verb,* **provided, providing.**
1. to give what is needed or wanted; supply: "Miss Cutler *provided* lunch, for those who asked for it, at one o'clock." (Kingsley Amis)
2. to take care of; support: "She has been *provided* for as if she were a little princess." (Frances Hodgson Burnett) **3.** to make plans; prepare for something: The campers carried extra food to *provide* for an emergency.

pro•vid•ed [prə vī′ did] *conjunction.* on the condition that; if: You can throw those old magazines away, *provided* Dad doesn't want to save any of them.

Boston Tea Party. ♦ Something that provokes is a **provocation** [präv′ və kā′ shən].

prow [prou] *noun, plural* **prows.** the front part of a boat or ship; the bow.

Pronunciation Key: G–N			
g	give; big	k	kind; cat; back
h	hold	l	let; ball
i	it; this	m	make; time
ī	ice; my	n	not; own
j	jet; gem; edge	ng	having

(Turn the page for more information.)

P

prowl [proul] *verb,* **prowled, prowling. 1.** of an animal, to move slowly and quietly while looking around for prey or food: "He knew that a fox *prowled* somewhere in the woods." (E.B. White) **2.** to move in a quiet, restless way: "Upstairs Mrs. Williton *prowled* uneasily round the room." (Barbara Pym) —*noun, plural* **prowls.** the act of prowling: a lion on the *prowl.*

pru•dent [proo′dənt] *adjective, more/most.* looking ahead to possible risks or problems; showing care and good judgment. ◆ The fact of being prudent is **prudence.**

prune¹ [proon] *noun, plural* **prunes.** a plum that is dried and used as food.

prune² *verb,* **pruned, pruning.** to cut off certain parts from a plant to help it grow or to make it look better: Fruit trees are often *pruned* so that they will produce better fruit.

pry¹ [prī] *verb,* **pried, prying.** to move or raise by force: "The thumbtack was still up there, and she *pried* it loose." (Shirley Jackson)

pry² *verb,* **pried, prying.** to be too curious or to ask personal questions about something that is not one's business: "She's always trying to *pry* into our affairs." (George Orwell)

psalm [säm] *noun, plural* **psalms. 1.** a sacred song or poem. **2. Psalms.** a collection of such poems in the Bible.

psy•chi•a•trist [sə kī′ ə trist] *noun, plural* **psychiatrists.** a doctor who is specially trained to treat people who are mentally ill or have serious mental problems. ◆ The treatment of mental illness is **psychiatry** [sə kī′ ə trē′].

psy•cho•log•i•cal [sī′ kə läj′ i kəl] *adjective.* **1.** having to do with psychology: Observing the behavior of babies is part of *psychological* research. **2.** having to do with the mind and feelings: to have *psychological* problems.

psy•chol•o•gy [sī käl′ ə jē] *noun.* the study of the human mind. Psychology studies how people think and why they act as they do. ◆ A person who is specially trained to practice psychology is a **psychologist** [sī käl′ ə jist].

pu•ber•ty [pyoo′ bər tē] *noun.* the age or time at which a person's body becomes physically mature and able to produce children.

pub•lic [pub′ lik] *adjective.* **1.** having to do with people as a group; of people in general: *Public* opinion is in favor of the President's new tax plan. **2.** serving or meant for everyone; not private: a *public* park, a *public* road, the *public* library. **3.** working or acting for the government: A police officer, a mayor, and a judge are known as *public* officials or *public* servants. **4.** done or presented in front of people: The art *public* speaking is called "oratory." —*noun.* people in general: Theodore Roosevelt's former home at Sagamore Hill is now open to the *public.* —**publicly,** *adverb.*

pub•li•ca•tion [pub′ lə kā′ shən] *noun, plural* **publications. 1.** something that is published; a magazine, newspaper, or other such printed material. **2.** the act or fact of publishing: The author John O'Hara often chose Thanksgiving Day as the official *publication* date for his new books.

pub•lic•i•ty [pub lis′ ə tē] *noun.* **1.** information that is given out so that the public will know more about something. Radio announcements, posters, and newspaper articles are types of publicity. **2.** the type of information that becomes known about a person or thing: That movie star has gotten a lot of bad *publicity* lately about being so rude to reporters.

public school a school that is open to all children living in its area, free of charge. The government pays for these schools with tax money that comes from the public.

public television television broadcasting that is supported by donations and public funds, rather than by commercials paid for by advertisers. Public TV usually broadcasts educational or cultural programs.

pub•lish [pub′ lish] *verb,* **published, publishing.** to produce a magazine, newspaper, book, or other such printed item and offer it to the public.

publishing The basic meaning of publish is "to make public." An author writes a book; a publisher publishes it. That is, the publisher gives an author a contract, and if he approves of the author's manuscript he gives the author advice and copy edits, designs the book, has it printed and bound, and sold to bookstores and libraries. About 40,000 new books are published each year in the U.S., of which about 15,000 are called "trade" books, meaning fiction and nonfiction addressed to the general reader. It is a sad but true fact that in the 1980's more than half of these books lose money for the publisher and earn very little money for the author. "Best Sellers" have become important because a best-selling book helps to pay for the publisher's losses on other books.

pub•lish•er [pub/lish ər] *noun, plural* **publishers.** a person or company that produces newspapers, magazines, books, or the like for sale to the public. ♦ The work or business of doing this is called **publishing.**

puck [puk] *noun, plural* **pucks.** a hard black rubber disk used in playing the game of ice hockey.

puck•er [puk/ ər] *verb,* **puckered, puckering.** to come together in small folds or wrinkles: "He *puckers* his lips and blows a kiss . . ." (Ann Beattie)

pud•ding [pood/ ing] *noun, plural* **puddings.** a sweet, creamy dessert made with milk, eggs, and flavorings.

pud•dle [pud/ əl] *noun, plural* **puddles.** a small pool of water or some other liquid on a surface.

pueb•lo [pweb/ lō] *noun, plural* **pueblos. 1.** an American Indian village of adobe and stone houses joined together in groups and having flat roofs. Pueblos can be found in New Mexico and Arizona. **2. Pueblo.** a member of a tribe that lives or once lived in pueblos.

pueblo The famous Taos pueblo in Taos, New Mexico shows an unusual combination of the Pueblo Indian, Plains Indian, and Spanish cultures.

Puer•to Ri•co [pôr/ tə rē/ kō] an island in the West Indies that is a commonwealth of the U.S. *Area:* 3,440 square miles. *Population:* 3,188,000. —**Puerto Rican,** *adjective; noun.*

puff [puf] *noun, plural* **puffs. 1.** a short, sudden blast of air, wind, smoke, and so on. **2.** anything soft, light, and fluffy: A cream *puff* is a type of food. —*verb,* **puffed, puffing. 1.** to give off a short blast of air or the like: to *puff* on a cigarette. **2.** to swell up: "He probably could not see very clearly anyway the way his eyes were *puffed* tight." (Ernest Hemingway) —**puffy,** *adjective: puffy* white clouds.

puf•fin [puf/ in] *noun, plural* **puffins.** a black-and-white sea bird with a plump body, a short,

puffin

thick neck, and a large, brightly-colored bill. Puffins live in large groups in northern areas.

Pu•lit•zer [pool/ it sər] **Joseph,** 1847–1911, American newspaper publisher, born in Hungary. He established a fund for the **Pulitzer Prizes,** which are given each year for outstanding writing of various kinds.

pull [pool] *verb,* **pulled, pulling. 1.** to hold something and move it toward or along with oneself: The boy *pulled* a wagon filled with his toy soldiers. **2.** to draw something up or out in this way: to *pull* weeds in a garden. **3.** to go or move to a certain place: A car *pulled* up in front of our house. **4.** to hurt or damage by stretching too hard: to *pull* a muscle. **5.** to do something, especially in a sudden or unexpected way: to *pull* a bank robbery, to *pull* a trick on someone. —*noun, plural* **pulls. 1.** the act or fact of pulling: The *pull* of the river's current made swimming dangerous. **2.** *Informal.* a special kind of influence or advantage: The senator tried to use his *pull* to keep his son in the army from being sent overseas.

pul•ley [pool/ ē] *noun, plural* **pulleys.** a wheel with a groove around it and a rope or chain that moves through the groove. A pulley is used to lift or lower heavy things, such as to raise the engine out of a car for repair.

pulp [pulp] *noun, plural* **pulps. 1.** the soft, juicy part of a fruit or vegetable. **2.** any wet, soft mass of material like this: Wood *pulp* is used to make newspapers.

Pronunciation Key. O–S			
ō	over; go	ou	out; town
ô	all; law	p	put; hop
oo	look; full	r	run; car
o͞o	pool; who	s	set; miss
oi	oil; boy	sh	show

(Turn the page for more information.)

pul•pit [pool′ pit] *noun, plural* **pulpits.** a separate, raised place in a church where a minister or priest may stand to give a sermon or to speak to the congregation.

pulse [puls] *noun, plural* **pulses. 1.** in the body, the steady beating of an artery that carries blood, caused by the heart pumping the blood. By feeling the pulse in your wrist, you can count the rate of your heartbeat. **2.** any steady or regular beat like this: the *pulse* of the bass drum in a marching band. —*verb,* **pulsed, pulsing.** to have or make a pulse; beat: "England after its great Victorian age was *pulsing* with new talent." (Barbara Tuchman)

pu•ma [pyōō′ mə] *noun, plural* **pumas.** a large, wild cat found in North and South America, more often called a MOUNTAIN LION.

pump [pump] *noun, plural* **pumps.** a machine that moves water, another liquid, or a gas into or out of something: A car's fuel *pump* moves gasoline from the gas tank into the engine. —*verb,* **pumped, pumping. 1.** to move a liquid or gas from one place to another with a pump. **2.** to blow air or other gas into: to *pump* up a bicycle tire. **3.** to swing something hard up and down, as if pumping water from a well: The pitcher *pumped* his arms over his head before throwing the ball to the batter. **4.** to try to get information by careful questioning: "As we chatted it suddenly occurred to me the fellow was trying to get at something—in fact *pumping* me." (Joseph Conrad)

pump•kin [pump′ kin] *noun, plural* **pumpkins.** a large, round yellow-orange fruit with a hard outer shell. People hollow out pumpkins and carve them into faces at Halloween.

pun [pun] *noun, plural* **puns.** a joking way of saying something by using a word or saying that has two different meanings. "The *late* Mr. Smith tried to jump on the train as it left the station" is a pun, because *late* means both "dead" and "not on time." *Grave* normally means "serious," but Shakespeare has a comic character who is about to die say that he soon will be "a *grave* man."

punch[1] [punch] *verb,* **punched, punching. 1.** to hit hard with the fist. **2.** to push or poke sharply at something: "Ramo began to *punch* at the earth with his stick." (Scott O'Dell) **3.** to poke or press something to make it work: "He *punched* the numbers on the square black computer." (James Houston) **4.** to herd or move cattle or sheep. —*noun, plural* **punches.** a blow with the fist. —**puncher,** *noun.*

punch[2] *noun, plural* **punches.** a tool for making holes or pressing a design in something. —*verb,* **punched, punching.** to make a hole or design with a punch.

punch[3] *noun, plural* **punches.** a sweet drink made by mixing different fruit juices, soda, and so on.

pumpkin

punc•tu•al [pungk′ chōō əl] *adjective, more/most.* at the proper or expected time; not late; prompt: "And once a year, *punctual* as clockwork, the stranger with the handsome buggy would come driving up." (Stephen Vincent Benét) —**punctually,** *adverb:* "Mrs. Wong comes back from the library *punctually* at four o'clock." (Ann Beattie)

punc•tu•ate [pungk′ chōō āt] *verb,* **punctuated, punctuating. 1.** to mark writing with periods, commas, and other symbols to make the mean-

puns John Nichols is noted for his books about the American Southwest, such as *The Milagro Beanfield War* and *If Mountains Die.* In his student days, he wrote a column for his college newspaper called "Just No Stories" (a takeoff on Rudyard Kipling's "Just So Stories"). Each column built up to its closing line, which was the worst, most outrageous pun Nichols could create. Puns are usually thought of as being silly, and an audience often groans rather than laughs. Why then do they appeal to people who are interested in serious writing? Poets are known for having a special interest in puns; Shakespeare used them often in his plays. Puns can be likened to crossword puzzles and other word games. Playing with words, twisting them around, searching for new uses of words—all this can be fun.

ing clear. **2.** to mark something as if using these symbols: "Mr. Heinz left his sentence unfinished, but from the way he *punctuated* it with the slam of the door even Paddington could see that he wasn't pleased . . ." (Michael Bond)

punc•tu•a•tion [pungk′chōō ā′shən] *noun.* the system of using periods, commas, and other symbols to make written material clear. ♦ A **punctuation mark** is used to do this.

punctuation This does for a writer what a speaker can do by pausing between words, lowering or raising the voice, and using other forms of emphasis. Let's say a speaker wants to show a break in thought. He or she just stops between words for a moment. But there's no sense of *time* in writing. So the writer must use a comma or semi-colon to create a short break, and a period for a more complete break. To show that a certain word stands out from the rest of the sentence, a speaker may say that word more loudly than the others. But in writing, all words look the same and would seem to have the same importance. So the writer underlines the word (or in print, uses *italics*). A rise in the tone of voice shows that a certain sentence is a question; in writing we use a question mark. Punctuation is not always related directly to speaking habits. A comma must be used at certain times: "Red, white, and blue are the colors of our country." "The Declaration of Independence was signed on July 4, 1776."

punc•ture [pung′chər] *verb,* **punctured, puncturing.** to make a hole in something with a sharp object; pierce: A piece of glass had *punctured* the tire. —*noun, plural* **punctures.** a hole made by a sharp object: Cathy had a *puncture* wound where the nail went into her foot.

pun•gent [pun′jənt] *adjective, more/most.* having a strong, sharp taste or smell: "The scent of the sun-warmed prairie came up to her, and the *pungent* smell of the sagebrush." (Edna Ferber)

pun•ish [pun′ish] *verb,* **punished, punishing. 1.** to make a person suffer for doing something wrong: For being so rude to her mother, she was *punished* by not being allowed to watch TV. **2.** to treat harshly or roughly. ♦ Usually used as an adjective: From here to the cabin is a *punishing* drive over old dirt roads.

pun•ish•ment [pun′ish mənt] *noun, plural* **punishments. 1.** the act or fact of punishing: The boy took his *punishment* without crying or complaining. **2.** the way in which someone is punished: Putting a person to death for a crime is called **capital punishment. 3.** rough treatment: The ads for these watches say they are made to take a lot of *punishment.*

punk [pungk] *noun, plural* **punks.** *Slang.* a young person who is rough and rude and who often breaks the law. —*adjective. Slang.* having to do with a rough, loud style of rock music, or with a style of dress that developed from this music, usually featuring loud colors and very unusual hairstyles and makeup.

punt [punt] *verb,* **punted, punting.** in football, a kick made by dropping the ball and kicking it before it hits the ground.

pu•ny [pyōō′nē] *adjective,* **punier, puniest.** small and weak: Other boys made fun of him for being short and said he had a *puny* build.

pup [pup] *noun, plural* **pups.** a young dog; a puppy. ♦ The young of some other animals are sometimes called pups, such as seals or sharks.

pu•pa [pyōō′pə] *noun, plural* **pupas.** an insect in a resting stage before it becomes an adult. A caterpillar is a pupa when it is in its cocoon.

pu•pil[1] [pyōō′pəl] *noun, plural* **pupils.** a person who is studying in school; a student.

pupil[2] *noun, plural* **pupils.** the opening in the center of the eye. The pupil looks like a black dot in the middle of the colored part of the eye. Light enters the eye through the pupil.

pup•pet [pup′it] *noun, plural* **puppets. 1.** a small figure of a person or animal that is used as a toy or in shows. Some puppets fit over the hand and are moved by moving the fingers; others have strings that are pulled to make them move. **2.** a person or group that is completely controlled by someone else. ♦ Also used as an adjective: East Germany has a *puppet* government that is actually under the power of the Soviet Union.

pup•py [pup′ē] *noun, plural* **puppies.** a young dog.

pur•chase [pur′chəs] *verb,* **purchased, purchasing.** to get something by paying money;

Pronunciation Key: T–Z

t	ten; date	v	very; live
th	think	w	win; away
<u>th</u>	these	y	you
u	cut; butter	z	zoo; cause
ur	turn; bird	zh	measure

(Turn the page for more information.)

613

P

buy: to *purchase* a car or a suit of clothes. —*noun, plural* **purchases. 1.** a thing that is purchased; something bought: In a supermarket people pay for their *purchases* at the check-out counter. **2.** the act of purchasing.

pure [pyoor *or* pyo͞or] *adjective,* **purer, purest. 1.** free from dirt, germs, or harmful substances; perfectly clean: *pure* drinking water from a mountain stream. **2.** not mixed with anything of lesser quality: a ring that is *pure* gold, a blouse of *pure* silk. **3.** free from evil or faults: a kindly, *pure*-hearted person. **4.** nothing other than; complete: I don't know how I picked the right number—it was *pure* luck.

pure•bred [pyoor′ bred′] *adjective.* of an animal, having ancestors that are all of the same breed or kind: Our dog is a *purebred* collie.

pur•i•fy [pyoor′ ə fī′] *verb,* **purified, purifying.** to make pure or clean: They attached a filter system to the faucet to *purify* their drinking water. ♦ The process of doing this is called **purification** [pyoor′ ə fə kā′ shən].

Pu•ri•tan [pyoor′ ə tən] *noun, plural* **Puritans. 1.** a member of a group in the 1500's and 1600's who wanted to "purify" the Church of England by making church services simpler and living strictly according to the teachings of the Bible. The PILGRIMS were Puritans. **2. puritan.** a person who follows very strict rules for living and does not approve of certain freedoms and pleasures. ♦ A person who has this attitude is **puritanical** [pyoor′ ə tan′ i kəl].

pur•ist [pyoor′ əst] *noun, plural* **purists.** a person who is very strict about the correct way of doing things: He's a *purist* in the use of language and always points out people's mistakes.

pu•ri•ty [pyoor′ ə tē] *noun.* the state of being pure: Diamonds are graded by their *purity.*

pur•ple [pur′ pəl] *noun, plural* **purples.** the color made up of red and blue mixed together.

pur•pose [pur′ pəs] *noun, plural* **purposes. 1.** the reason why something is made or done; a plan, goal, or use: The *purpose* of a football helmet is to protect the player's head. **2. on**

purpose. knowing what one is doing; not by accident: "He thinks the child knocked him over *on purpose.*" (Ann Beattie)

pur•pose•ly [pur′ pəs lē] *adverb.* for a reason; on purpose: Brian *purposely* left the phone off the hook; he didn't want to be disturbed.

purr [pur] *noun, plural* **purrs.** a soft, low sound such as is made by a cat. —*verb,* **purred, purring.** to make this sound: "The Lincoln's motor *purred* into life." (Stephen King).

purse [purs] *noun, plural* **purses. 1.** a bag used by women for carrying money, keys, a comb or brush, and other such small personal items; also called a handbag or pocketbook. **2.** a small bag or pouch used to hold money: a change *purse.* **3.** a sum of money given as a prize or gift: a horse race with a $100,000 *purse* for the winner. —*verb,* **pursed, pursing.** to pull or draw together, as if closing a purse: She *pursed* her lips as she tasted the sour medicine.

pur•sue [pər so͞o′] *verb,* **pursued, pursuing. 1.** to follow in order to catch up to or capture; chase: The howling dogs *pursued* the fox across the fields. ♦ A person or animal that does this is a **pursuer. 2.** to follow or carry out something: I could see that he was getting upset, so I decided not to *pursue* the matter.

pur•suit [pər so͞ot′] *noun, plural* **pursuits. 1.** the act of pursuing; chasing or following something: The bank robbers' car raced around the corner with two police cars in close *pursuit.* **2.** the act of making a continued effort to reach some goal: The Declaration of Independence says that all people have the right to the *pursuit* of happiness. **3.** a particular activity: Golf is a popular *pursuit* among retired people.

pus [pus] *noun.* a thick yellowish-white fluid that collects in a sore or infection.

push [poosh] *verb,* **pushed, pushing. 1.** to press against something in order to move it: They *pushed* the stalled car to the side of the road. **2.** to press or move forward with force: The man *pushed* his way through the crowd. **3.** to press with the finger: This lock is opened by

purpose of writing You might say, "The purpose of this letter is to thank Grandpa for the birthday present he sent me. The purpose of my English report is to get extra credit in the course." Teachers of writing would say that these are *motives* for writing, or *goals.* But a writer's purpose is the *effect* he or she hopes to have on the reader. If you write a science report, your purpose is to inform. You wouldn't include jokes, slang terms, made-up words, and so on. But suppose you wrote a note to cheer up a sick friend. Now your purpose is to entertain; jokes and made-up words do suit your purpose. Sometimes your purpose is to persuade, as in a letter to the editor. You'll be serious, as in the science paper. But now you need to give opinions as well as facts, so your approach will be different.

pushing a set of buttons. **4.** to try to make a person do something by urging or force: Billy doesn't like milk; Mom has to *push* him to drink it. **5.** to try to sell or promote something: The store is really *pushing* their new computer with a special sale. —*noun, plural* **pushes.** the act or fact of pushing. —**pushy,** *adjective.* too anxious to get ahead or to be noticed; very forward.

push•cart [poosh′ kärt′] *noun, plural* **pushcarts.** a small cart that is pushed by hand. People who sell flowers or hot dogs on the street often use pushcarts.

push-up [poosh′ up′] *noun, plural* **push-ups.** an exercise in which a person starts by lying face down, then raises and lowers himself by straightening and bending the arms while keeping the rest of the body straight.

pus•sy willow [poos′ ē] a small willow tree with silky-gray flower clusters that are thought to look like a cat's fur. These are known as **catkins.** They grow on long, straight branches.

put [poot] *verb,* **put, putting. 1.** to cause to be in a certain place: *Put* the milk in the refrigerator. He forgot to *put* a period after the sentence. **2.** to cause to be in a certain condition: You push this button to *put* on the TV. **3.** to say something in a certain way: Her taste in clothes is—how shall I *put* it?—very unusual.

putt [put] *verb,* **putted, putting.** in golf, to hit a ball that is on the green with a soft tap so that it will roll into or toward the hole. ♦ The golf club used to do this is called a **putter.**

put•ter [put′ ər] *verb,* **puttered, puttering.** to keep busy without doing anything important; work at small, minor tasks: On weekends Dad likes to *putter* around the yard, doing odd jobs.

put•ty [put′ ē] *noun, plural* **putties.** a mixture that is soft and moist like clay when put on and then slowly hardens. It is used to fill cracks in wood and hold panes of glass in place.

puz•zle [puz′ əl] *noun, plural* **puzzles. 1.** a game in which a person tries to solve some problem as a test of mental skill, such as a CROSSWORD PUZZLE or JIGSAW PUZZLE. **2.** something that is hard to understand; a mystery. —*verb,* **puzzled, puzzling.** to be a puzzle; be hard to understand; "The girl *puzzled* him. Try as he might he couldn't remember ever having heard of her." (P. D. James)

pyg•my [pig′ mē] *noun, plural* **pygmies. 1.** a person or thing that is much smaller than normal or usual. **2. Pygmy.** a member of a tribe of very short people living in central Africa. As adults, Pygmies are about four to five feet tall. —*adjective.* very small.

pyramid The Gizeh Pyramids near Cairo, Egypt were built in about 2680 B.C. The largest is the Great Pyramid of the Pharaoh (ruler) Khufu.

pyr•a•mid [pir′ ə mid] *noun, plural* **pyramids. 1.** a figure or object having a flat base and three or more triangles that slope upward to meet at the top. **2. Pyramid.** one of the huge stone structures with four triangle-shaped sides that were built thousands of years ago in Egypt.

py•thon [pī′ thän *or* pī′ thən] *noun, plural* **pythons.** a very large snake that is not poisonous, but that coils around its prey and crushes it to death. Pythons are found in Africa, Asia, and Australia.

python Among the world's largest snakes, pythons usually eat small animals. But they may hunt larger prey such as wild pig.

Pronunciation Key: [ə] Symbol

The [ə] or *schwa* sound occurs in syllables without an accent. It can be spelled with any vowel, such as **a** in above, **e** in listen, **i** in pencil, **o** in melon, **u** in circus. It can also be a combination of vowels, such as **io** in action, **ai** in mountain, **iou** in precious.

(Turn the page for more information.)

q, Q [kyōō] *noun, plural* **q's, Q's.** the seventeenth letter of the alphabet.

quack [kwak] *noun, plural* **quacks.** the sound that a duck makes. —*verb,* **quacked, quacking.** to make such a sound.

quail [kwāl] *noun, plural* **quail** or **quails.** a small bird with a plump body, short tail, and brownish feathers. It is often hunted as game. —*verb,*

qual·i·fy [kwäl′ə fī′] *verb,* **qualified, qualifying. 1.** to cause to be fit or suited for something; make able to do or have: The winner of this race will *qualify* for the state championship next week. **2.** to change so as to make less strong; limit or restrict: The governor had promised he wouldn't raise taxes, but he later *qualified* that by saying he'd do it "only if necessary."

---

qualifiers When you *qualify* a statement, you add something that weakens it. "She's a great tennis player" is an absolute statement. If you add "for her age" or "considering she's never had a lesson," then you've *qualified* it. E.B. White said: "Avoid the use of qualifiers. *Rather, very, little, pretty*—these are the leeches that infest [swarm all over] the pond of prose, sucking the blood of words." When you *qualify* a statement, you suck its strength, like a leech or mosquito sucking blood from the skin. "I was *a little* disappointed when I saw the Grand Canyon. It was *pretty* big, but not *quite* as big as I expected. It was *somewhat* crowded, and there wasn't much to do. I *sort of* wished there was *some kind of* amusement park. I ended up *rather* bored." This writer makes statements, but then backs away by adding a qualifier to each one. Is he saying that the Grand Canyon is boring? Then he's got a tiger by the tail—most people won't agree! He should write boldly and directly.

---

quailed, quailing. to shiver or draw back in fear, as a quail is thought to do when being hunted: "The man who *quails* or weakens in this fight of ours . . ." (Paul Laurence Dunbar)

quaint [kwānt] *adjective,* **quainter, quaintest.** interesting or attractive in an odd, old-fashioned way: a *quaint* little village with houses in the style of the 1890's.

quake [kwāk] *verb,* **quaked, quaking.** to shake or tremble: I could feel the ground *quake* when the heavy truck roared by. —*noun, plural* **quakes. 1.** the act of trembling or shaking. **2.** a short word for EARTHQUAKE.

qual·i·fi·ca·tion [kwal′ə fə kā′shən] *noun, plural* **qualifications. 1.** something that makes a person or thing suited for a job or task: Having good grades in your high school courses is the main *qualification* to get into college. **2.** something that limits or restricts: The boss accepted their plan, with one *qualification*—everything has to be ready by June instead of September.

qual·i·ty [kwäl′ə tē] *noun, plural* **qualities. 1.** something that makes a person or thing what it is; the nature or character of something: One *quality* that makes diamonds very valuable is their great hardness. "The most vital *quality* a soldier can possess is self-confidence." (George S. Patton) **2.** the amount of worth or value that something has: Silk is a high-*quality* fabric. "Now the *quality* of the houses improved, some large and attractive, with gardens full of flowers." (Bernard Malamud)

quan·ti·ty [kwän′tə tē] *noun, plural* **quantities. 1.** something that be counted or measured; a number or amount: In mathematics, the letter 'x' is often used to stand for an unknown *quantity*. **2.** a large number or amount: Supermarkets can charge lower prices than a small corner store because they buy and sell foods in *quantity*.

quar·an·tine [kwôr′ən tēn′] *noun, plural* **quarantines.** a period of time during which someone or something that may carry a dangerous disease is kept away from people, so that the disease will not spread. —*verb*, **quarantined, quarantining.** to put a person or thing in quarantine: In former times a ship coming into port would be *quarantined* in the harbor and not allowed to land for forty days if its crew was thought to be infected with disease.

quar•rel [kwôr′əl] *noun, plural* **quarrels.** an angry fight or disagreement with words; an argument. —*verb*, **quarreled, quarreling. 1.** to have a quarrel; argue. **2.** to find fault; disagree: The author did her research very carefully, and I really can't *quarrel* with any of her conclusions.

quar•ry[1] [kwôr′ē] *noun, plural* **quarries.** a place where stone is cut or blasted out to be used for building. —*verb*, **quarried, quarrying.** to cut and remove stone from a quarry.

quarry[2] *noun, plural* **quarries.** an animal that is being hunted; prey: "A faint splash told me the *quarry* had spotted me and slipped into the stream." (Russell Baker)

quart [kwôrt] *noun, plural* **quarts.** a unit of measure for liquids. A quart contains two pints, and four quarts make one gallon.

quar•ter [kwôr′tər] *noun, plural* **quarters. 1.** one of four equal parts; one-fourth: 440 yards is a *quarter* of a mile. **2.** a time of fifteen minutes, equal to one-fourth of an hour: 2:45 is a *quarter* to three. **3.** a coin of the United States and Canada that is worth twenty-five cents, or one-fourth of a dollar. **4.** one-fourth of a year; three months: Businesses usually report their sales and earnings for each *quarter*. **5.** one of the four equal time periods of play in football, basketball, and certain other games. **6.** a certain section or neighborhood of a city: The French *Quarter* in New Orleans is a historic and colorful part of the city. **7. quarters.** a place to live or stay: He has his office at the front of the building and his living *quarters* in the back. —*verb*, **quartered, quartering. 1.** to divide into four equal parts: to *quarter* a pie. **2.** to give a place to live or stay: to *quarter* soldiers at an army base.

quar•ter•back [kwôr′tər bak′] *noun, plural* **quarterbacks.** in football, the player who takes the ball from the center to start the play and either hands it off to another player, or passes it or runs with it himself.

quarter horse one of a breed of horses that were developed in the western United States to run short races up to a quarter of a mile.

quar•ter•ly [kwôr′tər lē] *adjective; adverb.*

happening or done once every quarter of the year: The bank pays *quarterly* interest on this savings account.

quar•tet [kwor tet′] *noun, plural* **quartets. 1.** a musical composition written for four voices or instruments. **2.** a group of four singers or musicians performing together: the Modern Jazz *Quartet*. **3.** any group of four persons or things: The Alexandria *Quartet* is a well-known series of four novels by Lawrence Durrell.

quartz A type of quartz known as *amethyst* [am′ə thist]. This specimen was found in Vera Cruz, Mexico.

quartz [kworts] *noun.* a very hard rock that is one of the most common minerals found on earth. It is colorless in its pure form but often appears in colored forms with other stones. Quartz crystals are used in watches and clocks and in transmitters for radios and TV sets.

quarter horse Quarter horses are often used to compete in rodeo events.

Pronunciation Key: A–F			
a	and; hat	ch	chew; such
ā	ate; stay	d	dog; lid
â	care; air	e	end; yet
ä	father; hot	ē	she; each
b	boy; cab	f	fun; off

(Turn the page for more information.)

qua•sar [kwā′ zär′] *noun, plural* **quasars.** a star-like heavenly body that sends out powerful radio waves or very bright light. Quasars are at very great distances from the earth, and it is not certain what their exact properties are.

quay [kē] *noun, plural* **quays.** a landing place, often built of stone, used for the loading and unloading of ships.

Quebec A view of Quebec City showing the famous Hotel Frontenac and a sightseeing boat on the St. Lawrence Seaway.

Que•bec [kwi bek′] **1.** a province of eastern Canada. *Area:* 595,000 square miles. *Population:* 6,234,000. **2.** *also,* **Quebec City.** the capital of Quebec, on the St. Lawrence River. *Population:* 177,000.

queen [kwēn] *noun, plural* **queens. 1.** a woman who rules a country as the head of a royal family. **2.** the wife or widow of a king. **3.** a woman or girl thought of as ruling like a queen: Elizabeth Taylor is a famous Hollywood movie *queen.* **4.** a female bee, ant, or other insect that is larger than the others of its kind and is usually the only one that lays eggs. **5.** a high-ranking playing card that has a picture of a queen on it. **6.** the most powerful piece in the game of chess.

queer [kwēr] *adjective,* **queerer, queerest.** not what is expected or normal; strange; odd: "You have a *queer* name, Daedalus, and I have a *queer* name too, Athy." (James Joyce)

quench [kwench] *verb,* **quenched, quenching. 1.** to put out a fire or light: ". . . the Fire Service who, instead of just *quenching* the flames, soaked the whole place with water." (Anne Frank) **2.** to put an end to; satisfy: He *quenched* his thirst with a glass of ice water.

que•ry [kwēr′ ē] *noun, plural* **queries.** a question: On the reporter's story her editor had written *queries* about several points he didn't understand. —*verb,* **queried, querying.** to ask a question: "During the meal, my young uncle would be *queried* as to how he had passed his day." (Mary McCarthy)

quest [kwest] *noun, plural* **quests.** the act of looking for something valuable or important; a search: The Spanish explorer Coronado roamed the American Southwest in a *quest* for gold. "You are still on a *quest*—a *quest* for knowledge." (Agatha Christie) —*verb,* **quested, questing.** to go in search of something; go on a quest.

ques•tion [kwes′ chən] *noun, plural* **questions. 1.** something that is said or written to get an answer, to find something out, or to test what a person knows. **2.** a matter to be thought about, discussed, or settled; an issue or problem: At tonight's meeting the school board will take up the *question* of whether Midland Avenue School should be closed. **3.** the fact of being uncertain or in doubt: Cindy didn't do very well on that test, but there's no *question* she's a good student. **4. out of the question.** not to be considered. —*verb,* **questioned, questioning. 1.** to ask a question or questions. **2.** to have or show doubts about: I'm not *questioning* his judgment, but I think we need more information to decide. ◆ Something that is **questionable** is uncertain or open to question: Quitting his job like that was a *questionable* decision.

questions English has two kinds of questions. One is called a *yes/no question,* because it asks for that kind of answer: "Is that your brother?" The other is an *information question*; it asks for some kind of information, rather than just *yes* or *no:* "*Who* was that on the phone?" "*Why* did Jimmy leave early?" A yes/no question can also be presented as a *tag question*—an extra phrase "tags along" at the end. We use this to invite the listener to respond, and also to soften the question: "You don't mind if I borrow your pen for a minute, *do you?*" A question normally has a question mark at the end, rather than a period. But an *indirect question* uses a period. "Jerry asked, 'Why was the talent show called off?'" BUT: "Jerry asked me why the talent show was called off." (Note the period.)

question mark a punctuation mark [?] that is put at the end of a sentence to show that it is a question.

ques•tion•naire [kwes′chən âr′] *noun, plural* **questionnaires.** a written or printed list of questions that is used to get information: To help them choose high-school courses, the 8th-grade students filled out a *questionnaire* about what they liked to do and learn about.

quib•ble [kwib′əl] *verb,* **quibbled, quibbling.** to argue about a very small point in order to avoid dealing with the main point or problem: The peace talks to end the Vietnam War were delayed by *quibbling* over the proper shape of the table used for the meetings.

quick [kwik] *adjective,* **quicker, quickest. 1.** moving or acting with speed; fast: A mongoose is able to kill poisonous snakes because its movements are so *quick* that it doesn't get bitten. **2.** done or happening in a short time; brief: Danny took a *quick* glance at the mail to see if there were any letters for him. **3.** able to understand and learn easily: a person with a *quick* mind. —*adverb.* in a quick way; fast: This book claims to show ways to get rich *quick.* ◆ Often combined with other words: *quick*-drying paint. A *quick*-witted person is clever and alert. —*noun, plural* **quicks.** the tender, sensitive skin under the fingernails. —**quickly,** *adverb.* —**quickness,** *noun.*

quick•sand [kwik′sand] *noun.* a soft, wet mixture of sand and water that will not hold up a heavy weight. A person who steps on quicksand will sink down into it.

qui•et [kwī′ət] *adjective,* **quieter, quietest. 1.** with little or no noise; silent: "It is so *quiet* you can hear the snow in the wind." (Ann Beattie) **2.** not loud: to speak in a *quiet* voice. **3.** without movement or activity; calm; peaceful: This is a *quiet* neighborhood without a lot of traffic or excitement. **4.** not standing out or making a show; modest: He always dresses in a very *quiet* way, with a gray suit and a plain dark tie. —*noun.* a lack of noise; silence: ". . . a large room very much like the library, with the same heavy *quiet* about it." (Louise Fitzhugh) —*verb,* **quieted, quieting.** to make or become quiet: Things *quieted* down in the house after the baby fell asleep. —**quietly,** *adverb.*

quill [kwil] *noun, plural* **quills. 1.** a bird's feather, especially one from the wing or tail. **2.** a pen made from such a feather. Quill pens were used by writers from ancient times up to the late 1800's. **3.** one of the sharp spines of a porcupine or other such animal.

quilt Women in Summers County, West Virginia, take part in a *quilting bee.*

quilt [kwilt] *noun, plural* **quilts.** a cover for a bed, made of two pieces of cloth stuffed with soft material and held together by stitching across the surface. ◆ A piece of clothing that is **quilted** is made in this same way: a *quilted* jacket. —*verb,* **quilted, quilting.** to make a quilt or something like this.

quin•tet [kwin tet′] *noun, plural* **quintets. 1.** a musical piece written for five voices or instruments. **2.** a group of five singers or five musicians performing together. ◆ A group of six is a **sextet,** seven is a **septet,** eight is an **octet.**

quill A portrait of the famous English author Charles Dickens writing with a quill pen.

Pronunciation Key: G–N

g	give; big	k	kind, cat, back
h	hold	l	let; ball
i	it; this	m	make; time
ī	ice; my	n	not; own
j	jet; gem; edge	ng	having

(Turn the page for more information.)

Q

Q

quintuplets *Quintuplets* are five children born at the same birth. These are the famous Dionne quintuplets of Canada on their first birthday, May 28, 1935.

quirt [kwurt] *noun, plural* **quirts.** a riding whip made of knotted rawhide thongs and having a short handle.

♦ Also used as a *noun:* "A *quiver* of activity ran through the crowd . . ." (Andrea Lee)

quiv•er² *noun, plural* **quivers.** a case for holding arrows.

quiz [kwiz] *noun, plural* **quizzes.** a short test: We had a ten-minute *quiz* today in our history class. —*verb,* **quizzed, quizzing.** to question: The coach *quizzed* him about why he hadn't been to football practice.

quo•rum [kwôr′əm] *noun, plural* **quorums.** in a club, lawmaking body, or other such group, the minimum number of members who must be present in order for a vote or an official meeting to take place.

quo•ta [kwō′tə] *noun, plural* **quotas. 1.** one part of a total amount that is due to or from a person or group: Each girl in the club has a *quota* of ten boxes of cookies to sell to raise money for the trip. **2.** the amount or percentage of a certain type of people or things allowed to enter a country, school, job, and so forth: The government put a *quota* on the number of foreign cars that could be imported, to try to help the sale of their own cars.

quotations A *quotation* is the direct use of someone else's words in your writing. You must use quotation marks to show this: While he was on a diet, he thought of how Oscar Wilde had said, "I can resist anything except temptation." Please note that when a quotation does not end the sentence, it is followed by a comma, not a period. This is true even if the quote would be a complete sentence on its own, as in the Wilde example. But if the punctuation is a question mark or exclamation mark, it is not replaced by a comma. "I've got to take a vacation soon!" he shouted. "Are you going to take a vacation soon?" she asked. Another tricky situation is a quotation within a quotation. Then you use single quote marks for the one inside, and double quote marks for the whole quotation. "Upon reaching Australia, MacArthur made a pledge that became famous: 'I shall return.'" *(World Book Encyclopedia)* The sentence as a whole is a quote from *World Book* (double quotes). Within it is a quote from MacArthur (single).

quit [kwit] *verb,* **quit, quitting. 1.** to stop doing something, especially something that is not wanted: My Uncle Marty is trying hard to *quit* smoking for good. **2.** to leave a job or position.
♦ A **quitter** is a person who gives up too easily in the face of problems or difficulty.

quite [kwīt] *adverb.* **1.** completely; entirely: Don't take out the roast yet—it's not *quite* done. **2.** more than usual; very; rather: They live next door to us and I know them *quite* well. **3. quite a.** very much; more than usual: "I get sent to the office *quite a* bit." (S.E. Hinton)

quiv•er¹ [kwiv′ər] *verb,* **quivered, quivering.** to shake slightly; tremble: "She stood in front of the door *quivering* with excitement." (Graham Greene)

quo•ta•tion [kwō tā′shən] *noun, plural* **quotations.** something that is quoted; the exact words of another person.

quotation mark one of a pair of punctuation marks [" "] used to show the beginning and ending of a quotation.

quote [kwōt] *verb,* **quoted, quoting. 1.** to repeat the exact words of another person: to *quote* Shakespeare. **2.** to name the price or cost of something. —*noun, plural* **quotes. 1.** the act of quoting another's words; a quotation. **2.** a price that is quoted: Mom got two *quotes* on the cost of having the house painted.

quo•tient [kwō′shənt] *noun, plural* **quotients.** a number obtained by dividing one number by another: If 8 is divided by 4, the *quotient* is 2.

Rr

r, R [är] *noun, plural* **r's, R's.** the eighteenth letter of the alphabet.

rab•bi [rab′ī] *noun, plural* **rabbis.** in the Jewish religion, a trained religious teacher who is usually the leader of a congregation.

rab•bit [rab′ it] *noun, plural* **rabbits.** a small animal that has soft fur, large front teeth, long ears, and a short tail. Rabbits usually live in fields and rest in a burrow or nest. They are found in most parts of the world.

ra•bid [rab′id] *adjective.* **1.** having rabies: A *rabid* dog may run wild and try to attack people. **2.** very intense or extreme: English soccer teams are known for their *rabid* fans.

rab•ies [rā′bēz] *noun.* a very serious disease that can cause death in warm-blooded animals, such as humans, dogs, squirrels, and bats. Rabies is caused by a virus, usually passed on by the bite of an animal that already has the disease.

rac•coon [ra koon′] *noun, plural* **raccoons.** an American animal with a plump body, a sharp pointed nose, a bushy tail, and markings on the face that look like a mask. Raccoons are mostly active at night and usually live near water. They can eat almost any kind of food.

race[1] [rās] *noun, plural* **races. 1.** a contest to decide who or what is fastest: a horse *race,* an auto *race.* The children had a *race* across the schoolyard. **2.** any contest thought of as being like this: Congresswoman Jones is entering the *race* for U.S. Senator. —*verb,* **raced, racing. 1.** to take part in a contest of speed: Ron *raced* his brother to the end of the block. **2.** to run fast, as if in a race. **3.** to do something very fast: Larry *raced* through dinner because he wanted to watch his favorite TV show.

race[2] *noun, plural* **races.** a large group of people who share certain physical features, such as the color of the skin, the shape of the body and face, and so on. These features are passed down from parent to child.

ra•cial [rā′shəl] *adjective.* having to do with a person's race: The Union of South Africa has had *racial* problems in recent years because of government policies that provide unfavorable treatment for black people. ♦ A person who opposes another or others because of their race is a **racist.** Such an attitude is called **racism.**

rack [rak] *noun, plural* **racks. 1.** a frame or stand for hanging or storing things: a towel *rack,* a luggage *rack* on the roof of a car. **2.** in earlier times, an instrument of torture that was used to stretch a person's body. —*verb,* **racked, racking. 1.** to suffer greatly, as if being tortured on a rack: She was *racked* with pain. **2. rack one's brain.** to make a great effort to remember or think of something: "Dorothy had *racked her brains* for a way to raise some money . . ." (George Orwell)

rack•et[1] [rak′ it] *noun, plural* **rackets. 1.** a loud, unpleasant noise: "He stormed out of the bedroom with a *racket* that woke me in my bed-

raccoon Because the raccoon was unknown in Europe, early American settlers borrowed its Indian name, which means "he scratches with his hands."

room across the hall . . ." (Russell Baker) **2.** *Informal.* a way to get money that is not honest or fair: The "numbers *racket*" is an illegal gambling game in which people bet on a certain number. ♦ A **racketeer** is a criminal who carries on some kind of illegal business.

racket² *noun, plural* **rackets.** (also spelled **racquet**) a round or oval frame having tightly-laced strings in a criss-cross pattern, and a long handle at the end. It is used to hit the ball in such games as tennis or badminton. ♦ **Racquetball** is a game for two or four players played on a four-walled court, in which the players hit a soft rubber ball with a short-handled racket.

ra•dar [rā′ där] *noun.* a device used to find out

R

> **radar** This is an ACRONYM—a word formed from the first letter or letters of several existing words. *Radar* comes from the phrase radio detection and ranging. *Radio* waves are aimed at an object, which is then located by the waves that bounce back to the sender. Then the range (distance) and location can be determined. *Radar* came into the language in the Second World War, along with many other acronyms, including *sonar* ("sound detection and ranging;" underwater radar), *GI* ("government issue;" a soldier), and *AWOL* ("absent without official leave;" away from one's post.)

where something is and where or how fast it is going. Radar works by sending out radio waves that bounce off objects and return to be displayed on a receiver. Radar is used by the military in locating enemy aircraft, by ships to stay on course, by airports to direct the movement of planes, and for many other purposes.

ra•di•ant [rā′ dē ənt] *adjective,* **more/most. 1.** giving off a bright light; shining or glowing: a *radiant* morning sky. **2.** glowing with happiness or joy: "Next moment, Tom himself emerged from the door, his whole face *radiant* with delight." (A. Conan Doyle) **3.** sent out in waves or made up of waves: Solar panels heat a house by collecting *radiant* heat from the sun. Heat, light, x-rays, and radio waves are forms of **radiant energy.** ♦ The quality of being radiant is **radiance:** "He was one of those red-haired people who seem to glow with an inner *radiance* that warms not only themselves but the surrounding air." (George Orwell)

ra•di•ate [rā′ dē āt′] *verb,* **radiated, radiating. 1.** to give off energy as rays: Heat *radiates* from a fire. **2.** to move or spread out from a central point: In Washington, D.C. many streets *radiate* from the center of town. "I loved the sense of family warmth that *radiated* through those long kitchen nights of talk." (Russell Baker)

ra•di•a•tion [rā′ dē ā′ shən] *noun.* **1.** the fact of radiating; light or other energy that travels through the air. The sun's rays are a form of

radiation. **2.** certain rays given off by RADIOACTIVE materials. Too much of this kind of radiation can be very dangerous.

ra•di•a•tor [rā′ dē ā′ tər] *noun, plural* **radiators. 1.** a device used for heating a room. A radiator is made up of a series of pipes or tubes through which hot water or steam passes. **2.** a device for cooling an engine or a machine, such as an automobile engine.

rad•i•cal [rad′ i kəl] *adjective,* **more/most. 1.** going to or affecting the most important part; extreme: Quitting his high-paying job and moving to the desert was a *radical* change in Mr. Butler's life. **2.** being in favor of or working toward extreme changes, especially in politics: "He's out to rebel against all authority, and so he grabs at everything *radical* to read . . ." (Eugene O'Neill) —*noun, plural* **radicals.** a person who has very extreme opinions in politics. ♦ The fact of being a political radical is **radicalism.** —**radically,** *adverb:* "She feels that there is something *radically* wrong with . . . her life."(Alice Adams)

ra•di•o [rā′ dē ō] *noun, plural* **radios. 1.** a way of sending and receiving sounds through the air by means of special electrical waves. **2.** a device that receives sounds which are produced or broadcast in this way. —*verb,* **radioed, radioing.** to send a message by radio: The captain of the ship *radioed* to the Coast Guard for help.

ra•di•o•ac•tive [rā′ dē ō ak′ tiv] *adjective.* caused by, having, or showing RADIOACTIVITY: Uranium is a *radioactive* mineral.

ra•di•o•ac•tiv•i•ty [rā′ dē ō ak tiv′ i tē] *noun.* the energy that is given off when the NUCLEUS of an atom breaks apart or decays. This usually causes the atom to give off particles in the form of invisible waves or rays called RADIATION. Some elements, such as radium and uranium, have natural radioactivity. Scientists cause radioactivity in other elements for use as fuel, as a source of energy, or for nuclear weapons.

rad•ish [rad′ ish] *noun, plural* **radishes.** a garden vegetable with a root that is usually eaten raw. The radish has a crisp white inside with a sharp taste and a thin red or white skin.

ra•di•um [rā′ dē əm] *noun.* a white metal that is highly RADIOACTIVE. Radium is a chemical element used in treating some types of cancer.

ra•di•us [rā′ dē əs] *noun, plural* **radii** [rā′ dē ī] or **radiuses. 1.** any line going straight from the center to the outside edge of a circle or sphere: A spoke of a bicycle wheel is a *radius.* ◆ Something that has to do with a radius is **radial. 2.** a circular area that is measured by the length of its radius: There are three big shopping centers within a twenty-mile *radius* of our house.

raft [raft] *noun, plural* **rafts.** a flat boat that is made up of a floating platform of logs, boards, or other materials fastened together.

rag [rag] *noun, plural* **rags. 1.** a small piece of old cloth, usually one that is worn-out or torn. **2. rags.** old, worn-out clothing.

rage [rāj] *noun, plural* **rages. 1.** a feeling of very strong, wild anger that one cannot control; fury: "In *rage,* Kunta snatched and kicked against the shackles that bound his wrists and ankles." (Alex Haley) **2.** something that is very popular at a certain time; a fad or fashion: The Beatles' music was all the *rage* in the 1960's. —*verb,* **raged, raging. 1.** to feel or show great anger. **2.** to act or move in a strong, violent way: "Fanned by the wind, the fire *raged* loudly." (Jerzy Kosinski)

rag•ged [rag′ id] *adjective, more/most.* **1.** worn or torn into rags: Dad has a *ragged* old jacket that he wears when he's painting or doing yard work. **2.** rough or uneven; not smooth: a *ragged* line of cliffs along the ocean.

rag•weed [rag′ wēd′] *noun, plural* **ragweeds.** a plant that is often found in North America. It produces large amounts of POLLEN which can cause HAY FEVER.

raid [rād] *noun, plural* **raids.** a sudden surprise attack: The police made a *raid* on an illegal gambling operation. —*verb,* **raided, raiding.** to make a raid. —**raider,** *noun.*

rail [rāl] *noun, plural* **rails. 1.** a long narrow piece of wood, metal, or other material used as a guard or support. Wooden rails are often held up by posts as part of a fence. Steel rails are placed in pairs on the ground to form a track for railroad cars. **2.** a railroad: A shipment of new cars was sent to the West Coast by *rail.*

rail•ing [rā′ ling] *noun, plural* **railings.** a fence made of a rail or rails, especially one used to keep people from falling or passing: a *railing* on a stairway, a *railing* along the edge of a bridge.

rail•road [rāl′ rōd′] *noun, plural* **railroads. 1.** a path or track made of two metal rails on which a train runs. **2.** a system of transportation in which people and goods are moved along railroad tracks, including all the trains, tracks, and stations, and the workers who operate the system. ◆ Also called a **railway.**

rain [rān] *noun, plural* **rains. 1.** drops of water that fall to the earth from the sky. **2.** the falling of such drops: a heavy *rain.* **3.** a heavy, fast fall of anything like rain: a *rain* of bullets. —*verb,* **rained, raining. 1.** to fall as rain: It *rained* so hard that the streets became flooded. **2.** to fall like rain: He shook the apple tree hard and fruit *rained* down all around him.

rain•bow [rān′ bō′] *noun, plural* **rainbows.** a band of colored light shaped like part of a circle, sometimes seen in the sky after or during a rain shower. It is caused by sunlight reflecting through tiny drops of water in the sky.

rainbow A summer rainbow showing the colors of the spectrum: red, orange, yellow, green, blue, indigo, violet.

rainbow trout a freshwater fish found in the streams and rivers of western North America.

rain•coat [rān′ kōt′] *noun, plural* **raincoats.** a coat made of waterproof material, used to keep a person dry when it rains.

rain•fall [rān′ fôl′] *noun, plural* **rainfalls. 1.** the falling of rain: There was a heavy *rainfall* last night. **2.** the amount of water that falls as rain, snow, sleet, or hail in a given area in a certain period of time.

rain forest a dense tropical forest in an area that has a high rainfall throughout the year.

Pronunciation Key: A–F			
a	and; hat	ch	chew; such
ā	ate; stay	d	dog; lid
â	care; air	e	end; yet
ä	father; hot	ē	she; each
b	boy; cab	f	fun; off
(Turn the page for more information.)			

R

rain•y [rān′ ē] *adjective,* **rainier, rainiest.** having a lot of rain: *rainy* weather.

raise [rāz] *verb,* **raised, raising. 1.** to move to a higher place or position; lift or push up: She *raised* her hand in class because she knew the answer. **2.** to move to a higher condition or amount: to *raise* your voice, to *raise* a worker's pay rate from $5.00 per hour to $6.00. **3.** to bring together; collect: The Red Cross *raised* money to help the victims of the flood. **4.** to bring up and take care of: to *raise* children, to *raise* tropical flowers. **5.** to ask or talk about: The mayor *raised* the question of how to pay for the new library. —*noun, plural* **raises. 1.** an increase in the rate of pay given to a worker. **2.** any increase in amount or value: In some card games, if you make a higher bet than another player it is called a *raise.*

rai•sin [rā′ zin] *noun, plural* **raisins.** a sweet dried grape that is eaten as a snack or used in cooking.

rake [rāk] *noun, plural* **rakes.** a garden tool having a long handle with a row of teeth or prongs attached at one end. Rakes are used to smooth dirt or to gather loose leaves, grass, and so on. —*verb,* **raked, raking. 1.** to gather or smooth with a rake: Richard *raked* up the fallen leaves in the back yard. **2.** to sweep or go over something with a movement like a rake.

ral•ly [ral′ ē] *verb,* **rallied, rallying. 1.** to bring back together; bring back in order: The general tried to *rally* his exhausted troops for one last attack on the enemy fort. **2.** to get back strength and health; recover: The patient has *rallied* from her illness and should be out of the hospital in a day or two. —*noun, plural* **rallies. 1.** the act of rallying: Behind by three runs in the last inning, the team put on a two-out *rally* to win the game. **2.** a gathering of many people to show support for some person or cause: a political *rally,* a protest *rally.*

ram [ram] *noun, plural* **rams. 1.** a male sheep. **2.** *also,* **battering ram. a.** a device used in ancient warfare to knock down the door of a fort or castle. It was made up of a long, heavy pole with an iron end in the shape of a ram's head. **b.** any similar device used in modern times to break down a door. —*verb,* **rammed, ramming.** to strike with great force; hit against: He had to stop short and the car behind *rammed* into his back bumper.

ram•ble [ram′ bəl] *verb,* **rambled, rambling. 1.** to go about without trying to get to any special place; wander. **2.** to grow or move in an irregular way: Some vines grow by *rambling*

along the ground. **3.** to talk or write without any order or purpose: The professor *rambled* on and on about his own college days and never did answer her question. ◆ Also used as an adjective: "Like all New Zealand houses, it was wooden, *rambling* over many squares . . ." (Colleen McCullough)

ramp [ramp] *noun, plural* **ramps.** a section of floor that slopes to connect a lower area with a higher one: Modern buildings have to have *ramps* as well as steps, for use by people in wheelchairs.

ram•page [ram′ pāj′] *noun, plural* **rampages.** a fit of violent or reckless behavior: The famous outlaws Bonnie and Clyde went on a *rampage* of bank robberies during the 1930's. —*verb,* **rampaged, rampaging.** to act in this way.

ran [ran] *verb.* the past tense of **run.**

ranch [ranch] *noun, plural* **ranches. 1.** a large farm on which herds of cattle, sheep, or horses are raised. **2.** any farm that is used to raise one particular animal or crop: a chicken *ranch.* **3.** a modern style of house developed from the old ranch houses of the American west, having one story and a long, low roof.

ran•dom [ran′ dəm] *adjective.* without any pattern, plan, or purpose; by chance: The contest winners were chosen by a *random* selection from all the postcards sent in. ◆ Often used in the phrase **at random:** The TV news show interviewed people *at random* on the street.

random-access [ran′ dəm ak′ ses] *adjective.* of a computer or similar device, having the ability to locate information at random rather than in a certain set order. ◆ In a computer, **RAM** stands for *"random-access memory."*

ram The idea for the battering ram came from the way the ram uses his horns to butt other animals.

rang [rang] *verb.* the past tense of **ring.**

range [rānj] *noun, plural* **ranges. 1.** the distance between certain limits: That car model has a price *range* of $10,000 to $17,000, depending on which extras you get. **2.** the longest distance that something can work or travel: The *range* of this jet is about 4,000 miles without stopping for fuel. **3.** a place to practice shooting a gun or a bow: a rifle *range.* **4.** a large open area of land on which farm animals can be kept. **5.** a row or series of mountains: The Teton *Range* is part of the Rocky Mountains. **6.** a stove for cooking: an electric *range.* —*verb,* **ranged, ranging. 1.** to go or extend between certain limits: Dinosaurs *ranged* in height from about two feet tall up to almost one hundred feet. **2.** to move through or over: "His troops had *ranged* deep into Russia . . ." (John Toland)

ran•ger [rān′jər] *noun, plural* **rangers. 1.** a person whose job is to guard and look after a forest; also called a **forest ranger. 2.** a member of a police force that patrols a certain area: The Texas *Rangers* were the state police force in the early days of Texas. **3.** a military force that is trained to make sudden, secret attacks.

rank[1] [rangk] *noun, plural* **ranks. 1.** a certain level within a group; a position or grade: Admiral is the highest *rank* of officer in the navy. **2.** a row or line of people placed side by side: The soldiers formed *ranks* on the parade ground. **3. ranks.** the common soldiers of an army, as opposed to the officers. **4. rank and file.** the ordinary members of a group, as opposed to its leaders: The new labor contract has to be approved by the union's *rank and file.* —*verb,* **ranked, ranking.** to have a certain rank. Alaska *ranks* first among the states in size but last in population.

rank[2] *adjective,* **ranker, rankest. 1.** having a strong, very unpleasant taste or smell. **2.** being a complete or extreme example of some bad quality; utter; total: a wrong answer that shows *rank* ignorance of the subject.

ran•sack [ran′sak′] *verb,* **ransacked, ransacking.** to search through something in a rough way: The burglars *ransacked* the house looking for hidden jewelry and money. "We might do what we pleased, *ransack* her desk and turn her drawers inside out . . ." (Charlotte Brontë)

ran•som [ran′səm] *noun, plural* **ransoms. 1.** money paid to set free some person who is being illegally held as a prisoner: The gang demanded a *ransom* of $100,000 to return the kidnapped man. **2.** the fact of holding someone captive in this way. —*verb,* **ransomed, ransom-**
ing. to set a prisoner free by paying a ransom.

rap [rap] *verb,* **rapped, rapping.** to knock or tap sharply. —*noun, plural* **raps.** a quick, sharp blow or knock; tap: Gary heard a *rap* on the door and got up to see who it was.

rap•id [rap′id] *adjective, more/most.* moving or done with great speed; very quick; fast: The famous pitcher Bob Feller was called *"Rapid Robert"* because he could throw the ball so fast. —**rapidly,** *adverb:* "The tracks were already *rapidly* disappearing in the snow." (Bret Harte) —**rapidity** [rə pid′ə tē], *noun.*

rapids River rafting through a stretch of rapids on the Klamath River in Oregon.

rap•ids [rap′idz] *noun.* a part of a river where the water flows very fast.

rapt [rapt] *adjective.* having the mind or feelings completely taken up by something: "Jack was over by the window . . . studying the view. He looked *rapt* and dreamy." (Stephen King) —**rapture,** *noun.*

rare[1] [râr] *adjective,* **rarer, rarest. 1.** not often seen or found; not happening often; unusual: Snow is *rare* in Florida. **2.** very valuable or special, because of not being common: a collection of *rare* old coins. ◆ Something that is rare is a **rarity.** —**rarely,** *adverb:* A mountain lion tries to avoid humans and is *rarely* seen in the wild.

rare[2] *adjective,* **rarer, rarest.** of meat, lightly cooked: *rare* roast beef, a steak cooked medium *rare.*

Pronunciation Key: G–N			
g	give; big	k	kind; cat; back
h	hold	l	let; ball
i	it; this	m	make; time
ī	ice; my	n	not; own
j	jet; gem; edge	ng	having

(Turn the page for more information.)

ras•cal [ras′ kəl] *noun, plural* **rascals.** a person who is naughty or full of mischief; someone who does bad things that are not really harmful.

rash[1] *noun, plural* **rashes.** a condition in which small red spots or patches break out on the skin, causing pain or itching. Poison ivy, measles, and allergies can cause a rash.

rash[2] [rash] *adjective,* **rasher, rashest.** in too much of a hurry; reckless or careless: The man made a *rash* decision and sold his house for a price that was much too low. "For if it is *rash* to walk into a lion's den unarmed . . ." (Virginia Woolf) —**rashly,** *adverb.*

rasp•ber•ry [raz′ ber′ ē] *noun, plural* **raspberries.** a sweet berry that grows on a prickly plant. Raspberries are usually red or black.

rat [rat] *noun, plural* **rats. 1.** an animal that looks like a mouse, but is larger. Rats have a long nose, round ears, and a long, thin tail. They are harmful to humans in several ways, such as by spreading disease germs, killing small farm animals, and damaging or destroying crops and food supplies. **2.** *Slang.* a person who is thought to have the bad qualities of a rat, as by being mean, sneaky, or destructive.

rate [rāt] *noun, plural* **rates. 1.** an amount or number that is measured against something else: The doctor showed us a chart where she's keeping track of the baby's growth *rate.* **2.** a fixed price or charge for something, especially some service: The electric company sent around a notice that they're raising their *rates.* **3.** a certain level of quality. ♦ Used in combinations such as first-*rate,* second-*rate,* and so on. —*verb,* **rated, rating.** to place at a certain level: That movie has been *rated* 'R.'

rath•er [rath′ ər] *adverb.* **1.** more willing to do one thing than another: Claire loves tennis — I think she'd *rather* play tennis than eat. **2.** to a certain amount or extent; somewhat: to be *rather* tired, a *rather* cold day. **3.** in the opposite or a different way: That car has the engine in back *rather* than in front. **4.** more correctly or more exactly: The artist Georgia O'Keeffe lived to be 100 years old, or *rather,* almost 100.

rat•i•fy [rat′ i fī′] *verb,* **ratified, ratifying.** to accept and approve in an official way: The U.S. Constitution became law after it was *ratified* by the states. —**ratification,** *noun.*

rat•ing [rā′ ting] *noun, plural* **ratings. 1.** a rank given to a TV or radio show to show how many people watch or listen to it: The Academy Award Show always gets a high *rating* each year. **2.** any grade or rank that shows position at a certain level: Newspapers publish a *rating* of the top 20 college football teams in the country. A person who wants to borrow money has to have a good credit *rating.*

ra•ti•o [rā′ shō *or* rā′ shē ō] *noun, plural* **ratios.** a comparison of the number or size of two different things. A ratio is the number of times the second thing can be divided into the first: Six girls and two boys are in Andrew's reading group, so the *ratio* of girls to boys is 3:1.

ra•tion [rash′ ən] *noun, plural* **rations.** a fixed amount or share of food allowed for one person or animal: Food given to soldiers at the battlefront is called *rations.* —*verb,* **rationed, rationing.** to limit food or other important supplies to a fixed amount: During World War II, the U.S. government *rationed* such things as meat, coffee, and gasoline. "Jimmy *rationed* himself so that toward the end of the week he still had some sugar left." (Frank O'Connor)

ra•tion•al [rash′ ən əl] *adjective, more/most.* **1.** able to think and reason: A human is a *rational* animal. **2.** having a sound mind; able to think clearly. **3.** based on sound thinking; reasonable: The thief must have worn gloves — that's the only *rational* explanation as to why no fingerprints were found. —**rationally,** *adverb.*

rat•tle [rat′ əl] *verb,* **rattled, rattling. 1.** to make a series of short, sharp sounds: "The window *rattled* madly in the wind, and she pulled the quilt close about her." (Madeleine L'Engle) **2.** to talk or say something quickly: Name any state in the Union, and Marty can *rattle* off its capital just like that. **3.** to make nervous or upset: The pitcher was *rattled* by the other team's yelling at him. —*noun, plural* **rattles.**

---

rather This is one of those adverbs that has two meanings, one strong, the other weak. Senator Henry Clay of Kentucky said, "I'd *rather* be right than be President." That is the strong sense. "It's *rather* cold today." "Those flowers look *rather* nice." These are typical weak uses of *rather.* Some experts on writing, E.B. White, William Zinsser, and James J. Kilpatrick, among others, argue that this use of *rather* should be abandoned. British critics, however, usually don't object to the weak use of the term. In British English, *rather* is considered to be polite. It's a way of softening a statement so it doesn't seem too extreme or boastful. "How do you like your new car?" An American answers: "I love it!" A Britisher: "I *rather* like it, actually."

1. a short, sharp sound. **2.** something that makes this sound: a baby's toy *rattle*.

rat•tle•snake [rat′ əl snāk′] *noun, plural* **rattlesnakes.** a poisonous American snake. A rattlesnake, has several horny rings at the end of its tail that rattle when shaken.

rattlesnake

rave [rāv] *verb,* **raved, raving. 1.** to talk in a very excited or wild way; say things that are crazy or that don't make sense: The man was *raving* about how creatures from outer space had taken control of his brain. **2.** to talk or write about something with great praise or approval. —*noun, plural* **raves.** very great praise or approval. ♦ Also used as an adjective: *"Rave* reviews greeted the book's publication both in America and in England." (Gay Talese)

rav•el [rav′ əl] *verb,* **raveled, raveling.** to separate into loose threads, as cloth does when it becomes worn out or torn. ♦ A more common form of this word is **unravel.**

ra•ven [rā′ vən] *noun, plural* **ravens.** a large black bird that is related to and looks very much like a crow, but is larger. Ravens have a harsh cry.

rav•en•ous [rav′ ən əs] *adjective, more/most.* very hungry. —**ravenously,** *adverb:* " . . . they were *ravenously* hungry from having worked hard all day . . ." (Mark Helprin)

ra•vine [rə vēn′] *noun, plural* **ravines.** a deep, narrow valley, usually formed by running water wearing down a space between two hills over a long period of time.

raw [rô] *adjective,* **rawer, rawest. 1.** not cooked: Oranges and other such fruits are usually eaten *raw.* **2.** in a natural condition; not processed: *raw* silk. **3.** not trained or experienced: Soldiers who are new to the army are called *raw* recruits. **4.** having the skin rubbed off: Jeff's knee was *raw* where he scraped it on the sidewalk. **5.** of weather, damp and cold: a *raw* north wind.

raw•hide [rô′ hīd′] *noun.* the hide of cattle or other animals that has not been tanned.

raw material a substance that is still in its natural state, and has not been refined, manufactured, or processed. Coal, wood, and cotton are important raw materials.

ray¹ [rā] *noun, plural* **rays. 1.** a narrow beam or line of light: The sun's *rays* feel very warm in the summer. **2.** any similar line or stream of some other form of energy: X-*rays* are used to photograph the inside of the body. **3.** one of a group of lines going out from a center. **4.** a very small amount: a *ray* of hope.

raven In Edgar Allan Poe's famous poem "The Raven," a lonely man is disturbed by a visit from a raven that speaks only one word, "nevermore."

ray² *noun, plural* **rays.** any one of a large group of saltwater fish that are related to sharks. A ray has a wide, flat body, broad fins, and a long tail. The **manta ray** and STINGRAY are often found in warm oceans.

ray•on [rā′ än′] *noun.* an artificial cloth or material made from the CELLULOSE fiber of wood or cotton.

ra•zor [rā′ zər] *noun, plural* **razors.** a small tool with a thin, sharp blade that is used for shaving hair from the face or body.

Pronunciation Key: O–S

ō	over; go	ou	out; town
ô	all; law	p	put; hop
oo	look; full	r	run; car
ōo	pool; who	s	set; miss
oi	oil; boy	sh	show

(Turn the page for more information.)

R

R

> **re—** One of the most often-used prefixes in English is *re-* meaning "again" or "another time." There are more words that use *re-* than you might think. In many cases the root word does not seem to be independent without the "re." Examples are *receive, reduce, remain, repair, and repeat.* Obviously there are no English verbs "ceive," "duce," "main," and so on. These words go back to Latin, as does *re-.* *Re-* was added to these verbs in Latin. When *re-* is added to a word beginning with *e,* the usual style is to use a hyphen: *re-elect, re-examine, re-enlistment, re-entry.* This is to avoid an awkward "ree-" form. However, our Word Survey shows that this distinction is fading away, and that many writers now do not use the hyphen.

reach [rēch] *verb,* **reached, reaching. 1.** to put out the hand to try to hold or touch something: The first baseman *reached* up to catch the throw. **2.** to stretch out as far as; extend to: "I was astounded to see how much light *reached* the ocean floor thirty feet below the surface." (Jules Verne) **3.** to come to a certain place; arrive at: "When she *reached* the gate no one was there." (Flannery O'Connor) **4.** to come to a certain point or condition: to *reach* a conclusion. **5.** to get in touch with someone; communicate: "He's been trying to *reach* Vixen, but the phone was busy." (Ishmael Reed) —*noun, plural* **reaches. 1.** the act of reaching, or the distance that can be covered by this: All the controls of the plane are within easy *reach* of the pilot. **2.** the distance that a person can extend the arms. **3.** a long stretch or extent: "His footsteps echoed through the vast silent *reaches* of the house." (Esther Forbes)

re•act [rē akt′] *verb,* **reacted, reacting. 1.** to act because something else happened or was done; respond: The firefighters *reacted* quickly to the alarm signal. **2.** to have a chemical reaction.

re•ac•tion [rē ak′shən] *noun, plural* **reactions. 1.** the fact of reacting; a response: What was Dad's *reaction* when you told him about the broken window? **2.** a condition in nature that occurs as a direct result of something else: One of Newton's laws of motion is that for every action, there is an equal and opposite *reaction.* **3.** in chemistry, a process by which substances are changed into new substances.

re•ac•tor [rē ak′tər] *noun, plural* **reactors.** a device that allows for the controlled splitting of atoms to create atomic energy; more often called a NUCLEAR REACTOR.

read [rēd] *verb,* **read** [red], **reading. 1.** to look at something that is written or printed and understand its meaning. **2.** to learn about something by reading: I *read* in the paper that there's a big storm coming. **3.** to get the meaning of; understand: She knows him so well she can almost *read* his mind. **4.** of an instrument, to give or show information in the form of letters, numbers, and so on: The thermometer *read* 80 degrees. **5.** of a computer, to locate information on a disk or other storage device and transfer it into the computer memory.

read•a•ble [rēd′ə bəl] *adjective, more/most.* able to be read easily. ◆ The measurement of how easy something is to read and understand is called its **reading level** or **readability.**

read•er [rē′dər] *noun, plural* **readers. 1.** a person who reads: She's a fast *reader.* **2.** a book used by students for learning and practicing the skill of reading.

read•i•ly [red′ə lē] *adverb.* **1.** in a willing way: "Miss Wilmarth . . . turned her big smile *readily* to each of them." (Dorothy Parker) **2.** without difficulty; easily.

read•ing [rē′ding] *noun, plural* **readings. 1.** the fact of reading: Mom went to a poetry *reading* given by a famous author. **2.** something to be read: This book makes good light *reading* for a vacation or plane trip. **3.** See READOUT.

read•out [rēd′out′] *noun.* information from a computer or other such device, appearing in a form that can be read by the user.

reactor Nuclear reactors inside these buildings give off steam from water used to cool the reaction.

read•y [red′ē] *adjective,* **readier, readiest. 1.** in the condition needed to go into use or action; prepared: I'll be *ready* to leave as soon as I find my notebook. **2.** likely or about to happen: You looked like you were *ready* to faint when she told us Bill invited her to the dance. **3.** able to be put into use quickly: a supply of *ready* cash kept on hand for an emergency. —*verb,* **readied, readying.** to make ready; prepare. ♦ The fact of being ready is **readiness:** Reading *readiness* helps young children prepare to start reading.

Rea•gan [rā′gən] **Ronald W.,** born 1911, the fortieth president of the United States, since 1981.

re•al [rēl] *adjective.* **1.** not imagined or made-up; true: "Marilyn Monroe" was the name she used in movies, but her *real* name was Norma Jean Baker. **2.** not artificial; genuine: Those flowers look *real,* but they're actually made of silk and paper. **3.** as is stated; actual: You're going to have a *real* problem with that tire if you don't get it replaced soon. —*adverb. Informal.* very. ♦ The fact of being real is **reality** [rē′al′ə tē].

a trout jumped up and swallowed the hook." (Jean Fritz) **2.** to make or become real: The company finally *realized* its goal of reaching 100 million dollars a year in sales. ♦ The act or fact of realizing is **realization** [rē′ə lə zā′shən].

re•al•ly [rē′ə lē *or* rē′lē] *adverb.* **1.** in fact; actually: Did Mom *really* say we could stay up until the end of the movie? "(He) wore thick glasses which made his eyes seem twice as big as they *really* were." (James Thurber) **2.** very much; very: It was *really* nice of her to help us. "There is hardly a night in England when it is *really* warm after midnight." (George Orwell)

realm [relm] *noun, plural* **realms. 1.** a kingdom: ". . . that Spain or any prince of Europe should dare to invade the borders of my *realm.*" (Queen Elizabeth I) **2.** an area of interest, knowledge, or activity: the *realm* of science.

reap [rēp] *verb,* **reaped, reaping. 1.** to cut down and gather wheat or a similar crop. **2.** to get as a reward: That singing group is *reaping* huge profits on their new hit record.

rear[1] [rēr] *noun, plural* **rears.** the part that is away from the front; the back. —*adjective.* at or in the back: a *rear*-view mirror.

---

real/really "Our PC Jr. program will be scaled back *real* fast." (William Gates) "Reagan came off *real* well in the debate." (Anne Armstrong) Can you spot the problem in these sentences? To be strictly correct, they should use *really,* not *real*—*really* fast, *really* well. In each case, the word called for is an adverb; *real* is an adjective. Some words have the same form for both the adjective and the adverb. (He's a *fast* runner. He ran *fast.*) But *real* and *really* follow the general rule: only the *-ly* form, *really,* can be used for the adverb. However, in our Word Survey, we did find a few examples of *real* used as an adverb by noted writers: "During *real* hard weather . . ." (Beatrix Potter) "He could cry *real* loud and moan *real* deep . . ." (Langston Hughes)

---

real estate land together with the buildings, plants, water, or other things that are on or in the land.

re•al•ism [rē′ə liz′əm] *noun.* the fact of seeing or showing things as they really are; being realistic. ♦ A writer or artist who is a **realist** presents life as it actually is in the real world.

re•al•is•tic [rē′ə lis′tik] *adjective,* **more/most. 1.** looking or seeming to be real; like real life: The toy gun was modeled after a hunting rifle and looked very *realistic.* **2.** dealing with real life; seeing things as they really are: She's hoping to win the contest, but she's *realistic* enough to know that there are thousands of other people hoping the same thing. —**realistically,** *adverb.*

re•al•ize [rē′ə līz′] *verb,* **realized, realizing. 1.** to notice or be aware of; know about; understand: "Before he *realized* what was happening,

rear[2] *verb,* **reared, rearing. 1.** to take care of and help a young person or animal while it is growing up; raise: Those children were *reared* very strictly by their parents. **2.** of an animal, to rise up on the hind legs: "The deer in the center *reared* and started in sudden fright." (Farley Mowat) **3.** to rise or lift up: "The distant lighthouse *reared* high." (Stephen Crane)

rea•son [rē′zən] *noun, plural* **reasons. 1.** a fact or cause that explains why something happens as it does: The *reason* that so few trees grow

Pronunciation Key: T–Z			
t	ten; date	v	very; live
th	think	w	win; away
<u>th</u>	these	y	you
u	cut; butter	z	zoo; cause
ur	turn; bird	zh	measure
(Turn the page for more information.)			

> **reason** "At first, Patrick Henry did not approve of the Constitution. The *reason* was *because* it did not give enough protection to individual rights." This would be better as "The reason was *that* it did not . . ." Why? "The reason is because" repeats the same idea twice. You could say "She doesn't watch much TV *because* she's too busy" or "The *reason* she doesn't watch much TV is that she's too busy," but not "The *reason* she doesn't watch much TV is *because* . . ." A few critics say "the reason is because" is acceptable. Bergen Evans in his *Dictionary of Contemporary American Usage* states that it is "used freely by the best modern writers." However, we didn't find that to be true in the selections we examined for our Word Survey. We agree with the majority of critics that "the reason is because" should be avoided.

around here is that it doesn't rain enough. The fight over slavery was one of the main *reasons* for the Civil War. **2.** the act or fact of thinking in a clear, sensible way: Animals do not have the power of *reason.* —*verb,* **reasoned, reasoning.** to give reasons to try to change someone's mind: Joe's parents tried to *reason* with him and talk him out of quitting school.

rea•son•a•ble [rēz′ nə bəl *or* rē′ zen ə bəl] *adjective, more/most.* **1.** acting with good reason; sensible; fair: The judge is a *reasonable* man who takes all the facts into consideration. Asking for time off from work because of a doctor's appointment was a *reasonable* request. **2.** not too much or too great: a restaurant with *reasonable* prices. "My raft was now strong enough to bear any *reasonable* weight." (Daniel Defoe) —**reasonably,** *adverb:* "I can't promise you, but you can be *reasonably* certain of having your evenings free." (Paul Theroux)

rea•son•ing [rē′ zən ing] *noun.* **1.** the process of using reason and facts to make a judgment; using the mind carefully and well. **2.** the reason or reasons for something.

re•as•sure [rē′ ə shoor′] *verb,* **reassured, reassuring.** to give confidence or courage to someone who is worried, afraid, or in doubt: "She pushed her glasses up on her nose to *reassure* herself that what she was seeing was real." (Madeleine L'Engle) —**reassurance,** *noun.*

re•bate [rē′ bāt′] *noun, plural* **rebates.** a part of the total sum of money paid for something, returned as a discount or refund: The car dealer is offering a $1000 *rebate* for anyone who buys a new car by the end of August. —*verb,* **rebated, rebating.** to give a rebate.

reb•el [reb′ əl] *noun, plural* **rebels. 1.** a person who fights against and will not obey the government or ruler that he is under: The Mexican War began when a group of Texas *rebels* declared their independence from Mexico. **2. Rebel.** a person who fought on the side of the South in the Civil War; a Confederate. **3.** any

person who goes against authority: Jane's a real *rebel* and is always getting in trouble for not obeying the dress code at her school. —[rə bel′] *verb,* **rebelled, rebelling. 1.** to fight against one's government or ruler. **2.** to go against authority or control.

re•bel•lion [ri bel′ yən] *noun, plural* **rebellions. 1.** an armed revolt against the government: In the Easter *Rebellion* of 1916, the Irish rose up to try to drive the English out of their country. **2.** the fact of rebelling against any authority or control: In 1985 many people stopped buying Coca-Cola as a form of *rebellion* against a change in the flavor. —**rebellious,** *adjective.*

re•call [ri kôl′] *verb,* **recalled, recalling. 1.** to bring back to memory; remember: "Seventy-five years is a long time to *recall* details and keep things straight in your head." (Ernie Pyle) **2.** to take back a product because of faults or problems: The car maker *recalled* all that year's models because of a weakness in the steering system. —[ri kôl′ *or* rē kôl′] *noun.* the fact of calling back: The ability to remember everything about a situation is called total *recall.*

re•cede [ri sēd′] *verb,* **receded, receding.** to go or move away: "A color so shaded that it seemed at any moment it would *recede* and disappear." (F. Scott Fitzgerald) ♦ Often used as an adjective: A person who is going bald is said to have a *receding* hairline.

re•ceipt [ri sēt′] *noun, plural* **receipts. 1.** a written statement that something has been received, such as money, mail, or merchandise: The clerk gave her a *receipt* showing how much she had paid for the dress. **2. receipts.** the amount of money received.

re•ceive [ri sēv′] *verb,* **received, receiving. 1.** to get or take on what is given; accept: "I have been traveling for some weeks and have not *received* any mail from England." (John Le Carré) **2.** to greet or welcome in a formal way: "At the gate of the castle the Prince was waiting to *receive* her." (Oscar Wilde)

re•ceiv•er [ri sē′ vər] *noun, plural* **receivers. 1.** a person or thing that receives: In football, a *receiver* is a player who catches a pass. **2.** the part of a telephone that is held up to the ear for hearing and speaking. **3.** a device that can receive a radio or TV signal and convert it to sound or sound and pictures.

re•cent [rē′ sənt] *adjective, more/most.* happening, done, or made just before the present; not old: There have been several accidents there in *recent* months. **—recently,** *adverb:* The car had been *recently* painted and looked new.

re•cep•ta•cle [ri sep′ tə kəl] *noun, plural* **receptacles.** a container used to hold something: a trash *receptacle.*

re•cep•tion [ri sep′ shən] *noun, plural* **receptions. 1.** the fact of receiving: The singer got a warm *reception* from the audience. **2.** a party or social gathering to welcome guests: After the wedding there was a large *reception* at the local country club. **3.** the quality of signals received by a radio or a television set.

re•cep•tion•ist [ri sep′ shə nist] *noun.* a person in business whose work is to greet visitors.

re•cess [rē′ ses *or* ri ses′] *noun, plural* **recesses. 1.** a time at elementary school when students stop their classes and are allowed to relax, play games, and so on. **2.** a time when work or other activity stops: The judge declared a *recess* in the trial because one of the lawyers was ill. **3.** *also,* **recesses.** a hidden or secret place: "All that night the two men hunted in the dark *recesses* of the canyon. "(Marguerite Henry) —*verb,* **recessed, recessing.** to stop school or work for a short time: The talks between the city and the unions have been *recessed* until Monday.

re•cit•al [ri sī′ təl] *noun, plural* **recitals. 1.** a public concert or performance, usually featuring the work of a single performer or composer: a piano *recital.* **2.** the act of reciting: the *recital* of a poem.

re•cite [ri sīt′] *verb,* **recited, reciting.** to repeat something from memory: The class *recited* the Pledge of Allegiance. "In a soft voice he *recited* the most important history of all the histories of our people." (Jamake Highwater)

reck•less [rek′ lis] *adjective, more/most.* not thinking or using care with something; careless: *Reckless* driving means not taking the proper care to avoid an accident. **—recklessly,** *adverb.* **—recklessness,** *noun.*

reck•on [rek′ ən] *verb,* **reckoned, reckoning. 1.** to find the value or amount of; count; calculate: The school board has plans for a new junior high school, but has not yet *reckoned* the total cost. **2.** *Informal.* to think or guess; suppose: Better set an extra place at the table; I *reckon* Uncle Dave will be staying for dinner.

re•cline [ri klīn′] *verb,* **reclined, reclining.** to lie down or lean back. ◆ A **recliner** is a stuffed chair on which a person can lie back.

rec•og•ni•tion [rek′ əg nish′ ən] *noun, plural* **recognitions.** the fact of recognizing or being recognized; being known: When Grandpa went back to his home town in Ireland, he found it had changed almost beyond *recognition.*

rec•og•nize [rek′ əg nīz′] *verb,* **recognized, recognizing. 1.** to see or hear a person and be able to tell who it is, because of something that was known before: "He *recognized* the two men because he'd seen their pictures in the newspaper from time to time." (Ishmael Reed) **2.** to

---

recession The noun *recession* comes from the verb to *recede,* meaning "to move back" or "to move away." When the word is used in business, the idea is that the economy is moving back, shrinking, falling off. There is no exact definition for the term *recession.* The one thing everyone agrees on is that it is not as serious as a *depression.* The term *recession* came into use so that people could talk about poor business conditions without saying *depression.* The Great Depression of the 1930's had such a bad effect on Americans that *depression* became a word to be avoided. Why such concern over words? If someone says that a depression is under way, people might stop spending and companies might stop investing. In short, words can sometimes affect reality, as well as describing it.

---

re•ces•sion [ri sesh′ ən] *noun, plural* **recessions.** a period of time when business conditions are bad. In a recession, sales and production fall, and there are fewer people working.

rec•i•pe [res′ ə pē] *noun, plural* **recipes. 1.** a set of directions for preparing something to eat or drink. **2.** any method or set of steps to reach a goal: a *recipe* for success in business.

Pronunciation Key: [ə] Symbol

The [ə] or *schwa* sound occurs in syllables without an accent. It can be spelled with any vowel, such as **a** in above, **e** in listen, **i** in pencil, **o** in melon, **u** in circus. It can also be a combination of vowels, such as **io** in action, **ai** in mountain, **iou** in precious.

(Turn the page for more information.)

know something for what it is; identify: "The handwriting of the one he *recognized* as Sir Edgar's." (Angus Wilson) **3.** to accept that a person or thing has a certain standing: The U.S. now *recognizes* the People's Republic of China as the official government of the country.

re•coil [ri koil′] *verb,* **recoiled, recoiling.** to draw back suddenly; move back: A rifle *recoils* when it is fired. "Estragon *recoils* in horror." (Samuel Beckett)

re•com•mend [rek′ ə mend′] *verb,* **recommended, recommending. 1.** to speak in favor of someone or something; give reasons or argue for: Mike's English teacher *recommended* him for a summer job on the town newspaper. **2.** to suggest or advise something as being a good idea: Dad *recommended* that I type the report because my handwriting is hard to read.

re•com•men•da•tion [rek′ ə men dā′ shən] *noun, plural* **recommendations.** the act or fact of recommending: Students can only take the advanced math course if they have the *recommendation* of their present teacher.

re•cord [rek′ ərd] *noun, plural* **records. 1.** a written statement of facts, events, or other such information: She checked her phone *records* to see how many long-distance calls she made last month. **2.** a plastic disk on which music or other sounds have been stored to be played back on a phonograph. **3.** a history of facts about someone or something: The man caught robbing the bank already had a long *record* of crime. **4.** a performance or action that is the highest, lowest, or best of its kind: The major-league *record* for most wins by a pitcher is 511, by Cy Young. ♦ Also used as an adjective: a *record* snowfall, a *record* crowd at a football game.
—[ri kôrd′] *verb,* **recorded, recording. 1.** to set down in writing: In her diary, Anne Frank *recorded* her secret thoughts about hiding from the Nazis. **2.** to keep track of or display: A special machine known as a seismograph *records* the size of earthquakes. **3.** to put sounds or a program on a record or tape.

re•cord•er [ri kôr′ dər] *noun, plural* **recorders. 1.** a machine that records something, such as a TAPE RECORDER or a VCR. **2.** a musical instrument that is blown through like a whistle or flute, having a wooden body and finger holes to change the pitch of the sound. **3.** a person who keeps records: a *recorder* of deeds for a county government.

re•cord•ing [ri kôr′ ding] *noun, plural* **recordings.** a disk or tape on which sound has been recorded.

re•cov•er [ri kuv′ ər] *verb,* **recovered, recovering. 1.** to get back something that was lost or stolen: The thieves had already sold one of the stolen diamonds, but the police *recovered* the others. **2.** to make up for; regain: The movie was not very popular and did not bring in enough money to *recover* the cost of making it. **3.** to get back to a normal state or condition: The doctors want to be sure he's *recovered* from his illness before he goes back to work.

re•cov•er•y [ri kuv′ rē] *noun, plural* **recoveries.** the fact of recovering.

re•cre•a•tion [rek′ rē ā′ shən] *noun, plural* **recreations.** something that is done for fun or relaxation; amusement; play: Our town swimming pool is run by the Department of Parks and *Recreation.* "His only *recreation,* he said, was listening to professional baseball games on the radio." (John Irving)

re•cruit [ri kroot′] *noun, plural* **recruits. 1.** a person who has recently joined the army or navy. **2.** any new member or newcomer: The company held a training session for its new sales *recruits.* —*verb,* **recruited, recruiting.** to get people to join: College basketball teams try to *recruit* outstanding high school players.

rec•tan•gle [rek′ tang′ gəl] *noun, plural* **rectangles.** a figure formed by four straight lines. A rectangle has four sides and four right angles. The opposite sides of a rectangle are parallel and equal in length. —**rectangular,** *adjective.*

re•cur [ri kur′] *verb,* **recurred, recurring.** to come or happen again: She has a *recurring* dream that she's falling out a window.

re•cy•cle [rē sī′ kəl] *verb,* **recycled, recycling.** to prepare or treat something so that it can be used again, instead of being thrown away: Glass bottles, aluminum cans, and paper are *recycled.* —**recycling,** *noun.*

red [red] *noun, plural* **reds;** *adjective.* a bright color that is the color of blood.

red blood cell a blood cell that carries oxygen from the lungs to other parts of the body. Red blood cells give blood its red color.

Red Cross an organization that helps people around the world who are wounded in a war or who are victims of floods, earthquakes, and other natural disasters. The symbol of this group is a red cross on a white square.

Red Sea a long, narrow sea between northeastern Africa and Arabia. It is connected to the Mediterranean by the Suez Canal.

re•duce [ri doos′] *verb,* **reduced, reducing. 1.** to make less or smaller in size or amount;

decrease: The price of that home has just been *reduced* from $120,000 to $110,000. **2.** to cause to lose weight from the body, as by dieting, exercise, and so on. **3. reduce to.** to make or bring into a lower or lesser state: "The house was no longer a house; it had been *reduced to* a pointed roof on which rain fell." (Patrick White) **—reduction,** *noun.*

red•wood [red′ wood′] *noun, plural* **redwoods.** a very large evergreen tree that grows along the Pacific coast of North America. The reddish-brown wood of this tree resists decay and insects and is often used for outdoor items such as decks and patio furniture.

reed [rēd] *noun, plural* **reeds. 1.** a tall slender grass plant with long, narrow leaves and hollow stems. Reeds grow in swamps and other wet places. **2.** a thin piece of wood or plastic that is used in the mouthpiece of certain musical instruments. The reed vibrates when a stream of air is blown over it, and this makes a musical sound. **3.** a musical instrument that uses a reed, such as a clarinet, a saxophone, or an oboe.

reef [rēf] *noun, plural* **reefs.** a chain or ridge of coral, rocks, or sand starting on the ocean bottom and often rising to the surface.

reef A colorful coral reef in the South Pacific.

reel¹ [rēl] *noun, plural* **reels.** a roller or spool on which something is wound. Fishing line, tape, rope, film, or string can be wound on a reel. **—***verb,* **reeled, reeling. 1.** to wind on a reel: When Sharon felt a jerk on her line, she *reeled* in the big fish. **2. reel off.** to say in a quick, easy way; rattle off.

reel² *verb,* **reeled, reeling. 1.** to be thrown off balance; sway or rock: "Mr. Clay *reeled* — there is no other word for the backward falling movement he made." (Gore Vidal) **2.** to turn around and around; whirl: Her mind *reeled* as she tried to keep straight all the information she'd been given.

redwood A typical redwood grows 200 to 275 feet high, with a trunk 8 to 12 feet in diameter.

reel³ *noun, plural* **reels.** a lively folk dance, often done in double time with circling movements. In the Virginia Reel, an old American dance, two rows of dancers face each other.

re•e•lect [re′ i lekt′] *verb,* **reelected, reelecting.** to elect again to the same office or position: In the 1984 election, President Ronald Reagan was *reelected* for a second term of office.

re•fer [ri fur′] *verb,* **referred, referring. 1.** to call by a certain name: "I noticed that they *referred* to Uncle Hal as 'the Colonel.'" (Russell Baker) **2.** to direct attention to; speak or write about: When Mom said Dan's room was a mess, she was *referring* to the fact that he left his papers and books all over the floor. **3.** to send or direct a person somewhere else for help or information: My doctor doesn't know what's causing my skin rash, so he *referred* me to a specialist at University Hospital.

ref•er•ee [ref′ ə rē′] *noun, plural* **referees.** in sports such as football, basketball, or hockey, an official who has charge of the game and sees that the rules are obeyed. The referee can call a foul or penalty if the rules are broken. **—***verb,* **refereed, refereeing.** to act as a referee: to *referee* a soccer game.

Pronunciation Key: Accent Marks

[′] is the normal accent mark. It shows where the main stress falls on a word.
[′] is a secondary accent mark. It shows a lighter stress than the primary accent. For example:

tel • e • vis • ion [tel′ə vizh′ən]
(Turn the page for more information.)

R

reference This word describes the relation between a pronoun and a noun. "Mrs. Cabot washed her diamonds and hung *them* out to dry." (John Cheever). "In the front room upstairs . . . were my mother and my brother Herman, who sometimes sang in *his* sleep, usually 'Marching Through Georgia' or 'Onward, Christian Soldiers.'" (James Thurber). Each of these situations is far from ordinary. A woman washes diamonds, and a boy sings in his sleep. Even so, because the reference is clear, we can easily understand. If Thurber had said "who sometimes sang while sleeping," we wouldn't be sure whether it was Herman, or both Herman and his mother. To be sure your reference is clear, substitute the noun being referred to for the pronoun in the sentence. "When we planted the tree in the middle of the lawn *it* didn't grow as well." Is "it" the tree, or the area of lawn? Try this: "The lawn didn't grow well after we planted a tree in the middle of it."

ref•er•ence [ref′ rəns *or* ref′ ər əns] *noun, plural* **references. 1.** the fact of referring to something: He began the business letter by saying, "*Reference* is made to your letter of June 3rd." ◆ Often used in the phrase **in reference to:** When she asked to speak to Mr. Lucas, his secretary asked her, "What is this *in reference to?*" **2.** something that refers a reader to another source of information: In this dictionary a word in small capitals LIKE THIS is a *reference* to another entry. ◆ This is also called a **cross reference. 3.** a standard source of useful information, such as a dictionary, encyclopedia, almanac, and so on. **4.** a statement about how suitable someone is for a certain job or position, or the person who can give such a statement. —*adjective.* used for reference or information: a *reference* library.

re•fill [rē fil′] *verb,* **refilled, refilling.** to fill again: Put the plant in the ground; then *refill* the hole. —[rē′ fil′] *noun, plural* **refills.** something that refills: Seeing that Karen had finished her soda, Dad asked if she wanted a *refill.*

re•fine [ri fīn′] *verb,* **refined, refining. 1.** to make pure or fine: When sugar cane is *refined,* the stalks and syrup are separated from the sugar, which is crushed into fine particles. **2.** to make more polished or elegant: "She knew it (her voice) sounded foolish and American and unlike the other *refined,* correct English ones at the table." (Paul Theroux) —**refinement,** *noun.*

re•fin•er•y [ri fī′ nə rē] *noun, plural* **refineries.** a place where a product is refined, especially one where crude oil is made into gasoline and other products.

re•flect [ri flekt′] *verb,* **reflected, reflecting. 1.** to turn or throw something back, such as light or heat: A dark shirt will tend to absorb heat from the sun, while a white shirt will *reflect* it. **2.** to show as a result: "(They) were discussing a subject that each considered important, and their serious faces *reflected* this." (John R.

Tunis) **3. reflect on. a.** to think carefully and seriously about: "For ten minutes he lay on his side *reflecting on* the events of the day." (Ian Fleming) **b.** to bring about a certain result or feeling: That new product has so many faults that it *reflects* badly *on* the whole company.

re•flec•tion [ri flek′ shən] *noun, plural* **reflections. 1.** an image that is reflected by a surface, such as a mirror or a pool of still water. **2.** careful and serious thinking: "On *reflection,* he decided that this was what he must do." (P.D. James) **3.** something that expresses or shows something else: The improvement in her work is a *reflection* of how much harder she's studying this year.

re•flex [rē′ fleks′] *noun, plural* **reflexes. 1.** an automatic action that takes place when certain nerves are touched; also called a **reflex action.** Pulling your hand away from a hot stove or blinking your eyes when you sneeze are reflex actions. **2. reflexes.** the ability of the body to react to some action or event. **3.** something done in an automatic way, as if by a reflex: "By now my shabby old *reflexes* would tell me it was time to buy an evening paper and bury my head in it." (S.J. Perelman)

refinery Oil refineries such as this one in Richmond, California, produce many products from petroleum.

re•form [ri fôrm´] *verb,* **reformed, reforming.** to make a change for the better; correct something that is wrong: In recent years, many states have *reformed* laws that were too easy on drunk drivers. ◆ A person who works for or favors reform is a **reformer.** —*noun, plural* **reforms.** a change for the better: This book says that the U.S. prison system needs *reform.*

re•form•a•to•ry [ri fôr´ mə tôr´ ē] *noun, plural* **reformatories.** a place to help or reform young people who have broken the law; also called a **reform school.**

re•frain¹ [ri frān´] *verb,* **refrained, refraining.** to hold back from; avoid: A sign on the railroad car door said, "Passengers in this car will please *refrain* from smoking."

refrain² *noun, plural* **refrains.** a phrase repeated regularly in a song or poem; a chorus.

re•fresh [ri fresh´] *verb,* **refreshed, refreshing.** **1.** to make fresh again; make fresh or relaxed: "His tiredness was gone. He looked completely *refreshed,* even happy." (John McGahern) **2. refresh one's memory.** to help a person remember; remind.

re•fresh•ment [ri fresh´ mənt] *noun, plural* **refreshments. 1. refreshments.** food or drink: Pizza and soda were the *refreshments* at Katie's birthday party. **2.** the fact of refreshing: "Even the air that pushed in from the sea was hot and held no *refreshment.*" (William Golding)

re•frig•er•ate [ri frij´ ə rāt´] *verb,* **refrigerated, refrigerating.** to keep something at a low temperature; keep cool or cold: Milk should be *refrigerated* to keep it from spoiling. ◆ The process of doing this is called **refrigeration.**

re•frig•er•a•tor [ri frij´ ə rā´ tər] *noun, plural* **refrigerators.** a device used to keep things cold, especially a kitchen appliance that is used to keep food from spoiling.

re•fuge [ref´ yōōj] *noun, plural* **refuges. 1.** protection from trouble or danger; a safe place or condition: They were caught in a rain shower and had to take *refuge* in a doorway. **2.** a place that gives such protection: a wildlife *refuge.*

ref•u•gee [ref´ yōō je´ *or* ref´ yōō jē´] *noun, plural* **refugees.** a person who flees from a place to find safety and protection somewhere else: After the war in Vietnam ended, many Vietnamese *refugees* came to the U.S.

re•fund [ri fund´] *verb,* **refunded, refunding.** to give or pay back: I returned the shirt to the store because it was the wrong size, and the salesman *refunded* my money. —[rē´ fund´] *noun, plural* **refunds.** the return of money that has already been paid.

re•fus•al [ri fyōō´ zəl] *noun, plural* **refusals.** the fact of refusing: The senator issued a statement explaining his *refusal* to meet the protesters.

re•fuse¹ [ri fyōōz´] *verb,* **refused, refusing. 1.** to decide not to do or allow something: "Aunt Christina . . . shut her mouth in a thin line and *refused* to say another word." (Noel Coward) **2.** to say no; turn down: The restaurant has a sign saying "We will *refuse* service to anyone who is not properly dressed."

re•fuse² [ref´ yōōs] *noun.* anything worthless that is thrown away; trash or garbage.

re•gain [ri gān´] *verb,* **regained, regaining.** to get back again; recover: The skater almost fell, but she *regained* her balance and kept going.

re•gard [ri gärd´] *verb,* **regarded, regarding. 1.** to think of in a certain way; consider to be: "He had always *regarded* himself as a really nice guy." (Stephen King) **2.** to look at closely; observe: "Then the two animals stood and *regarded* each other cautiously." (Kenneth Grahame) —*noun, plural* **regards. 1.** The fact of considering something: She jumped into the water to save the child with no *regard* for her own safety. **2.** a subject or situation to be considered: "He was here to ask what the warden had decided with *regard* to his friend." (John Gardner) **3. regards.** best wishes: When you visit your grandparents, give them my *regards.*

refugees Many refugees left Hungary in 1956 after an anti-Soviet revolt there failed. This family is getting their first look at their new country, the United States.

Pronunciation Key: A F			
a	and; hat	ch	chew; such
ā	ate; stay	d	dog; lid
â	care; air	e	end; yet
ä	father; hot	ē	she; each
b	boy; cab	f	fun; off

(Turn the page for more information.)

re•gard•ing [ri gärd′ ing] *preposition.* having to do with; about: There is a meeting tonight at City Hall *regarding* the plan for a dam on Boulder Creek.

reg•is•tra•tion [rej′ əs trā′ shən] *noun, plural* **registrations.** the fact of registering, or something that does this: The college is now holding *registration* for the fall term.

> **regardless** This is a useful word. It's a word that showed up often in our Word Survey. Its current sense is "not considering; not taking into account:" "In our youth soccer league every player has to play at least half the game, *regardless* of what the score is." But this useful word has a very unpopular cousin, *irregardless.* There is no such word in English. Why then do people make the mistake of using it? They probably think of similar word pairs—*relevant* means "to the point" and *irrelevant*, adding *ir-*, means "off the point." But *regardless* already carries the sense of "not" and doesn't need *ir-*.

re•gard•less [ri gärd′ lis] *adjective; adverb.* with no thought or regard for; in spite of: The boss said to get the job done right away, *regardless* of what it costs.

re•gime [ri zhēm′] *noun, plural* **regimes.** a system or way of government, or a time when a certain ruler or government is in power: From 1965 to 1986, the Philippine Islands were under the *regime* of Ferdinand Marcos.

reg•i•ment [rej′ ə mənt] *noun, plural* **regiments.** a large military unit, usually led by a colonel. —*verb,* **regimented, regimenting.** to act or think in a strict, unchanging way, as if part of a military unit: Several recent books have said that American business leaders are too *regimented* and resist new ideas.

Re•gi•na [ri jī′ nə] the capital of the province of Saskatchewan. Canada. *Population:* 162,000.

re•gion [rē′ jən] *noun, plural* **regions. 1.** any large area of land: Cactus plants grow in desert *regions.* The Highlands is a *region* of Scotland. **2.** an area of the body: a pain in the lower *region* of the back. —**regional,** *adjective.* being or happening in a region.

reg•is•ter [rej′ is tər] *noun, plural* **registers. 1.** an official list or record: Everyone who came to the wedding signed the guest *register.* **2.** a machine that automatically records the money that comes in from sales in a store, restaurant, or other such business; more often called a **cash register.** —*verb,* **registered, registering. 1.** to enter something on an official list or record: She just bought a new car and has to *register* it with the Motor Vehicle Bureau. **2.** to sign up as a student in a school or college: He just *registered* for the fall term. **3.** to show on a scale or meter: "He said the thermometer *registered* sixteen, that it was the coldest night in his memory . . ." (Harper Lee) **4.** to show or express: Several people in the office have *registered* complaints about the new parking rules.

re•gret [ri gret′] —*verb,* **regretted, regretting.** to feel sorry or disappointed about something: Dropping out of school may seem like a good idea to him now, but he's going to *regret* it later. —*noun, plural* **regrets.** a feeling of being sorry.

reg•u•lar [reg′ yə lər] *adjective, more/most.* **1.** being what is usual or expected; normal; standard: During the sale, this TV will sell for $50 less than the *regular* price. **2.** happening over and over at the same time, or in the same way: A healthy person should have a *regular* heartbeat. **3.** according to habit, custom, or usual behavior: My aunt is a *regular* customer at that restaurant. **4.** being part of a permanent or continuing group: This health plan is available to all *regular* employees of the company. ♦ The fact of being regular is **regularity:** The philosopher Immanuel Kant lived a life of complete *regularity* — it's said that people could set their watches by the time at which he took his walk each day. —*noun, plural* **regulars.** a person who is part of a regular group: Rip's Diner opens at 6:00 AM, but the *regulars* don't start to come in until about 7:00. —**regularly,** *adverb.*

reg•u•late [reg′ yə lāt′] *verb,* **regulated, regulating. 1.** to control or direct something according to a system or set of rules: Traffic signals *regulate* the flow of cars, trucks, and people crossing the streets. **2.** to adjust a machine or device so that it works in a certain way: The air conditioning in this office building is *regulated* so that it goes off at 8:00 each night.

reg•u•la•tion [reg′ yə lā′ shən] *noun, plural* **regulations. 1.** the fact of regulating. **2.** something that regulates, such as a law, rule, or order: Each new student at the high school got a booklet listing all of the school's *regulations.*

re•hears•al [ri hur′ səl] *noun, plural* **rehearsals.** a practice session before the actual performance of a play, concert, speech, or other such event.

R

re•hearse [ri hurs/] *verb,* **rehearsed, rehears-ing.** to practice or train for a play or the like before performing: The singer *rehearsed* the song for an hour before she recorded it.

reign [rān] *noun, plural* **reigns. 1.** the period of time when a king or queen rules: The *reign* of Queen Victoria was the longest in English history, lasting 64 years. **2.** a period of time when someone has great power or influence over others: The New York Yankees had a long *reign* as American League champions in the 1950's. —*verb,* **reigned, reigning. 1.** to hold power as a king or queen. **2.** to have great influence or power; rule: "Then the lights went out and darkness *reigned* once more . . ." (James Thurber)

rein [rān] *noun, plural* **reins. 1.** a long, narrow strap attached to a horse's bit at one end and held by the rider or driver at the other. The reins are used to control and guide the horse. **2.** any way of controlling or guiding something: Mary is trying to keep a tight *rein* on her eating habits so that she can lose weight. **3. reins.** a position of control or leadership: "In 1801, Thomas Jefferson took over the *reins* of the government . . ." (Robert Benchley) —*verb,* **reined, reining.** to control and guide with or as if with reins.

reindeer These animals are easily tamed by the Lapps in Arctic Europe, who use them to pull sleds and to provide meat, milk, and hides.

rein•deer [rān/ dēr/] *noun, plural* **reindeer.** a large deer that is found in cold northern areas of Europe, Asia, and North America. Reindeer are sometimes used as work animals and for food. The wild reindeer of North America are called CARIBOU.

re•in•force [rē/ in fôrs/] *verb,* **reinforced, rein-forcing.** to make something stronger, as by adding new or extra parts, making repairs, and so on: Building walls are often made of con-crete that has been *reinforced* with steel rods. —**reinforcement,** *noun:* The army sent *rein-forcements* from the rear to help the troops who were under attack.

re•ject [ri jekt/] *verb,* **rejected, rejecting. 1.** to refuse to use or accept: He *rejected* our offer to help and said he could do it all by himself. **2.** to throw away or put aside; discard: "She *rejected* the picture of herself doing this as quickly as it came to mind." (Barbara Pym) —[rē/ jekt/] *noun, plural* **rejects.** something that is rejected. —**rejection,** *noun:* She sent her story to a magazine hoping to get it published, but all she got back was a polite letter of *rejection.*

re•joice [ri jois/] *verb,* **rejoiced, rejoicing.** to show or feel great joy; be very happy: The waiting families *rejoiced* when they heard the news that the hijacked plane had been safely released.

re•lapse [rē/ laps] *noun, plural* **relapses.** the fact of falling back into a weaker or poorer condition: He was supposed to get out of the hospital last Sunday, but he had a *relapse* and had to stay another week. ♦ Also used as a verb: "He *relapsed* into a moody silence . . ." (A. Conan Doyle)

re•late [ri lāt/] *verb,* **related, relating. 1.** to tell the story of; give an account: "As they walked home Elizabeth *related* to Jane what she had seen pass between the two gentlemen . . ." (Jane Austen) **2.** to make or show a connection: In his talks to youth groups, the coach *relates* winning a football game with success in life. **3.** *Informal.* to understand and get along with other people; be connected to others: "She told me she just wishes Seymour would *relate* to more people." (J.D. Salinger)

re•lat•ed [ri lā/ tid] *adjective.* **1.** belonging to the same family: The leopard and the lion are *related* animals. **2.** having something in com-mon; connected: This book deals with the Mexican War, the Texas fight for independence, and other *related* events.

R

Pronunciation Key: G–N			
g	give; big	k	kind; cat; back
h	hold	l	let; ball
i	it; this	m	make; time
ī	ice; my	n	not; own
j	jet; gem; edge	ng	having

(Turn the page for more information.)

R

re•la•tion [ri lā′ shən] *noun, plural* **relations. 1.** the fact of being related; a connection between two or more things. **2.** the fact of understanding and getting along with one another: The U.S. and Great Britain have had friendly *relations* in recent years. **3.** the position or condition of one thing with respect to another: A fox has a long tail in *relation* to the size of its body. **4.** a person who belongs to the same family; a relative.

re•la•tion•ship [ri lā′ shən ship′] *noun, plural* **relationships. 1.** the fact of being related or connected to another person: They have a good working *relationship* but don't spend time together as friends. **2.** a connection between ideas or things: The *relationship* between water and ice is that ice is frozen water.

rel•a•tive [rel′ ə tiv] *noun, plural* **relatives.** a person who belongs to the same family. —*adjective.* **1.** having a connection with; being related: The judge wouldn't allow the evidence to be presented because it wasn't *relative* to the case. **2.** depending for its meaning or importance on something else: "Small" is a *relative* word; a black bear is a small kind of bear, but it is not small compared to other animals. —**relatively,** *adverb:* Colorado is a mountain state, but the Denver area is *relatively* flat.

horses. **2.** *also,* **relay race.** a race between teams in which each member of the team races a certain distance before being relieved by another member who continues the race. —[ri lā′ *or* rē lā′] *verb,* **relayed, relaying.** to pass along: Perry called and asked his little brother to *relay* a message to his mother.

relay The American team passes the baton in the women's 1600-meter relay race in the 1984 Olympics.

relative clauses A *relative clause* connects to—or affects—another part of the sentence. "Once she returned with a framed photograph of a beautiful woman *who was her mother* . . ." (Lillian Hellman) The sentence could stand without the relative clause ("who was her mother"), but the information would not be complete. A relative clause can be introduced by a *relative pronoun.* "The little man *who* came to the information desk in Nice airport . . ." (Graham Greene) The relative pronoun *who* deals with persons. For references to things, either *that* or *which* can be used: "It was this role *that* first brought him general recognition . . ." (Truman Capote) ". . . eight children in all crowded around the snake, *which* had been gliding slowly across the lawn . . ." (John McPhee) (Look up WHICH for more information.)

re•lax [ri laks′] *verb,* **relaxed, relaxing. 1.** to make loose or less tight: "Her hand clutched mine very hard and then *relaxed.*" (Noel Coward) **2.** to take it easy without work or worry; rest: His favorite way to *relax* is to go to the beach and lie in the sun. **3.** to be less strict or severe: The minimum height for a policeman in our city used to be 5′ 8″, but now they've *relaxed* the rule and made it 5′ 4″. ♦ The fact of relaxing, or something that relaxes, is **relaxation:** "His *relaxation* is playing golf." (John O'Hara)

re•lay [rē′ lā′] *noun, plural* **relays. 1.** a fresh supply of something to help or relieve another: Long ago Pony Express riders delivered mail across the country by using *relays* of fresh

re•lease [ri lēs′] *verb,* **released, releasing. 1.** to set free or let go: When the President's car drove up, the children in the crowd *released* hundreds of colorful balloons into the air. **2.** to provide to the public for use or sale: The movie *Snow White* was *released* in 1938. —*noun, plural* **releases. 1.** the fact of releasing: Miami quarterback Dan Marino is known for his quick *release* in passing the football. **2.** a letter or document granting freedom from something: When Mr. Jones applied for a loan, he had to sign a *release* allowing the bank to ask questions about his job and credit rating. **3.** something that is released: The candidate for mayor sent out a press *release* announcing that the former mayor had agreed to support him.

re•lent•less [ri lent′ lis] *adjective.* going on and on in a strict or harsh way; not stopping or letting up: "They went on steadily, Zeb Vance setting a *relentless* plowhorse pace." (Tom Wicker) —**relentlessly,** *adverb:* "The ants in Provence are almost as powerful as the flies, surging *relentlessly* from the red earth . . ." (M. F. K. Fisher)

> **relevant** When you say something is *relevant*, you mean it's to the point, it's meaningful. Let's make up an example. A lawyer questions a defendant and she asks, "Did you once keep a flock of pet pigeons?" The judge says, "How are pigeons *relevant* to a murder case, counselor?" The death of a person does not seem connected to a small matter of keeping pigeons. Let's say that the lawyer intends to prove that the man killed his pigeons in a fit of rage, which would suggest that he had a tendency toward violence. On the surface the question is *irrelevant*, so the lawyer has to tell how it relates to the case, why it is meaningful. If you write something that seems as if it might be off the topic, ask several questions: Does this matter occur several times? Does it settle a question? Does it affect anyone's life? Does it make a difference to the end of the story? In other words, be your own judge when you speak or write.

rel•e•vant [rel′ ə vənt] *adjective, more/most.* having to do with the subject or question being considered; related or connected: Don't worry now about what the title of your report should be—that isn't *relevant* until the teacher has approved the topic.

re•li•a•ble [ri lī′ ə bəl] *adjective, more/most.* that can be trusted or relied on; dependable: Jim needs a *reliable* car that will start in all kinds of weather. —**reliably,** *adverb.*

rel•ic [rel′ ik] *noun, plural* **relics.** something from the ancient past that has survived to the present time: The scientists found an Indian burial ground containing *relics* from hundreds of years ago.

re•lief[1] [ri lēf′] *noun, plural* **reliefs. 1.** something that brings freedom from pain, suffering, or sorrow; a form of comfort or help: I thought I had gotten 69 on the test but it was really an 89 — what a *relief*! ". . . clear, windy days, a *relief* after the cold rain of September." (Andrea Lee) **2.** help such as food, shelter, or medical care that is given to those in need. **3.** release from a job or duty: The security guard had to stay until 6:00 instead of 5:00, because his *relief* didn't get there on time.

relief[2] *noun, plural* **reliefs. 1.** a figure or design that is raised or carved to stand out from a flat background. **2. relief map.** a map that shows the height or depth of land and water areas.

re•lieve [ri lēv′] *verb,* **relieved, relieving. 1.** to make free from pain, suffering, or sorrow; give relief: ". . . the fireplace did little to *relieve* the night's fierce cold." (John Jakes) **2.** to make

free from worry or tension; relax: "He was *relieved* that Johnny had stepped in and settled matters." (Esther Forbes) **3.** to take over or free someone from a duty or job: In baseball a pitcher who is giving up a lot of runs will be *relieved* by another pitcher. "Doc and the girl worked steadily, one *relieving* the other from time to time." (Edward Abbey)

re•li•gion [ri lij′ ən] *noun, plural* **religions. 1.** a system of belief in something that cannot be known through the senses and that goes beyond human powers; belief in a God or gods. A religion usually teaches that there is life after death, that people should show their faith by

relief The three-dimensional effect of an ancient relief sculpture in Rome. In the background is the Roman Coliseum.

Pronunciation Key: O–S			
ō	over; go	ou	out; town
ô	all; law	p	put; hop
oo	look; full	r	run; car
o͞o	pool; who	s	set; miss
oi	oil; boy	sh	show

(Turn the page for more information.)

special acts and ceremonies, and that certain thoughts and actions are wrong. **2.** a particular branch or form of this belief, such as Christianity, Judaism, Islam, and so on. **3.** anything that is very strongly believed in or seriously practiced: Exercise is a *religion* with him; he runs five miles every morning and is always trying to get his friends to do the same.

re•li•gious [ri lij′ əs] *adjective, more/most.* **1.** having to do with religion: Many people came to America in early times seeking *religious* freedom. **2.** following the practices of a religion very closely: She's a very *religious* person and never misses church on Sunday.

re•lin•quish [ri ling′ kwish] *verb,* **relinquished, relinquishing.** to give up or put aside; yield: "We know that no one seizes power with the intention of *relinquishing* it." (George Orwell)

rel•ish [rel′ ish] *noun, plural* **relishes.** a mixture of chopped vegetables, spices, and other things used to add flavor to foods such as hot dogs, or eaten as a side dish. —*verb,* **relished, relishing.** to think of with pleasure; enjoy: It was a delicious meal, but she didn't *relish* the thought of cleaning up after. "King Sebastian *relished* the work he was doing." (John Jakes)

re•luc•tant [ri luk′ tənt] *adjective, more/most.* not wanting to do something; slow or unwilling to act or decide: "Leamas seemed *reluctant* to accept, but in the end he did." (John Le Carré) ◆ The fact of being reluctant is **reluctance.** —**reluctantly,** *adverb.*

re•ly [ri lī′] *verb,* **relied, relying.** to have trust or confidence in; depend on: "He *relied* on us to do our best and I don't want to let him down." (Anne Frank) "Since I could no longer see what was happening I had to *rely* upon my other senses." (Farley Mowat)

re•main [ri mān′] *verb,* **remained, remaining. 1.** to stay in the same place; not move or go away: "Throughout most of June 4 Eisenhower *remained* alone in his trailer." (Cornelius Ryan) **2.** to go on being; keep on; continue: "He pressed his back against the wall and *remained* motionless." (John Le Carré) **3.** to still be in a certain condition after other things have changed: "He counted the sheets which *remained* to be copied." (James Joyce)

re•main•der [ri mān′ dər] *noun, plural* **remainders. 1.** a part left over or remaining: It rained early this morning, but the *remainder* of the day was sunny. **2.** the number left when one number is subtracted from another: The *remainder* of 8 minus 2 is 6. **3.** the number left over when another number cannot be divided evenly.

re•mains [ri mānz′] *noun.* **1.** something that is left after other things change or move on: "Ralph was kneeling by the *remains* of the fire . . ." (William Golding) "The *remains* of last night's dinner clutter the table." (William Inge) **2.** a dead body.

re•mark [ri märk′] *noun, plural* **remarks.** something that is said; a short statement or opinion: The principal made a few opening *remarks* and then turned the meeting over to Mrs. Olsen. —*verb,* **remarked, remarking.** to say in a few words; mention: "Everyone in town *remarked* what nice people they were." (Walker Percy)

re•mark•a•ble [ri märk′ kə bəl] *adjective, more/most.* very much out of the ordinary; worth being noticed or spoken about; unusual: "His good looks are really quite *remarkable;* everybody notices them" (Oscar Wilde) —**remarkably,** *adverb.*

Rembrandt A self-portrait by Rembrandt, painted in 1669, shortly before his death.

Rem•brandt [rem′ brant] 1606-1669, Dutch painter.

re•me•di•al [ri mē′ dē əl] *adjective.* meant to improve or cure a problem: The junior high school has a *remedial* reading course that helps students become better readers.

rem•e•dy [rem′ ə dē] *noun, plural* **remedies. 1.** something that cures pain or illness: My grandmother says hot chicken soup is a good *remedy* for a cold. **2.** something that corrects a problem: He's found that the best *remedy* for being nervous when he gives a speech is to go over it carefully beforehand. —*verb,* **remedied, remedying.** to provide a remedy for; cure.

re•mem•ber [ri mem⁄ bər] *verb,* **remembered, remembering. 1.** to bring or call back to the mind; think of again: I know he used to go to our school, but I can't *remember* his name. **2.** to keep carefully in the memory: When you talk on the phone to Grandpa, *remember* to speak up so that he can hear you. **3.** to mention or bring greetings from: Please *remember* me to Mrs. Warren; she was my teacher last year. ♦ Something that is remembered is a **remembrance.**

re•mind [ri mīnd⁄] *verb,* **reminded, reminding. 1.** to cause a person to remember something: Tracey wrote a note on the calendar to *remind* herself of the Girl Scout meeting Friday. ♦ Something that helps a person to remember is a **reminder. 2.** to cause a person to think of someone or something else: "He *reminds* me of a boy I used to know in high school, Dutch McCoy." (William Inge)

re•mote [ri mōt⁄] *adjective,* **remoter, remotest. 1.** far away in place or time; distant: "Far off in the distance now I heard a rooster crow a faint call like a *remote* hurrah . . ." (William Styron) **2.** out of the way; secluded: He left the city and moved to a *remote* village upstate. **3.** slight or small: The ring is probably lost for good, but there's a *remote* chance that someone found it. —**remotely,** *adverb.* —**remoteness,** *noun.*

remote control the control of a machine or device from a distance by using radio waves, electricity, or a similar method. TV sets and model planes can be controlled this way.

re•mov•al [ri mōō⁄ vəl] *noun, plural* **removals.** the act or fact of removing: The builder has to take care of the *removal* of all the trash and spare lumber from the building site. The local newspaper called for the *removal* of the mayor from office because of a scandal.

re•move [ri mōōv⁄] *verb,* **removed, removing. 1.** to move away from one place to another; take off or take out: I have to *remove* all those weeds that have grown up around the mailbox. **2.** to get rid of: This confession should *remove* all doubts as to who the murderer was.

Ren•ais•sance [ren⁄ ə säns⁄] *noun.* **1.** a time in European history from about the 1300's to the 1600's, when learning and the arts became highly developed. Leonardo da Vinci and Michelangelo were important figures in the Italian Renaissance. **2.** *also,* **renaissance.** any period thought of as a high point of culture or learning: During the Harlem *Renaissance* of the 1920's, many outstanding black authors became well-known, such as the poet Langston Hughes.

ren•der [ren⁄ dər] *verb,* **rendered, rendering. 1.** to cause to be; make: "His father's misfortunes in trade *rendered* him unable to support his son . . ." (James Boswell) **2.** to give or present: We were all surprised when the jury *rendered* a verdict of not guilty. **3.** to create or perform: The artist *rendered* a very lifelike painting of the woman and her children. ♦ Something that is created or performed is a **rendition.**

ren•dez•vous [rän⁄ dā vōō⁄] *noun, plural* **rendezvous.** a plan to meet at a certain time and place: The soldiers had orders to parachute behind enemy lines and to arrange a *rendezvous* at an old farmhouse.

ren•e•gade [ren⁄ ə gād⁄] *noun, plural* **renegades.** a person who changes his loyalty from one group to another: Simon Girty, an American *renegade* of the Revolutionary War, led Indian warriors against the colonists.

re•new [ri nōō⁄] *verb,* **renewed, renewing. 1.** to make new or as if new again; restore: After a few days off from work, he felt completely rested and *renewed.* **2.** to begin again: After accidentally meeting at the train station, the two men *renewed* their old friendship that had started years earlier in high school. **3.** to extend the time or term of something: Alice *renewed*

Renaissance One of the greatest achievements of the Renaissance is Michelangelo's sculpture the *Pieta.*

Pronunciation Key: T–Z

t	ten, date	v	very; live
th	think	w	win; away
th	these	y	you
u	cut; butter	z	zoo; cause
ur	turn; bird	zh	measure

(Turn the page for more information.)

her driver's license before the old one expired. ◆ The fact of renewing something is **renewal**.

ren•o•vate [ren′ ə vāt′] *verb,* **renovated, renovating.** to restore to a better state: "The group earned money by painting and *renovating* Victorian houses." (Joe McGinniss) ◆ The act of doing this is **renovation**.

rent [rent] *noun, plural* **rents.** money paid for the use of something that someone else owns. Rent is usually based on the amount of time something is used. —*verb,* **rented, renting. 1.** to have or give the right to use something in exchange for paying rent: We *rented* a car for our vacation trip up the coast. **2.** to be available for rent: Apartments in that building *rent* for about $500 a month.

rent•al [ren′ təl] *noun, plural* **rentals.** something that is rented, or the amount of rent received or paid.

re•peat [ri pēt′] *verb,* **repeated, repeating.** to say, do, or happen again: "Say it again, *repeat* what you said." (Edward Albee) —[rē′ pēt′ *or* ri pēt′] *noun, plural* **repeats.** the act of repeating, or something that is repeated: I thought this was going to be a new show, but it's just a *repeat* of one I saw last fall. —**repeatedly** [ri pēt′ id lē], *adverb.*

re•pel [ri pel′] *verb,* **repelled, repelling. 1.** to drive back or force away: "The moss burned with a dim glow, producing smoke which *repelled* snakes and insects." (Jerzy Kosinski) **2.** to cause a very strong feeling of dislike or disgust: She was *repelled* by his bad table manners and rude remarks. ◆ Something that repels is **repellent:** The raincoat had been specially treated to make it water *repellent.* "He had a harsh voice and an unpleasant and *repellent* manner." (Paul Gallico)

repetition Repetition occurs needlessly in expressions like "a *tall giant* "or "an *expensive mansion.*" By definition a giant is tall and a mansion is expensive. A phrase like this is *redundant* [rē dun′ dənt]. You don't say *new innovation* because an innovation by definition is new. *Past history* is also redundant: history *is* the past. There is a tendency in English nowadays to say, "plan for the future." But of course you can't plan for the past—or even the present. However, there are also times when repetition does serve a purpose. Repeating a certain phrase is an effective way to give rhythm to your sentences. During World War II, Prime Minister Winston Churchill told the British after their troops were driven out of France and their cities were bombed daily by the Germans, "We shall fight on the beaches, we shall fight on the landing grounds, we shall fight in the fields and in the streets, we shall fight in the hills, we shall never surrender." Notice how he repeats "we shall." Note also the way the repetition works—the places are mentioned in the order that the enemy would reach them after invading England.

re•pair [ri pâr′] *verb,* **repaired, repairing. 1.** to put something that is broken or not working back in the proper condition; fix; mend: to *repair* a television set. **2.** to make up for some damage or wrong: "I can't help or *repair* the wrong I have done." (Anne Frank) —*noun, plural* **repairs. 1.** the fact of repairing: "*Repairs* were made on mud huts that had been damaged by the big rains . . ." (Alex Haley) **2.** the general condition of something: She always keeps her car in good *repair.* ◆ A man whose work is repairing things is a **repairman**.

re•pay [ri pā′] *verb,* **repaid, repaying.** to pay something back: to *repay* a car loan.

re•peal [ri pēl′] *verb,* **repealed, repealing.** to officially end or do away with something, especially a law: "The merchants agreed not to import any English goods until the Stamp Act was *repealed.*" (Esther Forbes) —*noun, plural* **repeals.** the act of repealing something.

rep•e•ti•tion [rep′ ə tish′ ən] *noun, plural* **repetitions.** the fact of repeating, or something that is repeated: He did some sit-ups and some push-ups, 10 *repetitions* of each.

re•place [ri plās′] *verb,* **replaced, replacing. 1.** to take the place of: Emily has a sore ankle and Carolyn is going to *replace* her as goalie for today's game. **2.** to put back into place: After glancing through the library book for a minute, Ellen *replaced* it on the shelf. **3.** to get or give something in the place of: "She saw that the hand towel was dusty . . . and *replaced* it with a fresh one." (James Agee)

re•place•ment [ri plās′ mənt] *noun, plural* **replacements. 1.** the act of replacing or being replaced: If these tires wear out within the first 5000 miles, there's no charge for *replacement.* **2.** someone or something that takes the place of another: The shower head is broken; we'll have to order a *replacement.*

rep•li•ca [rep′ lə kə] *noun, plural* **replicas.** a copy that is very close to the original: Beth has a statue on her dresser that's a *replica* of the Statue of Liberty.

re•ply [ri plī′] *verb,* **replied, replying.** to say or write something in return; give an answer: When I asked what she wanted for dinner, she *replied* that it was up to me to choose. —*noun, plural* **replies.** the act of replying; an answer or response: We sent her an invitation to the party, but we haven't had any *reply.*

re•port [ri pôrt′] *noun, plural* **reports. 1.** an account or statement telling the facts about something; a description in writing or speech: The weather *report* says that there may be snow tomorrow. **2.** a school assignment to give information about a certain thing: a book *report,* a science *report.* **3.** a loud noise like an explosion or shot: the *report* of a rifle. —*verb,* **reported, reporting. 1.** to give a report: The guard *reported* that he'd seen a white car driving back and forth outside the building. **2.** to present oneself to someone in charge: "Shortly before Christmas 1777, he *reported* to General Washington at Valley Forge." (Gore Vidal)

report card a regular, written report sent from a school to parents giving information on a student's marks, behavior, and so on.

re•port•er [ri pôr′ tər] *noun, plural* **reporters.** a person whose work is to gather and report the news for a newspaper, magazine, TV or radio station, and so on.

rep•re•sent [rep′ ri zent′] *verb,* **represented, representing. 1.** to stand for or be a symbol of: The stripes on the U.S. flag *represent* the thirteen original colonies. **2.** to speak or act for officially: A lawyer *represents* a client in court. **3.** to be an example of: "Plant life was *represented* by lovely floating seaweed . . ." (Jules Verne) —**representation** [rep′ ri zen tā′ shən] *noun:* This model is a *representation* of how the actual building will look when it's built.

rep•re•sent•a•tive [rep′ ri zen′ tə tiv] *noun, plural* **representatives. 1.** a person chosen to speak or act for others: A sales *representative* called at the school to show some of her company's textbooks to the teachers. **2. Representative.** a member of the U.S. House of Representatives, or a member of a state legislature. —*adjective,* **1.** being an example of a group or type; typical: This house is *representative* of the ones built by the Trent Company. **2.** having a government of elected representatives.

re•press [ri pres′] *verb,* **repressed, repressing.** to hold back or prevent: "She was struggling hard to *repress* the tears . . ." (Iris Murdoch) —**repression,** *noun.*

re•pro•duce [rē′ prə dōōs′] *verb,* **reproduced, reproducing. 1.** to make a copy; produce again: Our local newspaper is now able to *reproduce* color photos as well as black-and-white ones. **2.** to produce offspring: A cell *reproduces* by dividing itself into two new cells. —**reproduction,** *noun.*

rep•tile [rep′ təl *or* rep′ tīl′] *noun, plural* **reptiles.** one of a large group of cold-blooded animals that have backbones and dry, scaly skin. Most reptiles lay eggs. Snakes, lizards, alligators, and turtles are types of reptiles.

re•pub•lic [ri pub′ lik] *noun, plural* **republics. 1.** a form of government in which the citizens are governed by representatives whom they elect to manage the government. The head of a republic is a president. **2.** any country that has this form of government, such as the U.S.

Republican The first use of an elephant as the symbol of the Republican Party was in this drawing by the famous cartoonist Thomas Nast, in 1874.

re•pub•li•can [ri pub′ li kən] *adjective.* **1.** of or having to do with a republic: When Ireland was ruled by Great Britain, the Irish *Republican* Army fought for a separate Republic of Ireland. **2. Republican.** having to do with the Republican Party. —*noun, plural* **republicans. 1. Republican.** a person who belongs to or supports the Republican Party. **2.** anyone who supports a republic.

Pronunciation Key: [ə] Symbol

The [ə] or *schwa* sound occurs in syllables without an accent. It can be spelled with any vowel, such as a in above, e in listen, i in pencil, o in melon, u in circus. It can also be a combination of vowels, such as io in action, ai in mountain, iou in precious.

(Turn the page for more information.)

R

research papers In schools and colleges, teachers assign research papers, meaning reports that involve reading books and using encyclopedias and other reference books. What these teachers want is to teach students how to find information, how to discard unimportant facts, how to express ideas in a sensible order. But is this *original* material? No. Scholars refer to *primary* and *secondary* sources. Primary sources are letters, interviews, public records, old writings from the actual time of the subject. Secondary sources are those books, magazines, and newspapers that deal with a subject but do not gó back to the first documents, to original commentaries. For students in high school or college, the teacher will expect original research in a research paper.

Republican Party one of the two major political parties in the U.S., along with the DEMOCRATIC PARTY.

rep·u·ta·tion [rep′yə tā′shən] *noun, plural* **reputations.** a general opinion of someone or something that is held by the public; what others think a person or thing is like: "Jamie had the *reputation* of being a really mean person." (S.E. Hinton) ". . . the house had a *reputation* for being haunted." (Madeleine L'Engle)

re·quest [ri kwest′] *verb,* **requested, requesting.** to ask for something; ask in a polite way: She called the bank to *request* some information about their new savings plan. —*noun, plural* **requests. 1.** the act of requesting. **2.** something asked for: The disc jockey played the song "Misty," a *request* from one of his regular listeners.

re·quire [ri kwīr′] *verb,* **required, requiring. 1.** to have need of; need or demand: The main library has all the books you *require* for your project. **2.** to order or command someone to do something: The law *requires* drivers to carry their licenses when they drive. ◆ Also used as an adjective: American history is a *required* course in most high schools.

re·quire·ment [ri kwīr′mənt] *noun, plural* **requirements.** something that is required: Having a high-school diploma is a *requirement* for that job. One of these tablets will supply a person's daily *requirement* of Vitamin C.

res·cue [res′kyōo] *verb,* **rescued, rescuing.** to save or free from danger: A lifeguard's job is to *rescue* people who are drowning. —*noun, plural* **rescues.** the fact of rescuing someone. —**rescuer,** *noun.*

re·search [rē′surch′ *or* ri surch′] *noun, plural* **researches.** the careful study or testing of something to learn new facts: Doctors are carrying out a lot of *research* to try to find a cure for cancer. —*verb,* **researched, researching.** to do research on: Betty *researched* the history of her town for a social studies report.

—**researcher,** *noun:* News magazines have *researchers* who gather the facts for a story.

re·sem·ble [ri zem′bəl] *verb,* **resembled, resembling.** to look like or be like in some ways; be similar to: Brian *resembles* his father, especially because they both have red hair. "It is . . . cleverly designed to *resemble* a real airplane." (Ernest K. Gann) ◆ The fact of resembling something is a **resemblance.**

re·sent [ri zent′] *verb,* **resented, resenting.** to feel angry or annoyed toward; be bitter about: She *resents* having to share a room with her sister while each of her brothers has his own room. "I much *resented* that adult trick of talking about you as if you weren't there." (James Gould Cozzens) —**resentful,** *adjective.* —**resentment,** *noun.*

res·er·va·tion [rez′ər vā′shən] *noun, plural* **reservations. 1.** an arrangement to reserve something for someone: a hotel *reservation.* **2.** an uncertain feeling; a doubt: Mom had some *reservations* about letting Jackie drive all the way to the city alone. **3.** land that is set aside by the government for a particular purpose or use, especially for an Indian tribe to live on.

re·serve [ri zurv′] *verb,* **reserved, reserving. 1.** to arrange for something in advance: to *reserve* a seat for an airplane flight. **2.** to save or hold for some special purpose: He tried to *reserve* judgment until he had heard both sides of the story. "Her friends agreed that she ought to *reserve* her strength." (Elizabeth Bowen) **3.** to keep for oneself: The store had a sign saying, "We *reserve* the right to refuse service to anyone who is not properly dressed." —*noun, plural* **reserves. 1.** something set aside for future use: The U.S. has to be careful not to use up its oil *reserves* too quickly **2.** the quality of holding back one's thoughts or feelings: His *reserve* makes it hard for people to get to know him. ◆ Also used as an adjective: The judge is relaxed at home but very *reserved* in his courtroom. **3. reserves.** a group of soldiers who are not on actual duty but keep ready to serve if needed: the Navy or Marine Corps *Reserve.* **4.** public land set aside for a particular use: They hunted wild ducks on the game *reserve.*

reservoir Rio Grande Reservoir, in the San Juan Mountains of Colorado.

res•er•voir [rez′ ər vwär′] *noun, plural* **reservoirs.** a place where water or some other substance is stored for later use: New York City's drinking water comes from *reservoirs* in the mountains north of the city.

re•side [ri zīd′] *verb,* **resided, residing.** to have one's home at a certain place: To vote in the election for mayor you have to *reside* within the city limits.

res•i•dence [rez′ ə dəns] *noun, plural* **residences. 1.** the place where a person lives; one's home: "Owl lived at the Chestnuts, an old-world *residence* of great charm . . ." (A.A. Milne) **2.** the fact of living in a certain place: The college has a "writer-in-*residence*" program, which means that a famous author lives and teaches there for a year.

res•i•dent [rez′ ə dent] *noun, plural* **residents.** someone who lives in a certain place: The apartment swimming pool is for the use of *residents* only.

res•i•den•tial [rez′ ə den′ shəl] *adjective.* used as or suitable for residences: In our neighborhood only *residential* buildings can be built, not offices or businesses.

re•sign [ri zīn′] *verb,* **resigned, resigning. 1.** to give up a job, position, or office; quit: She *resigned* from her job to go to work for another company. **2. resign oneself.** to accept problems or difficulties patiently, without complaining: There are no seats left for the 8:00 show, so we'll just have to *resign ourselves* to waiting until 10:30. ◆ A person who is willing to accept suffering in this way is **resigned:** "She looked *resigned,* as if this sort of thing happened often." (Dick Francis)

res•ig•na•tion [rez′ ig nā′ shən] *noun, plural* **resignations. 1.** the fact of resigning: He's decided to leave his job and is going to hand in his letter of *resignation* today. **2.** the fact of accepting problems or difficulties patiently.

res•in [rez′ ən] *noun, plural* **resins.** a sticky substance that flows from pine, balsam, and other trees. Resin is used in medicine and in various paints, varnishes, and plastics.

re•sist [ri zist′] *verb,* **resisted, resisting. 1.** to fight or go against; oppose: The soldiers *resisted* the enemy attack. **2.** to keep from giving in to; not accept: He's supposed to be on a diet, but the cake was so good he couldn't *resist* a second helping. "No pilot alive can *resist* watching a plane take off or land." (Ernest K. Gann) **3.** to withstand the effects of: This paint *resists* the effects of dampness and rust. ◆ Someone or something that resists is **resistant:** chair covers made from stain-*resistant* fabric, a person who is *resistant* to new ideas.

resistance French resistance fighters on the streets of Paris, trying to block the advance of the Germans during World War II.

re•sist•ance [ri zis′ təns] *noun.* **1.** the fact of resisting: "They choose paths of least *resistance* over the land, often following in each other's tracks through deep snow." (Barry Lopez) **2.** the ability or power to resist: Because he hasn't been eating right or getting enough sleep lately, his *resistance* was low and he caught a bad cold. **3.** a force that goes against or prevents motion:

Pronunciation Key: Accent Marks

[′] is the normal accent mark. It shows where the main stress falls on a word.
[′] is a secondary accent mark. It shows a lighter stress than the primary accent. For example:

tel • e • vis • ion [tel′ə vizh′ən]
(Turn the page for more information.)

R

Cars and planes are designed to have low wind *resistance* in order to save fuel. **4.** in electricity, the power with which something resists an electrical current that is passing through it.

res•o•lu•tion [rez′ ə loo′ shən] *noun, plural* **resolutions. 1.** the fact of firmly deciding or promising to do something: She made a New Year's *resolution* to quit smoking. ♦ A person who decides something in this way is **resolute** [rez′ ə loot′]. **2.** something that has been officially decided: The city council passed a *resolution* that the new shopping center would not be allowed to have any fast-food restaurants. **3.** the fact of settling or solving something, such as a problem or a quarrel: The two parties in the lawsuit agreed to a *resolution* of the case. **4.** the sharpness or clearness of an image, such as a picture on a video screen.

re•solve [ri zolv′] *verb,* **resolved, resolving. 1.** to make up one's mind; make a firm decision about something; determine: "She *resolved* she would never speak to him again." (Lois Lenski) **2.** to find an answer to a problem or difficulty; settle: "Hardly was that ugly matter *resolved* . . . before a second crisis struck." (John Gardner) **3.** to decide by a vote: The committee *resolved* to cancel next week's meeting.

re•sound [ri zound′] *verb,* **resounded, resounding. 1.** to be filled with sound: "The house *resounded* with cries and the noise of slammed windows." (John Cheever) **2.** to make a loud, long sound.

re•source [ri sôrs′ *or* rē′ sôrs′] *noun, plural* **resources. 1.** someone or something to turn to for help; a source of aid or support: A dictionary is a good *resource* for a writer. ♦ A person who is good at making use of available resources is **resourceful. 2.** *also,* **resources.** a source of wealth: Oil is an important economic *resource.* ♦ See also NATURAL RESOURCE.

re•spect [ri spekt′] *noun, plural* **respects. 1.** a good opinion of the worth or value of something; high regard; admiration: I'm going to follow the teacher's advice because I have a lot of *respect* for her judgment. **2.** a polite attitude, as toward someone who is older, of higher rank, and so on: In Japan, people bow when they meet another person as a sign of *respect.* **3.** a certain point or detail to be considered: The dolphin and porpoise are different animals, but they are similar to each other in many *respects.* **4. respects.** a polite expression of greeting. —*verb,* **respected, respecting.** to have respect for someone or something.

respective Three different adjectives are formed from the noun *respect*. Two have a fairly obvious meaning. *Respectable* means that someone's personality or character allows—makes it *able*—for that person to be worthy of respect. Another use of *respect* is *respectful*. Here, a person shows that he or she admires or trusts others. But there's a tricky definition waiting in the bushes for an unwary writer! *Respective* has nothing to do with showing or having respect. It means "considering each one separately:" "Seymour and Buddy had moved into it in 1929, at the *respective* ages of twelve and ten." (J.D. Salinger) "After receiving their awards, the students returned to their *respective* classrooms." The students were *respectful* to their teacher, and the teacher was known as being *respectable*. But "*respective* classrooms" means "each to his or her own classroom."

res•o•nant [rez′ ə nənt] *adjective.* having a deep, rich, full tone or sound: an opera singer who is known for his *resonant* voice. ♦ The quality of being resonant is **resonance.**

re•sort [ri zôrt′] *noun, plural* **resorts. 1.** a place where people often go for a vacation or to relax: Acapulco, Mexico is a popular *resort* on the Pacific Ocean. **2.** someone or something used or appealed to for help: If I can't get the money any other way, as a last *resort* I could borrow it from Dad. —*verb,* **resorted, resorting.** to turn to something as a way of solving a problem: She was so worried about getting a good mark that she *resorted to* cheating.

re•spect•a•ble [ri spek′ tə bəl] *adjective, more/most.* **1.** worth being respected; having a good reputation: In earlier times it was not *respectable* for a young woman to travel alone or eat out by herself. ♦ The fact of being respectable is **respectability. 2.** fairly good or large: She's earned a *respectable* amount of money from her babysitting jobs. —**respectably,** *adverb.*

re•spect•ful [ri spekt′ fəl] *adjective, more/most.* having or showing respect; polite: The children always showed a *respectful* attitude toward their parents. —**respectfully,** *adverb:* The class secretary wrote at the end of her report, "*Respectfully* submitted by Janet Jones."

re•spec•tive [ri spek′ tiv] *adjective.* belonging to each; individual; separate: After summer vacation each of the boys returned to their *respective* schools and colleges. **—respectively,** *adverb:* in the order given: You and Ted and I will all be sitting together — we have seats 3A, 3B, and 3C, *respectively.*

res•pi•ra•tion [res′ pə rā′ shən] *noun.* the process of breathing. During respiration, OXYGEN is taken in from the air (or water) and CARBON DIOXIDE is given off as a waste product. In humans and other land animals, respiration occurs in the lungs; in fish it occurs through the gills. In plants, gases flow freely in and out of the cells.

res•pi•ra•to•ry [res′ prə tôr′ ē] *adjective.* having to do with breathing or the organs involved in breathing: A cough is sometimes caused by a *respiratory* infection. ◆ A machine or device used to help a person breathe is called a **respirator** [res′ pə rā′ tər].

res•pond [ri spänd′] *verb,* **responded, responding. 1.** to give an answer; reply: I called out to her, but she didn't *respond.* **2.** to act in return; react: When the Soviet Union tried to put missiles in Cuba in 1962, the U.S. *responded* by blocking Soviet shipping to Cuba.

re•sponse [ri späns′] *noun, plural* **responses.** something said or done as an answer: "I could get no *response* whatever to my knocks at the Warden's door." (John Gardner)

re•spon•si•bil•i•ty [ri spän′ sə bil′ ə tē] *noun, plural* **responsibilities. 1.** the fact of being responsible: He won't accept *responsibility* for his dog and lets it run loose all over the neighborhood. **2.** something that a person is responsible for: In the early grades, a homework assignment is often called a *responsibility* paper.

re•spon•si•ble [ri spän′ sə bəl] *adjective, more/ most.* **1.** having as a job, duty, or assignment: The treasurer is *responsible* for keeping track of the club's money. **2.** being the cause of: Who's *responsible* for leaving the kitchen in such a mess? **3.** able to be trusted or relied on; dependable: She would make a good babysitter because she's very *responsible.* **4.** having or requiring important duties: He's been with the bank for many years and has a very *responsible* position. **—responsibly,** *adverb.*

rest¹ [rest] *noun, plural* **rests. 1.** a time of sleep, relaxing, or not being active: After climbing halfway up the hill, the hikers took a *rest* under a tree. **2.** a state of not moving; a stop: The papers blew off the picnic table and came to *rest* in the corner of the yard. **3.** something used as a

support: Seats in an airliner have an arm *rest* on each side. **4.** in music, a period of silence between tones in a measure, or a symbol that shows this.
—verb, rested, resting. 1. to stop work or activity; take a rest. **2.** to give a rest to; allow to relax: "She had taken off her slippers and was *resting* her stockinged feet on the footstool." (Christopher Isherwood) **3.** to be at ease or at peace; be relaxed: The detective said he would not *rest* until all the gang members had been caught. **4.** to be placed on or against; sit or lie on: "She had taken the clock radio that always *rested* on the kitchen table." (Jeffery Paul Chan)

rest² *noun.* what is left over; the remainder: I'm going to watch this show and then do the *rest* of the cleaning up later. Over 2000 miles of ocean separates Hawaii from the *rest* of the U.S.

res•tau•rant [res′ tər ənt *or* res′ tränt′] *noun, plural* **restaurants.** a business where meals are prepared and served to customers.

rest•less [rest′ lis] *adjective, more/most.* **1.** not able to relax and be comfortable; continually moving in a nervous or impatient way: "Sometimes he seemed as *restless* as a Bengal tiger pacing back and forth inside its cage." (James Houston) **2.** causing or having such a feeling: She spent a *restless* night tossing in bed. **—restlessly,** *adverb:* "The baby slept *restlessly,* turning and turning." (Herman Wouk) **—restlessness,** *noun.*

re•store [ri stôr′] *verb,* **restored, restoring. 1.** to bring something back to an earlier and better condition: The carpenter *restored* the woodwork in the old house. ". . . the one whose duty was to *restore* the family to the glory it had known before Papa's death." (Russell Baker) **2.** to bring back into being or into use: "Witnesses for the defense *restored* my faith in human nature . . . because they were telling the truth." (James Weldon Johnson) ◆ Something that has been restored is a **restoration** [res′ tə rā′ shən]: Williamsburg, Virginia is a *restoration* of a village from early colonial times.

re•strain [ri strān′] *verb,* **restrained, restraining. 1.** to hold in or hold back: "Matcham could

R

Pronunciation Key: A–F

a	and; hat	ch	chow; such
ā	ate; stay	d	dog; lid
â	care; air	e	end; yet
ä	father; hot	ē	she; each
b	boy; cab	f	fun; off

(Turn the page for more information.)

not *restrain* a little cry." (Agatha Christie) ◆ Often used as an adjective: "Both of them were looking in our direction and speaking in carefully *restrained* tones, obviously about us." (Christopher Isherwood) **2.** to keep someone from acting in a certain way: "Jem *restrained* me from further questions." (Harper Lee)

re•straint [ri strānt/] *noun, plural* **restraints. 1.** the fact of being restrained, or something that is used to do this: Auto seat belts are a type of *restraint* because they prevent a person from being thrown out of the seat. **2.** the fact of restraining one's actions or feelings: "He moves nervously, and fast, but with a *restraint* which suggests that he is a cautious, thoughtful man." (John Hersey)

re•strict [ri strikt/] *verb,* **restricted, restricting.** to keep within certain limits; confine: Dad is on a diet that *restricts* the amount of red meat he's allowed to eat. ◆ Also used as an adjective: The movie rating 'R' means that a film is *restricted* as to who is allowed to see it.

tunnel and then *resumed* normal speed afterward. "After supper they would *resume* their homework . . ." (William F. Buckley) **2.** to take or occupy again: "The schoolmaster replaced the black notebook in his pocket and *resumed* his seat at the iron table." (John R. Tunis)

res•u•mé or **res•u•me** [rez/ ə mā/] *noun.* a paper or report that a person prepares when applying for a new job, listing past jobs held, educational background, and so on.

re•tail [re/ tāl] *noun.* the selling of goods directly to the general public, rather than selling them to a dealer or distributor who in turn makes the final sale to the public. ◆ A person who does this is a **retailer.** —*adjective.* having to do with the selling of products at retail, as opposed to WHOLESALE: a *retail* store. —*verb,* **retailed, retailing.** to sell goods in this way: In most stores this camera *retails* for about $300, but I bought it in a discount store for $229. ◆ The fact of doing this is **retailing.**

restrictive clauses If a sentence needs a certain clause in order to make sense, it is called a *restrictive* clause. A *nonrestrictive* clause adds an idea, but if you drop it, the sentence can still stand without it. "My little brother, <u>who hates to get up in the morning,</u> got a clock radio for his birthday." Note that the underlined clause is nonrestrictive. "My little brother got a clock radio for his birthday" would be a good, clear sentence without it. Look at the commas in the sentence above. Because a nonrestrictive clause causes a break in thought, it's set off by commas. But a restrictive clause ties directly to the rest of the sentence and does not need commas. "The new clock radio, which has a loud buzzer for an alarm, is sure to wake Ricky up." Note the commas to set off the nonrestrictive clause.

re•stric•tion [ri strik/ shən] *noun, plural* **restrictions. 1.** the fact of restricting: The soldier's punishment was *restriction* to his quarters for the entire weekend. **2.** anything that restricts, especially a law or rule: Dogs are allowed on this beach, with the *restriction* that they have to be kept on a leash.

re•sult [ri zult/] *noun, plural* **results. 1.** something that happens because of something else: One *result* of the Spanish-American War was that Spain lost almost all its colonies. **2.** something good that happens in this way: This weed killer promises noticeable *results* within three to five days. —*verb,* **resulted, resulting. 1.** to be a result of: His weight loss *resulted* from his being sick in bed for three weeks. **2.** to have as a result: Reckless driving often *results* in accidents.

re•sume [ri zoom/] *verb,* **resumed, resuming. 1.** to go on again after a break or interruption: The driver slowed down going through the

re•tain [ri tān/] *verb,* **retained, retaining. 1.** to keep or hold on to: He's lived in America for many years, but he still *retains* his German accent. **2.** to keep in a certain position or condition: The coals had *retained* just enough heat to start a new fire. ◆ The fact of retaining something is **retention** [ri ten/ shən].

ret•i•na [ret/ ə nə *or* ret/ nə] *noun, plural* **retinas.** the lining on the back of the eyeball, containing nerve cells that are sensitive to light. The retina sends images to the brain.

re•tire [ri tīr/] *verb,* **retired, retiring. 1.** to leave a job, business, or other work for good because of having reached a certain age, which is now usually 65 or 70. **2.** to give up one's work permanently; end a career: Actress Grace Kelly *retired* from movies after she became Princess Grace of Monaco. **3.** to go away to one's room or to a quiet place, as to sleep, relax, and so on: "My other uncle, yawning, would *retire* to his quarters." (Mary McCarthy)

re·tire·ment [ri tīr′ mənt] *noun, plural* **retirements.** the fact of being retired from work, or the time when this takes place.

re·tir·ing [ri tīr′ ing] *adjective, more/most.* wanting to avoid attention or notice; shy; reserved: Sam has a *retiring* nature and doesn't like to go to parties.

re·tort [ri tôrt′] *verb,* **retorted, retorting.** to answer or reply to what is said, especially in a quick or angry way: " 'Well, for a long time there was no reason to be sure.' Mary *retorted* with spirit." (James Agee) ♦ Also used as a *noun:* a sharp *retort.*

re·treat [ri trēt′] *verb,* **retreated, retreating.** to pull or move back; withdraw: The Emperor Napoleon's Grand Army almost conquered Russia, but then had to *retreat* because they were not prepared for the cold winter there. —*noun, plural* **retreats. 1.** the fact of retreating: The "Long March" is the name given to a famous *retreat* of 6000 miles across China by the Red Army. **2.** a place to get away to rest and relax: "He'd first met Jenny while visiting the *retreat* of some friends on a wooded mountainside . . ." (Philip Roth)

re·trieve [ri trēv′] *verb,* **retrieved, retrieving. 1.** to get back; recover: The golfer *retrieved* his ball from the edge of the lake and put it back into play. Computers store information and then *retrieve* it when it is needed by the user. **2.** in hunting, to find and bring back dead or wounded game. —**retrieval,** *noun.*

retriever Originally bred in England for hunting, the golden retriever is very popular in the U.S.

re·trie·ver [ri trē′ vər] *noun, plural* **retrievers.** a type of hunting dog that is trained to find and bring back dead or wounded game. The **Labrador retriever** and **golden retriever** are two popular breeds of this type.

re·turn [ri turn′] *verb,* **returned, returning. 1.** to come or go back: She's away on a business trip and plans to *return* on Friday. **2.** to take, bring, or send back: I'm going to *return* this sweater I bought because it's too big. **3.** to give back the same way: Connie was out, so I left a message for her to *return* my call. —*noun, plural* **returns. 1.** the act of returning: The tennis player made a great *return* of the other player's serve. **2.** an official record or statement: Anyone who earns a certain amount of money in a year has to file an income-tax *return.* **3. returns.** money made from a business; profits. **4.** a giving back; exchange: The thief was offered a light sentence in *return* for giving information about the leaders of the gang. —*adjective.* for or in return.

reunion Classmates gather for a college reunion at Harvard under signs showing the year of their class.

re·un·ion [rē yōōn′ yən] *noun, plural* **reunions.** a coming together of friends, family, or other groups of people who have not seen each other in some time.

re·veal [ri vēl′] *verb,* **revealed, revealing. 1.** to make known something that was hidden or unknown: "Sample *revealed* his plan at a secret meeting of the board of supervisors." (Art Buchwald) **2.** to show or display something; allow to be seen: "Eddie pulled off his shirt, *revealing* large arm muscles . . ." (Joe McGinniss) "His two daughters *revealed* a talent for music . . ." (William L. Shirer) ♦ Something that is revealed is a **revelation** [rev′ ə lā′ shən].

re·venge [ri venj′] *noun.* damage or injury done to another person to pay back the harm

Pronunciation Key: G–N			
g	give; big	k	kind, cat, back
h	hold	l	let; ball
i	it; this	m	make; time
ī	ice; my	n	not; own
j	jet; gem; edge	ng	having
(Turn the page for more information.)			

R

done by that person: "He does not forget even a petty slight and will wait years, if he has to, to get *revenge*." (Mike Royko) ◆ Also used as a verb: In Shakespeare's famous play, Hamlet sets out to *revenge* the murder of his father.

rev•e•nue [rev′ə nōō′] *noun, plural* **revenues. 1.** the income that a business takes in, especially money made from property and investments rather than from the sale of goods. **2.** the money taken in by the government from taxes, fees, and so on.

Re•vere [ri vēr′] **Paul,** 1735-1818, American patriot.

rev•er•ence [rev′rəns *or* rev′ər əns] *noun.* a feeling of great respect and honor, mixed with love: "Foremost among these models for the English writer stands Shakespeare . . . a name never to be mentioned without *reverence*." (Matthew Arnold)

rev•er•ent [rev′rənt *or* rev′ər ənt] *adjective, more/most.* feeling or showing reverence: to have a *reverent* attitude toward God. ◆ The word **Reverend** is used as a title for a religious leader: the *Reverend* Martin Luther King, Jr. —**reverently,** *adverb:* "They all *reverently* bowed their heads . . ." (Charles Dickens)

—*verb,* **reversed, reversing. 1.** to go backward or in the opposite way: In American restaurants a salad is served before the main meal; in France the order is *reversed.* **2.** to change to the opposite position: The Court of Appeals *reversed* the decision of the lower court.

re•view [ri vyōō′] *verb,* **reviewed, reviewing. 1.** to look over or study again: Lee quickly *reviewed* his notes just before the history test. **2.** to give an opinion as to the quality of a book, play, movie, or the like; act as a critic. ◆ A person who does this is a **reviewer. 3.** to inspect in a formal or official way: The colonel *reviewed* his troops. ◆ A **reviewing stand** at a parade is where important people stand to watch the marchers pass by.

—*noun, plural* **reviews. 1.** the act or fact of studying something again: At the end of each chapter of this textbook, there is a *review* of what was taught in the chapter. **2.** the fact of looking back: The *New York Times* publishes a summary of news called "The Week in *Review*." **3.** a report on a book, movie, or other work of art, giving its good and bad points. **4.** an official inspection: The general stood at attention as the soldiers passed in *review.*

revising "Revising is part of writing. Few writers are so expert that they can produce what they are after on the first try." (E. B. White) Some students have the mistaken idea that a professional writer can sit down and produce a finished piece of writing right away. Actually, if there's one principle of good writing that's accepted by all writers, it's that you must revise. The question, of course, is *how* you revise. That's a matter of opinion. However, here are some practical steps you can use: (1) Don't look back at the paper right away. Let it "cool off" for a while. (2) When you read over your paper, read it aloud. This will help you spot problems such as missing copy or awkward wording. (3) Check the sequence. Is information in the proper order? Is anything left out of the sequence? (4) Check to see if the paper goes straight from beginning to end. Does it always stay on the topic, or do some parts "detour" off the track?

re•verse [ri vurs′] *noun, plural* **reverses. 1.** something that is the exact opposite of something else: "It was the very *reverse* of a 'good' job. The hours were long, the pay was wretched . . . and there was no chance of advancement." (George Orwell) **2.** the gear position on a machine that causes it to move in a direction opposite to the usual: You put a car in *reverse* to make it back up. **3.** the back or rear part: A nickel shows Thomas Jefferson on the front and his home, Monticello, on the *reverse.* **4.** a change of luck for the worse; a setback: Abraham Lincoln suffered several *reverses* in his early political career. —*adjective:* turned backward; opposite: The students lined up in *reverse* order of height, with the shortest one first.

re•vise [ri vīz′] *verb,* **revised, revising. 1.** to check over a piece of writing before it is put in final form, in order to correct mistakes, add or take out material as needed, and make other improvements. **2.** to make changes in a finished book to correct errors, bring it up to date, and so on: Dictionaries are *revised* every few years to include new words that come into the language. **3.** to change something to meet new conditions: "New discoveries are constantly making us *revise* our ideas about the past." (V.S. Naipaul) ◆ Something that has been revised is a **revision** [ri vizh′ən].

re•vive [ri vīv′] *verb,* **revived, reviving. 1.** to bring back to life or activity; make healthy or conscious again: The police officers *revived* the woman who had fainted on the street. "In the center was a broken garden not yet *revived* by spring . . ." (Mark Helprin) **2.** to bring back into use or action: "The charm of this part of New Jersey is always *revived* for me by Winslow Homer's little painting, called *In June*." (Edmund Wilson) ♦ Something that is revived is a **revival:** a *revival* of a famous play.

re•voke [ri vōk′] *verb,* **revoked, revoking.** to officially take away or cancel: A person's driver's license can be *revoked* if he is convicted of drunken driving.

re•volt [ri vōlt′] *noun, plural* **revolts.** the act of rising up or fighting against a government or leader; a rebellion: In the Peasant *Revolt* of 1381, a large band of English farmers armed themselves and marched on London to make demands of the king. —*verb,* **revolted, revolting. 1.** to stage a revolt; rebel. **2.** to cause a feeling of sickness or disgust. ♦ Usually used as an adjective: a *revolting* smell of garbage. "Rarus P. Grigsby is yelling and swearing in a most *revolting* manner." (Damon Runyon)

rev•o•lu•tion [rev′ ə lōō′ shən] *noun, plural* **revolutions. 1.** the overthrow of one government in order to set up a new one: In the American *Revolution*, the thirteen colonies broke away from England to establish the United States. **2.** a great or complete change: The Industrial *Revolution* was the time when people began to use machines to make or move things. **3.** a complete movement in a circle around a certain point: The earth takes 365 days to make its *revolution* around the sun.

re•volve [ri välv′] *verb,* **revolved, revolving. 1.** to move in a circle around an object: The moon *revolves* around the earth. **2.** to turn or spin around something: Public buildings often have *revolving* doors to allow people to go in and out more quickly. **3.** to center on; have as a main point: All day long, his thoughts *revolved* around what was happening at the hospital.

re•volv•er [ri väl′ vər] *noun, plural* **revolvers.** a handgun that holds several bullets in a chamber that revolves each time the gun is shot.

re•ward [ri wôrd′] *noun, plural* **rewards. 1.** something given or gained in return for some work or service: The *rewards* of her job as a teacher go far beyond the money she earns. **2.** an offer of money made so that a criminal or missing person can be found, lost or stolen property recovered, and so on: Mrs. Carlyle paid a $1000 *reward* for the return of her diamond ring. —*verb,* **rewarded, rewarding.** to give a reward: The writer's efforts were finally *rewarded* when she had her book accepted by a publisher. ♦ Also used as an adjective: Beth's trip to Europe was a very *rewarding* experience.

re•write [rē rīt′] *verb,* **rewrote, rewritten, rewriting.** to write something again; greatly revise a piece of writing.

rhe•a [rē′ ə] *noun, plural* **rheas.** a large South American bird that cannot fly. It looks like an ostrich but is smaller.

rhet•o•ric [ret′ ə rik] *noun.* **1.** the art or talent of using language well, especially in public speaking or in formal writing. **2.** a false or exaggerated use of language.

rhetoric This is one of the "good—bad" words in English. It has one meaning that is positive, and a second that is negative. *Modern Rhetoric*, a widely-used textbook by the critic Cleanth Brooks and the novelist and poet Robert Penn Warren, gives this definition: "*Rhetoric* is the art of using language effectively." The writing articles in this dictionary fit that meaning of *rhetoric*, because they discuss the effective use of English. However, we hope that they won't be considered *rhetoric* in the other sense of the word, which is "fancy, but empty language; words that seem impressive but are not sincere or meaningful." In the Middle Ages, rhetoric was taught as a university subject. It was thought that someone trained in rhetoric would use grand, showy language to mislead his audience. It's too bad rhetoric is thought of this way; effective writing should not be fancy and complicated.

rev•o•lu•tion•ar•y [rev′ ə lōō′ shən er′ ē] *adjective, more/most.* **1.** of or having to do with a revolution: In the French *Revolutionary* Wars, France fought against foreign armies that opposed the French Revolution. **2.** leading to or causing a great change: Eli Whitney's cotton gin was a *revolutionary* new method of preparing cotton to make clothing.

Pronunciation Key: O–S			
ō	over; go	ou	out; town
ô	all; law	p	put; hop
oo	look; full	r	run; car
ōō	pool; who	s	set; miss
oi	oil; boy	sh	show

(Turn the page for more information.)

rheu•ma•tism [rōo′ mə tiz′ əm] *noun.* a disease that causes a painful stiffening and swelling of the muscles or joints.

rhi•noc•er•os [rī nos′ ər əs] *noun, plural* **rhinoceroses.** a very large, powerful animal that has thick, loose skin and either one or two horns rising from its nose. Different types of rhinoceroses live in Africa, India, and southeast Asia.

rhinoceros The horns of the rhinoceros are used for protection and to uproot bushes for food.

Rhode Island [rōd] a state on the northeastern coast of the U.S. *Capital:* Providence. *Nickname:* "Little Rhody." *Area:* 1,200 square miles. *Population:* 958,000.

rho•do•den•dron [rō′ də den′ drən] *noun, plural* **rhododendrons.** a shrub with large, shiny evergreen leaves and clusters of large, colorful flowers shaped like bells.

rhu•barb [rōo′ bärb′] *noun, plural* **rhubarbs.** a plant with thick, juicy reddish stems that are cooked for pies or sauces. The large leaves of the rhubarb plant are poisonous.

rhyme [rīm] *noun, plural* **rhymes. 1.** a word or line that has the same ending sound as another: Popular songs often use *rhymes* such as "June" and "moon" or "you," "blue," and "true." **2.** a poem or song that has such a pattern of sounds at the end of the lines. —*verb,* **rhymed, rhyming.** to sound alike or cause to sound alike.

rhythm [rith′ əm] *noun, plural* **rhythms. 1.** a regular repeating of sounds or movements in a certain pattern. Poetry, music, and dancing have rhythm. **2.** a similar repeating pattern in the way something happens: the *rhythm* of waves breaking on the seashore. ◆ Something that has rhythm is **rhythmic** or **rhythmical:** the *rhythmic* sound of a railroad train moving over the tracks.

rib [rib] *noun, plural* **ribs. 1.** one of the long bones that is attached to the backbone and curves around to the front of the body. The ribs enclose and protect the chest. **2.** a curved part that gives support like a rib: The timbers of a boat's frame and the supporting metal bars in an umbrella are called *ribs.*

rib•bon [rib′ ən] *noun, plural* **ribbons. 1.** a long, narrow strip of cloth, paper, or other material used for decoration or to tie something: The birthday present was wrapped with a red *ribbon.* **2.** something that looks like a ribbon: The strip of fabric that provides the ink in a typewriter is called a *ribbon.* **3.** a special ribbon given as a prize or award: Mike's pet rabbit won a blue *ribbon* at the county fair.

rice [rīs] *noun, plural* **rice.** a grain that is grown in warm, wet climates in many parts of the world. Rice is the main part of people's diet in China, India, and other countries of Asia.

rich [rich] *adjective,* **richer, richest. 1.** having a lot of money, property, or other valuable things. **2.** having a great supply of something; having a lot: The American Midwest is known for its *rich* soil. **3.** of food, containing a lot of sugar, cream, eggs, and so on: a *rich* chocolate cake. **4.** having a lot of a certain good quality: an expensive sports car with seats of dark, *rich* leather. "Sometimes Hugh would sing; he had a *rich* tenor voice." (Muriel Spark) —**richly,** *adverb:* "He was *richly* dressed in silk pajamas . . ." (Ishmael Reed)

rich•es [rich′ iz] *noun.* things that make a person rich, such as money or property; wealth.

Rich•ter scale [rik′ tər] a scale ranging from 1 to 10 that is used to measure the strength of earthquakes. An earthquake measuring 1.5 is considered mild, one measuring 4.5 would cause some damage, and one measuring 8.5 would cause very great damage. Each whole number on the scale represents an earthquake ten times as strong as the number below it. ◆ The scale is named for Charles *Richter,* the scientist who developed it.

ric•o•chet [rik′ ə shā′] *noun, plural* **richochets.** the act of bouncing back off a surface at an angle. —*verb,* **ricocheted, ricocheting.** to skip or glance off a surface in this way: "I clutched my chair while thoughts raced through my mind like *ricocheting* bullets." (Jerzy Kosinski)

rid [rid] *verb,* **rid** or **ridded, ridding. 1. rid of.** to do away with something that is not wanted: He bought some insect poison to *rid* the house *of* ants. **2. get rid of.** to become free of; do away with: I've got to *get rid of* those old newspapers that are piled up in the garage.

rid•den [rid′ ən] *verb.* the past participle of **ride.**

R

riddles What gets bigger the more you take away from it? A hole. What must you break in order to use it? An egg. When does Friday come ahead of the other days of the week? When it's in a dictionary. Now, all these are *riddles* in which the answers to the questions rely on tricks and turns of the language. Riddles appeal to us because they involve a creative use of words, such as: "What's black and white and red (read) all over?" (A newspaper) or "When is a door not a door?" (When it's ajar.) There are riddles in the Bible, and collections of riddles appear in literature from the time of the ancient Greeks through the Middle Ages. Many ancient folk tales tell of how someone gained a prize or honor by solving a riddle.

rid•dle¹ [rid′ əl] *noun, plural* **riddles. 1.** a tricky or difficult question to be answered by guessing. **2.** anything that is hard to understand; a mystery: Sir Winston Churchill said that the actions of the Soviet Union were a *riddle*.

riddle² *verb,* **riddled, riddling.** to put a lot of holes through something: The target was *riddled* with bullet holes.

ride [rīd] *verb,* **rode, ridden, riding. 1.** to sit on or in something and cause it to move: to *ride* a horse, to *ride* a bicycle. **2.** to travel in or on something: to *ride* in a car or an airplane. **3.** to float on or move over a surface: The surfer *rode* a wave in toward shore. Hawks can *ride* high in the sky on currents of wind. —*noun, plural* **rides. 1.** the act of riding: Tommy let me have a *ride* on his new bike. **2.** something ridden on or in for fun, as at an amusement park: My favorite *ride* at Playland is the Airplane Coaster. —**rider,** *noun.*

ridge [rij] *noun, plural* **ridges. 1.** a long, narrow hill or range of hills: The Blue *Ridge* Mountains are a famous area in Virginia. **2.** any long, thin part at the top of something: The cat's hair stood on end along the *ridge* of its back.

rid•i•cule [rid′ ə kyo͞ol′] *verb,* **ridiculed, ridiculing.** to make fun of a person or thing; laugh at in an unkind way: When he tried out for basketball, he was *ridiculed* by the other players because of his very small size. —*noun.* words or actions that make fun of someone.

ri•dic•u•lous [ri dik′ yə ləs] *adjective, more/most.* deserving to be laughed at; very foolish or silly: Clowns in the circus wear *ridiculous*-looking costumes. —**ridiculously,** *adverb.*

ri•fle [rī′ fəl] *noun, plural* **rifles.** a gun that has a long barrel with grooves cut within it. The grooves cause a bullet to spin when it is fired, giving the gun greater accuracy. A rifle is usually shot from the shoulder.

rig [rig] *verb,* **rigged, rigging. 1.** to equip a boat with the necessary ropes, sails, masts, and so on. **2.** to supply or equip something as needed: The station wagon was *rigged* out with an extra seat in the back. —*noun, plural* **rigs. 1.** an arrangement of sails on a ship. ♦ The ropes or cables that hold the sails are called the **rigging. 2.** equipment or machinery made for a certain purpose: an oil-drilling *rig.*

right [rīt] *adjective.* **1.** on the side opposite the left; on the side where cars go on the road or where a line of writing ends. **2.** without a mistake; correct: You get two points for each *right* answer. **3.** being fair, good, and just: It's just not *right* to invite all the boys in the class to the party except Kevin. **4.** suited for a certain purpose: The poster said "Smith for Mayor. He's the *right* man for the job."
—*noun, plural* **rights. 1.** the opposite of left; the right direction or side. **2.** what is fair, good, and just. **3.** something that is fair and proper for a person to do or have: Any person accused of a crime in this country has the *right* to a lawyer.
—*adverb.* **1.** to the right: Turn *right* at the next corner. **2.** in the right way: Ever since I dropped my watch it doesn't work *right*. **3.** in an exact way or place: Wait *right* here until I get back. —*verb,* **righted, righting.** to make right: Robert Kennedy was described as "a man who saw wrong and tried to *right* it." —**rightly,** *adverb:* "She guessed, *rightly,* that he was in his mid-thirties." (Margaret Drabble)

right angle an angle measuring 90 degrees and made by two lines that are straight up and down from each other. A square is made up of four right angles. ♦ A **right triangle** is a triangle with one angle that measures 90 degrees.

right•eous [rī′ chəs] *adjective, more/most.* acting in a way that is right or moral. —**righteously,** *adverb.* —**righteousness,** *noun.*

R

Pronunciation Key: T–Z			
t	ten; date	v	very; live
th	think	w	win; away
th	these	y	you
u	cut; butter	z	zoo; cause
ur	turn; bird	zh	measure

(Turn the page for more information.)

right-hand [rīt′ hand′] *adjective.* on or toward the right: Write your name in the upper *right-hand* corner of the paper.

right-hand•ed [rit′ han′ did] *adjective.* **1.** using the right hand more easily or more often than the left. **2.** done with or using the right hand: a *right*-handed pitcher in baseball.

rig•id [rij′ id] *adjective, more/most.* **1.** hard to bend or move; not flexible; stiff: Beams form a *rigid* support for a roof. **2.** not likely to change; fixed; strict: Soldiers in basic training in the army follow a very *rigid* schedule each day. **—rigidly,** *adverb:* "Kunta sat *rigidly* staring straight ahead . . . refusing to look back." (Alex Haley)

rim [rim] *noun, plural* **rims. 1.** the outer edge or border of something, especially something curved or round: the *rim* of a coffee cup. **2.** the outside part of a car or bicycle wheel to which a tire is fitted. *—verb,* **rimmed, rimming.** to go around the rim of: The ball *rimmed* the basket but did not go in. "The sky to the eastward was *rimmed* with red." (H. G. Wells)

rind [rīnd] *noun, plural* **rinds.** a hard, thick outer covering on certain fruits and other foods: watermelon *rind,* cheese *rind.*

ring¹ [ring] *noun, plural* **rings. 1.** a circle that is open in the center: There was a *ring* of trees around the cabin. **2.** a circular band worn on a finger as jewelry, or used to hold or fasten something: a diamond wedding *ring,* a key *ring* to hold car keys. **3.** an enclosed area used for sports, shows, and so on: a boxing *ring,* a three-*ring* circus. *—verb,* **ringed, ringing.** to form a circle or ring around.

ring² *verb,* **rang, rung, ringing. 1.** to make a sound like a bell: to *ring* a doorbell. **2.** to call someone with a bell, buzzer, or telephone. **3.** to be filled with a strong, clear sound: "When I swung my ax the whole forest *rang* out with the echoes of my work." (Jamake Highwater) **4.** of the ears, to seem to be filled with a steady buzzing or humming sound. *—noun, plural* **rings. 1.** a sound like that of a bell. **2.** a telephone call: Give me a *ring* when you get there so I'll know you arrived safely.

rink [ringk] *noun, plural* **rinks.** an enclosed area with a smooth surface that is used for ice skating or roller skating.

rinse [rins] *verb,* **rinsed, rinsing. 1.** to wash with clear water to remove soap or other matter: *Rinse* the soap off the car before you wax it. **2.** to wash lightly with water: Layne *rinsed* the dishes before putting them in the dishwasher. *—noun, plural* **rinses. 1.** the act of rinsing. **2.** a

liquid solution that temporarily changes the color of a person's hair.

Rio de Ja•nei•ro [rē′ ō dā zhə nâr′ ō] a city in southeastern Brazil. It is the second-largest city in South America. *Population:* 5,093,000.

Rio de Janeiro Considered one of the world's most beautiful cities, Rio de Janeiro lies between green mountains and white ocean beaches.

Rio Grande [grand] a river that flows from southwestern Colorado to the Gulf of Mexico, forming the border between Texas and Mexico.

ri•ot [rī′ ət] *noun, plural* **riots. 1.** a violent, noisy disturbance caused by a group of people: In the Draft *Riots* of 1863, hundreds of people in New York City were killed as armed mobs stormed through the city. **2.** a bright or colorful display: "He was a nice-looking boy with a *riot* of soft brown curls on his white forehead." (Margaret Mitchell) **3.** *Informal.* Something that is very funny. *—verb,* **rioted, rioting.** to take part in a riot; act in a violent and noisy way. ♦ A person who takes part in a riot is a **rioter. —riotous,** *adjective.*

rip [rip] *verb,* **ripped, ripping.** to split or cut open in a rough way; tear apart: Jacob *ripped* his shirt on a nail sticking out of the fence. *—noun, plural* **rips.** a ripped place; a tear.

ripe [rīp] *adjective,* **riper, ripest. 1.** of fruits and vegetables, fully grown and ready to be eaten: *Ripe* bananas are yellow, not green. **2.** fully developed or prepared; ready: He thinks the time is *ripe* to ask the boss for a raise. "It is no use to throw a good thing away merely because the market isn't *ripe* yet." (Mark Twain)

rip•en [rī′ pən] *verb,* **ripened, ripening.** to become ripe: If you let this tomato *ripen* a bit more, it will get softer.

rip•ple [rip′ əl] *noun, plural* **ripples. 1.** a tiny wave on the surface of water: Gary could tell from the *ripples* that there was a fish swimming

R

by. **2.** something that has small waves or ridges like this: "They watched the *ripple* of the smooth muscles as the horse walked . . ." (Marguerite Henry) **3.** anything that is thought of like the rippling of small waves on the shore: "A *ripple* of excitement . . . reached the room." (Anne Morrow Lindbergh) —*verb,* **rippled, rippling.** to form ripples: "The wind . . . *rippled* the tall grass and made the trees creak." (Walter Farley) "Anne felt jealousy *ripple* over her." (Mary Gordon)

rise [rīz] *verb,* **rose, risen, rising. 1.** to move from a lower to a higher place; go up: Smoke *rises* from a fire. The sun *rises* in the east. **2.** to stand up from a sitting, kneeling, or lying position; get up: An old saying speaks of being "early to bed and early to *rise.*" **3.** to increase in size or amount; become larger: The price of houses in our town has been *rising* steadily. —*noun, plural* **rises.** the act or fact of rising: a *rise* in temperature. Hitler made a sudden *rise* to power in Germany in the 1930's.

risk [risk] *noun, plural* **risks.** a chance of loss, harm, or injury; danger: The sign said, "No lifeguards on duty. Swim at your own *risk.*" —*verb,* **risked, risking. 1.** to take a chance of loss or harm; face danger: He *risked* his life to save the child from the fire. **2.** to take the risk of: to *risk* an accident by driving too fast.

risk•y [ris′ kē] *adjective,* **riskier, riskiest.** involving a risk; dangerous: Driving a racing car is a *risky* occupation.

rit•u•al [rich′ ōō əl] *noun, plural* **rituals. 1.** an action or set of actions that is always done in the same way, especially as part of a religious ceremony: the *ritual* of placing a ring on the bride's hand at a wedding. ◆ This is also called a **rite. 2.** any action that is often repeated in the same way: Shaving in the morning is a *ritual* for most men. ◆ Also used as an adjective: On hot summer days Mr. Grimes always makes his *ritual* remark, "Hot enough for you?"

ri•val [rī′ vəl] *noun, plural* **rivals.** a person who tries to do better at something than another; a competitor: Tim and I were on the same soccer team last season, but this year we're *rivals.* ◆ Often used as an adjective: The two *rival* candidates for mayor are going to appear on TV tomorrow. —*verb,* **rivaled, rivaling.** to be a rival for; be as good as: She's lived in many places, but she says nothing can *rival* the beauty of the Rocky Mountains. ◆ The fact of competing with another as a rival is **rivalry.**

riv•er [riv′ ər] *noun, plural* **rivers.** a large, natural stream of moving water that empties into a lake, an ocean, or a larger river.

riv•et [riv′ it] *noun, plural* **rivets.** a small piece of metal that is used to join two pieces of metal or other materials. A rivet is shaped like a large pin or bolt, with a rounded head at one end. The rivet is placed through holes in two metal plates and the pointed end is then hammered flat to make a second head that holds it in place. —*verb,* **riveted, riveting. 1.** to fasten with rivets. **2.** to fasten or fix firmly, as if with rivets: ". . . looking back over her shoulder, as if *riveting* me to the spot with her glance." (Iris Murdoch)

roach [rōch] *noun, plural* **roaches.** a small brown or black insect that is a household pest; more often known as a **cockroach.**

road [rōd] *noun, plural* **roads. 1.** a smooth path or way that has been specially prepared for travel by cars, trucks, and so on: She lives at 66 Milton *Road.* Cars in England drive on the left side of the *road.* **2.** a path or way that leads to some goal: the *road* to success, the *road* to ruin. Being the governor of a large state can be a *road* to the White House.

road•run•ner [rōd′ run′ ər] *noun, plural* **roadrunners.** a brownish-colored bird that lives in southwestern North America and is known for its ability to run at high speeds. It has long legs, a long, white-tipped tail, and a shaggy crest of feathers on top of its head.

road•side [rōd′ sīd] *noun, plural* **roadsides.** the land along the side of a road. ◆ Often used as an adjective: a *roadside* inn.

roam [rōm] *verb,* **roamed, roaming.** to travel widely around or through an area with no exact goal or purpose; wander: "Western New York was then a wilderness, where wolf packs still *roamed* . . ." (Fawn Brodie) "Give him some freedom, a chance to *roam* and be on his own again." (Walter Farley)

roar [rôr] *verb,* **roared, roaring. 1.** to make a very loud, deep noise: "The wind *roared* across Union Square, driving discarded newspapers before it . . ." (Pete Hamill) **2.** to laugh loudly: Randy *roared* when I told him the joke. —*noun, plural* **roars.** a very loud, deep sound: the *roar* of a lion, the *roar* of a subway train racing through the station.

R

Pronunciation Key: [ə] Symbol

The [ə] or *schwa* sound occurs in syllables without an accent. It can be spelled with any vowel, such as a in above, e in listen, i in pencil, o in melon, u in circus. It can also be a combination of vowels, such as io in action, ai in mountain, iou in precious.

(Turn the page for more information.)

R

roast [rōst] *verb,* **roasted, roasting. 1.** to cook food in an oven, over a fire, or on hot coals: to *roast* a turkey. **2.** to dry and brown by exposing to heat: Peanuts are usually *roasted* and salted before being canned. **3.** to make or be very hot: I've got to turn the air conditioner on — I'm *roasting* in this heat. *—noun, plural* **roasts.** a large cut of meat meant to be roasted.

rob [räb] *verb,* **robbed, robbing. 1.** to take someone else's money or goods in a way that is against the law: Two men *robbed* the jewelry store and took several gold watches. **2.** to keep a person from getting something in an unfair way: The soccer coach complained that his team was *robbed* after the referee wouldn't allow a goal to count. **—robber,** *noun.*

rob•ber•y [räb′ rē *or* räb′ ə rē] *noun, plural* **robberies.** the act of taking money or property that belongs to someone else.

robe [rōb] *noun, plural* **robes. 1.** a loose piece of clothing worn as a covering or for warmth: A bath*robe* is worn over pajamas or a nightgown. **2.** a long, flowing piece of clothing worn for ceremonies or to show rank or office: a judge's *robes. —verb,* **robed, robing.** to put on a robe.

rob•in [räb′ in] *noun, plural* **robins. 1.** a common North American songbird with a brown or black upper body, and a reddish-orange breast in the male. **2.** a similar but smaller European bird.

Rob•in•son [räb′ in sən] **Jackie,** 1919-1972, the first black player in major-league baseball.

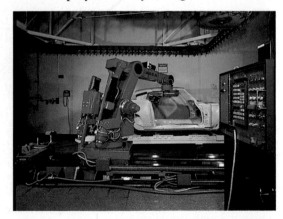

robot A modern factory in which robots do the work of putting a car together.

ro•bot [rō′ bät′] *noun, plural* **robots.** a machine that is designed to perform certain tasks that a human being can do. Robots are often shown in movies as looking somewhat like a human. ◆ The word *robot* first came into use in a 1921 play by Karel Capek.

ro•bust [rō bust′ *or* rō′ bəst] *adjective, more/ most.* full of energy; strong and healthy: Even though he is almost 75 years old, Grandpa is still a very *robust* man. **—robustly,** *adverb.*

rock [räk] *noun, plural* **rocks. 1.** a large mass of solid material forming part of the crust of the earth. Rock is usually made up of a combination of several different materials. Marble, granite, and slate are types of rocks. **2.** a small, separate piece of this material; a stone. **3.** a large mass of rock forming a cliff or hill: The *Rock* of Gibraltar stands high above the entrance to the Mediterranean Sea. **4.** someone or something thought of as like a rock, as by being very strong or dependable.

rock² *verb,* **rocked, rocking. 1.** to move back and forth or from side to side: The mother *rocked* her baby until it stopped crying. "A slight breeze *rocked* the tops of the pine trees." (Bret Harte) **2.** to cause to shake or sway in a sudden way: "Julius stepped on the brakes and the car *rocked* to a stop." (P.D. James) *—noun, plural* **rocks. 1.** a rocking movement. **2.** short for ROCK MUSIC.

Rock•e•fel•ler [räk′ ə fel′ ər] **John D.,** 1839-1937, American businessman in the oil and banking industries. Other members of his family were later important in politics and business.

rock•er [räk′ ər] *noun, plural* **rockers. 1.** a chair mounted on rockers or springs that allow it to rock back and forth; also called a **rocking chair. 2.** a curving piece of metal or wood on which an object rocks, such as a cradle or a rocking chair.

rock•et [räk′ it] *noun, plural* **rockets. 1.** a device that is moved at great speed by the force of burning gases being released from the rear. Very large and powerful rockets are used to launch spacecraft into space and to power guided missiles in warfare. A rocket engine differs from a jet engine in that it does not have to draw in outside air to create an explosion, which means that it can work in outer space while a jet cannot. **2.** a space vehicle or missile that is powered by a rocket engine. **3.** a type of firework that is shot through the air by gunpowder or another explosive, in a manner similar to a military or space rocket. *—verb,* **rocketed, rocketing.** to rise up or travel very fast: The racing car *rocketed* past the finish line.

rock music a modern form of popular music that began in the U.S. in the 1950's and is now widely played throughout the world. Rock music features a strong, steady beat, and usually a background of electric guitars and other electronic instruments.

rock 'n' roll or **rock and roll** rock music, especially in its early form in the 1950's.

Rock•well [räk′wel′] **Norman,** 1894-1978, American painter and illustrator.

rock•y[1] [räk′ē] *adjective,* **rockier, rockiest.** covered with or having many rocks: Farming was difficult for early settlers of New England because of the *rocky* soil there.

rocky[2] *adjective,* **rockier, rockiest.** likely to sway or fall; shaky: a *rocky* old picnic table.

Rocky Mountains Swiftcurrent Lake in Glacier National Park of the Montana Rocky Mountains.

Rocky Mountains a large mountain range of North America extending from Alaska to northern Mexico. ♦ Also known as **the Rockies.**

rod [räd] *noun, plural* **rods. 1.** a thin, straight bar of metal, wood, plastic, or such hard material: a curtain *rod,* a fishing *rod,* a piston *rod* in a car engine. **2.** in former times, a stick used to beat or punish a person. **3.** a unit of measure for length once used for measuring land. It is equal to 16-1/2 feet.

rode [rōd] *verb.* the past tense of **ride.**

ro•dent [rōd′ənt] *noun, plural* **rodents.** one of a large family of animals with large, sharp front teeth used for gnawing. There are nearly 2,000 different kinds of rodents, including mice, rats, squirrels, beavers, gophers, and porcupines.

ro•de•o [rō′dē ō *or* rō dā′ō] *noun, plural* **rodeos.** a public show that involves contests that test skills used by cowboys, such as cattle roping, horseback and bull riding, and steer wrestling.

rogue [rōg] *noun, plural* **rogues. 1.** a dishonest person; a cheat: The movie *Rogue Cop* told of a policeman who took payoff money from gangsters. **2.** an animal that is dangerous and hard to control, especially a wild elephant that lives apart from the herd.

role [rōl] *noun, plural* **roles. 1.** a certain character or part in a play, movie, or the like. **2.** a certain part or position taken by a person in some activity: Senator Jones played a key *role* in getting that bill passed by Congress. ♦ A **role model** is someone whom another person follows or imitates, as in doing a certain job.

roll [rōl] *verb,* **rolled, rolling. 1.** to move by turning over many times: The ball *rolled* into the street. **2.** to move on wheels or in a vehicle on wheels: The car *rolled* slowly to a stop. **3.** to turn something around on itself or on something else; wrap: Stan *rolled* up his sleeping bag. **4.** to move up, down, or from side to side: The storm clouds *rolled* in from the east. Nikki *rolled* her eyes when she heard the silly joke. **5.** to shape into a flat or even form with a roller: Ann *rolled* out the dough. **6.** to move or pass by in a smooth, steady way: The building project is *rolling* along and will be finished next month. **7.** to make a loud, deep sound; rumble: "'Madam' he said, in a voice that *rolled* like summer thunder." (Virginia Woolf)
—*noun, plural* **rolls. 1.** anything that is rolled up in the shape of a tube or cylinder: a *roll* of stamps, a *roll* of paper towels. **2.** a small, round piece of baked bread dough: hamburger *rolls.* **3.** a list of names: The substitute teacher called the *roll* at the beginning of class. **4.** a rolling motion: the *roll* of a boat on the waves. **5.** a deep, loud rumble: a drum *roll.*

rodeo Calf roping, a popular rodeo event, seen here at the Alaska State Fair in Palmer, Alaska.

Pronunciation Key: Accent Marks

[′] is the normal accent mark. It shows where the main stress falls on a word.

[′] is a secondary accent mark. It shows a lighter stress than the primary accent. For example:

tel • e • vis • ion [tel′ə vizh′ən]

(Turn the page for more information.)

roll•er [rō′lər] *noun, plural* **rollers. 1.** a rod or cylinder on which something is rolled up: a hair *roller,* a *roller* for a window shade. **2.** something that turns over and over and is used to smooth, flatten, or spread things: a paint *roller,* a cement *roller.* **3.** a small wheel or set of wheels attached to something so it can be moved: Heavy beds are often set on *rollers.*

roller coaster an amusement park ride in which a set of open cars travels very fast on tracks that form steep hills and sharp turns.

roller skate a shoe or boot that fastens to a plate with four wheels attached to the bottom. It is worn for skating on sidewalks or other hard, flat surfaces. —*verb,* **roller-skated, roller-skating.** to move along on roller skates.

rolling pin a kitchen tool shaped like a smooth cylinder with a handle on each end, usually made of wood. Rolling pins are used to flatten or roll out cookie dough, pie crusts, and so on.

Ro•man [rō′mən] *adjective.* **1.** having to do with the ancient or modern city of Rome, or with the people of Rome or their culture. **2.** *also,* **roman.** having to do with the usual style of printing, in which the letters are straight (like this). —*noun, plural* **Romans. 1.** a person living in Rome. **2.** Roman type or letters: This dictionary uses a typeface called Times *Roman.*

Roman Catholic Church a Christian church that is headed by the Pope. A member of this church is called a **Catholic** or **Roman Catholic.**

ro•mance [rō mans′ *or* rō′mans′] *noun, plural* **romances. 1.** a love story or love affair: The book *Windsor Story* describes the *romance* of the Duke and Duchess of Windsor. **2.** a story or poem about adventure, love, or great deeds, especially one that is set in a distant place or time: "King Arthur" is a *romance.* **3.** a quality of love, mystery, or adventure: "I had been in love with the *romance* of flying since first hearing about Charles A. Lindbergh, the Lone Eagle . . ." (Russell Baker)

Romance languages the modern languages that developed from Latin, the language of ancient Rome. Spanish, French, Italian, and Portuguese are Romance languages.

Ro•ma•nia [rō mā′nē yə] a country in southeastern Europe. *Capital:* Bucharest. *Area:* 91,700 square miles. *Population:* 22,742,000. —**Romanian,** *adjective; noun.*

Roman numeral a numeral in a numbering system that is based on the one used by the ancient Romans, in which letters are used instead of numbers. I = 1, V = 5, X = 10, L = 50, C = 100, D = 500, and M = 1,000.

ro•man•tic [rō man′ tik] *adjective, more/most.* **1.** having to do with or showing romance: They took a *romantic* cruise around the harbor under the full moon. **2.** having ideas or feelings suitable for a romance; not practical or realistic: In World War I many young men had a *romantic* view of war until they came under fire for the first time. —**romantically,** *adverb.*

Rome The Piazza (Square) of St. Peter's Church, the center of the Vatican City in Rome.

Rome [rōm] the capital of Italy, in the west-central part of the country. In ancient times it was the center of a large empire (the **Roman Empire**). *Population:* 2,868,000.

romanticism *Romantic* writing is contrasted with *naturalistic* writing. In general, romantic writing describes a pleasant, if not ideal world. It emphasizes things that are emotional, vivid, and heroic. Naturalism, on the other hand, describes the world as it appears and often concentrates on the harshness of life. Suppose a writer sets out to describe downtown Chicago at dusk. A romantic might show the skyline outlined against the setting sun, the lights of expensive hotels and restaurants, well-dressed crowds hurrying to the theater and other places. A naturalist might describe homeless people huddled in doorways, trash piles in the alleys, and the wail of police sirens and ambulances. Naturalism is like a wide-lens camera; it attempts to capture every harsh detail within sight. Romanticism is like a crystal and throws a narrow, brilliant light on its subject.

romp [rämp] *verb,* **romped, romping.** to run and play in a lively, noisy way: The dogs *romped* together in the open field. —*noun,* *plural* **romps.** a time of carefree and lively play.

roof [roof *or* ro͞of] *noun, plural* **roofs. 1.** the outer, top part covering a building. **2.** something like a roof: Terry burned the *roof* of her mouth with the hot soup. Tibet is called "The *Roof* of the World" because of its high mountains. —*verb,* **roofed, roofing.** to cover a building with a roof. —**roofer,** *noun.*

rook[1] [rook] *noun, plural* **rooks.** a large black European bird that is like a crow. Rooks live in large groups and build their nests together.

rook[2] *noun, plural* **rooks.** a piece used in the game of chess; also called a **castle.** A rook can move in a straight line parallel to the sides of the board.

rook•ie [rook′ē] *noun, plural* **rookies. 1.** a new soldier or a recruit in the armed services or on a police force. **2.** an athlete playing his first season on a professional sports team. **3.** any person without much experience; a beginner.

room [ro͞om *or* room] *noun, plural* **rooms. 1.** a space or area for a certain purpose: They have a big back yard with plenty of *room* to play ball. **2.** an area in a house or building that is enclosed by walls: a living *room,* a bed*room.* **3.** a chance or occasion to do something: Mr. Wilson's speech was put off because there wasn't enough *room* on today's schedule. —*verb,* **roomed, rooming. 1.** to live with another person as a ROOMMATE: At college Sharon *roomed* with two girls she knew from high school. **2.** to live in a rented room or set of rooms.

room•mate [ro͞om′ māt′ *or* room′ māt′] *noun, plural* **roommates.** a person who shares a room or rooms with someone else.

1884-1962, American writer and diplomat, the wife of Franklin D. Roosevelt.

roost [ro͞ost] *noun, plural* **roosts.** a place where a bird sleeps or rests. —*verb,* **roosted, roosting.** to rest or sleep on a roost.

roost•er [ro͞os′ tər] *noun, plural* **roosters.** a male chicken.

root[1] [ro͞ot *or* root] *noun, plural* **roots. 1.** the part of a plant that grows down into the ground. Roots hold the plant in place, and they draw water and minerals from the earth and send them up to the rest of the plant. The roots of some plants grow in air or water rather than in the ground. **2.** something like a root in the way it is formed or attached: the *root* of a tooth, the *root* of a hair. **3.** the part from which something grows or starts; the source or beginning: A famous saying from the Bible is, "The love of money is the *root* of all evil." **4.** the main part of a word to which other parts may be added. **5.** a number that when multiplied by itself a given number of times produces a certain quantity: 2 is the square *root* of 4 (2 × 2). **6. roots.** the feeling of belonging to a certain place: "The Barleys had no *roots* in the community . . ." (John O'Hara) —*verb,* **rooted, rooting. 1.** of a plant, to develop roots; grow. **2.** to pull out by the roots; uproot: They used a tractor to *root* up the big old tree. **3.** to keep from moving; fix in one place: When the famous movie star walked by, they stood *rooted* to the spot in surprise.

root[2] *verb,* **rooted, rooting. 1.** to dig in the soil with the nose, as a pig does. **2.** to look for something in a similar way; rummage: "Nobby *rooted* about under the hedge until he had collected an armful of dry sticks to get a fire going." (George Orwell)

root words The *root* of a word is the part from which other words develop. You can add to a root word either at the front, as in *un* kind or the back, as in *kind ness.* A root word can have many forms that carry the same basic idea as the root but have a different use. For example, *rough* can become *roughs, roughed, roughing, rougher, roughest, roughly, roughness,* even *semi-rough* or *non-rough.* In this dictionary, the entry for a certain term always begins with the root word. The other forms of the word then follow in the rest of the entry.

room•y [ro͞o′ mē] *adjective,* **roomier, roomiest.** having plenty of room; large: a *roomy* car that will hold six passengers comfortably.

Roo•se•velt [rō′ zə velt′] **1. Theodore,** 1858-1919, the twenty-sixth president of the United States, from 1901 to 1909. **2. Franklin Delano,** 1882-1945, the thirty-second president of the United States, from 1933 to 1945. **3. Eleanor,**

R

Pronunciation Key: A–F			
a	and; hat	ch	chew; such
ā	ate; stay	d	dog; lid
â	care; air	e	end; yet
ä	father; hot	ē	she; each
b	boy; cab	f	fun; off
(Turn the page for more information.)			

R

root³ *verb,* **rooted, rooting.** to cheer for or be in favor of one side in a game or contest: My dad grew up in New York and has always *rooted* for the New York Yankees. —**rooter,** *noun.*

root beer a soft drink that was originally flavored with the roots of certain plants.

rope [rōp] *noun, plural* **ropes. 1.** a thick, strong cord or line made by twisting together strands of such materials as plant fibers, nylon, or wire. **2.** a number of things twisted or strung together: a *rope* of pearls. —*verb,* **roped, roping. 1.** to tie or fasten something with a rope. Calf *roping* is an event in rodeos. **2. rope off.** to enclose an area with a rope.

rose A typical garden rose on a thorny stem (left), a smaller tea rose (top), and a wild rose (below).

rose¹ [rōz] *noun, plural* **roses. 1.** any one of a large group of plants that grow as a bush, vine, or small tree and have beautiful, sweet-smelling flowers and thorny stems. **2.** the flower of such a plant. Roses have several layers of large, colorful petals, usually red, pink, yellow, or white. **3.** a pinkish-red color.

rose² *verb.* the past tense of **rise.**

Rosh Ha•sha•nah [räsh hə shä′ nə] the Jewish New Year, celebrated in September or early October.

ros•y [rō′ zē] *adjective,* **rosier, rosiest. 1.** having a pinkish-red color: a healthy baby with *rosy* cheeks. **2.** full of cheer; bright and hopeful: a person with a *rosy* outlook on life.

rot [rät] *verb,* **rotted, rotting.** to become rotten or spoiled; decay: The roof of the old barn was *rotting* away. —*noun.* **1.** the process of rotting; a state of decay. **2.** any one of several plant diseases in which the plant decays, caused by

bacteria or fungi that infect the plant: Black *rot* attacks apples and other fruits.

ro•ta•ry [rō′ tər ē] *adjective.* turning around a center, or having parts that turn in a circle: a *rotary* lawn mower. "He stirred the tea with a rapid *rotary* motion of the spoon." (Paul Theroux)

ro•tate [rō′ tāt′] *verb,* **rotated, rotating. 1.** to turn or cause to turn in a circle, on a center called an AXIS: The earth *rotates* once each day. **2.** to take turns in a fixed order: Farmers often *rotate* the type of crops that they grow in a certain field from one year to the next.

ro•ta•tion [rō tā′ shən] *noun, plural* **rotations. 1.** the fact of rotating around a center: the *rotation* of an airplane propeller. **2.** the fact of taking turns, or one complete set of turns: A pitching *rotation* in baseball means that several different pitchers take turns starting games.

rote [rōt] *noun.* a way of doing something by repeating it from memory, usually without thinking about it or understanding it: He had learned by *rote* how many miles it was from his city to all the other major U.S. cities.

ro•tor [rō′ tər] *noun, plural* **rotors. 1.** the part of a machine or motor that turns or rotates. **2.** the large blades of a helicopter that rotate to lift and move it.

rot•ten [rät′ ən] *adjective,* **rottener, rottenest. 1.** of food, not fit to eat because of being spoiled or decayed: a *rotten* egg, *rotten* meat. **2.** old and worn out and likely to give way; weak: The old dock was closed because the timbers supporting it were *rotten.* **3.** *Informal.* very bad or poor; awful: You were sick in bed on your birthday? What *rotten* luck!

ro•tun•da [rō tun′ də] *noun, plural* **rotundas.** a round building or hall, especially one under a domed roof.

rotunda A funeral ceremony in the Rotunda of the Capitol Building in Washington, D.C.

rouge [roozh] *noun, plural* **rouges.** a pink or red makeup that is used to add color to the cheeks.

rough [ruf] *adjective,* **rougher, roughest. 1.** having a surface that is bumpy, scratchy, or jagged; not smooth or even: The car bounced and shook as we drove along the *rough* desert road. **2.** having or showing force or violence: Boxing is a very *rough* sport. **3.** not in a final or complete state; unfinished: A *rough* diamond is one that has not been cut and polished. **4.** not exact or detailed: Their *rough* estimate is that the project will take about two years. **5.** hard to deal with or get through; difficult or unpleasant: She had a *rough* day at the bank — there were long lines of customers all day. —*verb,* **roughed, roughing. 1.** to treat in a mean or violent way: The man claimed he'd been *roughed up* by the police after he was arrested. **2.** to make or plan in an unfinished way: She *roughed* out the plot of the story first and then filled in the details as she wrote. —*noun, plural* **roughs.** a thing that is rough: The area of high grass along the sides of a golf course is called a *rough.* —*adverb.* in a rough way; roughly: to play *rough* in a game. —**roughly,** *adverb.* **1.** in a rough way. **2.** about; approximately: Alaska is *roughly* twice the size of the next-largest state. —**roughness,** *noun.*

round [round] *adjective.* **1.** shaped like a ball or a globe: An orange is a *round* fruit. **2.** shaped like a circle or curve: Tires and rings are *round.* King Arthur and his knights sat at a *round* table. —*noun, plural* **rounds. 1.** something made into a round shape. **2.** a regular movement or route around a certain area: The night watchman at the factory checked all the doors and windows on his *rounds.* **3.** a complete game or contest, or a section of one: a *round* of golf, a ten-*round* boxing match. **4.** a series or set of things that happen: A *round* of applause means that many people are clapping at the same time. —*verb,* **rounded, rounding. 1.** to make or become round: The stone had been *rounded* by the action of the ocean waves. **2.** to pass around something; go to the other side: The racing car *rounded* the curve at high speed. —*adverb; preposition.* around: An old children's song is "Here We Go *Round* the Mulberry Bush." ◆ The use of *round* for *around* is common in British English but not in American English.

round•a•bout [round′ ə bout′] *adjective; more/ most.* in a way that is not straight or direct: The cab driver took a *roundabout* route to the airport. "He said several times in a mumbling *roundabout* way that he wished Dorothy were there to help him." (George Orwell)

round trip a trip that includes going to a place and then returning to the starting point. ◆ Also used as an adjective: The *round-trip* air fare between here and Chicago is $500.

round•up [round′ up′] *noun, plural* **roundups. 1.** a gathering together of farm animals such as cows, horses, or sheep, so that they can be counted, moved to another place, and so on. **2.** any similar gathering of people or things: a police *roundup* of suspected drug dealers.

rouse [rouz] *verb,* **roused, rousing. 1.** to disturb someone from sleep or rest: "He was nearly asleep when a clink of chain *roused* him." (John Jakes) **2.** to cause to move or become active; stir up: "The sense of danger at once *roused* me to action." (William Makepeace Thackeray) ◆ Also used as an adjective: The senator gave a *rousing* speech at the convention.

rout [rout] *noun, plural* **routs.** a complete defeat: The battle turned into a *rout* as the enemy soldiers ran away. —*verb,* **routed, routing.** to defeat completely: The soccer team *routed* the visiting team by a score of 9 to 0.

route [root *or* rout] *noun, plural* **routes. 1.** a way to get from one place to another; a road, course, or path: Running water will always take a downhill *route.* We drove on the scenic *route* that went along the edge of the ocean. **2.** a name for a highway: *Route* 66 was once the main road from the Midwest to California. **3.** a regular series of stops for a vehicle, delivery person, and so on: a bus *route,* a mail *route.* —*verb,* **routed, routing.** to send or be sent by a certain route: The shipping company *routed* the freighter through the Panama Canal.

rou•tine [roo tēn′] *noun, plural* **routines.** a regular or usual way of doing something; something that is repeated time after time: Washing, eating, and sleeping are part of a person's daily *routine.* **2.** an act or part of an act performed for a show: "Then during basketball practice I copied an old Harlem Globetrotters *routine* and got everybody laughing." (S.E. Hinton) —*adjective.* according to a routine; regular or repeated: "It's strictly *routine,* something they have to do, no matter where, no matter what." (Jerzy Kosinski) —**routinely,** *adverb.*

Pronunciation Key: G–N			
g	give; big	k	kind; cat; back
h	hold	l	let; ball
i	it; this	m	make; time
ī	ice; my	n	not; own
j	jet; gem; edge	ng	having

(Turn the page for more information.)

rove [rōv] *verb,* **roved, roving.** to move about from place to place; wander: ". . . to *rove* alone in the evening along the quiet avenue." (James Joyce) **—rover,** *noun.*

row¹ [rō] *noun, plural* **rows. 1.** a line of people or things: A *row* of houses faced the street. **2.** a line of chairs or seats in a theater, auditorium, stadium, or the like. **3.** a series of things, one right after the other, with no breaks in between: "Then all of a sudden she woke up and won six races in a *row*." (William Saroyan)

rowing Rowers in a racing boat called a *shell.* The person facing the rowers is the coxswain [käk′sən], who steers the boat and directs the oar strokes.

row² [rō] *verb,* **rowed, rowing.** to use oars to move a boat.

row³ [rou] *noun, plural* **rows.** a noisy quarrel or fight: "When the engagement came to an end Mattie and Aunt Tittie had a *row* and parted company." (Noel Coward)

row•boat [rō′bōt] *noun, plural* **rowboats.** a small boat that is moved by the use of oars.

row•dy [rou′dē] *adjective.* acting in a way that is noisy, rough, or rude; disorderly: A few *rowdy* people in the audience kept shouting out insults at the speaker.

roy•al [roi′əl] *adjective.* **1.** having to do with a king or queen: Prince Charles is part of the *royal* family of Great Britain. **2.** serving or belonging to a king or queen: a *royal* palace, the British *Royal* Air Force. **3.** suited for a king or queen: The fans gave the winning team a *royal* welcome at their victory parade. **—royally,** *adverb:* They dined *royally* at the fanciest restaurant in town.

roy•al•ty [roi′əl tē] *noun, plural* **royalties. 1.** a royal person such as a king, queen, prince, or princess. **2.** the position, rank, or powers of such a person: The color purple has long been a symbol of *royalty.* **3.** a share of the money earned from the sale or performance of a work such as a book, a play, or a piece of music.

Royalties are usually paid to the author or composer of such a work.

rub [rub] *verb,* **rubbed, rubbing. 1.** to press down on a surface while moving over it: She took the eraser and *rubbed* out what she'd written. **2.** to put on or spread over a surface: He *rubbed* some suntan lotion on his arms and neck. **3.** to move one thing over another, or two things against each other: to start a fire by *rubbing* two dry sticks very quickly together. **4.** to clean, polish, or smooth something by applying pressure to it.

rub•ber [rub′ər] *noun, plural* **rubbers. 1.** a strong substance that keeps out water and that can be easily stretched. Natural rubber is made from the milky sap of certain tropical plants, such as the **rubber tree.** Many kinds of artificial rubber are also made, using coal, oil, and chemicals. **2. rubbers.** waterproof overshoes made from this substance, used for wearing in the rain. **—rubbery,** *adjective.* like rubber in some way, as by being floppy or stretchy.

rub•bish [rub′ish] *noun.* **1.** things that are not wanted and are thrown away; useless or waste material; trash. **2.** foolish talk; nonsense.

rub•ble [rub′əl] *noun.* rough, broken pieces of stone, brick, and other solid material, such as the ruins of buildings that have been destroyed by an explosion or fire.

ru•by [rōō′bē] *noun, plural* **rubies.** a precious stone with a clear, red color.

rud•der [rud′ər] *noun, plural* **rudders. 1.** a wide, flat movable part attached to the back of a boat or ship and used for steering. **2.** a similar part attached to the tail of an aircraft.

rud•dy [rud′ē] *adjective,* **ruddier, ruddiest.** having a rich, healthy reddish color of the skin.

rude [rōōd] *adjective,* **ruder, rudest. 1.** showing or having bad manners; not polite: It is *rude* to interrupt another person who is talking. "All she did was to put her thumb to her nose and make a *rude* sign and put her tongue out." (John Fowles) **2.** made or done with little skill; crude or rough: a *rude* hut made of sticks and mud. **—rudely,** *adverb.* **—rudeness,** *noun.*

ruf•fle [ruf′əl] *noun, plural* **ruffles.** a strip of cloth, ribbon, or lace that has folds or waves at one edge, used for trimming. **—verb,** **ruffled, ruffling. 1.** to disturb something that was smooth or calm: The bird *ruffled* its feathers. "A faint stir of air *ruffled* the lace round her thin throat . . ." (John Galsworthy) **2.** to cause someone to become annoyed or upset: ". . . he's far too easy-going to allow her to *ruffle* him." (Noel Coward)

rules for writing George Orwell listed six rules for good writing, and said the last rule is: "Break any of these rules sooner than say anything outright barbarous." (*Barbarous* here means "not graceful and clear and precise.") There are lots of good principles to follow in writing. Orwell also said, "Never use a long word where a short word will do." In his book *The Philosophy of Composition*, E. D. Hirsch studied the recommendations made by five different writer's handbooks. He found that nine principles were common to all these books. The can be summed up as follows: (1) Keep to your subject. (2) Use simple, concrete words. (3) Don't pad—leave out needless words. (4) Organize your paper in complete paragraphs. (5) Vary between long and short sentences. (6) Make it clear how one sentence relates to the next. (7) Use natural word order in a sentence. (8) Choose the appropriate word for the situation. (9) Keep related words together.

rug [rug] *noun, plural* **rugs.** a piece of thick, heavy fabric that is used to cover a floor.

rug•by [rug′bē] *noun.* a form of football played by teams of 13 or 15 players, in which blocking and forward passing are not permitted.

rug•ged [rug′id] *adjective, more/most.* **1.** having a rough or broken surface or outline: a *rugged* range of mountains. The state of Maine has a *rugged* coastline. **2.** able to stand up to hard treatment; strong and sturdy: a *rugged* old oak table. **3.** hard to do or get through; severe; harsh: The soldiers faced six weeks of *rugged* training in the desert.

ruin [rōō′in] *noun, plural* **ruins. 1.** the fact of being completely destroyed; very great damage: The huge fire brought the *ruin* of a whole neighborhood. **2.** something that causes such a destruction or collapse. **3. ruins.** what is left of something that has been destroyed; remains: The police searched the *ruins* of the house to find out what had caused the explosion. —*verb,* **ruined, ruining. 1.** to bring or cause destruction or collapse: The Great Depression of the 1930's *ruined* many wealthy men. **2.** to spoil or harm: The rain *ruined* our picnic.

rule [rōōl] *noun, plural* **rules. 1.** a condition that controls how something is done; a statement telling what is allowed or not allowed: Using a metal bat is against the *rules* in big-league baseball. She has a *rule* that the children have to finish everything on their plates to get dessert. **2.** the regular or usual way that something is done: "As a *rule* they met before the game in the early afternoon." (John R. Tunis) **3.** the fact of being in control or governing: British *rule* in India lasted for almost 100 years. **4.** a straight line. —*verb,* **ruled, ruling. 1.** to have control over or govern: King Henry VIII *ruled* England from 1509 to 1547. **2.** to make a rule, or a decision about a rule: The referee *ruled* that the runner had stepped out of bounds.

rul•er [rōō′lər] *noun, plural* **rulers. 1.** a person who rules others, especially as the head of a country: Joseph Stalin was the *ruler* of the Soviet Union for many years. **2.** a strip of wood, plastic, or other material, used for measuring and for drawing straight lines.

rum [rum] *noun, plural* **rums.** a strong alcoholic drink, usually made from sugar cane or from molasses.

rum•ble [rum′bəl] *verb,* **rumbled, rumbling.** to make a deep, heavy, rolling sound: We could hear the traffic *rumbling* on the nearby highway. "The cart *rumbled* over the cobblestones and went out of sight." (Erskine Caldwell) —*noun, plural* **rumbles.** a deep, heavy rolling sound: "The night was close and thick, the stars were dim, and below us, under the cliff, we heard the *rumble* of the sea." (Henry James)

ru•mi•nant [rōō′mə nənt] *noun, plural* **ruminants.** a grass-eating animal that chews its cud and has hooves. Cows, goats, and sheep are ruminants; so are deer, giraffes, camels, and buffalo. Most ruminants have a special four-part stomach for digesting grasses.

rum•mage [rum′ij] *verb,* **rummaged, rummaging.** to search through something by moving things aside: Tommy *rummaged* through his toy chest looking for an old water pistol. "Vladimir *rummages* in his pockets, takes out a turnip and gives it to Estragon . . ." (Samuel Beckett)

rummage sale a sale of used clothes, furniture, and other household items.

R

Pronunciation Key: O–S

ō	over, go	ou	out; town
ô	all; law	p	put; hop
oo	look; full	r	run; car
ōō	pool; who	s	set; miss
oi	oil; boy	sh	show

(Turn the page for more information.)

R

ru•mor [rōō′mər] *noun, plural* **rumors. 1.** a story or report that is passed from person to person and believed to be true without any proof: There's a *rumor* going around town that the mayor and his secretary are going to get married. **2.** what people are saying in general; the general opinion: *Rumor* has it that the company is moving its headquarters to Arizona. —*verb,* **rumored, rumoring.** to spread or tell rumors: It's *rumored* that Mrs. Stevens will be the new principal.

rump [rump] *noun, plural* **rumps. 1.** the part of an animal's body where the back meets the legs. **2.** a cut of meat from this part.

rum•ple [rum′pəl] *verb,* **rumpled, rumpling.** to mess something by handling it roughly; wrinkle or crumple: While wrestling on the bed, the children *rumpled* the bedspread.

run [run] *verb,* **ran, run, running. 1.** to go by moving the legs more quickly than when walking. **2.** to take part in a race or contest: Who's *running* for class president this year? **3.** to travel regularly: This train *runs* between Los Angeles and San Diego. **4.** to make a small trip or trips to do routine things; do errands: Tammy says she's just going to *run* to the store for some milk and bread. **5.** to let something move freely: Water *runs* through pipes into a house. The engine *ran* better after the car had a tune-up. **6.** to pass into or bring to a place or condition: This road *runs* from Dallas to Houston. Be careful there, or you'll *run* into trouble. **7.** to happen or be in effect: The summer sale *runs* for two weeks. Blue eyes *run* in her family. **8.** to be in charge of: to *run* a business. **9.** to have the stitches of a fabric break: Della's stocking *ran* after she hooked it on the edge of the chair. **10.** to spread or leak out: The color of this red shirt will *run,* so you can't wash it with anything white. **11.** to experience something bad: to *run* a risk, or *run* a fever. **12.** to operate a program on a computer.
—*noun, plural* **run. 1.** the fact of running: The girls took a *run* around the school track. **2.** a

trip: The early train in the morning is called the milk *run* because it used to carry milk into the city. **3.** the freedom to move around or to use something: Their dog has the *run* of the house. **4.** a period of time when something continues to happen: a *run* of bad luck. The hit play had a two-year *run* on Broadway. **5.** a part of a knitted cloth where the stitches have broken and come undone. **6.** a score earned in baseball after a player has gone safely around every base and returned to touch home plate without being put out.

run•a•way [run′ə wā′] *noun, plural* **runaways.** a person, animal, or thing that runs away or runs out of control. —*adjective.* running away or moving without any control: a *runaway* horse. Ramps are built next to mountain highways to help stop *runaway* trucks.

run-on sentences "Run-on" refers to the error of having two separate thoughts that "run together" in one sentence: "They said the house would be finished in four months, it actually took seven." That's a run-on sentence. There are several ways you could fix it. You can add the word *but*: ". . . finished in four months, but it actually took seven." Or, you could have two separate sentences: ". . . finished in four months. It actually took seven." You could also change the comma to a semi-colon. Or, you could add a word at the front of the sentence to make the first part a clause: "Although they said the house would be finished in four months, it actually . . ." Student writers sometimes fall into the "run-on" pattern because they worry about having too many short sentences, and so connect sentences too carelessly.

run-down [run′ doun′] *adjective, more/most.* **1.** having bad health; sick or tired. **2.** needing to be fixed; falling apart: a *run-down* old house.

rung¹ [rung] *verb.* the past participle of **ring.**

rung² *noun, plural* **rungs. 1.** a crossing piece that forms the step of a ladder. **2.** a piece between the legs or within the framework of a chair that gives strength or support.

run•ner [run′ər] *noun, plural* **runners. 1.** a person or an animal that runs. **2.** the part on which an ice skate, sled, iceboat, or the like moves along the ice or snow. **3.** a narrow strip of carpeting in a hallway or on a stairway. **4.** a thin stem of a plant that crawls along the ground and roots in another place to make a new plant. **5.** a player in baseball who is on base or trying to reach base.

run•ner-up [run′ər up′] *noun, plural* **runners-up.** a person or team that finishes in second place in a race or contest.

runt [runt] *noun, plural* **runts.** *Informal.* an animal that is much smaller than normal.

run•way [run′wā] *noun, plural* **runways.** a long, narrow roadway where an airplane can take off and land.

rup•ture [rup′chər] *verb,* **ruptured, rupturing.** to break open; burst: After the water pipe *ruptured,* the floor was flooded. —*noun, plural* **ruptures.** the act or place of rupturing: A *rupture* of the appendix calls for an emergency operation.

ru•ral [roor′əl] *adjective.* having to do with or being in the country; away from cities or towns: That Congressman represents a *rural* district with no large cities.

rush¹ [rush] *verb,* **rushed, rushing. 1.** to hurry or move quickly: The doctor told the ambulance driver to *rush* the woman to the hospital. "He *rushed* past her like a football tackle, bumping her." (James Thurber) **2.** to do something in too much of a hurry: You might make careless mistakes on your paper if you *rush* your work. —*noun, plural* **rushes. 1.** the fact of rushing; quick or hurried movements. She was in a *rush* to get her work finished. **2.** the fact of many people rushing to do something: The California Gold *Rush* took place in 1849.

rush² *noun, plural* **rushes.** a grass-like plant that grows in very wet places. Most rushes have thin, hollow stems and bunches of little green or brown flowers. Their stems are used in weaving mats, baskets, and chair seats.

rush hour a time of day when many people are traveling, either going to or from work.

Mount Rushmore

Rush•more, Mount [rush′môr′] a mountain in western South Dakota on which the faces of Presidents Washington, Jefferson, Theodore Roosevelt, and Lincoln are carved.

Rus•sia [rush′ə] a former country in eastern Europe and western Asia that now makes up the main part of the SOVIET UNION. ♦ The Soviet Union is sometimes also called **Russia.**

rust [rust] *noun, plural* **rusts, 1.** a reddish-brown or orange coating that forms on iron when it is exposed to moisture or air for a long time. **2.** a plant disease that marks leaves and stems with reddish-brown or orange spots or streaks. **3.** a reddish-brown color. —*verb,* **rusted, rusting.** to become covered with rust.

rus•tle [rus′əl] *verb,* **rustled, rustling. 1.** to make a soft crackling or fluttering sound: "The dry leaves of the olive tree *rustled* crisply over their heads." (John Galsworthy) **2.** to lift or move something so that it makes a sound like this: "The fan had been shut off so as not to *rustle* the papers on his desk." (John Gregory Dunne) **3.** to steal cattle: Gangs of outlaws used to *rustle* cattle in the Old West. ♦ A person who does this is a **rustler.** —*noun, plural* **rustles.** a soft, whispering sound.

rust•y [rus′tē] *adjective,* **rustier, rustiest. 1.** covered with rust: The *rusty* nails gave way and the old gate fell apart. **2.** having the look or color of rust: ". . . the *rusty* pine needles gentle under their feet." (Madeline L'Engle) **3.** not as good as it should be, because of not being used or practiced: June's gotten a bit *rusty* at the piano since she hasn't played in so long.

rut [rut] *noun, plural* **ruts. 1.** a deep wheel track or groove made in the ground from repeated use: The logging trucks had left *ruts* in the dirt road. **2.** a way of living or doing things that is the same day after day; a boring routine: He's looking for a new job because he feels he's in a *rut* working at the gas station. —*verb,* **rutted, rutting.** to make ruts in something: ". . . the old Spanish trail, deeply *rutted* by the heavy wheels of Mexican carts." (Edna Ferber)

ruth•less [rooth′lis] *adjective, more/most.* having or showing no pity or kindness; harsh and cruel: Adolf Hitler was a *ruthless* dictator. —**ruthlessly,** *adverb* ". . . tramping *ruthlessly* on the sprouting seed that he had so carefully pressed into the earth." (Erskine Caldwell) —**ruthlessness,** *noun.*

rye [rī] *noun, plural* **ryes,** a grass plant with thin stems. Its grain is used to make flour, food for animals, and whiskey. **Rye bread** is made from this flour.

R

	Pronunciation Key: T–Z		
t	ten; date	v	very; live
th	think	w	win; away
th	these	y	you
u	cut; butter	z	zoo; cause
ur	turn; bird	zh	measure

(Turn the page for more information.)

S s

s, S [es] *noun, plural* **s's, S's.** the nineteenth letter of the alphabet.

Sab•bath [sab′əth] *noun, plural* **Sabbaths.** the day of the week that is set aside for worship and rest. The Sabbath is Sunday for Christians and Saturday for Jews.

sa•ber [sā′bər] *noun, plural* **sabers.** a long sword with a curved blade, used as a weapon by the cavalry in former times. Today it is used mainly in the sport of fencing.

sa•ber-toothed tiger [sā′bər tōōtht′] a large cat with two long curved eye-teeth. It lived during prehistoric times, but is now extinct.

saber-toothed tiger The huge teeth of the saber-toothed tiger measured up to eight inches.

sable [sā′bəl] *noun, plural* **sables.** a small four-legged animal of Europe and Asia that is somewhat like the mink. It is noted for its valuable dark fur, which is used for expensive coats.

sab•o•tage [sab′ə tazh′] *noun.* the destroying of factories, roads, or military bases by enemy agents working secretly. —*verb,* **sabotaged, sabotaging.** to damage or destroy something by sabotage. ◆ A *sabot* is a wooden shoe. In the early 1800's French workers would sabotage machinery by throwing their shoes into the working parts.

sac [sak] *noun, plural* **sacs.** a bag-like part of a plant or animal that usually holds liquid.

Sac•a•ja•we•a [sak′ə jə wē′ə] 1784?-1812?, American Indian woman who guided the Lewis and Clark expedition.

sack¹ [sak] *noun, plural* **sacks. 1.** a large bag made of strong, rough material. **2.** any bag: She brought her lunch to school in a paper *sack.* —*verb,* **sacked, sacking.** to put in a sack.

sack² *verb,* **sacked, sacking. 1.** to capture and rob a place; loot: In the 400's A.D. invaders from the north *sacked* the city of Rome. **2.** in football, to tackle the quarterback behind the line while he is trying to pass the ball. —*noun, plural* **sacks.** the act of sacking.

sa•cred [sā′krid] *adjective, more/most.* **1.** belonging to God; holy: "The first duty of every Moslem was to study the Koran, the *sacred* book of Islam." (T. E. Lawrence) **2.** worthy of special respect or honor: a *sacred* promise, a *sacred* duty.

sac•ri•fice [sak′rə fīs′] *noun, plural* **sacrifices. 1.** the act of offering something to God or a god as a form of worship: Ancient tribes often made a *sacrifice* by killing a sheep, goat, or other such animal in hope of pleasing the gods. **2.** the giving up of something one values for the sake of someone else: "It made us all realize how much Mother had done for us for years, and all the effort and *sacrifice* that she had made for our sake." (Stephen Leacock) **3.** a play in baseball in which the batter is put out but causes another runner to advance. —*verb,* **sacrificed, sacrificing. 1.** to make a religious sacrifice. **2.** to give up something for the sake of someone else: The soldier *sacrificed* his life to save the other men.

sad [sad] *adjective,* **sadder, saddest. 1.** not happy; feeling sorrow: The boy was *sad* to be all alone away from his home and family. **2.** causing or showing this feeling: *sad* news, a *sad* voice. —**sadly,** *adverb.* —**sadness,** *noun.*

sad•den [sad′ ən] *verb*, **saddened, saddening.** to make or become sad: "She was surprised and *saddened* to see that there were tears in his eyes." (Charles Dickens)

sad•dle [sad′ əl] *noun, plural* **saddles.** a seat for a rider on the back of a horse. —*verb*, **saddled, saddling. 1.** to put a saddle on: to *saddle* a horse. **2.** to put a load on; burden: "She wants an exciting father, and what's she got? She's *saddled* with me." (Graham Greene)

sa•fa•ri [sə fär′ ē] *noun, plural* **safaris.** a trip through wild country to hunt animals, especially in eastern or central Africa.

safe [sāf] *adjective*, **safer, safest. 1.** free from danger or harm: It's not *safe* to drive fast on a narrow, winding mountain road. **2.** not able or likely to cause harm: Dad keeps his tools in a *safe* place where the baby can't reach them. **3.** without the risk of being wrong or failing: It's *safe* to say the project will be finished by summer. **4.** in baseball, able to reach a base without being put out. —*noun, plural* **safes.** a strong box with a lock, used to keep money, jewelry, important papers, and other valuables from being lost or stolen. —**safely,** *adverb*.

safe•guard [sāf′ gärd′] *noun, plural* **safe-guards.** something that protects against harm or danger: Locking your car is a *safeguard* against theft. —*verb*, **safeguarded, safeguarding.** to keep safe.

sage [sāj] *noun, plural* **sages.** a person thought to be very wise: In his later years, after he was President, Thomas Jefferson was known as the *Sage* of Monticello. —*adjective*. having wisdom; wise: *sage* advice. —**sagely,** *adverb*.

sage•brush [sāj′ brush′] *noun*. a bushy shrub that commonly grows in the dry regions of western North America.

Sahara A Bedouin tribesman and his camel cross the sand dunes of the Sahara.

Sa•ha•ra [sə hâr′ ə] the largest desert in the world, stretching across northern Africa.

said [sed] the past form of **say.** "I have to leave now," Karen *said*.

said There are many words that are hard to avoid repeating. One of these is *said*. If you're writing a story in which characters are talking, you must use "she said," "he said," or "I said," even if, at times, you could be more precise by writing, "he declared," "she observed," or "I remarked." The simple form *said* works better than these substitutes. This doesn't mean you should never use other verbs for *said*. *Asked, answered, replied, shouted, cried,* or *called* can replace it, if they fit the situation. But remember, the speaker's words are what's important. The reader will focus on that and probably won't even notice if *said* is repeated.

safe•ty [sāf′ tē] *noun*. the fact of being safe; freedom from danger: The boat reached the *safety* of the harbor just before the storm.

safety pin a U-shaped pin with a special guard at one end to cover the sharp point.

sag [sag] *verb*, **sagged, sagging.** to bend or droop down loosely: "When they reached the top at last, they *sagged* against the sled exhausted." (James Houston) —*noun, plural* **sags.** the act of sagging, or a part that sags.

sa•ga [sä′ gə] *noun, plural* **sagas. 1.** an ancient story telling of the deeds of heroes of Norway and Iceland. **2.** any long story of adventure with many episodes: John Galsworthy wrote a famous series of novels called the *Forsyte Saga*.

sail [sāl] *noun, plural* **sails. 1.** a piece of heavy cloth attached to a boat or ship. It collects the force of the wind to make the boat move forward through the water. **2.** a trip on a boat or ship using sails. —*verb*, **sailed, sailing. 1.** to guide or control a boat with a sail. ◆ The sport of doing this is **sailing. 2.** to move or travel by

Pronunciation Key: A–F			
a	and; hat	ch	chew; such
ā	ate; stay	d	dog; lid
â	care; air	e	end; yet
ä	father; hot	ē	she; each
b	boy; cab	f	fun; off

(Turn the page for more information.)

S

ship: The *Pacific Princess* will *sail* for Hawaii at noon tomorrow. **3.** to move or glide smoothly, as if sailing on a boat: "Matthew was so hungry he felt light enough to take off and *sail* across the snow." (James Houston)

sail•boat [sāl′bōt′] *noun, plural* **sailboats.** a boat fitted with sails and powered by wind.

sail•or [sā′lər] *noun, plural* **sailors. 1.** a person who helps guide or control a boat or ship, especially someone who does this as a job. **2.** a member of the Navy, especially one who is not an officer.

saint [sānt] *noun plural* **saints. 1.** *also,* **Saint.** a very holy person. In certain religions, a saint is believed to have special powers, such as the ability to perform miracles. Saints of the Catholic Church are often honored after their death with prayers and special holidays. ◆ The fact of being a saint is **sainthood. 2.** a person thought of as having qualities like a saint, as by being very kind, patient, willing to help others, and so on. —**saintly**, *adjective.*

Saint Ber•nard [bər närd′] a very large, powerful dog with thick brown-and-white hair. ◆ These dogs were first bred by monks at the monastery of Saint Bernard, in the Swiss Alps, and were used there to find people lost in the snow.

St. Law•rence River [lôr′əns] a river in southeastern Canada, flowing northeast from Lake Ontario to the Gulf of St. Lawrence.

St. Lou•is [lōō′is *or* lōō′ē] a city in eastern Missouri, on the Mississippi River. *Population:* 453,000.

sake [sāk] *noun, plural* **sakes. 1.** benefit or good: Don't fix a whole meal just for my *sake,* unless you're going to eat too. **2.** reason or purpose: Just for the *sake* of argument, let's assume the house cost about $100,000.

sal•ad [sal′əd] *noun, plural* **salads. 1.** a dish of fruits or vegetables served cold, usually with dressing. **2.** a dish of cold meat or fish cut into small pieces and mixed with a dressing.

sal•a•man•der [sal′ə man′dər] *noun, plural* **salamanders.** a small animal that looks like a lizard, but is more closely related to frogs and toads. A salamander is an AMPHIBIAN that lives in or near damp places.

sal•a•ry [sal′rē] *noun, plural* **salaries.** a fixed amount of money paid for work performed. A salary is paid at regular times, such as by the week, month, or year, rather than by the hour or the job. ◆ This word is related to *salt.* It comes from the custom in the ancient Roman army of paying soldiers "salt money." At that

time salt was regarded as very important because it was expensive and hard to get.

sale [sāl] *noun, plural* **sales. 1.** an exchange of goods for money; the selling of something. **2.** the selling of goods or property at lower than usual prices: The supermarket had a *sale* on turkeys just before Thanksgiving.

sales•man [sālz′mən] *noun, plural* **salesmen.** a person, especially a man, whose work is selling something. ◆ The art or technique of selling is called **salesmanship.**

sales•per•son [sālz′pur′sən] *noun, plural* **salespeople** or **salespersons.** a salesman or saleswoman.

sales•woman [sālz′woom′ən] *noun, plural* **saleswomen.** a woman whose work is selling something.

sa•li•va [sə lī′və] *noun.* a clear, tasteless fluid given off into the mouth by special glands. Saliva helps moisten food as it is chewed and also helps in digestion.

Salk [sôlk] **Jonas E.,** born 1914, American medical scientist who developed a vaccine to prevent the dangerous disease POLIO.

sal•mon [sam′ən] *noun, plural* **salmon** or **salmons. 1.** a large, silver-colored fish that is hatched in fresh water but lives in the ocean as an adult. Salmon return to the fresh water where they were born to lay their eggs. The meat of salmon is widely used as food. **2.** an orange color like that of the flesh of a salmon.

salmon A salmon fights upstream to return to the waters of its birth; there it will have its young.

sa•loon [sə lōōn′] *noun, plural* **saloons.** a place where alcoholic drinks are served; a bar. ◆ *Saloon* is a more old-fashioned term than *bar.*

salt [sôlt] *noun, plural* **salts. 1.** *also,* **table salt.** a white crystal mined from the earth and taken from sea water. Its chemical name is **sodium**

chloride. Salt is used to season and preserve foods and is important in the diet of people and animals. **2.** a chemical compound formed under certain conditions, as when an acid is mixed with a base. **3.** any of various substances that look like salt: bath *salts.*—*verb,* **salted, salting. 1.** to season or preserve food with salt: to *salt* pork. **2. salt away.** to save for use at a later time.—**salty,** *adjective.* having a lot of salt: a *salty* food, the *salty* water of the Dead Sea. —**saline** [sā′ lēn′] *adjective.* having or containing salt: a *saline* solution.

salt•wat•er [sôlt′ wô′ tər] (*also,* **salt-water**) *adjective.* having to do with or living in the ocean, rather than in the fresh water of lakes, rivers, and so on: Sharks are *saltwater* fish.

sal•u•ta•tion [sal′ yōō tā′ shən] *noun, plural* **salutations.** an act or expression of greeting, especially the greeting used to begin a letter.

words or actions: "Today, as if to *salute* him on his first day in his new house, there was a letter from Medley." (Jean Stafford) —*noun, plural* **salutes.** the act or fact of saluting.

sal•vage [sal′ vij] *verb,* **salvaged, salvaging. 1.** to save something from being lost or damaged: The cargo from the sunken ship was *salvaged* by a crew of divers. **2.** to save from being thrown away or destroyed: "They emptied the waste-baskets, and Katie *salvaged* the longer bits of discarded chalk." (Betty Smith)—*noun.* the act or fact of salvaging something.

sal•va•tion [sal vā′ shən] *noun.* **1.** in the Christian religion, the saving of a person's soul from evil or sin, and protection against punishment for past sins. **2.** the fact of being saved from danger, destruction, or loss. ♦ The **Salvation Army** is an organization that brings religious services and aid to needy people.

---

salutation A *salutation* is the "Dear ____" part that comes just before the body of a letter. (It's also called the *greeting.*) *Salutation* comes from the idea that the writer *salutes* the reader—offers him or her a formal greeting. A salutation begins with a capital letter: "Dear Karen" "Friends" and so on. In business letters and other letters that are formal, it is punctuated by a colon: "Dear Ms. Alexander:" "Dear Sirs:" and so on. For friendly letters, the custom has been to use a comma: "Dear Grandma," "Dear Tommy," and so on. Today, business executives often receive letters from people they don't know that begin "Hello, Mr. Harper," or "Good Morning, Mr. Harper!" That is not a good idea. Most executives think of that sort of salutation as false cheer.

salute A U. S. Army war veteran salutes at a Memorial Day parade.

sa•lute [sə lōōt′] *verb,* **saluted, saluting. 1.** to show respect or honor in a formal way, especially by touching the open right hand to the forehead: Soldiers in the army are supposed to *salute* their officers. **2.** to greet with friendly

salve [sav] *noun, plural* **salves.** a creamy substance used to heal or soothe a sore or burn on the skin; an ointment.

same [sām] *adjective.* **1.** being the one and only and not another: Grandpa has lived in the *same* house ever since he was a boy. **2.** being exactly like another; identical: The twins wore the *same* dress at their birthday party. —*pronoun:* She ordered the fried chicken, and I had the *same.* —**sameness,** *noun.* the fact of being the same, especially in a boring or repetitive way.

sam•ple [sam′pəl] *noun, plural* **samples.** a small piece or amount that shows what the whole thing is like: She's getting new curtains for the bedroom, so she brought home *samples* of several different kinds of material. ♦ Also used

Pronunciation Key: G–N

g	give; big	k	kind; cat; back
h	hold	l	let; ball
i	it; this	m	make; time
ī	ice; my	n	not; own
j	jet; gem; edge	ng	having

(Turn the page for more information.)

as an adjective: a *sample* copy of a new magazine. —*verb*, **sampled, sampling.** to take a sample of; test a part or piece.

San An•to•ni•o [san′ an tō′ nē ō] a city in south-central Texas. *Population:* 786,000.

sanc•tion [sangk′ shən] *verb*, **sanctioned, sanctioning.** to approve of something in an official way: The President stated that he could not *sanction* any dealings with the terrorists. —*noun*, *plural* **sanctions. 1.** the fact of approving something officially. **2. sanctions.** an agreement by two or more countries to act against another country.

sanc•tu•ar•y [sangk′ choo er′ ē] *noun*, *plural* **sanctuaries. 1.** a holy or sacred place, such as a church. **2.** safety or protection: In the Middle Ages, an escaped criminal could seek *sanctuary* in a church. **3.** a natural area where wild animals are protected: a bird *sanctuary*.

papers. heavy paper that is coated with sand or other such rough material, used to smooth wood and other surfaces. —*verb*, **sandpapered, sandpapering:** to *sandpaper* a table before painting it.

sand•pi•per [sand′ pī′ pər] *noun*, *plural*, **sandpipers.** a small bird with a long, pointed bill, long legs, and brown or gray speckled feathers. Sandpipers live on or near the seashore.

sand•stone [sand′ stōn′] *noun*. a type of rock made of sand particles joined together.

sand•wich [sand′ wich] *noun*, *plural* **sandwiches.** slices of bread with a filling between them, such as meat, cheese, or peanut butter and jelly. —*verb*, **sandwiched, sandwiching.** to squeeze tightly between two things: "Once he spotted Simon passing the window, *sandwiched* between his parents." (Penelope Lively)

sand•y [san′ dē] *adjective*, **sandier, sandiest. 1.**

sandwich *Sandwich* is a city in southern England, on the English Channel, that was once a major seaport. The 4th Earl of Sandwich, John Montagu, was an English government official of the 1700's. It's said that the sandwich is named for him because he invented it, by putting meat between slices of bread so he could eat while taking part in an all-night card game. The Earl also gave his name to history in another way—the *Sandwich* Islands. This group of islands in the South Pacific was named for him by the British explorer Captain James Cook. As time went on, though, people began to call the islands by their native name—Hawaii.

S

sand [sand] *noun*, *plural* **sands.** loose, tiny grains of crushed or worn rock, often found in the desert or at the seashore. Sand is used to make products such as glass, cement, bricks, sandpaper, and explosives. —*verb*, **sanded, sanding. 1.** to smooth or polish with SANDPAPER: She *sanded* the desk top until it was smooth before she painted it. **2.** to sprinkle or spread over with sand: The highway department *sands* icy roads to help keep cars from skidding.

san•dal [san′ dəl] *noun*, *plural* **sandals.** an open shoe made up of a sole that is attached to the foot by straps.

sand•bar [sand′ bär′] *noun*, *plural* **sandbars.** a shallow place in a body of water, where sand has built up to form a ridge.

sand•box [sand′ bäks′] *noun*, *plural* **sandboxes.** a shallow box or enclosed area containing sand for children to play in.

Sand•burg [san′ burg′] **Carl,** 1878-1967, American poet.

San Di•e•go [dē ā′ gō] a port city in southern California, on the Pacific Ocean. *Population:* 876,000.

sand•pa•per [sand′ pā′ pər] *noun*, *plural* **sand-**

sandstorm A sandstorm makes travel dangerous on this road in California's Mojave Desert.

like or covered with sand: a *sandy* beach. **2.** light tan or reddish-blond: *sandy* hair.

sane [sān] *adjective*, **saner, sanest. 1.** having a mind that is healthy or normal; not crazy. **2.** showing good sense: The mayor called for a "safe and *sane*" Fourth of July celebration, with no one setting off dangerous fireworks.

San Fran•cis•co [fran sis′ kō] a city and port in west-central California, on San Francisco Bay. *Population:* 679,000.

sang [sang] *verb.* the past tense of **sing.**

san·i·tar·y [san′ ə ter′ ē] *adjective, more/most.* perfectly clean and free of germs: In motel rooms, drinking glasses are covered with a *sanitary* wrapper.

san·i·ta·tion [san′ ə tā′ shən] *noun.* the protection of the health of the public by keeping things clean. Sanitation includes such things as collecting garbage, providing safe drinking water, and building sewer systems.

San Jo·se [hō zā′] a city in west-central California, southeast of San Francisco. *Population:* 637,000.

sank [sangk] *verb.* the past tense of **sink.**

San·ta Claus [san′ tə klôs′] a man who represents the spirit of Christmas, shown as a fat, jolly old man wearing a white beard and a red suit, and believed by young children to give out presents on Christmas Eve.

San·ti·a·go [san′ tē ä′ gō] the capital and largest city of Chile. *Population:* 3,900,000.

São Paulo [sou pou′ lō] the largest city in South America, in southeastern Brazil. *Population:* 7,198,000.

sap¹ [sap] *noun, plural* **saps.** the liquid that flows through plants, carrying food and other materials throughout the plant.

sap² *verb,* **sapped, sapping.** to weaken by draining away; cause to lose power or energy.

oil in small, flat cans. **2. like sardines.** crowded very tight, like sardines in a can.

sa·ri [sä′ rē] *noun, plural* **saris.** a length of cotton or silk material wrapped around the body, as in the traditional outer clothing of Hindu women.

sash¹ [sash] *noun, plural* **sashes.** a broad length of cloth or ribbon worn around the waist or over the shoulder.

sash² *noun, plural* **sashes.** a frame into which the glass of a window or door is fitted.

Sas·katch·e·wan [sas kach′ ə wän] a province of central Canada. *Capital:* Regina. *Area:* 251,000 square miles. *Population:* 921,000.

sat [sat] *verb.* the past form of **sit.**

Sa·tan [sā′ tən] *noun.* another name for the Devil.

sat·el·lite [sat′ ə līt′] *noun, plural* **satellites. 1.** a heavenly body that revolves around a planet or another larger body in space. The moon is a satellite of the earth. **2.** an artificial body put into orbit from earth to provide weather information, send radio and TV signals, collect information on conditions in space, and so on. **3.** a country that is influenced or controlled by another, more powerful country: Bulgaria is a *satellite* of the Soviet Union.

sat·in [sat′ ən] *noun.* a smooth, shiny fabric made of silk or other material.

satire *Satire* is a sentence, a paragraph, an article, or a book that makes fun of something. A *satirist* sets out to criticize with humor. Satire is usually aimed at a person, a group of people, or an institution (government or business or church). It is one of the oldest forms of writing, highly developed by the Roman writers, Horace and Juvenal. Great satire is found throughout English literature. Its golden age in Britain was the late 1600's and 1700's, when Alexander Pope, John Dryden, and Jonathan Swift wrote. Swift's *Gulliver's Travels* (1726) is ranked as the greatest satire in English. Today's American satirists include Tom Wolfe, Art Buchwald, Fran Lebowitz, and Woody Allen. For a satire to be effective, it must contain a measure of truth. To poke fun at a trait of a person, such as his mispronouncing names, the readers have to recognize the trait. If they don't, there will be no "bite" to the satire.

sap·phire [saf′ īr] *noun, plural* **sapphires. 1.** a clear blue gemstone. **2.** a blue color like this.

sar·cas·tic [sär kas′ tik] *adjective, more/most.* using sharp, biting remarks or expressions to insult or make fun of someone. ♦ The use of such remarks or expressions is **sarcasm:** "Thanks so much for all your help," she said in *sarcasm* after he sat and watched her carry in all the packages. **—sarcastically,** *adverb.*

sar·dine [sär dēn′] *noun, plural* **sardines** or **sardine. 1.** a small herring or similar fish eaten as food. It is preserved by being packed tightly in

satire [sat′ īr] *noun, plural* **satires.** a written work that uses humor to show the foolishness or evil of some well-known custom or idea: The film *Dr. Strangelove* is a famous *satire* on the

Pronunciation Key: O–S

ō	over; go	ou	out, town
ô	all; law	p	put; hop
oo	look; full	r	run; car
ōō	pool; who	s	set; miss
oi	oil; boy	sh	show

(Turn the page for more information.)

U.S.-Soviet arms race. ♦ A person who writes or creates a satire is a **satirist** [sat′ ər ist].

sat•is•fac•tion [sat′ is fak′ shən] *noun.* the state of being satisfied, or something that causes this: "The house contained six rooms instead of four, much to my mother's *satisfaction,* and I had a room of my own." (Erskine Caldwell)

sat•is•fac•tory [sat′ is fak′ trē] *adjective, more/most.* **1.** giving satisfaction: "I grinned, for I had just arrived at a *satisfactory* explanation for his behaviour."(Christopher Isherwood) **2.** good enough but not outstanding; adequate: Danny got a mark of *Satisfactory* in reading this term. —**satisfactorily,** *adverb.*

sat•is•fy [sat′ is fī] *verb,* **satisfied, satisfying. 1.** to get what is wanted to fill a need or a desire: "We were very *satisfied* with the results of our hunting." (Jules Verne) **2.** to free from doubt; convince: "*Satisfied* that his room had not been searched while he was at the Casino . . ." (Ian Fleming)

sat•u•rate [sach′ ə rāt′] *verb,* **saturated, saturating.** to make as wet as possible; soak: "He squirmed over the wet moss, *saturating* his clothes and chilling his body." (Jack London) —**saturation,** *noun.*

Sat•ur•day [sat′ ər dā′] *noun, plural* **Saturdays.** the seventh day of the week. ♦ *Saturday* gets its name from the planet Saturn.

Saturn The planet is named for *Saturn,* the Roman god of farming.

Sat•urn [sat′ ərn] *noun.* the planet that is sixth in distance from the sun. Saturn is surrounded by large rings made up of particles of ice and water.

sauce [sôs] *noun, plural* **sauces.** a liquid mixture used to add flavor to certain foods, usually one that is poured or spooned on top of the food when it is served. ♦ *Sauce* is one of the many words for food from Latin *sal,* "salt." Others include *sausage, salami,* and *salad.*

sau•cer [sô′ sər] *noun, plural* **saucers.** a small shallow dish used to hold a cup.

Sau•di Arabia [sou′ dē] a country that occupies most of the Arabian Peninsula. *Capital:* Riyadh. *Area:* 830,000 square miles. *Population:* 11,100,000.

saun•ter [sôn′ tər] *verb,* **sauntered, sauntering.** to walk at a slow, easy pace.

sau•sage [sô′ sij] *noun, plural* **sausages.** chopped meat that is mixed with spices and then stuffed into a thin casing shaped like a tube. ♦ **Salami** [sə läm′ ē] is a kind of sausage made of pork or beef.

sav•age [sav′ ij] *adjective, more/most.* **1.** acting in a violent way; cruel or fierce: He swung a *savage* punch at the other man's head. **2.** not tamed; wild: *savage* animals, such as the tiger. —*noun, plural* **savages. 1.** a person from a primitive tribe; an uncivilized person. **2.** a cruel, violent person. ♦ The fact of being savage is **savagery** [sav′ ij rē′]. —**savagely,** *adverb.*

save [sāv] *verb,* **saved, saving. 1.** to make free from harm or danger; make safe: A lifeguard's job is to *save* people who are drowning. **2.** to put away for later use: The family is trying to *save* money so that they can buy a house. **3.** to keep from wasting or losing something: We'll *save* a lot of time on the drive to Grandma's once the new highway opens. —*noun, plural* **saves.** a play in hockey or soccer in which the goalie prevents a goal from being scored. —*preposition.* except for; but: "Without any light *save* what night glow came through the windows . . ." (Virginia Hamilton)

sav•ings [sā′ vingz] *noun.* money that is saved.

sav•ior [sāv′ yər] *noun, plural* **saviors. 1. Sav-ior.** another name for Jesus Christ. **2.** a person who saves another or others from harm.

sa•vor [sā′ vər] *verb,* **savored, savoring.** to enjoy in an intense way; take great pleasure in: "He wanted to *savor* the sights of his homecoming." (John Jakes) —**savory,** *adjective:* "He consumed a large plateful of the very *savory* stew." (Herman Wouk)

saw¹ [sô] *verb.* the past tense of **see.**

saw² *noun, plural* **saws. 1.** a tool having a thin, flat blade with V-shaped teeth on one edge, used for cutting wood, metal and other hard materials. Some saws are hand tools and others are powered by a motor. —*verb,* **sawed** or **sawn, sawing.** to cut with a saw.

saw•dust [sô′ dust′] *noun.* fine grains or dust that come from wood that has been sawed.

S

scale A teacher or critic may say that a writer should have a sense of *scale* (or "proportion" or "balance"). This means that the writer should choose statements and images that are in keeping with the real situations they describe. In other words, powerful or sweeping statements should not be used for small matters, and very serious matters should not be described in a light or trivial way. If a jet airliner crashes and a number of people are killed, it would not be appropriate to write as a lead sentence, "We've never had so much excitement around here. This was the first time our neighborhood was on TV." If you are writing about a new city law that prevents playing baseball on city streets, it would be out of scale to call it a "tragedy."

saw•horse [sô′ hôrs′] *noun, plural* **sawhorses.** a four-legged stand for holding wood to be sawed.

saw•mill [sô′ mil′] *noun, plural* **sawmills.** a place where logs are sawed into lumber.

sax•o•phone [sak′ sə fōn′] *noun, plural* **saxophones.** a musical wind instrument that has a curved metal body shaped something like the letter 'J.' Notes are played by blowing through a reed mouthpiece and pressing keys. ◆ The saxophone was invented in about 1840 by Adolphe *Sax,* a Belgian musician living in Paris.

say [sā] *verb,* **said, saying. 1.** to speak words out loud: to *say* 'hello,' to *say* 'yes.' **2.** to make known in words; express: He *says* he can't go with us. **3.** to guess or assume: I can choose any poet for my report—Robert Frost, let's *say.* —*noun, plural* **says.** a chance to speak: You'll get your *say* at the meeting.

say•ing [sā′ ing] *noun, plural* **sayings.** a well-known short phrase or expression containing some statement of common sense or wisdom, such as "Where there's smoke there's fire."

scab [skab] *noun, plural* **scabs.** a crust that forms over a cut or scrape on the skin to protect it as it is healing.

scaf•fold [skaf′ əld *or* skaf′ ōld′] *noun, plural* **scaffolds.** a platform used to support workmen who are working above the ground on a building, as to paint, clean, or repair it.

scale¹ [skāl] *noun, plural* **scales.** a device used to find out how much something weighs. A scale works by balancing the object that is being weighed against another weight or against the force of a spring.

scale² *noun, plural* **scales. 1.** a series of marks or numbers evenly spaced on a line to be used for measuring, as on a thermometer or a ruler. **2.** a series of steps or stages; a range: the pay *scale* for a job. **3.** an exact way of comparing the size of a plan, model, or map of something with the original: This house plan is drawn with a *scale* of one inch being equal to five feet of the actual house. **4.** in music, a series of notes that go up higher or lower in pitch in equal steps. A scale is usually made up of eight notes that form an OCTAVE. —*verb,* **scaled, scaling. 1.** to climb up: "Time after time, feet slipping . . . he tried to *scale* the rock, but it was no use." (Michael Bond) **2.** to make larger or smaller according to a certain measurement: to *scale* down a large recipe to serve a smaller number of people.

scale³ *noun, plural* **scales.** one of the thin, hard plates that cover the body of certain animals, such as fish, lizards, and snakes. —*verb,* **scaled, scaling.** to remove scales from: to *scale* a fish before cooking it.

scal•lion [skal′ yən] *noun, plural* **scallions.** a mild-flavored onion that is long and narrow, with a small white bulb and a green top.

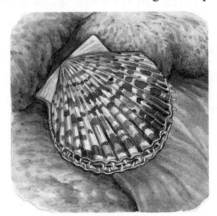

scallop The Atlantic Bay scallop is the one most commonly eaten in the U.S.

scal•lop [skäl′ əp *or* skal′ əp] *noun, plural* **scallops. 1.** a shellfish with a soft body enclosed in a double shell, each part of which has grooves

S

Pronunciation Key: T–Z

t	ten; date	v	very; live
th	think	w	win; away
<u>th</u>	these	y	you
u	cut; butter	z	zoo; cause
ur	turn; bird	zh	measure

(Turn the page for more information.)

that form a wavy edge. The body of the scallop is used for food. **2.** a wavy shape that looks like the edge of a scallop: The blouse had *scallops* around the neck. —*verb*, **scalloped, scalloping.** to make a wavy edge.

scalp [skalp] *noun, plural* **scalps.** the skin covering the area at the top the head.

scam•per [skam′ pər] *verb*, **scampered, scampering.** to run or hop quickly: "The child *scampered* into the bushes, and was lost to sight." (Aldous Huxley)

scan [skan] *verb*, **scanned, scanning. 1.** to look at carefully; examine closely: "Ned Hand *scanned* the ocean with his sharp eyes." (Jules Verne) **2.** to read over quickly: "About to *scan* the headlines, Corrigan paused first to note the paper's date." (Rod Serling) **3.** to use a special machine to check for certain information: Airline passengers are *scanned* by metal detectors to make sure they do not carry weapons. ◆ A machine that does this is a **scanner:** *Scanners* are used in stores to read a special code on an item that tells the price. —*noun, plural* **scans.** the fact of scanning: He was given a brain *scan* to see if he'd had any injury from the accident.

scan•dal [skan′ dəl] *noun, plural* **scandals.** something that shocks people and makes them feel a serious wrong has happened; a disgrace: In the famous Teapot Dome *Scandal* of the 1920's, a government official received secret payments for allowing valuable government land to be used by private businessmen. ◆ Something causing a scandal is **scandalous.**

Scan•di•na•vi•a [skan′ də nā′ vē ə] a region of northwestern Europe that includes the countries of Sweden, Norway, and Denmark, and usually Finland and Iceland as well. —**Scandinavian,** *adjective; noun.*

scant [skant] *adjective.* not quite enough of something, or just barely enough: Gasoline for private citizens was in *scant* supply during World War II. —**scanty,** *adjective:* "Dame Brinker earned *scanty* support for her family by raising vegetables." (Mary Mapes Dodge)

scar [skär] *noun, plural* **scars. 1.** a mark that is left when skin has healed from a cut or other injury. **2.** any such mark or sign of damage: The buildings of the town showed the *scars* of the recent tornado. —*verb*, **scarred, scarring.** to form a scar or become marked by a scar.

scarce [skârs] *adjective*, **scarcer, scarcest.** difficult to find; hard to get; rare: "The house took longer to build . . . because the wood which I needed was *scarce.*" (Scott O'Dell) ◆ The fact of being scarce is **scarcity** [skâr′ sə tē].

scarce•ly [skârs′ lē] *adverb.* **1.** almost not; barely: "He was short—*scarcely* five feet six inches tall . . ." (Russell Baker) **2.** definitely not; hardly: "The good dame could *scarcely* believe her eyes . . ." (Howard Pyle)

scare [skâr] *verb*, **scared, scaring.** to cause fear; make afraid; frighten: "Millicent sat up in bed, her heart pounding. Something had *scared* her awake." (Meindert DeJong) —*noun, plural* **scares.** something that causes fear: The plane made a sudden drop, giving us quite a *scare.*

scarecrow The crows don't seem to have any fear of this scarecrow.

scarf [skärf] *noun, plural* **scarves** or **scarfs.** a piece of cloth worn over the head or around the neck or shoulders.

scar•let [skär′ lit] *noun, plural* **scarlets.** a bright red color.

scar•y [skâr′ ē] *adjective*, **scarier, scariest.** causing fear or panic; frightening: a *scary* movie about an old house filled with ghosts.

scat•ter [skat′ ər] *verb*, **scattered, scattering. 1.** to go or cause to go in different directions; separate: "His friends were *scattered* through the audience, each standing alone." (Jean Fritz) **2.** to spread or toss in many different directions: "She picked up his shoes and socks and hung up the clothes *scattered* on the floor." (John Gregory Dunne)

scav•en•ger [skav′ in jər] *noun, plural* **scavengers. 1.** an animal having the habit of feeding on the remains of dead animals, such as a hyena. **2.** a person who looks through trash for useful objects that have been thrown away. ◆ The verb form of this word is **scavenge:** "Arctic foxes follow polar bears out onto the ice, where they *scavenge* the bear's winter kills." (Barry Lopez)

scene [sēn] *noun, plural* **scenes. 1.** the place where something happens: After a robbery, the police look for evidence at the *scene* of the crime. **2.** one part of a play or movie: In *Julius Caesar*, Caesar first comes on stage in Act One, *Scene* Two. **3.** the view of a certain place or area: The artist Toulouse-Lautrec often painted street *scenes* in the city of Paris. **4.** a public show of anger or strong feelings: The little boy made a *scene* in the restaurant when his mother wouldn't let him order dessert.

sce•ne•ry [sēn′rē *or* sē′nə rē] *noun.* **1.** the general way a place looks, especially an outdoor scene: Yellowstone National Park is famous for its beautiful *scenery*. **2.** on a stage, the painted screens and decorations that give an idea of the place where the action is happening.

scent [sent] *noun, plural* **scents. 1.** the smell of something: "The church was very old, with a *scent* of candle-wax and ancient dust." (George Orwell) **2.** an animal's sense of smell. **3.** a pleasant smell; perfume. —*verb*, **scented, scenting. 1.** to know or sense by scent; smell. **2.** to fill with a certain smell: "Blossoms *scented* the air and hung over the river." (John Knowles)

sched•ule [skej′ ōōl *or* skej′ ool] *noun, plural* **schedules. 1.** a record or list of events according to the times they happen: The magazine *TV Guide* gives a *schedule* of television programs. **2.** the normal or expected time for something to happen: The building of that house is behind *schedule;* it was supposed to be finished last month. —*verb*, **scheduled, scheduling.** to place or be on a schedule: Our plane to Dallas is *scheduled* to leave at two o'clock.

scheme [skēm] *noun, plural* **schemes. 1.** a plan of doing something; an idea: "I guess you could call us dreamers with these crazy *schemes* we've got to build our own boat and sail to Australia." (Joseph Wambaugh) **2.** a secret plan to do something wrong or bad; a *scheme* to avoid paying income taxes. **3.** an arrangement of things in an orderly or pleasing way: The color *scheme* for the room used the colors red and gray. —*verb*, **schemed, scheming.** to make up a scheme; to plot. —**schemer,** *noun.*

schol•ar [skäl′ ər] *noun, plural* **scholars. 1.** a person who has a great deal of knowledge from study or books: The first great modern encyclopedia was edited by the French *scholar* Denis Diderot. **2.** an older word for a student. ◆ A **scholarly** person is one who has spent much time studying or gaining knowledge.

schol•ar•ship [skäl′ ər ship′] *noun, plural* **scholarships. 1.** an amount of money that is given to a student to help pay the cost of studies. **2.** the practice of gaining knowledge.

scho•las•tic [skə las′ tik] *adjective.* having to do with students or with school: The high school runner's time set a national *scholastic* record.

school¹ [skōōl] *noun, plural* **schools. 1.** a place that holds regular classes for learning and teaching. **2.** the period of time that a person spends in such a place: At Taft High, *school* starts at 8:00. **3.** the students, teachers, and staff of a school. —*verb*, **schooled, schooling.** to train or teach: An ambassador to a foreign country must be well *schooled* in the customs of that country. ◆ This word is often used to form compounds such as **schoolteacher, schoolbook, schoolwork,** and so on.

school² *noun, plural* **schools.** a large group of fish or other water animals of the same kind swimming together: We saw a *school* of bluefish trailing behind the boat.

schoon•er [skōō′ nər] *noun, plural* **schooners.** a ship that has the masts and sails arranged so that the sails stretch back the length of the ship, rather than across from side to side.

Schweit•zer [shwīt′ sər] **Albert,** 1875-1964, French clergyman, philosopher, and doctor.

sci•ence [sī′ əns] *noun, plural* **sciences. 1.** a body of knowledge that results from the study

---

schedules Let's say you have to do a major writing assignment, a term paper for social studies. What you want to avoid, of course, is having all the work pile up on you at the last minute. The way to do this is to make a schedule for your writing. How do you know how much time to allow for each part of your schedule? Think back on how long it took to do each stage of your last paper, and allow similar amounts of time. If it's a new kind of assignment, get advice from a teacher, librarian, parent, older brother or sister, and so on. The main thing to remember is to allow enough time for the early steps of the paper.

Pronunciation Key: [ə] Symbol

The [ə] or *schwa* sound occurs in syllables without an accent. It can be spelled with any vowel, such as **a** in above, **e** in listen, **i** in pencil, **o** in melon, **u** in circus. It can also be a combination of vowels, such as **io** in action, **ai** in mountain, **iou** in precious.

(Turn the page for more information.)

science writing Scientists use exact words to name things, and the meaning of words is strictly controlled. For example, *mammal* and *vertebrate* have a single precise meaning in science, but *animal* does not. Scientists limit most of their writing to facts or factual procedures. They describe their research thoroughly and don't leave out any steps. How can these "scientific principles" be used by student writers? Vocabulary: Many science words are not familiar to the general reader. Explain your terms: "Others, like clams and oysters, are placed in a natural *estuary*, an area where the ocean extends into the mouth of a river." (Paul Brandwein) Facts: Be factual without being dull. For example, in discussing tigers it's not absurd to mention house cats. Detail: Don't just pile on details for the sake of "proof." For example, if you've said mammals are warm-blooded, it's not necessary to repeat this every time you mention a bear, a whale, or a deer.

of things in nature and in the universe, along with the forces that affect these things. Science consists of facts, which are based on experiments and careful observation, and also theories, in which a group of facts are combined to provide an explanation of something. **2.** a particular area of science, such as biology, chemistry, or physics. **3.** something thought of as like a science, as by being exact or carefully studied: The great baseball player Ted Williams wrote a book called *The Science of Hitting.*

sci•en•tif•ic [sī/ ən tif′ ik] *adjective, more/ most.* **1.** having to do with science: The fact that germs cause disease was an important *scientific* discovery. **2.** showing or using the methods or rules of science: That company takes a *scientific* approach to selling by testing people's reaction to each product. —**scientifically,** *adverb.*

sci•en•tist [sī/ ən tist] *noun, plural* **scientists.** a person who works in an area of science or who knows a great deal about science.

scis•sors [siz′ ərz] *plural noun.* a tool for cutting that is made up of two sharp blades that close against each other.

scold [skōld] *verb,* **scolded, scolding.** to blame someone with angry words; find fault with: The father *scolded* his son for running into the street without looking.

scoop [skoop] *noun, plural* **scoops.** a tool shaped like a bowl with a handle, used for shoveling or dipping. —*verb,* **scooped, scooping.** to take something with a scoop: to *scoop* ice cream out of a container.

scoot•er [skoo′ tər] *noun, plural* **scooters.** a toy that has a handlebar attached to a board with wheels on the bottom. The rider stands on the scooter and pushes it with one foot.

scope [skōp] *noun.* the area covered by an idea or action: The chairman said that to change the rules was outside the *scope* of their committee.

scorch [skôrch] *verb,* **scorched, scorching. 1.** to burn just slightly on the surface: The iron was

too hot and Laurie *scorched* her blouse. **2.** to be very hot: "During six *scorching* weeks of July and August . . ." (Studs Terkel) —*noun, plural* **scorches.** a slight burn; a surface burn.

score [skôr] *noun, plural* **scores. 1.** a set of numbers or points used to show how one person or thing compares with others in a game, contest, or test: We won the baseball game by a *score* of 4-2. **2.** written music that shows the parts for the musicians. **3.** a wrong or injury that must be taken care of. ◆ Usually used in the phrase **a score to settle. 4.** an older word for a group of twenty: Four *score* means four twenties, or eighty. **5.** a large number; a crowd: "All of these men, *scores* of them, dressed in red suits, big black belts, typing-paper white beards . . ." (Ishmael Reed) —*verb,* **scored, scoring. 1.** to have or record a certain score: Julie *scored* ten points in the basketball game. **2.** to cut lines or make marks on something.

scorn [skôrn] *noun.* a feeling that someone or something is very bad or of very low quality; a complete lack of respect. —*verb,* **scorned, scorning.** to treat with scorn; look down on. —**scornful,** *adjective.* —**scornfully,** *adverb.*

scorpion The sting of the scorpion can be extremely painful, but is not deadly.

scor•pi•on [skôr′ pē ən] *noun, plural* **scorpions.** a small animal related to the spider. Scorpions have a long tail with a poisonous stinger and a jointed body with powerful claws on the front legs. They are found mainly in hot, dry areas of the southwestern U.S. and Mexico.

Scotland [skät′lənd] a former country that is now part of Great Britain, located north of England. *Capital:* Edinburgh. *Area:* 30,400 square miles. *Population:* 5,100,000. —**Scottish** or **Scotch,** *adjective; noun.* —**Scot,** *noun.*

Scotland Dunnottar Castle, near the city of Stonehaven, on the east coast of Scotland.

scour[1] [skour] *verb,* **scoured, scouring.** to polish or clean by scrubbing: He *scoured* the dirty pan with a pad of steel wool.

scour[2] *verb,* **scoured, scouring.** to move over or through in a careful search: "We have been out most of the night *scouring* the countryside for signs of Odessa." (Sherley Anne Williams)

scout [skout] *noun, plural* **scouts. 1.** a member of an army unit who is sent out to get information, as about the nature of the land ahead, the location of the enemy, and so on: Kit Carson was a famous *scout* for the U.S. Army in Indian country. **2.** a person in sports who seeks out advance information, as about talented new players, the strategy of opposing teams, and so on. **3.** a member of the Girl Scouts or the Boy Scouts. —*verb,* **scouted, scouting.** to act as a scout: Football teams often send someone to *scout* the team they will play the following week.

scout•mas•ter [skout′mas′tər] *noun, plural* **scoutmasters.** the person in charge of a Boy Scout troop.

scowl [skoul] *noun, plural* **scowls.** an angry expression; a deep frown. —*verb,* **scowled, scowling.** to make an angry expression.

scram•ble [skram′bəl] *verb,* **scrambled, scrambling. 1.** to move quickly by climbing or crawling: "The lizards *scrambled* from shadow to shadow." (Saul Bellow) ◆ A quarterback in football is said to *scramble* when he moves around quickly in the backfield to avoid tacklers as he is trying to pass. **2.** to struggle to get something first: The children *scrambled* for the hidden Easter eggs. **3.** to mix or stir things together: Bill *scrambled* up the names in the hat for the contest. **4.** to cook eggs by stirring them together in a frying pan, blending the yolks and whites. —*noun.* the act or fact of scrambling.

scrap [skrap] *noun, plural* **scraps. 1.** a small piece or amount; a bit: She wrote the phone number down on a *scrap* of paper. **2.** something that is thrown away but may be used by someone else; a used item: When an old car no longer runs, its parts may be sold for *scrap.* **3. scraps.** bits of leftover food from a meal: to feed a dog *scraps.* **4.** *Informal.* a fight or quarrel. —*verb,* **scrapped, scrapping. 1.** to break up for use as scrap: Many old warships were *scrapped* by the Navy after World War II. **2.** give up something as useless or unwanted: The company decided to *scrap* the plan and start all over.

scrap•book [skrap′book′] *noun, plural* **scrapbooks.** a book with blank pages to which newspaper clippings, photos, and other such items can be attached.

scrape [skrāp] *verb,* **scraped, scraping. 1.** to damage or remove the surface of something by rubbing or scratching it: I *scraped* my elbow when I fell on the sidewalk. **2.** to make a harsh, unpleasant sound by rubbing or dragging something over a surface: He likes to annoy the teacher by *scraping* his chalk on the blackboard. **3.** to clean or smooth a surface by rubbing it against something: We *scraped* the mud off our shoes before going inside. **4.** to gather or collect something with difficulty: They just barely *scraped* together the money to pay this month's rent. —*noun, plural* **scrapes. 1.** the act of scraping, or the damage caused by this. **2.** *Informal.* a bad situation; a problem: to get in a *scrape* at school. ◆ A **scraper** is a tool that scrapes off paint or smooths a surface.

scratch [skrach] *verb,* **scratched, scratching. 1.** to cut, dig, or scrape a shallow mark with a

---

Pronunciation Key: Accent Marks

[′] is the normal accent mark. It shows where the main stress falls on a word.
[′] is a secondary accent mark. It shows a lighter stress than the primary accent. For example:

tel • e • vis • ion [tel′ə vizh′ən]
(Turn the page for more information.)

S

S

sharp, pointed object: She *scratched* her arm on a thorn while picking a rose. **2.** to rub or scrape the skin when it itches: The doctor told me not to *scratch* my poison ivy rash or it might get worse. **3.** to make a sound when rubbing or scraping something: He heard the dog *scratching* at the back door to get in. **4.** to remove or cancel: The runner had to be *scratched* from the race when he hurt his leg in the warmups. —*noun, plural* **scratches. 1.** a mark made by scratching. **2. from scratch.** *Informal.* from nothing; from the beginning: My grandmother doesn't make cake from a packaged mix; she starts *from scratch.* —**scratchy,** *adjective.*

scrawl [skrôl] *verb,* **scrawled, scrawling.** to write in a messy or hurried way: "She discovered two more addresses which were hastily *scrawled* over other numbers . . ." (Agatha Christie)

scraw•ny [skrô′nē] *adjective,* **scrawnier, scrawniest.** very thin; bony; skinny.

scream [skrēm] *verb,* **screamed, screaming.** to cry out with a sudden, loud, and high-pitched sound, usually in fright or in pain. —*noun, plural* **screams.** a sudden, loud sound or cry.

screech [skrēch] *verb,* **screeched, screeching.** to make a loud, shrill sound. —*noun, plural* **screeches:** the *screech* of tropical birds in a zoo.

screen [skrēn] *noun, plural* **screens. 1.** a frame holding wire netting, placed in a window or door to allow air in but keep insects from entering. **2.** a similar pattern of wire used to cover or protect something: Fireplaces often have a *screen* to keep sparks from flying out into the room. **3.** a curtain, wall, or frame used to separate or hide part of a room: In his office the file cabinets are behind a colorful Chinese *screen.* **4.** anything that acts like a screen to cover or hide something: "A thick *screen* of low cloud hid the moon and stars." (Ken Follett) **5.** a flat surface that reflects light, used to show movies or slides. **6.** the glass surface on a television set or computer where the images

appear. **7.** the movie business: a star of stage and *screen.* —*verb,* **screened, screening. 1.** to protect, hide, or shade with a screen: a house with a *screened* porch. **2.** to separate carefully, as if sifting through a wire screen: The secretary *screens* the boss's phone calls so that he'll only get the important ones.

screw [skrōō] *noun, plural* **screws.** a type of nail with a ridge that winds around its length. It is twisted into things to hold them together. A screw is usually turned by a SCREWDRIVER that fits into a slot in the head of the screw and pushes it into wood, metal, or other materials. —*verb,* **screwed, screwing. 1.** to join materials together with a screw. **2.** to tighten something with a twist or turn: Dean *screwed* the lid back on the jar. "She *screwed* up her eyes slightly as she faced the sun." (Kingsley Amis)

screw•driv•er [skrōō′drī′vər] *noun, plural* **screwdrivers.** a tool that turns the head of a screw.

scrib•ble [skrib′əl] *verb,* **scribbled, scribbling.** to draw or write in a quick, sloppy way. —*noun, plural* **scribbles.** The baby put *scribbles* all over my homework paper.

scribes In the Middle Ages, *scribes* did most of the writing for the whole society. *(Scribe comes from the Latin word meaning "to write.")* A number of scribes would work together in a *scriptorium,* or writing room. In a society where few people could read, the scribe was an important person—a keeper of treasures. Medieval scribes prepared new versions of famous books, such as the Bible or the great writings of ancient Greece and Rome. The scribes, in fact, made writing easier to read, even though they lived among very few readers. The Romans had used only capital letters, and they did not put punctuation or spacing between words. The scribes introduced lower-case letters, and also began the practice of putting spaces and punctuation marks after words.

scribe [skrīb] *noun, plural* **scribes.** in earlier times, a person who wrote or copied books and other writing by hand.

scribe Jean Mielot, a 15th-century French scribe.

scrim•mage [skrim′ ij] *noun, plural* **scrimmag-es. 1.** in sports, a practice game in the form of actual play. **2. line of scrimmage.** in football, the imaginary line that separates the two teams as they line up before a play.

> **scripts** A *script* is spoken by the actors in a play or movie or TV show. Certain style rules apply in scriptwriting. The name of the character who speaks always comes before the lines to be spoken. When a new character speaks, a new line begins. The character's name is set off by being in all capital letters, or else in black type, and the name is followed by a colon or a period. Scripts consist entirely of dialogue, except for two things: (1) *Stage directions* note how the actors should move on stage: (WILLY *enters*) (WILLY *moves left*) (2) *Acting directions* tell the actor how to read a certain line: WILLY (*with a big smile*) WILLY (FURIOUSLY) Note that both stage and acting directions are set off from the dialogue by parentheses: WILLY (*with increasing anger*): Howard, all I need to set my table is fifty dollars a week. (All examples are from Arthur Miller's *Death of a Salesman.*)

script [skript] *noun, plural* **scripts. 1.** a type of handwriting in which the letters are connected, as opposed to being separated as in printing. **2.** the written lines of a play, movie, television show, or other such spoken performance.

Scripture [skrip′ chər] *noun, plural* **Scriptures. 1.** *also,* **(the) Scriptures.** the Bible or a passage from the Bible. **2. scripture.** a holy book of another religion.

scroll [skrōl] *noun, plural* **scrolls.** a written piece of paper or parchment that is rolled up: The Dead Sea *Scrolls* are an ancient version of the early books of the Bible. —*verb,* **scrolled, scrolling.** in a computer, to search for information by using the controls to view different areas of a document.

scrub [skrub] *verb,* **scrubbed, scrubbing.** to rub hard or roughly, as in cleaning or drying something: June had to *scrub* the pan to get the burnt oatmeal off. —*noun.* the act of scrubbing.

scruff [skruf] *noun, plural* **scruffs.** the back part of the neck, or the loose skin that covers it.

scru•pu•lous [skroo′ pyə ləs] *adjective, more/most.* following what is right or what should be done; very careful and honest: "Gawain, the chief, made his round not once daily but twice, checking the treasures with *scrupulous* care." (William Steig) —**scrupulously,** *adverb.*

scu•ba [skoo′ bə] *noun.* the special air tanks worn by divers and swimmers for breathing under water. ◆ This word is an ACRONYM, formed from the words *s*elf-*c*ontained *u*nderwa-ter *b*reathing *a*pparatus.

scuff [skuf] *verb,* **scuffed, scuffing.** to scrape or scratch a surface: Max *scuffed* his new shoes by playing kickball on the playground.

scuf•fle [skuf′ əl] —*noun, plural* **scuffles.** a sud-den, confused fight or struggle, usually not long or serious: "But after a few noisy *scuffles* in which he knocked a picture off a wall, scratched the piano . . ." (Jean Kerr) —*verb,* **scuffled, scuffling.** to fight or struggle in this way.

sculp•tor [skulp′ tər] *noun, plural* **sculptors.** an artist who makes sculptures.

sculp•ture [skulp′ chər] *noun, plural* **sculp-tures. 1.** the art of making figures or designs out of stone, wood, metal, or other such materials. Sculpture is made by carving, molding, or otherwise changing the shape of the material into artwork. **2.** a piece of artwork made in this way, such as a statue. —*verb,* **sculptured, sculpturing.** to make figures or designs out of materials. ◆ The verb form is usually **sculpt.**

scum [skum] *noun.* a thin layer of material that rises to or forms on the surface of a liquid: *Scum* will form on still pond water.

scur•ry [skur′ ē] *verb,* **scurried, scurrying.** to move or run quickly; hurry: "Presently we heard his voice roaring orders and the *scurrying* of feet to obey them." (Rachel Field)

scur•vy [skur′ vē] *noun.* a disease caused by a diet that does not have enough vitamin C. This illness causes the person to have swollen and bleeding gums and to become weak. In former times, sailors on long sea voyages sometimes died from scurvy because they did not have fruits and vegetables on board to eat.

scut•tle [skut′ əl] *verb,* **scuttled, scuttling.** to move with quick, short motions: "A large gray rat *scuttled* around the corner of the house . . ." (Madeleine L' Engle)

Pronunciation Key: A–F			
a	and; hat	ch	chew; such
ā	ate; stay	d	dog; lid
â	care; air	e	end; yet
ä	father; hot	ē	she; each
b	boy; cab	f	fun; off

(Turn the page for more information.)

S

scythe [sīth] *noun, plural* **scythes.** a tool with a long handle and a long, curved blade, used to cut grasses or clear weeds.

sea [sē] *noun, plural* **seas. 1.** *also,* **the sea.** the large body of salt water that covers about three-fourths of the earth's surface; the ocean. **2.** the name of certain parts of this area of water: the Black *Sea*, the Caribbean *Sea*. **3.** the waves or heavy swell of the ocean: The fishing boat was made to stand up to rough *seas*. **4.** a great number; a huge amount: "He kept his eyes on the *sea* of black and white faces." (Richard Wright)

sea a•nem•o•ne [ə nem′ ə nē] a sea animal with a flexible body shaped like a tube and a mouth that is surrounded by many highly-colored, flowerlike tentacles.

sea•board [sē′ bôrd′] *noun, plural* **seaboards.** the land or region along or near the sea; also called the **seacoast.**

sea•food [sē′ fo͞od′] *noun, plural* **seafoods.** a fish or shellfish eaten as food.

sea gull (also spelled **seagull**) any gull that lives at or near the sea.

sea horse The male sea horse has a special pouch in its belly used to hatch the eggs passed by the female.

sea horse a type of fish with a head that looks something like a horse's head, and a curved tail that it uses to hang onto ocean plants.

seal[1] [sēl] *noun, plural* **seals.** a large animal having flippers and sleek shiny fur, found in cold ocean waters. Seals are mammals; they live mainly in the water and rest on land. The fur of seals is used to make expensive clothing.

seal[2] *noun, plural* **seals. 1.** a design on a mold or stamp that is pressed into ink, wax, paper, or other materials: In former times, a king or other ruler would put his *seal* on a letter to show that it was official. **2.** any similar design or mark of authority: Each U.S. state has an official state *seal*. **3.** something that keeps things tightly closed: Bottles of medicine come with a plastic *seal* around the cap. —*verb,* **sealed, sealing. 1.** to close or fasten tightly: The pipe was *sealed* to make sure water would not leak out. "Finally the bell became quiet . . . and their small world was *sealed* in silence." (Marguerite Henry) **2.** to put an official seal or stamp on.

sea level a measurement of the surface of the sea that is taken halfway between high tide and low tide. All measurements of the height or features of the earth are figured from sea level.

sea lion a very large seal that lives in the Pacific Ocean.

seam [sēm] *noun, plural* **seams. 1.** the line that is made when two pieces of cloth or other material are sewn together. **2.** any line like this where two things or parts come together, as in the hull of a ship. **3.** a line or layer of mineral in the earth: a *seam* of coal. —*verb,* **seamed, seaming.** to join together in a seam; make a seam.

sea•man [sē′ mən] *noun, plural* **seamen. 1.** a person who works on a ship; a sailor. **2.** a sailor in a navy who is not an officer. ◆ The ability to handle a ship at sea is called **seamanship.**

seam•stress [sēm′ stris] *noun, plural* **seamstresses.** a woman whose work is sewing, especially one who sews clothing.

sea•port [sē′ pôrt′] *noun, plural* **seaports.** a city on or near the ocean, with a harbor for ships; also called a **port.**

seal Three types of seals. The elephant seal (above), the harbor seal (center), and the northern fur seal (below).

search [surch] *verb*, **searched, searching.** to look carefully to find something; go over closely: "We *searched* high and low, but could find no sign of the man." (Robert Benchley) "On occasion he'd fool around with the piano . . . *searching* for new ways to express what was inside him." (Studs Terkel) —*noun, plural* **searches.** the act or fact of searching. —**searcher,** *noun.*

search·light [surch´līt´] *noun, plural* **searchlights.** a very large light that gives off a powerful beam, and that may be moved to shine in different directions for searching or signaling.

sea·shore [sē´shôr´] *noun, plural* **seashores.** the place where the land and sea meet.

sea·sick [sē´sik´] *adjective, more/most.* ill and dizzy from the rocking motion of a ship at sea.

sea·son [sē´zən] *noun, plural* **seasons. 1.** one of the four parts of the year; spring, summer, autumn, or winter. **2.** any period of time thought of as a separate part of the year: the baseball *season*, the hunting *season*, the harvest

seat·belt [sēt´belt´] *noun, plural* **seatbelts.** a strap or set of straps holding a person in place in the seat of a car, airplane, or other such moving vehicle, to help prevent injury in the case of an accident, bump, or sudden stop. ◆ Also called a **safety belt.**

Se·at·tle [sē at´əl] a city in northwestern Washington State, on Puget Sound. *Population:* 494,000.

sea·weed [sē´wēd´] *noun.* a general name for the many kinds of plants that grow in the ocean.

se·cede [si sēd´] *verb*, **seceded, seceding.** to withdraw officially from an organization: The Civil War came about when eleven Southern states *seceded* to form the Confederate States of America. —**secession** [si sesh´ən], *noun.*

se·clud·ed [si klōōd´id] *adjective, more/most.* **1.** alone or away from others; isolated: For many years the former movie star Greta Garbo led a *secluded* life, refusing to appear in public. **2.** hidden from view; private: We drove to a *secluded* spot in the woods for our picnic.

S

second person *You* had a cigarette while the man prayed, and all *you* could think of was what it would be like if *you* could throw away everything *you'd* ever done wrong . . ." (Jimmy Breslin) Ordinarily, when writers use the second-person pronoun *you*, they are referring to the reader. But in this case, it was the writer, Breslin, who smoked the cigarette and thought the thought. By using *you*, he placed the reader (you) right at the scene. Sportswriter Jimmy Cannon wrote whole columns in this style: "*Your* name is Sugar Ray Robinson. People call *you* the greatest fighter in the world . . ." Usually, though, second-person writing is limited to one part of a story. Ernest Hemingway's "In Another Country" is told in the first person. But it also has this passage: "Always, though, *you* crossed a bridge across the canal to enter the hospital. There was a choice of three bridges. On one of them a woman sold roasted chestnuts. It was warm, standing in front of her charcoal fire, and the chestnuts were warm afterward in *your* pocket."

season. —*verb*, **seasoned, seasoning.** to add spices or flavoring to food: The cooking of India is known for highly *seasoned* foods.

sea·son·ing [sē´zən ing] *noun, plural* **seasonings.** something that adds flavor to food, such as salt or pepper.

seat [sēt] *noun, plural* **seats. 1.** a place to sit on, such as a chair or bench. **2.** the part of the body that a person sits on, or the clothing that covers that part. **3.** a position as a member of a group or organization, thought of as a place where one sits: In this year's elections the Democrats gained three *seats* in the Senate. **4.** a special place that is the center of something: São Paolo is Brazil's largest city, but Brasilia is the *seat* of government. —*verb*, **seated, seating. 1.** to be taken to or placed on a seat. **2.** to have seats for: The school bus *seats* 63 people.

sec·ond¹ [sek´ənd] *adjective.* **1.** next after the first: *second* place in a race. **2.** below the first: Gene was on the *second* team in football. —*adverb.* coming after the first; next. —*noun, plural* **seconds. 1.** a person or thing that is next. **2.** a person who helps or supports another: A fighter in a boxing match is assisted by *seconds*. —*verb*, **seconded, seconding.** in a meeting, to support a motion or nomination so that it can be voted on. —**secondly,** *adverb.*

Pronunciation Key: G–N

g	give; big	k	kind; cat; back
h	hold	l	let; ball
i	it; this	m	make; time
ī	ice; my	n	not; own
j	jet; gem; edge	ng	having

(Turn the page for more information.)

second² *noun, plural* **seconds. 1.** a small unit of time. Sixty seconds equal one minute. **2.** any short period of time: Wait a *second* for me.

sec•ond•ar•y [sek′ ən der′ e] *adjective.* **1.** coming after the first; next in order, place, or time: Many *secondary* colors can be made by blending the primary colors red, yellow, and blue. **2.** not as important as the first or main thing: That's a *secondary* issue that will be discussed after the main meeting.

secondary school another name for **high school.**

sec•ond•hand *adjective.* having been used before; owned first by another: a *secondhand* car.

se•cre•cy [sē′ krə sē] *noun.* the fact of being secret or of keeping a secret: The plans for the D-Day attack in World War II were carried out in complete *secrecy.* ◆ A person who always wants to keep things secret is **secretive.**

se•cret [sē′ krit] *noun, plural* **secrets. 1.** information that is kept hidden and known only by one person or by a few: Want to know a *secret?* My parents got Billy a new bike for Christmas. **2.** a hidden reason or cause: This book claims to explain the *secret* of success in selling real estate. —*adjective, more/most.* known only to one person or a few; kept from most people: The spy sent the message in *secret* code so that the enemy could not read it. —**secretly,** *adverb.*

se•crete [si krēt′] *verb,* **secreted, secreting.** of an animal or plant, to give off a liquid from some part of the body: The stomach *secretes* certain juices to digest food. —**secretion,** *noun.*

sec•re•tar•y [sek′ rə ter′ ē] *noun, plural* **secretaries. 1.** a person in business whose job is to assist another person by doing such work as typing letters, answering the telephone, keeping records, and running office machines. ◆ The work done by a secretary is **secretarial** work. **2.** a person in a club or other organization who keeps the records of the group. **3.** a person who is officially in charge of a department of government: the *Secretary* of Defense. **4.** a piece of furniture with a surface to write on and drawers and shelves for papers and books. ◆ *Secretary* is related to *secret.* In early times, a secretary was a king's officer who dealt with secret papers and records.

sect [sekt] *noun, plural* **sects.** a smaller group within a larger religion, having certain special customs or beliefs: The Coptic Church of Egypt is a *sect* of the Christian Church.

sec•tion [sek′ shən] *noun, plural* **sections. 1.** one part of a whole thing: the *sections* of an orange or a grapefruit. **2.** a part of something that is written: She reads the food *section* of the newspaper to find new recipes. **3.** one certain part of a larger place: the business *section* of a city. —*verb,* **sectioned, sectioning.** to cut or separate into parts; divide. —**sectional,** *adjective; noun.*

sec•tor [sek′ tər] *noun, plural* **sectors.** a section or area: The city of Berlin is divided into West German and East German *sectors.*

sec•u•lar [sek′ yə lər] *adjective.* having to do with matters of the earth and mankind, rather than with God and religion: The mayor reacted to Father Murray's criticism of him by saying that priests should not comment on *secular* matters.

se•cure [si kyoor′] *adjective, more/most.* **1.** safe or protected against danger or loss: Castles of the Middle Ages had high walls to make them *secure* against attack. **2.** not likely to give way; firmly fastened; steady: Be careful on that ladder; it doesn't look too *secure.* **3.** free from fear or worry: It gave her a *secure* feeling to be safe inside the house on such a cold, stormy night. —*verb,* **secured, securing. 1.** to make secure: "He shut the door after him, and *secured* it with two bolts and a padlock." (Paul Theroux) **2.** to get, especially through some effort: to *secure* an appointment to the Air Force Academy.

se•cu•ri•ty [si kyoor′ ə tē] *noun, plural* **securities. 1.** the fact of being secure; protection against danger or loss: For the sake of *security,* she always keeps some extra money set aside in a separate bank account. **2.** the fact of protecting against attack, violence, crime, and so on: Very tight *security* will be in effect when the President visits the United Nations. ◆ Often used as an adjective: a *security* guard. **3.** property that is offered to make a loan secure, with the condition that if the money is not paid back the lender will gain ownership of the property. **4. securities.** stocks, bonds, or other such investments.

se•dan [si dan′] *noun, plural* **sedans.** a name for the standard design of an automobile body, with two or four doors, a front and back seat, a permanent roof, and a trunk.

sed•i•ment [sed′ ə mənt] *noun, plural* **sediments.** small pieces of matter that settle at the bottom of a liquid: There were dead leaves and other *sediment* at the bottom of the lake.

see [sē] *verb,* **saw, seen, seeing. 1.** to sense with the eyes; look at: Don't stand in front of the TV like that; I can't *see* the screen. **2.** to be able to use this sense: Grandpa can *see* much better with his new glasses. **3.** to sense with the mind;

S

understand: You don't have to explain; I *see* what you mean. **4.** to find out: Here's a new kind of soda—try it and *see* how you like it. **5.** to visit or meet: "The doctor will *see* you now," the nurse told her. **6.** to make sure: "Please try to *see* that the steak is rare and gets here hot." (James Gould Cozzens)

basketball game was a *seesaw* battle, with the lead changing between the two teams every few minutes. —*verb*, **seesawed, seesawing.** to move up and down on or as if on a seesaw.

seethe [sēth] *verb*, **seethed, seething.** to be very excited or angry: *Seething* with rage, he stormed out and slammed the door behind him.

> **seen/saw** The difference between these two verbs may seem obvious, but it's a serious mistake to confuse them. *Seen* and *saw* are both past forms of *see*. *Saw* is the form for the past tense: "I know he was at the baseball tryouts. I *saw* him there myself." The error that people make is to use *seen* in place of *saw*: "I *seen* him there myself." *Seen* is the past participle form. It has to be used with a form of BE or HAVE: "He's a Giants' fan; he'd never *be seen* in a Dodger cap." "I know he practices hitting at the batting cages because I've *seen* him there several times." You could say either "I *saw* him there several times" or "I *have seen* him there several times."

seed [sēd] *noun*, *plural* **seeds** or **seed. 1.** the part of a plant that can grow into a new plant. **2.** something thought of as being like a seed, because it is the source or beginning point: He had thought it was a good idea, but what she said planted *seeds* of doubt in his mind. —*verb*, **seeded, seeding. 1.** to plant land with seeds; sow: Chris *seeded* the back yard for a new lawn. **2.** to remove seeds from: to *seed* a watermelon.

seek [sēk] *verb*, **sought, seeking. 1.** to try to find; search for: "It was hot enough now to make us *seek* the shade." (Evelyn Waugh) **2.** to try to get or have: "Dear Prince, you must leave this castle at once and go *seek* your fortune in the wide world." (C. S. Lewis) **3.** to ask for; desire: Many people *seek* his advice on financial matters. —**seeker,** *noun*: "He started on the adventure trail by following the gold *seekers* to Alaska." (Ernie Pyle)

seem [sēm] *verb*, **seemed, seeming. 1.** to appear to be; look like: "Years of harsh work had made him *seem* older than he was." (John R. Tunis) **2.** to appear to be true; appear to exist: Something *seems* to be bothering you. Are you all right? **3.** to appear to oneself: I'm sorry; I *seem* to have forgotten your name. —**seemingly,** *adverb*. as far as one can tell; as it seems.

seen [sēn] *verb*. the past participle of **see.**

seep [sēp] *verb*, **seeped, seeping.** to spread or flow slowly: "(She) pushed an old towel against the bottom of the door to keep the water from *seeping* in." (J. M. Coetzee) "A little light *seeps* in dustily through cracks in the boards . . ." (Ursula K. LeGuin)

see•saw [sē′sô′] *noun*, *plural* **seesaws. 1.** a device used by children for play, made of a long board balanced in the middle so that when one end goes up the other goes down. **2.** a movement back and forth like that of a seesaw: The

seg•ment [seg′mənt] *noun*, *plural* **segments.** one of the parts into which a whole is or can be divided; a division or section: An insect's body is made up of three *segments*.

seg•re•ga•te [seg′rə gāt′] *verb*, **segregated, segregating.** to set apart from others: In that prison the most dangerous prisoners are *segregated* from the others. ♦ Often used as an adjective: Under a *segregated* school system, blacks and whites go to separate schools.

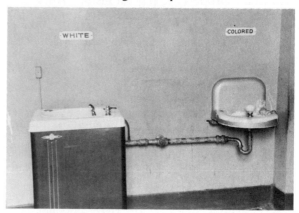

segregation When segregation was an official policy in the American South, black people (then called "colored") had to drink from a separate water fountain.

seg•re•ga•tion [seg′rə gā′shən] *noun*. the act or fact of separating, especially the separation of one racial group from another.

Pronunciation Key: O–S			
ō	over; go	ou	out; town
ô	all; law	p	put; hop
oo	look; full	r	run; car
o͞o	pool; who	s	set; miss
oi	oil; boy	sh	show

(Turn the page for more information.)

self The *self* pronouns (*myself, yourself, themselves,* and so on) are known as *reflexives.* A reflexive pronoun *reflects,* or looks back on, another word in the sentence: "Since Mom's sick *you'll* have to fix lunch for *yourself.*" Remember that *self* words reflect another word; they don't replace the word. Don't use *myself* in place of *I* or *me:* "Please send two tickets. My wife and *myself* both plan to attend." This should be "My wife and I . . ." "Please reserve two seats, one for Mrs. Brewer and one for *myself.*" This should be ". . . one for me." In these sentences, there is no earlier noun or pronoun for *myself* to connect with, so it's incorrect. *Self* can also appear as a prefix: "She enclosed a *self-addressed* envelope so that the refund could be mailed back to her." Notice that when *self* begins a word as it does in this example, it's spelled with a hyphen: *self-addressed.*

seis•mo•graph [sīz mə graf′] *noun, plural* **seismographs.** an instrument that records when and where an earthquake happens and how strong it is.

seize [sēz] *verb,* **seized, seizing. 1.** to take hold of suddenly; grab: "Cranly *seized* his arm and steered him round so as to head back towards Leeson Park." (James Joyce) **2.** to take by force or authority; capture: "We don't want our belongings to be *seized* by the Germans . . ." (Anne Frank)

sei•zure [sē′ zhər] *noun, plural* **seizures. 1.** the act of seizing: The court ordered a *seizure* of the man's property to pay off his tax debts. **2.** a sudden loss of control of the body: Epilepsy is a disease of the brain that causes violent *seizures.*

sel•dom [sel′ dəm] *adverb.* not often; rarely: "The pond Sam had discovered . . . was *seldom* visited by any human being." (E. B. White)

se•lect [si lekt′] *verb,* **selected, selecting.** to pick out from a group as the best or most fitting; choose: The teacher has to *select* someone to be the reader for the school play. —*adjective, more/ most.* **1.** picked or chosen specially: The Navy names a *select* group of men to train as fighter pilots. **2.** careful in choosing; exclusive: Harvard and Stanford are *select* colleges that admit only students with very high grades.

self [self] *noun, plural* **selves.** one's own person apart from all others: Dave is finally out of bed and feeling like his old *self* again.

self- a PREFIX meaning: "of, for, or by oneself or itself:" A *self-cleaning* oven is one that can be heated hot enough to clean itself. ◆ Among the common *self-* compounds are: **self-confident, self-conscious, self-control, self-defense, self-discipline, self-employed, self-government, self-help, self-interest, self-pity, self-respect, self-service, self-sufficient.**

sel•fish [sel′ fish] *adjective, more/most.* caring too much about one's own needs; acting to help oneself without regard for others: Even though she didn't want to read the magazine herself, she was too *selfish* to let her brother borrow it. —**selfishly,** *adverb.* —**selfishness,** *noun.*

sell [sel] *verb,* **sold, selling. 1.** to turn an item over to someone else in return for money: Barry *sold* his old car to his cousin for $1500. **2.** to offer a certain item in this way: a store that *sells* toys, a shirt that *sells* for $20. **3.** *Informal.* to agree to or approve of: The boss is really *sold* on that idea and wants to put it into action right away. **4. sell out.** to act in a disloyal way.

seller [sel′ ər] *noun, plural* **sellers. 1.** a person who sells something: The *seller* of the house met with the buyer's lawyer. **2.** a product that sells in a certain way: a book that is a best*seller.*

selection of words Here's a real-life illustration of how important it is to select your words carefully. When the marine park Sea World of Texas was planned, it was to include a walk along which 17 statues of famous Texans would stand. These were created by sculptors paid by Sea World. Someone wrote a draft of a brochure and called the statues "masterpieces." When told that works never yet seen could hardly be called that, the person changed the wording to "reproductions." What was their status? They were "commissioned, original works of art." Precision does count!

se•lec•tion [si lek′ shən] *noun, plural* **selections. 1.** the selecting of something; choice: The President made his *selection* of the people to serve in his Cabinet. **2.** a person or thing to be chosen.

selves [selvz] *noun.* the plural of **self.**

se•mes•ter [si mes′ tər] *noun, plural* **semesters.** one of the two terms into which a school year is divided. ◆ A school year can also be divided into three terms called **trimesters.**

S

semi- a PREFIX meaning: **1.** "partly; not completely:" That part of California is a *semi*desert area. **2.** "twice:" A *semi*annual event happens twice a year.

sem•i•cir•cle [sem′ ē sur′ kəl] *noun, plural* **semicircles.** half a circle.

---

semicolons These things usually apply in the use of a semicolon: (1) Each sentence part is complete in itself: "It was still raining outside in the street: a mild, gray, endless rain." (Carson McCullers) Note that the mark there is a *colon.* "A mild, gray endless rain" is not complete; it has no verb. (2) The parts are fairly short: "He held a pistol; he rose and faced the house." (William Faulkner) (3) The parts are closely related in thought, and show some contrast: "A train whistle caused him to lift his head. It was on time; he had hoped it would be late." (John Updike) (4) There is no connecting word such as *or, and,* or *but:* "His head knocked against something; a sharp pain dizzied him . . . .He was without light, *and* the water seemed to press upon him with the weight of rock." (Doris Lessing) Notice that when *and* appears in the second sentence, the mark is a comma.

---

sem•i•colon [sem′ ē kō′ lən] *noun, plural* **semicolons.** a mark of punctuation (;). It shows a greater break in thought than a comma, but less than a period.

sem•i•con•duc•tor [sem′ ē kən duk′ tər] *noun, plural* **semiconductors.** a material such as silicon, that conducts electricity much better when it is heated. Semiconductors are widely used in TV sets, radios, and computers.

sem•i•nar [sem′ ə när′] *noun, plural* **seminars. 1.** a small class or group of advanced students, as at a university, doing special study or research. **2.** a meeting for exchanging and discussing some kind of specialized information: Larry went to a *seminar* to learn more about the new computer his company would be using.

sem•i•nar•y [sem′ ə ner′ ē] *noun, plural* **seminaries.** a school that trains students to be priests, ministers, or rabbis.

Sem•i•nole [sem′ ə nōl′] *noun, plural* **Seminoles.** a member of a tribe of North American Indians that live in Florida and Oklahoma.

sen•ate [sen′ it] *noun, plural* **senates.** (usually **Senate**) **1.** the upper house of the United States Congress. The Senate has 100 members, two from each of the 50 states. **2.** the upper and smaller branch of a state legislature in the United States. **3.** any similar lawmaking or governing body: Student affairs at this college are managed by the Student *Senate.*

sen•a•tor [sen′ ə tər] *noun, plural* **senators. 1.** a member of a senate. **2. Senator.** a member of the United States Senate. **—senatorial** [sen′ ə tôr′ ē əl], *adjective.*

send [send] *verb,* **sent, sending. 1.** to cause a thing to move from one place to another: to *send* a letter to a friend. The fountain *sent* streams of water high in the air. **2.** to cause a person to go: He was *sent* off the field for arguing with the referee. **3.** to cause a certain feeling or condition: to *send* someone into a rage. Hearing the good news *sent* her spirits soaring. **—sender,** *noun.*

sen•ior [sēn′ yər] *adjective.* **1.** the older of two people with the same name: John Smith, *Senior,* and his son John, Junior. **2.** having higher rank or longer service: The *senior* Senator from a state is the one who has served longer in office. ♦ The fact of having this rank is **seniority** [sēn′ yôr′ ə tē]. **3.** having to do with the last year of high school or college. **—noun, plural** **seniors. 1.** a person who is older than another: Jim has one brother, who's his *senior* by four years. **2.** a student in the last year of high school or college.

senior citizen an older person, especially one who is retired from work.

Senate The meeting place of the U.S. Senate in the Capitol Building in Washington, D.C.

Pronunciation Key: T Z			
t	ten; date	v	very; live
th	think	w	win; away
th	these	y	you
u	cut; butter	z	zoo; cause
ur	turn; bird	zh	measure

(Turn the page for more information.)

sen•sa•tion [sen sā⁄ shən] *noun, plural* **sensa-tions. 1.** the use of the senses; the ability to see, hear, touch, taste, or smell. **2.** something known by one of the senses; a feeling: "He had exhausted his rocket fuel, and he was so high in such a vast space that there was no *sensation* of motion." (Tom Wolfe) **3.** great excitement or interest: "In 1964, the Beatles toured the U.S. and created a *sensation* everywhere they performed." (Jerry Grigadean)

sen•sa•tion•al [sen sā⁄ shən əl] *adjective, more/ most.* **1.** creating great excitement or interest: The center fielder made a *sensational* play as he reached high above the fence to catch the ball. **2.** trying to arouse great excitement or interest: Supermarket newspapers often print *sensational* headlines about scandals in Hollywood.

the cold weather will kill them. **5.** meaning: The book title *Man's Fate* uses "man" in the *sense* of "human beings; people." **6. senses.** a clear state of mind. —*verb,* **sensed, sensing.** to understand something without being told directly: "The bookshop man has many thoughts and feelings that I have, I *sense* that." (Russell Hoban) —**sensory,** *adjective.* having to do with the senses.

sense•less [sens⁄ lis] *adjective, more/most.* **1.** not having the use of the senses; unconscious. **2.** not showing proper use of the mind; foolish. —**senselessly,** *adverb.* —**senselessness,** *noun.*

sen•si•ble [sen⁄ sə bəl] *adjective, more/most.* having or showing good sense; reasonable: She was *sensible* enough to start her science report early, so she wouldn't be rushed at the end. —**sensibly,** *adverb.*

> **sense words** "Nick put the frying pan on the grill over the flames. He was hungrier. The beans and spaghetti warmed. Nick stirred them and mixed them together. They began to bubble, making little bubbles that rose with difficulty to the surface. There was a good smell." (Ernest Hemingway) The war novelist Ernest Hemingway and the children's-book author Laura Ingalls Wilder are not thought of as similar writers, but they use a similar style to describe things—words that call upon the *senses*. From Wilder's *Little House on the Prairie*, here is Sound: "Only the wind stirred and the grasses sighed. Then Pa lifted the fiddle to his shoulder and softly touched the bow to the strings. A few more notes fell like clear drops of water into the stillness." Touch: "The ground was hot under their bare feet. The sunshine pierced through their faded dresses and tingled on their arms and backs." Smell: "The air was really as hot as the air in an oven, and it smelled faintly like baking bread. Pa said the smell came from all the grass seeds parching in the heat."

sense [sens] *noun, plural* **senses. 1.** any of the powers by which a living being can be aware of itself and of what goes on around it; the ability to see, hear, feel, smell, or taste things. **2.** a feeling in the mind: a *sense* of pride. The expression "deja vu" means having a *sense* that something is happening just as it did before. **3.** the ability to use the physical senses or the mind to make judgments: She never gets lost when she's out hiking, because she has a good *sense* of direction. ♦ Often used in expressions such as a *sense* of humor or common *sense*. **4.** the proper use of the mind; good judgment: There's no *sense* putting the plants out now—

sen•si•tive [sen⁄ sə tiv] *adjective, more/most.* **1.** quick to show the effect of some physical force; sensing or responding quickly: Photos are developed on special paper that is *sensitive* to light. "Madame Defarge, being *sensitive* to cold, was wrapped in fur . . ." (Charles Dickens) **2.** easily hurt or upset; having delicate feelings: Tim is very *sensitive* and the teacher has to be careful about what she says to him. **3.** having deep feelings: The minister was very *sensitive* to the poor family's problems. —**sensitivity,** *noun.* —**sensitively,** *adverb.*

sent [sent] *verb.* the past form of **send.**

sen•tence [sen⁄ təns] *noun, plural* **sentences. 1.**

> **sentences** Our definition says a *sentence* is a group of words that has a noun and a verb and expresses a complete thought. But we admit this isn't totally satisfactory. It depends too much on the word *complete*. Usually, sentences have a subject-predicate (noun-verb) pattern—usually, but not always. "Why?" is a sentence. "Stop!" is a sentence. Another way to define a sentence is to say it is an ability (all human beings are born with a sentence-making ability) that allows a person to complete a statement. Sentences are to language what the will is to life, a basic element that is needed in order to make complex forms.

a group of words expressing a complete thought. A sentence has both a subject (a noun) and a verb. "Oranges and apples" is not a sentence. "Oranges and apples grow on trees" is a sentence, because it has the verb "grow." **2.** punishment given to a person who is found guilty by a court of law. —*verb*, **sentenced, sentencing.** to set the punishment of: The man was *sentenced* to three years in prison.

sen•ti•ment [sen′ tə mənt] *noun, plural* **sentiments. 1.** a thought based on feeling or emotion, especially tender or sensitive feelings: That coach really wants to win, and he won't keep a weaker player on the team just out of *sentiment.* **2.** *also,* **sentiments.** a mental attitude or point of view; an opinion.

sen•ti•men•tal [sen′ tə men′ təl] *adjective, more/most.* **1.** having or showing tender, sensitive feelings: "Never before had Orry been away from the family plantation at Christmas, and he got quite *sentimental* over the fact." (John Jakes) **2.** having or showing too much sentiment; too emotional: It was a *sentimental* story about a cute little orphan girl and a grouchy old man who adopts her. **—sentimentally,** *adverb.*

sen•try [sen′ trē] *noun, plural* **sentries.** a soldier or other person who is stationed at a place to keep watch and warn others of danger. ♦ Also called a **sentinel** [sen′ tə nəl].

Seoul [sōl] the capital and largest city of South Korea. *Population:* 11,900,000.

sep•a•rate [sep′ ə rāt] *verb,* **separated, separating. 1.** to keep apart; be between; divide: A fence *separates* our yard from our neighbors. **2.** to break into parts; set or place apart: *Separate* the magazines you want from the ones we can throw out. A newspaper reporter has to *separate* fact from opinion in writing a story. **3.** of a married couple, to make an agreement to live apart while still remaining legally married. —*adjective* [sep′ rit] **1.** apart from another or others: The two men ate together but asked for *separate* checks. **2.** different; distinct: In the 1800's men and women usually attended *separate* colleges. **—separately,** *adverb.*

sep•a•ra•tion [sep′ ə rā′ shən] *noun, plural* **separations. 1.** the act or fact of separating: The idea that religion and government should not influence each other is called "*separation* of church and state." **2.** something that separates.

Sep•tem•ber [sep tem′ bər] *noun.* the ninth month of the year. September has 30 days.

se•quel [sē′ kwəl] *noun, plural* **sequels. 1.** a complete story that continues from where an earlier story ended: The movie *Return of the Jedi* was a *sequel* to *Star Wars.* **2.** something that follows because of something else; a result.

se•quence [sē′ kwəns] *noun, plural* **sequences. 1.** the fact of one thing coming after another in a certain order: The houses on our block are numbered in *sequence* from 400 to 449. **2.** a series of connected things: The golf book had a *sequence* of photos that showed the complete act of swinging at a ball.

sequoia

se•quoi•a [si kwoi′ ə] *noun, plural* **sequoias.** a very large evergreen tree that bears cones and has a reddish-brown bark and pointed leaves. The **giant sequoia** is the largest tree on earth. Sequoias are found in California and Oregon.

Se•quoy•a [si kwoi′ ə] 1750?-1843, Cherokee Indian scholar and teacher. ♦ The *sequoia* tree is named in honor of him.

se•rene [si rēn′] *adjective, more/most.* calm and quiet; peaceful: "Above the open space of the graveyard, the full moon shone *serene,* mysterious." (John Gardner) **—serenity** [sə ren′ ə tē], *noun.* **—serenely,** *adverb.*

serf [surf] *noun, plural* **serfs.** in Europe in earlier times, a poor farm worker who was forced by law to work on a certain piece of land and pay rent to its owner. ♦ This custom was known as **serfdom.**

Pronunciation Key: [ə] Symbol

The [ə] or *schwa* sound occurs in syllables without an accent. It can be spelled with any vowel, such as **a** in above, **e** in listen, **i** in pencil, **o** in melon, **u** in circus. It can also be a combination of vowels, such as **io** in action, **ai** in mountain, **iou** in precious.

(Turn the page for more information.)

ser•geant [sär⁄ jənt] *noun, plural* **sergeants. 1.** an officer in the U.S. Army or Marine Corps ranking above a corporal but below a lieutenant. **2.** a police officer ranking next below a captain or sometimes below a lieutenant.

se•ri•al [sir⁄ē əl] *noun, plural* **serials.** a long story that is broken up into smaller parts that are published or broadcast one at a time.—*adjective.* arranged in a series.

serial number any one of a series of numbers that are given to the members of a large group to identify one from the others, as with cars of the same model, or soldiers in the Army.

se•ries [sir⁄ēz] *noun, plural* **series. 1.** a number of things of the same kind that come one after another: Police are concerned about the recent *series* of robberies in our neighborhood. **2.** a number of books, movies, etc. that deal with the same subject, or are otherwise related: She won an award for best comedy actress in a TV *series.* The "Dick and Jane" books were a widely-used reading *series* of the 1930's.

that separates from blood as a blood clot forms.

ser•vant [sur⁄vənt] *noun, plural* **servants.** a person whose job is to work regularly in another person's household, doing jobs such as cooking, cleaning, or gardening. ◆ People who work for the government are often called **public servants** or **civil servants.**

serve [surv] *verb,* **served, serving. 1.** to place food on the table for eating: to *serve* dinner. This recipe will *serve* four people. **2.** to be of use or help to: to *serve* your country, to *serve* a wealthy family as a cook. A cowboy hat has a wide brim that *serves* as protection against the sun. **3.** to carry out a certain job, duty, or obligation: to *serve* as governor of a state, to *serve* in the Navy, to *serve* two years in prison. **4.** to present in an official or legal way: Allen was *served* with a summons to appear in court for his traffic ticket. **5.** in tennis and similar games, to hit the ball to begin play. —*noun, plural* **serves.** the act of putting the ball in play in a game such as tennis or volleyball.

---

series comma Should you write "The special sale will be held on Friday, Saturday, and Sunday" or ". . . Friday, Saturday and Sunday"? That is, should a comma be placed after "Saturday"? This is called the *series comma* or *serial comma*. In this dictionary we do use the series comma, and we recommend it for your writing as well. Our Word Survey showed that both British and American authors use it: "The register of his burial was signed by the clergyman, the clerk, the undertaker, and the chief mourner." (Charles Dickens) ". . . a picture of Elkhart emerged for us that showed it as a flat place consisting chiefly of ball parks, poolrooms, and hardware stores." (Mary McCarthy)

---

se•ri•ous [sir⁄ē əs] *adjective, more/most.* **1.** not joking or acting in fun; not fooling: You say the math test is today, not tomorrow—are you *serious?* **2.** having a quiet, thoughtful manner; solemn; grave. **3.** that should not be dealt with lightly; important, difficult, or dangerous: a *serious* illness. That town has a *serious* drug problem. —**seriously,** *adverb:* "He was very nervous and thought *seriously* about turning back." (Toni Morrison) —**seriousness,** *noun.*

ser•mon [sur⁄mən] *noun, plural* **sermons. 1.** a talk on religion or good behavior given by a clergyman as part of a church service. **2.** *Informal.* any long, serious talk about how someone should behave.

ser•pent [sur⁄pənt] *noun, plural* **serpents.** a snake, especially a large poisonous snake. ◆ This word is used mainly in older writings, as in the Bible.

se•rum [sir⁄əm] *noun, plural* **serums. 1.** a liquid that is used to cure or treat a disease. It is made from the blood of an animal that is immune to the disease. **2.** the thin, clear liquid

ser•vice [sur⁄vis] *noun, plural* **services. 1.** the act or fact of helping others: The mayor gave Mrs. Evans an award for her many years of *service* to the community. **2. services.** professional help or advice: You need the *services* of a lawyer to handle that problem. **3.** the act of waiting on or helping customers: I don't like that restaurant, because the *service* is so slow. **4.** a system of providing things to the public: Our neighborhood has good bus *service* to the downtown area. **5.** a religious ceremony: a funeral *service.* **6.** the armed forces: My grandfather was in the *service* during World War II. **7.** a set of dishes for a meal: a *service* for twelve people. —*verb,* **serviced, servicing.** to put or keep in good condition: The dealer says that this car should be *serviced* every 5000 miles. —*adjective:* A *service* entrance to a store is used by workers rather than customers.

serv•ice•man [sur⁄vis man⁄] *noun, plural* **servicemen. 1.** a person in the armed forces. **2.** a person whose job is fixing things.

service station another term for a **gas station.**

setting The *setting* of a story is the place where the action happens. For example, in Scott O'Dell's *Island of the Blue Dolphins*, the setting is an island off the coast of California. But *time* is also a part of setting. The early 1800's is the time described in "Blue Dolphins." Not all stories have a realistic setting, of course. Ray Bradbury's "All Summer in a Day" is set in the future on the planet Venus. The place where Stephen Vincent Benét's "By the Waters of Babylon" is set is realistic—New York City. But the time is not realistic. The city has been destroyed by a war and no one lives there. In fact, the point of "Babylon" is how the reader gradually discovers what the setting is.

serv•ing [sur′ ving] *noun, plural* **servings.** a portion of food for one person: This package of frozen corn provides four *servings*.

ses•sion [sesh′ ən] *noun, plural* **sessions. 1.** a formal meeting of a club or organization: Please be seated—court is now in *session*. **2.** a series of such meetings, or the time when they take place: This *session* of Congress lasts until the summer break. **3.** any meeting at a fixed time: The rock group is practicing for a recording *session*.

set [set] *verb*, **set, setting. 1.** to put something in a certain place: *Set* the package down on the table. **2.** to put in a certain condition: to *set* a prisoner free, to *set* a house on fire. **3.** to put in the proper condition: to *set* the table. The doctor *set* her broken leg. **4.** to fix at a certain point or level: *Set* the oven at 300°. She *set* her alarm for six o'clock. **5.** to begin a trip or journey: The pioneer family *set* out for California. **6.** of the sun or another heavenly body, to go out of sight below the horizon. **7.** to make or become solid: After he put the model plane together, he put it aside to let the glue *set*. —*adjective*. **1.** fixed or decided: The restaurant has a *set* policy against smoking. **2.** ready; prepared: Are you all *set* for the camping trip? —*noun, plural* **sets. 1.** a group of things or people that belong together: a *set* of dishes, a *set* of encyclopedias. **2.** the scenery for a play, film, or television program. **3.** a device for receiving television signals. **4.** one part of a tennis match.

set•back [set′ bak′] *noun, plural* **setbacks.** a lack of progress or success; a reverse or defeat: The patient seemed to be getting better, but then suffered a *setback*.

Se•ton [sēt′ ən] **Elizabeth,** 1774-1821, American religious leader, the first person born in the U.S. to be declared a saint.

set•ter [set′ ər] *noun, plural* **setters. 1.** a large hunting dog with a long, silky coat and droopy ears, such as an **Irish setter** or **English setter. 2.** a person or thing that sets: Books are put into print by type*setters*.

set•ting [set′ ing] *noun, plural* **settings. 1.** the act of a person or thing that sets. **2.** a thing in which something else is set: a diamond ring with a gold *setting*. **3.** the place and time of the action in a book, play, or other such work.

set•tle [set′ əl] *verb*, **settled, settling. 1.** to agree or decide some issue or problem: to *settle* an argument. The lawyers for the two sides *settled* the case out of court. **2.** to make a home; live in a certain place: Australia was *settled* by people from Britain in the 1800's. **3.** to come to rest on something: "At eleven-thirty, as a light, cold drizzle *settled* over Luga, the first plane took off . . ." (John Toland) **4.** to sink slowly or gradually down: "Henry LaDoux *settled* into his usual chair at the Yankee Cafe." (Calvin Trillin) **5.** to make or become calm or less active: A long, hot bath *settles* her nerves after a busy day at the office. "After fifteen years on the road, he is finally *settling* down with the woman he loves." (Bobbie Ann Mason)

setter A setter was trained to remain still (*set*) when it saw game, rather than chasing the animal.

S

Pronunciation Key: Accent Marks

[′] is the normal accent mark. It shows where the main stress falls on a word.
[′] is a secondary accent mark. It shows a lighter stress than the primary accent. For example:

    tel • e • vis • ion [tel′ ə vizh′ ən]
(Turn the page for more information.)

set•tle•ment [set′əl mənt] *noun, plural* **settle-ments. 1.** the act or fact of settling. **2.** a small village or community: The city of Los Angeles began as a Spanish *settlement* in 1781.

set•tler [set′lər] *noun, plural* **settlers.** a person who goes to live in a new area or country, especially one who is among the first to live there.

sev•en [sev′ən] *noun, plural* **sevens;** *adjective.* one more than six; 7. —**seventh,** *adjective; noun.*

sev•en•ty [sev′ən tē] *noun, plural* **seventies;** *adjective.* seven times ten; 70. —**seventieth,** *adjective; noun.*

sev•er [sev′ər] **severed, severing.** to cut or break off, especially in a sharp, sudden way: Lightning struck the tree and *severed* the largest branch. "He was also greatly in favor of *severing* diplomatic ties with France." (John Mortimer)

sev•er•al [sev′rəl *or* sev′ər əl] *adjective; noun.* more than two, but not many: *Several* people have called about the car Mom has for sale. This sweater comes in *several* different colors.

se•vere [sə vir′] *adjective,* **severer, severest. 1.** not kind and gentle; strict; harsh: First-year students at the military school were subject to *severe* discipline. **2.** hard to bear or deal with; causing great pain, discomfort, or damage: a *severe* headache. "After an early autumn destroyed some of the crops, a *severe* winter set in." (Jerzy Kosinski) —**severely,** *adverb.* ◆ The state of being severe is **severity** [sə ver′ə tē].

sew [sō] *verb,* **sewed, sewed** or **sewn, sewing. 1.** to make or mend cloth or other such material with a needle and thread: Mom *sewed* up the torn sleeve on Eddie's jacket. ◆ The art or work of doing this is **sewing. 2. sew up.** *Informal.* to make certain of getting or having: "She already had a job *sewed up* at a private nursery school." (Mary McCarthy).

sew•age [sōō′ij] *noun.* waste matter from homes, factories, and other buildings. Sewage is carried off in sewers or drains.

sew•er [sōō′ər] *noun, plural* **sewers.** a pipe or channel located underground and used to carry away waste matter and dirty water.

sewing machine a mechanical device that sews, usually having an electric motor to run it.

sewn [sōn] *verb.* a past participle of **sew.**

sex [seks] *noun, plural* **sexes. 1.** one of the two groups, male or female, that humans, animals, and some plants are divided into. **2.** the fact or condition of being male or female: High schools

have two separate locker rooms that are divided by *sex.* —**sexual,** *adjective.* having to do with sex: For some birds, bright-colored feathers are a *sexual* trait found only in the male.

shab•by [shab′ē] *adjective,* **shabbier, shabbiest.** showing too much wear; faded and ragged: A man dressed in *shabby* clothes stopped us and asked for money. —**shabbily,** *adverb.*

shack [shak] *noun, plural* **shacks.** a small, roughly-built house or cabin: The old trapper lived in a rundown *shack* out in the woods.

shack•le [shak′əl] *noun, plural* **shackles.** a band or chain used to hold a prisoner, work animal, and so on in one place. —*verb,* **shackled, shackling.** to hold or confine with or as if with shackles: "Both Roosevelt and the Emperor wanted peace, but each was *shackled* by the restrictions of his own culture and political system." (John Toland)

shad [shad] *noun, plural* **shad** or **shads.** a small fish related to the herring. Shad live in the Atlantic Ocean and swim to fresh-water streams to lay their eggs. Both the shad itself and its eggs are valued as food.

shade [shād] *noun, plural* **shades. 1.** an area that is darker and cooler because sunlight is blocked off: They sat in the *shade* of a big oak tree. **2.** something that blocks off light: a lamp *shade,* window *shades.* **3.** the distinct nature of a color that makes it different from another similar one: Navy blue is a darker *shade* than sky blue. **4.** a small amount or difference; a little bit: I'd love to swim, but the water's still just a *shade* too cold. —*verb,* **shaded, shading. 1.** to keep direct light or heat away from something: The outfielder raised his hand to *shade* his eyes. **2.** to make or have different degrees of light and dark: The artist *shaded* parts of the drawing.

sewing machine This 1940's Singer machine got its power from a foot pedal instead of electricity.

shad•ow [shad′ō] *noun, plural* **shadows. 1.** a dark area caused by something blocking the sunlight. **2.** a person or thing that follows another very closely, as a person walking along seems to be followed by his own shadow: In soccer, a *shadow* is a player who is assigned to cover the other team's star player wherever he goes on the field. **3.** a small amount; a bit. ♦ Usually used in the phrase **(beyond) a shadow of a doubt.** —*verb,* **shadowed, shadowing. 1.** cover with a shadow; make a shadow on: "The room, *shadowed* well with awnings, was dark and cool." (F. Scott Fitzgerald) **2.** to follow very closely: Two police officers *shadowed* the suspect in hope that he would lead them to the stolen money. —**shadowy,** *adjective:* covered with or as if with shadows: In his later years, Howard Hughes was a mysterious, *shadowy* figure in American business.

shad•y [shā′dē] *adjective,* **shadier, shadiest. 1.** giving shade, or in the shade: a large, *shady* tree, a *shady* spot under a beach umbrella. **2.** *Informal.* not strictly honest or legal; doubtful: a *shady* deal to buy a stolen stereo.

shaft [shaft] *noun, plural* **shafts. 1.** the long, narrow part of an arrow or spear that is attached to the head. **2.** a similar part of a golf club, hockey stick, hammer, or the like. **3.** a bar in a machine that supports moving parts or sents motion to other parts of the machinery: the drive*shaft* or crank*shaft* of an automobile. **4.** a ray or beam of light: *shafts* of sunlight. **5.** a long, narrow, opening that goes up and down: an elevator *shaft,* a mine *shaft.*

quick movements: The directions on the medicine bottle said, "*Shake* well before using." **2.** to make a series of small, quick body movements because of illness, cold, fear, excitement, and so on; tremble: "Patty was *shaking* all over . . . Sweat ran off her, she was so scared." (Laura Ingalls Wilder) **3.** to upset, weaken, or disturb: The actor's confidence was *shaken* by the bad reviews his film got. **4.** to get rid of: "He stirred in his chair, trying to *shake* off his thoughts so that he could sleep." (Ken Follett) —*noun, plural* **shakes.** the act of shaking: They closed the deal with a hand*shake.*

Shakespeare One of the few existing portraits of William Shakespeare.

Shake•speare [shāk′spir′] **William,** 1564-1616, English dramatist and poet.

> **Shakespeare** "Shakespeare had it easy. He wrote his plays by using lots of famous quotations." That's an old joke, but there's a point to it. In a book of famous quotations, Shakespeare takes up about 65 pages. If you put together all the quotes from the *ten* writers quoted next most often—Milton, Pope, Johnson, Wordsworth, Byron, Emerson, Lincoln, Keats, Twain, and Churchill—they occupy about the same space as Shakespeare's alone. Here are some of those Shakespearean quotes: "Death lies on her like an untimely frost/Upon the sweetest flower of all the field." *(Romeo and Juliet)* "This was the noblest Roman of them all." *(Julius Caesar)* "This above all: to thine own self be true, And it must follow as the night the day, Thou canst not then be false to any man." *(Hamlet)* "All the world's a stage/And all the men and women merely players." *(As You Like It)*

shag•gy [shag′ē] *adjective,* **shaggier, shaggiest.** having hair, fur, wool, and so on that is long, rough, and thick: A sheepdog has a *shaggy* coat. "Under *shaggy* eyebrows the blue eyes of the little Scot brightened with interest . . ." (Barbara Tuchman)

shake [shāk] *verb,* **shook, shaken, shaking. 1.** to move up and down or from side to side in short,

Pronunciation Key: A–F			
a	and; hat	ch	chew; such
ā	ate; stay	d	dog; lid
â	care; air	e	end; yet
ä	father; hot	ē	she; each
b	boy; cab	f	fun; off

(Turn the page for more information.)

691

shak•y [shā′kē] *adjective*, **shakier, shakiest.** that shakes or is likely to shake; not steady: an old, *shaky* ladder. The witness told his story in a *shaky* voice. —**shakily,** *adverb.*

shale [shāl] *noun.* a rock formed from hardened clay or mud. It has thin layers that split easily.

shall [shal] a verb used with "I" or "we" to show the future.

> **shall** A language critic of the 1700's invented this rule for the use of *shall:* "When you talk about the future, write "I shall" or "we shall," but when you say that you are bound or determined to do something, use *will.*" This "rule" appeared in language books, but the actual use of *shall* is different. This is what our Word Survey shows: (1) The idea that "I (we) shall" means future plans, and "I (we) will" means determination, is generally ignored. In World War Two, the most famous examples of determination were General Douglas MacArthur's "I *shall* return" and Sir Winston Churchill's "We *shall* never surrender." (2) *Shall* is not common in any sense in American English. "I shall" is a British expression. (3) The main American use of *shall* is in formal statements: "A complete game *shall* consist of nine innings."

shal•low [shal′ō] *adjective*, **shallower, shallowest. 1.** not far from top to bottom; not deep: He wasn't a good swimmer, so he stayed in the *shallow* end of the pool. **2.** not deep in thought or feeling: He's a *shallow* person who judges others by how they dress or how much money they have. —**shallowness,** *noun.*

sham [sham] *noun, plural,* **shams.** something that is not true or real; a false imitation.

shame [shām] *noun.* **1.** a painful feeling that comes from doing something wrong or being connected with something bad: He felt *shame* for having cheated on the test. **2.** something that should not be; something bad or unwanted: "What a *shame* for such a nice young man to be ruining his life . . ." (Russell Baker) —*verb*, **shamed, shaming.** to cause shame: " It is up to you if you want to *shame* yourself by crying before him." (Wole Soyinka) —**shameless,** *adjective.* —**shamelessly,** *adverb.*

sham•poo [sham pōō′] *verb*, **shampooed, shampooing.** to wash the hair. —*noun, plural* **shampoos.** a special soap used for washing the hair.

sham•rock [sham′ räk′] *noun, plural* **shamrocks.** a small plant related to clover, having leaves with three leaflets. The shamrock is the national emblem of Ireland.

Shang•hai [shang′ hī′] the largest city in China, on the east coast at the mouth of the Yangtze River. *Population:* 8,367,000.

shape [shāp] *noun, plural* **shapes. 1.** the outer form or outline of something: A full moon appears to have a round *shape.* **2.** the physical condition of a person or thing, whether good or bad: "I'll call Sam this evening and see what *shape* his canoe's in." (James Dickey) **3.** good physical condition: Lee's doing a lot of running to get in *shape* for football.—*verb*, **shaped, shaping.** to give a certain shape to: a box of Valentine candy *shaped* like a heart.

share [shâr] *noun, plural* **shares. 1.** the part of a larger thing that belongs to one particular person: We got the garage cleaned quickly because everyone did his *share.* **2.** one of the equal parts of ownership of a company: 100 *shares* of stock in the Ford Motor Company. —*verb*, **shared, sharing. 1.** to use or take part in with others: Dave and his brother *share* a bedroom. The joke was on Larry, but he wasn't mad and he *shared* in the laughter. **2.** to divide into parts and give to others as well as to yourself: " 'Won't you take the pack and help me carry the gold? . . . We'll *share* it—half and half.'" (James Houston)

shark Three types of sharks. The hammerhead (above), the great white (center), and the thresher (below).

shark [shärk] *noun, plural* **sharks.** a saltwater fish that lives in warm seas and has rough, grayish skin and many rows of sharp teeth.

she/her Sailors think of their ship as feminine: "They could see the ship putting *her* side in the water and shouted all together, '*She's* going!'" (Joseph Conrad) Sailors have used *she* not only for their ships, but also for the forces of nature—the wind, the weather, the sea itself. That led to the practice of naming hurricanes for women—Hurricane Carol and so on. This practice has been abandoned because of complaints that it is unfair to women. Now, male names are mixed in. However, *she* can actually be regarded as sign of respect. No one uses *she* to refer to a pencil or a pocket calculator, but if a dam burst or an oil well gushed up, a worker might shout: "There *she* goes!"

Sharks attack other fish, and the larger kinds are dangerous to man.

sharp [shärp] *adjective,* **sharper, sharpest. 1.** having an edge or point that will cut easily: a *sharp* knife, a *sharp* point on a pencil. **2.** having a point or edge; not rounded: the *sharp* peaks of a mountain range, a face with *sharp* features. **3.** quick and exact in a way that is thought to be like the cutting of a knife: A hawk has *sharp* eyesight. Our new TV set gets a much *sharper* picture than the old one. **4.** having a sudden change in size, direction, amount, and so on: a *sharp* pain, a mountain road with *sharp* curves. There was a *sharp* increase in housing prices last year. —*adverb.* exactly; promptly: We'll meet at the school at seven o'clock *sharp.* —*noun, plural* **sharps.** in music, a tone or note that is one half note above its natural tone, or the symbol (♯) that indicates this. —**sharply,** *adverb:* "Miss Crail looked up *sharply* from her card index, as if she had heard a rude word." (John le Carré) —**sharpness,** *noun.*

sharp•en [shär′pən] *verb,* **sharpened, sharpening.** to make or become sharp or sharper: to *sharpen* an ax. "Math *sharpens* children's minds." (Kazuo Ishiguro)

shat•ter [shat′ər] *verb,* **shattered, shattering. 1.** to break into pieces in a sudden, violent way: The force of the blast *shattered* windows for several blocks around. "Being unused to the sound which *shattered* all the peace of my little garden . . ." (Graham Greene) **2.** to have a very bad effect on; damage or destroy: She was *shattered* by the terrible news.

shave [shāv] *verb,* **shaved, shaved** or **shaven, shaving. 1.** to cut hair from the body with a razor or other sharp blade. **2.** to cut off thin strips or pieces: "Billy brought some dead chestnut wood, *shaved* off some kindling with his knife and started the fire." (Lois Lenski) —*noun, plural* **shaves. 1.** the fact of shaving. **2. close shave.** a close call; a narrow escape.

shawl [shôl] *noun, plural* **shawls.** a piece of soft, heavy cloth that is worn over the shoulders or head, especially by women.

she [shē] *pronoun.* the girl, woman, or female animal being spoken or written about; that female one: Cathy lent me a book that *she* had finished reading. —*noun, plural* **she's.** a female.

shear [shēr] *verb,* **sheared, sheared** or **shorn, shearing.** to cut or clip something with a sharp tool: Sheep are *sheared* to remove their wool.— **shears,** *plural noun.* a cutting tool similar to scissors, only larger and heavier.

shed[1] [shed] *noun, plural* **sheds.** a small building or hut used for storing things: a tool*shed.*

shed[2] *verb,* **shed, shedding. 1.** of an animal or plant, to cast off or lose an outer covering: Many trees *shed* their leaves in autumn. Snakes *shed* their skin several times a year. **2.** to throw off some covering or burden in this way: "After a time they began to *shed* their knapsacks." (Stephen Crane) "He had *shed* his past fears and failures . . ." (Graham Greene) **3.** to let flow or cause to flow: "If you have tears, prepare to *shed* them now." (William Shakespeare) **4.** to send out; give off: ". . . it really is January, and by midafternoon the nearly invisible sun *sheds* no warmth." (Alice Adams)

she'd [shēd] the contraction for "she had" or "she would."

sheep [shēp] *noun, plural* **sheep.** a farm animal that is commonly raised for its wool and meat. Other kinds of sheep live wild in mountain areas of Asia, southern Europe, and western North America.

sheer [shēr] *adjective,* **sheerer, sheerest. 1.** very thin and light so that it can be seen through: *sheer* stockings for women. **2.** straight up or down; very steep: "He looked up at the gloomy walls that rose a thousand feet *sheer* above the

S

Pronunciation Key: G–N

g	give; big	k	kind; cat; back
h	hold	l	let; ball
i	it; this	m	make; time
ī	ice; my	n	not; own
j	jet; gem; edge	ng	having

(Turn the page for more information.)

circling pines around him." (Bret Harte) **3.** complete; total: to win a contest by *sheer* luck. ". . . many of the old folks have fallen asleep of *sheer* exhaustion." (Upton Sinclair)

sheet [shēt] *noun, plural* **sheets. 1.** *also,* **bedsheet.** one of a pair of large pieces of cloth used as a bed covering. **2.** any thin, wide piece of material like this: a *sheet* of paper, *sheets* of plywood. **3.** a broad thin, surface thought of as lying flat like a bedsheet: During the storm, the roads were a *sheet* of ice.

sheik [shēk] *noun, plural* **sheiks.** an Arab leader or ruler.

shelf [shelf] *noun, plural* **shelves. 1.** a thin, flat piece of wood, metal, glass, or other such material that is attached to a wall or frame and used to hold things, such as books. **2.** anything like a shelf: The Atlantic Ocean has a flat, shallow region called the Continental *Shelf.*

shell [shel] *noun, plural* **shells. 1.** a hard outer covering that protects the body of certain animals, such as turtles, clams, snails, and beetles. **2.** a similar covering of an egg, nut, seed, and so on. **3.** any outer covering or protection: The abandoned building was just a *shell,* with only the outer walls left standing. This year she's finally come out of her *shell* and gotten more friendly with the other girls. **4.** a metal case holding a bullet or explosive charge for a gun, or the bullet or charge itself. —*verb,* **shelled, shelling. 1.** to remove the shell from something: to *shell* peas. **2.** to attack with shells, cannons, or guns: The Civil War began when Southern troops *shelled* Fort Sumter.

she'll [shēl] the contraction for "she will" and "she shall."

shel•lac [shə lak′] *noun, plural* **shellacs.** a thick liquid that dries to form a shiny protective covering for furniture and floors, etc. ◆ Shellac is made from a solution of **lac** (a sticky substance given off by certain Asians insects) dissolved in alcohol. —*verb,* **shellacked, shellacking.** to cover or coat a surface with shellac.

shell•fish [shel′ fish′] *noun, plural* **shellfish** or **shellfishes.** any animal that lives in the water and has a shell to protect its body. Clams, oysters, crabs, and shrimp are shellfish.

shel•ter [shel′ tər] *noun, plural* **shelters. 1.** something that protects from the weather or from danger: A tent serves as a *shelter* for campers. It's said that man's three basic needs are food, clothing, and *shelter.* **2.** a place for homeless people to stay for a time: a Red Cross *shelter.* —*verb,* **sheltered, sheltering.** to give shelter to; protect: "The cove was partly shel-

tered from the wind . . ." (Scott O'Dell) —**sheltered,** *adjective.* away from harm or difficulty: She's been very protected by her parents and has led a *sheltered* life.

shelve [shelv] *verb,* **shelved, shelving. 1.** to put on a shelf: The librarian *shelved* the new books. **2.** to put aside to be considered later: The company *shelved* its plans to open a new office.

shelves [shelvz] *noun.* the plural of **shelf.**

Shep•ard [shep′ ərd] **Alan,** born 1923, American astronaut, the first American in space.

shep•herd [shep′ ərd] *noun, plural* **shepherds.** a person whose work is taking care of or herding sheep in the field. —*verb,* **shepherded, shepherding. 1.** to watch over or herd sheep. **2.** to guide or watch over something, as a shepherd does with his flock: The guide *shepherded* the tour group onto the bus.

shell The great beauty and variety of shells is shown in this colorful collection.

sher•bet [shur′ bit] *noun, plural* **sherbets.** a frozen dessert like ice cream, made mostly of fruit juice, water, and sugar.

sher•iff [sher′ if] *noun, plural* **sheriffs.** the chief law officer of a county.

she's [shēz] the contraction for "she is" and "she has."

shied [shīd] the past form of **shy.**

shield [shēld] *noun, plural* **shields. 1.** a heavy piece of armor that was carried on one arm by knights of the Middle Ages, to protect against blows or weapons during a battle. **2.** any similar object that protects in this way: The power saw had a metal *shield* to cover the blade. Judge Hugo Black called the U.S. Constitution a *shield* for the benefit of every American citizen. **3.** something shaped like a knight's shield, such as a police badge. —*verb,* **shielded, shielding.** to protect from harm or danger: "When we got into trouble we ran behind her and she *shielded* us." (Wole Soyinka)

shifts in tense A story set in the past should remain in the past. For example, if you write on General Custer and the Battle of Little Bighorn, use the past tense: "The Indian forces *camped* in the valley." "Several of Custer's best officers *were* not with him." "Chief Gall *was* a huge man who *weighed* over 240 pounds." If you then write, "On Sunday afternoon, June 25, the regiment *stops* to collect itself. Counting Indian scouts and guides, Custer *has* about 675 men," that's wrong. That is a shift in tense. The story line should stay within one tense—past, present, future. But there are variations, good ones, too. "The Bighorn River *flows* into the Yellowstone." This is not an incorrect shift—the river flowed into the Yellowstone in 1876, and it still does today. Also, a special use of the present can make a long-ago scene more dramatic: "The most famous battle of the Old West *is* about to begin."

shift [shift] *verb*, **shifted, shifting. 1.** to move or change from one to another: "Mrs. Verity's attention *shifted*. She had hardly noticed the boys up to this moment." (Penelope Lively) "The candles made a *shifting* pattern of light around him . . ." (Sherley Anne Williams) **2.** to change the gears in a car. —*noun, plural* **shifts. 1.** the act or fact of shifting: There's been a *shift* in public opinion on that issue. **2.** a part used for shifting: the gear*shift* of an automobile, a *shift* key on a typewriter. **3.** a certain group of workers, or the period of time that they work together: "He worked the night *shift* and Saturday was his only night off." (Zora Neale Hurston)

shil·ling [shil′ ing] *noun, plural* **shillings.** a coin once used in Britain that was equal to 1/20 of a pound.

shim·mer [shim′ ər] *verb*, **shimmered, shimmering.** to shine with a faint, waving light: "The tall trees that lined the road *shimmered* in silvery green." (Norton Juster)

shin [shin] *noun, plural* **shins.** the front part of the leg from the knee to the ankle. —*verb*, **shinned, shinning.** (*also,* **shinny**) to climb up something, using the arms and legs to hold on.

shine [shīn] *verb*, **shone** or **shined, shining. 1.** to give off a light; be bright; glow: "It was a beautiful warm summer night, and the stars shimmered and *shone* overhead." (James Jones) **2.** to make bright; polish: to *shine* shoes. **3.** to be outstanding: Carol's good in all her subjects, but English is where she really *shines*. —*noun, plural* **shines.** a bright reflection or light: She put a beautiful *shine* on the silver teapot.

shin·gle [shing′ gəl] *noun, plural* **shingles.** a thin piece of wood or other material that is used to cover a roof or wall in overlapping rows. Shingles protect against rain and weather. —*verb*, **shingled, shingling.** to put shingles on; cover with shingles.

shin·y [shī′ nē] *adjective*, **shinier, shiniest.** bright and shining: a *shiny* new car.

ship [ship] *noun, plural* **ships. 1.** a large sea-going boat. **2.** an airplane or spacecraft. —*verb*, **shipped, shipping. 1.** to send something by ship. **2.** to send by land or air: to *ship* a package. **3.** to go on a ship as a crew member.

-ship a SUFFIX meaning "the fact or condition of being." Member*ship* means the fact of being a member of something.

ship·ment [ship′ mənt] *noun, plural* **shipments.** the act of shipping, or something that is shipped: The store received a large *shipment* of toys just before the Christmas season.

ship·ping [ship′ ing] *noun.* **1.** the act or business of sending goods by water, land, or air. **2.** ships as a group: The canal has been closed to foreign *shipping*.

ship·wreck [ship′ rek′] *noun, plural* **shipwrecks.** the sinking or destruction of a ship at sea, or such a ship itself. —*verb*, **shipwrecked, shipwrecking.** to cause to suffer a shipwreck.

shirt [shurt] *noun, plural* **shirts.** a piece of clothing worn on the upper body, usually having sleeves and a collar.

shiv·er [shiv′ ər] *verb*, **shivered, shivering.** to shake from the cold or from fear; tremble: "I got out of bed, *shivering* as the icy air of the room gripped me, and pulled on my shirt . . ." (James Herriot) —*noun, plural* **shivers.** the act of shivering or trembling.

shoal [shōl] *noun, plural* **shoals.** a shallow place in a lake, river, or ocean.

Pronunciation Key: O–S

ō	over; go	ou	out; town
ô	all; law	p	put; hop
oo	look; full	r	run; car
ōō	pool; who	s	set; miss
oi	oil; boy	sh	show

(Turn the page for more information.)

S

shock¹ [shäk] *noun, plural* **shocks. 1.** a sudden, very strong blow to the mind and feelings that comes from some bad or unexpected event: Mr. Bell thought the boss called him in to give him a raise and instead he was fired—what a *shock!* **2.** a dangerous condition of the body caused by the blood suddenly failing to circulate properly. Shock can be brought on by an injury, by heavy bleeding, or by great fright or emotional distress. **3.** a feeling of pain caused by electricity passing through the body. **4.** a strong and sudden blow, jolt, or crash: An earthquake sends a violent *shock* along the surface of the earth. —*verb,* **shocked, shocking. 1.** to disturb or upset the mind and feelings: "Lola is *shocked* by his sudden appearance. She jumps and can't help showing her fright." (William Inge) **2.** to cause an electric shock.

shock² *noun, plural* **shocks. 1.** a bundle of grain stalks such as corn or wheat, set on end in a field to dry. **2.** a thick mass of hair.

shock•ing [shäk′ing] *adjective, more/most.* causing a shock; very wrong or bad: a *shocking* display of anger. —**shockingly,** adverb.

shod•dy [shäd′ē] *adjective,* **shoddier, shoddiest.** poorly made or of poor quality; inferior.

shoe [shoo] *noun, plural* **shoes. 1.** an outer covering worn on the foot. **2.** something like a shoe, such as a horseshoe.—*verb,* **shod** or **shoed, shoeing.** to put a shoe or shoes on.

shone [shōn] the past form of **shine.**

shook [shook] the past tense of **shake.**

shoot [shoot] *verb,* **shot, shooting. 1.** to fire a gun or other such weapon. **2.** to hit with a bullet, arrow, or the like: The hunter *shot* two ducks. **3.** to photograph or film something: Many of John Ford's Western movies were *shot* in Monument Valley. **4.** to move or grow quickly, as if sent from a gun: "Water *shoots* out of cracks in the rock . . ." (John McPhee) "Soon the Ford would be *shooting* back down the road in a cloud of dust . . ." (Langston Hughes) —*noun, plural* **shoots.** a new growth that comes out from a plant.

shop [shäp] *noun, plural* **shops. 1.** a small store where goods are sold: a card *shop,* a butcher *shop.* **2.** a public place where a certain kind of work is done: a barber *shop,* a repair *shop.* —*verb,* **shopped, shopping. 1.** to visit stores or shops to look for and buy goods. **2. shop around.** to compare prices in various stores before making a purchase.

shop•lift•er [shäp′lif′tər] *noun, plural* **shoplifters.** a person who steals goods from a store while pretending to be a customer.

shopping center a separate group of stores, restaurants, and other businesses, usually in the suburbs, that are connected or close together and have a common parking area.

shore [shôr] *noun, plural* **shores. 1.** the area of land along the ocean, a lake, or a river. **2.** dry land: The passengers went shopping on *shore* while the ship was docked.

short [shôrt] *adjective,* **shorter, shortest. 1.** not far from one end to the other; not long or tall: Men in the armed forces usually have *short* hair. **2.** not long in distance or time: a *short* walk around the block. **3.** not having enough; lacking: to be *short* of money or time. **4.** of a vowel, having a sound that is said more quickly and with less force. The *i* in "hit" is short, while the *i* in "mine" is long. —*adverb.* **1.** suddenly: The train stopped *short.* **2.** not quite as far as; on the near side of: The arrow fell *short* of the target. —*noun, plural* **shorts. 1.** something that is short, such as a movie lasting only a few minutes. **2.** pants that end above the knees. **3.** men's underpants.

short stories Because there are many different kinds of short stories, it's hard to identify common features. However, certain things are noticeable: <u>Character</u>: Short stories don't have a large cast of characters, not as many as a novel. Some tell only of relations between two people, as in Richard Connell's "The Most Dangerous Game" or O. Henry's "The Gift of the Magi." <u>Setting</u>: Short stories usually occur in one place, and within a limited amount of time. In Stephen Crane's "The Open Boat," the setting is a small lifeboat lost at sea. The events of one day make up Stephen Leacock's "How We Kept Mother's Day." <u>Plot</u>: The story quickly presents a problem or conflict. In Jack London's "To Build a Fire," the threat of freezing faces the character within the first few paragraphs. Similarly, the ending of a story often presents a quick twist, as in Shirley Jackson's "Charles" (there's no Charles) or Thomas Hardy's "The Three Strangers" (two strangers are really brothers). When you write a story, put it through these three tests: few characters, limited setting, and quickly-told plot.

short•age [shôr′ tij] *noun, plural* **shortages.** the fact of having less than is needed; too small an amount: The mayor asked people not to water their lawns because of the water *shortage.*

short circuit an electric circuit that allows too much current to flow through it. A short circuit usually happens when the insulation wears off wires that touch each other. A short circuit may blow a fuse or start a fire.

short•com•ing [shôrt′ kum′ ing] *noun, plural* **shortcomings.** a failure to reach the level needed; a fault or weakness: "As he drove on he discovered some of the car's *shortcomings.*" (Ken Follett)

short cut a quicker or shorter way to go somewhere or do something.

short•en [shôrt′ ən] *verb,* **shortened, shortening.** to make or become short: to *shorten* a pair of pants that are too long. "As the sun rose higher, *shortening* the shadows and drawing the dew from the grass . . ." (Richard Adams)

short•en•ing [shôrt′ ning] *noun.* any kind of fat that is used in baking or cooking, such as butter, lard, or vegetable oil.

short•hand [shôrt′ hand′] *noun.* a rapid method of writing that uses symbols or letters to take the place of longer words. It is used to write down quickly what someone else is saying, as by a secretary in a business office.

short•ly [shôrt′ lē] *adverb.* in a short time; soon: Mom went to the store; she left a note saying she'll be back *shortly.*

short•stop [shôrt′ stäp′] *noun, plural* **shortstops.** in baseball, the position between second and third base, or a player who plays there.

short story a work of fiction that is shorter than a novel.

shot[1] [shät] *noun, plural* **shots. 1.** the act of firing a gun, cannon, or other such weapon. **2.** a person who shoots a gun or other weapon: a soldier who is a good *shot.* **3.** *plural,* **shot.** a ball of lead or steel that is fired from a shotgun or cannon. **4.** the launching of a rocket or missile toward a target: a moon *shot.* **5.** an injection of medicine given with a needle: a penicillin *shot.* **6.** in games such as basketball, hockey, or soccer, an effort to score a goal. **7.** a photograph or view with a camera: The TV news crew tried to get a *shot* of the burning car. **8.** the heavy metal ball used in the SHOT PUT.

shot[2] *verb.* the past form of **shoot.**

shot•gun [shät′ gun′] *noun, plural* **shotguns.** a gun that is fired from the shoulder like a rifle, but that has a smooth barrel and fires a number of small metal balls (*shot*) for a short distance. It is used to hunt birds and small game.

shot put A member of the Canadian women's team prepares to release the shot during the 1984 Olympic Games.

shot put an event in track and field in which people compete to see how far they can throw a heavy metal ball. —**shotputter,** *noun.*

should In British English, *should* is used in place of *would,* just as *shall* is used for *will:* "We *should* be very happy if you joined us for dinner Friday evening." To Americans, this sounds fancy or old-fashioned; we say "We *would.*be happy . . ." In American English, *should* has two main uses: (1) To show that it's right or necessary to do something: "We *should* get that window fixed soon." (2) To show that something is likely or expected to happen: "We *should* get there about five o'clock, unless we run into heavy traffic."

should [shood] a verb used with other verbs to show: **1.** a duty or obligation: You *should* be careful when you drive in the rain. **2.** a condition that would lead to something else: If you *should* see Pete today, ask him to call me. **3.** what is expected: I *should* be back by noon.

Pronunciation Key: T–Z			
t	ten; date	v	very; live
th	think	w	win; away
<u>th</u>	these	y	you
u	cut; butter	z	zoo; cause
ur	turn; bird	zh	measure

(Turn the page for more information.)

shoul·der [shōl′dər] *noun, plural* **shoulders. 1.** the part on either side of the body between the neck and arm. ♦ The **shoulder blade** or **scapula** [skap′yə lə] is the large, flat bone at the rear of the shoulder. **2.** an edge or border alongside a road or highway. —*verb*, **shouldered, shouldering. 1.** to push with the shoulders: She *shouldered* her way through the crowd. **2.** to place a load on or as if on the shoulders: to *shoulder* the blame for something.

should·n't [shood′ənt] the contraction for "should not."

shout [shout] *verb*, **shouted, shouting.** to cry out loudly; yell: "'Answer me,' he *shouted*, as if miles separated him from his stepmother." (Jessamyn West) —*noun, plural* **shouts.** a loud cry; a yell.

shove [shuv] *verb*, **shoved, shoving.** to push or press roughly, especially in a rude way: "I *shoved* my way off the bleachers and ran to the locker room." (S. E. Hinton) —*noun, plural* **shoves.** a rough push.

shov·el [shuv′əl] *noun, plural* **shovels.** a tool with a handle and a broad scoop, used for digging and moving dirt, snow, and other loose matter. —*verb*, **shoveled, shoveling. 1.** to dig up and move with a shovel. **2.** to move or throw in large amounts, as with a shovel: The hungry boy *shoveled* the food into his mouth.

show [shō] *verb*, **showed, shown** or **showed, showing. 1.** to allow to be seen; bring into view: Melanie *showed* us her new dress. **2.** to be in sight; be able to be seen: "The sky is beginning to *show* some streaks of light over in the East there." (Thornton Wilder) **3.** to make known; reveal: Her angry comments *showed* how upset she was. **4.** to tell the proper way or course; guide or direct: The police officer *showed* us how to get to the museum. —*noun, plural* **shows. 1.** the act of showing: The vote was taken by a *show* of hands. **2.** something that is seen or presented to the public; an exhibition or display: a dog *show*, a flower *show*. **3.** a play, movie, television or radio program, or other such entertainment. **4.** a display that is intended to attract attention or to give a false impression: Even though he was scared, Sam put on a *show* of courage. —**showy**, *adjective.* putting on a show; attracting attention.

show·er [shou′ər] *noun, plural* **showers. 1.** a short rainfall. **2.** a bath in which water sprays down on a person from an overhead fixture with small holes in it. **3.** this fixture itself, or an enclosed space containing it. **4.** a fall of many small things like a rain shower: The burning log broke in half, sending up a *shower* of sparks. **5.** a party at which a woman's friends give her gifts to celebrate a happy event, such as a wedding or the birth of a baby. —*verb*, **showered, showering. 1.** to fall or cause to fall in a shower: "There was a big tree . . . which *showered* me, and only me, with a million white blossoms." (Kate Simon) **2.** to bathe in a shower. **3.** to give in large amounts; give generously: "The gods grow tired of *showering* their gifts on those who don't make use of them." (Angus Wilson)

shown [shōn] *verb.* the past participle of **show.**

shrank [shrangk] *verb.* the past tense of **shrink.**

shred [shred] *noun, plural* **shred. 1.** a narrow strip or small piece that has been torn or cut off: He tore the letter to *shreds* and threw it away. **2.** a small amount; a bit: The lawyer claimed there wasn't a *shred* of real evidence that his client was guilty. —*verb*, **shredded** or **shred, shredding.** to cut or tear into shreds. ♦ A machine that shreds paper is a **shredder.**

shrew The shrew, a fierce fighter, can kill animals larger than itself. This tiny creature eats three times its weight in food every day.

shrew [shrōō] *noun, plural* **shrews.** a very small animal somewhat like a mouse, having a long nose, short ears, and brownish fur.

shrewd [shrōōd] *adjective*, **shrewder, shrewdest.** clever and sharp, especially in acting for one's own benefit: He's a *shrewd* politician who knows how to keep his opponents off guard.— **shrewdly**, *adverb.* —**shrewdness**, *noun.*

shriek [shrēk] *noun, plural* **shrieks.** a loud, piercing sound or cry. —*verb*, **shrieked, shrieking.** to make such a sound: "Rhitta found his voice again and *shrieked* in horror." (Lloyd Alexander)

shrill [shril] *adjective*, **shriller, shrillest.** having a high, piercing sound: a *shrill* whistle, the *shrill* cries of a newborn baby.

S

shrimp Shrimp have special parts on the abdomen called *swimmerets*, which help them swim.

shrimp [shrimp] *noun, plural* **shrimp** or **shrimps.** a small shellfish with a long tail that is related to the lobster. Shrimp are highly valued as food.

shrine [shrīn] *noun, plural* **shrines. 1.** a holy place, such as the tomb of a saint, an altar in a church, or a box holding a holy object: Lourdes, France has a famous *shrine* of the Catholic Church where the Virgin Mary is believed to have appeared. **2.** a place or object that is respected or highly valued because of its history or memories: The Montreal Forum is often called "the *shrine* of hockey."

shrink [shringk] *verb,* **shrank** or **shrunk, shrunk** or **shrunken, shrinking. 1.** to make or become smaller in size: She used hot water to *shrink* her wool sweater. **2.** to draw back; move away from: "The circle of boys *shrank* away in horror." (William Golding)

shriv·el [shriv′əl] *verb,* **shriveled, shriveling.** to dry up; shrink: Some of the plants *shriveled* during the heat wave.

shroud [shroud] *noun, plural* **shrouds. 1.** a cloth used to cover a dead body for burying. **2.** something that covers or hides. —*verb,* **shrouded, shrouding.** to cover with or as if with a shroud: "In the early morning light the beaches of Normandy were *shrouded* in mist." (Cornelius Ryan)

shrub [shrub] *noun, plural* **shrubs.** a woody plant that is smaller than a tree, and that usually has several stems rather than a single trunk.
♦ A grouping of shrubs in a garden is **shrubbery** [shrub′rē].

shrug [shrug] *verb,* **shrugged, shrugging.** to raise the shoulders slightly to show doubt, dislike, or lack of interest. —*noun, plural* **shrugs.** the act of raising the shoulders in this way.

shud·der [shud′ər] *verb,* **shuddered, shuddering.** to shake or tremble: "She *shuddered* to think of her narrow escape . . ." (Jean Stafford) "The train *shuddered* to a halt at the small, ill-lit station . . ." (John Mortimer) —*noun, plural* **shudders.** the act of shuddering.

shuf·fle [shuf′əl] *verb,* **shuffled, shuffling. 1.** to walk by dragging the feet along the ground. **2.** to mix playing cards to change their order before dealing them out. **3.** to move things from one place to another: She *shuffled* the papers on her desk to look busy in case the boss was watching. —*noun, plural* **shuffles.** the act of dragging the feet along the ground.

shun [shun] *verb,* **shunned, shunning.** to avoid on purpose; stay away from: It's unusual that he's so healthy, because he completely *shuns* physical exercise.

shut [shut] *verb,* **shut, shutting. 1.** to move something so that it blocks an entrance or opening; close: He *shut* the screen door to keep the flies out. **2.** to bring together the parts of: to *shut* a book. She *shut* her eyes and went to sleep. **3.** to stop the operation or activity of. ♦ Used with a following adverb: to *shut off* a radio, to *shut down* a factory. "Winter darkness *shuts off* the far view." (Barry Lopez) **4. shut out.** in sports, to stop the opposing team from scoring. ♦ Also used as a noun: to pitch a *shutout.*

shut·ter [shut′ər] *noun, plural* **shutters. 1.** movable cover for a window or door, used to shut out light or to block the view from outside. **2.** a movable cover over a camera lens that lets in light for a very short time when a picture is taken. —*verb,* **shuttered, shuttering.** to close with or as if with shutters.

shut·tle [shut′əl] *noun, plural* **shuttles. 1.** in the weaving of cloth, a device that carries the thread back and forth across the piece that is being woven. **2.** a train, bus, or airplane that makes short trips between two places: He caught the 8:00 *shuttle* flight from Boston to New York. —*verb,* **shuttled, shuttling.** to move back and forth between two places.

S

Pronunciation Key: [ə] Symbol

The [ə] or *schwa* sound occurs in syllables without an accent. It can be spelled with any vowel, such as a in above, e in listen, i in pencil, o in melon, u in circus. It can also be a combination of vowels, such as io in action, ai in mountain, iou in precious.

(Turn the page for more information.)

S

shy [shī] *adjective,* **shyer, shyest** or **shier, shiest.**
1. not comfortable in public or in a group of people; bashful: Jamie doesn't talk much in class because she's too *shy.* **2.** of an animal, easily frightened; timid. **3.** *Informal.* short of; lacking: "Still four years *shy* of eighteen, I quickly calculated that the war would be over before it could take me." (Russell Baker) —*verb,* **shied, shying. 1.** to move back suddenly because of fear: The horse *shied* at the sight of the rattlesnake. **2.** to stay away from, out of doubt or dislike: He *shied* away from the business deal because he didn't trust the other man. —**shyly,** *adverb.* —**shyness,** *noun.*

sick [sik] *adjective, more/most.* **1.** not in good health; having a disease; ill. ♦ A person who is often sick is **sickly. 2.** having an upset stomach; feeling nausea. **3.** feeling strong dislike, unhappiness, or the like: I asked Mom to make me a different sandwich for lunch, because I'm *sick* of tuna fish. —**sickness,** *noun.*

sick•le [sik′ əl] *noun, plural* **sickles.** a tool with a sharp, curved blade on a short handle. It is used to cut tall grass and grain.

sickle-cell anemia [sik′ əl sel′] a serious disease caused by a harmful substance in the red blood cells. This disease can be inherited, and is found chiefly among black people.

side [sīd] *noun, plural* **sides. 1.** a surface or part of something, other than the front, top, bottom, or back: The doors of a car are on the *sides.* **2.** an outside line or surface: A square has four *sides.* **3.** one of the two similar surfaces of a flat object: Turn your paper over and write on the other *side.* **4.** a point or place away from the center of something: the east *side* of town. **5.** one of two opposing groups or points of view: Let's choose up *sides* for a game of basketball. Don't make up your mind until you've heard both *sides* of the argument. **6.** a certain quality that a person or thing has: He's serious at work, but he has a funny *side,* too. —*adjective.* **1.** at or near one side: a *side* door. **2.** less important; secondary: We had roast beef, with mashed potatoes as a *side* dish. —*verb,* **sided, siding. side with.** to take sides; support: Danny *sided* with his brother in the argument.

side•burns [sīd′ burnz′] *plural noun.* the hair that grows along the side of a man's face, next to the ears. ♦ Civil War General Ambrose *Burnside* was famous for his long side whiskers; his name was later reversed as *sideburns.*

side effect a secondary effect of a drug, chemical, or other medicine, besides the intended effect: Those pills really help Karen's allergies, but they have the *side effect* of making her sleepy.

side•walk [sīd′ wôk′] *noun, plural* **sidewalks.** a path or place alongside a street where people can walk. It is usually paved.

side•ways [sīd′ wāz′] (*also* **sidewise**) *adverb; adjective.* **1.** to one side; towards one side: to move *sideways.* **2.** with one side forward: to walk *sideways* through a narrow passageway.

siege [sēj] *noun, plural* **sieges.** the surrounding of a fort, city, or position for a long time by an army trying to capture it. During a siege, supplies are cut off from those who are surrounded, to force them to surrender.

Sierras Looking down from a peak in the High Sierras toward Lake Tahoe, California.

Si•er•ra Nevada [sē âr′ ə *or* sē er′ ə] a mountain range in eastern California; also known as the **Sierras.**

sideburns The Civil War general Ambrose Burnside.

sieve [siv] *noun, plural* **sieves.** a utensil that has many small holes in the bottom, used to separate liquid matter from solids or smaller pieces from larger ones.

sift [sift] *verb*, **sifted, sifting. 1.** to separate larger pieces from smaller ones by shaking through a sieve, net, or the like: Before they spread the dirt, they *sifted* it to remove unwanted stones and pebbles. **2.** to fall in a light, loose way, as if through a sieve: "Occasionally the wind will move a branch from a nearby tree and some snow will *sift* down through sunlight." (Alice Adams) **3.** to examine the individual items of a group, as if putting them through a sieve: The lawyer *sifted* through all the court records before preparing his argument.

sigh [sī] *verb*, **sighed, sighing. 1.** to let out a long, deep breathing sound to show that one is sad, tired, relieved, and so on. **2.** to make this sound: "Somewhere high above him he could hear the wind *sighing* through the mountain passes." (James Houston) —*noun, plural* **sighs.** the act or sound of sighing.

sight [sīt] *noun, plural* **sights. 1.** *also,* **eyesight.** the ability to see. **2.** the act or fact of seeing: "He caught *sight* of his own face in the wall-mirror . . ." (Kingsley Amis). **3.** the range or distance that one can see: We say that something is "out of *sight*," "in plain *sight*," and so on. **4.** something that is worth seeing: On her business trip to London she had time to visit the famous *sights* of the city. **5.** something that looks strange or unpleasant: They're just in the middle of moving, and the house is really a *sight.* **6.** *also,* **sights.** a device on a gun or other such object that helps in seeing and taking aim. —*verb*, **sighted, sighting. 1.** to sense with the eyes, observe: "Plans were therefore made to flee as soon as their ship was *sighted*." (Scott O'Dell) **2.** to look at a target through a sight.

sign [sīn] *noun, plural* **signs. 1.** a board or other such object that has words or numbers on it to give information: There was a large 'For Sale' *sign* in front of the house. **2.** a mark or object used to stand for something else; a symbol: The + *sign* means addition. **3.** a thing that shows or suggests some fact or quality: "All the doors and windows were open but there were no *signs* of life . . ." (John Cheever) **4.** a movement of the hand or body that carries some meaning; a signal: "He held up one hand as a *sign*, although Ben's father could clearly hear." (Virginia Hamilton) —*verb*, **signed, signing. 1.** to write one's name on: to *sign* a check. **2.** to use sign language. —**signer,** *noun.* a person who signs something.

sig·nal [sig′ nəl] *noun, plural* **signals. 1.** an action, sound, or object that is meant to give a warning or message: A police car puts on a flashing red light as a *signal* to a driver to pull over. **2.** a sign or action that causes something to happen: "Helen's eyes grew large and shiny; the *signal* of approaching tears." (Penelope Lively) —*verb* **signaled** or **signalled, signaling** or **signalling.** to give a signal: " . . . the slap of the old man's hand on the counter, which *signals* that he is preparing to leave." (Wright Morris)

sig·na·ture [sig′ nə chər] *noun, plural* **signatures. 1.** a person's name written in his or her own handwriting. **2.** a sign at the beginning of a section of music to show the key and meter.

sig·nif·i·cance [sig nif′ i kəns] *noun.* the fact of being significant; importance or meaning.

sig·ni·fi·cant [sig nif′ i kənt] *adjective, more/ most.* having special meaning; important: Easter Sunday is a *significant* day for Christians. —**significantly,** *adverb.*

sig·ni·fy [sig′ nə fī] *verb*, **signified, signifying.** to be a sign of; show: " . . . making a gesture with the other hand to *signify* that nothing serious had happened." (Alice Munro)

sign language a way of communicating by using hand and body movements to represent words and ideas. Indians on the Great Plains used sign language to communicate with other tribes. The **American sign language** is used by deaf people.

si·lence [sī′ ləns] *noun, plural* **silences. 1.** a lack of sound; complete quiet: "On a summer afternoon the whole place dozed in the sun, under *silences* broken only by the occasional cluck of a hen . . ." (Russell Baker) —*verb*, **silenced, silencing.** to make silent; keep quiet: "A youthful waiter had approached, his footfalls *silenced* by the carpet . . ." (Kingsley Amis)

silent [sī′ lənt] *adjective.* **1.** having or making no sound; quiet; still: "The big bird gave an angry hiss, rose and flew away on *silent* wings." (James Houston) "Our shouts echoed in the *silent* street." (James Joyce) **2.** not spoken out loud: a *silent* prayer. The "w" is *silent* in "answer." —**silently,** *adverb.*

S

Pronunciation Key: Accent Marks

[′] is the normal accent mark. It shows where the main stress falls on a word.
[′] is a secondary accent mark. It shows a lighter stress than the primary accent. For example:

tel • e • vis • ion [tel′ə vizh ′ən]
(Turn the page for more information.)

sil·hou·ette [sil′ ə wet′ *or* sil′ ōō wet′] *noun, plural* **silhouettes. 1.** a picture or drawing showing only the outline of the object filled in with a single color. **2.** a dark outline of something against a lighter background: "The *silhouette* of a moving cat wavered across the moonlight." (F. Scott Fitzgerald) —*verb*, **silhouetted, silhouetting.** to show a silhouette: "The lion looked huge, *silhouetted* on the rise of bank in the gray morning light . . ." (Ernest Hemingway)

sil·i·con [sil′ i kän′] *noun.* a nonmetallic element that exists as a brown powder or dark gray crystals and is the second most common element in the earth's crust. Silicon is widely used in making computers and other electronic devices. ◆ A compound of silicon and oxygen, **silicone** [sil′ i kōn], is used in oils and plastics.

silk [silk] *noun, plural* **silks. 1.** the soft, shiny thread that a silkworm produces, or the cloth made from this thread. Silk is noted for its great strength and for its deep, rich colors when dyed. **2.** anything like silk, such as the strands on an ear of corn. —**silken** or **silky,** *adjective.*

silk·worm [silk′ wurm′] *noun, plural* **silkworms.** a caterpillar that spins silk to make its cocoon.

sill [sil] *noun, plural* **sills.** the piece of wood or stone across the bottom of a door or window.

sil·ly [sil′ ē] *adjective,* **sillier, silliest. 1.** not serious or intelligent; not showing good sense; foolish: Instead of listening to the teacher, the boys giggled and made *silly* remarks to each other. —**silliness,** *noun.*

si·lo [sī′ lō] *noun, plural* **silos. 1.** a tall, round building used for storing food for farm animals. **2.** a deep hole in the ground used for the storing and launching of guided missiles.

silt [silt] *noun.* very fine particles of sand, clay, or other such matter that are carried along by flowing water and then settle at the bottom.

sil·ver [sil′ vər] *noun.* **1.** a shiny, white soft metal that is a chemical element. Silver is easily shaped to make such objects as coins, jewelry, or spoons, knives, and forks. ◆ A person who makes or repairs silver is a **silversmith. 2.** coins that are made of silver. **3.** short for SILVERWARE. **4.** a grayish-white color like silver. —*adjective.* made of, coated with, or having the color of silver. —*verb,* **silvered, silvering.** to coat with silver. —**silvery,** *adjective.*

sil·ver·ware [sil′ vər wâr′] *noun.* knives, forks, spoons, and the like, sometimes made of silver or containing silver.

silkworm A silkworm spins its valuable cocoon.

sim·i·lar [sim′ ə lər] *adjective, more/most.* not exactly the same but very much alike; of the same kind: Many animals have a body color that is *similar* to their surroundings. "Their voices were so *similar* that they could only be brothers." (Wole Soyinka) —**similarly,** *adverb.*

sim·i·lar·i·ty [sim′ ə lâr′ ə tē] *noun, plural* **similarities.** the fact of being similar; a likeness or resemblance.

sim·i·le [sim′ i lē] *noun.* a phrase or expression in which one thing is compared to another to suggest they are alike: "The lights of New York glowed on the skyline *like a dawn frozen in the act of breaking.*" (Arthur C. Clarke)

similes Whenever you compare a thing to something that is ordinarily thought of as different, you use *metaphor.* In a narrower sense, a *metaphor* states the comparison directly. "He was a tiger," you can say of a forceful man. *Similes* make a comparison less directly, by using "like or as." "At the end of the straight avenue of forests . . . the water that shone smoothly like a band of metal." (Joseph Conrad) Here Conrad calls the forest an "avenue," a metaphor, but then uses a simile to say that the water was *"like a band of metal."* In general, a metaphor is a stronger comparison, because it's more powerful to say that a thing *is* something than to say it's *like* something. Yet, similes can be very effective: ". . . behind them the sun was moving down slowly *as if it were descending a ladder.*" (Flannery O'Connor) "They could see across valleys and plains . . . A herd of sheep ten miles distant looked *like a tiny white glove resting on a mountainside.*" (Mark Helprin)

sim·mer [sim′ər] *verb*, **simmered, simmering. 1.** to cook below or just below the boiling point: Let the soup *simmer* for a while. **2.** to be just below the point of breaking out: "But the . . . irritation still *simmered* beneath the surface of her smile." (Colleen McCullough)

sim·ple [sim′pəl] *adjective*, **simpler, simplest. 1.** easy to understand or do; not difficult: First graders deal with *simple* math problems. **2.** without ornament or decoration; not fancy; plain: She likes to cook *simple* dishes of meat and potatoes. **3.** of the basic or ordinary kind; not complicated: "Fish swim" is a *simple* sentence. **4.** not intelligent; stupid or foolish: a *simple*-minded person. ◆ The fact of being simple is **simplicity** [sim plis′ ə tē].

simple machine see **machine.**

sim·pli·fy [sim′ plə fī′] *verb*, **simplified, simplifying.** to make easier or plainer; make simpler: The professor *simplified* his explanation to be sure the class would understand it. "At first she'd gotten over-dressed, so she had to *simplify* her outfit." (Paul Zindel)

sim·ply [sim′ plē] *adverb*. **1.** in a simple way: to explain a problem *simply*, to dress *simply*. **2.** only; just: I'm *simply* asking you to give me some help, not to write my whole paper. **3.** really; absolutely: "She *simply* did not want to learn her multiplication tables." (Beverly Cleary)

sim·u·late [sim′ yə lāt′] *verb*, **simulated, simulating.** to give a show or appearance of; imitate: "He played Indians, of course, patting his lips to *simulate* the Indian . . . yell." (Edna Ferber) —**simulation** [sim′ yə lā′ shən], *noun.*

si·mul·ta·ne·ous [sī′ məl tā′ nē əs] *adjective*. existing or happening at the same time: "The beginning of civilization and the appearance of temples are *simultaneous* in history." (H. G. Wells) —**simultaneously,** *adverb.*

sin [sin] *noun, plural* **sins. 1.** the act of breaking the law of God or going against God's will: the *sin* of murder, the *sin* of lying. **2.** any action that is thought of as very wrong or bad: Mom says it's a *sin* the way those people keep their dog chained up all the time without feeding him. —*verb*, **sinned, sinning.** to break the law of God or go against God's will. ◆ A person who sins is a **sinner.** —**sinful,** *adjective.*

since [sins] *adverb*. **1.** from then until now. She moved away last summer and I haven't seen her *since*. **2.** at some time between then and now: I didn't believe him at first, but I've *since* found out he was telling the truth. —*preposition*. from then until now: He's lived in California *since* 1981. —*conjunction*. **1.** after the time when: He's been looking for work *since* he was laid off from his job. **2.** because: "*Since* some children lived miles away from the nearest school, they might not attend classes at all until they were half grown." (Russell Freedman)

sin·cere [sin sēr′] *adjective*, **sincerer, sincerest.** telling or showing the truth; honest and real; not false: Joseph gave Larry a *sincere* apology for hurting his feelings. "She had been *sincere* when she described herself as happy." (Iris Murdoch) —**sincerely,** *adverb*: I'm glad you won the prize; I mean that *sincerely*. —**sincerity** [sin′ ser′ ə tē], *noun.*

sin·ew [sin′ yōō *or* sin′ ōō] *noun, plural* **sinews.** an older word for TENDON.

sing [sing] *verb*, **sang** or **sung, sung, singing. 1.** to make sounds or words with musical tones; produce music with the voice. **2.** to make a whistling, ringing, or humming sound that is like a song: "Agba could still feel the wind *singing* in his ears." (Marguerite Henry) **3.** to tell of or praise something in a song or poem: "Come near me, while I *sing* the ancient ways." (William Butler Yeats)

Singapore A view of Singapore Harbor.

Sin·ga·pore [sing′ gə pôr′] **1.** an island country in southeastern Asia, at the southern tip of the Malay Peninsula. *Area:* 238 square miles. *Population:* 2,577,000. **2.** the capital and chief port of this country. *Population:* 2,300,000.

S

Pronunciation Key: A–F			
a	and; hat	ch	chew; such
ā	ate; stay	d	dog; lid
â	care; air	e	end; yet
ä	father; hot	ē	she; each
b	boy; cab	f	fun; off

(Turn the page for more information.)

S

sing·er [sing′ ər] *noun, plural* **singers.** a person or bird that sings.

sin·gle [sing′ gəl] *adjective.* **1.** only one; one: Jimmy Carter served a *single* term as President. ◆ A line in which people stand one behind the other is called **single file. 2.** meant to be used by one person only: a *single* bed. **3.** not married: a *single* man or woman. —*noun, plural* **singles. 1.** a hit in baseball that allows the runner to reach first base safely. **2.** a person who is not married. —*verb,* **single, singling. 1. single out.** to pick or choose from a group: "What *singled* her *out* from those around her was her looks." (Kingsley Amis) **2.** to hit a single in baseball. —**single-handed,** *adjective.* without anyone else's help or support.

sin·gu·lar [sing′ gyə lər] *adjective.* **1.** showing only one person or thing: "Cat" is a *singular* noun; "cats" is *plural.* **2.** out of the ordinary; unusual: The sighting of the comet was a *singular* event that excited scientists around the world. —*noun, plural* **singulars.** the form of a word showing only one person or thing. —**singularly,** *adverb.*

sin·is·ter [sin′ i stər] *adjective, more/most.* evil or suggesting evil; threatening: The director of the horror movie chose that house for filming because of its strange, *sinister* appearance. ◆ The word *sinister* comes from the Latin word for "left." Because most people are right-handed, the idea of "left" was thought of in older times as standing for wrong or evil.

sink [singk] *verb,* **sank** or **sunk, sunk, sinking. 1.** to go down below water or another such surface: The car *sank* in the river after it went off the bridge. **2.** to become less or weaker: People's voices *sank* to a whisper when the judge entered the courtroom. **3.** to dig or drill into the earth: The men *sank* a hole for the telephone pole. **4.** to pass or fall gradually into a certain condition: to *sink* into a deep sleep, to let something *sink* into your mind. —*noun, plural* **sinks.** a basin of metal, porcelain, or the like, that is used for washing. Sinks have faucets that supply water, and a drain for emptying.

si·nus [sī′ nəs] *noun, plural* **sinuses.** one of the openings or air-filled spaces in the bones of the skull that connect to the nostrils. ◆ **Sinus trouble** or **sinusitis** means these sinus openings become swollen and cause painful pressure.

Sioux [so͞o] *noun, plural* **Sioux. 1.** a member of a group of North American Indian tribes that live in Minnesota, North and South Dakota, and Wyoming. These tribes are also called the **Dakota. 2.** the language spoken by these tribes.

sip [sip] *verb,* **sipped, sipping.** to drink in small amounts; take a little drink. —*noun, plural* **sips.** a little drink: She took a *sip* of tea.

si·phon [sī′ fən] *noun, plural* **siphons.** a bent tube or pipe that has the shape of an upside-down 'J'. Siphons are used to transfer liquid from one container to another by means of air pressure. —*verb,* **siphoned, siphoning.** to transfer liquid with a siphon: Mel *siphoned* some gas from his car to Leo's car.

sir [sur] *noun, plural* **sirs. 1.** a title or form of address used in place of a man's name: Excuse me, *sir,* can you tell me what time it is? **2. Sir.** a title used for a knight: *Sir* Francis Drake was a famous explorer. **3. Sire.** an old word for *Sir.*

si·ren [sī′ rən] *noun, plural* **sirens.** a device that makes a loud, shrill noise as a signal or warning, as on an ambulance, police car, or fire truck.

sis·ter [sis′ tər] *noun, plural* **sisters. 1.** a girl or woman who has the same parents as another person. **2.** a female member of a group or club. **3.** a female member of a religious order; a nun.

sis·ter·hood [sis′ tər hood′] *noun, plural* **sisterhoods. 1.** the state of being a sister or sisters. **2.** a group of women who are part of the same group or club.

sis·ter-in-law [sis′ tər ən lô′] *noun, plural* **sisters-in-law. 1.** the sister of a person's husband or wife. **2.** the wife of a person's brother.

sit [sit] *verb,* **sat, sitting. 1.** to be in the position in which the body is supported by the lower

Sioux A Sioux chief and his family in 1911, photographed by E. B. Fiske.

back where the hips and the legs join. **2.** to cause someone to be in this position: She *sat* her baby in the car seat. **3.** to occupy a certain place or position, as if sitting: Their house *sits* high up on the mountainside. That old car's just been *sitting* there on the corner for a week. **4.** to be a member of an official group: Senator Jones *sits* on the Banking Committee.

skate¹ [skāt] *noun, plural,* **skates. 1.** *also,* **ice skate.** a shoe or boot with a metal blade attached to the bottom, used for gliding over ice. **2.** *also,* **roller skate.** a shoe or boot with small wheels mounted on the bottom, used for moving over hard surfaces, such as streets and sidewalks. —*verb,* **skated, skating.** to move on skates.

> **sit/set** For many years language books have warned against confusing these two words. The problem still exists. *Sit* refers to what a person does when resting in a chair or riding in a car. *Set* means to put something down, to place it at rest. "I already had my answer in mind and I was just *setting* there, waiting for her to ask me." "Just *sit* it down over there, on the desk." Both of these are wrong; it should be "I was *sitting* there" and "Just *set* it down." You can *set* the table or *set* a package on the counter, but you can't in good English usage *set* and wait for someone or *set* down to rest.

Sit•ting Bull [sit′ ing bool′] 1831?-1890, Sioux Indian chief.

site [sīt] *noun, plural* **sites.** the position or location of something: The state put a historical marker at the *site* of the famous Civil War battle.

sit•u•at•ed [sich′ oo āt′ əd] *adjective.* in a certain place or position: "The empire of Blefescu is an island *situated* to the north-north-east side of Lilliput." (Jonathan Swift)

sit•u•a•tion [sich′ oo ā′ shən] *noun, plural* **situations.** any set of conditions that can apply at a given time; a state of affairs: The newscaster reported on the current *situation* in Iran.

six [siks] *noun, plural* **sixes;** *adjective.* one more than five; 6. —**sixth,** *adjective; noun.*

sixty [siks′ tē] *noun, plural* **sixties;** *adjective.* six times ten; 60. —**sixtieth,** *adjective; noun.*

size [sīz] *noun, plural* **sizes. 1.** the amount of space that a thing takes up; the height, width, or length that something has: An elephant is noted for its large *size.* **2.** a number or amount: The fire department is hoping for an increase in the *size* of their budget this year. **3.** a series of measurements that show how large clothing, shoes, and other such goods are: Dave wears a *size* 42 sweater. —*verb,* **sized, sizing. 1.** to have a certain size or number. **2. size up.** to form a judgment or opinion about: The president of the company is coming to the plant to *size up* the situation himself. —**sizeable,** *adjective:* fairly large: "A *sizeable* crowd had gathered to listen . . ." (Paul Theroux)

siz•zle [siz′ əl] *verb,* **sizzled, sizzling.** to make a hissing or crackling sound: —*noun, plural* **sizzles.** a hissing or crackling sound: "Over my shoulder comes the *sizzle* and smell of frying bacon." (Edward Abbey)

skate² *noun, plural* **skates** or **skate.** a flat fish that has two wide fins on the side of its body and a long, slender tail.

skate•board [skāt′ bôrd′] *noun, plural* **skateboards.** a low, flat board that has wheels mounted on the bottom, used for riding. It is usually ridden with the rider balanced in a standing position.

skel•e•ton [skel′ ə tən] *noun, plural* **skeletons. 1.** the complete set of bones that supports the body of a human or animal. **2.** a framework thought of as being like this: After the fire, all that remained was the *skeleton* of the house.

skep•ti•cal [skep′ ti kəl] *adjective, more/most.* having or showing doubt; not believing: Mom said we should be very *skeptical* about all those mail ads saying we've won cash or prizes. ◆ A person who is skeptical is a **skeptic.**

sketch [skech] *noun, plural* **sketches. 1.** a quick, rough drawing: The artist began by making a black-and-white *sketch* of her subject and then filled in colors and details later. **2.** a short piece of writing: Washington Irving's "*Sketch* Book" contained a series of articles on life in England. —*verb,* **sketched, sketching. 1.** to make a sketch. **2.** to show as if in a sketch: "Already dawn had *sketched* the outline of the mountains to the east in light gray." (Larry McMurtry) ◆ Something that is **sketchy** is quickly or roughly done, without enough detail.

Pronunciation Key: G–N

g	give; big	k	kind; cat; back
h	hold	l	let; ball
i	it; this	m	make; time
ī	ice; my	n	not; own
j	jet; gem; edge	ng	having

(Turn the page for more information.)

ski [skē] *noun, plural* **skis.** one of a pair of long, narrow runners made of wood, metal, or other material, worn to glide over snow or water. Snow skis are worn with special boots attached to the runner. Water skis have a rubber or plastic shoe into which the foot slides. —*verb*, **skied, skiing.** to move on skis: to *ski* down a hill. ◆ The sport of doing this is **skiing.**

ski jump The 70-meter ski jump event at the 1984 Winter Olympics in Sarajevo, Yugoslavia.

skid [skid] *noun, plural* **skids.** the act of slipping or sliding sideways on a wet or slippery surface: The car went into a *skid* as the driver tried to stop short on the icy road. —*verb*, **skidded, skidding.** to slip or slide sideways.

ski•er [skē′ ər] *noun, plural* **skier.** a person who uses skis.

skies [skīz] the plural of **sky.**

skiff [skif] *noun, plural* **skiffs.** a small, light boat, especially a rowboat.

skill [skil] *noun, plural* **skills.** an ability to do something well that comes from practice, training, or experience: The *skill* of the glass-blower could be seen from the beautifully-formed vases he created. Typing and operating a computer are office *skills.* —**skillful,** *adjective:* He picked up the oyster and opened the shell with one quick, *skillful* motion. —**skillfully,** *adverb.*

skilled [skild] *adjective, more/most.* **1.** having or showing special skill: Carpenters and plumbers are *skilled* workers

skil•let [skil′ it] *noun, plural* **skillets.** a shallow frying pan with a handle.

skim [skim] *verb,* **skimmed, skimming.** **1.** to remove floating matter from the surface of a liquid: The chef *skimmed* the fat from the gravy he had prepared. Their swimming pool has a machine to *skim* leaves off the water. ◆ A tool or machine that does this is a **skimmer. 2.** to read or examine quickly; scan: Mary *skimmed* over the chapter, reading only the introduction and the headings. **3.** to glide or move swiftly over a surface: " . . . all sorts of beautiful flowers were growing in the sun, with butterflies *skimming* over them." (Hugh Lofting)

skim milk or **skimmed milk** milk which has had the cream removed. Skim milk has fewer calories and less fat than whole milk.

skin [skin] *noun, plural* **skins. 1.** the outer layer of tissue that covers and protects the body. **2.** the outer covering or hide that is removed from the body of an animal. Animal skins are treated and used to make leather. **3.** any surface or outer layer that is like skin: Boil the potatoes and then remove their *skins.* —*verb,* **skinned, skinning. 1.** to injure by scraping or removing the skin from: Bobby *skinned* his elbow when he slid into home plate. **2.** to cut off the skin of an animal: to *skin* a deer.

skin diving an underwater swimming activity in which the diver stays under for long periods of time using a mask, flippers, and snorkel, and sometimes an artificial breathing tank. —**skin-dive,** *verb.* —**skin-diver,** *noun.*

skin•ny [skin′ ē] *adjective,* **skinnier, skinniest.** very thin, especially in an unhealthy or unattractive way: Dad says Mike is too *skinny* for football and wants him to gain weight.

skip [skip] *verb,* **skipped, skipping. 1.** to move with a springing step, hopping from one foot to another. **2.** to jump lightly over: Children *skip* rope as a playground game. **3.** to pass over; leave out: She was so busy at work that she *skipped* lunch. **4.** to bounce across a surface: The boys *skipped* stones across the pond. —*noun, plural* **skips.** a light, springing step.

skip•per [skip′ ər] *noun, plural* **skippers.** a nickname for the captain of a ship.

skirmish [skur′ mish] *noun, plural* **skirmishes.** a quick, brief fight involving two small groups: There was a *skirmish* at the border between the government troops and the rebels hiding in the hills. —*verb.* **skirmished, skirmishing.** to fight in this way.

skirt [skurt] *noun, plural* **skirts. 1.** a piece of woman's clothing that hangs down from the waist. **2.** the part of a dress or other longer piece of clothing that hangs down from the waist. —*verb,* **skirted, skirting.** to go around the edge of something rather than through it; avoid: The senator gave a light, humorous speech at the dinner and *skirted* controversial issues.

S

skull [skul] *noun*, *plural* **skulls.** the bony framework that forms the head of humans and other animals with a backbone. The skull protects the brain and supports the jaw and other bones of the face.

skunk [skungk] *noun*, *plural* **skunks.** a North American animal with black fur and a white stripe down its back. It is about the size of a house cat and has a long, bushy tail. Skunks spray a very strong, bad-smelling liquid when they are frightened or attacked.

skunk The striped skunk warns before it sprays by growling, stamping its feet, hunching its back, and raising its tail.

sky [skī] *noun*, *plural* **skies.** the upper space or atmosphere that appears above the earth.

sky•div•ing [skī′ dī′ ving] *noun.* a type of parachute jumping in which the jumper falls through the air for a long distance before opening the parachute.

sky•lark [skī′ lärk′] *noun*, *plural* **skylarks.** a small brown bird with black and white markings, that sings sweetly while in flight. Skylarks are found in Europe, Asia, and Africa.

sky•light [skī′ līt′] *noun*, *plural* **skylights.** a window in a ceiling or roof that lets in outside light.

sky•line [skī′ līn′] *noun*, *plural* **skylines. 1.** the line along which the sky and the earth seem to come together; the horizon. **2.** the outline of buildings, trees, or mountains against the sky: The Empire State Building is a famous feature of the New York City *skyline.*

sky•rock•et [skī′ räk it] *noun*, *plural* **skyrockets.** a firework that goes off high in the sky and showers colored sparks and lights. —*verb*, **skyrocketed, skyrocketing.** to rise, succeed, or become famous very quickly, like a skyrocket moving across the sky: Elvis Presley *skyrocketed* to world fame during the 1950's.

skyscraper The Chrysler Building is often thought of as New York City's most beautiful skyscraper.

sky•scrap•er [skī′ skrā′ pər] *noun*, *plural* **skyscrapers.** a very tall building, thought of as so high it touches (scrapes) the sky.

slab [slab] *noun*, *plural* **slabs.** a thick, flat piece of something: a *slab* of concrete.

slack [slak] *adjective*, **slacker, slackest. 1.** not tight or firm; loose: Grant realized that his dog had broken the leash when the chain suddenly went *slack.* **2.** not lively; slow: Business at the store had been *slack* since the holidays ended —*noun.* the part of something that hangs loose: Take up the *slack* in that rope.

slack•en [slak′ ən] *verb*, **slackened, slackening.** to make or become slack; let up: "M. Laruelle *slackened* his pace." (Malcolm Lowry) "The rain *slackened,* the clouds lifted a little." (V. S. Naipaul)

slacks [slaks] *plural noun.* trousers or pants, especially when worn as casual wear.

slain [slān] *verb.* the past participle of **slay.**

Pronunciation Key: O–S

o	over; go	ou	out; town
ô	all; law	p	put; hop
oo	look; full	r	run; car
o͞o	pool; who	s	set; miss
oi	oil; boy	sh	show

(Turn the page for more information.)

slam [slam] *verb*, **slammed, slamming. 1.** to shut with force, causing a loud sound: "She jumped out of the truck and *slammed* the door so hard it cracked the window right down the middle." (S. E. Hinton) **2.** to move or throw with force and a loud noise: She *slammed* on the brakes when the child ran out in front of her car. —*noun, plural* **slams.** a noisy closing or striking done with great force.

slan•der [slan′dər] *noun, plural* **slanders.** a false spoken statement that is made to damage another person's reputation. —*verb*, **slandered, slandering.** to talk in a false and harmful way about someone. —**slanderous**, *adjective.*

slang [slang] *noun.* a type of language that is much freer and more relaxed than standard language, and that is used in casual, everyday talk between friends, rather than in serious situations. Slang involves the use of new or made-up words, and of expressions that are humorous, exaggerated, impolite, and so on.

"Frozen branches *slashed* at their faces . . ." (John Jakes) **2.** to reduce sharply: Stores usually *slash* their prices on Christmas decorations after the holiday is over. —*noun, plural* **slashes.** the act or fact of slashing.

slat [slat] *noun, plural* **slats.** a thin, narrow strip of wood, metal, or other such material: Some of the *slats* in the fence have been broken.

slate [slāt] *noun.* **1.** a bluish-gray rock that splits easily into smooth, thin layers. Slate is used to make blackboards, roofs, and garden tiles. **2.** a small board used to write on with chalk, used in former times for school lessons.

slaugh•ter [slô′tər] *verb,* **slaughtered, slaughtering. 1.** to kill a farm animal for food: to *slaughter* a hog. ◆ A building where this is done is a **slaughterhouse. 2.** to kill many people in a cruel and brutal way. **3.** *Informal.* to defeat very badly: We played the first-place soccer team and got *slaughtered*, 12-0. —*noun, plural* **slaughters.** the act of slaughtering.

slang Poet Carl Sandburg said, "*Slang* is language that takes off its coat, spits on its hands, and gets down to work." Some slang words have been around for hundreds of years, but have never been accepted into the "club" of polite language. The idea that a brave person has a lot of *guts* is an example. Other slang words have made the club as time passed. The 19th-century poet and critic Samuel Coleridge attacked *talented*, which was a new slang term in his day. Today no one would think of it as slang. Some slang words are replaced by newer words. Something *good* has at various times been called *swell, keen, neat, cool, boss, radical*, even *bad*. This dictionary enters very few slang terms. Even if such terms are colorful (and useful) in everyday speech, they are out of place in *writing*. If you describe everything as "cool," you are not using the wonderful range of words that English offers to you.

slant [slant] *verb*, **slanted, slanting. 1.** to move or lie at an angle, rather than straight across or up and down: Roman type (like this) is upright, but italic *(like this) slants* to the right. "A ray of sunlight *slanting* through a window fell yellow on dusty tabletops." (George Orwell). **2.** to present facts or ideas so that they favor one side or point of view: The newspaper publisher was accused of *slanting* the election news to favor the candidate he was supporting. —*noun, plural* **slants.** a slanting line or direction.

slap [slap] *verb*, **slapped, slapping.** to strike quickly and sharply with the open hand or something flat: He *slapped* at the mosquito that landed on his arm. —*noun, plural* **slaps.** a sharp, quick blow.

slash [slash] *verb*, **slashed, slashing. 1.** to cut with a sweeping stroke of a knife or other sharp object: The man was arrested after he *slashed* the famous painting in an attempt to destroy it.

slave [slāv] *noun, plural* **slaves. 1.** a person who is legally owned by another person and who can be sold like a piece of property: Black *slaves* from Africa were brought to America and forced to work on Southern plantations. In ancient Greece and Rome, prisoners captured in war were often kept as *slaves*. **2.** a person who is completely controlled by some harmful habit or need: a *slave* to drugs. **3.** *Informal.* a person who works long and hard for little pay. —*verb*, **slaved, slaving.** to work like a slave; work long and hard: ". . . *slaving* at a killing job in Montana under the scorching sun and in the choking dust." (John Okada)

slav•er•y [slāv′rē] *noun.* **1.** the practice of owning another person as a slave: After the Civil War, *slavery* ended in the U. S. **2.** the condition of being a slave: to be sold into *slavery*.

Slav•ic [slä′vik] *adjective.* **1.** having to do with various related groups of people (**Slavs**) living in Eastern Europe, such as the Russians, Poles, Czechs, Bulgarians, and Serbians. **2.** having to do with the languages spoken by these people.

slay [slā] *verb*, **slew, slain, slaying.** to kill in a violent way; put to death: A famous legend tells of the *slaying* of a dragon by St. George.

sled [sled] *noun, plural* **sleds.** a wooden vehicle, mounted on metal runners, used to carry people and goods over the snow. —*verb*, **sledded, sledding.** to ride or travel by sled.

sledge•ham•mer [slej′ham′ər] *noun, plural* **sledgehammers.** a large, heavy hammer with a long handle, usually used with both hands, as to drive large posts into the ground or break up heavy surfaces such as concrete and rocks.

sleek [slēk] *adjective*, **sleeker, sleekest. 1.** soft and shiny; smooth: a champion race horse with a *sleek* coat. **2.** having a neat, smooth, or stylish appearance: the *sleek* lines of an expensive sports car.

sleep [slēp] *noun.* a natural state of rest for humans and animals that occurs at regular times from day to day. Sleep is a time for the mind and body to regain strength and energy. —*verb*, **slept, sleeping.** to be in this state.

sleeping bag a thickly padded, warm bag in which a person may sleep outdoors.

sleepless [slēp′lis] *adjective.* going without sleep; not sleeping: She spent a *sleepless* night worrying about her problems. —**sleeplessness,** *noun.*

sleep•y [slē′pē] *adjective*, **sleepier, sleepiest. 1.** needing sleep; drowsy. **2.** as if asleep; not active; quiet: "It was an empty, *sleepy* country station and there was hardly anyone on the platform . . ." (C. S. Lewis)

sleet [slēt] *noun.* frozen or partly-frozen rain. —*verb*, **sleeted, sleeting.** to come down as sleet: The roads were very slippery because it had *sleeted* all day.

sleeve [slēv] *noun, plural* **sleeves.** the part of an item of clothing that covers all or part of the arm.

sleigh [slā] *noun, plural* **sleighs.** a vehicle or carriage on runners, used to travel over snow and ice. A sleigh is usually pulled by a horse.

slen•der [slen′dər] *adjective*, **slenderer, slenderest. 1.** not big around; thin, especially in a graceful and attractive way: a *slender* fashion model or ballet dancer. **2.** small in size or amount; not as large as it could be: Peggy won the student election by a *slender* margin.

slept [slept] *verb.* the past form of **sleep.**

slew [sloo] *verb.* the past tense of **slay.**

slice [slīs] *noun, plural* **slices.** a thin, flat piece cut from something larger: a *slice* of bread —*verb*, **sliced, slicing. 1.** to cut into a thin, flat piece or pieces: to *slice* carrots, to *slice* roast beef. **2.** to cut or move like a knife: The motorboat *sliced* through the water.

slick [slik] *adjective.* **slicker, slickest. 1.** having a smooth or slippery surface: "The hilly, winding Scottish roads were *slick* with rain." (Ken Follett) **2.** clever or skillful; smooth: The mayor's new TV commercials are really *slick.* —*noun, plural* **slicks.** a smooth or slippery place. ◆ A place where spilled oil is floating in the water is called an **oil slick.** —*verb*, **slicked, slicking.** to make slick.

slid [slid] *verb.* the past form of **slide.**

slide [slīd] *verb*, **slid, sliding. 1.** to move smoothly and quickly across a surface: He took a run and *slid* across the puddle of ice. "A tear broke from his eye and slowly *slid* down his cheek." (Bernard Malamud) **2.** to shift or move suddenly: "He *slid* past the coat-room girl at the exit . . . disappearing through a swinging door at the end." (Robert Benchley) —*noun, plural* **slides. 1.** the act of sliding: The baseball player made a hard *slide* into second base. **2.** a piece of playground equipment with a smooth, slanting surface, used by children to slide down. **3.** the fall or slipping of a mass of earth, rocks, or snow down a hill. **4.** a small piece of photographic film viewed on a projector.

sleigh This Currier and Ives print of 1853 shows a type of sleigh that was then used in northeastern North America.

Pronunciation Key: T–Z			
t	ten; date	v	very; live
th	think	w	win; away
th	these	y	you
u	cut; butter	z	zoo; cause
ur	turn; bird	zh	measure

(Turn the page for more information.)

S

slight [slīt] *adjective*, **slighter, slightest. 1.** not much; small in amount or importance: Even though she had a *slight* cough, Abby was still able to sing in the school program. **2.** small in size; thin. —*verb*, **slighted, slighting.** to treat as unimportant; not pay attention to; insult: Andy felt *slighted* when the others went out for pizza and didn't invite him. —**slightly,** *adverb*.

slim [slim] *adjective*, **slimmer, slimmest. 1.** slender; thin: That diet must have worked, you look much *slimmer*. **2.** small in amount; slight: His chances of making the team are *slim* if he doesn't start playing better. —*verb*, **slimmed, slimming:** to *slim* down by exercising.

slime [slīm] *noun.* thick, slippery mud or a similar substance. —**slimy,** *adjective.*

sling [sling] *noun, plural* **slings. 1.** a hand-held device for throwing stones or other small objects: A famous Bible story tells of how David uses a *sling* to bring down the giant Goliath. **2.** a piece of cloth that is folded in a triangle and tied around the neck, to support an arm or shoulder while it is recovering from an injury. —*verb*, **slung, slinging. 1.** to hurl a stone or other small object. **2.** to hang or throw loosely: He took off his jacket and *slung* it over his shoulder.

sling•shot [sling′shät′] *noun, plural* **slingshots.** a Y-shaped piece of wood or metal that has an elastic band fastened to the ends of the prongs, used for shooting rocks or other small objects.

slink [slingk] *verb,* **slunk, slinking.** to move in a quiet, sneaking way, as if ashamed, trying to hide, and so on: "There was no way to tell what might be out in the night, *slinking* hungrily through the shadows . . ." (Stephen King)

slip[1] [slip] *verb,* **slipped, slipping. 1.** to slide or move suddenly, so as to lose control: to *slip* on an icy sidewalk. **2.** to move quietly, quickly, or smoothly: "(He) was ahead of us, *slipping* through the crowd easily, nobody touching him." (S. E. Hinton) **3.** to put on or take off clothing quickly: Laura got out of bed and *slipped* into her bathrobe. **4.** to make a mistake: The store *slipped* up and forgot to deliver the package. **5.** to fail to notice or remember: "But so many things were *slipping* away. It was getting so hard to remember." (Joseph Wambaugh) **6.** to become worse; decline: Sales have *slipped* in the past month. —*noun, plural* **slips. 1.** the act of slipping. **2.** a lightweight piece of cloth worn by women under a skirt or dress. **3.** an error; mistake: a *slip* of the tongue.

slip[2] *noun, plural* **slips. 1.** a small piece of paper, usually printed: You fill out a deposit *slip* when you put money in a bank account. **2.** a small twig cut from a plant to start a new plant.

slip•per [slip′ər] *noun, plural* **slippers.** a lightweight, low-cut shoe or sandal: bedroom *slippers,* ballet *slippers.*

slip•per•y [slip′rē] *adjective,* **slipperier, slipperiest. 1.** likely to slip or cause slipping: "The ramp was already *slippery* from the freezing rain." (Joe McGinniss) **2.** not to be trusted; sly; tricky: The police are sure he took the jewels, but he's too *slippery* to be caught with the evidence.

slit [slit] *noun, plural* **slits.** a long, narrow opening or cut: a *slit* up the side of a dress. —*verb,* **slit, slitting.** to make a slit or cut in something: to *slit* open an envelope.

slith•er [slith′ər] *verb,* **slithered, slithering.** to move with a slipping, twisting motion: "The soap *slithers* out of his grip and plunks into the water." (Robert Coover)

sliv•er [sliv′ər] *noun, plural* **slivers.** a small, thin piece of something that has been broken off to a sharp point; a splinter: The mirror broke and he got *slivers* of glass in his hand.

slo•gan [slō′gən] *noun, plural* **slogans.** a phrase or saying that expresses the goals or beliefs of some group. Slogans are often used to draw attention to something in politics or advertising: President Eisenhower's campaign *slogan* was "I Like Ike."

sloop *Sloop* is one of various words having to do with sailing that came into English from Dutch.

sloop [slo͞op] *noun, plural* **sloops.** a small sailboat with one mast.

slop [släp] *verb,* **slopped, slopping. 1.** to spill or splash a liquid in a careless manner. **2.** to give leftover food or garbage to farm animals.

S

slow "She was very old and small and she walked *slowly* in the dark pine shadows . . ." (Eudora Welty) "He worked *slowly* and carefully, keenly aware of his danger." (Jack London) Could you change the *slowly* here to *slow*? With some words, the adjective and adverb are the same: "She's a *fast* learner. She learns *fast.*" But most adverbs add the ending -ly: "He's a *quick* learner. He learns *quickly.*" Highway signs read "Slow." People tend to say "Go slow." Our view is that in serious writing it's best to use *slowly* as an adverb, not *slow*. We don't argue that traffic signs be changed, though—that usage is familiar to everyone and does very well.

slope [slōp] *verb*, **sloped, sloping.** to lie or move at an angle; not be straight across; slant: Their back yard *slopes* down a steep hill to the highway. —*noun, plural* **slopes.** land or any other surface that is not flat or level: a ski *slope.*

slop•py [släp′ē] *adjective*, **sloppier, sloppiest. 1.** very wet; wet and dirty: "His clothes were wet, clammy cold wet, and shoes *sloppy* with snow water." (Langston Hughes) **2.** not neatly done or made; careless; messy: *sloppy* handwriting.

slot [slät] *noun, plural* **slots. 1.** a straight and narrow opening in something; a groove: Pay phones and soda machines have *slots* for coins. **2.** a place or position: That TV show is moving to a different time *slot.*

sloth The claws of the sloth are so strong that it can sleep hanging upside down.

sloth [slôth *or* slōth] *noun, plural* **sloths. 1.** a slow-moving animal of South America. It uses its legs and long, curved claws to hang upside down from trees and can even sleep in this position. ♦ This word first meant "lazy; not willing to work." The animal was thought to be very lazy because of its lack of movement.

slouch [slouch] *verb*, **slouched, slouching.** to sit, stand, or walk in a loose, drooping position. —*noun, plural* **slouches.** a drooping of the head and shoulders.

slow [slō] *adjective*, **slower, slowest. 1.** not fast or quick; moving without much speed: A turtle is a *slow*-moving animal. **2.** taking longer than usual; taking a long time: a calm, easygoing person who is *slow* to anger. **3.** of a watch or clock, behind the correct time. **4.** not quick to learn or understand: a class for *slow* students. —*adverb.* in a slow manner; slowly: Drive *slow* when you pass the school. —*verb*, **slowed, slowing.** to make or become slow: The car *slowed* down and let the other car pass. —**slowly,** *adverb.* —**slowness,** *noun.*

slug[1] [slug] *noun, plural* **slugs. 1.** a slow-moving animal related to and resembling a snail, but usually without a shell. Some slugs live in gardens and others are ocean dwellers. **2.** a piece of lead or other metal that is fired from a gun. **3.** a coin-shaped piece of metal used illegally in place of a coin in a vending machine.

slug[2] *Informal. verb*, **slugged, slugging.** to hit hard, as with the fist or a weapon. —*noun, plural* **slugs.** a hard hit or punch. —**slugger,** *noun.*

slug•gish [slug′ish] *adjective*, **more/most.** slow to move or act: A car's engine is *sluggish* when it's first started on a very cold day. —**sluggishly,** *adverb.* —**sluggishness,** *noun.*

slum [slum] *noun, plural* **slums.** a poor section of a city, in which the buildings are in bad condition, the streets are dirty, and people live crowded together. Slum areas are associated with high rates of crime and disease.

slum•ber [slum′bər] *verb*, **slumbered, slumbering. 1.** to sleep or doze. **2.** to be quiet or inactive, as if sleeping. —*noun.* a sleep or rest: "Just before dawn he fell into a restless and dream-troubled *slumber.*" (Jim Kjelgaard)

Pronunciation Key: [ə] Symbol

The [ə] or *schwa* sound occurs in syllables without an accent. It can be spelled with any vowel, such as **a** in above, **e** in listen, **i** in pencil, **o** in melon, **u** in circus. It can also be a combination of vowels, such as **io** in action, **ai** in mountain, **iou** in precious.

(Turn the page for more information.)

S

slump [slump] *verb*, **slumped, slumping. 1.** to sink or fall heavily; slouch: "His body *slumped* on the curb as if all the muscles had gone out of it." (Stephen King) **2.** to go down in strength or quality; decline: Smith has been *slumping* at bat lately and his average is down to .200. —*noun, plural* **slumps.** the act or fact of slumping: Business in the beach town was in a bit of a *slump* because of the rainy weather.

slunk [slungk] the past form of **slink.**

slung [slung] the past form of **sling.**

slur[1] [slur] *verb*, **slurred, slurring.** to pronounce words in an unclear way, running together certain sounds: "Her speech was *slurred* and difficult to understand . . ." (Dick Francis)

having limited property or activity: *small* farmers, *small* businesses such as barber shops or pet stores. **4.** mean or bitter in a petty way: She made a *small* remark about how funny his shoes looked.

small letter a letter that is not a capital; a lowercase letter.

small•pox [smôl′ päks′] *noun.* a very serious, contagious disease marked by chills, fever, and headaches, and by small blisters that can leave deep, permanent scars on the skin. Smallpox was one of the most serious diseases in history and killed millions of people, but since the 1970's it has been considered to be under control.

---

smart "My dog is very *smart* and does lots of tricks." "He's a very *smart* dresser and always wears the latest styles." "Mom scolded me for making a *smart* remark to Grandma." "I spilled some lemon juice on my cut—it really *smarts*." All of these meanings can be related to an older use of *smart* to mean "sharp; quick." The idea is that a *smart* person has a quick, sharp mind, and so on. In recent years the term "street smart" has come to mean that a person in a city has skills and perhaps instincts that enable him to deal with all sorts of problems. A "street smart" person is not necessarily a good student; in fact, it's usually someone who is not well-educated in the traditional sense.

---

slur[2] *verb*, **slurred, slurring.** to say bad things about; criticize in an unfair way. —*noun, plural* **slurs.** an insulting remark or comment.

slush [slush] *noun.* partly melted snow; watery snow.

sly [slī] *adjective*, **slier, sliest,** or **slyer, slyest. 1.** able to fool or trick: cunning; shrewd: The fox has been called a *sly* animal because it is so good at escaping from hunters. **2.** full of mischief; playful in a clever way: He had a *sly* grin on his face when his sister found the frog in her lunch box. **3. on the sly.** in a sly way; secretly. —**slyly,** *adverb.* —**slyness,** *noun.*

smack [smak] *verb*, **smacked, smacking. 1.** to make a sharp sound by closing and opening the lips quickly. **2.** to strike or bump sharply making a loud noise: A sudden wind blew across the yard and the kitchen door *smacked* shut. —*noun, plural* **smacks. 1.** a noisy or sharp blow against a surface; a slap. **2.** a loud kiss. —*adverb.* straight into; directly: The branch swung back and hit me *smack* in the face.

small [smôl] *adjective*, **smaller, smallest. 1.** not large in size or number; little: Deserts get only a *small* amount of rain. Perfume is sold in *small* bottles. **2.** not important or serious: a *small* problem. They made *small* talk to pass the time while they waited for the bus. **3.** of a business,

smart [smärt] *adjective*, **smarter, smartest. 1.** having a good mind; quick to learn and understand; intelligent; bright. **2.** making good judgments; clever: She is a *smart* shopper who finds good bargains everywhere. **3.** quick and lively; brisk. **4.** in style; fashionable: "Graham and Carol both wear *smart* cross-country outfits." (Alice Adams) —*verb*, **smarted, smarting. 1.** to cause or feel a sharp, stinging pain: Don't touch my sunburn—it really *smarts!* **2.** to feel distress or hurt feelings: She is still *smarting* over what the other girls said about her. —**smartly,** *adverb:* "To the southwest an arctic hare rises up, immediately *smartly* alert." (Barry Lopez)

smash [smash] *verb*, **smashed, smashing. 1.** to break into many pieces with great force: At the launching of a new ship, it is a custom to *smash* a bottle of champagne against the bow. **2.** to strike or hit with a hard blow: "The wind *smashed* against the faces of Perce and Gay standing on the truck bed." (Arthur Miller) —*noun, plural* **smashes.** the act of something breaking in a violent way.

smear [smēr] *verb*, **smeared, smearing. 1.** to spread or stain using a sticky, dirty, or greasy substance: Young children like to fingerpaint because they can *smear* paint all over the paper. **2.** to be or cause to be blurred or messy: I couldn't read Mom's note because the ink got

S

smeared. **3.** to harm or spoil someone's reputation. —*noun, plural* **smears. 1.** a spot or stain caused by smearing: an oily *smear* on wallpaper. **2.** a false charge or criticism: The mayor accused the newspaper of using *smear* tactics against him.

smell [smel] *verb,* **smelled** or **smelt, smelling. 1.** to recognize or discover an odor by using the nose; use the sense of the nose. **2.** to have or give off an unpleasant odor: The boat's deck *smelled* of dead fish. —*noun, plural* **smells. 1.** the sense used to recognize odors. **2.** a particular odor or scent: I love the *smell* of freshly-ground coffee beans.

smelt[1] [smelt] *noun, plural* **smelts** or **smelt.** a small, silvery fish related to trout. Smelts live in cool waters of the Northern Hemisphere and are used for food.

smelt[2] *verb,* **smelted, smelting.** to melt ores to separate the metal from them: Iron ore must be *smelted* before it can be made into steel.

smelt[3] a past form of **smell.**

smile [smīl] *noun, plural* **smiles.** an expression of the face in which the corners of the mouth turn upward, to show a feeling of being happy, amused, or friendly. —*verb,* **smiled, smiling.** to have or show a smile.

smock [smäk] *noun, plural* **smocks.** a loosely fitting garment like a coat or shirt, worn over regular clothing to keep it from getting dirty. Artists and medical or laboratory workers often wear smocks while working.

smog A layer of smog over Chicago, along the lake front. *Smog* is formed from the words s<u>m</u>oke and f<u>og</u>.

smog [smag] *noun.* polluted air that is a mixture of smoke and fog. Smog is caused by the exhaust that comes from automobiles and factories in larger cities.

smoke [smōk] *noun, plural* **smokes.** a substance that is given off by something burning. Smoke is a combination of carbon particles and gases. It can be seen because it has tiny pieces of soot and ash in it. —*verb,* **smoked, smoking. 1.** to give off smoke: The flames are out, but the brush fire was still *smoking.* **2.** to take in and blow out smoke from a cigarette, cigar, or pipe. **3.** to preserve meat or fish by using smoke from certain kinds of wood: *Smoked* salmon and *smoked* ham are popular foods.

smoker [smō′kər] *noun, plural* **smokers.** a person who smokes cigarettes or other forms of tobacco.

smoke·stack [smōk′stak′] *noun, plural* **smoke-stacks.** a tall chimney for taking off smoke, as in a factory or on an ocean liner.

smok·y [smō′kē] *adjective,* **smokier, smokiest. 1.** giving off a lot of smoke, or filled with smoke: a *smoky* room. **2.** having the color or taste of smoke.

smol·der [smōl′dər] *verb,* **smoldered, smoldering. 1.** to burn or smoke with little or no flame. **2.** to show strong feelings that are just below the surface: He watched in silence as she left, his eyes *smoldering* with anger.

smooth [smo͞oth] *adjective,* **smoother, smoothest. 1.** having a surface that is not rough or uneven: A baby has *smooth* skin. The wind died down completely, and the lake was *smooth* and quiet. **2.** free from bumps or jolts; gentle: The pilot made a *smooth* landing. **3.** free from trouble or problems: The travel agent arranged everything so that our trip would be *smooth* and easy. **4.** not harsh or bitter to the taste: a cheese with a *smooth* flavor. —*verb,* **smoothed, smoothing. 1.** to level or make even; flatten: Ben *smoothed* the ground around the tree he had planted. **2.** to make easy or easier; take away troubles or problems. —**smoothly,** *adverb.* —**smoothness,** *noun.*

smoth·er [smuth′ər] *verb,* **smothered, smothering. 1.** to keep from getting enough air; suffocate. **2.** to cause a fire to go out by covering it: When the pan caught fire, Tracy quickly put the lid on to *smother* the flames. **3.** to cover thickly with something: "At times the wind blew so fiercely, it made one feel that the sand would eventually *smother* the tiny

---

Pronunciation Key: Accent Marks

[′] is the normal accent mark. It shows where the main stress falls on a word.
[′] is a secondary accent mark. It shows a lighter stress than the primary accent. For example:

tel • e • vis • ion [tel′ə vizh′ən]
(Turn the page for more information.)

settlement . . ." (John R. Tunis) **4.** to hide; conceal: "They talked and laughed, *smothering* their giggles under the bedclothes." (Eleanor Estes)

smudge [smuj] *verb*, **smudged, smudging.** to make dirty by smearing: She *smudged* ink all over her paper because the pen was leaking. —*noun, plural* **smudges.** a dirty mark or stain made by smearing.

smug [smug] *adjective*, **smugger, smuggest.** pleased with oneself to the point of annoying others, showing great self-satisfaction: "I got the only 'A' grade in the class," she said in a *smug* voice. —**smugly,** *adverb*.

smug•gle [smug′ əl] *verb*, **smuggled, smuggling. 1.** to take goods into a country in a secret and illegal way: When it was against the law to sell liquor in the U.S., Chicago gangsters *smuggled* it in from Canada. **2.** to carry or take secretly: He wasn't supposed to have candy while he was sick, but his friends *smuggled* some into the hospital. —**smuggler,** *noun*.

snack [snak] *noun, plural* **snacks.** a small amount of food or drink taken between regular meals; a light meal.

snag [snag] *noun, plural* **snags. 1.** a sharp or rough place on which things can be caught or torn, such as a branch or stump of a tree underwater. **2.** a hidden or unexpected problem that blocks progress: The plans for the new house hit a *snag* when he found that he needed a special permit to build on the land. —*verb*, **snagged, snagging.** to catch on a snag: Linda's knit dress was *snagged* by a rough spot on the chair.

snail [snāl] *noun, plural* **snails.** a small, slow-moving animal that has a soft body protected by a coiled shell. A snail moves by using a muscular body part called a *foot*. There are thousands of kinds of snails found throughout the world, both on land and in water.

snake [snāk] *noun, plural* **snakes.** a reptile that has a long, slender body with no limbs, a large mouth, and a covering of dry scales. It moves along the ground by tensing its powerful muscles. Some kinds of snakes have a poisonous bite. —*verb*, **snaked, snaking.** to move in a twisting or winding pattern, as a snake moves along the ground: The Mississippi River *snakes* back and forth as it flows to the sea.

snap [snap] *verb*, **snapped, snapping. 1.** to make a sharp, quick sound: to *snap* a whip, to *snap* your fingers. **2.** to break suddenly: The dry branch *snapped* in two when she stepped on it. **3.** to grab at or take quickly and eagerly: The

dog *snapped* at me when I tried to pet it. The sale prices were so low that the customers *snapped* up everything right away. **4.** to act or go with a quick, exact movement: "He went out the front door, *snapping* the lock behind him." (Lois Lenski) "The sentry *snapped* to attention as the great man appeared." (C. S. Forester) **5.** to take a photograph: Stand over by the fountain and I'll *snap* your picture. —*noun, plural* **snaps. 1.** the act or sound of snapping. **2.** a fastener that makes a clicking sound when opened or closed. **3.** a short period of very cold weather. **4.** *Informal.* something that is easy to do. —*adjective.* made suddenly without careful thought: When Mom buys a dress she looks at a lot of different ones rather than making a *snap* decision.

snap•dra•gon [snap′ drag′ ən] *noun, plural* **snapdragons.** a garden flower that grows in clusters on a long stalk and can be yellow, white, red, or pink in color.

snap•shot [snap′ shät′] *noun, plural* **snapshots.** a quick or informal photograph.

snare [snâr] *noun, plural* **snares.** a trap for catching small animals. A snare uses a rope or wire that jerks tightly around the animal when it steps into the trap. —*verb*, **snared, snaring.** to catch with or as if with a snare: to *snare* a rabbit. The robber was *snared* by the police as he tried to cross the border.

snail Four kinds of snails. Above, the periwinkle (left) and the common garden snail (right); below, the shark eye and the Helinca Margarite.

snarl¹ [snärl] *verb*, **snarled, snarling. 1.** of a dog or similar animal, to growl while showing the teeth. **2.** to speak in an angry or bad-tempered way: "'You said you'd lead me to some runaways,' the slavecatcher *snarled*." (Jean Fritz) —*noun, plural* **snarls.** an angry growl.

snarl² *noun, plural* **snarls. 1.** a mass of knots, twists, and so on; a tangled mess: She had just gotten out of bed and her hair was full of *snarls.* **2.** a tangled, confused situation or condition. —*verb,* **snarled, snarling.** to put into a snarl; make tangled or confused: The accident *snarled* traffic at the intersection all morning.

snatch [snach] *verb,* **snatched, snatching.** to grab suddenly: A thief tried to *snatch* her purse. "Then with a sudden swift spring he had *snatched* the piece of chocolate out of his sister's hand . . ." (George Orwell) —*noun, plural* **snatches. 1.** the act of grabbing or snatching. **2.** *usually,* **snatches.** a short period or amount; a little bit: "From the town came *snatches* of music." (Graham Greene)

sniff [snif] *verb,* **sniffed, sniffing. 1.** to breathe in through the nose in short quick breaths. **2.** to smell by sniffing: The dog *sniffed* the paper bag to see if there was food inside. —*noun, plural* **sniffs.** the act or sound of air being drawn quickly through the nose.

snif•fle [snif′əl] *verb,* **sniffled, sniffling.** to breathe loudly by sniffing through the nose, as when crying or when sick with a cold. —*noun, plural* **sniffles. 1.** the act or sound of sniffling. **2.** **sniffles.** a slight head cold.

snip [snip] *verb,* **snipped, snipping.** to cut with scissors in short, quick strokes: Betty *snipped* the ends of the flower stems before she put them in water. —*noun, plural* **snips.** the act of snipping, or a piece that is snipped off.

---

sneak You've probably heard the word *sneak* used as *snuck*: "I *snuck* right up behind him and yelled 'Boo!'" Although this form, *snuck*, is used by people in their everyday conversation, it's not a correct form for use in writing. The correct past tense form of *sneak* is *sneaked*: "When he thought the guard was looking the other way, he *sneaked* toward the door." It's hard to tell how *snuck* came to be used. In any event, it seems to be a fairly new word. Also, it seems to be confined to American English. Our survey of famous authors showed that they entirely avoid the term. So should you, in your own writing.

---

sneak [snēk] *verb,* **sneaked, sneaking. 1.** to move or act in a quiet, secret way, so as not to be seen or noticed: He didn't have enough money for the movie, so he tried to *sneak* in through a side door. **2.** to get or have in a secret way: " . . . Peter reached over her shoulder to *sneak* some popcorn." (John Barth) —*noun, plural* **sneaks.** a person who is dishonest or who acts in a secret way. —**sneaky,** *adjective.*

sneak•er [snē′kər] *noun, plural* **sneakers.** a light sports shoe with a rubber sole, worn to play tennis, basketball, and so on. ♦ The name comes from the idea that a person can walk quietly in sneakers.

sneer [snēr] *noun, plural* **sneers.** an expression like a twisted smile, showing anger, dislike or lack of respect. —*verb,* **sneered, sneering.** to have or say with a sneer.

sneeze [snēz] *verb,* **sneezed, sneezing.** to force air out through the nose and mouth in a sudden, violent way that cannot be stopped or controlled. People sneeze when the nerves of the nose are irritated by some object. —*noun, plural* **sneezes.** the act of sneezing.

snick•er [snik′ər] *noun, plural* **snickers.** a sly or cruel laugh that shows scorn, dislike, or disrespect; and so on. —*verb,* **snickered, snick•ering.** to laugh in this way: The boys in the other team's dugout *snickered* as Todd swung and missed the ball badly.

snipe [snīp] *noun, plural* **snipes.** a bird with a narrow, pointed bill and brown feathers with black and white spots. It lives in wet areas.

snip•er [snī′pər] *noun, plural* **snipers.** a rifleman who surprises an enemy by firing from a hidden place.

snob [snäb] *noun, plural* **snobs. 1.** someone who thinks he is better than others because of his wealth or position; someone who avoids or ignores people that he feels do not have the proper standing in society. **2.** a person who claims great knowledge or taste in some area, and who looks down on the taste of others: a wine *snob.*

snoop [snoop] *Informal. noun, plural* **snoops.** a person who looks secretly into other people's private affairs: She called her brother a *snoop* after she found him reading her diary. —*verb,* **snooped, snooping.** to go prying or sneaking in this way: "It's not decent to *snoop* around spying on people like that." (William Inge)

Pronunciation Key: A–F

a	and; hat	ch	chew; such
ā	ate; stay	d	dog; lid
â	care; air	e	end; yet
ä	father; hot	ē	she; each
b	boy; cab	f	fun; off

(Turn the page for more information.)

snooze [snōōz] *Informal. verb,* **snoozed, snooz-ing.** to sleep or nap; doze off. —*noun, plural,* **snoozes.** a quick nap or sleep.

snore [snôr] *verb,* **snored, snoring.** to make loud, rough breathing sounds while sleeping. —*noun, plural* **snores.** such a noise.

snor·kel [snôr′kəl] *noun, plural* **snorkels.** a short tube through which a person can breathe while swimming just under the surface of the water.

snort [snôrt] *verb,* **snorted, snorting.** to blow air through the nose with great force and noise. —*noun, plural* **snorts.** a loud, forceful noise made through the nose, as by a horse.

snout [snout] *noun, plural* **snouts.** in certain animals such as dogs, pigs, or crocodiles, the long front part of the head that extends outward.

snow [snō] *noun, plural* **snows. 1.** the white crystals or flakes of frozen water vapor that fall from the sky. **2.** a snowfall: We always have heavy *snows* this time of year in the mountains. —*verb,* **snowed, snowing. 1.** to fall as snow. **2.** to cover, block, or shut in with snow, or as if with snow: to be *snowed* in during a big storm. She was *snowed* under with homework during exam week. **3.** to fall like snow: "Above her head bits of sawdust *snowed* down from the wooden roof . . ." (Paul Theroux)

snowflake A greatly enlarged view of a snowflake clinging to a tiny leaf.

snow·ball [snō′bôl′] *noun, plural* **snowballs.** a small mass of snow that is packed together to resemble a ball. —*verb,* **snowballed, snowball-ing.** to grow bigger very quickly: After the company started advertising its new toy, orders for it began to *snowball.*

snow·bank [snō′bangk′] *noun, plural* **snow-banks.** a large mass of snow piled up against something; also called a **snowdrift.**

snow·fall [snō′fäl′] *noun, plural* **snowfalls.** the amount of snow that falls in a certain amount of time or at a particular place.

snow·flake [snō′flāk′] *noun, plural* **snow-flakes.** one of the small, six-sided ice crystals that fall as snow.

snow·man [snō′man′] *noun, plural* **snowmen.** a mass of snow shaped into the rough figure of a person.

snowmobile Snowmobile racing at Yellowstone National Park in Montana.

snow·mo·bile [snō′mō bēl′] *noun, plural* **snowmobiles.** a small open vehicle that travels over snow on ski-like runners. It is powered by an engine.

snow·plow [snō′plou′] *noun, plural* **snow-plows.** a large truck with a wide, curved blade mounted on the front, used to push snow off a road or other surface.

snow·shoe [snō′shōō′] *noun, plural* **snow-shoes.** one of a pair of flat, webbed frames that attach to shoes or boots, used to keep a person from sinking while walking on deep snow.

snow·y [snō′ē] *adjective,* **snowier, snowiest. 1.** covered with or having snow: a *snowy* day, *snowy* weather. **2.** like snow: The sky was bright blue and the clouds were *snowy* white.

snug [snug] *adjective,* **snugger, snuggest. 1.** warm and secure; comfortable; cozy: I went home early and was *snug* in bed before the snowstorm hit. **2.** tight or close-fitting: These shoes are a little *snug.* Could I try a larger size? —**snugly,** *adverb.*

snug·gle [snug′əl] *verb,* **snuggled, snuggling.** to move up against or lie close to someone, for warmth or out of love: "She *snuggled* down again beneath the coarse blankets, for it was very cold." (Herman Wouk) "She got their baby from the crib, and *snuggled* it up to him." (Ernie Pyle)

so There are a number of different ways to use this simple word. Here are a few points to remember: (1) *So* may be used either with the word *that* following or without it. It's considered more correct to include *that*: "Lake George is *so* clear *that* objects far below the surface can be seen in total definition." (John McPhee) (2) *So* can be used to begin a sentence. "*So* as soon as she got married and moved away from home the first thing she did was separate!" (Eudora Welty) (3) *So* is often used to mean *very*, as in "I'm *so* embarrassed!" Some critics, E.B. White for one, say that this use of the word so should be avoided. But in *Charlotte's Web*, White himself wrote: "All the animals trusted her, she was *so* quiet and friendly." A more practical rule seems to be that this use should be avoided in short sentences, such as "This is *so* confusing."

so [sō] *adverb*. **1.** to a certain extent or degree: It was *so* cold she wore her warmest coat. **2.** in a way stated or suggested: I didn't like it, and I told him *so*. **3.** in the same way; likewise; also: Margie got an 'A' and *so* did Bill. **4.** very much; extremely: Tina always seems *so* happy. **5.** most certainly; indeed: You did *so* say I could borrow your bike! —*adjective*. true: She thinks I don't like her, but that's just not *so*. —*conjunction*. with the result or purpose that: I missed the bus, *so* I had to walk. —*interjection*: So, it's you!

soak [sōk] *verb*, **soaked, soaking. 1.** to let sit in water or other liquid: He *soaked* the tablecloth overnight to get the grape juice out. **2.** to make very wet; wet completely: We'll be *soaked* to the skin if we go out in this downpour. **3.** to take or draw in; absorb: "He climbed a hill and lay on his back listening to the silence, feeling the warmth of the sun *soak* into his bones." (J. M. Coetzee)

soap [sōp] *noun, plural* **soaps.** a common cleaning substance usually made from fat and lye. Soap comes in the form of bars, liquids, powders, or flakes. —*verb*, **soaped, soaping.** to rub or cover with soap. —**soapy,** *adjective*.

soar [sôr] *verb*, **soared, soaring. 1.** to fly very high and seemingly without effort: The glider *soared* gracefully over the valley. "He *soared* over three fences like a bird, and disappeared down the road . . ." (Mark Twain) **2** to rise or greatly increase; go very high: a hot day on which the temperature *soars* into the 90's.

sob [säb] *verb*, **sobbed, sobbing.** to cry with short, quick catches of breath; cry hard. —*noun, plural* **sobs.** the act of crying in this way.

so•ber [sō′bər] *adjective*, **soberer, soberest. 1.** not drinking too much alcohol; not drunk. **2.** very serious; solemn; grave: Men who work for that bank are required to wear *sober* gray or blue suits. —*verb*, **sobered, sobering.** to make

sober: The girls laughed and giggled in their seats, but an angry look from the teacher had a *sobering* effect on them. —**soberly,** *adverb*.

so-called [sō′ kôld′] *adjective*. called such, but not actually so: It turned out that the *so-called* war hero had never even been near a battle.

soc•cer [säk′ ər] *noun*. a game played on a large field by two teams of eleven players each who try to get a round ball into a goal by kicking it or moving it with any part of the body but the hands and arms. ◆ The word *soccer* is short for As*soc*iation Football, the official name of the game in England, where soccer began. Most countries other than the U.S. still call this game *football*.

so•cia•ble [sō′ shə bəl] *adjective, more/most*. liking to be with other people; friendly: I wish he'd be more *sociable*, instead of spending so much time watching TV alone.

so•cial [sō′ shəl] *adjective*. **1.** having to do with society; having to do with people in groups or people in general: Great *social* changes came about in Europe when machines began to be used to make things. **2.** of animals, living together in groups, as humans do: Bees and ants are *social* insects. **3.** having to do with friends or friendly relations: Cindy is very popular at school and has an active *social* life. **4.** having to do with people who are rich, famous, fashionable, and so on: Her wedding was the *social* event of the year. —*noun, plural* **socials.** a friendly gathering; a party: a church *social*. —**socially,** *adverb*.

	Pronunciation Key: G–N		
g	give; big	k	kind; cat; back
h	hold	l	let; ball
i	it; this	m	make; time
ī	ice; my	n	not; own
j	jet; gem; edge	ng	having

(Turn the page for more information.)

so•cial•ism [sō′shəl iz′əm] (*also,* **Socialism**) *noun.* a system of economics and government in which the factories, land, businesses, and other means of producing goods are owned and managed by the government rather than by individual people or companies.

socialist [sō′shəl ist] (*also,* **Socialist**) *noun, plural* **socialists.** a person who believes in or practices socialism, or is a member of a socialist party or group.

social science 1. the study of human relationships and the way society works. History, government, economics, geography, sociology, and anthropology are social sciences. **2.** *usually,* **social studies.** the study of history, geography, and other social sciences as a subject in school.

social security 1. a government program to provide economic security to people who are unable to work, because of old age, illness, and so on. **2. Social Security.** a U. S. government program of this type. It uses payroll taxes paid by workers and employers to provide regular payments to retired workers and others.

social work a profession that brings social services and assistance to people in need, in areas such as health care, mental health, and family and child welfare. ◆ A person trained to do this work is a **social worker.**

so•ci•e•ty [sə sī′ə tē] *noun, plural* **societies. 1.** all human beings; people living and working together as a large group: The judge gave the man a long prison term because she considered him a threat to *society.* **2.** a certain group of people: Women have a less active role in Arab *society* than in Western countries. **3.** a group of people who share a common interest or purpose: the *Society* for the Prevention of Cruelty to Animals. At college Dad belonged to a club called the Emerson Literary *Society.* **4.** *also,* **high society.** people thought of as having a high rank in society; fashionable, rich, or famous people.

sock¹ [säk] *noun, plural* **socks.** a knitted or woven covering for the foot and lower leg.

sock² *verb,* **socked, socking.** *Informal.* to hit or punch.

sock•et [säk′it] *noun, plural* **sockets.** an opening or hollow place forming a holder for something: the eye *sockets,* an electric light *socket.*

Soc•ra•tes [säk′rə tēz] 469?-399 B.C., Greek philosopher and teacher.

sod [säd] *noun.* **1.** the surface of ground containing grass and its roots. **2.** a piece or layer of ground held together by grass and roots and not tightly secured to the earth: People who do not want to plant a new lawn from seed may use pieces of *sod* instead. —*verb,* **sodded, sodding.** to cover or plant with sod.

so•da [sō′də] *noun, plural* **sodas. 1.** a drink made with carbonated water and sweet flavoring. **2.** a similar drink containing ice cream. **3.** a white powder made with sodium. Soda is used in soap, in making glass, and in cooking and medicine.

so•di•um [sō′dē əm] *noun.* a soft, waxy, silvery element. Sodium occurs in nature only in combination with other substances. Table salt and sodas contain sodium.

so•fa [sō′fə] *noun, plural* **sofas.** a long, padded, cloth-covered seat or couch with a back and arms. Sofas can seat two or more people, and some can be converted into beds.

soft [sôft] *adjective,* **softer, softest. 1.** easily giving way to the touch: a *soft* feather pillow, a *soft* cotton ball. **2.** not rough or coarse; smooth and light to the touch: Rabbits and kittens have *soft* fur. **3.** not too strong or extreme; gentle; mild: *soft* music, *soft* lights, a *soft* breeze. **4.** not in good physical condition; lacking strength; weak. **5.** affected by the emotions; gentle and kind: Because of her *soft* heart, Beth feeds all the stray cats in the neighborhood. —**softly,** *adverb.* —**softness,** *noun.*

soft•ball [sôft′bôl′] *noun, plural* **softballs. 1.** a game like baseball but played with lighter bats and a larger, softer ball that is pitched underhand. **2.** the ball used in this game. ◆ **Fast-pitch softball** uses nine players and fast pitching. **Slow-pitch softball** uses ten players and requires the ball to be pitched in a high arc.

soft drink a sweet, carbonated drink made without alcohol; a soda.

sod house With few trees on the prairies for lumber, settlers dug sod out of the ground to build houses like this one in Nebraska (1886).

S

soft•en [sôf′ən] *verb*, **softened, softening.** to make or become softer: to *soften* butter by warming it. "Every year when the weather changed and the days *softened* into summer . . ." (Pete Hamill)

soft•ware [sôft′wâr′] *noun*, *plural* **software.** the programs that make a computer operate. Software is information and instructions for the computer. HARDWARE is machinery such as a keyboard, a display screen, or a printer.

sog•gy [säg′ē] *adjective*, **soggier, soggiest.** soaked with water; wet and heavy: The rain made the hiking trail *soggy* and difficult to walk on.

soil [soil] *noun*, *plural* **soils. 1.** the loose surface part of the earth in which plants grow; dirt; earth: The Midwestern region of the U.S. is known for its rich *soil*. **2.** country; land: "I have returned . . . our forces stand again on Philippine *soil*." (Douglas MacArthur) —*verb*, **soiled, soiling.** to make or become dirty; stain: The children *soiled* their clothes playing in the mud.

so•lar [sō′lər] *adjective*. having to do with the sun: *solar* energy. A *solar* eclipse is a blocking of the sun's rays from the earth's view.

solar system the sun and all the things that revolve around it, including planets, comets, and other heavenly bodies.

solar system A painting of the solar system by Helmut Wimmer, showing the sun with the planets in their orbits.

sold [sōld] *verb*. the past form of **sell.**

sol•der [säd′ər] *noun*. a metal that is melted and used to join two metal surfaces. A mixture of lead and tin is a common solder. —*verb*, **soldered, soldering.** to bind, fuse, or mend with solder.

sol•dier [sōl′jər] *noun*, *plural* **soldiers.** a person who serves in the army, especially one who is not an officer.
◆ The term *soldier* goes back to *solidus*, a gold coin that was used to pay soldiers in the ancient Roman army.

sole¹ [sōl] *noun*, *plural* **soles.** the bottom part of the foot, or of a shoe, slipper, or boot. —*verb*, **soled, soling.** to put a sole on a shoe or boot, or repair a sole: Mike had his hiking boots re-*soled* because the the tread was worn away.

sole² *adjective*. **1.** being the only one; single; alone: The famous novel *Last of the Mohicans* tells of an Indian who is the *sole* survivor among his tribe. **2.** limited to one person or group; exclusive: The Supreme Court has the *sole* responsibility for deciding if a law violates the Constitution. —**solely**, *adverb*.

sole The sole is one of the few creatures in nature that does not have a symmetrical body. It has both eyes on the top of its body.

sole³ *noun*, *plural* **sole** or **soles.** a flatfish related to the flounder, usually found near shore in warmer seas. The sole is a popular food fish.

sol•emn [säl′əm] *adjective*, *more/most*. very serious; grave: It is a *solemn* moment when a new President takes the oath of office. —**solemnly**, *adverb*: "They marched *solemnly*, silently up the stone steps of the main hall." (John Toland) ◆ The fact of being solemn is **solemnity** [sə lem′nə tē].

Pronunciation Key: O–S

ō	over; go	ou	out; town
ô	all; law	p	put; hop
oo	look; full	r	run; car
o͞o	pool; who	s	set; miss
oi	oil; boy	sh	show

(Turn the page for more information.)

sol·id [säl′id] *adjective, more/most.* **1.** having a definite shape and some amount of firmness; not a liquid or gas: Ice is the *solid* form of water. **2.** made entirely of one material or kind: a table of *solid* oak, a *solid* gold wedding ring. **3.** in firm agreement; united: In former times the southern states were called "the *Solid South*" because they all voted Democratic. **4.** without breaks; entire: She slept for twelve *solid* hours. —*noun, plural* **solids.** a substance that has shape and firmness and is not a liquid or gas. Wood, rocks, and metal are examples of solids. —**solidly,** *adverb:* The mayor favors the plan, and the council is *solidly* behind him. ♦ The fact of being solid is **solidity** [sə lid′ə tē].

solid-state [säl′id stāt′] *adjective.* having to do with the use of solid materials in electronic parts, such as transistors and certain kinds of circuits. *Solid-state* materials replaced vacuum tubes in radios, TV sets, and computers.

sol·i·taire [säl′ə târ] *noun, plural* **solitaires. 1.** a card game for one player. **2.** a single diamond or other gem set in a ring alone.

sol·i·tar·y [säl′ə ter′ē] *adjective.* **1.** being the only one; alone or single: "Mrs. Petrides was . . . a silent *solitary* thing like a tree alone in a field." (Kate Simon) **2.** by itself; isolated; lonely: "Orlando naturally loved *solitary* places, vast views . . ." (Virginia Woolf) ♦ The fact of being alone is **solitude** [säl′ə tood′].

so·lo [sō′lō] *noun, plural* **solos.** music played or sung by a single person: a piano *solo.* —*adjective; adverb.* done or performed by a single person: Charles Lindbergh was the first to fly *solo* across the Atlantic Ocean.

Sol·o·mon [säl′ə mən] died about 922 B.C., a king of the ancient Hebrews, the son of David.

sol·u·ble [säl′yə bəl] *adjective, more/most.* **1.** able to be dissolved in liquid: Sugar is *soluble* in water. **2.** able to be solved: "Many of the problems facing us may be *soluble* . . ." (Carl Sagan)

so·lu·tion [sə loo′shən] *noun, plural* **solutions.** **1.** an answer to a problem; an explanation: The newspaper prints a crossword puzzle one day and gives the *solution* in the next day's paper. **2.** a mixture of some substance dissolved in a liquid. ♦ A substance in which another can be dissolved is a **solvent.**

solve [sälv] *verb,* **solved, solving.** to find an answer or solution for; explain: The famous math problem known as Fermat's Last Theorem could not be *solved* for over 350 years. "If the Germans discovered Room 40 had *solved* their code they would never use it again." (Barbara Tuchman)

som·ber [säm′bər] *adjective, more/most.* dark, gloomy, and depressing: "The sunshiny open meadow was refreshing after the *somber* shade of the trees." (Beatrix Potter)

sombrero These men are wearing sombreros to represent the poor farmers who were led by the patriot Emiliano Zapata in the Mexican Revolution.

som·bre·ro [säm brâr′ō] *noun, plural* **sombreros.** a straw or felt hat with a very wide brim.

some [sum] *adjective.* being a thing that is referred to, but not named or known: Do you want *some* bread with your dinner? He said he'd call back *some* time tonight. —*pronoun:* I've read *some* of the book, but not all.

some·bod·y [sum′bud′ē] *pronoun.* **1.** a person; some person who is not known or named: *Somebody* called for you while you were out, but he didn't leave his name. **2.** an important person: Terry isn't content to stay around this little town; he wants to be *somebody.*

somebody "*Somebody* took my newspaper off the bench. I guess *they* thought I was through with it." According to strict rules of grammar, this should read "*Somebody* took my newspaper . . . I guess *he* thought . . ." because "somebody" is singular. In everyday conversation, people often break this rule because they want to express the idea that the "somebody" could be either a male or a female. "Every few months *somebody* writes me and asks if I will give *him* a name for *his* dog." (James Thurber) This would be awkward as ". . . if I will give *him or her* a name for *his or her* dog." And it would be confusing as, ". . . if I will give *them* a name for *their* dog."

some·day [sum′ dā′] *adverb*. at some time in the future: I hope to learn to fly a plane *someday*.

some·how [sum′ hou′] *adverb*. in a way that is not known or stated; in some way or another: I don't know how the dog got out; I guess *somehow* he pushed open the back door.

some·one [sum′ wun′] *pronoun*. some unknown or unnamed person; somebody.

som·er·sault [sum′ ər sôlt′] *noun*, *plural* **somersaults.** the act of rolling the body in a complete circle by bringing the feet up and over the head. —*verb*, **somersaulted, somersaulting.** to do a somersault.

some·thing [sum′ thing] *pronoun*. an unknown or unnamed thing: There's *something* wrong with the car—it's making a funny clicking noise. —*adverb*. to some degree; somewhat: A cheetah looks *something* like a leopard.

some·time [sum′ tīm′] *adverb*. at an indefinite time; at one time or another: He lives near us now—we'll have to visit him *sometime*.

some·times [sum′ tīmz′] *adverb*. now and then; at times: The winters are mild here, but *sometimes* we get a bit of frost.

some·what [sum′ wut′] *adverb*. to some amount; rather: They sold their house, but the price was *somewhat* lower than they'd wanted.

some·where [sum′ wâr′] *adverb*. **1.** in or to some unknown or unnamed place: If you're looking for the basketball, it's *somewhere* in the garage. **2.** at an unknown or unnamed point; about: The poet Chaucer died in 1400; he was born *somewhere* around 1340. **3. get somewhere.** to make progress; have some success.

son [sun] *noun*, *plural* **sons. 1.** a person's male child. **2.** a male thought of as being related to something like a son: The *Sons* of Liberty were patriots who opposed British rule of the American colonies.

so·nar [sō′ när] *noun*, *plural* **sonars.** an instrument that sends out and receives reflected sound waves in order to discover the location of objects under water. Sonar is used by fishing boats to find their catch, or by warships to detect submarines. ◆ This word comes from *so*und *na*vigation and *r*anging.

so·na·ta [sə nä′ tə] *noun*, *plural* **sonatas.** a musical composition written for one or two instruments and having three or four distinct sections that vary in rhythm or form.

song [sông] *noun*, *plural* **songs. 1.** a musical piece performed by the voice; music that is sung. **2.** music-like sounds made by a bird.

song·bird [sông′ burd′] *noun*, *plural* **songbirds.** any bird that sings or has a musical call.

son·ic [sän′ ik] *adjective*. having to do with or caused by sound waves. A **sonic boom** is an explosive sound occurring when an aircraft travels at speeds faster than sound.

son-in-law [sun′ in lô] *noun*, *plural* **sons-in-law.** the husband of a person's daughter.

son·net [sän′ it] *noun*, *plural* **sonnets.** a fourteen line poem that has ten syllables in each line, a certain rhythm, and a set pattern of rhyme.

soon [soon] *adverb*. **1.** in the near future; before long: Dad called from the store to say he'd be home *soon*. **2.** ahead of time; early: He took the meat out of the oven too *soon* and it wasn't cooked enough. **3.** quickly; fast: Billy *soon* tired of his new toy and began playing with something else. **4.** by choice; readily: I'd just as *soon* skip lunch so that we can get this finished now.

soot [soot] *noun*. a clinging, greasy black powder formed when fuel such as wood or coal is burned. Soot gives smoke a grayish or black color and makes the insides of chimneys and fireplaces dirty.

soothe [sooth] *verb*, **soothed, soothing. 1.** to calm down or quiet; comfort: The trainer *soothed* the frightened horse. **2.** to ease pain; relieve: He *soothed* his aching muscles with a heating pad. —**soothing,** *adjective*: "He sounded *soothing*, like a family doctor who feels his first job is to get the patient calmed down." (Helen MacInnes) —**soothingly,** *adverb*.

so·phis·ti·cat·ed [sə fis′ tə kā tid] *adjective*, *more/most*. **1.** having or showing much knowledge of the world; very cultured: a *sophisticated* style of dressing. TV movies are often set in *sophisticated* world capitals like New York and Paris. **2.** drawing on high levels of knowledge; complex; complicated: That software program is very *sophisticated* and can deal with advanced operations. — **sophistication,** *noun*.

soph·o·more [sôf′ môr′] *noun*, *plural* **sophomores.** a second-year student in a high school or college. ◆ *Sophomore* comes from a combination of the Greek words "wise" and "foolish."

S

	Pronunciation Key: T–Z		
t	ten; date	v	very; live
th	think	w	win; away
<u>th</u>	these	y	you
u	cut; butter	z	zoo; cause
ur	turn; bird	zh	measure

(Turn the page for more information.)

so•pran•o [sə prän′ ō] *noun, plural* **sopranos. 1.** the highest singing voice for women and boys, or a person who has such a voice. **2.** an instrument with such a range: a *soprano* saxophone.

sor•cer•er [sôr′ sər ər] *noun, plural* **sorcerers.** a person who practices magic or witchcraft. ◆ **Sorcery** is the use of witchcraft or magic.

sore [sôr] *adjective,* **sorer, sorest. 1.** causing pain; hurting: Karen has a *sore* leg from getting kicked in the soccer game. **2.** causing hurt feelings: Don't ask him how he did on the test; that's a *sore* subject with him. **3.** *Informal.* mad; angry.—*noun, plural* **sores.** an injured or painful place on the body.

so•ror•i•ty [sə rôr′ ə tē] *noun, plural* **sororities.** a social club for girls or women, especially one at a college or university.

sor•rel [sôr′ əl] *noun, plural* **sorrels.** a plant with long clusters of small green flowers and sour-tasting leaves that are used in salads and sauces.

sor•row [sär′ ō] *noun, plural* **sorrows.** a feeling of pain or unhappiness in the mind over some loss or bad event; sadness. —*verb,* **sorrowed, sorrowing.** to feel sorrow; be sad. —**sorrowful,** *adjective.* —**sorrowfully,** *adverb.*

sor•ry [sôr′ ē] *adjective,* **sorrier, sorriest. 1.** feeling or causing sorrow; sad: We're all *sorry* to hear that your mother is sick. **2.** feeling regret or shame over something one has done: I'm *sorry* I threw your magazine away; I thought you were finished with it. **3.** not very good; poor: Did you ever see the movie *Bad News Bears?* What a *sorry* collection of baseball players!

sort [sôrt] *noun, plural* **sorts.** a group of similar things; a type or kind: Stacy's having a friend stay for the weekend, and Mom asked what *sort* of food she likes to eat. He cuts people's lawns, takes care of their plants and trees—that *sort* of thing. —*verb,* **sorted, sorting.** to place by kind or group; arrange: A computer *sorts* the records it has and organizes them into fields of information. —*adverb.* **sort of.** *Informal.* a lit-

tle; somewhat: "I kept my jeans sorted by clean, *sort of* dirty, and real dirty." (S. E. Hinton)

SOS an international distress signal used to call for help: The sinking ship sent an urgent *SOS.*

sought [sôt] *verb.* the past form of **seek.**

soul [sōl] *noun, plural* **souls. 1.** the part of a person that is not the physical body; the spiritual force within a person that controls thoughts and feelings: Many people believe a person's *soul* lives forever. **2.** a person: "Indeed, with never a *soul* to talk to, the days dragged even more heavily than before." (George Orwell)

sound¹ [sound] *noun, plural* **sounds. 1.** something that can be heard; something that is sensed by the ear. Sound occurs when an object vibrates and causes pressure waves to travel outward from the object through the surrounding area. **2.** one of the distinct noises making up human speech: "City" begins with an "s" *sound.* —*verb,* **sounded, sounding. 1.** to make or cause something to make a noise: "At that moment a brown owl's call *sounded* from the opposite wood." (Richard Adams) **2.** to make an impression; seem to be: Grandma *sounded* happy when I spoke to her on the phone. **3.** to pronounce or be pronounced: "Rain" and "reign" *sound* alike.

sound² *adjective,* **sounder, soundest. 1.** free from illness, damage, or fault: a person with a *sound* mind and body. **2.** strong and safe; secure; solid: Buying stock in that company is a *sound* investment. **3.** wise or sensible: *sound* advice. —*adverb.* thoroughly; completely: to be *sound* asleep. —**soundly,** *adverb:* "I ate Eastern food and slept *soundly* in a soft Dutch bed." (Paul Theroux) —**soundness,** *noun.*

sound³ *verb,* **sounded, sounding. 1.** to measure the depth of a body of water by letting down a weighted rope or string until it touches the bottom. **2. sound out.** to try to discover a person's thoughts, feelings, or views: Carl *sounded out* his mother about his plan to buy a motorcycle.

sort It's often said that English doesn't have any true synonyms, that it's always possible to make some distinction even with the most closely-related words. One set of words that challenges this idea is *sort, kind,* and *type.* They all have the same basic meaning—"the group that something belongs to; what something is." How, then, are these words different? *Sort* is not as serious a word as *kind* or *type.* You might say to a friend, "They served soda, ice cream, and all *sorts* of cakes and pies." But in a science report, it would be better to write, "An elk is actually a *kind* of deer" or "The amount of rainfall that an area gets determines what *type* of grasses are able to grow there."

sound⁴ *noun, plural* **sounds.** a long, wide body of water that either connects two larger bodies or separates an island from the mainland.

sound•proof [sound′proof′] *adjective.* not allowing sound to pass in or out: *Recording studios are* soundproof *so that no outside noises get on the recordings.* —*verb,* **soundproofed, soundproofing.** to make a room or building soundproof.

soup [soop] *noun, plural* **soups.** a liquid food made by cooking meat, fish, or vegetables in milk, water, or another liquid, often with solid pieces of food in the liquid.

sour [sour] *adjective,* **sourer, sourest. 1.** having a sharp or biting taste: *Lemons and green apples are* sour. **2.** spoiled or decayed: *sour milk.* **3.** not happy or pleasant; having or showing bad feelings: *He listened to the teacher's comments with a* sour *expression on this face. "The whole journey seemed to turn* sour *then."* (V. S. Naipaul) —*verb,* **soured, souring.** to make or become sour: *The milk* soured *when I left it on the counter overnight.*

source [sôrs] *noun, plural* **sources.** the place or thing that something comes from; the origin: *The* source *of the Mississippi River is a small lake in Minnesota. The reporter was sure his story was right, because he had three reliable* sources *of information.*

sour cream a smooth, thick cream made sour with acids and used as an ingredient in soups, salads, and other dishes, or as a dressing, especially for baked potatoes.

south [south] *noun.* **1.** the direction that is on your left as you have face the sun at sunset; the opposite of north. **2.** *also,* **South.** a region or place located in this direction. **3.** *also,* **the South.** the southeastern U.S., especially the states that formed the Confederacy during the Civil War (Virginia, North Carolina, South Carolina, Georgia, Florida, Tennessee, Alabama, Mississippi, Louisiana, Arkansas, and Texas). —*adjective; adverb.* toward or at the south: *to travel* south.

South Africa a country in southern Africa, with coastlines on the Atlantic and Indian Oceans. *Capitals:* Pretoria; Cape Town. *Area:* 471,400 square miles. *Population:* 31,440,000.

South America the southern continent of the Western Hemisphere, lying mostly below the equator and between the Atlantic and Pacific Oceans. It is the fourth-largest continent.

South Carolina a state on the southeast coast of the U.S. *Capital:* Columbia. *Nickname:* "Palmetto State." *Area:* 31,100 square miles. *Population:* 3,203,000.

South Dakota a state in the north-central U.S. *Capital:* Pierre. *Nickname:* "Coyote State." *Area:* 77,000 square miles. *Population:* 691,000.

south•east [south′ēst′] *noun.* the direction between south and east. —*adjective; adverb.* at or in the southeast. —**southeastern,** *adjective.*

south•ern [suth′ərn] *adjective.* **1.** in, toward, or of the south. **2.** *also,* **Southern.** in or having to do with the American South.

south•ern•er [suth′ərn ər] *noun, plural* **southerners. 1.** a person born or living in the south part of a country or region. **2.** *also,* **Southerner.** someone who was born or lives in the American South.

South Korea a country in eastern Asia, occupying the southern part of the Korean Peninsula. *Capital:* Seoul. *Area:* 38,000 square miles. *Population:* 41,000,000.

South Pole the southernmost point on the earth, near the middle of Antarctica.

south•ward [south′wərd] *adjective; adverb.* toward or at the south.

S

> **sources** In *World of Our Fathers*, his autobiography, Irving Howe describes a scene from his school days in the early 1930's. Howe's English teacher always complained that his students tended to use only one source, an encyclopedia article, when writing an essay. That's still the case more than half a century later. (A *source* is any means of getting information for a paper, such as a book, a magazine article, or a person that you interview.) One reason to avoid a single source is the date of an encyclopedia or other reference work. If the source is, say, thirty years old, you would do well to look at other sources. Also, if an encyclopedia gives very little data, you really are forced to look elsewhere. Librarians are helpful here!

Pronunciation Key: [ə] Symbol

The [ə] or *schwa* sound occurs in syllables without an accent. It can be spelled with any vowel, such as **a** in above, **e** in listen, **i** in pencil, **o** in melon, **u** in circus. It can also be a combination of vowels, such as **io** in action, **ai** in mountain, **iou** in precious.

(Turn the page for more information.)

south•west [south′west′] *noun.* the direction between south and west. —*adjective, adverb.* toward or at the southwest.

sou•ve•nir [sōō′ və nēr′] *noun, plural* **souvenirs.** something kept as a reminder of a person, place, or event: She bought a stuffed panda as a *souvenir* from the Washington, D.C. Zoo.

sov•er•eign [säv′rən] *noun, plural* **sovereigns.** a king or queen. —*adjective.* **1.** having control or authority; ruling: His *Sovereign* Majesty, King Henry VIII. **2.** ruling itself; self-governing: India, once under British control, was made a *sovereign* state in 1947.

So•vi•et Union [sōv′ē et] another name for the UNION OF SOVIET SOCIALIST REPUBLICS. —**Soviet,** *adjective; noun.*

sow[1] [sō] *verb,* **sowed, sown** or **sowed, sowing.** to plant or scatter seeds in order to grow a crop: to *sow* wildflower seeds on a bare hillside.

sow[2] [sou] *noun, plural* **sows.** an adult female pig.

soy•bean [soi′bēn′] *noun, plural* **soybeans.** a protein-rich bean used in making flour and oil and eaten as food. Soybeans grow in pods on leafy green bushes.

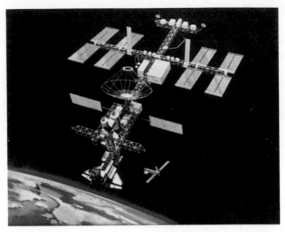

space station An artist at the John F. Kennedy Space Center shows a proposed space station.

space•craft [spās′kraft′] *noun, plural* **spacecrafts.** any vehicle used for traveling outside the earth's atmosphere; also called a **spaceship.**

space shuttle a vehicle that is launched into space by a rocket and used to carry people and supplies between earth and a spacecraft in orbit. It is able to return to earth, land on an airstrip as a plane does, and be used over again.

> **spacing a paper** The dimensions of the text you use in writing depend on whether the text is typed or handwritten. If you type on every line, without any extra space between lines, this is called *single spacing.* If you type on every other line, it's *double spacing.* In writing by hand, the final version should always be single spaced. In business the question of spacing is more important than most people assume. If you send a first draft of a report to your boss for approval, use double spacing. Why? You ought to give your boss room to change or add text. Typed lines are harder to edit when there's no extra space between them. By the way, word processors and most typewriters can be set so that the extra space is 1 1/2 lines.

space [spās] *noun, plural* **spaces. 1.** the area beyond the earth's air that has no known end or limits; the outer area where the sun, moon, planets, and stars are. **2.** the empty area of air that surrounds objects on the earth: She didn't answer me, but just stared off into *space.* **3.** an open distance or empty area between two things: Leave plenty of *space* on the sides of your paper. **4.** a place or area to be filled in some way: a parking *space.* When planes fly over a country, they are said to be in its air *space.* **5.** a period of time: He's made six business trips to Canada over the *space* of the last two years.—*verb,* **spaced, spacing.** to leave space between; keep apart; separate: There are only a few houses on that road and they're widely *spaced.*

space capsule a vehicle that can travel in space and then be recovered when it returns to earth.

space suit a special airtight suit that space travelers wear. It protects them from radiation and heat and provides oxygen.

spa•cious [spā′shəs] *adjective, more/most.* having a lot of space; large and open; roomy: a house with *spacious* rooms.

spade[1] [spād] *noun, plural* **spades.** a digging tool that has a long handle attached to a flat, metal blade, which is pushed into the ground with the foot. —*verb,* **spaded, spading.** to dig with a spade: *Spade* the garden to loosen the dirt before you plant those seeds.

spade[2] *noun, plural* **spades. 1.** a playing card marked with black figures like this [♠]. **2. spades.** the suit of cards with these figures.

spa•ghet•ti [spə get′ē] *noun.* very thin, long, string-like noodles that are cooked by boiling. Spaghetti is made of flour and water.

Spain [spān] a country in southwestern Europe, on the **Iberian Peninsula** [ī bēr′ ē ən]. *Capital:* Madrid. *Area:* 194,000 square miles. *Population:* 38,700,000.

Spain A statue of Miguel de Cervantes, Spain's greatest writer, stands in Madrid, Spain's capital. He is the author of the novel *Don Quixote.*

span [span] *noun, plural* **spans. 1.** the distance or section between two objects or supports: The Golden Gate Bridge has a *span* of 4200 feet between its two towers. **2.** a time period: A person's life *span* is the length of time the person is alive. —*verb* **spanned, spanning.** to reach or stretch across or over: "A high railroad bridge *spanned* the cliffs of a big river near the village." (Jerzy Kosinski)

Span•iard [span′ yərd] *noun, plural* **Spaniards.** a person who was born or is living in Spain.

span•iel [span′ yəl] *noun, plural* **spaniels.** a small or medium-sized dog that has long, wavy, silky hair and droopy ears.

Span•ish [span′ ish] *noun.* **1.** the people of Spain. **2.** the language that is spoken in Spain, Mexico, and most of Central and South America. —*adjective.* having to do with Spain, with its people and culture, or with the Spanish language.

spank [spangk] *verb,* **spanked, spanking.** to hit with a flat object or the open hand in order to punish: My mother *spanked* my little brother for running out in the street.

spare [spâr] *verb,* **spared, sparing. 1.** to keep from being hurt or punished; not harm or destroy: The tale of Androcles and the lion tells of how a lion *spared* his life because he had once helped it. **2.** to give up as not needed; allow: "All Henry could *spare* for her was a crew of ten men." (Irving Stone) "There were ten minutes to *spare* before the train left." (Katherine Mansfield) —*adjective.* **1.** more than is needed; extra: He goes fishing in his *spare* time. They have a *spare* bedroom now that their oldest son is married. **2.** not generous; scant: The hikers had only enough food for a *spare* breakfast. —*noun, plural* **spares. 1.** something extra or available as a replacement. **2.** *also,* **spare tire.** a tire that is carried in a car to replace one that goes flat on the road. **3.** in bowling, the knocking down of all ten pins with two balls.

spark [spärk] *noun, plural* **sparks. 1.** a tiny burning piece: *Sparks* from the fire could be seen rising out of the chimney. **2.** a small flash of light made when electricity jumps across open space. ♦ **Spark plugs** use sparks to explode the fuel mixture in an automobile engine. **3.** a small but important part: The crowd had seemed bored, but his speech really put the *spark* of life into them. —*verb,* **sparked, sparking. 1.** to produce or throw off sparks. **2.** to set off or cause to begin: That article about the mayor's family has *sparked* a lot of lively argument around town.

spar•kle [spär′ kəl] *verb,* **sparkled, sparkling. 1.** to give off small flashes of bright light: The diamond ring *sparkled* in the sunlight. "A few tiny flakes of snow *sparkled* on Parker's shoulders . . ." (George Plimpton) **2.** to be lively: a *sparkling* conversation. **3.** to give off bubbles of gas: Champagne is a *sparkling* wine. —*noun, plural* **sparkles.** a spark or glitter; a flash.

spar•row [spar′ ō] *noun, plural* **sparrows.** any of various kinds of small brownish or grayish songbirds commonly found in North America, such as the **house (English) sparrow.**

sparse [spärs] *adjective,* **sparser, sparsest.** scattered here and there; small in number or amount: "The grass near the hotel had been *sparse* and brown . . ." (Paul Theroux) "Her hair was so *sparse* her head looked shaved." (V. S. Naipaul) —**sparsely,** *adverb.*

spasm [spazm] *noun, plural* **spasms. 1.** a sudden and violent movement that cannot be controlled: a muscle *spasm.* "A *spasm* of coughing seized him." (William Styron) **2.** a sudden burst or outbreak: "He felt a *spasm* of irritation." (Walker Percy)

Pronunciation Key: Accent Marks

[′] is the normal accent mark. It shows where the main stress falls on a word.
[′] is a secondary accent mark. It shows a lighter stress than the primary accent. For example:

tel • e • vis • ion [tel′ə vizh′ən]

(Turn the page for more information.)

S

spat¹ [spat] *noun, plural* **spats.** a small or unimportant quarrel.

spat² *verb.* the past form of **spit.**

spat·ter [spat′ ər] *verb* **spattered, spattering.** to splash or scatter in small pieces: "Snow *spattered* against the windows like thrown sand." (Stephen King) "There was a *spattering* of applause." (E. L. Doctorow)

spat·u·la [spach′ ə lə] *noun, plural* **spatulas.** a kitchen tool with a long handle and a flat, wide blade, used to slide under foods that are being cooked in a pan, in order to turn them over.

spawn [spôn] *noun.* the eggs of water animals such as fish and frogs. —*verb,* **spawned, spawning. 1.** to lay eggs or produce offspring: Salmon travel many miles upstream in order to *spawn* in fresh water. **2.** to create a similar new idea or product; produce: A successful movie often *spawns* a TV series that imitates it.

speak [spēk] *verb,* **spoke, spoken, speaking. 1.** to use words; talk: The baby is just learning to *speak.* **2.** to mention in talking: Tom *spoke* to his Dad about borrowing the car. *Speaking* of Michelle, here she is now. **3.** to be able to use a certain language: to *speak* French. **4.** to give a speech: to *speak* in Congress.

head of a spear. Spearmint is used to give flavor to foods and to chewing gum.

spe·cial [spesh′ əl] *adjective, more/most.* **1.** different from others; unusual, especially in a good way: Christmas is a *special* day that many people celebrate by buying presents for each other. "He was not a *special* breed of dog . . . he was just a dog." (Booth Tarkington) **2.** meant for a certain use or situation; particular: The library owns a rare book that they keep in a *special* glass case in the lobby. —*noun, plural* **specials. 1.** something that is special: The restaurant offers ten regular dishes and two *specials* that change from day to day. **2.** a television show that is not part of a regular series. —**specially,** *adverb:* "My English leakproof shoes, *specially* bought for this trip . . ." (Paul Theroux)

spe·cial·ist [spesh′ əl ist] *noun, plural* **specialists. 1.** a doctor who deals with a particular area of medicine: Tony's broken finger was operated on by Dr. Lund, a hand *specialist.* **2.** anyone who concentrates on one limited area of a larger activity: The pro football squad had 22 offensive players, 21 defensive, and two kicking *specialists.*

---

speaking and writing English is English, whether spoken or written. The words are the same and the rules of grammar are the same. But when you speak, you have ways to indicate your meaning in addition to the words themselves. You can raise or lower your voice, speak quickly or slowly, change the expression of your face, make motions with your hands, and so on. In writing, the words themselves have to carry all the meaning—with a little help from punctuation symbols. When you speak, your audience is right in front of you and if your meaning is not coming across, you may soon know it from your listener's comments or facial expressions. As a writer, you still can find an audience—yourself. For that reason, we recommend you read a paper out loud to yourself. Sometimes, you will be surprised by what you hear!

---

speak·er [spē′ kər] *noun, plural* **speakers. 1.** a person who speaks, especially someone who gives a speech. **2.** the head officer of the United States House of Representatives or another law-making body. **3.** *also,* **loudspeaker.** a device or instrument that changes electrical signals into sounds: Our car radio has four *speakers.*

spear [spēr] *noun, plural* **spears. 1.** a weapon with a long, thin shaft and a sharp pointed head. **2.** the long, thin stalk of certain plants: Asparagus grows in *spears.* —*verb,* **speared, spearing.** to catch with or as if with a spear: The skin diver *speared* a fish. Joey reached out his fork and *speared* a piece of meat.

spear·mint [spēr′ mint′] *noun.* a pleasant-smelling plant whose leaves are shaped like the

spe·cial·ize [spesh′ ə līz′] *verb,* **specialized, specializing.** to study or work in one specific area of a larger field: She sings all kinds of songs in her act, but she *specializes* in folk songs. ◆ The fact of specializing is **specialization** [spesh′ ə li zā′ shən].

spe·cial·ty [spesh′ əl tē] *noun, plural* **specialties. 1.** a special product, attraction, or feature; something outstanding or unusual: They own a restaurant by the ocean whose *specialty* is fresh salmon. **2.** what a person specializes in; a special area of training or knowledge.

spe·cies [spē′ shēz *or* spē′ sēz] *noun.* a group of plants or animals that have certain common features which set them apart from others. The male and female of a species of animals can mate together to produce young that will resemble the parents. The wolf, the fox, and the coyote are different species of the canine family, which also includes the dog.

specifics Suppose you had to write a paper describing what someone is like—your aunt, let's say. To bring her to life on a page you need *specifics*, you need *details*. To say she is attractive doesn't mean much. What is the color of her eyes and her hair? How do you hear her voice? Is it shrill? Does she speak quietly? If you think she's very funny and clever, what are specific things she says that are funny? Does she imitate people? Is she a storyteller? George Washington was a tall, physically powerful man, but today few people know that, as a general point. However, most people have heard the legend of his throwing a silver dollar clear across the wide Rappahannock River. *That's* a detail that is memorable. Perhaps the best of all novelists in using details effectively was Charles Dickens. In describing persons, he stated the kind of clothing they wore, how they stood or gestured, how their speech gave a picture of themselves.

spe•cif•ic [spi sif′ ik] *adjective, more/most.* clearly stated; naming a certain one or ones; definite: Roosevelt's face is on Mt. Rushmore, or to be *specific*, Theodore Roosevelt, not Franklin. —*noun, plural* **specifics.** something that is exact and definite: The witness claimed he'd seen the whole thing, but the jury didn't believe him because he couldn't give any *specifics.* —**specifically,** *adverb.*

spec•i•fi•ca•tion [spes′ ə fə kā′ shən] *noun, plural* **specifications.** something specified; an exact or detailed statement: The publisher gave the printer a list of *specifications* for how the book should be made.

spec•i•fy [spes′ ə fī] *verb,* **specified, specifying.** to ask for or explain in a clear and precise way; say exactly: The federal government *specifies* April 15th as the date when income taxes are due.

spec•i•men [spes′ ə mən] *noun, plural* **specimens.** one person, animal, or thing that can represent and give information about the whole group: Eleanor has collected twenty different butterfly *specimens.* Doctors use blood *specimens* to determine the state of a person's health.

speck [spek] *noun, plural* **specks.** a small piece, spot, or mark: a *speck* of dust. —**speckled,** *adjective:* A *speckled* trout has small reddish spots on the sides of its body.

spec•ta•cle [spek′ tə kəl] *noun, plural* **spectacles. 1.** a very unusual or impressive sight: After the game there will be a large fireworks *spectacle.* **2.** a silly or embarrassing sight: I'm not going to go out there and ice skate—I'd make a *spectacle* of myself. **3. spectacles.** a pair of eyeglasses.

spec•tac•u•lar [spek tak′ yə lər] *adjective, more/*

most. sure to be noticed and remembered; very unusual or impressive: The real estate ad says the house has *spectacular* views of the ocean from every room.

spec•ta•tor [spek′ tā tər] *noun, plural* **spectators.** a person who watches a game or other such scheduled event: Most courtrooms have an area where *spectators* can sit.

spec•trum [spek′ trəm] *noun, plural* **spectrums. 1.** the bands of color that are separated and displayed together in a rainbow when sunlight passes through raindrops. A specially-shaped glass object called a **prism** [priz′ əm] is another tool for showing these individual colors. The colors of the spectrum are red, orange, yellow, green, blue, indigo, and violet. **2.** a wide range; a variety: The TV talk show had eight guests who represented a broad *spectrum* of opinion on the issue.

spec•u•late [spek′ yə lāt′] *verb,* **speculated, speculating. 1.** to think about something without having a body of facts or evidence; guess: It's not known why dinosaurs died out, so scientists can only *speculate* as to the reason. **2.** to take risks in business that may pay off in a good profit: to *speculate* in land in an unsettled area. —**speculation,** *noun:* "Their origin was still unknown . . . a source of endless *speculation.*" (Arthur C. Clarke) —**speculator,** *noun.*

sped [sped] *verb.* the past form of **speed.**

speech [spēch] *noun, plural* **speeches. 1.** the act of speaking; the use of spoken words to express thoughts and feelings. **2.** something that is

Pronunciation Key: A–F			
a	and; hat	ch	chew; such
ā	ate; stay	d	dog; lid
â	care; air	e	end; yet
ä	father; hot	ē	she; each
b	boy; cab	f	fun; off

(Turn the page for more information.)

spoken, especially a formal talk given by one person to a group: At the start of each year the President makes a *speech* to Congress called the State of the Union Address. **3.** the way a person or group speaks: The expression "G'day" is a common greeting in Australian *speech.*

speech•less [spēch′lis] *adjective.* unable to speak for a moment because of a shock or great surprise: He was *speechless* when he heard he had won a million dollars in the state lottery.

speed [spēd] *noun, plural* **speeds. 1.** fast movement or action; quickness: The cheetah is noted for its *speed.* **2.** any given rate of movement, whether fast or slow: Cars passing the school must reduce their *speed* to 15 miles per hour. —*verb,* **sped** or **speeded, speeding. 1.** to go at a fast rate; move quickly: He said a hurried good-bye and *sped* out the door. "I *speeded* up and passed him on a curve . . ." (Raymond Chandler) **2.** to drive a car, truck, or other such vehicle faster than the law allows (the **speed limit**).

speed•om•e•ter [spi däm′ ə tər] *noun, plural* **speedometers.** an instrument or device that shows how fast a car, truck, or bicycle is moving. Many speedometers also contain an **odometer** [ō′ däm′ ə tər] that shows how far the vehicle has traveled.

speed•y [spēd′ ē] *adjective,* **speedier, speediest.** going or able to go at a fast rate; swift: a pro football team with several *speedy* running backs. —**speedily,** *adverb.*

spell¹ [spel] *verb,* **spelled, spelling. 1.** to say or write the letters of a word in a certain order. The word "child" used to be *spelled* c-h-i-l-d-e. **2.** to say or write letters in the correct order: His writing shows good ideas, but he can't *spell* very well. **3.** to show or indicate; mean: The car engine just started knocking loudly—that *spells* trouble. **4. spell out.** to explain in a clear, simple way.

spell² *noun, plural* **spells. 1.** a magic power to control a person's actions: Folk tales often tell of witches who cast a *spell* over people to put them to sleep, make them fall in love, and so on. **2.** the words or action used to put a magic spell on someone. **3.** a power of great charm or attraction, like magic: Soon after coming to the island he fell under the *spell* of its beautiful warm sun and soft tropical breezes. ◆ A person who is controlled by a spell is **spellbound:** ". . . standing at the wall under the olive tree *spellbound* by the music she had been listening to." (Patrick White)

spell³ *noun, plural* **spells. 1.** a short, indefinite period of time: Let's stop and rest for a *spell.* **2.** a period of a certain action or condition: We finally got a warm day after that long cold *spell.*

spell•er [spel′ ər] *noun, plural* **spellers. 1.** a person who spells words: She's a good *speller.* **2.** a book that teaches spelling.

spell•ing [spel′ ing] *noun, plural* **spellings. 1.** the act of putting letters together to form words, or a school subject that teaches this. **2.** the correct written form of a word: Some words have two different *spellings,* such as "theater" and "theatre." ◆ A **spelling bee** is a contest to see who can spell the most words correctly.

spend [spend] *verb,* **spent, spending. 1.** to give money in return for something; pay out: to *spend* $5.00 to get into a movie. **2.** to use time for: "He *spends* hours in front of the mirror." (Ishmael Reed) **3.** to use up; wear out: At the end of the race the swimmers hung over the edge of the pool, completely *spent.* "Winter *spent* itself, and spring came, scattering wildflowers . . ." (Marguerite Henry) —**spender,** *noun:* He's a rich man and is known as a big *spender.*

sperm [spurm] *noun, plural* **sperms.** a cell produced by a male animal that can fertilize the egg of a female in order to produce new life.

spelling The English spelling system is more difficult than some other languages because it is not strictly *phonetic.* A phonetic language is one in which all letters have separate sounds, and spelling follows easily because of the letter-sound regularity. A speaker of those languages can listen to a word and tell how to spell it. In Spanish, the letter o is pronounced only in this way ("oh"). In English, there are six different "o" sounds. English has more than 40 sounds represented by only 26 letters. Not only does English derive from two separate sources—Germanic and Latin (through French)—but also English has taken on more foreign words than any other language. Often these words stay close to their original spellings but pick up an English-style pronunciation. This produces spelling oddities such as *pneumonia* and *psychology,* or *bologna* and *spaghetti.* All this helps to explain why dictionaries are a marvelous instrument: consult the dictionary because it teaches as it corrects.

sperm whale a large toothed whale of warm seas that has a huge flat head. Sperm whales have been hunted for their valuable **sperm oil.**

spew [spoo] *verb,* **spewed, spewing.** to pour out; move in a strong, quick flow: "At the front door, we saw fire *spewing* from Miss Mandie's dining-room windows." (Harper Lee) ". . . quarters, nickels, and dimes had *spewed* onto the floor." (Stephen King)

sphere [sfēr] *noun, plural* **spheres. 1.** a solid figure that has a round shape, or an object shaped like this. The earth and the moon are spheres. **2.** a certain area of interest or activity: The countries of Eastern Europe lie within the Soviet Union's *sphere* of influence. **—spherical,** *adjective.* having the shape of a sphere.

sphinx [sfingks] *noun, plural* **sphinxes.** an ancient Egyptian figure having the head of a man and the body of a lion.

spice [spīs] *noun, plural* **spices.** the seeds, leaves, or other parts of a plant that are used to flavor foods. Pepper, ginger, cinnamon, and sage are spices. **—verb,** **spiced, spicing.** to use spices to flavor foods. **—spicy,** *adjective.*

spi·der [spī′dər] *noun, plural* **spiders.** one of a large group of animals that have thin, jointed legs and can spin webs. Spiders differ from insects in that they have eight legs and a body with two parts, and in the fact that they lack wings. Spiders live mainly on insects which they trap in their webs. They have poison glands, and a few kinds are harmful to man.

spider Four common spiders, the daddy longlegs (top), grass and wolf spiders (middle), and the American house spider (below).

spied [spīd] *verb.* the past form of **spy.**

spike¹ [spīk] *noun, plural* **spikes. 1.** a large, pointed, thin piece of metal shaped like a nail.

Spikes are used for holding things in place, such as the rails and wooden ties on a railroad track. **2.** a sharp, pointed object or projection. Baseball players often wear shoes with spikes on the bottom.

spike² *noun, plural* **spikes. 1.** an ear of a grain plant such as corn or wheat. **2.** a long cluster of flowers on a single stem.

spill [spil] *verb,* **spilled, spilling. 1.** to let something flow, fall, or run out by accident: The baby *spilled* her milk on the table. **2.** to flow or fall: "The woman's long dark hair was *spilling* over her shoulders." (Andrea Lee) "Two cats *spilled* from her lap as she rose." (Ken Follett)

spin [spin] *verb,* **spun, spinning. 1.** to turn quickly around in circles: A car's wheels *spin* as it moves over the road. **2.** to feel dizzy from or as if from turning quickly around: All the noise and excitement made her head *spin.* **3.** to twist and draw out wool, cotton, or other fibers to make thread. **4.** of a spider, silkworm, or other such animal, to make a web or cocoon by giving off and stretching a special thread-like substance from its body. **—noun, plural** **spins. 1.** the act of spinning: The figure skater made a series of graceful *spins* on the ice. **2.** a short ride or trip for pleasure: Could I take your new bike for a *spin* around the block? **—spinner,** *noun.*

spinach A leafy spinach plant.

spin·ach [spin′ich] *noun.* a dark green vegetable leaf that is eaten raw in salads or cooked. Spinach is high in vitamin and mineral content.

Pronunciation Key: G N			
g	give; big	k	kind; cat; back
h	hold	l	let; ball
i	it; this	m	make; time
ī	ice; my	n	not; own
j	jet; gem; edge	ng	having

(Turn the page for more information.)

spi·nal cord [spī′nəl] the thick band of nerve tissue running through the center of the spine. It carries messages between the brain and the rest of the body.

spin·dle [spin′dəl] *noun, plural* **spindles. 1.** a thin stick or rod used in former times to twist fibers into thread. **2.** a machine part that turns or that holds another turning part.

spine [spīn] *noun, plural* **spines. 1.** the bones down the center of the back that serve to support the body and protect the nerves of the spinal cord; also called the backbone or **spinal column. 2.** the strip on the narrow edge of a book that joins the front cover to the back. The spine usually shows the name of the book and the author. **3.** a needle-like part that grows on some plants, such as cactus, and on some animals, such as a porcupine. —**spiny**, *adjective.* of an animal or plant, having spines: a *spiny* lobster.

S

spinning wheel A spinning wheel being used to spin wool into yarn.

spinning wheel a device used to spin thread by hand, used in former times before spinning machines were invented. It has a spindle and a large wheel set in a frame. The wheel is moved by hand or by a foot pedal to turn the spindle.

spi·ral [spī′rəl] *noun, plural* **spirals.** a curve that keeps winding in layers above or below itself. Screws and mattress springs take the shape of a spiral. A **spiral staircase** is one that turns on itself as it goes straight up, rather than rising at a slant. —*verb*, **spiraled, spiraling.** to move in a spiral.

spire [spīr] *noun, plural* **spires.** the narrow, pointed top of a building. Cathedrals in Europe are known for their very tall spires.

spir·it [spir′it] *noun, plural* **spirits. 1.** the part of a person's being that exists apart from the body; the soul: "All around me may be silence and darkness, yet within me, in the *spirit,* is music and brightness, and color flashes through all my thoughts." (Helen Keller) **2.** a dead person thought of as continuing to exist apart from the body: "I seemed to hear the *spirits* of those dead workmen who had returned each evening to the starlight . . ." (E. M. Forster) **3.** a force that gives life and energy: "He had answers to none of these questions and no *spirit* left to force himself to think about them." (Richard Adams) **4.** *also,* **spirits.** a state of mind; attitude: "He only starts telling it to him in a *spirit* of good clean fun . . ." (Damon Runyon) "Because of the lovely weather, Sally was in better *spirits* than I had seen her in for weeks." (Christopher Isherwood) **5. spirits.** a distilled alcoholic beverage such as whiskey or gin. —*verb,* **spirited, spiriting.** to move or take something away secretly: The letter was gone; someone had *spirited* it away.

spir·it·ed [spir′ə tid] *adjective, more/most.* **1.** full of spirit; lively, energetic, and so on. **2.** having a certain feeling or spirit: a grouchy, mean-*spirited* person.

spir·it·u·al [spir′ich ool *or* spir′i choo əl] *adjective, more/most.* having to do with the spirit, the mind, religion, and so on, as opposed to the body or the physical world: Father Barry's sermons often deal with family problems, as well as *spiritual* matters. —*noun, plural* **spirituals.** a type of religious song developed by black people of the southern United States in the 1800's. —**spiritually**, *adverb.*

spit[1] [spit] *verb,* **spit** or **spat, spitting.** to push or force saliva or other matter out of the mouth. —*noun, plural* **spits.** the watery fluid in the mouth; saliva.

spit[2] *noun, plural* **spits.** a thin rod on which meat is roasted, as in a fireplace or barbecue.

spite [spīt] *noun.* **1. in spite of.** even though there are opposing facts or conditions; despite: "It astonished me to find that *in spite of* the cold I was thirsty." (V. S. Naipaul) **2.** a feeling of wanting to hurt or annoy another person: He just rooted for the other team out of *spite,* because he wanted his sister's team to lose. —*verb,* **spited, spiting.** to show spite; act to hurt or annoy someone: ". . . just to *spite* her, I drank it all and left none for her." (Frank O'Connor) —**spiteful**, *adjective.*

splash [splash] *verb,* **splashed, splashing.** to cause water or other liquids to scatter or fly about: "Rain filled the gutters and *splashed* knee-high off the sidewalk." (Raymond Chandler) —*noun, plural* **splashes. 1.** the sound or feel of something hitting water: to dive into the water with a *splash*. **2.** a spot or patch of color made by splashing: The painting shows a few *splashes* of bright color against a gray background. **3.** something that creates excitement: That new rock group is causing a big *splash*.

splen•did [splen′did] *adjective, more/most.* **1.** very beautiful or impressive to look at; brilliant or magnificent: "The place . . . had a *splendid* view of the starlit Hudson . . ." (John Jakes) **2.** very good; excellent: "I hope you all had a *splendid* summer holiday." (Muriel Spark) —**splendidly**, *adverb.* —**splendor**, *noun.*

splint [splint] *noun, plural* **splints.** a straight piece of wood or other material that is used to hold a broken bone in place.

splin•ter [splin′tər] *noun, plural* **splinters.** a thin, sharp piece broken off from wood or other such material: Gary got a *splinter* in his hand when he picked up the board. —*verb,* **splintered, splintering.** to break into splinters.

split infinitive An infinitive is a verb form that begins with *to:* "She likes *to play* tennis." To "split an infinitive" means to put a word or words between *to* and the verb: "You have *to completely fill* the tank with water before you turn on the pump." To avoid that split, you'd write, "You have to fill the tank completely . . ." At one time, language critics believed that English should be modeled after Latin, which was regarded as a pure language representing great learning and achievement. In Latin, it is not possible to split an infinitive, because the infinitive is always a single word. Thus, it was thought wrong to split one in English. Nowadays, most teachers agree there is nothing wrong with splitting an infinitive as long as the words between are fairly short: "I'd like some of my friends *to just casually see* that we're homeowners." (Gwendolyn Brooks)

split [split] *verb,* **split, splitting. 1.** to break or divide along a length: to *split* wood into smaller pieces so that it will fit into a fireplace. **2.** to divide or go into parts: The Supreme Court was *split* on that case; the vote was 5-4. **3.** to divide into even parts; share: The two neighbors are going to *split* the cost of putting up a fence on their property line. —*noun, plural* **splits. 1.** the act or fact of splitting. **2.** a parting or division within a group: The Republican Party was formed after there was a *split* in the earlier Whig Party. **3.** an exercise in which the legs are spread wide apart.

spoil [spoil] *verb,* **spoiled** or **spoilt, spoiling. 1.** to hurt or ruin in some way: Let's go ahead with the picnic—a little rain won't *spoil* our fun. **2.** to become decayed or rotten: The fruit had *spoiled* from being left too long in the sun. **3.** to allow a person, especially a child, to become selfish or self-satisfied because of easy treatment: "You *spoil* him to death. You never correct him for anything." (Katherine Anne Porter) —**spoils**, *plural noun.* property that is

taken by force, as by the winning army in a battle. ◆ The **spoils system** is a practice in politics of giving government jobs to friends, fellow party members, and so on.

spoke¹ [spōk] *verb.* the past tense of **speak.** ◆ A person who speaks formally for another is a **spokesman** or **spokeswoman.**

spoke² *noun, plural* **spokes.** a thin rod or bar that connects the rim of a wheel to the hub, as on a bicycle tire.

spo•ken [spō′kən] *verb.* the past participle of **speak.** —*adjective.* **1.** expressed in speech; oral: A dictionary uses special symbols to represent *spoken* language. **2.** speaking in a certain way: a shy, soft-*spoken* person.

sponge [spunj] *noun, plural* **sponges. 1.** a water animal that lives attached to rocks or other solid objects. A sponge is full of holes and can absorb and hold large amounts of water. Sponges are dried and used for washing, bathing, wiping up liquids, and so on. **2.** an artificial cleaning pad that looks somewhat like a true sponge and is used in the same way. —*verb,* **sponged, sponging.** to clean or wipe off with a sponge. —**spongy**, *adverb.*

spon•sor [spän′sər] *noun, plural* **sponsors. 1.** a company, business, or other group that pays all or part of the cost of a television or radio program, in return for being allowed to advertise on the program. **2.** any person or group that pays to support some event or activity. **3.** a person who is responsible for or supports something: Senator Black is the *sponsor* of a new bill before Congress. —*verb,* **sponsored, sponsoring.** to act as a sponsor.

Pronunciation Key: O–S

ō	over; go	ou	out; town
ô	all; law	p	put; hop
oo	look; full	r	run; car
o͞o	pool; who	s	set; miss
oi	oil; boy	sh	show

(Turn the page for more information.)

spon•ta•ne•ous [spän tā′ nē əs] *adjective, more/ most.* happening by itself; not planned: "She was a silent woman, not given to *spontaneous* conversation." (Colleen McCullough) —**spontaneously,** *adverb:* "*Spontaneously,* boys and girls hopped off their seats and began to dance in the aisles." (Studs Terkel)

spool [spool] *noun, plural* **spools.** a rounded piece or cylinder of wood or plastic, used to hold thread, wire, or tape.

spoon [spoon] *noun, plural* **spoons.** a kitchen tool with a handle connected to a little bowl, used in eating, serving, stirring, or measuring foods. —*verb,* **spooned, spooning.** to use a spoon. —**spoonful,** *noun.* the amount held by a spoon.

spore [spôr] *noun, plural* **spores.** a tiny cell that can grow into a plant or animal. Ferns and fungi grow from spores.

small part or area that looks different from what is around it: Ladybugs are usually red with black *spots.* **3.** a particular place: The town roller-skating rink is a popular *spot* with teenagers. —*verb,* **spotted, spotting. 1.** to mark or stain with spots: The old sweatshirt was *spotted* with paint. "The sky was *spotted* with stars now . . ." (Jean Fritz) **2.** to catch sight of; see: "On a ridge of sand dune along the beach I *spot* an arctic fox." (Barry Lopez)

spot•less [spät′ lis] *adjective, more/most.* not having any marks, stains, flaws; completely clean: a *spotless* kitchen floor, a person with a *spotless* reputation. —**spotlessly,** *adverb.*

spot•light [spät′ līt′] *noun, plural* **spotlights. 1.** a bright light that is focused on a performer on stage. **2.** a position of public notice: The Senator's wife doesn't take part in his campaigns because she doesn't enjoy being in the *spotlight.*

sportswriting Sportswriting occurs in every daily newspaper, in many magazines, and in text read by television reporters on sports. Since so much sports copy is turned out under deadlines to get into print or onto the airwaves, it's not surprising that few sportswriters are regarded as outstanding writers. Ring Lardner and Damon Runyon were colorful writers in the 1920's, and Red Smith, Jimmy Cannon, and Roger Kahn stand out in the post-World War Two era. Roger Angell and Frank Deford are good writers in current times. Sports writing is hard to make vivid, since it usually is confined by the limits of the game itself—all baseball games are more or less alike. Another thing is that there are games played every day, yet only a few games are special or noteworthy, really. Some writers, to keep up reader interest, try to make a game seem more dramatic than it really was; this leads to a style that is marred by overstatement and clichés. A cure for this is knowledge. A sportswriter who truly knows a sport can always find interesting things to say.

sport [spôrt] *noun, plural* **sports. 1.** a game or other activity in which people actively use the body, play according to certain fixed rules, and compete to win. Baseball, football, and basketball are widely-played sports in the U. S. **2.** any other physical activity carried on for enjoyment or recreation, such as fishing, hiking, or mountain climbing. **3.** a person judged as to how fairly he plays a game and how he reacts to winning or losing: a good or bad *sport.* —*verb,* **sported, sporting.** to wear or display in public; show off: ". . . he *sported* a red rose instead of the customary carnation." (P. D. James)

sports car a small, low car seating one or two people, made for high speed and quick turns.

sports•man•ship [spôrts′ mən ship′] *noun.* the proper attitude and behavior in playing a sport; fair play. —**sportsmanlike,** *adjective.*

spot [spät] *noun, plural* **spots. 1.** a mark or stain left on clothes, furniture, and so on, by pieces of dirt, food, oil, paint, or other things. **2.** a

spouse [spous *or* spouz] *noun, plural* **spouses.** a wife or husband.

spout [spout] *verb,* **spouted, spouting. 1.** to force out water or liquid in a powerful stream; spray or spurt: A whale *spouts* water from a hole in its back. **2.** to pour forth a stream of words: Don't pay any attention to him; he's just *spouting* nonsense. —*noun, plural* **spouts.** a small opening, tube, or lip from which liquid is poured or flows out: the *spout* of a teapot.

sprain [sprān] *verb,* **sprained, spraining.** to hurt a joint of the body by twisting or straining it: Jackie *sprained* her ankle when she fell while playing basketball.

sprang [sprang] *verb.* the past participle of **spring.**

sprawl [sprôl] *verb,* **sprawled, sprawling. 1.** to sit or stretch out in a loose, awkward way: Bobby kicked off his shoes and *sprawled* out on the couch. **2.** to spread out or over an area in an uncontrolled way: "Here lies the *sprawling* section of the city known as El Hoyo." (Mario Suarez) —*noun, plural* **sprawls.** a sprawling position, or something that sprawls.

spray [sprā] *noun, plural* **sprays. 1.** drops of water or other liquid flying through the air: "Fireboats sent up *sprays* of water which misted in rainbows as the early morning sun rose over the city." (E. L. Doctorow) **2.** a stream of very tiny drops forced out from a can or container: to use hair *spray* to keep your hair in place, to kill ants with insect *spray.* —*verb,* **sprayed, spraying. 1.** to fall or cause to fall in a spray: to *spray* paint on a wall. **2.** to apply spray to: Farmers *spray* fruit trees to protect against disease and insects. —**sprayer,** *noun.*

spread [spred] *verb,* **spread, spreading. 1.** to open wide or stretch open: The bird *spread* its wings and flew away. "His father had maps *spread* out, covering half the floor." (James Houston) **2.** to put on or cover a surface: to *spread* peanut butter on a slice of bread. **3.** to reach out or extend over an area: "A puzzled smile *spread* slowly across her face." (Pete Hamill) "The song *spread* through the crowd until everyone was singing." (Ken Follett) —*noun, plural* **spreads. 1.** the amount or extent that something can stretch out or open: the wing*spread* of a jet plane. **2.** the covering or top cover of a bed. **3.** a soft food that can be spread on a piece of bread or cracker: a cheese *spread.*

spree [sprē] *noun, plural* **sprees.** a short burst of activity: They went on a shopping *spree* and bought all their school clothes in one day.

springs One of the many bubbling hot springs found in Yellowstone National Park.

spring [spring] *verb,* **sprang, sprung, springing. 1.** to move quickly up or out; jump; leap: A gazelle can *spring* high into the air to escape an animal that is chasing it. **2.** to open or close quickly and with force: "The streetcar stopped and the door *sprang* open." (Erskine Caldwell)

3. to come into being or appear quickly: We'd had two weeks of rain and weeds were *springing* up everywhere in the garden. **4.** to make happen suddenly: to *spring* a surprise on someone. —*noun, plural* **springs. 1.** the season of the year between winter and summer. **2.** a place where water comes out in a stream or flow from under the ground. **3.** a metal or plastic spiral that can be pulled or bent but that always returns to its first shape or position. **4.** the act of springing; a jump or leap.

springboard

spring·board [spring′bôrd′] *noun, plural* **springboards. 1.** a board used to spring high into the air. Divers use springboards to dive into the water. **2.** something that gets things moving quickly; a starting point: Business school was his *springboard* to success.

sprin·kle [spring′kəl] *verb,* **sprinkled, sprinkling. 1.** to scatter or spread around in tiny pieces or small drops: He *sprinkled* the chocolate bits all over the cake. "The stars shone very clear and big, like snow crystals *sprinkled* across the dark." (Rachel Field) **2.** to rain lightly or gently.

sprink·ler [spring′klər] *noun, plural* **sprinklers.** a device used to spray or sprinkle water over lawns and gardens.

Pronunciation Key: T–Z			
t	ten; date	v	very; live
th	think	w	win; away
<u>th</u>	these	y	you
u	cut; butter	z	zoo; cause
ur	turn; bird	zh	measure

(Turn the page for more information.)

S

sprint [sprint] *noun, plural* **sprints.** a short, fast race in which the runners run at top speed for the entire race. The 100-meter dash is a sprint. —*verb,* **sprinted, sprinting.** to run a sprint.

sprout [sprout] *verb,* **sprouted, sprouting. 1.** of a seed or plant, to start to grow. **2.** to come forth or out like a growing plant: ". . . a huge catfish with long whiskers stiffly *sprouting* from its snout." (Jerzy Kosinski) **3.** to arise or develop: "When opposition to some of his proposals *sprouted* . . ." (William L. Shirer) —*noun, plural* **sprouts.** a new growth on a plant.

spruce A tall spruce with a close-up of the needles and cone.

spruce [sproos] *noun, plural* **spruce** or **spruces.** an evergreen tree with short, needle-shaped leaves, light strong wood, and cones that carry seeds. Spruce grow in colder temperatures of the Northern Hemisphere.

sprung [sprung] *verb.* the past form of **spring.**

spry [sprī] *adjective,* **spryer, spryest.** active; lively: The *spry* old man walked at the pace of someone half his age. —**spryly,** *adverb.* —**spryness,** *noun.*

spun [spun] *verb.* the past form of **spin.**

spur [spur] *noun, plural* **spurs.** a sharply-pointed device worn on the heel of a rider's boot to get a horse to move faster. —*verb,* **spurred, spurring. 1.** to use spurs on a horse. **2.** to get someone to move faster or do better: His parents hope that putting Tony in the advanced class will *spur* him to study harder.

spurn [spurn] *verb,* **spurned, spurning.** to turn away from; reject: He *spurned* our offer of help and moved the heavy sofa all by himself.

spurt [spurt] *verb,* **spurted, spurting.** to pour or flow out in a strong stream; gush; spout: After

he shook the soda, it began to *spurt* out of the can. —*noun, plural* **spurts. 1.** a bursting out of water or some other liquid. **2.** a strong action or feeling that lasts only a short time: He did the paper in *spurts,* writing furiously for a few minutes and then slowing down. "Dessa felt a quick *spurt* of disappointment . . ." (Sherley Anne Williams)

sput•ter [sput′ ər] *verb,* **sputtered, sputtering. 1.** to make spitting, hissing, or popping noises; make a series of soft, rough noises: "We had a great wood-fire crackling and *sputtering* on the hearth." (A. Conan Doyle) ". . . a *sputtering* old Model T (car) coughed and died right beside the schoolyard." (Russell Baker) **2.** to speak in a rushed or confused way.

spy [spī] *noun, plural* **spies.** a person who secretly watches others and gathers information about them. A government may send spies to other countries to get secret information. —*verb,* **spied, spying. 1.** to watch others secretly; act as a spy: American patriot Nathan Hale disguised himself as a Dutch schoolteacher to *spy* on the British. **2.** to catch sight of; spot or see: "It was then that we *spied* the nest, hanging gray against the farther bank." (A. B. Guthrie)

squab•ble [skwab′ əl] *noun, plural* **squabbles.** a minor fight or argument. —*verb,* **squabbled, squabbling:** ". . . they used to *squabble* during playtime, and pull each other's hair and cry at the least thing." (Noel Coward)

squad [skwäd] *noun, plural* **squads. 1.** the smallest unit of soldiers in an army, made up of about 12 men. **2.** any small group that acts or works together: a football *squad.* ♦ A police patrol car is sometimes called a **squad car.**

squad•ron [skwäd′ rən] *noun, plural* **squadrons.** a unit of airplanes, warships, or other such forces that operate together.

squall[1] [skwäl] *noun, plural* **squalls.** a sudden and harsh windstorm, often with rain or snow.

squall[2] *noun, plural* **squalls.** a harsh cry or scream. —*verb,* **squalled, squalling.** to give out loud cries or screams.

squan•der [skwän′ dər] *verb,* **squandered, squandering.** to spend money in a foolish or careless way; waste money: "Peter had brought a month's allowance with him, simply to *squander.*" (Mary Gordon)

Squan•to [skwän′ tō] 1585-1622, American Indian who helped the Pilgrims when they first came to Massachusetts.

square [skwâr] *noun, plural* **squares. 1.** a figure that has four equal sides and angles, or an object or design with this shape: Checkers is played on a board with red and black *squares*. **2.** a four-sided open area that is surrounded by streets or buildings. **3.** in mathematics, the number that results when any number is multiplied by itself: The *square* of 5 is 25. —*adjective*, **squarer, squarest. 1.** having four equal sides and angles: a *square* box. **2.** making a right angle: Most rooms have *square* corners. **3.** measuring things in terms of a square area: A room that is 12 feet by 15 feet has an area of 180 *square* feet. **4.** honest, fair. The used-car dealer promised to give his customers a *square* deal. —*verb*, **squared, squaring. 1.** to make square: He stood up straight and *squared* his shoulders. **2.** to multiply a number by itself. —**squarely,** *adverb*. exactly or firmly: "She told him what was the matter, looking *squarely* into his face." (Frank Norris)

square dance a type of American folk dance that is done by four or more couples who form a square at the beginning of the dance.

square root a number that when multiplied by itself (squared), produces a certain other number. The square root of 16 is 4.

squash¹ [skwäsh *or* skwôsh] *verb*, **squashed, squashing. 1.** to press or force down into a flat mass; crush: He accidentally stepped on the tomato and *squashed* it on the ground. **2.** to put down or stop something: The government has *squashed* the military uprising. —*noun*. a game somewhat like tennis, played with a racket and a rubber ball in a walled court.

squash² *noun*, *plural* **squash** or **squashes.** a vegetable that grows on a vine along the ground and is related to the pumpkin. Squash may be orange, yellow, or green.

squat [skwät] *verb*, **squatted, squatting. 1.** to sit on the lower part of the legs while the knees are drawn close to the body: A catcher in baseball *squats* while waiting for the pitch to come in. **2.** to live on land without owning it or having a right to it. **3.** to live or settle on public land in order to become its owner. ◆ Much of the American West was settled by **squatters,** who farmed open lands that the government said they could keep under the claim of **squatter's rights.** —*adjective*. having a low, broad shape: The street was lined with row on row of *squat*, ugly warehouses.

squawk [skwôk] *verb*, **squawked, squawking. 1.** to make a loud, shrill cry. **2.** *Informal*. to complain noisily. —*noun*, *plural* **squawks:** the *squawk* of a parrot.

squeak [skwēk] *verb*, **squeaked, squeaking.** to make a short, sharp, high sound or cry. —*noun*, *plural* **squeaks:** the *squeak* of an old rusty door. —**squeaky,** *adjective*.

squeal [skwēl] *verb*, **squealed, squealing.** to make a loud shrill cry or sound: "Their heavy Arctic boots *squealed* on the polished floor . . ." (James Houston) —*noun*, *plural* **squeals:** There was a *squeal* of tires as the car raced away.

squeeze [skwēz] *verb*, **squeezed, squeezing. 1.** to push together the sides or parts of; press hard: to *squeeze* a lemon to get juice out of it, to *squeeze* toothpaste out of a tube. **2.** to force by pressing; force into a tight space: The subway car was full and we had to *squeeze* inside the door. The doctor was very busy, but she agreed to *squeeze* me in at the end of the day. —*noun*, *plural* **squeezes.** the act of squeezing.

squid The squid has ten tentacled arms plus two long arms with tentacles on the tips.

squid [skwid] *noun*, *plural* **squid** or **squids.** a sea animal that is like an octopus. Some squid are very small, but the **giant squid** can grow to be over 50 feet long.

squint [skwint] *verb*, **squinted, squinting. 1.** to look with the eyes slightly open: to *squint* in bright sunlight, to *squint* while reading a line of very small print. **2.** to give a quick look out of the corner of the eye. —*noun*, *plural* **squints.** the act of squinting.

Pronunciation Key: [ə] Symbol

The [ə] or *schwa* sound occurs in syllables without an accent. It can be spelled with any vowel, such as **a** in above, **e** in listen, **i** in pencil, **o** in melon, **u** in circus. It can also be a combination of vowels, such as **io** in action, **ai** in mountain, **iou** in precious.

(Turn the page for more information.)

squire [skwīr] *noun, plural* **squires. 1.** in the Middle Ages, a young man who acted as a servant to a knight while training to become a knight himself. **2.** at a later time in English history, a landowner or other wealthy man in a village or country area. —*verb,* **squired, squiring.** to escort a woman: "For two years he *squired* her about the country . . ." (Margaret Mitchell)

squirm [skwurm] *verb,* **squirmed, squirming. 1.** to twist or turn the body; wriggle: He tried to grab the dog, but it *squirmed* free and ran across the yard. **2.** to act or feel nervous or uneasy: The lawyer's sharp line of questioning made the witness *squirm.*

squirrel The common gray squirrel. They are about 20 inches long (half of which is tail) and weigh around one pound.

squir•rel [skwur′ əl] *noun, plural* **squirrels.** a small, furry animal with a long bushy tail and gray, reddish, or dark brown fur. Squirrels live in trees and feed mostly on nuts.

squirt [skwurt] *verb,* **squirted, squirting. 1.** to force out liquid through a narrow opening in a thin stream: He *squirted* oil on his bicycle chain. Water *squirted* out of the hole in the car radiator. **2.** to wet by squirting: It was so hot that we asked Mom to *squirt* us with the hose. —*noun, plural* **squirts.** the act of squirting.

Sri Lan•ka [srē läng′ kə] an island country off the southeast coast of India. *Capital:* Colombo. *Area:* 25,300 square miles. *Population:* 15,640,000. ◆ This country was formerly known as **Ceylon** [si län′].

stab [stab] *verb,* **stabbed, stabbing. 1.** to cut or wound with a knife or other pointed weapon. **2.** to strike with or as if with a pointed object: He *stabbed* his fork into the piece of meat. "Pain *stabbed* her arm, she had twisted it trying to break her fall." (Lloyd Alexander) —*noun, plural* **stabs. 1.** a wound or blow made with a pointed weapon. **2.** a sharp, brief feeling of

pain. **3.** an attempt; try: I don't know if I can do it, but I'll take a *stab* at it anyway.

sta•ble¹ [stā′ bəl] *noun, plural* **stables. 1.** a building where horses, cattle, or other such animals are kept and fed. **2.** a group of race horses belonging to a particular owner. —*verb,* **stabled, stabling.** to keep an animal in a stable.

stable² *adjective,* **stabler, stablest.** not easily moved, changed, or shaken; firm; steady: The supports of the old bridge are being checked to make sure they are *stable.* Great Britain has had a *stable* government for hundreds of years. ◆ The fact of being stable is **stability** [stə bil′ ə tē].

stack [stak] *noun, plural* **stacks. 1.** a large pile of straw or hay that is shaped like a cone or mound. **2.** a pile of things on top of one another: a *stack* of pancakes, a *stack* of magazines. **3.** short for SMOKESTACK. **4. stacks.** the area in a library where the books are kept on shelves. —*verb,* **stacked, stacking.** to put in a stack: He *stacked* the boxes against the wall.

sta•di•um [stā′ dē əm] *noun, plural* **stadiums.** a large structure that has many rows of seats built around an open field or playing area. Stadiums are used for sports events, concerts, rallies, and so on. ◆ In ancient Greece, a *stadium* was a length of about 200 yards, used as the distance for a race.

stadium One of the oldest big-league baseball stadiums, Boston's Fenway Park. In the background is the left-field wall, the famous "Green Monster."

staff [staf] *noun, plural* **staffs. 1.** a stick, rod, or pole: Shepherds used to use a *staff* to herd sheep. A flagpole is also called a flag*staff.* **2.** a group of people who work under a manager or other person of authority: Dr. Hill has just added two nurses to his *staff.* **3.** a group of officers who make plans for an army. **4.** a set of five lines and four spaces on which music is written. —*verb,* **staffed, staffing.** to provide with employees: The company is going to *staff* the new sales office with people just out of college.

stag [stag] *noun, plural* **stags.** a full-grown male deer; a buck.

stage [stāj] *noun, plural* **stages. 1.** the raised platform in a theater on which actors and other entertainers perform. **2.** *also,* **the stage.** the art or work of the theater. **3.** a step, period, or point in a process of development: A caterpillar must pass through the cocoon *stage* to become a butterfly. Germany won many important victories in the early *stages* of World War Two. **4.** short for a STAGECOACH. —*verb,* **staged, staging. 1.** to put on in a theater; present: to *stage* Shakespeare's play *Hamlet*. **2.** to put before the public; carry out: The auto union *staged* a strike. **3.** to act in an artificial way: What seemed to be an actual police raid had been *staged* for the TV news cameras.

stagecoach The stagecoach was an important form of transportation in the Old West. In 1887, this stage of the Concord line left from Fort Reno, Oklahoma for Caldwell, Kansas.

stage·coach [stāj′kōch′] *noun, plural* **stage-coaches.** a large closed coach drawn by horses. Stagecoaches were often used in former times to carry passengers and mail.

stag·ger [stag′ər] *verb,* **staggered, staggering. 1.** to move or walk in a weak, unsteady way, as if about to fall: "They *staggered* up with the fish between them, panting heavily, and dropped the dead weight of the great creature . . ." (Nadine Gordimer) **2.** to act strongly and suddenly on the mind or feelings; shock; stun: to be *staggered* by bad news. **3.** to schedule so as to begin at different times: The city wants businesses to *stagger* their work hours, so that everyone will not be on the road going to work at the same time. —*noun, plural* **staggers.** a weak, unsteady motion or walk.

stag·nant [stag′nənt] *adjective.* **1.** of water or air, being still rather than moving, especially so as to become foul or polluted: The old garbage can had a few inches of *stagnant* water at the bottom. **2.** not active; dull; lifeless: A new hit play has brought needed excitement to what had been a *stagnant* theater season.

stain [stān] *verb,* **stained, staining. 1.** to mark with an unwanted area of color that is hard to get out; soil; spot: She spilled grape juice and *stained* her new blouse. **2.** to color with a dye or tint: They *stained* the wooden dresser to make it darker. **3.** to mark by a wrong or dishonor; disgrace: The arrest for drunk driving *stained* the man's reputation. —*noun, plural* **stains. 1.** a place that is stained; a mark or spot: Timmy was playing on the lawn and got grass *stains* on his pants. **2.** a coloring or dye: to put wood *stain* on a bookcase. **3.** a mark of disgrace.

stainless steel a form of steel that does not rust or stain easily, often used for household products such as knives, forks, spoons, pots, pans, and so on.

stair [stâr] *noun, plural* **stairs. 1. stairs.** a series of steps, used to go from one floor or level to another. **2.** one of these steps: Watch it; there's a loose board on the top *stair*.

stair·case [stâr′kās′] *noun, plural* **staircases.** a flight of stairs.

stake [stāk] *noun, plural* **stakes. 1.** a stick or post pointed at one end for driving into the ground: We set *stakes* in the garden to hold up the tomato plants as they grew larger. **2.** something offered as a bet in a game, race, or contest: He wanted to play in the poker game, but the *stakes* were too high. **3.** an interest or share in a business, investment, or other such activity. **4. at stake.** in danger of being lost: There is a great deal of money at *stake* in producing a new movie. —*verb,* **staked, staking. 1.** to fasten or support with a stake. **2.** to gamble or risk; bet: I'm sure she's telling the truth; I'd *stake* my life on it. **3.** to mark off an area with or as if with stakes: The gold miner *staked* a claim to some land in the mountains.

sta·lac·tite [stə lak′tīt′] *noun, plural* **stalac-tites.** a formation that looks like an icicle and

Pronunciation Key: Accent Marks

[′] is the normal accent mark. It shows where the main stress falls on a word.
[′] is a secondary accent mark. It shows a lighter stress than the primary accent. For example:

tel • e • vis • ion [tel′ə vizh′ən]
(Turn the page for more information.)

hangs down from the ceiling of a cave. A stalactite is formed over a long period of time when water containing minerals drips down from the roof of the cave.

stalactite Stalactites in Luray Caverns, Virginia.

sta•lag•mite [stə lag′ mīt′] *noun, plural* **stalagmites.** a formation that is built up from the floor of a cave. ♦ A stalactite comes down from the ceiling of a cave; a stalagmite goes up from the ground.

stale expressions A *stale expression* is like day-old bread. (Another term for a stale expression is a *cliché.*) Obviously, you should avoid stale expressions such as "white as snow" or "cold as ice." But the question is: how can you tell whether something is stale or not? Most stale expressions are metaphors: "stone cold," "like a cat on a hot tin roof," "right as rain," "slick as oil." When you revise your report or story, look for expressions that are very familiar. Generally, those expression are clichés and therefore stale. Think of new expressions you can use. For example, "so cold the mercury didn't rise to make a degree," or "slick as soap in a tub," or "right as the final score." Some stale expressions can be turned around in humor. A speaker can say, instead of "to make a long story short," "I'll try not to make a long story longer."

stale [stāl] *adjective,* **staler, stalest. 1.** of air, water, or certain foods, not having the proper taste or quality; not fresh: I fed the birds some *stale* pieces of bread. **2.** having lost its energy or interest; worn-out; dull: The politician gave the same *stale* speech in every town he visited. **3.** not as lively or active as before: "He had gone *stale* on his novel and he did not sell enough stories that year . . ." (James Jones)

Stal•in [stä′ lin] **Joseph,** 1879-1953, the dictator of the Soviet Union from 1924 to 1953.

stalk[1] [stôk] *noun, plural* **stalks. 1.** the main stem of a plant: a bean*stalk*, a corn*stalk*. **2.** any long plant part that supports leaves or flowers.

stalk[2] *verb,* **stalked, stalking. 1.** to hunt or follow in a careful, quiet way, so as not to be seen or heard: "Bears *stalk* seals over the ice or ap-

proach by swimming quietly toward them." (Barry Lopez) **2.** to follow after something in a dangerous way, as if hunting prey: The boxer moved across the ring, *stalking* his opponent. **3.** to walk in a stiff or proud manner: "Instantly he leaped from his chair and *stalked* angrily from the room." (Ray Bradbury)

stall [stôl] *noun, plural* **stalls. 1.** a place in a stable for one animal. **2.** a small booth or counter where goods are sold: The two brothers sold T-shirts in a *stall* at the county fair. —*verb,* **stalled, stalling. 1.** to put an animal in a stall. **2.** to stop or bring to a stop: The car engine *stalled* at the intersection. **3.** to put off action; slow down; delay: The man tried to *stall* the bill collector by saying he'd pay next month.

stal•lion [stal′ yən] *noun, plural* **stallions.** a male horse.

sta•men [stā′ mən] *noun, plural* **stamens.** the part of a flower that produces pollen. The stamen is made up of a thin stalk with a pollen-bearing tip called the **anther** [an′ thər].

stam•i•na [stam′ ə nə] *noun.* the strength of body or mind to resist being tired and to keep going; endurance: It takes great *stamina* to run a marathon race.

stam•mer [stam′ ər] *verb,* **stammered, stammering.** to speak in a struggling way, repeating the same sound; stutter. —*noun, plural* **stammers:** a person with a nervous *stammer.*

stamp [stamp] *noun, plural* **stamps. 1.** a small piece of paper with a design on the front and a sticky substance on the back; also called a **postage stamp.** Stamps are put on letters and packages to show that a mailing charge has been paid. **2.** a similar piece of paper showing some mark or message: A tax *stamp* indicates that tax has been paid. ♦ Stores sometimes give out **trading stamps** which customers can exchange for merchandise. **3.** a tool for making a design or letters: The sales clerk used a *stamp* to mark 'Paid' on our copy of the bill. —*verb,* **stamped, stamping. 1.** to put a stamp on: The librarian *stamped* the book with the date it was due. **2.** to bring down the foot heavily and with force: to *stamp* the ground in anger. **3. stamp out.** to get rid of; do away with: The new mayor has promised to *stamp out* the illegal drug trade in the city.

stampede A stampede of wild horses at Camargue, in the south of France.

stam•pede [stam pēd′] *noun, plural* **stampedes. 1.** a sudden, wild rush of a frightened herd of animals. **2.** a sudden, wild rush of many people. —*verb*, **stampeded, stampeding. 1.** to be a part of or cause a stampede: A sudden loud noise can cause a herd of cattle to *stampede*. **2.** to force to act in a careless or thoughtless way: We need some time to think it over; we can't let the salesman *stampede* us into buying today. ♦ *Stampede* came from a word used in Mexican Spanish that meant "crash."

opinion or attitude: How does Senator Jones *stand* on the new tax bill? **5.** to put up with; bear: Turn off the TV; I can't *stand* that show! **6.** to carry out a certain duty or action: to *stand* guard, to *stand* trial.
—*noun, plural* **stands. 1.** the act of standing, or a place where something stands: Near the river there is a *stand* of cottonwood trees. **2.** an attitude or opinion: The mayor took a strong *stand* in favor of rent control. **3.** a stop for battle or resistance: The Battle of Little Bighorn is known as Custer's Last *Stand*. **4.** a rack or other structure for placing things: an umbrella *stand*. **5.** a booth, stall, or counter for selling things: a magazine *stand*, a fruit *stand*. **6. stands.** a raised structure where people can sit or stand: Our seat at the baseball game was high up in the *stands*. **7.** a place where a person performs an official duty: a witness *stand*.

stand•ard [stan′ dərd] *noun, plural* **standards. 1.** *usually,* **standards.** a certain level of quality or value: It's hard to get into that college, because they have very high *standards*. **2.** anything that is accepted as an example or used as a model: The U. S. has safety *standards* for cars which each auto company must follow. Mark Twain left school at the age of 11, but that wasn't unusual by the *standards* of his time. **3.** a flag or banner used as an emblem. —*adjective*. **1.** used as a model or guide: Water pipes come in *standard* sizes. **2.** generally accepted; usual; typical: You don't have to give a tip to a waiter in a restaurant, but it's *standard* practice in most places. **3.** used as a guide or authority: *standard* English.

S

standard English *Standard English* is the form of English that is accepted as correct by educated people. "He don't know nothin'" and "She ain't got no money" are not standard English. People do use them, of course, but they aren't accepted as correct in writing—unless you wish a character in a story to use "street talk." Some questions come to mind. Who decides what is standard? Is there a single book with a title like *Standard American English*? Is there an academy of scholars who are the authority on the use of the language? *No* to all of these. A number of dictionaries, language textbooks, and usage guides generally agree on what standard English is. The evidence for saying that something is standard English is the actual use of the language by respected speakers and writers. For example, in our research for this dictionary we examined the works of over 2000 authors.

stand [stand] *verb,* **stood, standing. 1.** to be on one's feet: A surfer sits or lies flat on the board to wait for a wave, then *stands* to ride on the wave. **2.** to be in an upright position: A huge fire swept through the area and only a few buildings were left *standing*. **3.** to be in a certain place or condition: Don't leave the paint can *standing* open like that. **4.** to have a certain

Pronunciation Key: A–F

a	and; hat	ch	chew; such
ā	ate; stay	d	dog; lid
â	care; air	e	end; yet
ä	father; hot	ē	she; each
b	boy; cab	f	fun; off

(Turn the page for more information.)

standard of living the level at which a country, group, or person lives, based on how well basic needs and wants are satisfied.

standard time the accepted measure of time in a certain region. States along the Atlantic coast follow Eastern Standard Time.

stand·ing [stan′ ding] *noun, plural* **standings.** a certain rank or position: This newspaper gives the *standings* for all college football leagues around the country. —*adjective.* **1.** that stands; in an upright or fixed position: The runners began the race from a *standing* start. **2.** not moving or changing; ongoing: Aunt Marge has a *standing* invitation to come and visit us if she's ever in Florida. "It was a *standing* joke in the family . . ." (Virginia Woolf)

stand·point [stand′ point′] *noun, plural* **standpoints.** a way of thinking about or judging things; a point of view.

stand·still [stand′ stil′] *noun.* a complete stop: "There was little traffic and life seemed to be at a *standstill*." (John Toland)

stank [stangk] a past form of **stink.**

Stanton Elizabeth Cady Stanton (seated) with another women's-rights leader, Susan B. Anthony.

Stan·ton [stan′ tən] **Elizabeth Cady,** 1815-1902, American women's-rights leader.

stan·za [stan′ zə] *noun, plural* **stanzas.** a group of lines that form one part of a poem or song.

staple¹ [stā′ pəl] *noun, plural* **staples. 1.** a U-shaped piece of metal with pointed ends. Staples are driven into a surface to hold a hook, pin, or bolt in place. **2.** a similar piece of thin metal that is used to hold papers and other thin materials together. —*verb,* **stapled, stapling.** to hold together or fasten with a staple. —**stapler,** *noun.*

staple² *noun, plural* **staples. 1.** a product or food that is used widely and often, such as salt, sugar, or flour. **2.** a major product or crop grown in a certain region.

star [stär] *noun, plural* **stars. 1.** a heavenly body that looks like a steady, bright point in the sky at night. Certain burning gases in stars produce the light that makes them shine. **2.** a figure in the shape that a star appears to have in the sky: She put a *star* on top of the Christmas tree. **3.** a person who is an outstanding performer in some field: a baseball *star,* an opera *star.* **4.** an actor or actress who plays a leading part in a movie, play, or television show. —*verb,* **starred, starring. 1.** to mark with a star: He *starred* the items on his list that needed to be done first. **2.** to play a leading role: to *star* in a Broadway play. —*adjective.* outstanding; excellent: He is the *star* runner on the track team.

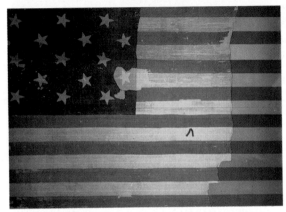

Stars and Stripes Francis Scott Key was inspired to write the "Star-Spangled Banner" when he saw this flag waving over Fort McHenry in the War of 1812.

star·board [stär′ bərd] *noun.* the right side of a boat or ship. —*adjective.* on the right side: The ship was having a problem with its *starboard* engine.

starch [stärch] *noun, plural* **starches. 1.** a white powdery food substance that has no taste or smell and is found in most green plants. Starch is an important element in the diet. Foods such as potatoes, corn, wheat, and rice contain starch. **2.** a form of this substance that is used to stiffen clothes or cloth. —*verb,* **starched, starching.** to make stiff by using starch: to *starch* a shirt collar. —**starchy,** *adjective:* Spaghetti and noodles are *starchy* foods.

stare [stâr] *verb,* **stared, staring.** to look long or hard with the eyes wide open: The people waiting for the bus *stared* angrily at the man who pushed ahead of the rest of the line. —*noun, plural* **stares.** a long, direct look.

star·fish [stär′fish] *noun, plural* **starfishes.** a sea animal with five arms and a body shaped like a star.

stark [stärk] *adjective.* **1.** in every way; absolute; complete. ♦ Usually used with negative words: *stark* terror, *stark* misery. **2.** bare and plain in appearance; harsh; bleak: The photograph showed a *stark* view of empty, frozen fields. —*adverb.* absolutely; completely: to be *stark*, raving mad. —**starkly,** *adverb.*

star·ling [stär′ling] *noun, plural* **starlings.** a bird with a plump body, pointed wings, and a short tail. Starlings live in large flocks and are found in great numbers in North America.

Star of David a six-pointed star that is the symbol of the Jewish religion and of Israel.

star·ry [stär′ē] *adjective,* **starrier, starriest. 1.** full of stars; lighted by stars: a clear, *starry* December night. **2.** shining like stars; bright: to gaze at something with *starry* eyes. **3. starry-eyed.** too hopeful or optimistic; dreamy.

Star-Span·gled Banner [stär′ spang′ gəld] the national anthem of the United States.

starfish

starve [stärv] *verb,* **starved, starving. 1.** to suffer or die from lack of food. **2.** to be very hungry: "We were both *starving,* neither of us having eaten since breakfast." (Dick Francis) **3.** to suffer from the lack of; want greatly: The lonely boy was *starving* for affection. "Everyone, *starved* for light through the darkness of December and January, is out strolling along the streets and canals." (Andrea Lee)

---

starter sentence Writing teachers use the term *starter sentence* to describe how a story or poem can be started from a single sentence. Ernest Hemingway wrote in *A Moveable Feast:* "So, finally, I would write one true sentence, and then go on from there." Poets who use this technique include Anne Sexton, Kenneth Rexroth, and James Merrill. Let's think of examples. "He knew he had only an hour left and it was to him like a death machine." "She said, 'There's no point in explaining how your car got dented since it's in the bay under water.'" "I never forget anything, but this morning I forgot the way to school." The sentence does not even have to relate directly to the plot; it may be just a description or an image: "The beach was empty and and the only motion was sand blowing across the boardwalk." "When you walk down the main street of town you're aware of the mountain, like someone reading the paper over your shoulder."

---

start [stärt] *verb,* **started, starting. 1.** to go into action; get moving; set out: Don't *start* running until I say 'Go.' **2.** to come into operation or being: The movie *starts* at 8:00. Let's finish this up—it's *starting* to rain. **3.** to cause to be in motion or in being: to *start* a car, to *start* a fire, to *start* a conversation with someone. **4.** to move suddenly, from surprise or fear. —*noun, plural* **starts. 1.** the act of starting: We should get an early *start* for the beach today. **2.** a sudden movement: "I would give a *start,* my eyes opening in alarm as I struggled to remember where I was." (James Fenimore Cooper)

star·tle [stär′təl] *verb,* **startled, startling.** to come upon without warning; frighten or excite suddenly: "They took the cat by surprise. In *startled* alarm it flew up the steps and crashed against the closed door." (Meindert DeJong)

star·va·tion [stär vā′shən] *noun.* the fact of starving; death or suffering from lack of food.

state [stāt] *noun, plural* **states. 1.** *also,* **State.** one of the fifty units of government within the United States: Alaska became a U. S. *state* in 1959. **2.** a similar unit of government in another country: Bahia is a *state* of Brazil. **3.** a group of people living together under one government; a nation: Many African *states* became indepen-

Pronunciation Key: G–N			
g	give; big	k	kind; cat; back
h	hold	l	let; ball
i	it; this	m	make; time
ī	ice; my	n	not; own
j	jet; gem; edge	ng	having
(Turn the page for more information.)			

S

dent in the 1950's and 1960's. **4.** the power or activity of government: In Communist countries businesses are owned by the *state*. **5. State.** the department of the U. S. government concerned with dealings with other governments. **6.** a certain condition of a person or thing: a *state* of excitement. The old shack was in a *state* of collapse. **7.** one of the three conditions (solid, liquid, or gas) in which all matter exists. —*verb*, **stated, stating.** to tell in speech or writing; express: The judge asked the witness to *state* his name and address.

sending out broadcast signals: Mom keeps the kitchen radio tuned to an all-news *station*. **3.** a building or place that is used for a particular purpose: a police *station*, a gas *station*. **4.** a person's place or rank in society: "I had dressed myself somewhat more suitable to my *station* in life . . ." (Robert Louis Stevenson) —*verb*, **stationed, stationing.** to assign to a certain position: While he was in the Army, my uncle was *stationed* at a base in Germany. "Mrs. Dubose was *stationed* on her porch when we went by." (Harper Lee)

stationary/stationery English has many "troublesome pairs"—words that are almost, but not quite, the same and that are often confused with each other. If you stay in one place and don't move, you are *stationary*. "Once he found himself *stationary*, staring out at the sea, and had no idea how long he had stopped." (Ken Follett) *Stationery*, with an *e*, is material used for writing, such as paper or envelopes. (The memory trick is "Pap*er* is station*ery*.")

state•ly [stāt′ lē] *adjective*, **statelier, stateliest.** grand and dignified in appearance or manner; elegant; majestic: The *stately* ocean liner slid gracefully out to sea.

state•ment [stāt′ mənt] *noun*, *plural* **statements. 1.** something that is stated; an idea expressed in speech or writing: You say computers actually make work go slower—what do you mean by that *statement?* **2.** a formal comment on something that has happened: The President issued a *statement* condemning the terrorist attack. **3.** a written summary or report of money owed, paid out, received, and so on: People who have checking accounts get a *statement* from the bank each month.

state-of-the-art [stāt′ əv thē ärt′] *adjective*. of the best or most advanced quality that is currently available: This computer system offers *state-of-the-art* printing quality.

states•man [stāts′ mən] *noun*, *plural* **statesmen.** a person who has great skill and experience in dealing with matters of government, especially with international affairs.

stat•ic [stat′ ik] *noun*. electrical charges in the air that are picked up by a television or radio and cause interference with the broadcast signal. —*adjective*. **1.** not moving; staying in one place or condition. ♦ **Static electricity** does not flow in a current. **2.** having to do with radio or television static: There were a lot of *static* noises on the car radio during the storm.

sta•tion [stā′ shən] *noun*, *plural* **stations. 1.** a stopping place along the route of a train, bus, or the like: We got on the subway at the 59th Street *station*. **2.** a company or location for

sta•tion•ar•y [stā′ shən er′ ē] *adjective*. **1.** not moving or changing; remaining still: Lift the weight overhead and then hold your arms *stationary* in that position for five seconds. **2.** not able to be moved; fixed: Attach the end of the rope to a tree, post, or other *stationary* object.

sta•tion•er•y [stā′ shən er′ ē] *noun*. **1.** writing paper and envelopes. **2.** materials used for writing, such as pens and pencils.

station wagon a car having a rear door that can be used for loading and unloading, and a rear seat or seats that can be folded down.

sta•tis•tics [stə tis′ tiks] *plural noun*. **1.** facts and figures that are collected to give information about a particular subject. **2. statistic.** a single number in a set of statistics.

stat•ue [stach′ ōō] *noun*, *plural* **statues.** a likeness of a person or animal that is made out of

statue A historic statue of George Washington in his uniform of the Revolutionary War.

S

stone, clay, metal, or other solid material. Statues are carved, molded, or cast into shape.

Statue of Liberty a huge statue of a woman wearing a crown and holding a torch, which stands in New York Harbor. The Statue of Liberty was given to the United States by France and has become a symbol for freedom.

Statue of Liberty

sta•ture [stach′ ər] *noun.* **1.** the height of the body: ". . . one man, huge, tall, and grownup to my child's *stature,* stood over me . . ." (James Jones) **2.** a level of achievement or development: In the 1800's Russia produced many writers of great *stature,* such as Tolstoy and Chekhov.

sta•tus [sta′ təs *or* stāt′ əs] *noun.* **1.** the condition or rank of a person or thing; state: The news magazine had a feature on the *status* of the nation's economy. What's the *status* of Smith's sore arm—can he pitch today? **2.** a person's rank or standing in society: They're very *status* conscious and are always seen at fancy parties.

stat•ute [stach′ o͞ot] *noun, plural* **statutes.** a law written down and put into effect by a legislature. A **statute of limitations** is a law stating that after a certain time limit a person cannot be brought to court for a crime. ◆ Something that is **statutory** [stach′ ə tôr′ ē] is fixed or controlled by a statute.

staunch [stönch] *adjective,* **stauncher, staunchest.** strong and solid; firm: Senator Jones is a *staunch* supporter of military spending. —**staunchly,** *adverb:* "Bertie had made a good home for them, she told herself *staunchly* . . ." (Sherley Anne Williams)

stave [stāv] *noun, plural* **staves. 1.** one of the long, curved strips of wood forming the sides of a barrel. **2.** a heavy rod or stick; a staff.

stay[1] [stā] *verb,* **stayed, staying. 1.** to continue to be in one place; not move on or leave; remain: Jerry has to *stay* in his room for an hour because he was fighting with his sister. **2.** to be in a certain position: We *stay* on this road until we get to Midland Avenue. **3.** to go on in the same manner or condition; continue: to *stay* up late, to *stay* on a diet. **4.** to live in or visit for a time: to *stay* in a motel, to *stay* over at a friend's house for the night. —*noun, plural* **stays. 1.** a short period of visiting or living in a place. **2.** a delay or putting off of an official action, especially of a criminal sentence.

stay[2] *noun, plural* **stays.** a strong rope or wire that is used to support the mast of a ship. —*verb,* **stayed, staying.** to secure with a stay.

stead•fast [sted′ fast′] *adjective, more/most.* not moving or changing; constant; fixed: "I would glance toward the fire and see those eyes upon me, a *steadfast* gaze . . ." (Mary O'Hara) —**steadfastly,** *adverb.*

stead•y [sted′ ē] *adjective,* **steadier, steadiest. 1.** firm in position; not likely to move, shake, or shift: You hold the ladder *steady* while I climb up. **2.** moving at an even rate; not changing: The windshield wipers swept back and forth with a *steady* beat. "A *steady* stream of employees was pouring through the gate." (Upton Sinclair) **3.** that can be relied on; regular or dependable: a *steady* customer, a *steady* job. **4.** not easily upset or excited; calm: Famous pilot Chuck Yeager was known for his *steady* nerves. —*verb,* **steadied, steadying.** to make or become steady: "He lifted his hands to his head, trying to *steady* himself." (George Eliot) —**steadily,** *adverb:* "I . . . worked *steadily* because there was nothing else to do." (M. F. K. Fisher) —**steadiness,** *noun.*

steak [stāk] *noun, plural* **steaks.** a slice of meat or fish for broiling or frying.

steal [stēl] *verb,* **stole, stolen, stealing. 1.** to take property that belongs to another in a way that is against the law: to *steal* a car, to *steal* money

Pronunciation Key: O–S			
ō	over; go	ou	out; town
ô	all; law	p	put; hop
o͞o	look; full	r	run; car
o͞o	pool; who	s	set; miss
oi	oil; boy	sh	show
(Turn the page for more information.)			

from a bank. **2.** to take or get in a dishonest way: He *stole* the idea for his new book from another writer. **3.** to act or move in a sly, secret way: "Simon came *stealing* out of the shadows by the shelters." (William Golding) "I *stole* glances at Mrs. Prentice's pretty, lively face." (James Gould Cozzens) **4.** to get or win by charm: "It was Rufel . . . whose heart she had *stolen* from the moment she smiled." (Sherley Anne Williams) **5.** in baseball, to run suddenly to the next base, without the ball being hit.

stealth [stelth] *noun.* the fact of moving in a quiet, secret way: ". . . our Indian-style fighting which relied on darkness, *stealth,* surprise." (Gore Vidal) —**stealthy,** *adjective.* —**stealthily,** *adverb.*

steam [stēm] *noun.* **1.** water that has changed into the form of gas or vapor by being heated to a boil. Steam is used for heating, cooking, and other forms of energy. **2.** the power produced by steam under pressure: In the 1800's railroad trains and ocean ships were driven by *steam.* **3.** *Informal.* a driving force or power: to do something under your own *steam.* She was angry and went for a walk to let off *steam.* —*verb,* **steamed, steaming. 1.** to give off steam: a *steaming* bowl of soup. **2.** to cook, soften, or work on with steam: to *steam* vegetables, to *steam* the wrinkles out of a shirt. **3.** to move by or as if by steam: The huge warship *steamed* into the harbor. **4.** *Informal.* to be very angry.

steamboat The 19th-century Ohio River steamboat "Fred Hartweg."

steam•boat [stēm′bōt′] *noun, plural* **steamboats.** a boat moved by steam. Steamboats are used mostly in bays, lakes, and rivers.

steam engine an engine that is powered by the force of expanding steam.

steam•er [stē′mər] *noun, plural* **steamers. 1.** a STEAMBOAT or STEAMSHIP. **2.** a special container in which food is steamed. **3.** a clam with a soft shell that is usually cooked by steaming.

steamroller This worker is using a steamroller to flatten asphalt on the road.

steam•roll•er [stēm′rō′lər] *noun, plural* **steamrollers.** a vehicle on heavy rollers that is used for crushing and smoothing road surfaces. Steamroller engines were originally powered by steam, but today use gasoline or diesel fuel.

steam•ship [stēm′ship′] *noun, plural* **steamships.** a steam-powered ship that sails on the open sea.

steam shovel a large machine that is used for digging. It has a large bucket or scoop at the end of a long beam. Steam shovels have been replaced by diesel-powered shovels.

steed [stēd] *noun, plural* **steeds.** a horse, especially a lively or high-spirited one. ◆ Used mostly in older writings.

steel [stēl] *noun.* a hard and strong metal that is made of iron mixed with carbon. Steel is used to make machines, automobiles, tools, the framework for large buildings, and many other things. —*verb,* **steeled, steeling.** to make oneself strong like steel: All day he's been *steeling* himself for when he has to see the principal. —**steely,** *adjective.* "The sun was a cold *steely* color as it dipped below the mountain." (Jean Craighead George)

steel wool a pad made of fine threads of steel, used for cleaning and polishing.

steep¹ [stēp] *adjective,* **steeper, steepest. 1.** having a sharp slope; rising at a sharp angle: a *steep* hill. **2.** very high; too high: $4000 for that old car—don't you think that's a bit *steep?*

steep² *verb*, **steeped, steeping. 1.** to soak in liquid: She *steeped* the tea leaves for several minutes to make the tea stronger. **2.** to be full of; involve deeply: "All that evening I sat by my fire at the Warwick Arms, *steeped* in a dream of the olden time . . ." (Mark Twain)

stee·ple [stē′ pəl] *noun, plural* **steeples.** a high tower that rises from the roof of a church or other building and narrows at the top.

steer¹ [stēr] *verb*, **steered, steering. 1.** to guide the course of a car, boat, or other such vehicle. **2.** of a vehicle, to be directed in a certain way: a car that *steers* easily. **3.** to follow a certain course; be guided: "Brady chose the most direct path into the woods, *steering* clear of the Hadleys." (Jean Fritz) "Thurber would gracefully *steer* the conversation around to asking whether anybody there had seen Hitchcock's film." (S. J. Perelman)

steer² *noun, plural* **steers.** a male animal of the cattle family that is raised for beef, rather than to produce young.

sheet of metal, paper, or other material that has letters or designs cut through it. When it is laid on a surface and ink or color is spread on it, these designs are made on the surface. —*verb*, **stenciled, stenciling.** to mark with a stencil.

steeplechase Horses and riders clearing a jump in a *steeplechase*, a race over a course with obstacles.

step-by-step writing "Step-by-step writing" means writing according to a schedule that is set beforehand, a 1,2,3 order. It might seem that such an approach would make writing easier—but is it possible? For a story, it's hard to set up a series of steps. Some writers actually begin with the ending of the story; Katherine Anne Porter and Toni Morrison are among those who've said they work this way. Joyce Cary and Vladimir Nabokov have said that they skip from place to place in writing a novel and only later fill in the gaps. Different writers choose different methods, according to their own individual talents. But almost all famous writers seem to agree that trying to follow a step-by-step order won't work. Even in a factual report, you can't use a strict sequence. Choosing a topic comes first, of course, but you may narrow or expand your topic as you work. Research comes before writing, but you may realize as you write you still don't have enough information and need to do more research. Sometimes, it's a good idea to write the introduction as the last thing. That way, you know what's in the rest of the report.

steg·o·sau·rus [steg′ ə sôr′ əs] *noun, plural* **stegosauruses.** a large dinosaur that had a spiked tail and two rows of bony plates standing upright on its back.

Stein·beck [stīn′ bek′] **John,** 1902-1968, American novelist.

stem¹ [stem] *noun, plural* **stems. 1.** the main part of a plant above the ground, from which leaves and flowers grow. **2.** a stalk supporting a leaf, flower, or fruit. **3.** something that is like the stem of a plant: the *stem* of a wine glass.

stem¹ *verb*, **stemmed, stemming. 1.** to stop the flow or movement of; check: to *stem* the flow of blood from a cut. **2. stem from.** to come from: It's thought that the story of John Henry and his hammer *stems from* a real incident.

sten·cil [sten′ səl] *noun, plural* **stencils.** a thin

step [step] *noun, plural* **steps. 1.** a movement made by lifting the foot and putting it down again in a new position: My aunt is really excited because her baby took his first *step* today. **2.** a short distance: Their home is right on the lake; their back door is just a few *steps* from the water. **3.** a place to put the foot on to go up or come down, such as a stair or a rung of a ladder. **4.** a sound or mark made by walking;

Pronunciation Key: T–Z			
t	ten; date	v	very; live
th	think	w	win; away
th	these	y	you
u	cut; butter	z	zoo; cause
ur	turn; bird	zh	measure
(Turn the page for more information.)			

S

745

a footstep or footprint. **5.** an action or actions to reach a goal: The company is laying off workers and taking other *steps* to save money. **6.** a grade or rank: Talk about a cheap car—that's barely one *step* above a bicycle! —*verb*, **stepped, stepping. 1.** to move by taking a step. **2.** to put or press the foot down: She hurt her foot when she *stepped* on a tack.

step•fath•er [step′fä′thər] *noun, plural* **step-fathers.** a man who has married someone's mother, after the person's father has died or been divorced from the mother.

step•lad•der [step′lad′ər] *noun, plural* **step-ladders.** a ladder that stands by itself on four legs and has flat steps instead of rungs.

step•moth•er [step′muth′ər] *noun, plural* **stepmothers.** a woman who has married some-one's father, after the person's mother has died or been divorced from the father.

steppe [step] *noun, plural* **steppes.** a dry, flat area with low grass and few trees, especially the large region of this type that is found in south-eastern Europe and parts of Asia.

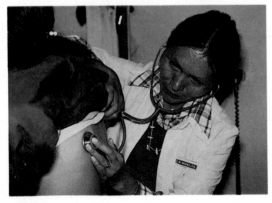

stethoscope A physician's assistant at New Mexico's Shiprock Indian Hospital uses a stethoscope.

ster•e•o [ster′ē o] *noun, plural* **stereos.** a re-cord or tape player that produces realistic sound by using two or more sets of loudspeak-ers placed in different locations.

ster•ile [ster′əl] *adjective.* **1.** free from harmful germs and dirt: Surgeons use *sterile* instruments when they operate on a patient. **2.** not able to produce young; not fertile: A mule is a *sterile* animal produced by mating a horse and a donkey. "After this came another *sterile* strip . . . where stone cropped out from the ground and nothing grew except the yellow-flowered thorn bushes." (W. H. Hudson) **3.** without life or energy; empty; barren: "A Woolworth's, a post office, a movie theater. Everything seemed *sterile* and deserted." (Joe McGinniss)

ster•i•lize [ster′ə līz′] *verb,* **sterilized, steriliz-ing. 1.** to make free from germs or dirt: You can *sterilize* drinking water by boiling it. **2.** to make unable to produce young.

ster•ling [stur′ling] *noun.* **1.** a valuable metal that is made of a mixture of 92.5% pure silver with 7.5% copper; also called **sterling silver. 2.** the British system of money: When we visited London, two U. S. dollars were worth about one pound *sterling.* —*adjective.* **1.** made of sterling silver. **2.** very fine or valuable: "He respected her for . . . all the *sterling* qualities she possessed." (Margaret Mitchell)

stern[1] [sturn] *adjective,* **sterner, sternest.** very strict and serious; not giving in easily: "The mayor stood very tall and *stern* at the head of his men. 'Stop!' he shouted." (Gore Vidal) "I'm talking to you as a friend, Stephen. I don't believe in playing the *stern* father." (James Joyce) —**sternly,** *adverb.*

stern[2] *noun, plural* **sterns.** the rear part of a boat or ship.

steth•o•scope [steth′ə skōp′] *noun, plural* **stethoscopes.** an instrument used by doctors to listen to sounds made by the heart, lungs, and other parts of the body.

stew [stoo] *noun, plural* **stews.** a dish made of a mixture of meat or fish with various vegetables, cooked slowly for a time in a liquid. —*verb,* **stewed, stewing.** to cook slowly in a liquid: to *stew* a chicken.

stereotypes In the printing industry, a *stereotype* is a metal plate used to print a page of type. It makes an exact copy of what is on the typeset page for transfer to a printing press. This meaning led to a figurative use of the word. A *stereotype* is an idea or opinion that is as fixed and unchanging as a metal copy of a page. The term is used in writing—a stereotyped character is one who keeps the exact same qualities regardless of the story in which he or she appears. If you watch TV situation comedies, you'll often see stereotyped characters (also called *stock characters*). These include the pretty but empty-headed "dumb blonde," the "nerd" who wears glasses and spouts computer terms, or the know-it-all kid who gives advice to his confused, ineffective dad. Using a stereotype is a short cut for the writer. He doesn't have to use his imagination to create a realistic, interesting person—he just presents the ready-made stereotype.

stew•ard [stoo′ ərd] *noun, plural* **stewards. 1.** a man in charge of food and other services on a ship, airplane, or train, or at a club or hotel. **2.** in former times, a man who was in charge of the household of a ruler or wealthy person.

> **stewardess** Originally, a *stewardess* was a woman aboard ship who served meals to female passengers. When airline travel came into being, the term *stewardess* was applied to the women who had served passengers on a plane. It was an-all female job. But in 1971 a federal court ruled that the airlines also had to hire men for this job. Within a short time, the term *stewardess* had been dropped by all the airlines in favor of *flight attendant*. However, people still do use *stewardess*: "Her first husband was a wealthy Texan who met her on a flight when she was an airline *stewardess*." (Carol Vogel, *New York Times Magazine*, 1988)

stew•ard•ess [stoo′ ər dis] *noun, plural* **stewardesses.** a woman who serves passengers on an airplane, ship, or train. ◆ An airline stewardess is now officially called a **flight attendant.**

stick [stik] *noun, plural* **sticks. 1.** a long, thin piece of wood: We found some *sticks* near our camp and used them to start a fire. ◆ Often used in compounds, such as drum*stick*, match*stick*, broom*stick*. **2.** something shaped like a stick: a *stick* of chewing gum.
—*verb*, **stuck, sticking. 1.** to push in with a pointed object: She *stuck* a fork into the turkey to see if it was done. **2.** to keep fixed in a certain spot; fasten or hold fast: Eddie spilled glue on his book and it *stuck* to the desk top. "The words *stuck* in his throat like two chunks of green apple." (Jean Fritz) **3.** to keep from moving or making progress; bring to a stop: The elevator got *stuck* between floors. I was *stuck* on the last problem and Mom had to help me. **4.** to stay in one place or condition; keep on: He wants to *stick* around after practice to talk to the coach. **5.** to move or cause to move in some way: He *stuck* his hands in his pockets. "She could *stick* anything in the ground and make it grow." (John Steinbeck)

stick•er [stik′ ər] *noun, plural* **stickers. 1.** a label or other printed paper that has glue or gum on the back. **2.** something that sticks, such as a sharp or rough part of a plant.

stick•y [stik′ ē] *adjective,* **stickier, stickiest. 1.** likely to stick, or covered with something that makes things stick: His hands were *sticky* from the candy cane. **2.** hot and humid: Florida weather can get very *sticky* in the summer.

stiff [stif] *adjective,* **stiffer, stiffest. 1.** not easily bent; not flexible: The shoes are brand new and the leather is still very *stiff*. **2.** not easy or natural in manner; very formal: That politician doesn't come across well on TV because he has a *stiff* manner of speaking. **3.** more extreme or

severe than usual: a *stiff* wind, a *stiff* price. That private school makes you pass a *stiff* test to get in. —*adverb. Informal.* completely; extremely: When I saw the movie *Jaws* I was scared *stiff*. —**stiffly,** *adverb*. —**stiffness,** *noun*.

stiff•en [stif′ ən] *verb,* **stiffened, stiffening.** to make or become stiff: "His body *stiffened* until he seemed to be made of white steel." (Farley Mowat)

sti•fle [stī′ fəl] *verb,* **stifled, stifling. 1.** to hold back a sound from the mouth or throat: "I caught sight of the woman behind the desk *stifling* a yawn." (Andrea Lee) **2.** to hold back; keep in: "And I don't know how long I shall be able to *stifle* my rage." (Anne Frank) **3.** to become or cause to become short of breath: "I must go out and sit in the garden. The air is *stifling* here." (Oscar Wilde)

stig•ma [stig′ mə] *noun, plural* **stigmas. 1.** a mark or sign of disgrace or dishonor: At one time students who did poorly in school had to bear the *stigma* of wearing a tall, pointed "Dunce Cap." **2.** the part of a flower that receives the pollen.

still [stil] *adjective,* **stiller, stillest. 1.** not moving; without motion: "He was never quite *still;* there was always a tapping foot somewhere, the impatient opening and closing of a hand." (F. Scott Fitzgerald) **2.** without sound; quiet; silent: "Only sometimes, if you listened on the *stiller* days, you might hear the sound of an axe . . ." (Patrick White) —*verb,* **stilled, stilling.** to make or become quiet. —*noun, plural* **stills.** the fact of being quiet: the *still* of the early morning. —*adverb.* **1.** not moving; without motion: "We dropped our little anchor, and lay *still* all night." (Daniel Defoe) **2.** now the

S

Pronunciation Key: [ə] Symbol

The [ə] or *schwa* sound occurs in syllables without an accent. It can be spelled with any vowel, such as **a** in above, **e** in listen, **i** in pencil, **o** in melon, **u** in circus. It can also be a combination of vowels, such as **io** in action, **ai** in mountain, **iou** in precious.

(Turn the page for more information.)

same as before; even now: Are you and Linda *still* mad at each other? —**stillness,** *noun:* "At that moment a long, loud roll of thunder broke the *stillness* of the afternoon." (Isak Dinesen)

still life a painting of objects that are not alive, such as cut flowers or a bowl of fruit.

stilt [stilt] *noun, plural* **stilts.** one of a long pair of slender poles with a small support for the foot that makes it possible to walk with the feet high above the ground.

stim•u•late [stim′yə lāt′] *verb,* **stimulated, stimulating.** to stir or rouse to action; excite: "The prospect of at last getting to grips with Le Chiffre *stimulated* him and quickened his pulse." (Ian Fleming) ◆ Something that can stimulate the activity of the body is a **stimulant:** Coffee and tea contain the *stimulant* caffeine. —**stimulation,** *noun.*

stim•u•lus [stim′yə ləs] *noun, plural* **stimuli** [stim′yə lī]. something that stimulates; something producing a reaction: Any living thing will be affected by a *stimulus* to its body, such as light or heat.

sting [sting] *verb,* **stung, stinging. 1.** to pierce or wound with a small, sharp point, as a bee or wasp does. **2.** to cause or suffer a quick, sharp pain: The cut *stung* a few seconds after he put the medicine on it. "The wind blew in *stinging* gusts and whipped the snow down the frigid streets." (Arthur Schlesinger) —*noun, plural* **stings. 1.** the sharp part of an insect or animal that is used for stinging; more often called a **stinger. 2.** a wound made by an insect or animal stinger: She had a bee *sting* on her arm.

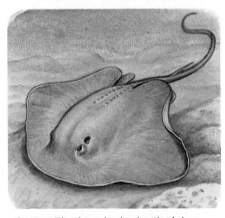

stingray The long barbed tail of the stingray gives a painful sting. It uses its "wings" in a sweeping motion to uncover shellfish buried in the sand.

sting•ray [sting′rā′] *noun, plural* **stingrays.** a large, flat, ocean fish that has a long whip-like tail with poisonous, stinging spines that can inflict a painful wound.

sting•y [stin′jē] *adjective,* **stingier, stingiest.** not willing to give or share something, especially money; not generous: In Dickens' *Christmas Carol,* the character of Scrooge is very *stingy* at the beginning of the story.

stink [stingk] *noun, plural* **stinks.** a strong, bad smell. —*verb,* **stank** or **stunk, stunk, stinking.** to have a strong, unpleasant smell.

stir [stur] *verb,* **stirred, stirring. 1.** to mix something by moving it in a circular motion with a spoon or similar tool: He kept *stirring* the sauce so that it wouldn't burn. **2.** to move or cause to move from a certain position: "Did you hear Rebecca *stirring* around upstairs?" (Thornton Wilder) "The sea was calm with small white-caps *stirred* by a slight breeze." (John Toland) **3.** to cause a certain thought or action; bring about: to *stir* up trouble. "The name Room 40, O. B. . . . *stirred* no curiosity . . ." (Barbara Tuchman) —*noun, plural* **stirs. 1.** the act of stirring. **2.** excitement or interest: "Although Bessie was unknown up north during those years, she was causing quite a *stir* on the southern circuit." (Studs Terkel)

stir•rup [stur′əp] *noun, plural* **stirrups.** a loop or ring that hangs from a saddle and supports the rider's foot, made of leather or metal.

stitch [stich] *noun, plural* **stitches. 1.** a single, complete movement of a thread and needle through a piece of cloth in sewing. **2.** any similar movement used in knitting, crocheting, or embroidering. **3.** the act of closing up a cut with a thread-like material, so that it can heal properly. ◆ The medical term for this is **suture** [soo′chər]. **4.** a sharp pain in the side. **5. in stitches.** laughing very hard. —*verb,* **stitched, stitching.** to make a stitch or stitches.

stock [stäk] *noun, plural* **stocks. 1.** a supply of things stored for future use or sale: This store won't have bathing suits in *stock* until next spring. **2.** animals raised or kept on a farm or ranch, such as cows, sheep, and pigs; also called **livestock. 3.** broth made from the liquid in which fish, meat, or poultry has been cooked: French onion soup is usually made from beef *stock.* **4.** shares of ownership in a business: to buy *stock* in Delta Air Lines. **5.** the handle of a firearm. —*verb,* **stocked, stocking.** to keep on hand; keep a supply: The refrigerator was well *stocked* with fruit juice and soda for the party. —*adjective.* **1.** on hand; in supply: The store has to order that specially for me; it's not a *stock* item. **2.** in common use: When he writes business letters he tries to make each one original instead of just repeating *stock* phrases.

stock•ade [stä kād′] *noun, plural* **stockades. 1.** an area surrounded and protected by strong, upright posts set in the ground. **2.** a military jail.

stock•brok•er [stäk′ brō′ kər] *noun, plural* **stockbrokers.** a persons who buys and sells shares of stock for others, in return for a fee.

stock•ing [stäk′ ing] *noun, plural* **stockings.** a close-fitting covering for the leg, usually reaching above the knee.

Stock•holm [stäk′ hōlm] the capital of Sweden, on the Baltic Sea. *Population:* 1,390,000.

stock market Crowds gather outside the New York Stock Exchange on the day of its great crash, "Black Thursday," October 24, 1929.

stock market or **stock exchange** a place where stocks and bonds are bought and sold.

stocks [stäks] *plural noun.* a wooden frame for a person to sit or stand in, with holes for the feet and sometimes the head and hands. In Colonial America people were punished for minor crimes by being put in the stocks.

stock•y [stäk′ ē] *adjective,* **stockier, stockiest.** having a short, heavy shape or build: a *stocky* football lineman.

stock•yard [stäk′ yärd′] *noun, plural* **stock-yards.** a place where livestock is kept in pens before being shipped to market or slaughtered.

stole [stōl] *verb.* the past tense of **steal.**

stom•ach [stum′ ək] *noun, plural* **stomachs. 1.** the bag-like part of the body located in the abdomen that holds food and begins digesting it. **2.** the area of the body between the middle of the chest and the hips. —*verb,* **stomached, stomaching.** to put up with something or someone; bear: I can't *stomach* the way he brags about all the money he has.

stomp [stämp] *verb,* **stomped, stomping.** to walk or step heavily and with force: "Sally picked up the basket and *stomped* out of Andrea's room." (Judy Blume) "She *stomped* the snow from her boots." (Margaret Atwood)

stone [stōn] *noun, plural* **stones. 1.** the hard mineral substance that makes up rocks. **2.** a piece of this material that is larger than a pebble but smaller than a boulder. **3.** a gem or jewel; also called a **precious stone. 4.** the hard pit of certain fruits, such as cherries and peaches. —*verb,* **stoned, stoning.** to throw stones at: The police were *stoned* by the rioters as they tried to clear out the area.

Stone Age the earliest known period of human history, when tools and weapons were made of stone rather than iron.

stood [stood] *verb.* the past tense of **stand.**

stool [stool] *noun, plural* **stools.** a seat without arms or a back.

stoop[1] [stoop] *verb,* **stooped, stooping. 1.** to bend the body forward and down: She *stooped* over to pick a flower. **2.** to stand or walk with the shoulders pushed forward. **3.** to lower oneself to do something one should not do: I know he was afraid he'd fail the test, but I didn't think he'd *stoop* to cheating. —*noun.* a bending forward of the head and shoulders.

stoop[2] *noun, plural* **stoops.** a small platform or porch with stairs leading up to the entrance of a house or other building.

stop [stäp] *verb,* **stopped, stopping. 1.** to keep from moving or going on: to *stop* a car for a red light. Mom told Katie to *stop* watching TV and start her homework. **2.** to keep from doing something: Mary *stopped* her little brother from climbing the fence so that he wouldn't hurt himself. **3.** to come to an end: The children went out to play after the rain *stopped*. **4.** to close up or block: We had to call a plumber after Lenny *stopped* up the sink with his modeling clay. —*noun, plural* **stops. 1.** the act of stopping or being stopped: The bus made a quick *stop* to avoid hitting the car. **2.** a place or location where a stop is made: He rode the train all the way to the last *stop*. **3.** something

S

Pronunciation Key: Accent Marks

[′] is the normal accent mark. It shows where the main stress falls on a word.
[′] is a secondary accent mark. It shows a lighter stress than the primary accent. For example:

tel • e • vis • ion [tel′ə vizh′ən]

(Turn the page for more information.)

used to stop or block: A door *stop* keeps a door from closing. **4.** a part that controls the tone and pitch on a musical instrument.

stop•per [stäp′ ər] *noun, plural* **stoppers.** something used to stop up or close the opening of a bottle, jar, or other container.

stop•watch [stäp′ wäch′] *noun, plural* **stopwatches.** a special watch that can be stopped to give the exact length of time that something takes, such as a race.

stor•age [stôr′ ij] *noun.* the act or fact of storing something: Ann didn't have room for all her furniture in the new apartment, so she put her sofa in *storage.*

store [stôr] *noun, plural* **stores. 1.** a place where things are sold to the public: a grocery *store,* a shoe *store.* **2.** a supply of things that are intended for future use: Squirrels often put away a *store* of nuts for the winter. —*verb,* **stored, storing. 1.** to put away and keep for future use: We packed up the Christmas ornaments to *store* them in the attic until next year. **2.** to put information into a computer memory, or onto a computer device such as a tape or disk.

store•house [stôr′ hous′] *noun, plural* **storehouses. 1.** a building or other place where things are stored for future use. **2.** a large supply or source: The *Guinness Book of World Records* is a *storehouse* of unusual facts.

stork [stôrk] *noun, plural* **storks.** a long-legged wading bird with a long neck and bill.

storm [stôrm] *noun, plural* **storms. 1.** a change in the weather that brings strong wind along with rain, snow, hail, or sleet. **2.** a sudden and strong outburst of noise or feeling: As the "bad guy" wrestler entered the ring, the crowd greeted him with a *storm* of boos. **3. by storm.** with a sudden and powerful attack: to take an enemy fort *by storm.* "A few days later came the news that took the plantation *by storm.*" (Alex Haley) —*verb,* **stormed, storming. 1.** to rain,

snow, or blow strongly. **2.** to rush or attack violently and quickly: "He often teased her till she'd *storm* out of the room." (John O'Hara)

storm•y [stôr′ mē] *adjective,* **stormier, stormiest. 1.** having to do with a storm or storms: *stormy* weather, a *stormy* day. **2.** like a storm; noisy, violent, angry, and so on: Baseball owner George Steinbrenner has had a *stormy* relationship with Billy Martin, hiring and firing him as manager many different times.

storywriting Why are third or fourth or fifth grade students given assignments to write stories? We all know, don't we, that almost all of the writing you do in high school and college and in a job or profession will be nonfiction. Why, then, assign storywriting? There is no doubt that most school reports and most business reports, however accurate, tend to lack inventiveness and liveliness. Writing stories can help you realize that your imagination should never take a vacation—use it for *anything* you write. Storywriting encourages you to use colorful and varied language. One rarely sees metaphors and images in nonfiction reports, and that's too bad, because those are techniques of writing you can use anywhere at all. Here's an example: "Our computers run. Nobody doubts that. But they are slow, like an old dog, and we all tend to feel comfortable with the familiar. We need speed in our data processing. We need a cheetah, not an old pet."

sto•ry¹ [stôr′ ē] *noun, plural* **stories. 1.** words telling about something that has happened: Did you read the *story* in the paper about yesterday's ice storm? **2.** an account or tale that is made up: the *story* of Cinderella. **3. a.** any piece of writing that is fiction rather than fact. **b.** see **short story. 4.** a lie: The little boy had a bad habit of telling *stories.*

story² *noun, plural* **stories.** one floor of a building that has different levels: a ten-*story* office building.

stork The wood stork is the only true stork native to the Americas. Florida suffered a great loss of these birds in recent years when many swamp areas were drained for human use.

stout [stout] *adjective*, **stouter, stoutest. 1.** large and heavy; fat: a person with a *stout* build. **2.** having courage; brave: In old stories, the hero might be said to be a "*stout* fellow" or **stout-hearted. 3.** strong and solid: ". . . inside the *stout* walls that kept out the howling blizzard." (Laura Ingalls Wilder)

stove [stōv] *noun, plural* **stoves.** a kitchen appliance that runs on gas or electricity and is used for cooking food. Some stoves can also use wood, coal, or oil for cooking and heating. ♦ A **stovepipe** is a large metal pipe used to carry smoke away from a stove.

stow [stō] *verb*, **stowed, stowing. 1.** to put or pack away: ". . . men were *stowing* away the cargo for its trip to England." (Langston Hughes) "Carefully *stowing* away his telescope in the closet . . ." (Walker Percy) **2. stow away.** to be a stowaway: "Once in London, he *stows away* aboard a freighter bound for the New World . . ." (Woody Allen)

stow•a•way [stō′ə wā′] *noun, plural* **stow-aways.** a person who hides on a ship or plane to avoid paying for a ticket.

Stowe [stō] **Harriet Beecher,** 1811-1896, American author who wrote *Uncle Tom's Cabin.*

strad•dle [strad′əl] *verb*, **straddled, straddling.** to have one leg or part on either side of something: "As I sat in an uptown streetcar, *straddling* my shiny new suitcase . . ." (William L. Shirer) "He let the car *straddle* the center of the road . . ." (Wright Morris)

strag•gle [strag′əl] *verb*, **straggled, straggling. 1.** to go off from the main group or main path; wander; stray: "They became widely separated as they *straggled* up the slope." (Richard Adams) **2.** to move in an uneven or crooked way: "The figures of these men and women *straggled* past the flower-bed with a curiously irregular movement . . ." (Virginia Woolf) **—straggler,** *noun:* "The crowds had gone, and only the *stragglers* like me were leaving now in twos and threes." (Dick Francis)

straight [strāt] *adjective*, **straighter, straightest. 1.** not curved or crooked; following one direction: Notebook paper is marked with *straight* lines. The pine tree had a tall, *straight* trunk. **2.** in the proper order or arrangement: Let me get this *straight*—the black dog is yours, but the white one isn't? **3.** honest and direct: "I can't make anything of you if you don't act *straight* by me." (Rudyard Kipling) **4.** not joking; serious: "A storm of laughter erupted. Wilson could not keep a *straight* face, though he tried." (George Plimpton) —*adverb.* **1.** in a straight manner or way: to stand up *straight;* to comb your hair *straight* back. **2.** without delay: She went *straight* home after school.

straight•en [strāt′ən] *verb*, **straightened, straightening.** to make or become straight: "She kept shaking her head and *straightening* her shoulders as though she had just rid herself of a tremendous burden." (Eleanor Estes)

straight•for•ward [strāt′fôr′wərd] *adjective, more/most.* acting or speaking in a direct way; honest; frank.

strain¹ [strān] *verb*, **strained, straining. 1.** to make a great effort; try hard: "Theo looked back, *straining* his eyes for a last sight of the ship." (Lloyd Alexander) "Byron *strained* to hear the low conversation of Aster and the captain in the tower." (Herman Wouk) **2.** to draw or pull tight; pull with force: "The dog *strained* at the leash and snarled but the thick rope did not loosen." (Jerzy Kosinski) **3.** to weaken or damage by stretching or putting too much pressure on: to *strain* a leg muscle while running. ". . . the kids played and the grown-ups sang songs by the fire, but there seemed something *strained* and forced about the day." (Joe McGinniss) **4.** to pour or press something through a strainer. —*noun, plural* **strains.** the fact or condition of being strained: "Despite the problems of the last five years, her face showed no *strain*." (John Toland)

strain² *noun, plural* **strains. 1.** a breed or type of animal: "An unusual *strain* of musk oxen with cream-colored guard hairs . . ." (Barry Lopez) **2.** a family line; ancestry. **3.** a piece of music; a melody or tune: ". . . the joyful *strains* of 'Tiger Rag' blared throughout the Beiderbecke house." (Studs Terkel)

strain•er [strā′nər] *noun, plural* **strainers.** a device for separating liquids from solids, with small holes to stop the solids as the liquids flow through.

strait [strāt] *noun, plural* **straits. 1.** a narrow channel between two larger bodies of water: The *Strait* of Gibraltar connects the Atlantic Ocean with the Mediterranean Sea. **2. straits.** a difficult situation: ". . . he was in *straits* about money." (Katherine Anne Porter)

Pronunciation Key: A–F			
a	and; hat	ch	chew; such
ā	ate; stay	d	dog; lid
â	care; air	e	end; yet
ä	father; hot	ē	she; each
b	boy; cab	f	fun; off

(Turn the page for more information.)

---

strategies for writing Textbooks on writing often refer to "strategies for writing." They tell you of methods for carrying out the task of writing. Perhaps a better term is "strategies for starting to write." Why? Because most strategies deal with getting started. The most widely-recommended strategy is to begin by arranging words in some kind of a list or chart, rather than in the form of ordinary sentences. A popular technique for this is CLUSTERING (see p. 147). Another strategy is to make a chart of the Five W's: Who ____? What ____? Where ____? When ____? Why ____? The traditional outline technique also falls into this category. Another strategy is to begin by talking about what you wish to write with other people—a friend, a teacher, or a parent. Remember you can always correct and revise, but to cut a cloth you need material!

---

strand¹ [strand] *verb*, **stranded, stranding.** to leave behind or in a helpless position: They ran out of gas and were *stranded* on a lonely mountain road for several hours.

strand² *noun*, *plural* **strands. 1.** one of the threads or wires that is twisted together to form a rope or cable. **2.** a hair or thread.

strange [strānj] *adjective*, **stranger, strangest. 1.** not known before; not familiar: I never sleep well the first night in a *strange* place. **2.** not normal or ordinary; odd; unusual: The TV's not working—it's just making a *strange* buzzing noise. Don't you think it's *strange* that she hasn't called us once since she moved? —**strangely,** *adverb.* —**strangeness,** *noun.*

strang•er [strānj′ ər] *noun*, *plural* **strangers. 1.** a person who is not known or is not familiar: I thought I saw my uncle on the street, but when the man turned around I realized it was a *stranger.* **2.** a person from another place: They asked her for directions, but she answered, "Sorry, I'm a *stranger* here myself."

stran•gle [strang′ gəl] *verb.* **strangled, strangling. 1.** to kill by squeezing the throat to cut off the breath. **2.** to be or feel unable to breathe; choke. —**strangulation,** *noun.*

strap [strap] *noun*, *plural* **straps.** a long, narrow strip of leather, cloth, or some other material used to tie or hold something: The *strap* on Susan's purse broke, spilling the contents on the floor. —*verb*, **strapped, strapping.** to fasten or hold with a strap.

stra•te•gic [strə tē′ jik] *adjective*, *more/most.* **1.** having to do with strategy: The Schlieffen Plan of 1905 was a *strategic* analysis of how Germany could attack and defeat France. **2.** important to strategy: Fort Pitt (Pittsburgh) was built in a *strategic* spot where three great rivers come together. **3.** carefully placed or done; well-chosen: Secret Service men were posted at *strategic* spots along the President's parade route.

strat•e•gy [strat′ ə jē] *noun*, *plural* **strategies. 1.** the technique of planning and directing troops and other forces during a war. ♦ *Strategy* deals with planning before a battle; TACTICS involves decisions made in or at the battle itself. **2.** a careful plan for reaching a goal: Deciding when to bring in a new pitcher is part of the *strategy* of baseball. I want to get the boss to change his mind about that—what's the best *strategy* to use?

straw [strô] *noun*, *plural* **straws. 1.** a narrow tube made of paper or plastic, used for sucking up liquids into the mouth. **2.** the thin, dried stalks of grains or grasses after they have been harvested and the seeds have been removed.

strawberry A close-up of the fruit of the strawberry. Also seen are the runners that come off the main plant to make a new plant.

straw•ber•ry [strô′ ber′ ē] *noun*, *plural* **strawberries.** a small, red berry with a sweet taste, growing on a plant that grows low to the ground.

stray [strā] *verb*, **strayed, straying.** to move off from a group or from the proper place; wander away: The horses *strayed* out of the corral and had to be rounded up again. Her paper had some interesting comments, but she kept *stray-*

ing from the main point. —*adjective.* **1.** wandering or lost: My sister is always bringing home *stray* cats that she finds around the neighborhood. **2.** scattered about: A few *stray* plants grew here and there on the hillside. —*noun, plural* **strays.** a lost or homeless animal.

streak [strēk] *noun, plural* **streaks. 1.** a long, thin mark that is usually a different color than the surrounding area: The old rag left *streaks* of dirt when I wiped the windshield. **2.** a continuing pattern or series of events: a ten-game winning *streak* in baseball. "We've had a *streak* of bad luck since we left Poker Flat." (Bret Harte) **3.** a small amount or trace of something: He's nice enough until you get him mad; then he's got a real mean *streak.* —*verb,* **streaked, streaking. 1.** to mark with streaks: "His shirt hung out and dirt *streaked* his cheeks and chin." (John Jakes) **2.** to move very fast: "Two aircraft *streaked* across the sky from south to north . . ." (J. M. Coetzee)

stream [strēm] *noun, plural* **streams. 1.** a small body of running water: We found a great fishing *stream* in the mountains when we went camping last fall. **2.** a steady flow or movement of something: "A mighty *stream* of people now emptied into the street, and came rolling slowly toward the church." (Nathaniel Hawthorne) —*verb,* **streamed, streaming. 1.** to flow steadily: "Tears were *streaming* down his face and his body was shaking with sobs." (Erskine Caldwell) "The light of a lamp *streamed* from an open window into the darkness . . ." (John Galsworthy) **2.** to wave or float in the air, as a flag does.

more efficient or able to work better: The airline has *streamlined* the check-in process so that people can get to the plane much faster.

streamlined A Japanese airport monorail shows the streamlining used in modern transportation.

street [strēt] *noun, plural* **streets.** a public road in a city or town. A street has houses or other buildings on one or both sides.

street•car [strēt′kär′] *noun, plural* **streetcars.** a vehicle that runs on rails in the streets and carries passengers.

strength [strengkth] *noun, plural* **strengths.** the quality of being strong; power or force: "There had been a time when M. C. hadn't the *strength* yet to ride the bike on the hills." (Virginia Hamilton) "The sun's rays appeared to lose their *strength* little by little." (Jules Verne)

strength•en [strengk′thən] *verb,* **strengthened, strengthening.** to make or grow stronger: The Senator felt the U. S. should *strengthen* its military forces in the Far East.

---

stream of consciousness This is a writing technique that is used in works such as James Joyce's *Ulysses* (1922) and William Faulkner's *The Sound and the Fury* (1929). The idea is that the writer puts down a "stream" or "flow" of thoughts on the page. Sentences are not complete and they jump from one idea to another, to represent the way our inner mind works. Even though Joyce and Faulkner are very advanced writers, something close to the stream-of-consciousness technique is useful for student writing. In *free writing,* the writer quickly puts down whatever thoughts come to mind about a topic. For example, *Kentucky:* "the Bluegrass State. Grass isn't really blue, though, just a darker shade of green. Dark . . . Dark and Bloody Ground was what the Indians called it. Tribes must have fought each other there . . ." Please note, though, that free writing is for the *first draft only.*

---

stream•er [strē′mər] *noun, plural* **streamers.** a long, ribbon-like flag or banner.

stream•line [strēm′līn′] *verb,* **streamlined, streamlining. 1.** to design and build something in the shape that offers the least resistance for moving through air or water. Cars that are streamlined can go faster on the highway and get better gas mileage. **2.** to make something

Pronunciation Key: G–N			
g	give; big	k	kind; cat; back
h	hold	l	let; ball
i	it; this	m	make; time
ī	ice; my	n	not; own
j	jet; gem; edge	ng	having
(Turn the page for more information.)			

753

stren•u•ous [stren′ yōō əs] *adjective*, *more/ most*. **1.** with great effort: "A man walks upright. For him it is *strenuous* to climb a steep hill." (Richard Adams) **2.** very active: There was *strenuous* opposition to the mayor's plan. **—strenuously,** *adverb:* "He had been *strenuously* occupied the whole day, going over hundreds of telegrams." (William L. Shirer)

throw. **2.** a straight or level area: ◆ The part of a race track just before the finish line is called the **home stretch.** "They looked out over the empty *stretches* of grass beyond." (Richard Adams) **3.** an unbroken period of time or activity: "When he was making a survey of the new Almaden mine he stayed underground for twenty hours at a *stretch.*" (Wallace Stegner)

stretching a paper Let's say you're working on a social studies report. It may be that no matter how well you plan the paper, you'll find yourself with just over three pages of text. If the assignment clearly called for a minimum of four pages, how can you stretch your paper to the assigned length? First, here's what you should *not* do: (1) Don't "pad" the paper by repeating yourself or adding unnecessary words. (2) Don't create a false appearance of length by allowing extra space between lines or making margins narrower. Here's what we *do* suggest: (1) Go back to your notes. You'll probably find some good information you have not used. (2) Search for good quotes by people involved in your paper. (3) Ask yourself if you can substitute specific details for certain generalizations. (4) Look at your conclusion. Can it be expanded by calling attention to contrary views? (5) Try to add complete new paragraphs rather than to build up within existing paragraphs. Finally, if you really can't find anything good to add, go with the paper, short as it is.

S

stress [stres] *noun*, *plural* **stresses. 1.** the force with which one body acts on another, as by pulling or pressing down: Materials used in buildings are tested to see how much *stress* they can withstand. **2.** pressure or strain on the mind and feelings: Important events in life, such as a new job or an illness in the family, may cause *stress*. **3.** a special meaning, emphasis, or importance: Our writing teacher puts great *stress* on having a good, strong opening for your paper. **4.** a stronger tone of voice used to emphasize a certain sound, word, or phrase: ◆ In the word *firefighter,* "fire" has **primary stress,** "fight" has **secondary stress,** and "er" has no stress.
—verb, **stressed, stressing. 1.** to give special meaning or importance to: The mayor's speech *stressed* the need for a new airport near the city. **2.** to *pronounce* a word or syllable of a word with greater emphasis: We *stress* the first syllable in the word "building."

stretch [strech] *verb*, **stretched, stretching. 1.** to draw out to become larger or wider: to *stretch* a rubber band. My cotton sweater *stretched* and now it's too big for me. **2.** to spread or reach out to full length: "I . . . pulled the canoe up on the bank and *stretched* out on a rock to wait for him." (James Dickey) **3.** to move or lie over an area; extend: "They saw before them now a dark and gloomy forest, *stretching* on and on . . ." (James Thurber) **—noun,** *plural* **stretches. 1.** the act of stretching: The first baseman made a long *stretch* to catch the low

stretch•er [strech′ ər] *noun*, *plural* **stretchers.** a frame or simple bed on which a sick or injured person can be carried.

strew [strōō] *verb*, **strewed, strewed** or **strewn, strewing.** to spread around by throwing or scattering: "His tools were *strewn* about the room." (Mark Helprin)

strick•en [strik′ ən] *verb*. a past participle of **strike. —adjective.** affected by sickness or trouble: "Her face was drained of all color and there was a *stricken,* despairing look in her eyes." (Edward S. Fox)

strict [strikt] *adjective*, **stricter, strictest. 1.** following or enforcing a rule in an exact, careful manner: "I was making my bed, having received *strict* orders from Bessie to get it arranged before she returned." (Charlotte Brontë) **2.** closely enforced; exact: The Soviet Union is often called "Russia," but in the *strict* sense Russia is one part of the Soviet Union. **3.** absolute or complete: My girlfriend shared her secret with me in *strict* confidence. **—strictly,** *adverb*. **—strictness,** *noun*.

stride [strīd] *verb*, **strode, striding.** to walk with long steps: "We saw the figure of a man *striding* along the road, walking fast and waving his arms . . ." (Virginia Woolf) **—noun,** *plural* **strides. 1.** a long step: "The three men moved across the park in step with Zeb Vance's firm *stride.*" (Tom Wicker) **2.** progress or improvement: That company has made great *strides* to improve safety conditions for its workers.

strike [strīk] *verb*, **struck, struck** or **stricken, striking. 1.** to contact with force; hit: "Halsey *struck* the desk with a bony gray-haired fist." (Herman Wouk) **2.** to come to the mind quickly or with force: "A new idea *struck* him. 'We'll go together, a double jump!'" (John Knowles) "When I first saw Richard Burton . . . I was *struck* by the promise this young actor held out." (John Simon) **3.** to affect the mind or feelings in a certain way: "I hope he *strikes* you as having talent." (Lewis Carroll) **4.** to show the time by sound: "The great bell of Saint Paul's was *striking* One in the cleared air . . ." (Charles Dickens) **5.** to set on fire by scratching: "Matthew saw a match *strike* in the darkest corner of the room." (James Houston) **6.** to discover suddenly: to *strike* gold. **7.** of workers, to stop work as a protest until certain demands are met, such as higher pay.
—*noun*, *plural* **strikes. 1.** the stopping of work as a method of forcing an employer to agree to certain demands. **2.** a sudden discovery: an oil *strike*. **3.** in baseball, a pitch that the batter swings at and misses, or hits in foul territory. ♦ A pitch is also a strike (**called strike**) if the batter does not swing but the ball passes over home plate and in the **strike zone.**

strike out 1. to make an out in baseball by getting three strikes. ♦ Also used as a *noun:* a pitcher who set a record for *strikeouts.* **2.** *Informal.* to fail completely. **3.** to begin to move or go; set out: "Dave *struck out* across the fields . . ." (Richard Wright)

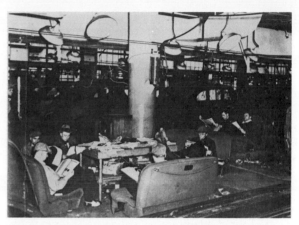

strike These General Motors auto workers are participating in a sit-down strike, in which they report to their jobs but don't do any work. The strike took place in 1937 at a plant in Michigan.

3. a series of persons, things, or events: The team finally won a game to break a long *string* of defeats. **4. strings.** musical instruments that have strings and are usually played with a bow, such as the violin or cello. —*verb*, **strung, stringing. 1.** to put on a string or provide with strings: to *string* pearls onto a necklace, to *string* a tennis racket. **2.** to arrange in a row or series. ♦ Used with a following adverb such as *out* or *together*: "The bridge lights were *strung out* in a burning necklace that can be seen for thirty miles." (Jimmy Breslin) "I never heard so many old, played out jokes *strung together* in my life." (Mark Twain)

"stringy" style "The town didn't take good care of the park. *And* weeds were growing up all over the field. *And so* people stopped playing ball there. *And then* the town didn't bother with it at all. *And so now* it's completely grown over with weeds and nobody goes there." This is referred to as a "stringy" style of writing by composition teachers. The writer "strings together" a series of sentences with conjunctions and adverbs: *and, and so, and then,* etc. Probably this style of writing is a carryover from speech. The "so this happened . . . and then this happened . . ." pattern is natural when you're talking to someone. But in writing you need to fit sentences more tightly together: "The town didn't take good care of the park; weeds were growing all over the field. Soon, people stopped playing ball there, and not long after that the town didn't bother to take care of it. Now it's merely an empty lot."

strik•ing [strī′ king] *adjective*, *more/most.* making a strong impression, as by being attractive or unusual: ". . . not so *striking* as Sylvia, who was the sort of girl people turn around to stare at in restaurants." (Noel Coward) —**strikingly,** *adverb.*

string [string] *noun*, *plural* **strings. 1.** a thin cord made of twisted fibers or wire. **2.** something that is like this in appearance or use: guitar *strings*, a *string* of Christmas tree lights.

string bean a long, green bean that is eaten in the pod.

Pronunciation Key: O–S			
ō	over; go	ou	out; town
ô	all; law	p	put; hop
oo	look; full	r	run; car
o͞o	pool; who	s	set; miss
oi	oil; boy	sh	show
(Turn the page for more information.)			

strip¹ [strip] *verb*, **stripped, stripping. 1.** to take off clothing; undress. **2.** to remove the covering or outer layer of something: "The force of the wind had *stripped* a maple of its red and yellow leaves . . ." (John Cheever)

strip² *noun, plural* **strips.** a long, narrow piece of some material: ·a *strip* of paper or cloth. This *strip* of land along the coast belongs to the National Park Service.

stripe [strīp] *noun, plural* **stripes.** a narrow, even band of color: The American flag has thirteen *stripes* on it. —*verb*, **striped, striping.** to mark with a stripe or stripes: a *striped* shirt.

strive [strīv] *verb*, **strove** or **strived, striving.** to make a great effort to get or do something; try hard: In her mystery stories that author always *strives* to create realistic, interesting characters.

strol·ler [strō′lər] *noun, plural* **strollers.** a baby carriage in which a child can sit upright.

strong [strông] *adjective*, **stronger, strongest. 1.** having much power or energy to lift or move things: Lifting weights is a test of how *strong* a person is. **2.** having much more than the usual power or force: a snowstorm with *strong* winds. "All Mediterranean fish seem much *stronger* in their smells and flavors than those of colder waters." (M. F. K. Fisher) **3.** able to stand up to strain or pressure; not easily damaged: Silk is a *strong* fabric. **4.** not easily moved or changed; firm: a person with a *strong* faith in God. —**strongly,** *adverb:* "The oysters had to be torn from the rocks to which they were so *strongly* attached." (Jules Verne)

strove [strōv] *verb.* the past tense of **strive.**

struck [struk] *verb.* the past form of **strike.**

> **structure** In writing, the term *structure* refers to the way a sentence, or an entire paper, is put together—how it is built, you might say. *Sentence structure* means the arrangement of words in a sentence. If a teacher says to a student, "That's poor *sentence structure*" or "Watch your *sentence structure*," this means the wording of the sentence needs to be improved. Common examples of poor sentence structure are the lack of a subject or a verb, or improperly joining two sentences as one. If you write, "Where were you when I called I was so worried?" that is a structural problem. The structure is a skeleton: it shows the way the paper is organized. Thus if your teacher says your history report has "*structural* problems," she does not mean that it does not have enough information, or that some of the information is incorrect. She means that there are too many short sections, or that the sections do not balance each other in length, or that the sections are not in the proper order. Without a proper skeleton, the paper cannot stay upright, cannot move along, no matter how much you flesh it out.

strode [strōd] *verb.* the past tense of **stride:** "Truman *strode* in like a conquering prince returning to his lands." (Alice Walker)

stroke¹ [strōk] *noun, plural* **strokes. 1.** the act of hitting or striking something: the *stroke* of a whip or an ax. **2.** the act of hitting the ball in a game: a backhand *stroke* in tennis. It took the golfer three *strokes* to get the ball on the green. **3.** a single motion that is repeated, as in swimming or in rowing a boat. **4.** the sudden breaking or blocking of a blood vessel in the brain.

stroke² *verb*, **stroked, stroking.** to rub or pat gently: Our cat likes to be *stroked* behind the ears and under the chin.

stroll [strōl] *verb*, **strolled, strolling.** to walk around in a slow and relaxed way: "He liked, if the weather was mild enough, to *stroll* across to the playing fields . . . and watch the games." (James Hilton) —*noun, plural* **strolls.** a slow, relaxed walk: "He went out for a *stroll* on the beach." (Charles Dickens)

struc·ture [struk′chər] *noun, plural* **structures. 1.** something that is built; a house or other building. **2.** the way in which the parts of something are organized into a whole: Biologists study the *structure* of living things. —*verb*, **structured, structuring.** to organize in a certain way: That company is *structured* so that there are three separate divisions with a vice-president in charge of each.

strug·gle [strug′əl] *verb*, **struggled, struggling. 1.** to make a great effort; try hard to get or do something: "Matthew had never worked so hard in his life, as he *struggled* to force the heavy machine forward." (James Houston) "*Struggling* for an education, the African child often must walk 15 or 20 miles . . . in his bare feet." (Paul Theroux) **2.** to fight or do battle. —*noun, plural* **struggles.** the fact of struggling.

strum [strum] *verb*, **strummed, strumming.** to stroke the strings of a musical instrument in an easy or relaxed way: to *strum* a guitar.

S

strung [strung] *verb*. the past form of **string**.

stub [stub] *noun, plural* **stubs**. the short part that remains when something is torn off or worn down: The man at the theater door tore our tickets in half and gave us the *stubs*. —*verb*, **stubbed, stubbing**. to bump one's toe or foot against something.

stub•ble [stub′ əl] *noun*. **1.** the short stalks of grain left standing in the ground after a crop is harvested. **2.** a short, rough growth of hair, especially on a man's face.

stub•born [stub′ ərn] *adjective, more/most*. **1.** not giving in easily; not willing to change or to go along with others: The coach us how to hold the bat, but Paul was very *stubborn* and kept doing it the way he always had. **2.** hard to change or deal with: I have a *stubborn* skin rash that just won't go away. —**stubbornly,** *adverb.* —**stubbornness,** *noun.*

stuck [stuk] *verb*. the past form of **stick**.

stud [stud] *noun, plural* **studs**. **1.** a small, round nail or other such object sticking out from a surface: Snow tires often have metal *studs* to grip the road better. **2.** one of the vertical posts in a wall to which boards and other materials are nailed or fastened. —*verb,* **studded, studding.** to cover with or as if with studs: The headland was *studded* with small limestone rocks." (P. D. James)

stu•dent [stoo′ dənt] *noun, plural* **students**. **1.** a person who goes to school. **2.** anyone who studies something: A novelist has to be a *student* of human nature.

stu•di•o [stoo′ dē ō] *noun, plural* **studios**. **1.** a place where an artist works. **2.** a place where movies are filmed or where radio and television programs are made.

stud•y [stud′ ē] *verb,* **studied, studying. 1.** to try to learn, know, or understand something by reading and thinking about it: to *study* for a math test. "Yurie has *studied* English for several years but had not had much practice in speaking it . . ." (Farley Mowat) **2.** to examine or look at something very closely: "He stood and *studied* the creek bed and its banks . . ." (Jack London) —*noun, plural* **studies. 1.** the act of studying: It requires years of *study* to become a doctor. **2.** a subject that is studied: He's been watching too much TV lately and neglecting his *studies.* **3.** a room used for studying. ◆ A **study hall** is a place in school where students can study. —**studious,** *adjective.* serious about one's studies; likely to spend time studying.

stuff [stuf] *noun*. **1.** things in a group; a mass or collection of things: Please pick up all the *stuff* you left on the living room floor. **2.** useless or unwanted things: We forgot to clean the pool and there was yellowish *stuff* all over the walls. **3.** *Informal.* something known about or mentioned, but not definitely named: Dad bought some new *stuff* to kill the weeds in the garden. —*verb,* **stuffed, stuffing. 1.** to pack full of; fill up: I can't eat another bite; I'm *stuffed.* **2.** to fill the skin of a dead animal to make it look natural: Hunters sometimes *stuff* animals they have killed. **3.** to put stuffing in food.

stuffing [stuf′ ing] *noun, plural* **stuffings. 1.** material that is used to fill or pack something: Be careful not to pull the *stuffing* out of that old chair. **2.** a seasoned mixture of food put inside some other kind of food: She cooked the turkey with a *stuffing* of bread crumbs and onions.

stuff•y [stuf′ ē] *adjective,* **stuffier, stuffiest. 1.** without enough fresh air: "I had spent most of the previous two years cooped up in a *stuffy* little workroom in New Jersey . . ." (Joe McGinniss) **2.** too serious and formal; dull; boring: The novel *Main Street* pictures the people of a small Midwestern town as narrow-minded and *stuffy.*

stum•ble [stum′ bəl] *verb,* **stumbled, stumbling. 1.** to trip or lose one's balance; fall or almost fall. **2.** to move in a clumsy and uncertain way: "They *stumbled* through the dark, using no light other than that of the stars." (Edward Abbey) **3.** to speak or act in a clumsy, hesitating way: He hadn't read over the list of students beforehand and he *stumbled* over some of the names. **4.** to discover accidentally or come upon by accident: "I came up . . . to try and get a moment's peace, and then *stumble* upon you fellows!" (Kenneth Grahame)

stump [stump] *noun, plural* **stumps. 1.** the lower part of a tree trunk left in the ground after the tree has been cut down. **2.** the part of something that is left after most of it has been used or worn down. —*verb,* **stumped, stumping.** to confuse someone: Will you help me with this crossword puzzle? It's got me *stumped.*

stun [stun] *verb,* **stunned, stunning. 1.** to make unconscious for a short time; daze. **2.** to make unable to act; shock or surprise greatly: "'En-

---

Pronunciation Key: O–S

ō	over; go	ou	out; town
ô	all; law	p	put; hop
oo	look; full	r	run; car
o͞o	pool; who	s	set; miss
oi	oil; boy	sh	show

(Turn the page for more information.)

gland had failed in India!' A *stunned* silence greeted his words." (William L. Shirer) —**stunning**, *adjective*. very attractive or stylish: The bride wore a *stunning* white gown.

stung [stung] *verb*. the past form of **sting**.

stunt[1] [stunt] *noun, plural* **stunts**. a difficult and daring act of skill: The drivers in the auto show did some amazing *stunts*. ♦ A **stunt man (stunt woman)** is employed to carry out dangerous actions in the filming of a movie.

stunt[2] *verb*, **stunted, stunting**. to stop or slow the growth of something: "There are no trees on the island except the small ones *stunted* by the winds." (Scott O' Dell)

speak in a jerky, uneven way, often repeating sounds. —*noun*. the act of stuttering.

style [stīl] *noun, plural* **styles**. **1.** a way of writing that makes one writer different from another; a particular way of writing. **2.** the particular qualities of a work of art that makes it distinct: the Greek *style* of architecture, a mystery film in the *style* of Alfred Hitchcock. **3.** any particular design, fashion, or way of doing things: to dress and wear your hair in 1950's *style*. **4.** the way of dressing and acting that is currently accepted; fashion: A beautiful coat like that will never go out of *style*. —**stylish**, *adjective*. showing the latest style; fashionable.

style A writer's *style* is the special way that he or she repeatedly uses language. If two writers both wrote on the same topic and presented the same ideas, their style would still distinguish one from the other. In *Writing the Natural Way*, Gabriele Rico analyzes the style of Ernest Hemingway and William Faulkner. As she points out, "It is nearly impossible to confuse a passage of Hemingway's with one of Faulkner's." In his *Writer's Guide*, Porter G. Perrin shows a difference In the style of George Orwell and Joseph Conrad. In *On Writing Well*, William Zinsser contrasts the style of John McPhee with that of Joan Didion. In each instance, the critic compares one writer who has a fairly plain, straight style—Hemingway, Orwell, McPhee—with one whose style is more complicated and "emotional"—Faulkner, Conrad, Didion. Use a style that's natural to you, that suits your personality. Whenever you are in doubt about style, *keep your writing simple* and do not strain to create effects.

stu•pid [stoo′ pid] *adjective, more/most*. not having intelligence or common sense; not smart. —**stupidly**, *adverb*. —**stupidity**, *noun*.

stur•dy [stur′ dē] *adjective*, **sturdier, sturdiest**. able to bear up to strain and hard use; strong: "It's the kind of *sturdy* brick house common to Chicago . . ." (Mike Royko) —**sturdily**, *adverb*. —**sturdiness**, *noun*.

stur•geon [stur′ jən] *noun, plural* **sturgeon** or **sturgeons**. a large food fish found in northern waters, having a long narrow body with bony scales. Its eggs are the source of CAVIAR.

stut•ter [stut′ ər] *verb*, **stuttered, stuttering**. to

sub- a *prefix* meaning "below" or "less than." *Subzero* temperatures are below zero. A *sub*topic is less important than the main topic.

sub•due [sub doo′] *verb*, **subdued, subduing**. **1.** to bring under control; conquer or defeat: The prisoner refused to get in the police car, and it took several officers to *subdue* him. **2.** to make less in force or strength; soften: ". . . the long dark hall of the apartment, the sound of *subdued* voices from the living room at the far end." (Helen MacInnes)

sub•ject [sub′ jikt] *noun, plural* **subjects**. **1.** something that is thought about, talked about,

subject The basic form of all English sentences is noun-verb, otherwise called subject-predicate. Think of it this way: Who or what is the subject of an action? The "who" (or "what") can be a noun or a pronoun. What action or condition affects this subject? That action can be a simple verb, or a more complicated verb form. "*He* forgot to put on the parking brake. *The car* rolled down the driveway." In these sentences, the subject comes first, and such an order is common in English. But if the sentence is a question rather than a statement, the order is reversed and the verb comes before the subject. "When does *the movie* start?" "Is *it* a comedy?" Sometimes, a writer will go against the usual order to create an effect: "Happy is *the house* that shelters a friend." (Ralph Waldo Emerson) A subject can include not only a noun or pronoun but also adjectives or adjective phrases: "*Our next-door neighbor Mr. Burns* loves to grow roses in his garden." In such sentences, the entire phrase is the *complete subject*.

or written about: The *subject* of Bruce Catton's book *Glory Road* is the Civil War. Dad didn't like us teasing Cathy about her new haircut, and he told us to change the *subject*. **2.** the word or words in a sentence that tell what the sentence is about. A complete sentence must have a subject, and a verb to show what the subject is or does. **3.** a course of study in school: Kelly's favorite *subject* is science. **4.** a person or thing who is under the control of a king or other such ruler: "Such duty as the *subject* owes the prince . . ." (William Shakespeare) **5.** a person or thing that is used in an experiment: The Russian scientist Pavlov often used dogs as the *subject* of his research. —*adjective.* **1.** under the control or influence of another: a *subject* land ruled by a foreign king. **2. subject to. a.** likely to have or be affected by: She's *subject to* colds and has to be careful not to get chilled. **b.** depending on: The plan is ready to go into effect, *subject to* final approval by the company president.
—[səb jekt**/**] *verb,* **subjected, subjecting. 1.** to rule or control: "They allowed a handful of foreigners to *subject* them." (James Joyce) **2.** to cause a person to experience something, especially something negative or unpleasant: Dictator Joseph Stalin arrested people who opposed him and *subjected* them to "Show Trials."

sub•mit [sub mit**/**] *verb,* **submitted, submitting. 1.** to give in to some power or authority; yield: A fierce fight had been expected, but instead the city *submitted* quietly to the attacking army. ♦ The fact of submitting is **submission,** and a person who submits easily is **submissive. 2.** to present or bring forward; offer: High school students have to *submit* applications to be accepted into college.

sub•or•di•nate [sə bôr**/** də nit] *adjective.* lower in rank or less important. ♦ In a sentence, a **subordinate clause** is not as important as the main clause, as in "When the phone rang (subordinate), we were eating dinner (main)." —*noun, plural* **subordinates.** a person who is lower in rank or importance: The chairman of the board will tour the new office today, along with several of his *subordinates.* —[sə bôr**/** də- nāt**/**] *verb,* **subordinated, subordinating.** to treat as less important. —**subordination,** *noun.*

sub•scribe [səb skrīb**/**] *verb,* **subscribed, subscribing. 1.** to pay for a magazine, newspaper, or other item that comes in the mail or to one's house at certain regular times: We used to *subscribe* to the *Daily News,* but now Mom buys it at her office. **2.** to agree with: People say that dogs can't see colors, but I don't *subscribe* to that theory. —**subscriber,** *noun.*

S

subjunctive *"If I were you,* I'd start my report tonight, not wait until the weekend." Somehow you can sense that "If I *was* you" would sound wrong in this case, even though "I *was*" is normally the correct form. "If I *were* you" is an example of what is called the *subjunctive mood* [səb jungk'tiv]. Here's another: "Bursting with ambition, he read law books as if he *were* renting them by the hour." (W. A. Swanberg) In language, verbs can be classified according to their *mood.* Mood is important in some languages, such as Latin, but not in English, because the form of an English verb does not change with mood. The only time there is a change is for the verb *was.* The subjunctive expresses a wish or states some condition that is contrary to the facts: "The floor glistened *as if it were* glass . . ." (Margaret Mitchell) "As they passed the Ferris Wheel, Fern gazed up at it and wished *she were* in the topmost car . . ." (E. B. White)

sub•mar•ine [sub**/** mə rēn**/**] *noun, plural* **submarines. 1.** a warship made to go under water in order to attack enemy ships. **2.** any ship that can travel under water. —*adjective.* under water: "*Submarine* volcanoes occasionally give rise to new land." (Thomas Huxley)

sub•merge [səb murj**/**] *verb,* **submerged, submerging. 1.** to put or go below water or down into another liquid: With this air tank a diver can remain *submerged* for about 30 minutes. **2.** to keep below the surface; cover or hide: ". . . The desire to write had not died, but was only *submerged.*" (V. S. Naipaul)

sub•scrip•tion [səb skrip**/** shən] *noun, plural* **subscriptions.** an agreement to pay for and receive a certain number of newspapers, magazines, theater tickets, and so on: Our family has a year's *subscription* to *Time* magazine.

Pronunciation Key: T–Z			
t	ten; date	v	very; live
th	think	w	win; away
<u>th</u>	these	y	you
u	cut; butter	z	zoo; cause
ur	turn; bird	zh	measure

(Turn the page for more information.)

sub•se•quent [sub′sə kwənt] *adjective.* happening as a result; coming after: There was a major accident on the road, and many people were delayed in the *subsequent* traffic jam. **—subsequently,** *adverb.*

sub•side [səb sīd′] *verb,* **subsided, subsiding. 1.** to go down or fall back to a lower level: "After the second day the sea *subsided* slowly to a glassy calm." (H. G. Wells) **2.** to become less; ease up; decrease: "The anger *subsided* and she felt a return of happiness." (John Mortimer)

sub•stance [sub′stəns] *noun, plural* **substances. 1.** the material that something is made of: Ice and snow are different forms of the same *substance,* water. **2.** the main idea or part; essence: I didn't hear the entire speech, but the *substance* of it was that he's decided to drop out of the race for President.

sub•stan•tial [səb stan′shəl] *adjective, more/most.* **1.** of a large or important amount: It's a *substantial* piece of land—big enough to build 20 or 30 houses on. **2.** strong and solid: The room was filled with *substantial* oak furniture in the early American style. **3.** having to do with the physical world; real. **—substantially,** *adverb:* If we fly first class, the cost will be *substantially* higher than a regular ticket.

sub•sti•tute [sub′stə toot′] *noun, plural* **substitutes.** a person or thing that takes the place of another: At the end of the first half the coach took out three of his starting players and put in *substitutes.* **—verb,** **substituted, substituting. 1.** to put or use in place of another: He made the recipe as it was in the book, except that he *substituted* milk for cream. **2.** to take the place of someone else: Mrs. Adams had to *substitute* for our regular teacher, who was out sick. **—substitution,** *noun.* The fact of substituting for another person or thing.

before he left, but then he became aware of some *subtle* changes. **—subtly** [sut′lē], *adverb:* That mystery writer develops her stories very *subtly* and it's hard to guess who the killer is.

sub•tract [səb trakt′] *verb,* **subtracted, subtracting.** to take one number away from another: If you *subtract* 4 from 9, you have 5.

sub•trac•tion [səb trak′shən] *noun, plural* **subtractions.** the subtracting of one number from another to figure the difference.

sub•tra•hend [sub′trə hend′] *noun, plural* **subtrahends.** a number that is subtracted from another: In the statement 10 − 3 = 7, 3 is the *subtrahend.*

sub•urb [sub′ərb] *noun, plural* **suburbs.** a town or area that is outside of but near a larger city. **—suburban,** *adjective:* The Long Island Railroad carries commuters from *suburban* areas to New York City.

subway The Boston Subway was the first American subway system, started in 1897.

sub•way [sub′wā′] *noun, plural* **subways.** an underground railroad that is powered by electricity. Subways serve the people of major cities, such as New York, Boston, and Chicago.

substitution Some teachers recommend *substitution* as a way to improve your writing. To do this, the writer goes through the paper in the revising stage. He or she underlines any words that have been repeated too often, when other words could have made the style more interesting. Usually it's verbs that need variety. For example, instead of repeating "He *walked,*" you can substitute more precise terms, depending on the context. "He *paced* back and forth on the station platform." "He *sauntered* (or *strolled*) along the street looking in store windows." "He *marched* (or *strode*) or *thundered* angrily up to her desk." If you use this technique, don't overdo it. If you're writing a story about a kangaroo that escaped from a zoo, just call it "the kangaroo" all the way through. You need not substitute "the escaped animal," or "the marsupial" or "the Australian beast," and so on.

sub•tle [sut′əl] *adjective,* **subtler, subtlest.** hard to see, notice, or understand; not obvious: At first his old home town seemed the same as

suc•ceed [sək sēd′] *verb,* **succeeded, succeeding. 1.** to do something very well, or to have something turn out well: Scientists have *suc-*

ceeded in controlling smallpox, once a deadly disease. The high jumper missed his first two tries but *succeeded* on the third. **2.** to come or be next: Prince Charles of England will *succeed* his mother, Queen Elizabeth II, on the throne of England.

suc•cess [sək ses′] *noun, plural* **successes. 1.** the fact of succeeding; a good result: There are many popular books offering ways to gain *success* in business. **2.** something that succeeds: The operation was a *success* and the patient is doing fine.

suc•cess•ful [sək ses′ fəl] *adjective, more/ most.* having or gaining a good result; resulting in success: John Wooden was a very *successful* college basketball coach who won the national championship ten times. —**successfully,** *adverb.*

suc•ces•sion [sək sesh′ ən] *noun, plural* **successions. 1.** a series of people or things coming one after another: Colorful fireworks exploded in the sky in quick *succession.* **2.** the following of one person by another to fill an office or position: If the U. S. President dies, the Vice President is next in the line of *succession.* —**successive** [sək ses′ iv] *adjective.* following one after the other; in succession: We've had a very dry summer for three *successive* years now. —**successively,** *adverb.*

such [such] *adjective.* **1.** of this kind; of the same kind: There are a lot of stories about unicorns, but there's actually no *such* animal. **2.** of the kind just mentioned, or about to be mentioned: Many Americans enjoy water sports, *such* as swimming, boating, and fishing. **3.** so much so: It was *such* a cold day that I stayed inside all day. —*pronoun.* someone or something of that kind: The shed was filled with garden tools—rakes, shovels, hoes, and *such.*

suck [suk] *verb,* **sucked, sucking. 1.** to draw up into the mouth: The baby *sucked* milk from his bottle. **2.** to hold or keep in the mouth and lick: to *suck* on a lollipop. **3.** to draw in: The vacuum cleaner *sucked* up the dirt.

suc•tion [suk′ shən] *noun.* the force of drawing or pulling a solid, liquid, or gas that is caused by lowering the air pressure on its surface. Vacuum cleaners use suction to lift dirt, pumps use it to draw water, and airplane wings use it to create lift in the air.

Sud•an [soo dan′] the largest country in Africa, in the northeastern part. *Capital:* Khartoum. *Area:* 967,500 square miles. *Population:* 20,250,000. —**Sudanese,** *adjective; noun.*

sud•den [sud′ ən] *adjective, more/most.* **1.** happening quickly and without warning; not ex-

pected: "I was awakened . . . by a *sudden,* blinding flash of light in my eyes." (Robert Louis Stevenson) **2. all of a sudden.** in a sudden way; suddenly: "Daddy's lamp blew a fuse, and *all of a sudden* we were sitting in darkness." (Anne Frank) —**suddenly,** *adverb:* "Suddenly something crashed against the fence in front of the boy's face." (William Armstrong) —**suddenness,** *noun:* "He turns and grabs her with great *suddenness* . . ." (Tom Stoppard)

suds [sudz] *noun.* the foam and bubbles found on top of and in soapy water.

sue [soo] *verb,* **sued, suing.** to begin a court case against someone; take a complaint before a judge or jury: The man is *suing* the city because he claims the police beat him up for no reason.

suede [swād] *noun.* very soft, somewhat fuzzy leather. Suede is used to make clothes, purses, shoes, and other items.

su•et [soo′ it] *noun.* the hard fat from the bodies of cattle and sheep. Suet is used in cooking.

Su•ez Canal [soo′ ez] a ship canal joining the Mediterranean Sea and the Red Sea.

suf•fer [suf′ ər] *verb,* **suffered, suffering. 1.** to feel pain or sadness: The doctor gave the injured man a pain-killing medicine so he wouldn't *suffer* so much. **2.** to experience something bad or unpleasant: "In ordinary shoes . . . I would have already *suffered* frostbite." (Joe McGinniss) "The Nautilus will be afloat and leave the Torres Strait without having *suffered* the slightest damage." (Jules Verne) **3.** to become worse; be hurt: Tim is spending too much time playing computer games and his schoolwork has *suffered.*

suf•fer•ing [suf′ ring] *noun, plural* **sufferings.** a feeling of pain or sadness: The movie *All Quiet On the Western Front* captures the horror and *suffering* of war.

suf•fi•cient [sə fish′ ənt] *adjective.* just as much as is needed or wanted; enough: He doesn't earn a big income, but it's *sufficient* for his needs. —**sufficiently,** *adverb:* ". . . as soon as the weather clears *sufficiently* for us to get a plane up." (Ken Follett)

Pronunciation Key: [ə] Symbol

The [ə] or *schwa* sound occurs in syllables without an accent. It can be spelled with any vowel, such as **a** in above, **e** in listen, **i** in pencil, **o** in melon, **u** in circus. It can also be a combination of vowels, such as **io** in action, **ai** in mountain, **iou** in precious.

(Turn the page for more information.)

S

suf•fix [suf′iks] *noun, plural* **suffixes.** a word ending that changes or adds to the meaning of the root word. *Painter, painted,* and *painting* are formed by adding suffixes to *paint.*

suf•fo•cate [suf′ə kāt′] *verb,* **suffocated, suffocating. 1.** to die or cause to die from lack of air. **2.** to keep from breathing well. **3.** to have or give a closed-in feeling: She says she's got to move away because she's *suffocating* in this small town. **—suffocation,** *noun.*

suf•frage [suf′rij] *noun.* the right to vote: The historic issue of women's *suffrage* was a dispute over whether women would be allowed to vote.

sug•ar [shoog′ər] *noun, plural* **sugars.** a white or brown sweet substance that usually comes in crystal or powder form, used to sweeten foods. Sugar is made from SUGARCANE or **sugar beets.** *—verb,* **sugared, sugaring.** to coat or mix food with sugar in order to sweeten it.

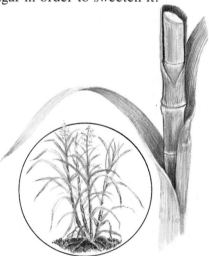

sugarcane A sugarcane plant. The cut piece shows the inner part of the stem from which the sugar juices are taken.

sug•ar•cane [shoog′ər kān′] *noun.* a tall grass with thick stalks that are cut down and pressed to squeeze out juices, which are dried into sugar. Sugarcane is grown best in hot tropical climates, in countries such as Cuba and India.

sug•gest [səg jest′] *verb,* **suggested, suggesting. 1.** to put forward an idea; say or write something: The boss wasn't sure what to call the new product and asked the sales people to *suggest* some names. **2.** to bring to mind; cause to think of: "The platform slept. The tracks were vacant, the signals up. There was little to *suggest* any train ever arrived at this station." (Malcolm Lowry)

sug•ges•tion [səg jes′chən] *noun, plural* **suggestions. 1.** the act of suggesting, or something that is suggested: Mom said, "I'm going to the store—any *suggestions* on what to have for dinner?" **2.** something that is indirectly brought to mind; a hint or trace: The word "slender" means "thin," but it also carries the *suggestion* of being trim and attractive.

su•i•cide [soo′ə sīd′] *noun, plural* **suicides. 1.** the act of killing oneself on purpose. **2.** someone who does this. **3. commit suicide.** to kill oneself.

suit [soot] *noun, plural* **suits. 1.** a set of clothes made to be worn together. Suits usually have trousers or a skirt and a matching jacket. **2.** *also,* **lawsuit.** a legal question that is brought before a judge or jury: The woman's *suit* charged that the newspaper had printed a false and damaging story about her. **3.** any of the four sets of playing cards in a deck. *—verb,* **suited, suiting. 1.** to be right for or meet the needs of: The students took a test to find out what kind of job they were best *suited* for. **2.** to be becoming to; flatter: "She had on a stiff turquoise-blue dress that *suited* her marvelously." (Esther Forbes) **3.** to please or satisfy: "You can draw and paint away . . . or do anything that *suits* you." (Lloyd Alexander)

suit•a•ble [soo′tə bəl] *adjective, more/most.* right or correct for the purpose; proper: The word "ain't" is not *suitable* for use in a school report. **—suitably,** *adverb.*

suit•case [soot′kās′] *noun, plural* **suitcases.** a flat, boxlike container for carrying clothes and other items while traveling.

suite [swēt] *noun, plural* **suites. 1.** a group of connected rooms in a hotel or motel: The company rented a large *suite* to hold a party for its customers. **2.** [*also,* sōot] a matching set of furniture. Each piece of a bedroom *suite* is made of the same wood or designed to go with the other pieces.

suit•or [sōo′tər] *noun, plural* **suitors.** a man who wants to date or marry a woman.

sul•fur [sul′fər] (also spelled **sulphur**) *noun.* a chemical element that appears in nature as a yellowish substance. Sulfur is found in underground deposits, and it occurs with coal, natural gas, and petroleum. It is used to make gunpowder, matches, insecticides, and other products. —**sulfuric** [sul fyoor′ik], *adjective.*

sulk [sulk] *verb,* **sulkier, sulkiest.** to be quiet while in a bad mood; refuse to talk: Eddie was *sulking* because his parents wouldn't let him go outside and play. —**sulky,** *adjective.* —**sulkily,** *adverb:* "When we were first alone, he appeared *sulkily* silent." (C. P. Snow)

sulk•y [sul′kē] *noun, plural* **sulkies.** a small, light carriage for one person. A sulky has two wheels and is drawn by one horse. Sulkies are used in horse races.

sul•len [sul′ən] *adjective,* **more/most. 1.** quiet and unhappy because of anger, dislike, and so on. **2.** dark and unpleasant; gloomy: It was a raw December day with a gray, *sullen* sky. —**sullenly,** *adverb:* "The boy glares *sullenly* at the babysitter, silently daring her to carry out the order." (Robert Coover)

sul•tan [sul′tən] *noun, plural* **sultans.** a title formerly used by rulers in Muslim countries.

sul•try [sul′trē] *adjective,* **sultrier, sultriest.** very hot, humid, and uncomfortable: "The air was thick and *sultry* with autumn heat." (Langston Hughes)

sum [sum] *noun, plural* **sums. 1.** a number that comes from adding two or more numbers together. The *sum* of 4+2+1 is 7. **2.** an amount of money: He paid them the *sum* of one hundred dollars. **3.** the full amount; the total: The report contains the *sum* of the doctors' findings about the new medicine. —*verb,* **summed, summing.**
sum up. to go over the main points; summarize: At the end of her talk, the speaker *summed up* what she had said.

su•mac [sōo′mak′] *noun, plural* **sumac** or **sumacs.** a small tree or shrub that has clusters of small flowers that turn into berries. Some kinds of sumac (**poison sumac**) have leaves that can cause a rash when touched.

sum•ma•rize [sum′ə rīz] *verb,* **summarized, summarizing.** to tell the main points briefly; make a summary: She began her report by *summarizing* the plot of the book.

> **summarizing** A summary comes at the end of a paper, when you draw together the main points. But you can summarize in many places, including within a paragraph. There's an old formula for public speaking: "Tell the listeners what you're going to say, then say it, then tell them what you said." This pattern also works for organizing paragraphs in descriptive writing: (1) Open with a general statement. (2) Follow this with a few good detail sentences. (3) Close with a summarizing sentence that looks at the situation from a different angle. Joan Didion's essay "Holy Water" deals with the Southern California water supply. One paragraph begins, "I have always wanted a swimming pool, and never had one." This is followed by three long sentences giving details. Then the summarizing point: "A pool is water, made available and useful, and is, as such, infinitely soothing to the western eye."

sum•ma•ry [sum′ər ē] *noun, plural* **summaries.** a short statement or brief account of the main points: Newspapers often print a *summary* of the day's news in a box on the front page. —*adjective.* **1.** having a brief account of the main points. **2.** done quickly and without delay. —**summarily** [sə mâr′ə lē], *adverb.* quickly: The mayor promised that the problem will be dealt with *summarily.*

sum•mer [sum′ər] *noun, plural* **summers.** the season of the year between spring and fall. —*verb,* **summered, summering.** to spend the summer in a certain place: They live in New York City but *summer* in Vermont. —*adjective.* suitable for the summer season: a lightweight *summer* suit.

sum•mit [sum′it] *noun, plural* **summits. 1.** the highest point of a mountain or hill. **2.** the

---

Pronunciation Key: Accent Marks

[′] is the normal accent mark. It shows where the main stress falls on a word.
[′] is a secondary accent mark. It shows a lighter stress than the primary accent. For example:
tel • e • vis • ion [tel′ə vizh′ən]
(Turn the page for more information.)

highest point or level; the top: That actor has reached the *summit* of his profession. **3.** meetings or talks that are held by the highest government officials: The U. S. President held a *summit* meeting with the Soviet leader.

sum•mon [sum′ ən] *verb*, **summoned, summoning. 1.** to call or send for someone, especially in an official or urgent way: ". . . one of the teachers called me out. I was being *summoned* to the office of the principal." (Jerzy Kosinski) "The desk-clerk hit his bell to *summon* the bag boy."(Hunter Thompson) **2.** *usually,* **summon up.** to gather together or call up; arouse: "She must have stood and watched before she could *summon up* all her courage to approach." (Isak Dinesen)

sum•mons [sum′ ənz] *noun, plural* **summonses.** an official order or notice to appear somewhere or do something, especially a written order to appear in court.

Sum•ter, Fort [sum′ tər] a fort in the harbor of Charleston, South Carolina. The Civil War began when Confederate forces fired on Union troops holding this fort.

sun [sun] *noun, plural* **suns. 1.** the star around which the earth and the other nine planets revolve. **2.** a similar star in another solar system. **3.** the light and heat that comes from the sun; sunshine. —*verb*, **sunned, sunning.** to put in the sunlight; be out in the sun: He spent the day relaxing, *sunning* himself by the pool.

Sun•belt or **Sun Belt** [sun′ belt′] *noun.* the southern and southwestern area of the U. S., where the weather is warmer than in other areas. ♦ The northeastern and midwestern U. S. are sometimes called the **Snow Belt** or **Frost Belt** in contrast with this.

sun•bathe [sun′ bāth′] *verb,* **sunbathed, sunbathing.** to lie in the sun; spend time in the sun.

sun•burn [sun′ burn′] *noun, plural* **sunburns.** a redness or burn on the skin caused by staying in the sun too long. A bad sunburn can cause serious damage to the skin. —*verb,* **sunburned** or **sunburnt, sunburning.** to be affected by sunburn.

sun•dae [sun′ dā] *noun, plural* **sundaes.** a serving of ice cream with syrup, fruits, whipped cream, or nuts on it.

Sun•day [sun′ dā] *noun, plural* **Sundays.** the first day of the week.

Sunday school a school held at a church on Sunday to teach children about religion.

sun•dial [sun′ dī′ əl] *noun, plural* **sundials.** a device that shows time by the movement of the

sun. It has a dial or plate marked with the hours and a pointer that casts a shadow from the sun onto the dial. Sundials were often used in ancient times before the development of modern clocks.

sundial A 17th-century English sundial.

sun•flow•er [sun′ flou′ ər] *noun, plural* **sunflowers.** a large flower that grows on a very tall stalk. The sunflower has bright yellow petals around a brownish center, and is thought to look like the sun. The seeds in the center of the flower are baked and eaten as food.

sung [sung] *verb.* the past participle of **sing.**

sun•glass•es [sun′ glas′ iz] *plural noun.* eyeglasses with lenses that are specially colored or shaded to protect the eyes from the sun's glare.

sunk [sunk] *verb.* a past form of **sink.**

sunk•en [sung′ kən] *adjective.* **1.** having gone to the bottom of water: *sunken* treasure from an old pirate ship. **2.** lower than other areas: A *sunken* living room is lower than other rooms on the same floor.

sun•light [sun′ līt′] *noun.* the light of the sun. —**sunlit,** *adjective.*

sun•ny [sun′ ē] *adjective,* **sunnier, sunniest. 1.** full of sunlight or warmth from the sun. **2.** bright and happy; cheerful: Marty has a *sunny* disposition and is always in a good mood.

sun•rise [sun′ rīz] *noun, plural* **sunrises.** the time of day when the sun appears to rise in the sky; early morning when the sun is first seen. ♦ Also called **sunup.**

sun•set [sun′ set′] *noun, plural* **sunsets.** the time of day when the sun appears to go down; evening when the sun goes out of sight. ♦ Also called **sundown.**

sun•shine [sun′ shīn′] *noun.* the light from the sun.

sun·spot [sun′spät′] *noun, plural* **sunspots.** a darker area on the surface of the sun, where the temperature is relatively cooler than in the surrounding areas. Scientists believe that sunspot activity may affect weather on earth.

sun·stroke [sun′strōk′] *noun, plural* **sunstrokes.** a condition caused by being exposed to too much heat from the sun for too long a time. A person affected by sunstroke has a high body temperature and feels dizzy and very weak. In some cases the victim may become unconscious or even die. ♦ Also called **heatstroke.**

su·per [soo′pər] *adjective. Informal.* very good; outstanding; excellent.

super The word *super* can be used as a prefix to mean "very great" or "very large." We say that "the U.S. and the Soviet Union are *superpowers*" or "Magic Johnson and Larry Bird are *superstars* of basketball." This is all right—even though "star" should be brilliant enough without being super. But using *super* alone is not good usage, as in "Michael Jordan is *super*." For "super" why not write "excellent" or "superb" or "outstanding" or "great"?

su·per·fi·cial [soo′pər fish′əl] *adjective, more/most.* on the surface; not deep or serious: A scratch on the skin is a *superficial* wound. The report gave only a *superficial* view of the problem and didn't deal with the real issues. —**superficially,** *adverb.*

su·perb [sə purb′ *or* soo purb′] *adjective.* excellent or outstanding; very fine: "She was *superb* with machinery. She could fix anything from a clock to a compass." (Gore Vidal) "We are having a *superb* spring after our long, lingering winter . . ." (Anne Frank) —**superbly,** *adverb.*

su·per·in·ten·dent [soop′rən ten′dənt *or* soo′pər in ten′dənt] *noun, plural* **superintendents. 1.** a person who is in charge or who manages something: The public schools in our town are under the direction of the *Superintendent* of Schools. **2.** someone who is responsible for the repair or cleaning of an apartment or office building.

su·pe·ri·or [sə pir′ē ər] *adjective, more/most.* **1.** better, higher, or greater than others of its kind; exceptional: He wore an expensive business suit made with a *superior* grade of wool. The travel guidebook gave this hotel its top rating of "Superior." **2.** having higher rank or office: The sergeant was punished for disobeying a *superior* officer. **3.** thinking oneself better than others; too proud: "He said it with an air of *superior* knowledge that irritated both of us." (Ernest Hemingway) —*noun, plural* **superiors.** a person who is higher in rank or office. The leader of an order of nuns often has the title Mother *Superior.*

Superior, Lake the largest and westernmost of the Great Lakes, on the U.S.-Canada border.

su·pe·ri·or·i·ty [sə pir′ē ôr′ə tē] *noun.* the fact of being superior: The first few chess matches were even, but then the champion began to show his *superiority* over the challenger.

superlatives An adjective in English can have three levels. If you say that a hill is a *high* point of land, that is the *positive* form of the adjective. Obviously, a hill is high compared to land in general, but no direct comparison is being made. If you say that one hill is *higher* than another, that is the *comparative* form. A direct comparison has been made to another hill. If you say that Lookout Hill is the *highest* point in the entire city, you are using the *superlative* form. You are comparing it to all other hills in the city. (For longer words, "more" and "most" are used instead of -er/-est: *more expensive, most expensive.*) Often, you do need the superlative to give force to your writing: "California is a state of extremes. It has the *most* people of any state. The *lowest* point in the continental U.S., Death Valley, and the *highest* point, Mt. Whitney, are both in California, only about 100 miles apart." The time to be careful is when the statement is an opinion: "That's the *funniest* show on TV."

su·per·la·tive [sə pur′lə tiv *or* soo pur′lə tiv] *noun, plural* **superlatives.** in grammar, the form of an adverb or adjective that describes the highest, the best, or the most of something. —*adjective.* **1.** above all others; supreme. **2.** describing the highest, the best, or the most.

Pronunciation Key: A–F			
a	and; hat	ch	chew; such
ā	ate; stay	d	dog; lid
â	care; air	e	end; yet
ä	father; hot	ē	she; each
b	boy; cab	f	fun; off

(Turn the page for more information.)

S

su•per•mar•ket [soo′ pər mär′ kit] *noun, plural* **supermarkets.** a large food store where customers serve themselves and then pay as they leave. Modern supermarkets also sell many non-food items for the house, such as cleaning products, health care items, and kitchen equipment.

su•per•nat•u•ral [soo′ pər nach′ ər əl] *adjective.* outside of the natural world; not part of normal human powers or understanding: God is a *supernatural* being. In old religious stories, saints perform *supernatural* feats such as being in two places at once. —*noun.* **the supernatural.** the world of supernatural beings, especially that of ghosts, spirits, and magic.

su•per•sti•tion [soo′ pər stish′ ən] *noun, plural* **superstitions.** a belief that the course of events can be affected by ordinary actions that are not important in themselves. Well-known superstitions say that bad luck can be brought on by walking under a ladder, breaking a mirror, or having a black cat cross your path, or that bad luck can be kept away by carrying a rabbit's foot.

su•per•sti•tious [soo′ pər sti′ shəs] *adjective, more/most.* caused by superstitions; likely to believe in superstitions: Some pro baseball players are *superstitious* and believe that it's bad luck to do such things as step on the foul lines or cross bats on the ground.

su•per•vise [soo′ pər viz′] *verb,* **supervised, supervising.** to watch over, direct, or manage: Four young men were loading the truck while an older man *supervised* their work. ♦ The fact of supervising is **supervision:** "At the age of three, I was . . . permitted to play outside our house without *supervision* by a parent." (Erskine Caldwell)

su•per•vi•sor [soo′ pər vi′ zər] *noun, plural* **supervisors.** a person who supervises; someone who is in charge: He's having a problem at work and is going to talk it over with his *supervisor.* —**supervisory,** *adjective.*

sup•per [sup′ ər] *noun, plural* **suppers.** the last meal of the day, especially a lighter meal when the main meal is eaten at midday.

sup•ple [sup′ əl] *adjective,* **suppler, supplest.** able to bend easily; flexible: Ballet dancers and gymnasts need *supple* bodies to perform their routines.

sup•ple•ment [sup′ lə mənt] *noun, plural* **supplements. 1.** something added to a thing to make it better: This pill is a vitamin *supplement* that you take once a day. **2.** a part added to a book, magazine, or newspaper to give further information or to concentrate on a special subject. —*verb,* **supplemented, supplementing.** to add to something; add as a supplement. —**supplementary** [sup′ lə men′ trē], *adjective:* She works as a teacher and earns a *supplementary* income writing textbook lessons.

sup•ply [sə plī′] *verb,* **supplied, supplying.** to give what is needed; provide: Their bakery *supplies* bread to many local stores and restaurants. Most of Southern California's water is *supplied* by rivers and lakes farther north in the state. —*noun, plural* **supplies. 1.** an amount of things ready for use: Japan must depend on foreign countries for its oil *supply.* **2. supplies.** food and other such necessary items: The campers had *supplies* for a two-week trip.

sup•port [sə pôrt′] *verb,* **supported, supporting. 1.** to hold the weight of something; keep from falling or collapsing; hold up: A table is *supported* by its legs. **2.** to take care of the needs of; provide for: The Bakers have three children and also *support* Mrs. Baker's mother, who lives with them. There isn't enough air on the moon to *support* human life. **3.** to help or back; favor: Both newspapers in town *support* Williams in the race for mayor. **4.** to help to prove true or correct: All the evidence so far *supports* the scientist's theory. —*noun, plural* **supports. 1.** the act of supporting: He walked slowly and with difficulty, using a cane for *support.* **2.** something that supports: the *supports* of a highway bridge. —**supporter,** *noun:* He's a strong *supporter* of gun control.

sup•pose [sə pōz′] *verb,* **supposed, supposing. 1.** to imagine or think to be possible; believe: I *suppose* that some day there will be a cure for the common cold. "People will learn that I was something quite different from what they *supposed.*" (Frank Herbert) **2.** to assume: Let's *suppose* that you drove off with the door open —this warning light will go on. **3.** to expect or require something: "Miss Ripper said everybody was *supposed* to do schoolwork and not sit around talking." (Paul Zindel) "There were *supposed* to be four hours and twenty-seven minutes of daylight in Fairbanks on this date . . ." (Joe McGinniss) —**supposedly** [sə pōz′ id lē], *adverb.* as is believed; as it appears: She is *supposedly* an expert swimmer, but I've never seen her anywhere near the water.

su•preme [sə prēm′] *adjective, more/most.* **1.** highest or greatest in authority: During World War Two General Eisenhower was appointed *Supreme* Commander of the Allied forces. One article of the U. S. Constitution says that it is "the *supreme* law of the land." **2.** greatest in importance; highest or most extreme: A soldier

S

who is killed in war is said to have made the *supreme* sacrifice for his country. —**supremely,** *adverb*. ♦ The fact of being supreme is **supremacy** [sə prem′ ə sē]: The government of South Africa has a policy of white *supremacy,* with lower status for black people.

Supreme Court the highest court in the United States, which acts as the final authority for any disputed court case. It consists of eight Associate Justices and one Chief Justice.

sup•press [sə pres′] *verb,* **suppressed, suppressing.** to hold back or keep down: In the early 1980's the Polish government acted harshly to *suppress* protests by Polish workers. "Bush's voice hinted at *suppressed* excitement." (C. S. Forester) —**suppression,** *noun.*

Supreme Court The entrance to the Supreme Court Building in Washington, D.C.

sure "If we switch to year-round schools, I'll have to go along with it. But I *sure* don't like the idea." Normally, *sure* is an adjective, as in "a *sure* bet" or "Are you *sure* you locked the back door?" But in everyday conversation people also use it as an adverb, as in the example above. However, in formal writing such as a school report, you should avoid this usage and use *surely:* "The school board *surely* could think of some other plan to deal with the problem of crowded schools" (not "*sure* could think of . . ."). The difference is in the situation where you're using the word.

sure [shoor] *adjective,* **surer, surest. 1.** having no doubt about something; certain: Yes, I'm *sure* Lincoln was born in Kentucky—I just read a book about him. **2.** certain to be or happen: Just watch Gail in this race—she's the *sure* winner. **3.** firm and steady: The water skier kept a *sure* grip on the tow line. —*adverb. Informal.* certainly: I don't know what's wrong—she *sure* is quiet today.

sure•ly [shoor′ lē] *adverb.* without doubt; certainly: "Mr. Godot told me to tell you he won't come this evening but *surely* tomorrow." (Samuel Beckett)

surf [surf] *noun.* the rise and swelling of ocean waves that break on the shore. —*verb,* **surfed,**

surfing Riding in the curl of the surf at San Diego, California.

surfing. to ride a wave to shore; take part in the sport of SURFING.

sur•face [sur′ fis] *noun, plural* **surfaces. 1.** the outside of a solid object or the upper level of a liquid: Sandpaper has a rough *surface.* A submarine travels below the *surface* of the water. **2.** the outer appearance of something: He seems cold on the *surface,* but underneath he's actually very nice. —*adjective.* having to do with a surface: Regular mail service is called *surface* mail to distinguish it from air mail. —*verb,* **surfaced, surfacing.** to come to or emerge on the surface: Some dolphins *surfaced* near our boat. Several serious problems have *surfaced* with the new computer.

surf•board [surf′ bôrd′] *noun, plural* **surfboards.** a long, flat board, usually made of a strong, light plastic covered with fiberglass. It is used to ride a wave into shore.

surf•ing [sur′ fing] *noun.* the sport of riding waves to shore on surfboards. ♦ A person who does this is a **surfer.**

Pronunciation Key: G–N			
g	give; big	k	kind; cat; back
h	hold	l	let; ball
i	it; this	m	make; time
ī	ice; my	n	not; own
j	jet; gem; edge	ng	having

(Turn the page for more information.)

surge [surj] *verb*, **surged, surging.** to move forward or swell up, like a powerful wave: "Under the full moon the tide was *surging* wildly against the breakwater." (Russell Hoban) "A Putney Bridge train came thundering in and the crowd began to *surge* forward." (Iris Murdoch) —*noun, plural* **surges.** the act of surging; a rushing movement: "He felt a *surge* of confidence and excitement." (P. D. James)

sur•geon [sur′jən] *noun, plural* **surgeons.** a medical doctor who has the special skill and training to perform operations.

sur•ger•y [sur′jər ē] *noun, plural* **surgeries. 1.** the branch of medicine that deals with treating disease and injury by cutting into the body to remove, repair, or replace affected parts. **2.** a place where a medical operation is performed. —**surgical,** *adjective.* having to do with surgery: *surgical* instruments, *surgical* procedures.

sur•ly [sur′lē] *adjective,* **surlier, surliest.** rude and unfriendly: His only reply to the question was a *surly* "Who cares?"

sur•name [sur′nām′] *noun, plural* **surnames.** a last name or family name.

sur•pass [sər pas′] *verb,* **surpassed, surpassing.** to do more than; be better or greater: Her acting in this movie *surpasses* all her earlier performances.

sur•plus [sur′plus′] *noun, plural* **surpluses.** an amount greater than what is needed: The printing company ordered too much paper and had a large *surplus* at the end of the year. —*adjective.* greater than is needed; left over.

sur•prise [sə prīz′ *or* sər prīz′] *noun, plural* **surprises. 1.** the fact of coming suddenly without warning: The rebels planned to steal up to the fort at night and take it by *surprise.* **2.** a feeling of wonder or amazement caused by something unexpected: I didn't know she went to our school—imagine my *surprise* when I met her in the hall. **3.** something that gives this feeling; something unexpected: Don't tell Billy about his birthday gift—it's supposed to be a *surprise.* —*verb,* **surprised, surprising. 1.** to cause to feel surprise: "Those Americans who had never seen Stalin before were *surprised* that he was so short." (John Toland) **2.** to come upon suddenly without warning. —**surprisingly,** *adverb:* It was a nice little hotel, and *surprisingly* cheap.

sur•ren•der [sə ren′dər] *verb,* **surrendered, surrendering. 1.** to give up in a fight or battle; accept defeat: The Revolutionary War ended when the British *surrendered* to General Washington. **2.** to give in; yield: After saying all along he'd oppose the bill, the senator finally *surrendered* to political pressure and voted for it. **3.** to give up a claim or right to: On his last day of work, he had to *surrender* his company I. D. card as he left the building. —*noun, plural* **surrenders.** the act of surrendering: Raising a white flag in battle is a sign of *surrender.*

sur•round [sə round′] *verb,* **surrounded, surrounding.** to make a circle around; close in on all sides: In the Battle of the Bulge, American troops in the town of Bastogne were *surrounded* by the Germans. "An old man was standing in the center *surrounded* by seagulls, pigeons, and robins." (William Saroyan)

sur•round•ings [sə roun′dingz] *plural noun.* the things or conditions that are around a person: Many animals have a brownish or grayish color that blends in with their *surroundings.*

sur•vey [sər vā′] *verb,* **surveyed, surveying. 1.** to study or examine in detail; look over: "Afterward she stood and *surveyed* herself in the full-length glass." (P. D. James) **2.** to measure the size, shape, or boundaries of a piece of land: The state government *surveyed* the highway to map out the new freeway. —[sur′vā′] *noun, plural* **surveys. 1.** a careful, detailed examination: "It was on the 15th of July that I began to take a more particular *survey* of the island itself." (Daniel Defoe) **2.** a gathering of detailed information about some topic or issue, as by asking questions: Advertising companies often take *surveys* to find out why people buy or don't buy certain products. **3.** a view or description of a broad subject: At that college, all freshman take a *survey* course in English Liter-

surprising the reader A good writer sometimes surprises a reader by approaching an obvious topic in an unexpected way. In 1965, Jimmy Breslin was one of many journalists who went to England to cover the funeral of Sir Winston Churchill. Instead of quoting heads of state and other famous people, he talked to the grave diggers at the cemetery, as well as people on the street watching the funeral procession. If you are writing about plastics, say, why not surprise the reader by discussing a world in which nothing is transparent, no glass to see through, no way to look inside a closed box or through a door. You then can discuss plastics that let light through and let images be seen.

ature. **4.** the act of surveying land, or the report of a survey.

sur•vey•or [sər vā′ ər] *noun, plural* **surveyors.** a person whose work is surveying land.

sur•viv•al [sər vī′ vəl] *noun.* the fact of surviving. ◆ The process in nature by which stronger animals live and weaker ones die out is called **survival of the fittest.**

sur•vive [sər vīv′] *verb,* **survived, surviving. 1.** to live or continue to live: All of the aircraft's passengers *survived* the crash. "The musk ox is one of the few large animals to have *survived* the ice ages in North America." (Barry Lopez) **2.** to continue to exist; remain: Few of the huge movie houses of the 1930's *survive* today. "Not a single letter to or from her has *survived.*" (Julian Barnes) —**survivor,** *noun.* a person or thing that survives.

sus•cep•ti•ble [sə sep′ tə bəl] *adjective, more/ most.* easily influenced or affected: The rich man was very *susceptible* to a hard-luck story and was always giving away money to people.

sus•pend [sə spend′] *verb,* **suspended, suspending. 1.** to hang down from above; be attached from above: "Vast chandeliers were *suspended* from the ceiling." (Ian Fleming) "Pete's dancing feet moved . . . as if his body were *suspended* like a puppet's from invisible wires." (John Gardner) **2.** to hang as if floating: "A butterfly *suspended* on an invisible breeze hovered over the sun-whitened clearing." (Jerzy Kosinski) **3.** to stop for a certain period of time: The rule against parking on this street will be *suspended* for the holiday tomorrow. **4.** to take away a privilege or rank: He was *suspended* from school for a week for bad behavior.

sus•pend•ers [sə spen′ dərz] *plural noun.* a pair of straps worn over the shoulders to hold up a pair of pants or a skirt.

sus•pense [sə spens′] *noun.* the condition of not knowing what will happen next; being uncertain: Dad wouldn't tell us what the surprise was and kept everybody in *suspense* until he got home.

suspense We all of us like suspense stories, stories of adventure, Westerns, thrillers about criminals and police, "private eye" stories, and "spy" stories. The great movie director Alfred Hitchcock said that the key to creating suspense was "the McGuffin." This was a complication or turn of events that was the key to the mystery. A famous example is Edgar Allan Poe's "The Purloined Letter." A letter is put in the most obvious place—and because the police are so intensely looking for it as a clue to a crime they don't bother to look in the obvious place. As much as any sensible person hates the existence of crime and the terrible cost of wars, the fact is that both crime and warfare are great settings for stories that are full of action and are excitingly suspenseful. Why is that so? Possibly a double answer is required. First, crime and wartime *always* involve action, physical danger, and movement of persons. Second, the good guys versus the bad guys is a story we can read over and over with satisfaction.

sus•pect [sə spekt′] *verb,* **suspected, suspecting. 1.** to think that someone is guilty without having proof: The store owner *suspected* the new clerk of stealing money from the cash drawer. **2.** to believe that something is true or possible; suppose: "Miss O'Hara kept her door slightly open and I *suspected* that she heard everything that went on in the building." (James Alan McPherson) **3.** to be aware of; realize or sense: He heard a strange noise outside and he *suspected* danger. "Neither his trainer nor his jockey . . . *suspected* the truth." (Marguerite Henry) —[sus′ pekt′] *noun, plural* **suspects.** someone who is suspected. —*adjective.* that can be doubted or mistrusted; uncertain: This treatment is supposed to restore a bald man's hair, but such claims are highly *suspect.*

sus•pen•sion [sə spen′ shən] *noun, plural* **suspensions.** the fact of suspending: The Giants announced the *suspension* of their star pitcher after he refused to report to training camp.

suspension bridge a bridge suspended from cables that are stretched between two towers.

sus•pi•cion [sə spish′ ən] *noun, plural* **suspicions. 1.** a feeling that something is wrong or bad; the doubting or distrusting of someone:

Pronunciation Key: O–S			
o	over; go	ou	out; town
ô	all; law	p	put; hop
oo	look; full	r	run; car
o͞o	pool; who	s	set; miss
oi	oil; boy	sh	show

(Turn the page for more information.)

"When he did not return after two hours, their *suspicions* were aroused." (S. J. Perelman) **2.** the condition of being suspected of a crime or wrongdoing: ". . . to avoid *suspicion*, I must immediately return in as private a manner as I came." (Jonathan Swift)

sus•pi•cious [sə spish′ əs] *adjective, more/most.* **1.** causing or arousing suspicion: Just before the store was robbed, I saw a *suspicious*-looking character hanging around outside. **2.** showing or expressing suspicion: "If anything at all were changed in the room, his father would be *suspicious*." (Jean Fritz) **—suspiciously,** *adverb:* "There was no obvious sign that the letter had been opened . . . But the glue was *suspiciously* weak." (P. D. James)

sus•tain [sə stān′] *verb,* **sustained, sustaining. 1.** to keep going in a certain way for an extended time; continue: "His wings had great power. The beat slowed as he settled into *sustained* flight." (E. B. White) **2.** to provide what is needed to keep on: "When Miss Truman brought two mince pies I accepted them both as though I needed them to *sustain* me for a long voyage." (Graham Greene) **3.** to suffer or undergo: "He had not played because of a knee injury *sustained* during the season." (George Plimpton) **—sustenance** [sus′ tə nəns], *noun.* something that provides life or strength.

swal•low[1] [swäl′ ō] *noun, plural* **swallows.** a small bird that has a forked tail and long wings. Swallows catch insects in the air and fly very gracefully.

swallow

swallow[2] *verb,* **swallowed, swallowing. 1.** to cause food to pass from the mouth down into the stomach. **2.** to take in or cover, as if by swallowing: I watched the log as it floated downstream and was *swallowed* up by the roaring waterfall. **3.** to hold back some feeling: Sandra *swallowed* her pride and asked the other girls to take her back in the club. **4.** *Informal.* to accept or believe without question: "No, every-

body *swallowed* these people's lies whole . . ." (Mark Twain) **—noun,** *plural* **swallows.** the act of swallowing.

swam [swam] *verb.* the past tense of **swim.**

swamp [swämp] *noun, plural* **swamps.** an area of wet, muddy land with a growth of trees and shrubs. **—verb,** **swamped, swamping. 1.** to fill with water or become soaked: A large wave *swamped* the rowboat. **2.** to cover or load with a large amount: I couldn't go to the game because I was *swamped* with homework.

swan [swän] *noun, plural* **swans.** a large bird that has a long, graceful neck, webbed feet, and usually, white feathers. Swans are related to ducks and geese but are larger.

swan

swap [swäp] *Informal. verb,* **swapped, swapping.** to trade or exchange one item for another: Dave and I *swapped* seats on the bus so that I could sit next to the window. **—noun,** *plural* **swaps.** a trade or exchange.

swarm [swôrm] *noun, plural* **swarms. 1.** a large colony of bees that leave a hive with a queen bee to start a new colony somewhere else. **2.** a large group or gathering: "Pigeons would come over in such *swarms* you couldn't even see the sun." (Jean Fritz) **—verb,** **swarmed, swarming. 1.** of bees, to fly off in a group to start a new colony. **2.** to move or gather in a large group: "Taxis *swarmed* the downtown section like flies." (Ernie Pyle)

swat [swät] *verb,* **swatted, swatting.** to hit or smack quickly or sharply: to *swat* a mosquito. **—noun,** *plural* **swats.** a sharp slap; a smack.

sway [swā] *verb,* **swayed, swaying. 1.** to swing slowly back and forth or from side to side: The branches of the willow tree *swayed* in the gentle wind. "She . . . stood between the seats, *sway-*

ing from side to side, waiting for the train to stop." (Penelope Lively) **2.** to change the thinking or opinion of; influence: The smooth style of the defense lawyer *swayed* the jury in favor of his client. —*noun, plural* **sways. 1.** the act of swaying. **2.** control or influence: a country that is under the *sway* of a dictator.

swear [swâr] *verb,* **swore, sworn, swearing. 1.** to make a formal or serious promise to do something: A witness in court has to *swear* to tell the truth. **2.** to say in a very definite way: "He always *swore* that he would not read John's articles . . ." (Angus Wilson) "I could have *sworn* that I heard shouts." (Samuel Beckett) **3.** to use bad language; curse.

sweat [swet] *noun.* **1.** salty liquid given off through the skin; perspiration. **2.** moisture that collects in drops on a surface. —*verb,* **sweated, sweating. 1.** to give off sweat; perspire. **2.** to gather drops of moisture: A glass of ice water *sweats* on a warm day. **3. sweat out.** *Informal.* to wait anxiously for something: He's finished the test and now he has to *sweat* it *out* waiting for the results. —**sweaty,** *adjective.*

sweat•er [swet′ ər] *noun, plural* **sweaters.** a piece of clothing that is knitted from wool or other fibers and worn on the upper part of the body. A sweater is often added to other clothes for warmth.

sweep [swēp] *verb,* **swept, sweeping. 1.** to clean with a broom, brush, or the like: to *sweep* the kitchen floor. **2.** to carry with force over a broad area: "Their eyes glanced level, and were fastened upon the waves that *swept* toward them." (Stephen Crane) **3.** to pass over or through in a quick, steady motion: "Once a white owl *swept* silently overhead . . ." (Richard Adams) "Headlights *swept* across him from the *passing* traffic." (Edward Abbey) —*noun, plural* **sweeps. 1.** a sweeping motion: The cat knocked over the glass with a *sweep* of its tail. **2.** an open area: "The aircraft goes in a wide *sweep* over the plain . . ." (Doris Lessing)

sweeping [swē′ ping] *adjective,* **more/most.** passing over a broad area: The company appointed a new president who made *sweeping* changes in the way its factories were run.

sweep•stakes [swēp′ stāks′] *noun.* a contest or race in which people pay money for tickets, and the winner receives that money or a prize.

sweet [swēt] *adjective,* **sweeter, sweetest. 1.** having a pleasing taste, like that of sugar or honey: the *sweet* taste of a ripe peach. **2.** pleasing to smell, hear, and so on: *sweet* music, a *sweet,* gentle spring breeze. **3.** pleasant or

kind; nice: I don't want to go, but it was *sweet* of you to ask me. **4.** not salty or sour: *Sweet* butter does not have salt added. —*noun, plural* **sweets.** something that is sweet, such as candy. —**sweetly,** *adverb.* —**sweetness,** *noun.*

sweet•en [swēt ən] *verb,* **sweetened, sweetening.** to make sweet or sweeter: to *sweeten* coffee by adding sugar. —**sweetener,** *noun.*

sweet•heart [swēt′ härt′] *noun, plural* **sweethearts.** a person who is loved by another.

sweet pea a climbing vine that has sweet-smelling flowers. Sweet peas may be red, white, pink, or purple in color.

sweet potato the sweet, thick root of a tropical plant that is cooked and eaten as a vegetable.

swell [swel] *verb,* **swelled, swelled** or **swollen, swelling. 1.** to grow or increase in size: My broken toe *swelled* up so much that I couldn't get my shoe on. "The little boy went on blowing and the balloon *swelled* steadily." (Katherine Anne Porter) **2.** to rise above the ordinary level; fill up: "Her heart *swelled* with love for this unhappy creature." (Paul Gallico) "The whole town, *swollen* by numbers of nearby farmers . . ." (William L. Shirer) —*noun, plural* **swells. 1.** a rolling wave on an ocean or lake. **2.** the act of swelling: ". . . Mark felt a *swell* of pride." (John Toland) —*adjective. Informal.* excellent or good; fine.

swell•ing [swel′ ing] *noun, plural* **swellings.** an enlarged or swollen part: She put ice on her sprained ankle to keep down the *swelling.*

swept [swept] *verb.* the past form of **sweep.**

swerve [swurv] *verb,* **swerved, swerving.** to turn or move to the side quickly: "The car came past his house, made a loud noise and *swerved* into a telephone pole." (E. L. Doctorow)

swift[1] [swift] *adjective,* **swifter, swiftest. 1.** moving or able to move with speed; fast: "The track was broad and beaten and they ran along at a *swift* trot." (William Golding) **2.** happening quickly: The company promised that all letters of complaint would get a *swift* reply. —**swiftly,** *adverb:* "They dashed through the night . . . gliding *swiftly* over the park's snow-covered trails." (Mark Helprin) —**swiftness,** *noun.*

Pronunciation Key: T–Z

t	ten; date	v	very; live
th	think	w	win; away
th	these	y	you
u	cut; butter	z	zoo; cause
ur	turn; bird	zh	measure

(Turn the page for more information.)

swift² *noun, plural* **swifts.** a bird similar to a swallow. It has narrow wings and is known for its ability to fly very fast.

swim [swim] *verb,* **swam, swum, swimming. 1.** to move through the water by using the arms and legs, or the fins, tail, and so on. **2.** to cross by swimming: to *swim* the English Channel. **3.** to be in or covered by a liquid: a plate of pancakes *swimming* in butter and syrup. **4.** to have a dizzy feeling; be light-headed: I can't believe this is happening—my head is *swimming* from all the excitement. *—noun, plural* **swims.** the act of swimming, or the distance covered: to take a *swim.* ♦ A **swimming pool** is a special indoor or outdoor pool for swimming.

swim•mer [swim′ ər] *noun, plural* **swimmers.** a person or animal that swims.

swin•dle [swin′ dəl] *verb,* **swindled, swindling.** to take someone's money or property in a dishonest way: He *swindled* people by selling them "rare" coins that actually had no extra value. *—noun, plural* **swindles.** the act of swindling. **—swindler,** *noun.*

swine [swīn] *noun, plural* **swine.** a pig or hog.

swing [swing] *verb,* **swung, swinging. 1.** to move back and forth with a steady motion: The children were *swinging* on a rope hanging from the tree. **2.** to move with a curving or sweeping motion: to *swing* at a pitch in baseball. The bus suddenly *swung* into his lane and he had to put on the brakes. *—noun, plural* **swings. 1.** the act of swinging. **2.** a seat that hangs by a rope or chain, in which a person can swing back and forth. **3.** activity; movement: After being out of school for a week, it was hard for her to get back into the *swing* of the things. **4. in full swing.** at the highest point of activity.

swirl [swurl] *verb,* **swirled, swirling.** to go around and around in a circular, twisting motion: A strong wind made dust *swirl* up on the desert road. *—noun, plural* **swirls.** a twisting motion or shape: ". . . the way a snowstorm looked as it moved across the harbor, with the Statue of Liberty lost in the grey *swirl* . . ." (Pete Hamill)

swish [swish] *verb,* **swished, swishing.** to make a soft, brushing sound; rustle: "The cows *swish* their tails beneath them on a hot afternoon . . ." (Virginia Woolf) *—noun, plural* **swishes.** a soft, rustling sound.

switch [swich] *noun, plural* **switches. 1.** a change or shift from one thing to another, especially a change that is not expected: The coach has made a *switch*—Holly's going to be goalie and Emily will play fullback. **2.** a device

for breaking an electrical circuit: a light *switch.* **3.** a long, thin rod or stick, especially one used for whipping. **4.** a device for changing a train from one track to another. *—verb,* **switched, switching. 1.** to change: After using the same phone service for many years, they just *switched* to another company. **2.** to turn on or off using an electrical switch: He *switched* on the porch light. **3.** to strike with a rod or switch: "The manager was *switching* his leg with a slender twig." (George Plimpton) **4.** to change a train from one track to another.

switch•board [swich′ bôrd′] *noun, plural* **switchboards.** a control panel with plugs or switches to connect and disconnect electrical circuits. Telephone systems are commonly operated by a switchboard.

Switzerland A view of the city of Spiez on Lake Thun, near Bern, Switzerland.

Switz•er•land [swit′ zər lənd] a mountainous country in west-central Europe. *Capital:* Bern. *Area:* 15,900 square miles. *Population:* 6,350,000. **—Swiss,** *adjective; noun.*

swiv•el [swiv′ əl] *noun, plural* **swivels.** a device linking two parts so that one or both can turn freely. Office chairs are often made to turn on a swivel. *—verb,* **swiveled, swiveling.** to turn on or twist freely, as if on a swivel.

swol•len [swō′ lən] *verb.* a past participle of **swell.** *—adjective.* made larger by swelling: to have a *swollen* finger because of an infected cut.

swoop [swōōp] *verb,* **swooped, swooping.** to move or go down suddenly and quickly, with a sweeping motion: "A blue-black crow *swoops* down from the roof of the house looking for its breakfast." (Paul Scott) *—noun, plural* **swoops. 1.** the act of swooping. **2. one fell swoop.** one

syllable division There are two different versions of how words should be divided at the end of a line. Some say you should break a word only at the end of a syllable. Others say it makes no difference how you break it, because end-of-line division is artificial anyway, having to do with printing, not with the basic structure of words. For example, *Communism* has four syllables [käm yə niz′ əm], but a usual end-of-line division shows only three, *com-mun-ism*. That's because *ism* has to be kept together in print to make sense. On the other hand, *camera* has two syllables [kam′ rə], but the usual end-of-line division shows three, *cam-er-a*. The reason that the end-of-line division and syllable division aren't always the same is that printers over the years have decided what looked best to them. Is this much of an issue? No. Just divide words in a manner that makes sense.

quick motion or action: "She knew it'd be easier on her meeting a couple of people at a time rather than . . . to face the whole party with *one fell swoop.*" (Paul Zindel)

sword [sôrd] *noun, plural* **swords.** a weapon used especially in former times, having a long, sharp blade set into a handle or hilt.

of a word. The word "go" has one syllable; "going" has two syllables. **2.** a division of a word in writing to show a syllable.

sym•bol [sim′ bəl] *noun, plural* **symbols.** something chosen to stand for something else: The eagle is a *symbol* of freedom in the United States. The *symbol* "&" stands for "and."

symbols Many times, when a writer mentions or describes some object, the object is a symbol—it has a meaning beyond what it actually is. The use of symbols in writing is called *symbolism.* Symbols are found much more often in poetry than in prose, but fiction writers use them also. Take the idea of using plants as a symbol, for example. In George Orwell's novel *Keep the Aspidistra Flying,* the character Gordon thinks of the aspidistra plant as a symbol of the settled middle-class life he's trying to avoid. When he finally gets married and settles down, he too puts an aspidistra in his window. In O. Henry's story "The Last Leaf," a girl is seriously ill and feels she will die once the last leaf falls off a vine outside her window. One leaf hangs on, she recovers, and she then discovers that an artist friend of hers had painted a leaf on the wall. This idea of a plant losing its leaves as winter comes is often used by writers as a symbol for death, just as the growth of new leaves in spring is a symbol of birth, or rebirth.

sword•fish [sôrd′ fish′] *noun, plural* **swordfish** or **swordfishes.** a large salt-water fish with a long upper jawbone shaped in a point like a sword. It is a popular food and game fish.

swore [swôr] *verb.* a past tense of **swear.**

sworn [swôrn] *verb.* the past participle of **swear.**

swum [swum] *verb.* the past participle of **swim.**

swung [swung] *verb.* the past form of **swing.**

syc•a•more [sik′ ə môr′] *noun, plural* **sycamores.** a North American tree with broad leaves and smooth bark that peels off in thin layers.

Syd•ney [sid′ nē] a port city in southeastern Australia, the country's largest city. *Population:* 2,880,000.

syl•la•ble [sil′ ə bəl] *noun, plural* **syllables. 1.** a single sound in speech that forms a word or part

sym•bol•ic [sim bäl′ ik] *adjective.* being or using a symbol: A twisted cross called a *swastika* was *symbolic* of Germany's Nazi Party. —**symbolically,** *adverb.*

sym•bol•ize [sim′ bəl īz′] *verb,* **symbolized, symbolizing.** to be a symbol; stand for something: In Robert Frost's poem "The Road Not Taken," a fork in the road *symbolizes* a choice in life.

sym•me•try [sim′ ə trē] *noun, plural* **symmetries. 1.** an exact match of the shape or form on

Pronunciation Key: [ə] Symbol

The [ə] or *schwa* sound occurs in syllables without an accent. It can be spelled with any vowel, such as **a** in above, **e** in listen, **i** in pencil, **o** in melon, **u** in circus. It can also be a combination of vowels, such as **io** in action, **ai** in mountain, **iou** in precious.

(Turn the page for more information.)

both sides of a body or object. **2.** a pleasing, balanced form resulting from such an arrangement. **—symmetrical,** *adjective.*

symmetry The butterfly shows symmetry. The detailed designs on each side are identical.

sym•pa•thet•ic [sim′ pə thet′ ik]   *adjective, more/most.* **1.** showing kindness or sympathy: "She didn't say anything *sympathetic*, didn't apologize, didn't try to make them feel better." (Cynthia Voigt) **2.** in favor of; supporting: At the business leaders' meeting, the President found a *sympathetic* audience for his new tax plan. **—sympathetically,** *adverb.*

sym•pa•thize [sim′ pə thīz′] *verb,* **sympathized, sympathizing.** to have or show sympathy: "I could understand and *sympathize* with S. J.'s dislike . . . because my own situation was not much different." (Erskine Caldwell)

sym•pa•thy [sim′ pə thē] *noun, plural* **sympathies. 1.** a feeling of sharing the troubles of others in an understanding way: When President Kennedy was killed, many Americans wrote to his wife to express their *sympathy.* **2.** support in thought or feelings; agreement: "He was trying to discover where my *sympathies* were. Would I give him an argument, or would I obey." (Paul Theroux)

sym•pho•ny [sim′ fə nē] *noun, plural* **symphonies. 1.** a long, musical piece written for an orchestra. Symphonies usually have four parts or movements. **2.** a large orchestra that plays symphonies or other such musical pieces. It usually consists of string, percussion, and wind instrument sections.

symp•tom [sim′ təm] *noun, plural* **symptoms. 1.** a change from the normal condition of the body, showing a disease or illness is present: A sore throat or a cough can be *symptoms* of a cold. **2.** a sign or indication of something bad: The streets were filled with trash and garbage, an obvious *symptom* of a dying neighborhood.

synagogue This synagogue in Prague, Czechoslovakia is one of the very few in Europe to survive World War II.

syn•a•gogue [sin′ ə gäg′] *noun, plural* **synagogues.** a place or building used for worship and instruction in the Jewish religion.

syn•o•nym [sin′ ə nim] *noun, plural* **synonyms.** a word that has the same or almost the same meaning as another word. "Courage" and "bravery" are synonyms.

syn•on•y•mous [si nän′ ə məs]   *adjective.* **1.** having the same or a similar meaning: "Swift" is *synonymous* with "fast." **2.** very closely connected: The song "Auld Lang Syne" has become *synonymous* with New Year's Eve.

syn•tax [sin′ taks] *noun.* the way in which words are put together to form sentences. "I the phone answered" is not proper *syntax,* because the verb "answered" is out of place.

syn•thet•ic [sin thet′ ik] *adjective.* made artificially with chemicals; not found in nature: Clothing is often made from *synthetic* fabrics.

Syr•i•a [sēr′ ē ə] a country in southwest Asia, on the Mediterranean. *Capital:* Damascus. *Area:* 72,000 square miles. *Population:* 9,800,000. **—Syrian,** *adjective; noun.*

syr•up [sir′ əp] *noun, plural* **syrups.** a thick, sweet liquid made by boiling sugar and water, or sometimes by boiling tree sap or fruit juice.

sys•tem [sis′ təm] *noun, plural* **systems. 1.** a group of things that are related and form a whole: the solar *system,* the human nervous *system.* **2.** a set of beliefs, laws, or principles: The U. S. has a democratic *system* of government. **3.** an orderly method of doing something: The company has a new computer *system* to keep track of its bills. **—systematic** [sis′ tə mat′ ik], *adjective.* following a strict or careful system: She arranged her notes in a *systematic* way. **—systematically,** *adverb.*

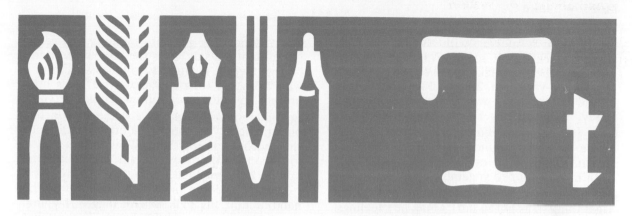

t, T [tē] *noun, plural* **t's, T's.** the 20th letter of the alphabet.

tab [tab] *noun, plural* **tabs.** a small flap or tag that is attached or stuck to some object: He pulled off the *tab* to open the can of soda.

ta·boo [ta bōō/] *noun, plural* **taboos.** a strong social or religious rule against doing certain things; a forbidden act or object: Among some American Indian tribes it was *taboo* to mention the name of a dead person.

---

table of contents When do you need a table of contents? None is needed for fiction, even if chapters are titled (which they rarely are these days). None is needed for a short report that is, in effect, a chapter in itself. Tables of contents serve well in a major piece of writing, such as a science project or a social studies report. A table of contents should be on a page by itself, coming after the title page and before the actual text. Set up the page so that the items line up with each other on the left and the page numbers on the right, not too far away.

---

ta·ble [tā/ bəl] *noun, plural* **table. 1.** a piece of furniture with a flat top, supported by one or more legs. **2.** the food served at a table. **3.** a short list of facts or information.

ta·ble·cloth [tā/ bəl klôth/] *noun, plural* **table-cloths.** a cloth that covers a table, used especially for meals.

ta·ble·spoon [tā/ bəl spōōn/] *noun, plural* **table-spoons. 1.** a large spoon that is used to serve food. **2.** a unit of measure used in cooking, equal to three teaspoons or one-half ounce.

tab·let [tab/ lit] *noun, plural* **tablets. 1.** a thin, flat slab of wood or stone that is used to write or draw on. People in ancient times used tablets before paper was invented. **2.** a number of sheets of paper held together at one edge. **3.** a small, flat piece of medicine or candy: aspirin *tablets.*

table tennis a game that is similar to tennis, played on a table with a small plastic ball and wooden paddles. ♦ Also called **ping-pong.**

tack [tak] *noun, plural* **tacks. 1.** a small, sharp-pointed nail with a wide, flat head. **2.** a change in the direction of a sailing ship. **3.** a course of action: Because its schools have gotten so crowded, the city is going to try a new *tack* and have year-round sessions. —*verb,* **tacked, tacking. 1.** to fasten with a tack or tacks: He *tacked* some photographs up on the bulletin board. **2.** of a sailing ship, to change direction: Sailboats moving into the wind *tack* back and forth to go forward. **3. tack on.** to add something extra at the end: Service charges were *tacked on* to the cost of the hotel room.

tack·le [tak/ əl] *noun, plural* **tackles. 1.** the equipment used for a certain activity or sport, especially the rod, reel, line, hooks, and so on used for fishing. **2.** a system of ropes and pulleys used for raising and lowering things, such as the sails of a ship. **3.** in football, a player whose position is between the guard and the end on offense, or in the middle of the line on defense. **4.** in football or soccer, the act of stopping a player who is moving with the ball. *—verb*, **tackled, tackling. 1.** to grab and force to the ground: The linebacker *tackled* the fullback after a two-yard gain. **2.** to deal with or take on: "Late in the year we *tackled* the informal essay." (Russell Baker) **—tackler,** *noun*.

ta•co [tä′kō] *noun, plural* **tacos.** a Mexican dish made of a flat round cake of cornmeal (a TORTILLA) rolled up or folded over and filled with meat, chopped vegetables, and so on.

tact [takt] *noun.* the ability to say and do the right thing so as not to hurt someone's feelings; dealing with people in a careful and sensitive way. ♦ A person who has this ability is **tactful:** The other girls knew Laurie wasn't invited to the party, so they were *tactful* and didn't talk about it in front of her. **—tactfully,** *adverb*.

tac•tic [tak′tik] *noun, plural* **tactics. 1. tactics.** the art or science of arranging troops and other military forces in battle and moving them during the battle. **2.** *also,* **tactics.** any plan or method of action to reach a goal: The senator didn't want the bill to pass, and used delaying *tactics* to keep it from coming to a vote. **—tactical,** *adjective*: a *tactical* error.

tadpole This tadpole of the spadefoot toad is beginning to look more like a toad than a fish. Notice the growing back legs.

tad•pole [tad′pōl′] *noun, plural* **tadpoles.** a very young frog or toad in the stage of development when it lives in the water and has gills, a tail, and no legs.

taf•fy [taf′ē] *noun, plural* **taffies.** a chewy candy made out of molasses or brown sugar that is mixed with butter and boiled until thick.

Taft [taft] **William Howard,** 1857-1930, the twenty-seventh president of the United States, from 1909 to 1913; also the Chief Justice of the Supreme Court from 1921 to 1930.

tag[1] [tag] *noun, plural* **tags.** a piece of paper, plastic, or other material that is attached to or hanging loosely from something. It is used to label, identify, or give information: A price *tag* on an item for sale gives the cost of the item. *—verb*, **tagged, tagging. 1.** to label with or as if with a tag. **2.** to follow closely: Dave's little brother *tags* along with him wherever he goes.

tag[2] *noun, plural* **tags. 1.** a game in which a player who is "it" chases the others until he or she touches one of them. The person who is touched then becomes "it" and must chase the others. **2.** in baseball, the act of putting out a runner by touching him with the ball or with the hand holding the ball. *—verb*, **tagged, tagging.** to touch or tap with the hand: The catcher *tagged* the runner out as he slid home.

tail [tāl] *noun, plural* **tails. 1.** the movable part of an animal's body that sticks out from the rear, usually having a long, thin shape. **2.** anything thought of as trailing behind or out like this: the *tail* of a shirt. **3.** the end, rear, or last part of something: the *tail* of an airplane. **4. tails.** one of the two sides of a coin, opposite the head. **5. tails.** a man's formal evening wear. *—verb*, **tailed, tailing.** to follow closely and watch: Two detectives have been *tailing* the suspect, hoping he'll lead them to the rest of the gang. *—adjective:* A wind coming from behind a plane is called a *tail* wind.

tail•or [tā′lər] *noun, plural* **tailors.** a person who makes, alters, or repairs clothing, especially men's suits and coats. *—verb*, **tailored, tailoring. 1.** to work on clothing as a tailor does: "His overcoat seemed to have been finely *tailored*, as if molded to his body." (Russell Baker) **2.** to make or adjust in a special way: The bank offers several savings plans that can be *tailored* to the needs of each customer.

Tai•wan [tī′wän′] an island country off the coast of mainland China. It was formerly known as **Formosa** [fôr mō′sə]. *Capital:* Taipei. *Area:* 13,900 square miles. *Population:* 18,600,000. **—Taiwanese,** *adjective; noun*.

take [tāk] *verb*, **took, taken, taking. 1.** to get hold of; get possession of: He *took* her arm and they walked out together. **2.** to go along with, or cause to go: *Take* this box out to the garage. Steve *took* Ellen to a movie. **3.** to deal with or experience in some way; get, use, have, and so on: to *take* a bath, to *take* a bus to school, to *take* notes in class, to *take* a person's advice. **4.** to need or require: His science project *took* a lot of work. **5.** to accept as true; assume: They look so much alike that people *take* them for sisters. *—noun, plural* **takes.** a scene of a movie, TV program, or recording that is photographed or recorded without interruption. **—taker,** *noun*.

take•off [tāk′ôf′] *noun, plural* **takeoffs. 1.** the act of an aircraft rising up in flight from the ground. ♦ Also used as a verb. Our plane *takes off* at 11:30. **2.** a copy or imitation of something, meant to amuse people: The TV show did a *takeoff* on the British royal family.

take•over [tāk′ō vər] *noun, plural* **takeovers.** in business, the act of taking control or ownership of a company by buying up a certain amount of the company's stock. ♦ Also used as a verb.

tale [tāl] *noun, plural* **tales. 1.** an imaginary story: Charles Dickens wrote a famous novel called *A Tale of Two Cities*. **2.** short for FOLK TALE. **3.** an account of real events: She told us a sad *tale* of all her illnesses and problems. **4.** a false story; a lie.

tall [tôl] *adjective,* **taller, tallest. 1.** higher than average; not short: A giraffe is a very *tall* animal. The Sears Tower in Chicago is a *tall* building. **2.** having a certain height: Suzy is five feet *tall*. ♦ A **tall tale** or **tall story** is one that is exaggerated and hard to believe.

tal•low [tal′ō] *noun.* melted fat from cattle and sheep, used in cooking and in making many products, such as candles and soap.

tal•ly [tal′ē] *noun, plural* **tallies.** a count of votes, points, and so on: The final *tally* showed the mayor winning by about 500 votes. —*verb,* **tallied, tallying.** to make or keep a tally.

tal•on [tal′ən] *noun, plural* **talons.** the claw of a bird or animal, especially an eagle, hawk, or other such bird of prey.

---

talent/skill Is talent something you can teach? No. It's thought to be inborn, something you inherit, at least to some degree. Are skills teachable? Of course they are. Whatever your talent is, it needs guiding, channeling, sharpening—somewhat in the way that piano practice is carried out daily by great pianists. In this dictionary we do not presume how much talent the reader may possess. We do care to make known writing skills—those are not inherited as much as taught and learned and practiced. Great writers, to repeat, are not writers who are great at writing skills. No, they are persons with unique and marvelous insights, thoughts, feelings, who are skilled at writing. Good writers can be self-taught, or taught in school. What they need is plain: to understand writing skills and use them. Someone asked Bobby Orr, the great hockey player of the 1960's and 1970's, "How is it you always pass to the right man as you come down the ice?" He replied, "I'm not sure. I didn't really learn." What we think is that he practiced his talent.

---

tal•ent [tal′ənt] *noun, plural* **talents. 1.** a special ability that is natural or inborn: It takes *talent* to be a great ballet dancer. "Gordon showed, almost from the start, a remarkable *talent* for copy-writing." (George Orwell) **2.** a person who has this special ability: Big-league baseball teams send scouts to high-school games looking for new *talent*. —**talented,** *adjective:* "Everybody said she was really very *talented* as a singer . . ." (James Joyce)

talk [tôk] *verb,* **talked, talking. 1.** to express words or ideas by using speech; speak: Babies usually learn to walk at around one year and *talk* at two. **2.** to speak about a certain subject; discuss: to *talk* politics. Carla wants to *talk* to the principal about changing her math class. **3.** to bring about or influence by speech: Eric *talked* his sister into lending him her camera. —*noun, plural* **talks. 1.** the act of talking: Dad had a *talk* with Bobby about not playing the radio too loud. **2.** a short or informal speech. ♦ A person who likes to talk a lot is **talkative.**

talk•er [tô′kər] *noun, plural* **talkers.** a person who talks in a certain way: a fast *talker*.

tam•bou•rine [tam′bə rēn′] *noun, plural* **tambourines.** a small drum with loose metal disks attached to the rim. The tambourine is played by shaking or striking it with the hand.

tame [tām] *adjective,* **tamer, tamest. 1.** of a wild animal, taken from nature and trained to live with man: The circus act featured a *tame* bear. **2.** not afraid of people; not wild or dangerous: "The square is full of pigeons, which are so *tame* that they perch on your hands and hat to eat corn." (Edmund Wilson) **3.** not lively or exciting; dull: He only likes the big roller coaster; the other rides are too *tame* for him. —*verb,* **tamed, taming.** to make or become tame: to *tame* a wild deer. —**tamely,** *adverb.* —**tamer,** *noun.*

Pronunciation Key: A–F			
a	and; hat	ch	chew; such
ā	ate; stay	d	dog; lid
â	care; air	e	end; yet
ä	father; hot	ē	she; each
b	boy; cab	f	fun; off

(Turn the page for more information.)

tam·per [tam′pər] *verb*, **tampered, tampering. tamper with.** to deal with in a harmful or careless way: Look at these scratches here—someone's been *tampering with* the lock.

tan [tan] *verb*, **tanned, tanning. 1.** to make animal skins into leather by soaking them in a special liquid. ◆ This is called **tanning,** and **tannin** is the liquid that is used. **2.** to have the skin become brown because of being out in the sun. —*noun, plural* **tans. 1.** a yellowish-brown color like that of leather that has been tanned. **2.** a brown color of the skin caused by the sun. —*adjective.* yellowish-brown.

tan·ge·rine [tan′jə rēn′] *noun, plural* **tangerines. 1.** a small, juicy fruit that is related to the orange. It has a skin that peels away easily. **2.** a reddish-orange color like the color of this fruit. —*adjective.* reddish-orange.

tan·gi·ble [tan′jə bəl] *adjective, more/most.* **1.** able to be sensed by touch; having a physical existence: Rocks are *tangible* objects. **2.** not imaginary; certain; real: Everyone seems to feel the man is guilty, but there's no *tangible* evidence that will prove it. —**tangibly,** *adverb.*

tan·gle [tang′gəl] *verb*, **tangled, tangling. 1.** to twist or mix together in a confused mass: "He's on the bed, asleep in a *tangled* net of blankets . . ." (Margaret Atwood) **2. tangle with.** to have a fight or dispute with. —*noun, plural* **tangles:** ". . . a *tangle* of plants as if someone had once tried to plant a small garden." (P. D. James)

tank The Sherman tank was the main U. S. battle tank in World War II.

tank [tangk] *noun, plural* **tanks. 1.** a large container for holding liquid or gas: Steam railroad engines used to draw water from *tanks* along the track. **2.** a large, heavy vehicle used in warfare, covered with thick metal plates and carrying a cannon and machine guns. A tank runs on two metal belts rather than on wheels.

tank·er [tangk′ər] *noun, plural* **tankers.** a ship, truck, or airplane that is built to carry large amounts of oil or other liquid.

tan·ner [tan′ər] *noun, plural* **tanners.** a person who tans hides to make them into leather. ◆ A **tannery** is a place where this work is done.

tan·ta·lize [tan′tə līz] *verb,* **tantalized, tantalizing.** to tease or disturb a person by keeping something that he wants just out of reach: the *tantalizing* smell of cookies baking in the oven.

tan·trum [tan′trəm] *noun, plural* **tantrums.** an outburst of temper; a fit of anger: Kelly had a *tantrum* when her mother told her to shut off the television.

Tanzania The Serengeti Plain in Tanzania.

Tan·za·ni·a [tan′zə nē′ə] a country in east-central Africa, on the Indian Ocean. *Capital:* Dar es Salaam. *Area:* 363,000 square miles. *Population:* 19,975,000.

tap¹ [tap] *verb,* **tapped, tapping.** to touch or strike lightly: "He *tapped* his fingers on the wheel, waiting for the light to change." (John Gregory Dunne) —*noun, plural* **taps.** a light or gentle blow: She heard a *tap* on the window.

tap² *noun, plural* **taps. 1.** a device for turning water or another liquid on or off; a faucet. **2.** a plug or cork that closes a hole in a barrel. —*verb,* **tapped, tapping. 1.** to make a hole in something to draw liquid out: Farmers in New England *tap* maple trees to get the sap for syrup. **2.** to cut in on a telephone line and secretly listen to another person's conversation.

tape [tāp] *noun, plural* **tapes. 1.** a long, narrow strip of paper, plastic, or other such material that is sticky on one side, used for wrapping, fastening, or sealing things. **2.** any long, narrow band like this. **3.** a long narrow piece of specially-treated plastic for recording sounds, or sounds and pictures. —*verb,* **taped, taping. 1.** to fasten with tape. **2.** to record sounds or images on tape: They *taped* the TV show on their VCR so they could watch it the next day.

tape measure a long, narrow piece of steel or cloth, marked off in units for measuring.

ta•per [tā′ pər] *verb*, **tapered, tapering. 1.** to make or become gradually smaller at one end: The Washington Monument *tapers* to a point at the top. **2.** to slowly become less and less; slowly decrease: "By midmorning the snow had *tapered* off. To the west, there was a faint hint of blue sky . . ." (Joe McGinniss)

tape recorder a machine that records sounds on specially-treated plastic tape so that they can be played back later.

---

tape recordings If you interview someone for a school writing assignment, should you tape-record the interview? The other choices are to trust your memory, or to take notes. Using a tape recorder produces an exact copy of the person's remarks. However, most interviewers still work from notes. Why? A person who is interviewed usually is more relaxed and open when not speaking into a microphone. When you use a notebook, you are in fact conducting a two-way conversation. And as you take notes, you begin to write your paper and see how the interview is taking shape on the page, allowing you to ask follow-up questions.

---

tap•es•try [tap′ is trē] *noun, plural* **tapestries.** a heavy fabric with design or pictures woven into it. Tapestries are hung on walls or laid over furniture as decoration.

tape•worm [tāp′ wurm′] *noun, plural* **tapeworms.** a long flat worm that can live in the intestines of people and animals. Tapeworms are PARASITES and can cause illness.

tap•i•o•ca [tap′ ē ō′ kə] *noun.* a starchy substance obtained from the root of a tropical plant. It is used to make pudding and sauces.

ta•pir [tā′ pər] *noun, plural* **tapirs.** a large animal with a heavy body and a long nose. It looks somewhat like a pig but is more closely related to the horse and rhinoceros. Tapirs live in tropical America and southern Asia.

taps [taps] *noun.* a bugle call played at night on an army base as a signal to put out all lights for the night. It is also played at military funerals.

tar [tär] *noun.* a thick, black sticky substance that is made from wood or coal. It is used to pave roads and waterproof roofs, and in making many industrial products. —*verb,* **tarred, tarring.** to cover or coat with tar: to *tar* a road.

ta•ran•tu•la [tə ran′ chə lə] *noun, plural* **tarantulas.** a large, hairy spider whose bite is painful but not dangerous. Tarantulas are found in tropical parts of the world.

tar•dy [tär′ dē] *adjective,* **tardier, tardiest.** coming or happening late; behind time: The stu-

dents who did not get to class on time were marked 'Tardy.' —**tardiness,** *noun.*

tar•get [tär′ git] *noun, plural* **targets. 1.** a mark or object that is aimed or fired at: His arrow hit the *target.* **2.** a person or thing that is attacked or made fun of: The senator has been the *target* of a lot of criticism for appointing his brother to a high-paying job. —*verb,* **targeted, targeting.** to set as a goal or target: Those funds are *targeted* for the African relief effort.

tar•iff [tar′ if] *noun, plural* **tariffs.** a tax or duty that a government puts on goods coming into a country: The car dealer paid a *tariff* on the cars he imported from Germany.

tar•nish [tär′ nish] *verb,* **tarnished, tarnishing. 1.** to dull the shine or color of: Salt water *tarnishes* silver. **2.** to lose its purity or quality: The senator's reputation has been *tarnished* by the scandals on his staff. —*noun.* a thin, dull coating; a loss of brightness or color.

tar•pau•lin [tär′ pə lin] *noun, plural* **tarpaulins.** a piece of waterproof canvas or other material that is used as a protective covering for playing fields, boats, and other objects exposed to the weather.

tar•pon [tär′ pən *or* tär′ pän′] *noun, plural* **tarpon** or **tarpons.** a large silvery fish that lives along the coast of the Atlantic Ocean.

tart[1] [tärt] *adjective,* **tarter, tartest. 1.** having a sharp or sour taste; not sweet. **2.** sharp or harsh in tone or meaning: She was angry and gave him a *tart* answer. —**tartness,** *noun.*

tart[2] *noun, plural* **tarts.** a pastry shell filled with fruit, jam, or custard.

tar•tan [tär′ tən] *noun, plural* **tartans. 1.** a plaid pattern or design, first made in Scotland. Each

---

Pronunciation Key: G–N

g	give; big	k	kind; cat; back
h	hold	l	let; ball
i	it; this	m	make; time
ī	ice; my	n	not; own
j	jet; gem; edge	ng	having

(Turn the page for more information.)

Scottish clan or family had its own special tartan. **2.** a piece of cloth having such a pattern.

tartan A Scottish bagpiper dressed in clan tartan.

tar·tar [tär′tər] *noun.* a yellowish substance that forms on the teeth. Tartar will form into a hard crust if it is not removed.

task [task] *noun, plural* **tasks.** a piece of work to be done; a job or duty: She had the difficult *task* of pulling out all the weeds without disturbing any of the flowers. ". . . he realized how hopeless was the *task* of finishing his copy of the contract before half past five." (James Joyce)

tas·sel [tas′əl] *noun, plural* **tassels.** a hanging bunch of threads or cords that are fastened together at one end.

taste [tāst] *noun, plural* **tastes. 1.** the sense felt in the mouth when food or drink is taken in: Sweet, sour, salty, and bitter are thought of as the four basic *tastes.* **2.** a particular sensation felt in the mouth; a flavor: The fish had an odd *taste* and he decided it wasn't fresh. **3.** a small amount of food or drink; a bit. **4.** a small amount or brief experience: Now that he's had a *taste* of life in the big city, he finds his little home town very boring. **5.** the ability to judge things and to appreciate what has beauty, style, and quality: She has great *taste* in furniture and her home is beautifully decorated.
—*verb,* **tasted, tasting.** to get the flavor of; have a certain flavor: This sauce *tastes* too salty. —**taster,** *noun.*

taste·ful [tāst′fəl] *adjective, more/most.* having or showing good taste. —**tastefully,** *adverb:* "His small house was . . . furnished *tastefully* with antiques." (A. B. Guthrie)

taste·less [tāst′lis] *adjective, more/most.* **1.** having little or no flavor: The only dessert was a watery, *tasteless* pudding. **2.** having or showing bad taste; rude; vulgar: a crude, *tasteless* remark. —**tastelessly,** *adverb.*

tast·y [tās′tē] *adjective,* **tastier, tastiest.** pleasing to the sense of taste; having a good flavor: The homemade pie was very *tasty.*

tat·tered [tat′ərd] *adjective, more/most.* torn or hanging in shreds (**tatters**); ragged: a *tattered* old shirt.

tat·tle [tat′əl] *verb,* **tattled, tattling.** of a child, to tell some minor wrong that another child has done: Jason *tattled* to his mother that his sister had taken some cookies. —**tattler** [tat′lər] or **tattletale** [tat′əl tāl′], *noun.*

tat·too [ta too′] *verb,* **tattooed, tattooing.** to mark the skin with permanent pictures or designs by pricking it with special needles that are dipped in colors. —*noun, plural* **tattoos.** such a picture or design on the skin.

taught [tôt] *verb.* the past form of **teach.**

taunt [tônt] *verb,* **taunted, taunting.** to make fun of; insult with bitter remarks: "'Cowards—babies,' he was *taunting* a group of young men . . ." (Anita Desai) —*noun, plural* **taunts.** an insulting or cruel remark.

taste How can you define good taste in writing? Partly, it depends on the times. Some words and expressions in today's novels would have horrified the critics and writers of fifty years ago. "Street talk" has come into fiction in a way that was not considered good taste in the 30's, 40's, and 50's. Even so, good taste persists, whatever the times. Clarity, politeness, and sensitivity are always in good taste.

taut [tôt] *adjective,* **tauter, tautest. 1.** stretched or drawn tight: "Nick swung the rod to make the line *taut* and tried to lead the trout toward the net . . ." (Ernest Hemingway) **2.** tense; strained: The defendant's nerves were *taut* as he waited for the jury to come in with the verdict.

tav·ern [tav′ərn] *noun, plural* **taverns. 1.** a place where alcoholic drinks are sold and drunk; a bar. **2.** in former times, a place where travelers could stay overnight; an inn.

taw•ny [tô′nē] *adjective*. brownish-yellow.

tax [taks] *noun, plural* **taxes.** money that people must pay to support the government: Workers pay a certain part of their income as *tax.* —*verb*, **taxed, taxing. 1.** to put a tax on: The U. S. government *taxes* the profits that companies earn from their business. ♦ Income that can be taxed is **taxable. 2.** to make a heavy demand on; tire out or strain: "Don't *tax* your memory trying to recall those ancient days of your youth." (Eugene O'Neill) —**taxpayer,** *noun.*

tax•a•tion [tak sā′shən] *noun.* the act or system of collecting taxes.

tax•i [tak′sē] *noun, plural* **taxis.** an automobile whose driver is paid to take passengers from place to place; also called a **taxicab.** —*verb*, **taxied, taxiing.** of an airplane, to move slowly over the ground before taking off or after landing.

Tchai•kov•sky [chī kôf′skē] **Peter Ilyich,** 1840-1893, Russian composer.

tea [tē] *noun, plural* **teas. 1.** a drink that is made by pouring boiling water over the leaves of a certain Asian plant. **2.** the dried leaves of this plant, or the plant itself. **3.** a similar drink made from another plant: herb *tea.* **4.** a light meal in the late afternoon at which tea is served.

tea•ket•tle [tē′ket′əl] *noun, plural* **teakettles.** a kettle with a handle and a spout, used to boil water, as for making tea.

teal [tēl] *noun, plural* **teal** or **teals.** a small wild duck that lives in rivers and marshes.

team [tēm] *noun, plural* **teams. 1.** in sports, a group of people who play together against other groups of the same kind: There are nine players on a baseball *team.* ♦ A person who belongs to the same team as another is a **teammate. 2.** a group of people who work or act together: A *team* of the nation's top doctors carried out the operation on the President. **3.** two or more horses or other animals joined or harnessed together to do work: Pioneers going West used *teams* of oxen to pull their covered wagons. —*verb*, **teamed, teaming. team up.** to work or join together as a team.

team•ster [tēm′stər] *noun, plural* **teamsters. 1.** a person who drives a team of animals. **2.** a person whose work is driving a truck.

team•work [tēm′wurk′] *noun.* the smooth working together of members of a team or group to reach the same goal.

tea•pot [tē′pät′] *noun, plural* **teapots.** a pot with a handle and spout, used to brew and serve tea.

teaching writing Teachers generally agree that writing *can* be taught. What they mean is that your vocabulary can be expanded, your usage improved, your grammar made accurate, your sense of order (or drama) sharpened. Teachers don't hope to discover geniuses in their classes—but indeed sometimes do, as did Ernest Hemingway's English teacher in Oak Park, Illinois. Two approaches are widely used in today's schools. The "part-to-whole" system was made popular in handbooks of grammar. Students start by studying single words, parts of speech. Then, lessons move on to groups of words, phrases and clauses. Then comes the sentence in several varieties, then paragraphs, ending with the study of the complete paper. Another method is the "writing process," which regards writing as having a series of guided, logical steps. (See WRITING PROCESS on p. 886.)

teach [tēch] *verb*, **taught, teaching. 1.** to cause a person to know something; give knowledge: to *teach* a child to read, to *teach* English to people who are new to this country. **2.** to show or explain how to perform some physical action or skill: to *teach* someone to swim. **3.** to show by example: The accident has *taught* him to be more careful with his driving. **4.** to give lessons as one's job; work as a teacher in school.

teach•er [tē′chər] *noun, plural* **teachers.** a person whose work is teaching in a school or giving lessons.

teak [tēk] *noun.* a strong, hard wood that comes from a tree of southeast Asia, used in furniture, floors, and shipbuilding.

tear¹ [târ] *verb*, **tore, torn, tearing. 1.** to pull apart in a rough, sudden way; split into pieces; rip: He *tore* up the paper and started over on a new page. Tricia *tore* her jacket climbing over the fence. **2.** to move quickly or with great force: "Then he *tore* down the road as fast as he could go." (Lois Lenski) **3.** to divide between

Pronunciation Key; O–S			
ō	over; go	ou	out; town
ô	all; law	p	put; hop
oo	look; full	r	run; car
o͞o	pool; who	s	set; miss
oi	oil; boy	sh	show

(Turn the page for more information.)

two sides; force apart: Two boys asked her to the dance, and she was *torn* over which one to go with. —*noun, plural* **tears.** a torn part.

tear² [tēr] *noun, plural* **tears. 1.** a drop of clear, salty liquid that comes from the eye; also called a **teardrop.** It is produced by glands called **tear ducts. 2. tears.** the fact of crying from pain or sadness: to burst into *tears.*

tease [tēz] *verb,* **teased, teasing. 1.** to annoy or bother someone in a playful way; make fun of: Todd *teases* his sister by calling her 'Miss Messy.' **2.** to comb the hair backwards to make it stand out and look fuller. —*noun, plural* **teases.** a person who teases someone.

tea•spoon [tē′ spo͞on′] *noun, plural* **teaspoons. 1.** a small spoon that is used for stirring liquids and eating soft food. **2.** a unit of measure used in cooking, equal to one-third of a tablespoon.

tech•ni•cal [tek′ ni kəl] *adjective, more/most.* **1.** having to do with the use of science to deal with practical problems: Students can train to become engineers in a *technical* college. **2.** having to do with one special field or profession: "Skin" is also known to doctors by the *technical* name "epidermis." **3.** in a strict and exact way: It's called the "Battle of Bunker Hill," but to be *technical,* it should be "Breed's Hill." —**technically,** *adverb.*

tech•ni•cian [tek nish′ ən] *noun, plural* **technicians. 1.** a person with special training in a technical field: a laboratory *technician.* **2.** a person skilled in the use of certain machinery.

and scientific principles to do work and solve problems. —**technological** [tek′ nə läj′ ə kəl], *adjective.* having to do with technology: The 1800's saw many great *technological* changes, such as the development of gasoline engines.

te•di•ous [tē′ dē əs] *adjective, more/most.* long and tiring; very boring: We had to stack all the newspapers and tie them up in bundles, a slow and *tedious* job. —**tediously,** *adverb.*

tee [tē] *noun, plural* **tees.** a small peg on which a golf ball may be placed for the first stroke in playing a hole. —*verb,* **teed, teeing. tee off.** to hit the ball off a tee to start a hole.

teem [tēm] *verb,* **teemed, teeming.** to be filled with; have in large numbers: "We are used to thinking of the North American plains as a place that *teemed* with life before the arrival of the Europeans . . ." (Barry Lopez)

teen•ag•er [tēn′ ā′ jər] *noun, plural* **teenagers.** a person who is between the ages of thirteen and nineteen. —**teenage** or **teenaged,** *adjective:* a family with two *teenaged* children.

teens [tēnz] *plural noun.* the years of a person's life between the ages of thirteen and nineteen.

tee•ter [tē′ tər] *verb,* **teetered, teetering.** to stand or move in an unsteady way: "A man *teetered* into the bar on a pair of platform shoes with soles about two inches thick." (V. S. Naipaul)

teeth [tēth] the plural of **tooth.** ♦ The fact or time of a baby growing teeth is called **teething** [tēth′ ing].

---

technique *Technique* is a way to produce a certain effect in writing. Let's say you want to write a story with a surprise ending, like Shirley Jackson's "Charles" or Ernest Hemingway's "A Day's Wait." You'll notice they use the technique of holding back key information until the very end of the story. For suspense, read Richard Connell's "The Most Dangerous Game," or A. Conan Doyle's "The Hound of the Baskervilles," or W.W. Jacobs' "The Monkey's Paw." Look for techniques they use, such as a strange, isolated place as the setting of the story; an unusual character (or object) at the center of the story; an unexpected event that the main character can't control or even explain. If your goal is to make the reader laugh, look at James Thurber's "The Night the Bed Fell." You will notice his characters have unusual names and act in odd ways. He uses exaggeration rather than describing things realistically. Thurber's characters seem not to notice the odd behavior of others, and they go on acting as if everything is normal.

---

tech•ni•que [tek nēk′] *noun, plural* **techniques.** a particular way of doing something or dealing with some problem; a method or plan of action: On his TV show the famous chef demonstrates basic cooking *techniques,* such as making bread dough or cutting up a chicken.

tech•nol•o•gy [tek näl′ ə jē] *noun, plural* **technologies.** the use of tools, machines, inventions,

Te•he•ran or **Teh•ran** [tā′ rän′] the capital of Iran. *Population:* 4,715,000.

tel•e•cast [tel′ ə kast′] *noun, plural* **telecasts.** a program broadcast by television.

tel•e•com•mu•ni•ca•tions [tel′ ə kə myo͞o′ nə ka′ shənz] *noun.* the process of sending messages or broadcasts by telephone, radio, television, computer, and so on.

T

tel•e•gram [tel′ ə gram] *noun, plural* **telegrams.** a message that is sent by telegraph.

tel•e•graph [tel′ ə graf′] *noun, plural* **telegraphs.** a method of sending and receiving messages over a long distance with electronic signals carried by wires or cables. —*verb*, **telegraphed, telegraphing.** to send a message by telegraph.

telephone A 1915 photo of a telephone operator using one of the earliest switchboards to direct calls.

tel•e•phone [tel′ ə fōn′] *noun, plural* **telephones.** an instrument used to send and receive sounds or speech over a distance. The sound is sent over wires or through the air by means of electricity. —*verb*, **telephoned, telephoning.** to call or talk by telephone.

tel•e•scope [tel′ ə skōp′] *noun, plural* **telescopes.** an instrument that makes distant objects seem much closer and larger. It uses a system of lenses or mirrors inside a long tube. Telescopes are used to study the stars and planets.

tel•e•vise [tel′ ə vīz′] *verb*, **televised, televising.** to send out a signal or program by television: to *televise* a pro football game.

tel•e•vi•sion [tel′ ə vizh′ ən] *noun, plural* **televisions. 1.** a system of sending pictures and sounds through the air by means of electronic signals, so that they can be seen and heard in other places. **2.** *also,* **television set.** a device used to receive such signals. **3.** programs broadcast in this way: She's not allowed to watch much *television* on school nights.

tell [tel] *verb*, **told, telling. 1.** to make known by words; say or write: *Tell* Matt there's someone on the phone for him. The story "The Open Boat" *tells* of a group of men lost at sea. **2.** to make known by some sign or indication: A

speedometer *tells* how fast a car is going. **3.** to know or sense; recognize: Can you *tell* the twins apart? "There's no way of *telling* what goes on inside that head of his." (Kingsley Amis) **4.** to order; command: Dad said, "I'm not asking you to clean your room—I'm *telling* you to do it."

tell•er [tel′ ər] *noun, plural* **tellers. 1.** a person who works in a bank and takes in, pays out, and counts money. **2.** a person who tells: She's a very amusing story*teller.*

tem•per [tem′ pər] *noun, plural* **tempers. 1.** a particular state of the mind or feelings: "Apparently he was in an evil *temper* with Montgomery." (H. G. Wells) **2.** an angry mood or state of mind: He's got quite a *temper* and gets mad whenever things don't go his way. **3.** control of the emotions: to keep or lose your *temper.* **4.** the degree of hardness of a metal. —*verb*, **tempered, tempering. 1.** to make less harsh; ease or soften: "A slight breeze *tempered* the air and made it cool and pleasant . . ." (W. H. Hudson) **2.** to make metal harder or more flexible: A knife blade of *tempered* steel.

tem•per•a•ment [tem′ prə mənt] *noun, plural* **temperaments. 1.** the normal state of the mind and feelings; a person's nature: The two sisters are close in age but have very different *temperaments*—one's calm and the other's a worrier.

telescope One of the world's largest telescopes, the Hale Telescope at Mt. Palomar, California.

Pronunciation Key: T–Z

t	ten; date	v	very; live
th	think	w	win; away
<u>th</u>	these	y	you
u	cut; butter	z	zoo; cause
ur	turn; bird	zh	measure

(Turn the page for more information.)

"He was a . . . cheerful young man by *temperament.*" (Doris Lessing) **2.** an angry or excited state of mind: "At times, as with all bands, there were outbursts of *temperament,* moments of tension." (Studs Terkel)

tem•per•a•men•tal [tem′ prə men′ təl] *adjective, more/most.* **1.** easily upset or made angry: That actor is very *temperamental* and walks off the set if someone interrupts his scene. **2.** having to do with temperament; caused by one's nature: ". . . the proper wolf dog, gray-coated and without any visible or *temperamental* difference from its brother, the wild wolf." (Jack London) **—temperamentally,** *adverb.*

tem•per•ate [tem′ pər it *or* tem′ prət] *adjective, more/most.* **1.** of weather, climate, and so on, not too hot nor too cold; not extreme: The *temperate* climate of the California coastline is much milder than the cold climate of Alaska. **2.** having or showing self-control, especially in the use of alcoholic drinks.

tem•per•a•ture [tem′ pər chur *or* tem′ prə-chər] *noun, plural* **temperatures. 1.** the level of heat or cold in a place or object, as measured by a thermometer: Water turns to ice at a *temperature* of 32 degrees Fahrenheit. **2.** the level of heat of the human body. Normal body *temperature* is 98.6 degrees Fahrenheit. **3.** a body temperature that is higher than normal; a fever: Jessica had to stay home from school because she had a slight *temperature.*

tem•pest [tem′ pist] *noun, plural* **tempests.** a very strong wind or storm.

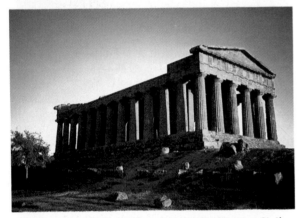

temple The Temple of Concordia in Agrigento, Sicily, built by the ancient Greeks in about 440 B.C.

tem•ple[1] [tem′ pəl] *noun, plural* **temples.** a building used for the worship of a god or gods: Buddhists and Hindus pray in temples. A Jewish synagogue is often called a temple.

tem•ple[2] *noun, plural* **temples.** the flat area on either side of the forehead, in front of the ear.

tem•po [tem′ pō] *noun, plural* **tempos. 1.** the speed at which music is played. **2.** the rate of speed of an activity: "Tsuji increased the *tempo* of the work . . ." (John Toland)

tem•po•rar•y [tem′ pə rer′ ē] *adjective, more/most.* lasting only for a short time; not permanent: She had a *temporary* job at the amusement park during her summer vacation. **—temporarily,** *adverb:* Their new house isn't finished yet, so they're *temporarily* living in a motel.

tempt [tempt] *verb,* **tempted, tempting. 1.** to lead to do something unwise or wrong: Seeing that the woman had left her purse open *tempted* him to reach in and take her wallet. "He spoke . . . very slowly, so that in conversation with him one always felt *tempted* to finish his sentences for him . . ." (Robert Graves) **2.** to appeal strongly to; attract: The cookbook featured many *tempting* color photos of Italian dishes. ". . . he had been *tempted* to take one down from the bookshelf and read out something to his wife." (James Joyce)

temp•ta•tion [temp tā′ shən] *noun, plural* **temptations.** the fact of being tempted, or something that tempts: "The *temptation* to try out some of my grandmother's beauty aids got the better of me when I was twelve." (Mary McCarthy)

ten [ten] *noun, plural* **tens;** *adjective.* one more than nine; 10. **—tenth,** *adjective; noun.*

te•na•cious [tə nā′ shəs] *adjective, more/most.* holding or grasping tight; not letting go or giving in: ". . . his memory was so *tenacious,* that he never forgot anything that he either heard or read." (James Boswell) ♦ The fact of being tenacious is **tenacity** [tə nas′ ə tē]. **—tenaciously,** *adverb.*

ten•ant [ten′ ənt] *noun, plural* **tenants.** a person who pays rent for the use of property owned by another person: The landlord painted the apartment before the new *tenant* moved in.

tend[1] [tend] *verb,* **tended, tending.** to move or develop in a certain way; be likely: Winter weather in this part of the country *tends* to be damp and cloudy. "He *tended* to pause and think before taking any important step." (John Jakes)

tend[2] *verb,* **tended, tending.** to take care of; look after: "Doctor Warren was in Roxbury *tending* a sick woman." (Esther Forbes)

ten•den•cy [ten′ dən sē] *noun, plural* **tendencies.** the way that something tends to be or go; a leaning: "Maggie's hair had a natural *tendency* to curl." (Colleen McCullough) "Orr had a *tendency* to assume that people knew what they were doing . . ." (Ursula K. LeGuin)

tense moment the bear stood his ground." (Jim Kjelgaard) —*verb*, **tensed, tensing.** to make or become tense. —**tensely,** *adverb*.

> **tense** The *tense* of a word indicates the time that the word refers to—present, past, or future. In English, only verbs show tense. We use the *present progressive tense* to tell about an action going on right now: "It's (It is) *raining* out." The *simple present* tells about a condition or habit that goes on in the present. "It *rains* a lot around here in the winter." For past time, the *simple past* tells about an action that began in the past and is now over: "It *rained* hard last night." The *past progressive* tells about a past action that was interrupted by something else: "We *were playing* ball when it suddenly started to rain." For future time, we use "going to" to tell about future plans: "I'm *going to* bring along an umbrella." We use "will" to show that something is bound to happen: "If you don't wear your raincoat *you'll* (you will) get soaked."

ten•der[1] [ten′dər] *adjective*, **tenderer, tenderest. 1.** of food, not tough; easily chewed: The meat was cooked in the oven until it was very *tender*. **2.** painful or sore; very sensitive: "Chance's leg was *tender;* a purple bruise covered almost the entire calf." (Jerzy Kosinski) **3.** not strong; delicate: *Tender* young plants that have just sprouted. **4.** showing love or kindness: She gave her son a *tender* pat on the head. —**tenderly,** *adverb*. —**tenderness,** *noun*.

tender[2] *verb*, **tendered, tendering.** to offer or present, especially in a formal way: ". . . I here *tender* him my apologies for my conduct to him." (William Makepeace Thackeray)

tender[3] *noun*, plural **tenders.** a person who tends or takes care of something: A bar*tender* serves drinks in a bar.

ten•don [ten′ dən] *noun*, *plural* **tendons.** a cord of tough tissue that connects muscles to bones.

ten•e•ment [ten′ ə mənt] *noun*, *plural* **tenements.** an old and badly-kept apartment building, usually in a poor section of a city.

Ten•nes•see [ten′ ə sē′] a state in the southeastern U.S. *Capital:* Nashville. *Nickname:* "Volunteer State." *Area:* 42,200 square miles. *Population:* 4,651,000.

ten•nis [ten′ is] *noun*. a game played by two or four persons. The players use rackets to hit a ball back and forth over a net stretched across a level playing surface called a *court*.

ten•or [ten′ ər] *noun*, *plural* **tenors. 1.** the highest adult male singing voice, or a singer who has this voice. **2.** an instrument having this range.

tense[1] [tens] *adjective*, **tenser, tensest. 1.** stretched or pulled out tightly; strained: John's face was *tense* as he waited for the teacher to give the signal to start the test. **2.** causing or showing strain, excitement, or worry: "For one

tense[2] *noun*, *plural* **tenses.** the form of a verb that shows the time of the action: The past *tense* of the verb "find" is "found."

tenement A New York City tenement known as "Bandit's Roost" is shown in this 1888 photo by the famous photographer Jacob Riis.

ten•sion [ten′ shən] *noun*, *plural* **tensions. 1.** the fact or condition of being strained or stretched out: People who go after big fish in the ocean use high-*tension* fishing line. **2.** mental strain or worry: She likes to walk home from work to relieve the *tension* that builds up during the day. **3.** an unfriendly or hostile feeling: "Now there was a *tension* between them and he hated to admit that his father was still the stronger." (Virginia Hamilton)

Pronunciation Key: [ə] Symbol

The [ə] or *schwa* sound occurs in syllables without an accent. It can be spelled with any vowel, such as **a** in above, **e** in listen, **i** in pencil, **o** in melon, **u** in circus. It can also be a combination of vowels, such as **io** in action, **ai** in mountain, **iou** in precious.

(Turn the page for more information.)

T

tent [tent] *noun, plural* **tents.** an outdoor shelter that can be put up and taken down, consisting of a fabric supported by poles and ropes. Tents are used by campers and by soldiers in the field.

ten·ta·cle [ten′ tə kəl] *noun, plural* **tentacles. 1.** a long, flexible part attached to the body of certain saltwater animals, used for holding things and for moving about. An octopus has eight tentacles, and a squid has ten. **2.** a thread-like growth extending from a plant.

ten·ta·tive [ten′ tə tiv] *adjective.* done or made as a suggestion or for a short trial period. —**tentatively,** *adverb:* "He never enters a room *tentatively* . . . always with a sense of purpose and direction." (Mike Royko)

ten·ure [ten′ yər] *noun.* the fact or right of holding some office or position: A teacher who has taught for a certain time can gain *tenure* and be protected from being fired.

te·pee [tē′ pē] *noun, plural* **tepees.** a cone-shaped tent made of animal skins or tree bark, used by certain North American Indians as a dwelling, especially among the Plains tribes.

term [turm] *noun, plural* **terms. 1.** a word or phrase having a certain meaning: Many *terms* used in real estate come from Old English law, such as "mortgage" and "tenant." ◆ The special terms used in a certain field are **terminology** [tur′ mə näl′ ə jē]. **2.** a certain period of time: The President of the United States is elected for a *term* of four years. **3. terms.** the conditions or requirements of an agreement: The *terms* of the contract say that you pay 20¢ for each mile you drive. **4. terms.** a relationship between people: to be on good or bad *terms* with someone. —*verb,* **termed, terming.** to call or name something: The President *termed* the summit meeting a great success.

ter·mi·nal [tur′ mə nəl] *noun, plural* **terminals. 1.** a station at either end of a route of travel for a train, bus, plane, and so on. **2.** a single keyboard and screen for a computer. **3.** any of the points in an electrical circuit where connections can be made. —*adjective.* **1.** at the end; coming last: The soldier's tour of duty is up and he was sent home on *terminal* leave. **2.** relating to an illness that will end in death.

ter·mi·nate [tur′ mə nāt′] *verb,* **terminated, terminating.** to bring to an end; stop; finish: The contract states that after one year either party may *terminate* the agreement without notice. —**termination,** *noun.*

ter·mite [tur′ mīt] *noun, plural* **termites.** a small insect that eats and destroys wood. Termites live in very large groups and can cause

severe damage to wooden buildings and furniture.

ter·race [tar′ is] *noun, plural* **terraces. 1.** a flat area made on the side of a hill or slope to provide a level surface for growing crops. **2.** a paved area next to a house; a patio. **3.** a small porch or balcony. —**terraced,** *adjective.*

tepee A tepee of the Assiniboin tribe, members of the Rocky Mountain Sioux Indian group.

ter·rain [tə rān′] *noun.* an area of land, especially in terms of its physical features: Few armies have invaded Switzerland over the centuries, because of its rugged mountain *terrain.*

ter·rar·i·um [tə rar′ ē əm] *noun, plural* **terrariums** or **terraria.** an enclosed glass container for keeping live plants and small animals.

ter·ri·ble [ter′ ə bəl] *adjective, more/most.* **1.** causing great fear or suffering; dreadful; horrible: a *terrible* car accident. The volcano erupted with a *terrible* roar. **2.** very damaging; very extreme: "Not getting into Radcliffe was *terrible* for me—it's why I never went to college at all." (Alice Adams) **3.** *Informal.* very bad or unpleasant: Dad thinks that TV show is *terrible* and doesn't want us watching it.

ter·ri·bly [ter′ ə blē] *adverb.* **1.** in a terrible way; very badly: to be *terribly* wounded in war. **2.** *Informal.* very much; very: We're out of that shirt in your size; I'm *terribly* sorry. "The range of human types and actions is not *terribly* wide." (Russell Hoban)

ter·ri·er [ter′ ē ər] *noun, plural* **terriers.** a breed of small, active dogs, once used to hunt rats and other animals that burrow in the ground.

ter·rif·ic [tə rif′ ik] *adjective, more/most.* **1.** causing great fear or suffering; terrible: President Franklin D. Roosevelt's last words before he died were, "I have a *terrific* headache." **2.** *Informal.* very good; excellent: a *terrific*-looking new car. —**terrifically,** *adverb.*

T

ter·ri·fy [ter′ ə fī] *verb*, **terrified, terrifying.** to frighten greatly; fill with terror: "We made frightful noises to *terrify* them still more . . ." (Emily Brontë) ◆ Often used as an adjective: "Rob heard the *terrified* screams of the little boys . . ." (Esther Forbes)

ter·ri·to·ri·al [ter′ ə tôr′ ē əl] having to do with a territory or territories: A nation's *territorial* waters are the ocean areas near its shores.

ter·ri·to·ry [ter′ ə tôr ē] *noun, plural* **territories. 1.** an area of land; a region: Wild animals such as the bighorn sheep defend a certain *territory* against other animals of the same kind. **2.** the land and waters that make up a state or nation: World War II began when German troops crossed the border into Polish *territory*. **3.** an area that is part of the United States but is not a state, with some amount of self-government. Alaska was a territory before it became a state.

ter·ror [ter′ ər] *noun, plural* **terrors. 1.** very great fear: "The wind from the open door blew out the light and the darkness added to her *terror*." (Zora Neale Hurston) **2.** a person or thing causing great fear.

ter·ror·ism [ter′ ə riz′ əm] *noun.* the use of terror or violence to gain some political goal. Terrorism involves tactics such as bombing, airplane hijacking, kidnapping, and murder. ◆ A person who uses such acts of terrorism is a **terrorist.**

ter·ror·ize [ter′ ə rīz] *verb,* **terrorized, terrorizing.** to make very frightened; terrify.

test [test] *noun, plural* **tests. 1.** a series of questions or problems to find out what someone knows or can do: Our class has a spelling *test* every Friday. To get a driver's license, you have to pass a driving *test*. **2.** any way to study or examine something to find out its nature or quality: Doctors give blood *tests* to patients to get information about their health. —*verb,* **tested, testing.** to give a test to: The company is *testing* a new soft drink in a few cities.

Tes·ta·ment [tes′ tə mənt] *noun, plural* **Testaments.** either of the two main parts of the Bible; the **Old Testament** or the **New Testament.**

tes·ti·fy [tes′ tə fī] *verb,* **testified, testifying. 1.** to make a formal statement giving proof or evidence about something: Witnesses in court *testify* as to what they know about the events connected with a crime. **2.** to show as proof; indicate: "He had survived torture—his scarred legs and chest *testified* to it." (John Jakes)

tes·ti·mo·ny [tes′ tə mō′ nē] *noun, plural* **testimonies. 1.** the fact of testifying; a formal statement made in a court of law. **2.** evidence or proof: The piles of notes and books were *testimony* to how hard she'd worked on her report.

test tube a small glass tube closed at one end, used in laboratory tests.

tet·a·nus [tet′ nəs] *noun.* a serious disease caused by bacteria. Tetanus causes the muscles to stiffen, especially the muscles of the jaw. It is also called **lockjaw.**

teth·er [teth′ ər] *noun, plural* **tethers.** a rope or chain used to tie an animal so that it can range only so far. —*verb,* **tethered, tethering.** to tie an animal in this way.

Texas The Rio Grande flows through Big Bend National Park on the border of Texas and Mexico.

Tex·as [tek′ səs] a state in the southwestern U.S., bordered by Mexico to the south. *Capital:* Austin. *Nickname:* "Lone Star State." *Area:* 267,300 square miles. *Population:* 15,280,000. —**Texan,** *noun.*

text [tekst] *noun, plural* **texts. 1.** a book used for studying; a textbook. **2.** the actual wording of something: I'm sure that's what the President said—the *text* of his interview was in today's paper. **3.** the words that form the main part of a book, as opposed to the introduction, pictures, index, and so on.

text·book [tekst′ book′] *noun, plural* **textbooks.** a book that provides facts, lessons, and so on for a class or course of study.

Pronunciation Key: Accent Marks

[′] is the normal accent mark. It shows where the main stress falls on a word.

[′] is a secondary accent mark. It shows a lighter stress than the primary accent. For example:

tel • e • vis • ion [tel′ə vizh′ən]

(Turn the page for more information.)

tex•tile [teks′ təl *or* teks′ tīl′] *noun, plural* **textiles.** fabric or cloth made by weaving or knitting fibers, such as cotton, wool, linen, or silk.

that Both *that* and *who* are used to introduce a clause: "Grover Cleveland is the only President *who* was voted out of office and then later elected again." "President Cleveland was not related to the man *that* founded Cleveland, Ohio." According to strict usage, though, only the first of these sentences is correct. *That* should not be used in a clause referring to a person. Only *who* is correct for such a clause: "Abraham Lincoln was the first President *who* was born outside the original thirteen colonies." The use of *that* should be restricted to clauses that deal with things, not persons: "Virginia and Ohio are the states *that* have produced the largest number of Presidents." (See also WHICH/THAT.)

tex•ture [teks′ chər] *noun, plural* **textures.** the way a surface feels to the touch; the roughness or smoothness of some object or fabric: Silk has a soft *texture.* The cake ingredients should be mixed until they have a smooth, even *texture.*

Thai•land [tī′ land] a country in southeastern Asia, between Burma and Cambodia. *Capital:* Bangkok. *Area:* 198,500 square miles. *Population:* 49,990,000. ♦ Formerly known as **Siam** [sī am′]. —**Thai** [tī], *adjective; noun.*

than [than *or* thən] *conjunction.* **1.** a word used to introduce the second part of a comparison: Gold is worth more *than* silver. **2.** a word used to show a preference: I'd rather have hamburgers *than* chicken for dinner tonight.

thank [thangk] *verb,* **thanked, thanking.** to say that one is pleased or grateful: *Thank* you for helping me with my work.

thank•ful [thangk′ fəl] *adjective,* more/most. feeling or showing thanks, grateful.

thanks [thangks] *interjection.* a word showing that one is pleased or grateful: *Thanks,* I'd love to come for dinner. —*plural noun:* Gail expressed *thanks* to all her classmates who had helped with her project.

Thanks•giv•ing [thangks′ giv′ ing] *noun, plural* **Thanksgivings.** **1.** a holiday celebrated by feasting and giving thanks to God. Thanksgiving is a national holiday in the U. S., on the fourth Thursday of November. **2. thanksgiving.** the act or fact of giving thanks: "We could make a little visit in *thanksgiving* of your coming home." (David Rabe)

that [that *or* thət] *adjective; pronoun, plural* **those.** **1.** being the one seen, named, or known: *That* was your mother on the phone. **2.** being the one at a greater distance: This sweater's too big; let me see *that* one in the back. —*adverb.* to a certain amount or degree: Don't give me so much; I'm hungry, but not *that* hungry.

—*conjunction.* used to begin another part of a sentence that gives a result or reason: Let me write it down so *that* I won't forget.

thatch [thach] *noun.* a type of roof made of straw, leaves, or grass. —*verb,* **thatched, thatching.** to cover a roof with thatch.

Thatch•er [thach′ ər] **Margaret,** born 1925, the prime minister of Great Britain since 1979.

Margaret Thatcher

that's [thats] the contraction for "that is."

thaw [thô] *verb,* **thawed, thawing. 1.** to change a solid to a liquid by raising the temperature; melt: I took the frozen orange juice out of the freezer and let it *thaw* out. **2.** to become warmer or more friendly. —*noun, plural* **thaws. 1.** the fact of thawing: After years of hatred between the two countries, there's been a *thaw* in their relations. **2.** a period when the weather is warm enough for ice and snow to thaw.

the [thē *or* thə] *definite article.* **1.** used to point out or name a certain person or thing: They served hot dogs and soda. *The* hot dogs were 50¢ each and *the* sodas were 25¢. **2.** being the only one or a special one: This is *the* dress for you—what a perfect color! —*adverb.* to that degree: *The* longer you take to do your homework, *the* less time you'll have to play.

T

theme The *theme* of a novel or short story is its central idea. John Steinbeck's *The Grapes of Wrath* tells of a family of poor Oklahoma farmers ("Okies") who are forced off their land during the dust storms and Depression of the 1930s and who travel west to California. This is the *plot* of Steinbeck's novel, but not the whole theme. Going to California reveals several themes. One is the idea that farmers had to fight nature on the dry, windy plains of America. Another theme is a direct contrast with the first: America is the land where great opportunities are still waiting for everyone, somewhere out West. A third theme is in the sense of living your dream. As in no other country, the word *dream* has an almost physical significance in America. Martin Luther King had a dream. The Joad family in *The Grapes of Wrath* had a dream. So did Jay Gatsby in *The Great Gatsby* and Willie Loman in *Death of a Salesman*.

the•a•ter [thē′ ə tər] *noun, plural* **theaters. 1.** *also,* **theatre.** a building or place where plays or motion pictures are presented. **2.** the art or work of presenting plays: She's always dreamed of having a career in the *theater*. **3.** an area where important military action takes place: Many large naval battles were fought in the Pacific *Theater* during World War II.

the•at•ri•cal [thē at′ ri kəl] *adjective, more/most.* **1.** having to do with the theater. **2.** like a play or drama; showy and dramatic: The player rolled on the ground in a very *theatrical* manner, but he really wasn't badly hurt. "The garden was full of flowers: he loved them for their *theatrical* display." (D. H. Lawrence)

thee [thē] *pronoun.* an old form of the word **you,** used as an object: "Shall I compare *thee* to a summer's day?" is the first line of a famous poem by William Shakespeare.

theft [theft] *noun, plural* **thefts.** the crime of stealing: Shoplifting is a form of *theft*.

their [thâr] *adjective.* belonging to them: *Their* house is across the street from ours.

theirs [thârz] *pronoun.* something belonging to

The *theme* of the short story "To Build a Fire" is the struggle between man and nature. **2.** a piece of writing done as an assignment for school. **3.** the main melody of a song. **4.** *also,* **theme song.** the main melody associated with a movie, a radio or television show, or a particular entertainer: The band played Bob Hope's *theme* song, "Thanks for the Memories," as he walked on stage. ◆ Something that has to do with a theme is **thematic** [thē mat′ ik].

them•selves [them selvz′ *or* thəm selvz′] *pronoun.* their own selves: The two boys painted the whole fence by *themselves*.

then [then] *adverb.* **1.** at that time: See this picture of my Cub Scout pack? I was in second grade *then*. **2.** next after that: First heat the pan, *then* put some butter in it. **3.** in that case: If you start your paper now, *then* you won't be rushed at the end. —*noun.* that time: Call back at six; she should be home by *then*.

thence [thens] *adverb.* from that place; from there on: "Heller led me down a great dark stairway to the first of the lower passages, and *thence* to a . . . large cell . . ." (John Gardner)

their *Their* is the correct spelling for the pronoun that means "belonging to them:" "Karen's team has won *their* last four games." *There* is the correct spelling for the adverb that points out a certain place: "I stopped by Steve's house, but he wasn't *there*." *There* is also used as a pronoun in statements with *is, are, was, were,* and so on: "From 1912 to 1959 *there* were 48 states in the Union." *They're* is the spelling for the contraction of "they are:" "The lion and tiger are related; *they're* both in the cat family." There are no tricks or memory games for keeping these words separated in your mind. You just have to look at the sentence and analyze it.

them: Our dog started to bark, and so did *theirs*.

them [them *or* thəm] *pronoun.* the form of **they** used as an object: Did you tell *them* you were going to stop over to their house for a visit?

theme [thēm] *noun, plural* **themes. 1.** the main subject or idea of a talk or a piece of writing:

Pronunciation Key: A–F

a	and; hat	ch	chew; such
ā	ate; stay	d	dog; lid
â	care; air	e	end; yet
ä	father; hot	ē	she; each
b	boy; cab	f	fun; off

(Turn the page for more information.)

T

the·ol·o·gy [thē äl′ ə jē] *noun, plural* **theologies.** the study of God and religion. —**theological** [thē′ ə läj′ ə kəl], *adjective.*

the·o·ret·i·cal [thē′ ə ret′ i kəl] *adjective.* having to do with or existing in theory, rather than actual practice: Absolute zero is a *theoretical* number that is thought to be the coldest temperature possible, but nothing has ever actually been this cold. —**theoretically,** *adverb.*

the·o·rize [thē′ ə rīz′] *verb,* **theorized, theorizing.** to form or express a theory.

the·o·ry [thir′ ē] *noun, plural* **theories. 1.** a set of facts or ideas generally accepted as an explanation of some event or condition in nature: The "germ *theory*" states that many diseases are caused by infection from germs. **2.** the rules and principles of an art or science, rather than the actual practice of it: ". . . how different the *theories* he had learned at St. Thomas's were from the practice of medicine in the sick rooms of Hartcombe and the Rapstone Valley." (John Mortimer) **3.** an idea or opinion that is presented without real proof: "They accepted it on the simple *theory* that whatever appeared in *The Times* must be true . . ." (Gay Talese)

ther·a·py [thar′ ə pē] *noun, plural* **therapies.** the treatment of an illness of the mind or body, especially in a way that does not involve drugs or operations. The doctor told her that swimming would be good *therapy* for her injured leg. ◆ A person who is trained to give a certain kind of therapy is a **therapist.**

way; by that means: They qualified for the safe driver program, *thereby* cutting their car insurance costs by 10%.

there·fore [thar′ fôr′] *adverb.* for that reason: The Supreme Court has nine members; *therefore* it's not possible for a vote to be a tie.

there's [thârz] the contraction for "there is."

ther·mal [thur′ məl] *adjective.* having to do with heat: *Thermal* windows hold heat inside a house.

ther·mom·e·ter [thər mäm′ ə tər] *noun, plural* **thermometers.** an instrument for measuring temperature. It usually consists of a glass tube containing mercury or another liquid, with a scale marked off in degrees on the side of the tube. The mercury rises or falls according to how hot or cold the temperature is.

ther·mos bottle [thur′ məs] an insulated container used to keep liquids either hot or cold.

ther·mo·stat [thur′ mə stat′] *noun, plural* **thermostats.** a device that automatically controls the temperature of something. The temperature inside a house can be raised by turning up the thermostat that is connected to the furnace.

the·sau·rus [thə sôr′ əs] *noun, plural* **thesauruses** or **thesauri.** a reference book that contains groups of words that share a similar meaning. Writers use it to find a synonym that will replace a word, or to choose the most suitable word from a group.

these [thēz] *adjective; pronoun.* the plural form of **this:** *These* cards are mine, not yours.

---

there is/there are These combinations are useful if you wish to state a general truth: *"There's* no place like home." "In war *there is* no substitute for victory." (Gen. Douglas MacArthur) *"There are* more things in heaven and earth, Horatio, than are dreamt of in your philosophy." (Shakespeare, *Hamlet*) Moreover, because "there" can carry a sense of one's being very definite, it also can give force to a physical description. This makes the details sound more like general truths than the personal thoughts of the writer: *"There was* not a house in sight . . . *There was* no use wishing he were back in bed, though." (Eudora Welty) *"There was* no sun nor hint of sun, though *there was* not a cloud in the sky." (Jack London) *"There was* a brick wall at the back and beyond the brick wall a church. *There was* a long smooth lawn, moon-silvered." (Raymond Chandler)

---

there [thâr] *adverb.* in, at, or to that place: Put the books on the table *there.* —*pronoun.* used to introduce a sentence in which the subject comes after the verb: *There* are 24 hours in a day. —*interjection.* used to express strong feelings: *There!* I'm finally finished!

there·af·ter [thar′ af′ tər] *adverb.* after that; from that time on.

there·by [thar′ bī′ *or* thâr′ bī′] *adverb.* in that

the·sis [thē′ sis] *noun, plural* **theses. 1.** a statement or position that is to be proved or defended. **2.** a long, formal report or essay written by a university student.

they [thā] *pronoun.* **1.** those persons or things previously named: Paul and Sandy couldn't go with us; *they* both had to study. **2.** people in general: *They* say we're in for a really hot summer this year.

they'd [thād] the contraction for "they had" or "they would."

they'll [thāl] the contraction for "they will."

they're [ther *or* thâr] the contraction for "they are."

they've [thāv] the contraction for "they have."

thick [thik] *adjective,* **thicker, thickest. 1.** with a large distance between its opposite sides or surfaces; not thin: Banks keep money in a special room with a very *thick* door. "The curtains were so *thick* they let in no light." (Margaret Drabble) **2.** having a certain size between its opposite sides: The floor boards were two inches *thick.* **3.** of a liquid, not flowing easily; not watery: a rich, *thick* pea soup. **4.** with many parts or objects close together; tightly packed: a dark, *thick* forest, *thick,* curly hair. —*adverb.* so as to be thick; thickly: Don't go light on the paint; put it on *thick.* —*noun.* the most active or dangerous part: Alexander the Great was brave in battle and was always in the *thick* of the fighting. —**thickly,** *adverb.* —**thickness,** *noun.*

thick•en [thik′ ən] *verb,* **thickened, thickening.** to make or become thicker: "By noon the cloud layer would *thicken* and the skies would become overcast again." (Cornelius Ryan)

thick•et [thik′ it] *noun, plural* **thickets.** a group of bushes or small trees growing close together.

thief [thēf] *noun, plural* **thieves.** a person who steals.

thigh [thī] *noun, plural* **thighs. 1.** the upper part of the leg, between the knee and the hip. **2.** the same part on the back leg of an animal.

and there was a *thin* layer of dust on it. **2.** not having a heavy body; not fat: All that walking she does helps to keep her *thin.* **3.** of a liquid, flowing easily, watery: If the gravy seems too *thin,* add more flour. **4.** with the parts far apart; not closely packed: The yard was bare except for a few *thin* patches of brown grass. **5.** lacking strength; weak: ". . . the *thin* warmth of the winter sun." (J. M. Coetzee) —*adverb.* so as to be thin; thinly: The clerk sliced the cheese *thin.* —*verb,* **thinned, thinning.** to make or become thin: "Gradually the crowd *thinned* out." (Ernie Pyle) —**thinly,** *adverb.* —**thinness,** *noun.*

thine [thīn] an old form of **yours:** "For *thine* is the kingdom, the power, and the glory" is part of a familiar Christian prayer.

thing [thing] *noun, plural* **things. 1.** an item that can be known to the senses but is not alive; a physical object: She treats her doll as if it were a real baby, not just a *thing.* **2.** an object that is not known or named: After you put the bread in the toaster, push down this black *thing* on the end. **3.** any idea or subject that is talked about or thought about: The best *thing* about that restaurant is its low prices. **4.** a person or animal thought of in a certain way: "She was a dear kind *thing,* always so nice to me . . ." (Henry James) **5. things. a.** personal belongings. **b.** the state of affairs; general conditions: So, how are *things* since the last time I saw you? **6.** an activity or interest that appeals to or suits a person: I don't like playing video games; it's just not my *thing.* "It was us against the world, and we had to do our own *thing.*" (Ernest Hemingway)

thing This is a useful word because it can refer to almost any object, idea, or action. "I'm not sure what controls the sprinklers; I think it's that green *thing* there." "Put your *things* in Gary's bedroom; you'll be sleeping there." "The first *thing* we have to do is clear away all the rocks and sticks." Because the word fits so many different situations, writers sometimes overuse it: "The *thing* about my uncle is that he'll do anything to avoid getting stuck in traffic." Make it: "My uncle will do anything . . ." "The first *thing* he does when he sees traffic ahead is to turn off onto a side road." Try instead: "As soon as he sees traffic up ahead, he turns off . . ." "The *thing* of it is, he actually takes longer to get there than if he'd stayed on the highway." Just take out that whole opening phrase: "He actually takes longer . . ."

thim•ble [thim′ bəl] *noun, plural* **thimbles.** a small cover made of metal or plastic that is worn when sewing, to protect the tip of the finger that pushes the needle.

thin [thin] *adjective,* **thinner, thinnest. 1.** with a small distance between its opposite sides or surfaces; not thick: He held the balloon by a *thin* string. The desk hadn't been used lately

Pronunciation Key: G–N			
g	give; big	k	kind; cat; back
h	hold	l	let; ball
i	it; this	m	make; time
ī	ice; my	n	not; own
j	jet; gem; edge	ng	having

(Turn the page for more information.)

think [thingk] *verb*, **thought, thinking. 1.** to use the mind to form an idea or opinion; have a thought: Don't start writing right away; *think* about your answer for a minute. **2.** to have a certain idea: Tim has to *think* of a title for his science report. Long ago people *thought* the earth was flat. **3.** to have an opinion; suppose: I *think* we'd better leave now. **—thinker,** *noun:* Albert Einstein was one of the great *thinkers* of the modern age.

third [thurd] *noun*, *plural* **thirds;** *adjective.* **1.** next after the second. **2.** one of three equal parts.

thirst [thurst] *noun*, *plural* **thirsts. 1.** a feeling of desire or need for something to drink. **2.** any strong desire for something: Michael has such a *thirst* for knowledge that he reads every book he can get his hands on.

thirst•y [thurs′tē] *adjective*, **thirstier, thirstiest. 1.** feeling thirst; having the desire or need to drink something. **2.** lacking water or moisture; very dry: *thirsty* desert plants.

thir•teen [thur′tēn′] *noun*, *plural* **thirteens;** *adjective.* one more than twelve; 13. **—thirteenth,** *adjective; noun.*

this [this] *adjective; pronoun*, *plural* **these. 1.** being the one seen, named, or known: *This* road goes right past the school. **2.** being the closer one of two things: *This* is a pear tree; that one back by the fence is a peach tree. **—adverb.** to the amount or extent mentioned; so: I expected it to be cold here, but not *this* cold.

thistle The very prickly leaves and stems of the thistle. It is considered to be the national flower of Scotland.

this•tle [this′əl] *noun*, *plural* **thistles.** a prickly wild plant with spiny leaves and purple, red, or yellow flowers, often growing as a weed in fields and pastures.

thong [thông] *noun*, *plural* **thongs.** a narrow strip of leather used to tie or fasten something. Sandals are held on the foot by thongs.

tho•rax [thôr′aks] *noun*, *plural* **thoraxes. 1.** the part of the body between the neck and the abdomen; the chest. **2.** the part of an insect's body between the head and abdomen.

Tho•reau [thə rō′] **Henry David,** 1817-1862, American author.

thorn [thôrn] *noun*, *plural* **thorns. 1.** a sharp point on a branch or stem of a plant. Roses have thorns. **2.** a tree or shrub that has thorns.

thorn•y [thôr′nē] *adjective*, **thornier, thorniest. 1.** full of thorns; prickly: a *thorny* bush. **2.** causing trouble; difficult: a *thorny* problem.

thor•ough [thur′ō] *adjective*, *more/most.* careful and complete; leaving nothing out: When Sue lost her watch she made a *thorough* search of her room, until she finally found it under the bed. **—thoroughly,** *adverb:* "She wiped his face *thoroughly* with the warm cloth." (Pearl Buck)

thoroughbred The thoroughbred Secretariat is often called the greatest race horse of all time.

thor•ough•bred [thur′ō bred′] *noun*, *plural* **thoroughbreds. 1.** a pet or farm animal that is of a pure breed, such as a horse or a dog. **2.** *also,* **Thoroughbred.** a special type of racing or jumping horse, originally bred in England. **—adjective.** of a pure or unmixed breed.

Thorpe [thôrp] **Jim,** 1888-1953, American athlete.

those [thōz] *adjective; pronoun.* the plural of **that:** *Those* cans go on the top shelf.

thou [thou] *pronoun.* an old form of the word **you:** "*Thou* shalt not kill" is one of the Ten Commandments in the Bible.

though [thō] *conjunction.* **1.** even if; although: Our new apartment is very nice, *though* it isn't as big as our old one. **2. as though.** as if: "He spoke very slowly and very correctly *as though* every word was costing him money." (V. S. Naipaul) —*adverb.* however; nevertheless: The movie was hard to follow; I did enjoy it *though.*

through: to *thread* a needle. **2.** to move in a winding, twisting way: "No other duck can dodge and *thread* its way through trees the way a wood duck can." (Jack Denton Scott)

though "I've never been mountain climbing, *though* I've always wanted to try it." (*although* I've always wanted to try it.) (*however,* I've always wanted to try it.) All of these three words, *though, although,* and *however,* can be used in this situation, as a way to connect two opposing or contrasting ideas. These words are much more common in writing than they are in speech. In ordinary conversation, a speaker would probably say ". . . *but* I've always wanted to try it." (Of course, *but* is a suitable choice for this sentence in writing also.) *However* carries the most serious tone of the three words. *Though* and *although* are almost identical, and can usually be used in place of one another. The only differences are that *although* is slightly more formal, and that only *though* can be used to end a sentence: "I've never been mountain climbing. I've always wanted to try it, *though.* "

thought [thôt] *verb.* the past form of **think:** "I *thought* I felt something behind us and turned to look." (John Gardner) —*noun, plural* **thoughts. 1.** the act or fact of thinking: She was lost in *thought* and didn't hear the doorbell ring. **2.** the result of thinking; ideas, feelings, or opinions: "She remembered her first *thoughts of* Africa, standing in the oval-domed lobby of the airport in New York . . ." (Paul Theroux)

thought•ful [thôt′fəl] *adjective, more/most.* showing the proper thought; having concern for other people: "It was *thoughtful* indeed of Barbara to buy them for him." (C. S. Forester) —**thoughtfully,** *adverb.* —**thoughtfulness,** *noun.*

thought•less [thôt′lis] *adjective, more/most.* showing a lack of thought; not thinking; careless or rude. —**thoughtlessly,** *adverb.* —**thoughtlessness,** *noun.*

thou•sand [thou′zənd] *noun, plural* **thousands;** *adjective.* ten times one hundred; 1,000. —**thousandth,** *adjective; noun.*

thrash [thrash] *verb,* **thrashed, thrashing. 1.** to beat hard or whip: In the book *David Copperfield,* David is *thrashed* by his cruel stepfather Mr. Murdstone. **2.** to move wildly; toss about: "He . . . got to *thrashing* around with his arms like the sails of a windmill." (Mark Twain)

thread [thred] *noun, plural* **threads. 1.** a very thin string or cord used in sewing and weaving cloth. **2.** anything thin and long like a thread: A gray *thread* of smoke rose from the small campfire. **3.** a narrow, winding ridge around a screw, nut, or bolt. The thread of a screw helps hold it in place. **4.** the main idea that connects different parts of a story, argument, and so on: The book has too many background details and it's hard to follow the *thread* of the story. —*verb,* **threaded, threading. 1.** to put a piece of thread

thread•bare [thred′bâr′] *adjective, more/most.* worn out so much that pieces of thread show; shabby: a *threadbare* old hunting jacket.

threat [thret] *noun, plural* **threats. 1.** a warning or plan of hurting someone: Someone sent the mayor a letter making *threats* to kill him. **2.** a person or thing that can be dangerous or harmful: The grass fire is out of control and is a *threat* to several houses nearby. **3.** a sign that something might be dangerous: "The day was grey with a *threat* of snow." (Graham Greene)

threat•en [thret′ən] *verb,* **threatened, threatening. 1.** to say that something will be done to hurt or punish: The gangsters *threatened* to wreck the man's restaurant if he didn't buy his supplies from them. "She wept and carried on and *threatened* to report him to his father . . ." (John O'Hara) **2.** to be the cause of danger or harm: "The ghost of Lacey Mahaffy was *threatening* him, it came nearer, growing taller as it came . . ." (Katherine Anne Porter) **3.** to be a sign of something dangerous: "The wind was howling past our cabin, and the wind *threatened* to burst in our window." (A. Conan Doyle)

three [thrē] *noun, plural* **threes;** *adjective.* one more than two; 3.

thresh [thresh] *verb,* **threshed, threshing.** to separate seeds or grain from plants by beating or striking. ◆ A **thresher** is a farm machine that does this.

Pronunciation Key: O–S

ō	over; go	ou	out; town
ô	all; law	p	put; hop
oo	look; full	r	run; car
ōō	pool; who	s	set; miss
oi	oil; boy	sh	show

(Turn the page for more information.)

T

thresh•old thresh/hōld/] *noun, plural* **thresh-olds. 1.** a piece of wood or stone at the base of a doorway. **2.** a point of beginning or entering: The scientist felt he was on the *threshold* of making an important new discovery.

threw [thrōō] *verb.* the past tense of **throw.**

thrice [thrīs] *adverb.* an older term meaning "three times."

thrift•y [thrif/tē] *adjective,* **thriftier, thriftiest.** careful in the use of money; likely to save; not wasteful: Mom's a *thrifty* shopper who always uses coupons and looks for special sales. ♦ The fact of being thrifty is **thrift.**

thrill [thril] *noun, plural* **thrills.** a strong sudden feeling of excitement or joy: It was a *thrill* for him to meet his favorite big-league ballplayer. —*verb,* **thrilled, thrilling.** to give a thrill to; fill with excitement or joy: "The marching and the music *thrilled* Orry . . ." (John Jakes) ♦ Often used as an adjective: "He should have been downstairs again by eight-thirty, but because the book was so *thrilling* he forgot the time . . ." (Anne Frank)

thrill•er [thril/ər] *noun, plural* **thrillers.** a person or thing that thrills, especially a story or movie that is full of suspense and excitement.

thrive [thrīv] *verb,* **thrived, thriving.** to be healthy or successful; grow or develop well: "You've eaten bluefish for years and *thrived* on it . . ." (Eugene O'Neill) ♦ Often used as an adjective: ". . . it became a *thriving* little city, and Rufus Woods published the paper and got rich." (Ernie Pyle)

throat [thrōt] *noun, plural* **throats. 1.** the front part of the neck. **2.** the passage from the mouth to the stomach.

throb [thräb] *verb,* **throbbed, throbbing.** to beat strongly or quickly; pound: "He could feel his temples *throbbing.* He blamed it on the heat and dust of the closed room." (Walter Farley) "Everything was *throbbing* with noise and music and energy." (S. E. Hinton) —*noun, plural* **throbs.** a quick or strong beat.

throne [thrōn] *noun, plural* **thrones. 1.** a large, decorated chair that a king or queen sits in for ceremonies or important decisions. **2.** the power or authority of a king or queen: King Edward VIII of England gave up the *throne* and his younger brother became king.

throng [thrông] *noun, plural* **throngs.** a large group of people; a crowd: "Chance pushed his way through the *throng* of dancing couples toward the exit." (Jerzy Kosinski) —*verb,* **thronged, thronging.** to move in a large group; crowd: "The streets were *thronged* with cars

seeming to rush in all directions." (Colleen McCullough)

throt•tle [thrät/əl] *noun, plural* **throttles.** a valve that controls the flow of fuel to an engine. —*verb,* **throttled, throttling.** to slow an engine by closing this valve.

through [thrōō] *preposition.* **1.** from one side or part to the other: "He looked *through* the window and saw Ruth digging in the garden." (Toni Morrison) **2.** from beginning to end: "All *through* breakfast, Anne worried about Laura . . ." (Mary Gordon) **3.** because of or by means of: You can order that book *through* the local bookstore. —*adverb.* **1.** from one side or end to the other: The road is blocked off and no one can get *through.* **2.** completely: "A cold rain fell; the wind blew in his face; he was wet *through* . . ." (Joseph Conrad) —*adjective.* **1.** finished; done: If you're *through* with the paper, I want to read it. **2.** going from one point to another in a direct way: Is this a *through* street, or a dead end?

through•out [thrōō out/] *preposition.* in every part of; from beginning to end: It rained *throughout* the night. "He became rich and famous, known *throughout* the United States." (Ernie Pyle)

throne The throne used by English kings and queens at Parliament in London.

throw [thrō] *verb,* **threw, thrown, throwing. 1.** to send something through the air with force, by a sudden movement of the arm and hand: to *throw* a baseball. **2.** to move suddenly and with force: "'Bobby!' I yelled, and *threw* both arms around him in a bear hug." (Stephen King) "A cab ran through the puddle and *threw* a spray of water." (Jimmy Breslin) **3.** to cause to go through the air: "He *threw* another proud and angry look at Deven . . ." (Anita Desai) **4.** to go suddenly or with force into a certain condition: "He *threw* himself into the business of sheep farming, tearing about the island in his jeep . . ." (Ken Follett) **5. throw away** or **throw out.** to get rid of something that is not wanted. —*noun, plural* **throws.** the act of throwing: The discus *throw* is an event in track and field.

thrown [thrōn] *verb.* the past participle of **throw.**

thrush The wood thrush.

thrush [thrush] *noun, plural* **thrushes.** one of a group of birds noted for their beautiful song. The **wood thrush** and **hermit thrush** are common in North America.

thrust [thrust] *verb,* **thrust, thrusting.** to push with force; shove: "Brady *thrust* the paper into his father's hand. 'Just look at that!' he cried." (Jean Fritz) —*noun, plural* **thrusts.** a sudden strong push or shove.

thud [thud] *noun, plural* **thuds.** a dull sound; a thump. —*verb,* **thudded, thudding.** to move or hit with a dull sound: ". . . her heart *thudded* against her ribs." (Sherley Anne Williams)

thug [thug] *noun, plural* **thugs.** a violent criminal or gangster. ◆ The *Thugs* were an old society of criminals in India, known for the many murders and robberies they committed.

thumb [thum] *noun, plural* **thumbs.** the short, thick finger on the end of the hand. —*verb,* **thumbed, thumbing.** to turn and look through the pages of: to *thumb* through a book. "He reached out and *thumbed* over the pile of magazines lying on the table." (John R. Tunis)

thumb•tack [thum′ tak′] *noun, plural* **thumbtacks.** a tack with a flat, round head that can be pressed into place with the thumb.

thump [thump] *noun, plural* **thumps.** a dull, heavy sound; a thud: The branch fell off the tree, hitting the car with a *thump.* —*verb,* **thumped, thumping.** to beat or hit with a dull, heavy sound: "Pa Forrester *thumped* the floor with his cane." (Marjorie Kinnan Rawlings)

thun•der [thun′ dər] *noun, plural* **thunders. 1.** the loud rumbling or crashing sound that follows lightning. Thunder is caused by the sudden heating and expanding of air. **2.** any very loud noise like thunder: "He could still hear the *thunder* of the train . . ." (Ross Lockridge) —*verb,* **thundered, thundering.** to make thunder or any noise like thunder: "The four engines of the . . . plane roared into life. It *thundered* down the airstrip . . ." (James Houston)

thun•der•bolt [thun′ dər bōlt] *noun, plural* **thunderbolts.** a flash of lightning together with a clap of thunder.

thun•der•head [thun′ dər hed′] *noun, plural* **thunderheads.** a rounded mass of dark cloud that often appears before a thunderstorm.

thunderhead A thunderhead cloud forming over the Grand Canyon area of northern Arizona.

thun•der•ous [thun′ dər əs] *adjective.* of or like thunder: "With the greatest of grace he returned to bow again to applause that was *thunderous.*" (Langston Hughes)

thun•der•storm [thun′ dər stôrm′] *noun, plural* **thunderstorms.** a storm having thunder and lightning.

Pronunciation Key: T–Z

t	ten; date	v	very; live
th	think	w	win; away
th	these	y	you
u	cut; butter	z	zoo; cause
ur	turn; bird	zh	measure

(Turn the page for more information.)

Thurs•day [thurz′dā′] *noun, plural* **Thursdays.** the fifth day of the week.

thus [thus] *adverb.* **1.** in this manner; in this way; so: "And *thus* speaking, the Reverend Mr. Clark bent forward to reveal the mystery of so many years." (Nathaniel Hawthorne) **2.** because of this; therefore: "*Thus,* any vision about the future is really based on visions of the past, because that is all we can know for certain." (Bruno Bettelheim)

for someone to pay a fine or go to court for breaking a traffic law: A driver who parks in the wrong place may get a parking *ticket.* **4.** a list of people running for office in an election: In the 1960 Presidential election, John Kennedy and Lyndon Johnson were on the Democratic *ticket.* —*verb,* **ticketed, ticketing. 1.** to put a card or tag on. **2.** to give a notice for someone to pay a fine or go to court: Mr. Sims was *ticketed* for going through a red light.

> **thus** *"Thus* the days and weeks passed without tidings." Thomas Hardy wrote that. In his day, the late 19th century, the use of *thus* was common (as was *tidings,* meaning "news"). *Thus* has lost ground over the past fifty years or so. "The small animals that the coyotes normally fed on began to disappear from the area. *Thus,* they had to find a new source of food." Yes, that's a good usage, but it's more common today to say, "That's why they had to find . . ." or "For that reason . . ." or "Therefore . . ." Are we discussing rules here? No. We are counting our blessings that English has so many words and phrases to choose from.

thwart [thwôrt] *verb,* **thwarted, thwarting.** to keep from doing or succeeding; oppose and defeat: "They did some more work on their hole, and then, finding themselves *thwarted* by a large root . . ." (Penelope Lively) "There had been no men strong enough to *thwart* his evil ways . . ." (James Thurber)

thy [thī] *pronoun.* an old form of the word **your:** "Love *thy* neighbor" is a famous saying from the Bible.

thyme [tīm] *noun.* a small plant with sweet-smelling leaves belonging to the mint family. Thyme leaves are used to flavor foods.

thy•roid [thī′roid′] *noun.* a large gland in the neck that controls the body's rate of growth and the rate at which it burns up food for energy.

tick[1] [tik] *noun, plural* **ticks.** a light, clicking sound such as is made by a clock or watch. —*verb,* **ticked, ticking. 1.** to make this sound. **2.** of time, to pass away: "The minutes *ticked* by; some say two minutes passed, others as many as five." (Cornelius Ryan) **3.** to mark with a check, dot, or slash: He *ticked* off the items on his grocery list as he put each one in the shopping cart.

tick[2] *noun, plural* **ticks.** a tiny animal with eight legs, related to the spider. A tick attaches itself to the skin of animals or people to suck their blood. In this way it can spread diseases.

tick•et [tik′it] *noun, plural* **tickets. 1.** a piece of paper or a card that gives a person certain services or rights. You pay money for a ticket to get into a movie or show, to get onto a plane or train, and so on. **2.** a tag that shows something, such as the price or size of clothing. **3.** a notice

tick•le [tik′əl] *verb,* **tickled, tickling. 1.** to touch the body lightly, causing a funny, tingling feeling: I *tickled* her ribs and she started to laugh. "The sun blazed down upon them, the sweat *tickled* his face." (George Orwell) **2.** *Informal.* to be delighted or pleased: My grandfather was really *tickled* that I sent him a birthday card. —*noun, plural* **tickles.** a funny, tingling feeling.

tick•lish [tik′lish] *adjective, more/most.* **1.** sensitive to tickling: My little brother's very *ticklish* and starts giggling as soon as you touch him. **2.** needing careful handling; difficult; delicate: She wants to invite one of the sisters to the party but not the other; it's a *ticklish* situation.

tid•al wave [tī′dəl] a huge, powerful ocean wave caused by an underwater earthquake or a heavy storm. Tidal waves can be as high as a tall building and can cause great damage.

tid•bit [tid′bit′] *noun, plural* **tidbits. 1.** a small, choice piece of food. **2.** an interesting bit of information or news.

tide [tīd] *noun, plural* **tides. 1.** the regular rise and fall in the level of the ocean or other large bodies of water. Tides are caused by the pull of gravity from the moon or sun on the earth, and they change from high to low and back to high about every twelve hours. **2.** anything thought to rise and fall like the tide: "Perhaps it was best . . . to drift along with the *tide* of events rather than trying to fight them." (Andre Norton) —*verb,* **tided, tiding. tide over.** to give help through a difficult period: "Perhaps five pounds of flour remained to *tide* them *over* two hundred miles of wilderness." (Jack London)

T

tiger The tiger is the largest of the cat family.

ti•dings [tī′ dingz] *plural noun.* information; news: The messenger brought sad *tidings* of the king's army having suffered a great defeat.

ti•dy [tī′ dē] *adjective,* **tidier, tidiest. 1.** clean and in good order; neat: His desk was very *tidy,* with papers, pens, and books all carefully arranged. **2.** fairly large: This painting would be worth a *tidy* sum of money if I ever decided to sell it. —*verb,* **tidied, tidying.** to make neat: "Bessie had now finished dusting and *tidying* the room." (Charlotte Brontë) —**tidily,** *adverb.* —**tidiness,** *noun.*

tie [tī] *verb,* **tied, tying. 1.** to fasten with string or rope: to *tie* your shoes, to *tie* up a pile of newspapers. **2.** to equal the score in a game or contest: The basketball game was *tied* at 68-68 with one minute to play. **3.** to join together; connect: Pollution from acid rain has been *tied* to the death of sea life along the Atlantic coast. **3. tie down** or **tie up.** to keep from moving or acting; limit; restrict: Dad called to say he was *tied up* at the office and wouldn't be home for dinner. ◆ Also used as a noun: a traffic *tie-up.* —*noun, plural* **ties. 1.** something that fastens or holds something together, such as a string or rope. **2.** a strip of cloth worn around the neck; a necktie. **3.** an equal score in a game or contest. **4.** something that joins or connects: The rebel group is believed to have *ties* to the Soviet Union. **5.** a piece of wood or metal that holds together and strengthens other parts. A railroad track has metal rails with wooden ties going across them.

tier [tēr] *noun, plural* **tiers.** a number of rows or layers arranged one above the other: Baseball stadiums often have several *tiers* of seats.

ti•ger [tī′ gər] *noun, plural* **tigers.** a large, powerful wild cat with orange-brown fur and black stripes. Tigers are found in Asia.

tight [tīt] *adjective,* **tighter, tightest. 1.** closely fastened, held, or tied; fixed firmly in place: a *tight* knot in a rope. Make sure all the screws are *tight* when you put the table together. **2.** fitting close to the body: a *tight* sweater. **3.** made so nothing can pass through. ◆ Used in combination: air*tight,* water*tight.* **4.** having little room or space; close or confined: It was a very *tight* race, with only two seconds between the winner and fourth place. ◆ A person who is in a difficult situation is said to be in a **tight spot,** a **tight squeeze,** and so on. **5.** not generous; stingy: a person who is *tight* with his money. —*adverb.* so as to be tight; firmly; securely: "The skin on her face was thin and drawn as *tight* as the skin on an onion." (Flannery O'Connor) —**tightly,** *adverb:* "She squeezed the water out of her jersey very *tightly.*" (Margaret Drabble) —**tightness,** *noun.*

tight•en [tīt′ ən] *verb,* **tightened, tightening.** to make or become tight: Water was leaking out where the hoses were joined, and I had to *tighten* the connection.

tightrope The famous performer Philippe Petit demonstrates some daring stunts on the tightrope.

tight•rope [tīt′ rōp′] *noun, plural* **tightropes.** a wire or rope that is stretched tight high above the ground. Circus stars and acrobats walk across tightropes to entertain people.

Pronunciation Key: [ə] Symbol

The [ə] or *schwa* sound occurs in syllables without an accent. It can be spelled with any vowel, such as **a** in above, **e** in listen, **i** in pencil, **o** in melon, **u** in circus. It can also be a combination of vowels, such as **io** in action, **ai** in mountain, **iou** in precious.

(Turn the page for more information.)

tights [tīts] *plural noun.* a tight-fitting garment covering the legs and lower part of the body. Tights stretch to fit the legs and are often worn by dancers and acrobats.

Ti•gris [tī′ gris] a river in southwest Asia that flows from eastern Turkey through Iraq to join the **Euphrates** [yōō frā′ tēz] near the Persian Gulf. The region near these two rivers was known in ancient times as MESOPOTAMIA, an early center of civilization.

tile [tīl] *noun, plural* **tiles.** a thin slab or piece of baked clay or other material. Tiles are usually square and are placed side by side on walls, floors, counter tops, and so on. —*verb,* **tiled, tiling.** to cover with tiles: to *tile* a kitchen floor.

hurried past." (Erskine Caldwell) —*noun, plural* **tilts. 1.** a slanting position. **2. full tilt.** full speed or force: "He ran *full tilt,* as if devils were chasing him . . ." (John Gardner)

tim•ber [tim′ bər] *noun, plural* **timbers. 1.** wood for building houses, boats, and other such items. **2.** a long, large piece of wood for building. **3.** a group of trees, or an area where trees grow; a forest. ♦ A **timberline** is the line on a mountain above which trees are not able to grow.

tim•bre [tim′ bər *or* tam′ bər] *noun.* the quality of a sound that makes it distinct from other sounds: "Her little-girl voice took on quite a hard *timbre.*" (Angus Wilson)

---

time order Normally you arrange information in a piece of writing according to the order in which the events happened—time passing. That is not always the best method, though. Suppose you wrote on Christopher Columbus. Since little is known about his boyhood, it's best to start with his dream of finding the rich and fabulous East by sailing westward. Your opening section might well be a description of Columbus's building his ships. You can even begin at the moment he and his sailors sight land in the New World. After this, you go back to his early life to tell the rest of the story in normal order. Suppose you're writing a story about a boy who's trying out for Little League baseball in hopes of reaching the Major division. If you begin there, you can then work in a section telling his thoughts about his last season in the Minors. This episode, called a *flashback,* gives a background for the present events.

T

till¹ [til] *preposition; conjunction.* up to the time of; until: Her birthday's today, but she's going to wait *till* Saturday for her party.

till² *verb,* **tilled, tilling.** to prepare and use farm land for growing crops: Farmers *till* the soil by churning it up with a plow. —**tiller,** *noun.*

till³ *noun, plural* **tills.** a small drawer for holding money, especially one under a counter in a store or shop.

till•er [til′ ər] *noun, plural* **tillers.** a handle or bar used to turn a rudder to steer a boat.

tilt [tilt] *verb,* **tilted, tilting.** to raise one end or side higher than the other; slant or tip: "A man with a gray hat *tilted* on the back of his head

time [tīm] *noun, plural* **times. 1.** a quality that goes on and on without end, separating things that happened before from those that will happen. Time is measured in hours, days, years, and so on. The moving of a clock's hands or the change from spring to summer show the passing of time. **2.** a way of measuring this quality: Boston is on Eastern Standard *Time.* **3.** a certain point or moment in the past, present, or future: The *time* now is 10:30 in the morning. **4.** a certain period of history: Cars and planes were not known in George Washington's *time.* **5.** an occasion or period having a certain purpose: It was *time* for the baby's nap. **6.** one of a number of occasions on which something hap-

---

timing In story writing, *timing* means a sense of the right spot in the story to present a certain piece of information. For example, suppose a story is a mystery in which one of the characters has stolen a valuable diamond. At what point in the story do the readers find out who the diamond thief is? Usually, this information is held back until the very end. However, the readers could learn at an earlier point who the thief was. Then the interest would lie in whether the police could catch him. Maybe the story is being told after the fact, by the diamond thief himself. As he tells it, we think he's escaped and is leading a life of ease on a remote tropical island. But as we read on we begin to get suspicious, and by the end we realize that he's actually living out on the street, without a penny, because his former partner cheated him out of the diamond.

---

pens: That's the third *time* today he's called. —*verb*, **timed, timing. 1.** to set to a certain time: The traffic light is *timed* to turn green once every 45 seconds. **2.** to measure the time of: The marathon winner was *timed* in 2 hours and 12 minutes.

time·less [tīm′ lis] *adjective.* not affected or limited by time: the *timeless* appeal of Shakespeare's plays.

time·ly [tīm′ lē] *adjective,* **timelier, timeliest.** happening or coming at a good or suitable time: Just as everyone in the meeting was getting restless, she made a *timely* suggestion that they take a short break. —**timeliness,** *noun.*

tim·er [tīm′ ər] *noun, plural* **timers.** a person or thing that keeps track of time. An oven timer is used to tell how long food has cooked.

times [tīms] *preposition.* multiplied by: Four *times* two is eight.

time·ta·ble [tīm′ tā′ bəl] *noun, plural* **timetables.** a list of the times when trains, buses, or the like arrive or leave.

tim·id [tim′ id] *adjective, more/most.* not brave or bold; easily frightened; shy: "I was *timid* about ringing the doorbells of strangers, relieved when no one came to the door, and scared when someone did." (Russell Baker) —**timidly,** *adverb.* —**timidity** [ti mid′ ə tē], *noun.*

tin [tin] *noun, plural* **tins. 1.** a soft, silver-white metal that is a chemical element. Tin is useful because it protects things from rust, and it is often used to coat other metals. **2.** something made out of tin. —*adjective.* made out of tin, or coated with tin: Soup is often sold in *tin* cans.

tin·der [tin′ dər] *noun.* any dry material that burns easily and is used to start a fire. Wood shavings, dry pine cones, and paper are tinder.

tin·foil [tin′ foil′] *noun.* a very thin sheet of tin, aluminum, or other metal used for wrapping.

tinge [tinj] *noun, plural* **tinges.** a slight amount; a trace: "The two ladies looked at each other again. This time with a *tinge* of smiling embarrassment . . ." (Edith Wharton) —*verb,* **tinged, tingeing. 1.** to give a slight amount of color to: "Her clear ivory skin was *tinged* now with a spot of red on either cheek." (Edna Ferber) **2.** to show a slight amount of some quality.

tin·gle [ting′ gəl] *verb,* **tingled, tingling.** to have a slight prickly, stinging feeling: His skin *tingled* as he ran warm water over his chilled hands. —*noun, plural* **tingles.** a tingling feeling.

tin·ker [tingk′ ər] *verb,* **tinkered, tinkering.** to fix or work with something in an unskilled or casual way: Tom likes to *tinker* with radios, trading parts between one and another. —*noun, plural* **tinkers.** in former times, a person who traveled around mending pots, pans, and other such household items.

tin·kle [ting′ kəl] *verb,* **tinkled, tinkling.** to make a light, clear ringing sound like the sound of tiny bells: ". . . the sleighbells *tinkled* off in the distance." (Eleanor Estes) "She laughed a *tinkling* little laugh." (E. B. White) —*noun, plural* **tinkles.** a light, clear ringing sound.

tin·sel [tin′ səl] *noun.* a thread or thin strip of shiny, glittering metal. Tinsel is hung as a decoration on Christmas trees.

tint [tint] *noun, plural* **tints.** a slight shade of color, especially a pale or delicate color. —*verb,* **tinted, tinting.** to give a tint to: ". . . a pair of *tinted* glasses hid her eyes." (Dick Francis)

ti·ny [tī′ nē] *adjective,* **tinier, tiniest.** very, very small: Fleas are *tiny* insects that can hardly be seen without a microscope.

tip[1] [tip] *noun, plural* **tips. 1.** the end or farthest point of anything: The *tip* of an arrow is sharp and pointed. **2.** a small piece on the end of something: a pen with a felt *tip.*

tip[2] *verb,* **tipped, tipping. 1.** to knock over; overturn or upset: The cat *tipped* over the plant, knocking dirt all over the floor. **2.** to raise one end or side; tilt or slant: The polite man *tipped* his hat in respect as the lady walked past.

tip[3] *noun, plural* **tips. 1.** a small amount of money given for service, beyond the normal amount due: People who eat in a restaurant usually add a *tip* to their bill for the waiter or waitress. **2.** a helpful hint; useful information: The soccer coach gave us some *tips* on how to control the ball better. —*verb,* **tipped, tipping. 1.** to give a small amount of money for a service: She paid the cab driver the fare of $12 and *tipped* him two dollars. **2.** *also,* **tip off.** to give someone private or secret information: He had been *tipped off* that the police were coming and he ran out the back door. —**tipper,** *noun.*

Pronunciation Key: Accent Marks

[′] is the normal accent mark. It shows where the main stress falls on a word.
[′] is a secondary accent mark. It shows a lighter stress than the primary accent. For example:

tel • e • vis • ion [tel′ ə vizh′ ən]
(Turn the page for more information.)

tip•toe [tip′tō′] *verb*, **tiptoed, tiptoeing.** to walk on the tip of one's toes. ♦ Also used as a noun: "She went out the door on *tiptoe* . . . going so softly down the stairs that no one behind a shut door could hear." (Graham Greene)

tire[1] [tīr] *verb*, **tired, tiring.** to make or become tired; "Do you never *tire* of sitting in one place and in one position . . . ?" (E. B. White) ♦ Often used as an adjective: It was a long, hot, *tiring* climb to the top of the hill.

tire[2] *noun, plural* **tires.** a covering for a wheel of a car, truck, bicycle, or other such vehicle. Tires are usually made of rubber. Most tires have air in them, but some are solid rubber.

cells in a plant or animal that are alike in what they do: The muscle *tissue* of an animal is what the muscle is made up of.

tissue paper a soft, thin paper used for wrapping or packing things.

ti•tle [tīt′əl] *noun, plural* **titles. 1.** the name of a book, song, movie, painting, or other such work. **2.** a word or name used with a person's name to show a rank or position, such as "Mrs.," "Doctor," or "Her Majesty." **3.** a championship: the heavyweight boxing *title*. **4.** the legal right a person has to own property, or a document that shows this right. —*verb*, **titled, titling.** to give a name or title to: The painting was *titled* "Pacific Sunset."

titles Tennessee Williams said, "The title comes last." A writing teacher, Donald Murray, argues that you should choose the title *first* and let it shape the writing. Whichever comes first, title or text, for a report it's probably better to choose a plain, descriptive title: "Lebanon's Civil War" or "The Issue of Acid Rain." Avoid long subtitles. Why? The editors of this dictionary believe that subtitles allow the writer to be either careless or overly clever in choosing titles. "Lebanon's Nightmare: The Civil War Between Moslems and Christians." "Death From Leaves: The Issue of Acid Rain as a Hazard." Usually, the best titles are short. The book *Fictions* is a collection of 100 outstanding short stories in which the average length of a title is three and a half words, even including *the, a,* or *of.*

T

tired [tīrd] *adjective, more/most.* feeling or showing a lack of energy in the mind or body; wanting to rest or sleep: ". . . standing on one foot to rest the other like a *tired* old horse . . ." (Katherine Anne Porter) **2.** no longer interested; bored or annoyed: "Alice was beginning to get very *tired* of sitting by her sister on the bank and of having nothing to do." (Lewis Carroll) ♦ Something that is **tiresome** is boring or annoying: "He turned often from his *tiresome* writing to gaze out of his office window." (James Joyce) —**tiredness,** *noun.*

tire•less [tīr′lis] *adjective.* never tiring; going on and on: a *tireless* worker. —**tirelessly,** *adverb:* ". . . his long legs pumping as *tirelessly* as the pistons of a railway engine." (Ken Follett)

Ti•to [tē′tō] **Josip Broz,** 1892-1980, the ruler of Yugoslavia from 1943 to 1980.

to [tōō] *preposition.* **1.** in the direction of; toward: The teacher walked *to* the back of the room. **2.** as far as the point or condition of: soaked *to* the skin, starving *to* death. The weather is changing from fall *to* winter. **3.** through and including: The library is open from ten *to* six. **4.** compared with: We won the game, 4 *to* 2. **5.** for the purpose of; for: She went *to* lunch. Is that the key *to* the top lock?

♦ **To** is also used: **1.** to introduce an indirect object: Give this note *to* Jennie. **2.** to show a relation to a noun or adjective: Why were you so rude *to* him? **3.** to indicate the INFINITIVE: I didn't know whether *to* laugh or *to* cry.

to/too *To* and *too* are responsible for common mistakes in writing. People should not write, "She went *too* the movies" or "The theater used *too* sell popcorn but now it doesn't." *To* is correct here. "The beginning of the movie was really funny, and I liked the happy ending. But the middle part was *to* slow." Use "too" here. "I thought there were *to* many characters in the story." Use "too" here, also. *Too* goes with a following adjective or adverb and refers to "*more*" or "*greater,*" a greater amount.

tis•sue [tish′ōō] *noun, plural* **tissues. 1.** a soft, thin paper used as a handkerchief. **2.** a group of

toad [tōd] *noun, plural* **toads.** an animal that is very much like a frog but has shorter legs, a thicker body, and dry, bumpy skin. A toad hatches and develops in water but spends most of its adult life on land.

toad•stool [tōd′ stool′] *noun, plural* **toadstools.** a MUSHROOM with an umbrella-shaped top, especially one that is poisonous.

toast[1] [tōst] *noun.* a crisp slice of bread that has been browned on both sides by heat. —*verb,* **toasted, toasting.** to brown by heating: Andy likes to *toast* marshmallows over a fire.

toast[2] *noun, plural* **toasts.** a short speech made before drinking in honor of someone: At the wedding party Uncle Stan made a *toast* to the good health and fortune of the married couple. —*verb,* **toasted, toasting.** to drink in honor of someone: People often *toast* the New Year by drinking champagne at the stroke of midnight.

toast•er [tōs′ tər] *noun, plural* **toasters.** an electric device for making bread into toast.

to•bac•co [tə bak′ ō] *noun.* **1.** a tall plant with pink and white flowers and broad, sticky leaves. **2.** the dried leaves of this plant used for smoking and chewing. Cigarettes and cigars are made of tobacco.

to•bog•gan [tə bäg′ ən] *noun, plural* **toboggans.** a long, flat wooden sled used for sliding down hills. The front of a toboggan is curled up. —*verb,* **tobogganed, tobogganing.** to ride on a toboggan.

to•day [tə dā′] *noun.* the present day or time: *Today* is a holiday and the schools are closed. —*adverb.* **1.** on or during the present day: Was there any mail for me *today?* **2.** at the present time; nowadays: *Today,* banks keep track of their records by computer.

tod•dler [täd′ lər] *noun, plural* **toddlers.** a small child who is learning to walk. ♦ Someone who walks with small, uncertain steps is said to **toddle.**

toe [tō] *noun, plural* **toes. 1.** one of the five parts at the end of the foot. **2.** the part of a sock, shoe, or boot that covers the toes.

to•ga [tō′ gə] *noun, plural* **togas.** a loose-fitting piece of clothing that was worn by men in ancient Rome.

to•geth•er [tə geth′ ər] *adverb.* **1.** with one another: ". . . a married couple who lived quiet and happy lives *together.*" (Agatha Christie) "The fellows were talking *together* in little groups here and there on the playground." (James Joyce) **2.** mixed or in contact with: Bobby put some blocks *together* to build a fort. **3.** in agreement: Before ending the meeting, the boss asked, "Are we all *together* on this?"

toil [toil] *noun, plural* **toils.** long, hard work:

"He had spent his youth and early life in the coal mines of Scotland, and after such *toil,* he found farming relatively easy . . ." (William L. Shirer) —*verb,* **toiled, toiling.** to work hard and long: "All summer long Husk and his son *toiled* over the rocks . . ." (Edward Albee)

toi•let [toi′ lit] *noun, plural* **toilets.** a bowl that is filled with water and has a seat attached to it. It is found in a bathroom and is used to carry away body wastes.

to•ken [tō′ kən] *noun, plural* **tokens. 1.** something that stands for another thing that is larger or greater; a sign or symbol: He gave her a silver heart as a *token* of their love. "Still, I should like to have some *token* of you while you are away . . ." (Virginia Woolf) **2.** a piece of metal or plastic that looks like a coin and is used in place of money: People pay with a *token* to ride on a city bus or a subway. —*adjective.* done only to meet a requirement; slight or insignificant: Instead of paying the entire $1000 he owed, he made a *token* payment of $50.

Tokyo The Imperial Palace is at the heart of the city.

To•ky•o [tō′ kē ō] the capital of Japan, on Tokyo Bay. *Population:* 8,220,000.

told [tōld] *verb.* the past form of **tell.**

To•le•do [tə lē′ dō] a city in northwestern Ohio, on Lake Erie. *Population:* 357,000.

tol•er•a•ble [täl′ ər ə bəl] *adjective.* that can be tolerated; acceptable. —**tolerably,** *adverb:* "I could now speak the language *tolerably* well." (Jonathan Swift)

Pronunciation Key: A–F			
a	and; hat	ch	chew; such
ā	ate; stay	d	dog; lid
â	care; air	e	end; yet
ä	father; hot	ē	she; each
b	boy; cab	f	fun; off

(Turn the page for more information.)

tol•er•ance [täl′ ər əns] *noun.* an attitude of allowing others to have ideas and beliefs that are different from one's own and of accepting people who are from a different background: A country that has religious *tolerance* allows different religions to exist, rather than insisting on one official religion. "She had a remarkable *tolerance* for us children and what she considered our wild schemes . . ." (William L. Shirer)

tol•er•ant [täl′ ər ənt] *adjective, more/most.* willing to accept other people's ideas and beliefs; showing tolerance: "Pete is a peace-loving person; he is *tolerant* and gives in very easily." (Anne Frank) —**tolerantly,** *adverb.*

tol•er•ate [täl′ ər āt′] *verb,* **tolerated, tolerating. 1.** to allow something that one does not agree with to be or be done: In a democracy the government has to *tolerate* criticism of its policies by the press. **2.** to be willing to accept or put up with: "I won't *tolerate* any more of your sloppy behavior." (Laurence Yep)

toll[1] [tōl] *noun, plural* **tolls. 1.** a fee paid for the right to do something, such as to travel on a road or bridge. **2.** serious loss or damage: the death *toll* from auto accidents. "My mother was a proud woman, and it took its *toll* on her that she was accepting charity." (Malcolm X)

toll[2] *verb,* **tolled, tolling.** of a bell, to ring in a slow, regular way. —*noun, plural* **tolls.** the slow, regular ringing of a bell.

Tol•stoy [tōl′ stoi] **Leo,** 1828-1910, Russian novelist and philosopher.

tom•a•hawk [täm′ ə hôk′] *noun, plural* **tomahawks.** a small, light ax used as a tool and weapon by North American Indians.

tomato Ripe tomatoes on the vine.

to•ma•to [tə mā′ tō *or* tə mä′ tō] *noun, plural* **tomatoes.** a juicy fruit, usually red in color, that grows on a vine. Tomatoes are widely eaten as a vegetable, either raw or cooked.

tomb [tōōm] *noun, plural* **tombs.** a place where a dead body is buried, especially a large decorated building in which the body is placed.

tomb Grant's Tomb in New York City is the burial place of former President and General U. S. Grant.

tom•boy [täm′ boi′] *noun, plural* **tomboys.** a girl who likes to do things that are usually of interest only to boys: She's considered a *tomboy* because she wants to play Little League baseball instead of playing in the girls' softball league. ◆ This word comes from the idea that a *tom* is a male animal, such as a *tomcat* or a *tom* turkey.

tomb•stone [tōōm′ stōn′] *noun, plural* **tombstones.** a marker for a grave, usually made of stone, giving the name and the dates of birth and death of the dead person.

to•mor•row [tə mär′ ō] *noun.* **1.** the day after today. **2.** the future: The show gave a preview of machines that will be used in the world of *tomorrow.* —*adverb.* on the day after today.

tom-tom [täm′ täm′] *noun, plural* **tom-toms.** a small drum played by beating the top with the hands, first used by native tribes in Africa or India.

ton [tun] *noun, plural* **tons.** a measure of weight used in the United States and Canada, equal to 2,000 pounds. ◆ This is also called a **short ton** to distinguish it from the **long ton** of 2,240 pounds that is used in Great Britain, or the **metric ton** of 1,000 kilograms used in most other countries.

tone [tōn] *noun, plural* **tones. 1.** the nature of a sound in terms of its pitch, loudness, length, and so on: The mother sang to her baby in soft, low *tones.* **2.** the difference in higher or lower pitch between two musical notes on a scale. **3.** the quality of the voice that shows some feeling

T

tone A writer's *tone* is in large part his attitude toward a subject, showing him to be angry, happy, serious, or humorous. Language is so self-revealing that a writer's tone can usually be sensed from a paragraph or two. An article about a new City Hall building might have the writer complaining that the building is too grand, it cost far too much, and uses money better spent on other needs. The tone here is negative and critical. Recognizing tone is especially important if there's a contrast between the tone the writer uses on the surface and his true thoughts that lie beneath. The classic example is Jonathan Swift's 1729 essay, *A Modest Proposal.* Swift seems to be arguing, quite seriously, that the way to deal with the problem of the poor people in Ireland who had too many children (because food was scarce) is to fatten them up and feed them to rich people. Try reading some Shakespeare, such as Marc Antony's famous speech after the death of Julius Caesar. "Friends, Romans, countrymen, lend me your ears . . ." How do you describe the tone of that speech?

or meaning: an angry *tone.* "For his *tone* seemed to have sharpened just a little at the question." (Louis L'Amour) **4.** a quality of a color that makes it distinct: She used several different *tones* of blue to make the painting of the sky look real. **5.** the style or character of something: "It was evident from the *tone* of his letter that he had forgiven Dorothy by this time." (George Orwell)

tongs [tôngz *or* tängz] *plural noun.* a tool used to hold or pick up something. Tongs have two long arms joined to form a handle at one end.

tongue [tung] *noun, plural* **tongues. 1.** the movable, muscular piece of flesh in the mouth, that is used in the tasting, chewing, and swallowing of food. When a person speaks, the tongue helps form certain sounds in words. **2.** the tongue of an animal used for food: beef *tongue.* **3.** a language: Joseph Conrad wrote his famous books in English, but his native *tongue* was Polish. **4.** the ability to speak: He was so surprised that he lost his *tongue* for a few moments. ◆ When this happens the person is said to be **tongue-tied. 5.** the narrow flat piece of leather located under the laces or buckle of a shoe. **6.** something shaped like a tongue: *Tongues* of flame rose from the fire.

ton·ic [tän′ik] *noun, plural* **tonics.** something that is meant to bring a person health or strength, such as a medicine.

to·night [tə nīt′] *noun.* the night of the present day. —*adverb.* on or during this night: I'm tired and I want to go to bed early *tonight.*

ton·sil [tän′səl] *noun, plural* **tonsils.** either of two small, oval pieces of flesh located on the inside back part of the throat. ◆ **Tonsillitis** [tän′sə lī′tis] is an infection of the tonsils.

too [tōō] *adverb.* **1.** also; besides: You can have another cookie if you give Eddie one *too.* **2.** more than enough; more than it should be: This box is *too* small to hold all those books. **3.** very; very much: I'll be only *too* glad to help you.

took [took] *verb.* the past tense of **take.**

tool [tōōl] *noun, plural* **tools. 1.** an instrument or device used for doing work, especially one that is held in the hand. Hammers, saws, and screwdrivers are types of tools. **2.** a person or thing that is used for a certain purpose: A dictionary can be a very useful *tool* for a writer. **3.** a person who is unfairly or dishonestly used by another. —*verb,* **tooled, tooling.** to use a tool on something: The book was bound in leather, with the title hand *tooled* on the side.

toot [tōōt] *noun, plural* **toots.** a short, loud blast of sound. —*verb,* **tooted, tooting.** to make or cause such a sound: The driver *tooted* his horn to get the car in front of him to move.

tooth [tōōth] *noun, plural* **teeth. 1.** one of a set of hard, bony parts in the mouth used for biting and chewing. Teeth are set in the gums and supported by the jaws. Animals also use their teeth to protect themselves and to kill prey. **2.** something that looks like or is used like a tooth: the *teeth* of a rake or a comb.

tooth·brush [tōōth′brush′] *noun, plural* **toothbrushes.** a small brush with a long handle, used to clean the teeth.

tooth·paste [tōōth′pāst′] *noun, plural* **toothpastes.** a paste used in cleaning the teeth.

tooth·pick [tōōth′pik′] *noun, plural* **toothpicks.** a small, thin piece of wood, plastic, or

Pronunciation Key: G–N

g	give; big	k	kind; cat; back
h	hold	l	let; ball
i	it; this	m	make; time
ī	ice; my	n	not; own
j	jet; gem; edge	ng	having

(Turn the page for more information.)

T

topic A writer has to deal with a topic in three stages: First is the selection of a topic. Second is the narrowing (or widening) of the topic so that it is suitable in length. Third is to keep the writing on the topic. It's far more likely that you will narrow a topic than widen it. If you're a baseball fan and want to write a science paper using baseball as a topic, the trick is to narrow "Baseball." For example, the topic might be "Do aluminum bats really hit the ball farther than the traditional wooden bats?" Does this point connect to the topic? "Many older fans prefer wood bats. They'd rather hear the bat make a good, solid 'crack' than a dull 'thunk.'" An interesting comment. But your experiment is to measure distance, not sound. This is off the topic.

other material, used for removing food from between the teeth.

top¹ [täp] *noun, plural* **tops. 1.** the highest part or point of something: The roof is the *top* of a building. ♦ Also used in combinations such as **mountaintop, hilltop,** and so on. **2.** the highest level or degree: to yell at the *top* of your voice. He started with that company as a mail boy and slowly worked his way to the *top*. **3.** something that goes on the higher or upper part: She wore gray slacks and a blue *top*. —*adjective*. of or at the top; highest: He keeps his socks in the *top* drawer. The Los Angeles Lakers are one of the *top* teams in pro basketball. —*verb*, **topped, topping. 1.** to cover or put a top on: The ice cream was *topped* with whipped cream and nuts. ♦ Something put on food in this way is a **topping. 2.** to be at or reach the top.

top² *noun, plural* **tops.** a toy, usually cone-shaped, that can be made to spin very fast on a point.

to•paz [tō′ paz] *noun, plural* **topazes.** a mineral, usually yellow or brown, that is valued as a gemstone.

top•ic [täp′ ik] *noun, plural* **topics.** something that is dealt with in speech or writing; the subject of a paper, book, discussion, and so on: Beth has to choose a *topic* for her social studies report. That new movie has been a big *topic* of conversation in school this week.

to•pog•ra•phy [tə päg′ rə fē] *noun.* **1.** the surface features of an area of land, such as mountains, hills, valleys, rivers, lakes, and so on. **2.** the science of showing these natural features on a map. —**topographical** [täp′ ə graf′ ə kəl], *adjective.*

top•ple [täp′ əl] *verb,* **toppled, toppling.** to push or fall over: ". . . he got to laughing so hard the chair started to *topple* over backwards." (John Dos Passos)

top•soil [täp′ soil′] *noun, plural* **topsoils.** a rich surface layer of soil that has most of the materials needed by plants to grow.

torch [tôrch] *noun, plural* **torches. 1.** a bright flame or light that is carried to light the way: Many people carried the Olympic *torch* across the United States to the 1984 Olympic Games in Los Angeles. **2.** a device that produces a very hot flame, such as a BLOWTORCH.

♦ In British English, a flashlight is called a *torch*.

tore [tôr] *verb.* the past tense of **tear:** "Rufus jumped out of bed and *tore* through the house like a cyclone." (Eleanor Estes)

tor•ment [tôr′ ment *or* tôr ment′] *verb,* **tormented, tormenting.** to cause great pain or suffering: ". . . with the mosquitos and other insects *tormenting* the people as they sat around the smoky night fires." (Alex Haley) —*noun, plural* **torments.** great pain or suffering.

topic sentences A *topic sentence* is a sentence that, if it begins a paragraph, states the central idea of that paragraph. It's possible that the last sentence or a sentence in the middle can be called a topic sentence, but usually it comes first in the paragraph. In Paul Fussell's book, *The Great War and Modern Memory,* he begins a paragraph on trenches at the battlefront: "There were normally three lines of trenches." That is a topic sentence, giving the main idea of the paragraph. Then he gives three sentences of detail, one for each type of trench. That is the classic pattern of a paragraph: topic sentence, then three or four sentences giving details to define and support it. Topic sentences have for a long time been a basic writing technique, yet this method is now argued against as being too confining. However, we found in our research that a majority of famous writers *do* use the topic-sentence technique—though of course not for every single paragraph.

torn [tôrn] *verb*. the past participle of **tear:** "The poor child, *torn* by a feeling which she hardly understood . . ." (Thomas Hardy)

tor•na•do [tôr nā′ dō] *noun, plural* **tornadoes** or **tornados.** a very strong wind storm that creates a dark, pipe-shaped cloud. This cloud, or *funnel*, twists around and around with great speed and force as it moves in a narrow path. Objects in the path of the tornado are often damaged or destroyed by the force of the wind.

To•ron•to [tə rän′ tō] the capital of the province of Ontario, Canada, on Lake Ontario. *Population:* 633,000.

tor•pe•do [tôr pē′ dō] *noun, plural* **torpedoes.** a weapon used to sink ships, made up of a long, tube-shaped metal shell that is filled with explosives. Torpedoes are fired from submarines, ships, or planes and then travel under the water to the target by their own power. —*verb*, **torpedoed, torpedoing.** to hit an object with a torpedo: During World War II, many Allied ships were *torpedoed* by German submarines.

tor•rent [tôr′ ənt] *noun, plural* **torrents. 1.** a heavy, fast-moving stream of water or other liquid: "The rain was falling in *torrents*." (Malcolm X) **2.** any strong, steady stream: ". . . bewildering him with a *torrent* of empty phrases . . ." (Frank Norris)

tor•so [tôr′ sō] *noun, plural* **torsos.** the upper part of the human body; the trunk.

tor•til•la [tôr tē′ yə] *noun, plural* **tortillas.** a round, flat cake made from corn or wheat flour, often used in Mexican cooking.

tortoise The Galapagos tortoise of the South American islands is the world's largest land turtle.

tor•toise [tôr′ təs] *noun, plural* **tortoise** or **tortoises.** a turtle, especially a land turtle.

tor•ture [tôr′ chər] *verb*, **tortured, torturing. 1.** to cause a person great pain or suffering, as a punishment or to force the person to do something: The spy was *tortured* by the enemy until

tornado The Oklahoma skies darken at mid-day as a tornado looms on the horizon.

he gave them the secret information they wanted. **2.** to cause suffering to; torment: She was *tortured* by the thought that she could have prevented the accident if she'd watched the road more closely. —*noun*. great pain or suffering.

toss [tôs] *verb*, **tossed, tossing. 1.** to make a quick or short throw: The players were warming up on the sidelines, *tossing* the ball back and forth. "The man . . . pulled out a silver coin and *tossed* it lightly into the air." (Jean Fritz) ◆ In a **tossed salad** the ingredients are quickly tossed or stirred to mix them together. **2.** to throw or move about quickly: "He had fallen asleep after what seemed hours of *tossing* and turning noisily . . ." (William Golding) —*noun, plural* **tosses. 1.** a quick or short throw: A coin *toss* decides which team kicks off in football. **2. toss-up.** an even chance: It's a *toss-up* whether Kim or Brooke will be named head cheerleader.

to•tal [tōt′ əl] *adjective*. making up the whole; complete: The *total* length of the Nile River is over 4,000 miles. The moon and stars were hidden by heavy clouds; we were in *total* darkness. —*noun, plural* **totals.** the complete amount. —*verb*, **totaled, totaling. 1.** amount to; come to as a total: Including tax, the bill *totaled* $42.20. **2.** *Informal.* to destroy completely: Her car was *totaled* in the accident.

Pronunciation Key: O–S			
ō	over; go	ou	out; town
ô	all; law	p	put; hop
oo	look; full	r	run; car
o͞o	pool; who	s	set; miss
oi	oil; boy	sh	show
(Turn the page for more information.)			

to•tal•i•tar•i•an [tō tal′ ə tãr′ ē ən]   *adjective.* having to do with a country in which the central government has complete power and greatly controls the lives of the citizens.

to•tal•ly [tō′ tə lē] *adverb.* completely; entirely: All her clothes were lost in the fire and she had to buy a *totally* new wardrobe.

tote [tōt] *verb*, **toted, toting.** *Informal.* to carry around or on one's person: "Hannah had *toted* Ben around since she was four and he was one." (Jessamyn West) ◆ A **tote bag** is used to carry small personal items.

totem pole An actual Northwest Indian totem pole, part of the Indian dwelling known as a long house.

to•tem [tō′ təm] *noun*, *plural* **totems.** in the beliefs of certain cultures, an animal, plant, or other natural object that is taken as the symbol for a family or tribe. ◆ A **totem pole** is a pole that has carved and painted images of totems. Totem poles were put up by certain Indian tribes of the Pacific Northwest.

tot•ter [tät′ ər] *verb*, **tottered, tottering.** to move in a shaky or unsteady way: "Suddenly Nur heaved himself out of his chair and stood *tottering* . . . as if he were about to fall." (Anita Desai)

tou•can [tōō′ kan] *noun*, *plural* **toucans.** a brightly-colored tropical bird with a large curving beak and a heavy body.

touch [tuch] *verb*, **touched, touching. 1.** to put a hand, finger, or other part of the body against: She accidentally *touched* the wet paint and got some on her hand. **2.** to put one thing against another so that there is no space between: The desk should be a few inches from the wall, not actually *touching* it. **3.** to affect the feelings: "The mole was so *touched* by his kind manner of speaking that he could find no voice to answer him . . ." (Kenneth Grahame) **4.** to

relate or refer to: ". . . but it did not concern her—in no way or relation did it *touch* her." (Rudyard Kipling) "I will just *touch* upon two other persons whom I have mentioned . . ." (Anne Brontë) **5. touch up.** to make small changes or improvements: "Ted found some paint in the shop and began *touching up* the trim on the house." (Erskine Caldwell) —*noun, plural* **touches. 1.** the sense by which objects are felt and known by the hands and other body parts. **2.** a particular feeling sensed in this way: The silk blouse had a soft, smooth *touch*. **3.** the act or fact of touching. **4.** a small amount: She's in bed with a *touch* of fever. "He got up and refilled the teapot, then his cup, adding a *touch* of skimmed milk . . ." (Kingsley Amis) **5.** communication between people: "I suppose you've lost *touch* with most of your old friends here." (Tennessee Williams)

touch•down [tuch′ doun′] *noun*, *plural* **touchdowns.** a score in football that is worth six points, made by carrying or catching the ball beyond the other team's goal line. ◆ Under the early rules of football, a player taking the ball past the goal had to *touch* it *down* to the ground for the score to count.

touch football a form of football in which the player with the ball is stopped by being tagged or touched, rather than tackled.

touch•y [tuch′ ē] *adjective*, **touchier, touchiest.** easily insulted or very sensitive.

tough [tuf] *adjective*, **tougher, toughest. 1.** not easily damaged by breaking, cutting, or tearing; strong: Elephants have a *tough* hide. The steak had been cooked too long and was very *tough*. **2.** able to put up with hardship and difficulty: Soldiers on the front line have to be brave and *tough*. **3.** likely to fight; mean and rough: The *tough* bullies in the neighborhood ganged up on the new boy. ◆ Also used as a noun: a gang of young *toughs*. **4.** hard to do; difficult: a *tough* math problem. Jack knew it would be a *tough* job moving the fallen tree by himself. —**toughness**, *noun*.

tough•en [tuf′ ən] *verb*, **toughened, toughening.** to make or become tough: New recruits in the army go through a harsh basic training course to *toughen* them up.

tou•pee [tōō pā′] *noun*, *plural* **toupees.** a small wig to cover a bald spot on the head.

tour [tōōr] *noun*, *plural* **tours. 1.** a trip where many places are visited for a short period of time: My parents went on a vacation *tour* of Europe last year. On the pro golf *tour*, players compete in a different city each week. **2.** a short trip around or through a place to see it: Our class took a *tour* of the City Art Museum. **3.** a period of time for fulfilling a required task or service: a *tour* of duty in the army. —*verb,* **toured, touring.** to travel in or through a place; make a tour: After that play finishes its run on Broadway, the actors will *tour* other cities in the U. S.

tour·ist [toor′ist] *noun, plural* **tourists.** a person who travels to visit a place for pleasure. ♦ The fact of doing this is **tourism.**

tour·na·ment [toor′ nə mənt] *noun, plural* **tournaments.** a series of contests involving two or more persons or teams: a tennis *tournament.*

tour·ni·quet [toor′ nə kit] *noun, plural* **tourniquets.** a bandage or cloth used to stop the flow of blood from a serious cut or wound. The bleeding is stopped by wrapping the cloth around the wound and twisting a short stick to tighten the cloth.

tow [tō] *verb,* **towed, towing.** to pull or drag behind something: After our car broke down, we had to have it *towed* to the dealer for repairs. —*noun, plural* **tows.** the act of towing.

to·ward [tôrd] (also spelled **towards**) *preposition.* in the direction of: After fishing all day, the crew headed the boat *toward* shore.

tow·el [toul] *noun, plural* **towels.** a piece of cloth or paper that is used for drying or wiping something. —*verb,* **toweled, toweling.** to wipe or dry with a towel: She stepped out of the shower and *toweled* herself dry.

tow·er [tou′ ər] *noun, plural* **towers.** a high structure that often is a narrow top portion of a larger building. Towers in buildings may hold large bells, clocks, or be used for a prison or a guard post. Two metal towers form the support for a suspension bridge. —*verb,* **towered, towering.** to rise or extend high into the air: ". . . a mountain *towered* over their heads so steep that the stones would often rumble down its sides . . ." (Nathaniel Hawthorne)

tow·er·ing [tou′ ər ing] *adjective.* **1.** very tall: ". . . a wall of *towering* cloud on the southern horizon . . ." (Farley Mowat) **2.** very great; outstanding: Sir Isaac Newton is a *towering* figure in the history of science.

town [toun] *noun, plural* **towns. 1.** an area with a group of houses and other buildings in which people live and work. ♦ The word *town* is used for a place than is smaller than a *city* but larger than a *village.* **2.** the people of a town: The whole *town* turned out for the big sale day at the mall. **3.** the downtown area of a city, or the city itself: He had a very late meeting and had

to spend the night in *town.* **4.** a unit of local government; more often called a TOWNSHIP.

town hall a meeting place in which the official business of a community takes place.

town·house [toun′ hous′] *noun, plural* **townhouses. 1.** a small house of two or three stories within a city, especially one of a row or group of such buildings. **2.** *also,* **town house.** a house in a city used by someone whose main home is in the suburbs or the country.

towns·people [tounz′ pē′ pəl] *plural noun.* those who live in towns or in a particular town.

town·ship [toun′ ship′] *noun, plural* **townships.** an area of local government within a county. A township may include only rural areas or have towns and cities within it.

tow truck a special truck used to tow disabled cars and trucks.

tower The Eiffel Tower in Paris, a famous symbol of France. It was built in 1889.

tox·ic [täk′ sik] *adjective,* *more/most.* having to do with or being a poison: A *toxic* gas. ♦ **Toxic waste** is the poisonous remains of certain industrial chemicals.

tox·in [täk′ sin] *noun, plural* **toxins.** any of various poisons produced by certain bacteria and viruses and causing diseases.

Pronunciation Key: T–Z			
t	ten; date	v	very; live
th	think	w	win; away
th	these	y	you
u	cut; butter	z	zoo; cause
ur	turn; bird	zh	measure

(Turn the page for more information.)

toy [toi] *noun, plural* **toys. 1.** something that is made to amuse or entertain children; an object that can be played with. **2.** a dog that is much smaller than one of the regular breed: a *toy* poodle. —*verb*, **toyed, toying. toy with. 1.** to play with to amuse oneself with: She *toyed with* her pencil as she listened on the phone. **2.** to think of in a light or casual way: "Now he was *toying with* the idea of going to America." (Bernard Malamud)

trace [trās] *noun, plural* **traces. 1.** a small amount left behind showing that something was there at one time: "Next he examined a faint *trace* of talcum powder on the . . . handle of the clothes cupboard." (Ian Fleming) "No *trace* of a smile on his face now . . ." (John Jakes) **2.** any small amount or quantity: "They had crossed more than half a mile of open pasture without a *trace* of cover . . ." (Richard Adams) "He heard a . . . voice with a *trace,* no more, of an Irish accent." (P. D. James) —*verb*, **traced, tracing. 1.** to follow the route, trail, or course of someone or something: The police *traced* the phone call and arrested the criminal as he was leaving the phone booth. "Miss Male's ills could be *traced* directly to the bad food . . ." (Paul Theroux) **2.** to copy something by following the lines as seen through a piece of paper. ♦ **Tracing paper** is special thin paper used to do this.

tra·che·a [trā′kē ə] *noun, plural* **tracheas.** the tube in the body that runs between the throat and the lungs; the windpipe.

track [trak] *noun, plural* **tracks. 1.** a mark or footprint left by a person, animal, or object as it moves over the ground: Jeff followed the rabbit *tracks* in the snow. **2.** a race course: Most horse races in the U. S. are run on a one-mile *track.* **3.** a set of rails that a train runs on. **4.** the continuous metal belts that tanks and tractors move on. **5. keep (lose) track of.** to keep (fail to keep) informed about or in communication with: "Francis had *lost track of* the men who had been with him in Vésey." (John Cheever) —*verb*, **tracked, tracking. 1.** to follow the marks or prints left by a person, animal, or thing. **2.** to follow the course or path of: The space center *tracked* the flight of the spacecraft. "It took Blyth about a week to *track* Dorothy down." (George Orwell) **3.** to make tracks on something: "He'll *track* mud all over her nice shiny kitchen floor . . ." (Margaret Atwood)

track and field a group of sporting events that involve running, jumping, and throwing. ♦ A **track meet** is a scheduled meeting of athletes to compete in track and field events.

tract [trakt] *noun, plural* **tracts. 1.** a large area of land: Our national parks are *tracts* of undeveloped land set aside for public use. **2.** a system of parts or organs in the body that work together: the digestive *tract.*

trac·tion [trak′shən] *noun.* the power to grip the surface of the road or ground and not slip while in motion: Cars have very little *traction* on snow or ice.

tractor A large tractor harvests hay near Florence, Montana.

trac·tor [trak′tər] *noun, plural* **tractors.** a work vehicle with large tires or continuous metal tracks. Tractors are used to pull farm machinery, pull loads over rough ground, or move other heavy objects.

trade [trād] *noun, plural* **trades. 1.** the act or business of buying and selling goods: The United States carries on *trade* with other nations in the world, such as Japan and Canada. ♦ A policy of **free trade** means that the government does not put restrictions or charges on goods coming into the country. **2.** a particular type of business: the book *trade.* The clothing business is nicknamed "the rag *trade.*" **3.** the exchange of one thing for another: I made a *trade* with my friend and got one of his video games for one of mine. —*verb*, **traded, trading. 1.** to give one thing for another; exchange: Major-league baseball teams often *trade* players between one team and another. **2. trade in.** to give something as part payment when buying a new item of the same kind. ♦ Also used as a noun: The dealer said he'd offer us $2000 on our old car as a *trade-in.* **3.** to buy and sell goods; carry on trade: Marco Polo made a famous trip to the Far East to *trade* for Chinese goods.

trade·mark [trād′märk′] *noun, plural* **trademarks. 1.** a picture, word, or symbol put onto an item so that it can be easily recognized as the product of a certain maker: The name "Chevrolet" is a *trademark* for a car sold by the General Motors Company. **2.** any distinctive feature that identifies a person or thing: The country singer Johnny Cash is known for wearing all-black outfits on stage; that's his *trademark.*

certain route: There's a lot of *traffic* going into the city on weekday mornings. ♦ Often used as an adjective: a *traffic* light, *traffic* accidents. **2.** the business of buying and selling goods, especially illegal goods: drug *traffic.* —*verb,* **trafficked, trafficking.** to buy, sell, or deal in goods, especially stolen or illegal goods.

> **tragedy** In the tragedies of the ancient Greeks, the main character—an important, powerful person—is brought down by a fault in his nature. This fault is called the *tragic flaw.* Shakespeare also wrote plays that were tragedies, such as *Hamlet, Othello, King Lear,* and *Macbeth.* Modern authors tend not to write about kings and emperors as Shakespeare and the ancient Greeks did, or even about modern equivalents of kings such as Presidents and generals. However, many modern authors do follow the basic plot line of a classic tragedy, by showing how the main character is carried along to destruction by his own flaws. Writers associated with this sort of "modern tragedy" include Graham Greene, Arthur Miller, and F. Scott Fitzgerald. In fact, Fitzgerald is famous for saying, "Show me a hero and I will write you a tragedy."

trad•er [trā′dər] *noun, plural* **traders. 1.** a person who takes part in trade: a fur *trader,* a *trader* on the stock exchange. **2.** a ship that is used to carry on trade. ♦ A **trade route** is a sea or land route used to go from one place to another for trade, especially in former times.

trading post a store in a frontier region where people can sell or exchange things for food and other supplies.

trag•e•dy [traj′ ə dē] *noun, plural* **tragedies. 1.** a very sad or unfortunate event; something that brings great unhappiness: The sinking of the ocean liner *Titanic* was a *tragedy* that took the lives of hundreds of people. **2.** a serious play in which the main character, an important or heroic person, meets death or ruin through fate or because of some fault in his nature. **3.** any story that has a sad ending.

> **traditional grammar** The form of grammar that was taught in American schools from about 1890 to today is called *traditional grammar.* It is based on the idea that a word can be classified (labeled) by its part of speech—for example, a house is a *noun*—and that this part of speech determines how the word is used in a sentence. However, in the 1960's and 70's this theory was strongly criticized by certain *linguists,* scholars who study the structure and uses of language. They argued that rules in traditional grammar were often artificial and did not reflect actual usage. Also, they criticized the definitions used by traditional grammar: "An *action verb* is a verb that shows action." Even so, the effect of such criticism has been to change and improve traditional grammar rather than to replace it.

tra•di•tion [trə dish′ ən] *noun, plural* **traditions.** a custom or belief that is passed from one generation to another: Thanksgiving dinner is a *tradition* celebrated by many families in the United States.

tra•di•tion•al [trə dish′ ən əl] *adjective, more/ most.* according to or following tradition; passed down over time: "Greensleeves" is a *traditional* English folk song. When our town had a Pioneer Day celebration, everyone dressed up in *traditional* frontier costumes. —**traditionally,** *adverb.*

traf•fic [traf′ ik] *noun.* **1.** the moving of cars, trucks, ships, planes, or other vehicles along a

trag•ic [traj′ ik] *adjective, more/most.* **1.** causing great suffering or sorrow; very sad: the *tragic* death of a child. The pilot made the *tragic* mistake of not checking his fuel level before he took off, and the plane run out of gas. **2.** having to do with a dramatic tragedy: Shakespeare's

---

Pronunciation Key: [ə] Symbol

The [ə] or *schwa* sound occurs in syllables without an accent. It can be spelled with any vowel, such as a in above, e in listen, i in pencil, o in melon, u in circus. It can also be a combination of vowels, such as io in action, ai in mountain, iou in precious.

(Turn the page for more information.)

characters Hamlet and Othello are famous *tragic* heroes. —**tragically,** *adverb.*

trail [trāl] *noun, plural* **trails. 1.** a path for moving through an area that is not settled or built up, such as a forest, desert, or mountain region. **2.** a mark, scent, or set of tracks made by an animal or person: The dogs followed the fox's *trail* into the woods. **3.** something that marks a trail or follows along behind: The truck left a *trail* of gravel as it pulled out of the driveway. —*verb,* **trailed, trailing. 1.** to follow the tracks or path of: "Two little men in brown suits, one twenty yards behind the other, *trailed* me along the seafront." (John Le Carré) **2.** to be behind in a race or game: The home team *trailed* by three runs going into the last inning. **3.** to grow along or over a surface: Watermelon plants grow by *trailing* along the ground. **4. trail off.** to become weaker and fade away: "His voice *trailed off* uneasily into silence." (Christopher Isherwood)

trail•er [trā′lər] *noun, plural* **trailers. 1.** an enclosed room or house on wheels that can be pulled behind a car. When parked, the trailer can be used as a home or office. ◆ People often live in a **trailer park** or **trailer camp,** where house trailers are set on permanent foundations called *pads.* **2.** a platform or box on wheels that is pulled behind a truck or car to move or carry something: a boat *trailer.*

trail The Oregon Trail was the main route to the West in the mid-1800's. This historic Currier & Ives painting shows pioneers crossing the Rocky Mountains through the South Pass.

train [trān] *noun, plural* **trains. 1.** a line of connected railroad cars being pulled by an engine. **2.** a group of vehicles, pack animals, or people traveling together: During the Civil War supplies were brought to the front by wagon *trains.* **3.** a connected series of ideas or events: The speaker lost his *train* of thought, and had to stop to check his notes. **4.** the part of a formal dress or gown that trails on the ground behind the wearer: Many wedding gowns have long *trains.*

—*verb,* **trained, training. 1.** to show or teach how to act in a certain way or carry out a particular task: Mike was *trained* to repair truck engines while he was in the army. ◆ Often used as an adjective: "He made me think of a *trained* baby elephant walking on hind-legs." (Joseph Conrad) ◆ A person who is being trained is called a **trainee. 2.** to get ready for some test or activity by repeated practice: She has been *training* for the marathon race by running at least five miles every day. **3.** to make something grow or go a certain way: Ralph *trained* his hair so that it would part on the left.

train•er [trā′nər] *noun, plural* **trainers. 1.** someone who helps an athlete exercise and get into condition for a sporting event. A trainer also treats minor injuries during a game or practice. **2.** someone who teaches animals to perform, as in a circus or zoo.

train•ing [trā′ning] *noun.* **1.** education or instruction in how to do something: Sally had three years of *training* to become a nurse. **2.** a program for good physical condition: He's on a soccer club that plays year-round and he has to stay in *training* all the time. ◆ All new soldiers in the army begin their service with a strict period of learning and exercise called **basic training.**

trait [trāt] *noun, plural* **traits.** a special feature or quality that sets one person or thing apart from others; a characteristic: "He was . . . deeply proud of what he produced, a *trait* rare in those war years when good workers were scarce." (Joseph Wambaugh)

trai•tor [trā′tər] *noun, plural* **traitors. 1.** a person who betrays his own country and helps its enemies: American general Benedict Arnold was a *traitor* who changed sides in the Revolutionary War to fight for the British. ◆ A person who acts in this way is **traitorous. 2.** anyone who betrays a cause or duty: He went to Rye High, but he's rooting for Harrison High to beat them in football—what a *traitor!*

tramp [tramp] *verb,* **tramped, tramping. 1.** to step or walk heavily: "Suddenly there was a growing murmur of voices and a great *tramping* of feet." (Joseph Conrad) **2.** to travel by foot; walk or hike: "We went in a different direction, and *tramped* for hours through woods where birds were scarce . . . ." (W. H. Hudson) —*noun, plural* **tramps. 1.** a person who has no home or job and wanders from place to place: In the Depression years, many men lost their jobs and became *tramps*. **2.** a heavy step, or the sound made by this.

tram•ple [tram′ pəl] *verb*, **trampled, trampling.** to walk heavily on, so as to crush or damage: A dog ran through the garden and *trampled* the flowers. "Lucky you didn't get *trampled* underfoot by the mob." (Lloyd Alexander)

tram•po•line [tram′ pə lēn′] *noun, plural* **trampolines.** a piece of strong netting or cloth that is attached by springs to a large metal frame. People bounce up and down and perform tumbling exercises on a trampoline.

tramway A *tramway* [tram′ wā′] has cars suspended on wires above the ground. This one is bringing skiers to Sandia Peak of New Mexico.

trance [trans] *noun, plural* **trances. 1.** a condition of the mind in which a person is only partly conscious and seems to be asleep: The magician hypnotized a man and put him in a *trance*. **2.** a state of mind in which a person is completely absorbed by something and not aware of what is happening: "Anne sat beside me in a *trance*, staring blankly ahead." (Iris Murdoch)

tran•quil [trang′ kwil] *adjective, more/most.* free from trouble or worry; calm; peaceful: "On Sunday morning the alarm clock dragged Miss Bramble out of a deep *tranquil* dream . . ." (Noel Coward) —**tranquillity** or **tranquility,** *noun.* —**tranquilly,** *adverb.*

tran•quil•iz•er [trang′ kwə lī zər] *noun, plural* **tranquilizers.** a drug used to calm the nerves or make a person less upset.

trans•ac•tion [tran zak′ shən] *noun, plural*

transactions. 1. the act of conducting a business deal or other such arrangement. **2. transactions.** the written record or minutes of a formal meeting.

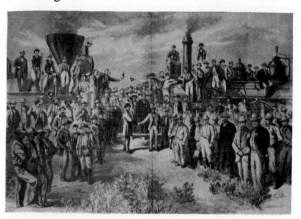

transcontinental The world's first transcontinental railroad was completed in 1869 when the tracks of the Central Pacific and Union Pacific met in the Promontory Mountains of northern Utah.

trans•con•ti•nen•tal [trans′ kän′ tə nen′ təl] *adjective.* going from one side of a continent to the other: a *transcontinental* railroad.

tran•scribe [tran skrīb′] *verb,* **transcribed, transcribing.** to make a written copy of something. —**transcription** [tran skrip′ shən], *noun.*

trans•fer [trans′ fər *or* trans fur′] *verb,* **transferred, transferring. 1.** to change or move from one place to another: "Mrs. B. *transferred* some of the soup to a smaller pot." (Wole Soyinka) **2.** to move a person officially from one job, position, or location to another: The company *transferred* him from Chicago to the San Francisco office. —*noun, plural* **transfers. 1.** the act or fact of transferring; a move from one place to another: A soldier who wants to be in a different unit can ask his commanding officer for a *transfer*. **2.** a ticket or pass that allows a person to change from one bus, train, or plane to another without paying an additional fare.

trans•fix [trans fiks′] *verb,* **transfixed, transfixing.** to make unable to move, as from shock or surprise: "I stood *transfixed* for what must have been several hours . . ." (Woody Allen)

Pronunciation Key: O–S			
ō	over; go	ou	out; town
ô	all; law	p	put; hop
oo	look; full	r	run; car
o͞o	pool; who	s	set; miss
oi	oil; boy	sh	show

(Turn the page for more information.)

811

trans•form [trans fôrm′] *verb*, **transformed, transforming.** to change greatly in form or appearance: The story of Cinderella tells of how she was *transformed* into a beautiful princess by her fairy godmother. ". . . with the aid of paste-pot and brush, I have *transformed* the walls into one gigantic picture." (Anne Frank) ◆ The fact of transforming is a **transformation.**

trans•form•er [trans fôr′mər] *noun, plural* **transformers. 1.** a person or thing that transforms. **2.** a device that changes the voltage of an electric current.

trans•fu•sion [trans fyo͞o′zhən] *noun, plural* **transfusions.** the transfer of blood from one person to another by medical means. People who need blood because of an accident or operation are given a transfusion.

tran•sis•tor [tran zis′tər] *noun, plural* **transistors.** a small, solid electronic device that is used to control the flow of electricity in computers, radios, televisions, and the like. Transistors replaced larger and less reliable vacuum tubes, so that many forms of electronic equipment could be made much smaller.

tran•sit [tran′sit] *noun.* the act of carrying or moving something: Our package hasn't arrived yet; the shipping company said it's still in *transit.*

tran•si•tion [tran zish′ən] *noun, plural* **transitions.** the fact of changing from one place or form to another: The *transition* from high school to college can be difficult for students.

words from one language to another: Constance Garnett was a famous *translator* who introduced English readers to the works of great Russian authors.

trans•la•tion [trans lā′shən] *noun, plural* **translations.** the changing of something spoken or written into another language: The announcement was given in English, followed by a Spanish *translation.*

trans•lu•cent [trans lo͞o′sənt] *adjective, more/most.* allowing some light to pass through, but not allowing what is on the other side to be seen clearly: Bathroom windows are often *translucent*, with glass that is cloudy rather than clear.

trans•mis•sion [trans mish′ən] *noun, plural* **transmissions. 1.** the act of transmitting; sending or passing something from one place to another: Certain insects can be dangerous to man because of their role in the *transmission* of disease. **2.** the broadcasting or sending out of radio and television signals. **3.** the series of gears that transfer power from the engine to the wheels of a car, truck, or other such vehicle.

trans•mit [trans mit′] *verb*, **transmitted, transmitting. 1.** to send or pass on from one person or place to another: "He pressed a button and *transmitted* an order to the ship's crew." (Jules Verne) "Mr. Effingham . . . *transmitted* to Marmaduke, for safe-keeping, all his valuable effects and papers . . ." (James Fenimore Cooper) **2.** to send out radio or television signals.

---

transition A *transition* is a movement from one point to another. In writing about events, you tend to organize your story or article by TIME ORDER. In that case you will probably make transitions by using words and phrases such as *first, second, after that, and then, later, next, before,* and *finally.* If places are described, your transitional expressions may be *next to, on, behind, around, in the middle, over, above,* and so on. If you organize a paper by joining ideas, you'll use *however, for example, therefore, yet, that is, because, actually, on the other hand,* etc. So far, we've said nothing about transitions from one paragraph to another. Suppose you were writing about deltas (the spread-out, fan-like land at the end of a large river where it meets the sea). You might start a new paragraph by saying "There are cities on deltas, and none is better known than New Orleans." The point is to connect to your main subject by using detail, especially *interesting* detail.

---

trans•late [trans′lāt] *verb*, **translated, translating. 1.** to change something spoken or written into another language: This novel was written in French and then *translated* into English for American readers. **2.** to explain or say in other words: "He took us to the dining hall for a 'little snack,' which *translated* itself into a five-course meal . . ." (Farley Mowat) **—translator,** *noun.* a person who translates

trans•mit•ter [trans mit′ər] *noun, plural* **transmitters.** an electronic device for sending out radio and television signals.

trans•par•ent [trans pâr′ənt] *adjective, more/most.* **1.** able to be seen through clearly: Eyeglasses are *transparent.* ◆ The fact of being transparent is **transparency. 2.** easily understood or detected; not able to hide or conceal: Danny's excuse was so *transparent* that I knew right away he wasn't telling the truth. **—transparently,** *adverb*.

trans•plant [trans plant/] *verb,* **transplanted, transplanting. 1.** to dig up and move a plant from one place to another: Because the bush had grown so quickly, it needed to be *transplanted* to a larger pot. **2.** to move from one place to another: He's a *transplanted* New Yorker who now lives in southern California. **3.** to transfer an organ or body part from one person to another by an operation: The doctor *transplanted* one of the mother's kidneys into her son's body because his kidneys were failing. ♦ Also used as a noun: a heart *transplant*.

transport In World War II, famous ocean liners were used as troop transports. Here the *Queen Elizabeth* brings soldiers home to New York at the war's end.

trans•port [trans pôrt/] *verb,* **transported, transporting.** to bring or carry someone or something from one place to another: "The track served mainly to *transport* timber from one station to another, a dozen miles apart." (Jerzy Kosinski) "It was as if I had suddenly been *transported* into another world." (S. J. Perlman) —[trans/ pôrt] *noun, plural* **transports. 1.** the act or fact of transporting: "For *transport* in and around Mayapore she rode a . . . Raleigh bicycle." (Paul Scott) **2.** a ship, truck, or airplane used to carry soldiers or military supplies.

trans•por•ta•tion [trans/ pər tā/ shən] *noun.* the fact of moving people or things from one place to another: Before the invention of cars and trains, riding on horseback was a common form of *transportation*.

trap [trap] *noun, plural* **traps. 1.** a device used to catch and hold a wild animal: People use mouse*traps* to rid a house of mice. African natives used to dig a large pit as an elephant *trap.* **2.** a trick used to catch someone by

surprise: The robbers walked right into a *trap*— the police were waiting for them inside the bank. —*verb,* **trapped, trapping.** to catch in a trap: Pioneers in early America used to *trap* animals such as beavers for their valuable fur. "I am usually happier alone than in company, and I felt *trapped* at this house." (Paul Theroux)

trap door a small door that is set in a ceiling, floor, or roof and that is slid or lifted to open.

tra•peze [tra pēz/] *noun, plural* **trapezes.** a strong, short bar hung between two ropes. A trapeze is used to swing on by acrobats in a circus or by performers in gymnastics.

trap•e•zoid [trap/ ə zoid/] *noun, plural* **trapezoids.** a figure having four sides, with only two sides being parallel to each other.

trap•per [trap/ ər] *noun, plural* **trappers.** a person who uses traps, especially someone who catches wild animals for their fur.

trapper "A Fur Trapper in the American West," by the famous frontier artist Frederic Remington.

trash [trash] *noun.* things that are of no use and are to be thrown away; rubbish: a pile of empty bottles, old newspapers, and other *trash.*

trau•ma [trô/ mə] *noun, plural* **traumas.** a serious physical injury or mental shock: A *trauma* center in a hospital gives emergency treatment to accident victims. **—traumatic,** *adjective.* being or causing a great injury or shock.

trav•el [trav/ əl] *verb,* **traveled, traveling** or **travelled, travelling. 1.** to go from one place to

Pronunciation Key: A–F			
a	and; hat	ch	chew; such
ā	ate; stay	d	dog; lid
â	care; air	e	end; yet
ä	father; hot	ē	she; each
b	boy; cab	f	fun; off
(Turn the page for more information.)			

another for business or pleasure: She wants to *travel* in Europe during her summer off from college. ◆ Also used as an adjective: a well-*traveled* path, a foreign news reporter who is widely-*traveled*. **2.** to pass or move from one point to another: "The news about Eddoes and the shoes *travelled* round the street pretty quickly." (V. S. Naipaul) —**traveler** or **traveller,** *noun.*

trav•erse [trav′ərs *or* trə vurs′] *verb,* **traversed, traversing.** to pass or go over or through: "He drove slowly downtown and . . . *traversed* the deserted streets of the business section . . ." (F. Scott Fitzgerald)

trawl [trôl] *noun, plural* **trawls.** a long fishing line with many hooks or a net that is dragged slowly along an ocean or lake bottom to catch fish. —*verb,* **trawled, trawling.** to fish with a trawl. ◆ A boat that fishes in this way is a **trawler.**

tray [trā] *noun, plural* **trays.** a flat, shallow dish with a small rim, used for carrying or displaying things: Waiters carry food and dishes on *trays.* The jeweler removed the *tray* of diamond rings from the display case.

treach•er•ous [trech′ ər əs] *adjective, more/most.* **1.** not to be trusted or relied on; disloyal: "I lead people on to trust me and then I turn on them. I'm well known for being *treacherous.*" (John Mortimer) ◆ The fact of being treacherous is **treachery. 2.** not as safe as it appears to be; dangerous: ". . . a perfect wilderness crossed by some of the most *treacherous* streams and fords that I have ever encountered." (Gore Vidal) —**treacherously,** *adverb.*

tread [tred] *verb,* **trod, trodden** or **trod, treading.** to walk on, along, or over something, especially in a rough way: American patriots in the Revolutionary War carried a flag with a picture of a snake and the motto, "Don't *Tread* on Me." —*noun, plural* **treads. 1.** the act or sound of walking. **2.** the grooved surface of a tire or the bottom of the shoe.

trea•son [trē′ zən] *noun.* the crime of betraying one's country by aiding its enemies. Acts of treason can include fighting against one's own country in wartime, or giving away a country's military secrets to the enemy.

treas•ure [trezh′ ər] *noun, plural* **treasures. 1.** wealth such as gold, silver, jewels, and so on, stored away or kept hidden: Pirates of the 1600's were known to hide or bury their stolen *treasure* on desert islands. **2.** anything that is very precious or valuable: "A clever child is a great *treasure* in an establishment like mine."

(Frances Hodgson Burnett) —*verb,* **treasured, treasuring.** to value highly; prize: ". . . the only one who kept and *treasured* a picture of his loved ones." (Colleen McCullough)

treas•ur•er [trezh′ ər ər] *noun, plural* **treasurers.** the person who is responsible for taking care of the money that belongs to a business, club, government, or other organization.

treas•ur•y [trezh′ ər ē] *noun, plural* **treasuries. 1.** the money belonging to a business, government, or other organization. **2. Treasury.** the department of the U. S. government that is in charge of manufacturing, collecting, and managing the country's money.

treat [trēt] *verb,* **treated, treating. 1.** to act or deal with in a particular way: "Sissy *treated* them like important human beings." (Betty Smith) ". . . black children here were trained to *treat* their elders with politeness and respect." (Alex Haley) **2.** to give medical care or treatment: The doctor *treated* the man's broken arm by putting a cast on it. **3.** to pay for the food or entertainment of another person: On Mom's birthday her friends *treated* her to lunch at her favorite restaurant. —*noun, plural* **treats.** anything that is a special or unexpected pleasure: For dessert we had fresh raspberries—a real *treat.*

treat•ment [trēt′ mənt] *noun, plural* **treatments.** the fact or way of treating a person or thing: The captured soldiers received cruel *treatment* in the prison camp.

treat•y [trē′ tē] *noun, plural* **treaties.** a formal agreement made between two or more groups or countries: Fighting in World War I was officially ended by the *Treaty* of Versailles.

tree [trē] *noun, plural* **trees.** a tall, woody plant that has a main stem or trunk from which branches and leaves or needles grow. —*verb,* **treed, treeing.** to chase up a tree: The hunting dogs had *treed* the raccoon and were barking wildly at the foot of the tree.

trek [trek] *noun, plural* **treks.** a long, difficult journey: The Arab travelers grew very short of water in their *trek* across the desert. —*verb,* **trekked, trekking.** to make a long, difficult journey: "He caught another train to Euston, *trekked* back to Charing Cross." (John Le Carré) ◆ *Trek* comes from a South African word meaning "a long journey by ox cart."

trel•lis [trel′ is] *noun, plural* **trellises.** a framework of wood or other material for plants to grow on.

trem•ble [trem′ bəl] *verb,* **trembled, trembling. 1.** to shake or shiver without control: "He was *trembling* and crying with sickness and fear." (John Cheever) **2.** to move quickly back and forth or shake: "He . . . danced around the room. The whole house seemed to *tremble* from his powerful weight." (James Houston)

tre•men•dous [tri men′ dəs] *adjective.* very large, strong, or great: The book *Moby Dick* tells of a hunt for a *tremendous* white whale. "He . . . seemed to have a *tremendous* desire to be nice and do the right thing." (Ernie Pyle) —**tremendously,** *adverb:* "Books impressed me *tremendously* . . ." (Jerzy Kosinski)

tre•mor [trem′ ər] *noun, plural* **tremors.** a shaking or vibrating movement: Did you feel the *tremors* from the earthquake this morning? "At the door of the new stall a *tremor* of fear shook her." (Marguerite Henry)

trem•u•lous [trem′ yə ləs] *adjective.* affected by trembling; shaking: "Jack's voice went on, *tremulous* yet determined . . ." (William Golding)

trench [trench] *noun, plural* **trenches. 1.** a long, narrow ditch: Workmen dug a *trench* along the road to allow the water to drain more quickly. **2.** a long ditch with earth piled high on one side, dug by soldiers for protection from enemy fire. **3.** a long, narrow depression in the ocean floor.

trench Much of World War I was fought in deep trenches across western France. This picture shows French soldiers in the early part of the war.

trend [trend] *noun, plural* **trends.** a particular direction or course that is being followed, as by a group of people: Shorter skirts for women are becoming a popular fashion *trend* this year. Recently there's been a *trend* in the U. S. toward eating less red meat.

trend•y [tren′ dē] *adjective,* **trendier, trendiest.** *Informal.* keeping up with or influenced by the latest styles: She's a *trendy* dresser who is sure to be seen wearing the newest 'in' look.

tres•pass [tres′ pas′ *or* tres′ pəs] *verb,* **trespassed, trespassing.** to break the law by entering or passing through someone else's property without permission: The farmer did not want deer hunters on his land and had posted large signs saying "No *Trespassing.*" ◆ A person who commits the crime of trespassing is a **trespasser.** —*noun, plural* **trespasses. 1.** in law, the act of trespassing. **2.** an older word for a sin or a wrong act: The Lord's Prayer asks God to "forgive us our *trespasses.*"

tress•es [tres′ iz] *plural noun.* long hair, especially a woman's hair worn long and loose.

trestle The Secrettown Trestle in the Sierra Nevada Mountains of California. It was built by Chinese laborers for the Central Pacific Railroad in 1877.

tres•tle [tres′ əl] *noun, plural* **trestles.** a wooden or metal framework that supports a bridge or other structure.

trial [trī′ əl] *noun, plural* **trials. 1.** the process of hearing and judging evidence in a court of law, to determine if a person is guilty of a crime, if someone should pay damages to another, and so on: to be on *trial* for murder. **2.** any test or study to determine the value or quality of a thing. ◆ Also used as an adjective: The new car was taken out for a *trial* run to make sure everything worked properly. **3.** something that causes suffering or is difficult to deal with: His long illness was a *trial* for the whole family.

trial and error a method of solving a problem by continuing to try different approaches until one is found that works.

	Pronunciation Key: G–N		
g	give; big	k	kind; cat; back
h	hold	l	let; ball
i	it; this	m	make; time
ī	ice; my	n	not; own
j	jet; gem; edge	ng	having

(Turn the page for more information.)

T

> **triangle style** The *triangle style*, or *pyramid style*, is associated with newspaper and magazine writing. The name comes from the idea that the story line of a piece of writing has the shape of an inverted triangle: ▽. That is, major points are made at the beginning of the piece, and it doesn't have a summary or "big ending." The writer teacher Donald Murray has said, "When I was on a newspaper I knew journalists who had never written an ending, whose stories just trailed off." This triangle style came about because of the nature of the newspaper story. Suppose a reporter writes a story that is ten column inches long. The actual length of the published piece might be only seven column inches, or even four. If this happens and the key to the story is in the tenth inch of copy, the story is in trouble.

tri•an•gle [trī′ ang′ gəl] *noun, plural* **triangles.** **1.** a figure having three sides and three angles, like this: △ **2.** a musical instrument made from a bent metal bar in the shape of a triangle. A triangle is struck with a small stick to make a bell-like sound.

tri•an•gu•lar [trī ang′ gyə lər] *adjective.* being or having to do with a triangle.

tri•bal [trī′ bəl] *adjective.* having to do with a tribe or tribes: a *tribal* custom.

tribe [trīb] *noun, plural* **tribes.** a group of people who live in the same area and have certain things in common, such as the same language, customs, and religious beliefs. ◆ *Tribe* has mainly been used to describe groups of native people in the Americas, Asia, and Africa.

trib•u•tar•y [trib′ yə ter′ ē] *noun, plural* **tributaries.** a smaller river or stream that flows into and joins a larger river: The Illinois River and Arkansas River are important *tributaries* of the Mississippi River.

trib•ute [trib′ yo͞ot′] *noun, plural* **tributes.** **1.** an act done to show respect or to honor someone: The Memorial Day holiday pays *tribute* to those who died in America's wars. "The terms changed—the Big Guy, the Leader . . . the Boss Man—whatever the title, it was one of *tribute*." (George Plimpton) **2.** a forced payment: The pirate captain demanded *tribute* from the merchant ship before he would allow it to pass.

trick [trik] *noun, plural* **tricks.** **1.** something done to fool or cheat a person: It seemed the prisoner was asleep in his cell, but it was a *trick*—he had put a dummy in the bed and escaped. **2.** an act that shows cleverness or skill; a stunt: Magicians often perform *tricks* such as pulling a rabbit out of a hat. —*verb,* **tricked, tricking.** to deceive someone with a trick; fool or cheat: The horse trader *tricked* them by switching the horse they'd bought for one that was sick and lame. ◆ The use of tricks to fool or cheat someone is **trickery.**

trick•le [trik′ əl] *verb,* **trickled, trickling. 1.** to flow or fall in drops or in a thin, slow, stream: ". . . a tear or two *trickled* down his cheek." (Lewis Carroll) **2.** to move slowly, a little at a time: They expected a lot of mail, but only a few letters have *trickled* in from day to day. —*noun, plural* **trickles:** "We can barely exist on the few *trickles* of oil we get out of the ground . . ." (Art Buchwald)

trick•y [trik′ ē] *adjective,* **trickier, trickiest. 1.** using tricks to fool or deceive; cunning; sly: The *tricky* salesman would promise customers anything to get them to agree to buy. **2.** requiring careful handling or skill: Be careful; some of the questions on the test are really *tricky.*

tri•cy•cle [trī′ sik əl] *noun, plural* **tricycles.** a child's vehicle that has three wheels and is usually moved by pedals.

tried [trīd] *verb.* the past form of **try.**

tri•fle [trī′ fəl] *noun, plural* **trifles. 1.** something of little value or importance: The waitress had added the bill wrong, but he didn't want to argue over a *trifle* of four cents difference. **2. a trifle.** a little bit: ". . . George, who was *a trifle* annoyed that his hook idea hadn't worked." (E. B. White) —*verb,* **trifled, trifling.** to treat something in a careless or joking way: "Essay did not *trifle* with reports of mischief in church or Sunday school." (Wole Soyinka)

trig•ger [trig′ ər] *noun, plural* **triggers.** a small lever pressed or pulled on by the finger to fire a gun. —*verb,* **triggered, triggering.** to cause or start something: The citizens' protest *triggered* a full-scale revolt.

trig•o•nom•e•try [trig′ ə näm′ ə trē] *noun.* a branch of mathematics that deals with the relations of the sides and angles of triangles.

tril•lion [tril′ yən] *noun, plural* **trillions;** *adjective.* a thousand billion, written as 1,000,000,000,000.

tril•o•gy [tril′ ə jē] *noun, plural* **trilogies.** a group of three novels, plays, or other works, each complete in itself but related to the others.

trim [trim] *verb,* **trimmed, trimming. 1.** to make something neat by cutting or chopping: The butcher *trimmed* the extra fat off the piece of beef. "His hair had been *trimmed* short with a clipper." (John R. Tunis) **2.** to decorate: to *trim* a Christmas tree. —*noun, plural* **trims. 1.** the state of being in good physical shape or condition: The boxer was in fighting *trim* for his big match. **2.** something used to decorate or finish. —*adjective,* **trimmer, trimmest.** in good condition or shape; neat: to keep a room *trim.*

trim•ming [trim′ ing] *noun, plural* **trimmings. 1.** something used as a decoration or ornament. **2. trimmings.** things that usually go along to accompany something else: My mother made Thanksgiving dinner with all the *trimmings.* **3.** something that has been trimmed.

trin•ket [tring′ kit] *noun, plural* **trinkets.** a small ornament, toy, or piece of inexpensive jewelry.

tri•o [trē′ ō] *noun, plural* **trios.** a group of three, especially a group of three musicians.

trip [trip] *noun, plural* **trips.** the act of traveling from one place to another, as in a car, train, bus, plane, and so on. Sam made a *trip* to his home town to visit his parents for Christmas. —*verb,* **tripped, tripping. 1.** to catch the foot and lose one's balance; fall or almost fall: "He hurried so fast that he *tripped* over a door mat and fell." (Lois Lenski) **2.** to walk with quick, light steps. **3. trip up.** to cause to make a mistake: He tried to *trip* her *up* by asking the question in a tricky, complicated way.

tripe [trīp] *noun.* **1.** the walls of the stomach of cattle used as food. **2.** something bad or useless: "Only five minutes ago his poem had still seemed to him a living thing; now he knew it . . . for the worthless *tripe* that it was." (George Orwell)

tri•ple [trip′ əl] *adjective.* **1.** having three parts: A **triple play** in baseball is one in which three outs are made on the same play. **2.** three times as much or as many: Those who work this Sunday will get *triple* pay. —*noun, plural* **tri-**

ples. a series or combination of three, especially a hit in baseball by which the batter reaches third base. —*verb,* **tripled, tripling.** to make or become three times as much: The company's profits have *tripled* since last year.

trip•let [trip′ lit] *noun, plural* **triplets. 1.** one of three children born to the same mother at the same time. **2.** a group of three lines of poetry.

tri•pod [trī′ päd′] *noun, plural* **tripods.** a three-legged support or stand used for holding a camera or telescope steady.

---

trite writing Suppose a writer is describing how he visited a city and took a taxicab to the airport. The writer says, "The area around the airport is growing *by leaps and bounds.* New buildings are *sprouting up like weeds.* The airport traffic was *all tied up in knots.* Then a car cut us off and the cab driver got *as mad as a wet hen.* He turned *as red as a beet.*" These are *trite* expressions (also called *clichés*). Not only are the expressions overused, but also complaining about taxi drivers is so frequent that it is trite in itself. Many people have ridden with an angry cabdriver. What would not be trite? "During a ten-minute cab ride today, I decided what I would do for the next four years of my life."

---

tri•umph [trī′ əmf] *verb,* **triumphed, triumphing.** to win or gain victory: After months of battle, the king's soldiers finally *triumphed* over the invading army. "They *triumphed* because they refused to be turned aside by difficulties or opposition." (Helen Keller) —*noun, plural* **triumphs.** a great victory: As the game ended the winning players carried their coach off the field in *triumph.*

tri•um•phant [trī um′ fənt] *adjective, more/most.* showing or being a triumph: "General Washington is to make his *triumphant* entry into the city." (Gore Vidal) —**triumphantly,** *adverb.*

triv•i•al [triv′ ē əl] *adjective, more/most.* not important; minor; insignificant: The newspaper was delivered later than usual today, but she shouldn't get so upset over such a *trivial* matter. ". . . a quarrel between Dussel and the Franks over something very *trivial:* the sharing out of the butter." (Anne Frank) —**trivia,** *noun.* **1.** things that are not important. **2.** a quiz or game of short factual questions about details of history, the arts, and so on. ◆ In the Middle Ages, the *trivium* were a group of school sub-

Pronunciation Key: O–S			
ō	over; go	ou	out; town
ô	all; law	p	put; hop
oo	look; full	r	run; car
o͞o	pool; who	s	set; miss
oi	oil; boy	sh	show

(Turn the page for more information.)

T

jects that were considered less important than other subjects.

trod [träd] *verb.* the past tense of **tread.**

trod•den [träd′ən] *verb.* a past participle of **tread:** "He came to a wide gap which had been *trodden* into mud by cattle." (Richard Adams)

Trojan Horse According to a famous legend, Greek soldiers hid inside the Trojan Horse, which the Trojans thought was a gift and brought inside the city walls.

Tro•jan [trō′jən] *noun, plural* **Trojans.** a person from ancient TROY. —*adjective.* of or having to do with Troy.

troll¹ [trōl] *verb,* **trolled, trolling.** to fish by moving a line and hook, as from a slow-moving boat.

troll² *noun, plural* **trolls.** in old folk tales, a dwarf or giant that lives underground or in a cave or hill.

trol•ley [träl′ē] *noun, plural* **trolleys. 1.** a small wheel that moves along an overhead electrical wire to run a streetcar, train, or bus. **2.** *also,* **trolley car.** an electric streetcar that gets its power from a trolley.

trom•bone [träm bōn′ or träm′ bōn′] *noun, plural* **trombones.** a brass musical instrument made up of two long, U-shaped tubes that are connected. The sound is changed by moving a sliding piece back and forth.

troop [trōop] *noun, plural* **troops. 1.** *also,* **troops.** a group of soldiers; a military unit, such as a unit of cavalry. **2.** a group or gathering of people doing something together: "Once a *troop* of children rushed in and chased each other noisily . . ." (J. M. Coetzee) **3.** a unit of Boy Scouts or Girl Scouts. —*verb,* **trooped, trooping.** to march or walk in a group: "At this time of summer evening, the cows are *trooping* down from the hills . . ." (William Makepeace Thackeray)

troop•er [trōo′pər] *noun, plural* **troopers. 1.** a state police officer. **2.** a cavalry soldier.

tro•phy [trō′fē] *noun, plural* **trophies.** a small statue, cup, or other object awarded to someone for winning an award or contest.

tropical [träp′i kəl] *adjective, more/most.* having to do with or found in the tropics: Bananas are a *tropical* fruit. Monkeys live mainly in *tropical* forests.

trop•ics [träp′iks] *plural noun.* the region of the earth that lies on or near the equator. The sun is strongest at the equator, so areas in the tropics have hot weather almost all the time.

trot [trät] *noun, plural* **trots.** a movement of a four-legged animal, between a walk and a run. When a horse moves at a trot, it lifts one front foot and the opposite rear foot off the ground at the same time. ♦ The sport of racing horses who run in this way is **trotting,** and such a horse is a **trotter.** —*verb,* **trotted, trotting. 1.** of an animal or a rider, to move or go at a trot. **2.** to move more quickly than walking: "The Motorcycle Boy was ready to move on again and we *trotted* along behind him." (S. E. Hinton)

Trot•sky [trät′skē] **Leon,** 1879-1940, Russian revolutionary leader.

trou•ble [trub′əl] *noun, plural* **troubles. 1.** something that causes danger, suffering, worry, and so on; a problem or difficulty: Jerry is in *trouble* because he was fighting with another boy at school. "That was the *trouble* with people those days—they didn't think . . ." (Flannery O'Connor) **2.** extra effort or work: Grandma went to a lot of *trouble* making sure everything was just right for our holiday dinner. **3.** an illness or ailment: heart *trouble,* stomach *trouble.* —*verb,* **troubled, troubling. 1.** to cause someone to be worried, anxious, upset, and so on; disturb; distress. **2.** to cause someone to do extra work: Can I *trouble* you to mail this package on your way downtown? **3.** to cause pain or illness: Mel has been *troubled* by a bad back for some time.

trou•ble•some [trub′əl səm] *adjective, more/most.* causing trouble; difficult or annoying: Crab grass is a *troublesome* weed that often grows up in lawns and gardens.

trough [trôf] *noun, plural* **troughs. 1.** a long, narrow box or container used for feeding or watering farm animals. **2.** any long, narrow, hollow place like this.

troupe [trōop] *noun, plural* **troupes. 1.** a group of actors or other performers. **2.** any such group or company: "It was the custom for the little girls . . . to walk to Penn Street School together, in a morning *troupe* that sometimes held fifteen or so." (M. F. K. Fisher)

T

trou•sers [trou′zərz] *plural noun.* a piece of clothing with two legs that covers the body from the waist to the ankles; pants. ◆ Usually used to refer to clothing for men or boys.

trout Three types of trout. Brown trout (back), brook trout (center), and rainbow trout (foreground).

trout [trout] *noun, plural* **trout** or **trouts.** any of several kinds of fish that live in cool, clear, fresh water. Trout are often eaten as food and are a very popular game fish.

Troy [troi] an ancient city in Asia, in what is now Turkey. Ancient Greek legends tell of the **Tro-jan War,** a great war thousands of years ago in which the army of Troy was defeated by the Greeks.

tru•ant [trōō′ənt] *adjective.* **1.** of a student, absent from school without permission. In for-mer times, a **truant officer** was someone whose job was to go around and find such students. —*noun, plural* **truants. 1.** a student who is absent from school without permission. **2.** a person who fails to do his work or duty. ◆ The fact of being a truant is **truancy** [trōō′ ən sē].

truce [trōōs] *noun, plural* **truces. 1.** a short time when fighting is halted; a break in a battle or war. A truce may be called so that those who are fighting can talk about how they can come to a peaceful settlement. **2.** any period of relief from fighting, conflict, and so on.

truck [truk] *noun, plural* **trucks. 1.** a motor vehicle that is larger, heavier, and more strong-ly built than a car, and that is used mainly for carrying goods rather than people. There are many types of trucks, from light **pickup trucks** that carry loads of one or two tons, to huge **trailer trucks** carrying 40 tons or more. **2.** *also,*

hand truck. a low frame or vehicle having wheels at one end and a handle at the other, used for moving heavy objects by hand, such as boxes in a store or warehouse. —*verb,* **trucked, trucking.** to drive a truck or carry something on a truck: Those cars are sent here by railroad and then *trucked* to the local dealers. ◆ A person whose work is driving a truck is a **trucker.**

Tru•deau [trōō′ dō′] **Pierre Elliot,** born 1919, Canadian political leader, prime minister of Canada from 1968 to 1979 and 1980 to 1984.

trudge [truj] *verb,* **trudged, trudging.** to walk in a slow, tired way: "They *trudged* across the sand, sweating in the windless air and the hot yellow sun." (Thomas Pynchon) —*noun, plural* **trudges:** "I started the long *trudge* across the fields . . ." (John Knowles)

true [trōō] *adjective,* **truer, truest. 1.** agreeing with the facts; not false or made up: I know that's a *true* story, because I was there myself and saw the whole thing. The statement read "Paris is the capital of France," so she marked *True* on her quiz paper. **2.** actually being what it is called; genuine; authentic: a *true* diamond. "Scientists divide trout into two groups: the *true* trout and the chars." (Carl Hubbs) **3.** faithful and loyal: He was *true* to his word and paid back every cent he borrowed. **4. come true.** to happen just as was dreamed, hoped, expected, and so on. —*adverb.* in a true way; truly.

tru•ly [trōō′ lē] *adverb.* **1.** in a true way; sin-cerely: Kenny's mother made him apologize, but I don't think he's *truly* sorry for what happened. **2.** in fact; indeed: If you read this book you'll agree she's *truly* a great writer.

Tru•man [trōō′ mən] **Harry S.,** 1884-1972, the thirty-third president of the United States, from 1945 to 1953.

trum•pet [trum′ pit] *noun, plural* **trumpets. 1.** a brass musical instrument, made up of a long tube that is curved into a loop and has a wide opening at one end. It is played by blowing into a mouthpiece at the other end and pressing down on valves on top of the tube. **2.** something that is shaped like a trumpet or that makes such

T

Pronunciation Key· T–Z			
t	ten; date	v	very; live
th	think	w	win; away
th	these	y	you
u	cut; butter	z	zoo; cause
ur	turn; bird	zh	measure

(Turn the page for more information.)

T

a sound. —*verb,* **trumpeted, trumpeting. 1.** to blow a trumpet or make a sound like that of a trumpet: *An elephant is said to* trumpet *when it blows air out from its trunk in a loud, shrill cry.*

trun•dle [trun′dəl] *verb,* **trundled, trundling.** to go along or roll on wheels: *"He remembered the years he had spent there* trundling *the heavy cars of ore in and out of the tunnel . . ."* (Frank Norris) ◆ A **trundle bed** is a low bed that can be pushed under another bed for storage.

trunk [trungk] *noun, plural* **trunks. 1.** the thick main stem of a tree, from which the branches and roots grow. **2.** the part of the human body from which the head, arms, and legs extend. **3.** a large, strong box used to store clothes and belongings, or carry them for travel. **4.** an enclosed area in a car, usually at the rear, for carrying or storing things. **5.** the long, flexible nose part of an elephant, used for drawing in air, food, and water, or for grasping objects. **6. trunks.** men's shorts or underwear: *swimming* trunks.

trust [trust] *verb,* **trusted, trusting. 1.** to believe that someone is honest, fair, reliable, and so

trustworthy. 2. property or money held and managed by one person or group for the benefit of another: *The child actor's earnings are being held in* trust *until he reaches the age of 18.* ◆ A **trust fund** is money or property held in this way. **3.** an agreement by which a group of different businesses or companies combine to control how much of a product is available and how much it costs. *Trusts of this kind are generally illegal in the U. S. (under* **antitrust laws**), *because they eliminate competition and drive up prices unfairly.* —**trustful,** *adjective.*

trus•tee [trus′tē′] *noun, plural* **trustees. 1.** a person who has the legal authority to manage the property of another. **2.** one of a group of people who manage the affairs of a college, church, or other such organization.

truth [trooth] *noun, plural* **truths. 1.** something that agrees with the facts; something that is true: *A witness in court is required by law to tell the* truth. *He wasn't really sick—the* truth *is, he just didn't want to go.* **2.** the fact or quality of being true: *There's a lot of* truth *in what she said.*

truthful writing A "truthful" story does not have to be a repeating of something that actually happened to you. But it should be true in these ways: (1) People should behave in a realistic way. You can make up a story of a flying saucer from outer space landing in someone's living room. But if the family doesn't notice this, or doesn't react to it, that isn't funny, it's just unrealistic. (2) Time should resemble real time. Don't take every funny thing your brother ever did in his life and write a story in which all those things happen before breakfast one morning. (3) Don't try to be more cute and clever than real life is. Among five boys in real life, one might have a colorful nickname like "the Badger." But don't have a story with five friends whose names are Badger, Speedo, Pie, Fuzzy, and Z.T. (4) Don't over-control the events in the story. The reader should not be able to say in advance, "Oh, I get it. While Fuzzy is doing his funny imitation of the teacher, she'll walk up behind him but he'll keep on without noticing her. I've seen this so many times on TV!"

on; have confidence in: *They didn't know how much the old painting was really worth, but they* trusted *her to pay them a fair price. "He had never* trusted *me to drive his father's car before . . ."* (John Updike) ◆ Often used as an adjective: *"Mrs. Aubrey has been Mr. Rand's* trusted *secretary at the First American Financial Corporation for years."* (Jerzy Kosinski) **2.** to believe in the strength or soundness of something; depend on: *I don't* trust *that elevator ever since someone got stuck in it for several hours.* **3.** to feel sure of; expect: *"I* trust *her mother brought along a few things on her own account."* (Irving Stone)

—*noun, plural* **trusts. 1.** the act or fact of trusting. ◆ A person who deserves trust is

truth•ful [trooth′fəl] *adjective, more/most.* telling the truth, or likely to tell the truth; honest: *This book is an accurate,* truthful *account of what life is like today in the Soviet Union.* —**truthfully,** *adverb.* —**truthfulness,** *noun.*

try [trī] *verb,* **tried, trying. 1.** to work toward doing something; make an effort: *He's* trying *to lose weight with a diet.* **2.** to use something in order to test its quality or effect: *Try* this new fruit drink and see how you like it. **3.** to strain a person's nerves, patience, and so on: *Patriot Thomas Paine said of the American Revolution, "These are the times that* try *men's souls."* **4.** to examine a case in a court of law; put a person on trial. **5. try on.** to put on clothing to see how it looks or fits. —*noun, plural* **tries.** an attempt to do something: In the high jump you get three *tries* to get over the bar.

try·out [trī′ out′] *noun, plural* **tryouts.** a test to see how well a person can do something: The drama club is having *tryouts* for the spring play.
♦ Also used as a verb: You can't play in our town soccer league unless you *try out* first.

T-shirt [tē′ shurt′] *noun, plural* **T-shirts.** a light, close-fitting shirt with short sleeves, worn under other clothes or as an outer shirt.

tub [tub] *noun, plural* **tubs. 1.** a large, open container for taking a bath; a bathtub. **2.** a small, round container used to keep or serve butter or other such foods.

tu·ba [tōō′ bə] *noun, plural* **tubas.** a very large brass musical instrument with a deep tone.

tube [tōōb] *noun, plural* **tubes. 1.** a hollow piece of rubber, plastic, glass, or metal that is shaped like a long pipe. Liquids and gases pass through or are held by tubes. **2.** any long, tubelike part or organ of the body, such as the BRONCHIAL TUBES. **3.** a container that is long and narrow and must be squeezed to get its contents out. Toothpaste and some shampoos come in tubes. **4.** an underground or underwater tunnel through which a train or subway runs.

tu·ber·cu·lo·sis [tə bur′ kyə lō′ sis] *noun.* a serious disease that affects the lungs or other parts of the body; also called **TB** or (formerly) **consumption.** It is caused by bacteria that can be passed from one person to another. Modern drugs can now prevent and treat this disease, but it is still a threat in some countries.

Harriet Tubman

Tub·man [tub′ mən]   **Harriet,**   1820?-1913, American anti-slavery leader.

tuck [tuk] *verb,* **tucked, tucking. 1.** to fold or push the ends or edges of something into place: "There were a couple of colored feathers *tucked* into the band of his hat . . ." (Raymond Chandler) **2.** to wrap or cover a person snugly in bed: "Every night he *tucked* her into the little crib that he had made with his hands for her." (Alex Haley) **3.** to hide or put into a safe or covered space: "I crept into my favorite hiding place, the little closet *tucked* under my stairs." (Jean Fritz) —*noun, plural* **tucks.** a fold of cloth that is sewn into a piece of clothing as a decoration or to make it fit better.

Tuc·son [tōō′ sän] a city in southeastern Arizona. *Population:* 331,000.

Tues·day [tōōz′ dā′] *noun, plural* **Tuesdays.** the third day of the week.

tuft [tuft] *noun, plural* **tufts.** a bunch of feathers, hair, grass, threads or other such material growing or fastened together at one end and loose at the other.

tug [tug] *verb,* **tugged, tugging.** to give a hard pull on something: The little girl reached up to her mother's arm and *tugged* on her sleeve. —*noun, plural* **tugs. 1.** a hard pull: He felt a *tug* at the end of the line and knew he'd hooked a fish. **2.** see **tugboat.**

tugboat A tugboat guiding a freighter into the harbor at the port of Baltimore, Maryland.

tug·boat [tug′ bōt′] *noun, plural* **tugboats.** a small but powerful boat that pushes or pulls larger boats, ships, or barges loaded with cargo.
♦ This boat is also called a **tug** or a **towboat.**

Pronunciation Key: [ə] Symbol

The [ə] or *schwa* sound occurs in syllables without an accent. It can be spelled with any vowel, such as **a** in above, **e** in listen, **i** in pencil, **o** in melon, **u** in circus. It can also be a combination of vowels, such as **io** in action, **ai** in mountain, **iou** in precious.

(Turn the page for more information.)

T

tu·i·tion [tōo ish′ ən] *noun.* the money that is paid for a student's instruction at a university or private school.

tu·lip [tōo′ lip] *noun, plural* **tulips.** a cup-shaped flower with thick petals. Each flower grows at the end of a long stem that comes out of the ground from a bulb. A tulip may be one of many bright colors, such as red, yellow, or pink.

Tul·sa [tul′ sə] a city in northeastern Oklahoma. *Population:* 361,000.

tum·ble [tum′ bəl] *verb,* **tumbled, tumbling. 1.** to lose one's balance and fall or roll over in an awkward way: "He lay on his face on the deck, *tumbling* around in salt water . . ." (Herman Wouk) **2.** to have a sudden or steep drop: "Wilberforce Falls on the Hood River suddenly *tumbles* 160 feet into a Wild Canyon . . ." (Barry Lopez) **3.** to move or go in a confused or disorganized way: "Books were *tumbled* all about the floor . . ." (Virginia Woolf) **4.** to do gymnastic or acrobatic exercises, such as flips or somersaults. —*noun, plural* **tumbles.** a fall: The baby took a *tumble* over one of her toys on the floor.

tum·bler [tum′ blər] *noun, plural* **tumblers. 1.** a person or thing that tumbles. **2.** a part inside a lock that holds the bolt until it is lifted by a key. **3.** a drinking glass that has no handle or stem.

tum·ble·weed [tum′ bəl wēd] *noun, plural* **tumbleweeds** or **tumbleweed.** any of several plants growing in dry areas of western North America. The branches of a tumbleweed break loose from the roots in a large ball which is rolled along by the wind, scattering seeds as it goes.

tu·mor [tōo′ mər] *noun, plural* **tumors. 1.** a swelling or abnormal growth in the body. A **benign tumor** [bə nīn′] is generally not harmful and usually does not spread to other parts of the body. A **malignant tumor** [mə lig′ nənt] is dangerous and can spread elsewhere in the body, destroying other tissue.

tu·mult [tōo′ məlt] *noun.* a loud noise or disturbance; confusion and excitement: "He was aroused at midnight by a thunderous *tumult* in his ears." (Armstrong Sperry) —**tumultuous** [tə mul′ chōo əs], *adjective:* The crowd at his campaign headquarters gave the winning candidate a *tumultuous* welcome.

tu·na [tōo′ nə] *noun, plural* **tuna** or **tunas.** any of several kinds of large ocean fish found in warm seas throughout the world. Tuna are caught in large numbers for use as food.

tun·dra [tun′ drə] *noun, plural* **tundras.** a large, flat area with no trees, found in arctic regions. Below the surface of the ground, tundra has a layer of soil that is always frozen. This soil layer is called **permafrost** [pur′ mə frôst′].

tune [tōon] *noun, plural* **tunes. 1.** the series of notes that make up a melody or piece of music: Our teacher made up a song for the party to the *tune* of "Happy Birthday." **2. in (out of) tune. a.** at (not at) the correct musical pitch or key. **b.** in (not in) agreement or sympathy. —*verb,* **tuned, tuning. 1.** to put into tune; fix the pitch of: to *tune* a guitar. **2.** *also,* **tune up.** to put into better working order; adjust the parts of: to have a car's engine *tuned.* ♦ Also used as a noun: The car doesn't need any major repairs, just a *tuneup.* **2.** to adjust a radio or television set so as to get a clearer sound or picture, or bring in a certain station.

tun·er [tōo′ nər] *noun, plural* **tuners. 1.** the part of a radio or television set that receives signals and changes them to sound or pictures. **2.** a person who tunes a musical instrument to the proper pitch: a piano *tuner.*

tung·sten [tung′ stən] *noun.* a hard, grayish metal that is a chemical element. Tungsten has a very high melting point and is added to steel to make it stronger and harder.

tu·nic [tōo′ nik] *noun, plural* **tunics. 1.** a piece of clothing reaching from the shoulders to the knees, somewhat like a long shirt. Tunics were worn by both men and women in ancient Greece and Rome. **2.** a modern item of clothing that looks something like this, such as a short, close-fitting jacket worn as part of a military uniform.

tuning fork a U-shaped metal object that always sounds the same tone when struck, used as a guide in tuning a musical instrument.

tuna A bluefin tuna feeds on a school of fish.

T

Tu•ni•sia [too nē´zhə] a country in northern Africa, on the Mediterranean Sea. *Capital:* Tunis. *Area:* 63,100 square miles. *Population:* 6,677,000. —**Tunisian,** *adjective; noun.*

tun•nel [tun´əl] *noun, plural* **tunnels.** a long, narrow passageway under the ground or the water: The Holland *Tunnel* and Lincoln *Tunnel* take cars under the Hudson River from New York City to New Jersey. —*verb,* **tunneled, tunneling.** to dig through or under something to make a tunnel: Miners *tunnel* into the earth to bring up coal, gold, and other minerals.

tur•ban [tur´bən] *noun, plural* **turbans.** a covering for the head made of a long scarf that is wound around and around, worn especially by men in Arab countries and in India.

tur•bine [tur´bīn´ *or* tur´bən] *noun, plural* **turbines.** a machine that turns its own blades by the force of a moving stream of air, steam, water, and so on. Turbines are used to power electric generators, water pumps, ship propellers, jet engines, and other devices.

tur•bu•lent [tur´byə lənt] *adjective, more/most.* causing or full of disorder, violence, or confusion: The late 1960's were a *turbulent* period in American history. ◆ The state of being turbulent is **turbulence:** We ran into a lot of air *turbulence* and the flight was very bumpy.

turf [turf] *noun.* **1.** the top layer of soil from which grasses and small plants grow. **2.** a grass course over which horses race. **3.** *Informal.* an area controlled by a certain person or group: Teenage gangs often consider their own neighborhood to be their *turf* and attack members of other gangs who come there.

between the Black Sea and the Mediterranean Sea. *Capital:* Ankara. *Area:* 301,400 square miles. *Population:* 48,000,000. —**Turkish,** *adjective; noun.* —**Turk,** *noun.*

tur•moil [tur´moil] *noun.* great disorder or confusion: "Our screams had arrived long before us and the whole household was—well, you can imagine the *turmoil.*" (Wole Soyinka)

turn [turn] *verb,* **turned, turning. 1.** to move in a circle or part of a circle: The wheels of a car *turn* as it goes along. You can open a door by *turning* the knob or *turning* a key in the lock. **2.** to move or go to a different direction or position: He *turned* his head to watch the girl walk by. **3.** to move or set a dial or other such control: I can't hear the TV; please *turn* up the sound. **4.** to change the condition or form of: As he got older, his black hair *turned* gray. Night fell and the rain *turned* to snow. **5.** to change one's attitude or feelings: The politician was involved in a big scandal and the voters *turned* against him. **6. turn on (off).** to cause a machine or device to operate (stop operating). **7. turn out. a.** to come out or gather for a meeting or event. ◆ Also used as a noun: a big *turnout* for a football game. **b.** to end up; prove to be: I didn't want to go to the party, but it *turned out* to be fun.
—*noun, plural* **turns. 1.** the act of turning: Cars have a flashing light to signal when the driver is going to make a *turn.* **2.** an act or deed. ◆ Usually used in the phrase **a good turn. 3.** a person's proper chance or time in a certain order: In baseball one team bats and then the other team gets its *turn.*

turning point The *turning point* in a story is a key moment, but it's not the same thing as the *climax.* The climax is the point just before the end when the reader learns how the conflict in the story will be settled. The turning point comes earlier. It's a point at which the story can go one way or another. But once a certain path is taken—because a character makes a decision or an event happens—then the story moves directly to its climax. For example, in Carl Stephenson's "Leiningen Verses the Ants," Leiningen realizes that the only hope against the ants is to open the dam and drown them, even though his reaching the dam seems impossible. The turning point is when he decides he'll risk his life to reach the dam. In the climax, he succeeds in flooding the land and the ants are defeated.

tur•key [tur´kē] *noun, plural* **turkeys.** a large reddish-brown bird with a spreading tail, a long neck and a head with no feathers. The turkey is a North American bird that is found in the wild and also widely raised as a domestic bird for food.

Tur•key [tur´kē] a country that lies partly in southwest Asia and partly in southeast Europe,

Pronunciation Key: Accent Marks

[´] is the normal accent mark. It shows where the main stress falls on a word.
[´] is a secondary accent mark. It shows a lighter stress than the primary accent. For example:

tel • e • vis • ion [tel´ə vizh´ən]
(Turn the page for more information.)

tur·nip [tur/ nip] *noun, plural* **turnips.** the white or yellow rounded root of a certain plant, cooked and eaten as a vegetable.

turn·o·ver [turn/ ō vər] *noun, plural* **turnovers. 1.** the number of times that something moves on or changes during a given period: That fast-food company has a big *turnover* of workers and is always hiring new people. **2.** a small pie made by filling half of a crust and turning the other half over on top.

turn·pike [turn/ pīk/] *noun, plural* **turnpikes.** a wide road, especially one where drivers have to pay a toll to use the road. ◆ In early America travelers on a turnpike had to stop to pay the tolls at a gate called a *turnpike* or *turnstile.*

turn·stile [turn/ stīl/] *noun, plural* **turnstiles.** a gate with horizontal bars that move around as people pass through one at a time, used at the entrance to a subway, stadium, or other such public area.

turn·ta·ble [turn/ tā/ bəl] *noun, plural* **turntables.** a round, flat platform that turns things around, especially the surface that spins around to play a record on a record player.

tur·pen·tine [tur/ pən tīn/] *noun.* a strong-smelling, oily liquid that is made from the sap of certain pine trees. Turpentine is used mainly to thin paints or to remove paint stains.

tur·quoise [tur/ kwoiz *or* tur/ koiz] *noun, plural* **turquoises. 1.** a bright-blue to greenish-blue mineral that is valued as a precious stone. **2.** the color of this stone. —*adjective.* having a turquoise color; greenish-blue.

tur·ret [tur/ it] *noun, plural* **turrets. 1.** a small tower that is built onto a house or other building. Castles of the Middle Ages often had turrets from which soldiers could fire down at the enemy. **2.** a structure on a military ship, tank, or aircraft, which has cannons or guns mounted inside it.

tur·tle [tur/ təl] *noun, plural* **turtles.** one of a large group of animals that have a low, flat body covered by a hard shell. A turtle can pull its head and legs inside its shell for protection. Turtles are reptiles; some types live on land, and others live in fresh or salt water.

turtle The red-eared turtle (top), Sonora mud turtle (center), western painted turtle (below).

tur·tle·neck [tur/ təl nek/] *noun, plural* **turtlenecks.** a sweater or shirt with a high, turned-down collar which fits closely around the neck.

tusk [tusk] *noun, plural* **tusks.** a very long, thick, and pointed tooth that grows out from the sides of some animals' mouths. Elephants, wild boars, and walruses have tusks.

tu·tor [tōō tər] *noun, plural* **tutors.** a teacher or helper who gives special lessons to a particular student or students outside of regular class time. —*verb,* **tutored, tutoring.** to act as a tutor: Jason's uncle is *tutoring* him in algebra because he's having trouble understanding it.

tux·e·do [tuk sē/ dō] *noun, plural* **tuxedos.** a man's dress jacket, usually all black, that is worn for serious formal occasions.

TV short for **television.**

Twain [twān] **Mark,** 1835-1910, American author. His real name was Samuel Langhorne Clemens.

Twain, Mark Ernest Hemingway wrote, "All modern American literature comes from one book by Mark Twain called *Huckleberry Finn.*" This is an interesting statement, since many other famous American authors came before Twain. Why, then, was Mark Twain especially American? He broke away from the earlier patterns of American literature in several important ways: Twain was born in the West and his books were set in the West. Earlier writers were from the Eastern seaboard—the area with close ties to Europe. They lived either in New York (Poe, Cooper, Melville, Whitman) or in Boston (Emerson, Longfellow, Thoreau, Hawthorne). Twain made the American dialect of the frontier a legitimate literary language. Huck Finn told his own story in his own native way. Twain's books had a rough-and-ready feeling, with coarse frontier humor. Huck Finn cannot be mistaken for anyone but an American!

tweed [twēd] *noun, plural* **tweed.** a rough cloth made of wool and woven with two or more colors of yarn. Tweed is used to make sport jackets, skirts, hats, and other clothes.

twelve [twelv] *noun, plural* **twelves;** *adjective.* one more than eleven; 12. —**twelfth,** *adjective; noun.*

twen·ty [twen′tē] *noun, plural* **twenties;** *adjective.* two times ten; 20. —**twentieth,** *adjective; noun.*

twice [twīs] *adverb,* two times: He liked the movie so much that he sat through it *twice.*

twig [twig] *noun, plural* **twigs.** a very small branch growing from a tree or woody shrub.

twi·light [twī′līt′] *noun.* **1.** a time just after sunset or just before sunrise when the sun's light is very soft and the sky appears somewhat gray. **2.** a time when a period of success or glory begins to fade away: In the *twilight* of his career, Babe Ruth was let go by the Yankees and played one year for the Boston Braves.

twin [twin] *noun, plural* **twins. 1.** one of two children born to the same mother at the same time. **Identical twins** are always the same sex and look very much alike. **Fraternal twins** [frə tur′ nəl] may or may not be the same sex and do not look so much alike. **2.** one of two things that are exactly alike. ♦ Also used as an adjective: He has a *twin* sister. The tallest structure in New York City is a two-part office building called the *Twin* Towers.

twine [twīn] *noun, plural* **twines.** a strong cord or string made of two or more strands twisted together. —*verb,* **twined, twining.** to twist or wind: Ivy *twined* around the tree trunk.

Mark Twain

twinge [twinj] *noun, plural* **twinges. 1.** a sudden, sharp pain: Jeff felt a *twinge* of pain when he bit his tongue. "On the way home he had felt a *twinge* of guilt for having spent the night away without telling his folks." (John Okada) —*verb,* **twinged, twinging.** to feel a twinge.

twin·kle [twing′kəl] *verb,* **twinkled, twinkling.** to shine or sparkle with short, quick flashes of light: "Stars *twinkled,* a brittle blue in the dark sky." (Ernie Pyle) —*noun, plural* **twinkles.** a flash or flicker of light.

twirl [twurl] *verb,* **twirled, twirling.** to cause to turn quickly; spin: The figure skater leaped off the ice and *twirled* in the air. High school bands have people who *twirl* batons as they march along. —**twirler,** *noun.*

twist [twist] *verb,* **twisted, twisting. 1.** to turn around something; wind around: ". . . blue dolphins, *twisting* their tails, leapt high now and again into the air." (Virginia Woolf) ♦ A tornado is called a **twister** because of the way it spins around as it moves. **2.** to move in a curving or winding course: "They had come to a stream which *twisted* and tumbled between high rocky banks . . ." (A. A. Milne) **3.** to move out of shape; change from its normal shape or position: "The corners of Agba's mouth *twisted* into a smile." (Marguerite Henry) **4.** to hurt a part of the body by turning it out of its normal position: Marty *twisted* his ankle when he fell off the ladder. **5.** to change the meaning of: Don't *twist* my words; you know that's not what I meant. —*noun, plural* **twists. 1.** something having a curled or bending shape. **2.** an unexpected change or development: The short stories of O. Henry often have a *twist* at the end to surprise the reader.

twitch [twich] *verb,* **twitched, twitching.** to move or pull with a sudden tug or jerk. —*noun, plural* **twitches.** a sharp, sudden movement: ". . . his eyes, dark and restless, and the mouth, nervously tense, *twitching* at the corner." (Penelope Lively) ". . . the big lion lay flattened out along the ground . . . his only movement was a slight *twitching* up and down of his long, black-tufted tail." (Ernest Hemingway)

	Pronunciation Key. A–F		
a	and; hat	ch	chew; such
ā	ate; stay	d	dog; lid
â	care; air	e	end; yet
ä	father; hot	ē	she; each
b	boy; cab	f	fun; off

(Turn the page for more information.)

two [tōō] *noun, plural* **twos;** *adjective.* one more than one; 2.

ty•coon [tī kōōn′] *noun, plural* **tycoons.** a wealthy and powerful business leader.

ty•ing [tī′ ing] *verb.* the present participle of **tie.**

Ty•ler [tī′ lər] **John,** 1790-1862, the tenth president of the United States, from 1841 to 1845.

tyrannosaurus The name *tyrannosaurus* actually means "tyrant-lizard king." It was the most ferocious meat-eater of its time.

T

type [tīp] *noun, plural* **types. 1.** a group or class of things that are alike in some way and different from others; a kind: Bermuda grass is a *type* of grass that grows well in hot climates. ◆ Hospitals must know a person's **blood type** in order to give the person blood during an operation. **2.** a piece of film, metal, wood, and so on, with a letter, number, or design on it, for use in printing: *This sentence is in italic type.* ◆ A particular style or design of type is called a **typeface.** —*verb,* **typed, typing. 1.** to write using a TYPEWRITER: Ben's teacher said the history report has to be *typed,* not handwritten. **2.** to find out what group a person or thing belongs to; classify as a certain type: It's easy to *type* that bird as belonging to the hawk family.

type•wri•ter [tīp′ rī′ tər] *noun, plural* **typewriters.** a machine that prints letters on paper. It has a set of keys which are pressed down to cause type letters to mark the paper. ◆ Something printed by a typewriter is **typewritten.**

ty•phoid fever [tī′ foid] a serious disease caused by bacteria in food, milk, or water. Typhoid fever shows up as spots on the skin, fever, great physical weakness, and disorders of the stomach and intestines.

ty•phoon [tī fōōn′] *noun, plural* **typhoons.** a violent hurricane that begins over tropical waters of the western Pacific Ocean and the China Seas.

typ•i•cal [tip′ i kəl] *adjective, more/most.* having qualities or characteristics that are common to a certain group: "Her hair was much darker than was *typical* in the family." (John Jakes) ". . . mild though, with a gentle breeze clearing the mist, *typical* Welsh weather." (Kingsley Amis) —**typically,** *adverb:* Wolves *typically* live in packs of about eight animals.

typ•ist [tī′ pist] *noun, plural* **typists.** a person who uses a typewriter.

ty•ran•no•saur•us [ti ran′ ə sôr′ əs] *noun, plural* **tyrannosauruses.** a huge, meat-eating dinosaur that lived in North America about 100 million years ago. The tyrannosaurus had a large head, small front legs, and powerful back legs that it walked on. ◆ This animal was also called **tyrannosaurus rex** or **tyrannosaur.**

tyr•an•ny [tir′ ə nē] *noun, plural* **tyrannies. 1.** a government in which one ruler has total power and control of all people and laws. **2.** total or absolute power that is used cruelly and unfairly. —**tyrannical** [ti ran′ ə kəl], *adjective:* The *tyrannical* leader ordered all those who disagreed with him to be sent to prison.

ty•rant [tī′ rənt] *noun, plural* **tyrants. 1.** a ruler who has absolute power over others and uses it in a cruel and unfair way. **2.** any person who uses power cruelly or unfairly: The movie director was a *tyrant* who constantly screamed at his actors and refused to listen to them.

type Until computers were common, *type* referred to two kinds of the mechanical making of letters: typewriting, and the typesetting of newspapers, magazines, and books. Word processors are, in effect, a widening of typewriting to include the use of computer memory. *Typeface* is the style of type to be used. The text you're now reading is set in Optima, a typeface only a few years old. An older typeface, Times Roman, is used here for the definitions. Once the typeface is chosen, then *points* have to be decided. This is the size of the letter of type. Newspapers generally use 9-point typeface; textbooks often use 10-point, or even larger. The space between one line of type and the next is *leading* [led′ ing]. Most books add extra leading between lines, so they will not appear dense.

u, U [yōō] *noun, plural* **u's, U's.** the twenty-first letter of the alphabet.

UFO [yōō′ ef′ ō′] *noun, plural* **UFO's.** an abbreviation for **Unidentified Flying Object.** A UFO is an object seen moving across the sky that cannot be explained or identified. UFO's are sometimes thought to be spacecraft from other planets.

Uganda Murchison Falls, on the upper reaches of the Nile River in western Uganda.

U•gan•da [yōō gän′ də] a country in central Africa, on the equator north of Lake Victoria. *Capital:* Kampala. *Area:* 91,100 square miles. *Population:* 14,630,000. **—Ugandan,** *adjective; noun.*

ug•ly [ug′ lē] *adjective,* **uglier, ugliest. 1.** not pleasing to look at; not pretty or attractive: The story of *Frankenstein* tells of an *ugly* monster. She had an *ugly* scar on her leg from the car accident. **2.** not pleasant; dangerous or disagreeable: He was in an *ugly* mood after his team lost the game in the last inning. An *ugly* storm was on the way and fishermen headed for shore. **—ugliness,** *noun.*

u•ku•le•le [yōō′ kə lā′ lē] *noun, plural* **ukeleles.** a small instrument like a guitar, having four strings and used in playing light music.

ul•cer [ul′ sər] *noun, plural* **ulcers.** an open sore which can be on the outside or inside of the body, and may be very painful. If a person's digestive system produces too much acid, he may get a stomach ulcer.

ul•ti•mate [ul′ tə mit] *adjective.* **1.** coming at the end; last or final: She's studying history in college now, but her *ultimate* goal is to become a lawyer. **2.** greatest or extreme: "He and his companions all agreed that diving among sharks was for them the *ultimate* challenge." (Russell Hoban) **—ultimately,** *adverb.* in the end; at last; finally: Trial lawyers select a jury very carefully because *ultimately* the jury will determine the outcome of the case.

ul•tra•vi•o•let [ul′ trə vī′ ə lit] *adjective.* of light rays, lying just beyond the violet end of the SPECTRUM and thus not able to be seen. The sun is the main source of ultraviolet rays.

um•brel•la [əm brel′ ə] *noun, plural* **umbrellas.** a circular piece of cloth or plastic stretched on a frame that can be folded up when not in use. It is held over the head by a handle or pole and used to give protection from the rain or sun.
♦ *Umbrella* comes from Latin *umbra,* meaning "shade."

ukelele The traditional musical instrument of the Hawaiian Islands is the ukelele, played here by women in native costume.

um·pire [um′ pīr′] *noun, plural* **umpires.** in baseball and other sports, a person who rules on plays: An *umpire* in baseball decides whether a runner is safe or out. —*verb,* **umpired, umpiring.** to act as an umpire: Our teacher *umpired* the softball game we had against Milton School.

UN or **U.N.** an abbreviation for **United Nations.**

un- a *prefix* meaning "not." *Un*happy means "not happy." *Un*married means "not married."

un·bear·a·ble [ən bar′ ə bəl] *adjective, more/ most.* not bearable: too harsh or extreme to bear: *unbearable* heat, *unbearable* pain.

un·be·liev·a·ble [un′ bi lē′ və bəl] *adjective, more/most.* **1.** that cannot be believed: The jury thought his story was *unbelievable* and found him guilty of the crime. **2.** very hard to believe; very surprising or shocking: In 1920 Babe Ruth hit more home runs by himself than any team in the league hit as a total, an *unbelievable* record.

un- The most common prefix in English is *un-*. The reason is obvious. *Un* means "not" or "contrary" or "otherwise"—the opposite of a condition or feeling or situation. There are two "not" words; the other is *non-*. *Un* is used with verbs (*undo, untie, unwind, uncover, unfold*) and with adjectives (*unhappy, uncomfortable, unafraid, unkind, unknown*). *Un* is generally not used with nouns (though it is possible to say, "He's a political unknown"). It's not a good idea to say that a certain soft drink is an "un-cola." That is tricky or catchy, perhaps, but it's a misuse of perfectly clear words. *Non* is the correct term with nouns: "This area is off limits to *non*-military personnel." "The insurance company offers lower rates for *non*-smokers." As you can see from these examples, *non* tends to be a more formal word than *un,* and it has a much wider range of uses.

un·able [ən ā′ bəl] *adjective.* not able: People who haven't registered in time will be *unable* to vote in this election.

un·ac·cep·ta·ble [un′ ak sep′ tə bəl] *adjective.* that will not or should not be accepted: The report must be typed; handwritten papers are *unacceptable.*

u·nan·i·mous [yoō nan′ ə məs] *adjective.* showing total agreement: Mark was elected as the new captain of the baseball team by a *unanimous* vote. —**unanimously,** *adverb.*

un·armed [ən ärmd′] *adjective.* not armed; not having a weapon: The medical officer wore a regular soldier's uniform but was *unarmed.*

un·a·ware [un′ ə wâr′] *adjective, adverb.* not knowing; not aware: He was *unaware* the schedule had changed and missed his train.

un·bal·anced [ən bal′ ənst] *adjective, more/ most.* not balanced; especially, not having a normal mind.

un·bro·ken [ən brō′ kən] *adjective.* **1.** not broken: The seal on the package was *unbroken.* **2.** not interrupted; continuous: Looking ahead, they saw mile after mile of *unbroken* desert.

un·can·ny [ən kan′ ē] *adjective, more/most.* seeming to be beyond normal powers; not natural or usual; mysterious: "His *uncanny* sense of timing ensured that both he and Odejimi met exactly at the back gate." (Wole Soyinka)

un·cer·tain [ən sur′ tən] *adjective, more/most.* not certain; doubtful: She was *uncertain* of her answer and decided not to raise her hand. —**uncertainly,** *adverb.* —**uncertainty,** *noun.*

un·changed [ən chānjd′] *adjective.* not changed or changing: The patient's condition is *unchanged* since yesterday.

un·cle [un′ kəl] *noun, plural* **uncles. 1.** the brother of one's father or mother. **2.** the husband of one's aunt.

un- words Here is a list of common *un-* words that we do not define in the dictionary. The meaning of these words can be understood by adding the idea of "not" to the meaning of the root word. Each of the words listed here occurs at a rate of at least once in every million words of English. For example, *uncontrolled* occurs three times per million.

unbreakable	undisturbed	unoccupied	unselfish
uncivilized	uneducated	unprofitable	unshaven
unclean	uninsured	unprotected	unsuitable
unconcerned	unintentional	unqualified	untrained
uncontrolled	uninteresting	unrestrained	untreated
undeveloped	uninterrupted	unrestricted	unyielding

U

un•clear [ən klēr/] *adjective, more/most.* not easy to understand; not clear: He didn't explain and it's *unclear* to me what he wants.

Uncle Sam 1. a figure who represents the United States, shown as a tall, thin man with gray hair and chin whiskers, usually wearing a high hat, a long tail coat, and striped trousers. **2.** the United States itself, or its government or people. ♦ The name *Uncle Sam* is said to come from the nickname of Samuel Wilson, a government inspector who stamped barrels of meat "U. S." during the War of 1812.

un•com•fort•a•ble [ən kum/ fər tə bəl *or* ən kumf/ tər bəl] *adjective, more/most.* not comfortable: The waiting room had only a hard, *uncomfortable* bench. "She simply said that Dean's temperature was still up and rising, that he had been *uncomfortable* much of the night." (John R. Tunis) —**uncomfortably,** *adverb.*

un•com•mon [ən käm/ ən] *adjective, more/most.* not common; unusual or different: "Making his way home by an *uncommon* route gave him the feeling that he was a pilgrim, an explorer . . ." (John Cheever) "During our short time in the USSR we had met an *uncommon* number of people who spoke English . . ." (Farley Mowat) —**uncommonly,** *adverb:* ". . . he was *uncommonly* tired and nervous." (Ivan Southall)

un•con•di•tion•al [un/ kən dish/ ən əl] *adjective.* not limited or restricted; without exception: An *unconditional* surrender means that the winning army does not grant any special terms to the defeated enemy.

un•con•scious [ən kän/ shəs] *adjective.* **1.** not fully awake; not conscious: He was *unconscious* for several minutes after falling and hitting his head on the pavement. **2.** not knowing; not aware: ". . . she was beautifully *unconscious* that she did any of these things." (John Galsworthy) —**unconsciously,** *adverb.*

un•con•sti•tu•tion•al [un/ kän sti tōō/ shən əl] *adjective.* not in keeping with or not following the constitution of a state or country, especially the U.S. Constitution: In 1954 the Supreme Court ruled it was *unconstitutional* to keep black students in separate schools.

un•con•ven•tion•al [un/ kən ven/ shən əl] *adjective, more/most.* out of the ordinary; not following the usual customs of society: The author Tom Wolfe is known for his *unconventional* style of wearing all-white suits even in winter. ". . . a girl who was so *unconventional* that she had not even bothered to have her own parents to her wedding . . ." (Mary McCarthy)

Uncle Sam One of the best-known painters of Uncle Sam was James Montgomery Flagg. This poster was done in World War I.

un•couth [ən kōōth/] *adjective, more/most.* not showing good manners; not polite; crude: Other people in the restaurant began staring at the *uncouth* way the boys were grabbing food off each other's plates and tossing it around.

un•cov•er [ən kuv/ ər] *verb,* **uncovered, uncovering. 1.** to take off a cover or top: They pulled away all the weeds and *uncovered* an old stone walkway. **2.** to discover and make known; reveal: The reporter said that he had *uncovered* a secret plan to give U.S. aid to the rebels.

un•daunt•ed [ən dôn/ tid] *adjective.* not frightened or discouraged: The storm was blowing waves over the deck of the ship, but the captain remained *undaunted.*

un•de•cid•ed [un/ di sī/ did] *adjective, more/most.* **1.** not having made up one's mind: She was *undecided* as to whether or not to invite Donna to her party. **2.** not yet settled: There are only three games left in the season, but it's still *undecided* who will finish in first place.

U

Pronunciation Key. A–F

a	and; hat	ch	chew; such
ā	ate; stay	d	dog; lid
â	care; air	e	end; yet
ä	father; hot	ē	she; each
b	boy; cab	f	fun; off

(Turn the page for more information.)

under A sportswriter once joked of a team that finished with a record of two wins, seven losses, and one tie: "They *overwhelmed* two opponents, *underwhelmed* seven others, and *whelmed* one." This joke plays on the common prefixes *over-* and *under-*. There is no such word as *underwhelm*. *Whelm* hasn't been commonly used for centuries. Our Word Survey found that common *under-* terms of this type include *underdeveloped, underemployed, undernourished, underpaid, underpopulated, understaffed,* and *undervalued*. Thus, *under* is a form that's suited to factual reporting, but it's not quite as forceful as some other expressions. When President Franklin D. Roosevelt described conditions during the Great Depression in 1933, he chose an old-fashioned term, *ill-*: "I see one-third of a nation ill-housed, ill-clad, ill-nourished."

un•der [un′ dər] *preposition.* **1.** lower than or down from; below; beneath: He jumped into bed and got *under* the covers. They were tired of walking and sat down *under* a tree to rest. **2.** less than a certain amount or level: Boys on this soccer team must be *under* 12 years old. **3.** controlled or affected by in some way: a matter that is *under* discussion, a person who is *under* the care of a doctor. **4.** in a certain group or category: Samuel Clemens wrote his books *under* the name Mark Twain. I found information about the America's Cup races *under* the article 'Sailing.' —*adverb.* in or to a lower place; below: The boat was taking on water and was in danger of going *under.* —*adjective.* lower in position or amount. ♦ Usually used in combination: *Undercooked* meat is not cooked enough. Someone who is *underage* is not the legal or proper age.

un•der•brush [un′ dər brush′] *noun.* low plants, bushes, and shrubs growing among larger trees in a woods or forest; also called **undergrowth.**

un•der•cov•er [un′ dər kuv′ ər] *adjective; adverb.* in a secret or hidden way: An *undercover* policeman wears ordinary street clothes rather than a uniform.

un•der•de•vel•oped [un′ dər di vel′ əpt] *adjective, more/most.* **1.** not properly developed: The child's body was *underdeveloped* from a poor diet and lack of exercise. **2.** of a country or region, behind other areas in the development of industry, standards of living, and so on. —**underdevelopment,** *noun.*

un•der•dog [un′ dər dôg′] *noun, plural* **underdogs. 1.** a person or team that is expected to lose a game or contest. **2.** a person or group treated in an unfair way by those in power.

un•der•foot [un′ dər foot′] *adverb.* **1.** under the feet: "The deck *underfoot* shook with the beat of the paddle wheels . . ." (John Dos Passos) **2.** in the way, as if under one's feet:

Their three little dogs were always getting *underfoot.*

un•der•go [un′ dər gō′] *verb,* **underwent, undergone, undergoing.** to go through or experience something, especially something difficult or unpleasant: She went into the hospital to *undergo* treatment for her injured back.

un•der•grad•u•ate [un′ dər graj′ ōo it] *noun, plural* **undergraduates.** a student in a college or university who has not yet graduated.

un•der•ground [un′ dər ground′] *adjective.* **1.** below the ground: That building has an *underground* parking garage. **2.** secret or hidden: The government controlled the official newspapers, but there was an *underground* press printing anti-government articles. —[*also,* un′ dər-ground′] *noun, plural* **undergrounds. 1.** an area below ground. **2.** a group that works in secret to oppose the government in power: When Germany occupied Denmark in World War II, members of the *underground* carried out attacks against the Germans. —*adverb.* **1.** below ground. **2.** secretly.

un•der•hand [un′ dər hand′] *adjective; adverb.* (also, **underhanded**) **1.** with the hand below the level of the shoulder: A pitcher in softball has to throw the ball *underhand.* **2.** in a dishonest or secret way: There's no way he could sell that worthless land—unless he pulled some *underhanded* trick to fool the buyer.

un•der•line [un′ dər līn′] *verb,* **underlined, underlining. 1.** to draw a line under something, like this: to *underline* an important word in a sentence. **2.** to show to be important; emphasize: Today's accident *underlines* the need for a stop light at that corner.

un•der•mine [un′ dər mīn′ *or* un′ dər mīn′] *verb,* **undermined, undermining. 1.** to dig out or wear away the ground under: The old dock is no longer safe because the constant action of the waves has *undermined* its supports. **2.** to weaken or ruin slowly: All those rumors about the mayor's personal life have *undermined* his ability to run the city effectively.

un•der•neath [un′ dər nēth′] *preposition; adverb.* under; below: He wore a heavy fur jacket and a wool sweater *underneath.* "*Underneath* the gentle saint (Gandhi) was a determined fighter . . ." (William L. Shirer)

un•der•pass [un′ dər pas′] *noun, plural* **underpasses.** a road that goes under another road or a bridge.

getting the meaning of something: Many areas of science require an *understanding* of mathematics. **2.** something assumed; a belief or opinion: It's my *understanding* that this car has only had one previous owner. **3.** a private agreement: They have an *understanding* that they will get married when they both finish college. —*adjective.* able to understand the feelings of others; I'd thought she'd be upset with what I did, but she was very *understanding.*

understatement Writers often use the technique of *understatement,* of saying less than could be said. Ernest Hemingway gives a long description of the smell of a delicious meal cooking and then closes with "It was a good smell." Raymond Chandler describes the face of a beautiful woman and then concludes: "It was a face you could get used to." Laura Ingalls Wilder often uses understatement in her "Little House" books. Once, she describes a Christmas scene, telling the presents that the girls got and giving sense details of the sounds, smells, and tastes of the Christmas celebration. Then the chapter ends with this line: "It was a happy Christmas." Note that she did *not* say: "That was the most wonderful Christmas I ever had! Was I happy!" She has given a half-page of details to *show* us that it was a very happy time. Then the understatement neatly wraps up the description.

un•der•priv•i•leged [un′ dər priv′ lijd] *adjective, more/most.* having fewer advantages or opportunities than others because of being poor.

un•der•score [un′ dər skôr′] *verb,* **underscored, underscoring.** another word for **underline.**

un•der•sea [un′ dər sē′] *adjective.* being or used under the sea. —*adverb.* (also, **underseas**) beneath the sea.

un•der•side [un′ dər sīd′] *noun, plural* **undersides.** the side underneath; the bottom.

un•der•stand [un′ dər stand′] *verb,* **understood, understanding. 1.** to get the meaning of; be clear about: The teacher made sure all the students *understood* the lesson before she went on to the next one. He studied Spanish in school, but when he went to Mexico he found it hard to *understand* what people were saying. **2.** to know a person's nature; be in sympathy with: The coach *understands* Jimmy and knows he needs extra praise to play well. **3.** to be informed; learn: "I *understand* you have some ideas about improving our phone system," the boss said to her. **4.** to assume or accept as true: If a book is a "limited edition," it's *understood* that only a certain number of copies will be sold. In the sentence, "Pass the salt, please," the subject "you" is *understood.*

un•der•stand•ing [un′ dər stan′ ding] *noun, plural* **understandings. 1.** the fact of knowing or

un•der•stood [un′ dər stood′] *verb.* the past form of **understand:** "Now that she was gone he *understood* how lonely her life must have been . . ." (James Joyce)

un•der•take [un′ dər tāk′] *verb,* **undertook, undertaken, undertaking.** to agree or attempt to do something; take on oneself: "When a man *undertakes* a job, he has to stick to it till he finishes it." (Laura Ingalls Wilder) —**undertaking,** *noun:* Writing a book can be quite an *undertaking.*

un•der•tak•er [un′ dər tā′ kər] *noun, plural* **undertakers.** a person whose job is to prepare a dead person for burying and to arrange the person's funeral.

un•der•tone [un′ dər tōn′] *noun, plural* **undertones. 1.** a low tone, as of the voice, a color, and so on. **2.** a feeling or thought that is partly hidden.

un•der•took [un′ dər took′] *verb.* the past form of **undertake:** "He *undertook* the hard work and confining hours of government service . . ." (Barbara Tuchman)

Pronunciation Key: G–N

g	give; big	k	kind; cat; back
h	hold	l	let; ball
i	it; this	m	make; time
ī	ice; my	n	not; own
j	jet; gem; edge	ng	having

(Turn the page for more information.)

U

un•der•tow [un/dər tō/] *noun, plural* **undertows.** in the ocean, a strong current below the surface of the water that flows back out to sea or along the beach while waves break on the shore.

un•der•wa•ter [un/dər wô/ tər] *adjective.* used, done, or lying below the surface of the water: At high tide these rocks are completely *underwater.* The "Chunnel" is a proposed *underwater* tunnel across the English Channel. —*adverb:* He dove in the pool and swam *underwater* to the other end.

un•der•wear [un/dər wâr/] *noun.* clothing worn next to the skin under one's outer clothing, such as an **undershirt** or **underpants.** ◆ Also called **underclothes** or **underclothing.**

un•der•weight [un/dər wāt/] *adjective.* below the usual, normal, or expected weight.

un•der•went [un/dər went/] *verb.* the past tense of **undergo.**

un•de•sir•a•ble [un/ di zīr/ ə bəl] *adjective, more/most.* not pleasing or wanted; disagreeable. —*noun, plural* **undesirables.** an undesirable person.

un•did [ən did/] *verb.* the past tense of **undo.**

un•do [ən dōō/] *verb,* **undid, undone, undoing.** **1.** to loosen or untie something: Her hair had come *undone* and was hanging loosely over her shoulders. **2.** to do away with something that has already been done: "Maybe he was trying to *undo* with them what he felt he had done wrong with his sons." (James Joyce) —**undoing,** *noun.* a cause of ruin or failure: He'd been trying not to snack, but when he smelled the cookies baking—that was his *undoing.*

un•done[1] [ən dun/] *adjective.* not done; not finished: ". . . there were a great many things left *undone* on this place." (Katherine Anne Porter)

un•done[2] *verb.* the past participle of **undo.**

un•doubt•ed•ly [ən dout/ id lē] *adverb.* without a doubt; certainly.

un•dress [ən dres/] *verb,* **undressed, undressing.** to remove the clothing; take off one's clothes.

un•eas•y [ən ē/ zē] *adjective, more/most.* not calm or relaxed; nervous; worried: "The child was *uneasy,* fluttering up and down, like a bird on the point of taking flight." (Nathaniel Hawthorne) —**uneasily,** *adverb:* "Dottie lowered her voice and glanced *uneasily* toward the far corner of the dining room." (Mary McCarthy) —**uneasiness,** *noun.*

un•em•ployed [un/ im ploid/] *adjective.* with-out a job; out of work. ◆ Also used as a noun: The government defines the *unemployed* as those who are without a job and are actively seeking to find one. ◆ **Unemployment** is the fact of being without a job.

un•e•qual [ən ē/ kwəl] *adjective.* not the same; not equal: It is now against the law to pay women an *unequal* amount from men for doing the same work.

un•e•ven [ən ē/ vin] *adjective, more/most.* **1.** not even: The old dirt road had a bumpy, *uneven* surface. **2.** not fair or balanced: It was an *uneven* contest because one team's players were much bigger and faster than the other's.

un•ex•pect•ed [un/ ik spek/ tid] *adjective, more/most.* not expected; coming or happening without notice: Mom was surprised when Dad brought an *unexpected* guest home for dinner, and she had to go out for some extra meat. —**unexpectedly,** *adverb:* We were prepared for lots of California sun and found the weather to be *unexpectedly* cloudy.

un•fair [ən fâr/] *adjective, more/most.* not fair; not right or proper: She watched the runners carefully to be sure no one got an *unfair* head start on the others. —**unfairly,** *adverb:* He complained that the teacher had treated him *unfairly* in giving him a 'C.'

un•fa•mil•iar [un/ fə mil/ yər] *adjective.* not familiar; not well-known: I thought she lived on this street, but all the houses look *unfamiliar.* The lawyer tried not to use special legal terms that the jury would be *unfamiliar* with.

un•fa•vor•a•ble [ən fāv/ rə bəl] *adjective, more/most.* not favorable: Business conditions looked *unfavorable,* and the company decided to put off its new project. She keeps trying to sell that article to a magazine, but so far she's had only *unfavorable* responses.

un•fin•ished [ən fin/ isht] *adjective.* not finished: When F. Scott Fitzgerald died, he left behind an *unfinished* novel, *The Last Tycoon.*

un•fit [ən fit/] *adjective, more/most.* not fit; not suited or qualified for something: "He was seized by fear that he was completely *unfit* for the project, the wrong choice for it." (Anita Desai)

un•fold [ən fōld/] *verb,* **unfolded, unfolding.** **1.** to open up or spread out: to *unfold* an umbrella. She sat down at the dinner table and *unfolded* her napkin. **2.** to come to be known; reveal: "That dream, as it *unfolds* in the following chapters . . ." (Barry Lopez)

un•for•get•ta•ble [un/ fər get/ ə bəl] *adjective, more/most.* impossible or difficult to forget;

U

unicorn "Lady with the Unicorn" is a French tapestry done in the late 1400's.

memorable: Her vacation trip to Paris and Rome was an *unforgettable* experience.

un•for•tu•nate [ən fôr′ chə nit] *adjective, more/most.* not fortunate; unlucky: "Its light might have the *unfortunate* effect of attracting some of the more dangerous inhabitants of these waters." (Jules Verne) **—unfortunately,** *adverb.*

un•friend•ly [ən frend′ lē] *adjective,* **un-friendlier, unfriendliest.** showing dislike or coldness towards others; not friendly.

un•gain•ly [ən gān′ lē] *adjective, more/most.* awkward or clumsy: "He was six feet four inches tall, and as a young man had been thin, *ungainly* . . ." (Barbara Tuchman)

un•grate•ful [ən grāt′ fəl] *adjective, more/most.* not thankful or grateful: "She did not want to appear *ungrateful* and tried to act as pleased as the rest." (Eleanor Estes)

un•hap•py [ən hap′ ē] *adjective,* **unhappier, un-happiest.** not happy; sad: "She had been very *unhappy* about a sister who had recently died." (Agatha Christie) **—unhappily,** *adverb.* **—unhappiness,** *noun.*

un•health•y [ən hel′ thē] *adjective,* **unhealthier, unhealthiest. 1.** not in good health; sick; ill. **2.** causing poor health: The doctor wants him to change his *unhealthy* eating habits.

un•heard-ot [ən hurd′ uv′] *adjective, more/most.* **1.** not heard of before; not previously known or done. **2.** not normally done; strange or unusual: "Looking at one another's letters to Santa Claus was usually an *unheard-of* procedure. They were for Santa's eyes alone." (Eleanor Estes)

u•ni•corn [yōō′ nə kôrn′] *noun, plural* **uni-corns.** an imaginary animal that looks like a white horse with a single, pointed horn in the middle of its forehead. Unicorns often appeared in art and stories of the Middle Ages.

u•ni•cy•cle [yōō′ nə sī kəl] *noun, plural* **unicy-cles.** a vehicle that is like a bicycle, but with only one wheel and a seat above.

unicycle A *unicyclist* performs at a Memorial Day parade in New City, N.Y.

un•i•form [yōō′ nə fôrm′] *noun, plural* **uni-forms.** a special set of clothes that identifies a person who wears it as belonging to a certain group. Soldiers, police officers, nurses, Girl Scouts, and members of sports teams wear uniforms. **—adjective.** being the same; having the same appearance, form, rate, and so on: The company's sales people all drive company cars with a *uniform* blue color. ♦ The fact of being uniform is **uniformity** [yōō′ nə fôr′ mə tē]. **—uniformly,** *adverb.*

un•i•formed [yōō′ nə fôrmd′] *adjective.* wearing a uniform: ". . . another pair of *uniformed* policemen entering with a handcuffed man." (Joseph Wambaugh)

un•im•por•tant [un′ im pôr′ tənt] *adjective, more/most.* having no special value or meaning; not important.

un•in•hab•ited [un′ in hab′ ə tid] *adjective.* not lived in; having no inhabitants: "He had been one of the first to settle on what was then a

U

Pronunciation Key: O–S

ō	over; go	ou	out; town
ô	all; law	p	put; hop
oo	look; full	r	run; car
ōō	pool; who	s	set; miss
oi	oil; boy	sh	show

(Turn the page for more information.)

lonely, almost *uninhabited* coast." (Louis L'Amour)

un·in·tel·li·gi·ble [un′ in tel′ ə jə bəl] *adjective, more/most.* not able to be understood: The plane was too far from the base and the pilot's radio message was *unintelligible.*

un·in·ter·est·ed [ən in′ tris tid] *adjective, more/most.* not interested: As the boring speech went on and on Mike gazed blankly out the window, completely *uninterested* in what was being said. ◆ See also DISINTERESTED on p. 229.

un·ion [yoon′ yən] *noun, plural* **unions. 1.** *also,* **labor union.** a group of workers who join together to deal with their company's management and to promote and protect their interests, as in trying to gain higher pay or better working conditions: Coal miners belong to the United Mine Workers *Union.* **2.** the fact of joining: the *union* of husband and wife in marriage. "All your strength is in your *union.*" (Henry Wadsworth Longfellow) **3.** a group of states or countries joined as one: the *Union* of South Africa. "We the People of the United States, in order to form a more perfect *Union* . . ." (U.S. Constitution) **4. the Union. a.** the United States of America. **b.** those states that remained part of the federal government during the Civil War.

Union of Soviet Socialist Republics the largest country in the world, in eastern Europe and northern Asia. It is made up mainly of the former country of Russia. It is also known as the SOVIET UNION. *Capital:* Moscow. *Area:* 8,603,000 square miles. *Population:* 269,600,000.

doing the same thing at the same time: "Children in another grade were reciting a lesson aloud *in unison.*" (Lois Lenski) "When the elevator door opened, I said good-bye, aloud, and their three heads turned *in unison* toward me." (J. D. Salinger)

Union The famous Union general William Tecumseh Sherman, sitting at the center surrounded by his staff.

u·nit [yoo′ nit] *noun, plural* **units. 1.** a single person, group, or thing that is part of a larger group: A squad is a military *unit* made up of about 12 soldiers. We're studying *Unit* Five of our American history book, which deals with the Civil War. **2.** a fixed amount that is used as a standard of measurement: Seconds, minutes, and hours are *units* of time. **3.** a piece of equipment or furniture having a special purpose: an air-conditioning *unit.* The new wall *unit* holds our TV, stereo, and video recorder.

unique Every snowflake is *unique.* So is every fingerprint. So is every DNA chain showing heredity. So is every killer whale's markings on its upper fin. In each case, no two or more instances are alike. Each is unique, unlike any other. If you see an ad that says: "A *most unique* car—the Buccaneer," you know the advertiser is struggling for effect—and using poor English. *Unique* is what is called an *absolute word.* It's no good saying that a thing is "almost unique" or "somewhat unique." "The boat's sails are arranged in a *rather unique* way." Here, the word called for is "different," not "unique." Why is it important, this distinction? Why throw away a "unique" word because you are too lazy to find other words that do fit properly?

u·nique [yoo nēk′] *adjective, more/most.* **1.** being the only one of its kind; different from all others: "The fame of this *unique* animal has spread to the far corners of the earth, attracting many valuable tourists to our great state." (E. B. White) **2.** *Informal.* very rare or unusual. **—uniquely,** *adverb.* **—uniqueness,** *noun.*

u·ni·son [yoo′ nə sən] *noun.* **in unison.** sounding the same notes, making the same sounds, or

u·nite [yoo nīt′] *verb,* **united, uniting.** to bring or join together; make one; combine: The six regions that make up the modern country of Yugoslavia were first *united* as an independent nation in 1918. **—united,** *adjective:* the *United* Auto Workers Union. *United* Airlines is a large company with flights to cities all over the U. S.

United Kingdom the official name of **Great Britain.**

U

United Nations The United Nations is located on the island of Manhattan in New York City, alongside the East River.

United Nations an organization that contains many nations from all over the world. The United Nations was formed after World War II to keep world peace and encourage countries to work together to solve problems. Over 150 different countries now belong to the United Nations.

United States of America a country in North America, made up of 50 states, the District of Columbia, Puerto Rico, and other territories. All the states lie between Canada and Mexico, except Hawaii in the Pacific and Alaska in northwestern North America. *Capital:* Washington, D.C. *Area:* 3,615,200 square miles. *Population:* 240,000,000.

admired him. **2.** being or happening everywhere: *Universal* time is the standard time calculated in Greenwich, England that serves as the basis for figuring time throughout the world. ◆The **Universal Product Code** is the series of black bars and lines appearing on food packages and other household products to allow them to be automatically identified by a computer. —**universally,** *adverb.*

u•ni•verse [yōō′ nə vurs′] *noun, plural* **universes.** all of the area that exists and everything that exists within it; the earth, planets, stars, and all other things.

u•ni•ver•si•ty [yōō′ nə vur′ sə tē] *noun, plural* **universities.** a place of higher learning where people study special fields such as medicine, law, the arts, and business. Students at a university may attend a college within the university, or they may be college graduates attending medical school, and so on.

un•just [ən just′] *adjective, more/most.* not fair or just. —**unjustly,** *adverb.*

un•kempt [ən kempt′] *adjective, more/most.* not neat, clean, in place, and so on: "In front of the sink stood an *unkempt* woman with gray hair stringing about her face." (Madeleine L'Engle)

un•kind [ən kīnd′] *adjective,* **unkinder, unkindest.** not kind; cruel or mean. —**unkindly,** *adverb.* —**unkindness,** *noun.*

un•known [ən nōn′] *adjective.* not known or familiar: The mysterious monument of Stonehenge in Britain was built by an *unknown* people thousands of years ago. ◆ Also used as

unity Books teaching writing often speak of how important it is to create *unity* within a paragraph—that is, to give a paragraph one subject, and not let its sentences wander off that subject. Of course, it's one thing to say this, and quite another thing to prove it. There are no rules to identify a sentence that's off the subject. Suppose Cathy, a student writer, is writing a science paper on the ways that food and other things are kept cold. Early in the paper, she mentions that she recently visited the Lincoln Memorial in Washington, D. C. Obviously, it seems Cathy has gone off the subject. But not if it turns out that the mention of the Memorial leads into a discussion of portable means of cooling, such as "dry ice" or small refrigeration units in carts, selling ice cream or soft drinks to tourists. A stronger point would be for Cathy to discuss how in the old days blocks of ice were cut from frozen rivers and kept from melting right away by packing them in snow.

u•ni•ty [yōō′ nə tē] *noun.* the fact of being united; British leader T. E. Lawrence brought *unity* to various Arab tribes that had formerly been enemies, and led their revolt against the Turks.

u•ni•ver•sal [yōō′ nə vur′ səl] *adjective.* **1.** of, for, or shared by everyone: There was *universal* sorrow in the world when President John Kennedy was killed because people everywhere

Pronunciation Key: T–Z

t	ten; date	v	very; live
th	think	w	win; away
th	these	y	you
u	cut; butter	z	zoo; cause
ur	turn; bird	zh	measure

(Turn the page for more information.)

a noun: Wendell Willkie was a political *unknown* who rose to challenge Franklin D. Roosevelt for President in 1940, even though he'd never run for office before.

Unknown Soldier The Tomb of the Unknown Soldier honors an unidentified American soldier killed in battle.

un•law•ful [ən lô′ fəl] *adjective,* *more/most.* against the law; illegal.

un•less [ən les′] *conjunction.* except in the case that; except that: "I know I'll never get a pet of my own *unless* I catch it myself." (Nancy Willard)

un•like [ən līk′] *preposition.* **1.** different from; not like: *Unlike* other deer, male and female caribou both have antlers. **2.** not typical of: I wonder where he is—it's *unlike* him to be so late. —*adjective.* not the same; different.

un•load [ən lōd′] *verb,* **unloaded, unloading.** to take off or remove a load from: They *unloaded* boxes of fruit from the truck. The hunter *unloaded* his gun and put the bullets away.

un•lock [ən läk′] *verb,* **unlocked, unlocking. 1.** to open the lock of: to *unlock* a door. ◆ Often used as an adjective: The thief got in through an *unlocked* window. **2.** to open something that is closed tight: "Florence knew that he could not *unlock* his lips to speak . . ." (James Baldwin) **3.** to make known something that was hidden or secret; reveal: By discovering bacteria, Louis Pasteur *unlocked* the mystery of how dangerous diseases spread.

un•luck•y [ən luk′ ē] *adjective,* **unluckier, unluckiest.** bringing or causing bad luck; not lucky: Many people think of 13 as an *unlucky* number.

un•manned [ən mand′] *adjective.* without a crew: an *unmanned* spacecraft.

un•mar•ried [ən mar′ ēd] *adjective.* not married; single.

un•mis•tak•a•ble [un′ mis tā′ kə bəl] *adjective.* not able to be mistaken or misunderstood; clear; obvious: I know she wrote that letter; her handwriting is *unmistakable.* —**unmistakably,** *adverb:* "We hear a small, high squeaking voice which is nevertheless *unmistakably* human." (Archibald MacLeish)

un•moved [ən mōōvd′] *adjective.* **1.** not affected by feelings of pity or sympathy: The police officer was *unmoved* by the man's excuses for

unlike "A seat in his boat was *not unlike* a seat upon a bucking bronco." (Stephen Crane) This use of *not* reverses the meaning, so *unlike* actually means *like.* "She had settled her life into a routine in which she was *not unhappy.*" (George Orwell) Note the effect achieved here. She's settled into a routine, isn't really sad, but she's not really happy either. She's in between—*not unhappy.* Look again at the Crane example. Crane makes a boat, which is very different from a bucking horse, somewhat like that horse. He's created an effect by comparing unlike things. If the school board decides to hold schools open year-round, and has been openly discussing the matter, you can reasonably say, "The decision was *not unexpected.*"

un•like•ly [ən līk′ lē] *adjective,* **unlikelier, unlikeliest. 1.** not expected or probable; not likely: She dropped her ring somewhere in the grass—she might find it, but it's highly *unlikely.* **2.** not likely to happen or be true: a far-fetched, *unlikely* scheme for making money.

un•lim•it•ed [ən lim′ it id] *adjective.* having no bounds or limits: When Grandpa retired from the bus company he got a gold pass that allows him *unlimited* free travel on all the city bus lines.

going too fast and calmly wrote out a speeding ticket. **2.** not changed in position; not moved.

un•nat•ur•al [ən nach′ ər əl] *adjective,* *more/most.* not natural or normal; strange: The paintings of Salvador Dali often feature strange, *unnatural* shapes and designs, such as melting watches.

un•nec•es•sar•y [ən nes′ ə ser′ ē] *adjective.* not needed; not necessary: The teacher pointed out several *unnecessary* sentences that I could cut out of my paper. —**unnecessarily,** *adverb.*

U

un·of·fi·cial [un/ ə fish/ əl] *adjective.* not formal or official: The village is too small to elect a mayor, but people consider Mr. Hale to be the *unofficial* mayor. —**unofficially,** *adverb.*

un·or·tho·dox [ən ôr/ thə däks] *adjective, more/most.* not usual or typical: Basketball star Rick Barry set records for free-throw shooting, even though he used the *unorthodox* method of shooting them underhanded.

un·paid [ən pād/] *adjective.* **1.** not yet paid or settled: an *unpaid* debt. **2.** without pay: He took an *unpaid* leave of absence from his job for six months.

un·pleas·ant [ən plez/ ənt] *adjective, more/ most.* not agreeable or pleasing; not pleasant: The assistant coach had the *unpleasant* job of telling players they'd been dropped from the team. —**unpleasantly,** *adverb:* "The lane was becoming *unpleasantly* slippery, for the mist was passing into rain." (George Eliot)

un·pop·u·lar [ən päp/ yə lər] *adjective, more/ most.* not generally liked; not popular.

un·pre·dict·able [ən pri dik/ tə bəl] *adjective, more/most.* not possible to predict; not able to be known or judged in advance: The currents at that beach are *unpredictable;* swimmers have to be very careful. "A mob was a dangerous beast: uncontrollable, *unpredictable.*" (Lloyd Alexander)

un·pre·pared [un/ prə pârd/] *adjective.* not ready: He came to class *unprepared* and couldn't answer the teacher's question.

un·real [ən rēl/ or ən rē/ əl] *adjective.* not true or real; imaginary. —**unrealistic,** *adjective.* not realistic or practical: You expect to sell that old bike for $100? You're being very *unrealistic.*

un·rea·son·a·ble [ən rēz/ nə bəl] *adjective, more/most.* not reasonable; not sensible or fair: "He said he would charge five dollars a lesson, which isn't *unreasonable* in my opinion." (Cynthia Voigt) —**unreasonably,** *adverb.*

un·re·li·a·ble [un/ ri lī/ ə bəl] *adjective, more/ most.* not to be trusted or depended on; not reliable: The king was convinced that the two generals were *unreliable* and were planning to overthrow him.

un·rest [ən rest/] *noun.* an uneasy or troubled state; lack of peace or ease: The late 1960's was a time of great *unrest* on college campuses, with protests and rioting.

un·ru·ly [ən rōō/ lē] *adjective,* **unrulier, un- ruliest.** hard to control; out of order: The soccer crowd became angry and *unruly* when the referee called a penalty shot against the home team.

un·safe [ən sāf/] *adjective, more/most.* dangerous and risky; not safe.

un·sat·is·fac·to·ry [un/ sat is fak/ trē] *adjective, more/most.* not good enough; not satisfactory: He received a grade of *Unsatisfactory* in reading and is going to have to take a special reading class.

un·scru·pu·lous [ən skrōō/ pyə ləs] *adjective, more/most.* not having the proper standards or principles; not careful about right and wrong: The *unscrupulous* lawyer gambled his clients' money in get-rich-quick schemes and bad investments.

un·seem·ly [ən sēm/ lē] *adjective, more/most.* not done with good manners or proper behavior; not polite.

un·seen [ən sēn/] *adjective.* not seen or noticed: The river is dangerous for boats because of its *unseen* rocks and shallows. "An owl glided past with great slow wings, and out of the swamp some *unseen* creature moved . . ." (Louis L'Amour)

un·set·tled [ən set/ əld] *adjective, more/most.* **1.** not lived in: Most of Alaska is *unsettled* wilderness. **2.** not decided: It's still *unsettled* who our new club president will be. **3.** not calm or peaceful. —**unsettling,** *adjective.* making uneasy or disturbed: Recent news about that company has been *unsettling,* and many people have sold their company stock.

un·skilled [ən skild/] *adjective, more/most.* not having or requiring a skill or special training: The city hired a group of *unskilled* workers and paid them to clean up vacant lots and unoccupied buildings.

un·sound [ən sound/] *adjective, more/most.* **1.** not strong or solid; weak. **2.** not based on truth or clear thinking: *unsound* reasoning.

un·speak·a·ble [ən spē/ kə bəl] *adjective, more/ most.* **1.** bad beyond description; horrible. **2.** not able to be said in words.

un·sta·ble [ən stā/ bəl] *adjective, more/most.* **1.** not firm or steady; shaky. **2.** not having a firm control of the mind or feelings.

un·stead·y [ən sted/ ē] *adjective,* **unsteadier, unsteadiest.** not firm or steady; shaky.

U

Pronunciation Key: [ə] Symbol

The [ə] or *schwa* sound occurs in syllables without an accent. It can be spelled with any vowel, such as **a** in above, **e** in listen, **i** in pencil, **o** in melon, **u** in circus. It can also be a combination of vowels, such as **io** in action, **ai** in mountain, **iou** in precious.

(Turn the page for more information.)

un•suc•cess•ful [ən sək ses′ fəl] *adjective, more/most.* not having a good result; not successful. —**unsuccessfully,** adverb.

un•sure [ən shoor′] *adjective, more/most.* not sure; doubtful: She's just started skating and is still very *unsure* of herself on the ice.

un•think•a•ble [ən thing′ kə bəl] *adjective, more/most.* not to be thought of or considered; not acceptable.

un•ti•dy [ən tī′ dē] *adjective,* **untidier, untidiest.** not in order; not tidy.

un•tie [ən tī′] *verb,* **untied, untying.** to unfasten a knot or something tied; loosen or undo: His shoelace came *untied* and he had to stop to tie it.

un•til [ən til′] *preposition; conjunction.* up to the time of; up to the stated time: "I've been at it all afternoon, from two o'clock *until* now." (Anne Frank)

un•to [un′ tōō] *preposition.* an older and more formal form of the word **to:** The "golden rule" is often stated as, "Do *unto* others as you would have them do *unto* you."

un•told [ən tōld′] *adjective.* **1.** not reported or told: Her book contains several previously *untold* stories about the ex-President. **2.** too great to be counted: World War II brought suffering to *untold* numbers of people.

un•touched [ən tuchd′] *adjective, more/most.* not touched: Sarah didn't want to eat the school lunch and left her plate *untouched.*

un•true [ən trōō′] *adjective, more/most.* not true or correct; false: It is *untrue* that being chilled will cause you to get a cold.

un•used [ən yōōzd′] *adjective, more/most.* **1.** not in use; not put to use: He cut off a piece of the butter and put the *unused* portion in the refrigerator. **2.** not used to; not accustomed to: Katie is *unused* to being in the house alone and was a bit nervous about it.

un•u•su•al [ən yōō′ zhōō əl] *adjective, more/most.* not ordinary or common; not usual: I haven't seen Dave at the park even once this week; it's very *unusual* for him not to be there. ". . . he watched his father filling his plate, piling it high with an *unusual* amount of food." (Jean Fritz) —**unusually,** *adverb:* "For her area and background, her I.Q. of 140 was *unusually* high." (Alice Walker)

un•veil [ən vāl′] *verb,* **unveiled, unveiling.** to remove a veil or covering from; reveal: "The airplane has *unveiled* for us the true face of the earth. For centuries, highways had been deceiving us." (Antoine de St. Exupéry)

un•want•ed [ən wän′ tid *or* ən wôn′ tid] *adjective, more/most.* not needed or wished for; not wanted.

un•wel•come [ən wel′ kəm] *adjective, more/most.* not well received; not welcome.

un•wil•ling [ən wil′ ing] *adjective, more/most.* not willing: He was *unwilling* to wait in line and decided to come back later. —**unwillingly,** *adverb.*

un•wind [ən wīnd′] *verb,* **unwound, unwinding. 1.** to loosen or undo something that has been wound up: The fishing line was *unwinding* rapidly as the fish carried the bait out to sea. **2.** to free from tension; relax: After a busy week teaching she likes to *unwind* by sitting on the beach with a good book.

un•wise [ən wīz′] *adjective, more/most.* showing poor judgment; not wise.

un•wor•thy [ən wur′ the] *adjective, more/most.* not worthy; not suitable: The director's new movie is very boring and *unworthy* of someone who has won so many honors in the past.

un•wound [ən wound′] *verb.* the past form of **unwind.**

un•wrap [ən rap′] *verb,* **unwrapped, unwrapping.** to remove the wrapping from; open or uncover: to *unwrap* a birthday present.

un•writ•ten [ən rit′ ən] *adjective.* not in writing; spoken: We had an *unwritten* agreement that he would pay me back for any repairs I made while I was renting his house. ♦ An **unwritten law** or **rule** is something that does not have legal force but is accepted as common practice: It's an *unwritten law* that when you take out a library book you don't write in it or tear out pages.

up [up] *adverb.* **1.** from a lower to a higher place: The cat jumped *up* on the table from the floor. **2.** in, at, or to a higher point or level: The price of gas has gone *up* since last month. Please turn *up* the radio; I can't hear it. **3.** to a place that is thought of as above, farther along, or farther away: They live in New York and have a summer home *up* in Canada. He went *up* to the movie star and asked for her autograph. **4.** out of bed: Ellen asked if she could stay *up* to watch the late movie. —*adjective.* **1.** going to or in a higher place or position: We want to get started before the sun is *up.* The temperature outside is *up* to almost 90°. ♦ Often used in combination: *Upland* is the hills or higher land in an area. **2.** out of bed. **3.** in baseball, at bat. —*preposition.* from a lower to a higher place or level: to climb *up* a hill. ♦ Often used with **to:** That school goes *up to* grade 8.

up *Up* is one of the few words in English that covers all the basic parts of speech. "Mom put Andy's drawing *up* on the refrigerator." (adverb) "Karen's house is *up* the hill from ours." (preposition) "Don't call so early; they won't be *up* yet." (adjective) Note that *up* has exactly the same sense as an adverb, adjective, or preposition. The way to identify the part of speech is by the different words that relate to *up*. If it begins a noun phrase—*up river, up a hill,* and so on—it's a preposition. If it ties directly to the noun, it's an adjective—*uptown, upstream, the sun is up.* If it is not directly connected to another word, but simply relates to a verb, then it's an adverb: "Is this elevator going *up* or down?" *Up* can also be used as a noun: "Every business has its *ups* and downs." It even has an informal use as a verb: "The Acme Company has *upped* the price of its portable computer," although better usage is to say *raise* or *increase* instead.

up•com•ing [up′ kum′ ing] *adjective.* coming up; coming near: The school band is practicing for the *upcoming* town parade.

up•date [up′ dāt′] *verb,* **updated, updating.** to bring up to date; make more modern or current: When a dictionary is *updated,* new words are added to it. ◆ Also used as a noun: The newspaper printed a short article as an *update* on last month's series about farm problems.

up•grade [up′ grād′ *or* up′ grād′] *verb,* **upgraded, upgrading.** to improve the quality or level of: The restaurant has been remodeled and *upgraded* to become a very fancy place. ◆ Also used as a noun: The airline allowed him an *upgrade* from a regular ticket to first class.

upheld the decision of the lower court and the law will stay in effect.

up•hol•ster [ə pōl′ stər] *verb,* **upholstered, upholstering.** to fit furniture with padding, cushions, or coverings. ◆ Often used as an adjective: an *upholstered* chair. ◆ The materials used to pad and cover furniture are called **upholstery** [ə pōl′ strē].

up•keep [up′ kēp′] *noun.* the keeping of something in good condition, or the cost of doing this: The *upkeep* on an old car can really get to be expensive.

up•lift [əp lift′] *verb,* **uplifted, uplifting. 1.** to raise or lift up: "The cat . . . stood with *uplifted* paw, pointing the direction of the wind."

upon "One of the boats dropped in the water, and walked toward us *upon* the sea with her long oars." (Joseph Conrad) *Upon* and *on* are a pair of words with the nearly the same basic meaning. *On* is by far the more common, appearing about fifteen times more often than *upon* in our Word Survey. Writers before the 1950's used *upon* frequently. "He reflected *upon* the mysterious dishes that were brought into the dining room . . ." (Willa Cather) Today, a modern writer would probably say "He reflected *on* . . ." *Upon* is also used by poets on occasion, because it offers a two-syllable word in place of a one-syllable one for the rhythm of a line: "Once *upon* a midnight dreary . . ." is the opening line of Edgar Allan Poe's "The Raven." As these examples indicate, *upon* has a formal, literary tone. Perhaps you should be cautious about using it in ordinary writing.

up•heav•al [up hē′ vəl] *noun, plural* **upheavals.** a time of great change or sudden disturbance: Law and order in France broke down completely during the period of *upheaval* that was the French Revolution.

up•hill [up′ hil′] *adverb; adjective.* **1.** going up a hill or toward a higher place; upward: Water cannot flow *uphill.* **2.** filled with obstacles; difficult: The home team fell behind 5-0 in the first inning and had to fight an *uphill* battle to win the game.

up•hold [əp hōld′] *verb,* **upheld, upholding.** to support or agree with: The Supreme Court has

(Meindert DeJong) **2.** to raise the spirit; encourage good feeling: "I felt rather *uplifted* as I marched away from the Grammar School; I was going there, that was settled." (Wole Soyinka)

Pronunciation Key: Accent Marks

[′] is the normal accent mark. It shows where the main stress falls on a word.
[′] is a secondary accent mark. It shows a lighter stress than the primary accent. For example:

tel • e • vis • ion [tel′ə vizh′ən]
(Turn the page for more information.)

up•on [ə pän´] *preposition.* on: "Baskets of green peas and one of beans I put *upon* the table in the dining room." (M. F. K. Fisher) "*Upon* the printed page, also by word of mouth, we have a record of it all." (Marianne Moore)

up•per [up´ər] *adjective.* higher in position: The house has two bedrooms downstairs and two on the *upper* floor. A middle school is for students in the *upper* elementary grades.

up•per•case [up´ər kās´] *adjective; noun.* in printing, the capital or larger letters. *A, B,* and *C* are uppercase.

up•right [up´rīt´] *adjective.* **1.** standing straight up. **2.** honest; trustworthy: "God knows, the old shoemaker earned an honest living and lived an *upright* life." (Carol Ryrie Brink) —*adverb.* standing straight up.

up•ris•ing [up´rī´zing] *noun, plural* **uprisings.** a revolt against a government or others with power; a rebellion: Cuba was a colony of Spain for 400 years, until the patriot José Martí began an *uprising* to free the country.

up•roar [up´rôr´] *noun, plural* **uproars.** a loud, confusing disturbance: A man in back suddenly shouted, "He didn't do it! I did!" This sent the courtroom into an *uproar.*

up•root [əp rōōt´] *verb,* **uprooted, uprooting. 1.** to tear or pull up by the roots: The huge windstorm *uprooted* two trees in our front yard. **2.** to send or force away; remove: John Steinbeck's *Grapes of Wrath* tells of a farm family that was *uprooted* from its home in Oklahoma.

up•set [əp set´] *verb,* **upset, upsetting. 1.** to tip or knock over: The boys were fooling around in the living room and *upset* the bowl of flowers. **2.** to disturb the order of; interfere with: Her travel plans were *upset* when her flight was cancelled. **3.** to make worried, nervous, or unhappy: The boys on the other team laughed when he went up to bat, which was very *upsetting.* **4.** to make slightly sick, especially in the stomach. **5.** to win a game or contest that one had been expected to lose. —[up´ set´ *or* up´ set´] *adjective.* **1.** worried, nervous, or unhappy. **2.** sick to one's stomach. —[up´ set] *noun, plural* **upsets.** the fact of upsetting: In the 1948 election for President, Harry Truman beat Thomas E. Dewey in a surprising *upset.*

upside down or **upside-down 1.** having the top part or side turned to the bottom part of something: The opossum can hang *upside down* by its tail to sleep. **2.** in disorder or confusion: We turned the house *upside down* trying to find Mom's missing car keys.

up•stairs [up´ stârz´] *adverb; adjective; noun.* up the stairs or on a higher floor: Please take this laundry basket *upstairs* to your bedroom. I heard someone walking around in the *upstairs* apartment.

up•stream [up´ strēm´] *adverb; adjective.* toward the start or source of a stream; up a stream: Salmon live in the ocean but move *upstream* to fresh water to bear their young.

up-to-date [up´ tə dāt´] *adjective, more/most.* keeping up with new or recent things; having the latest information.

up•ward [up´ wərd] *adverb; adjective.* from a lower to a higher place or stage: "Behind the houses the bare fields sloped *upward* . . . until they met the wide blankets of snow halfway up the sides of the mountains." (Erskine Caldwell) "It was *upward* of thirty days before I saw the mouth of the big river." (Joseph Conrad)

u•ra•ni•um [yoo rā´ nē əm] *noun.* a heavy, silver-white metal that is used to make nuclear energy. Uranium is a RADIOACTIVE chemical element.

U•ra•nus [yə rān´ əs] *noun.* **1.** the seventh planet from the sun. Uranus is the third-largest of the planets. It has five moons circling it. **2.** in the religion of the ancient Greeks, the god of the sky and the father of a race of giants.

ur•ban [ur´ bən] *adjective, more/most.* having to do with a city or with city life: Historically the Republican Party has appealed more to farmers, and the Democratic Party more to *urban* voters. ◆ **Urban renewal** is the fixing up of run-down city areas.

urge [urj] *verb,* **urged, urging. 1.** to push or force on: "Glorfindel still *urged* them on, and only allowed two brief halts during the day's march." (J. R. R. Tolkien) **2.** to try to convince or persuade; argue for: "Gandhi's friends had *urged* him to take one, but he refused." (William L. Shirer) —*noun, plural* **urges.** a strong desire or wish: "All at once I felt a strong *urge* to talk to her for hours and hours about everything." (Russell Hoban)

ur•gent [ur´ jənt] *adjective, more/most.* needing to be dealt with or taken care of right away; pressing; demanding: "As though in answer to her *urgent* prayer for relief, a knock sounded on the outside door . . ." (Elizabeth Speare) ◆ The fact of being urgent is **urgency. —urgently,** *adverb:* ". . . she sent *urgently* for a doctor." (Agatha Christie)

u•rine [yoor´ in] *noun.* a clear yellow fluid made of body wastes. Urine is given off by the kidneys and discharged from the body.

usage If you say, "They own two dog," your statement is clear; it is direct; but it is also wrong. "Two dogs" is correct. *Usage* says it's correct. But what is *usage* and who determines it? Earlier *lexicographers* (dictionary editors), such as Samuel Johnson and Noah Webster, decided that correct usage was found in the way the language was used by famous authors. They quoted these authors in their dictionaries. In general, that idea of correct usage was continued up until the early 1960's. Then dictionary makers began to argue that the definition was too narrow. They said that the language could only be judged by studying many, many writers, not a limited number of truly "great" authors. They used quotations not only from Shakespeare and Dickens, but also from magazine writers and newspaper reporters, and even from non-writers, such as actors, popular singers, and other celebrities. In this dictionary, we follow the older "Johnsonian" policy. We purposely limit our quotation list for examples of correct usage to about 500 famous authors.

urn [urn] *noun, plural* **urns. 1.** a large vase set on a base. Urns were often used in ancient Greece and Rome to hold the ashes of a dead person. Today urns are used mainly for decoration. **2.** a large metal container that holds several gallons of coffee or tea and that is used to serve large groups of people.

urn A Greek urn that was used for storing food, made about 520 B.C.

U•ru•guay [yoor′ə gwā′] a country in southeastern South America, on the Atlantic Ocean. *Capital:* Montevideo. *Area:* 72,000 square miles. *Population:* 2,960,000. **—Uruguayan,** *adjective; noun.*

us [us] *pronoun.* the pronoun **we** when used as an object: Naomi's mom gave *us* a ride home. My grandmother always brings *us* a treat when she comes to visit.

U. S. an abbreviation for **United States.**

U. S. A. an abbreviation for **United States of America.**

us•age [yoo′ sij] *noun, plural* **usages. 1.** a way of using or handling something; treatment: That delicate wristwatch won't last long with such rough *usage.* **2.** the way in which words are used in speaking or writing: The word "thee" meaning "you" is no longer a common *usage.*

use [yooz] *verb,* **used, using. 1.** to put into action or service for a special purpose: Sandy *used* a kitchen knife to cut the package open. In English, "the" is *used* more often than any other word. **2.** *also,* **use up.** to finish or consume: Cathy *used up* all the butter baking her cookies. **3.** to take advantage of: Ricky is just *using* Eddie; he's only nice to him so he can get to play all his video games. —[yoos] *noun, plural* **uses. 1.** the act or fact of being used: All the pay phones were in *use* and he had to wait to make his call. **2.** the quality of being useful or helpful: Let's wait until tomorrow morning; there's no *use* trying to find it in the dark. **3.** a need or purpose for which something is used: She's found that her computer has many *uses,* such as writing letters or keeping records. **4.** the power or right to use something: With this vacation plan you get the *use* of a rental car for a week.

used [yoozd′] *adjective.* having been owned by someone else; not new: a *used* car.

used to [yoost′ too′] **1.** having the habit of; accustomed to: "Some of the older children are *used to* coming to the mission school, but the smaller children are not." (Alice Walker) **2.** did

Pronunciation Key: A–F

a	and; hat	ch	chew; such
ā	ate; stay	d	dog; lid
â	care; air	e	end; yet
ä	father; hot	ē	she; each
b	boy; cab	f	fun; off

(Turn the page for more information.)

at one time or did in the past: "I was working in New York that spring, and I *used to* lunch with him at the Yale Club . . ." (F. Scott Fitzgerald)

use•ful [yōos′fəl] *adjective, more/most.* having a good use or purpose; helpful: I found that book to be very *useful* when I was doing my history report. **—usefulness,** *noun.*

use•less [yōos′lis] *adjective.* having no use; not helpful, worthless: "She clicked and clicked the *useless* flashlight, but it stayed dead." (Meindert DeJong)

us•er [yōo′zər] *noun, plural* **users.** a person who uses some stated thing: The lawnmower blades are covered to protect the *user* against getting cut.

us•er-friend•ly [yōoz′ər frend′lē] *adjective, more/most.* of a computer or computer program, easy to understand and operate for people who are not computer experts.

ush•er [ush′ər] *noun, plural* **ushers.** a person who shows people to their seats in a church, theater, stadium, and so on. *—verb,* **ushered, ushering. 1.** to act as an usher; escort someone: "'Mr. Desmond Burton-Cox,' announced George, *ushering* in the expected guest." (Agatha Christie) **2. usher in (out).** to cause something to come or go; lead the way: A week of mild weather *ushered in* the spring season.

U.S.S.R. or **USSR** an abbreviation for the **Union of Soviet Socialist Republics.**

u•su•al [yōo′zhōo əl] *adjective, more/most.* as is normal or to be expected; ordinary; common: "Lizzie woke up somewhere near her *usual* time—before daylight." (Jessamyn West) ◆ Often used in the phrase **as usual:** "Late that night, the phone rings. *As usual,* her mother has it on the first ring." (Ann Beattie)

u•su•al•ly [yōo′zhə lē *or* yōo′zhōo ə lē] in a way that is usual; normally: "Mr. Jeh *usually* ate his meals at the restaurant where he worked." (Laurence Yep)

U•tah [yōo′tô] a state in the west-central U.S. *Capital:* Salt Lake City. *Nickname:* "Beehive State." *Area:* 84,900 square miles. *Population:* 1,665,000.

u•ten•sil [yōo ten′səl] *noun, plural* **utensils.** a tool or small object that is useful and has a special purpose: Forks, knives, and spoons are kitchen *utensils.*

u•til•i•ty [yōo til′ə tē] *noun, plural* **utilities. 1.** a company that sells a basic service to the public. Telephone companies and gas and electric companies are utilities. **2.** the quality of being useful; usefulness.

u•ti•lize [yōo′tə līz′] *verb,* **utilized, utilizing.** to put into use; to make use of: "Eskimos *utilized* the caribou completely. They made clothing, bedding, and bags from its skin and tools and weapons from its bones and antlers." (Barry Lopez)

ut•most [ut′mōst′] *adjective.* greatest or most possible: He placed the tiny plants in the ground with the *utmost* care. ◆ Also used as a noun: "Lawyers always do their *utmost* to get men on the jury who are apt to decide in favor of their clients." (Clarence Darrow)

u•to•pi•a [yōo tō′pē ə] *noun, plural* **utopias.** (*also spelled* **Utopia**) an imaginary place offering a perfect life where complete happiness is enjoyed by all. **—utopian,** *adjective.* ◆ This word comes from the name of a book written in 1516 by Sir Thomas More, in which he describes an island of Utopia where all people are wise, healthy, and prosperous.

ut•ter[1] [ut′ər] *verb,* **uttered, uttering.** to say out loud; speak: "It was a strange, silent walk. Eisenhower *uttered* hardly a word." (Cornelius Ryan) **—utterance,** *noun.*

ut•ter[2] *adjective.* complete or total; absolute: "The young fool was set on a course of *utter* destruction." (Lloyd Alexander) "They would all have a good laugh over how she had made an *utter* fool of herself." (Brian Moore) **—utterly,** *adverb:* "When she was a child her mother had told her that she was *utterly* beautiful . . ." (Beryl Bainbridge)

Utah Utah's capital, Salt Lake City. Seen in the background are the Wasatch Mountains.

v, V [vē] *noun, plural* **v's, V's.** the twenty-second letter of the alphabet.

va•can•cy [vā′kən sē] *noun, plural* **vacancies.** the fact of being vacant or empty: If a motel has all its rooms rented it will put out a sign saying, "No *Vacancy*."

va•cant [vā′kənt] *adjective.* **1.** not in use; not occupied; empty: a *vacant* apartment. The boys played ball in a *vacant* lot at the end of the street. **2.** without expression or thought: "She looked around with the rather *vacant* expression of someone who is looking for something she has never heard of before . . ." (Agatha Christie) —**vacantly,** *adverb.*

va•cate [vā′kāt′] *verb,* **vacated, vacating.** to make vacant; leave empty: "An apartment on Buckingham Street was about to be *vacated*." (A. B. Guthrie)

va•ca•tion [vā kā′shən] *noun, plural* **vacations.** **1.** a period away from school, work, or other regular activity: School is closed for the summer and the children are on *vacation.* **2.** a time spent in travel or amusement; a pleasure trip. —*verb,* **vacationed, vacationing.** to take a vacation: to *vacation* in Hawaii.

vac•ci•nate [vak′sə nāt′] *verb,* **vaccinated, vaccinating.** to give a VACCINE in order to protect a person from disease: People are *vaccinated* against diseases such as smallpox and polio. —**vaccination,** *noun.*

vac•cine [vak′sēn′] *noun, plural* **vaccines.** a solution containing weakened or dead disease germs, injected into a person's bloodstream to help the person build up resistance against the actual disease. The use of vaccines has almost wiped out certain diseases that were previously very dangerous. ◆ *Vaccine* and *vaccinate* come from the Latin word *vacca,* meaning "cow." In the 1790's the English scientist Edward Jenner developed the first vaccine, a protection against smallpox, by taking germs from cows that had *cow-pox,* a mild disease.

vac•u•um [vak′yo͞om] *noun, plural* **vacuums.** **1.** a space that does not have anything in it, not even air. ◆ Since science is not able to make a perfect vacuum, the term is used to refer to a space that is almost empty of air and matter. **2.** short for **vacuum cleaner. 3.** an area or condition cut off from outside events and influences: Her office is in a different building from the main office and she's new to the company, so she's operating in a *vacuum* at this point. —*verb,* **vacuumed, vacuuming.** to clean with a vacuum cleaner: to *vacuum* a rug.

vacuum cleaner an electrical machine that is used to suck up dirt and dust from carpets, floors, furniture, and so on. A fan inside the machine creates a partial vacuum, and the suction from this draws air into the machine.

va•grant [vā′grənt] *noun, plural* **vagrants.** a person without a settled home or regular job. ◆ The fact of being a vagrant is **vagrancy.**

vague [vāg] *adjective,* **vaguer, vaguest.** not clear or definite: "Dorothy became *vague.* 'I can't

vague "My memory of my first day in kindergarten is *vague.* Was I too young or too scared?" This comment is *vague* on purpose. But if writing is vague because it does not interest and inform the reader, then it's simply *bad* writing. A broad statement such as "Washington was a great leader" is true and not vague by nature, but it becomes vague if left on its own. Use specifics—details, examples, comments. Try this, "It has been said by some historians that Washington was a poor general but a great politician. How can they say that? Consider this . . . Consider, also, that . . ." Also, use forceful language. Adverbs that weaken a statement (like *rather* or *somewhat)* are useless if you wish to avoid vagueness. So are "plain vanilla" adjectives like *nice, pretty,* or *fine.*

exactly remember.'" (John Mortimer) **—vaguely,** *adverb:* "She wanders around *vaguely,* trying to get her thoughts in order . . ." (William Inge)

vain [vān] *adjective,* **vainer, vainest. 1.** having too much pride in one's appearance or ability; conceited: "You met me, flattered me, and taught me to be *vain* of my good looks." (Oscar Wilde) **2.** not successful; useless. ◆ Usually used in the phrase **in vain:** "The people near Atkinson started trying to lift him up, but *in vain.*" (Kingsley Amis) **—vainly,** *adverb.*

val•e•dic•to•ri•an [val′ ə dik tôr′ ē ən] *noun, plural* **valedictorians.** the student who has the highest grades and gives the farewell speech at a graduation ceremony.

Valentine Valentine cards from the early 1800's.

val•en•tine [val′ ən tīn′] *noun, plural* **valentines. 1.** *also,* **Valentine.** a card, present, or greeting given to a sweetheart, friend, or family member on Valentine's Day. **2.** a person to whom such a card or gift is sent.

Valentine's Day February 14th, named after Saint Valentine, a Christian saint who lived in Rome in the 200's A.D. People send valentines to their sweethearts, friends, and relatives on this day.

val•iant [val′ yənt] *adjective, more/most.* full of bravery or courage; heroic: Clara Barton's *valiant* efforts saved many wounded soldiers during the Civil War. **—valiantly,** *adverb.*

val•id [val′ id] *adjective, more/most.* **1.** based on facts or truth; sound: He had a *valid* reason for handing his paper in late and the teacher didn't lower his mark. **2.** having force under the law: This driver's license is *valid* for a period of one year. ◆ The fact of being valid is **validity** [və lid′ ə tē].

val•ley [val′ ē] *noun, plural* **valleys.** an area of low land between hills or mountains, often with a river flowing through it: Egyptian civilization developed in the *valley* of the Nile River.

Valley Forge a village in southeastern Pennsylvania where General George Washington and his Continental Army camped during the harsh winter of 1777-78.

val•or [val′ ər] *noun.* great courage or bravery, especially in war.

val•u•a•ble [val′ yə bəl] *adjective, more/most.* **1.** worth a lot of money: Mink coats and diamond rings are *valuable* items. **2.** very important or useful: "So charming of you to have spared time—your very *valuable* time, I'm sure . . ." (Agatha Christie) **—noun, plural** **valuables.** something that is worth a lot of money or is of great importance: Guests at the hotel can keep their *valuables* in the hotel safe.

val•ue [val′ yōō] *noun, plural* **values. 1.** how much money, goods, or services a thing will bring in return; the worth of something when compared to other things: According to this used-car book, our car has a market *value* of about $3000. **2.** the quality of something that makes it important, useful, or helpful: The movie *It's a Wonderful Life* shows the *value* of having good friends. **3. values.** the standards or beliefs that someone has about how to act or to conduct one's life: He has a poor sense of *values* and doesn't accept the fact that cheating on a test is wrong. **—verb, valued, valuing. 1.** to set or estimate the worth of: Farm land in that area is *valued* at about $1000 an acre. **2.** to consider important or valuable; think highly of: "This period of her life passed so quickly she had not had time to properly *value* it." (Alice Walker)

valve [valv] *noun, plural* **valves. 1.** a movable part that can control the flow of a liquid or gas from one part of a machine or device to another: You open this *valve* to turn on the lawn sprinkler. In a car engine, burned gases leave the cylinder through the exhaust *valve.* **2.** a similar part in the body that controls the flow of blood or other fluids: the *valves* of the heart. **3.** one of the halves of the shell of an oyster or similar animal.

vam•pire [vam′ pīr] *noun, pural* **vampires. 1.** in folk tales, a dead body that rises from its grave at night to suck the blood of sleeping people. **2.** *also,* **vampire bat.** a bat of tropical America that sucks the blood of animals and that sometimes attacks sleeping humans.

van [van] *noun, plural* **vans. 1.** a large, covered truck that is used to haul goods or animals.

◆ A **moving van** is used to move furniture and household goods. **2.** a motor vehicle like a small truck, having several seats for passengers and extra room for carrying cargo.

Van Bur•en [van byŏor′ ən] **Martin**, 1782-1862, the eighth president of the United States, from 1837 to 1841.

Van•cou•ver [van koō′ vər] a city in southwestern British Columbia, Canada, on the Pacific Ocean. *Population:* 415,000.

vandalism An example of vandalism on the New York City subway system.

van•dal•ism [van′ də liz′ əm] *noun.* the crime of destroying or damaging someone's property on purpose. ◆ A person who does this is a **vandal**: *Vandals* did a lot of damage to our school last night—they broke windows, trampled flowers, and knocked over several young trees. ◆ In ancient times, the *Vandals* were a Germanic tribe who attacked Rome and destroyed many fine buildings and statues.

vane [vān] *noun, plural* **vanes. 1.** a blade that is moved around a center by water or wind. Windmills, propellers, and fans have *vanes*. **2.** see **weather vane**.

Van Gogh [van gō′] **Vincent**, 1853-1890, Dutch painter.

va•nil•la [və nil′ ə] *noun.* a liquid flavoring made from the dried seed pods of a certain tropical plant. Vanilla is used in ice cream, cookies, cakes, and other sweets.

van•ish [van′ ish] *verb,* **vanished, vanishing. 1.** to suddenly go out of sight; become invisible; disappear: "I was startled by a noise behind me, and turning suddenly saw the flapping white tail of a rabbit *vanishing* up the slope." (H. G. Wells) **2.** to stop existing; come to an end: "Do you really mean that Strider is one of the people of the old kings? . . . I thought they had all *vanished* long ago." (J.R.R. Tolkien)

van•i•ty [van′ ə tē] *noun, plural* **vanities.** the fact of being vain; too much pride in one's looks, accomplishments, or ability.

van•quish [vang′ kwish] *verb,* **vanquished, vanquishing.** to conquer or defeat: to *vanquish* an enemy in war. "The fire was rapidly being *vanquished*. There was no doubt about it." (Penelope Lively)

va•por [vā′ pər] *noun, plural* **vapors.** tiny particles of a liquid or gas that can be seen or smelled floating in the air. Clouds, steam, and gasoline fumes are kinds of vapor.

var•i•a•ble [vâr′ ē ə bəl] *adjective, more/most.* that varies; able or likely to change: If a loan has a *variable* rate of interest, it means the rate can change according to business conditions. —*noun, plural* **variables.** something that can change or be changed: Several *variables* could affect tomorrow's horse race, such as the weather or the condition of the track.

var•i•ant [vâr′ ē ənt] *noun, plural* **variants.** something that varies; a different form: The word "theatre" is a *variant* of "theater." ◆ Also used as an adjective: a *variant* spelling or pronunciation.

var•i•a•tion [vâr′ ē ā′ shən] *noun, plural* **variations. 1.** the fact of varying; a change from the normal or usual way: "Do it by the book. No

Van Gogh A self-portrait by the artist.

Pronunciation Key: A–F

a	and; hat	ch	chew; such
ā	ate; stay	d	dog; lid
â	care; air	e	end; yet
ä	father; hot	ē	she; each
b	boy; cab	f	fun; off

(Turn the page for more information.)

variations permitted." (John D. MacDonald) **2.** a similar but slightly different form of something: "He had an enormous number of stories about you, mostly *variations* on the same one . . ." (Malcolm Lowry)

var•ied [vâr′ ēd] *adjective, more/most.* that changes or has changed: "I hear America singing, the *varied* carols I hear . . ." (Walt Whitman) "The *varied* landscape afforded by the Andaman Islands . . ." (Jules Verne)

va•ri•e•ty [və rī′ ə tē] *noun, plural* **varieties. 1.** the fact of being different: "She had only one dress. She and her sisters swapped dresses each day so they might have at least this much *variety* . . ." (Alice Walker) **2.** things that are different; an assortment or collection: "All the people Ellen had known in Savannah might have been cast from the same mold . . . but here was a *variety* of people." (Margaret Mitchell) **3.** a particular type that is different from others: "Silver Queen" is a popular *variety* of white corn.

var•y [vâr′ ē] *verb,* **varied, varying.** to make or become different; change: "The cactus flowers are all much alike, *varying* only in color . . ." (Edward Abbey) "There is a chorus of *varying* sound—groans, curses, bursts of laughter and singing . . ." (George Orwell)

vase [vās *or* vāz] *noun, plural* **vases.** a container used to hold flowers or as a decoration.

vas•sal [vas′ əl] *noun, plural* **vassals.** in the Middle Ages, a person who held land and received protection from a lord. In return the vassal promised to be loyal to the lord, and to fight for him in war and give other service.

vast [vast] *adjective,* **vaster, vastest.** very large; huge: "For the next six hours they hurried across *vast* broken ice fields . . ." (James Houston) "They went through a dark tunnel and discovered a *vast* concealed court surrounded by perhaps a hundred buildings." (Mark Helprin) **—vastly,** *adverb.* very much: The team should be *vastly* improved over last season. **—vastness,** *noun.*

---

variety It's said to be the spice of life. It is also a spice in the brew of words. Variety in writing comes in several forms. Ernest Hemingway was famous for using short sentences, but he also warned a young writer, "If you use them too much you get a monotonous trip-hammer action that tires the reader." In a well-known passage, George Orwell used one sentence that was fifty words long and followed it with one of four words. Avoid a series of sentences that all have the same form, such as "There was . . ." "There was . . ." or "And then . . ." "And then . . ." This is not to say that writers don't ever repeat the same sentence opening. In Thomas Wolfe's "The Child by Tiger," he describes the room of an ex-army man, a very neat and orderly man. He uses a series of "There was . . ." sentences to help show this idea of strict order. What other ways do you know to add variety?

---

var•i•ous [vâr′ ē əs] *adjective.* **1.** not like each other; different: She made a fruit salad with *various* kinds of fruit. The Austro-Hungarian Empire was a collection of *various* national groups and it never acted as a strong, united nation. **2.** more than one; several or many: *Various* people stopped her to say they'd seen her TV interview. **—variously,** *adverb.*

var•nish [vär′ nish] *noun, plural* **varnishes.** a paint-like liquid spread on wood or another surface to give it a hard, shiny coating. It is usually made of RESINS dissolved in alcohol or mixed with oil. **—***verb,* **varnished, varnishing.** to cover with varnish: to *varnish* a table top.

var•si•ty [vär′ sə tē] *noun, plural* **varsities.** the main team representing a school, college, or club in a sport or other competition: Even though Kevin is only a freshman in high school, he's on the *varsity* soccer team. ♦ The team below the varsity is the **junior varsity (JV).**

vat [vat] *noun, plural* **vats.** a large tank or container for holding liquid. Vats may be used for holding grape juice to be made into wine, or dyes to color cloth.

Vat•i•can [vat′ i kən] **1. Vatican City.** an independent state within the city of Rome, Italy; also known as **the Vatican.** It is the residence of the Pope and the center of the Catholic Church. It is the smallest independent nation in the world. **2. the Vatican.** the office or power of the Pope.

vault¹ [vôlt] *noun, plural* **vaults.** a large compartment or room with strong walls and locks, used for storing valuable things and keeping them safe. Banks keep money in a vault.

vault² *verb,* **vaulted, vaulting.** to jump or leap over something: "Buck hurdled the fence and Jody *vaulted* it after him." (Marjorie Kinnan Rawlings) **—***noun, plural* **vaults.** a high leap or jump, as in the POLE VAULT.

VCR [vē/ sē/ är/] *noun, plural* **VCR's** or **VCRs.** a device that can connect to a television set to record or play programs on videotape. VCR's are used to show tapes of recorded TV programs, entertainment and educational films, home movies, and so on. ◆ The initials VCR stand for videocassette recorder.

VDT initials that stand for Visual Display Terminal, a screen that shows information as part of a computer system .

veal [vēl] *noun.* the meat from a calf.

veer [vēr] *verb,* **veered, veering.** to change direction; turn: "The car suddenly *veered* off the road and we came to a sliding halt in the gravel." (Hunter Thompson)

veg•e•ta•ble [vej/ tə bəl] *noun, plural* **vegetables.** any plant or plant part eaten for food, such as corn, peas, beans, lettuce, tomatoes, and potatoes. ◆ The term usually refers to plants eaten as part of a main meal or in a salad, as opposed to sweet fruits (apples, oranges, berries, and so on) eaten separately or for dessert. —*adjective.* made from or having to do with vegetables: a *vegetable* garden, *vegetable* oil.

veg•e•tar•i•an [vej/ ə târ/ ē ən] *noun, plural* **vegetarians.** a person who chooses not to eat meat or meat products. —*adjective:* a *vegetarian* meal, a *vegetarian* restaurant.

veg•e•ta•tion [vej/ ə tā/ shən] *noun.* plant life: The islands of the Caribbean are known for their beautiful tropical *vegetation.*

ve•hi•cle [vē/ ə kəl] *noun, plural* **vehicles.** anything that is used to move or carry people or goods: Cars and trucks are called motor *vehicles.*

ve•he•ment [vē/ ə mənt] *adjective, more/most.* marked by strong feeling or passion; intense: ". . . she got more *vehement,* less willing to compromise." (Ann Beattie) —**vehemence,** *noun.* —**vehemently,** *adverb.*

veil [vāl] *noun, plural* **veils. 1.** a very thin cloth or netting that a women wears over her head or face as a covering or decoration: The bride wore a lace *veil* with her long white gown. **2.** something that covers or hides: That dictator operates behind a *veil* of secrecy and people don't know what he is planning to do. —*verb,* **veiled, veiling.** to cover with or as if with a veil: Women in Arab countries often have their faces *veiled* when they appear in public. "The dust blew everywhere; the blue sky was *veiled* by dust." (Doris Lessing)

vein [vān] *noun, plural* **veins. 1.** one of the blood vessels that carry blood back to the heart from all parts of the body. **2.** a tube-like structure that carries food and water in a leaf, or provides support in an insect's wing. **3.** a long, narrow mineral deposit in a rock: a rich *vein* of gold. **4.** a streak of different color or texture in wood or marble. **5.** a certain style or mood: Canadian humorist Stephen Leacock wrote amusing stories about his family, in the same *vein* as those of James Thurber.

ve•loc•i•ty [və läs/ ə tē] *noun, plural* **velocities.** the rate of motion of an object; speed: We see lightning before we hear the thunder that goes with it, because the *velocity* of light is much greater than that of sound.

vel•vet [vel/ vit] *noun, plural* **velvets.** a kind of fabric that has a very soft, thick, raised surface. —*adjective.* **1.** made with velvet. **2.** *also,* **vel•vety.** very soft and smooth, like this fabric.

vend•ing machine [ven/ ding] a machine with a slot where money is deposited in order to get soft drinks, candy, stamps, and other such small items from the machine.

ven•dor [ven/ dər] *noun, plural* **vendors. 1.** a person who sells something on the street or from door to door: an ice cream *vendor.* "She walked down Ann Street with its jumble of cheap shops . . . and its loud crying fruit *vendors.*" (Brian Moore) **2.** anyone who sells something.

ve•neer [və nēr/] *noun, plural* **veneers. 1.** a thin sheet of fine wood glued or bonded to something of lesser material, to give it a nicer finish or a stronger structure. **2.** any outer covering or surface meant to hide some weakness or fault: "A *veneer* of . . . self-confidence thinly concealed his nervousness." (Aldous Huxley)

ven•er•a•ble [ven/ ər ə bəl] *adjective, more/most.* worthy of respect, because of age or good qualities: The *venerable* Professor Graves had been at the college for forty years.

Ve•ne•tian blind [və nē/ shən] a window shade that has many thin, horizontal slats made of wood, metal, or plastic. The slats can be adjusted at different angles to change the amount of light being let in. ◆ This type of shade became known through its use in the city of *Venice,* Italy.

V

Pronunciation Key: G–N			
ġ	give; big	k	kind; cat; back
h	hold	l	let; ball
i	it; this	m	make; time
ī	ice; my	n	not; own
j	jet; gem; edge	ng	having

(Turn the page for more information.)

Ven•e•zue•la [ven′ ə zwā′ lə] a country on the northern coast of South America. *Capital:* Caracas. *Area:* 352,100 square miles. *Population:* 14,900,000. —**Venezuelan,** *adjective; noun.*

venge•ance [ven′ jəns] *noun.* **1.** punishment given in return for a wrong or injury. **2. with a vengeance.** with great force or violent energy.

Venice This type of boat, a *gondola* [gän′ də lə], is the best way to travel on the Grand Canal of Venice, Italy.

Ven•ice [ven′ is] a city in Italy built on more than 100 small islands in the **Gulf of Venice,** which is part of the Adriatic Sea. Venice was a powerful city-state in the Middle Ages. *Population:* 367,000. —**Venetian,** *adjective; noun.*

ven•i•son [ven′ ə sən *or* ven′ ə zən] *noun.* the meat from a deer eaten as food. ♦ *Venison* goes back to a Latin word meaning "to hunt."

ven•om [ven′ əm] *noun, plural* **venoms. 1.** the poison that certain snakes, spiders, and other animals can pass on through a bite or sting. **2.** strong, bitter feelings; hatred. —**venomous,** *adjective.*

V

vent [vent] *noun, plural* **vents. 1.** an opening that allows gas or liquid to escape or enter: He opened the car's air *vents* to let fresh air in. **2.** a means of escape or release; an outlet: "Daddy doesn't understand that I need to give *vent* to my feelings over Mummy sometimes." (Anne Frank) —*verb,* **vented, venting.** to allow to escape through or as if through a vent: ". . . a stovepipe that *vented* the smoke from the fire through a hole in the wall." (Sherley Anne Williams)

ven•ti•la•tion [ven′ tə lā′ shən] *noun.* **1.** the movement of air through or around an area. **2.** a means of supplying fresh air to a place.

ven•ture [ven′ chər] *verb,* **ventured, venturing. 1.** to face a risk or danger; take a chance: "You folks should have stepped in at the Ranger station before *venturing* off on your own. This desert's no place to play around in." (Sam Shepard) **2.** to say something that may be objected to; dare to say: "She heard herself saying what she had intended to *venture* a while before . . ." (James Agee) —*noun, plural* **ventures.** the act of venturing; a course of action in which there is some risk: Mr. Selden is trying to find people to put up money for his new business *venture.*

Ve•nus [vē′ nəs] *noun.* **1.** the second-closest planet to the sun and sixth-largest planet in the solar system. Venus is slightly smaller than Earth. It is the brightest natural object in the sky after the sun and moon. **2.** the goddess of love in the religion of the ancient Romans.

ve•ran•da [və ran′ də] *noun, plural* **verandas.** a long, usually open porch with a roof that is attached to one or more sides of a house. Large homes built in the southern U. S. in earlier times often had verandas.

verb [vurb] *noun, plural* **verbs.** a word that expresses an action or a state of being. The words *jump, talk, plan, do, is,* and *have* are verbs.

verbs "All fine prose is based on the verbs carrying the sentences. They make the sentences move." (F. Scott Fitzgerald) Fitzgerald then referred to a line in the poem "The Eve of Saint Agnes," by John Keats: "The hare limped trembling through the frozen grass." Fitzgerald said that this line ". . . is so alive that you race through it . . . The limping, trembling, and freezing is going on before your own eyes." (Note that the hare does not "go," move," or "walk," it "limps trembling"—a very precise image.) In his story "The Dead," James Joyce writes: "The newspapers *were* right: snow *was* general all over Ireland. It *was falling* on every part of the dark central plain . . ." Then Joyce picks up the action verb, *fall:* ". . . *falling* softly upon the Bog of Allen" " . . . softly *falling* into the dark mutinous Shannon waves. It was *falling,* too, upon every part of the lonely churchyard where Michael Furey *lay* buried. It *lay* thickly drifted . . ." Notice how the verbs when repeated also link the sentences. Isn't English marvelous!

ver·bal [vur′bəl] *adjective.* of or having to do with words: Ernest Hemingway said that he wanted his writings about places in France to be the *verbal* equivalent of paintings by Cezanne.

ver·dict [vur′dikt] *noun, plural* **verdicts. 1.** the judgment or decision made by a judge or jury in a court trial: The jury decided on a *verdict* of guilty after considering all the evidence. **2.** any judgment or opinion: "She was by popular *verdict* one of the three most beautiful women of her day." (Robert Graves)

verge [vêrj] *noun.* the point at which some action or condition is just about to take place. ◆ Usually used in the phrase **on the verge of:** ". . . I was *on the verge of* collapse. I was leaning against the wall gasping for breath . . ." (James Herriot)

ver·i·fy [ver′ə fī′] *verb,* **verified, verifying.** to prove the truth of; show to be true: "Mrs. Oliver paused, opened the little address book in her hand, *verified* that she was in the place she thought she was . . ." (Agatha Christie) —**verification** [ver′ə fi kā′ shən], *noun.*

Ver·mont [vər mänt′] a state in the northeastern U. S. *Capital:* Montpelier. *Nickname:* "Green Mountain State." *Area:* 9,600 square miles. *Population:* 516,000.

James *Version.* **3.** a form of a written work or other work of art: The final *version* of the report must be typed. I've seen the movie *version* of *The Wizard of Oz,* but I've never read the book.

ver·sus [vur′səs] *preposition.* opposed to; against: Today's game features the Raiders *versus* the Chargers.

ver·te·bra [vur′tə brə] *noun, plural* **vertebrae** [vur′tə brā′] or **vertebras.** one of the bones in the backbone of a person or an animal.

ver·te·brate [vur′tə brāt′] *noun, plural* **vertebrates.** an animal with a backbone. Mammals, fish, reptiles, birds, and amphibians are vertebrates. ◆ Also used as an adjective: A cat is a *vertebrate* animal.

ver·ti·cal [vur′ti kəl] *adjective.* going straight up and down rather than across; upright: When you are standing, you are in a *vertical* position. —**vertically,** *adverb.*

ver·y [ver′ē] *adverb.* **1.** more than usual; to a high degree; extremely: New England has cold winters; Alaska has *very* cold winters. **2.** really; actually: Her clothes are made only from the *very* finest fabrics. —*adjective.* same; exact: As the ball dropped down, he ran to the *very* spot where it was about to fall.

very Some language critics say you should avoid *very* altogether, because it's a lazy word, vague and easy to use. We think that's too strong, yet there is the poor habit of trying to liven up sentences by sprinkling *very* here and there, like automatically putting salt on food without first tasting it. *Very tired* does go beyond *tired, very old* is stronger than *old,* and *very angry* is more than *angry.* But how about *exhausted? Ancient? Furious?* Also, some words are so strong that *very* weakens them! *Very great, very magnificent, very beautiful* add nothing and make *great, magnificent,* or *beautiful* sound as if they need help. Instead of using *very,* be precise. "His shoes were *very new,"* becomes: "His shoes, without a wrinkle or a speck of dust, were straight off the shelf."

ver·sa·tile [vur′sə təl] *adjective, more/most.* able to do a number of things well or be used for many purposes: He's a *versatile* performer who can sing, dance, and play several instruments. Cheese is a *versatile* food that can be used in appetizers, salads, and main dishes.

verse [vurs] *noun, plural* **verses. 1.** words put together in a certain pattern of sounds, often with rhyme; poetry. **2.** a group of lines within a poem or song; a stanza or section. **3.** a short, numbered section of the Bible.

ver·sion [vur′zhən] *noun, plural* **versions. 1.** an account or description given from one person's point of view: Each witness gave his own *version* of what had happened. **2.** a translation, especially a translation of the Bible: the King

ves·sel [ves′əl] *noun, plural* **vessels. 1.** a ship or large boat. **2.** a large, hollow container for holding liquids, such as a pitcher or tank. **3.** a long, narrow tube that carries fluids through the body of an animal or plant: a blood *vessel.*

vest [vest] *noun, plural* **vests.** a piece of clothing without sleeves or a collar, worn over a shirt or blouse and extending to the waist. —*verb,* **vest-**

Pronunciation Key: O–S			
ō	over; go	ou	out; town
ô	all; law	p	put; hop
oo	look; full	r	run; car
o͞o	pool; who	s	set; miss
oi	oil; boy	sh	show

(Turn the page for more information.)

ed, vesting. to give power or rights to: After workers have been with the company for seven years, they are *vested* and have full rights in the company pension plan.

vet·er·an [ve′ trən *or* vet′ ə rən] *noun, plural* **veterans. 1.** a person who has served in the armed forces, especially during wartime: My grandfather is a *veteran* of World War II. **2.** a person who has held a position for a long time or has a lot of experience: He's an experienced pilot, a *veteran* of 22 years with the airline. ♦ Also used as an adjective: Smith, the team's *veteran* catcher, is good at working with young pitchers.

vet·er·i·nar·i·an [vet′ rə när′ ē ən] *noun, plural* **veterinarians.** a person trained and licensed to be a doctor for animals. ♦ This type of medicine is known as **veterinary** medicine.

ve·to [vē′ tō] *noun, plural* **vetoes. 1.** the right or power of the President of the U. S. to reject a proposed law that has been passed by Congress. **2.** a similar authority held by a governor or other leader. —*verb,* **vetoed, vetoing. 1.** to stop the passage of a law with a veto: The President *vetoed* the new tax bill. **2.** to refuse to approve; forbid: I wanted to do a report on a book by Harold Robbins, but the teacher *vetoed* that idea. ♦ *Veto* comes from a Latin phrase meaning "I forbid." Officials in ancient Rome used this expression to block an action of the Senate.

vex [veks] *verb,* **vexed, vexing.** to bother or annoy; irritate. ♦ Usually used as an adjective: a *vexing* problem.

vi·a [vī′ ə *or* vē′ ə] *preposition.* by way of; through: The flight goes from San Diego to New York, *via* Dallas.

vi·a·ble [vī′ ə bəl] *adjective, more/most.* **1.** able to continue living and growing. **2.** able to succeed or function: a *viable* plan.

vi·brant [vī′ brənt] *adjective, more/most.* **1.** having vibrations; vibrating: "At this instant an adult wolf let loose a full-throated howl *vibrant* with alarm and warning . . ." (Farley Mowat) **2.** full of energy; lively: "His eyes were as bright as ever and his voice was *vibrant* . . ." (John P. Marquand) —**vibrantly,** *adverb.*

vi·brate [vī′ brāt′] *verb,* **vibrated, vibrating.** to shake back and forth quickly; quiver: "A soaking bumblebee . . . *vibrated* its wings for a few seconds and then flew away down the field." (Richard Adams) "The stone walls *vibrated* with the thudding of the sea." (P. D. James)

vi·bra·tion [vī brā′ shən] *noun, plural* **vibrations.** the act of vibrating; a quick moving back and forth, or up and down: "The elevator began to rise, with some *vibration* and clashing and banging from below at first." (Stephen King)

vice [vīs] *noun, plural* **vices.** a bad or evil habit or form of behavior: The *Vice* Squad of a police department deals with laws against gambling, improper use of drugs or alcohol, and so on.

vice- a *prefix* meaning "someone who ranks below and can take the place of another:" A *vice*-chairman directs the meeting if the chairman cannot serve or is absent.

vice president or **vice-president 1. Vice President.** the officer of the U. S. government who ranks next below the President, and who becomes President if that person dies, resigns from office, or is unable to serve. **2.** a person holding a similar office in other countries. **3.** an officer of a business or other organization, ranking below the president. A large business may have a number of vice presidents who are in charge of different operations.

vi·ce ver·sa [vī′ sə vur′ sə *or* vīs′ vur′ sə] *adverb.* in the opposite way; the other way around: "He used to meet me from school, and *vice versa,* I would meet him." (Anne Frank)

vi·cin·i·ty [vi sin′ ə tē] *noun, plural* **vicinities.** the area around or near a particular place: "In May 1899 there were only two hundred people in the *vicinity* of what soon would be Nome . . ." (Joe McGinniss)

vi·cious [vish′ əs] *adjective, more/most.* **1.** having or showing hate or cruelty; evil; mean: "They were as *vicious* as vultures. They had no feelings, understanding, compassion, or respect for my mother." (Malcolm X) **2.** likely or able to cause harm; dangerous; fierce: *Vicious* dogs protected the property from trespassers. —**viciously,** *adverb:* "The words came from Jack *viciously,* as though they were a curse." (William Golding) —**viciousness,** *noun.*

vic·tim [vik′ təm] *noun, plural* **victims. 1.** a living thing that is killed, injured, or made to suffer: The three accident *victims* have been taken to the hospital. "Unfortunately, most of the pinyon pines in the area are dead or dying, *victims* of another kind of pine—the porcupine." (Edward Abbey) **2.** a person who is cheated, fooled, or taken advantage of by another: "Except for a few *victims* of his sharp Irish wit, the students worshiped him." (John Toland) ". . . a businessman who has smelled a sale and does not intend to let the *victim* get away." (James Jones) ♦ A person who is fooled in this way is said to be **victimized.**

V

Queen Victoria Victoria had the longest reign of any English monarch, well over 60 years.

Vic•tor•i•a [vik tôr′ ē ə] 1819-1901, the queen of England from 1837 to 1901.

Vic•tor•i•an [vik tôr′ ē ən] *adjective.* **1.** of or having to do with the time during which Victoria was Queen of England: Charles Dickens was an important figure in *Victorian* literature. **2.** like the society of Queen Victoria's time: A person with a *Victorian* attitude is thought of as very respectable and proper, and opposed to social change and unusual behavior.

vic•to•ri•ous [vik tôr′ ē əs] *adjective.* having won a fight or struggle; having gained victory: Senator Jones was *victorious* in the election and gained a second term in office. ♦ A person who is victorious is a **victor.**

vic•to•ry [vik′ tər ē *or* vik′ trē] *noun, plural* **victories.** the act of winning a battle, struggle, or contest: V-E Day stands for *"Victory* in Europe,"* the day when German forces surrendered at the end of World War II.

vid•e•o [vid′ ē ō′] *adjective.* **1.** having to do with what is seen on a television or computer screen: We lost the *video* part of the TV program for several minutes, although we could still hear the sound. **2.** having to do with television or the television industry. —*noun, plural* **videos. 1.** the picture on a television or a computer screen. **2.** a short film that goes with the music of a popular song.

vid•e•o•cas•sette [vid′ ē ō kə set′] *noun, plural* **videocassettes.** a plastic case with a roll of VIDEOTAPE, on which pictures may be recorded or played using a special machine. This machine is called a **videocassette recorder** or **VCR.**

vid•e•o•disc [vid′ ē ō disk′] *noun, plural* **videodiscs.** a disk resembling a phonograph record, containing recorded pictures and sounds that can be played back on a television set. A videodisc can store much more information than a VIDEOTAPE and can refer to this information at random. But an existing disk cannot be used to make new recordings the way a videotape can.

video game an electronic game that is played by moving images around on a television or computer screen. It is operated by a small built-in computer. ♦ Also called a **computer game** or **electronic game.**

vid•e•o•tape [vid′ ē ō tāp′] *noun, plural* **videotapes.** a special type of magnetic tape that records television performances for later showing. It can also be used to record television broadcasts for home viewing. —*verb,* **videotaped, videotaping.** to record something on videotape: to *videotape* a movie.

Vi•en•na [vē en′ ə] the capital of Austria, on the Danube River. *Population:* 1,644,000. —**Viennese,** *adjective; noun.*

Viet•nam [vē′ et näm′] a country in southeast Asia, on the South China Sea. *Capital:* Hanoi. *Area:* 128,400 square miles. *Population:* 54,500,000. —**Vietnamese,** *adjective; noun.*

Vietnam War a war fought in Vietnam between 1957 and 1975, mainly involving North Vietnam and South Vietnamese rebels on one side and South Vietnamese regular troops and the United States on the other. An earlier phase of this war was fought from 1946 to 1954, between French colonial troops and Vietnamese forces.

view [vyo͞o] *noun, plural* **views. 1.** the act or fact of seeing something: A telescope is used to give a *view* of the stars and planets. A tall man sat in front of me and blocked my *view* of the stage. **2.** something that is seen: The house is on a cliff above the beach and has a beautiful ocean *view.* **3.** a way of thinking; an opinion: He has a radio talk show where people call in to give their *views* on politics and current events. **4. in view of.** because of; considering. —*verb,* **viewed, viewing. 1.** to look at; see: On the mountain road there's a place to pull off and *view* the valley below. **2.** to think about; consider: According to this poll, the public *views* the new City Hall project as a waste of money.

Pronunciation Key: T–Z			
t	ten; date	v	very; live
th	think	w	win; away
th	these	y	you
u	cut; butter	z	zoo; cause
ur	turn; bird	zh	measure

(Turn the page for more information.)

view•er [vyōō′ ər], *noun, plural* **viewers. 1.** a person who watches something, especially someone who watches television. **2.** a device to look through to see something, as on a camera.

view•point [vyōō′ point′] *noun, plural* **viewpoints.** a way of thinking; a point of view.

Bond spy novels are famous for their colorful *villains* such as Dr. No, Goldfinger, Mr. Big, and Sir Hugo Drax. **2.** a cruel, evil, or dishonest person. **—villainous,** *adjective:* "In history he cut a *villainous* path and there is very little good to be said for him." (Arthur Miller)

viewpoint How does a writer look at a subject? What is the *viewpoint*? Think of writing a paper on coal mining in the United States. If your viewpoint is engineering, then you'll discuss the depth of a mine, how its rooms are timbered, how the veins of coal are removed. If your viewpoint is economics, you'll point out that there are only a third as many coal miners today as there were forty years ago. If your viewpoint has to do with preserving the environment, you'll explain the problems of open-pit mining, slag heaps, and so on. If your viewpoint is geographical, you will point out that in the East hard coal (*anthracite*) is common, while in the Midwest and West soft, dusty coal (*bituminous*) is common. If your viewpoint is historical, you'll say that Polish, Italian, and Serbian miners were common in the West and in Pennsylvania but not in West Virginia, or that the Welsh are the great traditional coal miners not only in Britain but throughout the U.S.

vig•il [vij′ əl] *noun, plural* **vigils. 1.** a time of staying awake at night to keep watch or guard something. **2.** any such time of careful watching: "Although I continued my *vigil* at the observation tent well into July . . ." (Farley Mowat) ◆ A person who is watchful and alert is **vigilant.**

vig•or [vig′ ər] *noun.* the fact of being vigorous; healthy energy: "They had the *vigor* and alertness of country people who have spent all their lives in the open . . ." (Margaret Mitchell)

vig•or•ous [vig′ ər əs] *adjective, more/most.* **1.** full of energy; healthy and active: She's a lively, *vigorous* person who brings a spark of life to any group she's in. **2.** having force and strength: "He held *vigorous* opinions and had his own way of stating them." (A. B. Guthrie) **—vigorously,** *adverb.*

Vi•king [vī′ king] *noun, plural* **Vikings.** one of a group of Scandinavian warriors who raided the coasts of northern Europe from the late 700's to about 1100. The Vikings were feared for their swift surprise attacks. They were also highly-skilled sailors and shipbuilders.

vil•la [vil′ ə] *noun, plural* **villas.** a large and expensive house, especially one located in the country or at the seashore.

vil•lage [vil′ ij] *noun, plural* **villages.** a group of houses and other buildings located near each other, forming a community that is smaller than a town. **—villager,** *noun.*

vil•lain [vil′ ən] *noun, plural* **villains. 1.** in a story or play, an evil character who commits crimes or otherwise harms people: The James

vine [vīn] *noun, plural* **vines.** a plant with a long thin stem that crawls along or around something, such as a tree or fence, and holds on to it for support. Grapes and ivy grow as vines.

vin•e•gar [vin′ ə gər] *noun, plural* **vinegars.** a sour liquid made by FERMENTING cider, wine, or other liquids. Vinegar is used in salad dressing, to flavor foods, and to preserve foods such as pickles.

vine•yard [vin′ yərd] *noun, plural* **vineyards.** an area of land where grapes are grown to make wine.

vin•tage [vin′ tij] *noun, plural* **vintages.** a season's crop of wine grapes in a certain district or place, or a wine made from such a harvest. ◆ Also used as an adjective: *vintage* wine.

vi•nyl [vī′ nəl] *noun, plural* **vinyls.** any of several kinds of shiny, flexible plastic used to make floor tiles, phonograph records, raincoats, and many other products.

vi•o•la [vē ō′ lə] *noun, plural* **violas.** a stringed musical instrument that is like a violin, but slightly larger and with a deeper tone.

vi•o•late [vī′ ə lāt′] *verb,* **violated, violating.** to break a rule or law; fail to obey: She *violated* the law when she drove through a red light. "I *violated* one of my most sacred principles—never to borrow from a friend." (Christopher Isherwood) **—violator,** *noun:* The sign said, "No Trespassing. *Violators* Will Be Prosecuted."

vi•o•la•tion [vī′ ə lā′ shən] *noun, plural* **violations.** the fact of violating; breaking a law or rule: "Apparently it was some sort of serious *violation* of the air safety rules, flying too close to a commercial liner . . .'' (John D. Mac-Donald)

vi•o•lence [vī′ ə ləns] *noun.* **1.** the use of strong physical force to cause injury or damage: The movie shows fist fights, gun battles between outlaws and police, and other *violence.* **2.** great force or strength: the *violence* of a hurricane. "The blood rushed to my face and my heart beat with such *violence.*" (Iris Murdoch)

vi•o•lent [vī′ ə lənt] *adjective, more/most.* **1.** with strong physical force; rough and danger ous: The prisoner became *violent* and began kicking and punching the two police officers. **2.** caused by or showing strong, rough force: A person who is murdered is said to die a *violent* death. "There was a *violent* wind, as well as thunder, and either one or the other split a tree off at the corner of the building." (Emily Brontë)—**violently,** *adverb:* "Dante shoved her chair *violently* aside and left the table . . ." (James Joyce)

vi•o•let [vī′ ə lit] *noun, plural* **violets. 1.** a small plant with flowers that are usually bluish-purple but can be yellow or white. **2.** a bluish-purple color. —*adjective.* having this color.

vi•o•lin [vī′ ə lin′] *noun, plural* **violins.** a musical instrument that is played by drawing a bow across four strings. A violin is held under the chin with one arm as it is played. ♦ A **violinist** is a person who plays the violin.

vi•per [vī′ pər] *noun, plural* **vipers.** any of various poisonous snakes having a pair of sharp, hollow fangs, such as the rattlesnake.

vir•gin [vur′ jin] *adjective.* not yet touched, used, or marked; pure: ". . . the mansion he was building above the river, and the *virgin* land he was plowing." (Sherley Anne Williams)

Vir•gin•ia [vər jin′ yə] a state on the east coast of the U. S. *Capital:* Richmond. *Nickname:* "Old Dominion." *Area:* 40,800 square miles. *Population:* 5,941,000. —**Virginian,** *noun.*

vir•tu•al•ly [vur′ choo əl ē *or* vir′ chə lē] *adverb.* almost completely; practically: Although they saved a few belongings, the fire *virtually* destroyed their home. ". . . he was *virtually* certain that this must be the place." (John Gardner)

vir•tue [vur′ choo] *noun, plural* **virtues. 1.** the right way of thinking and acting; good living; morality. **2.** a certain good quality of character: "Patience is a *virtue*" is an old saying. **3.** something good; a benefit or advantage: "The business executive listening to a luncheon address on the *virtues* of free enterprise and the

evils of Washington . . .'' (John K. Galbraith) "Terrell Vaughan, by *virtue* of his marriage to Mary Lenore Reeves, owned three farms." (Sherley Anne Williams)

vir•tu•ous [vur′ choo əs] *adjective, more/most.* having or showing virtue; good; pure.

vi•rus [vī′ rəs] *noun, plural* **viruses.** a tiny living thing that grows in the cells of other living things. Viruses are smaller than bacteria. They can cause diseases, such as the common cold.

vi•sa [vē′ sə] *noun, plural* **visas.** an official mark placed on a person's passport in a foreign country to show that the person has permission to enter or leave that country.

vise [vīs] *noun, plural* **vises.** a tool with two heavy metal grips, or jaws, that hold wood or metal pieces tightly in place while they are being worked on.

vis•i•bil•i•ty [viz′ ə bil′ ə tē] *noun.* the ability to see, especially the distance at which an object can be seen: "For three days there had been a howling blizzard . . . with *visibility* reduced to zero by blinding snow squalls . . ." (Farley Mowat)

vis•i•ble [viz′ ə bəl] *adjective, more/most.* **1.** able to be seen: Bacteria are so small that they are only *visible* through the use of a microscope. "He looked around at the dark horizon of other hills, *visible* even in the darkness for miles." (William Faulkner) **2.** able to be understood or noticed; apparent: He says he's been

Virginia The Shenendoah Valley of Virginia.

Pronunciation Key: [ə] Symbol

The [ə] or *schwa* sound occurs in syllables without an accent. It can be spelled with any vowel, such as **a** in above, **e** in listen, **i** in pencil, **o** in melon, **u** in circus. It can also be a combination of vowels, such as **io** in action, **ai** in mountain, **iou** in precious.

(Turn the page for more information.)

studying harder, but there's been no *visible* improvement in his work. —**visibly**, *adverb:* The children were *visibly* upset by the loud thunderstorm.

vi•sion [vizh′ ən] *noun, plural* **visions. 1.** the power to see; the power of sight: Night *vision* is the ability to see things at night or in darkness. **2.** the range or distance of sight: "Gay headed the truck south toward where they knew the plane was, although it was still beyond their *vision*." (Arthur Miller) **3.** a thing that is seen, especially something of great beauty. **4.** the power or ability to think of what things will be like in the future: The builder had a *vision* of those dry, empty fields as tree-shaded streets lined with lovely homes. **5.** something imaginary that is seen in the mind, as in a dream: "There was a man who could make him see *visions* of the kingdom of God upon earth." (Fawn Brodie)

vis•it [viz′ it] *verb,* **visited, visiting.** to go to see a person or a place for a time: She doesn't live in this town; she's just *visiting* a friend. —*noun, plural* **visits.** a short stay with someone or at some place: a *visit* to the dentist.

vis•i•tor [viz′ ə tər] *noun, plural* **visitors.** a person who visits; a guest: This side door is for people who work at the museum; *visitors* use the front entrance.

vi•sor [vī′ zər] *noun, plural* **visors. 1.** a brim on the front of a hat to protect the eyes and face from the sun, as on a baseball cap. **2.** a wide flap inside a car that can be turned down over part of the windshield to block the sun.

vis•ta [vis′ tə] *noun, plural* **vistas.** a view, especially one that is seen through a long, narrow opening: ". . . nothing can be seen but a *vista* of distant hills, their summits crowned with thick groves of palm trees." (Eugene O'Neill)

vis•u•al [vizh′ ōō əl] *adjective.* **1.** having to do with the sense of sight: Painting and drawing are *visual* forms of expression. **2.** able to be seen; visible. ◆ In teaching, **visual aids** are things from which students can learn by seeing, such as pictures or maps. —**visually**, *adverb.*

vis•u•al•ize [vizh′ ōō əl īz] *verb,* **visualized, visualizing.** to form a mental picture of; see in the mind: "In my mind's eye I could *visualize* the wolf as if I had known him (or her) for years." (Farley Mowat)

vi•tal [vī′ təl] *adjective, more/most.* **1.** important or necessary to life: The heart and the lungs are called *vital* organs. ◆ In medicine, the **vital signs** are basic indications of a person's health, such as pulse rate and blood pressure. **2.** very important or needed; essential: Whether or not the town should raise its tax rate is the *vital* issue in this election. **3.** full of life and energy; lively. ◆ The fact of being vital or lively is **vitality** [vī tal′ ə tē]. —**vitally**, *adverb.*

vi•ta•min [vī′ tə min] *noun, plural* **vitamins. 1.** one of the natural substances that are found in small quantities in food, and that are necessary to keep the body healthy and functioning properly. Vitamins are identified by letters of the alphabet—for example, vitamin A comes from yellow vegetables, milk, and eggs. **2.** one or more of these substances concentrated in the form of a pill or liquid, taken as an aid to health.

viv•id [viv′ id] *adjective, more/most.* **1.** of color or light, bright and strong: "With her glowing cheeks, *vivid* black curly hair, and tawny hazel eyes . . ." (Mary McCarthy) **2.** full of life and energy; lively; active: "It was nice to see her face so *vivid* again and to hear her laugh . . ." (James Baldwin) "The storm that began with *vivid* lightning . . ." (V.S. Naipaul) **3.** giving a clear picture to the mind; lifelike: "I had lived in such a world only for the first ten years of my life, but it was as *vivid* as if I had never stepped out of it." (Ben Hecht) —**vividly**, *adjective:* "Very *vividly* she remembered the scene." (Joseph Wambaugh) —**vividness**, *noun.*

---

visual writing "A fearful man, all in coarse gray, with a great iron on his leg. A man with no hat, and with broken shoes, and with an old rag tied around his head. A man who had been soaked in water, and smothered in mud . . ." This is from Charles Dickens' *Great Expectations.* You see, suddenly, an escaped convict. Note the physical details—gray, iron, hatless, broken shoes, old rag for a cap, wet, muddy. Dickens is a *visual* writer—he makes you *see* the characters and the setting. Sometimes a writer avoids precise visual description. In Henry James' story, "The Tree of Knowledge," here's how he describes his main character's appearance: "He was . . . large and loose and ruddy and curly, with deep tones, deep eyes, deep pockets, to say nothing of the habit of long pipes, soft hats and brownish grayish weather-faded clothes . . ." Dickens wants to create exact effects, while James wants a general effect—"deep tones, deep eyes, deep pockets."

vocabulary There's nothing wrong with a common word like *look,* but sometimes it's better to use a more precise word. "He *looked* at the signature on the check." "He *glanced* at the signature . . ." (looked quickly, then looked away, not really noticing) "He *stared* . . ." (looked for some time in a fixed way, perhaps with surprise or disbelief) "He *peered* . . ." (looked closely, with effort, perhaps lifting his glasses and raising the check up to his eyes). Which of these is the right word? That depends—it's the one that best describes the action in a given situation. The key to vocabulary is not *range;* it's *exactness.* This dictionary has a much greater number of words than Shakespeare used to write all his plays. What counts is not how many different words a writer knows, but how well he or she chooses the right one. And how can you learn to do that? (1) Read a lot. (2) Use a dictionary. (3) Study your favorite writers. (4) Know your purpose as you write.

vo•cab•u•lar•y [vō kab′ yə lâr′ ē] *noun, plural* **vocabularies. 1.** all the words that a person uses and understands: It's said that the typical American adult has a *vocabulary* of about 10,000 words. **2.** all the words of a language: The *vocabulary* of English has many words that originally come from Latin. **3.** the particular set of words that is used by a certain group of people: the *vocabulary* of science or medicine. **4.** a list of words and their meanings, used in studying a language.

voice [vois] *noun, plural* **voices. 1.** the sound that is made through the mouth by a person in speaking or singing: Jerry didn't say who he was when he called, but I recognized his *voice.* **2.** the power or ability to produce sounds: a singer with a beautiful *voice.* **3.** the right to state an opinion: In a country ruled by a dictator, the people have no *voice.* —*verb,* **voiced, voicing.** to say or express in words: "Mrs. Garden kept *voicing* opinions, then looking at Faber for a reaction." (Ken Follett)

voice In grammar, *voice* is either active: "A car *hit* the *tree* and *knocked it* over," or it's passive: "That *tree was knocked* over by a car." (See also ACTIVE, PASSIVE.) *Voice* also shows a writer's personality in certain ways, because *voice* has another meaning that is close to *tone* and *style.* Teachers of writing speak of *voice* as a connection between speech and writing. They say that "talking into writing" allows you to rehearse, so that when your thoughts go onto the page the wording will be natural. Later, you can read your work out loud to yourself, to judge how your "written voice" compares to your normal speaking style.

vo•cal [vō′ kəl] *adjective, more/most.* having to do with the voice; using the voice.

vocal cords two pairs of MEMBRANES or folds of skin in the throat. As air passes through the vocal cords, the vibration creates voice sounds.

vo•ca•tion [vō kā′ shən] *noun, plural* **vocations. 1.** the work that a person does or is suited to do; a certain business or trade. **2.** a strong desire to enter a certain type of work, especially religious service. —**vocational** [vō kā′ shə nəl], *adjective.* having to do with a job or career. ♦ **Vocational education** trains high school students for work that does not require a college degree, such as auto repair, electronics, and secretarial work.

vod•ka [väd′ kə] *noun, plural* **vodkas.** a clear, colorless alcoholic drink that was first made in Russia. Vodka is produced from FERMENTED grain or potatoes.

void [void] *adjective.* **1.** not holding or having anything; empty or lacking: "He had watery gray eyes, oddly *void* of expression." (H. G. Wells) "I am cast upon a horrible, desolate island, *void* of all hope of recovery." (Daniel Defoe) **2.** having no power in law; not legally valid: The judge ruled the football player's contract *void* because the team had not paid him a bonus they promised. —*noun, plural* **voids.** an empty space or place.

vol•can•ic [väl kan′ ik] *adjective.* having to do

V

Pronunciation Key: Accent Marks

[′] is the normal accent mark. It shows where the main stress falls on a word.
[′] is a secondary accent mark. It shows a lighter stress than the primary accent. For example:

tel • e • vis • ion [tel′ə vizh′ən]
(Turn the page for more information.)

with or formed by a volcano: *volcanic* gases. Surtsey is a *volcanic* island in the North Atlantic formed by underwater eruptions in 1963.

vol•ca•no [väl kā′ nō] *noun, plural* **volcanoes** or **volcanos. 1.** an opening in the earth's crust from which hot gases, lava, and ashes are thrown up. A volcano creates a cone-shaped hill or mountain. There are many active volcanoes in the world, especially along the edges of the Pacific Ocean. **2.** the mountain or hill formed by a volcano.

vol•ley•ball [väl′ ē bôl′] *noun, plural* **volleyballs. 1.** a ball game between two teams who try to keep the ball in the air and return it over the net to the other team. A team can score when the other team lets the ball hit the ground or doesn't return it properly. **2.** the ball used in this game.

volt [vōlt] *noun, plural* **volts.** a unit used to measure the strength of an electric current. A volt is the amount of force necessary to carry a certain amount of current through a certain kind of material. ♦ The *volt* was named in honor of Alexander *Volta*, an Italian scientist of the 1800's who invented the electric battery.

vol•tage [vōl′ tij] *noun, plural* **voltages.** the force of an electric current as measured in volts.

vol•ume [väl′ yəm *or* väl′ yo͞om] *noun, plural* **volumes. 1.** the amount of sound; loudness: Mom said that Chris had his radio on too loud and told him to turn down the *volume*. **2.** the amount of space an object takes up, measured in terms of its height, width, and length: A box that is 3 feet by 3 feet by 3 feet has a *volume* of 27 cubic feet. **3.** a number of pages bound together as a book: He has a library of rare books, beautiful leather-bound *volumes*. **4.** one of a set of books: The article on 'Ants' is in the first *volume* of the encyclopedia.

vol•un•tar•y [väl′ ən tar′ ē] *adjective.* **1.** done by choice or of one's own free will, not forced: The museum does not charge a fee to get in, but people usually make a *voluntary* contribution. **2.** an action of the body, done by thought and controlled by the mind. —**voluntarily,** *adverb.*

vol•un•teer [väl′ ən tēr′] *noun, plural* **volunteers. 1.** a person who enters military service without being drafted or forced to join. **2.** a person who willingly does some job without pay: Linda is a *volunteer* at the local hospital to help with the patients. **3.** any person who agrees to take a difficult or unpleasant task: The soccer coach said, "I need someone to be team mother—any *volunteers?*"—*verb,* **volunteered, volunteering. 1.** to choose to join the armed

forces: to *volunteer* for the Marine Corps. **2.** to give help without being asked; offer to do something: "The manager asked if any member of the audience would *volunteer* to come upon the stage and be hypnotized." (Robert Benchley) —*adjective:* a *volunteer* firefighter.

vom•it [väm′ it] *verb,* **vomited, vomiting.** to become sick and throw up matter from the stomach. ♦ Also used as a noun.

vote [vōt] *verb,* **voted, voting. 1.** to show an opinion or choice in an election; choose one person or course of action. People may vote by marking a ballot in secret, or by speaking or raising their hand to show their choice. **2.** *Informal.* to make a choice or decision: Mom said we could pick what we want for dinner—I *vote* we have pizza. —*noun, plural* **votes. 1.** the act or fact of voting; a choice in an election: Tina was chosen as the new class president by a *vote* of 20 to 10. **2.** the right to take part in an election: It was not until 1920 that women were given the *vote* throughout the United States.

vow [vou] *noun, plural* **vows.** a serious promise that a person is determined to keep: When people get married, they make *vows* to love and be faithful to one another. —*verb,* **vowed, vowing.** to make a vow: "The new king *vowed* to conquer the land that was rightfully his." (Norton Juster)

vow•el [vou′ əl] *noun, plural* **vowels.** a sound in speech made by letting air pass freely through the open mouth, as opposed to a CONSONANT where the air is blocked in some way. In English the vowels are spelled with the letters *a, e, i, o, u,* and sometimes *y.* Every separate sound in English must have at least one vowel.

voy•age [voi′ ij] *noun, plural* **voyages.** a trip or journey, especially a long trip over water: an ocean *voyage.* —*verb,* **voyaged, voyaging.** to travel on a voyage. —**voyager,** *noun.*

vs. the abbreviation for **versus.**

vul•gar [vul′ gər] *adjective, more/most.* showing poor taste or bad manners; crude or disgusting. ♦ The fact of being vulgar is **vulgarity.**

vul•ner•a•ble [vul′ nər ə bəl] *adjective, more/most.* easily able to be hurt or injured; not strong or well protected: The army's attack was planned for dawn Sunday morning, because it was felt the enemy would be *vulnerable* then.

vul•ture [vul′ chər] *noun, plural* **vultures. 1.** a very large bird with dark feathers and a bare head and neck, related to hawks and eagles. It feeds on the decaying bodies of animals that it finds dead. **2.** a cruel, greedy person who gains from the troubles of others.

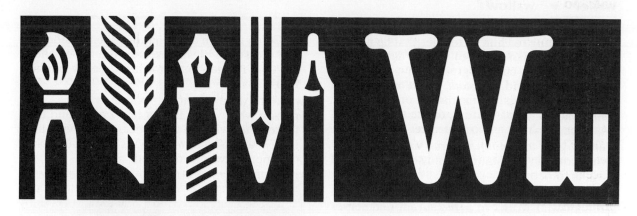

w, W [dub′əl yo͞o] *noun, plural* **w's, W's.** the twenty-third letter of the alphabet.

wad [wäd] *noun, plural* **wads. 1.** a small, soft mass: a *wad* of cotton. **2.** *Informal.* a large roll of paper money. —*verb,* **wadded, wadding.** to roll, squeeze, or crush into a wad: He *wadded* up the paper and threw it into the wastebasket.

wad•dle [wäd′əl] *verb,* **waddled, waddling.** to walk or move with short steps, with the body swaying from side to side, as a duck does: "Out of the darkness of the garden there came a peacock who *waddled* slowly into the long column of light . . ." (Anaïs Nin)

wade [wād] *verb,* **waded, wading. 1.** to walk in or through water, mud, snow, or another such substance that covers the feet and makes movement difficult. **2.** to move or make one's way slowly and with difficulty: She *waded* through a big pile of bills and letters on her desk.

wa•fer [wā′fər] *noun, plural* **wafers. 1.** a small, crisp cookie or cracker. **2.** a small, flat disk of bread used in the services of some churches, such as the Catholic Church.

waf•fle [wä′fəl] *noun, plural* **waffles.** a crisp cake made of batter. Waffles have little squares on them that are made by the special appliance that they are cooked in (called a **waffle iron**).

wag [wag] *verb,* **wagged, wagging.** to move back and forth or up and down with short, quick movements: Our dog always *wags* his tail when he's happy. —*noun, plural* **wags.** the act of moving in this way.

wage [wāj] *noun, plural* **wages.** payment for work done: The U. S. has a law that workers have to be paid a minimum hourly *wage.* —*verb,* **waged, waging.** to carry on a struggle or effort of some kind: "To Churchill, Tito was a gallant warrior *waging* a patriotic battle against Hitler." (John Toland)

wag•on [wag′ən] *noun, plural* **wagons. 1.** a large, heavy four-wheeled vehicle that is used for carrying heavy loads. It is pulled by horses, oxen, mules, and so on. **2.** a low, small four-wheeled vehicle like this that is pulled by hand, used as a child's toy.

wail [wāl] *verb,* **wailed, wailing. 1.** to make a long, loud cry because of sadness or pain. **2.** to make a long, mournful sound like this: "There was a ringing in her ears and another sound, a *wailing* siren-like cry." (Betsy Byars) —*noun, plural* **wails.** a long, loud cry: "And they both set up a heart breaking cry. I joined my *wail* to theirs, loud and bitter." (Emily Brontë)

waist [wāst] *noun, plural* **waists. 1.** the part of the human body between the ribs and the hips. **2.** a piece of clothing that covers this area: He wears trousers with a 34-inch *waist.*

wait [wāt] *verb,* **waited, waiting. 1.** to stay in a place or do nothing, until someone comes or something happens: "She stood *waiting* for a word, *waiting* for him to tell her that he needed her . . ." (Brian Moore) **2.** to delay or be delayed: Don't cut the grass today; it can *wait* until the weekend. **3.** *usually*, **wait on**. to attend to people's needs, as in a store or restaurant. —*noun*. the act of waiting, or the time spent in waiting: We have a two-hour *wait* for the flight.

wait•er [wā′tər] *noun, plural* **waiters.** a man who works in a restaurant and serves food and drinks to people.

wait•ress [wā′tris] *noun, plural* **waitresses.** a woman who works in a restaurant and serves food and drinks to people.

waive [wāv] *verb,* **waived, waiving.** to agree to give up a right or claim: The lawyer *waived* his usual fee and handled the case for free. —**waiver**, *noun*. the act or fact of waiving.

wake[1] [wāk] *verb,* **woke** or **waked, waked** or **woken, waking. 1.** to stop sleeping: "Eddie *woke* with a jump and stared out the window." (Bernard Malamud) "I had *waked* in my old bedroom . . ." (Paul Theroux) **2.** to cause to stop sleeping: Don't make so much noise or you'll *wake* the baby. **3. wake up. a**. to stop sleeping. **b**. to become active or aware.

wake[2] *noun, plural* **wakes.** a gathering to watch over the body of a dead person before burial and to pay last respects to the dead person.

wake[3] *noun, plural* **wakes. 1.** the track left by a ship, boat, or other object moving through water. **2.** any similar track or path that is left by something. **3. in the wake of**. following close behind; after.

wak•en [wā′kən] *verb,* **wakened, wakening. 1.** to wake up: "He had been *wakened* by the smell of burning . . ." (Patrick White) **2.** to make active; stir up: Watching that movie about Africa *wakened* his interest in going there.

Wales [wālz] a former country that is now part of Great Britain, located west of England. *Capital:* Cardiff. *Area:* 8,000 square miles. *Population:* 2,790,000. —**Welsh,** *adjective; noun.*

walk [wôk] *verb,* **walked, walking. 1.** to move on foot at the normal rate. **2.** to move over or through something on foot: She *walked* the floor for hours, trying to put the baby to sleep. **3.** to cause to walk: to *walk* a dog or a horse. **4.** in baseball, to allow a batter to go to first base by pitching four balls. —*noun, plural* **walks. 1.** the act of walking, especially for pleasure or exercise: Dad took the dog for a *walk* after dinner. **2.** the distance or time to be walked: Her house is about a ten-minute *walk* from here. **3.** a place that is set apart for walking: There were flowers on either side of the *walk*.

♦ Often used in combinations such as side*walk* and cross*walk*. **4.** in baseball, the act of allowing of a runner to go to first base by pitching four balls.

walk•er [wôk′ər] *noun, plural* **walkers. 1.** a person who walks: He's a fast *walker* and hard to keep up with on the street. **2.** a device used to help a person in walking, as for a young child or a person who is disabled.

wall The Great Wall of China was built entirely by hand between the years 400 and 1600. It is the longest structure in the world.

wall [wôl] *noun, plural* **walls. 1.** a solid, standing structure that divides or closes off an area, made of stone, brick, wood, plaster, or other materials. Walls form the sides of a building or room. **2.** something that looks or acts like a wall: "As each *wall* of water approached, it shut all else from the view of the men in the boat." (Stephen Crane) **3.** the side or inner surface of something, such as a body part: a cell *wall*, the *wall* of the stomach. **4.** something that separates or forms a barrier: The detective tried to ask the local people what had happened, but he was met with a *wall* of silence. "The First Amendment has erected a *wall* between church and state." (Hugo Black) —*verb,* **walled, walling.** to close off or protect with or as if with a wall: Cities of the Middle Ages were *walled* to protect against attack. "The three huge barns and the fence *walled* in the snug yard." (Laura Ingalls Wilder)

wal•let [wäl′it] *noun, plural* **wallets.** a small, flat folding case used for holding money, cards, photographs, and so on.

wal•low [wäl′ō] *verb,* **wallowed, wallowing. 1.** to roll about in deep mud, water, dirt, or the like: "Along the edge of the road, contented buffalo *wallowed* or grazed . . ." (Doris Lessing) **2.** to take too much pleasure in: She's been *wallowing* in self-pity ever since she lost her job.

wall•pa•per [wôl′ pā′ pər] *noun, plural* **wallpapers.** paper that is used to cover and decorate the walls of a room. Wallpaper is printed with colors and designs. —*verb,* **wallpapered, wallpapering.** to put wallpaper on: to *wallpaper* a kitchen.

wal•nut [wôl′ nut′] *noun, plural* **walnuts. 1.** a large nut that can be eaten, having a hard, thick shell that is evenly divided into two parts. **2.** the tree that this nut grows on. **3.** the hard, strong wood of the walnut tree, used to make furniture.

wal•rus [wôl′ rəs *or* wäl′ rəs] *noun, plural* **walrus** or **walruses.** a large sea animal of the Arctic region that looks like and is related to the seal. A walrus has a thick neck, two long tusks, and a thick, wrinkled hide.

waltz [wôltz] *noun, plural* **waltzes. 1.** a smooth, gliding dance for couples. **2.** music for this dance: The Blue Danube *Waltz* is a famous composition by Johann Strauss. —*verb,* **waltzed, waltzing. 1.** to dance a waltz. **2.** to move in a easy or confident way: He *waltzed* into the meeting as if he owned the place and sat down in an empty chair next to the boss.

wampum A wampum belt made by the Delaware Indians in the early 1700's. It later belonged to William Penn, founder of the colony of Pennsylvania.

wam•pum [wäm′ pəm] *noun.* small, colored beads made from shells and strung together into necklaces, belts, or bracelets. It was once used as money by the American Indians.

wand [wänd] *noun, plural* **wands.** a thin stick or rod, especially one held or waved around by a magician during a magic act.

wan•der [wän′ dər] *verb,* **wandered, wandering. 1.** to go or move around with no particular place to go: "For ten years I *wandered* upon the face of the earth, hearing the long sweet, sad, lost, lonesome cry of the train whistles in the night." (Frank Yerby) ♦ A person who wanders is a **wanderer. 2.** to lose one's way: The

bull got loose and *wandered* off onto a neighbor's farm. **3.** to move away from a certain point or place; move about without purpose: The coach told the goalie not to let his mind *wander* during the game. "She let her eyes *wander* around her son's room." (Stephen King)

wane [wān] *verb,* **waned, waning. 1.** to lose size gradually; become smaller: The moon is said to *wane* during the time after the full moon when it appears to be growing smaller in the sky. **2.** to lose power, strength, or importance: "The smile *waned* on Stephen's face." (James Joyce)

want [wänt] *verb,* **wanted, wanting. 1.** to wish to do or have; have a desire for: Bobby sent a letter to Santa Claus telling what he *wants* for Christmas. **2.** to have a need for; lack: The Bible contains the famous line "The Lord is my shepherd, I shall not *want.*" —*noun, plural* **wants. 1.** the fact of needing or lacking something: "She felt light-headed and terribly weak; it was the *want* of food, she was sure." (Brian Moore) **2.** *usually,* **wants.** something that is desired or needed.

wan•ton [wän′ tən] *adjective, more/most.* done without any reason or purpose; reckless: Smashing the windows was a *wanton* act.

war [wôr] *noun, plural* **wars. 1.** a large, continued fight between the armed forces of different countries or groups: The U. S. won its freedom from England in the Revolutionary *War.* **2.** a long, serious fight or struggle: a *war* against a deadly disease. President Lyndon Johnson called his program to help poor people "The *War* on Poverty." —*verb,* **warred, warring.** to take part in a war; fight: The United Nations finally got the two *warring* nations to agree to peace talks.

war•bler [wôr′ blər] *noun, plural* **warblers.** any of several small, brightly-colored birds noted for their song.

ward [wôrd] *noun, plural* **wards. 1.** a part of a hospital in which there are a number of patients of the same kind: Newborn babies and their mothers stay in the maternity *ward.* **2.** an election district or other such local division of a city. **3.** a person placed under the care or

Pronunciation Key: A–F			
a	and; hat	ch	chew; such
ā	ate; stay	d	dog; lid
â	care; air	e	end; yet
ä	father; hot	ē	she; each
b	boy; cab	f	fun; off

(Turn the page for more information.)

-**ward** Words such as *forward, backward, upward,* and *inward* each have another form that ends in "s" —*backwards, upwards,* and so on. When the word is used as an adverb, you may choose either form. "If the car starts to roll *forward,* pull this lever *backward.*" "He knows the list *backwards* and *forwards.*" But the "s" form cannot be used as an adjective; you can't say, "Take a *backwards* step" or "He made a *forwards* motion." Is this a hard point to keep straight? Then here's a suggestion: Just use the -*ward* form, without the "s." Our HBJ Word Survey shows that writers use this ending far more often than -*wards.*

supervision of a guardian or of a court: A child may be made a *ward* of the court if a judge rules that it is not be safe for him to live with his parents. —*verb,* **warded, warding. ward off.** to keep away; turn back: Knights in the Middle Ages carried shields to *ward off* the blows of an attacker.

war•den [wôr′ dən] *noun, plural* **wardens. 1.** a person who is in charge of a prison. **2.** an official who makes sure that certain laws are obeyed. ♦ **A game warden** enforces hunting and fishing laws.

ward•robe [wôrd′ rōb′] *noun, plural* **wardrobes. 1.** a person's clothes; a collection or supply of clothing: to buy a new summer *wardrobe.* Movie star Cary Grant was known for his stylish *wardrobe.* **2.** a large piece of furniture or a closet for hanging and keeping clothes.

ware [wâr] *noun, plural* **wares. 1. wares.** articles for sale: In early America, peddlers traveled from town to town selling their *wares.* **2.** manufactured items of a certain kind. ♦ Used in combinations such as kitchen*ware,* oven*ware,* house*wares.*

ware•house [wâr′ hous′] *noun, plural* **warehouses.** a building where goods are stored, especially one where items for sale are kept before being delivered to a store or a customer.

war•fare [wôr′ fâr′] *noun.* fighting between armed forces; war.

war•head [wôr′ hed′] *noun, plural* **warheads.** the front part of a torpedo, missile, or the like, which carries the explosive charge.

war•i•ly [wâr′ ə lē] *adverb.* in a wary manner; cautiously: "The boys ate *warily,* trying not to be seen or heard." (Katherine Anne Porter)

war•like [wôr′ līk′] *adjective, more/most.* ready for war; favoring or threatening war.

warm [wôrm] *adjective,* **warmer, warmest. 1.** somewhat hot; not cold: a *warm* spring day. **2.** giving off or holding in heat: to sit out in the *warm* sun. It's going to be a chilly day, so wear a *warm* coat. **3.** having or showing lively and friendly feeling: to give someone a *warm* smile or a *warm* welcome. "I felt *warm* inside at being able to load the table this way with so much food." (Laurence Yep) **4.** of a color, suggesting heat: Red, yellow, and orange are known as *warm* colors. —*verb,* **warmed, warming. 1.** to make or become warm: "There was something good and fine about her, so that I always *warmed* to her." (M. F. K. Fisher) **2. warm up. a.** to make or become warm: "Work hard and it will *warm* you *up* a little." (James Houston) **b.** to get a person or thing to perform or operate: Mom let the car engine *warm up* for a while before she left. ♦ Also used as a noun. —**warmly,** *adverb:* "The President greeted his old classmate *warmly,* stretching his arm across the table, grinning broadly." (John Toland)

warm-blood•ed [wôrm′ blud′ id] *adjective.* of an animal, having blood that stays at about the same temperature, even when the temperature of the surrounding air or water changes. Mammals and birds are warm-blooded; snakes are COLD-BLOODED.

warmth [wôrmth] *noun.* the fact of being warm: the *warmth* of a fire.

warn [wôrn] *verb,* **warned, warning. 1.** to give notice of something bad that might happen: The policeman fired a shot in the air to *warn* the robber that he should give up. **2.** to give advice about possible harm or danger: "She *warned* me that scratching the bites would leave scars on my skin . . ." (Tennessee Williams)

warn•ing [wôr′ ning] *noun, plural* **warnings.** a notice of harm or danger: Cigarette packs have to carry a *warning* which states that smoking is dangerous to your health. —*adjective.* that warns; serving to warn: "Jamie started to say something, caught a *warning* glance from Bob, and stopped for a second." (S.E. Hinton)

warp [wôrp] *verb,* **warped, warping. 1.** to bend or twist out of shape: The floor boards near the sink were *warped* from all the water that had been spilled on them. **2.** to turn from what is right: Some parents complain that TV advertising *warps* children's judgment about the importance of new clothes and toys.

war·rant [wôr′ənt] *noun, plural* **warrants.** an official written order that gives a person legal authority to do something: The police have to have a search *warrant* to search someone's home. —*verb,* **warranted, warranting.** to give or be a good reason for: "Used to focusing her attention on those among them who seemed to *warrant* it, . . ." (Colleen McCullough)

war·ran·ty [wôr′ən tē] *noun, plural* **warranties.** a written statement from the seller of some product to the buyer declaring that the product being sold is as described, and that for a certain period of time the seller will repair or replace the item if it fails to work as expected.

war·ri·or [wôr′yər] *noun, plural* **warriors. 1.** a person who is experienced in fighting wars or battles: At the Battle of Little Bighorn, U. S. Army forces were surrounded by Sioux and Cheyenne *warriors*. **2.** any person who takes part in a difficult struggle or conflict.

War·saw [wôr′sô′] the capital and largest city of Poland. *Population:* 1,615,000.

war·ship [wôr′ship′] *noun, plural* **warships.** a ship that is built and armed with weapons for use in war.

wart [wôrt] *noun, plural* **warts.** a small, hard lump that grows on the skin. Warts are caused by a virus.

wart·hog [wôrt′hôg′] *noun, plural* **warthogs.** a wild hog of Africa having long, curving tusks and large, wart-like growths sticking out from its head.

war·y [wâr′ē] *adjective,* **warier, wariest.** looking out for danger; on guard; alert: The deer were *wary* of us and would only come to the edge of the clearing.

washes over and over and around the stone, rolling it until it is round and perfect." (Patricia MacLachlan) —*noun, plural* **washes. 1.** the act of washing, or a place where this is done: He took his car to the car *wash*. **2.** the amount of clothes or other items that are washed at one time. **3.** a flow of water, or the sound made by this. **4.** an area in a desert or other dry place where water sometimes flows.

wash·er [wäsh′ər] *noun, plural* **washers. 1.** a person who washes: A window *washer* came to clean their office windows. **2.** another name for a WASHING MACHINE. **3.** a flat ring used to give a tighter fit to two parts that go together. A metal washer goes between a nut and a bolt.

washing machine an electric machine used for washing clothes, towels, and other such items automatically.

Washington, D. C.

Wash·ing·ton [wäsh′ing tən] **1. George,** 1732-1799, American general and the first president of the United States, from 1789 to 1797. **2.**

---

was/were The difference between these two forms of the verb BE is usually very obvious. *Was* is singular; *were* is plural. "When the power went off, I *was* working with my computer. Mom and Dad *were* watching TV." There is a special use of "I were" that is correct—the SUBJUNCTIVE verb. (See p. 759 for more information.) "If I *were* working with my computer, I'd be busy. But it's broken, so I'm waiting around." Notice that the person is saying something that is not a fact, but could be one, under other conditions. "If I *were* rich, I'd buy a Rolls Royce." The clue is that the statement is introduced by an expression that shows a condition, like *if* or *as if*.

---

was [wuz] *verb.* the past form of **am** and **is**: I *was* watching TV when Melissa called me.

wash [wäsh] *verb,* **washed, washing. 1.** to clear away dirt or stains by using water, or water and soap: to *wash* your hands, to *wash* the dishes after eating. **2.** to move or carry away by the action of water: Heavy rains *washed* away a lot of the dirt around the new house. "The sea

Pronunciation Key: G–N			
g	give; big	k	kind; cat; back
h	hold	l	let; ball
i	it; this	m	make; time
ī	ice; my	n	not; own
j	jet; gem; edge	ng	having

(Turn the page for more information.)

Booker T., 1845-1915, American educator. **3.** a state on the northwest coast of the U. S. *Capital:* Olympia. *Nickname:* "Evergreen State." *Area:* 68,200 square miles. *Population:* 4,245,000. **4.** the capital of the United States, forming the **District of Columbia** between Maryland and Virginia. *Population:* 638,000. ◆ Also known as **Washington, D.C.**

was•n't [wuz⁄ ənt] the contraction for "was not."

wasp The tiny mid-section of a wasp led to the term "wasp-waist," which was once used in women's fashions to mean a very slender waist.

wasp [wäsp] *noun, plural* **wasps.** a flying insect related to bees and ants, having a powerful sting and a slender body with a narrowed abdomen. Hornets and yellow jackets are types of wasps.

waste [wāst] *verb,* **wasted, wasting. 1.** to use or spend in a careless and foolish way: Don't leave all the lights on in the house when you go out—you're *wasting* electricity. "Every time they saw the coffee thrown away, they gave Mama a lecture about *wasting* things." (Betty Smith) **2.** to slowly lose health, strength, or force: ". . . an old man as bony and *wasted* as a person who's lived for years on just air and tea." (John Gardner) —*noun, plural* **wastes. 1.** the act or fact of wasting: "(I) decided it was a *waste* of time to read any more Trollope and have never since done so." (Edmund Wilson) **2.** things of no use or value; worthless material to be thrown away. **3.** material that is not digested for use as food and that is sent out from the body. —*adjective:* Ashes are a *waste* product of a fire. —**wasteful,** *adjective.*

waste•bas•ket [wāst⁄ bas⁄ kit] *noun, plural* **wastebaskets.** a basket or other container that is used to hold paper scraps **(waste paper)** and other things to be thrown away.

waste•land [wāst⁄ land⁄] *noun, plural* **waste-lands. 1.** an area of land where there are very few plants and animals and few people live, such as a desert or a polar region. **2.** an area that is without life or spirit: A famous critic once called television "a vast *wasteland,*" arguing that the quality of programs was very poor.

watch [wäch] *verb,* **watched, watching. 1.** to look carefully at some event or activity that is going on: to *watch* television, to *watch* a baseball game. **2.** to look at carefully; keep one's attention on: "All eyes *watched* her as she came in and sat down." (Brian Moore) "In the late afternoon they would walk away from town and *watch* the evening star come out." (Joan Didion) **3.** to keep guard over; look at so as to care for or protect: "There was no telling what Barney might do without me to *watch* him." (Laurence Yep) **4.** to be careful or concerned about: No dessert for me, thanks—I'm trying to *watch* my weight.
—*noun, plural* **watches. 1.** a small device that tells time, usually worn on the wrist or sometimes carried in a pocket. **2.** one or more people ordered to stay awake and alert to guard or protect others, as on a ship at night. **3.** the period of time when someone does this. **4.** the act or fact of looking carefully; close attention.

watch•dog [wäch⁄ dôg⁄] *noun, plural* **watch-dogs. 1.** a dog that is kept to guard a house or property and to warn of intruders. **2.** a person or group that tries to guard against loss, crime, and so on: a *watchdog* group that looks for areas of waste in government spending.

watch•ful [wäch⁄ fəl] *adjective.* carefully watching; alert. —**watchfully,** *adverb.*

watch•man [wäch⁄ mən] *noun, plural* **watch-men.** a person whose job is to watch and guard a factory, office building, or other such property at night or when the building is empty.

wa•ter [wô⁄ tər] *noun, plural* **waters.** the common liquid that is used for drinking and washing; the substance that falls from the sky as rain and forms the world's oceans, lakes, rivers, and so on. Water is a compound of hydrogen and oxygen. It has no color, smell, or taste in its pure form. —*verb,* **watered, watering. 1.** to supply with water: Please *water* the flowers every day while we're gone. The Arab travelers stopped at the oasis to *water* their camels. **2.** to give off a fluid like water: Cutting onions can make your eyes *water*. "Their mouths *watered* when they saw the food on the table." (V. S. Pritchett) **3. water down. a.** to make a liquid weaker by adding water. **b.** to make weaker or less effective: People often complain that modern textbooks have been *watered down,* with stories and lessons that are too simple.

wa•ter•bed [wô′tər bed′] *noun, plural* **waterbeds.** a type of bed that uses a plastic bag filled with water rather than an ordinary mattress.

water buffalo a large, powerful black buffalo found in Asia and Africa, having very wide horns that curve backward. It has been trained as a work animal in India and other countries.

water color 1. a paint that is made by mixing color with water instead of with oil. **2.** *also,* **watercolor.** a picture done with such paints, or the art of painting in this way.

wa•ter•cress [wô′tər kres′] *noun.* a type of plant that grows in water, having sharp-tasting leaves that are used in salads and sandwiches.

wa•ter•fall [wo′tər fôl′] *noun, plural* **waterfalls.** a stream of water that falls straight down from a high place, as over a cliff.

waterfall Water rushes over Chittenango Falls, in central New York State.

wa•ter•front [wô′tər frunt′] *noun, plural* **waterfronts. 1.** land that is at the edge of a body of water. **2.** the part of a city that is alongside a body of water, especially where there are docks.

Wa•ter•gate [wô′tər gāt′] a political scandal that involved illegal activities in the 1972 election for President, and that brought about Richard Nixon's resignation as President.

water lily a water plant that has flat floating leaves with showy, colorful flowers on top. Water lilies grow in freshwater ponds and lakes.

Wa•ter•loo [wô′tər loo] *noun.* **1.** a battle fought in 1815 in which the French emperor Napoleon suffered a great defeat and lost all his power. **2.** *also,* **waterloo.** a great or final defeat coming after a period of success.

watercolor A watercolor by the French painter Paul Cezanne, whose style greatly influenced later artists.

wa•ter•mel•on [wô′tər mel′ən] *noun, plural* **watermelons.** a large melon that has sweet, juicy red or pink flesh, many seeds, and a hard green outer skin. Watermelons grow on vines.

water moccasin a poisonous snake that lives in swamps and other wet areas on the southeastern United States; also called the COTTON-MOUTH.

water polo a water sport somewhat like soccer or hockey, played by two teams of swimmers who try to score by throwing or pushing a hollow rubber ball into the other team's goal.

wa•ter•proof [wô′tər proof′] *adjective.* keeping water from passing through: a *waterproof* raincoat. —*verb,* **waterproofed, waterproofing.** to make something waterproof.

wa•ter•shed [wô′tər shed′] *noun, plural* **watersheds. 1.** a ridge of mountains or other high land, separating two different river systems that flow in different directions. **2.** the total land area from which a river or lake drains its water. **3.** a crucial dividing point in the course of events.

wa•ter•ski [wô′tər skē′] *verb,* **water-skied, water-skiing.** to glide over water on skis (**water skis**) while holding on to a tow rope that is attached to a power boat.

wa•ter•way [wô′tər wā′] *noun, plural* **waterways.** a river, canal, or other such body of water that ships and boats travel on.

Pronunciation Key: O–S			
ō	over; go	ou	out; town
ô	all; law	p	put; hop
oo	look; full	r	run; car
oo	pool; who	s	set; miss
oi	oil; boy	sh	show

(Turn the page for more information.)

wa•ter•wheel [wô′tər wēl′] *noun, plural* **wa-terwheels.** a wheel that is turned by the weight of water falling on it. Waterwheels were often used in former times to provide power, as in grinding grain in a mill.

wa•ter•y [wô′tər ē] *adjective,* **waterier, wateriest.** full of water or containing too much water: a thin, *watery* soup.

watt [wät] *noun, plural* **watts.** a unit used to measure electrical power: She put a 60-*watt* bulb in her reading lamp. ◆ The *watt* is named for James Watt, a Scottish engineer of the late 1700's who invented the steam engine.

wave [wāv] *verb,* **waved, waving.** **1.** to move something in the air, such as the hand, as a signal or greeting: "They saw Jody's mother standing on the porch *waving* her apron in welcome." (John Steinbeck) **2.** to move freely back and forth in the air: The flag was *waving* in the breeze. **3.** to give a series of curls to the hair.
—*noun, plural* **waves. 1.** a moving ridge or high point on the surface of a body of water. **2.** any movement like the shape of an ocean wave. Sound and heat move in waves, and radio and TV programs travel through the air as waves. **3.** a strong feeling or condition that is thought of as moving like a wave: A period of hot weather is called a heat *wave.* "He felt a sudden *wave* of disgust sweep over him." (Arthur C. Clarke) **4.** the act of waving: The policeman signaled for us to go ahead with a *wave* of his hand. **5.** a curve or series of curves in the hair.

wave•length [wāv′lengkth′] *noun, plural* **wavelengths. 1.** the distance from a certain point on one wave to the same point of the next wave, especially from the top of one wave to the top of another. A radio signal can be sent out with a certain wavelength so that listeners can tune in to it. **2.** *Informal.* a certain way of thinking, in relation to how another or others think: Dad and I disagree about how I should dress; we're just not on the same *wavelength* at all when it comes to clothes.

wa•ver [wā′vər] *verb,* **wavered, wavering. 1.** to move back and forth in an unsteady way: "Helen's nervous head *wavered,* but her thoughts were steady." (Saul Bellow) **2.** to be uncertain; hesitate: "Older people have formed their opinions about everything, and don't *waver* before they act." (Anne Frank)

wav•y [wā′vē] *adjective,* **wavier, waviest.** having waves: a person with *wavy* hair.

wax¹ [waks] *noun, plural* **waxes. 1.** any of various thick, fatty substances that come from plants or animals and are also made artificially. Wax melts or becomes soft when it is heated. **2.** such a substance made by bees; more often called BEESWAX. **3.** any of various materials containing wax or a similar substance, used as a polish for floors and cars, to make candles, and for other items. —*verb,* **waxed, waxing.** to coat or polish with wax: The kitchen floor had a nice shine after she *waxed* it. —**waxy,** *adjective.*

wax² *verb,* **waxed, waxing.** to become larger or greater: The moon is said to *wax* during the time when it appears to grow larger in the sky as it gets closer to the full moon.

way [wā] *noun, plural* **ways. 1.** the certain manner or method in which something happens or is done: Put the forks on the table this *way,* to the left of the plate. **2.** a road or course going from one place to another; a route: Route 17 is the quickest *way* to the beach from here. **3.** a certain direction: I met John on my *way* to the library. **4.** a distance in space or time: Summer's still a long *way* off, but we're already having hot weather. **5.** what someone wants; a wish. ◆ Used mainly in the phrase **get (have) one's way.** —*adverb.* far: "Lem Peters was a friend from *way* back." (S. E. Hinton)

we [wē] *plural pronoun.* the person speaking or writing, and another or others thought of as in the same group: When I was a baby my family lived in Ohio, but then *we* moved to Texas.

weak [wēk] *adjective,* **weaker, weakest. 1.** not having the needed power or energy; not strong: The line was too *weak* to hold the heavy fish. "His eyes were *weak* and tired with tears so that he could not see." (James Joyce) **2.** lacking strength of character or will: British Prime Minister Neville Chamberlain was called a *weak* leader because he gave in too easily to the demands of Adolf Hitler.

weak•en [wē′kən] *verb,* **weakened, weakening.** to make or become weak: "The fear was *weakening* him and the pain was ferocious." (Joseph Wambaugh)

weak•ly [wēk′lē] *adverb.* in a weak manner: "There were at least eight dishes. I . . . sat for a minute looking *weakly* at the fork and spoon in my hand. " (M. F. K. Fisher)

weak•ness [wēk′nis] *noun, plural* **weaknesses. 1.** the fact of being weak; a lack of strength. **2.** a weak point; a fault or flaw: The pitchers like to throw him slow curve balls—that's his big *weakness.* **3.** a special liking that is hard to resist: "Her *weakness* was cats, and she loved to talk about how independent and smart and cute they were." (Ann Beattie)

wealth [welth] *noun.* **1.** a great amount of money, property, or valuable things; riches. **2.** a great amount: This book has a *wealth* of ideas on how to decorate your home.

wealth•y [wel′thē] *adjective,* **wealthier, wealthiest.** having wealth; rich.

weap•on [wep′ən] *noun, plural* **weapons. 1.** any tool or device used in fighting or killing, such as a gun, knife, and so on: The police say that a hammer was used as the murder *weapon.* **2.** anything used for attack or defense: A hawk's *weapons* are its sharp beak and claws. Dictator Joseph Stalin said that the printed word was the strongest *weapon* the Communist Party had.

wear [wâr] *verb,* **wore, worn, wearing. 1.** to have certain clothes on the body: Our soccer team *wears* blue-and-white uniforms. **2.** to have or show on the face or body: In the 1960's many people *wore* their hair long. "There are others besides you who have *worn* that look . . ." (Marianne Moore) **3.** to damage, weaken, or use up by rubbing or scraping, or by continued use. ♦ Usually used with a following adverb: to *wear out* a pair of shoes. The action of ocean waves can *wear away* rock. **4.** to hold up to such long use; last: That coat has *worn* well and still looks good on you. —*noun.* **1.** the act or fact of wearing. **2.** the damage caused by long use: Our living room rug is really showing signs of *wear.* **3.** things to be worn; clothing of a certain type. ♦ Used in combinations such as men's *wear,* sports*wear,* evening *wear.*

weasel This type of weasel is found all over North America. Its coat changes to white in winter. (See ERMINE for a picture of this.)

wea•sel [wē′zəl] *noun, plural* **weasels.** a small animal that has a long, slim body with soft, thick fur, short legs, and a long tail. Weasels eat small animals, such as rabbits, mice, and rats.

weath•er [weth′ər] *noun.* the condition of the outside air at a certain time and place, as to whether it is cold, hot, sunny, rainy, windy, and so on. —*verb,* **weathered, weathering. 1.** to change by being exposed to the air or weather: ". . . a two-story house, *weathered* and starting to fall apart . . ." (Elmore Leonard) **2.** to pass through a difficult experience safely, as if going through a storm: In 1980, the U. S. government made a huge loan to the Chrysler Corporation to help it *weather* a financial crisis.

weather Ernest Hemingway gave this advice to the novelist John Dos Passos: "Remember to get the weather into your book." In Hemingway's own stories, such as "Big Two-Hearted River" and "In Another Country," weather makes the setting dramatic and clear to the reader. Two authors for younger readers, Laura Ingalls Wilder and Patricia MacLachlan, are noted for bringing a sense of weather to their stories. Here are two chapter openings from MacLachlan's *Sarah, Plain and Tall.* "Sarah came in the spring. She came through green grass fields that bloomed with Indian paintbrush, red and orange, and blue-eyed grass." (Here, the family is excited about Sarah's arrival.) "The rain came and passed, but strange clouds hung in the northwest, low and black and green. And the air grew still." (Here, Sarah and Papa are about to have an argument.)

wea•ry [wir′ē] *adjective,* **wearier, weariest.** very tired: "He was very *weary* and often wished to rest—to lie down and sleep." (Jack London) "I grew *weary* of the sea, and intended to stay at home with my wife and family." (Jonathan Swift) —*verb,* **wearied, wearying.** to make or become tired. —**wearily,** *adverb.* —**weariness,** *noun.*

Pronunciation Key: T–Z			
t	ten; date	v	very; live
th	think	w	win; away
th	these	y	you
u	cut; butter	z	zoo; cause
ur	turn; bird	zh	measure

(Turn the page for more information.)

weath•er•man [weth′ ər mən′] *noun, plural* **weathermen. 1.** a person who studies the weather and predicts what it will be. **2.** a person who gives weather reports on television or radio.

weather vane a device that is moved by the wind and that has an arrow or pointer to show the direction in which the wind is blowing. ♦ A **weathercock** is a weather vane that has a design of a rooster on it.

weave [wēv] *verb,* **wove** or **weaved, woven** or **weaved, weaving. 1.** to pass threads or strips over and under each other to form cloth or other material: to *weave* a rug, to *weave* cotton for a shirt. American Indian tribes used to *weave* baskets out of straw or wood. **2.** of an insect, to spin a web or cocoon. **3.** to move quickly in and out; go by twisting or turning: The policeman noticed the car *weaving* from one lane to another and stopped it. —*noun, plural* **weaves.** a pattern or method of weaving: Men's dress shirts are often made in a style called a basket *weave.* ♦ A person who weaves is a **weaver.**

web Dewdrops hang from this delicate web as the garden spider waits in the center to trap an insect.

web [web] *noun, plural* **webs. 1.** the pattern of fine threads that is spun by a spider to catch its prey; also called a COBWEB or **spiderweb. 2.** a piece of cloth that is being woven. **3.** something that is thought of as being like a spider's web, as by being complicated, by trapping or deceiving someone, and so on. **4.** the skin between the toes of a swimming bird or animal, such as a duck, otter, or frog. ♦ Such a bird or animal is said to be **web-footed.**

Web•ster [web′ stər] **1. Daniel,** 1782-1852, American political leader and orator. **2. Noah,** 1758-1843, American dictionary editor and textbook author.

wed [wed] *verb,* **wedded, wedded** or **wed, wedding. 1.** to take a husband or wife; marry. **2.** to join a couple as husband and wife. **3.** to join or attach closely: I'm not *wedded* to that idea; I'm willing to try something different.

we'd [wēd] the contraction for "we had," "we should," and "we would."

wed•ding [wed′ ing] *noun, plural* **weddings.** a marriage ceremony, or a celebration that goes along with a marriage.

wedge [wej] *noun, plural* **wedges. 1.** a piece of wood or metal that is thick at one end and thin at the other. The thin end is forced into a narrow opening, usually by pounding on the thick end. Wedges are used to split objects apart, such as logs, to raise heavy objects, or to fill up a space between objects. **2.** anything that has the triangular shape of a wedge: a *wedge* of pie. —*verb,* **wedged, wedging. 1.** to split or separate with or as if with a wedge. **2.** to push or crowd into a tight space: "Leon squeezed into the booth himself and sat *wedged* there, hands folded . . ." (John Gardner)

Wed•nes•day [wenz′ dā′] *noun, plural* **Wednesdays.** the fourth day of the week.

weed [wēd] *noun, plural* **weeds.** a wild plant that grows where it is not wanted in a garden or field, harming the growth of other plants that are wanted. Crab grass and dandelions are common weeds in a lawn. —*verb,* **weeded, weeding. 1.** to take the weeds out of: to *weed* a flower garden. **2. weed out.** to remove something that is not wanted: Katie's closet is completely full, so she has to *weed out* the clothes that she never wears.

week [wēk] *noun, plural* **weeks. 1.** a period of seven days in a row, especially one starting with Sunday and ending with Saturday. **2.** the part of a seven-day period when a person works or goes to school.

week•day [wēk′ dā′] *noun, plural* **weekdays.** any day of the week except Saturday and Sunday.

week•end [wēk′ end′] *noun, plural* **weekends.** the time from the end of one work or school week to the beginning of the next.

week•ly [wēk′ lē] *adjective.* **1.** of or for a week: She made her *weekly* trip to the supermarket. **2.** done or happening once a week: *Time* is a *weekly* news magazine. —*noun, plural* **weeklies.** a newspaper or magazine published once a week. —*adverb.* once each week; every week.

weep [wēp] *verb,* **wept, weeping.** to cry; shed tears: "She *wept, wept* . . . until there were no more tears." (Brian Moore)

weeping willow a large, wide-spreading tree with light-green leaves and branches that hang down close to the ground. ◆ A tree is said to *weep* when its branches droop down, as if showing great sadness.

wee•vil [wē′vəl] *noun, plural* **weevils.** a type of small beetle that has a long snout. Weevils do great damage to grain and cotton crops.

weigh [wā] *verb,* **weighed, weighing. 1.** to find out how heavy someone or something is: She *weighed* herself on the bathroom scale. **2.** to have a certain weight: to *weigh* 150 pounds. **3.** to think about carefully; consider: The judge told the jury to *weigh* the evidence before making its decision: "He eyed me silently for a long pause, as though *weighing* whether I could be trusted . . ." (Russell Baker) **4. weigh down.** to put a heavy load or weight on: The tree branches were *weighed down* with snow.

weight [wāt] *noun, plural* **weights. 1.** how heavy a thing is: His *weight* is about 200 pounds. **2.** the quality of a thing caused by the pull of gravity on it. Weight tends to pull things toward the earth. **3.** A metal object that has a standard weight, used in the sport of WEIGHT LIFTING or for judging the weight of other objects on a balance scale. **4.** a heavy metal object used to hold something down. A **paperweight** is used to keep papers in place on a desk. **5.** something that bears down on a person like a heavy load: "Though as a rule he enjoyed the landscape, Yakov felt a *weight* on him. The buzz and sparkle of summer were gone." (Bernard Malamud) **6.** value or importance: Her opinion carries a lot of *weight* with the boss.
—*verb,* **weighted, weighting.** to put a load or weight on: Baseball players will often swing a *weighted* bat for practice before they go up to hit. ". . . her walk, not stumbling but heavy as though her feet were *weighted.*" (Sherley Anne Williams)

weight•less [wāt′lis] *adjective.* **1.** having little or no weight. **2.** free from the pull of gravity, as objects are in a spacecraft in outer space.

weight lifting an exercise or competition in which a person lifts an iron bar with heavy weights attached to it. ◆ A person who does this is a **weightlifter.**

weight•y [wāt′ē] *adjective,* **weightier, weightiest.** having great importance; serious: "At last the *weighty* matter of the board meeting was over." (Anita Desai)

weird [wērd] *adjective,* **weirder, weirdest. 1.** strange in a way that is frightening or disturbing: She had a *weird* feeling that something had

happened to her son, so she hurried home. "He threw back his head and made a *weird* howl, a howl that seemed to echo across the island." (Mary Norton) **2.** *Informal.* odd or unusual: "It was *weird* being lonesome in a place full of people." (S. E. Hinton)

wel•come [wel′kəm] *verb,* **welcomed, welcoming. 1.** to greet in a friendly way; meet with warm feelings: When the Navy ships returned from their cruise, the sailors were *welcomed* home by their friends and families. **2.** to be glad to accept; get with pleasure: ". . . he had *welcomed* the idea of a transfer to Base Fifteen . . ." (Colleen McCullough) —*noun, plural* **welcomes.** a friendly greeting: "He doesn't get a warm *welcome* from me when he comes . . ." (James Joyce) —*adjective.* **1.** greeted or received with pleasure: "Hale senses that he is no longer *welcome* in the house . . ." (Ann Beattie) "How bright and *welcome* the sun looked . . ." (Kenneth Grahame) **2.** free to have or use: You're *welcome* to take that book; I'm through with it. **3. You're welcome.** a polite remark made in answer to a person who has thanked you for something.

weightlifter American weightlifter Mario Martinez competing in the 1984 Olympic Games.

Pronunciation Key: [ə] Symbol

The [ə] or *schwa* sound occurs in syllables without an accent. It can be spelled with any vowel, such as **a** in above, **e** in listen, **i** in pencil, **o** in melon, **u** in circus. It can also be a combination of vowels, such as **io** in action, **ai** in mountain, **iou** in precious.

(Turn the page for more information.)

weld [weld] *verb,* **welded, welding.** to join two pieces of metal or other material by heating the pieces until they can be pressed together. ♦ This work is called **welding,** and a person who does it is a **welder.**

wel·fare [wel′fâr′] *noun.* **1.** the fact of being happy and healthy and of having what one needs to live comfortably: Her children's *welfare* is of the greatest importance to her. **2.** a government program to provide money, food, housing, medical care, or other forms of aid to poor people or those in need.

well[1] [wel] *adverb,* **better, best. 1.** in a good, proper, or favorable way: The team's been playing *well* lately and they've won six games in a row. All our neighbors are really nice and we get along *well* with them. ♦ Often used to form combinations, such as **well-balanced, well-behaved, well-defined, well-developed, well-dressed, well-educated, well-organized, well-trained,** and so on. **2.** to a great extent; very much: a football player who weighs *well* over 200 pounds. I've met him once or twice, but I don't know him *well.* —*adjective.* **1.** in good health; healthy: He looks very pale and tired; I don't think he's *well.* **2.** as it should be; in good order or condition: In olden times, a night watchman would call out "All's *well*" if there was nothing wrong. —*interjection.* **1.** used to show surprise: *Well!* I never thought that would happen! **2.** used to begin a new remark, or to continue with one after a pause or interjection: *Well,* I guess we'd better leave soon.

well[2] *noun, plural* **wells. 1.** a deep hole dug in the ground to bring up water. **2.** a similar hole to bring up oil or gas. **3.** a natural spring or fountain used as a source of water. —*verb,* **welled, welling.** to rise or flow, like water filling a well: His eyes *welled* with tears.

we'll [wēl] the contraction for "we will" and "we shall."

well-being [wel′bē′ing] *noun.* the fact of being healthy and happy.

well-done [wel′dun′] *adjective, more/most.* **1.** done well or properly: The firemen were congratulated for a job *well-done* in saving the building. **2.** thoroughly cooked: Mom likes her meat *well-done,* not rare.

well-known [wel′nōn′] *adjective, more/most.* generally or widely known: It's a *well-known* fact that water travels downhill. Johnny Carson is a *well-known* television personality.

well-mean·ing [wel′mē′ning] *adjective, more/most.* done with good intentions, though not always having the result wanted: He's very *well-meaning* around the house, but he sometimes gets in the way instead of helping.

well-to-do [wel′tə dōō′] *adjective, more/most.* having a lot of money or property; rich.

went [went] *verb.* the past tense of **go:** "Martha *went* out of her way to make me feel at home." (Frank Yerby)

wept [wept] *verb.* the past form of **weep.**

were [wur] *verb.* **1.** the plural past tense of **be:** They *were* already there when we arrived. **2.** the second person singular past tense of **be:** You *were* supposed to be here at 6:00, not 6:30.

we're [wēr] the contraction for "we are."

weren't [wurnt] the contraction for "were not."

west [west] *noun.* **1.** the direction that the sun goes in when it sets in the evening. **2.** usually, **West.** any place or region in this direction. **3. the West. a.** the western part of the United States, especially the area west of the Mississippi River. **b.** the countries west of Asia. **c.** the United States and the countries of Western Europe, as opposed to the Soviet Union and its allies in Eastern Europe. —*adjective.* **1.** toward the west: Billy lives on the *west* side of town. **2.** coming from the west: a *west* wind. —*adverb.* toward the west.

West Where is the American West? As America grew, as settlers founded towns and planted crops, the frontier —the edge of the West—kept being pushed across the Appalachians, across the prairie, across the high plains, over the Rockies, ending at the Pacific. In the late 1700's, Daniel Boone followed the Wilderness Road to the West—into what became the state of Kentucky. The West was centered in what we now call the Middle West through most of the 19th Century. The athletic league of Midwestern colleges (now the Big Ten) was called the Western Conference. The events of the "Wild West"—cattle drives, wagon trains, Indian fighting, land wars, and gunfights—took place mainly in the high plains area of the Dakotas, Nebraska, Missouri, Kansas, Oklahoma, and Texas. According to the official definition of the United States Census Bureau, the Western states now begin in the Rocky Mountains with Colorado.

west•ern [wes′tərn] *adjective*. **1.** toward the west: The city of Buffalo is in *western* New York State. **2.** coming from the west. **3. Western. a.** having to do with the western part of the U. S.: Nevada is a *Western* state. ◆ A **Westerner** is a person born or living in the West. **b.** having to do with the western part of the world: France is the largest country in *Western* Europe.
—*noun, plural* **westerns.** *also,* **Western.** a book, movie, or television show about life in the American West in the 1800's. Westerns deal with such stories as cowboys on the range, Indian fighting, lawmen and outlaws, and the lives of early settlers.

West Germany Neuschwanstein Castle in the Bavarian Alps of West Germany, built in the 19th century for King Ludwig of Bavaria.

West Germany the western and southern part of Germany, now a separate country. Its official name is the **Federal Republic of Germany.** *Capital:* Bonn. *Area:* 96,000 square miles. *Population:* 61,900,000.

West In•dies [in′dēz] a large group of islands between the Caribbean Sea and the Atlantic Ocean. Among the islands of the West Indies are Puerto Rico, Cuba, and Jamaica.

West Virginia a state in the east-central U. S. *Capital:* Charleston. *Nickname:* "Mountain State." *Area:* 24,200 square miles. *Population:* 1,948,000.

west•ward [west′wərd] *adverb; adjective*. toward the west.

wet [wet] *adjective*, **wetter, wettest. 1.** covered or soaked with water or another liquid: The grass was still *wet* from last night's rain. **2.** not yet dry or hardened: *wet* paint, *wet* cement. **3.** rainy: During the past month we had a lot of *wet* weather. —*verb,* **wet** or **wetted, wetting.** to cause to be wet: You have to *wet* the sponge first before you use it. —**wetness,** *noun.*

wet•land [wet′land′] *noun, plural* **wetlands.** *usually,* **wetlands.** a low-lying area that is partly covered with water and has very damp soil, such as a swamp or marsh. Wetlands are important as a home for animal and plant life.

we've [wēv] the contraction for "we have."

whack [wak] *Informal. verb,* **whacked, whacking.** to hit sharply; smack: "Sam *whacked* the leather with his fist." (Bernard Malamud) —*noun, plural* **whacks.** a loud or sharp blow.

whale [wāl] *noun, plural* **whales.** a very large sea animal that looks like a fish but is actually an air-breathing mammal. One type, the **blue whale,** can be up to 100 feet long and weigh as much as 150 tons. This makes it the largest animal that has ever lived on earth, larger even than the biggest dinosaurs.

whal•er [wā′lər] *noun, plural* **whalers.** a person whose job is hunting whales, or a special ship used for hunting whales.

whal•ing [wāl′ing] *noun.* the work or business of hunting whales for their meat, bone, and fat (called BLUBBER). This fat produces a valuable oil that was widely used in former times. Many countries now have laws against whaling because of the threat to the whale population.

wharf [wôrf] *noun, plural* **wharves** or **wharfs.** a structure that is built along the shore for the loading and unloading of ships. It usually is a platform set on pillars.

what [wut] *pronoun*. **1.** which thing or things: *What's* your favorite food? *What* does he do for a living? **2.** that or those which: Don't worry about the way the paint looks now; I know *what* I'm doing. —*adjective*. **1.** which or which type: *What* school does your sister go to? **2.** how surprising or unusual: *What* a beautiful day it is today! —*interjection*. used to show surprise or annoyance: *What!* You forgot to bring the hot dogs for the picnic?

what•ev•er [wut′ev′ər] *pronoun*. **1.** anything that: John did *whatever* he could to make his apartment look nice for his parents' visits. **2.** no matter what: *Whatever* you do, don't let the dog get out. —*adjective*. any and all: *Whatever* meat is left over we'll save for tomorrow night. **2.** of

---

Pronunciation Key; Accent Marks

[′] is the normal accent mark. It shows where the main stress falls on a word.
[′] is a secondary accent mark. It shows a lighter stress than the primary accent. For example:

tel • e • vis • ion [tel′ə vizh′ən]

(Turn the page for more information.)

any kind or type: She looked at me blankly, with no expression on her face *whatever*.

what's [wuts] a contraction for "what is" and "what has:" *What's* for dinner tonight? *What's* happened to that book I left on the table?

what•so•ev•er [wut′ sō ev′ ər] *pronoun; adjective.* of any kind; at all: There's no reason *whatsoever* why we can't finish this work today.

wheat [wēt] *noun.* a tall grass plant that has a thin stem and long leaves, and that is a very important source of food. The seeds (kernels) of wheat are ground up to make bread, breakfast cereal, spaghetti, noodles, and other foods.

wheat germ the center or inner part of a kernel of wheat. Wheat germ has a high amount of vitamins and is often added to other foods.

wheel [wēl] *noun, plural* **wheels. 1.** a round frame that can turn around a central point to allow a car, bicycle, or other such vehicle to move or machine to work. **2.** a machine or other thing that uses a wheel, such as a spinning wheel or water wheel. **3.** *also,* **steering wheel.** the circular frame used to control the movement of a car or other such vehicle: Dad was tired of driving, so Mom took the *wheel*. —*verb,* **wheeled, wheeling. 1.** to move on wheels: "A woman passed, *wheeling* a baby in a buggy." (Betty Smith) **2.** to turn or change direction: "Driving very fast, Darly *wheeled* the pickup around, spraying dirt." (Saul Bellow)

wheel•bar•row [wēl′ bâr′ ō] *noun, plural* **wheelbarrows.** a small vehicle with a wheel on the front, two handles in the back, and a flat container in which small loads of dirt or other materials can be carried.

wheel•chair [wēl′ châr′] *noun, plural* **wheelchairs.** a special chair mounted on wheels, used as a way of moving about by someone who cannot walk normally. A wheelchair may be rolled by the person in it, pushed by someone else from behind, or operated by motor.

wheeze [wēz] *verb,* **wheezed, wheezing.** to breathe with difficulty; breathe with a rough, whistling sound. —*noun, plural* **wheezes.** a wheezing sound.

whelk [welk] *noun, plural* **whelks.** a large saltwater snail that has a thick shell.

when [wen] *adverb.* **1.** at what time: *When* does the movie start? **2.** the time at which: He knows *when* to speak up and *when* to keep quiet. —*conjunction.* **1.** at the time that: I had just walked in the door *when* you called. **2.** at any time that: *When* he's at the beach, he likes to lie on the sand and rest. **3.** considering that; since: How can you buy that toy *when* you don't have

enough money? —*pronoun.* what or which time: Since *when* have you become a computer expert?

whence [wens] *adverb; conjunction.* from what place or cause: "If you know *whence* you came, there is really no limit to where you can go." (James Baldwin)

when•ev•er [wen′ ev′ ər] *adverb; conjunction.* at any time: The teacher is glad to help *whenever* one of the students has a problem.

where [wâr] *adverb.* at or in what place: *Where* are all the books you want me to take back to the library? —*conjunction.* **1.** in or at which place: See that house—that's *where* my friend Ellen lives. **2.** in that case or situation: He's getting to the point *where* he only wants to play video games all day.

where•a•bouts [wâr′ ə bouts′] *adverb.* near or in what location or place: You lost your jacket? *Whereabouts* did you last see it? —*noun, plural* **whereabouts.** the place where someone or something is: The robbers managed to get away, and their present *whereabouts* is unknown.

where•as [wâr′ az′] *conjunction.* on the other hand; while: Mammals give birth to live young, *whereas* birds hatch their young from eggs.

wheelchair President Franklin D. Roosevelt was crippled by polio as a young man. This is an unusual photo because he rarely used his wheelchair in public.

where•by [wâr′ bī′] *adverb; conjunction.* by means of which; through which: A new city law has gone into effect, *whereby* no smoking is allowed in office buildings.

where•fore [wâr′ fôr′] *adverb; conjunction.* for what reason; why. ◆ Used mainly in older writings: "*Wherefore* have all the people left their work today?" (Nathaniel Hawthorne)

which/that Both *which* and *that* can be used to set off a clause within a sentence. If the meaning of the complete sentence depends on this clause, the proper form is *that*: "Some of the creatures *that* lived with Molly needed her special attention even now." (John Balaban) If the clause is a "side note," and is not crucial to the sentence, it takes *which*: "Italy's land reform, *which* the Demo-Christians promised two years ago and *which* some Italians feel has been needed for centuries, actually got underway last Sunday, September 24th." (Janet Flanner) "Among the papers *that* Sarah laid out for me the other afternoon is the February 1879 issue of *Century* . . ." (Wallace Stegner) Here, the writer chose *that* because the clause presents important new information.

where•in [wâr′ in′] *adverb; conjunction.* **1.** in what way or manner. **2.** in which. ♦ *Wherein* and *whereby* are used mainly in literary or formal writing.

where•up•on [wâr′ ə pän′] *conjunction.* at which time: "It never thaws . . . until you build a house on it, *whereupon* the warmth seeping through the floor thaws the ground . . ." (Farley Mowat)

wher•ever [wâr′ ev′ ər] *conjunction; adverb.* **1.** in or to whatever place: We'll put the plant somewhere in the back yard—*wherever* it will get the most sun. **2.** where: You thought I didn't want to go? *Wherever* did you get that idea?

whet [wet] *verb,* **whetted, whetting. 1.** to sharpen a knife or blade, as by rubbing it against a sharpening stone. **2.** to make more keen or eager: "This so *whetted* my appetite that I spurred the horses . . ." (James Michener)

which•ev•er [wich′ ev′ ər] *pronoun; adjective.* any one of a group that; whatever one or ones: This sweater comes in six colors; you can get *whichever* one you like best.

whiff [wif] *noun, plural* **whiffs.** a light puff or breath, as of air or smoke: I got a *whiff* of the bacon cooking and suddenly felt hungry.

while [wīl] *noun.* **a while.** a period of time, especially a short time: Now that that's done, let's stop and rest for a *while*. I haven't seen Jeff around in quite a *while*—I wonder if he moved. —*conjunction.* **1.** during the time that: Your friend Dave called *while* you were out. Hold the log steady *while* I saw it. **2.** on the other hand; although: *While* I enjoyed camp last summer, I'm not sure I want to go back this year. **3.** whereas; but: This book seems to have more information, *while* the other one is much more up-to-date. —*verb,* **whiled, whiling. while**

whether This word is used to set up a choice: "We look the same way *whether* we're going to the PTA meeting, or going to get groceries, or to visit her parents." (Ann Beattie) At times *if* is used in place of *whether*: "Mason had time to wonder *if* he'd given her the wrong idea." (Anne Tyler) However, *whether* is generally considered to be better for serious writing. There are good reasons for that statement. "I doubt *whether* he heard you. And if he did, I doubt *whether* he knows or cares who you are." (John Knowles) Here, *whether* is the choice, because *if* is already in the sentence for a different purpose.

wheth•er [weth′ ər] *conjunction.* **1.** if it is likely that; if: She wants to know *whether* you are going to her party or not. **2.** if one or the other; in either or any case: I was so shocked I didn't know *whether* to laugh or cry.

whey [wā] *noun.* the clear, watery part of milk that separates when milk turns sour. Whey is used in making cheese.

which [wich] *pronoun.* **1.** what one or ones: I know you liked both movies, but *which* did you like better? **2.** the thing or things mentioned before: Our old car, *which* we no longer have, was the same make as this one. —*adjective.* what one or ones: *Which* desk do you sit at?

away. to spend time relaxing: "To *while away* time, she and her niece talked about the Chinese passengers." (Maxine Hong Kingston)

whim [wim] *noun, plural* **whims.** a sudden desire or wish to do something, especially something that is not serious or sensible: A *whim* to

Pronunciation Key. A–F

a	and; hat	ch	chew; such
ā	ate; stay	d	dog; lid
â	care; air	e	end; yet
ä	father; hot	ē	she; each
b	boy; cab	f	fun; off

(Turn the page for more information.)

go fishing made Dad rent a boat and equipment and take the whole family out on the lake.

whim•per [wim′ pər] *verb,* **whimpered, whimpering.** to cry in a low, broken sound: "Just then the hyena stopped *whimpering* in the night . . ." (Ernest Hemingway) —*noun, plural* **whimpers.** a whimpering sound.

whim•si•cal [wim′ zi kəl] *adjective, more/most.* full of humorous or lighthearted ideas: ". . . his mouth . . . *whimsical* as if he was teasing her." (Iris Murdoch)

whine [wīn] *verb,* **whined, whining. 1.** to cry in a complaining way: The dog was locked in the basement and he *whined* to be let out. **2.** to complain: "Her sisters call all the time, *whining* with unhappiness." (Ann Beattie) —*noun, plural* **whines.** the sound or act of whining.

whin•ny [win′ ē] *noun, plural* **whinnies.** a low, gentle sound like that made by a horse or a similar animal. —*verb,* **whinnied, whinnying.** to make this sound.

whip [wip] *noun, plural* **whips.** a device made up of a long cord or rope with a handle at one end. A rider in a race may hit a horse with a whip to get it to go faster. —*verb,* **whipped, whipping. 1.** to hit with a whip, strap, or other such device: In former times, prisoners were *whipped* as a punishment. **2.** to make go suddenly: "The catcher *whipped* the ball back at him . . ." (Roger Angell) "Curls of smoke rose from the chimney to be *whipped* away by the breeze." (Ken Follett) **3.** to move or pull out suddenly: "Then she *whipped* out a hairbrush and started to brush her long brown hair." (Judy Blume) **4.** to defeat: to *whip* another team in football. **5.** to beat cream, eggs, or other food into a foam. ♦ Cream treated this way is called **whipped cream.**

whip•lash [wip′ lash′] *noun, plural* **whiplashes. 1.** a blow from a whip. **2.** an injury to the neck caused by a sudden forward and backward movement of the head, such as can happen in an automobile accident.

whip•poor•will [wip′ ər wil′] *noun, plural* **whippoorwills.** a North American bird with brown and black feathers and an unusual whistling call that sounds like its name.

whir [wur] *verb,* **whirred, whirring.** to move or operate with a buzzing or humming sound. —*noun, plural* **whirs.** such a sound: the *whir* of an air conditioner.

whirl [wurl] *verb,* **whirled, whirling.** to turn or move quickly in a circle; spin around: "An electric fan is *whirling* on the end of the counter . . ." (Ernest K. Gann) —*noun, plural*

whirls. **1.** a quick, turning movement: "The wind rose and a *whirl* of snow swooped into the shelter . . ." (Marguerite Henry) **2.** a confused condition: "I felt in such a *whirl* after hearing a lot of sad news . . ." (Anne Frank)

whirl•pool [wurl′ pool′] *noun, plural* **whirlpools.** a strong current of water that moves quickly in a circle and pulls things below the surface.

whirl•wind [wurl′ wind′] *noun, plural* **whirlwinds.** a small windstorm in which a mass of air spins rapidly in a circle.

whisk [wisk] *verb,* **whisked, whisking. 1.** to brush off lightly: She *whisked* the crumbs off the table after dinner. **2.** to move or go quickly: "The door *whisked* open and this tall lady asked me to come on in . . ." (Jean Craighead George)

whisk•er [wis′ kər] *noun, plural* **whiskers. 1. whiskers.** the hair growing on a man's face. **2.** one hair of a man's beard. **3.** a stiff hair on the face of an animal, such as a cat.

whis•key [wis′ kē] *noun, plural* **whiskies.** a strong alcoholic drink made from corn, rye, barley, or other grains. ♦ *Whiskey* comes from Gaelic, an old language of Scotland and Ireland. It originally was an expression meaning "the water of life."

whis•per [wis′ pər] *verb,* **whispered, whispering.** to speak in a low or soft voice: "They would come together to *whisper* and laugh secretly if someone passed by who amused or interested them." (Joyce Carol Oates) —*noun, plural* **whispers.** a soft spoken sound.

whis•tle [wis′ əl] *verb,* **whistled, whistling. 1.** to make a clear, sharp, or musical sound by forcing air out through the closed lips or the teeth: to *whistle* a tune. **2.** to cause a similar sound: "A sharp and cutting fall wind had come up . . . it *whistled* across the parking lot." (Stephen King) —*noun, plural* **whistles. 1.** a small instrument that makes a clear, musical tune when air is blown through it. **2.** a whistling sound.

white [wīt] *noun, plural* **whites. 1.** the lightest of all colors; the color of milk or snow. **2.** *also,* **White.** a member of the race having light skin. —*adjective,* **whiter, whitest. 1.** being the opposite of black; the lightest of colors. **2.** light in color as compared to other things of the same kind: *white* wine, the *white* meat of a turkey. **3.** *also,* **White.** belonging to the race of people having light skin. —**whiteness,** *noun.*

white blood cell a colorless blood cell that acts as protection against disease and infection.

white-collar [wīt/ käl/ ər] *adjective.* having to do with jobs that are done in offices or indoors and that do not call for heavy physical activity: Working in a bank is a *white-collar* job. ◆ From the *white* dress shirts often worn by men who are office workers.

White House 1. the official home of the President of the United States in Washington, D.C. **2.** the authority of the President or the Executive branch: The *White House* will issue a statement today on the airline hijacking.

whit•en [wīt/ ən] *verb,* **whitened, whitening.** to make or become white or whiter.

white•wash [wīt/ wäsh/] *noun, plural* **white-washes.** a watery white paint made from lime and chalk, often used in former times to paint wooden fences or walls. —*verb,* **whitewashed, whitewashing. 1.** to cover a fence or other surface with whitewash. **2.** to cover up a crime or mistake: The newspaper accused the mayor of trying to *whitewash* a political scandal.

White House The White House in Washington, D.C. was rebuilt in 1814 after British forces set fire to the original Presidential house during the War of 1812.

who [hoo] *pronoun.* what or which person: *Who* was that on the phone just now? The man *who* lives next door to us just bought a new car.

who/whom *Who* is a subject pronoun; *whom* is an object pronoun: "Lee Iacocca is a figure *who* [subject] is in the news and *whom* [object] we cover in our newspaper." (Benjamin Bradlee) In ordinary conversation, you usually do not hear *whom.* "You know that secret you told me? I told somebody else about it." "What! *Who* did you tell?" In this situation, "*Whom* did you tell?" would sound stiff. But in writing, good writers do tend to observe the *who/whom* distinction: "He had a younger brother *whom* he was putting through college." (Saul Bellow) Especially, they use *whom* when it follows a preposition: "Beharry was the only person in Fuente Grove *with whom* Ganesh became friendly." (V. S. Naipaul) "There was even a female attendant, *to whom* she would have to announce her wants." (E. M. Forster) You wouldn't say, "to who."

whith•er [with/ ər] *adverb; conjunction.* to what or which place; where. ◆ Used mainly in literary writing: ". . . most of the boys had already gone into the village of Eastchester, *whither* Basil . . . was forbidden to follow." (F. Scott Fitzgerald)

Whit•man [wit/ mən] **Walt,** 1819-1892, American poet.

Whit•ney [wit/ nē] **1. Eli,** 1764-1825, American inventor who developed a new method to process cotton. **2. Mount Whitney.** the highest mountain in the continental United States, in the Sierra Nevadas of eastern California.

whit•tle [wit/ əl] *verb,* **whittled, whittling.** to cut away small pieces of wood with a knife, either as a pastime or to form some shape.

whiz [wiz] *verb,* **whizzed, whizzing.** to make a buzzing or humming sound while moving fast: He tried to get someone to stop, but the cars *whizzed* by without slowing down.

who'd [hood] the contraction for "who would" and "who had."

who•ev•er [hoo ev/ ər] *pronoun.* any person who; whatever person: *Whoever* took out the milk forgot to put it back in the refrigerator.

whole [hōl] *adjective.* being all that there is or should be; complete; entire: She spent the *whole* afternoon working in the yard. Are you really going to eat that *whole* pie all by yourself? —*noun.* **1.** all the parts that make up something; the complete amount. **2. on the whole** or **as a whole.** in general: A few critics

Pronunciation Key· G–N				
g	give; big		k	kind; cat; back
h	hold		l	let; ball
i	it; this		m	make; time
ī	ice; my		n	not; own
j	jet; gem; edge		ng	having

(Turn the page for more information.)

didn't like the movie, but *on the whole* the reviews were good.

whole number a number that does not contain a fraction or decimal, such as 33 or 98, as opposed to 33 1/3 or 98.6.

who's [hōōz] the contraction for "who is" and "who has."

whose [hōōz] *pronoun.* the possessive form of **who** or **which**: *Whose* roller skates are those lying in the driveway?

whose/who's *Whose* is possessive. "Goldilocks wondered, *Whose* house is this?" (Who is the owner of the house?) *Who's* is a contraction for *who is* or *who has:* "*Who's* been sleeping in my bed?" (Who has been sleeping?) "*Who's* that knocking at the door?" (Who is knocking?) In speaking, *whose* and *who's* are exactly the same in sound. But in writing, *who's* has a distinct use. If a man is interested in buying your car, it wouldn't make sense to write, "That's the man *whose* interested in buying our car."

whole•sale [hōl′ sāl′] *noun.* the selling of goods in large quantities, usually to store owners who then sell the goods to the public at a higher price (RETAIL). —*adjective; adverb.* **1.** having to do with the sale of goods in quantity: *wholesale* prices, to buy something *wholesale.* **2.** in too large an amount or quantity: In the late 1800's, hunters carried out a *wholesale* slaughter of buffalo. —**wholesaler**, *noun.*

whole•some [hōl′ sum′] *adjective, more/most.* **1.** good for the health; healthful: Mom always tries to get us to eat *wholesome* food and cut down on candy and soda. **2.** good for the mind or character: Walt Disney was known for producing films that provide *wholesome* family entertainment.

whole-wheat *adjective.* of bread or flour, made from the entire grain of wheat.

who'll [hōōl] the contraction for "who will" and "who shall."

whol•ly [hō′ lē] *adverb.* in a whole way; entirely; completely: to be *wholly* responsible or *wholly* to blame for something.

whom [hōōm] a form of **who,** used as the object of a verb or preposition: "The person to *whom* she is speaking is myself." (Truman Capote)

whoop [wōōp *or* hōōp] *noun, plural* **whoops.** a loud cry or shout. The shout given by American Indians going into battle was called a **war whoop.** —*verb,* **whooped, whooping.** to give a loud cry or shout: "He slid down and gave chase, *whooping* loudly." (Lois Lenski)

whooping cough a serious contagious disease of the lungs, causing violent coughing fits that end with a high-pitched whooping sound. This disease can be spread easily, but is now generally controlled by vaccination.

whooping crane a tall North American bird with long legs, a white body, and wings with black tips. The whooping crane is almost extinct. It is named for the loud cry it makes.

why [wī] *adverb; conjunction.* for what cause or reason: *Why* wasn't Eddie in school today? Was he sick? Tell me *why* you didn't like that movie—I thought it was great. —*interjection.* used to show surprise: *Why,* I had no idea that you could draw so beautifully!

wick [wik] *noun, plural* **wicks.** a cord or band of twisted fibers used in an oil lamp, candle, or lighter to draw up fuel for burning.

wick•ed [wik′ id] *adjective,* **wickeder, wickedest.** evil or bad: "Whoever that *wicked* murderer was . . ." (Agatha Christie) "He grinned, quick and *wicked* as a razor slash." (Colleen McCullough) —**wickedly**, *adverb.* —**wickedness**, *noun.*

wick•er [wik′ ər] *noun.* **1.** flexible twigs or reeds that are woven together. Furniture and baskets are sometimes made of wicker. **2.** *also,* **wickerwork.** an object made of wicker.

wide [wīd] *adjective,* **wider, widest. 1.** extending far from side to side; broad: a *wide* highway. The Amazon is a *wide* river. **2.** having a certain distance from one side to the other: The path was about four feet *wide.* **3.** large in range or amount: This book covers a *wide* range of topics. **4.** away from the target or goal: The throw to home plate was *wide* and the runner scored. —*adverb.* **1.** over a large area or space. ♦ Usually used in the expression **far and wide:** The movie director looked *far and wide* to find a new star for his film. **2.** to the full extent or amount: The front door was *wide* open. —**widely**, *adverb.* to a great extent: an author who is *widely* known. Someone who is *widely* read has read a lot of books.

wid•en [wī′ dən] *verb,* **widened, widening.** to make or become wide or wider: The road crew is *widening* that road so that it will have four lanes instead of two. "Father's beard slowly *widened* with a smile." (Laura Ingalls Wilder)

wide•spread [wīd′ spred′] *adjective, more/*

most. happening over or affecting a large area: The earthquake caused *widespread* damage throughout the county.

wid·ow [wid′ ō] *noun, plural* **widows.** a woman whose husband is dead and who has not married again.

wid·o·wer [wid′ ō ər] *noun, plural* **widowers.** a man whose wife is dead and who has not married again. ♦ It's correct to say either "She's a widow" or "She is Mr. Smith's *widow*" but not "He is Mrs. Smith's *widower.*" That can only be "He's a *widower.*"

width [width] *noun, plural* **widths.** the distance from one side of an object to the other: This book has a *width* of eight inches.

wield [wēld] *verb,* **wielded, wielding. 1.** to hold or use a weapon or tool: to *wield* a knife. **2.** to hold or use power or authority: That senator *wields* a lot of power in his home state.

wife [wīf] *noun, plural* **wives.** a woman who is married.

wig [wig] *noun, plural* **wigs.** a covering for the head made of artificial or real hair.

wig·gle [wig′ əl] *verb,* **wiggled, wiggling.** to move or twist from side to side in quick, short motions: The rabbit *wiggled* through the hole in the fence.

wig·wam [wig′ wäm′] *noun, plural* **wigwams.** a type of house or hut used by certain North American Indian tribes, made of a frame of wooden poles covered with bark or hides.

wild [wīld] *adjective,* **wilder, wildest. 1.** not under the care or control of people; living or growing in nature: A wolf is a *wild* animal; a dog is a tame one. ♦ A flower that grows in this way is a **wildflower. 2.** not lived in or settled: *wild* mountain country. **3.** rough or violent: "A *wild* river of air swept and swirled across the dark sky . . ." (Arthur Miller) **4.** not under proper control or discipline: a *wild* party. Don't listen to any of his *wild* ideas. **5.** not having the proper aim or direction: I don't have any idea of the answer—let me take a *wild* guess. —*adverb.* in a wild way; not under control: The fans went *wild* when the home team went ahead with two minutes to play. —*noun, plural* **wilds.** *usually,* **the wild** or **the wilds.** a natural area away from people; a wilderness. —**wildly,** *adverb:* "Then he began racing *wildly* up and down the bank, looking everywhere." (E.B. White) —**wildness,** *noun.*

wild·cat [wīld′ kat′] *noun, plural* **wildcats.** a name for various small, wild members of the cat family, such as the bobcat or lynx. —*adjective.* in business, done in an unusual or irregular

way: A *wildcat* strike is one that takes place without the permission of union leaders.

wildcat "Wildcat" is a general term, but it is most often used for the North American bobcat, *Lynx rufus.*

wil·der·ness [wil′ dər nis] *noun, plural* **wildernesses.** an area that is in its natural state, with wild animals and plants and with few people living there: Much of the state of Alaska is still *wilderness.*

wild·fire [wīld′ fīr′] *noun, plural* **wildfires. 1.** a fire that spreads quickly. **2. like wildfire.** in a very fast, uncontrolled way: The news that the company was being sold spread like *wildfire* among the workers.

wild·life [wīld′ līf′] *noun.* animals and plants that live naturally in a wild area.

will¹ [wil] a verb used with other verbs to show: **1.** something expected to happen in the future: I *will* be finished in a few minutes. **2.** something that should be done: You *will* clean up your room right now. **3.** something that is able to be done: This theater *will* seat 300 people. **4.** something that is done by habit or custom: Often when I ask her a question, she *will* just stare off into space without answering.

will² *noun, plural* **wills. 1.** the power that the mind has to make a decision and then select actions to carry it out: Something that a person purposely chooses to do is an act of *will.* ♦ Often used in the phrase **free will. 2.** a determination to make things happen in a certain way:

Pronunciation Key: O–S			
ō	over; go	ou	out; town
ô	all; law	p	put; hop
oo	look; full	r	run; car
o͞o	pool; who	s	set; miss
oi	oil; boy	sh	show

(Turn the page for more information.)

> **will** It's said that *will* is the future tense in English. It is so, but it's only one of various ways to show the future: I will leave in five minutes, I shall leave, I'm going to leave, I am leaving, I leave in five minutes. *Will* is a strong word; it shows that the person has definitely decided to do something or is certain about some future event. Here's an example from Arthur Miller's *Death of a Salesman*: "LINDA: Why don't you tell these things to Howard, dear? WILLY: I *will*, I definitely *will*." Or try this for the distinction: "There's *going* to be a softball game after school today." (plain statement, no special emphasis) "Mr. Lister said that the game *will* be played today, even if it rains." (strong statement, showing determination) (See also SHALL on p. 692.)

a tennis player with a *will* to win. British leader Margaret Thatcher has been called "The Iron Lady" because she is a person of very strong *will*. ◆ This is also called **willpower**: "She cured herself of being an invalid by sheer *willpower* . . ." (Mary McCarthy) **3.** a legal document that states what a person wants done with his money and property after he dies. —*verb*, **willed, willing. 1.** to use the power of the mind to control what goes on: Sandy *willed* herself to be calm when she made her speech. **2.** to give away one's property by a will.

will•ful [wil′fəl] *adjective, more/most.* determined to get one's own way, even at the expense of others; stubborn. —**willfully,** *adverb*.

William the Conqueror This 11th-century tapestry shows the court of King William. He appears on the right, seated between his two brothers.

Wil•liam or **William the Conqueror** [wil′yəm], 1028-1087, Duke of Normandy (a part of northern France) who defeated the English in a great battle at Hastings in 1066, and then was king of England from 1066 to 1087.

will•ing [wil′ing] *adjective, more/most.* ready or wanting to do something: Mr. Davis is always *willing* to come over and help Dad with work around the yard. —**willingly,** *adverb*. —**willingness,** *noun*.

wil•low [wil′ō] *noun, plural* **willows.** a tree or bush that has long, thin branches that droop. Willows have thin, pointed leaves and clusters of tiny flowers.

Wil•son [wil′sən] **Woodrow,** 1856-1924, the twenty-eighth president of the United States, from 1913 to 1921.

wilt [wilt] *verb,* **wilted, wilting. 1.** of a plant, to lose freshness; become limp or droopy: Cut flowers will *wilt* quickly if they aren't kept in water. **2.** to lose strength or energy: "Now she began to sing in a lower key, in a sad, *wilted* voice . . ." (Anita Desai)

win [win] *verb,* **won, winning. 1.** to be the best or first in a game or contest; come out ahead: to *win* a baseball game, to *win* an election, to *win* a spelling contest. **2.** to gain as a reward for success in a game or contest: to *win* $1000 in the state lottery, to *win* an Oscar for Best Actress. **3.** to get or achieve through an effort: The mayor has *won* the support of all the local newspapers in her campaign for reelection. —*noun, plural* **wins.** a victory or success: Our basketball team is in first place with a record of ten *wins* and one loss.

wince [wins] *verb,* **winced, wincing.** to draw back slightly or draw in the breath, as from pain or danger: "He stood up, *wincing* at the tightness of his shoes." (John Mortimer)

winch [winch] *noun, plural* **winches.** a device used for lifting or pulling heavy objects, made up of a large drum or pulley with a rope or chain that wraps around it. Winches can be operated by hand or by a motor.

wind[1] [wind] *noun, plural* **winds. 1.** the air that moves over the surface of the earth. **2.** the breath, or the ability to breathe: The football players did a lot of running to build up their *wind*. **3. winds.** WIND INSTRUMENTS as a group. —*verb,* **winded, winding.** to be or cause to be out of breath: "*Winded* after a quarter-mile run through the length of building . . ." (Kurt Vonnegut)

wind[2] [wīnd] *verb,* **wound, winding. 1.** to twist or wrap string, thread, wire, or the like around itself or around something else: "He took the rope off the saddle and *wound* the loops carefully in his left hand." (Lois Lenski) **2.** to turn a part on a watch or other such device to adjust it or make it work. **3.** to move in a series of twists and turns: "They *wound* down a hundred crooked alleys . . ." (Mark Helprin) "He turned his eyes to the grey gleaming river, *winding* along towards Dublin." (James Joyce) **4. wind up. a.** to bring to a close: Let's *wind up* the discussion and have a vote. **b.** of a pitcher in baseball, to move the arms and body before throwing the ball. ♦ Also used as a noun: a pitcher with a tricky *windup.*

wind•break•er [wind′brā′ kər] *noun, plural* **windbreakers.** a short, light jacket that protects against wind. ♦ The name **Windbreaker** is a trademark for a jacket of this type.

wind chill a way to measure how cold the wind feels to the surface of the skin. The **wind-chill factor** takes into account both the actual air temperature and the force of the wind. Thus if the temperature is 20° and there is a 20 mile-per-hour wind, the wind-chill factor is said to make a person feel as cold as if it were 9°.

wind•fall [wind′fôl′] *noun, plural* **windfalls.** an unexpected, lucky event: A *windfall* profit is one that comes from unusual changes in business conditions, rather than from the company's own good performance.

wind•ing [wīn′ding] *adjective, more/most.* full of bends or turns: a *winding* mountain road.

wind instrument any musical instrument that is played by blowing air into it, such as a bugle, trumpet, flute, or clarinet.

wind•mill [wind′mil′] *noun, plural* **windmills.** a machine that uses large blades to capture the power of the wind and turn it into mechanical energy. Windmills are now used mainly to pump water.

win•dow [win′dō] *noun, plural* **windows. 1.** an opening in a wall that is fitted with a frame and glass to let in light, and which usually can also be opened to let in air. **2.** a separate viewing area on a computer screen giving different information from the rest of the screen. ♦ *Window* goes back to an old word meaning "wind eye." The idea was that a window was like an eye, or hole, through which wind could enter.

win•dow•pane [win′dō pān′] *noun, plural* **windowpanes.** a sheet of glass used in a window.

wind•pipe [wind′pīp′] *noun, plural* **windpipes.** the tube that connects the throat to the lungs, carrying air in and out. In medical use it is called the TRACHEA.

wind•shield [wind′shēld′] *noun, plural* **wind-** shields. the clear window at the front of an automobile or other such vehicle. ♦ A **windshield wiper** is a device used to clear rain or dirt from a windshield.

wind•y [win′dē] *adjective,* **windier, windiest. 1.** having much wind: Chicago is called the *Windy City* because of the strong winds that often blow in off Lake Michigan. **2.** *Informal.* using a lot of wasteful talk: The audience was completely bored by the long, *windy* speech.

wine [wīn] *noun, plural* **wines. 1.** a drink containing alcohol, made from the juice of grapes. **2.** a similar drink made from another fruit or plant, such as apples or blackberries.

wing [wing] *noun, plural* **wings. 1.** one of the movable parts used by a bird, insect, or bat to move through the air. **2.** a flat structure extending out from either side of an airplane that helps it stay in the air as it moves forward. **3.** a smaller part that projects out from the main part of a building: The museum has just opened a new *wing.* **4.** an area to the side of a stage not visible to the audience: The singer waited in the *wings* until it was her turn to go on stage. **5.** in sports such as soccer and hockey, a player whose position is near the side of the playing area. —*verb,* **winged, winging. 1.** to use the

windmill A typical windmill of the Netherlands, attached to a farmhouse.

Pronunciation Key: T–Z			
t	ten; date	v	very; live
th	think	w	win; away
<u>th</u>	these	y	you
u	cut; butter	z	zoo; cause
ur	turn; bird	zh	measure

(Turn the page for more information.)

wings; fly. **2.** to wound slightly in the wing or arm: Even though the hunter *winged* the pheasant, it still got away.

winged [wingd *or* wing′id] *adjective.* having wings: Mosquitoes are *winged* insects.

wing•span [wing′span′] *noun, plural* **wingspans.** the distance between the tip of one extended wing and the other, used as a way to measure the size of a bird or an aircraft. ◆ Also called **wingspread.**

wink [wingk] *verb,* **winked, winking.** to close and open one eye quickly, usually as a private message or signal to someone: Dad *winked* at me to let me know that he wasn't really mad at Danny, but just pretending to be. —*noun, plural* **winks. 1.** the act of winking. **2.** a short period of time, especially a short sleep; a nap: The boys were so excited at the sleepover party that they didn't sleep a *wink.*

win•ner [win′ər] *noun, plural* **winners.** a person or thing that wins or is successful.

win•ning [win′ing] *adjective, more/most.* **1.** being the one that wins: The *winning* team in this game goes on to the Super Bowl. **2.** able to win favor or attention; charming; attractive: ". . . a young man with dark red hair and a *winning* smile . . ." (John McGahern) —*noun, plural* **winnings. 1.** the act of a person or thing that wins. **2.** **winnings.** something that is won, especially money won by betting or gambling.

Win•ni•peg [win′ə peg] the capital of the province of Manitoba, Canada. *Population:* 564,000.

win•ter [win′tər] *noun, plural* **winters.** the coldest season of the year; the season after fall and before spring.

win•ter•green [win′tər grēn′] *noun, plural* **wintergreens.** a shrub having red berries and evergreen leaves with a spicy scent. The oil from the leaves is used as a flavoring.

win•try [win′trē] *adjective,* **wintrier, wintriest.** having to do with or like winter: a cold, gray, *wintry* day.

wipe [wīp] *verb,* **wiped, wiping. 1.** to clean or dry by rubbing on or with something: Please *wipe* your shoes on the mat before you come inside. **2.** to remove by rubbing lightly: "He

ground his teeth and *wiped* away the tears." (John Gardner) **3. wipe out.** to kill or destroy completely: The beaver was almost *wiped out* in the late 1800's by hunters who wanted its fur.

wire [wīr] *noun, plural* **wires. 1.** a long, thin, flexible piece of metal that has a standard thickness for its entire length, often used to join or fasten things. **2.** such a piece of metal used to carry electricity. **3.** a message sent by telegraph wire; a telegram. —*verb,* **wired, wiring. 1.** to install wires for electricity: to *wire* a house for air conditioning. **2.** to fasten something with wire. **3.** to send a telegram.

wire•less [wīr′lis] *adjective.* without wires; not using wire. ◆ People used to call a radio a *wireless* or a *wireless set,* because it works by waves going through the air, rather than by electric wires, as the earlier telegraph did.

wire•tap [wīr′tap′] *noun, plural* **wiretaps.** the secret attachment of a listening device to telephone or telegraph wires in order to hear private conversations sent over them. —*verb,* **wiretapped, wiretapping.** to connect a wiretap.

wir•ing [wīr′ing] *noun, plural* **wiring.** a system of wires used to carry electricity.

wir•y [wīr′ē] *adjective,* **wirier, wiriest. 1.** like wire: *wiry* hair. **2.** thin, but strong: "Karl was always a *wiry* guy, and hard muscled . . ." (Joseph Wambaugh)

Wis•con•sin [wis kän′sən] a state in the north-central U. S. *Capital:* Madison. *Nickname:* "Badger State." *Area:* 56,200 square miles. *Population:* 4,765,000.

wis•dom [wiz′dəm] *noun.* good judgment as to what is true and right, gained through knowledge and experience: That book presents the *wisdom* of the Greek thinkers Aristotle, Plato, and Socrates. "He took it that Anne had accepted the *wisdom* of his decision." (W. Somerset Maugham)

wisdom tooth one of four teeth located at the very back of each side of the upper and lower jaws. ◆ These teeth are so called because they come in years later than the other teeth, when a person is older.

wise [wīz] *adjective,* **wiser, wisest. 1.** able to understand people and situations and choose

W

-wise The suffix *-wise* is misused by people who ought to know better—including advertising writers. It's a valid form in words such as *likewise* or *otherwise.* But to write, "It wasn't much of a vacation *weatherwise,*" is weak and lazy. "*Attendancewise,* this movie is the top film of the season." That's jargon, bad jargon. These two cars are about the same, gas *mileagewise.*" What's the rule here? Don't make up words with *wise*—even if you think it's "wise" to do so!

the right course of action; having knowledge and intelligence: The ancient King Solomon was a famous *wise* man who was known for his skill in dealing with people and solving problems. **2.** showing this ability to judge and decide; sensible: Peter made a *wise* decision not to go swimming alone. **3.** *Informal.* showing off one's knowledge in a rude or insulting way; fresh. ◆ A remark or joke of this kind is a **wisecrack. —wisely,** *adverb.*

wish [wish] *verb,* **wished, wishing. 1.** to want something that at present it is not possible to get; have a hope for: "He *wished* he had a dog like Grandma Hutto's." (Marjorie Kinnan Rawlings) **2.** to have a desire for; want to be or to happen: "I could not help *wishing* we were all there safe together." (Emily Brontë) "The shah *wishes* to know, please, where we are now, said Khashdrahr." (Kurt Vonnegut) —*noun, plural* **wishes.** the act of saying or thinking that one wants to get or have something: "All the detective's hopes and *wishes* were now centered on Hong Kong . . ." (Jules Verne) **—wishful,** *adjective.* based only on a wish. ◆ **Wishful thinking** means hoping that something will happen, even though it is not likely, because that is what one wants.

wisp [wisp] *noun, plural* **wisps.** a small bunch or bit: *wisps* of hair, a *wisp* of smoke.

wist•ful [wist′fəl] *adjective, more/most.* showing sadness because of a wish that did not come true or a memory of something lost; longing: "There was a *wistful* quality about the words which defeated me; a hint of a wild hope . . ." (James Herriot) **—wistfully,** *adverb.* **—wistfulness,** *noun.*

the soul of *wit.*" ◆ Now used mainly in combinations such as quick-*witted* or slow-*witted.* **4. wits.** the use of the mind. ◆ Used in special expressions such as "be scared out of your *wits,*" "keep your *wits* about you," "live by your *wits,*" and so on.

witch [wich] *noun, plural* **witches.** a woman thought to have magic powers and to use them for evil purposes. In former times people believed that a witch could bring illness, bad luck, and so on. ◆ The term *witch* was sometimes applied to men as well as women, but generally a male witch was known as a WIZARD, SORCERER, or **warlock** [wôr′läk′].

witch•craft [wich′kraft′] *noun.* the magic power of a witch, or the harmful events caused by a witch.

with [with *or* with] *preposition.* **1.** in the company of; beside or among: Glen went to the movies *with* his friend Larry. **2.** having or showing: See that girl *with* the blue jacket? That's my cousin. The dog was covered *with* mud. **3.** by means of: She put out the grass fire *with* a garden hose. **4.** because of or concerning: We have a problem *with* our new washing machine.

with•draw [with drô′] *verb,* **withdrew, withdrawn, withdrawing. 1.** to take money out of a bank account: He *withdrew* $300 from his savings account to buy a plane ticket. **2.** to move away or take something away: ". . . any wolf may . . . *withdraw* from the pack he belongs to." (Rudyard Kipling) **3.** to go away in order to be alone; stay to oneself: "He *withdrew* rapidly into the shelter of his room, deeply disturbed . . ." (Barbara Pym)

---

wit *Wit* can in some instances mean intelligence in the general sense. Expressions like "*outwit* someone" or "scared out of my *wits*" show an old-time use of *wit* for "mind." However, the modern sense of the word is narrower. *Wit* is used to refer to humor. To be *witty* is somewhat the same as being *funny,* although *wit* suggests sharp, polished comments—making just the right remark. *Wit* suggests writers such as Alexander Pope, Oscar Wilde, Noel Coward, and Dorothy Parker, writers who are known for famous quotes. President Calvin Coolidge was stone-faced and reserved, speaking little and rarely known to make small talk. When she heard that he had died, Dorothy Parker said, "How can they tell?" That's wit!

---

wit [wit] *noun, plural* **wits. 1.** the talent to describe things in a clever and funny way, a sense of humor. **2.** a person who has this talent: Statements such as "I can resist everything except temptation," are the product of the noted Irish *wit,* Oscar Wilde. **3.** the ability to know and understand things; intelligence: Shakespeare said that "brevity (being brief) is

---

Pronunciation Key: [ə] Symbol

The [ə] or *schwa* sound occurs in syllables without an accent. It can be spelled with any vowel, such as **a** in above, **e** in listen, **i** in pencil, **o** in melon, **u** in circus. It can also be a combination of vowels, such as **io** in action, **ai** in mountain, **iou** in precious.

(Turn the page for more information.)

with•draw•al [with drôl**/**] *noun, plural* **with-drawals. 1.** the act of withdrawing, especially taking out money from a bank account. **2.** the process of breaking the habit of using a certain drug. ♦ **Withdrawal symptoms** are the painful or unpleasant reactions caused by this.

with•drawn [with drôn**/**] *verb.* the past participle of **withdraw.** —*adjective.* wanting to be alone; not friendly: "The other men were still silent, watchful and *withdrawn* . . ." (Colleen McCullough)

with•er [with**/** ər] *verb,* **withered, withering.** of a plant, to dry up from lack of moisture: "The flowers were certainly past their best. Most of the leaves had *withered* . . ." (Barbara Pym)

with•hold [with hōld**/**] *verb,* **withheld, withholding.** to refuse to give; hold back: The policeman threatened to arrest the witness who was *withholding* information about the robbery. "Stephen parted his lips to answer yes and then *withheld* the word suddenly." (James Joyce)

with•in [with in**/** *or* with in**/**] *preposition.* **1.** in the limits of: There's no other house *within* a mile of theirs. **2.** in the inner part of: "Go outside, laugh, and take a breath of fresh air, a voice cries *within* me." (Anne Frank)

with•out [with out**/** *or* with out**/**] *preposition.* not having or doing; lacking: She drinks her coffee *without* sugar.

with•stand [with stand**/**] *verb,* **withstood, withstanding.** to hold out against; resist: ". . . the boat must be built to *withstand* such sudden summer gales." (Ken Follett) "More important, they *withstood* British cannon for eleven days." (James Michener)

wit•ness [wit**/** nis] *noun, plural* **witnesses. 1.** someone who is present and sees a crime, accident, or other such event: Several *witnesses* said they saw the blue car go through a red light just before the crash. **2.** a person who gives evidence in a court of law about something he knows or has seen. **3.** a person who is present at an important event to give proof that the event took place: a *witness* to a marriage ceremony. **4.** *Informal.* any person who is present when something takes place: You heard Jamie say she'd clean the kitchen tonight—you're my *witness.* —*verb,* **witnessed, witnessing.** to be a witness: to *witness* a crime.

wit•ty [wit**/** ē] *adjective,* **wittier, wittiest.** having a good wit; able to make clever, amusing remarks: Shakespeare's famous comic character Falstaff said, "I am not only *witty* in myself, but the cause that wit is in other men."

wives [wīvs] *noun.* the plural of **wife.**

wiz•ard [wiz**/** ərd] *noun, plural* **wizards. 1.** in old stories, a person thought to have magic powers. **2.** a person with great skill or cleverness: Helen is a real computer *wizard.*

wob•ble [wäb**/** əl] *verb,* **wobbled, wobbling.** to move from side to side in a shaky or unsteady way: The ladder wasn't set on level ground and it *wobbled* when he stood on it. —*noun, plural* **wobbles.** a wobbling movement. —**wobbly,** *adjective.*

woe [wō] *noun, plural* **woes.** sorrow or suffering. ♦ Used mainly in older writings: "For never was a story of more *woe,* than this of Juliet and her Romeo." (William Shakespeare) When the word *woe* is used today it is usually in a lighter way: "All right, sit down and tell me your sad tale of *woe.*" —**woeful,** *adjective.* —**woefully,** *adverb.*

wok [wäk] *noun, plural* **woks.** a wide, round-bottomed pot, used in Oriental cooking.

woke [wōk] *verb.* a past tense of **wake.**

woken [wōk**/** ən] a past participle of **wake.**

wolf The type of wolf that has become so well-known through folk tales and legends is this one, the gray wolf.

wolf [woolf] *noun, plural* **wolves.** a large, powerful wild animal that is related to the dog. Wolves kill and eat other animals, and band together in packs to hunt larger animals. At one time wolves lived over most of the northern half of the world, but hunting by man has driven them into a few remote regions. —*verb,* **wolfed, wolfing.** to eat quickly and hungrily: "He was *wolfing* down a heaping plate of thousand-mile beans . . ." (John Toland)

wolverine This animal is also called a *glutton*, because of its great appetite. A glutton is someone who eats huge amounts of food, far more than he needs.

wol•ver•ine [wool′ və rēn′] *noun, plural* **wolverines.** an animal with a heavy, powerful body, thick fur, and a bushy tail. Wolverines feed on other animals and live mostly in northern parts of the world.

which everything is in constant motion and every change seems an improvement." (Alexis de Tocqueville) ◆ In the ancient world, seven very large and impressive structures were chosen as the **Seven Wonders of the World**. **2.** a feeling of surprise and admiration: to gaze at something in *wonder*. **3.** something that is surprising or unusual: "'The Sioux loved this country,' Park said. 'No *wonder* they didn't want to give it up.'" (John McPhee)

won•der•ful [wun′ dər fəl] *adjective, more/ most.* **1.** causing wonder; amazing; marvelous: "All things wise and *wonderful*, the Lord God made them all." (Cecil Alexander) **2.** very good; excellent; fine: "I must tell you how very fond I am of reading your books and how *wonderful* I think they are." (Agatha Christie) **—wonderfully,** *adverb:* "The November California sun was *wonderfully* warm today." (Joseph Wambaugh)

won't [wōnt] the contraction of "will not:" Heather's sick and *won't* be able to go with us.

won't This is the contraction for *will not*. It may seem odd that the word *will* would be contracted as *won't*. Actually, the form *willn't* did exist in the past. However, it has faded out of use, probably because it's an awkward combination of letters that's hard to say. The main reason people use *will not* instead of *won't* is to make a statement stronger, to show that the person is absolutely determined: "I shall not seek, and I *will not* accept, the nomination of my party for another term as President." (Lyndon B. Johnson) The other common reason for chosing *will not* is that the writer wants to set up a pattern in which *will* and *will not* are contrasted: "all this *will not* be finished in the first one hundred days. Nor *will* it be finished in the first one thousand days . . ." (John F. Kennedy)

wolves [woolvz] *noun.* the plural of **wolf.**

wom•an [woom′ ən] *noun, plural* **women. 1.** a full-grown female person; a female who is no longer a girl. **2.** adult females as a group.

womb [woom] *noun, plural* **wombs.** the organ in a woman's body where a baby is developed and nourished before it is born. ◆ The medical term for the womb is the **uterus** [yo̅o̅t′ ər əs].

wom•en [wim′ in] *noun.* the plural of **woman.**

won [wun] *verb.* the past form of **win.**

won•der [wun′ dər] *verb,* **wondered, wondering.** to be curious or doubtful about; want to know: "She had not seen Barbara and *wondered* where she was." (Lois Lenski) "I hadn't seen that much food . . . for a long time, and I *wondered* where Mason got the money." (S. E. Hinton) *—noun, plural* **wonders. 1.** something that causes surprise or amazement, and also respect: "America is a land of *wonders*, in

wood [wood] *noun, plural* **woods. 1.** the hard material that makes up the trunk and branches of a tree or shrub. Wood can be cut up into various shapes and used as building material or burned as fuel. Furniture is often made of wood. **2.** *usually,* **woods.** an area having a thick growth of trees; a forest.

wood•chuck [wood′ chuk′] *noun, plural* **woodchucks.** a small animal having a thick body, short legs, and a broad tail. Woodchucks belong to the rodent family. They live in burrows that they dig in the ground, and they rest or

Pronunciation Key: Accent Marks

[′] is the normal accent mark. It shows where the main stress falls on a word.
[′] is a secondary accent mark. It shows a lighter stress than the primary accent. For example:
tel • e • vis • ion [tel′ə vizh ′ən]
(Turn the page for more information.)

sleep during the winter months. ◆ This animal is also known as a GROUNDHOG.

wood•ed [wood′ id] *adjective*. having trees; covered with many trees: *wooded* hills.

wood•en [wood′ ən] *adjective*. **1.** made of wood. **2.** like wood; stiff and lifeless: He was very nervous in his first acting role and spoke and moved in an odd, *wooden* manner.

wood•peck•er [wood′ pek′ ər] *noun, plural* **woodpeckers.** a bird with a long, pointed bill that it uses to peck holes in trees to find insects to eat. It is found in forest areas throughout North America and in many other parts of the world.

wood•wind [wood′ wind′] *noun, plural* **wood-winds.** a musical instrument, originally made of wood, that makes a sound when air is blown through the mouthpiece. Some woodwinds, such as the clarinet, have a reed in the mouthpiece that vibrates to make a sound. Others, such as the flute, have an opening in the mouthpiece.

wood•work [wood′ wurk′] *noun*. things made of wood, especially wooden parts on the inside of a house, such as a window or door frame or the strip along the lower part of a wall.

wood•work•ing [wood′ wur′ king] *noun*. the art or skill of making objects out of wood, especially furniture.

when used by itself. In speaking, a word is a sound or group of sounds with a short pause before and after it. In writing, a word is a letter or group of letters with a space before and after it. **2.** a certain one of these items, having its own particular sound, spelling, and meaning: "The" is the *word* most often used in English. "Milk" is the *word* for the liquid that comes from cows. **3.** a short talk or remark: Mom wants to have a *word* with my teacher after the meeting. Don't say a *word* to anyone about what happened today. **4.** a promise: He gave me his *word* he'd pay me back. **5.** information; news: I wonder how Gary's doing—we haven't had any *word* from him since he moved. **6.** **words.** an argument or quarrel. —*verb*, **worded, wording.** to say or write in words: Mark *worded* his answer very carefully.

word•ing [wur′ ding] *noun*. the way of expressing something in words: Clear *wording* of a report makes it easy to understand.

word processing the activity of producing written documents by means of a computer. Word processing differs from ordinary typing in that it allows the writer to change, add to, or reprint a document without re-typing it. ◆ A **word processor** is a machine used in word processing, or a person who uses one.

Words•worth [wurdz′ wərth] **William,** 1770-1850, English poet.

---

wordiness A wordy paper uses words that aren't needed, words that don't add information or that repeat what's said. And how do you cure wordiness? Mark Twain joked: "Editing is easy. All you have to do is cross out the wrong words." Actually, though, there is a good exercise you can try: Cut words out of a series of sentences. Here's an example: "He was going to that place near the Post Office, ~~well somewhat near~~ and he needed to buy some things ~~because he was short of some things~~, and he left without a raincoat because ~~he thought it might not rain and~~ the sky was clear."

---

wood•y [wood′ ē] *adjective,* **woodier, woodiest.** **1.** made of or containing wood: The *woody* part of a tree includes the trunk and branches, but not the leaves. **2.** having many trees; wooded.

wool [wool] *noun, plural* **wools. 1.** the thick, curly hair of sheep and some other animals that is used to make clothing, rugs, blankets, and other items. **2.** the fabric or yarn made from this hair. —*adjective*. made of wool; woolen.

wool•en [wool′ ən] *adjective*. having to do with or made of wool: a *woolen* sweater.

wool•ly [wool′ ē] *adjective*. made of, covered with, or like wool.

word [wurd] *noun, plural* **words. 1.** the smallest part of a language that can mean something

word•y [wurd′ ē] *adjective,* **wordier, wordiest.** using too many words; using more words than is necessary for the thought that is being expressed. —**wordiness,** *noun*.

wore [wôr] *verb*. the past tense of **wear.**

work [wurk] *noun, plural* **works. 1.** the use of the body or the mind to do something or to reach some goal: Cleaning out the garage was a lot of *work*. Sharon couldn't go out with her friends because she had too much *work* to do for school. **2.** what a person does regularly to earn money; a job: The high school students took a test to find out what kind of *work* they're best suited to do. **3.** something that is made or done: A painting is a *work* of art. **4. works.** the moving parts of a machine or instrument, such as a clock. —*verb*, **worked, working. 1.** to use the body or mind to do or get something: Mom is *working* late tonight at her office and Dad fixed us dinner. **2.** to do something for pay; have a job: He *works* in a bank. **3.** to cause to act in the proper way; operate: My sister showed me how to *work* the dishwasher. **4.** to act or operate in a certain way: We're in a new car pool this year and it's *working* out well.

work•a•ble [wur′kə bəl] *adjective, more/most.* able to work; that will work well: a *workable* machine, a *workable* plan.

work•book [wurk′book′] *noun, plural* **workbooks.** a book used for school studies, different from a textbook in that it has space on the pages for the student to answer questions.

work•er [wur′kər] *noun, plural* **workers. 1.** a person who works. **2.** a female bee, ant, or other insect that does most of the work of the hive or colony, but is unable to produce young.

work•man [wurk′mən] *noun, plural* **workmen.** a person who does work, especially someone who does work with the hands or with machines.

work•man•ship [wurk′mən ship′] *noun.* the skill with which a certain job or work is done: This cabinet shows beautiful *workmanship.*

work•out [wurk′out′] *noun, plural* **workouts.** a period of using the body in an active way, as a form of exercise for health or as training to improve athletic skill.

work•shop [wurk′shäp′] *noun, plural* **workshops. 1.** a room or building where work is done by hand or with machines. **2.** a meeting of people to work on or study a special subject: Our teacher went to a *workshop* last summer to learn about new methods of teaching writing.

world [wurld] *noun, plural* **worlds. 1.** the planet on which human beings live; the earth. **2.** a certain area or part of the earth: the Western *world,* the New *World.* **3.** an activity or way of life involving a large part of the earth or a large number of people: the business *world,* the plant *world.* **4.** all people; everyone: In Lincoln's Gettysburg Address, he said that the *world* would not remember what was said there that day. **5.** a large amount; a great deal: That vacation at the beach has certainly done her a *world* of good.

world•ly [wurld′lē] *adjective,* **worldlier, worldliest. 1.** of or having to do with the world or human existence, rather than with God and religion. **2.** knowing or caring a lot about the affairs of the world: He's a very *worldly* person

who has traveled a lot and had many different experiences. —**worldliness,** *noun.*

World War I a war fought from 1914 to 1918, involving Great Britain, France, Russia, the United States, and other countries on one side and Germany, Austria-Hungary, Turkey, and other countries on the other side.

World War II a war fought from 1939 to 1945, involving Great Britain, France, Russia, the United States, and other countries on one side and Germany, Italy, Japan, and other countries on the other side.

world•wide [wurld′wīd′] *adjective; adverb.* all over the world: Walt Disney's cartoon characters are famous *worldwide.*

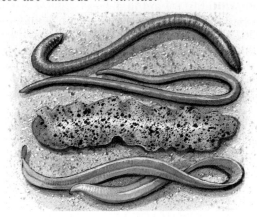

worm Four types of worms. The earthworm (top), the roundworm and the oval flatworm (center), the ribbon worm (below).

worm [wurm] *noun, plural* **worms.** a small animal with a long, thin body and no legs or backbone. —*verb,* **wormed, worming. 1.** to move by crawling or wriggling, as a worm does. **2. worm out.** to get something by a special trick or effort: "He . . . had *wormed out* of them what they had been doing." (Oscar Wilde)

worn [wôrn] *verb.* the past participle of **wear.** —*adjective, more/most.* **1.** damaged or made thin by long, hard use: "The pages were *worn* at the edges, and fell apart easily . . ." (George Orwell) **2.** looking tired or weak: "I saw her in front of me, clothed in rags, her face thin and *worn.*" (Anne Frank)

Pronunciation Key: A–F			
a	and; hat	ch	chew; such
ā	ate; stay	d	dog; lid
â	care; air	e	end; yet
ä	father; hot	ē	she; each
b	boy; cab	f	fun; off

(Turn the page for more information.)

worn-out [worn′ out′] *adjective, more/most.* **1.** having had such long and hard wear that it is no longer useful: *worn-out* clothing. **2.** *also,* **worn out.** very tired or weak; exhausted.

wor•ry [wur′ē] *verb,* **worried, worrying. 1.** to have a thought or feeling that something bad may happen; be uneasy or concerned: Laura can't relax because she keeps *worrying* about the big math test she has tomorrow. "She used to smoke, in those days, and the children were *worried* about her . . ." (Alice Munro) **2.** of an animal, to bite at or shake something with the teeth over and over again: a dog *worrying* a bone. —*noun, plural* **worries. 1.** the act or fact of worrying; a feeling of being anxious or uncomfortable: "I am in a great state of *worry* . . . and I would be grateful if you could see me." (Agatha Christie) **2.** something that causes this feeling: She's got everything ready for the concert; now her big *worry* is that not many people will come. —**worriedly,** *adverb.*

worse [wurs] the COMPARATIVE form of **bad.** —*adjective:* The weather was bad yesterday, but it's even *worse* today. ♦ Also used as a noun and an adverb.

wors•en [wurs′ ən] *verb,* **worsened, worsening.** to make or become worse: "The headache would *worsen* until it felt as if his head were being crushed . . ." (Stephen King)

wor•ship [wur′ ship] *verb,* **worshiped or worshipped, worshiping or worshipping. 1.** to show love and respect to God, as by taking part in a religious service. **2.** to love and respect a person greatly, often too greatly. —*noun.* **1.** great love and respect for God, or an action showing this. **2.** religious services: Churches and synagogues are called houses of *worship.*

worst [wurst] the SUPERLATIVE form of **bad.** —*adjective:* They have the *worst* record in the league—no wins and eight losses. ♦ Also used as a noun and an adverb.

worth [wurth] *preposition.* **1.** of the same value as: She stopped at the gas station and bought ten dollars *worth* of gas. **2.** having property or money amounting to: He lives in a small house and dresses simply, but he's actually *worth* over a million dollars. **3.** deserving of; good enough for: Are these paper bags *worth* saving? —*noun.* the value or importance of a person or thing: They took the painting to an art dealer to get an idea of its *worth.*

worth•less [wurth′ lis] *adjective, more/most.* having no worth; without value; useless: This shirt is completely worn out and it's *worthless* now except as a rag.

worth•while [wurth′ wīl′] *adjective, more/most.* having value or importance; worth spending time or money on: It's not *worthwhile* to get this radio fixed; we could buy a new one for almost the same cost.

wor•thy [wur′ thē] *adjective,* **worthier, worthiest. 1.** having value or importance; worthwhile: The hospital building project is a *worthy* cause to give money to. **2.** having merit; deserving support: "He would try to be *worthy* of Augustus's loving generosity." (Robert Graves)

would [wood] *verb.* the past tense of **will:** When I was little my parents *would* often take me to the town park to play. ♦ Also used in a polite request or question: *Would* you like some more dessert?

would•n't [wood′ ənt] the contraction for "would not."

wound[1] [woond] *noun, plural* **wounds.** an injury to the body caused by cutting or tearing the skin and flesh. —*verb,* **wounded, wounding. 1.** to harm the body by a cut or other injury: The U. S. gives a medal called the Purple Heart to soldiers who are *wounded* in battle. **2.** to hurt someone's feelings: His pride was *wounded* when his younger brother was picked for the team but he wasn't.

wound[2] [wound] *verb.* the past form of **wind:** "She threw open another door. A narrow crooked flight of stairs *wound* upward from it." (Mary E. Wilkins Freeman)

wove [wōv] *verb.* the past tense of **weave.**

wo•ven [wō′ vən] *verb.* a past participle of **weave.**

wrap [rap] *verb,* **wrapped or wrapt, wrapping. 1.** to cover by winding or folding something around: The Christmas presents were *wrapped* in bright green paper. "He . . . was *wrapped* in heavy furs, as the night was cold and foggy." (Oscar Wilde) **2.** to wind or fold about something: "She is sitting with her feet up and her arms *wrapped* around her knees." (Bobbie Ann Mason) **3. wrapped up in.** completely or only interested in: "Like many isolated people, they were *wrapped up in* themselves and not too interested in the world outside." (V.S. Naipaul) —*noun, plural* **wraps.** an outer garment worn for warmth, such as a coat.

wrap•per [rap′ ər] *noun, plural* **wrappers.** a covering, usually made of paper, used to wrap something: a candy *wrapper.*

wrap•ping [rap′ing] *noun, plural* **wrappings.** paper or other material used to wrap something.

wrath [rath] *noun, plural* **wraths.** great anger; rage.

wreath [rēth] *noun, plural* **wreaths.** a group of branches, leaves, or flowers woven together to form a ring: People often hang a *wreath* on their front door during the Christmas season.

wreck [rek] *noun, plural* **wrecks. 1.** the damaging or destroying of a car, train, ship, or other vehicle, by its striking heavily against another object: a *wreck* on the highway, a ship*wreck* at sea. **2.** the remains of something that has been damaged in this way: The junkyard was filled with abandoned cars and old *wrecks.* —*verb,* **wrecked, wrecking.** to damage badly or destroy; ruin: The crash at the intersection *wrecked* both cars. "The girl's nerves were *wrecked,* and she was forced to withdraw from the school for the rest of the term." (Alice Walker)

wreck•age [rek′ ij] *noun.* **1.** the fact of being wrecked. **2.** the broken parts of something that has been wrecked: *Wreckage* from the plane crash was scattered all over the mountain.

wren [ren] *noun, plural* **wrens.** a very small songbird having brown feathers with black and white markings.

wrench [rench] *noun, plural* **wrenches. 1.** a tool used to hold and turn nuts, bolts, or pipes, usually having two jaw-like parts that can be moved together to grip the object tight. **2.** a sharp twist or pull, or an injury caused by such a movement. —*verb,* **wrenched, wrenching.** to give a sudden, sharp twist to: Debbie is still limping from when she *wrenched* her ankle playing soccer.

wres•tle [res′ əl] *verb,* **wrestled, wrestling. 1.** to take part in the sport or contest of WRESTLING. **2.** to struggle in an attempt to hold a person or throw him to the ground: The policeman grabbed the robber and *wrestled* the gun out of his hand. **3.** to struggle to overcome: "All day and all night for nearly a whole week they *wrestled* with the problem." (Upton Sinclair)

wres•tler [res′ lər] *noun, plural* **wrestlers.** a person who takes part in wrestling, either as an amateur sport or a professional exhibition.

wres•tling [res′ ling] *noun.* **1.** a sport in which two opponents compete to try to force each other to the ground or hold each other in certain positions. **2.** a form of professional entertainment that developed from this sport, taking place in a roped and padded area like a boxing ring and involving competitors who have colorful nicknames and often wear unusual costumes.

wretch [rech] *noun, plural* **wretches. 1.** a very sad or unhappy person. **2.** a cruel person.

wretch•ed [rech′ id] *adjective, more/most.* **1.** very unfortunate or unhappy; suffering: ". . . the tears made dark spots on the red of my apron and I felt very *wretched.*" (Anne Frank) **2.** causing unhappiness or suffering: "In 1597 the icebound and shipwrecked Dutch explorer Willem Barents was . . . in *wretched* circumstances at the northern tip of Novaya Zemlya." (Barry Lopez) —**wretchedly,** *adverb.* **wretchedness,** *noun.*

wrig•gle [rig′ əl] *verb,* **wriggled, wriggling.** to move by twisting from side to side; squirm, as a worm or snake does: "It happened on the dusty road that begins at Prince Town and *wriggles* like a black snake . . ." (V.S. Naipaul)

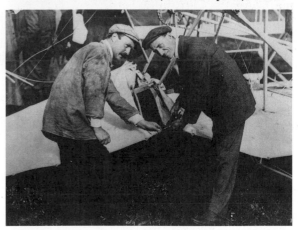

Wright Brothers The Wright brothers, Orville (left) and Wilbur (right), pose in front of their first plane.

Wright [rīt] **Orville,** 1871-1948, and his brother **Wilbur,** 1867-1912, American inventors, the first people to fly successfully in an airplane.

wring [ring] *verb,* **wrung, wringing. 1.** to twist or squeeze water from: to *wring* out a wet towel and hang it up to dry. **2.** to twist or squeeze: "The cook was *wringing* his hands, moving his shoulders back and forth as if his back ached." (John Gardner) **3.** to get by force or threat: "He spoke very slowly, and the words seemed *wrung* out of him almost against his will." (Oscar Wilde)

Pronunciation Key: G–N			
g	give; big	k	kind; cat; back
h	hold	l	let; ball
i	it; this	m	make; time
ī	ice; my	n	not; own
j	jet; gem; edge	ng	having
(Turn the page for more information.)			

wrin•kle [ring′kəl] *noun, plural* **wrinkles.** a small ridge or crease on a smooth surface, such as cloth or skin: Sheryl ironed out the *wrinkles* in her blouse. —*verb,* **wrinkled, wrinkling.** to have wrinkles: a person with dry, *wrinkled* skin.

wrist [rist] *noun, plural* **wrists.** the joint of the body that connects the hand and the arm.

writ [rit] *verb.* an older past form of **write.** —*noun, plural* **writs.** a legal document ordering a person to do or not do something.

write [rīt] *verb,* **wrote, written, writing. 1.** to put letters and words on paper or another such surface: Mary *wrote* a letter to her grandmother. He forgot to *write* his name on his homework paper. **2.** to create a book, article, or other work involving words: to *write* a song.

time is really 3:30. **2.** not according to what is good or proper: You were *wrong* to make fun of her like that. **3.** not suited to the purpose: Jack wore the *wrong* clothes to the party; everyone else was dressed up but he wasn't. —*adverb.* in an incorrect or improper way: to spell a word *wrong.* —*noun, plural* **wrongs.** something that is bad, incorrect, or improper. —*verb,* **wronged, wronging.** to treat in an unfair way: The man claimed that he'd been *wronged* and that he'd had nothing to do with the crime.

wrote [rōt] *verb.* the past participle of **write.**

wrought [rôt] an older past form of **work,** now used mainly in literature: "The planters had *wrought* immense beauty in the wilderness . . ." (Sherley Anne Williams)

wrung [rung] *verb.* the past form of **wring.**

> **writing process** The writing process is a method of creating a piece of writing by moving through a series of steps. This technique has become popular in schools in recent years. The steps vary from one teacher to another, but generally there is a *prewriting* step in which the writer carries out some preliminary thinking activity before putting finished sentences down on paper. This prewriting leads into the actual *writing* (or *composing*) of the paper. Then there is a *postwriting* stage in which the writer revises the paper, then edits and proofreads the final version. This process does not involve new ideas about what good writing is. Donald Murray, a teacher closely associated with the writing process, and William Zinsser, who's not connected with it, have each given a list of favorite prose writers. Several of the same names appear on both lists—George Orwell, E. B. White, Joseph Mitchell. (In fact, both quote passages from Mitchell as models of good writing.) What the writing process does do is take students away from the idea that they have to produce a final paper as soon as they start to write.

writ•er [rīt′ər] *noun, plural* **writers. 1.** any person who writes. **2.** someone who writes stories, articles, and so on as a job or for pay.

writhe [rīth] *verb,* **writhed, writhing.** to twist and turn because of pain: "Basil's spirit *writhed* with shame . . ." (F. Scott Fitzgerald)

writ•ing [rī′ting] *noun, plural* **writings. 1.** the fact of putting words on paper. **2.** something in the form of words on paper; something written: I have a hard time reading my brother's *writing.* You can't make your request by phone; it has to be in *writing.* **3.** the activity of creating a poem, story, play, article, or the like; the art of a writer: to take a school course in *writing.* **4.** a work of literature: the *writings* of William Shakespeare.

writ•ten [rit′ən] *verb.* the past participle of **write.** —*adjective.* in the form of writing: a *written* message, a *written* order.

wrong [rông] *adjective, more/most.* **1.** not agreeing with the facts; not correct: He had only one *wrong* answer and got an 'A' on the test. That clock is *wrong;* it says 3:10 but the

wry [rī] *adjective,* **wrier, wriest.** of a smile, remark, and so on, showing dislike or lack of feeling; forced or twisted. —**wryly,** *adverb.*

Wy•o•ming [wī ō′ming] a state in the west-central U. S. *Capital:* Cheyenne. *Nickname:* "Equality State." *Area:* 97,900 square miles. *Population:* 502,000.

Wyoming A view of Jackson Hole, with the Grand Teton Mountains in the background.

x, X [eks] *noun, plural* **x's, X's.** the twenty-fourth letter of the alphabet.

Xerox [zir′ äks] *noun, plural* **Xeroxes. 1.** a trademark name for a process of making photographic copies of written and printed material. **2.** a copy made in this way. **—Xeroxed, Xeroxing.** to make such a copy: to *Xerox* a letter. ♦ The Xerox Corporation often points out in its advertisements that this word applies only to machines made by their company, and they oppose the use of word in a general sense, as in "That's the original, not a *xerox* copy," or "I *xeroxed* the letter at the library."

Xmas [kris ′ məs *or* eks′ məs] *noun.* A short word for Christmas. ♦ It is often said that *Xmas* is an incorrect form of *Christmas*, and that it is insulting to Christians because it "takes Christ out of Christmas." It's thought that the word is a modern abbreviation created by advertisers to save space. Actually, *Xmas* is a very old word, going back to the 1500's. In Greek, Christ's name begins with the letter 'X'—which is spoken as *chi*.

X-ray [eks′ rā′] *noun, plural* **X-rays.** (also spelled **x-ray**) **1.** a powerful form of energy made up of waves of very short length. It is similar to ordinary light but has the power to pass through solid objects in a way that light cannot. **2.** a photographic film made with X-rays. X-rays are used to study the bones and the inside of the body. —*verb,* **X-rayed, X-raying.** to examine or photograph by the use of X-rays: When Dave hurt his leg in the football game, the doctor had it *X-rayed* to see if it was broken. ♦ 'X' stands for something that is not known. When the German scientist Wilhelm Roentgen discovered X-rays in 1895, at first he did not know what they were or why they acted in such an unusual way.

xylophone The most famous xylophone performer is American jazz musician Lionel Hampton.

xy•lo•phone [zī′ lə fōn′] *noun, plural* **xylophones.** a musical instrument that is made up of a series of flat wooden or metal bars of different sizes. It is played by striking the bars with small wooden mallets. ♦ This word comes from two Greek terms, *xylo* meaning "wood" and *phone* meaning "sound."

---

x The letter *x* has long been used in mathematics to stand for an unknown number or amount. This custom was started by René Descartes [dā′ kart′], a French mathematician and philosopher of the 1600's. His idea was that since the first three letters *a, b, c,* were used for known quantities, the last three, *x, y, z,* should represent the unknown. From this came the idea that *x* stands for anything unknown. Today, you find things like this in newspaper columns: "The whole town is buzzing about Mark Snyder's report that the Acme Company is broke. Rumor has it that Snyder's mysterious source, Mr. 'X,' is actually Acme's top executive." Then, there's this usage: "If a buyer tells us he has 'x' amount of money to spend, we'll direct him to the right car." In serious writing, you'd make that "*a certain* amount of money."

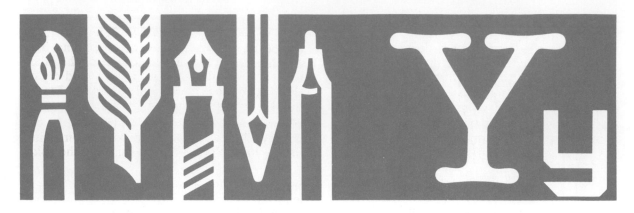

y, Y [wī] *noun, plural* **y's, Y's.** the twenty-fifth letter of the alphabet.

yacht [yät] *noun, plural* **yachts.** a large, expensive boat used for pleasure cruising or for racing. ♦ *Yacht* comes from a Dutch word meaning "hunting ship." The first type of yacht was a ship used to hunt for pirates and smugglers.

yacht The *Highlander,* a yacht owned by the wealthy American magazine publisher Malcolm Forbes.

yak [yak] *noun, plural* **yaks.** a long-haired animal that is a type of ox, living in the high mountains of central Asia. It is raised for meat and milk and used to pull heavy loads.

yam [yam] *noun, plural* **yams. 1.** a trailing tropical vine that has a thick root which can be eaten as a vegetable. **2.** a type of sweet potato.

yank [yangk] *verb,* **yanked, yanking.** to pull or jerk something suddenly: "He yanked the suitcase handle so hard, it was as if he was angry with it." (Paul Zindel) —*noun, plural* **yanks.** a sharp, sudden pull.

Yan·kee [yang′kē] *noun, plural* **Yankees.** ♦ **Yankee** or **Yank** is a nickname associated with the United States, and used for: **a.** a person from New England. **b.** a person who fought on the side of the Union in the Civil War. **c.** any person from the United States. In World War I and World War II American soldiers were often called *Yanks.*

yard[1] [yärd] *noun, plural* **yards. 1.** an area of ground around a house or other building: a home with a large back *yard.* ♦ Often used in combinations such as barn*yard,* school*yard,* and so on. **2.** an area used for a certain type of work: a ship*yard,* a railroad *yard.*

yard[2] *noun, plural* **yards. 1.** a way of measuring the length of something. A *yard* is equal to three feet, or 36 inches. **2.** a long pole set across the mast of a ship and used to support the top edge of the sails.

yard·stick [yärd′stik′] *noun, plural* **yardsticks. 1.** a measuring stick that is one yard in length. **2.** any way of measuring or comparing: Scores on a standard reading test are one *yardstick* for judging a school's success.

yak The wild yak has been hunted heavily and is in danger of becoming extinct.

yarn [yärn] *noun, plural* **yarns. 1.** twisted thread or fibers used for knitting or weaving, usually made from wool, cotton, silk, or an artificial material. **2.** an adventure story, especially one that is told for entertainment: Do you think Grandpa made up that wild *yarn* he told us about how he first came to this country?

yawn [yôn] *verb,* **yawned, yawning. 1.** to open the mouth wide and take a deep breath, as when one is tired, sleepy, or bored. **2.** to be or stand wide open: a *yawning* hole in the earth. —*noun, plural* **yawns.** the act of yawning.

ye [yē] *pronoun.* an old word for **you,** used in such writings as the Bible and Shakespeare: A famous saying by Jesus is, "Ask and it shall be given you; seek, and *ye* shall find."

loud voice; shout: I *yelled* to Bennie to jump out of the way when I saw the car coming. The coach *yelled* at the players for letting the other team score. —*noun, plural* **yells.** a loud cry or shout: They have a team *yell,* "Let's Go, Blue!" that the fans shout during a game.

yel·low [yel′ō] *noun, plural* **yellows. 1.** the color of butter or ripe lemons. **2.** something having this color. —*adjective.* having the color

yellow Words for colors are often used in negative ways: "He was *yellow!* He ran away when the man fell and needed help." "Cowardly; afraid" is an old slang meaning of *yellow. Yellow* journalism features glaring headlines and exaggerated, even false stories about crime and disasters. Communists are called *Reds* by those who oppose them. *Redneck* is a negative description for a poor white farm worker. To have the *blues* is to be sad or depressed. A *white elephant* is a large, elaborate object that is useless and unwanted. In addition to being *yellow,* a coward is said to show a *white feather*—that's British usage. Goods are sold illegally on the *black* market. A person others don't want in a club may be *blackballed.* Someone who is starting out at something and has no experience is said to be *green.* A jealous person is "*green* with envy."

year [yēr] *noun, plural* **years. 1.** the period of twelve months or 365 days from January 1st to December 31st, during which the earth moves around the sun once. **2.** any period of twelve months: Andrew will be nine *years* old next Sunday. We've lived in this house for seven *years.* **3.** a period of time, usually less than a year, used to measure some activity: The school *year* lasts from September to June. He's having a great *year* for the Yankees, leading the league in home runs.

year·book [yēr′book′] *noun, plural* **year-books. 1.** a book that is published once a year with information about the previous year. **2.** a book published once a year by a school with information about students, especially the students in the graduating class.

year·ling [yēr′ling] *noun, plural* **yearlings.** a racehorse or farm animal between one and two years of age.

year·ly [yēr′lē] *adjective.* **1.** happening or done once a year: The Super Bowl in football is a *yearly* event. **2.** lasting or for one year: a person's *yearly* income. —*adverb:* to pay taxes on a house *yearly.*

yearn [yurn] *verb,* **yearned, yearning.** to feel a strong desire for; want very much: ". . . a hopeful child *yearning* before a window of a candy store." (Ernest K. Gann)

yeast [yēst] *noun, plural* **yeasts.** a substance used to make bread rise and to brew beer. It is made of the tiny cells of a certain fungus plant.

yell [yel] *verb,* **yelled, yelling.** to cry out in a

yellow. —*verb,* **yellowed, yellowing.** to make or become yellow in color.

yellow fever a tropical disease that is carried by the bite of certain female mosquitoes. Yellow fever causes fever, chills, and sometimes death. It was once very common in areas of the Caribbean but is now largely under control. ◆ The name comes from the fact that this disease causes a person's skin to have a yellowish color.

yellow jacket or **yellowjacket** a type of wasp with bright yellow markings on its body.

yellow jacket

Pronunciation Key: O–S			
ō	over; go	ou	out; town
ô	all; law	p	put; hop
oo	look; full	r	run; car
o͞o	pool; who	s	set; miss
oi	oil; boy	sh	show

(Turn the page for more information.)

Y

Yel·low·stone National Park [yel′ ō stōn] the largest and oldest U.S. national park, located in northwestern Wyoming, eastern Idaho, and southern Montana.

Yem·en [yem′ ən] **1.** a country in southern Arabia, on the Arabian Sea. Its official name is the **People's Democratic Republic of Yemen**, and it is also called **Aden** or **Southern Yemen**. *Capital:* Aden. *Area:* 111,000 square miles. *Population:* 1,900,000. **2.** a country in southern Arabia, on the Red Sea. Its official name is the **Yemen Arab Republic**. *Capital:* San'a. *Area:* 75,300 square miles. Population: 6,120,000.

yen[1] [yen] *noun, plural* **yen.** the unit of money that is used in Japan.

yen[2] *noun. Informal.* a strong desire; an urge: He has a *yen* to travel and see the world.

yes [yes] *adverb; noun, plural* **yesses.** it is so; it is correct; the opposite of "no."

yes·ter·day [yes′ tər dā] *adverb; noun, plural* **yesterdays. 1.** the day before today. **2.** the past: The politician said, "We can't solve the problems of today with the solutions of *yesterday.* We need a change."

yet [yet] *adverb.* **1.** up to or at this time; so far: Stacy said she's going to play soccer, but she hasn't signed up *yet.* Did that letter you were waiting for come *yet?* —*conjunction.* even so; but; nevertheless: ". . . a husband who hates his wife *yet* would be lost if he deserted her." (James Michener)

yew [yōō] *noun, plural* **yews.** an evergreen tree that grows in Europe and Asia. It has reddish-brown bark and flat, needle-shaped leaves. Its wood is hard and fine-grained.

Yid·dish [yid′ ish] *noun.* a language that developed from German, spoken by Jews in central and eastern Europe and by Jewish immigrants in other places.

yield [yēld] *verb,* **yielded, yielding. 1.** to give up; surrender: The senator *yielded* to pressure from the party leaders and finally agreed to vote for the bill. "(He) ought not this once to have *yielded* so easily to the old doctor's opinion" (Isak Dinesen) **2.** to give way under force: "The last lock *yielded;* and Miss Mildred opened the door." (James Baldwin) **3.** to bring forth; produce: The state of Washington's orchards *yield* a large crop of apples each year. That investment should *yield* a good profit. —*noun, plural* **yields.** the amount yielded or obtained.

yo·gurt [yō′ gərt] *noun, plural* **yogurts.** a food prepared from milk that has been thickened by the addition and action of certain bacteria.

yoke [yōk] *noun, plural* **yokes.** a wooden crosspiece that is fastened over the necks of two oxen or other animals so that they can move together to pull a plow, wagon, or other device. —*verb,* **yoked, yoking.** to join or attach with a yoke: The oxen were *yoked* to the cart.

yolk [yōk] *noun, plural* **yolks.** the yellow part of an egg.

Yom Kip·pur [yäm kip′ ər] a Jewish holiday that falls in September or October, a day of not eating and of praying for forgiveness of sins. It is also called the **Day of Atonement.**

yon·der [yän′ dər] *adverb.* in that place; over there: "Next you'd see a raft sliding by, away off *yonder* . . . "(Mark Twain) ♦ Also used as an adjective, mainly in older writings: "What light through *yonder* window breaks?" (Shakespeare, *Romeo and Juliet*)

Yosemite A winter view of the Yosemite Valley, and the face of the mountain known as El Capitan.

Yo·sem·i·te National Park [yō sem′ i tē] a national park in east-central California, noted for its beautiful scenery.

you [yōō] *pronoun, plural* **you. 1.** the person or persons being spoken to: Mom, Dad's on the phone . . . he wants to talk to *you.* **2.** a person; anyone: *You* have to be 18 years old to vote in the United States.

you'd [yōōd] the contraction for "you had" and "you would."

you'll [yōōl] the contraction for "you will."

young [yung] *adjective,* **younger, youngest.** having lived or existed for a short period of time; not old: *Young* children may go to preschool before they start regular school. Israel is a fairly *young* country; it was founded in 1948. —*noun.* **1. the young.** young people as a group. **2.** an animal's young offspring: A mother bear is very careful to protect her *young.*

Yugoslavia Yugoslavia is made up of six different republics that once were separate states. This is the coastline of Montenegro, on the Adriatic Sea.

Young, Brigham, 1801-1877, American religious leader.

young•ster [yung′ stər] *noun, plural* **young-sters.** a young person; a child.

your [yôr *or* yo͞or] *adjective.* **1.** of or belonging to you: Put *your* name at the top of your paper. **2.** of or relating to any person: Go to the end of Elm Street; their house will be the last one on *your* right. **3.** *Informal.* any one; a or the: She's not exactly *your* typical housewife.

you're [yo͞or *or* yôr] the contraction for "you are."

yours [yôrz *or* yo͞orz] *pronoun.* belonging or relating to you: Someone left this book in our car. Is it *yours?*

your•self [yôr self′ *or* yo͞or self′] *pronoun, plural* **yourselves.** the one that you are; your own self: Don't worry; relax and try to enjoy *yourself.*

youth [yo͞oth] *noun, plural* **youths** *or* **youth. 1.** the time of being young, especially the part of life between early childhood and adulthood: Mark spent his *youth* on a farm in Iowa. **2.** a young man: The city honored two *youths* who saved a man from drowning. **3. the youth.** young people as a group. **4.** the fact of being young.

youth•ful [yo͞oth′ fəl] *adjective.* having youth or the qualities of youth; being young: a person with a *youthful* appearance. He's been playing big-league baseball for 20 years, but he still has a *youthful* enthusiasm for the game. **—youthfulness,** *noun.*

you've [yo͞ov] the contraction for "you have."

yo-yo [yō′ yō′] *noun, plural* **yo-yo's.** a toy that is made of two disks connected at the center by a piece which has a string wrapped around it. A yo-yo goes up and down as the string winds and unwinds around the center piece.

Yu•go•sla•vi•a [yo͞o′ gō slä′ vē ə] a country in southeastern Europe, on the Adriatic Sea. *Capital:* Belgrade. *Area:* 98,800 square miles. *Population:* 22,800,000. **—Yugoslavian,** *adjective; noun.*

Yu•kon [yo͞o′ kän] **1.** a territory in northwestern Canada. *Capital:* Whitehorse. *Area:* 207,000 square miles. *Population:* 22,000. **2.** a river that flows from the Yukon Territory across Alaska to the Bering Sea.

Yup•pie [yup′ ē] *noun, plural* **Yuppies.** *Informal.* a young adult who is thought to be very concerned about earning money and getting ahead in business, and very interested in keeping up with the latest trends in clothing, food, home furnishings, and so on. ♦ *Yuppie* comes from the phrase "Young Urban Professional."

---

you It's an old saying among advertising writers that the most powerful word in an ad is *you*. *You* is the reader! In general writing, there are two situations in which writers use *you*. One is when the writer is speaking directly to the reader as if having a conversation: "If *you* have never done any whittling, the first thing to learn is to sharpen *your* knife." The second use of *you* is to place the reader right in the middle of a story: ". . . the ball comes flying at them; and once it gets beyond them, 'It's mine,' you call, 'it's mine,' and then after it *you* go. For in center field, if *you* can get to it, it is *yours.*" (Philip Roth) Writers use this technique to make an experience more real to the readers. This is good, but it has to be controlled. *"You're* feeling very bored, and *you* check your watch. *You* realize that if *you* leave now *you'll* get home in time to catch a rerun of 'I Love Lucy.' *You* slide out the door without saying good-bye and . . ." Here, it's overdone, forced, artificial.

Pronunciation Key: T–Z			
t	ten; date	v	very; live
th	think	w	win; away
<u>th</u>	these	y	you
u	cut; butter	z	zoo; cause
ur	turn; bird	zh	measure

Y

Zz

z, Z [zē] *noun, plural* **z's, Z's.** the twenty-sixth letter of the alphabet.

Za·ire [zä ēr′] a country in central Africa, on the equator. *Capital:* Kinshasa. *Area:* 905,600 square miles. *Population:* 30,500,000.

zeal [zēl] *noun.* great interest and enthusiasm in working for some cause or goal: "In his *zeal* to convict, the prosecutor overstepped legal lines . . ." (James Weldon Johnson) —**zealous** [zel′ əs], *adjective.* having or showing zeal. —**zealously**, *adverb.*

zebra The zebra's unusual pattern of stripes helps it hide from its enemies.

ze·bra [zē′ brə] *noun, plural* **zebras** or **zebra.** an African animal that looks like a horse with a black-and-white or brown-and-white striped coat.

ze·nith [zē′ nith] *noun, plural* **zeniths. 1.** the point in the sky or heavens directly above where a person is standing. **2.** the highest or most important point; the peak: Ralph reached the *zenith* of his career at a very early age.

ze·ro [zir′ ō] *noun, plural* **zeros** or **zeroes. 1.** the number that leaves any other number the same when added to it; 0. **2.** point on a scale of measurement: In Celsius temperature, *zero* is the freezing point. **3.** nothing; none at all: The response was *zero*—not one person signed up. —*adjective.* of or at zero: The temperature was *zero* degrees Fahrenheit at seven o'clock this morning. They haven't won yet this season— their record is *zero* wins, six losses.

zest [zest] *noun.* an exciting or interesting quality. She's a lively, happy person with a real *zest* for life.

Zeus [zo͞os] *noun.* in the religion of the ancient Greeks, the chief god, ruling over all other gods.

zig·zag [zig′ zag′] *noun, plural* **zigzags.** a series of short, sharp turns or angles. —*verb,* **zigzagged, zigzagging.** to move or form a zigzag: ". . . the blue-green line that *zig-zagged* like a frozen streak of lightning across their path." (James Houston) "A station wagon shot past in the opposite direction, playfully *zig-zagging* on the deserted street . . ." (Kurt Vonnegut)

Zimbabwe The famous Victoria Falls of the Zambesi River on the Zimbabwe border.

Zim·ba·bwe [zim bäb′ wā] a country in south-central Africa, formerly known as **Rhodesia.**

Capital: Harare. *Area:* 150,800 square miles. *Population:* 10,500,000.

zinc [zingk] *noun.* a grayish-white metal that is a chemical element. Zinc is used to coat other metals and to make alloys such as brass.

zin·ni·a [zin′ ē ə] *noun, plural* **zinnias.** a garden plant with bright flowers that grow in various colors. ◆ This is one of the many flowers to be named for people. It gets its name from J.G. *Zinn,* a German plant scientist of the 1700's.

zip [zip] *verb,* **zipped, zipping.** to close or fasten something with a zipper: to *zip* up a jacket.

use: The streets around a hospital are called a hospital *zone.* An area where fighting is going on in a war is called a war *zone* or combat *zone.* **3.** a certain part of a city or town, classified by what kind of buildings are permitted there: In a residential *zone,* only private homes are permitted, not business or factories. ◆ The process of controlling land use in this way is called **zoning.** —*verb,* **zoned, zoning.** to divide land into zones: That area has been *zoned* for a shopping center.

zoo [zoo] *noun, plural* **zoos.** a special park or other place where wild animals are kept to be seen by the public.

> **zoo** The Greek form "zoo" creates terms in science, because it has the meaning "animal." *Zoology* is the study of animal life. Animals are displayed at the Bronx *Zoo* in New York, the San Diego *Zoo,* and so on. A 19th-century park in London where wild animals were displayed was called the *Zoological* Gardens. Later, this name came to be shortened to *Zoo.* The word now has an extended meaning: "The trading floor was a real *zoo.* Buyers wildly shouting orders, messengers running everywhere . . . " "Don't go to that store. It's a *zoo* on busy days!" The word is used to describe a place or situation that is rough, crowded, and confused. In reality, a zoo is tightly controlled and shows little activity. When people call a place a "zoo," they think instead of wild animals on the loose.

Zip Code a system of numbers used by the U.S. Postal Service to help in the delivery of mail, written after the state name in an address. Different locations within a city or other large area have different zip codes.

zip·per [zip′ ər] *noun, plural* **zippers.** a fastener made up of two rows of metal or plastic teeth that can be joined or separated by sliding a catch up or down. Zippers are used on clothing, suitcases, and other items.

zith·er [zith′ ər] *noun, plural* **zithers.** a musical instrument having thirty to forty strings stretched across a wooden sounding box.

zo·di·ac [zō′ dē ak′] *noun.* an imaginary belt in the sky along which the sun appears to travel. The zodiac is divided into twelve sections, called *signs,* each of which is named after a different group of stars. Certain periods of the year relate to certain signs of the zodiac. For example, a person born between December 22nd and January 19th is said to be under the sign of Capricorn, the goat.

zone [zōn] *noun, plural* **zones. 1.** any of the five regions of the earth's surface divided according to climate. Near the North and South Poles are the two **Frigid Zones.** The area on either side of the equator, with hot temperatures, is the **Torrid Zone.** Between these are the two **Temperate Zones,** which have a more mild climate. **2.** any area that has some special quality, condition, or

zo·ol·o·gy [zō äl′ ə jē] *noun.* the science that studies animals and animal life.

zither A zither player in a traditional German costume, shown at a restaurant in Milwaukee.

zoom [zoom] *verb,* **zoomed, zooming.** to move or go suddenly and quickly: "A bumblebee came *zooming* between them . . ." (T.H. White) "They had a borrowed motorcycle . . . and would go *zooming* down the back roads . . ." (Alice Walker)

zuc·chi·ni [zoo kē′ nē] *noun, plural* **zucchini** or **zucchinis.** a type of green-skinned squash that looks like a cucumber, often eaten as a vegetable.

Z

Authors Quoted in This Dictionary

Abbey, Edward (born 1927), American novelist.

Adams, Alice (born 1926), American short-story writer.

Adams, Richard (born 1920), English children's-book author.

Agee, James (l909-l955), American novelist and critic.

Aiken, Conrad (1889-1973), American poet.

Albee, Edward (born 1928), American dramatist.

Alcott, Louisa May (1832-1888), American novelist.

Alexander, Cecil (1818-1895), English poet.

Alexander, Lloyd (born 1924), American children's-book author.

Allen, Woody (born 1935), American humorist and film director.

Amis, Kingsley (born 1922), English novelist.

Anderson, Sherwood (1876-1941), American novelist and short-story writer.

Angell, Roger (born 1920), American sportswriter.

Angelou, Maya (born 1928), American author.

Armstrong, William (born 1914), American novelist.

Arnold, Matthew (1822-1888), English poet and critic.

Asimov, Isaac (born 1920), American science-fiction writer.

Atwood, Margaret (born 1939), Canadian poet and novelist.

Auden, W. H. (1907-1973), English poet.

Auel, Jean (born 1936), American novelist.

Austen, Jane (1775-1817), English novelist.

Bach, Richard (born 1936), American aviation writer.

Bainbridge, Beryl (born 1934), English novelist.

Baker, Russell (born 1925), American journalist and essayist.

Balaban, John (born 1943), American children's-book writer.

Baldwin, James (1924-1987), American novelist and essayist.

Barnes, Djuna (1892-1982), American novelist.

Barth, John (born 1930), American novelist.

Barthelme, Donald (born 1931), American novelist and short-story writer.

Baum, L. Frank (1856-1919), American children's-book author.

Beattie, Ann (born 1947), American novelist.

Beckett, Samuel (born 1906), Irish dramatist, living in France.

Behan, Brendan (1923-1964), Irish dramatist.

Bellow, Saul (born 1915), American novelist.

Benchley, Robert (1889-1945), American humorist.

Benét, Stephen Vincent (1898-1943), American poet.

Benét, William Rose (1886-1950), American poet and critic.

Bettelheim, Bruno (born 1903), American psychologist and author, born in Germany.

Bierce, Ambrose (1842-1914?), American short-story writer.

Bishop, Elizabeth (1911-1979), American poet.

Bishop, Jim (1907-1987), American author of popular biographies.

Black, Hugo (1886-1971), American judge and author.

Blake, William (1757-1827), English poet and critic.

Blume, Judy (born 1938), American children's-book author.

Bond, Michael (born 1926), English children's-book author.

Bontemps, Arna (1902-1973), American novelist and critic.

Boorstin, Daniel (born 1914), American historian.

Boston, L. M. (born 1892), English children's-book author.

Boswell, James (1740-1795), Scottish biographer.

Bowen, Elizabeth (1899-1973), British novelist and short-story writer.

Boyle, Kay (born 1903), American short-story writer.

Bradbury, Ray (born 1920), American science-fiction author.

Bradlee, Benjamin (born 1921), American journalist.

Brandeis, Louis (1856-1941), American judge and author.

Brandwein, Paul (born 1912), American textbook author.

Breslin, Jimmy (born 1930), American journalist and novelist.

Brink, Carol Ryrie (1895-1981), American children's-book author.

Brodie, Fawn (1915-1981), American historian.

Brontë, Anne (1820-1849), English novelist.

Brontë, Charlotte (1816-1855), English novelist.

Brontë, Emily (1818-1848), English novelist.

Brooks, Cleanth (born 1906), American critic.

Brooks, Gwendolyn (born 1917), American poet.

Brooks, Walter R. (1886-1958), American children's-book author.

Brown, Claude (born 1927), American author.

Brown, Margaret Wise (1910-1952), American children's-book author.

Buchwald, Art (born 1925), American humorist.

Buck, Pearl (1892-1973), American novelist.

Buckley, William F. (born 1925), American author.

Bunting, Eve (born 1928), American children's-book author.

Bunyan, John (1628-1688), English novelist.

Burgess, Anthony (born 1917), English novelist.

Burnett, Frances Hodgson (1849-1924), English children's-book author.

Burns, James MacGregor (born 1918), American historian.

Byars, Betsy (born 1928), American children's-book author.

Byron, Lord (1788-1824), English poet.

Cain, James M. (1892-1977), American novelist.

Caldwell, Erskine (1903-1987), American novelist and short story writer.

Callaghan, Morley (born 1903), Canadian novelist.

Camus, Albert (1913-1960), French novelist and essayist.

Cannon, Jimmy (1909-1973), American sportswriter.

Capote, Truman (1924-1984), American author.

Carroll, Lewis (1832-1898), English children's-book author.

Cary, Joyce (1888-1957), British novelist, born in Ireland.

Cather, Willa (1876-1947), American novelist and short-story writer.

Catton, Bruce (1899-1978), American historian.

Chan, Jeffery Paul (born 1942), American author.

Chandler, Raymond (1888-1959), American novelist and short-story writer.

Chaucer, Geoffrey (1340?-1400), English poet.

Cheever, John (1912-1982), American short-story writer and novelist.

Chesterfield, Lord (1694-1773) English author and political leader.

Christie, Agatha (1890-1976), English mystery-story writer.

Churchill, Winston (1874-1965), British political leader, orator, and author.

Clarke, Arthur C. (born 1917), English science-fiction writer.

Clavell, James (born 1924), British novelist.

Clay, Henry (1777-1852), American political leader.

Cleary, Beverly (born 1916), American children's-book author.

Cleaver, Bill (1920-1981), American children's-book author.

Cleaver, Vera (born 1919), American children's-book author.

Coatsworth, Elizabeth (born 1893), American children's-book author.

Coetzee, J. M. (born 1940), South African author.

Coleridge, Samuel Taylor (1772-1834), English poet and critic.

Connell, Evan S. (born 1924), American novelist and historian.

Connell, Richard (1883-1949), American short-story writer.

Conrad, Joseph (1857-1924), British novelist, born in Poland.

Cooper, James Fenimore (1789-1851), American novelist.

Coover, Robert (born 1932), American novelist.

Coward, Noël (1899-1973), English dramatist.

Cowley, Malcolm (born 1898), American critic and essayist.

Cozzens, James Gould (1903-1978), American novelist.

Crane, Stephen (1871-1900), American novelist and short-story writer.

Dahl, Roald (born 1916), British novelist and short-story writer.

Darrow, Clarence (1857-1938), American lawyer and author.

Defoe, Daniel (1660-1731), English novelist.

Deford, Frank (born 1938), American sportswriter.

DeJong, Meindert (born 1906), American children's-book author.

De La Mare, Walter (1873-1956), English author.

Desai, Anita (born 1937), British novelist and short-story writer, born in India.

De Tocqueville, Alexis (1805-1859), French philosopher and political writer.

Dickens, Charles (1812-1870), English novelist.

Dickey, James (born 1923), American poet and novelist.

Didion, Joan (born 1934), American essayist and novelist.

Dillard, Annie (born 1945), American naturalist and essayist.

Dinesen, Isak (1885-1962), Danish novelist and short-story writer.

Djilas, Milovan (born 1911), Yugoslavian political leader and author.

Doctorow, E. L. (born 1931), American novelist.

Dodge, Mary Mapes (1831-1905), American children's-book author.

Dos Passos, John (1896-1970), American novelist.

Doyle, A. Conan (1859-1930), English author of detective stories.

Drabble, Margaret (born 1939), English novelist and critic.

Dreiser, Theodore (1871-1945), American novelist.

Drury, Allen (born 1918), American novelist.

Dunbar, Paul Laurence (1872-1906), American poet.

Dunne, John Gregory (born 1932), American novelist.

Eliot, George (1819-1890), English novelist.

Eliot, T. S. (1888-1965), British poet and critic, born in the U. S.

Ellison, Ralph (born 1914), American novelist.

Emerson, Ralph Waldo (1803-1882), American essayist, critic, and poet.

Ephron, Nora (born 1941), American essayist and novelist.

Erdoes, Richard (born 1912), American children's-book author.

Estes, Eleanor (1906-1988), American children's-book author.

Farley, Walter (born 1920), American children's-book author.

Farrell, James T. (1904-1979), American novelist.

Faulkner, William (1897-1962), American novelist.

Ferber, Edna (1887-1968), American novelist.

Field, Rachel (1894-1942), American children's-book author.

Fielding, Henry (1707-1754), English novelist.

Fisher, M. F. K. (born 1908), American author and food critic.

Fitzgerald, F. Scott (1896-1940), American novelist and short-story writer.

FitzGerald, Frances (born 1940), American historian.

Fitzhugh, Louise (1928-1974), American children's-book author.

Flaherty, Joe (1936-1983), American journalist and novelist.

Flanner, Janet (1892-1978), American journalist and essayist.

Fleming, Ian (1908-1964), British author of spy novels.

Follett, Ken (born 1949), British author of suspense novels.

Forbes, Esther (1891-1967), American children's-book author.

Ford, Ford Madox (1873-1939), English author.

Forester, C. S. (1899-1966), English author of historical fiction.

Forster, E. M. (1879-1970), English novelist.

Fowler, Henry W. (1858-1933), British dictionary editor.

Fowles, John (born 1926), English novelist.

Fox, Edward (born 1911), American children's-book author.

Fox, Paula (born 1923), American children's-book author.

Francis, Dick (born 1920), English detective-story writer.

Frank, Anne (1929-1945), Dutch-Jewish author of a famous diary.

Franklin, Benjamin (1706-1790), American patriot and author.

Fritz, Jean (born 1915), American children's-book author.

Fuentes, Carlos (born 1923), Mexican novelist.

Fussell, Paul (born 1924), English critic and historian.

Galarza, Ernesto (1901-1984), American educator and author, born in Mexico.

Galbraith, John Kenneth (born 1908), American economist and author, born in Canada.

Gallico, Paul (1897-1976), American journalist and novelist.

Galsworthy, John (1867-1933), English novelist.

Gandhi, Mohandas K. (1869-1948), Indian nationalist leader.

Gann, Ernest K. (born 1910), American novelist.

Gardner, John (1933-1982), American novelist and critic.

George, Jean Craighead (born 1919), American children's-book author.

Ginsberg, Allen (born 1926), American poet.

Glanville, Brian (born 1931), British journalist and novelist.

Golding, William (born 1911), English novelist.

Gordimer, Nadine (born 1923), South African novelist and short-story writer.

Gordon, Mary (born 1949), American novelist.

Grahame, Kenneth (1859-1932), English children's-book author.

Graves, Robert (1895-1985), English poet, novelist, and critic.

Greeley, Andrew (born 1928), American novelist.

Greene, Graham (born 1904), English novelist.

Gunther, John (1901-1970), American journalist and author.

Guthrie, A. B., Jr. (born 1901), American novelist.

Halberstam, David (born 1934), American journalist and historian.

Haley, Alex (born 1921), American biographer.

Hamill, Pete (born 1935), American journalist and novelist.

Hamilton, Alexander (1755-1804), American political leader and author.

Hamilton, Virginia (born 1936), American children's-book author.

Hammett, Dashiell (1894-1961), American detective-story writer.

Hardy, Thomas (1840-1928), English novelist and poet.

Hart, Moss (1904-1961), American dramatist.

Harte, Bret (1836-1902), American short-story writer.

Hawthorne, Nathaniel (1804-1864), American novelist and short-story writer.

Hecht, Ben (1894-1964), American dramatist and screenwriter.

Heinlein, Robert (1907-1988), American science-fiction writer.

Heller, Joseph (born 1923), American novelist.

Hellman, Lillian (1905-1984), American dramatist.

Helprin, Mark (born 1947), American novelist and short-story writer.

Hemans, Felicia (1793-1835), English poet.

Hemingway, Ernest (1899-1961), American novelist and short-story writer.

Henley, Beth (born 1952), American dramatist.

Henry, Marguerite (born 1902), American children's-book author.

Henry, Patrick (1736-1799), American patriot and orator.

Henty, G. A. (1832-1902), English author of historical works for children.

Herbert, Frank (1920-1986), American science-fiction writer.

Herriot, James (born 1916), English veterinarian and author.

Hersey, John (born 1914), American novelist and historian.

Heyerdahl, Thor (born 1914), Danish explorer and author.

Higgins, George V. (born 1939), American author of crime novels.

Highet, Gilbert (1906-1978), American critic, born in Scotland.

Highwater, Jamake (born 1942), American children's-book author.

Hilton, James (1900-1954), English novelist.

Hinton, S. E. (born 1950), American author of teenage fiction.

Holling, Holling C. (1900-1973), American children's-book author and illustrator.

Houston, James (born 1921), Canadian children's-book author.

Hudson, W. H. (1841-1922), British author, born in Argentina.

Hughes, Langston (1902-1967), American poet and short-story writer.

Hurston, Zora Neale (1901-1960), American novelist and short-story writer.

Huxley, Aldous (1894-1963), English novelist.

Huxley, Thomas Henry (1825-1895), English scientist and author.

Inge, William (1913-1973), American dramatist.

Irving, John (born 1942), American novelist.

Irving, Washington (1783-1859), American author.

Isherwood, Christopher (1904-1986), English novelist.

Jackson, Shirley (1916-1965), American short-story writer.

Jacobs, W. W. (1863-1943), English short-story writer.

Jakes, John (born 1932), American author of historical fiction.

James, Henry (1811-1882), American novelist and critic.

James, P. D. (born 1930), English detective-story writer.

Jefferson, Thomas (1743-1826), third President of the U. S.

Johnson, James Weldon (1871-1938), American poet and editor.

Johnson, Samuel (1709-1784), English poet, essayist, and dictionary editor.

Jones, James (1921-1977), American novelist.

Joseph, Chief (1840?-1904), American Indian leader.

Jovanovich, William (born 1920), American publisher and author.

Joyce, James (1882-1941), Irish novelist and short-story writer.

Juster, Norton (born 1929), American children's-book author.

Kantor, MacKinlay (1904-1977), American novelist.

Kazin, Alfred (born 1915), American critic and essayist.

Keats, John (1795-1821), English poet.

Keillor, Garrison (born 1942), American humorist and radio personality.

Keller, Helen (1880-1968), American author and lecturer.

Kelley, William Melvin (born 1937), American novelist.

Kennedy, John F. (1917-1963), 35th President of the U. S.

Kennedy, William (born 1928), American novelist.

Kerouac, Jack (1922-1969), American novelist.

Kerr, Jean (born 1923), American humorist and dramatist.

Kesey, Ken (born 1935), American novelist.

Keyes, Daniel (born 1927), American short-story writer.

King, Martin Luther (1925-1968), American orator and civil-rights leader.

King, Stephen (born 1946), American writer of suspense novels.

Kingston, Maxine Hong (born 1940), American journalist and novelist.

Kipling, Rudyard (1865-1936), British author, born in India.

Kjelgaard, Jim (1910-1959), American children's-book author.

Knowles, John (born 1926), American novelist.

Konigsburg, E. L. (born 1930), American children's-book author.

Kosinski, Jerzy (born 1933), Polish novelist, living in the U. S.

Krumgold, Joseph (1908-1980), American children's-book author.

L'Amour, Louis (1908-1988), American author of western novels.

Lardner, Ring (1885-1933), American humorist.

Lawrence, D. H. (1885-1930), English novelist and critic.

Lawrence, T. E. (1888-1935), British military leader and author.

Lawson, Robert (1892-1957), American children's-book author.

Lazurus, Emma (1849-1887), American poet.

Leacock, Stephen (1869-1944), Canadian humorist.

le Carré, John (born 1931), English author of spy novels.

Lee, Andrea (born 1953), American journalist and novelist.

Lee, Harper (born 1926), American novelist.

LeGuin, Ursula K. (born 1929), American science-fiction writer.

L'Engle, Madeleine (born 1918), American children's-book author.

Lenski, Lois (1893-1974), American children's-book author.

Leonard, Elmore (born 1925), American author of detective novels.

Lessing, Doris (born 1919), British novelist, born in Persia.

Lewis, Anthony (born 1927), American political columnist.

Lewis, C. S. (1898-1963), English author.

Lewis, Sinclair (1885-1951), American novelist.

Lincoln, Abraham (1809-1865), 16th President of the U. S.

Lindbergh, Anne Morrow (born 1906), American author.

Lindbergh, Charles (1902-1974), American aviator and author.

Lippmann, Walter (1889-1974), American journalist and political writer.

Lively, Penelope (born 1933), British children's-book author.

Lockridge, Ross (1914-1948), American novelist.

Lofting, Hugh (1886-1947), English children's-book author.

London, Jack (1876-1916), American novelist and short-story writer.

Longfellow, Henry Wadsworth (1807-1882), American poet.

Lopez, Barry (born 1945), American author and naturalist.

Luce, Clare Boothe (1903-1987), American dramatist.

MacArthur, Douglas (1880-1964), American military leader.

MacDonald, John D. (born 1916), American detective-story writer.

MacInnes, Helen (1907-1985), American suspense-story writer, born in Scotland.

MacLachlan, Patricia (born 1938), American children's-book author.

Mailer, Norman (born 1923), American novelist and essayist.

Malamud, Bernard (1914-1986), American novelist.

Malcolm X (Malcolm Little) (1925-1965), American political leader and author.

Mamet, David (born 1947), American playwright.

Manchester, William (born 1922), American historian.

Mansfield, Katherine (1888-1923), British short-story writer, born in New Zealand.

Marquand, John P. (1893-1960), American novelist.

Mason, Bobbie Ann (born 1940), American short-story writer.

Maugham, W. Somerset (1874-1965), English novelist and short-story writer.

Maynard, Joyce (born 1953), American journalist.

McCarthy, Mary (born 1912), American novelist, essayist, and short-story writer.

McCullers, Carson (1917-1967), American novelist and short-story writer.

McCullough, Colleen (born 1938), Australian novelist.

McGahern, John (born 1934), Irish novelist.

McGinniss, Joe (born 1942), American journalist.

McKay, Claude (1890-1948), American poet and novelist.

McLuhan, Marshall (1911-1980), Canadian educator and author.

McMurtry, Larry (born 1936), American novelist.

McPhee, John (born 1931), American journalist and essayist.

McPherson, James Alan (born 1943), American short-story writer.

Melville, Herman (1819-1891), American novelist and short-story writer.

Mencken, H. L. (1880-1956), American journalist and critic.

Meredith, George (1828-1909), English novelist.

Merton, Thomas (1915-1969), American religious writer.

Michener, James (born 1907), American novelist.

Millay, Edna St. Vincent (1892-1950), American poet.

Miller, Arthur (born 1915), American dramatist.

Milne, A. A. (1882-1956), English children's-book author.

Mitchell, Joseph (born 1908), American essayist and journalist.

Mitchell, Margaret (1900-1949), American novelist.

Momaday, N. Scott (born 1934), American author.

Moore, Brian (born 1921), Canadian novelist, born in Ireland.

Moore, George (1852-1933), British novelist, born in Ireland.

Moore, Marianne (1887-1972), American poet.

Moravia, Alberto (born 1907), Italian novelist.

Morison, Samuel Eliot (1887-1976), American historian.

Morris, Willie (born 1934), American editor and author.

Morris, Wright (born 1910), American novelist.

Morrison, Toni (born 1931), American novelist.

Mortimer, John (born 1923), English novelist.

Mowat, Farley (born 1921), Canadian author and naturalist.

Munro, Alice (born 1931), Canadian novelist and short-story writer.

Murdoch, Iris (born 1919), English novelist.

Muro, Amado (1915-1971), American novelist and short-story writer.

Murrow, Edward R. (1908-1965), American journalist.

Nabokov, Vladimir (1899-1977), Russian novelist and critic, living in the U. S.

Naipaul, V. S. (born 1932), British-Indian novelist, born in Trinidad.

Nichols, John (born 1940), American novelist.

Nin, Anaïs (1903-1977), American author, born in France.

North, Sterling (1906-1974), American children's-book author.

Norton, Andre (born 1912), American science-fiction writer.

Norton, Mary (born 1903), English children's-book author.

Oates, Joyce Carol (born 1938), American author.

O'Casey, Sean (1880-1964), Irish dramatist.

O'Connor, Flannery (1925-1964), American novelist and short-story writer.

O'Connor, Frank (1903-1966), Irish novelist and short-story writer.

O'Dell, Scott (born 1903), American children's-book author.

Odets, Clifford (1906-1963), American dramatist.

O'Faolain, Julia (born 1932), Irish novelist and short-story writer.

O'Faolain, Sean (born 1900), Irish novelist and short-story writer.

O'Flaherty, Liam (1897-1984), Irish novelist and short-story writer.

O'Hara, John (1905-1970), American novelist and short-story writer.

O'Hara, Mary (1885-1980), American children's-book author.

O. Henry (William Sydney Porter) (1862-1910), American short-story writer.

Okada, John (1923-1971), American novelist.

O'Neill, Eugene (1888-1953), American dramatist.

Orwell, George (1903-1950), English novelist and essayist.

Osler, William (1849-1919), Canadian physician and author of medical works.

Paine, Thomas (1737-1809), American patriot and essayist, born in England.

Parker, Dorothy (1893-1967), American critic and short-story writer.

Pearce, Philippa (born 1920), English children's-book author.

Pepys, Samuel (1633-1703), English author of a famous diary.

Percy, Walker (born 1916), American novelist.

Pinter, Harold (born 1930), English dramatist.

Plath, Sylvia (1932-1963), American poet.

Plimpton, George (born 1927), American author.

Poe, Edgar Allan (1809-1849), American poet and short-story writer.

Pope, Alexander (1688-1744), English poet and critic.

Porter, Katherine Anne (1890-1980), American novelist and short-story writer.

Post, Laurens van der (born 1906), South African novelist and travel writer.

Potter, Beatrix (1866-1943), English children's-book author and illustrator.

Pritchett, V. S. (born 1900), English critic.

Pyle, Ernie (1900-1945), American war correspondent.

Pyle, Howard (1853-1911), American illustrator and author.

Pym, Barbara (1913-1980), English novelist.

Pynchon, Thomas (born 1937), American novelist.

Quiller-Couch, Arthur (1863-1944), English critic.

Rabe, David (born 1940), American dramatist.

Rawlings, Marjorie Kinnan (1896-1953), American novelist and short-story writer.

Reed, Ishmael (born 1938), American novelist.

Robinson, Edwin Arlington (1869-1935), American poet.

Roosevelt, Franklin D. (1882-1945), 32nd President of the U.S.

Rosten, Leo (born 1908), American humorist.

Roth, Philip (born 1933), American novelist and short-story writer.

Royko, Mike (born 1922), American journalist.

Runyon, Damon (1884-1946), American journalist and humorist.

Russell, Bertrand (1872-1970), British philosopher and author.

Ryan, Cornelius (1920-1974), American military historian.

Sagan, Carl (born 1934), American scientist and author.

Saint-Exupéry, Antoine de (1900-1944), French author and aviator.

Saki (H. H. Munro) (1870-1916), British author, born in Burma.

Salinger, J. D. (born 1919), American novelist and short-story writer.

Sanchez, Thomas (born 1944), American novelist.

Sandburg, Carl (1878-1967), American poet and biographer.

Saroyan, William (1908-1981), American author.

Schaefer, Jack (born 1907), American author of western novels.

Schlesinger, Arthur (born 1917), American historian.

Schulberg, Budd (born 1914), American novelist.

Scott, Jack Denton (born 1915), American nature writer.

Scott, Paul (1920-1978), British novelist.

Scott, Sir Walter (1771-1832), Scottish novelist and poet.

Sendak, Maurice (born 1928), American children's-book illustrator and author.

Serling, Rod (1924-1975), American science-fiction writer.

Sewell, Anna (1820-1878), English children's-book author.

Shaffer, Peter (born 1926), English dramatist.

Shaftesbury, Lord (1801-1885), English political leader and author.

Shah, Idries (born 1924), British author and folklorist.

Shakespeare, William (1564-1616), English dramatist and poet.

Shaw, George Bernard (1856-1950), British dramatist, born in Ireland.

Shaw, Irwin (1913-1984), American novelist and short-story writer.

Shepard, Sam (born 1943), American dramatist.

Shepherd, Jean (born 1929), American humorist.

Shirer, William L. (born 1904), American journalist and historian.

Silko, Leslie (born 1948), American poet and short-story writer.

Simon, John (born 1925), American critic, born in Yugoslavia.

Simon, Kate (1892-1969), American journalist.

Sinclair, Upton (1878-1968), American novelist.

Singer, Isaac Bashevis (born 1904), Polish-Jewish novelist, living in the U. S.

Smith, Betty (1904-1972), American novelist.

Smith, Red (1905-1982), American sportswriter.

Sobol, Donald J. (born 1924), American children's-book author.

Solzhenitsyn, Alexander (born 1918), Russian novelist.

Southall, Ivan (born 1921), Australian children's-book author.

Soyinka, Wole (born 1934), Nigerian dramatist and novelist.

Spark, Muriel (born 1918), Scottish novelist.

Speare, Elizabeth George (born 1908), American children's-book author.

Sperry, Armstrong (1897-1976), American children's-book author.

Stafford, Jean (1915-1979), American short-story writer and novelist.

Stegner, Wallace (born 1909), American novelist.

Steig, William (born 1907), American cartoonist and children's-book author.

Stein, Gertrude (1874-1946), American critic and novelist.

Steinbeck, John (1902-1968), American novelist and short-story writer.

Stephen, James F. (1829-1894), English critic.

Stephenson, Carl (born 1893), American short-story writer.

Sterne, Laurence (1713-1768), British novelist, born in Ireland.

Stevenson, Robert Louis (1850-1894), Scottish novelist and poet.

Stockton, Frank R. (1834-1902), American short-story writer.

Stone, Irving (born 1903), American novelist and biographer.

Stoppard, Tom (born 1937), British dramatist, born in Czechoslovakia.

Stuart, Jesse (1907-1984), American author.

Styron, Wiliam (born 1925), American novelist.

Swanberg, W. A. (born 1907), American biographer and historian.

Swift, Jonathan (1667-1745), English author, born in Ireland.

Talese, Gay (born 1932), American author.

Tarkington, Booth (1869-1946), American novelist.

Terhune, Albert Payson (1872-1942), American children's-book author.

Terkel, Studs (born 1912), American journalist and historian.

Thackeray, William Makepeace (1811-1863), English novelist.

Theroux, Paul (born 1941), American novelist and travel writer.

Thomas, Dylan (1914-1953), Welsh poet.

Thompson, Hunter (born 1939), American journalist.

Thoreau, Henry David (1817-1862), American naturalist and essayist.

Thurber, James (1894-1961), American humorist.

Toland, John (born 1912), American historian.

Tolkein, J. R. R. (1892-1973), English children's-book author.

Toomer, Jean (1894-1967), American poet and short-story writer.

Travers, P. L. (born 1906), English children's-book author.

Trevelyan, G. M. (1876-1962), English historian.

Trillin, Calvin (born 1935), American journalist and humorist.

Trilling, Lionel (1905-1975), American critic.

Trollope, Anthony (1815-1882), English novelist.

Truman, Harry (1884-1972), 33rd President of the U. S.

Tuchman, Barbara (born 1912), American historian.

Tunis, John R. (1889-1975), American children's-book author.

Twain, Mark (1835-1910), American author.

Tyler, Anne (born 1941), American novelist.

Uchida, Yoshiko (born 1921), American children's-book author.

Udall, Stewart (born 1920), American political leader and author.

Updike, John (born 1932), American novelist, critic, and short-story writer.

Valdez, Luis (born 1940), American dramatist.

Verne, Jules (1828-1905), French novelist.

Vidal, Gore (born 1925), American novelist.

Voigt, Cynthia (born 1942), American writer of teenage fiction.

Vonnegut, Kurt (born 1922), American novelist and short-story writer.

Vroman, Mary Elizabeth (1923-1967), American novelist.

Walker, Alice (born 1944), American novelist.

Walsh, Jill Paton (born 1937), English children's-book author.

Walton, Izaak (1593-1683), English author of a famous work on fishing.

Wambaugh, Joseph (born 1937), American novelist.

Warren, Robert Penn (born 1905), American novelist and critic.

Washington, George (1732-1799), first President of the U. S.

Waugh, Evelyn (1903-1966), English novelist.

Webster, Daniel (1782-1852), American orator and political leader.

Weidman, Jerome (born 1913), American novelist.

Wells, H. G. (1866-1946), English novelist and historian.

Welty, Eudora (born 1909), American short-story writer.

West, Jessamyn (1907-1984), American novelist.

West, Nathanael (1903-1940), American novelist.

Wharton, Edith (1862-1937), American novelist.

White, E. B. (1899-1986), American essayist and children's-book author.

White, T. H. (1906-1964), British author of historical fiction.

White, Theodore H. (1915-1986), American journalist and political writer.

Whitman, Walt (1819-1892), American poet.

Wicker, Tom (born 1926), American journalist and novelist.

Wilbur, Richard (born 1921), American poet.

Wilde, Oscar (1854-1900), Irish dramatist and novelist.

Wilder, Laura Ingalls (1867-1957), American author of historical fiction.

Wilder, Thornton (1897-1975), American dramatist.

Willard, Nancy (born 1936), American poet and children's-book author.

Williams, Margery (1880-1944), English children's-book author.

Williams, Sherley Anne (born 1944), American poet and novelist.

Williams, Tennessee (1911-1983), American dramatist.

Williams, William Carlos (1883-1963), American poet.

Wilson, Angus (born 1913), South African novelist.

Wilson, Edmund (1895-1972), American critic, essayist, and novelist.

Wilson, Lanford (born 1937), American dramatist.

Wolfe, Thomas (1900-1938), American novelist.

Wolfe, Tom (Thomas Kennerly) (born 1931), American essayist and novelist.

Woolf, Virginia (1882-1941), English novelist and critic.

Wordsworth, William (1770-1850), English poet.

Wouk, Herman (born 1915), American novelist.

Wright, Richard (1908-1960), American novelist.

Yeats, William Butler (1865-1939), Irish poet.

Yep, Laurence (born 1948), American children's-book author.

Yerby, Frank (born 1916), American novelist.

Zindel, Bonnie (born 1936), American children's book author.

Zindel, Paul (born 1936), American writer of teenage fiction.

Photo Credits

abbey: Shostal Associates; **aborigine:** P. Tweedie/Woodfin Camp & Associates; **accompany:** Frank Driggs; **acrobat:** Ray Shaw/The Stock Market; **admiral:** U.S. Navy; **adobe:** Franz Kraus/The Picture Cube; **aerial:** Bettmann Archive; **Africa:** R.S. Virdee/Shostal Associates; **airborne:** U.S. Army; **aircraft carrier:** U.S. Navy; **aisle:** Shostal Associates; **algae:** William E. Ferguson; **Alps:** Gilda Schiff/Photo Researchers; **Amazon:** S. Vidler/Leo de Wys, Inc.; **ameba:** SPL/Photo Researchers; **amphitheater:** Val & Alan Wilkerson/Valan Photos; **Andes:** F. Gohier/Photo Researchers; **Antarctica:** E. Stockins/Shostal Associates; **apprentice:** Bettmann Archive; **aqueduct:** Craig Collins/PhotoUnique; **arch:** Sally Weigand/The Picture Cube; **arena:** Balthazar Korab/Uniphoto; **Aristotle:** Metropolitan Museum of Art; **Arizona:** Spencer Swanger/Tom Stack & Associates; **armor:** SEF/Art Resource; **Louis Armstrong:** Frank Driggs; **asparagus:** HBJ Photo; **assembly:** Maggie Steber/Stock, Boston; **atlas:** SCALA/Art Resource; **atomic bomb:** Stern/Black Star; **auction:** Grant Heilman/Grant Heilman Photography; **bagpipes:** British Tourist Authority; **ballet:** Ken Regan/Camera 5; **balloon:** Brian Parker/Tom Stack & Associates; **Clara Barton:** HBJ Photo; **baton:** J.L. Atlan/Sygma; **battleship:** D.A.V.A.; **Beethoven:** Culver Pictures; **bell:** Robert Glander/Shostal Associates; **Berlin:** Walter Schmidt/Peter Arnold, Inc.; **Bible:** SCALA/Art Resource; **bison:** Richard Rowan; **blackout:** Ray Ellis/Photo Researchers; **blanket:** G. Adams/Stock Imagery; **bleachers:** Bob Glaze/Artstreet; **blizzard:** P. Conklin/Uniphoto; **bluff:** Rhode Island Dept. of Economic Development; **bobsled:** Jerry Cooke/Sports Illustrated; **bomber:** Bettmann Newsphotos; **Daniel Boone:** Washington U. Gallery of Art, St. Louis; **Boston:** Steve Dunwell/The Image Bank; **boulevard:** Metropolitan Museum of Art; **bow:** Steve Smith/Wheeler Pictures; **bowl:** Wheeler Pictures; **braces:** National Easter Seal Society; **braille:** Charles Gupton/The Stock Market; **breaker:** E.R. Degginger; **brick:** Rolly Desmarais; **bridge:** Steve Vidler/Leo de Wys, Inc.; **brook:** Ed Cooper; **Buddha:** E.R. Degginger; **bugle:** D.A.V.A.; **Burma:** E.R. Degginger/H. Armstrong Roberts, Inc.; **caboose:** Ernest H. Robl; **camel:** Mickey Gibson/Animals, Animals; **canal:** J. Hackett/Leo de Wys, Inc.; **canoe:** HBJ Photo; **canyon:** Arizona Office of Tourism; **Capitol:** Robert Glander/Shostal Associates; **cardinal:** Indiana Dept. of Commerce; **Caribbean:** V. Phillips/Leo de Wys, Inc.; **George Washington Carver:** National Portrait Gallery, by Betsey Graves Reyneau; **castle:** SEF/Art Resource; **cathedral:** Adam Woolfitt/Woodfin Camp & Associates; **cavalry:** Amon Carter Museum, Fort Worth, Texas; **cell:** Carroll H. Weiss/Camera M.D.; **cello:** Frank Driggs; **chariot:** Art Resource; **Chicago:** Cameramann International; **chip:** © Joel Gordon; **Churchill:** © Karsh, Ottawa/Woodfin Camp & Associates; **Cleopatra:** Granger Collection; **clipper ship:** Granger Collection; **cloud:** National Audubon Society/Photo Researchers; **coat of arms:** SCALA/Art Resource; **coin:** Nawrocki Stock Photo; **collie:** W. Hamilton/Shostal Associates; **colonial:** Joseph A. DiCello, Jr.; **Columbus:** Nawrocki Stock Photo; **comet:** Robert Provin, Courtesy of Astronomy Magazine; **compass:** Coco McCoy/Rainbow; **computer (1):** U. of Pennsylvania; **computer (2):** Tom Tracy; **Confederate:** Granger Collection; **confetti:** Randy Taylor/Sygma; **Congress:** Bettmann Archive; **conservation:** Philip Gould; **constellation:** California Inst. of Technology; **Constitution:** HBJ Photo; **control tower:** Ed Hall; **convoy:** U.S. Navy; **copper:** Laireille Soir/Gamma-Liaison; **cove:** Barbara Lowe Reed/Shostal Associates; **creek:** Tourism Quebec; **cricket:** Focus On Sports; **crow:** A. Schmidecker/FPG; **crown:** SCALA/Art Resource; **crystal:** Courtesy of Steuben Glass, **Curies:** Bettmann Archive; **curtsy:** Photoworld/FPG; **cypress:** E.R. Degginger; **dawn:** Walter Chandoha; **Death Valley:** Peter Menzel/Stock, Boston; **debate:** Culver Pictures; **delta:** General Electric Co. Space Systems; **Democratic:** Granger Collection; **derrick:** E.R. Degginger; **desert:** Franklin Wing/Stock, Boston; **destroyer:** D.A.V.A.; **Emily Dickinson:** Nawrocki Stock Photo; **dictionary:** Bettmann Archive; **dike:** Van Phillips/Leo de Wys, Inc.; **diner:** Jim Schaffer/Viewfinder; **diploma:** Hugh Rogers/Monkmeyer; **dirigible:** Culver Pictures; **disc jockey:** Van Bucher/Photo Researchers; **discus:** Focus On Sports; **dish:** Bob Thomason/Leo de Wys, Inc.; **dolphin:** E.R. Degginger/Animals, Animals; **donkey:** John Stevenson/Animals, Animals; **dragon:** SCALA/Art Resource; **driftwood:** V. Weinland/Photo Researchers; **drive-in:** Bett-

mann Archive; **drought:** Georg Gerster/Photo Researchers; **dugout:** Bettmann Newsphotos; **dunes:** National Park Service; **dust bowl:** Bettmann Archive; **earth:** NASA; **ebb tide:** Cotton Coulson/Woodfin Camp & Associates; **eclipse:** Terry Domico/Earth Images; **Egypt:** Cameramann International; **Einstein:** © Karsh, Ottawa/Woodfin Camp & Associates; **Elizabeth I:** British Services; **Elizabeth II:** Giorgio Nimatallah/Art Resource; **emerald:** E.R. Degginger; **engine:** HBJ Photo; **engraving:** Marburg/Art Resource; **eruption:** Camera Hawaii; **etching:** Guraudon/Art Resource; **Everglades:** Colour Library International/TPS; **exhaust:** Craig Aurness/West Light; **explosion:** Richard Pasley/Stock, Boston; **fable:** Bettmann Archive; **falcon:** Hans Reinhard/Bruce Coleman, Inc.; **fast food:** Courtesy of McDonald's Corp.; **fault:** James Balog/Black Star; **fawn:** Wisconsin Div. of Tourism; **fencing:** A. Boradulin/Leo de Wys, Inc.; **ferry:** Gerald Davis/Leo de Wys, Inc.; **fingerprint:** Don & Pat Valenti/Tom Stack & Associates; Lawrence S. Stepanowitz/Bruce Coleman, Inc.; **fireworks:** Bill Hickey/The Stock Market; **flamingo:** Laura Riley/Bruce Coleman, Inc.; **flats:** E.R. Degginger; **fleet:** Bettmann Archive; **float:** E.R. Degginger; **flood:** David W. Hamilton/The Image Bank; **Florence:** R. Srenco/Shostal Associates; **fog:** Idaho Div. of Economic Affairs; **folk art:** Philip Jon Bailey/The Picture Cube; **forest:** Rod Planck/Tom Stack & Associates; **fort:** National Archives; **fossil:** William E. Ferguson/Ulrich Fossil Gallery; **fountain:** Sapieha/Art Resource; **Benjamin Franklin:** © White House Historical Association/National Geographic Society; **frost:** Tom Bean; **fungus:** HBJ Photo; **furnace:** C. Aurness/West Light; **gargoyle:** Richard Rowan; **generic:** Artstreet; **geyser:** Richard Rowan; **glacier:** Tom Bean; **glider:** Bettmann Archive; **gnu:** Stephan Meyers/Animals, Animals; **gold:** Michael Ginsburg/Magnum Photos; **gold mine:** Karen Gilman/FPG; **graffiti:** Ancient Art & Architecture Collection; **gravestone:** Montana Travel Promotion; **Greece:** Colour Library International; **greyhound:** Edward Slater/Southern Stock Photos; **guard:** Ted Russell/The Image Bank; **guerrilla:** Steve McCurry/Magnum Photos; **gymnastics:** Focus On Sports; **halo:** John Shaw/Tom Stack & Associates; **hang glider:** ZEFA/H. Armstrong Roberts, Inc.; **harp:** Florida Symphony Orchestra; **harpoon:** Museum of Modern Art/Film Stills Archive; **Hawaii:** Hawaii Visitors Bureau; **hearth:** John Colwell/Grant Heilman Photography; **hedge:** Joe Viesti; **helicopter:** Em Ahart/Tom Stack & Associates; **Ernest Hemingway:** Culver Pictures; **heron:** National Park Service; **highlands:** Story Litchfield/Stock, Boston; **Himalayas:** Claude Shostal/Shostal Associates; **Hollywood:** D&J Heaton/Stock, Boston; **Hong Kong:** Heaton/After-Image; **hoop:** Brown Brothers; **Hopi:** Museum of the American Indian; **House of Representatives:** Architect of the Capitol; **Hungary:** Susan McCartney/Photo Researchers; **hurdle:** Focus On Sports; **hurricane:** Providence Journal; **hydrofoil:** Sea World; **iceberg:** E. Hummel/Leo de Wys, Inc.; **icicle:** Eric Sanford; **igloo:** David Hiser/Photographers Aspen; **immigrant:** Bettmann Archive; **inauguration:** Brown Brothers; **Inca:** Museum of the American Indian; **India:** Ray Manley/Shostal Associates; **infantry:** U.S. Army; **injection:** March of Dimes, Birth Defects Foundation; **inlet:** Richard Pasley/Stock, Boston; **insignia:** Ellis Herwig/Stock, Boston; **insulation:** E.R. Degginger; **integration:** Burt Glinn/Magnum Photos; **interceptor:** Bettmann Archive; **Ireland:** Eric Carle/Shostal Associates; **irrigation:** HBJ Photo; **ivory:** E.R. Degginger; **jack-o-lantern:** Terry E. Eiler/Stock, Boston; **javelin:** Heinz Kluetmeier/Sports Illustrated; **Jerusalem:** S. Vidler/Leo de Wys, Inc.; **Joan of Arc:** Nawrocki Stock Photo; **Benito Juarez:** Nawrocki Stock Photo; **juggler:** Jack Ward/The Image Bank; **junk:** T. Madison/The Image Bank; **kayak:** Shostal Associates; **Helen Keller:** Photo Researchers; **Kentucky:** Focus On Sports; **killer whale:** Sea World; **Martin Luther King:** Bob Adelman/Magnum Photos; **knight:** Art Resource; **lace:** Eric Carle/Shostal Associates; **lacrosse:** Anthony Neste/Focus On Sports; **landscape:** Wadsworth Atheneum, Hartford; **laser:** Bruce Frisch/Photo Researchers; **launch pad:** NASA; **lava:** Randy Hyman/Stock, Boston; **Leaning Tower:** Larry Lee/West Light; **Robert E. Lee:** U.S. Naval Academy Museum; **legend:** Bettmann Archive; **lei:** Werner Stoy/Camera Hawaii; **Leonardo:** SCALA/Art Resource; **Lewis & Clark:** Bettmann Archive; **lifeboat:** Rolly Desmarais; **lighthouse:** David Muench Photography; **lightning:** Viewfinder; **Charles & Anne Lind-**

bergh: Brown Brothers; **London:** Colour Library International; **longhorn:** Texas Tourist Development Agency; **Los Angeles:** Craig Aurness/West Light; **lumberjack:** Washington State Historical Society; **machete:** Jonathan Wilkens/FPG; **mainframe:** Steve Smith/Wheeler Pictures; **mall:** Margaret C. Berg/Berg & Associates; **marathon:** Focus On Sports; **Maryland:** U.S. Naval Academy; **Massachusetts:** John Coletti/Stock, Boston; **maze:** Dan Budnik/Woodfin Camp & Associates; **Mt. McKinley:** Tom Walker/Stock, Boston; **Mediterranean:** Colour Library International; **memorial:** E.C. Evans/Shostal Associates; **Mercury:** HBJ Photo; **mesa:** Miro Vintoniv/Stock, Boston; **Mexico City:** Vince Streano/After-Image; **microscope:** E.R. Degginger; **migration:** Stephen J. Kraseman/Valan Photos; **mill:** Granger Collection; **mint:** Malak/Shostal Associates; **mission:** Ed Cooper Photography; **moat:** Stuart Cohen/Stock, Boston; **mobile:** Paluan Mario Torino/Art Resource; **Monet:** SCALA/Art Resource; **monitor:** Michael Melford/Wheeler Pictures; **monument:** William Folsom/Uniphoto; **Moscow:** © Dilip Mehta/Contact/Camp; **mule:** L.L.T. Rhodes/Animals, Animals; **mural:** SCALA/Art Resource; **Napoleon:** Art Resource; **Navaho:** R.Y. Kaufman/Aperture Photobank; **needlepoint:** E.R. Degginger; **negative:** Lincoln Library & Museum, Ft. Wayne, Ind.; **neon:** Robert Garvey/The Stock Market; **Netherlands:** S. Vidler/Leo de Wys, Inc.; **New England:** Joseph A. DiChello, Jr.; **New Mexico:** Ed Cooper Photography; **northern lights:** Ned Haines/Photo Researchers; **Norway:** Messerschmidt/Leo de Wys, Inc.; **nucleus:** Alfred Lamme/Camera M.D. Studios; **observatory:** Tom Bean/DRK Photo; **Sandra Day O'Connor:** Supreme Court Historical Society; **oil well:** Library of Congress; **Ontario:** Ontario Ministry of Tourism; **opera:** Tom Lipton/Shostal Associates; **organ:** Tony Freeman Photographs; **outrigger:** John Penisten/The Travel Image; **pagoda:** V. Phillips/Leo de Wys, Inc.; **palace:** Luis Villota/The Stock Market; **Panama Canal:** Augusts Upitis/Shostal Associates; **paramecium:** Science Source/Photo Researchers; **parchment:** SCALA/Art Resource; **parka:** Bettmann Archive; **Louis Pasteur:** Brown Brothers; **pearl:** Shostal Associates; **Pearl Harbor:** Hawaii Visitors Bureau; **Peking:** S. Vidler/After-Image; **periscope:** Masterson Stock; **Peru:** S. Vidler/Leo de Wys, Inc.; **petrified:** Richard Kolar/Earth Scenes; **Picasso:** Reñ Burri/Magnum Photos; **pier:** Richard Rowan; **Pilgrims:** Culver Pictures; **pipeline:** Nancy Christensen/Berg & Associates; **pirates:** Granger Collection; **plantation:** Bettmann Archive; **plaza:** Luis Villota/The Stock Market; **plow:** Brown Brothers; **pole vault:** Paul Kennedy/Leo de Wys, Inc.; **portrait:** Bettmann Archive; **poster:** Granger Collection; **pottery:** Irish Tourist Board; **press:** Lou Jones/The Image Bank; **probe:** Tom McHugh, Science Source/Photo Researchers; **procession:** Cary Wolinsky/Stock, Boston; **produce:** Jeffrey Myers/Stock, Boston; **Prohibition:** Bettmann Archive; **promontory:** Craig Aurness/West Light; **pronghorn:** Marty Stouffer/Animals, Animals; **propeller:** Paul Bowen Photography; **pueblo:** Stewart Green/Tom Stack & Associates; **puffin:** Henry Ausloos/Animals, Animals; **pyramid:** Peter Morgan/Picture Group; **quarter horse:** Rob Brown/Focus On Sports; **quartz:** E.R. Degginger; **Quebec:** Tourism Quebec; **quill:** Brown Brothers; **quilt:** Linda Bartlett/Photo Researchers; **quintuplets:** Bettmann Newsphotos; **rainbow:** Index Stock; **rapids:** Keith Gunnar/Bruce Coleman, Inc.; **reactor:** George Lepp/Bruce Coleman, Inc.; **reef:** Carl Roesseler/Tom Stack & Associates; **refinery:** Lawrence Migdale/Photo Researchers; **refugees:** Bettmann Newsphotos; **relay:** Focus On Sports; **relief:** D. Forbert/Shostal Associates; **Rembrandt:** SCALA/Art Resource; **Renaissance:** SCALA/Art Resource; **Republican:** Granger Collection; **reservoir:** John Lemker/Earth Scenes; **resistance:** Bettmann Archive; **reunion:** Constantine Manas/Magnum Photos; **Rio de Janeiro:** Colour Library International; **robot:** Kim Steele/Wheeler Pictures; **Rockies:** D. Corson/Shostal Associates; **rodeo:** James B. Cudney/Nawrocki Stock Photo; **Rome:** Colour Library International; **rotunda:** Architect of the Capitol; **rowing:** Ellis Herwig/Stock, Boston; **Mt. Rushmore:** J. Blank/Leo de Wys, Inc; **Sahara:** H. Klein; **salute:** Bob Glaze/Artstreet; **sandstorm:** William E. Ferguson; **Saturn:** NASA; **scarecrow:** Hal H. Harrison/Grant Heilman Photography; **Scotland:** S. Vidler/Leo de Wys, Inc.; **scribe:** Bettmann Archive; **segregation:** Elliott Erwitt/Magnum Photos; **Senate:** Architect of the

Capitol; **sequoia:** Richard Rowan; **setter:** L. Willinger/FPG International; **sewing machine:** Culver Pictures; **Shakespeare:** The Folger Shakespeare Library, Washington, D.C.; **shell:** E.R. Degginger; **shot put:** Focus On Sports; **sideburns:** Bettmann Archive; **Sierras:** S. Wennberg/Black Star; **silkworm:** Hans Pfletschinger/Peter Arnold, Inc.; **Singapore:** Singapore Tourist Board; **Sioux:** Nawrocki Stock Photo; **ski jump:** Focus On Sports; **skyscraper:** Bob Glaze/Artstreet; **sleigh:** Granger Collection; **sloop:** Charles O'Rear/West Light; **smog:** Bob Glaze/Artstreet; **snowflake:** Clyde H. Smith/Peter Arnold, Inc.; **snowmobile:** Richard Rowan; **sod house:** Solomon D. Butcher Collection/Nebraska Historical Society; **solar system:** Hayden Planetarium; **sombrero:** Thomas Nebbia/Woodfin Camp & Associates; **space station:** NASA; **Spain:** Colour Library International; **spinning wheel:** Culver Pictures; **spring:** Eric Neurath/Stock, Boston; **springboard:** Focus On Sports; **stadium:** Peter Southwick/Stock, Boston; **stagecoach:** Western History Collections, U. of Oklahoma Library; **stalactite:** Virginia Div. of Tourism; **stampede:** H. Armstrong Roberts, Inc.; **Elizabeth Cady Stanton:** Library of Congress; **Stars and Stripes:** Smithsonian Institution Photo No. 83-7221; **statue:** Vernon Doucette/Stock, Boston; **Statue of Liberty:** R.S. Virdee/Grant Heilman Photography; **steamboat:** Bettmann Archive; **steamroller:** Owen Franken/Stock, Boston; **steeplechase:** Jerry Cooke/Sports Illustrated; **stethoscope:** Karl Kummels/Shostal Associates; **stock market:** Brown Brothers; **streamlined:** Air Pixies, N.Y.; **strike:** Library of Congress; **subway:** Peter Vandermark/Stock, Boston; **sundial:** Bettmann Archive; **Supreme Court:** Kay Chernush/The Image Bank; **surfing:** Choice Photos/Berg & Associates; **Switzerland:** Colour Library International; **synagogue:** SCALA/Art Resource; **tank:** D.A.V.A.; **Tanzania:** V. Harte/Taurua Photos; **tartan:** Steve Allen/Peter Arnold, Inc.; **telephone:** Courtesy of AT&T Corporate Archives; **telescope:** Courtesy of Hale Observatory; **temple:** John Snyder/The Stock Market; **tenement:** tory; **temple:** John Snyder/The Stock Market; **tenement:** Bettmann Archive; **tepee:** Library of Congress/E. Curtis Collection; **Texas:** Texas Tourist Development Agency; **Margaret Thatcher:** Peter Jordan/Gamma-Liaison; **thoroughbred:** Neil Leifer/Sports Illustrated; **throne:** Adam Woolfitt/Woodfin Camp & Associates; **thunderhead:** Emil Muench/Photo Researchers; **tightrope:** Johan Elbens/Sygma; **Tokyo:** Larry Lee/West Light; **tomb:** Jake Rajs/The Image Bank; **tornado:** © Howard Bluestein/Photo Researchers; **totem pole:** Terry Domico/Earth Images; **tower:** Luis Villota/The Stock Market; **tractor:** B. Olson/Leo de Wys, Inc.; **trail:** Granger Collection; **tramway:** Richard Rowan; **transcontinental:** Culver Pictures; **transport:** Bettmann Archive; **trapper:** Granger Collection; **trench:** Culver Pictures; **trestle:** Culver Pictures; **Trojan horse:** Granger Collection; **Harriet Tubman:** Library of Congress; **tugboat:** Roger Miller/The Image Bank; **Mark Twain:** Brown Brothers; **Uganda:** M. Philip Kahl, Jr./Black Star; **ukelele:** Douglas Peebles; **Uncle Sam:** Granger Collection; **unicorn:** Giraudon/Art Resource; **unicycle:** Martin M. Rotker/Taurus Photos; **Union:** United States Signal Corps; **United Nations:** Eric Carle/Shostal Associates; **Unknown Soldier:** Larry Lee/West Light; **urn:** Granger Collection; **Utah:** Craig Aurness/Woodfin Camp & Associates; **valentine:** E.T. Archive; **Van Gogh:** SCALA/Art Resource; **vandalism:** Francois Bota/Gamma-Liaison; **Venice:** Ray Manley/Shostal Associates; **Queen Victoria:** Granger Collection; **Virginia:** Linda Bartlett/Photo Researchers; **wall:** Ancient Art & Architecture Collection; **wampum:** Museum of the American Indian, Heye Foundation; **Washington:** Don A. Spark/The Image Bank; **watercolor:** SCALA/Art Resource; **waterfall:** New York State Dept. of Commerce; **web:** Grant Heilman/Grant Heilman Photography; **weightlifter:** S. Brown/Leo de Wys, Inc.; **wheelchair:** Franklin Delano Roosevelt Library (Margaret Suckley Collection); **White House:** Robert Glander/Shostal Associates; **William the Conqueror:** SCALA/Art Resource; **windmill:** Christopher Marsh/Bruce Coleman, Inc.; **Wright Brothers:** Bettmann Archive; **Wyoming:** Rod Allin/Tom Stack & Associates; **xylophone:** Stan Ries/Leo de Wys, Inc.; **yacht:** Dennis Brack/Black Star; **Yosemite:** Ronald R. Johnson/The Image Bank; **Yugoslavia:** E. Streichan/Colour Library International; **Zimbabwe:** Shostal Associates; **zither:** Milt & Joan Mann/Marilyn Gartman Agency.

Editing and Proofreading Symbols

Symbol	Example	Meaning of Symbol
℘	Don't blame it on me.	Take out a word, letter, or punctuation mark.
∧	*good* a book	Put in a missing word or punctuation mark.
∧	*a* station**e**ry	Change a letter.
∧—	*huge* the large pyramids	Change a word.
#	police#officer	Add a space.
⌒	fadeing light	Take out and close up the space.
⌒	some how	Close up the space.
⊙	Please sit down⊙	Add a period.
⌃	Oh, I did it again.	Add a comma.
⌃;	He isn't here, he left at two.	Add a semicolon.
⊙	these four items⊙	Add a colon.
=	old fashioned	Add a hyphen.
˅	the rock stars hit song	Add an apostrophe.
˵˵ ˵˵	She shouted, We won!	Add quotation marks.
≡	aunt Faye	Change a lowercase letter to a capital.
⊘	my Aunt	Change a capital letter to lowercase.
∩	foriegn	Change the order of these letters.
tr.	the best game in the new stadium of the year	Change the position of the circled words. (Write *tr.* in the margin nearby.)
⁋	⁋ "Look!" he exclaimed.	Begin a new paragraph.
No ⁋	The horse came closer. We reached out to pet it.	Run in, with no new paragraph.
[	[right after Bill got home.	Move flush left with the margin.
stet	a very hot day	Don't make the change shown; keep as written. (Write *stet* in the margin nearby.)